54th EDITION

vinitaly
INT'L WINE & SPIRITS EXHIBITION

PASSION IN BUSINESS

19-22
APRIL 2020
--> VERONA <--

WWW.VINITALY.COM
TRADE ONLY

TOGETHER WITH

SOL&AGRIFOOD
TASTE OF BUSINESS

ENOLITECH ▶▶▶
WINE / BEER / OLIVE OIL / EQUIPMENT

OperaWine
GRAND TASTING
FINEST ITALIAN WINES

vinitaly
AND THE CITY

5StarWines
THE BOOK

vinitalydesign
2020

Organized by

veronafiere
Trade shows & events since 1898

VERONAFIERE.IT

The advanced logistic solution for Wines & Spirits

www.ggori.com

Wine & Spirits Logistic Macrosystem Solution is a logistics package designed specif ically for the beverages industry. Giorgio Gori has achieved truly superlative standards in this sector in terms of expertise, partnerships, resources, organization and technology. Secure, modular transport systems, contracts with the most dependable carriers, excellent transport rates and optimum storage conditions will smooth the way for your products, from the bottling line to the consumer's table. Easily accessible web-enabled options combined with effective monitoring and forecasting instruments can provide real time information on the entire logistics process.

A DHL company

GORI
Wine and spirits logistics

Burberosso.
Riserva

Nobile
di Montepulciano

Azienda Agricola Metinella di Stefano Sorlini
Via Fontelellera 21/A - 53045 Montepulciano (SI)
Tel. (+39) 0305780877 www.metinella.it

Kellerei
Cantina **Terlan**

We let the
wine grow

Cantina Terlano • I-39018 Terlano • Tel. +39 0471 257 135
www.cantina-terlano.com

Innovative
tradition.
Since 1893.

Gambero Rosso

2020

ITALIAN WINES

VINI D'ITALIA 2020
GAMBERO ROSSO®

Senior Editors
Gianni Fabrizio
Marco Sabellico

Co-editor
Giuseppe Carrus

Technical Directors
William Pregentelli

Special Contributors
Stefania Annese
Antonio Boco
Paolo De Cristofaro
Lorenzo Ruggeri
Paolo Zaccaria

Regionali Coordinators
Nino Aiello
Francesco Beghi
Nicola Frasson
Massimo Lanza
Gianni Ottogalli
Nereo Pederzolli
Pierpaolo Rastelli

Contributors
Sergio Bonanno
Michele Bressan
Pasquale Buffa
Francesca Carlini
Dionisio Castello
Giacomo Mojoli
Elena Mozzini
Franco Pallini
Leonardo Romanelli
Giulia Sampognaro
Herbert Taschler
Cinzia Tosetti

Other Contributors
Edoardo Baracco
Stefano Barone
Dagoberto Basilico
Enrico Battistella
Lucio Chiesa
Pietro Chirco
Palmiro Ciccarelli
Mario Demattè
Franco Fusco
Davide Giachino
Giovanni Lanzillo
Alessandro Mancuso
Michele Muraro
Francesca Pagano
Alberto Parrinello
Dario Piccinelli
Nicola Piccinini
Massimo Ponzanelli
Mirko Rainer
Filippo Rapini
Giovanni Battista Rombo
Riccardo Rossetti
Maurizio Rossi
Simona Silvestri
Sabrina Somigli
Andrea Vannelli
Liliana Zanellato
Monia Zanette
Danilo Zannella

Editorial Secretary
Giulia Sciortino

Layout
Marina Proietti

Publisher
Gambero Rosso S.p.A.
via Ottavio Gasparri, 13/17
00152 Roma
tel. 06/551121 -fax 06/55112260
www.gamberorosso.it
email: gambero@gamberorosso.it

Managing Editor Books
Laura Mantovano

Graphics
Chiara Buosi

Commercial Director
Francesco Dammicco

**Editorial product distribution
and sales manager**
Eugenia Durando

Production
Angelica Sorbara

Translation
Jordan De Maio

Assistant translators
Jane Upchurch
Paul Bullard

Advertising Sales Agency:
Class Pubblicità SpA
Milano, Via Marco Burigozzo, 5
tel. +39 02 58219522
For sales information: mprestileo@class.it

Distribution
USA and Canada
by ACC ART BOOKS, 6 West 18th Street, Suite 4B
New York, NY 10011
UK and Australia
by ACC ART BOOKS Sandy Lane, Old Martlesham,
Woodbridge, Suffolk IP12 4SD - United Kingdom
Italy
by Messaggerie Libri S.p.A.
via Verdi, 8 - 20090 Assago (MI)

copyright © 2019
All rights reserved. No part of this publication may be
reproduced, stored in a retrieval system or
transmitted in any form or by any means, including
microfilm or photostatic copies

The final edit of Italian Wines was completed on
6 September 2019

ISBN 978-88-6641-048-5

Printed in Italy for
Gambero Rosso Holding S.p.A
in October 2019 by
FP Design Srl
Via Atto Tigri, 11
00197 Roma

SUMMARY

REGIONS

INDEXES

THE GUIDE

Italian Wines is now on its 33rd edition. It's an important milestone if you consider all the tasting, sorting and scoring that's been carried out over the past three decades. Over the years more than 300 collaborators have participated in an encyclopedia that's documented about half a million wines, making it an extremely important resource for laying out the modern history of Italian wine. What makes this enormous reference so unique is the fact that every wine has been reviewed and scored. Gambero Rosso, from its beginnings, adopted a scoring system that has become a benchmark for Italy and the world, for consumers and specialists in the field. It's a simple system, easy to interpret, though together with the tasting notes provided, it captures the complexity of our peninsula's wine industry. In the past we've laid out our tasting criteria, which treats the intrinsic characteristics of each wine as just as important as its overall pleasantness, so it's not necessary to do so again here. We'd just like to emphasize one thing. This year we evaluated something in the way of 45,000 wines, but in the guide you'll only find about 22,000. It's an important statistic. Half of the wines tasted don't make it into the guide! As a result, just being listed is an achievement in itself.

About 2,300 wines made it into our final round of tastings, the best of our regional commissions. These are our national elite, wines capable of representing the diversity, uniqueness and beauty of our vineyards. Among them 457 earned our highest honors, but it's important to remember that the difference between Tre Bicchieri and a mere finalist (Due Bicchieri in red) is truly small, a question of nuance and interpretation. Such statistics are even more striking if we consider that, despite the growing number of producers that partecipate in our tastings, and the increased number of wines tasted in recent years, the size of the guide has remained virtually the same. It follows that our criteria have become increasingly rigorous, especially in light of how much quality has grown of late — and continues to grow — throughout the country.

After a year of tastings, of trips and visits to wineries, we've got a snapshot of an industry in perfect health, one that's working to more fully express the unique identity of each terroir, and doing it through a truly fascinating variety of styles and philosophies. From reduced fermentation to the use of amphoras (increasingly common in Italian cellars), the rediscovery of concrete as an apt material for fermentation and aging, the rise of steel and computerized systems, the use of all types and sizes of barrels (with a constant and overall decline in the use of new barriques), nothing's missing in our wineries. And for that we're happy. There's no single recipe for producing quality wine, we've always said it — each producer just has to find its own direction.

Finally, it's important to underline that in every region and every district, producers have come to understand the complexity of the relationship between grower and environment. Estates are increasingly going organic and biodynamic, and there's a general focus on ecology (which we've always championed) that's resulting in an increasingly 'green', sustainable industry — environmentally, economically and socially. And this 33rd edition of our guide is available in English, German, Chinese and Japanese, testifying to a potentially unequalled commitment to raising global awareness about Italian wine.

Being in Gambero Rosso's Italian Wines, and receiving Tre Bicchieri, is by now a universal 'benchmark', an obligatory achievement that continues to favor Italian wines across the globe. We'd add that every year we're part of more than 50 international events, in both established and emerging markets, telling the stories of Italian wines both big and small, as well as their artificers. We meet with consumers, the press, sommeliers, importers and distributers. Our team has managed to build an important instrument for a fundamental part of our economy, one that has earned undisputed international credibility and consensus, and of this we're truly proud.

Our special awards are a snapshot of our vision of Italian wine, as well as a summary of the work done over the course of a year. Our

'Red of the Year' is Piaggia's Carmignano Riserva '16, an extremely elegant wine that's performed at the heights of excellence for some time now. Our 'White of the Year' is Lunae Bosoni's Colli di Luni Vermentino Etichetta Nera '18, forged by a tight-knit family of passionate winemakers. Our 'Sparkler of the Year' award goes to Sorelle Bronaca's Conegliano Valdobbiadene Brut Nature Particella 232 '18, a highly elegant blend made possible by a strong focus on the territory, underlining the success of Treviso's wine in a year in which it became a UNESCO World Heritage Site. Our 'Sweet of the Year' comes from Trentino, it's Cantina di Toblino's Vino Santo '03, a small gem that represents an endangered typology (sweet, meditation wines). Torre dei Beati's Cerasuolo d'Abruzzo Rosa-ae '18 takes home our 'Rosé of the Year' award. For 20 years this outstanding rosé, an increasingly popular and acclaimed typology, has been made with dedication and passion by winemakers Adriana Galasso and Fausto Albanesi. Our 'Winery of the Year' is Florence's Frescobaldi, a 700-year-old dynasty that has of late seen an exceptional growth in quality across all their estates.

Our 'Best Value for Money' is Pico Maccario's Barbera d'Asti Lavignone '18, an excellent wine available at an accessible price, and that does a nice job representing a great terroir. Our 'Grower of the Year' is Leopardo Felici, a true vigneron capable of interpreting every nuance of his land, Castelli di Jesi. Our 'Up-and-Coming Winery' award goes to Piedmont's Tenuta Santa Caterina, which debuts in the Tre Bicchieri club with a superb Grignolino d'Asti M '13. Once again a Puglia winery earns our 'Award for Sustainable Viticulture'. In addition to producing excellent wines for some years now, Cantina Produttori di Manduria is involved in an ambitious, certified sustainability project. Finally, our 'Solidarity Award' goes to the Sicilian Centopassi, the viticultural wing of Don Ciotti's Libera, which brings together various cooperatives to oversee land and vineyards confiscated from the mafia. Their wines are delicious, especially so when you think of the positive message behind them. You'll also find our Tre Bicchieri Verdi in green, those wines made by certified organic or biodynamic producers (some 121 this year). Finally, we also make note of those wines awarded that can be bought for €15 or less (84 in all, 20% of the wines awarded).

Gianni Fabrizio and Marco Sabellico

We would like to thank:
The Bolzano EOS Chamber of Commerce, the Oltrepò Pavese District of Quality Wine, the Arezzo Wine Road, the Marche Institute for Jesi Wine (IMT) and VINEA of Offida, Brescia Wine Association, The Carcare Training Consortium (Savona), Committee for the Tuscan Coast's Great Cru, Assovini Sicilia, the E. del Giudice Viticultural Innovation Centre in Marsala. We'd also like to thank the following protection consortiums: Gavi, Barolo, Barbaresco, Alba, Langhe and Dogliani, Wines of the Colli Tortonesi, Nebbiolo dell'Alto Piemonte, Caluso, Carema and Canavese, Valtellina, Oltrepò Pavese, Franciacorta, Valcalepio, Mantua Wines, Valcamonica Wines, San Colombano, Lugana, Valtenesi, Conegliano Valdobbiadene, Soave, Valpolicella, the Trento Wine Consortium, the Lambrusci Modenesi Historic Wines Consortium, as well as Lambrusco di Modena, Romagna Wines, Bolgheri, Brunello di Montalcino, Chianti Classico, San Gimignano, Montepulciano, Chianti Colli Fiorentini, Chianti Rufina, Morellino di Scansano, Maremma Toscana Wines, Montecucco, Carmignano, Orvieto, Montefalco, the Piceno Wines Consortium and, finally, the DOC Sicilia Wines Consortium.
We'd also like to thank the Enoteca Regionale of Roero and Nizza Monferrato, Canelli and Astesana, the Cantina Comunale I Söri in Diano d'Alba, the Bottega del Vino in Dogliani, Carpe Diem restaurant in Montaione, Calidario in Venturina, Tenuta Il Sassone in Massa Marittima, the City of Taste in Rome and Naples, the Enoteca Regionale of Basilicata in Venosa, Caneva in Mogliano Veneto, Da Nando restaurant in Mortegliano, Casa e Putia restaurant in Messina and, for Ticino, the Restaurant/winery Zoccolino in Bellinzona.
Finally, a sincere thanks to all our team, who showed true devotion in helping us realize Italian Wines, from local tastings to drafting the profiles, all the way to editing the volume itself, and to all those we've worked with down through the years. A special thanks to Danilo Zannella, director of all our tastings.

I TRE BICCHIERI 2020

VALLE D'AOSTA

Sopraquota 900 '18	Rosset Terroir	37
Valle d'Aosta Chambave Muscat Flétri '17	La Vrille	37
Valle d'Aosta Chardonnay Cuvée Bois '17	Les Crêtes	33
Valle d'Aosta Pinot Gris '18	Lo Triolet	35
Valle d'Aosta Pinot Noir L'Emerico '16	Elio Ottin	36
Valle d'Aosta Pinot Noir Semel Pater '17	Maison Anselmet	32

PIEDMONT

Alta Langa Extra Brut Millesimo2Mila15 '15	Marcalberto	119
Alta Langa Pas Dosé Zéro Ris. '13	Enrico Serafino	169
Barbaresco Albesani V. Borgese '15	Piero Busso	67
Barbaresco Asili '16	Ceretto	84
Barbaresco Asili Ris. '14	Bruno Giacosa	108
Barbaresco Crichët Pajé '11	Roagna	157
Barbaresco Currà Ris. '13	Bruno Rocca	158
Barbaresco Montaribaldi '15	Fiorenzo Nada	133
Barbaresco Ovello V. Loreto '16	Albino Rocca	157
Barbaresco Pajoré '16	Bel Colle	52
Barbaresco Pajoré '16	Sottimano	171
Barbaresco Rabajà '16	Giuseppe Cortese	95
Barbaresco Rio Sordo '16	Cascina delle Rose	76
Barbaresco Rombone Elisa '16	Ada Nada	132
Barbaresco Sorì Tildin '16	Gaja	104
Barbaresco Vallegrande '16	Ca' del Baio	68
Barbera d'Alba Ciabot dù Re '17	Giovanni Corino	93
Barbera d'Asti Lavignone '18	Pico Maccario	145
Barbera d'Asti Sup. La Luna e i Falò '17	Vite Colte	181
Barolo '15	Bartolo Mascarello	123
Barolo Aleste '15	Luciano Sandrone	163
Barolo Brea Vigna Ca' Mia '15	Brovia	66
Barolo Bricco delle Viole '15	G. D. Vajra	177
Barolo Briccolina '15	Batasiolo	51
Barolo Brunate '15	Giuseppe Rinaldi	155
Barolo Cannubi '15	Poderi Luigi Einaudi	98
Barolo Castelletto Ris. '13	Fortemasso	103
Barolo Cerretta '15	Garesio	105
Barolo Cerretta V. Bricco Ris. '13	Elio Altare	46
Barolo Ginestra Casa Maté '15	Elio Grasso	111
Barolo Ginestra Ris. '11	Paolo Conterno	91
Barolo Lazzarito Ris. '13	Ettore Germano	107
Barolo Monfortino Ris. '13	Giacomo Conterno	90
Barolo Monvigliero '15	F.lli Alessandria	44
Barolo R56 '15	Brandini	62
Barolo Ravera V. Elena Ris. '13	Elvio Cogno	88
Barolo Ris. '13	Paolo Manzone	118

Trento Brut Madame Martis Ris. '09 — Maso Martis — 300
Trento Brut Rotari Flavio Ris. '11 — Mezzacorona — 301
Trento Dosaggio Zero Letrari Ris. '12 — Letrari — 299
Trento Pas Dosé Balter Ris. '13 — Nicola Balter — 292

ALTO ADIGE
A. A. Cabernet Sauvignon Lafóa '16 — Cantina Colterenzio — 316
A. A. Gewürztraminer Auratus '18 — Tenuta Ritterhof — 332
A. A. Gewürztraminer Nussbaumer '17 — Cantina Tramin — 338
A. A. Gewürztraminer V. Kastelaz '18 — Elena Walch — 340
A. A. Lagrein Staffes Ris. '16 — Tenuta Kornell — 324
A. A. Lagrein Taber Ris. '17 — Cantina Bolzano — 313
A. A. Lagrein V. Klosteranger Ris. '15 — Cantina Convento Muri-Gries — 329
A. A. Müller Thurgau Feldmarschall von Fenner '17 — Tiefenbrunner — 337
A. A. Pinot Bianco Quintessenz '17 — Cantina Kaltern — 322
A. A. Pinot Bianco Sanct Valentin '17 — Cantina Produttori
San Michele Appiano — 333
A. A. Pinot Bianco Sirmian '18 — Nals Margreid — 330
A. A. Pinot Nero Trattmann Ris. '16 — Cantina Girlan — 319
A. A. Santa Maddalena Cl. Rondell '18 — Glögglhof - Franz Gojer — 319
A. A. Sauvignon Renaissance '16 — Gumphof - Markus Prackwieser — 321
A. A. Spumante Extra Brut 1919 Ris. '13 — Kettmeir — 323
A. A. Terlano Sauvignon Quarz '17 — Cantina Terlano — 337
A. A. Val Venosta Riesling Windbichel '17 — Tenuta Unterortl - Castel Juval — 339
A. A. Valle Isarco Riesling Praepositus '17 — Abbazia di Novacella — 312
A. A. Valle Isarco Sylvaner '18 — Kuenhof - Peter Pliger — 325
A. A. Valle Isarco Sylvaner R '17 — Köfererhof
Günther Kerschbaumer — 324
Manna '17 — Franz Haas — 321

VENETO
Amarone della Valpolicella '15 — Famiglia Cottini - Monte Zovo — 378
Amarone della Valpolicella Campo dei Gigli '15 — Tenuta Sant'Antonio — 411
Amarone della Valpolicella Case Vecie '13 — Brigaldara — 361
Amarone della Valpolicella Cl. '15 — Allegrini — 352
Amarone della Valpolicella Cl. '11 — Bertani — 356
Amarone della Valpolicella Cl. '11 — Giuseppe Quintarelli — 404
Amarone della Valpolicella Cl. '13 — Zymè — 431
Amarone della Valpolicella Cl.
 Campolongo di Torbe '12 — Masi — 390
Amarone della Valpolicella Cl. Casa dei Bepi '13 — Viviani — 428
Amarone della Valpolicella Cl. De Buris Ris. '09 — Tommasi Viticoltori — 419
Amarone della Valpolicella Cl. Sant'Urbano '15 — Speri — 414
Amarone della Valpolicella Leone Zardini Ris. '12 — Pietro Zardini — 429
Amarone della Valpolicella Mai Dire Mai '12 — Pasqua - Cecilia Beretta — 401
Capitel Croce '18 — Roberto Anselmi — 353

Collio Sauvignon '18	Tiare - Roberto Snidarcig	502
Desiderium I Ferretti '17	Tenuta Luisa	473
FCO Biancosesto '17	La Tunella	503
FCO Pinot Bianco Myò '18	Zorzettig	513
FCO Pinot Grigio '18	Torre Rosazza	503
FCO Sauvignon Zuc di Volpe '18	Volpe Pasini	511
Friuli Isonzo Pinot Bianco '17	Masùt da Rive	474
Friuli Isonzo Sauvignon Piere '17	Vie di Romans	506
Friuli Pinot Bianco '18	Vigneti Le Monde	471
Malvasia '15	Damijan Podversic	482
Ograde '17	Skerk	497
Ribolla Gialla Dosaggio Zero '15	Eugenio Collavini	455
Rosazzo Terre Alte '17	Livio Felluga	464
Tal Lùc 1.2	Lis Neris	472
Vintage Tunina '17	Jermann	469

EMILIA ROMAGNA

Callas Malvasia '17	Monte delle Vigne	535
Lambrusco di Sorbara del Fondatore '18	Cleto Chiarli Tenute Agricole	529
Lambrusco di Sorbara Leclisse '18	Alberto Paltrinieri	537
Lambrusco di Sorbara V. del Cristo '18	Cavicchioli	527
Reggiano Lambrusco Brut Cadelvento Rosé '18	Venturini Baldini	547
Reggiano Lambrusco Concerto '18	Ermete Medici & Figli	535
Romagna Albana Secco Vitalba '18	Tre Monti	545
Romagna Sangiovese Predappio Il Sangiovese '18	Noelia Ricci	539
Romagna Sangiovese Predappio Le Lucciole Ris. '16	Chiara Condello	530
Romagna Sangiovese Sup. Avi Ris. '16	San Patrignano	542
Romagna Sangiovese Sup. Predappio di Predappio V. del Generale Ris. '16	Fattoria Nicolucci	536
Romagna Sangiovese Sup. Primo Segno '17	Villa Venti	549
Romagna Sangiovese Sup. Tre Miracoli '18	Le Rocche Malatestiane	540

TUSCANY

Auritea '16	Tenuta Podernovo	649
Bolgheri Bianco Criseo '17	Guado al Melo	616
Bolgheri Rosso Sup. '16	Castello di Bolgheri	584
Bolgheri Rosso Sup. Grattamacco '16	Grattamacco	616
Bolgheri Rosso Sup. Le Gonnare '16	Fabio Motta	637
Bolgheri Rosso Sup. Orma '17	Orma	639
Bolgheri Rosso Sup. Ornellaia '16	Ornellaia	639
Bolgheri Rosso Sup. Sondraia '16	Poggio al Tesoro	650
Bolgheri Sup. Sassicaia '16	Tenuta San Guido	668
Brunello di Montalcino '14	Baricci	565
Brunello di Montalcino '14	Brunelli - Le Chiuse di Sotto	571
Brunello di Montalcino '14	Il Marroneto	627
Brunello di Montalcino '14	Pietroso	648

Offida Rosso Vignagiulia '16	Emanuele Dianetti	734
Piceno Sup. Morellone '15	Le Caniette	726
Rosso Piceno Sup. Roggio del Filare '16	Velenosi	757
Verdicchio dei Castelli di Jesi Cl. Sup. Origini '18	Fattoria Nannì	744
Verdicchio dei Castelli di Jesi Cl. Sup. V. V. '17	Umani Ronchi	756
Verdicchio dei Castelli di Jesi Cl. Sup. Vign. del Balluccio '17	Tenuta dell'Ugolino	753
Verdicchio di Matelica '18	Bisci	723
Verdicchio di Matelica Cambrugiano Ris. '16	Belisario	723
Verdicchio di Matelica Collestefano '18	Collestefano	729
Verdicchio di Matelica Jera Ris. '15	Borgo Paglianetto	724

UMBRIA

Adarmando Trebbiano Spoletino '17	Giampaolo Tabarrini	782
Cervaro della Sala '17	Castello della Sala	770
Il Roccafiore '16	Roccafiore	780
Montefalco Rosso Mattone Ris. '16	Briziarelli	768
Montefalco Rosso Pomontino '17	Tenuta Bellafonte	767
Montefalco Rosso Ris. '15	Antonelli - San Marco	766
Montefalco Rosso Ziggurat '17	Tenute Lunelli - Castelbuono	775
Montefalco Sagrantino '15	Terre de la Custodia	782
Montefalco Sagrantino 25 Anni '15	Arnaldo Caprai	769
Montefalco Sagrantino Sacrantino '15	F.lli Pardi	778
Orvieto Cl. Sup. Luigi e Giovanna '16	Barberani	767
Ramìci Ciliegiolo '16	Leonardo Bussoletti	769
Torgiano Rosso Pinturicchio Ris. '16	Terre Margaritelli	783
Torgiano Rosso Rubesco V. Monticchio Ris. '15	Lungarotti	775

LAZIO

Cesanese di Olevano Romano Silene '17	Damiano Ciolli	794
Faro della Guardia Biancolella '18	Casale del Giglio	792
Fiorano Bianco '17	Tenuta di Fiorano	801
Frascati Sup. '18	Castel de Paolis	793
Montiano '17	Falesco - Famiglia Cotarella	795
Poggio della Costa '18	Sergio Mottura	797
Roma Rosso Ed. Limitata '16	Poggio Le Volpi	800

ABRUZZO

Abruzzo Pecorino '18	Tenuta I Fauri	814
Cerasuolo d'Abruzzo Rosa-ae '18	Torre dei Beati	821
Montepulciano d'Abruzzo '18	Villa Medoro	824
Montepulciano d'Abruzzo Colline Teramane Notàri '17	Fattoria Nicodemi	817
Montepulciano d'Abruzzo Ilico '17	Dino Illuminati	816
Montepulciano d'Abruzzo Mo Ris. '15	Cantina Tollo	821
Montepulciano d'Abruzzo Organic '18	Feudo Antico	814

Don Antonio Primitivo '17	Coppi	885
Gioia del Colle Primitivo 17 Vign. Montevella '16	Polvanera	892
Gioia del Colle Primitivo		
Muro Sant'Angelo Contrada Barbatto '16	Tenute Chiaromonte	885
Idea '18	Varvaglione 1921	898
Negroamaro '17	Carvinea	883
Oltremé Susumaniello '18	Tenute Rubino	893
Primitivo di Manduria Lirica '17	Produttori di Manduria	892
Primitivo di Manduria		
Piano Chiuso 26 27 63 Ris. '16	Masca del Tacco	890
Primitivo di Manduria Raccontami '17	Vespa - Vignaioli per Passione	898
Primitivo di Manduria Sessantanni '16	San Marzano	894
Primitivo di Manduria		
Zinfandel Sinfarosa Terra Nera '17	Felline	887
Salice Salentino Rosso Donna Lisa Ris. '16	Leone de Castris	886
Salice Salentino Rosso Selvarossa Ris. '16	Cantine Due Palme	886
Taccorosso Negroamaro '15	Cantine Paolo Leo	889

CALABRIA

Cirò Rosso Cl. Sup. Duca San Felice Ris. '17	Librandi	911
Cirò Rosso Cl. Sup. Ris. '15	'A Vita	908
Grisara Pecorello '18	Roberto Ceraudo	909
Moscato Passito '18	Luigi Viola	913

SICILY

Cerasuolo di Vittoria Giambattista Valli '17	Feudi del Pisciotto	930
Contrada C '17	Passopisciaro	938
Eloro Nero d'Avola Fontanelle '14	Curto	928
Etna Bianco A' Puddara '17	Tenuta di Fessina	944
Etna Bianco Alta Mora '18	Alta Mora	921
Etna Bianco Cavanera Ripa di Scorciavacca '17	Firriato	932
Etna Rosato Mofete '18	Palmento Costanzo	937
Etna Rosso '17	Tornatore	945
Etna Rosso Arcurìa '17	Graci	934
Etna Rosso Contrada Monte Serra '17	Benanti	924
Etna Rosso Feudo di Mezzo '16	Cottanera	928
Etna Rosso V. Barbagalli '16	Pietradolce	939
Etna Rosso Vico Prephylloxera '16	Tenute Bosco	925
Etna Rosso Vign. Monte Gorna Ris. '13	Cantine Nicosia	935
Faro '17	Le Casematte	926
Malvasia delle Lipari Passito '18	Caravaglio	926
Noto Nero d'Avola Santa Cecilia '16	Planeta	939
Passito di Pantelleria Ben Ryé '16	Donnafugata	929
Sicilia Bianco Maggiore '18	Rallo	941
Sicilia Bianco Nozze d'Oro '17	Tasca d'Almerita	943
Sicilia Catarratto Terre Rosse di Giabbascio '18	Centopassi	927

Sicilia Grillo Shamaris '18	Cusumano	929
Sicilia Grillo V. di Mandranova '18	Alessandro di Camporeale	920
Sicilia Mandrarossa Cartagho '17	Cantine Settesoli	943
Sicilia Nero d'Avola Saia '17	Feudo Maccari	931
Sicilia Perricone Furioso '16	Assuli	921

SARDINIA

Alghero Torbato Terre Bianche Cuvée 161 '18	Tenute Sella & Mosca	973
Cannonau di Sardegna '17	Antonella Corda	961
Cannonau di Sardegna Cl. Dule '16	Giuseppe Gabbas	964
Cannonau di Sardegna Nepente di Oliena Pro Vois Ris. '14	F.lli Puddu	970
Capichera V. T. '16	Capichera	959
Carignano del Sulcis 6Mura Ris. '16	Cantina Giba	964
Carignano del Sulcis Sup. Terre Brune '15	Cantina di Santadi	971
Nuracada Bovale '17	Audarya	958
Terresicci '14	Cantine di Dolianova	962
Turriga '15	Argiolas	958
Vermentino di Gallura Sup. Costarenas '18	Masone Mannu	966
Vermentino di Gallura Sup. Sciala '18	Surrau	974
Vermentino di Gallura Sup. Soliànu - Tenuta Matteu '18	Andrea Ledda	965
Vermentino di Sardegna Stellato '18	Pala	969

THE BEST

RED OF THE YEAR

PIAGGIA - CARMIGNANO RIS. '16

WHITE OF THE YEAR

LUNAE BOSONI - COLLI DI LUNI VERMENTINO LUNAE ET. NERA '18

SPARKLER OF THE YEAR

SORELLE BRONCA
VALDOBBIADENE BRUT NATURE PARTICELLA 232 '18

SWEET OF THE YEAR

TOBLINO - TRENTINO VINO SANTO '03

ROSÈ OF THE YEAR

TORRE DEI BEATI - CERASUOLO D'ABRUZZO ROSA-AE '18

WINERY OF THE YEAR

FRESCOBALDI

BEST VALUE FOR MONEY

PICO MACCARIO - BARBERA D'ASTI LAVIGNONE '18

GROWER OF THE YEAR

LEOPARDO FELICI

UP-AND-COMING WINERY

TENUTA SANTA CATERINA

AWARD FOR SUSTAINABLE VITICULTURE

PRODUTTORI DI MANDURIA

SOLIDARITY AWARD

CENTOPASSI

TRE BICCHIERI VERDI

With our Tre Bicchieri Verdi we make note of those wines whose grapes are cultivated according to certified organic or biodynamic management (which we indicate in red). This year there are some 121 such wines, a record for our guide, testifying to how this positive trend is growing, year after year, from micro-wineries to large-scale producers, all taking on the challenge of moving towards sustainable practices.

A. A. Santa Maddalena Cl.		
Rondell '18	Glögglhof - Franz Gojer	Alto Adige
Abruzzo Pecorino '18	Tenuta I Fauri	Abruzzo
Aglianico del Vulture Gricos '17	Grifalco della Lucania	Basilicata
Alghero Torbato		
Terre Bianche Cuvée 161 '18	Tenute Sella & Mosca	Sardinia
Barbera d'Asti Lavignone '18	Pico Maccario	Piedmont
Barbera d'Asti Sup. La Luna e i Falò '17	Vite Colte	Piedmont
Campi Flegrei Falanghina '18	Agnanum	Campania
Cannonau di Sardegna '17	Antonella Corda	Sardinia
Capitel Croce '18	Roberto Anselmi	Veneto
Carmignano Santa Cristina in Pilli '16	Fattoria Ambra	Tuscany
Castel del Monte Rosso		
V. Pedale Ris. '16	Torrevento	Puglia
Castelli di Jesi Verdicchio Cl.		
Ambrosia Ris. '16	Vignamato	Marche
Cerasuolo d'Abruzzo Rosa-ae '18	Torre dei Beati	Abruzzo
Cesanese di Olevano Romano		
Silene '17	Damiano Ciolli	Lazio
Chianti Cl. '17	Riecine	Tuscany
Chianti Cl. Fontalpino '17	Fattoria Carpineta	
	Fontalpino	Tuscany
Chianti Cl.		
Lamole di Lamole Et. Bianca '16	Lamole di Lamole	Tuscany
Chianti Cl. Rocca di Castagnoli '17	Rocca di Castagnoli	Tuscany
Cirò Rosso Cl. Sup.		
Duca San Felice Ris. '17	Librandi	Calabria
Colli di Luni Vermentino Pianacce '18	Giacomelli	Liguria
Collio Bianco Fosarin '17	Ronco dei Tassi	Friuli Venezia Giulia
Collio Chardonnay '17	Ronco Blanchis	Friuli Venezia Giulia
Collio Pinot Bianco Santarosa '18	Castello di Spessa	Friuli Venezia Giulia
Conegliano Valdobbiadene		
Rive di Ogliano Brut Nature '18	BiancaVigna	Veneto
Custoza Sup. Amedeo '17	Cavalchina	Veneto
Custoza Sup. Ca' del Magro '17	Monte del Frà	Veneto
Dogliani Sup. Vigneti Dolci '17	San Fereolo	Piedmont
Don Antonio Primitivo '17	Coppi	Puglia
Etna Rosato Mofete '18	Palmento Costanzo	Sicily
Falanghina del Sannio		
Janare Senete '18	La Guardiense	Campania
Falanghina del Sannio Svelato '18	Terre Stregate	Campania
Falanghina del Sannio Taburno '18	Fontanavecchia	Campania
Falerio Pecorino Onirocep '18	Pantaleone	Marche
FCO Pinot Grigio '18	Torre Rosazza	Friuli Venezia Giulia
Frascati Sup. '18	Castel de Paolis	Lazio
Friuli Pinot Bianco '18	Vigneti Le Monde	Friuli Venezia Giulia
Grignolino d'Asti '18	Luigi Spertino	Piedmont
Idea '18	Varvaglione 1921	Puglia

Il Roccafiore '16	Roccafiore	**Umbria**
Lacrima di Morro d'Alba Sup. Orgiolo '17	Marotti Campi	**Marche**
Lambrusco di Sorbara del Fondatore '18	Cleto Chiarli Tenute Agricole	**Emilia Romagna**
Lambrusco di Sorbara Leclisse '18	Alberto Paltrinieri	**Emilia Romagna**
Lambrusco di Sorbara V. del Cristo '18	Cavicchioli	**Emilia Romagna**
Lugana Menasasso Ris. '15	Selva Capuzza	**Lombardy**
Montepulciano d'Abruzzo '18	Villa Medoro	**Abruzzo**
Montepulciano d'Abruzzo Ilico '17	Dino Illuminati	**Abruzzo**
Montepulciano d'Abruzzo Mo Ris. '15	Cantina Tollo	**Abruzzo**
Montepulciano d'Abruzzo Organic '18	Feudo Antico	**Abruzzo**
Moscato d'Asti Casa di Bianca '18	Gianni Doglia	**Piedmont**
Nobile di Montepulciano '16	Podere Le Bèrne	**Tuscany**
Offida Pecorino '18	Tenuta Santori	**Marche**
Offida Pecorino Artemisia '18	Tenuta Spinelli	**Marche**
Oltremé Susumaniello '18	Tenute Rubino	**Puglia**
Ovada Convivio '17	Gaggino	**Piedmont**
Parrina Sangiovese '18	Tenuta La Parrina	**Tuscany**
Pompeii Bianco '18	Bosco de' Medici	**Campania**
Primitivo di Manduria Lirica '17	Produttori di Manduria	**Puglia**
Reggiano Lambrusco Brut Cadelvento Rosé '18	Venturini Baldini	**Emilia Romagna**
Reggiano Lambrusco Concerto '18	Ermete Medici & Figli	**Emilia Romagna**
Riviera Ligure di Ponente Vermentino '18	Fontanacota	**Liguria**
Roero Arneis Renesio '18	Malvirà	**Piedmont**
Roero Arneis Sarun '18	Stefanino Costa	**Piedmont**
Romagna Sangiovese Predappio Il Sangiovese '18	Noelia Ricci	**Emilia Romagna**
Romagna Sangiovese Sup. Primo Segno '17	Villa Venti	**Emilia Romagna**
Romagna Sangiovese Sup. Tre Miracoli '18	Le Rocche Malatestiane	**Emilia Romagna**
Sicilia Bianco Maggiore '18	Rallo	**Sicily**
Sicilia Catarratto Terre Rosse di Giabbascio '18	Centopassi	**Sicily**
Sicilia Grillo Shamaris '18	Cusumano	**Sicily**
Sicilia Grillo V. di Mandranova '18	Alessandro di Camporeale	**Sicily**
Sicilia Mandrarossa Cartagho '17	Cantine Settesoli	**Sicily**
Soave Cl. Campo Vulcano '18	I Campi	**Veneto**
Soave Cl. Monte Carbonare '18	Suavia	**Veneto**
Soave Cl. Monte Fiorentine '17	Ca' Rugate	**Veneto**
Soave Sup. Il Casale '17	Agostino Vicentini	**Veneto**
Soave Sup. Runcata '17	Dal Cero Tenuta Corte Giacobbe	**Veneto**
Valdobbiadene Brut Ius Naturae '18	Bortolomiol	**Veneto**
Valdobbiadene Dosaggio Zero Vign. Del Faè '18	Canevel Spumanti	**Veneto**
Valdobbiadene Rive Di Refrontolo Brut Col Del Forno '18	Andreola	**Veneto**
Valpolicella Ca' Fiui '18	Corte Sant'Alda	**Veneto**
Verdicchio dei Castelli di Jesi Cl. Sup. Origini '18	Fattoria Nannì	**Marche**
Verdicchio di Matelica '18	Bisci	**Marche**
Verdicchio di Matelica Cambrugiano Ris. '16	Belisario	**Marche**
Verdicchio di Matelica Collestefano '18	Collestefano	**Marche**
Vernaccia di S. Gimignano Ostrea '17	Mormoraia	**Tuscany**

TABLE OF VINTAGES
FROM 1995 TO 2018

	ALTO ADIGE BIANCO		FRIULI BIANCO
2006	🍾🍾🍾	🍾🍾🍾	🍾🍾🍾🍾🍾
2007	🍾🍾🍾	🍾🍾🍾🍾	🍾🍾🍾🍾🍾
2008	🍾🍾🍾	🍾🍾🍾🍾	🍾🍾🍾
2009	🍾🍾🍾🍾	🍾🍾🍾🍾🍾	🍾🍾🍾🍾
2010	🍾🍾🍾🍾🍾	🍾🍾🍾🍾	🍾🍾
2011	🍾🍾🍾	🍾🍾🍾	🍾🍾🍾
2012	🍾🍾🍾🍾	🍾🍾🍾	🍾🍾🍾🍾
2013	🍾🍾🍾🍾	🍾🍾🍾🍾	🍾🍾🍾🍾
2014	🍾🍾	🍾🍾🍾	🍾🍾🍾
2015	🍾🍾🍾🍾	🍾🍾🍾🍾	🍾🍾🍾🍾🍾
2016	🍾🍾🍾🍾🍾	🍾🍾🍾🍾🍾	🍾🍾🍾🍾🍾
2017	🍾🍾🍾🍾	🍾🍾🍾🍾	🍾🍾🍾🍾
2018	🍾🍾🍾🍾	🍾🍾🍾🍾🍾	🍾🍾🍾🍾🍾

dispenser studio.it

cantina
FRENTANA
1958

Vini Costa del Mulino,
tutto il sapore
della nostra terra

www.cantinafrentana.it

SHARE OUR PASSION

 CAMPAGNA FINANZIATA AI SENSI DEL REGOLAMENTO CE N. 1308/13
CAMPAIGN FINANCED ACCORDING TO (EC) REGULATION N. 1308/13

TOP ITALIAN RESTAURANTS

www.gamberorosso.it/en/restaurants/

Follow us on:

f GamberoRossoInternational

◎ GamberoRossoInternational

GRECO DI TUFO

	BARBARESCO	BAROLO	AMARONE	CHIANTI CLASSICO
1995	🍾🍾🍾	🍾🍾🍾	🍾🍾🍾🍾🍾	🍾🍾🍾🍾
1996	🍾🍾🍾🍾🍾	🍾🍾🍾🍾🍾	🍾🍾🍾	🍾🍾🍾
1997	🍾🍾🍾	🍾🍾🍾	🍾🍾🍾🍾	🍾🍾🍾
1998	🍾🍾🍾	🍾🍾🍾🍾	🍾🍾🍾	🍾🍾🍾
1999	🍾🍾🍾🍾	🍾🍾🍾🍾🍾	🍾🍾🍾	🍾🍾🍾🍾
2000	🍾🍾🍾	🍾🍾🍾🍾	🍾🍾🍾🍾	🍾🍾🍾🍾
2001	🍾🍾🍾🍾🍾	🍾🍾🍾🍾🍾	🍾🍾🍾🍾🍾	🍾🍾🍾🍾🍾
2002	🍾🍾	🍾🍾	🍾🍾	🍾🍾
2003	🍾🍾	🍾🍾	🍾🍾	🍾🍾
2004	🍾🍾🍾🍾🍾	🍾🍾🍾🍾🍾	🍾🍾🍾🍾	🍾🍾🍾🍾
2005	🍾🍾🍾	🍾🍾🍾	🍾🍾🍾🍾	🍾🍾🍾
2006	🍾🍾🍾	🍾🍾🍾🍾	🍾🍾🍾	🍾🍾🍾
2007	🍾🍾🍾	🍾🍾🍾	🍾🍾🍾🍾🍾	🍾🍾🍾🍾🍾
2008	🍾🍾🍾🍾	🍾🍾🍾🍾	🍾🍾🍾🍾	🍾🍾🍾🍾
2009	🍾🍾	🍾🍾	🍾🍾🍾	🍾🍾🍾
2010	🍾🍾🍾🍾	🍾🍾🍾🍾🍾	🍾🍾🍾🍾	🍾🍾🍾🍾🍾
2011	🍾🍾🍾🍾	🍾🍾🍾🍾	🍾🍾🍾🍾	🍾🍾🍾
2012	🍾🍾🍾	🍾🍾🍾🍾	🍾🍾🍾	🍾🍾🍾
2013	🍾🍾🍾🍾	🍾🍾🍾🍾	🍾🍾🍾🍾	🍾🍾🍾🍾
2014	🍾🍾🍾	🍾🍾	🍾🍾	🍾🍾🍾🍾
2015	🍾🍾🍾🍾	🍾🍾🍾🍾	🍾🍾🍾🍾🍾	🍾🍾🍾🍾
2016	🍾🍾🍾🍾🍾			🍾🍾🍾🍾🍾
2017				🍾🍾🍾🍾

BRUNELLO DI MONTALCINO	BOLGHERI	TAURASI	MONTEPULCIANO D'ABRUZZO	ETNA ROSSO
5	3	3	5	3
2	3	3	4	2
4	4	4	4	3
3	4	1	4	3
5	3	5	2	3
3	3	1	3	3
5	5	4	5	5
2	2	2	2	2
3	2	4	3	3
4	3	4	4	3
2	3	4	4	4
4	4	3	4	4
4	5	3	5	5
3	4	5	3	5
1	5	3	2	2
5	3	4	2	4
3	4	2	4	5
3	4	3	3	4
5	5	4	4	3
2	2	2	2	5
	4	4	4	3
	4		3	5
				3

STARS

57
Gaja (Piedmont)

44
Ca' del Bosco (Lombardia)

38
Elio Altare (Piedmont)
La Spinetta (Piedmont)

35
Allegrini (Veneto)
Valentini (Abruzzo)

34
Castello di Fonterutoli (Tuscany)

31
Bellavista (Lombardia)
Giacomo Conterno (Piedmont)
Jermann (Friuli Venezia Giulia)
Tenuta San Guido (Tuscany)
Cantina Produttori San Michele
  Appiano (Alto Adige)

30
Castello della Sala (Umbria)
Ferrari (Trentino)
Masciarelli (Abruzzo)
Planeta (Sicily)

★★

28
Fèlsina (Tuscany)
Poliziano (Tuscany)
Tasca d'Almerita (Sicily)
Cantina Tramin (Alto Adige)
Vie di Romans
  (Friuli Venezia Giulia)

27
Marchesi Antinori (Tuscany)
Feudi di San Gregorio (Campania)
Bruno Giacosa (Piedmont)
Leonildo Pieropan (Veneto)

26
Livio Felluga
  (Friuli Venezia Giulia)
Ornellaia (Tuscany)

25
Argiolas (Sardinia)
Cantina Bolzano (Alto Adige)
Arnaldo Caprai (Umbria)
Castello di Ama (Tuscany)
Nino Negri (Lombardia)
Paolo Scavino (Piedmont)

Schiopetto (Friuli Venezia Giulia)
Villa Russiz (Friuli Venezia Giulia)

24
Falesco - Famiglia Cotarella
  (Lazio)
Fontodi (Tuscany)
Gravner (Friuli Venezia Giulia)
Tenute Sella & Mosca (Sardinia)
Cantina Terlano (Alto Adige)

23
Ca' Viola (Piedmont)
Cantina Colterenzio (Alto Adige)
Isole e Olena (Tuscany)
San Leonardo (Trentino)
Vietti (Piedmont)

22
Michele Chiarlo (Piedmont)
Domenico Clerico (Piedmont)
Les Crêtes (Valle d'Aosta)
Cantina Kaltern (Alto Adige)
Montevetrano (Campania)
Barone Ricasoli (Tuscany)
Volpe Pasini (Friuli Venezia Giulia)
Elena Walch (Alto Adige)

21
Ca' Rugate (Veneto)
Cascina La Barbatella (Piedmont)
Castellare di Castellina (Tuscany)
Castello del Terriccio (Tuscany)
Le Macchiole (Tuscany)
Montevertine (Tuscany)
Serafini & Vidotto (Veneto)

20
Luigi Cataldi Madonna (Abruzzo)
Cusumano (Sicily)
Donnafugata (Sicily)
Dorigo (Friuli Venezia Giulia)
Gioacchino Garofoli (Marche)
Elio Grasso (Piedmont)
Lis Neris (Friuli Venezia Giulia)
Ruffino (Tuscany)
Cantina di Santadi (Sardinia)
Sottimano (Piedmont)
Franco Toros
  (Friuli Venezia Giulia)
Venica & Venica
  (Friuli Venezia Giulia)

19
Abbazia di Novacella (Alto Adige)
Antoniolo (Piedmont)
Matteo Correggia (Piedmont)
Firriato (Sicily)
Livon (Friuli Venezia Giulia)
Masi (Veneto)
Monsupello (Lombardia)

Cantina Convento Muri-Gries
  (Alto Adige)
Fiorenzo Nada (Piedmont)
Palari (Sicily)
Giuseppe Quintarelli (Veneto)
Bruno Rocca (Piedmont)
Ronco dei Tassi
  (Friuli Venezia Giulia)
San Patrignano (Emilia Romagna)
Luciano Sandrone (Piedmont)
Umani Ronchi (Marche)
Le Vigne di Zamò
  (Friuli Venezia Giulia)

18
Roberto Anselmi (Veneto)
Brancaia (Tuscany)
Casanova di Neri (Tuscany)
Castello Banfi (Tuscany)
Conterno Fantino (Piedmont)
Coppo (Piedmont)
Kuenhof - Peter Pliger
  (Alto Adige)
Massolino (Piedmont)
Mastroberardino (Campania)
Doro Princic
  (Friuli Venezia Giulia)
Velenosi (Marche)
Fattoria Zerbina
  (Emilia Romagna)

17
Lorenzo Begali (Veneto)
Bertani (Veneto)
Bucci (Marche)
Fattoria Petrolo (Tuscany)
Pietracupa (Campania)
Querciabella (Tuscany)
Albino Rocca (Piedmont)
Suavia (Veneto)
Tenuta Unterortl - Castel Juval
  (Alto Adige)

16
Abbona (Piedmont)
Cavit (Trentino)
Aldo Conterno (Piedmont)
Romano Dal Forno (Veneto)
Di Majo Norante (Molise)
Grattamacco (Tuscany)
Librandi (Calabria)
Lungarotti (Umbria)
Bartolo Mascarello (Piedmont)
Miani (Friuli Venezia Giulia)
La Monacesca (Marche)
Rocca di Frassinello (Tuscany)
San Felice (Tuscany)
Tenuta Sant'Antonio (Veneto)
Speri (Veneto)
Vignalta (Veneto)
Viviani (Veneto)

15

F.lli Alessandria (Piedmont)
Biondi - Santi Tenuta Greppo
  (Tuscany)
Elvio Cogno (Piedmont)
Leone de Castris (Puglia)
Ferghettina (Lombardia)
Tenuta di Ghizzano (Tuscany)
Dino Illuminati (Abruzzo)
Malvirà (Piedmont)
Sergio Mottura (Lazio)
Piaggia (Tuscany)
Graziano Prà (Veneto)
Produttori del Barbaresco
  (Piedmont)
Aldo Rainoldi (Lombardia)
Russiz Superiore
  (Friuli Venezia Giulia)
Valle Reale (Abruzzo)
Roberto Voerzio (Piedmont)

14

Giulio Accornero e Figli
  (Piedmont)
Avignonesi (Tuscany)
Boscarelli (Tuscany)
Bricco Rocche - Bricco Asili
  (Piedmont)
Piero Busso (Piedmont)
Ca' del Baio (Piedmont)
Cavalchina (Veneto)
Tenute Cisa Asinari dei Marchesi
  di Grésy (Piedmont)
Eugenio Collavini
  (Friuli Venezia Giulia)
Poderi Luigi Einaudi (Piedmont)
Falkenstein Franz Pratzner
  (Alto Adige)
Tenute Ambrogio e Giovanni
  Folonari (Tuscany)
Frescobaldi (Tuscany)
Elena Fucci (Basilicata)
Ettore Germano (Piedmont)
Köfererhof - Günther
  Kerschbaumer (Alto Adige)
Mamete Prevostini (Lombardia)
Franco M. Martinetti (Piedmont)
Monchiero Carbone (Piedmont)
Nals Margreid (Alto Adige)
Oasi degli Angeli (Marche)
Fattoria Le Pupille (Tuscany)
Ronco del Gelso
  (Friuli Venezia Giulia)
Uberti (Lombardia)
Tenuta di Valgiano (Tuscany)
Villa Medoro (Abruzzo)
Villa Sparina (Piedmont)
Zenato (Veneto)

13

Braida (Piedmont)
Brovia (Piedmont)
Cascina Ca' Rossa (Piedmont)
Castello di Albola (Tuscany)
Castello di Volpaia (Tuscany)

Cavalleri (Lombardia)
Tenuta Col d'Orcia (Tuscany)
Cantine Due Palme (Puglia)
Le Due Terre
  (Friuli Venezia Giulia)
Foradori (Trentino)
Galardi (Campania)
Gini (Veneto)
Cantina Girlan (Alto Adige)
Edi Keber (Friuli Venezia Giulia)
Cantina Kurtatsch (Alto Adige)
Maculan (Veneto)
Marchesi di Barolo (Piedmont)
Vigneti Massa (Piedmont)
Pecchenino (Piedmont)
Salvioni (Tuscany)
Tormaresca (Puglia)
Torraccia del Piantavigna
  (Piedmont)
Torrevento (Puglia)
Tua Rita (Tuscany)

12

Gianfranco Alessandria
  (Piedmont)
Maison Anselmet (Valle d'Aosta)
Azelia (Piedmont)
Benanti (Sicily)
Brigaldara (Veneto)
Castello dei Rampolla (Tuscany)
Colle Massari (Tuscany)
Còlpetrone (Umbria)
Marisa Cuomo (Campania)
Dorigati (Trentino)
Franz Haas (Alto Adige)
Poggio di Sotto (Tuscany)
Dario Raccaro
  (Friuli Venezia Giulia)
Rocche dei Manzoni (Piedmont)
Tenute Rubino (Puglia)
Giampaolo Tabarrini (Umbria)
Tenute del Cerro (Tuscany)
G. D. Vajra (Piedmont)

11

Abate Nero (Trentino)
Guido Berlucchi & C. (Lombardia)
Borgo San Daniele
  (Friuli Venezia Giulia)
Cà Maiol (Lombardia)
I Campi (Veneto)
Tenuta di Capezzana (Tuscany)
Fattoria Carpineta Fontalpino
  (Tuscany)
Tenute Chiaromonte (Puglia)
F.lli Cigliuti (Piedmont)
Cleto Chiarli Tenute Agricole
  (Emilia Romagna)
Colli di Lapio (Campania)
Corte Sant'Alda (Veneto)
Cottanera (Sicily)
Feudi del Pisciotto (Sicily)
Feudo Maccari (Sicily)
Giuseppe Gabbas (Sardinia)
Giorgi (Lombardia)

Guerrieri Rizzardi (Veneto)
Lo Triolet (Valle d'Aosta)
Cantine Lunae Bosoni (Liguria)
La Massa (Tuscany)
Mastrojanni (Tuscany)
Ermete Medici & Figli
  (Emilia Romagna)
Poderi e Cantine Oddero
  (Piedmont)
Orma (Tuscany)
Ottella (Veneto)
Pio Cesare (Piedmont)
Prunotto (Piedmont)
Ruggeri & C. (Veneto)
Tenute San Sisto - Fazi Battaglia
  (Marche)
Luigi Spertino (Piedmont)
Tiefenbrunner (Alto Adige)

10

Badia a Coltibuono (Tuscany)
Nicola Balter (Trentino)
Enzo Boglietti (Piedmont)
Bruna (Liguria)
Capichera (Sardinia)
Castello di Monsanto (Tuscany)
Castello di Spessa
  (Friuli Venezia Giulia)
Cavallotto - Tenuta Bricco
  Boschis (Piedmont)
Ceretto (Piedmont)
Paolo Conterno (Piedmont)
Giovanni Corino (Piedmont)
Fontanafredda (Piedmont)
Gumphof - Markus Prackwieser
  (Alto Adige)
Hilberg - Pasquero (Piedmont)
Tenuta J. Hofstätter (Alto Adige)
Alois Lageder (Alto Adige)
Letrari (Trentino)
Giuseppe Mascarello e Figlio
  (Piedmont)
Cantina Meran (Alto Adige)
Monte del Frà (Veneto)
Monte Rossa (Lombardia)
Paternoster (Basilicata)
Pietradolce (Sicily)
Poggio Antico (Tuscany)
Poggio Le Volpi (Lazio)
Polvanera (Puglia)
Re Manfredi - Cantina Terre degli
  Svevi (Basilicata)
Podere Sapaio (Tuscany)
Tenuta Sette Ponti (Tuscany)
F.lli Tedeschi (Veneto)
Tenimenti Luigi d'Alessandro
  (Tuscany)
Tenuta delle Terre Nere (Sicily)
Villa Matilde (Campania)
Villa Sandi (Veneto)
Luigi Viola (Calabria)
Tenuta Waldgries
  (Alto Adige)
Conti Zecca (Puglia)

HOW TO USE THE GUIDE

WINERY INFORMATION
ANNUAL PRODUCTION
HECTARES UNDER VINE
VITICULTURE METHOD

N.B. The figures related here are provided annually by the producers.
The publisher is not responsible for eventual errors or inconsistencies.

SYMBOLS
O WHITE WINE
⊙ ROSÈ
● RED WINE

RATINGS

MODERATELY GOOD TO GOOD WINES IN THEIR RESPECTIVE CATEGORIES

VERY GOOD TO EXCELLENT WINES IN THEIR RESPECTIVE CATEGORIES

VERY GOOD TO EXCELLENT WINES THAT WENT FORWARD TO THE FINAL TASTINGS

EXCELLENT WINES IN THEIR RESPECTIVE CATEGORIES

WINES RATED IN PREVIOUS EDITIONS OF THE GUIDE ARE INDICATED BY WHITE GLASSES (♀, ♀♀, ♀♀♀),
PROVIDED THEY ARE STILL DRINKING AT THE LEVEL FOR WHICH THE ORIGINAL AWARD WAS MADE.

STAR ★
INDICATES WINERIES THAT HAVE WON TEN TRE BICCHIERI AWARDS FOR EACH STAR

PRICE RANGES
1 up to 5 euro	2 from € 5.01 to € 10.00
3 from € 10.01 to € 15.00	4 from € 15.01 to € 20.00
5 from € 20.01 to € 30.00	6 from € 30.01 to € 40.00
7 from € 40.01 to € 50.00	8 more than € 50.01

PRICES INDICATED REFER TO AVERAGE PRICES IN WINE STORES

ASTERISK *
INDICATES ESPECIALLY GOOD VALUE WINES

ABBREVIATIONS

A. A.	Alto Adige	P.R.	Peduncolo Rosso
C.	Colli		(red bunchstem)
Cl.	Classico	P.	Prosecco
C.S.	Cantina Sociale	Rif. Agr.	Riforma Agraria
	(co-operative winery)		(agrarian reform)
CEV	Colli Etruschi Viterbesi	Ris.	Riserva
Cons.	Consorzio	Sel.	Selezione
Coop.Agr.	Cooperativa Agricola	Sup.	Superiore
	(farming co-operative)	TdF	Terre di Franciacorta
C. B.	Colli Bolognesi	V.	Vigna (vineyard)
C. P.	Colli Piacentini	Vign.	Vigneto (vineyard)
Et.	Etichetta (label)	V. T.	Vendemmia Tardiva
FCO	Friuli Colli Orientali		(late harvest)
M.	Metodo (method)	V. V.	Vecchia Vigna/Vecchie Vigne
M.to	Monferrato		(old vine /old vines)
OP	Oltrepò Pavese		

VALLE D'AOSTA

Valle d'Aosta is a representative region when it comes to quality wine. Its appeal to tourists means that it offers wines in every price range, including daily-drinking selections, more approachable whites and reds. But you'd also expect outstanding, premium wines from a region with so few vineyards, wines capable of shining a light on Valle d'Aosta throughout Italy and even the world. And today that's the case — only production volumes prevent the region from increasing its exports. With a mountain climate that's unique for Italy, and with vineyards that range from the valley floor to considerable elevations (from 350 to more than 1100 meters above sea level), Valle d'Aosta gives rise to truly singular wines. Foremost, we have to consider its ampelography, in which international grapes (Chardonnay, Pinot Grigio or Malvoisie, Sauvignon, Viognier, Müller-Thurgau, Gamay, Pinot Nero, Merlot, Syrah, Grenache)are accompanied by lesser-known varieties (Moscato Bianco, Petite Arvine, Prié Blanc, Mebbiolo, Fumin, Petit Rouge, Vien de Nus, Prëmetta, Cornalin, Mayolet, Vuillermin). When we take into consideration the region's climate, the result is a richness and variety of wines that can't be found anywhere else, from subtle and taut whites to potent, sapid reds. But such a variety also risks creating confusion in the minds of consumers, and so it is that we're seeing vignerons and cooperative wineries moving in certain directions, while taking into account territorial tradition. In terms of its whites, fresh and fragrant Petite Arvines are making a name for themselves, contrasted by richer, fuller whites frequently vinified in barriques, like Chardonnay and Pinot Grigio. On the other hand, traditional Moscato di Chambave and Blanc de Morgex et de La Salle have maintained a presence (with sparkling versions as well). When it comes to the region's reds, we're seeing a desire to produce great, international Syrahs, and Pinot Neros especially. Nevertheless, full-bodied Fumins are still popular as well. The Tre Bicchieri awarded confirm these trends. The top-tier includes a Petite Arvine (the Sopraquota 900), a Chardonnay, a Pinot Grigio, two Pinot Neros and, finally, a Passito di Moscato, all produced by a strong hub of wineries that continue to make this small region known throughout the world.

★Maison Anselmet

FRAZ. VEREYTAZ, 30
11018 VILLENEUVE [AO]
TEL. +39 0165904851
www.maisonanselmet.it

CELLAR SALES
PRE-BOOKED VISITS
ANNUAL PRODUCTION 80,000 bottles
HECTARES UNDER VINE 11.50

Maison Anselmet is a shining light in Valle d'Aosta viticulture. Its management is entrusted to Giorgio, who can count on the full support of his family. Though attached to tradition, the winery has also adopted innovative technologies that both optimize production temperatures and regulate the terrain's condition by limiting the use of treatments, resulting in healthy, vital grapes. The Maison's prime location in the heart of Valle d'Aosta's symbolic Torrette DOC, allows it to produce a wide range with traditional varietals that is enjoyed in Italy and around the world. The Semel Pater is a splendid Pinot Nero offering a concentrated, delicate bouquet of spicy notes that harmonize with the fruity, majestic palate of tight-fitting tannins that gradually open in a long finish. Their Chardonnay is remarkable, with hints of sweet spices emerging from the buttery, honeyed opening notes and leading into a complex, fresh and balanced palate. Their interesting Syrah, delivers notes of black berries and pepper, proveing delicate and harmonious.

● Valle d'Aosta Pinot Noir Semel Pater '17	♟♟♟ 7
● Le Prisonnier '17	♟♟ 8
○ Valle d'Aosta Chardonnay Élevé en Fût de Chêne '17	♟♟ 5
● Valle d'Aosta Syrah Henri Élevé en Fût de Chêne '16	♟♟ 6
○ Valle d'Aosta Chardonnay Élevé en Fût de Chêne '15	♟♟♟ 5
○ Valle d'Aosta Chardonnay Élevé en Fût de Chêne '11	♟♟♟ 5
○ Valle d'Aosta Chardonnay Main et Cœur '16	♟♟♟ 6
● Valle d'Aosta Pinot Noir Semel Pater '13	♟♟♟ 8

Château Feuillet

LOC. CHÂTEAU FEUILLET, 12
11010 SAINT PIERRE
TEL. +39 3287673880
www.chateaufeuillet.it

CELLAR SALES
ACCOMMODATION AND RESTAURANT SERVICE
ANNUAL PRODUCTION 45,000 bottles
HECTARES UNDER VINE 6.00
VITICULTURE METHOD Certified Biodynamic

Torrette, a historic area of regional winemaking, is just a few kilometers from Aosta in the direction of Mont Blanc. Maurizio Fiorano's Château Feuillet is located here in Saint Pierre. He's shy but sunny and chatting with him is always very stimulating. The company is relatively young but in a short time it has earned a place among the other excellent regional wineries by respecting local traditions and mainting very high standards of quality. Their Petite Arvine, intense with floral and citrus notes, especially grapefruit, is refreshing and offers just a hint of sweetness. The Torrette Superiore pours an impenetrable ruby with aromas of jam and plum followed by still evident tannins in a full-bodied structure. The Fumin delivers rustic fruity scents and a harmonious palate with elegant tannins. Their beautiful ruby Syrah's greets the nose with intense, persistent red fruit and notes of white pepper leading to a refreshing, pulpy drink.

○ Valle d'Aosta Petite Arvine '18	♟♟ 3*
● Valle d'Aosta Fumin '18	♟♟ 4
● Valle d'Aosta Syrah '18	♟♟ 3
● Valle d'Aosta Torrette Sup. '17	♟♟ 3
○ Valle d'Aosta Petite Arvine '12	♟♟♟ 3*
○ Valle d'Aosta Petite Arvine '11	♟♟♟ 3*
○ Valle d'Aosta Petite Arvine '10	♟♟♟ 3*
● Valle d'Aosta Cornalin '16	♟♟ 4
● Valle d'Aosta Fumin '17	♟♟ 4
● Valle d'Aosta Fumin '16	♟♟ 4
○ Valle d'Aosta Petite Arvine '16	♟♟ 3
○ Valle d'Aosta Petite Arvine '15	♟♟ 3*
● Valle d'Aosta Syrah '17	♟♟ 3
● Valle d'Aosta Torrette Sup. '16	♟♟ 3*
● Valle d'Aosta Torrette Sup. '15	♟♟ 3
● Valle d'Aosta Torrette Sup. '14	♟♟ 3

★★Les Crêtes

LOC. VILLETOS, 50
11010 AYMAVILLES [AO]
TEL. +39 0165902274
www.lescretes.it

CELLAR SALES
PRE-BOOKED VISITS
ANNUAL PRODUCTION 200,000 bottles
HECTARES UNDER VINE 20.00
SUSTAINABLE WINERY

Les Cretes has always been a leader in Valle d'Aosta winemaking, though its creator, the poet of wine Constantine Charrère, is gradually exiting the stage. Giulio Corti's entry into the family, beside Elena and her sister Eleonora, has brought new vitality. The modern structure in Aymavilles represents everything that makes this winery intriguing, with new technology and innovative choices that are ahead of their time. The vineyards focus on traditional varietals, especially Chardonnay, which has carried the estate's name all over the world. The Chardonnay Cuvée Bois, their workhorse, stands out as a wine with an intense color, notes of acacia flowers, apricot and peach; elegantly spiced, it proves rich and refreshing with mineral notes and a long, enveloping finish. Even their entry-level Chardonnay offers perfumes of broom flowers enlivened by fine, sapid and complex mineral notes. The Syrah opens with delicate fruity notes that precede the rich, bold palate.

○ Valle d'Aosta Chardonnay Cuvée Bois '17	♟♟♟ 6
○ Valle d'Aosta Chardonnay '18	♟♟ 4
● Valle d'Aosta Syrah '17	♟♟ 4
● Valle d'Aosta Torrette Sup. '17	♟♟ 4
○ Valle d'Aosta Chardonnay Cuvée Bois '16	♟♟♟ 6
○ Valle d'Aosta Chardonnay Cuvée Bois '13	♟♟♟ 6
○ Valle d'Aosta Chardonnay Cuvée Bois '10	♟♟♟ 6
○ Valle d'Aosta Chardonnay Cuvée Bois '09	♟♟♟ 6
● Valle d'Aosta Nebbiolo Sommet '15	♟♟♟ 6
○ Valle d'Aosta Petite Arvine '13	♟♟♟ 3*
● Valle d'Aosta Syrah Côteau La Tour '14	♟♟♟ 4*

La Crotta di Vegneron

P.ZZA RONCAS, 2
11023 CHAMBAVE [AO]
TEL. +39 016646670
www.lacrotta.it

CELLAR SALES
PRE-BOOKED VISITS
RESTAURANT SERVICE
ANNUAL PRODUCTION 200,000 bottles
HECTARES UNDER VINE 31.00

The Crotta di Vegneron, located in Chambave, is a true touchstone of Valle d'Aosta wine. For a long time, the winery has followed a classic approach, including using traditional, local varieties, and has established itself firmly in both Italian and international markets. Sweet wines have long been the driving force, but now the range also embraces red and white wines, reaching consistently high levels of quality. The Moscato Passito Prieuré is always excellent: golden with very refined, layered hints of raisins and dried figs followed by a wonderful, balanced and enduring palate. The Syrah offers very elegant notes of spices, pepper and red berries with a well-defined, refreshing and lasting flavor. Their original Fumin combines notes of garden vegetables and fruit with a well-articulated, nuanced drink. The Nus Malvoisie proves very enjoyable, offering vivid aromas of pear, a complex palate of soft body typical of the variety and a finish with delicate nuances of bitterness.

○ Valle d'Aosta Chambave Moscato Passito Prieuré '17	♟♟ 5
● Valle d'Aosta Fumin Esprit Follet '17	♟♟ 5
● Valle d'Aosta Syrah Crème '17	♟♟ 5
○ Valle d'Aosta Nus Malvoisie '18	♟♟ 3
○ Valle d'Aosta Chambave Moscato Passito Prieuré '15	♟♟♟ 5
○ Valle d'Aosta Chambave Moscato Passito Prieuré '13	♟♟♟ 5
○ Valle d'Aosta Chambave Moscato Passito Prieuré '12	♟♟♟ 5
○ Valle d'Aosta Chambave Moscato Passito Prieuré '11	♟♟♟ 5
○ Valle d'Aosta Chambave Moscato Passito Prieuré '08	♟♟♟ 5
● Valle d'Aosta Fumin Esprit Follet '09	♟♟♟ 3

VALLE D'AOSTA

Caves Cooperatives de Donnas

VIA ROMA, 97
11020 DONNAS [AO]
TEL. +39 0125807096
www.donnasvini.it

CELLAR SALES
PRE-BOOKED VISITS
ANNUAL PRODUCTION 150,000 bottles
HECTARES UNDER VINE 26.00

Arriving in Valle d'Aosta from the south, Donnas is one of the first towns. The Cooperative was founded here in this long-established area because properties are extremely small. The varietals and training systems here are also different; the terrain is so difficult to work that a monorail had to be built to transport materials to and from the vineyards. Nebbiolo, locally called 'picotenner' or 'picotendro', is grown on overhead arbors in a form of truly heroic viticulture. The mountain people here are proud, tied to both tradition and traditional flavors. Their Napoléon, a brilliant garnet Nebbiolo, stands out with intense aromas of red fruit and great persistence with very fine-grained tannins. The Donnas is quite good, with notes of fruit macerated in alcohol and notable tannins with an intense, fleshy closure. The Vieilles Vignes continues to evolve, but with strong spicy notes covering the fruit it still needs time.

Cave Gargantua

FRAZ. CLOS CHATEL, 1
11020 GRESSAN [AO]
TEL. +39 3299271999
www.cavegargantua.it

ANNUAL PRODUCTION 25,000 bottles
HECTARES UNDER VINE 4.50

The Pila basin and its amphitheater overlook the city of Aosta. Gressan, at the foot of the famous tourist haven, is covered with vineyards cared for by many small producers who often sell the grapes. The Cuneaz brothers have chosen another route and their La Cave Gargantua has seen continuous growth over the years in terms of quality, reliability, and successful interpretation of the territory. Love for the work, the land and the vineyards is evident in their contagious enthusiasm. Their ruby red Torrette Supérieur Labié '17 proved very successful. The beautifully delicate aroma carries hints of red and black berries that harmonize with bark and tobacco, leading into a rich palate with elegant, gradually developing tannins. The Vin de la Fée is impressive, with fine, elegant aromas of mountain herbs followed by rose and spices, offering nice persistence and freshness. The Impasse, which opens with spicy, fruity scents and reveals its great complexity, is definitely worth a try.

● Valle d'Aosta Donnas Napoléon '16	♟♟ 4
● Valle d'Aosta Donnas '16	♟♟ 5
● Valle d'Aosta Donnas Sup. Vieilles Vignes '15	♟♟ 5
● Valle d'Aosta Donnas '15	♟♟ 4
● Valle d'Aosta Donnas '14	♟♟ 4
● Valle d'Aosta Donnas '13	♟♟ 4
● Valle d'Aosta Donnas '11	♟♟ 2*
● Valle d'Aosta Donnas Napoléon '15	♟♟ 5
● Valle d'Aosta Donnas Napoléon '14	♟♟ 5
● Valle d'Aosta Donnas Napoléon '13	♟♟ 5
● Valle d'Aosta Donnas Napoléon '11	♟♟ 3
● Valle d'Aosta Donnas Sup. V. V. '13	♟♟ 5
● Valle d'Aosta Donnas Sup. V. V. '12	♟♟ 5
● Valle d'Aosta Donnas Sup. Vieilles Vignes '14	♟♟ 5

● Valle d'Aosta Torrette Sup. Labiè '17	♟♟ 4
○ Spillo d'Oro	♟♟ 5
● Valle d'Aosta Rosso Impasse Elevée Fût de Chêne '16	♟♟ 5
● Valle d'Aosta Vin de la Fée '18	♟♟ 5
● Daphne '15	♟♟ 5
○ Valle d'Aosta Chardonnay Daphne '16	♟♟ 5
● Valle d'Aosta Pinot Noir '16	♟♟ 3*
● Valle d'Aosta Rosso Impasse '15	♟♟ 5
● Valle d'Aosta Torrette Sup. Labiè '16	♟♟ 4
● Vin de la Fée '16	♟♟ 5

★Lo Triolet

LOC. JUNOD, 7
11010 INTROD [AO]
TEL. +39 016595437
www.lotriolet.vievini.it

CELLAR SALES
PRE-BOOKED VISITS
ANNUAL PRODUCTION 42,000 bottles
HECTARES UNDER VINE 5.00

The Triolet has always been a flagship of viticulture in Valle d'Aosta. Over time, it has distinguished itself with production that respects the environment and concentrates on local cultivars, not just those with white berries. Owner Martin and his family's guest reception and accommodation give visitors not only the chance to learn about the winery and its wines but to discover the territory, the customs and traditions of a village that has hosted popes and cardinals. The Pinot Gris is unforgettable. Exciting scents of ripe pears and flowers lead into a remarkably structured drink with a long and pleasantly almond finish. Their Petite Arvine wafts with airy and refined notes of citrus, mandarin in particular, and a fresh, structured palate. The interesting Fumin delivers impenetrable color, fruity aromas preceding spicy quinine and licorice, and overall excellent structure. The Coteau Barrage needs further bottle aging .

○ Valle d'Aosta Pinot Gris '18	♥♥♥ 4*
○ Valle d'Aosta Petite Arvine '18	♥♥ 5
● Valle d'Aosta Coteau Barrage '17	♥♥ 4
● Valle d'Aosta Fumin '17	♥♥ 5
● Valle d'Aosta Fumin '16	♥♥♥ 5
○ Valle d'Aosta Pinot Gris '16	♥♥♥ 5
○ Valle d'Aosta Pinot Gris '15	♥♥♥ 5
○ Valle d'Aosta Pinot Gris '14	♥♥♥ 3*
○ Valle d'Aosta Pinot Gris '13	♥♥♥ 3*
○ Valle d'Aosta Pinot Gris '12	♥♥♥ 3*
○ Valle d'Aosta Pinot Gris '09	♥♥♥ 3
○ Valle d'Aosta Pinot Gris '08	♥♥♥ 3*
○ Valle d'Aosta Pinot Gris '05	♥♥♥ 3*
○ Valle d'Aosta Pinot Gris Élevé en Barriques '10	♥♥♥ 5

Cave Mont Blanc de Morgex et La Salle

FRAZ. LA RUINE
CHEMIN DES ÎLES, 31
11017 MORGEX [AO]
TEL. +39 0165800331
www.caveduvinblanc.com

CELLAR SALES
PRE-BOOKED VISITS
ANNUAL PRODUCTION 140,000 bottles
HECTARES UNDER VINE 19.00

On the slopes of Mont Blanc it's not uncommon to find someone rather curiously lying under a very low arbor. They are working the ground-hugging vineyards of Priè Blanc that produce the famous Blanc de Morgex, and La Salle, the appellation at the highest elevation in Europe. Snow can still be found in March or even April in this area, and the cultivated plots are truly microscopic. The varietal has a very short but remarkable growth cycle. Their sparkling wines again proved very impressive in this tasting. We recommend Pas Dosé Glacier with its very fine, persistent perlage, notes of fresh herbs and sour plum harmonized with hints of bread; it offers an elegant and persistent development. The still Rayon is quite good, with intense mountain herbs and delicate floral notes followed by rennet apple and a pleasant structure on the palate with a pulpy finish. The Extra Brut is very pleasant, perfumed with jasmine and orange blossom.

○ Valle d'Aosta Blanc de Morgex et de La Salle Pas Dosé Glacier M. Cl. '16	♥♥ 5
○ Valle d'Aosta Blanc de Morgex et de La Salle Brut Blanc du Blanc M. Cl. '16	♥♥ 5
○ Valle d'Aosta Blanc de Morgex et de La Salle Extra Brut 1187 M. Cl. '16	♥♥ 6
○ Valle d'Aosta Blanc de Morgex et de La Salle Rayon '18	♥♥ 3
○ Valle d'Aosta Blanc de Morgex et de La Salle Brut Blanc du Blanc M. Cl. '15	♥♥ 4
○ Valle d'Aosta Blanc de Morgex et de La Salle Extra Brut X.T. M.Cl. '15	♥♥ 6

Elio Ottin

FRAZ. POROSSAN NEYVES, 209
11100 AOSTA
TEL. +39 3474071331
www.ottinvini.it

CELLAR SALES
PRE-BOOKED VISITS
ANNUAL PRODUCTION 60,000 bottles
HECTARES UNDER VINE 8.00
SUSTAINABLE WINERY

Ottin, run by Elio and son Nicolas, is on the outskirts of Aosta. It marks the beginning of a new generation of great wines interpreted in a modern style that is refreshing, complex and fragrant. Wineries usually have a stand-out wine, but given its uniform high level of quality this isn't true at Ottin. In addition to its Petite Arvine, its interpretation of Pinot Nero (a moody variety but one that can deliver great results) improves every year. The impressive Pinot Noir L'Emerico, opens with pronounced and fine notes of fruit, raspberry, spices, tobacco and leather with a well-structured, harmonious and balanced palate. The remarkable Petite Arvine has intense and brilliant color, floral and citrusy aromas, and significant structure with a sapid and seemingly endless finish. Their interesting entry-level Pinot Noir delivers refined notes of strawberry and a velvety persistence. The Petite Arvine Nuances barrique version is also very interesting.

● Valle d'Aosta Pinot Noir L'Emerico '16	▼▼▼	6
○ Valle d'Aosta Petite Arvine '18	▼▼	4
○ Valle d'Aosta Petite Arvine Nuances '17	▼▼	5
● Valle d'Aosta Pinot Noir '17	▼▼	5
● Valle d'Aosta Fumin '12	♀♀♀	3*
○ Valle d'Aosta Petite Arvine '17	♀♀♀	4*
○ Valle d'Aosta Petite Arvine '16	♀♀♀	5
○ Valle d'Aosta Petite Arvine '15	♀♀♀	5
○ Valle d'Aosta Petite Arvine '14	♀♀♀	4*
○ Valle d'Aosta Petite Arvine '12	♀♀♀	3*
○ Valle d'Aosta Petite Arvine '11	♀♀♀	3*
○ Valle d'Aosta Petite Arvine '10	♀♀♀	3*

Ermes Pavese

S.DA PINETA, 26
11017 MORGEX [AO]
TEL. +39 0165800053
www.ermespavese.it

CELLAR SALES
PRE-BOOKED VISITS
ANNUAL PRODUCTION 32,000 bottles
HECTARES UNDER VINE 6.00
VITICULTURE METHOD Certified Organic

One of the last villages before reaching Mont Blanc, is Morgex, which is famous for its wine. Soil is almost non-existent at the foot of the massive mountain and viticulture would seem virtually impossible. But despite such harsh conditions, Ermes Pavese has carved out its own space with a limited production of stellar quality every year. Natural events over the last few years brought the wine production in Valle d'Aosta to its knees, but Pavese overcame the obstacles and once again his wines were worth the wait, paying off in both still and sparkling versions. Their successful Blanc de Morgex '18, with characteristic straw color and greenish reflections, offers pleasant hints of white flowers, proving well-structured with a refreshing, lasting finish and excellent overall harmony. The very enjoyable Metodo Classico pours with fine perlage and floral scents, delivering a juicy, spirited flavor. Their UnoPercento is a single release and definitely worth trying for the hints of chamomile and citrus that lead to a rich and complex palate with a bittersweet finish.

○ Valle d'Aosta Vin Blanc de Morgex et La Salle '18	▼▼	4
○ UnoPercento	▼▼	8
○ Valle d'Aoste Blanc de Morgex et de La Salle Pavese XXXVI Pas Dosé M. Cl. '14	▼▼	5
○ Valle d'Aosta Vin Blanc de Morgex et La Salle Pavese Pas Dosé M.Cl. XXIV '15	▼	5
○ Valle d'Aosta Vin Blanc de Morgex et La Salle '16	♀♀	4
○ Valle d'Aosta Vin Blanc de Morgex et La Salle Le Sette Scalinate Carlo Pavese '14	♀♀	4
○ Valle d'Aoste Blanc de Morgex et de La Salle Pavese XXXVI Pas Dosé M. Cl. '13	♀♀	5

Rosset Terroir

LOC. TORRENT DE MAILLOD, 4
11020 QUART [AO]
TEL. +39 0165774111
www.rosseterroir.it

CELLAR SALES
ANNUAL PRODUCTION 30,000 bottles
HECTARES UNDER VINE 7.00

Rosseterroir's attention to the smallest detail has enabled it to shine in the firmament of Italian winemaking. The winery's enologist was joined by an internationally acclaimed 'heavy-weight' consultant and the results are easy to recognizable. Year after year, the strong growth is evident in the new vineyards and the highly technological, avant-garde cellar where using wood barrels are used judiciously beside terra cotta jars. The Sopraquota 900 is superlative again this year; its intense straw-yellow with a fine, layered bouquet of white fruit and balanced spices lead into a rich, full yet still refreshing palate with a long finish that is in a class of its own. The Syrah is also not to be missed for its vibrant, concentrated nose of quinine, pepper, fruit and black berries followed by great structure and flavor. The very interesting Pinot Gris delivers a fruity nose with evident notes of ripe pear with a full, highly concentrated palate, both refreshing and harmonious. The Chardonnay opens on buttery notes that precede lightly spiced white fruit that proves well-balanced and zesty.

○ Sopraquota 900 '18	♛♛♛ 4*
● Valle d'Aosta Syrah '17	♛♛ 5
○ Vallée d'Aoste Pinot Gris '18	♛♛ 5
○ Valle d'Aosta Chardonnay '18	♛♛ 5
● Valle d'Aosta Cornalin '16	♛♛♛ 4*
● Valle d'Aosta Cornalin '15	♛♛♛ 4*
● Valle d'Aosta Syrah '13	♛♛♛ 4*
○ Valle d'Aosta Chambave Muscat '16	♛♛ 4
○ Valle d'Aosta Chardonnay '17	♛♛ 4
○ Valle d'Aosta Chardonnay '16	♛♛ 4
○ Valle d'Aosta Chardonnay '14	♛♛ 4
○ Valle d'Aosta Chardonnay '12	♛♛ 4
● Valle d'Aosta Cornalin '17	♛♛ 4
● Valle d'Aosta Syrah '15	♛♛ 4
● Valle d'Aosta Syrah '14	♛♛ 4
○ Vallée d'Aoste Pinot Gris '17	♛♛ 5

La Vrille

LOC. GRANGEON, 1
11020 VERRAYES [AO]
TEL. +39 0166543018
www.lavrille-agritourisme.com

CELLAR SALES
PRE-BOOKED VISITS
ACCOMMODATION AND RESTAURANT SERVICE
ANNUAL PRODUCTION 18,000 bottles
HECTARES UNDER VINE 3.90
VITICULTURE METHOD Certified Organic
SUSTAINABLE WINERY

Breathe in the new air. For the last few years attention had been divided between the diversification of other agricultural products, the vineyards and the agritourism. This year focus returned to winemaking , with obvious results that still fully respect the environment and follow organic dictates. Owner Hervè Deguillame is a shy, solid man who melts when he starts talking about his wines: a visit to the cellar is more than recommended. The dry version of the Muscat '17 is truly fantastic; it offers incomparable olfactory energy that passes from moss to rose to medicinal herbs, leading to a harmonious palate of great elegance with a long and vital finish. Their equally successful Muscat Flétri, a well-orchestrated and lively golden passito, delivers concentrated and refined notes of raisin, honey and dried fruit; the extraordinarily concentrated flavor closes with an intense, persistent finish. Their reds are also excellent, particularly the Vuillermin, which carries pleasant notes of alcohol-soaked red berries.

○ Valle d'Aosta Chambave Muscat Flétri '17	♛♛♛ 7
○ Valle d'Aosta Chambave Muscat '17	♛♛ 5
● Valle d'Aosta Vuillermin '16	♛♛ 5
● Valle d'Aosta Fumin '15	♛♛ 6
○ Valle d'Aosta Chambave Muscat '12	♛♛♛ 4*
○ Valle d'Aosta Chambave Muscat Flétri '16	♛♛♛ 7
○ Valle d'Aosta Chambave Muscat Flétri '15	♛♛♛ 7
○ Valle d'Aosta Chambave Muscat Flétri '14	♛♛♛ 7
○ Valle d'Aosta Chambave Muscat Flétri '11	♛♛♛ 6
○ Valle d'Aosta Chambave Muscat Flétri '10	♛♛♛ 5
○ Valle d'Aosta Chambave Muscat Flétri '07	♛♛♛ 4*

Grosjean

FRAZ. OLLIGNAN, 2
11020 QUART [AO]
TEL. +39 0165775791
www.grosjeanvins.it

CELLAR SALES
PRE-BOOKED VISITS
ANNUAL PRODUCTION 120,000 bottles
HECTARES UNDER VINE 12.00
VITICULTURE METHOD Certified Organic

● Valle d'Aosta Fumin V. Rovettaz '16	❦❦ 5
☉ Montmary Extra Brut Rosé M. Cl.	❦❦ 6
○ Valle d'Aosta Petite Arvine V. Rovettaz '18	❦❦ 4

Institut Agricole Régional

LOC. RÉGION LA ROCHÈRE, 1A
11100 AOSTA
TEL. +39 0165215811
www.iaraosta.it

CELLAR SALES
PRE-BOOKED VISITS
ANNUAL PRODUCTION 50,000 bottles
HECTARES UNDER VINE 7.30

● Valle d'Aosta Fumin '16	❦❦ 4
○ Valle d'Aosta Petite Arvine '18	❦❦ 4
○ Valle d'Aosta Pinot Gris '18	❦ 3

Cave des Onze Communes

LOC. URBAINS, 14
11010 AYMAVILLES [AO]
TEL. +39 0165902912
www.caveonzecommunes.it

CELLAR SALES
PRE-BOOKED VISITS
ANNUAL PRODUCTION 460,000 bottles
VITICULTURE METHOD Certified Organic

○ Valle d'Aosta Gewürztraminer '18	❦❦ 4
○ Valle d'Aosta Petit Arvine '18	❦❦ 4
○ Valle d'Aosta Muscat Petit Grain Flétry '18	❦ 5

André Pellissier

FRAZ. BUSSAN DESSOUS, 17
11010 SAINT PIERRE [AO]
TEL. +39 3405704029
andreperllissier@libero.it

CELLAR SALES
ANNUAL PRODUCTION 7,000 bottles
HECTARES UNDER VINE 2.00

● Valle d'Aosta Syrah '17	❦❦ 4
● Valle d'Aosta Torrette Sup. '17	❦❦ 4

Pianta Grossa

VIA ROMA, 213
11020 DONNAS [AO]
TEL. +39 3480077404
www.piantagrossadonnas.it

CELLAR SALES
PRE-BOOKED VISITS
ANNUAL PRODUCTION 10,000 bottles
HECTARES UNDER VINE 2.50

● Valle d'Aosta Donnas Georgos '16	❦❦ 7
● Valle d'Aosta Nebbiolo Dessus '17	❦❦ 5
● Valle d'Aosta Nebbiolo 396 '17	❦ 4

La Source

LOC. BUSSAN DESSOUS, 1
11010 SAINT PIERRE
TEL. +39 0165904038
www.lasource.it

CELLAR SALES
PRE-BOOKED VISITS
ANNUAL PRODUCTION 40,000 bottles
HECTARES UNDER VINE 7.00

○ Valle d'Aosta Bianco Ensemblo '17	❦❦ 3
● Valle d'Aosta Cornalin '16	❦ 3

PIEDMONT

Three cheers for Nebbiolo, Piedmont's crown prince, the grape behind some 46 of the wines awarded in the region, 26 Barolos, 13 Barbarescos, 3 Roeros and 4 Alto Piemonte reds. Such results were made possibile by excellent years (see the 2013 Barolo reserves and 2016 Barbarescos) brought out by increasingly attentive viticulture. Over the next years, Langa, rich in Barolo and to some extent Barbaresco as well, will find itself caught in a difficult battle with a worthy adversary: itself. Overall some 74 Tre Bicchieri were awarded in the region. With great pleasure we also note a certain international notoriety for their whites and for a solid number of cultivars long (and wrongfully) considered less important. Some eight dry whites earned top marks, from north to south, Erbaluce in the lake district and foothills of Caluso and Ivrea, Cortese shines in Gavi (an area that borders with Liguria). Tortona's Timorasso has, in a short time, become an absolute must, don't forget Arneis, Roero's undisputed king, either. Finally, we can't leave out Moscato Bianco, a grape that's as special as it is mistreated, that the world envies us for, even if 2018, with the cold and the rain, wasn't a great year for the grape. In terms of Metodo Classico, Piedmont is deploying a formidable platoon, bolstered by Canellese's long history and the peculiarities of the Belbo and Bormida valleys. Finally free of its self-imposed yoke, Alta Langa is becoming a top-quality and popular appellation. We close by mentioning Monferrato. To the west it's a land of outstanding Barberas that can be enjoyed immediately or after some time in the bottle, while the east is seeing the rebirth of a grape and a wine forgotten by consumers, Grignolino. Once considered noble for its innate class, Grignolino is regaining its footing, with three awarded wines also demonstrating its aging power. Finally, we welcome those wineries receiving their first Tre Bicchieri: Garesio, Fortemasso, Ada Nada, Cascina delle Rose and Platinetti. Among these, we also find the Girgnolino M 2013 produced by Santa Caterina, who received our prestigious 'Up-and-Coming Winery' award, while our award for 'Best Value for Money' goes to Pico Maccario's Barbera d'Asti Lavignone '18.

460 Casina Bric

LOC. CASCINA BRICCO
VIA SORELLO, 1A
12060 BAROLO [CN]
TEL. +39 335283468
www.casinabric-barolo.it

CELLAR SALES
PRE-BOOKED VISITS
ANNUAL PRODUCTION 45,000 bottles
HECTARES UNDER VINE 10.00

Cultivating Nebbiolo grapes at these altitudes (460 stands for the average elevation of La Morra's vineyards) has its benefits, considering the recent string of hot years. But it also requires a notable agronomic sensitivity, especially when it comes to the management of vegetation and sun exposure. And Gianluca Viberti, even more than a capable cellar man, is a passionate and expert farmer. Their selection is gradually expanding thanks both to their sparkling wines and their new property in Serralunga d'Alba. The Barolo Bricco delle Viole '15 is already quite open on notes of licorice and jammy echoes, while on the palate it proves delicately marked by tannins. The Barolo del Comune di Barolo '15 is more fruity and floral, not particularly muscular, but exhibits commendable balance. Highly pleasant berries, as well as refreshing sapidity, characterize the complex Nebbiolo d'Alba Spumante Brut Nature Rosé Metodo Classico.

★Abbona

B.GO SAN LUIGI, 40
12063 DOGLIANI [CN]
TEL. +39 0173721317
www.abbona.com

CELLAR SALES
PRE-BOOKED VISITS
ANNUAL PRODUCTION 350,000 bottles
HECTARES UNDER VINE 50.00

Marziano Abbona never stops. His doctor friend tries to remind him that, as he's been working since he was 14, the vigneron has now been at it for more than 50 years. But it's no use, his crus are looked after with the care that they deserve. In part it's because of increasing international attention, from Barolo Ravera to Dogliani Papà Celso, Barolo Cerviano and the exciting Viognier Cinerino. While this guide is going to print, they're preparing a new agritourism, elegant accommodations that will enrich their already prestigious underground cellar. The Barolo Pressenda '15 is rich in pulp and texture. The elegant Barolo Ravera '15, a wine redolent of incense and mint, is just a bit less firmly structured. Hints of cocoa powder and almond rise up off their splendid Dogliani Papà Celso '18, in a new, magnificent interpretation of the Dolcetto grape. The Barbera d'Alba Rinaldi '17 is still a bit wooded, while the aromatic Viognier Cinerino '18 proves pleasantly sapid and fresh.

● Barolo Bricco delle Viole '15	♈♈ 7
● Barolo del Comune di Barolo '15	♈♈ 6
⊙ Nebbiolo d'Alba Brut Rosè Origo Ginis Cuvée 970	♈♈ 5
⊙ Nebbiolo d'Alba Brut Rosè Origo Ginis M. Cl. '14	♈♈ 5
● Barolo del Comune di Serralunga d'Alba '15	♈ 6
● Ansì '14	♈♈ 4
● Barolo '13	♈♈ 6
● Barolo '12	♈♈ 6
● Barolo '11	♈♈ 6
● Barolo Bricco delle Viole '14	♈♈ 7
● Barolo Bricco delle Viole '13	♈♈ 7
● Barolo Bricco delle Viole '11	♈♈ 7
● Barolo Bricco delle Viole '10	♈♈ 7

● Dogliani Papà Celso '18	♈♈♈ 4*
● Barolo Pressenda '15	♈♈ 7
● Barolo Ravera '15	♈♈ 7
○ Langhe Bianco Cinerino '18	♈♈ 5
● Nebbiolo d'Alba Bricco Barone '17	♈♈ 4
● Barbera d'Alba Rinaldi '17	♈ 4
● Barolo Cerviano '10	♈♈♈ 7
● Barolo Terlo Ravera '08	♈♈♈ 6
● Barolo Terlo Ravera '06	♈♈♈ 6
● Dogliani Papà Celso '17	♈♈♈ 4*
● Dogliani Papà Celso '16	♈♈♈ 4*
● Dogliani Papà Celso '15	♈♈♈ 4*
● Dogliani Papà Celso '13	♈♈♈ 4*
● Dogliani Papà Celso '11	♈♈♈ 3*
● Dogliani Papà Celso '09	♈♈♈ 3
● Dogliani Papà Celso '07	♈♈♈ 3
● Dogliani Papà Celso '06	♈♈♈ 3

Anna Maria Abbona

FRAZ. MONCUCCO, 21
12060 FARIGLIANO [CN]
TEL. +39 0173797228
www.annamariabbona.it

CELLAR SALES
PRE-BOOKED VISITS
ANNUAL PRODUCTION 85,000 bottles
HECTARES UNDER VINE 20.00

Anna Maria Abbona has been overseeing her winery for 25 years. With great foresight, she's always made respect for nature a top priority. Starting with these principles, she makes aromatically focused wines, without too much oak, marked by perfect territorial expression. That's how it's been for her Doglianis and, for some years now, her Barolos as well, all crafted in her Monforte d'Alba cellar. Her husband is behind enology, helped by their son, who's already making a name for himself. Nebbiolo and Dolcetto are interpreted masterfully here, as demonstrated by the scorecard. In particular, the youthful, focused and fresh Barolo Bricco San Pieto '15 charms. It's a wine already endowed with exquisitely classical aromas of quinine, licorice and roses. Black berries, a touch of cocoa powder and an almond finish characterize the excellent Dogliani Superiore San Bernardo '16. The Riesling L'Alman '17, a floral wine of excellent acidity, is coming along well.

● Barolo Bricco San Pietro '15	♟♟ 7
● Dogliani Sup. San Bernardo '16	♟♟ 4
● Barbera d'Alba '18	♟♟ 3
● Barolo del Comune di Castiglione Falletto '15	♟♟ 6
● Dogliani Sup. Maioli '17	♟♟ 3
○ Langhe Nascetta Netta '17	♟♟ 3
● Langhe Nebbiolo '16	♟♟ 3
○ Langhe Riesling L'Alman '17	♟♟ 3
● Dogliani Sorì Dij But '18	♟ 3
● Langhe Dolcetto '18	♟ 2
● Dogliani Sup. San Bernardo '12	♟♟♟ 4*
● Dogliani Sup. San Bernardo '11	♟♟♟ 4*
● Barbera d'Alba '17	♟♟ 2*
● Barolo '14	♟♟ 6
● Barolo Bricco San Pietro '14	♟♟ 6
● Dogliani Sup. San Bernardo '15	♟♟ 4

F.lli Abrigo

LOC. BERFI
VIA MOGLIA GERLOTTO, 2
12055 DIANO D'ALBA [CN]
TEL. +39 017369104
www.abrigofratelli.it

CELLAR SALES
PRE-BOOKED VISITS
ANNUAL PRODUCTION 100,000 bottles
HECTARES UNDER VINE 27.00

The changes are notable, but quality remains high. As a result, those who know this important Diano producer have nothing to fear. The label designs have changed and the names shortened, but the goal is to offer more clarity and directness in identifying their wines — the outcome has been pleasant and precise. In all cases, Walter Abrigo remains an undisputed leader when it comes to Dolcetto di Diano d'Alba, even if the winery's size allows them to make whites and reds, from Alta Langa to their new Barolo Ravera. And this last took home a gold, proving open in its notes of licorice and quinine on a background of red berries. Nice structure and particularly elegant tannins means that it'll continue to evolve for many years. Blackberries and a hint of cocoa powder introduce the Diano d'Alba Sup. Pietrin '17, a wine that's quite warm in its alcohol and marked by a moderate length on the palate. The Diano d'Alba '18 is a high expression of classical style.

● Barolo Ravera '15	♟♟ 7
● Barbera d'Alba Sup. '17	♟♟ 3
● Diano d'Alba '18	♟♟ 2*
● Diano d'Alba Sup. Pietrin '17	♟♟ 3
● Nebbiolo d'Alba '17	♟ 3
● Barbera d'Alba Sup. '16	♟♟ 3
● Barolo Ravera '14	♟♟ 7
● Diano d'Alba Sorì dei Berfi '16	♟♟ 3
● Diano d'Alba Sorì dei Berfi '15	♟♟ 3*
● Diano d'Alba Sup. '16	♟♟ 3*
● Diano d'Alba Sup. Pietrin '13	♟♟ 3
● Dolcetto di Diano d'Alba '17	♟♟ 2*
● Dolcetto di Diano d'Alba Sup. Pietrin '15	♟♟ 3
● Nebbiolo d'Alba '16	♟♟ 3
● Nebbiolo d'Alba Tardiss '15	♟♟ 3
● Nebbiolo d'Alba Tardiss '14	♟♟ 3

Giovanni Abrigo

VIA SANTA CROCE, 9
12055 DIANO D'ALBA [CN]
TEL. +39 017369345
www.abrigo.it

CELLAR SALES
PRE-BOOKED VISITS
ANNUAL PRODUCTION 40,000 bottles
HECTARES UNDER VINE 10.00

Giulio and Sergio just graduated from the Alba School of Enology, but they're already active on their father's 15 hectares of vineyards. Their cellar was recently renovated and enlarged using sustainable methods, from the 'biomass' heating system (which also provides warmth for their house) to the use of an old well. Dolcetto di Diano takes center stage, giving rise to 30,000 bottles a year. As of 2013, it's been accompanied by two hectares of the magnificent Barolo Ravera cru. The Dolcetto di Diano d'Alba Superiore Garabei '17 exhibits an exquisite drinkability rooted in black berries, quinine and hints of tobacco. On the palate it's well-rounded, potent, with pleasant, fresh vegetal notes coming through on the finish. A balsamic touch revives their mouthfilling Barolo Ravera '15, a wine marked by delicate tannins, but that delivers pulp and pleasantness. A special mention for their Nebbiolo d'Alba '17, a wine of rare complexity. But all their selection performed well.

● Barolo Ravera '15	♟♟ 6
● Dolcetto Diano d'Alba Sup. Garabei '17	♟♟ 2*
● Barbera d'Alba Marminela '17	♟♟ 2*
● Nebbiolo d'Alba '17	♟♟ 3
● Dolcetto di Diano d'Alba Sorì dei Crava '18	♟ 2
● Barbera d'Alba Marminela '16	♟♟ 2*
● Barbera d'Alba Marminela '15	♟♟ 2*
● Barolo Ravera '14	♟♟ 6
● Diano d'Alba Sorì dei Crava '15	♟♟ 2*
● Diano d'Alba Sup. Garabei '15	♟♟ 2*
● Dolcetto di Diano d'Alba '17	♟♟ 2*
● Dolcetto di Diano d'Alba Sup. Garabei '16	♟♟ 2*
● Nebbiolo d'Alba '15	♟♟ 3

Orlando Abrigo

VIA CAPPELLETTO, 5
12050 TREISO [CN]
TEL. +39 0173630533
www.orlandoabrigo.it

CELLAR SALES
PRE-BOOKED VISITS
ACCOMMODATION
ANNUAL PRODUCTION 90,000 bottles
HECTARES UNDER VINE 22.00
SUSTAINABLE WINERY

As can be found in Alessandro Masnaghetti's Barbaresco MGA, the Meruzzano vineyard gives rise to particularly compact and vigorous wines. The Montersino cru also allows for wines rich in substance. Giovanni Abrigo's selection follows suit, with texture beating out elegance at all costs, even if his wines are never lacking in aromatic complexity. Much of their charming cellar is underground and covered by earth and roses, a fitting setting for their Foresteria Settevie to age in. The Riserva Rongalio '14, a wine decidedly rich in structure, sees oak still not entirely integrated with its enjoyable, fruity pulp. The youthful Barbaresco Meruzzano '16 features lovely aromas ranging from peach kernel to smoked wood, while it's still a bit stiff in its development. Kudos to their subtle and minty Nebbiolo Valmaggiore '15, while the pleasant Sauvignon D'Amblè '17 stands out for its sensations of citrus and apricot.

● Barbaresco Meruzzano '16	♟♟ 5
● Barbaresco Rongalio Ris. '14	♟♟ 8
○ Langhe Sauvignon D'Amblè '17	♟♟ 2*
○ Langhe Très Plus '17	♟♟ 3
● Nebbiolo d'Alba Valmaggiore '15	♟♟ 5
● Barbaresco Meruzzano '15	♟♟ 5
● Barbaresco Meruzzano '14	♟♟ 5
● Barbaresco Montersino '15	♟♟ 7
● Barbaresco Montersino '14	♟♟ 7
● Barbaresco Montersino '13	♟♟ 7
● Barbaresco Montersino '12	♟♟ 7
● Barbaresco Rongalio Ris. '13	♟♟ 8
● Barbaresco Rongalio Ris. '12	♟♟ 8
● Barbaresco Rongalio Ris. '11	♟♟ 8
○ Langhe Très Plus '16	♟♟ 3

★Giulio Accornero e Figli

CASCINA CA' CIMA, 1
15049 VIGNALE MONFERRATO [AL]
TEL. +39 0142933317
www.accornerovini.it

CELLAR SALES
PRE-BOOKED VISITS
ACCOMMODATION
ANNUAL PRODUCTION 100,000 bottles
HECTARES UNDER VINE 22.00
SUSTAINABLE WINERY

This Menferrina winery never stops growing. This year the project that sees Grignolino aged in wood barrels, the result of Ermanno's initiative, converges in Monferace, an association of Casalese and Asti producers who decided to lend a territorial identity to their products by dusting off a Monferrato appellation whose origins are documented as far back as the 16th century. A commitment to native grape varieties is the cornerstone of an approach that brings together tradition with a vision for the area's future. Theirs is an outstanding selection of wines, with the Bricco del Bosco Vigne Vecchie '15 in exquisite form, the best version yet, and worthy of Tre Bicchieri. The Bricco Battista '16 stirs the soul thanks to its nose-palate symmetry and masterful complexity. The Giulin '16 is harmonious and balance, bringing together aromatic complexity with a rich, full-bodied palate and great charm. The Bricco del Bosco '18 is another must.

● Grignolino del M.to Casalese Bricco del Bosco V. Vecchie '15	♟♟♟ 6
● Barbera del M.to Giulin '16	♟♟ 3*
● Barbera del M.to Sup. Bricco Battista '16	♟♟ 5
● Grignolino del M.to Casalese Bricco del Bosco '18	♟♟ 4
● Casorzo Brigantino '18	♟♟ 2*
● Grignolino del M.to Casalese Bricco del Bosco V. Vecchie '14	♟♟ 6
● M.to Girotondo '16	♟♟ 4
● Barbera del M.to Giulin '15	♟♟♟ 3*
● Barbera del M.to Sup. Bricco Battista '15	♟♟♟ 5
● Barbera del M.to Sup. Bricco Battista '13	♟♟♟ 5
● Barbera del M.to Sup. Bricco Battista '12	♟♟♟ 5

Marco e Vittorio Adriano

FRAZ. SAN ROCCO SENO D'ELVIO, 13A
12051 ALBA [CN]
TEL. +39 0173362294
www.adrianovini.it

CELLAR SALES
PRE-BOOKED VISITS
ANNUAL PRODUCTION 160,000 bottles
HECTARES UNDER VINE 27.00
SUSTAINABLE WINERY

Based in San Rocco Seno d'Elvio, not far from Alba and Barbaresco, this producer makes truly classic, charming wines. Marco and Vittorio's style privileges detail over power, large barrels over barriques, making for an exquisite aromatic precision that can be appreciated by those who love pure Nebbiolo, with soft extraction and subtle, intricate flavor. And that's not to mention their excellent prices, among the lowest of the area. We can taste all the freshness and finesse of the outstanding 2016 vintage in their Barbaresco Basarin, a wine marked by fragrant fruit (to say the least), and adorned by notes of quinine and licorice. On the palate it proves subtle, though complex, developing naturally and with character, only to close with length and vitality. The Barbaresco Sanadeive '16 is just a bit more mature in its aromas of herbs in the sun and flowers. The well-made Barbera d'Alba Superiore '17 and highly pleasant Ardì (made with Moscato) also stood out.

● Barbaresco Basarin '16	♟♟ 5
○ Ardì	♟♟ 2
● Barbaresco Sanadaive '16	♟♟ 5
● Barbera d'Alba Sup. '17	♟♟ 2*
● Barbera d'Alba '18	♟ 2
● Dolcetto d'Alba '18	♟ 3
● Langhe Nebbiolo Cainassa '17	♟ 3
○ Langhe Sauvignon Basarico '18	♟ 3
● Barbaresco Basarin '15	♟♟ 5
● Barbaresco Basarin '14	♟♟ 5
● Barbaresco Basarin Ris. '13	♟♟ 6
● Barbaresco Basarin Ris. '12	♟♟ 6
● Barbaresco Sanadaive '15	♟♟ 5
● Barbaresco Sanadaive '14	♟♟ 5
● Dolcetto d'Alba '15	♟♟ 2*
○ Langhe Sauvignon Basarico '15	♟♟ 3

Claudio Alario

VIA SANTA CROCE, 23
12055 DIANO D'ALBA [CN]
TEL. +39 0173231808
www.alarioclaudio.it

CELLAR SALES
PRE-BOOKED VISITS
ANNUAL PRODUCTION 46,000 bottles
HECTARES UNDER VINE 10.00

The winery that Claudio Alario took over in 1988 has been enlarged and modernized (and don't overlook the presence of young Matteo). Their style is focused on richness of flavor, as can be appreciated in their Dolcetto di Diano d'Alba and in their base level Nebbiolos. The Barolo Riva Roca, with its notable tannic traction, does a nice job demonstrating this, even if it comes from their delicate Verduno vineyards. Their solid, reliable selection should be on your list. Black berries and almond introduce their pleasant Sorì Montagrillo '18. The Sorì Pradurent '17, which undergoes a delicate stay in oak, proves very fruit-forward, while the Sorì Costa Fiore '18 is robust and youthful. The Barolo Riva Rocca '15, already guaranteed drinking, exhibits discernible, though not astringent, tannins, while the multi-award winning Barolo Sorano '15 is just a bit lacking in freshness. Pleasant notes of red berries and a touch of oak characterize their tasty Nebbiolo d'Alba Cascinotto '17.

● Barolo Riva Rocca '15	♛♛ 5
● Barbera d'Alba Valletta '17	♛♛ 4
● Barolo Sorano '15	♛♛ 6
● Dolcetto di Diano d'Alba Sorì Costa Fiore '18	♛♛ 2*
● Dolcetto di Diano d'Alba Sorì Montagrillo '18	♛♛ 2*
● Dolcetto di Diano d'Alba Sup. Sorì Pradurent '17	♛♛ 3
● Nebbiolo d'Alba Cascinotto '17	♛♛ 4
● Barolo Sorano '05	♛♛♛ 7
● Barolo Riva Rocca '14	♛♛ 5
● Barolo Riva Rocca '13	♛♛ 5
● Barolo Riva Rocca '12	♛♛ 5
● Barolo Sorano '14	♛♛ 6

★F.lli Alessandria

VIA B. VALFRÉ, 59
12060 VERDUNO [CN]
TEL. +39 0172470113
www.fratellialessandria.it

CELLAR SALES
PRE-BOOKED VISITS
ANNUAL PRODUCTION 90,000 bottles
HECTARES UNDER VINE 15.00

The notoriety enjoyed by the lovely winery overseen by Vittore Alessandria has been made possible thanks to a style centered on freshness and aromatic finesse. It's also the result of excellent vineyards, foremost their Monvigliero plots in Verduno and the high Gamolere in Monferte, both cultivated with the utmost respect for the environment. Even their so-called 'minor' wines are excellent, led by an enjoyable and fragrant Verduno Pelaverga Speziale. The Gramolere '15 is the proof of how Barolo's signature tannins can become a velvety force and its classic astringency can become enjoyable sapidity. Here they combine with elegant aromas of licorice, tobacco and red berries. The tasty Monvigliero, a wine that enchants in its length and complexity, is more delicate in its floral fragrances but surefooted on the palate. The Pelaverga Speziale '18 is characterized by a rare pleasantness, while the Nebbiolo Prinsiòt '17 stands out for its perfect drinkability.

● Barolo Monvigliero '15	♛♛♛ 6
● Barolo Gramolere '15	♛♛ 6
○ Verduno Pelaverga Speziale '18	♛♛ 3*
● Barolo '15	♛♛ 5
● Barolo San Lorenzo di Verduno '15	♛♛ 6
○ Langhe Favorita '18	♛♛ 2*
● Langhe Nebbiolo Prinsiot '17	♛♛ 3
● Barolo Gramolere '11	♛♛♛ 6
● Barolo Gramolere '10	♛♛♛ 6
● Barolo Gramolere '05	♛♛♛ 6
● Barolo Monvigliero '14	♛♛♛ 6
● Barolo Monvigliero '13	♛♛♛ 6
● Barolo Monvigliero '12	♛♛♛ 6
● Barolo Monvigliero '09	♛♛♛ 6
● Barolo Monvigliero '06	♛♛♛ 6
● Barolo S. Lorenzo '08	♛♛♛ 6

★Gianfranco Alessandria

Loc. Manzoni, 13
12065 Monforte d'Alba [CN]
Tel. +39 017378576
www.gianfrancoalessandria.com

CELLAR SALES
PRE-BOOKED VISITS
ANNUAL PRODUCTION 50,000 bottles
HECTARES UNDER VINE 7.00

Gianfranco embodies the qualities of a traditional producer because he's adopted a minimally-invasive approach. And he's an innovator — back in 1986 he chose small French wood to age his Nebbiolos and Barberas. His wife and their two daughters are involved at every stage of production, making for a selection that features Barolo San Giovanni and Barbera d'Alba Vittoria. This year a new Barolo, called Sgranà, is coming out (a local word meaning 'plucked grapes'). Mature cherry in the foreground and a delicate background of oak introduce their Complex Barolo San Giovanni '15, a wine that's potent and full-bodied on the palate, where a pleasant acidity also emerges. The subtle and mid-structured Barolo '15 is well-crafted in its balance of fruit. A small amount of oak and plenty of freshness characterize their enjoyable Barbera d'Alba Vittoria '16, a wine accompanied by a 'basic-level' 2017 version featuring sensations of wood resin and incense.

● Barbera d'Alba Vittoria '16	♛♛ 5
● Barolo San Giovanni '15	♛♛ 8
● Barbera d'Alba '17	♛♛ 3
● Barolo '15	♛♛ 6
● Barbera d'Alba Vittoria '15	♛♛♛ 5
● Barbera d'Alba Vittoria '11	♛♛♛ 5
● Barbera d'Alba Vittoria '98	♛♛♛ 5
● Barbera d'Alba Vittoria '97	♛♛♛ 4*
● Barbera d'Alba Vittoria '96	♛♛♛ 6
● Barolo '93	♛♛♛ 6
● Barolo S. Giovanni '04	♛♛♛ 7
● Barolo S. Giovanni '01	♛♛♛ 7
● Barolo S. Giovanni '00	♛♛♛ 7
● Barolo S. Giovanni '99	♛♛♛ 8
● Barolo S. Giovanni '98	♛♛♛ 7
● Barolo S. Giovanni '97	♛♛♛ 7

Marchesi Alfieri

P.zza Alfieri, 28
14010 San Martino Alfieri [AT]
Tel. +39 0141976015
www.marchesialfieri.it

CELLAR SALES
PRE-BOOKED VISITS
ACCOMMODATION
ANNUAL PRODUCTION 100,000 bottles
HECTARES UNDER VINE 21.00

Founded in the mid-1980s by sisters Emanuela, Antonella and Giovanna San Martino, this winery is dedicated entirely to the cultivation of red grapes. Accompanied by Mario Olivero, they oversee an estate that features primarily Barbera, with smaller shares of Pinot Nero, Grignolino and Nebbiolo. These give rise to a selection that's highly appreciated for its classic style and pleasantness. This time the Marchesi Alfieri submitted at least three first-rate wines. The Barbera La Tota '17 proves fragrant amidst echoes of plums, balsams, flowers and a darker touch of orange, sensations that reemerge on a harmonious, pervasive palate. It's an expressive quality that we also find in their Pinot Nero San Germano '16, while the Barbera Superiore Alfiera '16 features a more intense profile in its procession of cocoa powder, spices and plowed earth, not to mention its powerful palate.

● Barbera d'Asti La Tota '17	♛♛ 3*
● Barbera d'Asti Sup. Afiera '16	♛♛ 5
● Piemonte Pinot Nero San Germano '16	♛♛ 5
● Piemonte Grignolino Sansoero '18	♛♛ 3
● Terre Alfieri Nebbiolo Costa Quaglia '16	♛♛ 4
○ Blanc de Noir Extra Brut M.Cl. '15	♛ 5
● M.to Rosso Sostegno '17	♛ 2
● Barbera d'Asti Sup. Alfiera '07	♛♛♛ 5
● Barbera d'Asti Sup. Alfiera '05	♛♛♛ 5
● Barbera d'Asti Sup. Alfiera '01	♛♛♛ 5
● Barbera d'Asti Sup. Alfiera '00	♛♛♛ 5
● Barbera d'Asti Sup. Alfiera '99	♛♛♛ 5
● Barbera d'Asti La Tota '13	♛♛ 3*
● Barbera d'Asti Sup. Alfiera '15	♛♛ 5
● Barbera d'Asti Sup. Alfiera '14	♛♛ 5
● Barbera d'Asti Sup. Alfiera '13	♛♛ 5

Giovanni Almondo

VIA SAN ROCCO, 26
12046 MONTÀ [CN]
TEL. +39 0173975256
www.giovannialmondo.com

PRE-BOOKED VISITS
ANNUAL PRODUCTION 130,000 bottles
HECTARES UNDER VINE 18.00
SUSTAINABLE WINERY

For more than 40 years, Domenico Almondo's winery has offered classic territorial wines. Their vineyards, which are cultivated with an approach that looks to organic and biodynamic principles, are all situated in Montà d'Alba, host primarily Arneis. The terrain is characterized by Roero's trademark: mostly sandy with layers of clay for their Arneis and greater limestone for their Nebbiolo. They also cultivate Barbera, Brachetto, Freisa and Riesling, making for a sapid and elegant selection of notable character. The Roero Arneis Le Rive del Bricco delle Ciliegie '18 is intense on the nose with lovely notes of white-fleshed fruit, aromatic herbs and flint. Its vibrant, persistent palate is characterized by great finesse and rich pulp. Their Roero Arneis Bricco delle Ciligie '18 also put in a top-notch performance, opting more for fragrances of fresh herbs, dried fruit and nuts. On the palate it exhibits notable structure and fullness, coming through long and gutsy on the palate.

○ Roero Arneis Bricco delle Ciliegie '18	🍷🍷	3*
○ Roero Arneis Le Rive del Bricco delle Ciliegie '18	🍷🍷	4
● Roero Bric Valdiana '16	🍷🍷	5
○ Roero Arneis Le Rive del Bricco delle Ciliegie '16	🍷🍷🍷	4*
● Roero Bric Valdiana '11	🍷🍷🍷	5
● Roero Bric Valdiana '07	🍷🍷🍷	5
● Roero Bric Valdiana '03	🍷🍷🍷	5
● Roero Bric Valdiana '01	🍷🍷🍷	4
● Roero Bric Valdiana '00	🍷🍷🍷	4*
● Roero Giovanni Almondo Ris. '13	🍷🍷🍷	5
● Roero Giovanni Almondo Ris. '11	🍷🍷🍷	5
● Roero Giovanni Almondo Ris. '09	🍷🍷🍷	5

★★★Elio Altare

FRAZ. ANNUNZIATA, 51
12064 LA MORRA [CN]
TEL. +39 017350835
www.elioaltare.com

CELLAR SALES
PRE-BOOKED VISITS
ANNUAL PRODUCTION 70,000 bottles
HECTARES UNDER VINE 11.00

Nebbiolo is known all over the world for its particular elegance. In the case of Elio Altare they take things even further, with a selection of Barolos marked by elegance, grace, harmony and distinction, in addition to ageworthiness. And their Langhes are just as charming: the Giàrborina (Nebbiolo), Larigi (Barbera) and their La Villa (a blend of Nebbiolo and Barbera). For the first time, this year they're also releasing a small selection of Barolo (1500 bottles) from the area's most historic cru, Cannubi, a small plot of which Elio rented. Their superb Barolo Cerretta Vigna Bricco Ris. '13 is quite youthful, with red berries taking center stage and a gentle touch of oak lending complexity. On the palate it's rich and potent, marked by firm tannins and a finish made long and harmonious thanks to lovely, fruity pulp: Tre Bicchieri. Their 2017 Langhes, all first-rate, represent a masterful interpretation of Barbera and Nebbiolo. Their three 2018s are all, also, more than valid.

● Barolo Cerretta V. Bricco Ris. '13	🍷🍷🍷	8
● Barolo Arborina '15	🍷🍷	8
● Langhe La Villa '17	🍷🍷	8
● Langhe Larigi '17	🍷🍷	8
● Barbera d'Alba '18	🍷🍷	4
● Barolo '15	🍷🍷	8
● Dolcetto d'Alba '18	🍷🍷	3
● Langhe Giàrborina '17	🍷🍷	8
● Langhe Nebbiolo '18	🍷🍷	4
● Barolo Arborina '09	🍷🍷🍷	8
● Barolo Cerretta V. Bricco '11	🍷🍷🍷	8
● Barolo Cerretta V. Bricco '10	🍷🍷🍷	8
● Barolo Cerretta V. Bricco '06	🍷🍷🍷	8
● Langhe Larigi '13	🍷🍷🍷	8
● Langhe Rosso Giàrborina '16	🍷🍷🍷	8

Amalia Cascina in Langa

LOC. SANT'ANNA, 85
12065 CUNEO
TEL. +39 0173789013
www.cascinaamalia.it

CELLAR SALES
PRE-BOOKED VISITS
ACCOMMODATION
ANNUAL PRODUCTION 40,000 bottles
HECTARES UNDER VINE 8.00
SUSTAINABLE WINERY

Bolstered by nice vineyards and prestigious consultants both in the countryside and in the cellar, Cascina Amalia is an elegant destination for those in search of natural beauty and art, well represented here by an elegant B&B. Langa's classic wines are at the center of their selection, foremost Barolo. But it's not their only wine, indeed you could count the number of producers who make Rossese Bianco on one hand, and the Boffa family are one of them, making a sound contribution to proving its attributes. We suggest you try this crisp, floral white, whose origins are still mysterious, without delay. Though a warm 2017 made for a version that's a bit less fresh than usual. Their Barolo Bussia '15 is a masterpiece of elegance, adorned by notes of raspberry and licorice, silky tannins and plenty of alcohol. The Barolo Le Coste di Monforte '15 is a potent, warm wine characterized by aromas of bottled cherries, while the Barbera d'Alba 2017 proves surprisingly fresh and lively.

● Barolo Bussia '15	♟♟ 6
● Barbera d'Alba '17	♟♟ 4
● Barolo Le Coste di Monforte '15	♟♟ 6
○ Langhe Rossese Bianco '17	♟ 4
● Barbera d'Alba '15	♟♟ 4
● Barbera d'Alba Sup. '16	♟♟ 4
● Barbera d'Alba Sup. '15	♟♟ 4
● Barbera d'Alba Sup. '13	♟♟ 4
● Barolo '14	♟♟ 6
● Barolo '13	♟♟ 6
● Barolo '11	♟♟ 6
● Barolo Bussia '13	♟♟ 6
● Barolo Le Coste di Monforte '13	♟♟ 6
● Barolo Le Coste di Monforte '11	♟♟ 6
○ Langhe Rossese Bianco '15	♟♟ 4

Antichi Vigneti di Cantalupo

VIA MICHELANGELO BUONARROTI, 5
28074 GHEMME [NO]
TEL. +39 0163840041
www.cantalupo.net

CELLAR SALES
PRE-BOOKED VISITS
ANNUAL PRODUCTION 180,000 bottles
HECTARES UNDER VINE 35.00

The winery overseen by Alberto Arlunno represents a highly-valued and important interpreter of northern Piedmont's best wine. Theirs is a journey that's lasted 40 years, and earned them recognition throughout the world. Their style of winemaking is surely classic, inspired by the area's centuries-old history of viticulture, while their agronomic approach is highly respectful of the natural environment, forgoing the use of invasive chemicals. At the center of it all is Nebbiolo, which is proposed in various versions, foremost Ghemme. The Collis Carellae '11 opens on sensations of red berries and gentian, only to come through potent and assertive on the palate, where tannins are still pleasantly present. The spicy Abate di Cluny '11 moves along a similar track, just slightly more delicate. Lovely notes of apples and pears, along with a whiff of hazelnut, mark the succulent white Carolus, a wine made with Erbaluce, Arneis and Chardonnay.

● Ghemme Collis Carellae '11	♟♟ 6
● Colline Novaresi Abate di Cluny '11	♟♟ 5
○ Colline Novaresi Nebbiolo Il Mimo '18	♟ 2
○ Mia Ida Brut	♟ 3
● Ghemme '05	♟♟♟ 4
● Ghemme Collis Breclemae '00	♟♟♟ 6
● Colline Novaresi Vespolina Villa Horta '16	♟♟ 2*
● Ghemme Cantalupo Anno Primo '11	♟♟ 5
● Ghemme Cantalupo Anno Primo '10	♟♟ 5
● Ghemme Collis Breclemae '11	♟♟ 7
● Ghemme Collis Breclemae '10	♟♟ 6
● Ghemme Collis Carellae '10	♟♟ 6

★Antoniolo

c.so Valsesia, 277
13045 Gattinara [VC]
Tel. +39 0163833612
antoniolovini@bmm.it

CELLAR SALES
PRE-BOOKED VISITS
ANNUAL PRODUCTION 60,000 bottles
HECTARES UNDER VINE 12.00

Lorella Zoppis Antoniolo likes to remind people that it was Luigi Veronelli, the great philosopher of Italian artisanal wine, who convinced her to put the cru of origin on the label of her Gattinara. And so it was that in 1974 their Osso San Grato and San Francesco came to be, wines that would become celebrated expressions North Piedmont's Nebbiolo. They're characterized both by the territory's signature mineral presence and by splendid notes that call up wood resin and mint, with a palate that's never aggressive, always appealing. 2015 was an exemplary year for Antoniolo, with their Gattinara Osso San Grato taking home Tre Bicchieri thanks to its balance, and an elegance of sheer perfection. Notes of iodine and roots rise up on the nose, but it's recently ripened berry fruit that reigns supreme. The warm San Francesco, redolent of licorice, is just as rich, while the muscular Castelle, whose tannins are still a bit up-front, performs on similar levels.

● Gattinara Osso San Grato '15	♥♥♥	8
● Gattinara Le Castelle '15	♥♥	7
● Gattinara San Francesco '15	♥♥	8
● Coste della Sesia Nebbiolo Juvenia '12	♥♥	4
● Gattinara '15	♥♥	6
● Gattinara Osso S. Grato '11	♀♀♀	8
● Gattinara Osso S. Grato '10	♀♀♀	8
● Gattinara Osso San Grato '14	♀♀♀	8
● Gattinara Osso San Grato '13	♀♀♀	8
● Gattinara Osso San Grato '12	♀♀♀	8
● Coste della Sesia Nebbiolo Juvenia '16	♀♀	4
● Gattinara '14	♀♀	6
● Gattinara '13	♀♀	6
● Gattinara San Francesco '13	♀♀	8

Odilio Antoniotti

fraz. Casa del Bosco
v.lo Antoniotti, 5
13868 Sostegno [BI]
Tel. +39 0163860309
antoniottiodilio@libero.it

CELLAR SALES
PRE-BOOKED VISITS
ANNUAL PRODUCTION 15,000 bottles
HECTARES UNDER VINE 4.50

Increased interest in Nebbiolo is finally having an impact on appellations, like Bramaterra, that were at risk of being lost after the countryside was abandoned in the last century. Odilio Antoniotti, today accompanied by his son Mattia, is proving how, with natural spontaneity and without specific techniques in the cellar, the territory can give rise to great wines. Spontaneous fermentation in concrete vats is behind their perennially sound selection of Bramaterra is, along with a careful and measured use of wood, and Croatina, Vespolina and Uva Rara grapes, which leave their wines with a decidedly territorial mark. Licorice, golden-leaf tobacco and iodine fused on a lovely, fruit-forward nose introduce the Bramaterra 2015. On the palate it delivers excellent persistence characterized by tight-knit, but not aggressive, tannins. Their Nebbiolo is endowed with freshness both on the nose and the palate, as well as notable and appreciable structure.

● Bramaterra '15	♥♥	6
● Coste della Sesia Nebbiolo '16	♥♥	4
● Bramaterra '10	♀♀♀	3*
● Coste della Sesia Nebbiolo '15	♀♀♀	3*
● Bramaterra '14	♀♀	5
● Bramaterra '13	♀♀	4
● Bramaterra '12	♀♀	4
● Bramaterra '07	♀♀	3*

TENUTA DI
LILLIANO

www.lilliano.it

I VINE DI MASSIMO BASSA

Isola Aug

PALAZZOLO DELLO STELLA UI

LES ILES

CHARDONNAY
D.O.P.
FRIULI

ISOLA AUGUSTA

PRODUCT OF ITALY

AZIENDA AGRICOLA ISOLA AUGUSTA – CA
33056 PALAZZOLO DELLO STEL
www.isolaugusta.com info@iso

L'Armangia

FRAZ. SAN GIOVANNI, 122
14053 CANELLI [AT]
TEL. +39 0141824947
www.armangia.it

CELLAR SALES
PRE-BOOKED VISITS
ACCOMMODATION
ANNUAL PRODUCTION 95,000 bottles
HECTARES UNDER VINE 11.00
SUSTAINABLE WINERY

L'Armangia (a local word for 're-match') is much more than a brand for Ignazio Giovine. In 1988, he was inspired to create his winery in Canelli, where his family had been cultivating grapes and making wines since 1850. Supported by his wife, over the years he extended his estate with the vineyards of Moasca, San Marzano Oliveto and Castel Boglione. The result has been a contemporary style of wines grounded in Barbera, Chardonnay and Moscato, with smaller shares of Albarossa, Nebbiolo, Freisa, Merlot and Cab. It's a style perfectly expressed by their Nizza Titon '16. Fruity and meaty sensations are accompanied by floral whiffs and smoky touches, all anticipating a vivacious palate that never loses its cohesion or contrast thanks in part to its soft tannic weave. And once again it's the natural gustatory expression of their Lorenzo Maria Sole Dosaggio Zero Metodo Classico '13 to render the wine highly enjoyable, with its focused notes of black berries and licorice.

● Nizza Titon '16	♟♟ 4
○ Lorenzo MariaSole Dosaggio Zero M. Cl. '13	♟♟ 4
○ Piemonte Chardonnay Pratorotondo '18	♟♟ 2*
○ Mesicaseu	♟ 4
○ Moscato d'Asti Canelli '18	♟ 2
○ Lorenzo Mariasole Extra Brut M. Cl.	♟♟ 4
○ Lorenzo MariaSole Pas Dosé M. Cl.	♟♟ 4
○ Moscato d'Asti Canelli '17	♟♟ 2*
● Nizza Titon '15	♟♟ 4
● Nizza Titon '14	♟♟ 3*
● Nizza Vignali Ris. '15	♟♟ 5

★Azelia

VIA ALBA BAROLO, 143
12060 CASTIGLIONE FALLETTO [CN]
TEL. +39 017362859
www.azelia.it

CELLAR SALES
PRE-BOOKED VISITS
ANNUAL PRODUCTION 80,000 bottles
HECTARES UNDER VINE 16.00
SUSTAINABLE WINERY

While respecting the characteristics of each vintage, Luigi Scavino manages to consistently propose outstanding Barolos, making this small winery famous the world over. Much of the credit goes to their vineyards, but it's also important to note the care that goes into aging each wine, the use of various types of wood and for different lengths of time. In addition to their celebrated Bricco Fiasco, San Rocco, Margheria and Riserva Bricco Voghera, we recommend tasting one of the best Dolcetto d'Albas out there, their Bricco dell'Oriolo. Their 2015 Barolos are outstanding. We slightly preferred the Margheria, with its fresh spices and red berries. On the palate i's long, austere and rich in personality. Their fresher Bricco Fiasco is just a bit marked by acidity, while the firmly-structured San Rocco is an iota more mature in its hints of sun-dried herbs and touch of oak (the entry-level is also pleasant). Their Oriolo is absolutely one of 2017's best Dolcettos.

● Barolo '15	♟♟ 6
● Barolo Bricco Fiasco '15	♟♟ 8
● Barolo Margheria '15	♟♟ 8
● Barolo San Rocco '15	♟♟ 8
● Dolcetto d'Alba Bricco dell'Oriolo '17	♟♟ 3
● Langhe Nebbiolo '17	♟♟ 4
● Barolo '91	♟♟♟ 7
● Barolo Bricco Fiasco '12	♟♟♟ 8
● Barolo Bricco Fiasco '09	♟♟♟ 8
● Barolo Bricco Fiasco '01	♟♟♟ 7
● Barolo Bricco Fiasco '95	♟♟♟ 7
● Barolo Bricco Fiasco '93	♟♟♟ 6
● Barolo Margheria '06	♟♟♟ 7
● Barolo S. Rocco '11	♟♟♟ 8
● Barolo S. Rocco '08	♟♟♟ 8
● Barolo S. Rocco '99	♟♟♟ 7
● Barolo Voghera Brea Ris. '01	♟♟♟ 8

Barbaglia

VIA DANTE, 54
28010 CAVALLIRIO [NO]
TEL. +39 016380115
www.vinibarbaglia.it

CELLAR SALES
PRE-BOOKED VISITS
ANNUAL PRODUCTION 25,000 bottles
HECTARES UNDER VINE 4.50

The hope is that many young producers will follow the lead taken by Sergio Barbaglia and his daughter Silvia in reviving the vineyards of a territory that experienced a period of abandonment in the last century. The proof lies in the endless woods that surround their small family vineyards, today inhabited by numerous wild animals (and no longer cultivated by farmers). The model provided by the family also holds true for their wines, which are of high quality across their selection — from more approachable offeringslike the robust Il Silente and the fragrant Bianco Lucino, to their premium Boca. Warm, mature and pervasive, the Boca '15 offers up aromas of cherry and quinine before revealing a palate rich in pulp and marked by a creamy tannic weave. Among the rest of their sound selection the fresh and vital Bianco Lucino, whose suite of aromas is just a bit more subtle than usual, stood out, as did the pleasant Nebbiolo Il Silente '17.

● Boca '15	♟♟ 5
● Colline Novaresi Nebbiolo Il Silente '17	♟♟ 3
○ Colline Novaresi Bianco Lucino '18	♟ 3
● Colline Novaresi Vespolina Ledi '18	♟ 3
● Boca '13	♟♟ 5
● Boca '12	♟♟ 5
● Boca '11	♟♟ 5
● Boca '10	♟♟ 5
○ Colline Novaresi Bianco Lucino '17	♟♟ 3*
○ Colline Novaresi Bianco Lucino '15	♟♟ 3
● Colline Novaresi Nebbiolo Il Silente '15	♟♟ 3*
● Colline Novaresi Vespolina Ledi '17	♟♟ 3

Osvaldo Barberis

B.TA VALDIBÀ, 42
12063 DOGLIANI [CN]
TEL. +39 017370054
www.osvaldobarberis.com

CELLAR SALES
PRE-BOOKED VISITS
ANNUAL PRODUCTION 20,000 bottles
HECTARES UNDER VINE 8.00
VITICULTURE METHOD Certified Organic

Piedmont promoted 2019 as the 'Year of Dolcetto' so as to bring attention to the tasty drinkability of this regional wine, constituted of 2 DOCGs, 9 DOCs and 3,800 hectares of vineyards. Within this vast territory, there's no doubt that Dogliani DOCG occupies a place of honor, with its aromatically potent fruit and its rich, pervasive palate, which show a surprising capacity to improve over time. Osvaldo Barberis is an able interpreter who's absolutely respectful of tradition as well as nature, thanks to an organic cultivation approach. Commendable precision and typicality mark the youthful Dogliani Valdibà '18, a wine redolent of elegant notes of red berry fruit, quinine and almond. On the palate it's highly pervasive, both invigorating and juicy. Red berries and nice oak characterize the Barbera d'Alba Cesca '17, a wine made pleasant by a welcome acidity. The Nascetta Anì '18 calls up fresh peanuts and hazelnuts — in the mouth it's quite rich in pulp and highly drinkable.

● Dogliani Valdibà '18	♟♟ 2*
● Barbera d'Alba Cesca '17	♟♟ 3
○ Langhe Nascetta Anì '18	♟♟ 3
● Langhe Barbera Brichat '18	♟ 2
● Langhe Nebbiolo Visat '18	♟ 3
● Barbera d'Alba Cesca '16	♟♟ 3
● Barbera d'Alba Cesca '15	♟♟ 3
● Dogliani Puncin '17	♟♟ 3
● Dogliani Sup. Puncin '16	♟♟ 3
● Dogliani Valdibà '17	♟♟ 2*
● Dogliani Valdibà '16	♟♟ 2*
● Dogliani Valdibà '15	♟♟ 2*
● Langhe Barbera Brichat '16	♟♟ 2*
○ Langhe Nascetta Anì '16	♟♟ 3
● Langhe Nebbiolo Muntajà '16	♟♟ 3

Batasiolo

FRAZ. ANNUNZIATA, 87
12064 LA MORRA [CN]
TEL. +39 017350130
www.batasiolo.com

CELLAR SALES
PRE-BOOKED VISITS
ANNUAL PRODUCTION 2,500,000 bottles
HECTARES UNDER VINE 130.00

The array of plots available to the Dogliani family (more than 130 hectares) represents a rich viticultural patrimony, among the most prestigious in Langhe. This in addition to their Boscareto resort (which gets its name from the Serralunga d'Alba cru, and features a spectacular panoramic view of the estate) and gourmet food. Nebbiolo is cultivated along with Cortese, Arneis, Sauvignon, Pinot Bianco, Moscato, Brachetto, Barbera and Dolcetto. We start with a reserve that, 8 years after vintage, proves to be in excellent form, sophisticated in its lovely notes of tobacco and licorice, potent in its bold tannic weave, with excellent pulp and a long finish. The Briccolina '15 also put in a good performance, offering up fruit and dark spices refreshed by a vivid balsamic streak. On the palate it's rich, accessible, marked by perfectly mature, juicy fruit. The Dogliani '17 is fresh and elegant in its minty notes and whiffs of Mediterranean herbs.

● Barolo Briccolina '15	♈♈♈ 8
● Barolo Ris. '11	♈♈ 6
● Barbaresco '16	♈♈ 6
● Dogliani '17	♈♈ 3
○ Gavi del Comune di Gavi Granée '18	♈♈ 3
● Nebbiolo d'Alba Sup. '16	♈♈ 4
○ Langhe Chardonnay Vign. Morino '17	♈ 5
○ Roero Arneis '18	♈ 3
● Barolo Boscareto '05	♈♈♈ 7
● Barolo Corda della Briccolina '90	♈♈♈ 7
● Barolo Corda della Briccolina '89	♈♈♈ 7
● Barolo Corda della Briccolina '88	♈♈♈ 7

Bava

S.DA MONFERRATO, 2
14023 COCCONATO [AT]
TEL. +39 0141907083
www.bava.com

CELLAR SALES
PRE-BOOKED VISITS
ACCOMMODATION
ANNUAL PRODUCTION 490,000 bottles
HECTARES UNDER VINE 55.00

Owners of the Cocchi brand for 40 years, the Bava family's roots in wine go back to the early 20th century (the 17th century as vine growers). It all begins in Cocconato, in the hills of Monferrato, stretching outward to Agliano and Castiglione Falletto, in Langa. The result is an extremely varied selection of wines that highlights the attributes of more well-established grapes like Nebbiolo, Barbera and Moscato, as well as lesser-known typologies from Ruchè, Malvasia di Castelnuovo Don Bosco and Albarossa. The versatility of their selection was on full display during our recent round of tastings, starting with their Alta Langa Bruts. The TotoCorde '14 is harmonious and lively, while the Pas Dosé '12 is more austere and pulpy. The Nizza Piano Alto '17 amazes for its originality, introduced by sauvage notes that transform into more focused and fragrant suggestions of blackcurrant and orange. But it shows up it's best on palate, thanks to its sapid texture and tannic quality.

○ Alta Langa Pas Dosé '12	♈♈ 6
● Nizza Piano Alto '16	♈♈ 4
○ Alta Langa Brut TotoCorde '14	♈♈ 5
● Barolo Scarrone '14	♈♈ 7
○ Alta Langa Brut Bianc 'd Bianc '14	♈ 6
● Barbera d'Asti Libera '17	♈ 3
○ Piemonte Chardonnay Thou Bianc '18	♈ 3
○ Alta Langa Brut Bianc 'd Bianc Giulio Cocchi '12	♈♈ 6
○ Alta Langa Brut Bianc 'd Bianc Giulio Cocchi '10	♈♈ 6
● Nizza PianoAlto '15	♈♈ 4

Bel Colle

FRAZ. CASTAGNI, 56
12060 VERDUNO [CN]
TEL. +39 0172470196
www.belcolle.eu

CELLAR SALES
PRE-BOOKED VISITS
ANNUAL PRODUCTION 180,000 bottles
HECTARES UNDER VINE 14.00

In 1976 brothers Carlo and Franco Pontiglione, together with Giuseppe Priola, founded Bel Colle (as of 2015 the producer has been owned by Bosio Family Estates). It's headquartered in Borgo Castagni, in Verduno, but their vineyards span La Morra, Treiso and Barbaresco, comprising crus of absolute prestige, from the legendary Monvigliero, whose afternoon light confers its world-famous intricacy, to the spicy sensations of the Pajoré cru. They landed Tre Bicchieri thanks to an excellent Barbaresco Pajoré '16, which harmoniously brings together a vibrant, gutsy character with a gorgeous suite of spices, balsamic and Mediterranean whiffs, before a long, complex finish. The Barolo Mongigliero '15 is also exceptional, highly youthful in its aromas of wild strawberries, licorice and juniper. It's a classic, subtle wine with a flavorful marine profile. The Pelaverga '18 is delicious, delicate in its floral hints of rose and violent, the prelude to a light, tasty, jazzy palate.

● Barbaresco Pajoré '16	🍷🍷🍷	5
● Barolo Monvigliero '15	🍷🍷	6
● Verduno Pelaverga '18	🍷🍷	3*
● Barolo Simposio '15	🍷🍷	6
○ Roero Arneis '18	🍷🍷	3
● Barbera d'Alba Sup. Le Masche '17	🍷	3
○ Langhe Favorita '18	🍷	2
○ Langhe Nas-cëtta '18	🍷	3
● Nebbiolo d'Alba La Reala '17	🍷	3
● Barbaresco Pajoré '15	ΨΨΨ	5
● Barbaresco Roncaglie Ris. '08	ΨΨΨ	5
● Barolo Monvigliero '09	ΨΨΨ	5
● Barolo Monvigliero '07	ΨΨΨ	5
● Barolo Monvigliero '06	ΨΨΨ	5

Bera

LOC. CASCINA PALAZZO
VIA CASTELLERO, 12
12050 NEVIGLIE [CN]
TEL. +39 0173630500
www.bera.it

CELLAR SALES
PRE-BOOKED VISITS
RESTAURANT SERVICE
ANNUAL PRODUCTION 140,000 bottles
HECTARES UNDER VINE 26.00

Situated around their cellar at elevations of 320-280 meters, on tufaceous-clay soil rich in limestone, the Bera family's vineyards are some of the best in Neviglie. Theirs is an adventure that began many years ago, and that today sees Valter and Alida at the helm (the couple are also supported by their sons). Their selection is varied, to say the least, grounded in at least two crown jewels, Moscato and Nebbiolo, which are joined by Dolcetto, Barbera, Pinot Nero and Chardonnay. The outstanding overall performance put in by Bera's wines is rooted in their dynamic duo of Moscato d'Asti. The 2018 'entry-level' version comes through intense and precise, with citrusy notes, hints of dried herbs and white-fleshed fruit, the prelude to a harmonious and fleshy palate. The Su Reimond '18 represents a step forward in terms of complexity, proving irresistible in its procession of lime and medicinal herbs. On the palate it's rich and balanced, despite a pronounced final sweetness.

○ Moscato d'Asti Su Reimond '18	🍷🍷	3*
○ Alta Langa Bera Brut '12	🍷🍷	3
○ Moscato d'Asti '18	🍷🍷	2*
○ Asti '18	🍷	3
● Barbaresco '13	ΨΨ	5
● Barbaresco Basarin Ris. '11	ΨΨ	7
● Barbaresco Rabajà Ris. '12	ΨΨ	5
● Barbera d'Alba '17	ΨΨ	2*
○ Moscato d'Asti '17	ΨΨ	2*
○ Moscato d'Asti Su Reimond '17	ΨΨ	3*
○ Moscato d'Asti Su Reimond '16	ΨΨ	3*
○ Moscato d'Asti Su Reimond '15	ΨΨ	3*

Cinzia Bergaglio

VIA GAVI, 29
15060 TASSAROLO [AL]
TEL. +39 0143342203
www.vinicinziabergaglio.it

CELLAR SALES
PRE-BOOKED VISITS
ANNUAL PRODUCTION 30,000 bottles
HECTARES UNDER VINE 9.00

This small family-run producer is situated atop a hill in Rovereto and Tassarolo, two very interesting areas in terms of terrain types. On the one hand there's the marl clay of Rovereto, on the other there's the redder soil, more structured and iron-rich, that characterizes Tassarolo. These are perfect conditions for bringing out the unique attributes of Cortese, which the winery uses for much of their selection, from still wines to Metodo Classico sparklers and dessert wines. Their only red, the Rosaspina, is made with Barbera and Dolcetto. The Grifone delle Roveri '18 landed a place in our finals. Intense on the nose, it offers up lovely hints of fresh herbs and white-fleshed fruit accompanied by a light iodine note. On the palate it's powerful, with great structure and pulp giving way to a long, fresh finish. The Fornace '18 features nice aromatic complexity and a rich palate marked by pronounced acidity and a lingering finish.

○ Gavi del Comune di Gavi Grifone delle Roveri '18	♥♥ 2*
○ Gavi La Fornace '18	♥♥ 2*
○ Gavi del Comune di Gavi Grifone delle Roveri '15	♀♀ 2*
○ Gavi del Comune di Gavi Grifone delle Roveri '14	♀♀ 2*
○ Gavi del Comune di Gavi Grifone delle Roveri '12	♀♀ 2*
○ Gavi del Comune di Gavi Grifone delle Roveri '11	♀♀ 2*
○ Gavi La Fornace '13	♀♀ 2*
○ Gavi La Fornace '10	♀♀ 2*

Nicola Bergaglio

FRAZ. ROVERETO
LOC. PEDAGGERI, 59
15066 GAVI [AL]
TEL. +39 0143682195
nicolabergaglio@alice.it

CELLAR SALES
PRE-BOOKED VISITS
ANNUAL PRODUCTION 140,000 bottles
HECTARES UNDER VINE 17.00
SUSTAINABLE WINERY

Bergaglio is one of the appellation's most renowned family-run producers. Gianluigi and his son Diego oversee production with a clockwork precision that, year after year, gives rise to great Cortese di Gavi. Two wines are made. their Minaia cru and a base version made with grapes for other private vineyards. Their wines are aged in steel, thus leaving room for the cultivars' maximum expressivity, which here takes on an extraordinary elegance and a complexity that's even more appreciable after a few years in the bottle. Citrusy notes and floral hints introduce their entry-level Gavi, a more approachable and early-drinking wine whose fresh and enticing palate gives way to a long finish. The Gavi Minaia opens with aromas of fresh herbs accompanied by quite mature fruit and a mineral background. On the palate it proves rich and intense with lengthy flavor.

○ Gavi del Comune di Gavi Minaia '18	♥♥♥ 4*
○ Gavi del Comune di Gavi '18	♥♥ 2*
○ Gavi del Comune di Gavi Minaia '17	♀♀♀ 4*
○ Gavi del Comune di Gavi Minaia '15	♀♀♀ 4*
○ Gavi del Comune di Gavi Minaia '14	♀♀♀ 4*
○ Gavi del Comune di Gavi Minaia '11	♀♀♀ 4*
○ Gavi del Comune di Gavi Minaia '10	♀♀♀ 4
○ Gavi del Comune di Gavi '17	♀♀ 2*

Bersano

P.ZZA DANTE, 21
14049 NIZZA MONFERRATO [AT]
TEL. +39 0141720211
www.bersano.it

CELLAR SALES
PRE-BOOKED VISITS
ANNUAL PRODUCTION 1,500,000 bottles
HECTARES UNDER VINE 230.00

It's practically impossible to cram Bersano's agricultural and enological importance for Piedmont into just a few lines. The main plots of their private vineyards are to be found primarily in Monferrato and Langhe. But their well-rounded selection spans many of the region's most important appellations, from Nizza to Barolo, Barbaresco, Gavi, Moscato d'Asti and Alta Langa. It's a range of wines that shines constantly for its solidity and territorial personality. Once again they submitted a number of high quality wines, but it's worth focusing on the Nizza Generala Riserva. The 2016 impresses for its multifaceted citrus and balsamic sensations, the prelude to a spirited, flavorful, multidimensional palate. The Pinot Nero Le Prata '16 is just as firm and dynamic, marked by characteristic fruity, floral and spicy nuances, an atmosphere that amplifies across its full, surefooted palate before a refreshing finish.

● Nizza Generala Ris. '16	▼▼▼ 5
● Barbera d'Asti Costalunga '17	▼▼ 2*
● Barolo Badarina Ris. '12	▼▼ 7
○ Artur.O Brut Pas Dosè M. Cl.	▼▼ 4
● Barolo Badarina '13	▼▼ 7
● Piemonte Pinot Nero La Prata '16	▼▼ 4
○ Gavi del Comune di Gavi '18	▼ 3
○ Moscato d'Asti Monteolivo '18	▼ 3
● Ruché di Castagnole M.to San Pietro Realto '18	▼ 3
● Barbaresco Mantico '14	♈♈ 6
● Barbera d'Asti Sup. Cremosina '16	♈♈ 3*
○ Moscato d'Asti Monteolivo '17	♈♈ 3
● Nizza La Generala Ris. '14	♈♈ 5

Guido Berta

LOC. SALINE, 53
14050 SAN MARZANO OLIVETO [AT]
TEL. +39 0141856193
www.guidoberta.com

CELLAR SALES
PRE-BOOKED VISITS
ANNUAL PRODUCTION 50,000 bottles
HECTARES UNDER VINE 20.00

Situated in the heart of Nizza wine country, the producer overseen by Guido Berta for more than 20 years focuses primarily on Barbera reds. It's headquartered in San Marzano Oliveto, but the estate vineyards also comprise the Calamandrana and Agliano Terme plots, with considerable space dedicated to Chardonnay, Moscato and Nebbiolo. These give rise to an extremely competitive and versatile range of wines, which feature a combination of fruity exuberance and spirited vigor. It's an approach whose value was fully confirmed by our last round of tastings. The classic austerity of their Monferrato Rosso '16 was on full display, as was the earthy density of the Nizza Canto di Luna and the warm vivacity of their Barbera d'Asti Superiore (both 2016s). But it was the Barbera d'Asti '17 that most impressed. Wild blackberry, quinine, cocoa powder and the occasional toasty note don't overshadow a succulent mid palate that's both refreshing and rich in flavor.

● Barbera d'Asti '17	▼▼ 3*
● Barbera d'Asti Sup. '16	▼▼ 3
● M.to Rosso '16	▼▼ 4
● Nizza Canto di Luna '16	▼▼ 5
○ Moscato d'Asti '18	▼ 3
● Barbera d'Asti Le Rondini '16	♈♈ 3
○ Moscato d'Asti '17	♈♈ 3
○ Moscato d'Asti '16	♈♈ 3
● Nizza Canto di Luna '15	♈♈ 5
● Nizza Canto di Luna '14	♈♈ 5

Boasso Franco - Gabutti

B.TA GABUTTI, 3A
12050 SERRALUNGA D'ALBA [CN]
TEL. +39 0173613165
www.gabuttiboasso.com

CELLAR SALES
PRE-BOOKED VISITS
ACCOMMODATION
ANNUAL PRODUCTION 25,000 bottles
HECTARES UNDER VINE 7.00

Ezio Boasso has taken over the reins from his active and capable father, Franco, a vigneron with almost 50 harvests under his belt. Their vineyards, all in Serralunga, are among the most celebrated in Barolo, with the Gabutti cru standing out for its force, ageworthiness and aromatic richness (conferred by its sandy soil). Only red grapes are cultivated, primarily Nebbiolo, which is vinified in mid-size barrels, without added yeasts and without the use of chemicals in the vineyard. The Ris. di Margheria '13 put in a superlative performance, expressing Serralunga's greatness: it's complex, subtle, balanced, slow to open and enchanting. The Gabutti and the Margheria seem to have suffered from a hot 2015, proving undynamic and a bit tired. We found their first 2017s interesting. The Langhe Nebbiolo is floral, delicate and decidedly gradual in its development. The Barbera d'Alba Sup. offers up classic fruity aromas, exhibiting freshness and a small dose of tannins on the palate.

● Barolo Margheria Ris. '13	▾▾▾ 7
● Barbera d'Alba Sup. '17	▾▾ 2*
● Barolo del Comune di Serralunga d'Alba '15	▾▾ 5
● Barolo Gabutti '15	▾▾ 6
● Langhe Nebbiolo '17	▾▾ 3
● Barolo Margheria '15	▾ 6
● Dolcetto d'Alba '18	▾ 2
● Barolo Gabutti '13	▿▿▿ 6
● Barolo Margheria '05	▿▿▿ 5*
● Barolo del Comune di Serralunga d'Alba '14	▿▿ 5
● Barolo Gabutti '14	▿▿ 6
● Langhe Nebbiolo '16	▿▿ 3

★Enzo Boglietti

VIA FONTANE, 18A
12064 LA MORRA [CN]
TEL. +39 017350330
www.enzoboglietti.com

CELLAR SALES
PRE-BOOKED VISITS
ANNUAL PRODUCTION 100,000 bottles
HECTARES UNDER VINE 22.50
VITICULTURE METHOD Certified Organic
SUSTAINABLE WINERY

The Boglietti brothers' winery is about to turn 30. Over the years it has been said that their Barolos are 'international' in style, because of the use of French barrels, which have left their mark. But each time, Enzo repeated that his intention is to make appealing, elegant wines that can be enjoyed even a few years after vintage. By now we can say that history proved him right, considering his success in Italy (including this guide) and abroad. Nebbiolo gives rise to some six Barolos and a Brut Rosé Metodo Classico. Black berries and licorice characterize their spicy and elegant Barolo Case Nere '15, a wine whose lovely palate also features a pleasant freshness. Bottled cherries and golden-leaf tobacco rise up off their firmly-structured Arione '15, the prelude to a mouth-warming palate made possible by evident, pervasive alcohol. Charming minty notes introduce the supple Boiolo '15, while the 2016 versions of their Barbera d'Alba are more marked by oak.

● Barolo Arione '15	▾▾ 8
● Barolo Case Nere '15	▾▾ 8
● Barbera d'Alba '17	▾▾ 3
● Barolo Boiolo '15	▾▾ 7
● Barolo Brunate '15	▾▾ 8
● Barolo Fossati '15	▾▾ 8
● Barbera d'Alba Roscaleto '16	▾ 5
● Barbera d'Alba V. dei Romani '16	▾ 6
● Dolcetto d'Alba Tiglineri '16	▾ 3
● Langhe Nebbiolo '17	▾ 4
● Barolo Arione '06	▿▿▿ 8
● Barolo Arione '05	▿▿▿ 8
● Barolo Brunate '13	▿▿▿ 8
● Barolo Case Nere '04	▿▿▿ 8
● Barolo V. Arione '07	▿▿▿ 8

La Bollina

VIA MONTEROTONDO, 58
15069 SERRAVALLE SCRIVIA [AL]
TEL. +39 014361984
www.labollina.it

CELLAR SALES
PRE-BOOKED VISITS
ACCOMMODATION AND RESTAURANT SERVICE
ANNUAL PRODUCTION 200,000 bottles
HECTARES UNDER VINE 28.00

This historic Serravalle Scrivia estate is situated on the coast of the hills that dominate the skyline to the east, just by the renowned Outlet. In spans 120 hectares total, 28 of which are vineyards. In concert with their modern cellar, these give rise to seven wines: two Gavis (an entry-level and their Ventola), two Chardonnays (Armason and Beneficio), a Barbera (their Bricchetta), the Tinetta (a rosé), and a Chiaretto made with Nebbiolo. The Gavi '18 features a complex, vibrant aromatic profile. Elegant, fruity aromas and floral notes emerge on a mineral background, only to converge coherently on a fresh, sapid palate before giving way to an intense finish. The Armason is more focused in it its citrusy aromas and fragrances of tropical fruit, all accompanied by a slight note of sweet spices. On the palate it proves fresh and vibrant, with a nice sapid, length. The fresh and enticing Gavi Ventola is also noteworthy.

○ Gavi '18	♟♟ 3*
○ Gavi Ventola '18	♟♟ 3
○ M.to Bianco Armason '18	♟♟ 3
☉ M.to Chiaretto Tinetta '18	♟ 3
● M.to Rosso Bricchetta '16	♟ 3

Bondi

S.DA CAPPELLETTE, 73
15076 OVADA [AL]
TEL. +39 0131299186
www.bondivini.it

CELLAR SALES
PRE-BOOKED VISITS
ANNUAL PRODUCTION 20,000 bottles
HECTARES UNDER VINE 5.00

Small production volumes and excellent wines are the Bondi family's calling card. Their south-facing vineyards are situated in soil rich in white marl at considerable elevations, more than 700 meters. It's a solid foundation for an extremely reliable, notably ageworthy and territorial selection of wines. Dolcetto di Ovada and Barbera are the cornerstones of this modern-leaning winery, whose approach features the careful use of oak, measured extraction and pronounced primary aromas. Their D'Uien opens with lovely, fragrant fruit, and tertiaries of tobacco and cocoa powder. Dense and harmonious on the palate, it features a nice aromatic encore and a supple, persistent finish. The Barbera Banaiotta offers up a lovely mix of small black berries, slightly vegetal hints and well-crafted spicy aromas. In the mouth it proves austere, giving way to a persistent, harmonious finish.

● Ovada D'Uien '16	♟♟ 3*
● Barbera del M.to Banaiotta '17	♟♟ 4
● Dolcetto di Ovada Nani '17	♟♟ 2*
● Barbera del M.to Ruvrin '10	♟♟ 4
● Barbera del M.to Sup. Ruvrin '15	♟♟ 4
● Dolcetto di Ovada Nani '16	♟♟ 2*
● Dolcetto di Ovada Nani '15	♟♟ 2*
● M.to Rosso Ansensò '15	♟♟ 4
● M.to Rosso Ansensò '11	♟♟ 4
● Ovada D'Uien '15	♟♟ 3*
● Ovada D'Uien '13	♟♟ 3
● Ovada D'Uien '11	♟♟ 4

Marco Bonfante

S.DA VAGLIO SERRA, 72
14049 NIZZA MONFERRATO [AT]
TEL. +39 0141725012
www.marcobonfante.com

CELLAR SALES
PRE-BOOKED VISITS
ANNUAL PRODUCTION 250,000 bottles
HECTARES UNDER VINE 13.00
SUSTAINABLE WINERY

It was 2000 when Marco and Micaela
Bonfante decided to begin producing on
their own, after the death of their father
and the subsequent breaking up of the
winery he'd founded. Bolstered by an
8-generation family tradition, they have
managed to carve out an important place in
Asti (and beyond) in a short time. Indeed
their vast selection, which is divided into
various lines, is supported by a thriving
business as 'négoce' that covers all
Piedmont's primary appellations. The all
around completeness of their selection is
their strong point, even if some of their
wines prove capable of standing out from
the group. Their Nizza Bricco Bonfante
Riserva '15 is one example. Black berries,
quinine, cocoa powder and smoky touches
rise up out of the primaries. With aeration
come fresher, more floral and balsamic
registers, reviving its potent but invigorating
palate before a dynamic, long finish. It's
also worth mentioning the performance put
in by their Monferrato Rosso Duedidue '15.

● Nizza Bricco Bonfante Ris. '15	♀♀ 5
● Barolo Bussia '14	♀♀ 6
● Langhe Nebbiolo Imma '16	♀♀ 4
● M.to Rosso Duedidue '15	♀♀ 4
● Barbera d'Asti Sup. Stella Rossa '17	♀ 2
○ Roero Arneis Persté '18	♀ 2
● Barbera d'Asti Sup. Menego '15	♀♀ 4
● Barbera d'Asti Sup. Stella Rossa '16	♀♀ 2*
○ Moscato d'Asti '17	♀♀ 2*
● Nizza Bricco Bonfante Ris. '14	♀♀ 5

Gilberto Boniperti

VIA VITTORIO EMANUELE, 43/45
28010 BARENGO [NO]
TEL. +39 0321997123
www.bonipertivignaioli.com

CELLAR SALES
ANNUAL PRODUCTION 12,000 bottles
HECTARES UNDER VINE 3.50

Gilberto Boniperti started to breathe the
country air while accompanying his
grandfather in the vineyard. Then he
studied enology and, finally, in 2003,
began producing his own wines. The
winery is small enough where he can
personally oversee all stages of production,
including winemaking. Here steel is used
for their more approachable selections,
while French barrels of various sizes are
employed primarily for their Fara.
Obviously Gilberto's heart beats for
Nebbiolo, but he's done some excellent
work with the spicy Vespolina and fresh
Barbera as well. The Fara Bartön '16
exhibits exquisite finesse. It's already quite
complex thanks to the presence of fresh
herbs and more mature notes of tobacco.
Its rich palate is invigorated by slightly
grainy tannins that will soften in the bottle.
The Vespolina Favolalunga '17 is vivacious
and peppery, particularly tasty on the
palate. Both the Nebbiolo Carlin '17 and
the Barbera Barblin '17 are firm in the
mouth, austere on the nose.

● Fara Bartön '16	♀♀ 5
● Colline Novaresi Barbera Barblin '17	♀♀ 4
● Colline Novaresi Nebbiolo Carlin '17	♀♀ 4
● Colline Novaresi Vespolina Favolalunga '17	♀♀ 3
● Fara Bartön '15	♀♀♀ 5
● Colline Novaresi Barbera Barblin '16	♀♀ 4
● Colline Novaresi Nebbiolo Carlin '16	♀♀ 4
● Colline Novaresi Nebbiolo Carlin '15	♀♀ 4
● Colline Novaresi Vespolina Favolalunga '15	♀♀ 2*
● Fara Bartön '14	♀♀ 4
● Fara Bartön '13	♀♀ 4

Borgo Maragliano

VIA SAN SEBASTIANO, 2
14051 LOAZZOLO [AT]
TEL. +39 014487132
www.borgomaragliano.com

CELLAR SALES
PRE-BOOKED VISITS
ANNUAL PRODUCTION 365,000 bottles
HECTARES UNDER VINE 39.00
SUSTAINABLE WINERY

Couple Carlo Galliano and Silvia Quirico tend to a splendid estate on the Asti hills of Loazzolo, at about 450 meters elevation, where the soil is sandy, tufaceous and calcareous. Their flagship wines are Metodo Classico sparklers and natural, sweet Moscato. But the various positions of their plots allow them to play with Chardonnay, Riesling, Brachetto and Pinot Nero as well. It's an ampelographic diversity that gives rise to an extremely distinct selection, both for its expressive clarity and its sapid presence. Our tastings confirmed their selection's established internal hierarchy, starting with the Giovanni Galliano Brut Rosé '15, a wine characterized by aromas of red berries and spices of great elegance, harmony and pleasantness on the palate. Next up there's their Loazzolo V.T. '15, a wine redolent of raisins and a palate in which sweetness is supported by a pleasant citrus, sappy quality, and the Federico Galliano Brut Nature '16, a wine of nice grip and freshness.

⊙ Giovanni Galliano Brut Rosé M. Cl. '15	🍷🍷🍷 5
○ Federico Galliano Brut Nature M. Cl. '16	🍷🍷 5
○ Loazzolo V. T. '15	🍷🍷 5
○ Dogma Blanc de Noirs M. Cl. '15	🍷🍷 5
○ El Calié '18	🍷🍷 2*
○ Giuseppe Galliano Brut Nature M. Cl. '14	🍷🍷 5
○ Piemonte Chardonnay Crevoglio '18	🍷🍷 2*
○ Chardonnay Brut	🍷 3
○ Cuvée Germana Beltrame Brut Nature M. Cl.	🍷 5
○ Francesco Galliano Blanc de Blancs M. Cl. '16	🍷 4
○ Marajan Chardonnay '16	🍷 3
○ Giuseppe Galliano Brut Nature M. Cl. '13	🍷🍷🍷 5

Giacomo Borgogno & Figli

VIA GIOBERTI, 1
12060 BAROLO [CN]
TEL. +39 017356108
www.borgogno.com

CELLAR SALES
PRE-BOOKED VISITS
ANNUAL PRODUCTION 250,000 bottles
HECTARES UNDER VINE 16.00
SUSTAINABLE WINERY

Even if they offer a classic style of Barolo, it has to be recognized that Andrea Farinetti has brought about many changes here, from a return to the use of concrete, to organic certification of some of their vineyards, to acquiring new plots and increased white wine production. But Borgogno deservedly continues to be recognized the world over as one of Langa's great wineries, one that's capable of expressing, year after year, the essence of Nebbiolo. Their entire range is worth tasting, with their Barolo Riserva shining like a beacon, as usual. Even if it wasn't a particularly powerful year, the 2012 version of their Ris. di Barolo is masterful. Aromatically it's marked by fresh red berries, which join together with hints of licorice, while the palate proves long, tight, evenly developing, thrilling. Among their 2014 Barolos the Cannuni and Fossati stand out for their pleasant drinkability. The former is complex and harmonious while the latter is just a bit more vegetal.

● Barolo Ris. '12	🍷🍷 8
● Barbera d'Alba Sup. '17	🍷🍷 5
● Barbera d'Asti Sup. Cascina Valle Asinari '17	🍷🍷 6
● Barolo Cannubi '14	🍷🍷 8
● Barolo Fossati '14	🍷🍷 8
● Barolo Liste '14	🍷🍷 8
● Langhe Nebbiolo No Name '15	🍷🍷 6
● Nizza Cascina Valle Asinari '16	🍷🍷 5
● Barolo Liste '11	🍷🍷🍷 8
● Barolo Liste '10	🍷🍷🍷 8
● Barolo Liste '08	🍷🍷🍷 8
● Barolo Liste '07	🍷🍷🍷 7
● Barolo Ris. '11	🍷🍷🍷 8
● Barolo Ris. '10	🍷🍷🍷 8

Boroli

VIA PUGNANE, 4
12060 CASTIGLIONE FALLETTO [CN]
TEL. +39 017362927
www.boroli.it

CELLAR SALES
PRE-BOOKED VISITS
ACCOMMODATION AND RESTAURANT SERVICE
ANNUAL PRODUCTION 200,000 bottles
HECTARES UNDER VINE 32.00
SUSTAINABLE WINERY

The Boroli family operate in Castiglione Falletto, Barolo and La Morra, bolstered by crus that have become veritable international brands, like Cerequio and Villero (music to the ears of wine lovers). Their vines go back anywhere from 15 to 40 years, with Nebbiolo accompanied by various plots of Chardonnay, which gives rise to their only white. Rigorous attention is paid throughout all stages of production, while low yields and the use of small wood barrels make for reliable and modern wines. There's a sense of harmony and perfect balance in their Barolo Brunella '15. A vivid, brilliant color anticipates intense aromas of bottled cherries, floral sensations and a delicate spicy, vegetal streak. On the palate it's fresh and elegant, with a notable development and a long finish. The soft and juicy Barolo Villero '15 offers up silky sensations accompanied by graceful tannic extraction. The deep Barolo Cerequio '15 features more intense fragrances of sun-dried herbs and pepper.

● Barolo Brunella '15	🍷🍷 8
● Barolo Cerequio '15	🍷🍷 8
● Barolo Villero '15	🍷🍷 8
● Barolo Villero '01	🍷🍷🍷 6
● Barolo Villero '00	🍷🍷🍷 4*
● Barolo '14	🍷🍷 6
● Barolo '12	🍷🍷 6
● Barolo '11	🍷🍷 6
● Barolo Brunella '14	🍷🍷 8
● Barolo Brunella '13	🍷🍷 8
● Barolo Cerequio '14	🍷🍷 8
● Barolo Cerequio '13	🍷🍷 8
● Barolo Cerequio '12	🍷🍷 7
● Barolo Villero '13	🍷🍷 8
● Barolo Villero '12	🍷🍷 7
● Barolo Villero '11	🍷🍷 7
● Barolo Villero Ris. '09	🍷🍷 8

Agostino Bosco

VIA FONTANE, 24
12064 LA MORRA [CN]
TEL. +39 0173509466
www.barolobosco.com

CELLAR SALES
PRE-BOOKED VISITS
ANNUAL PRODUCTION 28,000 bottles
HECTARES UNDER VINE 5.50
SUSTAINABLE WINERY

Rightfully proud of his valued selection of Barolos, Andrea Bosco is celebrating his winery's 40th birthday by reaffirming his conviction that 'Barbera d'Alba is a wine that deserves worldwide appreciation, because great attention is shown both in the vineyard and when it comes to aging in wood'. Their two Barolos are perennial mainstays: the Neirane, which is cultivated on rather sandy soil, is more approachable and open, while La Serra is more austere and in need of aging. Their Barbera d'Alba Superiore Volupta is among 2017's best. Aromatically it's well-integrated amidst oak's signature spiciness, and the pronounced sensations of blackberries and plums for which the cultivar is known. The fruity, licorice-scented Barolo La Serra '15 proves firm in its structure, but delicate in its development, while their Neirane '15 is a bit smaller and more closed on its evanescent palate. The fruit-forward Nebbiolo Rurem '17 is enjoyably plush.

● Barbera d'Alba Sup. Volupta '17	🍷🍷 3*
● Barolo La Serra '15	🍷🍷 6
● Barolo Neirane '15	🍷🍷 5
● Langhe Nebbiolo Rurem '17	🍷🍷 3
● Barbera d'Alba Sup. Volupta '16	🍷🍷 3*
● Barbera d'Alba Sup. Volupta '15	🍷🍷 3
● Barbera d'Alba Sup. Volupta '14	🍷🍷 3
● Barbera d'Alba Sup. Volupta '13	🍷🍷 3
● Barolo La Serra '14	🍷🍷 6
● Barolo La Serra '13	🍷🍷 6
● Barolo La Serra '12	🍷🍷 6
● Barolo Neirane '14	🍷🍷 5
● Barolo Neirane '13	🍷🍷 5
● Dolcetto d'Alba Vantrin '15	🍷🍷 2*
● Langhe Nebbiolo Rurem '15	🍷🍷 3

Giacomo Boveri

FRAZ. MONTALE CELLI
VIA COSTA VESCOVATO, 15
15050 COSTA VESCOVATO [AL]
TEL. +39 0131838223
www.vignetiboveri.it

CELLAR SALES
PRE-BOOKED VISITS
ANNUAL PRODUCTION 25,000 bottles
HECTARES UNDER VINE 9.00

Giacomo Boveri's family have two centuries of farming tradition behind them. After many years in agriculture, in 1988 he decided to take control of the business, enlarging it and improving vinification processes. Their vineyards span three municipalities: Costa Vescovato, Cerreto True and Montegioco. In some cases they drew on already existing vines, while in others they've focused on vineyard aspect and terrain characteristics. This year it was the Timorasso Lacrime del Bricco that earned a place in our final round of tastings. It's a delicate, elegant wine, as complex on the nose as it is rich and balanced on the palate. We also found the Muntà l'è Ruma extremely interesting. At this stage it's less ready than the Lacrime del Bricco, but it exhibits great potential. We'll probably see it's true colors a bit further on.

○ Colli Tortonesi Timorasso Lacrime del Bricco '16	♈♈ 4
○ Colli Tortonesi Timorasso Muntà L'è Ruma '16	♈♈ 4
● Colli Tortonesi Barbera 19 Marzo 1878 '18	♈ 3
● Colli Tortonesi Barbera Sup. Bricco della Ginestra '14	♉♉ 3
● Colli Tortonesi Barbera Sup. Bricco della Ginestra '13	♉♉ 3
○ Colli Tortonesi Cortese Campo del Bosco '15	♉♉ 2*
○ Colli Tortonesi Timorasso Lacrime del Bricco '15	♉♉ 4
○ Colli Tortonesi Timorasso Muntà L'è Ruma '15	♉♉ 4
○ Colli Tortonesi Timorasso Muntà L'è Ruma '14	♉♉ 3

Luigi Boveri

LOC. MONTALE CELLI
VIA XX SETTEMBRE, 6
15050 COSTA VESCOVATO [AL]
TEL. +39 0131838165
www.boveriluigi.com

CELLAR SALES
PRE-BOOKED VISITS
ANNUAL PRODUCTION 80,000 bottles
HECTARES UNDER VINE 15.00

Luigi Boveri is a wine veteran, as well as a skilled artisan. Plenty of experience in the vineyard and cellar as well as excellent results over almost 30 years of activity have made him one of the area's most appreciated vignerons. His wines benefit form the peculiar characteristics of Costa Vescovato and Luigi's personal approach, which is aimed at bringing out Timorasso's power. We also shouldn't forget his knack for using wood barrels to age his reds. An outstanding selection of wines shines a line foremost on a single year, 2017, a great one for Timorasso. The Derthona is more accessible, rich and intense, while the Filari di Timorasso proves subtle and complex, with a bold structure and extremely long aromatic persistence. Their VIgnalunga is also in great form, proving extremely harmonious, with well-dosed oak. The 2016 version of their Croatina Sensazioni is another must.

● Colli Tortonesi Barbera Vignalunga '15	♈♈ 5
○ Colli Tortonesi Timorasso Derthona '17	♈♈ 4
○ Colli Tortonesi Timorasso Derthona Filari di Timorasso '17	♈♈ 5
● Colli Tortonesi Barbera Boccanera '18	♈♈ 2*
● Colli Tortonesi Croatina Sensazioni '16	♈♈ 4
○ Colli Tortonesi Cortese Terre del Prete '18	♈ 2
○ Colli Tortonesi Timorasso Derthona '11	♉♉♉ 4*
○ Colli Tortonesi Timorasso Filari di Timorasso '12	♉♉♉ 5
○ Colli Tortonesi Timorasso Filari di Timorasso '07	♉♉♉ 3

Gianfranco Bovio

FRAZ. ANNUNZIATA
B.TA CIOTTO, 63
12064 LA MORRA [CN]
TEL. +39 017350667
www.boviogianfranco.com

CELLAR SALES
PRE-BOOKED VISITS
ANNUAL PRODUCTION 55,000 bottles
HECTARES UNDER VINE 8.50

Gianfranco was one of Langa's great restaurateurs. In addition to his top-notch cooking (which continues today), he was a connoisseur of the area's Barolo, fond of opening a bottle with his customers and friends. There were many such bottles, in particular those made at his own winery (est. 1976), cultivated in the Gattera and Arborina crus. Today his daughter Alessandra manages both businesses with the same passion, having adopted a traditional approach and overseeing a consistently reliable selection. Their entire selection put in a sound performance. Their Barolo Ris. De-Rieumes, a new entry, is as firm as it is characteristic of a cool 2013, already open with forthright aromas of licorice and harmonious in its structure. The Arborina '15 is fruitier, endowed with clean oak, while the entry-level version is particularly well-made and already enjoyable. Both the Roccettevino '15 and the Gattera '15 prove splendid. Their Barbera Il Ciotto '18 exhibits gratifying drinkability.

● Barolo Arborina '15	♙♙	6
● Barolo Gattera '15	♙♙	6
● Barolo Rocchettevino '15	♙♙	5
● Barbera d'Alba Il Ciotto '18	♙♙	2*
● Barbera d'Alba Sup. Regiaveja '17	♙♙	4
● Barolo '15	♙♙	6
● Barolo De-Rieumes Ris. '13	♙♙	7
● Langhe Nebbiolo Firagnetti '17	♙♙	3
● Dolcetto d'Alba Dabbene '18	♙	2
○ Langhe Chardonnay Alessandro '17	♙	3
● Barolo Bricco Parussi Ris. '01	♙♙♙	6
● Barolo Gattera '11	♙♙♙	6
● Barolo Rocchettevino '06	♙♙♙	5*
● Barolo V. Arborina '90	♙♙♙	6

★Braida

LOC. CIAPPELLETTE
S.DA PROV.LE 27, 9
14030 ROCCHETTA TANARO [AT]
TEL. +39 0141644113
www.braida.it

CELLAR SALES
PRE-BOOKED VISITS
ACCOMMODATION
ANNUAL PRODUCTION 700,000 bottles
HECTARES UNDER VINE 70.00
SUSTAINABLE WINERY

Giuseppe and Raffaella have the honor, and burden, of overseeing a winery that's become a symbol of Piedmont. Founded by their grandfather and brought to the heights of excellence by their father, the estate spans five properties throughout Monferrato Astigiano and Langhe. In Rocchetta Tanaro they make classics like Bricco dell'Uccellone, Bricco della Bigotta, Ai Suma, La Monella and Montebruna. Castelnuovo Calcea and Costigliole d'Asti give rise to more approachable wines, while Trezzo Tinella and Mango d'Alba are dedicated to their white grapes and to Moscato. And once again it's their most important Barbera d'Astis that lead the way in what was yet another shining performance. Wild cherry, cassis cream and nutmeg introduce the Montebruna '17, which brings together texture and raciness, compensating for a slightly abrupt tannic close with quality of flavor. The Bricco della Bigotta '17, which is broader than it is linear, unfolds on more autumnal sensations.

● Barbera d'Asti Bricco dell'Uccellone '17	♙♙	7
● Barbera d'Asti Bricco della Bigotta '17	♙♙	7
● Barbera d'Asti Montebruna '17	♙♙	3*
● M.to Rosso Bacialé '17	♙♙	3
○ Moscato d'Asti Vigna senza Nome '18	♙♙	3
● Grignolino d'Asti Limonte '18	♙	3
● Barbera d'Asti Bricco dell'Uccellone '15	♙♙♙	7
● Barbera d'Asti Bricco dell'Uccellone '12	♙♙♙	7
● Barbera d'Asti Bricco dell'Uccellone '09	♙♙♙	6
● Barbera d'Asti Montebruna '11	♙♙♙	3*
● Barbera d'Asti Ai Suma '15	♙♙	7
● Barbera d'Asti Bricco dell'Uccellone '16	♙♙	7
● Barbera d'Asti Bricco della Bigotta '16	♙♙	7

PIEDMONT

Brandini

FRAZ. BRANDINI, 16
12064 LA MORRA [CN]
TEL. +39 017350266
www.agricolabrandini.com

CELLAR SALES
PRE-BOOKED VISITS
ACCOMMODATION AND RESTAURANT SERVICE
ANNUAL PRODUCTION 80,000 bottles
HECTARES UNDER VINE 15.00
VITICULTURE METHOD Certified Organic
SUSTAINABLE WINERY

In just a few years Sisters Giovanna and Serena Bagnasco have realized their dream: the ability to offer tourists hospitality, wine tastings, and the possibility to enjoy the best of Langhe. Indeed, their accommodations are fully operational while their wines, all organic, are made possible thanks to some four Barolo crus in La Morra and Serralunga d'Alba (in addition to vineyards in Alta Langa for their sparkling wines). A subtle harmony marks their Barolo R56 '15, a wine whose exquisite dynamism, made lively and vibrant thanks to nice acidity, complements its aromatic elegance, with fruit-driven fragrances emerging on a background of fresh herbs: Tre Bicchieri. The Cerretta di Serralunga cru gave rise to a Barolo '15 marked by a surprising roundness, with firm but not aggressive tannins and excellent robustness. Delicate minty notes and palate combine in their invigorating Barolo Annunziata '15, making for a juicy and dense drink.

Brangero

VIA PROVINCIALE, 26
12055 DIANO D'ALBA [CN]
TEL. +39 017369423
www.brangero.com

PRE-BOOKED VISITS
ANNUAL PRODUCTION 50,000 bottles
HECTARES UNDER VINE 9.00

Situated in the upper part of the hill opposite Diano d'Alba, Marco Brangero's winery is turning 20. In the vineyards around their cellar Piedmont's classic grapes are grown: Dolcetto, Barbera, Nebbiolo and Arneis, with a couple of plots dedicated to international varieties. But their real crown jewel is a small plot in Verduno, in the marvelous cru that is Monvigliero, which Marco transforms into two Barolos. Outside the region, in Liguria, Marco also manages La Ginestraia in the province of Imperia. A dense, impenetrable color, the Dolcetto di Diano d'Alba Sorì Cascina Soprano '17 opens on aromas of blackcurrant, cocoa powder and black olives. On the palate it's potent, mouthfilling, long and persistent. The Barolo Monvigliero '15 is a summery wine whose mature, intense profile nicely reflects the vintage. Their Barbera d'Alba Superiore La Soprana '17 comes through full-bodied and powerful.

● Barolo R56 '15	♥♥♥ 8
● Barolo Annunziata '15	♥♥ 8
● Barolo Cerretta '15	♥♥ 8
● Barbera d'Alba Sup. Rocche del Santo '16	♥♥ 5
● Barolo del Comune di La Morra '15	♥♥ 7
● Langhe Nebbiolo Filari Corti '16	♥♥ 4
○ Langhe Bianco Le Coccinelle '18	♥ 4
○ Langhe Bianco Rebelle '18	♥ 5
● Barolo del Comune di La Morra '14	♥♥♥ 8
● Barolo Resa 56 '13	♥♥♥ 8
● Barolo Resa 56 '12	♥♥♥ 8
● Barolo Resa 56 '11	♥♥♥ 7
● Barolo Resa 56 '10	♥♥♥ 7
● Barolo del Comune di La Morra '14	♥♥ 8
● Barolo del Comune di La Morra '13	♥♥ 8
● Barolo Meriame '14	♥♥ 8

● Barolo Monvigliero '15	♥♥ 6
● Dolcetto di Diano d'Alba Sörì Rabino Soprano '17	♥♥ 2*
● Barbera d'Alba Sup. La Soprana '17	♥ 3
● Barbera d'Alba La Soprana '13	♥♥ 3
● Barolo Monvigliero '14	♥♥ 6
● Barolo Monvigliero '12	♥♥ 6
● Barolo Monvigliero '11	♥♥ 6
● Dolcetto di Diano d'Alba Sörì Cascina Rabino '16	♥♥ 2*
● Dolcetto di Diano d'Alba Sörì Rabino Soprano '15	♥♥ 2*
○ Langhe Chardonnay Centofile '13	♥♥ 3
● Langhe Nebbiolo Quattro Cloni '16	♥♥ 4
● Langhe Nebbiolo Quattro Cloni '15	♥♥ 4
● Langhe Rosso Tremarzo '15	♥♥ 4
● Nebbiolo d'Alba Bricco Bertone '12	♥♥ 4

Brema

VIA POZZOMAGNA, 9
14045 INCISA SCAPACCINO [AT]
TEL. +39 014174019
www.vinibrema.com

CELLAR SALES
PRE-BOOKED VISITS
ANNUAL PRODUCTION 150,000 bottles
HECTARES UNDER VINE 25.00
SUSTAINABLE WINERY

Nizza Monferrato, Fontanile d'Asti, San
Marzano Oliveto, Incisa Scapaccino,
Sessame d'Asti, Mombaruzzo: some six
municipalities in Monferrato Astigiano host
the Brema family's vineyards. It's a
producer with more than 200 years of
history behind it, now on its fifth generation
of family in Umberto. Naturally the focus is
on Barbera, which is transformed into a
diverse selection. They're contemporary in
the best sense of the word, bringing
together varietal distinctness and territorial
character. This enological sensibility
emerged clearly in our last round of
tastings, in particular when it comes to
their Nizza A Luigi Veronelli '17. It's broad
and multifaceted wine aromatically, amidst
echoes of brandied fruit, topsoil and hot
spices. On the palate it's firm and coherent,
developing assertively. The Barbera
Superiore Volpettona '16 exhibits a more
modern profile in its sensations of vanilla
and coffee. But the palate features a
markedly taut and austere character.

● Barbera d'Asti Sup. Volpettona '16	♼♼ 5
● Nizza A Luigi Veronelli '16	♼♼ 6
● Barbera d'Asti Ai Cruss '17	♼♼ 2*
● Barbera d'Asti Sup. Nizza A Luigi Veronelli '12	♼♼♼ 6
● Barbera d'Asti Sup. Nizza A Luigi Veronelli '06	♼♼♼ 6
● Barbera d'Asti Sup. Nizza A Luigi Veronelli '13	♼♼ 6
● Barbera d'Asti Sup. Nizza A Luigi Veronelli '11	♼♼ 6
● Barbera d'Asti Sup. Volpettona '15	♼♼ 5
● Barbera d'Asti Sup. Volpettona '14	♼♼ 5
● Nizza A Luigi Veronelli '15	♼♼ 6

Giacomo Brezza & Figli

VIA LOMONDO, 4
12060 BAROLO [CN]
TEL. +39 0173560921
www.brezza.it

CELLAR SALES
PRE-BOOKED VISITS
ACCOMMODATION AND RESTAURANT SERVICE
ANNUAL PRODUCTION 100,000 bottles
HECTARES UNDER VINE 20.00
VITICULTURE METHOD Certified Organic
SUSTAINABLE WINERY

The bright color of tajarin, the unique
texture of agnolotti del plin, the penetrating
aromas of seasonal truffle … Brezza is
food, hospitality, wine (the first bottles
came in 1910). Their wines age slowly in
medium-size and large Slavonian oak,
while their vineyards can be found in
Barolo, as well as Monforte d'Alba,
Novello, Diano d'Alba and Alba. Their style
is exquisitely traditional, with wines rich in
edginess and acidity. The Barolo Sarmassa
Vigna Bricco Ris. '13 has the makings of a
great wine. It's classically-styled, marked
by subtle dried flowers, pepper and black
olives. Entering slowly, it closes with a
long, rising finish — it's got a bright
future. The Barolo '15 also delivers. It's
medium bodied, harmonious with light
fruit, perfectly calibrated on its firm, tannic
weave before giving way to a well-
sustained, lengthy finish. Echoes of quinine
and tobacco mark the Barolo Cannubi '15,
while their Langhe Nebbiolo '18 proves
highly pleasant on the palate.

● Barolo '15	♼♼ 5
● Barolo Cannubi '15	♼♼ 7
● Barolo Sarmassa V. Bricco Ris. '13	♼♼ 8
● Barolo Castellero '15	♼♼ 6
● Barolo Sarmassa '15	♼♼ 7
● Langhe Nebbiolo '18	♼♼ 3
● Dolcetto d'Alba '18	♼ 2
● Nebbiolo d'Alba V. Santa Rosalia '17	♼ 4
● Barolo Bricco Sarmassa '08	♼♼♼ 7
● Barolo Bricco Sarmassa '07	♼♼♼ 7
● Barolo Cannubi '01	♼♼♼ 6
● Barolo Cannubi '96	♼♼♼ 6
● Barolo Sarmassa '11	♼♼♼ 6
● Barolo Sarmassa '05	♼♼♼ 6
● Barolo Sarmassa '04	♼♼♼ 6
● Barolo Sarmassa '03	♼♼♼ 6
● Barolo Sarmassa V. Bricco Ris. '11	♼♼♼ 7

Gallino Domenico
Bric Castelvej

Madonna Loreto, 70
12043 Canale [CN]
Tel. +39 017398108
www.briccastelvej.com

CELLAR SALES
PRE-BOOKED VISITS
ANNUAL PRODUCTION 100,000 bottles
HECTARES UNDER VINE 12.40

Mario Repellino, along with his son (enologist and production manager), oversees Bric Castelvej, a winery founded by Domenico Gallino in 1956. Their vineyards, all of which are situated in Canale on loose, sandy soil with layers of silt and calcareous clay, give rise to the area's traditional grapes, starting with Arneis, Nebbiolo and Barbera. The result is a series of traditionally-styled wines that bring together structure, freshness and elegance. The wines submitted demonstrate a nice level of quality. Spicy hints and notes of red berries introduce their Roero Panera Alta Ris. '16 — on the palate it's juicy and taut. The Roero '16 is just a bit less rich, but fresh with elegant tannins. The Barbera d'Alba '18 is succulent, rich in fruit, while the Nebbiolo d'Alba Selezione il Pilone '18 features floral sensations and accents of black berries, coming through long, with nice texture on the palate. The fresh and pleasant Roero Arneis Vigna Bricco Novara '18 also performed well.

● Roero Panera Alta Ris. '16	♟♟ 6
● Barbera d'Alba '18	♟♟ 2*
○ Nebbiolo d'Alba Selezione Il Pilone '18	♟♟ 2*
● Roero '16	♟♟ 4
○ Roero Arneis V. Bricco Novara '18	♟♟ 3
○ Langhe Favorita '18	♟ 2
● Langhe Nebbiolo '18	♟ 3
● Roero '18	♟ 4
● Barbera d'Alba '17	♟♟ 2*
○ Roero Arneis '17	♟♟ 2*
● Roero Panera Alta '15	♟♟ 6

Bric Cenciurio

via Roma, 24
12060 Barolo [CN]
Tel. +39 017356317
www.briccenciurio.com

CELLAR SALES
PRE-BOOKED VISITS
ANNUAL PRODUCTION 50,000 bottles
HECTARES UNDER VINE 15.00

There are a number of wineries that operate in Langhe and that also produce classic Roero DOCGs like Arneis and red Nebbiolo Roero. Fiorella Sacchetto manages such a winery, along with her brother Carlo and, increasingly, her young enologist sons Alessandro and Alberto Pittatore. Indeed, Cenciurio is the name of a hill situated in Castellinaldo, while the rest of their private vineyards can be found in Magliano Alfieri, as well as Barolo. Their international fame came about as a result of both their Arneis and their Barolos (four of them, including a reserve). And it's their Riserva del Barolo Coste di Rose '13 that stood out during our tastings, thanks to complex aromas in which delicate balsamic hints combine with deep sensations of tar. On the mouth it plays more on balance than on power, with pleasant, sandy tannins. But all their Nebbiolos performed well, starting with the vanilla-scented Langhe '17, and moving on to their Barolo Base '15, and the soft Coste di Rose.

● Barolo Coste di Rose Ris. '13	♟♟ 7
● Barolo Monrobiolo di Bussia '15	♟♟ 6
● Barolo '15	♟♟ 5
● Barolo Coste di Rose '15	♟♟ 6
● Langhe Nebbiolo '17	♟♟ 4
○ Langhe Riesling '17	♟♟ 2*
○ Roero Arneis '18	♟♟ 3
○ Roero Arneis Sito dei Fossili '18	♟ 3
● Barolo '13	♟♟ 5
● Barolo Coste di Rose '14	♟♟ 6
● Barolo Coste di Rose Ris. '11	♟♟ 7
● Barolo Coste di Rose Ris. '09	♟♟ 7
● Barolo Monrobiolo di Bussia '14	♟♟ 6
● Barolo Monrobiolo di Bussia '13	♟♟ 6
● Langhe Nebbiolo '16	♟♟ 4
● Langhe Nebbiolo '15	♟♟ 4

Bricco Maiolica

FRAZ. RICCA
VIA BOLANGINO, 7
12055 DIANO D'ALBA [CN]
TEL. +39 0173612049
www.briccomaiolica.it

CELLAR SALES
PRE-BOOKED VISITS
ACCOMMODATION
ANNUAL PRODUCTION 110,000 bottles
HECTARES UNDER VINE 24.00
SUSTAINABLE WINERY

Diano d'Alba is a district that's rightfully known for the quality of its Dolcetto grapes. But few know that it also comprises a small hill zone that's part of Barolo. As of late Beppe Accomo, who's celebrating 35 years in the field this year, has been focusing on the typology, purchasing a plot of Nebbiolo that gives rise to their Barolo Contadin. Their large, spectacular estate is worth the visit, even more so thanks to the possibility of staying in their private agritourism, Casa Castella. Youthful and rich in flesh, the Barolo Contadin '15 stands in out particular for its array of aromas, which call up golden-leaf tobacco and dried flowers. The Nebbiolo Cumot '16 is one of the best of its kind, sophisticated and capable of improving for years in the bottle. Sweet spices, acacia flowers and toasted hazelnuts mark their mouthfilling and extremely well-crafted Chardonnay Pensiero Infinito '15.

● Barbera d'Alba Sup. V. Vigia '16	♟♟ 5
● Barolo del Comune di Diano d'Alba Contadin '15	♟♟ 8
○ Langhe Chardonnay Pensiero Infinito '15	♟♟ 6
● Nebbiolo d'Alba Sup. Cumot '16	♟♟ 5
● Langhe Pinot Nero Perlei '16	♟♟ 5
● Barbera d'Alba '17	♟ 3
● Langhe Rosso Tris '17	♟ 3
○ Langhe Sauvignon Castella '18	♟ 3
● Barbera d'Alba V. Vigia '98	♟♟♟ 4*
● Diano d'Alba Sup. Sòri Bricco Maiolica '07	♟♟♟ 3*
● Nebbiolo d'Alba Cumot '11	♟♟♟ 5
● Nebbiolo d'Alba Cumot '10	♟♟♟ 4*
● Nebbiolo d'Alba Cumot '09	♟♟♟ 4*
● Nebbiolo d'Alba Sup. Cumot '13	♟♟♟ 5

Francesco Brigatti

VIA OLMI, 31
28019 SUNO [NO]
TEL. +39 032285037
www.vinibrigatti.it

CELLAR SALES
PRE-BOOKED VISITS
ANNUAL PRODUCTION 25,000 bottles
HECTARES UNDER VINE 6.50

Francesco Brigatti has been at the helm for 25 years, bolstered by a deep enological sense and knowledge of the terrain, but this year marks the winery's 100th birthday. Nebbiolo takes center stage, obviously, finding its highest expression in their Ghemme Oltre il Bosco and their DOC Colline Novaresi: Möt Ziflon and Möt Frei. The former is more flowery and fruity, the latter a bit more austere and complex. Their spicy Vespolina is always a pleasure. Theirs is an extremely high quality selection. The Ghemme Oltre Il Boasco '15 exhibits great finesse. Aromas of tanned leather give way to orange, rust and blackcurrant. On the palate it's already enjoyable, promising to improve further for many years. The well-crafted Nebbiolo MötZiflon '16 is more youthfu, assertive, with fresh aromas of raspberry, licorice and rhubarb anticipating a sophisticated, juicy palate. Tasty drinkability marks their spicy, down-to-earth Vespolina Maria and the lively, robust Bianco Mottobello, both 2018s.

● Colline Novaresi Nebbiolo MötZiflon '16	♟♟ 3*
● Ghemme Oltre il Bosco '15	♟♟ 4
● Colline Novaresi Barbera Campazzi '18	♟♟ 3
○ Colline Novaresi Bianco Mottobello '18	♟♟ 3
● Colline Novaresi Nebbiolo Mötfrei '16	♟♟ 3
● Colline Novaresi Vespolina Maria '18	♟♟ 3
● Colline Novaresi Uva Rara Selvalunga '18	♟ 2
○ Colline Novaresi Bianco Mottobello '17	♟♟ 3
● Colline Novaresi Nebbiolo Mötfrei '15	♟♟ 3
● Colline Novaresi Nebbiolo MötZiflon '15	♟♟ 3
● Colline Novaresi Vespolina Maria '16	♟♟ 3*
● Ghemme Oltre il Bosco '13	♟♟ 4

★Brovia

VIA ALBA-BAROLO, 145
12060 CASTIGLIONE FALLETTO [CN]
TEL. +39 017362852
www.brovia.net

CELLAR SALES
PRE-BOOKED VISITS
ANNUAL PRODUCTION 60,000 bottles
HECTARES UNDER VINE 15.00
VITICULTURE METHOD Certified Organic

Founded in 1863 as a farm, in the 1950s Brovia established itself as one of the best producers of Barolo thanks to Giacinto's undisputed skill. He passed on the legacy to his passionate daughters, who've also proven their salt both in the vineyard and the cellar. Their splendid vineyards, from Villero to Brea and Rocche di Castiglione, careful selection of grapes, and a classic, meticulous approach in the cellar bring out the highest expression of richness and elegance. Their enchanting Barolo Brea Vigna Ca' Mia is full-bodied and rich on the palate, where a delicate tannic presence lends masterful balance, closing with an encore of red berry fruit, licorice and herbs: Tre Bicchieri. The rich and convincing Rocche di Castiglione '15 is just a bit less fruit-forward on the nose and a bit more austere on the palate, while velvety sophistication marks the softer Castiglione '15. Their Barbera d'Alba Sorì del Drago '17, one of the best of the vintage, exhibits a rare elegance.

G. B. Burlotto

VIA VITTORIO EMANUELE, 28
12060 VERDUNO [CN]
TEL. +39 0172470122
www.burlotto.com

CELLAR SALES
PRE-BOOKED VISITS
ACCOMMODATION
ANNUAL PRODUCTION 60,000 bottles
HECTARES UNDER VINE 15.00

You'd have to go back to the mid-19th century to probe the origins of Burlotto. Today the winery is overseen by Fabio Alessandria, who continues their work in pursuit of quality, following a traditional style aimed at bringing out the attributes of Langa's best crus. Their 15 hectares of property (the winery also serves as an agritourism) features vineyards like Monvigliero, Neirane, Breri and Rocche dell'Olmo in Verduno, which are accompanied by their Cannubi plots in Barolo. The Barolo Cannubi '15 is a high expression of this celebrated cru. It's particularly complex on the nose, with notes of iodine, tar and red berries followed by a full-bodied, warm, long, gratifying palate: Tre Bicchieri. The Monvigliero is spicier, tantalizing, with an invigorating, fresh palate, it's weighty and yet extremely delicate. The licorice-scented Barolo '15 is of extraordinary craft, exhibiting vitality and persistence. The floral Langhe Nebbiolo '17 is among the best of the year, hands down.

● Barolo Brea Vigna Ca' Mia '15	▼▼▼ 8
● Barbera d'Alba Sorì del Drago '17	▼▼ 4
● Barolo Rocche di Castiglione '15	▼▼ 8
● Barolo Villero '15	▼▼ 8
● Barolo '15	▼▼ 7
● Dolcetto d'Alba Vignavillej '17	▼▼ 3
● Barolo Brea V. Ca' Mia '10	▼▼▼ 8
● Barolo Ca' Mia '09	▼▼▼ 8
● Barolo Ca' Mia '00	▼▼▼ 8
● Barolo Rocche dei Brovia '06	▼▼▼ 7
● Barolo Rocche di Castiglione '12	▼▼▼ 8
● Barolo Villero '13	▼▼▼ 8
● Barolo Villero '11	▼▼▼ 8
● Barolo Villero '10	▼▼▼ 8
● Barolo Villero '08	▼▼▼ 7
● Barolo Villero '06	▼▼▼ 7

● Barolo '15	▼▼ 6
● Barolo Acclivi '15	▼▼ 6
● Barolo Cannubi '15	▼▼ 7
● Barolo Monvigliero '15	▼▼ 7
● Langhe Nebbiolo '17	▼▼ 3*
● Barbera d'Alba Aves '17	▼▼ 4
○ Langhe Sauvignon Dives '17	▼▼ 3
○ Langhe Sauvignon Viridis '18	▼▼ 3
● Verduno Pelaverga '18	▼▼ 3
● Barolo Acclivi '11	▼▼▼ 6
● Barolo Acclivi '07	▼▼▼ 6
● Barolo Cannubi '12	▼▼▼ 7
● Barolo Monvigliero '10	▼▼▼ 7
● Barolo '13	▼▼ 6
● Barolo Acclivi '13	▼▼ 6
● Barolo Cannubi '14	▼▼ 7
● Barolo Cannubi '13	▼▼ 7

★Piero Busso

VIA ALBESANI
12052 NEIVE [CN]
TEL. +39 017367156
www.bussopiero.com

CELLAR SALES
PRE-BOOKED VISITS
ACCOMMODATION
ANNUAL PRODUCTION 45,000 bottles
HECTARES UNDER VINE 11.50
SUSTAINABLE WINERY

For some 40 years now this strictly family-run winery has eschewed outside help and guidance, as well as the use of added yeasts and artificial chemicals in the vineyard. It's all been possible thanks to the undisputed skill of Piero, a producer recognized internationally as a faithful interpreter of pure, classic Barbaresco. Today that holds as true as ever, with the enlistment of his passionate son Pierguido. In addition to their perennially valid Gallina, San Stunet, Borgese and Mondino vineyards, in 2010 they added the rare and elegant Albesani Viti Vecchie. The enchanting Albesani Vigna Borgese '15 is a prototypical Barbaresco, harmonious and layered, complex and fresh, tannic and velvet-smooth: Tre Bicchieri. The balanced gustatory profile of their San Stunet '16 proves similar, though it's enriched by a delicious balsamic touch. Powerful structure marks the warm Barbaresco Gallina '15, with alcohol gently enveloping tannins and rendering the palate soft.

● Barbaresco Albesani V. Borgese '15	♛♛♛ 7
● Barbaresco Gallina '15	♛♛ 8
● Barbaresco S. Stunet '15	♛♛ 7
● Barbaresco Albesani Viti Vecchie Ris. '13	♛♛ 8
● Barbaresco Mondino '16	♛♛ 5
● Barbera d'Alba S. Stefanetto '17	♛♛ 5
● Langhe Nebbiolo '17	♛♛ 4
● Barbaresco Borgese '09	♛♛♛ 6
● Barbaresco Borgese '08	♛♛♛ 6
● Barbaresco Gallina '12	♛♛♛ 8
● Barbaresco Gallina '11	♛♛♛ 8
● Barbaresco Gallina '09	♛♛♛ 8
● Barbaresco Gallina '05	♛♛♛ 7
● Barbaresco S. Stefanetto '07	♛♛♛ 7
● Barbaresco S. Stefanetto '04	♛♛♛ 7
● Barbaresco S. Stefanetto '03	♛♛♛ 7

Ca' Bianca

REG. SPAGNA, 58
15010 ALICE BEL COLLE [AL]
TEL. +39 0144745420
www.cantinacabianca.it

CELLAR SALES
PRE-BOOKED VISITS
ANNUAL PRODUCTION 500,000 bottles
HECTARES UNDER VINE 24.00

In 2016 this Gruppo Italiano Vini producer bet on Andrea Autino, a young enologist with experience in Italy and abroad. A few years later, the winemaker's approach is bearing fruit. Their wines are more memorable, with more marked varietal characteristics and a solid structure that speaks to good aging power. Recently they've begun producing Turin Vermouth with the historic Calissano brand. Gavi serves as the base for their whites, while Langhe Nebbiolo is the cornerstone of their reds. The Barbera d'Asti Superiore Chersì made it back into our final tastings. A notable balance shines a light on clean aromas of fruit, all on a background made spicy by oak aging. The Barbera d'Asti Superiore '17 is delicate and complex. On the palate it proves rich and firmly-structured, sapid, before giving way to a fresh, persistent finish. The intriguing Moscato d'Asti '18 also performed well.

● Barbera d'Asti Sup. Chersì '16	♛♛ 4
● Barbera d'Asti Sup. Antè '17	♛♛ 2*
○ Gavi '18	♛♛ 3
○ Moscato d'Asti '18	♛♛ 2*
● Dolcetto d'Acqui '18	♛ 2
○ Roero Arneis '18	♛ 2
● Barbera d'Asti Sup. Antè '16	♛♛ 3
● Barbera d'Asti Sup. Antè '15	♛♛ 3
● Barbera d'Asti Sup. Chersì '15	♛♛ 5
● Barbera d'Asti Sup. Chersì '14	♛♛ 5
● Barbera d'Asti Teis '17	♛♛ 3
● Barbera d'Asti Teis '16	♛♛ 3
● Dolcetto d'Acqui '17	♛♛ 3
○ Gavi '17	♛♛ 3
○ Gavi '16	♛♛ 3
○ Roero Arneis '15	♛♛ 3

Ca' d' Gal

FRAZ. VALDIVILLA
S.DA VECCHIA DI VALDIVILLA, 1
12058 SANTO STEFANO BELBO [CN]
TEL. +39 0141847103
www.cadgal.it

CELLAR SALES
PRE-BOOKED VISITS
ACCOMMODATION AND RESTAURANT SERVICE
ANNUAL PRODUCTION 95,000 bottles
HECTARES UNDER VINE 12.00

If Valdivilla di Santo Stefano Belbo has become a familiar benchmark for those who love sweet and sparkling Moscato, much of the credit goes to the work carried out by Alessandro Boido and family. Some four wines are dedicated to the celebrated Piedmont grape, including their Vigna Vecchia which, year after year, aptly expresses the typology's incredible aging potential (a characteristic that's anything but well-known to the general public). Still wines made with Chardonnay, Sauvignon, Pinot Nero, Barbera and Freisa round out their selection The heart of Ca' d'Gal's selection turns on their various Moscato d'Astis. In this last round of tastings the Canelli Sant'Illario '18, in particular, stood out for its vibrant sensations of candied fruit and Mediterranean herbs, along with fresher, more delicate notes. On the palate it enters sweet and buttery, exhibiting a harmony made possible by a robust streak of citrus. The Lumine '18 is subtler but equally memorable.

○ Moscato d'Asti Canelli Sant'Ilario '18	🏆🏆	4
○ Moscato d'Asti Lumine '18	🏆🏆	3
○ Asti	🏆	3
○ Moscato d'Asti Canelli Sant'Ilario '16	🏆🏆🏆	4*
○ Moscato d'Asti Canelli Sant'Ilario '15	🏆🏆🏆	3*
○ Moscato d'Asti V. V. '11	🏆🏆🏆	3*
○ Moscato d'"Asti Vite Vecchia '14	🏆🏆	7
○ Moscato d'Asti Canelli Sant'Ilario '17	🏆🏆	4
○ Moscato d'Asti Lumine '17	🏆🏆	3
○ Moscato d'Asti Lumine '16	🏆🏆	3
○ Moscato d'Asti Lumine '15	🏆🏆	3*
○ Moscato d'Asti Lumine '14	🏆🏆	3
○ Moscato d'Asti Sant'Ilario '14	🏆🏆	3*
○ Moscato d'Asti V. Vecchia '14	🏆🏆	4
○ Moscato d'Asti V. Vecchia '10	🏆🏆	7
○ Moscato d'Asti Vite Vecchia '15	🏆🏆	7

★Ca' del Baio

VIA FERRERE SOTTANO, 33
12050 TREISO [CN]
TEL. +39 0173638219
www.cadelbaio.com

CELLAR SALES
PRE-BOOKED VISITS
ANNUAL PRODUCTION 130,000 bottles
HECTARES UNDER VINE 25.00

Giulio Grasso has managed to remain a true farmer, though he's enlarged his business and enlisted the help his daughters, all three of whom are now committed to the producer with a youthful passion. Their enological style is elegantly classical, with the use of large, French oak barrels dominating. Their entire selection is valid, with Barbarescos that are among the appellation's best and always commendable Riesling. Only Barbarescos were among the reds submitted. Mint, sweet tobacco and red berry fruit introduce a splendid Pora '15, a dense, full-bodied wine, but enjoyable, taut, vigorous and juicy. Tre Bicchieri for their magnificent Vallegrande '16, a potent but well-balanced wine whose freshness and vitality reflect the vintage and close with a balsamic encore. The complex and well-proportioned Autinbej '16 is just a bit more austere, with sensations of black fruits at the fore. Nice finesse, medicinal herbs and a reviving bitterness mark their firmly-structured Riesling '17.

● Barbaresco Vallegrande '16	🏆🏆🏆	5
● Barbaresco Asili '16	🏆🏆	6
● Barbaresco Pora '15	🏆🏆	6
● Barbaresco Autinbej '16	🏆🏆	5
○ Langhe Riesling '17	🏆🏆	3
● Barbaresco Asili '15	🏆🏆🏆	6
● Barbaresco Asili '12	🏆🏆🏆	6
● Barbaresco Asili '10	🏆🏆🏆	6
● Barbaresco Asili '09	🏆🏆🏆	5
● Barbaresco Asili Ris. '11	🏆🏆🏆	8
● Barbaresco Pora '10	🏆🏆🏆	6
● Barbaresco Pora '06	🏆🏆🏆	6
● Barbaresco Valgrande '08	🏆🏆🏆	5
● Barbaresco Vallegrande '14	🏆🏆🏆	5

Ca' Nova

VIA SAN ISIDORO, 1
28010 BOGOGNO [NO]
TEL. +39 0322863406
www.cascinacanova.it

CELLAR SALES
PRE-BOOKED VISITS
ACCOMMODATION
ANNUAL PRODUCTION 45,000 bottles
HECTARES UNDER VINE 10.00

It's rare to visit a winery whose adjacent vineyards are inside a golf course, but it's worth the trip. This is particularly true if you take into account the possibility of staying in one of their lovely rooms (named after their vineyards). Their wines are just as commendable, exhibiting stylistic precision thanks in part to the guidance that Giada Codecasa draws on. Other plots provide the grapes for their Ghemmes and for their other wines, including their notable Nebbiolos and Vespolinas. As last year they opted for an extra few months of aging, for this edition they presented two vintages of both their Nebbiolo San Quirico and their Ghemme Victor. It's the 2013 version of the San Quirico that that shone most brightly, a true marvel of sophistication and elegance, as aromatically focused as it is harmonious and balanced on the palate. The pleasant 2014 version is just a bit more contained and tannic, while the youthful Ghemme Victor '13 is still quite closed in and hard.

● Colline Novaresi Nebbiolo San Quirico '13	♛♛ 4
● Ghemme Victor '13	♛♛ 5
● Colline Novaresi Nebbiolo San Quirico '14	♛♛ 4
● Colline Novaresi Vespolina '18	♛♛ 2*
○ Colline Novaresi Bianco Rugiada '18	♛ 2
⊙ Colline Novaresi Nebbiolo Aurora '18	♛ 2
● Colline Novaresi Nebbiolo Bocciòlo '18	♛ 2
● Ghemme Victor '14	♛ 5
● Colline Novaresi Nebbiolo Melchior '11	♛♛ 3
● Colline Novaresi Vespolina '17	♛♛ 2*
● Ghemme '13	♛♛ 5
● Ghemme '12	♛♛ 5
○ Jad'or Brut M. Cl.	♛♛ 4

Ca' Rome'

S.DA RABAJÀ, 86
12050 BARBARESCO [CN]
TEL. +39 0173635126
www.carome.com

CELLAR SALES
PRE-BOOKED VISITS
ANNUAL PRODUCTION 30,000 bottles
HECTARES UNDER VINE 5.00

Its small size and the high percentage of wines exported mean that Ca' Romé is more well-known in New York than in Milan, and that Romano Marengo is rarely mentioned in Italian guides. But the fact is that this gem is among Langhe's best producers and that the entire family work to produce wines of extraordinary precision and quality year in, year out. Their 3,000 bottles of Barolo Rapet, which are as potent as they are elegant, are accompanied by 8,000 of the even more monolithic Cerretta, and 7,000 bottles of the alluring Barbaresco Maria di Brun. The splendid 2015 version of their Barbaresco Maria di Brün maintains its aromas and austere, multifaceted structure even in a rather warm year. On the nose it unveils black berries, cocoa powder and quinine, while on the palate it's a fantastic procession of warmth and caresses revived by a delicious astringency conferred by tannins. Rose petals, licorice and a hint of strawberry mark their classically-styled Barolo Rapet '15.

● Barbaresco Maria di Brün '15	♛♛ 8
● Barolo Rapet '15	♛♛ 7
● Barbaresco Chiaramanti '16	♛♛ 7
● Barolo Cerretta '15	♛♛ 7
● Barbaresco Maria di Brün '13	♛♛♛ 8
● Barbaresco Sorì Rio Sordo '06	♛♛♛ 6
● Barolo Rapet '14	♛♛♛ 7
● Barolo Rapet '11	♛♛♛ 7
● Barolo Rapet '08	♛♛♛ 7
● Barolo V. Cerretta '09	♛♛♛ 7
● Barbaresco Chiaramanti '15	♛♛ 7
● Barbaresco Rio Sordo '13	♛♛ 7
● Barbaresco Sorì Rio Sordo '13	♛♛ 6
● Barolo Cerretta '14	♛♛ 7

★★Ca' Viola

B.TA SAN LUIGI, 11
12063 DOGLIANI [CN]
TEL. +39 017370547
www.caviola.com

CELLAR SALES
PRE-BOOKED VISITS
ACCOMMODATION AND RESTAURANT SERVICE
ANNUAL PRODUCTION 70,000 bottles
HECTARES UNDER VINE 10.00

Beppe Caviola established himself as a
sensitive consultant, respectful of grapes
and different production styles, carefully
avoiding a uniform approach. Then he
gained attention for his tiny Montelupo
Albese winery's selection, especially
Dolcetto and Barbera d'Alba, which are
consistently among the best of their kind.
Today, with a splendid new operation in
Dogliani, we can affirm that he's a
prestigious producer of Barolo, having
purchased an excellent vineyard in the
Sottocastello di Novello cru, with results
that just keep getting better. Their complex,
classically-styled Barolo Sottocastello di
Novello '15 enchants with its harmony and
pure expression of Nebbiolo (partially the
result of maturation in large barrels). Red
fruits, quinine and licorice alternate towards
a long, succulent and austere finish: Tre
Bicchieri. Their sumptuous Nebbiolo '17
impressed during our blind tastings — it's
never been so elegant, rich in violet,
powerful and compact.

● Barolo Sottocastello di Novello '15	♟♟♟	8
● Dolcetto d'Alba Barturot '17	♟♟	4
● Langhe Nebbiolo '17	♟♟	5
○ Langhe Riesling Clem '17	♟♟	5
● Barbera d'Alba Brichet '17	♟♟	4
● Dolcetto d'Alba Vilot '18	♟♟	3
● Barbera d'Alba Bric du Luv '12	♟♟♟	5
● Barbera d'Alba Bric du Luv '10	♟♟♟	5
● Barolo Sottocastello di Novello '13	♟♟♟	8
● Barolo Sottocastello di Novello '12	♟♟♟	8
● Barolo Sottocastello di Novello '11	♟♟♟	8
● Barolo Sottocastello di Novello '10	♟♟♟	7
● Barolo Sottocastello di Novello '08	♟♟♟	7

Fabrizia Caldera

FRAZ. PORTACOMARO STAZIONE, 53

14100 ASTI
TEL. +39 0141296154
www.vinicaldera.it

CELLAR SALES
PRE-BOOKED VISITS
ACCOMMODATION
ANNUAL PRODUCTION 95,000 bottles
HECTARES UNDER VINE 22.00

Supported by her husband and son,
Fabrizia Caldera represents the fourth
generation to operate in the family winery
launched by Signor Prospero in the early
20th century. Mario Rodeglia oversees the
cellar, which spawns a broad catalogue of
wines made with local grapes. Barbera
makes up the lion's share, with three
versions (Balmèt, Harmonius, Il Giullare),
but they also get excellent results with
Moscato, Cortese, Viognier, Charodnnay,
Ruchè, Grignolino and Dolcetto. Their
Barbera d'Astis are once again at the top of
their game, thanks in particular to the
Balmèt '16. It's a little stifled on the
primaries, but opens gradually to charming
earthy and spicy notes, confirming its aging
power in a development that's hard but
never unrefined or dry. And freshness is a
key feature of their Grignolino Leserre '18
as well, a wine introduced by hints of citrus
and flowers. On the palate it's still youthful,
and in need of integration, but already racy
and lively.

● Barbera d'Asti Sup. Balmèt '16	♟♟	4
● Grignolino d'Asti Leserre '18	♟♟	3
● Ruché di Castagnole Monferrato Prevost '18	♟♟	4
● Barbera d'Asti Harmonius '16	♟	3
○ Gavi Reisì '18	♟	3
○ Monferrato Bianco Viò '18	♟	3
● Ruché di Castagnole Monferrato Xenio '17	♟	3
● Barbera d'Asti '15	♟♟	3
● Grignolino d'Asti Leserre '17	♟♟	2*
● Ruché di Castagnole Monferrato Prevost '17	♟♟	3

Cantina del Nebbiolo

VIA TORINO, 17
12050 VEZZA D'ALBA [CN]
TEL. +39 017365040
www.cantinadelnebbiolo.com

CELLAR SALES
PRE-BOOKED VISITS
ANNUAL PRODUCTION 300,000 bottles
HECTARES UNDER VINE 300.00
VITICULTURE METHOD Certified Organic

Founded in 1901 as Cantina Sociale Parrocchiale di Vezza d'Alba and rebuilt in 1959 under its current name, Cantina del Nebbiolo is one of Roero's most important cooperatives. It avails itself of 170 grower members who oversee vineyards both in Roero and Langhe. Their wines are made primarily with Nebbiolo, as the name suggests, but there's also Arneis, Barbera, Nascetta and Favorita, making for a selection of technically well-crafted wines that express the best characteristics of the territory. The Barbaresco Meruzzano Ris. '15 is a charming wine in its aromas of tobacco, red berries and licorice, and its expansive, pervasive, focused palate. The rest of their selection also proves well-made. We were particularly impressed with the fresh and approachable Barbaresco '16, an elegant wine with velvet-smooth tannins, the tightly-woven Barolo Perno '15, the vibrant, fruit-driven Roero Arneis '18 with its mineral nuances, and the aromatic Langhe Nascetta Riveverse '17.

● Barbaresco Meruzzano Ris. '15	♟♟ 5
● Barbaresco '16	♟♟ 4
● Barbaresco Meruzzano '16	♟♟ 5
● Barbera d'Alba Sup. '16	♟♟ 2*
● Barolo del Comune di Serralunga d'Alba '15	♟♟ 6
● Barolo Perno '15	♟♟ 5
○ Langhe Nascetta Riveverse '17	♟♟ 2*
○ Roero Arneis '18	♟♟ 2*
○ Roero Arneis Arenarium '18	♟♟ 2*
○ Langhe Favorita '18	♟ 2
● Nebbiolo d'Alba V. Valmaggiore '17	♟ 3
● Barbaresco '15	♟♟ 4
● Barolo '14	♟♟ 5
● Barolo Perno '14	♟♟ 5

Cantina del Pino

S.DA OVELLO, 31
12050 BARBARESCO [CN]
TEL. +39 0173635147
www.cantinadelpino.com

ANNUAL PRODUCTION 35,000 bottles
HECTARES UNDER VINE 7.00

A centuries-old maritime pine just outside Barbaresco, in the prestigious cru that is Ovello, inspired the name and foundation of this wine boutique, overseen with great passion by Renato Vacca. Established in 1997, today the producer's wines are known throughout the world thanks to a distinct style that highlights a unique territory, from Ovello to Gallina, forged in the bottle with a respectful, subtle hand when it comes to texture and flavor. Great care is shown, making for intricate and balanced wines. Seductive' is the right adjective for their Barbaresco Ovello '15, an extremely smooth wine in its tannic weave, silky and pervasive in its meaty fruit, with a use of oak that's sartorial, to say the least. The livelyBarbaresco '15 confirmed the excellent maturity of its fruit, combined with pronounced but never excessive spiciness and a sapid, multifaceted finish. The other two Barbarescos presented performed notably as well, making for a quality selection across the board.

● Barbaresco '15	♟♟ 5
● Barbaresco Ovello '15	♟♟ 7
● Barbaresco Albesani '15	♟♟ 7
● Barbaresco Gallina '14	♟♟ 7
● Barbaresco '04	♟♟♟ 5*
● Barbaresco '03	♟♟♟ 4*
● Barbaresco Albesani '14	♟♟♟ 7
● Barbaresco Albesani '05	♟♟♟ 6
● Barbaresco Ovello '13	♟♟♟ 7
● Barbaresco Ovello '07	♟♟♟ 6
● Barbaresco Ovello '99	♟♟♟ 5
● Barbaresco '14	♟♟ 5
● Barbaresco '13	♟♟ 5
● Barbaresco '12	♟♟ 5
● Barbaresco Albesani '13	♟♟ 7
● Barbaresco Ovello '14	♟♟ 7
● Barbaresco Ovello '12	♟♟ 6

La Caplana

VIA CIRCONVALLAZIONE, 4
15060 BOSIO [AL]
TEL. +39 0143684182
www.lacaplana.com

CELLAR SALES
PRE-BOOKED VISITS
ANNUAL PRODUCTION 120,000 bottles
HECTARES UNDER VINE 5.00

This family-run producer has wine in its DNA, cultivating steep hillside vineyards for generations and focusing on native grape varieties. Cortese, Dolcetto and Barbera, subdivided into two production lines, complete their selection, but there's also room for Chardonnay, both a monovarietal and a Brut Metodo Classico, where both Cortese and Moscato also contribute. Their wines are exceptionally well-crafted, especially their Gavi and Dolcetto, which on a number of occasions were contenders for Tre Bicchieri during our final tastings. The Dolcetto di Ovada Narcys is an excellent representative of the appellation. On the nose it offers up aromas of red berry fruits, delicate notes of almond and tobacco. On the palate it's harmonious, with decisive tannins and a long, persistent finish. The Gavi del Comune di Gavi '18 proves complex and subtle, with vegetal aromas meeting floral fragrances on a lovely, mineral backdrop. Acidity is crisp, the finish long and sapid.

● Dolcetto di Ovada Narcys '17	♟♟ 3*
○ Gavi del Comune di Gavi '18	♟♟ 2*
● Barbera d'Asti '17	♟♟ 3
● Barbera d'Asti Rubis '16	♟♟ 3
○ Gavi '18	♟♟ 2*
○ Gavi Villa Vecchia '18	♟♟ 2*
● Dolcetto di Ovada '18	♟ 2
● Dolcetto di Ovada Narcys '15	♟♟ 3*
● Dolcetto di Ovada Narcys '13	♟♟ 3*
○ Gavi del Comune di Gavi '17	♟♟ 2*
○ Gavi del Comune di Gavi '16	♟♟ 2*

La Casaccia

VIA D. BARBANO, 10
15034 CELLA MONTE [AL]
TEL. +39 0142489986
www.lacasaccia.biz

CELLAR SALES
PRE-BOOKED VISITS
ANNUAL PRODUCTION 25,000 bottles
HECTARES UNDER VINE 6.70
VITICULTURE METHOD Certified Organic

La Casaccia, has adopted a certified organic approach in which every part of production and business (including their agritourism) is carried out in accordance with ecological principles, in support of biodiversity. Their selection centers almost entirely on wines made with Monferrato's native grapes (Barbera, Grignolino, Freisa). It also includes a Chardonnay, the Charnò, while their La Casaccia Brut is a Metodo Classico made with Pinot Nero and Chardonnay. Aging takes place mostly in steel, with the exception of their Barbera del Monferrato Caliché, which sees a stay in barriques. We tasted the Poggeto '17 at a point in which it's aromatically rich, a decidedly classic profile for the typology. The palate is extraordinary for its fullness and tannic weave before giving way to a long finish. The Giuanìn '17 exhibits a leaner profile than usual, but maintains its balance and harmony. Their Metodo Classico is vibrant, with a pronounced acidity reemerging on its long finish.

● Grignolino del M.to Casalese Poggeto '17	♟♟ 2*
● Barbera del M.to Giuanìn '17	♟♟ 2*
○ La Casaccia Brut M.Cl. '15	♟♟ 4
● Barbera del M.to Bricco dei Boschi '15	♟♟ 3
● Barbera del M.to Calichè '15	♟♟ 3
● Barbera del M.to Giuanìn '15	♟♟ 2*
● Grignolino del M.to Casalese Ernesto '13	♟♟ 3
● Grignolino del M.to Casalese Ernesto '12	♟♟ 3*
● Grignolino del M.to Casalese Poggeto '16	♟♟ 2*
● Grignolino del M.to Casalese Poggeto '15	♟♟ 2*
● M.to Freisa Monfiorenza '16	♟♟ 3

Casalone

VIA MARCONI, 100
15040 LU [AL]
TEL. +39 0131741280
www.casalone.it

CELLAR SALES
PRE-BOOKED VISITS
ANNUAL PRODUCTION 50,000 bottles
HECTARES UNDER VINE 10.00

Tradition and history are part of this Lu Monferrato family's past. Their bond with the vineyards, which goes back to the 18th century, has resulted in wines of excellent craft. These speak primarily in Monferrato's local dialect, with Barbera, Grignolino, Freisa and Cortese on center stage. They also offer a particular selection of Malvasia Moscata (also known as Malvasia Greca, a variety known to the territory when Da Vinci was just a boy). Pinot Nero and Merlot are used along with Barbera in their Rus, while the Fandamat and Arnest are monovarietal Pinot Neros. A lovely version, fresh and enticing, of their Brut Metodo Classico 60 Mesi led their selection this year. The Grignolino I Canonici di Lu, on occasion of its debut, displays power and character. Its more youthful characteristics, moreover, guarantee that it will continue to improve with time. The balanced and multifaceted Rubermillo features fruity aromas accompanied by nice oak.

● Barbera del M.to Sup. Rubermillo '15	🏆🏆 3
○ Monvasia '18	🏆🏆 2*
○ Monvasia Brut M. Cl. 60 mesi '13	🏆🏆 4
● Piemonte Grignolino I Canonici di Lu '15	🏆🏆 4
● M.to Rosso Fandamat '17	🏆 3
● Piemonte Grignolino La Caplëtta '17	🏆 3
● Barbera d'Asti Rubermillo '11	🏆🏆 3*
● Barbera del M.to Sup. Bricco Morlantino '15	🏆🏆 3*
● Barbera del M.to Sup. Bricco Morlantino '13	🏆🏆 2*
● Monferrato Rosso Fandamat '14	🏆🏆 2*
● Piemonte Grignolino La Caplëtta '15	🏆🏆 3*

Cascina Barisél

REG. SAN GIOVANNI, 30
14053 CANELLI [AT]
TEL. +39 3394165913
www.barisel.it

CELLAR SALES
PRE-BOOKED VISITS
ANNUAL PRODUCTION 35,000 bottles
HECTARES UNDER VINE 4.50
SUSTAINABLE WINERY

Canelli's heavily calcareous soil sets the stage for the Penna family's charming estate, Cascina Barisél, a producer that's been active since 1985. Their best plots host the area's classic grapes: Barbera, Dolcetto and Moscato. But they also cultivate Favorita, Chardonnay and Pinot Nero (which is used to make a Metodo Classico sparkling wine). This varietal puzzle comes together harmoniously in a selection distinct for its rich, sunny character. The selection's dual track is well developed, as our last round of tastings testifies to. The Enrico Penna Extra Brut Metodo Classico '15 landed a place in our finals thanks to its fleshy black berry fruits, enriched by an elegant spiciness and supported by a close-woven, seductive palate. The same holds for the Barbera Sup. La Cappelletta '16, a wine rich in sylvan sensations and endowed with a flavorful palate in which fullness and style go hand in hand.

● Barbera d'Asti Sup. La Cappelletta '16	🏆🏆 4
○ Enrico Penna Brut M. Cl. '15	🏆🏆 5
● Barbera d'Asti '18	🏆🏆 2*
● Barbera d'Asti Sup. Listoria '17	🏆🏆 3
○ M.to Bianco Foravìa '18	🏆 2
○ Moscato d'Asti Canelli '18	🏆 2
● Barbera d'Asti Sup. La Cappelletta '15	🏆🏆 4
● Barbera d'Asti Sup. Listoria '16	🏆🏆 3*
● Barbera d'Asti Sup. Nizza V. dei Pilati '13	🏆🏆 6
● Moscato d'Asti Canelli '17	🏆🏆 2*
○ Moscato d'Asti Canelli '16	🏆🏆 2*

Cascina Bongiovanni

loc. UCCELLACCIO
VIA ALBA BAROLO, 3
12060 CASTIGLIONE FALLETTO [CN]
TEL. +39 0173262184
www.cascinabongiovanni.com

CELLAR SALES
PRE-BOOKED VISITS
ACCOMMODATION
ANNUAL PRODUCTION 50,000 bottles
HECTARES UNDER VINE 7.20
SUSTAINABLE WINERY

Firmly in the hands of Davide Mozzone, this historic Langa producer is bolstered by eight hectares of vineyards in the municipalities of Castiglione Falletto, Serralunga d'Alba, Monforte d'Alba, Diano d'Alba and San Pietro in Govone. Their selection is rich and varied, ranging from easy-drinking wines to great ageworthy reds, all proposed in a style that straddles the traditional and modern, with well-executed spiciness of oak that's never excessively toasty. The Barolo Riserva '13 has plenty to say. It's a deep wine in its notes of quinine, wood tar and tobacco, rich in fruit and spicy sensations. On the palate it's potent and multi-layered, austere in its tannic weave, with a finish so long that's it's still evolving. The Barolo '15 is intense in its toastiness, full-bodied and solidly built, just a bit drying at the end. The Langhe Rosso Faletto '17, elegant in its balsamic profile, comes through precise and rich on the palate, marked by a vibrant acidic freshness.

● Barolo Ris. '13	♟♟ 8
● Langhe Rosso Faletto '17	♟♟ 4
● Barolo '15	♟♟ 6
● Barolo Pernanno '15	♟♟ 7
● Langhe Nebbiolo '17	♟♟ 4
● Barbera d'Alba '17	♟ 4
● Dolcetto d'Alba '18	♟ 3
○ Langhe Arneis '18	♟ 3
● Barolo Pernanno '01	♟♟♟ 6
● Barolo '13	♟♟ 6
● Barolo Pernanno '14	♟♟ 7
● Barolo Pernanno '13	♟♟ 7
● Barolo Pernanno '12	♟♟ 7
● Barolo Pernanno '11	♟♟ 6
● Barolo Pernanno '10	♟♟ 6
● Dolcetto di Diano d'Alba '15	♟♟ 3*

★Cascina Ca' Rossa

loc. CASCINA CA' ROSSA, 56
12043 CANALE [CN]
TEL. +39 017398348
www.cascinacarossa.com

CELLAR SALES
PRE-BOOKED VISITS
ANNUAL PRODUCTION 90,000 bottles
HECTARES UNDER VINE 16.00
VITICULTURE METHOD Certified Organic

Over the years, the winery overseen by Angelo Ferrio and his son has established itself as a quality and style benchmark for Roero. Valmaggiore Audinaggio, Mompissano and the recently added Le Coste, all vineyards situated in Canale, Santo Stefano Roero and Vezza d'Alba, are doubtless among the highest expressions of Roero, proving elegant and utterly charming. They're joined by a Roero Arneis and Barbera d'Alba, two wines that are increasingly well-defined, brilliant, making for a selection matched by few. Their two classic crus are splendid. The Roero Valmaggiore Audinaggio '17 is elegant, with hints of wild berries and orange peel anticipating a coherent, juicy, fresh and taut palate. The Roero Ris. Mompissano '16 exhibits lovely complexity, proving subtle and multifaceted, rich in pulp, with a long finish. The complex and sapid Roero Arneis Merica '18 is well-made, as is the tannic but succulent Roero Le Coste '16, and the fruit-forward Barbera d'Alba Mulassa '17.

● Roero Valmaggiore V. Audinaggio '17	♟♟♟ 5
● Roero Mompissano Ris. '16	♟♟ 5
● Barbera d'Alba Mulassa '17	♟♟ 5
○ Roero Arneis Merica '18	♟♟ 3
● Roero Le Coste '16	♟♟ 5
● Roero Audinaggio '07	♟♟♟ 5
● Roero Mompissano Ris. '13	♟♟♟ 5
● Roero Mompissano Ris. '12	♟♟♟ 5
● Roero Mompissano Ris. '10	♟♟♟ 5
● Roero Mompissano Ris. '07	♟♟♟ 6
● Roero Valmaggiore V. Audinaggio '16	♟♟♟ 5
● Roero Valmaggiore V. Audinaggio '15	♟♟♟ 5

Cascina Chicco

VIA VALENTINO, 14
12043 CANALE [CN]
TEL. +39 0173979411
www.cascinachicco.com

CELLAR SALES
PRE-BOOKED VISITS
ANNUAL PRODUCTION 435,000 bottles
HECTARES UNDER VINE 50.00
SUSTAINABLE WINERY

Over the years the Faccenda brothers have managed to oversee notable growth in the family winery. Founded in the 1950s with the purchase of a hectare of vineyards in Canale, today the estate comprises some 40 hectares in Roero (Canale, Vezza d'Alba, Castellinald, Castagnito). These are accompanied by 5 hectares in Monforte d'Alba, which give rise to their Barolos. Their selection, which features technical precision, is increasingly focused on expressing the attributes of the territories of origin. Both Cascina Chicco's Barolos and their Barbera d'Albas were at the top of their game. The Barolo Rocche di Castelletto '15 features balsamic hints, notes of quinine and undergrowth, while on the palate it has nice texture and grip. The Barolo Ginestra Ris. '12 offers up floral notes and whiffs of tea leaves, anticipating a complex, mouthfilling palate. Their assertive, fruit-forward Barbera d'Alba Bric Loira '17 is marked by spicy nuances, along with red berries and rain-soaked earth.

● Barbera d'Alba Bric Loira '17	♟♟ 4
● Barolo Ginestra Ris. '12	♟♟ 8
● Barolo Rocche di Castelletto '15	♟♟ 5
○ Arcass	♟♟ 4
○ Cuvée Zero Extra Brut M. Cl. '15	♟♟ 4
⊙ Cuvée Zero Extra Brut M. Cl. Rosé '15	♟♟ 4
● Langhe Nebbiolo '18	♟♟ 3
○ Roero Arneis Anterisio '18	♟♟ 3
● Roero Valmaggiore Ris. '16	♟♟ 4
● Barbera d'Alba Granera Alta '18	♟ 3
○ Langhe Favorita '18	♟ 3
○ Arcàss Passito '04	♟♟♟ 3
● Barolo Ginestra Ris. '11	♟♟♟ 8
● Roero Valmaggiore Ris. '12	♟♟♟ 4*

Cascina Corte

FRAZ. SAN LUIGI
B.TA VALDIBERTI, 33
12063 DOGLIANI [CN]
TEL. +39 0173743539
www.cascinacorte.it

CELLAR SALES
PRE-BOOKED VISITS
ACCOMMODATION
ANNUAL PRODUCTION 30,000 bottles
HECTARES UNDER VINE 5.00
VITICULTURE METHOD Certified Organic
SUSTAINABLE WINERY

20 years ago, supported by his wife, Amalia, Sandro chose to create an artisanal winery that would exist in harmony with nature. Since then they've renovated the facility and vineyards, creating a lovely cellar and agritourism. They work hard and are constantly researching new paths, as long as they're ecological. To that end they've experimented with the use of amphoras (still limited for the moment). An homage to their Pirochetta Vecchie Vigne, a cornerstone of their selection, can be found in the interesting 'Vini da scoprire', published by Giunti. Aromas of quinine and oak on a raspberry background introduce their weighty Langhe Nebbiolo '17, one of the year's most true to type interpretations. On the palate it exhibits force, with discernible but never invasive tannins. Plums and a touch of cocoa powder characterize the Pirochetta Vecchie Vigne '17, an interpretation of the cultivar that's excellent thanks to its mouth-puckering grip and extraordinary, fruity flesh.

● Dogliani Sup. Pirochetta V. V. '17	♟♟ 3*
● Langhe Nebbiolo '17	♟♟ 4
● Dogliani '18	♟ 3
● Langhe Barbera '17	♟ 3
○ Langhe Nascetta Cecilia '18	♟ 3
○ Langhe Riesling '18	♟ 3
● Dogliani Vecchie V. Pirochetta '08	♟♟♟ 3*
● Dogliani '15	♟♟ 3*
● Dogliani '14	♟♟ 3
● Dogliani Sup. Pirochetta V. V. '15	♟♟ 3
● Dogliani Sup. Pirochetta V. V. '13	♟♟ 3
● Dogliani Sup. Pirochetta V. V. '12	♟♟ 3*
● Dogliani Sup. Pirochetta V. V. Anfora '17	♟♟ 3
● Langhe Nebbiolo '14	♟♟ 4
● Langhe Nebbiolo '13	♟♟ 4
● Langhe Nebbiolo Anfora '17	♟♟ 4

Cascina delle Rose

FRAZ. TRE STELLE
S.DA RIO SORDO, 58
12050 BARBARESCO [CN]
TEL. +39 0173638292
www.cascinadellerose.it

CELLAR SALES
PRE-BOOKED VISITS
ACCOMMODATION
ANNUAL PRODUCTION 20,000 bottles
HECTARES UNDER VINE 5.00
VITICULTURE METHOD Certified Organic

Cascina delle Rose is a producer that's as interesting as it is small — it's also a great destination for nature lovers. Here a traditional style reins, with wines rich in personality that have plenty to express when it comes to the territory and its grapes. For those interested in knowing more, Suzanne Hoffman's 'Labor of Love: Wine Family Women in Piedmont' offers a lovely portrait of Giovanna Rizzolio and her family. Barbaresco is at the center of their selection, but their Barbera d'Albas are also worth trying. The Barbaresco Rio Sordo exhibits a splendidly classical, pure style, perfectly expressing an outstanding 2016 by virtue of its considerable fruit and a perfect gustatory harmony in which freshness is accompanied by highly enjoyable drinkability. It's a Tre Bicchieri that nicely demonstrates the lightness and precision of fermentation and maturation in large barrels. The Barbaresco Tre Stelle '16 is slightly less rich but of precise and enjoyable craft.

● Barbaresco Rio Sordo '16	🍷🍷🍷	7
● Barbaresco Tre Stelle '16	🍷🍷	7
● Barbera d'Alba '17	🍷🍷	3
● Dolcetto d'Alba A Elizabeth '18	🍷🍷	3
● Langhe Nebbiolo '18	🍷🍷	4
● Barbera d'Alba Sup. Donna Elena '16	🍷	4
● Barbaresco Rio Sordo '15	🍷🍷	5
● Barbaresco Tre Stelle '15	🍷🍷	5
● Barbera d'Alba '16	🍷🍷	4
● Barbera d'Alba Sup. Donna Elena '15	🍷🍷	4
● Langhe Nebbiolo '16	🍷🍷	4

Cascina Fonda

VIA SPESSA, 29
12052 MANGO [CN]
TEL. +39 0173677877
www.cascinafonda.com

CELLAR SALES
PRE-BOOKED VISITS
ACCOMMODATION
ANNUAL PRODUCTION 110,000 bottles
HECTARES UNDER VINE 12.00

It was 1963 when Secondino Barbero founded the business that his sons Massimio and Marco consolidated in 1988 with the bottling of their own wines. From the outset they've focused on Moscato, which is proposed in various versions according to the geography of the hills spread throughout Mango and Neive. Over time it's been accompanied by other important regional grapes (Dolcetto, Brachetto and Barbaresco Nebbiolo), making for a selection that has become increasingly noteworthy for its consistent quality and stylistic coherence. The selection submitted for tasting is entirely dedicated to Moscato in all its multivariate interpretations. We chose to focus on the Moscato Spumante Tardivo, a wine introduced by delicate and complex nuances that range from pear to peach, from sage to mint, a profile that's alluring, to say the least. On the palate it even rises in intensity, proving dense but comfortably outside the reach of sugary excesses, lengthening with liveliness and flavor.

○ Moscato Spumante Tardivo	🍷🍷	3*
○ Asti Bel Piasì '18	🍷🍷	2*
○ Brut Nature	🍷🍷	4
○ Moscato d'Asti Bel Piano '18	🍷🍷	2*
○ Moscato Spumante Chiara Blanc	🍷🍷	2
○ Asti Bel Piasì '16	🍷🍷	2*
○ La Tardja '16	🍷🍷	3*
○ Moscato d'Asti Bel Piano '16	🍷🍷	2*
○ Moscato Spumante Tardivo '14	🍷🍷	3*
○ Moscato Spumante Tardivo '12	🍷🍷	3*

Cascina Fontana

Loc. Perno
v.lo della Chiesa, 2
12065 Monforte d'Alba [CN]
Tel. +39 0173789005
www.cascinafontana.com

CELLAR SALES
PRE-BOOKED VISITS
ANNUAL PRODUCTION 26,000 bottles
HECTARES UNDER VINE 5.00
SUSTAINABLE WINERY

Mario Fontana is on his 25th season, bolstered by a contagious enthusiasm that grows year after year, thanks in part to a growing number of successes and awards. His Barolo is made with grapes from both Monforte d'Alba and La Morra, while their other wines come from a lovely plot in Sinio. Both in the vineyard and in the cellar Mario pursues the highest expression of the individual grapes, achieving results that are always rich in personality. High elevations also confer excellent freshness. The Barolo '15 is intense, with classic notes of tobacco and red fruits accompanied by a delicate, jammy backdrop that's characteristic of the year. On the palate it's firm, with nice body and a robust, tannic backbone giving way to a harmonious finish (it's just a bit lacking in length). As is the want of skilled winemaker Mario Fontana, the rest of their selection plays more on substance than on elegance, all in pursuit of tradition and purity.

● Barolo '15	♼♼	6
● Barbera d'Alba '17	♼♼	3
● Dolcetto d'Alba '18	♼	2
● Langhe Nebbiolo '17	♼	4
● Barolo '12	♼♼♼	6
● Barolo '10	♼♼♼	7
● Barbera d'Alba '16	♀♀	3
● Barbera d'Alba '15	♀♀	3
● Barbera d'Alba '14	♀♀	3
● Barolo '14	♀♀	6
● Barolo '13	♀♀	6
● Barolo '11	♀♀	6
● Langhe Nebbiolo '16	♀♀	4
● Langhe Nebbiolo '15	♀♀	4
● Langhe Nebbiolo '14	♀♀	4
● Langhe Nebbiolo '13	♀♀	4

Cascina Gilli

via Nevissano, 36
14022 Castelnuovo Don Bosco [AT]
Tel. +39 0119876984
www.cascinagilli.it

CELLAR SALES
PRE-BOOKED VISITS
ACCOMMODATION
ANNUAL PRODUCTION 100,000 bottles
HECTARES UNDER VINE 15.00

Situated in Castelnuovo Don Bosco, Albugnano and Passerano Marmorito in lower Monferrato, the winery Cascina Gilli has been managed by Gianni Vergnano since 1983. Their journey began with Freisa and Malvasia-based wines, though over time they've gradually enlarged the estate to include other native cultivars, like Bonarda and, especially, Barbera. Today his son Paolo is involved, along with Giovanni Matteis and Gianpiero Gerbi, making for a close-knit staff and a reliable, original selection of wines. Intense aromas of pepper, tobacco and dried herbs, a broad and generous palate marked by vigorous tannins: the profile exhibited by their Freisa d'Asti Il Forno '17 is distinctive (to say the least) in terms of varietal correctness and natural expression (it's no coincidence that Cascina Gilli began with the typology). But their selection shines across the board, from the mouthfilling Barbera Superiore Dedica '16 to the flowery Malvasia di Castelnuovo Don Bosco '18.

● Freisa d'Asti Arvelé '15	♼♼	3*
● Freisa d'Asti Il Forno '17	♼♼	2*
● Barbera d'Asti Sup. Dedica '16	♼♼	3
● Malvasia di Castelnuovo Don Bosco '18	♼♼	2*
○ Piemonte Chardonnay Rafé '18	♼	2
● Barbera d'Asti Le More '15	♀♀	2*
● Barbera d'Asti Le More '11	♀♀	2*
● Freisa d'Asti Il Forno '16	♀♀	2*
● Malvasia di Castelnuovo Don Bosco '17	♀♀	2*
● Malvasia di Castelnuovo Don Bosco '16	♀♀	2*
● Piemonte Bonarda Sernù '16	♀♀	2*

★★Cascina La Barbatella

s.da Annunziata, 55
14049 Nizza Monferrato [AT]
Tel. +39 0141701434
www.labarbatella.com

CELLAR SALES
PRE-BOOKED VISITS
ANNUAL PRODUCTION 25,000 bottles
HECTARES UNDER VINE 4.00

In the early 1980s, Angelo Sonvico decided to bring a small producer to life, starting with a farmstead on the hills of Nizza Monferrato (aka La Barbatella) and the surrounding estate. As of 2010, Lorenzo and Cinzia Perego have also been part of the team. They've proven skilled and determined to relaunch a project that hinges on supple, linear Barberas made with grapes cultivated on the hills' trademark calcareous-sandy soil. The producer's ampelography is rounded out with other traditional grapes, as well as international varieties. Two versions of their Nizza Vigna dell'Angelo led their selection this year. The 2016 offers up vibrant, jammy notes of red and black berry fruits accompanied by hints of quinine and cocoa powder. On the palate it's warm and powerful, finding balance thanks to its lively and spirited contrasts. The sweetly spicy and gradually unfolding Nizza La Vigna dell'Angelo Riserva '15 is more clenched at this stage but guaranteed to age well.

● Nizza La V. dell'Angelo '16	♥♥	5
● Nizza La V. dell'Angelo Ris. '15	♥♥	5
● Barbera d'Asti La Barbatella '17	♥♥	3
○ M.to Bianco Non È '17	♥♥	3
● M.to Rosso Sonvico '14	♥♥	6
○ La Badessa Brut M. Cl. '14	♥	4
○ M.to Bianco Noè '17	♥	3
● Barbera d'Asti Sup. Nizza V. dell'Angelo '11	♥♥♥	5
● Barbera d'Asti Sup. Nizza V. dell'Angelo '07	♥♥♥	5
● M.to Rosso Sonvico '09	♥♥♥	6
● M.to Rosso Sonvico '06	♥♥♥	5
● Nizza La V. dell'Angelo '14	♥♥♥	5

Cascina Morassino

s.da Bernino, 10
12050 Barbaresco [CN]
Tel. +39 3471210223
morassino@gmail.com

CELLAR SALES
PRE-BOOKED VISITS
ANNUAL PRODUCTION 20,000 bottles
HECTARES UNDER VINE 4.50
SUSTAINABLE WINERY

A small but important winery in the world of Barbaresco, Cascina Morassino's selection exhibits consistently outstanding quality, a feat that's earned them awards both at home and internationally. Barbaresco Ovello, a wine they produce just over 3,000 bottles of, is their crown jewel. It's quite full-bodied and bold in structure, but their slightly fresher Morassino is also outstanding. Roberto Bianco is a main of few words but great enological skill. The lovely notes of red berries and licorice that open their magnificent, rose-scented Barbaresco Ovello '16, are still in their early stages of evolution. On the palate it exhibits perfect balance, proving succulent but without fattiness or excessive sweetness, and marked by a close-woven, gradual tannic weave. Their delicate Morassino, a wine that's particularly soft on the palate, is a bit simpler aromatically.

● Barbaresco Morassino '16	♥♥	5
● Barbaresco Ovello '16	♥♥	6
● Barbaresco Morassino '09	♥♥♥	5
● Barbaresco Ovello '14	♥♥♥	6
● Barbaresco Morassino '15	♥♥	5
● Barbaresco Morassino '14	♥♥	5
● Barbaresco Morassino '13	♥♥	5
● Barbaresco Ovello '15	♥♥	6
● Barbaresco Ovello '13	♥♥	6

Cascina Salicetti

via Cascina Salicetti, 2
15050 Montegioco [AL]
Tel. +39 0131875192
www.cascinasalicetti.it

CELLAR SALES
PRE-BOOKED VISITS
ANNUAL PRODUCTION 25,000 bottles
HECTARES UNDER VINE 16.00

Anselmo Franzosi inherited a legacy of
viticulture that spans generations, and
today his is still a family-run producer.
Anselmo's dynamism, along with his
technical skill, has allowed him to oversee
all aspects of production. Their wines are
made almost exclusively with native grape
varieties: Timorasso, Cortese, Barbera,
Bonarda Piemontese and Dolcetto.
Cabernet Sauvignon, which is vinified
separately for their Il Seguito, is the only
international grape present. The wines
presented for tasting represent only a part
of their selection, the others will be
submitted and reviewed in next year's
edition of the guide. The 2017 version of
the winery's flagship, the Timorasso Ombra
di Luna, exhibits nice nose-palate
symmetry, but it probably needs a bit more
time before it can offer up its best. Their
Seguito proves harmonious and balanced,
characterized by a fresh, expansive palate.

● Colli Tortonesi Rosso Il Seguito '16	♟♟ 2*
○ Colli Tortonesi Timorasso Ombra di Luna '17	♟♟ 4
● Colli Tortonesi Barbera Morganti '17	♟ 4
○ Colli Tortonesi Timorasso Ombra di Luna '15	♟♟♟ 4*
● Colli Tortonesi Barbera Morganti '13	♟♟ 4
○ Colli Tortonesi Cortese Montarlino '17	♟♟ 4
● Colli Tortonesi Dolcetto Di Marzi '12	♟♟ 2*
● Colli Tortonesi Dolcetto Mont'Effe '16	♟♟ 2*
● Colli Tortonesi Rosso Il Seguito '15	♟♟ 2*
● Colli Tortonesi Rosso Il Seguito '12	♟♟ 2*
○ Colli Tortonesi Timorasso Ombra di Luna '16	♟♟ 4
○ Colli Tortonesi Timorasso Ombra di Luna '13	♟♟ 4

Francesca Castaldi

via Novembre, 6
28072 Briona [NO]
Tel. +39 0321826045
www.cantinacastaldi.it

CELLAR SALES
PRE-BOOKED VISITS
ANNUAL PRODUCTION 20,000 bottles
HECTARES UNDER VINE 6.30
SUSTAINABLE WINERY

Francesca Castaldi's Fara has always been
characterized by a unique, multiform
personality. In addition to Nebbiolo's
classic fragrances of dried rose and tar,
you'll find both darker and fresher notes
calling up rhubarb and gentian. In addition
to careful work in the cellar, credit for this
notable complexity goes to mineral-rich
soil but also to the contribution (about
30%) of Vespolina, a native to north
Piedmont that exhibits spicy and floral
sensations, as well as nice acidity. A warm
2015 gave rise to a rather evolved Fara
whose color is already heading towards
garnet. On the nose it's marked more by
taut aromas of quinine and forest
undergrowth than by fresh red berries. The
palate proves supple, with moderate and
quite easy tannins. It's a sound wine,
though lacking the marks of great
vintages. The simple Nebbiolo Bigin '17 is
characterized by notable alcohol, while
their 2018 Uva Rara and Vespolina are
rather unruly in their youth.

● Fara '15	♟♟ 5
● Colline Novaresi Nebbiolo Bigin '17	♟ 3
⊙ Colline Novaresi Rosato Rosa Alba '18	♟ 3
● Colline Novaresi Uva Rara Valceresole '18	♟ 3
● Colline Novaresi Vespolina Nina '18	♟ 3
○ Colline Novaresi Bianco Lucia '17	♟♟ 3
● Colline Novaresi Nebbiolo Bigin '15	♟♟ 3
⊙ Colline Novaresi Rosato Rosa Alba '17	♟♟ 3
● Fara '14	♟♟ 5
● Fara '13	♟♟ 5
● Fara '12	♟♟ 5

Castellari Bergaglio

FRAZ. ROVERETO, 136R
15066 GAVI [AL]
TEL. +39 0143644000
www.castellaribergaglio.it

CELLAR SALES
PRE-BOOKED VISITS
ANNUAL PRODUCTION 90,000 bottles
HECTARES UNDER VINE 11.00

Marco Bergaglio's vineyards are situated in Gavi, Rovereto and Tassarolo. Here the terrain is characterized by varying pedoclimates, which are highlighted during production. Thus we get their Fornaci, made with grapes from Tassarolo, Rolona from vineyards in Gavi and Rovereto from 80-year old vineyards in the district of the same name. There's also their Pilin, a wine made with slightly-dried, choice grapes and fermented primarily in barriques. To round out their selection there's a base-level Gavi, a Metodo Classico that spends 18 months on the lees and a Passito. Their Vignavecchia pours a straw-yellow color bordering on gold, the prelude to intriguing aromas of peach and candied citrus (the result of quite marked barrrel maturation). On the palate it's rich and highly fresh, closing long. The delicate and complex Fornaci features elegant aromas of white-fleshed fruit and wild flowers, sensations that anticipate a powerful, generous palate and an extremely long finish.

○ Gavi del Comune di Gavi Rovereto Vignavecchia '16	▼▼ 3*
○ Gavi del Comune di Tassarolo Fornaci '18	▼▼ 2*
○ Gavi del Comune di Gavi Rolona '18	▼▼ 3
○ Gavi Brut Ardé M. Cl. '11	♀♀ 4
○ Gavi del Comune di Gavi Rolona '17	♀♀ 3*
○ Gavi del Comune di Tassarolo Fornaci '17	♀♀ 2*
○ Gavi del Comune di Tassarolo Fornaci '16	♀♀ 2*
○ Gavi del Comune di Tassarolo Fornaci '15	♀♀ 2*
○ Gavi Pilin '13	♀♀ 5

Castello di Castellengo

VIA CASTELLO, 31
13836 COSSATO [BI]
TEL. +39 3383543101
www.centovigne.it

ACCOMMODATION
ANNUAL PRODUCTION 25,000 bottles
HECTARES UNDER VINE 6.50

Situated in the lovely castle of Castellengo, Magda Zago and Alessandro Ciccioni's winery just recently turned 20. It's smaller in size, but the quality of their selection is high and diversified, thanks to the numerous small plots that provide their grapes. The most important variety grown is Nebbiolo, which is accompanied by Croatina and Vespolina for their reds, and Erbaluce for their whites. Their well-crafted and harmonious Nebbiolo Castellengo is just a bit marked by oak, though endowed with rich personality (not an easy feat for a vintage as difficult as 2014). Their robust Nebbiolo Centovigne '15 is highly pleasant, with lovely spicy aromas and a well-balanced palate. The Rosso della Motta '17, made with Nebbiolo, Vespolina and Croatina aged entirely in concrete, put in a forthright, lively performance. It's a splendid area, with a lovely cellar that we suggest visiting, in part for the castle's charming B&B.

● Coste della Sesia Nebbiolo Castellengo '14	▼▼ 4
● Coste della Sesia Nebbiolo Centovigne '15	▼▼ 4
● Rosso della Motta '17	▼▼ 3
⊙ Coste della Sesia Rosato Il Rosa '18	▼ 3
○ Miranda	▼ 3
● Coste della Sesia Nebbiolo Castellengo '13	♀♀ 4
● Rosso della Motta '16	♀♀ 3
● Rosso della Motta	♀♀ 3

Castello di Gabiano

VIA SAN DEFENDENTE, 2
15020 GABIANO [AL]
TEL. +39 0142945004
www.castellodigabiano.com

CELLAR SALES
PRE-BOOKED VISITS
ACCOMMODATION AND RESTAURANT SERVICE
ANNUAL PRODUCTION 130,000 bottles
HECTARES UNDER VINE 24.00

A charming residence and scenic landscape enrich this producer's main facility. Their primary resource are native grape varieties, like Barbera Fries and Grignolino, though their selection also features international cultivars, like Sauvignon and Chardonnay (both used for their Corte), while the Castello is a monovarietal Chardonnay and the Gavius an unusual blend of Barbera with a share of Pinot Nero. Their wines are consistent, ageworthy, endowed with an aromatic quality conferred by the Alps' cool night breeze. An outstanding Gabiano Riserva '12 opened our tastings. It pours a vivid ruby red, anticipating vibrant, complex aromas and a rich, powerful palate marked by trademark acidity, all in support of an extremely long finish. The Braja '17 is delicate and complex, with aromas of crisp fruit and vegetal notes emerging on the palate, where it comes through potent and full-flavoured before giving way to a long, sapid finish.

● Barbera d'Asti La Braja '17	♟♟♟4
● Gabiano Ris. A Matilde Giustiniani '12	♟♟♟8
● Grignolino del M.to Casalese Il Ruvo '18	♟♟♟4
⊙ M. to Chiaretto Castelvere '18	♟♟♟3
○ M.to Bianco Corte '18	♟♟♟4
○ Piemonte Chardonnay Castello '16	♟♟♟8
● Rubino di Cantavenna '16	♟♟♟5
● M.to Rosso Gavius '17	♟♟5
● Barbera d'Asti La Braja '16	♟♟2*
● Gabiano A Matilde Giustiniani Ris. '11	♟♟6
● Grignolino del M.to Casalese Il Ruvo '17	♟♟2*
● Grignolino del M.to Casalese Il Ruvo '16	♟♟2*
○ M. to Bianco Corte '17	♟♟3
⊙ M.to Chiaretto Castelvere '17	♟♟2*
● M.to Rosso Gavius '15	♟♟3
● Malvasia di Casorzo d'Asti Il Giardino di Flora '17	♟♟3

Castello di Neive

C.SO ROMANO SCAGLIOLA, 205
12052 NEIVE [CN]
TEL. +39 017367171
www.castellodineive.it

CELLAR SALES
PRE-BOOKED VISITS
ACCOMMODATION
ANNUAL PRODUCTION 170,000 bottles
HECTARES UNDER VINE 26.00
SUSTAINABLE WINERY

In 2019, wine lovers and journalists had the chance to enter the castle for the presentation of their 2016 Barbaresco. It's a splendid building and worth the visit, especially if you consider their increasingly popular tastings. To get an idea of the skill and foresight of its owner, Italo, it's enough to think that for decades they've been researching clones with the University of Turin. Their Barbaresco Stefano is masterful and ageworthy, the Gallina fruitier and more approachable. Excellent results for their premium 2016 Barbarescos. The Santo Stefano is still not quite open in its fruity aromas, relying for now on a delicious oaky backdrop, while the palate proves powerful and harmonious. The Gallina is more expansive in its aromas of red berries and licorice, and marked by a pronounced acidity on the palate. These two standouts are accompanied by a 2017 Barbera d'Alba that's as pleasurable as it is classically styled and focused, among the best of the year.

● Barbaresco Albesani Santo Stefano '16	♟♟8
● Barbaresco Gallina '16	♟♟8
● Barbera d'Alba Sup. '17	♟♟6
● Barbaresco '16	♟♟7
● Barbera d'Alba V. Santo Stefano '18	♟♟5
● Langhe Pinot Nero I Cortini '18	♟♟6
● Barbera d'Alba Free Sulphites '17	♟5
○ Langhe Arneis Monteberotto '18	♟5
● Barbaresco Albesani S. Stefano '12	♟♟♟6
● Barbaresco Albesani S. Stefano Ris. '12	♟♟♟8
● Barbaresco Albesani S. Stefano Ris. '11	♟♟♟8
● Barbaresco Albesani Santo Stefano Ris. '13	♟♟♟8
● Barbaresco S. Stefano Ris. '01	♟♟♟7
● Barbaresco S. Stefano Ris. '99	♟♟♟7

Castello di Tassarolo

LOC. ALBORINA, 1
15060 TASSAROLO [AL]
TEL. +39 0143342248
www.castelloditassarolo.it

CELLAR SALES
PRE-BOOKED VISITS
ANNUAL PRODUCTION 130,000 bottles
HECTARES UNDER VINE 20.00
VITICULTURE METHOD Certified Organic
SUSTAINABLE WINERY

For some time now this Tassarolo winery has been biodynamic, faithfully following a philosophy centered on nature and its rhythms. Their vineyards are adjacent to the cellar, where modern equipment allows for careful management of production. They use Barbera, Nebbiolo and Cabernet Sauvignon, with some six Corteses interpreted according to the vineyard of provenance, making for a selection of guaranteed quality. In this edition of our guide, the Gavi del Comune di Tassarolo Il Castello serves as their selection's flagship wine. On the nose it comes through intense and sophisticated, marked by a vegetal streak amidst aromas of fresh herbs, ferns and a note of white-fleshed fruit. On the palate it's potent and full, with nice acidity making for a sapid, very long finish. Their Titouan, a Barbera full of character, features vibrant fruit and a palate rich in flesh.

○ Gavi del Comune di Tassarolo Il Castello '18	♟♟ 3*
● M.to Rosso Cuvée '18	♟♟ 3
● Piemonte Barbera Titouan '18	♟♟ 3
○ Gavi del Comune di Tassarolo Alborina '17	♟ 3
○ Gavi del Comune di Tassarolo Spinola '18	♟ 2
☉ M.to Chiaretto Rosa Spinola '18	♟ 3
○ Gavi del Comune di Tassarolo Alborina '16	♟♟ 3*

Castello di Uviglie

VIA CASTELLO DI UVIGLIE, 73
15030 ROSIGNANO MONFERRATO [AL]
TEL. +39 0142488132
www.castellodiuviglie.com

CELLAR SALES
PRE-BOOKED VISITS
ANNUAL PRODUCTION 90,000 bottles
HECTARES UNDER VINE 25.00

Thanks to continued growth both in the numbers and the quality of their products, Simone Lupano's winery has transformed itself into a benchmark for the territory. Their Barberas are always extraordinary for elegance and finesse, but their born again Grignolino is no less, starting with the San Bastiano Terre Bianche, a wine for which the use of wood confers notable complexity of flavor. Their production style has a modern quality to it that's highly attentive to highlighting the attributes of their grapes, which is evident across their entire range. The exquisite selection presented saw three wines reach our final round of tastings: the Pico Gonzaga and Le Cave (territorial classics by now), along with their Grignolino San Bastiano. It's an outstanding trio whose varietal characteristics are on display. Their Bricco del Conte '18 proves pleasant and enticing, as does the Le Cave Metodo Classico. Their Passito Bricco del Ciliegio is another must.

● Barbera del M.to Sup. Le Cave '17	♟♟ 3*
● Barbera del M.to Sup. Pico Gonzaga '16	♟♟ 5
● Grignolino del M.to Casalese San Bastiano '18	♟♟ 3*
● Barbera del M.to Bricco del Conte '18	♟♟ 2*
○ Bricco del Ciliegio Passito '14	♟♟ 5
○ Le Cave Extra Brut M. Cl. '15	♟♟ 5
● Barbera del M.to Sup. Le Cave '16	♟♟♟ 3*
● Barbera del M.to Sup. Le Cave '13	♟♟♟ 3*
● Barbera del M.to Sup. Le Cave '09	♟♟♟ 3*
● Barbera del M.to Sup. Le Cave '07	♟♟♟ 3*
● Barbera del M.to Sup. Pico Gonzaga '13	♟♟♟ 5
● Barbera del M.to Sup. Pico Gonzaga '07	♟♟♟ 4*

Castello di Verduno

VIA UMBERTO I, 9
12060 VERDUNO [CN]
TEL. +39 0172470284
www.cantinecastellodiverduno.it

CELLAR SALES
PRE-BOOKED VISITS
ACCOMMODATION AND RESTAURANT SERVICE
ANNUAL PRODUCTION 68,000 bottles
HECTARES UNDER VINE 10.00
SUSTAINABLE WINERY

Castello di Verduno is a model winery with centuries of history behind it, a viticultural tradition in-step with the times, a first-rate hotel and a restaurant that serves local products. Gabriella and Franco are at the helm, supported by young Marcella and Giovanna, with about ten hectares of vineyards in Barbaresco and Barolo. Their focused and airy wines pursue a classical style, from Nebbiolo to the irreverent Pelaverga, which is proposed in some three versions. The Barolo Massara '15 unveils a rare, charming completeness. On the nose it's intense, with lovely, fresh notes of fruit, spices and a backdrop of violets. On the palate it's elegant, complex, rich and sapid, with a long, gradual finish. The Barbaresco Rabajà is deep, fresh in its aromas of watermelon and raspberries, young but promising. The Rabajà-Bas moves on the same track, it's just a bit weightier, spicier, marked by nice pace and contours. A couple more years in the bottle will bring out its fullest expression.

● Barbaresco Rabajà '16	♟♟ 6
● Barbaresco Rabajà-Bas '16	♟♟ 6
● Barolo Massara '15	♟♟ 6
● Verduno Basadone '18	♟♟ 3*
● Barbaresco '16	♟♟ 5
● Barolo '15	♟♟ 5
● Barolo Monvigliero Ris. '13	♟♟ 7
○ Bellis Perennis '18	♟ 3
● Barbaresco Rabajà '04	♟♟♟ 6
● Barolo Massara '08	♟♟♟ 6
● Barolo Massara '01	♟♟♟ 6
● Barolo Monvigliero Ris. '08	♟♟♟ 7
● Barolo Monvigliero Ris. '04	♟♟♟ 7
● Barbaresco Rabajà-Bas '15	♟♟ 6
● Barolo '13	♟♟ 5
● Barolo Massara '13	♟♟ 6
● Barolo Monvigliero Ris. '11	♟♟ 7

★ Cavallotto
Tenuta Bricco Boschis

LOC. BRICCO BOSCHIS
VIA ALBA-MONFORTE
12060 CASTIGLIONE FALLETTO [CN]
TEL. +39 017362814
www.cavallotto.com

CELLAR SALES
PRE-BOOKED VISITS
ANNUAL PRODUCTION 110,000 bottles
HECTARES UNDER VINE 25.00
VITICULTURE METHOD Certified Organic

Pursuing practices that don't harm human health or the environment can require sacrifices, as happened here when they decided to forgo Barolo production in 2014. But Alfio, Giuseppe and Laura are sure that it's necessary to reduce the impact of copper and sulfur, in addition to eliminating chemical fertilizers and substances, so as to obtain the healthiest and purest expression of their grapes. Their underground cellar hosts large barrels, no additives are used and sulfites are reduced to a minimum. The Barolo Vignolo Ris. '13 is superlative for finesse, complexity, rich in fragrances of rose and red berries, and majestic on the palate. Intense notes of raspberries and cherry join with hints of licorice, lending complexity and character to their magnificent Barolo Bricco Boschis '15, a wine whose austere palate is rich in gradual tannins, conferring a welcome austerity to the vintage. The Barbera d'Alba Sup. Vigna Cuculo '17 is a must, one of the best versions hands down.

● Barbera d'Alba Sup. V. Cuculo '17	♟♟ 5
● Barolo Bricco Boschis '15	♟♟ 8
● Barolo Vignolo Ris. '13	♟♟ 8
● Langhe Nebbiolo '17	♟ 5
● Barolo Bricco Boschis '12	♟♟♟ 8
● Barolo Bricco Boschis '05	♟♟♟ 6
● Barolo Bricco Boschis '04	♟♟♟ 7
● Barolo Bricco Boschis V. S. Giuseppe Ris. '05	♟♟♟ 8
● Barolo Bricco Boschis V. S. Giuseppe Ris. '01	♟♟♟ 7
● Barolo Bricco Boschis V. S. Giuseppe Ris. '00	♟♟♟ 7
● Barolo Vignolo Ris. '06	♟♟♟ 8
● Barolo Vignolo Ris. '04	♟♟♟ 8

Le Cecche

VIA MOGLIA GERLOTTO, 10
12055 DIANO D'ALBA [CN]
TEL. +39 3316357664
www.lececche.it

CELLAR SALES
PRE-BOOKED VISITS
ANNUAL PRODUCTION 35,000 bottles
HECTARES UNDER VINE 8.00

Jan Jules de Bruyne began producing in 2002, proceeding year after year to renovate and enlarge both his vineyards and cellar with the support of prestigious agronomic and enological experts. Their range of wines has grown over the years, but Dolcetto, which is cultivated in vineyards that can go back as far as 70 years, is at the center of their selection together with Nebbiolo, which gives rise to three Barolos. The wines presented this year are all of excellent quality, a laudable demonstration of the care shown for each product. The Diano d'Alba '18 is pleasantly almondy in its aromas, compelling on the palate with a nice, refreshing note — it's the year's best. Two new 2015 Barolos have also just been released: the Borzone (from Grinzane Cavour) and the Bricco San Pietro (Monforte d'Alba), which accompany an always reliable Barolo Sorano. The only concession to non-native grape varieties is the elegant and fruit-forward Merlot Fiammingo '17.

● Diano d'Alba '18	🍷🍷 2*
● Barbera d'Alba '17	🍷🍷 3
● Barolo Borzone '15	🍷🍷 6
● Barolo Bricco San Pietro '15	🍷🍷 6
● Barolo Sorano '15	🍷🍷 5
● Langhe Rosso '18	🍷🍷 3
● Langhe Rosso Fiammingo '17	🍷🍷 3
● Nebbiolo d'Alba '16	🍷🍷 3
● Barbera d'Alba '16	🍷🍷 3
● Barolo Sorano '14	🍷🍷 5
● Barolo Sorano '13	🍷🍷 5
● Barolo Sorano '11	🍷🍷 5
● Diano d'Alba '17	🍷🍷 2*
● Diano d'Alba '16	🍷🍷 2*
○ Langhe Riesling '15	🍷🍷 3
● Langhe Rosso Fiammingo '13	🍷🍷 3
● Nebbiolo d'Alba '15	🍷🍷 3

★ Ceretto

LOC. SAN CASSIANO, 34
12051 ALBA [CN]
TEL. +39 0173282582
www.ceretto.com

CELLAR SALES
PRE-BOOKED VISITS
RESTAURANT SERVICE
ANNUAL PRODUCTION 900,000 bottles
HECTARES UNDER VINE 130.00
VITICULTURE METHOD Certified Organic
SUSTAINABLE WINERY

The Ceretto family's history has been enriched over the years by great vineyards, important works of art, a prestigious restaurant and a literary prize, just to name a few milestones. And through the Cerettos, all of Langhe and Roero have benefited. Then, in 2010, Alessandro took over management of this large producer and decided to pay further homage to the territory by adopting biodynamic cultivation. It's been a successful decision in enological terms as well, as their various Barolos and Barbarescos have maintained their time-honored elegance while gaining in personality. Their splendid Barbaresco Asili '16 exhibits a delicate and sophisticated nose, with lovely notes of raspberries and oak moving in unison. On the palate it's perfectly structured, with plenty of flesh and freshness to round out a backbone of close-knit, gradually unfolding tannins. Tre Bicchieri. Their rich selection of wines also includes a 'base' Barbaresco '16, as well as the 2015 Barolo Prapò and Brunate.

● Barbaresco Asili '16	🍷🍷🍷 8
● Barbaresco '16	🍷🍷 6
● Barolo Brunate '15	🍷🍷 8
● Barolo Prapò '15	🍷🍷 8
● Barbaresco Bernardot '16	🍷🍷 8
● Barolo '15	🍷🍷 7
● Barolo Bricco Rocche '15	🍷🍷 8
● Barolo Bussia '15	🍷🍷 8
● Dolcetto d'Alba Rossana '18	🍷🍷 3
● Barbera d'Alba Piana '18	🍷 4
○ Langhe Arneis Blangé '18	🍷 4
○ Langhe Bianco Monsordo '18	🍷 5
● Nebbiolo d'Alba Bernardina '17	🍷 5
● Barbaresco Asili '15	🍷🍷🍷 8
● Barbaresco Asili '13	🍷🍷🍷 8
● Barolo Bricco Rocche '13	🍷🍷🍷 8

★★Michele Chiarlo

S.DA NIZZA-CANELLI, 99
14042 CALAMANDRANA [AT]
TEL. +39 0141769030
www.michelechiarlo.it

CELLAR SALES
PRE-BOOKED VISITS
ACCOMMODATION
ANNUAL PRODUCTION 1,100,000 bottles
HECTARES UNDER VINE 150.00
SUSTAINABLE WINERY

The winery founded by Michele Chiarlo took shape in the 1950s, in a socio-economic context very different from the one his sons Alberto and Stefano operate in today. The producer has grown tremendously, today comprising some of Langhe's, Monferrato's and Alessandrino's most prestigious vineyards: Cerequio, Cannubi, Asili, Faset for Barolo and Barbaresco; La Court for Nizza; Rovereto for Gavi (and more). But their success can be attributed to the overall quality of their wines. Yet another performance to remember by Chiarlo's selection, starting with the 2016 version of their Nizza La Court Riserva. It charms with its combination of floral and sylvan notes, sensations that explode on its well-sustained, penetrating palate. But it's hard to choose from among so many top-notch reds, from the elegant Barbaresco Asili '16 to the more austere Faset '16. And we shouldn't forget the Barolo Cerequio '15 or the Nizza La Court Vignaveja '13 either.

● Barbaresco Asili '16	🍷🍷 8
● Barbaresco Faset '16	🍷🍷 8
● Barolo Cerequio '15	🍷🍷 8
● Nizza La Court Ris. '16	🍷🍷 6
● Nizza La Court Vignaveja '13	🍷🍷 4
● Barolo Cannubi '15	🍷🍷 8
● Barolo Tortoniano '15	🍷🍷 7
● Nizza Cipressi '17	🍷🍷 4
○ Gavi del Comune di Gavi Rovereto '18	🍷 3
● Barbera d'Asti Sup. Nizza La Court '13	🍷🍷🍷 5
● Barolo Cerequio '10	🍷🍷🍷 7
● Nizza La Court Ris. '15	🍷🍷🍷 6

Chionetti

FRAZ. FRAZ. SAN LUIGI
B.TA VALDIBERTI, 44
12063 DOGLIANI [CN]
TEL. +39 017371179
www.chionettiquinto.com

CELLAR SALES
PRE-BOOKED VISITS
ANNUAL PRODUCTION 83,000 bottles
HECTARES UNDER VINE 15.00
VITICULTURE METHOD Certified Organic
SUSTAINABLE WINERY

Founded more than a century ago, Quinto Chionetti made this winery one of Langhe's most acclaimed, seeing to it that Dogliani DOCG has a place in important restaurants everywhere. Nicola carries on the work of his grandfather, gradually expanding their selection. Their Dogliani Briccolero (30,000 bottles a year) and San Luigi (43,000) represent the highest expression of Dolcetto. Plums and cherries emerge on the nose, great, pervasive flesh on the palate. Every year their Dogliani La Costa is released with an extra year of aging in large barrels. This year saw them obtain their first important results, with two 2015 Barolos from their Monforte d'Alba plots. The 'Primo' is open and rich, with aromas of raspberry and rose followed by a palate of remarkable harmony. The traditionally-styled Vigna Pianpolvere is a bit more lively, penetrating. Three Doglianis represent a precise and sound expression of Dolcetto, with the La Costa '17 proving particularly potent and full-bodied.

● Barolo Primo '15	🍷🍷 6
● Barolo Bussia V. Pianpolvere '15	🍷🍷 6
● Dogliani Briccolero '18	🍷🍷 3
● Dogliani La Costa '17	🍷🍷 4
● Dogliani San Luigi '18	🍷🍷 3
● Langhe Nebbiolo La Chiusa '17	🍷 4
● Dolcetto di Dogliani Briccolero '07	🍷🍷🍷 3*
● Dolcetto di Dogliani Briccolero '04	🍷🍷🍷 3*
● Dogliani Briccolero '17	🍷🍷 3*
● Dogliani Briccolero '16	🍷🍷 3
● Dogliani Briccolero '15	🍷🍷 3*
● Dogliani San Luigi '17	🍷🍷 3*
● Dogliani San Luigi '16	🍷🍷 3
● Dogliani San Luigi '15	🍷🍷 3*
● Langhe Nebbiolo La Chiusa '16	🍷🍷 4

Cieck

CASCINA CASTAGNOLA, 2
10090 SAN GIORGIO CANAVESE [TO]
TEL. +39 0124330522
www.cieck.it

CELLAR SALES
PRE-BOOKED VISITS
ANNUAL PRODUCTION 85,000 bottles
HECTARES UNDER VINE 12.00

Erbaluce gives rise to wines that exhibit excellent acidity and delicate aromas of flowers and herbs. Such is its versatility that it's suitable for still wines, sparklers and passitos. Remo Falconieri's winery, today managed by his daughter Lia and by Domenico Caretto, highlights the multifaceted nature of the grape, producing all three types. It's worth noting the recent release of their Caluso T Erbaluce, carefully aged in mid-sized French oak. The Caluso Alladium ages in wood and, with commendable consistency, demonstrates Erbaluce's predilection for being dried. The three Erbaluces made show commendable poise. All are high-quality sparklers, with the Brut San Giorgio '16 charming the nose with its aromas of fruit and bread crust, and a creamy, pleasantly acidic, palate. The alluring Passito Alladium offers up clear aromas of walnuts, incense, oak and coffee, while the palate is potent and sweet, but also fresh and multifaceted. Their Misobolo '18 is particularly well-made.

○ Erbaluce di Caluso Brut San Giorgio '16	♥♥ 4
○ Erbaluce di Caluso Passito Alladium '10	♥♥ 5
○ Erbaluce di Caluso '18	♥♥ 2*
○ Erbaluce di Caluso Brut Calliope '16	♥♥ 4
○ Erbaluce di Caluso Cieck Nature '16	♥♥ 5
○ Erbaluce di Caluso V. Misobolo '18	♥♥ 3
○ Erbaluce di Caluso Ingenuus '16	♥ 4
○ Erbaluce di Caluso Passito Alladium '06	♥♥♥ 5
○ Caluso Passito Alladium Ris. '05	♀♀ 5
○ Erbaluce di Caluso Brut San Giorgio '15	♀♀ 4
○ Erbaluce di Caluso Cieck Nature '13	♀♀ 5
○ Erbaluce di Caluso Misobolo '17	♀♀ 3
○ Erbaluce di Caluso Misobolo '16	♀♀ 3
○ Erbaluce di Caluso Passito Alladium '09	♀♀ 5
○ Erbaluce di Caluso San Giorgio '14	♀♀ 4
○ Erbaluce di Caluso T '16	♀♀ 3*

★F.lli Cigliuti

VIA SERRABOELLA, 17
12052 NEIVE [CN]
TEL. +39 0173677185
www.cigliuti.it

CELLAR SALES
PRE-BOOKED VISITS
ANNUAL PRODUCTION 30,000 bottles
HECTARES UNDER VINE 7.50

Claudia and Silvia Cigliuti continue to receive precious advice from their brilliant and tireless father, Renato, who at 80+ years (and with 45 seasons under his belt) remains one of Barbaresco's great and most recognized interpreters. Their two offerings are always solid, with the Serraboella more structured and slower to open, and the Vie Erte more approachable, floral and supple. It's a winery that's definitely worth a visit. This year they only submitted Barbaresco from 2015, a fruity and soft year. The Vie Erte is a true masterpiece, moving amidst red berries and licorice, on the palate it's close-knit and enfolding, with tannins that are as elegant and docile as they've ever been. The young and exuberant Serraboella, a wine rich in aromas of small black berries, is more potent in all respects, in particular when it comes to alcohol and astringency.

● Barbaresco Serraboella '15	♥♥ 8
● Barbaresco Vie Erte '15	♥♥ 6
● Barbaresco '83	♀♀♀ 6
● Barbaresco Serraboella '13	♀♀♀ 8
● Barbaresco Serraboella '11	♀♀♀ 7
● Barbaresco Serraboella '10	♀♀♀ 7
● Barbaresco Serraboella '09	♀♀♀ 7
● Barbaresco Serraboella '01	♀♀♀ 6
● Barbaresco Serraboella '00	♀♀♀ 6
● Barbaresco Serraboella '97	♀♀♀ 6
● Barbaresco Serraboella '96	♀♀♀ 7
● Barbaresco Serraboella '90	♀♀♀ 6
● Barbaresco V. Erte '04	♀♀♀ 6

★Tenute Cisa Asinari dei Marchesi di Grésy

LOC. MARTINENGA
S.DA DELLA STAZIONE, 21
12050 BARBARESCO [CN]
TEL. +39 0173635222
www.marchesidigresy.com

CELLAR SALES
PRE-BOOKED VISITS
ANNUAL PRODUCTION 200,000 bottles
HECTARES UNDER VINE 35.00
SUSTAINABLE WINERY

Tenute Cisa Asinary's crown jewel is, doubtless, Martinenga hill, 10 hectares that have for more than two centuries been owned by the marquis di Gresy family and give rise to their celebrated Camp Grow and Gaiun. Both are highly elegant Barberescos, subtle and luminous, made possible by at least partial aging in small barrels. These are accompanied by vineyards of Dolcetto, Chardonnay and Sauvignon in Treiso. But there's also Moscato, Barbera and Merlot from La Serra and Monferrato. The complex Barbaresco Martinenga Gaiun '15 shows nice vitality, rich in jammy notes of strawberries, medicinal herbs and licorice, exhibiting a pleasant balance on the palate and closing plush. As is fitting for the vintage, the taut, subtle Martinenga Camp Gros Ris. '14 doesn't draw on power. The fruit-forward Martinenga '16 is still slightly marked by oak, but already displays nice harmony on the palate. Their whites also performed well, including the sweet and fresh Moscato d'Asti La Serra '18.

● Barbaresco Martinenga '16	♟♟	8
● Barbaresco Martinenga Camp Gros Ris. '14	♟♟	8
● Barbaresco Martinenga Gaiun '15	♟♟	8
● Barbera d'Asti Monte Colombo '14	♟♟	5
● Barbera d'Asti '18	♟♟	3
○ Langhe Chardonnay Grésy '17	♟♟	5
○ Langhe Sauvignon '18	♟♟	4
● Langhe Virtus '11	♟♟	6
○ Moscato d'Asti La Serra '18	♟♟	3
● Dolcetto d'Alba Monte Aribaldo '17	♟	3
● Langhe Nebbiolo '18	♟	4
● Barbaresco Camp Gros Martinenga '09	♟♟♟	8
● Barbaresco Camp Gros Martinenga Ris. '13	♟♟♟	8
● Barbaresco Martinenga Camp Gros Ris. '12	♟♟♟	8

★★Domenico Clerico

LOC. MANZONI, 67
12065 MONFORTE D'ALBA [CN]
TEL. +39 017378171
www.domenicoclerico.com

PRE-BOOKED VISITS
ANNUAL PRODUCTION 110,000 bottles
HECTARES UNDER VINE 21.00

Domenico Clerico will always be remembered by Barolo lovers as a tireless researcher and a great interpreter of the wine's nuances. Immediately, when his first bottles appeared in the late 1970s, he was considered one of its most skilled innovators, a modernist who wanted to draw on history for the quality of his vineyards and grapes. In the cellar it was necessary to update and restore a tradition at risk of seeming dated. His wife, Giuliana Viberti, is continuing in this direction, bolstered by celebrated Monforte d'Alba crus such as Ginestra, Pajana and Mosconi. After a suite of youthful and still slightly oaky aromas, the Ciabot Mentin '15 impresses foremost for its palate. Its dense and weighty fruity flesh joins with a commendable acidity that's almost insuperable in this hot vintage. Their warm and substantive entry-level Barolo delivers with its charming notes of red fruits. Their nice overall selection also included a particularly notable Langhe Rosso Arte '16.

● Barolo '15	♟♟	6
● Barolo Ciabot Mentin '15	♟♟	8
● Barolo Aeroplanservaj '15	♟♟	7
● Barolo Pajana '15	♟♟	8
● Langhe Dolcetto Visadi '17	♟♟	2*
● Langhe Rosso Arte '16	♟♟	5
● Barolo Ciabot Mentin '08	♟♟♟	8
● Barolo Ciabot Mentin Ginestra '05	♟♟♟	8
● Barolo Ciabot Mentin Ginestra '04	♟♟♟	8
● Barolo Ciabot Mentin Ginestra '01	♟♟♟	7
● Barolo Ciabot Mentin Ginestra '99	♟♟♟	8
● Barolo Ciabot Mentin Ginestra '92	♟♟♟	8
● Barolo Ciabot Mentin Ginestra '86	♟♟♟	8
● Barolo Percristina '01	♟♟♟	8
● Barolo Percristina '99	♟♟♟	8
● Barolo Percristina '98	♟♟♟	8
● Barolo Percristina '97	♟♟♟	8

★Elvio Cogno

VIA RAVERA, 2
12060 NOVELLO [CN]
TEL. +39 0173744006
www.elviocogno.com

CELLAR SALES
PRE-BOOKED VISITS
ACCOMMODATION
ANNUAL PRODUCTION 90,000 bottles
HECTARES UNDER VINE 15.00
VITICULTURE METHOD Certified Organic
SUSTAINABLE WINERY

In thirty years, Nadia and Valter's small, elegant winery has reached the height's of excellence in Langhe, thanks to an exceptional enological sensibility that's brought forth great Barolos, year after year, without exception. A visit to their estate makes clear how much attention they dedicate to their wines, without forced practices, drawing on the use of various sizes of barrels, controlled temperatures, a flexible approach to aging depending on the cru, a well-studied and charming cellar, and a natural approach in the vineyard. Their Ravera Vigna Elena Ris. '13 sees lovely notes of tobacco, licorice dance on a backdrop of red fruits. In the mouth it's warm, richly structured, with elegant tannins and a juicy flesh giving way to a long, subtle finish: Tre Bicchieri. The Barolo Cascina Nuova '15 is as harmonious and balanced as ever, rich in clear notes of red berries, playing more on delicacy than on tannic power. The youthful Barolo Ravera '15 is tight-knit, full-bodied.

● Barolo Ravera V. Elena Ris. '13	♟♟♟ 8
● Barolo Cascina Nuova '15	♟♟ 6
● Barolo Ravera '15	♟♟ 8
● Barolo Ravera Bricco Pernice '14	♟♟ 8
● Barbaresco Bordini '16	♟♟ 5
● Barbera d'Alba Bricco dei Merli '17	♟♟ 4
○ Langhe Nascetta del Comune di Novello Anas-Cëtta '18	♟♟ 4
● Langhe Nebbiolo Montegrilli '18	♟♟ 4
● Dolcetto d'Alba Mandorlo '18	♟ 3
● Barolo Bricco Pernice '11	♟♟♟ 8
● Barolo Bricco Pernice '09	♟♟♟ 8
● Barolo Bricco Pernice '08	♟♟♟ 8
● Barolo Ravera '11	♟♟♟ 7
● Barolo Ravera Bricco Pernice '13	♟♟♟ 8
● Barolo Ravera Bricco Pernice '12	♟♟♟ 8
● Barolo V. Elena Ris. '06	♟♟♟ 8

Poderi Colla

FRAZ. SAN ROCCO SENO D'ELVIO, 82
12051 ALBA [CN]
TEL. +39 0173290148
www.podericolla.it

CELLAR SALES
PRE-BOOKED VISITS
ANNUAL PRODUCTION 150,000 bottles
HECTARES UNDER VINE 26.00

Our thoughts are with the family in remembering Beppe Colla, a true vigneron that left us last January at the age of 88. He was an authentic 'gentiluomo' that did so much for Piedmont's viticulture, bolstered by a winery with a centuries-old legacy, and a keen awareness of environmental issues. Manual labor, limited fertilizing, careful weeding and constant attention to diversity are all key features of their approach. Two outstanding parcels serve as the cornerstone of their selection: Roncaglie (Barbaresco), and Bussia Dardi Le Rose (Monforte d'Alba). Their Roncaglie '16 is a wine of great class and character, redolent of strawberries, raspberries, tobacco, licorice. It shows powerful structure, developing gradually towards a long, characterful finish. The Bussia Dardi Le Rose '15 also performed well, proving lovely and succulent in its fruit — it's guaranteed to age well, for those who can be patient. The Pian Balbo '18 is highly pleasant in its sensations of small wild berries.

● Barbaresco Roncaglie '16	♟♟ 6
● Barolo Bussia Dardi Le Rose '15	♟♟ 6
● Dolcetto d'Alba Pian Balbo '18	♟♟ 2*
● Barbera d'Alba Costa Bruna '17	♟ 3
○ Langhe Riesling '17	♟ 3
● Nebbiolo d'Alba Drago '17	♟ 3
● Barbaresco Roncaglie '14	♟♟♟ 6
● Barolo Bussia Dardi Le Rose '09	♟♟♟ 6
● Barolo Bussia Dardi Le Rose '99	♟♟♟ 6
● Barbaresco Roncaglie '15	♟♟ 6
● Barbaresco Roncaglie '13	♟♟ 6
● Barbaresco Roncaglie '12	♟♟ 6
● Barbaresco Roncaglie '11	♟♟ 6
● Barolo Bussia Dardi Le Rose '14	♟♟ 6
● Barolo Bussia Dardi Le Rose '13	♟♟ 6
● Barolo Bussia Dardi Le Rose '10	♟♟ 6

La Colombera

LOC. VHO
S.DA COMUNALE PER VHO, 7
15057 TORTONA [AL]
TEL. +39 0131867795
www.lacolomberavini.it

CELLAR SALES
PRE-BOOKED VISITS
ANNUAL PRODUCTION 80,000 bottles
HECTARES UNDER VINE 24.00
SUSTAINABLE WINERY

Over the years this family-run winery has carved out a position as one of the area's most representative producers. Timorasso takes center stage, but all their wines enjoy constant attention, with extremely well-made entry-levels confirming the overall quality of production. Even when it comes to Croatina, the Seminos have managed to square the circle. It's a difficult grape, tending towards exuberance but marked by invasive tannins, but here it's interpreted elegantly and with character. Cortese and Dolcetto are also used. This year their selection shone. The Derthona is more accessible, with sophisticated, subtle aromas and an extraordinary overall balance between freshness and depth. The Montino of the same vintage proves poignant in its aromas of medicinal herbs and citrus. It's got the depth and length of a real champion: a resounding Tre Bicchieri. The young Barbera Vegia Rampana is complex and elegant.

○ Colli Tortonesi Timorasso Il Montino '17	▼▼▼	5
○ Colli Tortonesi Timorasso Derthona '17	▼▼	4
○ Colli Tortonesi Cortese Bricco Bartolomeo '18	▼▼	2*
● Colli Tortonesi Croatina Arché '17	▼▼	4
● Colli Tortonesi Croatina La Romba '18	▼▼	3
● Colli Tortonesi Rosso Vegia Rampana '18	▼▼	3
● Colli Tortonesi Barbera Elisa '16	▼	4
● Colli Tortonesi Barbera Elisa '11	♀♀♀	3*
○ Colli Tortonesi Timorasso Il Montino '16	♀♀♀	5
○ Colli Tortonesi Timorasso Il Montino '13	♀♀♀	5
○ Colli Tortonesi Timorasso Il Montino '09	♀♀♀	5
○ Colli Tortonesi Timorasso Il Montino '06	♀♀♀	4

Colombo - Cascina Pastori

REG. CAFRA, 172B
14051 BUBBIO [AT]
TEL. +39 0144852807
www.colombovino.it

CELLAR SALES
PRE-BOOKED VISITS
ANNUAL PRODUCTION 40,000 bottles
HECTARES UNDER VINE 10.00
SUSTAINABLE WINERY

Cascina Pastori's vineyards can be found in Bubbio, a hamlet immersed in the heart of Langa. The winery was founded in 2004 by world-famous cardiologist Antonio Colombio, getting a boost in 2010 with the involvement of Riccardo Cotarella. Situated in an amphitheater of southeast-facing hills on calcareous-marl terrain, their vineyards host Pinot Nero, Chardonnay and Moscato, and are divided into the parcels Pratolungo, Pantalini, Il Fontanino, Le Banchine, Mo' Gheub and Il Brichetto. Their Pinot Nero Apertura '16 is extroverted and delectable in its play of strawberries, mandarin oranges and meadow herbs, confirming that it's a great interpretation, one capable of bringing together varietal and territorial identity. It may be just a bit lacking in breadth and complexity, but on the palate it proves pleasantly cohesive. Their Chardonnays also performed exceptionally well, both the Onisia '18 (a tropical and harmonious wine) and the Blanc de Blanc 48 Mesi Metodo Classico '14.

● Piemonte Pinot Nero Apertura '16	▼▼▼	4*
○ Piemonte Chardonnay Onisia '18	▼▼	2*
○ Piemonte Chardonnay Spumante Blanc de Blancs 48 Mesi M. Cl. '14	▼▼	5
● Piemonte Pinot Nero Apertura '15	♀♀♀	3*
○ Piemonte Chardonnay Spumante Blanc de Blancs Andrè M. Cl. '13	♀♀	5
● Piemonte Pinot Nero Apertura '14	♀♀	3*
● Piemonte Pinot Nero Apertura Maxima '12	♀♀	8
● Piemonte Pinot Nero Apertura Maxima Ris. '11	♀♀	8

Diego Conterno

VIA MONTÀ, 27
12065 MONFORTE D'ALBA [CN]
TEL. +39 0173789265
www.diegoconterno.it

CELLAR SALES
PRE-BOOKED VISITS
ANNUAL PRODUCTION 40,000 bottles
HECTARES UNDER VINE 7.50

The Conterno family has wine in their DNA. After founding Conterno Fantino in 1982 with his cousins, Diego ventured out on his own. Diego Conterno was established in 2000, bolstered by 7 hectares of vineyards, all well-developed amidst easy-drinking wines, like their Barbera d'Alba or Langhe Nascetta, and a line of excellent Monforte crus, like Le Coste and Ginestra, in some cases with outstanding results. Today Diego is accompanied by his son, who's increasingly active in producing a solid, rigorous selection. The Barolo Ginestra '15 is a hymn to Nebbiolo. Its ruby garnet color anticipates aromas of strawberries, aniseed, mint and licorice. On the palate it's sophisticated, subtle, complex, close-knit with gradual tannins and a long, rigorous finish. The Barolo '15, which also performed well, is more mature, fruit-forward, austere and spicy. The delectable Langhe Nascetta '18 is flowery and full-bodied — a restrained aromatic profile makes it a wine to drink, and then drink again.

● Barolo Ginestra '15	♟♟ 7
● Barolo '15	♟♟ 6
○ Langhe Nascetta '18	♟♟ 3
● Barbera d'Alba Ferrione '17	♟ 3
● Nebbiolo d'Alba Baluma '17	♟ 4
● Barolo Le Coste '09	♟♟♟ 6
● Barbera d'Alba Ferrione '16	♟♟ 3
● Barolo '14	♟♟ 6
● Barolo '13	♟♟ 6
● Barolo Ginestra '14	♟♟ 7
● Barolo Ginestra '13	♟♟ 7
● Barolo Ginestra '12	♟♟ 7
● Barolo Ginestra '11	♟♟ 6
○ Langhe Nascetta '17	♟♟ 3
○ Langhe Nascetta '16	♟♟ 3
● Nebbiolo d'Alba Baluma '15	♟♟ 3

★★★Giacomo Conterno

LOC. ORNATI, 2
12065 MONFORTE D'ALBA [CN]
TEL. +39 017378221
www.conterno.it

PRE-BOOKED VISITS
ANNUAL PRODUCTION 60,000 bottles
HECTARES UNDER VINE 23.00

Year after year this winery's fame grows throughout the world, thanks to the quality that Roberto Conterno continues to pursue with exceptional attention to detail both in the vineyard and in the cellar. And to all wine lovers, we strongly suggesting tasting not only his rare Monfortino, but the entire range offered by this gem of a producer. Indeed, his other Barolos are regularly excellent, as are his Barbera d'Albas from the Francia and Cerretta di Serralunga crus. This year saw the debut of the Barolo Arione, with a 2015 version that's tight, concentrated and austere, so much so that we suggest tasting after further aging in the bottle. The Monfortino '13 once again performed at impressive levels, exhibiting elegance, texture and a focused expression of Barolo's essence aromatically and in flavor — it amazes with its pervasiveness and length. The potent Francia and meaty Cerretta, both 2015s, also prove excellent, while the Barbera d'Alba '17 is at the top of its game.

● Barolo Monfortino Ris. '13	♟♟♟ 8
● Barbera d'Alba V. Cerretta '17	♟♟ 5
● Barbera d'Alba V. Francia '17	♟♟ 5
● Barolo Cerretta '15	♟♟ 8
● Barolo Francia '15	♟♟ 8
● Barolo Arione '15	♟♟ 8
● Barolo Cascina Francia '06	♟♟♟ 8
● Barolo Cascina Francia '05	♟♟♟ 8
● Barolo Cerretta '14	♟♟♟ 8
● Barolo Francia '12	♟♟♟ 8
● Barolo Francia '10	♟♟♟ 8
● Barolo Monfortino Ris. '10	♟♟♟ 8
● Barolo Monfortino Ris. '08	♟♟♟ 8
● Barolo Monfortino Ris. '06	♟♟♟ 8
● Barolo Monfortino Ris. '05	♟♟♟ 8
● Barolo Monfortino Ris. '04	♟♟♟ 8
● Barolo Monfortino Ris. '02	♟♟♟ 8

★Paolo Conterno

LOC. GINESTRA, 34
12065 MONFORTE D'ALBA [CN]
TEL. +39 017378415
www.paoloconterno.com

CELLAR SALES
PRE-BOOKED VISITS
ACCOMMODATION
ANNUAL PRODUCTION 180,000 bottles
HECTARES UNDER VINE 37.00
SUSTAINABLE WINERY

It was back in 1886 when Paolo Conterno founded this winery, choosing the best terrain for his Nebbiolo, Barbera and Dolcetto. His intuition paid off, and the legacy has passed down over four generations to Giorgio Conterno. In addition to the hillside vineyards of the legendary Ginestra cru (which gives rise to their Riva del Bric), Conterno manages the Antico Podere del Sant'Uffizio, in Asti and Monferrato, and Tenuta Ortaglia in Pratolino. The Barolo Ginestra '15 is warm, mature in its fruit and spices, with a finish that's still quite hard and rigorous. The Ginestra Ris. '11 takes home Tre Bicchieri with its fragrant, subtle and sophisticated character, its graceful spiciness, its tight-knit, dense palate, all making for a potent, long, austere red. Characteristic notes of rhubarb and wood tar introduce their Riva del Bric '15, which closes minty and harmonious. The well-made Barbera d'Alba La Ginestra '17 proves delectable in its fragrances of blackberries and coffee.

● Barolo Ginestra Ris. '11	♟♟♟ 8
● Barolo Ginestra '15	♟♟ 8
● Barbera d'Alba La Ginestra '17	♟♟ 4
● Barbera d'Asti Bricco '17	♟♟ 3
● Barolo Riva del Bric '15	♟♟ 6
○ Föra '16	♟♟ 4
○ Langhe Arneis A Val '18	♟♟ 4
● Dolcetto d'Alba L'Alto '17	♟ 3
● Langhe Nebbiolo A Mont '17	♟ 4
● Langhe Nebbiolo Bric Ginestra '17	♟ 5
● Barolo Ginestra '10	♟♟♟ 8
● Barolo Ginestra '06	♟♟♟ 8
● Barolo Ginestra Ris. '10	♟♟♟ 8
● Barolo Ginestra Ris. '09	♟♟♟ 8
● Barolo Ginestra Ris. '08	♟♟♟ 8
● Barolo Ginestra Ris. '06	♟♟♟ 8
● Barolo Ginestra Ris. '05	♟♟♟ 8

Contratto

VIA G. B. GIULIANI, 56
14053 CANELLI [AT]
TEL. +39 0141823349
www.contratto.it

CELLAR SALES
PRE-BOOKED VISITS
ANNUAL PRODUCTION 140,000 bottles
HECTARES UNDER VINE 21.00

The estate's origins go back to 1867, when Giuseppe Contratto began making his own wine in Canelli. Since the early 1900s they've specialized in Metodo Classico sparkling wines (including Moscato), finding notable success from the beginning both in Italy and abroad. In 2011 it passed into the hands of Giorgio Rivetti, already owner of La Spinetta, leading to a series of investments, including major acquisitions like 40 hectares of Pinot Nero and Chardonnay in Bossolasco. The calibrated, contemporary style of the wines presented for tasting is expressed in varying and complementary ways, though they all stand out for their complete, supple, crisp and spirited gustatory character. From the complex and deep Millesimato Pas Dosé 2014, to the alluring and linear Alta Langa Blanc de Blancs, the Extra Brut della Special Cuvée, which brings together force, freshness and elegance, they're all archetypes of a unique and well-suited territory.

○ Alta Langa Pas Dosé Blanc de Blancs '15	♟♟ 6
○ Millesimato Pas Dosé M. Cl. '14	♟♟ 5
○ Special Cuvée Extra Brut M. Cl. '11	♟♟ 5
○ Alta Langa Pas Dosé For England Blanc de Noir M. Cl. '15	♟♟ 6
⊙ Alta Langa Pas Dosé For England Rosé M. Cl '15	♟♟ 6
○ Cuvée Novecento Pas Dosé M. Cl. '10	♟♟ 5
○ Bacco d'Oro Brut '13	♟ 4
○ Asti De Miranda M. Cl. '00	♟♟♟ 5
● Barolo Cerequio '99	♟♟♟ 8
● Barolo Cerequio Tenuta Secolo '97	♟♟♟ 8

Vigne Marina Coppi

VIA SANT'ANDREA, 5
15051 CASTELLANIA [AL]
TEL. +39 0131837089
www.vignemarinacoppi.com

CELLAR SALES
PRE-BOOKED VISITS
ANNUAL PRODUCTION 25,000 bottles
HECTARES UNDER VINE 4.50

Since Francesco Bellocchio decided to dedicate himself to viticulture in the early 2000s, he's lived through a number of excellent seasons, earning Vigne Marina a reputation as one of the area's top producers. Production volumes are those of an artisanal winery, but Francesco's marketing skill and the quality of his products have allowed the brand to establish a worldwide presence. Their selection is made with the region's native grape varieties: Timorasso, Favorita, Barbera, Croatina and Nebbiolo. These give rise to eight wines, including a recently added, early-drinking Timorasso called Francesca. Their Fausto never disappoints. This year it features an elegant, complex aromatic profile of medicinal herbs and flint, anticipating a harmonious palate that lengthens fresh and sapid towards a long finish. The Francesca is more fruit-forward in its citrusy notes, while on the palate its flesh and lovely acidity emerge. The Marine, made with Favorita, proves harmonious and balanced.

○ Colli Tortonesi Timorasso Fausto '17	🍷🍷6
● Colli Tortonesi Barbera Sant'Andrea '18	🍷🍷3
○ Colli Tortonesi Favorita Marine '17	🍷🍷5
○ Colli Tortonesi Timorasso Francesca '18	🍷🍷3
● Colli Tortonesi Barbera Sup. I Grop '15	🍷5
● Colli Tortonesi Rosso Lindin '16	🍷5
○ Colli Tortonesi Timorasso Fausto '15	🍷🍷🍷6
○ Colli Tortonesi Timorasso Fausto '12	🍷🍷🍷6
○ Colli Tortonesi Timorasso Fausto '11	🍷🍷🍷6
○ Colli Tortonesi Timorasso Fausto '10	🍷🍷🍷6
○ Colli Tortonesi Timorasso Fausto '09	🍷🍷🍷6

★Coppo

VIA ALBA, 68
14053 CANELLI [AT]
TEL. +39 0141823146
www.coppo.it

CELLAR SALES
PRE-BOOKED VISITS
ANNUAL PRODUCTION 400,000 bottles
HECTARES UNDER VINE 52.00

Canelli's old cellars are veritable 'underground cathedrals' carved out of tuff. Here the Coppo family's sparkling wines lie in wait, in a uniquely beautiful place that expresses the producer's glorious history. Founded by Piero in the early 20th century, today Massimiliano and Luigi, the fourth generation, manage the winery with the help of their parents, aunts and uncles. But the core of their selection hasn't changed, with Metodo Classico sparkling wines accompanied by a Bordeaux-inspired Chardonnay and, especially, ambitious, ageworthy Barbera reds The commercial necessity of anticipating the release of their Pomorosso '17 and Monteriolo '17 made for a unique roster of wines and a number of standout performers. In the end we preferred the Pomorosso '17, with its exuberant, complex aromas of black berries and a pepper, and its generous, concentrated palate. It's followed by one of the best versions ever of the Riserva Coppo, and finally the 2011 version of their Alta Langa.

● Nizza Pomorosso '17	🍷🍷🍷7
○ Alta Langa Extra Brut Coppo Ris. '11	🍷🍷5
● Barbera d'Asti Camp du Rouss '17	🍷🍷3*
● Nizza Pomorosso '16	🍷🍷🍷7
○ Piemonte Chardonnay Monteriolo '17	🍷🍷6
○ Piemonte Chardonnay Monteriolo '16	🍷🍷6
● Barbera d'Asti L'Avvocata '18	🍷🍷3
● Barolo '15	🍷🍷8
○ Clelia Coppo Brut Rosé M. Cl. '14	🍷🍷5
○ Gavi Tenuta La Rocca '18	🍷🍷3
○ Luigi Coppo Brut M. Cl.	🍷🍷4
○ Piemonte Chardonnay Costebianche '18	🍷🍷3
● Barbera d'Asti L'Avvocata '17	🍷🍷🍷3*
● Barbera d'Asti Sup. Nizza Riserva della Famiglia '09	🍷🍷🍷8

★Giovanni Corino

FRAZ. ANNUNZIATA, 25B
12064 LA MORRA [CN]
TEL. +39 0173509452
www.corino.it

CELLAR SALES
PRE-BOOKED VISITS
ANNUAL PRODUCTION 50,000 bottles
HECTARES UNDER VINE 9.50

Giuliano Corino's winery began enjoying renown in the late 1980s (as part of the Barolo 'nouvelle vague'). Their approach sees careful selection of grapes, short fermentation in rotary macerators at controlled temperatures, and the use of small French barrels (some new). The same proven practices are followed today now that his children are on board, making for elegant Barolos rich in fruity, spicy sensations. In addition to their classic Giachini and Arborina crus, they've recently added the Barolo Bricco Manescotto. Their entire range dazzled, led by the best Barbera of 2017. The Ciabot dù Re opens with red berry notes and complex, delicate oak. On the palate it charms with its elegance, harmony, well-balanced flesh and acidity. Their Barolos are extraordinary. The newborn Bricco Manescotto '15 is sophisticated, subtle while the La Morra '15 joins fruit and oak exceptionally well. The potent, fresh Arborina '15 is notable, as is the spicy, licorice-scented Giachini '15 and the long, harmonious Ris. '13.

● Barbera d'Alba Ciabot dù Re '17	♥♥♥ 5
● Barolo Arborina '15	♥♥ 8
● Barolo Bricco Manescotto '15	♥♥ 7
● Barolo Giachini '15	♥♥ 8
● Barolo Ris. '13	♥♥ 8
● Barolo del Comune di La Morra '15	♥♥ 6
● Langhe Rosso L'Insieme '16	♥♥ 5
● Barbera d'Alba '17	♥ 3
● Barolo Giachini '12	♥♥♥ 7
● Barolo Giachini '11	♥♥♥ 7
● Barolo Rocche '01	♥♥♥ 7
● Barolo V. V. '99	♥♥♥ 8
● Barolo del Comune di La Morra '14	♥♥ 6
● Barolo Giachini '14	♥♥ 8

Renato Corino

FRAZ. ANNUNZIATA
B.GO POZZO, 49A
12064 LA MORRA [CN]
TEL. +39 0173500349
www.renatocorino.it

CELLAR SALES
PRE-BOOKED VISITS
ANNUAL PRODUCTION 50,000 bottles
HECTARES UNDER VINE 7.00

In addition to being elegant and pleasant, Renato Corino's Barolos feature well-integrated tannins that are never aggressive, even shortly after release. Aromatically they're notably expressive, with fragrances of violet and tar that have made the typology famous. Most of the credit still goes to the care with which vinification and aging are carried out, with restrained maceration periods and impeccably elegant use of French oak. We mustn't forget that Rocche dell'Annunziata and Arborina are two choice crus for Nebbiolo. The selection of Barolos tasted put in a rousing performance, all exhibiting a delicate, oaky background of rare finesse (and never invasive). The Arborina '15, the most austere on the palate, sees notes of tobacco and red berries on the nose. Their notable Barolo del comune di La Morra '15 proves pleasant, complex, while the exquisite, tannic Rocche dell'Annunziata '15 is still quite youthful, and the pleasantly fresh, succulent Ris. '13 is still marked by oak.

● Barolo Arborina '15	♥♥ 7
● Barolo del comune di La Morra '15	♥♥ 5
● Barolo Ris. '13	♥♥ 8
● Barolo Rocche dell'Annunziata '15	♥♥ 8
● Barbera d'Alba Pozzo '17	♥♥ 5
● Dolcetto d'Alba '18	♥ 3
● Barolo Rocche dell'Annunziata '14	♥♥♥ 8
● Barolo Rocche dell'Annunziata '11	♥♥♥ 8
● Barolo Rocche dell'Annunziata '10	♥♥♥ 7
● Barolo Rocche dell'Annunziata '09	♥♥♥ 7
● Barolo Vign. Rocche '06	♥♥♥ 7
● Barolo Vign. Rocche '04	♥♥♥ 8
● Barolo Vign. Rocche '03	♥♥♥ 8
● Barolo del Comune di La Morra '14	♥♥ 5
● Barolo Rocche dell'Annunziata '13	♥♥ 8
● Barolo Rocche dell'Annunziata '12	♥♥ 8

Cornarea

VIA VALENTINO, 150
12043 CANALE [CN]
TEL. +39 017365636
www.cornarea.com

CELLAR SALES
PRE-BOOKED VISITS
ACCOMMODATION
ANNUAL PRODUCTION 90,000 bottles
HECTARES UNDER VINE 14.00

Situated on the Cornarea hilltop just outside Canale, the Bovone family's historic winery should be considered a veritable benchmark for the territory, in particular when it comes to Roero Arneis. The estate vineyards, two-thirds of which are Arneis with the remaining part Nebbiolo, are a contiguous tract of land planted between 1975-1978 on calcareous-clay soil with a strong component of magnesium. Their wines exhibit great typicity and pronounced aromatic precision. The Bovone family submitted a series of high quality versions of their Arneis. The Roero Arneis '18 features notes of white-fleshed fruit and spices. On the palate it's subtle and fresh, with a sapid, citrusy finish. The velvety and extremely long Roero Arneis En Ritard '15 exhibits nice aromatic complexity amidst fragrances of fresh fruit, medicinal herbs and tobacco, while the Tarasco Passito '15, a wine redolent of walnuts, cinnamon and dried figs, stands out for its nice balance of sweetness and acidity.

○ Roero Arneis '18	♙♙ 3*
○ Roero Arneis En Ritard '15	♙♙ 3*
○ Tarasco Passito '15	♙♙ 5
● Roero '16	♙♙ 4
● Barbera d'Alba '16	♙ 4
● Nebbiolo d'Alba '17	♙ 3
● Roero '15	♙♙ 4
○ Roero Arneis '17	♙♙ 3*
○ Roero Arneis '16	♙♙ 3*
○ Roero Arneis '15	♙♙ 3*
○ Roero Arneis '14	♙♙ 3*
○ Tarasco Passito '12	♙♙ 5

★Matteo Correggia

LOC. GARBINETTO
VIA SANTO STEFANO ROERO, 124
12043 CANALE [CN]
TEL. +39 0173978009
www.matteocorreggia.com

CELLAR SALES
PRE-BOOKED VISITS
ANNUAL PRODUCTION 150,000 bottles
HECTARES UNDER VINE 20.00
VITICULTURE METHOD Certified Organic

Overseen for almost 20 years by Ornella Costa Correggia, now accompanied by her children Brigitta and Giovanni, Matteo Correggia is a national symbol of Roero. The estate vineyards are situated in Canale and Santo Stefano Roero, on Roero's signature sandy soil (lean in clay and loam, but rich in minerals), except for Ampsèj, where the soil mixes Asti and Tortonian typologies. Their wines are among Roero's most representative and charming. The Correggia family also chose to propose a selection of Arneis aged in their cellar over a number of years. The Roero Arneis La Val dei Preti '13 is vibrant in its notes of dried herbs and tropical fruit, all accompanied by saffron nuances and petrol. On the palate it's potent, long and characterful. The Roero Ròche d'Ampsèj Riserva '15 matches its reputation, proving long and fresh, with balsamic hints and citrus peel on the nose giving way to elegant tannins on the palate.

○ Roero Arneis La Val dei Preti '13	♙♙ 3*
● Roero Ròche d'Ampsèj Ris. '15	♙♙ 6
● Barbera d'Alba Sup. Marun '16	♙♙ 5
● Roero La Val dei Preti '16	♙♙ 5
● Roero Ròche d'Ampsèj '04	♙♙♙ 6
● Roero Ròche d'Ampsèj Ris. '14	♙♙♙ 6
● Roero Ròche d'Ampsèj Ris. '09	♙♙♙ 6
● Roero Ròche d'Ampsèj Ris. '07	♙♙♙ 6
● Roero Ròche d'Ampsèj Ris. '06	♙♙♙ 6
● Barbera d'Alba Marun '15	♙♙ 5
○ Roero Arneis '17	♙♙ 3
○ Roero Arneis '16	♙♙ 3
● Roero La Val dei Preti '15	♙♙ 5

Giuseppe Cortese

S.DA RABAJÀ, 80
12050 BARBARESCO [CN]
TEL. +39 0173635131
www.cortesegiuseppe.it

CELLAR SALES
PRE-BOOKED VISITS
ACCOMMODATION
ANNUAL PRODUCTION 58,000 bottles
HECTARES UNDER VINE 8.00
SUSTAINABLE WINERY

On Rabajà hill, one of the most celebrated and inspired Barbaresco crus, the Corteses make some of the most vibrant wines in the region. Evanescence and grace come together in rigorous atmospheres that open to depth and stratification of flavor. Their classic approach calls for medium and large oak barrels, making for wines that highlight the vineyards of origin. It's a solid selection, to say the least, starting with their Langhe Nebbiolos or Barberas, testifying to the producer's commitment to quality. The decidedly austere Barbaresco Rabajà '16 is intense in its notes of quinine and blackcurrant syrup. On the palate it's close-woven in its tannic weave, with fruity flesh, richness and acidity, all of which guarantee excellent aging prospects. The Langhe Nebbiolo '17 proves it's one of the best of its kind, fresh and delicate in its aromas of violet and watermelon, and closing cool, clear. The well-made Barbera d'Alba '18 is marked by greenness and a delicately herbaceous note.

● Barbaresco Rabajà '16	▼▼▼ 6
● Langhe Nebbiolo '17	▼▼ 3*
● Barbera d'Alba '18	▼▼ 3
● Barbaresco Rabajà '15	♀♀♀ 6
● Barbaresco Rabajà '11	♀♀♀ 5
● Barbaresco Rabajà '10	♀♀♀ 5
● Barbaresco Rabajà '08	♀♀♀ 5
● Barbaresco Rabajà Ris. '96	♀♀♀ 8
● Barbaresco Rabajà '14	♀♀ 6
● Barbaresco Rabajà '13	♀♀ 5
● Barbaresco Rabajà '12	♀♀ 5
● Barbaresco Rabajà Ris. '11	♀♀ 8
● Barbera d'Alba Morassina '15	♀♀ 3
● Barbera d'Alba Morassina '14	♀♀ 3
● Langhe Nebbiolo '16	♀♀ 3*
● Langhe Nebbiolo '15	♀♀ 3
● Langhe Nebbiolo '14	♀♀ 3*

Stefanino Costa

B.TA BENNA, 5
12046 MONTÀ [CN]
TEL. +39 0173976336
ninocostawine@gmail.com

CELLAR SALES
PRE-BOOKED VISITS
ANNUAL PRODUCTION 50,000 bottles
HECTARES UNDER VINE 9.50

Within Roero, the Costa family's winery has for some years now performed at the heights of excellence. The estate vineyards, situated in Canale, Montà and Santo Stefano Roero, rest in primarily sandy soil and host the area's classic grapes, from Arneis to Nebbiolo, Barbera and Brachetto. Their wines bring together a traditional style characterized by a strong attention to territorial expression and its characteristics with the pursuit of enological transparency and aromatic precision. The Costa family's selection once again put in a top-notch performance. The Arneis Sarun '18 is vibrant on the nose in its notes of fresh herbs and white-fleshed fruit, all on a mineral background. On the palate it proves assertive, with nice grip and length, playing more on elegance than on fullness. The Roero Gepin '15 features hints of red berries accompanied by spicy notes and white truffle, sensations that anticipate a taut, delicately tannic and fruit-forward palate.

○ Roero Arneis Sarun '18	▼▼▼ 3*
● Roero Gepin '15	▼▼ 4
○ Roero Arneis Seminari '18	▼▼ 3
○ Roero Arneis Sarun '17	♀♀♀ 3*
● Roero Gepin '13	♀♀♀ 4*
● Roero Gepin '12	♀♀♀ 4*
● Roero Gepin '11	♀♀♀ 4*
● Roero Gepin '10	♀♀♀ 4*
○ Roero Arneis Sarun '15	♀♀ 3*
○ Roero Arneis Sarun '13	♀♀ 3*
○ Roero Arneis Seminari '17	♀♀ 3*
● Roero Gepin '14	♀♀ 4

Tenuta Cucco

VIA MAZZINI, 10
12050 SERRALUNGA D'ALBA [CN]
TEL. +39 0173613003
www.tenutacucco.it

CELLAR SALES
PRE-BOOKED VISITS
ACCOMMODATION
ANNUAL PRODUCTION 70,000 bottles
HECTARES UNDER VINE 13.00

Owned by Rossi Cairo family, Tenuta Cucco produce a Barolo that's yet more proof that Serralunga Nebbiolo's potent tannic presence can be easily domesticated. All it takes is ripe grapes that can provide sufficient fruity flesh, thus creating a perfect harmony among its components. Tenuta Cucco has succeeded in the praiseworthy feat of producing excellent wines even during off years, such as 2014, while giving rise to a commendable selection of entry-levels (Serralunga d'Alba Barolo) that exhibits rare pleasantness. The Barolo del Comune di Serralunga d'Alba '15 has character, impressing with its aromatic breadth. It's mature, meaty in its fruit and true to type in its tannic grip, nicely balanced by freshness, with a balsamic finish. Notes of root and wood resin mark the Barolo Cerrati Vigna Cucco Ris. '13, whose spicy oakiness is still a bit dominant. The exuberant Barolo Cerrati '15 features aromas of quinine, and a notably austere palate that should get smoother over time.

● Barolo Cerrati V. Cucco Ris. '13	🏆🏆 8
● Barolo del Comune di Serralunga d'Alba '15	🏆🏆 6
● Barolo Cerrati '15	🏆🏆 7
● Barbera d'Alba '18	🏆 4
● Langhe Nebbiolo '18	🏆 4
● Barolo Cerrati '14	🏆🏆 7
● Barolo Cerrati '13	🏆🏆 7
● Barolo Cerrati V. Cucco Ris. '12	🏆🏆 8
● Barolo Cerrati V. Cucco Ris. '11	🏆🏆 8
● Barolo del Comune di Serralunga d'Alba '14	🏆🏆 6
● Barolo del Comune di Serralunga d'Alba '13	🏆🏆 6
○ Langhe Chardonnay '16	🏆🏆 3
● Langhe Rosso '16	🏆🏆 4

Giovanni Daglio

VIA MONTALE CELLI, 10
15050 COSTA VESCOVATO [AL]
TEL. +39 0131838262
www.vignetidaglio.com

CELLAR SALES
ANNUAL PRODUCTION 15,000 bottles
HECTARES UNDER VINE 10.00

The fact of running a small operation hasn't precluded Giovanni from achieving fame and recognition in top markets, successes earned in the field, like great athletes that reach great heights thanks to their talents and a life of sacrifice. The care he shows is almost obsessive and his passion uncontrollable. Over the years, the resulting wines have represented expressions of great finesse and elegance. And so it is that, in keeping with tradition, Giovanni has forged a style that interprets native grapes as few others can. Cantico goes in search of Tre Bicchieri with a lovely version that highlights their production style. It's potent and rich, with aromas of fresh herbs and a note of flint, all of which show ample room for improvement over time. Derthona exhibits a charming, complex aromatic profile and a full-bodied, extremely persistent palate. A special mention for their Nibiö 17, a wine with excellent nose-palate symmetry.

○ Colli Tortonesi Timorasso Cantico '17	🏆🏆 4
● Colli Tortonesi Barbera Basinas '17	🏆🏆 4
● Colli Tortonesi Dolcetto Nibiö '17	🏆🏆 3
○ Colli Tortonesi Timorasso Derthona '17	🏆🏆 4
○ Colli Tortonesi Cortese Vigna del Re '18	🏆 2
● Colli Tortonesi Barbera Basinas '16	🏆🏆 4
● Colli Tortonesi Dolcetto Nibiö '16	🏆🏆 3
○ Colli Tortonesi Timorasso Cantico '16	🏆🏆 4
○ Colli Tortonesi Timorasso Cantico '15	🏆🏆 4
○ Colli Tortonesi Timorasso Derthona '15	🏆🏆 4
○ Colli Tortonesi Timorasso Derthona Cantico '14	🏆🏆 4

Deltetto

c.so Alba, 43
12043 Canale [CN]
Tel. +39 0173979383
www.deltetto.com

CELLAR SALES
PRE-BOOKED VISITS
ANNUAL PRODUCTION 170,000 bottles
HECTARES UNDER VINE 21.00
VITICULTURE METHOD Certified Organic
SUSTAINABLE WINERY

The Deltetto family's winery, which has operated in Roero since 1953, has over time enlarged their selection. Today, in addition to the area's classic wines (grounded in traditional. grapes like Arneis, Favorita, Nebbiolo and Barbera), they also make a solid line of sparkling wines drawing primarily on Chardonnay and Pinot Nero, but also Nebbiolo and wines from other important regional appellations, such as Barolo and Gavi. Theirs is a modern style, always of high craftsmanship. The Roeros present are of excellent quality. The Gorrini '17 offers up lovely notes of raspberries and red berries with nuances of tobacco. On the palate it's harmonious and succulent, with velvety tannins and a long finish. The Braja Riserva '16 opts more for floral fragrances of violet followed by balsamic hints and quinine, sensations that anticipate a close-knit, round palate. Their perennially well-crafted Barolo Parussi and Metodo Classico are among the territory's best.

● Roero Braja Ris. '16	♟♟4
● Roero Gorrini '17	♟♟2*
● Barolo Parussi '14	♟♟6
○ Deltetto Brut M. Cl. '15	♟♟4
● Langhe Pinot Nero 777 '17	♟♟3
⊙ Deltetto Brut Rosé	♟5
○ Deltetto Extra Brut M. Cl. '13	♟5
○ Roero Arneis Daivej '18	♟3
○ Roero Arneis San Defendente '17	♟3
● Roero Braja Ris. '09	♟♟♟4*
● Roero Braja Ris. '08	♟♟♟4
● Roero Braja Ris. '07	♟♟♟4
● Barolo Parussi '13	♟♟6
⊙ Deltetto Rosé Brut M. Cl.	♟♟5

Gianni Doglia

via Annunziata, 56
14054 Castagnole delle Lanze [AT]
Tel. +39 0141878359
www.giannidoglia.it

CELLAR SALES
PRE-BOOKED VISITS
ANNUAL PRODUCTION 100,000 bottles
HECTARES UNDER VINE 12.00
SUSTAINABLE WINERY

The winery managed by Gianni Doglia, his sister, and his parents is a small family-run producer that's been making wines here in Castagnole delle Lanze (an important district for Asti) for three generations. It all centers on their private hillside vineyards, situated on calcareous-clay soil at 300 meters elevation, perfect conditions for the area's classic grapes. Barbera (presented in five versions) takes center stage, though we mustn't forget Grignolino, Ruchè, Merlot and Moscato. For the moment we'll go back to their new and magnificent Moscato d'Asti Casa di Bianca, with a 2018 whose subtle, harmonious and enticing aromas call up notes of medicinal herbs, peach and lime. The palate is marked by elegance and balance, with a mousse of great delicacy and finesse. Together with acidity it makes for an extremely fresh wine: Tre Bicchieri. Release of their barrel-aged Barbera was postponed until next year. So we'll have to wait until then.

○ Moscato d'Asti Casa di Bianca '18	♟♟♟3*
● Barbera d'Asti Sup. Genio '17	♟♟4
○ Moscato d'Asti '18	♟♟3*
○ Nizza V. V. '17	♟♟5
● Barbera d'Asti Bosco Donne '18	♟♟3
● Grignolino d'Asti '18	♟♟2*
● Piemonte Merlot '16	♟♟3
● Barbera d'Asti Sup. Genio '12	♟♟♟4*
○ Moscato d'Asti Casa di Bianca '17	♟♟♟5
○ Moscato d'Asti Casa di Bianca '16	♟♟♟3*
○ Moscato d'Asti Casa di Bianca '15	♟♟♟3*
● Barbera d'Asti Sup. Genio '16	♟♟6
● Grignolino d'Asti '17	♟♟4
○ Moscato d'Asti '17	♟♟4
○ Moscato d'Asti '16	♟♟2*
● Nizza '16	♟♟6

Dosio

REG. SERRADENARI, 6
12064 LA MORRA [CN]
TEL. +39 017350677
www.dosiovigneti.com

CELLAR SALES
PRE-BOOKED VISITS
ACCOMMODATION
ANNUAL PRODUCTION 65,000 bottles
HECTARES UNDER VINE 11.00

Beppe Dosio has been working in his lovely winery for 45 years. In 2010 it got a boost when the Lenci family became a partner and Marco Dotta came on board. Here in the highest part of Barolo (at almost 500 meters elevation), temperatures and ventilation guarantee freshness and nice fragrance, as can be appreciated when tasting their Serradenari cru. Their Barolo Fossati is perennially fruitier and more structured, with good tannic presence and good aging prospects. The greatness of 2016 can be appreciated right now, just by tasting their Langhe Momenti, a Nebbiolo and Barbera blend: sophisticated elegance, clear black berry sensations, a dense palate of perfect balance. And their balsamic Nebbiolo Barilà '16 is no less good, just a bit more enveloped by subtle oaky hints. Their licorice-scented Barolo Serradenari '15 is quite fresh, marked by a sophisticant tannic weave.

● Barolo Serradenari '15	♛♛ 7
● Langhe Momenti '16	♛♛ 5
● Barolo '15	♛♛ 6
● Barolo Fossati '14	♛♛ 7
● Dolcetto d'Alba '18	♛♛ 3
● Langhe Nebbiolo Barilà '16	♛♛ 5
● Dolcetto d'Alba Sup. Nassone '17	♛ 3
● Barbera d'Alba Sup. '16	♛♛ 4
● Barolo Fossati '13	♛♛ 7
● Barolo Fossati Ris. '12	♛♛ 8
● Barolo Fossati Ris. '11	♛♛ 8
● Barolo Serradenari '14	♛♛ 6
● Barolo Serradenari '13	♛♛ 6
● Barolo Serradenari '12	♛♛ 6
● Langhe Nebbiolo Barilà '15	♛♛ 5
● Langhe Rosso Momenti '15	♛♛ 5

★Poderi Luigi Einaudi

LOC. CASCINA TECC
B.TA GOMBE, 31/32
12063 DOGLIANI [CN]
TEL. +39 017370191
www.poderieinaudi.com

CELLAR SALES
PRE-BOOKED VISITS
ACCOMMODATION
ANNUAL PRODUCTION 350,000 bottles
HECTARES UNDER VINE 60.00
SUSTAINABLE WINERY

This large producer was founded by Italian president Luigi Einaudi. It's an estate that's grown in both size and beauty over time, with a particularly intense period of expansion coming of late under Matteo Sardagna. Indeed, in addition to their Barolo vineyards (including plots in Bussia, Cannubi and Terlo), they're about to add a new wine from the Monvigliero cru. Their selection, which comprises Dogliani naturally (led by their commendable Vigna Tecc), is worthy of the estate and its elegant relais. Their 2015 Barolos are just superb. The new Bussia is of splendid craft, elegant and spicy, with a succulent harmony. The Cannubi is a masterpiece, rich in nuances ranging from quinine to red berries, while on the palate it's fresh, pulpy with mature tannins. The magnificent Terlo Vigna Costa Grimaldi speaks in sweet tobacco and dried flower petals, followed by a palate that's already of rare harmony and balance. The Vigna Tecc '17 is among the best Doglianis of the year, hands down.

● Barolo Cannubi '15	♛♛♛ 8
● Barolo Bussia '15	♛♛ 8
● Barolo Terlo V. Costa Grimaldi '15	♛♛ 7
● Dogliani Sup. V. Tecc '17	♛♛ 3*
● Barolo '15	♛♛ 8
● Dogliani '18	♛♛ 3
● Langhe Barbera '17	♛♛ 3
● Langhe Nebbiolo '18	♛♛ 3
● Barolo Cannubi '11	♛♛♛ 8
● Barolo Cannubi '10	♛♛♛ 8
● Barolo Costa Grimaldi '05	♛♛♛ 8
● Barolo Costa Grimaldi '01	♛♛♛ 7
● Dogliani Sup. V. Tecc '10	♛♛♛ 3*
● Dogliani V. Tecc '06	♛♛♛ 4
● Langhe Rosso Luigi Einaudi '04	♛♛♛ 5

F.lli Facchino

LOC. VAL DEL PRATO, 210
15078 ROCCA GRIMALDA [AL]
TEL. +39 014385401
www.vinifacchino.it

CELLAR SALES
PRE-BOOKED VISITS
RESTAURANT SERVICE
ANNUAL PRODUCTION 80,000 bottles
HECTARES UNDER VINE 31.00

A growth in quality was already in the cards for some time. It was enough for the Facchino brothers to believe in themselves and in the quality of their grapes. But for those who want to make great wines, earning Tre Bicchieri shouldn't be an end in and of itself, but a starting point. Now the game gets hard, but the experience of generations of family, in the vineyard and in the cellar, overseeing extraordinary local grapes like Barbera and Dolcetto di Ovada, could make the difference. The road ahead is clear, it could become a highway. Their two Dolcetto di Ovadas, Poggiobello and and an entry-level Dolcetto, do the honors. The former highlights a generous aromatic profile, with varietal aromas emerging on an intense palate marked by still-evolving tannins. The entry-level Dolcetto features jammy aromas and evanescent notes, which reemerge on a firmly-structure palate only to give way to a long finish. The Barbera is an approachable, pleasant drink.

Tenuta Il Falchetto

FRAZ. CIOMBI
VIA VALLE TINELLA, 16
12058 SANTO STEFANO BELBO [CN]
TEL. +39 0141840344
www.ilfalchetto.com

CELLAR SALES
PRE-BOOKED VISITS
ANNUAL PRODUCTION 280,000 bottles
HECTARES UNDER VINE 50.00

Brothers Giorgio, Fabrizio and Andriano avail themselves of some six properties in the provinces of Cuneo (Santo Stefano Belbo and Castiglione Tinella) and Asti (Agliano Terme and Calosso). These areas are highly prized, especially for the cultivation of Moscato and Barbera, but Falchetto also produces interesting wines with Chardonnay, Dolcetto, Cab. Sauvignon, Merlot and Pinot Nero. It's a selection whose quality is constantly growing, both when it comes to their base line of wines and their premium wines. Three wines shone the brightest, starting with their Barbera Sup. Bricco Paradiso, a 2016 that's traditionally-styled in its aromas of black cherry, chocolate and quinine. Their Moscato d'Asti Canelli Ciombo '18 and Tenuta del Fant '18 both performed at high levels: the former is elegant in its aromas of lime, thyme and peach, the latter sees more tapered contours, aromas of citrus and medicinal herbs. In their Pian Craie '18 we discovered one of Italy's great Sauvignons.

● Dolcetto di Ovada '17	♟♟ 2*
● Dolcetto di Ovada Poggiobello '16	♟♟ 2*
● Barbera del M.to '18	♟♟ 2*
○ Cortese dell'Alto M.to Pacialan '18	♟ 2
● Piemonte Albarossa Note d'Autunno '15	♟ 4
● Barbera del M.to '16	♟♟♟ 2*
● Barbera del M.to '15	♟♟ 2*
● Barbera del M.to Terre del Re '15	♟♟ 2*
○ Cortese dell'Alto M.to Pacialan '16	♟♟ 2*
● Dolcetto di Ovada '16	♟♟ 2*
● Dolcetto di Ovada Poggiobello '15	♟♟ 2*
● Dolcetto di Ovada Poggiobello '14	♟♟ 2*
● M.to Rosso Note d'Autunno '11	♟♟ 3
● Ovada Carasöi '15	♟♟ 3
● Piemonte Albarossa Note d'Autunno '12	♟♟ 3

● Barbera d'Asti Sup. Bricco Paradiso '16	♟♟ 4
○ Moscato d'Asti Canelli Ciombo '18	♟♟ 2*
○ Moscato d'Asti Tenuta del Fant '18	♟♟ 2*
○ Piemonte Sauvignon Pian Craie '18	♟♟ 3*
● Barbera d'Asti Sup. Lurëi '16	♟♟ 3
● M.to Rosso La Mora '16	♟♟ 3
● Barbera d'Asti Pian Scorrone '18	♟ 2
● Piemonte Pinot Nero Solo '16	♟ 4
○ Moscato d'Asti Ciombo '15	♟♟♟ 2*
○ Moscato d'Asti Tenuta del Fant '11	♟♟♟ 2*
○ Moscato d'Asti Tenuta del Fant '09	♟♟♟ 2*
● Barbera d'Asti Sup. Bricco Paradiso '15	♟♟ 4
○ Moscato d'Asti Canelli Tenuta del Fant '17	♟♟ 2*

Benito Favaro

S.DA CHIUSURE, 1BIS
10010 PIVERONE [TO]
TEL. +39 012572606
www.cantinafavaro.it

CELLAR SALES
PRE-BOOKED VISITS
ANNUAL PRODUCTION 20,000 bottles
HECTARES UNDER VINE 3.50
VITICULTURE METHOD Certified Organic

The Erbaluce di Caluso 13 Mesi has become a symbol of this grape's aging power thanks to careful work aimed at bringing together its high acidity with enriched aromas, a feat made possible through mineral elements of rare finesse. Benito and Camillo's recipe is simple: reduce yields and use steel, concrete and little wood for aging. The winery's dimensions are a testament to the belief that 'small is beautiful'. White-fleshed fruit and medicinal herbs introduce their splendid Erbaluce di Caluso 13 Mesi '17, a wine whose palate impresses for its balance of rich texture and freshness: Tre Bicchieri. Their Le Chiusure '17 is quite similar, though with hints of incense lending further aromatic complexity. The spicy Rossomeraviglia '17, a Syrah, and the fruity Nebbiolo Ros '17, both made in limited quantities, are also worth noting.

○ Erbaluce di Caluso 13 Mesi '17	♟♟♟ 4*
○ Erbaluce di Caluso Le Chiusure '17	♟♟ 3*
● Ros '17	♟♟ 4
● Rossomeraviglia '17	♟♟ 5
● F2 '17	♟ 2
○ Erbaluce di Caluso 13 Mesi '16	♟♟♟ 3*
○ Erbaluce di Caluso Le Chiusure '16	♟♟♟ 2*
○ Erbaluce di Caluso Le Chiusure '13	♟♟♟ 2*
○ Erbaluce di Caluso Le Chiusure '12	♟♟♟ 2*
○ Erbaluce di Caluso Le Chiusure '11	♟♟♟ 2*
○ Erbaluce di Caluso Le Chiusure '10	♟♟♟ 2*
○ Erbaluce di Caluso 13 Mesi '15	♟♟ 3*
○ Erbaluce di Caluso 13 Mesi '11	♟♟ 3*
○ Erbaluce di Caluso 13 Mesi '10	♟♟ 3*
○ Erbaluce di Caluso Le Chiusure '15	♟♟ 2*
○ Erbaluce di Caluso Le Chiusure '14	♟♟ 2*

Giacomo Fenocchio

LOC. BUSSIA, 72
12065 MONFORTE D'ALBA [CN]
TEL. +39 017378675
www.giacomofenocchio.com

CELLAR SALES
PRE-BOOKED VISITS
ANNUAL PRODUCTION 90,000 bottles
HECTARES UNDER VINE 15.00
SUSTAINABLE WINERY

Claudio Fenocchio's selection adheres to a rigorously classical style, in particular through the use of large barrels for aging and long periods with skin and must contact, as made clear by the name '90 Dì' ('90 days') adopted for their Riserva Bussia. The resulting wines are characterized both by their aromatic cleanness and clearness and by the transparent expression of the crus of provenance, situated in excellent positions in Barolo, Castiglione Falletto and Monforte d'Alba. In the vineyard they've eliminated chemical products and abandoned fertilizer. Only Barolo was submitted for tasting this year. In terms of the 2015s, the Villero stands out in particular, proving subtle and unembellished, as does the Cannubi, a wine endowed with great character thanks to its aromas of raspberry and licorice. Spices and fresh red berries feature in the magnificent, though still austere, Bussia 90 Dì Riserva 2013. However, theirs is an extremely valid selection across the board.

● Barolo Bussia 90 Dì Ris. '13	♟♟ 8
● Barolo Cannubi '15	♟♟ 7
● Barolo Villero '15	♟♟ 7
● Barolo Bussia '15	♟♟ 6
● Barolo Castellero '15	♟♟ 6
● Barolo Bussia '11	♟♟♟ 6
● Barolo Bussia '09	♟♟♟ 6
● Barolo Bussia 90 Dì Ris. '12	♟♟♟ 8
● Barolo Bussia 90 Dì Ris. '10	♟♟♟ 8
● Barolo Brunate '14	♟♟ 5
● Barolo Bussia '14	♟♟ 6
● Barolo Bussia '13	♟♟ 6
● Barolo Bussia '12	♟♟ 6
● Barolo Bussia 90 Dì Ris. '11	♟♟ 8
● Barolo Cannubi '13	♟♟ 6
● Barolo Castellero '14	♟♟ 6
● Barolo Villero '14	♟♟ 7

Ferrando

VIA TORINO, 599
10015 IVREA [TO]
TEL. +39 0125633550
www.ferrandovini.it

CELLAR SALES
PRE-BOOKED VISITS
ANNUAL PRODUCTION 50,000 bottles
HECTARES UNDER VINE 5.00

Carema Etichetta Nera is a high expression of Nebbiolo: nice acidity, consistent but not dry tannins, elegant aromas, nice alcohol — what's more, it gets better over time. The only shame is that the few bottles produced get sent all over the world, so it's not easy to find one. But if you do, or if you happen to visit their winery, don't miss your chance. Today it's overseen by Roberto and Andrea, children of skilled winemaker Luigi Ferrando. They offer notable versions of Erbaluce di Caluso as well. A gorgeous 2015 Carema Etichetta Nera offers up intense aromas of raspberry, dried herbs and licorice on a background of bottled cherries. It's just a bit marked by toastiness, while tannins prove smooth, well-placed, making for a convincing, memorable drink. Their simpler Etichetta Bianca is warm, multifaceted, while the magnificent Erbaluce di Caluso Cariola '18 is redolent of apples, pears, candied lemon and a hint of ginger. On the palate it's rich and fresh, with excellent harmony.

● Carema Et. Nera '15	♟♟	7
○ Erbaluce di Caluso Cariola '18	♟♟	3*
● Carema Et. Bianca '15	♟♟	5
○ Erbaluce di Caluso La Torrazza '18	♟	3
● Carema Et. Bianca '12	♟♟♟	5
● Carema Et. Nera '11	♟♟♟	7
● Carema Et. Nera '09	♟♟♟	6
● Carema Et. Nera '08	♟♟♟	6
○ Caluso Passito '12	♟♟	5
● Carema Et. Bianca '13	♟♟	5
● Carema Et. Nera '13	♟♟	7
○ Erbaluce di Caluso Cariola '17	♟♟	3
○ Erbaluce di Caluso La Torrazza '17	♟♟	3*

Luca Ferraris

LOC. RIVI, 7
S.DA PROV.LE 14
14030 CASTAGNOLE MONFERRATO [AT]
TEL. +39 0141292202
www.ferrarisagricola.it

CELLAR SALES
PRE-BOOKED VISITS
ANNUAL PRODUCTION 220,000 bottles
HECTARES UNDER VINE 21.00
SUSTAINABLE WINERY

The winery managed by Luca Ferraris is without a doubt among those that have most contributed to highlighting the peculiarities of Castagnole Monferrato Ruchè. It's an especially notable feat if we consider how different a typology it is with respect to the intense, powerful, round wines enjoying so much popularity today. Founded in the 1920s by his grandmother Teresa and revived in 1999, today the producer avails itself of the support of Randall Grahm, and spans eight different vineyards in which Barbera, Grignolino, Viognier and Chardonnay are cultivated. 2018 proved particularly good for Ruchè. Dried flowers, forest undergrowth and licorice roots: the Clàsic is true to its name, while the Sant'Eufemia plays on floral and spicy notes, unfolding subtly but progressively across the palate. Their Vigna del Parroco distills the best qualities of both, coming through multifaceted and deep, with powerful tannins contrasted by bountiful succulence.

● Ruchè di Castagnole Monferrato V. del Parroco '18	♟♟	3*
● Ruchè di Castagnole Monferrato Clàsic '18	♟♟	2*
● Ruchè di Castagnole Monferrato Sant'Eufemia '18	♟♟	3
● Barbera d'Asti Sup La Regina '16	♟♟	3
● Ruchè di Castagnole M.to Clàsic '17	♟♟	2*
● Ruchè di Castagnole M.to Opera Prima per il Fondatore '16	♟♟	6
● Ruchè di Castagnole M.to Sant'Eufemia '17	♟♟	3

Roberto Ferraris

REG. DOGLIANO, 33
14041 AGLIANO TERME [AT]
TEL. +39 0141954234
www.robertoferraris.com

CELLAR SALES
PRE-BOOKED VISITS
ANNUAL PRODUCTION 60,000 bottles
HECTARES UNDER VINE 12.00
SUSTAINABLE WINERY

The winery founded almost a century ago by Stefano Ferrari (today managed by his grandson Roberto) is situated in Agliano Terme, a classic territory for Barbera. Not surprisingly, the grape is central to their selection, with some five different versions differentiated according to fermentation and aging. Only steel is used for their I Suôrí and Nobbio, mid-sized casks and barriques for Bisavolo and La Cricca, and 18 months in French oak for their Nizza Liberta (Castelnuovo Calcea). It's a solid, compact selection that's rounded out with two Grignolino and Nebbiolo reds. Their highly convincing selection includes a notable Barbera Sup. Bisavolo '17. It's expressive in its aromas of black fruits, cocoa powder and tobacco, unfolding on the palate with vivacity and measure, leaving an exquisite spicy streak in its wake. The Nizza Liberta '16 features a more mature profile, while the Barbera Sup. La Cricca '17 seems to possess adequate structure to integrate its share of oak.

● Barbera d'Asti Sup. Bisavolo '17	🍷🍷 3*
● Barbera d'Asti Nobbio '17	🍷🍷 3
● Barbera d'Asti Sup. La Cricca '17	🍷🍷 4
● Nizza Liberta '16	🍷🍷 5
● Barbera d'Asti I Suôrí '17	🍷 2
● Nizza Liberta '15	🍷🍷🍷 5
● Barbera d'Asti Nobbio '16	🍷🍷 3*
● Barbera d'Asti Nobbio '15	🍷🍷 3
● Barbera d'Asti Sup. Bisavolo '16	🍷🍷 3
● Barbera d'Asti Sup. Bisavolo '15	🍷🍷 4
● Barbera d'Asti Sup. La Cricca '16	🍷🍷 4
● Barbera d'Asti Sup. La Cricca '15	🍷🍷 5
● Barbera d'Asti Sup. La Cricca '13	🍷🍷 3*

Carlo Ferro

FRAZ. SALERE, 41
14041 AGLIANO TERME [AT]
TEL. +39 3282818967
www.ferrovini.com

CELLAR SALES
PRE-BOOKED VISITS
ANNUAL PRODUCTION 15,000 bottles
HECTARES UNDER VINE 12.00

The producer founded more than a century ago by the Ferro family on the hills of Agliano Terme (in Langhe and Monferrato) is entirely dedicated to producing red wines. Their estate vineyards, managed according to principles of sustainable agriculture, host Barbera, Dolcetto, Grignolino and Nebbiolo, all native grapes (except for a few rows of Cabernet Sauvignon). These give rise to a compact selection of intense and exuberant wines that have, in recent years, increasingly found themselves in the limelight. Their selection centers on various versions of Barbera d'Asti, foremost their Nizza La Corazziera '16. It's introduced by plum preserves, tobacco and cocoa powder on a smoky background, while on the palate its rich, mature character is confirmed, though without losing balance. Their Superiore Roche '16 moves on a similar track, it's just a bit lacking in freshness, while the Superiore Notturno '16 exhibits a racier profile, with nuances of red berries, black pepper and quinine.

● Nizza La Carrozziera '16	🍷🍷 4
● Barbera d'Asti Sup. Notturno '16	🍷🍷 3
● Barbera d'Asti Sup. Roche '16	🍷🍷 4
● Barbera d'Asti Giulia '17	🍷 2
● M.to Rosso Paolo '15	🍷 4
● Barbera d'Asti Sup. Giulia '16	🍷🍷 2*
● Barbera d'Asti Sup. Notturno '15	🍷🍷 3*
● Barbera d'Asti Sup. Notturno '11	🍷🍷 2*
● Nizza La Corazziera '15	🍷🍷 4

★Fontanafredda

LOC. FONTANAFREDDA
VIA ALBA, 15
12050 SERRALUNGA D'ALBA [CN]
TEL. +39 0173626111
www.fontanafredda.it

CELLAR SALES
PRE-BOOKED VISITS
ACCOMMODATION AND RESTAURANT SERVICE
ANNUAL PRODUCTION 8,500,000 bottles
HECTARES UNDER VINE 100.00
SUSTAINABLE WINERY

Bolstered by experience leading Giacomo Borgogno, Andrea has consolidated his role at the head of Fontanafredda and Casa E di Mirafiore. The production approach is the same: organic cultivation principles, use of large barrels, increased production of whites (here in Alta Langa, in particular). These combine with a continued attention for Barolo of increasingly high quality. The best way to learn about the winery's centuries-old history is to read two volumes rich in photography: Lorenzo Tablino's 'Fontanafredda: 125 Years of Vineyards and Cellars'. Paiagallo, rightfully considered one of Langa's best crus, gave rise to a commendable 2015 thanks to subtle, sophisticated and complex aromas of raspberries, rose petals, licorice and violets. A slow, splendid development is alluringly pervasive and devoid of harshness. If it's their Barolo 2015s that dominated, all it takes is a quick glance at the scorecard to see that quality is a priority for all their wines, without exception.

○ Alta Langa Brut Limited Edition '14	♥♥ 5
● Barolo Casa E. di Mirafiore Ris. '15	♥♥ 8
● Barolo Lazzarito Casa E. di Mirafiore '15	♥♥ 6
● Barolo Paiagallo Casa E. di Mirafiore '15	♥♥ 8
● Barolo '15	♥♥ 8
● Barolo del Comune di Serralunga d'Alba '15	♥♥ 7
● Barolo Fontanafredda V. La Rosa '15	♥♥ 8
● Barolo Silver '15	♥♥ 7
● Dolcetto d'Alba Casa E. di Mirafiore '18	♥♥ 4
● Langhe Rosso Pietra Magica Casa E. di Mirafiore '17	♥♥ 5
○ Roero Arneis Pradalupo '18	♥♥ 3
● Barolo Paiagallo Casa E. di Mirafiore '13	♥♥♥ 7
● Barolo Paiagallo Casa E. di Mirafiore '12	♥♥♥ 7

Fortemasso

LOC. CASTELLETTO, 21
12065 MONFORTE D'ALBA [CN]
TEL. +39 0173328148
www.fortemasso.it

CELLAR SALES
ANNUAL PRODUCTION 27,000 bottles
HECTARES UNDER VINE 5.20

Castelletto is a large vineyard in Monforte d'Alba. It enjoys a splendid, panoramic view, primarily of Serralunga's long, charming chain of hills. The Barolo cultivated here sees notable tannic presence and broad, fresh aromas (you can also detect delicate balsamic hints and notes of licorice). It's here that Agricole Gussalli Beretta built their cellar, the final node of a vast project that reaches into Abruzzo, Lombardy and Tuscany. Technical oversight is in good hands: Piero Ballario in the cellar and Gian Piero Romana in the vineyard. The 2013 Riserva Castelletto features a classically-styled and complex aromatic profile in which notes of quinine and tobacco are followed by licorice. On the palate it's supple, but it's got nice body too, with a tantalizing sapidity and a long, harmonious and lively finish: Tre Bicchieri. Raspberry, sun-dried herbs and licorice feature in their Barolo Castelletto '15, a wine of valid complexity whose delicate tannins favor an alluring softness.

● Barolo Castelletto Ris. '13	♥♥♥ 8
● Barolo Castelletto '15	♥♥ 6
● Barbera d'Alba '17	♥♥ 3
● Barbera d'Alba '16	♥♥ 3
● Barbera d'Alba '15	♥♥ 3
● Barolo Castelletto '14	♥♥ 6
● Barolo Castelletto '13	♥♥ 6
● Langhe Nebbiolo '17	♥♥ 3
● Langhe Nebbiolo '16	♥♥ 3

Gaggino

s.da Sant'Evasio, 29
15076 Ovada [AL]
Tel. +39 0143822345
www.gaggino.it

CELLAR SALES
PRE-BOOKED VISITS
ANNUAL PRODUCTION 150,000 bottles
HECTARES UNDER VINE 20.00

A growth in the quality of Gabriele's wines has gone hand in hand with the expansion of the estate, starting with new vineyard purchases and the renovation of Cascina Viola in Madonna Della Villa, a site destined to become the winery's future headquarters. At the moment Dolcetto di Ovada, with its history, its great potential and the elegance of simplicity, is the cornerstone of their selection. It's an extraordinary grape, here vinified in steel and aged in the bottle, whose attributes have yet to be fully recognized by international markets. Their Convivio confirms that it's one of Piedmont's great wines. The 2017 is characterized by extremely delicate and elegant fruit. On the palate we find close-knit and dense, though never aggressive, tannins that accompany its development towards an extremely long and characterful finish. The Ticco is back in our final round of tastings. It's a complex wine, with aromas of black berries accompanied by quinine, and a generous, potent palate.

● Ovada Convivio '17	♛♛♛ 3*
● Barbera del M.to Ticco '16	♛♛ 4
● Barbera del M.to La Lazzarina '18	♛♛ 2*
● Dolcetto di Ovada Sedici '18	♛♛ 2*
● Piemonte Rosso Passito '17	♛♛ 3
⊙ Piemonte Rosato Sedici Rosé '18	♛ 2
● Ovada Convivio '16	♛♛♛ 3*
● Ovada Convivio '13	♛♛♛ 2*
● Barbera del M.to La Lazzarina '16	♛♛ 2*
● Barbera del M.to La Lazzarina '15	♛♛ 2*
● Dolcetto di Ovada '17	♛♛ 2*
● Dolcetto di Ovada '16	♛♛ 2*
○ Gavi La Sverza '17	♛♛ 3
● Ovada Convivio '15	♛♛ 3*
● Ovada Convivio '14	♛♛ 3*
● Ovada Sant'Evasio '13	♛♛ 4

★★★★★ Gaja

via Torino, 18
12050 Barbaresco [CN]
Tel. +39 0173635158
info@gaja.com

ANNUAL PRODUCTION 350,000 bottles
HECTARES UNDER VINE 92.00

Vision, ambition, determination. Gaja's story is one of an osteria that became a winery, a family producer that, year after year, and great wine after great wine, built Italy's strongest brand, exported and managed with extraordinary care and professionalism the world over. It's a journey that spans 160 years and five generations, from Giovanni Gaja to Angelo's children: Gaia, Rosanna and Giovanni. The selection submitted was one of their best, marked by aromatic finesse and tannic texture. The San Lorenzo '16 is silk made into wine, with pure embroidery of fruit, subtle and delicate, and a long, balsamic finish. The Sorì Tildìn '16 enchants, and takes home a resounding Tre Bicchieri thanks to seductive fragrances of citron, mint, vivid fruit, making for an endless development and a close-woven, airy texture, closing weightlessly, ad infinitum. The rest of their wines perform at outstanding levels, including two Barolos (though we slightly preferred the Conteisa).

● Barbaresco Sorì Tildìn '16	♛♛♛ 8
● Barbaresco '16	♛♛ 8
● Barbaresco Costa Russi '16	♛♛ 8
● Barbaresco San Lorenzo '16	♛♛ 8
● Barolo Conteisa '15	♛♛ 8
● Barolo Sperss '15	♛♛ 8
● Barbaresco '09	♛♛♛ 8
● Barbaresco '08	♛♛♛ 8
● Barbaresco Costa Russi '13	♛♛♛ 8
● Barbaresco Sorì Tildìn '15	♛♛♛ 8
● Barbaresco Sorì Tildìn '14	♛♛♛ 8
● Langhe Darmagi '93	♛♛♛ 8
● Langhe Nebbiolo Costa Russi '10	♛♛♛ 8
● Langhe Nebbiolo Costa Russi '08	♛♛♛ 8
● Langhe Nebbiolo Costa Russi '07	♛♛♛ 8
● Langhe Nebbiolo Sorì Tildìn '11	♛♛♛ 8
● Langhe Nebbiolo Sperss '11	♛♛♛ 8

Filippo Gallino

FRAZ. VALLE DEL POZZO, 63
12043 CANALE [CN]
TEL. +39 017398112
www.filippogallino.com

CELLAR SALES
PRE-BOOKED VISITS
ACCOMMODATION
ANNUAL PRODUCTION 100,000 bottles
HECTARES UNDER VINE 14.00
SUSTAINABLE WINERY

The winery was founded in 1961 by the Gallinos has produced Barbera and Nebbiolo since the beginning of the last century. Today Filippo and his son oversee a producer that avails itself of vineyards like Briccola, Renesio and Mompissano, some of Roero's most famous, all situated in the municipality of Canale (primarily around their main facility). Their wines are made with the area's classic grapes — Arneis, Barbera and Nebbiolo — and are characterized by an approach that's both traditional and modern. This year they submitted a nice, compact selection of wines. The Roero Sorano Ris. '15 stood out with its aromas of quinine and tobacco, and a powerful palate marked by fresh pulp and still austere tannins. It's also worth noting the rich and nicely structured Roero Arneis 4 Luglio, a 2016 that's well-supported by a moderate freshness, and their Moda Veja, whose fragrances of yellow-fleshed fruit and almond anticipate a long, exuberant palate and nuanced tannic stroke.

● Roero Sorano Ris. '15	▼▼ 5
● Barbera d'Alba '17	▼▼ 2*
● Barbera d'Alba Sup. Bonora '15	▼▼ 4
● Langhe Nebbiolo '17	▼▼ 2*
○ Moda Veja	▼▼ 4
○ Roero Arneis 4 Luglio '16	▼▼ 3
○ Roero Arneis '18	▼ 2
● Barbera d'Alba Sup. '05	▽▽▽ 4*
● Barbera d'Alba Sup. '04	▽▽▽ 4*
● Roero '06	▽▽▽ 4*
● Roero Sup. '03	▽▽▽ 3
● Roero Sup. '01	▽▽▽ 5
● Roero Sup. '99	▽▽▽ 5

Garesio

LOC. SORDO, 1
12050 SERRALUNGA D'ALBA [CN]
TEL. +39 3667076775
www.garesiovini.it

CELLAR SALES
PRE-BOOKED VISITS
ANNUAL PRODUCTION 80,000 bottles
HECTARES UNDER VINE 19.00
VITICULTURE METHOD Certified Organic

The Garesio family operates both in Asti, with Barbera and two Nizza offerings, and Langa, where Nebbiolo dominates. In just a few years their goal of building an important winery, headquartered in Serralunga d'Alba, has been achieved. Two reputable experts were called on for technical support: Nicola Argamante for agriculture and Gian Luca Colombo for winemaking. The results are, if not yet entirely homogeneous, nevertheless magnificent, with both their Nizza and Barolo performing at top levels. Mint and medicinal herbs open the alluring aromatic profile of their Barolo del comune di Serralunga d'Alba '15, a notably sweet and pervasive wine on its long palate. Fresh red berries and even greater power characterize their elegant, warm and persistent Cerretta '15. The Nizza '16 is austere and concentrated, with spicy notes and oak harmonizing with its rich patrimony of black berries.

● Barolo Cerretta '15	▼▼▼ 7
● Barolo del Comune di Serralunga d'Alba '15	▼▼ 5
● Nizza '16	▼▼ 4
○ Garesio Pas Dosé M. Cl.	▼ 4
● Nizza Ris. '15	▼ 5
● Barbera d'Asti Superiore Nizza '13	▽▽ 4
● Barbera d'Asti Superiore Nizza '12	▽▽ 4
● Barbera d'Asti Superiore Nizza '11	▽▽ 5
● Barolo Cerretta '13	▽▽ 7
● Barolo del Comune di Serralunga d'Alba '14	▽▽ 5
● Barolo del Comune di Serralunga d'Alba '13	▽▽ 5
● Langhe Nebbiolo '16	▽▽ 3
● Langhe Nebbiolo '15	▽▽ 3
● Nizza '15	▽▽ 4

Cantine Garrone

VIA SCAPACCINO, 36
28845 DOMODOSSOLA [VB]
TEL. +39 0324242990
www.cantinegarrone.it

CELLAR SALES
PRE-BOOKED VISITS
ANNUAL PRODUCTION 50,000 bottles
HECTARES UNDER VINE 10.00

In thirty years of winemaking, the Garrone family have managed to put together a tract of land that's sizable for this northern Piedmont district. In addition to their 3 hectares of private vineyards, they draw on another dozen managed by some 50 local vigneron. The principal grape cultivated is Nebbiolo (here they call it Prünent), which, during the best years, gives rise to wines of rare elegance. It's combined with smaller quantities of Croatina, Barbera and Merlot. Balsamic aromas come together with red berries in the youthful aromatic profile of their Cà d'Maté '16, a wine that's rarely so poignant. The subtle and sophisticated Prünent '16 impresses foremost for its gustatory harmony, with tight-knit tannins already perfectly integrated in its rich, fruity flesh. The 2015 version of their Prünent diecibrente performs on similar levels (the name refers to the ancient unit of measurement for 50 liters), while we found the Tarlàp '17, a Merlot-based wine, simple and enjoyable.

● Valli Ossolane Nebbiolo Sup. Prünent '16	♟♟	5
● Valli Ossolane Nebbiolo Sup. Prünent diecibrente '15	♟♟	6
● Valli Ossolane Rosso Cà d'Maté '16	♟♟	4
● Tarlap '17	♟♟	3
● Munaloss '17	♟	2
● Valli Ossane Rosso Cà d'Maté '13	♟♟	3
● Valli Ossolane Nebbiolo Sup. Prünent '15	♟♟	4
● Valli Ossolane Nebbiolo Sup. Prünent '14	♟♟	4
● Valli Ossolane Nebbiolo Sup. Prünent '13	♟♟	4
● Valli Ossolane Nebbiolo Sup. Prünent '10	♟♟	3*
● Valli Ossolane Rosso Tarlàp '16	♟♟	2*

Gaudio - Bricco Mondalino

C.NE REG. MONDALINO, 5
15049 VIGNALE MONFERRATO [AL]
TEL. +39 0142933204
www.gaudiovini.it

CELLAR SALES
PRE-BOOKED VISITS
ANNUAL PRODUCTION 100,000 bottles
HECTARES UNDER VINE 19.50
SUSTAINABLE WINERY

This historic Vignale Monferrato winery draws on contributions from the whole family. Cellar management is in the hands of Beatrice (who holds a master's degree in viticulture and enology) and Matteo (enologist). Primarily native grapes are used, while the presence of international cultivars is limited to Chardonnay and Merlot, which contributes a quarter share to their Guadium Magnum. Barbera makes up the rest. But getting back to tradition, their Margot is a Grignolino Metodo Classico that almost disappeared after prospering around the turn of the century. In this edition of our guide, the Zerolegno earned a place in our finals thanks to a solid, convincing performance. On the nose a foreground of lovely fruit anticipates evanescent and spicy notes, which lengthen on a generous, sapid palate. Their Bricco Mondalino '17 is a balanced and harmonious Grignolino with nice structure. The Monte della Sala feature intense, varietal aromas, but these are obscured by still pronounced oak.

● Barbera d'Asti Zerolegno '17	♟♟	4
● Grignolino del M.to Casalese Bricco Mondalino '17	♟♟	3
● Grignolino del M.to Casalese Monte della Sala '16	♟♟	4
● Grignolino del M.to Casalese '18	♟	3
● Malvasia di Casorzo Dolce Stil Novo '18	♟	2
● Barbera d'Asti Il Bergantino '15	♟♟	4
● Barbera del M.to Sup. '16	♟♟	2*
● Barbera del M.to Sup. '15	♟♟	2*
● Grignolino del M.to Casalese '17	♟♟	3
● Grignolino del M.to Casalese '16	♟♟	3
● Grignolino del M.to Casalese Monte della Sala '13	♟♟	4
● Malvasia di Casorzo Dolce Stil Novo '16	♟♟	2*
● Malvasia di Casorzo Dolce Stil Novo '15	♟♟	2*

Generaj

B.TA TUCCI, 4
12046 MONTÀ [CN]
TEL. +39 0173976142
www.generaj.it

CELLAR SALES
PRE-BOOKED VISITS
ANNUAL PRODUCTION 50,000 bottles
HECTARES UNDER VINE 12.00
SUSTAINABLE WINERY

The Viglione family has been making wine in Roero for more than 70 years, and today Giuseppe is overseeing the producer. Their estate vineyards are situated in the northernmost part of the appellation, on various soils that range from sandier types to more calcareous and gravelly. Roero's classic grapes are cultivated, from Nebbiolo to Barbera, which is accompanied by smaller share of Bonarda and Croatina. Their wines exhibit a modern style that's attentive to freshness and richness of fruit. This year, they submitted two excellent Roeros for tasting. The Bric Aût Riserva '15 offers up spicy notes and aromas of fresh fruit, sensations that anticipate a palate characterized by great finesse, harmonious tannins and a long, juicy finish. The Roero Bric Aût '16 is more powerful, rich in flesh, with notes of black berries, wood tar, expansive tannins, and a finish of nice grip and traction. The rest of the selection also performed well.

● Roero Bric Aût '16	�wine♛ 4
● Roero Bric Aût Ris. '15	♛♛ 5
○ Generaj Brut M. Cl. '15	♛♛ 5
○ Roero Arneis Bric Varomaldo '18	♛♛ 2*
○ Roero Arneis Quindicilune Ris. '17	♛♛ 3
● Barbera d'Alba Sup. Cà d' Pistola '16	♛ 3
● Barbera d'Alba Sup. Ca' d' Pistola '13	♛♛ 3*
○ Roero Arneis Bric Varomaldo '17	♛♛ 2*
● Roero Bric Aût '15	♛♛ 4
● Roero Bric Aût Ris. '14	♛♛ 5
● Roero Bric Aût Ris. '13	♛♛ 5

★Ettore Germano

LOC. CERRETTA, 1
12050 SERRALUNGA D'ALBA [CN]
TEL. +39 0173613528
www.germanoettore.com

CELLAR SALES
PRE-BOOKED VISITS
ACCOMMODATION
ANNUAL PRODUCTION 90,000 bottles
HECTARES UNDER VINE 16.00

Sergio Germano, an expert in the vineyard and cellar, draws on Nebbiolo vineyards in Serralunga d'Alba. Cerretta, Prapò and Lazzarito are well-known to wine lovers, who'll soon have the chance to taste a new Vigna Rionda Barolo. The success of his Hèrzu isn't a coincidence either. In fact, Sergio has been tasting Riesling the world over for 30 years. The Cigliè hills, which give rise to their other whites as well as the Pinot Nero in their Alta Langa, have proven perfect for the grape's cultivation. Outstanding quality, across the board. Raspberries and spices mark their youthful, long Barolo Lazzarito Ris. '13, full-bodied and potent, though pleasantly supple. The Barolo Prapò '15, already open in its alluring notes of licorice, shows excellent acidic-tannic backbone. The 2016 is the best, most memorable version we can remember of the Barbera d'Alba Sup. della Madre, while the Hérzu '17 is harmonious, elegant. Their selection of sparkling wines is also notable.

● Barolo Lazzarito Ris. '13	♛♛♛ 8
● Barbera d'Alba Sup. della Madre '16	♛♛ 5
● Barolo del Comune di Serralunga d'Alba '15	♛♛ 6
● Barolo Prapò '15	♛♛ 7
○ Langhe Riesling Hérzu '17	♛♛ 4
○ Alta Langa Extra Brut '15	♛♛ 5
● Barolo Cerretta '15	♛♛ 7
● Langhe Nebbiolo '18	♛♛ 3
● Langhe Nebbiolo VR '14	♛♛ 6
◎ Rosanna Extra Brut Rosé M. Cl. '16	♛♛ 5
● Barolo Lazzarito Ris. '12	♛♛♛ 8
● Barolo Lazzarito Ris. '11	♛♛♛ 8
● Barolo Lazzarito Ris. '10	♛♛♛ 8
● Barolo Lazzarito Ris. '08	♛♛♛ 8
● Barolo Prapò '11	♛♛♛ 7
○ Langhe Bianco Hérzu '11	♛♛♛ 4*

La Ghibellina

FRAZ. MONTEROTONDO, 61
15066 GAVI [AL]
TEL. +39 0143686257
www.laghibellina.it

CELLAR SALES
PRE-BOOKED VISITS
RESTAURANT SERVICE
ANNUAL PRODUCTION 60,000 bottles
HECTARES UNDER VINE 17.00

Founded in 2000, this Monterotondo producer has rapidly and successfully established a place in the territory. Their Gavi have surprised right from the outset, serving as a cornerstone of their selection thanks to their ability to highlight the unique characteristics of Monterotondo's Cortese. It's all part of a modern production philosophy aimed at bringing out their grapes' potential. In the beginning their wines were lesser known, but they've opened up a new way of thinking about a cultivar that, when aged in the bottle, reveals ageworthiness and great tertiary aromas. Their complex Mainìn, with its austere aromatic profile, once again earns a place in our finals. Fragrances of almond and white-fleshed fruit emerge on a mineral background, anticipating a superbly structured palate and acidity that lengthens towards a full, weighty finish. Fruity aromas and vegetal notes feature in their Pituj, a wine whose palate proves quite close-knit, with tannins that are still evolving.

○ Gavi del Comune di Gavi Mainìn '18	♜♜	3*
● M.to Rosso Pituj '17	♜♜	4
○ Gavi del Comune di Gavi Brut Cuvée Marina '14	♜	5
● Piemonte Barbera Nero del Monte '16	♜	3
○ Gavi del Comune di Gavi Altius '16	♙♙	5
○ Gavi del Comune di Gavi Brut M. Cl. Cuvée Marina '12	♙♙	5
○ Gavi del Comune di Gavi Mainin '17	♙♙	3*
○ Gavi del Comune di Gavi Mainin '16	♙♙	3*

★★Bruno Giacosa

VIA XX SETTEMBRE, 52
12052 NEIVE [CN]
TEL. +39 017367027
www.brunogiacosa.it

ANNUAL PRODUCTION 300,000 bottles
HECTARES UNDER VINE 20.00
SUSTAINABLE WINERY

Bruno Giacosa, a master when it comes to knowledge of Langa and vinification of its wines, created two distinct entities. On the one hand there's Falletto, praised for its red reserves, bolstered by private vineyards in Serralunga (Falletto cru), in Barbaresco (Asili and Rabajà) and Vezza d'Alba in Roero (Valmaggiore). On the other there's Bruno Giacosa, which he draws on trusted growers for. With his experience and love for grapes (especially Nebbiolo), he's built a name that lives in the hearts of wine lovers the world over. The classically-styled Barbaresco Asili Ris. '14 delivers, with foregrounded notes of raspberries, fragrances of tobacco and violet. On the palate it's majestic, with velvety tannins supporting an extremely long finish: Tre Bicchieri. The Rabajà '15 is fruitier, more youthful, rich in flesh and vitality on the palate. Their elegant Barolo Falletto Vigna Le Rocche '15 proves particularly delicate and alluring.

● Barbaresco Asili Ris. '14	♜♜♜	8
● Barbaresco Rabajà '15	♜♜	8
● Barolo Falletto V. Le Rocche '15	♜♜	8
● Nebbiolo d'Alba V. Valmaggiore '17	♜♜	6
○ Roero Arneis '18	♜♜	4
● Barbaresco Asili '12	♙♙♙	8
● Barbaresco Asili Ris. '11	♙♙♙	8
● Barolo Falletto '07	♙♙♙	8
● Barolo Falletto V. Le Rocche Ris. '12	♙♙♙	8
● Barolo Falletto V. Le Rocche Ris. '11	♙♙♙	8
● Barolo Le Rocche del Falletto Ris. '08	♙♙♙	8
● Barolo Le Rocche del Falletto Ris. '07	♙♙♙	8

Carlo Giacosa

S.DA OVELLO, 9
12050 BARBARESCO [CN]
TEL. +39 0173635116
www.carlogiacosa.it

CELLAR SALES
PRE-BOOKED VISITS
ANNUAL PRODUCTION 42,000 bottles
HECTARES UNDER VINE 5.50
SUSTAINABLE WINERY

Domizio Cavazza is recognized as the father of the Barbaresco appellation, having contributed to founding Alba's school of enology and the territory's first cooperative producer. But few know that, among his private vineyards, he decided to keep a plot within the Montefico cru. It's here that Maria Grazia Giacosa cultivates the grapes for her premium wine, one vinified according to a pure, transparent style that best expresses the area's Nebbiolo. But her entire selection, which comprises two other Barbarescos, is absolutely faithful to the personality of the grapes used. You can't help but admire a small producer that so consistently manages to imbue its entire range of wines with such high quality. The Barbaresco Luca Riserva '14, which is devoid of the green, vegetal notes so common to the vintage, is a wonder of finesse and freshness, but complexity as well. The Montefico '16 is even fuller and more potent, proving almost exuberant in its richness of fruity flesh.

● Barbaresco Luca Ris. '14	♛♛ 7
● Barbaresco Montefico '16	♛♛ 6
● Barbaresco Narin '16	♛♛ 6
● Barbera d'Alba Sup. Lina '17	♛♛ 3
● Langhe Nebbiolo Maria Grazia '17	♛♛ 4
● Barbaresco Montefico '15	♛♛♛ 6
● Barbaresco Montefico '08	♛♛♛ 5*
● Barbaresco Montefico '14	♛♛ 5
● Barbaresco Montefico '13	♛♛ 5
● Barbaresco Narin '15	♛♛ 5
● Barbaresco Narin '14	♛♛ 5
● Barbaresco Narin '11	♛♛ 5
● Barbera d'Alba Mucin '16	♛♛ 3
● Barbera d'Alba Sup. Lina '16	♛♛ 4
● Barbera d'Alba Sup. Lina '15	♛♛ 3
● Langhe Nebbiolo Maria Grazia '15	♛♛ 4

F.lli Giacosa

VIA XX SETTEMBRE, 64
12052 NEIVE [CN]
TEL. +39 017367013
www.giacosa.it

CELLAR SALES
PRE-BOOKED VISITS
ANNUAL PRODUCTION 600,000 bottles
HECTARES UNDER VINE 51.00
VITICULTURE METHOD Certified Organic
SUSTAINABLE WINERY

Within the vast Basarin cru, the Gianmaté cru confers a particular robustness and expressivity to the wine, thanks to a position well exposed to the sun but protected from the wind. Here Maurizio and Paolo Giacosa cultivate the grapes for their premium wines, which are counterbalanced by the Vigna del Mandorlo in Barolo, in the Scarrone geographic mention. Notable production volumes are made possible by a sizable estate. Their commitment to protecting the environment is evidenced by the use of solar energy in their cellar. The Barolo Scarrone Vigna Mandorlo managed to distill only the best qualities from 2014, a poor growing year. It's fresh, elegant, not too full-bodied but well-balanced, endowed with nice acidity and a final encore of delicate balsamic hints. The Barolo Bussia '15 is fruit-forward and harmonious, already devoid of tannic asperity and quite round in its medium-structured palate, finishing on elegant sensations of tar.

● Barolo Scarrone V. Mandorlo '14	♛♛ 8
● Barbaresco Basarin V. Gianmatè '16	♛♛ 7
● Barolo Bussia '15	♛♛ 7
● Barbera d'Alba Maria Gioana '16	♛ 5
○ Langhe Chardonnay Rorea '18	♛ 4
● Barbaresco Basarin V. Gianmatè '15	♛♛ 7
● Barbaresco Basarin V. Gianmatè '14	♛♛ 7
● Barbaresco Basarin V. Gianmatè '11	♛♛ 6
● Barbera d'Alba Canavere '15	♛♛ 4
● Barbera d'Alba Maria Gioana '14	♛♛ 5
● Barbera d'Alba Maria Gioana '11	♛♛ 4
● Barolo Bussia '14	♛♛ 7
● Barolo Bussia '13	♛♛ 7
● Barolo Scarrone V. Mandorlo '11	♛♛ 8
○ Langhe Chardonnay Ca' Lunga '16	♛♛ 5

Giovanni Battista Gillardi

Cascina Corsaletto, 69
12060 Farigliano [CN]
Tel. +39 017376306
www.gillardi.it

CELLAR SALES
PRE-BOOKED VISITS
ANNUAL PRODUCTION 35,000 bottles
HECTARES UNDER VINE 7.00

The small winery founded by Giacolino Gillardi 10 years ago is flanked by the family's other winery in Farigliano, where his father has been bottling prestigious Dolcettos since 1980. Their wines are solid, pervasive, as drinkable now as they were back then, considering that Dogliani's pleasantness derives more from their vineyards than the cellar. Giacolino's creativity and skill have found a way to fully emerge thanks in part to the use of French grapes for his celebrated Harys (Syrah), Grané (Grenache) and Merlò (Merlot). The Barolo Vigname '15 offers up notes of sweet oak, lending complexity to a fruity, spicy ensemble topped off by a floral note. It's firmly-structured, with fair, focused length and plenty of satisfaction. The Barolo '15 is marked by warm alcohol and nice vitality. Commendable structure and mature fruit feature in their Dogliani Cursalet. The robust and persuasive Maestra '18 is noteworthy, as is the woody Langhe Harys '17, a full-bodied, chewy drink.

● Barolo Vignane '15	♟♟ 6
● Barolo '15	♟♟ 6
● Dogliani Cursalet '18	♟♟ 3
● Dogliani Maestra '18	♟♟ 3
● Langhe Harys '17	♟♟ 7
● Langhe Nebbiolo '17	♟♟ 4
● Dogliani Cursalet '11	♟♟♟ 3*
● Harys '00	♟♟♟ 6
● Harys '99	♟♟♟ 6
● Harys '98	♟♟♟ 6
● Barolo '14	♟♟ 6
● Barolo del Comune di Barolo '11	♟♟ 3*
● Barolo Vignane '13	♟♟ 6
● Dogliani Cursalet '17	♟♟ 3*
● Dogliani Cursalet '16	♟♟ 3*
● Langhe Harys '15	♟♟ 7

La Gironda

s.da Bricco, 12
14049 Nizza Monferrato [AT]
Tel. +39 0141701013
www.lagironda.com

CELLAR SALES
PRE-BOOKED VISITS
ANNUAL PRODUCTION 60,000 bottles
HECTARES UNDER VINE 9.00
SUSTAINABLE WINERY

Bricco di Nizza and Chiesavecchia di Calamandrana. These are the two great Barbera crus that have made La Gironda's brilliant rise possible. Guided passionately by Susanna Galandrino and Alberto Adamo, the winery was ahead of its time in terms of sustainability. Theirs is a somewhat modern, reliable selection made with Sauvignon, Moscato, Brachetto, Cabernet Sauvignon and Nebbiolo. And that's not to mention their Chardonnay and Pinot Nero Metodo Classico sparkling wines. Though once again it's their Barbera reds that occupy center stage. Take the Nizza Le Nicchie '16, a wine that plays on vibrant sensations of black fruits well-balanced by earthy and sylvan, foresty contrasts. On the palate it comes through warm and glyceric, though it preserves suppleness and balance in its development. The Superiore La Gena '17 moves on a similar track, though it opts for more sauvage sensations, and is surprisingly tight-knit on the palate.

● Barbera d'Asti Sup. La Gena '17	♟♟ 3*
● Nizza Le Nicchie '16	♟♟ 5
○ Galandrino Brut M. Cl. '14	♟♟ 3
● M.to Rosso Chiesavecchia '16	♟♟ 4
● Barbera d'Asti La Lippa '18	♟ 2
○ Moscato d'Asti '18	♟ 2
● Barbera d'Asti Sup. Nizza Le Nicchie '11	♟♟♟ 5
● Barbera d'Asti La Gena '15	♟♟ 3*
● M.to Rosso Chiesavecchia '06	♟♟ 2*
● M.to Rosso Soul '14	♟♟ 5
● Nizza Le Nicchie '15	♟♟ 5

Tenuta La Giustiniana

FRAZ. ROVERETO, 5
15066 GAVI [AL]
TEL. +39 0143682132
www.lagiustiniana.it

CELLAR SALES
PRE-BOOKED VISITS
ANNUAL PRODUCTION 200,000 bottles
HECTARES UNDER VINE 39.00

Giustiniana's new direction has led to this Rovereto winery becoming a leader among local producers, a role that reflects the Giustiniani family's importance to Gavi. Their presence in the territory is documented as far back as the 17th century, as evidenced by a historic villa that's been renovated over time but still has traces of the original structure. The property spans 110 hectares, 35% of which are vineyards, giving rise to a selection that comprises two historic wines, their Lugarara and Montessora, as well as the Terre Antiche di Giustiniana, a wine made with younger grapes. The excellent work done by enologist Crisian Pomo saw two superb wines land in our final round. The Montessora '18 greets with aromas of ferns and wild flowers on a mineral background. On the palate it's potent and rich, with an extremely long finish. The Lugara '18 features delicate and complex aromas of citrus on floral and mineral notes. Flesh and nice acidity support its long, sapid finish.

○ Gavi del Comune di Gavi Lugarara '18	♟♟	3*
○ Gavi del Comune di Gavi Montessora '18	♟	4
○ Gavi del Comune di Gavi Il Nostro Gavi '07	♟♟♟	4
○ Gavi del Comune di Gavi Il Nostro Gavi '12	♟♟	4
○ Gavi del Comune di Gavi Lugarara '16	♟♟	3*
○ Gavi del Comune di Gavi Montessora '17	♟♟	4
○ Gavi del Comune di Gavi Montessora '14	♟♟	4

★★Elio Grasso

LOC. GINESTRA, 40
12065 MONFORTE D'ALBA [CN]
TEL. +39 017378491
www.eliograsso.it

PRE-BOOKED VISITS
ANNUAL PRODUCTION 90,000 bottles
HECTARES UNDER VINE 18.00
SUSTAINABLE WINERY

Elio Grasso's story is one that began in the late 1970s, thanks to some 18 hectares of vineyards on plots in Monforte d'Alba. Here Nebbiolo is cultivated with care and passion, through a style that never neglects finesse and elegance, and clearly brings out the characteristics of the Ginestra Casa Matè, Gavarini Chiniera and Rüncot vineyards. These are accompanied by wines made with Dolcetto, Barbera and Chardonnay. The rousing Barolo Ginestra Casa Maté '15 opens with striking aromas of vivid and focused fruit, proceeding to notes of tobacco and raspberry, exhibiting the finesse, freshness and complexity of a truly outstanding wine. On the palate it proves exceptional for its close-knit, sweet tannic weave, which lengthen dramatically towards a highly elegant finish. The less vibrant Gavarini Chiniera is just a bit more austere, tending more to tar and quinine, with a rich palate and nice finesse. The Barbera d'Alba Vigna Martina '16 is fresh and lively, but still marked by oak.

● Barolo Ginestra Casa Maté '15	♟♟♟	8
● Barbera d'Alba V. Martina '16	♟♟	5
● Barolo Gavarini Chiniera '15	♟♟	8
● Barolo Gavarini Chiniera '09	♟♟♟	8
● Barolo Gavarini V. Chiniera '06	♟♟♟	8
● Barolo Gavarini V. Chiniera '01	♟♟♟	7
● Barolo Gavarini V. Chiniera '00	♟♟♟	7
● Barolo Gavarini V. Chiniera '99	♟♟♟	7
● Barolo Ginestra Casa Maté '12	♟♟♟	8
● Barolo Ginestra Casa Maté '07	♟♟♟	8
● Barolo Ginestra V. Casa Maté '05	♟♟♟	8
● Barolo Ginestra V. Casa Maté '04	♟♟♟	8
● Barolo Ginestra V. Casa Maté '03	♟♟♟	7
● Barolo Rüncot '01	♟♟♟	8
● Barolo Rüncot '00	♟♟♟	8
● Barolo Rüncot '99	♟♟♟	8

Silvio Grasso

FRAZ. ANNUNZIATA, 112
12064 LA MORRA [CN]
TEL. +39 3355273168
www.silviograsso.com

CELLAR SALES
PRE-BOOKED VISITS
ANNUAL PRODUCTION 80,000 bottles
HECTARES UNDER VINE 14.00

Federico Grasso has always been an advocate of a modern style of Barolo, meaning low yields in the vineyard and aging in French Barriques. But for those who love a more traditional, authentic style, there's the Turné, a wine that undergoes 40 days maceration on the skins and aging in Slavonian barrels. Their Barolo Bricco Luciani and Bricco manzoni are their most celebrated offerings, along with a splendid Barbera d'Alba Fontanile. Federico is supported by his brilliant wife and their sons. Only 2015 Barolos were presented. The Annunziata Vigna Plicotti cru stands out, proving rich in oak, which envelopes its initial, timid aromas of fruit and licorice. A full-bodied, well-balanced palate marked by pleasant sapidity follows. The Bricco Luciani exhibits excellent spiciness, but also notes of red berries. On the palate it features nice, warm alcohol and satisfying length. The Bricco Manzoni sees pronounced oak, while the Turné is more rugged and traditional.

● Barolo Annunziata V. Plicotti '15	▼▼ 7
● Barolo Bricco Luciani '15	▼▼ 7
● Barolo '15	▼▼ 5
● Barolo Bricco Manzoni '15	▼▼ 8
● Barolo Giachini '15	▼▼ 6
● Barolo Turné '15	▼▼ 7
● Barolo Bricco Luciani '04	▽▽▽ 7
● Barolo Bricco Luciani '01	▽▽▽ 6
● Barolo Bricco Luciani '96	▽▽▽ 6
● Barolo Bricco Luciani '95	▽▽▽ 6
● Barolo Bricco Luciani '90	▽▽▽ 6
● Barolo Bricco Manzoni '10	▽▽▽ 7
● Barbera d'Alba Fontanile '15	▽▽ 5
● Barolo Bricco Manzoni '13	▽▽ 8
● Barolo Turné '13	▽▽ 7
● Barolo Turne' '12	▽▽ 7

Bruna Grimaldi

VIA PAREA, 7
12060 GRINZANE CAVOUR [CN]
TEL. +39 0173262094
www.grimaldibruna.it

CELLAR SALES
PRE-BOOKED VISITS
ANNUAL PRODUCTION 70,000 bottles
HECTARES UNDER VINE 15.00
VITICULTURE METHOD Certified Organic

Simone Fiorino continues his estate training, bolstered by the schooling he received from his parents, who continue to participate actively. Their production approach sees to it that all wines are treated carefully, with equal dignity. As a result, the differences between their offerings come back to the grapes, the vineyards and length of aging. Naturally, the power of their Barolo Badarina di Serralunga is not the same as their elegant Bricco Ambrogio di Roddi or Camilla, which blends Grinzane and La Morra grapes. But we can recommend them all. Quinine, licorice and red berries introduce a well-made Barolo Badarina '15, whose palate is firm, convincing, with still discernible tannins. Refined elegance, dynamism and vigor characterize their Barbera d'Alba Sup. Scassa '16, which exhibits excellent balance both on the nose, bringing together red berries and smoky notes, and on the palate, where alcohol and acidic freshness interpenetrate perfectly. An outstanding set of wines.

● Barbera d'Alba Sup. Scassa '16	▼▼ 3*
● Barolo Badarina '15	▼▼ 6
● Barolo Bricco Ambrogio '15	▼▼ 6
● Barolo Camilla '15	▼▼ 5
● Dolcetto d'Alba '17	▼▼ 2*
○ Langhe Arneis '18	▼▼ 2*
● Barolo Badarina '14	▽▽ 6
● Barolo Badarina '13	▽▽ 6
● Barolo Badarina '12	▽▽ 6
● Barolo Badarina '11	▽▽ 6
● Barolo Badarina Ris. '11	▽▽ 7
● Barolo Badarina Ris. '10	▽▽ 7
● Barolo Bricco Ambrogio '14	▽▽ 5

Giacomo Grimaldi

VIA LUIGI EINAUDI, 8
12060 BAROLO [CN]
TEL. +39 0173560536
www.giacomogrimaldi.com

CELLAR SALES
PRE-BOOKED VISITS
ANNUAL PRODUCTION 50,000 bottles
HECTARES UNDER VINE 13.00

Situated in Barolo, Le Coste cru is one of the district's best, even it's fated to remain in the shadows because of it's size (fewer than 3 hectares). Nevertheless, thanks in part to a high share of sandy soil, it gives rise to broad aromas of red flowers and smooth tannins. Ferruccio Grimaldi, now supported by his son, also offers a selection of Barolo that's just a bit more austere, cultivated in their excellent Sotto Castello cru in Novello. Their Nebbiolo d'Alba Valmaggiore, from nearby Roero, is also enjoyable. The Barolo Le Coste '15 offers up sweet spices of oak and fruit, then pleasant chocolate. On the palate its nice structure is supported by acidity and still discernible but pleasant and not astringent tannins. The splendid Nebbiolo d'Alba Vigna Valmaggiore '17 is rich in flowers, especially violet. In combination with its rousing drinkability, it's surely one of the best of the year. The weighty Roero Arneis '18 is also notable with its pleasant sensations of fresh herbs.

● Barolo Le Coste '15	♟♟ 7
● Nebbiolo d'Alba V. Valmaggiore '17	♟♟ 4
● Barolo Sotto Castello di Novello '15	♟♟ 6
○ Roero Arneis '18	♟♟ 2*
● Barolo Sotto Castello di Novello '05	♟♟♟ 6
● Barbera d'Alba Pistin '15	♟♟ 3
● Barolo '13	♟♟ 6
● Barolo '12	♟♟ 6
● Barolo '11	♟♟ 6
● Barolo Le Coste '14	♟♟ 7
● Barolo Le Coste '13	♟♟ 7
● Barolo Le Coste '12	♟♟ 7
● Barolo Le Coste '11	♟♟ 7
● Barolo Sotto Castello di Novello '14	♟♟ 6
● Barolo Sotto Castello di Novello '13	♟♟ 6

Sergio Grimaldi
Ca' du Sindic

LOC. SAN GRATO, 15
12058 SANTO STEFANO BELBO [CN]
TEL. +39 0141840341
www.cadusindic.it

CELLAR SALES
PRE-BOOKED VISITS
ANNUAL PRODUCTION 100,000 bottles
HECTARES UNDER VINE 17.00
SUSTAINABLE WINERY

It was 1989 when Sergio Grimaldi decided to revive the family vineyards on the Santo Stefano Belbo hills. With the help of his parents, Ilario and Vittorina, he renovated the cellar and adopted its historic nickname, Ca' du Sindic ('The Mayor's House'). His wife, Angela, and young children Paolo and Ilaria are at his side. They're just as motivated in bringing out the unique attributes of each vineyard: San Grato, Bauda, San Maurizio, Moncucco. These give rise to Brachetto, Barbera, Dolcetto, Pinot Nero and Moscato grapes. The latest round of tastings saw their Alta Langa Brut at the fore. The 2015 delivers exuberant aromas of sweet cakes and white-fleshed fruit, all anticipating a rich, creamy palate that exhibits a well-sustained tension. Their flagship product, however, remains their Moscato d'Asti Ca' du Sindic '18, a wine redolent of rennet apple, sage and grapefruit, the prelude to a fresh and elegant palate made possible thanks to perfectly balanced sugars.

○ Moscato d'Asti Ca' du Sindic '18	♟♟ 3*
○ Alta Langa Brut '15	♟♟ 4
○ Moscato d'Asti V. Moncucco '18	♟♟ 3
○ Moscato d'Asti '18	♟ 2
○ Ventuno Brut	♟ 3
● Barbera d'Asti San Grato '15	♟♟ 2*
● Barbera d'Asti SanGrato '17	♟♟ 2*
● Dolcetto d'Alba '15	♟♟ 2*
○ Moscato d'Asti Ca' du Sindic '17	♟♟ 3
○ Moscato d'Asti Ca' du Sindic Capsula Oro '16	♟♟ 3
○ Moscato d'Asti Capsula Argento '16	♟♟ 3
○ Moscato d'Asti V. Moncucco '17	♟♟ 3*
○ Moscato d'Asti V. Moncucco '16	♟♟ 3*
○ Moscato d'Asti V. Moncucco '15	♟♟ 3*
○ Ventuno Brut '14	♟♟ 3

★Hilberg - Pasquero

VIA BRICCO GATTI, 16
12040 PRIOCCA [CN]
TEL. +39 0173616197
www.hilberg-pasquero.com

CELLAR SALES
PRE-BOOKED VISITS
ANNUAL PRODUCTION 24,000 bottles
HECTARES UNDER VINE 6.50
VITICULTURE METHOD Certified Organic

For more than twenty years, on the hills overlooking Priocca, Annette Hillberg and Michele Pasquero ('Miclo' to his friends) have overseen a winery that's earned itself a well-deserved reputation. The estate vineyards grow in silty, marly soil in Bricco Gatti, all around the cellar, and in the districts of Monteforche and Bricco Stella. Roero's classic grapes are grown, Barbera, Brachetto and Nebbiolo, making for a selection that highlights the typicity and attributes of the territory. The magnificent Barbera d'Alba '18 features focused aromas of plums and a full, fresh, dynamic palate rich in flesh. The other wines proposed also performed well. The Nebbiolo d'Alba '16 proves austere, tannic, long and sapid, while the powerful and firmly-structured Barbera d'Alba Sup. '16 offers up spicy notes and hints of black berries. Notes of tobacco and quinine, along with close-knit tannins, figure centrally in their Nebbiolo d'Alba Sul Monte '17, while the aromatic Vareij has nice flesh.

● Barbera d'Alba '18	♟♟ 3*
● Barbera d'Alba Sup. '16	♟♟ 5
● Nebbiolo d'Alba '16	♟♟ 5
● Nebbiolo d'Alba Sul Monte '17	♟♟ 5
● Vareij '18	♟♟ 3
● Barbera d'Alba Sup. '09	♟♟♟ 5
● Nebbiolo d'Alba '06	♟♟♟ 5
● Nebbiolo d'Alba '05	♟♟♟ 5
● Nebbiolo d'Alba '04	♟♟♟ 5
● Nebbiolo d'Alba '03	♟♟♟ 5
● Nebbiolo d'Alba '01	♟♟♟ 5
● Nebbiolo d'Alba '00	♟♟♟ 4

Icardi

LOC. SAN LAZZARO
S.DA COMUNALE BALBI, 30
12053 CASTIGLIONE TINELLA [CN]
TEL. +39 0141855159
www.icardivini.it

CELLAR SALES
PRE-BOOKED VISITS
ANNUAL PRODUCTION 290,000 bottles
HECTARES UNDER VINE 44.00
VITICULTURE METHOD Certified Biodynamic
SUSTAINABLE WINERY

Claudio Icardi confidently confirms that his adherence to biodynamic principles allows him to work his land without worry, as his vineyards regularly produce healthy, tasty grapes rich in substance. It's quite a sizable property for the area, with plots in Monferrato (Barolo) and Barbaresco. And its precisely this last that gives rise to the most noteworthy wines of an outstanding selection, both the recent Starderi and, more so, the Montubert '16, a wine that's truly impressive for its richness of fruit and perfect gustatory balance. The two 2015 Barolos also put in excellent performance, thanks to a delicate and balanced Parej and a just slightly more austere Fossati. The balsamic and plush Surìsjvan '17, also made with with Nebbiolo, exhibits perfect drinkability. Finally, it's worth noting their minty, succulent Dolcetto d'Alba, as well as to their Moscato La Rosa Selvatica with its enviable freshness and compelling aromatic profile.

● Barbaresco Montubert '16	♟♟ 5
● Barolo Parej '15	♟♟ 8
● Barbaresco Starderi '16	♟♟ 5
● Barolo Fossati '15	♟♟ 8
● Dolcetto d'Alba Rousori '18	♟♟ 3
● Langhe Nebbiolo Surìsjvan '17	♟♟ 4
● Langhe Rosso Dadelio '17	♟♟ 5
○ Moscato d'Asti La Rosa Selvatica '18	♟♟ 2*
○ Piemonte Bianco Pafoj '18	♟♟ 4
● Barbera d'Asti Sup. Nuj Suj '17	♟ 5
● Barbaresco Montubert '14	♟♟ 5
● Barolo Parej '13	♟♟ 8

Ioppa

fraz. Mauletta
via delle Pallotte, 10
28078 Romagnano Sesia [NO]
Tel. +39 0163833079
www.viniioppa.it

CELLAR SALES
PRE-BOOKED VISITS
ANNUAL PRODUCTION 140,000 bottles
HECTARES UNDER VINE 20.50

The first evidence of the Ioppas' activities goes back to 1852. It concerned what is today their flagship vineyard, Balsina, which gives rise to their prized Ghemme of the same name. Since then it's been a slow, gradual process of expanding their vineyards and cellar, the latter of which hosts small French and large Slavonian barrels. The young team that's recently come on board (Andrea, Luca and Marco) show great attention to Nebbiolo, as well as spicy Vespolina, which contributes to a version aged at length in oak. A splendid Ghemme Santa Fé '13 sees intense, complex nuances move from roots to tar on a background of raspberries. A rich palate perfectly expresses silky tannins. The firm, well-orchestrated Nebbiolo '16 is a small masterpiece, fresher and fruitier, characterized by hints of gentian and blackcurrant. The drinkable Nebbiolo Rusin '18 is a warm, citrusy rosé, while the San Grato proves soft, caressing and fresh.

● Colline Novaresi Nebbiolo '16	🍷🍷 3*
● Ghemme Santa Fé '13	🍷🍷 6
⊙ Colline Novaresi Nebbiolo Rusin '18	🍷🍷 2*
● Colline Novaresi Vespolina Coda Rossa '18	🍷🍷 3
○ San Grato Bianco	🍷🍷 2
● Ghemme '14	🍷 4
● Ghemme Balsina '13	🍷🍷🍷 6
● Colline Novaresi Nebbiolo '15	🍷🍷 3*
● Colline Novaresi Vespolina '12	🍷🍷 3*
● Colline Novaresi Vespolina Coda Rossa '15	🍷🍷 3*
● Ghemme Balsina '12	🍷🍷 6

Isolabella della Croce

loc. Saracchi
Regione Caffi, 3
14051 Loazzolo [AT]
Tel. +39 014487166
www.isolabelladellacroce.it

CELLAR SALES
PRE-BOOKED VISITS
ANNUAL PRODUCTION 90,000 bottles
HECTARES UNDER VINE 14.00

Loazzolo, which is often referenced for hosting the smallest Italian appellation, is a veritable crossroads of territories and cultures. The few producers operating here, in lower Langa (between Cuneese and Alessandrino), are valid ones. Among them are the Isolabella della Croce family: Luigi and Francesco (sons of its founder, Lodovico), who've been looking after this varied estate since 2001. Primarily Moscato, Chardonnay and Pinot Nero are cultivated, though they also grow Barbera in Calamdandrana, in Nizza. If Piedmont is proving increasingly promising for Pinot Nero, Isolabella della Croce's Bricco del Falco has made an important contribution. The 2015 impresses with its airy, multifaceted nose. On its supple, pervasive and flavorful palate spicy and balsamic registers emerge, along with a subtle tannic weave. The Nizza Augusta '15 is no less good by virtue of its integrity and dense fruit.

● Piemonte Pinot Nero Bricco del Falco '15	🍷🍷🍷 5
● Nizza Augusta '15	🍷🍷 4
○ Piemonte Chardonnay Solum '17	🍷🍷 4
● Barbera d'Asti Sup. Serena '16	🍷🍷 4
○ Moscato d'Asti Canelli Valdiserre '18	🍷🍷 3
○ Piemonte Sauvignon Blanc '18	🍷🍷 3
● Nizza Augusta '14	🍷🍷🍷 4*
● Barbera d'Asti Sup. Serena '15	🍷🍷 4
● Barbera d'Asti Sup. Serena '14	🍷🍷 4
○ Moscato d'Asti Canelli Valdiserre '17	🍷🍷 3*
○ Piemonte Chardonnay Solum '15	🍷🍷 4
● Piemonte Pinot Nero Bricco del Falco '14	🍷🍷 5

Tenuta Langasco

FRAZ. MADONNA DI COMO, 10
12051 ALBA [CN]
TEL. +39 0173286972
www.tenutalangasco.it

CELLAR SALES
PRE-BOOKED VISITS
ANNUAL PRODUCTION 60,000 bottles
HECTARES UNDER VINE 22.00

The Sacco family's lovely winery, active since 1979 in a lovely, panoramic location on the hills overlooking the towers of Alba, is definitely worth a visit. Claudio's selection of wines is wide and reliable, ranging from Langhe Arneis to Nebbiolo d'Alba, from Moscato d'Asti to Dolcetto Madonna di Como, Piemonte Branchetto and Langhe Favorita. They highlight the varietal character of the grapes used and are available at attractive prices. The Barbera d'Alba Sorì '17 stands out for its aromas of undergrowth, quinine and blackcurrant, with a highly intense spicy stroke. On the palate it's vivid and intense, characterized by nice acidity. The aromatically toasty and balsamic Barbera d'Alba Vigna Madonna di Como '17 is austere and rigorous in the mouth, with dark fruit and a coffee finish. Hints of almond and green tea feature in the linear Dolcetto d'Alba Vigna Miclet '18.

● Barbera d'Alba Sorì '17	🍷🍷 3
● Barbera d'Alba V. Madonna di Como '17	🍷🍷 2*
● Nebbiolo d'Alba Sorì Coppa '17	🍷🍷 4
● Dolcetto d'Alba V. Madonna di Como '18	🍷 2
● Dolcetto d'Alba V. Miclet '18	🍷 3
● Langhe Saccorosso '17	🍷 4
● Barbera d'Alba Sorì '14	🍷🍷 3
● Barbera d'Alba V. Madonna di Como '16	🍷🍷 2*
● Dolcetto d'Alba Madonna di Como V. Miclet '16	🍷🍷 3*
● Dolcetto d'Alba Madonna di Como V. Miclet '15	🍷🍷 3*
● Dolcetto d'Alba V. Madonna di Como '16	🍷🍷 2*
● Dolcetto d'Alba V. Miclet '17	🍷🍷 3
● Langhe Saccorosso '15	🍷🍷 4
● Nebbiolo d'Alba Sorì Coppa '13	🍷🍷 4

Ugo Lequio

VIA DEL MOLINO, 10
12057 NEIVE [CN]
TEL. +39 0173677224
www.ugolequio.it

CELLAR SALES
PRE-BOOKED VISITS
ANNUAL PRODUCTION 30,000 bottles
HECTARES UNDER VINE

The grapes this Molino di Neive winery purchases from trusted growers are always treated with care. Gallina, one of Barbaresco's most inspired crus, is their crown jewel. It's a wine that Ugo Lequio crafts with constance and a keen sensibility, paying homage to one of the noblest, most prestigious areas of Neive. Their approach calls for medium-long maceration and aging in mid-sized French oak. Intense and spicy in youth, their wines require time in the bottle to find the right rhythm. Their Barbaresco Gallina '16 is intense in its notes of tobacco and medicinal herbs, capable of exhibiting a well-orchestrated complexity of flavor, from mature red berries to balsamic sensations, with a long, broad, deep and characterful finish. The Barbera d'Alba Sup. Vigna Gallina '16 is spicy, redolent of pepper, cocoa powder, coming through warm, mature and gratifying on the palate. The fresh, pleasant Langhe Nebbiolo '17 is forthright in its fragrances of violet, blackcurrant.

● Barbaresco Gallina '16	🍷🍷 6
● Barbera d'Alba Sup. V. Gallina '16	🍷🍷 4
● Langhe Nebbiolo '17	🍷🍷 4
○ Langhe Arneis '18	🍷 3
● Barbaresco Gallina '15	🍷🍷 6
● Barbaresco Gallina '14	🍷🍷 6
● Barbaresco Gallina '13	🍷🍷 5
● Barbaresco Gallina '12	🍷🍷 5
● Barbaresco Gallina '11	🍷🍷 5
● Barbaresco Gallina Ris. '10	🍷🍷 6
● Barbera d'Alba Sup. '11	🍷🍷 4
● Barbera d'Alba Sup. Gallina '12	🍷🍷 4
● Barbera d'Alba Sup. V. Gallina '15	🍷🍷 4
● Barbera d'Alba Sup. V. Gallina '14	🍷🍷 4
○ Langhe Arneis '13	🍷🍷 3
● Langhe Nebbiolo '15	🍷🍷 4

Malabaila di Canale

VIA MADONNA DEI CAVALLI, 93
12043 CANALE [CN]
TEL. +39 017398381
www.malabaila.com

CELLAR SALES
PRE-BOOKED VISITS
ANNUAL PRODUCTION 100,000 bottles
HECTARES UNDER VINE 22.00
SUSTAINABLE WINERY

Founded in 1988 and owned by the
Carrega Malabaila family, together with
Valerio Falletti, Malabaila di Canale has
taken up and relaunched the viticultural
traditions of this historic patrimony. Their
vineyards, some of which go back more
than 60 years, are situated entirely within a
90-hectare estate that features steep
slopes and loose, marly and sandy soil.
Roero's classic grapes are cultivated:
Arneis, Nebbiolo, Favorita, Brachetto and
Dolcetto, making for wines that pursue a
faithful expression of the territory while
exhibiting great pleasantness. This year the
Roero Arneis Le Tre '18 particularly
impressed with its citrusy aromas, floral
nuances and hints of aromatic herbs. On
the palate it exhibits notable structure and
a lively acidity, with a long, fresh finish. The
Nebbiolo d'Alba Bric Merli '16 also stood
out by virtue of its notes of tobacco, licorice
and raspberry, and a superbly textured
palate in which close-woven tannins give
way to a long, succulent finish.

● Nebbiolo d'Alba Bric Merli '16	🍷🍷 3*
○ Roero Arneis Le Tre '18	🍷🍷 2*
● Barbera d'Alba Sup. Mezzavilla '16	🍷🍷 3
● Roero Castelletto Ris. '15	🍷🍷 5
○ Langhe Favorita Donna Costanza '18	🍷 2
● Langhe Nebbiolo '18	🍷 2
⊙ Langhe Rosato Donna Costanza '18	🍷 2
○ Roero Arneis Pradvaj '18	🍷 3
● Barbera d'Alba Giardino '16	🍷🍷 2*
○ Roero Arneis Pradvaj '17	🍷🍷 3
○ Roero Arneis Pradvaj '16	🍷🍷 3*
● Roero Bric Volta '13	🍷🍷 3*
● Roero Castelletto Ris. '14	🍷🍷 4

★Malvirà

LOC. CANOVA
VIA CASE SPARSE, 144
12043 CANALE [CN]
TEL. +39 0173978145
www.malvira.com

CELLAR SALES
PRE-BOOKED VISITS
ACCOMMODATION AND RESTAURANT SERVICE
ANNUAL PRODUCTION 300,000 bottles
HECTARES UNDER VINE 42.00

The Damonte family's Malvirà is one of
Roero's leading producers. Their vineyards
are situated primarily in Canale, in some of
the territory's most renowned crus, from
Mombeltramo to Renesio, Saglietto and
San Michele a Trinità, in addition to a plot
in La Morra (which gives rise to their
Barolo). The territory's classic grapes are
cultivated, foremost Arneis, Barbera and
Nebbiolo, making for charming, highly
territorial wines that exhibit a particular
predilection for aging. This year it was their
Roero Arneis that most impressed. The
splendid Renesio '18 proves intense in its
mineral notes and hints of fresh herbs,
sensations that anticipate a full palate in
which vibrant acidity gives way to a long
finish. The Trinità '18 opts more for aromas
of white-fleshed fruit followed by a
superbly structured and characterful
palate. Time will bring out its best qualities.
The traditionally-styled Barolo Boiolo '15
also proved excellent, rich and deep in its
aromas of quinine and tobacco.

○ Roero Arneis Renesio '18	🍷🍷🍷 3*
● Barolo Boiolo '15	🍷🍷 7
○ Roero Arneis S. S. Trinità '18	🍷🍷 3*
● Barbera d'Alba S. Michele '17	🍷🍷 3
● Roero '16	🍷🍷 3
● Roero Trinità Ris. '15	🍷🍷 5
● Roero V. Mombeltramo Ris. '15	🍷🍷 5
● Roero V. Renesio Ris. '15	🍷🍷 5
● Roero Mombeltramo Ris. '11	🍷🍷🍷 5
● Roero Mombeltramo Ris. '10	🍷🍷🍷 5
● Roero Renesio Ris. '05	🍷🍷🍷 5
● Roero Trinità Ris. '07	🍷🍷🍷 5
● Roero V. Mombeltramo Ris. '12	🍷🍷🍷 5

Giovanni Manzone

VIA CASTELLETTO, 9
12065 MONFORTE D'ALBA [CN]
TEL. +39 017378114
www.manzonegiovanni.com

CELLAR SALES
PRE-BOOKED VISITS
ANNUAL PRODUCTION 45,000 bottles
HECTARES UNDER VINE 7.50
SUSTAINABLE WINERY

Mirella and Mauro, both graduates of the Alba School of Enology, bring together their studies with the teachings of their still-active father, an expert who rebuilt the family's cellar for his children. Those who have the good fortune of passing through the high woodlands of Langhe mustn't forget to visit the balcony overlooking the winery (the view is worth it). Manzone's Barolo is always rich and structured, exhibiting excellent acidity and outstanding aging power. The Barolo Bricat is aromatically approachable, richly textured on the palate, introduced by notes of tobacco, oak and spices followed by licorice, black berries. In the mouth it's exquisite, rich in alcohol, with pronounced tannins. The Gramolere '15 follows a similar track — warm, long and succulent, although slightly astringent. The classically-styled, minty and lean-bodied Barolo Castelletto '15 is even fresher, while the Dolcetto d'Alba Le Ciliegie '17 exhibits notable freshness and pleasant pervasiveness.

● Barolo Bricat '15	🍷🍷 6
● Barolo Castelletto '15	🍷🍷 6
● Barolo Gramolere '15	🍷🍷 6
● Dolcetto d'Alba Le Ciliegie '17	🍷🍷 2*
● Barbera d'Alba Sup. La Marchesa '16	🍷 5
● Langhe Nebbiolo Il Crutin '17	🍷 3
● Barolo Bricat '05	🍷🍷🍷 6
● Barolo Castelletto '09	🍷🍷🍷 5
● Barolo Gramolere Ris. '05	🍷🍷🍷 7
● Barolo Le Gramolere '04	🍷🍷🍷 6
● Barolo Le Gramolere Ris. '01	🍷🍷🍷 7
● Barolo Le Gramolere Ris. '00	🍷🍷🍷 7
● Barolo Le Gramolere Ris. '99	🍷🍷🍷 7
● Barolo Bricat '14	🍷🍷 6
● Barolo Bricat '13	🍷🍷 6
● Barolo Castelletto '13	🍷🍷 6
● Barolo Gramolere '14	🍷🍷 6

Paolo Manzone

LOC. MERIAME, 1
12050 SERRALUNGA D'ALBA [CN]
TEL. +39 0173613113
www.barolomeriame.com

CELLAR SALES
PRE-BOOKED VISITS
ACCOMMODATION
ANNUAL PRODUCTION 85,000 bottles
HECTARES UNDER VINE 10.00
SUSTAINABLE WINERY

Luisella Corino and Paolo Manzone are joined together by love and their involvement in a multifaceted project that brings together enology, land management, entrepreneurship and tourism. Thus their lovely Meriame cru, one we've been hearing more and more about, now hosts a cellar and an agritourism (we strongly recommend enotourists have a visit). Their surrounding vineyards give rise to the winery's flagship Barolo, a perfect expression of Serralunga d'Alba Nebbiolo's power and elegance. Paolo Manzone is one of the best interpreters of reserve Barolos, and he proves it with an aromatically complex and sophisticated 2013. Notes of dried rose and licorice are the prelude to a velvety palate that's not without a touch of sapidity, with tannins lending flavor rather than hardness, thus earning it Tre Bicchieri. All their Nebbiolos and Barberas are valid, while their classic Roero white proves more than pleasant.

● Barolo Ris. '13	🍷🍷🍷 7
● Barolo Meriame '15	🍷🍷 7
● Barbera d'Alba Sup. Fiorenza '17	🍷🍷 3
● Barolo del Comune di Serralunga d'Alba '15	🍷🍷 6
● Nebbiolo d'Alba Mirinè '17	🍷🍷 3
○ Roero Arneis Reysù '18	🍷🍷 3
● Barolo Ris. '11	🍷🍷🍷 7
● Barolo del Comune di Serralunga d'Alba '14	🍷🍷 6
● Barolo Meriame '14	🍷🍷 7
● Barolo Meriame '13	🍷🍷 7
● Barolo Ris. '12	🍷🍷 7
● Langhe Rosso Luvì '16	🍷🍷 3

Marcalberto

VIA PORTA SOTTANA, 9
12058 SANTO STEFANO BELBO [CN]
TEL. +39 0141844022
www.marcalberto.it

CELLAR SALES
PRE-BOOKED VISITS
ANNUAL PRODUCTION 40,000 bottles
HECTARES UNDER VINE 6.50

"Small wineries grow" could sum up the Cane family's recent history. Alberto and Marco are at the helm while their father supervises, presiding over a constant process of transformation that's seen them grow from something they did in their spare time into a standard-bearer of national excellence dedicated to high quality Metodo Classico. Last year we mentioned the advent of a new, special press, this year the expansion of their cellar, as well as the begommomg of a few, cozy rooms next to the Cesare Pavese Museum (future accommodations for those who love the poetry and great wines of Alta Langa). Their Alta Langa Millesimo2Mila15 '15 is at the top of its game, handily bringing home Tre Bicchieri thanks to an aromatic complexity and gustatory stratification that can stand shoulder-to-shoulder with any of France's superb sparklers. Their Blanc de Blancs exhibits notable structure, drive and freshness, while the Sansannée proves supple and juicy.

○ Alta Langa Extra Brut Millesimo2Mila15 '15	♟♟♟ 5
○ Marcalberto Brut Sansannée M. Cl.	♟♟ 4
○ Marcalberto Pas Dosé Blanc de Blancs M. Cl.	♟♟ 4
⊙ Marcalberto Brut Rosé M. Cl.	♟♟ 4
○ Marcalberto Nature M. Cl. Senza Aggiunta di Solfiti	♟♟ 6
○ Marcalberto Extra Brut Millesimo2Mila12 M. Cl. '12	♟♟♟ 5
○ Marcalberto Extra Brut Millesimo2Mila13 M. Cl. '13	♟♟♟ 5
⊙ Marcalberto Brut Rosé M. Cl.	♟♟ 4
○ Marcalberto Pas Dosé Blanc de Blancs M. Cl.	♟♟ 4

Poderi Marcarini

P.ZZA MARTIRI, 2
12064 LA MORRA [CN]
TEL. +39 017350222
www.marcarini.it

CELLAR SALES
PRE-BOOKED VISITS
ACCOMMODATION
ANNUAL PRODUCTION 125,000 bottles
HECTARES UNDER VINE 20.00

At Marcarini, in La Morra, they're on the sixth generation of family, thanks to the work of siblings Andrea, Chiara and Elisa. The winery's roots go back to the mid-19th century, and today it avails itself of two of Langa's best crus, Brunate and La Serra, vineyards geographically close but different in terms of enological character. But by now they rely on some 20 hectares total, including their Sargentin plots in Neviglie and Muschiadivino in Mondaldo Roero, where Dolcetto, Barbera, Moscato and Arneis are cultivated. The 2015 version of their Barolo La Serra earned a place in our finals by virtue of its charming profile. A pale color is the prelude to aromas of wood resin and Mediterranean scrub. On the palate it exhibits delicate but surefooted grip, with creamy tannins and a long, balsamic finish on notes of mint and juniper. The Barolo Brunate '15 is darker in its spiciness, more firmly structured and powerful on the palate, making for a pepper and tobacco-scented finish.

● Barolo La Serra '15	♟♟ 7
● Barolo Brunate '15	♟♟ 7
● Barolo del Comune di La Morra '15	♟♟ 7
● Barolo Brunate '05	♟♟♟ 6
● Barolo Brunate '03	♟♟♟ 6
● Barolo Brunate '01	♟♟♟ 6
● Barolo Brunate '99	♟♟♟ 6
● Barolo Brunate '96	♟♟♟ 6
● Barolo Brunate Ris. '85	♟♟♟ 6
● Dolcetto d'Alba Boschi di Berri '96	♟♟♟ 4*
● Barbera d'Alba Ciabot Camerano '12	♟♟ 3*
● Barolo Brunate '13	♟♟ 7
● Barolo Brunate '12	♟♟ 7
● Barolo Brunate '11	♟♟ 6
● Barolo La Serra '12	♟♟ 7
● Barolo La Serra '10	♟♟ 6

★Marchesi di Barolo

VIA ROMA, 1
12060 BAROLO [CN]
TEL. +39 0173564400
www.marchesibarolo.com

CELLAR SALES
PRE-BOOKED VISITS
RESTAURANT SERVICE
ANNUAL PRODUCTION 1,500,000 bottles
HECTARES UNDER VINE 200.00

Marchesi di Barolo's roots coincide with modern Italian history. Indeed, it was 1861, the year of Italian unification, when this glorious winery was established. Today it continues to write important chapters in the history of Italian enology thanks to the tireless work of Anna and Ernesto and their children, who are increasingly involved in making Barolo known throughout the world, bolstered by the charm of Fallet Castle and a solid, 200-hectare estate that comprises blessed vineyards like Cannubi, Sarmassa and Costa di Rose. This year they submitted a notable selection. Their Nebbiolo d'Alba Roccheri that took full advantage of a strong 2016 for its finesse, balance and pleasantness. The perfectly balanced Barolo Coste di Rose '15 delivers delicate, graceful sensations, while the Cannubi '15 proves spicier and more firmly-structured. Finally, the quinine and gentian-scented Sarmassa '15 stands out for a powerful palate in which tannins are exceptionally well-balanced.

Marchesi Incisa della Rocchetta

VIA ROMA, 66
14030 ROCCHETTA TANARO [AT]
TEL. +39 0141644647
www.marchesiincisawines.it

CELLAR SALES
PRE-BOOKED VISITS
ACCOMMODATION AND RESTAURANT SERVICE
ANNUAL PRODUCTION 80,000 bottles
HECTARES UNDER VINE 17.00

The principal vineyards utilized by the Incisa della Rocchetta family are situated on the slopes of Rocchetta Tanaro. The park's sandy-clay soil gives rise to a territorial selection of wines made primarily with Barbera, though we shouldn't forget a historic presence of Pinot Nero and Grignolino (and smaller, residual shares of Merlot). They also realize wines from other districts, like Barolo, Roero Arneis and Moscato d'Asti. The versatility of their production range was fully confirmed by the last round of tastings. The Rollone '17, made with Pinot Nero and Barbera, is wholly true to the complementary characters of the two grapes, as evidenced by its notes of cherry and wild strawberries, and its sweetly spirited palate. The Valmorena '18 exhibits the pleasant transparency that we'd expect from a current-vintage Barbera, a quality that's further consolidated in terms of breadth and complexity in the Superiore Sant'Emiliano '17.

● Barolo Cannubi '15	♟♟ 8
● Barolo Coste di Rose '15	♟♟ 8
★ Barolo del Comune di Barolo '15	♟♟ 8
● Barolo Sarmassa '15	♟♟ 8
○ Langhe Bianco Bric Amel '18	♟♟ 4
● Nebbiolo d'Alba Roccheri '16	♟♟ 5
● Dolcetto d'Alba Madonna del Dono '18	♟ 3
● Barolo Cannubi '14	♟♟♟ 8
● Barolo Cannubi '12	♟♟♟ 8
● Barolo Cannubi '11	♟♟♟ 8
● Barolo Cannubi '10	♟♟♟ 8
● Barolo Sarmassa '09	♟♟♟ 8
● Barolo Sarmassa '08	♟♟♟ 7
● Barolo Sarmassa '07	♟♟♟ 7
● Barolo Sarmassa '06	♟♟♟ 7
● Barolo Sarmassa '05	♟♟♟ 7

● Barbera d'Asti Sup. Sant' Emiliano '17	♟♟ 5
● Barbera d'Asti Valmorena '18	♟♟ 3
● Grignolino d'Asti '18	♟♟ 3
● Piemonte Pinot Nero Barbera Rollone '17	♟♟ 3
● Piemonte Pinot Nero Marchese Leopoldo '17	♟ 5
⊙ Piemonte Rosato Futurosa '18	♟ 2
● Barbera d'Asti Sup. Sant' Emiliano '15	♟♟♟ 5
● Barbera d'Asti Sup. Sant' Emiliano '16	♟♟ 5
● Barbera d'Asti Sup. Sant'Emiliano '11	♟♟ 4
● Barbera d'Asti Valmorena '17	♟♟ 3
● Barbera d'Asti Valmorena '16	♟♟ 3
● Barbera d'Asti Valmorena '14	♟♟ 3*
● Grignolino d'Asti '17	♟♟ 3
● Grignolino d'Asti '16	♟♟ 3

Mario Marengo

LOC. SERRA DENARI, 2A
12064 LA MORRA [CN]
TEL. +39 017350115
marengo@cantinamarengo.it

CELLAR SALES
PRE-BOOKED VISITS
ANNUAL PRODUCTION 38,000 bottles
HECTARES UNDER VINE 7.50
SUSTAINABLE WINERY

This historic La Morra winery is turning 120, four generations working in the service of wine. Marco is leading the boutique producer, bolstered by seven hectares of estate vineyards cultivated with Langa's classic grapes: Nebbiolo, Barbera and Dolcetto. Among their most highly-prized vineyards, we find Brunate (in La Morra) and Bricco delle Viole (in Barolo). Their style is marked by innovation: short fermentation in vertical macerators and intense extraction, making for rich and potent wines with nice personality. An excellent Dolcetto d'Alba '18 features fragrances of almond and plums in a perfect tannic weave. Notes of bottled cherry and licorice introduce their Barolo '15, anticipating a long, elegant and noble palate. The Barolo Brunate '15 is austere and intense in its aromas of tobacco and pencil led, while on the palate it proves compact and rigorous, with a long finish, qualities that promise long evolution in the bottle. The Barolo Bricco delle Viole '15 is a bit behind.

● Barolo Brunate '15	♟♟ 7
● Barbera d'Alba V. Pugnane '17	♟♟ 3
● Barolo '15	♟♟ 5
● Barolo Bricco delle Viole '15	♟♟ 6
● Dolcetto d'Alba '18	♟♟ 2*
● Nebbiolo d'Alba V. Valmaggiore '17	♟♟ 4
● Barolo Brunate '12	♟♟♟ 7
● Barolo Brunate '11	♟♟♟ 7
● Barolo Brunate '09	♟♟♟ 6
● Barolo Brunate '07	♟♟♟ 6
● Barolo Brunate '06	♟♟♟ 6
● Barbera d'Alba V. Pugnane '16	♟♟ 3*
● Barolo '13	♟♟ 5
● Barolo Bricco delle Viole '14	♟♟ 6
● Barolo Bricco delle Viole '13	♟♟ 6
● Barolo Brunate '14	♟♟ 7

Claudio Mariotto

S.DA PER SAREZZANO, 29
15057 TORTONA [AL]
TEL. +39 0131868500
www.claudiomariotto.it

CELLAR SALES
PRE-BOOKED VISITS
ANNUAL PRODUCTION 100,000 bottles
HECTARES UNDER VINE 24.00

Claudio Mariotto has managed to skillfully bring together his inspired artistic inclinations with his winemaking business. Today his winery is a benchmark for Tortona, and his bottles are appreciated on more than one continent. Thanks to his production approach and a keen sensibility when it comes to Timorasso, Claudio's style has given rise to wines of great finesse and excellent aging potential over the years. His interpretations are capable of containing the grape's tendency to become exuberant, and highlighting its most valued attributes. The selection of wines presented confirms the good work being done. Their 2017 Timorassos are in great form, and even the Bricco San Michele, which is made from younger vineyards, debuted with a perfectly respectable score. What do the three wines that made it to our final round of tasting all share? Aromatic richness, complexity and a freshness that lengthens truly exquisite final aromatic persistence.

○ Colli Tortonesi Timorasso Derthona Pitasso '17	♟♟♟ 6
○ Colli Tortonesi Timorasso Cavallina '17	♟♟ 5
○ Colli Tortonesi Timorasso Derthona '17	♟♟ 5
● Colli Tortonesi Barbera Territorio '17	♟♟ 3
● Colli Tortonesi Freisa Braghè '17	♟♟ 3
○ Colli Tortonesi Timorasso Bricco San Michele '17	♟♟ 4
○ Colli Tortonesi Bianco Pitasso '06	♟♟♟ 5
○ Colli Tortonesi Bianco Pitasso '05	♟♟♟ 4
○ Colli Tortonesi Timorasso Pitasso '13	♟♟♟ 6
○ Colli Tortonesi Timorasso Pitasso '12	♟♟♟ 6
○ Colli Tortonesi Timorasso Pitasso '08	♟♟♟ 5

Marsaglia

VIA MADAMA MUSSONE, 2
12050 CASTELLINALDO [CN]
TEL. +39 0173213048
www.cantinamarsaglia.it

CELLAR SALES
PRE-BOOKED VISITS
ANNUAL PRODUCTION 80,000 bottles
HECTARES UNDER VINE 15.00

The Marsaglia family began bottling their wines in the 1980s. Their vineyards, some of which go back more than 50 years, are all situated in Castellinaldo on terrain that gets sandier as you approach Canale and more compact nearer to Castagnito. The territory's traditional grapes are cultivated, from Arneis to Barbera, Nebbiolo, Brachetto and Dolcetto. All their wines are well-made and geared towards pleasantness. On the nose the Roero Brich d'America '15 offers up austere notes of quinine and rain-soaked earth along with spicy nuances. On the palate it exhibits notable structure, with a long, assertive and juicy finish. The Roero Arneis Serramiana '18 follows original aromas of aniseed and aromatic herbs with an extremely tight-knit and dense palate, though without heaviness, and a long, flavorful finish.

○ Roero Arneis Serramiana '18	♥♥ 3*
● Roero Brich d'America '15	♥♥ 4
● Barbera d'Alba Sup. Castellinaldo '16	♥♥ 4
⊙ Langhe Rosato Rustichel '18	♥ 4
● Nebbiolo d'Alba San Pietro '17	♥ 3
● Barbera d'Alba Sup. Castellinaldo '15	♀♀ 4
● Nebbiolo d'Alba San Pietro '15	♀♀ 3
○ Roero Arneis Serramiana '17	♀♀ 3
● Roero Brich d'America '14	♀♀ 4
● Roero Brich d'America '12	♀♀ 4

★Franco M. Martinetti

VIA SAN FRANCESCO DA PAOLA, 18
10123 TORINO
TEL. +39 0118395937
www.francomartinetti.it

PRE-BOOKED VISITS
ANNUAL PRODUCTION 130,000 bottles
HECTARES UNDER VINE 5.00

Such is Franco Martinetti's passion for quality wine and food that his dinners have become famous. Here friends and experts meet to test the perfect food-wine pairings, with dishes prepared by his own trusted chefs. Guests may find themselves tasting one of his stupefying, 30-year Gavi Minaias or an elegant, cask-aged Timorasso, or one of his celebrated Barbera d'Astis, a selection that has few rivals in terms of drinkability. For 45 years he's been selecting grapes, and continues to pursue elegance and balance with each bottle. Their 2018 Biancofranco and Martin don't fall under the Colli Tortonesi DOC. The former is an alluring, well-balanced wine rich in fruit and medicinal herbs — magnificent. The Martin is a bit more vegetal, more relaxed in its development. The well-crafted Sul Bric '17 shows a certain aromatic austerity in which smoky notes join with quinine and ripe cherries. On the palate it's complex, acidulous, marked by tannins. It will age well for many years to come.

○ Biancofranco Timorasso '18	♥♥ 5
● M.to Rosso sul Bric '17	♥♥ 6
● Barbera d'Asti Sup. Bric dei Banditi '17	♥♥ 4
● Barbera d'Asti Sup. Montruc '17	♥♥ 6
● Barolo Marasco '15	♥♥ 8
● Barolo Marasco Ris. '13	♥♥ 8
○ Gavi del Comune di Gavi '18	♥♥ 4
○ Gavi Minaia '18	♥♥ 5
○ Martin Timorasso '18	♥♥ 6
● Barbera d'Asti Sup. Montruc '06	♀♀♀ 5
● Barbera d'Asti Sup. Montruc '01	♀♀♀ 5
● Barolo Marasco '01	♀♀♀ 7
● Barolo Marasco '00	♀♀♀ 7
○ Colli Tortonesi Timorasso Martin '12	♀♀♀ 6
○ Gavi Minaia '14	♀♀♀ 5
● M.to Rosso Sul Bric '10	♀♀♀ 6
● M.to Rosso Sul Bric '09	♀♀♀ 6

★Bartolo Mascarello

VIA ROMA, 15
12060 BAROLO [CN]
TEL. +39 017356125

CELLAR SALES
PRE-BOOKED VISITS
ANNUAL PRODUCTION 30,000 bottles
HECTARES UNDER VINE 5.00

Maria Teresa Mascarello is a cultured and disciplined person. Her knowledge of the world came to her through the teachings of her splendid parents (Franca Brezza and Bartolo Mascarello) and from the family's rich library. She's also an attentive interpreter of classic Barolo, bringing painstaking care and a 'natural' cultivation approach to her vineyards. After harvest, the Nebbiolo grapes from her four private vineyards are aged in carefully chosen wood barrels. For the winery's many fans, we suggest reading Kerin O'Keefe's history of 'Barolo and Barbaresco', published by the University of California Press. Mascarello's 2015 Barolo is surely one of the best of the year. Its core character is grounded in fruit, both on the nose and its round palate, where it's accompanied by licorice and a harmonious development, coming through lively, vigorous and racy thanks to its dense, tight and absolutely pleasing tannins: Tre Bicchieri.

● Barolo '15	♟♟♟ 8
● Barolo '13	♟♟♟ 8
● Barolo '12	♟♟♟ 8
● Barolo '11	♟♟♟ 8
● Barolo '10	♟♟♟ 8
● Barolo '09	♟♟♟ 8
● Barolo '07	♟♟♟ 8
● Barolo '06	♟♟♟ 8
● Barolo '05	♟♟♟ 8
● Barolo '01	♟♟♟ 8
● Barolo '99	♟♟♟ 8
● Barolo '98	♟♟♟ 8
● Barolo '89	♟♟♟ 8
● Barolo '85	♟♟♟ 8
● Barolo '84	♟♟♟ 8
● Barolo '83	♟♟♟ 8

★Giuseppe Mascarello e Figlio

VIA BORGONUOVO, 108
12060 MONCHIERO [CN]
TEL. +39 0173792126
www.mascarello1881.com

CELLAR SALES
PRE-BOOKED VISITS
ANNUAL PRODUCTION 60,000 bottles
HECTARES UNDER VINE 13.50

Visiting this winery means immersing yourself in history, in simplicity, forgoing any form of self-aggrandizement. Indeed, here we're light-years away from California, or even Langhe's most celebrated producers — no star architects, tasting rooms or panoramic views here, no barriques or concentrators. The only panorama that Mauro Mascarello is interested in is his vineyards, starting with his prized Monprivato plot, rightfully. His wines reflect this stripped-down style, offering enophiles the possibility to taste the essence of great Barolo. Despite the unremarkable year, the 2014 Barolo Monprivato stands out thanks to a notable harmony between Nebbiolo's classic fruit and the somewhat vegetal notes that characterize the vintage. The result is a wine of great pleasantness on a body of medium density. The Villero sees somewhat shy aromas accompanied by lively acidity and restrained structure, while we're seeing the first spicy notes emerge in their pleasantly fresh Vigna Santo Stefano.

● Barolo Monprivato '14	♟♟ 8
● Barolo Villero '14	♟♟ 8
● Barolo Perno V. Santo Stefano '14	♟♟ 8
● Barolo Monprivato '13	♟♟♟ 8
● Barolo Monprivato '12	♟♟♟ 8
● Barolo Monprivato '11	♟♟♟ 8
● Barolo Monprivato '10	♟♟♟ 8
● Barolo Monprivato '09	♟♟♟ 8
● Barolo Monprivato '08	♟♟♟ 8
● Barolo Monprivato '01	♟♟♟ 8
● Barolo Monprivato '85	♟♟♟ 8
● Barolo S. Stefano di Perno '98	♟♟♟ 8
● Barolo Villero '96	♟♟♟ 8

La Masera

s.da San Pietro, 32
10010 Piverone [TO]
Tel. +39 0113164161
www.lamasera.it

CELLAR SALES
PRE-BOOKED VISITS
ANNUAL PRODUCTION 25,000 bottles
HECTARES UNDER VINE 5.00
SUSTAINABLE WINERY

La Masera, a winery founded 15 years ago by five friends (all passionate for Canavese's wines), has experienced an increase in quality and recognition in our guide. The original idea was to focus on Caluso Passito, but business grew such that, today, they now produce some nine wines, all expressions of the territory's traditional grapes, from Erbaluce to Nebbiolo and Barbera. The selection submitted this year put in an admirable performance, including those Erbaluces that undergo longer maturation, with a particular applause for their Macaria '16. But the fresh Anima '18 also did well, proving clearly focused, potent, and fragrant of herbs and almond. The not too sweet Passito Venanzia '12 is complex and relaxed, more impressive on the palate than for its aromatic profile. The Canavese Rosso '17, a blend of primarily Barbera, Vespolina and Bonarda, also put in a good performance. It's just a bit simple but harmonious and fresh.

○ Caluso Passito Venanzia '12	♟♟ 5
● Canavese Rosso '17	♟♟ 2*
○ Erbaluce di Caluso Anima '18	♟♟ 3
○ Erbaluce di Caluso Anima d'Annata '16	♟♟ 3
○ Erbaluce di Caluso Macaria '16	♟♟ 3
● Canavese Barbera Monte Gerbido '16	♟ 2
○ Erbaluce di Caluso Pas Dosé Masilé	♟ 5
● Canavese Nebbiolo '13	♟♟ 3
● Canavese Nebbiolo '12	♟♟ 3
● Canavese Rosso '16	♟♟ 2*
○ Erbaluce di Caluso Anima '17	♟♟ 3*
○ Erbaluce di Caluso Anima '16	♟♟ 2*
○ Erbaluce di Caluso Anima '15	♟♟ 2*
○ Erbaluce di Caluso Brut Masilé '14	♟♟ 5
○ Erbaluce di Caluso Macaria '14	♟♟ 3

★Vigneti Massa

p.zza G. Capsoni, 10
15059 Monleale [AL]
Tel. +39 013180302
massa@vignetimassa.com

CELLAR SALES
PRE-BOOKED VISITS
ANNUAL PRODUCTION 120,000 bottles
HECTARES UNDER VINE 25.00
SUSTAINABLE WINERY

Walter Massa in an eclectic person, but he's also forward-thinking, considering the results he's achieved with Timorasso (which have affected the entire district). His commitment has shone a light on a territory rich in food and wine specialities and influenced its viticulture. In terms of the producer's style, it's notoriously rich and potent, with high concentrations of flavor. As a result, his wines need time to fully express their potential: decidedly ageworthy and complex, they're made exclusively with native grape varieties. The selection submitted saw 2017 turn out to be a very interesting year for Timorasso. Three of the producer's most representative wines earned a place in our final round of tastings, with a notable aromatic-gustatory profile accompanied by Massa's trademark richness — they're only missing that final push. The rest of their selection is also of excellent quality, including a noteworthy 2013 version of their Croatina Pertichetta.

○ Costa del Vento '17	♟♟ 6
○ Derthona '17	♟♟ 5
○ Montecitorio '17	♟♟ 6
○ Sterpi '17	♟♟ 6
○ Anarchia Costituzionale '18	♟♟ 3
● Pertichetta '13	♟♟ 4
● Pietra del Gallo '18	♟♟ 3
● Sentieri '18	♟♟ 4
● L'Avvelenata '15	♟ 4
○ Colli Tortonesi Timorasso Sterpi '08	♟♟♟ 7
○ Colli Tortonesi Timorasso Sterpi '07	♟♟♟ 7
○ Costa del Vento '15	♟♟♟ 6
○ Costa del Vento '12	♟♟♟ 6
○ Derthona '09	♟♟♟ 5
○ Derthona Sterpi '16	♟♟♟ 6
○ Montecitorio '11	♟♟♟ 6
○ Montecitorio '10	♟♟♟ 6

★Massolino

P.ZZA CAPPELLANO, 8
12050 SERRALUNGA D'ALBA [CN]
TEL. +39 0173613138
www.massolino.it

CELLAR SALES
PRE-BOOKED VISITS
ANNUAL PRODUCTION 257,000 bottles
HECTARES UNDER VINE 36.00
SUSTAINABLE WINERY

We start with the location: Paragada, Margheria, Vigna Rionda, all on the western side of Serralunga d'Alba; Parussi in Castiglione Falletto. These give rise to the Massolino family's most celebrated wines. Active since 1896, they focus on bringing together richness and power with tannic intensity and length. Their range is reliable across the board, drawing on Nebbiolo, Barbera, Dolcetto, Chardonnay and Moscato. A strong selection is only missing that one star performer. The Barbera d'Alba Gisep '17 and Dolcetto d'Alba are exemplary in their respective categories: fresh, juicy and elegant. The Barolo '15 has class, complexity. The Parafada is spicy, austere, the Parussi mouthfilling, penetrating. The long wait for their Vigna Rionda '13 made for sensations of truffle and tanned leather. On the palate it's muscular, sapid, rich in force and length, giving way to a proper finish just a bit dried by oak. It's lacking the bounce found in its best versions, but will still go far.

● Barbera d'Alba Gisep '17	♟♟ 5
● Barolo Parafada '15	♟♟ 8
● Barolo Parussi '15	♟♟ 8
● Barolo Vigna Rionda Ris. '13	♟♟ 8
● Dolcetto d'Alba '18	♟♟ 2*
● Barbera d'Alba '18	♟♟ 3
● Barolo '15	♟♟ 5
● Barolo Margheria '15	♟♟ 8
○ Langhe Riesling '17	♟♟ 4
○ Langhe Chardonnay '17	♟ 3
● Langhe Nebbiolo '17	♟ 4
● Barolo Parafada '11	♟♟♟ 8
● Barolo Vigna Rionda Ris. '11	♟♟♟ 8
● Barolo Vigna Rionda Ris. '10	♟♟♟ 8
● Barolo Vigna Rionda Ris. '08	♟♟♟ 8
● Barolo Vigna Rionda Ris. '06	♟♟♟ 8

Tiziano Mazzoni

VIA ROMA, 73
28010 CAVAGLIO D'AGOGNA [NO]
TEL. +39 3488200635
www.vinimazzoni.it

CELLAR SALES
PRE-BOOKED VISITS
ANNUAL PRODUCTION 20,000 bottles
HECTARES UNDER VINE 4.50
SUSTAINABLE WINERY

Tiziano Mazzoni's winery got its start almost as a lark in 1999. Since then it's been gradually enlarged, thanks to the purchase of vineyards and a concomitant expansion of the production facility. Today, finally, we can say that the cellar matches the quality of their wines. Their selection sees Ghemme on center stage, but for those who love Nebbiolo we can strongly suggest their Monteregio, a wine that's always received well during tastings thanks to its gentle minerality. Another standout is their Ricetto, a Vespolina endowed with a titillating note of white pepper. The Ghemme dei Mazzoni is a highly pleasant wine, despite a hot 2015 and its consequent tiredness, marked by herbs in the sun and pronounced tannins. The elegantly drinkable Nebbiolo del Monteregio '17 is richer in fruit. The most recent version of their mighty Iris, made with Erbaluce and unfortunately without a vintage (or indication thereof), is easily one of Piedmont's best whites.

● Colline Novaresi	
Nebbiolo del Monteregio '17	♟♟ 4
● Ghemme dei Mazzoni '15	♟♟ 8
○ Iris	♟♟ 4
● Colline Novaresi Vespolina	
Il Ricetto '18	♟♟ 4
● Elia	♟ 4
● Ghemme dei Mazzoni '12	♟♟♟ 5
● Colline Novaresi	
Nebbiolo del Monteregio '16	♟♟ 3
● Colline Novaresi Vespolina	
Il Ricetto '17	♟♟ 3
● Ghemme Ai Livelli '13	♟♟ 6
● Ghemme dei Mazzoni '14	♟♟ 5
● Ghemme dei Mazzoni '13	♟♟ 5

Tenuta La Meridiana

VIA TANA BASSA, 5
14048 MONTEGROSSO D'ASTI [AT]
TEL. +39 0141956172
www.tenutalameridiana.com

CELLAR SALES
PRE-BOOKED VISITS
ANNUAL PRODUCTION 100,000 bottles
HECTARES UNDER VINE 10.00
SUSTAINABLE WINERY

Tenuta La Meridiana's roots go back to the 19th century, and today Federico Primo represents the fifth generation of family to manage it. Situated in the heart of Monferrato, the winery specializes primarily in Barbera, a veritable benchmark for the area and the cornerstone of various wines differentiated according to vineyard of provenance and production approach. Their selection, however, has expanded over time to include a number of typologies based on Chardonnay, Cortese, Favorita, Arneis, Moscato, Nebbiolo and Malaga. Barbera d'Asti remains the cornerstone of their selection, in particular the 2017 Superiore versions. The Bricco Sereno is broad and multi-layered on notes of mature cherry, tobacco and licorice, the prelude to a potent yet mobile palate. The Tra la Terra e il Cielo is aromatically sweeter and more mature: cinnamon and toasted coffee rise up on the nose, while the palate comes through succulent and flavorful, with nice acidic tension.

● Barbera d'Asti Sup. Bricco Sereno '17	¥¥ 4
● Barbera d'Asti Le Gagie '17	¥¥ 3
● Barbera d'Asti Le Quattro Terre '18	¥¥ 2*
● Barbera d'Asti Sup. Tra la Terra e il Cielo '17	¥¥ 5
● M.to Rosso Rivaia '15	¥¥ 5
● Barbera d'Asti Vitis '18	¥ 2
○ M.to Bianco Puntet '18	¥ 3
○ Piemonte Bianco Le Quattro Terre '18	¥ 2
● Barbera d'Asti Le Quattro Terre '17	¥¥ 2*
● Barbera d'Asti Sup. Bricco Sereno '13	¥¥ 4
● Barbera d'Asti Sup. Tra la Terra e il Cielo '16	¥¥ 5
● Barbera d'Asti Vitis '17	¥¥ 2*
○ Joaçaba Brut M. Cl.	¥¥ 5

La Mesma

FRAZ. MONTEROTONDO, 7
15066 GAVI [AL]
TEL. +39 0143342012
www.lamesma.it

CELLAR SALES
PRE-BOOKED VISITS
ACCOMMODATION
ANNUAL PRODUCTION 52,000 bottles
HECTARES UNDER VINE 25.00
VITICULTURE METHOD Certified Organic

Having concluded a conversion to organic cultivation, La Mesma is carving out a place for itself among Gavi's most dynamic wineries. Theirs is a modern approach, both in terms of vineyard management and winemaking, aimed at protecting the environment and promoting sustainability over time. The result is wines that express this diverse terroir and the Rosina sisters' mission. Cortese is presented in every typology: still, sparkling and Metodo Classico (this last is available in a semi-dry version as well). They submitted a textbook selection, especially the Vigna della Rovere Verde reserve, an amazing wine for the complexity of its aromas, coming through bold and highly persistent on the palate. Notes of wisteria and lime blossom characterize the Indi, a sapid white with a fresh, vibrant palate. The density and harmony of the multifaceted Etichetta Gialla '18 is truly remarkable.

○ Gavi V. della Rovere Verde Ris. '17	¥¥¥ 5
○ Gavi del Comune di Gavi Et. Gialla '18	¥¥ 3*
○ Gavi del Comune di Gavi Indi '18	¥¥ 4
○ Gavi Brut M. Cl. '13	¥¥ 5
○ Gavi del Comune di Gavi 10 Anni '08	¥¥ 2*
○ Gavi del Comune di Gavi Et. Nera '18	¥¥ 3
○ Gavi V. della Rovere Verde Ris. '15	¥¥¥ 5
○ Gavi del Comune di Gavi Et. Gialla '15	¥¥ 2*
○ Gavi del Comune di Gavi Et. Nera '17	¥¥ 3*
○ Gavi del Comune di Gavi Et. Nera '16	¥¥ 3*
○ Gavi del Comune di Gavi Indi '17	¥¥ 4
○ Gavi V. della Rovere Verde Ris. '16	¥¥ 5

Moccagatta

S.DA RABAJÀ, 46
12050 BARBARESCO [CN]
TEL. +39 0173635228
www.moccagatta.eu

CELLAR SALES
PRE-BOOKED VISITS
ANNUAL PRODUCTION 65,000 bottles
HECTARES UNDER VINE 12.00
SUSTAINABLE WINERY

Martina Minuto continues to study the personality of her wines because, as she's fond of reminding you, 'The vineyard is the foundation, but the most important moment is when you put in the cork'. Her cousin oversees the vines, though it's important to note that their parents are still active, highly capable vigneron. Half the estate is cultivated with Nebbiolo, the other hosts Barbera, Dolcetto and, from as far back as 1983, Chardonnay. A firm support for organic principles hasn't resulted in any stylistic changes: here Barbaresco is, and always has been, fruity and rich, with a nice spiciness resulting from the use of French oak. And it is precisely aromas of wood, from vanilla to cocoa powder, charred oak to alcohol-steeped cherries, that dominate the 2016 versions of their Basarin and Bric Balin. As a result we recommend waiting a bit longer. The Cole '16 is more classically-styled: potent, tannic and juicy on the palate, with lovely hints of black berries and tobacco on the nose.

● Barbaresco Cole '16	♟♟7
● Barbaresco Basarin '16	♟♟6
● Barbaresco Bric Balin '16	♟♟6
● Barbaresco Bric Balin '05	♟♟♟6
● Barbaresco Bric Balin '04	♟♟♟6
● Barbaresco Bric Balin '01	♟♟♟6
● Barbaresco Bric Balin '90	♟♟♟6
● Barbaresco Cole '97	♟♟♟6
● Barbaresco Basarin '14	♟♟6
● Barbaresco Basarin '11	♟♟6
● Barbaresco Bric Balin '15	♟♟6
● Barbaresco Bric Balin '14	♟♟6
● Barbaresco Bric Balin '13	♟♟6
● Barbaresco Bric Balin '12	♟♟6
● Barbaresco Bric Balin '11	♟♟6
● Barbaresco Cole '12	♟♟7
● Barbaresco Cole '11	♟♟6

Mauro Molino

FRAZ. ANNUNZIATA GANCIA, 111A
12064 LA MORRA [CN]
TEL. +39 017350814
www.mauromolino.com

CELLAR SALES
PRE-BOOKED VISITS
ANNUAL PRODUCTION 95,000 bottles
HECTARES UNDER VINE 12.00
SUSTAINABLE WINERY

The southeast-facing, amphitheatrical Conca vineyard is as charming as it is small. Here, every year, just under 3,000 bottles are produced, wines that aptly represent the elegance and aromatic qualities of La Morra's Barolos. Along with his children, Mauro Molino oversees a winery situated not far from here, working the grapes from their various private crus, including a plot dedicated to Barbera d'Asti. Their production style calls for grapes that are always quite ripe, and the use of small, French oak casks. They only submitted 2015 Barolos for tasting. The Bricco Luciani delivers, proving long and precisely balanced, a development preceded by intense aromas of herbs, quinine and oak. Spices, red berries, oak and mint feature in the elegant Conca, a wine with marked tannic presence. The Gallinotto is a bit smaller, but of decidedly nice harmony, while the mid-structured, entry-level Barolo proves bewitching in its notes of rose and licorice.

● Barolo Bricco Luciani '15	♟♟6
● Barolo Conca '15	♟♟7
● Barolo Gallinotto '15	♟♟6
● Barolo '15	♟♟5
● Barbera d'Alba V. Gattere '00	♟♟♟5
● Barbera d'Alba V. Gattere '97	♟♟♟7
● Barbera d'Alba V. Gattere '96	♟♟♟7
● Barolo Gallinotto '11	♟♟♟6
● Barolo Gallinotto '03	♟♟♟6
● Barolo Gallinotto '01	♟♟♟6
● Barolo V. Conca '00	♟♟♟7
● Barolo V. Conca '97	♟♟♟7
● Barolo V. Conca '96	♟♟♟7
● Barolo Bricco Luciani '11	♟♟6
● Barolo Bricco Luciani '10	♟♟6
● Barolo Conca '12	♟♟7
● Barolo Conca '10	♟♟7

F.lli Monchiero

VIA ALBA MONFORTE, 49
12060 CASTIGLIONE FALLETTO [CN]
TEL. +39 017362820
www.monchierovini.it

CELLAR SALES
PRE-BOOKED VISITS
ANNUAL PRODUCTION 40,000 bottles
HECTARES UNDER VINE 12.00
SUSTAINABLE WINERY

Every year the winery managed by Vittorio Monchiero, which has been active since the 1970s, achieves increasingly notable results with their Barolo, thanks in part to the work of young Luca. Their most important vineyards are the celebrated Rocche di Castiglione and the more than valid Montanello, but their property spans plots in several Langhe municipalities, from La Morra to Alba, Roddi and Verduno. For enotourists there's a B&B, the Girasole, just next to the winery. This year we tasted three superb Barolos. The Ris. Montanello '13 exhibits aromatic complexity and contrast, ranging from raspberry notes to incense, showing exemplary harmony on the palate. The splendid Ris. Rocche di Castiglion '13 features tones of licorice accompanied by tannins just a bit more up front. The Barolo Rocche di Castiglione '15 is a good example of a delicate, harmonious, classical style grounded in focused, pleasant notes of red berries, as well as a pleasingly fresh palate.

● Barolo Montanello Ris. '13	▼▼	5
● Barolo Rocche di Castiglione '15	▼▼	5
● Barolo Rocche di Castiglione Ris. '13	▼▼	7
○ Langhe Arneis '18	▼▼	2*
● Langhe Nebbiolo '17	▼▼	3
⊙ Rosato Vignola	▼	2
● Barbera d'Alba Sup. '16	♀♀	3
● Barbera d'Alba Sup. '15	♀♀	3
● Barolo Montanello Ris. '10	♀♀	5
● Barolo Rocche di Castiglione '13	♀♀	5
● Barolo Rocche di Castiglione '12	♀♀	5
● Barolo Rocche di Castiglione '11	♀♀	5
● Barolo Rocche di Castiglione '12	♀♀	7
● Barolo Rocche di Castiglione Ris. '09	♀♀	5

★Monchiero Carbone

VIA SANTO STEFANO ROERO, 2
12043 CANALE [CN]
TEL. +39 017395568
www.monchierocarbone.com

CELLAR SALES
PRE-BOOKED VISITS
ANNUAL PRODUCTION 190,000 bottles
HECTARES UNDER VINE 30.00
SUSTAINABLE WINERY

The Monchiero family's winery is one of the most dynamic and committed to the territory of Roero and its wines. Their private vineyards, some of which can be found in the area's most famous crus (like Monbirone, Renesio or Sru), are situated in Canale, Vezza d'Alba, Monteu Roero and Priocca. The territory's traditional grapes are cultivated, from Arneis to Nebbiolo and Barbera. These give rise to wines that exhibit notable structure and complexity, along with close-focused aromas and noteworthy aging power. The Roero Printi Riserva '15 comes through generous on the nose, with notes of aromatic herbs, black berries, spices and tobacco preceding a nicely textured palate in which tannins are present but elegant. The Roero Arneis Cecu d'la Biunda '18 also exhibits notable finesse, proving assertive and sapid at the same time, redolent of citrus and hazelnut. The Roero Srü '16 offers up aromas of black wild berries and cocoa powder followed by a fresh and juicy palate of nice complexity.

● Roero Printi Ris. '15	▼▼▼	6
○ Roero Arneis Cecu d'La Biunda '18	▼▼	3*
● Roero Srü '16	▼▼	4
● Barbera d'Alba Monbirone '16	▼▼	5
● Barbera d'Alba Pelisa '17	▼▼	2*
○ Langhe Bianco Tamardi '18	▼▼	2*
○ Roero Arneis Recit '18	▼▼	3
● Langhe Nebbiolo Regret '18	▼	2
○ Roero Arneis Cecu d'la Biunda '17	♀♀♀	3*
○ Roero Arneis Cecu d'la Biunda '16	♀♀♀	3*
● Roero Printi Ris. '12	♀♀♀	5
● Roero Printi Ris. '11	♀♀♀	5
● Roero Printi Ris. '10	♀♀♀	5

La Montagnetta

FRAZ. BRICCO CAPPELLO, 4
14018 ROATTO [AT]
TEL. +39 0141938343
www.lamontagnetta.com

CELLAR SALES
PRE-BOOKED VISITS
ANNUAL PRODUCTION 50,000 bottles
HECTARES UNDER VINE 10.00

It's not easy to think of many producers that have invested so confidently in Freisa, the historic Piedmont grape that's gradually been relegated to the margins of the region's ampelography due to the success of Nebbiolo and Barbera. Domenico Capello's winery proposes it in practically every possible version, from still-dry to semi-sparkling, sparkling and rosés. Everything centers on their Roatto, San Paolo, Solbrito and Piovà Massaia vineyards, where Barbera, Bonarda, Chardonnay, Sauvignon and Viognier are also cultivated. This year their best Freisa appears to be the Superiore Bugianen '15. It enters on toasty notes of charred oak, and then a lovely weave of dark fruit follows through to an austere, crisp palate that's not lacking in flesh. The Barbera Pi-Cit '18 is more defined and complete with its aromas of mature black berries and a meaty, tantalizing palate that's well accompanied by fresh, supporting acidity.

● Barbera d'Asti Pi-Cit '18	♟♟ 2*
● Barbera d'Asti Sup. Piovà '16	♟♟ 4
● Freisa d'Asti Sup. Bugianen '15	♟♟ 4
○ M.to Bianco A Stim '18	♟♟ 3
● Freisa d'Asti Frizzante I Ronchi '18	♟ 2
⊙ Piemonte Rosato Il Ciarèt '18	♟ 2
● Barbera d'Asti Pi Cit '17	♟♟ 2*
● Barbera d'Asti Sup. Piova '15	♟♟ 4
● Barbera d'Asti Sup. Piovà '14	♟♟ 4
● Freisa d'Asti Sup. Bugianen '14	♟♟ 4
● Freisa d'Asti Sup. Bugianen '13	♟♟ 2*
● Piemonte Bonarda Frizzante Insolita '17	♟♟ 2*

Montalbera

VIA MONTALBERA, 1
14030 CASTAGNOLE MONFERRATO [AT]
TEL. +39 0119433311
www.montalbera.it

CELLAR SALES
PRE-BOOKED VISITS
ANNUAL PRODUCTION 650,000 bottles
HECTARES UNDER VINE 175.00
SUSTAINABLE WINERY

The Morando family's Agricola Montalbera spans a dual track. On the one hand there's their six hillside vineyards in Castagnole Monferrato, which host the area's most popular grapes: Viognier, Grignolino, Barbera and, especially, Ruchè (this last occupies 60% of the appellation's vineyards). On the other there's their property in Langa and, in particular Castiglione Tinella. Here, at 400 meters elevation, they cultivate Moscato, Barbera and Chardonnay on extremely favorable plots. Once again their Ruchè di Castagnole Monferratos shine, with two versions standing out. The Tradizione '18 features a classic style, both on the nose, where it's crossed by rich, fruity, spicy notes, and on the palate, where it's juicy, supported by a pervasive acidity. Laccento '18 is even more profuse in its hints of rose and licorice, which come through on its muscular palate, wrapped in tight-knit tannins and an elegant weave. Their Barbera Sup. Nuda '16 also performed well.

● Ruché di Castagnole M.to Laccento '18	♟♟♟ 4*
● Barbera d'Asti Sup. Nuda '16	♟♟ 5
● Ruché di Castagnole M.to La Tradizione '18	♟♟ 3*
● Grignolino d'Asti Grigné '18	♟♟ 2*
● Barbera d'Asti Solo Acciaio '18	♟ 2
● Barbera d'Asti Sup. Lequilibrio '16	♟ 3
● Barbera d'Asti Nuda '15	♟♟♟ 5
● Ruché di Castagnole M.to La Tradizione '15	♟♟♟ 3*
● Barbera d'Asti Sup. Lequilibrio '15	♟♟ 3
● Grignolino d'Asti Lanfora '16	♟♟ 3*
● Ruché di Castagnole M.to La Tradizione '17	♟♟ 3*
● Ruché di Castagnole M.to Laccento '17	♟♟ 4

Cecilia Monte

VIA SERRACAPELLI, 17
12052 NEIVE [CN]
TEL. +39 017367454
cecilia.monte@libero.it

CELLAR SALES
ANNUAL PRODUCTION 19,000 bottles
HECTARES UNDER VINE 3.50

Our last visit to Cecilia Monte's winery took place on a clear, sunny day in spring, when the profile of this outermost corner of Barbaresco emerged in all its glory, with the geometry of the vineyards enfolding a house-cellar that's truly unique for its position and style. A woman's touch marks the furnishings of their panoramic tasting area and the small but professional production facility. Because of a difficult 2014, their Barbaresco Serracapelli Dedicato a Paolo wasn't produced, and as a result the selection tasted this year was without their crown jewel. But it will be back for next year's edition. When it comes to 2015, their Barbaresco Serracapelli exhibits the best qualities of the vintage, proving powerful but complex in its notes of licorice, eucalyptus and violet, sensations that distinguish a truly succulent and pleasant palate. Their Langhe Nebbiolo Ca' di Monti '16 opts for mature, fruity tones.

● Barbaresco Serracapelli '15	❦❦	5
● Langhe Nebbiolo Ca' di Monti '16	❦❦	3
● Dolcetto d'Alba Montubert '18	❦	2
● Barbaresco Serracapelli '14	♀♀	5
● Barbaresco Serracapelli '13	♀♀	5
● Barbaresco Serracapelli Dedicato a Paolo '13	♀♀	6
● Barbaresco Serracapelli Dedicato a Paolo '11	♀♀	6
● Barbera d'Alba Maria Teresa '16	♀♀	3
● Dolcetto d'Alba Montubert '16	♀♀	2*

Tenuta Montemagno

VIA CASCINA VALFOSSATO, 9
14030 MONTEMAGNO [AT]
TEL. +39 014163624
www.tenutamontemagno.it

CELLAR SALES
PRE-BOOKED VISITS
ACCOMMODATION AND RESTAURANT SERVICE
ANNUAL PRODUCTION 140,000 bottles
HECTARES UNDER VINE 15.00
SUSTAINABLE WINERY

Montemagno's entire selection of wines is characterized by outstanding quality, a feat achieved in just a few years. With great class, their 15 wines express the varietal attributes of the grapes used: Timorasso and Sauvignon, blended or vinified separately, for their whites; Barbera, Grignolino, Syrah, Nebbiolo, Ruchè and Malvasia di Casorzo for their reds (among these their Violae, a blend of Barbera and Syrah). There's also room for a Metodo Classico made with Barbera, their TM Brut, which comes in two versions, 24 months on the lees and 36 months. Their quality selection features the Barbera Superiore Mysterium. Complex and elegant on the nose, it offers up intense, fruity aromas accompanied by spicy hints. On the palate it's powerful and rich, with a lovely, sapid and persistent finish. It's also worth noting a lovely 2018 version of their Solis Vis, a wine whose great potential is only partially expressed — time will do its part.

● Barbera d'Asti Sup. Mysterium '16	❦❦	4
● Barbera d'Asti Austerum '17	❦❦	3
● Grignolino d'Asti Ruber '18	❦❦	2*
○ M.to Bianco Musae '18	❦❦	3
○ M.to Bianco Nymphae '18	❦❦	2*
○ M.to Bianco Solis Vis '18	❦❦	3
○ TM24 Brut M. Cl.	❦❦	5
● M.to Rosso Violae '18	❦	2
● Barbera d'Asti Austerum '16	♀♀	3
● Barbera d'Asti Sup. Mysterium '15	♀♀	4
● Grignolino d'Asti Ruber '17	♀♀	2*
○ M.to Bianco Musae '17	♀♀	3
○ M.to Bianco Musae '17	♀♀	3
○ M.to Bianco Nymphae '17	♀♀	2*
○ M.to Bianco Nymphae '16	♀♀	2*
○ M.to Bianco Solis Vis '16	♀♀	3
○ M.to Bianco Solis Vis '15	♀♀	3

Paolo Monti

FRAZ. CAMIE
LOC. SAN SEBASTIANO, 39
12065 MONFORTE D'ALBA [CN]
TEL. +39 017378391
www.paolomonti.com

CELLAR SALES
PRE-BOOKED VISITS
ANNUAL PRODUCTION 50,000 bottles
HECTARES UNDER VINE 16.00

Paolo Monti, whose winery just passed the quarter century mark, is a skilled interpreter of the area's two most characteristic grapes, Nebbiolo and Barbera. We could say that his Barbera d'Alba Sup. has been so highly successful on international markets because their commitment to the grape is so strong here. Aged in new barriques, it's potent, aromatically rich, capable of evolving for years in the bottle. Their Barolo consistently exhibits the quality of crus such as Monforte d'Alba's Bussia and Bricco San Pietro. Elegant notes of wood and spices feature in their complex Barolo Bussia Ris. '13, a wine whose power is made possible, in part, by pronounced tannins. The elegant Barolo Bricco San Pietro '15 offers up hints of quinine and black berries. On the palate it's powerful, tight-knit, right up to a finish still dominated by oak. Fresh vegetal notes and plenty of oak mark their Barbera d'Alba '16, while the Nebbiolo d'Alba '16 stands out for its aromas of red and black berries.

● Barolo Bussia Ris. '13	🍷🍷 8
● Barbera d'Alba '16	🍷🍷 7
● Barolo Bricco San Pietro '15	🍷🍷 8
● Nebbiolo d'Alba '16	🍷🍷 4
● Barbera d'Alba '15	🍷🍷 5
● Barbera d'Alba '14	🍷🍷 5
● Barbera d'Alba '13	🍷🍷 5
● Barbera d'Alba Sup. '15	🍷🍷 7
● Barolo Bussia '14	🍷🍷 8
● Barolo Bussia Ris. '11	🍷🍷 8
● Barolo Bussia Ris. '10	🍷🍷 8
● Barolo del Comune di Monforte d'Alba '13	🍷🍷 7
● Barolo del Comune di Monforte d'Alba '11	🍷🍷 7
● Nebbiolo d'Alba '14	🍷🍷 4

Stefanino Morra

LOC. SAN PIETRO
VIA CASTAGNITO, 50
12050 CASTELLINALDO [CN]
TEL. +39 0173213489
www.morravini.it

CELLAR SALES
PRE-BOOKED VISITS
ANNUAL PRODUCTION 75,000 bottles
HECTARES UNDER VINE 12.00
SUSTAINABLE WINERY

For thirty years Stefanino Morra has overseen the family winery. The cornerstone of their estate is still in Castellinaldo, where the cellar and most important vineyards are located (like San Pietro and Sräi). These are accompanied by properties in Canale and Vezza d'Alba. Roero's traditional grapes are cultivated, from Arneis to Nebbiolo, Barbera and Favorita, making for traditionally styled wines that exhibit nice body and richness of fruit. Their Barbera d'Alba '16 is among the best Roero Barberas tasted this year. Notes of cherries and plums are accompanied by hints of bark and spices. A highly elegant and drinkable palate follows, supported by vibrant acidity, which lends energy and juice to its long finish. Their Roero '16 performs at truly high levels, offering up aromas of red berries and forest undergrowth, with a palate of notable body and close-woven tannins. Their Roero Arneis Vigna San Pietro '18 is also well-crafted.

● Barbera d'Alba '16	🍷🍷 3*
● Roero '16	🍷🍷 3*
○ Roero Arneis V. San Pietro '17	🍷🍷 3
● Barbera d'Alba Castellinaldo '16	🍷 4
● Barbera d'Alba Castlè '16	🍷 5
○ Roero Arneis '18	🍷 2
● Barbera d'Alba '15	🍷🍷 3*
● Barbera d'Alba Castellinaldo '15	🍷🍷 4
○ Roero Arneis '17	🍷🍷 2*
● Roero Sräi Ris. '15	🍷🍷 5

F.lli Mossio

FRAZ. CASCINA CARAMELLI
VIA MONTÀ, 12
12050 RODELLO [CN]
TEL. +39 0173617149
www.mossio.com

CELLAR SALES
PRE-BOOKED VISITS
ACCOMMODATION
ANNUAL PRODUCTION 50,000 bottles
HECTARES UNDER VINE 10.00
SUSTAINABLE WINERY

When it comes to quality, constance pays. Over almost 50 years this winery has managed to establish and consolidate its role as a flagship for Dolcetto d'Alba. Over time the wine has been joined by the area's other classic Nebbiolos and Barberas. Remo and Valerio Mossio are at the helm, celebrating the purchase of a major property that completes the range of services offered. Thus, in addition to the quality of their wines, enotourists have an extra reason to visit a pair of vigneron who are as skilled as they are courteous. The Mossio family are becoming increasingly skilled at crafting Nebbiolos as well, as demonstrated by their spicy, warm and well-balanced Luen '15 and their Rosso '16, a wine that includes Barbera and Dolcetto. Their two 2017 Dolcetto d'Albas were affected by the warm year, and lack the usual fresh, fruity exuberance, even if they're made with grapes cultivated in lovely, well-ventilated and high-elevation vineyards.

● Dolcetto d'Alba Piano delli Perdoni '17	¶¶ 2*
● Dolcetto d'Alba Sup. Bricco Caramelli '17	¶¶ 3
● Langhe Nebbiolo Luen '15	¶¶ 4
● Langhe Rosso '16	¶¶ 4
● Barbera d'Alba '17	¶ 4
● Dolcetto d'Alba Bricco Caramelli '00	¶¶¶ 3*
● Dolcetto d'Alba Bricco Caramelli '15	¶¶ 3*
● Dolcetto d'Alba Bricco Caramelli '14	¶¶ 3*
● Dolcetto d'Alba Piano delli Perdoni '16	¶¶ 2*
● Dolcetto d'Alba Sup. Bricco Caramelli '16	¶¶ 3
● Dolcetto d'Alba Sup. Gamus '13	¶¶ 4

Ada Nada

LOC. ROMBONE
VIA AUSARIO, 12
12050 TREISO [CN]
TEL. +39 0173638127
www.adanada.it

CELLAR SALES
PRE-BOOKED VISITS
ACCOMMODATION AND RESTAURANT SERVICE
ANNUAL PRODUCTION 45,000 bottles
HECTARES UNDER VINE 9.00

The lovely winery overseen by Elvio, his wife Anna Lisa, and daughters Elisa, Serena and Emma, is reaching an important milestone with the 100th anniversary of its founding. Est. 1919, today the estate comprises 9 hectares around their main facility, including prestigious crus like Valeirano and Rombone. Their Barberescos age in 3000 liter barrels, making for a style that seems to have achieved its full definition in recent years. For the first time, thanks to their Barbaresco Rombone Elisa, they earn Tre Bicchieri. The 2016 is an homage to classical style: aromatically elegant, supple, fragrant and evanescent, it's a racy wine, flavorful and vibrant in its freshness. On the palate its tannic weave is tightly woven, making for great cleanness, closing generous and sapid. The Barbaresco Valeirano '16 is warm and mature in its aromas of quinine, rhubarb and raspberries. It closes with a slightly pronounced share of alcohol, but it's complex and rich in nuances nevertheless.

● Barbaresco Rombone Elisa '16	¶¶¶ 5
● Barbaresco Valeirano '16	¶¶ 5
● Langhe Nebbiolo Serena '18	¶¶ 3
○ Langhe Sauvignon Neta '18	¶¶ 2*
● Dolcetto d'Alba Autinot '18	¶ 2
● Barbaresco Cichin Ris. '13	¶¶ 6
● Barbaresco Cichin Ris. '12	¶¶ 6
● Barbaresco Rombone Elisa '15	¶¶ 5
● Barbaresco Valeirano '15	¶¶ 5
● Barbera d'Alba Sup. Salgà '16	¶¶ 3

★Fiorenzo Nada

VIA AUSARIO, 12C
12050 TREISO [CN]
TEL. +39 0173638254
www.nada.it

CELLAR SALES
PRE-BOOKED VISITS
ANNUAL PRODUCTION 45,000 bottles
HECTARES UNDER VINE 10.00
SUSTAINABLE WINERY

Bruno Nada learned the secrets of the vineyards from his father, a skilled and wise vigneron who left us last June. In summing up the personalities of their various crus, we could say that their historic Rombone vineyard is rich, fresh and bold, Manzola more delicate and supple, and Montaribaldi, in Barbaresco, is decidedly harmonious — just to provide a brief sketch. The utmost care for each vine, and an approach in the cellar that's aimed at elegance, explain the well-deserved success of this winery, whose ageworthy Seifile has brought them further notoriety. Mint, raspberry and violet introduce their sensational Barbaresco Montaribaldi '15 only to return on a palate made extraordinary by its tannic density, elegance and slow, gradual development: Tre Bicchieri. The Rombone '15 is just as alluring, though slighty richer in alcohol. Their succulent, fresh, powerful and highly pleasant Seifile '15, made with Barbera and Nebbiolo, is also splendid.

● Barbaresco Montaribaldi '15	♟♟♟ 7
● Barbaresco Manzola '15	♟♟ 6
● Barbaresco Rombone '15	♟♟ 7
● Langhe Rosso Seifile '15	♟♟ 7
● Barbera d'Alba '17	♟♟ 4
● Langhe Nebbiolo '17	♟♟ 3
● Barbaresco Manzola '08	♟♟♟ 6
● Barbaresco Manzola '06	♟♟♟ 6
● Barbaresco Montaribaldi '14	♟♟♟ 7
● Barbaresco Montaribaldi '13	♟♟♟ 7
● Barbaresco Rombone '12	♟♟♟ 7
● Barbaresco Rombone '10	♟♟♟ 7
● Barbaresco Rombone '09	♟♟♟ 7
● Barbaresco Rombone '07	♟♟♟ 7
● Barbaresco Rombone '06	♟♟♟ 7
● Barbaresco Rombone '05	♟♟♟ 7
● Barbaresco Rombone '04	♟♟♟ 7

Cantina dei Produttori Nebbiolo di Carema

VIA NAZIONALE, 32
10010 CAREMA [TO]
TEL. +39 0125811160
www.caremadoc.it

CELLAR SALES
PRE-BOOKED VISITS
RESTAURANT SERVICE
ANNUAL PRODUCTION 65,000 bottles
HECTARES UNDER VINE 20.00

This courageous cooperative winery's problem isn't finding a market for its wines (unlike many coops), but rather finding enough grapes for its production! Indeed, in this scenic hamlet, on the border between Piedmont and the Aosta Valley, the difficulties with cultivation are such that the area they cover is down to a few dozen hectares (divided up between some 60 growers). Nevertheless, Carema represents a significant expression of the Nebbiolo grape, and deserves to be known by enophiles the world over. The Carema RIserva '15 is an intense wine full of character, with intense aromas of licorice and tobacco followed by embers and raspberry, sensations that lend finesse and complexity. On the palate it comes through potent and rich, harmonious and highly multifaceted, with nice tannic density. Their Carema '16, a wine characterized by smoky notes and an austere, slightly astringent palate, is also multi-layered and tantalizing.

● Carema Et. Bianca Ris. '15	♟♟ 4
● Canavese Nebbiolo Parè '17	♟♟ 2*
● Carema Et. Nera '16	♟♟ 3
● Carema Et. Bianca '07	♟♟♟ 3*
● Carema Et. Bianca Ris. '11	♟♟♟ 3*
● Carema Et. Bianca Ris. '09	♟♟♟ 3*
● Carema Et. Bianca Ris. '08	♟♟♟ 3*
● Carema Et. Bianca Ris. '12	♟♟ 3
● Carema Et. Bianca Ris. '10	♟♟ 3*
● Carema Et. Nera '15	♟♟ 3
● Carema Et. Nera '14	♟♟ 3
● Carema Et. Nera '13	♟♟ 2*
● Carema Et. Nera '12	♟♟ 2*
● Carema Et. Nera '11	♟♟ 2*
● Carema Et. Nera '10	♟♟ 2*
● Carema Et. Nera '08	♟♟ 2*
● Canavese Nebbiolo Parè '16	♟ 2

Negretti

FRAZ. SANTA MARIA, 53
12064 LA MORRA [CN]
TEL. +39 0173509850
www.negrettivini.com

CELLAR SALES
PRE-BOOKED VISITS
ANNUAL PRODUCTION 40,000 bottles
HECTARES UNDER VINE 13.00

Ezio and Massimo Negretti's winery is in excellent form, and it's clear that the brothers have fully developed the family business's potential. 13 hectares span the hills of La Morra (Rive and Bettolotti crus) and Roddi's Bricco Ambrogio. Their style is, by now, consolidated, with great vineyard care accompanied by intense, well-calibrated extraction, and balanced spiciness. In the cellar you'll find various barrel sizes (from 225 to 2500 liters) and types (French and Austrian). Their Barolo Rive '15 exhibits a classic, well-defined profile, proving vibrant in its notes of wood tar, licorice, dried flowers, and meaty fruit. On the palate it shows finesse, character, unfolding decisively, though softly, through a long finish. The Barolo Mirau '15 is toastier with notes of quinine and eucalyptus, needing time for oak to integrate. The Barolo '15 proves warm, rich and juicy, while the Bricco Ambrogio '15 has great character, with close-knit tannins and sweet wood harmonizing well.

● Barolo Rive '15	♟♟♟ 6
● Barolo '15	♟♟ 6
● Barolo Bricco Ambrogio '15	♟♟ 6
● Barolo Mirau '15	♟♟ 6
● Barbera d'Alba Sup. '16	♟♟ 3
● Nebbiolo d'Alba Minot '16	♟♟ 3
● Barolo Bricco Ambrogio '14	♟♟♟ 6
● Barbera d'Alba Sup. '15	♟♟ 3
● Barolo '14	♟♟ 6
● Barolo '13	♟♟ 6
● Barolo Bricco Ambrogio '13	♟♟ 6
● Barolo Mirau '13	♟♟ 6
● Barolo Rive '14	♟♟ 6
● Barolo Rive '13	♟♟ 6
○ Langhe Chardonnay Dadà '16	♟♟ 3
● Nebbiolo d'Alba Minot '15	♟♟ 3

Lorenzo Negro

FRAZ. SANT'ANNA, 55
12040 MONTEU ROERO [CN]
TEL. +39 017390645
www.negrolorenzo.com

CELLAR SALES
PRE-BOOKED VISITS
ANNUAL PRODUCTION 35,000 bottles
HECTARES UNDER VINE 8.00
SUSTAINABLE WINERY

Since 2006 Lorenzo Negro has overseen the family winery, situated atop the Serra Lupini hill, a property surrounded by the vineyards that dominate the whole area. The terrain here is sandy, with tracts of silt and clay. The area's traditional grapes are cultivated, from Arneis to Nebbiolo, Barbera, Bonarda and Dolcetto. Their wines seek to highlight the attributes of the territory, with a particular attention to aromatic freshness and clarity. This year he presented a high-quality selection. The Roero Prachiosso '16 features floral notes accompanied by nuances of black berries and forest undergrowth. On the palate it's juicy, nicely textured with velvety tannins and a long finish. The Roero S. Francesco Ris. '15 opts more for spicy notes and hints of aromatic herbs, while the palate exhibits delicate tannins, finishing long, juicy, harmonious. Finally, the excellent Barbera d'Alba '16 stands out for its richness of fruit, as well as its nice, fresh, supporting acidity.

● Roero Prachiosso '16	♟♟ 3*
● Roero S.Francesco Ris. '15	♟♟ 3*
● Barbera d'Alba '16	♟♟ 2*
○ Roero Arneis '18	♟♟ 2*
● Barbera d'Alba Sup. La Nanda '15	♟ 3
● Langhe Nebbiolo '16	♟ 2
○ Roero Arneis Brut M. Cl. '13	♟ 4
● Barbera d'Alba '15	♟♟ 2*
○ Roero Arneis Brut M. Cl. '12	♟♟ 4
● Roero Prachiosso '15	♟♟ 3*
● Roero San Francesco Ris. '14	♟♟ 3
● Roero San Francesco Ris. '13	♟♟ 3*

Angelo Negro e Figli

FRAZ. SANT'ANNA, 1
12040 MONTEU ROERO [CN]
TEL. +39 017390252
www.angelonegro.it

CELLAR SALES
PRE-BOOKED VISITS
ANNUAL PRODUCTION 350,000 bottles
HECTARES UNDER VINE 60.00
SUSTAINABLE WINERY

In recent years the Negro family, who've operated in the territory since the 17th century, enlarged its Langa estate. Its vineyards in Monteu Roero and Canale are now accompanied by two more properties, one in Neive, the other in Serralunga d'Alba. The numerous wines produced, including their sparklers, draw on the area's traditional grapes, like Arneis, Nebbiolo, Barbera, Brachetto, Dolcetto and Favorita, making for a range that aptly expresses the characteristics of the various territories, while maintaining nice aromatic clarity and precision. The Roero Sudisfà Ris. '16 features complex aromas, spicy and fruity notes. On the palate it's juicy, with soft tannins and a long finish well-supported by acidity. The Roero Arneis Sette Anni '12 is characterized by hints of saffron and citron, sensations that anticipate a sapid and surprisingly youthful palate. Finally the fresh, elegant and nicely-textured Barbaresco Basarin '16 offers up fragrances of licorice and tobacco.

Nervi Conterno

C.SO VERCELLI, 117
13045 GATTINARA [VC]
TEL. +39 0163833228
www.nervicantine.it

CELLAR SALES
PRE-BOOKED VISITS
ANNUAL PRODUCTION 120,000 bottles
HECTARES UNDER VINE 27.00

The renovation and upgrading work that Roberto Conterno decided to carry out after purchasing this prestigious, 113-year-old winery in 2018 is almost finished. For the moment there are no changes on the horizon in terms of their offerings, given that the first priority is to realize, both in the vineyard and in the cellar, a selection of outstanding quality that fully highlights the attributes of northern Piedmont's Nebbiolo. Despite the cool, rainy year, their Gattinara Vigneto Molsino '14 exhibits nice vitality, especially in its elegant aromas of quinine, tanned leather and roots. On the palate it's well-balanced and tasty, even absent a particularly muscular structure. The Vigna Valferana '14 moves on a similar track, though with more vegetal notes. The rounder, cosseting Gattinara '15 is characterized by fairly mature fruit.

● Roero Sudisfà Ris. '16	♟♟♟ 6
● Barbaresco Basarin '16	♟♟ 5
○ Roero Arneis Sette Anni '12	♟♟ 7
● Barbera d'Alba Bertù '17	♟♟ 5
● Barolo del Comune di Serralunga d'Alba '15	♟♟ 7
○ Roero Arneis Perdaudin '18	♟♟ 4
● Roero Ciabot San Giorgio '16	♟♟ 5
● Roero Prachiosso '16	♟♟ 4
○ Roero Arneis Serra Lupini '18	♟ 3
● Roero Sudisfà Ris. '13	♙♙♙ 6
● Roero Sudisfà Ris. '12	♙♙♙ 6
● Roero Sudisfà Ris. '10	♙♙♙ 6
● Roero Sudisfà Ris. '09	♙♙♙ 5

● Gattinara '15	♟♟ 4
● Gattinara V. Molsino '14	♟♟ 7
● Gattinara V. Valferana '14	♟♟ 6
⊙ Il Rosato '18	♟ 3
● Gattinara Podere dei Ginepri '01	♙♙♙ 5
● Gattinara Vign. Molsino '00	♙♙♙ 5
● Gattinara '15	♙♙ 5
● Gattinara Molsino '11	♙♙ 5
● Gattinara V. Molsino '12	♙♙ 5
● Gattinara V. Valferana '13	♙♙ 6

Cantina Sociale di Nizza

S.DA ALESSANDRIA, 57
14049 NIZZA MONFERRATO [AT]
TEL. +39 0141721348
www.nizza.it

CELLAR SALES
PRE-BOOKED VISITS
ANNUAL PRODUCTION 200,000 bottles
HECTARES UNDER VINE 560.00
VITICULTURE METHOD Certified Organic
SUSTAINABLE WINERY

About 200 vine growers make Cantina Sociale di Nizza a fundamental benchmark for Monferrato Asti's economy. Ever since its founded in 1955, it's managed to continuously evolve so as to respond to ever-changing market demands, though without losing its bond with tradition. Their ampelography continues to center on the area's traditional grapes (Barbera, Brachetto, Dolcetto, Freisa, Cortese, Moscato), with the occasional concession to international varieties like Chardonnay, making for a diverse selection of modern wines. Once again their Barberas are at the center of the selection submitted for tasting. The Superiore Magister '17 exhibits a fresh suite of black, forest berries, sweet spices and rain-soaked earth, sensations nurtured by a muscular palate in terms of flesh and length. The Nizza Riserva '16, which is even more powerful and chewy, is harmoniously enlivened by an exquisite sapid and spirited streak.

● Barbera d'Asti Sup. Magister '17	♟♟ 3*
● Nizza Ris. '16	♟♟ 5
● Barbera d'Asti Sup. 50 Vendemmie '17	♟♟ 3
● Nizza Ceppi Vecchi '17	♟♟ 5
● Barbera d'Asti '17	♟ 2
● Piemonte Barbera In Origine '18	♟ 2
● Barbera d'Asti Le Pole '16	♟♟ 2*
● Barbera d'Asti Sup. Magister '16	♟♟ 3
● Nizza Ceppi Vecchi '15	♟♟ 4
● Nizza Ris. '15	♟♟ 5
● Piemonte Rosso Baccherosse '15	♟♟ 2*

Silvano Nizza

FRAZ. BALLA LORA 29A
12040 SANTO STEFANO ROERO [CN]
TEL. +39 017390516
www.nizzasilvano.com

CELLAR SALES
PRE-BOOKED VISITS
ANNUAL PRODUCTION 65,000 bottles
HECTARES UNDER VINE 8.00

Silvano Nizza has taken up a 50-year tradition begun by his father, Sandro, and uncle Alfredo. He brings passion to his work of overseeing the family winery, situated in the municipality of Santo Stefano Roero, in the Ca' Boscarone farmstead. Their private vineyards are situated next to the farm itself, as well as in Canale and Montà. Their wines are made with the area's traditional grapes, from Arneis to Nebbiolo, Barbera and Brachetto, making for a selection of modern wines that seek to best highlight the territory's attributes. One of the best Roero Barberas tasted this year is the Barbera d'Alba Superiore Crua '16, with its lovely notes of licorice, tobacco, forest undergrowth and red berries, and a juicy palate that's rich in fruit and well supported by vibrant acidity. Their nicely-textured Roero Arneis '18, with its hints of tropical fruit and good acidity, proved well-crafted, as did their spicy, elegant Roero '16 with its hints of small black berry fruits.

● Barbera d'Alba Sup. Crua '16	♟♟ 4
● Roero '16	♟♟ 5
○ Roero Arneis '18	♟♟ 3
● Nebbiolo d'Alba '17	♟ 4
○ Roero Arneis Il Santo Stefano Limited Edition '16	♟ 3
● Roero Ca' Boscarone Limited Edition Ris. '15	♟ 6
● Barbera d'Alba '15	♟♟ 4
● Roero '15	♟♟ 5
○ Roero Arneis '17	♟♟ 3
○ Roero Ca' Boscarone Ris. '14	♟♟ 6

Noah

VIA FORTE, 48
13862 BRUSNENGO [BI]
TEL. +39 3201510906
info@noah.wine

CELLAR SALES
PRE-BOOKED VISITS
ANNUAL PRODUCTION 10,000 bottles
HECTARES UNDER VINE 4.50
SUSTAINABLE WINERY

In 10 years, without forcing nature's rhythms, Andrea Mosca and Giovanna Pepe Diaz showed confidence in their production project, purchasing vineyards, renovating their cellar and building up a selection for four wines. It's all been accompanied by a commercial and critical success that has stimulated their young enthusiasm even further. Obviously Nebbiolo takes center stage, giving rise to their Bramaterra (85%) and Lessona (100%), though here they also strongly believe in the more delicate and floral Croatina. The Lessona '15 put in an excellent performance. It's as elegant as it is varied in its rich aromatic suit, which ranges from fresh red fruit to rust and a touch of leather. On the palate it exhibits great balance, coming through flavorful, potent but drinkable as well. The robust Bramaterra '15 is a bit more austere and stiff, marked by warm alcohol and assertive tannins. Plums, licorice and black berries feature in their succulent and pleasant Croatina '15.

● Bramaterra '15	♟♟ 5
● Lessona '15	♟♟ 5
● Coste della Sesia Croatina '15	♟♟ 5
● Bramaterra '12	♟♟♟ 5
● Bramaterra '14	♟♟ 5
● Bramaterra '13	♟♟ 5
● Lessona '14	♟♟ 5

Figli Luigi Oddero

FRAZ. SANTA MARIA
LOC. TENUTA PARÀ, 95
12604 LA MORRA [CN]
TEL. +39 0173500386
www.figliluigioddero.it

CELLAR SALES
PRE-BOOKED VISITS
ANNUAL PRODUCTION 110,000 bottles
HECTARES UNDER VINE 20.00
SUSTAINABLE WINERY

Every year Luigi Oddero's wines get better, proving more defined and vibrant. After his experience in Poderi and Cantine Oddero, managed together with his brother, in 2006 Luigi went out on his own. Today he's helped in the best possible way by his wife and children, overseeing one of Langhe's leading producers. His is an exquisitely traditional style, made possible thanks to prestigious plots in Rive and Santa Maria, Scarrone, Vigna Rionda and Rombone. The rich, vibrant Barbera d'Alba '17, a true classic, is marked by focused, meaty fruit. The Barbaresco Rombone is intense in its notes of violet and quinine, while the palate proves austere, close-knit, rich in chiaroscuro. Their airy, enticing Barolo '15 also did well, but the real standout is their Barolo Vigna Rionda '13, which handily brought home Tre Bicchieri. It's tight-knit, potent and solid, characterized by outstanding tension, assertive flavor, complex and austere structure. Excellent today, it will be superb tomorrow.

● Barolo Vigna Rionda '13	♟♟♟ 8
● Barbaresco Rombone '16	♟♟ 6
● Barbera d'Alba '17	♟♟ 6
● Barolo '15	♟♟ 8
● Dolcetto d'Alba '18	♟♟ 2*
● Langhe Nebbiolo '16	♟♟ 6
● Barolo Vigna Rionda '10	♟♟♟ 8
● Barbaresco Rombone '15	♟♟ 6
● Barbaresco Rombone '14	♟♟ 8
● Barbaresco Rombone '13	♟♟ 5
● Barolo '13	♟♟ 8
● Barolo Rocche Ris. '11	♟♟ 8
● Barolo Rocche Rivera '13	♟♟ 6
● Barolo Rocche Rivera '10	♟♟ 6
● Barolo Specola '11	♟♟ 8
● Barolo Vigna Rionda '12	♟♟ 8

★Poderi e Cantine Oddero

FRAZ. SANTA MARIA
VIA TETTI, 28
12064 LA MORRA [CN]
TEL. +39 017350618
www.oddero.it

CELLAR SALES
PRE-BOOKED VISITS
ANNUAL PRODUCTION 150,000 bottles
HECTARES UNDER VINE 35.00
VITICULTURE METHOD Certified Organic
SUSTAINABLE WINERY

Mariacristina and Mariavittoria avail themselves of one of the region's most prestigious estates, thanks to the patrimony they inherited from their father: Villero and Rocche, Brunate, Vigna Mondoca di Bussia Soprana and Vignarionda, just to name a few of their many notable vineyards. Their wines pursue a classical, rigorous style, with a keen sensibility when it comes to extraction and the use of various sizes of barrels, making for a selection that evolves splendidly over time. The Bussia Vigneto Mondoca Ris. '13 does the honors, with its aromas of orange, raspberry and an extraordinary palate marked by superb flesh, tannic firmness and energy. The classically-styled Barolo Vignarionda Ris. '11 also performed well, offering up violet and licorice scents, coming through delicate and complex, full-bodied and tight-knit on the palate, with hints of roots and quinine adorning the finish. The delicate Barolo Villero '15, and warm, juicy Barolo Brunate '15 are also notable.

● Barbaresco Gallina '16	🏆🏆 6
● Barolo Brunate '15	🏆🏆 8
● Barolo Bussia V. Mondoca Ris. '13	🏆🏆 8
● Barolo Vignarionda Ris. '11	🏆🏆 8
● Barbera d'Asti Sup. Nizza '15	🏆🏆 4
● Barolo '15	🏆🏆 6
● Barolo Vignarionda '09	🏆🏆 8
● Barolo Villero '15	🏆🏆 8
○ Langhe Riesling '16	🏆🏆 3
● Langhe Nebbiolo '17	🏆 4
● Barbaresco Gallina '04	🏆🏆🏆 6
● Barolo Bussia V. Mondoca Ris. '12	🏆🏆🏆 8
● Barolo Bussia V. Mondoca Ris. '10	🏆🏆🏆 8
● Barolo Bussia V. Mondoca Ris. '08	🏆🏆🏆 8
● Barolo Mondoca di Bussia Soprana '04	🏆🏆🏆 7
● Barolo Rocche di Castiglione '09	🏆🏆🏆 7

Tenuta Olim Bauda

VIA PRATA, 50
14045 INCISA SCAPACCINO [AT]
TEL. +39 0141702171
www.tenutaolimbauda.it

CELLAR SALES
PRE-BOOKED VISITS
ANNUAL PRODUCTION 200,000 bottles
HECTARES UNDER VINE 30.00
SUSTAINABLE WINERY

Nizza Monferrato, Isola d'Asti, Fontanile, Castelnuovo Calcea and Gavi — these are the primary viticultural poles that serve Tenuta Oli Bauda's well-established production project. Founded in the 1960s by the Bertolino family and today overseen by Dino, Diana and Giovanni, it's a veteran estate both within Monferrato and beyond. The best plots are reserved for Barbera and Moscato, but Grignolino, Nebbiolo, Freisa, Cortese and Chardonnay also contribute to a selection that consistently brings together expressive purity and suppleness. The selection submitted by Tenuta Olim Bauda includes at least two points of excellence. The Barbera La Villa '18 is original, to say the least, in its suggestions of herb liquor and tamarind, alluring with its deliciously rustic, lively and flavorful palate. The Nizza Riserva '16 exhibits a more complete, elegant profile: cherry, blood orange and tobacco on the nose, while its juicy palate unfolds compact and taut.

● Nizza Ris. '16	🏆🏆🏆 5
● Barbera d'Asti La Villa '18	🏆🏆 3*
○ Moscato d'Asti Centive '18	🏆🏆 3*
● Freisa d'Asti '16	🏆🏆 4
○ Gavi del Comune di Gavi '18	🏆🏆 3
● Nebbiolo d'Alba San Pietro '17	🏆🏆 4
● Grignolino d'Asti Isolavilla '18	🏆 3
● Barbera d'Asti Sup. Nizza '13	🏆🏆🏆 5
● Barbera d'Asti Sup. Nizza '12	🏆🏆🏆 5
● Barbera d'Asti Sup. Nizza '11	🏆🏆🏆 5
● Barbera d'Asti Sup. Nizza '08	🏆🏆🏆 5
● Barbera d'Asti Sup. Nizza '07	🏆🏆🏆 5
● Barbera d'Asti Sup. Nizza '06	🏆🏆🏆 5
● Nizza '15	🏆🏆🏆 5

Orsolani

VIA MICHELE CHIESA, 12
10090 SAN GIORGIO CANAVESE [TO]
TEL. +39 012432386
www.orsolani.it

CELLAR SALES
PRE-BOOKED VISITS
ANNUAL PRODUCTION 140,000 bottles
HECTARES UNDER VINE 19.00

Gigi Orsolani is a firm supporter of a territory that, he'll tell you, can bring out the best of Erbaluce. Indeed, he was an active president of the DOCG Caluso Consortium (which comprises DOC Carema and Canavese as well) and is, foremost, a steady hand at making the three typologies in which the grape is used: a fresh and crisp still, a Metodo Classico sparkler and, finally, a sweet wine with partially-dried grapes. The result is a selection of outstanding quality across the board. Their Erbaluce di Caluso La Rustìa has been a flagship since its first year of production, 1985 (the name indicates the grapes have been sufficiently 'sun-roasted'). The 2018 is exceptionally well-crafted, redolent of flowers and herbs, sensations that precede a rich palate, clean and pleasantly fresh. The Canavese Rosso Acini Sparsi '17 exhibits lovely, red fruit. Made with Barbera and a touch of Nebbiolo, its pleasant palate is characterized by excellent balance.

○ Erbaluce di Caluso La Rustìa '18	▼▼ 3*
○ Caluso Extra Brut Cuvée Tradizione '15	▼▼ 5
● Canavese Rosso Acini Sparsi '17	▼▼ 3
○ Caluso Passito Sulé '12	▼ 5
○ Caluso Passito Sulé '04	♀♀♀ 5
○ Caluso Passito Sulé '98	♀♀♀ 5
○ Erbaluce di Caluso La Rustìa '15	♀♀♀ 3*
○ Erbaluce di Caluso La Rustìa '13	♀♀♀ 3*
○ Erbaluce di Caluso La Rustìa '12	♀♀♀ 3*
○ Erbaluce di Caluso La Rustìa '11	♀♀♀ 3*
○ Erbaluce di Caluso La Rustìa '10	♀♀♀ 2*
○ Erbaluce di Caluso La Rustìa '09	♀♀♀ 2*
○ Caluso Passito Sulé '10	♀♀ 5
○ Caluso Passito Sulé '09	♀♀ 5
○ Erbaluce di Caluso La Rustìa '16	♀♀ 3*
○ Erbaluce di Caluso La Rustìa '14	♀♀ 3*

Paitin

FRAZ. BRICCO DI NEIVE
VIA SERRABOELLA, 20
12052 NEIVE [CN]
TEL. +39 017367343
www.paitin.it

CELLAR SALES
PRE-BOOKED VISITS
ACCOMMODATION
ANNUAL PRODUCTION 80,000 bottles
HECTARES UNDER VINE 18.00
VITICULTURE METHOD Certified Organic
SUSTAINABLE WINERY

Even if the area's Nebbiolos have been appreciated for centuries, the decision to call the wine Barbaresco came in the late 19th century. It was then that the Pasquero Elia family's winery was founded, meaning they can claim to be among the appellation's original artificers. Giovanni and Silvano's approach is natural in the vineyards (no chemicals) and innovative in the cellar (rotary macerators, small French oak casks), making for Barbarescos that exhibit elegance and territorial expression. Their 2016 Barbarescos put in a brilliant performance. Finesse and freshness feature in their Serraboella Sorì Paitin, along with commendable harmony, even if it's still not particularly complex. The Serraboella is already more open, evolved in its notes of dried herbs and tobacco. The Sorì Paitin Ris. '14 is endowed with vegetal notes, hints of oak, while the not-to-be-missed Barbera d'Alba Sup. Campolive '16, with its nuances of tar and black berry fruits, proves to be of rare elegance.

● Barbaresco Serraboella Sorì Paitin '16	▼▼ 6
● Barbera d'Alba Sup. Campolive '16	▼▼ 5
● Barbaresco Serraboella '16	▼▼ 5
● Barbaresco Sorì Paitin Ris. '14	▼▼ 8
● Nebbiolo d'Alba Ca Veja '16	▼▼ 4
● Barbera d'Alba Serra '17	▼ 4
○ Roero Arneis Elisa '18	▼ 3
● Barbaresco Sorì Paitin '07	♀♀♀ 5
● Barbaresco Sorì Paitin '04	♀♀♀ 5
● Barbaresco Sorì Paitin '97	♀♀♀ 5
● Barbaresco Sorì Paitin '95	♀♀♀ 7
● Barbaresco Sorì Paitin V. V. '04	♀♀♀ 7
● Barbaresco Sorì Paitin V. V. '01	♀♀♀ 7
● Barbaresco Sorì Paitin V. V. '99	♀♀♀ 8
● Langhe Paitin '97	♀♀♀ 5

Palladino

p.zza Cappellano, 9
12050 Serralunga d'Alba [CN]
Tel. +39 0173613108
www.palladinovini.com

CELLAR SALES
ANNUAL PRODUCTION 180,000 bottles
HECTARES UNDER VINE 11.00

San Bernardo is a small, southeast-facing cru, and so slightly fresher than Serralunga's celebrated southwest-facing plots. This first gives rise to fewer than 3,000 bottles of a reserve that, in terms of elegance and balance, can stand shoulder-to-shoulder with Ornato and Parafada, where the grapes for their other two Barolos are cultivated. Maurilio Palladino, the true artificer of the winery's success, is accompanied by his granddaughter and her husband, with results that get better by the year. Their superb, classically-styled Barolo Ornato '15 sees licorice and tobacco scents, a hint of rose on a backdrop of fresh fruit. On the palate it shows magnificent structure, with harmony, tannic density and weighty pulp. The commendable, full-bodied Barolo Parafada '15, an austere wine, is just a bit less fresh, with aromas of truffle. Raspberry, rose and licorice feature in the traditionally-styled Barolo San Bernardo Riserva '13, a long, elegant wine worthy of Tre bicchieri.

● Barolo San Bernardo Ris. '13	▼▼▼ 8
● Barolo Ornato '15	▼▼ 6
● Barolo Parafada '15	▼▼ 6
● Barbera d'Alba Sup.	
Bricco delle Olive '16	▼▼ 3
● Barolo	
del Comune di Serraunga d'Alba '15	▼▼ 5
● Nebbiolo d'Alba '17	▼▼ 3
● Barolo San Bernardo Ris. '10	♀♀♀ 6
● Barolo Ornato '13	♀♀ 6
● Barolo Ornato '11	♀♀ 6
● Barolo Ornato '10	♀♀ 6
● Barolo Parafada '14	♀♀ 6
● Barolo Parafada '13	♀♀ 6
● Barolo Parafada '12	♀♀ 6
● Barolo Parafada '11	♀♀ 6
● Barolo Parafada '10	♀♀ 6

Armando Parusso

loc. Bussia, 55
12065 Monforte d'Alba [CN]
Tel. +39 017378257
www.parusso.com

CELLAR SALES
PRE-BOOKED VISITS
ANNUAL PRODUCTION 125,000 bottles
HECTARES UNDER VINE 23.00
SUSTAINABLE WINERY

Marco Parusso's method calls for every variable of each plot to be studied down to the last detail, taking into account soil type, climate, elevation and aspect, so as to obtain outstanding grapes. Their Nebbiolo is then dried for a few days before crushing, without added sulfites, and finally aged in small, French casks. Parusso's award-winning Barolo is always intense and mature, pervasive and assertive, often enriched by aromas of oak. And his Sauvignon Rovella is consistently among the best of its kind nationally. The spicy, exceptionally soft and warm Barolo Mosconi '15 is rich in pulp, devoid of tannic roughness, just a bit lacking in attack but highly enjoyable. The modern Mariondino '15 is marked by a backdrop of oak, with a richness of fruity flesh lending personality. The valid Bussia '15 is a bit marked by oak, though endowed with tannic thrust. Release of their new Sauvignon Rivella has been postponed, but in the meantime try their delicately saline Parusso Brut '14.

● Barolo Mariondino '15	▼▼ 7
● Barolo Mosconi '15	▼▼ 8
● Barolo '15	▼▼ 6
● Barolo Bussia '15	▼▼ 8
● Barolo Bussia Ris. '10	▼▼ 8
○ Parusso Brut M. Cl. '14	▼▼ 6
● Barbera d'Alba Sup. '00	♀♀♀ 5
● Barolo Bussia V. Munie '99	♀♀♀ 8
● Barolo Bussia V. Munie '97	♀♀♀ 8
● Barolo Bussia V. Munie '96	♀♀♀ 8
● Barolo Le Coste Mosconi '03	♀♀♀ 7
● Barolo V. V. in Mariondino Ris. '99	♀♀♀ 8
● Langhe Rosso Bricco Rovella '96	♀♀♀ 8

Agostino Pavia e Figli

LOC. MOLIZZO, 3
14041 AGLIANO TERME [AT]
TEL. +39 0141954125
www.agostinopavia.it

CELLAR SALES
PRE-BOOKED VISITS
ACCOMMODATION
ANNUAL PRODUCTION 75,000 bottles
HECTARES UNDER VINE 9.00

The winery overseen by Giuseppe and Mauro is situated in Bologna, Agliano Terme, an important agricultural center that serves as a territorial bridge between Langhe and Monferrato. Here they cultivate Barbera, mostly, on estate vineyards that partially extend into Montegrosso. Grignolino, Syrah and Dolcetto complete the puzzle, giving rise to an extremely versatile selection marked by continued growth, in recent years, in terms of the consistency of production and gastronomic potential. These impressions were confirmed by our recent tastings, which saw a Grignolino '18 stand out for its exemplary aromas of rose, pepper and rhubarb —on the palate it captivates with its tannic delicacy. Their Barbera reds are also at the top of their game. The Sup. La Marescialla '16 brings together juice and complexity governed by a refreshing acidity. The Blina '17 opts for a more mature aromatic profile of black cherry, nutmeg and licorice, sensations well-supported on a mouthfilling, flavorful palate.

● Barbera d'Asti Blina '17	▼▼ 2*
● Barbera d'Asti Sup. La Marescialla '16	▼▼ 4
● Grignolino d'Asti '18	▼▼ 2*
● Barbera d'Asti Sup. Moliss '16	▼▼ 3
● M.to Rosso Talin '16	▼▼ 3
☉ Piemonte Rosato '18	▼ 2
● Piemonte Rosso i Tre Volti '14	▼ 2
● Barbera d'Asti Bricco Blina '09	♀♀ 2*
● Barbera d'Asti La Marescialla '07	♀♀ 4

★Pecchenino

B.TA VALDIBERTI, 59
12063 DOGLIANI [CN]
TEL. +39 017370686
www.pecchenino.com

CELLAR SALES
PRE-BOOKED VISITS
ACCOMMODATION
ANNUAL PRODUCTION 130,000 bottles
HECTARES UNDER VINE 28.00
SUSTAINABLE WINERY

While they continue to develop their line of Barolos, Attilio and Orlando can boast having helped build a new image for Dogliani. Indeed, when it comes to the wine, they're experts in expressing its elegance and power. Most of the credit goes to their Sirì d'Jermu, which, as Orlando likes to remind you, proves that Dolcetto can do great things if yields are kept low and wood isn't invasive. In addition to hosting their charming cellar, the farmstead also includes a agritourism. This year their Dogliani San Luigi '18 took home a gold, thanks to its vibrant aromas of blackberry and cocoa powder on a background of almond. On the palate it exhibits nice structure, with plenty of flesh and balance, making for a wine joins classical style with finesse and complexity. The Sirì d'Jermu '17 is just a bit more austere, with excellent gustatory balance. Both their 2015 Barolos pursue the best qualities of tradition, with tannic astringency just a bit more pronounced in the San Giuseppe.

● Barolo Bussia '15	▼▼ 7
● Dogliani San Luigi '18	▼▼ 3*
☉ Alta Langa Pas Dosé Psea '15	▼▼ 5
● Barolo San Giuseppe '15	▼▼ 6
● Dogliani Sup. Bricco Botti '16	▼▼ 4
● Dogliani Sup. Sirì d'Jermu '17	▼▼ 4
○ Langhe Chardonnay Maestro '18	▼ 3
● Barolo Le Coste '05	♀♀♀ 8
● Dogliani Bricco Botti '07	♀♀♀ 4
● Dogliani Sirì d'Jermu '09	♀♀♀ 3*
● Dogliani Sirì d'Jermu '06	♀♀♀ 4
● Dogliani Sup. Bricco Botti '10	♀♀♀ 4*
● Dolcetto di Dogliani Sirì d'Jermu '03	♀♀♀ 3
● Dolcetto di Dogliani Sirì d'Jermu '01	♀♀♀ 3*
● Dolcetto di Dogliani Sup. Bricco Botti '04	♀♀♀ 4

Magda Pedrini

Loc. Cà' da' Meo
Via Pratolungo, 163
15066 Gavi [AL]
Tel. +39 0143667923
www.magdapedrini.it

CELLAR SALES
PRE-BOOKED VISITS
ANNUAL PRODUCTION 90,000 bottles
HECTARES UNDER VINE 11.50
SUSTAINABLE WINERY

It was 2006 when Magda Pedrini decided
to purchase Cà Da Meo, an estate in the
hills of Pratolungo. A lovely, scenic facility
and adjacent cellar were among the
investments made by the owner. This last is
equipped with the latest technology, both
when it comes to processing grapes and
aging. Four wines are produced: two
versions of Gavi del Comune di Gavi, a
Barbera and Cabernet Sauvignon
Monferrato Rosso, and a Cortese Metodo
Classico. Cristian Pomo, a careful and
skilled enologist, oversees winemaking.
Both their Gavis made it to our finals,
thanks to two outstanding performances.
The Magda is intense and complex on the
nose, with aromas of white-fleshed fruit
accompanied by vegetal notes tending to
more floral fragrances. On the palate it's
rich and powerful, with a lovely supporting
acidity balancing its very long finish. Ad
Lunam is a great classic, still quite youthful
but already endowed with amazing
nose-palate symmetry.

○ Gavi del Comune di Gavi ad Lunam '18	♟♟ 3*
○ Gavi del Comune di Gavi Magda '18	♟♟ 3*
○ Gavi del Comune di Gavi E' '17	♟♟ 3
○ Gavi del Comune di Gavi E' '16	♟♟ 3*
○ Gavi del Comune di Gavi E' '15	♟♟ 3
○ Gavi del Comune di Gavi La Piacentina '17	♟♟ 3*
○ Gavi del Comune di Gavi La Piacentina '16	♟♟ 3
○ Gavi del Comune di Gavi La Piacentina '15	♟♟ 3

Pelassa

B.go Tucci, 43
12046 Montà [CN]
Tel. +39 0173971312
www.pelassa.com

CELLAR SALES
ANNUAL PRODUCTION 80,000 bottles
HECTARES UNDER VINE 14.00

The Pelassa family avails itself of various
vineyards in Roero, in the northernmost
part of Montà d'Alba, in a fresh and woody
area where they cultivate the area's classic
grapes, from Arneis to Barbera and
Nebbiolo, and in Verduno, which gives rise
to their Barolo. Their selection comprises
wines made with other grapes as well, like
Brachetto, Favorita, Moscato, Cabernet
Sauvignon, Charonnay and Merlot, making
for a selection that expresses both the
territory and cultivar of origin. The wines
submitted for tasting put in a nice
performance, starting with their pleasant
and expansive Roero Antaniolo Riserva '16,
with its notes of red berries and
Mediterranean scrub, its elegant tannins
and its plucky finish. The Roero Arneis
San Vito '18 features notes of tropical
fruit and aromatic herbs, coming through
supple, sapid and energetic on the palate.
The spunky Barbera d'Alba Superiore
San Pancrazio '15 opts for fruity tones,
while the Barolo San Lorenzo '15 proves
full and austere.

● Roero Antaniolo Ris. '16	♟♟ 4
● Barbera d'Alba Sup. San Pancrazio '17	♟♟ 3
● Barolo San Lorenzo '15	♟♟ 6
○ Roero Arneis San Vito '18	♟♟ 3
● Barolo San Lorenzo di Verduno '13	♟♟ 6
● Nebbiolo d'Alba Sot '12	♟♟ 3
● Roero Antaniolo Ris. '15	♟♟ 4
● Roero Antaniolo Ris. '13	♟♟ 4
○ Roero Arneis San Vito '17	♟♟ 3*
○ Roero Arneis San Vito '16	♟♟ 2*

Pelissero

VIA FERRERE, 10
12050 TREISO [CN]
TEL. +39 0173638430
www.pelissero.com

CELLAR SALES
PRE-BOOKED VISITS
ANNUAL PRODUCTION 250,000 bottles
HECTARES UNDER VINE 43.00
SUSTAINABLE WINERY

Produced for the first time in 1960, Vanotu has become one of Barbaresco's most celebrated wines thanks to a stylistic continuity that has won over multitudes of enophiles. In addition to a lovely estate that draws on the Basarin, Marcarini and Tre Stelle crus, the credit goes to the constance with which Giorgio Pelissero has pursued an ideal of modern elegance based on short maceration with skin contact and a confident use of barriques. The estate's large dimensions allow the producer to forge some 16 different wines. This year, though, their Barbaresco Nubiola beat out their Vanotu '16 thanks to focused and elegant fruit followed by a youthful palate, rich in flesh and marked by lovely, docile tannins. Both their Barbera d'Albas put in excellent performances as well. The Tulin '16 is among the best of the vintage, hands down, exhibiting elegance, texture and freshness all at once. The Piani '17 is particularly round and supple, with just a touch of oak standing out.

● Barbaresco Nubiola '16	♥♥ 5
● Barbera d'Alba Piani '17	♥♥ 3*
● Barbera d'Alba Tulin '16	♥♥ 5
● Barbaresco Tulin '16	♥♥ 7
● Barbaresco Vanotu '16	♥♥ 8
● Langhe Nebbiolo '17	♥♥ 3
○ Langhe Favorita Le Nature '18	♥ 2
● Langhe Long Now '16	♥ 5
○ Langhe Riesling Rigadin '18	♥ 3
● Barbaresco Vanotu '08	♥♥♥ 8
● Barbaresco Vanotu '07	♥♥♥ 8
● Barbaresco Vanotu '06	♥♥♥ 8
● Barbaresco Vanotu '01	♥♥♥ 7
● Barbaresco Vanotu '99	♥♥♥ 7
● Barbaresco Vanotu '97	♥♥♥ 6

Pasquale Pelissero

CASCINA CROSA, 2
12052 NEIVE [CN]
TEL. +39 017367376
www.pasqualepelissero.com

CELLAR SALES
PRE-BOOKED VISITS
ANNUAL PRODUCTION 35,000 bottles
HECTARES UNDER VINE 8.00

Pasquale Pelissero was an expert vigneron — he knew Nebbiolo like the back of his hand. What's more, he sold his Barbaresco (produced for the first time in 1971) at a an almost laughably low price, considering the amount of work that went into each bottle. As of 2007 his determined daughter Ornella has been at the helm, renovating the cellar and enlarging the range of wines offered, while availing herself of valid enological guidance. Their vineyards are situated in the small cru of San Giuliano, not far from the more celebrated Albesani and Gallina crus and adjacent to the Crosa farmstead, where the winery is headquartered. Their Barbaresco San Giuliano Bricco '16 does a nice job expressing their traditional style. It's rich but also fresh, potent yet balanced, long and focused. The Cascina Crosa '16, which is a bit shorter and more astringent, is also spicier and endowed with focused sensations of oak. The pleasant Barbera d'Alba Anna '17 is vibrant and racy in its lovely freshness.

● Barbaresco San Giuliano Bricco '16	♥♥ 5
● Barbaresco Cascina Crosa '16	♥♥ 4
● Barbera d'Alba Anna '17	♥♥ 2*
● Langhe Freisa La Ferma '17	♥ 3
● Barbaresco Bricco San Giuliano '14	♥♥ 5
● Barbaresco Bricco San Giuliano '12	♥♥ 5
● Barbaresco Bricco San Giuliano '11	♥♥ 5
● Barbaresco Cascina Crosa '14	♥♥ 4
● Barbaresco Cascina Crosa '13	♥♥ 4
● Barbaresco Ciabot Ris. '13	♥♥ 4
● Barbaresco Ciabot Ris. '12	♥♥ 4
● Barbaresco Ciabot Ris. '10	♥♥ 4
● Barbaresco San Giuliano Bricco '15	♥♥ 5
● Barbaresco San Giuliano Bricco '13	♥♥ 5

Pertinace

LOC. PERTINACE, 2/5
12050 TREISO [CN]
TEL. +39 0173442238
www.pertinace.com

CELLAR SALES
PRE-BOOKED VISITS
ANNUAL PRODUCTION 700,000 bottles
HECTARES UNDER VINE 100.00

Pertinace is a cooperative winery that comprises 17 members, all of whom bring care and commitment to their work of cultivating 90 hectares of vineyards in Treiso. Founded by Mario Barbero in 1973, Petinace operates on high qualitative levels while maintaining advantageous prices — and their products can be found on major global markets. Nebbiolo, the primary grape cultivated, is accompanied by Dolcetto, Barbera, Chardonnay and Moscato, making for overall production volumes that surpass 600,000 bottles annually. Their Barbaresco Marcarini '16 landed a place in our final round. On the nose it offers up vibrant spices accompanied by meaty and mature red fruit. On the palate it exhibits a harmonious, delicate grip, closing long and with vitality. Their Barbaresco Castellizzano and Nervo, both 2016s, are more austere, leaving excellent margins for growth in the bottle. The highly enjoyable, juicy and balanced Dolcetto d'Alba '18 is true to type in its aromas of blackberry and almond.

● Barbaresco Marcarini '16	▼▼	5
● Barbaresco '16	▼▼	5
● Barbaresco Castellizzano '16	▼▼	5
● Barbaresco Nervo '16	▼▼	5
● Barbera d'Alba '17	▼▼	3
○ Dolcetto d'Alba '18	▼▼	3
● Langhe Nebbiolo '17	▼	4
● Barbaresco '15	♈♈	5
● Barbaresco '14	♈♈	5
● Barbaresco Castellizzano '15	♈♈	5
● Barbaresco Castellizzano '14	♈♈	5
● Barbaresco Castellizzano '12	♈♈	5
● Barbaresco Marcarini '15	♈♈	5
● Barbaresco Marcarini '14	♈♈	5
● Barbaresco Marcarini '13	♈♈	5
● Barbaresco Nervo '15	♈♈	5
● Dolcetto d'Alba '17	♈♈	3

Pescaja

VIA SAN MATTEO, 59
14010 CISTERNA D'ASTI [AT]
TEL. +39 0141979711
www.pescaja.com

PRE-BOOKED VISITS
ANNUAL PRODUCTION 200,000 bottles
HECTARES UNDER VINE 23.50

Giuseppe Guido's winery is based around two properties. One, which features sandy soils, was purchased in 1990 in Cisterna d'Asti, in the Roero and Terre Alfieri appellations. The other, acquired in 1998 in Nizza Monferrato, where the soil is more calcareous, lies in the Barbera d'Asti and Nizza appellations. They cultivate Arneis, Barbera, Nebbiolo, Bonarda and Chardonnay, making for modern wines of notable technical precision. Pescaja submitted a lovely selection of Arneis, starting with their Monferrato Bianco Solo Luna '17, redolent of peach, apricot and melon, bringing together richness and freshness on the palate. Their Roero Arneis '18 sees notes of aniseed anticipate a long, generous palate, while the Terre Alfieri Arneis Solei '18 plays more on acidity and freshness, all accompanied by hints of aromatic herbs. In terms of their Nizza Monferrato wines, the Soliter '18 is a fresh, succulent Barbera d'Asti, while their Nizza Solneri '16 proves gutsy, with notable structure.

○ Monferrato Bianco Solo Luna '17	▼▼	5
● Barbera d'Asti Soliter '18	▼▼	2*
● Monferrato Rosso Solis '16	▼▼	3
● Nizza Solneri '16	▼▼	4
⊙ Piemonte Rosato Le Fleury '18	▼▼	2*
○ Roero Arneis '18	▼▼	2*
○ Terre Alfieri Arneis Solei '18	▼▼	2*
● Terre Alfieri Nebbiolo Tuké '16	▼	3
● Barbera d'Asti Soliter '17	♈♈	2*
● Barbera d'Asti Soliter '16	♈♈	2*
● Nizza Solneri '15	♈♈	4
○ Roero Arneis '17	♈♈	2*
○ Terre Alfieri Arneis Sololuce '17	♈♈	2*

Le Piane

P.zza Matteotti, 1
28010 Boca [NO]
Tel. +39 3483354185
www.bocapiane.com

CELLAR SALES
PRE-BOOKED VISITS
ANNUAL PRODUCTION 45,000 bottles
HECTARES UNDER VINE 8.00
SUSTAINABLE WINERY

The old maggiorina system was re-elaborated by architect A. Antonelli, Ghemme native and designer of Turin's Mole, in the mid-19th century. The system only allowed for manual work, so it was almost entirely abandoned, and called for the presence of different grapes (primarily Nebbiolo, Croatina and Vespolina), as well as a pruning technique that allows the vines to bear fruit for more than 100 years. The great Christopf Künzli, who dedicated one of his wines to the method, is a firm supporter and credits it for a part of his extraordinary wines' success. The 2016 Mimmo, an homage to a former collaborator, is magnificent. The blend of grapes from younger vineyards, together with oak-aging, makes for a dynamic, vibrant wine with nice acidity, but also rich and long, offering up long notes of quinine and gentian on a delicate iodine background. Fresh fruit, rust and mint fuse in a splendid aromatic unison in their Boca '15, particularly commendable for its sumptuous, harmonious palate.

● Boca '15	♟♟♟ 8
● Mimmo '16	♟♟ 5
● La Maggiorina '18	♟♟ 3
● Boca '12	♟♟♟ 8
● Boca '11	♟♟♟ 8
● Boca '10	♟♟♟ 7
● Boca '08	♟♟♟ 7

Pico Maccario

via Cordara, 87
14046 Mombaruzzo [AT]
Tel. +39 0141774522
www.picomaccario.com

CELLAR SALES
PRE-BOOKED VISITS
ANNUAL PRODUCTION 650,000 bottles
HECTARES UNDER VINE 100.00

The winery founded in the late 1990s by ambitious brothers Pico and Vitaliano Maccario avails itself of a virtually contiguous 70-hectare estate. Here in Mombaruzzo, in the Nizza winemaking zone, we find a proper 'grand cru' for Barbera. Not coincidentally, it's their most cultivated grape (and gives rise to some four different wines). Wines made with Chardonnay, Sauvignon, Favorita, Freisa, Merlot and Cabernet grapes round out their selection. Among the many interesting options available, once again their Barbera-based reds stand out, starting with their Barbera Lavignone '18. It's contoured by fresh aromas of red berry and cooking spices, with lovely, fruity sweetness and suppleness on the palate. It's this edition's Best Value for the Money. We find the same expressive profile in their smooth Nizza Tre Roveri '17, though oak plays a greater role here, and in their excellent Barbera Superiore Epico '17.

● Barbera d'Asti Lavignone '18	♟♟♟ 3*
● Nizza Tre Roveri '17	♟♟ 4
● Barbera d'Asti Sup. Epico '17	♟♟ 6
● Barbera d'Asti Villa della Rosa '18	♟♟ 2*
○ M.to Bianco Vita '18	♟ 5
◉ Piemonte Rosato Lavignone '18	♟ 3
● Barbera d'Asti Lavignone '17	♟♟♟ 3*
● Barbera d'Asti Sup. Epico '15	♟♟♟ 5
● Barbera d'Asti Lavignone '16	♟♟ 3
● Barbera d'Asti Lavignone '15	♟♟ 3
● Barbera d'Asti Sup. Epico '16	♟♟ 5
● Barbera d'Asti Sup. Tre Roveri '16	♟♟ 4
● Barbera d'Asti Sup. Tre Roveri '15	♟♟ 4
● Barbera d'Asti Sup. Tre Roveri '14	♟♟ 4
● Barbera d'Asti Villa della Rosa '17	♟♟ 2*
● Barbera d'Asti Villa della Rosa '16	♟♟ 2*

★Pio Cesare

via Cesare Balbo, 6
12051 Alba [CN]
Tel. +39 0173440386
www.piocesare.it

ANNUAL PRODUCTION 420,000 bottles
HECTARES UNDER VINE 70.00

An underground cellar surrounded by 2000-year-old Roman walls, vineyards in magnificent crus, historical roots going back to 1881 — and, most importantly, the constant pursuit of the highest quality. These are the key features of a winery managed by the tireless Pio Boffa (who's supported by his grandson). It's another case where the pursuit of a classical style has gradually led to resizing the use of barriques, somewhat invasive in the 1990s, and large barrels, with absolutely notable results. Their so-called 'entry-level' wines are of such quality that, in many ways, they can be compared to their premium crus. The Bricco features commendable elegance and a palate as rich as it is harmonious. The fresh Barbaresco '15 exhibits equal complexity and power. It's the same story when it comes to Barolo. The basic version is, at the moment, more supple and fruity than those from the celebrated Ornato and Mosconi vineyards. Their Piodilei '16 continues to be one of Italy's best Chardonnays.

● Barbaresco '15	ΨΨ 8
● Barbaresco Il Bricco '15	ΨΨ 8
● Barolo '15	ΨΨ 8
● Barolo Ornato '15	ΨΨ 8
○ Langhe Chardonnay Piodilei '16	ΨΨ 6
● Barbera d'Alba V. Mosconi Fides '17	ΨΨ 5
● Barolo Mosconi '15	ΨΨ 8
● Barbaresco Il Bricco '97	ΨΨΨ 8
● Barolo Ornato '13	ΨΨΨ 8
● Barolo Ornato '12	ΨΨΨ 8
● Barolo Ornato '11	ΨΨΨ 8
● Barolo Ornato '10	ΨΨΨ 8
● Barolo Ornato '09	ΨΨΨ 8
● Barolo Ornato '08	ΨΨΨ 8
● Barolo Ornato '06	ΨΨΨ 8
● Barolo Ornato '05	ΨΨΨ 8

Luigi Pira

via XX Settembre, 9
12050 Serralunga d'Alba [CN]
Tel. +39 0173613106
pira.luigi@alice.it

CELLAR SALES
PRE-BOOKED VISITS
ANNUAL PRODUCTION 50,000 bottles
HECTARES UNDER VINE 12.00

The Pira family (actives in Langa since the 1950s) draw on a viticultural patrimony of estate vineyards concentrated primarily on the hills of Serralunga d'Alba. Luigi, the winery's founder, began by selling grapes and bulk wine. It was a business that, obviously, led him towards producing under his own brand. Today it's Gianpaolo, Romolo and Claudio who carefully oversee the estate's dozen hectares, which give rise to a 'comunale' Barolo and three cru wines: Margheria, Marenca and Vigna Rionda. Harmony, finesse and complexity figure centrally in their Barolo Margheria '15, a wine of sound structure that's already pleasantly drinkable. The valid VIgnarionda '15 is a bit astringent, less aromatically focused but endowed with excellent length. The mouthfilling Barolo del comune di Serralunga d'Alba '15 moves on a similar track, while their weighty Barolo Marenca '15 proves youthful, just tannic and fruity. Finally, kudos to their elegant and pleasant Barbera d'Alba Superiore '17.

● Barolo Marenca '15	ΨΨ 7
● Barolo Margheria '15	ΨΨ 6
● Barbera d'Alba Sup. '17	ΨΨ 3
● Barolo del Comune di Serralunga d'Alba '15	ΨΨ 5
● Barolo Vignarionda '15	ΨΨ 8
● Langhe Nebbiolo '17	ΨΨ 3
● Barolo Marenca '11	ΨΨΨ 7
● Barolo Marenca '09	ΨΨΨ 7
● Barolo Marenca '08	ΨΨΨ 7
● Barolo V. Marenca '01	ΨΨΨ 7
● Barolo V. Marenca '97	ΨΨΨ 8
● Barolo V. Rionda '06	ΨΨΨ 8
● Barolo V. Rionda '04	ΨΨΨ 8
● Barolo V. Rionda '00	ΨΨΨ 8
● Barolo Vignarionda '12	ΨΨΨ 8

E. Pira & Figli

VIA VITTORIO VENETO, 1
12060 BAROLO [CN]
TEL. +39 017356247
www.pira-chiaraboschis.com

CELLAR SALES
PRE-BOOKED VISITS
ANNUAL PRODUCTION 35,000 bottles
HECTARES UNDER VINE 8.50
VITICULTURE METHOD Certified Organic

For 30 years Chiara Boschis has been active in her small gem of a winery. All along she's shown faith in the future, made possible in part thanks to her excellent vineyards and her enviable willpower. Success came early, but she never let herself get carried away, limiting expansion to the purchase of almost a hectare in Monforte d'Alba, the lovely Mosconi cru. The style of her Barolos is thoroughly modern, always elegant and rich in substance. with the occasional hint of French barriques emerging in the early years of aging. The Barolo Cannubi '15 is a model of harmony. Even if it doesn't stand out for its power, aromatically it brings together fruit and spices masterfully, only to come through balanced, lively on the palate, with excellent, focused persistence. The Mosconi '15 exhibits a rather different profile, with oak tending to trap in Nebbiolo's classic aromas, even if the final result is one of sophisticated elegance. The Via Nuova '15 is just a bit more tannic and youthful.

● Barolo Cannubi '15	¥¥ 8
● Barolo Mosconi '15	¥¥ 8
● Barbera d'Alba Sup. '17	¥¥ 5
● Barolo Via Nuova '15	¥¥ 8
● Langhe Nebbiolo '17	¥ 6
● Barolo '94	¥¥¥ 7
● Barolo Cannubi '11	¥¥¥ 8
● Barolo Cannubi '10	¥¥¥ 8
● Barolo Cannubi '06	¥¥¥ 8
● Barolo Cannubi '05	¥¥¥ 8
● Barolo Cannubi '00	¥¥¥ 8
● Barolo Cannubi '97	¥¥¥ 8
● Barolo Cannubi '96	¥¥¥ 8
● Barolo Ris. '90	¥¥¥ 8

Guido Platinetti

VIA ROMA, 60
28074 GHEMME [NO]
TEL. +39 3389945783
www.platinettivini.com

CELLAR SALES
PRE-BOOKED VISITS
ANNUAL PRODUCTION 15,000 bottles
HECTARES UNDER VINE 5.50

This historic Ghemme winery, aptly managed by brothers Stefano and Andrea, has a long viticultural tradition behind it. Their five hectares of well-maintained vineyards are part of that tradition, especially Ronco al Maso, a southwest-facing hill rich in minerals. Nebbiolo takes center stage, though they also cultivate Barbera and Vespolina. Their wines exhibit great charm, and are available at attractive prices, making for a traditionally-styled selection that pays homage to the peculiarities of the DOCG zone. It's Platinetti's turn to take home Tre Bicchieri. It comes from an enchanting Ghemme Vigna Ronco al Maso '15, which offers up a variety of flavors and uncommon complexity. It's delicate, rich and potent, with superb gustatory cleanness, deep in its echoes of roots and licorice, extremely juicy in its fruit, closing long and rigorous. In short, it has the rhythm of a great wine. Hints of rhubarb and raspberry introduce the Nebbiolo '17, only to reemerge on a sapid, tasty palate.

● Ghemme V. Ronco al Maso '15	¥¥¥ 4*
● Colline Novaresi Nebbiolo '17	¥¥ 3
● Colline Novaresi Rosso Guido '18	¥¥ 3
● Colline Novaresi Vespolina '18	¥¥ 3
● Colline Novaresi Barbera Pieleo '17	¥ 3
● Colline Novaresi Nebbiolo '16	¥¥ 3
● Colline Novaresi Nebbiolo '14	¥¥ 3
● Colline Novaresi Vespolina '17	¥¥ 3
● Colline Novaresi Vespolina '16	¥¥ 2*
● Colline Novaresi Vespolina '14	¥¥ 2*
● Ghemme V. Ronco al Maso '13	¥¥ 4
● Ghemme V. Ronco Maso '12	¥¥ 4
● Ghemme V. Ronco Maso '10	¥¥ 4

Marco Porello

c.so Alba, 71
12043 Canale [CN]
Tel. +39 0173979324
www.porellovini.it

CELLAR SALES
PRE-BOOKED VISITS
ANNUAL PRODUCTION 130,000 bottles
HECTARES UNDER VINE 15.00

The Porello family's winery avails itself of vineyards in two Roero municipalities. In Vezza d'Alba they cultivate Arneis, Favorita and Nebbiolo on sandy, mineral-rich terrain. In Canale they grow Barbera, Brachetto and Nebbiolo on medium-density, calcareous-clay soil. The producer is divided into two parts: their headquarters, winemaking and bottling cavities are in Canale, while their aging cellar is situated adjacent to Guarene Castle. The Roero Torretta '17 is their flagship wine. It's redolent of fresh, floral fragrances and hints of red berry fruits, sensations accompanied by a tannic but juicy palate endowed with nice length. Other noteworthy performers include their Roero Arneis '18, with its mineral tones and sensations of white-fleshed fruit, the more delicate and compex Roero Arneis Camestrì '18, with its notable acidity, and the Roero San Michele Riserva '15, which is characterized by close-woven tannins and nice flesh adorned with toasty hints and notes of quinine.

● Roero Torretta '16	♥♥ 4
○ Roero Arneis '18	♥♥ 2*
○ Roero Arneis Camestri '18	♥♥ 3
○ Roero San Michele Ris. '15	♥♥ 3
● Barbera d'Alba Mommiano '18	♥ 2
● Langhe Nebbiolo '17	♥ 3
● Roero Torretta '06	♥♥♥ 3*
● Roero Torretta '04	♥♥♥ 3*
● Barbera d'Alba Filatura '15	♥♥ 4
○ Roero Arneis '17	♥♥ 2*
○ Roero Arneis Camestri '17	♥♥ 3*
● Roero Torretta '15	♥♥ 4
● Roero Torretta '14	♥♥ 4
● Roero Torretta '13	♥♥ 3*

Guido Porro

via Alba, 1
12050 Serralunga d'Alba [CN]
Tel. +39 0173613306
www.guidoporro.com

CELLAR SALES
PRE-BOOKED VISITS
ACCOMMODATION
ANNUAL PRODUCTION 35,000 bottles
HECTARES UNDER VINE 8.00

Guido Porro's work at his Serralunga d'Alba cellar is proceeding full speed ahead. Surrounded by a virtually contiguous, single set of vineyards in the heart of Lazzarito (their historic estate cru), here he makes sapid, balsamic wines. In all, four Barolos are proposed, the most recent of which is their prestigious Vigna Ruioda, the result of plots once owned by Tommaso Canale. Vinification is carried out in steel and concrete, followed by maturation in Slavonian barrels. Their Barolo Vigna Rionda '15 handily took home Tre Bicchieri, proving highly elegant in its aromatic profile, redolent of raspberries and wild strawberries, aniseed and pepper. On the palate it unfolds gradually, delicate and subtle, with excellent acidic grip, making for an extremely long drink. The rich and elegant Barolo Vigna Santa Caterina '15 is also harmonious in its characteristic fragrances of licorice and rose. We'll be closely following the evolution of their mature Laizzarasco and softer Gianetto '15.

● Barolo Vigna Rionda '15	♥♥♥ 8
● Barolo V. Lazzairasco '15	♥♥ 5
● Barolo V. Santa Caterina '15	♥♥ 5
● Barolo Gianetto '15	♥♥ 5
● Barbera d'Alba V. Santa Caterina '18	♥ 3
● Barolo V. Lazzairasco '13	♥♥♥ 5
● Barolo V. Lazzairasco '12	♥♥♥ 5
● Barolo V. Lazzairasco '11	♥♥♥ 5
● Barolo V. Lazzairasco '09	♥♥♥ 5
● Barolo V. Lazzairasco '07	♥♥♥ 5
● Barolo Gianetto '13	♥♥ 5
● Barolo Gianetto '11	♥♥ 5
● Barolo V. Lazzairasco '14	♥♥ 5
● Barolo V. Santa Caterina '12	♥♥ 5
● Barolo V. Santa Caterina '11	♥♥ 5
● Barolo V. Santa Caterina '10	♥♥ 5
● Barolo Vigna Rionda '14	♥♥ 8

Post dal Vin
Terre del Barbera

FRAZ. POSSAVINA
VIA SALIE, 19
14030 ROCCHETTA TANARO [AT]
TEL. +39 0141644143
www.postdalvin.it

CELLAR SALES
PRE-BOOKED VISITS
ANNUAL PRODUCTION 80,000 bottles
HECTARES UNDER VINE 100.00

Some 200 grower members make Post dal Vina, whose vineyards are situated primarily in the municipalities of Rocchetta Tanaro, Cortiglione and Masio, one of the most notable cooperative producers in Asti (and beyond). Founded in the late 1950s, the winery has two locations. Their main facility is equipped with the latest technology for winemaking and storage, while the other site features a retail point where their bottles and bulk wine are sold. Their Barbera reds have always been a cornerstone of their selection, and this year saw them on center stage. We're introduced to their supple and tasty Maricca '18 via a crescendo of complexity, despite its fermentative profile, before moving on to their Castagnassa '17, a wine that's slightly obscured on the nose but endowed with gustatory force and contrasts, only to close with the Rebarba '16, whose focused aromas of cherry and rain-soaked earth anticipate a broad, well-sustained palate.

● Barbera d'Asti Maricca '18	♈♈ 2*
● Barbera d'Asti Rebarba '16	♈♈ 2*
● Barbera d'Asti Sup. Castagnassa '17	♈♈ 3
● Barbera d'Asti '17	♈♈ 1*
● Barbera d'Asti Maricca '17	♈♈ 2*
● Barbera d'Asti Sup. Briccofiore '16	♈♈ 2*
● Barbera d'Asti Sup. BriccoFiore '11	♈♈ 2*
● Barbera d'Asti Sup. Castagnassa '16	♈♈ 3

La Prevostura

VIA CASCINA PREVOSTURA, 1
13853 LESSONA [BI]
TEL. +39 0158853188
www.laprevostura.it

CELLAR SALES
PRE-BOOKED VISITS
RESTAURANT SERVICE
ANNUAL PRODUCTION 15,000 bottles
HECTARES UNDER VINE 5.50

Both Lessona and Bramaterra risked becoming 'niche' wines, emblems of a great but long-gone past that goes all the way back to the ancient Romans' appreciation for the areas' wines. It's thanks to a small number of producers, including Marco and Davide Bellini's Prevostura, that the situation is improving, with once abandoned vineyards now revived along with a strong commitment to quality. Their Lessona is made entirely with Nebbiolo, while the Bramaterra sees small quantities of Robusta Croatina and spicy Vespolina. The latest version of their Bramaterra was still aging at the time of our tastings, so we focused on a superb 2015 Lessona. Its key qualities derive from its complexity and harmony. Aromatically it spans sensations of small red berries, medicinal herbs and pennyroyal mint, while on the palate it comes through rich, long and elegant, full of fruity flesh but in no way aggressive. The rest of their selection proved sound, without particular standouts.

● Lessona '15	♈♈ 5
● Rosso Muntacc	♈♈ 4
● Coste della Sesia Rosso Garsun '17	♈ 3
⊙ Piemonte Rosato Corinna '18	♈ 3
● Lessona '12	♈♈♈ 5
● Bramaterra '12	♈♈ 5
● Coste della Sesia Rosso Garsun '16	♈♈ 3
● Coste della Sesia Rosso Muntacc '15	♈♈ 4
● Coste della Sesia Rosso Muntacc '13	♈♈ 3*
● Coste della Sesia Rosso Muntacc '12	♈♈ 3*
● Lessona '14	♈♈ 5
● Lessona '13	♈♈ 5

Prinsi

VIA GAIA, 5
12052 NEIVE [CN]
TEL. +39 017367192
www.prinsi.it

CELLAR SALES
PRE-BOOKED VISITS
ANNUAL PRODUCTION 60,000 bottles
HECTARES UNDER VINE 14.50

Daniele Lequio, who's been with the winery since 1999, knows his various vineyards well. He also knows how to bring out their personalities in his Barbaresco. The Fausoni gives rise to assertive and tannic grapes that need time to find the right balance — and so it's used for their reserve. The Gaia Principe is less potent, but always aromatically elegant. Gallina, which derives from a larger cru in Neive, is of rare harmony and a bewitching roundness. This trio is accompanied by Langa's other classics, Nebbiolo, Arneis, Barbera and Dolcetto d'Alba, with small concessions for international grapes when it comes to their whites (Chardonnay and Sauvignon). Their 2019 releases prove solid, overall. The Barbaresco Gaia Principe '16 is marked by pronounced oakiness and notable fruitiness. The Gallina '16 moves on a similar track, with spicy aromas in evidence. Vegetal notes join with elegant oak in the rich and warm Barbera d'Alba Superiore Il Bosco '17.

● Barbaresco Gaia Principe '16	🍷🍷 5
● Barbaresco Gallina '16	🍷🍷 5
● Barbera d'Alba Sup. Il Bosco '17	🍷🍷 3
○ Langhe Arneis Il Nespolo '18	🍷 3
● Barbaresco Fausoni Ris. '11	🍷🍷 5
● Barbaresco Gaia Principe '15	🍷🍷 5
● Barbaresco Gaia Principe '14	🍷🍷 5
● Barbaresco Gaia Principe '13	🍷🍷 5
● Barbaresco Gallina '15	🍷🍷 5
● Barbaresco Gallina '14	🍷🍷 5
● Barbaresco Gallina '13	🍷🍷 5
● Barbera d'Alba Sup. Il Bosco '16	🍷🍷 3
○ Camp'd Pietru '16	🍷🍷 4

★Produttori del Barbaresco

VIA TORINO, 54
12050 BARBARESCO [CN]
TEL. +39 0173635139
www.produttoridelbarbaresco.com

CELLAR SALES
PRE-BOOKED VISITS
ACCOMMODATION
ANNUAL PRODUCTION 540,000 bottles
HECTARES UNDER VINE 105.00

We'll start with the numbers: 54 members work 105 hectares of Nebbiolo, giving rise to 540,000 bottles across 3 typologies. There's their vintage Barbaresco (240,000 bottles), 9 Barbaresco reserves (6,000-18,000 each), and Langhe Nebbiolo (140,000). The decision not to focus on other cultivars showed foresight, as it allowed the winery to become an international benchmark. A cooler 2014 was actually a valid year in Barbaresco, thanks to a temperature rebound in August and September, which allowed them to make all their reserves. As demonstrated by our latest round of tastings, in which a number of wines scored quite positively. The Muncagota leads the way, aptly expressing the vintage through aromas of dried herbs, spices and licorice, combined with greener, fresh vegetal notes. On the palate it exhibits excellent balance, coming through well-proportioned and harmonious. The Pora offers commendable flavor and fruit, proving rich, but also supple and without heaviness.

● Barbaresco Asili Ris. '14	🍷🍷 6
● Barbaresco Montestefano Ris. '14	🍷🍷 6
● Barbaresco Muncagota Ris. '14	🍷🍷 6
● Barbaresco Pora Ris. '14	🍷🍷 6
● Barbaresco Rio Sordo Ris. '14	🍷🍷 6
● Barbaresco '16	🍷🍷 5
● Barbaresco Montefico Ris. '14	🍷🍷 6
● Barbaresco Ovello Ris. '14	🍷🍷 6
● Barbaresco Paje' Ris. '14	🍷🍷 6
● Barbaresco Rabaja' Ris. '14	🍷🍷 6
● Barbaresco Asili Ris. '13	🍷🍷🍷 6
● Barbaresco Ovello Ris. '09	🍷🍷🍷 6

Cantina Produttori del Gavi

VIA CAVALIERI DI VITTORIO VENETO, 45
15066 GAVI [AL]
TEL. +39 0143642786
www.cantinaproduttoridelgavi.it

CELLAR SALES
PRE-BOOKED VISITS
ANNUAL PRODUCTION 300,000 bottles
HECTARES UNDER VINE 220.00

Cantina Produttori del Gavi's vineyards
span 220 hectares across 11 municipalities
in the area, making for a robust selection
that comprises all the best districts. The
vineyards' respective pedoclimatic
characteristics are wholly considered
thanks to the rigorous organization of their
95 grower members. Together they give
rise to a number of wines, with a nice line
of Corteses, including a Metodo Classico
sparkler. There are also three reds made
with native cultivars, specifically Barbera
and Dolcetto. The selection proposed points
up a particularly good vintage for Gavi.
Three of them earned a place in our finals,
all with notable aromatic-gustatory
qualities. They're joined by the extreme
aromatic complexity, as well as pronounced
acidity, which ably balances their richness
of their fruity pulp. We'll expect further
surprises over time. The rest of their
selection also proves well-made.

○ Gavi del Comune di Gavi Bio '18	🍷🍷 3*
○ Gavi del Comune di Gavi Mille951 '18	🍷🍷 3*
○ Gavi Maddalena '18	🍷🍷 2*
○ Gavi del Comune di Gavi GG '17	🍷🍷 3
○ Gavi del Comune di Gavi Primi Grappoli '18	🍷🍷 2*
○ Gavi G '17	🍷🍷 3
○ Gavi Il Forte '18	🍷🍷 2*
○ Gavi del Comune di Gavi Mille951 '17	🍷🍷 3*
○ Gavi G '15	🍷🍷 3*
○ Gavi Il Forte '17	🍷🍷 2*

★Prunotto

C.SO BAROLO, 14
12051 ALBA [CN]
TEL. +39 0173280017
www.prunotto.it

CELLAR SALES
PRE-BOOKED VISITS
ACCOMMODATION
ANNUAL PRODUCTION 800,000 bottles
HECTARES UNDER VINE 55.00

Founded in the early-20th century, this
important producer was purchased by
Marchesi Antinori thirty years ago. Since
then, they've steadily and strategically
enlarged the estate, thus reducing their
reliance on sourced grapes. The results can
be detected both in the vineyards, from
Monforte d'Alba to Agli Terme, Monteu
Roero and Barbaresco, and in the
extraordinary reliability of their wines
across the board (as testified to by the
below scorings). All of their extensive
list of wines are worth trying, though we
suggest a few less obvious options: the
tar-scented, mouthfilling and highly
pleasant Barolo '15, the exquisite and
alluring Monferrato Mompertone '16
(primarily Barbera and Syrah), the Nebbiolo
Occhetti, which is made with grapes
cultivated in one of Roero's most celebrated
crus, and finally their Barbaresco '16, an
entry-level wine endowed with elegant
spices and round, fruity pulp on the palate.

● Barbaresco '16	🍷🍷 4
● Barbaresco Bric Turot '16	🍷🍷 5
● Barbera d'Alba '18	🍷🍷 2*
● Barbera d'Alba Pian Romualdo '17	🍷🍷 3
● Barolo '15	🍷🍷 5
● Barolo Bussia '15	🍷🍷 8
● Barolo Bussia V. Colonnello Ris. '13	🍷🍷 8
● Dolcetto d'Alba Mosesco '17	🍷🍷 3
● Langhe Nebbiolo Occhetti '17	🍷🍷 3
● M.to Mompertone '16	🍷🍷 2*
● Nizza Costamiole Ris. '16	🍷🍷 4
○ Roero Arneis '18	🍷🍷 2*
● Barbera d'Asti Fiulot '18	🍷 2
● Dolcetto d'Alba '18	🍷 2
● Barolo Bussia '01	🍷🍷🍷 8
● Barolo Bussia '99	🍷🍷🍷 8

La Raia

S.DA MONTEROTONDO, 79
15067 NOVI LIGURE [AL]
TEL. +39 0143743685
www.la-raia.it

CELLAR SALES
PRE-BOOKED VISITS
ACCOMMODATION
ANNUAL PRODUCTION 150,000 bottles
HECTARES UNDER VINE 50.00
VITICULTURE METHOD Certified Biodynamic
SUSTAINABLE WINERY

Azienda di Novi Ligure avails itself of a
sizable estate, 180 hectares subdivided
into pastures, farmland, woods and
vineyards. Their production approach
centers on principles of biodynamic
agriculture, certified by Demeter in 2007.
When it comes to their wines, 3 of the 5
total are Corteses: a base level, theRiserva
Vigna della Madonnina and the Pisé. All are
fermented in steel, which is also used for
aging (6 months for the Riserva and 20 for
the Pisé). There are also 2 Barberas, a base
level and their Iq Largé, the latter of which
is aged in wood barrels. The Vigna della
Madonnina '17 delivered in our final
tastings with a highly elegant version.
Aromas of white-fleshed fruit and notes of
Alpine flowers converge on a fresh,
sophisticated palate, with a lovely sapid
phase and a lingering finish. The Gavi '18
is balanced and fresh, while the intense
Piemonte Barbera Largè sees somewhat
pronounced wood and the Barbera '18
proves delicate and subtle.

○ Gavi V. della Madonnina Ris. '17	♀♀ 3*
○ Gavi '18	♀♀ 3
● Piemonte Barbera '18	♀♀ 3
● Piemonte Barbera Largé '15	♀♀ 4
○ Gavi V. della Madonnina Ris. '16	♀♀♀ 3*
○ Gavi '17	♀♀ 3
○ Gavi '16	♀♀ 3*
○ Gavi Pisè '15	♀♀ 5
○ Gavi Ris. '15	♀♀ 3*

Renato Ratti

FRAZ. ANNUNZIATA, 7
12064 LA MORRA [CN]
TEL. +39 017350185
www.renatoratti.com

CELLAR SALES
PRE-BOOKED VISITS
ACCOMMODATION
ANNUAL PRODUCTION 350,000 bottles
HECTARES UNDER VINE 35.00

Founded 50 years ago by the great Renato
Ratti, this popular winery has seen some
changes of late. 2017 saw the new Langhe
Chardonnay Brigata, while the celebrated
Ochetti passes from Nebbiolo d'Alba to
Langhe Nebbiolo, with a significant volume
of about 90,000 bottles/year. Finally, their
Dolcetto d'Alba, originally made with
grapes from Mango only, now draws on a
parcel in Dogliani and is designated Langhe
Dolcetto. But their selection's core still lies
with their prized Barolo, made with grapes
from the Rocche dell'Annunziata, Conca
and Marcenasco crus. Their 2015 Barolos
prove excellent. The Rocche dell'Annunziata
unfolds on a gentle bed of oak, with scents
of flowers and red berries giving way to a
striking palate, rich and harmonious. The
delicious, soft Marcenasco exhibits even
more fruit and an initial accent of licorice,
while the Conca features added vegetal
notes, even truffle, together with dark hints
of quinine, and a tannic weave that's still
quite pronounced.

● Barolo Conca '15	♀♀ 8
● Barolo Marcenasco '15	♀♀ 6
● Barolo Rocche dell'Annunziata '15	♀♀ 8
● Barbera d'Alba Battaglione '18	♀♀ 3
● M.to Rosso Villa Pattono '16	♀♀ 5
○ Piemonte Sauvignon I Cedri '18	♀♀ 2*
○ Langhe Chardonnay Brigata '18	♀ 3
● Langhe Nebbiolo Ochetti '18	♀ 4
● Barolo Rocche '06	♀♀♀ 8
● Barolo Rocche Marcenasco '84	♀♀♀ 6
● Barolo Rocche Marcenasco '83	♀♀♀ 6
● Barolo Conca '14	♀♀ 8
● Barolo Marcenasco '14	♀♀ 6
● Barolo Rocche dell'Annunziata '14	♀♀ 8
● Barolo Rocche dell'Annunziata '13	♀♀ 8
● Langhe Nebbiolo Ochetti '16	♀♀ 4

Réva

LOC. SAN SEBASTIANO, 68
12065 MONFORTE D'ALBA [CN]
TEL. +39 0173789269
www.revamonforte.it

CELLAR SALES
PRE-BOOKED VISITS
ACCOMMODATION AND RESTAURANT SERVICE
ANNUAL PRODUCTION 35,000 bottles
HECTARES UNDER VINE 8.00
SUSTAINABLE WINERY

At just 8 years from its founding, 'The revolution never sleeps' might be a good slogan for Miroslav Lekes's winery. They've started with the building of a new winemaking facility, which will let them enlarge reception spaces for tourism at their current location, while continuing to expand their selection. New additions include their fresh Grey, a Langhe Bianco made with Sauvignon Bianco and Grigio that was recently the focus of major presentation events. But the core of their production still centers on reds, foremost Barolo — and enologist Gian Luca Colombo is an excellent interpreter, as demonstrated by their Ravera '15, a wine endowed with notable complexity amidst aromas of strawberry, rose and quinine. On the palate it's rich in alcohol and flesh, made assertive by nice tannic presence. A background of dried herbs and red fruit introduce their Barolo '15, a medium-structured wine that's still a bit austere on the palate. The floral Nebbiolo d'Alba '17 is supple and fresh, while the Grey '18 is clean, with lovely hints of tomato leaves.

● Barolo Ravera '15	♥♥ 7
● Barolo '15	♥♥ 5
○ Langhe Bianco Grey '18	♥♥ 3
● Nebbiolo d'Alba '17	♥♥ 3
● Dolcetto d'Alba '18	♥ 2
● Barbera d'Alba Sup. '15	♀♀ 3
● Barolo '14	♀♀ 5
● Barolo '13	♀♀ 5
● Barolo '12	♀♀ 5
● Barolo Ravera '13	♀♀ 7
● Barolo Ravera '12	♀♀ 7
○ Langhe Bianco Grey '17	♀♀ 3
● Nebbiolo d'Alba '16	♀♀ 3*
● Nebbiolo d'Alba '15	♀♀ 3

Carlo & Figli Revello

FRAZ. SANTA MARIA
12064 LA MORRA [CN]
TEL. +39 3356765021
www.carlorevello.com

PRE-BOOKED VISITS
ANNUAL PRODUCTION 25,000 bottles
HECTARES UNDER VINE 7.00

After a long experience in their father's winery, in 2016 Carlo and his brother Enzo decided to divide the operation. Carlo chose to leave more space to his children, in particular Erik (the oldest, a young enologist) and to adopt a new style. 7.5 hectares situated primarily in La Morra, in Annunziata's most famous crus (Rocche and Giachini), and Boiolo give rise to harmonious wines aged in barriques. As of 2016, their Barolos have also been aged in large barrels. In the future their separately fermented Rocche dell'Annunziata will come out as a reserve. The Barolo R.G., dedicated to father Giacomo Revello, is a blend of grapes from the Giachini and Boiolo crus. The 2015 exhibits a lovely, minty register that enriches an already elegant fruity foundation. Even without the structure of a top wine, on the palate it proves harmonious and elegant. The Barolo '15, made in part with grapes from their rented Serralunga d'Alba vineyards, is unquestionably endowed with balance and pleasantness.

● Barolo R.G. '15	♥♥ 7
● Barbera d'Alba Sup. '17	♥♥ 3
● Barolo '15	♥♥ 5
● Barbera d'Alba '16	♀♀ 3
● Barolo '14	♀♀ 5
● Barolo '13	♀♀ 5
● Barolo R.G. '14	♀♀ 7
● Barolo R.G. '13	♀♀ 7

F.lli Revello

FRAZ. ANNUNZIATA, 103
12064 LA MORRA [CN]
TEL. +39 017350276
www.revellofratelli.it

CELLAR SALES
PRE-BOOKED VISITS
ACCOMMODATION
ANNUAL PRODUCTION 45,000 bottles
HECTARES UNDER VINE 8.00
SUSTAINABLE WINERY

Lorenzo Revello is a perfect representation of Langa's family wineries: they started more than a century ago by selling their grapes to large wineries, then moved on to bottling their own wines and, finally, separate vinification of their various private crus. And it's all been carried out, over the last 30 yeas, with a firm adhesion to Barolo production regimes aimed at the highest expression of elegance and cleanness, with short maceration on the skins and the use of French barriques. Their Barolos comes from 4 La Morra crus and a recently purchased plot in the Cerretta vineyard in Serralunga d'Alba. This year's selection all proved to be of high quality, starting with their 2015 La Morra Barolos. Violet and licorice dominate the elegant aromatic profile of their Giachini, a vibrant and firmly-structured wine. The succulent and pleasantly acidic Conca is rich in character and highly enjoyable thanks to aromas of medicinal herbs and sweet spices, while the Gattera proves exceptionally elegant in its balsamic hints.

● Barolo Conca '15	♟♟7
● Barolo Giachini '15	♟♟7
● Barbera d'Alba Ciabot du Re '17	♟♟5
● Barolo '15	♟♟5
● Barolo Cerretta '15	♟♟7
● Barolo Gattera '15	♟♟6
● Langhe Nebbiolo '17	♟♟3
● Barbera d'Alba Ciabot du Re '05	♟♟♟5
● Barolo Rocche dell'Annunziata '01	♟♟♟8
● Barbera d'Alba Ciabot du Re '16	♟♟5
● Barolo '13	♟♟5
● Barolo Conca '13	♟♟7
● Barolo Gattera '13	♟♟6
● Barolo Giachini '14	♟♟7
● Langhe Nebbiolo '16	♟♟3

Michele Reverdito

FRAZ. RIVALTA
B.TA GARASSINI, 74B
12064 LA MORRA [CN]
TEL. +39 017350336
www.reverdito.it

CELLAR SALES
PRE-BOOKED VISITS
ANNUAL PRODUCTION 100,000 bottles
HECTARES UNDER VINE 24.00

Michele returned to the use of large casks, mostly 5000 liters, not out of fashion, but rather as part of his philosophy. It starts in the vineyards, where he's a firm supporter of the The Green Experience, and continues coherently in the cellar, where he pursues the purest expression of his grapes. So it is that even the amiable Nascetta forgoes the use of outside yeasts and the fragrant Pelaverga matures in amphoras. The core of their production, however, centers on Barolo, which is offered in 6 versions from La Morra, Monforte and Serralunga d'Alba. This year's selection is dominated by a brilliant performance by their Barolo Badarina '15. It's potent on the palate, as is the want of this classic Serralunga d'Alba grape, with tannins that are as dense as they are round and unaggressive. On the nose it's characterized by notes of licorice and dried herbs accompanied by mature red fruit. The Bricco Cogni is more austere on the palate, with excellent aromatic cleanness.

● Barolo Badarina '15	♟♟7
● Barolo Bricco Cogni '15	♟♟6
● Barolo Ascheri '15	♟5
○ Langhe Nascetta '17	♟3
● Langhe Nebbiolo Simane '17	♟3
● Verduno Pelaverga '17	♟3
● Barolo Bricco Cogni '04	♟♟♟6
● Barolo Ascheri '14	♟♟5
● Barolo Ascheri '13	♟♟5
● Barolo Badarina '12	♟♟6
● Barolo Bricco Cogni '14	♟♟8
● Barolo Bricco Cogni '13	♟♟6
● Barolo Bricco Cogni '12	♟♟6
● Barolo Castagni '14	♟♟7
● Langhe Nebbiolo Simane '16	♟♟4
● Langhe Nebbiolo Simane '15	♟♟3

Giuseppe Rinaldi

VIA MONFORTE, 5
12060 BAROLO [CN]
TEL. +39 017356156
rinaldimarta@libero.it

CELLAR SALES
PRE-BOOKED VISITS
ANNUAL PRODUCTION 35,000 bottles
HECTARES UNDER VINE 6.50

Beppe Rinaldi was a man of great sensibility, as honest as he was generous, in love with Langhe, a firm advocate of pure, classic Barolo. He was also the enemy of 'modern practices at any cost', from mobile phones to barriques, vineyard residences, email, excessive technology and 'international tastes'. Marta and Carlotta are continuing along this path of purity and tradition, pursuing the most natural grapes and wines, even if it means letting through the occasional quality that could be construed as a flaw. Lovely fruity harmony puts raspberries at the fore in the Barolo Brunate '15, then the complexity of licorice arrives followed by notes of camphor enriched by a bit of lift. On the palate it's majestic, with evident acidic freshness and a very long finish. The Tre Tine '15, made with grapes from the Le Coste, San Lorenzo and Ravera crus, is slightly more unruly and penetrating, with excellent structure and notable tannic density.

● Barolo Brunate '15	♀♀♀	8
● Barolo Tre Tine '15	♀♀	7
● Barolo Brunate '13	♀♀♀	7
● Barolo Brunate '11	♀♀♀	7
● Barolo Brunate-Le Coste '07	♀♀♀	7
● Barolo Brunate-Le Coste '06	♀♀♀	7
● Barolo Brunate-Le Coste '01	♀♀♀	6
● Barolo Cannubi S. Lorenzo-Ravera '04	♀♀♀	6
● Barolo Brunate '14	♀♀	7
● Barolo Tre Tine '14	♀♀	7
● Barolo Tre Tine '13	♀♀	7

Francesco Rinaldi & Figli

VIA CROSIA, 30
12060 BAROLO [CN]
TEL. +39 0173440484
www.rinaldifrancesco.it

CELLAR SALES
PRE-BOOKED VISITS
ACCOMMODATION
ANNUAL PRODUCTION 70,000 bottles
HECTARES UNDER VINE 11.00

Celebrated as far back as the 18th century as a vineyard of great quality, Cannubi is thought by many to square the circle in Barolo. In youth it's rich in fruity aromas, getting spicier with age — and yet it's highly balanced on the palate, where tannins are never hard or bitter. On the hill in front you'll find Brunate, whose wines are slightly more assertive, with aromas marked more by tar and dried violet. This is the area that Paola and Piera Rinaldi draw on for the lion's share of their Barolo, making for wines that are a high expression of tradition and classical style. Mature aromas of dried herbs are accompanied by fresher hints of small red berries in the complex Barolo Cannubi '15, a dense, rather plush wine with harmonious structure. The long, lingering Brunate '15 is classic in its aromas of raspberries, violets and spices, with a dynamic freshness. The well-made and well-gauged Cannubi Riserva '13 is redolent of red berries, with tannins in evidence on the palate.

● Barolo Brunate '15	♀♀	7
● Barolo Cannubi '15	♀♀	7
● Barolo Cannubi Ris. '13	♀♀	7
● Barbaresco '14	♀♀	5
● Barolo Brunate '13	♀♀	7
● Barolo Brunate '12	♀♀	7
● Barolo Cannubi '14	♀♀	7
● Barolo Cannubi '13	♀♀	7
● Barolo Cannubi '12	♀♀	7
● Nebbiolo d'Alba '16	♀♀	3

Massimo Rivetti

VIA RIVETTI, 22
12052 NEIVE [CN]
TEL. +39 017367505
www.rivettimassimo.it

CELLAR SALES
PRE-BOOKED VISITS
ANNUAL PRODUCTION 70,000 bottles
HECTARES UNDER VINE 25.00

Massimo is forthright, sincere, and that's how he wants his wines to be. It's why he eschews artificial products in his vineyards and outside yeasts in his cellar. Those who pay him a visit realize his philosophy doesn't look to the past (his only nostalgia is for a time when chemicals weren't so commonplace), but is rather focused on a future in which each wine represents its purest expression, better still if it's done through manual work. His whole family is involved in making a selection led by a line of Barbarescos. Certain wines weren't ready for our tastings, so they were postponed. The Ris. del Barbaresco Serraboella does a nice job expressing the 2014 vintage. On the nose it's rich in red berries and vegetal hints, sensations followed by a docile, linear palate of medium-force and devoid of harshness. The Barbaresco Froi '16 exhibits nice balance, with good, warm alcohol and soft tannins, while the valid Nebbiolo Avene '17 stands out for its fruit and well-gauged oak.

● Barbaresco Serraboella Ris. '14	▼▼	6
● Barbaresco Froi '16	▼▼	6
● Langhe Nebbiolo Avene '17	▼▼	3
● Barbaresco '14	♀♀	5
● Barbaresco '13	♀♀	5
● Barbaresco Froi '15	♀♀	6
● Barbaresco Froi '14	♀♀	6
● Barbaresco Froi '13	♀♀	5
● Barbaresco Froi '12	♀♀	5
● Barbaresco Serraboella '13	♀♀	7
● Barbera d'Alba Sup. Froi '16	♀♀	2*
● Barbera d'Alba Sup. V. Serraboella '16	♀♀	4
● Barbera d'Alba Sup. V. Serraboella '12	♀♀	4
● Langhe Nebbiolo Avene '15	♀♀	3
● Langhe Pinot Nero '15	♀♀	3

Rizzi

VIA RIZZI, 15
12050 TREISO [CN]
TEL. +39 0173638161
www.cantinarizzi.it

CELLAR SALES
PRE-BOOKED VISITS
ACCOMMODATION
ANNUAL PRODUCTION 70,000 bottles
HECTARES UNDER VINE 38.00
SUSTAINABLE WINERY

The Dellapiana family's winery is one of the most well known and appreciated in Barbaresco, an appellation that's gained increasing worldwide recognition. Behind their success are some of the best, most inspired crus, made possible thanks to painstaking care across all stages of production and a pricing policy that's extremely honest, despite the high demand. Four Barbarescos are made, all matured in mid-sized Slavonian oak barrels. Mouthfilling but cosseting, it lengthens with class, closing long, flavorful. The excellent Barbaresco Rizzi '16 proves fresh in its aromas of strawberries, raspberries enriched by tobacco and licorice. On the palate it's subtle, complex, with delicate tannic development and a penetrating, sapid finish. The mature, vivid Barbaresco Rizzi Bolto Ris. '14 is only partially impaired by the difficult year.

● Barbaresco Pajorè '16	▼▼	6
● Barbaresco Rizzi '16	▼▼	5
● Barbaresco Nervo '16	▼▼	6
● Barbaresco Rizzi Boito Ris. '14	▼▼	7
● Langhe Nebbiolo '17	▼▼	4
● Dolcetto d'Alba '18	▼	3
● Barbaresco Boito Ris. '10	♀♀♀	6
● Barbaresco Nervo '14	♀♀♀	6
● Barbaresco Boito Ris. '11	♀♀	7
● Barbaresco Nervo '15	♀♀	6
● Barbaresco Nervo '11	♀♀	5
● Barbaresco Pajorè '15	♀♀	6
● Barbaresco Pajorè '14	♀♀	6
● Barbaresco Pajorè '13	♀♀	6
● Barbaresco Pajorè '11	♀♀	6
● Barbaresco Pajorè '10	♀♀	6
● Barbaresco Rizzi Boito Ris. '13	♀♀	5

Roagna

LOC. PAJÉ
S.DA PAGLIERI, 7
12050 BARBARESCO [CN]
TEL. +39 0173635109
www.roagna.com

CELLAR SALES
PRE-BOOKED VISITS
ANNUAL PRODUCTION 50,000 bottles
HECTARES UNDER VINE 15.00

Walking with Luca in his property in the Asili cru is, in addition to being informative, amazing: no weeding, no fertilizers, no poisons — only old, unproductive vines, and plenty of insects. His approach departs from modern practices, privileging 'nature', even its wildest, chaotic elements. His father grounded his internationally successful wines in these principles, and Luca's not changing anything, making for a selection that highlights their artisanal philosophy. And that includes the work carried out in their new Castiglione Falletto cellar. Their outstanding selection features a sophisticated interpretation of 2014, playing on aromatic elegance and on a soft, but still assertive, grip. Fans of this celebrated winery will be pleased to see that three wines are debuting. The Crichët Pajé '11 is a masterpiece of harmony grounded in considerable gustatory richness and a freshness that opts more for sensations of incense and eucalyptus than acidity, making for irresistible charm.

● Barbaresco Crichët Pajé '11	♟♟♟	8
● Barbaresco Asili V. V. '14	♟♟	8
● Barbaresco Montefico V. V. '14	♟♟	8
● Barbaresco Pajè V. V. '14	♟♟	8
● Barolo del Comune di Barolo '14	♟♟	8
● Barolo Pira V. V. '14	♟♟	8
● Barbaresco Albesani '14	♟♟	8
● Barbaresco Faset '14	♟♟	8
● Barbaresco Gallina '14	♟♟	6
● Barbaresco Pajé '14	♟♟	8
● Barolo Pira '14	♟♟	8
○ Derthona Montemarzino '17	♟♟	8
● Langhe Rosso '14	♟♟	3
● Barbaresco Asili V. Viti '13	♟♟♟	8
● Barbaresco Crichët Pajé '08	♟♟♟	8

★Albino Rocca

S.DA RONCHI, 18
12050 BARBARESCO [CN]
TEL. +39 0173635145
www.albinorocca.com

CELLAR SALES
PRE-BOOKED VISITS
ANNUAL PRODUCTION 100,000 bottles
HECTARES UNDER VINE 18.00
SUSTAINABLE WINERY

Bolstered by a centuries-old tradition of winemaking, Paola, Daniela and Monica Rocca, and Paola's husband, oversee this celebrated Barbaresco producer. The estate comprises prestigious vineyards managed according to The Green Experience protocols. Their style pursues aromatic purity of Nebbiolo, which is fermented with elegance in mid-size oak casks. The only concession to the use of small, French barrels concerns their magnificent La Rocca, a sophisticated white made with Cortese. It's an essential benchmark for the entire area. At the end of our blind tastings, it's rare to discover that a producer earned stratospheric scores with all the wines presented. It happened this year with the Rocca family's 2016 Barolos, thanks to a series of first-rate performances. The Ovello Vigna Loreto took home Tre Bicchieri, proving extremely subtle in its aromas of raspberry and licorice, alluring and enjoyable on its truly outstanding palate.

● Barbaresco Ovello V. Loreto '16	♟♟♟	6
● Barbaresco Angelo '16	♟♟	5
★ Barbaresco Cottà '16	♟♟	5
● Barbaresco Montersino '16	♟♟	6
● Barbaresco Ronchi '15	♟♟	6
○ Piemonte Cortese La Rocca '17	♟♟	4
● Barbaresco Angelo '13	♟♟♟	5
● Barbaresco Ovello V. Loreto '11	♟♟♟	6
● Barbaresco Ovello V. Loreto '09	♟♟♟	6
● Barbaresco Ovello V. Loreto '07	♟♟♟	6
● Barbaresco Ronchi '10	♟♟♟	6
● Barbaresco Vign. Brich Ronchi Ris. '06	♟♟♟	8

★Bruno Rocca

s.da Rabajà, 60
12050 Barbaresco [CN]
Tel. +39 0173635112
www.brunorocca.it

CELLAR SALES
PRE-BOOKED VISITS
ANNUAL PRODUCTION 70,000 bottles
HECTARES UNDER VINE 15.00
VITICULTURE METHOD Certified Organic

Rabajà is one of Langhe's most important crus. It's here that Bruno founded his winery, adopting its name as well. The style is modern, with rigorous grape selection and the elegant use of French barrels, in addition to winemaking that's attentive to air contact, avoiding oxidation and drastically reducing the need for sulfites. Their selection, which has been enlarged to include a Ris. Barbaresco Currà, is of outstanding quality across the board, thanks in part to the contributions of Bruno's capable children. Only Barbaresco was submitted, with the new Ris. Rabajà '13 on center stage. It's vibrant, vivid in its aromas of red berries, which harmonize perfectly with licorice. On the palate it's majestic, with tannins both tight and delicate, and plenty of flesh to accompany a long, elegant finish. Their Ris. Currà '13 is similar in makeup and quality, it's just a bit spicier, with extraordinary density. The slightly fresher Rabajà '15 and more tannic Currà '15 are also superb.

● Barbaresco Currà Ris. '13	♟♟♟ 8
● Barbaresco Currà '15	♟♟ 8
● Barbaresco Rabajà '15	♟♟ 8
● Barbaresco Rabajà Ris. '13	♟♟ 8
● Barbaresco Coparossa '04	♟♟♟ 8
● Barbaresco Currà Ris. '12	♟♟♟ 8
● Barbaresco Maria Adelaide '07	♟♟♟ 8
● Barbaresco Maria Adelaide '04	♟♟♟ 8
● Barbaresco Maria Adelaide '01	♟♟♟ 8
● Barbaresco Rabajà '13	♟♟♟ 8
● Barbaresco Rabajà '12	♟♟♟ 8
● Barbaresco Rabajà '11	♟♟♟ 8
● Barbaresco Rabajà '10	♟♟♟ 8
● Barbaresco Rabajà '09	♟♟♟ 8
● Barbaresco Rabajà '01	♟♟♟ 8

Rocche Costamagna

via Vittorio Emanuele, 8
12064 La Morra [CN]
Tel. +39 0173509225
www.rocchecostamagna.it

CELLAR SALES
PRE-BOOKED VISITS
ACCOMMODATION
ANNUAL PRODUCTION 95,000 bottles
HECTARES UNDER VINE 15.80

Alessandro inherited a taste for beauty from his mother, Claudia, a celebrated painter and organizer of cultural events. And so he doesn't stop at personally crafting great wines — he's also stylishly renovated their cellar and realized the inimitable Art Suites, whose terrace offers one of the best views in all of Langhe. Their selection centers on Barolo, which is made with grapes cultivated in the magnificent Rocche dell'Annunziata cru. Here more than 5 hectares of private vineyards are overseen by agronomist Gian Piero Romana. Notes of quinine on a background of oak open the 2015 version of this Barolo, softened by its warm development, just punctuated by its tannins. Spices and a touch of tanned leather mark the entry-level version of the same vintage — it's just a bit more acidic. The robust, pleasantly sapid Barbera d'Alba '17 stands out for its fruit and undemanding drinkability, while the balsamic, delicate and well-proportioned Nebbiolo Roccardo '17 is highly enjoyable.

● Barbera d'Alba '17	♟♟ 3
● Barolo '15	♟♟ 5
● Barolo Rocche dell'Annunziata '15	♟♟ 6
● Langhe Nebbiolo Roccardo '17	♟♟ 3
● Dolcetto d'Alba '18	♟ 2
○ Langhe Arneis '18	♟ 3
● Barolo Rocche dell'Annunziata '04	♟♟♟ 5
● Barbera d'Alba '16	♟♟ 3
● Barbera d'Alba Sup. Rocche delle Rocche '15	♟♟ 4
● Barolo Rocche dell'Annunziata '14	♟♟ 6
● Barolo Rocche dell'Annunziata '13	♟♟ 6
● Barolo Rocche dell'Annunziata Bricco Francesco Ris. '12	♟♟ 8
● Langhe Nebbiolo Roccardo '16	♟♟ 3

★Rocche dei Manzoni

LOC. MANZONI SOPRANI, 3
12065 MONFORTE D'ALBA [CN]
TEL. +39 017378421
www.rocchedeimanzoni.it

CELLAR SALES
PRE-BOOKED VISITS
ANNUAL PRODUCTION 250,000 bottles
HECTARES UNDER VINE 40.00

Their first sparklers were produced in 1978, when Pinot Nero and Chardonnay were practically unknown in Langhe, by Valentino Migliorini. So it was that one of the area's most unorthodox wineries was founded, with its marble and frescoes overlooking rows of aging bottles and magnums. They were even innovative when it came to Barolo, with the use of new French barriques. Later these were accompanied by concrete vats, under his competent son Rodolfo, whose pursuit quality is further evidenced by the adoption of biodynamic practices. A fruit-heavy 2015 only allowed for an entry-level Barolo (the crus will come out next year). It's vivid, generous, already with nice tension despite a discernible background of oak, spices. It's dense and rich, though without being heavy, thanks to considerable flesh — a wine of excellent craft. The Bricco San Pietro Vigna d'la Roul '14, certainly pleasant for the typology, opts for a greater oak, while the Brut Elena '14 is extremely subtle, fresh, complex.

● Barolo '15	🍷🍷	8
○ Valentino Brut Elena M. Cl. '14	🍷🍷	7
● Barolo Bricco San Pietro V. d'la Roul '14	🍷🍷	8
● Barolo Perno V. Cappella di S. Stefano '14	🍷	8
● Barolo V. Big 'd Big '99	🍷🍷🍷	8
● Barolo V. Cappella di S. Stefano '01	🍷🍷🍷	8
● Barolo V. Cappella di S. Stefano '96	🍷🍷🍷	8
● Barolo V. d'la Roul '07	🍷🍷🍷	8
● Langhe Rosso Quatr Nas '99	🍷🍷🍷	6
● Langhe Rosso Quatr Nas '96	🍷🍷🍷	6
○ Valentino Brut Zero Ris. '98	🍷🍷🍷	5
○ Valentino Brut Zero Ris. '93	🍷🍷🍷	5
○ Valentino Brut Zerò Ris. '92	🍷🍷🍷	5

Il Rocchin

LOC. VALLEMME, 39
15066 GAVI [AL]
TEL. +39 0143642228
www.ilrocchin.it

CELLAR SALES
PRE-BOOKED VISITS
ANNUAL PRODUCTION 50,000 bottles
HECTARES UNDER VINE 20.00

The Zerbo family's winery has, over the years, improved the intrinsic quality of their wines, a path that's gone in step with growth in production volumes and the subsequent expansion/upgrade of their cellar. Today it's a dynamic, well-structured producer that makes classically styled wines, with both fermentation and aging carried out in steel. Their selection comprises a dozen wines, made primarily with three grapes: Cortese, Barbera and Dolcetto. Among these there's also a Moscato dessert wine and a Monferrato Bianco made with Sauvignon and Cortese. The 2017 version of their Il Basacco landed a place in our final round of tastings. It's a Barbera with an intense, complex aromatic profile amidst red berries and almost floral notes that meld with tertiaries of spices and tobacco. On the palate it's intense, rich in flesh with a long, lingering finish. The Bosco opens with sensations of candied citrus on a mineral background, while on the palate it comes through fresh and sapid.

● Barbera del M.to Il Basacco '17	🍷🍷	3*
○ Gavi del Comune di Gavi Il Bosco '18	🍷🍷	3
● Barbera del M.to Il Basacco '16	🍷🍷	3
● Dolcetto di Ovada '16	🍷🍷	2*
● Dolcetto di Ovada '15	🍷🍷	2*
○ Gavi del Comune di Gavi '17	🍷🍷	2*
○ Gavi del Comune di Gavi '16	🍷🍷	2*
○ Gavi del Comune di Gavi '15	🍷🍷	2*
○ Gavi del Comune di Gavi '14	🍷🍷	2*
○ Gavi del Comune di Gavi Il Bosco '17	🍷🍷	3*
○ Gavi del Comune di Gavi Il Bosco '16	🍷🍷	3*
○ Gavi del Comune di Gavi Il Bosco '15	🍷🍷	3*

Flavio Roddolo

FRAZ. BRICCO APPIANI
LOC. SANT'ANNA, 5
12065 MONFORTE D'ALBA [CN]
TEL. +39 017378535
info@roddolo.it

CELLAR SALES
PRE-BOOKED VISITS
ANNUAL PRODUCTION 25,000 bottles
HECTARES UNDER VINE 6.00

Flavio is one of Langa's most authentic vignerons, operating outside media and social events, marketing and communication plans. As a man of few words and clear ideas, he has no consultants, preferring to let his wines do the talking. These are made in his cellar in Monforte d'Alba only during the best years, and are released years after vintage. They're original, multifaceted wines, rich in edginess and character. Nebbiolo, the cornerstone of his legendary Ravera cru, is on center stage, followed by Dolcetto, Barbera and Cab. Sauvignon. The Barolo Ravera '12, aged at length in large barrels, maintains a gorgeous profile of raspberries and strawberries, with a classic touch of licorice and violet. Its tannic weave is already creamy, gratifying. The exuberant Nebbiolo d'Alba '12 is more rugged, austere in its notes of quinine and hay. 2016 delivered a fruity, succulent and complex Dolcetto, the wine that introduced us to Flavio in the 1980s.

● Barolo Ravera '12	♟♟7
● Barbera d'Alba Sup. Bricco Appiani '11	♟♟5
● Dolcetto d'Alba '16	♟♟3
● Nebbiolo d'Alba '12	♟♟5
● Dolcetto d'Alba Sup. '15	♟3
● Barolo Ravera '08	♟♟♟5
● Barolo Ravera '07	♟♟♟5
● Barolo Ravera '04	♟♟♟5
● Barolo Ravera '01	♟♟♟5
● Barolo Ravera '97	♟♟♟5
● Bricco Appiani '99	♟♟♟5
● Dolcetto d'Alba Sup. '11	♟♟3*
● Dolcetto d'Alba Sup. '10	♟♟3*
● Dolcetto d'Alba Sup. '09	♟♟3*
● Nebbiolo d'Alba '10	♟♟4
● Nebbiolo d'Alba '08	♟♟4
● Nebbiolo d'Alba '07	♟♟4

Giovanni Rosso

VIA RODDINO, 10/1
12050 SERRALUNGA D'ALBA [CN]
TEL. +39 0173613340
www.giovannirosso.com

CELLAR SALES
PRE-BOOKED VISITS
ANNUAL PRODUCTION 130,000 bottles
HECTARES UNDER VINE 18.00

110 years ago the family purchased plots in Serralunga. 50 years later saw Giovanni Rosso begin making wine. In 2001 Davide came on the scene, giving a major boost, building a new location and purchasing vineyards on Etna. It's a splendid history, but their biggest accomplishment lies in a range of extraordinary wines, foremost Barolo. Vigna Rionda gives rise to just 2,000 bottles, but their more accessible offerings, dedicated to Barolo Serra and Cerretta, are right up there. The Barolo Serra '15 is as complex as it is elegant, fresh in its scents of raspberries, strawberries and rose, dense, with tight-knit, supple tannins, and notable length. The enjoyable Cerretta, more licorice-scented, moves on a similar track. The exquisite 2015 Vigna Rionda Ester Canale Rosso is a monument to pervasiveness, finesse and drinkability. Vigna Rionda also gives rise to their fantastic Langhe Nebbiolo '16, made with younger vines. Soon we'll also be tasting bottles from their new Etna property.

● Barolo Serra '15	♟♟♟8
● Barolo Cerretta '15	♟♟8
● Barolo del Comune di Serralunga d'Alba '15	♟♟5
● Barolo Vigna Rionda Ester Canale Rosso '15	♟♟8
● Langhe Nebbiolo Ester Canale Rosso '16	♟♟8
● Barolo Cerretta '12	♟♟♟8
● Barolo La Serra '09	♟♟♟7
● Barolo La Serra '08	♟♟♟7
● Barolo Serra '10	♟♟♟7
● Barolo Vigna Rionda Ester Canale Rosso '14	♟♟♟8
● Barolo Vigna Rionda Ester Canale Rosso '13	♟♟♟8
● Barolo Vigna Rionda Ester Canale Rosso '11	♟♟♟8

Poderi Rosso Giovanni

P.ZZA ROMA, 36/37
14041 AGLIANO TERME [AT]
TEL. +39 0141954006
www.poderirossogiovanni.it

CELLAR SALES
PRE-BOOKED VISITS
ANNUAL PRODUCTION 53,000 bottles
HECTARES UNDER VINE 12.00

Lionello Rosso represents the third generation to work in the winery built by his family in Agliano Terme, a center of wine production in Monferrato. Spread throughout Cascina Perno and Cascina San Sebastiano, their vineyards are managed according to principles of sustainable agriculture and host primarily Barbera Astigiana, which is accompanied by a few plots of Cabernet Sauvignon. The result is an eclectic selection that draws on tailored approaches in terms of vinification and maturation, with steel, barriques and mid-size casks all used. And naturally it's their Barbera d'Asti Superiore to lead the group. The Gioco dell'Oca '16 impresses with its focused profile and rich, fruity flesh balanced by a vibrant freshness, while the Carlinet '16 comes across as warmer and more mature. But its the 2017 version of their Cascina Perno that squares the circle, with its aromas of cherry and blood orange, quinine and cocoa powder. This rigorous-relaxed dual track follows through on the palate.

● Barbera d'Asti Sup. Cascina Perno '17	♀♀	3*
● Barbera d'Asti Sup. Carlinet '16	♀♀	4
● Barbera d'Asti Sup. Gioco dell'Oca '16	♀♀	6
● Barbera d'Asti San Bastian '18	♀	2
● M.to Rosso Infine '16	♀	4
● Barbera d'Asti San Bastian '17	♀♀	2*
● Barbera d'Asti Sup. Carlinet '15	♀♀	4
● Barbera d'Asti Sup. Cascina Perno '16	♀♀	3*
● Barbera d'Asti Sup. Cascina Perno '15	♀♀	3
● Barbera d'Asti Sup. Gioco dell'Oca '15	♀♀	6

Josetta Saffirio

LOC. CASTELLETTO, 39
12065 MONFORTE D'ALBA [CN]
TEL. +39 0173787278
www.josettasaffirio.com

CELLAR SALES
PRE-BOOKED VISITS
ANNUAL PRODUCTION 30,000 bottles
HECTARES UNDER VINE 5.00
VITICULTURE METHOD Certified Organic
SUSTAINABLE WINERY

Sara transmits an infectious enthusiasm (check out her interesting, enjoyable blog) for her wines and, especially, her Langhe vineyards, including lesser known plots that will soon give rise to a sparkling Alta Langa DOCG made with Chardonnay and Pinot Nero. On that note, she's increasingly convinced of Nebbiolo's potential when it comes to Metodo Classico, and the grape is already being used for a 4,000-bottle/year selection. Though that shouldn't overshadow her full-bodied, classically-styled Barolos. The Barolo Persiera is from a vineyard in Castelletto di Monforte d'Alba. The 2015 offers up classic, focused aromas of red berries with accents of licorice. On the palate it shows good weight along with pleasant, tight but already velvety, tannins, lending personality. Their prestigious Barolo del comune di Monforte d'Alba '15 is marked by extraordinary aromatic complexity. An extremely small selection of Barolo Ris. Millenovecento48 '13 should also be of interest.

● Barolo del Comune di Monforte d'Alba '15	♀♀	5
● Barolo Millenovecento48 Ris. '13	♀♀	8
● Barolo Persiera '15	♀♀	8
○ Langhe Rossese Bianco '17	♀	3
● Barolo '89	♀♀♀	6
● Barolo '88	♀♀♀	6
● Barbera d'Alba Sup. '15	♀♀	3
● Barolo '13	♀♀	6
● Barolo Millenovecento48 Ris. '12	♀♀	8
● Barolo Millenovecento48 Ris. '11	♀♀	8
● Barolo Persiera '14	♀♀	8
● Barolo Persiera '13	♀♀	8
● Barolo Persiera '12	♀♀	8
● Langhe Nebbiolo '16	♀♀	3
● Langhe Nebbiolo '15	♀♀	3
○ Langhe Rossese Bianco '16	♀♀	3

San Fereolo

LOC. SAN FEREOLO
B.TA VALDIBÀ, 59
12063 DOGLIANI [CN]
TEL. +39 0173742075
www.sanfereolo.com

PRE-BOOKED VISITS
ANNUAL PRODUCTION 46,000 bottles
HECTARES UNDER VINE 12.00

Young Nicoletta arrived in Dogliani without experience in the field but with clear ideas: make respect for the environment a central part of this small winery's production philosophy. Her journey and pursuits haven't stopped — and so is that, with humility and perseverance, she's achieved what she has. The next step is biodynamic cultivation, and from there her sights are set on moving the territory and community closer towards sustainable integration with the local ecosystem. Her wines, whose adhesion to the La Renaissance des Appellations is marked on their labels, are a direct consequence of this direction, produced in the most natural way possible. This year, in addition to macerated, oxidative and 'imperfect' selections (in the style of her recently created 'Un Viaggio in Georgia') we find the Dogliani Superiore Vigneti Dolci 2017, an homage to the purity of fruit, buoyant drinkability, aromatic cleanness and most accessible yet complex expression of the Dolcetto grape.

● Dogliani Sup. Vigneti Dolci '17	♥♥♥ 3*
● Dogliani Sup. '17	♥♥ 3
● Langhe Rosso 1593 '07	♥♥ 5
● Dogliani Sup. San Fereolo '12	♥ 2
○ Langhe Bianco Coste di Riavolo '16	♥ 4
⊙ Langhe Rosato La Lupa '18	♥ 3
● Langhe Rosso Il Provinciale '15	♥ 6
○ Un Viaggio in Georgia '13	♥ 4
● Dogliani Valdibà '13	♥♥ 3*
○ Langhe Bianco Coste di Riavolo '11	♥♥ 3
● Langhe Rosso Il Provinciale '10	♥♥ 4

Tenuta San Sebastiano

CASCINA SAN SEBASTIANO, 41
15040 LU [AL]
TEL. +39 0131741353
www.dealessi.it

CELLAR SALES
PRE-BOOKED VISITS
ANNUAL PRODUCTION 70,000 bottles
HECTARES UNDER VINE 9.00

We can only call Roberto De Alessi a great wine artisan. Since 1992, the year in which he purchased the estate, he's been working to realize his enological projects, building on a family tradition that he decided to revive, so as to fulfill a longtime dream. His wines are like him, forthright and sincere, with a solidity and power that never lose their elegance, and are always rich and pleasant. His approach to winemaking and aging in wood barrels would suggest a modern style, but the attentive use of oak and judicious extraction allow for a full expression of the grapes. Their Mepari '17 once again earned a place in our final round of tastings. It features a youthful, striking profile, with a bold structure that speaks of good things to come. The Dalera '15 is balanced and harmonious, with fruity aromas that lean vegetal and a coherent palate rich in flesh. Their Grignolino and Monferrato Bianco Sperilium, both 2018s, also prove well-made.

● Barbera del M.to Sup. Mepari '17	♥♥ 4
○ M.to Bianco Sperilium '18	♥♥ 2*
● M.to Rosso Dalera '15	♥♥ 3
● Piemonte Grignolino '18	♥♥ 2*
● Barbera del M.to '17	♥ 2
● Barbera del M.to '16	♥♥ 2*
● Barbera del M.to Sup. Mepari '16	♥♥ 4
● Barbera del M.to Sup. Mepari '15	♥♥ 4
○ M.to Bianco Sperilium '16	♥♥ 2*
● M.to Rosso Capolinea '16	♥♥ 2*
● M.to Rosso Dalera '16	♥♥ 3
● Piemonte Grignolino '15	♥♥ 2*
● Piemonte Grignolino Monfiorato '13	♥♥ 4
● Piemonte Grignolino Monfiorato '12	♥♥ 4
● Piemonte Grignolino Monfiorato '11	♥♥ 4

★Luciano Sandrone

VIA PUGNANE, 4
12060 BAROLO [CN]
TEL. +39 0173560023
www.sandroneluciano.com

PRE-BOOKED VISITS
ANNUAL PRODUCTION 110,000 bottles
HECTARES UNDER VINE 27.00
SUSTAINABLE WINERY

Luciano Sandrone is a key figure for understanding Barolo's planetary success and evolution. Indeed, he was among the first (debuting in 1978) to use small wood barrels, proposing a highly original style that broke from tradition. In a few years that style set a precedent, spawning a healthy debate among producers. Luciano, with the fundamental support of his brother Luca and daughter Barbara, continue to propose neoclassic wines of great prestige that express in the glass the value of acclaimed vineyards like Cannubi Boschis (Barolo Aleste) or Le Vigne, which draws on grapes from Novello, Serralunga, Castiglione Falletto and Barolo. Their Barolo Aleste '15 exhibits a highly complex profile amidst aromas of red berries and spicier notes of wood tar and black pepper. It's a subtle, complex wine, both potent and austere, with superb, enlivening flesh and guaranteed aging power. Notes of quinine and tobacco characterize their rich Barolo Le Vigne '15.

● Barolo Aleste '15	♈♈♈ 8
● Barolo Le Vigne '15	♈♈ 8
● Nebbiolo d'Alba Valmaggiore '17	♈♈ 5
● Barbera d'Alba '17	♈ 5
● Barolo '84	♈♈♈ 8
● Barolo '83	♈♈♈ 7
● Barolo Cannubi Boschis '11	♈♈♈ 8
● Barolo Cannubi Boschis '10	♈♈♈ 8
● Barolo Cannubi Boschis '08	♈♈♈ 8
● Barolo Cannubi Boschis '07	♈♈♈ 8
● Barolo Cannubi Boschis '06	♈♈♈ 8
● Barolo Cannubi Boschis '05	♈♈♈ 8
● Barolo Cannubi Boschis '04	♈♈♈ 8
● Barolo Cannubi Boschis '03	♈♈♈ 8
● Barolo Cannubi Boschis '01	♈♈♈ 8
● Barolo Cannubi Boschis '00	♈♈♈ 8
● Barolo Le Vigne '99	♈♈♈ 8

Tenuta Santa Caterina

VIA GUGLIELMO MARCONI, 17
14035 GRAZZANO BADOGLIO [AT]
TEL. +39 0141925108
www.tenuta-santa-caterina.it

CELLAR SALES
PRE-BOOKED VISITS
ACCOMMODATION
ANNUAL PRODUCTION 50,000 bottles
HECTARES UNDER VINE 23.00

The Alleva family's winery is situated in a scenic location, thanks to excellent renovation work carried out on the estate's old buildings, and a splendid view of their vineyards. Here we find the cellar where their wines are aged in barrels of varying sizes, from barriques to 3000-liter casks. Their production centers on native grapes: Barbera, Freisa, Grignolino and Nebbiolo. Two wines are made with international cultivars: Salidoro (Chardonnay and Sauvignon Blanc) and Silente delle Marne (Chardonnay). Their selection put in a dazzling performance, earning the producer our Up-and-Coming Winery award, with three bottles making it to our final round. The Grignolino M features superb aromatic complexity and amazing flavor with tight-knit tannins and a vibrant, lingering finish. Arlandino is a Grignolino of great character, extremely complex on the nose, and just as rich, full-bodied on the palate. It's rare to find a Freisa like their Sorì di Giul '15, elegant yet potent and rich.

● Grignolino d'Asti M '13	♈♈♈ 5
● Freisa d'Asti Sorì di Giul '15	♈♈ 5
● Grignolino d'Asti Arlandino '17	♈♈ 3*
● Barbera d'Asti Sup. Setecàpita '15	♈♈ 5
● Barbera d'Asti Sup. V. Lina '16	♈♈ 3
○ Monferrato Salidoro '17	♈♈ 3
● Barbera d'Asti Sup. Setecàpita '13	♉♉ 5
● Barbera d'Asti Sup. Setecàpita '12	♉♉ 3
● Barbera d'Asti Sup. V. Lina '15	♉♉ 3*
● Barbera d'Asti Sup. V. Lina '14	♉♉ 3
● Barbera d'Asti Sup. V. Lina '13	♉♉ 3
● Freisa d'Asti Sorì di Giul '13	♉♉ 5
● Freisa d'Asti Sorì di Giul '12	♉♉ 3
● Grignolino d'Asti Arlandino '16	♉♉ 3
● Grignolino d'Asti M2012 '12	♉♉ 3*

Santa Clelia

REG. ROSSANA, 7
10035 MAZZÈ [TO]
TEL. +39 0119835187
www.santaclelia.it

CELLAR SALES
PRE-BOOKED VISITS
ANNUAL PRODUCTION 70,000 bottles
HECTARES UNDER VINE 12.00
VITICULTURE METHOD Certified Organic
SUSTAINABLE WINERY

Gabriella and Sergio Dezzuto's winery is on its 20th year of activity. The pair are the tireless artificers of a two-point philosophy. On the one hand there's their ecological (and organic) approach to cultivation in the vineyard, and on the other respect for the natural characteristics of Erbaluce, which means forgoing invasive production practices. Their vineyards are situated on marly hills, rich in sand, which sees to it that stagnant water doesn't form and guarantees broad aromas. The Essenthia '18 is subtle and complex, rich in aromas of flowers and white-fleshed fruit on a background of honey. On the palate it's generous and pervasive, but also fresh and dynamic, supple and highly pleasant. The Ypa '18 impresses on the palate, proving generous and multifaceted, though a bit less focused aromatically. Their Spumante Brut RIgore '11 is a bit worn down by its years. It's worth visiting the winery, both for the passion of its owners and for the area's natural beauty.

○ Erbaluce di Caluso Essenthia '18	🍷🍷	3*
○ Erbaluce di Caluso Ypa '18	🍷🍷	3
○ Erbaluce di Caluso Brut Rigore '11	🍷	5
○ Caluso Passito Dus '09	🍷🍷	4
○ Erbaluce di Caluso Essenthia '17	🍷🍷	3
○ Erbaluce di Caluso Essenthia '16	🍷🍷	3
○ Erbaluce di Caluso Ypa '17	🍷🍷	3*
○ Erbaluce di Caluso Ypa '16	🍷🍷	3

Paolo Saracco

VIA CIRCONVALLAZIONE, 6
12053 CASTIGLIONE TINELLA [CN]
TEL. +39 0141855113
www.paolosaracco.it

CELLAR SALES
PRE-BOOKED VISITS
ANNUAL PRODUCTION 600,000 bottles
HECTARES UNDER VINE 46.00

Castiglione Tinella is without a doubt Moscato d'Asti wine country. It's here that the Saracco family have operated since the early 20th century, specializing in the unmistakable sweet wines made with the region's widespread aromatic grape. The turning point came in the late 1980s, when, after completing his enological studies, Paolo decided to begin bottling. Thus their selection was enriched with Chardonnay, Riesling, Pinot Nero and Barbera as well. Saracco's selection once again proves that it's got a number of tricks up its sleeve. The Pinot Nero '17 brings together varietal identity and territorial identity. The Chardonnay Prasué '18 is no less good with its spicy aromatic suite, sensations amplified on its broad, pervasive palate. Both 2018 Moscatos live up to their fame. The DOCG offers up aromas of peach, sage and candied citrus, finding rhythm thanks to its vibrant acidity, while the d'Autunno is marked by hints of lime, sage and gustatory tension.

○ Moscato d'Asti '18	🍷🍷	3*
○ Piemonte Moscato d'Autunno '18	🍷🍷	3*
● Piemonte Pinot Nero '17	🍷🍷	5
○ Langhe Chardonnay Prasué '18	🍷🍷	3
○ Langhe Riesling '18	🍷	3
○ Moscato d'Asti '16	🍷🍷🍷	3*
○ Piemonte Moscato d'Autunno '09	🍷🍷🍷	3*
● Barbera d'Alba '16	🍷🍷	3
○ Langhe Chardonnay Prasué '16	🍷🍷	3
○ Moscato d'Asti '17	🍷🍷	3*
○ Moscato d'Asti '15	🍷🍷	3
○ Piemonte Moscato d'Autunno '17	🍷🍷	3*
○ Piemonte Moscato d'Autunno '16	🍷🍷	3*
○ Piemonte Moscato d'Autunno '15	🍷🍷	3*
○ Piemonte Moscato d'Autunno '14	🍷🍷	3*
○ Piemonte Moscato d'Autunno '13	🍷🍷	3*
● Piemonte Pinot Nero '13	🍷🍷	5

Roberto Sarotto

VIA RONCONUOVO, 13
12050 NEVIGLIE [CN]
TEL. +39 0173630228
www.robertosarotto.com

CELLAR SALES
PRE-BOOKED VISITS
ANNUAL PRODUCTION 700,000 bottles
HECTARES UNDER VINE 84.00
SUSTAINABLE WINERY

Roberto Sarotto's winery is among the largest and most diverse in the region, thanks to an estate that comprises more than 50 hectares (plus 30 hectares of rented plots). It stretches from Barolo to Barbaresco, Gavi and Asti, making for a selection that covers the classic appellations but also leaves space for innovative projects and new stylistic directions. Their approach centers on great intensity and aromatic richness, making for mature and spicy wines, pervasive and soft, all available at accessible prices. Among the wines presented this year, we point out the nice performance put in by their Chardonnay Puro '18, with its aromas of aniseed and vanilla, its elegant and creamy development and its long finish. It's a balsamic profile that we find in their harmonious, well-balanced, succulent and well-made Barolo Audace '15, with its sweet, mature aromas, and its sensations of red fruit and cocoa powder. Notes of bottled cherries and pepper mark their Barbaresco Currà Riserva '14.

● Barbaresco Currà Ris. '14	♟♟ 5
● Barbaresco Gaia Principe '16	♟♟ 6
● Barolo Audace '15	♟♟ 4
○ Gavi Aurora '18	♟♟ 2*
○ Gavi del Comune di Gavi Bric Sassi '18	♟♟ 2*
○ Langhe Arneis Runcneuv '18	♟♟ 2*
○ Piemonte Chardonnay Puro '18	♟♟ 3
● Barbera d'Alba Elena la Luna '17	♟ 4
● Barbaresco Gaia Principe '15	♟♟ 6
● Barolo Audace '14	♟♟ 4
● Barolo Briccobergera '13	♟♟ 4
○ Gavi Aurora '17	♟♟ 2*

Scagliola

VIA SAN SIRO, 42
14052 CALOSSO [AT]
TEL. +39 0141853183
www.scagliolavini.com

CELLAR SALES
PRE-BOOKED VISITS
ANNUAL PRODUCTION 200,000 bottles
HECTARES UNDER VINE 37.00

Scagliola's wines tell of a rich family history. Camillo founded the producer in the 1930s, and today young Martina and Federica represent the fifth generation. From the beginning, San Siro hill has been behind their success. It's a district of Calosso, a borderland between Monferrato and Langhe where the soil is a unique mix of sand, layers of tuff and calcareous pockets. The complexity of their vineyards' pedoclimate and personalities come through in an extremely rich selection, which sees Barbera reds and Moscato sweet wines at the fore. This year's scorings fully reflect the hierarchy of their selection. Their two Barbera Superiores, which are in many complementary, are excellent. The SanSì '17 brings together opulence, raciness, flavor with notes of cherry, sweet spices and tobacco. The SanSì Antologia '16 is a bit held back on the primaries by notes of oak, but is just as mobile, persistent over the long term. The fresh, balanced Moscato d'Asti Volo di Farfalle also stands out.

● Barbera d'Asti Sup. SanSì '17	♟♟ 6
● Barbera d'Asti Sup. SanSì Antologia '16	♟♟ 8
○ Moscato d'Asti Volo di Farfalle '18	♟♟ 3*
● M.to Rosso Azörd '17	♟♟ 5
○ Moscato d'Asti Primo Bacio '18	♟♟ 3
○ Piemonte Chardonnay Casot Dan Vian '18	♟♟ 3
● Barbera d'Asti Sup. SanSì Sel. '01	♟♟♟ 6
● Barbera d'Asti Sup. SanSì Sel. '00	♟♟♟ 6
● Barbera d'Asti Sup. SanSì Sel. '99	♟♟♟ 5
● Barbera d'Asti Frem '17	♟♟ 4
● Barbera d'Asti Frem '16	♟♟ 4
● Barbera d'Asti Sup. SanSì '16	♟♟ 6
● Barbera d'Asti Sup. SanSì '15	♟♟ 6
● Barbera d'Asti Sup. SanSì Antologia '15	♟♟ 8
○ Moscato d'Asti Volo di Farfalle '17	♟♟ 3*
○ Moscato d'Asti Volo di Farfalle '15	♟♟ 3*

Simone Scaletta

LOC. MANZONI, 61
12065 MONFORTE D'ALBA [CN]
TEL. +39 3484912733
www.simonescaletta.it

CELLAR SALES
PRE-BOOKED VISITS
ACCOMMODATION
ANNUAL PRODUCTION 35,000 bottles
HECTARES UNDER VINE 5.50

Here on his five hectares of property in Monforte d'Alba, Simone proposes wines of great personality. These bring together a strong territorial identity with a pronounced pleasantness and vibrant character. Behind it all is a minimally-invasive approach and the utmost respect for the environment in their vineyards: Viglioni, Sarsera, Chirlet and Autin 'd Madama. In the cellar, non-invasive extraction is privileged, making for a distinct style. And if the intrinsic quality of their wines is taken into account, their prices are very honest. This year they submitted another high-quality selection, with the Barolo Ris. '13 doing the honors. Redolent of Mediterranean scrub and blackcurrant, on the palate it's full and assertive, with a long, lively finish. The subtle and succulent Barolo Bussia '15 features sensations of small wild berries and harmonious development, closing with a nice, fresh resolution. A pale color and peppery whiffs characterize the pleasant Dolcetto d'Alba Viglioni '17.

● Barolo Bussia '15	♟♟ 8
● Barolo Ris. '13	♟♟ 7
● Barbera d'Alba Sup. Sarsera '17	♟♟ 5
● Barolo Chirlet '15	♟♟ 6
● Dolcetto d'Alba Viglioni '17	♟♟ 2*
● Langhe Nebbiolo Autin 'd Madama '17	♟ 4
● Barbera d'Alba Sup. Sarsera '16	♟♟ 5
● Barbera d'Alba Sup. Sarsera '15	♟♟ 4
● Barolo Bricco San Pietro Chirlet '14	♟♟ 8
● Barolo Bricco San Pietro Chirlet '12	♟♟ 6
● Barolo Bussia '14	♟♟ 8
● Barolo Chirlet '13	♟♟ 6
● Barolo Chirlet '11	♟♟ 6
● Barolo Ris. '11	♟♟ 7
● Langhe Nebbiolo Autin 'd Madama '16	♟♟ 5
● Langhe Nebbiolo Autin 'd Madama '15	♟♟ 4
● Langhe Nebbiolo Autin 'd Madama '13	♟♟ 3

Giorgio Scarzello e Figli

VIA ALBA, 29
12060 BAROLO [CN]
TEL. +39 017356170
www.barolodibarolo.com

CELLAR SALES
PRE-BOOKED VISITS
ANNUAL PRODUCTION 25,000 bottles
HECTARES UNDER VINE 5.50

For some time now this small winery has been deservedly famous, thanks to Giorgio's top-quality Barolos, which can age well in the bottle for decades. Today his son Federico is following the same path with enviable constance, realizing wines that, every year, prove to be among Barolo's best. His Sarmassa Vigna Merenda is a particularly noteworthy offering. About 5,000 bottles are released 5 years after vintage, and it's only made during the best years. But their Barolo del Comune di Barolo is just as pure and elegant. And, without a doubt, his potent and elegant Barbera d'Alba is another must. The splendid Merenda vineyard didn't take full advantage of a cool 2013, and so the resulting Barolo is a bit closed on the nose, with backgrounded notes of raspberries and white truffle, and a palate marked by austere tannins. Their well-crafted Barolo del comune di Barolo sees an analogous stylistic track.

● Barolo del Comune di Barolo '13	♟♟ 5
● Barolo Sarmassa V. Merenda '13	♟♟ 6
● Langhe Nebbiolo '17	♟♟ 3
● Barolo Sarmassa V. Merenda '10	♟♟♟ 6
● Barolo V. Merenda '99	♟♟♟ 5
● Barbera d'Alba Sup. '15	♟♟ 4
● Barolo del Comune di Barolo '14	♟♟ 5
● Barolo del Comune di Barolo '11	♟♟ 5
● Barolo del Comune di Barolo '10	♟♟ 5
● Barolo del Comune di Barolo '09	♟♟ 5
● Barolo Sarmassa V. Merenda '12	♟♟ 6
● Barolo Sarmassa V. Merenda '11	♟♟ 6
● Barolo Sarmassa V. Merenda '09	♟♟ 6
● Langhe Nebbiolo '16	♟♟ 3
● Langhe Nebbiolo '15	♟♟ 3
● Langhe Nebbiolo '13	♟♟ 3

★★Paolo Scavino

FRAZ. GARBELLETTO
VIA ALBA-BAROLO, 157
12060 CASTIGLIONE FALLETTO [CN]
TEL. +39 017362850
www.paoloscavino.com

CELLAR SALES
PRE-BOOKED VISITS
ANNUAL PRODUCTION 130,000 bottles
HECTARES UNDER VINE 29.00

This celebrated winery is about to turn 100. Founded in 1921, today it's masterfully overseen by Enrico Scavino, a man who's recognized by his colleagues as one of Barolo's great winemakers. His daughters actively contribute to managing this multifaceted estate, which comprises excellent vineyards in 5 different municipalities, and an extremely charming cellar that's worth visiting. Among the various selections proposed, their Barolo Bric dël Fiasc, cultivated in Castiglione Falletto, is a perennial standout, as is their Ris. Rocche dell'Annunziata, from La Morra. Enrico always manages to express with precision and the utmost quality the personality of each cru. The Rocche dell'Annunziata Ris. '13 is a model of harmony, with dried rose, licorice and red fruits fusing in a single, enchanting aroma. On the palate it's superb, as rich as it is fresh, elegant. We once again note their majestic Bric dël Fiasc, made with grapes from the lovely 2015 harvest.

● Barolo Bric dël Fiasc '15	♥♥ 8
● Barolo Cannubi '15	♥♥ 8
● Barolo Carobric '15	♥♥ 8
● Barolo Monvigliero '15	♥♥ 8
● Barolo Prapò '15	♥♥ 7
● Barolo Rocche dell'Annunziata Ris. '13	♥♥ 8
● Barbera d'Alba '18	♥♥ 3
● Barolo Bricco Ambrogio '15	♥♥ 8
● Barolo Enrico Scavino '15	♥♥ 7
● Barolo Ravera '15	♥♥ 7
● Langhe Nebbiolo '17	♥♥ 4
● Dolcetto d'Alba '18	♥ 3
○ Langhe Bianco Sorriso '18	♥ 3
● Barolo Bric dël Fiasc '12	♥♥♥ 8
● Barolo Novantesimo Ris. '11	♥♥♥ 8
● Barolo Rocche dell'Annunziata Ris. '11	♥♥♥ 8

Schiavenza

VIA MAZZINI, 4
12050 SERRALUNGA D'ALBA [CN]
TEL. +39 0173613115
www.schiavenza.com

CELLAR SALES
PRE-BOOKED VISITS
RESTAURANT SERVICE
ANNUAL PRODUCTION 46,000 bottles
HECTARES UNDER VINE 11.00
SUSTAINABLE WINERY

This small family-run winery, which comprises excellent vineyards in all of Serralunga d'Alba, follows a traditional approach. Luciano and Walter prove that, when you bring the right care to your work, pronounced tannic presence doesn't have to make for a hard, aggressive style of Barolo, but can stop at substance and texture. So it is that the large barrels in their old cellar host selections like their Prapò and Cerretta, two charming wines that exhibit exquisite harmony. They're already enjoyable upon release, and caressingly velvety after a decade in the bottle. Four wines and four bullseyes for their 2015 Barolos. The Broglio offers up licorice-scented complexity, bringing together close-knit, pleasant tannins with superb fruity flesh. The rich Cerretta is more youthful, perfectly harmonious. The Prapò sees added sensations of aniseed and mint, as well as delicate tannins. Their balsamic Barolo del comune di Serralunga d'Alba is just a bit less multifaceted.

● Barolo Broglio '15	♥♥ 6
● Barolo Cerretta '15	♥♥ 6
● Barolo Prapò '15	♥♥ 7
● Barolo del Comune di Serralunga d'Alba '15	♥♥ 5
● Langhe Nebbiolo '17	♥♥ 4
● Barbera d'Alba '17	♥ 3
● Barolo Broglio '11	♥♥♥ 5
● Barolo Broglio '05	♥♥♥ 5
● Barolo Broglio '04	♥♥♥ 5
● Barolo Broglio Ris. '08	♥♥♥ 7
● Barolo Broglio Ris. '04	♥♥♥ 5
● Barolo Prapò '08	♥♥♥ 6
● Barolo Broglio '14	♥♥ 6
● Barolo Prapò '14	♥♥ 6

PIEDMONT

Mauro Sebaste

FRAZ. GALLO D'ALBA
VIA GARIBALDI, 222BIS
12051 ALBA [CN]
TEL. +39 0173262148
www.maurosebaste.it

CELLAR SALES
PRE-BOOKED VISITS
ANNUAL PRODUCTION 150,000 bottles
HECTARES UNDER VINE 30.00

The heart of the winery is situated in Langa, which Mauro Sebaste chose for its celebrated crus (led by Prapò and Cerretta in Serralunga d'Alba). But his desire to offer a selection representative of southern Piedmont brought him to enlarge the estate, which is now turning in excellent results with both whites and reds (from Monferrato and Roero as well). Among their 14 wines, their Freisa (dedicated to his mother, Sylla, one of the most acclaimed interpreters of this rare grape) also deserves attention. The Barolo Cerretta '15, which brings together elegant notes of licorice with the winemaker's skill in conferring elegance, represents a perfect expression of the vintage, thanks to notes of perfectly mature red fruit and a precise, particularly potent and pervasive, interpretation of the cru. The recent purchase of the Costemonghisio cru made for a well-crafted wine that's modern in its freshness and delicate touch of oak.

● Barolo Cerretta '15	♀♀	6
● Barolo Trèsùri '15	♀♀	6
● Nizza Costemonghisio '16	♀♀	5
○ Langhe Bianco Centobricchi '17	♀	5
● Nebbiolo d'Alba Parigi '17	♀	4
● Barbera d'Alba Sup. Centobricchi '16	♀♀	5
● Barbera d'Alba Sup. Centobricchi '11	♀♀	4
● Barolo Cerretta '14	♀♀	6
● Barolo Ghè Ris. '12	♀♀	8
● Barolo Ghé Ris. '08	♀♀	8
● Barolo Prapò '11	♀♀	7
● Barolo Prapò '09	♀♀	7
● Barolo Prapò '08	♀♀	7
● Barolo Trèsùri '14	♀♀	6

F.lli Seghesio

LOC. CASTELLETTO, 19
12065 MONFORTE D'ALBA [CN]
TEL. +39 017378108
www.fratelliseghesio.com

CELLAR SALES
PRE-BOOKED VISITS
ANNUAL PRODUCTION 55,000 bottles
HECTARES UNDER VINE 10.00

Within the vast and prized area of Castelletto, the La Villa vineyard has the peculiarity of giving rise to a Barolo that's always quite structured and characterized by excellent freshness. These qualities, combined with the fact that the Seghesio family's vines are almost 50 years old and the use of small French oak barrels for aging, explain a selection that's as dense as it is elegant, as rich in fruity flesh as it is pleasantly drinkable. Their elegant Barbera d'Alba La Chiesa is perennially lively and bold as well. Only one wine was proposed for tasting this year, their admirable Barolo La Villa '15. It enters on graceful fruity notes on a background of tobacco and sweet spices. On the palate it exhibits bold structure, with delicate, gradually unfolding tannins that lend excellent pervasiveness. It's a delicate and complex Barolo that's destined to continue improving in the bottle for many years.

● Barolo La Villa '15	♀♀	7
● Barbera d'Alba Vign. della Chiesa '00	♀♀♀	4*
● Barbera d'Alba Vign. della Chiesa '97	♀♀♀	4*
● Barolo La Villa '10	♀♀♀	7
● Barolo Vign. La Villa '04	♀♀♀	6
● Barolo Vign. La Villa '99	♀♀♀	7
● Barolo Vign. La Villa '91	♀♀♀	6
● Barbera d'Alba '16	♀♀	3
● Barbera d'Alba La Chiesa '12	♀♀	4
● Barolo '14	♀♀	7
● Barolo '13	♀♀	7
● Barolo '12	♀♀	7
● Barolo '11	♀♀	7
● Barolo La Villa '14	♀♀	7
● Barolo La Villa '13	♀♀	7
● Barolo La Villa '12	♀♀	7
● Barolo La Villa '11	♀♀	7

Tenute Sella

VIA IV NOVEMBRE, 130
13060 LESSONA [BI]
TEL. +39 01599455
www.tenutesella.it

CELLAR SALES
PRE-BOOKED VISITS
ANNUAL PRODUCTION 70,000 bottles
HECTARES UNDER VINE 22.50
SUSTAINABLE WINERY

This worthy producer, whose wines are made under the skilled, resourceful guidance of Paolo Benassi, hasn't settled for having restored the glory of Lessona and Bramaterra. Indeed, they've now chosen to evidence their bond with Nebbiolo through a Metodo Classico. Their Lessona is cultivated on soil marked by a high-quantity of sand, thus it's powerful without ever being too austere. Their Bramaterra is from an area rich in porphyry, which confers structure. This is mitigated through the addition of Croatina and Vespolina to the final blend. The Lessona 2013 sees lovely aromatic contrasts, bringing together fresh fruits, dried herbs with rhubarb, tobacco. On the palate it's still quite youthful, with nice flesh well-contrasted by lively tannins. Harmony marks the Orbello '17, made with 50% Nebbiolo, added shares Barbera, Croatina, Vespolina, and a splash of Cab. Sauvignon. Tantalizing notes of pepper and herbs tickle the nose — on the palate is has lovely fullness, pleasant sapidity.

● Lessona '13	🍷🍷 5
● Coste della Sesia Rosso Orbello '17	🍷🍷 3
⊙ Coste della Sesia Rosato Majoli '18	🍷 3
○ Insubrico Pas Dosé M. Cl.	🍷 5
○ Piemonte Bianco Piandoro '18	🍷 3
● Bramaterra '12	🍷🍷 5
● Bramaterra I Porfidi '10	🍷🍷 5
● Lessona '12	🍷🍷 5
● Lessona S. Sebastiano allo Zoppo '10	🍷🍷 6
○ Piemonte Bianco Piandoro '17	🍷🍷 3

Enrico Serafino

C.SO ASTI, 5
12043 CANALE [CN]
TEL. +39 0173979485
www.enricoserafino.it

CELLAR SALES
PRE-BOOKED VISITS
ANNUAL PRODUCTION 400,000 bottles
HECTARES UNDER VINE 60.00
SUSTAINABLE WINERY

Founded in 1878 and today owned by the Krause family, Enrico Serafino was among the first producers in the region to make Metodo Classico. The winery avails itself of various vineyards situated in Canale, which host Nebbiolo, Barbera and Arneis (for classical Roero wines), while their sparkling Chardonnay and Pinot Nero are made with grapes provided by trusted growers. Their still wines are well crafted and modern, while their sparkling wines exhibit great finesse and aromatic precision. Their Alta Langa Pas Dosé Zéro Ris. '13 once again proves that it's top-notch: delicate, persistent beading anticipate generous floral notes and hints of white peach. On the palate it's long, complex, fruit-infused. The excellent Alta Langa Brut Oudeis '15 is rich in fruit, fresh and broad all at once, while the Alta Langa Blanc de Blancs Propago '15 stands out for its fragrances of damson, lemon peel and bread, and a supple, pleasant palate. Their selection of still wines also performs at high levels.

○ Alta Langa Pas Dosé Zéro Ris. '13	🍷🍷🍷 7
○ Alta Langa Brut Blanc de Blancs Propago '15	🍷🍷 7
○ Alta Langa Brut Oudeis '15	🍷🍷 5
⊙ Alta Langa Brut Rosé '15	🍷🍷 5
● Barbaresco Sanavento '16	🍷🍷 6
● Barbera d'Alba Pajena '17	🍷🍷 5
● Barolo '15	🍷🍷 7
● Barolo del Comune di Serralunga d'Alba '15	🍷🍷 7
● Barolo Monclivio '15	🍷🍷 6
● Nebbiolo d'Alba Tovasacco '16	🍷🍷 5
○ Roero Arneis Poggio di Caro '18	🍷🍷 4
● Roero Oesio '16	🍷🍷 4
○ Alta Langa Brut Zero Nature Sboccatura Tardiva '11	🍷🍷🍷 6
○ Alta Langa Zero Ris. '12	🍷🍷🍷 7

La Smilla

VIA GARIBALDI, 7
15060 BOSIO [AL]
TEL. +39 0143684245
www.lasmilla.it

CELLAR SALES
ANNUAL PRODUCTION 100,000 bottles
HECTARES UNDER VINE 5.00

This family-run winery has deep roots on the steep hills of Bosio. In the vineyard tradition reigns, with only native grape varieties cultivated. Cortese, Dolcetto and Barbera give rise to seven wines. Their four Corteses comprise a base level Gavi, a Gavi del Comune di Gavi and I Bergi, a wine made with select, cask-aged grapes. For some years now these have been accompanied by a commendably well-made Metodo Classico. Among their two Barberas the Calicanto (made with select grapes) stands out. Finally, they also produce an excellent Dolcetto di Ovada. Two 2018 Gavis, each with their own profile, led the selection of wines presented. The Gavi del Comune di Gavi is mature both in color and aromas, almost evolved, with a rich, buttery palate and an elegant finish. The Gavi is more approachable, intense in its fruit, with notes of flint and a weighty palate giving way to a nice, long finish. The Barbera d'Asti and Dolcetto di Ovada both prove well-made.

● Barbera d'Asti '17	♥♥ 2*
● Dolcetto di Ovada '17	♥♥ 2*
○ Gavi '18	♥♥ 2*
○ Gavi del Comune di Gavi '18	♥♥ 2*
○ Gavi Brut M. Cl. '15	♥ 3
○ M.to Bianco Bergi '17	♥ 3
● M.to Rosso Calicanto '16	♥ 3
○ Gavi '17	♥♥ 2*
○ Gavi del Comune di Gavi '17	♥♥ 2*
○ Gavi I Bergi '15	♥♥ 3*

Socré

S.DA TERZOLO, 7
12050 BARBARESCO [CN]
TEL. +39 3487121685
www.socre.it

CELLAR SALES
PRE-BOOKED VISITS
ANNUAL PRODUCTION 30,000 botties
HECTARES UNDER VINE 5.50

What might have seemed more like a hobby has transformed into a true passion, such that Marco Piacentino is significantly enlarging his vineyards, and preparing to offer a number of new wines. So it is that they've purchased plots in Barbaresco, in the magnificent Pajoré cru, in Dogliani and even Alta Langa, where they'll cultivate the grapes for a new sparkling wines. For the moment their selection, which is always precise and well-studied, comprises classically styled reds, from Barbaresco to Freisa, and a highly successful Chardonnay. The complex, elegant Barbaresco Roncaglie '15 sees plush tannins and lovely length, while the full, generous Barbaresco '16 is marked by muscular structure and bewitching scents of violet. The Freisa '17 brings charming roughness together with fragrances of blackberry and wet earth. Butter, honey, tropical fruit and oak make up the focused aromatic suite of their Chardonnay Paint It Black '17, a richly-textured, velvety and also rather dry, long drink.

● Barbaresco '16	♥♥ 5
● Barbaresco Roncaglie '15	♥♥ 6
○ Langhe Chardonnay Paint It Black '17	♥♥ 3*
● Langhe Freisa '17	♥♥ 3
● Barbaresco '15	♥♥ 5
● Barbaresco '14	♥♥ 5
● Barbaresco '13	♥♥ 5
● Barbaresco Roncaglie '14	♥♥ 6
● Barbaresco Roncaglie '13	♥♥ 6
● Barbaresco Roncaglie '12	♥♥ 6
● Barbera d'Alba Sup. '15	♥♥ 3
● Cisterna d'Asti De Scapin '13	♥♥ 2*
○ Langhe Chardonnay Paint It Black '16	♥♥ 3*
● Langhe Nebbiolo '15	♥♥ 3

Giovanni Sordo

FRAZ. GARBELLETTO
VIA ALBA BAROLO, 175
12060 CASTIGLIONE FALLETTO [CN]
TEL. +39 017362853
www.sordogiovanni.it

CELLAR SALES
PRE-BOOKED VISITS
ACCOMMODATION
ANNUAL PRODUCTION 350,000 bottles
HECTARES UNDER VINE 53.00

Their spectacular tasting room, which offers guests a rare view of Barolo's vineyards, is worthy of a winery more than a century old. Moreover, visitors can't help but be enchanted by a procession of some 110 large Slavonian oak barrels, which hold the Barolo from their 8 prized crus in 5 different municipalities. It's a winery that's not resting on its laurels and has, thanks in part to Giorgio Sordo's dynamic guidance, obtained increasingly noteworthy results. A nice selection saw their 2015 Barolos prove a bit less impressive than the 2013s. Scents of quinine, black berries in the Rocche di Castiglione — tannins still dominate on the palate. The Monvigliero is austere, close-knit. Licorice, berry scents mark the Gabutti, which is astringent, not particularly expansive. The harmonious, drinkable entry-level Barolo is floral, strawberry-scented, elegant. The valid Rapujé '10, made with mature Nebbiolo, Barbera and a splash of Dolcetto, is slightly oxidative but revived by minty hints.

● Barolo '15	▼▼ 5
● Barolo Gabutti '15	▼▼ 7
● Barolo Monvigliero '15	▼▼ 7
● Barolo Rocche di Castiglione '15	▼▼ 7
● Dolcetto d'Alba '18	▼▼ 3
● Langhe Rosso Rapujé '10	▼▼ 3
● Barolo '14	♀♀ 5
● Barolo Monvigliero '14	♀♀ 7
● Barolo Monvigliero '13	♀♀ 7
● Barolo Parussi '14	♀♀ 7
● Barolo Parussi '13	♀♀ 7
● Barolo Perno '14	♀♀ 7
● Barolo Perno '13	♀♀ 7
● Barolo Ravera '13	♀♀ 7
● Barolo Rocche di Castiglione '14	♀♀ 7
● Barolo Villero '14	♀♀ 8

★★Sottimano

LOC. COTTÀ, 21
12052 NEIVE [CN]
TEL. +39 0173635186
www.sottimano.it

CELLAR SALES
PRE-BOOKED VISITS
ANNUAL PRODUCTION 85,000 bottles
HECTARES UNDER VINE 18.00
VITICULTURE METHOD Certified Organic

In almost 40 years, Rino and Andrea Sottimano's winery has managed to earn a position among Langa's best known producers. And they've done it without the use of added yeasts, without must concentrators, without chemicals in the vineyard. Indeed, the secret lies in their great passion and the masterful use of French wood during aging. They offer six Barbarescos, including a rarely released reserve, all of consistently outstanding quality, but their entire range of reds exhibit notable personality. Their Barbaresco Pajoré is a splendid Tre Bicchieri. On the nose it's intense and elegant, with lovely notes of dried herbs and red fruit followed by tobacco and licorice. On the palate it proves striking, with plenty of flesh and a focused, extremely long finish. The Cottà exhibits excellent contrast between notes of sweet tobacco and licorice, with a compelling grip on the palate made possible thanks to bold fruity richness.

● Barbaresco Pajoré '16	▼▼▼ 7
● Barbaresco Cottà '16	▼▼ 7
● Barbaresco Fausoni '16	▼▼ 7
● Barbaresco Currà '14	▼▼ 8
● Langhe Nebbiolo '18	▼▼ 3
● Barbaresco Cottà '15	♀♀♀ 7
● Barbaresco Cottà '05	♀♀♀ 7
● Barbaresco Currà '12	♀♀♀ 8
● Barbaresco Currà '10	♀♀♀ 8
● Barbaresco Currà '08	♀♀♀ 7
● Barbaresco Currà '04	♀♀♀ 6
● Barbaresco Pajoré '14	♀♀♀ 7
● Barbaresco Pajoré '10	♀♀♀ 7
● Barbaresco Pajoré '08	♀♀♀ 7
● Barbaresco Ris. '10	♀♀♀ 8
● Barbaresco Ris. '05	♀♀♀ 8
● Barbaresco Ris. '04	♀♀♀ 8

★Luigi Spertino

VIA LEA, 505
14047 MOMBERCELLI [AT]
TEL. +39 0141959098
luigi.spertino@libero.it

CELLAR SALES
PRE-BOOKED VISITS
ANNUAL PRODUCTION 40,000 bottles
HECTARES UNDER VINE 9.00

In his early twenties, Luigi Spertino chose to break with the family tradition of vine growing and move to Turin, where he managed wine shops and restaurants for 20 years. He began producing Barbera and Grignolino in the late 1970s, and in a short time his experience and efforts paid off, allowing him to sell almost 20,000 bottles of Grignolino throughout the province. For many Luigi was the king of Grignolino. Today his son Mauro and grandchildren oversee the winery, which focuses on Barbera, but still has Girgnolino in its heart. Perhaps the planting of 2 hectares of Grignolino on the sandy part of the Mandorla hill was auspicious, though not to take anything away from their other wines, which all exhibit exceptional quality. Finally their flagship product takes home Tre Bicchieri: the Grignolino d'Asti '18 is a great, modern red, fragrant and well-gauged in its structure. It can even be enjoyed cool, together with a seafood.

● Grignolino d'Asti '18	♥♥♥	3*
● Barbera d'Asti Sup. V. La Mandorla '17	♥♥	8
● Grignolino d'Asti Margherita Barbero '18	♥♥	3*
○ Piemonte Pinot Nero Brut Nature M. Cl Cuvée della Famiglia '15	♥♥	7
● Barbera d'Asti '17	♥♥	4
● Barbera d'Asti Sup. La Mandorla '13	♥♥♥	8
● Barbera d'Asti Sup. La Mandorla '10	♥♥♥	8
● Barbera d'Asti Sup. V. La Mandorla '16	♥♥♥	8
● Barbera d'Asti Sup. V. La Mandorla '15	♥♥♥	8
● Barbera d'Asti Sup. V. La Mandorla '12	♥♥♥	8
● Barbera d'Asti Sup. V. La Mandorla Edizione La Grisa '14	♥♥♥	8

★★★La Spinetta

VIA ANNUNZIATA, 17
14054 CASTAGNOLE DELLE LANZE [AT]
TEL. +39 0141877396
www.la-spinetta.com

CELLAR SALES
PRE-BOOKED VISITS
ACCOMMODATION
ANNUAL PRODUCTION 500,000 bottles
HECTARES UNDER VINE 100.00
SUSTAINABLE WINERY

Giorgio is a firm believer in a modern style of winemaking and aging, thus, in pursuing the perfect wine, he avails himself of rotary macerators and new barriques, eschewing practices and materials unable to provide adequate aromatic elegance. But the real revolution came in the vineyard, convinced as he is that great grapes are more than just a slogan — they are at the foundation of any quality wine. Walking in his rows of Nebbiolo it's clear that they've researched the characteristics of each single plot. As usual, the Rivetti family's acclaimed estate proposed a first-class selection. Their 2016 Barbarescos dazzled, the Gallina with its hints of hazelnut, peach on an elegant oak backdrop. It's highly complex, just a bit austere, with a lovely balance between fruit, tannins, acidity. The Barolo Campè '15 is even richer in red fruits, endowed with weighty tannins well-integrated in a bold, muscular structure. The Pin del '15 is one of the most elegant versions in memory.

● Barbaresco Gallina '16	♥♥	8
● Barbaresco Starderi '16	♥♥	8
● Barbera d'Alba Gallina '16	♥♥	6
● Barolo Campè '15	♥♥	8
● M.to Rosso Pin '15	♥♥	6
● Barbaresco Valeirano '16	♥♥	8
● Barbaresco Vign. Bordini '16	♥♥	7
● Barbera d'Asti Ca' di Pian '16	♥♥	4
○ Langhe Bianco '16	♥♥	6
● Langhe Nebbiolo '16	♥♥	5
○ Moscato d'Asti Bricco Quaglia '18	♥♥	3
○ Piemonte Chardonnay Lidia '16	♥♥	6
● Barbaresco Gallina '11	♥♥♥	8
● Barbaresco Vign. Starderi '07	♥♥♥	8
● Barbera d'Asti Sup. Bionzo '09	♥♥♥	6
● Barbera d'Asti Sup. Bionzo '07	♥♥♥	6

Marchese Luca Spinola

FRAZ. ROVERETO DI GAVI
LOC. CASCINA MASSIMILIANA, 97
15066 GAVI [AL]
TEL. +39 0143682514
www.marcheselucaspinola.it

CELLAR SALES
PRE-BOOKED VISITS
ANNUAL PRODUCTION 30,000 bottles
HECTARES UNDER VINE 15.00
VITICULTURE METHOD Certified Organic

Marchese Luca Spinola's vineyards span plots in Tassarolo and Rovereto, historic areas for Cortese. The estate, which brings together territory and cultivar with the Spinola family's millennium-old history, gives rise to three wines. The Massimiliano isi marked by a more modern style, by virtue of fermentation in barriques, aimed at conferring complexity to this flagship wine. The Carlo, more traditionally-styled, occupies the lion's share of their production. And the Marchese col Fondo, made with Cortese, finishes with bottle fermentation, thus its slight sparkle. The Massimiliano '17 exhibits nice aromatic complexity, with fragrances of white-fleshed fruit melding rapidly with notes of licorice and tobacco. On the palate its attack is potent, fresh, with a lovely sapid stage giving way to an intense finish. The Carlo is a more classically-styled wine, redolent of fruit and flint. On the palate it's rich and full-flavored, with pronounced acidity lending vitality to a taut finish.

○ Gavi del Comune di Gavi Carlo '18	🍷🍷 3*
○ Gavi del Comune di Gavi Massimiliano '17	🍷🍷 3*
○ Gavi del Comune di Gavi '16	🍷🍷 2*
○ Gavi del Comune di Gavi '15	🍷🍷 2*
○ Gavi del Comune di Gavi Et. Blu '14	🍷🍷 2*
○ Gavi del Comune di Gavi Tenuta Massimiliana '16	🍷🍷 3*
○ Gavi del Comune di Gavi Tenuta Massimiliana '15	🍷🍷 3

Giuseppe Stella

S.DA BOSSOLA, 8
14055 COSTIGLIOLE D'ASTI [AT]
TEL. +39 0141966142
www.stellavini.com

CELLAR SALES
PRE-BOOKED VISITS
ANNUAL PRODUCTION 50,000 bottles
HECTARES UNDER VINE 12.00

The part of the business specialized in wine started with Giuseppe, the father of the estate's current owners. It took sacrifice for them to join the family's terrain together and plant the best plots. Today Massimo and Paolo cultivate 12 hectares, producing about 50,000 bottles/year, just a little over half of the total wine made. Paolo, their young enologist, loves wines that express Costigliole without embellishments. Traditional varieties (Barbera, Cortese, Grignolino, Freisa and Moscato) and Chardonnay give rise to wines with nice acidity and structure, and that naturally age well. Their selection of Barbera d'Asti exhibits plenty of personality and pluck, from the more youthful, approachable Stravisan '17 to the more complex Giaiet and the Maestro (dedicated to their grandfather, a music teacher). This year their Freisa '16 was at the head of the class, bringing together an elegant, complex nose (cherries, pepper, camphor) with an austere, succulent, extremely long palate.

● Freisa d'Asti Convento '16	🍷🍷 3*
● Barbera d'Asti Stravisan '17	🍷🍷 2*
● Barbera d'Asti Sup. Giaiet '16	🍷🍷 3
● Barbera d'Asti Sup. Il Maestro '16	🍷🍷 4
○ Piemonte Chardonnay Giaiet '17	🍷 3
● Barbera d'Asti Stravisan '13	🍷🍷 2*
● Barbera d'Asti Sup. Il Maestro '12	🍷🍷 4
● Grignolino d'Asti Sufragio '14	🍷🍷 3

Sulin

v.le Pininfarina, 14
14035 Grazzano Badoglio [AT]
Tel. +39 0141925136
www.sulin.it

CELLAR SALES
PRE-BOOKED VISITS
ANNUAL PRODUCTION 220,000 bottles
HECTARES UNDER VINE 19.50

Tradition and experience characterize a family history of winemaking that goes back to 1919. Today the Fracchia brothers oversee a dynamic winery, whose production is among the most solid and constant in the area. Their selection is dominated by wines made with native cultivars: Barbera, Grignolino, Dolcetto, Cortese and Malvasia di Casorzo. Among the international varieties used, a monovarietal Chardonnay stands out. It's fermented and briefly matured in 2500 liter casks, making for a surprising wine that's both ageworthy and varietal. Among the wines tasted, a new release stood out sharply: their Grignolino Monferace Brasal. It offers up intense tertiary aromas that anticipate a bold palate, rich and intense, with decisive and still-evolving tannins and a finish of notable length. The Ornella is a vibrant and multifaceted Barbera that exhibits well-calibrated oak before closing intense and long. Their Barbera '17 also put in an excellent performance.

● Piemonte Grignolino Monferace Brasal '15	♟♟ 5
● Barbera del M.to '17	♟♟ 2*
● Barbera del M.to Sup. Ornella '16	♟♟♟ 5
● Casorzo Voület '18	♟♟ 2*
● M.to Rosso Adriano '16	♟♟ 3
● Grignolino del M.to Casalese '18	♟ 2
○ Piemonte Chardonnay '18	♟ 2
● Barbera del M.to '16	♟♟ 2*
● Barbera del M.to '15	♟♟ 2*
● Barbera del M.to Sup. Ornella '15	♟♟ 5
● Barbera del M.to Sup. Ornella '13	♟♟ 5
● Casorzo '17	♟♟ 2*
● Casorzo '16	♟♟ 2*
● Grignolino del M.to Casalese '16	♟♟ 2*
○ Piemonte Chardonnay '17	♟♟ 2*
○ Piemonte Chardonnay '16	♟♟ 2*

Tacchino

via Martiri della Benedicta, 26
15060 Castelletto d'Orba [AL]
Tel. +39 0143830115
www.luigitacchino.it

CELLAR SALES
PRE-BOOKED VISITS
ANNUAL PRODUCTION 120,000 bottles
HECTARES UNDER VINE 12.00

Today Romina and Alessio Tacchino represent one of Ovada's viticultural mainstays. The experience of generations of family and the application of new technology allows them to regularly produce excellent wines that aren't afraid to age. Their premium offerings see the last part of alcoholic and malolactic fermentation carried out in barriques — from there maturation occurs according to the wine typology. It's a modern approach to vinification that takes nothing away from the peculiarities of the cultivars used, from Dolcetto di Ovada to Barbera. The Tacchino family's wines made an impact during our tastings, taking home Tre Bicchieri with their acclaimed Du Riva, and landing both their Barbera del Monferratos in our finals. The Du Riva '15 is intense, elegant, with lovely tannins and a memorable finish. The Albarola is quite youthful, with oak still dominant, but it enjoys a muscular structure and a long finish. The delicate, elegant Barbera '17 also performed well.

● Dolcetto di Ovada Sup. Du Riva '15	♟♟♟ 4*
● Barbera del M.to '17	♟♟ 3*
● Barbera del M.to Albarola '15	♟♟ 5
● Dolcetto di Ovada '17	♟♟ 2*
○ Gavi del Comune di Gavi '18	♟♟ 3
● M.to Rosso Di Fatto '16	♟♟ 4
● Dolcetto di Ovada '16	♟♟ 2*
● Dolcetto di Ovada '15	♟♟ 2*
● Dolcetto di Ovada Sup. Du Riva '13	♟♟♟ 4*
● Dolcetto di Ovada Sup. Du Riva '12	♟♟♟ 5
● Dolcetto di Ovada Sup. Du Riva '11	♟♟♟ 5
● Dolcetto di Ovada Sup. Du Riva '10	♟♟♟ 4*

Michele Taliano

c.so A. Manzoni, 24
12046 Montà [CN]
Tel. +39 0173975658
www.talianomichele.com

CELLAR SALES
PRE-BOOKED VISITS
ANNUAL PRODUCTION 60,000 bottles
HECTARES UNDER VINE 12.00

Brothers Alberto and Ezio oversee this historic family winery, which avails itself of private vineyards both in Roero (Montà) and in Barbaresco (San Rocco Seno d'Elvio). The territory's classic grapes are cultivated: Arneis, Nebbiolo, Barbera, Favorita, Dolcetto and Moscato, which are accompanied by small amounts of Sauvignon and Cabernet Sauvignon. Their wines are modern, balanced and, when it comes to the most important appellations, quite ageworthy. Their excellent Roero Roche dra Bossora Riserva '15 features aromas of raspberry, licorice and aromatic herbs on the nose. On the palate it makes a notable impact, coming through long and juicy, with velvety tannins. The Barbaresco Montersino Ad Altiora '15 is also excellent, with its fruity and spicy fragrances, its balance, lovely freshness and its rich flesh. The complex and full Roero Arneis Sernì '18 is well-crafted, as is the expansive and harmonious Barbaresco Montersino Tera Mia Riserva '12.

● Barbaresco Montersino Ad Altiora '15	♟♟ 5
● Roero Ròche dra Bòssora Ris. '15	♟♟ 3*
● Barbaresco Montersino Tera Mia Ris. '12	♟♟ 5
● Barbera d'Alba A Bon Rendre '18	♟♟ 2*
○ Roero Arneis Sernì '18	♟♟ 2*
● Barbera d'Alba Sup. Laboriosa '15	♟ 3
○ Langhe Favorita Fiori e Frutti '18	♟ 2
● Langhe Nebbiolo Blagheur '17	♟ 2
● Barbaresco Montersino Ad Altiora '14	♟♟ 5
● Barbaresco Montersino Ad Altiora '13	♟♟ 5
● Barbaresco Montersino Tera Mia Ris. '11	♟♟ 5
● Barbera d'Alba A Bon Rendre '16	♟♟ 3
● Barbera d'Alba Sup. '14	♟♟ 3
● Barbera d'Alba Sup. Laboriosa '13	♟♟ 3
○ Roero '14	♟♟ 2*
○ Roero Arneis '17	♟♟ 2*
○ Roero Arneis U R Nice '17	♟♟ 2*

Tenuta Tenaglia

s.da Santuario di Crea, 5
15020 Serralunga di Crea [AL]
Tel. +39 0142940252
www.tenutatenaglia.it

CELLAR SALES
PRE-BOOKED VISITS
ACCOMMODATION
ANNUAL PRODUCTION 100,000 bottles
HECTARES UNDER VINE 30.00
SUSTAINABLE WINERY

The accolades earned in the last edition of Italian Wines shone a light on a producer that for years has attained excellent results with its wines. Barbera and Grignolino serve as the cornerstone of their production. The former is available in a regular, standard-label version, or it's barrel-aged under the Barbera d'Asti or Barbera Monferrato appellations. Their Grignolino is always released within a year of vintage, but thanks to its nice longevity it can turn in surprising results after a few years in the bottle. Their Chiaretto Edenrose brings the two grapes together in a single wine. The 2018 version of their Grignolinosi also landed a place in our finals. It's a red with excellent varietal characteristics, peppery and fruity, just a bit held back by still-evolving tannins. The Monferace, a barrel-aged Grignolino, features gorgeous aromas of tanned leather and tobacco. On the palate it's highly elegant and intense, with a long finish.

● Grignolino del M.to Casalese '18	♟♟ 2*
● Grignolino del M.to Casalese Monferace '15	♟♟ 6
● Barbera d'Asti Bricco '18	♟♟ 3
● Barbera del M.to Sup. 1930 Una Buona Annata '15	♟♟ 5
● Barbera d'Asti Giorgio Tenaglia '16	♟ 4
⊙ M.to Chiaretto Edenrose '18	♟ 2
○ Piemonte Chardonnay '18	♟ 3
● Barbera d'Asti Emozioni '99	♟♟♟ 4*
● Grignolino del M.to Casalese '17	♟♟♟ 2*
● Barbera D'Asti Bricco '17	♟♟ 3
● Barbera del M.to Cappella III '17	♟♟ 2*
● Barbera del M.to Sup. 1930 Una Buona Annata '13	♟♟ 5
● Grignolino del M.to Casalese '16	♟♟ 2*
○ Piemonte Chardonnay '17	♟♟ 3

Terre del Barolo

VIA ALBA - BAROLO, 8
12060 CASTIGLIONE FALLETTO [CN]
TEL. +39 0173262053
www.arnaldorivera.com

CELLAR SALES
PRE-BOOKED VISITS
ANNUAL PRODUCTION 3,000,000 bottles
HECTARES UNDER VINE 600.00
VITICULTURE METHOD Certified Organic
SUSTAINABLE WINERY

'Prejudices die hard,' as the old saying goes. It's a rule that aptly applies to public perception of cooperative wineries, even the best ones, as is evidenced by the absence of Terre del Barolo from many wine guides. But we're convinced that this producer should be held in high regard for three reasons: its history (est. 1958), its size (with more than 300 grower members) and, finally, for its selection of Barolo. Dedicated to founder Arnaldo Rivera, every year it has something to offer. Their Barolo Monvigliero '15 is a precise interpretation of the vineyard of origin. Classic hints of rose and raspberry are accompanied by a characteristic note of white pepper. A sophisticated palate sees cosseting, silky tannins — simply enchanting. Their well-crafted Rocche di Castiglione '15 is more classic and structured, just a bit astringent but harmonious in its own way. The fresh Boiolo '15 opts more for elegance than for force, making for superb, approachable pleasantness.

● Barolo Boiolo '15	♟♟	5
● Barolo Castello '15	♟♟	6
● Barolo Monvigliero '15	♟♟	6
● Barolo Rocche di Castiglione '15	♟♟	7
● Barolo Undicicomuni '15	♟♟	5
● Barolo Vignarionda '15	♟♟	7
○ Langhe Nascetta del Comune di Novello '17	♟♟	3
● Barbera d'Alba Valdisera '17	♟	3
● Barolo Ravera '15	♟	6
● Barolo Vignarionda Arnaldo Rivera '13	♟♟♟	7
● Barolo Bussia '14	♟♟	6
● Barolo Castello '14	♟♟	6
● Barolo Undicicomuni '14	♟♟	5

★Torraccia del Piantavigna

VIA ROMAGNANO, 20
28074 GHEMME [NO]
TEL. +39 0163840040
www.torracciadelpiantavigna.it

CELLAR SALES
PRE-BOOKED VISITS
ANNUAL PRODUCTION 150,000 bottles
HECTARES UNDER VINE 38.00
SUSTAINABLE WINERY

In just over 20 years, Torraccia del Piantavigna has become synonymous with territory and quality. It's all thanks to a deep commitment by its owners, who've chosen expert winemakers to oversee production, mostly Nebbiolo, making for a selection of authentic, northern Piedmont wines that are repeatedly rewarded by both critics and consumers. A visit to their cellar gives you a good idea of how much care and attention are shown. Here you'll find historic, 15,000-liter Slavonian oak casks, barriques and 2500 liter French barrels (for their Ghemme and Gattinara). A rather warm year conferred commendable roundness on the Gattinara '15, a wine that's classic in its notes of forest undergrowth, rust and gentian. On the palate it exhibits enviable softness, length and pervasiveness. This year, from their lovely Pelizzane vineyard, they released a mature 2008 Ghemme of accomplished harmony. The gutsy Nebbiolo Ramale '16 features warm alcohol and quite lively tannins.

● Gattinara '15	♟♟♟	6
● Ghemme '14	♟♟	6
● Ghemme V. Pelizzane '08	♟♟	6
● Colline Novaresi Nebbiolo Ramale '16	♟♟	4
○ Colline Novaresi Bianco ErbaVoglio '18	♟	3
⊙ Colline Novaresi Nebbiolo Rosato Barlàn '18	♟	3
● Colline Novaresi Nebbiolo Tre Confini '17	♟	3
● Colline Novaresi Vespolina La Mostella '18	♟	3
● Gattinara '09	♟♟♟	5
● Ghemme '13	♟♟♟	6
● Ghemme '11	♟♟♟	5
● Ghemme '10	♟♟♟	5
● Ghemme V. Pelizzane '11	♟♟♟	6
● Ghemme V. Pelizzane '10	♟♟♟	6

Giancarlo Travaglini

VIA DELLE VIGNE, 36
13045 GATTINARA [VC]
TEL. +39 0163833588
www.travaglinigattinara.it

CELLAR SALES
PRE-BOOKED VISITS
ANNUAL PRODUCTION 250,000 bottles
HECTARES UNDER VINE 52.00
SUSTAINABLE WINERY

Their large estate does a nice job reflecting the viticultural attributes of upper Piedmont, bringing together Nebbiolo's classic spicy notes, hints of tar and fruit, with those aromas tasters often term as 'iron' and 'rust'. Cinzia Travaglini inherited the entire patrimony from her father, from its celebrated name to its original bottles. And she's proving up to the task, producing elegant Gattinara that's also robust and long-lived, and always among the best in the appellation. Their 2015 Gattinara is an excellent expression of the wine's aromatic peculiarities, from tobacco to quinine, red fruit and an iron-scented stroke. The palate is still evolving, with a nice contrast between the soft flesh and powerful tannins. The more firmly-structured 2014 version of their Tre Vigne is pleasant, playing on greener, vegetal tones. Oven-baked prunes and jammy notes feature in the mature Sogno '15, a wine made with Nebbiolo partially-dried on rush mats for more than three months.

● Gattinara '15	♛♛ 6
● Gattinara Tre Vigne '14	♛♛ 7
● Coste della Sesia Nebbiolo '18	♛♛ 3
● Il Sogno '15	♛♛ 8
○ Nebolé Dosaggio Zero M. Cl. '14	♛ 8
● Gattinara Ris. '13	♛♛♛ 7
● Gattinara Ris. '12	♛♛♛ 7
● Gattinara Ris. '06	♛♛♛ 6
● Gattinara Ris. '04	♛♛♛ 5
● Gattinara Ris. '01	♛♛♛ 5
● Gattinara Tre Vigne '04	♛♛♛ 5

★G. D. Vajra

FRAZ. VERGNE
VIA DELLE VIOLE, 25
12060 BAROLO [CN]
TEL. +39 017356257
www.gdvajra.it

PRE-BOOKED VISITS
ACCOMMODATION
ANNUAL PRODUCTION 350,000 bottles
HECTARES UNDER VINE 60.00
SUSTAINABLE WINERY

Founded during Barolo's 'annus horribilis', 1972 (a year voluntarily declassified by the territory's producers), G. D. Vajra proceeded with determination on a dual development path aimed at raising quality and quantity. The goal was ardently pursued by its founders, Aldo and Milena (who today have the support of their children). Despite the international success of their Barolos, we mustn't forget that Vajra make splendid Freisa and Barbera, as well as a Riesling that's paved the way for a new direction in Alta Langa. All their Barolos aptly interpret the 2015 vintage. The Bricco delle Viole earned Tre Bicchieri with its harmony of red fruit and licorice. It's properly austere, with tannins that aren't acidulous, but rather tight-knit right up to its long finish. The Ravera is a bit more assertive on the palate, exhibiting commendable aromatic finesse as well, while the youthful Baudana is well-fruited and pleasantly down-to-earth. The spicy and floral Coste di Rose also performed well.

● Barolo Bricco delle Viole '15	♛♛♛ 8
● Barolo Baudana Luigi Baudana '15	♛♛ 6
● Barolo Cerretta Luigi Baudana '15	♛♛ 6
● Barolo Ravera '15	♛♛ 8
● Barbera d'Alba Sup. '16	♛♛ 5
● Barolo Coste di Rose '15	♛♛ 8
● Dolcetto d'Alba Coste & Fossati '18	♛♛ 4
○ Langhe Bianco Dragon Luigi Baudana '18	♛ 4
● Barolo Baudana Luigi Baudana '09	♛♛♛ 6
● Barolo Bricco delle Viole '12	♛♛♛ 8
● Barolo Bricco delle Viole '10	♛♛♛ 8
● Barolo Cerretta Luigi Baudana '08	♛♛♛ 6

Mauro Veglio

FRAZ. ANNUNZIATA
LOC. CASCINA NUOVA, 50
12064 LA MORRA [CN]
TEL. +39 0173509212
www.mauroveglio.com

CELLAR SALES
PRE-BOOKED VISITS
ANNUAL PRODUCTION 80,000 bottles
HECTARES UNDER VINE 14.00
SUSTAINABLE WINERY

The first bottles came during the unfortunate 1992 season, when strong-willed winemaker Mauro Veglio understood that nature needs to be followed, not forced. An ecological approach to vineyard management and non-invasive production practices have given rise to wines of great purity and integrity. His wife has always been on the front lines, while 2019 saw the entrance of their already skilled grandson, who's brought with him the prospects of further expansion. In short, excellent wines made by exceptional people. All their 2015 Barolos performed well, from the potent and long Gattera, elegant in its toasty notes and hints of cocoa powder, to the potent, tight-knit and tannic Castelletto. Then there's the magnificent Rocche dell'Annunziata, which is fresh but not without scents of sweet spices and tobacco. The Arborina is admirable in its elegant intensity, but the minty, entry-level Barolo also deserves to be recognized. Their Barbera d'Alba Cascina Nuova is among the best of 2017.

● Barbera d'Alba Cascina Nuova '17	♟♟ 5
● Barolo Arborina '15	♟♟♟ 7
● Barolo Gattera '15	♟♟♟ 7
● Barolo Rocche dell'Annunziata '15	♟♟♟ 8
● Barbera d'Alba '18	♟♟♟ 3
● Barolo '15	♟♟ 5
● Barolo Castelletto '15	♟♟♟ 7
○ Dolcetto d'Alba '18	♟♟ 2*
● Langhe Nebbiolo Angelo '18	♟ 3
● Barbera d'Alba Cascina Nuova '99	♟♟♟ 5
● Barolo Arborina '10	♟♟♟ 6
● Barolo Rocche dell'Annunziata '12	♟♟♟ 8
● Barolo V. Rocche '96	♟♟♟ 8
● Barolo Vign. Arborina '01	♟♟♟ 6
● Barolo Vign. Arborina '00	♟♟♟ 6
● Barolo Vign. Gattera '05	♟♟♟ 6

Giovanni Viberti

FRAZ. VERGNE
VIA DELLE VIOLE, 30
12060 BAROLO [CN]
TEL. +39 017356192
www.viberti-barolo.com

CELLAR SALES
PRE-BOOKED VISITS
RESTAURANT SERVICE
ANNUAL PRODUCTION 100,000 bottles
HECTARES UNDER VINE 18.00
SUSTAINABLE WINERY

Claudio Viberti is seriously committed to creating Barolos that fully respect the potential of each single vineyard. To reach this goal he uses tailored practices in the vineyards, so as to avoid any excesses, the latest technology in the cellar, in particular when it comes to short maceration in rotary fermenters, and non-invasive methods for maturation, starting with the use of untoasted oak barrels of sizable dimensions. Among the 2013s produced, the Barolo Riserva Ravera stands out for its notable freshness and structure, while 2015 gave rise to a pleasant Barolo Buon Padre redolent of pennyroyal mint and tanned leather, all in a harmonious, mid-sized body. The fruity Dolbà '17, obviously a blend of Dolcetta and Barbera, proves highly pleasant, while the Dolcetto d'Alba Superiore 2017 is also highly enjoyable, especially for its soft notes of almond.

● Barolo Bricco delle Viole Ris. '13	♟♟♟ 7
● Barolo Buon Padre '15	♟♟ 6
● Barolo Ravera Ris. '13	♟♟ 8
○ Dolcetto d'Alba Sup. '17	♟♟ 3
● Langhe Dolbà '17	♟♟ 2*
● Langhe Nebbiolo '17	♟ 3
● Barbera d'Alba La Gemella '18	♟ 3
● Barbera d'Alba Sup. Bricco Airoli '16	♟ 4
● Barolo S. Pietro Ris. '13	♟ 7
○ Piemonte Chardonnay '18	♟ 3
● Barolo Bricco delle Viole Ris. '10	♟♟ 7
● Barolo La Volta Ris. '11	♟♟ 8

Vicara

VIA MADONNA DELLE GRAZIE, 5
15030 ROSIGNANO MONFERRATO [AL]
TEL. +39 0142488054
www.vicara.it

CELLAR SALES
PRE-BOOKED VISITS
ANNUAL PRODUCTION 200,000 bottles
HECTARES UNDER VINE 37.00
VITICULTURE METHOD Certified Biodynamic

It's full steam ahead for one of the
territory's largest wineries, a true
benchmark for their focus on native grapes
and an ecological approach that's
protective of the local ecosystem. Their
philosophy is aimed at bringing out the
qualities of the area's historic varieties.
Barbera and Grignolino are the
cornerstones, giving rise to both
standard-label and cask-aged versions. In
short, theirs is a versatile range built
around excellent grapes, which offer
beguiling varietal aromas in youth, but also
exhibit ageworthiness and classy tertiaries
when it comes to more long-lived
selections. With its debut, the Grignolino
Uccelletta Monferace earned a place in our
finals. It's a wine of fantastic balance,
opening on intense, complex aromas, while
on the palate is shows weighty structure,
then a fresh, sapid, long finish. The Cantico
della Crosia sees complex aromas of red
berries, tobacco and quinine, while the
Grignolino G. stands out for its considerable
structure and pleasantness.

● Barbera del M.to Sup.	
Cantico della Crosia '16	♥♥ 4
● Grignolino del M.to Casalese G '18	♥♥ 4
● Grignolino del M.to Casalese	
Uccelletta Monferace '15	♥♥ 4
● Barbera del M.to Volpuva '18	♥♥ 3
○ M.to Airales '18	♥ 3
● Grignolino del M.to Casalese '16	♥♥♥ 3*
● Grignolino del M.to Casalese °G '15	♥♥♥ 4*
● Barbera del M.to '17	♥♥ 2*
● Barbera del M.to	
Cascina La Rocca 33 '16	♥♥ 6
● Barbera del M.to Sup.	
Cantico della Crosia '15	♥♥ 4
● Barbera del M.to Volpuva '17	♥♥ 3*
● Grignolino del M.to Casalese '17	♥♥ 3*
○ M.to Bianco Sarnì '15	♥♥ 5

★★Vietti

P.ZZA VITTORIO VENETO, 5
12060 CASTIGLIONE FALLETTO [CN]
TEL. +39 017362825
www.vietti.com

CELLAR SALES
PRE-BOOKED VISITS
ANNUAL PRODUCTION 300,000 bottles
HECTARES UNDER VINE 40.00

The approach that made this winery great
is relatively simple: only the healthiest
grapes are used, rather lengthy
maceration, and clean but never excessive
use of oak. So it is that Luca Currado
produces a prestigious selection of Barolos
year after year. His wines are always
elegant, but never homogeneous, highly
structured but always respectful of the
vintage. Its new American owners have
embraced this style and are committed to
enlarging the estate, purchasing plots
everywhere from Barbaresco to Monleale,
in light of a forthcoming selection of
Timorasso. Their Barbaresco Masseria '15
is simply fantastic, sophisticated in its
notes of licorice, tobacco, endowed with a
body that's a model of harmony. But Tre
Bicchieri go to their Ris. Villero '12, a
masterpiece considering the difficult year.
The youthful Rocche di Castiglione '15,
made with grapes from one of Langhe's
best vineyards, is more tannic than it is
acidic, while the elegant Barbera d'Asti
La Crena '16 shouldn't be missed.

● Barolo Villero Ris. '12	♥♥♥ 8
● Barbaresco Masseria '15	♥♥ 8
● Barbera d'Asti La Crena '16	♥♥ 6
● Barolo Brunate '15	♥♥ 8
● Barolo Lazzarito '15	♥♥ 8
● Barolo Ravera '15	♥♥ 8
● Barolo Rocche di Castiglione '15	♥♥ 8
● Barbera d'Alba Scarrone	
V. Vecchia '17	♥♥ 6
● Barbera d'Alba Tre Vigne '17	♥♥ 5
● Barbera d'Alba V. Scarrone '17	♥♥ 5
● Barolo Castiglione '15	♥♥ 7
● Langhe Nebbiolo Perbacco '16	♥ 4
○ Roero Arneis '18	♥ 3
● Barolo Rocche di Castiglione '14	♥♥♥ 8
● Barolo Villero Ris. '09	♥♥♥ 8

Villa Giada

REG. CEIROLE, 10
14053 CANELLI [AT]
TEL. +39 0141831100
www.villagiada.wine

CELLAR SALES
PRE-BOOKED VISITS
ACCOMMODATION AND RESTAURANT SERVICE
ANNUAL PRODUCTION 180,000 bottles
HECTARES UNDER VINE 25.00
SUSTAINABLE WINERY

Situated in Canelli, the core of the cellar
that's still used by the Faccio family today
goes back to the late 18th century. Their
most important wines are made with
grapes cultivated on their Cascina Ceirole
plots (not far from their main facility, and
dedicated primarily to Moscato). These are
accompanied by parcels at Cascina del
Parrocco (Calosso) and Cascina Dani
(Agliano Terme), areas that are particularly
favorable to red grapes, especially Barbera.
It's a viticultural patrimony that's significant,
to say the least, and gives rise to a
stylistically varied selection of wines. Villa
Giada's selection is always quite diverse.
This year we find their unusual Gamba di
Pernice, a wine that plays on characteristic
notes of red berries, flowers and pepper,
and on a palate thick in harmonious tannic
presence. The Nizza Dedicato '16, which is
supported more by generous alcohol than
acidic backbone, offers up more mature,
jammy sensations and hints of red fruit
bottled in liquor.

● Gamba di Pernice	♟♟ 3*
● Nizza Dedicato '16	♟♟ 5
● Barbera d'Asti Sup. La Quercia '17	♟♟ 3
● Barbera d'Asti Surì '18	♟♟ 2*
● Barbera d'Asti Ajan '18	♟ 2
○ Moscato d'Asti Canelli '18	♟ 2
○ Moscato d'Asti Surì '18	♟ 2
● Barbera d'Asti Ajan '16	♟♟ 2*
● Barbera d'Asti Sup. La Quercia '16	♟♟ 3*
○ Moscato d'Asti Canelli '17	♟♟ 2*
○ Moscato d'Asti Canelli '16	♟♟ 2*
● Nizza Bricco Dani '15	♟♟ 4
● Nizza Dedicato '15	♟♟ 5
○ Piemonte Chardonnay Cortese Manè '17	♟♟ 2*

★Villa Sparina

FRAZ. MONTEROTONDO, 56
15066 GAVI [AL]
TEL. +39 0143633835
www.villasparina.it

PRE-BOOKED VISITS
ACCOMMODATION AND RESTAURANT SERVICE
ANNUAL PRODUCTION 550,000 bottles
HECTARES UNDER VINE 65.00

One of Gavi's renowned producers, Villa
Sparina has adopted an effective, modern
approach in terms of communication/
marketing, creating a brand that's come
into its own. Behind everything, naturally, is
an excellent product. In this case it's
Cortese, which thanks to a favorable
territory (Monterotondo) and a modern
production style, exhibits surprising
elegance and aging power. Their two Gavi
del Comune Gavi wines (Etichetta Gialla,
Cru Monterotondo) are forged here. Other
offerings include their Rivalta (a Barbera del
Monferrato Sup.) and the Villa Sparina Brut
Metodo Classico. Their Monterotondo '16
put in a standout performance. Intense
aromas of apricot, floral fragrances, evolve
into elegant spicy notes, making for a truly
harmonious palate. The Gavi del Comune di
Gavi '18 exhibits complexity, superb finesse.
Their Rivalta opens with vegetal hints on
spices, tobacco. It's fresh, harmonious on
the palate, closing with character. Their
Barbera '17 is splendidly fruity.

○ Gavi del Comune di Gavi Monterotondo '16	♟♟♟ 6
● Barbera del M.to '17	♟♟ 3*
● Barbera del M.to Sup. Rivalta '15	♟♟ 6
○ Gavi del Comune di Gavi '18	♟♟ 3*
○ Villa Sparina Brut M. Cl. '13	♟♟ 3
○ Gavi del Comune di Gavi Monterotondo '14	♟♟♟ 6
○ Gavi del Comune di Gavi Monterotondo '12	♟♟♟ 6
○ Gavi del Comune di Gavi Monterotondo '11	♟♟♟ 6
○ Gavi del Comune di Gavi Monterotondo '15	♟♟♟ 6

Viticoltori Associati di Vinchio Vaglio Serra

FRAZ. REG. SAN PANCRAZIO, 1
S.DA PROV.LE 40 KM. 3,75
14040 VINCHIO [AT]
TEL. +39 0141950903
www.vinchio.com

CELLAR SALES
PRE-BOOKED VISITS
ANNUAL PRODUCTION 1,200,000 bottles
HECTARES UNDER VINE 450.00

Founded in the late 1950s by some twenty vine growers, Cantina Sociale di Vinchio Vaglio Serra comprises almost 200 grower members who cultivate more than 450 hectares of land and produce some 50 wines. Such figures speak volumes about the winery's agricultural and economic importance to Monferrato Astigiano, a territory that's as charming as it is complex. In addition to the two municipalities after which it was named, they operate in Castelnuovo Belbo, Castelnuovo Calcea, Cortiglione, Incisa Scapaccino, Mombercelli and Nizza. It's a leading role that's been earned over time thanks to admirable performances, like this last. Their 2017 Barbera d'Astis need to be tried to be believed: the Sup. I Tre Vescovi is marked by a slightly unripe fruity note, but it's effectively balanced out on a well-sustained, penetrating palate. The Vigne Vecchie maintains juice and rhythm, despite a somewhat unresolved finish. Their Moscato Valmasca '18 showed excellent potential as well.

● Barbera d'Asti 50° Vigne Vecchie '17	♥♥ 3*
● Barbera d'Asti Sup. I Tre Vescovi '17	♥♥ 3*
● Barbera d'Asti Sup. Vigne Vecchie '16	♥♥ 5
○ Moscato d'Asti Valamasca '18	♥♥ 2*
● Nizza Laudana Ris. '15	♥♥ 4
● Barbera d'Asti La Leggenda '18	♥ 2
● Barbera d'Asti Sorì dei Mori '18	♥ 2
○ Piemonte Chardonay Le Masche '18	♥ 2
○ Roero Arneis Il Griso '18	♥ 3
● Ruché di Castagnole Monferrato Rebus '18	♥ 3
● Barbera d'Asti Sup. Vigne Vecchie '15	♥♥ 5
● Barbera d'Asti Sup. Vigne Vecchie '11	♥♥ 5

Vite Colte

VIA BERGESIA, 6
12060 BAROLO [CN]
TEL. +39 0173564611
www.vitecolte.it

CELLAR SALES
PRE-BOOKED VISITS
ANNUAL PRODUCTION 1,200,000 bottles
HECTARES UNDER VINE 300.00
VITICULTURE METHOD Certified Organic
SUSTAINABLE WINERY

The Vite Colte project, Terre da Vino's premium production range, continues to come into its own. It's grounded in a serious, shared agronomic policy that brings together 180 members (who cover a total of 300 hectares). Year after year, their wines prove increasingly rooted in their original, traditional characters, bolstered by prized plots within Barolo and Serralunga d'Alba. Indeed, theirs is a rich selection drawing on Nebbiolo, Barbera, Dolcetto, Arneis, Cortese and Moscato. The full-bodied, dark, juicy Barolo Essenze Ris. '10 impressed, true to type in its hints of violets, licorice. On the palate it's weighty, with plush tannins and an energetic, flavorful finish. The fresh Barolo del Comune di Barolo Essenze '15, redolent of raspberry, aniseed, licorice, also delivered, exhibiting firm structure, excellent tannic grip. Character, intensity, density mark the Barbera La Luna e Falo '17, a tight-knit wine, rich in fruit and properly tannic, closing long.

● Barbera d'Asti Sup. La Luna e i Falò '17	♥♥♥ 3*
● Barolo del Comune di Barolo Essenze '15	♥♥ 7
● Barolo Essenze Ris. '10	♥♥ 8
○ Piemonte Moscato Passito La Bella Estate '17	♥♥ 5
● Barbaresco La Casa in Collina '16	♥♥ 5
● Barolo Paesi Tuoi '15	♥♥ 6
● Barolo del Comune di Barolo Essenze '13	♥♥♥ 7
● Barolo del Comune di Barolo Essenze '12	♥♥♥ 6
○ Piemonte Moscato Passito La Bella Estate '16	♥♥♥ 5
● Barolo del Comune di Monforte d'Alba Essenze '13	♥♥ 7

499

LOC. CAMO
VIA ROMA, 3
12058 SANTO STEFANO BELBO [CN]
TEL. +39 0141840155
www.499vino.it

● Langhe Freisa '17	🍷🍷 3
○ Moscato d'Asti '18	🍷🍷 3
○ Enigma '18	🍷 3

Cantina Alice Bel Colle

REG. STAZIONE, 9
15010 ALICE BEL COLLE [AL]
TEL. +39 014474103
www.cantinaalicebc.it

CELLAR SALES
PRE-BOOKED VISITS
ANNUAL PRODUCTION 100,000 bottles
HECTARES UNDER VINE 370.00

● Barbera d'Asti Sup. Alix '16	🍷🍷 3*
○ Asti Classic M. Cl.	🍷🍷 4
● Barbera d'Asti Le Casette di Alice '18	🍷🍷 2*
○ Moscato d'Asti Paiè '18	🍷🍷 2*

Paolo Angelini

CASCINA CAIRO, 10
15039 OZZANO MONFERRATO [AL]
TEL. +39 3468549015
www.societaagricolaangelinipaolo.com

ANNUAL PRODUCTION 80,000 bottles
HECTARES UNDER VINE 40.00

● Barbera del M.to First '18	🍷🍷 3
● Barbera del M.to Jenerosa '16	🍷🍷 3
● Barbera del M.to Sup. Adamant '16	🍷🍷 3
● Grignolino del M.to Casalese Arpian '18	🍷🍷 2*

Antica Cascina dei Conti di Roero

LOC. VAL RUBIAGNO, 2
12040 VEZZA D'ALBA [CN]
TEL. +39 017365459
www.oliveropietro.it

CELLAR SALES
PRE-BOOKED VISITS
ANNUAL PRODUCTION 100,000 bottles
HECTARES UNDER VINE 13.50
SUSTAINABLE WINERY

● Nebbiolo d'Alba '17	🍷🍷 3*
● Roero V. Sant'Anna Ris. '15	🍷🍷 4
○ San Giovanni Dosaggio Zero M. Cl. '13	🍷🍷 4
○ Roero Arneis Vezza d'Alba '18	🍷 3

F.lli Aresca

VIA PONTETTO, 8A
14047 MOMBERCELLI [AT]
TEL. +39 0141955128
www.arescavini.it

CELLAR SALES
PRE-BOOKED VISITS
ANNUAL PRODUCTION 180,000 bottles
HECTARES UNDER VINE 12.00
SUSTAINABLE WINERY

● Nizza San Luigi '16	🍷🍷 5
● Barbera d'Asti La Moretta '17	🍷🍷 2*
● Grignolino d'Asti Testabalorda '18	🍷🍷 2*
● Barbera d'Asti Superiore La Rossa '16	🍷 3

L'Astemia Pentita

VIA CROSIA, 40
12060 BAROLO [CN]
TEL. +39 0173560501
www.astemiapentita.it

CELLAR SALES
PRE-BOOKED VISITS
ANNUAL PRODUCTION 70,000 bottles
HECTARES UNDER VINE 15.00
SUSTAINABLE WINERY

● Barolo Cannubi Ris. '13	🍷🍷 8
● Barolo Cannubi '15	🍷🍷 8
● Barolo Terlo '15	🍷🍷 8
● Barolo Terlo Ris. '13	🍷🍷 8

Baldissero

VIA ROMA, 29
12050 TREISO [CN]
TEL. +39 3334420201
www.baldisserovini.it

ANNUAL PRODUCTION 10,000 bottles
HECTARES UNDER VINE 7.00

● Barbaresco '16	♛♛ 6
● Langhe Nebbiolo '16	♛♛ 4
● Langhe Rosso Ancò '17	♛♛ 4
● Dolcetto d'Alba '18	♛ 2

Cantina Sociale Barbera dei Sei Castelli

VIA OPESSINA, 41
14040 CASTELNUOVO CALCEA [AT]
TEL. +39 0141957137
www.barberaseicastelli.it

CELLAR SALES
PRE-BOOKED VISITS
ANNUAL PRODUCTION 80,000 bottles
HECTARES UNDER VINE 620.00

● Nizza '16	♛♛ 5
○ Piemonte Chardonnay Gavarra '18	♛♛ 2*
● Barbera d'Asti 50 Anni di Barbera '17	♛ 3
● Barbera d'Asti Ventiforti '18	♛ 2

Fabrizio Battaglino

LOC. BORGONUOVO
VIA MONTALDO ROERO, 44
12040 VEZZA D'ALBA [CN]
TEL. +39 0173658156
www.battaglino.com

CELLAR SALES
PRE-BOOKED VISITS
ANNUAL PRODUCTION 25,000 bottles
HECTARES UNDER VINE 5.00

● Nebbiolo d'Alba Paradi '17	♛♛ 3
● Nebbiolo d'Alba Colla '16	♛♛ 4
○ Roero Arneis Bastia '18	♛♛ 3
● Roero Sergentin Riserva '15	♛♛ 5

Battaglio - Briccogrilli

LOC. BORBORE
VIA SALERIO, 15
12040 VEZZA D'ALBA [CN]
TEL. +39 017365423
www.battaglio.com

CELLAR SALES
PRE-BOOKED VISITS
ANNUAL PRODUCTION 35,000 bottles
HECTARES UNDER VINE 4.00

● Barbaresco Serragrilli '16	♛♛ 7
● Barbera d'Alba Madunina '17	♛♛ 3
○ Roero Arneis Piasì '18	♛♛ 3
● Roero Ris. '15	♛♛ 6

Antonio Bellicoso

FRAZ. MOLISSO, 5A
14048 MONTEGROSSO D'ASTI [AT]
TEL. +39 0141953233
antonio.bellicoso@alice.it

CELLAR SALES
PRE-BOOKED VISITS
ANNUAL PRODUCTION 15,000 bottles
HECTARES UNDER VINE 4.00
SUSTAINABLE WINERY

● Barbera d'Asti Merum '17	♛♛ 4
● Freisa d'Asti '18	♛♛ 3
● Barbera d'Asti Amormio '18	♛ 2

Piero Benevelli

LOC. SAN GIUSEPPE, 13
12065 MONFORTE D'ALBA [CN]
TEL. +39 017378416
www.barolobenevelli.com

ANNUAL PRODUCTION 50,000 bottles
HECTARES UNDER VINE 10.00

● Barolo Le Coste di Monforte '15	♛♛ 6
● Barolo Ravera di Monforte '15	♛♛ 7

Silvano Bolmida

LOC. BUSSIA 30
12065 MONFORTE D'ALBA [CN]
TEL. +39 0173789877
www.silvanobolmida.com

CELLAR SALES
PRE-BOOKED VISITS
ANNUAL PRODUCTION 30,000 bottles
HECTARES UNDER VINE 6.00

● Barolo Bussia '15	▼▼ 5
● Barolo Bussia V. dei Fantini '15	▼▼ 5
● Barolo Le Coste di Monforte '15	▼▼ 5

F.lli Serio & Battista Borgogno

LOC. CANNUBI
VIA CROSIA, 12
12060 BAROLO [CN]
TEL. +39 017356107
www.borgognoseriobattista.it

CELLAR SALES
PRE-BOOKED VISITS
ANNUAL PRODUCTION 60,000 bottles
HECTARES UNDER VINE 7.50

● Barolo '15	▼▼ 5
● Barolo Cannubi '15	▼▼ 6
● Barolo Cannubi Ris. '13	▼▼ 7
● Nebbiolo d'Alba '16	▼ 3

Francesco Boschis

B.TA PIANEZZO, 57
12063 DOGLIANI [CN]
TEL. +39 017370574
www.boschisfrancesco.it

CELLAR SALES
PRE-BOOKED VISITS
ANNUAL PRODUCTION 35,000 bottles
HECTARES UNDER VINE 10.00

● Dogliani Sup. V. del Ciliegio '16	▼▼ 3
● Dogliani Sup. V. Sorì San Martino '17	▼▼ 2*
● Langhe Freisa Bosco delle Cicale '18	▼▼ 3
● Dogliani Sup. V. dei Prey '17	▼ 2

F.lli Botto

S.DA PROV. S. STEFANO ROERO, 9
12046 MONTÀ [CN]
TEL. +39 0173976015
www.bottovini.it

CELLAR SALES
PRE-BOOKED VISITS
ANNUAL PRODUCTION 10,000 bottles
HECTARES UNDER VINE 3.00
SUSTAINABLE WINERY

○ Roero Arneis Valnebiera '18	▼▼ 2*
● Roero Valnebiera '16	▼▼ 4

Bricco dei Guazzi

VIA VITTORIO VENETO, 23
15030 OLIVOLA [AL]
TEL. +39 0422864511
www.briccodeiguazzi.it

PRE-BOOKED VISITS
ANNUAL PRODUCTION 100,000 bottles
HECTARES UNDER VINE 35.00
SUSTAINABLE WINERY

● Piemonte Albarossa '16	▼▼ 5
● Barbera d'Asti '16	▼▼ 2*
● M.to Rosso La Presidenta '17	▼▼ 3
○ Piemonte Chardonnay '18	▼▼ 3

La Briccolina

VIA RODDINO, 7
12050 SERRALUNGA D'ALBA [CN]
TEL. +39 3282217094
labriccolina@gmail.com

ANNUAL PRODUCTION 3,000 bottles
HECTARES UNDER VINE 5.50

● Barolo Briccolina '15	▼▼ 5

Broccardo

LOC. MANZONI, 22
12065 MONFORTE D'ALBA [CN]
TEL. +39 017378180
www.broccardo.it

CELLAR SALES
PRE-BOOKED VISITS
ANNUAL PRODUCTION 50,000 bottles
HECTARES UNDER VINE 13.00
SUSTAINABLE WINERY

● Barolo Bricco San Pietro '15	🍷🍷 6
● Barolo I Tre Pais '15	🍷🍷 5
● Langhe Nebbiolo Il Giò Pì '17	🍷🍷 3
● Barolo Paiagallo '15	🍷 7

Bussia Soprana

LOC. BUSSIA, 88A
12065 MONFORTE D'ALBA [CN]
TEL. +39 039305182
www.bussiasoprana.it

CELLAR SALES
PRE-BOOKED VISITS
ANNUAL PRODUCTION 40,000 bottles
HECTARES UNDER VINE 14.00

● Barbaresco Basarin '15	🍷🍷 6
● Barolo Bussia V. Colonnello '14	🍷🍷 7
● Nizza '16	🍷🍷 5

Oreste Buzio

VIA PIAVE, 13
15049 VIGNALE MONFERRATO [AL]
TEL. +39 0142933197
www.orestebuzio.altervista.org

CELLAR SALES
PRE-BOOKED VISITS
ANNUAL PRODUCTION 25,000 bottles
HECTARES UNDER VINE 6.00
VITICULTURE METHOD Certified Organic

● Barbera del M.to Sup. Riccardo II '15	🍷🍷 4
● M.to Freisa '18	🍷🍷 2*
● Barbera del M.to '18	🍷 2
● Grignolino del M.to Casalese '18	🍷 3

F.lli Calorio

VIA MARCONI, 54-56B
12046 MONTÀ [CN]
TEL. +39 0173975636
/www.fratellicalorio.it

PRE-BOOKED VISITS
ANNUAL PRODUCTION 35,000 bottles
HECTARES UNDER VINE 6.00

● Barbera d'Alba '18	🍷🍷 3
○ Roero Arneis Kalipè '18	🍷🍷 3
○ Roero Casette '15	🍷🍷 5
● Barbera d'Alba Sup. La Corona '17	🍷 5

Marco Canato

FRAZ. FONS SALERA
LOC. CA' BALDEA, 19/3
15049 VIGNALE MONFERRATO [AL]
TEL. +39 00393409193882
www.canatovini.it

CELLAR SALES
PRE-BOOKED VISITS
ANNUAL PRODUCTION 30,000 bottles
HECTARES UNDER VINE 11.00

● Grignolino del M.to Casalese Celio '18	🍷🍷 3*
● Barbera del M.to Gambaloita '18	🍷🍷 3
● Grignolino del M.to Casalese Primo Canato '15	🍷🍷 4

Pierangelo Careglio

LOC. APRATO, 15
12040 BALDISSERO D'ALBA [CN]
TEL. +39 3339905448
www.cantinacareglio.it

CELLAR SALES
PRE-BOOKED VISITS
ANNUAL PRODUCTION 35,000 bottles
HECTARES UNDER VINE 9.00
SUSTAINABLE WINERY

● Barbera d'Alba '17	🍷🍷 4
● Roero '16	🍷🍷 5
○ Roero Arneis Savij '15	🍷🍷 5
○ Roero Arneis '18	🍷 3

Tenuta Carretta

LOC. CARRETTA, 2
12040 PIOBESI D'ALBA [CN]
TEL. +39 0173619119
www.tenutacarretta.it

CELLAR SALES
PRE-BOOKED VISITS
ACCOMMODATION AND RESTAURANT SERVICE
ANNUAL PRODUCTION 480,000 bottles
HECTARES UNDER VINE 70.00

● Barolo Cannubi Selezione Franco Miroglio Ris. '13	♥♥ 8
● Barbaresco Garassino '15	♥♥ 5
● Barbera d'Asti Sup. Gaiana '16	♥ 3

Casavecchia

VIA ROMA, 2
12055 DIANO D'ALBA [CN]
TEL. +39 017369321
www.cantinacasavecchia.com

CELLAR SALES
PRE-BOOKED VISITS
ANNUAL PRODUCTION 45,000 bottles
HECTARES UNDER VINE 10.00

● Barolo del Comune di Castiglione Falletto Ris. '11	♥♥ 7
● Diano d'Alba Sörì Bruni '18	♥♥ 3
● Nebbiolo d'Alba V. Piadvenza '15	♥♥ 4

Cascina Adelaide

VIA AIE SOTTANE, 14
12060 BAROLO [CN]
TEL. +39 0173560503
www.cascinaadelaide.com

CELLAR SALES
PRE-BOOKED VISITS
ANNUAL PRODUCTION 50,000 bottles
HECTARES UNDER VINE 9.50

● Barolo Cannubi '15	♥♥ 8
● Barolo Fossati '14	♥ 8
○ Langhe Nascetta del Comune di Novello '17	♥ 3

Cascina Alberta

VIA ALBA, 5
12050 TREISO [CN]
TEL. +39 0173638047
www.calberta.it

CELLAR SALES
PRE-BOOKED VISITS
ACCOMMODATION
ANNUAL PRODUCTION 28,000 bottles
HECTARES UNDER VINE 9.00
VITICULTURE METHOD Certified Organic
SUSTAINABLE WINERY

● Barbaresco Giacone '16	♥♥ 5
● Langhe Nebbiolo '17	♥♥ 3
● Barbera d'Alba '17	♥ 2
● Barbera d'Alba Sup. Tres '16	♥ 4

Cascina Ballarin

FRAZ. ANNUNZIATA, 115
12064 LA MORRA [CN]
TEL. +39 017350365
www.cascinaballarin.it

CELLAR SALES
PRE-BOOKED VISITS
ACCOMMODATION
ANNUAL PRODUCTION 60,000 bottles
HECTARES UNDER VINE 9.00
VITICULTURE METHOD Certified Organic
SUSTAINABLE WINERY

● Barbera d'Alba Giuli '16	♥♥ 5
● Barolo Bricco Rocca '15	♥♥ 7
● Barolo Bricco Rocca Tistot Ris. '13	♥♥ 8
● Barolo Tre Ciabót '15	♥ 6

Cascina Castlet

S.DA CASTELLETTO, 6
14055 COSTIGLIOLE D'ASTI [AT]
TEL. +39 0141966651
www.cascinacastlet.com

CELLAR SALES
PRE-BOOKED VISITS
ANNUAL PRODUCTION 250,000 bottles
HECTARES UNDER VINE 30.00
SUSTAINABLE WINERY

● Barbera d'Asti '18	♥♥ 2*
● Barbera d'Asti Sup. Litina '16	♥♥ 3
○ Moscato d'Asti '18	♥♥ 2*
● Barbera d'Asti Sup. Passum '16	♥ 5

Cascina del Monastero

LOC. LA MORRA
FRAZ. ANNUNZIATA, 112A
12064 LA MORRA [CN]
TEL. +39 0173509245
www.cascinadelmonastero.it

CELLAR SALES
PRE-BOOKED VISITS
ACCOMMODATION
ANNUAL PRODUCTION 40,000 bottles
HECTARES UNDER VINE 12.00
VITICULTURE METHOD Certified Organic
SUSTAINABLE WINERY

● Barolo Annunziata '09	♟♟ 7
● Barolo Bricco Luciani '15	♟♟ 6
● Barolo Perno '14	♟♟ 5

Cascina Galarin

VIA CAROSSI, 12
14054 CASTAGNOLE DELLE LANZE [AT]
TEL. +39 0141878586
www.galarin.it

CELLAR SALES
ANNUAL PRODUCTION 30,000 bottles
HECTARES UNDER VINE 6.00
VITICULTURE METHOD Certified Organic

● Barbera d'Asti Le Querce '17	♟♟ 2*
● Barbera d'Asti Sup. Tinella '16	♟♟ 5
○ Langhe Arneis Barivel '18	♟ 2
○ Moscato d'Asti Prá Dône '18	♟ 2

Cascina Garitina

VIA GIANOLA, 20
14040 CASTEL BOGLIONE [AT]
TEL. +39 0141762162
www.cascinagaritina.it

CELLAR SALES
PRE-BOOKED VISITS
ANNUAL PRODUCTION 150,000 bottles
HECTARES UNDER VINE 23.00

● Nizza 900 Neuvsent Vecchia '15	♟♟ 6
● Barbera d'Asti Sup. Caranti '16	♟♟ 4
● Nizza 900 Neuvsent Margherita '15	♟♟ 6
● Piemonte Pinot Nero Alfero '15	♟♟ 4

Cascina Gentile

S.DA PROV.LE PER SAN CRISTOFORO. 11
15060 CAPRIATA D'ORBA [AL]
TEL. +39 0143468975
www.cascinagentile.tumblr.com

CELLAR SALES
PRE-BOOKED VISITS
ANNUAL PRODUCTION 30,000 bottles
HECTARES UNDER VINE 10.00
SUSTAINABLE WINERY

● Barbera del M.to Barberrique '15	♟♟ 3
○ Cascina Gentile Brut M. Cl. '15	♟♟ 3
○ Gavi '18	♟♟ 2*
● Ovada Tre Passi Avanti '17	♟♟ 3

Cascina Massara Gian Carlo Burlotto

VIA CAPITANO LANERI, 6
12060 VERDUNO [CN]
TEL. +39 0172470152
www.cantinamassara.it

ANNUAL PRODUCTION 75,000 bottles
HECTARES UNDER VINE 9.50

● Barolo '14	♟♟ 6
● Barolo '13	♟♟ 6
● Langhe Nebbiolo '17	♟♟ 4
● Verduno Pelaverga '18	♟♟ 3

Cascina Melognis

VIA SAN PIETRO, 10
12036 REVELLO [CN]
TEL. +39 0175257395
cascina.melognis@gmail.com

ANNUAL PRODUCTION 15,000 bottles
HECTARES UNDER VINE 4.00

● Colline Saluzzesi Divicaroli '18	♟♟ 3
⊙ Sinespina '18	♟♟ 3
● Colline Saluzzesi Ardy '17	♟ 3
● Novamen	♟ 4

Cascina Montagnola

S.DA MONTAGNOLA, 1
15058 VIGUZZOLO [AL]
TEL. +39 3480742701
www.cascinamontagnola.com

CELLAR SALES
PRE-BOOKED VISITS
ANNUAL PRODUCTION 30,000 bottles
HECTARES UNDER VINE 10.00

○ Colli Tortonesi Timorasso Morasso '17	♟♟ 4
● Colli Tortonesi Rosso Zemira '16	♟ 3
● Donaldo '17	♟ 3
○ Sornione '17	♟ 4

Cascina Mucci

LOC. MUCCI, 2
12050 RODDINO [CN]
TEL. +39 3496201920
www.cascinamucci.it

CELLAR SALES
PRE-BOOKED VISITS
ANNUAL PRODUCTION 13,000 bottles
HECTARES UNDER VINE 1.85

● Barbera d'Alba Sup. '16	♟♟ 4
● Barbera d'Alba Sup. Meros '16	♟♟ 4
● Langhe Nebbiolo Però '16	♟♟ 4
○ Langhe Chardonnay '18	♟ 3

Cascina Rabaglio

S.DA RABAJÀ, 8
12050 BARBARESCO [CN]
TEL. +39 3388885031
www.cascinarabaglio.com

● Barbaresco Gaia Principe '16	♟♟ 5
● Barbera d'Alba '18	♟♟ 3
● Dolcetto d'Alba '18	♟ 2

Cascina Val del Prete

S.DA SANTUARIO, 2
12040 PRIOCCA [CN]
TEL. +39 0173616534
www.valdelprete.com

CELLAR SALES
PRE-BOOKED VISITS
ANNUAL PRODUCTION 55,000 bottles
HECTARES UNDER VINE 11.00
VITICULTURE METHOD Certified Organic

● Barbera d'Alba Serra de' Gatti '18	♟♟ 3
● Roero Bricco Medica '16	♟♟ 3
○ Roero Arneis Luèt '18	♟♟ 2*
● Roero Ris. '16	♟ 5

Pietro Cassina

VIA IV NOVEMBRE, 171
13583 LESSONA [BI]
TEL. +39 3332518903
www.pietrocassina.com

CELLAR SALES
PRE-BOOKED VISITS
ACCOMMODATION
ANNUAL PRODUCTION 18,000 bottles
HECTARES UNDER VINE 6.00
SUSTAINABLE WINERY

● Coste della Sesia Nebbiolo Ciuèt '12	♟♟ 5
● Coste della Sesia Nebbiolo Severina '16	♟♟ 5
● Coste della Sesia Vespolina Tèra Rùssa '11	♟♟ 7
● Lessona Tanzo '09	♟♟ 8

Renzo Castella

VIA ALBA, 15
12055 DIANO D'ALBA [CN]
TEL. +39 017369203
renzocastella@virgilio.it

CELLAR SALES
PRE-BOOKED VISITS
ANNUAL PRODUCTION 20,000 bottles
HECTARES UNDER VINE 8.00

● Dolcetto di Diano d'Alba '18	♟♟ 2*
● Dolcetto di Diano d'Alba Sorì della Rivolta '18	♟♟ 2*
● Langhe Nebbiolo Madonnina '17	♟♟ 2*

Cavalier Bartolomeo

VIA ALBA BAROLO, 55
12060 CASTIGLIONE FALLETTO [CN]
TEL. +39 017362866
www.cavalierbartolomeo.com

ANNUAL PRODUCTION 15,000 bottles
HECTARES UNDER VINE 3.50

● Barolo Altenasso '15	♟♟ 6
● Barolo San Lorenzo '15	♟♟ 6

Davide Cavelli

VIA PROVINCIALE, 77
15010 PRASCO [AL]
TEL. +39 0144375706
www.cavellivini.com

ANNUAL PRODUCTION 60,000 bottles
HECTARES UNDER VINE 10.50

● Ovada Bricco Le Zerbe '16	♟♟ 3*
● Barbera del M.to Sup. Le Muraglie '15	♟♟ 3

Cerutti

VIA CANELLI, 205
14050 CASSINASCO [AT]
TEL. +39 0141851286
www.cascinacerutti.it

CELLAR SALES
PRE-BOOKED VISITS
ANNUAL PRODUCTION 20,000 bottles
HECTARES UNDER VINE 7.00
SUSTAINABLE WINERY

○ Alta Langa Brut Cuvée Enrico Cerutti '15	♟♟ 3
● Barbera d'Asti Sup. Föje Rùsse '16	♟♟ 4
○ Moscato d'Asti Canelli Surì Sandrinet '18	♟♟ 2*
○ Piemonte Chardonnay Riva Granda '17	♟♟ 3

La Chiara

LOC. VALLEGGE, 24
15066 GAVI [AL]
TEL. +39 0143642293
www.lachiara.it

CELLAR SALES
PRE-BOOKED VISITS
ANNUAL PRODUCTION 110,000 bottles
HECTARES UNDER VINE 26.00

○ Gavi del Comune di Gavi '18	♟♟ 2*
○ Gavi del Comune di Gavi Et. Nera '17	♟♟ 3
○ Gavi del Comune di Gavi Groppella '17	♟♟ 2*

Paride Chiovini

VIA GIUSEPPE GARIBALDI, 20
28070 SIZZANO [NO]
TEL. +39 3394304954
www.paridechiovini.it

CELLAR SALES
PRE-BOOKED VISITS
ANNUAL PRODUCTION 10,000 bottles
HECTARES UNDER VINE 3.00

● Ghemme '15	♟♟ 4
● Colline Novaresi Uva Rara Briseide '18	♟ 3
● Colline Novaresi Vespolina Afrodite '17	♟ 2
● Sizzano '14	♟ 4

Ciabot Berton

FRAZ. SANTA MARIA, 1
12064 LA MORRA [CN]
TEL. +39 017350217
www.ciabotberton.it

CELLAR SALES
PRE-BOOKED VISITS
ANNUAL PRODUCTION 70,000 bottles
HECTARES UNDER VINE 14.00

● Barbera d'Alba Fisetta '17	♟♟ 3
● Barbera d'Alba V. Bricco S. Biagio '17	♟♟ 4
● Barolo Rocchettevino '14	♟♟ 6
● Barolo Roggeri '14	♟ 6

Aldo Clerico

LOC. MANZONI, 69
12065 MONFORTE D'ALBA [CN]
TEL. +39 017378509
www.aldoclerico.it

CELLAR SALES
PRE-BOOKED VISITS
ANNUAL PRODUCTION 30,000 bottles
HECTARES UNDER VINE 8.00

● Barbera d'Alba '17	♥♥ 3
● Barolo '15	♥♥ 6
● Barolo Ginestra '15	♥♥ 8
● Dogliani '18	♥ 2

Colle Manora

S.DA BOZZOLA, 5
15044 QUARGNENTO [AL]
TEL. +39 0131219252
www.collemanora.it

CELLAR SALES
PRE-BOOKED VISITS
ACCOMMODATION
ANNUAL PRODUCTION 90,000 bottles
HECTARES UNDER VINE 21.00

● Barbera del M.to Pais '18	♥♥ 2*
○ M.to Bianco Mimosa '18	♥♥ 2*
● Piemonte Albarossa Ray '16	♥♥ 3
○ M.to Bianco Mila '16	♥ 4

Comero

VIA GIUSEPPE CORNA, 8
28070 SIZZANO [NO]
TEL. +39 3332575651
www.cantinacomero.it

CELLAR SALES
ANNUAL PRODUCTION 7,000 bottles
HECTARES UNDER VINE 6.00

○ Colline Novaresi Bianco La Grazia del Marchese '18	♥♥ 2*
● Colline Novaresi Nebbiolo '18	♥♥ 3
● Sizzano '15	♥♥ 4

Col dei Venti

S.DA COMUNALE BALBI, 25
12053 CASTIGLIONE TINELLA [CN]
TEL. +39 0141793071
www.coldeiventi.com

PRE-BOOKED VISITS
ANNUAL PRODUCTION 30,000 bottles
HECTARES UNDER VINE 10.00

● Barbaresco Túfoblu '16	♥♥ 6
● Barolo Debútto '15	♥♥ 7
● Langhe Nebbiolo Lampio '17	♥♥ 4
○ Moscato d'Asti Cométe '18	♥ 3

Colombera & Garella

VIA CASCINA COTTIGNANO, 2
13866 MASSERANO [BI]
TEL. +39 01596967
colomberaegarella@gmail.com

CELLAR SALES
PRE-BOOKED VISITS
ANNUAL PRODUCTION 20,000 bottles
HECTARES UNDER VINE 9.00

● Bramaterra Cascina Cottignano '15	♥♥ 5
● Lessona Pizzaguerra '15	♥♥ 5

Clemente Cossetti

VIA GUARDIE, 1
14043 CASTELNUOVO BELBO [AT]
TEL. +39 0141799803
www.cossetti.it

CELLAR SALES
PRE-BOOKED VISITS
ACCOMMODATION AND RESTAURANT SERVICE
ANNUAL PRODUCTION 500,000 bottles
HECTARES UNDER VINE 28.00

● Barbera d'Asti Sup. La Vigna Vecchia '17	♥♥ 2*
● Grignolino d'Asti Gelsomora '18	♥♥ 2*
● Barbera d'Asti Gelsomora '17	♥ 2
● Ruché di Castagnole M.to '18	♥ 3

Costa Catterina

VIA CASTELLINALDO, 14
12050 CASTAGNITO [CN]
TEL. +39 0173213403
www.costacatterina.com

CELLAR SALES
PRE-BOOKED VISITS
ACCOMMODATION
ANNUAL PRODUCTION 70,000 bottles
HECTARES UNDER VINE 15.00

● Roero '16	♟♟ 5
○ Roero Arneis Arsivel '18	♟♟ 3
● Barbera d'Alba Sup. '16	♟ 3
● Nebbiolo d'Alba Sup. '16	♟ 3

Cantine Crosio

VIA ROMA, 75
10010 CANDIA CANAVESE [TO]
TEL. +39 0119836048
www.cantinecrosio.it

CELLAR SALES
RESTAURANT SERVICE
ANNUAL PRODUCTION 45,000 bottles
HECTARES UNDER VINE 7.50

○ Erbaluce di Caluso Primavigna '18	♟♟ 3
● Canavese Rosso '18	♟ 2
○ Erbaluce di Caluso Costaparadiso '16	♟ 4
○ Erbaluce di Caluso Erbalus '18	♟ 2

Cuvage

STRADALE ALESSANDRIA, 90
15011 ACQUI TERME [AL]
TEL. +39 0144371600
www.cuvage.com

ANNUAL PRODUCTION 80,000 bottles
HECTARES UNDER VINE 200.00

○ Alta Langa Brut '15	♟♟ 4
○ Brut Blanc de Blancs M. Cl.	♟♟ 3
⊙ Nebbiolo d'Alba Brut Rosé M.Cl.	♟♟ 3
○ Pas Dosé Cuvage de Cuvage M. Cl.	♟♟ 3

Dacapo

S.DA ASTI MARE, 4
14041 AGLIANO TERME [AT]
TEL. +39 0141964921
www.dacapo.it

CELLAR SALES
PRE-BOOKED VISITS
ANNUAL PRODUCTION 50,000 bottles
HECTARES UNDER VINE 8.50

● Barbera d'Asti Sanbastiàn '17	♟♟ 2*
● Barbera d'Asti Sup. Valrionda '16	♟♟ 3
● Ruchè di Castagnole M.to Majoli '18	♟♟ 3
● Nizza '15	♟ 4

Duilio Dacasto

FRAZ. VIANOCE, 26
14041 AGLIANO TERME [AT]
TEL. +39 3339828612
www.dacastoduilio.com

ANNUAL PRODUCTION 24,000 bottles
HECTARES UNDER VINE 8.00

● Barbera d'Asti La Maestra '17	♟♟ 3
● Barbera d'Asti Sup. Camp Riond '17	♟♟ 3
● Nizza Moncucco '16	♟♟ 4
○ Piemonte Chardonnay Bourg '18	♟ 3

Fabio Fidanza

VIA RODOTIGLIA, 55
14052 CALOSSO [AT]
TEL. +39 0141826921
a.a.fidanza@gmail.com

CELLAR SALES
PRE-BOOKED VISITS
ANNUAL PRODUCTION 20,000 bottles
HECTARES UNDER VINE 10.00

● Barbera d'Asti '17	♟♟ 2*
● Barbera d'Asti Sup. Sterlino '17	♟♟ 4
○ Moscato d'Asti '18	♟♟ 2*

Fontanabianca

loc. Bordini, 15
12057 Neive [CN]
Tel. +39 017367195
www.fontanabianca.it

CELLAR SALES
PRE-BOOKED VISITS
ANNUAL PRODUCTION 85,000 bottles
HECTARES UNDER VINE 16.00

- ● Barbaresco Serraboella '16 — 🍷🍷 6
- ● Barbaresco '16 — 🍷🍷 5
- ● Barbaresco Bordini '16 — 🍷🍷 6
- ● Barbera d'Alba Sup. '17 — 🍷🍷 3

Forteto della Luja

reg. Candelette, 4
14051 Loazzolo [AT]
Tel. +39 014487197
www.fortetodellaluja.it

CELLAR SALES
PRE-BOOKED VISITS
ANNUAL PRODUCTION 50,000 bottles
HECTARES UNDER VINE 11.00
VITICULTURE METHOD Certified Organic

- ● Barbera d'Asti Mon Ross '18 — 🍷🍷 2*
- ○ Loazzolo V. T. Piasa Rischei '15 — 🍷🍷 6
- ● M.to Rosso Le Grive '17 — 🍷 4

Davide Fregonese

via Roddino, 10/1
12050 Serralunga d'Alba [CN]
Tel. +39 3409643637
www.davidefregonese.com

ANNUAL PRODUCTION 5,000 bottles
HECTARES UNDER VINE 1.00

- ● Barolo Cerretta '15 — 🍷🍷 7
- ● Barolo Prapò '15 — 🍷🍷 7

La Fusina - Luigi Abbona

fraz. Santa Lucia, 33
12063 Dogliani [CN]
Tel. +39 017370488
www.lafusina.com

CELLAR SALES
PRE-BOOKED VISITS
ANNUAL PRODUCTION 80,000 bottles
HECTARES UNDER VINE 20.00
SUSTAINABLE WINERY

- ● Barolo Perno '15 — 🍷🍷 6
- ○ Alta Langa Extra Brut '16 — 🍷🍷 5
- ● Barbera d'Alba '18 — 🍷🍷 3
- ● Dogliani Sup. Cavagnè '17 — 🍷 3

Le Ginestre

s.da Grinzane, 15
12050 Grinzane Cavour [CN]
Tel. +39 0173262910
www.leginestre.com

SUSTAINABLE WINERY

- ● Barbera d'Alba '16 — 🍷🍷 3
- ● Barolo Sotto Castello di Novello '15 — 🍷🍷 6
- ● Dolcetto d'Alba '17 — 🍷 3

La Giribaldina

fraz. San Vito, 39
14042 Calamandrana [AT]
Tel. +39 0141718043
www.giribaldina.com

CELLAR SALES
PRE-BOOKED VISITS
ACCOMMODATION
ANNUAL PRODUCTION 65,000 bottles
HECTARES UNDER VINE 11.00

- ● Barbera d'Asti Sup. Valsarmassa '17 — 🍷🍷 3
- ● Nizza Cala delle Mandrie Ris. '16 — 🍷🍷 5
- ● Barbera d'Asti Montedelmare '18 — 🍷 2

Gozzelino

S.DA BRICCO LÙ, 7
14055 COSTIGLIOLE D'ASTI [AT]
TEL. +39 0141966134
www.gozzelinovini.com

CELLAR SALES
PRE-BOOKED VISITS
ANNUAL PRODUCTION 100,000 bottles
HECTARES UNDER VINE 30.00

● Barbera d'Asti Sup. Ciabot d'la Mandorla '16	♟♟ 3
○ Moscato d'Asti Bruna '18	♟♟ 2*
○ Piemonte Moscato Passito '12	♟♟ 4

Clemente Guasti

C.SO IV NOVEMBRE, 80
14049 NIZZA MONFERRATO [AT]
TEL. +39 0141721350
www,clemente.guasti.it

CELLAR SALES
PRE-BOOKED VISITS
ANNUAL PRODUCTION 120,000 bottles
HECTARES UNDER VINE 10.00

● Barbera d'Asti Sup. Boschetto Vecchio '15	♟♟ 4
● Barbera d'Asti Sup. Severa '15	♟♟ 3
● Barbera d'Asti Desideria '17	♟ 3
○ Moscato d'Asti Santa Teresa '18	♟ 3

Franco Ivaldi

S.DA CARANZANO, 211
15016 CASSINE [AL]
TEL. +39 348 7492231
www.francoivaldivini.com

ANNUAL PRODUCTION 40,000 bottles
HECTARES UNDER VINE 7.00

● Barbera d'Asti La Guerinotta '18	♟♟ 2*
○ Moscato d'Asti Douss '18	♟♟ 2*
● Piemonte Albarossa '16	♟♟ 3
● Dolcetto d'Acqui La Moschina '18	♟ 2

La Guardia

POD. LA GUARDIA, 74
15010 MORSASCO [AL]
TEL. +39 014473076
www.laguardiavilladelfini.it

CELLAR SALES
PRE-BOOKED VISITS
ANNUAL PRODUCTION 100,000 bottles
HECTARES UNDER VINE 35.00

● Ovada V. Il Gamondino Ris. '16	♟♟ 4
● Lucifero	♟♟ 3
● M.to Rosso Sacroprofano '15	♟♟ 5
● Monferrato Rosso Leone '15	♟ 3

Paride Iaretti

VIA PIETRO MICCA, 23B
13045 GATTINARA [VC]
TEL. +39 0163826899
www.parideiaretti.it

CELLAR SALES
PRE-BOOKED VISITS
ANNUAL PRODUCTION 15,000 bottles
HECTARES UNDER VINE 5.00

● Coste della Sesia Nebbiolo Velut Luna '17	♟♟ 3
● Gattinara Pietro '15	♟♟ 4
● Uvenere	♟ 2

Lagobava

FRAZ. CA' BERGANTINO, 5
15049 VIGNALE MONFERRATO [AL]
TEL. +39 3476900656
www.lagobava.it

CELLAR SALES
PRE-BOOKED VISITS
ANNUAL PRODUCTION 14,000 bottles
HECTARES UNDER VINE 6.00
VITICULTURE METHOD Certified Organic
SUSTAINABLE WINERY

● Barbera del M.to Sup. L'Ago '12	♟♟ 5
● Piemonte Barbera '17	♟♟ 3
● Solorosso '15	♟♟ 3
● M.to Rosso L'Amo '15	♟ 4

Maccagno

VIA BONORA, 29
12043 CANALE [CN]
TEL. +39 0173979438
www.cantinamaccagno.it

CELLAR SALES
PRE-BOOKED VISITS
ANNUAL PRODUCTION 50,000 bottles
HECTARES UNDER VINE 10.00

● Barbera d'Alba Sup. Arcalè '16	▼▼ 3
○ Roero Arneis '18	▼▼ 3
● Roero S. Michele '15	▼▼ 3

Podere Macellio

VIA ROMA, 18
10014 CALUSO [TO]
TEL. +39 0119833511
www.erbaluce-bianco.it

CELLAR SALES
PRE-BOOKED VISITS
ANNUAL PRODUCTION 25,000 bottles
HECTARES UNDER VINE 3.50

○ Erbaluce di Caluso '18	▼▼ 2*
○ Erbaluce di Caluso Extra Brut	▼ 3

Marenco

P.ZZA VITTORIO EMANUELE II, 10
15019 STREVI [AL]
TEL. +39 0144363133
www.marencovini.com

CELLAR SALES
PRE-BOOKED VISITS
ACCOMMODATION
ANNUAL PRODUCTION 250,000 bottles
HECTARES UNDER VINE 80.00
SUSTAINABLE WINERY

● Barbera d'Alba Sup. Ciresa '16	▼▼ 5
● Brachetto d'Acqui Pineto '18	▼▼ 3
○ Moscato d'Asti Scrapona '18	▼▼ 3
● Barbera d'Asti Bassina '17	▼ 3

Le Marie

VIA SAN DEFENDENTE, 6
12032 BARGE [CN]
TEL. +39 0175345159
www.lemarievini.eu

CELLAR SALES
PRE-BOOKED VISITS
RESTAURANT SERVICE
ANNUAL PRODUCTION 45,000 bottles
HECTARES UNDER VINE 9.50

○ Blanc de Lissart '18	▼▼ 2*
● Pinerolese Rosso Debárges '15	▼▼ 3
○ Sant'Agostino	▼▼ 2*
● Pinerolese Rosso Rouge de Lissart '17	▼ 2

Molino

VIA AUSARIO, 5
12050 TREISO [CN]
TEL. +39 0173638384
www.molinovini.com

CELLAR SALES
PRE-BOOKED VISITS
ANNUAL PRODUCTION 8,000 bottles
HECTARES UNDER VINE 16.00
SUSTAINABLE WINERY

● Barbaresco Teorema '16	▼▼ 6
● Barbaresco Ausario '15	▼▼ 7
● Piemonte Rosso Selvaggia '18	▼▼ 3

Mongioia

FRAZ. VALDIVILLA, 40
12058 SANTO STEFANO BELBO [CN]
TEL. +39 0141847301
www.mongioia.com

CELLAR SALES
PRE-BOOKED VISITS
ANNUAL PRODUCTION 50,000 bottles
HECTARES UNDER VINE 10.00
VITICULTURE METHOD Certified Organic

○ Moscato d'Asti L'Astralis '17	▼▼ 3*
○ Moscato d'Asti La Moscata '18	▼▼ 3
○ Meramente Brut Nature M. Cl. Primo Tempo '16	▼ 5

Diego Morra

VIA CASCINA MOSCA, 37
12060 VERDUNO [CN]
TEL. +39 3284623209
www.morrawines.com

CELLAR SALES
PRE-BOOKED VISITS
ANNUAL PRODUCTION 25,000 bottles
HECTARES UNDER VINE 32.00

● Barolo Monvigliero '15	♟♟ 7
● Barbera d'Alba '16	♟♟ 3
● Dolcetto d'Alba '17	♟♟ 2*

Musso

VIA D. CAVAZZA, 5
12050 BARBARESCO [CN]
TEL. +39 0173635129
www.mussobarbaresco.it

CELLAR SALES
PRE-BOOKED VISITS
ANNUAL PRODUCTION 80,000 bottles
HECTARES UNDER VINE 10.00

● Barbaresco Pora '16	♟♟ 6
● Barbaresco Rio Sordo '16	♟♟ 6
● Barbera d'Alba Sup. Brua '16	♟♟ 4
● Langhe Nebbiolo '18	♟♟ 4

Oltretorrente

VIA CINQUE MARTIRI
15050 PADERNA [AL]
TEL. +39 3398195360
www.oltretorrente.com

CELLAR SALES
PRE-BOOKED VISITS
ANNUAL PRODUCTION 20,000 bottles
HECTARES UNDER VINE 7.00
VITICULTURE METHOD Certified Organic
SUSTAINABLE WINERY

○ Colli Tortonesi Timorasso Derthona '17	♟♟ 5
● Colli Tortonesi Barbera Sup. '16	♟ 6
○ Colli Tortonesi Bianco '18	♟ 3
● Colli Tortonesi Rosso '18	♟ 2

Pace

FRAZ. MADONNA DI LORETO
LOC. CASCINA PACE, 52
12043 CANALE [CN]
TEL. +39 0173979544
www.pacevini.it

CELLAR SALES
PRE-BOOKED VISITS
ANNUAL PRODUCTION 60,000 bottles
HECTARES UNDER VINE 22.00

○ Roero Arneis Giuan da Pas '10	♟♟ 7
● Barbera d'Alba '17	♟♟ 2*
○ Langhe Favorita '18	♟ 2
○ Roero Arneis '18	♟ 2

Massimo Pastura
Cascina La Ghersa

VIA CHIARINA, 2
14050 MOASCA [AT]
TEL. +39 0141856012
www.laghersa.it

CELLAR SALES
PRE-BOOKED VISITS
ACCOMMODATION
ANNUAL PRODUCTION 150,000 bottles
HECTARES UNDER VINE 23.00

● Barbera d'Asti Sup. Camparò '17	♟♟ 2*
○ Colli Tortonesi Timorasso Derthona Sivoy '17	♟♟ 4
● Nizza Vignassa '16	♟♟ 5

Elio Perrone

S.DA SAN MARTINO, 3BIS
12053 CASTIGLIONE TINELLA [CN]
TEL. +39 0141855803
www.elioperrone.it

CELLAR SALES
PRE-BOOKED VISITS
ANNUAL PRODUCTION 250,000 bottles
HECTARES UNDER VINE 16.00
SUSTAINABLE WINERY

● Barbera d'Asti Sup. Mongovone '17	♟♟ 5
○ Moscato d'Asti Sic '18	♟♟ 3
○ Moscato d'Asti Sourgal '18	♟♟ 2*
● Barbera d'Asti Tasmorcan '18	♟ 3

Le Pianelle

S.DA FORTE, 24
13862 BRUSNENGO [BI]
TEL. +39 3478772726
www.lepianelle.com

PRE-BOOKED VISITS
ANNUAL PRODUCTION 12,000 bottles
HECTARES UNDER VINE 3.00

⊙ Coste della Sesia Rosato Al Posto dei Fiori '18	🍷🍷 3
● Coste della Sesia Rosso Al Forte '16	🍷 5

Armando Piazzo

FRAZ. SAN ROCCO DI SENO D'ELVIO, 31
12051 ALBA [CN]
TEL. +39 017335689
www.piazzo.it

CELLAR SALES
PRE-BOOKED VISITS
ACCOMMODATION
ANNUAL PRODUCTION 500,000 bottles
HECTARES UNDER VINE 70.00
SUSTAINABLE WINERY

● Barbaresco Nervo V. Giaia Ris. '13	🍷🍷 6
● Barolo Sottocastello di Novello Ris. '13	🍷🍷 7
● Barbaresco '16	🍷 5

Poderi dei Bricchi Astigiani

FRAZ. REPERGO
VIA RITANE, 7
14057 ISOLA D'ASTI [AT]
TEL. +39 0141958974
www.bricchiastigiani.it

CELLAR SALES
PRE-BOOKED VISITS
ANNUAL PRODUCTION 40,000 bottles
HECTARES UNDER VINE 15.00
VITICULTURE METHOD Certified Organic

● Barbera d'Asti '17	🍷🍷 2*
● Barbera d'Asti Sup. Bricco del Perg '16	🍷🍷 3
● M.to Rosso Bricco Preje '16	🍷🍷 2*
⊙ Piemonte Rosato Bricco Preje '18	🍷 2

Paolo Giuseppe Poggio

VIA ROMA, 67
15050 BRIGNANO FRASCATA [AL]
TEL. +39 0131784929
www.cantinapoggio.com

CELLAR SALES
PRE-BOOKED VISITS
ANNUAL PRODUCTION 18,000 bottles
HECTARES UNDER VINE 3.50

● Colli Tortonesi Barbera Campo La Bà '17	🍷🍷 2*
○ Colli Tortonesi Timorasso Ronchetto '17	🍷🍷 3
● Colli Tortonesi Croatina Prosone '16	🍷 2

Pomodolce

VIA IV NOVEMBRE, 7
15050 MONTEMARZINO [AL]
TEL. +39 0131878135
www.pomodolce.it

CELLAR SALES
PRE-BOOKED VISITS
RESTAURANT SERVICE
ANNUAL PRODUCTION 14,000 bottles
HECTARES UNDER VINE 4.00
VITICULTURE METHOD Certified Organic

○ Colli Tortonesi Timorasso Diletto '17	🍷🍷 3*
● Colli Tortonesi Barbera Marsèn '12	🍷🍷 4

Giovanni Prandi

FRAZ. CASCINA COLOMBÈ
VIA FARINETTI, 5
12055 DIANO D'ALBA [CN]
TEL. +39 017369248
www.prandigiovanni.it

CELLAR SALES
PRE-BOOKED VISITS
ANNUAL PRODUCTION 20,000 bottles
HECTARES UNDER VINE 5.00
SUSTAINABLE WINERY

● Barbera d'Alba '18	🍷🍷 2*
● Dolcetto di Diano d'Alba Sörì Cristina '18	🍷🍷 2*
● Dolcetto di Diano d'Alba Sörì Colombè '18	🍷 2
● Nebbiolo d'Alba '17	🍷 3

Diego Pressenda
La Torricella
LOC. SANT'ANNA, 98
12065 MONFORTE D'ALBA [CN]
TEL. +39 017378327
www.diegopressenda.it

CELLAR SALES
PRE-BOOKED VISITS
ACCOMMODATION AND RESTAURANT SERVICE
ANNUAL PRODUCTION 50,000 bottles
HECTARES UNDER VINE 13.00
SUSTAINABLE WINERY

● Barolo Bricco San Pietro '15	♟♟ 7
○ Langhe Riesling '17	♟♟ 3
● Nebbiolo d'Alba Il Donato '17	♟♟ 4
● Barbera d'Alba Sup. Ariota '17	♟ 4

Raineri
LOC. PANEROLE, 24
12060 NOVELLO [CN]
TEL. +39 3396009289
www.rainerivini.com

CELLAR SALES
PRE-BOOKED VISITS
ANNUAL PRODUCTION 40,000 bottles
HECTARES UNDER VINE 6.00
SUSTAINABLE WINERY

● Barolo '15	♟♟ 6
● Barolo Perno '15	♟♟ 8
● Dogliani Zovetto '18	♟♟ 2*
○ Langhe Bianco Elfobianco '18	♟♟ 3

Ressia
VIA CANOVA, 28
12052 NEIVE [CN]
TEL. +39 0173677305
www.ressia.com

CELLAR SALES
PRE-BOOKED VISITS
ANNUAL PRODUCTION 3,000 bottles
HECTARES UNDER VINE 5.50
SUSTAINABLE WINERY

● Barbaresco Canova '16	♟♟ 5
● Barbera d'Alba V. Canova '18	♟♟ 3
● Dolcetto d'Alba V. Canova '18	♟♟ 2*
● Langhe Nebbiolo Gepù '16	♟♟ 4

Pietro Rinaldi
FRAZ. MADONNA DI COMO
12051 ALBA [CN]
TEL. +39 0173360090
www.pietrorinaldi.com

CELLAR SALES
PRE-BOOKED VISITS
ACCOMMODATION
ANNUAL PRODUCTION 70,000 bottles
HECTARES UNDER VINE 10.00

● Barbaresco Massirano '15	♟♟ 5
● Barbaresco San Cristoforo '16	♟♟ 5
● Barolo Monvigliero '15	♟♟ 6
● Dolcetto d'Alba Madonna di Como '18	♟♟ 2*

Silvia Rivella
LOC. MONTESTEFANO, 17
12050 BARBARESCO [CN]
TEL. +39 0173635040
www.agriturismorivella.it

CELLAR SALES
PRE-BOOKED VISITS
ACCOMMODATION AND RESTAURANT SERVICE
ANNUAL PRODUCTION 10,000 bottles
HECTARES UNDER VINE 1.50

● Barbaresco Fausoni '16	♟♟ 8
● Barbaresco '16	♟♟ 7

Rivetto dal 1902
LOC. LIRANO, 2
12050 SINIO [CN]
TEL. +39 0173613380
www.rivetto.it

CELLAR SALES
PRE-BOOKED VISITS
ACCOMMODATION
ANNUAL PRODUCTION 100,000 bottles
HECTARES UNDER VINE 20.00
VITICULTURE METHOD Certified Organic

● Barbaresco Marcarini '16	♟♟ 6
● Barolo Leon Ris. '13	♟♟ 8
● Barolo del Comune di Serralunga D'Alba '15	♟ 6

Tenuta Rocca

LOC. ORNATI, 19
12065 MONFORTE D'ALBA [CN]
TEL. +39 017378412
www.tenutarocca.com

CELLAR SALES
PRE-BOOKED VISITS
ACCOMMODATION
ANNUAL PRODUCTION 90,000 bottles
HECTARES UNDER VINE 15.00

- Barolo Bussia '15 ♟♟ 6
- Barbera d'Alba '18 ♟♟ 3
- Barbera d'Alba Sup. Roca Neira '17 ♟♟ 4
- Langhe Rosso Or Nati '17 ♟♟ 5

Rolfo - Ca' di Cairè

B.GO VALLE CASETTE, 52
12046 MONTÀ [CN]
TEL. +39 0173971263
www.emanuelerolfo.it

PRE-BOOKED VISITS
ANNUAL PRODUCTION 38,000 bottles
HECTARES UNDER VINE 5.00

- ○ Roero Arneis Menelic '16 ♟♟ 2*
- ● Roero Ris. '15 ♟♟ 3
- ○ Roero Arneis '18 ♟ 2

Rossi Contini

S.DA SAN LORENZO, 20
15076 OVADA [AL]
TEL. +39 0143822530
www.rossicontini.com

CELLAR SALES
PRE-BOOKED VISITS
ANNUAL PRODUCTION 17,000 bottles
HECTARES UNDER VINE 4.50
SUSTAINABLE WINERY

- Dolcetto di Ovada San Lorenzo '18 ♟♟ 3

Podere Ruggeri Corsini

LOC. BUSSIA BOVI 18
12065 MONFORTE D'ALBA [CN]
TEL. +39 017378625
www.ruggericorsini.com

CELLAR SALES
PRE-BOOKED VISITS
ANNUAL PRODUCTION 75,000 bottles
HECTARES UNDER VINE 9.80
SUSTAINABLE WINERY

- Barbera d'Alba Sup. Armujan '16 ♟♟ 3
- Barolo Bricco San Pietro '15 ♟♟ 5
- Barolo Bussia Corsini '15 ♟♟ 5
- Piemonte Albarossa Autenzio '16 ♟ 4

San Bartolomeo

LOC. VALLEGGE
CASCINA SAN BARTOLOMEO, 26
15066 GAVI [AL]
TEL. +39 0143643180
www.sanbartolomeogavi.com

CELLAR SALES
PRE-BOOKED VISITS
ANNUAL PRODUCTION 50,000 bottles
HECTARES UNDER VINE 21.00
SUSTAINABLE WINERY

- ○ Gavi del Comune di Gavi Pelöia '18 ♟♟ 3*

San Biagio

FRAZ. SANTA MARIA
SAN BIAGIO, 98
12064 LA MORRA [CN]
TEL. +39 017350214
www.barolosanbiagio.com

CELLAR SALES
PRE-BOOKED VISITS
ANNUAL PRODUCTION 45,000 bottles
HECTARES UNDER VINE 20.00

- Barbaresco Montersino '16 ♟♟ 5
- Barolo Bricco San Biagio '15 ♟♟ 5
- Barolo Rocchettevino '15 ♟ 5

Cantine Sant'Agata

REG. MEZZENA, 19
14030 SCURZOLENGO [AT]
TEL. +39 0141203186
www.santagata.com

CELLAR SALES
PRE-BOOKED VISITS
RESTAURANT SERVICE
ANNUAL PRODUCTION 150,000 bottles
HECTARES UNDER VINE 12.00

● Barbera d'Asti Sup. Altea '17	▼▼ 3
● Barolo La Fenice '15	▼▼ 6
● Ruchè di Castagnole M.to Il Cavaliere '18	▼▼ 2*
● Ruchè di Castagnole M.to Pro Nobis '16	▼▼ 4

Sassi - San Cristoforo

VIA PASTURA, 10
12057 NEIVE [CN]
TEL. +39 0173677122
www.sassisancristoforo.com

CELLAR SALES
PRE-BOOKED VISITS
ANNUAL PRODUCTION 10,000 bottles
HECTARES UNDER VINE 1.30

● Barbaresco '16	▼▼ 6
● Dolcetto d'Alba '18	▼ 2

Giacomo Scagliola

REG. SANTA LIBERA, 20
14053 CANELLI [AT]
TEL. +39 0141831146
www.scagliola-canelli.it

CELLAR SALES
ANNUAL PRODUCTION 70,000 bottles
HECTARES UNDER VINE 15.00

○ Alta Langa Blanc de Blancs Brut Cuvée Alessandro '14	▼▼ 4
● Barbera d'Asti Sup. Bric dei Mandorli '15	▼▼ 4
○ Moscato d'Asti Canelli Sifasol '18	▼▼ 2*

Segni di Langa

LOC. RAVINALI, 25
12060 RODDI [CN]
TEL. +39 3803945151
www.segnidilanga.it

CELLAR SALES
PRE-BOOKED VISITS
ACCOMMODATION
ANNUAL PRODUCTION 6,000 bottles
HECTARES UNDER VINE 0.90
SUSTAINABLE WINERY

● Nebbiolo d'Alba '17	▼▼ 4
● Barbera d'Alba Sup. '17	▼▼ 4
● Langhe Pinot Nero '17	▼▼ 4

Collina Serragrilli

FRAZ. SERRAGRILLI, 30
12052 NEIVE [CN]
TEL. +39 0173677010
www.serragrilli.it

CELLAR SALES
PRE-BOOKED VISITS
ANNUAL PRODUCTION 100,000 bottles
HECTARES UNDER VINE 15.00

● Barbaresco Serragrilli '16	▼▼ 6
● Barbaresco Starderi '16	▼▼ 7
● Barbera d'Alba Grillaia '16	▼▼ 4
○ Langhe Bianco Grillobianco '18	▼ 2

Vini Silva

CASCINE ROGGE, 1B
10011 AGLIÉ [TO]
TEL. +39 3473075648
www.silvavini.com

CELLAR SALES
PRE-BOOKED VISITS
ANNUAL PRODUCTION 50,000 bottles
HECTARES UNDER VINE 12.00

○ Erbaluce di Caluso Dry Ice '18	▼▼ 2*
○ Erbaluce di Caluso Tre Ciochè '18	▼ 2

Francesco Sobrero

VIA PUGNANE, 5
12060 CASTIGLIONE FALLETTO [CN]
TEL. +39 017362864
www.sobrerofrancesco.it

CELLAR SALES
PRE-BOOKED VISITS
ACCOMMODATION
ANNUAL PRODUCTION 90,000 bottles
HECTARES UNDER VINE 16.00

● Barolo Parussi '15	♟♟ 7
● Barolo Pernanno Ris. '13	♟♟ 8
● Barolo Ciabot Tanasio '15	♟ 6

Le Strette

VIA LE STRETTE, 1F
12060 NOVELLO [CN]
TEL. +39 0173744002
www.lestrette.com

CELLAR SALES
PRE-BOOKED VISITS
ANNUAL PRODUCTION 23,000 bottles
HECTARES UNDER VINE 7.00
VITICULTURE METHOD Certified Organic
SUSTAINABLE WINERY

○ Langhe Nas-Cëtta del Comune di Novello Pasinot '17	♟♟ 4
● Barolo Bergeisa '15	♟♟ 6
● Barolo Bergera-Pezzole '15	♟♟ 7

Cantina Stroppiana

FRAZ. RIVALTA SAN GIACOMO, 6
12064 LA MORRA [CN]
TEL. +39 0173509419
www.cantinastroppiana.com

CELLAR SALES
PRE-BOOKED VISITS
ANNUAL PRODUCTION 35,000 bottles
HECTARES UNDER VINE 7.00

● Barolo Leonardo '15	♟♟ 5
● Barolo Bussia '14	♟♟ 6
● Barolo Bussia Ris. '12	♟♟ 6
● Barolo San Giacomo '15	♟♟ 6

Terre Astesane

VIA MARCONI, 42
14047 MOMBERCELLI [AT]
TEL. +39 0141959155
www.terreastesane.it

CELLAR SALES
PRE-BOOKED VISITS
ANNUAL PRODUCTION 100,000 bottles
HECTARES UNDER VINE 240.00

● Barbera d'Asti La '17	♟♟ 2*
● Grignolino d'Asti Ganassa '18	♟♟ 2*
● Barbera d'Asti Anno Domini '16	♟ 3
● Barbera d'Asti Maniman '18	♟ 2

Terre di Sarizzola

FRAZ. SARIZZOLA
VIA APPENNINI, 41
15050 COSTA VESCOVATO [AL]
TEL. +39 3381222128
www.terredisarizzola.com

○ Derthona Biancornetto '17	♟♟ 4
● Colli Tortonesi Rosso Gambarasca '15	♟♟ 3
○ Colli Tortonesi Timorasso Derthona '17	♟♟ 4
● Colli Tortonesi Barbera Sup. M.....e '15	♟ 3

Tibaldi

S.DA SAN GIACOMO, 49
12060 POCAPAGLIA [CN]
TEL. +39 0172421221
www.cantinatibaldi.com

CELLAR SALES
ANNUAL PRODUCTION 35,000 bottles
HECTARES UNDER VINE 7.00

● Barbera d'Alba '17	♟♟ 3
○ Langhe Favorita '18	♟♟ 3
● Roero '16	♟♟ 3

La Toledana

LOC. SERMOIRA,5
15066 GAVI [AL]
TEL. +39 0141837211
www.latoledana.it

CELLAR SALES
PRE-BOOKED VISITS
ANNUAL PRODUCTION 160,000 bottles
HECTARES UNDER VINE 28.00

○ Gavi del Comune di Gavi V.Rade Foglio 46 '18	♈♈ 5
● Barolo Lo Zoccolaio '15	♈♈ 5
○ Gavi del Comune di Gavi La Toledana '18	♈♈ 5

Tradiberri

B.TA TORRIGLIONE, 4
12064 LA MORRA [CN]
TEL. +39 3391605470
www.trediberri.com

CELLAR SALES
PRE-BOOKED VISITS
ANNUAL PRODUCTION 50,000 bottles
HECTARES UNDER VINE 8.00
VITICULTURE METHOD Certified Organic

● Barolo '15	♈♈ 5
● Barolo Rocche dell'Annunziata '15	♈♈ 7
● Barbera d'Alba '18	♈ 2
● Langhe Nebbiolo '18	♈ 2

Poderi Vaiot

BORGATA LAIONE, 43
12046 MONTÀ [CN]
TEL. +39 0173976283
www.poderivaiot.it

ANNUAL PRODUCTION 25,000 bottles
HECTARES UNDER VINE 4.00

● Barbera d'Alba Lupestre '17	♈♈ 2*
○ Roero Arneis Franco '18	♈♈ 2*
● Roero Pierin '16	♈ 2

Valdinera

VIA CAVOUR, 1
12040 CORNELIANO D'ALBA [CN]
TEL. +39 0173619881
www.valdinera.com

CELLAR SALES
PRE-BOOKED VISITS
ANNUAL PRODUCTION 160,000 bottles
HECTARES UNDER VINE 20.00

● Roero San Carlo Ris. '15	♈♈ 5
● Nebbiolo d'Alba '16	♈♈ 3
○ Roero Arneis '18	♈♈ 3
● Barbera d'Alba Sup. '16	♈ 3

Valfaccenda

FRAZ. MADONNA LORETO
LOC. VAL FACCENDA, 43
12043 CANALE [CN]
TEL. +39 3397303837
www.valfaccenda.it

CELLAR SALES
PRE-BOOKED VISITS
ACCOMMODATION
ANNUAL PRODUCTION 22,000 bottles
HECTARES UNDER VINE 3.50
VITICULTURE METHOD Certified Organic
SUSTAINABLE WINERY

● Roero Ris. '15	♈♈ 6
● Roero V. Valmaggiore Ris. '16	♈♈ 6
● Roero '17	♈ 5
○ Roero Arneis '18	♈ 3

La Vecchia Posta

VIA MONTEBELLO, 2
15050 AVOLASCA [AL]
TEL. +39 0131876254
www.lavecchiaposta-avolasca.com

CELLAR SALES
PRE-BOOKED VISITS
ACCOMMODATION AND RESTAURANT SERVICE
ANNUAL PRODUCTION 10,000 bottles
HECTARES UNDER VINE 2.70
VITICULTURE METHOD Certified Organic

○ Colli Tortonesi Timorasso Il Selvaggio '17	♈♈ 3*
● Colli Tortonesi Barbera Lolita '18	♈♈ 2*
○ Poggio dello Scagno '15	♈ 3

I Vignaioli di Santo Stefano
loc. Marini, 26
12058 Santo Stefano Belbo [CN]
Tel. +39 0141840419
www.ivignaiolidisantostefano.it

CELLAR SALES
PRE-BOOKED VISITS
ANNUAL PRODUCTION 275,000 bottles
HECTARES UNDER VINE 32.00
SUSTAINABLE WINERY

○ Moscato d'Asti '18	🍷🍷 3
○ Asti '18	🍷 3

Villa Guelpa
via Francesco Cesone, 52
13853 Lessona [BI]
Tel. +39 3403850385
www.villaguelpa.it

ANNUAL PRODUCTION 25,000 bottles
HECTARES UNDER VINE 4.00

● Sizzano '16	🍷🍷 6
● Lessona '16	🍷🍷 7
⊙ Rosato Longitudine 8.11	🍷🍷 3
● Rosso Longitudine 8.26	🍷🍷 4

Virna
via Alba, 24
12060 Barolo [CN]
Tel. +39 017356120
www.virnabarolo.it

CELLAR SALES
PRE-BOOKED VISITS
ANNUAL PRODUCTION 60,000 bottles
HECTARES UNDER VINE 12.00

● Barbera d'Alba La '17	🍷🍷 3
● Barolo Cannubi '15	🍷🍷 8
● Barolo del Comune di Barolo '15	🍷🍷 6
● Barolo Sarmassa '15	🍷🍷 8

Alberto Voerzio
b.go Brandini, 1a
12064 La Morra [CN]
Tel. +39 3333927654
www.albertovoerzio.com

CELLAR SALES
ANNUAL PRODUCTION 13,000 bottles
HECTARES UNDER VINE 6.00
SUSTAINABLE WINERY

● Barbera d'Alba '16	🍷🍷 3
● Barolo Castagni '15	🍷🍷 6
● Barolo La Serra '15	🍷🍷 7
● Langhe Nebbiolo '16	🍷 6

Voerzio Martini
s.da Loreto, 3
12064 La Morra [CN]
Tel. +39 0173509194
voerzio.gianni@tiscali.it

CELLAR SALES
PRE-BOOKED VISITS
ANNUAL PRODUCTION 54,000 bottles
HECTARES UNDER VINE 12.00

● Barolo La Serra '15	🍷🍷 8
● Barbera d'Alba Ciabot della Luna '17	🍷🍷 5
● Barolo '15	🍷🍷 6
○ Langhe Arneis Bricco Cappellina '18	🍷 3

La Zerba
loc. Zerba, 1
15060 Tassarolo [AL]
Tel. +39 0143342259
www.la-zerba.it

CELLAR SALES
PRE-BOOKED VISITS
ANNUAL PRODUCTION 90,000 bottles
HECTARES UNDER VINE 12.00
VITICULTURE METHOD Certified Organic

○ Gavi del Comune di Tassarolo Anfora '17	🍷🍷 3
○ Gavi del Comune di Tassarolo Terrarossa '18	🍷🍷 2*
○ Gavi del Comune Tassarolo Primin '17	🍷🍷 3

LIGURIA

The quality of Liguria's wines is highly notable, even if, in the past, producers often preferred easy shortcuts. By now, however, as tasters and consumers are discovering, a group of wineries are offering a well-rounded range of regional wines, and increasingly we're seeing a qualitative hierarchy emerge in the sector. We're not just talking about those wineries that have managed to create brand loyalty, but also lesser known producers who are proving more and more capable of high-quality wines. This long, narrow strip of land running from Sanremo to Sarzana, delimited by the sea on one side, the mountains on the other, is capable of delivering absolutely first-rate bottles. Traditional Ligurian grapes, Vermentino and Pigato (even if DNA tests certify that they're the same), give rise to very different types of whites. At the risk of generalizing, Pigato is richer in edges and personality, while Vermentino is more elegant and linear. In truth, western Liguria made a marketing choice. That is, Pigato is the great wine to which the best vineyards are dedicated, while Vermentino is considered second-tier (even if there's no genetic basis for it). Things change dramatically when we go east of Genoa. At this point Vermentino, absent competition from Pigato, is the most important cultivar planted. In this edition the region earned one additional Tre Bicchieri (with respect to last year) making for a total of eight wines awarded, equally divided between Ponente and Levante. Dolceacqua affirms its top-tier status with two historic Rossese wineries (Maccario Dringenberg and Terre Bianche) getting our highest honors. We'd like to mention Fontanacota, a highly qualified producer that's back on top after seven years. But our biggest round of applause goes to Zangani, who are taking home their first Tre Bicchieri and, especially, a magnificent Colli di Luni Vermentino Etichetta Nera that allows Lunae Bosoni to earn one of our guide's most sought after awards, 'White of the Year'.

Massimo Alessandri

VIA COSTA PARROCCHIA, 42
18020 RANZO [IM]
TEL. +39 018253458
www.massimoalessandri.it

CELLAR SALES
PRE-BOOKED VISITS
RESTAURANT SERVICE
ANNUAL PRODUCTION 35,000 bottles
HECTARES UNDER VINE 7.00

Massimo Alessandri personally manages this Ranzo winery, while his father Luciano and mother Nicoletta run the family restaurant in Albenga. Pigato, the main variety, grows high in the red soil hills, rich in iron and clay, while Vermentino is planted in the pebble and sand soil found at a lower range along the river bed. The farm's patchwork of 30-or-so small plots make for very hard work, kept going by great passion. Many of their wines came out early, especially their Vermentino Costa de Vigne '18. Aromas of fruit and fresh herbs meet a harmonic body with nice acidity. Their Granaccia '17 proved excellent, pouring a vibrant color with violet highlights. On the palate fruity notes unfold on a velvety and harmonic body, with a pleasant aftertaste.

○ Riviera Ligure di Ponente Vermentino Costa de Vigne '18	🍷🍷 3*
● Riviera Ligure di Ponente Granaccia '17	🍷🍷 4
○ Riviera Ligure di Ponente Pigato Costa de Vigne '18	🍷🍷 3
● Riviera Ligure di Ponente Rossese Costa de Vigne '17	🍷🍷 4
○ Riviera Ligure di Ponente Pigato Vigne Vëggie '17	🍷 4
○ Viorus '17	🍷 5
● Ligustico '15	🍷🍷 6
● Riviera Ligure di Ponente Granaccia '16	🍷🍷 4
○ Riviera Ligure di Ponente Pigato Vigne Vëggie '16	🍷🍷 4
○ Riviera Ligure di Ponente Vermentino Costa de Vigne '17	🍷🍷 3
○ Riviera Ligure di Ponente Pigato Costa de Vigne '17	🍷 3

Tenuta Anfosso

C.SO VERBONE, 175
18036 SOLDANO [IM]
TEL. +39 0184289906
www.tenutaanfosso.it

CELLAR SALES
ACCOMMODATION
ANNUAL PRODUCTION 23,000 bottles
HECTARES UNDER VINE 4.50

The estate was founded in 2002 thanks to Alessandro's strong determination to transform the work started by his father Luciano Anfosso. However, it really took root in 1998 when additional vineyards in Poggio Pini were purchased, merged with those already owned and then replanted. Subsequently, the new winery was built, bottling began and the winery came to national and international markets. For some years now, son Lorenzo's presence has further strengthened things in terms of quality and the productive personality. Their Dolceacqua Superiore '17 proved excellent. It pours a vibrant color, with a nose that features intense aromas of pepper and tobacco on a light, vegetal background. The body is bold, close-knit, with a delicate, though present tannic weave that accompanies its elegant structure. Their Luvaira '17 offers up intense sensations of red, mature berries and pepper, with an elegant tannic weave. It's just a bit young.

● Dolceacqua Sup. '17	🍷🍷 4
● Dolceacqua Sup. Luvaira '17	🍷🍷 5
○ Antea '17	🍷 4
● Dolceacqua Sup. Fulavin '17	🍷 5
● Dolceacqua Sup. Poggio Pini '17	🍷 5
● Dolceacqua '15	🍷🍷 4
● Dolceacqua Sup. '16	🍷🍷 4
● Dolceacqua Sup. '13	🍷🍷 4
● Dolceacqua Sup. Fulavin '16	🍷🍷 4
● Dolceacqua Sup. Fulavin '13	🍷🍷 4
● Dolceacqua Sup. Luvaira '16	🍷🍷 5
● Dolceacqua Sup. Luvaira '13	🍷🍷 4
● Dolceacqua Sup. Poggio Pini '16	🍷🍷 5
● Dolceacqua Sup. Poggio Pini '15	🍷🍷 4
● Dolceacqua Sup. Poggio Pini '12	🍷🍷 4

Arrigoni

VIA SARZANA, 224
19126 LA SPEZIA
TEL. +39 0187504060
www.arrigoni1913.it

CELLAR SALES
PRE-BOOKED VISITS
ACCOMMODATION AND RESTAURANT SERVICE
ANNUAL PRODUCTION 150,000 bottles
HECTARES UNDER VINE 18.00
SUSTAINABLE WINERY

The history of the Arrigoni family is long. In 1913, grandfather Gervasio Pagni left the Altopascio countryside in Tuscany for La Spezia with the aim of going to the Americas. But he set down roots in this Ligurian city, creating a future for himself and his family. As a small merchant of porridge and bulk wine, he opened a shop, began to produce wine from the Tuscan countryside and married Lina, a widow with a son, Bruno Arrigoni. In the 1960s the reins passed to his son Riccardo and the company grew, rooting itself even more firmly in Liguria. Their Tra i Monti '18 exhibits great territorial character. Intense aromas of fresh fruit and delicately salty flavors of great personality and complexity emerge on the nose. These give way to a highly pleasant palate supported by an intense, long finish. Their Cascina dei Peri '18 features an intensely elegant body with a fresh finish.

○ Cinque Terre Tra I Monti '18	♥♥ 3*
○ Colli di Luni Vermentino La Cascina dei Peri '18	♥♥ 3
○ Colli di Luni Vermentino V. del Prefetto '18	♥♥ 3
○ Cinque Terre Sciacchetrà Passito Rosa di Maggio '09	♀♀ 8
○ Cinque Terre Sciacchetrà Rosa di Maggio '16	♀♀ 8
○ Cinque Terre Sciacchetrà Tramonti '09	♀♀ 8
○ Cinque Terre Tramonti '17	♀♀ 3*
○ Cinque Terre Tramonti '16	♀♀ 3
○ Colli di Luni Vermentino La Cascina Dei Peri '12	♀♀ 2*
○ Colli di Luni Vermentino V. del Prefetto '17	♀♀ 3

Laura Aschero

P.ZZA VITTORIO EMANUELE, 7
18027 PONTEDASSIO [IM]
TEL. +39 0183710307
www.lauraaschero.it

CELLAR SALES
PRE-BOOKED VISITS
ANNUAL PRODUCTION 65,000 bottles
HECTARES UNDER VINE 50.00

The estate is secure and looking towards the future thanks to Bianca's decision to follow in her father Marco's footsteps. A recently purchased disused olive grove in the Pontedassio area borders its existing patrimony and has been replanted with grapevines. Work continues to grow along with vineyard demands, particularly those given to Pigato, the native variety par excellence of the Italian Riviera, the Ponente. Wine tourism is also strong and the renovated winery has expanded its reception capabilities while also struggling to meet demand with the number of bottles produced. Their most intriguing wine is the Pigato '18. The nose offers up aromas of ripe fruit and exotic hints. The body, which is well-structured, supported and made harmonious by adequate pulp and acidity, gives way to a pleasant, almondy finish. Their Vermentino '18 pours a lively color, with flavors that play on white fruit in a broad and pleasantly persistent body.

○ Riviera Ligure di Ponente Pigato '18	♥♥ 3*
○ Riviera Ligure di Ponente Vermentino '18	♥♥ 3
○ Riviera Ligure di Ponente Vermentino '10	♀♀♀ 3*
○ Riviera Ligure di Ponente Pigato '17	♀♀ 3
○ Riviera Ligure di Ponente Pigato '16	♀♀ 3
○ Riviera Ligure di Ponente Pigato '15	♀♀ 3*
○ Riviera Ligure di Ponente Vermentino '17	♀♀ 3
○ Riviera Ligure di Ponente Vermentino '16	♀♀ 3
○ Riviera Ligure di Ponente Vermentino '15	♀♀ 3
○ Riviera Ligure di Ponente Vermentino '14	♀♀ 3

La Baia del Sole - Federici

FRAZ. LUNI ANTICA
VIA FORLINO, 3
19034 LUNI [SP]
TEL. +39 0187661821
www.cantinefederici.com

CELLAR SALES
PRE-BOOKED VISITS
ANNUAL PRODUCTION 180,000 bottles
HECTARES UNDER VINE 35.00

La Baia del Sole's founder, Giulio Federici still works, together with mother Isa, coordinating and directing the all-round activities of the estate. However, the new spirit(s) of the winery are sons, Andrea, who studied agronomy and manages the vineyards, and Luca, an enologist, mainly responsible for winemaking. Together they work the vineyards located in the hilly area of Luni and Castelnuovo Magra. Apart from Sarticola, the only cru, wines are made from careful selection of harvested grapes. 2018 made for a Solaris rich in aromas. A vibrant color is the prelude to close-knit aromas of ripe white fruit and dried herbs. On the palate it exhibits intensity of alcohol, which accompanies its lengthy aftertaste. Their Sarticola also has plenty to say, with its notes of dried herbs, Mediterranean shrub and a slightly iodine. It finishes complex and harmonious.

○ Colli di Luni Vermentino Sarticola '18	♟♟5
○ Colli di Luni Vermentino Solaris '18	♟♟3*
○ Colli di Luni Bianco Gladius '18	♟♟3
● Colli di Luni Rosso Eutichiano '18	♟♟3
○ Colli di Luni Vermentino Oro d'Isèe '18	♟♟4
○ Colli di Luni Vermentino Sarticola '15	♟♟♟4*
○ Colli di Luni Bianco Gladius '17	♟♟2*
● Colli di Luni Eutichiano '16	♟♟3
● Colli di Luni Rosso Eutichiano '17	♟♟3
○ Colli di Luni Vermentino Gladius '16	♟♟2*
○ Colli di Luni Vermentino Oro d'Isée '17	♟♟4
○ Colli di Luni Vermentino Oro d'Isée '16	♟♟4
○ Colli di Luni Vermentino Sarticola '17	♟♟5
○ Colli di Luni Vermentino Sarticola '16	♟♟4
○ Colli di Luni Vermentino Solaris '17	♟♟3*
○ Muri Grandi '17	♟♟2*

Maria Donata Bianchi

VIA MEREA, 101
18013 DIANO ARENTINO [IM]
TEL. +39 0183498233
www.aziendaagricolabianchi.it

CELLAR SALES
PRE-BOOKED VISITS
ACCOMMODATION
ANNUAL PRODUCTION 30,000 bottles
HECTARES UNDER VINE 4.00

Maria Donata Bianchi and Emanuele Trevia's daughter Marta is taking her first independent steps. The estate works its own vineyards, which center around the two white Ligurian 'princes' of Pigato and Vermentino. Pigato is the first to reflect the changes implemented by Marta; on approximately 4,000 square meters of land in Diano Castello, the old vines were removed and, after a year of cover cropping, new vines have been planted. Their Vermentino '18 is a lively, vibrant wine. On the nose it offers up aromas of white fruit and dried herbs along with a light, delicately salty sensation. On the palate it proves balanced, elegant and complex, expanding harmoniously towards a long finish. Their Antico Sfizio '18 is a different wine, featuring aromas of white fruit, a bold, mineral body and well-structured freshness.

○ Riviera Ligure di Ponente Vermentino '18	♟♟3*
○ Antico Sfizio '18	♟♟4
○ Riviera Ligure di Ponente Pigato '18	♟♟3
○ Riviera Ligure di Ponente Pigato '12	♟♟♟3*
○ Riviera Ligure di Ponente Vermentino '09	♟♟♟3
○ Riviera Ligure di Ponente Vermentino '07	♟♟♟3*
○ Riviera Ligure di Ponente Pigato '17	♟♟3
○ Riviera Ligure di Ponente Vermentino '17	♟♟3
○ Riviera Ligure di Ponente Vermentino '16	♟♟3

BioVio

FRAZ. BASTIA
VIA CROCIATA, 24
17031 ALBENGA [SV]
TEL. +39 018220776
www.biovio.it

CELLAR SALES
PRE-BOOKED VISITS
ACCOMMODATION
ANNUAL PRODUCTION 60,000 bottles
HECTARES UNDER VINE 6.00
VITICULTURE METHOD Certified Organic

The young Cateriana Vio, with the
assistance of boyfriend Vincenzo
Sorrentino, has a firm grasp of the reins in
both the vineyards and the cellar. She
continues to use organic methods, diversify
production and bottle single-variety wines,
while contemporaneously revising the
timing of harvests and late harvests as well
as the selection of grapes. Father Aimone
still supervises and mother Chiara manages
guest reception. Sisters Carolina and
Camilla focus on agritourism, and on the
aromatic herb department and accounting,
respectively. Constant quality distinguishes
this producer. Concerning the 2018 vintage
we point out two wines. Their Ma René
offers up intense aromas of white fruit,
dried flowers, aniseed and notes of
Mediterranean shrub. The body is firmly
structured and harmonious with great,
fresh grip. Their Bon in da Bon appeals for
its rich style and long finish.

○ Riviera Ligure di Ponente Bon in da Bon '18	♟♟ 5
○ Riviera Ligure di Ponente Pigato Ma René '18	♟♟ 3*
● Riviera Ligure di Ponente Rossese U Bastiò '18	♟♟ 3
○ Riviera Ligure di Ponente Vermentino Aimone '18	♟♟ 3
○ Riviera Ligure di Ponente Vermentino Grand Père '17	♟ 5
○ Riviera Ligure di Ponente Pigato Bon in da Bon '17	♟♟♟ 5
○ Riviera Ligure di Ponente Pigato Bon in da Bon '16	♟♟♟ 5
○ Riviera Ligure di Ponente Pigato Bon in da Bon '15	♟♟♟ 2*

Bregante

VIA UNITÀ D'ITALIA, 47
16039 SESTRI LEVANTE [GE]
TEL. +39 018541388
www.cantinebregante.it

CELLAR SALES
PRE-BOOKED VISITS
ANNUAL PRODUCTION 120,000 bottles
HECTARES UNDER VINE 1.00

Still managed by Simona, who takes care
of the shop, and husband Sergio Bregante,
the winery is located in the historic center
of the beautiful, small village of Sestri
Levante. Simona's great-grandfather
started the family's commercial activities,
while her father, Ferdinando, started
'production' by establishing vineyards.
Sergio, took over in the 1980s and boosted
the winery's growth, making it one of the
area's important businesses. Traditional
Bianchetta Genovese, Vermentino, Ciliegiolo
varieties are cultivated. There is also
Muscato, which produces a sweet wine
and, according to the vintage, a natural
passito. Their Bianco '18 pours a vibrant
straw-yellow color, a prelude to notes of
fresh herbs and wild flowers. Its mineral
body features structure and great harmony.
Their Moscato '18 is young and vibrant,
pervasive in the mouth with nice balance
between sweetness and freshness. Their
Clliegiolo '18 is a pleasant and elegant
wine with intense fruit and Mediterranean
sensations.

○ Golfo del Tigullio Portofino Bianco '18	♟♟ 2*
● Golfo del Tigullio Portofino Ciliegiolo '18	♟♟ 2*
○ Golfo del Tigullio Portofino Dosaggio Zero Baia delle Favole M. Cl.	♟♟ 5
○ Golfo del Tigullio Portofino Moscato '18	♟♟ 3
○ Golfo del Tigullio Portofino Bianchetta Genovese '18	♟ 2
○ Golfo del Tigullio Portofino Vermentino '18	♟ 2
○ Golfo del Tigullio Portofino Bianchetta Genovese '17	♟♟ 2*
○ Golfo del Tigullio Portofino Bianco '17	♟♟ 2*
○ Golfo del Tigullio Portofino Moscato '17	♟♟ 3
○ Golfo del Tigullio Portofino Vermentino '16	♟♟ 2*
○ Sole della Costa Passito '16	♟♟ 5

★Bruna

FRAZ. BORGO
VIA UMBERTO I, 81
18020 RANZO [IM]
TEL. +39 0183318082
www.brunapigato.it

CELLAR SALES
PRE-BOOKED VISITS
ANNUAL PRODUCTION 40,000 bottles
HECTARES UNDER VINE 8.50

2018 marked a serious loss for the Bruna family: Riccardo, who founded the winery in 1970, passed away. It was a great emotional loss for his wife Maddalena, daughter Francesca and son-in-law Roberto, but it was also difficult for the whole area of the Riviera Ligure di Ponente, which had thrived in part due to his contributions. Intelligent and far-sighted, in 1972 he used Pigato grapes from the old vineyard that he bought from the curia, and produced the first wines bearing the place name of origin, Russeghine. Their vibrant straw-yellow Pigato Majé '18 offers up classic aromas of Mediterranean shrub on notes of quinine. A wine of notable character, on the palate it's sapid with plenty of fullness and excellent freshness. Their Russeghine '18 stands out for its youthful liveliness. It's an intense wine with complex notes of dried herbs — on the palate it proves rich, with nice harmony and a pleasant finish.

○ Riviera Ligure di Ponente Pigato Le Russeghine '18	🍷🍷 4
○ Riviera Ligure di Ponente Pigato Majé '18	🍷🍷 3
○ Riviera Ligure di Ponente Pigato U Baccan '17	🍷🍷 5
● Riviera Ligure di Ponente Rossese '18	🍷🍷 3
● Pulin '17	🍷 5
○ Riviera Ligure di Ponente Pigato U Baccan '16	🍷🍷🍷 5
○ Riviera Ligure di Ponente Pigato U Baccan '15	🍷🍷🍷 5
○ Riviera Ligure di Ponente Pigato U Baccan '13	🍷🍷🍷 5
○ Riviera Ligure di Ponente Pigato U Baccan '12	🍷🍷🍷 5
○ Riviera Ligure di Ponente Pigato U Baccan '11	🍷🍷🍷 5

Cantine Calleri

LOC. SALEA
REG. FRATTI, 2
17031 ALBENGA [SV]
TEL. +39 018220085
www.cantinecalleri.com

ANNUAL PRODUCTION 55,000 bottles
HECTARES UNDER VINE 6.00

With great determination, Marcello continues the work that his father Paolo Calleri began in 1968. The winery is in Salea, a small village in the hamlet of Albenga, an area known for excellent Pigato. The grapes are harvested from the best areas: Salea, Leca and the neighbouring municipality of Cisano sul Neva. Vermentino on the other hand loves heat and tuffaceous soil and therefore grows best in Pietra Ligure. One of the territory's historic estates, the winery is authorized by derogation to vinify and bottle Ormeasco grapes. Their Saleasco '18 is intense with broad aromas of tobacco and dried herbs enriched by a light and elegant spiciness. On the palate it features a delicately salty flavor with iodine notes, closing with a long, pleasant finish. Their Vermentino '18 sees citrusy notes, along with hints of fresh fruit and Mediterranean aromas — the palate is harmonious and fresh.

○ Riviera Ligure di Ponente Pigato di Albenga Saleasco '18	🍷🍷 3*
● Ormeasco di Pornassio '17	🍷🍷 3
○ Riviera Ligure di Ponente Vermentino '18	🍷🍷 3
● Rossese di Dolceacqua '17	🍷🍷 3
○ Riviera Ligure di Ponente Vermentino I Müzazzi '18	🍷 3
● Ormeasco di Pornassio '16	🍷🍷 3
○ Riviera Ligure di Ponente Pigato di Albenga '17	🍷🍷 3
○ Riviera Ligure di Ponente Pigato di Albenga Saleasco '17	🍷🍷 3*
○ Riviera Ligure di Ponente Vermentino '17	🍷🍷 3
○ Riviera Ligure di Ponente Vermentino '16	🍷🍷 3
○ Riviera Ligure di Ponente Vermentino I Müzazzi '17	🍷🍷 3*
○ Riviera Ligure di Ponente Vermentino I Müzazzi '16	🍷🍷 3*

Cheo

via Brigate Partigiane, 1
19018 Vernazza [SP]
Tel. +39 0187821189
www.cheo.it

CELLAR SALES
PRE-BOOKED VISITS
ANNUAL PRODUCTION 13,000 bottles
HECTARES UNDER VINE 2.00
SUSTAINABLE WINERY

It's possible to admire Lise and Bartolomeo Lercari's vineyards from Vernazza's castle tower to the height of the church's bell tower; they cover a wide east-west radius and circumscribe the entire small Cinqueterre village. The plots are cultivated using techniques with low environmental impact, there are no tractors or machinery, and harvesting is done by hand from the steep stairs of the dry stone walls. The wines are made with different varietal blends: Cheo uses Bosco, Vermentino and a bit of Albarola, while Perciò uses Bosco, Vermentino and local 'Piccabon'. Intense with notes of dried herbs and tobacco on the background and a lovely iodine sensation — their Mavà '17 is rich in character and personality, exhibiting harmony on the palate and closing with a long, elegant finish. Their Perciò '18 also delivers with its intense aromas of Mediterranean shrub and dried herbs. On the palate it's classic and fresh, expanding with elegance and harmony.

○ Cinque Terre Mavà '17	♟♟	4
○ Cinque Terre Perciò '18	♟♟	4
○ Cheo Bianco '18	♟♟	3
● Cheo Rosso '17	♟♟	4
○ Cinque Terre Sciacchetrà '16	♟♟	8
○ Cinque Terre Cheo '18	♟	3
○ Cinque Terre Cheo '17	♟♟	3
○ Cinque Terre Cheo '16	♟♟	3
○ Cinque Terre Cheo '15	♟♟	3
○ Cinque Terre Perciò '17	♟♟	4
○ Cinque Terre Perciò '16	♟♟	4
○ Cinque Terre Perciò '15	♟♟	4
○ Cinque Terre Perciò '14	♟♟	4
○ Cinque Terre Sciacchetrà '15	♟♟	8
○ Cinque Terre Sciacchetrà '14	♟♟	8
○ Cinque Terre Sciacchetrà '13	♟♟	8

Cantina Cinque Terre

fraz. Manarola
loc. Groppo
19010 Riomaggiore [SP]
Tel. +39 0187920435
www.cantinacinqueterre.com

PRE-BOOKED VISITS
ANNUAL PRODUCTION 200,000 bottles
HECTARES UNDER VINE 45.00

It's difficult to maintain a consistent supply of grapes in the Cinqueterre. The fairytale environment offers not only enchanting, sweeping views towards the open sea, but also real challenges for winemaking: steep walls perched above the sea must be preserved, and the grapevines, traditionally trained on low arbors, require continuous care and attention. Winegrowers often abandon the terraces, which can be a lucky break for audacious newcomers. In Volastra, where Costa da Posa is made, several small producers are bringing new life to the area and contributing grapes to the winery. Their Vigne Alte '18 offers up intense notes of sea salt and iodine across a youthful and fresh body. It's a wine rich in Mediterranean sensations and fresh fruit, with a velvety, sapid and elegant structure. Their Cinqueterre '18 is intense and rich in character, with delicately salty aromas and fruity notes. On the palate it's distinct for its pleasant and fresh character.

○ Cinque Terre Vigne Alte '18	♟♟	3*
○ Cinque Terre '18	♟♟	2*
○ Cinque Terre Costa da' Posa '18	♟♟	3
○ Cinque Terre Costa de Campu '18	♟♟	3
○ Cinque Terre Sciacchetrà '17	♟♟	6
○ Cinque Terre Costa de Sèra '18	♟	3
○ Cinque Terre Pergole Sparse '18	♟	3
○ Cinque Terre '17	♟♟	2*
○ Cinque Terre '16	♟♟	2*
○ Cinque Terre Costa da Posa '16	♟♟	3*
○ Cinque Terre Costa da' Posa '17	♟♟	3
○ Cinque Terre Costa de Campu '17	♟♟	3
○ Cinque Terre Pergole Sparse '17	♟♟	3
○ Cinque Terre Pergole Sparse '16	♟♟	3
○ Cinque Terre Sciacchetrà '15	♟♟	6
○ Cinque Terre Sciacchetrà Ris. '12	♟♟	6
○ Cinque Terre Vigne Alte '17	♟♟	3*

Fontanacota

FRAZ. PONTI
VIA PROVINCIALE, 137
18100 PORNASSIO [IM]
TEL. +39 3339807442
www.fontanacota.it

CELLAR SALES
PRE-BOOKED VISITS
ANNUAL PRODUCTION 40,000 bottles
HECTARES UNDER VINE 6.00

New forces are emerging at Fontanacota. Supporting Marina in the cellar and with guest reception is son Andreas; after completing his enological studies, son Ludovico will help in the vineyards currently run by brother Fabio. In the future, the young men will carry on this beautiful small estate, which, given growing market demands, has recently acquired an additional plot of about five hectares in Dolcedo. This new single body of land will be planted and merged with their existing, historic vineyard of established Pigato. Their Vermentino '18 offers up intense aromas, proving capable of exploding into infinite sensations of fresh herbs, lemon and Mediterranean shrub. On the palate it exhibits plenty of pulp and a rich freshness before giving way to a pervasive, spicy finish. Elegant, intense and rich, their Pigato '18 shows a notable and balanced structure with a long, sapid finish.

○ Riviera Ligure di Ponente Vermentino '18	▼▼▼ 3*
○ Riviera Ligure di Ponente Pigato '18	▼▼ 3*
● Ormeasco di Pornassio '17	▼▼ 3
● Ormeasco di Pornassio Sup. '17	▼▼ 3
☉ Ormeasco di Pornassio Sciac-trà '18	▼ 3
● Riviera Ligure di Ponente Rossese '18	▼ 3
○ Riviera Ligure di Ponente Pigato '11	♀♀♀ 3*
○ Riviera Ligure di Ponente Pigato '17	♀♀ 3
● Riviera Ligure di Ponente Rossese '17	♀♀ 3
○ Riviera Ligure di Ponente Vermentino '17	♀♀ 3
○ Riviera Ligure di Ponente Vermentino Sup. Barbazenà '16	♀♀ 3

Giacomelli

VIA PALVOTRISIA, 134
19030 CASTELNUOVO MAGRA [SP]
TEL. +39 3496301516
www.azagricolagiacomelli.com

CELLAR SALES
PRE-BOOKED VISITS
ANNUAL PRODUCTION 100,000 bottles
HECTARES UNDER VINE 12.00
SUSTAINABLE WINERY

Roberto Petacchi, owner of Giacomelli, continues to replant his vineyards in the prestigious Villa Baracchini. After the first plot (which has already been put into production), he's concluded planting of a second, one-hectare plot of Vermentino. It's part of a constant push for growth aimed at identifying the best areas for cultivating the native white grapes called for by DOC protocols. Their Pinacce '18 is an outstanding wine, intense with notes of rosemary, peach and apricot on a background of medicinal herbs. On the palate it exhibits plenty of richness with a long, fresh finish of great elegance. Their fresh and elegant Boboli '18 is far behind, nor is their Giardino dei Vescovi '17, a complex but well-balanced wine with a long finish.

○ Colli di Luni Vermentino Pianacce '18	▼▼▼ 3*
○ Colli di Luni Vermentino Boboli '18	▼▼ 4
○ Colli di Luni Vermentino Giardino dei Vescovi '17	▼▼ 5
○ Colli di Luni Vermentino Paduletti '18	▼▼ 2*
☉ Gorgonia Rosato '18	▼▼ 2*
● Pergole Basse '18	▼ 3
○ Colli di Luni Vermentino Boboli '17	♀♀♀ 4*
○ Colli di Luni Bianco Paduletti '16	♀♀ 2*
○ Colli di Luni Vermentino Boboli '15	♀♀ 4
○ Colli di Luni Vermentino Boboli '13	♀♀ 4
○ Colli di Luni Vermentino Boboli '11	♀♀ 4
○ Colli di Luni Vermentino Pianacce '17	♀♀ 3
○ Colli di Luni Vermentino Pianacce '16	♀♀ 2*
○ Colli di Luni Vermentino Pianacce '15	♀♀ 2*
○ Colli di Luni Vermentino Pianacce '14	♀♀ 2*
☉ Gorgonia Rosato '16	♀♀ 2*

La Ginestraia

VIA STERIA
18100 CERVO [IM]
TEL. +39 3482613723
www.laginestraia.com

ANNUAL PRODUCTION 50,000 bottles
HECTARES UNDER VINE 7.00

The connections between Marco Brangero and Mauro Leporieri continue to grow and strengthen, in step with their investments in the winery in Liguria and in new plots. Varieties native to the Ligurian DOC zone are cultivated: Pigato in primis, as well as Vermentino and Rossese. Vineyards are distributed in various municipalities to provide suitable conditions for different cultivars: Vermentino in Cervo, about 500 meters from the sea and Pigato in Ortovero, close to the wide Albenga plain, in the Arroscia Valley. 2018 also made for a first-rate selection. The vibrant color of their Le Marige is the prelude to aromas of dried herbs and apricots, sensations that emerge on an elegant palate of great structure. It's a velvety and somewhat austere wine that unfolds with true class. Their fresh Pigato is redolent of white fruit and citrus, with a harmonious body and a long finish.

○ Riviera Ligure di Ponente Pigato Le Marige '18	♛♛♛ 5
○ Riviera Ligure di Ponente Pigato '18	♛ 3*
○ Riviera Ligure di Ponente Vermentino '18	♛ 3
○ Riviera Ligure di Ponente Pigato Le Marige '15	♛♛♛ 3*
○ Riviera Ligure di Ponente Pigato Via Maestra '16	♛♛♛ 5
○ Riviera Ligure di Ponente Pigato Le Marige '17	♛♛ 3
○ Riviera Ligure di Ponente Pigato Le Marige '16	♛♛ 3
○ Riviera Ligure di Ponente Pigato Via Maestra '15	♛♛ 3*
○ Riviera Ligure di Ponente Vermentino '16	♛♛ 3

Ka' Manciné

FRAZ. SAN MARTINO
VIA MACIURINA, 7
18036 SOLDANO [IM]
TEL. +39 339 3965477
www.kamancine.it

CELLAR SALES
PRE-BOOKED VISITS
ANNUAL PRODUCTION 20,000 bottles
HECTARES UNDER VINE 3.00

Guided by Maurizio Anfosso, Kà Mancinè is located in the Verbone valley in Soldano, one of the municipalities best suited for the production of Rossese. The grapes come from two main vineyards located near the winery: Beragna faces north-east on largely calcareous soil, Galeae looks east-southeast with a prevalence of clay soil. From the latter also comes Angé, which is vinified without temperature control and spends six to eight months in small oak casks before bottle aging. 2018 was a great year for the producer, starting with their Beragna, a wine with lovely aromas of pepper and red fruit on a slightly vegetal background. In the mouth its body is warm and well-balanced, thanks to sapidity and the freshness of its tannins. Their Galeae l'Angé '17 is just as good. It's rich in fruit with light spices, quinine and a warm finish that extends its harmony.

● Dolceacqua Galeae Angè Ris. '17	♛♛ 3*
● Dolceacqua Beragna '18	♛♛ 3
● Dolceacqua Galeae '18	♛♛ 3
☉ Sciakk '18	♛ 3
○ Tabaka '18	♛ 3
● Dolceacqua Beragna '17	♛♛♛ 3*
● Dolceacqua Beragna '16	♛♛♛ 3*
● Dolceacqua Galeae '13	♛♛♛ 3*
● Dolceacqua Beragna '15	♛♛ 3*
● Dolceacqua Galeae '17	♛♛ 3*
● Dolceacqua Galeae '16	♛♛ 3*
● Dolceacqua Galeae '15	♛♛ 3
● Dolceacqua Galeae Angè Ris. '16	♛♛ 3*
● Dolceacqua Galeae Angè Ris. '15	♛♛ 3
● Dolceacqua Galeae Angè Ris. '14	♛♛ 3*

Ottaviano Lambruschi

VIA OLMARELLO, 28
19030 CASTELNUOVO MAGRA [SP]
TEL. +39 0187674261
www.ottavianolambruschi.com

CELLAR SALES
PRE-BOOKED VISITS
ANNUAL PRODUCTION 36,000 bottles
HECTARES UNDER VINE 10.00

Father Ottaviano may have celebrated his 89th birthday, but his vigilance in the vineyard remains as constant as ever. In 2018, a new hectare entered into production planted with the area's main variety, Vermentino, some of which will expand the Costa Marina cru. Agronomic management is entrusted to son Fabio, while young niece Ylenia is implementing a new corporate vision focusing more on wine tourism made possible by expanding the guest reception areas. Lambruschi once again submitted an excellent selection, in particular their Costa Marina '18. It's an intense wine with lovely notes of rosemary and iodine on a fruity background. In the mouth it comes through complex, with nice balanced between freshness and sapidity. Their Maggiore '18 is also excellent, with its Mediterranean and mineral sensations, and a nice freshness that persists right up through its long finish.

○ Colli di Luni Vermentino Costa Marina '18	♥♥ 4
○ Colli di Luni Vermentino Il Maggiore '18	♥♥ 5
○ Colli di Luni Vermentino '18	♥♥ 3
○ Ottaviano '18	♥♥ 3
○ Colli di Luni Vermentino Costa Marina '16	♥♥♥ 4*
○ Colli di Luni Vermentino Costa Marina '11	♥♥♥ 4*
○ Colli di Luni Vermentino Il Maggiore '15	♥♥♥ 5
○ Colli di Luni Vermentino Il Maggiore '14	♥♥♥ 5
○ Colli di Luni Vermentino Il Maggiore '13	♥♥♥ 5
○ Colli di Luni Vermentino Il Maggiore '12	♥♥♥ 4*

★Cantine Lunae Bosoni

VIA PALVOTRISIA, 2
19030 CASTELNUOVO MAGRA [SP]
TEL. +39 0187669222
www.cantinelunae.com

CELLAR SALES
PRE-BOOKED VISITS
ANNUAL PRODUCTION 550,000 bottles
HECTARES UNDER VINE 80.00

Diego Bosoni is working more and more with his father Paolo: he was the one who started working some of the vineyards organically in preparation for a full conversion in the future. At the same time, he has intensified his study of local indigenous varieties such as Vermentino Nero, Pollera Nero and Massaretta. In the winery's structures as well, the reins are being passed to the next generation, where Debora Bosoni welcomes wine tourists on visits enhanced by a museum of farming and with the production of liqueurs and preserves. Their Etichetta Nera '18 is an aromatically explosive wine. It unfolds with great harmony and elegant fruit accompanied by a vibrant note of dried grass. Deep, rich and gratifying: it's our 'White of the Year'. Their Cavagino '18 also delivered, proving complex with nice alcohol, as did their Albarola '18, a white whose aromas of white flowers evolve towards honey — it's a vibrant, extremely well-made wine.

○ Colli di Luni Vermentino Lunae Et. Nera '18	♥♥♥ 4*
○ Colli di Luni Vermentino Albarola '18	♥♥ 4
○ Colli di Luni Vermentino Cavagino '18	♥♥ 5
○ Colli di Luni Bianco Fior di Luna '18	♥♥ 3
● Colli di Luni Rosso Niccolò V '15	♥♥ 4
○ Colli di Luni Vermentino Et. Grigia '18	♥♥ 3
○ Colli di Luni Vermentino Numero Chiuso '15	♥♥ 6
● Colli di Luni Rosso Niccolò V Ris. '12	♥ 5
○ Colli di Luni Vermentino Et. Nera '15	♥♥♥ 4*
○ Colli di Luni Vermentino Lunae Et. Nera '17	♥♥♥ 4*
○ Colli di Luni Vermentino Lunae Et. Nera '16	♥♥♥ 4*

Maccario Dringenberg

VIA TORRE, 3
18036 SAN BIAGIO DELLA CIMA [IM]
TEL. +39 0184289947
maccariodringenberg@yahoo.it

CELLAR SALES
PRE-BOOKED VISITS
ANNUAL PRODUCTION 23,000 bottles
HECTARES UNDER VINE 4.00

After meticulously mapping the geography of their terroir, Giovanna Maccario and Goetz Dringenberg decided against laying claim to Superiore and Riserva, adopting the name of the cru of provenance. The vineyards are distributed among the most prestigious areas of the territory: in the Nervia valley of San Biagio della Cima, Luvaira is cultivated on soils characterized by sedimentary marl and clay, while Posaù comes from a beautiful amphitheater facing south-east on marine limestone. Il Brae, on the other hand, comes from Perinaldo. Their Posaù Biamonti '17 performed spectacularly. A wine that pours a dense ruby red, highlighting its youth, it shows great character and complex structure. On the palate, amidst notes of cocoa and licorice, tannins taper towards a long, pleasant finish. Red berries, dried herbs and pleasant notes of black pepper characterize the elegant Dolceacqua '18.

● Rossese di Dolceacqua Posaù Biamonti '17	▼▼▼ 5
● Rossese di Dolceacqua '18	▼▼ 3*
● Rossese di Dolceacqua Sup. Posaù '17	▼▼ 3*
● Rossese di Dolceacqua Sup. Brae '18	▼▼ 3
● Rossese di Dolceacqua Sup. Luvaira '17	▼▼ 4
○ L'Amiral '18	▼ 3
● Dolceacqua Sup. Vign. Posaù '13	♈♈♈ 3*
● Rossese di Dolceacqua Sup. Vign. Luvaira '07	♈♈♈ 4*
● Rossese di Dolceacqua Sup. V ign. Posaù '10	♈♈♈ 3*
● Rossese di Dolceacqua Sup. Vign. Posaù '08	♈♈♈ 3
● Rossese di Dolceacqua Sup. '17	♈♈ 3*
● Rossese di Dolceacqua Sup. Posaù Biamonti '16	♈♈ 5

Maixei

LOC. PORTO
18035 DOLCEACQUA [IM]
TEL. +39 0184205015
www.maixei.it

CELLAR SALES
PRE-BOOKED VISITS
ANNUAL PRODUCTION 45,000 bottles
HECTARES UNDER VINE 10.00

Maixei is based in Dolceacqua, the productive heart of west Liguria's great red wine. The Rossese-planted vineyards are in the Verbone Valley (Soldano) and the Nervia Valley (Camporosso, Dolceacqua and Pigna) at elevations ranging from 200 to 400 meters above sea level on sub-alkaline soils with traditional head-trained vines. The estate is run by director, jack-of-all-trades and enologist, Fabio Corradi along with its president, Gianfranco Croese. Their Dolceacqua '18 is an excellent wine, offering up fruity, elegant notes enriched by sensations of tobacco and black pepper. On the palate it proves elegant and complex, as well as pleasantly persistent. Their Vermentino '18 sees intense aromas of herbs and white fruit. Its body is fresh and velvety, pleasant and persistent. Their Barbadirame '17 is intense and warm with elegant tannins.

● Dolceacqua '18	▼▼ 3*
● Dolceacqua Sup. Barbadirame '17	▼▼ 4
○ Riviera Ligure di Ponente Vermentino '18	▼▼ 3
● Dolceacqua '15	♈♈ 3
● Dolceacqua '14	♈♈ 3*
● Dolceacqua Sup. '16	♈♈ 4
● Dolceacqua Sup. '15	♈♈ 4
● Dolceacqua Sup. '14	♈♈ 4
● Dolceacqua Sup. '13	♈♈ 4
● Dolceacqua Sup. '12	♈♈ 4
● Dolceacqua Sup. Barbadirame '16	♈♈ 4
● Dolceacqua Sup. Barbadirame '15	♈♈ 4
● Mistral '15	♈♈ 4
○ Riviera Ligure di Ponente Riviera dei Fiori Vermentino '17	♈♈ 3

La Pietra del Focolare

VIA ISOLA, 76
19034 LUNI [SP]
TEL. +39 0187662129
www.lapietradelfocolare.it

CELLAR SALES
PRE-BOOKED VISITS
ANNUAL PRODUCTION 30,000 bottles
HECTARES UNDER VINE 6.00
SUSTAINABLE WINERY

La Pietra del Focolare is a small town in Luni, at the easternmost part of Liguria, on the border of Tuscany. Owners Laura Angelini and Stefano Salvetti personally follow the entire production process: from care of the vineyards (about fifteen small plots cultivated with only local, traditional vines, distributed between Sarzana, Castelnuovo Magra and Ortonovo) to winemaking. Recently, they have purchased two amphorae for long macerations without cultured yeasts or added sulphites. Their selection of 2018s put in a splendid performance, starting with their Villa Linda, a wine that opens on notes of dried herbs and apricot before embracing mineral hints. On the palate it's rich in freshness with a pleasant, long finish. Their Augusto features vegetal aromas along with tobacco and dried herbs, while the Saltamasso convinces with its bold extract rich in red fruit.

Poggio dei Gorleri

FRAZ. DIANO GORLERI
VIA SAN LEONARDO
18013 DIANO MARINA [IM]
TEL. +39 0183495207
www.poggiodeigorleri.com

CELLAR SALES
PRE-BOOKED VISITS
ACCOMMODATION
ANNUAL PRODUCTION 80,000 bottles
HECTARES UNDER VINE 10.50

2018 was a year of significant change in Poggio dei Gorleri's organization: Matteo Merano, who worked in the vineyard for years, left the family business and the young Manuele Priolo now works in enological management alongside Beppe Caviola. Davide Merano remains, managing the estate with the full support of his father Giampiero, who coordinates work in the vineyards. Mother Rosella and wife Cristina take care of the 22-room agritourism and fully operational restaurant during the high season. Rich in freshness, the Cycnus '18 features broad fruity aromas and sensations of medicinal herbs. The body is intense and balanced, persistent, with a pleasant, harmonious finish. Their Sorì '18 is also excellent in its vibrant aromas: notes of melon and apricot, and a finish of dried herbs. On the palate the wine proves complex, sapid and fresh, characterized by a pleasant harmony.

○ Colli di Luni Vermentino Sup. Villa Linda '18	♟♟ 4
● Colli di Luni Rosso Saltamasso '16	♟♟ 4
○ Colli di Luni Vermentino Augusto '18	♟♟ 3
○ Colli di Luni Vermentino Sup. Solarancio '18	♟♟ 4
○ Colli di Luni Vermentino Augusto '17	♟♟ 3
○ Colli di Luni Vermentino Augusto '16	♟♟ 3
○ Colli di Luni Vermentino Sup. Villa Linda '17	♟♟ 4
○ Colli di Luni Vermentino Sup. Villa Linda '16	♟♟ 4
○ Solarancio '17	♟♟ 5
○ Vigna delle Rose '17	♟♟ 3*

○ Riviera Ligure di Ponente Pigato Cycnus '18	♟♟ 3*
○ Riviera Ligure di Ponente Vermentino V. Sorì '18	♟♟ 3*
● Riviera Ligure di Ponente Granaccia Shalok '16	♟♟ 5
● Ormeasco di Pornassio Peinetti '18	♟ 3
○ Riviera Ligure di Ponente Vermentino Blu di Mare '18	♟ 3
○ Riviera Ligure di Ponente Pigato Albium '13	♟♟♟ 5
○ Riviera Ligure di Ponente Pigato Albium '10	♟♟♟ 5
○ Riviera Ligure di Ponente Pigato Cycnus '13	♟♟♟ 5
○ Riviera Ligure di Ponente Pigato Cycnus '12	♟♟♟ 3*

Terenzuola

via Vercalda, 14
54035 Fosdinovo [MS]
Tel. +39 0187670387
www.terenzuola.it

PRE-BOOKED VISITS
ANNUAL PRODUCTION 180,000 bottles
HECTARES UNDER VINE 18.00

Once realized, Ivan Giuliani's 'Historical Lunigiana' project will allow him work in three areas in Liguria and Tuscany: Cinqueterre, Colli di Luni and Candia. A new half-hectare plot at Riomaggiore in the Cinqueterre, between the Sanctuary of Montenero and Il Telegrafo of Riomaggiore means that the dream is almost fulfilled. The vineyards are planted with Vermentino, Bosco and Ruzzese, an indigenous variety that suffers from abortive flower problems but withstands winds and high temperatures. Intense in its notes of tropical fruit and dried herbs, their Fosso di Corsano '18 is a regal wine, highly complex and elegant. Its juicy palate exhibits a nice acidic staying power that balances and lengthens the finish. Their pale straw-yellow colored Cinqueterre '18 features a vibrant and intense flavor of apples and pears with lovely mineral notes.

○ Colli di Luni Vermentino Sup. Fosso di Corsano '18	¶¶¶ 4*
● Merla della Miniera '16	¶¶ 4
● Vigne Basse '17	¶¶ 3*
○ Cinque Terre '18	¶¶ 4
○ Colli di Luni Bianco Permano '17	¶¶ 5
● Permano Vermentino Nero '15	¶¶ 8
○ Colli di Luni Vermentino Sup. Fosso di Corsano '17	♀♀♀ 3*
○ Colli di Luni Vermentino Sup. Fosso di Corsano '16	♀♀♀ 3*
○ Colli di Luni Vermentino Sup. Fosso di Corsano '11	♀♀♀ 3*
○ Cinque Terre '17	♀♀ 4
○ Cinque Terre Sciacchetrà Ris. '16	♀♀ 8
○ Colli di Luni Bianco Permano '16	♀♀ 5

Terre Bianche

loc. Arcagna
18035 Dolceacqua [IM]
Tel. +39 018431426
www.terrebianche.com

CELLAR SALES
PRE-BOOKED VISITS
ACCOMMODATION
ANNUAL PRODUCTION 55,000 bottles
HECTARES UNDER VINE 8.50
SUSTAINABLE WINERY

Terre Bianche is one of the most deeply rooted and best known wineries in the Dolceacqua area. Filippo Rondelli and Franco Locani's energy and drive to improve find expression that starts in their park of vineyards: the new planting of about half a hectare in the Terrabianca area at 300 to 400 meters above sea level brings them close to their ten-hectare goal. The incremental increase in size goes hand in hand with their process of conversion to certified organic methods. This agronomic and stylistic growth is increasingly tangible in the quality of the entire range. Their selection of 2017s put in an excellent performance. Vibrant and elegant with a fruity note of great harmony and complexity, their Bricco Arcagna opens on tobacco and a slight hint of quinine. On the palate it exhibits close-knit tannins on magnificent fruity flesh. Their Terrabianca is just as good, with its charming palate, enriched and made more complex by hints of vanilla.

● Rossese di Dolceacqua Bricco Arcagna '17	¶¶¶ 6
● Rossese di Dolceacqua Terrabianca '17	¶¶ 5
○ Riviera Ligure di Ponente Pigato '18	¶¶ 3
● Rossese di Dolceacqua '18	¶¶ 3
○ Riviera Ligure di Ponente Vermentino '18	¶ 3
● Dolceacqua Bricco Arcagna '14	♀♀♀ 5
● Dolceacqua Bricco Arcagna '12	♀♀♀ 5
● Rossese di Dolceacqua '12	♀♀♀ 3*
● Rossese di Dolceacqua Bricco Arcagna '09	♀♀♀ 4
● Rossese di Dolceacqua Bricco Arcagna '16	♀♀ 6
● Rossese di Dolceacqua Terrabianca '16	♀♀ 5

Vis Amoris

LOC. CARAMAGNA
S.DA PER VASIA, 1
18100 IMPERIA
TEL. +39 3483959569
www.visamoris.it

CELLAR SALES
PRE-BOOKED VISITS
ANNUAL PRODUCTION 24,000 bottles
HECTARES UNDER VINE 3.50
VITICULTURE METHOD Certified Organic
SUSTAINABLE WINERY

Vis Amoris has been certified organic for years and now it has moved to biodynamic management in some of the vineyards. The wine produced is macerated for about three months on the skins without selected yeasts and is neither clarified nor filtered. Moreover, after two years of experimenting with spontaneous fermentation, Roberto and Danilo Tozzi have introduced sparkling wines without added sulphites and using indigenous yeasts. These are the first steps toward an increasingly 'natural' process. Their Sogno '17 exhibits an explosion of olfactive sensations that call up Mediterranean shrub, white fruit and sea water. On the palate it proves rich, full and exceptionally persistent. Their Verum '18 intrigues for its complex body, unleashing exotic notes, hints of cocoa and red pepper as it moves towards a highly elegant finish.

○ Riviera Ligure di Ponente Pigato Sogno '17	♟♟ 4
○ Riviera Ligure di Ponente Pigato Verum '18	♟♟ 3*
○ Regis '17	♟♟ 5
○ Vis Amoris Brut M.Cl.	♟♟ 5
○ Pepp-one '16	♟ 5
○ Riviera Ligure di Ponente Pigato Domè '18	♟ 4
○ Riviera Ligure di Ponente Pigato Sogno '16	♟♟ 4
○ Riviera Ligure di Ponente Pigato Sogno '15	♟♟ 4
○ Riviera Ligure di Ponente Pigato Verum '17	♟♟ 3*
○ Riviera Ligure di Ponente Pigato Verum '16	♟♟ 3

Zangani

LOC. PONZANO SUPERIORE
VIA GRAMSCI, 46
19037 SANTO STEFANO DI MAGRA [SP]
TEL. +39 0187632406
www.zangani.it

CELLAR SALES
PRE-BOOKED VISITS
ACCOMMODATION AND RESTAURANT SERVICE
ANNUAL PRODUCTION 40,000 bottles
HECTARES UNDER VINE 10.00

Grandfather Alberto, who worked the vineyards and produced wine in bulk, laid the groundwork for the winery in the 1960s. It has been bottling its wine since 1995, but it was in 2014 that Zangani took on its present form. Sons Paolo and Roberto, have left the reins in the hands of Paolo's son Filippo, a young winemaker and entrepreneur, responsible for the estate's agricultural management. And it's working. All ten hectares of vineyards will soon be productive, adding to the already active olive groves, restaurant and hotel, located in and around Santo Stefano Magra. A wine whose color speaks of great freshness, the Boceda '18 offers up pervasive aromas of white fruit and delicately salty hints. On the palate, it proves classically styled, exhibiting the right balance between acidity and sapidity. The Mortedo '18 features ripe and intense fruit, which expand and enrich the palate, finishing on a pleasantly bitter note.

○ Colli di Luni Vermentino Sup. Boceda '18	♟♟♟ 4*
○ Colli di Luni Vermentino Mortedo '18	♟♟ 3*
○ Marfi Bianco '18	♟♟ 2*
● Marfi Rosso '18	♟♟ 2*
○ Boceda '16	♟♟ 3
○ Colli di Luni Il Mortedo '12	♟♟ 2*
○ Colli di Luni Vermentino Boceda '14	♟♟ 3
○ Colli di Luni Vermentino Il Mortedo '13	♟♟ 3
○ Colli di Luni Vermentino La Boceda '13	♟♟ 3
○ Colli di Luni Vermentino Mortedo '17	♟♟ 3
○ Colli di Luni Vermentino Sup. Boceda '17	♟♟ 4
○ Marfi Bianco '16	♟♟ 2*
○ Mortedo '16	♟♟ 2*

Michele Alessandri

VIA UMBERTO I, 15
18020 RANZO [IM]
TEL. +39 0183318114
az.alessandricarlo@libero.it

CELLAR SALES
PRE-BOOKED VISITS
ANNUAL PRODUCTION 23,000 bottles
HECTARES UNDER VINE 2.13

● Pornassio '18	♟ 3
● Pornassio Sciac-Trà '18	♟ 3
○ Riviera Ligure di Ponente Pigato '18	♟ 3
○ Riviera Ligure di Ponente Vermentino '18	♟ 2

aMaccia

FRAZ. BORGO
VIA UMBERTO I, 54
18020 RANZO [IM]
TEL. +39 0183318003
www.amaccia.it

CELLAR SALES
PRE-BOOKED VISITS
ACCOMMODATION
ANNUAL PRODUCTION 25,000 bottles
HECTARES UNDER VINE 3.80
SUSTAINABLE WINERY

○ Riviera Ligure di Ponente Pigato Collezione '17	♟♟ 3
○ Riviera Ligure di Ponente Vermentino '18	♟♟ 3
○ Riviera Ligure di Ponente Pigato '18	♟ 3

Berry and Berry

VIA MATTEOTTI, 2
17020 BALESTRINO [SV]
TEL. +39 3332805368
www.berryandberry.it

CELLAR SALES
PRE-BOOKED VISITS
ANNUAL PRODUCTION 8,500 bottles
HECTARES UNDER VINE 2.00

○ Baitinin '18	♟♟ 4
○ Campulou '17	♟♟ 5
● Poggi del Santo '16	♟♟ 5
⊙ Lappazucche '18	♟ 4

Bisson

C.SO GIANELLI, 28
16043 CHIAVARI [GE]
TEL. +39 0185314462
www.bissonvini.it

CELLAR SALES
PRE-BOOKED VISITS
ANNUAL PRODUCTION 80,000 bottles
HECTARES UNDER VINE 12.00

○ Portofino Cimixà V. Rovente '17	♟♟ 3
○ Portofino Passito Acinirari '09	♟♟ 6
● Braccorosso '09	♟ 5
○ Intrigoso Vermentino '17	♟ 3

Samuele Heydi Bonanini

VIA SAN ANTONIO, 72
19017 RIOMAGGIORE [SP]
TEL. +39 0187920959
www.possa.it

CELLAR SALES
PRE-BOOKED VISITS
ANNUAL PRODUCTION 7,000 bottles
HECTARES UNDER VINE 1.50

○ Cinque Terre Sciacchetrà Ris. '15	♟♟ 8
○ Parmea '18	♟♟ 3
○ Cinque Terre '18	♟ 5
○ Er Giancu '18	♟ 4

Cantine Bondonor

VIA ISOLA ALTA, 53
19034 LUNI [SP]
TEL. +39 3488713641
www.cantinebondonor.it

ANNUAL PRODUCTION 15,000 bottles
HECTARES UNDER VINE 3.00

○ Colli di Luni Vermentino Aegidius Vintage Et. Bianca '17	♟♟ 4
○ Colli di Luni Vermentino Lunaris '18	♟♟ 3

Andrea Bruzzone

VIA BOLZANETO, 96R
16162 GENOVA
TEL. +39 0107455157
www.andreabruzzonevini.it

CELLAR SALES
PRE-BOOKED VISITS
ANNUAL PRODUCTION 10,000 bottles
HECTARES UNDER VINE 2.00
SUSTAINABLE WINERY

○ La Superba '18	▼▼ 3*
● Treipaexi '18	▼▼ 3
○ Bunassa '18	▼ 3

Luca Calvini

VIA SOLARO, 76/78A
18038 SANREMO [IM]
TEL. +39 0184660242
www.luigicalvini.com

CELLAR SALES
PRE-BOOKED VISITS
ANNUAL PRODUCTION 50,000 bottles
HECTARES UNDER VINE 3.50
SUSTAINABLE WINERY

○ Riviera Ligure di Ponente Pigato '18	▼▼ 3*
○ Riviera Ligure di Ponente Moscatello di Taggia '18	▼▼ 5
○ Riviera Ligure di Ponente Vermentino '18	▼▼ 3

La Cappelletta di Portofino

VIA DEL FONDACO, 30
16034 PORTOFINO [GE]
TEL. +39 3482551501
info@lacappellettadiportofino.it

ANNUAL PRODUCTION 3,700 bottles
HECTARES UNDER VINE 1.00
SUSTAINABLE WINERY

○ Portofino Vermentino '18	▼▼ 5

I Cerri

VIA GARIBOTTI
19012 CARRO [SP]
TEL. +39 3485102780
www.icerrivaldivara.it

ANNUAL PRODUCTION 8,000 bottles
HECTARES UNDER VINE 1.00

○ Cian dei Seri '18	▼▼ 3*
● Fonte Dietro il Sole '18	▼▼ 3
○ Poggio alle Api '18	▼▼ 3
○ Campo Grande '18	▼ 3

Durin

VIA ROMA, 202
17037 ORTOVERO [SV]
TEL. +39 0182547007
www.durin.it

CELLAR SALES
PRE-BOOKED VISITS
ACCOMMODATION AND RESTAURANT SERVICE
ANNUAL PRODUCTION 150,000 bottles
HECTARES UNDER VINE 17.50
SUSTAINABLE WINERY

○ Riviera Ligure di Ponente Pigato Braie '18	▼▼ 3*
○ Riviera Ligure di Ponente Vermentino '18	▼▼ 3

E Prie

C.SO VERBONE, 175
18036 SOLDANO [IM]
TEL. +39 3383116590
www.eprie.it

ANNUAL PRODUCTION 5,000 bottles
HECTARES UNDER VINE 1.00

● Dolceacqua '18	▼▼ 3*

Dario Enrico

FRAZ. BASTIA
VIA MASSARI, 8
17031 ALBENGA [SV]
TEL. +39 3205510946

○ Riviera Ligure di Ponente Pigato Sup.		
U Baletta '17		🍷🍷 3*
○ Passito di Pigato Amé '16		🍷🍷 5
○ Riviera Ligure di Ponente Pigato '18		🍷🍷 3

Gajaudo

LOC. BUNDA
S.DA PROV.LE 7
18035 ISOLABONA [IM]
TEL. +39 0184208095
www.gajaudo.it

CELLAR SALES
PRE-BOOKED VISITS
ANNUAL PRODUCTION 110,000 bottles
HECTARES UNDER VINE 10.00

● Dolceacqua '18		🍷🍷 3*
○ Riviera Ligure di Ponente		
Vermentino '18		🍷🍷 3
○ Riviera Ligure di Ponente Pigato '18		🍷 3

Guglierame

VIA CASTELLO, 4
18024 PORNASSIO [IM]
TEL. +39 3475696718
www.ormeasco-guglierame.it

CELLAR SALES
ANNUAL PRODUCTION 15,000 bottles
HECTARES UNDER VINE 2.50

● Ormeasco di Pornassio '17		🍷🍷 4
⊙ Ormeasco di Pornassio Sciac-trà '18		🍷🍷 4
● Ormeasco di Pornassio Sup. '16		🍷🍷 5

Il Monticelio

VIA GROPPOLO, 7
19038 SARZANA [SP]
TEL. +39 0187621432
www.ilmonticello.it

CELLAR SALES
PRE-BOOKED VISITS
ACCOMMODATION
ANNUAL PRODUCTION 68,000 bottles
HECTARES UNDER VINE 10.00
VITICULTURE METHOD Certified Biodynamic

○ Colli di Luni Vermentino Groppolo '18		🍷🍷 3*
● Colli di Luni Rosso		
Poggio dei Magni Ris. '16		🍷🍷 3
● Rupestro '18		🍷🍷 2*

Gino Pino

FRAZ. MISSANO
VIA PODESTÀ, 31
16030 CASTIGLIONE CHIAVARESE [GE]
TEL. +39 0185408036
pinogino.az.agricola@tin.it

ANNUAL PRODUCTION 25,000 bottles
HECTARES UNDER VINE 3.50

○ Missanto '17		🍷🍷 3*
● Ciliegiolo '18		🍷🍷 3
○ Bianchetta Genovese '18		🍷 3
○ Vermentino '18		🍷 3

Podere Grecale

LOC. BUSSANA
VIA CIOUSSE
18038 SANREMO [IM]
TEL. +39 01841955158
www.poderegrecale.it

CELLAR SALES
PRE-BOOKED VISITS
ANNUAL PRODUCTION 18,000 bottles
HECTARES UNDER VINE 3.00

○ Riviera Ligure di Ponente		
Vermentino Maèn '17		🍷🍷 3
● Riviera Ligure di Ponente Sup.		
Granaccia Beusi '17		🍷 4

Edoardo Primo

VIA AURELIA, 190
19030 CASTELNUOVO MAGRA [SP]
TEL. +39 340 6739118
www.edoardoprimo.it

CELLAR SALES
ANNUAL PRODUCTION 30,000 bottles
HECTARES UNDER VINE 7.00

○ Colli di Luni Vermentino Ma Teo '18	♟♟ 3*
○ Colli di Luni Vermentino Cà' Duà '18	♟♟ 3

Podere Lavandaro

VIA CASTIGLIONE
54035 FOSDINOVO [MS]
TEL. +39 018768202
www.poderelavandaro.it

CELLAR SALES
PRE-BOOKED VISITS
ANNUAL PRODUCTION 25,000 bottles
HECTARES UNDER VINE 5.00

○ Colli di Luni Vermentino '18	♟♟ 3*
⊙ Merlarosa '18	♟♟ 3
● Vermentino Nero '18	♟♟ 3
● Vignanera '17	♟♟ 3

Rossana Ruffini

VIA TIROLO, 58
19020 BOLANO [SP]
TEL. +39 0187939988
g.brandani@libero.it

ANNUAL PRODUCTION 10,000 bottles
HECTARES UNDER VINE 3.00

○ Colli di Luni Vermentino Portolano '18	♟♟ 3

Natale Sassarini

LOC. PIAN DEL CORSO 1
19016 MONTEROSSO AL MARE [SP]
TEL. +39 0187818063
cantinasassarini@alice.it

○ Cinque Terre Bucce '17	♟♟ 3*
○ Cinque Terre Cian du Corsu '18	♟♟ 4
○ Cinque Terre Campo al Sole '17	♟♟ 3
○ Cinque Terre Sciacchetrà '17	♟♟ 5

Terre di Levanto

LOC. SAN GOTTARDO, 1
19015 LEVANTO [SP]
TEL. +39 3395432482
www.terredilevanto.com

CELLAR SALES
PRE-BOOKED VISITS
ANNUAL PRODUCTION 2,500 bottles
HECTARES UNDER VINE 2.50
SUSTAINABLE WINERY

○ Giaè '18	♟ 3
○ Gianco '18	♟ 3

Innocenzo Turco

VIA BERTONE, 7A
17040 QUILIANO [SV]
TEL. +39 0192000026
www.innocenzoturco.it

CELLAR SALES
PRE-BOOKED VISITS
ACCOMMODATION AND RESTAURANT SERVICE
ANNUAL PRODUCTION 6,000 bottles
HECTARES UNDER VINE 2.50

● Granaccia '18	♟♟ 4
● Granaccia Cappuccini '16	♟♟ 5
○ Riviera Ligure di Ponente Pigato '18	♟ 3

LOMBARDY

When we talk about regions that are part of Italy's 'emerging' wine trends, we rarely (or almost never) think of Lombardy. But that's just wrong. With extraordinary progress, over these past twenty years, Lombardy's producers have achieved a series of important goals and gained considerable market share both in Italy and abroad. The first appellation that comes to mind when we think of Lombardy is Franciacorta, which, through tireless promotion efforts, has managed to earn its cuvées national and international renown while obtaining notable success. But promotion wouldn't be adequate if there weren't solid quality behind it, vanguard techniques and enormous efforts by many producers (in addition to the natural attributes of the terroir). In Franciacorta it's all there, as is the case throughout the region. Just think of another celebrated appellation, Lugana (even if its shared with nearby Veneto) — it's a bestseller in Italy and northern Europe. Once again Valtellina delivered reds of superb character, the result of heroic viticulture, while we're seeing good things happening in Oltrepò Pavese, a territory that's starting to realize the extraordinary potential of its many excellent terroirs, whether it be with Metodo Classico or outstanding reds and whites. But our analysis doesn't finish here. The smaller appellations are growing, like the Brescia side of Garda (Valtènesi foremost). And there are plenty of encouraging signs coming from lesser known districts, like Valcalepio, Valcamonica and even the province of Lecco. Lombardy's healthy pragmatism sees to it that the region's wineries are managed carefully, with an attentive eye to innovation and marketing. And this applies not only to its most important brands, but to its small and medium-sized businesses as well. Finally, it's a region where we continue to see new wineries popping up throughout its various districts. This means that it's attractive to investors and capable of bringing in important human and capital resources. To top off a historic year in terms of Tre Bicchieri awarded, we'd like to greet the newest members of the top tier: Cantina Scuropasso with their Pas Dosé Roccapietra '13, Fiamberti with the Buttafuoco Storico Vigna Sacca del Prete '15 (both in Oltrepò), then Podere Selva Capuzza and their Lugana Menasasso Riserva '15 and Perla del Garda with the Lugana Superiore Madonna della Scoperta '17.

Marchese Adorno

via Garlassolo, 30
27050 Retorbido [PV]
Tel. +39 0383374404
www.marcheseadorno-wines.it

CELLAR SALES
PRE-BOOKED VISITS
ANNUAL PRODUCTION 250,000 bottles
HECTARES UNDER VINE 85.00

Owned by the Cattaneo Adorno family since 1834, the winery is currently overseen by Marquis Marcello, who has brought about significant qualitative improvements. A new, splendid cellar has been built, the property has been renovated and their 60 hectares of vineyards, located on very different terroirs on the hills behind Retorbido, have been mapped. Under the guidance of young Filippo Prè and Enrico Rovino, a number of the wines, starting with Riesling, Barbera and Pinot Nero, are reaching remarkable levels. Their Rile Nero '16 affirmed its status as one of the territory's best Pinot Neros. Elegant and vibrant, it offers up notes of toasted coffee and blueberries, with spicy nuances and herbs. On the palate it exhibits transparent texture, graceful and precise tannins, with a long, close-focused finish. Their Arcolaio '17, is a 'doppia maturazione' monovarietal Renano of rare finesse and focus — and it's only at the beginning of its evolution. Their varietal, vibrant, fragrant and juicy Brugherio is an early-drinking Pinot Nero vinified without the use of wood.

● OP Pinot Nero Brugherio '17	ΨΨ 2*
● OP Pinot Nero Rile Nero '16	ΨΨ 5
○ OP Riesling Arcolaio '17	ΨΨ 3*
● OP Barbera V. del Re '16	ΨΨ 4
● OP Barbera Poggio Marino '17	Ψ 3
● OP Bonarda Costa del Sole '18	Ψ 3
○ Pinot Grigio '18	Ψ 3
● OP Pinot Nero Rile Nero '15	ΥΥΥ 5
● Cliviano '15	ΥΥ 3
● OP Barbera V. del Re '15	ΥΥ 4
● OP Bonarda Vivace Costa del Sole '16	ΥΥ 2*
● OP Pinot Nero Brugherio '16	ΥΥ 2*
● OP Pinot Nero Brugherio '15	ΥΥ 2*
○ OP Riesling Arcolaio '16	ΥΥ 3*

F.lli Agnes

via Campo del Monte, 1
27040 Rovescala [PV]
Tel. +39 038575206
www.fratelliagnes.it

CELLAR SALES
PRE-BOOKED VISITS
ANNUAL PRODUCTION 120,000 bottles
HECTARES UNDER VINE 21.00

If Rovescala is the undisputed kingdom of Bonarda, brothers Sergio and Cristiano Agnes are its most rigorous and significant interpreters. Tenacity, passion, the wisdom handed down from Luigi and Alberto of the previous generation, and lands that are among the area's best come together to produce a range of always impeccable single-variety wines that are rigorous and exhibit great personality. The Croatina, or rather the 'Pignola', a small variety with compact clusters, is available in every possible version (still and sparkling, sweet and dry, young and aged), all with a commendable qualitative consistency. As usual, their Campo del Monte '18 is at the top of its game. It's a mature Bonarda, complete, harmonious and extraordinarily drinkable. The Cresta del Ghiffi '18 is no less good, with a fruitier, 'likable' style made possible by notably higher residual sugars. The Millennium '15, a potentially highly ageworthy, barrel-aged still wine, will require some more patience.

● OP Bonarda Frizzante Campo del Monte '18	ΨΨ 2*
● OP Bonarda Frizzante Cresta del Ghiffi '18	ΨΨ 2*
● OP Bonarda Millennium '15	ΨΨ 4
● Loghetto '17	Ψ 5
● Possessione del Console '17	Ψ 3
● OP Bonarda Vivace Campo del Monte '15	ΥΥΥ 2*
● OP Bonarda Frizzante Campo del Monte '17	ΥΥ 2*
● OP Bonarda Frizzante Cresta del Ghiffi '17	ΥΥ 2*
● OP Bonarda Millennium '13	ΥΥ 4
● OP Bonarda Vivace Campo del Monte '16	ΥΥ 2*
● OP Bonarda Vivace Cresta del Ghiffi '16	ΥΥ 2*
● OP Bonarda Vivace Cresta del Ghiffi '15	ΥΥ 2*

Antica Fratta

VIA FONTANA, 11
25040 MONTICELLI BRUSATI [BS]
TEL. +39 030652068
www.anticafratta.it

CELLAR SALES
PRE-BOOKED VISITS
ANNUAL PRODUCTION 350,000 bottles
HECTARES UNDER VINE 35.00

Monticelli Brusati is in the heart of Franciacorta and for years the winery has been making Franciacorta of excellent quality. The company is in the orbit of the Ziliani family, and therefore of Guido Berlucchi, but functions independently as far as the management and heritage of the vineyards are concerned. The headquarters, a beautiful nineteenth century building restored at the end of the 1970s by the family, has always been known as 'il Cantinon' because of its suggestive vaulted underground cellars, which form a Greek cross. The manor house was the residence of a wealthy wine merchant and today is used for events and receptions. Their Extra Brut Riserva '09 is a Franciacorta of sophisticated elegance. On the nose it's alluring in its aromas of fruit, aromatic herbs, cookies and yeast, which release elegant citrusy nuances, while the palate offers a truly creamy effervescence, limpid, fruity flesh and a long finish. Their Brut confirms the outstanding level of quality the winery has achieved.

○ Franciacorta Extra Brut Quintessence Ris. '09	♟♟ 7
○ Franciacorta Brut	♟♟ 5
○ Franciacorta Essence Noir '14	♟♟ 6
○ Franciacorta Brut Essence '14	♙♟ 5
○ Franciacorta Brut Essence '13	♙♟ 5
○ Franciacorta Extra Brut Quintessence Ris. '07	♙♟ 7
○ Franciacorta Extra Brut Quintessence Ris. '07	♙♟ 7
○ Franciacorta Nature Essence '14	♙♟ 5
○ Franciacorta Nature Essence '13	♙♟ 5
○ Franciacorta Nature Essence '11	♙♟ 5
⊙ Franciacorta Rosé Essence '14	♙♟ 5
○ Franciacorta Rosé Essence '11	♙♟ 5
○ Franciacorta Satèn Essence '11	♙♟ 5
○ Franciacorta Satèn Essence '10	♙♟ 5

Antinori - Tenuta Montenisa

FRAZ. CALINO
VIA PAOLO VI, 62
25046 CAZZAGO SAN MARTINO [BS]
TEL. +39 0307750838
www.tenutamontenisa.it

CELLAR SALES
ANNUAL PRODUCTION 300,000 bottles
HECTARES UNDER VINE 60.00

The array of Antinori estates in Italy was enriched by a beautiful winery in Franciacorta some years ago; it has been managing the Conti Maggi family's beautiful Calino estate since 1999. The new life of Tenuta Montenisa thus began with renovating the vineyards and the historic villa. Production is divided into two lines, one of which is dedicated to single-vintages and to reserve wines produced only during the best years. The single-vintage 2011 Contessa Maggi put in a good performance during our finals. It pours a lovely, brilliant straw-yellow with green highlights, accompanied by extremely delicate perlage, the prelude to aromas of white flowers, vanilla and mature fruit. On the palate it's full, soft, and extremely long. The Brut Cuvée Royale proves succulent, harmonious and elegant in its freshness. The rest of their selection is also notable, with the obligatory special mention for their sapid rosé.

○ Franciacorta Brut Contessa Maggi '11	♟♟ 7
○ Franciacorta Brut Cuvée Royale	♟♟ 5
○ Franciacorta Brut Blanc de Blancs	♟♟ 5
○ Franciacorta Brut Rosé	♟♟ 5
○ Franciacorta Brut Conte Aimo '07	♙♟ 8
○ Franciacorta Brut Conte Aimo Ris. '09	♙♟ 8
○ Franciacorta Brut Contessa Maggi '06	♙♟ 7
○ Franciacorta Brut Contessa Maggi '02	♙♟ 7
○ Franciacorta Brut Contessa Maggi Ris. '07	♙♟ 7
○ Franciacorta Brut Satèn Donna Cora '11	♙♟ 6
○ Franciacorta Satèn '09	♙♟ 6
○ Franciacorta Satèn '06	♙♟ 6
○ Franciacorta Satèn '04	♙♟ 6
○ Franciacorta Satèn '04	♙♟ 6

Ar.Pe.Pe.
VIA DEL BUON CONSIGLIO, 4
23100 SONDRIO
TEL. +39 0342214120
www.arpepe.com

CELLAR SALES
PRE-BOOKED VISITS
ANNUAL PRODUCTION 100,000 bottles
HECTARES UNDER VINE 13.00

The Pelizzati Perego family's wines are increasingly seen on the shelves of the world's best wine bars and on the menus of great restaurants. This is their reward for a vision carried out consistently over time and with an unmistakable style. Opened after a long rest in the bottle, their wines reveal the elegance and complexity of the great Nebbiolo. The seriousness of the winery carries through in the airy mountain traits and a strong, vibrant sapidity that characterize the range, from the Grumello or deep Sassella to the entry-level versions. There's the mountain and biodiversity in this magnificent Sassella Riserva Rocce Rosse '09. It's intense and multifaceted, with aromas of fruit, tobacco, nuances of mint and dried flowers. On the palate it's rich, nicely harmonizing tannins and acidity before giving way to an extremely long finish. The Sassella Stella Retica '15 features aromas of dried herbs melded with lovely, fresh raspberry. On the palate it exhibits class, with invigorating flesh lending character, and a long finish.

● Valtellina Sup. Grumello Rocca De Piro '15	♟♟ 5	
● Valtellina Sup. Sassella Rocce Rosse Ris. '09	♟♟ 7	
● Valtellina Sup. Sassella Stella Retica '15	♟♟ 5	
● Rosso di Valtellina '17	♟♟ 4	
● Valtellina Sup. Il Pettirosso '16	♟♟ 5	
● Valtellina Sup. Inferno Fiamme Antiche '15	♟♟ 6	
● Valtellina Sup. Grumello Buon Consiglio Ris. '07	♟♟♟ 6	
● Valtellina Sup. Sassella Rocce Rosse Ris. '07	♟♟♟ 8	
● Valtellina Sup. Sassella Rocce Rosse Ris. '05	♟♟♟ 7	
● Valtellina Sup. Sassella V. Regina Ris. '09	♟♟♟ 8	

Ballabio
VIA SAN BIAGIO, 32
27045 CASTEGGIO [PV]
TEL. +39 0383805728
www.ballabio.net

CELLAR SALES
PRE-BOOKED VISITS
ANNUAL PRODUCTION 100,000 bottles
HECTARES UNDER VINE 60.00

The winery founded by Angelo Ballabio in 1905 in the center of Casteggio has long been a landmark in the history of Oltrepò Pavese wines, being one of the first to have faith in Metodo Classico made from Pinot Nero. Things have changed significantly over the years. The very beautiful, well-equipped headquarters is now located in the hills of Casteggio and its activities focus on the production of sparkling wine, showing vertical growth in both quality and the number of bottles produced. Elegance is the key word when describing Ballabio's selection of sparkling wines. Zero Dosage is their crown jewel, a wine redolent of wild berries, with extremely fine and creamy bead; it's ripe, lively, crisp, mineral and very long. Their full-bodied and generous Extra Brut features vigor and personality, while their Rosé, a wine that pours a lovely pale onion skin hue, is sapid, citrusy and deep.

○ Farfalla Zero Dosage M. Cl.	♟♟♟ 4	
○ Farfalla Brut M. Cl. Rosé	♟♟ 4	
○ Farfalla Extra Brut M. Cl.	♟♟ 4	
● OP Bonarda V. delle Cento Pertiche '15	♟♟ 3	
● OP Bonarda V. delle Cento Pertiche '13	♟♟ 3	
● OP Bonarda V. delle Cento Pertiche '11	♟♟ 2*	
○ OP Pinot Grigio Clastidium '15	♟♟ 3	
○ Pinot Grigio Clastidium '16	♟♟ 2*	

Barone Pizzini

via San Carlo, 14
25050 Provaglio d'Iseo [BS]
Tel. +39 0309848311
www.baronepizzini.it

CELLAR SALES
PRE-BOOKED VISITS
ACCOMMODATION
ANNUAL PRODUCTION 290,000 bottles
HECTARES UNDER VINE 55.00
VITICULTURE METHOD Certified Organic
SUSTAINABLE WINERY

Barone Pizzini is one of the most important producers in Franciacorta's crowded, competitive landscape. This is a result of the commitment of its members and the enlightened vision of Silvano Brescianini, deus ex machina of the winery and now president of the Consorzio della Franciacorta. Silvano's work over the years has made him a leader in the Italian organic, biodynamic and sustainability sectors. Excellent cuvées are impressive in their own right, but the modern cellar, an example of sustainable architecture and respect for the land, is also worth a visit. Their selection is extremely vast, but this year the Bagnadore Dosaggio Zero '11 stands out over the rest, bewitching with its elegance, complexity and depth, all expressed with a harmony worthy of Tre Bicchieri. But from the citrusy verve of the Animante Extra Brut to the soft pleasantness of the Satèn Edizione 2015, each of their wines deserves an attentive taste.

○ Franciacorta Dosaggio Zero Bagnadore Ris. '11	♟♟♟ 7
○ Curtefranca Bianco Polzina '18	♟♟ 3
○ Franciacorta Brut Golf 1927	♟♟ 5
○ Franciacorta Brut Satèn Edizione '15	♟♟ 5
○ Franciacorta Extra Brut Animante	♟♟ 5
● San Carlo '16	♟♟ 5
● Curtefranca Rosso '17	♟ 3
○ Franciacorta Dosage Zero Naturae '15	♟ 5
☉ Franciacorta Extra Brut Rosé Edizione '15	♟ 5
○ Franciacorta Brut Naturae '13	♟♟♟ 5
○ Franciacorta Brut Naturae '11	♟♟♟ 5
○ Franciacorta Brut Nature '10	♟♟♟ 5
○ Franciacorta Brut Nature '09	♟♟♟ 5
○ Franciacorta Brut Nature '08	♟♟♟ 5

★★★Bellavista

via Bellavista, 5
25030 Erbusco [BS]
Tel. +39 0307762000
www.bellavistawine.it

CELLAR SALES
PRE-BOOKED VISITS
ANNUAL PRODUCTION 1,400,000 bottles
HECTARES UNDER VINE 190.00
SUSTAINABLE WINERY

There's no resting on your laurels here. This large group is divided into various estates in Lombardy, Tuscany and Sardinia. But it's the Franciacorta Bellavista that leads as one of the most famous brands of the territory and of Italian wines. The close-knit family team is led by Vittorio Moretti, who, never satisfied with past achievements, works to bring out the value of each territory through new wines, acquisitions and renovations. The Convento della SS. Annunciata is an example; restored to its former glory and equipped with an evocative cellar, it produces an excellent white. The crisp-fruit scented Cuvée Alma Non Dosato is a Franciacorta of extraordinary freshness. It's made with Chardonnay and Pinot Nero grapes carefully selected from their best vineyards and aged for more than thirty months on the lees. It enchants with its citrusy nuance, linearity and its delicate iodine notes. A special mention for their excellent Teatro alla Scala '14 (subtle and elegant), and their Rosé '15 (linear, sapid and complex).

○ Franciacorta Non Dosato Alma	♟♟♟ 5
○ Curtefranca Convento SS. Annunciata '15	♟♟ 6
○ Franciacorta Brut Rosé '15	♟♟ 7
○ Franciacorta Brut Teatro alla Scala '14	♟♟ 7
○ Curtefranca Alma Terra '18	♟♟ 4
○ Curtefranca Uccellanda '15	♟♟ 6
○ Franciacorta Brut Gran Cuvée Alma	♟♟ 6
○ Franciacorta Pas Operé '13	♟♟ 8
○ Franciacorta Satèn '15	♟♟ 7
○ Franciacorta Brut Teatro alla Scala '13	♟♟♟ 7
○ Franciacorta Pas Operé '10	♟♟♟ 7
○ Franciacorta Pas Operé '09	♟♟♟ 7

F.lli Berlucchi

FRAZ. BORGONATO
VIA BROLETTO, 2
25040 CORTE FRANCA [BS]
TEL. +39 030984451
www.fratelliberlucchi.it

CELLAR SALES
PRE-BOOKED VISITS
ANNUAL PRODUCTION 380,000 bottles
HECTARES UNDER VINE 70.00

A very well curated range of Franciacorta wines is found in the cellars of the sixteenth-century Casa delle Colonne on the ancient Berlucchi family's estate in Borgonato di Cortefranca. It was created by Tilli Rizzo and her mother Pia Donata Berlucchi on behalf of this ancient family. Only grapes grown on their 70 hectares of local vineyards are used to produce the two lines: the Franciacorta Riserva, Casa delle Colonne, and the vintage, Freccia Nera. Brut 25 is the only non-vintage sparkling wine made here. Their Casa delle Colonne Zero is one of the most convincing interpretations of the typology. The 2012 is an impressive mix of fresh, fruity, lively notes melded with more linear, evolved and deep sensations, all made possible by lengthy maturation on the lees. It closes elegant on tertiary nuances of saffron. Their Casa delle Colonne Brut '12 is more relaxed and expansive, with lovely notes of vanilla and citrus. The truly delicious Freccianera Satèn '15 is also notable.

○ Franciacorta Casa delle Colonne Zero Ris. '12	♥♥ 8
○ Franciacorta Brut 25	♥♥ 6
○ Franciacorta Brut Casa delle Colonne Ris. '12	♥♥ 8
○ Franciacorta Brut Freccianera '14	♥♥ 6
○ Franciacorta Nature Freccianera '15	♥♥ 7
⊙ Franciacorta Rosé Freccianera '15	♥♥ 6
○ Franciacorta Satèn '15	♥♥ 7
○ Franciacorta Brut Casa delle Colonne Ris. '11	♀♀ 8
○ Franciacorta Brut Freccianera '12	♀♀ 6
○ Franciacorta Casa delle Colonne Zero Ris. '11	♀♀ 8
○ Franciacorta Nature Freccianera '14	♀♀ 6
⊙ Franciacorta Rosé Freccianera Rosa '14	♀♀ 6
○ Franciacorta Satèn Freccianera '14	♀♀ 6
○ Franciacorta Satèn Freccianera '13	♀♀ 7

★Guido Berlucchi & C.

LOC. BORGONATO
P.ZZA DURANTI, 4
25040 CORTE FRANCA [BS]
TEL. +39 030984381
www.berlucchi.it

CELLAR SALES
PRE-BOOKED VISITS
ACCOMMODATION
ANNUAL PRODUCTION 4,400,000 bottles
HECTARES UNDER VINE 550.00
VITICULTURE METHOD Certified Organic
SUSTAINABLE WINERY

In little more than a decade, enologist and president of Guido Berlucchi, Arturo Ziliani, has transformed the company that his father Franco founded into one of the most important brands of French and Italian wine. Siblings Cristina and Paolo, respectively involved in marketing and sales, have contributed significantly to making the winery a leader in the production of Franciacorta, successfully exporting it around the world. While the reserves of their Palazzo Lana line age in their Borgonato cellars, we tasted a series of outstanding wines from their line 61 (the year in which Berlucchi & C. and Franciacorta were established). The 2012 version of their Nature beat out the rest and took home Tre Bicchieri by virtue of its exemplary focus and stylistic cleanness. It has balanced, fruity pulp and a touch of complexity that enlivens its linear purity. The 61 Rosé and Blanc de Blancs, both 2012s, also deserve an applause.

○ Franciacorta Nature 61 '12	♥♥♥ 7
⊙ Franciacorta Brut Rosé 61 '12	♥♥ 5
○ Franciacorta Nature Blanc de Blancs 61 '12	♥♥ 6
○ Franciacorta Brut 61	♥♥ 5
○ Franciacorta Satèn 61	♥♥ 5
⊙ Franciacorta Rosé 61	♥ 5
○ Franciacorta Brut Cellarius '08	♀♀♀ 5
○ Franciacorta Nature 61 '10	♀♀♀ 7
○ Franciacorta Brut Extrême Palazzo Lana Ris. '06	♀♀♀ 6
○ Franciacorta Extra Brut Extreme Palazzo Lana Ris. '07	♀♀♀ 7
○ Franciacorta Nature 61 '11	♀♀♀ 7
○ Franciacorta Nature 61 '09	♀♀♀ 5
○ Franciacorta Satèn Palazzo Lana '06	♀♀♀ 6

Cantina Bersi Serlini

VIA CERETO, 7
25050 PROVAGLIO D'ISEO [BS]
TEL. +39 0309823338
www.bersiserlini.it

CELLAR SALES
PRE-BOOKED VISITS
ACCOMMODATION AND RESTAURANT SERVICE
ANNUAL PRODUCTION 200,000 bottles
HECTARES UNDER VINE 30.00
VITICULTURE METHOD Certified Organic

This beautiful estate's origins emerge from the mist of the Middle Ages. The oldest building, built by the Cluniac monks from nearby San Pietro in Lamosa, is the grange they used to vinify grapes and store agricultural products coming from their abbey's lands. Since 1886 the estate has been owned by the Bersi Serlini family, who have constantly modernized it and now produce a complete range from their own vineyards. It's also an important location for conferences, events and wine tourism. Their Rosa Rosae is a lovely, antique rose-colored Franciacorta Brut redolent of wild berries, sensations that merge with more evolved notes before giving way to a sapid, linear palate. The Anteprima Brut is characterized by vitality, freshness and an effervescent creaminess while lovely notes of white fruit feature on the nose. The soft Satèn, an excellent representative of this Franciacorta typology, proves alluring in its notes of vanilla and peach.

○ Franciacorta Brut Anniversario	♀♀ 5	
○ Franciacorta Brut Anteprima	♀♀ 5	
○ Franciacorta Brut Cuvée n. 4 '15	♀♀ 6	
⊙ Franciacorta Brut Rosé Rosa Rosae	♀♀ 5	
○ Franciacorta Brut Satèn	♀♀ 5	
○ Franciacorta Demi Sec Nuvola	♀♀ 4	
○ Franciacorta Extra Brut '15	♀♀ 6	
○ Franciacorta Brut Cuvée n. 4 '13	♀♀ 6	
○ Franciacorta Brut Cuvée n. 4 '12	♀♀ 5	
⊙ Franciacorta Brut Rosé Rosa Rosae '10	♀♀ 5	
○ Franciacorta Extra Brut '14	♀♀ 6	
○ Franciacorta Extra Brut '13	♀♀ 6	
○ Franciacorta Extra Brut '12	♀♀ 6	
○ Franciacorta Non Dosato Mia Ris. '05	♀♀ 6	

Bertè & Cordini

VIA CAIROLI, 67
27043 BRONI [PV]
TEL. +39 038551028
www.bertecordini.it

CELLAR SALES
PRE-BOOKED VISITS
ACCOMMODATION
ANNUAL PRODUCTION 700,000 bottles
HECTARES UNDER VINE 18.00
SUSTAINABLE WINERY

The Bertè and Cordini families acquired the winery in the 1970s but its history dates to 1895. For some years now, the newest generation, represented by two young enologists Matteo Bertè and Luca Cordini with sister Marzia, has been moving decisively towards quality production, a trend already started by Matteo's father, Natale. Typical of this area, the winery produces a wide range, all of which are very good, with the best results coming from their Metodo Classico made with Pinot Nero. Among their sparkling wines, the Cuvée della Casa is the one that most convinced. Notes of spices, white chocolate, bay leaf, ripe tropical fruit feature on the nose, while on the palate it comes through quite generous, with an open finish. Their Cuvée Tradizione '15 is a classic Pinot Nero. It pours gold with coppery highlights and proves correct in its residual sugars. Among the rest of their selection, we point out the highly fragrant and mineral Sauvignon Masaria '17.

○ OP Cuvée Tradizione Brut M. Cl. '15	♀♀ 5	
○ OP Pinot Nero Brut M. Cl. Cuvée della Casa	♀♀ 5	
○ OP Sauvignon Masaria '17	♀♀ 2*	
● OP Buttafuoco '18	♀ 2	
○ OP Pinot Nero Brut Cuvée Nero d'Oro M. Cl.	♀ 5	
● OP Pinot Nero Nuval '15	♀ 3	
● OP Bonarda Sabion '15	♀♀ 2*	
● OP Buttafuoco Bertè & Cordini '13	♀♀ 2*	
○ OP Cuvée Tradizione Brut M. Cl. '14	♀♀ 5	
○ OP Pinot Nero Brut Cuvée Tradizione '12	♀♀ 4	
○ OP Pinot Nero Dosage Zéro Oblio M. Cl. '10	♀♀ 7	

F.lli Bettini

LOC. SAN GIACOMO
VIA NAZIONALE, 4A
23036 TEGLIO [SO]
TEL. +39 0342786068
www.vinibettini.it

CELLAR SALES
PRE-BOOKED VISITS
ANNUAL PRODUCTION 200,000 bottles
HECTARES UNDER VINE 15.00

This Teglio winery is a cornerstone of Valtellina winemaking. It can boast a tradition of over 130 years of activity. The range focuses on the character of the unique territory, offering fragrant, alpine wines that also have enviable power and aromatic fullness. The winery features a rich, mature style, and shows the skillful use of small wood barrels in its most important wines. The results are dense and spicy wines capable of long bottle aging, where they find rhythm and balance. The Sforzato Fruttaio di Spina '15 is a great classic. It's elegant, marked by aromas of plums and bottled cherries, notes of tobacco and quinine. On the palate it's rich, with lovely harmony in its tannic development before a long finish. Their 2009 reserve, La Botte Ventitrè, put in a good presence. It's subtle, with lovely sensations of licorice and tobacco lending complexity to its still-evident fresh fruit. On the palate it's harmonious and pervasive, closing long and soft.

● Sforzato di Valtellina Fruttaio di Spina '13	♟♟ 7
● Valtellina Sup. Inferno Prodigio '15	♟♟ 5
● Valtellina Sup. La Botte Ventitrè Ris. '09	♟♟ 3
● Valtellina Sup. Sassella Reale '15	♟♟ 5
● Sforzato di Valtellina '13	♟♟ 6
● Sforzato di Valtellina Fruttaio di Spina '13	♟♟ 7
● Sforzato di Valtellina Vign. di Spina '11	♟♟ 7
● Valtellina Sfursat '10	♟♟ 5
● Valtellina Sup. Inferno Prodigio '13	♟♟ 5
● Valtellina Sup. Inferno Prodigio '11	♟♟ 5
● Valtellina Sup. Sant'Andrea '13	♟♟ 5
● Valtellina Sup. Sassella Reale '13	♟♟ 5
● Valtellina Sup. Valgella V. La Cornella '13	♟♟ 5

Bisi

LOC. CASCINA SAN MICHELE
FRAZ. VILLA MARONE, 70
27040 SAN DAMIANO AL COLLE [PV]
TEL. +39 038575037
www.aziendagricolabisi.it

CELLAR SALES
PRE-BOOKED VISITS
ANNUAL PRODUCTION 90,000 bottles
HECTARES UNDER VINE 30.00

Claudio Bisi is so passionately 'integrated' into his role as a winemaker that year after year his wines take on some of his personality: firm, tenacious, a bit closed initially while at the same time generous. This is particularly true of his wines meant for aging. Never banal or predictable, they strongly express the vintage, sometimes releasing themselves reluctantly; but, once opened they reveal depth, insight and complexity and offer enduring interest. These are wines that are to be understood slowly, with time and dedication. The Roncolongo '16 is Barbera according to Bisi. It's intense, vigorous and characterful, redolent of spices, chocolate, morello cherry, wild berries. On the palate it proves mouth-filling and persistent, with an endless finish. Their Ca' Longa '16, a Pinot Nero with class and personality, also delivered. There's not enough space to describe the value and completeness of their Senz'Aiuto (a Barbera without yeasts and added sulfites) or their Ultrapadum (a Barbera and Croatina that undergoes a second fermentation in the bottle).

● Ca' Longa Pinot Nero '16	♟♟ 5
● Roncolongo Barbera '16	♟♟ 5
○ LaGrà Riesling '18	♟♟ 2*
● OP Bonarda Vivace La Peccatrice '18	♟♟ 2*
● Pezzabianca Barbera '17	♟♟ 3
● Senz'Aiuto Barbera '17	♟♟ 3
● Ultrapadum '17	♟♟ 3
○ Villa Marone Malvasia Passita '16	♟♟ 5
● Barbera Pezzabianca '15	♟♟ 3
● Ca' Longa Pinot Nero '15	♟♟ 5
○ LaGrà Riesling Renano '17	♟♟ 2*
● OP Bonarda Vivace La Peccatrice '17	♟♟ 2*
○ Riesling LaGrà '16	♟♟ 2*
● Roncolongo Barbera '15	♟♟ 5
○ Villa Marone Malvasia Passita '15	♟♟ 5

Castello Bonomi

VIA SAN PIETRO, 46
25030 COCCAGLIO [BS]
TEL. +39 0307721015
www.castellobonomi.it

CELLAR SALES
PRE-BOOKED VISITS
ANNUAL PRODUCTION 100,000 bottles
HECTARES UNDER VINE 24.00
SUSTAINABLE WINERY

Brothers Carlo and Roberto Paladin have long roots in Veneto. However, in addition to Paladin, the family also owns Bosco del Merlo in Friuli, Castelvecchi at Radda in Chianti and a few years ago they acquired Castello Bonomi in Coccaglio, at the foot of Mount Orfano. The winery gets its name from the beautiful Art Nouveau villa at the entrance of the estate. It has 24 hectares of vineyards facing south on calcareous soils, where Pinot Nero, in addtion to Chardonnay, develops its character and fullness. Some two of Bonomi's wines earned a place in our final tastings. They're two single-vintages, the Cuvée Lucrezia Etichetta Bianca '08 and the CruPerdu '11, confirming the aging power and longevity of the producer's wines. The first features creamy fruit, vitality and harmony before closing long, sapid and vibrant, while the second stands out for its transparent notes of white fruit and lovely overall cleanness.

○ Franciacorta Brut Cru Perdu '11	⚑⚑ 7
○ Franciacorta Extra Brut Cuvée Lucrezia Et. Bianca Ris. '08	⚑⚑ 8
○ Franciacorta Brut Gran Cuvée	⚑⚑ 7
○ Franciacorta Satèn	⚑⚑ 6
● Curtefranca Rosso Cordelio '12	⚑ 7
⊙ Franciacorta Brut Rosé	⚑ 7
○ Franciacorta Brut Cru Perdu '04	⚑⚑⚑ 7
○ Franciacorta Extra Brut Lucrezia Et. Nera '04	⚑⚑⚑ 8
○ Franciacorta Brut CruPerdu Ris. '09	⚑⚑ 7
○ Franciacorta Dosage Zéro '12	⚑⚑ 7
○ Franciacorta Dosage Zero '10	⚑⚑ 8
○ Franciacorta Dosage Zéro Gran Cuvée del Laureato '10	⚑⚑ 8
○ Franciacorta Extra Brut Cuvée Lucrezia '06	⚑⚑ 8

Bosco Longhino

FRAZ. MOLINO MARCONI
27047 SANTA MARIA DELLA VERSA [PV]
TEL. +39 0385798049
www.bosco-longhino.it

PRE-BOOKED VISITS
ACCOMMODATION AND RESTAURANT SERVICE
ANNUAL PRODUCTION 200,000 bottles
HECTARES UNDER VINE 29.00

Edoardo Faravelli founded the family estate in 1895 with just over 6.5 hectares in the Molino Marconi area. As was customary at the time, there were also arable lands, fodder and cattle. After the war, Edoardo's son, Tullio changed direction by planting Barbera and Croatina. Today, the fourth generation produces wines that year after year are distinguished by their quality and precision. La Bonarda '18 is extremely well made, austere, with vigor, fine-grained tannins and residual sugar that hits the mark. We appreciated their Riesling '18 even more than last year. It's a slightly overripe Renano redolent of tropical fruit and citrus. La Rivetta '17 is a fragrant and supple Barbera, redolent of morello cherry, mouthfilling and persistent in its finish. The Pinot Grigio Campo dei Fitti '18 proves pleasant fresh, while the Buttafuoco has nice mouthfeel but is lacking a bit in pluck.

● La Rivetta Barbera '17	⚑⚑ 3
● OP Bonarda '18	⚑⚑ 2*
● Riesling '18	⚑⚑ 3
○ Campo dei Fitti Pinot Grigio '18	⚑ 3
● OP Buttafuoco '16	⚑ 3
○ Campo dei Fitti Pinot Grigio '17	⚐⚐ 3
● OP Bonarda Prete Bertino '15	⚐⚐ 3
● OP Buttafuoco '11	⚐⚐ 2*
● Pinot Nero Campo dei Graci '16	⚐⚐ 3
○ Riesling '17	⚐⚐ 3

Bosio

FRAZ. TIMOLINE
VIA M. GATTI, 4
25040 CORTE FRANCA [BS]
TEL. +39 0309826224
www.bosiofranciacorta.it

CELLAR SALES
PRE-BOOKED VISITS
ANNUAL PRODUCTION 100,000 bottles
HECTARES UNDER VINE 30.00
VITICULTURE METHOD Certified Organic
SUSTAINABLE WINERY

Bosio, one of Franciacorta's most solid wineries, was founded years ago with a small vineyard plot owned by the family. Thanks to the commitment of siblings Cesare and Laura, respectively, agronomist (who consults at many other appellation wineries) and brilliant manager, Bosio has reached an important level both qualitatively and quantitatively. Grapes are obtained from their own thirty hectares of vineyards and are processed with great care in the modern cellar, where they are transformed into a complete range of Franciacorta and territorial wines. The Dosaggio Zero Girolamo Bosio is their premium vineyard selection. The 2012 features a brilliant straw-yellow color and extremely subtle beading. On the nose it exhibits evolved notes of nice complexity, with fruit joined by nuances of aromatic herbs, citrus, yeast and tobacco, while on the palate it proves complex and subtle, with nice structure and a long, harmonious finish. Lovely toasty and mineral sensations characterize their Boschedòr '13.

○ Franciacorta Pas Dosè Girolamo Bosio Ris. '12		♙♙ 8
○ Franciacorta Brut		♙♙ 5
○ Franciacorta Extra Brut Boschedòr '13		♙♙ 6
⊙ Franciacorta Pas Dosè Rosè Girolamo Bosio Ris. '11		♙♙ 8
⊙ Franciacorta Rosé Extra Brut '15		♙♙ 5
⊙ Franciacorta Satèn		♙♙ 5
○ Franciacorta Pas Dosé Girolamo Bosio Ris. '09		♙♙♙ 5
○ Franciacorta Dosaggio Zero B.C. Ris. '07		♙♙ 8
⊙ Franciacorta Extra Brut Rosé '14		♙♙ 5
○ Franciacorta Nature '13		♙♙ 5
○ Franciacorta Pas Dosè Girolamo Bosio Ris. '11		♙♙ 8

Alessio Brandolini

FRAZ. BOFFALORA, 68
27040 SAN DAMIANO AL COLLE [PV]
TEL. +39 038575232
www.alessiobrandolini.com

CELLAR SALES
PRE-BOOKED VISITS
ANNUAL PRODUCTION 70,000 bottles
HECTARES UNDER VINE 11.00
SUSTAINABLE WINERY

Alessio Brandolini may be young but he's already experienced. He's leading the family winery with passion and rigor along a path aimed at bringing out the best from the land by planting varieties according to the characteristics of each vineyard. The area is ideal for not only Croatina and Carbera, but also Malvasia (Piacentino, after all, is only a stone's throw) and above all, Pinot Nero, used in the two classic versions, namely red wine and sparkling Metodo Classico. The Bardughino '18 is a dry Malvasia redolent of citrus and wild flowers, intense in its tasty and fragrant palate. Their Beneficio '15 is a blend of Croatina and Barbera aged in barriques. It's still dominated by tannins and just needs some time before it can fully express its ripe fruit. The Croatina Il Soffio features delicate hints of overripe fruit and an almondy finish.

○ Il Bardughino Malvasia '18	♙♙ 2*
● Il Beneficio '15	♙♙ 4
● Il Soffio Croatina '18	♙♙ 2*
● Al Negres Pinot Nero '17	♙ 4
○ Luogo d'Agosto Brut Nature M. Cl.	♙ 5
⊙ Note d'Agosto Brut M. Cl. Rosé	♙ 5
● OP Bonarda Frizzante Il Cassino '18	♙ 2
⊙ Brut M. Cl. Rosé Note d'Agosto '13	♙♙ 5
○ Il Bardughino '16	♙♙ 2*
○ Il Bardughino '15	♙♙ 2*
● Il Beneficio '14	♙♙ 4
● Il Beneficio '13	♙♙ 4
● Il Beneficio '12	♙♙ 2*
● Il Soffio Croatina '17	♙♙ 2*

★Cà Maiol

VIA COLLI STORICI, 119
25015 DESENZANO DEL GARDA [BS]
TEL. +39 0309910006
www.camaiol.it

CELLAR SALES
PRE-BOOKED VISITS
ANNUAL PRODUCTION 1,500,000 bottles
HECTARES UNDER VINE 160.00
SUSTAINABLE WINERY

Several harvests have passed since Ca'
Maiol merged into the Marzotto family's
Santa Margherita group, giving further
commercial and qualitative impetus to
production. The winery is one of the area's
most significant, boasting 150 hectares of
vineyards on several estates between
Valtènesi and Lugana. It's truly a benchmark
in the latter appellation. The Riserva Fabio
Contato '17 is one of the appellation's
benchmark wines. It has character and
expressive richness, as well as great, fruity
flesh that turns on smoky and mineral
notes, while on the palate it exhibits a truly
noteworthy balance and harmony. Even if it
can't boast the same level of concentration,
the Lugana Molin '18 features remarkable
freshness and typicity with its sensations of
fresh fruit and citrus, all supported by a
lively acidic streak in its long finish. The
excellent Prestige '18, a sapid and taut
wine, completes an important trio for the
DOC zone.

○ Lugana Molin '18	♟♟ 3*
○ Lugana Sel. Fabio Contato Ris. '17	♟♟ 5
○ Lugana Prestige '18	♟♟ 3
○ Lugana Molin '16	♟♟♟ 3*
○ Lugana Molin '15	♟♟♟ 3*
○ Lugana Molin '14	♟♟♟ 3*
○ Lugana Molin '13	♟♟♟ 3*
○ Lugana Molin '12	♟♟♟ 3*
○ Lugana Sel. Fabio Contato '16	♟♟♟ 5
○ Lugana Sup. Sel. Fabio Contato '11	♟♟♟ 5
○ Lugana Sup. Sel. Fabio Contato '10	♟♟♟ 5
○ Lugana Sup. Sel. Fabio Contato '09	♟♟♟ 5

Cà Tessitori

VIA MATTEOTTI, 15
27043 BRONI [PV]
TEL. +39 038551495
www.catessitori.it

CELLAR SALES
PRE-BOOKED VISITS
ANNUAL PRODUCTION 120,000 bottles
HECTARES UNDER VINE 40.00

With the support of sons Giovanni and
Francesco, Luigi Giorgi has made various
adjustments over the years that have helped
this classic Oltrepò Pavese winery achieve
considerable levels of quality. With passion
and expertise they work mostly traditional
cultivars on two plots at Montecalvo
Versiggia (Ca 'Tessitori) and Montalto
Pavese (Finigeto). Every year, the vineyards
enable them to produce wines of
uncompromising character using very
traditional vinification, predominantly in
cement tanks. Their sparkling Metodo
Classico is also definitely worth trying. And
their LB9 '14 just falls short of Tre Bicchieri,
with a new, undosed version that highlights
linear energy, vigor and an aromatic breadth
featuring citrus and aromatic herbs.
Oltremodo '17 is a Croatina that undergoes
a second fermentation in the bottle. It's
vibrant, deep, properly rustic and highly
persistent. The Bonarda Frizzante '18 is a
pleasant, fresh wine that's on the mark.

● Oltremodo '17	♟♟ 3*
○ OP Pinot Nero M. Cl. Dosaggio Zero LB9 '14	♟♟ 5
○ Agòlo '18	♟♟ 2*
● OP Bonarda Frizzante '18	♟♟ 2*
● Borghesa Rosso '18	♟ 3
○ Agòlo '17	♟♟ 2*
● Borghesa Rosso '17	♟♟ 3
● Marona Barbera '15	♟♟ 4
● OP Bonarda Avita '16	♟♟ 3
● OP Bonarda Frizzante '17	♟♟ 2*
● OP Bonarda Vivace '16	♟♟ 2*
● OP Bonarda Vivace '15	♟♟ 2*
○ OP Pinot Nero Brut M. V. '12	♟♟ 4
● OP Rosso Borghesa '16	♟♟ 2*

★★★★Ca' del Bosco

VIA ALBANO ZANELLA, 13
25030 ERBUSCO [BS]
TEL. +39 0307766111
www.cadelbosco.com

CELLAR SALES
PRE-BOOKED VISITS
ACCOMMODATION
ANNUAL PRODUCTION 0 bottles
HECTARES UNDER VINE 245.40
VITICULTURE METHOD Certified Organic
SUSTAINABLE WINERY

Maurizio Zanella's created the estate at the end of the 1960s. He transformed Ca' del Bosco, a family holiday home, into one of Italy's most important wineries. The process underwent a great acceleration when Ca' entered the Marzotto family's Santa Margherita group, but certain things remain firm: Maurizio is still president and Stefano Capelli, enologist, is responsible for production. Their two Annamaria Clementi select blends are among the best sparkling wines produced in Italy in recent years. The Rosé '09 is a deep, elegant and multifaceted wine in its aromas of yellow peach, in its perfectly integrated prickle, and in its mineral hints (which lend complexity), but we confidently hand Tre Bicchieri to their Bianco '09. It's a Dosaggio Zero blend (Chardonnay 50%, Pinot Bianco 25% and Pinot Nero 25%) from the best vineyards that rests nine years on the lees before disgorgement, making for absolutely charming depth, complexity and development.

○ Franciacorta Dosaggio Zero Cuvée Annamaria Clementi Ris. '09	▼▼▼ 8
○ Curtefranca Chardonnay '15	▼▼ 8
⊙ Franciacorta Extra Brut Rosé Cuvée Annamaria Clementi Ris. '09	▼▼ 8
● Carmenero '12	▼▼ 8
○ Curtefranca Bianco Corte del Lupo '17	▼▼ 7
● Curtefranca Rosso Corte del Lupo '16	▼▼ 6
○ Franciacorta Brut Cuvée Prestige	▼▼ 8
○ Franciacorta Brut Vintage Collection '14	▼▼ 8
○ Franciacorta Dosage Zéro Vintage Collection '14	▼▼ 8
○ Franciacorta Dosage Zéro Vintage Collection Noir '10	▼▼ 8
○ Franciacorta Satèn Vintage Collection '14	▼▼ 8

Ca' del Gè

FRAZ. CA' DEL GÈ, 3
27040 MONTALTO PAVESE [PV]
TEL. +39 0383870179
www.cadelge.com

CELLAR SALES
PRE-BOOKED VISITS
ANNUAL PRODUCTION 160,000 bottles
HECTARES UNDER VINE 45.00

Enzo Padroggi founded the winery in 1985. He passed away a few years ago but would certainly have been very proud of his children Carlo, Stefania and Sara, who run the 36 hectares with low environmental impact. The vineyards are divided between Montalto Pavese, where mainly Riesling and Pinot Nero benefit from gypsum soils, and Cigognola, planted with the area's traditional red varietals. The commitment and humility of the siblings are rewarded by high levels of quality at very low prices. We quite enjoyed their Italici Filagn Long and Brinà, both 2018s. They're sapid and mineral wines, the former deeper and more structured, the second flowery and tropical, exhibiting a more accessible style. Their Buttafuoco Fajro '15 debuted this year on aromas of vanilla and white chocolate. Dense and robust, it needs time to reach full aromatic expression.

○ Brinà Riesling '18	▼▼ 2*
○ Filagn Long Riesling '18	▼▼ 3
○ Brut M. Cl. '14	▼ 5
○ Il Marinoni Riesling '18	▼ 3
● OP Bonarda Frizzante La Fidela '17	▼ 4
● OP Buttafuoco Fajro '15	▼ 4
○ Brinà Riesling '17	♈♈ 2*
○ Brut M. Cl. '13	♈♈ 5
○ Il Marinoni '15	♈♈ 3
● OP Bonarda Frizzante La Fidela '16	♈♈ 4
○ OP Brut Cà del Gé '13	♈♈ 5
○ OP Pinot Nero Brut M. Cl. '11	♈♈ 3
○ OP Riesling Brinà '16	♈♈ 2*
○ OP Riesling Brinà '15	♈♈ 2*

Ca' di Frara

via Casa Ferrari, 1
27040 Mornico Losana [PV]
Tel. +39 0383892299
www.cadifrara.com

CELLAR SALES
PRE-BOOKED VISITS
ANNUAL PRODUCTION 400,000 bottles
HECTARES UNDER VINE 46.00

The winery was one of Oltrepò Pavese's first to impose strict qualitative criteria. Luca Bellani took charge of the estate twenty years ago while still quite young, counting on his mother Daniela's support and his father Tullio's experience. The land is particularly suitable for producing several cultivars for wines that have made their mark in the story of the area. The style has undergone changes over the years in a search for enhanced elegance with firm structure. At the same time its very successful interpretations of Metodo Classico has made it an important player in sparkling wines. This year their selection performed at a truly high level. Two outstanding rosé sparklers handily landed a place in our finals: the Pas Dosé Centoventi Luca Bellani is vibrant, generous in its fruit, fresh and extremely elegant; the Extra Brut Oltre il Classico is flowery and extremely harmonious. Their Extra Brut is taut and mineral, while the deep, multifaceted Pinot Nero Parcella 4 stands out among the rest of their selection.

⊙ Oltre il Classico Extra Brut M. Cl. Rosé	🍷🍷 5
⊙ OP Pinot Nero M. Cl. Pas Dosé Luca Bellani Centoventi Rosé	🍷🍷 5
● Il Frater '15	🍷🍷 5
○ Oliva Riesling Ris. '17	🍷🍷 4
○ Oltre il Classico Extra Brut M. Cl.	🍷🍷 4
● OP Pinot Nero Mornico Parcella 4 Ris. '16	🍷🍷 5
○ OP Riesling '18	🍷 2
○ OP Riesling Oliva Ris. '16	🍷🍷🍷 4*
● Io Rosso '15	🍷🍷 5
● Mornico Pinot Nero '15	🍷🍷 5
● OP Bonarda La Casetta '15	🍷🍷 3
● OP Bonarda Vivace Monpezzato '15	🍷🍷 2*
○ OP Riesling '15	🍷🍷 4
○ OP Riesling Sup. '16	🍷🍷 2*

Ca' Lojera

loc. Rovizza
via 1866, 19
25019 Sirmione [BS]
Tel. +39 0457551901
www.calojera.com

CELLAR SALES
PRE-BOOKED VISITS
RESTAURANT SERVICE
ANNUAL PRODUCTION 120,000 bottles
HECTARES UNDER VINE 20.00

If you were to ask anyone in the territory the name of the winery that best embodies respect for Lugana's land, traditions, and craftsmanship, there is no doubt that the answer would be Ca' Lojera (House of the Wolves). And they would be justified; Franco and Ambra Tiraboschi have dedicated themselves to their vineyards and cellar with genuine passion for decades. Their vines are on a flat plot near the lake with their roots in the classic white clay that is preferred by the local Trebbiano, here known as Turbiana. Convinced of this superb white's aging power, when a great vintage comes the Tiraboschis wait years and years before releasing their bottles to the public, as with a 1999 that only just came out just last year. It's worth it. Their Riserva del Lupo '16 is a wine of great richness, proving soft, balanced and complex, endowed with vitality. The Superiore '16 is more evolved but it exhibits lovely and pleasant softness. As always, their Lugana '18 proves fresh, sapid and meaty.

○ Lugana Riserva del Lupo '16	🍷🍷 5
○ Lugana '18	🍷🍷 3
○ Lugana Sup. '16	🍷🍷 3
○ Lugana '17	🍷🍷 3
○ Lugana '16	🍷🍷 3
○ Lugana '15	🍷🍷 3
○ Lugana '14	🍷🍷 3
○ Lugana Annata Storica '99	🍷🍷 4
○ Lugana Riserva del Lupo '15	🍷🍷 5
○ Lugana Riserva del Lupo '14	🍷🍷 5
○ Lugana Riserva del Lupo '13	🍷🍷 5
○ Lugana Riserva del Lupo '12	🍷🍷 5
○ Lugana Sup. '15	🍷🍷 3
○ Lugana Sup. '14	🍷🍷 3
○ Lugana Sup. '13	🍷🍷 3

Calatroni

LOC. CASA GRANDE, 7
27040 MONTECALVO VERSIGGIA [PV]
TEL. +39 038599013
www.calatronivini.it

CELLAR SALES
PRE-BOOKED VISITS
RESTAURANT SERVICE
ANNUAL PRODUCTION 70,000 bottles
HECTARES UNDER VINE 15.00
SUSTAINABLE WINERY

Cristian and Stefano Calatroni are the fourth generation to run the winery their great-grandfather Luigi founded in 1964, when he bought the vineyards that the family had been renting. In a short time, the wines produced by these two young men came to the attention of the public and critics. They are wines that fully bring out and represent the characteristics of the land, bringing out the minerality and personality imbued by mainly white soil, especially with Riesling and Pinot Nero based sparklers. The location is splendid and the adjoining agritourism Calice dei Cherubini certainly merits a visit. Their Norema '10 Dosaggio Zero is a work of art, once again proving that Oltrepò Pavese's Pinot Nero, if well managed, needs time more than anything else. A pale onion skin hue anticipates broad, elegant and ripe aromas, creamy bead and sapidity — it's a rosé with great personality. Once again their Brut 64 '15 proves to be of high quality, while the Pinot Nero Fioravanti '18 stands out for its fragrance and varietal coherence.

⊙ Norema 90 Dosaggio Zero M. Cl. Rosé '10	♈♈ 5
● OP Pinot Nero Fioravanti '18	♈♈ 3
○ Pinot Nero Brut 64 M. Cl. '15	♈♈ 4
● OP Bonarda Frizzante Vigiò '18	♈ 2
○ OP Riesling Campo Dottore '17	♈ 3
● OP Sangue di Giuda Siliquastro '18	♈ 2
⊙ OP Pinot Nero Rosé M. Cl. NorEma '13	♈♈♈ 4*
○ Pinot Nero Brut 64 '11	♈♈♈ 5
● OP Bonarda Frizzante Vigiò '17	♈♈ 2*
○ OP Riesling Viticoltori in Montecalvo '14	♈♈ 5
○ Pinot Nero Brut 64 '13	♈♈ 4
○ Pinot Nero Brut 64 M. Cl. '14	♈♈ 4

Il Calepino

VIA SURRIPE, 1
24060 CASTELLI CALEPIO [BG]
TEL. +39 035847178
www.ilcalepino.it

CELLAR SALES
PRE-BOOKED VISITS
ANNUAL PRODUCTION 230,000 bottles
HECTARES UNDER VINE 15.00

Every year, we praise the work of the brothers Franco and Marco Plebani, who preach in a territory struggling to find its own defined identity. Il Calepino has found it primarily in Metodo Classico; the right bank of the River Oglio is quite literally a stone's throw away from Franciacorta. The environment is essentially the same, so meticulous work in the vineyard and cellar bear visible results. The winery's main characteristic, above all, is the extended time its Metodo Classico spend refining on the lees. This year we tasted two crown jewels of their sparkling wine selection, and they didn't disappoint. We were partial to the Non Dosato '11, a rich, creamy wine redolent of cake and recently baked bread crust that's delicate and penetrating on the palate, long and elegant. As per tradition, the Fra' Ambrogio '10 exhibits a more opulent style. Its gold color serves as the prelude to sensations of vanilla and wood spices, candied fruit and almond. On the palate it comes through mature (in keeping with more oxidative profiles), full, extremely delicate in its bead, before giving way to an endless finish.

○ Brut M. Cl. Non Dosato '11	♈♈ 4
○ Brut M. Cl. Fra' Ambrogio Ris. '10	♈♈ 4
● Kalòs Cabernet '15	♈♈ 5
○ Terre del Colleoni B.D.B. Brut M. Cl.	♈♈ 4
○ Brut Cl. Il Calepino '12	♈ 3
● Valcalepio Rosso '16	♈ 2
● Valcalepio Rosso Surìe Ris. '13	♈ 3
○ Brut Cl. Il Calepino '11	♈♈ 3
○ Brut M. Cl. Fra' Ambrogio Ris. '09	♈♈ 4
○ Brut M. Cl. Non Dosato '10	♈♈ 4
⊙ Brut M. Cl. Rosé '11	♈♈ 3
● Kalòs Cabernet '13	♈♈ 5

Camossi

VIA METELLI, 5
25030 ERBUSCO [BS]
TEL. +39 0307268022
www.camossi.it

CELLAR SALES
PRE-BOOKED VISITS
ANNUAL PRODUCTION 60,000 bottles
HECTARES UNDER VINE 30.00

Dario and Claudio Camossi are passionate winemakers. They run the family estate founded by their grandfather Pietro at the beginning of the 20th century. Wine production began in 1996, but for some years now their wines have undergone a second fermentation using the must from the same grapes, without added sucrose. The Camossi only work grapes from their 24 hectares of vineyards divided into three areas: Erbusco, where the cellar also is,; Paratico, from which comes Pinot Nero; and, Provaglio d'Iseo, mostly located in Provezze. Cleanness, expressive focus and stylistic rigor are the qualities that join the Camossi family's blends. Their Rosé, one of the best in the appellation, is the proof. Its enticing, pale rose color is the prelude to aromas of red berries, citrus and Mediterranean herbs, sensations that follow through punctually on the palate, where the wine proves sapid, elegant and harmonious. It's a lovely expression of Pinot Nero (which forms 90% of the blend). As with the rest of their selection, the Extra Brut '14 is characterized by vigor and elegance.

○ Franciacorta Brut Satèn	🍷🍷 5
○ Franciacorta Dosaggio Zero	🍷🍷 5
○ Franciacorta Extra Brut '14	🍷🍷 6
○ Franciacorta Extra Brut	🍷🍷 6
⊘ Franciacorta Rosé Extra Brut	🍷🍷 5
○ Franciacorta Brut Satèn '11	🍷🍷 6
○ Franciacorta Extra Brut '12	🍷🍷 6
○ Franciacorta Extra Brut '11	🍷🍷 6
○ Franciacorta Extra Brut '09	🍷🍷 6
○ Franciacorta Extra Brut '08	🍷🍷 6
○ Franciacorta Extra Brut '08	🍷🍷 6
○ Franciacorta Extra Brut Pietro Camossi Ris. '07	🍷🍷 8
○ Franciacorta Extra Brut Ris. '10	🍷🍷 6
○ Franciacorta Extra Brut Ris. '09	🍷🍷 6
○ Franciacorta Extra Brut Ris. '08	🍷🍷 6

Cantrina

VIA COLOMBERA, 7
25081 BEDIZZOLE [BS]
TEL. +39 3356362137
www.cantrina.it

CELLAR SALES
ANNUAL PRODUCTION 35,000 bottles
HECTARES UNDER VINE 7.90
VITICULTURE METHOD Certified Organic

Cantrina is a tiny Valtènesi village in the municipality of Bedizzole, between Lake Garda and Brescia. But it's also the name of Cristina Inganni and Diego Lavo's beautiful winery, which first brought its bottles to the general market in 1999. It's a small but high-profile, strictly family-run operation. The vineyards extend for about eight hectares on morainic hills and are divided into three different plots. The Rosso Zerdi '15, a Rebo (a blend of Teroldego and Merlot), is an elegant mix of concentration and elegance, rich in fruit and fine-grained tannins, harmonious, creamy and lingering. It's probably the best Valtènesi red tasted this year, and brought the producer back into our main section. But it's not an only child. Cristina and Diego offer a notable selection of reds and whites that do an excellent job expressing this terroir.

● Zerdì '15	🍷🍷 3*
● Nepomuceno '15	🍷🍷 5
○ Sole di Dario Passito '15	🍷🍷 5
○ Riné '17	🍷 3
● Riviera del Garda Cl. Rosso '17	🍷 3
⊘ Rosanoire '18	🍷 2
⊙ Valtènesi Chiaretto '18	🍷 3
● Nepomuceno '13	🍷🍷 5
● Nepomuceno '11	🍷🍷 5
○ Riné '16	🍷🍷 3
⊙ Rosanoire '14	🍷🍷 2*
○ Sole di Dario Passito '12	🍷🍷 5
● Valtènesi Rosso '16	🍷🍷 3
● Zerdì '13	🍷🍷 3

CastelFaglia - Monogram

FRAZ. CALINO
LOC. BOSCHI, 3
25046 CAZZAGO SAN MARTINO [BS]
TEL. +39 0307751042
www.cavicchioli.it

CELLAR SALES
PRE-BOOKED VISITS
ANNUAL PRODUCTION 350,000 bottles
HECTARES UNDER VINE 22.00

Enologist Sandro Cavicchioli comes from an established wine family in Modena. He creates Metodo Classico sparkling wines in both Bellei di Bomporto and Castelfaglia in Franciacorta. Here, in a cellar dug into the hillside, are born cuvées divided into two lines, CastelFaglia and Monogram (the latter dedicated to single-vintages and selections). The 22 hectares of mostly terraced vineyards are at the foot of the ancient Faglia Castle in Calino. It's evident that Sandro has a gift for Blanc de Blancs, given that every year, like clockwork, their Monogram stands out during our tastings. Its brilliant straw-yellow color, tinted green, anticipates delicate and elegant aromas of white-fleshed fruit, with peach and damson in the fore. These give way to fragrances of aromatic herbs and fresh, citrus notes. On the palate it's alluring, sapid and coherent in its aromas. Their Dosaggio Zero '15 features a tantalizing, delicately balsamic streak.

○ Franciacorta Brut Blanc de Blancs Monogram	♛♛ 5
○ Franciacorta Brut	♛♛ 4
○ Franciacorta Brut Monogram '12	♛♛ 5
○ Franciacorta Dosage Zéro '15	♛♛ 5
○ Franciacorta Dosage Zero Monogram '15	♛♛ 5
⊙ Franciacorta Monogram Brut Rosé	♛♛ 5
○ Franciacorta Monogram Zero '15	♛♛ 5
○ Franciacorta Extra Brut	♛ 4
○ Franciacorta Brut Monogram '11	♛♛ 5
○ Franciacorta Brut Monogram '10	♛♛ 5
○ Franciacorta Dosage Zero Monogram '13	♛♛ 5
○ Franciacorta Dosage Zero Monogram '12	♛♛ 5
○ Franciacorta Satèn Monogram '12	♛♛ 5
○ Franciacorta Satèn Monogram Zero '14	♛♛ 5

Castello di Cigognola

P.ZZA CASTELLO, 1
27040 CIGOGNOLA [PV]
TEL. +39 0385284828
www.castellodicigognola.com

CELLAR SALES
PRE-BOOKED VISITS
ANNUAL PRODUCTION 75,000 bottles
HECTARES UNDER VINE 30.00

The Castle of Cigognola guards the entrance to the Scuropasso Valley. It was founded at the height of feudalism in 1212, later housed a Renaissance court and by the beginning of the 1800s had already become a place of wine production. Some years ago, the very beautiful and well-maintained estate embarked on a path of producing quality wines with the help of capable Oltrepò enologist Emilio Defilippi, who has honed the style and personality of the wines, particularly the Metodo Classico. The winery has also become a research facility in collaboration with the University of Milan. In honor of Angelo Moratti, we get a highly promising Pas Dosé '12, wine that handily earned a place in our finals by virtue of its ripe notes of cake, its lengthy persistence, its vital structure and fine bead. The 'More is a linear Brut redolent of candied fruits, with creamy bubbles and a juicy, round finish. Their Barbera La Maga '16 is subtler than usual — there's room to improve in the bottle.

○ Pas Dosé M. Cl. Riserva dell'Angelo '12	♛♛ 5
○ 'More Brut M. Cl.	♛♛ 4
○ 'More Cuvée Brut M. Cl. '15	♛♛ 4
● La Maga Barbera '16	♛♛ 4
● Nebbiolo per Papà '14	♛ 5
○ Brut 'More '11	♛♛♛ 4*
○ Brut 'More '10	♛♛♛ 4*
● OP Barbera Castello di Cigognola '07	♛♛♛ 6
● OP Barbera Castello di Cigognola '06	♛♛♛ 6
● OP Barbera Dodicidodici '11	♛♛♛ 3*
○ OP Brut 'More '12	♛♛♛ 4*
○ OP Brut Pinot Nero 'More '13	♛♛♛ 4*
○ OP Brut Pinot Nero 'More '08	♛♛♛ 4*

Castello di Gussago La Santissima

VIA MANICA, 8
25064 GUSSAGO [BS]
TEL. +39 0302525267
www.castellodigussago.it

CELLAR SALES
PRE-BOOKED VISITS
ANNUAL PRODUCTION 130,000 bottles
HECTARES UNDER VINE 21.00
VITICULTURE METHOD Certified Organic
SUSTAINABLE WINERY

Gozio is a long-established name in Franciacorta. In the early 2000s, the family renovated an ancient Dominican convent on the Colle della Santissima in Gussago and built a modern winery. The estate only processes grapes from its twenty-hectare patchwork of vineyards in the municipality, some of which are next to the abbey at an elevation of 450 meters. In recent years, our tastings have shown great effort and constant growth in quality from the estate, which is also committed to sustainability. Their growth in quality is tangible, as testified to by this year's tastings. Their two Noble wines, in particular, earned the highest praise. The Nobleblanc landed a place in our finals by virtue of its complex floral aromas and a lovely balance between freshness and fruit, prickle and structure. The Noblenoir exhibits a nice, linear and deep character.

○ Franciacorta Brut Nobleblanc	♟♟ 5
○ Franciacorta Brut Noblenoir	♟♟ 5
○ Franciacorta Club Cuvée Satèn	♟♟ 5
⊙ Franciacorta Extra Brut Rosé '14	♟♟ 5
○ Curtefranca Bianco Malandrino '15	♟♟ 5
○ Curtefranca Bianco Malandrino '14	♟♟ 5
● Curtefranca Rosso Pomaro '15	♟♟ 4
● Curtefranca Rosso Pomaro '13	♟♟ 4
○ Franciacorta Brut	♟♟ 5
○ Franciacorta Brut Sel. Gozio '13	♟♟ 6
⊙ Franciacorta Extra Brut Rosé '12	♟♟ 5
○ Franciacorta Pas Dosé '12	♟♟ 5
○ Franciacorta Pas Dosé 800 '14	♟♟ 5
○ Franciacorta Satèn '12	♟♟ 5

★Cavalleri

VIA PROVINCIALE, 96
25030 ERBUSCO [BS]
TEL. +39 0307760217
www.cavalleri.it

PRE-BOOKED VISITS
ANNUAL PRODUCTION 200,000 bottles
HECTARES UNDER VINE 42.00
VITICULTURE METHOD Certified Organic

The Cavalleri are a historic Franciacorta family whose name already appears in a notarial deed of the territory in 1450. In 1968, Gian Paolo and son Giovanni started producing wine and, later, Franciacorta. Half a century later, we find Giovanni's daughters, Maria and Giulia, and his grandchildren, Francesco and Diletta, at the helm of the winery, supported by a staff of valuable employees. The company boasts 42 hectares of vineyards in Erbusco that are managed using natural practices. Giovanni Cavalleri was among the founders of Franciacorta and the Consortium. As a result, they've dedicated their most prestigious line to him. The Riserva '08, a Blanc de Blancs, is one of their top offerings. The base wine is matured mostly in steel, but also in large barrels and used barriques, before bottle fermentation, which last some nine years. The result is a wine of great complexity and depth that caps off an outstanding overall selection.

○ Franciacorta Brut Collezione Esclusiva Giovanni Cavalleri Ris. '08	♟♟ 8
○ Franciacorta Brut Blanc de Blancs	♟♟ 5
○ Franciacorta Satèn '15	♟♟ 6
⊙ Franciacorta Brut Rosé '14	♟ 6
○ Franciacorta Brut Collezione '05	♟♟♟ 6
○ Franciacorta Brut Collezione Esclusiva Giovanni Cavalleri '05	♟♟♟ 8
○ Franciacorta Brut Collezione Esclusiva Giovanni Cavalleri '04	♟♟♟ 7
○ Franciacorta Brut Collezione Esclusiva Giovanni Cavalleri '01	♟♟♟ 7
○ Franciacorta Collezione Grandi Cru '08	♟♟♟ 6
○ Franciacorta Pas Dosé '07	♟♟♟ 5
○ Franciacorta Pas Dosé R. D. '06	♟♟♟ 6

Citari

FRAZ. SAN MARTINO DELLA BATTAGLIA
LOC. CITARI, 2
25015 DESENZANO DEL GARDA [BS]
TEL. +39 0309910310
www.citari.it

CELLAR SALES
PRE-BOOKED VISITS
ANNUAL PRODUCTION 150,000 bottles
HECTARES UNDER VINE 21.00
SUSTAINABLE WINERY

Citari's vineyards are at the foot of the San Martino della Battaglia's commemorative tower. Founded in 1975 by Francesco Gettuli, it's now run by his grandchildren, Francesco and Maria Giovanna. Of its 25 hectares straddling the Lugana and San Martino appellations, 21 are vineyards. Mixed morainic soils, with calcareous clays rich in mineral salts, lend sapidity and aromatic finesse, while more calcareous soils give the wines elegance and longevity. The estate uses low-impact cultivation, harvests by hand and has a modern cellar. This year they submitted a nice trio of Luganas, all 2018s. The Conchiglia is made with grapes cultivated in old vineyards and fermented for six months on the fine lees. It exhibits depth and fullness, proving rich in fruity notes and admirable freshness. The Sorgente is more casual, coming through fresh, spirited and highly pleasant. Finally, their Torre (made with overripe grapes) is characterized by a rich, opulent and fruity structure, qualities that don't overpower its freshness and pleasantness.

○ Lugana Conchiglia '18	♟♟ 4
○ Lugana Sorgente '18	♟♟ 3
○ Lugana Torre '18	♟♟ 2*
⊙ Garda Cl. Chiaretto 18 e Quarantacinque '18	♟ 3
● Riviera del Garda Cl. Bigoncio '16	♟ 3
○ San Martino della Battaglia '18	♟ 2
○ Eretico '16	♟♟ 2*
○ Lugana Conchiglia '17	♟♟ 4
○ Lugana Conchiglia '15	♟♟ 4
○ Lugana Sorgente '17	♟♟ 3
○ Lugana Sorgente '16	♟♟ 3
○ Lugana Terre Bianche '16	♟♟ 3
○ Lugana Torre '15	♟♟ 2*

Battista Cola

VIA INDIPENDENZA, 3
25030 ADRO [BS]
TEL. +39 0307356195
www.colabattista.it

CELLAR SALES
PRE-BOOKED VISITS
ANNUAL PRODUCTION 70,000 bottles
HECTARES UNDER VINE 10.00
SUSTAINABLE WINERY

Stefano Cola passionately leads the family winery that was officially founded in 1985 by his father Battista, though his grandfather Giovanni had been growing grapes and produced wine on a small scale. Today, Cola has 10 hectares of beautiful vineyards on Monte Alto di Adro, and production exceeds 70,000 bottles yearly. Cola's Franciacorta and other wines have maintained that genuine 'récoltant' character, espressing proudly artisanal methods used in the vineyard and cellar. Their quality keeps improving year after year. After a nice performance put in by their Non Dosato last year, this year it's the Brut '13 that most impressed. It has a brilliant straw-yellow color, extremely fine beading, and is the epitome of style, with complex and delicate aromas of yeast, bonbon anglais and white-fruit. On the palate it's sapid, creamy, rich in fruit, mineral and long. Their tantalizing Rosé '15 is one of the best tasted this year.

○ Franciacorta Brut '13	♟♟ 5
○ Franciacorta Brut	♟♟ 4
○ Franciacorta Brut Satèn '15	♟♟ 5
⊙ Franciacorta Brut Satèn Athena '15	♟♟ 5
○ Franciacorta Dosaggio Zero '14	♟♟ 5
○ Franciacorta Extra Brut	♟♟ 4
○ Franciacorta Brut '12	♟♟ 5
○ Franciacorta Brut '11	♟♟ 5
○ Franciacorta Brut Satèn '12	♟♟ 5
○ Franciacorta Non Dosato '13	♟♟ 5
○ Franciacorta Non Dosato '12	♟♟ 5
○ Franciacorta Non Dosato '11	♟♟ 5
⊙ Franciacorta Rosé Athena '12	♟♟ 5
○ Franciacorta Satèn '14	♟♟ 5

Contadi Castaldi

LOC. FORNACE BIASCA
VIA COLZANO, 32
25030 ADRO [BS]
TEL. +39 0307450126
www.contadicastaldi.it

CELLAR SALES
PRE-BOOKED VISITS
ANNUAL PRODUCTION 1,000,000 bottles
HECTARES UNDER VINE 150.00
SUSTAINABLE WINERY

The winery was born in the 1990s out of Vittorio Moretti's idea of transforming the abandoned Adro furnaces into a modern, well-equipped cellar. It makes Franciacorta from its own grapes but also uses those selected from among the territory's many growers. In other words, what the French refer to as a 'maison récoltant-manipulant'. Over the years, Contadi Castaldi has reached enviable levels of quality, harvesting from over 90 vineyards of a more than 130 hectare-park. The Franciacorta are refreshing, gutsy and contemporary. All the blends tasted this year put in an excellent performance, with a particular applause for their Satèn '15, which took home a gold. It pours a lovely, brilliant, straw-yellow color tinted green, with fine and creamy beading. On the nose it offers up an alluring and enticing bouquet of mature, white fruit and vanilla. On the palate it's soft, but with lovely tension, proving rich in fruity and citrusy notes, and very long. The non-vintage Brut also delivered, as did the rest of their selection.

○ Franciacorta Satèn '15	♟♟♟ 6
○ Franciacorta Zero '15	♟♟ 5
⊙ Franciacorta Brut	♟♟ 5
⊙ Franciacorta Brut Rosé	♟♟ 5
○ Franciacorta Brut Satèn Soul '11	♟♟♟ 6
○ Franciacorta Satèn Soul '06	♟♟♟ 6
○ Franciacorta Satèn Soul '05	♟♟♟ 6
○ Franciacorta Zero '14	♟♟♟ 5
○ Franciacorta Zero '12	♟♟♟ 5
○ Franciacorta Zero '09	♟♟♟ 5
○ Franciacorta Brut Satèn '12	♟♟ 6
○ Franciacorta Pinònero Natura '11	♟♟ 7
○ Franciacorta Satèn '14	♟♟ 6
○ Franciacorta Zero '13	♟♟ 5

Conte Vistarino

FRAZ. SCORZOLETTA, 82
27040 PIETRA DE' GIORGI [PV]
TEL. +39 038585117
www.contevistarino.it

CELLAR SALES
PRE-BOOKED VISITS
ANNUAL PRODUCTION 400,000 bottles
HECTARES UNDER VINE 200.00

The estate consists of 800 hectares (virtually the entire Rocca de' Giorgi municipality) and 120 of these are vineyards, mostly Pinot Nero. The Scuropasso Valley area has proved to have the ideal soil for the variety since its introduction here almost 150 years ago. In particular it is the best cru from which to obtain Pinot Nero for high profile reds and, in higher areas as the base for sparkling wines. Thanks to Ottavia's drive and the completion of the splendid new cellar next to Villa Fornace the family's residence, things only continue to improve. Because of an excessively hot year, we're missing their Pernice and Bertone cru this year. Thus it's the Tavernetto '16 that vies for a place as Oltrepò Pavese's best Pinot Nero. Complex in its aromas of wild berries, spices and aromatic herbs, it's a close-focused, deep, pervasive wine that can still continue to evolve. The Cépage tasted is, quite possibly, the best version yet, proving juicy and redolent of wild berries, accompanied by a tropical note. The sapidity and tension of their Riesling Renano Ries '17 is also worth pointing out.

● Tavernetto Pinot Nero '16	♟♟♟ 3*
○ Cépage Brut M. Cl.	♟♟ 4
○ OP Pinot Nero M. Cl. Brut 1865 '14	♟♟ 5
○ Ries Riesling '17	♟♟ 3
● Costa del Nero Pinot Nero '17	♟ 4
● OP Bonarda L'Alcova '18	♟ 3
● Bertone Pinot Nero '15	♟♟♟ 5
● Bertone Pinot Nero '13	♟♟♟ 5
○ OP Pinot Nero Brut Conte Vistarino 1865 '08	♟♟♟ 4*
● OP Pinot Nero Pernice '06	♟♟♟ 4*
● OP Buttafuoco '16	♟♟ 3
● Pernice Pinot Nero '15	♟♟ 5
○ Ries Riesling '16	♟♟ 3
● Tavernetto Pinot Nero '15	♟♟ 3*

Corte Aura

VIA COLZANO, 13
25030 ADRO [BS]
TEL. +39 030 7357281
www.corteaura.it

CELLAR SALES
PRE-BOOKED VISITS
ANNUAL PRODUCTION 100,000 bottles
HECTARES UNDER VINE 6.00

Corte Aura is a rapidly growing brand in Franciacorta, and owner Federico Fossati loves both this territory and Franciacorta. A few years ago he decided to invest in creating an ambitious winery and enrolled Pierangelo Bonomi, an enologist with a great deal of experience in making Franciacorta, for this adventure. Federico renovated an old farmhouse, transformed it into a cellar, and passionately cultivates six hectares (for now) of vineyards. He integrates carefully selected acquired grapes into his own, resulting in a product that has already distinguished itself in quality and numbers. Their excellent Rosé pours a pale, antique rose color, anticipating sapid and creamy flavors rich in notes of red berries before coming through structured, full, harmonious and deep on the palate. The Satèn is quite notable with its classic hints of ripe white peach enlivened by citrus fragrances and herbs. The Satèn '13 is creamy and pleasant, the Dosaggio Zero Insé complex and rich in balsamic notes.

○ Franciacorta Brut	♟♟	5
○ Franciacorta Brut Satèn '13	♟♟	5
○ Franciacorta Brut Satèn	♟♟	5
○ Franciacorta Brut Rosè	♟♟	5
○ Franciacorta Pas Dosé Insé	♟♟	5
○ Franciacorta Pas Dosé Armonia Ris.	♀♀	5
○ Franciacorta Pas Dosé Insè '12	♀♀	7
○ Franciacorta Satèn '10	♀♀	6

La Costa

FRAZ. COSTA
VIA GALBUSERA NERA, 2
23888 PEREGO [LC]
TEL. +39 0395312218
www.la-costa.it

CELLAR SALES
PRE-BOOKED VISITS
RESTAURANT SERVICE
ANNUAL PRODUCTION 30,000 bottles
HECTARES UNDER VINE 12.00
VITICULTURE METHOD Certified Organic

In the heart of the Montevecchia regional park and the Curone Valley, in Lecco's Brianza region, is a noteworthy winery that continues to surprise. The Crippa family cares for twelve vineyards in the middle of the woods as if they they were gardens. They use organic methods and much of the energy consumed comes from solar panels. International varieties grown on soils rich in limestone are the stars. Their Serìz '16 represents a nice interpretation of the wine, made with Merlot and Syrah. Flickering notes of pepper and black berries rise up on the nose, while on the palate it's firm, with lovely pulp on display and a long finish. The Solesta '16 is intense, with nuances of aniseed and medicinal herbs fused elegantly with fruity fragrances of apricot. On the palate it's lively and firmly-structured, with notable length to its vivid finish. Lovely fruity notes, along with slight hints of bread crust, feature in their Extra Brut Incrediboll, a Riesling Italico and Renano. On the palate it's harmonious, with nicely integrated prickle, closing fresh and sapid.

○ Solesta '16	♟♟	5
○ Incrediboll Extra Brut M. Cl. '16	♟♟	5
● Serìz '16	♟♟	4
● Vino del Quindici '15	♟♟	6
○ Brigante Bianco '17	♀♀	3
● Brigante Rosso '16	♀♀	3
● San Giobbe '16	♀♀	5
● San Giobbe '15	♀♀	4
● San Giobbe '13	♀♀	4
○ Solesta '15	♀♀	4
○ Solesta '14	♀♀	4
○ Solesta '13	♀♀	4

Costaripa

VIA COSTA, 1A
25080 MONIGA DEL GARDA [BS]
TEL. +39 0365502010
www.costaripa.it

CELLAR SALES
PRE-BOOKED VISITS
ANNUAL PRODUCTION 400,000 bottles
HECTARES UNDER VINE 40.00

With a great deal of research and experimentation, Mattia Vezzola has turned his winery into one of the most interesting in Lombardy. Costaripa is a benchmark not only in Valtènesi, but for all Italian wineries that produce rosé. In fact, Molmenti, made from Groppello, is not only the appellation's best rosé but also the first to have successfully explored the aging potential of this type in Italy. Renowned enologist Mattia is also passionate about making sparkling wine and his children Nicole and Gherardo collaborate with him on a permanent basis. The Molmenti '16 didn't disappoint our expectations. Its pale rose color is the prelude to a complex, charming bouquet of red berries, citrus and Mediterannean scrub, which give way to elegant, spicy notes of cloves and almond. These follow through coherently on the palate, where the wine exhibits complex structure, proving rich but also extraordinarily enjoyable. The Brut Grande Annata '14 is excellent, as are the rest of their wines.

⊙ Valtènesi Chiaretto Molmenti '16	♟♟♟ 5
○ Brut Grande Annata '14	♟♟ 5
○ Mattia Vezzola Brut	♟♟ 5
⊙ Mattia Vezzola Brut Rosé	♟♟ 5
⊙ Valtènesi Chiaretto RosaMara '18	♟♟ 2*
○ Mattia Vezzola Crémant	♟ 4
⊙ Valtènesi Chiaretto Molmenti '15	♟♟♟ 3*
○ Brut Grande Annata '13	♟♟ 5
○ Lugana Pievecroce '15	♟♟ 2*
○ Mattia Vezzola Brut '11	♟♟ 5
⊙ Valtènesi Chiaretto Molmenti '13	♟♟ 2*
⊙ Valtènesi Chiaretto Molmenti '12	♟♟ 2*
⊙ Valtènesi Chiaretto RosaMara '17	♟♟ 3
⊙ Valtènesi Chiaretto RosaMara '16	♟♟ 2*
⊙ Valtènesi Chiaretto RosaMara '15	♟♟ 2*

Derbusco Cives

VIA PROVINCIALE, 83
25030 ERBUSCO [BS]
TEL. +39 0307731164
www.derbuscocives.com

CELLAR SALES
PRE-BOOKED VISITS
RESTAURANT SERVICE
ANNUAL PRODUCTION 96,000 bottles
HECTARES UNDER VINE 12.00

Dario and Giuseppe Vezzoli, Luigi Dotti, Paolo Brescianini and Vanni Bordiga, all friends from Erbusco, decided to found this beautiful winery in 2004. They chose the very simple name 'cittadini di Erbusco' (citizens of Erbusco) to underscore the centrality and peculiarities of the terroir of Erbusco, the capital of Franciacorta. The winery has a 12-hectare park of vineyards (all in Erbusco, of course) and works using modern methods but following tradition, such as second fermentation with must from Franciacorta grapes (and, therefore, without added sugar) and late disgorgement. They are greatly committed to sustainability. Doppio Erre Di stands for 'delayed disgorgement' and 'recently disgorged', just one of the particularities that distinguishes this excellent Franciacorta, which ages for more than thirty months on the lees. Made with Chardonnay and a 15% share of Pinot Nero, it's a harmonious, complex Brut, rich in fruit and freshness, with a lovely linear development that closes citrusy and long.

○ Franciacorta Brut Doppio Erre Di	♟♟ 5
○ Franciacorta Brut Doppio Erre DV	♟♟ 5
⊙ Franciacorta Rosé '14	♟♟ 6
○ Franciacorta Brut '12	♟♟ 6
○ Franciacorta Brut '11	♟♟ 6
○ Franciacorta Brut '10	♟♟ 6
○ Franciacorta Brut '09	♟♟ 6
○ Franciacorta Brut Crisalis '12	♟♟ 6
○ Franciacorta Brut Crisalis '11	♟♟ 6
○ Franciacorta Extra Brut '12	♟♟ 8
○ Franciacorta Extra Brut '11	♟♟ 8
○ Franciacorta Extra Brut '10	♟♟ 8

Dirupi

LOC. MADONNA DI CAMPAGNA
VIA GRUMELLO, 1
23020 MONTAGNA IN VALTELLINA [SO]
TEL. +39 3472909779
www.dirupi.com

CELLAR SALES
PRE-BOOKED VISITS
ANNUAL PRODUCTION 35,000 bottles
HECTARES UNDER VINE 7.00
SUSTAINABLE WINERY

Davide Fasolini and Pierpaolo di Franco's enthusiasm were needed to reveal a handful of plots on steep slopes in Valtellina. At the same time, the duo planted new vineyards in strategic positions. Their wines have the lightness of the mountain air given freedom from constraints by those who want to do something different with wine. Technical knowledge and a truly enviable territory result in the type of glou glou wines sought around the world. The Riserva '16, a bona fide Grumello cru, is bursting with freshness, complexity and elegance. Sensations of raspberry and tobacco rise up off a gorgeous background of iron and gentian. On the palate it's rich and succulent, with vibrant acidity and a first-class finish. The Dirupi '17 is less complex but extraordinarily pleasant and vigorous. Superb balance and personality characterize their Sforzato '17, with its notes of tobacco, spices and red berries, and a firmly-structured palate in which subtle tannins give way to a long finish.

● Valtellina Sup. Grumello Dirupi Ris. '16	▼▼▼ 7
● Sforzato di Valtellina Vino Sbagliato '17	▼▼ 6
● Valtellina Sup. Dirupi '17	▼▼ 4
● Rosso di Valtellina Olè '18	▼▼ 3
● Valtellina Sup. Grumello Gess '16	▼▼ 5
● Valtellina Sup. Dirupi '16	♀♀♀ 4*
● Valtellina Sup. Dirupi Ris. '14	♀♀♀ 6
● Valtellina Sup. Dirupi Ris. '12	♀♀♀ 6
● Valtellina Sup. Dirupi Ris. '11	♀♀♀ 6
● Valtellina Sup. Dirupi Ris. '09	♀♀♀ 6

Luca Faccinelli

VIA MEDICI, 3A
23030 CHIURO [SO]
TEL. +39 3470807011
www.lucafaccinelli.it

CELLAR SALES
PRE-BOOKED VISITS
ANNUAL PRODUCTION 20,000 bottles
HECTARES UNDER VINE 3.00
SUSTAINABLE WINERY

The worthy winery founded by Luca Faccinelli in 2007 makes it into this section of our guide for the first time. Chiuro is located in the intriguing Valtellina territory at the foot of the Alps, an area that is quite challenging for growing grapes. The vineyards are in the sub-area of Grumello between 400 and 650 meters above sea level, with slopes that can reach angles of 70 degrees. Work can only be done here by hand, which requires the passion and enthusiasm expressed across a range that improves every year. This year they presented a promising and lively exposition of Grumello. Their Riserva '16 is complex and rich in red fruit, with nuances of quinine and licorice. On the palate it's powerful, velvety, with a long, characterful finish. The other two, the Ortensio Lando '06 and the Tell '15, are multifaceted and fresh. The former features fruity notes and iron sensations. On the palate it's full and harmonious, with nice sapidity. The second is redolent of rhubarb, with notes of crisp, red fruit, making for a rich palate marked by lively acidity and considerable length.

● Valtellina Sup. Grumello Ris. '16	▼▼ 6
● Rosso di Valtellina Matteo Bandello '17	▼▼ 4
● Valtellina Sup. Grumello Ortensio Lando '16	▼▼ 5
● Valtellina Sup. Grumello Tell '15	▼▼ 5
● Rosso di Valtellina Matteo Bandello '16	♀♀ 4
● Valtellina Sup. Grumello Ortensio Lando '15	♀♀ 5
● Valtellina Sup. Ortensio Lando '13	♀♀ 5

Sandro Fay

LOC. SAN GIACOMO DI TEGLIO
VIA PILA CASELLI, 1
23030 TEGLIO [SO]
TEL. +39 0342786071
www.vinifay.it

CELLAR SALES
PRE-BOOKED VISITS
ANNUAL PRODUCTION 38,000 bottles
HECTARES UNDER VINE 13.00

Sandro Fay established this noteworthy Valtellina winery in the heart of the Valgella sub-zone in 1973 — since then it's managed to keep in step with the times. Studies carried out over the years on environmental sustainability and the effect of altimetry have kept the winery ahead of the competition. Marco Fay, a great interpreter of the territory's different voices, is at the helm. Their Sforzato Ronco del Picchio '16 put in a superb performance. It's intense and sophisticated, with notes of tobacco, a background of mature red berries, even licorice and mint. On the palate it's elegant and succulent, with a long, first-class finish. Freshness, red fruit and immense drinkability mark their two Valgellas, the Riserva Carteria '15 and the Cà Morei '16, with both wines exhibiting fine tannins, a harmonious palate and notable development. The Chardonnay Sottocastello '17 is promising and subtle, aromatically intense. The vineyard is situated at 830 meters elevation and, for this reason as well, on the palate there's no lack of character.

● Sforzato di Valtellina Ronco del Picchio '16	♛♛♛ 6
● Valtellina Sup. Valgella Ca' Morèi '16	♛♛ 5
● Valtellina Sup. Valgella Carterìa Ris. '15	♛♛ 6
○ Sottocastello Chardonnay '17	♛♛ 4
● Valtellina Sup. Costa Bassa '16	♛♛ 4
● Valtellina Sup. Sassella Il Glicine '16	♛♛ 5
● Valtellina Sforzato Ronco del Picchio '10	♛♛♛ 6
● Valtellina Sforzato Ronco del Picchio '09	♛♛♛ 6
● Valtellina Sforzato Ronco del Picchio '02	♛♛♛ 6
● Valtellina Sup. Valgella Cà Moréi '13	♛♛♛ 5
● Sforzato di Valtellina Ronco del Picchio '14	♛♛ 6
● Valtellina Sup. Valgella Carterìa Ris. '14	♛♛ 6

★Ferghettina

VIA SALINE, 11
25030 ADRO [BS]
TEL. +39 0307451212
www.ferghettina.it

CELLAR SALES
PRE-BOOKED VISITS
ANNUAL PRODUCTION 400,000 bottles
HECTARES UNDER VINE 160.00
VITICULTURE METHOD Certified Organic
SUSTAINABLE WINERY

A visit to this beautiful winery in Adro always promises a surprise of some sort: a novelty, an extension, a modernization of equipment, the acquisition of new vineyards. The Gatti family has achieved brilliant results so far and every day puts great effort into the seemingly unceasing growth in quality and quantity. In short, a first-class winery. Yet another feather in the cap for their Riserva 33, this time with the 2012. It's a cuvée of the best Chardonnay batches fermented in steel and then blended the following spring. Bottle fermentation can last more than 80 months, making for incredible depth of flavor. You'll be bowled over by its creaminess, the freshness of its vegetal and citrus tones woven in with focused and creamy fruit, by its depth and overall harmony. Each of their wines is of outstanding quality, however.

○ Franciacorta Pas Dosè Riserva 33 Ris. '12	♛♛♛ 7
○ Franciacorta Extra Brut '13	♛♛ 6
○ curtefranca Bianco '18	♛♛ 2*
● Curtefranca Rosso '17	♛♛ 2*
○ Franciacorta Brut	♛♛ 4
○ franciacorta Brut Milledì '15	♛♛ 5
⊙ Franciacorta Brut Rosé '15	♛♛ 5
○ Franciacorta Brut Satèn '15	♛♛ 5
○ Franciacorta Extra Brut '09	♛♛♛ 5
○ Franciacorta Extra Brut '05	♛♛♛ 5
○ Franciacorta Pas Dosé 33 Ris. '10	♛♛♛ 6
○ Franciacorta Pas Dosé 33 Ris. '09	♛♛♛ 6
○ Franciacorta Pas Dosé 33 Ris. '07	♛♛♛ 6
○ Franciacorta Pas Dosé 33 Ris. '06	♛♛♛ 6
○ Franciacorta Pas Dosé Riserva 33 '11	♛♛♛ 6

Fiamberti

via Chiesa, 17
27044 Canneto Pavese [PV]
Tel. +39 038588019
www.fiambertivini.it

CELLAR SALES
PRE-BOOKED VISITS
ANNUAL PRODUCTION 140,000 bottles
HECTARES UNDER VINE 18.00

Ambrogio Fiamberti and his son Giulio run this long-established family winery. It has some of the most suitable vineyards in the 'Stradella Spur', the foothills separating the Versa and Scuropasso Valleys. The territory's traditional wines come to life here, particularly reds in the various interpretations that characterize the zone: sparkling, still, young, aged. Giulio's very actively involved in the Club del Buttafuoco Storico (presenting two cru this year) and shows constant growth in Metodo Classico. The first Buttafuoco Storico to gain a place among the Tre Bicchieri elite is Fiamberti's Vigna Sacca del Prete '15. It's an aromatically rich and generous wine whose fragrances span wild berries, balsamic and spicy hints. On the palate it's juicy, energetic and racy while also exhibiting harmony. The Solenga '15 falls a bit short on this first release after replanting: the vineyard is still too young, but it's got potential in spades.

● OP Buttafuoco Storico V. Sacca del Prete '15	▼▼▼ 5
⊙ OP Cruasé	▼▼ 4
● OP Bonarda La Briccona '18	▼▼ 2*
● OP Buttafuoco Il Cacciatore '16	▼▼ 3
● OP Buttafuoco Storico V. Solenga '15	▼▼ 4
○ OP Pinot Nero Brut M. Cl.	▼ 3
● OP Buttafuoco Cacciatore '15	♈ 3
● OP Buttafuoco Storico V. Sacca del Prete '13	♈ 4
● OP Buttafuoco Storico V. Sacca del Prete '12	♈ 4
○ OP Riesling Ida '16	♈ 2*
● OP Sangue di Giuda Lella '16	♈ 2*

Enrico Gatti

via Metelli, 9
25030 Erbusco [BS]
Tel. +39 0307267999
www.enricogatti.it

CELLAR SALES
PRE-BOOKED VISITS
ANNUAL PRODUCTION 120,000 bottles
HECTARES UNDER VINE 17.00

The winery was founded by Enrico Gatti in 1975 and has firmly occupied one of Franciacorta's top positions for years. Credit must go to Lorenzo and Paola Gatti, a tight-knit family team completed by Paola's husband, Enzo Balzarini. They work with the care of artisans in the modern cellar that has been enlarged several times just to accommodate the fruit from their vineyards. The winery's seventeen hectares are all in Erbusco, which gives them special structure, fullness and a lovely minerality. Once again, Gatti's blends put in an excellent performance. Needless to say, their Nature led the way, earning a place in our final round of tastings. On the nose it proves dynamic, fresh, extremely focused and lively in its fruity and mineral aromas — with just a bit more depth it could take home top marks. The Rosé is also among the best in the appellation. A lovely pale rose color anticipates elegant aromas of small berries accompanied by delicately spicy notes and vanilla. On the palate it's taut, linear, assertive and highly enjoyable.

○ Franciacorta Nature	▼▼ 5
○ Franciacorta Brut	▼▼ 5
⊙ Franciacorta Brut Rosé	▼▼ 5
○ Franciacorta Brut Satèn '15	▼▼ 5
○ Franciacorta Nature '13	▼▼ 6
○ Franciacorta Brut '05	♈♈ 6
○ Franciacorta Nature '07	♈♈ 5
○ Franciacorta Satèn '05	♈♈ 5
○ Franciacorta Satèn '03	♈♈ 5
○ Franciacorta Satèn '02	♈♈ 4
○ Franciacorta Satèn '01	♈♈ 4
○ Franciacorta Satèn '00	♈♈ 5
○ Franciacorta Brut Satèn '14	♈ 5
○ Franciacorta Brut Satèn '13	♈ 6
○ Franciacorta Nature '11	♈ 6

I Gessi

FRAZ. CASCINA FOSSA, 8
27050 OLIVA GESSI [PV]
TEL. +39 0383896606
www.cantineigessi.it

CELLAR SALES
PRE-BOOKED VISITS
ACCOMMODATION
ANNUAL PRODUCTION 160,000 bottles
HECTARES UNDER VINE 41.00

As indicated by the name of the winery and district ('gesso' means chalk), I Gessi's vineyards and agritourism are characterized by gypsum, limestone soil. Led by Fabbio Defilippi with the support of his brother, expert Oltrepò enologist Emilio, the Gessi winery is producing increasingly interesting wines, the top versions coming from grapes best adapted to the soil's characteristics, namely Riesling and Pinot Nero. The latter, in particular, is used for very respectable sparkling wines. A faint straw-yellow color, the undosed Maria Cristina offers up hints of rosemary and mint, sensations that reemerge on a fresh, clean palate. Among their Metodo Classicos, the Dieffe made it's debut this year. It's a monovarietal Chardonnay redolent of citrus and tropical fruit. The Rosé Non Dosato '11 opens slowly, revealing a rather complex aromatic profile. Their Fasarda '16, a red made with Croatina, exhibits a solid structure.

● Fasarda Croatina '16	♟♟ 3
○ Maria Cristina Pas Dosé M. Cl.	♟♟ 5
● 1907 Pinot Nero '16	♟ 4
● Croatina Frizzante '18	♟ 3
○ Dieffe Brut M. Cl.	♟ 4
○ Maria Cristina Brut M. Cl.	♟ 3
○ Maria Cristina Pas Dosé M. Cl. Rosé '11	♟ 5
○ Riesling '18	♟ 3
● 1907 Pinot Nero '15	♟♟ 6
● OP Bonarda Frizzante '17	♟♟ 2*
○ OP Pinot Nero Pas Dosé M. Cl. Maria Cristina '12	♟♟ 8
○ OP Pinot Nero Pas Dosé Maria Cristina '11	♟♟ 5
○ OP Riesling I Gessi '16	♟♟ 1*

★Giorgi

FRAZ. CAMPONOCE, 39A
27044 CANNETO PAVESE [PV]
TEL. +39 0385262151
www.giorgi-wines.it

CELLAR SALES
PRE-BOOKED VISITS
ANNUAL PRODUCTION 1,600,000 bottles
HECTARES UNDER VINE 60.00

The new generation, represented by Fabiano Giorgi, his sister Eleonora and his wife Ileana, under the careful supervision of their father Antonio, has revolutionized this winery over the years. It has brought the quality higher and higher to the point of reaching absolute excellence, particularly with the Pinot Nero-based Metodo Classico. 100,000 bottles of the latter alone are now produced annually. In the cellar, enologist Matteo Olcelli has been joined by Andrea Bonfanti, who carries with him a great deal of experience from Alto Adige. And once again we sing the praises of the Top Zero, an undosed sparkling wine made possible through lengthy aging on the lees. It's linear and opulent, as punchy as ever. Their multi-award winning 1870 is of a different, broader style. The 2015 comes through creamy, elegant, citrusy. The well-made Casa del Corno '15 is a juicy wine that hits the mark. When it comes to the rest of their selection the graphic speaks for itself, with a special mention for their Riesling Renano Il Bandito and the Clilele, an early-drinking Buttafuoco.

○ Top Zero Pas Dosé M. Cl.	♟♟♟ 6
● OP Buttafuoco Storico V. Casa del Corno '15	♟♟ 3*
○ OP Pinot Nero Brut M. Cl. 1870 '15	♟♟ 5
○ Gerry Scotti Extra Brut M. Cl.	♟♟ 4
● OP Bonarda Vivace La Brughera '18	♟♟ 2*
● OP Buttafuoco Clilele '17	♟♟ 3
○ OP Pinot Nero Brut M. Cl. Gianfranco Giorgi '16	♟♟ 5
○ OP Riesling Il Bandito '18	♟♟ 4
● OP Sangue di Giuda '18	♟♟ 3
● OP Pinot Nero Monteroso '17	♟ 3
● Vigalòn '18	♟ 2
○ OP Pinot Nero Brut 1870 '12	♟♟♟ 5
○ OP Pinot Nero Brut 1870 '11	♟♟♟ 5
○ OP Pinot Nero Brut 1870 '10	♟♟♟ 5

Isimbarda

Fraz. Castello
Cascina Isimbarda
27046 Santa Giuletta [PV]
Tel. +39 0383899256
www.isimbarda.com

CELLAR SALES
PRE-BOOKED VISITS
ANNUAL PRODUCTION 130,000 bottles
HECTARES UNDER VINE 40.00

This Oltrepò winery is both beautiful and historic; the story of wine production by the Marquises Isimbardi on the hills of Santa Giuletta dates back to the 17th century. The estate has clayey soils but, even more so, calcareous and marly soils particularly suitable for the cultivation of white varietals (starting with the Riesling Renano) and Pinot Nero. The latter, for several years now, has also been used for the production of sparkling wine, with often interesting results expressing the territory and its character. The 2018 version of their Vigna Martina also stands out as one of Oltrepò's best Riesling Renanos. It's a wine of substance, redolent of chamomile and aromatic herbs, though it gives up its best a few years after harvest, when those tertiaries that make it a singular grape rise up slowly. Among their Metodo Classico sparklers, some of which are debuting in our guide, the Sniper stands out. It's a gutsy yet elegant monovarietal Pinot Nero.

Lantieri de Paratico

Loc. Colzano
via Videtti (ingresso da via 2 Agosto)
25031 Capriolo [BS]
Tel. +39 030736151
www.lantierideparatico.it

CELLAR SALES
PRE-BOOKED VISITS
ACCOMMODATION AND RESTAURANT SERVICE
ANNUAL PRODUCTION 140,000 bottles
HECTARES UNDER VINE 20.00
VITICULTURE METHOD Certified Organic

The Lantieri de Paratico family has been in Franciacorta since 930 CE. They settled in Capriolo in 1500 and even then their wine was prized in Italy and in European courts. Fabio Lantieri has created a modern cellar in the historic family home, making excellent Franciacorta from the grapes of the winery's twenty hectares of vineyards, which have long been organically cultivated. In our final round of tastings the Arcadia Brut '15 put in an excellent performance, one worthy of the producer. It offers up complex aromas of lovely finesse, with fresh notes of fruit weaving with more complex sensations of aromatic herbs and elegant citrus. On the palate it's soft and succulent. The Origines '13 is also excellent, proving deep and complex though not as transparent as the previous year.

○ OP Pinot Nero Brut M. Cl. Première Cuvée	♟♟ 4
○ OP Pinot Nero Pas Dosé M. Cl. Sniper	♟♟ 5
○ OP Riesling Renano V. Martina '18	♟♟ 3
● OP Barbera Montezavo '16	♟ 3
⊙ OP Cruasé	♟ 4
○ OP Pinot Nero Brut M. Cl. Blanc de Noir	♟ 4
● OP Bonarda Vivace V. delle More '15	♟♟ 2*
● OP Pinot Nero V. dei Giganti '16	♟♟ 3
● OP Pinot Nero V. del Cardinale '16	♟♟ 4
○ OP Riesling Renano V. Martina '17	♟♟ 3*
○ OP Riesling Renano V. Martina '16	♟♟ 2*
○ OP Riesling V. Martina '15	♟♟ 3

○ Franciacorta Brut Arcadia '15	♟♟ 5
○ Curtefranca Bianco '18	♟♟ 2*
● Curtefranca Rosso '16	♟♟ 2*
○ Franciacorta Brut	♟♟ 5
○ Franciacorta Brut Bio Gemmae	♟♟ 5
○ Franciacorta Extra Brut	♟♟ 5
○ Franciacorta Nature	♟♟ 4
○ Franciacorta Nature Origines Ris. '13	♟♟ 7
⊙ Franciacorta Brut Rosé	♟ 5
○ Franciacorta Brut Arcadia '13	♟♟♟ 5
○ Franciacorta Nature Origines Ris. '12	♟♟♟ 7
○ Franciacorta Brut Arcadia '14	♟♟ 5
○ Franciacorta Nature Origines Ris. '11	♟♟ 7
● L'Enio '15	♟ 5

Lazzari

VIA MELLA, 49
25020 CAPRIANO DEL COLLE [BS]
TEL. +39 0309747387
www.lazzarivini.it

CELLAR SALES
PRE-BOOKED VISITS
ANNUAL PRODUCTION 40,000 bottles
HECTARES UNDER VINE 9.50
VITICULTURE METHOD Certified Organic
SUSTAINABLE WINERY

It's a pleasure to walk through the vineyard with Davide Lazzari. He's the fourth generation of winemakers to cling with tenacity to Monte Netto, a small hill in the vast Po Valley south of Brescia. The winery is run on organic methods, photovoltaic power and engaging passion. The care taken in the vineyards and cellar, including risktaking and experimentation, is perceivable first in the man and then in the wines, into which his personality is inevitably transferred. We start with their Bastian Contrario '16. It's made with 'Turbiana' (as Trebbiano is known in these parts) harvested late with botrytis, then fermented and aged in barriques. It's honey colored and extremely fragrant, reminiscent of blue cheese even, while on the palate it proves full and savory. It's entirely faithful to its name, but definitely worth trying. The Riserva degli Angeli '16 is a great red, calibrated in its fruit and oak, full of detail. The fragrant, tropical Bianco dedicated to grandfather Fausto is also well-made.

● Capriano del Colle Rosso Riserva degli Angeli Ris. '16	♟♟ 5
○ Capriano del Colle Bianco Fausto '18	♟♟ 2*
○ Capriano del Colle Bianco Sup. Bastian Contrario '16	♟♟ 6
● Capriano del Colle Marzemino Berzamì '18	♟ 2
● Capriano del Colle Rosso Adagio '16	♟ 2
○ Adamah Extra Brut '12	♟♟ 4
○ Capriano del Colle Bianco Fausto '16	♟♟ 2*
● Capriano del Colle Rosso Riserva degli Angeli '15	♟♟ 4

★Mamete Prevostini

LOC. SAN VITTORE
VIA DON PRIMO LUCCHINETTI, 63
23020 SONDRIO
TEL. +39 034341522
www.mameteprevostini.com

CELLAR SALES
PRE-BOOKED VISITS
RESTAURANT SERVICE
ANNUAL PRODUCTION 180,000 bottles
HECTARES UNDER VINE 20.00
SUSTAINABLE WINERY

Mamete Prevostini is a central player in the world of Valtellina wine, whose reputation and recognition he has helped to enhance with great wines. Also important in this regard is the vital sharing and planning work done within the Consorzio Vini Valtellina. His wine cellar in Valchiavenna offers very successfully styled wines that perfectly combine fragrance and richness. There's no doubt about it. Supreme elegance is the best way to describe their Sforzato Corte di Cama '17. Lovely notes of tobacco and dried herbs rise up off a subtle background of red fruit. On the palate it exhibits perfect harmony between acidity and tannins, all well-balanced with pulp. Their Sassella Sommarovina '17 put in an excellent performance, with aromas reminiscent of mature red fruits, nuances of rhubarb and dried flowers. On the palate it proves elegantly structured, with gradually unfolding, pervasive tannins and an endless finish. The Sforzato Albareda '17 is decidedly weighty, with strong personality, characterized by complex aromas and a powerful palate.

● Valtellina Sforzato Corte di Cama '17	♟♟♟ 6
● Valtellina Sforzato Albareda '17	♟♟ 6
● Valtellina Sup. Sassella Sommarovina '17	♟♟ 5
● Valtellina Sup. Inferno La Cruus '17	♟♟ 5
● Valtellina Sup. Sassella San Lorenzo '17	♟♟ 6
● Valtellina Sforzato Albareda '15	♟♟♟ 6
● Valtellina Sforzato Albareda '13	♟♟♟ 6
● Valtellina Sup. Ris. '09	♟♟♟ 5
● Valtellina Sup. Sassella San Lorenzo '16	♟♟♟ 6
● Valtellina Sup. Sassella San Lorenzo '10	♟♟♟ 5
● Valtellina Sup. Sassella Sommarovina '13	♟♟♟ 5

Le Marchesine

VIA VALLOSA, 31
25050 PASSIRANO [BS]
TEL. +39 030657005
www.lemarchesine.it

CELLAR SALES
PRE-BOOKED VISITS
ANNUAL PRODUCTION 450,000 bottles
HECTARES UNDER VINE 43.00
SUSTAINABLE WINERY

The Biatta family and name have been
present in Lombardy for centuries and
always connected to wine. Le Marchesine,
however, was born in 1985 when Giovanni
started vinifying grapes from three hectares.
A lot of time has passed and today this
impressive winery, run by his son Loris with
the help of his grandchildren Alice and
Andrea, has reached prestigious heights of
quality. Enologist Jean Pierre Valade brings
international experience in Metodo Classico
and is a trusted consultant. They're back
with Tre Bicchieri thanks to a seductive
version of their Secolo Novo, the Dosage
Zero Riserva '11, a Franciacorta of
unembellished, sophisticated elegance. It's
a brilliant straw-yellow color with golden
highlights and extremely fine beading. Its
elegant bouquet is characterized by
medicinal herbs, white fruit and yeast,
sensations that introduce a decidedly sapid
palate, crisp and linear. It's a wine that
marvelously brings together stylistic rigor,
richness of fruit and pleasantness. The
Secolo novo Brut '11 is also excellent, as is
the rest of their selection.

○ Franciacorta Dosage Zero Secolo Novo Ris. '11	🍷🍷🍷 8
○ Franciacorta Brut	🍷🍷 4
⊙ Franciacorta Brut Rosé '15	🍷🍷 6
○ Franciacorta Brut Satèn '15	🍷🍷 6
○ Franciacorta Brut Secolo Novo '11	🍷🍷 8
○ Franciacorta Extra Brut	🍷🍷 5
○ Franciacorta Extra Brut Blanc de Noirs '15	🍷🍷 6
○ Franciacorta Brut Blanc de Noir '09	🍷🍷🍷 5
○ Franciacorta Brut Secolo Novo '05	🍷🍷🍷 7
○ Franciacorta Dosage Zero Secolo Novo Ris. '08	🍷🍷🍷 8
○ Franciacorta Brut Blanc de Blancs '11	🍷🍷 8
⊙ Franciacorta Brut Rosé '13	🍷🍷 6
○ Franciacorta Satèn '14	🍷🍷 6

Tenuta Mazzolino

VIA MAZZOLINO, 34
27050 CORVINO SAN QUIRICO [PV]
TEL. +39 0383876122
www.tenuta-mazzolino.com

CELLAR SALES
PRE-BOOKED VISITS
ANNUAL PRODUCTION 100,000 bottles
HECTARES UNDER VINE 20.00

Do not miss an opportunity to visit
Mazzolino in Oltrepò Pavese. Since 1980,
this beautiful winery, consisting of a
nineteenth-century village with villa,
Italian-style garden and enchanting view of
the Po Valley, has been owned by the
Braggiotti family, which turned it into one of
the area's most important. The plots of land
surrounding the estate are largely planted
with Pinot Nero and Chardonnay, a result of
the Burgundian approach favored by
Kyriakos Kynigopoulos, who was brought in
directly from Beaune. Management is
entrusted to Piacenza enologist Stefano
Malchiodi. We tasted the Noir '16 at a
stage when close-focused, ripe fruit are in
the foreground. It's a wine with substance,
redolent of red and black red fruits, spices,
chocolate and forest undergrowth. Their
two Metodo Classicos gain in quality year
after year: the extremely floral Cruasé and
a Blanc de Blanc whose aromas of citrus
and ripe tropical fruit anticipate a fine bead.
The Blanc '17 is a Chardonnay fermented
in barriques that's for laying down, thanks
to outstanding aging power.

● OP Pinot Nero Noir '16	🍷🍷 5
○ Chardonnay Blanc '17	🍷🍷 3
○ Mazzolino Blanc de Blancs Brut M. Cl. '15	🍷🍷 4
⊙ OP Cruasé Mazzolino	🍷🍷 4
● Terrazze Pinot Nero '18	🍷🍷 3
○ Camarà Chardonnay '18	🍷 2
● OP Pinot Nero Noir '12	🍷🍷🍷 5
● OP Pinot Nero Noir '10	🍷🍷🍷 5
● OP Pinot Nero Noir '09	🍷🍷🍷 5
● OP Pinot Nero Noir '08	🍷🍷🍷 5
● OP Pinot Nero Noir '07	🍷🍷🍷 5
● OP Pinot Nero Noir '06	🍷🍷🍷 5
○ OP Chardonnay Blanc '16	🍷🍷 3
○ OP Chardonnay Blanc '15	🍷🍷 3
● OP Pinot Nero Noir '15	🍷🍷 5
● OP Pinot Nero Noir '14	🍷🍷 5

Mirabella

VIA CANTARANE, 2
25050 RODENGO SAIANO [BS]
TEL. +39 030611197
www.mirabellafranciacorta.it

CELLAR SALES
PRE-BOOKED VISITS
ACCOMMODATION
ANNUAL PRODUCTION 350,000 bottles
HECTARES UNDER VINE 50.00
SUSTAINABLE WINERY

Mirabella was born in 1979, the brainchild of enologist Teresio Schiavi, who brought a group of vigneron friends in on the adventure. Today the winery can boast of its beautiful location, 50 hectares of vineyards and a cellar with modern equipment. At the helm are the administrator, Francesco Bracchi, and Teresio's sons, enologist Alessandro and commercial director Alberto. Production levels are high (nearly half a million bottles) and the winery's reputation continues to grow thanks to its commitment to sustainability and to wines with low or no sulphur content. A blend of Chardonnay (80%) and Pinot Bianco, the Edea ages for more than 30 months on the lees before disgorgement. It features brilliant, fine beading, fresh aromas of white fruit that alternate with citrus, closing on aromatic herbs. On the palate it's sapid, succulent, fresh and lively, thus earning itself a place in our final tastings. The Døm, a Dosaggio Zero Riserva '11, is also excellent, proving sapid, complex, deep and mineral.

○ Franciacorta Brut Edea	♟♟5
○ Franciacorta Brut Satèn	♟♟5
○ Franciacorta Dosaggio Zero Døm Ris. '11	♟♟7
○ Franciacorta Pinot Nero Brut Nature '15	♟♟6
● TdF Rosso Maniero '15	♟♟2*
⊙ Franciacorta Brut Rosé	♟5
○ Franciacorta Extra Brut Elite	♟7
○ Franciacorta Dosaggio Zero Dom '06	♟♟6
○ Franciacorta Dosaggio Zero Dom '04	♟♟6
○ Franciacorta Dosaggio Zero Dom Ris. '09	♟♟6
○ Franciacorta Exra Brut Demetra '12	♟♟5
○ Franciacorta Extra Brut '09	♟♟5

★Monsupello

VIA SAN LAZZARO, 5
27050 TORRICELLA VERZATE [PV]
TEL. +39 0383896043
www.monsupello.it

CELLAR SALES
PRE-BOOKED VISITS
ANNUAL PRODUCTION 260,000 bottles
HECTARES UNDER VINE 50.00

In the panorama of wine, not only in Lombardy but in all Italy, it is difficult to find a family winery capable of producing consistent high-quality wines of all types: Metodo Classico, white, red, dessert, sparkling. However, if there is a criticism to be made about Pierangelo and Laura, children of the great Carlo Boatti, it's that of creating (in typical Oltrepò style) too many labels. Marco Bertelegni has been managing the cellar (and more) for many years and plays a key role in the overall organization and in the production of wines, among which the Metodo Classico stands out as among Italy's best. The Nature di Monsupello, with its trademark copper highlights, is back at the top of its game. It's a sapid wine, clear, taut and meaty, redolent of flowers and raspberries, long in its finish. The Millesimato '14 also delivered, with its crisp fruit enriched by spicy wood, and its fine bead. Their fruit-forward 'base' Brut is anything but a 'base level' wine, while the Ca' del Tava features lovely texture. It may just be a bit dominated by the vanilla of new barriques.

○ Nature M. Cl.	♟♟♟4
○ Brut M. Cl. '14	♟♟5
○ Brut M. Cl.	♟♟5
○ Brut M. Cl. Rosé	♟♟4
○ Ca' del Tava Brut M. Cl.	♟♟6
● OP Bonarda Vivace Vaiolet '18	♟2
○ Riesling '18	♟2
○ Senso Chardonnay '13	♟5
○ Brut '11	♟♟♟5
○ Brut '08	♟♟♟5
○ Brut M. Cl. '13	♟♟♟5
○ OP Brut Classese '06	♟♟♟5
○ OP Brut Classese '04	♟♟♟5
○ Brut '11	♟♟5

★Monte Rossa

FRAZ. BORNATO
VIA MONTE ROSSA, 1
25040 CAZZAGO SAN MARTINO [BS]
TEL. +39 030725066
www.monterossa.com

CELLAR SALES
PRE-BOOKED VISITS
ANNUAL PRODUCTION 500,000 bottles
HECTARES UNDER VINE 70.00

Monte Rossa helped write the story of Franciacorta wine. Guided by Paolo, the Rabotti family began to market wine and sparkling Franciacorta in the early 1970s. Today, his son Emanuele, together with Oscar Farinetti, maintains the prestige of this famous Cazzago San Martino estate. It has 70 hectares of vineyards with different exposures that supply grapes for about 500,000 excellent quality bottles each year. The cuvée Riserva, which has been aged on the lees for a long time, is successful all over the world. The PR Brut, which bears the initials of the winery's founders (Paolo Rabotti and Paola Rovetta), is a Blanc de Blancs that's made with their best Chardonnay. 35% of the wine is older vintage grapes aged in steel and oak before bottle fermentation, which can last for more than two years. The result is a Franciacorta with character, marked by fresh vegetal tones amidst fruit and more complex, toasty, spicy and mineral nuances. Their Prima Cuvée stands out for its finesse and cleanness.

○ Franciacorta Brut P. R.	♟♟5
○ Franciacorta Brut Cabochon Fuoriserie '14	♟♟8
○ Franciacorta Brut Prima Cuvée	♟♟5
○ Franciacorta Brut Satèn Sansevé	♟♟5
⊙ Franciacorta Rosé Flamingo	♟♟5
○ Franciacorta Extra Brut Salvadék '15	♟6
○ Franciacorta Non Dosato Coupé	♟5
○ Franciacorta Brut Cabochon '05	♟♟♟6
○ Franciacorta Brut Cabochon '04	♟♟♟6
○ Franciacorta Brut Cabochon '03	♟♟♟6
○ Franciacorta Brut Cabochon '01	♟♟♟6
○ Franciacorta Brut Cabochon '99	♟♟♟7
○ Franciacorta Satèn	♟♟♟5
○ Franciacorta Satèn	♟♟♟5

Mosnel

FRAZ. CAMIGNONE
C.DA BARBOGLIO, 14
25050 PASSIRANO [BS]
TEL. +39 030653117
www.mosnel.com

CELLAR SALES
PRE-BOOKED VISITS
RESTAURANT SERVICE
ANNUAL PRODUCTION 250,000 bottles
HECTARES UNDER VINE 40.00
VITICULTURE METHOD Certified Organic

Mosnel is a historic Camignone property: a perfectly restored sixteenth-century village, with adjoining villa, open to visitors and events. The winery complex, which houses the modern cellars, is at the center of 40 hectares of a single body of organically cultivated vineyards. Giulio and Lucia Barzanò, the fifth generation of the family to manage these lands, work with the same passion and commitment as their mother, Emanuela Barboglio, a pioneer in Franciacorta. The Mosnel range is truly excellent. If last year it was the Pas Dosé that most impressed, this year it was a lovely 2015 interpretation of their Satèn that stood out, thus affirming the producer's already-established stylistic maturity. This cuvée pours a lovely, brilliant straw-yellow color tinted green. On the nose it's intense, with lovely notes of fresh herbs, white peach and lime, while on the palate it comes through creamy, alluring, but not without mineral sensations and a certain complexity. Their sapid and crisp Extra Brut EBB '14 also performed at a high level, though their entire selection is notable.

○ Franciacorta Satèn '15	♟♟♟6
○ Franciacorta Extra Brut EBB '14	♟♟7
○ Curtefranca Bianco Campolarga '18	♟♟3
○ Franciacorta Brut	♟♟5
⊙ Franciacorta Brut Rosé	♟♟5
○ Franciacorta Nature Bio	♟♟4
⊙ Franciacorta Pas Dosé	♟♟5
⊙ Franciacorta Pas Dosè Parosé '14	♟♟7
○ Franciacorta Extra Brut EBB '09	♟♟♟5
○ Franciacorta Pas Dosé QdE Ris. '04	♟♟♟8
○ Franciacorta Pas Dosé Ris. '08	♟♟♟5
○ Franciacorta Satèn '05	♟♟♟5
⊙ Franciacorta Pas Dosè Parosé '12	♟♟7

★★Nino Negri

VIA GHIBELLINI
23030 CHIURO [SO]
TEL. +39 0342485211
www.ninonegri.it

CELLAR SALES
PRE-BOOKED VISITS
RESTAURANT SERVICE
ANNUAL PRODUCTION 750,000 bottles
HECTARES UNDER VINE 160.00
SUSTAINABLE WINERY

Valtellina's story can be found in the cellars carved out of the rock at historic Nino Negri. The winery made the territory known first in Italy and then in the world. Inside Castello Quadrio the splendid current vintages prove just how far this incredible district has come. What's there to say about a Sforzato 5 Stelle that's been recognized by more than 20 editions of Italian Wines? With the 2016 it declares itself 'glocal'. That is, it's a territorial wine but also capable of international reach. It's traditional yet modern, marked by pleasant fruit. On the palate it exhibits great finesse and harmony, close-knit but without excesses, with elegant tannins and a long finish. Their Sassella Le Tense '16 is an homage to Nebbiolo delle Alpi, with its sensations of red fruits, tobacco and medicinal herbs. On the palate it's extraordinary for its finesse, before giving way to a long finish. Mature fruit, pepper and licorice feature in their Sforzato C. Negri '16, a generous wine, long and full of character, that exhibits surprising acidity for the typology.

● Valtellina Sfursat 5 Stelle '16	▼▼▼ 8
● Valtellina Sfursat Carlo Negri '16	▼▼ 6
● Valtellina Sup. Sassella Le Tense '16	▼▼ 5
● Valtellina Sup. Vign. Fracia '16	▼▼ 6
● Valtellina Sup. Grumello Sassorosso '16	▼▼ 5
● Valtellina Sup. Inferno Carlo Negri '16	▼▼ 5
● Valtellina Sup. Mazer '16	▼▼ 5
● Valtellina Sfursat 5 Stelle '15	♀♀♀ 8
● Valtellina Sfursat 5 Stelle '13	♀♀♀ 8
● Valtellina Sfursat 5 Stelle '11	♀♀♀ 8
● Valtellina Sfursat 5 Stelle '10	♀♀♀ 7
● Valtellina Sfursat 5 Stelle '09	♀♀♀ 7
● Valtellina Sfursat Carlo Negri '15	♀♀♀ 6
● Valtellina Sfursat Carlo Negri '11	♀♀♀ 8

Noventa

LOC. MATTINA
VIA MERANO, 28
25080 BOTTICINO [BS]
TEL. +39 0302691500
www.noventabotticino.it

CELLAR SALES
PRE-BOOKED VISITS
ANNUAL PRODUCTION 45,000 bottles
HECTARES UNDER VINE 11.00
VITICULTURE METHOD Certified Organic

This beautiful company, internationally recognized as a face of Botticino DOC, continues to grow without setbacks. For over 40 years, Pierangelo Noventa, his daughter Alessandra and the rest of the family have been passionately working their now organically run vineyards. The plots have a panoramic position 450 meters above sea level and with perfect exposure. The Noventa family's range of red wines from the most recent vintages, in which excessive maturation has been abandoned, shows truly remarkable elegance and finesse. The 2017 version of their Gobbio was also up to our expectations. It's a firmly-structured, powerful red made with grapes from the vineyard of the same name, a veritable estate cru wine that pours a lovely garnet ruby. On the nose it proves complex and enticing in its aromas of cocoa powder, berries and spicy nuances. On the palate it comes through rich and deep, delivering healthy, fruity flesh and burnished tannins. The Pià della Tesa '17 is spicy and very well balanced, while their rosé Aura '18, made with Schiava Gentile, also proves notable.

● Botticino Gobbio '17	▼▼▼ 5
● Botticino Colle degli Ulivi '17	▼▼ 2*
● Botticino Pià della Tesa '17	▼▼ 3
⊙ L'Aura Schiava '18	▼▼ 3
● Botticino Gobbio '16	♀♀♀ 5
● Botticino Colle degli Ulivi '16	♀♀ 2*
● Botticino Gobbio '15	♀♀ 5
● Botticino Pià de la Tesa '15	♀♀ 3
● Botticino Pià de la Tesa '12	♀♀ 3
● Botticino Pià della Tesa '16	♀♀ 3
● Botticino V. del Gobbio '11	♀♀ 5
● Botticino V. del Gobbio '10	♀♀ 5
● Botticino V. del Gobbio 50 '12	♀♀ 5

Oltrenero

LOC. BOSCO
27049 ZENEVREDO [PV]
TEL. +39 0385245326
www.ilbosco.com

CELLAR SALES
PRE-BOOKED VISITS
ANNUAL PRODUCTION 1,000,000 bottles
HECTARES UNDER VINE 152.00

The Zonin Group's estate is undergoing organizational restructuring and has, rather suddenly, replaced skilled director Piernicola Olmo. Olmo helped the winery achieve excellent results in recent years, in particular with the Metodo Classico which we awarded twice in different interpretations and that is destined to improve, taking the range to the highest possible level. While waiting for new developments we had the pleasure tasting a high profile range that focused on Oltrepò's Pinot Nero and its high potential for refreshing, vibrant character. The Nature '14 features fine bead, close-focused aromas of lime with tropical hints. It's a lively, crisp, sapid wine. The non-vintage Brut is characterized by hints of very ripe tropical fruit, with a presence of residual sugars that's quite evident. The Cruasé pours a radiant rose color, anticipating clear hints of red wild berries and citrus peel. On the palate it too plays on soft, sweetish tones.

○ OP Pinot Nero Nature M. Cl Oltrenero '14	♀♀ 6
○ OP Pinot Nero Brut M. Cl. Oltrenero	♀♀ 5
⊙ OP Cruasé Oltrenero	♀ 5
○ OP Pinot Nero Nature M. Cl Oltrenero '13	♀♀♀ 6
● OP Bonarda '13	♀♀ 2*
● OP Bonarda Vivace '15	♀♀ 2*
● OP Bonarda Vivace '14	♀♀ 2*
○ OP Pinot Nero Nature Oltrenero '10	♀♀ 6

Pasini San Giovanni

FRAZ. RAFFA
VIA VIDELLE, 2
25080 PUEGNAGO SUL GARDA [BS]
TEL. +39 0365651419
www.pasinisangiovanni.it

CELLAR SALES
PRE-BOOKED VISITS
RESTAURANT SERVICE
ANNUAL PRODUCTION 300,000 bottles
HECTARES UNDER VINE 36.00
SUSTAINABLE WINERY

Cousins Luca, Sara, Laura and Paolo Pasini have been running the family winery for over twenty years. Founded by Andrea Pasini in 1958, it embraces both Lugana and Valtenesi. They work passionately, with the drive to do more than produce good wines: for years they have also focused on environmental protection and sustainability. Their wines were among the first in the area to be certified organic and the core of the winery functions autonomously in terms of energy. While waiting for the release of their Buso Caldo, their Lugana estate cru, we tasted an excellent Valtènesi Arzane '15, a premium Groppello that pours a lovely, brilliant ruby red. On the nose it proves subtle and fresh in its fragrances of small red and black berries, aromatic herbs and a slight almond touch. On the palate it exhibits a lean body, subtle tannins, nice overall integrity and a long finish of fruit. The Lugana Bio '18 is fruity and fresh, with nice acidic vigor. Their Chiaretto '18 is highly valid, as is their Extra Brut 100%, made with Groppello vinified off the skins.

○ 100% Extra Brut M. Cl.	♀♀ 4
○ Lugana Bio '18	♀♀ 2*
● Valtènesi Arzane '15	♀♀ 3
⊙ Valtènesi Chiaretto Rosagreen '18	♀♀ 3
● Valtènesi Il Groppello '17	♀♀ 3
⊙ Ceppo 326 Brut Rosé M. Cl.	♀ 4
○ Lugana '17	♀♀ 2*
○ Lugana Buso Caldo '17	♀♀ 3
○ Lugana Il Lugana '16	♀♀ 3
● Valtènesi '16	♀♀ 2*
● Valtènesi Arzane '14	♀♀ 3
⊙ Valtènesi Chiaretto '16	♀♀ 2*
⊙ Valtènesi Il Chiaretto '16	♀♀ 3

Perla del Garda

VIA FENIL VECCHIO, 9
25017 LONATO [BS]
TEL. +39 0309103109
www.perladelgarda.it

CELLAR SALES
PRE-BOOKED VISITS
ANNUAL PRODUCTION 120,000 bottles
HECTARES UNDER VINE 30.00
VITICULTURE METHOD Certified Organic
SUSTAINABLE WINERY

The Prandini siblings, Giovanna and Ettore, have been working hard since 2000 and it's paid off: in 2006 they began vinifying grapes from 30 hectares of vineyards on the family estate. Located on the morainic hills of lower Garda, the plots are mainly dedicated to the Turbiana, and therefore the Lugana DOC. The moderny equipped winery is very committed to a certified path of sustainability and low environmental impact. Giovanna is also president of the Strada del vino e dei Sapori del Garda. The Lugana Madonna della Scoperta is their flagship wine. Made with the oldest vines (more than 20 years), it's fermented in steel but aged at length in large barrels before further maturation in fiberglass. The 2017 is in great form, pouring a brilliant color, and offering up focused, complex aromas of white fruit, aromatic herbs and flowery sensations accompanied by a delicate vegetal stroke. On the palate it proves fresh, sapid and crisp in its fruit. The Lugana Perla Bio '18 is characterized by clear, focused fruit and nice vigor.

○ Lugana Sup. Madonna della Scoperta '17	♟♟♟ 4*
● Garda Merlot Leonatus '15	♟♟ 4
○ Lugana Madreperla '16	♟♟ 4
○ Lugana Perla Bio '18	♟♟ 2*
○ Lugana Perla '18	♟ 3
○ Lugana Bio '16	♟♟ 2*
○ Lugana Brut Nature M. Cl. '11	♟♟ 7
○ Lugana Perla '17	♟♟ 3
○ Lugana Perla '16	♟♟ 3
○ Lugana Perla '15	♟♟ 3
○ Lugana Perla '13	♟♟ 3
○ Lugana Sup. Madonna della Scoperta '13	♟♟ 4
○ Lugana V. T. '13	♟♟ 4

Andrea Picchioni

FRAZ. CAMPONOCE, 4
27044 CANNETO PAVESE [PV]
TEL. +39 0385262139
www.picchioniandrea.it

CELLAR SALES
PRE-BOOKED VISITS
ACCOMMODATION
ANNUAL PRODUCTION 70,000 bottles
HECTARES UNDER VINE 10.00
VITICULTURE METHOD Certified Organic
SUSTAINABLE WINERY

At 52, Andrea Picchioni can look back with satisfaction on his work so far. Over 30 years ago, while still young, he founded the winery that he built from the ground up and now runs with the stubbornness of those born to make wine. It's been forged on the impervious ridge of Val Solinga, where once-abandoned vineyards have allowed him to create wines with an increasingly assertive character. We are certain that the recent death of his father, an unconditional supporter, will not alter Andrea's approach. It's with pleasure that we finally award the Riva Bianca, the wine dearest to Picchioni's heart, a Tre Bicchieri. The 2016 is a dense Buttafuoco, potent yet elegant, with fruit perfectly expressed both on the nose and on the palate, where it's precise in its tannins and destined to improve for years. Their fragrant, juicy, enticing Rosso d'Asia '16 is no less good. The Da Cima A Fondo '17, a blend of Croatina and Uva Rara that undergoes second fermentation in the bottle, is as rustic as it is delectable. And what a Pinot Nero!

● OP Buttafuoco Bricco Riva Bianca '16	♟♟♟ 4*
● Da Cima a Fondo '17	♟♟ 3*
● Rosso d'Asia '16	♟♟ 4
● Arfena Pinot Nero '17	♟♟ 4
● OP Bonarda Vivace Ipazia '18	♟♟ 2*
● OP Buttafuoco Cerasa '18	♟♟ 3
● Arfena Pinot Nero '15	♟♟♟ 4*
● Arfena Pinot Nero '16	♟♟ 4
● Da Cima a Fondo '16	♟♟ 3*
● OP Bonarda Vivace Ipazia '17	♟♟ 2*
● OP Buttafuoco Bricco Riva Bianca '15	♟♟ 4
● OP Buttafuoco Bricco Riva Bianca '13	♟♟ 4
● OP Buttafuoco Cerasa '17	♟♟ 3
● Rosso d'Asia '15	♟♟ 4
● Rosso d'Asia '13	♟♟ 4

Prime Alture

VIA MADONNA, 109
27045 CASTEGGIO [PV]
TEL. +39 038383214
www.primealture.it

CELLAR SALES
PRE-BOOKED VISITS
ACCOMMODATION AND RESTAURANT SERVICE
ANNUAL PRODUCTION 40,000 bottles
HECTARES UNDER VINE 8.00

Roberto Lechiancole has created a
beautiful resort in the Casteggio hills
complete with a tasting area, panoramic
terrace, six themed rooms and a salt
water pool. Our interest is primarily wines,
however, so we are pleased to say that
these have shown significant improvement
in quality between the first tastings and
now, attributable to a small but functional
cellar and the care taken during the
strictly by-hand harvest into baskets.
Sopra Riva '18 is a crisp white made with
Moscato Bianco and Chardonnay. On the
nose, lovely fragrances of citrus peel and
tropical fruit give way to wild flowers. The
Io Per Te is a well-crafted and highly
pleasant Brut made exclusively with Pinot
Nero grapes. It's creamy in its bead,
redolent of small red berries with tropical
hints, and mineral on the palate. Their
Monsieur '16 is an interesting Pinot Nero
with clear, flowery nuances. The Merlot
L'Altra Metà del Cuore '16 is a varietal
and pleasant wine, as is the early-drinking
Pinot Nero Bordo Bosco '18.

○ OP Pinot Nero Brut M. Cl. Io per Te	♟♟ 6
● Pinot Noir Monsieur '16	♟♟ 5
○ Sopra Riva '18	♟♟ 3
● L'Altra Metà del Cuore '16	♟ 5
● Pinot Noir Bordo Bosco '18	♟ 4
○ Il Bianco 60&40 '17	♟♟ 4
● Merlot L'Altra Metà del Cuore '12	♟♟ 3
● Pinot Noir Centopercento '15	♟♟ 5
● Pinot Noir Centopercento '14	♟♟ 5
● Pinot Noir Centopercento '13	♟♟ 5
● Pinot Noir Centopercento '12	♟♟ 4

Quadra

VIA SANT'EUSEBIO, 1
25033 COLOGNE [BS]
TEL. +39 0307157314
www.quadrafranciacorta.it

CELLAR SALES
PRE-BOOKED VISITS
RESTAURANT SERVICE
ANNUAL PRODUCTION 170,000 bottles
HECTARES UNDER VINE 32.00

In 2003, entrepreneur Ugo Ghezzi
established this Franciacorta winery with
the support and passion of his children
Cristina and Marco. In 2008, Mario Falcetti,
enologist and researcher, became a partner
and took over management. Today Quadra
boasts 32 hectares of organic vineyards.
The cuvées place great importance on
Pinot Bianco, for which three strongly
complementary areas were identified, and
to Pinot Nero, which was planted in very
suitable hillside plots. The Brut QBlack
stood out during our final tastings for its
lovely balance and a complexity that
emerges both on the nose and on the
palate. It's a classic Chardonnay cuvée with
14% Pinot Nero and a splash of Pinot
Bianco. 30 months of aging before
disgorgement makes for a complex wine,
redolent of fruit, yeast, citrus and mineral
strokes. On the palate it's generous, crisp,
caressing and deep. Their entire selection,
however, is excellent.

○ Franciacorta Brut QBlack	♟♟ 5
⊙ Franciacorta Brut QRosé	♟♟ 5
○ Franciacorta QSatèn '14	♟♟ 5
○ Franciacorta Dosaggio Zero EretiQ '11	♟♟ 6
○ Franciacorta Dosaggio Zero EretiQ '10	♟♟ 6
○ Franciacorta Dosaggio Zero EretiQ '10	♟♟ 6
○ Franciacorta Dosaggio Zero QZero '11	♟♟ 5
○ Franciacorta Dosaggio Zero QZero '10	♟♟ 5
○ Franciacorta Extra Brut Cuvée 55 '10	♟♟ 5
○ Franciacorta Extra Brut Quvée 58 Ris. '11	♟♟ 5
○ Franciacorta QSatèn '12	♟♟ 5
○ Franciacorta QSatèn '11	♟♟ 5
○ Franciacorta QSatèn '10	♟♟ 5
○ Franciacorta Quvée 46 '09	♟♟ 5
○ Franciacorta Satèn QSatèn '13	♟♟ 5

Francesco Quaquarini

LOC. MONTEVENEROSO
VIA CASA ZAMBIANCHI, 26
27044 CANNETO PAVESE [PV]
TEL. +39 038560152
www.quaquarinifrancesco.it

CELLAR SALES
PRE-BOOKED VISITS
ANNUAL PRODUCTION 650,000 bottles
HECTARES UNDER VINE 60.00
VITICULTURE METHOD Certified Organic

Francesco Quaquarini and his children
Umberto and Maria Teresa run this classic,
family-owned Oltrepò winery. It offers
numerous selections of the territory's
traditional wines and pays close attention
to value for money (average prices for very
good level wines). The wines fall just short
of the absolute excellence that they are
capable of given the quality of the
organically managed land, the winery's
structures and equipment, and the great
skills of enologist Umberto. The Selezione
Unica FQ '18 is a red with nice structure,
redolent of black wild berries, forest
undergrowth and aromatic herbs. On the
palate, delicate residual sugars render it
quaffable and fragrant. Ripe fruit, jammy
hints and California plums rise up off their
Vigna Pregana '15, a muscular and
well-balanced Buttafuoco Storico. Their
always pleasant Sangue di Giuda '18 offers
up aromas of raspberries and wild
strawberries.

● OP Buttafuoco Storico V. Pregana '15	♟♟♟ 6
● OP Sangue di Giuda '18	♟♟ 2*
● Selezione Unica FQ '18	♟♟ 3
● OP Bonarda Riva di Sass '18	♟ 3
○ OP Pinot Nero Brut Classese '12	♟ 4
● OP Bonarda Riva di Sass '17	♟♟ 3
● OP Buttafuoco Storico V. Pregana '13	♟♟ 6
● OP Pinot Nero Blau '14	♟♟ 3
○ OP Riesling '16	♟♟ 2*
● OP Sangue di Giuda '17	♟♟ 2*
● OP Sangue di Giuda '16	♟♟ 2*
● OP Sangue di Giuda '15	♟♟ 2*

★Aldo Rainoldi

FRAZ. CASACCE
VIA STELVIO, 128
23030 CHIURO [SO]
TEL. +39 0342482225
www.rainoldi.com

CELLAR SALES
PRE-BOOKED VISITS
ANNUAL PRODUCTION 180,000 bottles
HECTARES UNDER VINE 9.60

Aldo Rainoldi forges ahead, and since 2018
he has also presided over the Consorzio
Vini Valtellina. Active since 1925, Rainoldi is
one of the territory's most well-established
wineries and has a valuable park of
vineyards, including some with the best
exposures in the area, which have been
acquired over time. The 2020 edition of
Italian Wines is the year of Grumello. The
Grumello Riserva '13 is truly special. It
starts intense, complex, with an explosion
of red berries in concert with spicy notes.
On the palate it's close-knit, juicy, with a
sapid finish — all signs point to great
future prospects. Their Sassella Riserva '15
is excellent, with notes of quinine and
tobacco anticipating a fruity raciness
adorned by nuances of rhubarb. In the
mouth it comes through full and
harmonious before giving way to a long,
lingering finish. Herbs and dried flowers
together with brandied fruit and quinine
mark their elegant Sforzato Cà Rizzieri '16.
On the palate it proves muscular, with
subtle, pleasant pulp and a lengthy finish.

● Valtellina Sup. Grumello Ris. '13	♟♟♟ 6
● Valtellina Sfursat Ca' Rizzieri '16	♟♟ 6
● Valtellina Sup. Sassella Ris. '15	♟♟ 5
○ Valtellina Sup.Sassella V. degli Apostoli '13	♟♟ 3
● Valtellina Sfursat Fruttaio Ca' Rizzieri '15	♟♟♟ 6
● Valtellina Sfursat Fruttaio Ca' Rizzieri '11	♟♟♟ 6
● Valtellina Sfursat Fruttaio Ca' Rizzieri '10	♟♟♟ 6
● Valtellina Sfursat Fruttaio Ca' Rizzieri '09	♟♟♟ 6
● Valtellina Sup. Sassella Ris. '13	♟♟♟ 5
● Valtellina Sup. Sassella Ris. '12	♟♟♟ 5

Ricci Curbastro

VIA ADRO, 37
25031 CAPRIOLO [BS]
TEL. +39 030736094
www.riccicurbastro.it

CELLAR SALES
PRE-BOOKED VISITS
ACCOMMODATION
ANNUAL PRODUCTION 200,000 bottles
HECTARES UNDER VINE 27.00
SUSTAINABLE WINERY

Many years ago, Riccardo Ricci Curbastro took over the estate founded by his father Gualberto. Gradually he has brought it to a position of importance in Franciacorta. An agronomist, Riccardo has constantly modernized and added to the winery, while also bringing the style of its wines and Franciacorta ever more up-to-date. Today is his son Gualberto Jr. manages national and international sales and the family's Romagna estate, the Rontana. For years they've been debating stylistic interpretations of Satèn (Blanc de Blancs with less pressure in the bottle) in Franciacorta. We're really fond of this producer, which emphasizes softness, stylistic cleanness and freshness. We find these qualities punctually in their Satèn '15. It's sapid, elegant, rich in clear, focused aromas of golden delicious apples and white peach, with delicate citrusy nuances and hints of aromatic herbs that follow through coherently on the palate. In the mouth it proves succulent and soft, but endowed with a nice acidic vigor that accompanies it through a long finish.

○ Franciacorta Satèn '15	▼▼▼ 5
○ Franciacorta Extra Brut Museum Release '08	▼▼ 6
○ Brolo dei Passoni Passito '12	▼▼ 4
○ Franciacorta Brut	▼▼ 4
⊙ Franciacorta Rosé	▼▼ 5
● Pinot Nero '11	▼▼ 4
○ Sebino Pinot Bianco '18	▼▼ 2*
○ Curtefranca Bianco '18	▼ 2
● Curtefranca Rosso '16	▼ 2
○ Franciacorta Demi Sec	▼ 4
○ Franciacorta Brut Museum Release '07	♀♀♀ 6
○ Franciacorta Dosaggio Zero Gualberto '06	♀♀♀ 6
○ Franciacorta Extra Brut '12	♀♀♀ 5
○ Franciacorta Satèn '14	♀♀♀ 5

Ronco Calino

LOC. QUATTRO CAMINI
FRAZ. TORBIATO
VIA FENICE, 45
25030 ADRO [BS]
TEL. +39 0307451073
www.roncocalino.it

CELLAR SALES
PRE-BOOKED VISITS
ANNUAL PRODUCTION 70,000 bottles
HECTARES UNDER VINE 13.00
VITICULTURE METHOD Certified Organic
SUSTAINABLE WINERY

In 1996, Paolo Radici bought the estate of pianist Arturo Benedetti Michelangeli, and entrusted it to the passionate care of his wife Laura. The highly-regarded winery has ten hectares of vineyards in a spectacular morainic amphitheater. It benefits from Leonardo Valenti's enological advice with the assistance of agronomist Pierluigi Donna. A range of Franciacortas and excellent territorial wines are produced in the beautiful, well-equipped underground cellar. This year their Brut Rosé Radijan proves to be among the best in the appellation. It's a cuvée of Pinot Nero that ages for more than three years on the lees. It has extremely low dosage and pours a truly enticing, pale rose color. On the nose and on the palate it won't disappoint, with a complex, focused bouquet playing on floral hints and wild berries accompanied by citrusy notes. On the palate it's firm and assertive, as expected, caressing in its sparkle, sapid and deep. The rest of their selection also performed excellently.

⊙ Franciacorta Brut Rosé Radijan	▼▼ 5
○ Curtefranca Bianco Leànt '18	▼▼ 3
● Curtefranca Rosso Ponènt '16	▼▼ 4
○ Franciacorta Brut '12	▼▼ 5
○ Franciacorta Brut	▼▼ 5
○ Franciacorta Satèn	▼▼ 5
○ Franciacorta Brut Nature '15	▼ 5
○ Curtefranca Bianco Leànt '17	♀♀ 3
● Curtefranca Rosso Ponènt '15	♀♀ 4
○ Franciacorta Brut '11	♀♀ 5
○ Franciacorta Brut '10	♀♀ 5
○ Franciacorta Brut Nature '12	♀♀ 5
○ Franciacorta Brut Nature '11	♀♀ 5
○ Franciacorta Extra Brut Centoventi Ris. '07	♀♀ 8
● L'Arturo Pinot Nero '15	♀♀ 5

Rossetti & Scrivani

VIA COSTAIOLA, 23
27054 MONTEBELLO DELLA BATTAGLIA [PV]
TEL. +39 038383169
www.rossettiescrivani.it

ANNUAL PRODUCTION 100,000 bottles
HECTARES UNDER VINE 10.00

A few years ago, the Rossetti and Scrivani families inaugurated the winery that bears their name and is exclusively dedicated to the production of sparkling Metodo Classico based on Pinot Nero. Year after year, the hard work of enologist Michele Rossetti, brother Fabio, and cousin Simona Scrivani, is showing increasingly interesting results. It follows a period of some difficulty due mainly to corporate restructuring and the pains associated with separating from the 'mother' company, La Costaiola, on the hills above Casteggio. The signature style is increasingly clean, assertive and impactful. And this year we tasted their best Nature yet, a wine that handily landed a place in our finals thanks in part to close-focused aromas of small fruits and medicinal herbs. On the palate it exhibits fine, creamy bead, with a linear vigor that energetically accompanies it through its long, open finish. The Blanc de Noir opts more for aromas of ripe tropical fruit, while the Rosé de Noir is redolent of small red fruits, with a delicate vegetal hint.

○ Brut Nature M. Cl.	♟♟ 4
○ Brut Blanc de Noir M. Cl.	♟♟ 4
○ Brut Rosé de Noir M. Cl.	♟ 4

San Cristoforo

FRAZ. VILLA D'ERBUSCO
VIA VILLANUOVA, 2
25030 ERBUSCO [BS]
TEL. +39 0307760482
www.sancristoforo.eu

CELLAR SALES
PRE-BOOKED VISITS
ANNUAL PRODUCTION 80,000 bottles
HECTARES UNDER VINE 10.00
SUSTAINABLE WINERY

In 1997 Bruno and Claudia Dotti took over a small winery. In little more than twenty years of passionate work they have increased the size of their vineyards to ten hectares and renovated the cellar, equipping it with the most up-to-date equipment. They keep their production small and intimate, like real 'récoltant', but the quality of San Cristoforo's cuvées is constantly growing. Their daughter Celeste now works beside them full time. Their Franciacorta Brut dei Dotti is probably the most captivating among the versions tried this year, earning itself a place in our final tastings. It's the epitome of style, impressing for its cleanness and freshness, for the elegance of its fruity flavors, both aromatically and on the palate, where it's fresh and creamy in its prickle, succulent and sapid. The Pas Dosé '14 is also excellent in its subtle aromas of white fruit and citron, qualities that it shares with the softer Brut of the same vintage.

○ Franciacorta Brut	♟♟ 4
○ Franciacorta Brut '14	♟♟ 6
○ Franciacorta Pas Dosé '14	♟♟ 6
○ Franciacorta Brut '13	♟♟ 6
○ Franciacorta Brut '11	♟♟ 6
○ Franciacorta Dosaggio Zero '11	♟♟ 6
○ Franciacorta Dosaggio Zero Celeste '08	♟♟ 8
○ Franciacorta Pas Dosé '13	♟♟ 6
○ Franciacorta Pas Dosé '12	♟♟ 6
○ Franciacorta Pas Dosé '10	♟♟ 6
○ Franciacorta Pas Dosé '09	♟♟ 6
○ Franciacorta Pas Dosé Celeste '10	♟♟ 8
○ Franciacorta Pas Dosé Celeste '09	♟♟ 8

Scuropasso

FRAZ. SCORZOLETTA, 40/42
27043 PIETRA DE' GIORGI [PV]
TEL. +39 038585143
www.scuropasso.it

CELLAR SALES
PRE-BOOKED VISITS
ANNUAL PRODUCTION 200,000 bottles
HECTARES UNDER VINE 15.00

Fabio Marazzi's winery, run with the help of his young daughter Flavia, just gets better and better. Fifteen hectares of vineyards are being converted to organic methods, the cellar is totally powered by renewable energy, and they have clear objectives. This is specially true regarding two types of wine: the territory's traditional red Buttafuoco (Fabio has recently joined the Club del Buttafuoco Storico) and Fabio's favorite as a great fan of sparkling wines, Pinot Nero-based Metodo Classico. The Roccapietra Zero '13 won us over and earned itself Tre Bicchieri for its unique, slightly evolved style, its aromas of cakes and ripe fruit, its integrity and substance, its creamy bubbles, and its extremely long, precise finish. The lively and robust Lunapiena '13, a wine recently admitted to the Buttafuoco Storico club, also performed well. It's also worth highlighting the compactness and ripe fruit of their Buttafuoco Scuropasso '16.

○ Roccapietra Pas Dosé M. Cl. '13	▼▼▼ 4*
● OP Buttafuoco Storico Lunapiena '13	▼▼ 3*
● OP Buttafuoco Scuropasso '16	▼▼ 3
⊙ OP Cruasé Roccapietra '13	▼▼ 4
○ Roccapietra Brut M. Cl. '12	▼ 4
○ Brut Roccapietra Zero '10	♀♀ 3
● OP Buttafuoco '15	♀♀ 4
● OP Buttafuoco Lunapiena '13	♀♀ 3
⊙ OP Cruasé '11	♀♀ 4
⊙ OP Cruasé Roccapietra '12	♀♀ 4
○ OP Pinot Nero Brut Roccapietra '10	♀♀ 4
○ Roccapietra Brut M. Cl. '11	♀♀ 4
○ Roccapietra Pas Dosé M. Cl. '12	♀♀ 4

Selva Capuzza

FRAZ. SAN MARTINO DELLA BATTAGLIA
LOC. SELVA CAPUZZA
25010 DESENZANO DEL GARDA [BS]
TEL. +39 0309910381
www.selvacapuzza.it

CELLAR SALES
PRE-BOOKED VISITS
ACCOMMODATION AND RESTAURANT SERVICE
ANNUAL PRODUCTION 300,000 bottles
HECTARES UNDER VINE 25.00
SUSTAINABLE WINERY

Luca Formentini's beautiful Selva Capuzza estate is south of Lake Garda nestled amid the Lugana, San Martino della Battaglia and Garda appellations. Its 50 hectares extend through woods, vineyards and olive groves in the morainic amphitheater. Luca manages the century-old estate with competence, passion, and great attention to the environment and sustainability. Selva Capuzza specializes in traditional wines and only uses grapes from its own vineyards. There is also an agritourism, a restaurant and catering facilities. Their Lugana Menasasso Riserva '15 is a wine of extraordinary finesse. It's the result of an attentive selection of their vineyards' grapes, harvested when slightly overripe, then fermented and aged for two years in steel (even if a small share mature in oak with frequent lees stirring). After another six months, the final blend goes in the bottle, where it continues to mature at length. Thanks to an excellent 2015, this version is already in outstanding shape, overwhelmingly taking home Tre Bicchieri. Ad meliora!

○ Lugana Menasasso Ris. '15	▼▼▼ 3*
○ Lugana San Vigilio '18	▼▼ 3
○ Lugana Selva '18	▼▼ 4
○ San Martino della Battaglia Campo del Soglio '18	▼▼ 4
⊙ Valtènesi Chiaretto San Donino '18	▼▼ 2*
● Garda Cl. Dunant '16	▼ 2
● Garda Cl. Dunant '15	♀♀ 2*
● Garda Cl. Groppello San Biagio '17	♀♀ 3
● Garda Cl. Groppello San Biagio '16	♀♀ 3
● Garda Cl. Sup. Rosso Madèr '13	♀♀ 3
○ Lugana Menasasso Ris. '13	♀♀ 3
○ Lugana San Vigilio '17	♀♀ 3
○ Lugana Selva '17	♀♀ 4
○ San Martino della Battaglia Campo del Soglio '17	♀♀ 4

Le Sincette

Loc. Picedo di Polpenazze del Garda
via Rosario, 44
25080 Polpenazze del Garda [BS]
Tel. +39 0365651471
www.lesincette.it

CELLAR SALES
PRE-BOOKED VISITS
ANNUAL PRODUCTION 30,000 bottles
HECTARES UNDER VINE 11.00
VITICULTURE METHOD Certified Biodynamic

A few years ago, successful entrepreneur Ruggero Brunori decided to produce wine according to his philosophy of natural systems with low environmental impact. Thanks to the valuable contribution of Andrea Salvetti, who runs it, this trend has become more and more established over the years. Currently, the roughly fourteen hectares of Cascina vineyards are cultivated according to the rules of biodynamics. The morainic hills overlooking Lake Garda contain a lot of clay, which imbue the wines with structure and freshness. It's well known that , when it comes to rosé, Valtenesi and Groppello are an excellent combination. Their Chiaretto '18, a classic field blend that features Groppello, testifies to the fact. It pours a lovely pale rose color, anticipating aromas of berries accompanied by herbs and Mediterranean scrub. On the palate it's sapid and succulent, exhibiting tension and length. The Ronco del Garda '17, made with Merlot and Marzemino, is excellent, as is the Groppello '18.

⊙ Valtenesi Chiaretto '18	♟♟ 2*
● Garda Cl. Groppello '18	♟♟ 2*
● Ronco del Garda '17	♟ 2
● Garda Cl. Groppello '14	♟♟ 2*
● Garda Cl. Groppello '13	♟♟ 2*
● Ronco del Garda '13	♟♟ 2*

Lo Sparviere

via Costa
25040 Monticelli Brusati [BS]
Tel. +39 030652382
www.losparviere.com

CELLAR SALES
PRE-BOOKED VISITS
ANNUAL PRODUCTION 120,000 bottles
HECTARES UNDER VINE 30.00

Ugo Gussalli Beretta heads the world's oldest industrial dynasty, which has been documented since 1526. He shares the great passion that his wife Monique and son Piero have for the land and wine. Starting in Franciacorta, the family built a group of estates that now embraces Tuscany's Castello di Radda in Chianti Classico, Abruzzo's Orlandi Contucci Ponno, Piedmont's ForteMasso in Monforte d'Alba, and Alto Adige's Steinhauserhof in Pochi di Salorno. Lo Sparviere covers 150 hectares, 30 of which are vineyards. Their Extra Brut '13 put in an excellent performance, opening with a complex bouquet of chestnut honey and spices, followed by delicate hints of yeast, and healthy, crisp fruit with notes of golden delicious apples and citrusy nuances. It's a profile that reemerges on the palate, where the wine unfolds harmonious and sapid, creamy in its sparkle and truly long in its sensations of fruit and spices. Their balanced and deep Dosaggio Zero Riserva '12 also performed at a high level.

○ Franciacorta Extra Brut '13	♟♟♟ 6
○ Franciacorta Dosaggio Zero Riserva '12	♟♟ 6
○ Franciacorta Brut '14	♟♟ 5
⊙ Franciacorta Brut Rosé Monique	♟ 5
○ Franciacorta Satèn	♟ 6
○ Franciacorta Brut '13	♟♟♟ 5
○ Franciacorta Brut '12	♟♟♟ 5
○ Franciacorta Dosaggio Zero Ris. '08	♟♟♟ 6
○ Franciacorta Extra Brut '09	♟♟♟ 5
○ Franciacorta Extra Brut '08	♟♟♟ 5
○ Franciacorta Extra Brut '07	♟♟♟ 5
○ Franciacorta Brut '11	♟♟ 5
○ Franciacorta Dosaggio Zero Ris. '09	♟♟ 6
○ Franciacorta Extra Brut '12	♟♟ 6

Torrevilla

VIA EMILIA, 4
27050 TORRAZZA COSTE [PV]
TEL. +39 038377003
www.torrevilla.it

CELLAR SALES
PRE-BOOKED VISITS
ANNUAL PRODUCTION 3,000,000 bottles
HECTARES UNDER VINE 650.00

This exemplary cooperative, chaired by
Massimo Barbieri, draws on its contributing
members' best plots for the production of a
range with a remarkable level of quality.
This success can be attributed to the
renewal projects started in 2008, 100 years
after the Cantina Sociale of Torrazza Coste
was founded. The works included updated
equipment, the start of a collaboration with
the University of Milan and the Riccagioia
Research Center, and serious and accurate
zoning work done with the support of four
meteorological survey stations. The Nature
Riserva 110 '14 is a classy sparkling wine,
redolent of aromatic herbs and small fruits,
full and rich on the palate, with fine bead
and a close-focused, mineral, persistent
finish. The two 2017 versions of their La
Genisia Bio wine also delivered. The still
Bonarda is ripe, well-calibrated, redolent of
blackberries, while the Barbera offers up
notes of cherry and black cherry. This latter
has vigor and intensity, a great drink. The
highly fruity and pleasant Bonarda '18 is
worth noting, as is their Riesling '18, a
sophisticated Renano.

○ OP Pinot Nero Brut Nature M. Cl. 110 Ris. '14	🍷🍷 5
● OP Barbera La Genisia '18	🍷🍷 2*
● OP Barbera La Genisia Bio '17	🍷🍷 2*
● OP Bonarda La Genisia Bio '17	🍷🍷 2*
○ OP Pinot Grigio La Genisia Ramato '18	🍷🍷 3
○ OP Riesling Sup. La Genisia '18	🍷🍷 3
⊙ OP Cruasé La Genisia	🍷 4
○ OP Pinot Nero Brut Nature M. Cl. La Genisia	🍷 5
● OP Bonarda Vivace La Genisia '16	🍷🍷 2*
○ OP Pinot Nero Brut Nature M. Cl. La Genisia '13	🍷🍷 5
○ OP Riesling Sup. La Genisia '17	🍷🍷 3

Pietro Torti

FRAZ. CASTELROTTO, 9
27047 MONTECALVO VERSIGGIA [PV]
TEL. +39 038599763
www.pietrotorti.it

CELLAR SALES
PRE-BOOKED VISITS
ACCOMMODATION
ANNUAL PRODUCTION 40,000 bottles
HECTARES UNDER VINE 18.00
VITICULTURE METHOD Certified Organic

As we said last year, the winery that Sandro
Torti, Pietro's son, has been running for
many years inevitably has its ups and
downs. This is largely due to the fact that
Sandro does practically everything by
himself, though in recent years his
daughter Chiara has begun to make her
own important contributions. Nevertheless,
wines of absolute quality, in rotation so to
speak, do emerge every year, always
characterized by strong personality that
expresses the vintage. This year their
Cruasé '13, a lovely, rose-colored Metodo
Classico, stood out. On the nose it proves
vibrant in its aromas of red fruits, while the
palate is juicy, fine in its bead and
persistent in length. The Campo Rivera '16
is a Barbera with ripe fruit, foremost
morello cherry, and spicy hints. The mouth
proves full and weighty. The Verzello '17 is
a still Bonarda characterized by nice, fruity
flesh — it's quite deceptive by virtue of
evident residual sugars.

● OP Barbera Campo Rivera '16	🍷🍷 4
● OP Bonarda Verzello '17	🍷🍷 2*
⊙ OP Cruasé '13	🍷🍷 4
● Castelrosso '15	🍷 4
● OP Pinot Nero Mobi '15	🍷 4
○ Fagù '16	🍷🍷 2*
● OP Barbera Campo Rivera '15	🍷🍷 4
● OP Barbera Campo Rivera '12	🍷🍷 4
● OP Bonarda Frizzante '17	🍷🍷 2*
● OP Bonarda Vivace '16	🍷🍷 2*
⊙ OP Cruasé '12	🍷🍷 4
○ OP Pinot Nero Brut M. Cl. Torti '13	🍷🍷 4
● Uva Rara '15	🍷🍷 3

Travaglino

LOC. TRAVAGLINO
27040 CALVIGNANO [PV]
TEL. +39 0383872222
www.travaglino.it

CELLAR SALES
PRE-BOOKED VISITS
ACCOMMODATION AND RESTAURANT SERVICE
ANNUAL PRODUCTION 200,000 bottles
HECTARES UNDER VINE 80.00

The Comi family's long-established Oltrepò Pavese winery boasts of land particularly suited to the cultivation of white varieties and Pinot Nero, for both sparkling and red wines. In the 1960s, and well ahead of his time, Vincenzo Comi had already identified the best soils and crus. His niece Cristina Cerri now leads the estate with the support of enologist Achille Bergami, and the quality of the wines continues to rise year after year. The Gran Cuvée is a Metodo Classico with substance, offering up notes melon and small wild berries. On the palate it's juicy, with fine bead and a pleasant, almondy finish. Campo di Fojada is the name of the historic cru where their Riesling Renano is cultivated. Today it's offered in two versions, the current vintage (redolent of flowers) and the reserve. The 2016 of this latter proves sapid and energetic, still fragrant of tropical fruit but already heading towards a more mineral evolution. Once again their Poggio della Buttinera '16, a Pinot Nero with notable personality, performed well.

○ OP Pinot Nero Brut M. Cl. Gran Cuvée	♟♟ 4
○ OP Riesling Campo della Fojada Ris. '16	♟♟ 3*
○ OP Pinot Nero Brut M. Cl. Monteceresimo Rosé '12	♟♟ 4
● OP Pinot Nero Pernero '18	♟♟ 3
● OP Pinot Nero Poggio della Buttinera '16	♟♟ 5
○ OP Riesling Campo della Fojada '18	♟♟ 3
● OP Pinot Nero Poggio della Buttinera '15	♟♟ 5
○ OP Riesling Campo della Fojada '17	♟♟ 3*
○ OP Riesling Campo della Fojada Ris. '15	♟♟ 3

★Uberti

LOC. SALEM
VIA E. FERMI, 2
25030 ERBUSCO [BS]
TEL. +39 0307267476
www.ubertivini.it

PRE-BOOKED VISITS
ANNUAL PRODUCTION 180,000 bottles
HECTARES UNDER VINE 26.00
VITICULTURE METHOD Certified Organic
SUSTAINABLE WINERY

In 1793, a certain Agostino Uberti became owner of a manor and surrounding vineyards it near Salem di Erbusco. 40 years ago, his descendent (also named Agostino) began a brilliant adventure in winemaking, specifically of Franciacorta. The excellent shape of the winery today can be attributed to the commitment and talent of Agostino, steadily assisted by his wife Eleonora. At their side for a few years now are daughters, enologist Silvia, and Francesca, who oversees administration. We don't always manage to decipher Uberti's stylistic direction, but this year we appreciated the Magnificentia, their 2015 Satèn. It's opens with a floral bouquet adorned by white-fleshed fruit and meadow herbs. On the palate it enters full, with nice fruit, coming through juicy and fairly long. Their Riserva Sublimis '11 delivered for its lovely and evolved complexity, as did their Dequinque, a blend of 10 vintages that's only available in magnums and that highlight's the winery's unique style.

○ Franciacorta Satèn Magnificentia '15	♟♟ 6
○ Curtefranca Bianco Maria Medici '16	♟♟ 4
○ Franciacorta Brut Francesco I	♟♟ 5
○ Franciacorta Dosaggio Zero Sublimis Ris. '11	♟♟ 7
○ Franciacorta Extra Brut Dequinque Magnum	♟♟ 8
○ Franciacorta Extra Brut Francesco I	♟♟ 5
○ Franciacorta Brut Rosé Francesco I	♟ 5
○ Franciacorta Extra Brut Quinque	♟ 8
○ Franciacorta Extra Brut Comarì del Salem '03	♟♟♟ 6
○ Franciacorta Extra Brut Comarì del Salem '02	♟♟♟ 6
○ Franciacorta Extra Brut Comarì del Salem '01	♟♟♟ 6

Vanzini

FRAZ. BARBALEONE, 7
27040 SAN DAMIANO AL COLLE [PV]
TEL. +39 038575019
www.vanzini-wine.com

CELLAR SALES
PRE-BOOKED VISITS
ANNUAL PRODUCTION 600,000 bottles
HECTARES UNDER VINE 27.00

The Vanzini brothers have always run the family winery with a respect for tradition and hard work. The range offers excellent value for money that is particularly appealing for those who love the Oltrepò Pavese's most typical wines that 'buscia' or 'frizza' (sparkle or fizz, in local dialect). Enologist Pierpaolo's sure hand during the second fermentation in autoclave serves as a guarantee both for the array of lively wines and for the sparkling Metodo Martinotti (made exclusively with the property's own Pinot Nero grapes). The Bonarda '18 performed quite well during our tastings. Aromas of blackcurrant and wild berries rise up off the nose. On the palate it's lively, healthy in its fruit and precise in its tannins, vibrant and quaffable all at once. For years now their two Martinotti Extra Drys have been an absolute guarantee, with the rosé earning our preference by virtue of its lovely, close-focused and harmonic fruit. Their spicy, elegant and balanced Barbaleone '15 put in a convincing performance as well, proving plucky yet supple on the palate.

● OP Bonarda Frizzante '18	♟♟ 2*
● OP Rosso Barbaleone '15	♟♟ 5
● OP Sangue di Giuda '18	♟♟ 3
○ Pinot Nero Extra Dry	♟♟ 3
⊙ Pinot Nero Extra Dry Rosé	♟♟ 3
● La Desiderata Barbera '18	♟ 2
○ Moscato Spumante Dolce	♟ 3
● OP Barbera La Desiderata '17	♟♟ 2*
● OP Bonarda '16	♟♟ 2*
● OP Sangue di Giuda '17	♟♟ 3
● OP Sangue di Giuda '16	♟♟ 3

Bruno Verdi

VIA VERGOMBERRA, 5
27044 CANNETO PAVESE [PV]
TEL. +39 038588023
www.brunoverdi.it

CELLAR SALES
PRE-BOOKED VISITS
ANNUAL PRODUCTION 90,000 bottles
HECTARES UNDER VINE 12.00

We truly admire winemaker Paolo Verdi. Passionate, talented and tenacious, he took on the weight of the winery when he was only twenty and led it step by step to become what is now: one of the territory's most skillful and highly acclaimed. This has been achieved by producing a vast array of every type (white, red, sparkling, still, dry, dessert, for holding) at a consistently high level and with instances of absolute excellence. He has never ceased trying to improve and has been benefiting for some years now from the support of his son Jacopo. No one knows better than Paolo Verdi how to make absolutely first-rate sparkling wines (Vergomberra '14: rich, full, creamy, redolent of thyme, small fruits, fine and persistent bead, traction), ageworthy reds (Cavariola '15: vibrant and deep in its notes of mint, chocolate and wild berries), as well as early-drinking reds. The delicious Buttafuoco '18 surprised for its juiciness and frank drinkability, while the Campo del Marrone '17, a Barbera, features notes of morello cherry and a captivating palate.

● OP Barbera Campo del Marrone '17	♟♟ 4
● OP Buttafuoco '18	♟♟ 2*
○ OP Pinot Nero M. Cl. Dosage Zero Vergomberra '14	♟♟ 5
● OP Rosso Cavariola Ris. '15	♟♟ 5
● OP Bonarda Frizzante Possessione di Vergomberra '18	♟♟ 2*
● OP Sangue di Giuda Frizzante Paradiso '18	♟♟ 2*
○ OP Dosage Zero Vergomberra '12	♟♟♟ 5
○ OP Pinot Nero Dosage Zéro M. Cl. Vergomberra '13	♟♟♟ 5
● OP Rosso Cavariola Ris. '10	♟♟♟ 5
● OP Rosso Cavariola Ris. '07	♟♟♟ 4

Vigne Olcru

Via Buca, 26
27047 Santa Maria della Versa [PV]
Tel. +39 0385799958
www.vigneolcru.com

PRE-BOOKED VISITS
ANNUAL PRODUCTION 190,000 bottles
HECTARES UNDER VINE 29.00
SUSTAINABLE WINERY

A great debut for the estate founded in 2013 by brothers Massimiliano and Matteo Brambilla with the construction of a futuristic structure on the steep ridges of the Alta Valle Versa. Its establishment coincided with the signing of an agreement with the agricultural department of the University of Milan focusing on a study coordinated by Professor Leonardo Valenti of numerous different Pinot Nero clones. The winery has now entered into its maturity, and the results are palpable. The Victoria '14 is a faintly hued, undosed rosé that landed a place in our finals thanks to close-focused aromas of red fruits and medicinal herbs. These give way to an airy, sapid, plucky palate rich in substance, full and long in its finish. Their Verve '13, a deep, vital and highly gratifying Extra Brut, also features sapidity and minerality, while we found the Coppiere Nero '16 interesting — it's a very spicy Pinot Nero with nice fruit that's sure to age well.

⊙ Victoria Pas Dosé M. Cl. Rosé '14	▼▼	7
● Coppiere Nero Pinot Nero '16	▼▼	4
○ Verve Extra Brut M. Cl. '13	▼▼	4
● Antico Tralcio '16	▼	4
● Enigma Nero Pinot Nero '18	▼	3
○ Virtus Pas Dosé M. Cl. '14	▼	4
● Enigma Nero Pinot Nero '17	♀♀	3
● OP Bonarda Buccia Rossa '15	♀♀	4
● OP Bonarda Buccia Rossa '16	♀♀	4
○ Virtus Brut M. Cl. '13	♀♀	4

Villa Crespia

Via Valli, 31
25030 Adro [BS]
Tel. +39 0307451051
www.villacrespia.it

PRE-BOOKED VISITS
ANNUAL PRODUCTION 360,000 bottles
HECTARES UNDER VINE 55.00
VITICULTURE METHOD Certified Organic
SUSTAINABLE WINERY

The Muratori family has created one of the most significant wineries of the appellation. Villa Crespia has its own estate of over 60 hectares within each of the territory's six districts, resulting in wines of unquestionable quality. A modern, underground cellar gives rise to a well-crafted selection that expresses the diverse facets of Franciacorta. Here cuvées are frequently non-dosed, vineyards are fermented separately and long maturation confers complexity. Their Riserva Millè '07 is a Blanc de Blancs made with Chardonnay cultivated in various vineyards. The base blend matures for 30 years in steel, on the fine lees, after which it's bottle fermented for some 130 months. The result is a fine Franciacorta of great finesse. Freshness and complexity come together with flowery and fruity notes, as well as more evolved sensations of yeast, hazelnut and vanilla. Their Rosé Extra Brut Brolese, the Millè '11 also performed at high levels, as did the rest of their selection.

○ Franciacorta Brut Millè Ris. '07	▼▼	5
○ Franciacorta Brut Millè '11	▼▼	5
○ Franciacorta Brut Novalia	▼▼	5
○ Franciacorta Brut Satèn Cesonato	▼▼	5
○ Franciacorta Extra Brut Rosé Brolese	▼▼	5
○ Franciacorta Dosaggio Zero Cisiolo	▼	5
○ Franciacorta Dosaggio Zero Numerozero	▼	5
○ Franciacorta Dosaggio Zero Francesco Iacono Ris. '04	♀♀♀	7
○ Franciacorta Brut Millè '10	♀♀	5
○ Franciacorta Dosaggio Zero Francesco Iacono Ris. '11	♀♀	7

Villa Franciacorta

FRAZ. VILLA
VIA VILLA, 12
25040 MONTICELLI BRUSATI [BS]
TEL. +39 030652329
www.villafranciacorta.it

PRE-BOOKED VISITS
ACCOMMODATION AND RESTAURANT SERVICE
ANNUAL PRODUCTION 300,000 bottles
HECTARES UNDER VINE 37.00

40 years ago, Alessandro Bianchi restored the sixteenth-century village of Villa, in Monticelli Brusati, turning it into a luxurious relais. The terraced vineyards on Monte della Madonna della Rosa have also been replanted. Today the estate covers 100 hectares, 40 of which are vineyards, boasts a totally underground cellar, and has one million bottles of wine resting before the rémuage. The winery is currently managed by Alessandra Bianchi and her husband Paolo Piziol. To celebrate 40 years of vintage Franciacorta production, Villa created the Emozione 40, a 2008 reserve of excellent quality. It's a blend dominated by Chardonnay with smaller shares of Pinot Nero and Bianco from more than 20 plots. It's vinified partially in steel and partially in oak, and matures for more than 100 months on the lees. The result is a rich, deep, complex and multi-layered wine that's also fresh and lively at the same time. Their Emozione '15 is also excellent, as is the rest of their rich selection.

○ Franciacorta Brut Emozione 40 Ris. '08	♥♥	5
○ Franciacorta Brut Cuvette '12	♥♥	5
○ Franciacorta Brut Emozione '15	♥♥	5
○ Franciacorta Mon Satèn '15	♥♥	5
○ Franciacorta Pas Dosé Diamant '13	♥♥	6
⊙ Franciacorta Brut Rosé Boké '15	♥	5
⊙ Franciacorta Brut Rosé Bokè Noir '15	♥	5
○ Franciacorta Brut Emozione '09	♥♥♥	5
⊙ Franciacorta Brut Rosé Boké '12	♥♥♥	5
○ Franciacorta Extra Brut '98	♥♥♥	4*
○ Franciacorta Brut Emozione '14	♥♥	5
○ Franciacorta Brut Emozione '13	♥♥	5
○ Franciacorta Extra Brut Extra Blu '13	♥♥	6
○ Franciacorta Mon Satèn '14	♥♥	5

Chiara Ziliani

VIA FRANCIACORTA, 7
25050 PROVAGLIO D'ISEO [BS]
TEL. +39 030981661
www.cantinachiaraziliani.it

PRE-BOOKED VISITS
ANNUAL PRODUCTION 400,000 bottles
HECTARES UNDER VINE 26.00
SUSTAINABLE WINERY

Chiara Ziliani's beautiful estate sits on top of a hill in Provaglio, providing an expansive view over its 22 hectares. Chiara uses the raw material from seventeen of these to fashion more than 20 different Franciacorta and territorial wines, which are divided into five lines. The vineyards, facing south and south-east at an elevation of 250 meters, are cultivated with low environmental impact and high-density planting (over 7000 vines per hectare). The range is of excellent quality. This year's tastings saw their Brut Noir '15, from the Ziliani C line, reach our final round of tasting. It's made with estate-grown Pinot Nero that matures for more than three years on the lees before disgorgement. It pours a lovely, brilliant straw-yellow gold color, with intensely fruity aromas arriving up on the nose, enlivened by spicy notes and hints of white pepper. On the palate it's sapid, taut and mineral, with nice length. As is tradition, they also submitted two excellent Satèn interpretations from the same line.

○ Franciacorta Brut Noir Ziliani C '15	♥♥	4
○ Franciacorta Brut Conte di Provaglio	♥♥	3
⊙ Franciacorta Brut Rosé Conte di Provaglio	♥♥	3
⊙ Franciacorta Brut Rosé Ziliani C '14	♥♥	5
○ Franciacorta Brut Satèn Conte di Provaglio	♥♥	3
○ Franciacorta Brut Satèn Ziliani C '15	♥♥	4
○ Franciacorta Brut Ziliani C	♥♥	3
○ Franciacorta Extra Brut Ziliani C '15	♥♥	4
○ Franciacorta Satèn Ziliani C	♥♥	3
○ Franciacorta Brut Gran Cuvée Italo Ziliani Ris. '12	♥♥	5
○ Franciacorta Brut Ziliani C '13	♥♥	4
○ Franciacorta Pas Dosé Ziliani C '13	♥♥	4
○ Franciacorta Satèn Maria Maddalena Cavalieri Ris. '12	♥♥	5

1701

P.zza Marconi, 6
25046 Cazzago San Martino [BS]
Tel. +39 0307750875
www.1701franciacorta.it

CELLAR SALES
PRE-BOOKED VISITS
ANNUAL PRODUCTION 60,000 bottles
HECTARES UNDER VINE 10.50
VITICULTURE METHOD Certified Biodynamic

○ Franciacorta Brut Rosé	♟♟ 6
○ Franciacorta Dosaggio Zero	♟♟ 7
○ Franciacorta Satèn	♟♟ 6

Elisabetta Abrami

via Vicinale delle Fosche
25050 Provaglio d'Iseo [BS]
Tel. +39 0306857185
www.vinielisabettaabrami.it

CELLAR SALES
ACCOMMODATION
ANNUAL PRODUCTION 60,000 bottles
HECTARES UNDER VINE 15.00
VITICULTURE METHOD Certified Organic

○ Franciacorta Brut '14	♟♟ 5
○ Franciacorta Extra Brut Blanc de Noirs Ris. '12	♟♟ 5
○ Franciacorta Pas Dosé '14	♟♟ 6

Annibale Alziati

loc. Scazzolino, 55
27040 Rovescala [PV]
Tel. +39 038575261
www.gaggiarone.it

CELLAR SALES
PRE-BOOKED VISITS
ANNUAL PRODUCTION 100,000 bottles
HECTARES UNDER VINE 19.00
VITICULTURE METHOD Certified Organic
SUSTAINABLE WINERY

● Gaggiarone Dintorni '16	♟♟ 4
● OP Bonarda Gaggiarone V. V. '14	♟♟ 4
● OP Bonarda Gaggiarone Ris. '08	♟ 4

Tenuta degli Angeli

fraz. Santo Stefano
via Fara, 2
24060 Carobbio degli Angeli [BG]
Tel. +39 035687130
www.tenutadegliangeli.it

CELLAR SALES
PRE-BOOKED VISITS
ANNUAL PRODUCTION 12,000 bottles
HECTARES UNDER VINE 2.00

○ Moscato Giallo Colle degli Angeli '18	♟♟ 6
● Valcalepio Moscato Passito di Carobbio '13	♟♟ 6
○ Oro degli Angeli Passito '15	♟ 5

Giovanni Avanzi

via Trevisago, 19
25080 Manerba del Garda [BS]
Tel. +39 0365551013
www.avanzi.net

CELLAR SALES
PRE-BOOKED VISITS
RESTAURANT SERVICE
ANNUAL PRODUCTION 600,000 bottles
HECTARES UNDER VINE 63.00

○ Garda Dorobianco '18	♟♟ 3
● Rosso Montecorno '16	♟♟ 5
○ Lugana '18	♟ 3
◐ Valtènesi Chiaretto Il Vino di una Notte '18	♟ 3

Balgera

c.so M. Quadrio, 26
23030 Chiuro [SO]
Tel. +39 0342482203
www.vinibalgera.it

CELLAR SALES
PRE-BOOKED VISITS
ANNUAL PRODUCTION 75,000 bottles

● Valtellina Sforzato '01	♟♟ 7
● Valt. Sup. Grumello Ris. '04	♟♟ 6
● Valt. Sup. Valgella Ca' Fracia '02	♟♟ 5
● Valtellina Sup. Valgella '03	♟♟ 5

Barbacarlo - Lino Maga

S.DA BRONESE, 3
27043 BRONI [PV]
TEL. +39 038551212
barbacarlodimaga@libero.it

CELLAR SALES
PRE-BOOKED VISITS
ANNUAL PRODUCTION 20,000 bottles
HECTARES UNDER VINE 12.00

● Barbacarlo '17	♟♟ 5

Barboglio De Gaioncelli

FRAZ. COLOMBARO
VIA NAZARIO SAURO
25040 CORTE FRANCA [BS]
TEL. +39 0309826831
www.barbogliodegaioncelli.it

CELLAR SALES
PRE-BOOKED VISITS
RESTAURANT SERVICE
ANNUAL PRODUCTION 90,000 bottles
HECTARES UNDER VINE 60.00

○ Franciacorta Brut	♟♟ 4
○ Franciacorta Brut '14	♟♟ 4
○ Franciacorta Extra Dry 1875	♟♟ 4

I Barisei

VIA BELLAVISTA, 1A
25030 ERBUSCO [BS]
TEL. +39 0307356069
www.ibarisei.it

ANNUAL PRODUCTION 90,000 bottles
HECTARES UNDER VINE 40.00

○ Franciacorta Brut Sempiterre	♟♟ 6
○ Franciacorta Natura '13	♟♟ 6
○ Franciacorta Rosé '13	♟♟ 6
○ Franciacorta Satèn '14	♟♟ 6

Belon du Belon

VIA PIAVE
25030 ADRO [BS]
TEL. +39 3351433774
www.franciacortabelon.it

ANNUAL PRODUCTION 35,000 bottles
HECTARES UNDER VINE 5.60

○ Franciacorta Brut	♟♟ 5
○ Franciacorta Pas Dosé Et. Bianca 48	♟♟ 5
○ Franciacorta Pas Dosé Et. Nera 80	♟ 5

Cantina Sociale Bergamasca

VIA BERGAMO, 10
24060 SAN PAOLO D'ARGON [BG]
TEL. +39 035951098
www.cantinabergamasca.it

CELLAR SALES
PRE-BOOKED VISITS
ANNUAL PRODUCTION 650,000 bottles
HECTARES UNDER VINE 90.00

○ Terre del Colleoni Brut Colleoni '14	♟♟ 4
○ Terre del Colleoni Incrocio Manzoni 6013 '18	♟♟ 5
● Valcalepio Rosso Orologio '16	♟ 2

Bertagna

LOC. BANDE
S.DA MADONNA DELLA PORTA, 14
46040 CAVRIANA [MN]
TEL. +39 037682211
www.cantinabertagna.it

CELLAR SALES
PRE-BOOKED VISITS
ANNUAL PRODUCTION 160,000 bottles
HECTARES UNDER VINE 17.00

○ Montevolpe Bianco '17	♟♟ 3
● Rosso del Barone '17	♟♟ 3
● Rosso del Chino '16	♟ 3

Bonfadini

FRAZ. CLUSANE
VIA L. DI BERNARDO, 85
25049 ISEO [BS]
TEL. +39 0309826721
www.bonfadini.it

CELLAR SALES
PRE-BOOKED VISITS
ANNUAL PRODUCTION 120,000 bottles
HECTARES UNDER VINE 12.00

○ Franciacorta Brut Nobilium	♥♥ 5
○ Franciacorta Nature Veritas	♥♥ 5
○ Franciacorta Satèn Carpe Diem	♥♥ 5
⊙ Franciacorta Brut Rosé Opera	♥ 5

La Boscaiola Vigneti Cenci

VIA RICCAFANA
25033 COLOGNE [BS]
TEL. +39 0307156386
www.vigneticenci.com

CELLAR SALES
PRE-BOOKED VISITS
ANNUAL PRODUCTION 50,000 bottles
HECTARES UNDER VINE 6.00

○ Franciacorta Brut La Capinera	♥♥ 4
○ Franciacorta Extra Brut Nelson Cenci	♥♥ 6
○ Franciacorta Rosé La Capinera	♥♥ 4

Bulgarini

LOC. VAIBÒ, 1
25010 POZZOLENGO [BS]
TEL. +39 030918224
www.vini-bulgarini.com

CELLAR SALES
ANNUAL PRODUCTION 750,000 bottles
HECTARES UNDER VINE 40.00

○ Lugana '18	♥♥ 2*
○ Lugana 010 '17	♥♥ 3

Ca d'Or

FRAZ. TIMOLINE
VIA BRESCIA, 3A
25040 CORTE FRANCA [BS]
TEL. +39 0309826562
www.cadorwine.it

CELLAR SALES
PRE-BOOKED VISITS
ACCOMMODATION AND RESTAURANT SERVICE
ANNUAL PRODUCTION 200,000 bottles
HECTARES UNDER VINE 30.00

○ Franciacorta Noble Cuvée	♥♥ 5
○ Franciacorta Pas Dosé Ris. '11	♥♥ 7
○ Franciacorta Satèn	♥ 5

Ca' del Santo

ILOC. CAMPOLUNGO, 4
27040 MONTALTO PAVESE [PV]
TEL. +39 0383870545
www.cadelsanto.it

CELLAR SALES
PRE-BOOKED VISITS
ANNUAL PRODUCTION 25,000 bottles
HECTARES UNDER VINE 6.00

● OP Bonarda Grand Cuvée '18	♥♥ 2*
⊙ OP Cruasé Brut '11	♥♥ 4
○ Mon Amì Brut Nature M. Cl.	♥ 4
● OP Rosso Carolo Ris. '15	♥ 3

Andrea Calvi

FRAZ. VIGALONE, 13
27044 CANNETO PAVESE [PV]
TEL. +39 038560034
www.andreacalvi.it

CELLAR SALES
PRE-BOOKED VISITS
ANNUAL PRODUCTION 100,000 bottles
HECTARES UNDER VINE 26.00

● OP Bonarda Frizzante '18	♥♥ 2*
○ OP Pinot Nero M. Cl. Brut	♥ 4

Davide Calvi

FRAZ. PALAZZINA, 24
27040 CASTANA [PV]
TEL. +39 038582136
www.vinicalvi.it

CELLAR SALES
PRE-BOOKED VISITS
ANNUAL PRODUCTION 45,000 bottles
HECTARES UNDER VINE 8.00

● Brut Civia M. Cl.	🍷🍷 2*
● OP Buttafuoco V. Montarzolo '15	🍷 4

Camillucci

VIA DELLE SELVE, 1
25038 PADERNO FRANCIACORTA [BS]
TEL. +39 0307702739
www.camilucci.it

PRE-BOOKED VISITS
ANNUAL PRODUCTION 50,000 bottles
HECTARES UNDER VINE 6.00

○ Franciacorta Brut	🍷🍷 5
○ Franciacorta Satèn '14	🍷🍷 5
○ Franciacorta Extra Brut Anthologie Blanc '13	🍷 6

Le Cantorìe

FRAZ. CASAGLIO
VIA CASTELLO DI CASAGLIO, 24/25
25064 GUSSAGO [BS]
TEL. +39 0302523723
www.lecantorie.it

ANNUAL PRODUCTION 75,000 bottles
HECTARES UNDER VINE 12.00

○ Franciacorta Brut Armonia	🍷🍷 4
⊙ Franciacorta Rosé Rosi delle Margherite	🍷🍷 4
○ Franciacorta Satèn Armonia	🍷🍷 5

Cascina Belmonte

FRAZ. MONIGA DEL BOSCO
LOC. TOPPE
25080 MUSCOLINE [BS]
TEL. +39 3335051606
www.cascinabelmonte.it

PRE-BOOKED VISITS
ANNUAL PRODUCTION 50,000 bottles
HECTARES UNDER VINE 10.00

○ Manzoni Bianco '18	🍷🍷 3
○ Riesling '18	🍷 3
⊙ Valtenesi Chiaretto '18	🍷 3

Cascina Clarabella

VIA ENRICO MATTEI
25040 CORTE FRANCA [BS]
TEL. +39 0309821041
www.cascinaclarabella.it

CELLAR SALES
PRE-BOOKED VISITS
ANNUAL PRODUCTION 70,000 bottles
HECTARES UNDER VINE 11.00
VITICULTURE METHOD Certified Organic

○ Franciacorta Pas Dosé '11	🍷🍷 6
○ Franciacorta Satèn	🍷🍷 5

Cascina Gnocco

FRAZ. LOSANA, 45
27040 MORNICO LOSANA [PV]
TEL. +39 038383499
www.cascinagnocco.it

CELLAR SALES
PRE-BOOKED VISITS
ANNUAL PRODUCTION 60,000 bottles
HECTARES UNDER VINE 13.00

● Orione '13	🍷🍷 4

Castello di Grumello

VIA FOSSE, 11
24064 GRUMELLO DEL MONTE [BG]
TEL. +39 0354420817
www.castellodigrumello.it

CELLAR SALES
PRE-BOOKED VISITS
ACCOMMODATION
ANNUAL PRODUCTION 100,000 bottles
HECTARES UNDER VINE 18.00
SUSTAINABLE WINERY

● Valcalepio Rosso Colle del Calvario Ris. '11	♟♟ 5	
○ Valcalepio Bianco '18	♟♟ 2*	
● Valcalepio Rosso Colle del Calvario Ris. '13	♟ 5	

Castello di Luzzano

LOC. LUZZANO, 5
27040 ROVESCALA [PV]
TEL. +39 0523863277
www.castelloluzzano.com

CELLAR SALES
PRE-BOOKED VISITS
ACCOMMODATION AND RESTAURANT SERVICE
ANNUAL PRODUCTION 120,000 bottles
HECTARES UNDER VINE 76.00

● OP Bonarda Carlino '17	♟♟ 2*
● OP Bonarda Frizzante Sommossa '18	♟ 2
● OP Pinot Nero Umore Nero '18	♟ 3

Castelveder

VIA BELVEDERE, 4
25040 MONTICELLI BRUSATI [BS]
TEL. +39 030652308
www.castelveder.it

CELLAR SALES
PRE-BOOKED VISITS
ANNUAL PRODUCTION 70,000 bottles
HECTARES UNDER VINE 11.00

○ Franciacorta Brut '13	♟♟ 6
○ Franciacorta Brut	♟♟ 4
○ Franciacorta Extra Brut	♟♟ 5
○ Franciacorta Satèn	♟ 5

Cantine Cavallotti

VIA VALLESCUROPASSO, 92
27040 CIGOGNOLA [PV]
TEL. +39 0290848829
www.cantinecavallotti.it

CELLAR SALES
PRE-BOOKED VISITS
ANNUAL PRODUCTION 12,000 bottles
HECTARES UNDER VINE 8.00

● OP Bonarda Passo Gaio '18	♟♟ 2*
○ OP Cruasé	♟♟ 4

Le Chiusure

FRAZ. PORTESE
VIA BOSCHETTE, 2
25010 SAN FELICE DEL BENACO [BS]
TEL. +39 0365626243
www.lechiusure.net

CELLAR SALES
PRE-BOOKED VISITS
ACCOMMODATION
ANNUAL PRODUCTION 22,000 bottles
HECTARES UNDER VINE 4.00

● Malborghetto '16	♟♟ 5
● Valtenesi Groppello '17	♟♟ 3
☉ Valtenesi Riviera del Garda Cl. Chiaretto '18	♟ 3

Il Cipresso

FRAZ. TRIBULINA
VIA CERRI, 2
24020 SCANZOROSCIATE [BG]
TEL. +39 0354597005
www.ilcipresso.info

CELLAR SALES
PRE-BOOKED VISITS
ANNUAL PRODUCTION 20,000 bottles
HECTARES UNDER VINE 4.00

● Moscato di Scanzo Serafino '15	♟♟ 6
○ Valcalepio Bianco Melardo '18	♟ 2
● Valcalepio Rosso Dionisio '16	♟ 3

Corte Fusia

VIA DEGLI ORTI, 2
25030 COCCAGLIO [BS]
TEL. +39 3288471276
www.cortefusia.com

CELLAR SALES
ANNUAL PRODUCTION 30,000 bottles
HECTARES UNDER VINE 7.00

○ Franciacorta Brut	♟♟ 5
○ Franciacorta Satèn	♟♟ 5

De Toma

VIA BATTISTI, 7
24020 SCANZOROSCIATE [BG]
TEL. +39 035657329

CELLAR SALES
PRE-BOOKED VISITS
ANNUAL PRODUCTION 5,000 bottles
HECTARES UNDER VINE 2.50

● Moscato di Scanzo '15	♟♟ 7

Diana

VIA ROMA 63
27040 CASTANA [PV]
TEL. +39 0385249618
www.dianawine.it

CELLAR SALES
PRE-BOOKED VISITS
ANNUAL PRODUCTION 35,000 bottles
HECTARES UNDER VINE 9.00

● OP Buttafuoco Storico V. Ca' Cagnoni '15	♟♟ 3

Due Pini

LOC. PICEDO
VIA NOVAGLIO, 16
25080 POLPENAZZE DEL GARDA [BS]
TEL. +39 0365675123
www.viniduepini.it

PRE-BOOKED VISITS
ANNUAL PRODUCTION 40,000 bottles
HECTARES UNDER VINE 6.00
VITICULTURE METHOD Certified Organic

● Garda Cl. Groppello Sara '18	♟♟ 3
○ Martina Dosaggio Zero	♟♟ 3
● San Vincenzo '16	♟♟ 5
● Riviera del Garda Cl. Paola '16	♟ 2

Lorenzo Faccoli

VIA CAVA, 7
25030 COCCAGLIO [BS]
TEL. +39 0307722761
www.faccolifranciacorta.it

CELLAR SALES
PRE-BOOKED VISITS
ANNUAL PRODUCTION 55,000 bottles
HECTARES UNDER VINE 5.50

○ Franciacorta Brut	♟♟ 5
○ Franciacorta Extra Brut	♟♟ 4
⊙ Franciacorta Rosè	♟♟ 5

Feliciana

LOC. FELICIANA
25010 POZZOLENGO [BS]
TEL. +39 030918228
www.feliciana.it

ANNUAL PRODUCTION 220,000 bottles
HECTARES UNDER VINE 20.00

○ Lugana Sercè Ris. '16	♟♟ 4
○ Lugana Felugan '18	♟ 3

Il Feudo Nico

VIA SAN ROCCO, 63
27040 MORNICO LOSANA [PV]
TEL. +39 0383892452

ANNUAL PRODUCTION 40,000 bottles
HECTARES UNDER VINE 16.00

● Edoardo '17	♟♟ 4
○ Maria Antonietta Brut M. Cl. '12	♟♟ 4
○ Maria Antonietta Blanc de Blanc Extra Brut M. Cl.	♟ 4

Finigeto

LOC. CELLA, 27
27040 MONTALTO PAVESE [PV]
TEL. +39 328 7095347
www.finigeto.com

CELLAR SALES
PRE-BOOKED VISITS
ACCOMMODATION
ANNUAL PRODUCTION 80,000 bottles
HECTARES UNDER VINE 42.00

○ Chardonnay Il Fermo '18	♟♟ 3
● OP Pinot Nero Il Nirò '16	♟♟ 5
○ OP Riesling Lo Spavaldo '18	♟♟ 2*
● OP Bonarda Frizzante Il Baldo '18	♟ 3

La Fiòca

FRAZ. NIGOLINE
VIA VILLA, 13B
25040 CORTE FRANCA [BS]
TEL. +39 0309826313
www.lafioca.com

CELLAR SALES
PRE-BOOKED VISITS
ACCOMMODATION AND RESTAURANT SERVICE
ANNUAL PRODUCTION 40,000 bottles
HECTARES UNDER VINE 5.00
VITICULTURE METHOD Certified Organic

○ Franciacorta Brut	♟♟ 5
○ Franciacorta Dosaggio Zero '11	♟♟ 6
○ Franciacorta Extra Brut '10	♟♟ 6
⊙ Franciacorta Rosé	♟♟ 5

La Fiorita

VIA MAGLIO, 10
25020 OME [BS]
TEL. +39 030652279
www.lafioritafranciacorta.com

CELLAR SALES
PRE-BOOKED VISITS
ACCOMMODATION AND RESTAURANT SERVICE
ANNUAL PRODUCTION 94,000 bottles
HECTARES UNDER VINE 10.00

○ Franciacorta Brut	♟♟ 4
⊙ Franciacorta Brut Rosé	♟♟ 5
○ Franciacorta Dosaggio Zero	♟♟ 4
○ Franciacorta Zerozerosette +5 '12	♟♟ 6

Le Fracce

FRAZ. MAIRANO
VIA CASTEL DEL LUPO, 5
27045 CASTEGGIO [PV]
TEL. +39 038382526
www.lefracce.com

CELLAR SALES
PRE-BOOKED VISITS
ANNUAL PRODUCTION 180,000 bottles
HECTARES UNDER VINE 40.00

● OP Bonarda Vivace Rubiosa '18	♟♟ 3
○ OP Pinot Nero Extra Brut M. Cl. Special Cuvée Bussolera '16	♟♟ 4
○ OP Riesling Landò '18	♟♟ 3

Giorgio Gianatti

VIA DEI PORTICI, 82
23020 MONTAGNA IN VALTELLINA [SO]
TEL. +39 0342380033
gianatti.giorgio@alice.it

CELLAR SALES
PRE-BOOKED VISITS
ANNUAL PRODUCTION 8,000 bottles
HECTARES UNDER VINE 2.00

● Valtellina Sup. Grumello San Martino '12	♟♟ 6
● Valtellina Rosso '17	♟♟ 4

Cantina Sociale di Gonzaga

via Stazione, 39
46023 Gonzaga [MN]
Tel. +39 037658051
www.cantinagonzaga.it

CELLAR SALES
ANNUAL PRODUCTION 1,000,000 bottles
HECTARES UNDER VINE 170.00

- ● Lambrusco Mantovano Rosso della Signoria '18 — 🍷🍷 3
- ● Lambrusco Mantovano Rosso della Signoria Bio '18 — 🍷 3

Tenuta La Vigna

Cascina La Vigna
25020 Capriano del Colle [BS]
Tel. +39 0309748061
www.tenutalavigna.it

CELLAR SALES
PRE-BOOKED VISITS
ANNUAL PRODUCTION 35,000 bottles
HECTARES UNDER VINE 6.00

- ○ Capriano del Colle Bianco Torrazza '18 — 🍷🍷 3
- ● Capriano del Colle Montebruciato Ris. '15 — 🍷🍷 5
- ○ Brut M. Cl. Nature Ugo Botti — 🍷 5

Lebovitz

fraz. Governolo
v.le Rimembranze, 4
46037 Roncoferraro [MN]
Tel. +39 0376668115
www.lebovitz.it

CELLAR SALES
PRE-BOOKED VISITS
ANNUAL PRODUCTION 1,000,000 bottles

- ● Al Scagarün '18 — 🍷🍷 1*
- ● Lambrusco Mantovano Rosso dei Concari '18 — 🍷🍷 2*
- ● Sedamat '18 — 🍷🍷 1*

Francesco Maggi

fraz. Costiolo, 87
27044 Canneto Pavese [PV]
Tel. +39 038560233
www.maggifrancesco.it

- ● OP Buttafuoco Storico V. Costera '15 — 🍷 3
- ● OP Riesling '18 — 🍷 2

Majolini

loc. Valle
via A. Manzoni, 3
25050 Ome [BS]
Tel. +39 0306527378
www.majolini.it

CELLAR SALES
PRE-BOOKED VISITS
ANNUAL PRODUCTION 150,000 bottles
HECTARES UNDER VINE 24.00
VITICULTURE METHOD Certified Organic
SUSTAINABLE WINERY

- ○ Franciacorta Brut Electo '11 — 🍷🍷 5
- ○ Franciacorta Brut Satèn '15 — 🍷🍷 5
- ⊙ Franciacorta Rosé — 🍷🍷 5
- ⊙ Franciacorta Rosé Altera — 🍷🍷 6

Manuelina

fraz. Ruinello di sotto, 3a
27047 Santa Maria della Versa [PV]
Tel. +39 0385278247
Fraz. Ruinello di Sotto 3/a

CELLAR SALES
PRE-BOOKED VISITS
ANNUAL PRODUCTION 230,000 bottles
HECTARES UNDER VINE 22.00

- ○ Brut Pas Dosè '15 — 🍷🍷 3
- ⊙ OP Pinot Nero Brut M. Cl. Rosè 145 '13 — 🍷🍷 3
- ○ OP Pinot Nero Brut M. Cl. 137 '15 — 🍷 4

Marangona

LOC. MARANGONA 1
25010 POZZOLENGO [BS]
TEL. +39 030919379
www.marangona.com

CELLAR SALES
PRE-BOOKED VISITS
ANNUAL PRODUCTION 30,000 bottles
HECTARES UNDER VINE 30.00

○ Lugana '18	♥♥ 2*
○ Lugana Cemento '18	♥♥ 4
○ Lugana Tre Campane '17	♥♥ 3

Alberto Marsetti

VIA SCARPATETTI, 15
23100 SONDRIO
TEL. +39 0342216329
www.marsetti.it

ANNUAL PRODUCTION 20,000 bottles
HECTARES UNDER VINE 5.00

● Sforzato di Valtellina '14	♥♥ 6
● Valtellina Sup. Grumello '15	♥♥ 5
● Valtellina Sup. Le Prudenze '15	♥♥ 5

Martilde

FRAZ. CROCE, 4A
27040 ROVESCALA [PV]
TEL. +39 0385756280
www.martilde.it

CELLAR SALES
PRE-BOOKED VISITS
ANNUAL PRODUCTION 30,000 bottles
HECTARES UNDER VINE 15.00
VITICULTURE METHOD Certified Organic

● OP Barbera '17	♥♥ 2*
● OP Bonarda '15	♥♥ 2*

Marzaghe Franciacorta

FRAZ. ZOCCO
VIA PARLAMENTO, 28
25030 ERBUSCO [BS]
TEL. +39 0307267245
www.marzaghefranciacorta.it

CELLAR SALES
PRE-BOOKED VISITS
ACCOMMODATION
ANNUAL PRODUCTION 40,000 bottles
HECTARES UNDER VINE 7.00
VITICULTURE METHOD Certified Organic
SUSTAINABLE WINERY

○ Franciacorta Brut LM 1935	♥♥ 5
○ Franciacorta Brut Nature Aureum Ris. '09	♥♥ 8
○ Franciacorta Dosaggio Zero Superno	♥♥ 6

Medolago Albani

VIA REDONA, 12
24069 TRESCORE BALNEARIO [BG]
TEL. +39 035942022
www.medolagoalbani.it

CELLAR SALES
PRE-BOOKED VISITS
ANNUAL PRODUCTION 200,000 bottles
HECTARES UNDER VINE 23.00

⊙ Brut Rosè M. Cl. '16	♥♥ 3
● Valcalepio Rosso I Due Lauri Ris. '15	♥♥ 4
● Valcalepio Rosso '17	♥ 3

Il Molino di Rovescala

LOC. MOLINO, 2
27040 ROVESCALA [PV]
TEL. +39 339 4739924
www.ilmolinodirovescala.it/

CELLAR SALES
PRE-BOOKED VISITS
ANNUAL PRODUCTION 40,000 bottles
HECTARES UNDER VINE 23.00
SUSTAINABLE WINERY

○ Malvasia Madone '14	♥♥ 4
○ Riesling Felice '14	♥♥ 4
● OP Bonarda '15	♥ 5

Monte Cicogna

VIA DELLE VIGNE, 6
25080 MONIGA DEL GARDA [BS]
TEL. +39 0365503200
www.montecicogna.it

CELLAR SALES
PRE-BOOKED VISITS
ACCOMMODATION
ANNUAL PRODUCTION 150,000 bottles
HECTARES UNDER VINE 30.00

○ Garda Riesling Vasca 59 '17	♥♥ 3
⊘ Riviera del Garda Cl. Chiaretto Siclì '18	♥♥ 3
● Riviera del Garda Cl. Groppello Beana '17	♥♥ 3

Tenuta Monte Delma

VIA VALENZANO, 23
25050 PASSIRANO [BS]
TEL. +39 0306546161
www.montedelma.it

CELLAR SALES
PRE-BOOKED VISITS
ANNUAL PRODUCTION 100,000 bottles
HECTARES UNDER VINE 20.00

○ Franciacorta Brut	♥♥ 4
⊘ Franciacorta Brut Rosé	♥♥ 5
○ Franciacorta Brut Satèn	♥♥ 5

Montelio

VIA D. MAZZA, 1
27050 CODEVILLA [PV]
TEL. +39 0383373090
montelio.gio@alice.it

CELLAR SALES
PRE-BOOKED VISITS
ACCOMMODATION AND RESTAURANT SERVICE
ANNUAL PRODUCTION 130,000 bottles
HECTARES UNDER VINE 27.00

● OP Pinot Nero Costarsa '16	♥♥ 4
● OP Bonarda La Grangia '17	♥ 2
○ OP Riesling Il Nadòt '18	♥ 2

Monterucco

VIA VALLE CIMA, 38
27040 CIGOGNOLA [PV]
TEL. +39 038585151
www.monterucco.it

PRE-BOOKED VISITS
ANNUAL PRODUCTION 200,000 bottles
HECTARES UNDER VINE 20.00

○ Malvasia Valentina '18	♥♥ 2*
○ OP Pinot Nero Brut Nature M. Cl. '12	♥♥ 3
● OP Bonarda Frizzante V. Il Modello '18	♥ 2

La Montina

FRAZ. BAIANA, 17
25040 MONTICELLI BRUSATI [BS]
TEL. +39 030653278
www.lamontina.com

CELLAR SALES
PRE-BOOKED VISITS
RESTAURANT SERVICE
ANNUAL PRODUCTION 400,000 bottles
HECTARES UNDER VINE 70.00
VITICULTURE METHOD Certified Organic

○ Franciacorta Brut	♥♥ 5
○ Franciacorta Demi Sec	♥♥ 4
○ Franciacorta Pas Dosé Baiana Ris. '11	♥♥ 5
○ Franciacorta Extra Brut	♥ 4

Montonale

LOC. CONTA, 4A
25015 DESENZANO DEL GARDA [BS]
TEL. +39 0309103358
www.montonale.it

ANNUAL PRODUCTION 100,000 bottles
HECTARES UNDER VINE 25.00

○ Lugana Orestilla '17	♥♥ 5
○ Lugana Montunal '18	♥ 3
⊘ Valtènesi Chiaretto Rosa di Notte '18	♥ 3

Monzio Compagnoni

VIA NIGOLINE, 98
25030 ADRO [BS]
TEL. +39 0307457803
www.monziocompagnoni.com

CELLAR SALES
PRE-BOOKED VISITS
ANNUAL PRODUCTION 170,000 bottles
HECTARES UNDER VINE 17.00

○ Franciacorta Brut '14	♥♥ 5
○ Curtefranca Bianco Ronco della Seta '18	♥ 3
○ Franciacorta Brut Cuvée alla Moda	♥♥ 5

Nettare dei Santi

VIA CAPRA, 17
20078 SAN COLOMBANO AL LAMBRO [MI]
TEL. +39 0371200523
www.nettaredeisanti.it

CELLAR SALES
PRE-BOOKED VISITS
ANNUAL PRODUCTION 600,000 bottles
HECTARES UNDER VINE 40.00

● Franco Riccardi '13	♥♥ 4
○ Solitaire '16	♥ 3

Panigada - Banino

VIA DELLA VITTORIA, 13
20078 SAN COLOMBANO AL LAMBRO [MI]
TEL. +39 037189103
www.banino.it

CELLAR SALES
PRE-BOOKED VISITS
ANNUAL PRODUCTION 30,000 bottles
HECTARES UNDER VINE 5.00
SUSTAINABLE WINERY

○ Aureum '16	♥♥ 4
● San Colombano Banino V. La Merla Ris. '15	♥♥ 4
● San Colombano Banino Tranquillo '16	♥ 2

La Perla

LOC. TRESENDA
VIA VALGELLA, 29B
23036 TEGLIO [SO]
TEL. +39 3462878894
www.vini-laperla.com

CELLAR SALES
PRE-BOOKED VISITS
ANNUAL PRODUCTION 20,000 bottles
HECTARES UNDER VINE 3.30

○ La Perla Extra Brut M. Cl.	♥♥ 5
● Sforzato di Valtellina Quattro Soli '14	♥♥ 7
● Valtellina Sup. Elisa Ris. '13	♥♥ 5
● Valtellina Sup. La Mossa '14	♥♥ 5

Pian del Maggio

VIA ISEO, 108
25030 ERBUSCO [BS]
TEL. +39 3355638610
www.piandelmaggio.it

CELLAR SALES
PRE-BOOKED VISITS
ANNUAL PRODUCTION 25,000 bottles
HECTARES UNDER VINE 1.80

○ Franciacorta Nature Furente '11	♥♥ 5
○ Franciacorta Brut Proscenio '14	♥♥ 4
⊙ Franciacorta Rosé ...e Anna Sorrise	♥♥ 5
○ Franciacorta Satèn Capriccio	♥♥ 5

Piccolo Bacco dei Quaroni

FRAZ. COSTAMONTEFEDELE
27040 MONTÙ BECCARIA [PV]
TEL. +39 038560521
www.piccolobaccodeiquaroni.it

CELLAR SALES
PRE-BOOKED VISITS
RESTAURANT SERVICE
ANNUAL PRODUCTION 35,000 bottles
HECTARES UNDER VINE 10.00
VITICULTURE METHOD Certified Organic

● Campasso Il Moreè '17	♥♥ 2*
● OP Pinot Nero Vign. La Fiocca '17	♥ 3
○ OP Riesling Vign. del Pozzo '14	♥ 2

Pilandro

FRAZ. SAN MARTINO DELLA BATTAGLIA
LOC. PILANDRO, 1
25015 DESENZANO DEL GARDA [BS]
TEL. +39 0309910363
www.pilandro.it

CELLAR SALES
PRE-BOOKED VISITS
ANNUAL PRODUCTION 300,000 bottles
HECTARES UNDER VINE 33.00

○ Lugana Terecrea '18	🍷🍷 3
○ Lugana '18	🍷 2
○ Lugana Sup. Arilica '17	🍷 3

Plozza

VIA CAPPUCCINI, 26
23037 TIRANO [SO]
TEL. +39 0342701297
www.plozza.com

CELLAR SALES
PRE-BOOKED VISITS
ANNUAL PRODUCTION 450,000 bottles
HECTARES UNDER VINE 28.00

● N°1 '15	🍷🍷 8
● Sforzato di Valtellina Blackedition '15	🍷🍷 5
● Valtellina Sup. Sassella Rededition Ris. '15	🍷🍷 4

Pratello

VIA PRATELLO, 26
25080 PADENGHE SUL GARDA [BS]
TEL. +39 0309907005
www.pratello.com

CELLAR SALES
ACCOMMODATION AND RESTAURANT SERVICE
ANNUAL PRODUCTION 600,000 bottles
HECTARES UNDER VINE 70.00
VITICULTURE METHOD Certified Organic

● Valtènesi Torrazzo '17	🍷🍷 3
○ Lugana 90+10 '18	🍷 3
○ Lugana Catulliano '18	🍷 4
◉ Valtènesi Chiaretto Sant'Emiliano '18	🍷 3

Quattro Terre

FRAZ. BORGONATO
VIA RISORGIMENTO, 11
25040 CORTE FRANCA [BS]
TEL. +39 030984312
www.quattroterre.it

CELLAR SALES
PRE-BOOKED VISITS
ACCOMMODATION AND RESTAURANT SERVICE
ANNUAL PRODUCTION 50,000 bottles
HECTARES UNDER VINE 10.00

○ Franciacorta Brut Grano Salis	🍷🍷 5
○ Franciacorta Dosaggio Zero Genius Loci '14	🍷🍷 6
○ Franciacorta Extra Brut Sinequal	🍷🍷 5

Cantina Sociale Cooperativa di Quistello

VIA ROMA, 46
46026 QUISTELLO [MN]
TEL. +39 0376618118
www.cantinasocialequistello.it

CELLAR SALES
PRE-BOOKED VISITS
ANNUAL PRODUCTION 1,000,000 bottles
HECTARES UNDER VINE 330.00
SUSTAINABLE WINERY

● Gran Rosso del Vicariato di Quistello '18	🍷🍷 2*
◉ 80 Vendemmie Rosato '18	🍷 2

Tenuta Quvestra

LOC. CASE NUOVE 9
27047 SANTA MARIA DELLA VERSA [PV]
TEL. +39 3476014109
www.quvestra.it

CELLAR SALES
PRE-BOOKED VISITS
ACCOMMODATION
ANNUAL PRODUCTION 35,000 bottles
HECTARES UNDER VINE 12.00

● OP Bonarda Frizzant '17	🍷🍷 2*
○ OP Pinot Nero Brut Symposium	🍷🍷 4
◉ OP Pinot Nero Cruasé Zephiro	🍷 3
● Sinfonia in Rosso '16	🍷 3

Rebollini

LOC. SBERCIA
27040 BORGORATTO MORMOROLO [PV]
TEL. +39 0383872295
www.rebollini.it

CELLAR SALES
PRE-BOOKED VISITS
ANNUAL PRODUCTION 100,000 bottles
HECTARES UNDER VINE 35.00
SUSTAINABLE WINERY

○ Brut Nature M. Cl. '12	♀♀ 5
○ Cuvée Brut M. Cl.	♀♀ 4
⊙ OP Cruasé '12	♀ 4
○ OP Riesling '18	♀ 2

La Riccafana

VIA F.LLI FACCHETTI, 91
25033 COLOGNE [BS]
TEL. +39 0307156797
www.riccafana.com

CELLAR SALES
ANNUAL PRODUCTION 100,000 bottles
HECTARES UNDER VINE 12.00
VITICULTURE METHOD Certified Organic

○ Franciacorta Brut	♀♀ 5
○ Franciacorta Satèn	♀♀ 5

Ricchi

FRAZ. RICCHI
VIA FESTONI, 13D
46040 MONZAMBANO [MN]
TEL. +39 0376800238
www.cantinaricchi.it

CELLAR SALES
PRE-BOOKED VISITS
ANNUAL PRODUCTION 300,000 bottles
HECTARES UNDER VINE 40.00

● Garda Cabernet Ribò '16	♀♀ 3
○ Le Cime '17	♀♀ 5

La Rifra

LOC. PILANDRO, 2
25010 DESENZANO DEL GARDA [BS]
TEL. +39 0309108023
claudiofraccaroli@virgilio.it

ANNUAL PRODUCTION 90,000 bottles
HECTARES UNDER VINE 14.00

○ Lugana Il Bepi Ris. '16	♀♀ 3
○ Lugana Libiam '18	♀♀ 2*
○ San Martino '18	♀ 2

Ruinello

FRAZ. RUINELLO DI SOPRA, 15
27047 SANTA MARIA DELLA VERSA [PV]
TEL. +39 0385278057
www.ruinello.it

ANNUAL PRODUCTION 500,000 bottles
HECTARES UNDER VINE 20.00

○ OP Pinot Nero Brut Gran Cuvée M. Cl.	♀♀ 4
○ OP Extra Dry Martinotti	♀ 2
○ Riesling	♀ 2

San Michele

VIA PARROCCHIA, 57
25020 CAPRIANO DEL COLLE [BS]
TEL. +39 0309444091
www.sanmichelevini.it

CELLAR SALES
PRE-BOOKED VISITS
ANNUAL PRODUCTION 70,000 bottles
HECTARES UNDER VINE 16.00
VITICULTURE METHOD Certified Organic

○ Capriano del Colle Bianco Netto '18	♀♀ 2*
● Capriano del Colle Rosso Carme '17	♀♀ 2*
● Capriano del Colle Marzemino '18	♀ 2

Poderi di San Pietro

VIA STEFFENINI 2/6
20078 SAN COLOMBANO AL LAMBRO [MI]
TEL. +39 0371208054
www.poderidisanpietro.it

CELLAR SALES
PRE-BOOKED VISITS
ANNUAL PRODUCTION 300,000 bottles
HECTARES UNDER VINE 80.00

○ Cuvée Brut San Pietro M. Cl. '16	🍷🍷 4
● San Colombano Monastero di Valbissera Ris. '13	🍷🍷 3
◉ Nuè Rosato '17	🍷 4

Santa Lucia

VIA VERDI, 6
25030 ERBUSCO [BS]
TEL. +39 0307769814
www.santaluciafranciacorta.it

CELLAR SALES
PRE-BOOKED VISITS
ANNUAL PRODUCTION 100,000 bottles
HECTARES UNDER VINE 28.00
VITICULTURE METHOD Certified Organic

○ Franciacorta Brut	🍷🍷 5
○ Franciacorta Extra Brut '08	🍷🍷 8
○ Franciacorta Brut Satèn	🍷 5

Santus

VIA BADIA, 68
25060 CELLATICA [BS]
TEL. +39 0308367074
www.santus.it

CELLAR SALES
PRE-BOOKED VISITS
ANNUAL PRODUCTION 50,000 bottles
HECTARES UNDER VINE 9.50
VITICULTURE METHOD Certified Organic

○ Franciacorta Brut	🍷🍷 4
◉ Franciacorta Extra Brut Rosé	🍷🍷 4

Tenuta Scerscé

VIA STELVIO, 18
23037 TIRANO [SO]
TEL. +39 3461542970
www.tenutascersce.it

CELLAR SALES
PRE-BOOKED VISITS
ANNUAL PRODUCTION 22,000 bottles
HECTARES UNDER VINE 2.50
SUSTAINABLE WINERY

● Valtellina Sforzato Infinito '16	🍷🍷 6
● Valtellina Sup. Essenza '15	🍷🍷 5

Sullali

VIA COSTA DI SOPRA, 22
25030 ERBUSCO [BS]
TEL. +39 3930206080
info@sullali.com

ANNUAL PRODUCTION 10,000 bottles
HECTARES UNDER VINE 3.50

○ Franciacorta Brut Satèn	🍷🍷 4
○ Franciacorta Dosaggio Zero	🍷🍷 4
○ Franciacorta Extra Brut	🍷 4

Tenute del Garda

VIA BURAGO, 2
25080 CALVAGESE DELLA RIVIERA [BS]
TEL. +39 0309919000
www.tenutedelgarda.it

ANNUAL PRODUCTION 50,000 bottles
HECTARES UNDER VINE 23.00

○ Garda Riesling '16	🍷🍷 2*
● Valtènesi Groppello Vistalago Ris. '16	🍷🍷 6
○ Brut Sottosopra	🍷 4
◉ Valtènesi Chiaretto '18	🍷 3

Terre d'Oltrepò

VIA TORINO, 96
27045 CASTEGGIO [PV]
TEL. +39 038551505
www.bronis.it

CELLAR SALES
PRE-BOOKED VISITS
ANNUAL PRODUCTION 4,000,000 bottles
HECTARES UNDER VINE 4500.00

● OP Bonarda Frizzante Dolium '18	🏆🏆 2*
○ OP Brut M. Cl. Svic	🏆🏆 3
○ OP Riesling Clefi '17	🏆 2

Conti Thun

VIA MASSERINO 2
25080 PUEGNAGO SUL GARDA [BS]
TEL. +39 0365651757
www.contithun.com

ANNUAL PRODUCTION 25,000 bottles
HECTARES UNDER VINE 12.00

⊙ Valtenesi Chiaretto Michaela '18	🏆🏆 4
⊙ Brut Rosé Bolle di Michaela '18	🏆 4
⊙ Riesling Gioia '18	🏆 4
⊙ Vinorosa '18	🏆 5

Togni Rebaioli

FRAZ. ERBANNO
VIA ROSSINI, 19
25047 DARFO BOARIO TERME [BS]
TEL. +39 0364529706

● 1703 '17	🏆🏆 4
● Brut Pas Dosè Attaccabrighe	🏆🏆 4
● San Valentino '17	🏆 6

La Torre

FRAZ. MOCASINA DI CALVAGESE
25080 CALVAGESE DELLA RIVIERA [BS]
TEL. +39 030601034
www.pasini-latorre.com

CELLAR SALES
PRE-BOOKED VISITS
ANNUAL PRODUCTION 35,000 bottles
HECTARES UNDER VINE 9.50

● Riviera del Garda Cl. Sup Il Torrione '13	🏆🏆 6
⊙ Valtenesi Chiaretto Sinigol '18	🏆🏆 2
● Garda Cl. Groppello di Mocasina '17	🏆 2

Tosi

VIA PIANAZZA, 45
27040 MONTESCANO [PV]
TEL. +39 3384781752
www.vinitosi.com

ANNUAL PRODUCTION 50,000 bottles
HECTARES UNDER VINE 12.00

● OP Bonarda Frizzante Podere La Guardia '18	🏆🏆 3
○ OP Pinot Nero Brut Nirfea M. Cl. '15	🏆🏆 3
● Pinot Nero Sax '18	🏆 3

La Travaglina

FRAZ. CASTELLO
VIA TRAVAGLINA, 1
27046 SANTA GIULETTA [PV]
TEL. +39 0383899195
www.latravaglina.it

CELLAR SALES
PRE-BOOKED VISITS
ANNUAL PRODUCTION 230,000 bottles
HECTARES UNDER VINE 30.50

● OP Bonarda Frizzante Zavola '18	🏆🏆 2*
● OP Pinot Nero Casaia '14	🏆 3
○ OP Riesling Rugiadè '18	🏆 2

Turra

VIA PREDARI SNC
25033 COLOGNE [BS]
TEL. +39 3383655489
info@turrafranciacorta.it

ANNUAL PRODUCTION 30,000 bottles
HECTARES UNDER VINE 12.00

○ Franciacorta Brut	🍷🍷 4
○ Franciacorta Pas Dosé '12	🍷🍷 4

Valdamonte

FRAZ. VALDAMONTE, 58
27047 SANTA MARIA DELLA VERSA [PV]
TEL. +39 038579665
www.valdamonte.it

ANNUAL PRODUCTION 17,000 bottles
HECTARES UNDER VINE 16.00
VITICULTURE METHOD Certified Organic
SUSTAINABLE WINERY

○ 347 M.S.L.M '18	🍷🍷 3
● 347 M.S.L.M '18	🍷🍷 2*
● OP Bonarda Frizzante Novecento '18	🍷 2

Vercesi del Castellazzo

VIA AURELIANO, 36
27040 MONTÙ BECCARIA [PV]
TEL. +39 0385262098
www.vercesidelcastellazzo.it

CELLAR SALES
PRE-BOOKED VISITS
ANNUAL PRODUCTION 80,000 bottles
HECTARES UNDER VINE 13.00

● Pezzalunga '18	🍷🍷 2*
● OP Bonarda Fatila '13	🍷 4
○ OP Pinot Nero in Bianco Gugiarolo '18	🍷 2

Giuseppe Vezzoli

VIA COSTA SOPRA, 22
25030 ERBUSCO [BS]
TEL. +39 0307267579
www.vezzolivini.it

CELLAR SALES
PRE-BOOKED VISITS
ANNUAL PRODUCTION 200,000 bottles
HECTARES UNDER VINE 63.00

○ Franciacorta Brut '14	🍷🍷 5
○ Franciacorta Brut	🍷🍷 4
○ Franciacorta Extra Brut Nefertiti Dizeta '12	🍷🍷 6

Vigna Dorata

FRAZ. CALINO
VIA SALA, 80
25046 CAZZAGO SAN MARTINO [BS]
TEL. +39 0307254275
www.vignadorata.it

CELLAR SALES
PRE-BOOKED VISITS
ANNUAL PRODUCTION 70,000 bottles
HECTARES UNDER VINE 8.00

● Curtefranca Rosso Runcat '15	🍷🍷 5
○ Franciacorta Nature	🍷🍷 5
○ Franciacorta Satèn	🍷🍷 5

Zatti

VIA LANFRANCHI, 10
25080 CALVAGESE DELLA RIVIERA [BS]
TEL. +39 3464273907
www.cantinazatti.it

ANNUAL PRODUCTION 10,000 bottles
HECTARES UNDER VINE 2.00

● Garda Marzemino Verrone '15	🍷🍷 3
○ Garda Riesling Gep '16	🍷🍷 3
⊙ Brut Rosé Sandriolè M. Cl. '16	🍷 5

CANTON TICINO

For many Ticino is the 'land of Merlot'. Today changes in climate have notably diversified its ampelography, such that in a few years we'll be looking at a considerably transformed territory. These changes have gone hand-in-hand with an increasing number of visitors who come to appreciate Canton Ticino's beauty, with its vineyards peeping out not far from the more densely inhabited lake districts, enjoying the terraced slopes overlooking the valleys. It's a scenic landscape, enriched by the charm of viticulture, and possesses a particular allure, a potent attraction for a tourism industry in constant growth. Geographically speaking, Ticino is divided into two areas: the northern Sopraceneri and the southern Sottoceneri, which vary in terms of climate and soil. To the north, in the Sopraceneri, light, sandy, rocky terrain dominates, making for a permeability that's important in a region that sees so much precipitation. In the valleys, Ticino's viticulture becomes even more alpine and scenic. Here the granitic terrain gives rise to wines that show even greater aging power. In the Sottoceneri, to the south, where the landscape is more Mediterranean, the territory becomes flatter, the soil heavier and more fertile, rich in limestone and clay. And now on to our awards, which this year are equally divided (one for the north and one for the south). Two Tre Bicchieri recognize the value of the work being done by producers skilled in interpreting the unique characteristics of the territory and its grapes. Luigi Panini's Castello Luigi '16 truly bewitched with its extremely elegant body, thrilling us today but promising more good things to come. It was the decisive character and generous of bouquet of Angelo Delea's Carato '16 that most surprised us, pointing to a constantly evolving and growing region. Year after year, thanks in part to a new generation of vine growers, we're sure that the territory will continue to establish itself with new, original products.

Agriloro

VIA PRELLA, 14
6852 GENESTRERIO
TEL. +39 +41916405454
www.agriloro.ch

CELLAR SALES
PRE-BOOKED VISITS
ANNUAL PRODUCTION 200,000 bottles
HECTARES UNDER VINE 23.00

Meinrad Perler, a farmer's son, came to Ticino in 1960. After a career in finance, he decided to focus on vinegrowing and purchased Tenimento dell'Ör, with 11 hectares of vineyards in an enviable hillside location. In 2002 he also bought Tenimento La Prella in Genestrerio, which is the main winery today. His foresight and research in the sector led him to create an ampelographic garden around the new estate, containing over 600 vine varieties trained for experimental purposes. It is one of the most important collections in Switzerland and possibly in Europe. The Sottobosco '16 made a very good impression. Leading with intense aromas of black plum and blackberry, it envelops the mouth in decisive tannins and delicacy at the same time. Their Casimiro '15, on the other hand, reveals a complex bouquet of fruit and a variety of aromatic herbs with a balanced body supported by a fine suite of tannins and a gutsy finish.

● Casimiro '15	♟♟ 5
● Ticino Sottobosco '16	♟♟ 6
○ Ticino Bianco Granito '17	♟ 5
● Ticino Syrah '15	♟ 6
○ Ticino Bianco Granito '16	♟♟ 5
● Ticino Merlot La Prella Ris. '16	♟♟ 6
● Ticino Merlot La Prella Ris. '15	♟♟ 6
● Ticino Rosso Sottobosco '15	♟♟ 6

Castello Luigi

VIA BELVEDERE, 1
6863 BESAZIO
TEL. +39 +41916300808
www.zanini.ch

CELLAR SALES
PRE-BOOKED VISITS
ANNUAL PRODUCTION 12,000 bottles
HECTARES UNDER VINE 12.50

The Castello Luigi winery was founded in Besazio in 1988 by Luigi Zanini. The building is of architectural interest because it was inspired by a famous Bordeaux château. The unusual feature of this structure is the spiral-shaped cellar (the only one in Ticino). It reaches a depth of 18.5 metres, which means that all the cellar work is done by means of natural gravity, without mechanical intervention or causing trauma. The winery only produces two wines: a monovarietal Chardonnay, which spends a period in barriques, and a red wine made with Merlot and Cabernet Sauvignon grapes. Their very memorable Castello Luigi Rosso '16, is in the top tier of Ticino wines. Its bouquet is rich with hints of berries and beautiful toasted notes. Its delicate entrance in the mouth gives way to an extremely refined body which returns to a fruity finish. The Castello Luigi Bianco '16 also features pleasant, corpulent aromas and great character.

● Ticino Rosso Castello Luigi '16	♟♟♟ 8
○ Ticino Bianco Castello Luigi '16	♟♟ 8
● Ticino Rosso Castello Luigi '15	♟♟ 8

F.lli Corti

VIA SOTTOBISIO, 13A
6828 BALERNA
TEL. +39 +41916833702
www.fratellicorti.ch

CELLAR SALES
PRE-BOOKED VISITS
ANNUAL PRODUCTION 60,000 bottles
HECTARES UNDER VINE 7.00

Fratelli Corti began business back in 1972.
Today the brilliant winemaker Nicola Corti
runs the family winery with great passion
and dedication. His contribution brought
about exciting results right from the start.
Thanks to continual research on the
subject and the territory, Nicola has
significantly extended his range of wines
over the years, following a philosophy that
aims to enhance the elegance and
structure that Merlot has to offer:
medium-long maceration and a careful
choice of French barriques produce
prestigious wines. The Salorino '16, which
combines Merlot and Cabernet Sauvignon,
delivers well-harmonized fruits and spices,
a balanced and soft body, pleasant acidity
and a surefooted finish. Their Merlot
Lénéo '16 offers pleasant enjoyability,
featuring refreshing aromas and a smooth
palate. The Stria Bianca '18 may still be a
little young, but proves supple and really
well-crafted despite its simplicity.

● Ticino Merlot Lenéo '16	♟♟ 8
● Ticino Rosso Salorino '16	♟♟ 5
● Ticino Merlot Tre Corti '17	♟ 5
○ Ticino Stria Bianca '18	♟ 5
○ Ticino Chardonnay Sileno '15	♟♟ 7
○ Ticino Chardonnay Sileno Ris. '16	♟♟ 7
● Ticino Merlot Lenéo '15	♟♟ 8
● Ticino Merlot Lenéo '14	♟♟ 8
○ Ticino Stria Bianca '16	♟♟ 5

Vini Angelo Delea

VIA ZANDONE
6616 LOSONE
TEL. +39 +41917910817
www.delea.ch

CELLAR SALES
PRE-BOOKED VISITS
ANNUAL PRODUCTION 550,000 bottles
HECTARES UNDER VINE 24.00

The Delea winery was founded in 1983
with the aim of creating high-quality wines.
Angelo Delea's foresight and passion led
him to follow his instinct and search for
products that were innovative but retained
their traditional nature at the same time.
For instance, he was one of the first to
produce sparkling wine in this territory.
Today his sons Cesare and David have
joined the winery, which now focuses on
young, modern products. However, they
always show great substance and never
neglect their fundamental philosophy. Their
Carato '16, definitely a Merlot to remember,
is truly the highest expression of elegance.
It offers a succession of fruity aromas from
plum to cherry that anticipate a rich yet
delicate palate with a balanced finish. The
Diamante '15 is complex and enveloping
with a very powerful finish and notable
wood. The winery truly knows how to
create wines that exhibit great depth.

● Ticino Merlot Carato '16	♟♟♟ 5
● Ticino Diamante '15	♟♟ 8
● Ticino Merlot Carato Ris. '16	♟♟ 6
● Ticino Merlot Saleggi '16	♟♟ 4
○ Ticino Il Chardonnay '18	♟ 4
○ Ticino Il Sauvignon '18	♟ 4
○ Ticino Carato Bianco '17	♟♟ 4
○ Ticino Carato Bianco '15	♟♟ 4
● Ticino Diamante '13	♟♟ 8
○ Ticino Il Sauvignon '17	♟♟ 3
○ Ticino Il Sauvignon '16	♟♟ 3
● Ticino Merlot Carato Ris. '15	♟♟ 6

Fawino Vini & Distillati

VIA BORROMINI, 20
6850 MENDRISIO
TEL. +39 +491763695829
www.fawino.ch

CELLAR SALES
PRE-BOOKED VISITS
ANNUAL PRODUCTION 40,000 bottles
HECTARES UNDER VINE 6.00

Great synergy exists between the two winemakers Simone Favini and Claudio Widmer. It is a meeting of passion and research on the territory, to create more well-orchestrated products. Their work is scrupulously done to obtain virtually impeccable raw materials. Their extremely attentive winemaking produces wines that encompass the characteristics intrinsic to the terroir. Each and every process is carefully supervised by both winemakers and done with extreme delicacy to guarantee extreme freshness and excellent characteristics. The virtually equivalent and unanimous scores testify to wines that hold their own against previous vintages. The Merlot Musa '17, always a stand out, proved captivating and satisfying. The noteworthy Merlot Meride '18, perhaps still a little young having just been bottled, is destined to excite when it reaches its best.

● Ticino Merlot Musa '17	♟♟ 5
● Ticino Merlot Meride '18	♟ 5
● Ticino Merlot Musa '14	♟♟♟ 5
● Ticino Merlot Musa '15	♟♟ 5

Roberto e Andrea Ferrari

LOC. CAPOLAGO
VIA BELLA CIMA, 2
6855 STABIO
TEL. +39 +41765662255
www.viniferrari.ch

ANNUAL PRODUCTION 50,000 bottles
HECTARES UNDER VINE 9.00

Andrea Ferrari was born in 1979 and, after studying at Changins School (Canton of Vaud), he decided to follow in his father's footsteps and joined the family winery. His important contribution has takne the winery towards important objectives. They have always been innovative but careful to maintain a high level of quality. Most of their production is dedicated to Merlot, but they also produce interesting wines with Chardonnay, Syrah, Viognier, Carminoir, Marselan, Caladac and Petit Verdot grapes. They were the first in Switzerland to produce this latter variety as a monovarietal in 2011. Their Castanar Rosso Riserva '11 reaches the finals with its rich bouquet of plums, currants, and spicy notes that end with roasting coffee. Rich and juicy, it offers good continuity through the finish. The surprising Merlot Castanar '15 opens on intense aromas of cherry jam and a mild vegetality that lead to full flavor with a long finish.

● Ticino Castanar Ris. '11	♟♟ 8
● Ticino Merlot Castanar '15	♟♟ 7
● Ticino Merlot Seseglio '16	♟ 4
● Ticino Merlot Castanar '13	♟♟♟ 7
● Ticino Castanar Ris. '10	♟♟ 7
● Ticino Syrah Loto '12	♟♟ 5

Gialdi Vini - Brivio

VIA VIGNOO, 3
6850 MENDRISIO
TEL. +39 +41916403030
www.gialdi.ch

CELLAR SALES
PRE-BOOKED VISITS
ANNUAL PRODUCTION 1,000,000 bottles
HECTARES UNDER VINE 120.00

Gialdi, which was founded in 1953, is an integral part of the Brivio brand. Feliciano Gialdi leads the winery today with great charisma. Continual investments in the Mendrisio and Bodio cellars make for a noteworthy and cutting-edge winery, which uses the very best technology. Their wines are all high quality and expertly created by the winemaker Alfred Demartin. Barrique aging is done in hundred-year-old cellars dug out of the Monte Generoso rock, where the constantly cool climate guarantees ideal maturation conditions. Truly refelcting the Ticino territory, only red wines were presented. One of their selections reaches the finals each year and this year that honor goes to the Merlot Sassi Grossi '16. The elegant olfactory profile is embellished with fruity notes and sweet spices, while in the mouth it is extremely soft. The Platinum '15, with velvety tannins, is another very well-made wine.

● Ticino Merlot Sassi Grossi '16	♟♟ 7
● Ticino Merlot Platinum '15	♟♟ 8
● Ticino Brivio Merlot Riflessi d'Epoca '15	♟♟ 5
● Ticino Merlot Arzo '15	♟♟ 5
● Ticino Merlot Arzo '13	♟♟ 5
● Ticino Merlot Riflessi d'Epoca '16	♟♟ 5
● Ticino Merlot Sassi Grossi '15	♟♟ 6
● Ticino Merlot Sassi Grossi '13	♟♟ 6
● Ticino Merlot Trentasei '13	♟♟ 7
● Ticino Merlot Trentasei '10	♟♟ 7

Moncucchetto

VIA MARIETTA CRIVELLI TORRICELLI, 27
6900 LUGANO
TEL. +39 +41919677060
www.moncucchetto.ch

CELLAR SALES
PRE-BOOKED VISITS
RESTAURANT SERVICE
ANNUAL PRODUCTION 30,000 bottles
HECTARES UNDER VINE 6.50

This unique and beautiful location with its breath-taking views, is far from city traffic but still in the heart of Lugano. The spectacular Moncucchetto winery, designed on three levels by the architect Mario Botta, is situated here, where nature, culture and high-quality products all live together. Cristina Monico, the famous winemaker from Ticino, diligently looks after each and every product. Her aim is to obtain great wines, while bearing in mind the quality of the raw materials and respecting an evolving tradition that looks toward new market trends. All of the wines coming from this cellar are elegant and show great respect for the territory. The Bianco dell'Arco '18, predominantly Chardonnay with some Pinot Noir, proved their best interpretation this year for its wonderful combination of aromatic refinement and beautiful, progressive flavor. The Bianco Moncucchetto '17, also excellent, delivers great balance and elegance.

○ Ticino Bianco dell'Arco '18	♟♟ 5
○ Ticino Bianco Moncucchetto '17	♟♟ 4
● Ticino Merlot L'Arco '17	♟♟ 5
● Ticino Merlot Moncucchetto '17	♟♟ 6
○ Ticino Sauvignon '18	♟ 5
● Ticino Merlot Moncucchetto '16	♟♟ 6
○ Ticino Sauvignon '17	♟♟ 5

Pelossi

VIA CARONA, 8
6912 PAZZALLO
TEL. +39 +41919945677
s.pelossi@gmail.com

CELLAR SALES
PRE-BOOKED VISITS
ANNUAL PRODUCTION 35,000 bottles
HECTARES UNDER VINE 6.00

Sacha Pelossi's winery, founded in 1987, is in continual development. With the help of his brother Christian, they never cease to amaze us with their wines. In 2013 they took over Tenuta San Matteo in Cagiallo, started a new range of products and significantly increased production. Sacha's is a distinctive line: an outstanding search for elegance and great balance, thanks to a careful choice and precise use of barriques, further enhances their wines. The range presented for this edition was truly of uniformly high level. The graceful Agra Riserva '16 offers a delicate bouquet of small wild berries, great expressiveness and a long finish. Their Lamone '16 proves lovely and subtle with mature, delicately spiced aromas. The Riva del Tasso '16, features more pronounced notes of wood and a hint of vegetality, which contribute equally to its overall enjoyability.

● Ticino Merlot Agra Ris. '16	♟♟ 6
● Ticino Merlot Lamone '16	♟♟ 6
● Ticino Rosso Riva del Tasso '16	♟♟ 6
○ Ticino Bianco della Piana '16	♟♟ 5
○ Ticino Bianco della Piana '15	♟♟ 5
● Ticino Merlot Agra Ris. '14	♟♟ 6
● Ticino Merlot Lamone '15	♟♟ 6
● Ticino Merlot Lamone '14	♟♟ 6
● Ticino Rosso Riserva del Ronco '15	♟♟ 6
● Ticino Rosso Riserva del Ronco '14	♟♟ 6
● Ticino Rosso Riva del Tasso '14	♟♟ 6

Tamborini Vini

VIA SERTA, 18
6814 LAMONE
TEL. +39 +41919357545
www.tamborinivini.ch

CELLAR SALES
PRE-BOOKED VISITS
ANNUAL PRODUCTION 700,000 bottles
HECTARES UNDER VINE 30.00

The Tamborini winery's history is continually developing and is marked by remarkable dynamism. Since he started out at this winery, Claudio Tamborini has focused on the excellence of his products: he takes extreme care in the vineyards and adopts innovative techniques in the cellar. This winery always comes across as daring, partly for its wines but even more so for the dynamic and enthusiastic people who contribute to its overall success. Today it is run by the third generation: Claudio, his daughter Valentina and Mattia carry forward their constantly-increasing work. The winery's signature style results in wines of great character that highlight their close connection to the territory. The splendid Merlot Tenuta San Rocco '16 pours with beautiful ruby tones and rich aromas. In the mouth the wine finds its strength, developing vigorously and continuously until arriving at a delicate finish. Their Merlot San Domenico '16 and Castelrotto '16 also prove very elegant.

● Ticino Merlot Tenuta San Rocco '16	♟♟ 4
● Ticino Merlot Castelrotto '16	♟♟ 6
● Ticino Merlot San Domenico '16	♟♟ 4
● Ticino Merlot San Zeno Trentalune '16	♟♟ 7
● Ticino Credi '16	♟ 6
● Ticino Merlot Comano '16	♟ 7
○ Ticino Vivi '18	♟ 6
● Ticino Credi '15	♟♟ 7
● Ticino Merlot Comano '15	♟♟ 7
● Ticino Merlot San Domenico '15	♟♟ 7
● Ticino Merlot San Zeno Costamagna '15	♟♟ 7
● Ticino Merlot V. V. '15	♟♟ 4
○ Ticino Vivi '17	♟♟ 5

Tenuta Vitivinicola Trapletti

VIA P. F. MOLA, 34
6877 COLDRERIO
TEL. +39 +41916301150
www.avvt.ch

CELLAR SALES
PRE-BOOKED VISITS
ANNUAL PRODUCTION 50,000 bottles
HECTARES UNDER VINE 13.60

An inseparable link binds Enrico Trapletti to the land. As a young man he divided his time between school and the fields, before taking a break to go and work for the railroads. But this separation didn't last long because the call of the land was too strong. In 2004 he began his winemaking venture, following in his father's footsteps. Right from the start his flair and assertive character took him along the path to success and impressive wines. In addition to the classic Merlot, he grows 15 other varieties and always experiments with new and innovative techniques. Enrico's wines prove modern and of great quality, exploiting a technical precision that creates charming wines with excellent drinkability and longevity. The Merlot Culdrée '17 starts on notes of berries and sweet spices that anticipate the compact, powerful development and very long finish.

● Ticino Merlot Culdrée '17	♟♟ 7
● Ticino Vino del Monte S. Giorgio '17	♟♟ 5
● Ticino Merlot Terra Creda '17	♟ 4
● Ticino Merlot Culdrée '15	♟♟ 7
● Ticino Merlot Culdrée '13	♟♟ 7
● Trapletti Rosso '13	♟♟ 5
● Ticino Bianco Avigia '17	♟ 5
● Ticino Merlot Terra Creda '16	♟ 5
● Ticino Merlot Terra Creda '15	♟ 5

Valsangiacomo Vini

V.LE ALLE CANTINE, 6
6850 MENDRISIO
TEL. +39 +41916836053
www.valswine.ch

CELLAR SALES
PRE-BOOKED VISITS
ANNUAL PRODUCTION 250,000 bottles
HECTARES UNDER VINE 20.00

Valsangiacomo was initially known for wine imports and sales, before starting to specialize in production at the start of the 1900s and going on to become a key player in Canton Ticino. Today Uberto Valsangiacomo carries on the family business. The winery produces high-quality wines that have become classics in Switzerland. Maturation and aging take place in characteristic cellars in Mendrisio, which enjoy perfect natural temperature and humidity conditions. Great care and attention is paid to the vineyards and winemaking processes, to best enhance their character and territoriality. Their Merlot Loverciano '16, debuted in the Guide and really surprised with its subtle yet captivating character, offering a well-balanced and low-key tannic presence, with a natural, easy drink. The Piccolo Ronco '15, once again surprises with its seductive nose, extreme elegance, and the slightly minty finish that makes it even more appealing.

● Ticino Merlot Loverciano '16	♟♟ 5
● Ticino Merlot Piccolo Ronco '15	♟♟ 5
○ Ticino Gransegreto Fondo del Bosco '16	♟♟ 5
● Ticino Merlot Piccolo Ronco '13	♟♟ 5

Vinattieri

VIA COMI, 4
6853 LIGORNETTO
TEL. +39 +41916472332
www.zanini-vinattieri.ch

CELLAR SALES
PRE-BOOKED VISITS
ANNUAL PRODUCTION 500,000 bottles
HECTARES UNDER VINE 100.00

The Zanini family have an important history. Luigi came to Ticino in 1957, full of hopes and dreams. He and his wife Liliana set up the family business, but now the running has passed to their son, Luigi Zanini Jr, who leads a sound and truly state-of-the-art group. His care of the land and vineyards is exemplary, and grape selection is meticulous: this enables him to produce sought-after wines, with great substance. Vinattieri is an icon of excellence and the jewel in the crown of both Ticino and Switzerland. Three wines made it to the final and credit certainly goes to the meticulous attention paid to each of the selections. The Vinattieri '16, among the best, first offers beautiful notes of red berries, a touch of leather and cigar, and then reveals all its sophistication and complexity in a development with a very noticeable and long yet delicate finish. The very surprising Roncaia Riserva '16, proves an absolute must-try wine.

● Ticino Merlot Ligornetto '16	🍷🍷 6
● Ticino Merlot Roncaia Ris. '16	🍷🍷 5
● Ticino Merlot Vinattieri '16	🍷🍷 8
○ Ticino Vinattieri '18	🍷 5
● Ticino Merlot Vinattieri '15	🍷🍷🍷 8
● Ticino Merlot Vinattieri '13	🍷🍷🍷 8
● Ticino Merlot Ligornetto '15	🍷🍷 6
● Ticino Merlot Ligornetto '13	🍷🍷 6
● Ticino Merlot Roncaia Ris. '15	🍷🍷 5

Vini Rovio Ronco Gianfranco Chiesa

VIA IN BASSO, 21
6921 ROVIO
TEL. +39 +41916495831
www.vinirovio.ch

CELLAR SALES
PRE-BOOKED VISITS
ANNUAL PRODUCTION 35,000 bottles
HECTARES UNDER VINE 6.00

Gianfranco Chiesa's winery in Rovio is modern and up-to-date. It is located on a beautiful terrace, where you can enjoy an incomparable view of Lake Lugano, framed by mountains surrounding Monte San Giorgio (a UNESCO World Heritage Site). Vine rows on terraces and Merlot and Chardonnay vineyards grow in full respect of the terroir. His vineyards are located in Rovio, Pugerna and Ligornetto. He also cultivates other varieties, such as Gamaret, Syrah, Cabernet Franc and Sauvignon and Chasselas, which go to producing truly elegant and well-orchestrated wines. The Chardonnay Rovio Riserva '17 debuts in the best possible manner as an outstanding expression of the famous white variety. The pervasive yet delicate nose opens buttery and slightly citrusy, leading into a sapid, lingering and gutsy palate with a very pleasant finish. The Merlot Rovio '17, still a bit young, nonetheless delivers a good overall sensory impact and a delicate finish.

○ Ticino Chardonnay Rovio Ris. '17	🍷🍷 5
● Ticino Merlot Rovio '17	🍷🍷 5
● San Vigilio '15	🍷🍷 5
● San Vigilio 75.25 '13	🍷🍷 5
● Ticino Merlot Rovio Ris. '16	🍷🍷 5
● Ticino Merlot Rovio Ris. '15	🍷🍷 5

Bianchi
S.DA DA RÖV, 24
6822 AROGNO
TEL. +39 +4176 2732050
www.bianchi.bio

CELLAR SALES
PRE-BOOKED VISITS
ANNUAL PRODUCTION 12,000 bottles
HECTARES UNDER VINE 6.00

● Ticino Syrah BioPiaz '17		♟♟ 5
○ Ticino Bianco None '18		♟ 5
● Ticino Merlot BioPiaz '17		♟ 6

Cagi - Cantina Giubiasco
VIA LINOLEUM, 12
6512 GIUBIASCO
TEL. +39 +41918572531
www.cagivini.ch

PRE-BOOKED VISITS
ANNUAL PRODUCTION 600,000 bottles
SUSTAINABLE WINERY

● Ticino Bondola Tera Negra '16		♟♟ 3
● Ticino Merlot Montecarasso '16		♟♟ 6
● Ticino Merlot Camorino '16		♟ 5

Castello di Cantone
LOC. RANCATE
VIA CANTONE, 8
6862 MENDRISIO
TEL. +39 +41916404434
www.castellodicantone.ch

● Ticino Rosso Negromante '16		♟♟ 6
○ Ticino Merlot Bianco Galanthus '18		♟ 6
● Ticino Merlot Castello di Cantone '16		♟ 8

I Fracc
I FRACC, 26A
6513 MONTE CARASSO
TEL. +39 +4179 7723735
www.ifracc.ch

ANNUAL PRODUCTION 30,000 bottles
HECTARES UNDER VINE 2.50

● Duetto '17		♟♟ 5
● Ido '17		♟♟ 5

Cantine Ghidossi
VIA RONCO REGINA, 2
6988 CROGLIO
TEL. +39 +4179 6193133
www.cantine-ghidossi.ch

ANNUAL PRODUCTION 10,000 bottles
HECTARES UNDER VINE 5.00

● Ticino Merlot Saetta '16		♟♟ 7
○ Ticino Bianco Dialogo '17		♟♟ 6
● Ticino Merlot Saetta San Martino '16		♟♟ 5
● Ticino Merlot Terra del Sole '17		♟ 4

Luigina
VIA BRUCIATA, 2
8655 STABIO
TEL. +39 +41916821543
www.tenutaluigina.ch

● Ticino Merlot Ronco dei Profeti '17		♟♟ 7
● Ticino Merlot Ronco delle Noci '17		♟♟ 7
● Ticino Sono Rosso '17		♟♟ 8
● Ticino Merlot Gemma dell'Est '16		♟ 8

F.lli Matasci

VIA VERBANO
6598 TENERO
TEL. +39 +41917356011
www.matasci.com

CELLAR SALES
PRE-BOOKED VISITS
ANNUAL PRODUCTION 80,000 bottles
SUSTAINABLE WINERY

● Ticino Rose Rosse '17	♟♟ 3
● Ticino Merlot Loco Coste '16	♟ 5

F.lli Meroni

VIA VECCHIO BORGO, 3
6710 BIASCA
TEL. +39 +41918623964
www.fratellimeroni.ch

● Ticino Merlot Le Pergole '15	♟♟ 7
● Ticino Merlot Rampèda '15	♟♟ 6
● Ticino Merlot Biasca '16	♟ 5

Mondò

VIA AL MONDÒ
6514 SEMENTINA
TEL. +39 +41918574558
www.aziendamondo.ch

ANNUAL PRODUCTION 40,000 bottles
HECTARES UNDER VINE 6.30

● Ticino Scintilla '16	♟ 4

Tenuta Pian Marnino

AL GAGGIOLETTO, 2
6515 GUDO
TEL. +39 +41918590960
pianmarnino@bluewin.ch

PRE-BOOKED VISITS
ANNUAL PRODUCTION 20,000 bottles
HECTARES UNDER VINE 5.00

● Ticino Merlot Tenuta Pian Marnino '17	♟♟ 4
● Ticino Tre Ori di Gudo '13	♟♟ 6
○ Ticino Bianco Vignabianca '18	♟ 5

Ronchi Biaggi

VIA INDUSTRIE, 18
6593 CADENAZZO
TEL. +39 +41919106353
www.ronchibiaggi.ch

PRE-BOOKED VISITS
ANNUAL PRODUCTION 20,000 bottles
HECTARES UNDER VINE 4.00
SUSTAINABLE WINERY

● Ticino Rosso Eos '16	♟♟ 4
● Ticino Rosso Torlem Minusio '16	♟♟ 4
○ Ticino Bianco Verdabbio '18	♟ 4

Tenuta San Giorgio

VIA AL BOSCO, 40
6990 TICINO
TEL. +39 +41916055868
www.tenutasangiorgio.ch

PRE-BOOKED VISITS
ANNUAL PRODUCTION 30,000 bottles
HECTARES UNDER VINE 7.00
SUSTAINABLE WINERY

● Ticino Rosso Crescendo '17	♟ 5
● Ticino Rosso Sottoroccia '17	♟ 4

TRENTINO

On the one hand there's Trento's sparklers, on the other its still wines. Trentino's growing quality is discernible across all typologies, even if sparkling wine continues to drive its reputation. Its bubbles impress more and more, and not just for their organoleptic qualities — they've shown an ability to transmit the essence of the territory, one constituted of highland vineyards and a mountain microclimate. So it is that TrentoDOC Metodo Classicos exhibit such originality and can stand shoulder to shoulder with our country's best. In terms of its still wines, we once again highlight the exploit put in by Teroldego Rotaliano, which proves that it's a superb regional red (as evidenced by the Tre Bicchieri awarded, but also by increased quality by all its producers). It seems to us that there's a considerable disconnect with the region's other reds and whites, but the hope is that this will only push producers to concentrate more on other grapes, especially traditional varieties. Certainly Teroldego is finding its direction, thanks in part to the Teroldego Revolution (founded in 2018 to create a regime for top-quality production). In terms of its whites, we especially appreciated its increasingly precise and clean Müller Thurgaus. While we expect more from dry Nosiola, its sweet versions (made with dried grapes) represent a true resource for the region, and, even if Vino Santo still isn't particularly popular, it's important to keep believing in the wine's potential. This year we believed so much in Toblino's 2003 that we chose it as our 'Sweet of the Year'. We're particularly pleased to announce the award in light of the fact that it's going to a cooperative producer (cooperatives are wineries that represent a number of growers and wine families, all working to protect the region's agriculture and rural landscapes). There's no doubt that Trentino's cooperatives produce wines of outstanding quality at the right prices, while also exhibiting territorial expression and originality. But most importantly, they've adopted a management style that fully recognizes the value of all aspects of production and, especially, their growers.

★Abate Nero

FRAZ. GARDOLO
S.DA TRENTINA, 45
38121 TRENTO
TEL. +39 0461246566
www.abatenero.it

CELLAR SALES
PRE-BOOKED VISITS
ANNUAL PRODUCTION 65,000 bottles
HECTARES UNDER VINE 65.00

There's new life at this historic sparkling wine producer. For a few months, founder Luciano Lunelli has been flanked by his daughter Laura and by Roberto Sebastiani, who brings international experience to the position. Together they intend to bolster the characteristics of the Trentos made in their cellar just outside Lavis, on the banks of the Avisio river. Grapes are cultivated on the surrounding hills and selected under the supervision of Luciano, one of Trentino's wine patriarchs. The Domini Rosé stood out during the tastings. Its soft color evokes the pinkish tones of Pinot Noir, with exotic fruit and strawberries in both its aromas and its playful drinkability. Equally satisfying is their Domini Nero, with coppery gold highlights and a rhythmic perlage of caressing softness followed by an equally flavorful drink. The extrabrut is uncomplicated and approachable.

⊙ Trento Brut Domini Rosé '13	♈♈ 5
○ Trento Brut Domini Nero '13	♈♈ 5
○ Trento Extra Brut Abate Nero	♈♈ 4
⊙ Trento Brut Rosé Abate Nero	♈ 5
○ Trento Brut Domini '10	♈♈♈ 5
○ Trento Brut Domini '07	♈♈♈ 5
○ Trento Brut Domini Nero '10	♈♈♈ 5
○ Trento Brut Domini Nero '08	♈♈♈ 5
○ Trento Domini Nero '09	♈♈♈ 5
○ Trento Brut	♈♈ 4
○ Trento Brut Rosé	♈♈ 4
○ Trento Extra Brut	♈♈ 5

★Nicola Balter

VIA VALLUNGA II, 24
38068 ROVERETO [TN]
TEL. +39 0464430101
www.balter.it

CELLAR SALES
PRE-BOOKED VISITS
ANNUAL PRODUCTION 80,000 bottles
HECTARES UNDER VINE 10.00

The Balter family have transformed the vineyards that surround their rustic castelliere into a landscape worthy of Burgundy, with plots nested among woods on the uplands overlooking Rovereto. Cultivation is carried out according the principles of organic agriculture. Nicola Balter is accompanied by his son, who oversees the cellar, and daughter, who takes care of sales. Their wines demonstrate a pronounced personality, especially their TrentoDoc sparkling wines, which for years have been among the best in Trentino, and beyond. The same holds for some of their reds as well. Pas Dosé is yet more proof of Balter's authoritativeness. This top Trento Doc is a classic Dolomites sparkling wine that offers good aromatic pluck with the right suppleness and just as much taste. Tre Bicchieri. Their Brut and Rosé are also quite good. The winemaker's expert hand can also be sensed in the house Bordeaux, the Barbanico, with its soft and enveloping structure. Their unusual Lagrein/Merlot is refreshing and pleasant, while the other whites are uncomplicated.

○ Trento Pas Dosé Balter Ris. '13	♈♈♈ 6
● Barbanico '16	♈♈ 5
● Trentino Cabernet Sauvignon '16	♈♈ 4
○ Trento Brut Balter	♈♈ 4
⊙ Trento Rosé Balter	♈♈ 5
● Lagrein Merlot '17	♈ 2
○ Sauvignon '18	♈ 4
○ Traminer '18	♈ 4
○ Trento Balter Ris. '06	♈♈♈ 5
○ Trento Dosaggio Zero Ris. '10	♈♈♈ 7
○ Trento Pas Dosé Balter Ris. '12	♈♈♈ 6
○ Trento Pas Dosé Balter Ris. '11	♈♈♈ 5
○ Trento Pas Dosé Balter Ris. '09	♈♈♈ 5

Barone de Cles

VIA G. MAZZINI, 18
38017 MEZZOLOMBARDO [TN]
TEL. +39 0461601081
www.baronedecles.it

CELLAR SALES
PRE-BOOKED VISITS
ANNUAL PRODUCTION 80,000 bottles
HECTARES UNDER VINE 39.00

The dynastic de Cles family have left their mark on the history of Trentino in various fields: religious, social and viticultural. As far back as 1700, the family gave the go ahead to the cardinal of Concilio di Trento, and to a series of innovative farmers (who were among the first), to cultivate Teroldego. Today it's young Giorgio de Cles who's carrying forward the values of his ancestors and developing the family farms situated in the valley floor around the scenic Cles castle, on the banks of the lake that's become a symbol of the Non Valley. The harvests of recent years have focused on strengthening their Teroldego's identity and have helped it reach high levels of quality. Tre Bicchieri for this fresh and juicy 2016 version. It plays on elegance, is approachable, and stretches out with velvety richness into a persistent and tasty finish. The Riserva Maso Scari '13 proves denser and more structured, and the Lagrein Riserva '16, excellent.

● Teroldego Rotaliano '16	♛♛♛ 4*
● Teroldego Rotaliano Sup. Maso Scari Ris. '13	♛♛ 5
● Trentino Lagrein Ris. '16	♛♛ 4
● Teroldego Rotaliano '14	♛♛ 3
● Teroldego Rotaliano Cardinale '12	♛♛ 5
● Teroldego Rotaliano Sup. Cardinale '13	♛♛ 5
● Trentino Lagrein '14	♛♛ 3

Bellaveder

LOC. MASO BELVEDERE
38010 FAEDO [TN]
TEL. +39 0461650171
www.bellaveder.it

CELLAR SALES
PRE-BOOKED VISITS
ANNUAL PRODUCTION 70,000 bottles
HECTARES UNDER VINE 12.00
SUSTAINABLE WINERY

The winery avails itself of two distinct, but not opposed, properties. One overlooks Lake Garda. The other (where the cellar is located) stretches along the steep hills of Faedo, near the Cembra Valley. The strategic choice was aimed at diversifying their selection while maintaining a highly pleasant style. At the center of it all is Tranquillo Lucchetta, a self-taught vigneronwho's nevertheless adept at experimentation. In his vineyards he's adopted organic cultivation, with grapes destined (depending on the vineyard of origin) for classic TrentoDocs and a group of powerful reds. But the showstopper is the decidedly racy, intriguing and intense Riesling. Their Pinot Noir Faedi, a Riserva that has been at the top of quality in Dolomite wines for years, follows along the same vein. The Lagrein Mansum, the prototype of the category, and the Müeller Thurgau, both perform admirably. Their Sauvignon and Nature di Trento DOC versions, though exquisitely executed, trail slightly.

● Trentino Pinot Nero Faedi Ris. '16	♛♛ 5
○ Trentino Riesling '16	♛♛ 3*
● Trentino Lagrein Mansum '16	♛♛ 5
○ Trentino Müller Thurgau San Lorenz '18	♛♛ 5
○ Trentino Sauvignon '17	♛ 2
○ Trento Brut Nature '14	♛ 6
● Trentino Lagrein Mansum '15	♛♛ 5
○ Trentino Müller Thurgau San Lorenz '17	♛♛ 4
○ Trentino Müller Thurgau San Lorenz '16	♛♛ 3
● Trentino Pinot Nero Faedi '15	♛♛ 6
○ Trento Brut Nature Ris. '12	♛♛ 5
○ Trento Brut Nature Ris. '12	♛♛ 6

Borgo dei Posseri

LOC. POZZO BASSO, 1
38061 ALA [TN]
TEL. +39 0464671899
www.borgodeiposseri.com

CELLAR SALES
PRE-BOOKED VISITS
ANNUAL PRODUCTION 60,000 bottles
HECTARES UNDER VINE 21.00
VITICULTURE METHOD Certified Organic
SUSTAINABLE WINERY

The official maps document vineyards on the hills over Ala as far back as 1774, amidst arduous woods where at one time they hunted with arquebus rifles. Today in the Ronchi Valley, on the left side of the Adige and on the mountain border with Veneto, the heart of the terrain is expertly cultivated by Borgo dei Possèri, a winery led by Martin Mainenti and Maria Marangoni (and families). Some ten wines are produced, each from a specific vineyard, which can be visited through a scenic enotour. Their Pinot Noir is new this year and it has been very well looked after: Paradis Plus, opens with a somewhat rustic character while still being graceful and captivating. The same can be said of their Trento Brut and fragrant Quaron made with Müeller Thurgau grapes cultivated high in the hills. The Sauvignon and Traminer exhibit some aromatic uncertainty, while the white Malusèl proves properly smooth and ready to drink.

○ Malusèl '16	♥♥ 3
● Paradis Plus Pinot Nero '16	♥♥ 3
○ Quaron Müller Thurgau '18	♥♥ 4
● Rocol Merlot '16	♥♥ 3
○ Trento Brut Tananai '15	♥♥ 5
○ Arliz Gewürztraminer '18	♥ 3
○ Furiel '18	♥ 4
○ Cuvée Malusel '15	♀♀ 4
○ Cuvée Malusel '14	♀♀ 3
○ Müller Thurgau Quaron '16	♀♀ 3
○ Sauvignon Furiel '16	♀♀ 3
○ Trento Brut Tananai '14	♀♀ 5
○ Müller Thurgau Quaron '17	♀ 4

Bossi Fedrigotti

VIA UNIONE, 43
38068 ROVERETO [TN]
TEL. +39 0456832511
www.masi.it

CELLAR SALES
PRE-BOOKED VISITS
ANNUAL PRODUCTION 120,000 bottles
HECTARES UNDER VINE 40.00
SUSTAINABLE WINERY

The count Bossi Fedrigotti family recently donated their historic agrarian archive, which goes back to 1500, to the Rovereto public library. Here they keep a record of Vallagrina's agronomic development, important viticultural references and advice, like the practice that led to Fojaneghe, a Bordeaux red, or the harvest of 'Champagne grapes' (dated 1838). For some ten harvests now, management of the winery has been entrusted to Masi, who've expanded their production of sparkling wine, though without neglecting the legendary Fojaneghe. Again this year it proved to be the winery's symbolic wine: a red with a strong personality and a structure that guarantees interesting development. The equally successful classic Conte Federico, a sparkling Trento of grace and power opens with hints of almond and a touch of lemon intertwined with the aroma of freshly baked brioche. The Vign'Asmara, a blend of aromatic grapes, delivers uncompromising simplicity.

● Fojaneghe Rosso '15	♥♥ 5
○ Trento Brut Conte Federico Ris. '15	♥♥ 5
○ Trentino Vign'Asmara '17	♥♥ 4
● Fojaneghe Rosso '12	♀♀♀ 5
○ Trento Brut Conte Federico Ris. '12	♀♀♀ 5
● Fojaneghe Rosso '13	♀♀ 5
○ Trentino Bianco Vign'Asmara '16	♀♀ 4
● Trentino Teroldego Mas'Est '16	♀♀ 3
○ Trento Brut Conte Federico Ris. '13	♀♀ 5
○ Vign'Asmara '15	♀♀ 4

★Cavit

VIA DEL PONTE, 31
38040 TRENTO
TEL. +39 0461381711
www.cavit.it

CELLAR SALES
PRE-BOOKED VISITS
ANNUAL PRODUCTION 70,000,000 bottles
HECTARES UNDER VINE 5500.00

Cavit is a lovely operation that brings together the work of almost 5,000 vine growers. They produce bottles capable of satisfying various market demands, though without compromising in typicity and territorial adherence. The primary focus is on meticulously differentiating the various types of wines, starting with their classic Trentodoc. Though they also offer the occasional surprise, like Pinot Nero, Riesling, Nosiola or Schiava. Their prices are truly competitive and decidedly affordable. Tre Bicchieri to their undisputed champion, the sparkling Altemasi Graal, a decidedly authoritative Riserva representative of both the grace and gustatory power of Trento wines. Three other sparklers stand out: Pas Dosè, Brut Millesimato and Rosé. The Pinot Noir Brusafer and Riesling Una Tantum (a one-off in name and fact) offer great drinkability. Their wide range of Cavit wines always proves excellent, from the new Nosiola Conzal to the traditional Quattro Vicariati Bordeaux.

○ Trento Brut Altemasi Graal Ris. '12	♥♥♥ 6
● Trentino Pinot Nero Sup. Brusafer '16	♥♥ 5
○ Trentino Riesling Una Tantum '14	♥♥ 3*
○ Trentino Nosiola Bottega Vinai '18	♥♥ 2*
○ Trentino Nosiola Conzal '18	♥♥ 4
● Trentino Rosso Quattro Vicariati '16	♥♥ 4
○ Trento Altemasi Pas Dosé '13	♥♥ 5
⊙ Trento Altemasi Rosé	♥♥ 4
○ Maso Torresella Cuvée '17	♥ 4
○ Trento Brut Altemasi Graal Ris. '10	♀♀♀ 6
○ Trento Brut Altemasi Graal Ris. '09	♀♀♀ 6
○ Trento Brut Altemasi Graal Ris. '08	♀♀♀ 6

Cesarini Sforza

FRAZ. RAVINA
VIA STELLA, 9
38123 TRENTO
TEL. +39 0461382200
www.cesarinisforza.com

CELLAR SALES
PRE-BOOKED VISITS
ANNUAL PRODUCTION 1,300,000 bottles
HECTARES UNDER VINE 800.00

Cesarini Sforza has half a century of experience under its belt, all in sparkling wine. Situated in Trento, in the so-called 'sparkling triangle', it was one of the first producers to bet on Trentino's viticulture and mountain bubblies. Indeed, here 3 esteemed wineries produce almost 8 million bottles of Metodo Classico. Moreover, a partnership with Cantina Lavis has been strategic and fundamental, allowing Cesarini Sforza to produce some of the Dolomites' most important cuvèes while competing with estates situated further on high. Six Trentos were proposed at our tastings and these included some absolute treats. The 1673 Riserva '12 and Aquila Reale '09 both made it to the finals, with the latter receiving the higher commendation. Their other wines, especially those of the 1673 line, deliver vibrance and versatility: their Noir Nature proves juicy and their Rosé gratifying.

○ Trento Brut Aquila Reale Ris. '09	♥♥♥ 6
○ Trento Extra Brut 1673 Ris. '12	♥♥ 5
○ Trento Brut Nature Noir 1673 '13	♥♥ 5
⊙ Trento Rosè 1673 '13	♥♥ 5
○ Trento Brut	♥ 4
⊙ Trento Brut Rosé	♥ 4
○ Trento Aquila Reale Ris. '05	♀♀♀ 7
○ Trento Aquila Reale Ris. '02	♀♀♀ 7
○ Trento Extra Brut 1673 Ris. '11	♀♀♀ 5
○ Trento Extra Brut Tridentum '09	♀♀♀ 4*
○ Trento Brut Nature Noir 1673 '12	♀♀ 5
⊙ Trento Brut Rosé Ris. '11	♀♀ 4
○ Trento Brut Tridentum '12	♀♀ 4
○ Trento Extra Brut 1673 Ris. '10	♀♀ 5

TRENTINO

Corvée

LOC. BEDIN, 1
38034 LISIGNAGO [TN]
TEL. +39 3440260170
www.corvee.wine

CELLAR SALES
PRE-BOOKED VISITS
ANNUAL PRODUCTION 50,000 bottles
HECTARES UNDER VINE 13.60

Corvée has broken out in Trentino with great determination, and done it with wines that are decidedly 'of the mountains'. Moreover, entrepreneurial skill and innovation have resulted in a selection that's of high quality. Indeed the producer has, from the outset, held a top place, overturning antiquated modes of management. The technical side is entrusted to expert enologist Beppe Caviola, a Piedmont native who knows Trentino well. He's helped by Trentino native Moreno Nardin, who has agronomic experience in Veneto and Tuscany. It's only taken a few harvests for the Lisignago winery to reach the top of Trentino production. All ten of the wines presented proved to be exceptional. Tre Bicchieri for their Müller Thurgau Viach, once again unbeatable with its variegated floral notes and focused presence of flavor. Next come two Trento wines, a Brut and a Rosé, true novelties for this newborn winery. The Pinot Noir, a red of great class and elegance, also deserves mention.

○ Trentino Müller Thurgau Vìach '18	▼▼▼ 4*
● Trentino Pinot Nero Agole '17	▼▼ 6
○ Trentino Chardonnay Quaràs '18	▼▼ 5
● Trentino Lagrein Passo della Croce '17	▼▼ 5
○ Trentino Pinot Bianco Còr '18	▼▼ 5
○ Trentino Pinot Grigio Corvaia '18	▼▼ 4
○ Trentino Sauvignon Bisù '18	▼▼ 5
○ Trentino Traminer Clongiàn '18	▼▼ 5
○ Trento Brut	▼▼ 5
⊙ Trento Rosè	▼▼ 5
○ Trentino Müller Thurgau Vìach '17	♈♈♈ 4*
● Trentino Lagrein Passo della Croce '16	♈♈ 5
○ Trentino Pinot Bianco Cor '17	♈♈ 5
● Trentino Pinot Nero Agole '16	♈♈ 6

De Vescovi Ulzbach

P.ZZA GARIBALDI, 12
38016 MEZZOCORONA [TN]
TEL. +39 04611740050
www.devescoviulzbach.it

CELLAR SALES
PRE-BOOKED VISITS
ANNUAL PRODUCTION 20,000 bottles
HECTARES UNDER VINE 3.50

Giulio De Vescovi has affirmed his status as one of Teroldego Rotaliano's best interpreters. His passion for the wine has allowed him to take on other promotional challenges, like TeroldeGO(R)evolution, a group of friends who oversee nearby wineries connected to Teroldego. Great attention is paid to the estate's vineyards, which bring out the highest possible character of the territory. Some of these are high-elevation, terraced plots, which they use to experiment with Metodo Classico and whites of a singular complexity. We were presented with three serious interpretations of Teroldego of great class that proved almost equal and were all met with applause. This year it wasn't the younger version or the exclusive Vigilius that took Tre Bicchieri, but their Le Fron, the most recent version and perhaps for this reason the most carefully managed of the three. It won with relative ease thanks to its portentous sophistication: a thoroughbred's grace and elegance dominate the palate and the finish is exquisitely Rotaliano.

● Teroldego Rotaliano V. Le Fron '16	▼▼▼ 6
● Teroldego Rotaliano Vigilius '16	▼▼ 5
● Teroldego Rotaliano '17	▼▼ 3
● Teroldego Rotaliano '15	♈♈♈ 3*
● Teroldego Rotaliano Vigilius '12	♈♈♈ 5
● Kino Nero '15	♈♈ 4
● Teroldego Rotaliano '16	♈♈ 3*
● Teroldego Rotaliano '14	♈♈ 3*
● Teroldego Rotaliano Vigilius '15	♈♈ 5
● Teroldego Rotaliano Vigilius '13	♈♈ 5

★Dorigati

VIA DANTE, 5
38016 MEZZOCORONA [TN]
TEL. +39 0461605313
www.dorigati.it

CELLAR SALES
PRE-BOOKED VISITS
ANNUAL PRODUCTION 100,000 bottles
HECTARES UNDER VINE 10.00
SUSTAINABLE WINERY

Cousins Michele and Paolo Dorigati are volcanic wine producers, (volcanic, like much of the mountain soil surrounding their vineyards on the valley floor). Fresh off their university studies, they're carrying forward a family-run producer that has 170 vintages under its belt, all of which passed through their deep cellar. The primary focus is on Teroldego, the area's prince grape. It's no coincidence that they also promote TeroldeGO(R)evolution, a decidedly innovative project aimed at sharing highly valuable undertakings. This year though we only tasted three versions of Teroldego Rotaliano and all proved splendid. Their Luigi Riserva '15 fell just short of the highest possible rating. The vigorous Diedri demands attention with a pulpy juiciness that has perhaps never before been so successful, as does their more traditional version (from the 2017 vintage) of this symbolic Campo Rotaliano wine/vine.

● Teroldego Rotaliano Luigi Ris. '15	♟♟6
● Teroldego Rotaliano Cl. '17	♟♟4
● Teroldego Rotaliano Diedri Ris. '16	♟♟5
● Teroldego Rotaliano Luigi Ris. '13	♟♟♟6
○ Trento Brut Methius Ris. '09	♟♟♟6
○ Trento Brut Methius Ris. '08	♟♟♟6
○ Trento Brut Methius Ris. '06	♟♟♟6
○ Trento Brut Methius Ris. '05	♟♟♟6
○ Trento Brut Methius Ris. '04	♟♟♟6
○ Trento Brut Methius Ris. '03	♟♟♟6
○ Trento Brut Methius Ris. '02	♟♟♟6
○ Trento Brut Methius Ris. '00	♟♟♟6

Endrizzi

LOC. MASETTO, 2
38010 SAN MICHELE ALL'ADIGE [TN]
TEL. +39 0461650129
www.endrizzi.it

CELLAR SALES
PRE-BOOKED VISITS
ANNUAL PRODUCTION 600,000 bottles
HECTARES UNDER VINE 55.00
SUSTAINABLE WINERY

The keyword here is 'eco-sustainability'. The Endrici family have been practicing it for more than thirty years, overseeing a winery they've owned since 1885. Respect for the environment, experimentation and a new focus on promotion are the principles guiding Lisa and Daniele (who are supported by their young children, Cristine and Paolo, as well as enologist Vito Pigger). They're also committed to culture, holding art exhibitions and musical performances at their winery, activities that accompany a production philosophy aimed at quality. The sparkling wines prove varied, impressive and international while also showing territoriality. Their Rosé, for example, opens very finely and develops Mediterranean aromas. The robust, complex Gran Masetto, a deliberately concentrated wine made from overripe grapes, delivers notes of cherry jam, cocoa and spices encouraging a leisurely, meditative sip. The Teroldego proves jovial and the two Masetto wines, containing Teroldego paired with either Cabernet or Merlot, very approachable.

● Gran Masetto '14	♟♟8
● Teroldego Rotaliano Sup. Leocorno Ris. '16	♟♟4
○ Trento Brut Piancastello Rosè Ris. '13	♟♟5
○ Trento Masetto Privè '09	♟♟8
● Masetto Due '17	♟6
● Masetto Nero '16	♟4
● Gran Masetto '13	♟♟8
● Gran Masetto '12	♟♟8
○ Masetto Bianco '15	♟♟3
● Teroldego Rotaliano Leoncorno Ris. '15	♟♟5
○ Trento Masetto Privè '08	♟♟6
○ Trento Piancastello '13	♟♟5

★★★Ferrari

VIA PONTE DI RAVINA, 15
38123 TRENTO
TEL. +39 0461972311
www.ferraritrento.it

CELLAR SALES
PRE-BOOKED VISITS
RESTAURANT SERVICE
ANNUAL PRODUCTION 5,500,000 bottles
HECTARES UNDER VINE 120.00
SUSTAINABLE WINERY

The Lunelli family occupy a leading place among sparkling winemakers. Undisputed pioneers of signature wines appreciated the world over, Camilla, Alessandro, Matteo and Marcello have brought together territorial values with the charm of Italian style, a commitment passed down over generations. Their cultivation practices in Trentino (as with their estates in Umbria and Tuscany) are aimed at eco-sustainability. Their range of Trentodocs, which are produced under the supervision of Ruben Larentis, prove more engaging by the year. The most recent addition is their Giulio Ferrari Rosé. Many Trento wines made it with ease to our final tastings, and all placed among the top. The legendary Giulio, however, thanks to its incredible elegance, proved the most impressive and gets Tre Bicchieri. The creamy mousse, leaving a refreshing, intriguing trail, offers an almost indescribable overall goodness. The very lively Rosé version suggests further aging potential. Applause also for the Perlé Nero and the Riserva Lunelli. In truth, the whole range is worthy of mention.

○ Trento Brut Giulio Ferrari Riserva del Fondatore '08	♟♟♟ 8
○ Trento Brut Giulio Ferrari Riserva del Fondatore Rosè '07	♟♟ 8
○ Trento Extra Brut Lunelli Ris. '10	♟♟ 7
○ Trento Extra Brut Perlé Nero Ris. '11	♟♟ 8
○ Trento Brut Perlé Bianco Ris. '10	♟♟ 7
○ Trento Perlè Zero Cuvèe 12	♟♟ 6
○ Trento Brut Giulio Ferrari Riserva del Fondatore '06	♟♟♟ 8
○ Trento Brut Giulio Ferrari Riserva del Fondatore '05	♟♟♟ 8
○ Trento Brut Giulio Ferrari Riserva del Fondatore '04	♟♟♟ 8
○ Trento Extra Brut Lunelli Ris. '07	♟♟♟ 7
○ Trento Perlé Zero Cuvée Zero '11	♟♟♟ 8

La Vis - Valle di Cembra

VIA CARMINE, 7
38015 LAVIS [TN]
TEL. +39 0461440111
www.la-vis.com

CELLAR SALES
PRE-BOOKED VISITS
ACCOMMODATION AND RESTAURANT SERVICE
ANNUAL PRODUCTION 1,000,000 bottles
HECTARES UNDER VINE 850.00
SUSTAINABLE WINERY

La Vis - Valle di Cembra was one of the first Trentino cooperatives to focus on precision, thanks to a series of high-quality selections. At times this commitment was put to the test by managerial uncertainties, but these were overcome by the determination of their members and new, competent management. Their range of wines is vast, with particular attention to white grapes cultivated in the high hills. They also work with native grapes and more well-known international varieties. Of the 20 wines proposed, almost all earned Due Bicchieri and two reached the finals. The Riesling '18 offers just the right amount of spirit, proving smooth yet powerful (it's also great value for the money). The same goes for their Kerner and Traminer Clinga, not to mention the Vigna delle Forche, a Müller Thurgau from the upper Cembra valley. Their Pinot Noir Saosent, Lagrein Greggi and certain Chardonnays, particularly the cru Diaol, all put in fine showings. The lean, captivating Pinot Bianco did well, as did the Nosiola and white Maso Franch.

○ Trentino Müller Thurgau V. delle Forche '17	♟♟ 3*
○ Trentino Riesling '18	♟♟ 2*
● Maso Franch '15	♟♟ 4
● Trentino Cabernet Sauvignon '15	♟♟ 4
○ Trentino Chardonnay Diaol '17	♟♟ 3
○ Trentino Kerner V. Cembra '18	♟♟ 3
● Trentino Lagrein Greggi '15	♟♟ 5
○ Trentino Nosiola '18	♟♟ 5
○ Trentino Pinot Bianco '18	♟♟ 4
○ Trentino Pinot Grigio '18	♟♟ 4
● Trentino Pinot Nero V. di Saosent '16	♟♟ 5
○ Trentino Riesling V. Cancor '18	♟♟ 4
○ Trentino Sauvignon '18	♟♟ 4
○ Trentino Traminer Clinga '18	♟♟ 4

★Letrari

VIA MONTE BALDO, 13/15
38068 ROVERETO [TN]
TEL. +39 0464480200
www.letrari.it

CELLAR SALES
PRE-BOOKED VISITS
ANNUAL PRODUCTION 160,000 bottles
HECTARES UNDER VINE 23.00

Lucia Letrari is carrying forward with great determination and a constant commitment learnt from her father, the unforgettable Nello, one of Trentino's most respected sparkling winemakers. Lucia is a tireless 'lady of wine', as ready to explain her production philosophy at any number of promotional tastings as she is busy in her Vallagarina vineyards and family winery. Her perennially reliable and precise selection of Trentodocs are accompanied by the occasional still wine (foremost Marzemino) and a Teroldego from outside the district. We had no hesitation awarding Tre Bicchieri to the powerful Dosaggio Zero Riserva, this worthy Rovereto winery's most coddled Trento. It delivers tight flavor, splendid acidity and a persistent finish. The Quore, a monovarietal Chardonnay, offers very delicate fabric and assertive substance. Versatility and solid flavor distinguish the rest of the range, including the simple Marzemino, an hommage to the traditions of Vallagarina.

○ Trento Dosaggio Zero Letrari Ris. '12	♟♟♟ 6
○ Trento Brut Quore Ris. '12	♟♟ 6
○ Trento Brut '16	♟♟ 5
○ Trento Brut Ris. '13	♟♟ 5
● Trentino Marzemino '18	♟ 3
○ Trento Cuvèe Blance	♟ 4
○ Trento Brut 976 Riserva del Fondatore '05	♟♟♟ 8
○ Trento Brut Letrari Ris. '09	♟♟♟ 5
○ Trento Brut Letrari Ris. '08	♟♟♟ 5
○ Trento Brut Letrari Ris. '07	♟♟♟ 5
○ Trento Brut Ris. '10	♟♟♟ 5
○ Trento Brut Rosé +4 '09	♟♟♟ 6
○ Trento Dosaggio Zero Ris. '11	♟♟♟ 6

Mas dei Chini

FRAZ. MARTIGNANO
VIA BASSANO, 3
38121 TRENTO
TEL. +39 0461821513
www.cantinamasdeichini.it

CELLAR SALES
ANNUAL PRODUCTION 55,000 bottles
HECTARES UNDER VINE 30.00

We could call Mas dei Chini an 'urban' agricultural business inasmuch as their vineyards are nested among Trento's hillside dwellings, on the sunnier side of Monte Calisio, a symbol of the territory. Graziano Chini is a well-known dealer of industrial vehicles and automobiles who's made a decisive turn to winemaking, especially sparkling wines. The winery is constantly growing in terms of production (not just Metodo Classico, there are also still wines made with native grapes). There are also guest accommodations and a restaurant. Two Trento wines reached the top during our tastings. The Inkino Nature Rosé, opens with delicious hints of berries blended with pastries. The Inkino Brut Carlo V Riserva '10, a carbonic sparkling wine, perfectly balances acidity and sapidity. The other sparklers presented also prove impressive. Among still versions their juicy, dynamic red Lagrein '18 stands out.

○ Trento Inkino Carlo V Ris. '10	♟♟♟ 6
○ Trento Inkino Rosè Nature	♟♟♟ 6
● Trentino Lagrein '18	♟♟ 4
○ Trento Inkino Brut	♟♟ 6
○ Trento Inkino Nature '11	♟♟ 6
○ Theodor '18	♟ 4
○ Trentino Traminer '18	♟ 4
○ Inkino Brut Riserva '10	♟♟ 5
○ Trento Inkino Carlo V '08	♟♟ 6
○ Trento Inkino Rosè Nature	♟♟ 6

Maso Cantanghel

VIA CARLO SETTE, 21
38015 LAVIS [TN]
TEL. +39 0461246353
www.masocantanghel.eu

CELLAR SALES
PRE-BOOKED VISITS
ANNUAL PRODUCTION 20,000 bottles
HECTARES UNDER VINE 8.50
VITICULTURE METHOD Certified Organic
SUSTAINABLE WINERY

The Simoni family's premium wine bottles
feature an image of a formidable, late-19th
century fort. The image is closely tied to the
origin of the grapes used, which are
cultivated in vineyards around the
Cantanghel fort, between Trento and
Valsugana. It's here that the prestigious
Lavis winery's most important grapes are
harvested and then used for a small,
exclusive selection of wines. Among these
still wines is one of the Dolomites' most
important Pinot Neros. Their Trentodoc
sparkling wines are sold under the family's
under brand, Monfort. Tre Bicchieri to their
Pinot Noir thanks to its aromatic austerity,
elegant color and just as juicy palate. The
wine exhibits a decidedly clear style tied to
the constant attention paid to it by Federico
Simoni at his country residence. The Cuvèe
Sotsàs also stands out along with an agile
Sauvignon and two other traditional whites.

● Trentino Pinot Nero	
Maso Cantanghel '16	♟♟♟ 5
○ SotSàs Cuvée '17	♟♟ 3
○ Trentino Sauvignon	
Maso Cantanghel '18	♟♟ 4
○ Pinot Grigio Maso Papa '17	♟ 3
○ Trentino Traminer Aromatico	
Vigna Caselle '18	♟ 3
● Trentino Pinot Nero V. Cantanghel '15	♟♟♟ 5
○ Blanc de Sers '16	♟♟ 4
○ Trentino Nosiola Corylus '16	♟♟ 4
● Trentino Pinot Nero V. Cantanghel '11	♟♟ 5
○ Trentino Sauvignon	
Maso Cantanghel '17	♟♟ 4
○ Trento Brut Ris. Monfort '12	♟♟ 6

Maso Martis

LOC. MARTIGNANO
VIA DELL'ALBERA, 52
38121 TRENTO
TEL. +39 0461821057
www.masomartis.it

CELLAR SALES
PRE-BOOKED VISITS
ANNUAL PRODUCTION 65,000 bottles
HECTARES UNDER VINE 12.00
VITICULTURE METHOD Certified Organic

A feminine touch can be detected in each of
this producer's wines. Indeed, Antonio
Stelzer is leaving more room to his wife,
Roberta, and their young daughters,
Alessandra and Maddalena. They operate
out of the family's lovely residence, amidst
vineyards that crawl up the slopes of Calisio,
the sunniest of the mountains overlooking
Trento. Antonio concerns himself primarily
with these, working among the flowers and
vegetation that make evident their
commitment to organic cultivation and
biodiversity. Elegance and finesse are the
primary features of Maso Martis's Trendocs.
Madame Martis may have impeccable form
but is, above all, elegant. A truly wonderful,
vivid gold sparkling wine, it delivers very fine
mousse, hints of shortbread and dried
peaches, as well as notes of pineapple and
candied citron that carry through on the
palate. An exceptionally well-deserved Tre
Bicchieri. The other Trento wines from the
organic Casa Stelzer also hit very close to
the bullseye, in particular the increasingly
powerful and complex Zero Dosage and their
tried and true Rosé.

○ Trento Brut Madame Martis Ris. '09	♟♟♟ 8
○ Trento Dosaggio Zero	
Maso Martis Ris. Bio '15	♟♟ 5
○ Trento Brut Maso Martis Bio	♟♟ 5
○ Trento Brut Maso Martis Rosè Bio '15	♟♟ 5
○ Trento Brut Madame Martis Ris. '08	♟♟♟ 8
○ Trento Dosaggio Zero Ris. '12	♟♟♟ 6
○ Trento Dosaggio Zero Ris. '11	♟♟♟ 5
○ Trentino Chardonnay L'Incanto '15	♟♟ 3
○ Trento Brut Maso Martis Ris. '13	♟♟ 6
○ Trento Brut Ris. '11	♟♟ 5
○ Trento Dosaggio Zero '13	♟♟ 5

Maso Poli

LOC. MASI DI PRESSANO, 33
38015 LAVIS [TN]
TEL. +39 0461871519
www.masopoli.com

CELLAR SALES
PRE-BOOKED VISITS
ANNUAL PRODUCTION 75,000 bottles
HECTARES UNDER VINE 13.00

Three young sisters, Martina, Romina and Valentina, form the axis of the winery founded by their father, Luigi Togn. Luigi was one of Trentino's wine 'patriarchs' and a longtime leading member of local wine associations. Today, all the sisters have specific roles, proving as competent as they are determined to improve their already highly-valued selection. It's a variegated range that comprises wines made with grapes cultivated near the farmstead, on the hills of Lavis, and selections from their other winery, Gajerhof di Roverè della Luna, which operates between Trento and Bolzano. The Trento Brut Riserva immediately stood out during the tastings for its particularly aggressive mousse and delicate yet invigorating drink. The gentle Riesling opens with hints of citrus and hits the palate with peppery tones, agility and just the right amount of linearity. Their aromatic Traminer is also impressive, hitting the nose with moderately spicy tones that vaguely recall curry. Among the reds, the Marmoran (Teroldego and Lagrein) proves increasingly dense and deep.

● Trentino Marmoram '16	▼▼	5
○ Trentino Riesling '18	▼▼	4
○ Trentino Traminer '18	▼▼	3
○ Trento Brut Ris. '13	▼▼	6
○ Trentino Nosiola '18	▼	3
● Trentino Pinot Nero '16	▼	3
○ Trentino Gewürztraminer '17	♀♀	4
● Trentino Marmoram '15	♀♀	5
○ Trentino Nosiola '16	♀♀	3
○ Trentino Pinot Grigio '16	♀♀	3
○ Trento Maso Poli	♀♀	5

Mezzacorona

VIA DEL TEROLDEGO, 1E
38016 MEZZOCORONA [TN]
TEL. +39 0461616399
www.mezzacorona.it

CELLAR SALES
PRE-BOOKED VISITS
ACCOMMODATION
ANNUAL PRODUCTION 48,000,000 bottles
HECTARES UNDER VINE 2800.00

A high quality selection of wines testify to their level of mastery, but they've proven they can succeed when it comes to quantity as well. The Mezzacorona group are one of Italy's most important producers thanks to a diversified management approach involving thousands of regional growers and properties that extend all the way to Sicily. It's all aimed at highlighting the attributes of each territory through increasingly green methods, both in the vineyards and in their cellars. Teroldego Rotaliano remains a cornerstone, though a series of Trentodocs are also making their mark. Virtually all of the thirteen wines presented at the tastings were of high quality. Their sparkling Flavio confirms its place as a champion and this year again wins Tre Bicchieri. Credit goes to its expression of citrus and its enfolding drink which proves bright, snappy and absolutely enjoyable. This same kind of sparkling panache also emerges in their Rosé, which is decidedly gratifying. The Teroldego Nòs and Marzemino, perhaps the best interpretations of each that we tasted this year, also deserve praise.

○ Trento Brut Rotari Flavio Ris. '11	▼▼▼	8
○ Trento Brut Rosé AlpeRegis '14	▼▼	6
● Nerofino '16	▼▼	4
● Teroldego Rotaliano Castel Firmian Ris. '15	▼▼	2*
● Teroldego Rotaliano Nòs '13	▼▼	4
○ Trentino Chardonnay Castel Firmian Ris. '17	▼▼	5
● Trentino Marzemino Castel Firmian '17	▼▼	3
○ Trentino Pinot Grigio Castel Firmian '17	▼▼	5
○ Trento Pas Dosé Rotari AlpeRegis '13	▼▼	6
○ Trentino Gewürztraminer Castel Firmian '18	▼	3
○ Trentino Sauvignon Castel Firmian '18	▼	5
○ Trento Brut Rotari Flavio Ris. '10	♀♀♀	8
○ Trento Brut Rotari Flavio Ris. '09	♀♀♀	8
○ Trento Brut Rotari Flavio Ris. '08	♀♀♀	5

Moser

FRAZ. GARDOLO DI MEZZO
VIA CASTEL DI GARDOLO, 5
38121 TRENTO
TEL. +39 0461990786
www.cantinemoser.com

CELLAR SALES
PRE-BOOKED VISITS
ACCOMMODATION
ANNUAL PRODUCTION 120,000 bottles
HECTARES UNDER VINE 17.00

Supple, but with some pluck. In a nutshell (and in perfect keeping with their author), that's how you could define the wines produced by Francesco Moser, a cycling champion who transformed his youthful passion for vine growing into a modern winery. Helped by his children Carlo, Francesca and Ignazio, as well as his enologist grandson Matteo, he completely renovated and implemented a vast property over Gardolo di Trento through management of other plots in the Cembra Valley, near the cyclist's birthplace. Their Trentodocs are notable, as are their still white wines. Their Nature once again proved excellent, a champion of the category, though this year, penalized for its uncontrolled energy, it didn't manage to again capture Tre Bicchieri. The Rosé, too, looks well positioned for a possible future win. Other stars included their Trento 51.151 (named after Franceso's 1984 Olympic record) as well as the Chardonnay and Traminer, both of which offer excellent drinkability.

○ Trento Brut Nature '13	🏆 5
○ Trentino Chardonnay '18	🏆 2*
○ Trentino Traminer Aromatico '18	🏆 3
○ Trento Brut 51,151	🏆 5
⊙ Trento Extra Brut Rosé '15	🏆 5
○ Trento Brut Nature '12	🏆 5
○ Trentino Chardonnay '17	🏆 2*
○ Trento Brut 51,151	🏆 5
○ Trento Brut Nature '11	🏆 5

Pojer & Sandri

LOC. MOLINI, 4
38010 FAEDO [TN]
TEL. +39 0461650342
www.pojeresandri.it

CELLAR SALES
PRE-BOOKED VISITS
ACCOMMODATION
ANNUAL PRODUCTION 200,000 bottles
HECTARES UNDER VINE 26.00
VITICULTURE METHOD Certified Organic

Mario Pojer and Fiorentino Sandri aren't tired in the least bit. They bring youthful vigor to their work, spurred on by the continued pursuit of new agronomic solutions, and by a desire to improve and innovate while making wines that maintain a bond with the territory. Their vineyards are situated both in Faedo and on high, on the steepest slopes of the property purchased along the Avisio river, in the Cembra Valley. The latest technology is used in the cellar, but it's also a pleasure to know that their wines can amaze without the use of chemicals in their vineyards. This year, too, the tastings revealed an absolutely delightful selection of wines with strong personality. Their Rosé proves among the most exciting, as does their Pinot Noir, perennially at the top of the category. The particularly dense, rich Faye has all it needs to be even more promising at future tastings. Among their other satisfying wines, the perfectly supple Traminer leads the pack, along with the Palai, made Müller Thurgau grapes.

● Rodel Pianezzi Pinot Nero '16	🏆 5
⊙ Spumante Brut Rosé	🏆 5
● Faye Rosso '15	🏆 6
○ Palai '18	🏆 3
○ Trentino Traminer Covelli '17	🏆 4
○ Nosiola '18	🏆 3
○ Trentino Riesling '18	🏆 4
● Bianco Faye '08	🏆🏆 5
● Bianco Faye '01	🏆🏆 5
● Pinot Nero Rodel Pianezzi '09	🏆🏆 5
● Rosso Faye '05	🏆🏆 5
● Rosso Faye '00	🏆🏆 5
○ Cuveé Extra Brut 13/14	🏆 6
○ Faye Bianco '15	🏆 5
● Faye Rosso '13	🏆 6

Pravis

Loc. Le Biolche, 1
38076 Lasino [TN]
Tel. +39 0461564305
www.pravis.it

CELLAR SALES
PRE-BOOKED VISITS
ANNUAL PRODUCTION 200,000 bottles
HECTARES UNDER VINE 32.00

Founded by three friends in the mid-1970s, today the winery is under the guidance of their children (Pedrini, Chistè, Zambarda). Pravis's philosophy centers on eco-sustainability, and enologist Erika Pedrini has decided to work with interspecific grapes as well, vines that are disease-resistant and don't require chemical treatment. It was for many years a low-key project, but now they're offering experimental wines, accompanied by a praised selection of traditional 'Valle dei Laghi' wines. We were most impressed with their red Syrae, which proved compact and very elegant despite it power. The Shiraz it's based on has been masterfully raised for years in this sun-kissed area. The Madruzzo (a Pinot Noir) envelopes the palate and has nose full of wild berries. White wines coming from high hillside vineyards play a compelling supporting role. The San Thomà (a Müller Thurgau) has traditional gutsy aromas, while their Le Frate (a Nosiola) offers herbaceous grace in its delicate simplicity. The Kerner and Rebo are both quite pleasing.

● Syrae '16	♈♈ 5
● Madruzzo Pinot Nero '16	♈♈ 3
○ Müller Thurgau San Thomà '18	♈♈ 2*
○ Nosiola Le Frate '18	♈♈ 2*
○ Kerner '18	♈ 4
● Rebo '16	♈ 4
● Fratagranda '10	♈♈♈ 4*
● Fratagranda '09	♈♈♈ 4*
● Fratagranda '07	♈♈♈ 4
○ Vino Santo Arèle '06	♈♈♈ 6
● Fratagranda '13	♈♈ 4
○ l'Ora '14	♈♈ 5
○ Soliva '12	♈♈ 6
○ Stravino di Stravino '13	♈♈ 4
● Syrae '15	♈♈ 5

Revì

via Florida, 10
38060 Aldeno [TN]
Tel. +39 0461843155
www.revispumanti.com

CELLAR SALES
PRE-BOOKED VISITS
ANNUAL PRODUCTION 20,000 bottles
HECTARES UNDER VINE 1.70
VITICULTURE METHOD Certified Organic

The name Revì represents an homage to the 're del vino' ('king of wine'), as agricultural tradition has it here in Aldeno, a viticultural district on the right back of the Adige river between Trento and Rovereto. Since 1982, Paolo Malfer has been making exclusively sparkling wine in his cellar here. His commitment is constant and his work, which is continually evolving and highly artisanal, is supported by his sons Giacomo and Stefano. Meticulous attention is shown in cultivating the grapes used, both when it comes to their estate vineyards and those overseen by trusted growers. Organic agriculture and carefully designed bottles make the difference. Their Trento wines stood out this year, starting with the Rosé, which proved truly enjoyable with a solid backbone of flavor; truly one of the best we've recently tasted. Their very elegant Paladino opens on notes of plums and passionfruit that leads to a gentle herbaceous boost. More subtly versatile, the Dosaggio Zero offers hints of honey and exotic spices. The Cavaliere Nero, an ideal cuvée with a harmonious and unfolding drink, also deserves a mention.

⊙ Trento Brut Rosé '15	♈♈ 5
⊙ Trento Dosaggio Zero '15	♈♈ 5
⊙ Trento Extra Brut Paladino '13	♈♈ 7
⊙ Trento Brut '15	♈ 4
⊙ Trento Brut Rosé '13	♈♈ 5
○ Trento Dosaggio Zero '14	♈♈ 5
○ Trento Dosaggio Zero '13	♈♈ 5
○ Trento Extra Brut Bio Paladino '12	♈♈ 7
○ Trento Extra Brut Cavaliere Nero '10	♈♈ 5
○ Trento Extra Brut Paladino Ris. '11	♈♈ 5

Agraria Riva del Garda

LOC. SAN NAZZARO, 4
38066 RIVA DEL GARDA [TN]
TEL. +39 0464552133
www.agririva.it

CELLAR SALES
PRE-BOOKED VISITS
ANNUAL PRODUCTION 250,000 bottles
HECTARES UNDER VINE 280.00

For many years, the coop Agraria Riva del Garda has interpreted the countryside here along the 46° parallel, the northernmost limit for the cultivation of olives. It's no coincidence that they're renowned for their excellent extra-virgin, among Europe's most recognized. Their growers show just as much care when it comes to their vineyards, situated along Garda, an area with a Mediterranean microclimate, and day-night temperature swings characteristic of the Dolomites. International grapes cultivated amidst olive trees give rise to a noteworthy selection of wines. The cooperative immediately caught our attention when it presented its pride and joy, the modern, refreshing Lagrein Sasèra '17. The white Loré '17 made from Chardonnay also surprised, proving as sapid as it is lean. The Riv'aldego, an interpretation of Terodego with a fruity nose and palate alive with youthful energy, hits the mark once again. The other proposed wines also deliver great enjoyability, with the Bordeaux-based Gère leading the pack.

○ Trentino Chardonnay Loré '18	♚♚	3
● Trentino Gère '16	♚♚	3
● Trentino Lagrein Sasèra '17	♚♚	4
● Trentino Riva'Ldego '17	♚♚	2*
○ Trentino Gewürztraminer Prea '17	♚	4
● Trentino Merlot Crèa '16	♚	4
● Maso Lizzone '16	♟♟	4
○ Trentino Chardonnay Loré '16	♟♟	3
● Trentino Sup. Pinot Nero Elesi '15	♟♟	4
○ Trentino Traminer Aromatico La Prea '16	♟♟	3

★★San Leonardo

LOC. SAN LEONARDO, 1
38063 AVIO [TN]
TEL. +39 0464689004
www.sanleonardo.it

CELLAR SALES
PRE-BOOKED VISITS
ANNUAL PRODUCTION 270,000 bottles
HECTARES UNDER VINE 40.00
VITICULTURE METHOD Certified Organic
SUSTAINABLE WINERY

Marquis Carlo and Anselmo Guerrieri Gonzaga's San Leonardo is a small temple of wine and good sense. Everything here is in harmony with a historic estate whose terrain has been cultivated for wine grapes since the late-11th century. It's an area that has long contributed to Trentino's historic and agronomic evolution, making it a cornerstone of 'culture' in all senses. Each vineyard receives the same attention and the same respect for ecological balance. The same holds for their approach in the cellar, resulting in wines that are increasingly thrilling, authoritative and bold. San Leonardo has an edge over many Bordeaux-style wines produced both within Italy and beyond. Its formidable sensory progression proves intense and tireless (absolutely capable of defying time) without ever pushing. The Villa Gresti gives similar synergy, though perhaps a leaner body makes it much more accessible in its sophisticated drinkability. The Terre (another Bordeaux blend) is perennially noteworthy, alongside the Vette, made with Sauvignon.

● San Leonardo '15	♚♚♚	8
● Villa Gresti di San Leonardo '15	♚♚	5
● Terre di San Leonardo '16	♚♚	3
○ Vette di San Leonardo '18	♚♚	3
● Carmenère '07	♟♟♟	8
● San Leonardo '14	♟♟♟	8
● San Leonardo '13	♟♟♟	8
● San Leonardo '11	♟♟♟	8
● San Leonardo '10	♟♟♟	7
● San Leonardo '08	♟♟♟	7
● San Leonardo '07	♟♟♟	7
● San Leonardo '06	♟♟♟	7
● San Leonardo '05	♟♟♟	7

Toblino

FRAZ. SARCHE
VIA LONGA, 1
38076 MADRUZZO
TEL. +39 0461564168
www.toblino.it

PRE-BOOKED VISITS
RESTAURANT SERVICE
ANNUAL PRODUCTION 400,000 bottles
HECTARES UNDER VINE 700.00
VITICULTURE METHOD Certified Organic
SUSTAINABLE WINERY

Toblino is seeking to be Trentino's most innovative cooperative producer, thanks to vineyard management grounded in organic principles and the contribution of its 636 growers. Their philosophy centers on low yields and, consequently, the attributes of the various vineyards spread throughout the 'Valley of the Lakes'. Great attention is shown to the area's exclusive cultivar, Nosiola, which is presented in two classic versions, as an early-drinking white and, after partial drying, as a rare Vino Santo. The rest of their selection of traditional regional wines is just as reliable. Their passito par excellence really took us by surprise. This long-lived, charming wine of gentle concentration testifies to the passion of the valley's growers. With an exciting balance between acidity and sweetness, it merits not only Tre Bicchieri, but it's also our 'Sweet of the Year'. The Largiller also proves a lovely interpretation of super-ripe Nosiola, both savory and unusual. The rosé Lagrein, fresh and full of character, may be easy-going but it's in no way banal.

○ Trentino Vino Santo '03	▼▼▼ 6
○ Kerner '18	▼▼ 2*
● Teroldego Bio '16	▼▼ 2*
⊙ Trentino Lagrein Kretzer '18	▼▼ 2*
⊙ Trentino Nosiola Largiller '12	▼▼ 3
● Trentino Rebo Elimarò '17	▼▼ 2*
○ L'Ora '14	▼ 3
○ Trentino Moscato Giallo '17	▼ 2
● Trentino Rebo '17	▼ 2
○ Goldtraminer '16	♈♈ 3
○ Trentino Manzoni Bianco Bio '17	♈♈ 5
○ Trentino Nosiola '17	♈♈ 2*
● Trentino Pinot Nero '16	♈♈ 2*
○ Trentino Vino Santo '02	♈♈ 6

Vallarom

LOC. VO' SINISTRO
FRAZ. MASI, 21
38063 AVIO [TN]
TEL. +39 0464684297
www.vallarom.it

CELLAR SALES
PRE-BOOKED VISITS
ACCOMMODATION AND RESTAURANT SERVICE
ANNUAL PRODUCTION 35,000 bottles
HECTARES UNDER VINE 7.00
VITICULTURE METHOD Certified Organic
SUSTAINABLE WINERY

Science and nature coexist harmoniously at this lower Vallagarina winery. Situated in Campi Sarni and Terra dei Forti, along the Adige river, Filippo and Barbara Scienza's family estate is cultivated according to rigorous organic methods aimed at environmental sustainability. The vineyards around the farmstead are a triumph of biodiversity, safeguarded at vintage and exalted by technical skill, resulting in wines that are unabashedly territorial, unique in their texture and drinkability. In short, they're traditional wines, with a verve reminiscent of the area's classic sparklers. We were immediately won over by the Fuflus (which means 'floating river'), the winery's most notable Bordeaux-style red wine. Its full nose contains hints of currants, subtle mint and juniper. The lively Vadum Cesaris is a jubilant pairing of Pinot Bianco left on the lees. The Trentatrè, a blend of Muscat, Nosiola and Verdealbara, stands out among their other uncomplicated but very well made selections.

● Fuflus '15	▼▼ 4
○ Trentatrè '18	▼▼ 3
● Trentino Marzemino '18	▼ 3
⊙ Vadum Caesaris '18	▼ 3
○ Trentatrè '16	♈♈ 3
● Trentino Marzemino Bio '15	♈♈ 3
⊙ Vadum Caesaris '17	♈♈ 3*
⊙ Vadum Caesaris '16	♈♈ 3
● Vallagarina Pinot Nero '15	♈♈ 4
○ Vo' '14	♈♈ 4
○ Vo' '13	♈♈ 4
⊙ Vo' Rosé de Saignée	♀ 4

Villa Corniole

FRAZ. VERLA
VIA AL GREC', 23
38030 GIOVO [TN]
TEL. +39 0461695067
www.villacorniole.com

CELLAR SALES
PRE-BOOKED VISITS
ACCOMMODATION
ANNUAL PRODUCTION 75,000 bottles
HECTARES UNDER VINE 10.00
SUSTAINABLE WINERY

The winery is embedded among the porphyry rocks of the Cembra Valley, a mineral of volcanic origin with a distinctive red color. There's also porphyry in the vineyards, gravity-defying terraces whose steep slopes may limit the quantity of wine produced, but not their quality. The property is owned by the Pellegrini family, pa Onorio who tends to his vineyards along with his wife, Maddalena, and three young daughters, Sara, Linda and Sabina. Enology is entrusted to Mattia Clementi, an expert in winemaking, especially when it comes to whites. Kròz (the local name for the red porphyry rock of the Cembra valley), a lovely white wine made from Chardonnay and Müller Thurgau grapes, delivered excellent aroma with good sapidity, depth and assertiveness. Their Müller Thurgau '17 makes a fine showing, as always. The sparkling Salísa proves convincing, as does the version of Teroldego, from vineyards at the bottom of the valley. The other wines are quite good.

○ Kròz '17	▼▼ 5
● Teroldego Rotaliano 7 Pergole '15	▼▼ 6
● Trentino Lagrein Petramonis '17	▼▼ 4
○ Trentino Müller Thurgau Sup. Petramonis '18	▼▼ 3
○ Trento Brut Salísa '15	▼▼ 5
○ Trentino Chardonnay Pietramontis '18	▼ 3
○ Trentino Traminer '18	▼ 3
○ Kròz '16	♀♀ 5
○ Kroz '15	♀♀ 4
● Teroldego Rotaliano 7 Pergole '13	♀♀ 6
○ Trentino Müller Thurgau Petramontis '17	♀♀ 4
○ Trento Brut Salísa '13	♀♀ 5
○ Trento Dosaggio Zero Salísa '14	♀♀ 6
○ Trento Dosaggio Zero Salísa '13	♀♀ 5

Roberto Zeni

FRAZ. GRUMO
VIA STRETTA, 2
38010 SAN MICHELE ALL'ADIGE [TN]
TEL. +39 0461650456
www.zeni.tn.it

CELLAR SALES
PRE-BOOKED VISITS
ANNUAL PRODUCTION 150,000 bottles
HECTARES UNDER VINE 14.00
VITICULTURE METHOD Certified Organic

They're known as the 'Zeni di Grumo', a dynasty of vine growers, master distillers, and for some years now, also brewers. They are artisan experimenters who operate in a facility built on Maso Nero, a splendid hillside estate over Lavis and near to the Cembra Valley. It's here that they cultivate the grapes for their whites, including a classic sparkler. On the valley floor, near their cellar and in the heart of Campo Rotaliano, they cultivate primarily Teroldego. All their wines exhibit notable personality. The bright garnet Pini is a truly invigorating interpretation of Teroldego; it offered aromatic notes, balsamic tones with sweet spices and a spacious palate. We prefer it to the next Teroldego they presented, their Ternet di Schwarzhof. Their Lealbere, yet another Teroldego, however, proves delicious, demonstrating all of its intrinsic youthfulness. The Nosiola and the Maso Nero Dosaggio Zero, a single-varietal Trento made from Pinot Bianco, also impress.

● Teroldego Rotaliano Lealbere '18	▼▼ 3*
● Teroldego Rotaliano Pini '15	▼▼ 6
● Teroldego Rotaliano Ternet Schwarzhof '16	▼▼ 5
○ Trentino Nosiola Schwarzhof '18	▼▼ 2*
○ Trento Maso Nero Dosaggio Zero '13	▼▼ 5
● Trentino Lagrein '16	▼ 4
● Teroldego Rotaliano Pini '13	♀♀♀ 6
● Teroldego Rotaliano Pini '12	♀♀♀ 6
● Teroldego Rotaliano Pini '09	♀♀♀ 6
● Teroldego Ternet Schwarzhof '10	♀♀♀ 5
○ Nosiola Schwarzhof '17	♀♀ 3

Cantina Aldeno

VIA ROMA, 76
38060 ALDENO [TN]
TEL. +39 0461842511
www.cantinaaldeno.com

CELLAR SALES
PRE-BOOKED VISITS
ANNUAL PRODUCTION 240,000 bottles
HECTARES UNDER VINE 340.00

○ San Zeno Rosso Ris. '14	♟♟	4
○ Trentino Traminer Bio-Vegan '18	♟♟	2*
○ Trento Blanc de Blancs Altinate Bio '15	♟♟	5
○ Trento Pas Dosé Altinum '15	♟♟	5

Bolognani

VIA STAZIONE, 19
38015 LAVIS [TN]
TEL. +39 0461246354
www.bolognani.com

CELLAR SALES
PRE-BOOKED VISITS
ANNUAL PRODUCTION 60,000 bottles
HECTARES UNDER VINE 4.40

● Armìlo Teroldego '17	♟♟	3
● Gabàn '13	♟♟	5
○ Nosiola '18	♟	3
○ Trentino Gewürztraminer SanRòc '17	♟	3

Cantina Sociale di Trento

VIA DEI VITICOLTORI, 2/4
38123 TRENTO
TEL. +39 0461920186
www.cantinasocialetrento.it

CELLAR SALES
PRE-BOOKED VISITS
ANNUAL PRODUCTION 250,000 bottles
HECTARES UNDER VINE 50.00
SUSTAINABLE WINERY

● Mori Vecio '16	♟♟	4
○ Santacolomba '18	♟♟	3
○ Trento Brut Zèll	♟♟	5
○ Trento Brut Zèll Rosé	♟♟	5

Cantina De Vigili

VIA MOLINI, 28
38017 MEZZOLOMBARDO [TN]
TEL. +39 3495543239
www.cantinadevigili.it

ANNUAL PRODUCTION 20,000 bottles
HECTARES UNDER VINE 3.00

● Teroldego Rotaliano Sup. Ottaviano Ris. '16	♟♟	5
● Teroldego Rotaliano '17	♟♟	4
○ Teroldego Rosato '18	♟♟	5
○ Trentino Chardonnay Terre Bianche '18	♟	5

Marco Donati

VIA CESARE BATTISTI, 41
38016 MEZZOCORONA [TN]
TEL. +39 0461604141
www.cantinadonatimarco.it

CELLAR SALES
PRE-BOOKED VISITS
ANNUAL PRODUCTION 100,000 bottles
HECTARES UNDER VINE 20.00
SUSTAINABLE WINERY

● Teroldego Rotaliano Bagolari '17	♟♟	4
● Teroldego Rotaliano Sangue di Drago '16	♟♟	6
○ Trentino Müller Thurgau Albeggio '18	♟♟	4
○ Trentino Traminer Tramonti '18	♟	4

Etyssa

LOC. MOIA, 4
38121 TRENTO
TEL. +39 3938922784
www.etyssaspumanti.it

ANNUAL PRODUCTION 3,500 bottles
HECTARES UNDER VINE 14.00

○ Trento Extra Brut Cuvée N. 3 '14	♟♟	5

Gaierhof

VIA IV NOVEMBRE, 51
38030 ROVERÈ DELLA LUNA [TN]
TEL. +39 0461658514
www.gaierhof.com

CELLAR SALES
PRE-BOOKED VISITS
ANNUAL PRODUCTION 500,000 bottles
HECTARES UNDER VINE 150.00
SUSTAINABLE WINERY

● Teroldego Rotaliano '17	♟♟	2*
○ Trentino Traminer '18	♟♟	3
○ Trento Siris	♟♟	4
● Trentino Lagrein '18	♟	4

Grigoletti

VIA GARIBALDI, 12
38060 NOMI [TN]
TEL. +39 0464834215
www.grigoletti.com

CELLAR SALES
PRE-BOOKED VISITS
ANNUAL PRODUCTION 60,000 bottles
HECTARES UNDER VINE 6.00

● Trentino Merlot Antica Vigna '16	♟♟	4
● Trentino Marzemino '18	♟♟	3
○ Trentino Chardonnay L'Opera '18	♟	3
○ Trentino Pinot Grigio '18	♟	3

Cantina d'Isera

VIA AL PONTE, 1
38060 ISERA [TN]
TEL. +39 0464433795
www.cantinaisera.it

CELLAR SALES
PRE-BOOKED VISITS
ANNUAL PRODUCTION 500,000 bottles
HECTARES UNDER VINE 246.00
VITICULTURE METHOD Certified Organic

● Trentino Lagrein '17	♟♟	3
● Trentino Marzemino Et. Verde '17	♟♟	3
○ Trento Brut Ris. '13	♟♟	5
○ Trento Extra Brut '13	♟♟	5

Lagertal

VIA A. PESENTI, 1
38060 VILLA LAGARINA [TN]
TEL. +39 0422836790
info@lagertal.com

ANNUAL PRODUCTION 25,000 bottles
HECTARES UNDER VINE 2.00

○ Trentino Chardonnay Merum '17	♟♟	4
● Trentino Pinot Nero Dextrum '16	♟♟	5
○ Trento Brut Ris. '13	♟♟	5
○ Trentino Goldtraminer '18	♟	4

Martinelli

VIA CASTELLO, 10
38016 MEZZOCORONA [TN]
TEL. +39 3388288686
www.cantinamartinelli.com

ANNUAL PRODUCTION 12,000 bottles
HECTARES UNDER VINE 3.00

● Teroldego Rotaliano Ris. '16	♟♟	5
○ Trentino Chardonnay '18	♟♟	4
● Trentino Lagrein Ris. '16	♟♟	5

Maso Grener

LOC. MASI DI PRESSANO
38015 LAVIS [TN]
TEL. +39 0461871514
www.masogrener.it

CELLAR SALES
PRE-BOOKED VISITS
ANNUAL PRODUCTION 18,000 bottles
HECTARES UNDER VINE 3.00

○ Maso Grener '18	♟♟	4
○ Nosiola '18	♟♟	4
● Trentino Pinot Nero V. Bindesi '17	♟♟	5
○ Trentino Chardonnay V. Tratta '18	♟	4

Cantine Monfort

VIA CARLO SETTE, 21
38015 LAVIS [TN]
TEL. +39 0461246353
www.cantinemonfort.it

CELLAR SALES
PRE-BOOKED VISITS
ANNUAL PRODUCTION 170,000 bottles
HECTARES UNDER VINE 45.00
SUSTAINABLE WINERY

○ Trento Brut Monfort Ris. '13	♟♟ 5
○ Blanc de Sers Brut Nature M. Cl. '17	♟♟ 3
○ Trentino Nosiola Corylus '17	♟♟ 4
● Trentino Pinot Nero Casata Monfort '17	♟♟ 3

Pedrotti Spumanti

VIA ROMA, 2A
38060 NOMI [TN]
TEL. +39 0464835111
www.predottispumanti.it

CELLAR SALES
ANNUAL PRODUCTION 30,000 bottles
HECTARES UNDER VINE 3.00
SUSTAINABLE WINERY

○ Trento Brut Nature	♟♟ 5
⊙ Trento Brut Rosé '14	♟♟ 5
○ Trento Pas Dosé Ris. 111 '14	♟♟ 6
○ Trento Brut	♟ 4

Pisoni

LOC. SARCHE
FRAZ. PERGOLESE DI LASINO
VIA SAN SIRO, 7A
38076 MADRUZZO
TEL. +39 0461564106
www.pisoni.net

CELLAR SALES
PRE-BOOKED VISITS
ANNUAL PRODUCTION 23,500 bottles
HECTARES UNDER VINE 16.00

○ Trentino Vino Santo '05	♟♟ 7
○ Trento Extra Brut Erminia Segalla '10	♟♟ 6
○ Trentino Nosiola '18	♟♟ 4
● Trentino Pinot Nero Bio '16	♟♟ 5

Cantina Rotaliana

VIA TRENTO, 65B
38017 MEZZOLOMBARDO [TN]
TEL. +39 0461601010
www.cantinarotaliana.it

CELLAR SALES
PRE-BOOKED VISITS
ACCOMMODATION
ANNUAL PRODUCTION 800,000 bottles
HECTARES UNDER VINE 330.00
SUSTAINABLE WINERY

○ Trento Brut Ris. '11	♟♟ 6
○ Trentino Pinot Bianco '18	♟♟ 3
● Trentino Pinot Nero '17	♟♟ 5
○ Trento Extra Brut	♟♟ 4

Arcangelo Sandri

VIA VANEGGE, 4A
38010 FAEDO [TN]
TEL. +39 0461650935
www.arcangelosandri.it

CELLAR SALES
PRE-BOOKED VISITS
ANNUAL PRODUCTION 22,000 bottles
HECTARES UNDER VINE 3.00

○ Kerner '18	♟♟ 4
● Trentino Lagrein Capòr '16	♟♟ 4
○ Trentino Müller Thurgau Cosler '18	♟♟ 4
○ Trentino Traminer Aromatico Razer '18	♟ 2

Armando Simoncelli

VIA NAVICELLO, 7
38068 ROVERETO [TN]
TEL. +39 0464432373
www.simoncelli.it

CELLAR SALES
PRE-BOOKED VISITS
ANNUAL PRODUCTION 90,000 bottles
HECTARES UNDER VINE 10.50

● Trentino Marzemino '18	♟♟ 4
● Trentino Navesèl '16	♟♟ 5
○ Trentino Pinot Grigio '18	♟♟ 4
○ Trento Simoncelli Brut '15	♟♟ 4

Enrico Spagnolli

VIA G. B. ROSINA, 4A
38060 ISERA [TN]
TEL. +39 0464409054
www.vinispagnolli.it

CELLAR SALES
PRE-BOOKED VISITS
ANNUAL PRODUCTION 85,000 bottles
HECTARES UNDER VINE 18.00

● Trentino Marzemino '17	♟♟ 4
● Trentino Marzemino Don Giovanni '17	♟♟ 4
● Lagrein '17	♟ 2
○ Trentino Pinot Grigio '18	♟ 2

Marco Tonini

LOC. FOLASO
VIA ROSMINI, 8
38060 ISERA [TN]
TEL. +39 3404991043

CELLAR SALES
PRE-BOOKED VISITS
ANNUAL PRODUCTION 8,000 bottles
HECTARES UNDER VINE 4.00

○ Trento Brut Nature Ris. '16	♟♟ 5
○ Trento Nature Le Grile '16	♟♟ 5
● Trentino Marzemino '17	♟ 4

Vin de la Neu

FRAZ. COREDO
VIA SAN ROMEDIO, 8
38012 PREDAIA
TEL. +39 3474116854
www.vindelaneu.it

ANNUAL PRODUCTION 508 bottles
HECTARES UNDER VINE 0.35

○ Vin de la Neu '17	♟♟ 8

Vivallis

VIA PER BRANCOLINO, 4
38068 NOGAREDO [TN]
TEL. +39 0464834113
www.vivallis.it

CELLAR SALES
PRE-BOOKED VISITS
ANNUAL PRODUCTION 1,000,000 bottles
HECTARES UNDER VINE 730.00
VITICULTURE METHOD Certified Organic

● Trentino Pinot Nero '16	♟♟ 4
● Trentino Lagrein '16	♟♟ 2*
● Trentino Rebelèr '17	♟♟ 5
● Trentino Marzemino dei Ziresi '17	♟ 3

Luigi Zanini

VIA DE GASPERI, 42
38017 MEZZOLOMBARDO [TN]
TEL. +39 0461601496
www.zaniniluigi.com

CELLAR SALES
PRE-BOOKED VISITS
ANNUAL PRODUCTION 90,000 bottles
HECTARES UNDER VINE 8.50

● Teroldego Rotaliano Le Cervare '17	♟♟ 4
● Trentino Lagrein '18	♟ 4
○ Trentino Traminer '18	♟ 4

Zanotelli

V.LE 4 NOVEMBRE, 52
38034 CEMBRA [TN]
TEL. +39 0461683131
www.zanotelliwines.com

CELLAR SALES
PRE-BOOKED VISITS
ANNUAL PRODUCTION 40,000 bottles
HECTARES UNDER VINE 11.00

● Trentino Pinot Nero Silvester Ris. '16	♟♟ 3
○ Trentino Riesling Le Strope '16	♟♟ 4
○ Trentino Kerner '18	♟ 4
● Trentino Pinot Nero '17	♟ 3

ALTO ADIGE

If we had to choose a single word to describe
the essence of Adige's viticulture it would be
"light'. Patches of vineyards spread out across
the plains just a stone's throw from Trentino,
quickly rising to elevations of over 1000 meters,
reaching the high plateaus of Corniano and Appiano Monte,
the sunny slopes of Mazzon, Bolzano's warm and gravelly highlands, and the
more rugged valleys where vines literally cling to the mountainside, like Eisack
and Vinschgau. Behind it all is that crystalline light that shines over the growers
cultivating vineyards that often span just a few thousand meters, and that give
rise to selections ranging from just a few bottles to more sizable figures in the
case of cooperatives and historic producers. Considering the suitability of Alto
Adige's terrain and the technical skill of its winemakers, the region's producers
are pursuing a more territorial style in the name of bringing out that grape-
vineyard relationship that represents the highest form of expression. And thus
we have Mazzon's Pinot Nero, Grits's Lagrein, Söll's Gewürztraminer, the Eisack
Valley's Sylvaner. It's a small but complex puzzle, with each piece constituted
of a different soil type, climate, position and, naturally, cultivar. And so it's no
coincidence that this year, among the wines awarded, most were made with
grapes cultivated in what are considered their most well-suited territories, as with
the Lagreins made by Cantina di Bolzano, Muris and Tenuta Kornell. The same
holds for Elena Walch, Cantina Tramin and Ritterhof and their Gewürztraminers.
The region's sparkling wines are proving more interesting, with Kettmeir serving
as a benchmark, but Metodo Classico is also taking hold. If Girlan was the only
producer to deliver an award-winning Pinot Nero, the Eisack Valley recovered
from a difficult 2017 with a series of top-notch wines, from Peter Pliger's and
Günther Kerschbaumer's Sylvaner to Abazia di Novacella's Riesling. The territory's
value, however, is reflected less in those that earned our highest honors, than in
the high number of wines that made it into our final round of tastings, a veritable
sea of exquisite wines that represent the best of Italy's northernmost region.

★Abbazia di Novacella

FRAZ. NOVACELLA
VIA DELL'ABBAZIA, 1
39040 VARNA/VAHRN [BZ]
TEL. +39 0472836189
www.abbazianovacella.it

CELLAR SALES
PRE-BOOKED VISITS
RESTAURANT SERVICE
ANNUAL PRODUCTION 650,000 bottles
HECTARES UNDER VINE 20.00

Abbazia di Novacella is situated in Vahrn, in an enchanting area where the last vineyards of the Eisack Valley can be found, that is before the landscape becomes an Alpine enclave. Stone walls line strips of land dedicated to cultivating white grapes, a recently-enlarged and reorganized cellar, a top-notch staff … It all serves as the backbone for a producer that's further supported by many smalltime vine growers who sell them their crop. Their Praepositus line is the crown jewel of a selection without weak points, starting with an energetic Riesling '17. The cultivar's unmistakable aromatic profile is interpreted through a territorial lens. In the mouth it proves firm with sapid tension accompanying its long palate. Their Veltliner '17 of the same line pours vibrant and enticing, marked by smoky fragrances and yellow fruit, which reemerge on its rich, dynamic palate.

○ A. A. Valle Isarco Riesling Praepositus '17	♥♥♥ 4*
○ A. A. Valle Isarco Veltliner Praepositus '17	♥♥ 3*
● A. A. Lagrein Praepositus Ris. '16	♥♥ 5
● A. A. Moscato Rosa Praepositus '17	♥♥ 5
● A. A. Pinot Nero Praepositus Ris. '16	♥♥ 4
○ A. A. Sauvignon Praepositus '18	♥♥ 4
○ A. A. Valle Isarco Gewürztraminer '18	♥♥ 3
○ A. A. Valle Isarco Kerner '18	♥♥ 3
○ A. A. Valle Isarco Müller Thurgau Praepositus '18	♥♥ 4
○ A. A. Valle Isarco Riesling '18	♥♥ 3
○ A. A. Valle Isarco Sylvaner Praepositus '18	♥♥ 4
○ A. A. Valle Isarco Veltliner '18	♥♥ 3
○ A. A. Valle Isarco Veltliner Praepositus '17	♀♀ 3*

Tenuta Baron Di Pauli

VIA CANTINE, 12
39052 CALDARO/KALTERN [BZ]
TEL. +39 0471963696
www.barondipauli.com

CELLAR SALES
PRE-BOOKED VISITS
ANNUAL PRODUCTION 46,000 bottles
HECTARES UNDER VINE 15.00

Following the road that leads from Cortaccia up towards Caldaro, one has the impression that it's an unvaried landscape, with east-facing vineyards that gradually slope towards the valley floor and then clamber up towards the Oltradige plateau. But in reality, the southern part is perfectly suited to all those grapes in need of warmth. And once past the lake, the conditions prove ideal for subtler, more delicate varieties. It's here that Baron di Pauli operate, making wines with great expressive force that undergo a lengthy stay in the cellar before their release to the public. Caldaro's most convincing wine is a 2018, their Gewürztraminer Exil. Closed aromas gradually open up, revealing an aromatic profile of great substance and depth. In the mouth the wine lets through the force of the vineyard, transmitting fullness, generosity and power to a palate that's supported more by sapidity than acidity.

○ A. A. Gewürztraminer Exil '18	♥♥ 6
○ A. A. Gewürztraminer Exilissi '15	♥♥ 6
○ A. A. Gewürztraminer Passito Exilissi Sell '15	♥♥ 6
● A. A. Lagrein Carano Ris. '16	♥♥ 5
● A. A. Merlot Cabernet Sauvignon Arzio Ris. '16	♥♥ 6
○ A. A. Sauvignon Kinesis '18	♥♥ 4
○ Enosi '18	♥♥ 3
○ A. A. Gewürztraminer Elix '17	♀♀ 6
● A. A. Lago di Caldaro Cl. Sup. Kalkofen '17	♀♀ 3*
● A. A. Merlot Cabernet Arzio Ris. '15	♀♀ 6
○ Enosi '17	♀♀ 3

Bessererhof - Otmar Mair

LOC. NOVALE DI PRESULE, 10
39050 FIÈ ALLO SCILIAR/VÖLS AM SCHLERN [BZ]
TEL. +39 0471601011
www.bessererhof.it

CELLAR SALES
PRE-BOOKED VISITS
ANNUAL PRODUCTION 40,000 bottles
HECTARES UNDER VINE 4.50

Otmar Mair and his wife, Rosmarie, oversee an estate situated at the entrance of the Eisack Valley, where the heat of Bolzano is suddenly cooled by the winds coming down off the valley and the Sciliar. Most of their vineyards are in Fié, near the family farmstead of about 350 meters. But they have plots that reach all the way up to 900 meters at their Tiso estate in the Funes valley. Their selection centers primarily on whites, with the only exceptions between Schiava and the traditional Zweigelt. It's their Sauvignon '18 leading the way this year, a wine made with grapes cultivated at elevations of 400 meters elevation, on a well-ventilated, west-facing vineyard. Subtle aromas call up white fruit and almonds, letting through flowery notes and delicate spices. In the mouth it delivers thanks to harmony and tension rather than power.

○ A. A. Sauvignon '18	♔♔ 4
○ A. A. Chardonnay Fellis Ris. '16	♔♔ 4
○ A. A. Gewürztraminer Fellis '18	♔♔ 4
○ A. A. Pinot Bianco Fellis Ris. '17	♔♔ 4
⊙ Roansé '18	♔♔ 3
○ A. A. Moscato Giallo '18	♔ 4
○ A. A. Pinot Bianco '18	♔ 3
○ A. A. Valle Isarco Kerner '18	♔ 4
● Roan '15	♔ 4
○ A. A. Chardonnay Ris. '15	♔♔ 3
○ A. A. Chardonnay Ris. '13	♔♔ 3
○ A. A. Chardonnay Ris. '14	♔♔ 3
○ A. A. Pinot Bianco '17	♔♔ 3
○ A. A. Pinot Bianco '16	♔♔ 3*
○ A. A. Sauvignon '16	♔♔ 4
○ A. A. Valle Isarco Kerner '17	♔♔ 4
○ A. A. Valle Isarco Kerner '16	♔♔ 4

★★Cantina Bolzano

P.ZZA GRIES, 2
39100 BOLZANO/BOZEN
TEL. +39 0471270909
www.cantinabolzano.com

CELLAR SALES
PRE-BOOKED VISITS
ANNUAL PRODUCTION 3,000,000 bottles
HECTARES UNDER VINE 350.00
SUSTAINABLE WINERY

The winery managed by Stefan Filippi isn't just one of the largest cooperative wineries in Bolzano, it's also managed to distinguish itself among South Tyrol's competitive producers. It's situated in the one of the region's warmest basins, surrounded by vineyards, at 250 meters elevation in the Gries plains and almost 1,000 meters in Renon. Their new facility can be found at the northwestern border of the capital, perfectly immersed in vineyards, just by the mountains that separate the Sarentino and Adige valleys. Their Lagrein Taber is a reserve made with 80-year-old vineyards situated in Gries. Stefan interpreted 2017 in pursuit of tension and elegance, with smoky and foresty notes perfectly expressed on a crisp palate of great balsamic freshness. Their Kleinstein '18 is a potent, charming wine, while Huck am Bach '18 is the usual harmonious, exhilarating red.

● A. A. Lagrein Taber Ris. '17	♔♔♔ 6
● A. A. Santa Maddalena Cl. Huck am Bach '18	♔♔ 3*
● A. A. Cabernet Mumelter Ris. '17	♔♔ 6
○ A. A. Gewürztraminer Kleinstein '18	♔♔ 5
● A. A. Lagrein - Merlot Mauritius '16	♔♔ 5
● A. A. Lagrein Prestige Line Ris. '17	♔♔ 4
● A. A. Merlot Siebeneich Ris. '17	♔♔ 5
○ A. A. Moscato Giallo Passito Vinalia '17	♔♔ 3
○ A. A. Pinot Bianco Dellago '18	♔♔ 4
● A. A. Pinot Nero Ris. '17	♔♔ 5
○ A. A. Sauvignon Mock '18	♔♔ 4
○ A. A. Sauvignon Ris. '17	♔♔ 4

Josef Brigl

LOC. SAN MICHELE
VIA MADONNA DEL RIPOSO, 3
39057 APPIANO/EPPAN [BZ]
TEL. +39 0471662419
www.brigl.com

CELLAR SALES
PRE-BOOKED VISITS
ACCOMMODATION
ANNUAL PRODUCTION 1,000,000 bottles
HECTARES UNDER VINE 50.00
SUSTAINABLE WINERY

The Brigl family's winery has been operating for centuries in South Tyrol, bolstered by deep roots in the territory, vineyards that span some of the region's best areas and a tight network of vine growers who passionately cultivate the estate's small plots. In their cellar, modern technology and tradition come together, making for a wide range of wines that highlight the close-focused aromas of the area's local grapes. Haselhof vineyard, one of the winery's crown jewels, provides the grapes for this fragrant Pinot Bianco '18. Visually vibrant, its aromas are dominated by ripe, pulpy yellow fruit, sensations that reemerge on the palate. Here the wine lengthens supple and sapid, revealing perfectly integrated oak. Their Caldaro Windegg vineyard gave rise to their Gewürztraminer of the same vintage. It's an aromatically exuberant wine endowed with a crisp, elegant palate.

○ A. A. Gewürztraminer V. Windegg '18	♟♟	3*
○ A. A. Pinot Bianco V. Haselhof '18	♟♟	3*
● A. A. Lago di Caldaro Cl. V. Windegg '18	♟♟	3
● A. A. Lagrein Ris. '16	♟♟	5
○ A. A. Pinot Grigio V. Windegg '18	♟♟	3
● A. A. Pinot Nero Ris. '16	♟♟	4
● A. A. Santa Maddalena V. Rielerhof '18	♟♟	3
○ A. A. Sauvignon V. Rielerhof '18	♟♟	3
● A. A. Schiava V. Haselhof '18	♟	2
○ A. A. Pinot Grigio Windegg '11	♟♟♟	3*

Brunnenhof
Kurt Rottensteiner

LOC. MAZZON
VIA DEGLI ALPINI, 5
39044 EGNA/NEUMARKT [BZ]
TEL. +39 0471820687
www.brunnenhof-mazzon.it

CELLAR SALES
PRE-BOOKED VISITS
ANNUAL PRODUCTION 35,000 bottles
HECTARES UNDER VINE 5.50
VITICULTURE METHOD Certified Organic

Johanna and Kurt Rottensteiner's winery is situated in Mazzon, in the heart of one of Alto Adige's prized territories for Pinot Nero. Their vineyards grow in calcareous-clay terrain that also features a significant presence of sand. Elevations range from 400 meters all the way up to the woods of Königswiese. Most of the property is here, around the farmstead, while a small number of plots can also be found along the valley floor, where old parcels of Lagrein enjoy the warmer climate and extremely gravelly soil. At Rottensteiner they're only missing a standout, with two Pinot Neros that exalt the fruity and potent profile that's the Mazzon cru's trademark. Their reserve plays more on fruit, while their Vigna Zis is deeper and more complex. Their Lagrein is a notable wine made with grapes from very old vineyards. On the nose it offers up its signature aromas of wild fruit, spices and undergrowth, only to liberate itself on a palate well-sustained by acidic vigor.

● A. A. Lagrein V. V. '17	♟♟	4
● A. A. Pinot Nero Ris. '16	♟♟	5
● A. A. Pinot Nero V. Zis Ris. '16	♟♟	5
○ Eva '18	♟♟	4
○ A. A. Gewürztraminer '18	♟♟	4
○ A. A. Pinot Nero Rosé '18	♟	4
○ A. A. Gewürztraminer '14	♟♟	4
● A. A. Lagrein V. V. '16	♟♟	5
● A. A. Lagrein V. V. '15	♟♟	4
● A. A. Pinot Nero Mazzon Ris. '15	♟♟	5
● A. A. Pinot Nero Mazzon V. Zis Ris. '15	♟♟	5
● A. A. Pinot Nero Ris. '14	♟♟	5
● A. A. Pinot Nero Ris. '13	♟♟	5
● A.A. Lagrein '13	♟♟	5
○ Eva '17	♟♟	4
○ Eva '16	♟♟	4
○ Eva '15	♟♟	4

Castel Sallegg

v.lo di Sotto, 15
39052 Caldaro/Kaltern [BZ]
Tel. +39 0471963132
www.castelsallegg.it

CELLAR SALES
PRE-BOOKED VISITS
ANNUAL PRODUCTION 170,000 bottles
HECTARES UNDER VINE 30.00

The Kuenburg family's winery avails itself of a rather sizable estate that stretches throughout Caldaro, from the vineyards that line the lake (where clay and sand fuse harmoniously) to higher plots in Prey (where the soil is made up of porphyry and sandstone). Wines are made in the splendid edifices that also host their main Caldaro offices. Built in various periods, the cellars are dedicated specifically to various stages of production, from fermentation to maturation in wooden barrels and in barriques. All the potential of the vineyards facing Lake Caldaro is expressed through their Merlot Riserva '16 and Lago di Caldaro Bischofsleiten '18. The former features intense, ripe fruit on the nose and a sapid, generous palate that's refreshed by a final touch of spices. The latter exhibits greater finesse in its aromas of flowers and wild fruit, while on the palate it unfolds gracefully and with a juicy lightness.

● A. A. Lago di Caldaro Cl. Sup. Bischofsleiten '18	♟♟ 3*
● A. A. Merlot Ris. '16	♟♟ 4
○ A. A. Bianco Ars Lyrica '16	♟♟ 4
● A. A. Cabernet Sauvignon Ris. '16	♟♟ 5
○ A. A. Gewürztraminer '18	♟♟ 3
● A. A. Lagrein Ris. '16	♟♟ 5
● A. A. Merlot Cabernet Chorus Madrigal Ris. '16	♟♟ 5
● A. A. Moscato Rosa V. T. '16	♟♟ 7
● A. A. Pinot Nero '17	♟♟ 3
● A. A. Sauvignon '18	♟♟ 3
○ A. A. Terlano Pinot Bianco Pratum '16	♟♟ 5
○ A. A. Moscato Giallo '18	♟ 3
● A. A. Lago di Caldaro Scelto Sup. Bischofsleiten '15	♟♟♟ 2*
● A. A. Cabernet Sauvignon Ris. '15	♟♟ 5

Castelfeder

via Portici, 11
39040 Egna/Neumarkt [BZ]
Tel. +39 0471820420
www.castelfeder.it

CELLAR SALES
PRE-BOOKED VISITS
ANNUAL PRODUCTION 400,000 bottles
HECTARES UNDER VINE 20.00

The Giovannett family's winery is situated in the heart of the Adige Valley, in Cortina, along the 'Wine Trail', where the valley narrows and then emerges a few more miles south in Trentino. Their large estate is concentrated in the Bassa Atesina wine district, from the valley floor to higher elevations dedicated to Müller Thurgau, which can reach up to almost 1,000 meters. Their Pinot Nero is cultivated in their Glen vineyards, where the Dolomites' fresh winds confer fragrance and elegance to the grapes. Their selection is divided into multiple levels, with Borgum Novum representing their top wines. 2016 brought great aromatic depth to the fore, a quality that we find in the Sauvignon, a wine that goes all in on fullness and harmony. Their Pinot Nero '16 highlights an elegant, stratified olfactory profile, opening little by little before unfolding on the palate with tension, and finishing with a blast of sapidity.

● A. A. Pinot Nero Burgum Novum Ris. '16	♟♟ 5
○ A. A. Sauvignon Burgum Novum '16	♟♟ 4
○ A. A. Chardonnay Burgum Novum Ris. '16	♟♟ 4
○ A. A. Chardonnay Doss '18	♟♟ 3
● A. A. Lagrein Burgum Novum Ris. '16	♟♟ 4
○ A. A. Pinot Bianco Tecum '17	♟♟ 3
○ A. A. Pinot Bianco Vom Stein '18	♟♟ 3
○ A. A. Pinot Grigio 15 '18	♟♟ 3
○ Raif Sauvignon '18	♟♟ 3
○ A. A. Gewürztraminer Vom Lehm '18	♟ 3
● A. A. Pinot Nero Glener '17	♟ 3
● A. A. Schiava Alte Reben '18	♟ 3
○ A. A. Gewürztraminer Vom Lehm '15	♟♟♟ 3*
○ A. A. Pinot Bianco Tecum '10	♟♟♟ 3*
○ A. A. Chardonnay Burgum Novum Ris. '15	♟♟ 4

★★Cantina Colterenzio

LOC. CORNAIANO/GIRLAN
S.DA DEL VINO, 8
39057 APPIANO/EPPAN [BZ]
TEL. +39 0471664246
www.colterenzio.it

CELLAR SALES
PRE-BOOKED VISITS
ANNUAL PRODUCTION 1,600,000 bottles
HECTARES UNDER VINE 300.00
SUSTAINABLE WINERY

Despite just sixty years of experience, Cantina di Colterenzio's importance to Alto Adige's wine sector has been fundamental. All from the area of Colterenzio, a few founding members have now become three hundred. They cultivate plots primarily in the area of Oltradige, even if there are also vineyards to the north, moving towards Bolzano, and to the south towards Salorno. Their cellar, which was renovated in recent years and uses gravity techniques, hosts all stages or production, making for a selection that brings together sophistication and varietal identity. This year Colterenzio submitted a flawless selection. Their Cabernet Sauvignon Lafòa '16 opens deep and complex in its aromas, only to conquer the palate with its extraordinary elegance. Their Chardonnay Lafòa '17 proves rich and complex, yet approachable at the same time. It's a white of rare elegance and harmony. It's also worth pointing out the excellent performance put in by their Pinot Bianco Berg '17.

Hartmann Donà

VIA RAFFEIN, 8
39010 CERMES/TSCHERMS [BZ]
TEL. +39 3292610628
hartmann.dona@rolmail.net

ANNUAL PRODUCTION 35,000 bottles
HECTARES UNDER VINE 4.65

Before talking about his vineyards or winemaking approach, you have to mention Hartmann Donà's path of growth, which saw him move from experiences with important producers to founding his own winery. What hasn't changed over the years is his curiosity and desire to understand how the bond between cultivar, vineyard, climate and winemaker come together in a balanced way and result in the highest form of expression. His selection is dedicated to wines that reflect the varietal identity of each cultivar, with three reserve wines that represent the sum total of his philosophy. A 2013, their Chardonnay Donà Blanc starts out closed on the nose, almost hesitant to reveal its aromas. It slowly emerges with a never invasive fruit and a delicate, charming minerality that's perfectly fused with nuances of oak. The palate is crisp, slender, gutsy and elegant all at the same time, convincing in its tension and elegance.

● A. A. Cabernet Sauvignon Lafóa '16	♛♛♛ 7
○ A. A. Chardonnay Lafóa '17	♛♛ 5
○ A. A. Gewürztraminer Lafóa '17	♛♛ 5
○ A. A. Chardonnay Altkirch '18	♛♛ 2*
○ A. A. Gewürztraminer Perelise '18	♛♛ 3
● A. A. Lagrein Sigis Mundus Ris. '16	♛♛ 5
○ A. A. Pinot Bianco Berg '17	♛♛ 4
● A. A. Pinot Nero St. Daniel Ris. '16	♛♛ 4
● A. A. Pinot Nero Villa Nigra Ris. '16	♛♛ 5
○ A. A. Sauvignon Lafóa '17	♛♛ 5
○ A. A. Sauvignon Prail '18	♛♛ 3
● A. A. Cabernet Sauvignon Lafóa '10	♛♛♛ 7
● A. A. Cabernet Sauvignon Lafóa '12	♛♛♛ 7
● A. A. Cabernet Sauvignon Lafóa '11	♛♛♛ 7
○ A. A. Chardonnay Lafóa '16	♛♛♛ 5
○ A. A. Chardonnay Lafóa '15	♛♛♛ 5
○ A. A. Sauvignon Lafóa '14	♛♛♛ 5

○ Donà Blanc '13	♛♛ 5
○ A. A. Chardonnay '18	♛♛ 3
○ A. A. Chardonnay Donà D'Or '11	♛♛ 5
○ A. A. Gewürztraminer '18	♛♛ 4
○ A. A. Pinot Bianco '18	♛♛ 3
● A.A. Pinot Nero Donà Noir '13	♛♛ 8
● Donà Rouge '12	♛♛ 5
○ A. A. Sauvignon '18	♛ 4

Tenuta Donà

FRAZ. RIVA DI SOTTO
39057 APPIANO/EPPAN [BZ]
TEL. +39 0473221866
www.weingut-dona.com

CELLAR SALES
PRE-BOOKED VISITS
ACCOMMODATION
ANNUAL PRODUCTION 30,000 bottles
HECTARES UNDER VINE 6.00

After a long career as cellar master in an important regional cooperative, Hansjörg Donà created his own winery. He's bolstered by a few hectares of vineyards in the area that stretches from Missiano to Andriano, and the precious support of his entire family. Indeed, his wife, Marina, and sons Josef and Martin are increasingly involved at all stages of production. Their selection is limited to just a few cultivars, which are interpreted with an eye towards varietal fragrance and territorial identity. Their Terlano Chardonnay '18 put in an excellent performance. It opens with fresh aromas of white fruit and flowers, caressed by a delicate hint of oak. On the palate it unfolds with tension, lengthening towards a crisp, elegant finish. Among their reds, we appreciated the forthrightness of their Schiava '18, a cultivar that Hansjörg is particularly adept with. If its aromas are simple and approachable, on the palate it impresses for its character and fragrance.

● A. A. Merlot - Lagrein '17	🏆🏆 4
○ A. A. Pinot Bianco '18	🏆🏆 3
● A. A. Schiava '18	🏆🏆 3
○ A. A. Terlano Chardonnay '18	🏆🏆 4
○ A. A. Sauvignon '18	🏆 5
● A. A. Lagrein '15	🍷 5
● A. A. Lagrein '14	🍷 4
○ A. A. Sauvignon '17	🍷 5
○ A. A. Sauvignon '16	🍷 5
○ A. A. Sauvignon '15	🍷 3
● A. A. Schiava '17	🍷 3
● A. A. Schiava '16	🍷 3
● A. A. Schiava '14	🍷 2*
○ A. A. Terlano Chardonnay '16	🍷 4
○ A. A. Terlano Chardonnay '15	🍷 3
○ A. A. Terlano Chardonnay '14	🍷 3
● Merlot - Lagrein '16	🍷 4

Tenuta Ebner
Florian Unterthiner

FRAZ. CAMPODAZZO, 18
39054 RENON/RITTEN [BZ]
TEL. +39 0471353386
www.weingutebner.it

CELLAR SALES
PRE-BOOKED VISITS
RESTAURANT SERVICE
ANNUAL PRODUCTION 20,000 bottles
HECTARES UNDER VINE 4.50

Florian and Brigitte Unterthiner's winery is situated near Campodazzo, at the beginning of the Eisack Valley, atop a kind of rocky ridge at 500 meters elevation. The terrain here, which hosts red grape varieties, is rich in porphyry and enjoys a southern exposure. Their white grapes are cultivated in cooler, more ventilated, southeast-facing plots. Their selection focuses primarily on white wines, with the exception of traditional Zweigelt and Pinot Nero. Their Veltliner '18 leads a highly commendable selection this year. Its delicate aromas open slowly on notes of chamomile, exotic fruit and dried flowers. In the mouth it reveals nice fullness, lengthening with sapidity and harmony. It's also worth noting their Pinot Nero '18, a wine that's pleasantly smoky on the nose and endowed with a supple, long palate.

○ A. A. Valle Isarco Veltliner '18	🏆🏆 3*
○ A. A. Pinot Bianco '18	🏆🏆 3
● A. A. Pinot Nero '17	🏆🏆 3
● A. A. Schiava '18	🏆🏆 2*
○ A. A. Valle Isarco Gewürztraminer '18	🏆🏆 4
● Zweigelt '17	🏆 4
○ A. A. Pinot Bianco '17	🍷 3*
○ A. A. Pinot Bianco '16	🍷 3
● A. A. Pinot Nero '16	🍷 3
● A. A. Pinot Nero '16	🍷 3
○ A. A. Sauvignon '17	🍷 3
○ A. A. Sauvignon '16	🍷 3
● A. A. Schiava '17	🍷 2*
○ A. A. Valle Isarco Gewürztraminer '17	🍷 3
○ A. A. Valle Isarco Gewürztraminer '16	🍷 4
○ A. A. Valle Isarco Grüner Veltliner '17	🍷 3

Erbhof Unterganzner
Josephus Mayr

FRAZ. CARDANO
VIA CAMPIGLIO, 15
39053 BOLZANO/BOZEN
TEL. +39 0471365582
www.mayr-unterganzner.it

CELLAR SALES
PRE-BOOKED VISITS
ANNUAL PRODUCTION 65,000 bottles
HECTARES UNDER VINE 9.00

Josephus Mayr's farmstead is situated in the northeastern limits of Bolzano, practically at the entrance to the Eisack Valley, at 285 meters elevation. The terrain here is rich in porphyry and caressed by the wind. Their vineyards span plots in the immediate vicinity of the farm as well as higher positions in Kampenn, where all their white grapes are cultivated. There are also small parcels dedicated to red grapes, which confer finesse and grip. The cornerstone of their selection, however, is undoubtedly Lagrein, a variety grown in the warmer, sunnier positions. Their Riserva '16 pours dark. Aromatically it opens subdued and closed only to open gradually on notes of undergrowth, ripe fruit, pepper and nuances of violet. On the palate it's full, powerful and long. Their Santa Maddalena '17 moves on an entirely different track, with a ripe, pervasive nose and palate that's surprisingly supple, sustained by an enthralling sapidity.

★Falkenstein
Franz Pratzner

VIA CASTELLO, 19
39025 NATURNO/NATURNS [BZ]
TEL. +39 0473666054
www.falkenstein.bz

CELLAR SALES
PRE-BOOKED VISITS
ANNUAL PRODUCTION 90,000 bottles
HECTARES UNDER VINE 12.00

This year marks Bernadette and Franz Pratzner's thirtieth season. It's an adventure that began back in 1989 with the decision to abandon apples and begin wine-growing, a move followed by the construction of a cellar above Naturno castle. The vineyards were gradually enlarged to what is today a dozen hectares, dedicated almost exclusively to white grapes, among which their Riesling stands out for its quality and volumes. The parcels are situated on south-facing slopes, at elevations ranging from 600 to 900 meters. And it's a Riesling that once again leads their selection. It's a 2017 that offers up braod, multifaceted aromas of dry flowers and Mediterranean shrub only to give way to fruit and initial mineral hints. The palate is firm and gutsy, Pratzner's trademark. Their Pinot Bianco '17 is an aromatically complex wine, energetic and succulent on the palate.

● A. A. Lagrein Ris. '16	🍷🍷 5
● A. A. Santa Maddalena Cl. '17	🍷🍷 3*
● A. A. Cabernet Ris. '16	🍷🍷 5
○ A. A. Chardonnay Platt & Pignat '18	🍷🍷 3
○ A. A. Sauvignon Platt & Pignat '18	🍷🍷 3
● Composition Reif '16	🍷🍷 6
● Lamarein '16	🍷🍷 6
⊙ A. A. Lagrein Kretzer Rosato V. T. '18	🍷 3
● A. A. Lagrein Ris. '13	🍷🍷🍷 5
● A. A. Lagrein Ris. '11	🍷🍷🍷 5
● A. A. Lagrein Scuro Ris. '05	🍷🍷🍷 4
● A. A. Lagrein Scuro Ris. '01	🍷🍷🍷 4
● A. A. Lagrein Scuro Ris. '00	🍷🍷🍷 4
● A. A. Lagrein Scuro Ris. '99	🍷🍷🍷 4
● Lamarein '05	🍷🍷🍷 6
● A. A. Santa Maddalena Cl. '17	🍷🍷 3

○ A. A. Val Venosta Pinot Bianco '17	🍷🍷 4
○ A. A. Val Venosta Riesling '17	🍷🍷 5
● A. A. Val Venosta Pinot Nero '17	🍷🍷 5
○ A. A. Val Venosta Sauvignon '17	🍷🍷 4
○ A. A. Val Venosta Pinot Bianco '07	🍷🍷🍷 4
○ A. A. Val Venosta Riesling '15	🍷🍷🍷 5
○ A. A. Val Venosta Riesling '14	🍷🍷🍷 5
○ A. A. Val Venosta Riesling '13	🍷🍷🍷 5
○ A. A. Val Venosta Riesling '12	🍷🍷🍷 5
○ A. A. Val Venosta Riesling '11	🍷🍷🍷 5
○ A. A. Val Venosta Riesling '10	🍷🍷🍷 5
○ A. A. Val Venosta Riesling '09	🍷🍷🍷 5
○ A. A. Val Venosta Riesling '08	🍷🍷🍷 5
○ A. A. Val Venosta Riesling '07	🍷🍷🍷 5
○ A. A. Val Venosta Riesling '06	🍷🍷🍷 5
○ A. A. Val Venosta Riesling '05	🍷🍷🍷 5
○ A. A. Val Venosta Riesling '00	🍷🍷🍷 3

★Cantina Girlan

LOC. CORNAIANO
VIA SAN MARTINO, 24
39057 APPIANO/EPPAN [BZ]
TEL. +39 0471662403
www.girlan.it

CELLAR SALES
PRE-BOOKED VISITS
ANNUAL PRODUCTION 1,500,000 bottles
HECTARES UNDER VINE 220.00

Cantina Girlan is a cooperative winery founded almost a century ago. Today it's made up of about 200 grower members who cultivate 200 hectares of vineyards in the southern part of the province, in Oltradige and Bassa Atesina. At their main facility, which underwent major renovations in 2010, modern and historic spaces alternate in a kind of labyrinth situated beneath the courtyard and historic medieval buildings. In the vineyards they continue to improve their approach, working to bring about the perfect union of grape and terroir. The wine that best represents this approach is most certainly their Pinot Nero Trattmann, a 2016 reserve that goes beyond the cultivar's innate aromatic expression to evince notes of undergrowth and spices, unafraid of bringing its close-knit tannic weave to the fore so as to lend rigor and depth to the palate. Their Sauvignon Flora '17, a sapid and harmonious wine, performed well, while their Schiava Gschleier '17 proves austere and rigorous.

● A. A. Pinot Nero Trattmann Ris. '16	▼▼▼ 8
○ A. A. Sauvignon Flora '17	▼▼ 4
● A. A. Schiava Gschleier Alte Reben '17	▼▼ 3*
○ A. A. Bianco Cuvée Flora '17	▼▼ 4
○ A. A. Chardonnay Flora '17	▼▼ 5
○ A. A. Gewürztraminer V.T. Pasithea Oro '17	▼▼ 6
● A. A. Moscato Rosa V. T. Pasithea Rosa '17	▼▼ 5
○ A. A. Pinot Bianco Flora '17	▼▼ 3
○ A. A. Pinot Bianco Platt&Riegl '18	▼▼ 3
○ A. A. Pinot Bianco Sandbichler H. Lun '18	▼▼ 3
● A. A. Pinot Nero Sandbichler H. Lun '16	▼▼ 6
● A. A. Schiava Fass N° 9 '18	▼▼ 3
● A. A. Pinot Nero Trattmann Mazon Ris. '15	♀♀♀ 8

Glögglhof - Franz Gojer

FRAZ. SANTA MADDALENA
VIA RIVELLONE, 1
39100 BOLZANO/BOZEN
TEL. +39 0471978775
www.gojer.it

CELLAR SALES
PRE-BOOKED VISITS
ACCOMMODATION
ANNUAL PRODUCTION 55,000 bottles
HECTARES UNDER VINE 7.40

Santa Maddalena hill stands out prominently in outer Bolzano. Literally blanketed with vineyards (punctuated only by a few sporadic farms), it's here that Franz Gojer, a historic interpreter of Bolzano's reds, operates, overseeing historic plots of traditional, pergola-trained vines. These give rise to wines that manage to bring together approachability and complexity, proving both elegant and full. Their whites are partially made with grapes cultivated in new plots in Cornedo, situated at the entrance to the Eisack Valley. Their oldest vineyards, which are situated on the southeast side of the hill, give rise to their Vigna Randell '18. It's a Santa Maddalena redolent of cherries and spices — on the palate sapidity takes center stage. Their Lagrein Riserva '16 is another wine altogether, deep in its notes of forest undergrowth and dark fruit, on the palate it proves tonic and powerful, perfectly supported by acidity and a close-knit tannic weave.

● A. A. Santa Maddalena Cl. Rondell '18	▼▼▼ 3*
● A. A. Lagrein Ris. '16	▼▼ 4
● A. A. Santa Maddalena Cl. '18	▼▼ 2*
● A. A. Schiava Alte Reben '18	▼▼ 2*
○ A. A. Pinot Bianco Karneid '18	▼▼ 4
○ A. A. Kerner Karneid '18	▼ 3
● A. A. Santa Maddalena Cl. Rondell '16	♀♀♀ 3*
● A. A. Santa Maddalena Cl. Rondell '15	♀♀♀ 3*
○ A. A. Kerner Karneid '17	♀♀ 3
● A. A. Lagrein '14	♀♀ 3*
● A. A. Lagrein Ris. '15	♀♀ 4
● A. A. Santa Maddalena Cl. '17	♀♀ 2*
● A. A. Santa Maddalena Cl. Rondell '17	♀♀ 3*
○ A. A. Sauvignon Karneid '17	♀♀ 2*
● A. A. Schiava Alte Reben '17	♀♀ 2*
● A. A. Schiava Alte Reben '16	♀♀ 2*

Griesbauerhof
Georg Mumelter

VIA RENCIO, 66
39100 BOLZANO/BOZEN
TEL. +39 0471973090
www.griesbauerhof.it

CELLAR SALES
PRE-BOOKED VISITS
ANNUAL PRODUCTION 30,000 bottles
HECTARES UNDER VINE 3.80

The Mumelter family's estate is situated in one of South Tyrol's wine-growing cradles, the hills of Santa Maddalena and Santa Glustina. Even if it's facing the entrance to the Eisack Valley, it's one of the region's warmest enclaves, an area historically dedicated to Schiava and Lagrein. Over the years their estate has enlarged to include small shares of Merlot and Cabernet, while Georg had to go all the way to Appiano to find the best conditions for his Pinot Bianco and Pinot Grigio. Lagrein is still the cornerstone of their selection, as testified to by their Riserva '16. Its compact, vibrant color anticipates aromas of dark gruit, licorice and medicinal herbs. On the palate the wine reveals great force and fullness, proving ripe and pervasive, capable of delivering length and sunniness. Their Cabernet Sauvignon Riserva '16 brings together aromatic maturity with nice tension and suppleness.

● A. A. Lagrein Ris. '16	♟♟ 5
● A. A. Cabernet Sauvignon Ris. '16	♟♟ 3
● A. A. Merlot Spitz '17	♟♟ 3
○ A. A. Pinot Grigio '18	♟♟ 3
● A. A. Santa Maddalena Cl. '18	♟♟ 2*
● A. A. Lagrein '18	♟ 3
⊙ A. A. Merlot Rosé '18	♟ 3
● Isarcus Schiava '17	♟ 3
● A. A. Lagrein Ris. '09	♟♟♟ 5
● A. A. Lagrein Scuro Ris. '99	♟♟♟ 5
● A. A. Cabernet Sauvignon Ris. '15	♟♟ 3
● A. A. Lagrein '16	♟♟ 3
● A. A. Lagrein Ris. '15	♟♟ 3
● A. A. Merlot Spitz '16	♟♟ 3
○ A. A. Pinot Grigio '17	♟♟ 3
● A. A. Schiava Isarcus '16	♟♟ 3
● Schiava Isarcus '15	♟♟ 3

Gummerhof - Malojer

VIA WEGGESTEIN, 36
39100 BOLZANO/BOZEN
TEL. +39 0471972885
www.malojer.it

CELLAR SALES
PRE-BOOKED VISITS
ANNUAL PRODUCTION 100,000 bottles
HECTARES UNDER VINE 18.00

Gummerhof's winemaking business began in the late 19th century and has been passed down, generation after generation, ever since. Today, as back then, their selection is made possible by private vineyards and the contribution of local growers, all of which allows for high production volumes rooted in the Bolzano basin and Renon. The winery, which is still situated along Via Weggestein, also comprises office spaces and a welcoming wine bar/patio. Their original blend of Cabernet and Lagrein, Cuvée Bautzanum, is at the top of its game. On the nose it offers up Largein's deep, dark aromas, which find the right support in Cabernet's nuances of medicinal herbs and pencil lead. On the palate it comes through decisively, only to gain in tension and finesse. Among their whites we appreciated the aromatic finesse of their Sauvignon Gur zu Sand '18, which convinces for its elegance, sapidity and length.

○ A. A. Bianco Cuvée Bautzanum '18	♟♟ 4
● A. A. Cabernet Lagrein Cuvée Bautzanum Ris. '16	♟♟ 4
● A. A. Cabernet Sauvignon Ris. '16	♟♟ 4
○ A. A. Gewürztraminer Kui '18	♟♟ 3
● A. A. Lagrein Gummerhof zu Gries '18	♟♟ 4
● A. A. Lagrein Ris. '16	♟♟ 4
○ A. A. Pinot Grigio Gur zu Sand '18	♟♟ 3
○ A. A. Sauvignon Gur zu Sand '18	♟♟ 3
○ A. A. Valle Isarco Sylvaner Kreiter '18	♟♟ 2*
○ A. A. Pinot Bianco Kreiter '18	♟ 3
● A. A. Pinot Nero Ris. '16	♟ 4
● A. A. Santa Maddalena Cl. Loamer '18	♟ 2
● A. A. Lagrein Gries '09	♟♟♟ 2*
● A. A. Cabernet Ris. '15	♟♟ 4
● A. A. Lagrein Gummerhof zu Gries '16	♟♟ 4
● A. A. Lagrein Ris. '15	♟♟ 4

★Gumphof
Markus Prackwieser

LOC. STRADA DI FIÈ, 11
FRAZ. NOVALE DI PRESULE
39050 FIÈ ALLO SCILIAR/VÖLS AM SCHLERN [BZ]
TEL. +39 0471601190
www.gumphof.it

CELLAR SALES
PRE-BOOKED VISITS
ANNUAL PRODUCTION 45,000 bottles
HECTARES UNDER VINE 5.00

Markus Prackwieser's winery is located in Novale di Presule, a small town at the entrance to the Eisack Valley. Interestingly, their vineyards occupy a kind of borderland, where the warmth of the Bolzano basin is mitigated by the fresh winds of the valley, making for generous, ripe grapes that, at the same time, exhibit finesse and fragrance. Their small cellar, formed out of rock, offers a cool, humid space for aging a selection centered primarily on white grapes. Their Sauvignon Renaissance '16 is at the top of its game. It's a wine that ages at length in Markus's cellar before seeing the light of day. On the nose it opens up slowly, with exotic fruit accompanied by floral notes, all of which reemerge on its crisp palate, where oak proves perfectly integrated. Their Pinot Bianco Renaissance follows a similar track, one constituted of aromatic delicacy and finesse of flavor, while their Pinot Bianco Praesulis '18 plays on the vitality and energy of its palate.

○ A. A. Sauvignon Renaissance '16	♛♛♛ 4*
○ A. A. Pinot Bianco Praesulis '18	♛♛ 4
○ A. A. Pinot Bianco Renaissance '16	♛♛ 6
○ A. A. Gewürztraminer Praesulis '18	♛♛ 5
○ A. A. Pinot Bianco Mediaevum '18	♛♛ 3
● A. A. Pinot Nero Praesulis '17	♛♛ 5
● A. A. Pinot Nero Renaissance Ris. '16	♛♛ 6
○ A. A. Sauvignon Praesulis '18	♛♛ 5
● A. A. Schiava Mediaevum '18	♛♛ 4
○ A. A. Pinot Bianco Praesulis '17	♛♛♛ 4*
○ A. A. Pinot Bianco Praesulis '15	♛♛♛ 3*
○ A. A. Pinot Bianco Praesulis '14	♛♛♛ 3*
○ A. A. Pinot Bianco Praesulis '06	♛♛♛ 3*
○ A. A. Sauvignon Praesulis '13	♛♛♛ 4*
○ A. A. Sauvignon Praesulis '09	♛♛♛ 3
○ A. A. Sauvignon Praesulis '07	♛♛♛ 3*
○ A. A. Sauvignon Renaissance '14	♛♛♛ 4*

★Franz Haas

VIA VILLA, 6
39040 MONTAGNA/MONTAN [BZ]
TEL. +39 0471812280
www.franz-haas.it

CELLAR SALES
PRE-BOOKED VISITS
ANNUAL PRODUCTION 350,000 bottles
HECTARES UNDER VINE 55.00
SUSTAINABLE WINERY

Franz Haas was destined to the role of vigneron, having inherited a veritable dynasty that goes back generations on the Montagna hills. Today the estate has been enlarged, in particular moving towards the Aldino range, with vineyards that initially ranged up to 850 meters elevation but have since broken the 1,000 meter mark. The result can be experienced in the grip and increasingly sophisticated aromatic expression of his wines. Their Manna '17 is an original blend of aromatic grapes that offers up broad, charming fragrances amidst notes of exotic fruit, hints of dried rose and a subtle, mineral vein. In the mouth it lengthens decisively, proving sapid and harmonious. Their Sauvignon '17 also delivered with its intense aromas of wild fruit and medicinal herbs. Aged in steel and barriques, it features an energetic, racy palate.

○ Manna '17	♛♛♛ 5
○ A. A. Sauvignon '17	♛♛ 5
● A. A. Pinot Nero '17	♛♛ 5
● A. A. Pinot Nero Schweizer '15	♛♛ 6
○ Moscato Giallo '18	♛♛ 5
● A. A. Moscato Rosa '12	♛♛♛ 5
● A. A. Moscato Rosa '11	♛♛♛ 5
● A. A. Moscato Rosa Schweizer '00	♛♛♛ 4
● A. A. Moscato Rosa Schweizer '99	♛♛♛ 4
● A. A. Pinot Nero Schweizer '13	♛♛♛ 6
● A. A. Pinot Nero Schweizer '02	♛♛♛ 5
● A. A. Pinot Nero Schweizer '01	♛♛♛ 5
○ A. A. Sauvignon '13	♛♛♛ 5
○ Manna '07	♛♛♛ 4
○ Manna '05	♛♛♛ 4
○ Manna '04	♛♛♛ 4

Haderburg

FRAZ. POCHI
VIA ALBRECHT DÜRER, 3
39040 SALORNO/SALURN [BZ]
TEL. +39 0471889097
www.haderburg.it

CELLAR SALES
PRE-BOOKED VISITS
ANNUAL PRODUCTION 100,000 bottles
HECTARES UNDER VINE 12.00
VITICULTURE METHOD Certified Biodynamic

Arriving in Alto Adige from the south, a small plateau suddenly opens up on the eastern side of the valley at Pochi di Salorno. It's an area that ranges from 400 to 600 meters elevation and is dedicated almost exclusively to viticulture. Here we find Alois Ochsenreiter's winery and a part of his vineyards, which also comprise plots in the Eisack Valley purchased in the early 2000s. Without taking anything away from their excellent still wines, the true speciality here is Metodo Classico, a selection that does an excellent job expressing the brilliance and freshness of the territory. Their Riserva Hausmannhof '09 is a Brut made with Chardonnay aged for a year in barriques before second fermentation. Its complex aromas alternate fruity notes with hints of dried flowers and torrefaction, closing on whiffs of Mediterranean shrub. In the mouth it expresses firmness and tension perfectly supported by creamy bubbles.

○ A. A. Spumante Hausmannhof Brut Ris. '09	♟♟ 5
○ A. A. Chardonnay V. Hausmannhof '18	♟♟ 3
● A. A. Merlot Cabernet Erah '15	♟♟ 5
● A. A. Pinot Nero Hausmannhof '15	♟♟ 6
● A. A. Pinot Nero V. Hausmannhof '17	♟♟ 5
○ A. A. Spumante Brut	♟♟ 5
○ A. A. Spumante Pas Dosé '15	♟♟ 5
○ A. A. Gewürztraminer '17	♟ 3
○ A. A. Spumante Hausmannhof Ris. '97	♟♟♟ 6
○ A. A. Valle Isarco Sylvaner Obermairlhof '05	♟♟♟ 3*
● A. A. Merlot Cabernet Erah '14	♟♟ 5
○ A. A. Pinot Grigio Salurn Pfatten '17	♟♟ 5
● A. A. Pinot Nero Hausmannhof '16	♟♟ 5
○ A. A. Spumante Hausmannhof Brut Ris. '08	♟♟ 5

★★Cantina Kaltern

VIA CANTINE, 12
39052 CALDARO/KALTERN [BZ]
TEL. +39 0471963149
www.kellereikaltern.com

CELLAR SALES
PRE-BOOKED VISITS
ANNUAL PRODUCTION 3,400,000 bottles
HECTARES UNDER VINE 480.00

In an agricultural milieu characterized by extreme fragmentation, the presence of small producers and few large estates, Cantina di Caldaro represents a kind of juggernaut. It's bolstered by almost 500 hectares of terrain and more than 600 grower members who contribute to their production. The staff, led by Andrea Moser, oversee a selection that comprises a a simpler, more fragrant base line of wines and a premium line of fuller, more complex wines. Quintessenz represents the top of their selection, Their Pinot Bianco '17 is a wine of great fragrance while the palate draws you in with its tension and continuity. Their Lago di Caldaro '18 also put in an excellent performance. It's a red that features aromas of small fruits and spices, and a supple, sapid palate that's a pleasure to quaff. Finally, we close with their Sauvignon Stern '18, a white that exhibits elegant, enthralling fragrances.

○ A. A. Pinot Bianco Quintessenz '17	♟♟♟ 5
● A. A. Lago di Caldaro Cl. Sup. Quintessenz '18	♟♟ 3*
○ A. A. Bianco Solos '18	♟♟ 3
○ A. A. Brut Nature '13	♟♟ 5
● A. A. Cabernet Sauvignon Quintessenz Ris. '16	♟♟ 5
○ A. A. Gewürztraminer Campaner '18	♟♟ 3
● A. A. Lagrein Lareith Ris. '16	♟♟ 5
○ A. A. Moscato Giallo Passito Quintessenz '15	♟♟ 6
○ A. A. Pinot Bianco Vial '18	♟♟ 3
○ A. A. Sauvignon Quintessenz '17	♟♟ 5
○ A. A. Sauvignon Stern '18	♟♟ 3
● A. A. Lago di Caldaro Cl. Sup. Quintessenz '17	♟♟♟ 3*

Kettmeir

VIA DELLE CANTINE, 4
39052 CALDARO/KALTERN [BZ]
TEL. +39 0471963135
www.kettmeir.com

CELLAR SALES
PRE-BOOKED VISITS
ANNUAL PRODUCTION 330,000 bottles
HECTARES UNDER VINE 41.00

Kettmeir, the historic Caldaro brand, debuted exactly one hundred years ago. Since the 1980s the producer has been part of the Santa Margherita group, and today Josef Romen oversees management of a vast estate based primarily in Bassa Atesina and Oltradige (though they also cultivate small parcels on the Renon plateau). In the cellar, their selection comprises the regional's principal wines and an increasingly significant presence of Metodo Classico sparkling wines. The 2013 reserve version of their Brut 1919 excelled during our tastings. It's a sparkling wine that, year after year, gains in clarity, with notable aromatic integrity and, especially, a firm, refined palate. In terms of their still wines, we were impressed with their Müller Thurgau Athesis '17, made with grapes cultivate on the hill of Renon. It offers up mineral, citrus fragrances, which we find on its energetic, flavorful palate. Their Pinot Bianco Athesis '17 is also excellent.

○ A. A. Spumante Extra Brut 1919 Ris. '13	♥♥♥	6
○ A. A. Müller Thurgau Athesis '17	♥♥	4
○ A. A. Pinot Bianco Athesis '17	♥♥	4
○ A. A. Chardonnay '18	♥♥	3
○ A. A. Chardonnay V. Maso Reiner '17	♥♥	4
○ A. A. Gewürztraminer '18	♥♥	3
○ A. A. Pinot Bianco '18	♥♥	3
● A. A. Pinot Nero V. Maso Reiner '16	♥♥	4
○ A. A. Sauvignon '18	♥♥	3
○ A. A. Spumante Brut Athesis '16	♥♥	4
○ A. A. Spumante Brut Athesis Rosé '16	♥♥	5
● A. A. Moscato Rosa Athesis '15	♥	5
○ A. A. Spumante Brut 1919 M. Cl. Ris. '11	♥♥♥	6
○ A. A. Spumante Extra Brut 1919 Ris. '12	♥♥♥	6
○ A. A. Chardonnay V. Maso Reiner '16	♀♀	4
○ A. A. Pinot Bianco Athesis '16	♀♀	4

Tenuta Klosterhof
Oskar Andergassen

LOC. CLAVENZ, 40
39052 CALDARO/KALTERN [BZ]
TEL. +39 0471961046
www.garni-klosterhof.com

CELLAR SALES
PRE-BOOKED VISITS
ACCOMMODATION AND RESTAURANT SERVICE
ANNUAL PRODUCTION 38,000 bottles
HECTARES UNDER VINE 5.00

The Klosterhof estate is situated in the northernmost part of Caldaro, where houses suddenly give way to hillside vineyards. Their business centers on hospitality and winemaking, as well as distilling for some years now. Their vineyards are entirely based in Oltradige, especially in Trifall, Panigl and Platanditsch, making for a selection centered on Schiava and Pinot Nero. Their Pinot Nero Schwarze Madonna '16 led their selection this year. It's a wine with an aromatic profile of great maturity, with red fruit on center stage, accompanied by a refreshing whiff of spicy notes and aromatic herbs. The palate is soft, almost creamy, supported by fresh acidity. Their Merlot Riserva '16, a wine character by a sunny, full palate, plays on warmer notes.

● A. A. Merlot Ris. '16	♥♥	4
○ A. A. Moscato Giallo Birnbaum '18	♥♥	3
● A. A. Pinot Nero Schwarze Madonna '16	♥♥	5
○ A. A. Pinot Nero Rosé '18	♥	4
● A. A. Lago di Caldaro Cl. Sup. Plantaditsch '17	♀♀	2*
● A. A. Lago di Caldaro Cl. Sup. Plantaditsch '16	♀♀	2*
● A. A. Merlot Ris. '15	♀♀	4
○ A. A. Moscato Giallo Birnbaum '17	♀♀	3
○ A. A. Pinot Bianco Acapella '17	♀♀	3
○ A. A. Pinot Bianco Acapella '16	♀♀	3
○ A. A. Pinot Bianco Ris. '15	♀♀	3*
● A. A. Pinot Nero Panigl '14	♀♀	5
● A. A. Pinot Nero Panigl '13	♀♀	5
● A. A. Pinot Nero Ris. '14	♀♀	4
● A. A. Pinot Nero Schwarze Madonna '15	♀♀	5

★Köfererhof
Günther Kerschbaumer

FRAZ. NOVACELLA
VIA PUSTERIA, 3
39040 VARNA/VAHRN [BZ]
TEL. +39 3474778009
www.kofererhof.it

CELLAR SALES
PRE-BOOKED VISITS
RESTAURANT SERVICE
ANNUAL PRODUCTION 80,000 bottles
HECTARES UNDER VINE 10.00

Günther Kerschbaumer's estate is situated in the heart of the Eisack Valley, in Novacella to be precise, in what we could call the northernmost outpost of Italian viticulture. Here sunny days alternate with cool, windy nights, and the vines are literally latched on to plots held up by stone walls. The small but efficient cellar hosts numerous medium-sized wooden barrels, which are used for their premium wines, and steel containers, employed for their simpler lines. With his wines, Günther manages to transmit the sunniness of the area, as testified to once again by his Sylvaner R. The 2017 exhibits intense aromas calling up yellow fruit and dried flowers. In the mouth the wine changes gears, delivering for its fullness, tension and backbone. Their Riesling '17 follows a similar track, while their Pinot Grigio '18 proves to be an intense, potent and pervasive drink.

Tenuta Kornell

FRAZ. SETTEQUERCE
VIA COSMA E DAMIANO, 6
39018 TERLANO/TERLAN [BZ]
TEL. +39 0471917507
www.kornell.it

CELLAR SALES
PRE-BOOKED VISITS
ANNUAL PRODUCTION 120,000 bottles
HECTARES UNDER VINE 15.00

Florian Brigl oversees the family winery in Settequerce, a small village situated between Bolzano and Terlano, an area where apples and vineyards fight for the best positions. At the woods' edge we find their cellar and adjacent house, as well as most of their vineyards, in a particularly sunny and warm area that consistently confers a notable richness its grapes. Their more delicate and subtle wines are made with grapes grown in Appiano Monte. The result is a selection that succeeds in bringing together varietal identity with elegance and firmness. Their Lagrein Staffes Ris. '16 exhibits all the warm sunniness of the area, underlined by the presence of forest undergrowth and spices. These bring out a full, powerful palate supported more by vigor than tannins. Their Merlot Staffes '16 follows a similar track, while their Kressfeld vineyard gives rise to a Merlot '15 characterized by even riper aromas and a robust, broad palate.

○ A. A. Valle Isarco Sylvaner R '17	♟♟♟ 5
○ A. A. Valle Isarco Pinot Grigio '18	♟♟ 3*
○ A. A. Valle Isarco Riesling '17	♟♟ 5
○ A. A. Valle Isarco Gewürztraminer '18	♟♟ 4
○ A. A. Valle Isarco Kerner '18	♟♟ 3
○ A. A. Valle Isarco Müller Thurgau '18	♟♟ 3
○ A. A. Valle Isarco Sylvaner '18	♟♟ 3
○ A. A. Valle Isarco Veltliner '17	♟♟ 4
○ A. A. Valle Isarco Pinot Grigio '15	♟♟♟ 3*
○ A. A. Valle Isarco Pinot Grigio '13	♟♟♟ 3*
○ A. A. Valle Isarco Pinot Grigio '12	♟♟♟ 3*
○ A. A. Valle Isarco Pinot Grigio '11	♟♟♟ 3*
○ A. A. Valle Isarco Riesling '16	♟♟♟ 5
○ A. A. Valle Isarco Riesling '10	♟♟♟ 4
○ A. A. Valle Isarco Sylvaner '16	♟♟♟ 3*
○ A. A. Valle Isarco Sylvaner R '13	♟♟♟ 5
○ A. A. Valle Isarco Sylvaner R '09	♟♟♟ 4

● A. A. Lagrein Staffes Ris. '16	♟♟♟ 5
● A. A. Merlot V. Kressfeld Ris. '15	♟♟ 5
○ A. A. Bianco Aichberg '17	♟♟ 4
○ A. A. Cabernet Sauvignon Staffes Ris. '16	♟♟ 5
○ A. A. Gewürztraminer Damian '18	♟♟ 4
● A. A. Lagrein Greif '18	♟♟ 3
● A. A. Merlot Staffes Ris. '16	♟♟ 5
○ A. A. Pinot Bianco Eich '18	♟♟ 4
○ A. A. Pinot Grigio Gris '18	♟♟ 4
○ A. A. Sauvignon Cosmas '18	♟♟ 3
○ A. A. Sauvignon Oberberg '17	♟♟ 6
● A. A. Pinot Nero Marith '18	♟ 6
● A. A. Lagrein Staves Ris. '14	♟♟♟ 5
● A. A. Lagrein Staves Ris. '12	♟♟♟ 5
● A. A. Merlot Kressfeld Ris. '13	♟♟ 5
● A. A. Merlot Staves Ris. '15	♟♟ 5

★Kuenhof - Peter Pliger

LOC. LA MARA, 110
39042 BRESSANONE/BRIXEN [BZ]
TEL. +39 0472850546
pliger.kuenhof@rolmail.net

CELLAR SALES
PRE-BOOKED VISITS
ANNUAL PRODUCTION 38,000 bottles
HECTARES UNDER VINE 6.00
SUSTAINABLE WINERY

Peter Pliger's winery is situated in La Mara, one of the Eisack Valley's most notable districts. A handful of hectares climb along the steep slopes of Lahner, a crisp and sunny area that Peter and his wife, Brigitte, lined with strong stone walls. These are indispensable for cultivating the land and the valley's traditional grapes, which give rise to Sylvaner, Riesling and Veltliner, the backbone of their entire selection. Their Sylvaner '18 has delicate aromas that are almost hesitant to give themselves up — first simple notes of apple, then dried flowers, licorice root and a subtle smoky note. On the palate it's true to the typology, rich, sapid and enthralling. Their Kaiton '18 follows a similar track aromatically, though it's enriched by aromatic herbs and a slight citrusy note. In the mouth it reveals greater length and acidic tension.

★Cantina Kurtatsch

LOC. BREITBACH
S.DA DEL VINO, 23
39040 CORTACCIA/KURTATSCH [BZ]
TEL. +39 0471880115
www.cantina-kurtatsch.it

CELLAR SALES
PRE-BOOKED VISITS
ANNUAL PRODUCTION 1,500,000 bottles
HECTARES UNDER VINE 190.00
SUSTAINABLE WINERY

Cantina di Cortaccia is one of South Tyrol's small and historic cooperative wineries. Founded by a handful of members in 1900, it has always maintained a strong bond with the territory. Still today their vineyards span a wide range of elevations, from 200 to 900 meters, situated entirely in Cortaccia and organized according to the needs of each cultivar. Their selection is carefully overseen by Othmar Donà, an expert cellar master who transforms the cooperative's grapes into wines of great character. The force of the territory expresses itself perfectly in their Gewürztraminer Brenntal '17, a wine with intense aromas that range from sulfurous notes to candied citrus, wild rose and licorice, only to release itself onto a crisp palate of splendid tension. Their Merlot Brenntal '17 is a rich, ripe wine, while their Pinot Grigio Penóner '17 and Chardonnay Freienfeld '17, two whites that bring together vigor and power, impress for their finesse and harmony.

○ A. A. Valle Isarco Sylvaner '18	♟♟♟ 3*
○ A. A. Valle Isarco Riesling Kaiton '18	♟♟ 4
○ A. A. Valle Isarco Veltliner '18	♟♟ 4
○ A. A. Valle Isarco Gewürztraminer '18	♟♟ 3
○ A. A. Valle Isarco Grüner Veltliner '15	♟♟♟ 3*
○ A. A. Valle Isarco Riesling Kaiton '16	♟♟♟ 3*
○ A. A. Valle Isarco Riesling Kaiton '12	♟♟♟ 4*
○ A. A. Valle Isarco Riesling Kaiton '11	♟♟♟ 4*
○ A. A. Valle Isarco Riesling Kaiton '10	♟♟♟ 4
○ A. A. Valle Isarco Riesling Kaiton '07	♟♟♟ 3*
○ A. A. Valle Isarco Riesling Kaiton '05	♟♟♟ 3*
○ A. A. Valle Isarco Sylvaner '14	♟♟♟ 3*
○ A. A. Valle Isarco Sylvaner '13	♟♟♟ 3*
○ A. A. Valle Isarco Sylvaner '08	♟♟♟ 3
○ A. A. Valle Isarco Sylvaner '06	♟♟♟ 3*
○ A. A. Valle Isarco Sylvaner V.T. '04	♟♟♟ 3*
○ A. A. Valle Isarco Veltliner '09	♟♟♟ 3*

○ A. A. Gewürztraminer Brenntal Ris. '17	♟♟ 5
● A. A. Merlot Brenntal Ris. '16	♟♟ 6
○ A. A. Pinot Grigio Penóner '17	♟♟ 4
○ A. A. Bianco Amos '17	♟♟ 5
● A. A. Cabernet Sauvignon Freienfeld Ris. '15	♟♟ 6
○ A. A. Chardonnay Freienfeld Ris. '16	♟♟ 7
● A. A. Lagrein Frauenrigl Ris. '16	♟♟ 5
● A. A. Müller Thurgau Graun '18	♟♟ 3
● A. A. Pinot Nero Mazon Ris. '16	♟♟ 6
○ A. A. Sauvignon Kofl '17	♟♟ 4
● A. A. Schiava Sonntaler Alte Reben '18	♟♟ 3
○ Aruna V. T. '17	♟♟ 6
○ A. A. Gewürztraminer Brenntal Ris. '16	♟♟♟ 5
○ A. A. Gewürztraminer Brenntal Ris. '15	♟♟♟ 5
○ A. A. Gewürztraminer Brenntal Ris. '14	♟♟♟ 5
○ A. A. Gewürztraminer Brenntal Ris. '12	♟♟♟ 5

Laimburg

LOC. LAIMBURG, 6
39040 VADENA/PFATTEN [BZ]
TEL. +39 0471969590
www.laimburg.bz.it

CELLAR SALES
PRE-BOOKED VISITS
ANNUAL PRODUCTION 100,000 bottles
HECTARES UNDER VINE 20.00
SUSTAINABLE WINERY

If South Tyrol's wines are enjoying great success today, and its producers are held in high esteem throughout the world, it's partially thanks to the Laimburg Institute. This agricultural research center put great effort into understanding and promoting the best suited viticultural practices for the region. In their Vadena cellar, they produce a selection made with grapes cultivated throughout the entire territory. Such a rich viticultural patrimony makes for a wide range of wines, led once again this year by their Lagrein Barbagòl, a 2016 reserve that pours dark and is, initially, aromatically a bit bashful — it needs time. After a few moments it bursts forth, dominated by timbres of dark fruit accompanied by notes of undergrowth and spices, all of which follow through on an energetic, close-knit and decidedly generous palate. Among their whites we especially appreciated the elegance of their Pinot Bianco Musis '18.

Klaus Lentsch

S.DA REINSPERG, 18A
39057 APPIANO/EPPAN [BZ]
TEL. +39 0471967263
www.klauslentsch.eu

CELLAR SALES
PRE-BOOKED VISITS
ANNUAL PRODUCTION 50,000 bottles
HECTARES UNDER VINE 6.00

Klaus Lentsch inherited a legacy of viticulture that goes back generations. But it was only some twenty years ago that he managed to realize his dream and purchase the Amperg estate in Campodazzo. Three hectares in the Eisack Valley were rapidly expanded with purchases in Oltradige, where in 2013 he built a new cellar in San Paolo. Today the estate spans these two territories, making for a selection that comprises Amperg's taut, energetic whites and reds arising from more mild areas. The Eisack Valley gave rise to their most convincing wine this year, their Veltliner Eichberg '17. It's a white that alternates sulphur with exotic notes and citrus, unfolding gracefully on the palate only to close with a long, harmonious finish. Their two Pinot Nero Bachgarts also put in a good performance. Both are 2016s characterized by aromas of wild fruit and fines herbes. We preferred the reserve for exhibiting greater character on the palate.

● A. A. Lagrein Barbagòl Ris. '16	♟♟ 5
○ A. A. Pinot Bianco Musis '18	♟♟ 3*
● A. A. Cabernet Sauvignon Sass Roà Ris. '16	♟♟ 5
○ A. A. Sauvignon Oyèll '16	♟♟ 4
● Col de Réy '15	♟♟ 6
○ Dòa '16	♟♟ 4
○ A. A. Gewürztraminer Elyònd '16	♟ 4
○ A. A. Gewürztraminer '94	♟♟♟ 5
● A. A. Lagrein Scuro Barbagòl Ris. '00	♟♟♟ 5
● A. A. Cabernet Sauvignon Sass Roà Ris. '15	♟♟ 5
● A. A. Lagrein Barbagòl Ris. '15	♟♟ 5
● A. A. Merlot Ris. '16	♟♟ 4
○ A. A. Pinot Bianco '17	♟♟ 2*
○ A. A. Sauvignon Passito Saphir '16	♟♟ 6

○ A. A. Valle Isarco Veltliner Eichberg '17	♟♟ 4
● A. A. Pinot Nero Bachgart '16	♟♟ 4
● A. A. Pinot Nero Bachgart Ris. '16	♟♟ 5
○ A. A. Moscato Giallo Amperg '18	♟ 3
○ A. A. Pinot Bianco Amperg '18	♟ 3
○ A. A. Sauvignon Amperg '18	♟ 3
● A. A. Pinot Nero Bachgart '13	♟♟♟ 4*
○ A. A. Bianco Cuvée Syvi '16	♟♟ 3
○ A. A. Gewürztraminer Fuchslahn '16	♟♟ 2*
○ A. A. Grüner Veltliner Eichberg '16	♟♟ 3
● A. A. Lagrein Amperg Ris. '15	♟♟ 4
○ A. A. Pinot Grigio '17	♟♟ 2*
● A. A. Pinot Nero Bachgart '15	♟♟ 4
● A. A. Pinot Nero Bachgart Ris. '14	♟♟ 3
○ A. A. Sauvignon Amperg '16	♟♟ 3
○ A. A. Valle Isarco Grüner Veltliner Eichberg '15	♟♟ 3

Loacker Schwarhof

LOC. SANKT JUSTINA, 3
39100 BOLZANO/BOZEN
TEL. +39 0471365125
www.loacker.bio

CELLAR SALES
PRE-BOOKED VISITS
ANNUAL PRODUCTION 60,000 bottles
HECTARES UNDER VINE 7.00
VITICULTURE METHOD Certified Organic
SUSTAINABLE WINERY

The Loacker family were certainly among the first to contemplate sustainable viticulture, an approach in keeping with nature's rhythms and rules. It was first put into practice with organic management and later with biodynamic. Their cellar is situated in the heart of the Santa Maddalena production zone, surrounded by vineyards of Schiava and Lagrein. These were eventually joined by plots of Bordeaux varieties and some whites, resulting in energetic wines that transmit the area's heat, and the force of its terrain. Their Gran Lareyn '16 put in a top performance. It's a Lagrein reserve that brings intensely fruity notes and medicinal herbs to the fore, sensations that are amplified across its generous yet elegant palate, which closes with a charming smoky note. Their Merlot Ywain '16 offers up aromas dominated by sweet and ripe red fruit, while on the palate it proves full, supported by pleasantly rough tannins.

● A. A. Lagrein Gran Lareyn Ris. '16	▼▼	5
○ A. A. Gewürztraminer Atagis '17	▼▼	4
● Kastlet '15	▼▼	5
● Lagrein Gran Lareyn '17	▼▼	4
● Ywain '16	▼▼	4
○ Tasnim '18	▼	4
● A. A. Merlot Ywain '04	▼▼▼	4*
● A. A. Lagrein Gran Lareyn Ris. '15	▽▽	4
● A. A. Santa Maddalena Cl. Morit '17	▽▽	3
● A. A. Santa Maddalena Cl. Morit '16	▽▽	3
○ Chardonnay Ateyon '16	▽▽	4
○ Chardonnay Ateyon '15	▽▽	4
● Kastlet '14	▽▽	5
● Lagrein Gran Lareyn '16	▽▽	4
● Lagrein Gran Lareyn '15	▽▽	4
● Merlot Ywain '14	▽▽	4
○ Sauvignon Blanc Tasnim '16	▽▽	4

Manincor

LOC. SAN GIUSEPPE AL LAGO, 4
39052 CALDARO/KALTERN [BZ]
TEL. +39 0471960230
www.manincor.com

CELLAR SALES
PRE-BOOKED VISITS
ANNUAL PRODUCTION 330,000 bottles
HECTARES UNDER VINE 50.00
VITICULTURE METHOD Certified Biodynamic
SUSTAINABLE WINERY

The count Göess-Enzemberg family are among Oltradige's leaders. Theirs is a large estate based primarily in Caldaro, though it also reaches into the Terlano hills. Virtually hidden in the landscape, just a stone's throw from the lake, their cellar sees all stages of production carried out with the utmost respect for the environment, working with gravity and respecting the times necessary for wines to reach maturity. Biodynamic vineyard management and the great skill of Helmuth Zozin in interpreting each vintage provide the rest. Their Eichorn '17 is a splendid Pinot Bianco redolent of ripe fruit and flowers, with a curious nuance of white pepper that lends lightness. The palate it rich and juicy, well-supported by acidity. Their Chardonnay Sophie '17 expresses perfectly integrated oak, which reemerges on its crisp, elegant palate. Finally, we mention the excellent performances put in by their Sauvignon Lieben Aich '17 and Passit Le Petit '17.

○ A. A. Terlano Chardonnay Sophie '17	▼▼	6
○ A. A. Terlano Pinot Bianco Eichhorn '17	▼▼	5
○ A. A. Terlano Sauvignon Lieben Aich '17	▼▼	8
○ Le Petit '17	▼▼	8
● A. A. Pinot Nero Mason '17	▼▼	6
● A. A. Pinot Nero Mason di Mason '17	▼▼	8
○ A. A. Terlano Réserve della Contessa '18	▼▼	4
○ A. A. Terlano Sauvignon Tannenberg '17	▼▼	5
● Castel Campan '16	▼▼	8
○ A. A. Terlano Pinot Bianco Eichhorn '16	▽▽▽	5
○ A. A. Terlano Pinot Bianco Eichhorn '15	▽▽▽	5
○ A. A. Terlano Pinot Bianco Eichhorn '13	▽▽▽	5
○ A. A. Terlano Pinot Bianco Eichhorn '12	▽▽▽	5
○ A. A. Terlano Sauvignon Tannenberg '13	▽▽▽	5

Lorenz Martini

LOC. CORNAIANO/GIRLAN
VIA PRANZOL, 2D
39057 APPIANO/EPPAN [BZ]
TEL. +39 0471664136
www.lorenz-martini.it

CELLAR SALES
PRE-BOOKED VISITS
ANNUAL PRODUCTION 15,000 bottles
HECTARES UNDER VINE 2.00

Lorenz Martini's relationship with sparkling winemaking goes back many years, when fresh off his first job in a historic local winery he began to experiment with the typology. It was a long journey though Lorenz was convinced that with time and passion he'd go far. Today he cultivates a handful of prized hectares in Cornaiano, Appiano Monte and Cologna, where Chardonnay, Pinot Bianco and Pinot Nero can preserve the sapidity and acidity that are so essential to Comitissa. 2015 added an intensely fruit expression to its typically honed and gutsy profile, resulting in enticing aromas that follow through coherently on the palate. Here their Comitissa Pas Dosé Riserva unfolds gracefully, perfectly supported by a creamy carbonic weave and by an acidity that's decisive but never excessively so. Sapidity, harmony and length complete the picture, making for an exquisitely territorial sparkling wine.

K. Martini & Sohn

LOC. CORNAIANO
VIA LAMM, 28
39057 APPIANO/EPPAN [BZ]
TEL. +39 0471663156
www.martini-sohn.it

CELLAR SALES
PRE-BOOKED VISITS
ANNUAL PRODUCTION 230,000 bottles
HECTARES UNDER VINE 30.00

Active for forty years now, the Martini family's winery comprises a thirty-hectare estate situated primarily in Oltradige, where the cellar is also located. In addition to their Cornaiano vineyards, they have well-positioned plots in Caldaro and Appiano Monte. When it comes to Lagrein, cultivation is concentrated in Gries, naturally, while their Eisack Valley varieties are grown in Chiusa. It's a small puzzle of vineyards that makes for a selection composed of various lines, both varietals and more ambitious wines. As always, they submitted a wide selection to our tastings, captained by an excellent 2018 Gewürztraminer from their Palladium line. In addition to its signature flowery and exotic aromas, there's a curious note of flint. It does particularly well in the mouth, where it's characterized by an extraordinary sapidity and an approachable, juicy palate. Their Lagrein Maturum '16 also put in a good performance. It's a wine dominated by notes of undergrowth and licorice, sensations exalted on its pervasive, delicately salty palate.

○ A. A. Spumante Pas Dosé Comitissa Ris. '15	♟♟♟ 5
○ A. A. Brut Comitissa Ris. '10	♟♟ 5
○ A. A. Brut Comitissa Ris. '09	♟♟ 5
○ A. A. Spumante Brut Comitissa Gold Gran Riserva '06	♟♟ 5
○ A. A. Spumante Brut Comitissa Ris. '12	♟♟ 5
○ A. A. Spumante Brut Comitissa Ris. '11	♟♟ 5
○ A. A. Spumante Comitissa Brut Ris. '08	♟♟ 5
○ A. A. Spumante Comitissa Brut Ris. '07	♟♟ 5
○ A. A. Spumante Comitissa Brut Ris. '06	♟♟ 5
○ A. A. Spumante Comitissa Brut Ris. '01	♟♟ 5
○ A. A. Spumante Comitissa Brut Ris. '00	♟♟ 5
○ A. A. Spumante Pas Dosé Comitissa Ris. '13	♟♟ 5
○ A. A. Spumante Pas Dosé Comitissa Ris. '13	♟♟ 5

○ A. A. Gewürztraminer Palladium '18	♟♟♟ 4
○ A. A. Kerner Palladium '18	♟♟ 2*
● A. A. Lagrein Maturum Ris. '16	♟♟ 5
○ A. A. Müller Thurgau Palladium '18	♟♟ 3
○ A. A. Pinot Bianco Alte Reben '16	♟♟ 3
○ A. A. Pinot Bianco Palladium '18	♟♟ 2*
● A. A. Pinot Nero Palladium '17	♟♟ 3
○ A. A. Sauvignon Palladium '18	♟♟ 3
● A. A. Schiava Palladium '17	♟♟ 3
○ A. A. Chardonnay Maturum '17	♟ 4
○ A. A. Moscato Giallo '18	♟ 4
● Coldirus Palladium '17	♟ 3
○ A. A. Sauvignon Palladium '04	♟♟♟ 2*
○ A. A. Chardonnay Maturum '16	♟♟ 4
● A. A. Lagrein Maturum Ris. '15	♟♟ 5
○ A. A. Moscato Giallo '17	♟♟ 4
● Coldirus Palladium '16	♟♟ 3

★Cantina Meran

via Cantina, 9
39020 Marlengo/Marling [BZ]
Tel. +39 0473447137
www.cantinamerano.it

CELLAR SALES
PRE-BOOKED VISITS
ANNUAL PRODUCTION 1,600,000 bottles
HECTARES UNDER VINE 265.00

Founded in 2010 as a fusion of the historic cooperative wineries of Burggräfler and Merano, this large producer now avails itself of more than 400 grower members operating throughout the spa town and neighboring municipalities (and reaching all the way to the Vinschgau Valley). In their modern Marlengo cellar, renovated in 2013, Stefan Kapfinger and his staff give rise to a selection that does a nice job representing the territory, from simpler wines to more ambitious versions, not to mention their Sonnenberg line, which is dedicated entirely to Vinschgau. Their Sissi '16 is a Moscato Giallo passito that pours gold, and offers up aromas of candied group and dried flowers. The palate, which possesses a measured sweetness, closes long and crisp. Their Gewürztraminer Graf '18 also had a good day. Exotic in its aromas, on the palate it manages to govern exuberance with sapidity and finesse. Finally, their Pinot Bianco Tyrol '17 proves ripe in its olfactive profile, with a sapid, harmonious palate.

○ A. A. Gewürztraminer Graf '18	🍷🍷 3*
○ A. A. Moscato Giallo Passito Sissi '16	🍷🍷 6
○ A. A. Pinot Bianco Tyrol '17	🍷🍷 4
● A. A. Cabernet Graf Ris. '16	🍷🍷 4
● A. A. Lagrein Segen Ris. '16	🍷🍷 4
● A. A. Meranese Schickenburg Graf '18	🍷🍷 3
● A. A. Merlot Freiherr Ris. '16	🍷🍷 5
● A. A. Pinot Nero Zeno Ris. '16	🍷🍷 4
○ A. A. Sauvignon Mervin '17	🍷🍷 4
○ A. A. Val Venosta Kerner '18	🍷🍷 4
○ A. A. Val Venosta Pinot Bianco '18	🍷🍷 3
○ A. A. Pinot Bianco Tyrol '16	🍷🍷🍷 4*
○ A. A. Pinot Bianco Tyrol '15	🍷🍷🍷 4*
○ A. A. Pinot Bianco Tyrol '13	🍷🍷🍷 4*
○ A. A. Sauvignon Mervin '14	🍷🍷🍷 4*
○ A. A. Valle Venosta Pinot Bianco Sonnenberg '13	🍷🍷🍷 3*

★Cantina Convento Muri-Gries

p.zza Gries, 21
39100 Bolzano/Bozen
Tel. +39 0471282287
www.muri-gries.com

CELLAR SALES
ANNUAL PRODUCTION 700,000 bottles
HECTARES UNDER VINE 55.00
SUSTAINABLE WINERY

It's as if the winery situated in Piazza Gries hides the Klosteranger vineyard from prying eyes, enclosed as it is by the abbey and its surrounding walls — features of an agricultural past that once characterized all of Bolzano. Today cellar master Christian Werth is accompanied in the fields by Walter Bernard and oversees a large estate based primarily in Gries Moritzing (where Schiava and Lagrein are grown), as well as Appiano (where mostly white varieties are cultivated). And their Klosteranger vineyard gave rise to the most interesting wine tasted this year. It's a vibrantly-colored Lagrein '15 whose aromas of dark fruit are broadened by spices, medicinal herbs and licorice roots. On the palate it's close-woven, energetic and enthralling. Their Lagrein Abtei Muri Ris. '16 is a more approachable wine, while their Pinot Bianco Abtei Muri proves elegant and balanced.

● A. A. Lagrein V. Klosteranger Ris. '15	🍷🍷🍷 8
● A. A. Lagrein Abtei Muri Ris. '16	🍷🍷 5
○ A. A. Terlano Pinot Bianco Abtei Muri Ris. '16	🍷🍷 5
● A. A. Lagrein '18	🍷🍷 3
● A. A. Moscato Rosa V.T. Abtei Muri '17	🍷🍷 5
● A. A. Pinot Nero Abtei Muri Ris. '16	🍷🍷 5
● A. A. Santa Maddalena '18	🍷🍷 2*
○ A. A. Terlano Pinot Bianco '18	🍷🍷 3
⊙ A. A. Lagrein Kretzer '18	🍷 3
● A. A. Lagrein Abtei Muri Ris. '14	🍷🍷🍷 5
● A. A. Lagrein Abtei Muri Ris. '12	🍷🍷🍷 5
● A. A. Lagrein Abtei Muri Ris. '11	🍷🍷🍷 5
● A. A. Lagrein Abtei Muri Ris. '10	🍷🍷🍷 5
● A. A. Lagrein Abtei Muri Ris. '09	🍷🍷🍷 5
● A. A. Pinot Nero Abtei Muri Ris. '15	🍷🍷🍷 5

★Nals Margreid

VIA HEILIGENBERG, 2
39010 NALLES/NALS [BZ]
TEL. +39 0471678626
www.kellerei.it

CELLAR SALES
PRE-BOOKED VISITS
ANNUAL PRODUCTION 980,000 bottles
HECTARES UNDER VINE 165.00
SUSTAINABLE WINERY

Nals Margreid is one of the region's
smallest cooperatives, but its vineyards
occupy a bit of each of South Tyrol's
wine-growing districts. Over the past
twenty years the area cultivated has
increased while production volumes have
remained the same, testifying to an
approach that's increasingly selective. If
Gottfried Pollinger made their wines famous
the world over, Harald Schraffl discerningly
interprets the grapes cultivated in some of
the province's best crus, like Sirmian's
Pinot Bianco and Punggl's Pinot Grigio, with
the aim of bringing out the deep bond
between grape, vineyard and human effort.
And these are the wines that lead among
the producer's 2018s. Their Sirmian offers
up aromas of white damson and flowers,
while the palate proves crisp and elegant. If
their Punggl '18 is more pervasive and
meatier, their Sauvignon Mantele '18
expresses itself with suppleness and
tension, while their Baron Salvadori '16 is
an elegant, deep Chardonnay. But their
entire selection shines for varietal and
territorial coherence.

○ A. A. Pinot Bianco Sirmian '18	🏆🏆🏆 5
○ A. A. Chardonnay Baron Salvadori '16	🏆🏆 6
○ A. A. Sauvignon Mantele '18	🏆🏆 5
○ A. A. Chardonnay Magred '18	🏆🏆 4
○ A. A. Gewürztraminer Lyra '18	🏆🏆 5
● A. A. Lagrein Gries Ris. '16	🏆🏆 5
● A. A. Merlot Cabernet Anticus Ris. '16	🏆🏆 7
○ A. A. Moscato Giallo Passito Baronesse '16	🏆🏆 7
○ A. A. Pinot Bianco Penon '18	🏆🏆 3
○ A. A. Pinot Grigio Punggl '18	🏆🏆 5
● A. A. Schiava Galea '18	🏆🏆 3
● A. A. Pinot Nero Jura Ris. '16	🏆 6
○ A. A. Pinot Bianco Sirmian '17	🏆🏆🏆 5
○ A. A. Pinot Bianco Sirmian '16	🏆🏆🏆 5
○ A. A. Pinot Bianco Sirmian '14	🏆🏆🏆 5

Ignaz Niedrist

LOC. CORNAIANO/GIRLAN
VIA RONCO, 5
39057 APPIANO/EPPAN [BZ]
TEL. +39 0471664494
www.ignazniedrist.com

CELLAR SALES
PRE-BOOKED VISITS
ANNUAL PRODUCTION 50,000 bottles
HECTARES UNDER VINE 10.00
SUSTAINABLE WINERY

Ignaz and Elisabeth Niedrist have some 30
vintages under their belt. Their adventure
began with the few vineyards situated
around their home. Over time these grew to
include purchases in Ronco, Appiano Monte
and Gries. The first two see elevations of
around 500 meters, but feature very
different pedoclimatic conditions, such that
Ignaz interprets his Pinot Nero, Pinot Bianco
and Sauvignon differently according to the
vineyard of origin. Their plots in Gries can
be found in the warm Bolzano basin, and
host solely Lagrein. An excellent 2016 gave
rise to a Lagrein Berger Gei Riserva whose
rich expression of fruit finds freshness in
medicinal herbs and spices. In the mouth
the wine is compact and powerful, with
tannins lending stillness to the palate. Their
Pinot Nero Nom Kalk '16 moves in an
entirely different register, proving broad and
graceful in its expressions of wild fruit and
forest undergrowth, delicate and balanced
on the palate.

● A. A. Lagrein Berger Gei Ris. '16	🏆🏆 5
● A. A. Pinot Nero Vom Kalk '16	🏆🏆 8
● A. A. Pinot Nero Ris. '16	🏆🏆 6
○ A. A. Riesling Berg '18	🏆🏆 4
○ A. A. Sauvignon Limes '17	🏆🏆 5
○ A. A. Pinot Bianco Limes '17	🏆 5
○ A. A. Riesling Berg '11	🏆🏆🏆 4*
○ A. A. Terlano Pinot Bianco '12	🏆🏆🏆 3*
○ A. A. Terlano Sauvignon '10	🏆🏆🏆 3
○ A. A. Terlano Sauvignon '00	🏆🏆🏆 3*
○ Trias '14	🏆🏆🏆 4*
● A. A. Lagrein Berger Gei Ris. '15	🏆🏆 4
○ A. A. Pinot Bianco Limes '16	🏆🏆 4
● A. A. Pinot Nero Ris. '15	🏆🏆 5
○ A. A. Riesling Berg '16	🏆🏆 4
○ A. A. Sauvignon Limes '16	🏆🏆 4
○ Trias '16	🏆🏆 4

Pacherhof - Andreas Huber

RAZ. NOVACELLA
.LO PACHER, 1
39040 VARNA/VAHRN [BZ]
EL. +39 0472835717
www.pacherhof.com

CELLAR SALES
PRE-BOOKED VISITS
ACCOMMODATION AND RESTAURANT SERVICE
ANNUAL PRODUCTION 90,000 bottles
HECTARES UNDER VINE 8.50

Andreas Huber oversees one of the Eisack Valley's loveliest estates, one whose roots go back to the 12th century (wine production began in the late 19th century). Their vineyards are concentrated around the farmstead, in a sunny position that's continually cooled by rapid winds moving down towards Bolzano. Their lovely cellar, which comprises both historic and modern spaces, was built with the utmost respect for the environment. In addition to steel containers, there's a sizable collection of mid-sized wooden barrels here, which are used for their more ambitious wines. As usual the selection submitted had no weak points, though we appreciated three wines in particular. Their Sylvaner Alte Reben '17 offers up aromas of great personality, dominated by smoky and sulfurous notes that let through exotic hints. In the mouth it proves firm and continuous. Their Riesling '18 is aromatically finer and honed on the palate, while their Pinot Grigio '18 expresses maturity and harmony.

○ A. A. Valle Isarco Pinot Grigio '18	TT 4
○ A. A. Valle Isarco Sylvaner Alte Reben '17	TT 5
○ Riesling '18	TT 4
○ A. A. Valle Isarco Kerner '18	TT 4
○ A. A. Valle Isarco Sylvaner '18	TT 4
○ A. A. Valle Isarco Veltliner '18	TT 4
○ Private Cuvée Andreas Huber '17	TT 6
○ A. A. Valle Isarco Grüner Veltliner '16	YYY 4*
○ A. A. Valle Isarco Riesling '04	YYY 3
○ A. A. Valle Isarco Sylvaner '13	YYY 3*
○ A. A. Valle Isarco Sylvaner Alte Reben '16	YYY 5
○ A. A. Valle Isarco Sylvaner Alte Reben '05	YYY 4
○ A. A. Valle Isarco Grüner Veltliner '17	YY 4
○ A. A. Valle Isarco Sylvaner '17	YY 4

Pfannenstielhof Johannes Pfeifer

VIA PFANNESTIEL, 9
39100 BOLZANO/BOZEN
TEL. +39 0471970884
www.pfannenstielhof.it

CELLAR SALES
PRE-BOOKED VISITS
ANNUAL PRODUCTION 43,000 bottles
HECTARES UNDER VINE 4.00

In a winemaking district like Alto Adige, where even smaller producers cultivate many different varieties, it's striking to come across a winery like that led by Hannes Pfeifer and his wife, Margareth. They've dedicated themselves entirely to two grapes that have characterized the territory since time immemorial: Schiava and Lagrein. Here on Santa Maddalena hill, the vineyards descend slowly down to Eisack, with Schiava growing in soil rich in porphyry and dolomitic limestone, while Lagrein finds ideal conditions in deeper soils characterized by sand and gravel. Pfeifer's Santa Magdalena Classico is always one of their most convincing wines. It succeeds in the difficult work of bringing together aromatic approachability and depth with a simple, racy and rich palate, though without betraying the essence of the typology. 2018 brought out lovely nuances of medicinal herbs, which lend lightness to notes of ripe cherry and spices, sensations that reemerge on a juicy, pleasantly rough palate.

● A. A. Santa Maddalena Cl. '18	TT 3*
● A. A. Lagrein Ris. '16	TT 5
● A. A. Lagrein vom Boden '18	TT 3
● A. A. Santa Maddalena Cl. Annver '17	TT 3
⊙ Lagrein Rosé '18	T 3
● A. A. Santa Maddalena Cl. '14	YYY 3*
● A. A. Santa Maddalena Cl. '09	YYY 2*
● A. A. Lagrein Ris. '15	YY 5
● A. A. Lagrein Ris. '14	YY 5
● A. A. Lagrein Ris. '13	YY 5
⊙ A. A. Lagrein Rosé '17	YY 3
● A. A. Lagrein vom Boden '17	YY 3
● A. A. Lagrein vom Boden '16	YY 3
● A. A. Santa Maddalena Cl. '17	YY 3*
● A. A. Santa Maddalena Cl. '16	YY 3*
● A. A. Santa Maddalena Cl. '15	YY 3*
⊙ Lagrein Rosé '16	YY 2*

Tenuta Pfitscher

VIA DOLOMITI, 17
39040 MONTAGNA/MONTAN [BZ]
TEL. +39 04711681317
www.pfitscher.it

CELLAR SALES
PRE-BOOKED VISITS
ANNUAL PRODUCTION 60,000 bottles
HECTARES UNDER VINE 7.00

The Pfitscher family has been active in
Montagna for more than a century and a
half. Initially they had a hands-off approach,
but today they oversee every stage of
production, with a selection of wines that's
both high profile and environmentally
sustainable. Their estate, which is based
almost exclusively in Bassa Atesina,
comprises plots around their new cellar,
their lower Egna and Ora vineyards and
stretches all the way to Cortaccia, on the
other side of the valley. The only exception
is their steep Fiè also Sciliar vineyards
where Müller Thurgau and Sauvignon are
cultivated. And it's Fiè, the Kathreinerfelder
vineyard to be precise (900 meters
elevation) that provides the grapes for their
Mathias '17, a Sauvignon that offers up
exotic aromas of candied citrus and licorice,
sensations that are amplified on the palate,
where the wine proves crisp and sapid,
governed by a penetrating acidity. Their
Pinot Nero Matan '16 is deep in its notes of
undergrowth and wild fruit, while the palate
delivers for its tension and finesse.

Tenuta Ritterhof

LOC. CALDARO
S.DA DEL VINO, 1
39052 CALDARO/KALTERN [BZ]
TEL. +39 0471963298
www.ritterhof.it

CELLAR SALES
PRE-BOOKED VISITS
RESTAURANT SERVICE
ANNUAL PRODUCTION 300,000 bottles
HECTARES UNDER VINE 7.50

Ludwig Kaneppele brings passion and
persistence to his work at the Roner family's
winery, one of the loveliest estates in
Caldaro, Oltradige. The vineyards are based
primarily in the area, with a few exceptions
that comprise some of the region's most
interesting districts for wine-growing, like
Gries for Lagrein, Cortaccia for
Gewürztraminer, and Mazzon for Pinot Nero,
on the other side of the Adige Valley. In the
cellar they work to bring out the clear
varietal expression of their wines. Their
Gewürztraminer Auratus '18, however, goes
beyond the cultivar's typical aromatic
scheme, evidencing all the attributes of the
territory (the best positions in Tramin). It's a
wine with a buoyant olfactive profile, a rich
and potent palate. Their Pinot Bianco
Versus '18 and Pinot Nero Dignus '15, two
interpretations featuring sophisticated
aromas and an energetic, juicy palate, also
put in good performances.

○ A. A. Sauvignon Mathias Ris. '17	▼▼ 4
○ A. A. Chardonnay Arvum '18	▼▼ 3
○ A. A. Gewürztraminer Rutter Ris. '17	▼▼ 4
○ A. A. Gewürztraminer Stoass '18	▼▼ 4
● A. A. Lagrein Griesfeld '16	▼▼ 5
● A. A. Pinot Nero Matan Ris. '16	▼▼ 5
○ A. A. Sauvignon Saxum '18	▼▼ 4
○ A. A. Spumante Brut Ris. '14	▼▼ 5
● Cortazo '16	▼▼ 5
○ A. A. Müller Thurgau Dola '18	▼ 4
○ A. A. Pinot Bianco Langefeld '18	▼ 3
● A. A. Pinot Nero Fuchsleiten '17	▼ 4
○ A. A. Chardonnay Arvum '17	♈♈ 3
○ A. A. Gewürztraminer Rutter '16	♈♈ 4
● A. A. Lagrein Ris. '15	♈♈ 5
○ A. A. Pinot Bianco Langefeld '17	♈♈ 3
○ A. A. Sauvignon Saxum '17	♈♈ 4

○ A. A. Gewürztraminer Auratus '18	▼▼▼ 5
● A. A. Pinot Nero Dignus Crescendo '15	▼▼ 5
● A. A. Cabernet Merlot Ramus '15	▼▼ 4
○ A. A. Gewürztraminer '18	▼▼ 3
○ A. A. Lago di Caldaro Cl. Sup. Novis '18	▼▼ 3
● A. A. Lagrein Manus Ris. '16	▼▼ 5
○ A. A. Pinot Bianco '18	▼▼ 2*
○ A. A. Pinot Bianco Verus '18	▼▼ 3
● A. A. Santa Maddalena Perlhof '18	▼▼ 2*
○ A. A. Sauvignon '18	▼▼ 2*
○ A. A. Sauvignon Paratus '18	▼▼ 2*
● A. A. Lagrein '18	▼ 3
○ A. A. Gewürztraminer Auratus '17	♈♈♈ 5
○ A. A. Gewürztraminer Auratus '16	♈♈♈ 4*
○ A. A. Gewürztraminer Auratus Crescendo '15	♈♈♈ 4*

Tenuta Hans Rottensteiner

FRAZ. GRIES
VIA SARENTINO, 1A
39100 BOLZANO/BOZEN
TEL. +39 0471282015
www.rottensteiner-weine.com

CELLAR SALES
PRE-BOOKED VISITS
ANNUAL PRODUCTION 450,000 bottles
HECTARES UNDER VINE 90.00

Toni and Hannes Rottensteiner are leading the family's winery, a business that began many years ago and that's managed to renew itself in a short period of time. They've abandoned their focus on quantity, a distant memory by now, and concentrated on bringing out the best of their well-positioned vineyards. In their historic Gries cellar, a wide-ranging selection comprises all the region's wines. Their premium versions, which are made with grapes cultivated in their private vineyards near the capital, are dedicated to the Bolzano basin's most representative cultivars. Their southeast-facing Premstallerhof is situated in Santa Maddalena at elevations ranging from 400-500 meter. Gertrud Vogel manages the vineyard according to the principles of biodynamic viticulture. The grapes cultivated here give rise to one of the most convincing wines of the typology: aromas of wild fruit are enriched by a subtle, smoky presence. On the palate it features a pronounced sapidity in its lovely, juicy and gratifying stride.

● A. A. Santa Maddalena Cl. V. Premstallerhof '18	▼▼ 3*
○ A. A. Gewürztraminer Passito Cresta '17	▼▼ 6
○ A. A. Müller Thurgau '18	▼▼ 3
● A. A. Pinot Nero Select Ris. '16	▼▼ 5
○ A. A. Sauvignon '18	▼▼ 3
● A. A.Lagrein Grieser Select Ris. '16	▼▼ 5
○ A.A. Pinot Grigio '18	▼▼ 3
○ A .A. Gewürztraminer Cancenai '18	▼ 4
⊙ A. A. Lagrein Rosé '18	▼ 3
○ A. A. Pinot Bianco Carnol '18	▼ 3
○ A. A. Valle Isarco Sylvaner '18	▼ 3
● A. A. Lagrein Ris. '02	▼▼▼ 2*
● A. A. Cabernet Select Ris. '15	▼▼ 5
● A. A. Lagrein Grieser Select Ris. '15	▼▼ 5
○ A. A. Pinot Bianco Carnol '17	▼▼ 3

★★★Cantina Produttori San Michele Appiano

VIA CIRCONVALLAZIONE, 17/19
39057 APPIANO/EPPAN [BZ]
TEL. +39 0471664466
www.stmichael.it

CELLAR SALES
PRE-BOOKED VISITS
ANNUAL PRODUCTION 2,200,000 bottles
HECTARES UNDER VINE 380.00

It's difficult to talk about Alto Adige's wines without referring to the important promotion and development work done by Hans Terzer and Cantina di San Michele Appiano. The cooperative is one of the region's largest, bolstered by a small army of vine growers who passionately and skillfully cultivate their private vineyards, contributing to a range of wines based primarily in Oltradige. These stand out for their close-focused, fragrant character, while their line of premium wines exhibits an original complexity. It's difficult to choose their best wine this year — some four from their Sanct Valentin line stood out. Their Pinot Bianco '17 is a solid wine of great integrity. Their Chardonnay '17 opts more for ripe fruit and a supple, juicy palate. Among their reds, the Pinot Nero '16 is the usual thoroughbred, while their Cabernet Merlot '16 reveals a full and powerful, yet also supple palate.

○ A. A. Pinot Bianco Sanct Valentin '17	▼▼▼ 5
● A. A. Cabernet Merlot Sanct Valentin Ris. '16	▼▼ 5
● A. A. Pinot Nero Sanct Valentin Ris. '16	▼▼ 5
○ A. A. Chardonnay Sanct Valentin '17	▼▼ 5
○ A. A. Gewürztraminer Passito Comtess '17	▼▼ 7
○ A. A. Gewürztraminer Sanct Valentin '18	▼▼ 5
○ A. A. Pinot Bianco Schulthauser '18	▼▼ 3
○ A. A. Pinot Grigio Sanct Valentin '17	▼▼ 5
○ A. A. Sauvignon Sanct Valentin '18	▼▼ 5
○ A. A. Pinot Bianco Sanct Valentin '15	▼▼▼ 6
○ A. A. Pinot Bianco St. Valentin '13	▼▼▼ 5
○ A. A. Pinot Grigio Sanct Valentin '14	▼▼▼ 5
● A. A. Pinot Nero Sanct Valentin Ris. '15	▼▼▼ 5

Cantina Produttori San Paolo

LOC. SAN PAOLO
VIA CASTEL GUARDIA, 21
39057 APPIANO/EPPAN [BZ]
TEL. +39 0471662183
www.stpauls.wine

CELLAR SALES
PRE-BOOKED VISITS
ANNUAL PRODUCTION 1,200,000 bottles
HECTARES UNDER VINE 175.00
SUSTAINABLE WINERY

Cantina San Paolo is situated just a stone's throw from the district of the same name in Appiano. Here vineyards abound, stretching into Oltradige. Thanks to its grower members, the cooperative is able to oversee a vast estate that includes some of the territories best positions. For example there's the vineyard dedicated to their flagship wine, Sanctissimus, a dizzying, east-facing slope that hosts historic plots of Pinot Bianco. In the cellar their production is divided between varietal wines and their premium Passion selection. Their house sparkler, Praeclarus, fully convinced. It's a Brut, vibrant in color, that exhibits aromas of white fruit, toasted hazelnut and croissant. On the palate its bubbles caress delicately, accompanying the palate in a lengthy development characterized by pronounced sapidity. Their Pinot Grigio '18 and Pinot Bianco Plötzner '18 both performed at high levels as well.

○ A. A. Brut Praeclarus	♟♟ 5
○ A. A. Pinot Bianco Plötzner '18	♟♟ 3*
○ A. A. Pinot Grigio '18	♟♟ 3*
○ A. A. Gewürztraminer Justina '18	♟♟ 3
● A. A. Lagrein Passion Ris. '17	♟♟ 5
● A. A. Merlot Passion Ris. '16	♟♟ 7
○ A. A. Pinot Bianco Passion Ris. '17	♟♟ 5
○ A. A. Pinot Grigio Kössler '18	♟♟ 3
● A. A. Pinot Noir Passion Ris. '17	♟♟ 5
○ A. A. Sauvignon Passion '17	♟♟ 5
● A. A. Schiava Missianer '18	♟♟ 2*
● A. A. Schiava Passion '17	♟♟ 4
○ A. A. Pinot Bianco Passion '09	♟♟♟ 4
○ A. A. Pinot Bianco Passion Ris. '11	♟♟♟ 4*
○ A. A. Pinot Bianco Plötzner '17	♟♟ 3
○ A. A. Pinot Bianco Sanctissimus Ris. '15	♟♟ 8

Peter Sölva & Söhne

VIA DELL'ORO, 33
39052 CALDARO/KALTERN [BZ]
TEL. +39 0471964650
www.soelva.com

CELLAR SALES
PRE-BOOKED VISITS
ANNUAL PRODUCTION 75,000 bottles
HECTARES UNDER VINE 12.00

Ten generations of Sölva family have overseen this historic winery, though the turning point came during World War II. Indeed, it was then that the producer took a major step in terms of quality, abandoning bulk wine and dedicating all their efforts to bottled wines. Today the project is propelled by a dozen hectares of land in the southern part of the province, in Bassa Atesina, Oltradige and the Bolzano basin, where each variety is cultivated in the best possible position. Their Cuvée Amistar is a blend of Chardonnay and Sauvignon from vineyards in Cornaiano and Caldaro, with a small share of grapes harvested late. Heavy in oak, it opens with aromas of sunny yellow fruit, which find a whiff of freshness in mineral notes and delicate spices. In the mouth it proves rich and pervasive, characterized by a nice juiciness and great pleasantness.

○ Amistar Cuvée Bianco '17	♟♟ 6
● A. A. Lago di Caldaro Cl. Sup. Peterleiten DeSilva '18	♟♟ 2*
● A. A. Lagrein I Vigneti '17	♟♟ 3
○ A. A. Sauvignon DeSilva '17	♟♟ 4
○ A. A. Gewürztraminer I Vigneti '18	♟ 5
○ A. A. Terlano Pinot Bianco DeSilva '18	♟ 3
○ A. A. Terlano Pinot Bianco DeSilva '10	♟♟♟ 3
● A. A. Cabernet Franc Amistar '15	♟♟ 5
● A. A. Lagrein '16	♟♟ 3
○ A. A. Pinot Bianco DeSilva '16	♟♟ 4
○ A. A. Sauvignon DeSilva '16	♟♟ 4
○ Amistar Bianco '16	♟♟ 6
○ Amistar Bianco '15	♟♟ 6
● Amistar Edizione Rossa Serie A6 '13	♟♟ 6
● Amistar Rosso '15	♟♟ 5
● Amistar Rosso '14	♟♟ 5

Stachlburg - Baron von Kripp

VIA MITTERHOFER, 2
39020 PARCINES/PARTSCHINS [BZ]
TEL. +39 0473968014
www.stachlburg.com

CELLAR SALES
PRE-BOOKED VISITS
ANNUAL PRODUCTION 30,000 bottles
HECTARES UNDER VINE 7.00
VITICULTURE METHOD Certified Organic

The Vinschgau Valley is one of South Tyrol's least developed, with just a few dozen hectares in an area characterized by little rain, notable day-night temperature swings and southern exposures. At the entrance to the valley we find the Kripp family's estate, which is divided between wine production and apples, the area's principal crop. Organic management gives rise to a varied and reliable selection of wines. Their Merlot Ris. '16 is from their Andriano vineyards. The use of oak is evident from the outset, from their the wine opens quickly to notes of ripe red fruit and medicinal herbs. In the mouth it unfolds broad and pervasive, exalted by riper notes. It finishes well supported by acidity and by delicately salty suggestions that lend suppleness to its crisp palate.

Strasserhof
Hannes Baumgartner

FRAZ. NOVACELLA
LOC. UNTERRAIN, 8
39040 VARNA/VAHRN [BZ]
TEL. +39 0472830804
www.strasserhof.info

CELLAR SALES
PRE-BOOKED VISITS
ACCOMMODATION
ANNUAL PRODUCTION 45,000 bottles
HECTARES UNDER VINE 5.50

Going up the Eisack Valley you realize that shortly after Varna township viticulture suddenly ceases and gives way to a classic Alpine landscape. Here, at the edge of wine country, we find Hannes Baumgarnter, a young and stubborn vigneron who's proven to be one of the area's most inspired producers. His small estate features plots supported by stone walls and dedicated entirely to the area's traditional varieties. These are interpreted in pursuit of elegance and aromatic freshness, thus highlighting the territory's signature style. Their Veltliner '18 pours a light straw-yellow, introducing an aromatic profile in which finesse and personality merge perfectly, with smoky and flowery notes alternating with citrus. In the mouth the wine is held together by a sapid acidity. Their Riesling '18 impressed as well. It's finer and tangier on the nose, delivering on the palate with succulence and length. The rest of their gamma also performed well.

● A. A. Merlot Ris. '16	♟♟ 5
○ A. A. Pinot Grigio '17	♟♟ 2*
○ A. A. Val Venosta Chardonnay '18	♟♟ 4
○ A. A. Val Venosta Pinot Bianco '18	♟♟ 3
● A. A. Val Venosta Pinot Nero '16	♟♟ 5
● A. A. Val Venosta Pinot Nero Eustachius Ris. '15	♟♟ 6
○ Praesepium V. T. '16	♟♟ 5
⊙ A. A. Lagrein Rosé '18	♟ 3
○ A. A. Terlano Sauvignon '18	♟ 3
○ A. A. Valle Venosta Pinot Bianco '13	♟♟♟ 3*
○ A. A. Valle Venosta Pinot Bianco '10	♟♟♟ 3*
● A. A. Merlot Ris. '14	♙♙ 5
● A. A. Merlot Wolfsthurn R '15	♙♙ 4
○ A. A. Pinot Grigio Wolfsthurn R '17	♙♙ 2*
○ A. A. Terlano Sauvignon Wolfsthurn '17	♙♙ 4
○ A. A. Val Venosta Pinot Nero '15	♙♙ 5

○ A. A. Valle Isarco Riesling '18	♟♟ 4
○ A. A. Valle Isarco Veltliner '18	♟♟ 3*
○ A. A. Sauvignon '18	♟♟ 3
○ A. A. Valle Isarco Gewürztraminer '18	♟♟ 4
○ A. A. Valle Isarco Kerner '18	♟♟ 3
○ A. A. Valle Isarco Müller Thurgau '18	♟♟ 3
○ A. A. Valle Isarco Sylvaner '18	♟♟ 3
○ A. A. Valle Isarco Sylvaner Anjo V. V. '17	♟♟ 4
○ A. A. Valle Isarco Riesling '12	♟♟♟ 3*
○ A. A. Valle Isarco Riesling '11	♟♟♟ 3*
○ A. A. Valle Isarco Veltliner '10	♟♟♟ 3*
○ A. A. Valle Isarco Veltliner '09	♟♟♟ 3*
○ A. A. Valle Isarco Grüner Veltliner '17	♙♙ 3
○ A. A. Valle Isarco Kerner '17	♙♙ 3
○ A. A. Valle Isarco Riesling '17	♙♙ 4
○ A. A. Valle Isarco Sylvaner '17	♙♙ 3
○ A. A. Valle Isarco Sylvaner Anjo '16	♙♙ 4

Stroblhof

LOC. SAN MICHELE
VIA PIGANÒ, 25
39057 APPIANO/EPPAN [BZ]
TEL. +39 0471662250
www.stroblhof.it

CELLAR SALES
PRE-BOOKED VISITS
ANNUAL PRODUCTION 40,000 bottles
HECTARES UNDER VINE 5.20

Oltradige doesn't offer much variation in terms of elevation. Vineyards range from 400 meters above sea level in the lower zones to 600 meters along Mendola hill. What changes, however, is the composition of the terrain and, even more notably, the day-night temperature swings that characterize the cooler areas near the woods. Here Rosa Hanny and Andreas Nicolussi-Leck oversee Stroblhof, one of Appiano Monte's most noteworthy producers, dedicating their attention to just four cultivars: Pinot Nero, Pinot Bianco, Sauvignon and Chardonnay. The grapes for their Pinot Nero find a fantastic territory in the areas just by the woods, making for a wine that features aromatic complexity and suppleness. Their Riserva '16 moves perfectly in this register: juicy and racy, it doesn't renounce a gutsy tannic presence either. Their Pigeno '17 opts for greater fruit, resulting in a more approachable, transparent interpretation. Their Pinot Bianco Strahler '18 is graceful, almost subtle.

● A. A. Pinot Nero Ris. '16	♛♛ 6
○ A. A. Chardonnay Schwarzhaus '18	♛♛ 4
○ A. A. Pinot Bianco Strahler '18	♛♛ 4
● A. A. Pinot Nero Pigeno '16	♛♛ 5
○ A. A. Sauvignon Nico '18	♛ 4
○ A. A. Pinot Bianco Strahler '09	♛♛♛ 3*
● A. A. Pinot Nero Ris. '15	♛♛♛ 6
● A. A. Pinot Nero Ris. '05	♛♛♛ 5
○ A. A. Chardonnay Schwarzhaus '17	♛♛ 4
○ A. A. Chardonnay Schwarzhaus '16	♛♛ 4
○ A. A. Pinot Bianco Strahler '17	♛♛ 4
● A. A. Pinot Nero Pigeno '15	♛♛ 5
● A. A. Pinot Nero Pigeno '14	♛♛ 5
● A. A. Pinot Nero Pigeno '13	♛♛ 5
● A. A. Pinot Nero Ris. '13	♛♛ 6
○ A. A. Sauvignon Nico '17	♛♛ 4
○ A. A. Sauvignon Nico '16	♛♛ 4

Taschlerhof - Peter Wachtler

LOC. MARA, 107
39042 BRESSANONE/BRIXEN [BZ]
TEL. +39 0472851091
www.taschlerhof.com

CELLAR SALES
PRE-BOOKED VISITS
ANNUAL PRODUCTION 30,000 bottles
HECTARES UNDER VINE 4.20

Peter Wachtler oversees the family winery in La Mara, a small district of Bressanone situated in the heart of the Eisack Valley. Thanks to a recent renovation and expansion of their cellar, all stages of production can be carried out carefully, but their true strength lies in their splendid vineyards, which literally climb up Lahner as if they were hanging gardens. Their selection, which centers entirely on the area's white grapes, is characterized by clear varietal expression and a crisp, slender profile. Their Riesling '18 put in an excellent performance. It immediately offers up its sulfureous aromas and notes of white fruit, sensations that we find on the palate along with flowers and shrub. The palate is crisp, lengthening decisively. Their Sylvaner Lahner '17 is slower in revealing its smoky aromas and notes of dried flowers. On the palate it proves larger and more pervasive, supported perfectly by a pronounced sapidity.

○ A. A. Valle Isarco Riesling '18	♛♛ 4
○ A. A. Valle Isarco Sylvaner Lahner '17	♛♛ 5
○ A. A. Valle Isarco Gewürztraminer '18	♛♛ 4
○ A. A. Valle Isarco Kerner '18	♛♛ 4
○ A. A. Valle Isarco Sylvaner '18	♛♛ 3
○ A. A. Valle Isarco Riesling '14	♛♛♛ 4*
○ A. A. Valle Isarco Sylvaner '15	♛♛♛ 3*
○ A. A. Valle Isarco Sylvaner Lahner '16	♛♛♛ 5
○ A. A. Riesling V. T. '15	♛♛ 4
○ A. A. Valle Isarco Kerner '17	♛♛ 4
○ A. A. Valle Isarco Kerner '16	♛♛ 4
○ A. A. Valle Isarco Riesling '17	♛♛ 4
○ A. A. Valle Isarco Riesling '16	♛♛ 4
○ A. A. Valle Isarco Riesling '15	♛♛ 4
○ A. A. Valle Isarco Sylvaner '17	♛♛ 3*
○ A. A. Valle Isarco Sylvaner '16	♛♛ 3*
○ A. A. Valle Isarco Sylvaner Lahner '15	♛♛ 4

★★Cantina Terlano

VIA SILBERLEITEN, 7
39018 TERLANO/TERLAN [BZ]
TEL. +39 0471257135
www.cantina-terlano.com

CELLAR SALES
PRE-BOOKED VISITS
ANNUAL PRODUCTION 1,500,000 bottles
HECTARES UNDER VINE 190.00

Cantina di Terlano is one of the region's most well-known producers, bolstered by a history of quality that goes back many years, and increasingly high expectations for the future. Vineyard management is carried out by 140 grower members, and only when a grower's abilities, the cultivar and location line up perfectly are the grapes used for their premium wines. The red, porphyry-rich soil of Terlano and calcareous-clay of Andriano give rise to a selection that Rudi Kofler endows with character. Their Sauvignon Quarz is at the top of its game. 2017 gave rise to a particularly fresh and elegant version aromatically, with greener, more floral notes still hiding fruit a bit. In the mouth it proves energetic, supported by sapid acidity. Their Rarity '06 is an extraordinarily young and dynamic wine, while their Vorber '16 and Pinot Nero Monticol Riserva bring together richness and elegance.

★Tiefenbrunner

FRAZ. NICLARA
VIA CASTELLO, 4
39040 CORTACCIA/KURTATSCH [BZ]
TEL. +39 0471880122
www.tiefenbrunner.com

CELLAR SALES
PRE-BOOKED VISITS
RESTAURANT SERVICE
ANNUAL PRODUCTION 650,000 bottles
HECTARES UNDER VINE 78.00

The Tiefenbrunner family's winery is situated in Niclara, in Bassa Atesina. Don't let the name mislead you, this is the area with the greatest day-night temperature swings, with hillside slopes that range from 200 meters elevation in the valley floor up to 1,000 in Favogna. Their selection is divided into four lines, from their monovarietal premium versions to fresher and more simpler varietals, allowing for virtually ideal vineyard management. It's truly difficult to say which of Tiefenbrunner's wines put in the best showing this year. At the end their Feldmarshall '17, Vigna Rachtl and Vigna Au '16 prevailed. The first is a Müller Thurgau made in Favogna and redolent of candied citrus and spices. In the mouth it proves enthralling, with sapidity and acidity lending pleasantness to the palate. The second is a full, juicy Sauvignon, while the third is a Chardonnay of great depth and elegance.

○ A. A. Terlano Sauvignon Quarz '17	♟♟♟ 6
○ A. A. Terlano Pinot Bianco Rarity '06	♟♟ 8
○ A. A. Terlano Pinot Bianco Vorberg '16	♟♟ 5
○ A. A. Chardonnay Doran Andriano '16	♟♟ 3
○ A. A. Gewürztraminer '18	♟♟ 3
● A. A. Lagrein Porphyr Ris. '16	♟♟ 6
● A. A. Merlot Gant Andriano Ris. '16	♟♟ 4
● A. A. Pinot Nero Anrar Andriano Ris. '17	♟♟ 5
● A. A. Pinot Nero Monticol Ris. '16	♟♟ 5
○ A. A. Sauvignon Andrius Andriano '17	♟♟ 5
○ A. A. Terlano Cuvée '18	♟♟ 5
○ A. A. Terlano Sauvignon Winkl '18	♟♟ 3
○ A. A. Terlano Nova Domus Ris. '15	♟♟♟ 6
○ A. A. Terlano Nova Domus Ris. '13	♟♟♟ 6
○ A. A. Terlano Nova Domus Ris. '12	♟♟♟ 6
○ A. A. Terlano Nova Domus Ris. '11	♟♟♟ 6
○ A. A. Terlano Sauvignon Quarz '15	♟♟♟ 6

○ A. A. Müller Thurgau Feldmarschall von Fenner '17	♟♟♟ 6
○ A. A. Sauvignon V. Rachtl '16	♟♟ 4
● A. A. Cabernet Merlot Linticlarus Cuvée Ris. '16	♟♟ 6
● A. A. Cabernet Sauvignon V. Toren Ris. '15	♟♟ 8
○ A. A. Chardonnay V. Au '16	♟♟ 3
○ A. A. Gewürztraminer Linticlarus V.T. '15	♟♟ 6
○ A. A. Gewürztraminer Turmhof '17	♟♟ 5
● A. A. Lagrein Linticlarus Ris. '16	♟♟ 5
● A. A. Pinot Bianco Anna '17	♟♟ 3
● A. A. Pinot Nero Linticlarus Ris. '16	♟♟ 6
○ A. A. Sauvignon Turmhof '17	♟♟ 4
○ A. A. Müller Thurgau Feldmarschall von Fenner '16	♟♟♟ 6

★★Cantina Tramin

S.DA DEL VINO, 144
39040 TERMENO/TRAMIN [BZ]
TEL. +39 0471096633
www.cantinatramin.it

CELLAR SALES
PRE-BOOKED VISITS
ANNUAL PRODUCTION 1,500,000 bottles
HECTARES UNDER VINE 250.00

Usually Alto Adige's cooperatives draw on all of the region's grapes. Willi Sturz's is no exception, even if the Tramin winery is primarily identified with Gewürztraminer, the aromatic cultivar whose homeland is Cortaccia and Termeno. The winery's almost 300 grower members cultivate, on average, less than a hectare each, making for a veritable viticultural puzzle. They give rise to a selection that brings together the fullness of Bassa Atesina with a more 'nordic' finesse. Once again their Nussmabumer earned the highest applause. 2017 saw the Gewürztraminer manage its exuberant force with a rare touch of elegance. Their Pinot Grigio Unterebner '17 expresses broad and deep fruit, which develops across a crisp, gutsy palate. Their Stoan '17 doesn't rely on aromatic shortcuts and impresses with its class, while their Terminum '16 proves to be a passito of great harmony.

Untermoserhof Georg Ramoser

VIA SANTA MADDALENA, 36
39100 BOLZANO/BOZEN
TEL. +39 0471975481
untermoserhof@rolmail.net

CELLAR SALES
PRE-BOOKED VISITS
ACCOMMODATION
ANNUAL PRODUCTION 30,000 bottles
HECTARES UNDER VINE 3.70

The winery managed by Georg Ramoser and his son Florian is situated in the heart of Santa Maddalena, immersed in the vineyards and literally watched over by a small church perched on the hilltop. Here you can sense the bond with tradition, one that's deep (to say the least): just a few hectares are reserved almost exclusively for its two most representative grapes, Lagrein (cultivated in the lower, warmer areas) and Schiava (cultivated at higher elevations). It all takes place on small plots spread throughout the hill at elevations ranging from 280 to 400 meters Their Santa Maddalena Hueb '17 once again demonstrates how indispensable power and structure are to a great wine. Its aromas range from smoky notes to wild berries, while the palate impresses for its sapidity and harmony. Their Lagrein Ris. 16 is diametrically opposed. It pours thick, while on the nose it features aromas of wet earth, undergrowth and spices. The fullness of its palate is perfectly supported by acidic vigor.

○ A. A. Gewürztraminer Nussbaumer '17	♟♟♟ 5
○ A. A. Bianco Stoan '17	♟♟ 4
○ A. A. Gewürztraminer Terminum V. T. '16	♟♟ 7
○ A. A. Pinot Grigio Unterebner '17	♟♟ 5
● A. A. Cabernet Merlot Loam Ris. '16	♟♟ 5
○ A. A. Gewürztraminer Roen V. T. '17	♟♟ 5
● A. A. Lagrein Urban Ris. '17	♟♟ 5
○ A. A. Pinot Bianco Moriz '18	♟♟ 2*
● A. A. Pinot Nero Maglen Ris. '16	♟♟ 5
○ A. A. Sauvignon Pepi '18	♟♟ 3
● A. A. Schiava Freisinger '18	♟♟ 3
○ A. A. Gewürztraminer Nussbaumer '16	♟♟♟ 5
○ A. A. Gewürztraminer Nussbaumer '15	♟♟♟ 5
○ A. A. Gewürztraminer Nussbaumer '14	♟♟♟ 5
○ A. A. Gewürztraminer Nussbaumer '13	♟♟♟ 5
○ A. A. Gewürztraminer Nussbaumer '12	♟♟♟ 5
○ A. A. Gewürztraminer Nussbaumer '11	♟♟♟ 5

● A. A. Lagrein Ris. '16	♟♟ 4
● A. A. Santa Maddalena Cl. Hueb '17	♟♟ 3*
● A. A. Santa Maddalena Cl. '18	♟♟ 3
● A. A. Lagrein '18	♟ 3
● A. A. Lagrein Scuro Ris. '03	♟♟♟ 4*
● A. A. Lagrein Scuro Ris. '97	♟♟♟ 4*
● A. A. Santa Maddalena Cl. Hueb '16	♟♟♟ 4*
○ A. A. Chardonnay '16	♟♟ 3
○ A. A. Chardonnay '15	♟♟ 3
● A. A. Lagrein Ris. '15	♟♟ 4
● A. A. Lagrein Ris. '13	♟♟ 5
● A. A. Lagrein Ris. '12	♟♟ 5
● A. A. Lagrein Untermoserhof Ris. '11	♟♟ 5
● A. A. Merlot Ris. '15	♟♟ 4
● A. A. Merlot Ris. '13	♟♟ 5
● A. A. Santa Maddalena Cl. '17	♟♟ 3
● A. A. Santa Maddalena Cl. '14	♟♟ 3

★Tenuta Unterortl Castel Juval

LOC. JUVAL, 1B
39020 CASTELBELLO CIARDES/KASTELBELL TSCHARS [BZ]
TEL. +39 0473667580
www.unterortl.it

CELLAR SALES
PRE-BOOKED VISITS
ANNUAL PRODUCTION 33,000 bottles
HECTARES UNDER VINE 4.00

Unterortl, the estate overseen by Martin and Gisela Aurich, is situated on the north side of the Vinschgau Valley, by the small village of Castelbello. Their vineyards, which cling atop astonishingly steep slopes, appear as if they're hanging from the sky. They enjoy a southern exposure, warm daytime temperatures and cool evening winds that come down from the hilltop. In the cellar all their work is aimed at bringing out the bond between cultivar and territory, with a limited range of primarily white wines. Great attention is reserved for Riesling, probably the variety that best expresses itself in these parts. Their Unterortl '18 offers up faint aromas that hesitate to open, but in the mouth it changes gears. The palate is decisive, gusty and highly sapid. Their Windbichel '17 sees mineral hints alternative with citrus and saffron, sensations that reemerge on its taut, very long palate.

○ A. A. Val Venosta Riesling Windbichel '17	▼▼▼ 5
○ A. A. Val Venosta Riesling Unterortl '18	▼▼ 4
○ A. A. Val Venosta Müller Thurgau '18	▼▼ 3
○ A. A. Val Venosta Pinot Bianco '18	▼▼ 2*
● A. A. Val Venosta Pinot Nero '16	▼▼ 5
○ A. A. Val Venosta Riesling Gletscherschliff '18	▼▼ 4
○ A. A. Val Venosta Pinot Bianco Castel Juval '13	♀♀♀ 3*
○ A. A. Val Venosta Pinot Bianco Castel Juval '12	♀♀♀ 3*
○ A. A. Val Venosta Riesling '14	♀♀♀ 4*
○ A. A. Val Venosta Riesling '10	♀♀♀ 4
○ A. A. Val Venosta Riesling Castel Juval '11	♀♀♀ 4*
○ A. A. Val Venosta Riesling Unterortl '15	♀♀♀ 4*

Cantina Produttori Valle Isarco

VIA COSTE, 50
39043 CHIUSA/KLAUSEN [BZ]
TEL. +39 0472847553
www.cantinavalleisarco.it

CELLAR SALES
PRE-BOOKED VISITS
ANNUAL PRODUCTION 900,000 bottles
HECTARES UNDER VINE 150.00
SUSTAINABLE WINERY

Cantina Produttori Valle Isarco is surely this subzone's most important producer, bolstered by an estate that reaches throughout the territory, from the outer limits of Bolzano to Novacella. Most of its 130 grower members, however, operate in the enclave of Chiusa, the steep slopes that reach almost 1,000 meters elevation. Here they oversee the area's classic cultivars, making for a selection characterized primarily by taut, precise white wines. Only a Sylvaner and Veltliner could be the cooperative's most representative wines. Both belong to their Aristos line, and both are 2018s. They perfectly express gutsy determination marked by noteworthy acidic and sapid thrust. The first features complex aromas and a harmonious, elegant palate. The latter moves on a more audacious and penetrating register aromatically, with a palate that proves energetic and direct.

○ A. A. Valle Isarco Sylvaner Aristos '18	▼▼ 4
○ A. A. Valle Isarco Veltliner Aristos '18	▼▼ 3*
○ A. A. Pinot Bianco Aristos '18	▼▼ 4
○ A. A. Sauvignon Aristos '18	▼▼ 4
○ A. A. Valle Isarco Gewürztraminer Aristos '18	▼▼ 4
○ A. A. Valle Isarco Kerner Aristos '18	▼▼ 4
○ A. A. Valle Isarco Kerner Passito Nectaris '17	▼▼ 6
○ A. A. Valle Isarco Müller Thurgau Aristos '18	▼▼ 4
○ A. A. Valle Isarco Pinot Grigio Aristos '18	▼▼ 4
○ A. A. Valle Isarco Riesling Aristos '18	▼▼ 4
○ A. A. Valle Isarco Kerner Aristos '05	♀♀♀ 3*
○ A. A. Valle Isarco Sylvaner Aristos '16	♀♀♀ 4*
○ A. A. Valle Isarco Sylvaner Aristos '15	♀♀♀ 4*

Von Blumen

FRAZ. POCHI, 18/BULCHOLZ, 18
39040 SALORNO/SALURN [BZ]
TEL. +39 0457230110
www.vonblumenwine.com

CELLAR SALES
PRE-BOOKED VISITS
ANNUAL PRODUCTION 44,000 bottles
HECTARES UNDER VINE 11.00
SUSTAINABLE WINERY

The Fugatti brothers' winemaking
adventure in Alto Adige began a few years
ago, even if in the past they had an
important family nursery in Salorno, the
same territory in which they now oversee
12 hectares in the Pochi highlands. From
the first harvest, their choices centered on
low-impact viticulture. The grapes
cultivated give rise to a range of wines
characterized by clear varietal expression,
enriched by the presence of a more
ambitious selection, named Flowers, that's
made with Pinot Bianco and Sauvignon And
it's a Pinot Bianco '17 from this line that
most convinced this year. Aged at length in
oak, on the nose it offers up clear notes of
white fruit and flowers, with sweet oak just
detectable in the background. In the mouth
it amazes for the way in which it transforms
its particular aromatic delicacy into energy
and rhythm. On the palate it's racy, to say
the least, and very long. But their entire
selection is showing positive signs.

○ A. A. Pinot Bianco Flowers Selection '17	♀♀ 5
○ A. A. Gewürztraminer '18	♀♀ 4
● A. A. Lagrein '17	♀♀ 4
○ A. A. Pinot Bianco '18	♀♀ 3
○ A. A. Sauvignon '18	♀♀ 3
○ A. A. Sauvignon Flowers Selection '17	♀♀ 5
● A. A. Pinot Nero '18	♀ 4
○ A. A. Gewürztraminer '17	♀♀ 4
● A. A. Lagrein '16	♀♀ 4
● A. A. Lagrein '15	♀♀ 4
○ A. A. Pinot Bianco '17	♀♀ 3
○ A. A. Pinot Bianco Flowers '16	♀♀ 5
○ A. A. Pinot Bianco Flowers Selection '15	♀♀ 5
● A. A. Pinot Nero '17	♀♀ 3
○ A. A. Sauvignon '17	♀♀ 3
○ A. A. Sauvignon Flowers '16	♀♀ 5
○ A.A. Sauvignon '16	♀♀ 3

★★Elena Walch

VIA A. HOFER, 1
39040 TERMENO/TRAMIN [BZ]
TEL. +39 0471860172
www.elenawalch.com

CELLAR SALES
PRE-BOOKED VISITS
RESTAURANT SERVICE
ANNUAL PRODUCTION 500,000 bottles
HECTARES UNDER VINE 33.00

Elena Walch's winery is one of the leaders of
the South Tyrol wine renaissance. From the
beginning they've focused on highlighting
the bond between cultivar and vineyard,
thanks to a large estate that hasn't grown in
any single, particular direction over the
years, but has been organized according to
the disposition and potential of each
vineyard, making for a notable viticultural
patrimony. Among their vineyards, there's
certainly a place of honor for Castel
Ringberg (Caldaro) and Kastelaz (Termeno).
The particular microclimate that this last
enjoys allows cultivars in need of warmth to
mature perfectly, as testified to by their
Merlot Ris. '16 and Gewürztraminer '18. The
former offers up intense notes of red fruit
and spices, while on the palate it's refreshed
by balsamic hints, lengthening decisively.
The latter is aromatically exuberant and
sapid on the palate. Their Cuvée Beyond The
Clouds '17 is a deep, harmonious wine.

○ A. A. Gewürztraminer V. Kastelaz '18	♀♀♀ 5
○ A. A. Bianco Grande Cuvée Beyond the Clouds '17	♀♀ 7
○ A. A. Chardonnay V. Castel Ringberg Ris. '16	♀♀ 7
● A. A. Lagrein V. Castel Ringberg Ris. '16	♀♀ 5
● A. A. Merlot V. Kastelaz Ris. '16	♀♀ 6
○ A. A. Pinot Bianco Kristallberg '17	♀♀ 4
○ A. A. Pinot Grigio V. Castel Ringberg '18	♀♀ 4
● A. A. Pinot Nero Ludwig '16	♀♀ 5
○ A. A. Sauvignon V. Castel Ringberg '18	♀♀ 4
○ A. A. Bianco Beyond the Clouds '16	♀♀♀ 7
○ A. A. Gewürztraminer Kastelaz '13	♀♀♀ 5
○ A. A. Gewürztraminer Kastelaz '12	♀♀♀ 5
○ A. A. Gewürztraminer Kastelaz '11	♀♀♀ 5
● A. A. Lagrein Castel Ringberg Ris. '11	♀♀♀ 5

★Tenuta Waldgries

LOC. SANTA GIUSTINA, 2
39100 BOLZANO/BOZEN
TEL. +39 0471323603
www.waldgries.it

CELLAR SALES
PRE-BOOKED VISITS
ANNUAL PRODUCTION 65,000 bottles
HECTARES UNDER VINE 8.20

Christian Plattner is the man behind Waldgries, a gorgeous estate situated in the heart of the Santa Maddalena appellation. The manor is surrounded by vineyards that face the city of Bolzano on the one side and Sciliar on the other, a position that allows them to benefit from the basin's warmth and the cool alpine air. Over time the estate has been enlarged with plots in Appiano, where at 600 meters elevation they cultivate white grapes, and in Furggl di Ora, where Lagrein is grown. Antheos '18 is a Santa Maddalena made with old plots of Schiava and a touch of Lagrein, a combination that confers aromas of red fruit broadened by smoky notes and spices. In the mouth it's firm while conserving the typology's racy drinkability. Their Lagrein Mirell '16 is aromatically richer and even more so on the palate, while their Sauvignon Myra '17 brings together fresher, flowery notes with exotic suggestions — on the palate it proves elegant and very long.

● A. A. Lagrein Mirell '16	▼▼ 6
● A. A. Santa Maddalena Cl. Antheos '18	▼▼ 5
○ A. A. Sauvignon Myra '18	▼▼ 4
● A. A. Lagrein Ris. '16	▼▼ 5
● A. A. Lagrein Roblinus de Waldgries '16	▼▼ 8
● A. A. Moscato Rosa '17	▼▼ 5
○ A. A. Pinot Bianco Isos '16	▼▼ 4
● A. A. Santa Maddalena Cl. '18	▼▼ 3
● A. A. Lagrein Mirell '09	▽▽▽ 6
● A. A. Lagrein Mirell Ris. '15	▽▽▽ 6
● A. A. Lagrein Scuro Mirell '08	▽▽▽ 6
● A. A. Lagrein Scuro Mirell '07	▽▽▽ 6
● A. A. Lagrein Scuro Mirell '01	▽▽▽ 6
● A. A. Santa Maddalena Cl. Antheos '16	▽▽▽ 5
● A. A. Santa Maddalena Cl. Antheos '13	▽▽▽ 4*
● A. A. Santa Maddalena Cl. Antheos '12	▽▽▽ 4*
● A. A. Santa Maddalena Cl. Antheos '11	▽▽▽ 4*

Josef Weger

LOC. CORNAIANO/GIRLAN
VIA CASA DEL GESÙ, 17
39050 APPIANO/EPPAN [BZ]
TEL. +39 0471662416
www.wegerhof.it

CELLAR SALES
PRE-BOOKED VISITS
ACCOMMODATION AND RESTAURANT SERVICE
ANNUAL PRODUCTION 80,000 bottles
HECTARES UNDER VINE 8.00

The Weger family have been making wine in South Tyrol for six generations, since Josef founded the winery in 1820 and it passed down from one Weger to the next up to modern day. Now Johannes is at the helm, bolstered by an estate situated primarily in the southern part of the province (Bassa Altesina and Oltradige), with the exception of plots in Bolzano (Gries), for their Lagrein. Their range is comprises simpler wines of more authentic varietal expression and their premium, Maso delle Rose line. And this line includes their Pinot Nero '16, a wine redolent of forest undergrowth, wet leaves and wild fruit. On the palate it opens up with richness and an unexpected determination supported by pleasantly rough tannins. Among their whites we point out their Pinot Grigio Ried '18, a wine that's aromatically simple and approachable, but capable of changing gears in the mouth, revealing a firm body and a crisp, splendidly sapid palate.

○ A. A. Gewürztraminer Artyo '18	▼▼ 3
○ A. A. Müller Thurgau Pursgla '18	▼▼ 3
○ A. A. Pinot Grigio Ried '18	▼▼ 3
● A. A. Pinot Nero Maso delle Rose '16	▼▼ 5
○ A. A. Sauvignon Myron '18	▼▼ 3
○ A. A. Pinot Bianco Lithos '18	▼ 3
● A. A. Schiava Kol '18	▼ 3
○ A. A. Gewürztraminer Maso delle Rose '16	▽▽ 3
● A. A. Lagrein Stoa '15	▽▽ 3
● A. A. Merlot Maso delle Rose '15	▽▽ 5
○ A. A. Pinot Bianco Lithos '16	▽▽ 3
○ A. A. Pinot Bianco Maso delle Rose '16	▽▽ 4
○ A. A. Sauvignon Maso delle Rose '16	▽▽ 4
○ A. A. Sauvignon Myron '17	▽▽ 2*
○ A. A. Sauvignon Myron '16	▽▽ 2*
● Joanni Maso delle Rose '16	▽▽ 4

Weingut Niklas - Dieter Sölva

LOC. SAN NICOLÒ
VIA DELLE FONTANE, 31A
39052 CALDARO/KALTERN [BZ]
TEL. +39 0471963434
www.niklaserhof.it

CELLAR SALES
PRE-BOOKED VISITS
ANNUAL PRODUCTION 50,000 bottles
HECTARES UNDER VINE 7.00

Sölva is a common surname among Caldaro's vine growers. Today the family oversee an estate situated entirely in Oltradige, with plots that occupy some of the area's best positions, both in the warmer part of the territory, near the lake (like Prutznai and Schweiggeregg) and in the cooler area near the Mendola massif (Vial and Kardatsch). Only a few grapes are cultivated, and these are chosen for their suitability to the area, making for a solid selection characterized by a strong territorial identity. The grapes for their Pinot Bianco Hos '18 are cultivated in the fresh areas of Vial, Salt and Planitzing. It's a wine redolent of flowers and white fruit, while on the palate it proves supple with sustained sapidity. Their Merlot DJJ '16 plays on ripeness of fruit and fullness of the palate. It's a reserve made with grapes from an old vineyard situated closer to Lake Caldaro, where the heat and clay-rich soils allow Bordeaux varieties to ripen perfectly.

○ A. A. Pinot Bianco Hos '18	🍷🍷 3*
○ A. A. Kerner Libellula Mondevinum '16	🍷🍷 4
○ A. A. Kerner Luxs '18	🍷🍷 3
● A. A. Lago di Caldaro Cl. Sup. Hect Klaser '18	🍷🍷 2*
● A. A. Lagrein Bos Taurus Mondevinum Ris. '16	🍷🍷 4
● A. A. Lagrein Cabernet Klaser Ris. '16	🍷🍷 4
● A. A. Merlot DJJ Ris. '16	🍷🍷 4
○ A. A. Pinot Bianco Salamander Klaser Ris. '16	🍷🍷 4
○ A. A. Sauvignon Doxs '18	🍷 3
○ Kerner Without '17	🍷 3
○ A. A. Pinot Bianco Klaser Ris. '15	🍷🍷🍷 4*
○ A. A. Kerner Mondevinum Ris. '15	🍷🍷 4
● A. A. Lago di Caldaro Cl. Sup. Klaser '17	🍷🍷 2*

Peter Zemmer

S.DA DEL VINO, 24
39040 CORTINA SULLA STRADA DEL VINO/KURTINIG [BZ]
TEL. +39 0471817143
www.peterzemmer.com

CELLAR SALES
PRE-BOOKED VISITS
ANNUAL PRODUCTION 500,000 bottles
HECTARES UNDER VINE 65.00

Peter Zemmer oversees the family winery situated along the 'Wine Trail', in Cortina. The province's smallest municipality, Cortina enjoys a perfect position in the valley center, without nearby mountains or woods. The large estate spans both sides of the valley and rises to elevations of 1,000 meters. Each grape is cultivated according to the most desirable conditions, with Pinot Grigio and Gewürztraminer enjoying warmer positions, and cooler plots reserved for Pinot Nero and Müller Thurgau. Among the selection submitted we preferred their Pinot Grigio Giatl '17, a white made with grapes from the calcareous and sandy vineyards situated near the cellar. Fermented in oak, on the nose it offers up intense notes of williams pears, sensations that reemerge on its full, powerful and gutsy palate. Their Chardonnay Vigna Crivelli '17 is even sunnier and riper, playing on sweet, fruity aromas and a generous palate.

○ A. A. Chardonnay V. Crivelli Ris. '17	🍷🍷 4
○ A. A. Pinot Grigio Giatl Ris. '17	🍷🍷 3*
○ A. A. Chardonnay '18	🍷🍷 2*
● A. A. Lagrein Fruggl Ris. '17	🍷🍷 4
○ A. A. Pinot Grigio '18	🍷🍷 3
● A. A. Pinot Nero V. Kofl Ris. '17	🍷🍷 5
○ Cortinie Bianco '18	🍷🍷 3
● Cortinie Rosso '16	🍷🍷 3
● A. A. Müller Thurgau Caprile '18	🍷 3
● A. A. Pinot Nero Rolhütt '18	🍷 4
○ A. A. Riesling '18	🍷 2
○ A. A. Sauvignon '18	🍷 3
○ A. A. Pinot Grigio Giatl Ris. '15	🍷🍷🍷 3*
○ A. A. Chardonnay Crivelli Ris. '16	🍷🍷 4
● A. A. Lagrein Fruggl Ris. '16	🍷🍷 4
○ A. A. Pinot Grigio Giatl Ris. '16	🍷🍷 3*
○ A. A. Riesling '17	🍷🍷 2*

Baron Longo

VIA VAL DI FIEMME 30
39044 EGNA/NEUMARKT [BZ]
TEL. +39 0471 820007
www.baronlongo.com

ANNUAL PRODUCTION 30,000 bottles
HECTARES UNDER VINE 17.00

● Friedberg Lagrein '17	♟♟ 3
○ Meanberg Pinot Grigio '17	♟♟ 3
○ Solaris Sichlburg '18	♟♟ 3
○ A. A. Gewürztraminer Hohenstein '17	♟ 3

Baron Widmann

ENDERGASSE, 3
39040 CORTACCIA/KURTATSCH [BZ]
TEL. +39 0471880092
www.baron-widmann.it

CELLAR SALES
PRE-BOOKED VISITS
ANNUAL PRODUCTION 35,000 bottles
HECTARES UNDER VINE 15.00

● A. A. Cabernet Merlot '16	♟♟ 4
○ A. A. Gewürztraminer '17	♟♟ 3
● A. A. Schiava '18	♟♟ 3

Bergmannhof

LOC. SAN PAOLO
RIVA DI SOTTO, 46
39050 APPIANO/EPPAN [BZ]
TEL. +39 0471637082
www.bergmannhof.it

CELLAR SALES
PRE-BOOKED VISITS
ANNUAL PRODUCTION 13,000 bottles
HECTARES UNDER VINE 2.20

● A. A. Merlot '17	♟♟ 2*
● A. A. Schiava '18	♟♟ 2*
● Kalch '15	♟♟ 3
● A.A. Lagrein Ris. '16	♟ 4

Castello Rametz

LOC. MAIA ALTA
VIA LABERS, 4
39012 MERANO/MERAN [BZ]
TEL. +39 0473211011
www.rametz.com

CELLAR SALES
PRE-BOOKED VISITS
RESTAURANT SERVICE
ANNUAL PRODUCTION 400,000 bottles
HECTARES UNDER VINE 8.00

○ A. A. Sauvignon '18	♟♟ 3*
● A. A. Merlot '16	♟♟ 3
○ A. A. Gewürztraminer '18	♟ 2
○ A. A. Riesling '18	♟ 3

Eberlehof - Zisser

SANTA MAGDALENA, 26
39100 BOLZANO/BOZEN
TEL. +39 0471978607
www.gojer.it

CELLAR SALES
PRE-BOOKED VISITS
ANNUAL PRODUCTION 50,000 bottles
HECTARES UNDER VINE 10.00

● A. A. Lagrein Ris. '16	♟♟ 3
● A. A. Santa Maddalena Cl. '18	♟♟ 2*
● A. A. Lagrein Merlot Mabon '16	♟ 3

Egger-Ramer

VIA GUNCINA, 5
39100 BOLZANO/BOZEN
TEL. +39 0471280541
www.egger-ramer.com

CELLAR SALES
PRE-BOOKED VISITS
ANNUAL PRODUCTION 120,000 bottles
HECTARES UNDER VINE 14.00

● A. A. Lagrein Kristan '17	♟♟ 3*
● A. A. Lagrein Gries '18	♟♟ 2*
● A. A. Lagrein Kristan Ris. '16	♟♟ 3
● A. A. Santa Maddalena Cl. Reisegger '18	♟♟ 2*

Eichenstein

Katzensteinstrasse, 34
39012 Merano/Meran [BZ]
Tel. +39 3442820179
www.eichenstein.it

ANNUAL PRODUCTION 25,000 bottles
HECTARES UNDER VINE 4.50
SUSTAINABLE WINERY

○ A. A. Chardonnay '18	♟♟ 3
○ A. A. Chardonnay Seppelaia Fass 66 '14	♟♟ 3
○ A. A. Sauvignon Stein '17	♟ 3
○ Gloria Dei '18	♟ 3

Fliederhof - Stefan Ramoser

Loc. Santa Maddalena di Sotto, 33
39100 Bolzano/Bozen
Tel. +39 0471979048
www.fliederhof.it

CELLAR SALES
PRE-BOOKED VISITS
ANNUAL PRODUCTION 25,000 bottles
HECTARES UNDER VINE 2.40

● A. A. Lagrein Ris. '16	♟♟ 5
● A. A. Santa Maddalena Cl. Gran Marie '17	♟♟ 4
○ Moscato Giallo Peperum '18	♟ 3

Himmelreichhof

Via Convento, 15a
39020 Castelbello Ciardes/Kastelbell Tschars [BZ]
Tel. +39 0473624417
www.himmelreich-hof.info

ANNUAL PRODUCTION 20,000 bottles
HECTARES UNDER VINE 3.50

○ A.A. Val Venosta Pinot Bianco '18	♟♟ 4
○ A.A. Val Venosta Riesling Geieregg '17	♟♟ 4

Lehengut

Via delle Fonti, 2
39020 Colsano
Tel. +39 3487562676
www.lehengut.it

ANNUAL PRODUCTION 10,000 bottles
HECTARES UNDER VINE 3.00
VITICULTURE METHOD Certified Organic

○ A. A. Val Venosta Pinot Bianco '18	♟♟ 3
● A. A. Val Venosta Pinot Nero Ris. '17	♟♟ 3
○ A. A. Val Venosta Riesling '18	♟♟ 3

Lieselehof
Werner Morandell

Via Kardatsch, 6
39052 Caldaro/Kaltern [BZ]
Tel. +39 3299011593
www.lieselehof.com

CELLAR SALES
PRE-BOOKED VISITS
ACCOMMODATION
ANNUAL PRODUCTION 20,000 bottles
HECTARES UNDER VINE 3.00
VITICULTURE METHOD Certified Organic

○ Julian Orange '17	♟♟ 3
○ Vino del Passo '18	♟♟ 6
● Feldherr '15	♟ 5

Marinushof - Heinrich Pohl

Loc. Maragno
S.da Vecchia, 9b
39020 Castelbello Ciardes/Kastelbell Tschars [BZ]
Tel. +39 0473624717
www.marinushof.it

CELLAR SALES
PRE-BOOKED VISITS
ACCOMMODATION
ANNUAL PRODUCTION 8,000 bottles
HECTARES UNDER VINE 1.20

● A. A. Val Venosta Pinot Nero '17	♟♟ 5
○ A. A. Val Venosta Riesling '18	♟♟ 4
● Zweigelt Primus '17	♟ 5

Maso Thaler

VIA GLENO, 59
39040 MONTAGNA/MONTAN [BZ]
TEL. +39 3388483363
www.masothaler.it

CELLAR SALES
PRE-BOOKED VISITS
ANNUAL PRODUCTION 20,000 bottles
HECTARES UNDER VINE 3.50

○ A. A. Gewürztraminer '18	♟♟ 3
● A. A. Pinot Nero 680 Ris. '15	♟♟ 5
○ Manzoni Bianco '18	♟♟ 2*
● A. A. Pinot Nero Ris. '16	♟ 5

Tenuta Nicolussi-Leck

VIA KREITH, 2
39051 CALDARO/KALTERN [BZ]
TEL. +39 3382963793
www.wein.kaltern.com

○ A. A. Lago di Caldaro Cl. Sup. 1917 Alexander '18	♟♟ 4
● A. A. Lagrein 1921 Sepp '17	♟♟ 3
○ A. A. Pinot Bianco 1957 Verena '18	♟♟ 4

Nusserhof - Heinrich Mayr

VIA MAYR NUSSER, 72
39100 BOLZANO/BOZEN
TEL. +39 0471978388

CELLAR SALES
PRE-BOOKED VISITS
ANNUAL PRODUCTION 15,000 bottles
HECTARES UNDER VINE 2.50
VITICULTURE METHOD Certified Organic

● A. A. Lagrein Ris. '13	♟♟ 4
● Elda '14	♟♟ 4
● Gloria '13	♟♟ 4
● Tyr.....o '14	♟ 4

Obermoser
H. & T. Rottensteiner

FRAZ. RENCIO
VIA SANTA MADDALENA, 35
39100 BOLZANO/BOZEN
TEL. +39 0471973549
www.obermoser.it

CELLAR SALES
PRE-BOOKED VISITS
ANNUAL PRODUCTION 30,000 bottles
HECTARES UNDER VINE 3.80

● A. A. Lagrein Grafenleiten Ris. '16	♟♟ 5
● A. A. Santa Maddalena Cl. '18	♟♟ 2*
● A. A. Santa Maddalena Cl. Nobilis '17	♟♟ 2*
● A. A. Lagrein '18	♟ 3

Bergkellerei Passeier

VIA DEI LEGNAI, 5A
39015 SAN LEONARDO IN PASSIRIA/SANKT LEONHARD [BZ]
TEL. +39 3479982554
www.bergkellerei.it

ANNUAL PRODUCTION 8,000 bottles
HECTARES UNDER VINE 1.50

● A. A. Lagrein Ris. '16	♟♟ 4
○ A. A. Pinot Bianco Burgunder '17	♟♟ 3
○ A. A. Sauvignon '17	♟♟ 3
○ Giovo '17	♟ 3

Thomas Pichler

FRAZ. VILLA DI MEZZO
VIA DELLE VIGNE, 4A
39052 CALDARO/KALTERN [BZ]
TEL. +39 0471963094
www.thomas-pichler.it

CELLAR SALES
PRE-BOOKED VISITS
ANNUAL PRODUCTION 15,000 bottles
HECTARES UNDER VINE 2.00

● A. A. Lago di Caldaro Cl. Sup. Olte Reben '18	♟♟ 3
● A. A. Lagrein Sond Ris. '17	♟♟ 5
○ Mitanond '18	♟ 3

Pitzner

via Cornedo, 15
39053 Cornedo all'Isarco/Karneid [BZ]
Tel. +39 3384521694
www.pitzner.it

ANNUAL PRODUCTION 16,000 bottles
HECTARES UNDER VINE 3.00

● A. A. Merlot MR 17 '17	🍷🍷 4
○ A. A. Pinot Grigio Finell '18	🍷🍷 4
● A. A. Santa Maddalena Malanders '18	🍷🍷 3
● A. A. Lagrein Scharfegg '18	🍷 5

Plonerhof - Erhard Tutzer

via Tramontana, 29
39020 Marlengo/Marling [BZ]
Tel. +39 0473490525
www.weingut-plonerhof.it

ANNUAL PRODUCTION 30,000 bottles
HECTARES UNDER VINE 5.00

● A. A. Pinot Nero Exclusiv Ris. '16	🍷🍷 3
○ A. A. Sauvignon Exclusiv '17	🍷🍷 4
○ Nörder Cuvée Blanc '18	🍷🍷 4
○ Solaris '18	🍷🍷 5

Weingut Plonerhof Simon Geier

loc. Untermagdalena, 29
39100 Bolzano/Bozen
Tel. +39 0471975559
www.magdalenerwein.it

ANNUAL PRODUCTION 10,000 bottles
HECTARES UNDER VINE 3.00

● A. A. Lagrein Lagralena Ris. '16	🍷🍷 4
● A. A. Santa Maddalena Cl. Vite Antica '18	🍷🍷 2*
● Weissgold '16	🍷🍷 4

Prackfolerhof

via Spiegelweg, 9
39050 Fiè allo Sciliar/Völs am Schlern [BZ]
Tel. +39 0471601532
www.prackfolerhof.it

ANNUAL PRODUCTION 18,000 bottles
HECTARES UNDER VINE 4.50

● A. A. Pinot Nero '16	🍷🍷 3
○ A. A. Sauvignon '18	🍷🍷 3
● A. A. Schiava '18	🍷🍷 3

Rielingerhof

Siffianer Leitach, 7
39054 Renon/Ritten [BZ]
Tel. +39 0471356274
www.rielinger.it

ANNUAL PRODUCTION 20,000 bottles
HECTARES UNDER VINE 3.00

○ A. A. Val Venosta Riesling V. Stein '18	🍷🍷 3
○ Kerner '18	🍷 3
○ Müller Thurgau '18	🍷 3

Röckhof - Konrad Augschöll

via San Valentino, 22
39040 Villandro/Villanders [BZ]
Tel. +39 0472847130
roeck@rolmail.net

CELLAR SALES
PRE-BOOKED VISITS
RESTAURANT SERVICE
ANNUAL PRODUCTION 20,000 bottles
HECTARES UNDER VINE 3.50

○ A. A. Valle Isarco Riesling Viel Anders '17	🍷🍷 3
○ A. A. Valle Isarco Veltliner Gail Fuass '18	🍷🍷 3
○ Caruess Weiß '17	🍷🍷 3
○ A. A. Valle Isarco Müller Thurgau '18	🍷 3

Rynnhof

VIA SCHNECKENTHALER, 13
39040 TERMENO/TRAMIN [BZ]
TEL. +39 0471860293
www.rynnhof.com

○ A. A. Pinot Bianco '18	♟♟ 3
● A. A. Schiava '18	♟♟ 3
○ A. A. Gewürztraminer '18	♟ 3
● A. A. Lagrein '17	♟ 3

Schloss Englar

LOC. PIGENO, 42
39057 APPIANO/EPPAN [BZ]
TEL. +39 0471662628
www.weingut-englar.com

ANNUAL PRODUCTION 15,000 bottles
HECTARES UNDER VINE 7.00

○ A. A. Chardonnay '16	♟♟ 4
● A. A. Pinot Nero Ris. '16	♟♟ 4
● A. A. Schiava R '16	♟♟ 3
○ A. A. Sauvignon '17	♟ 4

Schloss Plars

FRAZ. PLARS DI MEZZO, 25
39022 LAGUNDO/ALGUND [BZ]
TEL. +39 0473448472
www.schlossplars.com

CELLAR SALES
PRE-BOOKED VISITS
ACCOMMODATION
ANNUAL PRODUCTION 12,000 bottles
HECTARES UNDER VINE 2.00

● A. A. Merlot Lagrein Yhrn '17	♟♟ 3
○ A. A. Pinot Bianco Pataun '18	♟ 3
○ A. A. Sauvignon Marzan '17	♟ 3

Andi Sölva

VIA BARLEIT, 24
39052 CALDARO/KALTERN [BZ]
TEL. +39 3493233246
www.andisoelva.com

ANNUAL PRODUCTION 8,000 bottles
HECTARES UNDER VINE 1.30

● A. A. Lago di Cladaro Cl. Sea '18	♟♟ 3
● Genration K '16	♟♟ 4
○ A. A. Pinot Bianco Wir Mussten Künstler Sein '18	♟ 3

Thurnhof - Andreas Berger

LOC. ASLAGO
VIA CASTEL FLAVON, 7
39100 BOLZANO/BOZEN
TEL. +39 0471288460
www.thurnhof.com

CELLAR SALES
PRE-BOOKED VISITS
ANNUAL PRODUCTION 25,000 bottles
HECTARES UNDER VINE 3.50

● A. A. Cabernet Sauvignon Weinegg Ris. '16	♟♟ 5
● A. A. Lagrein Merlau '18	♟♟ 2*
● A. A. Lagrein Ris. '16	♟♟ 4
● A. A. Santa Maddalena '18	♟♟ 2*

Tröpfltalhof

VIA GARNELLEN, 17
39052 CALDARO/KALTERN [BZ]
TEL. +39 0471964126
www.bioweinhof.it

ANNUAL PRODUCTION 10,000 bottles
HECTARES UNDER VINE 2.30

○ Sauvignon Anfora '15	♟♟ 3
● Cabernet Sauvignon Anfora '15	♟ 4
○ LeViogn '17	♟ 4

Thomas Unterhofer

LOC. PIANIZZA DI SOPRA, 5
39052 CALDARO/KALTERN [BZ]
TEL. +39 0471669133
www.weingut-unterhofer.com

CELLAR SALES
PRE-BOOKED VISITS
ANNUAL PRODUCTION 12,000 bottles
HECTARES UNDER VINE 3.00

● A. A. Lago di Caldaro Cl. Sup. Leitn '18	🍷🍷	3
○ A. A. Pinot Bianco Spalier '18	🍷🍷	2*
● A. A. Schiava Campenn '18	🍷🍷	2*
○ A. A. Chardonnay '18	🍷	3

Vivaldi - Arunda

VIA JOSEF-SCHWARZ, 18
39010 MELTINA/MÖLTEN [BZ]
TEL. +39 0471668033
www.arundavivaldi.it

CELLAR SALES
PRE-BOOKED VISITS
ANNUAL PRODUCTION 90,000 bottles
HECTARES UNDER VINE 12.00

○ A. A. Spumante Extra Brut Cuvée Marianna	🍷🍷	5
○ A. A. Spumante Extra Brut Ris. '13	🍷🍷	7
○ A. A. Spumante Brut	🍷	5

Wassererhof

LOC. NOVALE DI FIÈ, 21
39050 FIÈ ALLO SCILIAR/VÖLS AM SCHLERN [BZ]
TEL. +39 0471724114
www.wasservererhof.com

CELLAR SALES
PRE-BOOKED VISITS
RESTAURANT SERVICE
ANNUAL PRODUCTION 35,000 bottles
HECTARES UNDER VINE 4.00

● A. A. Cabernet Ris. '16	🍷🍷	3
○ A. A. Pinot Bianco '17	🍷🍷	3
○ A. A. Pinot Grigio '17	🍷🍷	3

Villscheiderhof Florian Hilpold

PIAN DI SOTTO, 13
39042 BRESSANONE/BRIXEN [BZ]
TEL. +39 0472832037
villscheider@akfree.it

CELLAR SALES
PRE-BOOKED VISITS
ANNUAL PRODUCTION 4,500 bottles
HECTARES UNDER VINE 1.50

○ A. A. Valle Isarco Kerner '18	🍷🍷	3
○ A. A. Valle Isarco Riesling '18	🍷🍷	3
○ A. A. Valle Isarco Sylvaner '18	🍷🍷	3
● Zweigelt '18	🍷	3

Wilhelm Walch

VIA A. HOFER, 1
39040 TERMENO/TRAMIN [BZ]
TEL. +39 0471860172
www.walch.it

CELLAR SALES
PRE-BOOKED VISITS
ANNUAL PRODUCTION 600,000 bottles
HECTARES UNDER VINE 73.00

○ A. A. Chardonnay Pilat '18	🍷🍷	2*
○ A. A. Pinot Bianco '18	🍷🍷	3
○ A. A. Sauvignon Krain '18	🍷🍷	2*

Weinberghof Christian Bellutti

IN DER AU, 4A
39040 TERMENO/TRAMIN [BZ]
TEL. +39 0471863224
www.weinberg-hof.com

ANNUAL PRODUCTION 20,000 bottles
HECTARES UNDER VINE 2.80

○ A. A. Gewürztraminer '18	🍷🍷	3
○ A. A. Lago di Caldaro Cl. '18	🍷🍷	3
● A. A. Lagrein Ris. '16	🍷🍷	3
○ A. A. Pinot Grigio '18	🍷🍷	3

VENETO

Even a region with great commercial success, like Veneto, has its new tendencies. They may be hidden, but they're laying the groundwork for future directions. If for years producers have been focusing on sustainability (in not only economic terms, but also energy conservation, resources and the use of chemicals in the vineyard), it's the idea of wine itself that's changing. The pursuit of concentration, density and power that characterized the previous decades is increasingly seen as a limit; but rather than trying to surpass it entirely, producers are attempting to manage it for the purpose of expressing the terrain, vintage and originality of the grapes cultivated. Valpolicella is emblematic in this sense. It's an area whose success has been made possible thanks to richness of flavors, but that's turned to making more delicate, elegant wines, supported more by acidity than by alcohol and tannins. Then there's the historic sparkling wine appellation Conegliano Valdobbiadene, which is focusing on crisper, less sugary wines that can win over consumers only if the grapes used are of the highest possible quality. Soave is experiencing great success, once again demonstrating the extraordinary bond between Garganega and Veneto's best vineyards (brought out through the work of the region's most discerning winemakers). If the wines awarded to Scaligera were 6, a huge number were right behind them, testifying on the one hand to the rigorous criteria applied, and on the other to the appellation's potential. Colli Euganei also put in an excellent performance by virtue of wines that respect the area's Mediterranean qualities, but also the finesse and elegance that characterize northern territories. And then there are the many wines that fall outside the region's more well-known appellations, Serafini & Vidotto's Montello, Cescon's Treviso plains, the Fugatti brothers' Vallagarina, or Monte del Frà's and Cavalchina's Custoza. It's a veritable puzzle in which each piece is not just important, but in its own way contributes to creating an overall picture of the region.

A Mi Manera

FRAZ. LISON
VIA CADUTI PER LA PATRIA, 29
30026 PORTOGRUARO [VE]
TEL. +39 336592660
www.vinicolamimanera.com

CELLAR SALES
PRE-BOOKED VISITS
ANNUAL PRODUCTION 42,000 bottles
HECTARES UNDER VINE 7.00

Toni Bigai's estate is situated in inner Veneto, along the Adriatic coast, between the Livenza and Tagliamento rivers, where the soil of the Padana plains is heavy in clay. The property, which spans just a few hectares, hosts the area's traditional varieties, like Tai and Malvasia, as well as international grapes that have, for a century, been cultivated in this corner of the region. Their selection, which is quite varied, features primarily monovarietal wines, apart from a white and red blend. This year, the wine that most convinced us was their Pinot Nero '17. Despite the territory's heat, it offers up multilayered, fine aromas dominated by notes of wild fruit and medicinal herbs. These qualities reemerge on the palate, which proves dynamic and highly pleasant. In terms of their whites, we appreciated the fullness of their 2018 Tai, a white that never ceases to amaze.

○ A Mi Manera Bianco	♼♼	2*
● A Mi Manera Rosso	♼♼	3
● Pinot Nero '17	♼♼	5
○ Tai '18	♼♼	3
○ Chardonnay '18	♼	3
○ Malvasia '18	♼	3
● Cabernet '17	♼♼	3
○ Malvasia '17	♼♼	3
○ Malvasia '16	♼♼	3
○ Malvasia '15	♼♼	3
○ Malvasia Anfora '17	♼♼	4
● Merlot '17	♼♼	2*
○ Tai '18	♼♼	3
○ Tai '17	♼♼	3
○ Tai '16	♼♼	3
○ Tai '15	♼♼	3

Stefano Accordini

FRAZ. CAVALO
LOC. CAMPAROL, 10
37022 FUMANE [VR]
TEL. +39 0457760138
www.accordinistefano.it

CELLAR SALES
PRE-BOOKED VISITS
ANNUAL PRODUCTION 120,000 bottles
HECTARES UNDER VINE 13.00

The Accordini family's winery is situated in the highest part of Valpolicella, where the terraces and slopes, abandoned by vine growers decades ago, are thriving again, taking advantage of the cool, fine air that only comes at higher elevations. The cellar, which has been designed to be as eco-friendly as possible, gives rise to a range of wines that centers on tradition (apart from their Paxxo), pointing up richness of fruit and firmness. After lengthy aging in the cellar, their Amarone Il Fornetto '12 proves warm and ripe in color. On the nose sweet, meaty fruit dominate, while on the palate spicy and mineral notes emerge, making for an energetic wine that's well supported by acidity. Their Ripasso Aciatico '17 offers up aromas of ripe fruit, while on the palate it reveals greater crispness and a suppler dynamic of flavor.

● Amarone della Valpolicella Cl. Il Fornetto Ris. '12	♼♼	8
● Amarone della Valpolicella Cl. Acinatico '15	♼♼	7
● Paxxo '17	♼♼	4
● Valpolicella Cl. Sup. Ripasso Acinatico '17	♼♼	3
● Valpolicella Sup. Stefano '17	♼♼	3
● Valpolicella Cl. '18	♼	2
● Recioto della Valpolicella Cl. Acinatico '04	♼♼♼	6
● Amarone della Valpolicella Cl. Acinatico '14	♼♼	7
● Recioto della Valpolicella Cl. Acinatico '16	♼♼	5

Adami

fraz. Colbertaldo
via Rovede, 27
31020 Vidor [TV]
Tel. +39 0423982110
www.adamispumanti.it

CELLAR SALES
PRE-BOOKED VISITS
ANNUAL PRODUCTION 700,000 bottles
HECTARES UNDER VINE 12.00

In a territory like Valdobbiadene, which has seen overwhelming success, Franco and Armando Adami's winery has managed to remain firmly rooted in tradition and focused on their best vineyards. Eschewing unwarranted expansion, they've grounded their selection in their private vineyards and trusted suppliers. Their entire range is dedicated to sparkling wine, balancing perfectly approachability and personality. The size of a wine district is made evident during more complicated years, when the sensibility of a producer combines with their vineyards to result in small gems. That's the case with their Vigneto Giardino '18, a Valdobbiadene that offers up wide, sophisticated aromas in which citrus merges with white fruit and flowers. On the palate the wine impresses for its delicate sweetness, closing perfectly crisp and sustained by sapidity.

○ Valdobbiadene Rive di Colbertaldo Asciutto Vign. Giardino '18	🍷🍷 3*
○ Cartizze	🍷🍷 5
○ Prosecco Frizzante sul Lievito	🍷🍷 2
○ Valdobbiadene Brut Bosco di Gica	🍷🍷 3
○ Valdobbiadene Extra Dry Dei Casel	🍷🍷 3
○ Valdobbiadene Rive di Farra di Soligo Brut Col Credas '18	🍷🍷 3
○ Prosecco di Treviso Extra Dry Garbel	🍷 2
○ Valdobbiadene Rive di Colbertaldo Asciutto Vign. Giardino '16	🍷🍷🍷 3*
○ Valdobbiadene Rive di Farra di Soligo Brut Col Credas '13	🍷🍷🍷 3*
○ Valdobbiadene Rive di Farra di Soligo Brut Col Credas '12	🍷🍷🍷 3*
○ Valdobbiadene Rive di Colbertaldo Asciutto Vign. Giardino '17	🍷🍷 3*

Ida Agnoletti

loc. Selva del Montello
via Saccardo, 55
31040 Volpago del Montello [TV]
Tel. +39 0423621555
www.agnoletti.it

CELLAR SALES
PRE-BOOKED VISITS
ANNUAL PRODUCTION 50,000 bottles
HECTARES UNDER VINE 7.00

Ida Agnoletti is one of Montello's most beloved interpreters. It's a kind of large hill situated north of Treviso that blocks the path of the Piave, forcing the river to go around it on its way to the sea. Here the iron-rich earth gives rise to grapes whose acidity is notable for racy, supple wines that never give in to breadth and force. In addition to Bordeaux varieties, long cultivated in the area, they grow Glera, Recantina and Manzoni Bianco. Their Seneca '16 is a Bordeaux blend made with grapes from their oldest vineyards. In addition to notes of ripe red fruit, it offers a fresh whiff of medicinal herbs and flowers. In the mouth these are even more clearly expressed, with a firm palate that uses acidity to gain in length and elegance. Their Vita Life is Red '16, a Bordeaux enriched by a splash of Syrah, opts for greater fruit and a richer, softer palate.

● Montello e Colli Asolani Recantina '17	🍷🍷 2*
● Montello e Colli Asolani Rosso Seneca '16	🍷🍷 3
○ PSL Always Frizzante	🍷🍷 2
● Vita Life is Red '16	🍷🍷 3
● Montello e Colli Asolani Merlot La Ida '17	🍷 2
● Montello e Colli Asolani Cabernet Sauvignon Love Is... '15	🍷🍷 2*
● Montello e Colli Asolani Merlot '14	🍷🍷 2*
● Montello e Colli Asolani Merlot '13	🍷🍷 2*
● Montello e Colli Asolani Merlot La Ida '16	🍷🍷 2*
● Montello e Colli Asolani Merlot La Ida '15	🍷🍷 2*
● Montello e Colli Asolani Merlot La Ida '15	🍷🍷 2*
● Montello e Colli Asolani Recantina '15	🍷🍷 2*
● Montello e Colli Asolani Rosso Seneca '15	🍷🍷 3
● Seneca '13	🍷🍷 3
● Vita Life is Red '12	🍷🍷 3

★★★Allegrini

VIA GIARE, 5
37022 FUMANE [VR]
TEL. +39 0456832011
www.allegrini.it

CELLAR SALES
PRE-BOOKED VISITS
ACCOMMODATION AND RESTAURANT SERVICE
ANNUAL PRODUCTION 1,000,000 bottles
HECTARES UNDER VINE 150.00
SUSTAINABLE WINERY

The Allegrini family's winery is a cornerstone of modern Valpolicella history thanks to a large estate that comprises some of the territory's best areas and a style that brings out the integrity and aromatic of Freshness of Valpolicella's native grapes. And that's not to mention the international reach of their range of wines. If Amarone and Valpolicella form a large part of their selection, La Gola and La Poja pursue the highest expression of each single vineyard of origin. It's a hill that forms the border between Valpolicella and Valdadige, the top of which gives rise to their La Poja, while the lower ridges provide the grapes for their La Grola. The former is full and elegant, the second fresher and dynamic, perfect examples of how this area can fully expressive itself even without partial drying. Their Amarone '15 is deep, sophisticated in its expression of wild fruit and spices, winning over the palate with decisiveness and substance.

● Amarone della Valpolicella Cl. '15	♟♟♟	8
● La Grola '16	♟♟	5
● La Poja '15	♟♟	8
● Palazzo della Torre '16	♟♟	3
○ Soave '18	♟♟	3
● Valpolicella Cl. '18	♟♟	3
● Amarone della Valpolicella Cl. '14	♛♛♛	8
● Amarone della Valpolicella Cl. '13	♛♛♛	8
● Amarone della Valpolicella Cl. '12	♛♛♛	8
● Amarone della Valpolicella Cl. '11	♛♛♛	8
● Amarone della Valpolicella Cl. '10	♛♛♛	8
● Amarone della Valpolicella Cl. '09	♛♛♛	8
● Amarone della Valpolicella Cl. '08	♛♛♛	8
● Amarone della Valpolicella Cl. '07	♛♛♛	8
● Amarone della Valpolicella Cl. '06	♛♛♛	8
● Amarone della Valpolicella Cl. '05	♛♛♛	7
● Amarone della Valpolicella Cl. '04	♛♛♛	7

Andreola

FRAZ. COL SAN MARTINO
VIA CAVRE, 19
31010 FARRA DI SOLIGO [TV]
TEL. +39 0438989379
www.andreola.eu

CELLAR SALES
PRE-BOOKED VISITS
ANNUAL PRODUCTION 900,000 bottles
HECTARES UNDER VINE 77.00
SUSTAINABLE WINERY

Stefano Pola inherited the legacy passed down by his father Nazzareno, and in just a few years he's had a major impact on the family winery. Today, between their own private estate and land covered by suppliers, they cover 75 hectares, which gives Stefano and his staff the opportunity to ground their production in the quality and characteristics of each batch. Their entire selection is dedicated to sparklers, with Glera on center stage, obviously, making for a complete and consistent range of wines. Great attention is paid to the steepest, best vineyards, with some four wines designated in the Rive appellation. The most convincing is from Refrontolo — it's their Col del Forno Brut '18. Its fragrances are dominated by trademark sensations of apple, pear and lime blossom, while the palate seems to rely more on sapidity than on acidity, finishing long and pleasantly gutsy. Their Cartizze '18 is a ripe, creamy, pervasive wine.

○ Valdobbiadene Rive Di Refrontolo Brut Col Del Forno '18	♟♟♟	3*
○ Cartizze '18	♟♟	5
○ Valdobbiadene Brut Dirupo '18	♟♟	3
○ Valdobbiadene Extra Dry Dirupo	♟♟	3
○ Valdobbiadene Rive di Col San Martino Brut 26° Primo '18	♟♟	3
○ Valdobbiadene Rive di Rolle Dry Vigne di Piai '18	♟♟	3
○ Valdobbiadene Rive di Soligo Extra Dry Mas de Fer '18	♟♟	3
○ Valdobbiadene Dry Sesto Senso	♟	3
○ Valdobbiadene Prosecco Frizzante Casilir '18	♟	3
○ Valdobbiadene Prosecco Tranquillo Romit '18	♟	3
○ Valdobbiadene Brut Dirupo '17	♛♛♛	3*

★Roberto Anselmi

VIA SAN CARLO, 46
37032 MONTEFORTE D'ALPONE [VR]
TEL. +39 0457611488
www.anselmi.eu

CELLAR SALES
PRE-BOOKED VISITS
RESTAURANT SERVICE
ANNUAL PRODUCTION 700,000 bottles
HECTARES UNDER VINE 70.00

Even if for more than twenty years he's renounced the Soave appellation, Roberto Anselmi, along with his children Lisa and Tomasso, is one of the most careful winemakers working along the volcanic hills that surround Soave and Monteforte. In addition to historic Garganega, over the years they've cultivated other grapes. These prove indispensable to Roberto's approach, which centers on the highest possible expression, managing to be current while also respecting the natural disposition of the territory. Their Capitel Croce '18 is a bright, straw-yellow color that transmits vitality. Its fragrances open on notes of ripe yellow fruit that gradually give way to flowers and mineral hints. On the palate what impresses is its extraordinary sapidity, and an unfolding of flavor that lengthens with tension and balance. Their Capitel Foscarino '18 opts for an intenser, more immediate aromatic profile, which follows through to a racy, compelling palate.

○ Capitel Croce '18	♟♟♟ 3*
○ Capitel Foscarino '18	♟♟ 3*
○ I Capitelli Passito '16	♟♟ 6
○ San Vincenzo '18	♟♟ 2*
○ Capitel Croce '17	♟♟♟ 3*
○ Capitel Croce '15	♟♟♟ 3*
○ Capitel Croce '09	♟♟♟ 3*
○ Capitel Croce '06	♟♟♟ 3
○ Capitel Croce '05	♟♟♟ 3
○ Capitel Croce '04	♟♟♟ 3
○ Capitel Croce '03	♟♟♟ 3
○ Capitel Croce '02	♟♟♟ 3*
○ Capitel Croce '01	♟♟♟ 3
○ Capitel Croce '00	♟♟♟ 3
○ Capitel Croce '99	♟♟♟ 3*
○ Recioto dei Capitelli '85	♟♟♟ 8
○ Recioto di Soave I Capitelli '96	♟♟♟ 5

Antolini

VIA PROGNOL, 22
37020 MARANO DI VALPOLICELLA [VR]
TEL. +39 0457755351
www.antolinivini.it

CELLAR SALES
PRE-BOOKED VISITS
ACCOMMODATION
ANNUAL PRODUCTION 60,000 bottles
HECTARES UNDER VINE 9.00
SUSTAINABLE WINERY

Even if Valpolicella is a highly successful and continually evolving territory, here you'll find small wineries that perfectly bring together past and future, where a producer is foremost a farmer, and then a businessperson, following the traditions and rhythms that represent an essential value for the appellation. This is Antolini: ten hectares of historic vineyards where the use of chemicals is kept to a minimum and wines are full of character. Two Amarones are produced in different valleys. Their Moròpio is from Marano and their Ca' Coato from Negrar (both are vintage 2015). The former delivers for an aromatic sophistication that distinguishes the territory's grapes. On the palate it proves energetic, racy and pleasantly rough. The latter is more open and sunnier, both on the nose and the palate. It's a pervasive, mature wine. Their Valpolicella Persegà '17, a dynamic and linear red, is another interesting contender.

● Amarone della Valpolicella Cl. Ca' Coato '15	♟♟ 8
● Amarone della Valpolicella Cl. Moròpio '15	♟♟ 8
● Recioto della Valpolicella Cl. '17	♟♟ 6
● Valpolicella Cl. Sup. Persegà '17	♟♟ 3
● Valpolicella Cl. Sup. Ripasso '16	♟ 5
● Amarone della Valpolicella Cl. Moròpio '14	♟♟ 8
● Amarone della Valpolicella Cl. Moròpio '13	♟♟ 8
● Corvina '15	♟♟ 4
● Corvina '13	♟♟ 4
● Recioto della Valpolicella Cl. '15	♟♟ 6
● Recioto della Valpolicella Cl. '13	♟♟ 6
● Theobroma '12	♟♟ 4
● Valpolicella Cl. '16	♟♟ 3
● Valpolicella Cl. Sup. Persegà '16	♟♟ 3*
● Valpolicella Cl. Sup. Ripasso '15	♟♟ 5
● Valpolicella Cl. Sup. Ripasso '14	♟♟ 5

Albino Armani

VIA CERADELLO, 401
37020 DOLCÈ [VR]
TEL. +39 0457290033
www.albinoarmani.com

CELLAR SALES
PRE-BOOKED VISITS
ANNUAL PRODUCTION 900,000 bottles
HECTARES UNDER VINE 220.00
SUSTAINABLE WINERY

Albino Armani was one of Valdadige's pioneers or, to put it plainly, one of the few in the territory who didn't abandon his vineyards to the invasion of Pinot Grigio that arrived a few decades ago. Indeed, Albino sought to stay true to the appellation, rediscovering historic cultivars and bringing out the best of international varieties. Today the estate has been enlarged to include some of the northeast's most important appellations, from nearby Valpolicella to Grave Friulane and a partnership with Maurizio Donadi in Piave. This year the selection submitted was reduced to the essentials, all dedicated to the province of Verona. Their Amarone Classico '15, the result of an excellent vintage, opens with an aromatic profile in which ripe fruit dominates, leaving only a small amount of room for mineral hints and spices. In the mouth the fullness of its palate is well managed by acidity and tannins, and the wine lengthens decisively and harmoniously.

● Amarone della Valpolicella Cl. '15	▼▼ 5
● Valpolicella Cl. Sup. Egle '17	▼▼ 2*
● Valpolicella Cl. Sup. Ripasso '16	▼▼ 3
○ Lugana '18	▼ 3
● Amarone della Valpolicella Cl. '12	♀♀ 5
● Amarone della Valpolicella Cl. Cuslanus '13	♀♀ 6
● Amarone della Valpolicella Cl. Cuslanus '12	♀♀ 6
○ Campo Napoleone Sauvignon '17	♀♀ 2*
● Valdadige Terra dei Forti Foja Tonda '14	♀♀ 3
● Valdadige Terra dei Forti Foja Tonda Casetta '13	♀♀ 3
● Valpolicella Cl. Sup. Egle '14	♀♀ 2*
● Valpolicella Cl. Sup. Ripasso '15	♀♀ 3

Balestri Valda

VIA MONTI, 44
37038 SOAVE [VR]
TEL. +39 0457675393
www.vinibalestrivalda.com

CELLAR SALES
PRE-BOOKED VISITS
ACCOMMODATION
ANNUAL PRODUCTION 65,000 bottles
HECTARES UNDER VINE 16.00
VITICULTURE METHOD Certified Organic
SUSTAINABLE WINERY

The Rizzotto family's winery is situated in the eastern part of Soave's 'zona classica', almost hidden among the hills, surrounded by vineyards and the rare wooded patches where the slopes are too steep to be cultivated. Laura's entrance as a member of staff has brought about a change not so much in quality, which is always high, but in management of their vineyards and cellar. Indeed, today they're much more attentive to the ecosystem and reducing the environmental impact of their production. Their Soave Sengialta '16, which is just now being released after a long stay in the cellar, offers up complex aromas in which ripe fruit find flashes of freshness in mineral notes, all on a background on Mediterranean shrub. In the mouth it's firm, well supported by acidity, and closes with a vibrant tannic presence. Their Libertate '16 is intriguing in its tension and sapidity. It's a monovarietal Trebbiano di Soave that ages in steel tanks and amphoras.

○ Libertate '16	▼▼ 3
○ Soave Cl. '18	▼▼ 2*
○ Soave Cl. Vign. Sengialta '16	▼▼ 3
○ Recioto di Soave Cl. '16	▼ 5
○ Soave Cl. '17	♀♀ 2*
○ Soave Cl. '16	♀♀ 2*
○ Soave Cl. '12	♀♀ 2*
○ Soave Cl. Lunalonga '12	♀♀ 3*
○ Soave Cl. Lunalonga '11	♀♀ 3
○ Soave Cl. Vign. Sengialta '15	♀♀ 3
○ Soave Cl. Vign. Sengialta '14	♀♀ 2*
○ Soave Cl. Vign. Sengialta '13	♀♀ 2*
○ Soave Cl. Vign. Sengialta '12	♀♀ 2*

Barollo

VIA RIO SERVA, 4B
31022 PREGANZIOL [TV]
TEL. +39 0422633014
www.barollo.com

CELLAR SALES
PRE-BOOKED VISITS
ANNUAL PRODUCTION 88,000 bottles
HECTARES UNDER VINE 45.00
SUSTAINABLE WINERY

Marco and Nicola Barollo understood how to take a lesser-known territory like lower Treviso and create a space for exploring the area's historic grapes. A large estate is only partially cultivated for their own private production, allowing the Barollo brothers to rigorously select only the best batches. The result is a range of wines that are never banal, and every year has something interesting to offer. Their selection's frontman is Frank! '17, a Cabernet Franc that pursues elegance rather than fullness and opulence. Aromatically it opens timidly, with fresh fruit rapidly giving way to flowery notes, pepper and faint vegetal nuances that bestow a freshness to the region's most interesting Bordeauxs. The palate follows a similar stylistic trajectory. Sapid and crisp, it's supported by a fresh acidity.

● Frank! '17	▼▼▼ 4*
○ Piave Chardonnay '17	▼▼ 5
○ Venezia Chardonnay Frater '18	▼▼ 3
● Venezia Merlot Frater '18	▼▼ 3
○ Prosecco di Treviso Brut '18	▼ 2
○ Sauvignon '18	▼ 3
○ Alfredo Barollo M. Cl. Brut Ris. '12	♀♀ 5
○ Alfredo Barollo M. Cl. Brut Ris. '11	♀♀ 5
○ Chardonnay '16	♀♀ 4
● Frank! '16	♀♀ 4
● Frank! '15	♀♀ 4
○ Manzoni Bianco '16	♀♀ 3
○ Piave Chardonnay '15	♀♀ 4
● Venezia Merlot Frater '17	♀♀ 3

Le Battistelle

FRAZ. BROGNOLIGO
VIA SAMBUCO, 110
37032 MONTEFORTE D'ALPONE [VR]
TEL. +39 0456175621
www.lebattistelle.it

CELLAR SALES
PRE-BOOKED VISITS
ANNUAL PRODUCTION 22,000 bottles
HECTARES UNDER VINE 9.00
SUSTAINABLE WINERY

The hills of classic Soave stand out over the Padana plain. Dense as they are with vineyards, they are the landscape's dominant feature. If you go inside and explore the less visible sections, you'll discover a territory made up of steep vineyards lined with boundaries of black earth. It's here that we find Gelmino and Cristina Dal Bosco's property, just under 10 hectares subdivided into small plots characterized by the presence of numerous historic vineyards. There are no creative variations here in Via Sambuco, only Soave interpreted with a keen eye to bringing out the best of their plots. It's the case with their Roccolo del Durlo, a Soave Classico that drew on the 2017 vintage for its fragrances of ripe fruit, flowers and, at the same time, Garganega's rustic vegetal profile, which lends character and identity. The palate is firm, gutsy and compelling. Their Le Battistelle '17 follows a similar stylistic vein, opting however for a juicy and more approachable palate.

○ Soave Cl. Le Battistelle '17	▼▼ 3*
○ Soave Cl. Roccolo del Durlo '17	▼▼ 3*
○ Soave Cl. Montesei '18	▼▼ 2*
○ Soave Cl. Battistelle '14	♀♀ 3
○ Soave Cl. Le Battistelle '16	♀♀ 3
○ Soave Cl. Le Battistelle '15	♀♀ 3
○ Soave Cl. Montesei '17	♀♀ 2*
○ Soave Cl. Montesei '16	♀♀ 2*
○ Soave Cl. Montesei '10	♀♀ 2*
○ Soave Cl. Roccolo de Durlo '09	♀♀ 3
○ Soave Cl. Roccolo del Durlo '16	♀♀ 3*
○ Soave Cl. Roccolo del Durlo '15	♀♀ 3*
○ Soave Cl. Roccolo del Durlo '14	♀♀ 3

★Lorenzo Begali

VIA CENGIA, 10
37020 SAN PIETRO IN CARIANO [VR]
TEL. +39 0457725148
www.begaliwine.it

CELLAR SALES
PRE-BOOKED VISITS
ANNUAL PRODUCTION 90,000 bottles
HECTARES UNDER VINE 12.00

Situated in the southernmost part of
Valpolicella Classica, Lorenzo Begali's
winery is among the appellation's most
notable interpreters. The owners were in no
hurry to enlarge the estate, even when the
Amarone phenomenon literally exploded.
Instead they waited to purchase small plots
in the best areas, as was the case for
Masua. Their range of wines, which is firmly
rooted in tradition, is characterized by a rich,
elegant style. Their new Valpolicella
Superiore, debuting with the 2016 vintage,
is made with grapes cultivated in recently
purchased vineyards, a part of which are
then briefly dried. Fragrances of sweet,
crisp fruit refreshed by notes of flowers and
medicinal herbs emerge on the nose. The
palate is decisive, pleasantly spirited and
perfectly supported by acidity. Their
Armarone '15 proves approachable and
pervasive in its aromas of overripe fruit and
spices, while its fine palate comes through
powerful and rigorous.

● Amarone della Valpolicella Cl. '15	♟♟ 6
● Recioto della Valpolicella Cl. '15	♟♟ 6
● Valpolicella Cl. Sup. '16	♟♟ 2*
● Tigiolo '15	♟♟ 5
● Valpolicella Cl. Sup. Ripasso Vign. La Cengia '17	♟♟ 3
● Valpolicella Cl. '18	♟ 2
● Amarone della Valpolicella Cl. Monte Ca' Bianca '13	♟♟♟ 8
● Amarone della Valpolicella Cl. Monte Ca' Bianca '12	♟♟♟ 8
● Amarone della Valpolicella Cl. Monte Ca' Bianca '11	♟♟♟ 8
● Amarone della Valpolicella Cl. Monte Ca' Bianca '10	♟♟♟ 8
● Amarone della Valpolicella Cl. Vign. Monte Ca' Bianca '09	♟♟♟ 8

★Bertani

VIA ASIAGO, 1
37023 GREZZANA [VR]
TEL. +39 0458658444
www.bertani.net

CELLAR SALES
PRE-BOOKED VISITS
ANNUAL PRODUCTION 2,100,000 bottles
HECTARES UNDER VINE 200.00
SUSTAINABLE WINERY

The historic winery of Grezzana has
managed to maintain a strong identity, even
when it passed into the hands of the
Angelini group, becoming its main brand.
It's all thanks to a forward-thinking staff led
by Emilio Pedron, who prevented Bertani
from falling into the modish whims of the
market and allowed it to stay true to the
territory and its grapes. Their wines have
an unmistakable style, one that highlights
the elegance and age-worthiness of
Verona's traditional cultivars. The desire to
highlight the bond between territory and
cultivar inspired their new Valpolicella Le
Miniere, which debuts with the 2018
vintage, and interprets the appellation's
most elegant and charming qualities. It's
redolent of wild fruit, wild rose and spices.
In the mouth it impresses for its sapidity,
indicating a line of development that could
prove very interesting for the territory and
the entire appellation. The Amarone '11 is
the usual thoroughbred, complex in its
aromas and highly elegant on the palate.
Tre Bicchieri.

● Amarone della Valpolicella Cl. '11	♟♟♟ 8
● Valpolicella Cl. Le Miniere '18	♟♟ 4
● Valpolicella Cl. Sup. Ognisanti '17	♟♟ 5
● Amarone della Valpolicella Valpantena '16	♟♟ 7
● Secco Bertani Vintage '16	♟♟ 4
○ Soave Vintage '17	♟♟ 4
● Valpolicella '18	♟♟ 3
● Valpolicella Ripasso '17	♟♟ 3
● Valpolicella Ripasso Cl. Sup. Catullo '16	♟♟ 5
○ Soave Sereole '18	♟ 3
● Amarone della Valpolicella Cl. '10	♟♟♟ 8
● Amarone della Valpolicella Cl. '09	♟♟♟ 8

BiancaVigna

LOC. OGLIANO
VIA MONTE NERO, 8
31015 CONEGLIANO [TV]
TEL. +39 0438788403
www.biancavigna.it

CELLAR SALES
PRE-BOOKED VISITS
ANNUAL PRODUCTION 600,000 bottles
HECTARES UNDER VINE 30.20
SUSTAINABLE WINERY

Elena and Enrico Moschetta founded Biancavigna a few years ago, developing a family business who's roots go back to the early 20th century. In just a few years, the estate grew in the Prosecco DOCG zone, starting from San Gallo and moving towards Ogliano and Collalto. The result is a selection of Proseccos that, today, derives entirely from their own private vineyards. Their wines feature a noteworthy supporting acidity that's especially prevalent in their drier versions. Their two Rive '18s exhibit very different profiles. The Ogliano expresses all the aromatic delicacy and harmony of flavor that the territory can offer, with a palate that's characterized by sapidity and elegance. Their Soligo is more spirited. If it's more fruit-forward on the nose, in the mouth it reveals a firm body and a prominent acidity that confers a kind of restlessness by virtue of a lack of sugars.

○ Conegliano Valdobbiadene Rive di Ogliano Brut Nature '18	♀♀♀ 3*
○ Conegliano Valdobbiadene Rive di Soligo Dosaggio Zero '18	♀♀ 3*
○ Conegliano Valdobbiadene Brut '18	♀♀ 3
○ Conegliano Valdobbiadene Brut Bio	♀♀ 3
○ Conegliano Valdobbiadene Extra Dry '18	♀♀ 3
○ Brut Nature Sui Lieviti	♀ 3
○ Conegliano Valdobbiadene Prosecco Frizzante	♀ 2
⊙ Cuvée 1931 Brut Rosé	♀ 2
○ Conegliano Valdobbiadene Rive di Ogliano Brut Nature '17	♀♀♀ 3*
○ Conegliano Valdobbiadene Rive di Ogliano Brut Nature '16	♀♀♀ 3*
○ Conegliano Valdobbiadene Rive di Soligo Dosaggio Zero '17	♀♀ 3*

Bisol 1542

FRAZ. SANTO STEFANO
VIA FOLLO, 33
31049 VALDOBBIADENE [TV]
TEL. +39 0423900138
www.bisol.it

CELLAR SALES
PRE-BOOKED VISITS
ANNUAL PRODUCTION 4,500,000 bottles
HECTARES UNDER VINE 55.00

Known and appreciated for decades, Bisol is one of the Lunelli family's gems. A producer rooted in Valdobbiadene, they oversee an estate that spans various hectares within the historic part of the territory and beyond. Their range is dedicated entirely to Prosecco, which, when it comes to their premium wines, is divided up according to their vineyards of origin, while their more commercial wines pursue the right balance of sweetness, freshness and bubbles. Their best vineyards in the splendid district of Guia give rise to their Relio, a Brut that delivers for its close-focused, exotic aromas and hints of ripe fruit. These follow through on a palate that surprises for its freshness and acidic tension, qualities underlined by a faint aromatic return. Their Cartizze plays its best cards when it comes to mature aromas and a sapid dynamic of taste, with creamy, caressing bubbles.

○ Valdobbiadene Brut Rive di Guia Relio '18	♀♀ 4
○ Cartizze '18	♀♀ 5
○ Valdobbiadene Brut Crede '18	♀♀ 3
○ Valdobbiadene Brut Jeio	♀♀ 2*
○ Valdobbiadene Extra Dry Molera '18	♀♀ 3
○ Valdobbiadene Extra Dry Jeio	♀ 2
○ Cartizze '17	♀♀ 4
○ Cartizze Brut Private Fermentato in Bottiglia '14	♀♀ 5
○ Valdobbiadene Brut Crede '17	♀♀ 4
○ Valdobbiadene Brut Rive di Guia Relio '17	♀♀ 4
○ Valdobbiadene Extra Dry Molera '16	♀♀ 3
○ Valdobbiadene Extra Dry Rive di Campea '17	♀♀ 4

Bolla

FRAZ. PEDEMONTE
VIA A. BOLLA, 3
37029 SAN PIETRO IN CARIANO [VR]
TEL. +39 0456836555
www.bolla.it

CELLAR SALES
PRE-BOOKED VISITS
ANNUAL PRODUCTION 9,000,000 bottles
HECTARES UNDER VINE 185.00

Bolla is a large producer that answers to Gruppo Italiano Vini. In recent years it's taken major steps forward in terms of representing Verona's wine throughout the world. Under the guidance of Christian Zulian, Bolla launched an initiative aimed at rethinking their wines, resulting in a selection of outstanding quality. It's all thanks to painstaking effort in their sizable vineyards and their cellar, working to select the best batches for each wine. Two great Amarones, the Rhetico and Le Origini, both 2013s, are the top of their game. The first offers up intense expressions of ripe, sweet fruit on the nose, yet in the mouth the wine changes gears, highlighting fullness, harmony and length. The second is a more traditional reserve, aromatically complex and evolved in its aromas of forest undergrowth and macerated fruit. This endows the palate with an expansive quality, accompanied by finely worked tannins, lightness and sophistication.

● Amarone della Valpolicella Cl. Le Origini Ris. '13	▼▼ 7
● Amarone della Valpolicella Cl. Rhetico '13	▼▼ 7
● Amarone della Valpolicella Cl. '14	▼▼ 5
⊙ Bardolino Chiaretto La Canestraia '18	▼▼ 2*
○ Soave Cl. Sup. Tufaie '17	▼▼ 2*
● Valpolicella Cl. Sup. Ripasso Le Poiane '16	▼▼ 4
○ Soave Cl. '18	▼ 2
● Valpolicella Cl. Il Calice '18	▼ 2
● Amarone della Valpolicella Cl. '13	♈ 5
● Amarone della Valpolicella Cl. Le Origini Ris. '12	♈ 7
● Amarone della Valpolicella Cl. Le Origini Ris. '11	♈ 6
● Bardolino Cl. La Doria '17	♈ 2*

Borgo Stajnbech

VIA BELFIORE, 109
30020 PRAMAGGIORE [VE]
TEL. +39 0421799929
www.borgostajnbech.com

CELLAR SALES
PRE-BOOKED VISITS
ANNUAL PRODUCTION 90,000 bottles
HECTARES UNDER VINE 15.00

Giuliano Valent is one of the most appreciated producers operating in this large Venetian appellation, an expanse of plains that stretches from the Adriatic to the borders of Friuli and Grave. The terrain is highly varied, with sand, silt and clay alternating as it approaches the waterways, but Giuliano and his wife, Adriana, know how to interpret the area carefully and attentively. As is often the case in this corner of Veneto, their selection draws primarily on international grape varieties, which are enriched by historic Tai and Refosco. It's a quality that we find perfectly expressed in their Sauvignon Bosco della Donna '18, a wine that offers delicate aromatic notes adorned with exotic, flowery nuances. In the mouth the wine proves expansive and commendably harmonious. Force, however, comes through in their Lison 150 '17, a wine that opens with deep, stratified aromas — first Mediterranean shrub, then almond and, finally, iodine. On the palate it expresses fullness and richness governed by a sapid and gutsy acidity.

○ Bosco della Donna Sauvignon '18	▼▼ 3
○ Lison Cl. 150 '17	▼▼ 3
● Lison-Pramaggiore Refosco P. R. '17	▼▼ 3
● Malbech '17	▼▼ 2*
● Merlot '17	▼▼ 3
○ Pinot Grigio delle Venezie '18	▼ 2
● Pinot Nero '17	▼ 3
○ Traminer Aromatico '17	▼ 2
○ Lison Cl. 150 '15	♈ 3
● Malbech '16	♈ 2*
● Merlot '16	♈ 3
○ Pinot Grigio '17	♈ 2*
● Refosco P. R. '16	♈ 2*
● Refosco P. R. '14	♈ 2*
● Rosso Stajnbech '13	♈ 3
○ Stajnbech Bianco '16	♈ 3
○ Stajnbech Bianco '15	♈ 3

Borgoluce

Loc. Musile, 2
31058 Susegana [TV]
Tel. +39 0438435287
www.borgoluce.it

CELLAR SALES
PRE-BOOKED VISITS
ACCOMMODATION AND RESTAURANT SERVICE
ANNUAL PRODUCTION 250,000 bottles
HECTARES UNDER VINE 70.00

Susegana is a large estate made up of terrain that stretches for hundreds of hectares in the foothills to the north of Treviso, running all the way up to the Adriatic coast. Only a small part of the party is dedicated to viticulture. In their new, gorgeous winery, designed so as to have minimal environmental impact, attention centers on the wine that most represents the territory, Prosecco. Here easy, sugary workarounds are eschewed in favor of personality and pluck. Their Rive di Collalto Brut '18 is a Prosecco that eschews more fragrant expressions in favor of close-focused notes of pear, golden apple and wisteria, all characteristic of the grape. On the palate, a low presence of residual sugars is compensated for by a force that's almost unexpected for a Prosecco, proving crisp, sapid and endowed with nice grip. Their Extra Dry exhibits greater fruit and a caressing, delicate palate.

Borin Vini & Vigne

Fraz. Monticelli
via dei Colli, 5
35043 Monselice [PD]
Tel. +39 042974384
www.viniborin.it

CELLAR SALES
PRE-BOOKED VISITS
ANNUAL PRODUCTION 105,000 bottles
HECTARES UNDER VINE 28.00

The Borin family have been working here in Euganeo for half a century, on vineyards that span the southern part of the appellation, partially in the Monticelli foothills and partially along the Arquà slopes. Every plot hosts the grape that's best suited to particular climatic conditions and, as is particularly true of the Euganean hill's volcanic terrain, the different soil types. Today Francesco and his father Gianni focus on production while Gianpaolo and mother Teresa oversee marketing and client relations. Their Zuàn '16 is a Bordeaux blend with slightly larger share of Merlot followed by Cabernet Sauvignon and Franc. On the nose intense notes of sweet, ripe fruit emerge accompanied by fresh nuances of medicinal herbs. On the palate it opens with fullness and generosity only to gradually gain in elegance and grip as it unfolds towards a long, crisp finish. Their Chardonnay Vigna Costa '17, a harmonious white with nice vitality, also delivered.

○ Valdobbiadene Rive di Collalto Brut '18	♟♟ 3*
○ Valdobbiadene Brut	♟♟ 3
○ Valdobbiadene Extra Dry	♟♟ 3
○ Valdobbiadene Rive di Collalto Extra Dry '18	♟♟ 3
○ Valdobbiadene Prosecco Frizzante Gaiante	♟ 3
○ Valdobbiadene Rive di Collalto Brut '17	♟♟ 3*
○ Valdobbiadene Rive di Collalto Brut '16	♟♟ 2*
○ Valdobbiadene Rive di Collalto Brut '15	♟♟ 2*
○ Valdobbiadene Rive di Collalto Brut '14	♟♟ 2*
○ Valdobbiadene Rive di Collalto Extra Dry '17	♟♟ 3
○ Valdobbiadene Rive di Collalto Extra Dry '16	♟♟ 2*
○ Valdobbiadene Rive di Collalto Extra Dry '14	♟♟ 2*

● Colli Euganei Rosso Zuàn '16	♟♟ 3*
○ Colli Euganei Chardonnay V. Bianca '17	♟♟ 3
○ Colli Euganei Fior d'Arancio Spumante	♟♟ 3
○ Colli Euganei Manzoni Bianco Corte Borin '17	♟♟ 3
○ Sauvignon '18	♟♟ 3
● Colli Euganei Cabernet Sauvignon V. Costa '16	♟ 3
○ Colli Euganei Fior d'Arancio Fiore di Gaia '18	♟ 2
○ Colli Euganei Pinot Bianco Monte Archino '18	♟ 2
● Colli Euganei Cabernet Sauvignon Mons Silicis Ris. '15	♟♟ 4
○ Colli Euganei Manzoni Bianco Corte Borin '16	♟♟ 3*
● Colli Euganei Merlot Rocca Chiara Ris. '15	♟♟ 4

Bortolomiol

VIA GARIBALDI, 142
31049 VALDOBBIADENE [TV]
TEL. +39 04239749
www.bortolomiol.com

CELLAR SALES
PRE-BOOKED VISITS
RESTAURANT SERVICE
ANNUAL PRODUCTION 1,800,000 bottles
HECTARES UNDER VINE 5.00
SUSTAINABLE WINERY

The Bortolomiol family's winery is one of
the best known and most appreciated in
Prosecco Superiore. Today managed by
Maria Elena, Elvira, Luisa and Giuliana, only
a small part of their grapes are cultivated
on their own private vineyards. For the rest
they avail themselves of a strong network
of growers who've been collaborating
closely with the winery for many years.
Their range centers primarily on Prosecco
Superiore, but in recent years the family
has also purchased a vineyard in Tuscany,
in the area bordering the Montalcino DOCG
zone. The Ius Naturae project started way
back, with a desire to convert their small
private vineyards to organic so as to
produce wines that represent the
appellation's purest qualities. 2018
conferred a fine, captivating aromatic
profile dominated by white fresh and
enriched by nuances of flowers and shrub.
In the mouth the wine proves firm,
characterized by a spirited, racy palate.

○ Valdobbiadene Brut Ius Naturae '18	♟♟♟ 3*
● Il Segreto di Giuliano '16	♟♟ 6
○ Valdobbiadene Brut Rive San Pietro di Barbozza Grande Cuvée del Fondatore Motus Vitae '17	♟♟ 5
○ Valdobbiadene Dry Maior '18	♟♟ 3
○ Valdobbiadene Extra Dry Banda Rossa '18	♟♟ 3
○ Valdobbiadene Extra Dry Banda Rossa Special Reserve '18	♟♟ 3
○ Valdobbiadene Extra Dry Senior '18	♟♟ 3
○ Cartizze '18	♟ 5
⊙ Filanda Brut Rosé Ris. '18	♟ 3
○ Riserva del Governatore Extra Brut '17	♟ 3
○ Valdobbiadene Brut Audax 3.0 '18	♟ 3
○ Valdobbiadene Brut Prior '18	♟ 3

Carlo Boscaini

VIA SENGIA, 15
37015 SANT'AMBROGIO DI VALPOLICELLA [VR]
TEL. +39 0457731412
www.boscainicarlo.it

CELLAR SALES
PRE-BOOKED VISITS
ACCOMMODATION
ANNUAL PRODUCTION 60,000 bottles
HECTARES UNDER VINE 14.00

The Boscaini family's winery is situated in
Sant'Ambrogio, Valpolicella, along the
slopes that lead to San Giorgio. Here the
nearby Adige valley gives rise to winds that
guarantee the health of the grapes, evening
during difficult years, as well as beneficial
day-night temperature swings. Grapes are
cultivated here and then transformed
according to an approach that's deeply tied
to tradition. The result is a range of wines in
which a rich, generous palate serves as the
common thread. Their Amarone Classico, a
result of the excellent 2015 vintage, is an
intensely colored wine, though it leaves
room for vitality. Aromatically it opens with
overripe red fruit only to explore roads less
traveled (for the typology), like mineral
notes, forest undergrowth and macerated
leaves. In the mouth it proves reassuring,
dominated by soft, pervasive sensations and
refreshed by its characteristic acidity. Their
Ripasso Zane '16 exhibits ripe aromas and
an energetic, gutsy palate.

● Amarone della Valpolicella Cl. San Giorgio '15	♟♟ 6
● Valpolicella Cl. Sup. Ripasso Zane '16	♟♟ 4
● Valpolicella Cl. Sup. La Preosa '16	♟ 3
● Amarone della Valpolicella Cl. San Giorgio '13	♟♟ 6
● Amarone della Valpolicella Cl. San Giorgio '12	♟♟ 6
● Recioto della Valpolicella Cl. La Sengia '14	♟♟ 4
● Valpolicella Cl. Ca' Bussin '16	♟♟ 2*
● Valpolicella Cl. Sup. La Preosa '14	♟♟ 3
● Valpolicella Cl. Sup. La Preosa '12	♟♟ 3
● Valpolicella Cl. Sup. Ripasso Zane '15	♟♟ 4
● Valpolicella Cl. Sup. Ripasso Zane '13	♟♟ 4
● Valpolicella Cl. Sup. Ripasso Zane '11	♟♟ 4

Bosco del Merlo

VIA POSTUMIA, 12
30020 ANNONE VENETO [VE]
TEL. +39 0422768167
www.boscodelmerlo.it

CELLAR SALES
PRE-BOOKED VISITS
ANNUAL PRODUCTION 950,000 bottles
HECTARES UNDER VINE 90.00

The Paladin family have been operating here along the border between Venice and Udine for more than half a century, first with Valentino, and now with Lucia, Carlo and Roberto, who oversee a veritable juggernaut of Venetian wine. Over time the producer has always acquired wineries in Chianti Classico and Franciacorta, but their beating heart remains closely tied to the clay that characterizes the vineyards of Lison. Their style privileges elegance over excessive concentration, a quality that doesn't represent the territory. Their Roggio dei Roveri, a 2016 reserve, put in an excellent performance, impressing for aromas that gradually unfold: first fruit, then spicy hints and, finally, the cultivar's signature floral fragrances. In the mouth the wine unabashedly releases its notes of wild berry, closing with a crisp, slender finish. In terms of their whites, we appreciated the aromatic expressivity of their 2018 Sauvignon Turranio.

● Lison Pramaggiore Refosco P. R. Roggio dei Roveri Ris. '16	♟♟ 6
● Lison Pramaggiore Merlot Campo Camino Ris. '16	♟♟ 6
● Lison Pramaggiore Rosso Vineargenti Ris. '16	♟♟ 7
○ Lison-Pramaggiore Sauvignon Turranio '18	♟♟ 6
○ Lison-Pramaggiore Verduzzo Passito Soandre '16	♟♟ 5
● Malbech Gli Aceri Paladin '16	♟♟ 6
○ Iside Ribolla Gialla '18	♟ 5
○ Pinot Grigio delle Venezie '18	♟ 3
○ Pinot Grigio delle Venezie Tudajo '18	♟ 5
○ Prosecco Brut '18	♟ 5
○ Valdobbiadene Brut	♟ 3
● Lison-Pramaggiore Rosso Vineargenti Ris. '15	♟♟ 6

★Brigaldara

FRAZ. SAN FLORIANO
VIA BRIGALDARA, 20
37029 SAN PIETRO IN CARIANO [VR]
TEL. +39 0457701055
www.brigaldara.it

CELLAR SALES
PRE-BOOKED VISITS
ANNUAL PRODUCTION 300,000 bottles
HECTARES UNDER VINE 50.00
SUSTAINABLE WINERY

Stefano Cesari began his winemaking adventure here in Valpolicella some 40 years ago. The few hectares around his splendid home in San Pietro in Cariano have gradually grown to fifty, a veritable puzzle of vineyards that span the valleys of Marano, Grezzana and Marcellise, across various elevations, positions and terrains, which allow for a range that's full of personality. Only traditionally styled wines are made here at Cesari, and these seek to bring out the peculiarities of each area of origin. This year they submitted an excellent selection, with some three wines reaching our finals. Their Amarone Classico '15 offers up highly delicate aromas of dried fruit and spices. It's a subtlety we find on a balanced palate that expands with lightness and charm. Their Case Vecie '13 is fuller, more intense and deep, proving to be an Amarone with substance and character. We close with their Valpolicella '17, a wine with an intact profile and a firm, crisp, juicy palate.

● Amarone della Valpolicella Case Vecie '13	♟♟♟ 6
● Amarone della Valpolicella Cl. '15	♟♟ 6
● Valpolicella Sup. Case Vecie '17	♟♟ 3*
● Amarone della Valpolicella Cavolo '13	♟♟ 6
○ Soave '18	♟♟ 3
● Valpolicella Sup. Ripasso Il Vegro '17	♟♟ 4
● Valpolicella '18	♟ 3
● Amarone della Valpolicella Case Vecie '07	♟♟♟ 7
● Amarone della Valpolicella Cl. '13	♟♟♟ 6
● Amarone della Valpolicella Cl. '10	♟♟♟ 7
● Amarone della Valpolicella Cl. '06	♟♟♟ 6
● Amarone della Valpolicella Cl. '05	♟♟♟ 6
● Amarone della Valpolicella Ris. '07	♟♟♟ 8

Sorelle Bronca

FRAZ. COLBERTALDO
VIA MARTIRI, 20
31020 VIDOR [TV]
TEL. +39 0423987201
www.sorellebronca.com

CELLAR SALES
PRE-BOOKED VISITS
ACCOMMODATION
ANNUAL PRODUCTION 350,000 bottles
HECTARES UNDER VINE 24.00

Ersiliana and Antonella Bronca are two stubborn sisters deeply tied to the land, those steep and rugged hills that have, since anyone can remember, hosted Glera. It's a land that's as generous as it is delicate and in need of continued care. That's why they've chosen to reduce invasive agriculture practices to a minimum, facilitating the development of biodiversity and eschewing the idea of cultivating exclusively for Prosecco. Instead, they've left room for red grapes, and even olive trees and small woods. Nevertheless, two Proseccos impressed our panels most, starting with their Particella 232. It's a 2018 Brut Nature that offers up aromas of exotic fruit and flowers, which prove even more close-focused on its energetic, crisp and extraordinarily sapid palate. Tre Bicchieri and for us the 'Sparkler of the Year'. Their Particella 68 is a more gentle wine in its classic aromas of apple, pear and wisteria followed by a commendably harmonious palate and bubbles that provide elegant support.

○ Valdobbiadene Brut Nature Particella 232 '18	♟♟♟ 5
○ Valdobbiadene Brut Particella 68	♟♟ 4
○ Colli di Conegliano Bianco Delico '18	♟♟ 3
● Colli di Conegliano Rosso Ser Bele Ris. '16	♟♟ 5
○ Valdobbiadene Brut	♟♟ 3
○ Valdobbiadene Extra Dry	♟♟ 3
● Colli di Conegliano Rosso Ser Bele '09	♟♟♟ 5
○ Valdobbiadene Brut Particella 68 '15	♟♟♟ 4*
○ Valdobbiadene Brut Particella 68 '13	♟♟♟ 4*
○ Colli di Conegliano Bianco Delico '17	♟♟ 3
○ Colli di Conegliano Bianco Delico '15	♟♟ 3
● Colli di Conegliano Rosso Ser Bele '15	♟♟ 5
● Colli di Conegliano Rosso Ser Bele '13	♟♟ 5
○ Valdobbiadene Brut Particella 68 '16	♟♟ 4
○ Valdobbiadene Brut Particella 68 '14	♟♟ 4

Luigi Brunelli

VIA CARIANO, 10
37029 SAN PIETRO IN CARIANO [VR]
TEL. +39 0457701118
www.brunelliwine.com

CELLAR SALES
PRE-BOOKED VISITS
ACCOMMODATION
ANNUAL PRODUCTION 120,000 bottles
HECTARES UNDER VINE 14.00

The years and generations pass, and today Alberto Brunelli is at the helm. Here on Via Cariano, under the attentive watch of his father, Luigi, and mother, Luciana, he manages one of Valpolicella's most notable producers. Their vineyards, the winery's real patrimony, enjoy a climate in which the heat of Padana plains is mitigated by the influx of air from nearby Lake Garda. Both the traditional pergola system (reworked and shrunk) and guyot are used so as to allow each vineyard to produce the best grapes possible. Campo Inferi provides the grapes, and name, for one of their Amarones. It's a 2013 reserve that offers up intense aromas of wild fruit and pepper, fragrances highlighted on the wine's full, pervasive palate. Their Amarone Classico '15 opts for a more relaxed, supple profile, managing its bold flavor with delicacy and harmony.

● Amarone della Valpolicella Cl. Campo Inferi Ris. '13	♟♟ 8
● Amarone della Valpolicella Cl. '15	♟♟ 8
● Corte Cariano '16	♟♟ 2*
● Valpolicella Cl. Sup. '16	♟♟ 3
● Valpolicella Cl. '17	♟ 2
● Amarone della Valpolicella Cl. '14	♟♟ 8
● Amarone della Valpolicella Cl. Campo del Titari Ris. '13	♟♟ 8
● Recioto della Valpolicella Cl. '17	♟♟ 5
● Valpolicella Cl. Sup. '15	♟♟ 3

Buglioni

FRAZ. CORRUBBIO
VIA CAMPAGNOLE, 55
37029 SAN PIETRO IN CARIANO [VR]
TEL. +39 0456760681
www.buglioni.it

CELLAR SALES
PRE-BOOKED VISITS
ACCOMMODATION
ANNUAL PRODUCTION 170,000 bottles
HECTARES UNDER VINE 48.00

Mariano Buglioni's winery spans three main tracts: Sant'Ambrogio and San Pietro in Cariano, where viticulture is clearly geared towards high quality, and the vineyards around their cellar in Corrubio, where the traditional double pergola is used. Having an almost fifty-hectare estate available allows Mariano and his trusted winemaker, Diego Bertoni, to carry out a rigorous selection of only the best batches for their wines. Their Amarone Lussurioso '15 offers up intense aromas dominated by fruity notes, with a distinct, though resolute procession of spices, aromatic herbs and macerated flowers. In the mouth it comes through full and powerful, gaining in rigor and tension thanks to a close-knit tannic weave. Their Buggiardo '16, on the other hand, is a Ripasso that opts for riper and sweeter aromas of fruit, which give way to a palate characterized by pleasant acidic tension and sapidity.

● Amarone della Valpolicella Cl.	
Il Lussurioso '15	🍷🍷 7
● Valpolicella Cl. Sup. L'(Im)perfetto '16	🍷🍷 4
● Valpolicella Cl. Sup. Ripasso	
Il Bugiardo '16	🍷🍷 5
○ Lugana Musa '18	🍷 2
● Amarone della Valpolicella Cl.	
Il Lussurioso '13	🍷🍷 7
● Amarone della Valpolicella Cl.	
Il Lussurioso Ris. '12	🍷🍷 7
● Amarone della Valpolicella Cl.	
Teste Dure Ris. '10	🍷🍷 8
● Valpolicella Cl. Sup. L'Imperfetto '15	🍷🍷 4
● Valpolicella Cl. Sup. L'Imperfetto '14	🍷🍷 5
● Valpolicella Cl. Sup. Ripasso	
Il Bugiardo '15	🍷🍷 5

Ca' La Bionda

FRAZ. VALGATARA
VIA BIONDA, 4
37020 MARANO DI VALPOLICELLA [VR]
TEL. +39 0456801198
www.calabionda.it

CELLAR SALES
PRE-BOOKED VISITS
ACCOMMODATION
ANNUAL PRODUCTION 150,000 bottles
HECTARES UNDER VINE 29.00
VITICULTURE METHOD Certified Organic

Few Valpolicella producers have managed to face the great success that the territory is enjoying in a way that balances growth and respect for nature's rhythms, or often unpredictable market demand and the re-elaboration of a traditional style with modern expression. Alessandro and Nicola Castellani have endowed their winery with these qualities, bolstered by a deep bond with the territory and a visceral love for its wines. Their Valpolicella Campo Casal Vegri '17 is an extraordinary wine, one orchestrated by elegance and tension, one that doesn't opt for opulence and can stand shoulder-to-shoulder with some of the best wines in the world. Their elegant and firm Bianco del Casal, a white in a land of reds, is like a rabbit pulled out of a hat, a commendable blend of Trebbiano and Garganega aged in oak. Finally, their Amarone Ravazzol '15 proves to be a characterful, harmonious red.

● Valpolicella Cl. Sup.	
Campo Casal Vegri '17	🍷🍷🍷 6
● Amarone della Valpolicella Cl.	
Vign. di Ravazzol '15	🍷🍷 8
○ Bianco del Casal '18	🍷🍷 3*
● Valpolicella Cl. Sup.	
Campo Casal Vegri Decennale '08	🍷🍷 7
● Valpolicella Cl. Sup. Ripasso	
Malavoglia '17	🍷🍷 4
● Valpolicella Cl. '18	🍷 5
● Amarone della Valpolicella Cl.	
Vign. di Ravazzol '13	🍷🍷🍷 8
● Amarone della Valpolicella Cl.	
Vign. di Ravazzol '11	🍷🍷🍷 8
● Valpolicella Cl. Sup.	
Campo Casal Vegri '15	🍷🍷🍷 6
● Valpolicella Cl. Sup.	
Campo Casal Vegri '11	🍷🍷🍷 5

Ca' Lustra - Zanovello

LOC. FAEDO
VIA SAN PIETRO, 50
35030 CINTO EUGANEO [PD]
TEL. +39 042994128
www.calustra.it

CELLAR SALES
PRE-BOOKED VISITS
ANNUAL PRODUCTION 160,000 bottles
HECTARES UNDER VINE 25.50
VITICULTURE METHOD Certified Organic
SUSTAINABLE WINERY

After the premature death of his father, Franco (a passionate vine grower whose deep knowledge of the territory made him a point of reference among his peers), Marco Zanovello has taken over the reins of the family winery. It's a lovely estate of more than forty hectares, half of which are dedicated to viticulture. Here, in the Euganean regional park, a variety of elevations, positions and terrain types mean that every cultivar can find the right conditions. In the countryside the utmost respect for the environment is shown while their approach in the cellar is as minimally invasive as possible. Present since the mid-19th century, Merlot and Cabernet have found the perfect habit in the Euganean hills, as testified to by their Girapoggio and Sassonero '15. The former is a blend of Cabernet Sauvignon and Carmenère that delivers for its aromatic complexity and sapid palate. The latter is a monovarietal Merlot with intense aromas and a full, taut, very long palate.

● Colli Euganei Cabernet Girapoggio '15	♟♟ 3*
● Colli Euganei Merlot Sassonero '15	♟♟ 3*
○ 'A Cengia '17	♟♟ 2*
○ Colli Euganei Fior d'Arancio Passito '17	♟♟ 4
● Colli Euganei Rosso Moro Polo '15	♟♟ 2*
○ Olivetani '17	♟♟ 3
⊙ Aganoor Rosato '17	♟ 2
● Marzemino Passito '16	♟ 3
○ Pedevenda '17	♟ 3
● Colli Euganei Cabernet Girapoggio '05	♟♟♟ 3
○ Colli Euganei Fior d'Arancio Passito '07	♟♟♟ 4
● Colli Euganei Merlot Sassonero Villa Alessi '05	♟♟♟ 3
○ Colli Euganei Fior d'Arancio Passito '16	♟♟ 4
● Colli Euganei Merlot Sassonero '13	♟♟ 3*

Ca' Orologio

VIA CA' OROLOGIO, 7A
35030 BAONE [PD]
TEL. +39 042950099
www.caorologio.com

CELLAR SALES
PRE-BOOKED VISITS
ACCOMMODATION
ANNUAL PRODUCTION 30,000 bottles
HECTARES UNDER VINE 10.00
VITICULTURE METHOD Certified Organic
SUSTAINABLE WINERY

Even if she's highly familiar with the territory, Mariagioia Rosellini has been working in viticulture for fewer than twenty years, having fallen in love with the area and its expressions. Her cellar is situated in the 16th-century Villa Ca' Orologio in Baone, a small hamlet situated in the southernmost part of the appellation. A small part of their vineyards, which have been organically cultivated for twenty years, can be found around the villa, while the rest grow along the slopes of the surrounding hills. Their Calaóne is a Bordeaux blend (primarily Merlot) made with spontaneously fermented grapes from the Cecilia and Castello hills. On the nose it offers up intense notes of ripe, wild fruit refreshed by the presence of spicy, balsamic notes. On the palate the wine delivers for its fullness and generosity, with acidity and tannins conferring a welcome rigor. Their Relógio is a deeper, more mature and complex wine on the nose. It's a Carmenère with a smaller share of Cabernet Sauvignon that's endowed with a close-knit, powerful palate.

● Colli Euganei Rosso Calaóne '17	♟♟ 4
● Relógio '17	♟♟ 5
○ Salaróla '18	♟♟ 3
● Lunisóle '17	♟ 4
⊙ Salarosa '18	♟ 3
● Colli Euganei Rosso Calaóne '05	♟♟♟ 3*
● Relógio '09	♟♟♟ 4*
● Relógio '07	♟♟♟ 4
● Relógio '06	♟♟♟ 4
● Relógio '04	♟♟♟ 4*
● Colli Euganei Rosso Calaóne '16	♟♟ 4
● Lunisóle '16	♟♟ 4
● Relógio '16	♟♟ 5
○ Salaróla '17	♟♟ 3

★★Ca' Rugate

VIA PERGOLA, 36
37030 MONTECCHIA DI CROSARA [VR]
TEL. +39 0456176328
www.carugate.it

CELLAR SALES
PRE-BOOKED VISITS
ACCOMMODATION
ANNUAL PRODUCTION 650,000 bottles
HECTARES UNDER VINE 72.00
SUSTAINABLE WINERY

In just a few years Michele Tessari has moved the family winery even further ahead so that now the estate is almost evenly balanced between Soave and Valpolicella. Their vineyards span some of the appellation's best positions, as well as a corner of Lessinia that gives rise to their house sparkling wines. Their vineyards are currently being converted to organic while in the cellar maximum care is shown for each stage of production, making for a selection of wines featuring elegance and longevity. Aging in the cellar conferred their Monte Fiorentine '17 with aromatic depth and a relaxed palate, making for a wine that brings together richness and elegance. Their Monte Alto '17 opts for greater aromatic maturity and elegance of taste. Their Amedeo is an increasingly persuasive wine, a 2014 sparkler that proves well-integrated on the nose and racy on the palate. Their Amarone Punta 470 '15 is full, powerful and yet supple at the same time.

○ Soave Cl. Monte Fiorentine '17	♟♟♟ 3*
● Amarone della Valpolicella Punta 470 '15	♟♟ 7
○ Lessini Durello Pas Dosé M. Cl. Amedeo Ris. '14	♟♟ 5
○ Soave Cl. Monte Alto '17	♟♟ 3*
○ Studio '17	♟♟ 4
● Recioto della Valpolicella L'Eremita '16	♟♟ 5
○ Soave Cl. San Michele '18	♟♟ 2*
○ Soave Cl. Sup. Bucciato '17	♟♟ 3
● Valpolicella Rio Albo '18	♟♟ 2*
● Valpolicella Sup. Campo Lavei '17	♟♟ 4
● Valpolicella Sup. Ripasso Campo Bastiglia '17	♟♟ 3
○ Soave Cl. Monte Alto '16	♟♟♟ 3*
○ Studio '15	♟♟♟ 4*

Giuseppe Campagnola

FRAZ. VALGATARA
VIA AGNELLA, 9
37020 MARANO DI VALPOLICELLA [VR]
TEL. +39 0457703900
www.campagnola.com

CELLAR SALES
PRE-BOOKED VISITS
ANNUAL PRODUCTION 5,000,000 bottles
HECTARES UNDER VINE 155.00

For many years, Giuseppe Compagnola has been at the head of the family's winery, an operation that manages to bring together high production volumes and the character of Valpolicella. Over the years their estate has grown in three directions: Valpolicella, Lake Garda and the Friuli plains. In addition to their private vineyards, they rely on fifty growers from the Marano valley who, after close supervision over the course of the year, bring their crop to the producer's modern cellar on Via Agnella. Their Tenuta di Missoj, a handful of hectares in Mizzole, gives rise to their new Amarone. The 2013 version is redolent of overripe fruit and spices, while in the mouth it exhibits its enormous potential: power, suppleness and rigor coexist in a palate of notable substance, one that could win over even the most cunning taster. A cool 2014 conferred their Amarone Caterina Zardini with grip and juiciness.

● Amarone della Valpolicella Tenuta di Missoj Ris. '13	♟♟ 6
● Amarone della Valpolicella Cl. Caterina Zardini Ris. '14	♟♟ 6
● Amarone della Valpolicella Cl. Vign. Vallata di Marano '16	♟♟ 6
● Recioto della Valpolicella Cl. Casotto del Merlo '16	♟♟ 5
● Roccolo del Lago Corvina Veronese V. T. '17	♟♟ 3
● Valpolicella Cl. Sup. Caterina Zardini '17	♟♟ 4
● Valpolicella Cl. Sup. Ripasso '17	♟♟ 3
● Bardolino Cl. Roccolo del Lago '18	♟ 2
○ Soave Cl. Vign. Monte Foscarino Le Bine '18	♟ 3
● Valpolicella Cl. Le Bine '18	♟ 3

★I Campi

LOC. ALLODOLA
FRAZ. CELLORE D'ILLASI
VIA DELLE PEZZOLE, 3
37032 ILLASI [VR]
TEL. +39 0456175915
www.icampi.it

CELLAR SALES
PRE-BOOKED VISITS
ANNUAL PRODUCTION 80,000 bottles
HECTARES UNDER VINE 12.00

Over the years Flavio Prà has gradually reduced the time he spends consulting so as to dedicate himself exclusively to his winery, a 12-hectare estate straddling the Soave and Valpolicella appellations. He's bolstered by a deep knowledge of the area and a profound understanding of its grapes. Only a few wines are offered, all faithfully tied to local tradition and interpreted so as to reflect the best qualities of the two territories: the finesse and grip of Soave, the fullness and generosity of fruit of Valpolicella's reds. The selection that Flavio proposed this year provided plenty of satisfying moments. His Valpolicella Superiore '17 debuts with a bang. On the nose notes of ripe wild fruit, still crisp, emerge. They're refreshed by the presence of medicinal herbs and a faint spicy note that resurfaces on its racy, succulent palate. Their Campo Ciotoli '17 is deeper and more stratified, while their Soave Campo Vulcano '18 expresses the qualities of elegance and tension on a supple, very long palate.

○ Soave Cl. Campo Vulcano '18	♟♟♟ 3*
● Valpolicella Sup. '17	♟♟ 3*
● Valpolicella Sup. Ripasso Campo Ciotoli '17	♟♟ 3*
○ Lugana Campo Argilla '17	♟ 2
○ Soave Cl. Campo Vulcano '15	♟♟♟ 3*
○ Soave Cl. Campo Vulcano '13	♟♟♟ 3*
○ Soave Cl. Campo Vulcano '12	♟♟♟ 3*
○ Soave Cl. Campo Vulcano '11	♟♟♟ 5
○ Soave Cl. Campo Vulcano '10	♟♟♟ 3*
○ Soave Cl. Campo Vulcano '09	♟♟♟ 3*
○ Soave Cl. Campo Vulcano '08	♟♟♟ 3*
● Valpolicella Sup. Ripasso Campo Ciotoli '16	♟♟♟ 3*
● Valpolicella Sup. Ripasso Campo Ciotoli '15	♟♟♟ 3*

Canevel Spumanti

FRAZ. SACCOL
VIA ROCCAT E FERRARI, 17
31049 VALDOBBIADENE [TV]
TEL. +39 0423975940
www.canevel.it

CELLAR SALES
PRE-BOOKED VISITS
ANNUAL PRODUCTION 900,000 bottles
HECTARES UNDER VINE 26.00
VITICULTURE METHOD Certified Organic
SUSTAINABLE WINERY

Like many of the territory's producers, Canevel relies on the precious work carried out by numerous local vine growers. Collectively they constitute the appellation's agricultural fabric, delivering their crop to sparkling winemakers. But the Masi group has chosen to involve these growers even further, asking them not only to meet quality standards but also to embrace the producer's philosophy, which is aimed at bringing out the best of the territory and its traditions. Vigneto del Faè gives rise to their Valdobbiadene Dosaggio Zero, a wine with great aromatic depth. On the nose, ripe fruit takes center stage, accompanied by flowery and citrusy notes. A firm, gutsy palate compensates for a lack of sugars with a pronounced sapidity that's well-balanced by acidic freshness. The work done in the cellar (they slowed refermentation) conferred the palate with fullness of flavor and nice aging potential.

○ Valdobbiadene Dosaggio Zero Vign. Del Faè '18	♟♟♟ 3*
○ Cartizze '18	♟♟ 4
○ Valdobbiadene Brut Campofalco '18	♟♟ 3
○ Valdobbiadene Brut Setàge '18	♟♟ 4
○ Valdobbiadene Extra Dry Il Millesimato '18	♟♟ 5
⊙ Rosa del Faè Brut Rosé '18	♟ 3
○ Valdobbiadene Extra Dry Setàge '18	♟ 4
○ Valdobbiadene Brut Campofalco Vign. Monfalcon '18	♟♟♟ 5
○ Valdobbiadene Dosaggio Zero Vign. del Faè '17	♟♟ 4
○ Valdobbiadene Extra Dry Il Millesimato '17	♟♟ 5

Cantina del Castello

V.LO CORTE PITTORA, 5
37038 SOAVE [VR]
TEL. +39 0457680093
www.cantinacastello.it

CELLAR SALES
PRE-BOOKED VISITS
ANNUAL PRODUCTION 120,000 bottles
HECTARES UNDER VINE 13.00

Arturo Stocchetti oversees the family winery in the heart of Soave Classico, a dozen hectares situated primarily on the northeastern face of Monte Foscarino and in Pressoni. The presence of black, basalt earth immediately makes its origins clear. It's not particularly steep terrain, but it manages to give rise to aromatically rich, sugary grapes. In their Corte Pittora cellar all stages of production are carried out with an eye towards painting the delicate, fragrant character of that historic typology, Scaligera. Great attention is paid to their Soave Castello '18, a Garganega (with a smaller share of Trebbiano di Soave) that represents their most important wine in terms of production volumes. On the nose it offers up close-focused flowery sensations and notes of white fruit. These reemerge on the palate, where the wine gracefully expands, supported by acidity and the territory's trademark sapidity.

○ Soave Cl. Castello '18	♟♟ 2*
○ Brut	♟ 2
○ Tentazioni '17	♟ 4
○ Soave Cl. Sup. Monte Pressoni '01	♟♟♟ 3
○ Soave Cl. Carniga '14	♟♟ 3
○ Soave Cl. Carniga '13	♟♟ 3*
○ Soave Cl. Carniga '11	♟♟ 3*
○ Soave Cl. Carniga '10	♟♟ 3
○ Soave Cl. Castello '16	♟♟ 2*
○ Soave Cl. Castello '15	♟♟ 2*
○ Soave Cl. Castello '12	♟♟ 2*
○ Soave Cl. Pressoni '17	♟♟ 3
○ Soave Cl. Pressoni '15	♟♟ 3*
○ Soave Cl. Pressoni '14	♟♟ 3
○ Soave Cl. Pressoni '13	♟♟ 3

La Cappuccina

FRAZ. COSTALUNGA
VIA SAN BRIZIO, 125
37032 MONTEFORTE D'ALPONE [VR]
TEL. +39 0456175036
www.lacappuccina.it

CELLAR SALES
PRE-BOOKED VISITS
RESTAURANT SERVICE
ANNUAL PRODUCTION 310,000 bottles
HECTARES UNDER VINE 42.00
VITICULTURE METHOD Certified Organic

The Tessari siblings, Elena, Sisto and Pietro, have transformed the family winery into one of Soave's most striking organic estates, bolstered by vast vineyards that span the eastern part of the appellation. Here primarily Garganega is cultivated in the black soil of volcanic origin, along with traditional cultivars like Oseleta and Trebbiano di Soave, as well as classic Bordeaux varieties. Their two Soaves take on the duty of representing the winery's top quality, the San Brizio '17 and Monte Stelle '18. The former, aged in oak and then a year more in the bottle, is made with grapes cultivated behind their cellar. It impresses for the maturity of its aromas and its delicate palate. The latter, which is made with grapes cultivated on the high hills of the area's classic heart, exhibits a fine aromatic profile and a supple, juicy palate.

○ Soave Cl. Monte Stelle '18	♟♟ 3*
○ Soave San Brizio '17	♟♟ 3*
○ Basaltik Sauvignon '18	♟♟ 2*
● Campo Buri '15	♟♟ 4
○ Recioto di Soave Arzimo '16	♟♟ 5
○ Soave '18	♟♟ 2*
○ Soave Fontègo '18	♟♟ 3
○ Villa Buri Brut M. Cl. '09	♟♟ 5
○ Filòs Brut	♟ 2
● Madégo '17	♟ 2
● Camp Buri Cabernet Sauvignon '95	♟♟♟ 5
○ Basaltik Sauvignon '17	♟♟ 2*
● Campo Buri '13	♟♟ 4
○ Recioto di Soave Arzimo '15	♟♟ 5
○ Soave Fontègo '17	♟♟ 3
○ Soave Cl. Monte Stelle '17	♟♟ 3
○ Soave San Brizio '16	♟♟ 3*

Le Carline

VIA CARLINE, 24
30020 PRAMAGGIORE [VE]
TEL. +39 0421799741
www.lecarline.com

CELLAR SALES
PRE-BOOKED VISITS
ANNUAL PRODUCTION 400,000 bottles
HECTARES UNDER VINE 18.00
VITICULTURE METHOD Certified Organic

Daniele Piccinin, a passionate vigneron driven by a desire to continually experiment, is a pioneer of organic viticulture in the region's plains. Tasting Le Carine's wines is a bit like taking part in the journey, from the version produced in the Venetian island of Santa Cristina, to those made without sulfites. Then there's his most recent creation, made with a grape that's resistant to cryptogamic diseases. The vines don't require treatments and so, in a certain way, their cultivation goes even further than the idea of organic. Their Resiliens is a 2018 white redolent of citrus and exotic fruit, with a subtle, flowery note. On the palate it offers up fullness and a vibrant acidic thrust. Their Dogale operates on an entirely different level. It's a late-harvest Verduzzo that enchants with its aromas of candied fruit and spices. It wins you over, thanks to the right amount sweetness and a palate that privileges sapidity over acidic tension.

Carpenè Malvolti

VIA ANTONIO CARPENÉ, 1
31015 CONEGLIANO [TV]
TEL. +39 0438364611
www.carpene-malvolti.com

CELLAR SALES
PRE-BOOKED VISITS
ANNUAL PRODUCTION 5,300,000 bottles
HECTARES UNDER VINE 26.00
SUSTAINABLE WINERY

This historic Conegliano winery is a legend for those who love wine. It's a veritable emblem of Italian sparkling wine, and among the first to promote their product on television. Many years have passed since those images of Prosecco being poured into a crystal glass circulated on TV, but still today Carpené Malvoti is among the territory's most representative producers, bolstered by close relationships with a large number of local growers. Their PVXINVM is the result of a selection carried out among their best vineyards, those older than 50 years and that produce a limited amount of grapes rich in aromas and flavor. In the cellar, production is aimed at preserving aromatic finesse, which follow through on the palate in a perfect fusion of sweetness, acidity and bubbles. Their Brut, a wine dedicated to the founder and identifiable by its historic 1924 label, also delivered.

○ Dogale Passito	🍷🍷	3
● Lison-Pramaggiore Refosco P. R. '18	🍷🍷	2*
○ Resiliens '18	🍷🍷	3
● Lison-Pramaggiore Cabernet '18	🍷	2
○ Venezia Pinot Grigio '18	🍷	2
● Carline Rosso '12	🍷🍷	3
● Carline Rosso '11	🍷🍷	3
● Carline Rosso '10	🍷🍷	3
● Carline Rosso '07	🍷🍷	4
● Carline Rosso '07	🍷🍷	4
○ Diana Brut M. Cl. '16	🍷🍷	4
○ Diana Brut M. Cl. '15	🍷🍷	4
○ Diana Brut M. Cl. '15	🍷🍷	4
○ Lison Cl. '12	🍷🍷	2*
● Lison-Pramaggiore Merlot '16	🍷🍷	2*
● Lison-Pramaggiore Refosco P. R. senza solfiti aggiunti '13	🍷🍷	2*

○ Conegliano Valdobbiadene 1924 Brut	🍷🍷	3*
○ Conegliano Valdobbiadene Extra Dry PVXINVM '17	🍷🍷	8
○ Cartizze 1868	🍷	5
○ Conegliano Valdobbiadene Extra Dry 1868	🍷	3
○ Conegliano Valdobbiadene Extra Dry PVXINVM '14	🍷🍷	5

Casa Cecchin

VIA AGUGLIANA, 11
36054 MONTEBELLO VICENTINO [VI]
TEL. +39 0444649610
www.casacecchin.it

CELLAR SALES
PRE-BOOKED VISITS
ANNUAL PRODUCTION 30,000 bottles
HECTARES UNDER VINE 7.00

Along with her father, Renato, Roberta Cecchin oversees one of the Lessinia's most historic and loveliest wineries. Lessinia is a hilly district that joins and serves as the border between Vicenza and Verona. Here Durella takes center stage, though there's a limited presence of Garganega along the easternmost slopes of the appellation. The result is a selection focused primarily on Metodo Classico sparkling wines and takes advantage of the grape's pronounced acidity. Nostrum '14 is an Extra Brut that comes from an old vineyard called Spianata. Situated at 250 meters elevation with southeast exposure, the plot features black, basalt soil from which the vine roots extract extraordinary mineral force. Fragrances range from golden apple to toasted bread, with a faint flowery note in the background that becomes clearer on the palate. In the mouth the wine lengthens with decisiveness and pluck, proving perfectly supported by bubbles.

○ Lessini Durello Brut M. Cl. Nostrum '14	♟♟	4
○ Pietralava '18	♟♟	3
○ Durello Passito Montebello '15	♟♟	5
○ Gambellara San Nicolò '15	♟♟	2*
○ Il Durello '16	♟♟	2*
○ Lessini Durello Brut M. Cl. Nostrum '13	♟♟	4
○ Lessini Durello Dosaggio Zero M. Cl. '11	♟♟	5
○ Lessini Durello Extra Brut M. Cl. Nostrum '12	♟♟	4
○ Lessini Durello Il Durello '14	♟♟	2*
○ Lessini Durello Pietralava '14	♟♟	2*
○ Pietralava '17	♟♟	3
○ Pietralava '15	♟♟	3
○ San Nicolò '16	♟♟	2*

Casa Roma

VIA ORMELLE, 19
31020 SAN POLO DI PIAVE [TV]
TEL. +39 0422855339
www.casaroma.com

CELLAR SALES
PRE-BOOKED VISITS
ANNUAL PRODUCTION 200,000 bottles
HECTARES UNDER VINE 15.00

The territory of Piave had to deal with two high-impact phenomena only a few years apart. The first was Pinot Grigio, today it's Prosecco. Many producers were unable to manage these revolutions. Luigi Peruzzetto, however, was unafraid, respecting their importance though without giving up on or betraying a selection in which varietal wines play a central role. Raboso, the historic grape that represents the territory more than any other, serves as a cornerstone. It's accompanied by Bordeaux varieties. Their Malanotte '12 is made with partially-dried Raboso. It's a lovely, intense ruby-red wine with aromas that call up stewed wild fruit, only to broaden to warmer, more Mediterranean notes, carob and sweet spices. In the mouth, the wine's fullness is managed by a structure in which acidity and tannins figure centrally, making for a full, sapid palate. Their Raboso '13 is fresher, more spirited and honed.

● Piave Carmènere Peruzzet '18	♟♟	2*
● Piave Malanotte '12	♟♟	6
○ Piave Manzoni Bianco Peruzzet '18	♟♟	2*
● Piave Manzoni Bianco San Dordi '17	♟♟	3
● Piave Raboso Peruzzet '13	♟♟	4
○ Pinot Grigio delle Venezie Peruzzet '18	♟	2
● Venezia Cabernet Sauvignon Peruzzet '18	♟	2
○ Venezia Chardonnay Peruzzet '18	♟	2
● Venezia Merlot Peruzzet '18	♟	2
○ Peruzzet Marzemina Bianca '17	♟♟	2*
● Piave Carmènere Peruzzet '17	♟♟	2*
○ Piave Manzoni Bianco '16	♟♟	2*
● Piave Raboso '12	♟♟	4
● Piave Raboso '10	♟♟	4
● Piave Raboso Indigeno '07	♟♟	6
● Sestier Raboso '17	♟♟	2*
○ Venezia Pinot Grigio Peruzzet '17	♟♟	2*

Case Paolin

via Madonna Mercede, 55
31040 Volpago del Montello [TV]
Tel. +39 0423871433
www.casepaolin.it

CELLAR SALES
PRE-BOOKED VISITS
ANNUAL PRODUCTION 130,000 bottles
HECTARES UNDER VINE 15.00
VITICULTURE METHOD Certified Organic
SUSTAINABLE WINERY

Diego, Adelino and Mirco Pozzobon are among the most important figures operating in one of Veneto's smallest appellations, Montello and Colli Asolani, an area that's well-suited to the production of great red wines, but that today is seeing Glera spread like wildfire. Without taking anything away from Treviso's sparkling wines, Case Paolin continues undaunted in the production of still wines, the simplest are made with grapes cultivated in the flat, gravelly terrain are their cellar, while their premium wines are cultivated along the Montello hills. And from these vineyards, in San Carlo, we get the grapes destined for their most important wine, a Bordeaux that, with the 2015 vintage, features a lovely, ruby-red color. This anticipates aromas of wild fruit and spices, with a subtle oaky note in the background. In the mouth the wine proves full, with nice pulp, a palate supported by close-knit tannins and lively acidity. Their Asolo Brut, an energetically and pleasantly firm wine, also performed well.

● Montello e Colli Asolani Rosso San Carlo '15	▼▼ 5
○ Asolo Brut	▼▼ 3
○ Costa degli Angeli Manzoni Bianco '18	▼▼ 3
● Rosso del Milio '17	▼▼ 3
● Cabernet '18	▼ 2
○ Prosecco di Treviso Extra Dry	▼ 2
● Cabernet '17	▽▽ 2*
○ Costa degli Angeli Manzoni '16	▽▽ 3*
○ Manzoni Bianco Costa degli Angeli '15	▽▽ 3
● Montello e Colli Asolani Rosso San Carlo '13	▽▽ 4
● Rosso del Milio '16	▽▽ 3
● Rosso del Milio '15	▽▽ 3
● Rosso del Milio '14	▽▽ 3

Michele Castellani

fraz. Valgatara
via Granda, 1
37020 Marano di Valpolicella [VR]
Tel. +39 0457701253
www.castellanimichele.it

CELLAR SALES
PRE-BOOKED VISITS
ANNUAL PRODUCTION 300,000 bottles
HECTARES UNDER VINE 50.00

Sergio Castellani's winery is situated in Valgatara, a district of Marano di Valpolicella that marks the passage from the valley floor to the hills. Their vineyards, which comprise private property and directly managed plots, span some 15 hectares of hills in the classic heart of the area. But Sergio and his children, Michele, Martina and Mara, also rely on partnerships with numerous growers who provide the winery with additional crop. Their winemaking style privileges the fullness and power that comes with using partially-dried grapes. It's a style that's perfectly expressed in their Amarone Cinquestelle, the producer's crown jewel. They use the best grapes harvested in their Ca' del Pipa vineyard. These are then dried at length, and the wine ages in oak for three years. The result is an intensely colored wine that's redolent of red fruit preserves and sweet spices, all refreshed by a subtle balsamic vein. In the mouth its impact is powerful and warm, governed by a close-knit tannic weave.

● Amarone della Valpolicella Cl. Cinquestelle Collezione Ca' del Pipa '15	▼▼ 7
● Amarone della Valpolicella Cl. Campo Casalin I Castei '16	▼▼ 6
● Recioto della Valpolicella Cl. Monte Fasenara I Castei '17	▼▼ 5
● Valpolicella Cl. Campo del Biotto I Castei '18	▼ 2
● Valpolicella Cl. Sup. Ripasso Costamaran I Castei '17	▼ 3
● Recioto della Valpolicella Cl. Le Vigne Ca' del Pipa '99	▽▽▽ 6
● Amarone della Valpolicella Cl. Campo Casalin I Castei '15	▽▽ 6
● Recioto della Valpolicella Cl. Monte Fasenara I Castei '16	▽▽ 5
● Valpolicella Cl. Sup. Ripasso Costamaran I Castei '16	▽▽ 3

★ Cavalchina

LOC. CAVALCHINA
FRAZ. CUSTOZA
VIA SOMMACAMPAGNA, 7
37066 SOMMACAMPAGNA [VR]
TEL. +39 045516002
www.cavalchina.com

CELLAR SALES
PRE-BOOKED VISITS
ANNUAL PRODUCTION 445,000 bottles
HECTARES UNDER VINE 50.00

Siblings Piona, Luciano and Franco oversee a complex estate founded in the early 20th century in Custoza. In recent decades, especially, it's grown in four different directions, resulting in a kind of viticultural puzzle that stretches from Custoza to Mincio, with their La Prendina, then towards Valpolicella with Torre d'Orti, and finally towards southern Lake Garda with 'L Lac. Their range of wines is grounded in solid principles: respect for the natural disposition of the vineyards, the potential of each cultivar and, finally, great technical skill. Once again their Custoza Amedeo leads their selection. 2017 endowed the wine with a sophisticated aromatic profile dominated by flowery notes and hints of white fruit. In the mouth the wine offers up all its extraordinary youthfulness with lightness and sapidity. Their Bardolino Casella '15, a wine that explores the deepest, hidden qualities of the appellation, had an excellent debut.

○ Custoza Sup. Amedeo '17	♟♟♟ 3*
● Bardolino Casella '15	♟♟ 5
● Amarone della Valpolicella Torre D'Orti '15	♟♟ 6
● Bardolino '18	♟♟ 2*
⊙ Bardolino Chiaretto '18	♟♟ 2*
○ Custoza '18	♟♟ 2*
● Garda Cabernet Sauvignon Falcone Prendina '16	♟♟ 4
○ Garda Riesling '18	♟♟ 3
○ Lugana 'L Lac '18	♟♟ 3
● Valpolicella Sup. Morari Torre d'Orti '16	♟♟ 5
● Valpolicella Sup. Ripasso Torre d'Orti '17	♟♟ 3
● Garda Merlot Faial Prendina '16	♟ 5
○ Garda Pinot Grigio Prendina '18	♟ 2
○ Custoza Sup. Amedeo '16	♟♟♟ 3*

Cavazza

C.DA SELVA, 22
36054 MONTEBELLO VICENTINO [VI]
TEL. +39 0444649166
www.cavazzawine.com

CELLAR SALES
PRE-BOOKED VISITS
ACCOMMODATION
ANNUAL PRODUCTION 860,000 bottles
HECTARES UNDER VINE 150.00
SUSTAINABLE WINERY

The Cavazza family's winery got its start almost a century ago. Today, as back then, the family itself oversees all stages of production, from vineyard management to winemaking and sales. If their commitment hasn't changed, the estate today is very different in size and location. In addition to their historic Bocara vineyard, purchased in 1928, they've added large plots in the area of Gambellara and, as of 1987, in Colli Berici. And this system of hills south of Vicenza has given rise to an important new wine. It's their Merlot Cicogna '16, a red that's redolent of ripe fruit and spices, with a fresh flowery note in the background that confers lightness. In the mouth its fullness is ably managed by a fresh acidity. Their Gambellara Creari '16 also performed well. It opts more for aromatic maturity and fullness in the mouth, proving pervasive and soft on the palate, and supported by a pronounced sapidity.

● Colli Berici Merlot Cicogna '16	♟♟ 5
○ Gambellara Cl. Creari '16	♟♟ 3*
● Syrhae Cicogna '16	♟♟ 4
○ Gambellara Cl. Bocara '18	♟ 2
● Cicogna Syrah '15	♟♟ 5
● Colli Berici Cabernet Cicogna '15	♟♟ 4
● Colli Berici Cabernet Cicogna '13	♟♟ 4
● Colli Berici Merlot Cicogna '13	♟♟ 5
● Colli Berici Tai Rosso Corallo '16	♟♟ 3
● Fornetto '16	♟♟ 3
○ Gambellara Cl. Bocara '17	♟♟ 2*
○ Gambellara Cl. La Bocara '16	♟♟ 2*
○ Gambellara Cl. La Bocara '15	♟♟ 2*
○ Recioto di Gambellara Cl. Capitel '15	♟♟ 4

Giorgio Cecchetto

FRAZ. TEZZE DI PIAVE
VIA PIAVE, 67
31028 VAZZOLA [TV]
TEL. +39 043828598
www.rabosopiave.com

CELLAR SALES
PRE-BOOKED VISITS
ANNUAL PRODUCTION 200,000 bottles
HECTARES UNDER VINE 73.00
SUSTAINABLE WINERY

Situated in historic Piave, Giorgio Cecchetto's winery is an indispensable benchmark for those who love the territory's most representative grape, Raboso. Today their vineyards span several hectares in the appellation, but only a small part of these contribute to a range of wines whose style is firmly rooted in the pursuit of the fullest expression of each cultivar. Things are a bit different when it comes to Raboso, which is presented in various ways so as to highlight its most interesting qualities. After a few years off, their Gelsaia is back in a new, sumptuous version, the Malanotte, a 2016 that draws on the vintage for its intense sensations of overripe fruit supported by spicy and mineral notes. In the mouth its fullness is buoyant, while a close-knit tannic weave brings the wine back to rigor and vigor. Their Raboso '16, a sophisticated wine both on the nose and the palate, also delivered.

● Carmenère '18	🍷🍷 2*
● Piave Malanotte Gelsaia '16	🍷🍷 5
● Piave Raboso '16	🍷🍷 3
○ Manzoni Bianco '18	🍷 2
● Passito RP	🍷 4
● Malanotte Gelsaia '13	🍷🍷 5
○ Manzoni Bianco '15	🍷🍷 2*
● Piave Raboso '15	🍷🍷 3
● Piave Raboso '13	🍷🍷 3
⊙ Rosa Bruna Cuvée 21 Brut M. Cl. '12	🍷🍷 3
● Sante Rosso '16	🍷🍷 4

Gerardo Cesari

LOC. SORSEI, 3
37010 CAVAION VERONESE [VR]
TEL. +39 0456260928
www.cesariverona.it

CELLAR SALES
PRE-BOOKED VISITS
ANNUAL PRODUCTION 1,500,000 bottles
HECTARES UNDER VINE 120.00
SUSTAINABLE WINERY

The large producer Cavaion Veronese divides up its time and efforts between Valpolicella and the appellations along the banks of Garda, Lugana and Bardolino. Their vineyards span many hectares in these two areas, as well as comprising land in Grave del Friuli, and give rise to a range of precisely styled wines. Their simplest offerings are defined by their varietal expression and fragrance, while their rich and complex premium wines are only released after lengthy aging. Their Amarone Bosan '10, is a reserve that's released only after a very lengthy stay in the cellar. On the nose it offers up aromas of overripe fruit enriched by notes of tobacco, dried flowers and spices. In the mouth it comes through warm and pervasive, though there's also a suppleness by virtue of the cultivars' trademark acidity. The Amarone Il Bosco '13 expresses greater aromatic freshness and a crisper, pluckier palate.

● Amarone della Valpolicella Cl. Bosan Ris. '10	🍷🍷 8
● Amarone della Valpolicella Cl. '15	🍷🍷 5
● Amarone della Valpolicella Cl. Il Bosco '13	🍷🍷 6
● Valpolicella Sup. Ripasso Bosan '16	🍷🍷 4
● Jèma Corvina Veronese '15	🍷 5
○ Lugana Cento Filari '18	🍷 3
● Valpolicella Sup. Ripasso Mara '17	🍷 3
● Amarone della Valpolicella Bosan Ris. '08	🍷🍷 8
● Amarone della Valpolicella Cl. '14	🍷🍷 5
● Amarone della Valpolicella Cl. Bosan Ris. '09	🍷🍷 8
● Amarone della Valpolicella Cl. Il Bosco '12	🍷🍷 6
● Valpolicella Sup. Ripasso Bosan '15	🍷🍷 4

Italo Cescon

FRAZ. RONCADELLE
P.ZZA DEI CADUTI, 3
31024 ORMELLE [TV]
TEL. +39 0422851033
www.cesconitalo.it

CELLAR SALES
PRE-BOOKED VISITS
ANNUAL PRODUCTION 930,000 bottles
HECTARES UNDER VINE 115.00
VITICULTURE METHOD Certified Organic
SUSTAINABLE WINERY

Immersed in the gravelly, clay plains of the
Piave appellation, in just a few years the
Cescon family's winery has profoundly
revolutionized its approach to viticulture. In
the past they were focused on more simpler
wines. But today, under siblings Domenico,
Gloria and Graziella, the winery has
abandoned more conventional methods and
embraced organic viticulture, giving rise to a
range of wines that offers flashes of great
personality. That Manzoni Bianco is a
cultivar with tremendous potential is nothing
new, but we didn't expect to find a winery
that managed to bring out its potential
based on the season's climate conditions.
Madre '17 is a delicately cloudy white, the
result of not being filtered. It's redolent of
citrus and exotic fruit, while on the palate
proves energetic and sapid, only to
conclude with an impressively long finish.

○ Madre '17	♚♚♚	5
● Amaranto 72 Ris. '13	♚♚	6
● Chieto '16	♚♚	4
● Tralcetto Merlot '17	♚♚	3
○ Tralcetto Pinot Grigio '18	♚♚	3
● Piave Raboso Rabìa Ris. '12	♚	7
● Tralcetto Pinot Noir '18	♚	3
○ Madre '16	♔♔♔	5
○ Madre '14	♔♔♔	4*
○ Choku Rei Pinot Grigio '16	♔♔	4
○ Madre '15	♔♔	5

Coffele

VIA ROMA, 5
37038 SOAVE [VR]
TEL. +39 0457680007
www.coffele.it

CELLAR SALES
PRE-BOOKED VISITS
ANNUAL PRODUCTION 120,000 bottles
HECTARES UNDER VINE 25.00
VITICULTURE METHOD Certified Organic

In Castelcerino, the territory of Soave has
one of its most original enclaves. Its
elevation and soil type, which alternates
basalt and limestone, allow for a production
of great personality. Chiara and Alberto
Coffele oversee the family estate, a
contiguous tract of 25 hectares in the area
that's accompanied by a small vineyard in
Campiano where they cultivate the grapes
for their Valpolicella reds. Their wines are
dedicated primarily to the region's historic
appellations, interpreted with precision and
elegance. Their Alzari '17 is made with
grapes cultivated in the vineyard of the
same name. A part of these are dried for
about a month, and then it ages in oak for
almost a year. Its aromas call up ripe white
fruit, dried flowers and spices, while in the
mouth it delivers for the harmony of its
sensations. Its full palate finds the right
acidic support, making for a long,
sophisticated wine. Their Ca' Visco '18 is a
fresher wine aromatically and dynamic on
the palate.

○ Soave Cl. Alzari '17	♚♚	3*
○ Soave Cl. Ca' Visco '18	♚♚	3*
○ Recioto di Soave Cl. Le Sponde '17	♚♚	5
○ Soave Cl. Castel Cerino '18	♚♚	3
○ Recioto di Soave Cl. Le Sponde '09	♔♔♔	5
○ Soave Cl. Ca' Visco '14	♔♔♔	3*
○ Soave Cl. Ca' Visco '05	♔♔♔	3*
○ Soave Cl. Ca' Visco '04	♔♔♔	2
○ Soave Cl. Ca' Visco '03	♔♔♔	2
○ Recioto di Soave Cl. Le Sponde '16	♔♔	5
○ Soave Cl. Alzari '16	♔♔	3*
○ Soave Cl. Ca' Visco '17	♔♔	3
○ Soave Cl. Ca' Visco '16	♔♔	3*
○ Soave Cl. Castel Cerino '17	♔♔	3

Col Vetoraz

FRAZ. SANTO STEFANO
S.DA DELLE TRESIESE, 1
31040 VALDOBBIADENE [TV]
TEL. +39 0423975291
www.colvetoraz.it

CELLAR SALES
PRE-BOOKED VISITS
ANNUAL PRODUCTION 1,200,000 bottles
HECTARES UNDER VINE 130.00

More than a quarter century has passed since this Santo Stefano winery was founded by Francesco Miotto along with partners Loris Dall'Acqua and Paolo De Bortoli, but the bond shared between the Miotto family and the territory goes back more than a century. Today Col Vetoraz is one of the appellation's most notable producers, thanks in part to the harmony that's developed between the three owners and the numerous growers who guarantee the high quality standards the winery offers. Their selection, just five wines (all from the last vintage) knows no weak points. They perfectly represent the world of Prosecco Superiore. Il Cartizze opens with delicate aromas of citrus and white fruit caressed by a subtle hint of flowers. In the mouth it impresses more for its sapidity than for its sweetness, proving supple, succulent and sophisticated. Their Dosaggio Zero, a pure, slender Prosecco is more energetic and pluckier.

○ Cartizze '18	▼▼	4
○ Valdobbiadene Brut '18	▼▼	3
○ Valdobbiadene Dosaggio Zero '18	▼▼	3
○ Valdobbiadene Dry '18	▼▼	3
○ Valdobbiadene Extra Dry '18	▼▼	3
○ Cartizze '17	♀♀	4
○ Cartizze '16	♀♀	4
○ Valdobbiadene Brut '17	♀♀	3
○ Valdobbiadene Brut '16	♀♀	3
○ Valdobbiadene Dosaggio Zero '17	♀♀	3*
○ Valdobbiadene Dosaggio Zero '16	♀♀	3*
○ Valdobbiadene Extra Dry '17	♀♀	3
○ Valdobbiadene Extra Dry '16	♀♀	3

Conte Collalto

VIA XXIV MAGGIO, 1
31058 SUSEGANA [TV]
TEL. +39 0438435811
www.cantine-collalto.it

CELLAR SALES
PRE-BOOKED VISITS
ANNUAL PRODUCTION 850,000 bottles
HECTARES UNDER VINE 164.00
SUSTAINABLE WINERY

This historic Susegana winery is one of the loveliest and most sizable estates in Coneglianese. Isabella Collalto De Croÿ oversees their 160-hectare vineyard, which is situated in a hillside rich in biodiversity. Here viticulture doesn't dominate but rather integrates with pastures, woods, occasionally olive groves, and, even more occasionally, dwellings. In recent years the producer has launched a gradual makeover of their production, which increasingly centers on Conegliano Valdobbiadene. Their new sparkling wine, Isabella '17, put in a nice performance. It's a wine made with grapes from their best plots in Collalto, a brut with low amounts of residual sugars that stands out for the finesse of its varietal aromas: apple, pear, acacia blossoms. On the palate it expresses fullness and firmness, peculiar characteristics of Conegliano's grapes which allow for a reduced use of sugars. Their VInciguerra '13 is mature on the nose, broad and silky on the palate.

● Colli di Conegliano Rosso Vinciguerra '13	▼▼	5
○ Conegliano Valdobbiadene Brut Ponte Rosso '18	▼▼	3
○ Conegliano Valdobbiadene Dry Dame '18	▼▼	3
○ Conegliano Valdobbiadene Extra Dry Gaio '18	▼▼	3
○ Conegliano Valdobbiadene Rive di Collalto Isabella Brut '17	▼▼	3
○ Conegliano Valdobbiadene Brut San Salvatore '18	▼	3
● Incrocio Manzoni 2.15 '17	▼	2
○ Manzoni Bianco '18	▼	2
○ Rosabianco '18	▼	2
⊙ Sogno Rosarossa '18	▼	2
⊙ Violette Rosé Extra Dry	▼	2
● Wildacher '16	▼	2

Le Colture

LOC. SANTO STEFANO
VIA FOLLO, 5
31049 VALDOBBIADENE [TV]
TEL. +39 0423900192
www.lecolture.com

CELLAR SALES
PRE-BOOKED VISITS
ACCOMMODATION
ANNUAL PRODUCTION 750,000 bottles
HECTARES UNDER VINE 40.00

Generally Valdobbiadene works a bit like Champagne, with numerous vine growers supplying grapes to producers whose own land holdings are quite small. The Ruggeri family have always gone in the opposite direction, purchasing sizable tracts of land so as to directly oversee all stages of producing. Today more than half of their production comes from their own private vineyards, giving rise to a range of wines in which Prosecco figures centrally. Gerardo is a Brut made with grapes from their oldest plots in Santo Stefano, those with the best positions where they seem literally suspended from the sky. Refermentation is carried out very slowly and carefully, resulting in a wine that's redolent of pear and flowers, capable of drawing you in for its sapidity. It lengthens delicately while perfectly balancing bubbles and acidity. Their Cartizze, a wine that's sunnier on the nose and pervasive on the palate, also impressed.

○ Valdobbiadene Rive di Santo Stefano Brut Gerardo '18	🏆🏆 3*
○ Cartizze	🏆🏆 5
○ Valdobbiadene Brut Fagher	🏆🏆 3
○ Valdobbiadene Dry Cruner	🏆🏆 3
○ Valdobbiadene Extra Dry Pianer	🏆🏆 3
⊙ Rosé Brut	🏆 2
○ Valdobbiadene Prosecco Frizzante Mas	🏆 3
○ Valdobbiadene Brut Fagher	🏆🏆 3
○ Valdobbiadene Brut Rive di Santo Stefano Gerardo '16	🏆🏆 3
○ Valdobbiadene Dry Cruner	🏆🏆 3
○ Valdobbiadene Extra Dry Pianer	🏆🏆 3
○ Valdobbiadene Extra Dry Prime Gemme	🏆🏆 3
○ Valdobbiadene Rive di Santo Stefano Brut Gerardo '15	🏆🏆 3

Corte Adami

CIRCONVALLAZIONE ALDO MORO, 32
37038 SOAVE [VR]
TEL. +39 0456190218
www.corteadami.it

CELLAR SALES
PRE-BOOKED VISITS
ANNUAL PRODUCTION 170,000 bottles
HECTARES UNDER VINE 38.00
SUSTAINABLE WINERY

Giulia, Martina and Andrea Adami have revolutionized the family winery. In fewer than 15 years, they've gone from supplying grapes to a local cooperative, to becoming a full-fledged producer that makes wines for two of Verona's most important appellations, Valpolicella and Soave. Their Garganega and Trebbiano di Soave vineyards are situated along the hills north of Soave and in the flatlands around their cellar, while their Ferrazze estate gives rise to their Valpolicella grapes. Their Soave Decennale '16 performed very well. It was made to celebrate the winery's 10-year birthday, but considering its success, they produce it almost every year. On the nose it offers up notes of flint and dried flowers while on the palate it highlights fullness and acidic tension, all accompanied by a pronounced sapidity conferred by the territory. In terms of their reds, we appreciated their Ripasso '16, a wine that goes in on ripeness of fruit and fullness of the palate.

● Amarone della Valpolicella '15	🏆🏆 6
○ Soave Decennale '16	🏆🏆 3
○ Soave Sup. V. della Corte '17	🏆🏆 3
● Valpolicella Sup. Ripasso '16	🏆🏆 4
○ Soave '18	🏆 2
○ Soave Cl. Cimalta '18	🏆 2
● Amarone della Valpolicella '14	🏆🏆 6
○ Soave '17	🏆🏆 2*
○ Soave '16	🏆🏆 2*
○ Soave Cl. Cimalta '17	🏆🏆 2*
○ Soave Sup. V. della Corte '16	🏆🏆 3
○ Soave V. della Corte '15	🏆🏆 3*
● Valpolicella Sup. '14	🏆🏆 3
● Valpolicella Sup. Ripasso '14	🏆🏆 3

Corte Gardoni

LOC. GARDONI, 5
37067 VALEGGIO SUL MINCIO [VR]
TEL. +39 0456370270
www.cortegardoni.it

CELLAR SALES
PRE-BOOKED VISITS
ANNUAL PRODUCTION 180,000 bottles
HECTARES UNDER VINE 25.00

Whether under father Gianni, or under his children Mattia, Stefano and Andrea, the Piccoli family winery has always represented a sure bet for those who want to explore Lake Garda's numerous appellations. The property is situated along the morainic hills that line the Garda basin, stretching for almost fifty hectares, half of which are vineyards. Their entire range of wines is defined by a style that pursues finesse and elegance, both aromatically and on the palate. Their Rosso di Corte is a Cabernet Franc with a substantial share of Merlot that expresses the qualities of the lake. If it impresses on the nose for its aromas of red fruit and aromatic herbs, in the mouth it highlights all the attributes of the territory, with a palate that's never exaggerated in its fullness and constantly supported by acidity and sapidity, making for a highly pleasant drink. Their Custoza Greoto '18, a simple and highly drinkable wine, also performed well.

● Bardolino Le Fontane '18	♟♟ 2*
● Becco Rosso '17	♟♟ 3
○ Custoza Greoto '18	♟♟ 2*
○ Fenili Passito '16	♟♟ 5
● Rosso di Corte '16	♟♟ 3
⊙ Bardolino Chiaretto Nichesole '18	♟ 2
● Bardolino Sup. Pràdicà '16	♟♟♟ 3*
○ Bianco di Custoza Mael '09	♟♟♟ 2*
○ Bianco di Custoza Mael '08	♟♟♟ 2*
○ Custoza Mael '13	♟♟♟ 3*
○ Custoza Mael '11	♟♟♟ 3*
● Bardolino Le Fontane '17	♟♟ 2*
● Becco Rosso '16	♟♟ 3
○ Custoza '17	♟♟ 2*
○ Custoza Mael '16	♟♟ 3*

Corte Moschina

VIA MOSCHINA, 1
37030 RONCÀ [VR]
TEL. +39 0457460788
www.cortemoschina.it

CELLAR SALES
PRE-BOOKED VISITS
ANNUAL PRODUCTION 95,000 bottles
HECTARES UNDER VINE 35.00
SUSTAINABLE WINERY

Patrizia Niero and her husband, Silvano, purchased the villa that houses Corte Moschina in the early 1990s, but it was under their children Alessandro and Giacomo that the winery turned a corner. The estate is situated in the eastern part of Soave and stretches along Calvarina, the old volcano that, along with nearby Crocetta, defines the geography of this hillside. Here in the area straddling Verona and Vincenza, Garganega has occupied a primary place for some time now. Their Soave Evaos '17 explores the most authentic and gutsy side of Garganega, pursuing the healthy rusticity of the region's grape, rather than great aromatic expressions. Here it's interpreted with an eye towards the grip, length and lively acidity conferred by the territory of Roncà. I Tarai, rather, goes in the exact opposite direction. It's mature on the nose, enriched by a curious fragrance, while on the palate it proves appealing, creamy and pervasive, making for a soft, succulent drink.

○ Soave Evaos '17	♟♟ 3*
○ Lessini Durello Brut M. Cl. 60 Mesi Ris. '12	♟♟ 5
○ Soave Roncathe '18	♟♟ 2*
○ Soave Sup. I Tarai '17	♟♟ 3
● Colle Alto '16	♟ 4
○ Lessini Durello Brut M. Cl. '14	♟ 4
○ Lessini Durello Brut M. Cl. '13	♟♟ 4
○ Lessini Durello Brut Nature M. Cl. Ris. '11	♟♟ 5
○ Recioto di Soave Incanto '15	♟♟ 4
○ Soave Evaos '16	♟♟ 3
○ Soave Roncathe '17	♟♟ 2*
○ Soave Roncathe '16	♟♟ 2*
○ Soave Sup. I Tarai '16	♟♟ 3*
○ Soave Sup. I Tarai '15	♟♟ 3*

Corte Rugolin

FRAZ. VALGATARA
VIA RUGOLIN, 1
37020 MARANO DI VALPOLICELLA [VR]
TEL. +39 0457702153
www.corterugolin.it

CELLAR SALES
PRE-BOOKED VISITS
ANNUAL PRODUCTION 80,000 bottles
HECTARES UNDER VINE 13.00
SUSTAINABLE WINERY

Elena and Federica Coati's winery gets its name from the district in which its situated, at the entrance to Marano, where the valley floor quickly becomes a series of terraces and buttresses leading up to the highest vineyards. Throughout the estate, which also comprises plots in nearby San Giorgio and Castelrotto, we find only traditional grapes, making for a selection whose style, year after year, proves increasingly centered on firmness and finesse. All the wines tasted this year delivered, making for another step towards a stylistic identity constituted of finesse and tension. Their San Giorgio '16 features an aromatic profile of wild fruit, medicinal herbs and pepper, all of which follows through perfectly on the palate. Here the wine reveals a firm body and great suppleness. Their Valpolicella Rugolin '18 is fresh in its aromatic expression, a relaxed red that delivers for its supple palate and great pleasantness.

● Valpolicella Cl. Sup. San Giorgio '16	♥♥ 5
● Recioto della Valpolicella Cl. '17	♥♥ 5
● Valpolicella Cl. Rugolin '18	♥♥ 3
● Valpolicella Cl. Sup. Ripasso '16	♥♥ 5
● Amarone della Valpolicella Cl. Crosara de le Strie '13	♀♀ 7
● Amarone della Valpolicella Cl. Crosara de le Strie '12	♀♀ 7
● Amarone della Valpolicella Cl. Monte Danieli Ris. '12	♀♀ 8
● Recioto della Valpolicella Cl. '15	♀♀ 5
● Valpolicella Cl. Rugolin '17	♀♀ 3
● Valpolicella Cl. Sup. Ripasso '15	♀♀ 5
● Valpolicella Cl. Sup. Ripasso '14	♀♀ 5
● Valpolicella Cl. Sup. San Giorgio '15	♀♀ 5

★Corte Sant'Alda

LOC. FIOI
VIA CAPOVILLA, 28
37030 MEZZANE DI SOTTO [VR]
TEL. +39 0458880006
www.cortesantalda.it

CELLAR SALES
PRE-BOOKED VISITS
ACCOMMODATION
ANNUAL PRODUCTION 90,000 bottles
HECTARES UNDER VINE 19.00
VITICULTURE METHOD Certified Biodynamic

The lengthy journey undertaken by producer Marinella Camerani is foremost a personal one in pursuit of harmony. Over these thirty years, the vineyards have grown denser, while the right soil and position for each cultivar have been chosen. She's embraced biodynamic viticulture, while in the cellar no invasive techniques are used. The result is a style that pursues the highest expression of the cultivar-territory bond. Kudos to their Valpolicella Ca' Fiui, a wine made with grapes from 15-year-old vineyards and aged in oak. It expresses great aromatic finesse, with wild fruit merging with Corvina's signature spicy notes. On the palate it's sapid, juicy and dynamic, a truly territorial wine made with fresh grapes. Their Campi Magri '16 is richer and more stratified on the nose, while their Mithas '15 proves to be the highest expression of their Macie vineyard — Corvina and Corvinone are harvested only when perfectly ripe, making for a wine of substance and character.

● Valpolicella Ca' Fiui '18	♥♥♥ 3*
● Valpolicella Sup. Mithas '15	♥♥ 8
● Valpolicella Sup. Ripasso Campi Magri '16	♥♥ 5
⊙ Agathe '18	♥♥ 4
● Amarone della Valpolicella Ruvain Adalia '14	♥♥ 8
● Amarone della Valpolicella Valmezzane '13	♥♥ 8
● Recioto della Valpolicella '16	♥♥ 6
● Valpolicella Laute Adalia '18	♥♥ 3
● Valpolicella Sup. Ripasso Balt Adalia '17	♥♥ 4
○ Inti '18	♥ 3
● Amarone della Valpolicella '10	♀♀♀ 8
● Amarone della Valpolicella '06	♀♀♀ 7
● Valpolicella Sup. Mithas '12	♀♀♀ 8

Famiglia Cottini
Monte Zovo

Loc. Zovo, 23A
37013 Caprino Veronese [VR]
Tel. +39 0457281301
www.montezovo.com

CELLAR SALES
PRE-BOOKED VISITS
ACCOMMODATION AND RESTAURANT SERVICE
ANNUAL PRODUCTION 1,000,000 bottles
HECTARES UNDER VINE 140.00
SUSTAINABLE WINERY

The Cottini family's winery is situated in the northeastern part of Valpolicella, in the Valdadige valley, where the climate cools quickly and the vineyards are refreshed daily by beneficial winds. Their vineyards span more than 100 hectares in two clearly defined areas. The terrain around their winery is dedicated to Bardolino and wines with geographic indication, while their plots in Tregnago, in the Issasi valley, give rise to their Valpolicella reds. Aromatic richness of fruit and firmness on the palate are defining characteristics of their selection. Their Amarone '15 took advantage of a great vintage to confer fruity fragrances, with red fruit preserves in the foreground followed by spicy notes and hints of medicinal herbs. In the mouth the wine opens with fullness and power, only to gradually gain in tension and sapidity and finally close with a long, crisp finish. Their Calinverno '15, a red made with overripe grapes that are subsequently dried, stands out for the fullness of its palate.

● Amarone della Valpolicella '15	♟♟♟ 8
● Calinverno '15	♟♟ 5
○ Oltremonte Sauvignon '18	♟♟ 4
● Valpolicella Sup. Ripasso '17	♟♟ 5
● Amarone della Valpolicella '14	♟♟♟ 8
● Amarone della Valpolicella '13	♟♟ 7
● Amarone della Valpolicella '12	♟♟ 6
● Ca' Linverno '14	♟♟ 4
● La Sogara Comis '13	♟♟ 3
○ Sauvignon '17	♟♟ 4
○ Sauvignon '16	♟♟ 4
● Valpolicella Sup. '15	♟♟ 4
● Valpolicella Sup. Ripasso '16	♟♟ 5
● Valpolicella Sup. Ripasso '15	♟♟ 4

Dal Cero
Tenuta Corte Giacobbe

Via Moschina, 11
37030 Roncà [VR]
Tel. +39 0457460110
www.dalcerofamily.it

CELLAR SALES
PRE-BOOKED VISITS
ANNUAL PRODUCTION 300,000 bottles
HECTARES UNDER VINE 40.00

Don't be misled by the size of their vineyards and production volumes, the Dal Cero's winery is firmly rooted to the land and its traditions. Their vineyards are situated along the eastern slopes of Calvarina, the extinct volcano overlooking Soave, and are managed with the utmost respect for the environment. The result is a small but select range of wines. When it comes to Valpolicella, the producer prefers to work with growers on a contract basis, so as to have more control during the various stages of production. Calvarina's force shines through in the Soave Runcata '17, a wine that offers up faint flowery hints and notes of white fruit, all of which might give you the idea of a delicate, light wine. But on the palate it amazes for its richness and, especially, its blast of acidity, the true signature of these hills' soil. Their Augusto '13 is a sparkling wine rich in aromas of fruit and croissant that impresses for its rigor, sapidity and pluck.

○ Soave Sup. Runcata '17	♟♟♟ 3*
○ Lessini Durello Dosaggio Zero Cuvée Augusto M. Cl. '13	♟♟ 5
○ Brut M. Cl.	♟♟ 4
○ Soave '18	♟♟ 2*
● Valpolicella Sup. Ripasso '16	♟♟ 3
● Valpolicella '16	♟ 3
○ Soave Sup. Vign. Runcata '14	♟♟♟ 2*
● Amarone della Valpolicella '13	♟♟ 7
● Amarone della Valpolicella '12	♟♟ 7
○ Pino Grigio delle Venezie Ramato '17	♟♟ 2*
○ Soave '17	♟♟ 2*
○ Soave Sup. Vign. Runcata '16	♟♟ 5
● Valpolicella Sup. Ripasso '15	♟♟ 4

Dal Maso

C.DA SELVA, 62
36054 MONTEBELLO VICENTINO [VI]
TEL. +39 0444649104
www.dalmasovini.com

CELLAR SALES
PRE-BOOKED VISITS
RESTAURANT SERVICE
ANNUAL PRODUCTION 300,000 bottles
HECTARES UNDER VINE 30.00
SUSTAINABLE WINERY

Last year we mentioned how Dal Maso is moving from Gambellara to the Colli Berici hills. Today it's worth noting how they're also gaining a foothold on the Lessinia hills, testifying to the attention that Nicola and his sisters Anna and Silvia are paying to the entire area around their Selva cellar. If Colli Berici gives rise to tight, energetic wines, those from Gambellara and Lessinia are defined by their finesse and grip. Their Merlot Casara Roveri '16 pours a lovely, intense ruby-red. On the nose it offers up aromas of sweet, ripe fruit enriched by the presence of medicinal herbs and flowers. In the mouth the wine proves full and forceful, bold even, endowed with a succulent palate that seems to go on endlessly. Their Pas Dosé '15 had a very interesting debut indeed. It's a sparkling wine with sophisticated, fresh aromas that unfold across a crisp, dynamic palate supported by the cultivar's trademark acidity.

● Colli Berici Merlot Casara Roveri '16	♟♟ 5
● Colli Berici Tai Rosso Colpizzarda '16	♟♟ 5
○ Lessini Durello Pas Dosé M. Cl. Ris. '15	♟♟ 5
● Cabernet Casara Roveri '16	♟♟ 4
● Cabernet Montebelvedere '17	♟♟ 3
● Colli Berici Tai Rosso Montemitorio '17	♟♟ 3
○ Gambellara Cl. Riva del Molino '17	♟♟ 3
○ Recioto di Gambellara Cl. Riva dei Perari '17	♟♟ 5
○ Gambellara '18	♟ 2
○ Gambellara Ca' Fischele '18	♟ 3
○ Lessini Durello Brut	♟ 3
● Colli Berici Merlot Casara Roveri '15	♟♟♟ 5
○ Gambellara Cl. Riva del Molino '07	♟♟♟ 2*
○ Gambellara Ca' Fischele '17	♟♟ 3

De Stefani

VIA CADORNA, 92
30020 FOSSALTA DI PIAVE [VE]
TEL. +39 042167502
www.de-stefani.it

CELLAR SALES
PRE-BOOKED VISITS
ANNUAL PRODUCTION 500,000 bottles
HECTARES UNDER VINE 60.00
SUSTAINABLE WINERY

Alessandro De Stefani has clear-headedly navigated Piave's wine sector, eschewing the easy commercial success of Prosecco and dedicating himself to making still wines that bring together fullness and character. The estate comprises three historic parcels, the Refrontolo hillside, Monastier and Fossalta, where native grape varieties and more recently planted cultivars are overseen with a keen eye towards minimizing the use of chemicals. Olmera is an original blend of slightly dried Tai, which is aged in oak, and Sauvignon that's matured in steel. The result is an aromatically intense wine that calls up hints of exotic fruit and flowers on the nose, while on the palate it proves energetic, sapid and long. Another wine that did well was their Kreda, a Refosco made with grapes from the clay-rich terrain of Le Ronche. It opts for a mature profile and a buoyant fullness.

○ Olmera '17	♟♟ 5
● Colli di Conegliano Rosso Stefen 1624 '15	♟♟ 8
● Kreda '15	♟♟ 6
● Piave Malanotte '13	♟♟ 3
● Solèr '16	♟♟ 4
○ Valdobbiadene Brut Nature Rive di Refrontolo '18	♟♟ 2*
○ Venezia Pinot Grigio '18	♟♟ 3
○ Valdobbiadene Brut	♟ 2
○ Vènis '18	♟ 3
● Kreda '15	♟♟ 5
○ Olmera '16	♟♟ 5
● Piave Merlot Plavis '15	♟♟ 4
● Solèr '15	♟♟ 4
● Stefen 1624 '13	♟♟ 8

Conte Emo Capodilista La Montecchia

via Montecchia, 16
35030 Selvazzano Dentro [PD]
Tel. +39 049637294
www.lamontecchia.it

CELLAR SALES
PRE-BOOKED VISITS
ACCOMMODATION
ANNUAL PRODUCTION 144,000 bottles
HECTARES UNDER VINE 30.00
SUSTAINABLE WINERY

Giordano Emo Capodilista's estate is situated in the Euganean regional park, with historic vineyards in the northern part of the area and more recent acquisitions to the extreme south. There are fewer than ten kilometers between the two sites, but they feature very different climatic conditions, from the almost pre-Alpine territory of Selvazzano to the decidedly more Mediterranean area of Baone. Merlot, Carmenère and white varieties are cultivated around their Villa Emo Capodilista, while Cabernet Sauvignon grows along the slopes of Monte Castello. And it's precisely this last that gives rise to their Ireneo '16, a Cabernet Sauvignon with a sunny, deep profile. On the nose aromas of dark fruit find a blast of freshness in Mediterranean shrub and balsamic whiffs. On the palate the wine reveals a full body and a rigorous dynamic of flavor. Their Donna Daria '16 is a more mature and complex wine. It's a supple, well-balanced passito that's redolent of candied fruit and spices.

● Colli Euganei Cabernet Sauvignon Ireneo '16	♥♥ 4
○ Colli Euganei Fior d'Arancio Passito Donna Daria '16	♥♥ 5
● Ca' Emo '17	♥♥ 3
○ Colli Euganei Fior d'Arancio Spumante '18	♥♥ 2*
● Colli Euganei Merlot Carlotto '16	♥♥ 3
● Godimondo Cabernet Franc '17	♥♥ 2*
○ Piùchebello '18	♥♥ 2*
○ Colli Euganei Pinot Bianco Rolandino '18	♥ 2
● Baon '15	♥♥♥ 7
● Colli Euganei Cabernet Sauvignon Ireneo '12	♥♥♥ 4*
○ Colli Euganei Fior d'Arancio Passito Donna Daria '06	♥♥♥ 5

Farina

loc. Pedemonte
via Bolla, 11
37029 San Pietro in Cariano [VR]
Tel. +39 0457701349
www.farinawines.com

CELLAR SALES
PRE-BOOKED VISITS
ANNUAL PRODUCTION 800,000 bottles
HECTARES UNDER VINE 45.00

Today the Farina family winery is managed by Claudio, Elena and Alessandro. It's bolstered by a deep past, but with the entrance of Elena and Claudio it's turned a corner, with a selection that's increasingly defined by, and true to, Valpolicella's historic wines. To reach higher production volumes, the Pedemonte producer draws on its own private plots as well as the support of numerous growers who deliver their crop to the winery. Amarone Montefante is their crown jewel, a wine that, with the 2013 vintage, calls up overripe fruit, vegetal notes and spices. On the palate the wine reveals a character closely tied to tradition — it's pervasive and soft in its warmer sensations, and endowed with a characteristic acidity. Their Ripasso Montecorna '17, a highly fruit forward wine rich in balsamic whiffs, goes in more for suppleness.

● Amarone della Valpolicella Cl. Montefante Ris. '13	♥♥ 8
● Amarone della Valpolicella Cl. '16	♥♥ 5
● Amarone della Valpolicella Cl. Famiglia Farina '15	♥♥ 5
● Valpolicella Cl. Sup. Ripasso '17	♥♥ 2*
● Valpolicella Cl. Sup. Ripasso Montecorna '17	♥♥ 3
● Nodo d'Amore	♥ 3
● Recioto della Valpolicella Cl. '17	♥ 5
● Amarone della Valpolicella Cl. '15	♀♀ 5
● Amarone della Valpolicella Cl. Montefante Ris. '12	♀♀ 8
● Valpolicella Cl. Sup. Ripasso Remo Farina '16	♀♀ 2*

Fattori

FRAZ. TERROSSA
VIA OLMO, 6
37030 RONCÀ [VR]
TEL. +39 0457460041
www.fattoriwines.com

CELLAR SALES
PRE-BOOKED VISITS
ANNUAL PRODUCTION 280,000 bottles
HECTARES UNDER VINE 72.00
SUSTAINABLE WINERY

Antonio Fattori has brought about major developments at this Terrossa producer. A winery originally focused on Soave's whites, today, thanks to insightful purchases in Valpolicella and a new facility in Col de la Bastia, they also make great regional red wines. Their estate also comprises plots in Lessinia, which give rise to monovarietals and sparklers made with the hillside's traditional grape, Durella. The grapes of their Motto Piane '17 rest for about a month in their drying loft, after which the wine ages both in steel and in oak only to be blended. On the nose it's dominated by ripe and pulpy yellow fruit while in the mouth it reveals fullness and softness, finding the right tension in acidity and sapidity. Among their reds we particularly appreciated their Ripasso '17, its expression of whole, ripe fruit and its supple, racy palate.

● Amarone della Valpolicella Col de La Bastia '15	▼▼ 6
○ Soave Motto Piane '17	▼▼ 4
● Valpolicella Sup. Ripasso Col de la Bastia '17	▼▼ 5
● Amarone della Valpolicella '15	▼ 8
○ Lessini Durello Brut 60 M. Cl. '12	▼ 6
○ Roncha '18	▼ 3
○ Soave Cl. Runcaris '18	▼ 2
○ Soave Danieli '18	▼ 2
● Amarone della Valpolicella Col de La Bastia '14	♀♀ 6
○ Lessini Durello Brut Roncà M. Cl. 36 Mesi	♀♀ 4
○ Soave Cl. Runcaris '17	♀♀ 2*

Il Filò delle Vigne

VIA TERRALBA, 14
35030 BAONE [PD]
TEL. +39 042956243
www.ilfilodellevigne.it

CELLAR SALES
PRE-BOOKED VISITS
ANNUAL PRODUCTION 50,000 bottles
HECTARES UNDER VINE 22.00

Carlo Giordani's winery is one of the loveliest here on the Euganean hills. Situated in the southernmost part of the appellation, the estate spans more than 20 hectares, most of which are dedicated to red Bordeaux varieties. The sunny, crisp climate allows Cabernet Sauvignon to ripen perfectly, and in this corner of Veneto it takes a quality that's at once Mediterranean and fresh. Matteo Zanaica has been integral, personally overseeing the vineyards and cellar, making for a range of wines that features noteworthy territorial expression. Renowned for their selection of powerful, gusty Cabernets, Filò delle Vigne offers a Merlot Casa del Merlo '16 of rare stylistic precision. On the nose it's dominated by sensations of fruit accompanied by medicinal herbs and spices. These follow through on its full, sapid and juicy palate, which lengthens decisively towards its finish. Their Cecilia di Baone '16, a wine aged in concrete vats, brings together the ripe, fruity richness of its aromas with a supple and highly drinkable palate.

● Colli Euganei Merlot Casa del Merlo '16	▼▼▼ 5
○ Calto delle Fate '16	▼▼ 4
● Colli Euganei Cabernet Cecilia di Baone '16	▼▼ 3
● Io di Baone '13	▼▼ 3
○ Terralba di Baone '18	▼▼ 3
● Volo '18	▼▼ 3
● Colli Euganei Cabernet Borgo delle Casette Ris. '12	♀♀♀ 5
● Colli Euganei Cabernet Borgo delle Casette Ris. '10	♀♀♀ 5
● Colli Euganei Cabernet Borgo delle Casette Ris. '06	♀♀♀ 5
● Colli Euganei Cabernet Borgo delle Casette Ris. '15	♀♀ 5

Silvano Follador

LOC. FOLLO
FRAZ. SANTO STEFANO
VIA CALLONGA, 11
31040 VALDOBBIADENE [TV]
TEL. +39 0423900295
www.silvanofollador.it

CELLAR SALES
PRE-BOOKED VISITS
ANNUAL PRODUCTION 20,000 bottles
HECTARES UNDER VINE 3.50

In a panorama in which even the smallest wineries produce at least 200-300,000 bottles per year, Alberta and Silvano Follador's estate is a rarity. If you consider their more than admirable commitment to avoid becoming a slave to numbers, the greatness of this winery lies in their stubborn attachment to their steep family vineyards. These are cultivated with the utmost respect for the environment, and interpreted without relying on sugars or fermentative aromas, but rather in pursuit of the most authentic territorial expression. Their Valdobbiadene Brut Nature '18 is a charmat that offers up faint fragrances of apple and flowers enriched by a curious vegetal nuance. On the palate the absence of residual sugars is compensated for by a pronounced sapidity, making for a long, elegant drink in which acidity and bubbles are perfectly balanced. Their intriguing Bianco Fermo is a Glera accompanied by a splash of Verdiso, Bianchetta and Perera. The result is a simple though highly pleasant wine.

○ Valdobbiadene Brut Nature '18	♛♛♛ 5
○ Bianco Fermo '18	♛♛ 3
○ Valdobbiadene Brut Nature M. Cl. '17	♛♛ 3
○ Cartizze Brut '08	♛♛♛ 4
○ Valdobbiadene Brut Nature '16	♛♛♛ 5
○ Bianco Fermo '17	♛♛ 3
○ Bianco Fermo '16	♛♛ 3
○ Cartizze Brut Nature M. Cl. '16	♛♛ 4
○ Valdobbiadene Brut Nature '17	♛♛ 5
○ Valdobbiadene Brut Nature '15	♛♛ 4
○ Valdobbiadene Brut Nature '14	♛♛ 4
○ Valdobbiadene Brut Nature '13	♛♛ 4
○ Valdobbiadene Sup. Brut Dosaggio Zero M. Cl. '12	♛♛ 3

Le Fraghe

LOC. COLOMBARA, 3
37010 CAVAION VERONESE [VR]
TEL. +39 0457236832
www.fraghe.it

CELLAR SALES
PRE-BOOKED VISITS
ACCOMMODATION
ANNUAL PRODUCTION 120,000 bottles
HECTARES UNDER VINE 28.00
VITICULTURE METHOD Certified Organic

Matilde Poggi's estate is situated in an area where climate and terrain figure centrally. Here in Cavaion Veronese, the narrow Adige Valley arrives from the north with its fresh air and suddenly opens onto the marly hills that surround Lake Garda to the south, making for a milder climate. The terrain here is characterized by a notable presence of gravel, and the vineyards primarily host the traditional grapes that make up Bardolino wine. Organic cultivation gives rise to a selection for which elegance and tension are key traits. Their Rod?n '18 is a light and lively colored Bardolino Chiaretto. On the nose it's dominated by sensations of wild berries and flowers, which prove enticing and endow the wine with a certain freshness. On the palate it reveals a lean body supported by acidity and sapidity, making for an appealing drink overall. Their Bardolino '18, on the other hand, goes in more for ripe, approachable fruit, finding freshness in Corvina's pepperiness. It's also characterized by a pronounced sapidity.

⊙ Bardolino Chiaretto Ròdon '18	♛♛ 2*
● Bardolino '18	♛♛ 2*
○ Camporengo Garganega '18	♛♛ 2*
● Bardolino Cl. Brol Grande '15	♛♛♛ 3*
● Bardolino Cl. Brol Grande '12	♛♛♛ 3*
● Bardolino Cl. Brol Grande '11	♛♛♛ 3*
● Bardolino '17	♛♛ 2*
● Bardolino '16	♛♛ 2*
⊙ Bardolino Chiaretto Rodon '16	♛♛ 2*
● Bardolino Cl. Brol Grande '16	♛♛ 3*
○ Camporengo Garganega '17	♛♛ 2*
● Quaiare Cabernet '16	♛♛ 4
● Quaiare Cabernet '15	♛♛ 4

Franchetto

FRAZ. TERROSSA
VIA BINELLI, 2
37030 RONCÀ [VR]
TEL. +39 0457460287
www.cantinafranchetto.com

ANNUAL PRODUCTION 35,000 bottles
HECTARES UNDER VINE 15.00

In recent years, the hillside to the east of Monteforte d'Alpone has become a new frontier for Soave. The vineyards, many of which are quite old, integrate in a territory that's less exploited for viticulture and have the opportunity to explore the sides of the Calvarina, Duello and Crocetta ridges, the ancient volcanoes that gave rise to Soave's noblest district. Here the Franchetto family have been working for generations, first as vine growers and then, as of the 1980s, as producers in their own right. Their most interesting wine is their Soave Recorbian '16. Made with Garganega and a splash of Chardonnay, it impresses for its aromatic complexity and gutsy tension. For their Durello sparkling ones, the vineyards are situated in the heart of Lessinia, in Vestenanova, at about 600 meters elevation. Their 2014 reserve is a Metodo Classico sparkling that's complex in its mineral notes. On the palate it features a crisp, cutting profile, lengthening with sapidity and a long finish.

○ Lessini Durello Brut M.Cl. Ris. '14	♟♟	5
○ Soave La Capelina '18	♟♟	3
○ Soave Recorbian '16	♟♟	3
○ Delle Venezie Pinot Grigio Val Serina '18	♟	3
○ Lessini Durello Brut Borgoletto '17	♟	5

Marchesi Fumanelli

FRAZ. SAN FLORIANO
VIA SQUARANO, 1
37029 SAN PIETRO IN CARIANO [VR]
TEL. +39 0457704875
www.squarano.com

CELLAR SALES
PRE-BOOKED VISITS
RESTAURANT SERVICE
ANNUAL PRODUCTION 50,000 bottles
HECTARES UNDER VINE 23.00

Tenuta di Squarano is situated on a tiny hill in San Pietro in Cariano, in a splendid villa built on Roman ruins. Today it's surrounded by cypress trees with vineyards sloping on the horizon down towards the plains. Most of their estate is situated directly around the villa, though there are smaller plots spread throughout Valpolicella's classic heart, making for a selection defined by the lean, elegant quality of the appellation's historic grapes. Only a few wines were presented this year, but there weren't any weak points. Octavius '12 is an Amarone reserve of great aromatic depth, with overripe fruit gradually giving way to aromatic herbs. On the palate it impresses for its soft and pervasive impact, with acidity conferring lightness — the result is a supple, long drink. Their Amarone '15, a wine endowed with a flavorful sapidity, is more approachable and fragrant.

● Amarone della Valpolicella Cl. Octavius Ris. '12	♟♟	8
● Amarone della Valpolicella Cl. '15	♟♟	5
● Valpolicella Cl. Sup. Squarano '16	♟♟	3
● Amarone della Valpolicella Cl. '13	♟♟	5
● Amarone della Valpolicella Cl. '11	♟♟	5
● Amarone della Valpolicella Cl. Octavius Ris. '10	♟♟	8
● Amarone della Valpolicella Cl. Octavius Ris. '07	♟♟	8
● Valpolicella Cl. Sup. '15	♟♟	3*
● Valpolicella Cl. Sup. '14	♟♟	3
● Valpolicella Cl. Sup. Squarano '14	♟♟	3

Gamba

VIA GNIREGA, 19
37020 MARANO DI VALPOLICELLA [VR]
TEL. +39 0456801714
www.vinigamba.it

CELLAR SALES
PRE-BOOKED VISITS
ANNUAL PRODUCTION 80,000 bottles
HECTARES UNDER VINE 15.00

The Aldrighetti family's winery is situated in the classic heart of the appellation, the Marano Valley, an area that's managed to maintain its agriculture without selling its terrain off for development (even when the appellation was navigating in shallow waters). Their selection draws in part on their private vineyards and in part on outside suppliers, all local, and pursues the territory's trademark suppleness and pressure rather than power. Their Amarone Campedel Riserva '12, a wine aged at length, is only released during the best years. On the nose it offers up aromas of overripe fruit, which intersect with spicy and mineral expression. In the mouth it reveals a full body and pleasantly rough tannins. Their Amarone Campedel '15, on the other, plays on lighter, more fragrant notes. It's an aromatically fruit forward wine, while on the palate it opens with fullness only to taper around a precious acidity.

● Amarone della Valpolicella Cl. Campedel '15	⚱⚱ 7
● Amarone della Valpolicella Cl. Campedel Ris. '12	⚱⚱ 8
● Amarone della Valpolicella Cl. Le Quare '15	⚱⚱ 6
● Valpolicella Cl. Sup. Ripasso Campedel '16	⚱⚱ 5
● Valpolicella Cl. Le Quare '18	⚱ 2
● Valpolicella Cl. Sup. Ripasso Le Quare '16	⚱ 3
● Amarone della Valpolicella Cl. Campedel Ris. '11	⚱⚱ 8
● Amarone della Valpolicella Cl. Le Quare '14	⚱⚱ 6
● Amarone della Valpolicella Le Quare Cl. '13	⚱⚱ 5

★Gini

VIA MATTEOTTI, 42
37032 MONTEFORTE D'ALPONE [VR]
TEL. +39 0457611908
www.ginivini.com

CELLAR SALES
PRE-BOOKED VISITS
ANNUAL PRODUCTION 200,000 bottles
HECTARES UNDER VINE 58.00
VITICULTURE METHOD Certified Organic

Sandro and Claudio Gini are among the most highly valued producers operating here in Soave, the large appellation that stretches along the volcanic hills lying to the north of Soave and Monteforte d'Alpone. The two brothers manage a sizable estate here that, as with Salvarenza, features century-old vines, as well as plots in Campiano where Chardonnay, Sauvignon and Pinot Nero are cultivated, together with vineyards for their new venture in the world of Valpolicella wines. Once again the Salvarenza '16 leads their large selection. It's a Soave that offers up complex aromas of ripe fruit, flowery notes and medicinal herbs. These reemerge on the palate, where exotic fruit and licorice are guided by acidity and, especially, sapidity, making for an energetic and yet highly elegant drink. Their new Amarone '10, from Tenuta Scajari, impresses right from the outset. It's a red with rich, mature aromas and a firm, tonic palate.

● Amarone della Valpolicella Tenuta Scajari '10	⚱⚱ 8
○ Soave Cl. Contrada Salvarenza V. V. '16	⚱⚱ 5
● Campo alle More '15	⚱⚱ 5
○ Maciete Fumé '16	⚱⚱ 4
○ Sorai '16	⚱⚱ 3
● Valpolicella Sup. Le Mattoline Tenuta Scajari '13	⚱⚱ 6
○ Soave Cl. '18	⚱ 3
○ Soave Cl. Contrada Salvarenza V. V. '14	⚱⚱⚱ 5
○ Soave Cl. Contrada Salvarenza V. V. '09	⚱⚱⚱ 5
○ Soave Cl. Contrada Salvarenza V. V. '08	⚱⚱⚱ 5
○ Soave Cl. La Froscà '11	⚱⚱⚱ 4*

Giusti Wine

VIA DEL VOLANTE, 4
31040 NERVESA DELLA BATTAGLIA [TV]
TEL. 0422720198
www.giustiwine.com

CELLAR SALES
PRE-BOOKED VISITS
ACCOMMODATION
ANNUAL PRODUCTION 200.000 bottles
HECTARES UNDER VINE 75.00
SUSTAINABLE WINERY

Some years back Ermenegildo Giusti, a businessman active in Canada, founded Giusti Wine, an estate situated in his homeland, Montello. International grape varieties alternate with local cultivars like Glera and the lesser-known Recantina across his 75-hectare property, and give rise to a selection that sees Prosecco as its cornerstone. The vineyards, which are spread throughout the Montello hillside, host the grapes that are best suited to each plot's soil and climate, allowing for ideal management of cultivation. Their Umberto I° '15 is a Bordeaux blend dominated by fruity sensations among which plum and cherry play a central role. In the mouth the wine's impact is rich and substantive, gaining in tension gradually as the palate unfolds. In terms of their Proseccos, we appreciated their Asolo Extra Brut, an elegant sparkling wine that finds its highest expression in its crisp, determined palate.

● Montello e Colli Asolani Rosso Umberto I° '15	♟♟ 8
○ Asolo Extra Brut	♟♟ 2*
● Montello e Colli Asolani Recantina Augusto '17	♟♟ 5
○ Pinot Grigio delle Venezie Longheri '18	♟♟ 3
○ Asolo Brut	♟ 2
○ Asolo Extra Dry	♟ 2
○ Chardonnay Dei Carni '18	♟ 3
● Valpolicella Cl. Sup. Ripasso '16	♟ 4
● Amarone della Valpolicella Cl. '14	♟♟ 8
● Antonio '15	♟♟ 5
○ Longheri Pinot Grigio '17	♟♟ 3
● Montello e Colli Asolani Recantina '15	♟♟ 5
● Montello e Colli Asolani Recantina Augusto '16	♟♟ 5
● Valpolicella Cl. Sup. '16	♟♟ 5

La Giuva

VIA TREZZOLANO, 20C
37141 VERONA
TEL. +39 3421117089
www.lagiuva.com

CELLAR SALES
PRE-BOOKED VISITS
ANNUAL PRODUCTION 20,000 bottles
HECTARES UNDER VINE 9.50
VITICULTURE METHOD Certified Organic

Alberto Malesani, who's accompanied by his daughters Giulia and Valentina, came to run a winery in the upper Val Squaranto valley solely because of his passion for wine and a deep bond with his homeland. Trezzolano is a pure, uncontaminated district where viticulture don't dominate, but rather alternates with pastures and woods, making for a classic, authentic landscape. The vineyards, which benefit in part from northern exposures, are cultivated with an eye towards preserving aromatic freshness while also respecting the environment. Their Amarone '15 took advantage of a great vintage to highlight the attributes of their hillside vineyards, bringing together intense fruitiness with a fresh blast of spices and aromatic herbs. In the mouth it comes through rich and soft, revived by acidity at the end, making for a juicy, long palate. As usual, their current vintage Valpolicella performed very well. This year, the 2018 proves fresh, peppery and highly drinkable.

● Amarone della Valpolicella '15	♟♟ 7
● Valpolicella Il Valpo '18	♟♟ 3
● Valpolicella Sup. Il Rientro '16	♟♟ 5
● Amarone della Valpolicella '13	♟♟ 7
● Amarone della Valpolicella '12	♟♟ 7
● Recioto della Valpolicella '16	♟♟ 6
● Recioto della Valpolicella '15	♟♟ 6
● Valpolicella Il Valpo '17	♟♟ 3
● Valpolicella Il Valpo '16	♟♟ 3
● Valpolicella Il Valpo '15	♟♟ 3
● Valpolicella Sup. Il Rientro '15	♟♟ 5
● Valpolicella Sup. Il Rientro '14	♟♟ 5
● Valpolicella Sup. Il Rientro '13	♟♟ 5

Gorgo

FRAZ. CUSTOZA
LOC. GORGO
37066 SOMMACAMPAGNA [VR]
TEL. +39 045516063
www.cantinagorgo.com

ANNUAL PRODUCTION 350,000 bottles
HECTARES UNDER VINE 50.00

Roberta Bricolo is heading the family winery. Founded almost 50 years ago, from the outset it has focused on making the wines for which this corner of Veneto is known: Custoza and Bardolino. The cellar is situated in a small facility immersed in the vineyards. Today the property is managed organically by a young, dynamic staff that's earned attention and respect among Verona's often competitive producers thanks to a selection of wines in which finesse is a defining trait. Summa is a Custoza made with grapes cultivated when super-ripe. It's characterized by an aromatic profile in which exotic fruit is accompanied by an elegant flowery expression and a timid mineral note that's waiting to emerge. In the mouth its fullness is governed by sapidity and a fresh acidity that lengthens the palate. Their Custoza San Michelin, a gutsy and almost cutting wine, also performed very well.

○ Custoza Sup. Summa '17	♀♀ 2*
● Bardolino '18	♀♀ 2*
⊙ Bardolino Chiaretto '18	♀♀ 2*
○ Custoza '18	♀♀ 2*
○ Custoza San Michelin '18	♀♀ 2*
⊙ Rosa di Monte Torre '16	♀♀ 2*
⊙ Bardolino Chiaretto Brut Perlato Rosa	♀ 2
● Bardolino Sup. Monte Maggiore '16	♀ 3
○ Chardonnay '18	♀ 2
○ Custoza Brut Perlato	♀ 3
○ Delle Venezie Pinot Grigio '18	♀ 2
○ Custoza '17	♀♀ 2*
○ Custoza San Michelin '17	♀♀ 2*
○ Custoza Sup. Summa '16	♀♀ 2*

Gregoletto

FRAZ. PREMAOR
VIA SAN MARTINO, 83
31050 MIANE [TV]
TEL. +39 0438970463
www.gregoletto.com

CELLAR SALES
PRE-BOOKED VISITS
ANNUAL PRODUCTION 200,000 bottles
HECTARES UNDER VINE 18.00

Luigi Gregoletto's winery is situated on the northern border of Conegliano Valdobbiadene, where the climate is cooler and vineyards gradually give way to chestnut trees. Despite the great success that Prosecco has enjoyed in recent years, Luigi has preferred to focus on a range of wines, not only sparklers. As a result, in his vineyards, one finds various grapes that have over the years been important to the territory, from international varieties to the historic Verdiso. Their Prosecco Tranquillo '18 explores the most authentic expression of the historic Treviso vineyard, without help from residual sugars or bubbles. On the nose it offers up faint notes of golden apple and wild flowers. In the mouth it's light-bodied and lean, and yet an intense sapidity confers tension and pleasantness. Their Colli di Conegliano Rosso '15 expresses fragrances of wild fruit and pepper, while the firm and juicy palate unfolds with elegance.

○ Conegliano Valdobbiadene Prosecco Tranquillo '18	♀♀ 2*
● Colli di Conegliano Rosso '15	♀♀ 5
○ Manzoni Bianco '18	♀♀ 3
● Merlot '17	♀♀ 3
○ Pinot Bianco '18	♀♀ 3
○ Verdiso '18	♀♀ 3
○ Chardonnay '18	♀ 3
○ Colli di Conegliano Bianco Albio '18	♀ 3
○ Conegliano Valdobbiadene Brut	♀ 3
○ Conegliano Valdobbiadene Extra Dry	♀ 3
○ Prosecco di Treviso Frizzante sui Lieviti '18	♀ 3
○ Conegliano Valdobbiadene Prosecco Tranquillo '17	♀♀ 2*
○ Manzoni Bianco '17	♀♀ 3

★Guerrieri Rizzardi

S.DA CAMPAZZI, 2
37011 BARDOLINO [VR]
TEL. +39 0457210028
www.guerrieri-rizzardi.it

CELLAR SALES
PRE-BOOKED VISITS
ANNUAL PRODUCTION 700,000 bottles
HECTARES UNDER VINE 100.00
SUSTAINABLE WINERY

Few wineries have an estate at their disposal that crosses so many appellations, with such varied soil types, climates and cultivars. Today Agostino and Giuseppe are leading the Rizzardis' winery, and in just a short time they've managed to revive the family's property, starting with Valpolicella, then Bardolino and Soave. Insight in the cellar allows them to produce wines capable of expressing the territory and highlighting its attributes. This year some of their workhorses are missing — their Amarones (because of a brutal 2014) and their Bardolino Tacchetto (because it's still aging). Their Ripasso Pojega '17 still put in an excellent performance. It's a wine with a full, juicy, highly pleasant palate and an aromatic profile that has, in recent years, acquired greater expression of fruit. Their Clos Roareti, a Merlot, also delivered, thanks to intensely fruity aromas and a palate that's both energetic and elegant at the same time.

● Valpolicella Cl. Sup. Ripasso Pojega '17	♟♟ 3*
● Bardolino Cl. '18	♟♟ 2*
● Clos Roareti '16	♟♟ 5
⊙ Rosa Rosae '18	♟♟ 2*
○ Soave Cl. Costeggiola '18	♟♟ 2*
○ Soave Cl. Ferra '16	♟♟ 3
⊙ Bardolino Chiaretto Cl. '18	♟ 2
○ Soave Cl. '18	♟ 2
● Valpolicella Cl. '18	♟ 2
● Amarone della Valpolicella Cl. Calcarole '13	♟♟♟ 8
● Amarone della Valpolicella Cl. Calcarole '11	♟♟♟ 8
● Amarone della Valpolicella Cl. Villa Rizzardi '13	♟♟♟ 7

Latium Morini

VIA FIENILE, 2
37030 MEZZANE DI SOTTO [VR]
TEL. +39 0457834648
www.latiummorini.it

CELLAR SALES
PRE-BOOKED VISITS
ANNUAL PRODUCTION 150,000 bottles
HECTARES UNDER VINE 40.00
SUSTAINABLE WINERY

If Valpolicella Classica confers fragrance and suppleness to its wines, the eastern part, by virtue of its heat and greater day-night temperature swings, endows its wines with greater fullness and a firmer tannic weave. It's just here, in the Illasi and Mezzane valleys to be precise, that we find the Morini brother's large estate. Their vineyards run from the gravelly valley floor all the way up to the surrounding hills at elevations spanning 100-300 meters. Smack in the center of the Mezzane Valley you find Campo Leon, a vineyard destined to one of their most important wines, an Amarone reserve that, with the 2014 vintage, is particularly fresh and penetrating in its aromas, with wild fruit crossing spicy and balsamic notes. On the palate the wine is full and energetic, pervasive in its softest notes, with alcohol and sugars taking on a central role. Their Soave Campo Le Calle '18 goes in on the fullness of ripe fruit.

● Amarone della Valpolicella Campo Leon '14	♟♟♟ 6
○ Soave '18	♟♟ 2*
○ Soave Campo Le Calle '18	♟♟ 2*
○ Amitor '18	♟ 2
⊙ Forziello '13	♟ 3
● Valpolicella '17	♟ 2
● Valpolicella Sup. Campo Prognai '15	♟ 4
● Valpolicella Sup. Ripasso Campo dei Ciliegi '16	♟ 3
● Amarone della Valpolicella Campo Leon '13	♟♟ 6
● Amarone della Valpolicella Campo Leon '12	♟♟ 6
○ Soave '17	♟♟ 2*
○ Soave Campo Le Calle '17	♟♟ 2*

Conte Loredan Gasparini

FRAZ. VENEGAZZÙ
VIA MARTIGNAGO ALTO, 23
31040 VOLPAGO DEL MONTELLO [TV]
TEL. +39 0423870024
www.loredangasparini.it

CELLAR SALES
ACCOMMODATION
ANNUAL PRODUCTION 450,000 bottles
HECTARES UNDER VINE 60.00

Lorenzo Palla oversees this historic Venegazzù producer, one of the first wineries to exhibit the great potential of Montello, an area that was valued as early as the late 1960s for its Merlot and Cabernet reds. Today the vineyards are spread out in different territories, starting with their historic Centopiante plot near their cellar and reaching all the way to Giavera, where primarily Glera is cultivated. Their range centers mostly on Bordeaux reds and Prosecco. Their Capo di Stato, a classically styled Bordeaux, put in an outstanding performance. Thanks to an excellent 2015, its fragrance open timid and hidden, only to gradually reveal a procession of wild wild, medicinal herbs and spices. These reemerge on the palate, in which Montello's trademark acidic tension shines forth. It's a wine that brings together power and rigor with character and elegance. Their Venegazzù della Casa '15 proves endowed with a full, succulent palate.

● Montello e Colli Asolani Venegazzù Sup. Capo di Stato '15	🍷🍷🍷 6
● Montello e Colli Asolani Cabernet Sauvignon '16	🍷🍷 3
● Montello e Colli Asolani Merlot Falconera '16	🍷🍷 3
● Montello e Colli Asolani Venegazzù Rosso della Casa '15	🍷🍷 4
● Montello e Colli Asolani Cabernet Sauvignon '15	🍷🍷 3
● Montello e Colli Asolani Rosso Capo di Stato '13	🍷🍷 7
● Montello e Colli Asolani Rosso Capo di Stato '12	🍷🍷 7
● Montello e Colli Asolani Rosso Venegazzù della Casa '13	🍷🍷 4

★Maculan

VIA CASTELLETTO, 3
36042 BREGANZE [VI]
TEL. +39 0445873733
www.maculan.net

CELLAR SALES
PRE-BOOKED VISITS
ANNUAL PRODUCTION 650,000 bottles
HECTARES UNDER VINE 50.00

Angela and Maria Vittoria Maculan are working alongside their father, Fausto, in managing the family winery. Theirs is a historic Breganze producer that has for more than sixty years promoted quality Italian wine throughout the world. The various plots are situated along the hills that from the plains seem almost to reach the Sette Comuni plateau, gentle slopes that host vineyards, cherry trees, olives and small woods. It's an area that enjoys sunny days cooled by the northern mountain breeze. Their Crosara is a Merlot that, with 2015, put in a high-caliber performance. On the nose it unleashes intense aromas of sweet, ripe fruit made light by notes of spices and medicinal herbs. In the mouth it comes through rich and powerful, with its tannic weave bringing the wine back to rigor and precision. The Torcolato is a mature, complex, enticing wine in which sweetness is perfectly contrasted by savoriness.

○ Breganze Torcolato '15	🍷🍷🍷 6
● Crosara '16	🍷🍷🍷 8
● Breganze Cabernet Sauvignon Palazzotto '16	🍷🍷 4
● Breganze Pinot Nero Altura '15	🍷🍷 5
○ Breganze Vespaiolo Valvolpara '18	🍷🍷 2*
● Brentino '17	🍷🍷 3
○ Chardonnay Ferrata '17	🍷🍷 4
○ Dindarello '18	🍷🍷 4
○ Tre Volti Brut M. Cl.	🍷🍷 3
○ Bidibi '18	🍷 2
● Breganze Pinot Nero '17	🍷 3
● Cabernet '17	🍷 2
⊙ Costadolio '18	🍷 2
○ Pino & Toi '18	🍷 2
○ Sauvignon Ferrata '18	🍷 4
● Speaia '15	🍷 3

Manara

LOC. SAN FLORIANO
VIA DON CESARE BIASI, 53
37029 SAN PIETRO IN CARIANO [VR]
TEL. +39 0457701086
www.manaravini.it

CELLAR SALES
PRE-BOOKED VISITS
ANNUAL PRODUCTION 150,000 bottles
HECTARES UNDER VINE 11.00
SUSTAINABLE WINERY

Valpolicella's agricultural fabric is made up of many different types of producers — small and medium-sized businesses, bottlers and large cooperatives. It's a sector that's exploited Amarone's great success, transforming the territory and the economy. The winery led by the Manara brothers, Lorenzo, Fabio and Giovanni, is among those who've stayed true to their private vineyards and the appellation's classic wines, proving capable of bringing out the best of their vineyards' positions. Their Amarone Postera '13 comes from a vineyard situated on a windy hilltop in the Marano Valley, a position that enjoys sun from morning to night. On the nose it offers up notes of fruit preserves and spices, with a curious nuance of coffee in the background. In the mouth its maturity is managed with tension and suppleness. Aromatically, their Ripasso le Morete '17 is dominated by sensations of ripe, intact fruit, while on the palate it proves soft.

● Amarone della Valpolicella Cl. Postera '13	♈♈ 6
● Valpolicella Cl. Sup. Ripasso Le Morete '17	♈♈ 3
● Amarone della Valpolicella Cl. Corte Manara '15	♈ 5
● Guido Manara '13	♈ 6
● Recioto della Valpolicella Cl. El Rocolo '17	♈ 5
● Valpolicella Cl. Val Polesela '18	♈ 2
● Amarone della Valpolicella Cl. Corte Manara '13	♉♉ 5
● Amarone della Valpolicella Cl. Postera '12	♉♉ 6
● Recioto della Valpolicella Cl. El Rocolo '15	♉♉ 5

Masari

LOC. MAGLIO DI SOPRA
C.DA BEVILACQUA, 2A
36078 VALDAGNO [VI]
TEL. +39 0445410780
www.masari.it

CELLAR SALES
PRE-BOOKED VISITS
ANNUAL PRODUCTION 55,000 bottles
HECTARES UNDER VINE 10.00
VITICULTURE METHOD Certified Organic
SUSTAINABLE WINERY

Founded in the late 1990s, Massimo Dal Lago and Arianna Tessari's winery is pioneering a rediscovery of the Agno valley, an area that stretches from Montecchio Maggiore up to the 'Piccole Dolomiti'. It's an intact landscape worth exploring, where intensive agriculture doesn't exist and the hills alternate between pastures and woods, the occasional vineyard and even rarer tracts of farmland. Their property extends along the eastern side of the valley, an area characterized by calcareous soils, and to the west, where basalt predominates. Their Masari '16 is a Bordeaux blend made primarily with Cabernet Sauvignon. On the nose it's deep, dominated by ripe red fruit, with spices and balsamic notes gradually gaining in force, enriching and bringing lightness to its aromatic profile. In the mouth it comes through full and powerful, perfectly supported by acidity and a close-knit, smooth tannic weave. Their Pinot Neros do a nice job interpreting the two sides of the valley with precision and finesse.

● Masari '16	♈♈ 6
○ Agnobianco '18	♈♈ 3
● Pinot Nero Costa Nera '17	♈♈ 4
● Pinot Nero San Lorenzo '16	♈♈ 7
○ Agnobianco '17	♉♉ 3
○ AgnoBianco '15	♉♉ 2*
○ Antico Pasquale Passito Bianco '08	♉♉ 8
○ Doro Passito '15	♉♉ 5
○ Doro Passito Bianco 10 Anni '07	♉♉ 5
● Masari '15	♉♉ 6
● Monte Pulgo '11	♉♉ 8
● Monte Pulgo '09	♉♉ 8
● Vicenza Rosso San Martino '15	♉♉ 3
● Vicenza Rosso San Martino '13	♉♉ 3*

★Masi

FRAZ. GARGAGNAGO
VIA MONTELEONE, 26
37015 SANT'AMBROGIO DI VALPOLICELLA [VR]
TEL. +39 0456832511
www.masi.it

CELLAR SALES
PRE-BOOKED VISITS
ACCOMMODATION
ANNUAL PRODUCTION 4,300,000 bottles
HECTARES UNDER VINE 670.00
SUSTAINABLE WINERY

The juggernaut being led by Sandro Bascaini's steady hand is one of Veneto's, and Italy's, most important wineries. A large estate stretches from Lake Garda to Valpolicella, extending to Soave and the Friuli plains. In addition to managing these properties, there are also collaborations with important Valdadige and Valdobbiadene producers and a large tract of land in Argentina. It's a complex business, but it's carefully overseen by a technical group led by Sandro's son Raffaele, who is supported by enologists, agronomists and market experts. The winery's beating heart, however, remains with Valpolicella's noblest son, Amarone. Their Campolongo di Torbe '12 offers up aromas of overripe red fruit enriched by the presence of medicinal herbs and pepper. In the mouth it proves powerful, bold and extraordinarily young in its palate, supported by firm, close-knit tannins. Their Vaio Armaron '13 expresses greater freshness and suppleness.

- Amarone della Valpolicella Cl.
  Campolongo di Torbe '12 ♟♟♟ 8
- Amarone della Valpolicella Cl.
  Vaio Armaron Serègo Alighieri '13 ♟♟ 8
- Amarone della Valpolicella Cl. '13 ♟♟ 7
- Recioto della Valpolicella Cl.
  Mezzanella Amandorlato '13 ♟♟ 8
- Valpolicella Cl. Sup. Toar '16 ♟♟ 4
- ○ Possessioni Bianco
  Serègo Alighieri '18 ♟ 3
- Valpolicella Cl. Sup.
  Monte Piazzo Serègo Alighieri '16 ♟ 5
- Amarone della Valpolicella Cl.
  Campolongo di Torbe '11 ♟♟♟ 8
- Amarone della Valpolicella Cl.
  Costasera Ris. '13 ♟♟♟ 8
- Amarone della Valpolicella Cl.
  Vaio Armaron Serègo Alighieri '11 ♟♟♟ 8

Masottina

LOC. CASTELLO ROGANZUOLO
VIA BRADOLINI, 54
31020 SAN FIOR [TV]
TEL. +39 0438400775
www.masottina.it

CELLAR SALES
PRE-BOOKED VISITS
ANNUAL PRODUCTION 1,000,000 bottles
HECTARES UNDER VINE 230.00

In the face of the great commercial success that's overwhelmed Conegliano Valdobbiadene, the Dal Bianco family have always maintained a low profile, dedicating themselves to developing their large estate, building a splendid, eco-friendly cellar and eschewing the limelight. It's an approach that's reflected in their selection, which is grounded primarily in Prosecco but also leaves room for a small but important line of still wines that bring out the best of Conegliano and Veneto. However, it's up to their loveliest Ogliano vineyards to provide the greats for Dal Bianco's most interesting wine, their Extra Dry '18. On the nose its close-focused fruitiness, accompanied by faint citrus and flowery nuances, proves enticing. In the mouth the wine exhibits the perfect fusion of bubbles, sweetness and acidity. Their Rizzardo '15 offers up intensely fruity aromas while on the palate it's supported by fullness and acidity.

- ○ Conegliano Valdobbiadene
  Rive di Ogliano Extra Dry '18 ♟♟ 5
- ○ Colli di Conegliano Bianco Rizzardo '15 ♟♟ 8
- Colli di Conegliano Rosso Montesco '15 ♟♟ 6
- ○ Conegliano Valdobbiadene Extra Dry ♟♟ 4
- ○ Conegliano Valdobbiadene
  Rive di Ogliano Brut
  Contrada Granda '18 ♟♟ 5
- ○ Aether Ai Palazzi '17 ♟ 4
- ○ Conegliano Valdobbiadene Brut ♟ 4
- ○ Delle Venezie Pinot Grigio
  Dorsoduro Ai Palazzi '18 ♟ 4
- ○ Conegliano Valdobbiadene
  Rive di Ogliano Brut
  Contrada Granda '17 ♟♟ 5
- ○ Conegliano Valdobbiadene
  Rive di Ogliano Extra Dry '17 ♟♟ 5

Roberto Mazzi e Figli

Loc. San Peretto
via Crosetta, 8
37024 Negrar [VR]
Tel. +39 0457502072
www.robertomazzi.it

CELLAR SALES
PRE-BOOKED VISITS
ACCOMMODATION AND RESTAURANT SERVICE
ANNUAL PRODUCTION 50,000 bottles
HECTARES UNDER VINE 8.00

Antonio and Stefano Mazzi's estate is situated in the Negrar valley, San Peretto to be precise, along its eastern side. The entire property, which is fewer than ten hectares, is divided up according to the characteristics of the plots — Poiega, Villa, Castel and Calcarole — with only the best grapes used. Their cellar, which integrates perfectly with the ancient, rural farmstead, hosts all stages of production, making for wines of notable precision and clarity. Their Sanperetto '16 is a one of Valpolicella Superiore's most interesting interpretations, a wine free of partial-drying that highlights the aromatic finesse and tension that are the trademark of the territory's grapes. Aromatically it's dominated by wild fruit and pepper, while the palate moves supplely and succulently, perfectly supported by sapidity and acidity. Their Poiega '16, a ripe and harmoniously drinkable wine, plays on Valpolicella's richness and pervasiveness.

Menegotti

Loc. Acquaroli, 7
37069 Villafranca di Verona [VR]
Tel. +39 0457902611
www.menegotticantina.com

CELLAR SALES
PRE-BOOKED VISITS
ACCOMMODATION
ANNUAL PRODUCTION 250,000 bottles
HECTARES UNDER VINE 30.00
SUSTAINABLE WINERY

Antonio and Andrea Mengotti are overseeing the family winery, a property founded in the early 1970s and today comprising some thirty hectares along the morainic hills that extend to the south of Lake Garda, particularly on mount Mamaor. Even if they operate in the area's two most important appellations (Bardolino for reds, Custoza for whites), Antonio and Andrea have managed to carve out a role as leaders in the production of Metodo Classico sparkling wines. Their intensely straw-yellow colored Custoza Elianto '17 ages at length in steel containers before being bottled. On the nose it ranges from notes of ripe yellow fruit to shrub, only to close with a lovely nuance of flint. In the mouth it proves rich and decisive, lengthening well towards its finish by virtue of acidity. Their Brut '15, half Chardonnay and half Corvina (vinified without the skins), features delicate aromas and a decisive, determined palate.

● Valpolicella Cl. Sup. Poiega '16	♟♟ 4
● Valpolicella Cl. Sup. Sanperetto '16	♟♟ 3*
● Amarone della Valpolicella Cl. Punta di Villa '14	♟♟ 7
● Valpolicella Cl. '18	♟♟ 3
● Valpolicella Cl. Sup. Sanperetto '11	♟♟♟ 3*
● Amarone della Valpolicella Cl. Castel '13	♟♟ 7
● Amarone della Valpolicella Cl. Punta di Villa '13	♟♟ 7
● Amarone della Valpolicella Cl. Punta di Villa '12	♟♟ 7
● Recioto della Valpolicella Cl. Le Calcarole '13	♟♟ 5
● Valpolicella Cl. '17	♟♟ 3
● Valpolicella Cl. Sup. Poiega '14	♟♟ 4

○ Custoza Sup. Elianto '17	♟♟ 3*
⊙ Bardolino Chiaretto '18	♟♟ 2*
○ Brut M. Cl. '15	♟♟ 4
○ Custoza '18	♟♟ 2*
● Bardolino '18	♟ 2
○ Biancospino Frizzante	♟ 2
○ Extra Dry M. Cl.	♟ 3
● Geodoro '15	♟ 5
○ Lugana '18	♟ 3
○ Brut M. Cl. '14	♟♟ 4
○ Custoza '16	♟♟ 2*
○ Custoza Sup. Elianto '16	♟♟ 3*
● Mezzacosta '15	♟♟ 3

Merotto

Loc. Col San Martino
via Scandolera, 21
31010 Farra di Soligo [TV]
Tel. +39 0438989000
www.merotto.it

CELLAR SALES
PRE-BOOKED VISITS
ANNUAL PRODUCTION 610,000 bottles
HECTARES UNDER VINE 28.00

Graziano Merotto has affirmed his status as one of Prosecco di Valdobbiadene's most important interpreters, bolstered by a vineyard that spans some of the appellation's best positions and a insight into the potential of the area's grapes. This year there's plenty of news at Via Scandolera, from enlarging their cellar to the creation of a shop immersed in their vineyards. The latter was made possible by renovations of an old farmhouse, thus allowing visitors to enjoy the fragrance of the vineyards, their peace and quiet. Their most interesting new release this year is a Brut Integral, an elegant wine in its pure aromas and palate that explores the hidden, more austere qualities of the appellation. But their Graziano Merotto, made with grapes from their best Col San Martino vineyards, once again leads the selection. Intoxicating aromas of flowers and white fruit are accompanied by a background note of citrus. On the palate it's sapid and delicate, revealing the perfect fusion between sweetness, acidity and bubbles. Their Dry La Primavera di Barbera is a ripe, pervasive and creamy wine.

○ Valdobbiadene Brut Rive di Col San Martino Cuvée del Fondatore Graziano Merotto '18	♛♛♛ 4*
○ Cartizze '18	♛♛ 5
○ Le Fare Extra Brut	♛♛ 3
● Rosso Dogato '15	♛♛ 4
○ Valdobbiadene Brut Bareta	♛♛ 3
○ Valdobbiadene Brut Integral '18	♛♛ 3
○ Valdobbiadene Dry La Primavera di Barbara '18	♛♛ 3
○ Valdobbiadene Extra Dry Castèl '18	♛♛ 4
○ Valdobbiadene Extra Dry Colbelo	♛♛ 3
⊙ Grani Rosa di Nero Brut	♛ 3
○ Valdobbiadene Brut Rive di Col San Martino Cuvée del Fondatore Graziano Merotto '17	♛♛♛ 4*

Ornella Molon

fraz. Campodipietra
via Risorgimento, 40
31040 Salgareda [TV]
Tel. +39 0422804807
www.ornellamolon.it

CELLAR SALES
PRE-BOOKED VISITS
RESTAURANT SERVICE
ANNUAL PRODUCTION 500,000 bottles
HECTARES UNDER VINE 42.00
SUSTAINABLE WINERY

This Campodipietra winery represents a sure bet for those who love wines from the plains of Venice, Treviso and Udine. It's a generous land in which gravel and deep layers of clay alternate. Here Ornella and Giancarlo Traverso, along with their children Stefano, Alex and Loris, devote themselves to cultivating more than 40 hectares of terrain, transforming the grapes into forthright, authentic wines. Their selection features early-drinking wines and more ambitious versions, where richness is never for its own sake but an instrument for realizing the territory's potential. Their Piave Malanotte '12 is a Raboso made with old vineyards and that avails itself of a small share of dried grapes, then aged at lengthen oak. Today it offers up aromas in which fruit, fresh hints and more evolved, deeper notes alternate in turn. On the palate it impresses for its fullness and power, refreshed by notes of medicinal herbs and its trademark acidity. Their Rosso di Villa '15 opts instead for greater aromatic finesse and elegance on the palate.

○ Bianco di Ornella '15	♛♛ 5
● Piave Malanotte '12	♛♛ 8
● Piave Merlot Rosso di Villa '15	♛♛ 5
● Piave Raboso '13	♛♛ 5
○ Prosecco di Treviso Brut	♛ 2
○ Prosecco di Treviso Extra Dry	♛ 3
○ Traminer '18	♛ 3
● Vite Rossa '15	♛ 5
○ Bianco di Ornella '14	♛♛ 5
○ Bianco di Ornella '13	♛♛ 4
● Piave Malanotte '12	♛♛ 8
● Piave Merlot Rosso di Villa '12	♛♛ 5
○ Traminer '17	♛♛ 3
● Venezia Merlot Rosso di Villa '13	♛♛ 6
● Vite Rossa '13	♛♛ 4

Monte Cillario

FRAZ. PARONA DI VALPOLICELLA
VIA SANTA CRISTINA, 1B
37124 VERONA
TEL. +39 045941387
www.montecillariovini.com

CELLAR SALES
PRE-BOOKED VISITS
ANNUAL PRODUCTION 22,000 bottles
HECTARES UNDER VINE 30.00
SUSTAINABLE WINERY

Some 10 years ago, the Marchesini family moved on from a collaboration with a large, local cooperative to launch their own production. They're bolstered by extensive experience in viticulture and a large estate that alternates the plains vineyards of Quar and Parona (used for their whites and simpler wines), with the hillside plots of San Dionigi and Monte Cillario, which provide the partially-dried grapes for their premium wines. The luminous shine of their Amarone Ego Sum '15 anticipates close-focused aromas in which fruit takes center stage, enriched by mineral nuances and medicinal herbs. On the palate it succeeds in the difficult work of conferring power and drinkability, thanks to its sapidity and a particularly smooth tannic weave. Their Valpolicella Euphoria '16, a wine that feature ripe fruit accompanied by a hint of oak, also did well, even if it possesses less character.

● Amarone della Valpolicella Casa Erbisti '15	♟♟ 6
● Amarone della Valpolicella Ego Sum '15	♟♟ 6
● Valpolicella Essentia '17	♟♟ 3
● Valpolicella Sup. Euphoria '16	♟♟ 3
● Valpolicella Sup. Ripasso Excellentia '16	♟♟ 4
● Recioto della Valpolicella San Dionigi '17	♟ 4
● Valpolicella Marchesini '18	♟ 3
● Valpolicella Sup. Borgo Antico '16	♟ 3
● Valpolicella Sup. Ripasso Berari '16	♟ 4
● Amarone della Valpolicella Casa Erbisti '14	♟♟ 6
● Amarone della Valpolicella Casa Erbisti '13	♟♟ 6
● Amarone della Valpolicella Rinaldo Marchesini Ris. '12	♟♟ 7
● Valpolicella Marchesini '17	♟♟ 3

Monte dall'Ora

LOC. CASTELROTTO
VIA MONTE DALL'ORA, 5
37029 SAN PIETRO IN CARIANO [VR]
TEL. +39 0457704462
www.montedallora.com

CELLAR SALES
PRE-BOOKED VISITS
ANNUAL PRODUCTION 35,000 bottles
HECTARES UNDER VINE 6.00
VITICULTURE METHOD Certified Organic

Carlo Venturini is one of Valpolicella's most notable producers. He's a man committed to his small estate situated on Castelrotto, one of Valpolicella Classica's southernmost hillsides, on a stretch of land that runs right up to the Adige's left bank. Along with his wife, Alessandra, he oversees a handful of organically managed hectares, making for a selection entirely dedicated to the area's traditional wines, interpreted with a keen eye to the dynamic, elegant character of its historic grapes. The long wait for their Amarone Stropa '11 was worth it. It's a deep wine, aromatically stratified, in which complexity hides an almost unexpected freshness characterized by sweet cherry and thyme, plums and pepper, making for a palate that's both energetic and relaxed at the same time. Their buoyant Recioto Sant'Ulderico '12 also delivered, while their Camporenzo '16, a Valpolicella Superiore, brings together generous aromas of fruit with an elegant palate.

● Amarone della Valpolicella Cl. Stropa '11	♟♟ 8
● Recioto della Valpolicella Cl. Sant' Ulderico '12	♟♟ 6
● Valpolicella Cl. Sup. Camporenzo '16	♟♟ 4
● Valpolicella Cl. Sup. Ripasso Saustò '16	♟♟ 5
● Valpolicella Cl. Sup. San Giorgio Alto '15	♟♟ 5
● Valpolicella Cl. Saseti '18	♟ 2
● Valpolicella Cl. Sup. Camporenzo '15	♟♟♟ 4*
● Valpolicella Cl. Sup. Camporenzo '13	♟♟♟ 4*
● Valpolicella Cl. Sup. Camporenzo '11	♟♟♟ 4*
● Valpolicella Cl. Sup. Camporenzo '10	♟♟♟ 4*
● Valpolicella Cl. Sup. Ripasso Saustò '07	♟♟♟ 5

★Monte del Frà

S.DA PER CUSTOZA, 35
37066 SOMMACAMPAGNA [VR]
TEL. +39 045510490
www.montedelfra.it

CELLAR SALES
PRE-BOOKED VISITS
ANNUAL PRODUCTION 1,000,000 bottles
HECTARES UNDER VINE 197.00

The Bonomo family's winery began operating more than sixty years ago, first along the morainic hills of Custoza and Bardolino, and now with plots in Valpolicella Classica, thus establishing itself as one of area's most notable producers. They avail themselves of several private vineyards, situated in some of the best parts of their respective appellations, making for a range of wines long defined by their pursuit of finesse and character, both when it comes to their fresher lake wines and their richer Valpolicellas. Their Custoza Ca' del Magro put in a performance for the ages. It's a 2017 that offers up rich fruit and flowery hints enriched by a subtle, spicy nuance. On the palate it unfolds with finesse, accompanied by sapidity and a vibrant acid tension. Their Amarone Lena di Mezzo '15 also did well. It's a wine that doesn't opt for banal softness, exhibiting richness and rigor instead.

○ Custoza Sup. Ca' del Magro '17	♟♟♟ 3*
● Amarone della Valpolicella Cl. Lena di Mezzo '15	♟♟ 8
● Amarone della Valpolicella Cl. Scarnocchio Lena di Mezzo Ris. '17	♟♟ 8
● Bardolino '18	♟♟ 2*
⊙ Bardolino Chiaretto '18	♟♟ 2*
○ Custoza '18	♟♟ 2*
● Valpolicella Cl. Sup. Lena di Mezzo '17	♟♟ 3
● Valpolicella Cl. Lena di Mezzo '18	♟ 3
○ Custoza Sup. Ca' del Magro '16	♟♟♟ 3*
○ Custoza Sup. Ca' del Magro '15	♟♟♟ 3*
○ Custoza Sup. Ca' del Magro '14	♟♟♟ 3*
○ Custoza Sup. Ca' del Magro '13	♟♟♟ 3*
○ Custoza Sup. Ca' del Magro '12	♟♟♟ 2*
○ Custoza Sup. Ca' del Magro '11	♟♟♟ 2*

Monte Santoccio

LOC. SANTOCCIO, 6
37022 FUMANE [VR]
TEL. +39 3496461223
www.montesantoccio.it

CELLAR SALES
ANNUAL PRODUCTION 40,000 bottles
HECTARES UNDER VINE 6.00

Nicola Ferrari, along with his wife, Laura, oversees this small estate situated along the ridge that divides the valley of Marano from Fumane. Their vineyards alternate between overhead trellis and VSP systems. In the cellar tradition reigns supreme, less in the choice of containers and length of maceration than in the style of the wines, whose fullness is always well-balanced with the acidity that comes with the territory's grapes. Their Recioto '15 has two distinct characters. On the one hand there's its aromatic profile, dominated by notes of dried fruit, dates, strawberry preserves and spices. On the other its palate reveals a measured sweetness that's never overwhelming, finding its balance through its vibrant acidity. Their Amarone '15 opts for greater fragrance and suppleness.

● Amarone della Valpolicella Cl. '15	♟♟ 7
● Recioto della Valpolicella Cl. '15	♟♟ 5
● Valpolicella Cl. '18	♟ 2
● Valpolicella Cl. Sup. '17	♟ 2
● Valpolicella Cl. Sup. Ripasso '17	♟ 4
● Amarone della Valpolicella Cl. '13	♛♟ 7
● Amarone della Valpolicella Cl. '12	♛♟ 7
● Recioto della Valpolicella Cl. Amandorlato '14	♛♟ 5
● Valpolicella Cl. Sup. '15	♛♟ 2*
● Valpolicella Cl. Sup. '14	♛♟ 2*
● Valpolicella Cl. Sup. Ripasso '15	♛♟ 4
● Valpolicella Cl. Sup. Ripasso '13	♛♟ 4
● Valpolicella Cl. Sup. Ripasso '12	♛♟ 4

Monte Tondo

LOC. MONTE TONDO
VIA SAN LORENZO, 89
37038 SOAVE [VR]
TEL. +39 0457680347
www.montetondo.it

CELLAR SALES
PRE-BOOKED VISITS
ACCOMMODATION
ANNUAL PRODUCTION 200,000 bottles
HECTARES UNDER VINE 32.00

The years go by but Gino Magnabosco is still firmly in control at Monte Tondo, a producer that has, over time, managed to enlarge its horizons to Valpolicella while also maintaining its headquarters in Soave. Their vineyards span more than thirty hectares in the two territories, with highly-prized positions on Monte Foscarino and Monte Tondo. Their range features young wines with a relaxed and fragrant style, and premium wines that more thoroughly explore the character each vineyard bestows. Casette Foscarin and Foscarin Slavinus, both 2017s, are made with grapes from two plots on Monte Foscarino, where the black earth makes its volcanic origins evident. The former is redolent of ripe, yellow fruit and citrus, with well-integrated notes of oak. The palate proves firm, succulent, and closes with a long finish. The latter expresses more delicate fragrances, which follow through well on an elegant palate characterized by nice acidic tension.

○ Soave Cl. Casette Foscarin '17		♟♟ 3*
○ Soave Cl. Sup. Foscarin Slavinus '17		♟♟ 4
● Amarone della Valpolicella '15		♟♟ 6
● Amarone della Valpolicella Ris. '11		♟♟ 6
○ Brut '18		♟ 3
○ Garganega Bru M. Cl. '16		♟ 3
○ Soave Cl. Monte Tondo '18		♟ 2
● Valpolicella Ripasso Campo Grande '16		♟ 4
● Valpolicella Sup. San Pietro '17		♟ 2
○ Soave Cl. Monte Tondo '06		♟♟♟ 2*
● Amarone della Valpolicella '14		♟♟ 6
○ Recioto di Soave Nettare di Bacco '16		♟♟ 4
○ Soave Cl. Casette Foscarin '16		♟♟ 3*
○ Soave Cl. Sup. Foscarin Slavinus '16		♟♟ 4

Cantina Sociale di Monteforte d'Alpone

VIA XX SETTEMBRE, 24
37032 MONTEFORTE D'ALPONE [VR]
TEL. +39 0457610110
www.cantinadimonteforte.it

CELLAR SALES
PRE-BOOKED VISITS
ANNUAL PRODUCTION 3,000,000 bottles
HECTARES UNDER VINE 1300.00

Look at the amount of land cultivated versus bottles produced and one immediately understands what type of producer Cantina Sociale di Monteforte is. It's bolstered by more than fifty years of experience and a sizable tract of land, though Gaetano Tobin sees to it that only a small part of the grapes end up bottled, using only the best plots cultivated by the most trusted growers. Their approach to viticulture is increasingly concerned with environmental impact, making for a selection in which simple, fragrant wines alternate with more ambitious, sophisticated versions. Their Soave Castellaro '17 is a monovarietal Garganega made with grapes cultivated on the hill of the same name. The wine is aged half in steel and half in oak. On the nose it offers up notes of ripe white fruit, which give way to fresh, flowery sensations and hints of citrus. In the mouth it unfolds with tension and sapidity, proving elegant and very long. Their Soave Foscarino '17, a fresher, racier wine, also delivered.

○ Soave Cl. Sup. Castellaro '17		♟♟ 2*
● Amarone della Valpolicella Tolotti '16		♟♟ 5
○ Soave Cl. Foscarino '17		♟♟ 3
○ Soave Cl. Il Vicario '18		♟♟ 2*
● Valpolicella Ripasso Clivus '17		♟♟ 2*
● Clivus Rosso '16		♟ 3
○ Garda Pinot Grigio Clivus '18		♟ 3
○ Soave Cl. Clivus '18		♟ 2
○ Soave Cl. Sup. Vign. di Castellaro '15		♟♟♟ 2*
○ Recioto di Soave Cl. Sigillo '15		♟♟ 3
○ Soave Cl. Clivus '17		♟♟ 2*
○ Soave Cl. Foscarino '16		♟♟ 3*
○ Soave Cl. Sup. Castellaro '16		♟♟ 2*
○ Soave Cl. Vicario '17		♟♟ 2*

Montegrande

VIA TORRE, 2
35030 ROVOLON [PD]
TEL. +39 0495226276
www.vinimontegrande.it

CELLAR SALES
PRE-BOOKED VISITS
ANNUAL PRODUCTION 250,000 bottles
HECTARES UNDER VINE 30.00

The Euganean hills, an area of volcanic origin, suddenly sprout up out of the Padana plains. It's a complex territory where just a few kilometers can make a difference in terms of climatic conditions. The same is true of soil types, which can be dramatically different from one area to the next. Raffaele Cristofanon oversees the family winery in Rovolon, in the northwestern part of the appellation, working to produce reds characterized by pluck and decisiveness. Ottomano is a 2016 Bordeaux reserve blend that offers up intense, fruit-forward aromas accompanied by mineral notes and sweet spices. A delicate nuance of oak emerges on the palate, where the wine proves compact and firm. Their Vigna delle Roche is from the same vintage but it's a fresher wine that's juicy and supple on the palate. Their Sereo '16 is a gutsy, satisfying Cabernet.

● Colli Euganei Cabernet Borgomoro '17	♟♟	3
● Colli Euganei Cabernet Sereo Ris. '16	♟♟	3
● Colli Euganei Merlot Corterocco '17	♟♟	3
● Colli Euganei Rosso Ottomano Ris. '16	♟♟	4
● Colli Euganei Rosso V. delle Roche Ris. '16	♟♟	3
○ Colli Euganei Bianco Erto '18	♟	3
○ Colli Euganei Fior d'Arancio Spumante '18	♟	2
○ Colli Euganei Moscato Castearo	♟	3
○ Colli Euganei Pinot Bianco Marani '18	♟	2
● Colli Euganei Rosso Momi '17	♟	3
○ Serenissima Brut M. Cl. '14	♟	4
● Colli Euganei Cabernet Sereo Ris. '15	♟♟	3
● Colli Euganei Rosso Ottomano Ris. '15	♟♟	4
● Colli Euganei Rosso V. delle Roche Ris. '15	♟♟	3

Monteversa

VIA MONTE VERSA, 1024
35030 VO' [PD]
TEL. +39 0499941092
www.monteversa.it

CELLAR SALES
PRE-BOOKED VISITS
ANNUAL PRODUCTION 23,000 bottles
HECTARES UNDER VINE 17.00
VITICULTURE METHOD Certified Organic

The Voltazza family only recently began growing wine grapes, coming off an experience in industry carried out a few kilometers from the Euganean hills. The idea to create a high-profile producer brought them to choose the area of Monte Versa, of the appellation's most renowned hills, where Bordeaux red grapes ripen well. Their range of products, made with organically cultivated grapes, is limited to a small number of select wines. Animaversa Rosso '16 is a Bordeaux blend that highlight's the territory's warmth. It's guided by a ripe, meaty red fruit accompanied by spicy notes and Mediterranean shrub, which confer freshness. On the palate it's full and juicy, well supported by acidity and a lively tannic weave. When it comes to their whites, we appreciated their Animaversa Manzoni '17, a wine whose aromas play on the fullness of yellow fruit, and whose palate features sapidity together with a commendable harmony.

● Colli Euganei Rosso Animaversa '16	♟♟	4
○ Colli Euganei Fior d'Arancio Spumante '18	♟♟	4
○ Colli Euganei Manzoni Bianco Animaversa '17	♟♟	3
○ Colli Euganei Chardonnay Animaversa '17	♟	4
○ Primaversa Frizzante '18	♟	3
○ Colli Euganei Fior d'Arancio Spumante '16	♟♟	4
● Colli Euganei Rosso Animaversa '15	♟♟	4
● Colli Euganei Rosso Animaversa '13	♟♟	4
● Colli Euganei Rosso Versacinto '16	♟♟	3
○ Versavò '17	♟♟	2*
○ Versavò '15	♟♟	2*

Le Morette

Fraz. San Benedetto di Lugana
v.le Indipendenza, 19d
37019 Peschiera del Garda [VR]
Tel. +39 0457552724
www.lemorette.it

CELLAR SALES
PRE-BOOKED VISITS
ANNUAL PRODUCTION 380,000 bottles
HECTARES UNDER VINE 32.00
SUSTAINABLE WINERY

Fabio and Paolo Zenato are carrying forward in their parents' footsteps, continuing to develop a somewhat atypical winery. Founded by their grandfather as a nursery after World War II, it gradually focused more and more on winemaking, first almost as an experiment and then with greater conviction. Today winemaking is the most important part of their business, though they continue to operate as a highly-specialized nursery, especially when it comes to the territory's traditional varieties. Their Lugana Riserva '16 is the result of the estate's best grapes aged at length in oak barrels. On the nose it offers up subtle, sophisticated aromas in which white fruit is only one sensation among many. It's accompanied by flowery notes and spices, with a subtle minerality that waits before fully emerging. The palate is full and juicy, extremely long and elegant. Their Lugana Benedictus, a white that features character and tension, also performed well.

○ Lugana Ris. '16	♙♙ 4
○ Accordo Passito '16	♙♙ 4
⊙ Bardolino Chiaretto Cl. '18	♙♙ 2*
● Bardolino Cl. '18	♙♙ 2*
○ Lugana Benedictus '17	♙♙ 3
○ Lugana Mandolara '18	♙♙ 3
● Perseo '16	♙ 5
⊙ Bardolino Chiaretto Cl. '17	♟♟ 2*
⊙ Bardolino Chiaretto Cl. '16	♟♟ 2*
○ Lugana Benedictus '16	♟♟ 3
○ Lugana Benedictus '15	♟♟ 3
○ Lugana Mandolara '17	♟♟ 3
○ Lugana Mandolara '16	♟♟ 3
○ Lugana Ris. '15	♟♟ 4

Marco Mosconi

via Paradiso, 5
37031 Illasi [VR]
Tel. +39 0456529109
www.marcomosconi.it

CELLAR SALES
PRE-BOOKED VISITS
ANNUAL PRODUCTION 25,000 bottles
HECTARES UNDER VINE 10.00

Eastern Valpolicella is characterized by higher average elevations with respect to the appellation's classic heart, as well as a warmer, crisper climate. These conditions are reflected in highly sophisticated, energetic wines that Marco Mosconi has managed to endow with unexpected suppleness and finesse. Their vineyards span some ten hectares on the valley floor, around the winery, stretching up to the nearby hills at 300 meters elevation. Their selection comprises both Soave whites and Valpolicella reds. Their Soave Superiore '15 took advantage of an excellent year to express its fruit immediately, almost explosively, while its full palate, supported by sapidity, lengthens with suppleness and finesse. Marco's journey in the world of Soave also takes an interesting turn with his Corte Paradiso, a wine that explores the fresher, zestier side of the appellation, while his Rosetta features richer, deeper aromas that reemerge on a firm, juicy palate.

● Valpolicella Sup. '15	♙♙ 5
● Amandorlato '15	♙♙ 3
○ Soave Corte Paradiso '18	♙♙ 2*
○ Soave Rosetta '18	♙♙ 3
● Turan '15	♙♙ 3
● Valpolicella Montecurto '17	♙ 3
● Valpolicella Sup. '13	♟♟♟ 5
● Valpolicella Sup. '12	♟♟♟ 5
● Amarone della Valpolicella '13	♟♟ 8
○ Soave Corte Paradiso '17	♟♟ 2*
○ Soave Rosetta '15	♟♟ 3
● Turan '13	♟♟ 3
● Valpolicella Montecurto '16	♟♟ 3
● Valpolicella Sup. '14	♟♟ 5

Mosole

LOC. CORBOLONE
VIA ANNONE VENETO, 60
30029 SANTO STINO DI LIVENZA [VE]
TEL. +39 0421310404
www.mosole.com

CELLAR SALES
PRE-BOOKED VISITS
ANNUAL PRODUCTION 230,000 bottles
HECTARES UNDER VINE 30.00

Lucio Mosole is a dynamic producer, but one who's also deeply connected to the territory and the cultivars that have defined it for centuries. In addition to traditional Tai and Refosco, the last century saw the introduction of Bordeaux varieties, Chardonnay and, especially, Pinot Grigio, which are often interpreted with lightness and fragrance. Lucio manages to express the power of the clay that dominates his vineyards' soil, and the character of the marine breeze that cross them, offering a wide, consistent range of wines. Hora Prima is made with Chardonnay aged in oak, Tai and Sauvignon (both of which are aged in steel). The result is a white that brings together aromas of ripe fruit with flowery, citrusy nuances. On the palate it proves crisp, taught and elegant. Merlot Ad Nonam and Cabernet Hora Sexta (both 2016s) opt for different profiles. The former is rich, fruity and generous, while the second is a quintessential Venetian wine thanks to its spicy, dynamic expressions.

Il Mottolo

LOC. LE CONTARINE
VIA COMEZZARA, 13
35030 BAONE [PD]
TEL. +39 3479456155
www.ilmottolo.it

CELLAR SALES
PRE-BOOKED VISITS
ANNUAL PRODUCTION 30,000 bottles
HECTARES UNDER VINE 8.00

Sergio Fortin, along with Roberto Dalla Libera, created this winery 15 years ago with the intention of producing exclusively high-profile wines that could express the territory of the Euganean hills. Inevitably, they chose the southern part of Baone, the warmest and sunniest in the district, which guarantees the perfect climate for Bordeaux grape varieties to mature. Gradually the winery has developed its estate and today they manage almost ten hectares in the enclave, with red grapes at the center of their production. Two reds for the ages, both 2016s. Their Serro is a Bordeaux, primarily Merlot, that succeeds in the difficult task of bringing together fruity richness with aromatic freshness. In the mouth it's sapid, succulent and elegant. Their Vignànima is a sunny, deep, spicy and satisfyingly drinkable monovarietal Carmenère that features smooth tannins and energy.

○ Hora Prima '17	♟♟ 4
● Lison-Pramaggiore Cabernet Hora Sexta '16	♟♟ 4
● Lison-Pramaggiore Merlot Ad Nonam '16	♟♟ 5
○ Ad Nonam Passito '17	♟♟ 4
○ Lison Eleo '18	♟♟ 3
● Venezia Cabernet Franc '18	♟♟ 2*
○ Venezia Chardonnay '18	♟♟ 2*
● Venezia Merlot '18	♟♟ 2*
○ Sauvignon '18	♟ 2
○ Tai '18	♟ 2
○ Venezia Pinot Grigio '18	♟ 2
○ Hora Prima '16	♟♟ 4
○ Lison Eleo '17	♟♟ 3*
● Lison-Pramaggiore Cabernet Hora Sexta '15	♟♟ 4

● Colli Euganei Rosso Serro '16	♟♟♟ 4*
● Vignànima '16	♟♟ 4
○ Colli Euganei Fiori d'Arancio Passito Luna del Pozzo '16	♟♟ 3
● Merlot Comezzara '17	♟♟ 2*
● V. Marè Cabernet '17	♟♟ 2*
○ Le Contarine '18	♟ 3
● Colli Euganei Rosso Serro '11	♟♟♟ 3*
● Colli Euganei Rosso Serro '10	♟♟♟ 3*
● Colli Euganei Rosso Serro '09	♟♟♟ 3*
○ Le Contarine '17	♟♟ 2*
○ Le Contarine '16	♟♟ 2*
● Serro '15	♟♟ 4
● V. Marè Cabernet '16	♟♟ 4
● Vignànima '15	♟♟ 4

Mulin di Mezzo

via Molin Di Mezzo,16
30020 Annone Veneto [VE]
Tel. +39 0422 769398
www.mulindimezzo.com

PRE-BOOKED VISITS
ANNUAL PRODUCTION 40,000 bottles
HECTARES UNDER VINE 6.00

Today one of eastern Veneto's most noteworthy winemakers, Paolo Lazzarin has managed to develop his winery, which started out as a producer of easy, simple wines, a common occurrence in the Lison Pramaggiore appellation. High density vineyards, low yields and careful grape selection bring out the richness of the territory, conferring substance and especially sapidity to their wines. Their range comprises a limited number of wines interpreted with vigor and energy. Great attention is paid to the cultivar that represents this territory more than any other, Tai (called Lison within the appellation). Their Classico '18 offers up aromas of yellow fruit refreshed by a flowery nuance. The palate is succulent, sapid and supple. Their Blanc '18 features deeper, characterful aromas, with notes of Mediterranean shrub meeting almond and exotic fruit. Its delicately salty palate is supported by a gutsy acidity.

○ Lison Cl. '18	🍷🍷 2*
○ Lison Cl. Blanc '18	🍷🍷 2*
● Lison Pramaggiore Merlot '16	🍷🍷 2*
● Rosso Molino '17	🍷🍷 2*
○ Lison Pramaggiore Chardonnay '18	🍷 2
○ Sauvignon '18	🍷 2
● Venezia Cabernet Sauvignon '17	🍷 2
● Il Priore '10	🍸🍸 4
○ Lison Cl. '17	🍸🍸 2*
○ Lison Cl. '16	🍸🍸 2*
○ Lison Pramaggiore Chardonnay '17	🍸🍸 2*
● Rosso Molino '15	🍸🍸 2*

Daniele Nardello

via IV novembre, 56
37032 Monteforte d'Alpone [VR]
Tel. +39 0457612116
www.nardellovini.it

CELLAR SALES
PRE-BOOKED VISITS
ANNUAL PRODUCTION 75,000 bottles
HECTARES UNDER VINE 16.00
SUSTAINABLE WINERY

Soave's classic heart is naturally delimited to the south by the hills outside Soave and Monteforte d'Alpone. Right in the middle you'll find Daniele and Federica Nardello's two most important properties, situated on two nearby hills, Zoppega and Tenda. The plots have very different characteristics. The first is balsalt, more yellow, while the second is rich in sand and silt, conditions that allow for wines that do a nice job expressing the territory, exploiting the different terrains so as to bring out each's unique attributes. Their Soave is made with grapes from Monte Zoppega. It offers up fruit-forward aromas enriched by the presence of dried flowers and a subtle hint of flint. 2017 gave rise to a full, mature palate characterized by a long, crisp finish. Their Turbian '18 is an entirely different wine, expressing great aromatic freshness and a palate whose backbone features notable acidity.

○ Soave Cl. Monte Zoppega '17	🍷🍷 4
○ Recioto di Soave Suavissimus '16	🍷🍷 4
○ Soave Cl. Meridies '18	🍷🍷 2*
○ Soave Cl. Turbian '18	🍷🍷 3
○ Blanc de Fe' '18	🍷 3
○ Recioto di Soave Suavissimus '14	🍸🍸 4
○ Recioto di Soave Suavissimus '11	🍸🍸 4
○ Soave Cl. Meridies '17	🍸🍸 2*
○ Soave Cl. Meridies '15	🍸🍸 2*
○ Soave Cl. Monte Zoppega '16	🍸🍸 4
○ Soave Cl. Monte Zoppega '15	🍸🍸 3*
○ Soave Cl. Monte Zoppega '14	🍸🍸 3*
○ Soave Cl. V. Turbian '17	🍸🍸 3*
○ Soave Cl. V. Turbian '16	🍸🍸 2*
○ Soave Cl. V. Turbian '15	🍸🍸 2*

Nicolis

VIA VILLA GIRARDI, 29
37029 SAN PIETRO IN CARIANO [VR]
TEL. +39 0457701261
www.vininicolis.com

CELLAR SALES
PRE-BOOKED VISITS
ANNUAL PRODUCTION 220,000 bottles
HECTARES UNDER VINE 42.00

The Nicolis family's historic winery has been active for more than half a century in the classic heart of Valpolicella, bolstered by a more than 40-hectare estate that alternates hillside vineyards with plots along the valley floor. It's a circumstance that allows Giuseppe, who oversees all stages of production, to use the best batches for each wine. Their selection is grounded almost exclusively in traditional wines and features elegance, grip. Amarone Ambrosan '10 is being released after a very lengthy stay in the cellar. On the nose it exhibits all the complexity that time has to offer, with fruit coming through overripe, almost stewed, and revived by the presence of medicinal herbs and a faint minerality. On the palate the wine achieves the perfect balance between alcohol, acidity and tannins, proving long, relaxed and juicy. Their Amarone '13 follows a similar aromatic profile, revealing a richer palate, however, that plays more on softness.

● Amarone della Valpolicella Cl. '13	♟♟ 6
● Amarone della Valpolicella Cl. Ambrosan '10	♟♟ 7
● Valpolicella Cl. '18	♟ 2
● Valpolicella Cl. Sup. Ripasso Seccal '16	♟ 3
● Amarone della Valpolicella Cl. Ambrosan '06	♟♟♟ 7
● Amarone della Valpolicella Cl. Ambrosan '98	♟♟♟ 7
● Amarone della Valpolicella Cl. Ambrosan '93	♟♟♟ 6
● Amarone della Valpolicella Cl. '12	♟♟ 6
● Amarone della Valpolicella Cl. '11	♟♟ 6
● Amarone della Valpolicella Cl. Ambrosan '09	♟♟ 7
● Testal '15	♟♟ 4
● Valpolicella Cl. Sup. Ripasso Seccal '15	♟♟ 3

Novaia

VIA NOVAIA, 1
37020 MARANO DI VALPOLICELLA [VR]
TEL. +39 0457755129
www.novaia.it

CELLAR SALES
PRE-BOOKED VISITS
ANNUAL PRODUCTION 50,000 bottles
HECTARES UNDER VINE 7.00
VITICULTURE METHOD Certified Organic
SUSTAINABLE WINERY

Marcello Vaona and his cousin Cristina oversee the winery founded by Giampaolo and Cesare more than fifty years ago. Situated in the heart of Valpolicella Classica, in the high Marano valley, everything here turns on the idea of balance, sustainability and authenticity. Their estate, which has been organically cultivated for some years now, features the traditional pergola system and more recent guyot vineyards, while their new cellar integrates harmoniously with the surrounding land. Wines are made in their new facility and the historic manor. Their Amarone Le Balze '13 begins closed on the nose only to reveal itself gradually with tones of overripe fruit, macerated flowers and pepper. In the mouth the wine changes gears. Governed by a close-knit tannic weave, it wins over the palate decisively, without concessions to sweetness. Their Recioto Le Novaje '17, on the other hand, opts for a supple, racy palate, impressing for its measured sweetness and pleasantness in the mouth.

● Amarone della Valpolicella Cl. Le Balze Ris. '13	♟♟ 7
● Recioto della Valpolicella Cl. Le Novaje '17	♟♟ 4
● Valpolicella Cl. '18	♟♟ 3
● Valpolicella Cl. Sup. I Cantoni '16	♟♟ 4
● Valpolicella Cl. Sup. Ripasso '16	♟♟ 4
● Amarone della Valpolicella Cl. Corte Vaona '13	♟♟ 6
● Amarone della Valpolicella Cl. Corte Vaona '12	♟♟ 6
● Amarone della Valpolicella Cl. Le Balze '11	♟♟ 8
● Recioto della Valpolicella Cl. Le Novaje '16	♟♟ 4
● Recioto della Valpolicella Cl. Le Novaje '15	♟♟ 4
● Valpolicella Cl. '17	♟♟ 3
● Valpolicella Cl. '16	♟♟ 2*
● Valpolicella Cl. Sup. Ripasso '14	♟♟ 3

★ Ottella

FRAZ. SAN BENEDETTO DI LUGANA
LOC. OTTELLA
37019 PESCHIERA DEL GARDA [VR]
TEL. +39 0457551950
www.ottella.it

CELLAR SALES
PRE-BOOKED VISITS
ANNUAL PRODUCTION 350,000 bottles
HECTARES UNDER VINE 40.00

Step-by-step, Francesco and Michele Montresor have been growing the family winery. Founded on the southern banks of Lake Garda, it has gradually been enlarged to include additional plots in the area, in Ponti sul Mincio and, recently, a precious presence in Valpolicella. These three components are overseen with passion, in pursuit of the best expression for each territory: the harmony and aromas of Lugana, the firmness of Lombard reds, and finally the power and rigor of Valpolicella. Their Lugana Molceo '17 is a reserve wine that explores the deepest qualities of the typology. On the nose it offers up tones of white flowers and citrus, with a delicate almondy note in the background. In the mouth the wine unfolds with tension and pluck, finishing crisp and juicy. Their Le Creete '18 features a similar style, with fresh and penetrating aromas and a crisp, balanced palate. When it comes to their reds, their Valpolicella Ripa della Volta '18 put in an excellent performance.

○ Lugana Molceo Ris. '17	♀♀♀ 4*
○ Lugana Le Creete '18	♀♀ 3*
● Amarone della Valpolicella Ripa della Volta '15	♀♀ 6
● Campo Sireso '16	♀♀ 4
○ Lugana '18	♀♀ 2*
○ Lugana Back to Silence '18	♀♀ 2*
⊙ RosesRoses Brut M. Cl.	♀♀ 4
● Valpolicella Ripasso Ripa della Volta '18	♀♀ 4
● Gemei '18	♀ 2
○ Nasomatto '18	♀ 2
⊙ RosesRoses '18	♀ 2
○ Lugana Molceo Ris. '16	♀♀♀ 4*
○ Lugana Molceo Ris. '15	♀♀♀ 4*
○ Lugana Molceo Ris. '14	♀♀♀ 4*
○ Lugana Molceo Ris. '13	♀♀♀ 4*

Pasqua - Cecilia Beretta

LOC. SAN FELICE EXTRA
VIA BELVEDERE, 135
37131 VERONA
TEL. +39 0458432111
www.pasqua.it

CELLAR SALES
PRE-BOOKED VISITS
ANNUAL PRODUCTION 15,000,000 bottles
HECTARES UNDER VINE 322.00

In just a few seasons, the Pasqua family have revolutionized their production, passing from reliable and technically impeccable wines to wines that can tell a story, express a territory and a vision of tradition. This change in gears was pushed for by Riccardo Pasqua, whose steady hand guides the winery today while also encouraging his technical staff to explore the potential of the territory and its grapes. Their Amarone Mai dire Mai '12, a wine intended as an interpretation of tradition, perfectly represents the new direction. Aromatic depth serves its crisp, powerful palate, one that's almost austere, putting the wine on an absolutely new level. Hey French is a new creation and even more intriguing. It's a blend dominated by Garganega with smaller shares of Sauvignon and Pinot Bianco. Produced on the Calvarina volcano, it brings together four vintages, making for great aromatic complexity and an elegant palate.

● Amarone della Valpolicella Mai Dire Mai '12	♀♀♀ 8
● Amarone della Valpolicella Famiglia Pasqua '15	♀♀ 6
○ Hey French	♀♀ 6
● Amarone della Valpolicella Cecilia Beretta '15	♀♀ 7
○ Soave Cl. Brognoligo Cecilia Beretta '18	♀♀ 4
● Valpolicella Sup. Mizzole Cecilia Beretta '17	♀♀ 5
● Amarone della Valpolicella Pasqua Mai dire Mai '11	♀♀♀ 8
● Amarone della Valpolicella Famiglia Pasqua Ris. '10	♀♀ 8
● Valpolicella Sup. Pasqua Mai dire Mai '13	♀♀ 8

★★Leonildo Pieropan

VIA CAMUZZONI, 3
37038 SOAVE [VR]
TEL. +39 0456190171
www.pieropan.it

CELLAR SALES
PRE-BOOKED VISITS
ANNUAL PRODUCTION 550,000 bottles
HECTARES UNDER VINE 70.00
VITICULTURE METHOD Certified Organic

Andrea and Dario Pieropan's winery is among those that have done the most over past decades to promote Soave and its wine. Their 70 hectares of organically cultivated vineyards have for some time also comprised plots in nearby Valpolicella, making for a limited selection of wines that highlight the extraordinary bond that exists between grape, vineyard and winemaker. Their new cellar in Soave, situated on the ridge by the town's outer wall, hosts all stages of production for the area's wines, while their Valpolicella reds are made in their Villa Cipolla cellar in Tregnago. Their Soave Calvarino '17 put in a performance for the ages. Made with grapes cultivated on the western side of the appellation's 'classic' district, it exploits a noteworthy presence of Trebbiano di Soave for its intensely fruity and flowery perfumes. These reemerge on its taut, juicy and very long palate. Their La Rocca '17, a monovarietal Garganega Soave, joins great finesse with richness and maturity. Their excellent Amarone '15 is a red that brings together power and tension.

○ Soave Cl. Calvarino '17	▼▼▼ 4*
● Amarone della Valpolicella '15	▼▼ 6
○ Soave Cl. La Rocca '17	▼▼ 5
○ Soave Cl. '18	▼▼ 3
● Valpolicella Sup. Ruberpan '16	▼▼ 4
○ Soave Cl. Calvarino '09	♀♀♀ 4*
○ Soave Cl. Calvarino '08	♀♀♀ 4
○ Soave Cl. Calvarino '07	♀♀♀ 4
○ Soave Cl. Calvarino '06	♀♀♀ 4
○ Soave Cl. Calvarino '05	♀♀♀ 3
○ Soave Cl. Calvarino '04	♀♀♀ 3
○ Soave Cl. Calvarino '03	♀♀♀ 3
○ Soave Cl. Calvarino '02	♀♀♀ 3
○ Soave Cl. La Rocca '10	♀♀♀ 5
○ Soave Cl. La Rocca '02	♀♀♀ 5

Albino Piona

FRAZ. CUSTOZA
VIA BELLAVISTA, 48
37060 SOMMACAMPAGNA [VR]
TEL. +39 045516055
www.albinopiona.it

CELLAR SALES
PRE-BOOKED VISITS
ANNUAL PRODUCTION 350,000 bottles
HECTARES UNDER VINE 77.00

The Piona brothers' winery can be found at the foot of the Custoza hills, immersed in the vineyards and somewhat off the beaten track with respect to more popular producers. It's equipped with facilities and technology that guarantee respect for the environment and Garda's historic wines. Their vineyards are spread out on various parcels, from Sommacampagna to Valeggio, Sona and Villafranca, and every plot hosts the cultivars best suited to the climatic conditions and territory. Their Bardolino SP '16 explores the hidden qualities of this regional wine thanks to the great care taken in the cellar and the patience with which its released. Its pale color anticipates aromas in which fruit emerges gradually and then merge with smoky notes, hints of dried flower and pepper. On the palate it's crisp, supported by trademark acidity and endowed with a captivating length that brings out its sapidity.

● Bardolino SP '16	▼▼ 2*
● Bardolino '18	▼▼ 2*
⊙ Bardolino Chiaretto '18	▼▼ 2*
○ Custoza '18	▼▼ 2*
○ Verde Piona Frizzante	▼ 2
● Bardolino '13	♀♀♀ 2*
● Bardolino '17	♀♀ 2*
⊙ Bardolino Chiaretto '17	♀♀ 2*
⊙ Bardolino Chiaretto '16	♀♀ 2*
● Bardolino SP '15	♀♀ 2*
● Campo Massimo Corvina Veronese '15	♀♀ 2*
○ Custoza '18	♀♀ 2*
○ Custoza SP '15	♀♀ 2*
○ Custoza Sup. Campo del Selese '15	♀♀ 2*
○ Gran Cuvée Pas Dosé M. Cl.	♀♀ 4

Piovene Porto Godi

FRAZ. TOARA DI VILLAGA
VIA VILLA, 14
36021 VILLAGA [VI]
TEL. +39 0444885142
www.piovene.com

CELLAR SALES
PRE-BOOKED VISITS
ACCOMMODATION
ANNUAL PRODUCTION 120,000 bottles
HECTARES UNDER VINE 40.00
SUSTAINABLE WINERY

Tomaso Piovene is one of Berico's great interpreters, highlighting the attributes of a generous land in which viticulture doesn't dominate but rather alternates with woods, grasslands and, along the valley floor, farmland as well. The decidedly warm and dry climate allows for the perfect maturation of grapes, which Toara transforms into a selection that expresses the sunniness of the area and its natural disposition for varieties like Tai Rosso. Their sizable estate is situated entirely on the hills that surround their historic villa. Their Pozzare vineyard is situated on south-facing, calcareous terrain at 240 meters elevation and provides the grapes for their Cabernet '16. The microclimate here gives rise to rich, fruity aromas revived by notes of medicinal herbs and spices. In the mouth the wine opens soft and pervasive, only to find tension thanks to a pronounced sapidity and acidic thrust that lightens and lengthens the palate. Their simpler Polveriera '17, a lively and succulent Bordeaux, also put in a nice performance.

● Colli Berici Cabernet Vign. Pozzare '16	♛♛ 4
○ Colli Berici Pinot Bianco Polveriera '18	♛♛ 4
○ Colli Berici Sauvignon Vign. Fostine '18	♛♛ 2*
● Polveriera Rosso '17	♛♛ 2*
○ Sauvignon Campigie '17	♛♛ 3
○ Colli Berici Garganega Vign. Riveselle '18	♛ 2
● Colli Berici Tai Rosso '18	♛ 5
● Colli Berici Cabernet Vign. Pozzare '12	♛♛♛ 4*
● Colli Berici Cabernet Vign. Pozzare '07	♛♛♛ 3
○ Colli Berici Pinot Bianco Vign. Polveriera '17	♛♛ 2*
○ Colli Berici Sauvignon Vign. Fostine '17	♛♛ 2*
● Colli Berici Tai Rosso Vign. Riveselle '17	♛♛ 2*

★Graziano Prà

VIA DELLA FONTANA, 31
37032 MONTEFORTE D'ALPONE [VR]
TEL. +39 0457612125
www.vinipra.it

CELLAR SALES
PRE-BOOKED VISITS
ACCOMMODATION
ANNUAL PRODUCTION 350,000 bottles
HECTARES UNDER VINE 35.00
VITICULTURE METHOD Certified Organic
SUSTAINABLE WINERY

Graziano Prà has increasingly focused on developing his winery. Founded on Monte Grande as a producer dedicated to the wines of Soave, in the area's classic heart, it has gradually expanded in Monte Bisson, a kind of island of hills in the plains that separate Soave from Colognola. Their selection of reds is deeply bound to the hills that divide the Tregnago and Mezzane valleys, an estate situated on limestone-rich terrain at 500 meters. The vineyards here are very dense and characterized by decidedly low yields. Their Soave Staforte '17 is redolent of ripe fruit and flowers, while in the mouth Garganega's pluckier and pleasantly rustic qualities emerge, making for a crisp, sapid palate of nice length. If their Monte Grande '17 is the usual thoroughbred white, their splendid Amarone Morandina '13 came through in spades. It begins closed and hidden, only to open on a dynamic and extraordinarily fresh palate.

● Amarone della Valpolicella Morandina '13	♛♛ 7
○ Soave Cl. Monte Grande '17	♛♛ 4
○ Soave Cl. Staforte '17	♛♛ 3*
○ Soave Cl. Otto '18	♛♛ 3
● Valpolicella Morandina '18	♛♛ 3
● Valpolicella Sup. Ripasso Morandina '17	♛♛ 4
○ Soave Cl. Monte Grande '16	♛♛♛ 4*
○ Soave Cl. Monte Grande '11	♛♛♛ 4*
○ Soave Cl. Monte Grande '08	♛♛♛ 4
○ Soave Cl. Staforte '15	♛♛♛ 3*
○ Soave Cl. Staforte '14	♛♛♛ 4*
○ Soave Cl. Staforte '13	♛♛♛ 4*
○ Soave Cl. Staforte '11	♛♛♛ 4*
○ Soave Cl. Staforte '08	♛♛♛ 4

★Giuseppe Quintarelli

VIA CERÈ, 1
37024 NEGRAR [VR]
TEL. +39 0457500016
vini@giuseppequintarelli.it

CELLAR SALES
PRE-BOOKED VISITS
ANNUAL PRODUCTION 60,000 bottles
HECTARES UNDER VINE 10.00

The Quintarelli family's winery, today managed by Francesco and Lorenzo along with their parents, is an icon of Valpolicella and its wines. The estate isn't particularly large, and they've never produced single-vineyard wines, but they've always performed the difficult work of blending different plots so as to produce the best possible wine. They're bolstered by a deep knowledge of the territory and its cultivars, how they exalt and compensate for one other, how partial drying and the use of oak affect a wine that pursues complexity and harmony rather than power. The new direction remains faithful to grandpa Giuseppe's idea of a wine, with just a tiny bit more integrity and freshness, as their Amarone '11 testifies to. Here super-ripe fruit is supported by a mineral, spicy background while on the palate it proves sapid and elegant. Their extraordinary Recioto, dedicated to their friend Roberto Ferrarini, is a delicate and highly characterful passito.

● Amarone della Valpolicella Cl. '11	▼▼▼ 8
● Recioto della Valpolicella Cl. A Roberto '07	▼▼ 8
● Valpolicella Cl. Sup. '12	▼▼ 7
● Amarone della Valpolicella Cl. '09	♀♀♀ 8
● Amarone della Valpolicella Cl. '06	♀♀♀ 8
● Amarone della Valpolicella Cl. '03	♀♀♀ 8
● Amarone della Valpolicella Cl. '98	♀♀♀ 8
● Amarone della Valpolicella Cl. Ris. '07	♀♀♀ 8
● Amarone della Valpolicella Cl. Sup. Monte Cà Paletta '00	♀♀♀ 8
● Recioto della Valpolicella Cl. '01	♀♀♀ 8
● Recioto della Valpolicella Cl. Monte Ca' Paletta '97	♀♀♀ 8

Quota 101

VIA MALTERRENO, 12
35038 TORREGLIA [PD]
TEL. +39 0425410922
www.quota101.com

PRE-BOOKED VISITS
ACCOMMODATION
ANNUAL PRODUCTION 45,000 bottles
HECTARES UNDER VINE 18.00
VITICULTURE METHOD Certified Organic
SUSTAINABLE WINERY

Roberto Gardina purchased Quota 101 a few years, having fallen in love with the Euganean hills and the landscape. The estate, which is surrounded by woods, vineyards and olive groves, spans some 20 hectares in Torreglia, in the northeastern part of the Colli Euganei Regional Park. Already certified as a 'Biodiversity Friend', they're now working towards organic. Even the old cellar was renovated with an eye towards optimizing the spaces and limiting its impact on the environment. Ortone '16 is half Merlot, a quarter Cabernet Franc and a quarter Sauvignon. On the nose it offers up intense notes of red fruit and medicinal herbs, which are even more evident on the palate. Here the wine offers up all the territory's warmth, proving rich, soft and pervasive. Their very interesting Gelso di Lapo '16, a passito made with Yellow Moscato, offers up close-focused varietal notes and endears for its full palate.

○ Colli Euganei Fior d'Arancio Passito Il Gelso di Lapo '16	▼▼ 5
○ Colli Euganei Manzoni Bianco '18	▼▼ 3
● Colli Euganei Rosso Ortone '16	▼▼ 4
○ Colli Euganei Fior d'Arancio '18	▼ 3
○ Colli Euganei Fior d'Arancio Spumante '18	▼ 3
○ Colli Euganei Tai '18	▼ 3
○ Colli Euganei Fior d'Arancio '16	♀♀ 3
○ Colli Euganei Fior d'Arancio Passito Il Gelso '13	♀♀ 5
○ Colli Euganei Fior d'Arancio Passito Il Gelso di Lapo '15	♀♀ 5
○ Colli Euganei Fior d'Arancio Passito Il Gelso di Lapo '14	♀♀ 5
○ Colli Euganei Manzoni Bianco '16	♀♀ 3
● Colli Euganei Rosso Ortone '15	♀♀ 4

Le Ragose

FRAZ. ARBIZZANO
VIA LE RAGOSE, 1
37024 NEGRAR [VR]
TEL. +39 0457513241
www.leragose.com

CELLAR SALES
PRE-BOOKED VISITS
ANNUAL PRODUCTION 120,000 bottles
HECTARES UNDER VINE 18.00

The Galli family's winery is one of Valpolicella's historic wineries. Founded half a century ago, it's not among the oldest, but their wines pursue an adherence to tradition while also remaining faithful to the expression of the wines. It's an approach that makes the producer a benchmark for those in search of a classic style. The estate's vineyards extend along the ridge that separates the Negrar and Quinzano valleys, immersed among woods at altitudes ranging from 300 to 300 meters. This year Galli submitted a selection without weak points. The only thing missing was a standout. Their Amarone Marta Galli '09 begins closed, almost hesitant to reveal itself. Slowly sweet, overripe fruit emerges, sensations rounded out by spices and hints of wet earth. The palate is full and powerful, broadening on more relaxed notes, proving harmonious and very long indeed. Their Recioto '15 is a complex wine that exhibits a measured sweetness.

● Amarone della Valpolicella Cl. '09	♥♥ 7
● Amarone della Valpolicella Cl. Marta Galli '09	♥♥ 7
● Recioto della Valpolicella Cl. '15	♥♥ 5
● Valpolicella Cl. Sup. Marta Galli '15	♥♥ 5
● Amarone della Valpolicella Cl. '08	♀♀ 7
● Amarone della Valpolicella Cl. Caloetto '08	♀♀ 7
● Amarone della Valpolicella Cl. Caloetto '07	♀♀ 7
● Recioto della Valpolicella Cl. '14	♀♀ 5
● Valpolicella Cl. Sup. Marta Galli '14	♀♀ 5
● Valpolicella Cl. Sup. Ripasso Le Sassine '14	♀♀ 4
● Valpolicella Cl. Sup. Ripasso Le Sassine '13	♀♀ 4

F.lli Recchia

LOC. JAGO
VIA CA' BERTOLDI, 30
37024 NEGRAR [VR]
TEL. +39 0457500584
www.recchiavini.it

CELLAR SALES
PRE-BOOKED VISITS
ANNUAL PRODUCTION 250,000 bottles
HECTARES UNDER VINE 100.00

If you exclude cooperatives, few producers in Valpolicella can boast operating on an estate as large as the Recchia family's. And not only, some of their vineyards can be found in the appellation's most sought after positions. Historic plots alternate with new ones along the best slopes, where rebuilt stone walls have given back the territory its unique character. Their selection is divided into two lines. Their Masua di Jago line comprises more traditional wines, like their Amarone '15, a red with mature, pervasive aromas and a sapid, light palate. Their premium wines are associated with their vineyard of origin. For example, there's their Amarone Ca' Bertoldi '12, a reserve that impresses for the complexity of its aromas and for a palate that explores the richer, more powerful side of the typology only to finish crisp and long.

● Amarone della Valpolicella Cl. Ca' Bertoldi Ris. '12	♥♥ 5
● Amarone della Valpolicella Cl. Masua di Jago '15	♥♥ 5
● Recioto della Valpolicella Cl. Masua di Jago '17	♥♥ 4
● Korvilot '17	♥ 5
● Valpolicella Cl. Masua di Jago '18	♥ 2
● Amarone della Valpolicella Cl. Masua di Jago '14	♀♀ 5
● Recioto della Valpolicella Cl. Masua di Jago '16	♀♀ 4
● Recioto della Valpolicella Cl. La Guardia '15	♀♀ 4
● Valpolicella Cl. Sup. Masua di Jago '16	♀♀ 2*
● Valpolicella Cl. Sup. Masua di Jago '15	♀♀ 2*

Roccolo Grassi

VIA SAN GIOVANNI DI DIO, 19
37030 MEZZANE DI SOTTO [VR]
TEL. +39 0458880089
www.roccolograssi.it

PRE-BOOKED VISITS
ANNUAL PRODUCTION 49,000 bottles
HECTARES UNDER VINE 14.00
SUSTAINABLE WINERY

Moving from gentle, east and west-facing hills, the large Mezzane valley narrows suddenly and then rises as if in search of cooler temperatures. It's here at this straight that you'll find Francesca and Marco Sartori's winery. Their vineyards are spread out on multiple plots, hills and soil types, from the calcareous-clay of Valpolicella to the extremely gravelly terrain of Soave. Only a few types of wine are produced, making for a selection of great precision and rigor. Their Soave La Broia '17 is a truly commendable wine that moves away from the idea of a fresh, juicy white, opting instead for a cautiously managed and firm palate governed by bold acidity. 100% Garganega, aged mostly in oak, makes for a gutsy, territorial wine. When it comes their reds their Amarone '15 offers up ripe, deep aromas, which reemerge on a powerful palate supported by close-knit tannins.

● Amarone della Valpolicella '15	♟♟8
○ Soave La Broia '17	♟♟3*
● Valpolicella Sup. '15	♟♟5
● Amarone della Valpolicella Roccolo Grassi '07	♟♟♟8
● Amarone della Valpolicella Roccolo Grassi '00	♟♟♟7
● Amarone della Valpolicella Roccolo Grassi '99	♟♟♟7
● Valpolicella Sup. '13	♟♟♟5
● Valpolicella Sup. '11	♟♟♟5
● Valpolicella Sup. Roccolo Grassi '09	♟♟♟5
● Valpolicella Sup. Roccolo Grassi '07	♟♟♟5
● Valpolicella Sup. Roccolo Grassi '04	♟♟♟5

Roeno

VIA MAMA, 5
37020 BRENTINO BELLUNO [VR]
TEL. +39 0457230110
www.cantinaroeno.com

CELLAR SALES
PRE-BOOKED VISITS
ACCOMMODATION AND RESTAURANT SERVICE
ANNUAL PRODUCTION 400,000 bottles
HECTARES UNDER VINE 80.00
SUSTAINABLE WINERY

Cristina and Giuseppe Fugatti have carried on the legacy of their father, Rolando, and breathed new life into the family's winery (and we shouldn't forget the precious support of Roberta, either). It's a journey that began many years ago and saw the family living through historic transformations of the Adige valley, while staying firmly tied to the land and its traditions. Today the estate's vineyards extend along the river, spanning the sandy valley floor where their historic plots of Enantio are situated and more recent parcels in the high hills dedicated to Riesling and aromatic varieties. Their Riesling Collezione di Famiglia '15 is aged at length in the cellar, first in large oak barrels, then in the bottle, only to be released just now. On the nose aromas of petrol merge with chamomile and exotic notes, while on the palate the come proves rich and juicy, with a fresh vein of acidity. Their Cristina '16 is an elegant and harmonious late-harvest wine, while their Pre Fillossera '13 is smoky, powerful and sapid.

○ Riesling Renano Collezione di Famiglia '15	♟♟♟6
○ Cristina V. T. '16	♟♟5
● Valdadige Terra dei Forti Enantio 1865 Pre Fillossera Ris. '13	♟♟4
● Marzemino La Rua '18	♟♟2*
○ Riesling Praecipuus '17	♟♟6
○ Valdadige Pinot Grigio Tera Alta '18	♟♟2*
● Valdadige Terra dei Forti Enantio '16	♟♟4
○ Valdadige Terra dei Forti Pinot Grigio Rivoli '16	♟♟2*
○ Cristina V. T. '13	♟♟♟5
○ Cristina V. T. '12	♟♟♟5
○ Cristina V. T. '11	♟♟♟5
○ Cristina V. T. '08	♟♟♟5
○ Riesling Renano Collezione di Famiglia '13	♟♟♟6

Rubinelli Vajol

FRAZ. SAN FLORIANO
VIA PALADON, 31
37029 SAN PIETRO IN CARIANO [VR]
TEL. +39 0456839277
www.rubinellivajol.it

CELLAR SALES
PRE-BOOKED VISITS
ACCOMMODATION
ANNUAL PRODUCTION 50,000 bottles
HECTARES UNDER VINE 10.00

Even if they can't boast a historic presence as regional winemakers, the Rubinelli family have been in the Vajol basin for about a century and are deeply tied to Valpolicella and its wines. Their vineyards are situated entirely in a kind of south-facing amphitheater, ten hectares dedicated exclusively to the area's traditional grapes. Here they enjoy constant sun during daytime and cool breezes at night, making for a production that brings out the subtlest and most elegant expression of the appellation. Their Amarone '13 follows precisely this direction. It's delicate and light in its aromas of ripe cherry and flowers, with medicinal herbs conferring additional freshness. On the palate it's impresses more for its supple and sapid stride than for power or exuberance. Their Ripasso '15 exhibits a softer, more pervasive palate that finishes with a lovely return of overripe fruit.

● Amarone della Valpolicella Cl. '13	♀♀	7
● Valpolicella Cl. Sup. '15	♀♀	4
● Valpolicella Cl. Sup. Ripasso '15	♀♀	4
● Amarone della Valpolicella Cl. '12	♀♀	7
● Amarone della Valpolicella Cl. '11	♀♀	7
● Amarone della Valpolicella Cl. '10	♀♀	6
● Recioto della Valpolicella Cl. '13	♀♀	6
● Recioto della Valpolicella Cl. '12	♀♀	6
● Recioto della Valpolicella Cl. '11	♀♀	6
● Valpolicella Cl. '13	♀♀	2*
● Valpolicella Cl. Sup. '14	♀♀	4
● Valpolicella Cl. Sup. '12	♀♀	4
● Valpolicella Cl. Sup. '11	♀♀	4
● Valpolicella Cl. Sup. Ripasso '14	♀♀	5
● Valpolicella Cl. Sup. Ripasso '12	♀♀	5

★Ruggeri & C.

FRAZ. ZECCHEI
VIA PRÀ FONTANA, 4
31049 VALDOBBIADENE [TV]
TEL. +39 04239092
www.ruggeri.it

CELLAR SALES
PRE-BOOKED VISITS
ANNUAL PRODUCTION 1,600,000 bottles
HECTARES UNDER VINE 28.00
SUSTAINABLE WINERY

The large winery situated at Via Prà Fontana is among the appellation's most attentive interpreters of Treviso sparkling wine, bolstered by collaborations with a sizable network of vine growers who provide Ruggeri with their grapes. The fact that they work with one grape, and have limited time to manage the crop, means that winemaker Paolo Bisol works with two delivery channels and numerous presses. In that way they can better manage the harvest, selecting and setting aside the best batches. Their Giustino B. '18 is a textbook Extra Dry that brings together everything you could desire in a top-quality Prosecco. The cleanness of its aromas makes for a broad and highly fresh, fruity and flowery expression. In the mouth it's sapid and succulent, with bubbles that caress the palate. Their Vecchie Viti '18, a wine made with grapes cultivated by reliable growers in various centuries-old vineyards, is an edgier wine aromatically, while on the palate it delivers with decisiveness and pluck.

○ Valdobbiadene Extra Dry Giustino B. '18	♀♀♀	5
○ Valdobbiadene Brut Vecchie Viti '18	♀♀	4
○ Cartizze	♀♀	5
○ Cartizze Brut	♀♀	5
○ Valdobbiadene Brut Quartese	♀♀	4
○ Valdobbiadene Dry S. Stefano	♀♀	4
○ Valdobbiadene Extra Brut Saltèr	♀♀	4
○ Valdobbiadene Extra Dry Giall'Oro	♀♀	4
○ Valdobbiadene Brut V. V. '14	♀♀♀	4*
○ Valdobbiadene Brut Vecchie Viti '13	♀♀♀	4*
○ Valdobbiadene Extra Dry Giustino B. '17	♀♀♀	5
○ Valdobbiadene Extra Dry Giustino B. '16	♀♀♀	4*
○ Valdobbiadene Extra Dry Giustino B. '15	♀♀♀	4*
○ Valdobbiadene Extra Dry Giustino B. '12	♀♀♀	3*

Le Salette

VIA PIO BRUGNOLI, 11c
37022 FUMANE [VR]
TEL. +39 0457701027
www.lesalette.it

CELLAR SALES
PRE-BOOKED VISITS
ANNUAL PRODUCTION 130,000 bottles
HECTARES UNDER VINE 20.00

Franco Scamperle oversees the family winery in the heart of Valpolicella Classica, in Fumane, just beneath the La Salette Sanctuary. Here the valley suddenly gets narrower and is practically free of viticulture, thus returning to a rustic landscape dominated by woods and cypress trees. It's here that we find Salette's cellar, divided into multiple spaces in the courtyard and connected by underground tunnels. The vineyards are situated on the hills around the cellar, as well as nearby Sant'Ambrogio and San Floriano. Their Amarone Pergole Vece is made only when the vintage is exceptional, as was the case in 2015. It's the result of painstaking selection of the best grape bunches from very old vineyards. On the nose it offers up aromas of overripe fruit and spices, while on the palate it comes through rich, unfolding generously and well supported by its signature acidity. Their Amarone La Marega '15 is from the vineyard of the same name, in Fumane, and opts for a suppler, racier profile.

● Amarone della Valpolicella Cl. La Marega '15	▼▼ 6
● Amarone della Valpolicella Cl. Pergole Vece '15	▼▼ 8
● Valpolicella Cl. Sup. Ripasso I Progni '17	▼▼ 3
● Ca' Carnocchio '16	▼ 4
⊙ Lamolinara '18	▼ 2
● Recioto della Valpolicella Cl. Le Traversagne '16	▼ 5
● Valpolicella Cl. '18	▼ 2
● Amarone della Valpolicella Cl. Pergole Vece '95	▼▼▼ 8
● Amarone della Valpolicella Cl. Pergole Vece '13	▼▼ 8
● Recioto della Valpolicella Cl. Le Traversagne '15	▼▼ 5

Tenute SalvaTerra

VIA CENGIA, 8
37029 SAN PIETRO IN CARIANO [VR]
TEL. +39 0456859025
www.tenutesalvaterra.it

CELLAR SALES
PRE-BOOKED VISITS
ANNUAL PRODUCTION 80,000 bottles
HECTARES UNDER VINE 16.00

The village of Cengia is characterized by a handful of dwellings interspersed among vineyards, and the presence of Villa Giona, a 16th-century manor whose 'brolo' (a kind of enclosed park) hosts a splendid Italian garden and a vineyard. It's here that we find Tenute Salvaterra, one of Valpolicella's most interesting producers. In addition to the brolo, the estate spans property in Prun, Mezzane and Montorio, all of which give rise to a selection of red wines. They also have plots in Oliosi, San Martino Buon Albergo and Vescovana. Their premium wines are made with grapes cultivated on their Campocroce estate, in the Mezzane Valley. Their Valpolicella Superiore '17 is a prime example, a wine that pursues aromatic integrity and tension rather than fullness and opulence. Aromatically it expresses wild berry and pepper, while on the palate it proves crisp, slender and racy. Their Amarone '15 opts for an entirely different profile, featuring fruity exuberance and softness on the palate.

● Amarone della Valpolicella Campocroce '15	▼▼ 8
● Valpolicella Sup. Campocroce '17	▼▼ 4
● Valpolicella Campocroce '18	▼▼ 3
● Valpolicella Cl. Sup. Ripasso '16	▼▼ 5
● Falia Bianco	▼ 3
⊙ Falia Rosé	▼ 3
● Falia Rosso	▼ 3
○ Pinot Grigio delle Venezie '18	▼ 5
○ Prosecco Extra Dry '18	▼ 3
● Valpolicella Sup. Tenuta Campocroce '16	▼▼▼ 4*
● Amarone della Valpolicella Cl. '11	▼▼ 8
● Amarone della Valpolicella Cl. Cave di Prun Ris. '08	▼▼ 8
● Valpolicella Tenuta Campocroce '17	▼▼ 3

Marco Sambin

LOC. VALNOGAREDO
VIA FATTORELLE, 20A
35030 CINTO EUGANEO [PD]
TEL. +39 3456812050
www.vinimarcus.com

CELLAR SALES
PRE-BOOKED VISITS
RESTAURANT SERVICE
ANNUAL PRODUCTION 20,000 bottles
HECTARES UNDER VINE 3.00
VITICULTURE METHOD Certified Organic
SUSTAINABLE WINERY

Valnogaredo is a small hamlet situated on the eastern part of the Euganean hills, just a few dwellings lost among the vineyards, woods and the occasional olive tree. A bit further on, bordering the plains, you'll find Marco Sambin's small estate, a property that extends along the foot of Monte Versa. Here the terraced plots, supported by stone and perfectly exposed to the south, host primarily Bordeaux varieties. But there's also the occasional reminder of a deeper past, like Garganega, or newer experiment, like Syrah. Their vineyards are cultivated organically with an eye towards biodynamic approaches, and give rise to a selection in which their Marcus '16, a Bordeaux blend made with a splash of Syrah, figures centrally. On the nose it evinces ripe fruit refreshed by balsamic notes. In the mouth the sunniness of their vineyards gives rise to a generous palate with close-knit tannins. Long maceration in amphoras endows their Psyche '18, a monovarietal Garganega, with elegance and harmony.

○ Helena Passito '16	🍷🍷 5
● Le Femminelle '18	🍷🍷 3
● Marcus '16	🍷🍷 5
○ Psyché '18	🍷🍷 3
○ Sarah '18	🍷 3
● Alter '15	🍷🍷 4
● Alter '14	🍷🍷 4
○ Helena Passito '15	🍷🍷 5
● Le Femminelle '17	🍷🍷 3
● Marcus '15	🍷🍷 5
● Marcus '13	🍷🍷 5
● Marcus al Quadrato '13	🍷🍷 6
○ Sarah '17	🍷🍷 3

San Cassiano

VIA SAN CASSIANO, 17
37030 MEZZANE DI SOTTO [VR]
TEL. +39 0458880665
www.cantinasancassiano.it

CELLAR SALES
PRE-BOOKED VISITS
ANNUAL PRODUCTION 50,000 bottles
HECTARES UNDER VINE 14.00
SUSTAINABLE WINERY

Mirko Sella has managed to grow what was once a small estate revived by his grandfather Albino in the 1960s. Today the winery avails itself of 15 hectares of vineyards and a 10-hectare olive grove, the two products that most represent the territory. Various parcels are spread throughout the valley at elevations of around 300 meters. Their product range, which is bound closely to the territory's appellations, is the result of painstaking care in the vineyards and an approach to winemaking that privileges richness. Their Amarone '13 is a reserve with intense, mature aromas in which fruit preserves meet spicy and balsamic notes. In the mouth the wine maintains the same stylistic track, revealing a full, generous and pervasive palate. Their Amarone '15 features a fresher aromatic profile, once again dominated by overripe fruit that we find on its palate, where the wine exhibits impeccable balance grounded in softer notes.

● Amarone della Valpolicella '15	🍷🍷 6
● Amarone della Valpolicella Ris. '13	🍷🍷 6
● Valpolicella '17	🍷 2
● Valpolicella Sup. Le Aléne '13	🍷 4
● Valpolicella Sup. Ripasso '16	🍷 3
● Amarone della Valpolicella '14	🍷🍷 6
● Amarone della Valpolicella '13	🍷🍷 6
● Amarone della Valpolicella '11	🍷🍷 6
● Recioto della Valpolicella '15	🍷🍷 5
○ Soave '17	🍷🍷 3
● Valpolicella '16	🍷🍷 2*
● Valpolicella '15	🍷🍷 2*
● Valpolicella Sup. Ripasso '14	🍷🍷 3
● Valpolicella Sup. Ripasso '12	🍷🍷 2*

La Sansonina

LOC. SANSONINA
37019 PESCHIERA DEL GARDA [VR]
TEL. +39 0457551905
www.sansonina.it

CELLAR SALES
ANNUAL PRODUCTION 35,000 bottles
HECTARES UNDER VINE 13.00

The clay terrain that surrounds Lake Garda to the south and penetrates the morainic hills up towards San Martino della Battaglia and Madonna della Scoperta is a prized territory for Lugana wines. In addition to the area's traditional white grapes, at Carla Prospero's Sansonina they've devoted significant efforts to cultivating Bordeaux red grapes, in particular Merlot, a variety that's had a presence here for many years. The few wines they produce are characterized by a style that brings together fullness and elegance. Sansonina '17, their house Merlot, pours a luminous ruby red, anticipating aromas of ripe red fruit accompanied by deep mineral notes and strains of forest undergrowth. On the palate the wine proves full and powerful, made taut and lean by its vibrant acidity. Their Lugana Fermentazione Spontanea is an intriguing white that impresses for its ability to bring together lightness and tension with riper, more pervasive fruit.

○ Lugana Fermentazione Spontanea '17	▼▼ 3
● Sansonina '17	▼▼ 6
● Garda Evaluna '17	▼ 4
● Garda Cabernet Evaluna '16	♈ 4
● Garda Cabernet Evaluna '15	♈ 4
● Garda Evaluna '14	♈ 4
○ Lugana Fermentazione Spontanea '16	♈ 3*
○ Lugana Sansonina '13	♈ 3
○ Lugana Sansonina '12	♈ 3
○ Lugana V. del Morano Verde '15	♈ 4
○ Lugana V. del Morano Verde '14	♈ 3
● Sansonina '16	♈ 6
● Sansonina '14	♈ 6
● Sansonina '13	♈ 6
● Sansonina '12	♈ 6

Tenuta Sant'Anna

FRAZ. LONCON
VIA MONSIGNOR P. L. ZOVATTO, 71
30020 ANNONE VENETO [VE]
TEL. +39 0422864511
www.tenutasantanna.it

CELLAR SALES
PRE-BOOKED VISITS
ANNUAL PRODUCTION 2,800,000 bottles
HECTARES UNDER VINE 140.00

The historic winery of Tenuta Sant'Anna, a part of Generali's agricultural business, spans 140 hectares along the Adriatic coast. As far back as anyone can remember, they've grown wine grapes here in an area where clay alternates with deep layers of gravel. In addition to Prosecco, which is the area's most commonly produced wine, they also cultivate native grape varieties like Tai. These are interpreted with fragrance and suppleness, stylistic features that have always defined this corner of Veneto. And Tai gives rise to their Lison Bianco '18, a wine redolent of flowery fragrances and white fruit, aromas that find development across a fresh, pleasant palate. Their Merlot '18 also delivers. It's a red aged entirely in concrete, making for aromas of ripe, juicy fruit. In the mouth it moves with lightness and suppleness, proving harmonious and relaxed. Their line of Valdobbiadenes featured a fresh, sapid Extra Dry and a valid Cartizze.

○ Cartizze '18	▼▼ 5
○ Lison-Pramaggiore Bianco '18	▼▼ 2*
○ Valdobbiadene Extra Dry '18	▼▼ 3
● Venezia Cabernet Sauvignon '18	▼▼ 2*
● Venezia Merlot '18	▼▼ 2*
○ Brut di Pinot	▼ 2
○ Cuvée Blanche Extra Dry	▼ 2
⊙ Cuvée Rosé Brut	▼ 2
○ Moscato Spumante Dolce	▼ 2
○ Prosecco Brut	▼ 3
○ Prosecco Brut Mill. '18	▼ 3
○ Prosecco Extra Dry	▼ 3
○ Venezia Chardonnay '18	▼ 2
○ Venezia Pinot Grigio '18	▼ 2
● Lison-Pramaggiore Merlot Poderi '16	♈ 2*
● Venezia Cabernet Sauvignon Poderi '17	♈ 2*
○ Venezia Pinot Grigio '16	♈ 2*

★Tenuta Sant'Antonio

LOC. SAN ZENO
VIA CERIANI, 23
37030 COLOGNOLA AI COLLI [VR]
TEL. +39 0457650383
www.tenutasantantonio.it

CELLAR SALES
PRE-BOOKED VISITS
ANNUAL PRODUCTION 700,000 bottles
HECTARES UNDER VINE 100.00

The Castagnedi brothers' estate extends along the ridge that separates the Mezzane and Marcellise valleys. They also have vineyards extending east, towards the Illasi valley. The surface of this large marly expanse is white, almost blindingly so, deprived as it is of nutrients. As a result the vine roots are forced to go deeper down in search of richer soil. Their cultivation approach is increasingly centered on reducing environmental impact, and in the cellar they're also working to limit the presence of chemicals. Their Amarone Campo dei Gigli '15, the producer's most representative wine, comes from a vineyard that goes back more than 40 years. It opens with aromas dominated by overripe red fruit, exalted on a rich, decisive palate of notable tension. Their Recioto Argille Biance '11 is a buoyant and gutsy wine at the same time, while their La Bandina '16 is an aromatically deep and mature Valpolicella Superiore that expresses great richness.

Santa Margherita

VIA ITA MARZOTTO, 8
30025 FOSSALTA DI PORTOGRUARO [VE]
TEL. +39 0421246111
www.santamargherita.com

CELLAR SALES
PRE-BOOKED VISITS
ANNUAL PRODUCTION 13,500,000 bottles
HECTARES UNDER VINE 50.00

More than eighty years have passed since Gaetano Marzotto founded Santa Margherita, a large property that, at the time, served the agricultural needs of a rapidly growing population. At almost 100, it's become a wine-growing estate that spans three different territories: the plains between Fossalta and the sea, historic Prosecco, and Alto Adige. A close-knit staff follow each stage of production in pursuit of the highest possible territorial expression. Their Pinot Grigio Impronta del Fondatore '18, the winery's cornerstone, fully convinced our tasters with its close-focused aromas of pear and flowers, and smoky notes. On the palate it gracefully unfolds, supported by the sapid acidity that characterizes Atesina. Their Rive di Refrontolo Brut '18 also performed well. It's a Prosecco that perfectly expresses the territory, with aromas dominated by fruity sensations and a crisp, firm palate.

● Amarone della Valpolicella Campo dei Gigli '15	▼▼▼ 8
● Recioto della Valpolicella Argille Bianche '11	▼▼ 5
● Valpolicella Sup. La Bandina '16	▼▼ 5
○ Soave Monte Ceriani '18	▼▼ 3
○ Soave V. V. '17	▼▼ 3
● Valpolicella Sup. Ripasso Monti Garbi '17	▼▼ 3
● Amarone della Valpolicella Sel. Antonio Castagnedi '15	▼ 6
● Amarone della Valpolicella Campo dei Gigli '12	♔♔♔ 8
● Amarone della Valpolicella Campo dei Gigli '11	♔♔♔ 8
● Amarone della Valpolicella Campo dei Gigli '10	♔♔♔ 8

○ A. A. Pinot Grigio Impronta del Fondatore '18	▼▼ 3*
○ Cartizze Extra Dry	▼▼ 5
○ Valdobbiadene Brut	▼▼ 3
○ Valdobbiadene Brut 52	▼▼ 3
○ Valdobbiadene Brut Rive di Refrontolo '18	▼▼ 3
⊙ Stilrose '18	▼ 3
○ Stilwhite '18	▼ 3
○ Valdadige Pinot Grigio '18	▼ 3
○ Valdobbiadene Extra Dry	▼ 2
○ A. A. Bianco Luna dei Feldi '16	♔♔ 3
○ A. A. Pinot Grigio Impronta del Fondatore '17	♔♔ 3*
○ Valdobbiadene Brut Rive di Refrontolo '17	♔♔ 3

Santa Sofia

FRAZ. PEDEMONTE DI VALPOLICELLA
VIA CA' DEDÉ, 61
37029 SAN PIETRO IN CARIANO [VR]
TEL. +39 0457701074
www.santasofia.com

CELLAR SALES
PRE-BOOKED VISITS
ANNUAL PRODUCTION 550,000 bottles
HECTARES UNDER VINE 53.00

Thanks to Luciano Begnoni, the winery founded by his father Giancarlo in the 1960s has turned a corner. Situated just below and next to the Palladian villa of Santa Sofia, the producer has always relied on numerous vine growers for its grapes, even if in recent years they've purchased and planted a sizable property in eastern Valpolicella. Their selection spans all the area's appellations, though their beating heart remains closely tied to Valpolicella. Their Amarone '13, a wine that pours an enticing, compact, vivid ruby red, put in a performance for the ages. On the nose fruit takes center stage, though it leaves room for flowery notes and hints of medicinal herbs, which bring a touch of lightness. On the palate it comes through full and potent, with its well-crafted tannic weave offering the right support. Their Montegradella '16 also convinced. It's a Valpolicella Superiore that plays on generosity of fruit.

● Amarone della Valpolicella Cl. '13	♟♟ 7
● Valpolicella Cl. Sup. Montegradella '16	♟♟ 4
● Valpolicella Sup. Ripasso '16	♟♟ 4
● Recioto della Valpolicella Cl. '15	♟ 5
● Valpolicella Cl. '18	♟ 3
● Amarone della Valpolicella Cl. '12	♟♟ 7
● Amarone della Valpolicella Cl. '12	♟♟ 7
● Amarone della Valpolicella Cl. '11	♟♟ 7
● Recioto della Valpolicella Cl. '11	♟♟ 5
● Valpolicella Cl. '16	♟♟ 3
● Valpolicella Cl. Sup. Montegradella '15	♟♟ 4
● Valpolicella Cl. Sup. Montegradella '14	♟♟ 4
● Valpolicella Sup. Ripasso '15	♟♟ 4
● Valpolicella Sup. Ripasso '14	♟♟ 4

Santi

VIA UNGHERIA, 33
37031 ILLASI [VR]
TEL. +39 0456529068
www.cantinasanti.it

CELLAR SALES
PRE-BOOKED VISITS
ANNUAL PRODUCTION 1,400,000 bottles
HECTARES UNDER VINE 53.00

The arrival of Cristian Ridolfi at Santi has coincided with the reopening of their historic cellar in Illasi, a building that was renovated and equipped for the production of high-profile wines. Their technical choices have been decisive, starting with the use of only large wooden barrels and then, for only a small part of their production, small local wood like cherry, chestnut and acacia. Their selection is characterized by a style that we could call classic, with elegance and grip figuring centrally. If we're used to outstanding performances from their Amarone Proemio, as was the case with their 2013, it's their Valpolicella Ventale that wowed us with its surge in quality. Their approach seeks to bring out the attributes of traditional grapes without relying on partial-drying. The result is a Ventale '17 of great aromatic expressivity, with fruit crossed by spicy notes — sensations that reemerge on a crisp, balanced palate.

● Amarone della Valpolicella Cl. Proemio '13	♟♟ 7
● Valpolicella Sup. Ventale '17	♟♟ 3*
● Amarone della Valpolicella Cl. '14	♟♟ 6
● Valpolicella Cl. Sup. Ripasso Solane '16	♟♟ 3
● Amarone della Valpolicella Proemio '05	♟♟♟ 6
● Amarone della Valpolicella Proemio '03	♟♟♟ 6
● Amarone della Valpolicella Proemio '00	♟♟♟ 5
● Valpolicella Cl. Sup. Ripasso Solane '09	♟♟♟ 3*
● Amarone della Valpolicella Cl. '13	♟♟ 6
● Amarone della Valpolicella Cl. Proemio '12	♟♟ 7
● Amarone della Valpolicella Cl. Proemio '11	♟♟ 6
● Valpolicella Sup. Ventale '16	♟♟ 3*

Sartori

FRAZ. SANTA MARIA
VIA CASETTE, 4
37024 NEGRAR [VR]
TEL. +39 0456028011
www.sartorinet.com

CELLAR SALES
PRE-BOOKED VISITS
ANNUAL PRODUCTION 16,000,000 bottles
HECTARES UNDER VINE 120.00
SUSTAINABLE WINERY

This large winery is a faithful interpreter of
the region's historic appellations, bolstered
by a privileged relationship with the
territory's institutions and a network of
growers whose grapes give rise to a solid,
contemporary selection of wines. In their
Santa Maria di Negrar cellar, they produce
wines that, rather than pursue easy
commercial success, promote the
marvelous bond that exists between
vineyard, cultivar and winemaker. The result
is a selection in which elegance figures
more prominently than power. Their
Amarone Classico Corte Bra '12 is a wine
whose color isn't too intense, which reflects
the fainter hues of the traditional grapes
used. It's redolent of dried fruit and spices,
while in the mouth it delivers for its sapid
lightness and crisp, supple finish. Their
eastern Valpolicella vineyard gives rise to
their Amarone I Saltari '12, a wine that's
aromatically deeper and more stratified. On
the palate it comes through energetic, solid
and pleasantly rough.

● Amarone della Valpolicella Cl. Corte Brà '12	♟♟ 7
● Amarone della Valpolicella Cl. Reius '13	♟♟ 7
● Amarone della Valpolicella I Saltari '12	♟♟ 8
● Valpolicella Cl. Sup. Montegradella '15	♟♟ 3
● Valpolicella Sup. I Saltari '14	♟♟ 5
● Cent'Anni '15	♟ 4
○ Marani '17	♟ 3
○ Recioto di Soave Vernus '16	♟ 4
● Valpolicella Sup. Ripasso Regolo '16	♟ 3
● Amarone della Valpolicella Cl. Corte Brà '11	♟♟ 7
● Amarone della Valpolicella I Saltari '11	♟♟ 8
● Recioto della Valpolicella Cl. Rerum '15	♟♟ 5
● Valpolicella Sup. I Saltari '13	♟♟ 5

Secondo Marco

VIA CAMPOLONGO, 9
37022 FUMANE [VR]
TEL. +39 0456800954
www.secondomarco.it

CELLAR SALES
PRE-BOOKED VISITS
ACCOMMODATION
ANNUAL PRODUCTION 75,000 bottles
HECTARES UNDER VINE 15.00

Marco Speri founded his winery some 12
years ago. Today it features a new cellar,
perfectly integrated with the Fumane
valley floor, which also hosts his vineyards.
It's an area characterized by alternating
gravel and alluvial deposits. Constant
winds channeled through the valley here
guarantee healthy grapes, which are
cultivated on pergolas that have been
revisited and shrunk so as to obtain richer,
perfectly ripe fruit. The direction that
Marco's taking in the cellar means that
time is needed before his wines express
their full potential. That's why, this year,
we only had the chance to taste his
Ripasso '15 while the rest of the selection
ages. On the nose it offers up intense
fruity notes that quickly give way to
balsamic nuances and spices, with
pepper gradually rising to prominence.
On the palate it proves crisp, sapid and
commendably long.

● Valpolicella Cl. Sup. Ripasso '15	♟♟ 5
● Amarone della Valpolicella Cl. '11	♟♟♟ 8
● Amarone della Valpolicella Cl. '12	♟♟ 8
● Amarone della Valpolicella Cl. '10	♟♟ 7
● Recioto della Valpolicella Cl. '13	♟♟ 6
● Recioto della Valpolicella Cl. '12	♟♟ 6
● Solo per un Amico '12	♟♟ 8
● Valpolicella Cl. '16	♟♟ 3
● Valpolicella Cl. '15	♟♟ 3
● Valpolicella Cl. '14	♟♟ 3
● Valpolicella Cl. '13	♟♟ 3
● Valpolicella Cl. Sup. Ripasso '14	♟♟ 5
● Valpolicella Cl. Sup. Ripasso '13	♟♟ 5
● Valpolicella Cl. Sup. Ripasso '12	♟♟ 5

★★Serafini & Vidotto

VIA LUIGI CARRER, 8
31040 NERVESA DELLA BATTAGLIA [TV]
TEL. +39 0422773281
www.serafinividotto.it

CELLAR SALES
PRE-BOOKED VISITS
ANNUAL PRODUCTION 250,000 bottles
HECTARES UNDER VINE 23.00
SUSTAINABLE WINERY

In a region where Glera seems to have taken over all the vineyards, Francesco Serafini and Antonello Vidotto's vineyards represent a life-preserver for all those who love wines that, in addition to quality, maintain an extraordinary bond with the territory. Today the winery, founded in the late 1980s, comprises a lovely cellar on Via Carrer and an estate that stretches along the southern slopes of Montello, cultivated according to an approach that minimizes the use of chemicals. Their Rosso dell'Abazia led the selection proposed this year. It's a Bordeaux blend, primarily Cabernet Sauvignon, that features intense aromas of wild fruit and spices. On the palate it impresses for its harmony and delicate tannins. Following the Bordeaux track, their Phigaia '16 serves as the perfect 'second vin', a little brother that exhibits a similar style, though with greater freshness and easiness. It's also worth noting the fruity pleasantness of their Recantina '18.

★Speri

LOC. PEDEMONTE
VIA FONTANA, 14
37029 SAN PIETRO IN CARIANO [VR]
TEL. +39 0457701154
www.speri.com

CELLAR SALES
PRE-BOOKED VISITS
ANNUAL PRODUCTION 350,000 bottles
HECTARES UNDER VINE 60.00
VITICULTURE METHOD Certified Organic
SUSTAINABLE WINERY

The history of wine in Valpolicella goes way back, but the success and notoriety that it's enjoyed as of late are thanks to a handful of wineries. Among these, the Speri family have performed, and continue to perform, a lead role, providing modern interpretations of time-honored traditions while navigating fashions and tendencies without losing their balance. Their vineyards span the gravelly valley floor and hills of rare beauty, making for a selection of wines centered solely on the appellation, all interpreted with firmness and elegance. Their Amarone Sant'Urbano '15 expresses all the value of an excellent year and a splendid vineyard, exhibiting an aromatic profile in which fruit takes center stage, but leaves plenty of room for gladiolus and pepper. In the mouth its full palate is governed with precision by acidity and tannins, making for a wine of great tension. Their Valpolicella '16 features fresher aromas and a juicy, racy palate.

● Montello e Colli Asolani Il Rosso dell'Abazia '16	▼▼▼	6
○ Asolo Extra Dry Bollicine di Prosecco	▼▼	3
● Montello e Colli Asolani Phigaia '16	▼▼	4
○ Phigaja El Blanco '17	▼▼	4
● Pinot Nero '16	▼▼	7
● Recantina '18	▼▼	3
○ Montello e Colli Asolani Manzoni Bianco '18	▼	3
○ Prosecco di Treviso Bollicine di Prosecco	▼	3
● Montello e Colli Asolani Il Rosso dell'Abazia '15	♀♀♀	6
● Montello e Colli Asolani Il Rosso dell'Abazia '13	♀♀♀	6
● Montello e Colli Asolani Il Rosso dell'Abazia '12	♀♀♀	5
● Montello e Colli Asolani Il Rosso dell'Abazia '11	♀♀♀	6

● Amarone della Valpolicella Cl. Sant'Urbano '15	▼▼▼	7
● Valpolicella Cl. Sup. Sant'Urbano '16	▼▼	4
● Recioto della Valpolicella Cl. La Roggia '16	▼▼	6
● Valpolicella Cl. '18	▼▼	3
● Valpolicella Cl. Sup. Ripasso '17	▼▼	4
● Amarone della Valpolicella Cl. Vign. Monte Sant'Urbano '12	♀♀♀	7
● Amarone della Valpolicella Cl. Vign. Monte Sant'Urbano '09	♀♀♀	7
● Amarone della Valpolicella Cl. Vign. Monte Sant'Urbano '08	♀♀♀	7
● Amarone della Valpolicella Cl. Vign. Sant'Urbano '11	♀♀♀	7
● Amarone della Valpolicella Vign. Monte Sant'Urbano '13	♀♀♀	7

David Sterza

VIA CASTERNA, 37
37022 FUMANE [VR]
TEL. +39 3471343121
www.davidsterza.it

CELLAR SALES
PRE-BOOKED VISITS
ANNUAL PRODUCTION 40,000 bottles
HECTARES UNDER VINE 4.50

Casterna is a tiny district that extends across the eastern side of the Fumane valley. A handful of houses here are surrounded by vineyards that gently rise up out of the valley floor along the side of Sant'Urbano hill. David Sterza and his cousin Paolo Mascanzoni personally oversee the vineyards, transforming the grapes into wines of great integrity and pleasantness. Their small but well-equipped cellar hosts all stages of production, from partial-drying of the grapes to bottling. Their Amarone '15 is one of those wines that interprets tradition with an eye towards the most vibrant, rigorous qualities of the typology, eschewing softer, more pervasive sensations. Aromatically it's dominated by notes of wild fruit and medicinal herbs, which give way to pepper. In the mouth the wine comes through rich and powerful, finding tension and suppleness thanks to noteworthy acidity and a close-knit tannic weave that bring out its crisp, almost austere character.

● Amarone della Valpolicella Cl. '15	♟♟ 6
● Valpolicella Cl. Sup. Ripasso '17	♟♟ 3
● Valpolicella Cl. '18	♟ 2
● Amarone della Valpolicella Cl. '13	♟♟♟ 6
● Amarone della Valpolicella Cl. '12	♟♟♟ 6
● Amarone della Valpolicella Cl. '14	♟♟ 6
● Amarone della Valpolicella Cl. '11	♟♟ 6
● Amarone della Valpolicella Cl. '10	♟♟ 6
● Recioto della Valpolicella Cl. '15	♟♟ 5
● Recioto della Valpolicella Cl. '13	♟♟ 5
● Valpolicella Cl. '17	♟♟ 2*
● Valpolicella Cl. '14	♟♟ 2*
● Valpolicella Cl. Sup. Ripasso '16	♟♟ 3
● Valpolicella Cl. Sup. Ripasso '15	♟♟ 3
● Valpolicella Cl. Sup. Ripasso '14	♟♟ 3
● Valpolicella Cl. Sup. Ripasso '13	♟♟ 3*

★Suavia

FRAZ. FITTÀ DI SOAVE
VIA CENTRO, 14
37038 SOAVE [VR]
TEL. +39 0457675089
www.suavia.it

CELLAR SALES
PRE-BOOKED VISITS
ANNUAL PRODUCTION 100,000 bottles
HECTARES UNDER VINE 12.00

In Fittà, the high hills of Soave's classic heart have one of their best districts. It's an area marked by black basalt terrain, steep slopes facing every which way, old vineyards that make for unforgettable scenery and constant winds that caress the hills. Here we find Meri, Valentina and Alessandra Tessari, three female vine growers respectful of the territory and its traditions. Only Garganega and Trebbiano di Soave are cultivated, making for a selection of wines that's full of character. You can feel the force of the territory in Tessari's wines, with their Soave Monte Carbonare '17 exploring its deepest, most elegant qualities. On the nose flowery fragrances find fullness and generosity together with fruit. In the mouth sapidity confers rigor to the palate. Their Massifitti '16 is elegant on the nose, only to amaze for its acidic thrust and rigidity. Le Rive '16 proves mature and pervasive in its aromas, while on the palate it succeeds in bringing together power and lightness.

○ Soave Cl. Monte Carbonare '17	♟♟♟ 3*
○ Massifitti '16	♟♟ 3*
○ Le Rive '16	♟♟ 4
○ Opera Semplice Dosaggio Zero M. Cl.	♟♟ 4
○ Soave Cl. '18	♟♟ 2*
○ Soave Cl. Monte Carbonare '16	♟♟♟ 3*
○ Soave Cl. Monte Carbonare '15	♟♟♟ 3*
○ Soave Cl. Monte Carbonare '14	♟♟♟ 3*
○ Soave Cl. Monte Carbonare '12	♟♟♟ 3*
○ Soave Cl. Monte Carbonare '11	♟♟♟ 3*
○ Soave Cl. Monte Carbonare '10	♟♟♟ 3*
○ Soave Cl. Monte Carbonare '09	♟♟♟ 3*
○ Soave Cl. Monte Carbonare '08	♟♟♟ 3*
○ Soave Cl. Monte Carbonare '07	♟♟♟ 3*
○ Soave Cl. Monte Carbonare '06	♟♟♟ 3*
○ Soave Cl. Monte Carbonare '05	♟♟♟ 3*
○ Soave Cl. Monte Carbonare '04	♟♟♟ 3

Sutto

LOC. CAMPODIPIETRA
VIA ARZERI, 34/1
31040 SALGAREDA [TV]
TEL. +39 0422744063
www.sutto.it

CELLAR SALES
PRE-BOOKED VISITS
ACCOMMODATION AND RESTAURANT SERVICE
ANNUAL PRODUCTION 461,000 bottles
HECTARES UNDER VINE 75.00

In just a few years, Stefano and Luigi Sutto have brought a new dimension to the winery founded by their father, Ferruccio, such that today they're one of lower Piave's most noteworthy producers. Their many vineyards are situated primarily in the gravel and clay-rich plains between Venice and Friuli Venezia Giulia, with a smaller share of plots cultivated along the hills of Prosecco. In their modern cellar at Via Arzeri they only use the best grapes, making for wines that bring together varietal character with a firmness conferred by the territory. Campo Sella is a Merlot made with grapes from a single vineyard. On the nose it features elegant aromas, with ripe fruit accompanied by notes of medical herbs and sweet spices. These are even more prominent on the palate, where the wine brings together richness and suppleness. Their Dogma draws on a share of Cabernet for greater freshness and a palate that goings suppleness with vibrant, pleasantly rough tannins.

● Campo Sella '16	♥♥ 5
○ Bianco di Sutto '18	♥♥ 2*
● Cabernet '18	♥♥ 2*
● Dogma Rosso '16	♥♥ 4
● Merlot '18	♥♥ 2*
○ Pinot Grigio '18	♥♥ 2*
○ Chardonnay '18	♥ 2
● Piave Raboso '15	♥ 4
○ Prosecco Brut	♥ 2
● Campo Sella '15	♥♥♥ 5
○ Bianco di Sutto '17	♥♥ 2*
○ Bianco di Sutto '16	♥♥ 2*
● Cabernet '17	♥♥ 2*
● Cabernet '16	♥♥ 2*
● Merlot '17	♥♥ 2*
○ Venezia Pinot Grigio '17	♥♥ 2*

Tamellini

FRAZ. COSTEGGIOLA
VIA TAMELLINI, 4
37038 SOAVE [VR]
TEL. +39 0457675328
piofrancesco.tamellini@tin.it

CELLAR SALES
PRE-BOOKED VISITS
ANNUAL PRODUCTION 250,000 bottles
HECTARES UNDER VINE 27.00

Soave's classic heart spans the hills that surround the townships of Soave and Monteforte d'Alpone. If the eastern slope of the appellation sees soil made dark by its volcanic origins, moving west the presence of limestone gradually becomes more prominent. Just on the western side you'll find Gaetano and Pio Francesco Tamellini's estate. For more than twenty years the brothers have been considered valued interpreters of Soave's white wine, the result of painstaking care in the cellar so as to bring out all the clarity of Garganega. Le Bine de Costiola '17 is their most important wine, a Soave made exclusively with Garganega that offers up aromas of nice clarity. Aromatically it's dominated by yellow fruit, which leaves the work of conferring additional freshness to echoes of citrus and flowers. Only steel is used for aging, making for a palate in which dynamism the main stylistic feature. Their Soave '18 is fresher, juicier and more approachable.

○ Soave Cl. Le Bine de Costiola '17	♥♥ 3*
○ Soave '18	♥♥ 2*
○ Soave Cl. Le Bine '04	♥♥♥ 3*
○ Soave Cl. Le Bine de Costiola '14	♥♥♥ 3*
○ Soave Cl. Le Bine de Costiola '13	♥♥♥ 3*
○ Soave Cl. Le Bine de Costiola '11	♥♥♥ 3*
○ Soave Cl. Le Bine de Costiola '06	♥♥♥ 3*
○ Soave Cl. Le Bine de Costiola '05	♥♥♥ 3*
○ Extra Brut M. Cl. '10	♥♥ 5
○ Soave '17	♥♥ 2*
○ Soave Cl. '16	♥♥ 2*
○ Soave Cl. Le Bine de Costiola '16	♥♥ 3*
○ Soave Cl. Le Bine de Costiola '15	♥♥ 3*

Giovanna Tantini

FRAZ. OLIOSI
LOC. I MISCHI
37014 CASTELNUOVO DEL GARDA [VR]
TEL. +39 3488717577
www.giovannatantini.it

CELLAR SALES
PRE-BOOKED VISITS
ACCOMMODATION
ANNUAL PRODUCTION 30,000 bottles
HECTARES UNDER VINE 11.50

Giovanni Tantini founded her winery at the turn of the millennium, an estate situated to the south of Lake Garda where the clay lake terrain gives way to the morainic hills that have historically been cultivated for Bardolino and Custoza wines. The former are guyot, making for close-focused wines with an emphasis on lightness, while the latter are cultivating according to region's classic pergola system and give rise to the producer's only white. For Giovanna, time plays an important role in wine production. Even with a fresh wine like Bardolino, they take their time before releasing it. 2017 brought intensely flowery notes to the fore, enriched by spicy echoes of pepper. In the mouth the wine unfolds with lightness and tension, proving supple and gratifying. Ettore '14, a blend of slightly dried Corvina and Merlot with aromas of forest undergrowth and spices, delivers for its harmony.

★F.lli Tedeschi

FRAZ. PEDEMONTE
VIA G. VERDI, 4
37029 SAN PIETRO IN CARIANO [VR]
TEL. +39 0457701487
www.tedeschiwines.com

CELLAR SALES
PRE-BOOKED VISITS
ANNUAL PRODUCTION 500,000 bottles
HECTARES UNDER VINE 46.00
SUSTAINABLE WINERY

The Tedeschi brand is one of Valpolicella's most highly valued, bolstered by a vast estate and roots that go back more than a century (even if it was during the World War II, under Lorenzo, that it took on the configuration that we know today). The original vineyard on Monte Olmi has now been joined by Fabriseria in Pontare and, more recently, Maternigo, a splendid property surrounded by woods on the Mezzane hills. At Maternigo their vineyards are getting to the right age for prized fruit. These are interpreted by Riccardo with greater finesse and tension (with respect to the past), as is evidenced by their Valpolicella '16. On the nose wild fruit comes through ripe and crisp, enriched by flowery suggestions and fines herbes. In the mouth the impact is firm, with acidity and tannins reviving the palate. Both their Amarone Monte Olmi '13 and their Marne '15 also proved excellent.

● Bardolino '17	🍷🍷 2*
⊙ Bardolino Chiaretto '18	🍷🍷 2*
● Ettore '14	🍷🍷 4
○ Custoza '18	🍷 2
● Garda Corvina Ma.Gi.Co. '18	🍷 2
● Greta '13	🍷 5
● Bardolino '15	🍷🍷 2*
● Bardolino '14	🍷🍷 2*
⊙ Bardolino Chiaretto '16	🍷🍷 2*
⊙ Bardolino Chiaretto '15	🍷🍷 2*
○ Custoza '17	🍷🍷 2*
● Ettore '12	🍷🍷 4
● Ettore '11	🍷🍷 4
● Garda Corvina Ma.Gi.Co. '17	🍷🍷 2*

● Valpolicella Sup. Maternigo '16	🍷🍷🍷 5
● Amarone della Valpolicella Cl. Capitel Monte Olmi Ris. '13	🍷🍷 8
● Amarone della Valpolicella Marne 180 '15	🍷🍷 6
● Amarone della Valpolicella Marne 180 '16	🍷🍷 6
● Valpolicella Cl. Sup. La Fabriseria '16	🍷🍷 5
● Valpolicella Sup. Capitel Nicolò '17	🍷🍷 3
● Valpolicella Sup. Ripasso Capitel San Rocco '17	🍷🍷 4
● Valpolicella Cl. Lucchine '18	🍷 2
● Amarone della Valpolicella Cl. Capitel Monte Olmi '11	🍷🍷🍷 8
● Amarone della Valpolicella Cl. La Fabriseria Ris. '11	🍷🍷🍷 8

Le Tende

via Tende, 35
37017 Lazise [VR]
Tel. +39 0457590748
www.letende.it

CELLAR SALES
PRE-BOOKED VISITS
ANNUAL PRODUCTION 100,000 bottles
HECTARES UNDER VINE 12.50
VITICULTURE METHOD Certified Organic

Le Tende gets its name from the western Garda villa around which a part of the Fortuna and Lucillini's property is situated. Their other vineyards can be found in Cavaion, where the the lake's mild climate meets the cooler, windier climate of Valdadige. Organic cultivation, which has been a feature for years now, gives rise to highly prized grapes and allows Mauro Fortuna to forge an elegant selection of wines that perfectly expresses the character of tradition. Their Bardolino Classico '18 is a wine of great stylistic precision. A vibrant color anticipates fresh aromas, with pepper dominating, supported by flowery notes and hints of wild berries. In the mouth the wine proves fresh and racy, but what really impresses is its extraordinary sapidity, Garda's true trademark. Their Chiaretto '18, one of the most convincing in the appellation, is also a delicious wine.

⊙ Bardolino Chiaretto Cl. '18	🍷🍷 2*
● Bardolino Cl. '18	🍷🍷 2*
● Corvina '18	🍷🍷 3
○ Custoza '18	🍷🍷 3
⊙ Bardolino Chiaretto Brut Voluttà '18	🍷 3
● Bardolino Cl. Sup. '17	🍷 3
● Cicisbeo '17	🍷 5
○ Sabia '18	🍷 2
⊙ Bardolino Chiaretto Cl. '17	🍷🍷 2*
● Bardolino Cl. '17	🍷🍷 2*
● Bardolino Cl. Sup. '16	🍷🍷 3
● Bardolino Cl. Sup. '15	🍷🍷 3
● Corvina '16	🍷🍷 3
○ Custoza '16	🍷🍷 2*
○ Sabia '16	🍷🍷 2*

Gianni Tessari

via Prandi, 10
37030 Roncà [VR]
Tel. +39 0457460070
www.giannitessari.wine

CELLAR SALES
PRE-BOOKED VISITS
ANNUAL PRODUCTION 450,000 bottles
HECTARES UNDER VINE 55.00

Gianni Tessari is overseeing a complex winery, taken over only recently and active on three distinct fronts. First there's Soave, then Lessinia (with its sparkling wines) and finally Colli Berici, which is focused primarily on reds. If familiarity with Soave has made for wines that, from the outset, have proven convincing, the other two territories have shown themselves to be even more interesting. They're explored with the delicacy of one moving in a lesser-known land, but with the awareness that comes with great technical skill. Amarone Brolo delle Giare '12 is a generous reserve with very ripe aromas. On the palate it proves full, powerful and warm, underlined by the presence of oak and spices. Their Amarone Corte Majoli '15, on the other hand, offers up overripe fruit and still crispy fruit on the nose. These unfold in the mouth, where its powerful impact is followed by an energetic, supple unfolding of flavor. Among their Ripassos, we appreciate the suppleness of their Corte Majoli '17.

○ Lessini Durello Extra Brut M. Cl. 120 Mesi '08	🍷🍷 5
● Colli Berici Tai Rosso '17	🍷🍷 2*
○ Lessini Durello Extra Brut M. Cl. 36 Mesi	🍷🍷 5
○ Soave Cl. Pigno '17	🍷🍷 3
● Colli Berici Rosso Pian Alto '15	🍷 5
○ Due Bianco	🍷 2
● Due Rosso '16	🍷 2
○ Rebellis '18	🍷 3
○ Soave Cl. Monte Tenda '18	🍷 3
○ Soave Cl. Pigno Gianni Tessari '13	🍷🍷🍷 3*
○ Lessini Durello Brut 36 Mesi	🍷🍷 3
○ Soave Cl. Pigno '16	🍷🍷 3*
○ Soave Cl. Pigno '15	🍷🍷 3*

Tezza

FRAZ. POIANO DI VALPANTENA
VIA STRADELLA MAIOLI, 4
37142 VERONA
TEL. +39 045550267
www.tezzawines.it

CELLAR SALES
PRE-BOOKED VISITS
ANNUAL PRODUCTION 200,000 bottles
HECTARES UNDER VINE 28.00

The Tezza cousin's estate is situated in Valpolicella's only subzone, Valpantena, a large valley characterized by a gravelly floor that runs at 100 meters elevation only to slope upwards and suddenly close off after Grezzana. Here the wind passes through the valley, guaranteeing healthy grapes that give rise to a large selection. This is subdivided into three lines: Brolo delle Giare represent their premium wines, then there's Tezza and, finally, Corte Majoli for their simpler offerings. Their Durello '08 is an Extra Brut that's released more than 10 years after vintage. On the nose it features complex, stratified aromas, with an initial fruity whiff followed by notes of dry flowers, toasted hazelnut and bread. In the mouth the cultivar's trademark acidity lends tension and suppleness, while the palate finishes crisp and very long. Their energetic and balanced Soave Pigno '17, a monovarietal Garganega that ages in oak, also performed well.

● Amarone della Valpolicella Corte Majoli '18	♟♟ 5
● Amarone della Valpolicella Valpantena Brolo delle Giare Ris. '12	♟♟ 7
● Valpolicella Sup. Ripasso Corte Majoli '17	♟♟ 3
● Valpolicella Sup. Ripasso Ma Roat '17	♟♟ 2*
● Valpolicella Corte Majoli '18	♟ 2
● Valpolicella Valpantena Sup. Ripasso '16	♟ 3
● Valpolicella Valpantena Sup. Ripasso Brolo delle Giare '15	♟ 5
● Amarone della Valpolicella Valpantena '12	♟♟ 6
● Recioto della Valpolicella Valpantena '15	♟♟ 5

Tommasi Viticoltori

LOC. PEDEMONTE
VIA RONCHETTO, 4
37029 SAN PIETRO IN CARIANO [VR]
TEL. +39 0457701266
www.tommasi.com

CELLAR SALES
PRE-BOOKED VISITS
ACCOMMODATION AND RESTAURANT SERVICE
ANNUAL PRODUCTION 1,500,000 bottles
HECTARES UNDER VINE 205.00
SUSTAINABLE WINERY

In the late 1990s the Tommasi family began investing with persistence and foresight in new vineyards, creating an estate that today spans more than two hundred hectares. Of these, more than half are situated in Valpolicella Classica, while the rest can be found in other important regional appellations. Naturally, such a sizable estate has forced the winery to enlarge its cellar on multiple occasions, making it into what is today one of the territory's largest. Year after year, the new De Buris project is proving increasingly well defined, and with their 2009 the wine has reached another milestone in terms of quality. On the nose it evinces the deepest notes for a wine of its kind, with intact, crisp fruit crossed by spicy notes and hints of medicinal herbs (that reveal an unexpected youthfulness). In the mouth the wine exhibits decisiveness and softness, revived at the end by a sapidity and tension that characterize the best Amarones. Their Lugana Fornaci '18 is a fresh, racy and pleasant wine.

● Amarone della Valpolicella Cl. De Buris Ris. '09	♟♟♟ 8
● Amarone della Valpolicella Cl. '15	♟♟ 7
○ Lugana Le Fornaci '18	♟♟ 3
● Valpolicella Cl. Sup. Ripasso '17	♟♟ 4
● Crearo '16	♟ 5
● Valpolicella Cl. Sup. Rafael '17	♟ 3
● Amarone della Valpolicella Cl. De Buris Ris. '08	♟♟♟ 7
● Amarone della Valpolicella Cl. '13	♟♟ 7
● Amarone della Valpolicella Cl. Ca' Florian Ris. '11	♟♟ 7
● Crearo della Conca d'Oro '15	♟♟ 4
● Valpolicella '16	♟♟ 3
● Valpolicella Cl. Sup. Rafael '15	♟♟ 3
● Valpolicella Cl. Sup. Ripasso '16	♟♟ 4
● Valpolicella Cl. Sup. Ripasso '15	♟♟ 4

La Tordera

via Alnè Bosco, 23
31020 Vidor [TV]
Tel. +39 0423985362
www.latordera.it

CELLAR SALES
PRE-BOOKED VISITS
ANNUAL PRODUCTION 1,200,000 bottles
HECTARES UNDER VINE 70.00
VITICULTURE METHOD Certified Organic
SUSTAINABLE WINERY

The Vettoretti siblings, Gabriella, Paolo and Renato, have grown the family winery founded in 2001. Today they avail themselves of a large estate that covers some of the area's best positions, as well as the support of local growers who deliver their grapes to the winery. With a view towards its environmental impact, the new cellar is certified CasaClima Wine, while their vineyards are organically managed. Their Brut Otreval '18 put in a strong showing. It's a wine made with grapes from an old vineyard in Guia. On the nose signature flowery aromas emerge along with apple. These follow through on the palate, where the absence of residual sugars confers tension and pluck. Their Extra Dry Serrai, which originates in the lower part of Vidor, exhibits more intense, ripe aromas dominated by fruity sensations. In the mouth a delicate sugariness makes for a pleasurable palate.

○ Valdobbiadene Extra Dry Serrai	🍷🍷 3
○ Valdobbiadene Rive di Guia Brut Otreval '18	🍷🍷 3
○ Cartizze	🍷 4
⊙ Gabry Brut Rosé	🍷 2
○ Valdobbiadene Brut Brunei '18	🍷 3
○ Valdobbiadene Rive di Vidor Dry Tittoni '18	🍷 3
○ Valdobbiadene Brut Brunei '17	🍷🍷 3
○ Valdobbiadene Extra Dry Serrai '16	🍷🍷 3
○ Valdobbiadene Rive di Guia Brut Otreval '17	🍷🍷 3
○ Valdobbiadene Rive di Guida Brut Otreval '16	🍷🍷 3
○ Valdobbiadene Rive di Vidor Dry Tittoni '17	🍷🍷 3

Trabucchi d'Illasi

loc. Monte Tenda
37031 Illasi [VR]
Tel. +39 0457833233
www.trabucchidillasi.it

CELLAR SALES
PRE-BOOKED VISITS
ANNUAL PRODUCTION 120,000 bottles
HECTARES UNDER VINE 25.00
VITICULTURE METHOD Certified Organic

The Trabucchi family's winery is situated in one of eastern Valpolicella's loveliest areas, specifically on the Monte Tenda ridge separating the Tramigna and Illasi valleys. From here you can see the vineyards of Valpolicella and the northern mountains of Lessinia, while the eastern side slopes down towards the Illasi Valley and the western drops off suddenly towards Cazzano. Their vineyards, which have been organically cultivated for many years now, provide the grapes for a selection characterized by a rich, generous style. Their Amarone Cent'Anni is a 2010 reserve that exhibits unexpected freshness underpinned by ripe, but still vibrant and crisp wild fruit. There's also Corvinone's trademark pepperiness, which lends lightness. In the mouth the wine follows a similar tract, impacting soft and pervasive only to be gradually refreshed by acidity. Their Valpolicella Superiore '13 is a fresher wine characterized by a crisp, pleasantly rough finish.

● Amarone della Valpolicella Cent'Anni Ris. '10	🍷🍷 8
● Valpolicella Sup. '13	🍷🍷 3
● Amarone della Valpolicella '04	🍷🍷🍷 8
● Recioto della Valpolicella Cereolo '05	🍷🍷🍷 8
● Valpolicella Sup. Terre di S. Colombano '03	🍷🍷🍷 4*
● Amarone della Valpolicella '10	🍷🍷 8
● Amarone della Valpolicella '09	🍷🍷 8
● Valpolicella Sup. Terre del Cereolo '09	🍷🍷 5
● Valpolicella Sup. Terre di S. Colombano '10	🍷🍷 3*
● Valpolicella Sup. Terre di San Colombano '12	🍷🍷 3

Spumanti Valdo

VIA FORO BOARIO, 20
31049 VALDOBBIADENE [TV]
TEL. +39 04239090
www.valdo.com

CELLAR SALES
PRE-BOOKED VISITS
ANNUAL PRODUCTION 9,000,000 bottles
HECTARES UNDER VINE 155.00

Founded in 1926, Società Anonima Vini
Superiori was bought by Verona's Bolla
family a few years later, but it wasn't until
1951 that the Valdo brand first appeared.
And so the Bolla family have managed this
historic Valdobbiadene winery for more
than 90 years, and today Pierluigi is at the
helm, a captain who's transformed it into
one of the territory's most reliable
producers. Within Prosecco Superiore they
don't have a substantial property, relying
instead on the precious work of a dense
network of growers who deliver their
grapes to the winery. Their Brut Nature '18
is made with the best grapes from their
San Pietro di Babozza vineyards. On the
nose it offers up delicate notes of flowers
and white fruit, which are even clearer on a
crisp and pleasantly tense palate. The
almost total absence of sugars allows a
pronounced sapidity to emerge, a quality
that's common to the territory's best
districts. Thus the wine unfolds perfectly
sustained by acidity and bubbles.

○ Valdobbiadene Rive di San Pietro di Barbozza Brut Nature '18	♈♈ 3*
○ Cartizze Cuvée Viviana	♈♈ 5
○ Valdobbiadene Brut Cuvée del Fondatore '18	♈♈ 3
○ Valdobbiadene Brut Cuvée di Boj '18	♈♈ 2*
○ Valdobbiadene Brut Numero 10 M. Cl. '17	♈ 4
○ Valdobbiadene Extra Dry Cuvée 1926	♈ 2
○ Valdobbiadene Brut Cuvée del Fondatore '17	♈♈ 3*
○ Valdobbiadene Brut Cuvée del Fondatore '14	♈♈ 3
○ Valdobbiadene Brut M. Cl. Numero 10 '15	♈♈ 4
○ Valdobbiadene Brut M. Cl. Numero 10 '14	♈♈ 4
○ Valdobbiadene Rive di San Pietro di Barbozza Brut Nature '17	♈♈ 3

Cantina Produttori di Valdobbiadene - Val d'Oca

VIA SAN GIOVANNI, 45
31030 VALDOBBIADENE [TV]
TEL. +39 0423982070
www.valdoca.com

CELLAR SALES
PRE-BOOKED VISITS
ANNUAL PRODUCTION 13,000,000 bottles
HECTARES UNDER VINE 950.00
VITICULTURE METHOD Certified Organic

Founded after WW II, this large
Valdobbiadene cooperative boasts more
than 60 years of experience, making it
what is today one of Prosecco Superiore's
leading producers. More than a thousand
hectares of land are covered by a small
army of growers who, day after day,
cultivate a territory recently designated a
world patrimony and dedicated to a single
grape, Glera. Indeed, more than 600
grower members provide the ingredients
for a selection that features their premium
Val D'Oca wines. Great attention has been
paid to their Rive line, as testified to by the
presence of some two wines made with
grapes from their best San Pietro di
Barbozza and Santo Stefano vineyards. The
former give rise to a fresh and nicely sapid
Brut, while the latter make for a Brut Nature
with elegant aromas dominated by
characteristic expressions of golden apples
and flowers. These follow through on a
crisp, pleasantly tense and very long palate.

○ Valdobbiadene Extra Dry Jos '18	♈♈ 3
○ Valdobbiadene Rive di San Pietro di Barbozza Brut '18	♈♈ 4
○ Valdobbiadene Rive di Santo Stefano Brut Nature '18	♈♈ 4
● Marzemino Spumante Dolce Zoj	♈ 4
○ Valdobbiadene Dry Uvaggio Storico	♈ 3
○ P. di Valdobbiadene Dry Millesimato Val d'Oca '06	♈♈ 3
○ P. di Valdobbiadene Extra Dry Uvaggio Storico Val d'Oca	♈♈ 3
○ Valdobbiadene Rive di Colbertaldo Extra Dry '17	♈♈ 4
○ Valdobbiadene Rive di Santo Stefano Brut '17	♈♈ 4
○ P. di Valdobbiadene Extra Dry Val d'Oca '05	♈ 2

Cantina Valpantena Verona

LOC. QUINTO
VIA COLONIA ORFANI DI GUERRA, 5B
37142 VERONA
TEL. +39 045550032
www.cantinavalpantena.it

CELLAR SALES
PRE-BOOKED VISITS
ANNUAL PRODUCTION 9,000,000 bottles
HECTARES UNDER VINE 750.00
SUSTAINABLE WINERY

This large cooperative winery, situated just outside Verona, is going through a period of transformation. If for years their goals were rooted in high production volumes and an easily recognizable style, today Luca Degani and his staff are raising the bar. They're pursuing the same goals (recognizability and quality) but with an eye towards expressing the beauty and unique attributes of the territory. La Cantina avails itself of 250 grower members who oversee vineyards situated primarily in eastern Valpolicella. Their vineyard in the heart of Valpolicella gives rise to their premium wines, an Amarone '11 and a Valpolicella Superiore '13 named Brolo dei Giusti. The former features aromas of overripe fruit, dried leaves and pepper. On the palate it opens strong but gradually finds suppleness, thanks to acidity and the support of smooth tannins. The latter offers an aromatic profile centered on a fruit and a well-balanced palate.

Cantina Valpolicella Negrar

VIA CA' SALGARI, 2
37024 NEGRAR [VR]
TEL. +39 0456014300
www.cantinanegrar.it

CELLAR SALES
PRE-BOOKED VISITS
RESTAURANT SERVICE
ANNUAL PRODUCTION 7,000,000 bottles
HECTARES UNDER VINE 700.00

Founded in the interwar period, today Cantina Valpolicella Negrar avails itself of more than 200 grower members who oversee vineyards situated primarily in Valpolicella Classica, in all five of its valleys. If in the vineyard work is still carried out according to tradition, at Via Ca' Salgari there's plenty of news, from the building of a new grape drying facility to a new aging cellar, where their Amarone undergoes a lengthy stay in large wooden barrels. The grapes for Collezione Pruviniano come exclusively from vineyards in the Marano Valley. It's a new line that interprets Valpolicella with an eye towards the fitness and tension that are trademarks of the valley. Their Amarone '14 offers up intense notes of red fruit refreshed by a balsamic presence. On the palate it's crisp and slender with a nice tannic presence that lends vigor and pluck.

- Amarone della Valpolicella Brolo dei Giusti '11 — 8
- Amarone della Valpolicella '16 — 6
- Amarone della Valpolicella Torre del Falasco '15 — 7
- Recioto della Valpolicella Tesauro '16 — 5
- Valpolicella Sup. Brolo dei Giusti '13 — 2*
- Valpolicella Sup. Torre del Falasco '17 — 2*
- Valpolicella Valpantena Ripasso Ritocco '17 — 4
- Chardonnay Baroncino '18 — 2
- Corvina Torre del Falasco '18 — 2
- Garganega Torre del Falasco '18 — 2
- Lugana Torre del Falasco '18 — 3
- Valpolicella Sup. Ripasso Torre del Falasco '17 — 4

- Amarone della Valpolicella Cl. Pruviniano Domini Veneti '14 — 5
- Amarone della Valpolicella Cl. Vign. Jago Domini Veneti '13 — 6
- Valpolicella Cl. Sup. Ripasso La Casetta Domini Veneti '16 — 4
- Valpolicella Cl. Sup. Verjago Domini Veneti '13 — 4
- Recioto della Valpolicella Cl. Amardorlato Amando Domini Veneti '12 — 6
- Valpolicella Cl. Sup. Coll. Pruviano Domini Veneti '16 — 3
- Amarone della Valpolicella Cl. S. Rocco Domini Veneti '08 — 8
- Amarone della Valpolicella Cl. Villa Domini Veneti '05 — 8
- Recioto della Valpolicella Cl. Vigneti di Moron Domini Veneti '01 — 5

Odino Vaona

LOC. VALGATARA
VIA PAVERNO, 41
37020 MARANO DI VALPOLICELLA [VR]
TEL. +39 0457703710
www.vaona.it

CELLAR SALES
PRE-BOOKED VISITS
ANNUAL PRODUCTION 70,000 bottles
HECTARES UNDER VINE 10.00
SUSTAINABLE WINERY

Alberto Vaona leads his family's winery in the Marano Valley, about 10 hectares along the hills that surround the cellar, at elevations spanning 200-250 meters (a couple of vineyards situated at lower elevations provide the grapes for their simpler wines). In their small but efficient cellar in Paverno, all stages of production are carried out according to tradition, including their choice of cultivars and the style of their wines. The grapes from their Pegrandi vineyard give rise to their most interesting wine, their Amarone '15. Its lovely ruby-red color anticipates aromas of sweet, ripe red fruit. In the mouth the wine is rich and supple, revived by an acidity that lengthens and lightens the palate. The Riserva '13, however, exhibits a deeper, more complex aromatic profile. It's a quality that's particularly pronounced on the palate, where power and exuberance dominate.

- Amarone della Valpolicella Cl. Pegrandi '15 — ♟♟ 6
- Amarone della Valpolicella Cl. Pegrandi Ris. '12 — ♟♟ 8
- Recioto della Valpolicella Cl. Le Peagnè '16 — ♟♟ 4
- Valpolicella Cl. Sup. Ripasso Pegrandi '17 — ♟♟ 3
- Valpolicella Sup. '17 — ♟♟ 3
- Amarone della Valpolicella Cl. Paverno '15 — ♟ 5
- Amarone della Valpolicella Cl. Pegrandi '09 — ♟♟♟ 5
- Amarone della Valpolicella Cl. Pegrandi '08 — ♟♟♟ 5
- Amarone della Valpolicella Cl. Pegrandi '13 — ♟♟ 6

Venturini

FRAZ. SAN FLORIANO
VIA SEMONTE, 20
37029 SAN PIETRO IN CARIANO [VR]
TEL. +39 0457701331
www.viniventurini.com

CELLAR SALES
PRE-BOOKED VISITS
ANNUAL PRODUCTION 130,000 bottles
HECTARES UNDER VINE 15.00
SUSTAINABLE WINERY

The Venturini siblings, Giuseppina, Daniele and Mirco, have left their historic headquarters at San Floriano and moved to a cellar perched along the ridge that separates the Negrar and Marano valleys, a strip of land that from upper Valpolicella stretches towards Verona. The vineyards can be found on various plots, traditional pergolas situated along tracts supported by stone walls. Just a few wines are made, all of them traditional classics. The winery proposed two Amarones, their Classico '15 and their Campomasua '13. The former is a traditionally styled wine marked by aromas of overripe fruit accompanied by vegetal and mineral notes. These introduce a generous palate with a finish of notable finesse. The latter is aromatically richer, deeper and more stratified, while the palate is powerful but unafraid to show its soft side.

- Amarone della Valpolicella Cl. '15 — ♟♟ 5
- Amarone della Valpolicella Cl. Campomasua '13 — ♟♟ 6
- Recioto della Valpolicella Cl. '16 — ♟♟ 5
- Massimino '15 — ♟ 5
- Valpolicella Cl. Sup. Ripasso Semonte Alto '15 — ♟ 4
- Amarone della Valpolicella Cl. Campomasua '07 — ♟♟♟ 6
- Amarone della Valpolicella Cl. Campomasua '05 — ♟♟♟ 6
- Recioto della Valpolicella Cl. Le Brugnine '97 — ♟♟♟ 5
- Amarone della Valpolicella Cl. Ris. '07 — ♟♟ 8
- Recioto della Valpolicella Cl. Le Brugnine '13 — ♟♟ 6

Agostino Vicentini

FRAZ. SAN ZENO
VIA C. BATTISTI, 62C
37030 COLOGNOLA AI COLLI [VR]
TEL. +39 0457650539
www.vinivicentini.com

CELLAR SALES
PRE-BOOKED VISITS
ANNUAL PRODUCTION 100,000 bottles
HECTARES UNDER VINE 20.00

Colognola ai Colli is situated at the entrance to the Illasi valley. It's a small plateau that slopes rapidly towards a valley floor rich in gravel and clay. Here we find Agostino Vicentini's winery, surrounded by vineyards that clamber up Illasi's slopes. It's an estate that straddles both the Soave and Valpolicella appellations, and gives rise to exclusively traditional grapes. These are interpreted by Agostino with an eye towards bringing out their purity of character. A year in the cellar treated their Soave Il Casale '17 well. On the nose it offers up delicate aromas with ripe yellow fruit finding support in a hint of almond, dried flowers and shrub. In the mouth the wine changes gears, proving approachable and rich, supported by an extraordinary sapidity. Here the wine unfolds supplely, making for a crisp, gutsy finish. Their Terre Lunghe '18, a Soave that relies on a small share of Trebbiano, is all fragrance, tension and juice.

Vigna Ròda

FRAZ. CORTELÀ
VIA MONTE VERSA, 1569
35030 Vo' [PD]
TEL. +39 0499940228
www.vignaroda.com

CELLAR SALES
PRE-BOOKED VISITS
ANNUAL PRODUCTION 52,000 bottles
HECTARES UNDER VINE 17.00

Gianni Strazzacappa's winery is situated on the western side of the Euganean hills, on an estate that comprises some twenty hectares. For more than a century these gentle hills have hosted primarily historic Bordeaux red grapes. Their selection still doesn't use all the grapes cultivated, allowing Gianni and his wife, Elena, to choose only the best batches for their wines, making for a selection that features an approachable, generous style. This year they presented a limited selection due to the decision to give their younger wines more time to find the right harmony. Their Scarlatto '16 is a Bordeaux blend, primarily Merlot, that pursues a style in which concentration serves elegance and pleasantness. Its aromas call up ripe, crisp red fruit, while in the mouth the wine unfolds with lightness, supported by a commendable sapid presence.

○ Soave Sup. Il Casale '17	♛♛♛ 3*
○ Soave Vign. Terre Lunghe '18	♛♛ 3
● Valpolicella Sup. '16	♛♛ 3
● Valpolicella Boccascalucce '17	♛ 3
○ Soave Sup. Il Casale '16	♛♛♛ 3*
○ Soave Sup. Il Casale '15	♛♛♛ 3*
○ Soave Sup. Il Casale '14	♛♛♛ 3*
○ Soave Sup. Il Casale '13	♛♛♛ 3*
○ Soave Sup. Il Casale '12	♛♛♛ 3*
○ Soave Sup. Il Casale '09	♛♛♛ 3*
○ Soave Sup. Il Casale '08	♛♛♛ 3*
○ Soave Sup. Il Casale '07	♛♛♛ 3*
○ Recioto di Soave '15	♛♛ 5
○ Soave Vign. Terre Lunghe '17	♛♛ 3
○ Soave Vign. Terre Lunghe '16	♛♛ 2*
● Valpolicella Sup. '15	♛♛ 3
● Valpolicella Sup. Idea Bacco '13	♛♛ 5

○ Colli Euganei Fior d'Arancio Passito Petali d'Ambra '13	♛♛ 4
● Colli Euganei Rosso Scarlatto '16	♛♛ 3
○ Aroma 2.0 '18	♛ 2
● Colli Euganei Cabernet Espero '16	♛♛ 2*
○ Colli Euganei Fior d'Arancio Passito Petali d'Ambra '12	♛♛ 4
● Colli Euganei Rosso '17	♛♛ 2*
● Colli Euganei Rosso '16	♛♛ 2*
● Colli Euganei Rosso Scarlatto '15	♛♛ 3*
● Colli Euganei Rosso Scarlatto '14	♛♛ 3
● Merlot Il Damerino '17	♛♛ 2*
● Merlot Il Damerino '16	♛♛ 2*

Vignale di Cecilia

Loc. Fornaci
via Croci, 14
35030 Baone [PD]
Tel. +39 042951420
www.vignaledicecilia.it

PRE-BOOKED VISITS
ANNUAL PRODUCTION 20,000 bottles
HECTARES UNDER VINE 8.00
VITICULTURE METHOD Certified Organic

Paolo Brunello came to viticulture almost by accident, taking over the family winery and transforming what was initially a hobby into a complex estate that explores the great potential of the Euganean hills. Originally just four hectares and a cellar, today their vineyards span various plots. Bordeaux grapes are cultivated along with Moscato and varieties that call up a distant past, like Garganega and Tai. In the cellar, wines are made in keeping with nature's rhythms, making for a plucky selection that shows some character. El Moro is a blend of equal parts Cabernet Franc and Sauvignon cultivated on calcareous terrain and aged in large wooden barrels. On the nose it exhibits a splendid presence of fruit enriched by notes of medicinal herbs and pencil lead, all of which seem to explode in its vibrant and lengthy palate. It's a wine that perfectly expresses the Euganean hills, with a sapidity and creaminess that are the trademarks of the territory.

● El Moro Cabernet '16	♟ 3*
● Colli Euganei Rosso Covolo '16	♟♟ 3
○ Poldo	♟♟ 3
○ Benavides '17	♟ 2
○ Prosecco Campo Nicoletta	♟ 2
○ Benavides '16	♟♟ 2*
○ Benavides '15	♟♟ 2*
○ Cocài '16	♟♟ 3
○ Cocài '12	♟♟ 3
● Colli Euganei Rosso Covolo '15	♟♟ 3
● Colli Euganei Rosso Covolo '14	♟♟ 3
● Colli Euganei Rosso Covolo '13	♟♟ 3
● Colli Euganei Rosso Passacaglia '15	♟♟ 4
● Colli Euganei Rosso Passacaglia '13	♟♟ 4
● Colli Euganei Rosso Passacaglia '12	♟♟ 4
● El Moro Cabernet '15	♟♟ 3

★Vignalta

via Scalette
35032 Arquà Petrarca [PD]
Tel. +39 0429777305
www.vignalta.it

CELLAR SALES
PRE-BOOKED VISITS
ANNUAL PRODUCTION 230,000 bottles
HECTARES UNDER VINE 35.00
SUSTAINABLE WINERY

Situated in the southern part of the Euganean hills, Vignalta is one of the territory's most representative producers, bolstered by a sizable estate and a history that goes back thirty years. A winery that began almost as a lark now comprises an enlarged cellar, making it possible for all stages of production, including aging, to be followed more easily. The estate's prized vineyards can be found in Monte Gemola. It's an area that enjoys an excellent southeast aspect and crumbly trachyte soils, making it the ideal place to cultivate the grapes for their most important reds. The wine that most impressed this year, however, was their Alpianae '16, a vibrant gold Fior d'Arancio (Moscato Giallo). It explodes on the nose with notes of citrus, licorice and exotic fruit seeming to grow in intensity. Its rich, buoyant palate exhibits great concentration of sugars, but it's tamed by an acidity and sapidity that lend softness.

○ Colli Euganei Fiori d'Arancio Passito Alpianae '16	♟♟♟ 5
● Colli Euganei Rosso Gemola '12	♟♟ 6
● Agno Tinto '13	♟♟ 5
○ Brut Nature M. Cl.	♟♟ 4
○ Chardonnay '17	♟♟ 4
● Colli Euganei Rosso Ris. '14	♟♟ 3
○ Moscato L.H. '17	♟♟ 3
⊙ Pinot Grigio delle Venezie '18	♟♟ 4
○ Sirio '18	♟♟ 2*
○ Agno Casto '17	♟ 4
○ Colli Euganei Fior d'Arancio Passito Alpianae '12	♟♟♟ 5
● Colli Euganei Rosso Gemola '13	♟♟♟ 6
● Colli Euganei Rosso Gemola '09	♟♟♟ 5
● Colli Euganei Rosso Gemola '08	♟♟♟ 5

Le Vigne di San Pietro

VIA SAN PIETRO, 23
37066 SOMMACAMPAGNA [VR]
TEL. +39 045510016
www.levignedisanpietro.it

CELLAR SALES
PRE-BOOKED VISITS
ANNUAL PRODUCTION 70,000 bottles
HECTARES UNDER VINE 10.00

Carlo Nerozzi's winery gets its name from the hill road along which the cellar and vineyards are situated (though they also manage plots in Balconi Rossi). An architect who's fond of viticulture, Nerozzi has always pursued the idea that wine should express the territory, in this case that means privileging elegance and personality over force. The choice to operate within Garda's historic appellations, Custoza and Bardolino, has allowed the producer to make wines that explore their deepest, most privileged qualities. In fact, rather than a fresh, varietal wine, their Bardolino Superiore '17 expresses the typology's hidden qualities. Spices and wild fruit reemerge on a palate that evidences tannins, making for a crisp wine of great stylistic precision. Their most recent creation, Come un Pino Nero, is an interesting monovarietal Corvina. As the name suggests, it's interpreted as if it were it's noble Burgundian cousin.

● Bardolino Sup. '17	♟♟	3*
☉ Bardolino Chiaretto CorDeRosa '18	♟♟	2*
● Come un Pino Nero '16	♟♟	4
○ Custoza Sup. Sanpietro '18	♟♟	4
○ Custoza '18	♟	2
● Bardolino '14	♟♟♟	2*
● Bardolino '11	♟♟♟	2*
○ Custoza Sanpietro '16	♟♟♟	4*
● Refolà Cabernet Sauvignon '04	♟♟♟	6
○ Sud '95	♟♟♟	6
● Bardolino '17	♟♟	2*
☉ Bardolino Chiaretto CorDeRosa '17	♟♟	2*
☉ Bardolino Chiaretto CorDeRosa '16	♟♟	2*
● Bardolino Sup. '16	♟♟	3*
● Bardolino Sup. '15	♟♟	3*
○ Custoza Sup. Sanpietro '15	♟♟	3*

Vigneto Due Santi

V.LE ASIAGO, 174
36061 BASSANO DEL GRAPPA [VI]
TEL. +39 0424502074
www.vignetoduesanti.it

CELLAR SALES
PRE-BOOKED VISITS
ANNUAL PRODUCTION 100,000 bottles
HECTARES UNDER VINE 18.00
SUSTAINABLE WINERY

The Zonta family's winery is situated in the northwestern part of Bassano, where the houses suddenly become less frequent and give way to hillside vineyards. The property, which is situated practically at the entrance to the Valsugana valley, enjoys the area's cool winds, giving rise to healthy, generous grapes. The sizable tract of land covered allows for a rigorous grape selection process, making for a selection of full, juicy and highly supple wines. Their Cabernet Due Santi '16 took advantage of an excellent year to express an aromatic profile of great precision and freshness, one in which wild fruit is crossed by spicy notes and cut flowers. The palate impresses for the way it brings together richness and acidic tension, making for a wine of great suppleness and elegance. Their Pinot Bianco '18 had a nice debut. It's a wine with elegant aromas and a fine, long palate.

● Breganze Cabernet Due Santi '16	♟♟	4
○ Breganze Bianco Rivana '18	♟♟	2*
● Breganze Cabernet '17	♟♟	3
● Breganze Merlot '17	♟♟	2*
○ Breganze Pinot Bianco '18	♟♟	2*
○ Malvasia Campo di Fiori '18	♟♟	2*
○ Breganze Torcolato '16	♟	5
○ Prosecco Extra Dry	♟	2
● Breganze Cabernet Due Santi '14	♟♟♟	4*
● Breganze Cabernet Vign. Due Santi '12	♟♟♟	4*
● Breganze Cabernet Vign. Due Santi '08	♟♟♟	4*
● Breganze Cabernet Vign. Due Santi '07	♟♟♟	4
● Breganze Cabernet Vign. Due Santi '05	♟♟♟	4
● Breganze Cabernet Vign. Due Santi '04	♟♟♟	4*
● Breganze Cabernet Vign. Due Santi '03	♟♟♟	4*

★Villa Sandi

VIA ERIZZO, 113/A
31035 CROCETTA DEL MONTELLO [TV]
TEL. +39 04238607
www.villasandi.it

CELLAR SALES
PRE-BOOKED VISITS
ACCOMMODATION AND RESTAURANT SERVICE
ANNUAL PRODUCTION 5,500,000 bottles
HECTARES UNDER VINE 560.00
VITICULTURE METHOD Certified Organic
SUSTAINABLE WINERY

Few wineries have managed to navigate the world of Prosecco with as much lucidity as Villa Sandi. It's a producer that has, in a few short decades, managed to significantly increase its range of influence, purchasing vineyards both in the historic appellation and in nearby ones, reaching all the way to Asolo. In addition to Prosecco, the producer has developed a noteworthy line of Metodo Classico sparklers and still wines made with grapes cultivated along the northwestern side of Montello. Contrary to what happens traditionally, their Cartizze La Rivetta is interpreted in a Brut version, but limiting the presence of sugars and relying on the richness of the grapes used. Its aromas are delicate and light, calling up golden apple and wild flowers with delicate citrusy notes. In the mouth it proves commendably made. Its bubbles caress the palate, while sapidity and firmness find suppleness in its juicy, acidic stride.

○ Cartizze Brut V. La Rivetta	♔♔♔ 6
○ Amalia Moretti Brut M. Cl. Opere Ris.	♔♔ 8
○ Asolo Brut	♔♔ 3
○ Montello e Colli Asolani Manzoni Bianco '18	♔♔ 3
● Montello e Colli Asolani Merlot Còrpore '16	♔♔ 5
○ Serenissima Brut Opere M. Cl.	♔♔ 5
○ Valdobbiadene Rive di San Pietro di Barbozza Dry '18	♔♔ 3
○ Cartizze Brut V. La Rivetta '11	♔♔♔ 4*
○ Cartizze Brut V. La Rivetta '10	♔♔♔ 4
○ Cartizze Brut V. La Rivetta '09	♔♔♔ 4
● Montello Colli Asolani Cabernet Filio '15	♔♔ 4
○ Valdobbiadene Dry Rive di San Pietro di Barbozza '17	♔♔ 4

Villa Spinosa

LOC. JAGO
VIA JAGO DALL'ORA, 14
37024 NEGRAR [VR]
TEL. +39 0457500093
www.villaspinosa.it

CELLAR SALES
PRE-BOOKED VISITS
ACCOMMODATION
ANNUAL PRODUCTION 45,000 botties
HECTARES UNDER VINE 20.00
SUSTAINABLE WINERY

In a territory like Valpolicella, which lived through a frenzied period of success, Villa Spinosa is something of a rarity. Enrico Cascella has been able to manage the family winery lucidly and slowly, respecting the rhythms set out by nature. Today Villa Spinosa is one of the region's most noteworthy producers, bolstered by an estate that spans the valleys of Marano and Negrar and a selection that brings together tradition with the modern world. Here force is never employed for its own sake but instead serves to express each vineyard. The grapes for their Ripasso '16 are cultivated in one of the Negar Valley's most interesting districts, Jago. This Valpolicella lets through all the austerity that characterizes the vineyard's grapes, with fruit never serving as a solo act, but always accompanied by a chorus of mineral notes, spices and medicinal herbs. The palate is crisp and gutsy, delineated and reinvigorated by tannins and acidity.

● Valpolicella Cl. Sup. Ripasso Jago '16	♔♔ 3*
● Amarone della Valpolicella Cl. '15	♔♔ 6
● Valpolicella Cl. Sup. Figari '16	♔♔ 3
● Valpolicella Cl. '18	♔ 2
● Amarone della Valpolicella Cl. '08	♔♔♔ 7
● Amarone della Valpolicella Cl. Albasini '11	♔♔♔ 7
● Amarone della Valpolicella Cl. Albasini '10	♔♔♔ 7
● Valpolicella Cl. Sup. Ripasso Jago '11	♔♔♔ 3*
● Amarone della Valpolicella Cl. '14	♔♔ 6
● Amarone della Valpolicella Cl. Guglielmi di Jago 20 anni '08	♔♔ 8
● Recioto della Valpolicella Cl. Francesca Finato Spinosa '13	♔♔ 5
● Valpolicella Cl. '15	♔♔ 2*
● Valpolicella Cl. Sup. Ripasso Jago '15	♔♔ 3*

Vigneti Villabella

Fraz. Calmasino di Bardolino
Loc. Canova, 2
37011 Bardolino [VR]
Tel. +39 0457236448
www.vignetivillabella.com

CELLAR SALES
PRE-BOOKED VISITS
ACCOMMODATION
ANNUAL PRODUCTION 500,000 bottles
HECTARES UNDER VINE 220.00

Founded in the 1970s by the Cristoforetti and Delibori families, Vigneti Villabella has managed to enlarge their estate along the banks of Garda, such that, at hundreds of hectares, it now comprises the region's primary appellations. Villa Cordevigo is their crown jewel, a viticultural pearl of natural beauty that extends for several hectares and, gradually, is being converted to organic. They offer a wide range of wines characterized by a clear, close-focused style centered on drinkability. Their Bardolino Morlongo '17 proved an emblematic drink. It's a red whose aromatic profile is dominated by suggestions of forest undergrowth and spices, which follow through on a palate that doesn't dwell on the freshness of the typology, but rather enriches it with character and pluck. Their Bardolino Chiaretto Villa Cordevigo '18 is a rosé with fresh and flowery aromas and a palate that stands out for its sapidity.

⊙ Bardolino Chiaretto Cl. Villa Cordevigo '16	🍷🍷 2*
● Bardolino Cl. Morlongo '17	🍷🍷 2*
● Amarone della Valpolicella Cl. '13	🍷🍷 5
● Amarone della Valpolicella Cl. Fracastoro Ris. '10	🍷🍷 7
⊙ Bardolino Chiaretto Heaven Scent '18	🍷🍷 2*
○ Fiordilej Villa Codervigo Passito '15	🍷🍷 3
● Montemazzano '16	🍷🍷 3
⊙ Bardolino Chiaretto Cl. '18	🍷 2
○ Lugana '18	🍷 3
● Valpolicella Cl. Sup. Ripasso '17	🍷 3
○ Villa Cordevigo Bianco '16	🍷 4
● Villa Cordevigo Rosso '12	🍷 5
● Bardolino Cl. V. Morlongo '14	🍷🍷🍷 2*

★Viviani

via Mazzano, 8
37020 Negrar [VR]
Tel. +39 0457500286
www.cantinaviviani.com

CELLAR SALES
PRE-BOOKED VISITS
ANNUAL PRODUCTION 80,000 bottles
HECTARES UNDER VINE 10.00
SUSTAINABLE WINERY

Moving up the Negrar Valley along the eastern ridge towards Lessinia, we find the small hamlet of Mazzano. At 480 meters elevation it represents a kind of borderland between the viticultural zone and the area once dedicated to pastures (but has now been reclaimed by nature). It's here that Claudio Viviani, a gifted producer who never wanted to abandon his agricultural roots, operates, faithful to his few hectares of property situated largely in the higher part of the appellation. Even more careful management of their vineyards is starting to bear fruit and their Amarone Casa dei Bepi '13 is one of the best tasted yet. On the nose it calls up overripe red fruit, spices and balsamic nuances. In the mouth it impresses for the way in which its full palate relies more on sapidity and tannins than on sugars. Their Campo Morar '16 is the usual Valpolicella thoroughbred, while their Amarone '15 surprises for its integrity and vibrance.

● Amarone della Valpolicella Cl. Casa dei Bepi '13	🍷🍷🍷 8
● Amarone della Valpolicella Cl. '15	🍷🍷 6
● Valpolicella Cl. Sup. Campo Morar '16	🍷🍷 5
● Valpolicella Cl. '18	🍷🍷 2*
● Amarone della Valpolicella Cl. Casa dei Bepi '12	🍷🍷🍷 8
● Amarone della Valpolicella Cl. Casa dei Bepi '11	🍷🍷🍷 8
● Amarone della Valpolicella Cl. Casa dei Bepi '10	🍷🍷🍷 8
● Amarone della Valpolicella Cl. Casa dei Bepi '09	🍷🍷🍷 8
● Amarone della Valpolicella Cl. Casa dei Bepi '05	🍷🍷🍷 8
● Valpolicella Cl. Sup. Campo Morar '09	🍷🍷🍷 5

Pietro Zanoni

FRAZ. QUINZANO
VIA ARE ZOVO, 16D
37125 VERONA
TEL. +39 0458343977
www.pietrozanoni.it

CELLAR SALES
PRE-BOOKED VISITS
ANNUAL PRODUCTION 25,000 bottles
HECTARES UNDER VINE 7.50

Pietro Zanoni's winery is situated in a lesser-known part of Valpolicella, the Quinzano Valley, a territory of extraordinary natural beauty whose vineyards stretch almost to the southern outskirts of Verona. The property can be found entirely in this area, guyot vineyards destined to an extremely limited selection of wines. In his cellar, Pietro takes care of the rest, bringing skill to a line of wines characterized by richness and fullness. Zanoni's Amarone '14 offers up aromas dominated by stewed red fruit, enriched by oaky notes and spices, all of which we find well-expressed on the palate. A difficult vintage limited its palate, which is just a bit closed between its initial, full and generous impact, and a crisp, spirited finish. Time will surely balance things out. Their Campo Denari '16 is an anthem to maturity, an intoxicating glass of sweet red fruit whose palate features alcohol and softness.

● Amarone della Valpolicella '14	♟♟♟ 7
● Valpolicella Sup. Campo Denari '16	♟♟ 4
● Valpolicella Sup. Ripasso '16	♟ 4
● Amarone della Valpolicella Zovo '13	♟♟ 7
● Amarone della Valpolicella Zovo '12	♟♟ 7
● Amarone della Valpolicella Zovo '11	♟♟ 7
● Amarone della Valpolicella Zovo '10	♟♟ 6
● Recioto della Valpolicella '11	♟♟ 5
● Recioto della Valpolicella '09	♟♟ 4
● Valpolicella Sup. '16	♟♟ 3
● Valpolicella Sup. '15	♟♟ 2*
● Valpolicella Sup. '14	♟♟ 2*
● Valpolicella Sup. '13	♟♟ 2*
● Valpolicella Sup. Campo Denari '15	♟♟ 4
● Valpolicella Sup. Campo Denari '11	♟♟ 4
● Valpolicella Sup. Ripasso '15	♟♟ 4
● Valpolicella Sup. Ripasso '13	♟♟ 4

Pietro Zardini

VIA DON P. FANTONI, 3
37029 SAN PIETRO IN CARIANO [VR]
TEL. +39 0456800989
www.pietrozardini.it

CELLAR SALES
PRE-BOOKED VISITS
ANNUAL PRODUCTION 60,000 bottles
HECTARES UNDER VINE 10.00

Pietro Zardini's winery is part of a dense network of producers that have, in recent years, come to the forefront, contributing to the international success of the region's red wines. But the Zardini family's bond with the territory's viticulture goes much further back. Indeed, Pietro's grandfather made wine on these hills and Pietro himself, before going out on his own, studied the territory, its grapes and traditions at other, important producers in the region. Today their Amarone Leone Zardini '12 is a reserve that brings together modernity and history. Its aromas are dominated by overripe and almost decadent fruit which find vitality in balsamic notes and spices. In the mouth it impresses for the way it unfolds, seductive and enticing, only to find a whiff of freshness in its acidic backbone, lengthening and stretching the palate. Their Ripasso '16, a crisper, fresher wine, also delivered.

● Amarone della Valpolicella Leone Zardini Ris. '12	♟♟♟ 8
○ Lugana '18	♟♟ 2*
● Valpolicella Sup. Ripasso Pietro Junior '16	♟♟ 4
● 70 30 Corvina Cabernet '15	♟ 4
● Austero	♟ 3
⊙ Rosignol Rosato Brut	♟ 3
● Amarone della Valpolicella Leone Zardini Ris. '11	♟♟♟ 8
● Amarone della Valpolicella Cl. Leone Zardini Ris. '10	♟♟ 6
● Amarone della Valpolicella Pietro Junior '13	♟♟ 6
● Recioto della Valpolicella Pietro Junior '16	♟♟ 4
● Valpolicella Sup. Ripasso Pietro Junior '15	♟♟ 3

★Zenato

VIA SAN BENEDETTO, 8
37019 PESCHIERA DEL GARDA [VR]
TEL. +39 0457550300
www.zenato.it

CELLAR SALES
PRE-BOOKED VISITS
ANNUAL PRODUCTION 2,000,000 bottles
HECTARES UNDER VINE 95.00

This historic winery was founded by Sergio Zenato in the early 1960s. One of the region's most important producers, it operates in two of its most well-known appellations, Lugana and Valpolicella. Today it's managed by Sergio's children, Nadia and Alberto, who oversee a large estate that comprises vineyards in the clay-rich plains (for their white wines) and the hills of Sant'Ambrogio (for their Valpolicella reds). The two appellations may be close geographically, but they're very different in stylistic terms. In both cases, however, here they're interpreted with precision and sensitivity. Their Lugana Riserva 'Sergio Zenato' was at the top of its game this year. It's a wine that, over the years, has found an elegant, complex profile that reemerges in the 2016. Their Amarone '13 is diametrically opposed, playing on aromatic richness of fruit and a palate in which concentration and generosity are governed and stretched by its tannic weave.

○ Lugana Sergio Zenato Ris. '16	♔♔♔ 5
● Amarone della Valpolicella Cl. Sergio Zenato Ris. '13	♔♔ 8
● Amarone della Valpolicella Cl. '15	♔♔ 7
● Cresasso Corvina Veronese '13	♔♔ 6
○ Lugana Brut M. Cl. '15	♔♔ 4
○ Lugana Massoni S. Cristina '18	♔♔ 3
● Recioto della Valpolicella Cl. '13	♔♔ 6
● Valpolicella Sup. Ripasso Ripassa '15	♔♔ 4
○ Soave Cl. Colombara '18	♔ 2
● Amarone della Valpolicella Cl. Sergio Zenato Ris. '11	♔♔♔ 8
● Amarone della Valpolicella Cl. Sergio Zenato Ris. '10	♔♔♔ 8
● Amarone della Valpolicella Cl. Sergio Zenato Ris. '09	♔♔♔ 8
○ Lugana Sergio Zenato Ris. '15	♔♔♔ 5

Zeni 1870

VIA COSTABELLA, 9
37011 BARDOLINO [VR]
TEL. +39 0457210022
www.zeni.it

CELLAR SALES
PRE-BOOKED VISITS
ANNUAL PRODUCTION 1,000,000 bottles
HECTARES UNDER VINE 25.00

Elena, Federica and Fausto Zeni oversee the family winery in Bardolino, on the hills overlooking Lake Garda. Even if it was founded in the late 1800s, it was with their father, Gaetano (otherwise known as 'Nino'), that the producer turned a corner, moving the cellar from the center of Bardolino to its current hillside position, and shifting the focus to the quality and provenance of their wines. Today, as back then, all their efforts are aimed at producing wines that express the territory in which their grapes are cultivated. Two wines stand out among the many tasted this year: their Amarone Vigne Alte '15 and a Bardolino (dedicated to their father), I Filari del Nino '18. The former is a red that impresses for its softness and fullness on the palate. The latter pursues maximum expressivity, even without added sulfites. It's marked by aromas of forest undergrowth and a crisp, juicy, highly pleasant palate.

● Amarone della Valpolicella Cl. Vigne Alte '15	♔♔ 6
● Bardolino Cl. I Filari del Nino '18	♔♔ 5
● Amarone della Valpolicella Cl. '16	♔♔ 6
● Corvina '18	♔♔ 3
○ Lugana Vigne Alte '18	♔♔ 2*
● Valpolicella Sup. Ripasso Marogne '17	♔♔ 3
● Valpolicella Sup. Vigne Alte '17	♔♔ 2*
⊙ Bardolino Chiaretto Cl. Inanfora '17	♔ 2
⊙ Bardolino Chiaretto Cl. Vigne Alte '18	♔ 2
● Bardolino Cl. Sup. '17	♔ 3
● Bardolino Cl. Vigne Alte '18	♔ 2
○ Lugana Marogne '18	♔ 3
● Amarone della Valpolicella Cl. Nino Zeni '13	♔♔ 8

Zonin

VIA BORGOLECCO, 9
36053 GAMBELLARA [VI]
TEL. +39 0444640111
www.zonin1821.it

CELLAR SALES
PRE-BOOKED VISITS
ANNUAL PRODUCTION 38,000,000 bottles
HECTARES UNDER VINE 2000.00

Gambellara is one of Italy's largest producers, bolstered by a veritable mosaic of vineyards that stretches from Veneto to Friuli, Lombardy, Piedmont, Tuscany, Puglia, and Sicily. Their heart, however, remains firmly rooted in their homeland, Veneto, with particular attention paid to the appellations that, more than any other, represent the territory: Amarone and Prosecco. Their style centers on pleasantness and varietal expression. Their Amarone '16 pursues this style. Redolent of ripe cherry and spices, on the palate it proves fragrant and supple, lengthening decisively towards the finish. Their Ripasso '17 expresses greater aromatic integrity, while on the palate the wine brings together richness of flavor and tension. In terms of their Proseccos, we appreciated their Valdobbiadene Extra Dry, a sparkling wine whose delicate, fruity aromas are followed by a sapid, creamy palate that's perfectly accompanied by bubbles.

● Amarone della Valpolicella '16	♥♥	6
○ Valdobbiadene Extra Dry Prestige 1821	♥♥	3
● Valpolicella Cl. '18	♥♥	2*
● Valpolicella Sup. Ripasso '17	♥♥	4
○ Lugana '18	♥	3
○ Prosecco Brut Cuvée 1821	♥	4
○ Soave Cl. '18	♥	2
● Amarone della Valpolicella '14	♀♀	6
○ Friuli Aquileia Pinot Grigio '16	♀♀	2*
○ Gambellara Cl. Il Giangio '17	♀♀	3
○ Gambellara Cl. Il Giangio '16	♀♀	2*
● Valpolicella Sup. Ripasso '16	♀♀	3
● Valpolicella Sup. Ripasso '15	♀♀	3

Zymè

LOC. SAN FLORIANO
VIA CA' DEL PIPA, 1
37029 SAN PIETRO IN CARIANO [VR]
TEL. +39 0457701108
www.zyme.it

CELLAR SALES
PRE-BOOKED VISITS
ANNUAL PRODUCTION 80,000 bottles
HECTARES UNDER VINE 30.00
SUSTAINABLE WINERY

For about twenty 20 years Celestino Gaspari's winery has been active in the territory. An adventure that began humbly with just a few hectares of family vineyards has grown into a much larger operation, with most of their plots situated in Valpolicella. The cellar was built by enlarging and adapting a 15th-century sandstone mine, thus supporting the bond that exists between land and wine, past and future, a constantly evolving bond grounded in balance and harmony. Their Amarone '13 is simply splendid. It opens with hidden aromas that gradually reveal themselves, leaving it up to ripe fruit to initiate a procession followed by notes of undergrowth and pepper. On the palate it highlights great richness, managed with precision and lightness, only to finish elegant and long. Their Valpolicella Superiore '16 is a more approachable wine, both aromatically and on the palate, proving soft and pervasive, while playing on generosity of fruit.

● Amarone della Valpolicella Cl. '13	♥♥♥	8
● Valpolicella Cl. Sup. '16	♥♥	5
● Valpolicella Reverie '18	♥♥	3
○ Il Bianco From Black to White '18	♥	3
● Amarone della Valpolicella Cl. '06	♀♀♀	8
● Amarone della Valpolicella Cl. La Mattonara Ris. '03	♀♀♀	8
● Amarone della Valpolicella Cl. La Mattonara Ris. '01	♀♀♀	8
● Amarone della Valpolicella Cl. '11	♀♀	8
● Harlequin '09	♀♀	8
○ Il Bianco From Black to White '17	♀♀	3
○ Il Bianco From Black to White '16	♀♀	3
● Kairos '15	♀♀	8
● Valpolicella Cl. Sup. '15	♀♀	5
● Valpolicella Reverie '16	♀♀	3

Ai Galli

VIA LOREDAN, 28
30020 PRAMAGGIORE [VE]
TEL. +39 0421799314
www.aigalli.it

CELLAR SALES
PRE-BOOKED VISITS
ACCOMMODATION AND RESTAURANT SERVICE
ANNUAL PRODUCTION 600,000 bottles
HECTARES UNDER VINE 60.00

○ Lison Cl. '18	♥♥ 3
○ Venezia Chardonnay '17	♥♥ 3
○ Lison-Pramaggiore Sauvignon '18	♥ 3
○ Tai '18	♥ 2

Beato Bartolomeo
da Breganze

VIA ROMA, 100
36042 BREGANZE [VI]
TEL. +39 0445873112
www.cantinabreganze.it

CELLAR SALES
ANNUAL PRODUCTION 2,500,000 bottles
HECTARES UNDER VINE 700.00

● Breganze Cabernet Kilò Ris. '15	♥♥ 4
○ Breganze Torcolato '14	♥♥ 5
● Breganze Cabernet Bosco Grande Ris. '15	♥ 3
● Breganze Cabernet Sup. Savardo '17	♥ 2

Bellussi Spumanti

VIA ERIZZO, 215
31049 VALDOBBIADENE [TV]
TEL. +39 0423983411
www.bellussi.com

CELLAR SALES
PRE-BOOKED VISITS
ANNUAL PRODUCTION 1,300,000 bottles

○ Cartizze Belcanto	♥♥ 4
○ Valdobbiadene Extra Dry Belcanto	♥♥ 3
○ Valdobbiadene Brut Belcanto	♥ 3
○ Valdobbiadene Extra Dry	♥ 3

Bacio della Luna

VIA ROVEDE, 36
31020 VIDOR [TV]
TEL. +39 0423983111
www.baciodellaluna.it

ANNUAL PRODUCTION 12,500,000 bottles
HECTARES UNDER VINE 25.00
VITICULTURE METHOD Certified Organic

○ Conegliano Valdobbiadene Brut '18	♥♥ 3*
○ Conegliano Valdobbiadene Brut Nature '18	♥♥ 3
○ Cartizze '18	♥ 3
○ Conegliano Valdobbiadene Extra Dry '16	♥ 3

Ornella Bellia

VIA ROMA, 117
30020 PRAMAGGIORE [VE]
TEL. +39 0421200679
www.ornellabellia.it

ANNUAL PRODUCTION 500,000 bottles
HECTARES UNDER VINE 28.00

○ Manzoni Bianco '18	♥♥ 3
● Carmenère Filo d'Erba '17	♥ 3
● G 1928 '16	♥ 3
○ Pensiero d'Amore Passito '17	♥ 3

Bergamini

LOC. COLÀ
VIA CÀ NOVA, 3
37017 LAZISE [VR]
TEL. +39 0456490407
www.bergaminivini.it

CELLAR SALES
PRE-BOOKED VISITS
ANNUAL PRODUCTION 65,000 bottles
HECTARES UNDER VINE 13.00

● Bardolino Sup. '17	♥♥ 2*
○ Custoza Sup. '18	♥♥ 2*
● Bardolino '18	♥ 2
○ Custoza '18	♥ 2

Borgo Antico

FRAZ. OGLIANO
S.DA DELLE SPEZIE, 39
31015 CONEGLIANO [TV]
TEL. +39 0438788111
www.borgoanticovini.com

CELLAR SALES
PRE-BOOKED VISITS
ANNUAL PRODUCTION 120,000 bottles
HECTARES UNDER VINE 20.00

○ Valdobbiadene Brut	♀♀ 3
○ Valdobbiadene Dry	♀ 3
○ Valdobbiadene Extra Dry	♀ 3

Borgo Molino

FRAZ. RONCADELLE
VIA FONTANE, 3
31034 ORMELLE [TV]
TEL. +39 0422851625
www.borgomolino.it

ANNUAL PRODUCTION 4,000,000 bottles
HECTARES UNDER VINE 100.00

○ Valdobbiadene Extra Dry	♀♀ 3
○ Pinot Grigio delle Venezie Ciari '18	♀ 2
○ Valdobbiadene Brut 09 '18	♀ 3
● Venezia Cabernet Sauvignon Scuri '18	♀ 3

F.lli Bortolin

FRAZ. SANTO STEFANO
VIA MENEGAZZI, 5
31049 VALDOBBIADENE [TV]
TEL. +39 0423900135
www.bortolin.com

CELLAR SALES
PRE-BOOKED VISITS
ANNUAL PRODUCTION 300,000 bottles
HECTARES UNDER VINE 20.00

○ Valdobbiadene Brut Rù '18	♀♀ 3
○ Valdobbiadene Extra Dry	♀♀ 2
○ Valdobbiadene Brut	♀ 2
○ Valdobbiadene Dry	♀ 2

Ca' Bianca

LOC. FONTANAFREDDA
VIA CINTO, 5
35030 CINTO EUGANEO [PD]
TEL. +39 042994288

CELLAR SALES
RESTAURANT SERVICE
ANNUAL PRODUCTION 80,000 bottles
HECTARES UNDER VINE 20.00

● Colli Euganei Rosso Rossura dei Briganti Ris. '13	♀♀ 4
● Colli Euganei Cabernet Ritocchino 42 '14	♀ 3
● Colli Euganei Merlot Bumagro '14	♀ 3

Ca' Ferri

VIA CA' FERRI, 43
35020 CASALSERUGO [PD]
TEL. +39 049655518
www.vinicaferri.com

CELLAR SALES
PRE-BOOKED VISITS
ANNUAL PRODUCTION 10,000 bottles
HECTARES UNDER VINE 8.00

● Colli Euganei Rosso Taurilio '16	♀♀ 2*
● Corti Benedettine del Padovano Cabernet Ser Ugo '17	♀ 2

Campion

VIA CAMPION, 2
31049 VALDOBBIADENE [TV]
TEL. +39 0423980432
www.campionspumanti.it

ANNUAL PRODUCTION 180,000 bottles
HECTARES UNDER VINE 20.00

○ Cartizze	♀♀ 3
○ Valdobbiadene Brut	♀♀ 2*
○ Valdobbiadene Extra Dry '18	♀♀ 2*

Canoso

LOC. MONTEFORTE D'ALPONE
VIA ROMA, 97
37032 VERONA
TEL. +39 0456101981
www.canoso.it

CELLAR SALES
PRE-BOOKED VISITS
ANNUAL PRODUCTION 40,000 bottles
HECTARES UNDER VINE 15.00

○ Soave Cl. Fonte '18		♟♟ 2*
● Valpolicella Sup. Terra '15		♟ 3

Case Bianche Tenuta Col Sandago

VIA BARRIERA, 41
31058 SUSEGANA [TV]
TEL. +39 043864462
www.colsandago.com

CELLAR SALES
PRE-BOOKED VISITS
ANNUAL PRODUCTION 500,000 bottles
HECTARES UNDER VINE 30.00

○ Valdobbiadene Brut Nature '18		♟♟ 4
● Wildbacher '13		♟♟ 5

Castello di Roncade

VIA ROMA, 141
31056 RONCADE [TV]
TEL. +39 0422708736
www.castellodironcade.com

CELLAR SALES
PRE-BOOKED VISITS
ANNUAL PRODUCTION 200,000 bottles
HECTARES UNDER VINE 45.00

● Piave Raboso dell'Arnasa '15		♟♟ 3
○ Venezia Chardonnay dell'Arnasa '17		♟♟ 2*
● Baronessa Ilaria Raboso Passito '14		♟ 5
● Piave Merlot Rosso dell'Arnasa '16		♟ 2

Cirotto

VIA BASSANESE,51
31011 ASOLO [TV]
TEL. +39 0423952396
www.cirottovini.com

ANNUAL PRODUCTION 80,000 bottles
HECTARES UNDER VINE 9.00

○ Asolo Brut '18		♟♟ 2*
○ Asolo Extra Brut '15		♟♟ 3
● Montello e Colli Asolani Rosso Costalunga '13		♟♟ 3

Vignaioli Contrà Soarda

S.DA SOARDA, 26
36061 BASSANO DEL GRAPPA [VI]
TEL. +39 0424505562
www.contrasoarda.it

CELLAR SALES
PRE-BOOKED VISITS
RESTAURANT SERVICE
ANNUAL PRODUCTION 80,000 bottles
HECTARES UNDER VINE 20.00
VITICULTURE METHOD Certified Organic
SUSTAINABLE WINERY

○ Breganze Vespaiolo Vignasilan '16		♟♟ 5
● Terra Musso '15		♟♟ 4
● Breganze Rosso Terre di Lava Ris. '13		♟ 5
○ Breganze Vespaiolo Soarda '18		♟ 3

Corte Canella

FRAZ. CELLORE
VIA CANELLA, 14
37031 ILLASI [VR]
TEL. +39 0457834869
www.cortecanella.it

CELLAR SALES
PRE-BOOKED VISITS
ANNUAL PRODUCTION 30,000 bottles
HECTARES UNDER VINE 16.00

○ Soave La Vero '18		♟♟ 3
● Amarone della Valpolicella '14		♟ 6
● Valpolicella Sup. '15		♟ 3

Corte Figaretto

FRAZ. POIANO
VIA CLOCEGO, 48A
37142 VERONA
TEL. +39 0458700753
www.cortefigaretto.it

CELLAR SALES
PRE-BOOKED VISITS
ANNUAL PRODUCTION 49,500 bottles
HECTARES UNDER VINE 7.50

● Amarone della Valpolicella Valpantena Graal '15	♟♟ 6
● Valpolicella Valpantena Sup. Ripasso Acini Ameni '17	♟ 3

Corte Mainente

V.LE DELLA VITTORIA, 45
37038 SOAVE [VR]
TEL. +39 0457680303
www.cortemainente.com

CELLAR SALES
PRE-BOOKED VISITS
ANNUAL PRODUCTION 37,000 bottles
HECTARES UNDER VINE 12.00
SUSTAINABLE WINERY

○ Soave Cl. Vigne del Tenda '17	♟♟ 4
○ Soave Netteroir '17	♟♟ 5
○ Soave Cengelle '18	♟ 3
○ Soave Cl. Tovo al Pigno '18	♟ 4

Corte San Benedetto

FRAZ. ARBIZZANO
VIA CASA ZAMBONI, 10A
37024 NEGRAR [VR]
TEL. +39 0456020531
www.cortesanbenedetto.it

● Amarone della Valpolicella Cl. '12	♟♟ 7
● Amarone della Valpolicella Cl. Camporal Ris. '09	♟♟ 8
● Valpolicella Cl. Sup. Ripasso '14	♟ 5

Paolo Cottini

FRAZ. CASTELROTTO
VIA BELVEDERE, 29
37029 VERONA
TEL. +39 0456837293
www.paolocottini.it

CELLAR SALES
PRE-BOOKED VISITS
ANNUAL PRODUCTION 40,000 bottles
HECTARES UNDER VINE 3.50

● Amarone della Valpolicella Cl. '15	♟♟ 6
● Valpolicella Cl. Sup. Ripasso '16	♟♟ 4
● Castrum '15	♟ 3
● Valpolicella Cl. '18	♟ 2

Valentina Cubi

VIA CASTERNA, 60
37022 FUMANE [VR]
TEL. +39 0457701806
www.valentinacubi.it

CELLAR SALES
PRE-BOOKED VISITS
ANNUAL PRODUCTION 40,000 bottles
HECTARES UNDER VINE 10.00
VITICULTURE METHOD Certified Organic

● Amarone della Valpolicella Cl. Ris. '06	♟♟ 8
● Valpolicella Cl. Sup. Il Tabarro '16	♟♟ 3
● Sin Cero '18	♟ 2
● Valpolicella Iperico '17	♟ 2

Cantina di Custoza

LOC. CUSTOZA
VIA STAFFALO, 1
37066 SOMMACAMPAGNA [VR]
TEL. +39 045516200
www.cantinadicustoza.it

CELLAR SALES
PRE-BOOKED VISITS
ANNUAL PRODUCTION 4,000,000 bottles
HECTARES UNDER VINE 1000.00
VITICULTURE METHOD Certified Organic

○ Custoza Sup. Custodia '17	♟♟ 3
○ Custoza Val dei Molini '18	♟♟ 2*
⊙ Bardolino Chiaretto Cl. Val dei Molini '18	♟ 3
● Bardolino Cl. Val dei Molin '18	♟ 3

La Dama

FRAZ. SAN VITO
VIA GIOVANNI QUINTARELLI, 39
37024 NEGRAR [VR]
TEL. +39 0456000728
www.ladamavini.com

ANNUAL PRODUCTION 50,000 bottles
HECTARES UNDER VINE 10.00
VITICULTURE METHOD Certified Organic

● Amarone della Valpolicella Cl. '15	♥♥ 7
● Recioto della Valpolicella Cl. '16	♥♥ 6
● Valpolicella Cl. '18	♥♥ 3
● Valpolicella Cl. Sup. Ca' Besi '16	♥ 5

Sandro De Bruno

VIA SANTA MARGHERITA, 26
37030 MONTECCHIA DI CROSARA [VR]
TEL. +39 0456540465
www.sandrodebruno.it

ANNUAL PRODUCTION 80,000 bottles
HECTARES UNDER VINE 22.00

○ Soave Colli Scaligeri '16	♥♥ 2*
○ Soave Sup. Monte San Piero '16	♥♥ 3
● Rosso Fumo '16	♥ 3
○ Soave '18	♥ 3

Diesel Farm

VIA SAN BENEDETTO, 2
36036 MAROSTICA [VI]
TEL. +39 042475224
www.dieselfarm.it

CELLAR SALES
PRE-BOOKED VISITS
ANNUAL PRODUCTION 27,000 bottles
HECTARES UNDER VINE 5.00
VITICULTURE METHOD Certified Organic

○ Bolle di Rosso Brut Celebrating 55 M. Cl. '15	♥♥ 6
● Breganze Rosso di Rosso '12	♥♥ 6
○ Breganze Chardonnay Bianco di Rosso '13	♥ 5

Fraccaroli

FRAZ. SAN BENEDETTO
LOC. BERRA VECCHIA, 1
37019 PESCHIERA DEL GARDA [VR]
TEL. +39 0457550949
www.fraccarolivini.it

CELLAR SALES
PRE-BOOKED VISITS
ANNUAL PRODUCTION 280,000 bottles
HECTARES UNDER VINE 50.00

○ Lugana Sup. Campo Serà '17	♥♥ 2*
○ Lugana 1912 Ris. '15	♥ 4
○ Lugana Pansere '18	♥ 2

Garbara

LOC. S.STEFANO
VIA MENEGAZZI, 19
31049 VALDOBBIADENE [TV]
TEL. +39 0423900155
www.garbara.it

CELLAR SALES
PRE-BOOKED VISITS
ANNUAL PRODUCTION 21,000 bottles
HECTARES UNDER VINE 0.90

○ Cartizze Brut Zero	♥♥ 4
○ Cartizze Extra Dry	♥♥ 4
○ Quinto Vino Brut Nature	♥ 4

Fattoria Garbole

LOC. GARBOLE
VIA FRACANZANA, 6
37039 TREGNAGO [VR]
TEL. +39 0457809020
www.fattoriagarbole.it

CELLAR SALES
PRE-BOOKED VISITS
ANNUAL PRODUCTION 15,000 bottles
HECTARES UNDER VINE 6.00

● Amarone della Valpolicella Hatteso '09	♥♥ 8
● Hurlo '11	♥♥ 8

Gentili

VIA S. ANTONIO, 271
37013 CAPRINO VERONESE [VR]
TEL. +39 3391651823
www.cantinagentili.com

ANNUAL PRODUCTION 10,000 bottles
HECTARES UNDER VINE 43.00

⊙ Bardolino Chiaretto '18	🍷🍷 2*
● Bardolino Cl. '17	🍷🍷 3
⊙ San Verolo '17	🍷 3
⊙ Trebianel '18	🍷 2

Io Mazzucato

VIA SAN GAETANO, 21
36042 BREGANZE [VI]
TEL. +39 0445308348
www.iomazzucato.it

ANNUAL PRODUCTION 70,000 bottles
HECTARES UNDER VINE 25.00

⊙ Breganze Torcolato '14	🍷🍷 5
● Land Merlot '15	🍷🍷 3
⊙ Land Bianco '17	🍷 3
⊙ Pas Dosé Rosé M. Cl.	🍷 4

La Farra

VIA SAN FRANCESCO, 44
31010 FARRA DI SOLIGO [TV]
TEL. +39 0438801242
www.lafarra.it

CELLAR SALES
ANNUAL PRODUCTION 200,000 bottles
HECTARES UNDER VINE 20.00

⊙ Valdobbiadene Extra Dry '18	🍷🍷 2*
⊙ Valdobbiadene Rive di Farra di Soligo Extra Dry '18	🍷🍷 3

Lenotti

VIA SANTA CRISTINA, 1
37011 BARDOLINO [VR]
TEL. +39 0457210484
www.lenotti.com

CELLAR SALES
PRE-BOOKED VISITS
ANNUAL PRODUCTION 1,400,000 bottles
HECTARES UNDER VINE 105.00

● Amarone della Valpolicella Cl. Di Carlo '11	🍷🍷 7
⊙ Bardolino Chiaretto Cl. Decus '18	🍷🍷 3
● Bardolino Cl. '18	🍷 2

Manera

LOC. SALVATRONDA
VIA SILE, 50
31033 CASTELFRANCO VENETO [TV]
TEL. +39 0423490602
www.vinimanera.com

CELLAR SALES
PRE-BOOKED VISITS
ANNUAL PRODUCTION 50,000 bottles
HECTARES UNDER VINE 11.00

● Recantina '18	🍷🍷 3
⊙ Incrocio Manzoni 6.0.13 '18	🍷 2
● Merlot '18	🍷 2
● Rossomanera '17	🍷 3

Le Manzane

LOC. BAGNOLO
VIA MASET, 47B
31020 SAN PIETRO DI FELETTO [TV]
TEL. +39 0438486606
www.lemanzane.com

CELLAR SALES
PRE-BOOKED VISITS
ANNUAL PRODUCTION 1,000,000 bottles
HECTARES UNDER VINE 72.00

⊙ Conegliano Rive di Formeniga Brut Springo Blue '18	🍷🍷 4
⊙ Conegliano Valdobbiadene Extra Dry 20.10 '18	🍷 3

Le Marognole

LOC. VALGATARA
VIA MAROGNOLE, 7
37020 MARANO DI VALPOLICELLA [VR]
TEL. +39 0457755114
www.lemarognole.it

CELLAR SALES
PRE-BOOKED VISITS
ANNUAL PRODUCTION 15,000 bottles
HECTARES UNDER VINE 5.50

● Amarone della Valpolicella Cl. Campo Rocco '15	♛♛ 5
● Recioto della Valpolicella Cl. Campo Gerico '16	♛♛ 4

Marsuret

LOC. GUIA DI VALDOBBIADENE
VIA BARCH, 17
31049 VALDOBBIADENE [TV]
TEL. +39 0423900139
www.marsuret.it

CELLAR SALES
PRE-BOOKED VISITS
ANNUAL PRODUCTION 600,000 bottles
HECTARES UNDER VINE 50.00

○ Cartizze	♛♛ 4
○ Valdobbiadene Rive di Guia Brut '18	♛♛ 3
○ Valdobbiadene Brut San Boldo	♛ 3
○ Valdobbiadene Dry Agostino '18	♛ 3

Maschio

LOC. VISNÀ
VIA CADORE MARE, 2
31020 VAZZOLA [TV]
TEL. +39 0438794115
www.cantinemaschio.it

PRE-BOOKED VISITS
ANNUAL PRODUCTION 20,000,000 bottles
HECTARES UNDER VINE

○ Valdobbiadene Brut Maschio dei Cavalieri	♛♛ 3
○ Valdobbiadene Extra Dry Maschio dei Cavalieri	♛♛ 3

Natalino Mattiello

FRAZ. COSTOZZA
VIA VOLTO, 57
36023 LONGARE [VI]
TEL. +39 0444555258
www.cantinamattiello.it

CELLAR SALES
PRE-BOOKED VISITS
ANNUAL PRODUCTION 40,000 bottles
HECTARES UNDER VINE 10.00

● Colli Berici Cabernet Franc Ris. '15	♛♛ 3
● Colli Berici Cabernet Sauvignon I Covoli Rosso Ris. '16	♛♛ 3
○ Colli Berici Bianco I Covoli '18	♛ 3

Firmino Miotti

VIA BROGLIATI CONTRO, 53
36042 BREGANZE [VI]
TEL. +39 0445873006
www.firminomiotti.it

CELLAR SALES
PRE-BOOKED VISITS
ANNUAL PRODUCTION 25,000 bottles
HECTARES UNDER VINE 5.00

● Breganze Rosso '16	♛♛ 3
○ Sampagna Frizzante	♛♛ 2
⊙ Fondo 53 Rosato Frizzante	♛ 2
● Gruajo	♛ 3

Mongarda

FRAZ. COL SAN MARTINO
VIA CANAL NUOVO, 8
31010 FARRA DI SOLIGO [TV]
TEL. +39 0438989168
www.mongarda.it

HECTARES UNDER VINE 16.00

○ Valdobbiadene Brut	♛♛ 3
○ Valdobbiadene Extra Dry	♛♛ 3
○ Glera Frizzante '17	♛ 3
○ Valdobbiadene Dosaggio Zero	♛ 3

Montecariano

VIA VALENA, 3
37029 SAN PIETRO IN CARIANO [VR]
TEL. +39 0456838335
www.montecariano.it

CELLAR SALES
PRE-BOOKED VISITS
ANNUAL PRODUCTION 20,000 bottles
HECTARES UNDER VINE 21.00

● Amarone della Valpolicella Cl. '13	♟♟ 7
● Puntara '15	♟♟ 5

Montelvini

FRAZ. VENEGAZZÙ
VIA CAL TREVIGIANA, 51
31040 VOLPAGO DEL MONTELLO [TV]
TEL. +39 042387778777
www.montelvini.it

CELLAR SALES
ANNUAL PRODUCTION 5,200,000 bottles
HECTARES UNDER VINE 35.00
SUSTAINABLE WINERY

○ Asolo Brut	♟♟ 2*
○ Asolo Extra Brut '18	♟♟ 2*
○ Asolo Frizzante Colfondo Il Brutto	♟ 2
○ Asolo Frizzante Extra Dry Serenitatis	♟ 2

Walter Nardin

LOC. RONCADELLE
VIA FONTANE, 5
31024 ORMELLE [TV]
TEL. +39 0422851622
www.vinwalternardin.it

PRE-BOOKED VISITS
ANNUAL PRODUCTION 350,000 bottles
HECTARES UNDER VINE 30.00

○ Putél Brut M. Cl. La Zerbaia '14	♟♟ 3
● Rosso della Ghiaia La Zerbaia '15	♟♟ 4
○ Tai La Zerbaia '17	♟♟ 3
● Refosco P. R. La Zerbaia '15	♟ 3

Perlage

LOC. FARRA DI SOLIGO
VIA CAL DEL MUNER, 16
31020 FARRA DI SOLIGO [TV]
TEL. +39 0438900203
www.perlagewines.com

CELLAR SALES
PRE-BOOKED VISITS
ANNUAL PRODUCTION 2,300,000 bottles
HECTARES UNDER VINE 100.00
VITICULTURE METHOD Certified Biodynamic
SUSTAINABLE WINERY

○ Valdobbiadene Brut Canah '18	♟♟ 3
○ Valdobbiadene Extra Dry Quorum '18	♟♟ 3
○ Valdobbiadene Extra Dry Col di Manza '18	♟ 5

Pian delle Vette

FRAZ. PREN DI FELTRE
VIA TEDA, 11
32032 BELLUNO
TEL. +39 0439302803
www.piandellevette.it

SUSTAINABLE WINERY

○ Pas Dosé Mat'55 M.Cl '11	♟♟ 7
● Pinot Nero '16	♟♟ 6
● Granpasso '12	♟ 5

Poggio delle Grazie

VIA MILANO, 199
37014 CASTELNUOVO DEL GARDA [VR]
TEL. +39 347 8608785
www.poggiodellegrazie.it

ANNUAL PRODUCTION 40,000 bottles
HECTARES UNDER VINE 15.00
SUSTAINABLE WINERY

● Bardolino '17	♟♟ 3
● Quadrivium '14	♟♟ 5
⊙ Bardolino Chiaretto '18	♟ 3

Viticoltori Ponte

VIA VERDI, 50
31047 PONTE DI PIAVE [TV]
TEL. +39 0422858211
www.viticoltoriponte.it

CELLAR SALES
ANNUAL PRODUCTION 15,000,000 bottles
HECTARES UNDER VINE 2000.00

○ Manzoni Bianco Campe Dhei '18	♟♟	2*
○ Prosecco Extra Dry '18	♟	3
○ Sauvignon Campe Dhei '18	♟	2
○ Venezia Pinot Grigio Campe Dhei '18	♟	2

PuntoZero

VIA MONTE PALÙ, 1
36045 LONIGO [VI]
TEL. +39 049659881
www.puntozerowine.it

CELLAR SALES
PRE-BOOKED VISITS
ANNUAL PRODUCTION 16,000 bottles
HECTARES UNDER VINE 11.00

● Merlot Punto '13	♟♟	8
● Colli Berici Cabernet Souvignon Idea '18	♟	3
○ Colli Berici Pinot Bianco Trasparenza '18	♟	3

Rechsteiner

FRAZ. PIAVON
VIA FRASSENÈ, 2
31046 ODERZO [TV]
TEL. +39 0422752074
www.rechsteiner.it

CELLAR SALES
PRE-BOOKED VISITS
ACCOMMODATION AND RESTAURANT SERVICE
ANNUAL PRODUCTION 150,000 bottles
HECTARES UNDER VINE 50.00
SUSTAINABLE WINERY

● Malanotte '13	♟♟	4
○ Domenicale Passito '18	♟	3
● Piave Carmenère '18	♟	2
○ Piave Manzoni Bianco '18	♟	2

San Nazario

LOC. CORTELÀ
VIA MONTE VERSA, 1519
35030 VO' [PD]
TEL. +39 0499940194
www.vinisannazario.it

CELLAR SALES
PRE-BOOKED VISITS
ANNUAL PRODUCTION 50,000 bottles
HECTARES UNDER VINE 10.00
VITICULTURE METHOD Certified Organic

○ Colli Euganei Fior d'Arancio Passito Messalino '15	♟♟	5
○ Colli Euganei Fior d'Arancio Spumante '18	♟♟	4
○ Colli Euganei Bianco Ca' Suppiej '18	♟	2

San Rustico

FRAZ. VALGATARA
VIA POZZO, 2
37020 MARANO DI VALPOLICELLA [VR]
TEL. +39 0457703348
www.sanrustico.it

CELLAR SALES
PRE-BOOKED VISITS
ANNUAL PRODUCTION 250,000 bottles
HECTARES UNDER VINE 22.00

● Amarone della Valpolicella Cl. Gaso '12	♟♟	8
● Valpolicella Cl. Sup. Ripasso Gaso '16	♟♟	4
● Valpolicella Cl. '18	♟	2
● Valpolicella Cl. Sup. '17	♟	2

Sandre

FRAZ. CAMPODIPIETRA
VIA RISORGIMENTO, 16
31040 SALGAREDA [TV]
TEL. +39 0422804135
www.sandre.it

CELLAR SALES
PRE-BOOKED VISITS
ANNUAL PRODUCTION 100,000 bottles
HECTARES UNDER VINE 33.00

● Cuor di Vigna '15	♟♟	4
○ Acini Bianchi '18	♟	2
○ Manzoni Bianco '18	♟	2
● Piave Merlot '17	♟	2

Tenuta Santa Maria

FRAZ. PIEVE
VIA CAVOUR, 34
37030 COLOGNOLA AI COLLI [VR]
TEL. +39 0456152087
www.tenutapieve.com

PRE-BOOKED VISITS
ANNUAL PRODUCTION 25,000 bottles
HECTARES UNDER VINE 19.00

● Amarone della Valpolicella Cl. Ris. '13	▼▼ 8
● Valpolicella Cl. Sup. Ripasso '16	▼▼ 7
● Decima Aurea '10	▼ 6
● Valpolicella Cl. Sup. '17	▼ 7

T.E.S.S.A.R.I.

LOC. BROGNOLIGO
VIA FONTANA NUOVA, 86
37032 MONTEFORTE D'ALPONE [VR]
TEL. +39 0456176041
www.cantinatessari.com

CELLAR SALES
PRE-BOOKED VISITS
ANNUAL PRODUCTION 40,000 bottles
HECTARES UNDER VINE 17.00

○ Recioto di Soave Tre Colli '17	▼▼ 5
○ Soave Cl. Grisela '18	▼▼ 2*
○ Soave Cl. Le Bine Longhe '17	▼▼ 5
○ Garganega Frizzante Sur Lie Avus '18	▼ 3

Terra Felice

VIA MARLUNGHE 19
35032 ARQUÀ PETRARCA [PD]
TEL. +39 0429718143
agri.terrafelice@gmail.com

CELLAR SALES
PRE-BOOKED VISITS
ACCOMMODATION
ANNUAL PRODUCTION 36,000 bottles
HECTARES UNDER VINE 10.00
SUSTAINABLE WINERY

● Cabernet '15	▼▼ 6
● Pianoro '15	▼▼ 3
○ Chardonnay '17	▼ 3

Terre di Leone

LOC. PORTA
37020 MARANO DI VALPOLICELLA [VR]
TEL. +39 0456895040
www.terredileone.it

CELLAR SALES
PRE-BOOKED VISITS
ANNUAL PRODUCTION 36,000 bottles
HECTARES UNDER VINE 10.00

● Valpolicella Cl. Sup. '15	▼▼ 5
● Valpolicella Cl. Sup. Ripasso '15	▼▼ 4
● Dedicatum '13	▼ 6

Terre di San Venanzio Fortunato

VIA CAPITELLO FERRARI, 1
31049 VALDOBBIADENE [TV]
TEL. +39 0423974083
Via Capitello Ferrari, 1

ANNUAL PRODUCTION 300,000 bottles

○ Asolo Extra Brut '18	▼▼ 4
○ Cartizze Brut '18	▼▼ 4
○ Valdobbiadene Brut '18	▼ 2
○ Valdobbiadene Extra Dry	▼ 2

Davide Vignato

VIA CAPO DI SOPRA, 39
36053 GAMBELLARA [VI]
TEL. +39 0444 444144
www.davidevignato.it

ANNUAL PRODUCTION 28,000 bottles
HECTARES UNDER VINE 14.00
SUSTAINABLE WINERY

○ Cuvée dei Vignato Brut Non Dosato M.Cl '15	▼▼ 5
○ Gambellara El Gian '17	▼▼ 3

Vigneti di Ettore

VIA CASETTA DI MONTECCHIO, 2
37024 NEGRAR [VR]
TEL. +39 0457540158
www.vignetidiettore.it

ACCOMMODATION
ANNUAL PRODUCTION 60,000 bottles
HECTARES UNDER VINE 15.00
VITICULTURE METHOD Certified Organic
SUSTAINABLE WINERY

● Valpolicella Cl. Sup. Ripasso '17	♟♟ 4
● Valpolicella Cl. Sup. Pavaio '17	♟♟ 3
● Amarone della Valpolicella Cl. '15	♟ 7
● Valpolicella Cl. '18	♟ 3

Villa Angarano

FRAZ. SANT'EUSEBIO
VIA CONTRÀ CORTE S.EUSEBIO, 15
36061 BASSANO DEL GRAPPA [VI]
TEL. +39 0424503086
www.villaangarano.com

CELLAR SALES
PRE-BOOKED VISITS
ANNUAL PRODUCTION 30,000 bottles
HECTARES UNDER VINE 8.00
VITICULTURE METHOD Certified Organic

● Breganze Rosso Angarano '16	♟♟ 3
○ Breganze Torcolato San Biagio '16	♟♟ 5
○ Breganze Vespaiolo Bianco Angarano '18	♟ 3
○ Ca' Michiel '16	♟ 4

Villa Canestrari

VIA DANTE BROGLIO, 2
37030 COLOGNOLA AI COLLI [VR]
TEL. +39 0457650074
www.villacanestrari.com

CELLAR SALES
PRE-BOOKED VISITS
ANNUAL PRODUCTION 150,000 bottles
HECTARES UNDER VINE 15.00

● Amarone della Valpolicella '14	♟♟ 5
● Amarone della Valpolicella Plenum Ris. '12	♟♟ 7
● Valpolicella Terre di Lanoli '18	♟ 2

Villa Medici

VIA CAMPAGNOL, 9
37066 SOMMACAMPAGNA [VR]
TEL. +39 045515147
www.cantinavillamedici.it

ANNUAL PRODUCTION 220,000 bottles
HECTARES UNDER VINE 32.00

⊙ Bardolino Chiaretto '18	♟♟ 2*
○ Custoza Sup. '18	♟♟ 2*
● Bardolino Sup. '16	♟ 3
○ Custoza '18	♟ 2

Villa Minelli

VIA POSTIOMA, 66
31020 VILLORBA [TV]
TEL. +39 0422912355
www.villaminelli.it

CELLAR SALES
PRE-BOOKED VISITS
ANNUAL PRODUCTION 65,000 bottles
HECTARES UNDER VINE 9.50
SUSTAINABLE WINERY

○ Chardonnay '18	♟♟ 3
● Merlot Cabernet '15	♟♟ 2*
○ Delle Venezie Pinot Grigio '18	♟ 2
○ Malvasia '18	♟ 3

Zardetto

VIA MARTIRI DELLE FOIBE, 18
31015 CONEGLIANO [TV]
TEL. +39 0438394969
www.zardettoprosecco.com

CELLAR SALES
ANNUAL PRODUCTION 2,000,000 bottles
HECTARES UNDER VINE 40.00
VITICULTURE METHOD Certified Organic

○ Conegliano Valdobbiadene Brut Refosso '18	♟♟ 3
○ Conegliano Valdobbiadene Brut Rive di Ogliano Tre venti '18	♟ 3

FRIULI VENEZIA GIULIA

The 2018 climate proved practically ideal for vineyard cultivation and grape maturation in Friuli Venezia Giulia and surpassed even the best expectations — it was certainly the best of the century.

Quantity and quality normally don't go hand in hand, but when everything goes perfectly, higher production volumes don't effect quality in the least bit. The region's 2018s express considerable vigor and complexity for their young age. This year again saw 26 wines breaking into the top tier, and 12 of them were from last year's production. The territory's most representative wine, Friulano, earned our highest honors thanks to three historic Collio Goriziano producers: Schiopetto, Toros and Livon (whose Manditocai pays homage to the loss of the cultivar's name). Livio Felluga's Rosazzo Bianco Terre Alte '17 and Jermann's Vintage Tunina '17 affirm their roles as ambassadors of the region'sblends. They're accompanied by acclaimed wines such as Ronco dei Tassi's Collio Bianco Fosarin '17, Angoris's Collio Bianco Riserva '17, and La Tunella's BiancoSesto '17, and Tenuta Luisa's Desiderium '17 (from their I Ferretti line). Villa Russiz's Malvasia '18 is from Collio, as is Ronco Blanchis's Chardonnay '18, Tiare's Sauvignon '18 (which earns its sixth consecutive Tre Bicchieri), and some three versions of Pinot Bianco '18: Doro Princic, Russiz Superiore and Castello di Spessa with their Santarosa. We'd like to highlight how this year this last grape earned a greater number of awards. In addition to those cited we should add Zorzettig's Pinot Bianco Myò '18, Vigneti Le Monde's Pinot Bianco '18 and Masut da Rive's Pinot Bianco '17. Torre Rosazza confirms its excellence with their Pinot Grigio '18, Volpe Pasini with the Sauvignon Zuc di Volpe '18 and Vie di Romans with their Sauvignon Pière '17. The intriguing macerated whites that characterize Oslavia and Karst are represented by Primosic's Ribolla Gialla Riserva '16, Podversic's Malvasia '15 and Skerk's Ograde. The region's sparkling wines also delivered thanks to Collavini and their Ribolla Gialla '15, in its new Brut Nature version. It's always best to close with something sweet, and so a special mention for Lis Neris's Tal Lùc cuvée .1.2.

Antonutti

FRAZ. COLLOREDO DI PRATO
VIA D'ANTONI, 21
33037 PASIAN DI PRATO [UD]
TEL. +39 0432662001
www.antonuttivini.it

CELLAR SALES
PRE-BOOKED VISITS
ANNUAL PRODUCTION 780,000 bottles
HECTARES UNDER VINE 51.00
SUSTAINABLE WINERY

Even if they boast high production volumes, this important regional winery continues to be family operated. Founded by Ignazio in 1921, today it's managed by his granddaughter Adriana Antonutti along with her husband Lino and children Caterina and Nicola. One of the most important turning points came when their historic vineyards in Colloredo di Prato, Udine, were joined by various plots owned by Lino, situated throughout the rugged, stony flatlands of Barbeano, in Spilimbergo. Among their 2018s, the Traminer Aromatico '18 stands out both on the nose and on the palate for its delicious sensations of peach, while the Pinot Grigio Ramato '18 impresses on the palate by virtue of refreshing whiffs of pink grapefruit. Among their reds, we appreciated the Poppone '16, a blend of Merlot and Pignolo. It's considered a meditation wine but lends itself well to various gastronomic pairings. The Pinot Nero '17 is decidedly more delicate.

○ Ant Brut M. Cl. '15	▼▼ 5
○ Friuli Pinot Grigio Ramato '18	▼▼ 3
○ Friuli Traminer Aromatico '18	▼▼ 3
● Poppone '16	▼▼ 5
○ Friuli Friulano '18	▼ 3
● Friuli Grave Refosco P. R. '17	▼ 3
● Friuli Pinot Nero '17	▼ 3
○ Ant Brut M. Cl. '13	♀♀ 5
○ Friuli Grave Friulano '16	♀♀ 3
○ Friuli Grave Pinot Grigio Ramato '16	♀♀ 3
○ Friuli Grave Traminer Aromatico '17	♀♀ 3
○ Lindul '15	♀♀ 6
● Ros di Murì '15	♀♀ 5

Bastianich

LOC. GAGLIANO
VIA DARNAZZACCO, 44/2
33043 CIVIDALE DEL FRIULI [UD]
TEL. +39 0432700943
www.bastianich.com

CELLAR SALES
PRE-BOOKED VISITS
ACCOMMODATION AND RESTAURANT SERVICE
ANNUAL PRODUCTION 270,000 bottles
HECTARES UNDER VINE 35.00

When Joe Bastianich founded this winery in Friuli, he was inspired by a desire to return to his roots. In 1997 he took the plunge, purchasing first a group of vineyards in Buttrio and Premariacco, and later other plots closer to the winery itself, in Gagliano, in Cividale del Friuli. Trusting in an experienced staff, right from the outset the producer began making wines of outstanding structure, like the Vespa, Plus and Calabrone, all perfect for restaurants, as well as a selection of lively, engaging vintage offerings. Three wines, all labeled 'Solo' Riserva, expand their already rich range a Friuliano '17, a Refosco '16 and a Pinot Bianco '17, all of which earned full approval from our panel. At the top of the rankings sit the winery's historic blends; the Vespa Bianco '16 (a splendid combination of Chardonnay, Sauvignon and Picolit), and the Vespa Rosso '16, made with Merlot, Refosco and Schioppettino.

○ Vespa Bianco '16	▼▼ 5
● Vespa Rosso '15	▼▼ 5
○ FCO Friulano '18	▼▼ 3
○ FCO Friulano Solo Ris. '17	▼▼ 4
○ FCO Pinot Bianco Solo Ris. '17	▼▼ 4
○ FCO Pinot Grigio '18	▼▼ 3
● FCO Refosco P. R. Solo Ris. '16	▼▼ 5
● FCO Ribolla Gialla '18	▼▼ 3
● FCO Schippettino '17	▼▼ 3
○ FCO Sauvignon '18	▼ 3
○ COF Tocai Friulano Plus '02	♀♀♀ 3*
○ Vespa Bianco '04	♀♀♀ 4
○ Vespa Bianco '03	♀♀♀ 4
○ Vespa Bianco '01	♀♀♀ 4
○ Vespa Bianco '00	♀♀♀ 3
○ Vespa Bianco '99	♀♀♀ 3*

Tenuta Borgo Conventi

S.DA DELLA COLOMBARA, 13
34072 FARRA D'ISONZO [GO]
TEL. +39 0481888004
www.borgoconventi.it

CELLAR SALES
PRE-BOOKED VISITS
ACCOMMODATION
ANNUAL PRODUCTION 300,000 bottles
HECTARES UNDER VINE 35.00

Borgo Conventi gets its name from a legend according to which Rizzardo di Srassoldo, a local feudal lord, donated a plot of land to Dominican monks who erected a convent there. Founded in 1975 by Gianni Vescovo, the winery was taken over in 2001 by the Folonari family. Recently the estate was purchased by the Moretti Polegato family, who've always been on the front line in the fight for sustainability and environmental protections, thus the decision to apply low-impact agricultural practices over the years. The change in management has had positive effects right out of the gate, as testified to by a number of favorable ratings. Among these two wines earned a place in our final round tastings. The Ribolla Gialla '18 proves to one of the best in its category, especially aromatically. The Braida Nuova '12, a blend of Merlot and Refosco dal Penduncolo Rosso, is a well-crafted wine, to say the least.

● Braida Nuova '12	♈♈ 5
○ Collio Ribolla Gialla '18	♈♈ 3*
● Braida Nuova '13	♈♈ 5
○ Collio Chardonnay '18	♈♈ 3
○ Collio Friulano '18	♈♈ 3
○ Collio Pinot Grigio '18	♈♈ 3
○ Collio Sauvignon '18	♈♈ 3
○ Friuli Isonzo Friulano '18	♈♈ 2*
○ Friuli Isonzo Pinot Grigio '18	♈♈ 3
○ Friuli Isonzo Sauvignon '18	♈♈ 2*
● Schioppettino '14	♈♈ 4
○ Friuli Isonzo Chardonnay '18	♈ 3
○ Ribolla Gialla '18	♈ 2
● Braida Nuova '91	♈♈♈
○ Collio Friulano '17	♈♈ 3
○ Collio Ribolla Gialla '17	♈♈ 3

Borgo delle Oche

VIA BORGO ALPI, 5
33098 VALVASONE ARZENE [PN]
TEL. +39 0434840640
www.borgodelleoche.it

CELLAR SALES
PRE-BOOKED VISITS
ACCOMMODATION
ANNUAL PRODUCTION 35,000 bottles
HECTARES UNDER VINE 7.00
SUSTAINABLE WINERY

Luisa Menini and Nicola Pittini make a splendid couple, one joined in life and work. In 2004 they founded Borgo delle Oche, a small producer that in a few years has affirmed its status a model winery — a concrete example of how it's possible to draw out of the region's plains full wines with character and personality. Low yields and painstaking care are owner Luisa's guiding principles. She's always loved the outdoors and has taken on the responsibility of cultivating quality grapes that are then entrusted to winemaker Nicola. The Traminer Passito Alba '17 overcame a lot of competition in the regional category of sweet wines and landed a place in our finals, delighting the palate with its fragrant notes of spices and candied citrus. The Lupi Terrae '16 (Malvasia Istriana, Tocai Friulano and Verduzzo Friulano) also put in an excellent performance, bolstered by a variegated aromatic weave wrought of floral wafts, pine resin, summer hay, hazelnuts, honey and malt cookies.

○ Traminer Passito Alba '17	♈♈ 5
○ Friuli Pinot Grigio '18	♈♈ 2*
○ Lupi Terrae '16	♈♈ 3
● Merlot '16	♈♈ 2*
● Refosco P. R. '15	♈♈ 3
○ Traminer Aromatico '18	♈♈ 2*
○ Friuli Sauvignon '18	♈ 2
○ Malvasia '17	♈ 2
○ Friuli Friulano '17	♈♈ 2*
○ Friuli Friulano '16	♈♈ 2*
○ Friuli Pinot Grigio '17	♈♈ 2*
○ Malvasia '16	♈♈ 2*
○ Malvasia '15	♈♈ 2*
● Merlot '15	♈♈ 2*
○ Pinot Grigio '16	♈♈ 2*
○ Terra e Cielo Extra Brut '14	♈♈ 5

★Borgo San Daniele

VIA SAN DANIELE, 28
34071 CORMÒNS [GO]
TEL. +39 048160552
www.borgosandaniele.it

CELLAR SALES
PRE-BOOKED VISITS
ACCOMMODATION
ANNUAL PRODUCTION 60,000 bottles
HECTARES UNDER VINE 19.00
VITICULTURE METHOD Certified Organic
SUSTAINABLE WINERY

Borgo San Daniele gets its name from the district where the winery, and the old house lived in by grandfather Antonio, are situated. In 1990 Antonio left a few hectares of vineyards to his grandchildren Mauro and Alessandra. Mauro's skills and insight vaulted the winery to the heights of regional excellence in just a short time. Their production guidelines are clear: high density vineyards with low vigor, grassing, late harvests, various types of maceration, malolactic fermentation, a long stay on the lees and, finally, bottling without filtering. Borgo San Daniele submitted only three wines this year, all of which proved capable of performing at high levels and earned places in the upper rankings of their respective categories. The Malvasia '17 and Pinot Grigio '17, in particular, but also their excellent Friulano of the same vintage. It's also worth noting an intriguing Vermouth that wasn't reviewed here, but that represents the producer's commitment to continued research.

○ Friuli Isonzo Malvasia '17	♥♥ 4
○ Friuli Isonzo Pinot Grigio '17	♥♥ 4
○ Friuli Isonzo Friulano '17	♥♥ 4
○ Arbis Blanc '10	♥♥♥ 4*
○ Arbis Blanc '09	♥♥♥ 4
○ Arbis Blanc '05	♥♥♥ 4
○ Friuli Isonzo Arbis Blanc '02	♥♥♥ 4
○ Friuli Isonzo Friulano '08	♥♥♥ 4*
○ Friuli Isonzo Friulano '07	♥♥♥ 4*
○ Friuli Isonzo Pinot Grigio '04	♥♥♥ 4
○ Friuli Isonzo Tocai Friulano '03	♥♥♥ 3
● Gortmarin '03	♥♥♥ 5

Borgo Savaian

VIA SAVAIAN, 36
34071 CORMÒNS [GO]
TEL. +39 048160725
Via Savaian

CELLAR SALES
PRE-BOOKED VISITS
ANNUAL PRODUCTION 100,000 bottles
HECTARES UNDER VINE 18.00

It's an old story but a current one as well. A family of farmhands dedicated to wine-growing that finds new life, energy and enthusiasm with each generational shift. Now it's Stefano and Rosanna Bastiani's turn to over see the winery they inherited from their father Mario. Putting to use his enological studies, as well as the experience gained year after year, Stefano is showing that he's capable of bringing out Collio's extraordinary potential. Though he's also managed to produce excellent wines in the flatlands of the Friuli Isonzo appellation. The Malvasia '18 is a concrete example of how important it is for the plains and hills to be treated as equals. It excels both on the nose and on the palate, with close-focused notes of medicinal herbs and tropical fruit. It proves to be one of the best in its category and earned itself a place in our final round of tastings. The rest of their 2018s are all excellent, with a final note for their decidedly curious Aransat, made with white grapes that undergo prolonged maceration.

○ Friuli Isonzo Malvasia '18	♥♥ 3*
○ Aransat	♥♥ 3
○ Collio Friulano '18	♥♥ 3
○ Collio Pinot Grigio '18	♥♥ 3
○ Collio Ribolla Gialla '18	♥♥ 3
● Friuli Isonzo Merlot '17	♥♥ 3
○ Friuli Isonzo Sauvignon '18	♥♥ 3
○ Friuli Isonzo Traminer Aromatico '18	♥ 3
○ Collio Friulano '17	♥♥ 3
○ Collio Friulano '16	♥♥ 3
○ Collio Pinot Grigio '17	♥♥ 3
○ Collio Pinot Grigio '16	♥♥ 3
○ Collio Ribolla Gialla '17	♥♥ 3
○ Collio Sauvignon '16	♥♥ 3*
○ Friuli Isonzo Malvasia '17	♥♥ 3
○ Friuli Isonzo Sauvignon '17	♥♥ 3

Cav. Emiro Bortolusso

via Oltregorgo, 10
33050 Carlino [UD]
Tel. +39 043167596
www.bortolusso.it

CELLAR SALES
PRE-BOOKED VISITS
ACCOMMODATION
ANNUAL PRODUCTION **120,000 bottles**
HECTARES UNDER VINE **40.00**

Sergio and Clara Bortolusso's winery is one of the most thriving and representative of the Friuli Annia appellation, a strip of terrain situated in a landscape of great natural beauty. Their vineyards span the vast clearings of Friuli's plains, areas that are often surrounded by coppice woods overlooking the Adriatic sea. The mild climate guarantees excellent ripening of the grapes, while the beneficial sea breeze contributes to consolidating their natural varietal aromas. Consistent quality and good prices have been decisive in earning the producer success and accolades. The Bortolusso family's selection essentially replicated last year's performance, yet more proof of how, within a territory, every cultivar can express its potential even in the face of very different years in terms of climatic and agronomic conditions. The Friulano '18 and the Malvasia '18 lead the way, but all excel for their drinkability.

○ Friuli Friulano '18	TT 2*
○ Friuli Pinot Grigio '18	TT 2*
○ Malvasia '18	TT 2*
○ Sauvignon '18	TT 2*
○ Chardonnay '18	T 2
○ Traminer Aromatico '18	T 2
○ Chardonnay '16	YY 2*
○ Friuli Annia Friulano '17	YY 2*
○ Friuli Annia Malvasia '17	YY 2*
○ Friuli Annia Pinot Grigio '17	YY 2*
○ Malvasia '17	YY 2*
○ Malvasia '16	YY 2*
○ Pinot Grigio '16	YY 2*
○ Pinot Grigio '15	YY 2*
○ Sauvignon '17	YY 2*
○ Sauvignon '16	YY 2*

Branko

loc. Zegla, 20
34071 Cormòns [GO]
Tel. +39 0481639826
www.brankowines.com

CELLAR SALES
PRE-BOOKED VISITS
ANNUAL PRODUCTION **45,000 bottles**
HECTARES UNDER VINE **9.00**

Igor Erzetic, the estate's current owner, deserves credit for transforming a small, family-run winery into a regional enological pearl. His father, Branko, officially founded the producer in 1950, but its roots go back before anyone can remember, as is to be expected considering that the close bond between farmer and land is a time-honored tradition in Collio. The small size of the estate and its limited selection of wines allow Igor to dedicate all his attention to caring for the vineyards and making wine. Their Chardonnay '18 is entirely in line with the quality registered in previous years. It excels for typicality, delighting the notes with its notes of vanilla, passion fruit, pineapple and candied citron. It's on par with their Friulano '18, a wine redolent of summer hay and whose palate exhibits enviable drinkability. Their notable Capo Branko '18 (Malvasia Istriana, Tocai Friulano and Sauvignon) is characterized by an intriguing sweetness.

○ Collio Chardonnay '18	TT 4
○ Collio Friulano '18	TT 4
○ Capo Branko '18	TT 4
○ Collio Pinot Grigio '18	TT 4
○ Collio Pinot Grigio '14	YYY 4*
○ Collio Pinot Grigio '08	YYY 3*
○ Collio Pinot Grigio '07	YYY 3
○ Collio Pinot Grigio '06	YYY 3
○ Collio Pinot Grigio '05	YYY 3
○ Capo Branko '17	YY 4
○ Collio Chardonnay '17	YY 4
○ Collio Chardonnay '16	YY 4
○ Collio Friulano '17	YY 4
○ Collio Pinot Grigio '17	YY 4
○ Collio Sauvignon '16	YY 4
● Red Branko '15	YY 4

Livio e Claudio Buiatti

VIA LIPPE, 25
33042 BUTTRIO [UD]
TEL. +39 0432674317
www.buiattivini.it

CELLAR SALES
PRE-BOOKED VISITS
ANNUAL PRODUCTION 35,000 bottles
HECTARES UNDER VINE 8.00

Claudio Buiatti, now joined by his son Matteo, oversees a classic family-run winery where everyone has a hand in looking after everything. The winery is situated in the town of Buttrio, while the vineyards span the gentle, sunny slopes of the eocenic hill range that extends towards Premariacco, in the splendid district of 'In Mont e Poanis'. Their entire range centers on outstanding quality, with points of excellence that highlight their deep commitment to making great wine at affordable prices. An excellent day for their overall selection (all wines true to their varietal profiles), and a noteworthy performance by their Merlot '16, is capped off by their Rosso Momom Ros Ris. '15. This Merlot and Cabernet Sauvignon blend pours an elegant garnet red, the prelude to intriguing aromas of small black berries, sweet spices, licorice and coffee. On the palate it unfolds self-assuredly and pervasively.

○ FCO Friulano '18	♟♟ 3
○ FCO Malvasia '18	♟♟ 3
● FCO Merlot '16	♟♟ 3
● FCO Momom Ros Ris. '15	♟♟ 4
○ FCO Pinot Grigio '18	♟♟ 3
○ FCO Friulano '17	♟♟ 3*
○ FCO Friulano '16	♟♟ 3
○ FCO Friulano '15	♟♟ 3
● FCO Merlot '15	♟♟ 3
● FCO Momom Ros Ris. '13	♟♟ 4
○ FCO Pinot Grigio '17	♟♟ 3
○ FCO Pinot Grigio '16	♟♟ 3
● FCO Refosco P. R. '15	♟♟ 3
○ FCO Sauvignon '17	♟♟ 3
○ FCO Sauvignon '16	♟♟ 3*
○ FCO Sauvignon '15	♟♟ 3

La Buse dal Lôf

VIA RONCHI, 90
33040 PREPOTTO [UD]
TEL. +39 0432701523
www.labusedallof.com

CELLAR SALES
PRE-BOOKED VISITS
ANNUAL PRODUCTION 100,000 bottles
HECTARES UNDER VINE 25.00

It was 1972 when Giuseppe Pavan formally founded this lovely Prepotto winery, naming it after the area: La Buse dal Lôf, which in local dialect means 'the wolf's den'. Today its managed by his son Michele, a worthy heir to a winery rooted foremost in its vineyards, which span the Friuli Colli Orientali appellation. The eocenic terrain here, primarily marl and sandstone, is protected by the Julian Alps while also benefiting from the breeze of the nearby Adriatic. This year they didn't present the Schioppettino di Prepotto, widely recognized as the area's most representative wine (it has to age for a while longer). Its absence is felt, inasmuch as we've always referred to as their flagship product, but the overall performance put in by their 2018s, and their fruity, pleasantly spicy and promising Merlot '17, is more than up to snuff.

○ FCO Chardonnay '18	♟♟ 3
○ FCO Friulano '18	♟♟ 3
● FCO Merlot '17	♟♟ 3
○ FCO Sauvignon '18	♟♟ 3
○ FCO Ribolla Gialla '18	♟ 3
○ FCO Chardonnay '16	♟♟ 3
● FCO Merlot '16	♟♟ 3
○ FCO Pinot Bianco In Bocca al Lupo '15	♟♟ 3
● FCO Refosco P. R. '15	♟♟ 3
○ FCO Ribolla Gialla '16	♟♟ 3
○ FCO Sauvignon '15	♟♟ 3
● FCO Schioppettino di Prepotto '15	♟♟ 4
● FCO Schioppettino di Prepotto '13	♟♟ 4

Valentino Butussi

VIA PRÀ DI CORTE, 1
33040 CORNO DI ROSAZZO [UD]
TEL. +39 0432759194
www.butussi.it

CELLAR SALES
PRE-BOOKED VISITS
ACCOMMODATION
ANNUAL PRODUCTION 120,000 bottles
HECTARES UNDER VINE 18.00
VITICULTURE METHOD Certified Organic
SUSTAINABLE WINERY

The Butussi family's roots run deep in the marl-sandy terrain of Prà di Corte, in Corno di Rosazzo. The winery is the cumulation of experiences, knowledge and little secrets passed down over the ages, ever since Valentino Butussi first set in motion their work in the early 20th century. He was followed by Angelo, who consolidated the winery's reputation as one of the most important in the region. The new generation is represented by Tobia, Filippo, Mattia and Erika, who offer a selection of wines that, however vast, manages to express the character of each grape variety. Their 2018s didn't betray expectations, but it was their vintage wines that earned the highest praise. The Rosso Santuari Ris. '13 (Cabernet Sauvignon and Merlot) amazes for its fragrance and gustatory exuberance. The Bianco WhiteAngel '14 (Chardonnay, Sauvignon and Pinot Bianco) excels for its structure and opulence, while the Sauvignon Genesis '15 stands out for its varietal profile.

● FCO Rosso Santuari Ris. '13	♟♟ 5
○ COF Picolit '12	♟♟ 6
○ FCO Bianco White Angel '14	♟♟ 4
○ FCO Chardonnay '18	♟♟ 2*
○ FCO Friulano '18	♟♟ 2*
○ FCO Sauvignon '18	♟♟ 2*
○ FCO Sauvignon Genesis '15	♟♟ 4
○ FCO Pinot Grigio Ramato '18	♟ 2
○ COF Picolit '11	♟♟ 6
○ FCO Bianco di Corte '16	♟♟ 3
● FCO Cabernet Sauvignon '16	♟♟ 3
○ FCO Chardonnay '17	♟♟ 2*
● FCO Merlot '16	♟♟ 3
○ FCO Pinot Grigio '17	♟♟ 2*
○ FCO Pinot Grigio Et. Storica '14	♟♟ 5
○ Ribolla Gialla Brut	♟♟ 5

Maurizio Buzzinelli

LOC. PRADIS, 20
34071 CORMÒNS [GO]
TEL. +39 048160902
www.buzzinelli.it

CELLAR SALES
PRE-BOOKED VISITS
ACCOMMODATION
ANNUAL PRODUCTION 120,000 bottles
HECTARES UNDER VINE 35.00

For three generations the Buzzinelli family have passed down knowledge and experience, year after year. Now it's Maurizio's job to oversee the vineyards that extend across the hills of Collio Goriziano, an area renowned for its white wines. From the gentle slopes here, one's gaze gets lost in the plains below, which stretch all the way to the nearby Adriatic sea. Their other plots form part of the Friuli Isonzo appellation and host primarily red grapes, which take advantage of the area's iron and mineral-rich subsoil. The small number of wines submitted for tasting doesn't allow for a complete analysis of the producer's overall capacities. Nevertheless, those tasted performed quite well, starting with their Friulano '18, which landed a place in our finals. On the nose it calls up summer hay, the blossoming of the acacia, white-fleshed fruit and honey, only to enchant on the palate for its pleasantness. Both the Ribolla Gialla '18 and the Malvasia '18 also prove excellent.

○ Collio Friulano '18	♟♟ 3*
○ Collio Malvasia '18	♟♟ 2*
○ Collio Ribolla Gialla '18	♟♟ 3
○ Collio Müller Thurgau '18	♟ 2
○ Collio Chardonnay '15	♟♟ 3
○ Collio Friulano '17	♟♟ 3
○ Collio Friulano '16	♟♟ 3*
○ Collio Friulano '15	♟♟ 3
○ Collio Malvasia '16	♟♟ 2*
○ Collio Malvasia '15	♟♟ 2*
○ Collio Pinot Grigio '17	♟♟ 3
○ Collio Ribolla Gialla '15	♟♟ 3
○ Collio Sauvignon '17	♟♟ 3
○ Collio Sauvignon '16	♟♟ 3
○ Collio Sauvignon '15	♟♟ 3
○ Collio Traminer Aromatico '17	♟♟ 3

Ca' Bolani

VIA CA' BOLANI, 2
33052 CERVIGNANO DEL FRIULI [UD]
TEL. +39 043132670
www.cabolani.it

CELLAR SALES
PRE-BOOKED VISITS
ANNUAL PRODUCTION 2,700,000 bottles
HECTARES UNDER VINE 550.00

Tenuta Cà Bolani belonged to the Cà Bolani family until 1970, when it was taken over by the Venetian Zonin group. The estate also comprises the vineyards of Cà Vescovo and Molin di Ponte, which were purchased in 1980 and 1998 respectively. With its 2,000 kilometers of vineyards, Cà Bolani is one of the region's, and northern Italy's, most sizable estates. Aquilis and Opimio are the crus that guarantee the best grapes, and represent the producer's crown jewels. But quality is guaranteed across their entire range, including their less expensive offerings. This year an excellent Pinot Grigio '18 leads their selection, highlighting the territorial potential of a grape long cultivated in the region. It earned a place in our final tastings by virtue of its delicate, floral nuances of acacia and elder, accompanied by medicinal herbs and citron peel. On the palate it unfolds fully, proving juicy and mineral, as well as fragrant. The Sauvignon Aquilis '17 also performed commendably.

○ Friuli Aquileia Pinot Grigio '18	▼▼ 3*
○ Friuli Aquileia Pinot Bianco '18	▼▼ 3
● Friuli Aquileia Refosco P. R. '17	▼▼ 3
○ Friuli Aquileia Sauvignon Aquilis '17	▼▼ 5
○ Friuli Aquileia Traminer Aromatico '18	▼▼ 3
○ Friuli Aquileia Friulano '18	▼ 4
○ Friuli Aquileia Sauvignon '18	▼ 3
○ Prosecco Brut	▼ 3
○ Friuli Aquileia Pinot Bianco '09	▼▼▼ 2*
○ Friuli Aquileia Pinot Bianco Opimio '16	▼▼ 5
○ Friuli Aquileia Pinot Grigio '17	▼▼ 3
● Friuli Aquileia Refosco P. R. Alturio '15	▼▼ 4
○ Friuli Aquileia Sauvignon Aquilis '16	▼▼ 5

Ca' Tullio

VIA BELIGNA, 41
33051 AQUILEIA [UD]
TEL. +39 0431919700
www.catullio.it

CELLAR SALES
PRE-BOOKED VISITS
ANNUAL PRODUCTION 200,000 bottles
HECTARES UNDER VINE 100.00

Owner Paolo Calligaris brought together under one banner two completely different wine-growing territories in terms of soil and microclimate. About half of the vineyards fall within the Friuli Aquileia appellation, a famously flat land by the Adriatic sea. The other half enjoy the splendid position made possible by the Manzano hills. These two areas complement one another, making for a selection of wines that are extremely representative of the region's potential. Most of the wines presented hail from the hillside, and these were the ones that elicited the most favorable reactions. The Traminer Viola '18, however, was neck-in-neck, confirming the lowlands' suitability for the grape. The Friulano '18 offers up intense aromas of helichrysum and lemon wafer, unfolding supple and tasty on the palate. The Pinot Grigio '18 calls up the aromas of the summer hay harvest.

○ FCO Chardonnay '18	▼▼ 2*
○ FCO Friulano '18	▼▼ 2*
○ FCO Pinot Grigio '18	▼▼ 2*
○ FCO Ribolla Gialla '18	▼▼ 3
○ Friuli Aquileia Traminer Viola '18	▼▼ 2*
● FCO Pignolo '15	▼ 3
● Patriarca Refosco P. R. '17	▼ 3
○ FCO Chardonnay '17	▼▼ 2*
○ FCO Chardonnay '16	▼▼ 2*
○ FCO Friulano '17	▼▼ 2*
● FCO Pignolo '14	▼▼ 3
○ FCO Pinot Grigio '17	▼▼ 2*
○ FCO Pinot Grigio '16	▼▼ 2*
● FCO Schioppettino '15	▼▼ 3

Cadibon

LOC. CASALI GALLO, 1
33040 CORNO DI ROSAZZO [UD]
TEL. +39 0432759316
www.cadibon.com

CELLAR SALES
PRE-BOOKED VISITS
ACCOMMODATION
ANNUAL PRODUCTION 55,000 bottles
HECTARES UNDER VINE 13.00
VITICULTURE METHOD Certified Organic

For generations, the Bon family dedicated themselves to cultivating vines in Corno di Rosazzio. After a long journey, in 1977, Gianni officially founded the winery, which is now managed by young Luca and Francesca. In addition to bringing a blast of innovation and energy, they've undergone a conversion to organic and biodynamic management. Their vineyards span three separate appellations (Friuli Colli Orientali, Friuli Grave and Collio), all different but bound together by the expressive purity of the wines drawn from them. Their Malvasia '18 leads a competitive group of wines and earned itself a place in our final round of tastings. Notes of citrus and peppermint rise up on the nose, interspersed with whiffs of aromatic herbs and Mediterranean scrub. On the palate it's harmonious, fresh, plush and pleasantly sapid. The Sauvignon Lavoron '18 confirms last year's accolades. It's a wine of great character, elegance and personality.

○ FCO Malvasia '18	♚♚	3*
○ Collio Chardonnay '18	♚♚	3
○ Collio Sauvignon '18	♚♚	3
○ Collio Sauvignon Lavoron '18	♚♚	3
○ FCO Friulano '18	♚♚	3
● FCO Merlot '17	♚♚	3
○ FCO Ribolla Gialla '18	♚♚	3
○ Verduzzo Friulano '17	♚	3
○ Collio Chardonnay '17	♚♚	3
○ Collio Pinot Grigio '17	♚♚	3
○ Collio Sauvignon '17	♚♚	3
○ Collio Sauvignon Lavoron '17	♚♚	3
● Epoca '16	♚♚	5
● FCO Merlot '16	♚♚	3
● FCO Refosco P. R. '16	♚♚	3
○ FCO Ribolla Gialla '17	♚♚	3

Canus

LOC. CASALI GALLO
VIA GRAMOGLIANO, 21
33040 CORNO DI ROSAZZO [UD]
TEL. +39 0432759427
www.canus.it

CELLAR SALES
PRE-BOOKED VISITS
ANNUAL PRODUCTION 60,000 bottles
HECTARES UNDER VINE 18.00

After extensive work experience in the industrial sector, in 2015 Otto Casonato began making wine. He was a neophyte to the field, inspired by the desire to create a small though important winery. Out of a pragmatic need, and considering the scope of his ambitions he decided to avail himself of the experience of enologist Gianni Bignucolo, entrusting him with a selection of wines that brings together quality and character. Consider Otto's choice as one aimed at beginning anew, and a sense of freedom he doesn't intend to give up. The producer's philosophy requires wines to be released only after appropriate aging. As a result, this year we only tasted 2017s, as they have reached the ideal aromatic and gustatory maturity. The Chardonnay '17 and Pinot Grigio '17 competed for the title of best of the lot, and both earned a place in our finals, just beating out the rest.

○ FCO Chardonnay '17	♚♚	4
○ FCO Pinot Grigio '17	♚♚	4
○ FCO Bianco Gramogliano '17	♚♚	4
○ FCO Friulano '17	♚♚	4
○ FCO Ribolla Gialla '17	♚♚	4
○ COF Pinot Grigio '15	♚♚	3
○ FCO Bianco Gramogliano '16	♚♚	4
○ FCO Bianco Gramogliano '15	♚♚	4
○ FCO Chardonnay '16	♚♚	4
○ FCO Friulano '15	♚♚	3
● FCO Merlot '12	♚♚	5
● FCO Merlot '11	♚♚	4
● FCO Pignolo '11	♚♚	6
● FCO Pignolo '10	♚♚	5
○ FCO Pinot Grigio '16	♚♚	4
● FCO Rosso Mezzo Secolo '10	♚♚	5

Fernanda Cappello

S.DA DI SEQUALS, 15
33090 SEQUALS [PN]
TEL. +39 042793291
www.fernandacappello.it

CELLAR SALES
PRE-BOOKED VISITS
RESTAURANT SERVICE
ANNUAL PRODUCTION 100,000 bottles
HECTARES UNDER VINE 126.00
SUSTAINABLE WINERY

Just beneath the hills of Sequals, on the right bank of the Tagliamento river, you'll find Fernanda Cappello's estate, which in 1988 she took over from her family, plunging in to what Fernanda herself calls an 'exciting adventure'. With more than 100 hectares of vineyards, the estate is among western Friuli's largest. The terrain here is made up of lean, rocky, arid alluvial sediment, notoriously well-suited to vine growing. For some time now Fabio Coser has served an important role as enological consultant. Their selection of 2018s, true to their varietal characteristics, exhibit an enviable freshness, proving highly drinkable and appealing. Those aged at length excel in structure and complexity. Their Chardonnay Perla dei Sassi '15 deserves a special mention, delighting the nose with its aromas of candied fruit, Catalan cream and vanilla, and enveloping the palate with velvety, juicy sensations. Great value as well.

Il Carpino

LOC. SOVENZA, 14A
34070 SAN FLORIANO DEL COLLIO [GO]
TEL. +39 0481884097
www.ilcarpino.com

CELLAR SALES
PRE-BOOKED VISITS
ANNUAL PRODUCTION 70,000 bottles
HECTARES UNDER VINE 16.00

It was 1987 when Anna and Franco Sosol founded their winery in Borgo del Carpino, in the district of Sovenza. Here the old and the new come together with enviable synergy. The tendency to return to the past is still alive and, as is custom, grapes are macerated on the skins for several days (white grapes as well). Modern technology is reserved for grapes from their younger vineyards, which are fermented in steel tanks. The wines presented in this edition all belong to their brilliant Vigna Runc line (we'll have to wait for next year to taste their new macerated whites, as the producer has chosen to adopt an additional, supplementary period of aging). We once again appreciated the eclectic mastery of the Sasol family, whose wines have risen to the heights of regional excellence as of late, including their steel-aged selections.

● Friuli Grave Cabernet Sauvignon '16	♟♟ 2*
○ Friuli Grave Chardonnay Perla dei Sassi '15	♟♟ 3
○ Friuli Grave Friulano '18	♟♟ 2*
● Friuli Grave Merlot '14	♟♟ 2*
○ Friuli Grave Pinot Bianco '18	♟♟ 2*
○ Friuli Grave Pinot Grigio '18	♟♟ 2*
○ Friuli Grave Traminer Aromatico '18	♟♟ 2*
● Friuli Grave Refosco P. R. '16	♟ 2
○ Friuli Grave Sauvignon '18	♟ 2
○ Prosecco Extra Dry	♟ 2
○ Ribolla Gialla '18	♟ 2
○ Ribolla Gialla Brut	♟ 2
● Friuli Grave Cabernet Franc '16	♟♟ 2*
○ Friuli Grave Pinot Grigio '17	♟♟ 2*
○ Friuli Grave Sauvignon '17	♟♟ 2*
○ Ribolla Gialla '17	♟♟ 2*

○ Collio Friulano V. Runc '17	♟♟ 3*
○ Collio Malvasia V. Runc '17	♟♟ 3
○ Collio Pinot Grigio V. Runc '18	♟♟ 3
○ Collio Bianco V. Runc '10	♟♟♟ 3*
○ Collio Malvasia V. Runc '11	♟♟♟ 3*
○ Malvasia '15	♟♟♟ 5
○ Malvasia '11	♟♟♟ 5
● Rubrum '99	♟♟♟ 3*
○ Chardonnay '12	♟♟ 5
○ Exordium '15	♟♟ 5
○ Exordium '13	♟♟ 5
○ Friuli Isonzo Friulano V. Runc '15	♟♟ 3
○ Sauvignon '15	♟♟ 4
○ Vis Uvae '15	♟♟ 5
○ Vis Uvae '13	♟♟ 5

Castello di Buttrio

VIA DEL POZZO, 5
33042 BUTTRIO [UD]
TEL. +39 0432673015
www.castellodibuttrio.it

CELLAR SALES
PRE-BOOKED VISITS
ACCOMMODATION AND RESTAURANT SERVICE
ANNUAL PRODUCTION 60,000 bottles
HECTARES UNDER VINE 25.00

Alessandra Felluga comes from a winemaking family. Thanks to patient renovation she's restored the ancient walls of Buttrio Castle to their former glory. It's an area that's rich in history and that today hosts both the winery and their administrative center, both harmoniously enclosed in the estate purchased by her father, Marco, in 1994. Castello di Buttrio wines immediately ascended to the heights of regional excellence, especially thanks to the agronomic and enological support of expert Hartmann Donà. The even distribution of the scores awarded, both whites and reds, testifies to the validity of their entire range. The Merlot '16 delights the palate, offering up pleasant, fruity hints of blackberry and blackcurrant, then dark chocolate and tobacco. Their Bianco Mon Blanc '17 (a blend of Tocaì Friulano, Malvasia Istriana and Ribolla Gialla) is also excellent, proving intensely fragrant and creamy.

○ FCO Friulano '18	▼▼	4
● FCO Merlot '16	▼▼	4
● FCO Refosco P. R. '16	▼▼	4
○ FCO Sauvignon '18	▼▼	3
○ Mon Blanc '17	▼▼	3
○ FCO Ribolla Gialla '18	▼	4
○ FCO Friulano '16	♀	4

★Castello di Spessa

VIA SPESSA, 1
34070 CAPRIVA DEL FRIULI [GO]
TEL. +39 048160445
www.castellodispessa.it

CELLAR SALES
PRE-BOOKED VISITS
ACCOMMODATION AND RESTAURANT SERVICE
ANNUAL PRODUCTION 300,000 bottles
HECTARES UNDER VINE 83.00

Loretto Pali is the current owner of Castello di Spessa, a splendid manner that displays a subtle charm both for the elegance of the edifice itself and for its millennium-old history, which is rich in personages and stories. In the bunker that connects the castle and the winery, which was used by occupying troops during World War II, wines are left to age in naturally cool temperatures and constant humidity. The support of Enrico Paternoster rounds out a winery that has already reached the heights of excellence, but have no intention of resting on their laurels. With three wines in our final round of tastings, Castello di Spessa confirms its status as one of the region's best producers. The Pinot Bianco Santarosa '18 excels for its elegant aromas and pervasive palate. The Sauvignon Segrè '18 features pronounced varietal characteristics, while the Friulano Rassauer '18 delights with its pleasantness. The Collio Bianco San Serff '12 affirms the aging power of the region's whites.

○ Collio Pinot Bianco Santarosa '18	▼▼▼	3*
○ Collio Friulano Rassauer '18	▼▼	3*
○ Collio Sauvignon Segrè '18	▼▼	5
○ Collio Bianco San Serff '12	▼▼	4
○ Collio Ribolla Gialla Yellow Hills '18	▼▼	3
○ Ribolla Gialla Brut Perté '18	▼▼	3
○ Collio Pinot Grigio Joy '18	▼	4
○ Collio Pinot Bianco '14	♀♀♀	3*
○ Collio Pinot Bianco '13	♀♀♀	3*
○ Collio Pinot Bianco '11	♀♀♀	3*
○ Collio Pinot Bianco '06	♀♀♀	3*
○ Collio Pinot Bianco '01	♀♀♀	3
○ Collio Sauvignon Segrè '03	♀♀♀	5
○ Collio Sauvignon Segrè '02	♀♀♀	5
○ Collio Tocai Friulano '05	♀♀♀	3*

Castello Sant'Anna

LOC. SPESSA
VIA SANT'ANNA, 9
33043 CIVIDALE DEL FRIULI [UD]
TEL. +39 0432716289
www.castellosantanna.it

CELLAR SALES
PRE-BOOKED VISITS
ANNUAL PRODUCTION 25,000 bottles
HECTARES UNDER VINE 7.00
VITICULTURE METHOD Certified Organic

Once the summer home of a noble Friulian family, Sant'Anna castle was purchased by Giuseppe Giaiotti in 1966. Vineyards surround its outer walls, which house 17th-century structures, while the perimeter is delimited by two cylindrical towers, renovated in the 17th century but whose foundations go back to the 13th-15th centuries. Today the winery is managed by the third generation of family, Andrea Giaiotti. The fact of being a smaller estate with a limited selection of wines allows the producer to personally and painstakingly oversee the entire production cycle. With their reds locked away in the cellar (so as to enjoy a further stint of aging), this year we dealt exclusively with their 2017 whites. Our impressions were positive, to say the least, thanks especially to their Pinot Grigio '17: an aromatic profile wrought of pear juicy, ripe melon and strawberry gives way to a succulent, mouthfilling palate. Their Friulano of the same year is also excellent.

○ FCO Pinot Grigio '17	♟♟	3*
○ FCO Friulano '17	♟♟	3
○ FCO Ribolla Gialla '17	♟♟	3
○ FCO Sauvignon '17	♟♟	3
● FCO Cabernet Franc '16	♟♟	4
○ FCO Friulano '16	♟♟	3
○ FCO Friulano '15	♟♟	3
● FCO Merlot '15	♟♟	4
● FCO Merlot Ris. '13	♟♟	4
○ FCO Pinot Grigio '16	♟♟	3
○ FCO Pinot Grigio '15	♟♟	3*
● FCO Refosco P. R. '13	♟♟	4
○ FCO Ribolla Gialla '16	♟♟	3
○ FCO Sauvignon '16	♟♟	3
○ FCO Sauvignon '15	♟♟	3
● FCO Schioppettino '12	♟♟	5

Castelvecchio

VIA CASTELNUOVO, 2
34078 SAGRADO [GO]
TEL. +39 048199742
www.castelvecchio.com

CELLAR SALES
PRE-BOOKED VISITS
ACCOMMODATION AND RESTAURANT SERVICE
ANNUAL PRODUCTION 120,000 bottles
HECTARES UNDER VINE 35.00
SUSTAINABLE WINERY

Castelvecchio is situated in the southernmost part of Carso Goriziano, on a hilltop from which it enjoys an extraordinary panoramic view of the regional territory. The rocky subsoil, a thin layer of red, iron and limestone-rich topsoil, the area's particular wind patterns and a late harvest make for a limited selection of wines with absolutely unique characteristics. In 1978 the estate was purchased by the Terraneo family, who've managed to harness this special environment through exceptional technical choices. And once again the Malvasia Dileo leads a prestigious selection of whites and reds, a group that has proved capable of expressing the best of Karst from one year to the next. The 2018 reached our final round of tastings for the fourth year in a row, just falling short of our highest honors. It's refined in all respects, standing out for its intriguing style, apparently simple but delicately complex and compelling.

○ Carso Malvasia Dileo '18	♟♟	4
● Carso Cabernet Franc '16	♟♟	3
○ Carso Malvasia '18	♟♟	3
○ Carso Pinot Grigio '18	♟♟	3
● Carso Refosco P. R. '16	♟♟	3
○ Carso Sauvignon '18	♟♟	3
○ Carso Traminer Aromatico '18	♟♟	3
○ Carso Vitovska '18	♟♟	3
● Carso Cabernet Sauvignon '16	♟	3
● Carso Terrano '17	♟	3
○ Carso Malvasia Dileo '15	♟♟♟	4*
○ Carso Malvasia '17	♟♟	3
○ Carso Malvasia Dileo '17	♟♟	4
○ Carso Pinot Grigio '17	♟♟	3
○ Carso Traminer Aromatico '17	♟♟	3
○ Carso Vitovska '17	♟♟	3

Tenimenti Civa

FRAZ. BELLAZOIA
VIA SUBIDA, 16
33040 POVOLETTO [UD]
TEL. +39 04321770382
www.tenimenticiva.com

CELLAR SALES
ANNUAL PRODUCTION 1,000,000 bottles
HECTARES UNDER VINE 60.00

Tenimenti Civa continues its formidable march forward. It was just 2016 when Valerio Civa made his winemaking debut in the region, taking over a winery an a significant number of vineyards in the Friuli Colli Orientali appellation, specifically Bellazoia di Povoletto and the surrounding area. In addition to their completely renovated winery, in August of 2018 they opened a new production facility equipped with the latest technology, both storage tanks and twenty-some autoclaves for sparkling winemaking. The elevated number of wines submitted for tasting allows us to provide a thorough analysis of the producer's capacities. To that end, we very much appreciated their Sauvignon '18, a wine rich in sophisticated aromatic nuances and pleasantly lean on the palate. The Ribolla Gialla Biele Zôe Cuvèe '18 enjoys a small share of Chardonnay and other traditional, regional grapes, which contribute to the quality of its aromatic weave.

★Eugenio Collavini

LOC. GRAMOGLIANO
VIA DELLA RIBOLLA GIALLA, 2
33040 CORNO DI ROSAZZO [UD]
TEL. +39 0432753222
www.collavini.it

CELLAR SALES
PRE-BOOKED VISITS
RESTAURANT SERVICE
ANNUAL PRODUCTION 1,200,000 bottles
HECTARES UNDER VINE 140.00
SUSTAINABLE WINERY

Manlio Collavini, along with his sons Luigi and Giovanni, manages a winery founded in 1896 by the family's progenitor Eugenio. In the 1970s he began making gradual improvements as part of a larger project aimed at modernizing the vineyards and creating partnerships with growers, who are continuously supervised by the winery's agronomist. Their high production volumes and the consistent level of quality across their entire product range makes them one of the region's most important producers, a global ambassador of the territory's potential. The decision to grant another year of aging to the Collio Bianco Broy, their flagship wine, in no way detracted from the performance put in by the rest of Collavini's selection. In particular, two splendid sparkling wines excelled. The Ribolla Gialla Brut Nature '15 even debuted with Tre Bicchieri, standing out for its vivacity and fragrance. The Ribolla Gialla Brut '15 is no less excellent.

○ FCO Sauvignon '18	♙♙ 3*
○ FCO Friulano '18	♙♙ 3
● FCO Merlot V. Bellazoia '17	♙♙ 3
● FCO Refosco P. R. V. Bellazoia '17	♙♙ 3
○ FCO Ribolla Gialla Biele Zôe Cuvèe '18	♙♙ 3
○ FCO Sauvignon V. Bellazoia '17	♙♙ 3
● FCO Schioppettino '17	♙♙ 3
○ FCO Ribolla Gialla '18	♙ 3
○ Ribolla Gialla Extra Brut '18	♙ 2
○ FCO Friulano '17	♗♗ 3
● FCO Merlot '16	♗♗ 3
● FCO Refosco P. R. '17	♗♗ 3
○ FCO Ribolla Gialla '17	♗♗ 3*
○ FCO Ribolla Gialla '16	♗♗ 3
○ FCO Sauvignon '17	♗♗ 3
○ FCO Sauvignon '16	♗♗ 3*

○ Ribolla Gialla Dosaggio Zero '15	♙♙♙ 5
○ Ribolla Gialla Brut '15	♙♙ 5
○ Collio Friulano T '18	♙♙ 3
● Collio Merlot dal Pic '15	♙♙ 5
○ Collio Ribolla Gialla Turian '18	♙♙ 5
○ Collio Sauvignon Blanc Fumat '18	♙♙ 3
● FCO Pignolo '12	♙♙ 8
○ Collio Bianco Broy '17	♙♙♙ 6
○ Collio Bianco Broy '15	♙♙♙ 5
○ Collio Bianco Broy '14	♙♙♙ 5
○ Collio Bianco Broy '13	♙♙♙ 5
○ Collio Bianco Broy '11	♙♙♙ 4*
○ Collio Bianco Broy '10	♙♙♙ 4
○ Collio Bianco Broy '09	♙♙♙ 4*
○ Collio Bianco Broy '08	♙♙♙ 4*
○ Ribolla Gialla Brut '13	♙♙♙ 5

Colle Duga

LOC. ZEGLA, 10
34071 CORMÒNS [GO]
TEL. +39 048161177
www.colleduga.com

CELLAR SALES
PRE-BOOKED VISITS
ANNUAL PRODUCTION 50,000 bottles
HECTARES UNDER VINE 9.00

By now Colle Duga is an established brand in Collio Goriziano. It's a small producer with a human dimension that allows Damian Princic to oversee all stages of production. The vineyards are situated in Zegla, and are divided into four parcels that vary according to microclimate and terrain, conditions that bring out the grapes' unique characteristics. It's a heritage that is gracefully moving into the hands of a new generation. Indeed, for some time now, Karin has been collaborating closely while Patrik, fresh off his enological studies, will soon take over winemaking. The Friulano '18 and Collio Biano '18 lead the compact but extremely valid selection that we've grown used to seeing from Damian over time. The former is a sunny wine redolent of summer wheat, dried medicinal herbs and pistachios. On the palate it proves velvety, broad and long. The second is a sophisticated mix of Chardonnay, Malvasia Istriana, Sauvignon and Tocai Friulano, all in equal shares. On the palate it unfolds more softly but just as elegantly.

○ Collio Bianco '18	♟♟ 4
○ Collio Friulano '18	♟♟ 3*
○ Collio Chardonnay '18	♟♟ 3
● Collio Merlot '17	♟♟ 4
○ Collio Pinot Grigio '18	♟♟ 3
○ Collio Sauvignon '18	♟♟ 3
○ Collio Bianco '16	♟♟♟ 4*
○ Collio Bianco '11	♟♟♟ 4*
○ Collio Bianco '08	♟♟♟ 3*
○ Collio Bianco '07	♟♟♟ 3
○ Collio Friulano '09	♟♟♟ 3*
○ Collio Tocai Friulano '06	♟♟♟ 3*
○ Collio Tocai Friulano '05	♟♟♟ 3*

Colli di Poianis

VIA POIANIS, 23
33040 PREPOTTO [UD]
TEL. +39 0432713444
www.collidipoianis.it

CELLAR SALES
PRE-BOOKED VISITS
ACCOMMODATION
ANNUAL PRODUCTION 80,000 bottles
HECTARES UNDER VINE 11.00
SUSTAINABLE WINERY

The Marinig family settled in Prepotto in the early part of the 20th century, but the turning point came in 1991 when Gabriele decided to upgrade the winery founded by his father in Colli di Poianis. He proceeded to revive their vineyards of native grapes, closely following tradition and respecting the historic configuration of the hills (considered to be among the best in the district). The area and the winery get their name from the predatory birds that fly among the woods and vineyards, protected by a favorable and harmonious habitat. A blend of Merlot and Refosco dal Pendunculo Rosso, the Rosso Ronco della Poiana '16 ranks among the best in its category and earned a place in our final round of tastings. On the nose it calls up aromas of ripe morello cherries, with sensations of dark chocolate, pepper, coffee grind and smoky notes to accompany the palate. Their 2018 whites are all excellent, as is the Schioppettino di Prepotto '16, which opens spicy and closes fruity.

● FCO Rosso Ronco della Poiana '16	♟♟ 5
○ FCO Chardonnay '18	♟♟ 4
○ FCO Friulano '18	♟♟ 4
○ FCO Malvasia '18	♟♟ 4
○ FCO Sauvignon '18	♟♟ 4
● FCO Schioppettino di Prepotto '16	♟♟ 5
○ FCO Chardonnay '17	♟♟ 4
○ FCO Chardonnay '16	♟♟ 4
○ FCO Friulano '17	♟♟ 4
○ FCO Friulano '16	♟♟ 4
○ FCO Malvasia '17	♟♟ 4
○ FCO Malvasia '16	♟♟ 4
○ FCO Ribolla Gialla '17	♟♟ 4
● FCO Rosso Ronco della Poiana '15	♟♟ 4
○ FCO Sauvignon '16	♟♟ 4
● FCO Schioppettino di Prepotto '15	♟♟ 5

Colmello di Grotta

LOC. GROTTA
VIA GORIZIA, 133
34072 FARRA D'ISONZO [GO]
TEL. +39 0481888445
www.colmello.it

CELLAR SALES
PRE-BOOKED VISITS
ANNUAL PRODUCTION 75,000 bottles
HECTARES UNDER VINE 15.00
SUSTAINABLE WINERY

Colmello di Grotta has been a female-managed winery for three generations. Luciana Bennati founded the producer in 1965. Her daughter Francesca Bortolotto then took over, and now Francesca is accompanied by her daughter Olimpia Possati. Half of the vineyards are situated on the gravelly-calcareous terrain of Friuli Isonzo, while the other have enjoy the marl and sandstone soil of Collio. When it comes to style, their whites are never aged in wood barrels as the producers prefer the latest generation of microporous, ceramic amphoras. In last year's edition we were unable to taste those wines thought unready. The wait was worth it thanks to an expressiveness, in terms of aromatic complexity and gustatory substance, surely brought about by the extra time spent aging in fiberglass. Moreover, the excellent results obtained testify to the care given to each territory and cultivar, both their hillside vineyards and their property in the lowlands.

○ Collio Pinot Grigio '17	♟♟	3
○ Collio Sauvignon '17	♟♟	3
○ Friuli Isonzo Friulano '17	♟♟	3
○ Friuli Isonzo Pinot Brut '18	♟♟	3
● Friuli Isonzo Merlot '17	♟	3
● Friuli Isonzo Rosso Rondon '16	♟	5
○ Collio Chardonnay '15	♟♟	3
○ Collio Friulano '15	♟♟	3
○ Collio Pinot Grigio '16	♟♟	3
○ Collio Pinot Grigio '15	♟♟	3
○ Collio Sauvignon '16	♟♟	3
○ Collio Sauvignon '15	♟♟	3
○ Friuli Isonzo Bianco Sanfilip '16	♟♟	4
○ Friuli Isonzo Sauvignon '16	♟♟	3

Gianpaolo Colutta

VIA ORSARIA, 32A
33044 MANZANO [UD]
TEL. +39 0432510654
www.coluttagianpaolo.com

CELLAR SALES
PRE-BOOKED VISITS
ANNUAL PRODUCTION 100,000 bottles
HECTARES UNDER VINE 30.00

Elisabetta Colutta, daughter of Gianpaolo, serves as the lead figure at this lovely estate whose agricultural roots go back millennia. Their vineyards spans the northeastern foothills, the best exposed to the breeze coming in off the nearby Adriatic and part of a natural amphitheater that's common to the region's rural landscapes. They cover some thirty hectares and host plots that go back more than thirty years. It's a heritage that's well cared for thanks to attentive management aimed at preserving the varietal characteristics of each grape. The lovely array of whites and reds presented for tasting allows us to appreciate the key features of their entire selection: elegance, lightness and drinkability. The best impressions concern their Friulano '18, which seems to have all the qualities necessary to compete with the best in its category. Among the reds we particularly appreciated both the Schioppettino '17 and the Cabernet '17.

○ FCO Friulano '18	♟♟	3*
● FCO Cabernet '17	♟♟	3
○ FCO Pinot Grigio '18	♟♟	3
○ FCO Sauvignon '18	♟♟	3
● FCO Schioppettino '17	♟♟	5
● FCO Pignolo '17	♟	7
● FCO Pinot Nero '17	♟	4
○ Ribolla Gialla Brut	♟	4
○ FCO Bianco Prariòn '16	♟♟	4
● FCO Cabernet '16	♟♟	3
○ FCO Friulano '16	♟♟	3
○ FCO Pinot Grigio '17	♟♟	3
○ FCO Pinot Grigio '16	♟♟	3
○ FCO Ribolla Gialla '17	♟♟	4
○ FCO Sauvignon '17	♟♟	3

Giorgio Colutta

VIA ORSARIA, 32
33044 MANZANO [UD]
TEL. +39 0432740315
www.colutta.it

CELLAR SALES
PRE-BOOKED VISITS
ACCOMMODATION
ANNUAL PRODUCTION 140,000 bottles
HECTARES UNDER VINE 21.00

Giorgio Colutta's winery is situated in
Manzano, in an old 18th-century manor
that was purchased by the family in the
early 20th century, and still houses a
winery. Their selection has always featured
wines of exemplary precision and linearity,
with the best vintages highlighting the
potential of a group of noteworthy crus.
Additionally Giorgio, who's always attentive
to market demand, has for some time now
produced certified Kosher wines that are
aimed at Jewish consumers. A favorable
year particularly benefited the whites
recently presented for tasting — these
proved exemplary in the way they reflect
the varietal characteristics of each grape,
and stood out for their drinkability. The
results are quite evenly distributed, but the
Pinot Grigio '18 excelled, earning itself a
place in our final round of tastings. Rich in
aromas, primarily fruit (apple, pear,
banana), it comes through tasty and
coherent on the palate.

○ FCO Pinot Grigio '18	♟♟ 3*
● FCO Cabernet '16	♟♟ 3
○ FCO Chardonnay '18	♟♟ 3
○ FCO Friulano '18	♟♟ 3
○ FCO Verduzzo Friulano '14	♟♟ 4
● FCO Pignolo '12	♟ 7
○ FCO Sauvignon '18	♟ 3
○ Prosecco Brut	♟ 2
● FCO Cabernet '15	♀♀ 3
○ FCO Friulano '17	♀♀ 3*
○ FCO Friulano '16	♀♀ 3
● FCO Merlot '15	♀♀ 3
○ FCO Pinot Grigio '17	♀♀ 3
○ FCO Pinot Grigio '16	♀♀ 3
○ FCO Ribolla Gialla '17	♀♀ 3
○ FCO Sauvignon '16	♀♀ 3

Paolino Comelli

B.GO CASE COLLOREDO, 8
33040 FAEDIS [UD]
TEL. +39 0432711226
www.comelli.it

CELLAR SALES
PRE-BOOKED VISITS
ACCOMMODATION
ANNUAL PRODUCTION 60,000 bottles
HECTARES UNDER VINE 12.50
SUSTAINABLE WINERY

The Comelli family's winery is named
after the estate's founder, who purchased
Case Colloredo, a rural farmstead in
disrepair, in the years after World War I.
Today Paolino Comelli is a model producer,
one of Friuli Colli Orientali's crown jewels,
thanks in part to a skilled and close-knit
staff. When it comes to winemaking, they
avail themselves of the technical guidance
of Emilio Del Medico, while vineyard
management is entrusted to Giovanni
Bigot and his Perleuve VTS project
(wine, territory, sustainability). Not only did
their selection repeat last year's
outstanding performance, but it's been
enriched by two wines that deservedly
earned a place in our final round of
tastings. The Sauvignon '18 delivers on the
nose with exotic suggestions of lychee and
passion fruit, while on the palate freshness
and softness form a harmonious contrast.
The Mavlasia '17 excels on the palate for
its structure, balance and full mouthfeel.

○ FCO Malvasia '17	♟♟ 3*
○ FCO Sauvignon '18	♟♟ 3*
○ COF Picolit '16	♟♟ 5
○ FCO Bianco Soffumbergo '17	♟♟ 3
○ FCO Friulano '18	♟♟ 3
● FCO Pignolo '12	♟♟ 5
○ FCO Pinot Grigio Amplius '18	♟♟ 3
● Soffumbergo '16	♟♟ 4
○ COF Picolit '15	♀♀ 5
○ FCO Bianco Soffumbergo '16	♀♀ 3
○ FCO Friulano '17	♀♀ 3
○ FCO Malvasia '16	♀♀ 3
● FCO Merlot Jacò '16	♀♀ 3
● FCO Pignolo '11	♀♀ 5
○ FCO Pinot Grigio Amplius '17	♀♀ 3
○ FCO Sauvignon '17	♀♀ 3

Dario Coos

LOC. RAMANDOLO, 5
33045 NIMIS [UD]
TEL. +39 0432790320
www.dariocoos.it

CELLAR SALES
PRE-BOOKED VISITS
ANNUAL PRODUCTION 80 bottles
HECTARES UNDER VINE 12.00

The Coos have been producing wine on the steep hills in the extreme northern part of the Friuli Colli Orientali appellation since the early 19th century. Dario founded the winery in 1986, and it still bears his name, even if its managed by a small group of passionate partners. Their selection, which in the past centered on dried-grape wines, has been enlarged to include various offerings, primarily made with native grape varieties. It's a well-rounded range that has had success on the most important markets and earned the brand prestige. Once again their selection exhibited high quality across the board, and we found the current year's wines on par with those of previous vintages. The Schioppettino '17 calls up bottled cherries and various clear spices on the nose, while in the mouth it proves pleasant and gratifying. The Malvasia '18 is pleasantly aromatic and soft to drink, while the Ribolla Gialla '18 is redolent of white peach, refreshing on the palate.

○ Friuli Friulano '18	♟♟ 3
○ Friuli Malvasia '18	♟♟ 3
○ Friuli Sauvignon '18	♟♟ 3
● Refoso P.R. '15	♟♟ 4
○ Ribolla Gialla '18	♟♟ 3
○ Ribolla Gialla Brut	♟♟ 3
● Schioppettino '17	♟♟ 4
○ Friuli Pinot Grigio '18	♟ 3
● Pignolo '15	♟ 4
○ Ramandolo Il Longhino '16	♟ 4
☉ Rosato '18	♟ 3
○ COF Picolit '16	♟♟ 6
○ COF Picolit '15	♟♟ 6
○ Friuli Sauvignon '16	♟♟ 3
● Pignolo '14	♟♟ 4
○ Ramandolo V.T. '16	♟♟ 4

Cantina Produttori Cormòns

VIA VINO DELLA PACE, 31
34071 CORMÒNS [GO]
TEL. +39 048162471
www.cormons.com

CELLAR SALES
PRE-BOOKED VISITS
ACCOMMODATION AND RESTAURANT SERVICE
ANNUAL PRODUCTION 2,250,000 bottles
HECTARES UNDER VINE 400.00
SUSTAINABLE WINERY

Cantina Produttori di Cormòns is made up of more than 120 vine-growers who formed their cooperative back in 1968. They established a statute with exhaustive guidelines for performing their work, one which they still must adhere to. This thriving operation boasts a number of wines, though their famous 'Vino della Pace' has been the most notable and newsworthy as of late. Created as a message of peace and brotherhood, and made with the best grapes, it also serves as the cooperative's flagship product. And it's the new version of their Vino della Pace '17 that most convinced our tasting panel. A decidedly strong debut opened with floral whiffs of broom, delighting the nose and giving way to hints of tropical fruit, cream and vanilla. On the palate it exhibits a fragrant freshness and notable structure supported by a pleasant, glycerine softness. The rest of their selection proves exceptionally well-made and highly drinkable.

○ Collio Bianco '18	♟♟ 3
○ Collio Friulano '18	♟♟ 3
○ Collio Pinot Grigio '18	♟♟ 3
● Collio Pinot Nero '17	♟♟ 4
○ Collio Sauvignon '18	♟♟ 3
○ Friuli Isonzo Malvasia '18	♟♟ 2*
○ Vino della Pace '17	♟♟ 5
○ Collio Bianco Collio & Collio '17	♟♟ 3
○ Collio Bianco Collio & Collio '15	♟♟ 3
○ Collio Chardonnay '16	♟♟ 2*
○ Collio Chardonnay n.108 '16	♟♟ 2*
○ Collio Friulano '16	♟♟ 3
○ Friuli Isonzo Malvasia '16	♟♟ 2*
○ Friuli Isonzo Malvasia n.68 '16	♟♟ 2*

Crastin

LOC. RUTTARS, 33
34070 DOLEGNA DEL COLLIO [GO]
TEL. +39 0481630310
www.vinicrastin.it

CELLAR SALES
PRE-BOOKED VISITS
ANNUAL PRODUCTION 35,000 bottles
HECTARES UNDER VINE 6.00

It was 1990 when Sergio Collarig began bottling his own wine, offering it to visitors at his farmstay, which he'd opened with his sister Vilma on the splendid hills of Ruttars in Collio Goriziano. The excellent quality of their entire selection immediately earned the attention of even the most demanding palates, and that's not to mention their prices. The fact of being a smaller producer has allowed Sergio to personally oversee his vineyards, drawing on traditional, time-honored agricultural methods. Year after year we point out Sergio's abilities as an interpreter of the expressive peculiarities of each grape. The Friulano '18 emanates sweet aromas of chamomile flowers and calls up hints of sun-dried mountain grass, rich in floral notes and aromatic plants. On the palate it's compelling; fresh, soft and balanced. The Sauvignon '18 excels for its fragrance and mineral character.

di Lenardo

LOC. ONTAGNANO
P.ZZA BATTISTI, 1
33050 GONARS [UD]
TEL. +39 0432928633
www.dilenardo.it

CELLAR SALES
PRE-BOOKED VISITS
ANNUAL PRODUCTION 750,000 bottles
HECTARES UNDER VINE 60.00
SUSTAINABLE WINERY

The Di Lenardo's winery's roots go back to 1878, making it a historic estate, but its best years have been made possible thanks to its current owner, Massimo, who's increasingly helped by his son Vittorio. Their wines, which often feature original names, stand out for being simple and linear yet also rich in nuances that render them particularly enticing. It's a style that's also had success abroad, with foreign markets accounting for around 80% of their business. Their white, Thanks, continues its streak of quality, earning, for the third year in a row, a place in our final round of tastings by virtue of a well-crafted 2018. It's most certainly an important wine, produced in honor of the winery's founders and capable of delighting the most discriminating palates with its fullness and vigor. It's a qualitative trend that's detectable across all their selection of monovarietals, both whites and reds.

● Collio Cabernet Franc '17	♟♟ 3
○ Collio Friulano '18	♟♟ 3
● Collio Merlot '16	♟♟ 4
○ Collio Pinot Grigio '18	♟♟ 3
○ Collio Ribolla Gialla '18	♟♟ 3
○ Collio Sauvignon '18	♟♟ 3
● Collio Cabernet Franc '15	♟♟ 3
○ Collio Friulano '17	♟♟ 3
○ Collio Friulano '16	♟♟ 3
● Collio Merlot '15	♟♟ 4
○ Collio Pinot Grigio '17	♟♟ 3
○ Collio Pinot Grigio '16	♟♟ 3
○ Collio Ribolla Gialla '17	♟♟ 3
○ Collio Sauvignon '17	♟♟ 3
○ Collio Sauvignon '16	♟♟ 3
○ Verduzzo Friulano '15	♟♟ 3

○ Thanks '18	♟♟ 4
○ Chardonnay '18	♟♟ 2*
○ Father's Eyes Chardonnay '18	♟♟ 3
○ Friuli Pinot Grigio '18	♟♟ 2*
○ Friulia Pinot Grigio Ramato Gossip '18	♟♟ 2*
● Just Me Merlot '16	♟♟ 4
● Ronco Nolè '17	♟♟ 2*
● Cabernet '18	♟ 2
○ Comemivuoi Ribolla Gialla '18	♟ 2
○ Friuli Friulano Toh! '18	♟ 2
● Merlot '18	♟ 2
● Pass The Cookies!	♟ 3
○ Sarà Brut M. Cl.	♟ 3
○ Chardonnay '15	♟♟♟ 2*

★★Dorigo

S.DA PROV.LE 79
33040 PREMARIACCO [UD]
TEL. +39 0432634161
www.dorigowines.com

CELLAR SALES
PRE-BOOKED VISITS
ANNUAL PRODUCTION 120,000 bottles
HECTARES UNDER VINE 20.00
SUSTAINABLE WINERY

Some years ago Alessio Dorigo began a reshuffling of his business that concluded with the purchase of a new, modern, architecturally avant-guard facility along the road connecting Udine and Cividale. Passionate and curious, Alessio has honored the brand created by his father, Girolamo, fifty years ago. His innate skills have allowed for a selection that has in no way been altered by the changes, instead his wines are increasingly defined by their balance and clear character. Once again their entire range put in a superlative performance. This year even saw some new wines making it into our final round of tastings, testifying to the strong overall quality of Dorigo's selection. The decidedly varietal Friulano '18, among the best in its category, is soft and substantive. Their Rosso Montsclapade '15, a blend of Merlot and Cabernet, is back at the levels that made it famous.

Draga - Miklus

LOC. SCEDINA, 8
34070 SAN FLORIANO DEL COLLIO [GO]
TEL. +39 0481884182
www.draga-miklus.com

CELLAR SALES
PRE-BOOKED VISITS
ANNUAL PRODUCTION 50,000 bottles
HECTARES UNDER VINE 14.00
SUSTAINABLE WINERY

When Milan Miklus took over management in 1982, he had just one hectare of vineyards. And so it was that he began converting and planting the remaining terrain, with the first wines bottled 10 years later. From the outset his wines earned surprising success, thanks in part to the choice to adopt both modern methods and time-honored ones, all aimed at sustainability. Draga comprises fresh and aromatic wines fermented in steel tanks, while their Miklus line includes forthright, traditional interpretations with some personality. The Malvasia Miklus '16 once again leads their selection, confirming that it's one of the best of its kind. It's redolent of macaroons, marron glacé, green tea and golden-leaf tobacco, an original olfactive profile that envelops the palate, closing with sophisticated aromatic quality. Their Ribolla Gialla Miklus Natural Art '14 is a wine of noteworthy character, citrusy and tasty though still a bit astringent.

○ FCO Friulano '18	♟♟ 3*
● FCO Rosso Montsclapade '15	♟♟ 6
○ Blanc de Blancs Pas Dosé	♟♟ 5
○ Blanc de Noir Dosage Zéro	♟♟ 5
○ Dorigo Brut Cuvée	♟♟ 5
● Dorigo Rosso	♟♟ 4
○ FCO Chardonnay Ronc di Juri '17	♟♟ 5
○ FCO Pinot Grigio '18	♟♟ 3
○ FCO Pinot Grigio Pinorigo '18	♟♟ 3
○ FCO Ribolla Gialla '18	♟♟ 3
○ FCO Sauvignon '18	♟♟ 3
○ COF Chardonnay Vign. Ronc di Juri '96	♟♟♟ 5
○ COF Picolit Passito '95	♟♟♟ 5
● COF Rosso Montsclapade '06	♟♟♟ 6
● COF Rosso Montsclapade '04	♟♟♟ 6
● COF Rosso Montsclapade '98	♟♟♟ 6

○ Collio Malvasia Miklus '16	♟♟ 5
○ Collio Malvasia '18	♟♟ 3
○ Collio Ribolla Gialla Miklus Natural Art '14	♟♟ 5
○ Collio Friulano '18	♟ 3
● Collio Merlot '14	♟ 5
○ Collio Malvasia Miklus '10	♟♟♟ 7
○ Collio Friulano '17	♟♟ 3
○ Collio Friulano '16	♟♟ 3
○ Collio Malvasia Miklus '15	♟♟ 5
○ Collio Malvasia Miklus '14	♟♟ 4
○ Collio Pinot Grigio '16	♟♟ 3
○ Collio Pinot Grigio Miklus '16	♟♟ 6
○ Collio Pinot Grigio Miklus '11	♟♟ 4
○ Collio Sauvignon Miklus '15	♟♟ 5
○ Ribolla Gialla Miklus '12	♟♟ 6

Drius

VIA FILANDA, 100
34071 CORMÒNS [GO]
TEL. +39 048160998
www.drius.it

CELLAR SALES
PRE-BOOKED VISITS
ANNUAL PRODUCTION 50,000 bottles
HECTARES UNDER VINE 15.00
SUSTAINABLE WINERY

Mauro Drius is a proud and stubborn vigneron working in Cormòns, an area that spans the appellations of Friuli Isonzo and Collio. When it comes to management, he avails himself of the help of the female family component, while he's already passed on much of his experience and knowledge to his young son Denis, entrusting him with winemaking. Their wines highlight the enviable forthrightness and personality of the area's grapes. This year two wines from the Friuli Isonzo appellation led their selection and earned a place in our final round of tastings, thus testifying to the care Mario shows for both his hillside vineyards and those in the lowlands. One is their Chardonnay '18, the other is their Pinot Bianco '18, both extremely elegant with slim-bodied palates and flowery aromas of lilly of the valley and hawthorn. Their Bianco Vignis di Siris '17 is also excellent.

★Le Due Terre

VIA ROMA, 68B
33040 PREPOTTO [UD]
TEL. +39 0432713189
fortesilvana@libero.it

CELLAR SALES
PRE-BOOKED VISITS
ANNUAL PRODUCTION 18,000 bottles
HECTARES UNDER VINE 5.00

When Flavio Basilicata and Silvana Forte decided to found their winery back in 1984, they were inspired by the subsoil of the hills and decided to call it Le Due Terre. Flavio always loves a challenge and, in the homeland of white wines, he's decided to focus primarily on red grapes, both native and international varieties. Only spontaneous fermentation is used while wines undergo a long stay in barriques, without racking, so as to preserve their structure integrity and varietal expression. The Sacrisassi Rosso '17 is a blend of equal parts Schioppettino and Refosco dal Peduncolo Rosso. On the nose it offers up suggestions of small black berries, with spicy notes of black pepper, star anise and cloves. On the palate it proves rich in flavor, closing with balsamic wafts. The Sacrisassi Bianco '17, primarily Tocai Friulano with a smaller share of Ribolla Gialla, amazes both for its array of aromas and for the grace with which it caresses the palate.

○ Friuli Isonzo Chardonnay '18	♟♟	3*
○ Friuli Isonzo Pinot Bianco '18	♟♟	3*
○ Collio Friulano '18	♟♟	3
○ Collio Sauvignon '18	♟♟	3
○ Friuli Isonzo Bianco Vignis di Siris '17	♟♟	3
● Friuli Isonzo Cabernet Sauvignon '17	♟♟	4
○ Friuli Isonzo Malvasia '18	♟♟	3
○ Friuli Isonzo Pinot Grigio '18	♟♟	3
○ Friuli Isonzo Friulano '18	♟	3
● Friuli Isonzo Merlot '17	♟	4
○ Collio Tocai Friulano '05	♟♟♟	3*
○ Collio Tocai Friulano '02	♟♟♟	2*
○ Friuli Isonzo Bianco Vignis di Siris '02	♟♟♟	3*
○ Friuli Isonzo Friulano '07	♟♟♟	3
○ Friuli Isonzo Malvasia '08	♟♟♟	3*
○ Friuli Isonzo Pinot Bianco '09	♟♟♟	3*

○ FCO Bianco Sacrisassi '17	♟♟	5
● FCO Rosso Sacrisassi '17	♟♟	5
● FCO Merlot '17	♟♟	5
● FCO Pinot Nero '17	♟♟	5
○ COF Bianco Sacrisassi '05	♟♟♟	5
● COF Merlot '03	♟♟♟	5
● COF Merlot '02	♟♟♟	5
● COF Merlot '00	♟♟♟	5
● COF Rosso Sacrisassi '12	♟♟♟	5
● COF Rosso Sacrisassi '11	♟♟♟	5
● COF Rosso Sacrisassi '10	♟♟♟	5
● COF Rosso Sacrisassi '09	♟♟♟	5
● COF Rosso Sacrisassi '08	♟♟♟	5
● COF Rosso Sacrisassi '07	♟♟♟	5
● FCO Rosso Sacrisassi '13	♟♟♟	5

Ermacora

FRAZ. IPPLIS
VIA SOLZAREDO, 9
33040 PREMARIACCO [UD]
TEL. +39 0432716250
www.ermacora.it

CELLAR SALES
PRE-BOOKED VISITS
ANNUAL PRODUCTION 180,000 bottles
HECTARES UNDER VINE 47.00
SUSTAINABLE WINERY

In the panorama of regional winemaking, the Ermacora brand is synonymous with absolute quality. Early in the 20th century, the founding family showed great foresight in choosing the Ipplis hills to plant their vines, well aware of the area's excellent pedoclimate. Indeed, the calcareous-clay subsoil here is lean but rich in mineral salts. Over time the winery established itself, with Dario and Luciano now at the helm and a new generation ready to carry on the legacy. First-rate wines and others close behind feature in Ermacora's selection. It's a feat that doesn't surprise us in the least, and testifies to the care shown for their entire range. Once again their Pinot Bianco '18 stands out, making a name for itself during our final round of tastings. Space prohibits us from describing their other wines, but the rankings speak for themselves.

○ FCO Pinot Bianco '18	♛♛ 3*
○ COF Picolit '15	♛♛ 6
○ FCO Friulano '18	♛♛ 3
○ FCO Malvasia '18	♛♛ 3
● FCO Pignolo '13	♛♛ 5
○ FCO Pinot Grigio '18	♛♛ 3
○ FCO Ribolla Gialla '18	♛♛ 3
○ FCO Sauvignon '18	♛♛ 3
● COF Pignolo '00	♛♛♛ 5
○ FCO Friulano '17	♛♛ 3
○ FCO Pinot Bianco '17	♛♛ 3*
● FCO Refosco P. R. '16	♛♛ 3
○ FCO Ribolla Gialla '17	♛♛ 3
● FCO Rosso Rîul '14	♛♛ 4
○ FCO Sauvignon '17	♛♛ 3
● FCO Schioppettino '16	♛♛ 3

Fantinel

FRAZ. TAURIANO
VIA TESIS, 8
33097 SPILIMBERGO [PN]
TEL. +39 0427591511
www.fantinel.com

CELLAR SALES
PRE-BOOKED VISITS
RESTAURANT SERVICE
ANNUAL PRODUCTION 5,000,000 bottles
HECTARES UNDER VINE 300.00
SUSTAINABLE WINERY

The Fantinel family's winery is situated in Tauriano, Spilimbergo, literally immersed in the vineyards. It's a classic example of art, culture and functionality that gives rise to a vast collection of wines, all capable of satisfying the needs of every type of consumer (thanks in part to a distribution network that gives them a presence in more than ninety countries throughout the world). Most of their plots are located in the vast flatlands that stretch across the right bank of the Tagliamento river, but their crown jewel is Tenuta Sant'Elena in Collio Goriziano. The Prosecco Brut One & Only '18 and the Ribolla Gialla Brut pursue a cutting-edge style, one aimed at an engaging and almost thirst-quenching freshness. But their Collio selection goes above and beyond. Their supporting structure renders the palate long and captivating. In particular, the Pinot Grigio Sant'Helena '18 stands out for its floral and fruity whiffs of rare pleasantness, benefiting from excellent freshness and closing on a marked mineral streak.

● Cabernet Sauvignon '14	♛♛ 3
○ Collio Friulano Sant'Helena '18	♛♛ 3
○ Collio Pinot Grigio Sant'Helena '18	♛♛ 3
○ Collio Sauvignon Sant'Helena '18	♛♛ 3
○ Prosecco Brut One&Only '18	♛♛ 3
○ Ribolla Gialla Sant'Helena '18	♛♛ 3
○ Ribolla Gialla Brut	♛ 3
○ Collio Bianco Frontiere Sant'Helena '16	♛♛ 4
○ Collio Friulano Sant'Helena '17	♛♛ 3
○ Collio Friulano Sant'Helena '16	♛♛ 3
○ Collio Pinot Grigio Sant'Helena '16	♛♛ 3
○ Collio Pinot Grigio Tenuta Sant'Helena '17	♛♛ 3
○ Prosecco Brut One&Only '17	♛♛ 3
○ Prosecco Brut One&Only '16	♛♛ 3
○ Ribolla Gialla Tenuta Sant'Helena '17	♛♛ 3

FRIULI VENEZIA GIULIA

★★Livio Felluga

FRAZ. BRAZZANO
VIA RISORGIMENTO, 1
34071 CORMÒNS [GO]
TEL. +39 048160203
www.liviofelluga.it

PRE-BOOKED VISITS
ANNUAL PRODUCTION 800,000 bottles
HECTARES UNDER VINE 170.00
SUSTAINABLE WINERY

The history of Felluga is the history of a family that straddled the Austro-Hungarian empire and then Italian unification, moving from the rocky coast of the Istrian peninsula to the Grado lagoon and finally settling on the slopes of Friuli. These were the hills that founder Livio printed on his labels: the famous 'geographic map' that can be found in wine bars the world over. Today his four children manage a brand that has driven the entire region's wine industry, a guarantee of commitment and absolute quality. Their historic wines, which have written and continue to write some of the region's best chapters in enology, lead the usual outstanding selection. The renowned Rosazzo subzone gave rise to their Terre Alte '17 and their 2016 grape blend, named after the abbey that sits above it. Their Bianco Illivio '16, dedicated to the winery's founder, is spectacular, as is their Picolit '15, which convinces with its pleasant sweetness.

Marco Felluga

VIA GORIZIA, 121
34072 GRADISCA D'ISONZO [GO]
TEL. +39 048199164
www.marcofelluga.it

CELLAR SALES
PRE-BOOKED VISITS
RESTAURANT SERVICE
ANNUAL PRODUCTION 600,000 bottles
HECTARES UNDER VINE 100.00
SUSTAINABLE WINERY

The Felluga's bond with wine goes back to the second half of the 19th century and began on the island of Istria. Good fortune brought the family to the other side of the gulf, to Grado, and then to Friuli. Then, in 1956, Marco founded the winery that bears his name, dedicating himself full time to highlighting the attributes of Collio Goriziano. For years he also oversaw his beloved territory's protection consortium. Marco's son Roberto, who inherited his father's reputation as an innovator, currently owns this splendid estate. Once again we most appreciated a wine that's released after a long period of aging. It's a winery policy stubbornly upheld by the Felluga family, resulting in a selection that's already mature when it hits the market and that demonstrates the aging power of Collio's whites. The Bianco Molamatta '15 has to be tasted to be believed. It's a perfectly balanced, sapid and tasty blend of Pinot Bianco, Tocai Friulano and Ribolla Gialla.

○ Rosazzo Terre Alte '17	♔♔♔ 7
○ COF Picolit '15	♔♔ 8
○ FCO Bianco Illivio '16	♔♔ 5
○ Rosazzo Abbazia di Rosazzo '16	♔♔ 6
○ FCO Friulano '18	♔♔ 4
○ FCO Pinot Grigio '18	♔♔ 4
● FCO Rosso Sossó Ris. '15	♔♔ 7
○ FCO Sauvignon '18	♔♔ 4
○ COF Bianco Illivio '10	♔♔♔ 5
○ COF Rosazzo Bianco Terre Alte '09	♔♔♔ 7
○ COF Rosazzo Bianco Terre Alte '08	♔♔♔ 7
○ FCO Bianco Illivio '14	♔♔♔ 5
○ Rosazzo Terre Alte '16	♔♔♔ 7
○ Rosazzo Terre Alte '12	♔♔♔ 7
○ Rosazzo Terre Alte '11	♔♔♔ 7

○ Collio Bianco Molamatta '15	♔♔ 5
○ Collio Chardonnay '18	♔♔ 5
○ Collio Friulano Amani '18	♔♔ 3
○ Collio Ribolla Gialla Maralba '18	♔♔ 3
○ Collio Pinot Grigio Mongris Ris. '16	♔♔♔ 5
○ Collio Chardonnay '17	♔♔ 5
○ Collio Chardonnay '16	♔♔ 5
○ Collio Friulano '17	♔♔ 3
○ Collio Friulano '16	♔♔ 3*
○ Collio Pinot Grigio Mongris '17	♔♔ 5
○ Collio Pinot Grigio Mongris '16	♔♔ 5
○ Collio Pinot Grigio Mongris Ris. '15	♔♔ 5
○ Collio Pinot Grigio Mongris Ris. '13	♔♔ 5
○ Collio Ribolla Gialla '17	♔♔ 3
● Collio Rosso Carantan '10	♔♔ 7
● Refosco P.R. Ronco dei Moreri '13	♔♔ 3

Feudi di Romans

FRAZ. PIERIS
VIA CÀ DEL BOSCO, 16
34075 SAN CANZIAN D'ISONZO [GO]
TEL. +39 048176445
www.ifeudidiromans.it

CELLAR SALES
ANNUAL PRODUCTION 500,000 bottles
HECTARES UNDER VINE 70.00

Founded by Enzo Lorenzon in 1974 as a
small agricultural producer, over time, with
the purchase of other vineyards, it carved
out a place for itself as a major winery. But
the turning point came in the mid-1990s,
when it was taken over by his sons Davide
and Nicola who made Feudi di Romans one
of the most important producers operating
on the left bank of the So?a river. Their
plots extend across calcareous-clay terrain
accompanied by red, iron gravel. A lovely
series of wines were led by their Bianco
Sontium '17, a blend of Pinot Bianco, Tocai
Friulano and Malvasia Istriana with a touch
of aromatic Traminer. It delights the nose
with its floral whiffs, followed by sensations
of lemon cream, acacia honey and
pennyroyal mint. On the palate it proves
highly balanced, closing balsamic and
delicately salty. We also appreciated their
Pinot Grigio '18 for its linear, evenly
developing palate.

Fiegl

FRAZ. OSLAVIA
LOC. LENZUOLO BIANCO, 1
34170 GORIZIA
TEL. +39 0481547103
www.fieglvini.com

CELLAR SALES
PRE-BOOKED VISITS
ANNUAL PRODUCTION 180,000 bottles
HECTARES UNDER VINE 30.00
SUSTAINABLE WINERY

Originally from nearby Austria, the Fiegls
settled in the northernmost part of Collio
back in 1782, in the district of Oslavia.
Their presence is testified to by a bill of
purchase of the vineyard Meja by Valentino.
In recent decades, brothers Alessio,
Giuseppe and Rinaldo have invested heavily
both in the vineyard and winery so as to
further improve the quality of their
products. The new generation, Martin,
Robert and Matej, who are already fully
involved in the business, will inherit a
healthy and competitive producer. The
Ribolla Gialla Oslavia '17 is the result of
prolonged skin maceration with must
contact. The technique makes for an
intense, antique gold-yellow color and an
aromatic complexity in which jammy notes
meet fragrances of almond brittle. On the
palate its softness is enlivened by a
pronounced mineral salinity. Their Leopold
Cuvée Blanc '17, a blend of Malvasia
Istriana, Ribolla Gialla and Tocai Friulano, is
also excellent.

○ Friuli Isonzo Bianco Sontium '17	♙♙ 5
○ Friuli Isonzo Malvasia '18	♙♙ 3
○ Friuli Isonzo Pinot Bianco '18	♙♙ 3
○ Friuli Isonzo Pinot Grigio '18	♙♙ 3
● Friuli Isonzo Pinot Nero '17	♙♙ 3
○ Friuli Isonzo Sauvignon '18	♙♙ 3
● Friuli Isonzo Refosco P. R. '17	♙ 3
○ Ribolla Gialla '18	♙ 3
○ Friuli Isonzo Bianco Sontium '16	♙♙ 5
○ Friuli Isonzo Chardonnay '17	♙♙ 3
○ Friuli Isonzo Friulano '16	♙♙ 3
○ Friuli Isonzo Malvasia '17	♙♙ 3
● Friuli Isonzo Merlot Alfiere Rosso '15	♙♙ 3
● Friuli Isonzo Pinot Bianco '17	♙♙ 3
● Friuli Isonzo Pinot Nero '16	♙♙ 3
○ Ribolla Gialla '16	♙♙ 3

○ Ribolla Gialla di Oslavia '17	♙♙ 5
○ Collio Bianco Leopold Cuvée Blanc '17	♙♙ 4
○ Collio Friulano '18	♙♙ 3
○ Collio Malvasia '18	♙♙ 3
● Collio Merlot Leopold '12	♙♙ 5
○ Collio Pinot Bianco '18	♙♙ 3
○ Collio Pinot Grigio '18	♙♙ 3
○ Collio Ribolla Gialla '18	♙♙ 3
● Collio Rosso Leopold Cuvée Rouge '12	♙♙ 5
○ Collio Sauvignon '18	♙ 3
○ Collio Friulano '15	♙♙♙ 3*
○ Collio Pinot Grigio '04	♙♙♙ 2*
○ Collio Chardonnay '17	♙♙ 2*
○ Collio Friulano '17	♙♙ 3
○ Collio Ribolla Gialla '17	♙♙ 3
○ Collio Sauvignon '17	♙♙ 3

Gigante

VIA ROCCA BERNARDA, 3
33040 CORNO DI ROSAZZO [UD]
TEL. +39 0432755835
www.adrianogigante.it

CELLAR SALES
PRE-BOOKED VISITS
ACCOMMODATION
ANNUAL PRODUCTION 100,000 bottles
HECTARES UNDER VINE 25.00

Adriano Gigante's winery, which has been among the region's top producers for many years now, has always distinguished itself for the high quality of its entire selection. It began with grandfather Ferruccio, at the time a miller. In 1957 he noticed that from an extant and already historic vineyard of Tocai Friulano he was able to make excellent wine. Though it may be a somewhat predictable pun, we can affirm that Adriano is truly 'gigantic' when it comes to his role as an artisan winemaker. The wide range of wines submitted for tasting allows for a complete overview of their selection, and their outstanding overall performance is in keeping with the standards we've grown used to over time. The Malvasia '18 was a lovely surprise, earning itself a place in our final round of tastings for the first time. The Pignolo Ris. '09 speaks volumes about the aging power of this native grape variety.

● FCO Pignolo Ris. '09	♈♈ 5
○ Friuli Malvasia '18	♈♈ 3*
○ COF Picolit '11	♈♈ 6
○ FCO Friulano Vign. Storico '18	♈♈ 4
● FCO Merlot '16	♈♈ 3
● FCO Merlot Ris. '13	♈♈ 5
○ FCO Pinot Grigio '18	♈♈ 3
● FCO Refosco P. R. Ris. '15	♈♈ 3
○ FCO Ribolla Gialla '18	♈♈ 3
○ FCO Sauvignon '18	♈♈ 3
⊙ Prima Nera Brut Rosé	♈ 3
○ Ribolla Gialla Brut	♈ 3
○ COF Tocai Friulano Vign. Storico '06	♈♈♈ 4
○ COF Tocai Friulano Vign. Storico '05	♈♈♈ 4
○ FCO Picolit '08	♈♈♈ 6

Gori Wines

VIA G.B. GORI, 14
33045 NIMIS [UD]
TEL. +39 0432878475
www.goriagricola.it

PRE-BOOKED VISITS
ANNUAL PRODUCTION 50,000 bottles
HECTARES UNDER VINE 18.00

La Gori Wines was founded in 2009 thanks to Gianpiero Gori's love for the land. This successful entrepreneur decided to dedicate himself full time to wine production here in Nimis, in the westernmost part of the Friuli Colli Orientali DOC appellation (an area known as the cradle of Ramandolo). The modern cellar, which is carved in a hill so as to reduce its environmental impact, unfolds across three floors, which allows them to use gravity during vinification. Agronomy and enology are entrusted to well-prepared staff like Giovanni Bigot and Natale Favretto. Once again their Friulano Bonblanc '17 put in an excellent performance, handily earning itself a place in our final round of tastings (a feat it just missed out on last year). It impresses for the pleasantness of its aromas, but especially for its rich, fragrant and flavorful palate. The rest of their selection is right up there, testifying to a consolidated level of quality across their entire range, both whites and reds.

○ FCO Friulano Bonblanc '17	♈♈ 3*
○ FCO Chardonnay Giùgiù '17	♈♈ 3
○ FCO Pinot Grigio Pipinot '17	♈♈ 3
○ FCO Sauvignon Busseben '17	♈♈ 3
● FCO Schioppettino TitaG '16	♈♈ 3
○ Ramandolo OrodiNemas '16	♈♈ 4
○ FCO Chardonnay Giùgiù '16	♈♈ 3
○ FCO Chardonnay Giugiù '15	♈♈ 3
○ FCO Friulano Bonblanc '16	♈♈ 3
○ FCO Friulano Bonblanc '15	♈♈ 3*
● FCO Merlot Toni Vasut '15	♈♈ 3
● FCO Pinot Nero Nemas I° '15	♈♈ 3
○ FCO Sauvignon Busseben '16	♈♈ 3
○ FCO Sauvignon Busseben '15	♈♈ 3
○ Ramandolo OrodiNemas '15	♈♈ 4
● Refosco P. R. Redelbosco '13	♈♈ 3*

Gradis'ciutta

LOC. GIASBANA, 10
34070 SAN FLORIANO DEL COLLIO [GO]
TEL. +39 0481390237
www.gradisciutta.eu

CELLAR SALES
PRE-BOOKED VISITS
ANNUAL PRODUCTION 100,000 bottles
HECTARES UNDER VINE 20.00

In 1997 Robert Princic founded Gradis'ciutta, taking the name from a small village in Giasbana, San Floriano del Collo. In medieval times the area was called Monvinoso, which speaks to the long tradition of wine-growing in these hills, and their suitability to cultivation. The age of vineyards varies from fifty to ninety years, guaranteeing consistent quality in their production, independent of an individual year's climate. Moreover, they can be found in various districts and at different elevations, where each variety finds its ideal habitat. On the nose, the Chardonnay '18 comes across as an important, sophisticated wine, with aromas of white peach and yellow plum, only to delight the palate with enviable fragrance. The Friulano '18 matches the qualitative levels we've grown used to over time, while the Collio Bianco Ris. '15, a blend of Ribolla Gialla, Malvasia Istriana and Tocai Friulano, does everything you could ask for from an ageworthy white.

○ Collio Chardonnay '18	♟♟ 3*
○ Collio Bianco Bratinis '16	♟♟ 3
○ Collio Bianco Ris. '15	♟♟ 4
○ Collio Friulano '18	♟♟ 3
○ Collio Malvasia '18	♟♟ 3
○ Collio Pinot Grigio '18	♟♟ 3
○ Collio Sauvignon '18	♟♟ 3
○ Collio Ribolla Gialla '18	♟ 3
○ Collio Chardonnay '17	♟♟ 3
○ Collio Friulano '17	♟♟ 3
○ Collio Friulano '16	♟♟ 3*
○ Collio Malvasia '17	♟♟ 3*
○ Collio Pinot Grigio '17	♟♟ 3
○ Collio Ribolla Gialla '17	♟♟ 3
○ Collio Sauvignon '17	♟♟ 3
○ Collio Sauvignon '16	♟♟ 3*

Anna Grillo

VIA ALBANA, 60
33040 PREPOTTO [UD]
TEL. +39 0432713201
www.vinigrillo.it

CELLAR SALES
PRE-BOOKED VISITS
ACCOMMODATION
ANNUAL PRODUCTION 40,000 bottles
HECTARES UNDER VINE 9.00

Accompanied by her husband Andrea, Anna Grillo manages her lovely winery in Albana, Prepotto, in an old 18th century manor whose cellar features splendid, now restored, stone walls. Their vineyards stretch throughout a lovely valley crossed by the Judrio river, which also serves as the border with Collio, and are cooled by relatively fresh winds. Such climatic conditions are particularly favorable for cultivating healthy, crisp, ripe grapes. An excellent overall performance from their entire selection is topped off by a splendid Sauvignon '17. With its stylish elegance, it exhibits the grape's classic varietal qualities: sensations of tomato leaf, sage, green peppers, box hedge and lychee.The Schioppettino di Prepotto '16 stands out for its pleasantness, but especially for its perfect nose-palate symmetry. The rest of their selection proves aromatically enticing.

○ FCO Il Sauvignon '17	♟♟ 4
● FCO Cabernet Sauvignon '15	♟♟ 3
○ FCO Friulano '18	♟♟ 3
● FCO Merlot Ris. '15	♟♟ 3
○ FCO Ribolla Gialla '18	♟♟ 3
○ FCO Sauvignon '18	♟♟ 3
● FCO Schioppettino di Prepotto '16	♟♟ 3
● FCO Cabernet Franc '16	♟♟ 3
○ FCO Friulano '17	♟♟ 3
○ FCO Il Sauvignon '16	♟♟ 4
● FCO Merlot Ris. '13	♟♟ 3
○ FCO Sauvignon '17	♟♟ 3
○ FCO Sauvignon '16	♟♟ 3
○ FCO Sauvignon Blanc '15	♟♟ 3*
● FCO Schioppettino di Prepotto '15	♟♟ 3
● FCO Schioppettino di Prepotto '14	♟♟ 3

Albano Guerra

LOC. MONTINA
V.LE KENNEDY, 39A
33040 TORREANO [UD]
TEL. +39 0432715479
www.guerraalbano.it

CELLAR SALES
PRE-BOOKED VISITS
ANNUAL PRODUCTION 60,000 bottles
HECTARES UNDER VINE 10.00

Dario Guerra is a jack-of-all-trades at this lovely, family-run winery, as well its owner. Raised among the vines, he loves to repeat how in these parts viticulture is a lifestyle, something that you carry within you from brith and that's passed down from one generation to the next together with the local culture and history. Like a true artisan, he's also adopted a production philosophy that takes the environment into account, cover cropping and intervening only when necessary. Their entire selection put in a strong overall performance, with the Ribolla Gialla Bruta Giuliet '16, a Metodo Classico, standing out in particular. Golden highlights adorn close-woven bead. On the nose it unleashes intense aromas of ripe fruit, broom and honey. We like to underline their excellent prices as well, in light of quality. They represent excellent value for the consumer.

Jacùss

FRAZ. MONTINA
V.LE KENNEDY, 35A
33040 TORREANO [UD]
TEL. +39 0432715147
www.jacuss.it

CELLAR SALES
PRE-BOOKED VISITS
ANNUAL PRODUCTION 50,000 bottles
HECTARES UNDER VINE 11.00

Brothers Sandro and Andrea Iacuzzi have been working in perfect harmony since they founded their winery, Jacùss, in 1990. As is often the case with small, family-run operations, together they personally tend to their vineyards in the Montina hills, in the district of Torreano, Cividale, and the same holds for the winemaking process itself. The pleasing results have been a catalyst for continuous, further improvements. Their wines are forthright, varietal and sincere, and have won over the palates of enophiles. The Friulano '18 ranks at the top of their range, earning accolades for its perfect varietal correctness. It's redolent of spring flowers, honey and rosemary, but it's on the palate that it offers up its best. The Merlot '15, Cabernet Sauvignon '16 and Tazzelenghe '14 all confirm the territory's wine-growing suitability, including for reds, while their Sauvignon '18 and Pinot Bianco '18 round out the selection.

○ Ribolla Gialla Brut Giuliet M. Cl. '16	♟♟ 3*
○ FCO Friulano '18	♟♟ 2*
● FCO Pignolo Matteo I '10	♟♟ 5
○ FCO Pinot Grigio '18	♟♟ 2*
● FCO Refosco P. R. Ris. '16	♟♟ 3
● FCO Rosso Gritul Ris. '11	♟♟ 4
○ FCO Sauvignon '18	♟♟ 2*
○ FCO Malvasia '18	♟ 2
● COF Rosso Gritul Ris. '09	♟♟ 4
○ FCO Friulano '17	♟♟ 2*
○ FCO Malvasia '17	♟♟ 2*
○ FCO Malvasia '16	♟♟ 2*
○ FCO Pinot Grigio '17	♟♟ 2*
○ FCO Pinot Grigio '16	♟♟ 2*
○ FCO Sauvignon '16	♟♟ 2*
○ Ribolla Gialla Brut Giuliet M. Cl. '15	♟♟ 3

● FCO Cabernet Sauvignon '16	♟♟ 3
○ FCO Friulano '18	♟♟ 3
● FCO Merlot '15	♟♟ 3
○ FCO Pinot Bianco '18	♟♟ 3
○ FCO Sauvignon '18	♟♟ 3
● FCO Tazzelenghe '14	♟♟ 3
● FCO Refosco P. R. '14	♟ 3
○ Bianco Forment '16	♟♟ 3
○ Bianco Forment '15	♟♟ 3*
○ COF Picolit '12	♟♟ 6
● FCO Merlot '14	♟♟ 3
● FCO Merlot '13	♟♟ 3
○ FCO Pinot Bianco '16	♟♟ 3
○ FCO Sauvignon '17	♟♟ 3
● FCO Tazzelenghe '12	♟♟ 3
○ FCO Verduzzo Friulano '16	♟♟ 3

★★★Jermann

FRAZ. RUTTARS
LOC. TRUSSIO, 11
34072 DOLEGNA DEL COLLIO [GO]
TEL. +39 0481888080
www.jermann.it

CELLAR SALES
PRE-BOOKED VISITS
ANNUAL PRODUCTION 900,000 bottles
HECTARES UNDER VINE 160.00

The Jermann brand is known the world over as a synonym of absolute quality. Today Silvio is at the helm, with the producer's free spirit coming through in the personality of their wines: pure and authentic, but free of production regimes imposed by the appellation. In 1975 he created the Vintage Tunina (a celebrated blend of Chardonnay, Malvasia Istriana, Picolit, Ribolla Gialla and Sauvignon), which still serves as the winery's flagship product, even if it's gradually been accompanied by interpretations of equal prestige and character. And in no way did the 2017 deny us, earning yet another Tre Bicchieri. It's a satisfying and complete Vintage Tunina that is, in many respects, perfect. Though its might shouldn't overpower the performance put in by the Capo Martino '17 (last year's 'White of the Year'), and the W... Dreams... '17, two splendid companions on an upward journey of excellence. But once again the entire selection shines.

○ Vintage Tunina '17	♟♟♟	7
○ Capo Martino '17	♟♟	7
○ W.... Dreams.... '17	♟♟	8
○ Chardonnay '18	♟♟	4
○ Pinot Grigio '18	♟♟	4
● Red Angel Pinot Nero '16	♟♟	4
○ Sauvignon '18	♟♟	4
○ Vinnae Ribolla Gialla '18	♟♟	4
○ Capo Martino '16	♟♟♟	7
○ Capo Martino '10	♟♟♟	8
○ Pinot Grigio '15	♟♟♟	4*
○ Vintage Tunina '15	♟♟♟	7
○ Vintage Tunina '13	♟♟♟	6
○ Vintage Tunina '12	♟♟♟	6
○ Vintage Tunina '11	♟♟♟	6
○ W... Dreams... ... ... '12	♟♟♟	8

Kante

FRAZ. SAN PELAGIO
LOC. PREPOTTO, 1A
34011 DUINO AURISINA [TS]
TEL. +39 040200255
www.kante.it

ANNUAL PRODUCTION 45,000 bottles
HECTARES UNDER VINE 13.00

In Karst, Edi Kante is considered by everyone as a forefather, a pioneer of modern wine-growing in an area that appears complicated, if not impossible, when it comes to agriculture and winemaking. In his splendid cellar, which is entirely carved out of rock, orderly rows of barrels and barriques follow the ecliptic geometry of the charming, jagged, glistening walls. Here in the silent depths of Karst, wines continue to breathe the salty air of the mysterious, subterranean coves that guarantee constant humidity and temperature. This producer was among the first in Karst to establish itself using international grape varieties, with gratifying results. But the heart of their selection is still tied to tradition: Malvasia Istriana, Terrano and Vitovska come together in a splendid 2016 that earns itself a place at the top of their range and lands a place in a our final round of tasting. On the nose it's redolent of Mediterranean shrubs, while on the palate it comes through lean and continuous.

○ Vitovska '16	♟♟	4
○ Chardonnay '16	♟♟	4
○ Chardonnay La Bora di Kante '09	♟♟	5
○ Malvasia '16	♟♟	4
○ Sauvignon '16	♟♟	4
○ Carso Malvasia '07	♟♟♟	5
○ Carso Malvasia '06	♟♟♟	5
○ Carso Malvasia '05	♟♟♟	5
○ Carso Malvasia '98	♟♟♟	5
○ Carso Sauvignon '92	♟♟♟	5
○ Carso Sauvignon '91	♟♟♟	5
○ Chardonnay '94	♟♟♟	5
○ Chardonnay '90	♟♟♟	5
○ Malvasia '12	♟♟♟	4*

★Edi Keber

LOC. ZEGLA, 17
34071 CORMÒNS [GO]
TEL. +39 048161184
www.edikeber.it

CELLAR SALES
PRE-BOOKED VISITS
ACCOMMODATION
ANNUAL PRODUCTION 50,000 bottles
HECTARES UNDER VINE 12.00

The Keber family's producer is a classic
frontier story. Their origins are in Slovenia,
in Medana, while the winery is situated in
Zegla, Cormòns, in the heart of Collio. For
almost twenty years now, Edi has been at
the helm, accompanied full-time by his son
Kristian. Together they're carrying forward
in their mission of identifying their territory
through a single wine, called simply 'Collio'.
It's a characteristic blend of Friulano,
Malvasia Istriana and Ribolla Gialla with
unmistakable style of expression. In last
year's edition we didn't get the chance to
taste Keber's celebrated house blend, as
they decided to delay its release. It was a
courageous decision for a winery that
produces one wine only, but it was
obviously a deliberate one. And so it is that
their Collio '17 enjoyed a longer period of
bottle ageing with respect to previous
vintages, with positive effects on its
amalgam of aromas, gustatory harmony
and territorial adherence.

○ Collio '17	♟♟ 3*
○ Collio Bianco '10	♟♟♟ 3*
○ Collio Bianco '09	♟♟♟ 3
○ Collio Bianco '08	♟♟♟ 3*
○ Collio Bianco '04	♟♟♟ 3*
○ Collio Bianco '02	♟♟♟ 3
○ Collio Tocai Friulano '07	♟♟♟ 3
○ Collio Tocai Friulano '06	♟♟♟ 3
○ Collio Tocai Friulano '05	♟♟♟ 3
○ Collio Tocai Friulano '03	♟♟♟ 3*
○ Collio Tocai Friulano '01	♟♟♟ 3
○ Collio Tocai Friulano '99	♟♟♟ 3*
○ Collio Tocai Friulano '97	♟♟♟ 3*
○ Collio Tocai Friulano '95	♟♟♟ 3*

Alessio Komjanc

LOC. GIASBANA, 35
34070 SAN FLORIANO DEL COLLIO [GO]
TEL. +39 0481391228
www.komjancalessio.com

CELLAR SALES
PRE-BOOKED VISITS
ANNUAL PRODUCTION 80,000 bottles
HECTARES UNDER VINE 24.00
SUSTAINABLE WINERY

The Komjanc family's history in San
Floriano del Collio goes back as far as
anyone can remember. It's known that
Alessio's grandparents were already
producing wine in the late 19th century, but
the first bottles of Alessio Komjanc can be
traced back to 1973. The true turning point
came in 2000, when all their male children
definitively became part of the winery's
staff. It's a family joined together by the
values of tradition, but that's looking
towards the future with enthusiasm. Recent
consultations have given a further boost to
the quality of their selection. All their wines,
rigorously monovarietal, perform at the
highest levels, with freshness, verve and
drinkability serving as the common thread
between them. Two gained access to our
final round of tastings. The Friulano '18 is
redolent of elderflower, medicinal herbs and
golden apple, with a fragrant, symmetrical
palate. The Pinot Nero Dedica '16 is a
lovely find, a real treat. It's also worth
mentioning the great value of their Pinot
Grigio '18.

○ Collio Friulano '18	♟♟ 3*
● Pinot Nero Dedica '16	♟♟ 4
○ Collio Ribolla Gialla '18	♟♟ 3
○ Collio Chardonnay '18	♟♟ 3
○ Collio Picolit '16	♟♟ 6
○ Collio Pinot Bianco '18	♟♟ 3
○ Collio Pinot Grigio '18	♟♟ 3
○ Collio Sauvignon '18	♟♟ 3
○ Collio Chardonnay '17	♟♟ 3
○ Collio Chardonnay '16	♟♟ 3
○ Collio Friulano '17	♟♟ 3
○ Collio Friulano '16	♟♟ 3
○ Collio Pinot Grigio '17	♟♟ 2*
○ Collio Ribolla Gialla '17	♟♟ 3
○ Collio Sauvignon '17	♟♟ 3
○ Collio Sauvignon '16	♟♟ 3
○ Malvasia '17	♟♟ 2*

Kurtin

LOC. NOVALI
LOC. NOVALI
34071 CORMÒNS [GO]
TEL. +39 3488672297
www.kurtin.it

CELLAR SALES
PRE-BOOKED VISITS
ANNUAL PRODUCTION 65,000 bottles
HECTARES UNDER VINE 10.00

It was 1906 when the Kurtin family founded their winery in the district of Novali, in Cormòns. Already back then, the natural amphitheater facing Slovenia was considered ideal for making quality white wines. After the early death of Albino Kurtin, a few years ago management passed to a business group that embraced the producer's artisanal spirit. Now production is entrusted to Isacco Curtarello while agronomy is still in the hands of young Alessio Kurtin. Among their 2018s, an excellent Ribolla Gialla stands out. It's a trend-setting wine that excels for its citrusy notes of mandarin orange, set in a highly pleasant, floral atmosphere, proving fragrant and long. Structure and character distinguish their Collio Rosso '15, a blend of Merlot and Cabernet Franc that alternates herbaceous notes with sensations of forest undergrowth, dark chocolate, ground coffee and licorice.

○ Collio Bianco Opera Prima '16	♟♟ 3
○ Collio Friulano '18	♟♟ 3
○ Collio Ribolla Gialla '18	♟♟ 3
● Collio Rosso '15	♟♟ 3
○ Collio Sauvignon '18	♟♟ 3
● Diamante Nero '16	♟♟ 3
○ Risposta 110 Ribolla Gialla Brut	♟ 3
○ Collio Chardonnay '17	♥♥ 3
○ Collio Friulano '17	♥♥ 3
○ Collio Friulano '16	♥♥ 3
○ Collio Pinot Grigio '17	♥♥ 3
○ Collio Pinot Grigio '16	♥♥ 3
○ Collio Ribolla Gialla '17	♥♥ 3
○ Collio Ribolla Gialla '16	♥♥ 3
○ Collio Sauvignon '17	♥♥ 3
○ Collio Sauvignon '16	♥♥ 3

Vigneti Le Monde

LOC. LE MONDE
VIA GARIBALDI, 2
33080 PRATA DI PORDENONE [PN]
TEL. +39 0434622087
www.lemondewine.com

CELLAR SALES
PRE-BOOKED VISITS
ANNUAL PRODUCTION 400,000 bottles
HECTARES UNDER VINE 80.00
SUSTAINABLE WINERY

Vigneti Le Monde is one of the region's most important wineries. Founded in 1970 in Villa Giustinian, Portobuffolè, in 2008 the estate was taken over by Alex Maccan, a young and dynamic entrepreneur who endowed the producer with a modern cellar and entrusted winemaking to enologist Giovanni Ruzzene. Their vineyards are situated in the plains, in an area particularly well-suited to cultivation thanks to a mix of gravel and clay terrain, favorable climatic conditions and the presence of vines planted more than thirty years ago. A number of wines were submitted for tasting, allowing us a panoramic view of their production philosophy. Whites, reds and sparkling wines are all treated with equal dignity and attention, without excesses or cutting corners. The common denominator is aromatic and gustatory clarity, as well as pleasantness. Among them the Pinot Bianco '18 stands out, once again finding itself at the head of its class. During our final round it bowled over our tasting panel, taking home Tre Bicchieri.

○ Friuli Pinot Bianco '18	♟♟♟ 2*
● Friuli Cabernet Franc '17	♟♟ 2*
○ Friuli Friulano '18	♟♟ 2*
● Friuli Grave Rosso Inaco Ris. '15	♟♟ 4
● Friuli Merlot '17	♟♟ 3
○ Friuli Pinot Grigio '18	♟♟ 2*
● Friuli Refosco P. R. '17	♟♟ 2*
○ Friuli Sauvignon '18	♟♟ 2*
○ Ribolla Gialla Brut	♟♟ 3
⊙ Pinot Nero Rosé Brut	♟ 2
○ Friuli Chardonnay '17	♥♥♥ 3*
○ Friuli Grave Pinot Bianco '15	♥♥♥ 2*
○ Friuli Grave Pinot Bianco '14	♥♥♥ 2*
○ Friuli Grave Pinot Bianco '13	♥♥♥ 2*
○ Friuli Grave Pinot Bianco '12	♥♥♥ 2*
○ Friuli Pinot Bianco '16	♥♥♥ 2*

★★Lis Neris

VIA GAVINANA, 5
34070 SAN LORENZO ISONTINO [GO]
TEL. +39 048180105
www.lisneris.it

CELLAR SALES
PRE-BOOKED VISITS
ACCOMMODATION
ANNUAL PRODUCTION 400,000 bottles
HECTARES UNDER VINE 74.00
SUSTAINABLE WINERY

Since 1879, in San Lorenzo Isontino four generations of Pecorari family have put tenacity and passion into creating one of the region's most representative producers. Alvaro took over management in 1981 and since then they've grown exponentially. Their vineyards are situated not far from their main facility, on a small plateau between the Slovenian border and the right bank of the Isonzo river. The plateau is made up of deep layers of gravel that were pulled down into the valley from the eastern Alps by melting water. The high quality of the wines submitted always makes it difficult to choose the best. The Tal Luc Cuvèe features a juicy, captivating sweetness with clear notes of citrus caramel. The Sauvigon Picol '17 calls up sensations of sage, box hedge and green pepper, coming through buoyant on the palate. The Pinot Grigio Gris '17 is among the best in its category, excellent in every respect.

○ Tal Lùc Cuvée .1.2	▼▼▼	8
○ Friuli Isonzo Pinot Grigio Gris '17	▼▼	5
○ Friuli Isonzo Sauvignon Picol '17	▼▼	5
○ Confini '16	▼▼	6
○ Lis '16	▼▼	6
○ Fiore di Campo '06	♀♀♀	3
○ Friuli Isonzo Pinot Grigio Gris '13	♀♀♀	4*
○ Friuli Isonzo Pinot Grigio Gris '12	♀♀♀	4*
○ Friuli Isonzo Pinot Grigio Gris '11	♀♀♀	4*
○ Friuli Isonzo Pinot Grigio Gris '10	♀♀♀	4*
○ Friuli Isonzo Pinot Grigio Gris '09	♀♀♀	4*
○ Lis '15	♀♀♀	5
○ Pinot Grigio Gris '08	♀♀♀	4*
○ Pinot Grigio Gris '04	♀♀♀	4*
○ Sauvignon Picòl '06	♀♀♀	3*

★Livon

FRAZ. DOLEGNANO
VIA MONTAREZZA, 33
33048 SAN GIOVANNI AL NATISONE [UD]
TEL. +39 0432757173
www.livon.it

CELLAR SALES
PRE-BOOKED VISITS
ACCOMMODATION
ANNUAL PRODUCTION 850,000 bottles
HECTARES UNDER VINE 180.00

The Livon brand is one of Italy's great powerhouses, a veritable ambassador of national excellence throughout the world. Founded in 1964 by Dorino, today Valneo and Tonino are at the helm. Their entrepreneurial skills have allowed the producer to expand beyond regional borders and acquire prestigious wineries like Borgo Salcetino in Chianti Classico and Colsanto in Umbria. And the new generation, represented by Matteo (Valneo's son) and Francesca (Tonino's daughter) are already an integral part of the business. The Braide Alte is without a doubt their most well-known and internationally recognized wine. But the high quality of their entire range sees to it that various typologies alternate in turn as their brightest stars. Last year it was the Bianco Solarco '17 that outperformed the competition. This year the Braide Alte '17 earned a place in the finals, along with the Sauvignon Valbuins '18 and the Friulano Manditocai '17.

○ Collio Friulano Manditocai '17	▼▼▼	5
○ Braide Alte '17	▼▼	6
○ Collio Sauvignon Valbuins '18	▼▼	4
○ Collio Bianco Solarco '18	▼▼	4
○ Collio Pinot Grigio Ramato Clas '18	▼▼	4
○ Braide Alte '13	♀♀♀	5
○ Braide Alte '11	♀♀♀	5
○ Braide Alte '09	♀♀♀	5
○ Braide Alte '07	♀♀♀	5
○ COF Picolit '12	♀♀♀	6
○ COF Verduzzo Friulano Casali Godia '94	♀♀♀	5
○ Collio Bianco Solarco '17	♀♀♀	3*
○ Collio Bianco Solarco '15	♀♀♀	3*
○ Collio Braide Alte '08	♀♀♀	3
○ Collio Friulano Manditocai '12	♀♀♀	5
○ Collio Friulano Manditocai '10	♀♀♀	5

Tenuta Luisa

FRAZ. CORONA
VIA CAMPO SPORTIVO, 13
34070 MARIANO DEL FRIULI [GO]
TEL. +39 048169680
www.tenutaluisa.it

CELLAR SALES
PRE-BOOKED VISITS
ACCOMMODATION
ANNUAL PRODUCTION 350,000 bottles
HECTARES UNDER VINE 100.00
SUSTAINABLE WINERY

Tenuta Luisa is a lovely winery immersed in the green vineyards that occupy the right bank of the Isonzo river. The producer is led by a major regional player, Eddi, who has a tight-knit supporting cast behind him. For some time now his sons have been on board with Michele focusing on winemaking and Davide serving as agronomist. Painstaking care for every detail testifies to the passion that drives the business, and is reflected in the quality of their wines. As usual, two mainstays from the I Ferretti line earned a place in our final round of tastings. This year they were accompanied by a notable Friulano '18, a wine that's seemingly simple, but firm and substantive. But the role of star performer once again goes to their Desiderium, a blend of Chardonnay, Tocai Friulano and Sauvignon. The 2017 earns Tre Bicchieri by virtue of its variegated nose and velvety, penetrating palate.

Magnàs

LOC. BOATINA
VIA CORONA, 47
34071 CORMÒNS [GO]
TEL. +39 048160991
www.magnas.it

CELLAR SALES
PRE-BOOKED VISITS
ACCOMMODATION AND RESTAURANT SERVICE
ANNUAL PRODUCTION 25,000 bottles
HECTARES UNDER VINE 10.00

Magnàs is an artisanal winery, which allows Andrea Visintin to personally oversee all stages of production. It was founded in the early 1970s by his father, Luciano, who decided to draw on the family's centuries-old agricultural roots while giving a personal identity to an entirely new project. Firm in his principles, he never let himself be swayed by fashion, stubbornly maintaining an original hands-on approach tied to tradition and territorial values. On a number of occasions we've stressed how Magnàs shows equal attention to each variety cultivated, independent of the area of origin. But it's almost always their Collio wines that go that extra mile. The last round of tastings was no exception, but a splendid Malvasia '18 also stood out for its intriguing aromas and a pervasive palate that unfolds with a velvety delicateness.

○ Desiderium I Ferretti '17	♥♥♥ 4*
○ Friuli Isonzo Friulano '18	♥♥ 3*
○ Friuli Isonzo Friulano I Ferretti '17	♥♥ 4
○ Friuli Isonzo Chardonnay '18	♥♥ 3
○ Friuli Isonzo Pinot Bianco '18	♥♥ 3
○ Friuli Isonzo Sauvignon '18	♥♥ 3
● I Ferretti Cabernet Sauvignon '15	♥♥ 4
● I Ferretti Refosco P. R. '15	♥♥ 4
○ Rôl I Ferretti '15	♥♥ 5
○ Ribolla Gialla '18	♥ 3
○ Desiderium I Ferretti '16	♥♥♥ 4*
○ Desiderium I Ferretti '13	♥♥♥ 4*
○ Desiderium Sel. I Ferretti '09	♥♥♥ 4*
○ Friuli Isonzo Friulano I Ferretti '15	♥♥♥ 3*
○ Friuli Isonzo Tocai Friulano '03	♥♥♥ 2*

○ Malvasia '18	♥♥ 3*
○ Collio Bianco '17	♥♥ 3
○ Collio Friulano '18	♥♥ 3
● Merlot Neri dal Murzùl '16	♥♥ 3
○ Pinot Grigio '18	♥♥ 3
○ Sauvignon '18	♥ 3
● Cabernet Franc '15	♥♥ 3
○ Chardonnay '17	♥♥ 3
○ Chardonnay '16	♥♥ 3*
○ Collio Bianco '16	♥♥ 3
○ Collio Friulano '17	♥♥ 3
○ Friuli Isonzo Pinot Grigio '17	♥♥ 3
○ Malvasia '16	♥♥ 3
● Merlot Neri dal Murzùl '15	♥♥ 3
○ Pinot Grigio '16	♥♥ 3

Marinig

VIA BROLO, 41
33040 PREPOTTO [UD]
TEL. +39 0432713012
www.marinig.it

CELLAR SALES
PRE-BOOKED VISITS
ANNUAL PRODUCTION 25,000 bottles
HECTARES UNDER VINE 9.00
SUSTAINABLE WINERY

It was 1921 when great-grandfather Luigi, owner of a small agricultural business, purchased a second one, bringing all his experience as a vine grower to the venture. Just a few hectares were enough to set in motion a journey that later generations were able to develop, maintaining a constance in quality terms that's made for a solid winery rooted firmly in the territory. Valerio, who's still flanked by his father Sergio in the vineyard, oversees the project with the same passion and commitment passed down from his ancestors, looking after both the agronomic and enological side of things. Three whites and three reds were scored almost identically, confirming the quality of their entire range. The Rosso Biel Cûr '16 (Refosco dal Peduncolo Rosso, Schioppettino and Pignolo) offers up notes of pipe tobacco, dark spicy hints, aromas of prunes and pencil led. On the palate it's glyceric with vibrant tannins. The Sauvignon '18 is fragrant and varietal, as are the Pinot Bianco '18 and the Schioppettino di Prepotto '16.

○ FCO Friulano '18	🍷🍷 2*
○ FCO Pinot Bianco '18	🍷🍷 2*
● FCO Refosco P. R. '16	🍷🍷 3
● FCO Rosso Biel Cûr '16	🍷🍷 4
○ FCO Sauvignon '18	🍷🍷 3
● FCO Schioppettino di Prepotto '16	🍷🍷 4
○ FCO Friulano '17	🍷🍷 2*
○ FCO Friulano '16	🍷🍷 2*
● FCO Pignolo '13	🍷🍷 4
○ FCO Pinot Bianco '17	🍷🍷 2*
● FCO Refosco P. R. '15	🍷🍷 3
● FCO Rosso Biel Cûr '15	🍷🍷 4
○ FCO Sauvignon '17	🍷🍷 3
○ FCO Sauvignon '16	🍷🍷 3
● FCO Schioppettino di Prepotto '15	🍷🍷 4
● FCO Schioppettino di Prepotto '13	🍷🍷 4

Masùt da Rive

VIA MANZONI, 82
34070 MARIANO DEL FRIULI [GO]
TEL. +39 048169200
www.masutdarive.com

CELLAR SALES
PRE-BOOKED VISITS
ANNUAL PRODUCTION 120,000 bottles
HECTARES UNDER VINE 25.00
SUSTAINABLE WINERY

Masùt da Rive comes from a local nickname given to the Gallos, a family whose roots in Mariano del Friuli go back to the early 20th century. The family understood how to bring out the attributes of a subsoil rich in minerals, especially iron, thanks to the presence of the Isonzo river. Today the winery is managed by Fabrizio and Marco, though the turning point came in 1979 when their father, Silvano, began bottling the first wines. He's also to thank for believing in the potential of Pinot Nero and for having passed down his passion and conviction to this children. More than once we've emphasized the growth in quality that's brought Masùt da Rive to the heights of regional excellence. Last year we praised the exceptional performance put in by their entire selection, and especially the Pinot Bianco '16, which scored Tre Bicchieri. Such a feat can be satisfying, but in many ways it's even more satisfying to duplicate it. And that's just what the 2017 version did. Kudos.

○ Friuli Isonzo Pinot Bianco '17	🍷🍷🍷 5
○ Friuli Isonzo Chardonnay Maurus '17	🍷🍷 5
○ Friuli Isonzo Pinot Grigio '18	🍷🍷 3
○ Friuli Isonzo Pinot Grigio Jesimis '17	🍷🍷 5
● Friuli Isonzo Pinot Nero '17	🍷🍷 5
● Friuli Isonzo Rosso Sassirossi '17	🍷🍷 3
○ Friuli Isonzo Friulano '18	🍷 3
○ Friuli Isonzo Sauvignon '18	🍷 3
○ Friuli Isonzo Pinot Bianco '16	🍷🍷🍷 5
○ Friuli Isonzo Tocai Friulano '04	🍷🍷🍷 3*
○ Friuli Isonzo Chardonnay Maurus '16	🍷🍷 5
○ Friuli Isonzo Pinot Grigio '17	🍷🍷 3
○ Friuli Isonzo Pinot Grigio Jesimis '16	🍷🍷 5
● Friuli Isonzo Pinot Nero '16	🍷🍷 5
● Friuli Isonzo Pinot Nero Maurus '15	🍷🍷 6
● Friuli Isonzo Sassirossi '16	🍷🍷 3

Davino Meroi

VIA STRETTA, 7B
33042 BUTTRIO [UD]
TEL. +39 0432673369
www.meroi.wine

CELLAR SALES
PRE-BOOKED VISITS
RESTAURANT SERVICE
ANNUAL PRODUCTION 45,000 bottles
HECTARES UNDER VINE 19.00
SUSTAINABLE WINERY

Meroi bears the name of its founder, even if for many years management has been entrusted to his son Paolo, who works in the family vineyards. Primarily older plots give rise to thoroughly mature grapes, making for an elegant, personal style. Their wines are structured, flavorful, long-lived, the result of extensive experience and an uncommon skill in the use of wood barrels during various stages of production. Mirko Degan provides precious support both in the vineyards and in the cellar. Once again we dealt with a smaller selection, but two wines earned a place in our finals, nonetheless, as with last year. The Malvasia Zitelle Durì '16 emanates notes of tropical fruit, ripe melon and custard, unfolding harmoniously on a palate that's bursting with elegant, lingering aromas. The Chardonnay V. Dominin '16 is no less good, proving potent and penetrating on the nose, firm and elegant on the palate.

○ FCO Chardonnay V. Dominin '16	♥♥	5
○ FCO Malvasia Zitelle Durì '16	♥♥	5
○ FCO Friulano Zitelle Pesarin '16	♥♥	5
○ FCO Sauvignon Zitelle Barchetta '17	♥♥	4
○ COF Friulano '11	♥♥♥	5
○ COF Friulano '10	♥♥♥	5
○ COF Verduzzo Friulano '08	♥♥♥	5
○ FCO Chardonnay '16	♀♀	5
○ FCO Chardonnay '15	♀♀	5
○ FCO Friulano '15	♀♀	5
● FCO Merlot Ros di Buri '13	♀♀	5
● FCO Merlot V. Dominin '13	♀♀	8
○ FCO Ribolla Gialla '16	♀♀	5
● FCO Rosso Nèstri '16	♀♀	3
○ FCO Sauvignon '16	♀♀	4
○ FCO Sauvignon '15	♀♀	4

Modeano

FRAZ. MODEANO
VIA CASALI MODEANO, 1
33056 PALAZZOLO DELLO STELLA [UD]
TEL. +39 043158244
www.modeano.it

CELLAR SALES
PRE-BOOKED VISITS
ANNUAL PRODUCTION 40,000 bottles
HECTARES UNDER VINE 32.00
SUSTAINABLE WINERY

At Palazzolo dello Stella, in the heart of the 'Friulian Riviera', the ancient village of Modeano hosts a lovely producer whose roots back back to the early 20th century. It was then that Norberto Marzotto, a student of agronomy and viticulture, laid the groundwork for vineyard planting and a cellar. Today Gabriele Vialetto and his wife, Emanuela, own the estate, renovating the vineyards (and subsequently upgrading their main facility). Their efforts have brought the winery to the attention of global markets thanks to a line of authentic, deeply territorial wines. Almost all their wines are designated within the Friuli appellation, which comprises the region's best wine-growing districts. Their vintage 2018s seem to have benefited from the nearby Adriatic breeze, which confers iodine sensations on the nose, and lends its mineral character. The Friulano '18 is particularly elegant and balsamic, while the Pinot Grigio '18 proves floral, juicy and balanced.

○ Friuli Friulano '18	♥♥	2*
○ Friuli Malvasia '18	♥♥	2*
○ Friuli Pinot Grigio '18	♥♥	2*
● Friuli Refosco P. R. '17	♥♥	2*
● Friulia Merlot '17	♥♥	2*
○ Avril Ribolla Gialla Brut	♀	3
● Friuli Cabernet Sauvignon '17	♀	2
○ Friuli Chardonnay '18	♀	2
○ Ribolla Gialla '18	♀	2
● Friuli Cabernet Sauvignon '16	♀♀	2*
○ Friuli Chardonnay '17	♀♀	2*
○ Friuli Friulano '17	♀♀	2*
○ Friuli Malvasia '16	♀♀	2*
○ Friuli Pinot Grigio '17	♀♀	2*
○ Ribolla Gialla '17	♀♀	2*
● Rosso Peng '15	♀♀	3

Murva - Renata Pizzulin

VIA CELSO MACOR, 1
34070 MORARO [GO]
TEL. +39 0432713027
www.murva.it

CELLAR SALES
PRE-BOOKED VISITS
ANNUAL PRODUCTION 15,000 bottles
HECTARES UNDER VINE 4.00
SUSTAINABLE WINERY

Even if this small winery was founded only recently, Murva has quickly found success thanks to the quality of their wines, but especially for an approach that's at the vanguard. Much of the credit goes to Alberto Pelos who, bolstered by experiences in prestigious wineries, immediately aimed high. Vineyards are distinguished based on specific pedoclimatic conditions and positions, thus bringing out the expressive characteristics of the grapes cultivated. This year we only tried four wines, but it was enough to confirm the accolades that Alberto has accumulated over previous editions. Though they exhibit different facets of the grape, the Sauvignon Teolis and Corvatis '17 both highlight its aromatic qualities, benefiting from a supple, pleasant palate. Their Chardonnay Paladis '17 also impressed, bringing together structure and elegance with freshness and length.

○ Friuli Isonzo Chardonnay Paladis '17	♥♥ 4
○ Friuli Isonzo Malvasia Melaris '17	♥♥ 4
○ Friuli Isonzo Sauvignon Corvatis '17	♥♥ 3
○ Friuli Isonzo Sauvignon Teolis '17	♥♥ 4
○ Friuli Isonzo Bianco Teolis '15	♀♀ 4
○ Friuli Isonzo Chardonnay Monuments '16	♀♀ 3
○ Friuli Isonzo Chardonnay Monuments '15	♀♀ 3
○ Friuli Isonzo Chardonnay Paladis '16	♀♀ 4
○ Friuli Isonzo Chardonnay Paladis '15	♀♀ 4
○ Friuli Isonzo Malvasia Melaris '15	♀♀ 4
○ Friuli Isonzo Sauvignon Corvatis '16	♀♀ 4
○ Friuli Isonzo Sauvignon Teolis '16	♀♀ 4
● Refosco P. R. Murellis '15	♀♀ 4

Muzic

LOC. BIVIO, 4
34070 SAN FLORIANO DEL COLLIO [GO]
TEL. +39 0481884201
www.cantinamuzic.it

CELLAR SALES
PRE-BOOKED VISITS
ANNUAL PRODUCTION 90,000 bottles
HECTARES UNDER VINE 21.00
SUSTAINABLE WINERY

The winery is managed by Giovanni 'Ivan' Muzic, a lover of the outdoors who found his ideal work environment in the vineyards The future is guaranteed by his young children Elija and Fabijan, who have diligently divided their responsibilities and have for some time now worked in perfect harmony. Mother Orieta, the winery's beating heart, looks after their scenic, 16th-century underground cellar. Its stone walls and vaulted ceilings host the barriques in which their red wines are aged. A splendid overall performance by their entire selection testifies to the care and attention reserved for each grape cultivar. Once again the Collio Bianco Stare Brajde '17 is at the head of the class. It's made according to tradition, with native grapes, Tocai Friulano, Malvasia Istriana and Ribolla Gialla. It's a summery wine that offers up wafts of harvested wheat and, from one sip to the next, offers up a procession of aniseed and rosemary.

○ Collio Bianco Stare Brajde '17	♥♥ 3*
○ Collio Chardonnay '18	♥♥ 3
○ Collio Friulano V. Valeris '18	♥♥ 3
○ Collio Malvasia '18	♥♥ 3
○ Collio Pinot Grigio '18	♥♥ 3
○ Collio Ribolla Gialla '18	♥♥ 3
○ Collio Sauvignon V. Pàjze '18	♥♥ 3
● Friuli Isonzo Merlot '17	♥♥ 3
○ Collio Bianco Stare Brajde '16	♀♀ 3*
○ Collio Chardonnay '17	♀♀ 3*
○ Collio Friulano V. Valeris '17	♀♀ 3
○ Collio Friulano V. Valeris '16	♀♀ 3*
○ Collio Malvasia '17	♀♀ 3
○ Collio Pinot Grigio '17	♀♀ 3
○ Collio Ribolla Gialla '17	♀♀ 3
○ Collio Sauvignon V. Pàjze '17	♀♀ 3

Alessandro Pascolo

LOC. RUTTARS, 1
34070 DOLEGNA DEL COLLIO [GO]
TEL. +39 048161144
www.vinipascolo.com

CELLAR SALES
PRE-BOOKED VISITS
ANNUAL PRODUCTION 25,000 bottles
HECTARES UNDER VINE 7.00
SUSTAINABLE WINERY

Having concluded his enological and agronomic studies, in 2006 Alessandro Pascolo decided to put to work the insights of his grandfather Angelo, who in the 1970s chose to invest in the countryside, purchasing a farmstead and vineyards on the sunny slopes of the Ruttàrs hills, a pearl of Dolegna del Collio. Alessandro now personally oversees the estate, masterfully interpreting the territory and concentrating all his efforts on making forthright, personal wines. This year their Pascal '17 earned the highest accolades. It's a red made primarily with Cabernet Sauvignon, and a smaller share of Merlot. On the nose it's still redolent of grape skin, before opening to wild blackberries, licorice and printer's ink. On the palate it proves potent but graceful. Their Collio Bianco Agnul '17 (dedicated to grandfather Angelo) is excellent, as is their Friulano '18, a wine that's fragrant on the nose, crisp on the palate. The rest of their selection is also entirely convincing.

○ Collio Bianco Agnul '17	♟♟ 4
○ Collio Friulano '18	♟♟ 3
○ Collio Pinot Bianco '18	♟♟ 3
○ Collio Sauvignon '18	♟♟ 3
● Pascal '17	♟♟ 4
○ Collio Malvasia '18	♟ 3
○ Collio Bianco Agnul '16	♟♟ 4
○ Collio Bianco Agnul '14	♟♟ 4
○ Collio Friulano '16	♟♟ 3
○ Collio Malvasia '16	♟♟ 3
● Collio Merlot Sel. '15	♟♟ 5
● Collio Merlot Sel. '14	♟♟ 5
○ Collio Sauvignon '17	♟♟ 3
○ Collio Sauvignon '16	♟♟ 3
○ Collio Sauvignon '15	♟♟ 3
● Pascal '16	♟♟ 4

Pierpaolo Pecorari

VIA TOMMASEO, 56
34070 SAN LORENZO ISONTINO [GO]
TEL. +39 0481808775
www.pierpaolopecorari.it

CELLAR SALES
PRE-BOOKED VISITS
ANNUAL PRODUCTION 150,000 bottles
HECTARES UNDER VINE 30.00

Pierpaolo Pecorari is a viticultural pioneer in the region. He was little more than an adolescent when, in 1970, with ambition and foresight, he founded the winery that he still manages today (together with his son Alessandro). His vineyards are situated in the Isonzo plains, between Cormòns and Gradisca, where the soil is pebbly, shallow, well-drained and rich in mineral salts. Their selection comprises multiple lines, divided chiefly according to vineyard age. Their reserve wines are matured in wood barrels and named after the vineyard place names. This year we had the chance to try their Sauvignon Kolaus '17, a wine that has, for some time, been missing from our guide. It intrigues with the sophistication of its varietal aromas of green pepper, pennyroyal mint and sage, all adorned by spicy hints of white pepper and vanilla. The steel-aged version of their Sauvignon '18 stands out for its citrusy fragrances and supple palate.

○ Adsum	♟♟ 4
● Merlot '16	♟♟ 3
● Merlot Baolar '16	♟♟ 5
○ Sauvignon '18	♟♟ 3
○ Sauvignon Kolaus '17	♟♟ 5
○ Chardonnay '18	♟ 3
○ Friuli Pinot Grigio '18	♟ 3
● Gildo Cabernet Franc '16	♟ 3
○ Sauvignon Kolàus '96	♟♟♟ 3*
○ Chardonnay '16	♟♟ 3
○ Chardonnay Sorjs '15	♟♟ 5
○ Malvasia '15	♟♟ 3*
● Merlot Baolar '13	♟♟ 5
○ Pinot Grigio Olivers '14	♟♟ 5
○ Sauvignon Kolaus '14	♟♟ 5
○ Traminer Aromatico '16	♟♟ 4

Perusini

LOC. GRAMOGLIANO
VIA DEL TORRIONE, 13
33040 CORNO DI ROSAZZO [UD]
TEL. +39 0432759151
www.perusini.com

CELLAR SALES
PRE-BOOKED VISITS
ACCOMMODATION AND RESTAURANT SERVICE
ANNUAL PRODUCTION 100,000 bottles
HECTARES UNDER VINE 15.00
VITICULTURE METHOD Certified Organic
SUSTAINABLE WINERY

The Perusinis, a family of noble origins, founded this historic winery in 1700, spawning over the years important figures for the region's political and social life. Teresa Perusini, the estate's current owner, has brought further value to her family's legacy, proving capable of interpreting the territory and transmitting her enthusiasm to a new generation of winemakers. Indeed Carlo, Tommaso and Michele have been serving as an integral part of the business for some time now. Their selection is of outstanding quality, with Picolit serving as their crown jewel. This last always require a lengthy period of aging, the reason why we didn't get a chance to taste it for this year's edition of the guide. This allowed us to focus on the rest of their selection, where our impressions were virtually unanimous. Among their whites, the Sauvignon '18 stands out for its freshness and elegance, while their reds are led by the Refosco dal Peduncolo Rosso '16, a wine rich in spicy nuances and aromas of wood resin.

● FCO Cabernet Franc '16	♈♈	3
● FCO Cabernet Sauvignon '16	♈♈	3
○ FCO Friulano '18	♈♈	3
● FCO Merlot '16	♈♈	3
○ FCO Pinot Grigio '18	♈♈	3
● FCO Refosco P.R. '16	♈♈	3
○ FCO Sauvignon '18	♈♈	3
○ FCO Ribolla Gialla '18	♈	3
○ COF Picolit '15	♈♈	8
○ FCO Chardonnay '16	♈♈	3
○ FCO Friulano '17	♈♈	3
○ FCO Friulano '16	♈♈	3
● FCO Merlot '15	♈♈	3
○ FCO Ribolla Gialla '17	♈♈	3
● FCO Rosso del Postiglione '15	♈♈	3

Petrucco

VIA MORPURGO, 12
33042 BUTTRIO [UD]
TEL. +39 0432674387
www.vinipetrucco.it

CELLAR SALES
PRE-BOOKED VISITS
ANNUAL PRODUCTION 80,000 bottles
HECTARES UNDER VINE 25.00

Paolo Petrucco took over this Buttrio di Monte winery in 1981, an estate already rich in history. Indeed, many of the vineyards were planted just before World War II by Italo Balbo, a well-known politician and fearless aviator of the time. Their Ronco del Balbo is dedicated to him. It's a wine that ages in barriques, the result of careful selection of the best grapes. Production is entrusted to the enological and agronomic guidance of Flavio Cabas, who brings years of experience to overseeing every stage of production and guaranteeing the finest quality. Once again virtually all their wines rank on the same level, testifying to a commendably consistent level of quality. Among their reds, a special mention for their Refosco Ronco del Balbo '17 thanks to its absolute varietal correctness and excellent craftsmanship. The Bianco cabas Ronco del Balbo '17 (Tocai Friulano, Chardonnay, Malvasia Istriana and Sauvignon) is intriguing on the nose, while on the palate it develops well and closes even better.

○ FCO Bianco Cabas Ronco del Balbo '17	♈♈	4
○ FCO Friulano '18	♈♈	3
● FCO Merlot Ronco del Balbo '16	♈♈	4
● FCO Pignolo Ronco del Balbo '13	♈♈	5
○ FCO Pinot Bianco '18	♈♈	3
● FCO Refosco P. R. Ronco del Balbo '17	♈♈	4
○ FCO Malvasia '18	♈	3
○ FCO Pinot Grigio '18	♈	3
○ FCO Bianco Cabas Ronco del Balbo '16	♈♈	4
○ FCO Friulano '17	♈♈	3
○ FCO Malvasia '17	♈♈	3
○ FCO Pinot Bianco '17	♈♈	3
○ FCO Pinot Bianco '16	♈♈	3
● FCO Refosco P. R. Ronco del Balbo '15	♈♈	4
○ FCO Ribolla Gialla '17	♈♈	3
○ FCO Sauvignon '16	♈♈	3

Petrussa

VIA ALBANA, 49
33040 PREPOTTO [UD]
TEL. +39 0432713192
www.petrussa.it

CELLAR SALES
PRE-BOOKED VISITS
ACCOMMODATION
ANNUAL PRODUCTION 45,000 bottles
HECTARES UNDER VINE 10.00

Gianni and Paolo Petrussa are firm
supporters of simple, minimally-invasive
winemaking based on the traditional values
they inherited from their ancestors. In 1986
they took over the family business, and still
today they operate in perfect harmony in the
district of Albana, Prepotto. It's an area
whose terrain and microclimate are
renowned, especially for red wines,
Schioppettino foremost. The two brothers
have shown, however, that they're capable
of producing outstanding whites as well,
despite the few hectares they have available.
This year an excellent Sauvignon '18 just
beat out the rest of their selection, which is
nevertheless impeccable in all respects. The
Schioppettino di Prepotto '16 and Rosso
Petrussa '16 (a monovarietal Merlot) see to
it that their reds are well-represented. Then
there's the extremely sweet Pensiero '16, a
wine that's among the highest expressions
of Verduzzo Friulano's potential. As the
rankings make clear, their whites drew on
two outstanding years.

○ FCO Chardonnay S. Elena '17	♙♙ 4
○ FCO Friulano '18	♙♙ 3
○ FCO Pinot Bianco '18	♙♙ 3
● FCO Rosso Petrussa '16	♙♙ 5
○ FCO Sauvignon '18	♙♙ 3
● FCO Schioppettino di Prepotto '16	♙♙ 5
○ Pensiero '16	♙♙ 5
○ FCO Ribolla Gialla '18	♙ 3
○ FCO Chardonnay S. Elena '16	♙♙ 4
○ FCO Friulano '17	♙♙ 3
○ FCO Pinot Bianco '17	♙♙ 3
○ FCO Ribolla Gialla '17	♙♙ 3
● FCO Rosso Petrussa '15	♙♙ 5
○ FCO Sauvignon '17	♙♙ 3
● FCO Schioppettino di Prepotto '15	♙♙ 5
○ Pensiero '15	♙♙ 5

Norina Pez

VIA ZORUTTI, 4
34070 DOLEGNA DEL COLLIO [GO]
TEL. +39 0481639951
www.norinapez.it

CELLAR SALES
PRE-BOOKED VISITS
ANNUAL PRODUCTION 40,000 bottles
HECTARES UNDER VINE 7.00

The Bernardis family, based along the
Dolegna del Collio hills, boast an almost
century-old tradition of winemaking. The
early 1980s marked a turning point, when
Giuseppe Bernardis and his wife, Norina
Pez, formalized the founding of the winery
(in her name). They began with just a few
wines, only to establish themselves and
create a lovely producer for their son
Stefano to manage. It's a small operation,
which allows for personal oversight of all
production stages and calls for the use of
exclusively estate-grown grapes. Made with
Merlot and Schioppettino that's dried over a
period of weeks, the El Neri di Norino offers
up an intriguing aromatic profile that
ranges from black cherry jam to sweet
spices, sensations that give way to a
vigorous palate and a balsamic finish. Their
white 2018s stand out for their fragrance
and drinkability. It's also worth noting their
exceptional prices, especially in light of the
quality offered.

● Collio Cabernet Franc '16	♙♙ 2*
● Collio Merlot '16	♙♙ 2*
○ Collio Pinot Grigio '18	♙♙ 2*
○ Collio Sauvignon '18	♙♙ 2*
● El Neri di Norina '13	♙♙ 5
● Schioppettino '16	♙♙ 3
○ Collio Friulano '18	♙ 2
○ Collio Ribolla Gialla '18	♙ 3
○ Collio Chardonnay '17	♙♙ 2*
○ Collio Chardonnay '16	♙♙ 2*
○ Collio Pinot Grigio '17	♙♙ 2*
○ Collio Pinot Grigio '16	♙♙ 2*
○ Collio Sauvignon '17	♙♙ 2*
○ Collio Sauvignon '16	♙♙ 2*
● El Neri di Norina '12	♙♙ 5
● Schioppettino '15	♙♙ 3
● Schioppettino '14	♙♙ 3

Roberto Picéch

LOC. PRADIS, 11
34071 CORMÒNS [GO]
TEL. +39 048160347
www.picech.com

CELLAR SALES
PRE-BOOKED VISITS
ACCOMMODATION
ANNUAL PRODUCTION 30,000 bottles
HECTARES UNDER VINE 8.00
VITICULTURE METHOD Certified Organic

Roberto Picéch is an established leader of regional viticulture and winemaking. His is a small winery situated in Pradis, in Cormòns, a home to many prestigious producers. Even if he's operated at the heights of excellence for some time, Picéch has proven open to innovation in the continued pursuit of new horizons. This has led to a distinctive and personal enological style, a faithful expression of his character: pure, authentic, decisive and not always necessarily straightforward. The violent hailstorm that struck Pradis in July of 2018 forced Roberto to make a hard call: bring the remaining grapes to maturation and produce only one wine. It was a courageous decision that led to the desired outcome. Indeed, the Collio Bianco Atto Unico '18 excels for its elegant fragrances of wild flowers and aromatic herbs, sensations that point up a palate of exemplary balance.

○ Collio Bianco Atto Unico '18	¶¶ 3*
○ Collio Bianco Athena '05	¶¶¶ 7
○ Collio Bianco Jelka '11	¶¶¶ 4*
○ Collio Bianco Jelka '99	¶¶¶ 7
○ Collio Pinot Bianco '13	¶¶¶ 3*
○ Collio Bianco Athena Magnum '16	¶¶ 7
○ Collio Bianco Athena Magnum '15	¶¶ 7
○ Collio Friulano '17	¶¶ 3
○ Collio Malvasia '17	¶¶ 3
○ Collio Malvasia '16	¶¶ 3*
○ Collio Malvasia '14	¶¶ 3*
○ Collio Pinot Bianco '17	¶¶ 3*
○ Collio Pinot Bianco '16	¶¶ 3*
● Collio Rosso '14	¶¶ 3*
● Collio Rosso Ruben Ris. '15	¶¶ 6

Pitars

VIA TONELLO, 10
33098 SAN MARTINO AL TAGLIAMENTO [PN]
TEL. +39 043488078
www.pitars.it

CELLAR SALES
PRE-BOOKED VISITS
ANNUAL PRODUCTION 800,000 bottles
HECTARES UNDER VINE 150.00
SUSTAINABLE WINERY

The Pitars come from a long line of vignerons that stretches all the way back to 1510. Theirs can be defined a 'small, ancient world', one rich in authentic Friulian values. Their vineyards, which are carefully cultivated and of low yield per hectare, extend broadly throughout the provinces of Udine and Pordenone, straddling the Tagliamento river, on terrain rich in calcareous-dolomitic material. Their modern cellar, which brings together beauty and functionality, was built according to the principles of 'green construction' and so in perfect harmony with the surrounding environment. Their multifaceted range covers every market need, and benefits further from their competitive prices. Their estate-bottled selection of sparkling wines is particularly varied. This year a special mention for their Sauvignon '18, which stands out for its subtle, sophisticated varietal notes of white peach, grapefruit, lychee and pennyroyal mint. On the palate it unfolds supplely, with extremely fresh notes of iodine and sea salt.

○ Friuli Sauvignon '18	¶¶ 2*
○ Angelo '16	¶¶ 6
● Friuli Rosso Brumal '16	¶¶ 3
○ Friuli Traminer Aromatico '18	¶¶ 2*
○ Malvasia '18	¶¶ 2*
● Naos '15	¶¶ 4
○ Tureis '16	¶¶ 4
○ Prosecco Extra Dry	¶ 2
○ Ribolla Gialla Brut	¶ 2
○ Friuli Friulano '17	¶¶ 2*
● Friuli Grave Cabernet Franc '16	¶¶ 2*
● Friuli Grave Merlot '16	¶¶ 2*
○ Friuli Grave Traminer Aromatico '17	¶¶ 2*
○ Friuli Pinot Grigio '17	¶¶ 2*
○ Friuli Sauvignon '17	¶¶ 2*

Vigneti Pittaro

VIA UDINE, 67
33033 CODROIPO [UD]
TEL. +39 0432904726
www.vignetipittaro.com

CELLAR SALES
PRE-BOOKED VISITS
ACCOMMODATION
ANNUAL PRODUCTION 300,000 bottles
HECTARES UNDER VINE 90.00
SUSTAINABLE WINERY

Piero Pittaro comes from an old family of vigneron who've been working the region's terrain for more than 450 years. Most of the vineyards can be found around their splendid cellar in Codroipo, in the immense stony expanses that characterize the Friuli Grave appellation. Other plots are situated on the northernmost hills of Friuli, in the area of Ramandolo. Their diverse selection of wines is rounded out by a noteworthy line of Metodo Classico sparklers, made possible by cellar director Stefano Trinco's extensive experience. For some time now sparkling wines have served as the winery's strong point. Every year they're among the best available, achieving results that go beyond those typically attributed to the typology. This year two wines made it into our final round of tastings: the Brut Et. Oro '12 and the Ribolla Gialla Brut. But we're compelled to mention the performance put in by their Friulano '17, which ranks among the best in its category.

○ Pittaro Et. Oro Brut M. Cl. '12	♔♔ 5
○ Ribolla Gialla Brut	♔♔ 5
○ FCO Friulano '17	♔♔ 3
○ Pittaro Brut Et. Argento	♔♔ 4
⊙ Pittaro Brut Rosé Pink	♔♔ 5
○ Pittaro Et. Oro Pas Dosé '11	♔♔ 6
● FCO Refosco P. R. '16	♔ 3
⊙ Valzer in Rosa Moscato Rosa '18	♔ 3
○ FCO Friulano Ronco Vieri '16	♕♕ 3
● FCO Refosco P. R. Ronco Vieri '15	♕♕ 3
○ Manzoni Bianco '16	♕♕ 3
○ Pittaro Brut Et. Oro '10	♕♕ 5
○ Pittaro Brut Et. Oro Pas Dosé '09	♕♕ 6
○ Pittaro Et. Oro Brut M. Cl. '11	♕♕ 5
○ Ramandolo Ronco Vieri '15	♕♕ 3

Denis Pizzulin

VIA BROLO, 43
33040 PREPOTTO [UD]
TEL. +39 0432713425
www.pizzulin.com

CELLAR SALES
PRE-BOOKED VISITS
ANNUAL PRODUCTION 30,000 bottles
HECTARES UNDER VINE 11.00
SUSTAINABLE WINERY

Denis Pizzulin is owner and 'jack-of-all-trades' at this lovely winery in Prepotto, a territory that boasts a millennium-old wine-growing tradition. The area is characterized by a unique microclimate, with the hills guaranteeing just the right amount of sunlight and the Julian Alps offering protection from the cold northern winds. The terrain is made up of a mix of marl and sandstone, perfect for cultivating grapes, while the estate's smaller size allows for painstaking care across every stage of production. This year we tasted the usual, lovely selection of wines, with only small differences registered between the first and last-place candidates. We wanted to focus, in particular, on the performance putin by their Bianco Rarisolchi '17, a blend of primarily Pinot Bianco with a small but important share of Sauvignon. It excels for the elegance of its aromas, enriched by smooth whiffs of vanilla and aromatic herbs. On the palate it's plush, balanced, taut and progressive in its development.

○ FCO Bianco Rarisolchi '17	♔♔ 3*
○ FCO Friulano '18	♔♔ 3
● FCO Merlot Scaglia Rossa Ris. '16	♔♔ 5
○ FCO Pinot Grigio '18	♔♔ 3
● FCO Refosco P. R. Ris '16	♔♔ 5
○ FCO Sauvignon '18	♔♔ 3
● FCO Schioppettino di Prepotto '16	♔♔ 5
○ Pinot Bianco '18	♔♔ 3
○ FCO Friulano '17	♕♕ 3
● FCO Merlot Scaglia Rossa Ris. '15	♕♕ 5
○ FCO Pinot Bianco '17	♕♕ 3
● FCO Pinot Nero '18	♕♕ 5
● FCO Refosco P. R. Ris '15	♕♕ 5
○ FCO Sauvignon '17	♕♕ 3
● FCO Schioppettino di Prepotto '15	♕♕ 5
● FCO Schioppettino di Prepotto '13	♕♕ 4

Damijan Podversic

VIA BRIGATA PAVIA, 61
34170 GORIZIA
TEL. +39 048178217
www.damijanpodversic.com

CELLAR SALES
PRE-BOOKED VISITS
ANNUAL PRODUCTION 28,200 bottles
HECTARES UNDER VINE 10.00
VITICULTURE METHOD Certified Organic
SUSTAINABLE WINERY

Damijan Podversic is one of the most
fervent supporters of sustainable
wine-growing and aims for an approach
that respects wildlife in and around the
vineyards. He's always been at the frontline
when it comes to courageous decisions,
starting with low yields and fermentation
with skin contact that can last for months.
It all makes for wines that are often
extreme, difficult to understand. But in our
view there's nothing to read into them —
we love them, period. Wines of great
organoleptic complexity, they're for sipping
slowly while enjoying their surprising
easiness. Damijan's wines always garner
more than just flattering praise. Certain
descriptors always come up (toasted
hazelnuts, custard, green tea, candied
orange peel, cookies, honey), and yet their
selection is very diverse. Logically, it's the
grape that makes the difference, but it's
difficult to say which is the best among
their Malvasia '15, Nekaj '15 and the
Ribolla Gialla '15. In the end we chose the
Malvasia: Tre Bicchieri.

○ Malvasia '15	⬤⬤⬤ 8
○ Nekaj '15	⬤⬤ 6
○ Ribolla Gialla '15	⬤⬤ 8
○ Kaplja '15	⬤⬤ 6
● Prelit '15	⬤⬤ 6
○ Kaplja '08	⬤⬤⬤ 6
○ Malvasia '13	⬤⬤⬤ 8
○ Malvasia '10	⬤⬤⬤ 6
○ Malvasia '09	⬤⬤⬤ 6
○ Nekaj '14	⬤⬤⬤ 6
○ Ribolla Gialla '12	⬤⬤⬤ 8
○ Kaplja '14	⬤⬤ 6
○ Malvasia '14	⬤⬤ 8
● Prelit '14	⬤⬤ 6
○ Ribolla Gialla '14	⬤⬤ 8
○ Ribolla Gialla '13	⬤⬤ 8

Isidoro Polencic

LOC. PLESSIVA, 12
34071 CORMÒNS [GO]
TEL. +39 048160655
www.polencic.com

CELLAR SALES
PRE-BOOKED VISITS
ACCOMMODATION
ANNUAL PRODUCTION 120,000 bottles
HECTARES UNDER VINE 28.00

Young siblings Elisabetta, Michele and Alex
Polencic have shown a commendable ease
in managing the winery they inherited from
their father, Isidoro. Most of their vineyards
can be found around their cellar in
Plessiva, in Cormòns, while the others are
spread out in surrounding districts Ruttars,
Novali, Mossa e Castelletto. The winery's
crown jewel is their Fisc, a wine that
undergoes a stay in large wood barrels.
The grapes come from a plot replanted
with rooting from more than century-old
Tocai Friulano vines. This year the Fisc
wasn't presented, evidently because it's in
need of further bottle aging. And so it is
that we turn our attention to the rest of
their selection, and the Pinot Grigio '18 in
particular. On the nose it offers up
multifaceted fruity notes, while on the
palate it's sapid, benefiting from perfect
equilibrium. The rest of the wines
proposed, which all score virtually the
same, also prove excellent.

○ Collio Pinot Grigio '18	⬤⬤ 3*
○ Collio Chardonnay '18	⬤⬤ 3
○ Collio Friulano '18	⬤⬤ 3
○ Collio Pinot Grigio '18	⬤⬤ 3
○ Collio Sauvignon '18	⬤⬤ 3
○ Oblin Blanc '17	⬤⬤ 4
○ Collio Friulano Fisc '07	⬤⬤⬤ 3*
○ Collio Pinot Bianco '07	⬤⬤⬤ 3
○ Collio Pinot Grigio '98	⬤⬤⬤ 3*
○ Collio Tocai Friulano '04	⬤⬤⬤ 3*
○ Collio Friulano '17	⬤⬤ 3
○ Collio Friulano Fisc '16	⬤⬤ 4
○ Collio Pinot Grigio '17	⬤⬤ 3
○ Oblin Blanc '16	⬤⬤ 4
○ Oblin Blanc '13	⬤⬤ 4

Polje

LOC. NOVALI, 11
34071 CORMÒNS [GO]
TEL. +39 047160660
www.polje.com

CELLAR SALES
PRE-BOOKED VISITS
ANNUAL PRODUCTION 64,000 bottles
HECTARES UNDER VINE 12.00

Venetian entrepreneurs who already owned the Sutto e Batiso brand, brothers Luigi and Stefano Sutto fell in love with Collio Goriziano while visiting in the first decade of the new millennium. They seized the occasion to purchase a winery in Novali, Cormòns, a district well-known for its south-facing, particularly favorable terrain. And the Polje brand, inspired by the characteristic sinkholes formed by the erosion of the Julian Pre-Alps, came to be. This emerging winery has literally taken off, managing to carve out a place for itself among the region's already-crowded roster of major producers. Vintage after vintage, they've been offering an increasingly impressive and noteworthy selection of wines, starting with their Pinot Grigio '18, which repeated last year's exploit and landed a place in our finals. It stands out for its fragrance and lightness, while exhibiting a notable softness and aromatic complexity.

○ Collio Pinot Grigio '18	♼♼ 4
○ Collio Friulano '18	♼♼ 4
○ Collio Ribolla Gialla '18	♼♼ 4
● Collio Rosso '17	♼♼ 4
○ Collio Sauvignon '18	♼♼ 4
○ Fantazija '18	♼♼ 4
○ Ribolla Gialla Brut '18	♼ 4
○ Collio Friulano '17	♼♼ 3
○ Collio Friulano '16	♼♼ 3
○ Collio Pinot Grigio '17	♼♼ 3*
○ Collio Pinot Grigio '16	♼♼ 3
○ Collio Ribolla Gialla '17	♼♼ 3
○ Collio Ribolla Gialla '16	♼♼ 3
○ Collio Sauvignon '17	♼♼ 3*
○ Collio Sauvignon '16	♼♼ 3*
○ Collio Sauvignon '14	♼♼ 3

Pradio

FRAZ. FELETTIS
VIA UDINE, 17
33050 BICINICCO [UD]
TEL. +39 0432990123
www.pradio.it

CELLAR SALES
PRE-BOOKED VISITS
ANNUAL PRODUCTION 300,000 bottles
HECTARES UNDER VINE 33.00

The flourishing Friuli producer Pradio belongs to the Cielo family, who've been involved in winemaking as far back as anyone can remember. Founded in 1974, it's managed by cousins Luca and Pierpaolo, who share the same passion for the land and wine. They're convinced of the territory's potential and focusing on making quality wines that can fully express the Friuli Grave appellation's stony, dry, sunny terrain. Director Enrico Della Mora oversees agronomy while enology has been entrusted to Gianni Menotti. The Bianco Starz '18, a Chardonnay accompanied by small brushstrokes of Sauvignon and Tocai Friuliano, proves that it's a wine of great class and personality. Tropical fruit, honey and mandarin orange emerge from a floral background, sensations that reemerge on the palate and across its long finish. The correctness and linearity of the rest of their selection testifies to the producer's focus on safeguarding their wines' varietal characteristics.

○ Starz Bianco '18	♼♼ 5
○ Priara Pinot Grigio '18	♼♼ 3
● Roncomoro Merlot '17	♼♼ 2*
○ Teraje Chardonnay '18	♼♼ 3
● Tuaro Refosco P. R. '17	♼♼ 3
○ Gaiare Friulano '18	♼ 3
○ Sobaja Sauvignon '18	♼ 3
● Friuli Grave Cabernet Sauvignon Crearo '16	♼♼ 3
○ Friuli Grave Friulano Gaiare '16	♼♼ 2*
○ Friuli Grave Pinot Grigio Priara '17	♼♼ 3
○ Friuli Grave Pinot Grigio Priara '16	♼♼ 2*
● Friuli Grave Refosco P. R. Tuaro '15	♼♼ 2*
● Friuli Grave Refosco P.R. Tuaro '16	♼♼ 3
○ Friuli Grave Starz Bianco '16	♼♼ 2*
● Friuli Grave Starz Rosso '13	♼♼ 2*

Primosic

FRAZ. OSLAVIA
LOC. MADONNINA DI OSLAVIA, 3
34070 GORIZIA
TEL. +39 0481535153
www.primosic.com

CELLAR SALES
PRE-BOOKED VISITS
ANNUAL PRODUCTION 210,000 bottles
HECTARES UNDER VINE 32.00

Oslavia hill, a stalwart of Collio, enjoys a unique microclimate that's particularly well-suited to time-honored techniques, like long maceration with skin contact (whites as well). Marko and Boris Primosic don't stop here, offering a range of high-quality wines. Moreover they've launched a project aimed at identifying the best areas for each cultivar and the area where the grapes were cultivated are frequently a central feature of their wine labels. Once again the wines submitted performed at their usual level of excellence — and it's no coincidence that the highest scoring among them are the traditional selections that made this corner of the region famous throughout the world. An excellent Pinot Grigio Skin '16 has the appearance and aroma of a red berry tea, but it's the Ribolla Gialla di Oslavia Ris. '16 that truly shines with its aromas of apricot preserves and walnutskin: Tre Bicchieri.

○ Collio Ribolla Gialla di Oslavia Ris. '16	♟♟♟	6
○ Collio Bianco Klin '15	♟♟	6
○ Collio Pinot Grigio Skin '16	♟♟	6
○ Collio Sauvignon Gmajne '17	♟♟	5
○ Refosco P. R. '15	♟♟	3
○ Collio Chardonnay Gmajne '15	♟♟♟	5
○ Collio Chardonnay Gmajne '11	♟♟♟	4*
○ Collio Ribolla Gialla di Oslavia Ris. '13	♟♟♟	5
○ Collio Ribolla Gialla di Oslavia Ris. '12	♟♟♟	5
○ Collio Ribolla Gialla di Oslavia Ris. '11	♟♟♟	5

★Doro Princic

LOC. PRADIS, 5
34071 CORMÒNS [GO]
TEL. +39 048160723
doroprincic@virgilio.it

CELLAR SALES
PRE-BOOKED VISITS
ANNUAL PRODUCTION 60,000 bottles
HECTARES UNDER VINE 10.00

Princic is emblematic of hospitality. Here you're always welcome and you'll find a desire to dialogue and share that's in many ways unique for the region, and beyond. Alessandro, the charismatic son of Doro, loves to surprise visitors, liberally opening bottles with a cheery smile. Accompanied by his son Carlo, he manages to impress character on all his wines, which are rigorously monovarietal, respecting and highlighting the attributes of each cultivar. The Pinot Bianco di Princic is, by now, an icon, and the 2018 proves explosive, demonstrating how power and elegance can coexist harmoniously. In its tight and well-integrated aromatic weave, wafts of cardamom emerge along with lemon wafer, white peach and honey. On the palate it's a juicy concentrate of aromas, amplified across its long finish thanks to spectacular balance. Their Friulano '18 and Sauvignon '18 are also excellent.

○ Collio Pinot Bianco '18	♟♟♟	5
○ Collio Friulano '18	♟♟	5
○ Collio Sauvignon '18	♟♟	5
○ Collio Malvasia '18	♟♟	5
○ Collio Pinot Grigio '18	♟♟	5
○ Collio Ribolla Gialla '18	♟♟	5
○ Collio Friulano '15	♟♟♟	5
○ Collio Malvasia '14	♟♟♟	5
○ Collio Malvasia '13	♟♟♟	5
○ Collio Malvasia '12	♟♟♟	5
○ Collio Malvasia '11	♟♟♟	5
○ Collio Malvasia '10	♟♟♟	4
○ Collio Malvasia '09	♟♟♟	4*
○ Collio Malvasia '08	♟♟♟	4
○ Collio Pinot Bianco '17	♟♟♟	5
○ Collio Pinot Bianco '16	♟♟♟	5

Puiatti

LOC. ZUCCOLE, 4
34076 ROMANS D'ISONZO [GO]
TEL. +39 0481909608
www.puiatti.com

CELLAR SALES
PRE-BOOKED VISITS
ANNUAL PRODUCTION 450,000 bottles
HECTARES UNDER VINE 50.00
SUSTAINABLE WINERY

For some years now the Puiatti brand has
joined with Bertani Domains, but the
winery's philosophy, set out by the great
Vittorio Puiatti, hasn't changed. A figure
who wrote an important chapter in the
region's wine-growing history, in 1967
Vittorio founded the estate and was among
the first to use technology unknown at the
time. A firm supporter of maturation
without the use of wood, he's endowed all
his wines with an unmistakable style, one
aimed at respecting the characteristics of
each cultivar while limiting alcohol content
on behalf of drinkability. The Ribolla Gialla
Archetipi '17 seduces right out of the gate,
with its golden highlights adorning a
lustrous straw-yellow color. On the nose
notes of candied fruit emerge along with
honey and medicinal herbs, while on the
palate its softness serves to contrast a
fresh, lemony stroke. Their Sauvignons
(a 2018 'basic-level' versionand the
Archetipi '17) offer up fragrant nuances of
citrus and elderflower, accompanied by a
palate that's pleasantly minty.

○ Friuli Sauvignon '18	♀♀ 3
○ Ribolla Gialla Archetipi '17	♀♀ 5
○ Sauvignon Archetipi '17	♀♀ 3
○ Friuli Pinot Grigio '18	♀ 3
○ Ribolla Gialla '18	♀ 3
○ Collio Sauvignon Archetipi '88	♀♀♀ 5
○ Friuli Isonzo Friulano Vuj '16	♀♀ 3
○ Friuli Pinot Grigio '17	♀♀ 3
○ Fun Sauvignon '17	♀♀ 3
○ Ribolla Extra Brut M. Cl.	♀♀ 4
○ Ribolla Gialla Archetipi '16	♀♀ 5
○ Ribolla Gialla Archetipi '15	♀♀ 5
○ Ribolla Gialla Archetipi '14	♀♀ 5
○ Ribolla Gialla Extra Brut M. Cl.	♀♀ 4
○ Sauvignon Archetipi '16	♀♀ 3

La Rajade

LOC. PETRUS, 2
34070 DOLEGNA DEL COLLIO [GO]
TEL. +39 0481639273
www.larajade.it

CELLAR SALES
PRE-BOOKED VISITS
ANNUAL PRODUCTION 50,000 bottles
HECTARES UNDER VINE 6.50

In local dialect 'La Rajade' means 'Ray of
light'. The winery, owned by the Campeotto
and Faurlin families, is situated at the
eastern foothills of Friuli, in the valley of the
Judrio river. Here, in the northernmost part
of Collio, nature dominates and sets out the
rhythms of life. The particular microclimate,
in combination with the geography of the
hills, creates the groundwork for excellent
day-night temperature swings, which are
perfect for creating distinctive aromas. For
some time now winemaking has been
entrusted to Diego Zanin. The Bianco
Caprizi Ris. '16 continues to garner praise
and leads the selection in this year's
tastings. Mostly a Malvasia Istriana, with a
share of Chardonnay and Tocai Friulano, on
the nose it calls up medicinal herbs,
polyflora honey, sage and mint tea, only to
caress the palate with grace and nobility.
The Cabernet Sauvignon Ris. '16 is also
excellent, opening on fruity tones and
evolving across a pleasant spiciness.

○ Collio Bianco Caprizi Ris. '16	♀♀ 5
● Collio Cabernet Sauvignon Ris. '16	♀♀ 5
○ Collio Sauvignon '18	♀♀ 3
○ Collio Friulano '18	♀ 3
● Collio Merlot Ris. '15	♀ 5
○ Collio Ribolla Gialla '18	♀ 3
○ Collio Bianco Caprizi Ris. '15	♀♀ 5
○ Collio Bianco Caprizi Ris. '14	♀♀ 3*
● Collio Cabernet Sauvignon Ris. '15	♀♀ 5
● Collio Cabernet Sauvignon Ris. '14	♀♀ 5
○ Collio Friulano '16	♀♀ 3
● Collio Merlot Ris. '14	♀♀ 5
● Collio Rosso '16	♀♀ 3
○ Collio Sauvignon '17	♀♀ 3
○ Collio Sauvignon '16	♀♀ 3
● Schioppettino '15	♀♀ 3

Rocca Bernarda

FRAZ. IPPLIS
VIA ROCCA BERNARDA, 27
33040 PREMARIACCO [UD]
TEL. +39 0432716914
www.sagrivit.it

CELLAR SALES
PRE-BOOKED VISITS
ANNUAL PRODUCTION 100,000 bottles
HECTARES UNDER VINE 38.50

Founded in 1559, Rocca Bernarda is situated on the hill of the same name and housed in an ancient manor. On the outer wall a stone engraving testifies to the fact that the cellar was built even before the villa. The winemaking tradition was maintained over the centuries thanks to the count Perusini family, who in 1977 handed over the entire property to the Knights of Malta. As of 2006, the estate has been managed by the Società Agricola Vitivinicola Italiana. One of the nation's largest agricultural groups, S.Agri.V.It manages 14 historic producers throughout the country. It's been a long time since we last tasted their Picolit, one of Rocca Bernarda's most prestigious wines. This year it's back in the limelight, and the 2016 version immediately proves worthy of its fame. It pours an antique gold, the prelude to aromas of custard, stewed pear, dates and beeswax. On the palate it's no less impressive with its delicious play on sweetness and freshness. The rest of their selection is also excellent.

○ COF Picolit '16	♈♈ 8
● FCO Cabernet Franc '17	♈♈ 3
○ FCO Friulano '18	♈♈ 3
● FCO Merlot Centis '16	♈♈ 6
● FCO Refosco P. R. '17	♈♈ 3
○ FCO Ribolla Gialla '18	♈♈ 3
○ FCO Sauvignon '18	♈ 3
● COF Merlot Centis '99	♈♈♈ 7
○ COF Picolit '03	♈♈♈ 7
○ COF Picolit '98	♈♈♈ 7
○ COF Picolit '97	♈♈♈ 7
○ FCO Friulano '16	♈♈ 3
● FCO Merlot '16	♈♈ 3
● FCO Merlot Centis '15	♈♈ 6
● FCO Refosco P. R. '16	♈♈ 3
● FCO Refosco P. R. '15	♈♈ 3

Paolo Rodaro

LOC. SPESSA
VIA CORMONS, 60
33043 CIVIDALE DEL FRIULI [UD]
TEL. +39 0432716066
www.rodaropaolo.it

CELLAR SALES
PRE-BOOKED VISITS
ANNUAL PRODUCTION 250,000 bottles
HECTARES UNDER VINE 64.00
SUSTAINABLE WINERY

Paolo Rodaro, a resourceful and dynamic wine artisan, inherited an ancestral love for the land. Even if he's already reached important milestones, he continues to pursue new horizons that will allow him to enrich his already formidable selection of wines with new products. For some time now the producer has offered the prestigious Romain line, which comprises highly sophisticated, first-rate reds. Now he's focusing on a pair of Metodo Classico sparklers (Bianco and Rosé), which found immediate success. The Malvasia '18 stands out for its lovely aromatic weave, but especially for its pervasive creaminess on the palate. The Friulano '18 proves to be one of the best in its category for its perfect varietal correctness, both on the nose and on the palate, with that signature touch of bitterness marking the finish. The Friulano l'Evoluto '14 also put in an excellent performance, proving redolent of wheat and honey — it's a summery wine that's 'evolved' decidedly well.

○ FCO Friulano '18	♈♈ 3*
○ FCO Friulano L' Evoluto '14	♈♈ 6
○ FCO Malvasia '18	♈♈ 4
○ FCO Chardonnay '18	♈♈ 4
● FCO Pignolo Romain '11	♈♈ 6
○ FCO Pinot Grigio '18	♈♈ 4
● FCO Refosco P. R. Romain '10	♈♈ 6
○ FCO Sauvignon '18	♈♈ 4
⊙ Nature M. Cl. Rosé '14	♈♈ 5
● COF Refosco P. R. Romain '03	♈♈♈ 6
○ COF Sauvignon Bosc Romain '96	♈♈♈ 4*
○ FCO Malvasia '16	♈♈♈ 4*
○ Ronc '00	♈♈♈ 3

La Roncaia

FRAZ. CERGNEU
VIA VERDI, 26
33045 NIMIS [UD]
TEL. +39 0432790280
www.laroncaia.it

CELLAR SALES
PRE-BOOKED VISITS
ANNUAL PRODUCTION 60,000 bottles
HECTARES UNDER VINE 25.00

Roncaia stands out as among the best producers in the extreme north of the Friuli Colli Orientali appellation. It was founded in 1998 by the Fantinel family, who decided to expand into the territory with the goal of maintaining continuity, but especially of bringing further value to a business already active for thirty years and already well-versed in modern enological approaches. Dense vineyards host international cultivars. These alternate with much older vineyards of more prized, native varieties, all of which are then entrusted to the enological experience of Gabriele Tami. Their entire selection put in a decidedly brilliant performance this year, with a special mention reserved for their sweet wines, thanks to a splendid Picolit '15. On the nose it calls up macaroons, raisins, dates, dried orange peel, peach tea and lime blossom honey, while on the palate it unfolds smooth and velvety. Their Merlot Fusco '14, a red of notable structure, is also excellent. It's dark and deep, somewhat difficult to read but extremely pleasant.

○ COF Picolit '15	♟♟ 5
○ FCO Friulano '17	♟♟ 4
● FCO Merlot Fusco '14	♟♟ 5
○ FCO Pinot Grigio '17	♟♟ 5
● FCO Refosco P.R. '14	♟♟ 5
○ Ramandolo '15	♟♟ 5
● FCO Cabernet Franc '16	♟ 4
○ FCO Ribolla Gialla '17	♟ 4
○ Eclisse '12	♟♟♟ 4*
○ Bianco Eclisse '16	♈♈ 5
○ Bianco Eclisse '15	♈♈ 5
○ Bianco Eclisse '14	♈♈ 5
○ COF Picolit '13	♈♈ 5
○ FCO Friulano '16	♈♈ 4
○ FCO Friulano '15	♈♈ 4
● FCO Merlot Fusco '13	♈♈ 5

Il Roncal

FRAZ. COLLE MONTEBELLO
VIA FORNALIS, 148
33043 CIVIDALE DEL FRIULI [UD]
TEL. +39 0432730138
www.ilroncal.it

CELLAR SALES
PRE-BOOKED VISITS
ANNUAL PRODUCTION 80,000 bottles
HECTARES UNDER VINE 20.00

Roncal gets its name from 'ronchi', which in local dialect identifies the terraced tracts of farmland situated along the hills here. It's a brand that has established itself among the region's winemakers thanks to Martina Moreale, who completed a project begun in 1986 by her husband, Roberto Zorzettig, an expert vigneron and founder of the estate. They're situated in a splendid villa atop Montebello hill, adjacent to the cellar and a hospitality resort where style and nature come together in an environmentally-friendly approach. This year their Bianco Ploe di Stelis '17, a commendable mix of equal parts Chardonnay, Riesling and Tocai Friulano, led their selection. On the nose it reveals tropical notes along with peach tea, hawthorn, wisteria and vanilla. On the palate softness and sapidity balance, making for a general harmony. Their 2018s also impressed, with the Malvasia '18 offering up sophisticated sensations both on the nose and the palate.

○ FCO Bianco Ploe di Stelis '17	♟♟ 4
○ FCO Friulano '18	♟♟ 4
○ FCO Malvasia '18	♟♟ 4
● FCO Refosco P. R. '16	♟♟ 4
○ FCO Schioppettino '16	♟♟ 5
○ FCO Bianco Ploe di Stelis '16	♈♈ 4
○ FCO Bianco Ploe di Stelis '15	♈♈ 4
○ FCO Friulano '17	♈♈ 3*
○ FCO Friulano '16	♈♈ 3
● FCO Merlot '15	♈♈ 3
● FCO Pignolo '11	♈♈ 5
○ FCO Pinot Grigio '17	♈♈ 3
○ FCO Pinot Grigio '16	♈♈ 3*
○ FCO Ribolla Gialla '17	♈♈ 3
○ FCO Sauvignon '16	♈♈ 3
● FCO Schioppettino '15	♈♈ 4

Il Roncat - Giovanni Dri

FRAZ. RAMANDOLO
VIA PESCIA, 7
33045 NIMIS [UD]
TEL. +39 0432790260
www.drironcat.com

CELLAR SALES
PRE-BOOKED VISITS
ANNUAL PRODUCTION 40,000 bottles
HECTARES UNDER VINE 10.00

Some maintain that Il Roncat means Ramandolo, others argue that Ramandolo means Il Roncat. But the substance doesn't change. The wine's and territory's destiny coincide with the period in which Giovanni Dri began promoting them to the world. It comes from Verduzzo Giallo, a somewhat unproductive local cultivar that risked extinction, but that the winery was able to save with a tenacity common to those born among the rocks, on the steep slopes of Monte Bernadia, in the extreme north of the Fiuli Colli Orientali appellation. The Picolit '15 and Ramandolo Uve Decembrine '13 testify to the territory's propensity for sweet wines. They delight the palate with indelible notes of barley sugar, dried fruit and nuts, dried apricot, candied orange peel, honey and marron glacé. Their reds are also excellent, especially the Schioppettino Monte dei Carpini '16, a wine that's fragrant and herbaceous, yet delicately spicy and ageworthy.

○ COF Picolit '15	♟♟	7
● FCO Merlot '14	♟♟	3
● FCO Pignolo Monte dei Carpini '14	♟♟	5
● FCO Rosso Il Roncat '13	♟♟	4
○ FCO Sauvignon '17	♟♟	4
● FCO Schioppettino Monte dei Carpini '16	♟♟	4
○ Ramandolo Uve Decembrine '13	♟♟	5
● FCO Cabernet '15	♟	3
● FCO Refosco P. R. '14	♟	3
○ Ramandolo '15	♟	4
○ COF Picolit '14	♟♟	7
● FCO Cabernet '14	♟♟	3
● FCO Pignolo Monte dei Carpini '13	♟♟	5
○ Ramandolo Il Roncat '12	♟♟	5
○ Ramandolo Uve Decembrine '12	♟♟	5

Ronchi di Manzano

VIA ORSARIA, 42
33044 MANZANO [UD]
TEL. +39 0432740718
www.ronchidimanzano.com

CELLAR SALES
PRE-BOOKED VISITS
ANNUAL PRODUCTION 200,000 bottles
HECTARES UNDER VINE 60.00

Ronchi di Manzano is a splendid all-female winery managed by Roberta Borghese and her young daughters Lisa and Nicole. It's a producer deeply bound to an area rich in history, one chosen in past centuries by the count Trento family to produce wines for the nobility of the Austro-Hungarian empire. In 1984 the family purchased the property, entrusting it to the then young Roberta who immediately showed innate entrepreneurial skill. The vineyards are situated in three separate plots: Ronc di Scossai, Ronc di Subule and Ronc di Rosazzo. Bianco Ellégri, a blend of Tocai Friulano, Chardonnay, Sauvignon andtouch of Picolit, is a regular contender in our final tasting rounds. The 2018 features an aromatic profile in which elegant hints of jasmine stand out along with notes of lilly of the valley, white peach, grapefruit and wisteria, sensations that accompany the palate as it moves towards a fresh, minty finish. Their Pinot Grigio Ramato '18, which unveils a fruity, mineral texture, is a lovely surprise.

○ Bianco Ellègri '18	♟♟	3*
○ FCO Pinot Grigio Ramato '18	♟♟	3*
○ FCO Chardonnay '18	♟♟	3
○ FCO Friulano '18	♟♟	3
● FCO Merlot Ronc di Subule '15	♟♟	3
● FCO Rosso Brauros '15	♟♟	4
○ FCO Sauvignon '18	♟♟	3
○ Rosazzo Bianco '16	♟♟	3
○ COF Ellegri '13	♟♟♟	3*
○ COF Friulano '10	♟♟♟	3*
○ COF Friulano '09	♟♟♟	3*
● COF Merlot Ronc di Subule '99	♟♟♟	3*
● COF Merlot Ronc di Subule '96	♟♟♟	3*
○ COF Rosazzo Bianco Ellégri '11	♟♟♟	3*
○ Rosazzo Bianco '13	♟♟♟	3*

Ronco Blanchis

VIA BLANCHIS, 70
34070 MOSSA [GO]
TEL. +39 048180519
www.roncoblanchis.it

PRE-BOOKED VISITS
ANNUAL PRODUCTION 60,000 bottles
HECTARES UNDER VINE 14.00
SUSTAINABLE WINERY

For some time now Lorenzo Palla has managed the family winery, and it was his choices that led to its current success. For example, there was the decision to only produce white wines, almost as if to justify their name. They're wines of unique character, tied to the particular microclimate that characterizes Blanchis hill, one of the highest in Collio. In the lower valley, day-night temperature swings and high humidity make for thick fog, and the formation of noble rot, which contributes notably to their wines' aromatic qualities. The Chardonnay '17 leads their selection. It's an extremely elegant, intriguing white redolent of fruit and flowers, all tied together in a nice weave. Their Friulano '18 is also excellent, standing out once again for the complexity of its fragrances, adorned by tropical whiffs. Their Collio Bianco Ris. '17, a calibrated mix of Chardonnay, Tocai Friulano, Malvasia Istriana and Sauvignon, also deserves a mention.

○ Collio Chardonnay '17	♟♟♟ 3*
○ Collio Friulano '18	♟♟ 4
○ Collio Bianco Ris. '17	♟♟ 4
○ Collio Malvasia '18	♟♟ 3
○ Collio Pinot Grigio '18	♟♟ 4
○ Collio Sauvignon '18	♟♟ 4
○ Collio '13	♟♟♟ 3*
○ Collio '12	♟♟♟ 3*
○ Collio Bianco Ris. '16	♟♟ 4
○ Collio Blanc de Blanchis '16	♟♟ 3*
○ Collio Chardonnay '16	♟♟ 3
○ Collio Friulano '17	♟♟ 4
○ Collio Malvasia '17	♟♟ 3
○ Collio Pinot Grigio '17	♟♟ 4
○ Collio Sauvignon '17	♟♟ 4
○ Collio Sauvignon '16	♟♟ 4

★Ronco dei Tassi

LOC. MONTONA, 19
34071 CORMÒNS [GO]
TEL. +39 048160155
www.roncodeitassi.it

CELLAR SALES
PRE-BOOKED VISITS
ANNUAL PRODUCTION 110,000 bottles
HECTARES UNDER VINE 18.00

Enrico and Matteo Coser belong to a generation of young vine growers who grew up alongside their father and benefitted from his decades of experience and precious advice. Fabio Coser founded Ronco dei Tassi in 1989 when he decided to purchase a farmstead at the edge of a natural park of rare beauty in Cormons, in the district of Montona. The name was inspired by the badgers that inhabit the woods around their vineyards and love to eat the sweet bunches of grapes. Some three wines earned a place in our final round of tastings, all contending for our highest honors. Once again it's the Collio Bianco Fosarin '17 that stands out for the way it brings together the elegance of Pinot Bianco with the power of Tocai Friulano and the fragrance of Malvasia Istriana. The Malvasia '18 also exhibit its usual, high level of quality, though it was matched this year by the Sauvignon '18, which performed splendidly in pursuit of charm and substance.

○ Collio Bianco Fosarin '17	♟♟♟ 3*
○ Collio Malvasia '18	♟♟ 3*
○ Collio Sauvignon '18	♟♟ 3*
○ Collio Friulano '18	♟♟ 3
○ Collio Pinot Grigio '18	♟♟ 3
○ Collio Ribolla Gialla '18	♟♟ 3
● Collio Rosso Cjarandon Ris. '15	♟♟ 5
○ Collio Bianco Fosarin '16	♟♟♟ 3*
○ Collio Bianco Fosarin '15	♟♟♟ 3*
○ Collio Bianco Fosarin '10	♟♟♟ 3
○ Collio Bianco Fosarin '09	♟♟♟ 3*
○ Collio Malvasia '15	♟♟♟ 3*
○ Collio Malvasia '14	♟♟♟ 3*
○ Collio Malvasia '13	♟♟♟ 3*
○ Collio Malvasia '12	♟♟♟ 3*
○ Collio Malvasia '11	♟♟♟ 3*

Ronco delle Betulle

LOC. ROSAZZO
VIA ABATE COLONNA, 24
33044 MANZANO [UD]
TEL. +39 0432740547
www.roncodellebetulle.it

CELLAR SALES
PRE-BOOKED VISITS
ANNUAL PRODUCTION 60,000 bottles
HECTARES UNDER VINE 12.00
VITICULTURE METHOD Certified Organic
SUSTAINABLE WINERY

Even if the winery is today managed by her
son, Ivana Adami still has a hand in
overseeing production. Indeed, she's passed
on to Simone her simple philosophy, which
centers on making high quality wines. A
stubborn and resourceful woman, she
contributed to promoting the Ronco delle
Betulle brand, keeping it in the competitive
Friuli Colli Orientali appellation's pantheon
of excellence for more than thirty years. Her
prestigious Rosazzo vineyards surround the
famous abbey that was and still is a prime
area for vine growing. The even distribution
of the scorings testifies to the excellent
quality of their entire range, even if we're
slightly partial to two of their renowned
blends. A calibrated mix of Tocai Friulano,
Charonnay and Sauvignon gives rise to their
Rosazzo '17, a decidedly fruity wine on the
nose, gratifying on the palate. Their best
Merlot and Cabernet Franc grapes are used
for the harmonious Rosso Narciso '16, a
wine redolent of small wild berries.

● FCO Merlot '16	♟♟ 3
● FCO Cabernet Franc '16	♟♟ 3
○ FCO Friulano '18	♟♟ 3
○ FCO Pinot Grigio '18	♟♟ 3
● FCO Refosco P. R. '16	♟♟ 3
● FCO Rosso Narciso '16	♟♟ 5
○ FCO Sauvignon '18	♟♟ 3
○ Rosazzo '17	♟♟ 5
● FCO Pignolo di Rosazzo '13	♟ 6
○ FCO Ribolla Gialla '18	♟ 3
● Narciso Rosso '94	♟♟♟ 4*
○ FCO Friulano '17	♟♟ 3
● FCO Merlot '15	♟♟ 3
○ FCO Pinot Grigio '17	♟♟ 3
○ FCO Sauvignon '17	♟♟ 3*
○ Rosazzo '16	♟♟ 5

Ronco Scagnet

LOC. CIME DI DOLEGNA, 7
34070 DOLEGNA DEL COLLIO [GO]
TEL. +39 0481639870
www.roncoscagnet.it

CELLAR SALES
PRE-BOOKED VISITS
ANNUAL PRODUCTION 80,000 bottles
HECTARES UNDER VINE 12.50

In Friuli, the terraced hill vineyards are
called 'ronchi'. On one of these, specifically
among the slopes that overlook the district
of Lonzano in Dolegna del Collio, stands
Ronco Scagnet. The winery is owned by
Valter Cozzarolo, who's accompanied by his
son Dimitri. The producer recently rose to
prominence, vaulting forward with a
commendable selection of wines that
caught our eye. It's a brand that can stand
shoulder-to-shoulder with other standout
Collio producers, those who have
historically worked to bring out the
territory's potential. Competitive prices are
a further boon to a wide-ranging and
diverse selection of whites and reds. The
Friulano '18 convinces for the elegance of
its aromas, sensations consolidated on the
palate, while the Sauvignon '18 features
classic varietal characteristics, which are
pronounced but not invasive. The Pinot
Grigio '18 delights the nose with fruity
hints, while the palate features fragrance
and mineral tension.

● Collio Cabernet Franc '16	♟♟ 2*
○ Collio Friulano '18	♟♟ 2*
● Collio Merlot '17	♟♟ 2*
○ Collio Pinot Grigio '18	♟♟ 2*
● Collio Refosco P. R. '17	♟♟ 2*
● Collio Ribolla Gialla '18	♟♟ 2*
○ Collio Sauvignon '18	♟♟ 2*
○ Collio Chardonnay '18	♟ 2
● Collio Cabernet Franc '15	♟♟ 2*
○ Collio Friulano '17	♟♟ 2*
○ Collio Malvasia Istriana '17	♟♟ 2*
● Collio Merlot '16	♟♟ 2*
○ Collio Pinot Grigio '17	♟♟ 2*
○ Collio Ribolla Gialla '17	♟♟ 2*
○ Collio Sauvignon '17	♟♟ 2*
● Schioppettino '16	♟♟ 2*

Ronco Severo

VIA RONCHI, 93
33040 PREPOTTO [UD]
TEL. +39 04337133440
www.roncosevero.it

CELLAR SALES
PRE-BOOKED VISITS
ANNUAL PRODUCTION 22,000 bottles
HECTARES UNDER VINE 8.00
VITICULTURE METHOD Certified Organic

Stefano Novello is the heart and soul of this small estate, just a few hectares, which allows him to personally look after his grapes. He brings painstaking care and great passion to his work, trusting in an organic and biodynamic approach. Even if he's well-versed in modern cellar techniques, learned while working with other producers in various territories, Stefano loves making wine according to the traditional methods of his predecessors. He practices long maceration, uses select yeasts and enzymes, and doesn't use chemicals or sulphur dioxide. Ronco Severo's wines are not always easily intelligible, but the most careful and curious tasters are, by now, used to appreciating their most appealing peculiarities. Theirs are juicy, richly extracted, captivating wines, like their Friulano Ris. '17, which once again earned a place in our finals. On the nose it offers up suggestions of dried medicinal herbs, lavender, saffron, bee's wax and pine resin. On the palate it's alluring and flavorful, with an extremely long finish.

○ FCO Friulano Ris. '17	♆♆ 4
○ FCO Pinot Grigio '17	♆♆ 4
● FCO Schioppettino di Prepotto '16	♆♆ 4
○ Ribolla Gialla '17	♆♆ 4
○ Severo Bianco '17	♆♆ 4
○ Severo Bianco '12	♆♆♆ 4*
○ FCO Friulano Ris. '16	♆♆ 4
○ FCO Friulano Ris. '15	♆♆ 4
● FCO Merlot Artiûl Ris. '13	♆♆ 5
● FCO Merlot Ris. '15	♆♆ 5
● FCO Schioppettino di Prepotto '15	♆♆ 4
○ Pinot Grigio '16	♆♆ 4
○ Pinot Grigio '15	♆♆ 4
○ Ribolla Gialla '16	♆♆ 4
○ Ribolla Gialla '14	♆♆ 4
○ Severo Bianco '16	♆♆ 4

Roncùs

VIA MAZZINI, 26
34076 CAPRIVA DEL FRIULI [GO]
TEL. +39 0481809349
www.roncus.it

CELLAR SALES
PRE-BOOKED VISITS
ACCOMMODATION
ANNUAL PRODUCTION 40,000 bottles
HECTARES UNDER VINE 10.00

Roncùs is run by Marco Perco, a meticulous vigneron who resolutely pursues a production philosophy aimed at bringing out the grapes' varietal aromas and the great aging potential of these wines, starting with a lengthy stay on the lees. Such interpretations require further aging even after their release, which usually comes at least a year and a half after harvest. Underlying everything is a noteworthy patrimony of old vineyards, which guarantees consistent quality and naturally limited yields. This year, among their monovarietals, we only tasted the Ribolla Gialla '18, a wine we appreciated for its pronounced fragrance. Their three blends all delivered, starting with their Collio Bianco V.V. '15 (Malvasia Istriana, Tocai Friulano and Ribolla Gialla). It's a wine that's complex on the nose and harmonious on the palate. Their fresher Collio Bianco '17 (Pinot Bianco, Tocai Friulano and Savignon) is notable, as is their Val di Miez '16 (Merlot and Cabernet Franc), a well-crafted wine to say the least.

○ Collio Bianco V. V. '15	♆♆ 5
○ Collio Bianco '17	♆♆ 3
○ Ribolla Gialla '18	♆♆ 3
● Val di Miez '16	♆♆ 5
○ Collio Bianco V. V. '08	♆♆♆ 5
○ Roncùs Bianco V. V. '01	♆♆♆ 5
○ Collio Bianco '16	♆♆ 3
○ Collio Bianco '15	♆♆ 3*
○ Collio Bianco V. V. '14	♆♆ 5
○ Collio Bianco V. V. '13	♆♆ 5
○ Collio Bianco V. V. '12	♆♆ 5
○ Collio Friulano '16	♆♆ 4
○ Malvasia '17	♆♆ 3
○ Pinot Bianco '16	♆♆ 4
○ Pinot Bianco '15	♆♆ 4
● Val di Miez '15	♆♆ 5

★Russiz Superiore

VIA RUSSIZ, 7
34070 CAPRIVA DEL FRIULI [GO]
TEL. +39 048180328
www.marcofelluga.it

CELLAR SALES
PRE-BOOKED VISITS
ACCOMMODATION
ANNUAL PRODUCTION 180,000 bottles
HECTARES UNDER VINE 50.00
SUSTAINABLE WINERY

Russiz Superiore is managed by Roberto Felluga, but you can't talk about the producer without mentioning his father, Marco, who purchased the estate way back in 1966. Marco, who's still active and involved, is a considered a pioneer in quality regional wine-growing, having created a benchmark for all of Collio. Roberto is following in his father's footsteps with courage and continuity, launching a project aimed at raising consumer awareness about ageworthy white wines, thanks in part to reserve wines offered after some years of aging in the bottle. This year no reds or reserves were submitted — evidently they're in need of further aging. And so it is that we concentrated on their whites, appreciating the Collio Bianco Col Disôre '16 in particular (it's a blend of Pinot Bianco, Tocai Friulano, Sauvignon and Ribolla Gialla). But we were even more impressed with their splendid Pinot Bianco '18, a true thoroughbred that takes home Tre Bicchieri.

○ Collio Pinot Bianco '18	♟♟♟	4*
○ Collio Bianco Col Disôre '16	♟♟	5
○ Collio Friulano '18	♟♟	4
○ Collio Pinot Grigio '18	♟♟	4
○ Collio Sauvignon '18	♟♟	4
○ Collio Bianco Russiz Disôre '01	♟♟♟	5
○ Collio Bianco Russiz Disôre '00	♟♟♟	4
○ Collio Friulano '16	♟♟♟	4*
○ Collio Friulano '15	♟♟♟	4*
○ Collio Friulano '14	♟♟♟	4*
○ Collio Pinot Bianco '07	♟♟♟	4
○ Collio Pinot Grigio '11	♟♟♟	4*
○ Collio Sauvignon '05	♟♟♟	3
○ Collio Sauvignon '04	♟♟♟	5
○ Collio Sauvignon Ris. '13	♟♟♟	5
○ Collio Tocai Friulano '99	♟♟♟	3*

Sant'Elena

VIA GASPARINI, 1
34072 GRADISCA D'ISONZO [GO]
TEL. +39 048192388
www.sant-elena.com

CELLAR SALES
PRE-BOOKED VISITS
ANNUAL PRODUCTION 130,000 bottles
HECTARES UNDER VINE 30.00

Cosimo Nocerino is to thank for reviving this historic winery whose roots go back to the late 19th century. The agricultural terrain was only converted to vineyards in the mid-1960s and in 1997 Dominic Nocerino, a well-known US importer of Italian wines, purchased the property. In 2015 the involvement of Vincenzo Mercurio led to further innovations (including conversion to organic), which are having an increasing impact on the style of their product range. The wide range of wines submitted for tasting allowed us to provide a more complete assessment of their offerings, and the even distribution of the scoring testifies to the attention paid to each single product. Their whites highlight the varietal peculiarities of the grapes used, and excel for their fragrance and gustatory simplicity. Their reds feature spicy nuances, conferred by lengthy aging.

● Cabernet Franc '13	♟♟	4
● Cabernet Sauvignon '13	♟♟	4
○ Friuli Isonzo Friulano Rive Alte '18	♟♟	3
○ Friuli Isonzo Pinot Grigio Rive Alte '18	♟♟	3
○ Friuli Isonzo Sauvignon Rive Alte '18	♟♟	4
● Merlot '13	♟♟	4
● Merlot Ròs di Rôl '13	♟♟	5
● Tato '14	♟♟	5
○ Friuli Isonzo Chardonnay Rive Alte '18	♟	3
● Friuli Isonzo Pignolo Quantum '14	♟	7
○ Friuli Isonzo Friulano Rive Alte '16	♟♟	3
● Friuli Isonzo Pignolo Quantum '13	♟♟	7
○ Friuli Isonzo Pinot Grigio Rive Alte '17	♟♟	3
○ Friuli Isonzo Pinot Grigio Rive Alte '16	♟♟	3
● Tato '13	♟♟	5

Marco Sara

FRAZ. SAVORGNANO DEL TORRE
VIA DEI MONTI, 3A
33040 POVOLETTO [UD]
TEL. +39 0432666066
www.marcosara.com

CELLAR SALES
PRE-BOOKED VISITS
ANNUAL PRODUCTION 25,000 bottles
HECTARES UNDER VINE 8.00
VITICULTURE METHOD Certified Organic

Marco Sara's winery is situated in Savorgnano del Torre, in the easternmost and coolest part of the Friuli Colli Orientali appellation. The fact of having vineyards spread out in various areas means that the producers are able to take advantage of different conditions and, consequently, the different characters of the grapes. It's also important to note the decision to adopt an organic approach in the vineyard and cellar back in 2005, with certification coming 2011. Their wines are made almost entirely with native grape varieties, except for an old plot of Cabernet Franc. It's no longer news: Marco Sara's Picolit dei Colli Orientali del Friuli has proven that it's one of the best in its category. The 2017 shines like pure gold, emanating intriguing wafts of canned peach, almond brittle, dates, orange peel and lavender honey. Its pronounced sweetness is dampened by a balsamic freshness that limits any type of redundancy, enlivening the palate.

○ COF Picolit '17	🍷🍷 6
○ FCO Friulano Erba Alta '16	🍷🍷 4
● FCO Schioppettino '17	🍷🍷 4
○ FCO Verduzzo Friulano '17	🍷🍷 4
● FCO Refosco P. R. El Re '17	🍷 4
○ COF Picolit '16	🍷🍷 6
○ COF Picolit '15	🍷🍷 6
○ FCO Bianco Erba Alta '16	🍷🍷 4
○ FCO Bianco Erba Alta '15	🍷🍷 5
○ FCO Friulano '15	🍷🍷 3
○ FCO Picolit '14	🍷🍷 5
● FCO Refosco P. R. el Rè '16	🍷🍷 4
● FCO Schioppettino '16	🍷🍷 4
● FCO Schioppettino '15	🍷🍷 4
○ FCO Verduzzo Friulano '16	🍷🍷 4
○ FCO Verduzzo Friulano '15	🍷🍷 4

Sara & Sara

FRAZ. SAVORGNANO DEL TORRE
VIA DEI MONTI, 5
33040 POVOLETTO [UD]
TEL. +39 3393859042
www.saraesara.com

CELLAR SALES
PRE-BOOKED VISITS
ANNUAL PRODUCTION 25,000 bottles
HECTARES UNDER VINE 7.50
SUSTAINABLE WINERY

Sara & Sara is a true pearl of regional winemaking, a tiny producer that's managed to quickly establish itself thanks to the artisanal talent of Alessandro Sara, who's accompanied by his brother Manuele. Together they offer impressive and pleasant wines, drawing on meticulously cared for vineyards that stretch along the steep northern slopes of Friuli. Here the cool wind guarantees noteworthy day-night temperature swings. Verduzzo and Picolit find their perfect habit here and give rise to a range of highly prized sweet wines. The few wines tasted for this year's edition doesn't allow us a complete overview of their selection. Nevertheless, we highly appreciated the Rio Falcone '13, a blend of Refosco dal Peduncolo Rosso and Pinot Nero. It's dense in color, vibrant on the nose and vigorous on the palate. Their highly notable Verduzzo Friulano '17 proves elegant and intoxicating on the nose, caressing and harmonious across its long finish.

○ FCO Friulano '17	🍷🍷 6
● Il Rio Falcone '13	🍷🍷 4
○ Verduzzo Friulano '17	🍷🍷 5
○ COF Verduzzo Friulano Crei '10	🍷🍷🍷 5
○ COF Friulano '12	🍷🍷 3
○ COF Picolit '13	🍷🍷 6
○ COF Picolit '12	🍷🍷 6
○ COF Picolit '10	🍷🍷 5
○ COF Verduzzo Friulano Crei '11	🍷🍷 5
○ FCO Friulano '16	🍷🍷 6
○ FCO Picolit '11	🍷🍷 6
○ FCO Verduzzo Friulano Crei '13	🍷🍷 5
○ FCO Verduzzo Friulano Crei '12	🍷🍷 5
○ SaraGialla '17	🍷🍷 3
○ Sauvignon '12	🍷🍷 2*

★★Schiopetto

VIA PALAZZO ARCIVESCOVILE, 1
34070 CAPRIVA DEL FRIULI [GO]
TEL. +39 048180332
www.schiopetto.it

CELLAR SALES
PRE-BOOKED VISITS
ANNUAL PRODUCTION 190,000 bottles
HECTARES UNDER VINE 30.00
SUSTAINABLE WINERY

Promise kept: the renovation work at the splendid Capriva estate is already in its final stages. The trails among these legendary vineyards that enotourists will be able to traverse will feature a stop in a splendid facility renovated according to modern, 'green building' techniques. The 'Osteria dei Pompieri' will be inaugurated in memory of the historic Udine site where, more than sixty years ago, Mario Schiopetto began a journey that saw him become one of the founders of regional enology. The future of this great brand is assured by young Alessandro Rotolo. There are always a number of Schiopettos in our finals. This year the Blanc des Rosis '18, a blend of Sauvignon, Pinot Bianco and Pinot Grigio, proves newsworthy, standing out for its aromatic elegance, but especially for its gustatory energy. As usual, however, it's the Friulano '18 to emerge as the clear front runner, taking home Tre Bicchieri.

○ Collio Friulano '18	♟♟♟	4*
○ Blanc des Rosis '18	♟♟	4
○ Collio Pinot Bianco '18	♟♟	4
○ Collio Sauvignon '18	♟♟	4
○ Collio Malvasia '18	♟♟	4
○ Collio Pinot Grigio '18	♟♟	4
● Podere dei Blumeri Rosso '17	♟♟	5
● Rivarossa '17	♟♟	4
○ Blanc des Rosis '07	♟♟♟	4
○ Blanc des Rosis '06	♟♟♟	4
○ Collio Friulano '17	♟♟♟	4*
○ Collio Friulano '16	♟♟♟	4*
○ Collio Friulano '15	♟♟♟	4*
○ Collio Friulano '14	♟♟♟	4*
○ Collio Friulano '13	♟♟♟	4*
○ Mario Schiopetto Bianco '08	♟♟♟	5
○ Mario Schiopetto Bianco '07	♟♟♟	5

La Sclusa

LOC. SPESSA
VIA STRADA DI SANT'ANNA, 7/2
33043 CIVIDALE DEL FRIULI [UD]
TEL. +39 0432716259
www.lasclusa.it

CELLAR SALES
PRE-BOOKED VISITS
ACCOMMODATION
ANNUAL PRODUCTION 160,000 bottles
HECTARES UNDER VINE 30.00

Spessa has long been known for quality wine-growing. Here in the south of Cividale del Friuli the Zorzettig family has been operating for many generations. For some time now, Germano, Maurizio and Luciano have been at the helm, skillfully overseeing the winery founded by their father, Gino, back in 1971. Their approach is unabashedly inspired by tradition, in concert with the rhythms of nature and working to bring out the territory's unique attributes. They never force their bottles, resulting in fresh and aromatic whites and full-bodied, smooth reds. Once again we make note of a selection that's in good form overall, and is available at excellent prices. Their Schioppettino '18, in particular, shines. Even if it's young, it benefits from exemplary softness and drinkability. The excellent Friulano 12 Viti '18 stands out for its aromatic complexity and gustatory typicality, while the Chardonnay '18 distinguishes itself for its elegance and succulence. The rest of their selection all performed at a high level.

○ COF Picolit '15	♟♟	6
○ FCO Chardonnay '18	♟♟	3
○ FCO Friulano 12 Viti '18	♟♟	4
○ FCO Pinot Grigio '18	♟♟	3
○ FCO Ribolla Gialla '18	♟♟	3
○ FCO Sauvignon '18	♟♟	3
● FCO Schioppettino '18	♟♟	3
● FCO Cabernet Franc '18	♟	3
○ COF Picolit '14	♟♟	6
○ FCO Chardonnay '17	♟♟	3
○ FCO Chardonnay '16	♟♟	3
○ FCO Friulano '17	♟♟	3
○ FCO Friulano '16	♟♟	3*
○ FCO Friulano 12 Viti '16	♟♟	4
○ FCO Pinot Grigio '17	♟♟	3
○ FCO Ribolla Gialla '17	♟♟	3

Marco Scolaris

VIA BOSCHETTO, 4
34070 SAN LORENZO ISONTINO [GO]
TEL. +39 0481809920
www.scolaris.it

CELLAR SALES
PRE-BOOKED VISITS
ANNUAL PRODUCTION 600,000 bottles
HECTARES UNDER VINE 20.00
SUSTAINABLE WINERY

In its almost century of history, Scolaris has always aimed for authentic winemaking. In recent decades they had the support of Marco, a serious and professional leader who embraced a modest but concrete philosophy: lead an innovative winery that's proud of its history, rooted in the present and geared towards the future. His recent death was felt deeply, and now his son Gianmarco, active in the winery for some time, represents the fourth generation to carry the venture forward. The fact of having a large group of internal and external collaborators at their disposal makes for an extremely diverse range of wines, even if they're focused primarily on Collio whites. The Ribolla Gialla '18 is freshness in a bottle, calling up lemon peel and green apple, teasing the palate with thirst-quenching notes. The Pinot Grigio '18 is highly fruity on the nose, with frequent whiffs of flowering hay and chamomile. On the palate it proves soft and pervasive.

○ Collio Chardonnay '18	🍷🍷 3
○ Collio Friulano '18	🍷🍷 3
● Collio Merlot '18	🍷🍷 3
○ Collio Pinot Grigio '18	🍷🍷 3
○ Collio Ribolla Gialla '18	🍷🍷 3
● Collio Cabernet Franc '18	🍷 3
○ Traminer Aromatico '18	🍷 3
○ Collio Chardonnay '17	🍷🍷 3
○ Collio Friulano '17	🍷🍷 3
○ Collio Malvasia '16	🍷🍷 3
○ Collio Malvasia '15	🍷🍷 3
● Collio Merlot '16	🍷🍷 3
○ Collio Pinot Grigio '16	🍷🍷 3
○ Collio Ribolla Gialla '17	🍷🍷 3
○ Collio Sauvignon '16	🍷🍷 3
○ Traminer Aromatico '17	🍷🍷 3

Roberto Scubla

FRAZ. IPPLIS
VIA ROCCA BERNARDA, 22
33040 PREMARIACCO [UD]
TEL. +39 0432716258
www.scubla.com

CELLAR SALES
PRE-BOOKED VISITS
ANNUAL PRODUCTION 50,000 bottles
HECTARES UNDER VINE 11.00

Roberto Scubla is the founder of this lovely estate situated on the Rocca Bernarda foothills, one of Colli Orientali's most important historic sites. Taking advantage of his enological skills and a deep friendship with Gianni Menotti, his winery has established itself as among the region's best. The pair are fond of remembering how they created the blend for their Pomèdes, undoubtedly one of Italy's greatest whites. The wine got its name from the Alpine lodge they were stuck in during a snowstorm. A sizable set of wines put in a sumptuous performance during our last round. It's certainly not just a coincidence, considering that for some years now the results have been quite the same. The Verduzzo Friulano Passito Cràtis '16 is always a top-notch performer in its category, while the Pinot Bianco '18 repeats last year's exploit. A nice piece of news is their Sauvignon '18, a wine of great elegance and personality.

○ FCO Pinot Bianco '18	🍷🍷 4
○ FCO Sauvignon '18	🍷🍷 4
○ FCO Verduzzo Friulano Passito Cràtis '16	🍷🍷 6
○ FCO Bianco Pomédes '17	🍷🍷 5
● FCO Cabernet Sauvignon '17	🍷🍷 4
○ FCO Friulano '18	🍷🍷 4
○ FCO Malvasia Lo Speziale '18	🍷🍷 4
● FCO Merlot '17	🍷🍷 4
● FCO Refosco P. R. '17	🍷🍷 4
● FCO Rosso Scuro '16	🍷🍷 5
○ COF Bianco Pomèdes '04	🍷🍷🍷 4
○ COF Bianco Pomèdes '99	🍷🍷🍷 4*
○ COF Verduzzo Friulano Cràtis '09	🍷🍷🍷 5
○ COF Verduzzo Friulano Cràtis '06	🍷🍷🍷 5
○ COF Verduzzo Friulano Cràtis '04	🍷🍷🍷 5
○ COF Verduzzo Friulano Graticcio '99	🍷🍷🍷 5

Simon di Brazzan

FRAZ. BRAZZANO
VIA SAN ROCCO, 17
34070 CORMÒNS [GO]
TEL. +39 048161182
www.simondibrazzan.com

CELLAR SALES
PRE-BOOKED VISITS
ANNUAL PRODUCTION 70,000 bottles
HECTARES UNDER VINE 13.00
VITICULTURE METHOD Certified Organic

They're celebrating at Simon di Brazzan. Last year, owner Enrico Veliscig turned 100, but the real news is that at 100 (almost 101 by now) he still works in the vineyards from morning to night. His contribution is important for his grandson Daniele Drius, who for more than twenty years has been managing the winery. A firm supporter of organic viticulture, Daniele has embraced all its tenets, eschewing the use of chemicals and employing only natural methods, both when it comes to managing the terrain and to handling vegetation. The Friulano Blanc di Simon '18 lands in our final round of tastings for the third year in a row, leading their selection once again. Don't let the creative name fool you, the wine perfectly expresses its varietal attributes. The excellent Sauvignon '18 proves rich in citrusy and balsamic tones. And we mustn't forget their Merlot Centenario '16, a wine made in honor of grandfather Enrico's 100th birthday.

○ Friuli Friulano Blanc di Simon '18	▼▼ 3*
○ Sauvignon '18	▼▼ 3*
○ Friuli Pinot Grigio '18	▼▼ 3
○ Malvasia '18	▼▼ 3
● Merlot Centenario '16	▼▼ 4
○ Ri.nè Blanc '17	▼▼ 3
○ Friuli Friulano Blanc di Simon '17	♀♀ 3*
○ Friuli Friulano Blanc di Simon '16	♀♀ 3*
○ Friuli Pinot Grigio '17	♀♀ 3
○ Malvasia '17	♀♀ 3
○ Malvasia '16	♀♀ 3
● Merlot '15	♀♀ 4
○ Pinot Grigio '16	♀♀ 3
○ Ri.nè Blanc '16	♀♀ 3*
○ Ri.nè Blanc '15	♀♀ 3*
○ Sauvignon '17	♀♀ 3

Sirch

VIA FORNALIS, 277/1
33043 CIVIDALE DEL FRIULI [UD]
TEL. +39 0432709835
www.sirchwine.com

CELLAR SALES
PRE-BOOKED VISITS
ANNUAL PRODUCTION 450,000 bottles
HECTARES UNDER VINE 80.00

Sirch recently launched a major initiative aimed at enlarging their estate, purchasing new plots so as to render their range of regional products more complete. It's an ambitious project made possible in part thanks to the involvement of an export powerhouse with international reach, Feudi di San Gregorio. To that end, their partnership with this Campana producer, who's already been handling distribution of Luca Sirch's wines in Friuli, has been essential. 2018 turned out to be once of the century's best years yet, a season whose climatic conditions allowed for quality and quantity to be reconciled. The Sirch family's selection is the proof, with whites that enjoy a fragrance of exemplary suppleness and pronounced varietal character. Their Pinot Nero '18 also exhibits a lovely softness and pleasant mouthfeel.

○ FCO Chardonnay '18	▼▼ 3
○ FCO Friulano '18	▼▼ 3
○ FCO Pinot Grigio '18	▼▼ 3
● FCO Pinot Nero '18	▼▼ 3
○ FCO Sauvignon '18	▼▼ 3
○ FCO Traminer Aromatico '18	▼▼ 3
○ FCO Ribolla Gialla '18	▼ 3
○ COF Friulano '07	♀♀♀ 2*
○ FCO Bianco Cladrecis '15	♀♀ 3*
○ FCO Chardonnay '16	♀♀ 3
○ FCO Friulano '17	♀♀ 3
○ FCO Friulano '16	♀♀ 3
○ FCO Pinot Grigio '17	♀♀ 3
○ FCO Ribolla Gialla '17	♀♀ 3
○ FCO Ribolla Gialla '16	♀♀ 3
○ FCO Sauvignon '17	♀♀ 3

Skerk

FRAZ. SAN PELAGIO
LOC. PREPOTTO, 20
34011 DUINO AURISINA [TS]
TEL. +39 040200156
www.skerk.com

CELLAR SALES
PRE-BOOKED VISITS
RESTAURANT SERVICE
ANNUAL PRODUCTION 22,000 bottles
HECTARES UNDER VINE 7.00
VITICULTURE METHOD Certified Organic

By now Sandi Skerk is one of Karst's established producers. Here rocks dominate and arable land is limited, but the area's thin layer of red earth is rich in limestone and iron. Production is grounded in local tradition: lengthy maceration on the skins that go on for weeks, followed by a simple racking during the first days of the waning moon, without clarification or filtration. These time-honored techniques endow their wines with character and personality, rich flavor and aromatic nuances of rare elegance. By now we're accustomed to the masterpieces offered by Skerk year in, year out. If there was a time that we were amazed by his splendid interpretations, now we find ourselves facing the difficult task of having to choose among the Malvasia '17, the Vitovska '17 and the Ograde '17. They represent the best of this splendid territory's gifts, where the vines breathe in the salty sea area, and wines rest in karst caves at constant humidity year-round. Tre Bicchieri for their Ograde.

○ Ograde '17	♛♛♛ 5
○ Malvasia '17	♛♛ 5
○ Vitovska '17	♛♛ 5
● Terrano '17	♛♛ 5
○ Carso Malvasia '08	♛♛♛ 4
○ Malvasia '13	♛♛♛ 5
○ Ograde '16	♛♛♛ 5
○ Ograde '15	♛♛♛ 5
○ Ograde '12	♛♛♛ 5
○ Ograde '11	♛♛♛ 5
○ Ograde '10	♛♛♛ 4
○ Ograde '09	♛♛♛ 4*

Edi Skok

LOC. GIASBANA, 15
34070 SAN FLORIANO DEL COLLIO [GO]
TEL. +39 3408034045
www.skok.it

CELLAR SALES
PRE-BOOKED VISITS
ANNUAL PRODUCTION 38,000 bottles
HECTARES UNDER VINE 11.00

In the past fifty years, here on the splendid slopes of San Floriano almost all families working in agriculture have specialized in cultivating grapes. And so it is that a number of outstanding wineries have emerged and risen to heights of regional excellence. Among these we surely must count Edi and Orietta Skok's operation, a producer that's proved capable of admirably interpreting the potential of Collio, in particular when it comes to white wines. A year as favorable as 2018 certainly couldn't betray our expectations, and in fact the consensus concerning the quality of all their wines was unanimous. The Sauvignon '18, in particular, exhibits notable varietal stamping, proving elegant on the nose and closing well on the palate. Their Collio Bianco Pe Ar '17 (Chardonnay, Pinot Grigio and Sauvignon) is excellent, as is the Friulano Zabura '18, one of the best in its category.

○ Collio Bianco Pe Ar '17	♛♛ 3
○ Collio Chardonnay '18	♛♛ 2*
○ Collio Friulano Zabura '18	♛♛ 3
○ Collio Pinot Grigio '18	♛♛ 3
○ Collio Sauvignon '18	♛♛ 3
○ Collio Bianco Pe Ar '16	♛♛ 3*
○ Collio Bianco Pe Ar '15	♛♛ 3*
○ Collio Chardonnay '17	♛♛ 2*
○ Collio Chardonnay '16	♛♛ 2*
○ Collio Friulano Zabura '17	♛♛ 3
● Collio Merlot '16	♛♛ 3
● Collio Merlot '15	♛♛ 3
● Collio Merlot Villa Jasbinae '13	♛♛ 3
○ Collio Pinot Grigio '16	♛♛ 3
○ Collio Sauvignon '17	♛♛ 3
○ Collio Sauvignon '16	♛♛ 3

Specogna

FRAZ. ROCCA BERNARDA, 4
33040 CORNO DI ROSAZZO [UD]
TEL. +39 0432755840
www.specogna.it

CELLAR SALES
PRE-BOOKED VISITS
ACCOMMODATION
ANNUAL PRODUCTION 120,000 bottles
HECTARES UNDER VINE 25.00
SUSTAINABLE WINERY

The death of Graziano left a void at the Specogna family's winery, but his sons Michele and Cristian never miss the chance to honor his memory. For some time the two enologists have collaborated in perfect harmony, making wines that stand out for their fragrance and linearity. In recent years, a group of reserve wines have further enriched their selection and earned high praise. Their Pinot Grigio Ramato, a blend of five consecutive vintages, has provoked curiosity among wine lovers. In the last edition we emphasized the splendid performance put in by their entire selection, with some four wines gaining access to our final round of tastings. Well, they've repeated the feat — actually, they may have surpassed it. The Rosso Oltre '16 (Refosco dal Peduncolo Rosso, Pignolo and Schioppettino) put in a superb performance, highlighting the potential of the region's indigenous red grapes.

○ FCO Malvasia Ris. '16	♟♟ 4
● FCO Rosso Oltre '16	♟♟ 6
○ FCO Sauvignon Blanc Duality '17	♟♟ 3*
○ Pinot Grigio Ramato	♟♟ 6
○ COF Picolit '15	♟♟ 6
○ FCO Bianco Identità '17	♟♟ 7
○ FCO Friulano '18	♟♟ 3
● FCO Merlot Ris. '15	♟♟ 4
○ FCO Pinot Grigio '18	♟♟ 3
○ FCO Sauvignon '18	♟♟ 3
○ FCO Bianco Identità '15	♟♟♟ 7
○ FCO Bianco Identità '16	♟♟ 7
○ FCO Chardonnay '17	♟♟ 3
○ FCO Friulano Ris. '16	♟♟ 3
○ FCO Malvasia Ris. '15	♟♟ 4
○ FCO Sauvignon Blanc Duality '16	♟♟ 3*

Stanig

VIA ALBANA, 44
33040 PREPOTTO [UD]
TEL. +39 0432713234
www.stanig.it

CELLAR SALES
ACCOMMODATION AND RESTAURANT SERVICE
ANNUAL PRODUCTION 45,000 bottles
HECTARES UNDER VINE 9.00

It was 1920 when Giuseppe Stanig launched his winemaking venture in Albana di Prepotto. A century of love and dedication for the land and for local tradition has been passed down to brothers Federico and Francesco, who are carrying on with the same enthusiasm. Prepotto is a small district in the extreme northeastern part of the Friuli Colli Orientali appellation, bordering Slovenia on the one side and Collio Goriziano on the other. It's a territory that, by virtue of its soil and unique microclimate, is considered ideal for producing red wines, foremost Schioppettino. The even distribution of the scoring plays in favor of their entire selection. Their Schioppettino di Prepotto '16 is highly varietal, redolent of raspberries and black pepper, drawing on the linearity of its poised tannins. The Ribolla Gialla '18 is extremely flowery, with the occasional hint of wild strawberries. Their Bianco del Gelso '16 is a sweet wine made with Picolit and Verduzzo Friulano partially dried in small cases.

○ Bianco Del Gelso '16	♟♟ 5
○ FCO Malvasia '18	♟♟ 3
○ FCO Ribolla Gialla '18	♟♟ 3
○ FCO Sauvignon '18	♟♟ 3
● FCO Schioppettino di Prepotto '16	♟♟ 5
● FCO Cabernet '17	♟ 3
○ FCO Friulano '18	♟ 3
○ FCO Friulano '17	♟♟ 3
○ FCO Friulano '15	♟♟ 3
○ FCO Malvasia '17	♟♟ 3
○ FCO Malvasia '16	♟♟ 3
● FCO Merlot '15	♟♟ 3
○ FCO Ribolla Gialla '17	♟♟ 3
○ FCO Sauvignon '17	♟♟ 3
● FCO Schioppettino di Prepotto '15	♟♟ 3

Tenuta Stella

LOC. SCRIÒ
VIA SDENCINA, 1
34070 DOLEGNA DEL COLLIO [GO]
TEL. +39 0481639895
www.tenutastellacollio.it

CELLAR SALES
PRE-BOOKED VISITS
ANNUAL PRODUCTION 35,000 bottles
HECTARES UNDER VINE 12.00
VITICULTURE METHOD Certified Organic
SUSTAINABLE WINERY

Founded by Sergio Stevanato less than a decade ago, Tenuta Stella immediately distinguished itself for the high quality of its entire product range, made strictly with native grape varieties, including their Metodo Classico sparklers. Erika Barbieri and Alberto Faggiani form part of a highly skilled staff whose approach features organic management. It's their job to get the best out of their prized, older vineyards while also planting new ones in ways that are in line with local tradition. Tenuta Stella's performance this year is one for the ages, thanks foremost to two splendid wines that earned places in our final round of tastings. The Ribolla Gialla Brut, a Metodo Classico, features extremely delicate but lively bead. It penetrates the nostrils with floral notes and fragrant whiffs of citrus, while magically satisfying the palate. Their Friulano '17 is also excellent. Sapid and creamy, it's among the best in its category.

○ Collio Friulano '17	♟♟ 4
○ Ribolla Gialla Brut	♟♟ 5
○ Collio Malvasia '17	♟♟ 4
○ Collio Ribolla Gialla '17	♟♟ 4
○ Cuvée Tanni Brut	♟♟ 5
● Rosso '16	♟♟ 4
○ Collio Friulano '16	♟♟ 4
○ Collio Friulano '15	♟♟ 3*
○ Collio Malvasia '16	♟♟ 4
○ Collio Malvasia '15	♟♟ 4
○ Collio Malvasia '14	♟♟ 4
○ Collio Ribolla Gialla '16	♟♟ 4
○ Collio Ribolla Gialla '15	♟♟ 4
○ Collio Ribolla Gialla '14	♟♟ 4
○ Collio Ribolla Gialla '13	♟♟ 4

Stocco

VIA CASALI STOCCO, 12
33050 BICINICCO [UD]
TEL. +39 0432934906
www.vinistocco.it

CELLAR SALES
PRE-BOOKED VISITS
RESTAURANT SERVICE
ANNUAL PRODUCTION 250,000 bottles
HECTARES UNDER VINE 49.00

In medieval Italian the word 'stocco' meant 'sword'. For the Stocco family, the symbol has represented their values for more than a century: strength, rigor and respect for the land. Today it's the fourth generation's turn, Andrea, Daniela and Paola, to keep the flag of their wide-ranging, authoritative selection flying high, and so demonstrating that the Friulian plains are capable of standing shoulder-to-shoulder with the most prestigious hillside vineyards. As Andrea says, their goal is to capture the nuance and elegance of Grave in every bottle. All the wines submitted for tasting this year stood out for their accessibility, adherence to varietal characteristics, and for their fantastic value for the money. The Malvasia '18 calls up aromas of ripe fruit and dry mountain hay, rich in flowers and medicinal herbs. The Traminer Aromatico '18 is redolent of lemon cream, honey and barley sugar.

● Cabernet Sauvignon '17	♟♟ 2*
○ Chardonnay '18	♟♟ 5
○ Friuli Grave Friulano '18	♟♟ 2*
○ Malvasia '18	♟♟ 2*
○ Ribolla Gialla Botis '17	♟♟ 2*
○ Sauvignon '18	♟♟ 2*
○ Traminer Aromatico '18	♟♟ 5
○ Pinot Bianco '18	♟ 2
○ Prosecco Extra Dry '18	♟ 2
○ Ribolla Gialla '18	♟ 2
○ Ribolla Gialla Brut	♟ 3
○ Chardonnay '17	♟♟ 5
○ Friuli Grave Friulano Doghis '16	♟♟ 2*
○ Friuli Grave Sauvignon '17	♟♟ 2*
● Merlot '16	♟♟ 4
○ Sericus '16	♟♟ 3
○ Sericus '15	♟♟ 3

Subida di Monte

LOC. SUBIDA
VIA SUBIDA, 6
34071 CORMÒNS [GO]
TEL. +39 048161011
www.subidadimonte.it

CELLAR SALES
PRE-BOOKED VISITS
ACCOMMODATION
ANNUAL PRODUCTION 45,000 bottles
HECTARES UNDER VINE 9.00

Cristian and Andrea Antonutti, children of legendary Luigi Antonutti, are Subida di Monte's current owners. It's a lovely winery situated along a hill of Collio Goriziano, between two rivers, the Isonzo and Judrio. In addition to its unique microclimate, the area also enjoys favorable soil (made up of clay, limestone and a small share of sand), or 'ponca' as it's known in local dialect. The two brothers have always practiced sustainable agriculture, using natural, organic fertilizer and keeping anti-parassite treatments to a minimum. Last year we were unable to try their reds, which apparently needed more time to age. Our recent tastings saw them performing well, along with a well-crafted selection of 2018 whites. We found the Collio Rosso Poncaia '16 noteworthy. It's almost entirely Merlot, there's just a small share of Cabernet Franc that contributes to its aromatic profile and gustatory development.

● Collio Rosso Poncaia '16	♟♟ 4
● Collio Cabernet '17	♟♟ 3
○ Collio Friulano '18	♟♟ 3
○ Collio Malvasia '18	♟♟ 3
● Collio Merlot '17	♟♟ 3
○ Collio Pinot Grigio '18	♟♟ 3
○ Collio Sauvignon '18	♟♟ 3
● Collio Cabernet Franc '15	♟♟ 3
○ Collio Friulano '17	♟♟ 3
○ Collio Friulano '16	♟♟ 3
○ Collio Malvasia '17	♟♟ 3*
○ Collio Malvasia '16	♟♟ 3
○ Collio Pinot Grigio '17	♟♟ 3
○ Collio Pinot Grigio '16	♟♟ 3
● Collio Rosso Poncaia '13	♟♟ 4
○ Collio Sauvignon '17	♟♟ 3

Tenuta di Angoris

LOC. ANGORIS, 7
34071 CORMÒNS [GO]
TEL. +39 048160923
www.angoris.com

CELLAR SALES
PRE-BOOKED VISITS
RESTAURANT SERVICE
ANNUAL PRODUCTION 500,000 bottles
HECTARES UNDER VINE 85.00
SUSTAINABLE WINERY

The Locatelli family's Tenuta di Angoris has roots that go back to 1648. It's headquartered in Cormòns, but the estate comprises vineyards in Isontino, near the property's manor house, and along the hills of Collio Goriziano and Colli Orientali del Friuli. Today Marta Locatelli is guiding the winery and under her direction they've reached important milestones. Their entire range demonstrates quality, bringing out the best of each cultivar and the territory itself. Once again the Collio Bianco Giulio Locatelli Ris. '17 is at the top of its game, taking home Tre Bicchieri for the third year in a row. It's a territorial wine, made with best grapes cultivated in their prestigious Ronco Antico vineyards. It impresses on the nose with its elegant, fruity and floral whiffs, while delighting the palate with velvety, sweet notes of honey. The Chardonnay Spìule Giulio Locatelli Ris. '17 also put in an excellent performance.

○ Collio Bianco Giulio Locatelli Ris. '17	♟♟♟ 4*
○ FCO Chardonnay Spìule Giulio Locatelli Ris. '17	♟♟ 4
○ Collio Pinot Grigio '18	♟♟ 3
○ FCO Friulano '18	♟♟ 3
● FCO Merlot Ravòst Giulio Locatelli Ris. '16	♟♟ 4
● FCO Pignolo Giulio Locatelli Ris. '14	♟♟ 5
● FCO Refosco P. R. '16	♟♟ 3
○ FCO Ribolla Gialla '18	♟♟ 3
● Friuli Isonzo Pinot Nero Albertina '17	♟♟ 4
○ Friuli Isonzo Sauvignon '18	♟ 2
○ Collio Bianco Giulio Locatelli Ris. '16	♟♟♟ 4*
○ Collio Bianco Giulio Locatelli Ris. '15	♟♟♟ 4*
○ FCO Chardonnay Spìule '13	♟♟♟ 4*
○ FCO Friulano '15	♟♟♟ 3*

Matijaž Terčič

LOC. BUCUIE, 4A
34070 SAN FLORIANO DEL COLLIO [GO]
TEL. +39 0481884920
www.tercic.com

CELLAR SALES
PRE-BOOKED VISITS
ANNUAL PRODUCTION 30,000 bottles
HECTARES UNDER VINE 9.50

The winery founded and managed by
Matijaž Terčič has established itself as one
of San Floriano del Collio's most
accomplished. Matijaž oversees his prized
vineyards with the painstaking care of a true
artisan, and releases his wines only when
properly aged. These exhibit an
unmistakable personal style grounded in
forthrightness, approachability and
drinkability. The balance of aromas is
favored by a unique microclimate, made
possible by the cool winds coming in off the
Vipacco valley, and the breeze of the nearby
Adriatic. This year the Planta '14, a
monovarietal Chardonnay, led their
selection. It's a mature wine that fully
conserves its fruity fragrances, unfolding
complex and alluring both on the nose and
on the palate. The Sauvignon '17 stands out
for its varietal correctness, and especially
for a pleasant, minty finish. We should also
mention their Ribolla Gialla '17, one of the
best interpretations of the typology.

○ Planta '14	♟♟ 4
● Collio Merlot '15	♟♟ 4
○ Collio Pinot Grigio '17	♟♟ 3
○ Collio Sauvignon '17	♟♟ 3
○ Friuli Isonzo Friulano '17	♟♟ 3
○ Ribolla Gialla '17	♟♟ 3
○ Collio Pinot Grigio '07	♟♟♟ 3*
○ Collio Pinot Grigio '16	♟♟ 3
○ Collio Pinot Grigio '15	♟♟ 3
○ Collio Ribolla Gialla '15	♟♟ 4
○ Collio Sauvignon '16	♟♟ 3*
○ Collio Sauvignon '15	♟♟ 3*
○ Collio Sauvignon '14	♟♟ 3
○ Friuli Isonzo Friulano '14	♟♟ 3
○ Vino degli Orti '16	♟♟ 3
○ Vino degli Orti '13	♟♟ 3*

Terre di Ger

LOC. FRATTINA
S.DA DELLA MEDUNA, 17
33076 PRAVISDOMINI [PN]
TEL. +39 0434644452
www.terrediger.it

CELLAR SALES
PRE-BOOKED VISITS
ANNUAL PRODUCTION 100,000 bottles
HECTARES UNDER VINE 70.00

Owned by the Spinazzè family, Terre di Ger
is one of Friuli Occidentale's thriving
wineries. Their vineyards are situated
between the Lemene and Livenza rivers,
bordering Veneto. Their main facility is
surrounded by their Frattina plots, but the
property also includes Baite, Villaraccolta
and Arcane. Gianluigi Spinazzè and his son
Robert have, for some years now, been
working on a project called 'hyper-organic',
using the latest generation of resistant
grapes obtained by cross-breeding vitis
vinifera, which allows them to drastically
reduce vineyard treatment. Already in last
year's edition we sang the praises of the
blends made with recently added grape
varieties. And once again, this year it's the
Limine '18 that garners the highest
accolades. Made primarily with Soreli,
accompanied by a small (though important)
share of Sauvignon Kretos, it's a summery
wine that calls up wild flowers and wheat in
a cloud of vanilla, proving fresh, soft and
mouthfilling on the palate.

○ Arconi '18	♟♟ 5
○ Brut M. Cl.	♟♟ 5
● Friuli Cabernet Franc '17	♟♟ 3
○ Friuli Pinot Grigio '18	♟♟ 3
○ Limine '18	♟♟ 6
● Friuli Grave Merlot '17	♟ 3
● Friuli Grave Refosco P. R. '17	♟ 3
○ Sauvignon Blanc '18	♟ 3
○ Brut M. Cl.	♟♟ 4
● El Masut '16	♟♟ 3
○ Friuli Grave Chardonnay '16	♟♟ 2*
○ Friuli Grave Chardonnay '15	♟♟ 2*
● Friuli Grave Merlot '16	♟♟ 2*
○ Limine '17	♟♟ 5
○ Limine '16	♟♟ 3
○ Limine '13	♟♟ 3*

Tiare - Roberto Snidarcig

FRAZ. VENCÒ
LOC. SANT'ELENA, 3A
34070 DOLEGNA DEL COLLIO [GO]
TEL. +39 048162491
www.tiaredoc.com

CELLAR SALES
PRE-BOOKED VISITS
RESTAURANT SERVICE
ANNUAL PRODUCTION 90,000 bottles
HECTARES UNDER VINE 10.00
SUSTAINABLE WINERY

For Roberto Snidarcig moving from managing just a hectare of land to his current success was a true accomplishment. He decided to call his winery Tiare, a tribute to the land that allowed him to realize his desire to establish his estate among the region's top producers and contribute to promoting Dolegna del Collio. It's an area in which tough grapes like Sauvignon, which figures in most of his production, enjoy the temperature changes of the cool eastern winds. This year the same two wines as last year made it into our finals, though they were accompanied by a splendid 2018 version of the Ribolla Gialla, which just fell short of our highest honors. The Malvasia '18 is also excellent, proving elegant on the nose and pervasive on the palate. But on the throne, once again we find their flagship Sauvignon '18, which was awarded Tre Bicchieri for the sixth year in a row.

○ Collio Sauvignon '18	♛♛♛ 5
○ Collio Malvasia '18	♛♛ 3*
○ Collio Ribolla Gialla '18	♛♛ 4
○ Collio Bianco Rosemblanc '16	♛♛ 5
○ Collio Chardonnay '18	♛♛ 3
○ Collio Friulano '18	♛♛ 4
○ Collio Pinot Grigio '18	♛♛ 4
○ Friuli Sauvignon Il Tiare '18	♛♛ 3
○ Collio Sauvignon '17	♛♛♛ 5
○ Collio Sauvignon '16	♛♛♛ 5
○ Collio Sauvignon '15	♛♛♛ 5
○ Collio Sauvignon '14	♛♛♛ 5
○ Collio Sauvignon '13	♛♛♛ 3*

★★Franco Toros

LOC. NOVALI, 12
34071 CORMÒNS [GO]
TEL. +39 048161327
www.vinitoros.com

CELLAR SALES
PRE-BOOKED VISITS
ANNUAL PRODUCTION 60,000 bottles
HECTARES UNDER VINE 11.00

A lover of the great outdoors, Franco Toros painstakingly looks after his vineyards. He's not a man for boasting, preferring instead to let his wines do the talking. He chisels these using modern technological tools, supported by that ancient knowledge passed down ever since his grandfather Edoardo settled in Novali (near Cormòns) in the early 20th century. Even back then they made a wine whose marked personality attracted the attention of wine lovers throughout Italy and Austria. The Pinot Bianco '18 is a true thoroughbred in Franco's stable, a combination of elegance and power whose aromatic impact is extraordinary and whose gustatory pleasantness is indelible. The Sauvignon '18 is also excellent, always a standout despite the fierce competition. But this year it's their sumptuous Friulano '18 that earns Tre Bicchieri. Pleasantly fruit on the nose, it exhibits balance and harmony on the palate. The rest of their selection, both their whites and their reds, all also performed at high levels.

○ Collio Friulano '18	♛♛♛ 4*
○ Collio Pinot Bianco '18	♛♛ 4
○ Collio Sauvignon '18	♛♛ 4
○ Collio Chardonnay '18	♛♛ 4
● Collio Merlot '15	♛♛ 4
○ Collio Pinot Grigio '18	♛♛ 4
○ Collio Friulano '12	♛♛♛ 4*
○ Collio Friulano '11	♛♛♛ 4*
○ Collio Friulano '10	♛♛♛ 4
○ Collio Friulano '09	♛♛♛ 4*
○ Collio Friulano '08	♛♛♛ 4*
○ Collio Pinot Bianco '17	♛♛♛ 4*
○ Collio Pinot Bianco '14	♛♛♛ 4*
○ Collio Pinot Bianco '13	♛♛♛ 4*
○ Collio Pinot Bianco '08	♛♛♛ 4*
○ Collio Pinot Bianco '07	♛♛♛ 4

Torre Rosazza

FRAZ. OLEIS
LOC. POGGIOBELLO, 12
33044 MANZANO [UD]
TEL. +39 0422864511
www.torrerosazza.com

CELLAR SALES
PRE-BOOKED VISITS
ANNUAL PRODUCTION 200,000 bottles
HECTARES UNDER VINE 90.00
SUSTAINABLE WINERY

Torre Rosazza is a regional gem when it comes to winemaking, a historic producer situated on the hills of Manzano and headquartered in the 18th-century Palazzo De Marchi. It's part of Genagricola, a solid, established group that brings together prestigious wineries from throughout Italy. As far back as the 1970s they were studying and researching the territory so as to identify the best plots, in terms of position and geological characteristics, for bringing out the attributes of each cultivar. Another year to remember for this historic winery, which manages to land some two wines in our final round of tastings. The Ribolla Gialla '18 is a pleasant surprise, proving fresh and summery at the same time, both fragrant and creamy. Their Pinot Grigio '18 also put in a noteworthy performance, one worthy of Tre Bicchieri. Aromas of lime blossom and acacia are accompanied by white peach and mint, sensations that give way to a graceful, alluring palate. But their entire selection proves compelling.

○ FCO Pinot Grigio '18	♙♙♙ 3*
○ FCO Ribolla Gialla '18	♙♙ 3*
○ Blanc di Neri Brut	♙♙ 5
● FCO Cabernet Sauvignon '16	♙♙ 3
○ FCO Friulano '18	♙♙ 3
○ FCO Pinot Bianco '18	♙♙ 3
● FCO Pinot Nero Ronco del Palazzo '15	♙♙ 4
● FCO Refosco P. R. '17	♙♙ 3
● FCO Rosso Altromerlot '15	♙♙ 5
○ FCO Sauvignon '18	♙♙ 3
● FCO Pignolo '15	♙ 5
○ COF Pinot Grigio '13	♙♙♙ 3*
○ COF Pinot Grigio '12	♙♙♙ 3*
○ FCO Pinot Bianco '17	♙♙♙ 3*
○ FCO Pinot Bianco '14	♙♙♙ 3*

La Tunella

FRAZ. IPPLIS
VIA DEL COLLIO, 14
33040 PREMARIACCO [UD]
TEL. +39 0432716030
www.latunella.it

CELLAR SALES
PRE-BOOKED VISITS
ANNUAL PRODUCTION 400,000 bottles
HECTARES UNDER VINE 70.00
SUSTAINABLE WINERY

Massimo and Marco Zorzettig belong to a family of winemakers. They were still adolescents when the early death of their father, Livio, forced them to jump the gun and take over the family business (which back then had only recently taken shape). Mother Gabriella supported them and spurned them on, and today Tunella is a modern, dynamic, model producer. Winemaker Luigino Zamparo has grown along with the two brothers and serves as an integral part of a young, tight-knit staff that's come so far and done so much with such humility and passion. Once again we find two indigenous grape blends in our finals. The Arcione '13 is a red made with equal parts Pignolo and Schioppettino. It's complex on the nose in its sanguine and spicy hints, while on the palate it comes through juicy and well-balanced. The 2017 version of their BiancoSesto, a classic blend of Tocai Friulano and Ribolla Gialla, proves complete, once again scoring Tre Bicchieri.

○ FCO Biancosesto '17	♙♙♙ 5
● L'Arcione '13	♙♙ 5
○ FCO Malvasia Valmasia '18	♙♙ 3
○ FCO Pinot Grigio '18	♙♙ 3
○ FCO Ribolla Gialla Col de Bliss '17	♙♙ 4
○ FCO Ribolla Gialla Rjgialla '18	♙♙ 3
○ FCO Sauvignon Col Matiss '17	♙♙ 4
○ Noans '17	♙♙ 5
● Schioppettino '16	♙♙ 5
○ COF BiancoSesto '11	♙♙♙ 4*
○ COF BiancoSesto '07	♙♙♙ 3
○ COF BiancoSesto '06	♙♙♙ 3*
○ FCO Bianco LaLinda '14	♙♙♙ 4*
○ FCO BiancoSesto '16	♙♙♙ 4*
○ Noans '12	♙♙♙ 5

Valchiarò

FRAZ. TOGLIANO
VIA DEI LAGHI, 4C
33040 TORREANO [UD]
TEL. +39 0432715502
www.valchiaro.it

CELLAR SALES
PRE-BOOKED VISITS
ANNUAL PRODUCTION 45,000 bottles
HECTARES UNDER VINE 14.00
SUSTAINABLE WINERY

In the late 20th century, six small Torreano di Cividale producers, each of whom owned just a few hectares, decided to join together and form a single brand so as to have a greater impact and firmer foundation. They called it Valchiarò after the Chiarò river that crosses the valley. Trusting in highly reputable ecological guidance, they quickly established themselves as a top producer in the already-crowded Colli Orientali appellation, an area where the Adriatic sea breeze gives way to continental winds blowing in from the northeast. By now it's customary to find their Friulano Nexus '17 at the top of the scorecard. Once again it lands in our final round of tastings, demonstrating that it's one of the best of its kind. Their Rosso Torre Qual Ris. '16, another first-rate wine, is a grape blend of Merlot, Refosco dal Peduncolo Rosso and Cabernet that unleashes jammy whiffs of cherries, golden-leaf tobacco and clear spices, coming juicy and symmetrical on the palate.

○ FCO Friulano Nexus '18	🏆🏆 3*
○ FCO Friulano '18	🏆🏆 3
● FCO Merlot Ris. '16	🏆🏆 3
○ FCO Pinot Grigio '18	🏆🏆 3
● FCO Refosco P. R. '15	🏆🏆 3
● FCO Rosso Torre Qual Ris. '16	🏆🏆 3
○ FCO Sauvignon '18	🏆🏆 3
○ FCO Verduzzo Friulano '16	🏆🏆 4
○ FCO Friulano Nexus '17	🏆🏆 3*
○ FCO Friulano Nexus '16	🏆🏆 3*
○ FCO Pinot Grigio '17	🏆🏆 3
○ FCO Pinot Grigio '16	🏆🏆 3
● FCO Rosso Torre Qual Ris. '15	🏆🏆 3
○ FCO Sauvignon '16	🏆🏆 3
○ FCO Verduzzo Friulano '15	🏆🏆 4

Valpanera

VIA TRIESTE, 5A
33059 VILLA VICENTINA [UD]
TEL. +39 0431970395
www.valpanera.it

CELLAR SALES
PRE-BOOKED VISITS
ANNUAL PRODUCTION 450,000 bottles
HECTARES UNDER VINE 55.00

Founded in 1972 by Giampietro Dal Vecchio and now managed mostly by his son Giovanni, Valpanera is a model winery that pays homage to the Friuli Aquileia appellation. Its enormous entrance is emblazoned with the words 'Casa del Refosco', a clear indication of their desire to champion the region's most representative, native cultivar. Naturally, other wines are produced as well, both whites and reds, rounding out a selection aimed at satisfying any market demand. Once again the Refosco dal Peduncolo Rosso leads an excellent performance, both the Superiore '16 and the Riserva '13. We also appreciated the Sauvignon '18. On the nose it's varietal and true to type in its herbaceous and tropical nuances, while on the palate it proves fresh and taut, closing pleasantly crisp and linear. The rest of their selection also delivers.

○ Album '18	🏆🏆 2*
● Atrum '16	🏆🏆 2*
● Friuli Aquileia Refosco P. R. Ris. '13	🏆🏆 5
● Friuli Aquileia Refosco P. R. Sup. '16	🏆🏆 3
○ Friuli Aquileia Sauvignon '18	🏆🏆 3
○ Friuli Aquileia Chardonnay '18	🏆 2
○ Friuli Aquileia Verduzzo Friulano '17	🏆 4
○ Album '17	🏆🏆 2*
● Atrum '15	🏆🏆 2*
○ Friuli Aquileia Chardonnay '17	🏆🏆 3
● Friuli Aquileia Refosco P. R. '14	🏆🏆 2*
● Friuli Aquileia Refosco P. R. Ris. '12	🏆🏆 5
● Friuli Aquileia Refosco P. R. Sup. '14	🏆🏆 3
● Friuli Aquileia Refosco P. R. Sup. '13	🏆🏆 3
● Friuli Aquileia Rosso Alma '13	🏆🏆 5
○ Friuli Aquileia Sauvignon '17	🏆🏆 3

★★Venica & Venica

LOC. CERÒ, 8
34070 DOLEGNA DEL COLLIO [GO]
TEL. +39 048161264
www.venica.it

CELLAR SALES
PRE-BOOKED VISITS
ACCOMMODATION
ANNUAL PRODUCTION 310,000 bottles
HECTARES UNDER VINE 40.00
SUSTAINABLE WINERY

In the early part of the 20th century, the
Venica family settled on the hills of Dolegna
del Collio, the highest in the district,
founding a brand that is, by now, an
established international player. Indeed,
Venica is a true ambassador of the
territory's potential, especially when it
comes to white wines. Today Gianni and
Giorgio Venica oversee a tight, dynamic
team, with each member making a
contribution to a winery that brings together
the farmer's spirit with notable
entrepreneurial skill. Finding their flagship
offerings at the top of the scorecard is
certainly not unexpected. The Friulano
Ronco delle Crime '18 exhibits elegant
whiffs of flowers and Alpine grass, only to
offer up citrusy hints and notes of tropical
fruit, sensations that accompany the palate
towards a balsamic finish. The Sauvignon
Ronco delle Mele '18 is a milestone in its
category, highly varietal, fragrant on the
nose and minty on the back palate.

○ Collio Friulano Ronco delle Cime '18	♟♟ 5
○ Collio Sauvignon Ronco delle Mele '18	♟♟ 6
○ Collio Chardonnay Ronco Bernizza '18	♟♟ 4
○ Collio Malvasia Pètris '18	♟♟ 4
○ Collio Pinot Bianco Tàlis '18	♟♟ 4
○ Collio Pinot Grigio Jesera '18	♟♟ 4
○ Collio Sauvignon Ronco del Cerò '18	♟♟ 5
○ Collio Traminer Aromatico '18	♟♟ 4
● FCO Schioppettino '12	♟♟ 6
○ Collio Sauvignon Ronco delle Mele '16	♟♟♟ 6
○ Collio Sauvignon Ronco delle Mele '13	♟♟♟ 6
○ Collio Sauvignon Ronco delle Mele '12	♟♟♟ 6
○ Collio Sauvignon Ronco delle Mele '11	♟♟♟ 6
○ Collio Sauvignon Ronco delle Mele '10	♟♟♟ 5

La Viarte

VIA NOVACUZZO, 51
33040 PREPOTTO [UD]
TEL. +39 0432759458
www.laviarte.it

CELLAR SALES
PRE-BOOKED VISITS
ACCOMMODATION
ANNUAL PRODUCTION 100,000 bottles
HECTARES UNDER VINE 27.00
SUSTAINABLE WINERY

La Viarte sits atop a Prepotto hill that's
been skillfully divided into terraced plots.
It's a true gem, one of which Colli Orientali
is proud. Founded in the 1960s by the
Ceschin family, it's earned a place among
the region's top producers. And thanks to
Alberto Piovan, who's owned the winery for
almost ten years now, it's enjoying its
greatest success yet. Both in the vineyard
and in the cellar, he's accompanied by a
top-notch staff that's managed to revitalize
operations, bringing a breath of fresh air
that's evident in all their wines. In local
dialect 'liende' means legend. And the
wines that make up this line are the result
of careful selection of the best grapes. The
scorecard highlights the validity of their
entire selection, with some three wines
earning a place in our finals. The Sauvignon
Liende '17 leads the way, followed by an
excellent Friulano '18 and an elegant Pinot
Bianco '18. We also found their white
grape blend Arteus '18 interesting.

○ FCO Friulano '18	♟♟ 4
○ FCO Pinot Bianco '18	♟♟ 4
○ FCO Sauvignon Liende '17	♟♟ 5
○ Arteus '18	♟♟ 4
○ FCO Chardonnay Liende '18	♟♟ 4
○ FCO Pinot Grigio '18	♟♟ 4
○ FCO Sauvignon '18	♟♟ 4
○ FCO Friulano Liende '17	♟♟♟ 5
○ FCO Friulano Liende '16	♟♟♟ 5
○ FCO Sauvignon Liende '15	♟♟♟ 5
○ FCO Chardonnay '17	♟♟ 4
○ FCO Friulano '17	♟♟ 4
○ FCO Pinot Bianco '17	♟♟ 4
○ FCO Pinot Grigio '17	♟♟ 4
○ FCO Riesling '17	♟♟ 4
○ FCO Sauvignon '17	♟♟ 4

Vidussi

VIA SPESSA, 18
34071 CAPRIVA DEL FRIULI [GO]
TEL. +39 048180072
www.vinimontresor.it

CELLAR SALES
PRE-BOOKED VISITS
ANNUAL PRODUCTION 500,000 bottles
HECTARES UNDER VINE 30.00

The winery founded in the 1980s by Ferruccio Vidussi had been rented and managed by Vinicola Giacomo Montresor from 1999 to 2018. The historic Verona group was then purchased by three of Italy's most important producers: Terre Cevico, Cantina Valpantena and Vitevis. And so this lovely winery, literally tucked away in a small corner of paradise in Collio Goriziano, is ready for a new beginning. Technical oversight is still entrusted to enologist Luigino De Giuseppe, who's been with the winery for twenty years and has earned the trust of the new ownership. In no way has the change in management affected the quality of their selection, which is entirely in line with previous editions of the guide, starting with the Sauvignon '18. It landed in our final tastings by virtue of its characteristic notes of sage, green pepper and tomato leaf, as well as its elegant, pleasant palate. The rest of their rigorously monovarietal selection also performed at high levels.

○ Collio Sauvignon '18	♟♟ 2*
○ Collio Friulano '18	♟♟ 3
○ Collio Malvasia '18	♟♟ 2*
○ Collio Pinot Grigio '18	♟♟ 2*
○ Collio Ribolla Gialla '18	♟♟ 2*
○ Collio Traminer Aromatico '18	♟♟ 2*
● Schioppettino '18	♟♟ 3
○ Collio Chardonnay '18	♟ 2
● FCO Refosco P. R. '18	♟ 3
○ Collio Chardonnay '17	♟♟ 2*
○ Collio Friulano '17	♟♟ 3
○ Collio Friulano '16	♟♟ 3
○ Collio Malvasia '17	♟♟ 2*
○ Collio Pinot Grigio '17	♟♟ 2*
○ Collio Ribolla Gialla '17	♟♟ 2*
● Ribolla Nera o Schioppettino '17	♟♟ 3

★★Vie di Romans

LOC. VIE DI ROMANS, 1
34070 MARIANO DEL FRIULI [GO]
TEL. +39 048169600
www.viediromans.it

CELLAR SALES
PRE-BOOKED VISITS
ANNUAL PRODUCTION 300,000 bottles
HECTARES UNDER VINE 60.00
SUSTAINABLE WINERY

Gianfranco Gallo is the author of Vie di Romans' production style, constituted of a rigorous approach to vineyard management and careful winemaking. His wines (especially his whites), which are released at least two years after vintage, embody pronounced territorial expression supported by bold structure. Their vineyards lie entirely within the Friuli Isonzo appellation, on flatlands characterized by mineral-rich subsoils. Situated just a few kilometers from the Gulf of Trieste, it's an area where the continental climate merges with that of the Mediterranean. A sumptuous performance by their entire selection is yet more proof of the quality of their production approach. The scorecard found here speaks for itself, the rest is a question of splitting hairs. In the end it was their most representative wine, the Sauvignon Piere '17, that earned Tre Bicchieri. It's a superb version, a distillation of flavor, pleasantness and emotions.

○ Friuli Isonzo Sauvignon Piere '17	♟♟♟ 5
○ Dut'Un '16	♟♟ 7
○ Friuli Isonzo Chardonnay Ciampagnis '17	♟♟ 5
○ Friuli Isonzo Pinot Grigio Dessimis '17	♟♟ 5
○ Friuli Isonzo Sauvignon Vieris '17	♟♟ 5
○ Friuli Isonzo Bianco Flors di Uis '17	♟♟ 5
○ Friuli Isonzo Chardonnay '17	♟♟ 5
○ Friuli Isonzo Bianco Flors di Uis '09	♟♟♟ 4*
○ Friuli Isonzo Chardonnay Ciampagnis Vieris '13	♟♟♟ 4*
○ Friuli Isonzo Friulano Dolée '12	♟♟♟ 5
○ Friuli Isonzo Friulano Dolée '11	♟♟♟ 4*
○ Friuli Isonzo Sauvignon Piere '16	♟♟♟ 5
○ Friuli Isonzo Sauvignon Piere '15	♟♟♟ 5
○ Friuli Isonzo Sauvignon Piere '10	♟♟♟ 4*
○ Friuli Isonzo Sauvignon Piere '08	♟♟♟ 4*

Vigna del Lauro

LOC. MONTONA, 19
34071 CORMÒNS [GO]
TEL. +39 0481629549
www.vignadellauro.it

CELLAR SALES
PRE-BOOKED VISITS
ANNUAL PRODUCTION 60,000 bottles
HECTARES UNDER VINE 10.00

Vigna del Lauro came out of a project by Fabio Coser (already owner of a prestigious producer) in the late-20th century. He wanted to differentiate production so as to serve a market demand for simple, drinkable wines that are characteristic of the territory but also affordable. To that end he identified an old vineyard of Tocai Friulano surrounded almost entirely by old bay laurel trees (which inspired the winery's name). The project's success led to the acquisition of additional plots and a wider range of wines. Vigna del Lauro's selection draws on grapes cultivated both in the hills and the lowlands. In both cases the results score similarly, even if their Collio offerings regularly seem to go the extra mile. The Pinot Grigio and the Ribolla Gialla '18 lead the way, followed by a Friulano and Sauvignon of the same vintage. But their entire selection, both reds and whites, convince for their varietal correctness and drinkability.

○ Collio Friulano '18	🍷🍷 3
○ Collio Pinot Grigio '18	🍷🍷 3
○ Collio Sauvignon '18	🍷🍷 3
○ Friuli Isonzo Chardonnay '18	🍷🍷 2*
● Friuli Isonzo Merlot '17	🍷🍷 2*
○ Friuli Isonzo Traminer Aromatico '18	🍷🍷 2*
● Novaj Pinot Nero '16	🍷🍷 3
○ Ribolla Gialla '18	🍷🍷 3
● Friuli Isonzo Cabernet Franc '18	🍷 2
○ Friuli Isonzo Friulano '18	🍷 2
○ Collio Sauvignon '99	🍷🍷🍷 2*
○ Collio Friulano '17	🍷🍷 3
○ Collio Pinot Grigio '17	🍷🍷 3
○ Collio Sauvignon '17	🍷🍷 3
● Pinot Nero Novaj '15	🍷🍷 3
○ Ribolla Gialla '17	🍷🍷 3

Vigna Petrussa

VIA ALBANA, 47
33040 PREPOTTO [UD]
TEL. +39 0432713021
www.vignapetrussa.it

CELLAR SALES
PRE-BOOKED VISITS
ANNUAL PRODUCTION 30,000 bottles
HECTARES UNDER VINE 7.00

In 1995 Hilde Petrussa took over the reigns of the family business. It had been neglected for some time, and was falling short of its potential. A true lady of wine, she showed determination in facing the difficult challenge, trusting agronomic management and winemaking to experienced experts. When it came time to replant the estate's vineyards, they focused on native grape varieties, privileging Ribolla Nera, which gives rise to their Schioppettino. It's a wine whose name is bound up with Prepotto, an area that, thanks to Hilde and other winegrowers, is now recognized as a subzone. Some three Schioppettinos stood out during this year's tastings. The Prepotto Ris. '15 is the most firmly structured, while its 2016 counterpart proves more accessible and highly varietal. But it's the Richenza '17, a blend of Tocai Friulano, Riesling Renano, Malvasia Istriana and Picolit that leads their selection, offering up aromas of golden apple, wild flowers, honey and lavender.

○ Richenza '17	🍷🍷 4
○ FCO Friulano '18	🍷🍷 3
● FCO Schioppettino di Prepotto '16	🍷🍷 5
● FCO Schioppettino di Prepotto Ris. '15	🍷🍷 5
● FCO Schioppettino RiNera '17	🍷🍷 3
○ FCO Ribolla Gialla '18	🍷 3
○ COF Picolit '15	🍷🍷 6
○ COF Picolit '13	🍷🍷 6
○ FCO Friulano '17	🍷🍷 3
○ FCO Friulano '16	🍷🍷 3
○ FCO Ribolla Gialla '17	🍷🍷 3
● FCO Schioppettino di Prepotto '15	🍷🍷 5
● FCO Schioppettino RiNera '16	🍷🍷 3
● Refosco P. R. '16	🍷🍷 4
○ Richenza '16	🍷🍷 4
○ Richenza '15	🍷🍷 4

Vigna Traverso

VIA RONCHI, 73
33040 PREPOTTO [UD]
TEL. +39 0422804807
www.vignatraverso.it

CELLAR SALES
PRE-BOOKED VISITS
RESTAURANT SERVICE
ANNUAL PRODUCTION 100,000 bottles
HECTARES UNDER VINE 22.00
SUSTAINABLE WINERY

The winery founded by Giancarlo Traverso in 1998 is now managed by his son Stefano, a young but experienced vine grower. He's begun converting and reviving the oldest vineyards, collaborating with vine physiologist Stefano Zaninotti. Stefano is an innovator in practice but traditionalist in his heart. Indeed, the winery's historic concrete tanks still occupy an importance place in their new cellar, which integrates perfectly with the steep hillside. The Bianco Sottocastello '16 earned the best score, confirming its position at the top of their selection. It's a well-calibrated mix of Chardonnay and Sauvignon that features a complex, harmonious aromatic profile, and a fragrant, firmly-structured palate. Their excellent Rosso Troj '15, a blend of Merlot, Refosco dal Peduncolo Rosso and Schioppettino, is intriguing in its hints of Provence herbs and forest undergrowth.

○ FCO Bianco Sottocastello '16	▼▼	5
● FCO Rosso Troj '15	▼▼	4
● FCO Cabernet Franc '15	▼▼	4
○ FCO Friulano '18	▼▼	3
● FCO Refosco P. R. '15	▼▼	4
● FCO Rosso Sottocastello '15	▼▼	5
● FCO Schioppettino di Prepotto '15	▼▼	5
○ FCO Pinot Grigio '18	▼	3
○ FCO Sauvignon '18	▼	3
○ Ribolla Gialla Brut '18	▼	5
○ FCO Bianco Sottocastello '15	▽▽	5
○ FCO Friulano '17	▽▽	3
● FCO Refosco P. R. '14	▽▽	4
○ FCO Ribolla Gialla '17	▽▽	3
● FCO Rosso Sottocastello '13	▽▽	5
○ FCO Sauvignon '17	▽▽	3

★Le Vigne di Zamò

LOC. ROSAZZO
VIA ABATE CORRADO, 4
33044 MANZANO [UD]
TEL. +39 0432759693
www.levignedizamo.com

CELLAR SALES
PRE-BOOKED VISITS
ANNUAL PRODUCTION 280,000 bottles
HECTARES UNDER VINE 42.00
SUSTAINABLE WINERY

Vigne di Zamo is a historic brand that brings out the best of Rosazzo's well-known attributes. It was the last stop on Tullio Zamò's winemaking journey, before the legendary pioneer of Friuli wine went on to work with Oscar Farinetti's Fontanafredda. The change in management, which has been concluded for some time now, didn't affect the winery's philosophy at all. To the contrary, it served as an opportunity for consolidation and growth on international markets, a feat made possible thanks primarily to a highly distinct selection of wines. The Chardonnay Ronco Acacie '16 leads a high quality selection that does a nice job honoring this prestigious brand. On the nose it evokes aromas of medicinal herbs, Mediterranean scrub, candied citrus and bee's wax. On the palate it proves juicy, but supple and graceful. We also make note of their Rosso Ronco dei Roseti '16, a classic Bordeaux blend of Merlot and Cabernet, and their Pinot Bianco Tullio Zamò '16, an homage to their founder.

○ FCO Chardonnay Ronco delle Acacie '16	▼▼	7
○ FCO Pinot Bianco Tullio Zamò '16	▼▼	7
○ FCO Pinot Grigio '18	▼▼	5
○ FCO Ribolla Gialla '18	▼▼	5
● FCO Rosso Ronco dei Roseti '16	▼▼	8
○ FCO Sauvignon '18	▼▼	5
○ COF Friulano V. Cinquant'Anni '09	▽▽▽	5
○ COF Friulano V. Cinquant'Anni '08	▽▽▽	5
● COF Merlot V. Cinquant'Anni '09	▽▽▽	5
● COF Merlot V. Cinquant'Anni '06	▽▽▽	5
○ COF Tocai Friulano V. Cinquant'Anni '06	▽▽▽	5
○ FCO Friulano No Name '15	▽▽▽	5
○ Friuli Friulano No Name '16	▽▽▽	4*

Villa de Puppi

VIA ROMA, 5
33040 MOIMACCO [UD]
TEL. +39 0432722461
www.depuppi.it

CELLAR SALES
PRE-BOOKED VISITS
ANNUAL PRODUCTION 70,000 bottles
HECTARES UNDER VINE 25.00
SUSTAINABLE WINERY

In the small hamlet of Moimacco, just a stone's throw from Cividale del Friuli, the count de Puppi family oversee an agricultural business whose roots go back as far as anyone can remember. In 1991 Luigi de Puppi proceeded to reorganize the old vineyards so as to turn them over to his young children Caterina and Valfredo. Today it's mostly the dynamic Caterina who looks after things, having assumed responsibility both for winemaking and agronomic management. Most of their vineyards surround the main villa, but their best extend along the splendid hills of Rosazzo. Their diverse selection includes their prestigious Rosa Bosco offerings, and this year it was precisely the Merlot il Boscorosso '13 to lead the way, earning itself a position in our final tasting round. On the nose notes of quinine and licorice emerge amidst frequent whiffs of spices, dark chocolate and coffee, sensations that accompany the palate towards a lovely, balsamic finish.

● Il Boscorosso di Rosa Bosco Merlot '13	♟♟♟ 6
○ Blanc de Blancs Rosa Bosco	♟♟ 4
○ Chardonnay '17	♟♟ 3
○ Friuli Friulano '17	♟♟ 3
○ Friuli Pinot Grigio '17	♟♟ 3
● Refosco P. R. '15	♟♟ 3
○ Sauvignon '17	♟♟ 3
● Merlot '15	♟ 3
○ Ribolla Gialla '17	♟ 3
○ Ribolla Gialla Brut	♟ 3
● Merlot Il Boscorosso di Rosa Bosco '12	♟♟ 6
○ Pinot Grigio '16	♟♟ 3
● Refosco P.R. Cate '13	♟♟ 5
○ Ribolla Gialla di Rosa Bosco '15	♟♟ 4
○ Sauvignon '16	♟♟ 3
○ Sauvignon Blanc di Rosa Bosco '15	♟♟ 5

★★Villa Russiz

LOC. ITALIA
VIA RUSSIZ, 4/6
34070 CAPRIVA DEL FRIULI [GO]
TEL. +39 048180047
www.villarussiz.it

CELLAR SALES
PRE-BOOKED VISITS
ANNUAL PRODUCTION 220,000 bottles
HECTARES UNDER VINE 45.00
SUSTAINABLE WINERY

For many years now, the Villa Russiz brand has been synonymous with quality. Its selection of wines is known throughout the world for its consistently outstanding level craftsmanship. We like to remind readers that in the late 19th century, lacking any heirs, the count De La Tour family left their patrimony to a state institution that would support disadvantaged children. To that end, the Villa Russiz foundation continues to operate today, serving as a concrete example of how solidarity and viticulture can come together when the cause is enthusiastically supported by the right people. An excellent performance by their 2018s was accompanied by an equally outstanding Cabernet Sauvignon Dèfi de la Tour '13. It opens with Mediterranean notes of myrtle and rhubarb, then cloves, licorice and balsamic hints of eucalyptus. The Sauvignon de La Tour '18 enters on the tips of its toes, only to expand with explosive fragrance. The Malvasia '18 is highly floral, smooth, sophisticated and delicious, both on the nose and the palate.

○ Collio Malvasia '18	♟♟♟ 4*
● Collio Cabernet Sauvignon Défi de La Tour '13	♟♟ 8
○ Collio Sauvignon de La Tour '18	♟♟ 6
○ Collio Chardonnay '15	♟♟ 3
○ Collio Pinot Bianco '18	♟♟ 4
○ Collio Pinot Grigio '18	♟♟ 4
○ Collio Chardonnay Gräfin de La Tour '14	♟♟♟ 7
○ Collio Friulano '09	♟♟♟ 4*
Collio Merlot Graf de La Tour '94	♟♟♟ 4
○ Collio Pinot Bianco '16	♟♟♟ 4*
○ Collio Pinot Bianco '07	♟♟♟ 3
○ Collio Sauvignon de La Tour '08	♟♟♟ 5
Collio Sauvignon de La Tour '90	♟♟♟ 8
Collio Sauvignon de La Tour '89	♟♟♟ 8
○ Collio Tocai Friulano '95	♟♟♟ 3

Tenuta Villanova

LOC. VILLANOVA DI FARRA
VIA CONTESSA BERETTA, 29
34072 FARRA D'ISONZO [GO]
TEL. +39 0481889311
www.tenutavillanova.com

CELLAR SALES
PRE-BOOKED VISITS
ANNUAL PRODUCTION 400,000 bottles
HECTARES UNDER VINE 105.00

Tenuta Villanova's roots go back to 1499, making it one of the region's oldest producers. There are many charming historic anecdotes, for example, Louis Pasteur's visit in 1869 (when Alberto Levi owned the property), in which the famous frenchman had the chance to ascertain that the quality of Friuli's wines was in no way inferior to those of his homeland. Today the winery is led by Giuseppina Grossi Bennati, who's accompanied by her grandson Alberto in managing their sizable estate in the Collio and Friuli Isonzo appellations. This year we tasted their Fraia '13, a mature, powerful and structured blend of Merlot and Cabernet Sauvignon. It's redolent of wild berries, plums, dark tobacco, dark chocolate and coffee, sensations that reemerge on the palate all the way through its long finish. The rest of their selection was almost unanimously appreciated, though, understandably, their Collio offerings perform at a level that's a cut above the rest.

● Fraia '13		♟♟5
○ Collio Picolit Ronco Cucco '17		♟♟5
○ Collio Pinot Grigio Ronco Cucco '18		♟♟3
○ Collio Ribolla Gialla Ronco Cucco '18		♟♟3
● Friuli Isonzo Cabernet Franc '17		♟♟3
● Friuli Isonzo Merlot '17		♟♟3
○ Friuli Isonzo Chardonnay '18		♟2
○ Collio Chardonnay Monte Cucco '97		♟♟♟3*
○ Collio Friulano Ronco Cucco '17		♟♟4
○ Collio Friulano Ronco Cucco '16		♟♟4
○ Collio Picolit Ronco Cucco '15		♟♟5
○ Collio Pinot Grigio Ronco Cucco '17		♟♟3
○ Collio Sauvignon Ronco Cucco '16		♟♟4
○ Friuli Isonzo Friulano '17		♟♟3
● Friuli Isonzo Refosco P. R. '16		♟♟2*

Andrea Visintini

VIA GRAMOGLIANO, 27
33040 CORNO DI ROSAZZO [UD]
TEL. +39 0432755813
www.vinivisintini.com

CELLAR SALES
PRE-BOOKED VISITS
ANNUAL PRODUCTION 140,000 bottles
HECTARES UNDER VINE 35.00
VITICULTURE METHOD Certified Organic
SUSTAINABLE WINERY

For some time now, Oliviero Visintini, along with his sisters Cinzia and Palmira, oversee the family estate inherited from their father, Andrea. It's one of Corno di Rosazzo's most flourishing wineries, a true crown jewel of the Friuli Colli Orientali appellation. The property stands on the remains of the historic feudal castle of Gramogliano, a structure destroyed and rebuilt more than once. A splendid circular watchtower, built in 1560 and perfectly preserved, testifies to its ancient origins. It's the first time that we've tasted their new Amphora line of wines, which are worked in 800 liter terracotta containers from fermentation to bottling. Right out of the gate they've distinguished themselves as some of the producer's best offerings. In particular, we appreciate the Friulano '17, with its aromas of mature fruit, white chocolate and acacia honey, and a palate that delights the taste buds. But their Pignolo '13 also stood out, delivering herbaceous notes of forest undergrowth and hints of mature morello cherries, all supported by a bold structure.

○ FCO Friulano Amphora '17		♟♟4
○ FCO Friulano '18		♟♟2*
● FCO Pignolo Amphora '13		♟♟4
○ FCO Pinot Bianco '18		♟♟2*
○ FCO Sauvignon '18		♟♟2*
○ Friuli Pinot Grigio '18		♟♟2*
○ FCO Riesling '18		♟2
○ FCO Friulano '15		♟♟2*
○ FCO Friulano Toriòn '15		♟♟2*
○ FCO Pinot Bianco '16		♟♟2*
○ FCO Pinot Grigio '16		♟♟2*
● FCO Refosco P. R. '15		♟♟2*
○ FCO Ribolla Gialla '16		♟♟2*
○ FCO Sauvignon '16		♟♟2*
○ Malvasia '16		♟♟2*

★★Volpe Pasini

FRAZ. TOGLIANO
VIA CIVIDALE, 16
33040 TORREANO [UD]
TEL. +39 0432715151
www.volpepasini.it

CELLAR SALES
PRE-BOOKED VISITS
ACCOMMODATION
ANNUAL PRODUCTION 400,000 bottles
HECTARES UNDER VINE 52.00
SUSTAINABLE WINERY

By now Volpe Pasini doesn't just charm us, it amazes year after year. It's not just painstakingly maintained vineyards and ancient edifices returned to their former splendor. Over the last year Emilio and Alessandro Rotolo pushed their obsession with quality even further through technological upgrades both in the cellar and in the vineyard. Their investments are aimed at environmental sustainability and work safety, putting human well-being at the center of their project as well. This year their Volpe Pasini wines gave the more prestigious Zuc di Volpe line a run for its money. The small difference between them points up the quality work being done here, and the great value for the money you're getting with their wines. Nevertheless, their premium offerings prove a cut above the rest, with their captain, the Sauvignon Zuc di Volpe '18, handily earning Tre Bicchieri.

○ FCO Sauvignon Zuc di Volpe '18	♛♛♛ 5
○ FCO Friulano Zuc di Volpe '18	♛♛ 3*
● FCO Merlot Zuc di Volpe '15	♛♛ 4
○ FCO Pinot Bianco Zuc di Volpe '18	♛♛ 5
○ FCO Pinot Grigio Zuc di Volpe '18	♛♛ 4
○ FCO Ribolla Gialla Zuc di Volpe '18	♛♛ 4
○ FCO Chardonnay Volpe Pasini '18	♛♛ 3
○ FCO Pinot Grigio Grivò Volpe Pasini '18	♛♛ 3
● FCO Refosco P. R. Volpe Pasini '16	♛♛ 3
○ COF Pinot Bianco Zuc di Volpe '12	♛♛♛ 4*
○ COF Sauvignon Zuc di Volpe '13	♛♛♛ 4*
○ COF Sauvignon Zuc di Volpe '12	♛♛♛ 4*
○ COF Sauvignon Zuc di Volpe '11	♛♛♛ 4*
○ FCO Sauvignon Zuc di Volpe '17	♛♛♛ 5
○ FCO Sauvignon Zuc di Volpe '16	♛♛♛ 5
○ FCO Sauvignon Zuc di Volpe '15	♛♛♛ 5
○ FCO Sauvignon Zuc di Volpe '14	♛♛♛ 5

Francesco Vosca

FRAZ. BRAZZANO
VIA SOTTOMONTE, 19
34071 CORMÒNS [GO]
TEL. +39 048162135
www.voscavini.it

CELLAR SALES
PRE-BOOKED VISITS
ANNUAL PRODUCTION 60,000 bottles
HECTARES UNDER VINE 10.00
SUSTAINABLE WINERY

At Francesco Vosca's winery time seems to stand still. Proud of his agricultural roots, he's always keen to remind visitors that in the 1960s the territory experienced severe hardship. Many had to leave, but he, still a child, was forced to stay and work the field. Today he's joined by his son Gabriele, who's responsible for vinification. The avail themselves of vineyards both on the Collio hills and the Isonzo plains, which allows them to express the qualities of each of the two terroirs through their wines. More than once we've pointed out how Vosca pays equal attention to its lowland and hillside vineyards, as this round of tastings once again confirmed. If we had to express a preference, it would be for the Malvasia '18, one of their classic offerings. Hints of bay leaf, dried sage, rhubarb and honey emerge from its lovely aromatic weave, while on the palate it proves fragrant, juicy, pervasive and long.

○ Collio Friulano '18	♛♛ 3
○ Collio Malvasia '18	♛♛ 3
○ Collio Ribolla Gialla '18	♛♛ 3
○ Friuli Isonzo Pinot Grigio '18	♛♛ 3
○ Friuli Isonzo Sauvignon '18	♛♛ 3
○ Collio Friulano '17	♕♕ 3
○ Collio Friulano '16	♕♕ 3
○ Collio Malvasia '17	♕♕ 3
○ Collio Malvasia '16	♕♕ 3
● Collio Merlot '15	♕♕ 4
○ Collio Ribolla Gialla '17	♕♕ 3
○ Collio Ribolla Gialla '16	♕♕ 3
○ Friuli Isonzo Chardonnay '17	♕♕ 3
○ Friuli Isonzo Chardonnay '16	♕♕ 3
○ Friuli Isonzo Pinot Grigio '16	♕♕ 3
○ Friuli Isonzo Sauvignon '17	♕♕ 3

Zaglia

LOC. FRASSINUTTI
VIA CRESCENZIA, 10
33050 PRECENICCO [UD]
TEL. +39 0431510320
www.zaglia.com

CELLAR SALES
PRE-BOOKED VISITS
ANNUAL PRODUCTION 100,000 bottles
HECTARES UNDER VINE 15.00

Founded by Aldo Zaglia in 1970, the estate spans the municipalities of Precenicco and Pocenia, both situated in the Friuli Latisana appellation, an area with a centuries-old tradition of viticulture. In the early 1980s management was entrusted to Giorgio, who undertook major agronomic and enological changes aimed at the pursuit of quality while maintaining the utmost respect for the environment. Their vineyards are situated between the Stella and Tagliamento rivers, where the terrain is rich in clay and mineral salts. An early 20th-century farmhouse hosts their main facility, their cellar and guest accomodations. Their selection is diverse, to say the least, meeting every market need. Whites, rosés, reds and sparkling wines are all offered, and share in their linear profile, respect for their varietal characteristics, fragrance and, especially, drinkability. The cherry on top is their competitive prices which, in light of quality, are surely a boon to consumers.

○ Friuli Friulano '18	♟♟ 2*
● Friuli Merlot '18	♟♟ 2*
○ Friuli Pinot Grigio '18	♟♟ 2*
● Friuli Refosco P.R. '18	♟♟ 2*
● Friuli Cabernet Franc '18	♟ 2
○ Friuli Chardonnay '18	♟ 2
☉ Rosato '18	♟ 2
○ Solis Chardonnay	♟ 2
● FCO Cabernet Franc Amanti Ris. '15	♟♟ 2*
● FCO Cabernet Franc Amanti Ris. '14	♟♟ 2*
○ Friuli Chardonnay '16	♟♟ 2*
○ Friuli Friulano '17	♟♟ 2*
○ Friuli Friulano '16	♟♟ 2*
● Friuli Latisana Cabernet Franc V. degli Amanti Ris. '10	♟♟ 2*
● Friuli Merlot '17	♟♟ 2*
● Friuli Merlot '16	♟♟ 2*

Zidarich

LOC. PREPOTTO, 23
34011 DUINO AURISINA [TS]
TEL. +39 040201223
www.zidarich.it

CELLAR SALES
PRE-BOOKED VISITS
ANNUAL PRODUCTION 28,000 bottles
HECTARES UNDER VINE 8.00

It was 1988 when Beniamino Zidarich decided to revolutionize his father's winery in the heart of the Karst Plateau. After gradual expansion, it now comprises a sizable hectarage, especially considering the morphology of the terrain, which is rich in rock and lean in red earth. The cellar, which is entirely carved out of rock (a feat that only locals can do this well), maintains the cool temperatures of the undersoil, while from on high you can enjoy a splendid view of the Gulf of Trieste. Vitovska, Malvasia and Terrano are historic cultivars in Karst, thanks to their ability to hold up through drought and withstand violent blasts of northern winds. Beniamino dedicates a couple of interpretations to each, which often prove to be veritable works of art: marked, loud colors, complex and intriguing aromas, but especially unusual flavors, delicately salty with spicy, balsamic hints.

○ Malvasia Lehte '15	♟♟ 6
○ Vitovska '17	♟♟ 5
○ Vitovska Kamen '17	♟♟ 7
○ Malvasia '17	♟♟ 5
● Ruje '13	♟♟ 7
● Terrano '17	♟♟ 5
○ Carso Malvasia '09	♟♟♟ 5
○ Carso Malvasia '06	♟♟♟ 5
○ Carso Vitovska V. Collezione '09	♟♟♟ 8
○ Prulke '10	♟♟♟ 5
○ Prulke '08	♟♟♟ 5
○ Malvasia '16	♟♟ 5
○ Malvasia '15	♟♟ 5
○ Vitovska '16	♟♟ 5
○ Vitovska Kamen '16	♟♟ 7
○ Vitovska Kamen '14	♟♟ 7

Zorzettig

FRAZ. SPESSA
S.DA SANT'ANNA, 37
33043 CIVIDALE DEL FRIULI [UD]
TEL. +39 0432716156
www.zorzettigvini.it

CELLAR SALES
PRE-BOOKED VISITS
ACCOMMODATION
ANNUAL PRODUCTION 800,000 bottles
HECTARES UNDER VINE 115.00
SUSTAINABLE WINERY

Annalisa Zorzettig is a classic example of successful female entrepreneurship, while her brother Alessandro loves contact with nature and the silence of the vineyards. Together they oversee the winery founded by their father, Giuseppe. Back in 1986 he purchased the historic farmstead, settling in with his family and, in a short time, transforming it into a modern, operational producer. Even if they maintain a low profile that's in keeping with their agricultural roots, Annalisa and Alessandro have always aimed high and never lost sight of quality. The high number of wines submitted for tasting allows us a full overview of the producer's capacities. The wines of their Myò line, the result of careful grape selection, are a cut above the rest, naturally. In particular, we appreciated the Friulano '18, which landed in our final round of tastings. The 2018 version of the Pinot Bianco from the same line repeated last year's exploit and once again took home Tre Bicchieri.

○ FCO Pinot Bianco Myò '18	♟♟♟ 5
○ FCO Friulano Myò '18	♟♟ 5
○ FCO Malvasia Myò '18	♟♟ 5
○ FCO Pinot Bianco '18	♟♟ 3
○ FCO Ribolla Gialla Myò '18	♟♟ 5
● FCO Rosso Cunfins Segno di Terra '15	♟♟ 5
○ FCO Sauvignon Myò '18	♟♟ 5
● FCO Schioppettino '17	♟♟ 4
○ Optimum Ribolla Gialla Brut '18	♟♟ 4
○ FCO Chardonnay '18	♟ 3
○ FCO Donzel Segno di Terra '17	♟ 4
○ FCO Pinot Bianco Myò '17	♟♟♟ 4*
○ FCO Pinot Bianco Myò '16	♟♟♟ 4*
○ FCO Pinot Bianco Myò '15	♟♟♟ 4*
○ FCO Pinot Bianco Myò '14	♟♟♟ 4*

Zuani

LOC. GIASBANA, 12
34070 SAN FLORIANO DEL COLLIO [GO]
TEL. +39 0481391432
www.zuanivini.it

CELLAR SALES
PRE-BOOKED VISITS
ACCOMMODATION
ANNUAL PRODUCTION 75,000 bottles
HECTARES UNDER VINE 15.00

After a long stint in her father's winery, in 2001 Patrizia Felluga decided to go out on her own, getting her young children Antonio and Caterina involved as well. She identified an old vineyard clinging to the splendid slopes of San Floriano del Collio, in Giasbana, that's showered by the sun from morning to night, adopting its place name, Zuani, for her winery. The grapes cultivated give rise to a single wine, the Collio Bianco, an expression of the territory. It's an ambitious project that she's pursued for many years and that's now been enlarged with the creation of their Sodevo line. The Collio Bianco Zuani Vigne '18, a blend of equal parts Chardonnay, Pinot Grigio, Sauvignon and Tocai Friulano, confirms its title as leader of the pack and once again participated in our final tasting round. Its aromatic profile encompasses fruity notes of citrus, white peach and gooseberry, all rounded out with nuances of aromatic herbs. On the palate it proves rich and gratifying, exhibiting the perfect synergy of freshness, softness and sapidity.

○ Collio Bianco Zuani Vigne '18	♟♟ 4
○ Collio Bianco Zuani Ris. '16	♟♟ 5
○ Collio Ribolla Gialla Sodevo '18	♟♟ 3
○ Friuli Pinot Grigio Sodevo '18	♟♟ 3
○ Collio Bianco Zuani Vigne '10	♟♟♟ 3
○ Collio Bianco Zuani Vigne '07	♟♟♟ 3
○ Collio Bianco Zuani Ris. '15	♟♟ 5
○ Collio Bianco Zuani Ris. '14	♟♟ 5
○ Collio Bianco Zuani Ris. '13	♟♟ 5
○ Collio Bianco Zuani Ris. '12	♟♟ 5
○ Collio Bianco Zuani Vigne '17	♟♟ 4
○ Collio Bianco Zuani Vigne '16	♟♟ 4
○ Collio Bianco Zuani Vigne '15	♟♟ 4
○ Collio Bianco Zuani Vigne '14	♟♟ 4
○ Collio Ribolla Gialla '17	♟♟ 3
○ Friuli Pinot Grigio '17	♟♟ 3

Amandum

VIA F. PETRARCA, 40
34070 MORARO [GO]
TEL. +39 335242566
www.amandum.it

ANNUAL PRODUCTION 35,000 bottles
HECTARES UNDER VINE 2.00

○ Friuli Isonzo Chardonnay '17	♟♟ 4
○ Friuli Isonzo Friulano '17	♟♟ 4
○ Friuli Isonzo Pinot Bianco '17	♟♟ 4
○ Friuli Isonzo Sauvignon '17	♟♟ 4

Maurizio Arzenton

FRAZ. SPESSA
VIA CORMONS, 221
33043 CIVIDALE DEL FRIULI [UD]
TEL. +39 0432716139
www.arzentonvini.it

CELLAR SALES
PRE-BOOKED VISITS
ANNUAL PRODUCTION 30,000 bottles
HECTARES UNDER VINE 10.00

○ COF Picolit '15	♟♟ 6
○ FCO Chardonnay '18	♟♟ 3
○ FCO Friulano '18	♟♟ 3
○ FCO Sauvignon '18	♟♟ 3

Ascevi - Luwa

LOC. UCLANZI, 24
34070 SAN FLORIANO DEL COLLIO [GO]
TEL. +39 0481884140
www.asceviluwa.it

CELLAR SALES
PRE-BOOKED VISITS
ANNUAL PRODUCTION 200,000 bottles
HECTARES UNDER VINE 30.00

○ Collio Pinot Grigio Grappoli '18	♟♟ 4
○ Collio Sauvignon Ronco dei Sassi '18	♟♟ 3
○ Collio Chardonnay Rupis '18	♟ 4
○ Collio Ribolla Gialla '18	♟ 3

Attems

FRAZ. CAPRIVA DEL FRIULI
VIA AQUILEIA, 30
34070 GORIZIA
TEL. +39 0481806098
www.attems.it

CELLAR SALES
PRE-BOOKED VISITS
ANNUAL PRODUCTION 420,000 bottles
HECTARES UNDER VINE 44.00

○ Collio Sauvignon Cicinis '17	♟♟ 5
○ Chardonnay '18	♟♟ 3
○ Collio Pinot Grigio '18	♟♟ 2*
○ Collio Pinot Grigio Ramato '18	♟♟ 3

Bajta - Fattoria Carsica

VIA SALES, 108
34010 SGONICO [TS]
TEL. +39 0402296090
www.bajta.it

CELLAR SALES
PRE-BOOKED VISITS
ACCOMMODATION AND RESTAURANT SERVICE
ANNUAL PRODUCTION 30,000 bottles
HECTARES UNDER VINE 4.00

○ Malvasia '18	♟♟ 3
⊙ Mediterraneo Extra Brut M. CL.	♟♟ 4
⊙ Terra Roza Brut M. Cl.	♟♟ 4
○ Vitovska Ragionata '15	♟♟ 4

Baroni del Mestri

SALITA AL MONTE QUARIN, 22
34071 CORMÒNS [GO]
TEL. +39 040313177
www.baronidelmestri.it

ANNUAL PRODUCTION 10,000 bottles
HECTARES UNDER VINE 2.00

○ Collio Bianco '16	♟♟ 4
● Collio Rosso Barone di Schoenberg '16	♟♟ 4
○ Ribolla Gialla Extra Brut '18	♟♟ 3
⊙ Theresia Brut Rosé '18	♟♟ 3

La Bellanotte

S.DA DELLA BELLANOTTE, 3
34072 FARRA D'ISONZO [GO]
TEL. +39 0481888020
www.labellanotte.it

CELLAR SALES
PRE-BOOKED VISITS
ANNUAL PRODUCTION 100,000 bottles
HECTARES UNDER VINE 14.00

○ Collio Friulano '18	♟♟ 3
● Friuli Isonzo Merlot Rojadelsonzo '13	♟♟ 5
○ Conte Lucio Pinot Grigio Ramato '15	♟ 5
○ Friuli Pinot Grigio Armonico '18	♟ 2

Tenuta Beltrame

FRAZ. PRIVANO
LOC. ANTONINI, 4
33050 BAGNARIA ARSA [UD]
TEL. +39 0432923670
www.tenutabeltrame.it

CELLAR SALES
PRE-BOOKED VISITS
ANNUAL PRODUCTION 80,000 bottles
HECTARES UNDER VINE 25.00

○ Friuli Friulano '18	♟♟ 3
○ Friuli Pinot Grigio '18	♟♟ 3
● Friuli Merlot '16	♟ 3
● Pinot Nero '17	♟ 3

Bidoli

FRAZ. ARCANO SUPERIORE
VIA FORNACE, 19
33030 RIVE D'ARCANO [UD]
TEL. +39 0432810796
www.bidolivini.com

CELLAR SALES
PRE-BOOKED VISITS
ANNUAL PRODUCTION 1,000,000 bottles
SUSTAINABLE WINERY

○ Friuli Grave Friulano '18	♟♟ 2*
○ Friuli Grave Traminer Aromatico '18	♟♟ 2*
● Friuli Refosco P. R. '17	♟♟ 2*
○ Pinot Grigio '18	♟♟ 2*

Tenuta di Blasig

VIA ROMA, 63
34077 RONCHI DEI LEGIONARI [GO]
TEL. +39 0481475480
www.tenutadiblasig.it

CELLAR SALES
PRE-BOOKED VISITS
RESTAURANT SERVICE
ANNUAL PRODUCTION 80,000 bottles
HECTARES UNDER VINE 12.00

○ Friuli Isonzo Pinot Grigio '17	♟♟ 3
○ Friuli Isonzo Malvasia '17	♟ 3

Blason

LOC. BRUMA
VIA ROMA, 32
34072 GRADISCA D'ISONZO [GO]
TEL. +39 048192414
www.blasonwines.com

CELLAR SALES
PRE-BOOKED VISITS
ANNUAL PRODUCTION 60,000 bottles
HECTARES UNDER VINE 18.00

● Friuli Isonzo Bruma Rosso '16	♟♟ 4
○ Friuli Isonzo Friulano '18	♟♟ 2*
○ Malvasia '18	♟♟ 3
○ Ribolla Gialla '18	♟ 2

Borgo dei Sapori

S.DA DI PLANEZ, 60
33043 CIVIDALE DEL FRIULI [UD]
TEL. +39 0432732477
www.borgodeisapori.net

CELLAR SALES
PRE-BOOKED VISITS
ANNUAL PRODUCTION 27,000 bottles
HECTARES UNDER VINE 4.00
VITICULTURE METHOD Certified Organic

● FCO Cabernet Franc '17	♟♟ 3
○ FCO Friulano '17	♟♟ 2*
● FCO Sauvignon '17	♟♟ 3
● FCO Merlot '17	♟ 3

Borgo Magredo

Fraz. Tauriano
Via Basaldella, 5
33090 Spilimbergo [PN]
Tel. +39 0422864511
www.borgomagredo.it

CELLAR SALES
PRE-BOOKED VISITS
ANNUAL PRODUCTION 450,000 bottles
HECTARES UNDER VINE 105.00
SUSTAINABLE WINERY

○ Friuli Grave Pinot Grigio '18	♟♟ 2*
○ Friuli Grave Chardonnay '18	♟ 2
● Friuli Grave Merlot '18	♟ 2
○ Friuli Grave Sauvignon '18	♟ 2

Borgo Sant'Andrea

Fraz. Brazzacco
Via Sant'Andrea
33030 Moruzzo [UD]
Tel. +39 0432642015
www.borgosantandrea.com

CELLAR SALES
PRE-BOOKED VISITS
RESTAURANT SERVICE
ANNUAL PRODUCTION 30,000 bottles
HECTARES UNDER VINE 21.00

○ Friuli Chardonnay '17	♟♟ 3
○ Friuli Friulano '17	♟♟ 3
● Friuli Refosco P. R. '17	♟♟ 3
○ Prosecco Brut '17	♟♟ 2*

Tenuta Bosco Albano

Loc. Pasiano
Fraz. Cecchini
Via Bosco di Cecchini, 27B
33087 Pasiano di Pordenone [PN]
Tel. +39 0434628678
www.boscoalbano.com

CELLAR SALES
PRE-BOOKED VISITS
ACCOMMODATION
ANNUAL PRODUCTION 100,000 bottles
HECTARES UNDER VINE 45.00

○ Friuli Friulano '18	♟♟ 3
○ Pinot del Bosco Brut M. Cl.	♟♟ 4
○ Friuli Ribolla Gialla '18	♟ 3
○ Friuli Traminer Aromatico '18	♟ 3

Braidot

Loc. Versa
Via Palmanova, 20 B
34076 Romans d'Isonzo [GO]
Tel. +39 0481908970
www.braidotwines.it

CELLAR SALES
PRE-BOOKED VISITS
ANNUAL PRODUCTION 400,000 bottles
HECTARES UNDER VINE 60.00

○ Friuli Friulano '18	♟♟ 3
○ Friuli Pinot Grigio '18	♟♟ 3
○ Ribolla Gialla '18	♟♟ 2*

Ca' dei Faggi

Fraz. Raschiacco
Via Città di Nave, 10
33040 Faedis [UD]
Tel. +39 3207460693
www.cadeifaggi.it

PRE-BOOKED VISITS
ACCOMMODATION
ANNUAL PRODUCTION 100,000 bottles
HECTARES UNDER VINE 20.00

○ FCO Friulano Perabò '17	♟♟ 3
● FCO Refosco di Faedis '15	♟♟ 5
● FCO Rosso Tre Fadis Neri '16	♟♟ 5
○ FCO Sauvignon Perabò '17	♟♟ 3

I Clivi

Loc. Gramogliano, 20
33040 Corno di Rosazzo [UD]
Tel. +39 3287269979
www.iclivi.wine

CELLAR SALES
PRE-BOOKED VISITS
ANNUAL PRODUCTION 50,000 bottles
HECTARES UNDER VINE 12.00
VITICULTURE METHOD Certified Organic

○ FCO Verduzzo Friulano '17	♟♟ 4
○ Collio Friulano San Pietro '18	♟♟ 3
○ RBL Brut Nature '18	♟♟ 3
○ Ribolla Gialla '18	♟♟ 3

Cornium

VIA AQUILEIA, 79
33040 CORNO DI ROSAZZO [UD]
TEL. +39 0432755896
info@viniborgojudrio.it

CELLAR SALES
PRE-BOOKED VISITS
ANNUAL PRODUCTION 20,000 bottles
HECTARES UNDER VINE 12.00

○ FCO Malvasia '17	♟♟ 2*
○ FCO Friulano '17	♟♟ 2*
● FCO Refosco P. R. '16	♟♟ 2*
○ FCO Sauvignon '17	♟♟ 2*

La Cricca

LOC. CRAORETTO, 2
33040 PREPOTTO [UD]
TEL. +39 3275618717
www.vinilacricca.it

CELLAR SALES
PRE-BOOKED VISITS
ANNUAL PRODUCTION 4,000 bottles
HECTARES UNDER VINE 2.50
SUSTAINABLE WINERY

○ Busart '18	♟♟ 4
○ FCO Friulano '18	♟♟ 3
○ Pinot Bianco '18	♟ 4

Marina Danieli

VIA BELTRAME, 77
33042 BUTTRIO [UD]
TEL. +39 0432674421
www.marinadanieli.estate

ANNUAL PRODUCTION 100,000 bottles
HECTARES UNDER VINE 35.00

● FCO Merlot '16	♟♟ 4
○ FCO Pinot Grigio '16	♟♟ 3
● FCO Schioppettino '17	♟♟ 4
○ Feralta Bianco '17	♟♟ 3

Viticoltori Friulani La Delizia

VIA UDINE, 24
33072 CASARSA DELLA DELIZIA [PN]
TEL. +39 0434869564
www.ladelizia.com

CELLAR SALES
PRE-BOOKED VISITS
ANNUAL PRODUCTION 16,000,000 bottles
HECTARES UNDER VINE 1,950.00

○ Friuli Pinot Grigio Sass Ter' '18	♟♟ 2*
○ Friuli Refosco P. R. Sass Ter' '16	♟♟ 3
○ Jadèr Cuvée Brut	♟♟ 2
○ Ribolla Gialla Brut Naonis	♟♟ 2

Le Favole

LOC. TERRA ROSSA
VIA DIETRO CASTELLO, 7
33070 CANEVA [PN]
TEL. +39 0434735604
www.lefavole-wines.com

CELLAR SALES
PRE-BOOKED VISITS
ACCOMMODATION
ANNUAL PRODUCTION 70,000 bottles
HECTARES UNDER VINE 20.00

○ Friuli Friulano '18	♟♟ 2*
● Friuli Merlot '17	♟♟ 2*
○ Friuli Pinot Grigio '18	♟♟ 2*
○ Giallo di Roccia Brut	♟♟ 4

Flaibani

VIA CASALI COSTA, 7
33043 CIVIDALE DEL FRIULI [UD]
TEL. +39 0432730943
www.flaibani.it

CELLAR SALES
PRE-BOOKED VISITS
ANNUAL PRODUCTION 10,000 bottles
HECTARES UNDER VINE 3.50
VITICULTURE METHOD Certified Organic
SUSTAINABLE WINERY

○ FCO Bianco Riviere '17	♟♟ 4
● FCO Cabernet Franc '15	♟♟ 5
⊙ FCO Pinot Grigio '17	♟♟ 4
● Tentazione '12	♟♟ 5

Foffani

FRAZ. CLAUIANO
P.ZZA GIULIA, 13
33050 TRIVIGNANO UDINESE [UD]
TEL. +39 0432999584
www.foffani.com

CELLAR SALES
PRE-BOOKED VISITS
ACCOMMODATION AND RESTAURANT SERVICE
ANNUAL PRODUCTION 80,000 bottles
HECTARES UNDER VINE 10.00
SUSTAINABLE WINERY

○ Friuli Pinot Grigio Sup. '18	🍷🍷 3
○ Friuli Sauvignon Sup. '18	🍷🍷 3
○ Friuli Friulano '18	🍷 3
○ Merlot Bianco '18	🍷 3

Forchir

LOC. CASALI BIANCHINI
33030 CAMINO AL TAGLIAMENTO [UD]
TEL. +39 0432821525
www.forchir.it

CELLAR SALES
PRE-BOOKED VISITS
ANNUAL PRODUCTION 1,200,000 bottles
HECTARES UNDER VINE 240.00
VITICULTURE METHOD Certified Organic
SUSTAINABLE WINERY

○ Ethos '18	🍷🍷 2*
○ Friuli Grave Pinot Bianco Maraveis '17	🍷🍷 3
○ Friuli Grave Traminer Aromatico Glère '18	🍷🍷 2*
● Refoscone Refosco P. R. '15	🍷🍷 3

Fossa Mala

VIA BASSI, 81
33080 FIUME VENETO [PN]
TEL. +39 0434957997
www.fossamala.it

CELLAR SALES
PRE-BOOKED VISITS
ACCOMMODATION AND RESTAURANT SERVICE
ANNUAL PRODUCTION 130,000 bottles
HECTARES UNDER VINE 37.00

● Friuli Grave Merlot Refossa '16	🍷🍷 2*
○ Friuli Grave Pinot Grigio '18	🍷🍷 2*
○ Friuli Grave Sauvignon Refossa '18	🍷🍷 2*
○ Friuli Grave Traminer Aromatico '18	🍷🍷 2*

Humar

LOC. VALERISCE, 20
34070 SAN FLORIANO DEL COLLIO [GO]
TEL. +39 0481884197
www.humar.it

CELLAR SALES
PRE-BOOKED VISITS
ANNUAL PRODUCTION 60,000 bottles
HECTARES UNDER VINE 12.00

● Collio Cabernet Franc '17	🍷🍷 3
● Collio Cabernet Franc Rogoves '15	🍷🍷 4
○ Collio Ribolla Gialla '18	🍷🍷 3
○ Collio Sauvignon '18	🍷🍷 2*

Isola Augusta

VIA CASALI ISOLA AUGUSTA, 4
33056 PALAZZOLO DELLO STELLA [UD]
TEL. +39 043158046
www.isolaugusta.com

CELLAR SALES
PRE-BOOKED VISITS
ACCOMMODATION AND RESTAURANT SERVICE
ANNUAL PRODUCTION 270,000 bottles
HECTARES UNDER VINE 65.00
SUSTAINABLE WINERY

○ Friuli Latisana Chardonnay Les Iles '16	🍷🍷 4
○ Chardì Extra Brut	🍷🍷 3
○ Friuli Friulano '18	🍷🍷 3
● Schioppettino '18	🍷🍷 3

Rado Kocjancic

FRAZ. DOLINA
VIA DOLINA, 528
34018 SAN DORLIGO DELLA VALLE [TS]
TEL. +39 3483063298
www.radokocjancic.eu

CELLAR SALES
PRE-BOOKED VISITS
ANNUAL PRODUCTION 15,000 bottles
HECTARES UNDER VINE 5.00

○ Carso Bianco Brejanka '15	🍷🍷 5
○ Carso Malvasia '17	🍷🍷 2*
○ Carso Vitovska '17	🍷🍷 3
○ Pasik '15	🍷🍷 4

Lupinc

FRAZ. PREPOTTO, 11B
34011 DUINO AURISINA [TS]
TEL. +39 040200848

CELLAR SALES
PRE-BOOKED VISITS
ANNUAL PRODUCTION 15,000 bottles
HECTARES UNDER VINE 3.00

○ Malvasia '17	♟♟ 3*
○ Stara Brajda '17	♟♟ 3
○ Vitovska '17	♟♟ 3
● Terrano '16	♟ 3

Mulino delle Tolle

FRAZ. SEVEGLIANO
VIA MULINO DELLE TOLLE, 15
33050 BAGNARIA ARSA [UD]
TEL. +39 0432924723
www.mulinodelletolle.it

CELLAR SALES
PRE-BOOKED VISITS
ACCOMMODATION AND RESTAURANT SERVICE
ANNUAL PRODUCTION 100,000 bottles
HECTARES UNDER VINE 22.00

○ Friuli Aquileia Friulano '18	♟♟ 3
○ Friuli Aquileia Malvasia '18	♟♟ 3
● Friuli Aquileia Refosco P. R. '16	♟♟ 3
● Friuli Aquileia Rosso Sabellius '16	♟♟ 3

Cantina Odoni

FRAZ. LONGERA
34100 TRIESTE
TEL. +39 3409317794
www.cantinaodoni.com

CELLAR SALES
PRE-BOOKED VISITS
RESTAURANT SERVICE
ANNUAL PRODUCTION 50,000 bottles
HECTARES UNDER VINE 6.00

○ Aurum Quindici Giorni	♟♟ 5
● Lignum ruber	♟♟ 5
○ Malvasia '18	♟♟ 3
○ Vitovska '18	♟♟ 3

Monviert

VIA STRADA DI SPESSA, 8
33043 CIVIDALE DEL FRIULI [UD]
TEL. +39 0432716172
www.monviert.com

CELLAR SALES
PRE-BOOKED VISITS
ANNUAL PRODUCTION 400,000 bottles
HECTARES UNDER VINE 70.00
SUSTAINABLE WINERY

○ FCO Friulano Martagona '18	♟♟ 2*
○ FCO Ribolla Gialla '18	♟♟ 2*
○ FCO Ribolla Gialla Martagona '18	♟♟ 3
○ FCO Sauvignon '18	♟♟ 2*

Obiz

B.GO GORTANI, 2
33052 CERVIGNANO DEL FRIULI [UD]
TEL. +39 043131900
www.obiz.it

CELLAR SALES
PRE-BOOKED VISITS
ANNUAL PRODUCTION 100,000 bottles
HECTARES UNDER VINE 40.00
SUSTAINABLE WINERY

● Friuli Aquileia Refosco P. R. Teodoro '17	♟♟ 2*
○ Friuli Friulano '18	♟♟ 2*
○ Natissa Bianco '17	♟♟ 3
○ Friuli Ribolla Gialla '18	♟ 2

Ostrouska

LOC. SAGRADO, 1

34010 SGONICO [TS]
TEL. +39 0402296672
www.ostrouska.it

ANNUAL PRODUCTION 5,000 bottles
HECTARES UNDER VINE 1.50

○ Carpe Diem Brut	♟♟ 4
○ Malvasia '17	♟♟ 5
○ Vitovska '17	♟♟ 5
● Terrano '17	♟ 5

Parovel

LOC. CARESANA, 81
34018 SAN DORLIGO DELLA VALLE [TS]
TEL. +39 040227050
www.parovel.com

ANNUAL PRODUCTION 35,000 bottles
HECTARES UNDER VINE 11.00
SUSTAINABLE WINERY

○ Carso Vitovska '11	🍷🍷 3*
○ Carso Malvasia '12	🍷🍷 3
● Refosco P. R. Imà '12	🍷🍷 5
○ Visavì '16	🍷🍷 3

Piè di Mont

LOC. PIEDIMONTE DEL CALVARIO
VIA MONTE CALVARIO, 30
34170 GORIZIA
TEL. +39 0481391338
www.piedimont.it

CELLAR SALES
PRE-BOOKED VISITS
ANNUAL PRODUCTION 10,000 bottles
HECTARES UNDER VINE 1.20

○ Piè di Mont Brut '15	🍷🍷 6

Pighin

FRAZ. RISANO
V.LE GRADO, 11/1
33050 PAVIA DI UDINE [UD]
TEL. +39 0432675444
www.pighin.com

CELLAR SALES
PRE-BOOKED VISITS
ANNUAL PRODUCTION 800,000 bottles
HECTARES UNDER VINE 160.00
SUSTAINABLE WINERY

○ Collio Chardonnay '18	🍷🍷 3
○ Collio Malvasia '18	🍷🍷 3
○ Collio Pinot Grigio '18	🍷🍷 3
○ Collio Ribolla Gialla '18	🍷 3

Tenuta Pinni

VIA SANT' OSVALDO, 3
33098 SAN MARTINO AL TAGLIAMENTO [PN]
TEL. +39 0434899464
www.tenutapinni.com

CELLAR SALES
PRE-BOOKED VISITS
ANNUAL PRODUCTION 27,000 bottles
HECTARES UNDER VINE 27.00
SUSTAINABLE WINERY

● Cabernet Sauvignon '16	🍷🍷 2*
○ Chardonnay '18	🍷🍷 2*
○ Sauvignon '18	🍷🍷 2*
○ Traminer Aromatico '18	🍷🍷 2*

Flavio Pontoni

VIA PERUZZI, 8
33042 BUTTRIO [UD]
TEL. +39 0432674352
www.pontoni.it

CELLAR SALES
PRE-BOOKED VISITS
ACCOMMODATION
ANNUAL PRODUCTION 30,000 bottles
HECTARES UNDER VINE 4.50

● FCO Cabernet Sauvignon '17	🍷🍷 2*
○ FCO Chardonnay '18	🍷🍷 2*
○ FCO Friulano '18	🍷🍷 2*
○ FCO Malvasia '18	🍷🍷 2*

Teresa Raiz

LOC. MARSURE DI SOTTO
VIA DELLA ROGGIA, 22
33040 POVOLETTO [UD]
TEL. +39 0432679556
www.teresaraiz.it

CELLAR SALES
PRE-BOOKED VISITS
ANNUAL PRODUCTION 80,000 bottles
HECTARES UNDER VINE 11.50

○ FCO Pinot Grigio '18	🍷🍷 3
○ FCO Ribolla Gialla '18	🍷🍷 3
● FCO Rosso Decano '16	🍷🍷 5
○ Friuli Chardonnay '18	🍷🍷 3

Reguta

VIA BASSI, 16
33050 POCENIA [UD]
TEL. +39 0432779157
www.reguta.it

CELLAR SALES
PRE-BOOKED VISITS
ACCOMMODATION AND RESTAURANT SERVICE
ANNUAL PRODUCTION 2,000,000 bottles
HECTARES UNDER VINE 277.00

● Altropasso Rosso '17	❦❦ 4
○ Collio Sauvignon '18	❦❦ 4
○ Prediale '18	❦❦ 4
○ Collio Ribolla Gialla '18	❦ 4

Ronco dei Pini

VIA RONCHI, 93
33040 PREPOTTO [UD]
TEL. +39 0432713239
www.roncodeipini.it

CELLAR SALES
PRE-BOOKED VISITS
ANNUAL PRODUCTION 90,000 bottles
HECTARES UNDER VINE 15.00

○ FCO Friulano '18	❦❦ 3
● FCO Merlot '17	❦❦ 3
○ FCO Sauvignon '18	❦❦ 5
● FCO Schioppettino di Prepotto '16	❦❦ 5

Ronco Margherita

VIA XX SETTEMBRE, 106A
33094 PINZANO AL TAGLIAMENTO [PN]
TEL. +39 0432950845
www.roncomargherita.it

CELLAR SALES
PRE-BOOKED VISITS
ANNUAL PRODUCTION 150,000 bottles
HECTARES UNDER VINE 36.00
SUSTAINABLE WINERY

○ Friuli Friulano '18	❦❦ 3
● Friuli Refosco P. R. '16	❦❦ 3
● Ovalis '16	❦❦ 4

Russolo

VIA SAN ROCCO, 58A
33080 SAN QUIRINO [PN]
TEL. +39 0434919577
www.russolo.it

CELLAR SALES
PRE-BOOKED VISITS
ANNUAL PRODUCTION 165,000 bottles
HECTARES UNDER VINE 16.00
SUSTAINABLE WINERY

○ Chardonnay '18	❦❦ 3
● Refosco P.R. Collezione '16	❦❦ 3
○ Ribolla Gialla '18	❦❦ 3
○ Pinot Grigio '18	❦ 3

San Simone

LOC. RONDOVER
VIA PRATA, 30
33080 PORCIA [PN]
TEL. +39 0434578633
www.sansimone.it

CELLAR SALES
PRE-BOOKED VISITS
ANNUAL PRODUCTION 900,000 bottles
HECTARES UNDER VINE 85.00
SUSTAINABLE WINERY

● Friuli Grave Cabernet Sauvignon Nexus Ris. '16	❦❦ 4
● Friuli Grave Merlot Evante Ris. '16	❦❦ 4
○ Friuli Grave Pinot Grigio '18	❦❦ 3

Scarbolo

FRAZ. LAUZACCO
V.LE GRADO, 4
33050 PAVIA DI UDINE [UD]
TEL. +39 0432675612
www.scarbolo.com

CELLAR SALES
PRE-BOOKED VISITS
RESTAURANT SERVICE
ANNUAL PRODUCTION 200,000 bottles
HECTARES UNDER VINE 28.00
SUSTAINABLE WINERY

● Campo del Viotto Merlot '15	❦❦ 4
○ Friuli Grave Chardonnay Lara '16	❦❦ 4
○ Friuli Pinot Grigio '18	❦❦ 3
○ Friuli Pinot Grigio Mattia '15	❦❦ 4

Ferruccio Sgubin

VIA MERNICO, 8
34070 DOLEGNA DEL COLLIO [GO]
TEL. +39 048160452
www.ferrucciosgubin.it

CELLAR SALES
PRE-BOOKED VISITS
ANNUAL PRODUCTION 100,000 bottles
HECTARES UNDER VINE 20.00

○ Collio Friulano '18	♟♟ 3
○ Collio Pinot Bianco '18	♟♟ 3
○ Collio Ribolla Gialla '18	♟♟ 3
● Mirnik '16	♟♟ 4

Tarlao

VIA SAN ZILI, 41
33051 AQUILEIA [UD]
TEL. +39 043191417
www.tarlao.eu

CELLAR SALES
PRE-BOOKED VISITS
ANNUAL PRODUCTION 18,000 bottles
HECTARES UNDER VINE 5.00

○ Friuli Aquileia Malvasia Ninive '18	♟♟ 3
○ Friuli Aquileia Pinot Bianco Poc ma Bon '18	♟♟ 3
○ Friuli Aquileia Sauvignon Giona '18	♟♟ 3

Terre del Faet

FRAZ. FAET
V.LE ROMA, 82
34071 CORMÒNS [GO]
TEL. +39 3470103325
www.terredelfaet.it

CELLAR SALES
PRE-BOOKED VISITS
ANNUAL PRODUCTION 24,000 bottles
HECTARES UNDER VINE 4.50

○ Collio Bianco del Faet '17	♟♟ 3*
○ Collio Friulano '18	♟♟ 3
○ Collio Malvasia '18	♟♟ 3
○ Collio Pinot Bianco '18	♟♟ 3

Valle

VIA NAZIONALE, 3
33042 BUTTRIO [UD]
TEL. +39 0432674289
www.valle.it

CELLAR SALES
PRE-BOOKED VISITS
ANNUAL PRODUCTION 150,000 bottles
HECTARES UNDER VINE 20.00

● FCO Cabernet Ris. '13	♟♟ 4
○ FCO Friulano San Blâs '18	♟♟ 3
○ FCO Sauvignon '18	♟♟ 3
○ Ribolla Gialla Brut	♟ 3

Venchiarezza

VIA UDINE, 100
33043 CIVIDALE DEL FRIULI [UD]
TEL. +39 3496829576
www.venchiarezza.it

ANNUAL PRODUCTION 50,000 bottles
HECTARES UNDER VINE 8.00

● Refosco P. R. '17	♟♟ 3
○ Vigna del Tempo '18	♟♟ 3
○ Friuli Pinot Grigio Grey e Rosé '18	♟ 3
● Merlot '17	♟ 3

Villa Parens

VIA DANTE, 69
34072 FARRA D'ISONZO [GO]
TEL. +39 0481888198
www.villaparens.com

CELLAR SALES
PRE-BOOKED VISITS
ANNUAL PRODUCTION 50,000 bottles
HECTARES UNDER VINE 6.00

○ Gran Noir Dosage Zero M. Cl. '13	♟♟ 5
○ Ribolla Gialla Privé '15	♟♟ 6
⊙ Rosé de Noirs Dosage Zero M. Cl. '15	♟♟ 6
● Pinot Nero '17	♟ 4

EMILIA ROMAGNA

There's nothing like traveling through Emilia when it comes to appreciating the territory's wealth of producers, which vary drastically from province to province, from the Piacenza hills to those of Bologna and the vast lands of Lambrusco. If Bologna is by now well-established in the production of Pignoletto, in all its forms (with sub-zones and expansion of the appellation), in Piacenza the most interesting things are happening with Malvasia di Candia Aromatica and Metodo Classico, which shouldn't surprise given its proximity to Oltrepò Pavese. When it comes to Gutturnio, as long as there is a semi-sparkling version (more traditional) and still version (both of which can be quite interesting when done well), it will be difficult to promote it effectively, especially in light of the consortium's chronic absence. On the Parma hills things are a bit more of a patchwork, with international grapes accompanied by native cultivars — some producers are doing good work, but there's a lack of a single, coherent vision. Such a vision is certainly not lacking in Lambrusco, Reggio Emilia and, especially, Modena, where it's Sorbara (albeit 2018 wasn't a great year) playing a leading role, bringing together large-scale producers and small, family-run wineries. This dialectical and complementary relationship between the territory's diverse set of producers (diverse especially in terms of volume and size) is, obviously, also a part of its identity. Large groups working alongside medium-small businesses, at times minuscule, makes for a colorful situation that's moving forward in all respects. We're in full-blown Sangiovese wine country — it's indisputable that for some years now many ideas and efforts have centered on this great cultivar, such that the region is now a detailed map of geographic mentions, which some of the region's most interesting producers rely on. Swapping out maps for bottles, it's increasingly clear the various directions and shifts that are taking place (while maintaining a solid, common base, obviously). Many other grapes, some rare indigenous varieties, some almost forgotten until a few years ago, some international, are also established in the region. It's worth mentioning among its increasingly widespread white grapes the growing popularity of Albana and the intriguing Rebola.

Ancarani

FRAZ. ORIOLO
VIA SAN BIAGIO ANTICO, 14
48018 FAENZA [RA]
TEL. +39 3338314188
www.viniancarani.it

CELLAR SALES
PRE-BOOKED VISITS
RESTAURANT SERVICE
ANNUAL PRODUCTION 30,000 bottles
HECTARES UNDER VINE 14.00

Claudio Ancarani and his wife Rita Babini are key players in one of the most intriguing, original and highly artisanal wineries in Romagna. It is located in Torre di Oriolo, near Faenza, an area known for quality wine production, especially using traditional grapes. Work in the vineyard respects nature and organic protocols as much as possible, with only copper and sulfur used for treatments. This is carried over into the cellar, where intervention is kept to a minimum to safeguard grapes and vintages. It was something of an off year for Ancarani's wines, amidst absences and underperforming contenders. In the end their best offerings seemed to be two whites made with native cultivars: their Albana Sânta Lusa 2016 is delicately iodine, with an iron nuance on the palate, somewhere between mineral and gratifying sensations of ripe fruit. The finish comes through tannic and flavorful with nice acidity. The Famoso Signore '18 is made with white grapes of the same name.

○ Famoso Signore '18	⚏⚏ 3
○ Romagna Albana Secco Sânta Lusa '16	⚏⚏ 4
● Romagna Sangiovese Sup. Biagio Antico '16	⚏⚏⚏ 2*
● Centesimino '17	⚏⚏ 3
○ Famoso Signore '17	⚏⚏ 2*
○ Romagna Albana Secco Sânta Lusa '15	⚏⚏ 3
○ Romagna Albana Secco Sânta Lusa '14	⚏⚏ 3
● Romagna Sangiovese Sup. Biagio Antico '15	⚏⚏ 2*
● Sangiovese di Romagna Oriolo '16	⚏⚏ 2*
● Sangiovese di Romagna Oriolo '15	⚏⚏ 2*
● Uvappesa Centesimino '12	⚏⚏ 4

Francesco Bellei & C.

FRAZ. CRISTO DI SORBARA
VIA NAZIONALE, 132
41030 BOMPORTO [MO]
TEL. +39 059902009
www.francescobellei.it

CELLAR SALES
PRE-BOOKED VISITS
ANNUAL PRODUCTION 70,000 bottles
HECTARES UNDER VINE 103.00

Francesco Bellei's winery, right at the heart of Cristo di Sorbara, is an unusual one. Giuseppe Bellei, a great Champagne enthusiast, planted Pinot Nero and Chardonnay here in the 1970s, with the aim of producing a Metodo Classico sparkler. Thirty years on, traditional grapes, such as Sorbara and Pignoletto, are also being bottle-fermented, using the Ancestral Method without disgorgement. The Cavicchioli family have now owned it for some years and Sandro Cavicchioli personally oversees winemaking. The Nature '15 is a Metodo Classico with plenty of substance. Redolent of white flowers, vanilla and tropical fruit, it's mature and fresh, with delicate, creamy bead and a long finish. Their Cuvée Rosso '11 moves on a different track. It's more evolved, with aromas of cake and mature fruit. On the palate it's elegant and complex, with verve and assertiveness. The Cuvée Rosso '16, made entirely with Sorbara, offers up fragrances of citrus and pomegranate, with slightly vegetal notes. In the mouth it's supported by notable personality.

○ Brut Nature M. Cl. '15	⚏⚏ 6
○ Brut M. Cl. Cuvée Speciale '11	⚏⚏ 6
⊙ Brut Rosé M. Cl. '15	⚏⚏ 6
● Brut Rosso M. Cl. '16	⚏⚏ 4
● Blanc de Noirs Brut M. Cl. '12	⚏ 6
⊙ Lambrusco Ancestrale '17	⚏ 3
⊙ Cuvée Brut M. Cl. Rosé '14	⚏⚏ 5
⊙ Cuvée Brut Rosé M.Cl. '12	⚏⚏ 5
● Cuvée Brut Rosso M. Cl. '14	⚏⚏ 3*
● Lambrusco di Modena Rifermentazione Ancestrale '15	⚏⚏ 3*
● Modena Lambrusco Rifermentazione Ancestrale '16	⚏⚏ 3
● Modena Pignoletto Rifermentazione Ancestrale '15	⚏⚏ 3

Stefano Berti

LOC. RAVALDINO IN MONTE
VIA LA SCAGNA, 18
47121 FORLÌ
TEL. +39 0543488074
www.stefanoberti.it

CELLAR SALES
PRE-BOOKED VISITS
ANNUAL PRODUCTION 40,000 bottles
HECTARES UNDER VINE 6.00

The winery came into being in 1963 with the purchase of two farms in Ravaldino in Monte, in the hills near Forlì. At the end of the 1960s, the first two hectares of Sangiovese were planted; then in 1982, Stefano Berti, who currently runs the show, arrived on the scene. This was a turning point for the winery which would lead to a radical transformation. Today it is one of the most important wineries for quality and style in Predappio, an interesting terroir that is currently gaining awareness. The Calisto Ris. '15 is a Predappio Sangiovese that's charming to say the least, despite the fact that it's anything but easy. Aromatically it's in perfect keeping with its pronounced tertiaries, but after a few minutes it intrigues. On the palate it removes any doubt, proving extremely flavorful and lively, as tight as it is rich in flavor. The Ravaldo '17 is more open and airy, the Bartimeo '17 more streamlined.

● Romagna Sangiovese Predappio Calisto Ris. '15	♟ 4
● Romagna Sangiovese Bartimeo '17	♟♟ 2*
● Romagna Sangiovese Predappio Ravaldo '17	♟♟ 3
● Romagna Sangiovese Nonà '18	♟ 3
● Romagna Sangiovese Sup. Bartimeo '16	♟♟♟ 2*
● Sangiovese di Romagna Sup. Calisto '01	♟♟♟ 4
● Romagna Sangiovese Bartimeo '15	♟♟ 2*
● Romagna Sangiovese Predappio Ravaldo '15	♟♟ 2*
● Romagna Sangiovese Sup. Nonà '16	♟♟ 2*
● Romagna Sangiovese Sup. Nonà '15	♟♟ 2*

Ca' di Sopra

LOC. MARZENO
VIA FELIGARA, 15
48013 BRISIGHELLA [RA]
TEL. +39 3284927073
www.cadisopra.com

CELLAR SALES
PRE-BOOKED VISITS
ANNUAL PRODUCTION 30,000 bottles
HECTARES UNDER VINE 28.00
SUSTAINABLE WINERY

Ca' di Sopra, located in Marzeno, in the foothills of Faenza, was founded in the late 1960s. The soils are calcareous-clay, while elevations skim 240 meters above sea level. The winery has belonged to the Montanari family since its foundation and underwent decisive modernization in the early 2000s. The wines, with their clear style and precise winemaking, are the jewel in the crown of this medium-small, family-run, artisan winery. The 2018 version of their Albana Secco Sandrona delivered, impressing for its finesse and energy, elegance and lively flavor. Aromas of yellow fruit and dried lemon give way to an elegant mouth marked by fine, flavorful tannins. The Romagna Sangiovese Superiore Crepe '18 is rich, lush and full-bodied, offering up aromas of dark fruit with an herbaceous touch.

○ Romagna Albana Secco Sandrona '18	♟♟ 3*
● Romagna Sangiovese Sup. Crepe '18	♟♟ 2*
● Remel '16	♟ 3
○ Uait '18	♟ 2
○ Romagna Albana Secco '15	♟♟ 3
○ Romagna Albana Secco Sandrona '17	♟♟ 3
● Romagna Sangiovese Marzeno '15	♟♟ 3
● Romagna Sangiovese Marzeno Cà del Rosso '15	♟♟ 3
● Romagna Sangiovese Sup. Crepe '17	♟♟ 2*
● Romagna Sangiovese Sup. Crepe '15	♟♟ 2*
● Sangiovese di Romagna Marzeno Cadisopra Ris. '11	♟♟ 4

Cantina della Volta

VIA PER MODENA, 82
41030 BOMPORTO [MO]
TEL. +39 0597473312
www.cantinadellavolta.com

CELLAR SALES
PRE-BOOKED VISITS
ANNUAL PRODUCTION 130,000 bottles
HECTARES UNDER VINE 16.00
VITICULTURE METHOD Certified Organic

Now in its fourth generation, this family has been producing Lambrusco di Sorbara in Bomporto since 1920. Christian Bellei set up his winery with some friends in 2010, on the strength of experience and expertise gained on his family's estate. His main aim was to produce high-level, bottle-fermented Lambrusco and he seems to have hit the bullseye, given the quality and personality of his wines. Their Prima Volta '15 is a Metodo Classico made with Lambrusco di Sorbara harvested by hand in cases. It's a blush color, and features aromas of small wild berries, wild flowers and aromatic herbs, while in the mouth citrusy sensations emerge. Their Rimosso is a highly characteristic wine, fragrant in its notes of wild strawberries, sapid and supple on the palate. And there's not just Lambrusco. The Mattaglio Blanc de Blancs '13, a monovarietal made with Chardonnay cultivated at 650 meters elevation, is redolent of flowers and mature tropical fruit.

⊙ La Prima Volta Brut Rosé M. Cl. '15	🍷🍷 5
● Lambrusco di Sorbara Rimosso	🍷🍷 3
○ Il Mattaglio Blanc de Blancs Brut M. Cl. '13	🍷 6
⊙ Lambrusco di Modena Brut Rosé M. Cl. '13	🍷🍷🍷 5
⊙ Lambrusco di Modena Brut Rosé M. Cl. '12	🍷🍷🍷 5
● Lambrusco di Modena Brut M. Cl. Trentasei '13	🍷🍷 4
● Lambrusco di Modena Brut M. Cl. Trentasei '12	🍷🍷 4
⊙ Lambrusco di Sorbara Brut Rosé M. Cl. '14	🍷🍷 5
● Lambrusco di Sorbara Brut Trentasei M. Cl. '14	🍷🍷 4
● Lambrusco di Sorbara Secco Rimosso '15	🍷🍷 3*

Cantina di Santa Croce

FRAZ. SANTA CROCE
S.DA ST.LE 468 DI CORREGGIO, 35
41012 CARPI [MO]
TEL. +39 059664007
www.cantinasantacroce.it

CELLAR SALES
ANNUAL PRODUCTION 400,000 bottles
HECTARES UNDER VINE 600.00

This cooperative was founded in 1907, in the place Lambrusco Salamino is named after: Santa Croce di Carpi. Although the premises have been renovated several times, they have never moved in over 100 hundred years of history. 250 growers mostly cultivate Salamino di Santa Croce, as well as other varieties of Lambrusco. Winemaker Maurizio Boni manages to bring out authentic, powerful and territorial interpretations of Salamino, which is grown on mainly clayey soils in the plain. Once again, Cantina di Santa Croce submitted a selection of classy Sorbaras, fruity and floral, taut in their citrusy flesh, supple and balanced. The Rosso 100 Vendemmie did well. It's a Brut made entirely with Salamino grapes redolent of black wild berries and forest undergrowth, coming through taut and meaty on the palate. The Salamino Secco has nice, clean fruit and well-integrated tannins, while the filtered sweet version is a highly pleasant blueberry extract.

● Lambrusco di Sorbara	🍷🍷 1'
● 100 Vendemmie Rosso Brut	🍷🍷 2'
● Lambrusco Grasparossa di Castelvetro	🍷🍷 1'
● Lambrusco Salamino di Santa Croce Secco Tradizione	🍷🍷 1'
● Lancellotta Filtrato Dolce	🍷🍷 1'
○ 100 Vendemmie Pignoletto Brut	🍷 2'
● Lambrusco Salamino di Santa Croce Amabile	🍷 1'
● Il Castello Lambrusco Semisecco '17	🍷🍷 1'
● Il Castello Rosso Lambrusco '17	🍷🍷 1'
● Lambrusco di Sorbara '17	🍷🍷 1'
● Lambrusco Salamino di Santa Croce Secco Tradizione '17	🍷🍷 1'

Cantina Sociale di Carpi e Sorbara

VIA CAVATA
41012 CARPI [MO]
TEL. +39 059 643071
www.cantinadicarpiesorbara.it

ANNUAL PRODUCTION 2,300,000 bottles
HECTARES UNDER VINE 2300.00

Over a thousand members, 45 million liters of wine produced each year and 6 winemaking and bottling structures. These are the numbers for the winery created in 2012 by the merger of two historic cooperatives in Carpi (founded in 1903) and Sorbara (1923). They were among the pioneers of cooperation that formed the cornerstone of the agroalimentary sector in Emilia. Gino Friedmann was one of its founders, which is why their two most prestigious wines are dedicated to him. The Salamino di Santa Croce 903 Terre dei Pio is quite good, generous in its fruity notes of black cherry, raspberries and cherry. On the palate it's fragrant, driven by residual sugars towards an almondy finish. Among their two Sorbara Gino Friedmann selections, this year we slightly preferred the one that undergoes a second fermentation in autoclaves, proving pulpy and focused in its red fruit. The entry-level Salamino also exhibits nice, ripe fruit with jammy notes.

● Lambrusco Salamino di Santa Croce 903 Terre dei Pio	♥♥ 2*
● Lambrusco di Sorbara Secco Omaggio a Gino Friedmann '18	♥♥ 3
● Lambrusco Mantovano 1946	♥♥ 2*
● Lambrusco Salamino di S. Croce	♥♥ 2*
● Lambrusco di Sorbara Amabile Emma	♥ 2
● Lambrusco di Sorbara Secco Omaggio a Gino Friedmann FB '18	♥ 3
⊙ Piazza Grande Lambrusco Brut Rosé	♥ 1*
● Lambrusco di Sorbara Secco Omaggio a Gino Friedmann '16	♥♥♥ 3*
● Lambrusco di Sorbara Secco Omaggio a Gino Friedmann '13	♥♥♥ 3*
● Lambrusco di Sorbara Secco Omaggio a Gino Friedmann FB '14	♥♥♥ 3*

Cavicchioli

VIA CANALETTO, 52
41030 SAN PROSPERO [MO]
TEL. +39 059812412
www.cavicchioli.it

CELLAR SALES
PRE-BOOKED VISITS
ANNUAL PRODUCTION 10,000,000 bottles
HECTARES UNDER VINE 90.00

Umberto Cavicchioli founded this winery in San Prospero in 1928. Over the years, it has managed to garner fame beyond national borders. Part of the colossus GIV since 2011, it is now run by Umberto's grandsons, Sandro and Claudio, who have given substantial new drive to wines. This is especially true for Sorbara, the noblest of Modena's Lambruscos, where high-level results have been achieved by selecting the best terrains and grapes, as well as using the Metodo Classico winemaking method. The Vigna del Cristo is at the top of its game. It's an elegant Sorbara, sapid, fragrant, rich and creamy, somewhere between citrus and wild berries, long and deep. We also like the Robanera Abboccato, a wine redolent of blueberry. It's pulpy and fruity, supple and fluid. Another mainstay is their Tre Medaglie, a precise Sorbara with pleasant notes of forest undergrowth. As usual their Brut Metodo Classico delivers as well.

● Lambrusco di Sorbara V. del Cristo '18	♥♥♥ 3*
⊙ Lambrusco di Sorbara Brut Rosé del Cristo M. Cl. '15	♥♥ 5
● Lambrusco di Sorbara Tre Medaglie	♥♥ 2*
● Robanera Abboccato	♥♥ 2*
● Lambrusco di Sorbara Millenovecentoventotto	♥ 2
● Lambrusco di Sorbara V. del Cristo '17	♥♥♥ 3*
● Lambrusco di Sorbara V. del Cristo '16	♥♥♥ 2*
● Lambrusco di Sorbara V. del Cristo '15	♥♥♥ 2*
● Lambrusco di Sorbara V. del Cristo '14	♥♥♥ 2*
● Lambrusco di Sorbara V. del Cristo '13	♥♥♥ 2*
● Lambrusco di Sorbara V. del Cristo '12	♥♥♥ 2*
● Lambrusco di Sorbara V. del Cristo '11	♥♥♥ 2*

Caviro

via Convertite, 12
48018 Faenza [RA]
Tel. +39 0546629111
www.caviro.it

CELLAR SALES
ANNUAL PRODUCTION 25,000,000 bottles
HECTARES UNDER VINE 31.00

Caviro is an Italian wine giant that manages to bring together 32 cooperatives and 12 thousand vine growers, located in 8 regions from north to south. Naturally, such a colossus emcompasses several projects, levels, product lines and numerous wines of all shapes and sizes. Tavernello is just one example. Alongside commercial wines, however, there's no lack of more sought-after projects, produced in limited editions with grapes grown in the best vineyards in Romagna. Their 1502 Da Vinci in Romagna line was inspired by the trip the genius took that year, crossing various cities and places throughout the region. Their Sangiovese Sup. Rocca di Cesena Ris. '16 offers up intense notes of berries (blackcurrant, strawberries and pomegranate), while the palate is placid and supple, well-balanced. The Rosato '18 is delicious in its hints of medlar and mandarin orange peel, while the round and thick Sangiovese Appassimento '17 features jammy sensations and hints of violet.

⊙ Romagna Sangiovese Rosato Portocanale di Cesenatico '18	🍷🍷 2*
● Romagna Sangiovese Sup. Rocca di Cesena Ris. '16	🍷🍷 4
● Romagna Sangiovese Appassimento '17	🍷 3
○ Romagna Albana Secco Romio '17	🍷🍷 2*
○ Romagna Albana Secco Romio '16	🍷🍷 2*
○ Romagna Albana Secco Romio '15	🍷🍷 2*
○ Romagna Albana Secco Romio '14	🍷🍷 2*
● Romagna Sangiovese Sup. Terragens Ris. '12	🍷🍷 4
○ Romagna Trebbiano Terre Forti '15	🍷🍷 1*

Celli

v.le Carducci, 5
47032 Bertinoro [FC]
Tel. +39 0543445183
www.celli-vini.com

CELLAR SALES
PRE-BOOKED VISITS
ANNUAL PRODUCTION 300,000 bottles
HECTARES UNDER VINE 35.00
SUSTAINABLE WINERY

The Celli winery belongs to the Sirri and Casadei families. Their vineyard located in Bertinoro, is divided between plots at Tenuta Maestrina, Tenuta La Massa and Campi di Bracciano, where calcareous soils contain seabed tufa. Renewal works begun in 1985 are giving excellent results, both in terms of wine quality and typicity. They grow several international and local grapes to produce numerous wines: results with Albana, a rather unusual traditional white cultivar, are particularly interesting. Their Albana Secco I Croppi didn't miss a beat. Even if the 2018 is a bit lacking in pulp and density of taste, it maintains its 'macerated' originality while gaining in vigor, drinkability and length. Their Sangiovese surprised with their nice texture and flavor. The Bron&Rusèval Ris. '16 is brilliant in its aromas of fresh flowers and spices, while the Le Grillaie Ris. '16 proves sapid and even.

○ Romagna Albana Secco I Croppi '18	🍷🍷 2*
● Romagna Sangiovese Bertinoro Bron & Ruseval Ris '16	🍷🍷 3
● Romagna Sangiovese Sup. Le Grillaie Ris. '16	🍷🍷 2*
○ Romagna Albana Secco I Croppi '17	🍷🍷🍷 2*
○ Romagna Albana Secco I Croppi '16	🍷🍷🍷 2*
○ Romagna Albana Secco I Croppi '15	🍷🍷🍷 2*
○ Romagna Albana Dolce Le Querce '15	🍷🍷 2*
○ Romagna Albana Passito Solara '15	🍷🍷 4
○ Romagna Albana Secco I Croppi '14	🍷🍷 2*
● Romagna Sangiovese Sup. Le Grillaie '15	🍷🍷 2*
● Romagna Sangiovese Sup. Le Grillaie '14	🍷🍷 2*
● Romagna Sangiovese Sup. Le Grillaie Ris. '14	🍷🍷 2*

★Cleto Chiarli Tenute Agricole

VIA BELVEDERE, 8
41014 CASTELVETRO DI MODENA [MO]
TEL. +39 0593163311
www.chiarli.it

CELLAR SALES
PRE-BOOKED VISITS
ANNUAL PRODUCTION 900,000 bottles
HECTARES UNDER VINE 100.00

1860 could be considered year zero for the history of Modena's Lambrusco. After opening and running Osteria dell'Artigliere in the center of Modena ten years earlier, where he served his own wine by the glass, Cleto Chiarli decided to focus exclusively on producing wine. He was the first to understand the importance of bottling Lambrusco and fermenting it in the bottle. Later on, pressure tanks, grape selection and a return to the Ancestral Method came along, resulting in long-lived wines with a strong personality. This year Chiarli submitted a formidable selection. As usual the Lambrusco del Fondatore is unbeatable, redolent of fruits and herbs, from raspberry to mint, strawberry, rosemary and citrus, sensations that come together in a supple palate, driven and full of vitality. The Vecchia Modena Premium is less complex but precise and focused in its fruit. The two Cialdinis, Grasparossas redolent of blackberry and blueberry, also deliver.

● Lambrusco di Sorbara del Fondatore '18	♈♈♈ 3*
● Lambrusco di Sorbara Vecchia Modena Premium '18	♈♈ 3*
● Lambrusco Grasparossa di Castelvetro Vign. Cialdini '18	♈♈ 3*
● Lambrusco Grasparossa di Castelvetro Villa Cialdini '18	♈♈ 2*
⊙ Rosé de Noir Brut '18	♈♈ 3
● Pruno Nero Dry '18	♈ 3
● Lambrusco di Sorbara del Fondatore '17	♈♈♈ 3*
● Lambrusco di Sorbara del Fondatore '16	♈♈♈ 3*
● Lambrusco di Sorbara del Fondatore '15	♈♈♈ 3*
● Lambrusco di Sorbara del Fondatore '14	♈♈♈ 3*
● Lambrusco di Sorbara del Fondatore '12	♈♈♈ 3*
● Lambrusco di Sorbara del Fondatore '11	♈♈♈ 2*
● Lambrusco di Sorbara Vecchia Modena Premium '13	♈♈♈ 2*

Condé

LOC. FIUMANA DI PREDAPPIO
VIA LUCCHINA, 27
47016 PREDAPPIO [FC]
TEL. +39 0543940860
www.conde.it

CELLAR SALES
PRE-BOOKED VISITS
ACCOMMODATION AND RESTAURANT SERVICE
ANNUAL PRODUCTION 150,000 bottles
HECTARES UNDER VINE 77.00
SUSTAINABLE WINERY

Founded in 2001, Francesco Condello's winery boasts vast vineyards in this important Predappio subzone, with elevations ranging from 150 to 350 meters. Sangiovese, the main regional variety, has also come to represent this family, both for the quantity they produce, as well as their quality and care. They also cultivate Merlot, but it's wines made with Romagna's traditional red variety that prove the most iconic. We think their wine style has grown in awareness in recent vintages. Their Romagna Sangiovese Predappio Raggio Brusa Riserva, a child of a blessed 2016, performed well during tastings. It's a red of great finesse, streamlined and long, marked by a delicious palate and density of flavor that doesn't renounce persistence and dynamism. It's already excellent but the sense is that it will only continue to improve.

● Romagna Sangiovese Predappio Raggio Brusa Ris. '16	♈♈ 8
● Romagna Sangiovese Predappio '12	♈♈ 3
● Romagna Sangiovese Predappio Ris. '13	♈♈ 6
● Romagna Sangiovese Predappio Ris. '12	♈♈ 6
● Romagna Sangiovese Sup. '12	♈♈ 3

Chiara Condello

LOC. FIUMANA DI PREDAPPIO
VIA LUCCHINA, 27
47016 PREDAPPIO [FC]
TEL. +39 0543940860
www.chiaracondello.com

CELLAR SALES
PRE-BOOKED VISITS
ANNUAL PRODUCTION 17,000 bottles
HECTARES UNDER VINE 4.80
SUSTAINABLE WINERY

Chiara Condello's winery has been a real discovery this year in Romagna. She wanted to give individual direction to wines produced in her area, with the excellent winemaking subzone of Predappio as a starting point. She cultivates vines on the edge of a wood, between 150 and 300 meters of elevation, on poor calcareous-clay soils, rich in tufaceous-sandstone rock. Naturally the focus is on Sangiovese, to produce wines that whisper an aery and refined language, while maintaining a rich flavor. Such qualities are perfectly embodied by their Romagna Sangiovese Predappio Le Lucciole '16, one of the best in its category. The toasty notes with which it opens, in no way invasive and exceptionally well-executed, surround a bright fruity weave, making for a multifaceted aromatic profile, rich in detail. In the mouth it proves appealing and deep, offering up hints of black fruits and pencil led in the mid-palate, with a tight finish that tops off a great wine.

● Romagna Sangiovese Predappio Le Lucciole Ris. '16	💯💯💯 7
● Romagna Sangiovese Predappio Chiara Condello '16	💯💯 4

Costa Archi

LOC. SERRA
VIA RINFOSCO, 1690
48014 CASTEL BOLOGNESE [RA]
TEL. +39 3384818346
costaarchi.wordpress.com

CELLAR SALES
PRE-BOOKED VISITS
ANNUAL PRODUCTION 16,000 bottles
HECTARES UNDER VINE 11.00

Gabriele Succi is a vinegrower with clear ideas and a strong desire to express them. He manages to do things his own way without fear or compromise. His winery was founded in Castel Bolognese in the 1960s, but recently it has really begun to take off. The vineyards are divided into two plots, at an elevation of 160 meters, on red and yellow clay soils rich in limestone. Work in the fields and cellar proves coherent, sensitive and well-balanced, which is reflected in wines displaying intensity, flavor and territorial expression. This year Costa Archi submitted three excellent wines, including the vibrant white Le Barrosche '17. But, as usual, it was two thoroughbred Sangioveses that led their selection. The Assiolo is delicious, full-bodied and flavorful, never heavy, even with the hot 2017. The Monte Brullo Ris. '15 is earthier, almost fluvial, with a nice, thick and juicy, long palate — it may be just a bit stiff in its tannic finish.

● Romagna Sangiovese Serra Monte Brullo Ris. '15	💯💯 2*
● Romagna Sangiovese Serra Assiolo '17	💯💯 3
○ Le Barrosche '17	💯 3
● Romagna Sangiovese Sup. Assiolo '13	💯💯💯 4*
● GS Sangiovese '14	💯💯 5
● GS Sangiovese '13	💯💯 5
● GS Sangiovese '12	💯💯 5
● Romagna Sangiovese Serra Assiolo '16	💯💯 3*
● Romagna Sangiovese Serra Assiolo '15	💯💯 2*
● Romagna Sangiovese Serra Monte Brullo Ris. '12	💯💯 2*
● Romagna Sangiovese Sup. Assiolo '14	💯💯 2*
● Sangiovese di Romagna Sup. Monte Brullo Ris. '10	💯💯 2*

Drei Donà Tenuta La Palazza

LOC. MASSA DI VECCHIAZZANO
VIA DEL TESORO, 23
47121 FORLÌ
TEL. +39 0543769371
www.dreidona.it

CELLAR SALES
PRE-BOOKED VISITS
ANNUAL PRODUCTION 130,000 bottles
HECTARES UNDER VINE 27.00
SUSTAINABLE WINERY

Drei Donà is a historic winery in Romagna that belongs to the family it was named after at the start of the last century. It boasts land in the best winemaking hills in the region, between Forlì, Castrocaro and Predappio, where the valleys of the Rabbi and Montone rivers meet. It is now run by Claudio Drei Donà and his son Enrico, who have managed to instill substantial change and enter a cautious management phase. Their wines display a modern style, especially those made with their favorite variety: Sangiovese. The Romagna Sangiovese Predappio Notturno '17 delivered. Toasty notes emerge, remaining in the foreground, though they never overwhelm brilliant, fresh and punchy fruit. On the palate it proves dense and linear, with texture, balance and character sure to evolve positively in the bottle. Their Tornese '18 is at the top of its game, while the Magnificat '15 proves well made.

● Romagna Sangiovese Predappio Notturno '17	♟♟ 3*
○ Il Tornese '18	♟♟ 3
● Magnificat '15	♟ 5
○ Il Tornese Chardonnay '95	♟♟♟ 3*
● Magnificat Cabernet Sauvignon '94	♟♟♟ 3*
● Sangiovese di Romagna Sup. Pruno Ris. '07	♟♟♟ 5
● Sangiovese di Romagna Sup. Pruno Ris. '06	♟♟♟ 5
● Sangiovese di Romagna Sup. Pruno Ris. '01	♟♟♟ 4*
● Sangiovese di Romagna Sup. Pruno Ris. '00	♟♟♟ 4
● Magnificat '13	♟♟ 5
● Romagna Sangiovese Sup. Pruno Ris. '15	♟♟ 7

Emilia Wine

VIA 11 SETTEMBRE 2001, 3
42019 SCANDIANO [RE]
TEL. +39 0522989107
www.emiliawine.eu

ANNUAL PRODUCTION 300,000 bottles
HECTARES UNDER VINE 1900.00

Emilia Wine was founded relatively recently. It was created in 2014 from the merger of three cooperatives already existing in the area (Arceto, Correggio and Prato di Correggio) and serves to illustrate the strength of cooperation in Emilia. Its 700 members cultivate very different terrains, from the plain, the kingdom of Lambrusco, to the hills of Reggio Emilia, between the Enza and Secchia rivers, which are more suitable for white grapes. Right from the start the fundamental principle was to analyze and get the best out of each terrain. The excellent results have not been long in the waiting. Among Emilia Wine's vast selection, the Migliolungo della Cantina di Arceto stands out. It's a blend of Reggio's traditional grapes, highly redolent of red berries and meaty on the palate. The 1077 Rosso is a full-bodied sparkling Lambrusco. On the nose it offers up aromas of plum, black wild berries, sensations accompanied by a tantalizing, bitter note. We also found the Cardinale Pighin notable for its fragrances of small red and black berry fruits.

● Migliolungo Lambrusco Cantina di Arceto	♟♟ 2*
● 1077 Rosso Brut	♟♟ 2
● Colli di Scandiano e Canossa Lambrusco Grasparossa Cardinale Pighini Cantina di Arceto	♟♟ 1*
○ Colli di Scandiano e di Canossa Spergola Brut 1077	♟ 2
● Reggiano Lambrusco Il Perdono Cantina di Arceto	♟ 2
⊙ Colli di Scandiano e di Canossa Lambrusco Rosaspino Cantina di Arceto '17	♟♟ 2*
● Reggiano Lambrusco Il Correggio '17	♟♟ 2*

Stefano Ferrucci

VIA CASOLANA, 3045
48014 CASTEL BOLOGNESE [RA]
TEL. +39 0546651068
www.stefanoferrucci.it

CELLAR SALES
PRE-BOOKED VISITS
ANNUAL PRODUCTION 130,000 bottles
HECTARES UNDER VINE 16.00

Ferrucci is a family-run enterprise dating from 1932. More recently, however, it has seen a decisive growth spurt, with substantial investments that are redesigning its new look. The cellar, where winemaking and aging is done, has been created from a Roman building: ancient charm combines with up-to-date technology and expertise. Their wines exhibit good personality and are impressively made. The names of the wines sold are clearly inspired by the place where they're produced and stored. The Albana Passito Domus Aurea '17 put in a noteworthy performance, proving aromatically nuanced, as complex as it is elegant. The same holds for the palate, where it proves pleasant, flavorful and long in its final aromatic echoes. We also found the Romagna Sangiovese Superiore Centurione '18 interesting. It's still quite young and primary in its aromas. The mouth is tapered, racy, punctuated by nice stuffing.

○ Romagna Albana Passito Domus Aurea '17	▾▾ 5
● Romagna Sangiovese Sup. Centurione '18	▾▾ 2*
○ Romagna Albana Passito Domus Aurea '15	▿▿ 5
○ Romagna Albana Passito Domus Aurea '13	▿▿ 5
● Romagna Sangiovese Auriga '15	▿▿ 2*
● Romagna Sangiovese Sup. Centurione '17	▿▿ 2*
● Romagna Sangiovese Sup. Centurione '14	▿▿ 2*
● Romagna Sangiovese Sup. Domus Caia Ris. '13	▿▿ 5
● Romagna Sangiovese Sup. Domus Caia Ris. '12	▿▿ 5

Paolo Francesconi

LOC. SARNA
VIA TULIERO, 154
48018 FAENZA [RA]
TEL. +39 054643213
www.francesconipaolo.it

CELLAR SALES
PRE-BOOKED VISITS
ANNUAL PRODUCTION 20,000 bottles
HECTARES UNDER VINE 8.00
VITICULTURE METHOD Certified Biodynamic
SUSTAINABLE WINERY

Paolo Francesconi's winery is a model of charming, authentic style, though sometimes a bit variable. But that's the beauty of artisan wine and we salute this kind of approach, which respects nature and its fruits and never overly manipulates or intervenes. It is located on the slopes of the foothills of the Faenza Apennines, at an elevation of about 85 meters and a just few kilometers from the city. The silty-clay soils guarantee flavorsome wines with a certain verve: the southwestern exposure and warm-dry climate complete the picture. In general their selection convinced, especially considering their production philosophy. We start with the Sangiovese Le Iadi Ris. '16, an open wine with fruity notes and delicate spices — it's a bit rustic, but with nice spontaneity. The D'Incanto '16, made with partially-dried grapes, proves delicious, exhibiting extraordinary aromatic vibrance and intensity of flavor, calling up chopped black fruits.

● D'Incanto '16	▾▾ 5
● Romagna Sangiovese Sup. Le Iadi Ris. '16	▾▾ 5
● Rosso '18	▾ 3
● Romagna Sangiovese Sup. Limbecca '14	▿▿▿ 3*
● Sangiovese di Romagna Sup. Limbecca '11	▿▿▿ 3*
● Sangiovese di Romagna Sup. Limbecca '10	▿▿▿ 3*
○ Arcaica '15	▿▿ 3
● Romagna Sangiovese Le Iadi Ris. '13	▿▿ 5
● Romagna Sangiovese Sup. Limbecca '16	▿▿ 3
● Vite in Fiore '15	▿▿ 3

Gallegati

VIA LUGO, 182
48018 FAENZA [RA]
TEL. +39 0546621149
www.aziendaagricolagallegati.it

CELLAR SALES
PRE-BOOKED VISITS
ACCOMMODATION
ANNUAL PRODUCTION 15,000 bottles
HECTARES UNDER VINE 6.00

The Gallegati family's beautiful winery in Faenza is run by brothers Antonio and Cesare. They are both wine enthusiasts and graduates in agricultural science. Well-trained vineyards grow on the classic local silty-clay soils, with a high presence of limestone. The winery's approach centers on environmental sustainability, which translates into methods that respect grapes and winemaking during production. This results in authentic wines that are unwilling to compromise and proudly express their territory. The Corallo Rosso '17 is one of the best Romagna Sangioveses tasted this year. A toasty note, with the occasional hint of wood resin, opens the dance, but fruit confidently emerges from a distance. Then come the spices and dried flowers, accompanying a procession of fresh cherries. As aromatically intense as it is flavorful. A wonder.

- ● Romagna Sangiovese Brisighella
  Corallo Rosso '17 — 🍷🍷 2*
- ○ Romagna Albana Secco
  Corallo Giallo '18 — 🍷 3
- ● Romagna Sangiovese Brisighella
  Corallo Nero Ris. '16 — 🍷 4
- ○ Albana di Romagna Passito
  Regina di Cuori Ris. '10 — 🍷🍷🍷 4*
- ○ Albana di Romagna Passito
  Regina di Cuori Ris. '09 — 🍷🍷🍷 4*
- ○ Romagna Albana Passito
  Regina di Cuori Ris. '12 — 🍷🍷🍷 4*
- ● Sangiovese di Romagna Sup.
  Corallo Nero Ris. '06 — 🍷🍷🍷 3

Lombardini

VIA CAVOUR, 15
42017 NOVELLARA [RE]
TEL. +39 0522654224
www.lombardinivini.it

CELLAR SALES
PRE-BOOKED VISITS
ANNUAL PRODUCTION 800,000 bottles
HECTARES UNDER VINE

Chiara, Cecilia and Virginia have become a permanent fixture at the family winery, alongside their father Marco. The Lombardinis have been producing Lambrusco for four generations, ever since 1925 when Angelo decided to add winemaking to his bar business in the center of Novellara. However, the decision to do away with vineyards and focus on the cautious selection of grapes and must, as well as winemaking, dates from the 1970s. This led to a range of drinkable, approachable and fruity wines that proves to be their trump card. The Signor Campanone is a superb Lambrusco Reggiano, a ruby red blend of Salamino and Sorbara exploding with clear, crisp fruit. On the palate it's soft and spirited, a great drink. The Del C'era uno Volta proves sapid, compact, fresh and drinkable. The Spumante 1925, a monovarietal Sorbara, is complex with vegetal streaks and hints of red berries.

- ● Reggiano Lambrusco
  Il Signor Campanone '18 — 🍷🍷 2*
- ● Lambrusco di Sorbara Brut 1925 '18 — 🍷🍷 2*
- ● Reggiano Lambrusco
  Del C'era Una Volta '18 — 🍷🍷 2*
- ● Reggiano Lambrusco Il Campanone '18 — 🍷 2
- ● Reggiano Lambrusco Nubilaia '18 — 🍷 2
- ● Lambrusco della Dama '16 — 🍷🍷 1*
- ● Lambrusco di Sorbara
  C'era Una Volta '17 — 🍷🍷 2*
- ● Reggiano Lambrusco Il Campanone '17 — 🍷🍷 2*
- ● Reggiano Lambrusco
  Il Signor Campanone '16 — 🍷🍷 2*

Luretta

loc. Castello di Momeliano
29010 Gazzola [PC]
Tel. +39 0523971070
www.luretta.com

CELLAR SALES
PRE-BOOKED VISITS
ANNUAL PRODUCTION 300,000 bottles
HECTARES UNDER VINE 50.00
VITICULTURE METHOD Certified Organic

Felice Salamini is a theatrical vinegrower, globe-trotter and French wine enthusiast. In 2002, his winery moved to the fourteenth-century castle of Momeliano, which used to stand guard over the territory, in the hills of the Luretta valley. Felice and his son Lucio produce wines with grapes grown under strict organic management. They then age in the charming underground vaulted cellar. Felice and his wife Carla Asti's creativity gives rise to unusually made and named wines. The Selìn dl'armari '17, a Chardonnay fermented and matured in new oak barriques, is anything but banal, offering up aromas of pineapple and spices. On the palate it's broad and succulent, supported by a healthy acidic vigor. The Sauvignon Blanc I Nani e le Ballerina '18 features all the cultivar's classic fragrances, from cut grass to yellow citrus and tropical fruit. On the palate it's racy and graceful, with well-defined flesh. We tasted the Pantera '16, a blend of Croatina, Barbera and Cabernet Sauvignon redolent of plums and spices, in a phase in which it's still settling. Patience is in order.

○ C. P. Chardonnay Selín dl'Armari '17	♥♥ 4
○ C. P. Sauvignon I Nani e le Ballerine '18	♥♥ 3
○ C. P. Malvasia Boccadirosa '18	♥ 3
● C. P. Pinot Nero Achab '16	♥ 5
● Gutturnio Sup. L'Ala del Drago '15	♥ 3
● Pantera '16	♥ 4
● C. P. Cabernet Sauvignon Corbeau '00	♥♥♥ 4*
● C. P. Barbera Carabas '15	♥♥ 3
⊙ C. P. Brut Rosé On Attend les Invités '11	♥♥ 4
○ C. P. Chardonnay Selín dl'Armari '15	♥♥ 4
○ C. P. Sauvignon I Nani e le Ballerine '16	♥♥ 3
● Gutturnio Sup. '12	♥♥ 3
● Pantera '15	♥♥ 4
○ Principessa Pas Dosé Brut M. Cl. '09	♥♥ 4
○ Principessa Pas Dosé M. Cl. '10	♥♥ 4

Tenuta Mara

via Ca' Bacchino, 1665
47832 San Clemente [RN]
Tel. +39 0541988870
www.tenutamara.com

CELLAR SALES
PRE-BOOKED VISITS
ACCOMMODATION AND RESTAURANT SERVICE
ANNUAL PRODUCTION 35,000 bottles
HECTARES UNDER VINE 11.00
VITICULTURE METHOD Certified Biodynamic

Dream, vision and passionate tension towards a romantic idea of wine and meticulous planning of the winery: this is the essence of Tenuta Mara pursued by Giordano Emendatori, who named the estate after his wife. Land was purchased in 2000, then vineyards were planted near the hillside town of San Clemente, in the Rimini area. Their preferred variety is Sangiovese, their wine style is highly artisanal and outside of the box. We start with their most important red, the Maramia '16. It's a unique version that offers up conspicuous aromas of red fruit, sanguine notes and hints of sweet spices. Its charming nose anticipates a creamy palate made rhythmic by slightly pronounced tannins and a freshness that softens a slight sweetness at the end. The Guiry is younger, a kind of 'second vin', but in light of its substance we can't consider it second-rate. It's a close-woven wine, lean and supple, with acidity conferring a certain vivacity to the palate, and a finish that comes through extremely clean and deep.

● Guiry Sangiovese '17	♥♥ 5
● MaraMia Sangiovese '16	♥♥ 6
● Guiry '16	♥♥ 5
● Maramia Sangiovese '15	♥♥ 7
● Maramia Sangiovese '13	♥♥ 7
● Maramia Sangiovese '12	♥♥ 4

★Ermete Medici & Figli

LOC. GAIDA
VIA I. NEWTON, 13A
42124 REGGIO EMILIA
TEL. +39 0522942135
www.medici.it

CELLAR SALES
PRE-BOOKED VISITS
ANNUAL PRODUCTION 800,000 bottles
HECTARES UNDER VINE 75.00
SUSTAINABLE WINERY

The Medici family is a key figure in Lambrusco's history in Reggio Emilia. Remigio founded the winery at the end of the 1800s, but it was his son Ermete (who it is named after) who brought expansion and the basis for it to become a benchmark after four generations. Alberto Medici has managed to develop his best terrains to produce quality wines, by choosing the most suitable clones and lowering yields in vineyards. And the Ancestral Method still manages to give high-level results. As usual, their Concerto is among the region's top Lambruscos. Its lovely violet highlights are the prelude to clear, fragrant notes of blackcurrant, strawberry and raspberry. On the palate it exhibits vigor, personality and substance, with precise tannins and a long finish. Their Reggiano I Quercioli is a different style but of outstanding quality, opting more for dark wild berry notes with shades of forest undergrowth, and a taut, close-woven palate. On its second version, we found the Phermento '18 quite interesting indeed.

● Reggiano Lambrusco Concerto '18	♟♟♟ 2*
● Modena Lambrusco Phermento Metodo Ancestrale '18	♟♟ 3*
● Reggiano Lambrusco I Quercioli	♟♟ 2*
● Reggiano Lambrusco Dolce I Quercioli	♟♟ 2*
● Lambrusco di Sorbara I Quercioli	♟ 2
○ Nebbie d'Autunno Malvasia Dolce '18	♟ 2
● Reggiano Lambrusco Assolo '18	♟ 2
● Reggiano Lambrusco Concerto '17	♟♟♟ 2*
● Reggiano Lambrusco Concerto '16	♟♟♟ 2*
● Reggiano Lambrusco Concerto '15	♟♟♟ 2*
● Reggiano Lambrusco Concerto '14	♟♟♟ 2*
● Reggiano Lambrusco Concerto '13	♟♟♟ 2*
● Reggiano Lambrusco Concerto '12	♟♟♟ 2*
● Reggiano Lambrusco Concerto '11	♟♟♟ 2*

Monte delle Vigne

LOC. OZZANO TARO
VIA MONTICELLO, 22
43046 COLLECCHIO [PR]
TEL. +39 0521309704
www.montedellevigne.it

CELLAR SALES
PRE-BOOKED VISITS
ACCOMMODATION
ANNUAL PRODUCTION 350,000 bottles
HECTARES UNDER VINE 60.00

When Andrea Ferrari founded this estate in 1983, he started out with 15 hectares, seven of which were planted with vines. His aim was to produce quality still wines in an area mostly dedicated to sparkling winemaking. Between 2003 and 2004 he met builder Paolo Pizzarotti, whose bordering land stretched over 100 hectares. At the end of 2006, the new undergound cellar was officially opened. Now the organically-grown vineyards cultivate traditional as well as international varieties; in recent years an important sparkling wine project has gotten underway. Despite a hot 2017, the Malvasia Callas managed to duplicate last year's success and took home Tre Bicchieri by virtue of a sophisticated, varietal aromatic profile, in which white flowers merge with tropical fruits. On the palate it enjoys a sapid freshness that drives its development towards a long and elegant herbaceous finish. The Colli di Parma Rosso '18 is a tight, firm wine.

○ Callas Malvasia '17	♟♟♟ 4*
● Colli di Parma Rosso MDV '18	♟♟ 3
● Colli di Parma Lambrusco I Calanchi '18	♟ 5
○ Callas Malvasia '15	♟♟♟ 4*
● Colli di Parma Rosso MDV '16	♟♟♟ 3*
● Colli di Parma Rosso MDV '14	♟♟♟ 2*
○ Callas Malvasia '14	♟♟ 4
○ Colli di Parma Malvasia Frizzante '15	♟♟ 2*
○ Colli di Parma Malvasia Frizzante '14	♟♟ 2*
○ Colli di Parma Malvasia Poem '14	♟♟ 2*
● Colli di Parma Rosso MDV '17	♟♟ 3
● Lambrusco Emilia '14	♟♟ 2*
● Nabucco '16	♟♟ 5
● Nabucco '15	♟♟ 5

Fattoria Monticino Rosso

VIA MONTECATONE, 7
40026 IMOLA [BO]
TEL. +39 054240577
www.fattoriadelmonticinorosso.it

CELLAR SALES
PRE-BOOKED VISITS
ANNUAL PRODUCTION 70,000 bottles
HECTARES UNDER VINE 18.00

Founded in 1965 by Antonio Zeoli, Fattoria Monticino Rosso is named after the farm neighboring the original one, which was purchased in the mid-1980s. The terroir is located in the Imola hills, overlooking nearby Emilia. Today, Luciano and Gianni Zeoli run the winery with uncommon sensitivity in cultivating grapes, followed by attentive winemaking in order to preserve their characteristics. The Albana variety stands out for the way it manages to work its magic here in Romagna and in this particular winery. The Passito '15 is among the best tasted this year. Complex aromas of pineapple, mixed fruit and nuts are balanced by mineral notes. On the palate it follows a similar track, exhibiting lush pulp and superb sweetness. Among the reds we preferred the Sangiovese S '18, a delicately fruity and floral wine.

○ Romagna Albana Passito '15	▼▼ 4
○ 8Venti	▼▼ 4
○ Romagna Albana Secco Codronchio Special Edition '16	▼▼ 3
● Romagna Sangiovese Sup. S '18	▼▼ 2*
○ Romagna Albana Secco A '18	▼ 2
● Romagna Sangiovese Sup. S Zero Solfiti Aggiunti '18	▼ 2
○ Albana di Romagna Secco Codronchio '08	♈♈♈ 3*
○ Albana di Romagna Passito '16	♈♈ 4
○ Romagna Albana Secco A '17	♈♈ 2*
○ Romagna Albana Secco A '16	♈♈ 2*
○ Romagna Albana Secco Codronchio '15	♈♈ 3
● Romagna Sangiovese Sup. Le Morine Ris. '15	♈♈ 3

Fattoria Nicolucci

VIA UMBERTO I, 21
47016 PREDAPPIO [FC]
TEL. +39 0543922361
www.vininicolucci.com

CELLAR SALES
PRE-BOOKED VISITS
ANNUAL PRODUCTION 70,000 bottles
HECTARES UNDER VINE 10.00
SUSTAINABLE WINERY

Founded as far back as 1885, the Nicolucci Farm can boast a long history. However, far from being an old-style winery, it is one of the most dynamic, modern and prestigious estates in Romagna. It expresses the Predappio Alta area (an excellent subzone for Sangiovese) with class and clear style. Meager calcareous and stony soils, combined with maturation in concrete vats and large wooden barrels, lend their reds an elegant, intense and nuanced, but full-bodied quality. The Sangiovese Vigna del Generale '16 brings together fruit that's as relaxed as it is dense with toasty notes that are still awaiting full integration, but of nice grain. It's a complex wine that just needs a bit more time in the bottle to find the right balance. The Tre Rocche '18 also features spicy notes, while I Mandorli '18 exhibits a delicious palate that calls up watermelon. Oaky notes are more foregrounded in the Nero di Predappio '18.

● Romagna Sangiovese Sup. Predappio di Predappio V. del Generale Ris. '16	▼▼▼ 5
● Romagna Sangiovese Sup. I Mandorli '18	▼▼ 2*
● Romagna Sangiovese Sup. Tre Rocche '18	▼▼ 3
● Nero di Predappio '18	▼ 5
● Romagna Sangiovese Sup. Predappio di Predappio V. del Generale Ris. '15	♈♈ 5
● Romagna Sangiovese Sup. V. del Generale Ris. '13	♈♈ 5
● Romagna Sangiovese Sup. V. del Generale Ris. '12	♈♈ 5
● Sangiovese di Romagna Predappio di Predappio V. del Generale Ris. '11	♈♈ 5

Enio Ottaviani

LOC. SANT'ANDREA IN CASALE
VIA PIAN DI VAGLIA, 17
47832 SAN CLEMENTE [RN]
TEL. +39 0541952608
www.enioottaviani.it

CELLAR SALES
PRE-BOOKED VISITS
ANNUAL PRODUCTION 130,000 bottles
HECTARES UNDER VINE 12.00

Enio Ottaviani boasts a long past in the wine world, despite being more recently remodeled. Today, the business is run by Davide and Massimo Lorenzi, with their cousins Marco and Milena Tonelli. And they're doing a great job, judging by the diverse wines they produce and sell each year. Their grapes grow in San Clemente near Rimini, on clay-loam soils which benefit from the vicinity of the sea. Their winemaking style focuses mainly on precise extraction and well-defined aromas. Dado is a project dedicated to the area's Sangiovese, starting with four different plots (worked and vinified separately). The 2018, fermented in concrete and aged in large wood barrels, offers up iron, mineral notes, with bark and wet earth balanced by fruit. On the palate it's smooth, enjoyable, just a bit rough in its clenched tannic finish. The Sangiovese Sup. Caciara '18 is delicious in its delicacy and flavor.

● Romagna Sangiovese Dado '18	♀♀♀ 6
● Romagna Sangiovese Sup. Caciara '18	♀♀ 3
○ Romagna Pagadebit Strati '18	♀ 3
○ Clemente Primo '15	♀♀ 2*
● Merlot '13	♀♀ 2*
○ Romagna Pagadebit Strati '17	♀♀ 2*
● Romagna Sangiovese Caciara '15	♀♀ 3
● Romagna Sangiovese Primalba '14	♀♀ 2*
● Romagna Sangiovese Primalba Bio '17	♀♀ 2*
● Romagna Sangiovese Sup. Caciara '17	♀♀ 3
● Romagna Sangiovese Sup. Caciara '16	♀♀ 3
● Romagna Sangiovese Sup. Sole Rosso Ris. '15	♀♀ 4
● Romagna Sangiovese Sup. Sole Rosso Ris. '13	♀♀ 4

Alberto Paltrinieri

FRAZ. SORBARA
VIA CRISTO, 49
41030 BOMPORTO [MO]
TEL. +39 059902047
www.cantinapaltrinieri.it

CELLAR SALES
PRE-BOOKED VISITS
ANNUAL PRODUCTION 150,000 bottles
HECTARES UNDER VINE 17.00

Here at the heart of Cristo di Sorbara, on alluvial soil surrounded by the Secchia and Panaro rivers, lies the best area for cultivating Lambrusco di Sorbara. Alberto Paltrinieri and his wife Barbara have taken up the legacy of his father Gianfranco and his grandfather Achille Paltrinieri, a chemist and pharmacist with a passion for wine who founded the winery. Their mission is to produce Lambrusco with the savoriness and elegance that this terroir is capable of. Cru selection and the adoption of different kinds of second fermentation are giving extraordinary results. Their Leclisee always has plenty of personality. It's a citrusy and floral Sorbara, elegant, open and deep. Theirspirited and sapid, drinkable and fragrant Sant'Agata, another citrusy wine, exhibits nice fruit. Lariserva is a Sorbara sparkler vinified off the skins that surprises for its clear minerality, notes of lime and aromatic herbs, and the tension of its bead. Their Solco, a more 'appealing' Lambrusco also proves well-made.

⊙ Lambrusco di Sorbara Leclisse '18	♀♀♀ 3*
● Lambrusco di Sorbara Sant'Agata '18	♀♀ 2*
⊙ Lambrusco di Sorbara Brut Lariserva '17	♀♀ 3
⊙ Solco Lambrusco '18	♀♀ 2*
● Lambrusco di Sorbara Piria '18	♀ 2
⊙ Lambrusco di Sorbara Radice '18	♀ 3
● Lambrusco di Sorbara Leclisse '17	♀♀♀ 3*
● Lambrusco di Sorbara Leclisse '16	♀♀♀ 3*
● Lambrusco di Sorbara Leclisse '10	♀♀♀ 3*
● Lambrusco di Sorbara Radice '18	♀♀♀ 2*
● Lambrusco di Sorbara Leclisse '15	♀♀ 2*
● Lambrusco di Sorbara Piria '17	♀♀ 2*
● Lambrusco di Sorbara Piria '16	♀♀ 2*
● Lambrusco di Sorbara Radice '15	♀♀ 2*
● Lambrusco di Sorbara Sant'Agata '16	♀♀ 2*
● Lambrusco di Sorbara Sant'Agata '15	♀♀ 2*

Pandolfa

FRAZ. FIUMANA
VIA PANDOLFA, 35
47016 PREDAPPIO [FC]
TEL. +39 0543940073
www.pandolfa.it

CELLAR SALES
ANNUAL PRODUCTION 120,000 bottles
HECTARES UNDER VINE 30.00
SUSTAINABLE WINERY

Tenuta Pandolfa manages to combine a prestigious past with a dynamic present. The modern era began when Paola Piscopo purchased it, and continues under the current management of her son Marco Cirese. Their vineyards cover 140 hectares in Fiumana di Predappio, in the Tuscan-Emilian Apennines, where Sangiovese boasts a long tradition. The vineyards are located at elevations between 150 and 400 meters, on sandstone and calcareous-marl soils. The resulting wines are delicate and polished with an original style. Their Sangiovese Pandolfo '16 embodies this production style. It's a wine aged mostly steel with the remaining share in Slavonian oak. Autumnal in its aromas, sylvan notes alternate with dried herbs and small berries. On the palate it proves elegant, just slightly bitter in its tannic weave, but long and tasty at the finish. This linear character will certainly do well over time.

● Romagna Sangiovese Sup. Pandolfo Ris. '18	♟♟ 2*
● Romagna Sangiovese Federico '17	♟♟ 2*
○ Battista '18	♟ 2
⊙ Ginevra '18	♟ 2
● Romagna Sangiovese Sup. Federico '16	♟♟ 2*
● Romagna Sangiovese Sup. Pandolfo '16	♟♟ 2*
● Romagna Sangiovese Sup. Pandolfo Ris. '15	♟♟ 3*

Fattoria Paradiso

FRAZ. CAPOCOLLE
VIA PALMEGGIANA, 285
47032 BERTINORO [FC]
TEL. +39 0543445044
www.fattoriaparadiso.com

CELLAR SALES
PRE-BOOKED VISITS
ACCOMMODATION AND RESTAURANT SERVICE
ANNUAL PRODUCTION 200,000 bottles
HECTARES UNDER VINE 150.00
VITICULTURE METHOD Certified Organic
SUSTAINABLE WINERY

Fattoria Paradiso is a historic winemaking brand in Romagna. It was one of the first wineries to manage to express regional wines and to attract the attention of critics and enthusiasts. Run by the Pezzi family, it is located near Bertinoro: they only process their own grapes, which are cultivated in distinct plots containing some very old vines. The development of native varieties has always been a distinctive feature of the winery, while their wines, which were innovative in the past, now stand out among the most reliable classics. Their Spugnone '18 is made with an original grape called Barbarossa, which Fattoria Paradiso has purposefully bet on. Aromatically it's delicate while on the palate it's elegant, subtle and pleasant. The Sangiovese Sup. Peti Tufi '18 also performed well. Blackberry juice emerges up off the nose, while the palate proves full, clean and juicy, with a nice finish of gingerbread. Their Albana Dolce Vigna del Viale '18 calls up flint, dried fruit and nuts.

○ Lo Spugnone '18	♟♟ 3
○ Romagna Albana Dolce V. del Viale '18	♟♟ 3
● Romagna Sangiovese Sup. Peti Tufi '18	♟♟ 3
○ Romagna Albana Secco V. dell'Olivo '18	♟ 2
● Barbarossa Il Dosso '13	♟♟ 4
● Il Dosso '14	♟♟ 4
● Mito '13	♟♟ 6
● Romagna Sangiovese Bertinoro V. delle Lepri Ris. '15	♟♟ 4
● Romagna Sangiovese Sup. V. del Molino Maestri di Vigna '16	♟♟ 2*
● Romagna Sangiovese Sup. V. del Molino Maestri di Vigna '15	♟♟ 2*
● Romagna Sangiovese Sup. V. delle Lepri Ris. '13	♟♟ 3

Quarticello

VIA MATILDE DI CANOSSA, 1A
42027 MONTECCHIO EMILIA [RE]
TEL. +39 0522866220
www.quarticello.it

CELLAR SALES
PRE-BOOKED VISITS
ANNUAL PRODUCTION 45,000 bottles
HECTARES UNDER VINE 5.00
VITICULTURE METHOD Certified Organic

Compared to the overall statistics for Lambrusco, the winery Roberto Maestri founded in 2001 is a relatively small one. Its five hectares of vineyards are located on the Reggio Emilia side of the Enza river, at the foot of the Apennines, in the heart of Cannossa. If we take a look at quality, however, the situation changes dramatically. Roberto graduated in enology and began vinifying traditional grapes grown in his organic vineyards in 2006. Careful selection and use of the Metodo Classico winemaking method result in interesting and unusual wines. The Malvasia Frizzante is highly pleasant and fragrant, generous in its citrus aromas and notes of tropical fruit, subtle in its bead, with nice backbone. The Caschinaronchi '16 is a sparkler made with 85% Spergola and 15% Malvasia di Candia Aromatica. This unfiltered, golden wine exhibits substance, with a nice aromatic and acidic drive. The Fiordiligi Bruscnature '16 is a rosé sparkling wine made entirely with Salamino grapes that spend 24 months on the lees. It's dark in its notes of undergrowth and black berries.

○ Cascinaronchi Brut Nature M. Cl. '16	♥♥ 4
○ Despina Malvasia Frizzante	♥♥ 2*
◉ Fiordiligi Bruscnature Brut M. Cl. '16	♥♥ 4
◉ Ferrando Lambrusco	♥ 3
○ Incia	♥ 2
● Neromaestri	♥ 3
○ Despina '14	♀♀ 2*
◉ Despina Rifermentato in Bottiglia '15	♀♀ 2*
◉ Ferrando '14	♀♀ 2*
◉ Ferrando Rifermentato in Bottiglia '15	♀♀ 2*
◉ Fiordiligi Bruscnature Pas Dosé M. Cl. '15	♀♀ 4
○ Stradora '15	♀♀ 3

Noelia Ricci

FRAZ. FIUMANA
VIA PANDOLFA, 35
47016 PREDAPPIO [FC]
TEL. +39 0543940073
www.noeliaricci.it

CELLAR SALES
PRE-BOOKED VISITS
ACCOMMODATION
ANNUAL PRODUCTION 58,000 bottles
HECTARES UNDER VINE 9.00
SUSTAINABLE WINERY

The Noelia Ricci winery appears to be growing each year in terms of both quality and awareness. This is thanks to an innovative style for this area, which has not damped down field studies and the quest for an increasingly authentic and impressive interpretation of Romagna's Sangiovese. We get the impression that recent vintages are much more mature when it comes to the personality, substance and flavor of wines: they prove airy and elegant but slightly more territorial and complete than in the past. This year their selection was without their Godenza, but the Sangiovese '18 rose to the occasion, exhibiting outstanding quality in terms of stylistic maturity and awareness. Among Romagna's reds (and not only), it's one of the most intriguing expressions we tasted: elegant and airy, as delicately floral as it is lively — it seems to tiptoe endlessly on the palate, without renouncing tension and flavor.

● Romagna Sangiovese Predappio Il Sangiovese '18	♥♥♥ 3*
○ Brò '18	♥ 3
● Romagna Sangiovese Predappio Godenza '16	♀♀♀ 4*
● Romagna Sangiovese Sup. Godenza '14	♀♀♀ 3*
● Romagna Sangiovese Sup. Il Sangiovese '16	♀♀♀ 3*
● Romagna Sangiovese Sup. Il Sangiovese '14	♀♀♀ 2*
● Romagna Sangiovese Predappio '17	♀♀ 2*
● Romagna Sangiovese Sup. Godenza '15	♀♀ 4

Cantine Riunite & Civ

VIA G. BRODOLINI, 24
42040 CAMPEGINE [RE]
TEL. +39 0522905711
www.riuniteciv.com

CELLAR SALES
ANNUAL PRODUCTION 130,000,000 bottles
HECTARES UNDER VINE 3500.00
SUSTAINABLE WINERY

There's no need to point out that this is Italy's largest cooperative in terms of turnover and number of bottles produced. It includes over 2600 members and commands a total of 3500 hectares of vineyards. However, this giant manages to live alongside much smaller wineries. Throughout the years, the group has brought out certain wines of absolute quality, by selecting the best batches of grapes, as well as focussing on still wines and organic viticulture. It's difficult to choose from a selection this wide and of such high average quality. The Cuvée 1950 stands out thanks to its generous bouquet of blueberries, raspberries and citrus. On the palate it has flesh and balance, closing supple and broad. The lively, crisp Semisecco Righi offers up aromas of blueberry, it's delectable but also perfectly balanced. The Grasparossa Righi is rich in mouthfeel, punctuated by pleasant tannic sensations.

- Reggiano Lambrusco Cuvée 1950 ⚑⚑ 1*
- Lambrusco Grasparossa di Castelvetro Righi ⚑⚑ 1*
- Modena Lambrusco Semisecco Righi ⚑⚑ 1*
- Lambrusco di Sorbara Gaetano Righi '16 ⚑⚑ 2*
- Lambrusco di Sorbara Semisecco '16 ⚑⚑ 1*
- Lambrusco Grasparossa di Castelvetro Amabile Il Fojonco '17 ⚑⚑ 2*
- Lambrusco Grasparossa di Castelvetro Amabile Il Fojonco '16 ⚑⚑ 2*
- Lambrusco Grasparossa di Castelvetro Secco Gaetano Righi '16 ⚑⚑ 1*
- Lambrusco Salamino di Santa Croce Secco '16 ⚑⚑ 1*
- Lambrusco Senzatempo RF '16 ⚑⚑ 1*
- Modena Lambrusco Semisecco Righi '17 ⚑⚑ 1*

Le Rocche Malatestiane

VIA EMILIA, 104
47900 RIMINI
TEL. +39 0541743079
www.lerocchemalatestiane.it

CELLAR SALES
PRE-BOOKED VISITS
ANNUAL PRODUCTION 700,000 bottles
HECTARES UNDER VINE 800.00

The Malatestas were an important family of condottieri and patrons in Rimini. They carried out great building works, including some of the most magnificent strongholds and fortresses that dominate the area. This important winery was inspired by and named after them. It brings together 500 vignerons, who cultivate a total of 800 hectares between Alta Val Marecchia and Cattolica, towards the boundary with the Marche region. This winery has grown over the years, as shown by the quality of their range, which has been developed since 2011 and focusses on Sangiovese. Among the wines made with Romagna's classic red cultivar, their Sangiovese Sup. Tre Miracoli '18 stands out for its style and quality. It's a 'faux simple' wine inasmuch as, in reality, it's an elegant delight redolent of fresh, May cherries and small wild berries. The palate is racy, linear, with the occasional hint of unripe fruit enhancing tension and drinkability. Their Sigismondo '18 is another excellent wine.

- Romagna Sangiovese Sup. Tre Miracoli '18 ⚑⚑⚑ 2*
- Romagna Sangiovese Sup. Sigismondo '18 ⚑⚑ 2*
- Colli di Rimini Cabernet Sauvignon E Nèr Ris. '16 ⚑ 3
- Colli di Rimini Sangiovese Mons Iovis '16 ⚑ 3
- Romagna Sangiovese Sup. I Diavoli '18 ⚑ 2
- Romagna Sangiovese Sup. Sigismondo '17 ⚑⚑⚑ 2*
- Romagna Sangiovese Sup. Sigismondo '16 ⚑⚑⚑ 2*
- Romagna Sangiovese Sup. I Diavoli '17 ⚑⚑ 2*

Cantine Romagnoli

LOC. VILLÒ
VIA GENOVA, 20
29020 VIGOLZONE [PC]
TEL. +39 0523870904
www.cantineromagnoli.it

CELLAR SALES
PRE-BOOKED VISITS
ANNUAL PRODUCTION 300,000 bottles
HECTARES UNDER VINE 45.00
SUSTAINABLE WINERY

The beautiful courtyard of this farm founded in the mid-nineteenth century and taken over by the Romagnoli family in 1926, is well worth visiting. The current owners have decided to keep the original name. Now it has been completely renovated, with the old buildings in full view next to the more recent cellar, complete with temperature-controlled rooms and underground barrique cellar. Carefully run by young Alessandro Perini, it was the first winery to produce and sell Metodo Classico wines in Piacenza. These are still one of their flagship products, alongside more traditional local wines. The producer submitted a notable selection, starting with the Pigro Dosaggio Zero '16. Aromas of small, red fruits and aromatic herbs rise up on the nose, the prelude to creamy prickle and a taut, racy palate. Their other two Metodo Classicos also delivered, the delicately mineral and iodine Brut and the Rosé, a clear wine in its faded rose color and fragrance of fruit. The Gutturnio Superiore Ciccotto '18 also performed well. It's a mature and intense wine with notes of herbs.

○ Cuvée Il Pigro Dosaggio Zero M. Cl. '16	♥♥ 4
● Gutturnio Sup. Colto Vitato del Cicotto '17	♥♥ 2*
● Caravaggio '17	♥♥ 5
○ Colto Vitato della Filanda n. 3 '17	♥♥ 3
○ Cuvée Il Pigro Brut M. Cl. '16	♥♥ 4
☉ Cuvée Il Pigro Brut M. Cl. Rosé '16	♥♥ 4
● Gutturnio Sup. Colto Vitato della Bellaria '18	♥♥ 2
● Vibo '17	♥ 2
● C. P. Gutturnio Sup. Colto Vitato della Bellaria '16	♀♀ 2*
● Colto Vitato del Cicotto '16	♀♀ 2*
○ Colto Vitato della Filanda n. 3 '16	♀♀ 3*
○ Cuvée Il Pigro Brut M. Cl. '15	♀♀ 4
● Gutturnio Sup. Colto Vitato della Bellaria n. 15 '17	♀♀ 2*

Tenuta Saiano

FRAZ. MONTEBELLO DI POGGIO TORRIANA
VIA CASONE, 35
47825 TORRIANA [RN]
TEL. +39 0541675515
www.tenutasaiano.it

CELLAR SALES
PRE-BOOKED VISITS
ACCOMMODATION AND RESTAURANT SERVICE
ANNUAL PRODUCTION 20,000 bottles
HECTARES UNDER VINE 11.00
VITICULTURE METHOD Certified Organic

This is an extraordinary place in every respect, displaying undeniable natural charm and high-quality intensive work: a visit to Tenuta Saiano certainly gladdens your heart. The territory is in the Rimini hills near Torriana, a setting that sees vines snatch portions of land from woods and share the scene with olives. There are also some animals, which form a kind of oasis that respects the natural life cycle of flora and fauna. The vineyard slopes down toward the valley, on Monte Scorticata: the wines express all these environmental features. The impact isn't entirely transparent, but their Sangiovese Sup. Gianciotto '18 makes itself appreciated. It opens slowly, both on the nose and the palate, exhibiting a background rich in charm and flavor. Their Animo '18 is a Rebola that's at once vibrant and delicate, quite impressive, while the Rosanita '17 is an original Brut redolent of wild fennel, medlar and orange peel.

○ Colli di Rimini Rebola L'Animo '18	♥♥ 3
● Romagna Sangiovese Sup. Gianciotto '18	♥♥ 2*
☉ Rosanita Brut Rosé	♥♥ 3
● Romagna Sangiovese Sup. Gianciotto '15	♀♀ 2*
● Romagna Sangiovese Sup. Gianciotto '14	♀♀ 2*
● Romagna Sangiovese Sup. Gianciotto '13	♀♀ 2*
● Saiano '16	♀♀ 3
● Saiano Rosso '15	♀♀ 2*
● Saiano Rosso '14	♀♀ 2*
● Saiano Rosso '13	♀♀ 2*

★San Patrignano

VIA SAN PATRIGNANO, 53
47853 CORIANO [RN]
TEL. +39 0541362111
www.spaziosanpa.com

PRE-BOOKED VISITS
RESTAURANT SERVICE
ANNUAL PRODUCTION 500,000 bottles
HECTARES UNDER VINE 110.00
VITICULTURE METHOD Certified Organic

This is more than just a winery, it's a benchmark social project that has created a complex organization able to encompass several fronts: San Patrignano, in fact, belongs to a drug rehabilitation community founded by Vincenzo Muccioli in 1978. It is located in the Colli di Rimini, where plots are planted with Bordeaux varieties, which have proved to root well, as well as Sangiovese. Their modern range focusses on ripeness, fullness and good roundness, with aging in small wooden casks reserved for the more serious wines. 2016 was good to their Sangiovese Avi Riserva, making for one of the best versions in recent memory. Toasty notes open the dance, but a mix of fruit nicely balances its components. Its riper sensations, even opulent at times, are a signature of the territory, as are penetrating but integrated tannins. Their Montepirolo '16 also performed well.

● Romagna Sangiovese Sup. Avi Ris. '16	♟♟♟ 4*
○ Aulente Bianco '18	♟♟ 2*
● Colli di Rimini Cabernet Sauvignon Montepirolo '16	♟♟ 4
○ Vie '18	♟ 3
● Colli di Rimini Cabernet Sauvignon Montepirolo '15	♟♟♟ 4*
● Colli di Rimini Cabernet Sauvignon Montepirolo '13	♟♟♟ 4*
● Colli di Rimini Cabernet Sauvignon Montepirolo '12	♟♟♟ 4*
● Romagna Sangiovese Sup. Avi Ris. '11	♟♟♟ 5
● Sangiovese di Romagna Sup. A vi Ris. '08	♟♟♟ 5
● Sangiovese di Romagna Sup. Ora '12	♟♟♟ 3*
● Sangiovese di Romagna Sup. Ora '11	♟♟♟ 3*

Tenuta Santa Lucia

VIA GIARDINO, 1400
47025 MERCATO SARACENO [FC]
TEL. +39 054790441
www.santaluciavinery.it

CELLAR SALES
PRE-BOOKED VISITS
ACCOMMODATION
ANNUAL PRODUCTION 90,000 bottles
HECTARES UNDER VINE 17.00
VITICULTURE METHOD Certified Biodynamic
SUSTAINABLE WINERY

This is an intriguing winery and a worthy standard bearer for an original area like the upper Savio valley. Here in Mercato Saraceno, vineyards are cultivated with respect and passion according to the principles of biodynamics. The grapes are almost exclusively local ones, such as Albana, Famoso, Centesimino and, of course, Sangiovese. Their wines exhibit a marked personality and are about as good as they get in this production area. Kudos to their Albana Secco Albarara '18, a fantastic wine that pours a vibrant yellow. On the nose it enchants for its aromas of ripe fruit and flowers, tea, fresh citrus and flint. It also proves intriguing on the palate, aromatically coherent, full and as structured as it is dynamic, closing on an extraordinary sweet-savory contrast. Their 100-year anniversary wine, the Centuplo '18, is fun in its delicate primaries and light palate.

○ Romagna Albana Secco Albarara '18	♟♟ 3*
● Centuplo '18	♟ 3
● Romagna Sangiovese Sup. Taibo '17	♟ 3
○ Vensamè	♟ 4
○ Albana di Romagna Secco Alba Rara '15	♟♟ 2*
● Centuplo Centesimino '13	♟♟ 3
○ Romagna Albana Passito Albarara '11	♟♟ 4
○ Romagna Albana Secco Alba Rara '17	♟♟ 3
○ Romagna Albana Secco Albarara '16	♟♟ 3*

Tenuta Santini

FRAZ. PASSANO
VIA CAMPO, 33
47853 CORIANO [RN]
TEL. +39 0541656527
www.tenutasantini.com

CELLAR SALES
PRE-BOOKED VISITS
ANNUAL PRODUCTION 40,000 bottles
HECTARES UNDER VINE 22.00

The estate is located in the Coriano hills, behind Rimini and Riccione, between San Marino and Val Marecchia. Founded in the 1960s by two brothers, Giuseppe and Primo Santino, today the winery features a modern tone. Their vineyards are planted on calcareous-clay soils and benefit from a typical Mediterranean climate. They cultivate Bordeaux grapes, as well as Sangiovese. Their wines are structured, well-crafted, intense and succulent. It seems as if their reds are missing a bit of personality, at least not enough to reach our highest honors. Their Sangiovese Beato Enrico '17 goes all in on notes of dark fruit, from blackberries to blueberries, sensations that reemerge on a pleasant palate that closes with a not entirely integrated tannic presence. The Cornelianum '16 is dominated by toasty notes while the Rebola Isotta '18 proves simple but enjoyable.

● Romagna Sangiovese Sup. Beato Enrico '17	♟♟ 2*
○ Colli di Rimini Rebola Isotta '18	♟ 2
● Romagna Sangiovese Sup. Cornelianum Ris. '16	♟ 4
● Battarreo '15	♟♟ 3
● Battarreo '14	♟♟ 3*
● Romagna Sangiovese Sup. Beato Enrico '16	♟♟ 2*
● Romagna Sangiovese Sup. Beato Enrico '15	♟♟ 2*
● Romagna Sangiovese Sup. Cornelianum Ris. '15	♟♟ 4
● Romagna Sangiovese Sup. Orione '15	♟♟ 4

Terre Cevico

VIA FIUMAZZO, 72
48022 LUGO [RA]
TEL. +39 0545284711
www.gruppocevico.com

CELLAR SALES
PRE-BOOKED VISITS
ANNUAL PRODUCTION 50,000,000 bottles
HECTARES UNDER VINE 7000.00

Cevico is a large-scale cooperative that brings together a good 4500 vignerons and 6700 hectares of vineyards. Their activities extend well beyond the borders of Romagna. A winery of this size naturally involves numerous productive and commercial subsets, as well as many brands and wines. Their top brands include Terre Cevico, Vigneti Galassi, Sancrispino, Ronco, Romandiola and Bernardi: all projects with limited numbers, at least as far as the parent company is concerned, which aim to promote their territory and unique vineyards. And the Romandiola project gave rise to the best results based on our most recent tastings. The dark fruit and herbaceous notes of their Sangiovese Malatesta '18 proved excellent, while we were fully convinced by the characteristically macerated and tannic Albana Nova Luna '18, a wine endowed with excellent freshness. Good signs from their Sangiovese Vigneti Galassi '18 as well.

○ Albana di Romagna Secco Nova Luna '18	♟♟ 3
● Romagna Sangiovese La Romandiola Il Malatesta '18	♟♟ 3
● Romagna Sangiovese La Romandiola Nova Luna '18	♟♟ 3
● Romagna Sangiovese Vign. Galassi '18	♟ 2
○ Albana di Romagna Secco Romandiola '15	♟♟ 3
○ Colli di Imola Pignoletto Frizzante Romandiola '15	♟♟ 2*
● Romagna Sangiovese Sup. Vign. Galassi '17	♟♟ 2*
● Romagna Sangiovese Sup. Vign. Galassi '16	♟♟ 2*
● Romagna Sangiovese Sup. Vign. Galassi '15	♟♟ 2*

Torre San Martino

VIA MORANA, 14
47015 MODIGLIANA [FC]
TEL. +39 0546940102
www.torre1922.it

CELLAR SALES
PRE-BOOKED VISITS
ANNUAL PRODUCTION 45,000 bottles
HECTARES UNDER VINE 15.00

Torre San Martino is a benchmark for winemaking in Romagna and a leading representative of the Modigliana terroir. The property boasts a legacy of old vines, some dating back to the 1920s, along the Acerreta valley, one of three valleys that rise towards the Apennines. The vine rows are laid out like an amphitheater, at an elevation of 300 meters and on soils with good amounts of clay. Their wines prove as elegant as they are intense, with excellent structure, and evolve well over time. The Sangiovese Vigna 1922, a child of a blessed 2016, performed well during our tastings. The year gave rise to a version of great balance, exhibiting elegance and nice verb — though it still manages an aromatic impact with nice presence. Spices dominate, making for intriguing fragrances and a spicy palate. Among the whites, their flavorful and macerated Vigna della Signora '18 stood out.

● Romagna Sangiovese Modigliana V. 1922 '16	⬤⬤ 7
○ Colli Di Faenza Bianco V. Della Signora '18	⬤⬤ 5
● Romagna Sangiovese Modigliana Gemme '18	⬤ 5
● Romagna Sangiovese Modigliana Sup. V. 1922 Ris. '13	⬤⬤⬤ 6
● Romagna Sangiovese Sup. Gemme '14	⬤⬤⬤ 3*
● Sangiovese di Romagna V. 1922 Ris. '11	⬤⬤⬤ 6
● Romagna Sangiovese Modigliana Gemme '16	⬤⬤ 3
● Romagna Sangiovese Modigliana V. 1922 '15	⬤⬤ 5

La Tosa

LOC. LA TOSA
29020 VIGOLZONE [PC]
TEL. +39 0523870727
www.latosa.it

CELLAR SALES
PRE-BOOKED VISITS
RESTAURANT SERVICE
ANNUAL PRODUCTION 110,000 bottles
HECTARES UNDER VINE 19.00

Stefano and Ferruccio Pizzamiglio were born in Milan and destined to a medical career, but the call of family brought them back to their mother's land in Piacenza's hills. Back in the 1980s they purchased their first plots of land (almost just for the fun of it), including the farm that the estate is named after. Four years later they founded the winery, which has become a benchmark over the years in Val Nure and the whole Piacenza area. They have since added accommodation, a library and a wine museum. The Malvasia Secca Sorriso di Cielo is always a sure bet, and that includes the 2018. It's a varietal wine, redolent of tropical fruits, citrus and aromatic herbs. On the palate it's sapid, flavorful, juicy and racy. The Luna Selvatica '17, a spicy Cabernet Sauvignon that features fragrant fruit, aromas of hay, stuffing and precise tannins, proved well-crafted. The Vignamorello '17 is a fruit forward and palpably sapid Gutturnio Superiore. Their Riodeltordo, a white made with Malvasia, Ortrugo, Trebbiano and Sauvignon, proves highly pleasant in its kaleidoscope of tropical fruit.

● C. P. Cabernet Sauvignon Luna Selvatica '17	⬤⬤ 5
○ C. P. Malvasia Sorriso di Cielo '18	⬤⬤ 3
● Gutturnio Sup. Vignamorello '17	⬤⬤ 4
○ Riodeltordo '18	⬤⬤ 2*
○ C. P. Sauvignon '18	⬤ 3
● Gutturnio Frizzante Terrafiaba '18	⬤ 2
● Gutturnio Sup. TerredellaTosa '18	⬤ 2
● C. P. Gutturnio Sup. TerredellaTosa '16	⬤⬤ 2*
● C. P. Gutturnio Sup. Vignamorello '15	⬤⬤ 4
○ C. P. Malvasia Sorriso di Cielo '17	⬤⬤ 3
○ C. P. Malvasia Sorriso di Cielo '12	⬤⬤ 3
○ C. P. Valnure Riodeltordo '16	⬤⬤ 2*
● Gutturnio Sup. Vignamorello '16	⬤⬤ 4

Tre Monti

FRAZ. BERGULLO
VIA LOLA, 3
40026 IMOLA [BO]
TEL. +39 0542657116
www.tremonti.it

CELLAR SALES
PRE-BOOKED VISITS
ANNUAL PRODUCTION 180,000 bottles
HECTARES UNDER VINE 40.00
VITICULTURE METHOD Certified Organic
SUSTAINABLE WINERY

This now historic winery was set up in the 1970s and is run by the founder's children today. Tre Monti underwent a substantial modernization phase in the late 1980s: this was a decisive step for the recent life of this company, which achieves excellent results in terms of critique and market. It is divided into two main estates located between Bergullo (in the Imola hills) and Petrignone, in the Forlì area. The star performers in their wide range of wines are the native Sangiovese, Albana and Pignoletto grapes. Their Albana Secco Vitalba '18 is a truly charming and original wine made possible thanks to spontaneous fermentation, maturation in 470 liter Georgian amphoras, and maceration on the skins for 70-120 days. Its mature, oxidative tones are never over-the-top, calling up sensations of pollen, honey, burnt wheat, dates and dried citrus. On the palate it's a wonder of extractive measure, intensity and depth. Their 'dry' Vigna Rocca '18 is right up there as well.

○ Romagna Albana Secco Vitalba '18	▼▼▼ 4*
○ Romagna Albana V. Rocca '18	▼▼ 2*
● Romagna Sangiovese Sup. Petrignone Ris. '16	▼▼ 3
○ Anablà '18	▼ 3
● Colli di Imola Boldo '97	▼▼▼ 3*
● Sangiovese di Romagna Sup. Petrignone Ris. '08	▼▼▼ 3*
● Sangiovese di Romagna Sup. Petrignone Ris. '07	▼▼▼ 4
● Sangiovese di Romagna Sup. Petrignone Ris. '06	▼▼▼ 3
○ Romagna Albana V. Rocca '17	▼▼ 2*
● Romagna Sangiovese Sup. Campo di Mezzo '17	▼▼ 2*
● Romagna Sangiovese Sup. Thea Ris. '15	▼▼ 4
○ Thea Bianco '16	▼▼ 4

Trerè

LOC. MONTICORALLI
VIA CASALE, 19
48018 FAENZA [RA]
TEL. +39 054647034
www.trere.com

CELLAR SALES
PRE-BOOKED VISITS
ACCOMMODATION AND RESTAURANT SERVICE
ANNUAL PRODUCTION 150,000 bottles
HECTARES UNDER VINE 35.00
SUSTAINABLE WINERY

Treré is a veteran winery, located in the beautiful hills of Faenza. It displays a modern façade, in terms of both the graphics and style of their numerous wines. Podere Saccona is the heart of the winery, where it all began back in the 1960s. Then other land came along, for instance Podere Ca' Lunga. Their wine range proves constantly praiseworthy for its interpretative precision and its ability to never lose touch with the grapes and territorial character, while maintaining a modern outlook. The Romagna Sangiovese Sup. Sperone '18 is redolent of blackberry and dark wild berries, with a delicate but pleasant smoky sensation in the background. Its varietal brother, the Lona Bona '18, is more approachable but moves on a similar track, with fruit as intense as it is fresh and licorice emerging both on the nose and on the palate. It's a delectable wine and great drinking.

○ Re Famoso '18	▼▼ 2*
● Romagna Sangiovese Lona Bona '18	▼▼ 2*
● Romagna Sangiovese Sup. Sperone '18	▼▼ 2*
○ Re Bianco '18	▼ 2
○ Romagna Albana Armarcord d'un Bianc '17	▼ 3
○ Romagna Albana Secco Arlùs '18	▼ 2
○ Albana di Romagna Passito Mrosa '15	▼▼ 4
○ Romagna Albana Secco Arlùs '17	▼▼ 2*
● Romagna Sangiovese Lôna Bôna '17	▼▼ 2*
● Romagna Sangiovese Sup. Amarcord d'un Ross Ris. '15	▼▼ 3
● Sangiovese di Romagna Sup. Sperone '15	▼▼ 2*

Marta Valpiani

VIA BAGNOLO, 158
47011 CASTROCARO TERME E TERRA DEL SOLE [FC]
TEL. +39 0543769598
www.vinimartavalpiani.it

CELLAR SALES
PRE-BOOKED VISITS
ANNUAL PRODUCTION 19,000 bottles
HECTARES UNDER VINE 11.50

The Marta Valpiani winery has certainly established itself as one of the most original and innovative in Romagna, especially if we consider what has happened in this area in recent years. Although it is named after the founder, today her daughter Elisa Mazzavillani is the modern face of the winery. Their vineyards are concentrated in the Castrocaro Terme subzone. Their style of interpreting wines is familiar: airy and elegant, with precise extraction, nuanced aromas and they go down easily. Their flagship Sangiovese, the Crete Azzurre '16, offers up complex fragrances of wild berries, bark and leaves crossed by an almost smoky stroke. Its not totally transparent on the primaries, these open and characterize a linear palate, first welcoming and then quite spirited. The Sangiovese Sup. '17 is delicious highly elegant, while the Albana Madonna dei Fiori is just as gratifying.

● Romagna Sangiovese Castrocaro e Terra del Sole Crete Azzurre '16	▼▼ 3*
○ Romagna Albana Secco Madonna dei Fiori '18	▼▼ 3
● Romagna Sangiovese Sup. '17	▼▼ 2*
● Romagna Sangiovese Castrocaro e Terra del Sole Crete Azzurre '15	▽▽▽ 3*
○ Bianco '15	▽▽ 2*
● LaFarfalla '16	▽▽ 2*
○ Marta Valpiani Bianco '17	▽▽ 3
● Romagna Sangiovese Sup. '16	▽▽ 2*
● Romagna Sangiovese Sup. '15	▽▽ 2*
● Romagna Sangiovese Sup. '14	▽▽ 2*

Cantina Valtidone

VIA MORETTA, 58
29011 BORGONOVO VAL TIDONE [PC]
TEL. +39 0523846411
www.cantinavaltidone.it

CELLAR SALES
PRE-BOOKED VISITS
ANNUAL PRODUCTION 6,500,000 bottles
HECTARES UNDER VINE 1100.00
VITICULTURE METHOD Certified Organic
SUSTAINABLE WINERY

Compared to many cooperatives founded at the start of the last century, Cantina Valtidone is young. It was founded by 16 members in 1966, just outside Borgonovo Val Tidone, where they're still based. Then they began upgrading and growing. It now numbers 220 members who produce 90 thousand quintals of grapes per year, 80% of which are used for DOCs. 50 Vendemmie is their flagship line, with Alba's, Francesco Fissore bringing out the best of Piacenza's traditional wines. First a clarification. Even it's not on the label, their two Metodo Classico Perlages originate in two different vintages. The 2012, bottled only as a magnum, spends 3 extra years on the lees and you can taste it. It's evolved, delicate in its bead, sapid, taut and fragrant. It has verve and depth. The supper (but also simpler) 2015 is more mineral, with citrus notes. The Bollo Rosso '15 is a Gutturnio Ris. with substance — full and generous, it offers up jammy aromas. Their entire 50 Vendemmie line delivers, with a special mention for the Gutturnio Classico Sup.

○ Perlage Brut M. Cl. Magnum	▼▼ 6
● Gutturnio Bollo Rosso Ris. '15	▼▼ 4
● Gutturnio Cl. Sup 50 Vendemmie '18	▼▼ 3
○ Colli Piacentini Malvasia 50 Vendemmie '18	▼ 3
● Gutturnio Frizzante 50 Vendemmie '18	▼ 3
○ Perlage Brut M. Cl.	▼ 4
○ Venus Malvasia Dolce '17	▼ 3
○ C. P. Malvasia 50 Vendemmie '17	▽▽ 2
● Gutturnio Frizzante 50 Vendemmie '17	▽▽ 2

Podere Vecciano

VIA VECCIANO, 23
47852 CORIANO [RN]
TEL. +39 0541658388
www.poderevecciano.it

CELLAR SALES
PRE-BOOKED VISITS
ANNUAL PRODUCTION 100,000 bottles
HECTARES UNDER VINE 15.00
VITICULTURE METHOD Certified Organic
SUSTAINABLE WINERY

Podere Vecciano is located in the inland hills of Rimini, where the vineyards enjoy good exposure, excellent sunlight and sea breezes. Rows of vines share the scene with a variety of flora and are cultivated using methods that respect the environment and with an eye to biodynamics. They grow Sangiovese, Rebola, Pagadebit and Famoso, but also Montepulciano and international varieties such as Chardonnay, Merlot and Petit Verdot. Their winemaking experiments in amphorae prove interesting. This year's tastings confirmed the winery's strong bill of health and its persuasive stylistic approach. Their selection is led by the Sangiovese Superiore d'Enio Ris. '16, an introverted wine that's as pure and essential as it is charming, taut and linear. Their Sangiovese Monte Tauro '18 also enchants with its aromas of pomegranate and fresh cherry, while among their whites the full and floral Rebola Vigna Le Ginestre '18 stands out.

○ Colli di Rimini Rebola V. La Ginestra '18	♟♟♟ 3
● Romagna Sangiovese Sup. D'Enio Ris. '16	♟♟ 4
● Romagna Sangiovese Sup. Monte Tauro '18	♟♟ 2*
○ Pian delle Marne '18	♟ 2
○ Romagna Pagadebit Vigna delle Rose '18	♟ 2
● Romagna Sangiovese Sup. Vignalmonte '17	♟ 3
● Colli di Rimini Sangiovese Montetauro '14	♟♟ 2*
○ Ramante Rosé Brut '15	♟♟ 2*
● Romagna Sangiovese Sup. Vignalmonte '13	♟♟ 3
● Sangiovese di Romagna Sup. D'Enio Ris. '11	♟♟ 4
● Vignalavolta '12	♟♟ 2*

Venturini Baldini

FRAZ. RONCOLO
VIA TURATI, 42
42020 QUATTRO CASTELLA [RE]
TEL. +39 0522249011
www.venturinibaldini.it

CELLAR SALES
PRE-BOOKED VISITS
RESTAURANT SERVICE
ANNUAL PRODUCTION 90,000 bottles
HECTARES UNDER VINE 35.00
VITICULTURE METHOD Certified Organic
SUSTAINABLE WINERY

A splendid estate surrounds Villa Manodori, which was built in the early 1500s on even older foundations dating back to the time of Matilda of Canossa. 30 hectares of vineyards are cultivated under organic management (one of the first wineries in Emilia to obtain certification), at an elevation of 370 meters, as well as over 100 hectares of woods, meadows and springs. The current winery was founded in 1976 and now belongs to a foreign owner that decided to invest in Lambrusco made in Emilia, in these hills between Parma and Reggio Emilia. The Cadelvento, a sparkler made with Sorbara and Grasparossa fermented after brief maceration on the skins, offers up aromas of citrus, flowers and aromatic herbs. On the palate it's lively, supple, focused and persistent. Made with Salamino grapes, their Montelocco is a semidry that features slightly overripe aromas of black cherry, while the Rubino del Cerro (Montericco, Salamino, Grasparossa) is dry and redolent of small berries and mountain herbs.

⊙ Reggiano Lambrusco Brut Cadelvento Rosé '18	♟♟♟ 3*
● Montelocco Lambrusco	♟♟ 3
● Reggiano Lambrusco Spumante Brut Rubino del Cerro	♟ 3
⊙ Reggiano Lambrusco Brut Cadelvento Rosé '17	♟♟♟ 3*
● Reggiano Lambrusco Marchese Manodori '16	♟♟♟ 3*
● Reggiano Lambrusco Brut Rubino del Cerro '17	♟♟ 3
● Reggiano Lambrusco Marchese Manodori '17	♟♟ 3*
● Reggiano Lambrusco Marchese Manodori '15	♟♟ 3*
⊙ Reggiano Lambrusco Rosato Spumante Secco Cadelvento '15	♟♟ 3

Francesco Vezzelli

FRAZ. SAN MATTEO
VIA CANALETTO NORD, 878A
41122 MODENA
TEL. +39 059318695
aavezzelli@gmail.com

CELLAR SALES
PRE-BOOKED VISITS
ANNUAL PRODUCTION 120,000 bottles
HECTARES UNDER VINE 15.00

This interesting little winery, founded in the Lambrusco di Sorbara area in 1958, has reached its third generation of vinegrowers. Their vineyards lie in a characteristic position along the left bank of the Secchia River, in the municipality of Soliera, opposite Bomporto and Cristo di Sorbara on the other bank. These loose and stony floodplain soils are ideal for growing Sorbara, which achieves its best expression here, making for elegant, taut and mineral wines. It is also made as a sparkling wine. Redolent of citrus and small wild berries, the Soldino is a vigorous semidry Sorbara, extremely pleasant and precise in its balancing of sweetness and acidity. Their Bollabianca is a sparkling Pignoletto with aromas of flowers and white-fleshed fruits, delicate in its fresh and fragrant simplicity. Morosa is a rosé whose color is quite vibrant and whose aromas recall wild strawberries and freshly cut grass. The Selezione is a sapid and mineral sparkling Sorbara, while the Grasparossa Rive dei Ciligi features hints of small wild berries.

○ Bollabianca Brut	🍷🍷 3
● Lambrusco di Sorbara Soldino '18	🍷🍷 2*
● Lambrusco di Sorbara Brut Il Selezione	🍷 2
⊙ Lambrusco di Sorbara Brut MoRosa M. Cl.	🍷 3
● Lambrusco Grasparossa di Castelvetro Rive dei Ciliegi '18	🍷 2
● Lambrusco di Sorbara Brut Il Selezione '17	🍷🍷 2*
● Lambrusco di Sorbara Il Selezione '15	🍷🍷 2*
● Lambrusco di Sorbara Il Selezione '14	🍷🍷 2*
● Lambrusco di Sorbara Secco Soldino '15	🍷🍷 2*
● Lambrusco di Sorbara Soldino '16	🍷🍷 2*
⊙ Lambrusco di Sorbara Spumante Brut MoRosa Rosé '15	🍷🍷 2*

Villa di Corlo

LOC. BAGGIOVARA
S.DA CAVEZZO, 200
41126 MODENA
TEL. +39 059510736
www.villadicorlo.com

CELLAR SALES
PRE-BOOKED VISITS
ANNUAL PRODUCTION 100,000 bottles
HECTARES UNDER VINE 16.50
VITICULTURE METHOD Certified Organic

This lovely winery, headed by Maria Antonietta Munari, runs entirely on photovoltaic panels. It is located just outside Modena, to the southwest of the city, on the best soils for producing Lambrusco Grasparossa di Castelvetro. International varieties, such as Cabernet Sauvignon, Merlot and Chardonnay are grown at an elevation of about 320 meters, on the south/southeastern-facing slopes of the hills. Chardonnay is used to produce a Metodo Classico sparkling wine. Two types of Traditional Balsamic Vinegar are produced in the attic of the villa, as per tradition in Modena. We very much appreciated their Grasparossa Secco, with its healthy, fragrant fruit (blackberries and blueberries, plus a hint of medicinal herbs). On the palate it shows vigor and pulp, coming through fresh and characterized by a nice, racy finish. The Olimpia semidry features similar aromas, with blueberry in the foreground and a nice balance of sweet fruit, acidity and tannins. Their Corleto exhibits an earthier style, with aromas of forest undergrowth.

● Lambrusco Grasparossa di Castelvetro Villa di Corlo '18	🍷🍷 2*
○ Ghiareto Pignoletto Extra Dry	🍷🍷 2*
● Lambrusco di Sorbara Primevo '18	🍷🍷 2*
● Lambrusco Grasparossa di Castelvetro Corleto '18	🍷🍷 2*
● Lambrusco Grasparossa di Castelvetro Semisecco Olimpia Bio '18	🍷🍷 2*
● Lambrusco di Sorbara Primevo '14	🍷🍷 2*
● Lambrusco Grasparossa di Castelvetro '16	🍷🍷 2*
● Lambrusco Grasparossa di Castelvetro Corleto '17	🍷🍷 2*
● Lambrusco Grasparossa di Castelvetro Corleto '16	🍷🍷 2*
● Lambrusco Grasparossa di Castelvetro Corleto '15	🍷🍷 2*

Villa Papiano

VIA IBOLA, 24
47015 MODIGLIANA [FC]
TEL. +39 3381041271
www.villapapiano.it

CELLAR SALES
PRE-BOOKED VISITS
ANNUAL PRODUCTION 50,000 bottles
HECTARES UNDER VINE 10.00
VITICULTURE METHOD Certified Organic
SUSTAINABLE WINERY

The origins of this estate date far back to the 15th century and the times of Papiano, the Medici family's lieutenant. However, it was in the early 2000s that this winery found new drive and set out on a more modern path. The Modigliana territory is characterized by poor soils, significant differences in elevation and vineyards surrounded by woods and vegetation. This prestigious environment, combined with the winery's style, makes for pure, delectable wines with excellent finesse and good complexity. The Sangiovese Modigliana Probi Ris. '16 proves highly charming. Aromatically it sacrifices a bit of transparency in favor of delicate sylvan sensations, quite intriguing in their own way. The palate is airy and graceful, but tannins clench and cage in the finish, impeding it from a full expansion. Their Sangiovese Papesse '18 was just as convincing. It's an elegantly spicy wine imbued with sensations of red fruits, making for a juicy, streamlined palate.

● Romagna Sangiovese Modigliana I Probi Ris. '16	♟♟ 6
● Romagna Sangiovese Sup. Le Papesse '18	♟♟ 4
○ Strada Corniolo '18	♟ 5
● Romagna Sangiovese I Probi di Papiano Ris. '12	♟♟♟ 3*
● Romagna Sangiovese Modigliana I Probi di Papiano Ris. '15	♟♟♟ 4*
● Romagna Sangiovese Modigliana I Probi di Papiano Ris. '14	♟♟♟ 4*
● Romagna Sangiovese Modigliana I Probi di Papiano Ris. '13	♟♟♟ 3*
● Sangiovese di Romagna I Probi di Papiano Ris. '11	♟♟♟ 3*

Villa Venti

LOC. VILLAVENTI DI RONCOFREDDO
VIA DOCCIA, 1442
47020 FORLÌ
TEL. +39 0541949532
www.villaventi.it

CELLAR SALES
PRE-BOOKED VISITS
ACCOMMODATION
ANNUAL PRODUCTION 27,500 bottles
HECTARES UNDER VINE 7.00
VITICULTURE METHOD Certified Organic

Mauro Giardini and Davide Castellucci's winery is a benchmark. Their style combines the old with the modern, managing to sever with the recent past in order to embrace a modern model based on elegance, approachability and great drinkability. Sangiovese, Famoso and Centesimino are grown between Roncofreddo and Longiano, on the left bank of the Rubicon River, where the soils are clayey, sandy and calcareous, and elevations favor excellent ventilation. Their Sangiovese Superiore Primo Segno '17 shone during our tastings. It brings together a trademark finesse with excellent structure and ripeness (foremost sweet cherries). Even if the palate is still extremely crisp, linear and taut it's never immature or bitter — complete and delicious! Their fragrant Riserva Longiano '16 is also notable.

● Romagna Sangiovese Sup. Primo Segno '17	♟♟♟ 3*
● Romagna Sangiovese Longiano Ris. '16	♟♟ 5
○ Serenaro '18	♟ 3
● Sangiovese di Romagna Longiano Primo Segno '11	♟♟♟ 3*
● Sangiovese di Romagna Sup. Primo Segno '09	♟♟♟ 3*
● Sangiovese di Romagna Sup. Primo Segno '08	♟♟♟ 3*
● Centesimino A '16	♟♟ 4
● Romagna Sangiovese Sup. Primo Segno '16	♟♟ 3*
● Sangiovese di Romagna Sup. Primo Segno '15	♟♟ 3
● Sangiovese di Romagna Sup. Primo Segno '13	♟♟ 3*

★Fattoria Zerbina

FRAZ. MARZENO
VIA VICCHIO, 11
48018 FAENZA [RA]
TEL. +39 054640022
www.zerbina.com

CELLAR SALES
PRE-BOOKED VISITS
ANNUAL PRODUCTION 220,000 bottles
HECTARES UNDER VINE 33.00

Fattoria Zerbina is one of the most solid and mature wineries in Romagna. It demonstrates the unmistakable aptitude of this area for producing excellent wines of various types and nature. It belongs to the Geminiani family, who have followed some increasingly interesting paths since 1966 in the Marzeno subzone, with its red clay soils and alberello-trained vineyards. However, quality received a real boost in 1987, when Vincenzo's granddaughter Cristina took over. Their style is not static and the long tradition does not hinder new ideas and positive developments. Matured in concrete for about six months, the Bianco di Ceparano '18 (made with Albana grapes) is close-focused and vibrant with a pronounced smoky stroke. Their delicious Rosa di Ceparano '18 is a Sangiovese and Syrah redolent of raspberries and medlar. The Ceregio '18 is an accessible Sangiovese fermented entirely in steel and concrete. Tasting of some of their flagship reds and sweet wines was postponed.

○ Romagna Albana Secco Bianco di Ceparano '18	♟♟ 2*
⊙ Rosa di Ceparano '18	♟♟ 2*
● Romagna Sangiovese Sup. Ceregio '18	♟ 2
○ Albana di Romagna Passito AR Ris. '06	♟♟♟ 8
● Marzieno '08	♟♟♟ 4*
● Marzieno '04	♟♟♟ 5
○ Romagna Albana Passito Scacco Matto '13	♟♟♟ 6
● Sangiovese di Romagna Sup. Pietramora Ris. '11	♟♟♟ 5
● Sangiovese di Romagna Sup. Pietramora Ris. '08	♟♟♟ 6
● Sangiovese di Romagna Sup. Pietramora Ris. '06	♟♟♟ 6
● Sangiovese di Romagna Sup. Pietramora Ris. '04	♟♟♟ 6

Cantina Zucchi

LOC. SAN LORENZO
VIA VIAZZA, 64
41030 SAN PROSPERO [MO]
TEL. +39 059908934
www.vinizucchi.it

CELLAR SALES
PRE-BOOKED VISITS
ANNUAL PRODUCTION 130,000 bottles
HECTARES UNDER VINE 10.00
SUSTAINABLE WINERY

In the 1950s, the forefather Bruno Zucchi first began vinifying his own grapes in San Prospero, one of the best areas for producing Sorbara. He handed down this passion for wine to his son Davide and his wife Maura. The third generation, his daughter Silvia, has recently appeared on the scene to give new drive to production. She graduated in enology at Conegliano and has significant experience from working in Italy and abroad. Now they produce different types of Sorbara wine with a strong territorial character. This year Zucchi submitted a Metodo Classico Sorbara that we found decidedly interesting. It's a brilliantly colored (almost red) undosed 2016 with generous, transparent fruit and bead of nice finesse. It's evolved well, exhibiting vigor and substance — a truly well made wine. The Ancestrale '17 is very different (it couldn't be otherwise), more rustic, redolent of strawberry, raspberry and lime with earthy sensations. We also found the Sorbara '18 pleasant.

● Lambrusco di Sorbara Dosaggio Zero M. Cl. '16	♟♟ 5
● Lambrusco di Sorbara Fermentato in Questa Bottiglia '17	♟♟ 3
● Lambrusco di Sorbara Brut Rito '18	♟ 3
● Lambrusco di Sorbara Et. Bianca '18	♟ 2
● Modena Lambrusc Marascone '18	♟ 2
● Lambrusco di Sorbara Rito '14	♟♟♟ 2*
● Lambrusco di Sorbara Secco Rito '15	♟♟♟ 2*
● Lambrusco di Modena Marascone '16	♟♟ 2*
● Lambrusco di Sorbara Et. Bianca '17	♟♟ 2*
● Lambrusco di Sorbara Rito '16	♟♟ 3
● Modena Lambrusco Marascone '17	♟♟ 2*

Agrintesa

VIA G. GALILEI, 15
48018 FAENZA [RA]
TEL. +39 0546941195
www.cantineintesa.it

CELLAR SALES
PRE-BOOKED VISITS
ANNUAL PRODUCTION 350,000 bottles
HECTARES UNDER VINE 44.00

○ Romagna Albana Secco Poderi delle Rose '18	🍷🍷 2*
● Romagna Sangiovese Poderi delle Rose '18	🍷🍷 2*

Albinea Canali

FRAZ. CANALI
VIA TASSONI, 213
42123 REGGIO EMILIA
TEL. +39 0522569505
www.albineacanali.it

ANNUAL PRODUCTION 440,000 bottles
HECTARES UNDER VINE 150.00
VITICULTURE METHOD Certified Organic

● 1936 Lambrusco Bio	🍷🍷 2*
● Ottocentonero	🍷🍷 2*
○ Ottocentorosa Extra Dry Rosé	🍷🍷 2*

Podere dell'Angelo

VIA RODELLA, 38/40
47923 RIMINI
TEL. +39 0541727332

ANNUAL PRODUCTION 30,000 bottles
HECTARES UNDER VINE 10.00

● Colli di Rimini Cabernet Sauvignon Novanta '16	🍷🍷 2*
● Romagna Sangiovese Sup. Angelico '16	🍷🍷 2*
● Romagna Sangiovese Sup. Luis Ris. '15	🍷 2

Ariola Vigne e Vini

LOC. CALICELLA DI PILASTRO
FRAZ. PILASTRO
S.DA DELLA BUCA, 5A
43010 LANGHIRANO [PR]
TEL. +39 0521637678
www.viniariola.it

CELLAR SALES
PRE-BOOKED VISITS
RESTAURANT SERVICE
ANNUAL PRODUCTION 1,200,000 bottles
HECTARES UNDER VINE 70.00
SUSTAINABLE WINERY

○ Forte Rigoni Malvasia '18	🍷🍷 3
● Marcello Dry '18	🍷🍷 3

Balìa di Zola

VIA CASALE, 11
47015 MODIGLIANA [FC]
TEL. +39 0546940577
www.baliadizola.com

CELLAR SALES
PRE-BOOKED VISITS
ANNUAL PRODUCTION 30,000 bottles
HECTARES UNDER VINE 5.00

● Romagna Sangiovese Sup. Balitore '18	🍷🍷 3
● Romagna Sangiovese Modigliana Redinoce Ris. '16	🍷 4

Conte Otto Barattieri di San Pietro

VIA DEI TIGLI, 100
29020 VIGOLZONE [PC]
TEL. +39 0523875111
ottobarattieri@libero.it

CELLAR SALES
PRE-BOOKED VISITS
ANNUAL PRODUCTION 120,000 bottles
HECTARES UNDER VINE 34.00

○ C. P. Vin Santo Albarola '08	🍷🍷 5
● Gutturnio Sup. '17	🍷🍷 2*
● La Berganzina Barbera '18	🍷 2

Piccolo Brunelli

S.DA SAN ZENO, 1
47010 GALEATA [FC]
TEL. +39 3468020206
www.piccolobrunelli.it

CELLAR SALES
PRE-BOOKED VISITS
ACCOMMODATION
ANNUAL PRODUCTION 23,000 bottles
HECTARES UNDER VINE 20.00
SUSTAINABLE WINERY

● Romagna Sangiovese Sup.
  Dante 1872 Ris. '15   ♟♟ 4
● Romagna Sangiovese Predappio
  Cesco 1938 '17   ♟ 2

Cantina di Soliera

VIA CARPI RAVARINO, 529
41011 SOLIERA [MO]
TEL. +39 0522942135
www.cantinadisoliera.it

ANNUAL PRODUCTION 20,000 bottles
HECTARES UNDER VINE 5.00
SUSTAINABLE WINERY

● Lambrusco di Sorbara   ♟♟ 2*
● Lambrusco Grasparossa di Castelvetro
  Dolce Bocciolo   ♟♟ 2*

Casali Viticultori

FRAZ. PRATISSOLO
VIA DELLE SCUOLE, 7
42019 SCANDIANO [RE]
TEL. +39 0522855441
www.casalivini.it

CELLAR SALES
PRE-BOOKED VISITS
ANNUAL PRODUCTION 1,500,000 bottles
HECTARES UNDER VINE 48.00

● Feudi del Boiardo Lambrusco '18   ♟♟ 2*
● Reggiano Lambrusco Pra di Bosso '18 ♟♟ 2*
⊙ Rosa Casali Brut M. Cl.   ♟♟ 3

Castelluccio

LOC. POGGIOLO DI SOTTO
VIA TRAMONTO, 15
47015 MODIGLIANA [FC]
TEL. +39 0546942486
www.ronchidicastelluccio.it

CELLAR SALES
PRE-BOOKED VISITS
ACCOMMODATION
ANNUAL PRODUCTION 85,000 bottles
HECTARES UNDER VINE 16.00

○ Lunaria '18   ♟ 2
● Romagna Sangiovese Sup. Le More '18 ♟ 3
● Ronco dei Ciliegi '15   ♟ 3

Cantine Ceci

VIA PROVINCIALE, 99
43030 TORRILE [PR]
TEL. +39 0521810252
www.lambrusco.it

CELLAR SALES
PRE-BOOKED VISITS
ANNUAL PRODUCTION 1,500,000 bottles
HECTARES UNDER VINE 12.00

● In Moto con Bruno Ceci Brut   ♟♟ 2*
● Otello Nero di Lambrusco   ♟♟ 2*
● Terre Verdiane 1813 Lambrusco   ♟♟ 2*

Tenuta Colombarola

LOC. COLOMBAROLA
FRAZ. TREVOZZO
S.DA PROV.LE 412
29031 PIACENZA
TEL. +39 0523863932
www.tenutacolmbarola.com

ANNUAL PRODUCTION 100,000 bottles
HECTARES UNDER VINE 37.00

○ Extra Brut M. Cl.   ♟♟ 4
○ Pietragaia '16   ♟♟ 3
⊙ Brut M. Cl. Rosé   ♟ 4

Donelli

VIA CARLO SIGONIO, 54
41124 MODENA
TEL. +39 0522908715
www.donellivini.it

CELLAR SALES
PRE-BOOKED VISITS
ACCOMMODATION
ANNUAL PRODUCTION 30,000,000 bottles
HECTARES UNDER VINE 120.00
VITICULTURE METHOD Certified Organic

● Lambrusco di Sorbara Brut Sergio Scaglietti	♈♈ 2*
● Reggiano Lambrusco Brut Sergio Scaglietti	♈ 2

Maria Letizia Gaggioli

VIA F. RAIBOLINI IL FRANCIA, 55
40069 ZOLA PREDOSA [BO]
TEL. +39 051753489
www.gaggiolivini.it

CELLAR SALES
PRE-BOOKED VISITS
ACCOMMODATION AND RESTAURANT SERVICE
ANNUAL PRODUCTION 160,000 bottles
HECTARES UNDER VINE 21.00
SUSTAINABLE WINERY

● C.B. Merlot M '17	♈♈ 3
● C.B. Rosso Bologna '16	♈♈ 3
● C. B. Cabernet Sauvignon '16	♈ 3

Maria Galassi

FRAZ. PADERNO
VIA CASETTA, 688
47522 CESENA [FC]
TEL. +39 054721177
www.galassimaria.it

CELLAR SALES
PRE-BOOKED VISITS
ANNUAL PRODUCTION 18,000 bottles
HECTARES UNDER VINE 20.00
VITICULTURE METHOD Certified Organic

● Romagna Sangiovese Sup. La Ca' Storta Bio '18	♈♈ 2*
● Romagna Sangiovese Sup. Smembar '17	♈♈ 3

Fiorentini

VIA SADURANO, 6
47011 CASTROCARO TERME E TERRA DEL SOLE [FC]
TEL. +39 0543769123
www.fiorentini vini

CELLAR SALES
ANNUAL PRODUCTION 15,000 bottles
HECTARES UNDER VINE 6.50

○ Romagna Albana Secco Cleonice '18	♈♈ 4
● Romagna Sangiovese V. dei Dottori Ris. '15	♈♈ 2*

Podere Gaiaschi

LOC. CÀ DI SOTTO, 1
29010 NIBBIANO [PC]
TEL. +39 0523990346
www.poderegaiaschi.it

ANNUAL PRODUCTION 50,000 bottles
HECTARES UNDER VINE 6.00

○ C. P. Malvasia '18	♈♈ 2*
○ Orodolce MIavasia '18	♈♈ 2*
● C. P. Barbera Frizzante Diamante di Silvia '18	♈ 2

Garuti

FRAZ. SORBARA
VIA PER SOLARA, 6
41030 BOMPORTO [MO]
TEL. +39 059902021
www.garutivini.it

ANNUAL PRODUCTION 130,000 bottles
HECTARES UNDER VINE 30.00

● Lambrusco di Sorbara Podere Ca' Bianca	♈♈ 2*
○ Lambrusco di Sorbara Rosato Rosà	♈♈ 2*
● Lambrusco di Sorbara Fermentazione Naturale	♈ 2

La Grotta

LOC. SAIANO
VIA CIMADORI, 621
47023 CESENA [FC]
TEL. +39 0547326368
www.lagrottavini.it

CELLAR SALES
PRE-BOOKED VISITS
ANNUAL PRODUCTION 30,000 bottles
HECTARES UNDER VINE 12.00
SUSTAINABLE WINERY

○ Romagna Albana Secco Damadora '18	♟♟ 2*
● Romagna Sangiovese Sup. Mazapegul '18	♟♟ 2*
● Romagna Sangiovese Sup. Sallius '17	♟♟ 2*

Tenuta La Viola

VIA COLOMBARONE, 888
47032 BERTINORO [FC]
TEL. +39 0543445496
www.tenutalaviola.it

CELLAR SALES
PRE-BOOKED VISITS
ANNUAL PRODUCTION 44,000 bottles
HECTARES UNDER VINE 11.00
VITICULTURE METHOD Certified Organic
SUSTAINABLE WINERY

● Romagna Sangiovese Bertinoro P. Honorii Ris. '15	♟♟ 4
● Romagna Sangiovese Sup. In Terra '17	♟♟ 4

Lusvardi

LOC. MOLINO DI GAZZATA
VIA CANALE PER REGGIO, 2
42018 SAN MARTINO IN RIO [RE]
TEL. +39 0522646516
www.lusvardi.it

ANNUAL PRODUCTION 35,000 bottles
HECTARES UNDER VINE 3.50
VITICULTURE METHOD Certified Organic

○ Lusvardi Blanc Brut	♟♟ 3
● Senzafondo Lambrusco	♟♟ 3
● Grato Lambrusco Fermentazione in Bottiglia	♟ 3

Giovanna Madonia

LOC. VILLA MADONIA
VIA DE' CAPPUCCINI, 130
47032 BERTINORO [FC]
TEL. +39 0543444361
www.giovannamadonia.it

CELLAR SALES
PRE-BOOKED VISITS
RESTAURANT SERVICE
ANNUAL PRODUCTION 60,000 bottles
HECTARES UNDER VINE 14.00

● Romagna Sangiovese Bertinoro Ombroso Ris. '16	♟♟ 5
● Sterpigno '18	♟ 5
● Tenentino '18	♟ 2

Tenuta Masselina

LOC. SERRÀ
VIA POZZE, 1030
48014 CASTEL BOLOGNESE [RA]
TEL. +39 0545284711
www.masselina.it

ACCOMMODATION
ANNUAL PRODUCTION 50,000 bottles
HECTARES UNDER VINE 16.00

● Romagna Sangiovese Sup. Centotrentotto '18	♟♟ 2*
● Romagna Sangiovese Serra Ris. '15	♟ 4

Merlotta

VIA MERLOTTA, 1
40026 IMOLA [BO]
TEL. +39 054241740
info@merlotta.com

ANNUAL PRODUCTION 400,000 bottles
HECTARES UNDER VINE 45.00
SUSTAINABLE WINERY

○ Colli di Imola Chardonnay Grifaia '18	♟♟ 2*
● Romagna Sangiovese Sup. Ris. '16	♟♟ 3
● Romagna Albana Secco Fondatori '18	♟ 2

Poderi Morini

LOC. ORIOLO DEI FICHI
VIA GESUITA
48018 FAENZA [RA]
TEL. +39 0546634257
www.poderimorini.com

ANNUAL PRODUCTION 100,000 bottles
HECTARES UNDER VINE 26.00
SUSTAINABLE WINERY

○ Romagna Albana Passito Innamorato '12	♥♥ 4
○ Romagna Albana Secco Sette Note '18	♥♥ 3
● Nadèl '15	♥ 5

I Muretti

VIA SARCIANO, 5
47854 MONTESCUDO [RN]
TEL. +39 3356780500
www.imuretti.it

CELLAR SALES
PRE-BOOKED VISITS
ACCOMMODATION AND RESTAURANT SERVICE
ANNUAL PRODUCTION 23,000 bottles
HECTARES UNDER VINE 5.00
VITICULTURE METHOD Certified Organic
SUSTAINABLE WINERY

○ Colli di Rimini Rebola Libera '18	♥♥ 3
● Colli di Rimini Sangiovese Sup. Complice '17	♥♥ 3

Opera 02 di Ca' Montanari

FRAZ. LEVIZZANO RANGONE
VIA MEDUSIA, 32
41014 CASTELVETRO DI MODENA [MO]
TEL. +39 059741019
www.opera02.it

CELLAR SALES
PRE-BOOKED VISITS
ACCOMMODATION AND RESTAURANT SERVICE
ANNUAL PRODUCTION 75,000 bottles
HECTARES UNDER VINE 20.00
VITICULTURE METHOD Certified Organic
SUSTAINABLE WINERY

● Lambrusco di Modena Amabile	♥♥ 2*
● Lambrusco Grasparossa di Castelvetro Brut Operapura	♥♥ 3

Podere Palazzo

VIA ORTE, 120
47521 CESENA [FC]
TEL. +39 340 959 2725
www.poderepalazzo.it

ANNUAL PRODUCTION 60,000 bottles
HECTARES UNDER VINE 10.00
SUSTAINABLE WINERY

● Romagna Sangiovese Sup. Augustus Ris. '16	♥♥ 3
● Romagna Sangiovese Sup. Don Pasquale '17	♥♥ 2*

Pertinello

VIA ARPINETO PERTINELLO, 2
47010 GALEATA [FC]
TEL. +39 0543983156
www.tenutapertinello.it

CELLAR SALES
PRE-BOOKED VISITS
ANNUAL PRODUCTION 70,000 bottles
HECTARES UNDER VINE 14.00
VITICULTURE METHOD Certified Organic

○ Extra Brut M. Cl.	♥ 4
● Pinot Nero di Pertinello '17	♥ 5
● Romagna Sangiovese Il Bosco di Pertinello '18	♥ 2

Poderi dal Nespoli 1929

LOC. NESPOLI
VILLA ROSSI, 50
47012 CIVITELLA DI ROMAGNA [FC]
TEL. +39 0543989911
www.poderidalnespoli.com

CELLAR SALES
PRE-BOOKED VISITS
ACCOMMODATION
ANNUAL PRODUCTION 1,000,000 bottles
HECTARES UNDER VINE 180.00
SUSTAINABLE WINERY

● Romagna Sangiovese Sup. Ris. '16	♥♥ 4
● Romagna Sangiovese Sup. Prugneto '18	♥ 3

Il Poggiarello

LOC. SCRIVELLANO DI STATTO
29020 TRAVO [PC]
TEL. +39 0523957241
www.ilpoggiarellovini.it

CELLAR SALES
PRE-BOOKED VISITS
ANNUAL PRODUCTION 100,000 bottles
HECTARES UNDER VINE 18.00

● Gutturnio Frizzante Spago '18	♟♟ 2*
○ L'Alba e la Pietra Annoquattordici	♟♟ 5
● Gutturnio Sup. La Barbona '16	♟ 3

Quinto Passo

LOC. SOZZIGALLI DI SOLIERA
VIA CANALE, 267
41019 SOLIERA [MO]
TEL. +39 0593163311
www.quintopasso.it

CELLAR SALES
ANNUAL PRODUCTION 40,000 bottles
HECTARES UNDER VINE 12.00

⊙ Modena Brut Rosé M. Cl. '15	♟♟ 4
○ Pas Dosé M. Cl. '15	♟♟ 5

Podere il Saliceto

VIA ALBONE, 10
41011 CAMPOGALLIANO [MO]
TEL. +39 3491459612
www.podereilsaliceto.com

ANNUAL PRODUCTION 13,000 bottles
HECTARES UNDER VINE 4.00

● Lambrusco di Sorbara Brut Nature M. Cl. Ring Adora '16	♟♟ 3
● Lambrusco di Sorbara Falistra	♟♟ 2*

Tenuta de' Stefenelli

FRAZ. FRATTA TERME
VIA FRATTA, KM 1,800
47032 BERTINORO [FC]
TEL. +39 3332182466
www.destefenelli.it

CELLAR SALES
PRE-BOOKED VISITS
ACCOMMODATION
ANNUAL PRODUCTION 16,000 bottles
HECTARES UNDER VINE 10.00

○ Capriccio Italiano '15	♟♟ 4
○ Swing '18	♟♟ 2*
● Romagna Sangiovese Sup. Armonia '15	♟ 4

Cantina Sociale Vicobarone

FRAZ. VICOBARONE
VIA CRETA, 60
29010 ZIANO PIACENTINO [PC]
TEL. +39 0523868522
www.cantinavicobarone.com

CELLAR SALES
PRE-BOOKED VISITS
ANNUAL PRODUCTION 2,700,000 bottles
HECTARES UNDER VINE 800.00

○ C. P. Malvasia Spumante Dolce Cassiopea '18	♟♟ 2*
⊙ Duevì Extra Dry Rosé	♟♟ 2*
○ C. P. Malvasia Theta '18	♟ 2

Consorzio Vini di San Marino

LOC. BORGO MAGGIORE
FRAZ. VALDRAGONE - S.DA SERRABOLINO, 89
47893 SAN MARINO
TEL. +39 0549903124
www.consorziovini.sm

CELLAR SALES
PRE-BOOKED VISITS
ANNUAL PRODUCTION 650,000 bottles
HECTARES UNDER VINE 120.00
SUSTAINABLE WINERY

○ Biancale di San Marino '18	♟♟ 2*
○ Caldese di San Marino '17	♟♟ 4
○ Ribolla di San Marino '18	♟♟ 2*

TUSCANY

In terms of numbers and quality, this edition of Italian Wines is a record for Tuscany. In addition to a fortuitous succession of good years (like 2015 and 2016), which made for good results everywhere, it should be noted that Tuscany's vine growers have exhibited extraordinary sensibility towards their appellations' territories, both classic and emerging ones. Across the region there's enthusiasm, bolstered by favorable markets (both domestic and international), which, like yeast in bread, have set in motion a general rise in quality and number of producers. Large-scale wineries are growing and consolidating their production, like Antinori and Frescobaldi, and we're seeing considerable investment from outside groups as well. It's the case with Constellation Brands and Ruffino, the Bulgheroni Family Vineyards, Kendall Jackson with Arceno and Arcanum, the French EPI group with Biondi Santi, and the Saverys family with Avignonesi (to name a few) — many more are at the door. And that's not to mention other Italian groups, like Gaja, Masi, Bertani Domains, Zonin, Agricole Beretta, the Paladin family or Livon, which now have a stake in Tuscany's terroirs. These are positive signs that testify to the importance of Tuscany, a region that stands shoulder-to-shoulder with global powerhouses like Bordeaux and California. And if at one time it was Chianti Classico, Montalcino and Bolgheri leading the way, in recent years we've seen Maremma, Montecucco and Cortona step into the limelight, not to mention the Apennines, which are starting to host vineyards of Pinot Nero. But in all this fervor we mustn't forget our special awards — Tuscany took home two big ones. Our 2020 'Red of the Year' is yet another superb version, the 2016 of Silvia Vannucci's Carmignano Riserva di Piaggia di Mauro. And our 'Winery of the Year' is Florence's Frescobaldi, a historic brand that has, in recent years, seen an exponential growth in quality on each of its many estates. We close by greeting those producers that have obtained their first Tre Bicchieri: Maurizio Alongi, Badia di Morrona, Il Borro, I Fabbri, Pianirossi, Tenute Piccini, Tenuta Podernovo, Podere Le Ripi, Vallepicciola.

Abbadia Ardenga

FRAZ. TORRENIERI
VIA ROMANA, 139
53028 MONTALCINO [SI]
TEL. +39 0577834150
www.abbadiardengapoggio.it

CELLAR SALES
PRE-BOOKED VISITS
ANNUAL PRODUCTION 40,000 bottles
HECTARES UNDER VINE 10.00

Once a Benedictine monastery, an outpost of the Francigena Way and a museum of rural culture, Abbadia Ardenga currently belongs to the Siena 'Esecutori di Pie Disposizioni'. The winery is situated in Torrenieri, an important district in northeastern Montalcino characterized by a distinct pedoclimate. It's here that we also find their principal plots of Sangiovese, which give rise to classic reds. Their Brunello is made with medium-long maceration and maturation in large wooden barrels, both when it comes to their 'vintage' and to their Vigna Piaggia cru version. Even in a year as difficult as 2014 their Abbadia Ardenga line didn't disappoint. The Brunello unfolds harmoniously and freshly, it's only a bit limited in terms of length and complexity. Their Vigna Piaggia opts more for smoky and spicy tones, and, more notably, a closer-knit mouthfeel accompanied by a lovely grain of tannins. Their Brunello Ris. '13 is airy and austere at the same time.

● Brunello di Montalcino '14	▼▼ 5
● Brunello di Montalcino Ris. '13	▼▼ 6
● Brunello di Montalcino V. Piaggia '14	▼▼▼ 5
● Rosso di Montalcino '17	▼ 3
● Brunello di Montalcino '08	♀♀ 5
● Brunello di Montalcino '07	♀♀ 5
● Brunello di Montalcino '06	♀♀ 5
● Brunello di Montalcino '05	♀♀ 5
● Brunello di Montalcino Ris. '12	♀♀ 6
● Brunello di Montalcino V. Piaggia '13	♀♀ 5
● Brunello di Montalcino V. Piaggia '12	♀♀ 5
● Brunello di Montalcino V. Piaggia '10	♀♀ 5
● Brunello di Montalcino V. Piaggia '09	♀♀ 5
● Brunello di Montalcino V. Piaggia '08	♀♀ 5
● Brunello di Montalcino V. Piaggia '07	♀♀ 5
● Rosso di Montalcino '10	♀♀ 3

Maurizio Alongi

LOC. MONTI DI SOTTO
53013 GAIOLE IN CHIANTI [SI]
TEL. +39 3389878937
www.maurizioalongi.it

ANNUAL PRODUCTION 4,500 bottles
HECTARES UNDER VINE 1.30
SUSTAINABLE WINERY

Maurizio Alongi's winery was founded around plots of Sangiovese, Malvasia Nera and Canaiolo. His two small vineyards are surrounded by woods in the Gaiole in Chianti subzone, with vines that go back more than thirty years on average. Here along the backbone of the so-called 'Macigno del Chianti', the territory and crus are characterized by sandstone soil and unique climatic conditions. Indeed, it's the birthplace of a single wine, one of impeccable craftsmanship that exhibits stylistic precision and, especially, an extremely coherent territorial identity. Their Chianti Classico Vigna Barbischio RIserva '16 exhibits a coherently Chianti character. Clear aromas of fresh cherry rise up on the nose, along with hints of forest undergrowth and spices. On the palate it's vibrant, with precise, flavorful tannins and a decisive development that comes through elegant and balanced amidst gustatory chiaroscuro and an almost spicy hot finish. Simply superb.

● Chianti Cl. V. Barbischio Ris. '16	▼▼▼ 5
● Chianti Cl. V. Barbischio Ris. '15	♀♀ 5

Fattoria Ambra

VIA LOMBARDA, 85
59015 CARMIGNANO [PO]
TEL. +39 3358282552
www.fattoriaambra.it

CELLAR SALES
PRE-BOOKED VISITS
ANNUAL PRODUCTION 80,000 bottles
HECTARES UNDER VINE 20.00
VITICULTURE METHOD Certified Organic

Fattoria Ambra is situated in the historic 'microzone' of DOCG Carmignano. The Romei Rigoli family has owned the estate since the mid-19th century, with plots dominated primarily by Sangiovese and smaller shares of Canaiolo, Trebbiano, Vermentino and Cabernet Sauvignon. This last is called 'Uva Francesca' here, especially among older vigneron, in reference to the legend that Caterina de' Medici brought it here from France as queen in the 16th century. Their selection put in a good overall performance, but it's their Carmignano Santa Cristina in Pilli '16 that stands out. It's an elegant wine in its aromas of raspberry and plums, with minty and mineral hints. A supplely structured, well-defined body features silky, fine tannins and an enticing, fresh finish. Their Carmignano Montefortini Podere Lombarda '16 also delivered with its tertiary aromas of tobacco and tanned leather, close-knit, firm structure and a flavorful, lingering finish.

● Carmignano Santa Cristina in Pilli '16	♟♟♟ 3*
● Barco Reale '18	♟♟ 2*
● Carmignano Elzana Ris. '15	♟♟ 5
● Carmignano Montalbiolo Ris. '15	♟♟ 5
● Carmignano Montefortini Podere Lombarda '16	♟♟ 3
● Barco Reale Vin Ruspo '18	♟ 2
○ Trebbiano '18	♟ 2
● Carmignano Santa Cristina in Pilli '15	♟♟♟ 3*
● Carmignano Elzana Ris. '13	♟♟ 5
● Carmignano Montalbiolo Ris. '13	♟♟ 5
● Carmignano Montalbiolo Ris. '12	♟♟ 5
● Carmignano Montefortini Podere Lombarda '15	♟♟ 3
● Carmignano Santa Cristina in Pilli '13	♟♟ 3
○ Vin Santo di Carmignano '09	♟♟ 5

Stefano Amerighi

LOC. POGGIOBELLO DI FARNETA
52044 CORTONA [AR]
TEL. +39 0575648340
www.stefanoamerighi.it

CELLAR SALES
PRE-BOOKED VISITS
ANNUAL PRODUCTION 35,000 bottles
HECTARES UNDER VINE 8.50
VITICULTURE METHOD Certified Biodynamic
SUSTAINABLE WINERY

If we can use the word 'natural' to describe wine and winemakers, then this winery can wholeheartedly describe itself as such. Passion and sustainability are the hallmarks that inspire vigneron Stefano Amerighi. And the same holds for the cultivation of grains, vegetables, animal breeding and, of course, grapes, primarily Syrah, which is cultivated along the hills of Cortona. Trimming, cultivation and plant-health are all carried out in accordance with the rhythms and ways of nature. Both their wines landed a place in our finals. The Syrah '16 opens with a complex bouquet amidst spices and tanned leather, then concentrated notes of red berries, sanguine hints and a shade of thyme. On the palate it enters meaty, with nice flesh and fine tannins giving way to a flavorful finish. Their Syrah Apice '15 stands out on the nose for its notes of black cherry and vegetal hints, exhibiting a firm but dynamic body on the palate, as well as measured freshness.

● Cortona Syrah '16	♟♟♟ 5
● Cortona Syrah Apice '15	♟♟ 6
● Cortona Syrah '15	♟♟♟ 5
● Cortona Syrah '14	♟♟♟ 5
● Cortona Syrah '11	♟♟♟ 5
● Cortona Syrah '10	♟♟♟ 5
● Cortona Syrah '09	♟♟♟ 5
● Cortona Syrah '13	♟♟ 5
● Cortona Syrah '12	♟♟ 5
● Cortona Syrah Apice '14	♟♟ 6
● Cortona Syrah Apice '13	♟♟ 6
● Cortona Syrah Apice '11	♟♟ 6
● Cortona Syrah Apice '10	♟♟ 6

Antico Colle

VIA PROVINCIALE, 9
53040 MONTEPULCIANO [SI]
TEL. +39 0578707828
www.anticocolle.it

CELLAR SALES
PRE-BOOKED VISITS
ANNUAL PRODUCTION 150,000 bottles
HECTARES UNDER VINE 30.00

Andrea Frangiosa brings passion to the work of managing his winery. It's situated in the eastern part of the appellation, though his vineyards occupy various tracts of land throughout Montepulciano. The stylistic approach here is precise and balanced, bringing together a mix of time-honored practices with the measured use of technology. Maturation is carried out in barriques, mid-size casks and large barrels, with a nice, balanced use of oak making for dynamic wines marked by character and personality. Their Nobile di Montepulciano '16 is a solid wine, with fruity aromas accompanied by hints of talcum powder and a light smokiness rising up on the nose. On the palate it exhibits nice balance and density, with a crisp, rising finish. Their Rosso di Montepulciano '17 is extremely spicy on the nose, finding its strong point in a truly compelling drinkability. The Rosso Tosscana '18, made with Sangiovese, Merlot and Cabernet Sauvignon, is just as pleasant.

● Nobile di Montepulciano '16	♙♙♙ 3*
● Rosso di Montepulciano '17	♙♙ 2*
● Rosso Toscana '18	♙♙ 1*
● Nobile di Montepulciano '15	♙♙ 3
● Nobile di Montepulciano '10	♙♙ 3
● Nobile di Montepulciano '09	♙♙ 3
● Nobile di Montepulciano Il Saggio Ris. '13	♙♙ 5
● Nobile di Montepulciano Il Saggio Ris. '07	♙♙ 5
● Rosso di Montepulciano '16	♙♙ 2*

★★Marchesi Antinori

P.ZZA ANTINORI, 3
50123 FIRENZE
TEL. +39 05523595
www.antinori.it

CELLAR SALES
PRE-BOOKED VISITS
ACCOMMODATION AND RESTAURANT SERVICE
ANNUAL PRODUCTION 2,000,000 bottles
HECTARES UNDER VINE 2350.00

Antinori is the only business that has a winery in each Tuscan appellation, from Montalcino to Bolgheri, the hills of Florence, Sovana and Castiglione della Pescaia, Montepulciano and Cortona (the only one missing is San Gimignano). They also have a significant presence in Chianti Classico, with their Tignanello vineyards and Bargino cellar. The Florentine brand is most tied to this last. Its philosophy and strategy may be in keeping with other producers in the territory, but it's marking out a way forward for others to follow. Everyone seems to agree about the Chianti Classico Marchese Antinori Riserva '16, those who prefer a more modern profile, and those partial to more territorial wines. The Chianti Classico Badia a Passignano Gran Selezione '16 also had a good today, though it's marked by one too many notes of oak. The impeccable Solaia '16, a blend of Cabernet Franc, Cabernet Sauvignon and Sangiovese, is full, deep, complex and extremely long. Tre Bicchieri.

● Solaia '16	♙♙♙ 8
● Chianti Cl. Gran Selezione Badia a Passignano '16	♙♙ 6
● Chianti Cl. Marchese Antinori '16	♙♙ 6
● Chianti Cl. Pèppoli '17	♙♙ 3
● Chianti Cl. Villa Antinori Ris. '16	♙♙ 4
● Tignanello '16	♙ 8
● Chianti Cl. Marchese Antinori Ris. '15	♙♙♙ 5
● Solaia '07	♙♙♙ 8
● Solaia '06	♙♙♙ 8
● Solaia '03	♙♙♙ 8
● Tignanello '13	♙♙♙ 8
● Tignanello '09	♙♙♙ 8
● Tignanello '08	♙♙♙ 8
● Tignanello '05	♙♙♙ 8
● Tignanello '04	♙♙♙ 8
● Tignanello '82	♙♙♙ 8

Tenuta di Arceno - Arcanum

LOC. ARCENO
FRAZ. SAN GUSMÉ
53010 CASTELNUOVO BERARDENGA [SI]
TEL. +39 0577359346
www.tenutadiarceno.com

CELLAR SALES
PRE-BOOKED VISITS
ANNUAL PRODUCTION 250,000 bottles
HECTARES UNDER VINE 92.00

Tenuta di Arceno is the Chianti 'branch' of the American juggernaut Kendall-Jackson (who also have wineries in France, Chile, South Africa and Australia). Headquartered in Castelnuovo Berardenga, the southern part of Chianti Classico, the winery is characterized by the area's climate and a generally modern organizational approach that's resulted, nevertheless, in wines of increasing clarity. This shift is having a favorable impact on their designated wines, as has already been the case with their selections made with international cultivars. Their Chianti Classico '17 features focused aromas ranging from lush fruit to spicy hints. On the palate it's simply delicious, unfolding juicy, full and fragrant. Darker, more mature notes characterize their Arcanum '15, a blend of Cabernet Sauvignon, Cabernet Franc, Merlot and Petit Verdot. It's pervasive and tasty on the palate, though marked by just a bit too much oak.

● Chianti Cl. '17	▼▼▼ 4*
● Arcanum '15	▼▼ 8
● Chianti Cl. Ris. '16	▼▼ 5
● Valadorna '13	♀♀♀ 8
● Arcanum '13	♀♀ 8
● Chianti Cl. '16	♀♀ 4
● Chianti Cl. '15	♀♀ 3
● Chianti Cl. '13	♀♀ 3
● Chianti Cl. Gran Selezione Strada al Sasso '15	♀♀ 6
● Chianti Cl. Ris. '15	♀♀ 5
● Chianti Cl. Ris. '14	♀♀ 5
● Chianti Cl. Ris. '12	♀♀ 5
● Il Fauno di Arcanum '14	♀♀ 6
● Valadorna '11	♀♀ 7

Tenuta Argentiera

LOC. I PIANALI
FRAZ. DONORATICO
VIA AURELIA, 412A
57022 CASTAGNETO CARDUCCI [LI]
TEL. +39 0565773176
www.argentiera.eu

CELLAR SALES
PRE-BOOKED VISITS
ANNUAL PRODUCTION 450,000 bottles
HECTARES UNDER VINE 76.00

Wedged in between the sea and the hills, Tenuta Argentiera gets its name from the silver mines once found in this part of Alta Maremma. Today the Austrian industrialist Stanislao Turnauer owns a majority share in this benchmark Bolgheri winery. He's accompanied by CEO Federico Zileri and new GM Leonardo Raspini. Their estate, which impresses for its breadth and beauty, consistently gives rise to one of the appellation's best selections. Thanks in part to a favorable year, their Bolgheri Sup. is back in form. The 2016 is an intense, complex wine. It opens on autolytic notes and hints of berry fruit, with the occasional jammy sensation that doesn't compress a dynamic aromatic profile and a full, meaty, deep palate. Their two 2017 Bolgheri Rossos also prove excellent, though we're somewhat partial to the Poggio ai Ginepri.

● Bolgheri Rosso Sup. '16	▼▼ 8
● Bolgheri Rosso Poggio ai Ginepri '17	▼▼ 4
● Bolgheri Rosso Villa Donoratico '17	▼▼ 5
● Bolgheri Sup. '11	♀♀♀ 8
● Bolgheri Sup. Argentiera '10	♀♀♀ 7
● Bolgheri Sup. Argentiera '06	♀♀♀ 7
● Bolgheri Sup. Argentiera '05	♀♀♀ 7
● Bolgheri Sup. Argentiera '04	♀♀♀ 7
● Bolgheri Rosso Poggio ai Ginepri '13	♀♀ 3
● Bolgheri Rosso Sup. '14	♀♀ 8
● Bolgheri Rosso Sup. '13	♀♀ 8
● Bolgheri Rosso Villa Donoratico '15	♀♀ 5
● Bolgheri Sup. Argentiera '15	♀♀ 8
● Bolgheri Villa Donoratico '13	♀♀ 5
○ Poggio ai Ginepri Bianco '17	♀♀ 3

Artimino

FRAZ. ARTIMINO
V.LE PAPA GIOVANNI XXIII, 1
59015 CARMIGNANO [PO]
TEL. +39 0558751423
www.artimino.com

CELLAR SALES
PRE-BOOKED VISITS
ACCOMMODATION AND RESTAURANT SERVICE
ANNUAL PRODUCTION 420,000 bottles
HECTARES UNDER VINE 88.00

Since the 1980s, Tenuta di Artimino has been owned by the Olmo family (famous for making bicycles). It's situated in a territory of rare beauty, in the heart of Tuscany and Carmignano wine country. The town's history is lost in time, it was first an Etruscan settlement, then a medieval village and finally a haunt of the De' Medicis. And that's where we find Artimino, headquartered in one of their most important villas, 'dei Cento Camini' ('100 fireplaces'), otherwise known as La Ferdinanda. The Iris '15, made with Cabernet Sauvignon and Merlot, performed very well, delivering jammy, cherry notes adorned by hints of tobacco, leather and cloves. On the palate it's warm, broad and expansive, with a subtle and well-integrated tannic weave and a delicious finish. Their Vin Santo Occhio di Pernice '12 offers up a classic bouquet of hazelnut and dried figs, anticipating a broad, velvety and creamy body, relaxed, big and deep in flavor, with long aromatic persistence.

● Iris '15	♟♟ 5
● Vin Santo di Carmignano Occhio di Pernice '12	♟♟ 5
● Barco Reale Ser Biagio '18	♟ 2
☉ Barco Reale Vin Ruspo Rosato '18	♟ 2
● Carmignano Poggilarca '16	♟ 3
● Chianti Montalbano '17	♟ 2
● Carmignano Poggilarca '15	♟♟ 3
● Carmignano Poggilarca '14	♟♟ 3
● Carmignano V. Grumarello Ris. '13	♟♟ 4
● Carmignano V. Grumarello Ris. '12	♟♟ 4
● Vin Santo di Carmignano Occhio di Pernice '11	♟♟ 5
● Vin Santo di Carmignano Occhio di Pernice '10	♟♟ 5

Assolati

FRAZ. MONTENERO
POD. ASSOLATI, 47
58040 CASTEL DEL PIANO [GR]
TEL. +39 0564954146
www.assolati.it

CELLAR SALES
PRE-BOOKED VISITS
ACCOMMODATION
ANNUAL PRODUCTION 18,000 bottles
HECTARES UNDER VINE 5.00

Floriano Giannetti's winery has unflinchingly embraced the philosophy of DOC Montecucco, focusing on Sangiovese. Here in the hills of Montenero d'Orcia, the grape often gives rise to noteworthy wines. Assolati's selection, which is certainly not lacking in character, centers on earthy aromas, at times almost too decisive but characteristic of the area's Sangiovese. Their wines are austere and at times less discernible, the distinctive traits of a style in pursuit of personality. Dark and spicy aromatic sensations mark their Montecucco Sangiovese '16, a wine that unfolds sweet and generally juicy on the palate. Well-profiled fragrances of red fruits and herbs characterize their Montecucco Sangiovese Riserva '16, a wine that comes through supple, well-sustained and tasty on the palate. The Montecucco Rosso '16 is sweet and pleasant, while the Dionysos '18, a monovarietal Vermentino, is fragrant and simple, but well-made nonetheless.

● Montecucco Sangiovese '16	♟♟ 3
● Montecucco Sangiovese Ris. '16	♟♟ 4
○ Dionysos '18	♟ 2
● Montecucco Rosso '16	♟ 2
○ Dionysos '16	♟♟ 2*
● Montecucco Rosso '15	♟♟ 2*
● Montecucco Rosso '14	♟♟ 2*
● Montecucco Rosso '12	♟♟ 2*
● Montecucco Sangiovese '15	♟♟ 3
● Montecucco Sangiovese '14	♟♟ 3
● Montecucco Sangiovese '13	♟♟ 3
● Montecucco Sangiovese Ris. '15	♟♟ 4
● Montecucco Sangiovese Ris. '13	♟♟ 4
● Montecucco Sangiovese Ris. '12	♟♟ 3

★Avignonesi

FRAZ. VALIANO DI MONTEPULCIANO
VIA COLONICA, 1
53045 MONTEPULCIANO [SI]
TEL. +39 0578724304
www.avignonesi.it

CELLAR SALES
PRE-BOOKED VISITS
ACCOMMODATION AND RESTAURANT SERVICE
ANNUAL PRODUCTION 500,000 bottles
HECTARES UNDER VINE 169.00
VITICULTURE METHOD Certified Organic

This Valiano producer, whose ambitious enological project is still being finalized, draws on an estate of respectable dimensions for its selection of wines. Virgine Saverys's philosophy centers on the environment and biodynamic certification for all their vineyards. Thus Avignonesi continues to be one of Montepulciano's most important symbols, thanks to balanced wines with nice personality. Part of the credit also goes to the rigorous study of the best terroirs and a multifaceted zoning system. The 2016 Nobile once again proves that, when it comes to quality, it's one of the most solid of its kind, aromatically well-profiled amidst flowers and fruits, toastiness and spiciness, supple and tasty on the palate. Their Da-Di '18, a fragrant and flavorful Sangiovese aged in amphoras, is marked by a clear aromatic profile. The 2015 version of their 50 & 50, a historic Supertuscan produced in partnership with the Chianti's Capannelle, also did well.

● Nobile di Montepulciano '16	♟♟	5
● 50 & 50 '15	♟♟	8
● Da-Di '18	♟♟	6
● Cantaloro '16	♟	2
● Grifi '16	♟	3
● Nobile di Montepulciano '12	♟♟♟	4*
● Nobile di Montepulciano Ris. '85	♟♟♟	8
○ Vin Santo '98	♟♟♟	8
○ Vin Santo '96	♟♟♟	8
○ Vin Santo '95	♟♟♟	8
● Vin Santo Occhio di Pernice '97	♟♟♟	8
● Nobile di Montepulciano Caprile '15	♟♟	5
● Nobile di Montepulciano Progetto Alleanza '15	♟♟	5

★Badia a Coltibuono

LOC. BADIA A COLTIBUONO
53013 GAIOLE IN CHIANTI [SI]
TEL. +39 0577746110
www.coltibuono.com

CELLAR SALES
PRE-BOOKED VISITS
ACCOMMODATION AND RESTAURANT SERVICE
ANNUAL PRODUCTION 240,000 bottles
HECTARES UNDER VINE 62.00
VITICULTURE METHOD Certified Organic
SUSTAINABLE WINERY

Interpreting a territory's deepest spirit is the most important goal that a winery can set out for itself. In the case of Badia a Coltibuono, in addition to reaching that goal, we also find an ability to maintain it over time. It's a fact that puts this Gaiole in Chianti producer in an exclusive club of wineries that 'mustn't be missed'. Their quality is consistently very high and their signature style features an uncommon level of finesse and personality that's can be found throughout their selection. Their Chianti Classico Riserva '16 reaffirms the producer's style, with subtly whispered notes of fresh cherry, floral accents, undergrowth and smoky hints. On the palate it proves well-balanced, well-sustained and flavorful. Their Chianti Classico '17 follows a similar track, even if it performs on a lower level, aiming for pleasant accessibility.

● Chianti Cl. '17	♟♟	4
● Chianti Cl. Ris. '16	♟♟	5
● Sangioveto '15	♟♟	7
● Cancelli '18	♟	3
● Montebello '15	♟	7
● Chianti Cl. '15	♟♟♟	4*
● Chianti Cl. '13	♟♟♟	3*
● Chianti Cl. '12	♟♟♟	3*
● Chianti Cl. '06	♟♟♟	3*
● Chianti Cl. Cultus Boni '15	♟♟♟	4*
● Chianti Cl. Cultus Boni '09	♟♟♟	4*
● Chianti Cl. Ris. '09	♟♟♟	5
● Chianti Cl. Ris. '07	♟♟♟	5
● Chianti Cl. Ris. '04	♟♟♟	5
● Sangioveto '95	♟♟♟	6

Badia di Morrona

VIA DEL CHIANTI, 6
56030 TERRICCIOLA [PI]
TEL. +39 0587658505
www.badiadimorrona.it

CELLAR SALES
PRE-BOOKED VISITS
ACCOMMODATION AND RESTAURANT SERVICE
ANNUAL PRODUCTION 350,000 bottles
HECTARES UNDER VINE 110.00

The property has been in the hands of the Glaslini Alberti family since 1939, but the turning point in quality and style came more recently. Its beauty, on the other hand, is nothing new, starting with an 11th-century Benedictine abbey and a 600-hectare estate in Terricciola (straddling Pisa and Volterra). For some years now their wines have shown improvement in terms of consistency and awareness, with advances made throughout their selection and not just when it comes to their premium wines. Two thoroughbreds were in our final tastings. The VignaAlta '16 exhibits noteworthy personality, thanks in part to foresty sensations that merge with red fruit and fade on toasty nuances. On the palate it's lush and compact, with a nice, youthful hardness. The N'Antia '16, a blend of Cabernet Sauvignon, Franc and Merlot, has a more even direction to it, both aromatically and on the palate, but it's still exquisite, with tantalizing notes of blackberries and licorice.

● Terre di Pisa Sangiovese VignaAlta '16	▼▼▼	5
● N'antia '16	▼▼	5
● Taneto '16	▼▼	3*
● Chianti I Sodi del Paretaio '18	▼▼	2*
○ Vin Santo del Chianti '13	▼▼	4
○ Felciaio '18	▼	2
● Chianti I Sodi del Paretaio '17	♀♀	2*
● Chianti I Sodi del Paretaio '16	♀♀	2*
● Chianti I Sodi del Paretaio '15	♀♀	2*
● N'antia '15	♀♀	5
● Taneto '15	♀♀	3*
● Taneto '13	♀♀	3
● VignaAlta '15	♀♀	5
● VignaAlta '13	♀♀	5
○ Vin Santo del Chianti '11	♀♀	4

Baracchi

LOC. CEGLIOLO, 21
52044 CORTONA [AR]
TEL. +39 0575612679
www.baracchiwinery.com

CELLAR SALES
PRE-BOOKED VISITS
ACCOMMODATION AND RESTAURANT SERVICE
ANNUAL PRODUCTION 140,000 bottles
HECTARES UNDER VINE 32.00
SUSTAINABLE WINERY

In this winery, situated on the hills around Cortona, they've been making wines for 160 years. The current owner, Riccardo Baracchi (who's accompanied by his son Benedetto), hasn't left behind traditional grapes like Trebbiano and Sangiovese, but he's working in a different direction, as his sparkling wines demonstrate. In other cases he's focused on Syrah, which has found a perfect home in the territory, or on a more demanding grape like Pinot Nero. Some of his vineyards are situated on the estate around his cellar, which is also accompanied by a hotel, restaurant and spa. Their Syrah Smeriglio '16 offers up enticing aromas, while on the palate it proves relaxed and soft, with silky tannins and a pleasant, full finish. Their interesting Astore '18, a monovarietal Trebbiano macerated on the skins, features aromas of tea and chamomile, then ripe apple with almond, the prelude to a juicy, long gustatory profile.

● Ardito '15	▼▼	6
○ Astore '18	▼▼	3
● Cortona Syrah Smeriglio '16	▼▼	4
● Pinot Nero '16	▼	6
⊙ Sangiovese Brut Rosé '16	▼	5
○ Trebbiano Brut '16	▼	5
○ Brut Trebbiano '14	♀♀	5
● Cortona Cabernet Ris. '15	♀♀	6
● Cortona Cabernet Ris. '13	♀♀	6
● Cortona Pinot Nero '14	♀♀	4
● Cortona Smeriglio Syrah '13	♀♀	4
● Cortona Syrah Ris. '15	♀♀	6
● Cortona Syrah Ris. '13	♀♀	6
● Cortona Syrah Smeriglio '15	♀♀	4
● Cortona Syrah Smeriglio '14	♀♀	4
● Pinot Nero '13	♀♀	6

Fattoria dei Barbi

Loc. Podernovi, 170
53024 Montalcino [SI]
Tel. +39 0577841111
www.fattoriadeibarbi.it

CELLAR SALES
PRE-BOOKED VISITS
ACCOMMODATION AND RESTAURANT SERVICE
ANNUAL PRODUCTION 600,000 bottles
HECTARES UNDER VINE 66.00

Fattoria dei Barbi was among the first wineries to export Brunello throughout Europe and America. It's a winery that's always proven capable of bringing together a proud awareness of their long history with a true pioneering spirit. Here in Podernovi, a benchmark district for mideast Montalcino, we find the cellar-museum, a tavern and most of their Sangiovese vineyards. This last has proven to be the cornerstone grape of a selection that features tailored fermentation and maturation paired with an equally austere touch. You can add the 2013 to Fattoria dei Barbi's list of more successful Brunello reserves. It features a multifaceted profile of quinine and summer fruit with a touch of incense. On the palate it confirms its austere, though not excessively, character, despite unpolished tannins. Their Brunello '14 put in a brilliant performance, proving light-bodied but substantive. And don't forget their subtle and earthy Rosso '17.

● Brunello di Montalcino Ris. '13	♟♟	7
● Brunello di Montalcino '14	♟♟	5
● Rosso di Montalcino '17	♟♟	3
● Brunello di Montalcino '13	♟♟	5
● Brunello di Montalcino '11	♟♟	5
● Brunello di Montalcino '10	♟♟	5
● Brunello di Montalcino Ris. '12	♟♟	7
● Brunello di Montalcino Ris. '11	♟♟	7
● Brunello di Montalcino Ris. '10	♟♟	7
● Brunello di Montalcino V. del Fiore '13	♟♟	7
● Brunello di Montalcino V. del Fiore '12	♟♟	7
● Brunello di Montalcino V. del Fiore '11	♟♟	7
● Brunello di Montalcino V. del Fiore '10	♟♟	7
● Morellino di Scansano '15	♟♟	3
● Rosso di Montalcino '16	♟♟	3
● Rosso di Montalcino '15	♟♟	3
● Rosso di Montalcino '14	♟♟	3

Baricci

Loc. Colombaio di Montosoli, 13
53024 Montalcino [SI]
Tel. +39 0577848109
www.baricci.it

CELLAR SALES
PRE-BOOKED VISITS
ANNUAL PRODUCTION 30,000 bottles
HECTARES UNDER VINE 5.00

Power and vigor, warmth and contrast, juice and flavor: at Podere Colombia di Montosoli they've carved out a veritable 'signature Baricci style'. For more than 60 years this north Montalcino cru 'par excellence' was incarnated by legendary Nello, while in recent years their work has been honed with extraordinary coherence by his son-in-law Pietro Buffi, and grandsons. At the center of it all are the plots surrounding the cellar, fermented separately with long maceration and maturation in 2000 and 4000 liter Slavonian oak, resulting in their Rosso and Brunello wines. The most recent versions of a great couple prove even more splendid. The warm year made for a slight lack of vigor and alcohol finish, but their Rosso '17 is still a must for its flavorful, foresty profile. And so it is that their Brunello '14 takes on the role of leader, thanks to its meaty impact (blueberries, bergamot, resin), sensations amplified in its firm, vigorous palate.

● Brunello di Montalcino '14	♟♟♟	6
● Rosso di Montalcino '17	♟♟	4
● Brunello di Montalcino '10	♟♟♟	6
● Brunello di Montalcino '09	♟♟♟	5
● Brunello di Montalcino '07	♟♟♟	5
● Brunello di Montalcino '83	♟♟♟	5
● Brunello di Montalcino Nello Ris. '10	♟♟♟	6
● Rosso di Montalcino '16	♟♟♟	4*
● Rosso di Montalcino '15	♟♟♟	4*
● Brunello di Montalcino '13	♟♟	6
● Brunello di Montalcino '12	♟♟	6
● Brunello di Montalcino '11	♟♟	6
● Brunello di Montalcino Nello Ris. '12	♟♟	6
● Rosso di Montalcino '14	♟♟	4
● Rosso di Montalcino '13	♟♟	4
● Rosso di Montalcino '11	♟♟	3*

Basile

POD. MONTE MARIO
58044 CINIGIANO [GR]
TEL. +39 0564993227
www.basilessa.it

CELLAR SALES
PRE-BOOKED VISITS
ANNUAL PRODUCTION 50,000 bottles
HECTARES UNDER VINE 8.00
VITICULTURE METHOD Certified Organic
SUSTAINABLE WINERY

Giovanbattista Basile's winery got its start in 1999. The decision to focus on organic cultivation from the outset was an important part of their success, though not the only contributing factor. Consistently considered to be one of Montecucco's most important wineries, this small producer's selection tends to be well-defined, clearly modern, capable of bringing out the best of the area's Sangiovese, as well as international grapes that come across as somewhat particular while expressing a decisive personality. Like clockwork their Montecucco Sangiovese Ad Agio Riserva '15 stands out as one of the best. Here it features rich and fragrant aromas, as well as the solid and dynamic gustatory development of a great red. Their Montecucco Sangiovese Cartacanta '16 is fruity and lush on the palate, juicy and pervasive. The flavorful and rhythmic Maremma Toscana Rosso Comandante '16 also proves well-made.

● Montecucco Sangiovese Ad Agio Ris. '15	♟♟♟ 5
● Maremma Toscana Rosso Comandante '16	♟♟ 4
● Montecucco Sangiovese Cartacanta '16	♟♟ 3
● Montecucco Sangiovese Ad Agio Ris. '14	♟♟♟ 5
● Montecucco Sangiovese Ad Agio Ris. '12	♟♟♟ 5
● Maremma Comandante '12	♟♟ 3
● Montecucco Cartacanta '11	♟♟ 3
● Montecucco Sangiovese Ad Agio Ris. '13	♟♟ 5
● Montecucco Sangiovese Ad Agio Ris. '11	♟♟ 5
● Montecucco Sangiovese Cartacanta '15	♟♟ 3
● Montecucco Sangiovese Cartacanta '13	♟♟ 3

Pietro Beconcini

FRAZ. LA SCALA
VIA MONTORZO, 13A
56028 SAN MINIATO [PI]
TEL. +39 0571464785
www.pietrobeconcini.com

CELLAR SALES
PRE-BOOKED VISITS
ANNUAL PRODUCTION 95,000 bottles
HECTARES UNDER VINE 12.00

A new territory, at least in terms of viticultural renown, and old, defunct vineyards. These are the defining characteristics of San Miniato, and of one of its wineries. Here Leonardo and Eva Bellagamba, who are carrying on the legacy of their father, Pietro, offset a lack of a long tradition with vivacity and originality. Theirs is a selection that deliberately eschews the usual schema, resulting in an increased presence of Malvasia Nera and the rediscovery of Tempranillo, a cultivar of Spanish origin. Their Reciso '16, a monovarietal Sangiovese, is marked by ripe aromas of cherry and plum, then tertiary notes of tobacco and leather. On the palate it enters pleasant and soft, with nicely integrated tannins, lovely freshness and a convincing finish. The Vin Santo Caratello '09 unveils bitter notes, then dried fruits, like dates and figs. In the mouth it's warm and firm, tasty, delicately sweet, finishing long.

● IXE Tempranillo '17	♟♟ 3
● Reciso '16	♟♟ 5
○ Vin Santo del Chianti Caratello '09	♟♟ 6
● Chianti Ris. '16	♟ 3
● Maurleo '17	♟ 3
○ Vea Trebbiano Anno Zero '18	♟ 4
● Vigna Le Nicchie '15	♟ 6
● Chianti Ris. '13	♟♟ 2*
● IXE '15	♟♟ 3
● IXE '14	♟♟ 3
● Ixe Tempranillo '16	♟♟ 3
● Maurleo '16	♟♟ 3
● Maurleo '15	♟♟ 2*
● Reciso '13	♟♟ 5
● Vigna alle Nicchie '12	♟♟ 6
○ Vin Santo del Chianti Caratello '08	♟♟ 5

Bibbiano

VIA BIBBIANO, 76
53011 CASTELLINA IN CHIANTI [SI]
TEL. +39 0577743065
www.bibbiano.com

CELLAR SALES
PRE-BOOKED VISITS
ACCOMMODATION
ANNUAL PRODUCTION 140,000 bottles
HECTARES UNDER VINE 30.00
VITICULTURE METHOD Certified Organic
SUSTAINABLE WINERY

Tenuta di Bibbiano boasts more than sixty years of experience in winemaking. Here in the Castellina in Chianti subzone, they embody a territorial stylistic model that's clearly inspired by the appellation, one without the useless frills or forced techniques. Today the winery is managed by brothers Tommaso and Federico Marrocchesi Marzi, whose work is centered primarily on the noble aim of conserving a classic production style. It's one that, especially recently, has returned to prominence and distinguishes Chianti Classico's best wines. Their Chianti Classico Riserva '16 is characterized by aromatic cleanness and gustatory poise. On the nose lush fruit takes center stage, accompanied by spices and slightly smoky notes. On the palate it's tight enough, allowing fragrance and flavor to emerge as well. Their Chianti Classico '17 is more approachable, with subtle and balanced flavor, though just a bit too heavy in vegetal sensations.

● Chianti Cl. Ris. '16	♥♥♥ 4
● Chianti Cl. '17	♥♥ 3
● Chianti Cl. '16	♀♀ 3*
● Chianti Cl. '15	♀♀ 3
● Chianti Cl. '13	♀♀ 3*
● Chianti Cl. '11	♀♀ 3*
● Chianti Cl. '10	♀♀ 3
● Chianti Cl. Gran Selezione V. del Capannino '15	♀♀ 5
● Chianti Cl. Montornello '11	♀♀ 3
● Chianti Cl. Montornello '10	♀♀ 3
● Chianti Cl. Montornello Ris. '13	♀♀ 4
● Chianti Cl. Montornello Ris. '12	♀♀ 4
● Chianti Cl. Ris. '15	♀♀ 4
● Chianti Cl. V. del Capannino Ris. '10	♀♀ 5

Bindella

FRAZ. ACQUAVIVA
VIA DELLE TRE BERTE, 10A
53045 MONTEPULCIANO [SI]
TEL. +39 0578767777
www.bindella.it

CELLAR SALES
PRE-BOOKED VISITS
ANNUAL PRODUCTION 170,000 bottles
HECTARES UNDER VINE 42.50

Acquavivia di Montepulciano, a winery managed by Rudolf Bindella, has proven capable of a splendid range of wines and an established, consistent level of quality. It's all thanks to discerning choices that, over thirty years, never fell prey to fashion, but focused instead on the typicity and ageworthiness of their wines. Their vineyards are situated on various soil types, in different districts, Vallocaia, Santa Maria and Fossolupaio, in short, some of Nobile's most important crus. Their main selections are aged in large and small wood barrels. Their Nobile di Montepulciano '16 offers up aromas of fruit, aromatic herbs and highly distinct iron notes, making for a superbly fragrant profile. On the palate it's dynamic, exhibiting nice contrast and superb sapidity. Their well-made Nobile I Quadri '16 is a bit more marked by oak, though this doesn't interfere with the wine's energy. The Nobile Vallocaia Riserva '15 proves full-bodied and austere.

● Nobile di Montepulciano I Quadri '16	♥♥♥ 5
● Nobile di Montepulciano '16	♥♥ 4
⊙ Gemella Rosato '18	♥♥ 3
● Nobile di Montepulciano Vallocaia Ris. '15	♥♥ 6
● Rosso di Montepulciano Fossolupaio '17	♥♥ 3
● Nobile di Montepulciano I Quadri '13	♀♀♀ 5
● Nobile di Montepulciano I Quadri '12	♀♀♀ 5
● Nobile di Montepulciano '15	♀♀ 4
● Nobile di Montepulciano '14	♀♀ 4
● Nobile di Montepulciano I Quadri '15	♀♀ 5

★Biondi - Santi
Tenuta Greppo

Loc. Villa Greppo, 183
53024 Montalcino [SI]
Tel. +39 0577848023
www.biondisanti.it

HECTARES UNDER VINE 26.00

Giampiero Bertolini is the new CEO of the
French EPI Group, owner of the Biondi Santi
brand. It's his job to bring definitive
international recognition to Montalcino's
most celebrated producer, while also
preserving the philosophy and style that
made Greppo Brunello a legendary wine.
The choice to further delay the release of
their Riserva 2012 is a step in this
direction, as is their focus on more mature
vintages and soil study of the various
vineyard blocks. We find the selection's
other 'classic' wines, which, as usual,
performed at high levels. Their Rosso '15
features its trademark airy profile amidst
small red fruit and medicinal herbs,
sensations supported by soft, eager
mouthfeel. Their Brunello '13 is just a bit
more algid. A procession of balsam, roots
and wild berries anticipates a palate that
plays primarily on vibrant acidity.

● Brunello di Montalcino '13	♟♟ 8
● Rosso di Montalcino '15	♟♟ 6
● Brunello di Montalcino '12	♟♟♟ 8
● Brunello di Montalcino '10	♟♟♟ 8
● Brunello di Montalcino '09	♟♟♟ 8
● Brunello di Montalcino '06	♟♟♟ 7
● Brunello di Montalcino '04	♟♟♟ 8
● Brunello di Montalcino '03	♟♟♟ 8
● Brunello di Montalcino '01	♟♟♟ 8
● Brunello di Montalcino '83	♟♟♟ 8
● Brunello di Montalcino Ris. '10	♟♟♟ 8
● Brunello di Montalcino Ris. '07	♟♟♟ 8
● Brunello di Montalcino Ris. '06	♟♟♟ 8
● Brunello di Montalcino Ris. '04	♟♟♟ 8
● Brunello di Montalcino Ris. '01	♟♟♟ 8
● Brunello di Montalcino Ris. '99	♟♟♟ 8
● Brunello di Montalcino Ris. '95	♟♟♟ 8

Tenuta di Biserno

Loc. Palazzo Gardini
P.zza Gramsci, 9
57020 Bibbona [LI]
Tel. +39 0586671099
www.biserno.it

ANNUAL PRODUCTION 160,000 bottles
HECTARES UNDER VINE 99.00

Biserno is Lodovico and Piero Antinori's
umpteenth endeavor, and in this case
they're accompanied by Umberto Mannoni.
It's a bet on the terroir of Bibbona, a truly
beautiful place, clearly well-suited to the
task of hosting an established producer.
But most importantly they have a clear
vision in pursuit modern and
internationally-styled wines. To this end the
contribution of Michel Rolland is evident,
and their various wines are the proof.
Chromatic, aromatic and gustatory
concentration figure centrally in their Pino
di Biserno '16, a blend of Cabernet Franc,
Merlot and Cabernet Sauvignon. Aromas of
black berry fruit and coffee give way to a
decisive herbaceous stroke that calls up
peppers. The same monumental structure
and aromas characterize their Biserno '15.
SOF '18 is a claret-red colored wine
redolent of wild berries and aromatic herbs.
The Insoglio del Cinghiale '17 is decidedly
mature and plush.

● Il Pino di Biserno '16	♟♟ 6
● Biserno '15	♟♟ 8
⊙ Sof '18	♟♟ 3
● Insoglio del Cinghiale '17	♟ 4
● Biserno '10	♟♟♟ 8
● Biserno '08	♟♟♟ 6
● Il Pino di Biserno '09	♟♟♟ 6
● Biserno '13	♟♟ 8
● Biserno '12	♟♟ 8
● Biserno '11	♟♟ 8
● Il Pino di Biserno '14	♟♟ 6
● Il Pino di Biserno '11	♟♟ 6
● Insoglio del Cinghiale '16	♟♟ 4
● Insoglio del Cinghiale '15	♟♟ 4

Borgo Salcetino

Loc. Lucarelli
53017 Radda in Chianti [SI]
Tel. +39 0577733541
www.livon.it

PRE-BOOKED VISITS
ANNUAL PRODUCTION 95,000 bottles
HECTARES UNDER VINE 15.00
SUSTAINABLE WINERY

The Livon family of Friuli are well-known in the world of white wine. But they've diversified their selection with two estates for the cultivation of reds: the Umbrian Colsanto and the Tuscan Borgo Salcetino. This latter, purchased in the Radda in Chianti subzone in the mid-1990s, is giving rise to truly noteworthy wines, among the region's best. Their style is modern but true to the time-honored codes of Chianti Classico, starting with aging in large oak barrels. Their wines, which pursue energy of taste, do a superb job expressing the territory Their Chianti Classico Lucarello Riserva '15 exhibits a rich, complex aromatic profile characterized by a cross between fruit and flowers, peppery hints and smoky notes. On the palate it unfolds airy, with nice contrast and a lovely full-bodied density. The Chianti Classico '17 goes all in on enjoyability. Aromatically it's more fleeting, but juicy, sapid and dynamic to drink.

● Chianti Cl. Lucarello Ris. '15	♟♟♟ 4*
● Chianti Cl. '17	♟♟ 3
● Chianti Cl. '16	♟♟♟ 3*
● Chianti Cl. '15	♟♟♟ 3*
● Chianti Cl. '14	♟♟♟ 3*
● Chianti Cl. '13	♟♟♟ 3*
● Chianti Cl. '11	♟♟♟ 3*
● Rossole '12	♟♟♟ 3*
● Chianti Cl. '10	♟♟ 3
● Chianti Cl. Gran Selezione I Salci '15	♟♟ 6
● Chianti Cl. Lucarello Ris. '13	♟♟ 4
● Chianti Cl. Lucarello Ris. '12	♟♟ 4
● Chianti Cl. Lucarello Ris. '11	♟♟ 4
● Chianti Cl. Lucarello Ris. '10	♟♟ 4

Il Borro

Fraz. San Giustino Valdarno
Loc. Il Borro, 1
52020 Loro Ciuffenna [AR]
Tel. +39 055977053
www.ilborro.it

CELLAR SALES
PRE-BOOKED VISITS
ACCOMMODATION AND RESTAURANT SERVICE
ANNUAL PRODUCTION 160,000 bottles
HECTARES UNDER VINE 45.00
VITICULTURE METHOD Certified Organic
SUSTAINABLE WINERY

Ferruccio Ferragmo purchased this historic estate in 1993. Along with his son Salvatore, he began the complex work of renovating and developing its buildings and villas, but especially its vineyards. For some years now these have been organically managed and are also currently undergoing biodynamic conversion. In addition to Sangiovese, the dominant regional grape, they also cultivate Merlot, Cabernet Sauvignon and Petit Verdot. Their medieval underground cellar, carved out of the earth, unfolds beneath the main villa. Their Borro '16 is made with Merlot and smaller shares Syrah, Petit Verdot and Cabernet Sauvignon. Aromatically it's truly elegant, with notes of black cherry and plums followed by spicy hints of cloves and cinnamon. On the palate it enters soft, smooth in its tannins and balanced, truly long and gratifying. Tre Bicchieri. Their Alessandro Dal Borro '15, a monovarietal Merlot, also performed well, proving alluring in its aromas and rich on the palate.

● Il Borro '16	♟♟♟ 7
● Alessandro Dal Borro '15	♟♟ 8
● Petruna Sangiovese in Anfora '17	♟♟ 6
● Pian di Nova '16	♟♟ 3
● Polissena '16	♟♟ 5
⊙ Brut Bolle di Borro '13	♟ 8
⊙ Rosé del Borro '18	♟ 3
● Il Borro '15	♟♟ 7
● Il Borro '13	♟♟ 7
● Petruna '14	♟♟ 7
● Petruna Sangiovese in Anfora '16	♟♟ 6
● Pian di Nova '15	♟♟ 3
● Pian di Nova '13	♟♟ 3
● Polissena '15	♟♟ 5

★Boscarelli

LOC. CERVOGNANO
VIA DI MONTENERO, 28
53045 MONTEPULCIANO [SI]
TEL. +39 0578767277
www.poderiboscarelli.com

CELLAR SALES
PRE-BOOKED VISITS
ANNUAL PRODUCTION 100,000 bottles
HECTARES UNDER VINE 14.00

At times Italian history contains
unexpected turns of events. Indeed, it was
the De Ferrari Corradi family who, upon
arriving in Tuscany from Genoa, created
one of Nobile di Montepulciano's most
representative estates. In them an ancient
territory and wine in need of a 'makeover'
found exceptional craftsmen. The estate
isn't situated in some anonymous district,
but in one of its best terroirs: Cervognano.
It's an area with peculiar characteristics,
which give rise to elegant wines with lovely
character and pronounced fragrance. Their
elegant Nobile di Montepulciano '16 is
dominated by floral scents, which meet
slight spiciness and smoky notes. On the
palate it exhibits vitality, proving deep and
tasty. Aromatic herbs and hints of dried
flowers mark their Nobile Riserva '15, a
wine characterized by elegant contrast
on the palate. The Nobile Sottocasa
Riserva '14 is pleasant and fragrant, while
the Rosso di Montepulciano Prugnolo '18
proves delicious and quaffable.

● Nobile di Montepulciano '16	🍷🍷🍷 5
● Nobile di Montepulciano Ris. '15	🍷🍷 5
● Nobile di Montepulciano Sottocasa Ris. '14	🍷🍷 6
● Rosso di Montepulciano Prugnolo '18	🍷🍷 3
● Nobile di Montepulciano Il Nocio '13	🍷🍷🍷 8
● Nobile di Montepulciano Il Nocio '12	🍷🍷🍷 8
● Nobile di Montepulciano Il Nocio '11	🍷🍷🍷 8
● Nobile di Montepulciano Nocio dei Boscarelli '10	🍷🍷🍷 8
● Nobile di Montepulciano Nocio dei Boscarelli '09	🍷🍷🍷 8
● Nobile di Montepulciano Nocio dei Boscarelli '08	🍷🍷🍷 8
● Nobile di Montepulciano Nocio dei Boscarelli '07	🍷🍷🍷 8

★Brancaia

LOC. POPPI, 42
53017 RADDA IN CHIANTI [SI]
TEL. +39 0577742007
www.brancaia.it

CELLAR SALES
PRE-BOOKED VISITS
ACCOMMODATION
ANNUAL PRODUCTION 725,000 bottles
HECTARES UNDER VINE 80.00
SUSTAINABLE WINERY

With vineyards spread throughout
Castellina and Radda in Chianti, as well as
property in Maremma, over its almost forty
years of history Brancaia has established
itself as one of Tuscany's foremost
producers. And it did it thanks primarily to
wines that offer a consistent level of quality
and a modern style, one distinguished by
aromatic intensity and structural power, but
also, always, a lovely elegance. It's a style
that still convinces and that represents one
of the best compromises between
approachable appeal and the territory's
more complex offerings. Aromatically their
Chianti Classico '17 mostly features
sensations of violet, which are adorned by
hints of undergrowth and smoky accents.
On the palate it proves very enjoyable, with
broad, balanced and fragrant development.
Darker notes characterize their Chianti
Classico Riserva '16, a wine that's a bit
more marked by oak. On the palate it's
more surefooted by virtue of smooth
tannins and full, juicy flavor.

● Chianti Cl. '17	🍷🍷 4
● Chianti Cl. Ris. '16	🍷🍷 5
● Brancaia Il Blu '16	🍷 7
● Ilatraia '16	🍷 7
● Brancaia Il Blu '08	🍷🍷🍷 8
● Brancaia Il Blu '07	🍷🍷🍷 7
● Brancaia Il Blu '06	🍷🍷🍷 8
● Brancaia Il Blu '05	🍷🍷🍷 6
● Brancaia Il Blu '04	🍷🍷🍷 6
● Brancaia Il Blu '03	🍷🍷🍷 6
● Brancaia Il Blu '01	🍷🍷🍷 6
● Chianti Cl. Brancaia '13	🍷🍷🍷 4*
● Chianti Cl. Ris. '14	🍷🍷🍷 5
● Chianti Cl. Ris. '13	🍷🍷🍷 5
● Chianti Cl. Ris. '11	🍷🍷🍷 5
● Chianti Cl. Ris. '10	🍷🍷🍷 4*
● Chianti Cl. Ris. '09	🍷🍷🍷 7

Brunelli - Le Chiuse di Sotto

LOC. PODERNOVONE, 157
53024 MONTALCINO [SI]
TEL. +39 0577849337
www.giannibrunelli.it

CELLAR SALES
PRE-BOOKED VISITS
ACCOMMODATION AND RESTAURANT SERVICE
ANNUAL PRODUCTION 30,000 bottles
HECTARES UNDER VINE 6.50
SUSTAINABLE WINERY

The journey that made Gianni Brunelli's Sangiovese one of the most distinctive continues uninterrupted, despite the winemaker's early death. The credit goes to his wife, Maria Laura Vacca, who's accompanied by Adriano Brunelli and family. A rigorous and elegant sensibility binds together vineyards of somewhat different temperaments. Le Chiuse di Sotto is a contiguous tract situated in the northeast part of Montalcino, while Podernovone (to the southeast) hosts the cellar and the block of vineyards subsequently taken over. The pair of Brunellos submitted for tasting this year proved to be one of the best in recent memory. The Ris. '13 is just a bit restricted in terms of expansion, but its procession of roots and earth combines perfectly with its elegant, extractive weave. The 'vintage' 2014 moves on a similar track amidst notes of wild strawberries, topsoil and mint, with the added support of aromatic brilliance, continuity of flavor and sapidity.

Brunello di Montalcino '14	▼▼▼ 6
● Brunello di Montalcino Ris. '13	▼▼ 8
Amor Costante '15	▼▼ 5
● Rosso di Montalcino '17	▼▼ 4
● Amor Costante '05	♀♀♀ 5
Brunello di Montalcino '12	♀♀♀ 6
● Brunello di Montalcino '10	♀♀♀ 6
Amor Costante '10	♀♀ 5
Brunello di Montalcino '13	♀♀ 6
● Brunello di Montalcino '11	♀♀ 6
Brunello di Montalcino '09	♀♀ 6
● Brunello di Montalcino '08	♀♀ 6
Brunello di Montalcino Ris. '10	♀♀ 8
Brunello di Montalcino Ris. '07	♀♀ 8
● Rosso di Montalcino '16	♀♀ 4
● Rosso di Montalcino '13	♀♀ 4
● Rosso di Montalcino '12	♀♀ 4

Bruni

FRAZ. FONTEBLANDA
S.DA VIC.LE MIGLIORINA, 6
58015 ORBETELLO [GR]
TEL. +39 0564885445
www.aziendabruni.it

CELLAR SALES
ANNUAL PRODUCTION 500,000 bottles
HECTARES UNDER VINE 48.00

Moreno and Marco Bruni built one of Maremma's most dynamic wineries, wisely interpreting both market trends and stylistic challenges and producing impeccable wines that manage to bring together the primary traits of a generous territory. Their selection is rooted in Morellino, but it's been with the recent Maremma DOC appellation that their wines have earned the most recognition. This is especially true of their Oltreconfine, a Grenache that's proven to be one of Maremma's most intriguing wines of late. Their Maremma Toscana Grenache Oltreconfine impresses more and more. Even with a year like 2017, this red exhibits first-rate tannic finesse, and an energy and pleasantness that few can express with such consistency, even in other production zones. The rest of their selection performed well, with the Perlaia '18 leading among their whites.

● Maremma Toscana Oltreconfine '17	▼▼▼ 5
○ Maremma Toscana Vermentino Perlaia V. T. '18	▼▼ 3*
○ Maremma Toscana Vermentino Plinio '18	▼▼ 2*
● Morellino di Scansano Marteto '18	▼▼ 3
● Morellino di Scansano Laire Ris. '16	▼ 4
● Grenache Oltreconfine '13	♀♀♀ 2*
● Maremma Toscana Alicante Oltreconfine '15	♀♀♀ 6
● Maremma Toscana Grenache Oltreconfine '16	♀♀♀ 6
● Morellino di Scansano Laire Ris. '15	♀♀ 4
○ Vermentino Perlaia '17	♀♀ 3

Alejandro Bulgheroni Family Vineyards

FRAZ. VAGLIAGLI
LOC. DIEVOLE, 6
53019 CASTELNUOVO BERARDENGA [SI]
TEL. +39 0577322613
www.dievole.it

CELLAR SALES
PRE-BOOKED VISITS
ACCOMMODATION AND RESTAURANT SERVICE
ANNUAL PRODUCTION 350,000 bottles
HECTARES UNDER VINE 80.00

The Bulgheroni family's mosaic of regional wineries has taken on a definitive shape: two estates in Montalcino, two more in Bolgheri, and one in Chianti. These constitute a major production network that's already geared for superb quality. For now the best results are coming out of the Chianti subzone of Castelnuovo Berardenga, which, having had a head start, has gotten more attention. It's a selection that's well-known by now, and has proven capable of standing shoulder-to-shoulder with the best. Their Chianti Classico Novecento Riserva '16 possesses aromas of great definition, exhibiting equal complexity and clarity on the palate, where it comes through elegant and delectable, full of contrasts. Their Chianti Classico Vigna di Sessina Gran Selezione '16 is a step below, with its gustatory and aromatic qualities still in the process of evolving. The wines from their other estates proved excellent as well.

● Chianti Cl. Novecento Ris. Dievole '16	♟♟ 5
● Bolgheri Rosso Sup. Maestro di Cava Tenuta Meraviglia '16	♟♟ 6
● Bolgheri Rosso Sup. Tenuta Le Colonne '17	♟♟ 6
● Bolgheri Rosso Tenuta Meraviglia '17	♟♟ 4
● Brunello di Montalcino Ris. Podere Brizio '13	♟♟ 6
● Chianti Cl. Dievole '17	♟♟ 4
● Chianti Cl. Gran Selezione V. di Sessina Dievole '16	♟♟ 7
● Rosso di Montalcino Podere Brizio '17	♟♟ 4
● Brunello di Montalcino Podere Brizio '14	♟ 6
● Chianti Cl. Novecento Ris. Dievole '14	♟♟♟ 5
● Bolgheri Rosso Tenuta Meraviglia '16	♟♟ 4
● Chianti Cl. Dievole '15	♟♟ 4

Buondonno Casavecchia alla Piazza

LOC. LA PIAZZA, 37
53011 CASTELLINA IN CHIANTI [SI]
TEL. +39 0577749754
www.buondonno.com

CELLAR SALES
PRE-BOOKED VISITS
ACCOMMODATION
ANNUAL PRODUCTION 40,000 bottles
HECTARES UNDER VINE 11.00
VITICULTURE METHOD Certified Organic
SUSTAINABLE WINERY

Starting in 1988, Gabriele Buondonno and Valeria Sodana (both agronomists) began building a business and a winery according to a specific philosophy. Virtually from the outset their vineyards were managed in organic, while in the cellar they maintained important traditional practices, like aging their wine in large wooden barrels. The result is a selection of decidedly 'Chianti' wines, pleasant yet complex, at times austere, and always capable of offering up their best over time. A bit too much oak doesn't impede their Chianti Classico Riserva '16 from expressing its aromatic intensity and coherence. On the palate the wine finds its strength, unfolding enticingly and complexly, presided over by sapidity. Their Lemme Lemme '16, a field blend of Sangiovese, Canaiolo, Malvasia Nera and Colorino, is a lovely red in terms of craft and character while their Chianti Classico '17 proves small but decidedly well-made.

● Chianti Cl. Casavecchia alla Piazza Ris. '16	♟♟ 3*
● Lemme Lemme '16	♟♟ 2*
● Chianti Cl. Casavecchia alla Piazza '17	♟♟ 3
● Chianti Cl. Casavecchia alla Piazza '15	♟♟♟ 3*
● Chianti Cl. Casavecchia alla Piazza '16	♟♟ 3*
● Chianti Cl. Casavecchia alla Piazza Ris. '15	♟♟ 3
● Chianti Cl. Ris. '13	♟♟ 5

Caiarossa

Loc. Riparbella
Loc. Serra all'Olio, 59
56046 Riparbella [PI]
Tel. +39 0586699016
www.caiarossa.com

CELLAR SALES
PRE-BOOKED VISITS
ANNUAL PRODUCTION 130,000 bottles
HECTARES UNDER VINE 32.00
VITICULTURE METHOD Certified Biodynamic

This producer has existed for more than
20 years, but its purchase by Eric Albada
Jelgersma, owner of Chateau Giscours and
du Terte in Bordeaux, represented a
turning point. While in the vineyards
principles of biodynamic agriculture are
followed, the cellar was built according to
the Asian philosophy of Feng Shui. The
name derives from the red color of its
diaspore-rich soil. The tasty and enticing
Caiarossa '16 is a blend of seven grapes,
predominantly Merlot and Cabernet Franc.
It opens on minty and balsamic hints, only
to give way to notes of blueberries and
blackcurrant, followed by pencil lead. On
the palate it's elegant, marked by juicy but
measured pervasiveness, delicate tannins
and a sapid, lengthy finish.Their Aria di
Caiarossa '15, which is also made with
Bordeaux varieties, offers up toasty notes
of coffee followed by juniper, eucalyptus
and nutmeg. Acidity is pronounced on its
round, well-structured body.

● Caiarossa '16	♟♟ 6
● Aria di Caiarossa '15	♟♟ 5
○ Bianco '17	♟♟ 4
● Pergolaia '15	♟♟ 3
● Aria di Caiarossa '13	♟♟ 5
● Aria di Caiarossa '12	♟♟ 5
● Caiarossa '13	♟♟ 6
● Caiarossa '12	♟♟ 6
○ Oro di Caiarossa '14	♟♟ 6
● Pergolaia '13	♟♟ 3
● Pergolaia '12	♟♟ 3

Tenuta Le Calcinaie

Loc. Santa Lucia, 36
53037 San Gimignano [SI]
Tel. +39 0577943007
www.tenutalecalcinaie.it

CELLAR SALES
PRE-BOOKED VISITS
ANNUAL PRODUCTION 60,000 bottles
HECTARES UNDER VINE 9.50
VITICULTURE METHOD Certified Organic

Just a few kilometers from San Gimignano,
Simone Santini is living his passion, tending
to every small detail of his winery with
painstaking care. The first vineyards were
planted in 1986 while winemaking began
in 1993. Conversion to organic cultivation
followed a couple years later and, in 2001,
winemaking was also certified organic. In
his extremely well-equipped underground
cellar, which is designed to maintain
constant temperatures and humidities,
particular attention is shown for the use of
hydraulic resources. Their Vernaccia Vigna
Al Sassi Riserva '16 opens with subtle
mineral hints accompanied by vegetal
accents of chives and sage, all followed by
fruity notes of white peach and damson. On
the palate it enters fresh and lively with
nice juiciness and a pleasantly long finish
marked by sapid notes. Their Vernaccia '18
plays on citrusy aromas of mandarin
orange and lemon, then fresh fruits like
kiwi — on the palate it's long and fresh.

● Chianti Colli Senesi '18	♟♟ 2*
○ Vernaccia di S. Gimignano '18	♟♟ 2*
○ Vernaccia di S. Gimignano V. ai Sassi Ris. '16	♟♟ 3
● Teodoro '15	♟ 4
● Chianti Colli Senesi '12	♟♟ 4
● Teodoro '13	♟♟ 4
○ Vernaccia di S. Gimignano '17	♟♟ 2*
○ Vernaccia di S. Gimignano '15	♟♟ 2*
○ Vernaccia di S. Gimignano '13	♟♟ 2*
○ Vernaccia di S. Gimignano Benedetta di San Donato Ris. '14	♟♟ 3
○ Vernaccia di S. Gimignano V. ai Sassi Ris. '15	♟♟ 3
○ Vernaccia di S. Gimignano V. ai Sassi Ris. '14	♟♟ 3

Camigliano

LOC. CAMIGLIANO
VIA D'INGRESSO, 2
53024 MONTALCINO [SI]
TEL. +39 0577844068
www.camigliano.it

CELLAR SALES
PRE-BOOKED VISITS
ANNUAL PRODUCTION 350,000 bottles
HECTARES UNDER VINE 92.00
SUSTAINABLE WINERY

You can't fully appreciate Camigliano's wines without talking about the beautiful landscape from which they arise, a historic village situated along the western border of Montalcino, just a stone's throw from Alta Maremma. Today it's thriving, thanks primarily to the Ghezzi family, who took over the estate in the 1950s and then made it the hub of their wine production business. Their work centers on Sangiovese da Brunello, a distinctly Mediterranean wine that's aged in medium-large French oak barrels. Their selection proved to be in top form, starting with a Brunello '14 that's original, to say the least, in its aromas of dark citrus, shrubs and resin. Despite the difficult year, it's close-knit and juicy on the palate, with a development that's slowed only by austere tannins. Their Gualto Ris. '13 is just as rigorous, though more expansive on the palate. Clear sensations of blackcurrant, curing spices and wet earth give way to a meaty, penetrating palate.

● Brunello di Montalcino '14	♟♟ 6
● Brunello di Montalcino Gualto Ris. '13	♟♟ 8
● Rosso di Montalcino '17	♟♟ 3
● Brunello di Montalcino Gualto Ris. '12	♟♟♟ 8
● Brunello di Montalcino '13	♟♟ 6
● Brunello di Montalcino '12	♟♟ 6
● Brunello di Montalcino '11	♟♟ 6
● Brunello di Montalcino '10	♟♟ 6
● Brunello di Montalcino '09	♟♟ 6
● Brunello di Montalcino Gualto Ris. '10	♟♟ 7
● Brunello di Montalcino Gualto Ris. '09	♟♟ 7
● Brunello di Montalcino Paesaggio Inatteso '12	♟♟ 7
● Brunello di Montalcino Ris. '11	♟♟ 6
● Rosso di Montalcino '15	♟♟ 3
● Rosso di Montalcino '13	♟♟ 3

Antonio Camillo

LOC. PIANETTI DI MONTEMERANO
58014 MANCIANO [GR]
TEL. +39 3391525224
www.antoniocamillo.it

CELLAR SALES
PRE-BOOKED VISITS
ANNUAL PRODUCTION 95,000 bottles
HECTARES UNDER VINE 17.00
VITICULTURE METHOD Certified Organic

If we were asked to name a figure who can express the most intimate part of Maremma's past through his wines, it would have to be Antonio Camillo. He brought the virtues of Ciliegiolo to the territory, presenting the wine as no one had thought to in recent times. Free of small wood barrels, his Ciliegiolo stands out for a style that comes through clearly. It's one in which a rustic character is abandoned in favor of pleasantness, and qualities not lacking in originality or complexity. They also make a Sangiovese del Morellino and white wines. The most glaring aspect of this year's tastings was the absence of their Vallerana Alta, the flagship wine that made Antonio Camillo a production leader in Maremma. Their Ciliegiolo '18, however, maintains its delicious and approachable character adorned by aromas of wild herbs and small wild berries. The Morellino di Scansano '18, with its nuanced aromas and decisive flavor, is small but very well-crafted.

● Ciliegiolo '18	♟♟ 3
● Morellino di Scansano '18	♟♟ 3
● Maremma Toscana Ciliegiolo V. Vallerana Alta '16	♟♟♟ 5
● Maremma Toscana Ciliegiolo V. Vallerana Alta '15	♟♟♟ 6
● Maremma Toscana Ciliegiolo V. Vallerana Alta '14	♟♟♟ 3*
● Maremma Toscana Ciliegiolo '17	♟♟ 3
● Maremma Toscana Ciliegiolo Principio '15	♟♟ 2*
● Maremma Toscana Ciliegiolo Principio '14	♟♟ 2*
● Maremma Toscana Ciliegiolo V. Vallerana Alta '13	♟♟ 3*
● Morellino di Scansano Cotozzino '15	♟♟ 3

Campo alle Comete

Loc. Sughericcio
Via Fornacelle, 249
57022 Castagneto Carducci [LI]
Tel. +39 0565766056
www.campoallecomete.it

CELLAR SALES
PRE-BOOKED VISITS
ACCOMMODATION
ANNUAL PRODUCTION 120,000 bottles
HECTARES UNDER VINE 21.00
VITICULTURE METHOD Certified Organic

The Bolgheri branch of the Feudi di San Gregorio group (a leader of the Campania wine renaissance), Campo all Comete definitely got off on the right foot. Credit goes to the Capaldo family, who've quickly revived a lovely patrimony of vineyards and proven apt winemakers. The grapes used are the territory's classics: Merlot, Cabernet Sauvignon, Cabernet Franc and Petit Verdot. Their wines are well-crafted, Mediterranean and contemporary in the best sense of the term. The Bolgheri Rosso Stupore '17 put in an excellent performance, proving dense and close-woven in its fruity weave, well supported by a delicately spicy presence and crossed by refreshing vegetal, balsamic strokes. It's still young, but already intelligible, it just needs greater tannic cohesion. It's joined by their Podere 277 in charm, quality and vintage. This 2017 is a juicy red, dark in its aromas of blueberries and forest undergrowth. The Bolgheri Sup. '16 proves well-crafted but oak-laden.

⊙ Bolgheri Rosato '18	🍷🍷 3
● Bolgheri Rosso Stupore '17	🍷🍷 4
● Bolgheri Rosso Sup. '16	🍷🍷 5
● Cabernet Sauvignon '17	🍷🍷 4
● Podere 277 Syrah '17	🍷🍷 3
● Bolgheri Rosso Stupore '16	🍷🍷 4
● Bolgheri Rosso Sup. '15	🍷🍷 4
● Cabernet Sauvignon '15	🍷🍷 4
○ Vermentino '17	🍷🍷 5

Canalicchio di Sopra

Loc. Casaccia, 73
53024 Montalcino [SI]
Tel. +39 0577848316
www.canalicchiodisopra.com

CELLAR SALES
PRE-BOOKED VISITS
ACCOMMODATION
ANNUAL PRODUCTION 55,000 bottles
HECTARES UNDER VINE 15.00

Founded in 1961 by Primo Pacenti and subsequently managed by his son-in-law, Pier Luigi Ripaccioli, Canalicchio di Sopra is a veteran producer with a young spirit. Siblings Simonetta, Marco and Francesco oversee the winery today, bringing a modern sensibility and further anchoring it to the two prestigious districts that host its vineyards, both in the northern part of Montalcino. Indeed, their vineyards in Canalicchi and Montosoli come together to produce vigorous Rosso and Brunello wines. Aged primarily in 3000 liter oak barrels, they're generally very ageworthy.. Our most recent tastings highlight the aging potential of their Riserva '13. Blackberries, juniper and pepper hold together power and verve, though it seems to need a bit more time to integrate its vigorous extractive substance. Their Rosso '17 is also showing excellent signs, playing on sweet notes of red fruit and caramel. It's just a bit dry at the finish but endowed with juice.

● Brunello di Montalcino Ris. '13	🍷🍷 8
● Rosso di Montalcino '17	🍷🍷 3
● Brunello di Montalcino '14	🍷 6
● Brunello di Montalcino '10	🍷🍷🍷 6
● Brunello di Montalcino '07	🍷🍷🍷 6
● Brunello di Montalcino '06	🍷🍷🍷 6
● Brunello di Montalcino '04	🍷🍷🍷 6
● Brunello di Montalcino Ris. '10	🍷🍷🍷 8
● Brunello di Montalcino Ris. '07	🍷🍷🍷 8
● Brunello di Montalcino Ris. '04	🍷🍷🍷 7
● Brunello di Montalcino Ris. '01	🍷🍷🍷 7
● Brunello di Montalcino '13	🍷🍷 6
● Brunello di Montalcino '12	🍷🍷 6
● Brunello di Montalcino '09	🍷🍷 6
● Brunello di Montalcino '08	🍷🍷 6
● Rosso di Montalcino '15	🍷🍷 3*

Cantalici

FRAZ. CASTAGNOLI
VIA DELLA CROCE, 17-19
53013 GAIOLE IN CHIANTI [SI]
TEL. +39 0577731038
www.cantalici.it

CELLAR SALES
PRE-BOOKED VISITS
ANNUAL PRODUCTION 46,000 bottles
HECTARES UNDER VINE 30.00

Antica Fornace di Ridolfo, name after the 16th-century furnace present on the property when it was purchased in the 1970s, is situated along the Giaole in Chianti hillside. It's a young producer, founded in the late 1990s by brothers Carlo and Daniele Cantalici, who draw on the teachings of their father, Loris, as well as their experience in forestry, wine-growing and olive cultivation throughout Chianti. Their Gran Selezione Baruffo '15 features a complex aromatic profile in which broad-based notes of cherry and plums are followed by hints of forest undergrowth. On the palate it's solid, elegant and fresh, with resolved tannins and a nice, long finish. Their Chianti Classico Baruffo '16 stands out on the nose for its intense bouquet of wild berries and mature cherry, as well as its fresh nuances of aromatic herbs. In the mouth it's elegant, balanced, with a well-integrated acidity, and a juicy, long finish.

● Chianti Cl. Baruffo '16	♈♈ 3*
● Chianti Cl. Gran Sel. Baruffo '15	♈♈ 3*
○ Cantavento '17	♈♈ 4
● Tangano '15	♈♈ 4
● Chianti Cl. '15	♈ 3
⊙ Petali Rosa '18	♈ 3
○ Cantavento '16	♉♉ 4
● Chianti Cl. Baruffo '13	♉♉ 4
● Chianti Cl. Baruffo Ris. '13	♉♉ 5
● Chianti Cl. Baruffo Ris. '11	♉♉ 3
● Chianti Cl. Gran Sel. Baruffo '13	♉♉ 3*
● Petali Rosso '17	♉♉ 3
● Tangano '13	♉♉ 4
○ Vin Santo del Chianti Cl. Baruffo '11	♉♉ 6

Capanna

LOC. CAPANNA, 333
53024 MONTALCINO [SI]
TEL. +39 0577848298
www.capannamontalcino.com

CELLAR SALES
PRE-BOOKED VISITS
ANNUAL PRODUCTION 70,000 bottles
HECTARES UNDER VINE 21.00

At Podere Capanna they don't only produce superb Brunellos. Recently they also began a new Wine Relais activity that comprises both a spa and restaurant. It's one more reason to visit the Cencioni family, who settled on this scenic estate overlooking Montosoli hill in the late 1950s. The territory gives rise to wines that bring together warmth, austerity and sapid strength, explored through a traditional winemaking approach, starting with lengthy maturation in 1000 and 3000 liter oak. A brilliant overall performance was made more interesting by the presence of wines that are in many ways harmonious in their expression. While the Rosso '17 shows a warm and expansive dimension, the Brunello '14 impresses with its light, almost minimalist stride. But it is, as usual, the Riserva '13 that pulls things together, with its twin poles: a placid and enveloping opening, a robust and appealing finish.

● Brunello di Montalcino 50° Vendemmia Ris. '13	♈♈ 8
● Brunello di Montalcino '14	♈♈ 6
● Rosso di Montalcino '17	♈♈ 3
● Brunello di Montalcino Ris. '10	♉♉♉ 8
● Brunello di Montalcino Ris. '06	♉♉♉ 7
● Brunello di Montalcino Ris. '04	♉♉♉ 7
● Brunello di Montalcino Ris. '90	♉♉♉ 6
● Rosso di Montalcino '15	♉♉♉ 3*
● Brunello di Montalcino '13	♉♉ 6
● Brunello di Montalcino '12	♉♉ 6
● Brunello di Montalcino '11	♉♉ 6
● Brunello di Montalcino '10	♉♉ 6
● Brunello di Montalcino Ris. '12	♉♉ 8
○ Moscadello di Montalcino V. T. '15	♉♉ 4
○ Moscadello di Montalcino V. T. '12	♉♉ 4
● Rosso di Montalcino '16	♉♉ 3

Caparsa

LOC. CASE SPARSE CAPARSA, 47
53017 RADDA IN CHIANTI [SI]
TEL. +39 0577738174
www.caparsa.it

CELLAR SALES
PRE-BOOKED VISITS
ACCOMMODATION
ANNUAL PRODUCTION 40,000 bottles
HECTARES UNDER VINE 12.08
VITICULTURE METHOD Certified Organic
SUSTAINABLE WINERY

Since 1982, Paolo Cianferoni and his family have managed Caparsa. Situated in the Radda in Chianti subzone, the producer (founded by his father, Reginaldo Cianferoni, in 1965) makes wines that enthusiastically draw on tradition, with all its consequences. In the vineyard organic principles are followed rigorously, to say the least, while their winemaking approach could be characterized as bare-bones, with fermentation in concrete and aging in large wood barrels. The 2016 version of their Chianti Classico Caparsino Riserva is truly extraordinary for its character and expressiveness, highlighting scents of earth, flowers, fruit and spices. On the palate it's invigorating, close-woven but at the same time generous, with a juicy, rhythmic palate. A bit too much oak and tannic hardness characterize the gustatory profile of their Chianti Classico Doccio a Matteo Riserva '16, a wine that stands out for the nice personality of its aromas.

● Chianti Cl. Caparsino Ris. '16	♥♥ 6
● Chianti Cl. Doccio a Matteo Ris. '16	♥♥ 7
● Chianti Cl. Caparsa '16	♥ 5
● Chianti Cl. Doccio a Matteo Ris. '00	♀♀♀ 5
● Chianti Cl. Caparsino Ris. '15	♀♀ 5
● Chianti Cl. Caparsino Ris. '10	♀♀ 5
● Chianti Cl. Doccio a Matteo Ris. '15	♀♀ 5
● Chianti Cl. Doccio a Matteo Ris. '11	♀♀ 5

★Tenuta di Capezzana

LOC. SEANO
VIA CAPEZZANA, 100
59015 CARMIGNANO [PO]
TEL. +39 0558706005
www.capezzana.it

CELLAR SALES
PRE-BOOKED VISITS
ACCOMMODATION AND RESTAURANT SERVICE
ANNUAL PRODUCTION 400,000 bottles
HECTARES UNDER VINE 75.00
VITICULTURE METHOD Certified Organic

Theirs is a family history that continues with enthusiasm and commitment. In Carmignano they've been making wine for more than a millenium but the Contini Bonaccossi family have been in the business since the 1920s, with a group of farms that came together as a single estate. Credit goes primarily to Ugo Contini who, after WW II, focused on viticulture. His work continued with his children, and now his grandchildren. The interesting historical record preserved in their cellar testifies to the territory's viticultural potential. Their Vin Santo '12 is a spectacular wine. Aromas of orange peel dominate, followed by almonds and apricots. On the palate it proves broad, creamy, dense and velvety, with a finish of extraordinary length in its after-scents of dried fruit and nuts. Their Ghiaie della Furba '16, made with Cabernet, Merlot and Syrah, opens with floral notes of geranium, then peppers and wild berries. An elegant, soft and well-sustained palate follows.

○ Vin Santo di Carmignano Ris. '12	♥♥♥ 6
● Carmignano Villa di Capezzana '16	♥♥ 5
● Ghiaie della Furba '16	♥♥ 6
● Carmignano Villa di Capezzana '07	♀♀♀ 4
● Carmignano Villa di Capezzana '05	♀♀♀ 4
● Carmignano Villa di Capezzana '99	♀♀♀ 5
● Ghiaie della Furba '01	♀♀♀ 5
● Ghiaie della Furba '98	♀♀♀ 5
○ Vin Santo di Carmignano Ris. '10	♀♀♀ 6
○ Vin Santo di Carmignano Ris. '09	♀♀♀ 6
○ Vin Santo di Carmignano Ris. '08	♀♀♀ 6
○ Vin Santo di Carmignano Ris. '07	♀♀♀ 6
○ Vin Santo di Carmignano Ris. '05	♀♀♀ 5

Caprili

FRAZ. TAVERNELLE
LOC. CAPRILI, 268
53024 MONTALCINO [SI]
TEL. +39 0577848566
www.caprili.it

CELLAR SALES
PRE-BOOKED VISITS
ACCOMMODATION
ANNUAL PRODUCTION 75,000 bottles
HECTARES UNDER VINE 21.00
SUSTAINABLE WINERY

Originally owned by the Castelli-Martinozzi family (also owners of Villa Santa Restituta), Podere Caprili was taken over by the Barolommei family in the 1960s, when it became the headquarters of one of southeastern Montalcino's loveliest wineries. Their decidedly lush, summery Brunellos are made with grapes cultivated and vinified separately from Vigna Madre, Ceppo Nero, Testucchiaia, Quadrucci, del Pino and Palazzetto. The resulting blend comes together after lengthy maturation in large wooden barrels. In the latest tastings, their Brunello '14 does a nice job compensating for the absence of a reserve. Despite some vegetal and evolved notes, it proves to be an energetic wine endowed with multifaceted aromas (roots, curing spices, plowed earth), but especially sweetness and warmth. Their Rosso '17 seems a bit lacking in suppleness — however it's a large and meaty wine in its jammy hints and aromas of forest undergrowth.

● Brunello di Montalcino '14	▼▼ 6
● Rosso di Montalcino '17	▼ 3
● Brunello di Montalcino '13	▼▼▼ 6
● Brunello di Montalcino '10	▼▼▼ 6
● Brunello di Montalcino '06	▼▼▼ 7
● Brunello di Montalcino AdAlberto Ris. '10	▼▼▼ 8
● Brunello di Montalcino Ris. '08	▼▼▼ 7
● Brunello di Montalcino Ris. '06	▼▼▼ 7
● Brunello di Montalcino Ris. '04	▼▼▼ 5
● Brunello di Montalcino '12	▽▽ 6
● Brunello di Montalcino '11	▽▽ 6
● Brunello di Montalcino '09	▽▽ 5
● Brunello di Montalcino AdAlberto Ris. '12	▽▽ 8
● Rosso di Montalcino '16	▽▽ 3*
● Rosso di Montalcino '15	▽▽ 3

Tenuta Carleone

LOC. CASTIGLIONI
53017 RADDA IN CHIANTI [SI]
TEL. +39 0577735613
www.carleone.it

CELLAR SALES
PRE-BOOKED VISITS
ANNUAL PRODUCTION 35,000 bottles
HECTARES UNDER VINE 15.00
VITICULTURE METHOD Certified Organic

Karl Egger is an Austrian industrialist and head of Ke Kelit group (manufacturers of cooling systems). Since 2012 he and enologist Sean O'Callaghan have been working on a project that's become one of the most interesting to emerge in Chianti Classico. Their vineyards are situated in the Radda in Chianti subzone, and their wines already express all the area's charm. It's a selection full of character, bringing out all the subtlety of Chianti Sangiovese: delicate wines marked by distinct finesse, vitality, extraordinary energy and precision. The 2016 version of their Uno, a monovarietal Sangiovese, dazzles. Right from the outset it exhibits finesse and character. Its floral fragrances, joined with notes of wild herbs, are a prelude to an invigorating and juicy development on the palate. Their Chianti Classico '16 is equally intriguing, with its earthy aromatic profile and fragrant palate. Their Guercio '17, made with Sangiovese, proves fresh and delectable.

● Uno '16	▼▼▼ 8
● Chianti Cl. '16	▼▼ 5
● Il Guercio '17	▼▼ 7
● Chianti Cl. '15	▼▼▼ 5
● Il Due '15	▽▽ 6
● Il Guercio '16	▽▽ 7
● Il Guercio '15	▽▽ 7

★Fattoria Carpineta Fontalpino

FRAZ. MONTAPERTI
LOC. CARPINETA
53019 CASTELNUOVO BERARDENGA [SI]
TEL. +39 0577369219
www.carpinetafontalpino.it

CELLAR SALES
PRE-BOOKED VISITS
ACCOMMODATION
ANNUAL PRODUCTION 100,000 bottles
HECTARES UNDER VINE 23.00
VITICULTURE METHOD Certified Organic

Owned by Gioia and Filippo Cresti, Carpineta Fontalpino can be found in Castelnuovo Berardenga, in the south of Chianti Classico. The winery, which has achieved a solid level of quality, offers a range of wines that are modern, but not lacking in balance and character. Generous, full wines that are in keeping with the pedoclimatic characteristics of the territory, they exhibit bold structure, accompanied, however, by grip and freshness, and characterized by a carefully pursued maturity of fruit. While waiting for their Chianti Classico Montaperto and Dofana, wisely left to age a while longer, their Chianti Classico Fontalpino '17 once again proves that it's a well-made wine with nice personality. Aromatically it calls up red berries, earth and spices, while on the palate it unfolds sapid, well-sustained and fragrant. Their Do Ut Des '16, a generous blend of Sangiovese, Cabernet Sauvignon and Merlot, also delivered.

● Chianti Cl. Fontalpino '17	♟♟♟ 3*
● Do ut des '16	♟♟ 5
● Chianti Cl. Dofana '16	♟♟♟ 4*
● Chianti Cl. Montaperto '15	♟♟♟ 4*
● Do ut des '13	♟♟♟ 5
● Do ut des '12	♟♟♟ 5
● Do ut des '11	♟♟♟ 5
● Do ut des '10	♟♟♟ 5
● Do ut des '09	♟♟♟ 5
● Do ut des '07	♟♟♟ 5
● Dofana '10	♟♟♟ 7
● Dofana '07	♟♟♟ 8

Casa alle Vacche

FRAZ. PANCOLE
LOC. LUCIGNANO, 73A
53037 SAN GIMIGNANO [SI]
TEL. +39 0577955103
www.casaallevacche.it

CELLAR SALES
PRE-BOOKED VISITS
ACCOMMODATION AND RESTAURANT SERVICE
ANNUAL PRODUCTION 120,000 bottles
HECTARES UNDER VINE 28.00
SUSTAINABLE WINERY

It's a name that recalls local history: Casa all Vacche was the name of the place where, in the 19th century, farm animals (oxen and cows) were kept. In the oldest part of the property you'll notice stone ceilings, common to the period's buildings. For some time now the Ciappi family have dedicated themselves to cultivating vineyards and olives, activities integrated with the opening of an agritourism, thanks to the work of Silvano. His sons Fernando and Lorenzo now oversee the estate. Their Vernaccia di S. Gimignano Crocus Riserva '16 performed well with its aromatic profile characterized by spices and vanilla, sensations that fade to buttery hints and tropical fruit. On the palate it proves smooth, full, with nice acidic vigor and a sapid, graceful finish. Their interesting Merlot '16 opens with classic cherry and raspberry fruit aromas adorned with spicy notes of pepper and clove. On the palate it enters soft, with smooth, enjoyable tannins.

○ Vernaccia di S. Gimignano Crocus Ris. '16	♟♟ 3*
● Merlot '16	♟♟ 2*
○ Vernaccia di S. Gimignano I Macchioni '18	♟♟ 2*
● Chianti Colli Senesi Cinabro Ris. '15	♟ 3
⊙ Raffy Rosato '18	♟ 2
● Aglieno '12	♟♟ 2*
● Canaiolo '16	♟♟ 2*
○ Vernaccia di S. Gimignano Crocus Ris. '14	♟♟ 3
○ Vernaccia di S. Gimignano Crocus Ris. '13	♟♟ 3
○ Vernaccia di S. Gimignano I Macchioni '16	♟♟ 2*
○ Vernaccia di S. Gimignano I Macchioni '15	♟♟ 2*
○ Vernaccia di S. Gimignano I Macchioni '14	♟♟ 2*

★Casanova di Neri

POD. FIESOLE
53024 MONTALCINO [SI]
TEL. +39 0577834455
www.casanovadineri.com

PRE-BOOKED VISITS
ACCOMMODATION
ANNUAL PRODUCTION 225,000 bottles
HECTARES UNDER VINE 63.00

A special mix of territory and skill makes
Giacomo Neri's Brunellos unique. Helped by
his sons Gianlorenzo and Giovanni, he
produces wines characterized by a notable
compactness that's brought out by aging in
new and old wood barrels. We should also
take into consideration the position of their
plots, situated throughout Montalcino, in
Torrenieri, Sesta, Cava dell'Onice and
Podernuovo (just to name the most
well-known). These give rise to a 'vintage'
version, as well as their Tenuta Nuova,
which includes grapes from their Cerretalto
cru. Even if the selection submitted has
seen significant changes, and is missing
their top wines, Casanova di Neri managed
to carve out a prominent place in our latest
tastings. The Rosso '17 is a commendable
combination of pleasantness and
performance. Their Brunello '14 is even
more surprising for its slightly salty
exuberance combined with a delicate
extraction that amplifies lovely notes of
sage and licorice.

● Brunello di Montalcino '14	♟♟ 6
● Rosso di Montalcino '16	♟♟ 5
● Brunello di Montalcino '09	♟♟♟ 6
● Brunello di Montalcino '06	♟♟♟ 5
● Brunello di Montalcino Cerretalto '07	♟♟♟ 8
● Brunello di Montalcino Cerretalto '06	♟♟♟ 8
● Brunello di Montalcino Cerretalto '04	♟♟♟ 8
● Brunello di Montalcino Cerretalto '01	♟♟♟ 8
● Brunello di Montalcino Cerretalto '99	♟♟♟ 8
● Brunello di Montalcino Tenuta Nuova '13	♟♟♟ 8
● Brunello di Montalcino Tenuta Nuova '06	♟♟♟ 8
● Brunello di Montalcino Tenuta Nuova '05	♟♟♟ 7
● Brunello di Montalcino Tenuta Nuova '01	♟♟♟ 6
● Brunello di Montalcino Tenuta Nuova '99	♟♟♟ 6
● Pietradonice '05	♟♟♟ 8
● Sant'Antimo Pietradonice '01	♟♟♟ 8
● Sant'Antimo Pietradonice '00	♟♟♟ 8

Casisano

LOC. CASISANO
53024 MONTALCINO [SI]
TEL. +39 0577835540
www.casisano.it

ANNUAL PRODUCTION 11,000 bottles
HECTARES UNDER VINE 22.00

A veritable natural terrace hosts the
Casisano estate, a historic property that
has for some years now formed part of the
Tommasi Family Estates group. Situated in
the southeast of Montalcino, between
Sant'Antimo abbey and the Orcia river
valley, it's a sunny, ventilated area that
gives rise to pervasive Sangiovese da
Brunello that's rich in fibre. Their premium
wines mature slowly in 1800 and 2500
liter Slavonian oak, starting with their
Colombaiolo Riserva, a wine made with
grapes cultivated on one of the
appellation's highest plots. And it's
precisely Casisano's premium wine that
authoritatively earns itself a place
Montalcino's elite. The 2013 opens with
multifaceted aromas of light fruit, pine
needles and inflorescences, sensations
well-supported by a supple, juicy palate
thanks to its soft tannic endowment.
Natural expression is also a feature of their
Rosso '17, despite its generous alcohol.

● Brunello di Montalcino Colombaiolo Ris. '13	♟♟ 8
● Rosso di Montalcino '17	♟♟ 4
● Brunello di Montalcino '12	♟♟ 7
● Brunello di Montalcino '01	♟♟ 5
● Brunello di Montalcino '99	♟♟ 5
● Brunello di Montalcino Colombaiolo Ris. '11	♟♟ 8
● Brunello di Montalcino Ris. '01	♟♟ 8
● Brunello di Montalcino Ris. '99	♟♟ 8
● Brunello di Montalcino V. del Colombaiolo '99	♟♟ 8
● Rosso di Montalcino '16	♟♟ 4
● Rosso di Montalcino '15	♟♟ 4
● Rosso di Montalcino '02	♟♟ 3
● Rosso di Montalcino Colombaiolo '02	♟♟ 4

Tenuta Casteani

LOC. CASTEANI
POD. FABBRI
58023 GAVORRANO [GR]
TEL. +39 0566871050
www.casteani.it

CELLAR SALES
PRE-BOOKED VISITS
ACCOMMODATION AND RESTAURANT SERVICE
ANNUAL PRODUCTION 80,000 bottles
HECTARES UNDER VINE 14.00
SUSTAINABLE WINERY

Mario Pelosi has been cultivating his vineyards in Gavoranno (today part of the Maremma appellation) since 2004. The area's traditional grapes are grown (Sangiovese, Vermentino, Alicante and Aleatico), along with international varieties (Syrah, Merlot and Viognier). Their style centers on aromatic precision, and flavor that's never over-the-top. Part of their success comes back to the use of new, small wood barrels for aging, with second and third stages in large wood barrels and terra-cotta. Multifaceted aromas of red berries, herbs and spices characterize their Maremma Toscana Terra di Casteani '15, a wine that finds its strong point on the palate, where it comes through well-sustained and succulent. The Maremma Toscana Sessanta '15 also did well, with its more nuanced aromas, and its dense, pervasive gustatory development. The Maremma Toscana Syrah Marujo '16 is compact and less discernible, but well-crafted nonetheless.

● Maremma Toscana Rosso Sessanta '15	♟♟ 3
● Maremma Toscana Rosso Terra di Casteani '15	♟♟ 5
● Maremma Toscana Syrah Marujo '16	♟ 5
○ Maremma Toscana Vermentino Serin '18	♟ 2
● Maremma Toscana Rosso Terra di Casteani '13	♟♟ 5
● Maremma Toscana Sessanta '14	♟♟ 3
○ Maremma Toscana Vermentino Spirito Libero '17	♟♟ 2*
● Terra di Casteani '08	♟♟ 5

Castell'in Villa

LOC. CASTELL'IN VILLA
53019 CASTELNUOVO BERARDENGA [SI]
TEL. +39 0577359074
www.castellinvilla.com

CELLAR SALES
PRE-BOOKED VISITS
ANNUAL PRODUCTION 100,000 bottles
HECTARES UNDER VINE 54.00

At Castell'In Villa no exceptions are made, despite the dictates of fashion. Here they only make classic Tuscan wines with grapes cultivated around their small winery. It was Riccardo Pignatelli della Leonessa's idea to buy a property in Chianti, near Castelnuovo Berardenga, in 1967. Today Coralia Ghertsos, 'the princess', manages the estate herself. Their vintage wines are often thrilling for those who know wine well. But their more recent releases are also impressing, both for their adherence to the past and for their current virtues. Charming notes of slightly dried flowers mark their Chianti Classico Riserva '13. These gradually gets fresher and more lively before giving way to spices and smoky hints, which lend aromatic complexity. On the palate the wine exhibits character and assertiveness, proving rhythmic and well-sustained before closing on a lovely sapid note.

● Chianti Cl. Ris. '13	♟♟ 6
● Chianti Cl. '11	♟♟♟ 5
● Chianti Cl. '09	♟♟♟ 5
● Chianti Cl. '08	♟♟♟ 5
● Chianti Cl. Ris. '85	♟♟♟ 6
● Chianti Cl. '14	♟♟ 5
● Chianti Cl. '13	♟♟ 5
● Chianti Cl. '12	♟♟ 5
● Chianti Cl. '10	♟♟ 5
● Chianti Cl. Poggio delle Rose Ris. '10	♟♟ 8
● Chianti Cl. Ris. '11	♟♟ 6
● Chianti Cl. Ris. '10	♟♟ 6

★★Castellare di Castellina

LOC. CASTELLARE
53011 CASTELLINA IN CHIANTI [SI]
TEL. +39 0577742903
www.castellare.it

CELLAR SALES
PRE-BOOKED VISITS
ACCOMMODATION
ANNUAL PRODUCTION 200,000 bottles
HECTARES UNDER VINE 28.00

The owner of this producer is also a shareholder of Gambero Rosso spa. To avoid any conflict of interest, Paolo Panerai has subordinated the possible awarding of Tre Bicchieri (which, in any case, only occurs through a blind tasting) to the attainment of the same rating of excellence (upwards of 90/100) by an independent, international panel. This was the case here.

In its 2015 version, once again their Sodi di San Niccolò, a blend of Sangiovese and Malvasia Nera, proves that it's a benchmark wine for Chianti. Aromatically it's defined and multifaceted, while on the palate the wine comes through juicy and well-sustained. Their Chianti Classico '17 is also highly enjoyable, with lush fruit making up virtually the whole of its aromatic profile before developing fragrantly, rhythmically and sapid on the palate.

★★Castello del Terriccio

LOC. TERRICCIO
VIA BAGNOLI, 16
56040 CASTELLINA MARITTIMA [PI]
TEL. +39 050699709
www.terriccio.com

CELLAR SALES
PRE-BOOKED VISITS
ANNUAL PRODUCTION 150,000 bottles
HECTARES UNDER VINE 60.00

Gian Annibale Rossi di Medelana created a winery that's particularly attentive to the territory, managing to carry out important renovation work when he carefully oversaw the change from sharecropping to single ownership. Today wine takes center stage, but they continue with other activities, like raising sheep and cattle, and producing oil. The Lupicaia '15, made with Cabernet Sauvignon, Merlot and Petit Verdot, offers up complex aromas, with toasty hints of coffee closing and giving way to intense fruity fragrances of cherry and blackcurrant before shifting, finally, to spicy notes. On the palate it enters pleasant, proving soft, juicy, properly fresh, then closing long and gratifying. The Castello del Terriccio '15, a blend of mostly Syrah and Petit Verdot, proves enticing in its sea and iodine scents. On the palate it's initially austere, but then expands, gaining in depth and harmony.

● I Sodi di San Niccolò '15	♟♟♟ 8
● Chianti Cl. '17	♟♟ 4
● Chianti Cl. Ris. '16	♟♟ 5
● Poggio ai Merli '17	♟♟ 8
● Chianti Cl. Il Poggiale Ris. '16	♟ 6
● Coniale '15	♟ 8
● I Sodi di S. Niccolò '13	♟♟♟ 8
● I Sodi di S. Niccolò '12	♟♟♟ 8
● I Sodi di S. Niccolò '11	♟♟♟ 8
● I Sodi di S. Niccolò '10	♟♟♟ 8
● I Sodi di S. Niccolò '09	♟♟♟ 8
● I Sodi di S. Niccolò '08	♟♟♟ 7
● I Sodi di S. Niccolò '07	♟♟♟ 7
● I Sodi di S. Niccolò '06	♟♟♟ 7
● I Sodi di S. Niccolò '05	♟♟♟ 7
● I Sodi di S. Niccolò '04	♟♟♟ 7
● I Sodi di San Niccolò '14	♟♟♟ 8

● Castello del Terriccio '15	♟♟ 8
● Lupicaia '15	♟♟ 8
○ Con Vento '17	♟♟ 4
○ Rondinaia	♟♟ 4
● Tassinaia '16	♟♟ 6
● Castello del Terriccio '11	♟♟♟ 8
● Castello del Terriccio '07	♟♟♟ 8
● Castello del Terriccio '04	♟♟♟ 8
● Castello del Terriccio '03	♟♟♟ 8
● Lupicaia '13	♟♟♟ 8
● Lupicaia '11	♟♟♟ 8
● Lupicaia '10	♟♟♟ 8
● Lupicaia '07	♟♟♟ 8
● Lupicaia '06	♟♟♟ 8
● Lupicaia '05	♟♟♟ 8
● Lupicaia '04	♟♟♟ 8

Castello del Trebbio

VIA SANTA BRIGIDA, 9
50065 PONTASSIEVE [FI]
TEL. +39 0558304900
www.castellodeltrebbio.it

CELLAR SALES
PRE-BOOKED VISITS
ACCOMMODATION AND RESTAURANT SERVICE
ANNUAL PRODUCTION 350,000 bottles
HECTARES UNDER VINE 60.00
SUSTAINABLE WINERY

Saffron, wine and oil-based beauty
products, extra-virgin oil and, especially,
wine. That's what they make in this hillside
over Pontassieve, an area that hosts a
castle where the Pazzi family plotted to
assassinate Lorenzo de' Medici in 1478.
Anna Baj Macario and her husband
Stefano are the brains, heart and brawn of
this estate, cultivated with a biointegral
approach, and more. They also run
Tecnovite, a business specialized in
agricultural systems/management, as well
as Tenuta Casa Dei in Maremma and
Olianas in Sardinia. Their interesting
Lastricato '15 features mineral hints, iron
and leather scents, then plum and cherry.
On the palate it's sapid, luscious, closing
flavorful. The Pazzesco '16, a blend of
almost equal parts Merlot and Syrah,
exhibits fresh aromas of aromatic herbs
and wild fruit. On the palate it enters
meaty, broad and full, with a long finish.
The Vin Santo '12 features a bouquet of
dried figs and almonds followed by a soft,
sweet, long body.

● Chianti Rufina Lastricato Ris. '15	▼▼ 5
○ Congiura '16	▼▼ 4
● Pazzesco '16	▼▼ 5
○ Vin Santo del Chianti '12	▼▼ 5
● De' Pazzi '16	▼ 4
● Chianti Rufina Lastricato Ris. '11	♀♀♀ 4*
● Chianti Rufina Lastricato Ris. '14	♀♀ 5
● Chianti Rufina Lastricato Ris. '12	♀♀ 5
● Chianti Sup. '15	♀♀ 3*
● Chianti Sup. '14	♀♀ 2*
● De' Pazzi '15	♀♀ 4
● De' Pazzi '14	♀♀ 4
○ Vin Santo del Chianti '11	♀♀ 5

★Castello di Albola

LOC. PIAN D'ALBOLA, 31
53017 RADDA IN CHIANTI [SI]
TEL. +39 0577738019
www.albola.it

CELLAR SALES
PRE-BOOKED VISITS
ANNUAL PRODUCTION 800,000 bottles
HECTARES UNDER VINE 125.00
VITICULTURE METHOD Certified Organic

Since 1821 Castello d'Abola has been part
of the Zonin group, standing out among the
Veneto juggernaut's roster of wineries for
its quality and stylistic coherence. It would,
however, be an error not to consider the
estate on its own terms. It's no coincidence
that the producer operates in one of the
appellation's best districts, Radda in
Chianti, a territory that gives rise to wines
of great charm, possibly Zonin's best,
wines capable of remaining firmly rooted in
the soil, climate and traditions of the area.
The Chianti Classico Riserva '16 opens on
focused and complex aromas, anticipating
a lean, juicy development. The Acciaiolo '16
is almost as good. It's a Sangiovese and
Cabernet Sauvignon blend redolent of
intense fruit, coming through denser and
more approachable on the palate.
Abundant toasty notes mark the tight and
decisive Chianti Classico Solatio Gran
Selezione '16.

● Chianti Cl. Ris. '16	▼▼▼ 5
● Acciaiolo '16	▼▼ 8
● Chianti Cl. Gran Selezione Il Solatio '16	▼▼ 8
● Chianti Cl. Gran Selezione Santa Caterina '16	▼▼ 6
● Chianti Cl. '17	▼ 4
● Acciaiolo '06	♀♀♀ 6
● Acciaiolo '04	♀♀♀ 6
● Chianti Cl. '14	♀♀♀ 3*
● Chianti Cl. Gran Sel. '13	♀♀♀ 5
● Chianti Cl. Il Solatio Gran Sel. '11	♀♀♀ 5
● Chianti Cl. Il Solatio Gran Sel. '10	♀♀♀ 5
● Chianti Cl. Le Ellere '08	♀♀♀ 3
● Chianti Cl. Ris. '14	♀♀♀ 4*
● Chianti Cl. Ris. '09	♀♀♀ 4*
● Chianti Cl. Ris. '08	♀♀♀ 4*

★★Castello di Ama

LOC. AMA
53013 GAIOLE IN CHIANTI [SI]
TEL. +39 0577746031
www.castellodiama.com

CELLAR SALES
PRE-BOOKED VISITS
ANNUAL PRODUCTION 300,000 bottles
HECTARES UNDER VINE 90.00

At Castello di Ama, a bond with the territory has always been of the utmost importance and Chianti Classico has always been Lorenza Sebasti and Marco Pallanti's first wine. But they've also managed to bring originality to their non-denominational wines with a coherence that has always been a pronounced feature of Ama's wines. Despite a few small stumbles, they've promptly recovered and seen to it that their wines are among the territory's best. The Chianti Classico Ama '17 proves well-made, delivering clean, fragrant aromas, and a rhythmic, invigorating, sapid development. We found the Chianti Classico Vigneto Bellavista Gran Selezione '16 interesting, with its complex aromas and its deep, juicy palate — there's just a bit too much oak. The Haiku '16, a field blend of Sangiovese, Cabernet Franc and Merlot, is fragrant and dense.

● Chianti Cl. Ama '17	♚♚ 4
● Chianti Cl. Gran Selezione Vign. Bellavista '16	♚♚ 8
● Haiku '16	♚♚ 6
● Chianti Cl. Gran Selezione San Lorenzo '16	♚ 6
● Chianti Cl. Gran Selezione Vign. La Casuccia '16	♚ 8
● Chianti Cl. Ama '11	♚♚♚ 4*
● Chianti Cl. Bellavista '01	♚♚♚ 8
● Chianti Cl. Castello di Ama '05	♚♚♚ 5
● Chianti Cl. Castello di Ama '03	♚♚♚ 5
● Chianti Cl. Gran Sel. San Lorenzo '13	♚♚♚ 6
● Chianti Cl. La Casuccia '04	♚♚♚ 8
● Chianti Cl. La Casuccia '01	♚♚♚ 8
● Chianti Cl. San Lorenzo '83	♚♚♚ 8
● L'Apparita '01	♚♚♚ 8

Castello di Bolgheri

LOC. BOLGHERI
S.DA LAURETTA, 7
57020 CASTAGNETO CARDUCCI [LI]
TEL. +39 0565762110
www.castellodibolgheri.eu

CELLAR SALES
PRE-BOOKED VISITS
ACCOMMODATION
ANNUAL PRODUCTION 80,000 bottles
HECTARES UNDER VINE 50.00

Castello di Bolgheri's roots go back to the 16th century, when it was part of the the count Gherardesca's vast estate. Situated in the inner part of the district, today the winery is a modern operation expertly managed by the Zileri Dal Verme family and proud of its noble past. Their vineyards span good positions for cultivation, and grow in sandy-clay terrain that's rich in stones and limestone. When it comes to winemaking, their wines exhibit the rigor, style and precision that we've grown used to over time. A fantastic Bolgheri Rosso Superiore '16 earned itself a place among the best wines tasted this year, at least when it comes to the district and appellation of origin. It is in many ways still evolving, crossed by dark notes that time will work out, but already of sensational finesse, deriving a truly great palate for its texture and class, coming through silky and deep. Their Rosso Varvara '17 is also excellent.

● Bolgheri Rosso Sup. '16	♚♚♚ 7
● Bolgheri Varvàra '17	♚♚ 4
● Bolgheri Sup. Castello di Bolgheri '12	♚♚♚ 6
● Bolgheri Sup. Castello di Bolgheri '10	♚♚♚ 6
● Bolgheri Sup. Castello di Bolgheri '09	♚♚♚ 6
● Bolgheri Sup. Castello di Bolgheri '07	♚♚♚ 6
● Bolgheri Rosso Sup. '15	♚♚ 7
● Bolgheri Rosso Sup. '13	♚♚ 7
● Bolgheri Sup. Castello di Bolgheri '11	♚♚ 6
● Bolgheri Varvàra '16	♚♚ 4
● Bolgheri Varvàra '15	♚♚ 4
● Bolgheri Varvàra '13	♚♚ 4

★★★Castello di Fonterutoli

LOC. FONTERUTOLI
VIA OTTONE III DI SASSONIA, 5
53011 CASTELLINA IN CHIANTI [SI]
TEL. +39 057773571
www.mazzei.it

CELLAR SALES
PRE-BOOKED VISITS
ACCOMMODATION AND RESTAURANT SERVICE
ANNUAL PRODUCTION 800,000 bottles
HECTARES UNDER VINE 117.00
SUSTAINABLE WINERY

Theirs is an approach in pursuit of intense fruit and bold structure, but marked by pressure, dynamism, balance and elegance as well: the Mazzei family's signature style. The historic Chianti producer's selection exhibits an immediately recognizable, well-defined character made possible by aging in barriques, in their Castellina in Chianti cellar. Then there's the great precision that comes together with vanguard technology and the expressive potential of one of the appellation's best districts. Even if it's a bit held back by excessive oak, the Mix 36 '16 is an exceptionally tasty bottle. It's a monovarietal Sangiovese redolent of violet and forest undergrowth adorned by smoky touches. We also tasted an excellent version of their Maremma Toscana Rosso di Tenuta Belguardo, a Cabernet Sauvignon with a small share of Franc. It's an intense, Mediterranean wine, close-knit and superbly structured. The rest of their selection also proves well-crafted.

● Maremma Toscana Rosso Tenuta Belguardo '16	♥♥ 6
● Mix36 '16	♥♥ 8
● Chianti Cl. Fonterutoli '17	♥♥ 5
● Chianti Cl. Ser Lapo Ris. '16	♥♥ 5
● Concerto '16	♥♥ 8
● Philip '15	♥♥ 6
● Poggio Badiola '17	♥♥ 3
● Mix36 '15	♥♥♥ 8
● Mix36 '11	♥♥♥ 8
● Mix36 '08	♥♥♥ 8
● Siepi '15	♥♥♥ 8
● Siepi '13	♥♥♥ 8
● Siepi '11	♥♥♥ 8
● Siepi '10	♥♥♥ 8
● Siepi '08	♥♥♥ 8

★Castello di Monsanto

VIA MONSANTO, 8
50021 BARBERINO VAL D'ELSA [FI]
TEL. +39 0558059000
www.castellodimonsanto.it

CELLAR SALES
PRE-BOOKED VISITS
ANNUAL PRODUCTION 450,000 bottles
HECTARES UNDER VINE 72.00

Monsanto is one of Chianti Classico's most charming wineries. Owned by the Bianchi family since 1962, today they're proving capable of representing the territory's traditions and classic style in all their coherence and rigor. Their wines, which are aged primarily in large wooden barrels, have proven they can stand the test of time like few others. They're sophisticated and elegant, even if, at times, a bit too austere and not always approachable. But such qualities only increase the charm of a selection that aptly interprets the territory of Barberino Val d'Elsa. The Chianti Classico '17 features dark aromas in which red fruit meets spicy hints, sensations that introduce a succulent development characterized by nice rhythm. The Chianti Classico Riserva '16 is more concentrated, with oak influencing its aromatic and flavor profile more heavily. The Chianti Classico Il Poggio Gran Selezione '14, aromatically marked by abundant toastiness, isn't lacking in sapidity.

● Chianti Cl. '17	♥♥ 3*
● Chianti Cl. Gran Selezione Il Poggio '14	♥♥ 7
● Chianti Cl. Ris. '16	♥♥ 3
● Nemo '15	♥♥ 6
● Chianti Cl. '15	♥♥♥ 3*
● Chianti Cl. '11	♥♥♥ 3*
● Chianti Cl. Cinquantenario Ris. '08	♥♥♥ 6
● Chianti Cl. Il Poggio Ris. '13	♥♥♥ 7
● Chianti Cl. Il Poggio Ris. '10	♥♥♥ 8
● Chianti Cl. Il Poggio Ris. '06	♥♥♥ 6
● Chianti Cl. Il Poggio Ris. '88	♥♥♥ 5
● Chianti Cl. Ris. '11	♥♥♥ 5
● Nemo '01	♥♥♥ 6
● Sangioveto '10	♥♥♥ 7

Castello di Radda

LOC. IL BECCO, 101A
53017 RADDA IN CHIANTI [SI]
TEL. +39 0577738992
www.castellodiradda.it

CELLAR SALES
PRE-BOOKED VISITS
ANNUAL PRODUCTION 100,000 bottles
HECTARES UNDER VINE 33.00

The Beretta family's winery has gained a solid reputation in Chianti Classico, distinguishing itself for coherently interpreting Radda and consistently earning a place among the area's top wines. It's all thanks to a clear stylistic approach that's rooted in Chianti, one that privileges elegance, finesse and drinkability. In the cellar forced tactics are eschewed, while the attentive use of small and large wood barrels proves well-suited to the excellent raw materials with which they begin. The 2017 version of this Raddese producer's Chianti Classico proves well-crafted. An enticing, multifaceted aromatic suite offers up floral hints on a fruity backdrop, all adorned with sweet spices. The Gran Selezione Vigna il Corno '15 is a deeper, more austere wine that's still evolving. Black fruits, spices and sensations of roots infused with oak characterize both the nose and the palate, with a long finish to follow.

● Chianti Cl. Gran Selezione V. Il Corno '15	🍷🍷🍷 3*
● Chianti Cl. '17	🍷🍷 3*
● Chianti Cl. '15	♈♈♈ 3*
● Chianti Cl. Gran Selezione V. Il Corno '14	♈♈♈ 6
● Chianti Cl. Ris. '13	♈♈♈ 5
● Chianti Cl. Ris. '12	♈♈♈ 5
● Chianti Cl. Ris. '11	♈♈♈ 6
● Chianti Cl. Ris. '07	♈♈♈ 5
● Chianti Cl. '16	🍷🍷 3
● Chianti Cl. '14	🍷🍷 3
● Chianti Cl. Gran Selezione '13	🍷🍷 3
● Chianti Cl. Gran Selezione '12	🍷🍷 3*
● Chianti Cl. Gran Selezione '11	🍷🍷 3
● Chianti Cl. Ris. '14	🍷🍷 5

★Castello di Volpaia

LOC. VOLPAIA
P.ZZA DELLA CISTERNA, 1
53017 RADDA IN CHIANTI [SI]
TEL. +39 0577738066
www.volpaia.com

CELLAR SALES
PRE-BOOKED VISITS
ACCOMMODATION AND RESTAURANT SERVICE
ANNUAL PRODUCTION 200,000 bottles
HECTARES UNDER VINE 46.00
VITICULTURE METHOD Certified Organic
SUSTAINABLE WINERY

The Mascheroni Stianti family not only deserve credit for having protected one of Chianti Classico's most scenic areas, but also for producing wines that reflect the image and character of the estate. Theirs is an impeccable selection, modern yet capable of expressing the Radda in Chianti subzone's trademark personality and traits. The careful use of oak makes for lively wines that never obscure the natural properties of grapes cultivated at 500 meters elevation. In addition to outstanding balance, the Chianti Classico Riserva '16 delivers extremely delicate aromas in which flowers meet spices. On the palate it exhibits firmness, portrayed with grace and suppleness, making for a juicy, sapid drink. The modern and decidedly well-crafted Chianti Classico Coltassala Gran Selezione '16 is also denser, more darker aromatically.

● Chianti Cl. Ris. '16	🍷🍷🍷 5
● Chianti Cl. Gran Selezione Coltassala '16	🍷🍷 7
● Chianti Cl. '17	🍷🍷 4
● Balifico '16	🍷 7
● Chianti Cl. Gran Selezione Il Puro Vign. Casanova '15	🍷 8
● Chianti Cl. '16	♈♈♈ 4*
● Chianti Cl. '15	♈♈♈ 4*
● Chianti Cl. '13	♈♈♈ 3*
● Chianti Cl. Coltassala Ris. '04	♈♈♈ 6
● Chianti Cl. Il Puro Vign. Casanova Ris. '08	♈♈♈ 8
● Chianti Cl. Il Puro Vign. Casanova Ris. '06	♈♈♈ 8
● Chianti Cl. Ris. '13	♈♈♈ 5
● Chianti Cl. Ris. '10	♈♈♈ 5

Castello Romitorio

LOC. ROMITORIO, 279
53024 MONTALCINO [SI]
TEL. +39 0577847212
www.castelloromitorio.com

CELLAR SALES
PRE-BOOKED VISITS
ACCOMMODATION
ANNUAL PRODUCTION 150,000 bottles
HECTARES UNDER VINE 30.00

The generational shift that made Castello Romitorio a benchmark for western Montalcino has been completed for some time. By now Filippo, son of world-famous winemaker Sandro Chia (the winery's owner since the 1980s) and Stefano Martini (son of master winemaker Franco) are firmly established at the producer. But the estate, which comprises Ghiaccio Forte (in Scansano), Romitorio and Poggio di Sopra, remains unchanged. It's a territory that proves perfect for cultivating enchanting, robust 'Tyrrhenian' Sangiovese. In short, the lovely story narrated by Castello Romitorio's Brunello Ris. '13 is one of a relaxed aromatic impact, with red fruits, sylvan herbs and red pepper. Placid and mouthfilling in the mouth, it plays on slightly salty vigor towards the midpalate, more than on extractive volume. Without a doubt it's one of the vintage's most convincing wines. Their Rosso '17 and Toro '16, blends of Syrah and Petit Verdot, also showed good signs.

● Brunello di Montalcino Ris. '13	♟♟ 8
● Il Toro '16	♟ 3
● Rosso di Montalcino '17	♟ 5
● Brunello di Montalcino '10	♟♟♟ 8
● Brunello di Montalcino '05	♟♟♟ 8
● Brunello di Montalcino Ris. '97	♟♟♟ 8
● Brunello di Montalcino '13	♟♟ 8
● Brunello di Montalcino '12	♟♟ 8
● Brunello di Montalcino '11	♟♟ 8
● Brunello di Montalcino Filo di Seta '13	♟♟ 8
● Brunello di Montalcino Filo di Seta '12	♟♟ 8
● Brunello di Montalcino Filo di Seta '11	♟♟ 8
● Brunello di Montalcino Filo di Seta '10	♟♟ 8
● Brunello di Montalcino Ris. '12	♟♟ 8
● Brunello di Montalcino Ris. '10	♟♟ 8
● Rosso di Montalcino '16	♟♟ 5
● Rosso di Montalcino '15	♟♟ 5

Castello Vicchiomaggio

LOC. LE BOLLE
VIA VICCHIOMAGGIO, 4
50022 GREVE IN CHIANTI [FI]
TEL. +39 055854079
www.vicchiomaggio.it

CELLAR SALES
PRE-BOOKED VISITS
ACCOMMODATION AND RESTAURANT SERVICE
ANNUAL PRODUCTION 300,000 bottles
HECTARES UNDER VINE 38.00
SUSTAINABLE WINERY

Castello di Vicchiomaggio, owned by the Matta family since 1964, began focusing on quality in 1982, a course that led the winery to become one of Greve in Chianti's most important. Today Vicchiomaggio's wines exhibit a precise physiognomy and a notable consistence in quality, though they're not lacking in character either. Made with impeccable technical skill, their selection brings together excellent raw material with a style that's modern, but never excessively. Depending on the wine, they use large wood barrels or barriques for aging. The fresh and intense Chianti Classico Guado Alto '17 stood out during our tastings. It's intelligible aromatically, featuring lush fruit on a spicy and smoky backdrop. On the palate the wine proves well-sustained, balanced and not without sapidity. The Chianti Classico Agostino Petri Riserva '16 exhibits nice definition as well, with its nuanced aromas and flavorful development. It's maybe just a bit too dry at the finish.

● Chianti Cl. Guado Alto '17	♟♟ 3*
● Chianti Cl. Agostino Petri Ris. '16	♟♟ 5
● Chianti Cl. Gran Selezione Le Bolle '16	♟♟ 8
● Ripa delle More '16	♟♟ 6
● Chianti Cl. San Jacopo '17	♟ 3
● FSM '16	♟ 8
● Ripa delle Mandorle '18	♟ 2
● Chianti Cl. Gran Sel. Vigna La Prima '10	♟♟♟ 7
● FSM '07	♟♟♟ 8
● FSM '04	♟♟♟ 5
● Ripa delle More '97	♟♟♟ 6
● Ripa delle More '94	♟♟♟ 7
● Chianti Cl. Agostino Petri Ris. '15	♟♟ 5
● Chianti Cl. San Jacopo da Vicchiomaggio '15	♟♟ 3

Castelvecchio

LOC. SAN PANCRAZIO
VIA CERTALDESE, 30
50026 SAN CASCIANO IN VAL DI PESA [FI]
TEL. +39 0558248032
www.castelvecchio.it

CELLAR SALES
PRE-BOOKED VISITS
ACCOMMODATION
ANNUAL PRODUCTION 100,000 bottles
HECTARES UNDER VINE 24.00
VITICULTURE METHOD Certified Organic
SUSTAINABLE WINERY

Filippo and Stefania are the third generation of Rocchis to oversee Castelvecchio. 60 years ago, their grandfather purchased the estate, renovated its buildings (part of which are used for hospitality), and gave life to its winemaking business by building a cellar and planting vineyards. It made a name for itself by focusing on traditional grapes (Sangiovese, Canaiolo Nero, Malvasia del Chianti, Trebbiano), but also interpreting international cultivars (Merlot, Cabernet Sauvignon, Petit Verdot). Their Brecciolino '16 blend offers up broad aromas in which wild berries meet cloves and cinnamon. In the mouth it enters full, with nice acidity followed by the right sapidity and raciness. Their Ris. Vigna La Quercia '16 opens with slightly tertiary notes of leather, then mineral hints and blackberries. On the palate it's tasty, with mellow, well-integrated tannins and good length. Citrusy sensations of lime, and a pleasant, enticing body feature in their San Lorenzo '18.

● Il Brecciolino '16	♟♟ 5
● Chianti Colli Fiorentini V. La Quercia Ris. '16	♟♟ 4
● Numero Otto '16	♟♟ 4
○ San Lorenzo Trebbiano '18	♟♟ 2*
● Chianti Colli Fiorentini Il Castelvecchio '17	♟ 2
● Chianti Santa Caterina '17	♟ 2
● Il Brecciolino '15	♟♟♟ 5
● Il Brecciolino '11	♟♟♟ 5
● Chianti Colli Fiorentini V. La Quercia Ris. '13	♟♟ 4
● Chianti S. Caterina '15	♟♟ 2*
● Il Brecciolino '13	♟♟ 5
● Orme in Rosso '15	♟♟ 4
● Solo Uno '15	♟♟ 6

Castiglion del Bosco

LOC. CASTIGLION DEL BOSCO
53024 MONTALCINO [SI]
TEL. +39 05771913750
www.castigliondelbosco.com

CELLAR SALES
PRE-BOOKED VISITS
ACCOMMODATION AND RESTAURANT SERVICE
ANNUAL PRODUCTION 250,000 bottles
HECTARES UNDER VINE 62.00
VITICULTURE METHOD Certified Organic

Gauggiole and Capanna are the two principal parcels of Sangiovese that give rise to Castiglion del Bosco's Brunellos. These are situated in the heart of Northwest Montalcino, just a stone's throw from the enchanting hamlet that has belonged to the Ferragamo family since 2003. Here you'll find their cellar as well as restaurants, a resort, a wellness spa, a golf club and much more. This 'exclusive hospitality' project is increasingly integrated with a selection of wines that continues to improve in pleasantness and balance. In this round of tastings only two wines were presented, with their Brunello '14 impressing most. It's an interpretation that's decidedly faithful to the vintage. Almost stripped down fruit gives way to hints of caramel and herbs. This pure minimalism characterizes the palate as well, though the wine finds juice and continuity without ambiguous wanderings. Their Rosso Gauggiole '16, on the other hand, comes across as a little too closed and rugged.

● Brunello di Montalcino '14	♟♟ 6
● Rosso di Montalcino Gauggiole '16	♟ 4
● Brunello di Montalcino '12	♟♟ 6
● Brunello di Montalcino 1100 Ris. '12	♟♟ 6
● Brunello di Montalcino 1100 Ris. '11	♟♟ 6
● Brunello di Montalcino Campo del Drago '13	♟♟ 8
● Brunello di Montalcino Campo del Drago '12	♟♟ 8
● Brunello di Montalcino Campo del Drago '11	♟♟ 8
● Brunello di Montalcino Campo del Drago '10	♟♟ 8
● Brunello di Montalcino Campo del Drago '08	♟♟ 8
● Brunello di Montalcino Ris. 1100 '10	♟♟ 6
● Rosso di Montalcino '11	♟♟ 3

Famiglia Cecchi

LOC. CASINA DEI PONTI, 56
53011 CASTELLINA IN CHIANTI [SI]
TEL. +39 057754311
www.famigliacecchi.net

CELLAR SALES
PRE-BOOKED VISITS
RESTAURANT SERVICE
ANNUAL PRODUCTION 8,500,000 bottles
HECTARES UNDER VINE 385.00
SUSTAINABLE WINERY

Since 1893 the Cecchi family have been leaders in the regional and national wine industry. Originally wine merchants, they subsequently (and with increasing commitment) shifted to a focus on quality. To that end they began gradually purchasing vineyards and estates like Castello di Montauto (in San Gimignano) and Val delle Rose (in Maremma). Production volumes are those of a large winery, but with a comforting consistency it's possible to identify wines capable of offering notable personality. Their Chianti Classico Riserva di Famiglia '16 delivers with its aromas of fruits and flowers accompanied by hints of undergrowth, earth and spices. On the palate it's docile, juicy and superbly flavorful. The Chianti Classico Villa Rosa Gran Selezione '16 is even better, exhibiting equal detail but proving even more complex and elegant. We found the rest of their reliable selection well-made and balanced.

● Chianti Cl. Gran Selezione Villa Rosa '16	▼▼▼ 6
● Chianti Cl. Villa Cerna Ris. '16	▼▼ 5
● Chianti Cl. Gran Selezione Valore di Famiglia '16	▼▼ 6
● Chianti Cl. Riserva di Famiglia '16	▼▼ 5
● Coevo '16	▼▼ 8
● Chianti Cl. Riserva di Famiglia '15	♀♀♀ 5
● Chianti Cl. Riserva di Famiglia '07	♀♀♀ 5
● Chianti Cl. Villa Cerna Ris. '13	♀♀♀ 5
● Chianti Cl. Villa Cerna Ris. '12	♀♀♀ 5
● Chianti Cl. Villa Cerna Ris. '08	♀♀♀ 5
● Coevo '11	♀♀♀ 8
● Coevo '10	♀♀♀ 7
● Coevo '06	♀♀♀ 7
● Chianti Cl. Gran Selezione Valore di Famiglia '15	♀♀ 6

Centolani

LOC. FRIGGIALI
S.DA MAREMMANA
53024 MONTALCINO [SI]
TEL. +39 0577849454
www.tenutafriggialiepietranera.it

CELLAR SALES
PRE-BOOKED VISITS
ACCOMMODATION
ANNUAL PRODUCTION 260,000 bottles
HECTARES UNDER VINE 70.00

The Peluso-Centolani's property is situated in parts of Montalcino that are somewhat diverse. To the west there's Tenuta Friggiali, which comprises plots cultivated in sandy soil at elevations ranging from 250 to 450 meters. Pietranera lies further to the south, near the Sant'Antimo abbey, where lower elevations and firmer soils prevail (as well as higher shares of marl and clay). Such variables emerge in an eclectic winemaking style that draws on the use of medium-sized and large barrels. This year they were missing a standout, but Centolani's selection is certainly a reliable one. To that end, their Rosso '17 is emblematic, proving pleasantly balanced with close-focused aromas of fruit and balsamic whiffs, sensations that we find further enriched in their Brunello Pietranera '14. Here sweet spices and hints of undergrowth are even more evident, with a palate that's quite fluent, only a bit clenched at the end due to somewhat dusty tannins.

● Brunello di Montalcino Pietranera '14	▼▼ 5
● Rosso di Montalcino Tenuta Friggiali '17	▼▼ 3
● Brunello di Montalcino Tenuta Friggiali '14	▼ 6
● Brunello di Montalcino Pietranera '13	♀♀ 5
● Brunello di Montalcino Pietranera '12	♀♀ 5
● Brunello di Montalcino Pietranera '11	♀♀ 5
● Brunello di Montalcino Pietranera Ris. '12	♀♀ 6
● Brunello di Montalcino Pietranera Ris. '10	♀♀ 6
● Brunello di Montalcino Tenuta Friggiali '12	♀♀ 6
● Brunello di Montalcino Tenuta Friggiali Ris. '11	♀♀ 6
● Rosso di Montalcino Pietranera '16	♀♀ 3
● Rosso di Montalcino Tenuta Friggiali '16	♀♀ 3

Vincenzo Cesani

LOC. PANCOLE, 82D
53037 SAN GIMIGNANO [SI]
TEL. +39 0577955084
www.cesani.it

CELLAR SALES
PRE-BOOKED VISITS
ACCOMMODATION
ANNUAL PRODUCTION 100,000 bottles
HECTARES UNDER VINE 21.00
VITICULTURE METHOD Certified Organic

Maria Luisa and Letizia Cesani are the women behind a multifaceted project driving the family business. It ranges from a line of natural beauty products to an agritourism, cultivating saffron, olives and, of course, wine grapes. In short, since moving from Marche to Tuscany in the 1950s, Cesani has come a long way, and today they're undisputed leaders among San Gimignano's producers. The Riserva Sanice '15 is a pleasant wine, opening on mineral notes before proceeding to mature apple, dried fruit and nuts (almond in particular), as well as aromatic herbs like sage and aniseed. On the palate it enters gratifyingly and pervasively, with a graceful sapidity giving way to a rising finish. Their intriguing Chianti Colli Senesi '18 is redolent of vibrant fruit like cherry and strawberry, then pepper. In the mouth it proves lively, supported by nice acidity.

○ Vernaccia di S. Gimignano Sanice Ris. '16	♟♟ 3*
● Chianti Colli Senesi '18	♟♟ 2*
○ Vernaccia di S. Gimignano Clamys '17	♟♟ 2*
⊙ Rosato '18	♟ 2
○ Vernaccia di S. Gimignano '18	♟ 2
● Luenzo '99	♟♟♟ 4
● Luenzo '97	♟♟♟ 4*
○ Vernaccia di S. Gimignano Sanice Ris. '15	♟♟♟ 3*
○ Vernaccia di S. Gimignano Sanice Ris. '14	♟♟♟ 3*
● Chianti Colli Senesi '15	♟♟ 2*
● Luenzo '12	♟♟ 4
○ Vernaccia di S. Gimignano '17	♟♟ 2*
○ Vernaccia di S. Gimignano Clamys '16	♟♟ 2*
○ Vernaccia di S. Gimignano Clamys '15	♟♟ 2*

Giovanni Chiappini

LOC. FELCIAINO
VIA BOLGHERESE, 189C
57020 BOLGHERI [LI]
TEL. +39 0565765201
www.giovannichiappini.it

CELLAR SALES
PRE-BOOKED VISITS
ANNUAL PRODUCTION 70,000 bottles
HECTARES UNDER VINE 23.00
VITICULTURE METHOD Certified Organic
SUSTAINABLE WINERY

The history of Chiappini follows a pattern that's common among Tuscany's producers. Originally from Marche, the family moved to Bolgheri in search of good fortune. But surely at the time they couldn't have imagined what they'd find. Today their business centers exclusively on vineyards and wine, and they're enjoying increasing success both in Italy and abroad. Despite the attention they've earned, Chiappini is a family-run winery, and deeply artisanal in size, style and spirit. Their splendid Bolgheri Rosso Felciaino '17 is one of the category's best for this vintage. It plays on aromatic contrasts, amidst colored fruits and medicinal herbs, while on the palate it exhibits vigor and presence, flavor and length. Their Liena Cabernet Franc '16, which once again proves excellent, comes through spicy and delicately minty in its finish. Their Rosso Sup. Guado de' Gemoli '16 is decidedly toasty and needs more time in the bottle.

● Bolgheri Rosso Felciaino '17	♟♟ 4
● Lienà Cabernet Franc '16	♟♟ 8
● Bolgheri Rosso Sup. Guado de' Gemoli '16	♟♟ 8
● Bolgheri Felciaino '13	♟♟ 4
● Bolgheri Rosso Felciaino '16	♟♟ 4
● Bolgheri Rosso Felciaino '15	♟♟ 3
● Bolgheri Rosso Sup. Guado de' Gemoli '15	♟♟ 8
● Bolgheri Sup. Guado de' Gemoli '13	♟♟ 8
● Bolgheri Sup. Guado de' Gemoli '12	♟♟ 8
● Lienà Cabernet Franc '15	♟♟ 8
● Lienà Cabernet Franc '13	♟♟ 8
● Lienà Cabernet Franc '12	♟♟ 8
● Lienà Cabernet Sauvignon '15	♟♟ 7
● Lienà Cabernet Sauvignon '11	♟♟ 7

Le Chiuse

LOC. PULLERA, 228
53024 MONTALCINO [SI]
TEL. +39 055597052
www.lechiuse.com

CELLAR SALES
PRE-BOOKED VISITS
ACCOMMODATION
ANNUAL PRODUCTION 30,000 bottles
HECTARES UNDER VINE 8.00
VITICULTURE METHOD Certified Organic

Le Chiuse is practically a single, contiguous tract of Sangiovese surrounded by north Montalcino's best districts, from Montosoli to Canalicchio. It passed from the hands of the late Fiorella Biondi Santi to Simonetta Valiani, who's helped by her husband and son. For more than 30 years they've been offering classic (to say the least) Brunellos that are universally appreciated for their finesse and personality. They avail themselves of organic vineyard management, spontaneous fermentation and maturation in 2000, 3000 and 5000 liter oak barrels. Yet another pair to remember from Le Chiuse, despite problematic vintages. Clear and juicy, their Rosso '17 quickly settles on noble notes of wild berries, nutmeg, licorice and bergamot orange. Their Brunello '14 is only a bit lacking in expansion and depth, though it remains one of the most notable of its kind by virtue of a vibrant combination of citrus and spices, but especially thanks to its tonic, delicately salty verve.

● Brunello di Montalcino '14	♀♀ 7
● Rosso di Montalcino '17	♀♀ 4
● Brunello di Montalcino '12	♀♀♀ 7
● Brunello di Montalcino '11	♀♀♀ 7
● Brunello di Montalcino '10	♀♀♀ 7
● Brunello di Montalcino '07	♀♀♀ 7
● Brunello di Montalcino Ris. '07	♀♀♀ 8
● Brunello di Montalcino '13	♀♀ 7
● Brunello di Montalcino '09	♀♀ 7
● Brunello di Montalcino '08	♀♀ 7
● Brunello di Montalcino Ris. '09	♀♀ 8
● Rosso di Montalcino '16	♀♀ 4
● Rosso di Montalcino '15	♀♀ 4
● Rosso di Montalcino '14	♀♀ 4
● Rosso di Montalcino '13	♀♀ 4
● Rosso di Montalcino '12	♀♀ 4
● Rosso di Montalcino '11	♀♀ 4

Ciacci Piccolomini D'Aragona

FRAZ. CASTELNUOVO DELL'ABATE
LOC. MOLINELLO
53024 MONTALCINO [SI]
TEL. +39 0577835616
www.ciaccipiccolomini.com

CELLAR SALES
PRE-BOOKED VISITS
ACCOMMODATION
ANNUAL PRODUCTION 200,000 bottles
HECTARES UNDER VINE 40.00

Siblings Lucia and Paolo Bianchini are carrying forward the work begun by their father in the mid 1980s, when he inherited the historic property from the Ciacci Piccolomini d'Aragona family. Situated in southeastern Montalcino, equidistant from Castelnuovo dell'Abate and the celebrated Sant'Antimo abbey, the estate comprises the vineyards of Ferraiole, Egle, Contessa and Colombaio. Grapes are fermented separately and give rise to their three Brunellos after a stay in Slavonian oak barrels of various sizes (from 750 to 7500 liters). Without a doubt, their premium wines put in one of its best performances in recent memory. Their Rosso '17 is already complete in its stratification and volume — it's almost capable of standing shoulder-to-shoulder with the more intense and complex Vigna di Pianrosso Ris. '13. But it's their Brunello '14 that leads the selection thanks to a version that's surprising, to say the least, for its elegant medicinal herbs and delicate saltiness.

● Brunello di Montalcino '14	♀♀ 5
● Brunello di Montalcino V. di Pianrosso Ris. '13	♀♀ 7
● Rosso di Montalcino '17	♀♀ 4
● Brunello di Montalcino '13	♀♀ 5
● Brunello di Montalcino '06	♀♀ 5
● Brunello di Montalcino '04	♀♀ 5
● Brunello di Montalcino Santa Caterina d'Oro Ris. '04	♀♀ 7
● Rosso di Montalcino Rossofonte '15	♀♀ 4
● Sant'Antimo Fabius '07	♀♀ 3

Cigliano

VIA CIGLIANO, 17
50026 SAN CASCIANO IN VAL DI PESA [FI]
TEL. +39 055820033
www.villadelcigliano.it

CELLAR SALES
PRE-BOOKED VISITS
ANNUAL PRODUCTION 40,000 bottles
HECTARES UNDER VINE 25.00

Of late this San Casciano Val di Pesa producer has amply demonstrated that it is one of Gallo Nero's most significant wineries, especially when it comes to the rigor with which they carry out production, making for bottles whose Chianti character is unequivocal. Their wines are appreciated with increasing constance for their balance and elegance, delivering a classic style made possible by apt choices like, for example, the use of a traditional mix of concrete and large wood barrels for aging. Their Chianti Classico Villa del Cigliano Riserva '16 exhibits great aromatic elegance, with floral notes emerging in the foreground just supported by spicy notes. On the palate it's delicate, tasty and rhythmic. Their delicious Chianti Classico '16 opens more on fragrant fruit, unfolding delectably and enticingly on the palate. The Chianti Classico '17 is simpler but no less pleasant.

● Chianti Cl. Villa del Cigliano Ris. '16	♈♈♈ 5
● Chianti Cl. '16	♈♈ 3*
● Chianti Cl. '17	♈♈ 3
● Chianti Cl. Cigliano '13	♈♈♈ 3*
● Chianti Cl. '15	♈♈ 3*
● Chianti Cl. '14	♈♈ 3
● Chianti Cl. '10	♈♈ 2*
● Chianti Cl. Cigliano '12	♈♈ 3*
● Chianti Cl. Cigliano '11	♈♈ 3
● Chianti Cl. Ris. '15	♈♈ 4
● Chianti Cl. Villa Cigliano Ris. '13	♈♈ 4
● Chianti Cl. Villa Cigliano Ris. '11	♈♈ 4
● Chianti Cl. Villa Cigliano Ris. '09	♈♈ 4

Cinciano

LOC. CINCIANO, 2
53036 POGGIBONSI [SI]
TEL. +39 0577936588
www.cinciano.it

CELLAR SALES
PRE-BOOKED VISITS
ACCOMMODATION AND RESTAURANT SERVICE
ANNUAL PRODUCTION 140,000 bottles
HECTARES UNDER VINE 24.00

Since 1983 the Garré family have owned this estate, which is situated near Poggibonsi but also comprises vineyards in the Barberino Val d'Elsa subzone. In the cellar they avoid force, opting for large barrels that are used in moderation, while fermentation is carried out both in steel and in concrete. The result is a notable selection of wines that masterfully brings together drinkability and elegance, offering up a distinct and frank character that's also coherent with the territory. The Chianti Classico Gran Selezione '15 offers up fragrant, fruity aromas joined with smoky notes and hints of undergrowth. On the palate it exhibits a dense but nicely rhythmic and tasty development. There's no lack of supporting oak in their Pietra Forte '14, a blend of Sangiovese, Merlot and Cabernet Sauvignon that proves supple and pleasant nonetheless. We found their Chianti Classico Riserva '16 to be well-crafted.

● Chianti Cl. Gran Selezione '15	♈♈ 6
● Chianti Cl. Ris. '16	♈♈ 5
● Pietraforte '14	♈♈ 3
● Chianti Cl. '17	♈ 4
● Chianti Cl. '16	♈♈♈ 4
● Chianti Cl. '15	♈♈ 3
● Chianti Cl. '12	♈♈ 3
● Chianti Cl. Gran Sel. '12	♈♈ 5
● Chianti Cl. Gran Sel. '11	♈♈ 5
● Chianti Cl. Gran Selezione '14	♈♈ 6
● Chianti Cl. Ris. '15	♈♈ 5
● Chianti Cl. Ris. '14	♈♈ 3
● Chianti Cl. Ris. '13	♈♈ 3
● Chianti Cl. Ris. '12	♈♈ 3
● Chianti Cl. Ris. '11	♈♈ 3

Le Cinciole

VIA CASE SPARSE, 83
50020 PANZANO [FI]
TEL. +39 055852636
www.lecinciole.it

CELLAR SALES
PRE-BOOKED VISITS
ANNUAL PRODUCTION 45,000 bottles
HECTARES UNDER VINE 11.00
VITICULTURE METHOD Certified Organic
SUSTAINABLE WINERY

Organic vineyard management, notable elevations (over 400 meters), aging in large and small wood barrels: this is a brief description of this small but interesting winery. It's also important to note that the producer (managed by Luca and Valeria Orsini) is situated in one of Chianti Classico's most charming subzones, Panzano. Their production style comes across as well-defined, with fresh and lively wines that also exhibit a consistent level of quality, and not infrequently, a pleasant hardness and ageworthiness. The Petresco '15, a monovarietal Sangiovese, features generous aromas of mature red fruit and spices, coming through dense, detailed and succulent on the palate. The Cinciorosso '17, a blend of Sangiovese, Merlot and Syrah also did well. A flavorful, delectable palate gives way to an almost spicy hot finish, while aromatically it calls up pepper on a fragrant cherry backdrop. There's no lack of supporting oak in their Chianti Classico A Luigi Riserva '14.

● Petresco '15	♟♟ 5
● Chianti Cl. A Luigi Ris. '14	♟♟ 3
● Cinciorosso '17	♟♟ 3
● Chianti Cl. '16	♟ 3
● Camalaione '04	♟♟♟ 7
● Chianti Cl. '14	♟♟♟ 3*
● Chianti Cl. '12	♟♟♟ 3*
● Chianti Cl. Petresco Ris. '01	♟♟♟ 5
● Petresco '12	♟♟♟ 5
● Chianti Cl. '15	♟♟ 3*
● Chianti Cl. '13	♟♟ 3
● Chianti Cl. A Luigi Ris. '12	♟♟ 3
● Cinciorosso '16	♟♟ 3
● Cinciorosso '13	♟♟ 3
● Cinciorosso '12	♟♟ 3
● Petresco '13	♟♟ 5
● Petresco '10	♟♟ 5

Donatella Cinelli Colombini

LOC. CASATO, 17
53024 MONTALCINO [SI]
TEL. +39 0577662108
www.cinellicolombini.it

CELLAR SALES
PRE-BOOKED VISITS
ACCOMMODATION AND RESTAURANT SERVICE
ANNUAL PRODUCTION 140,000 bottles
HECTARES UNDER VINE 34.00

After leaving the family business in 1998, Donatella Cinelli Colombini planned two new ones: Casato Prime Donne, whose cellar and vineyards are situated in northern Montalcino, and Fattoria del Colle in Trequanda, transforming an old property into a gorgeous agritourism and creating a winery whose vineyards were re-planted with old local grapes like Foglia Tonda and dedicated to DOC Orcia. Today both the winery and hospitality businesses are primarily in the hands of women. For example, their enologist is Valérie Lavigne, a well-known specialist based in Bordeaux. Among Casato Prime Donne's selection, their Riserva '13 stands out for its harmony amidst freshness and power. It's a wine that's particularly complex on the nose due to long aging in oak barrels (almost 42 months). The Cenerentola '16is a blend of Sangiovese (65%) and Foglia Tonda. It requires maturation in mid-sized casks to tame the power of the latter, which lends support to the finesse of Sangiovese.

● Brunello di Montalcino Ris. '13	♟♟ 8
● Brunello di Montalcino '14	♟♟ 6
● Orcia Rosso Cenerentola '16	♟♟ 5
● Orcia Leone Rosso '16	♟ 2
● Brunello di Montalcino Prime Donne '01	♟♟♟ 6
● Brunello di Montalcino '10	♟♟ 5
● Brunello di Montalcino '09	♟♟ 5
● Brunello di Montalcino Prime Donne '13	♟♟ 7
● Brunello di Montalcino Ris. '12	♟♟ 8
● Brunello di Montalcino Ris. '10	♟♟ 8
● Rosso di Montalcino '15	♟♟ 3
● Rosso di Montalcino '12	♟♟ 3

Podere della Civettaja

VIA DI CASINA ROSSA, 5A
52100 AREZZO
TEL. +39 3397098418
www.civettaja.it

CELLAR SALES
PRE-BOOKED VISITS
ANNUAL PRODUCTION 7,000 bottles
HECTARES UNDER VINE 3.00
VITICULTURE METHOD Certified Organic

Agronomist by trade, owner Vincenzo
Tommasi had the skill and courage to start
cultivating Pinot Nero in Casentino again.
The grape had been abandoned in the
mid-20th century due to its low
productivity. But after closely studying the
terrain, this lover of Burgundy decided to
try to apply French cultivation techniques in
a territory considered by many to be
unsuited to quality wine-growing. He
perseverance paid off and the results have
been excellent. In the cellar the most
natural methods of vinification possible are
adopted. The Pinot Nero '16 features an
intense aromatic profile in which fruity
notes of cherry and blackcurrant are just a
bit overripe but still pleasing thanks in part
to the presence of elegant oak, with
aromatic thyme and mint completing the
picture. On the palate it's harmonious from
the outset, with lovely finesse and nice
flesh accompanied by elegant, tailored
tannins. It's a gratifying, highly charming
wine with lengthy persistence.

● Pinot Nero '16	▼▼▼ 6
● Pinot Nero '14	♈♈♈ 6
● Pinot Nero '13	♈♈♈ 6
● Pinot Nero '15	♈♈ 6
● Pinot Nero '12	♈♈ 3
● Pinot Nero '11	♈♈ 3

★Tenuta Col d'Orcia

VIA GIUNCHETI
53024 MONTALCINO [SI]
TEL. +39 057780891
www.coldorcia.it

CELLAR SALES
PRE-BOOKED VISITS
ANNUAL PRODUCTION 800,000 bottles
HECTARES UNDER VINE 142.00
VITICULTURE METHOD Certified Organic
SUSTAINABLE WINERY

The historic estate taken over by the count
Marone Cinzano family in the 1970s is
situated on the southern border with
Montalcino, between Sant'Angelo in Colle
and the Orcia river. It's a brand that
established itself quickly, thanks in part to
several memorable versions of their Poggio
al Vento Riserva. Aged for almost four years
in 2500 and 7500 liter Allier and Slavonian
oak barrels, it's a model Brunello in its
palpably gentle character, which pervades
their entire range, not just their
Sangioveses. The selection submitted by
Col d'Orcia put in a performance for the
ages, with some six wines earning more
than Due Bicchieri. Among these are their
Poggio al Vento Riserva, with a 2012 that
comes across as a bit less precise than
usual due to alcohol and tannic presence.
To compensate, their Brunello '14 is
multi-layered, to say the least, in its aromas
of black cherry, pencil lead and topsoil,
while on the palate it proves full, flavorful
and persistent.

● Brunello di Montalcino '14	▼▼ 7
● Brunello di Montalcino Nastagio '13	▼▼ 8
● Brunello di Montalcino Poggio al Vento Ris. '12	▼▼ 8
● Rosso di Montalcino '17	▼▼ 5
● Rosso di Montalcino Banditella '16	▼▼ 5
● Sant'Antimo Cabernet Olmaia '14	▼▼ 6
● Brunello di Montalcino Poggio al Vento Ris. '10	♈♈♈ 8
● Brunello di Montalcino Poggio al Vento Ris. '06	♈♈♈ 8
● Brunello di Montalcino Poggio al Vento Ris. '04	♈♈♈ 8
● Brunello di Montalcino Poggio al Vento Ris. '99	♈♈♈ 8
● Brunello di Montalcino Poggio al Vento Ris. '83	♈♈♈ 7
● Olmaia '01	♈♈♈ 7

Col di Bacche

FRAZ. MONTIANO
S.DA DI CUPI
58051 MAGLIANO IN TOSCANA [GR]
TEL. +39 0564589538
www.coldibacche.com

CELLAR SALES
PRE-BOOKED VISITS
ANNUAL PRODUCTION 80,000 bottles
HECTARES UNDER VINE 13.50

Col di Bacche is a small winery passionately managed by the Carnasciali family. Founded in 1998 not far from Magliano in Toscana, this Cupi producer has managed to stand out in Maremmano's complex wine panorama. Their approach calls for quality raw materials to be transformed into wines rich in the area's trademark fruit, with an added sapidity that results in increased complexity and pleasantness. Over time their use of wood for aging has also proven more balanced and precise. The Poggio alle Viole '15 is a monovarietal Sangiovese that doesn't hide its ambitions. Extremely clear, focused and detailed Mediterranean aromas anticipate a succulent, well-sustained and deep palate. The Morellino di Scansano Rovente Riserva '16 is just as good, with its slightly peppery, lush fruit and a palate that exhibits close-woven, vivid structure.

● Poggio alle Viole '15	🍷🍷🍷 5
● Morellino di Scansano Rovente Ris. '16	🍷🍷 5
● Morellino di Scansano '18	🍷🍷 3
○ Vermentino '18	🍷🍷 3
● Cupinero '09	🍷🍷🍷 5
● Morellino di Scansano Rovente '05	🍷🍷🍷 4
● Morellino di Scansano Rovente Ris. '15	🍷🍷🍷 5
● Cupinero '15	🍷🍷 5
● Cupinero '13	🍷🍷 5
● Morellino di Scansano '17	🍷🍷 3
● Morellino di Scansano '16	🍷🍷 3
● Morellino di Scansano '15	🍷🍷 3*
● Morellino di Scansano Rovente Ris. '13	🍷🍷 5
● Poggio alle Viole '14	🍷🍷 5

Fattoria Collazzi

LOC. TAVARNUZZE
VIA COLLERAMOLE, 101
50023 IMPRUNETA [FI]
TEL. +39 0552374902
www.collazzi.it

CELLAR SALES
PRE-BOOKED VISITS
ANNUAL PRODUCTION 80,000 bottles
HECTARES UNDER VINE 32.00

In the early 1930s, the Marchi family purchased 400 hectares not far from Florence, around the estate's historic villa. More than 50 years later, siblings Carlo and Bona Marchi set in motion a new, more modern production stage that included olive groves, beekeeping and, gradually, a resuscitation of the vineyards. New varieties were planted alongside Sangiovese, like Cabernet Sauvignon and Franc, Merlot, Petit Verdot, Syrah, Malvasia Nera and Fiano. The Collazzi '16 is a Bordeaux blend of Cabernet Franc and Sauvignon, Merlot and Petit Verdot. Vegetal tones of roasted pepper are garnished with wild berries, then minty notes. On the palate it enters pleasant, creamy, broad and smooth before giving way to a relaxed, lingering finish. The Ottomuri '18, made with Fiano grapes, intrigues with its fresh and citrusy bouquet, its dynamic, lean body, and a lively back palate of appetizing sapidity.

● Collazzi '16	🍷🍷 6
● Ferro '16	🍷🍷 5
● Libertà '17	🍷🍷 3
○ Otto Muri '18	🍷🍷 3
● Chianti Cl. I Bastioni '17	🍷 3
● Collazzi '15	🍷🍷 6
● Collazzi '13	🍷🍷 6
● Collazzi '11	🍷🍷 6
● Collazzi '10	🍷🍷 6
● Ferro '15	🍷🍷 5
● Ferro '13	🍷🍷 5
● Ferro '12	🍷🍷 5
● Libertà '16	🍷🍷 3
● Libertà '13	🍷🍷 3
○ Otto Muri '17	🍷🍷 3
○ Otto Muri '15	🍷🍷 3

Colle di Bordocheo

LOC. SEGROMIGNO IN MONTE
VIA DI PIAGGIORI BASSO, 123
55012 CAPANNORI [LU]
TEL. +39 0583929821
www.colledibordocheo.com

CELLAR SALES
PRE-BOOKED VISITS
ACCOMMODATION
ANNUAL PRODUCTION 30,000 bottles
HECTARES UNDER VINE 10.00

Colle di Bordocheo is situated in a splendid location, along the Lucchesi hills of Segromigno in Monte. The estate comprises an agritourism surrounded by organically cultivated vineyards and olive groves. When it comes to their reds, primarily Sangiovese, Ciliegiolo and Merlot are used. For their whites it's Trebbiano, Vermentino and Chardonnay. Their wines are technically well-crafted, but also exhibit a notable personality that renders them enjoyable and captivating. We can unhesitatingly confirm that virtually their entire selection put in an excellent performance. It's hard to choose the best, starting with their Sangiovese Picchio Rosso '16, a wine that's as spicy and Mediterranean as it is racy, linear and deep on the palate. It's joined by the Mille968 in vintage and quality, in addition to its similar stylistic qualities. Their Sestilia '18, a rosé redolent of medlars and citrus, is of high quality, as are their two Bordocheos (Bianco '18 and Rosso '17).

● Colline Lucchesi Rosso Mille968 '16	♟♟ 5
● Colline Lucchesi Sangiovese Picchio Rosso '16	♟♟ 3*
○ Colline Lucchesi Bianco Bordocheo '18	♟♟ 2*
● Colline Lucchesi Rosso Bordocheo '17	♟♟ 2*
⊙ Sestilia '18	♟♟ 3
○ Bianco dell'Oca '17	♟♟ 3
○ Bianco dell'Oca '16	♟♟ 3
○ Bianco dell'Oca '15	♟♟ 3
○ Colline Lucchesi Bordocheo Bianco '14	♟♟ 2*
● Colline Lucchesi Picchio Rosso '13	♟♟ 3
● Colline Lucchesi Picchio Rosso '12	♟♟ 3
● Colline Lucchesi Rosso Mille968 '15	♟♟ 5

★Colle Massari

LOC. POGGI DEL SASSO
58044 CINIGIANO [GR]
TEL. +39 0564990496
www.collemassari.it

CELLAR SALES
PRE-BOOKED VISITS
ACCOMMODATION
ANNUAL PRODUCTION 500,000 bottles
HECTARES UNDER VINE 110.00
VITICULTURE METHOD Certified Organic
SUSTAINABLE WINERY

Collemassari took its first steps in 1998, starting with a series of important investments aimed at developing this corner of Maremma. Today it's one of the area's most significant wineries, an achievement made possible by the solid and continued growth of their wines, consistently among Maremma's best. Behind this highly ambitious project is explosive winemaker Claudio Tipa, who's also president of the Montecucco Consortium, a role in which he's managed to give a further boost to the appellation. The Montecucco Rosso Riserva '16 is a truly intriguing wine. On the palate it's marked by great contrast while airy and well-defined aromas reminiscent of fresh cherry and pepper rise up on the nose. Their Montecucco Sangiovese Poggio Lombrone Riserva '15 also delivered, with its vibrant aromas and dense, close-woven gustatory development (which still needs time to settle). The Canaiolo Tenuta Montecucco '18 is truly a model of pleasantness.

● Montecucco Rosso Ris. '16	♟♟♟ 4*
● Montecucco Sangiovese Poggio Lombrone Ris. '15	♟♟ 6
● Canaiolo Tenuta di Montecucco '18	♟♟ 2*
● Montecucco Rosso Rigoleto '17	♟♟ 3
○ Montecucco Vermentino Irisse '17	♟♟ 4
● Montecucco Rosso Colle Massari Ris. '08	♟♟♟ 3
● Montecucco Rosso Ris. '13	♟♟♟ 3*
● Montecucco Sangiovese Lombrone Ris. '11	♟♟♟ 6
● Montecucco Sangiovese Lombrone Ris. '10	♟♟♟ 6
● Montecucco Sangiovese Lombrone Ris. '09	♟♟♟ 6
● Montecucco Sangiovese Lombrone Ris. '08	♟♟♟ 6

Colle Santa Mustiola

ᴠ ᴅᴇʟʟᴇ Torri, 86ᴀ
3043 Cʜɪᴜsɪ [SI]
ʟ. +39 057820525
ᴡᴡ.poggioaichiari.it

CELLAR SALES
PRE-BOOKED VISITS
ANNUAL PRODUCTION 18,000 bottles
HECTARES UNDER VINE 5.00
SUSTAINABLE WINERY

abio Cenni is one of Tuscany's most
important vigneron, a key figure in the
region's wine renaissance. He brings
valuable experience to the work of
managing his vineyards and cellar, having
ever succumbed to the trends that
fluenced the world of wine over the years.
s Poggio ai Chiari might be the best
xample of how to produce Sangiovese
utside the region's classic districts. Full of
haracter and stylistically well defined, his
election is a benchmark for its ability to
ge and reach the heights of absolute
xcellence, even in the most difficult years.
mong the wines tasted we mention their
pecial edition' Poggio ai Chiari 2004
ithout properly reviewing it, considering
e wine's unique status — once again it
oints up the class and age-worthiness of
e producer's Sangiovese. Their fantastic
gna Flavia '13 put in a noteworthy
erformance as well, proving tasty and
eep, magnificent in its texture and
romatic complexity.

Vigna Flavia '13	▼▼ 5
Kernos '15	▼▼ 4
Poggio ai Chiari '06	▼▼▼ 6
Kernos '15	♀♀ 4
Poggio ai Chiari '11	♀♀ 6
Poggio ai Chiari '10	♀♀ 6

Fattoria Colle Verde

ꜰʀᴀᴢ. Mᴀᴛʀᴀɪᴀ
ʟᴏᴄ. Cᴀsᴛᴇʟʟᴏ
55012 Lᴜᴄᴄᴀ
Tᴇʟ. +39 0583402310
www.colleverde.it

CELLAR SALES
PRE-BOOKED VISITS
ANNUAL PRODUCTION 30,000 bottles
HECTARES UNDER VINE 7.50
VITICULTURE METHOD Certified Organic

Piero Tartagni and Francesca Pardini made
a deliberate choice when they moved to the
countryside some years ago. Shortly
thereafter a full-fledged agricultural
business was born, one that has proven,
over time, to be one of Lucca's most
noteworthy, thanks to a lovely cellar and a
veritable wine resort. It's all situated on the
gorgeous Matraia hills, where the terrain is
cultivated with biodynamic methods and
gives rise to extremely precise and rigorous
wines, technically impeccable and apt in
their territorial expressiveness. Their Brania
delle Ghiandaie, a blend of Sangiovese and
Syrah, is among the territory's best reds,
and the 2016 offers up its best. Aromas of
cocoa and licorice rise up off the nose.
There's still a bit too much oak here, due to
barrel maturation, but its fruit is superb,
healthy and swollen. In short, there's little
doubt about its excellent aging power. Their
Nero della Spinosa '16 proves rich in dark
sensations.

● Brania delle Ghiandaie '16	▼▼ 5
● Nero della Spinosa '16	▼▼ 5
● Terre di Matraja Rosso '18	▼ 3
● Brania delle Ghiandaie '15	♀♀ 5
● Brania delle Ghiandaie '14	♀♀ 5
● Colline Lucchesi Rosso Brania delle Ghiandaie '13	♀♀ 5
● Colline Lucchesi Rosso Brania delle Ghiandaie '12	♀♀ 5
● Nero della Spinosa '14	♀♀ 5
● Nero della Spinosa '13	♀♀ 5
● Sinòpia '13	♀♀ 8
● Terre di Matraja Rosso '17	♀♀ 3
● Terre di Matraja Rosso '16	♀♀ 3

Collemattoni

FRAZ. SANT'ANGELO IN COLLE
LOC. COLLEMATTONI, 100
53024 MONTALCINO [SI]
TEL. +39 0577844127
www.collemattoni.it

CELLAR SALES
PRE-BOOKED VISITS
ANNUAL PRODUCTION 60,000 bottles
HECTARES UNDER VINE 11.00
VITICULTURE METHOD Certified Organic
SUSTAINABLE WINERY

Marcello Bucci is the face of Collemattoni, as well as its driving force. It all starts with a farmstead situated in southwest Montalcino, a stone's throw from Sant'Angelo in Colle. It's accompanied by Fontelontano (for their Brunello Riserva), Sesta, Cava (in Castelnuovo dell'Abate) and Orcia (near Sant'Angelo Scalo). This patchwork of vineyards gives rise to compact, succulent Sangiovese reds that have proven increasingly convincing as of late. It's an impression that was fully confirmed by out tastings, with their Brunello '14 standing out in particular: timid notes of mandarin orange peel, plowed earth and dried herbs anticipate a tonic and taut (though not unrefined) palate that's just a bit lacking in flavor at the end. Their Rosso '17, a wine that's at once generous and measured, also delivered, as did their Vigna Fontelontano Ris. '13 with its aromas of dark fruit preserves and roots, a prelude to a large, ripe palate.

● Brunello di Montalcino '14	♈♈ 6
● Brunello di Montalcino V. Fontelontano Ris. '13	♈♈ 8
● Rosso di Montalcino '17	♈♈ 4
● Adone '17	♈ 3
● Brunello di Montalcino '01	♈♈♈ 5
● Brunello di Montalcino Fontelontano Ris. '01	♈♈♈ 6
● Brunello di Montalcino '13	♈♈ 6
● Brunello di Montalcino '10	♈♈ 6
● Brunello di Montalcino '09	♈♈ 6
● Brunello di Montalcino '08	♈♈ 6
● Rosso di Montalcino '16	♈♈ 4
● Rosso di Montalcino '15	♈♈ 4
● Rosso di Montalcino '14	♈♈ 4
● Rosso di Montalcino '13	♈♈ 3*

Colognole

LOC. COLOGNOLE
VIA DEL PALAGIO, 15
50065 PONTASSIEVE [FI]
TEL. +39 0558319870
www.colognole.it

CELLAR SALES
PRE-BOOKED VISITS
ACCOMMODATION AND RESTAURANT SERVIC
ANNUAL PRODUCTION 90,000 bottles
HECTARES UNDER VINE 27.00

Cesare and Mario, sons of a countess and descendants of the Spalletti Trivellis, took over the family business in 1990. In their vineyards, on the right bank of the Sieve (Chianti Rufina wine country), they grow Sangiovese and smaller quantities of Colorino, Merlot and Chardonnay. They also produce extra-virgin olive oils and are quite strong when it comes to hospitality, offering visitor accommodations in the estate's villas and farmhouses. The Vigna Le Rogaie '15 intrigues with its vegetal, floral and earthy hints. On the palate it proves juicy and warm, with soft tannins and an enticing finish. The surprising Syrah '17 offers up captivating vegetal aromas together with slight hints of pepper and cinnamon, then blackcurrant. On the palate it's rich, unfolding well, with elegant tannins and a nice, sapid back palate. The Quattro Chiacchiere '17, a monovarietal Chardonnay, moves from toasty notes to white peach. Pervasive and fresh, it closes delicately salty.

● Chianti Rufina Collezione '16	♈♈ 3
● Chianti Rufina V. Le Rogaie '15	♈♈ 3
○ Quattro Chiacchiere a Oltrepoggio '17	♈♈ 4
● Syrah '17	♈♈ 4
● Chianti Rufina '16	♈ 3
● Chianti Sup. Sinopie '18	♈ 2
● Chianti Rufina '15	♈♈ 3
● Chianti Rufina '12	♈♈ 2
● Chianti Rufina Riserva del Don '15	♈♈ 5
● Chianti Rufina Riserva del Don '12	♈♈ 5
● Chianti Sinopie '15	♈♈ 2
● Le Lastre '15	♈♈ 4
○ Quattro Chiacchiere a Oltrepoggio '15	♈♈ 4

Colombaio di Santa Chiara

ᴄ. Racciano
ᴀ San Donato, 1
3037 San Gimignano [SI]
ᴇʟ. +39 0577942004
ww.colombaiosantachiara.it

ᴇLLAR SALES
ᴘRE-BOOKED VISITS
ᴄCCOMMODATION
ᴀNNUAL PRODUCTION 98,000 bottles
ᴇCTARES UNDER VINE 22.00
ᴛTICULTURE METHOD Certified Organic
USTAINABLE WINERY

Tuscan" grapes like Vernaccia,
angiovese, Canaiolo and Colorino, as well
s less classic varieties like Cabernet Franc
nd Merlot: this is the mix that thrives on a
istoric estate just outside San Gimignano.
here's also a church and a tuff edifice
ɔlus cellar) now used for elegant guest
ccommodations. The Logi brothers
versee the vineyards and olive groves they
nherited from their father, bringing passion
nd care to their work, as well as the
tmost respect for the environment. A
ibrant, lively Ris. Albereta '16 sees citrusy
ɔotes and aromatic herbs meld with
ragrances of white peach. Subtle and
complex, it exhibits harmony and bold
structure together with nice acidity. A long
nish caps off a performance worthy of Tre
Bicchieri. The Vernaccia Selvabianca '18,
vhich sees fruity hints of mango and citron
dominate on the nose along with basil, also
mpressed. On the palate it enters
liscretely only to gain in strength and
'nally exhibit great vitality.

○ Vernaccia di San Gimignano L'Albereta Ris. '16	🍷🍷🍷 5
○ Vernaccia di San Gimignano Selvabianca '18	🍷🍷 3*
● Chianti Colli Senesi Il Priore '15	🍷 4
○ Cremisi Rosato '18	🍷 3
○ Vernaccia di San Gimignano Campo della Pieve '17	🍷 5
○ Vernaccia di S. Gimignano Albereta Ris. '13	🍷🍷🍷 3*
○ Vernaccia di S. Gimignano Albereta Ris. '12	🍷🍷🍷 5
○ Vernaccia di S. Gimignano Albereta Ris. '11	🍷🍷🍷 4*
○ Vernaccia di S. Gimignano Campo della Pieve '11	🍷🍷🍷 3*
○ Vernaccia di S. Gimignano Selvabianca '17	🍷🍷🍷 3*

Corte dei Venti

Loc. Piancornello, 35
53024 Montalcino [SI]
Tel. +39 3473653718
www.lacortedeiventi.it

CELLAR SALES
PRE-BOOKED VISITS
ANNUAL PRODUCTION 20,000 bottles
HECTARES UNDER VINE 5.00

Fresh, penetrating, subtle and essential
even: the expressiveness of Corte dei
Venti's reds certainly isn't what we'd
expect from an area as characteristically
Mediterranean as Piancornello. Here in the
heart of south Montalcino, the vineyards
grow in iron-rich soil at elevations ranging
from 100 to 300 meters. It's the constant
wind that gives rise to various types of
Brunellos, a microclimatic feature that's
highlighted by the name Clara Monaci and
Maurizio Machetti chose for their brilliant
adventure. Corte dei Venti doesn't only
make excellent monovarietal Sangiovese. In
this edition of the guide we discovered the
attributes of their Sant'Antimo Rosso
Poggio dei Lecci '16, a blend of Merlot,
Cabernet Sauvignon and Syrah that
impresses for its delectably Mediterranean
character and its meaty, resolved palate.
But their Brunello also performed at high
levels, once again. The 2014 version is just
a bit held back by tannic clench.

● Brunello di Montalcino '14	🍷🍷 8
● Sant'Antimo Poggio dei Lecci '16	🍷🍷 3*
● Rosso di Montalcino '17	🍷🍷 5
● Brunello di Montalcino '13	🍷🍷🍷 8
● Brunello di Montalcino '12	🍷🍷🍷 8
● Brunello di Montalcino '11	🍷🍷 8
● Brunello di Montalcino Donna Elena Ris. '10	🍷🍷 8
● Brunello di Montalcino Ris. '12	🍷🍷 8
● Rosso di Montalcino '16	🍷🍷 5
● Rosso di Montalcino '15	🍷🍷 5
● Sant'Antimo Poggio dei Lecci '14	🍷🍷 3

Cortonesi

LOC. LA MANNELLA, 322
53024 MONTALCINO [SI]
TEL. +39 0577848268
www.lamannella.it

PRE-BOOKED VISITS
ANNUAL PRODUCTION 35,000 bottles
HECTARES UNDER VINE 8.00

The winery identified by many with La
Mannella hasn't just changed its name.
The decision further underlines the
Cortonesi family's gifts as producers.
Indeed, for some time now, Marco has
been accompanied by his son Tommaso,
and the level of their wines continues to
strengthen in personality and quality,
vintage after vintage. This is particularly
true of their two Brunellos, which are
cultivated in two areas that are almost the
mirror-image of each other: Poggiarelli
(from Castelnuovo dell'Abate, in the
southeast) and La Mannella (situated
around their cellar, on the north side).
During a difficult 2014, they only produced
a Brunello La Mannella, which reinforced
our impressions of the producer's positive
stylistic path. It takes a minute for the nose
to open, then it settles on fresh sensations
of wild berries and spring flowers, with a
delicate spiciness accompanying its light
but assertive palate. Their Rosso '17
exhibits a crisper, warmer profile.

● Brunello di Montalcino La Mannella '14	❦❦ 5
● Rosso di Montalcino '17	❦ 3
● Brunello di Montalcino '10	❦❦ 5
● Brunello di Montalcino '09	❦❦ 5
● Brunello di Montalcino '08	❦❦ 5
● Brunello di Montalcino Ris. '10	❦❦ 6
● Brunello di Montalcino I Poggiarelli '13	❦❦ 5
● Brunello di Montalcino I Poggiarelli '12	❦❦ 5
● Brunello di Montalcino I Poggiarelli '11	❦❦ 5
● Brunello di Montalcino I Poggiarelli '10	❦❦ 5
● Brunello di Montalcino La Mannella '13	❦❦ 5
● Brunello di Montalcino La Mannella '12	❦❦ 5
● Rosso di Montalcino '15	❦❦ 3*
● Rosso di Montalcino '14	❦❦ 3
● Rosso di Montalcino '13	❦❦ 3

Andrea Costanti

LOC. COLLE AL MATRICHESE
53024 MONTALCINO [SI]
TEL. +39 0577848195
www.costanti.it

CELLAR SALES
PRE-BOOKED VISITS
ANNUAL PRODUCTION 60,000 bottles
HECTARES UNDER VINE 12.00

Divided into the plots of Casottino and
Calbello, Colle al Matrichese's vineyards
are situated on the eastern offshoot of the
slope that host this Montalcino winery. The
estate, which is historically well suited to
viticulture (thanks to its soil, rich in marl,
and elevations of over 400 meters),
became Andrea Costanti's headquarters in
1983. Their Brunellos are a benchmark for
those who love rigorous, yet well-crafted
Sangiovese, brought out by aging in
mid-sized casks and 3000 liter oak barrels
For this edition we tasted only one wine,
their Rosso '17. It presents itself as a
convincing interpretation of a year that was
anything but easy, considering the heat and
mugginess that characterized most of the
summer. Crisp and mobile on the nose, it
centers on smoky tones, sensations that
revive a potent but vigorous palate, where
the wine is supported by mature tannins.

● Rosso di Montalcino '17	❦❦ 4
● Brunello di Montalcino '06	❦❦❦ 6
● Brunello di Montalcino '88	❦❦❦ 6
● Brunello di Montalcino '13	❦❦ 6
● Brunello di Montalcino '12	❦❦ 6
● Brunello di Montalcino '11	❦❦ 6
● Brunello di Montalcino '10	❦❦ 6
● Brunello di Montalcino '09	❦❦ 6
● Brunello di Montalcino '08	❦❦ 6
● Brunello di Montalcino '07	❦❦ 6
● Brunello di Montalcino Ris. '12	❦❦ 8
● Brunello di Montalcino Ris. '10	❦❦ 8
● Brunello di Montalcino Ris. '07	❦❦ 8
● Brunello di Montalcino Ris. '06	❦❦ 8
● Rosso di Montalcino '15	❦❦ 4
● Rosso di Montalcino '11	❦❦ 4
● Rosso di Montalcino Vermiglio '14	❦❦ 5

La Cura

Loc. Cura Nuova, 12
58024 Massa Marittima [GR]
Tel. +39 0566918094
www.cantinalacura.it

CELLAR SALES
PRE-BOOKED VISITS
ANNUAL PRODUCTION 30,000 bottles
HECTARES UNDER VINE 15.00
SUSTAINABLE WINERY

Situated in Cura Nova, almost equidistant between Massa Marittima and Follonica, this winery operates in the image of its owner, Enrico Corsi. He brings passion and the occasional creative touch to his work. Vineyards are organically managed, while in the cellar, where they aren't afraid to experiment, only small barrels are used. Their modern and Mediterranean wines exhibit a well-defined character and a consistent level of quality that, year after year, make this one of Maremma's most notable producers. Their Cabernets '17, a blend of Cabernet Sauvignon and Cabernet Franc, offers up discernible varietal aromas that merge with toasty notes and spicy hints. On the palate it's mouthfilling but doesn't lose its rhythm or suppleness. The Maremma Toscana Collebruno '17, a Mediterranean wine, features a juicy, almost spicy hot gustatory profile. The Monteregio di Massa Marittima Breccerosse '17 is sapid on the palate, iron-scented on the nose.

● Cabernets '17	♀♀ 5
● Maremma Toscana Rosso Colle Bruno '17	♀♀ 2*
● Maremma Toscana Sangiovese Cavaliere d'Italia '18	♀♀ 2*
● Monteregio di Massa Marittima Rosso Breccerosse '17	♀♀ 3
○ Monteregio di Massa Marittima Bianco Falco Pescatore '18	♀ 2
○ Trinus '18	♀ 2
● Maremma Toscana Cabernet Sauvignon Cabernets '15	♀♀ 5
● Maremma Toscana Sangiovese Cavaliere d'Italia '16	♀♀ 2*
● Merlot '16	♀♀ 5
● Predicatore '17	♀♀ 3
○ Valdemàr Vermentino '17	♀♀ 2*
● Vedetta '16	♀♀ 4

De' Ricci

Fraz. S.Albino
Fraz. via Fontecornino, 15
53045 Montepulciano [SI]
Tel. +39 0578798152
www.dericci.it

CELLAR SALES
PRE-BOOKED VISITS
RESTAURANT SERVICE
ANNUAL PRODUCTION 90,000 bottles
HECTARES UNDER VINE 32.00
SUSTAINABLE WINERY

Cantine De' Ricci comprises two sites, as the plural form of their name suggests. One is the historic palazzo Ricci, their retail point in the Montepulciano city center. The other is situated in Sant'Albino, where their wines are produced with grapes from the Ascianello, Croce and Fontecornino subzones. Their selection also follows a dual track. Their designated wines are monovarietal Sangioveses (with varying degrees of complexity), aged in large wood barrels. International varieties, which are aged in barriques, are used for their IGT wines. Their Nobile di Montepulciano '16 is marked by fruity, meaty and spicy aromas, exhibiting gorgeous detail on the palate where it brings together acidic freshness and sweetness, density and flavor. Their Nobile SorAldo '16 is more influenced by oak, but juicy and fragrant nonetheless. The Rosso di Montepulciano '17 is enjoyable and gratifying, while the Severo '16, a monovarietal Petit Verdot, proves intense and soft.

● Nobile di Montepulciano '16	♀♀ 5
● Nobile di Montepulciano SorAldo '16	♀♀ 6
● Il Severo '16	♀♀ 3
● Rosso di Montepulciano '17	♀♀ 3
● Nobile di Montepulciano '15	♀♀ 5
● Nobile di Montepulciano SorAldo '15	♀♀ 6
● Rosso di Montepulciano '16	♀ 3

Maria Caterina Dei

VIA DI MARTIENA, 35
53045 MONTEPULCIANO [SI]
TEL. +39 0578716878
www.cantinedei.com

CELLAR SALES
PRE-BOOKED VISITS
ACCOMMODATION
ANNUAL PRODUCTION 230,000 bottles
HECTARES UNDER VINE 60.00
SUSTAINABLE WINERY

In 1964 Alibrando Dei bought terrain in Bossona, planting the first vineyard. The 1960s saw the purchase of their Martiena estate and its villa. In 1985 came the first 'Dei' brand Nobile di Montepulciano. Today Caterina Dei oversees the property, which comprises the vineyards of Martiena, Bossona, La Ciarliana and La Piaggia. Their selection features some of the most sumptuous Nobiles out there, wines capable of standing the test of time like few others. Stylistically focused and compact, they aren't lacking in character and finesse either. Lush fruitiness, aromas of ground coffee, vanilla and licorice characterize their Nobile Madonna della Querce '15, a wine marked by dense, soft and gratifying flavor. Nuanced fragrances open their Nobile di Montepulciano '16, while on the palate it's still influenced by oak, though well-contoured and broad. Strawberry sensations feature in their Rosso di Montepulciano '18 anticipating an approachably fresh and sweet palate.

● Nobile di Montepulciano Madonna della Querce '15	♟♟♟ 8
● Nobile di Montepulciano '16	♟♟ 5
● Rosso di Montepulciano '18	♟♟ 3
● Nobile di Montepulciano '14	♟♟♟ 4*
● Nobile di Montepulciano '13	♟♟♟ 4*
● Nobile di Montepulciano Bossona Ris. '13	♟♟♟ 6
● Nobile di Montepulciano Bossona Ris. '04	♟♟♟ 5
● Nobile di Montepulciano Bossona Ris. '15	♟♟ 4
● Nobile di Montepulciano Bossona Ris. '12	♟♟ 6

Fabrizio Dionisio

FRAZ. OSSAIA, 87
LOC. IL CASTAGNO
52040 CORTONA [AR]
TEL. +39 063223391
www.fabriziodionisio.it

CELLAR SALES
PRE-BOOKED VISITS
ANNUAL PRODUCTION 45,000 bottles
HECTARES UNDER VINE 15.00
VITICULTURE METHOD Certified Biodynamic
SUSTAINABLE WINERY

A deep respect for the land is this winery's defining characteristic. Over the past 20 years, they've focused on Syrah, a grape that, here on the hills facing Cortona, has gradually substituted Sangiovese and Trebbiano (considering just how well it's done since its introduction, possibly during French occupation in the Napoleonic era). Fabrizio's wines, which he himself calls 'artisanal', are 'territorial capsules' that conserve the best characteristics of each vintage. The Syrah Il Castagno '16 performed well, with its distinct aromas of blackcurrant and cherry, then spicy hints of pepper and vanilla. On the palate it proves flavorful, generous, juicy and elegant, with a long finish. The pleasant Syrah Castagnino '18 features notes of blackcurrant, then strawberry and nuances of white pepper. In the mouth it's supple, fresh and dynamic — an excellent drink. The aromatically austere Syrah Cuculaia '15 stands out for its tertiary aromas and its potent structure.

● Cortona Syrah Il Castagno '16	♟♟ 5
● Cortona Syrah Castagnino '18	♟♟ 3
● Cortona Syrah Cuculaia '15	♟♟ 7
● Cortona Syrah Il Castagno '12	♟♟♟ 5
● Cortona Syrah Il Castagno '11	♟♟♟ 5
● Cortona Syrah Il Castagno '10	♟♟♟ 5
● Cortona Syrah Castagnino '17	♟♟ 3
● Cortona Syrah Castagnino '16	♟♟ 3
● Cortona Syrah Castagnino '15	♟♟ 3*
● Cortona Syrah Castagnino '14	♟♟ 3
● Cortona Syrah Cuculaia '13	♟♟ 7
● Cortona Syrah Cuculaia '10	♟♟ 7
● Cortona Syrah Il Castagno '15	♟♟ 5
● Cortona Syrah Il Castagno '14	♟♟ 5
● Cortona Syrah Il Castagno '13	♟♟ 5

Donna Olimpia 1898

FRAZ. BOLGHERI
LOC. MIGLIARINI, 142
57020 CASTAGNETO CARDUCCI [LI]
TEL. +39 0302279601
www.donnaolimpia1898.it

CELLAR SALES
ACCOMMODATION AND RESTAURANT SERVICE
ANNUAL PRODUCTION 250,000 bottles
HECTARES UNDER VINE 45.00
SUSTAINABLE WINERY

This winery is part of the Guido Folonari group (famous in Tuscan and Italian wine). Olimpia Alliata, who inspired the undertaking, was the lady of Biserno, wife of celebrated Gherardo della Gherardesca. Their vineyards are the result of serious research into clones, carried out in collaboration with professor Attilio Scienza. We find Cabernet Sauvignon, Cabernet Franc, Merlot, Syrah and Petito Verdot among their reds, Vermentino, Viognier and Petit Manseng for their whites, making for modern wines aged in small oak barrels. Their Superiore Millepassi '16 just fell short of excellence. This time its toastiness too forward, especially when considering the favorable vintage (which should guarantee elegance). It's highly likely that over time it will improve by virtue of its firm structure. The Campo alla Giostra '16 is redolent of ripe red and black berry fruits, adorned by lovely herbaceous sensations. Among their whites we appreciated the pleasant Obizzo '18.

Bolgheri Rosso Sup. Millepassi '16	🍷🍷 7
Bolgheri Rosso Campo alla Giostra '16	🍷🍷 5
Obizzo Vermentino '18	🍷🍷 2*
Orizzonte '15	🍷 7
Tageto '17	🍷 2
Bolgheri Rosso Sup. Millepassi '15	🍷🍷🍷 7
Bolgheri Rosso Sup. Millepassi '13	🍷🍷🍷 6
Bolgheri Rosso Sup. Millepassi '11	🍷🍷🍷 8
Bolgheri Rosso '15	🍷🍷 5
Bolgheri Rosso '13	🍷🍷 5
Bolgheri Rosso Campo alla Giostra '15	🍷🍷 5
Bolgheri Rosso Sup. Millepassi '12	🍷🍷 6
Millepassi '13	🍷🍷 6
Obizzo Vermentino '17	🍷🍷 2*
Tageto '16	🍷🍷 2*

Duemani

LOC. ORTACAVOLI
56046 RIPARBELLA [PI]
TEL. +39 0583975048
www.duemani.eu

CELLAR SALES
PRE-BOOKED VISITS
ANNUAL PRODUCTION 50,000 bottles
HECTARES UNDER VINE 12.00
VITICULTURE METHOD Certified Biodynamic
SUSTAINABLE WINERY

Elena and Luca's approach to viticulture is extremely precise. It couldn't be otherwise, considering their desire to bring the best out of their grapes while also respecting the environment. Luca handles vineyard planning and management for numerous producers, not just his own, while also overseeing production processes. Situated on the hills of Riparbella, peppered with Mediterranean shrub, Duemani overlooks the sea, spawning Cabernet Franc, Syrah and Merlot. Their Suisassi '16, a monovarietal Syrah, opens with intense, complex aromas, pepper, tobacco, balsamic nuances all on a background of raspberry and cherry. On the palate it's powerful, tight, with superb flesh and a long, characterful finish. The Duemani '16, a Cab Franc, offers up vibrant fragrances of blackberry coulis adorned by rich spices and flowers. A complex nose is followed by a big, full-flavoured palate, with harmonious and close-woven tannins joined by superb flesh and lengthy aromatic persistence.

● Suisassi '16	🍷🍷🍷 8
● Duemani '16	🍷🍷 8
● Altrovino '16	🍷🍷 6
● Cifra '17	🍷🍷 5
⊙ Si '18	🍷 6
● Altrovino '15	🍷🍷🍷 6
● Duemani '15	🍷🍷🍷 8
● Duemani '13	🍷🍷🍷 8
● Duemani '12	🍷🍷🍷 8
● Duemani '09	🍷🍷🍷 8
● Suisassi '10	🍷🍷🍷 8
● Cifra '16	🍷🍷 5
● Cifra '15	🍷🍷 5
● Cifra '13	🍷🍷 5
● Duemani '14	🍷🍷 8
● Suisassi '15	🍷🍷 8

L'Erta di Radda

Case Sparse Il Corno, 25
53017 Radda in Chianti [SI]
Tel. +39 3284040500
www.ertadiradda.it

ANNUAL PRODUCTION 22,000 bottles
HECTARES UNDER VINE 5.00
VITICULTURE METHOD Certified Organic

Diego Finocchi, owner of this small Chianti producer (founded in 2006, in the Radda in Chianti subzone) has brought skill and passion to his work. First he decided to focus on organic viticulture, which is rigorously practiced, then he adopted a minimally-invasive approach to winemaking. The first bottles hit the market in 2009 and, despite the inevitable uncertainties brought about by youth, they immediately had an impact. Indeed, especially of late, they exhibit unwavering territorial coherence and increased quality, particularly in terms of personality and energy. The Chianti Classico Riserva '16 offers up focused aromas that aren't without personality. On the palate it delivers spirited tannins and contrast of flavor, coming through fragrant before a finish marked by an encore of fruit on earthy sensations. Independent of the occasional aromatic impurity and a bit of tannic stiffness, the Chianti Classico '17 stands out for its highly pleasant palate, assertive and flavorful.

● Chianti Cl. '17	🍷🍷 3*
● Chianti Cl. Ris. '16	🍷🍷 5

Eucaliptus - Dario Di Vaira

loc. Bolgheri
via Bolgherese, 275a
57022 Castagneto Carducci [LI]
Tel. +39 0565763511
www.agriturismoeucaliptus.com

CELLAR SALES
PRE-BOOKED VISITS
ACCOMMODATION AND RESTAURANT SERVIC
ANNUAL PRODUCTION 30,000 bottles
HECTARES UNDER VINE 7.00

The winery is managed and owned by Dario Di Vaira, who succeeded his father 2008. The vineyards, which were planted in 1998, are situated along the Via Bolgherese: high-density plots divided up according to a rather common ampelography (Cabernet Sauvignon and Franc, Merlot, Sangiovese, Petit Verdot ar a small share of Syrah). When it comes to their whites they cultivate Vermentino, Viogner and Chardonnay. It's an around farm business that also produces vegetables sold directly the public and prepared for guests in their 'kilometer zero' restaurant. Their Bolgheri Sup. Ville Rustiche '16 is extraordinary in its finess and complexity. It's truly a personal, complete, delectable and tasty red that enchants with its aromatic weave of wild berries and Mediterranean shrub, spicy nuances and a gorgeous suite of herbaceous notes that fade to bay leaves. Their exceptionally stylish and smooth Bolgheri Rosso Clarice '17 is just as convincing.

● Bolgheri Rosso Clarice '17	🍷🍷
● Bolgheri Rosso Sup. Ville Rustiche '16	🍷🍷
○ Bolgheri Vermentino Le Pinete '18	🍷🍷
● Bolgheri Rosso Clarice '16	🍷🍷
● Bolgheri Rosso Clarice '14	🍷🍷
● Bolgheri Rosso Clarice '13	🍷🍷
● Bolgheri Rosso Clarice '12	🍷🍷
● Bolgheri Rosso Clarice '11	🍷🍷
● Bolgheri Rosso Sup. Ville Rustiche '15	🍷🍷
● Bolgheri Sup. Ville Rustiche '13	🍷🍷
● Bolgheri Sup. Ville Rustiche '12	🍷🍷
● Bolgheri Sup. Ville Rustiche '11	🍷🍷
● Bolgheri Sup. Ville Rustiche '10	🍷🍷

Fabbri

LOC. LAMOLE
VIA CASOLE, 52
50022 GREVE IN CHIANTI [FI]
TEL. +39 339412622
www.ifabbrichianticlassico.it

CELLAR SALES
PRE-BOOKED VISITS
ANNUAL PRODUCTION 35,000 bottles
HECTARES UNDER VINE 11.00
VITICULTURE METHOD Certified Organic

Fabbri, a name that goes back to the workshop of the estate's ancient hamlet, has been making wines since 2000, thanks to the efforts of sisters Susanna and Maddalena Grassi. Situated in the unique subzone of Lamole, in Greve in Chianti, the winery avails itself of organic management. The resulting wines exhibit a definite style, one that's honed and recognizable, not always immediately intelligible but certainly coherent with a territory as unique as Chianti Classico, and capable of withstanding the tests of time. The Chianti Classico Lamole '17 stands out for its gustatory development, exhibiting linearity, flavor and superb fragrance, making for a truly impressive drink. Aromas are backgrounded, but highly complex, delicate and subtle. The Chianti Classico Riserva '16 also delivered. It's more marked by oak but aromatically well-defined and spirited, flavorful on the palate.

Chianti Cl. Lamole '17	♟♟♟ 4*
Chianti Cl. Ris. '16	♟♟ 4
Chianti Cl. Terra di Lamole '16	♟♟ 3
Chianti Cl. Olinto '17	♟ 4
Chianti Cl. '16	♟♟ 4
Chianti Cl. '13	♟♟ 4
Chianti Cl. '12	♟♟ 4
Chianti Cl. Gran Sel. '11	♟♟ 6
Chianti Cl. Gran Selezione '15	♟♟ 6
Chianti Cl. Olinto '15	♟♟ 4
Chianti Cl. Olinto '14	♟♟ 4
Chianti Cl. Olinto '12	♟♟ 4
Chianti Cl. Ris. '13	♟♟ 4
Chianti Cl. Ris. '11	♟♟ 4
Chianti Cl. Terra di Lamole '15	♟♟ 3
Chianti Cl. Terra di Lamole '13	♟♟ 3*

Fabbrica Pienza

LOC. BORGHETTO
53026 PIENZA [SI]
TEL. +39 0578810030
info@fabbricapienza.com

CELLAR SALES
PRE-BOOKED VISITS
ANNUAL PRODUCTION 20,000 bottles
HECTARES UNDER VINE 35.00
VITICULTURE METHOD Certified Organic
SUSTAINABLE WINERY

Swiss couple Antonie and Philippe Bertherat, inspired primarily by a passion for their work, have been making wines in Tuscany for thirty years. They may operate in an area not particularly known for viticulture (Pienza), but they've got very clear ideas. Their well-defined style centers on a minimalist approach, without comprises: vineyards are organically managed and in the cellar they use small, carefully selected wooden barrels. The result is a selection of precise wines, complex and not lacking in personality. They certainly leave their mark. The Sangiovese '16 features vibrant aromas of red berries and spices, sensations that anticipate a lively gustatory development, closing sweet and compact, with the occasional immoderate oaky note. The Syrah '16 stands out for its vigorous and balanced palate, while on the nose there's a bit too much toastiness obscuring its fragrant fruit. The Bianco '17 is an aromatically complex wine, rhythmic and deep on the palate.

● Sangiovese '16	♟♟ 5
● Syrah '16	♟♟ 5
○ Bianco di Fabbrica '17	♟♟ 6
○ Bianco di Fabbrica '16	♟♟ 6
● Prototipo 470.1 '13	♟♟ 5
● Prototipo 470.2 '14	♟♟ 5
● Prototipo 470.3 Sangiovese '15	♟♟ 8

Tenuta Fanti

Fraz. Castelnuovo dell'Abate
Podere Palazzo, 14
53020 Montalcino [SI]
Tel. +39 0577835795
www.tenutafanti.it

CELLAR SALES
PRE-BOOKED VISITS
ANNUAL PRODUCTION 200,000 bottles
HECTARES UNDER VINE 50.00

Father and daughter Filippo and Elisa Fanta oversee one of Montalcino's most appealing estates to visit. Situated just a stone's throw from Castelnuovo dell'Abate, this is a veritable center of gravity in the territory's southeast. It's a district perfect for making succulent, caressing Brunellos that also exhibit some backbone. The style is further explored by an innovative approach in the cellar, one that completely respects that special mix of sunniness, ventilation and day-night temperature swings (due to nearby Amiata) that makes them so unmistakable. The Fanti family puts their best foot forward with their delectable Rosso '17, a wine that's almost springy in its aromas of flowers, cooking herbs and balsams. These help drive a development that's more characterized by a fresh, slightly salty vein and a soft tannic weave than by fullness. Their Brunello Vigna le Macchiarelle Ris. 13 is just as mobile and multifaceted in its aromas of topsoil and aromatic herbs.

● Rosso di Montalcino '17	♚♚ 3*
● Brunello di Montalcino	
V. Le Macchiarelle Ris. '13	♚♚ 6
● Brunello di Montalcino '07	♚♚♚ 5
● Brunello di Montalcino '00	♚♚♚ 6
● Brunello di Montalcino '97	♚♚♚ 5
● Brunello di Montalcino Ris. '95	♚♚♚ 5
● Brunello di Montalcino Vallocchio '13	♚♚♚ 7
● Brunello di Montalcino '13	♚♚ 6
● Brunello di Montalcino '12	♚♚ 6
● Brunello di Montalcino '11	♚♚ 6
● Brunello di Montalcino '10	♚♚ 6
● Brunello di Montalcino	
V. Le Macchiarelle Ris. '10	♚♚ 6
● Brunello di Montalcino Vallocchio '11	♚♚ 6
● Rosso di Montalcino '16	♚♚ 3

Tenuta Le Farnete/Cantagallo

Fraz. Comeana
via Macia
59100 Carmignano [PO]
Tel. +39 0571910078
www.tenutacantagallo.it

CELLAR SALES
PRE-BOOKED VISITS
ACCOMMODATION AND RESTAURANT SERVIC
ANNUAL PRODUCTION 65,000 bottles
HECTARES UNDER VINE 40.00
SUSTAINABLE WINERY

Cantagallo spans 200 hectares on the hills of Vinci, while the 50-hectare Farnete is situated in Carmignano. These two properties, owned by the Pierazzuoli family, were purchased 20 years apart. In both cases vineyards alternate with woods and olive groves. In both cases there's a restaurant, an area for guests and a cellar. The former hosts Sangiovese and smaller shares of Merlot, Syrah, Trebbiano, Malvasia and Colorino. The latter hosts Sangiovese, Cabernet Sauvignon and Aleatico. Once again their Carmignano Riserva '16 takes home Tre Bicchieri, with its notes of aromatic herbs, earth, tanned leather, tobacco and red fruits, like cherry, in the foreground. On the palate it comes through sapid and tasty, fresh, lively in its velvety tannins, with a long and enjoyable finish. The Ris. Il Fondatore '16 plays on clear, focused aromas of wild berries, balsamic hints, then a rich and balanced structure marked by good acidity, subtle tannins and a flavorful, long finish.

● Carmignano Ris. '16	♚♚♚
● Chianti Montalbano Tenuta Cantagallo	
Il Fondatore Ris. '16	♚♚
● Carmignano '17	♚♚
● Chianti Montalbano	
Tenuta Cantagallo '18	♚♚
● Chianti Montalbano T	
enuta Cantagallo Ris. '16	♚♚
● Gioveto Tenuta Cantagallo '16	♚♚
○ Vin Santo Chianti	
Montalbano Millarium '13	♚♚
● Barco Reale Le Farnete '18	♚
● Carmignano Ris. '15	♚♚♚
● Carmignano Ris. '14	♚♚♚
● Chianti Montalbano Tenuta Cantagallo	
Il Fondatore Ris. '15	♚♚
● Gioveto Tenuta Cantagallo '15	♚♚

Fattoi

Loc. Santa Restituta
Pod. Capanna, 101
53024 Montalcino [SI]
Tel. +39 0577848613
www.fattoi.it

CELLAR SALES
PRE-BOOKED VISITS
ANNUAL PRODUCTION 50,000 bottles
HECTARES UNDER VINE 9.00

The producer created by Ofelio Fattoi and sons (Lamberto, Leonardo, and young Lucia) is one of Montalcino's loveliest artisanal wineries. In a way they were just feeling their way until they decided to change gears and aim high. They're particularly appreciated by those in search of spontaneity and drinkability, though without compromising the meaty, visceral qualities of the best Brunellos. It's a style closely tied to Santa Restituta's pedoclimate, one of the southeast's great crus, and brought out through aging in medium sized-large oak barrels. Even during a year as complicated as 2014, Fattoi's Brunello exhibits an unmistakable vigor. Wild berries, roots, topsoil and a touch of black olives rise up off the nose, tying in harmoniously with a vigorous and lip-smacking palate. It's a highly drinkable wine, despite a slightly diluted finish. Their Rosso '17 also proves faithful to its standards. It's aromatically fragrant, lively and fluttering in its development.

● Brunello di Montalcino '14	▼▼ 5
● Rosso di Montalcino '17	▼▼ 4
● Rosso della Toscana '16	▼ 4
● Brunello di Montalcino '10	▼▼▼ 5
● Brunello di Montalcino Ris. '12	▼▼▼ 7
● Brunello di Montalcino '13	▽▽ 5
● Brunello di Montalcino '12	▽▽ 5
● Brunello di Montalcino '11	▽▽ 5
● Brunello di Montalcino '09	▽▽ 5
● Brunello di Montalcino Ris. '10	▽▽ 7
● Brunello di Montalcino Ris. '08	▽▽ 7
● Brunello di Montalcino Ris. '07	▽▽ 7
● Rosso di Montalcino '16	▽▽ 3
● Rosso di Montalcino '15	▽▽ 3
● Rosso di Montalcino '14	▽▽ 3
● Rosso di Montalcino '13	▽▽ 3
● Rosso di Montalcino '12	▽▽ 3

Fattoria Fibbiano

via Fibbiano, 2
56030 Terricciola [PI]
Tel. +39 0587635677
www.fattoria-fibbiano.it

CELLAR SALES
PRE-BOOKED VISITS
ACCOMMODATION AND RESTAURANT SERVICE
ANNUAL PRODUCTION 185,000 bottles
HECTARES UNDER VINE 17.00

This winery and agritourism, whose origins go back to the 12th century, is situated on a sunny slope bound by two streams on the hills between Pisa and Volterra. Since the late 1990s the estate has been owned by the Cantoni family. The terrain is treated with organic substances and using minimally-invasive methods. Great attention is paid to energy consumption, thanks to solar energy (used to produce clean water), and a heating system powered by plant clippings. Their excellent Ciliegiolo '17 is decisive and intense on the nose, with aromas of blackberries and plums, then blackcurrant and finally aromatic herbs. Its docile, succulent, elegant and full palate features discernible, well-integrated tannins, closing with nice density. The Sanforte '15, made with grapes from a revived vineyard, is a curious wine whose bouquet opts first for medicinal herbs, then notes of cherry, with hints of thyme to top it off. On the palate it exhibits body, volume and nice acidity.

● Ciliegiolo '17	▼▼ 4
○ Fonte delle Donne '18	▼▼ 3
● Sanforte '15	▼▼ 5
● Chianti Sup. Casalini '16	▼ 2
⊙ Sofia Rosato '18	▼ 2
● Chianti Sup. Casalini '15	▽▽ 2*
● Ciliegiolo '16	▽▽ 4
● Ciliegiolo '15	▽▽ 3
○ Fonte Delle Donne '15	▽▽ 3
● L'Aspetto '15	▽▽ 5
● L'Aspetto '13	▽▽ 4
● Le Pianette '16	▽▽ 2*
● Le Pianette '15	▽▽ 2*
● Sanforte '14	▽▽ 5
● Terre di Pisa Ceppatella '13	▽▽ 6

★Tenute Ambrogio e Giovanni Folonari

LOC. PASSO DEI PECORAI
VIA DI NOZZOLE, 12
50022 GREVE IN CHIANTI [FI]
TEL. +39 055859811
www.tenutefolonari.com

CELLAR SALES
PRE-BOOKED VISITS
ACCOMMODATION
ANNUAL PRODUCTION 1,400,000 bottles
HECTARES UNDER VINE 200.00

Ambrogio and Giovanni Folonari have inherited a legacy that traverses a significant part of Italian wine history. Nino Folonari purchased Chianti's Tenuta del Cabreo in 1967 and Tenuta di Nozzole in 1971. In 2000, Ambrogio and Giovanni Folonari (son and grandson of Nino, respectively), found their winery, carrying forward the family tradition. Today the producer has a presence in some of Tuscany's most important terroir, from Bolgheri to Montalcino. Nevertheless, it's not difficult to see that its beating heart lies in Chianti. Their Chianti Classico La Forra Riserva '15 is a decidedly modern wine, but well-crafted. Aromatically its fruity fragrances are supported by nice oak, the prelude to a dense, soft development marked by good rhythm. Their Chianti Classico '17 is a fragrant, pleasant, highly drinkable wine, while the Cabreo Il Borgo '16, a blend of Sangiovese, Cabernet Sauvignon and Merlot, proves solid and well-crafted, fragrant, succulent and tasty.

● Cabreo Il Borgo '16	▼▼▼	6
● Chianti Cl. La Forra Ris. '15	▼▼	4
● Chianti Cl. '17	▼▼	3
● Black '16	▼	5
● Il Pareto '16	▼	8
● Cabreo Il Borgo '06	♀♀♀	5
● Chianti Cl. La Forra Ris. '90	♀♀♀	4*
● Il Pareto '15	♀♀♀	8
● Il Pareto '09	♀♀♀	7
● Il Pareto '07	♀♀♀	7
● Il Pareto '04	♀♀♀	7
● Il Pareto '01	♀♀♀	7
● Il Pareto '00	♀♀♀	7
● Il Pareto '98	♀♀♀	7
● Il Pareto '97	♀♀♀	7
● Il Pareto '93	♀♀♀	7

★★Fontodi

FRAZ. PANZANO IN CHIANTI
VIA SAN LEOLINO, 89
50020 GREVE IN CHIANTI [FI]
TEL. +39 055852005
www.fontodi.com

CELLAR SALES
PRE-BOOKED VISITS
ACCOMMODATION
ANNUAL PRODUCTION 300,000 bottles
HECTARES UNDER VINE 80.00
VITICULTURE METHOD Certified Organic

If Panzano's celebrated 'Conca d'Oro' is recognized as one of Chianti Classico's best subzones, most of the credit must go to the Manetti family. In 1968 they took over this estate and since then they've managed to impress their Sangioveses with an absolutely authentic style. Today Fontodi's journey still hasn't finished. On the contrary, an organic approach to cultivation is bringing the producer closer to a style defined by character and personality, even if, at times, that expressiveness can be a bit too liberal. The Chianti Classico Vigna del Sorbo Gran Selezione '16 exhibits a generous character, starting with its fruity aromatic suite adorned by spicy hints. On the palate it comes through pervasive and full of contrast, with a rising finish. The Chianti Classico '16 proves well-made, aromatically clean and sapid on the palate. The Chianti Classico Filetta di Lamole '16 is more rustic, but no less interesting.

● Chianti Cl. Gran Selezione V. del Sorbo '16	▼▼▼	6
● Chianti Cl. '16	▼▼	4
● Chianti Cl. Filetta di Lamole '16	▼▼	3
● Flaccianello della Pieve '16	▼	8
● Syrah '16	▼	6
● Chianti Cl. '10	♀♀♀	4
● Chianti Cl. Gran Sel. V. del Sorbo '14	♀♀♀	6
● Chianti Cl. V. del Sorbo Ris. '01	♀♀♀	6
● Flaccianello della Pieve '12	♀♀♀	8
● Flaccianello della Pieve '09	♀♀♀	8
● Flaccianello della Pieve '08	♀♀♀	8
● Flaccianello della Pieve '07	♀♀♀	8
● Flaccianello della Pieve '05	♀♀♀	6
● Flaccianello della Pieve '03	♀♀♀	6
● Flaccianello della Pieve '01	♀♀♀	6
● Flaccianello della Pieve '85	♀♀♀	8

Fontuccia

VIA PROVINCIALE, 54
58012 ISOLA DEL GIGLIO [GR]
TEL. +39 0564809576
www.fontuccia.it

ANNUAL PRODUCTION 6,500 bottles
HECTARES UNDER VINE 3.00

Simone and Giovanni Rossi are celebrating ten years of winemaking. It's a significant achievement, if you think that they operate on the island of Giglio, where viticulture is heroic, to say the least. In the total absence of mechanization, vineyards must be climbed to be reached and are entirely cultivated by hand. Here they make 'vin de garage' in the truest sense of the term, considering that a couple old depots serve as their cellar. Pure and characterized by pronounced personality, their wines exhibit excellent technical precision and a definite saline quality. The 2018 is one of the best versions of their Caperrosso Senti Oh! yet. It's a monovarietal Ansonica redolent of iodine, eucalyptus and flint, the prelude to outstanding development in terms of rhythm and flavor, and a finish marked by a characterful, delicately salty note. Their Senti Oh! '18 follows a similar stylistic track, though it's noticeably less complex.

○ Capperrosso Senti Oh! '18	♥♥ 4
○ N'antro Po' Ansonica Passito '18	♥♥ 6
○ Senti Oh! '18	♥♥ 4
○ Capperrosso Senti Oh! '16	♀♀ 4
○ Capperrosso Senti Oh! '15	♀♀ 4
○ N'antro Po' '13	♀♀ 6
● Saracio '16	♀♀ 6
○ Senti Oh! '17	♀♀ 4
○ Senti Oh! '16	♀♀ 4

Fornacelle

LOC. FORNACELLE, 232A
57022 CASTAGNETO CARDUCCI [LI]
TEL. +39 0565775575
www.fornacelle.it

CELLAR SALES
PRE-BOOKED VISITS
ANNUAL PRODUCTION 35,000 bottles
HECTARES UNDER VINE 9.00

The Billi-Battistoni family's winery gets its name from the unique subzone of Bolgheri in which it's located (an area where several furnaces once operated). In the 1990s, an ambitious renovation effort was carried out, both in the vineyards and the cellar. Their grapes are cultivated along the plains, on various types of medium-texture terrain characterized by stones, sandy-loam and gravel. Precise and highly expressive, their wines perform at high levels. Their Bolgheri Sup. Guardaboschi '16 is quite good, even if its fruit is obscured by foregrounded herbaceous sensations and by slightly powdery tannins (details that aren't particularly significant considering an overall profile that just falls short of excellence). Their other Bolgheri Sup. Foglio 38 '15 is excellent, proving creamy and full-bodied with lovely extraction — and it never loses its verve. Their Rosso Zizzolo '18 is also worth mentioning.

● Bolgheri Rosso Sup. Guardaboschi '16	♥♥ 6
● Bolgheri Rosso Sup. Foglio 38 '15	♥♥ 7
● Bolgheri Rosso Zizzolo '18	♥ 3
● Bolgheri Rosso Sup. Guarda Boschi '15	♀♀ 6
● Bolgheri Rosso Zizzolo '16	♀♀ 3
● Bolgheri Rosso Zizzolo '13	♀♀ 3
● Bolgheri Rosso Zizzolo '12	♀♀ 3
● Bolgheri Sup. Foglio 38 '14	♀♀ 7
● Bolgheri Sup. Foglio 38 '13	♀♀ 6
● Bolgheri Sup. Guarda Boschi '13	♀♀ 6
● Bolgheri Sup. Guarda Boschi '12	♀♀ 6
● Bolgheri Sup. Guarda Boschi '11	♀♀ 6
○ Bolgheri Vermentino Zizzolo '14	♀♀ 3

Podere Forte

LOC. PETRUCCI, 13
53023 CASTIGLIONE D'ORCIA [SI]
TEL. +39 05778885100
www.podereforte.it

CELLAR SALES
PRE-BOOKED VISITS
ANNUAL PRODUCTION 12,000 bottles
HECTARES UNDER VINE 15.00
VITICULTURE METHOD Certified Biodynamic
SUSTAINABLE WINERY

It's difficult to think of an operation like Pasquale Forte's. More than a farm, his is a lifestyle applied to work, where each operation has a purpose and nothing is done unnecessarily. Modeled on the Roman farm, a number of activities are carried out, creating an ecosystem that balances each crop. For this reason, in addition to viticulture, they raise animals, bees and are setting the stage for biodynamic cultivation. The Guardiavigna '15 blend stands out for its complex bouquet, with meaty, mineral notes followed by focused cherry and blackcurrant, all softened by juniper. On the palate it proves dynamic and long. The clean, fresh Petruccino '16 enchants. It's a vibrant Sangiovese marked by notes of tobacco and red fruit, then a hint of herbs and mint, making for a delicate, complex aromatic profile. On the palate it's harmonious, characterized by juicy sensations of blueberry and blackcurrant, lovely acidic freshness and length. In short, Tre Bicchieri.

● Orcia Petruccino '16	♆♆♆	7
● Guardiavigna '15	♆♆	8
● Orcia Anfiteatro '16	♆♆	8
● Orcia Melo '16	♆♆	8
● Orcia Guardiavigna '01	♆♆♆	8
● Guardiavigna '14	♆♆	8
● Guardiavigna '13	♆♆	8
● Guardiavigna '12	♆♆	8
● Guardiavigna '11	♆♆	8
● Orcia Petrucci '10	♆♆	8
● Orcia Petruccino '15	♆♆	6
● Orcia Petruccino '13	♆♆	8
● Orcia Rosso Petrucci '11	♆♆	8
● Orcia Rosso Petruccino '12	♆♆	8

Podere Fortuna

VIA SAN GIUSTO A FORTUNA, 7
50038 SCARPERIA E SAN PIERO [FI]
TEL. +39 0558487214
www.poderefortuna.com

CELLAR SALES
PRE-BOOKED VISITS
ACCOMMODATION
ANNUAL PRODUCTION 25,000 bottles
HECTARES UNDER VINE 6.00
SUSTAINABLE WINERY

Since the time of the Medicis they've been making wine here. The farmstead was part of Cafaggiolo castle and historical archives date viticulture here all the way back to 1465, though there wasn't any Pinot Nero then (the cultivar chosen by Alessandro Brogi, who founded the winery in the early part of the century). Entrepreneur Alfredo Lowenstein purchased the property after buying the castle, showing constant care and attention for this unique grape. The 1465 landed a place in our finals thanks to its fresh notes of aromatic herbs, like pennyroyal mint and thyme, then hints of blackcurrant and blueberries. On the palate it enters impressively, proving decisive and highly fresh, even if the body remains compact and linear up through a lively, vibrant finish. The Podere Fortuni '15 features a more mature bouquet, with foregrounded fruit and spicy notes anticipating a nice body, though without excesses, subtle tannins and a sapid back palate.

● 1465 MCDLXV '15	♆♆	8
● Coldaia '16	♆♆	5
● Fortuni '15	♆♆	5
● 1465 MCDLXV '10	♆♆♆	8
● 1465 MCDLXV '12	♆♆	8
● 1465 MCDLXV '11	♆♆	8
● Coldaia '14	♆♆	5
● Coldaia '13	♆♆	5
● Coldaia '12	♆♆	5
● Coldaia '11	♆♆	5
● Fortuni '14	♆♆	5
● Fortuni '12	♆♆	5
● Fortuni '11	♆♆	6
● Fortuni '10	♆♆	6
○ Greto alla Macchia '16	♆♆	5
○ Greto alla Macchia '12	♆♆	5

Tenuta La Fortuna

LOC. LA FORTUNA, 83
53024 MONTALCINO [SI]
TEL. +39 0577848308
www.tenutalafortuna.it

CELLAR SALES
PRE-BOOKED VISITS
ANNUAL PRODUCTION 60,000 bottles
HECTARES UNDER VINE 18.00

Two main blocks of vineyards constitute the estate managed by siblings Angelo and Romina, the sixth generation of family to work at La Fortuna. The farmstead that lends its name to the winery is situated in the northeast part of Montalcino, while parcels acquired later can be found near Castelnuovo dell'Abate (to the southeast). These two areas, very different in pedoclimate, come together in a multivariate selection and intense, dynamic Brunellos (aged both in barriques and mid-sized barrels). The selection submitted by La Fortuna this year provides plenty of noteworthy wines, to say the least. We begin with a fresh and poised Rosso '17, a red that's far from the overripe suggestions that characterized many of the year's wines. Their Brunello '14 is just as nuanced in its hints of light fruit and medicinal herbs, it's pure but mobile palate. For those who prefer greater volume and tannic presence, there's the Brunello '13, Giobi and Riserva.

● Brunello di Montalcino '14	♟♟ 6
● Brunello di Montalcino Giobi '13	♟♟ 6
● Brunello di Montalcino Ris. '13	♟♟ 7
● Rosso di Montalcino '17	♟♟ 3
● Brunello di Montalcino '06	♟♟♟ 6
● Brunello di Montalcino '04	♟♟♟ 6
● Brunello di Montalcino '01	♟♟♟ 5
● Brunello di Montalcino '13	♟♟ 6
● Brunello di Montalcino '12	♟♟ 6
● Brunello di Montalcino '08	♟♟ 6
● Brunello di Montalcino Giobi '12	♟♟ 6
● Brunello di Montalcino Giobi '10	♟♟ 6
● Brunello di Montalcino Ris. '07	♟♟ 7
● Brunello di Montalcino Ris. '06	♟♟ 6
● Rosso di Montalcino '16	♟♟ 3
● Rosso di Montalcino '11	♟♟ 3

La Fralluca

LOC. BARBICONI, 153
57028 SUVERETO [LI]
TEL. +39 0565829076
www.lafralluca.com

CELLAR SALES
PRE-BOOKED VISITS
ANNUAL PRODUCTION 45,000 bottles
HECTARES UNDER VINE 10.00
SUSTAINABLE WINERY

Fralluca stands for Francesca and Luca (she from Pisa, he from Milan). Twelve years ago they married off into a hill near Suvereto. After renovating the property and its vineyards, they built a cellar and began producing wine with Sangiovese, Cabernet Franc, Syrah, Alicante, Bouschet, Viognier and Vermentino. Their wines, which are named after mythological characters who transformed into trees that grow in the area, are made with grapes cultivated according to sustainable principles. The Filemone '18 is a highly interesting Vermentino characterized by fresh, citrusy aromas of mandarin orange and lime accompanied by vegetal strokes of basil. On the palate it proves pleasant by virtue of a fresh acidity and nice structure, giving way to a sapid, well-sustained finish. The Pitis '15 is a monovarietal Syrah marked by intriguing aromas of pencil lead and quinine, hints of pepper and red berries. In the mouth it's dynamic, juicy and long, with crunchy tannins.

○ Elice '16	♟♟ 5
○ Filemone '18	♟♟ 3
● Pitis '15	♟♟ 5
● Suvereto Sangiovese Ciparisso '15	♟ 5
● Suvereto Sangiovese Ciparisso '12	♟♟ 5
○ Bauci '15	♟♟ 3
○ Bauci '14	♟♟ 3
● Cabernet Franc '15	♟♟ 6
● Cabernet Franc '14	♟♟ 5
● Cabernet Franc '13	♟♟ 5
● Fillide '15	♟♟ 3
● Fillide '14	♟♟ 3
● Fillide '12	♟♟ 3
● Pitis '14	♟♟ 5
○ Viognier Bauci '13	♟♟ 3

Frascole

LOC. FRASCOLE, 27A
50062 DICOMANO [FI]
TEL. +39 0558386340
www.frascole.it

CELLAR SALES
PRE-BOOKED VISITS
ACCOMMODATION
ANNUAL PRODUCTION 65,000 bottles
HECTARES UNDER VINE 16.00
VITICULTURE METHOD Certified Organic

We find Frascole on a small plateau between Val di Sieve and Mugello. It's a medieval hamlet built on pre-existing Etruscan/Roman settlements, surrounded by vineyards and olive groves tended to by Enrico and his wife, Elisa. Their selection centers on the Chianti Rufina appellation, and on extra-virgin oil. But there's also a bit of room for Merlot, Trebbiano and Pinot Nero, which are starting to bear fruit on this rough yet gentle land. The Pinot Nero '16 put in a strong debut in our finals. Aromatic herbs fuse with wild berries, generating fresh, subtle fragrances, while a pleasant, racy entry gives makes for a rich, though not opulent palate and an assertive finish. Their Chianti Rufina Riserva '16 is enticing, mineral. It has body and balance, as well as nice persistence. The 2017 features vegetal notes and cherry, then a substantive structure, coming through broad and harmonious. The Albis sulle bucce '16 is a meaty, flavorful monovarietal Trebbiano.

● Chianti Rufina Ris. '16	♛♛♛ 3*
● Pinot Nero '16	♛♛♛ 4
● Chianti Rufina '17	♛♛ 2*
○ In Albis '16	♛♛ 3
○ In Albis sulle bucce '16	♛♛ 5
● Bitornino '16	♛♛ 2*
● Bitornino '15	♛♛ 2*
● Chianti Rufina '16	♛♛ 2*
● Chianti Rufina '14	♛♛ 2*
● Chianti Rufina '13	♛♛ 2*
● Chianti Rufina Ris. '15	♛♛ 3
● Chianti Rufina Ris. '14	♛♛ 3
● Chianti Rufina Ris. '12	♛♛ 3*
○ In Albis sulle bucce '15	♛♛ 5
○ Passito '02	♛♛ 8

★Frescobaldi

VIA SANTO SPIRITO, 11
50125 FIRENZE
TEL. +39 05527141
www.frescobaldi.it

CELLAR SALES
PRE-BOOKED VISITS
ANNUAL PRODUCTION 7,500,000 bottles
HECTARES UNDER VINE 923.00
SUSTAINABLE WINERY

An ancient coat of arms represents a millennium-long tradition (winemaking began 300 years after its founding). In subsequent centuries, 6 more estates in Tuscany would follow, and today the commitment continues. In addition to their vineyards and wines, which express the region's diversity, they have other initiatives. For example, there's their island winemaking project on Gorgona, whose social value is another feather in the cap for the family. The intriguing Ris. Vecchie Viti '16 features notes of earth, tanned leather, Mediterranean scrub and cherry. On the palate it's delicate, elegant and well-balanced, closing long and full. Tre Bicchieri. The Montesodi '16, a monovarietal Sangiovese, unfolds with spicy notes accompanying wild berries. In the mouth it's pervasive, juicy and delicately tannic. The Pinot Nero '16 impresses for its fragrances of blueberry and aromatic herbs. Considering all the family's accomplishments, for us Frescobaldi is the the 'Winery of the Year'.

● Chianti Rufina Nipozzano V. V. Ris. '16	♛♛♛ 5
● Montesodi '16	♛♛ 6
● Mormoreto '16	♛♛ 8
● Pomino Pinot Nero '16	♛♛ 4
● Castiglioni '16	♛♛ 4
● Chianti Cl. Gran Selezione Rialzi Tenuta Perano '16	♛♛ 5
● Chianti Cl. Tenuta Perano Ris. '16	♛♛ 5
● Chianti Rufina Nipozzano Ris. '16	♛♛ 4
● Giramonte '15	♛♛ 8
● Lamaione '14	♛♛ 8
○ Pomino Bianco Benefizio Ris. '17	♛♛ 5
○ Pomino Brut Leonia '15	♛♛ 6
Pomino Vin Santo '10	♛♛ 6
● Chianti Rufina Nipozzano V. V. Ris. '13	♛♛♛ 5
● Montesodi '15	♛♛♛ 6

Fuligni

VIA SALONI, 33
53024 MONTALCINO [SI]
TEL. +39 0577848710
www.fuligni.it

CELLAR SALES
PRE-BOOKED VISITS
ANNUAL PRODUCTION 52,000 bottles
HECTARES UNDER VINE 12.00

Elevations of almost 450 meters are well protected by the nearby sea's humid air currents, while the soil is lean and stony — the Fulgini family operates in a unique territory. Here in Cottimelli, which connects the Montalcino hills to the northern slopes, pedoclimatic conditions make for an area well suited to vine growing. Indeed, the various parcels are fermented separately, making for dense, expressive Sangiovese reds aged in mid-size casks and barrels. This year Fulgini's selection exhibits a nice crescendo. If their Rosso Ginestreto '17 features youthful impetuosity, their Brunello '14 expresses the house style with great coherence, offering up aromas of light fruit, medicinal herbs, laurel and a citrus vein that's even more pronounced on its tapered palate. It's a profile that's even more deeply expressed in their Brunello Ris. 13, a wine that's only a bit held back by rough acidity and tannins.

● Brunello di Montalcino Ris. '13	♟♟ 8
● Brunello di Montalcino '14	♟♟ 6
○ Rosso di Montalcino Ginestreto '17	♟ 4
● Brunello di Montalcino '10	♟♟♟ 6
● Brunello di Montalcino Ris. '01	♟♟♟ 8
● Brunello di Montalcino Ris. '97	♟♟♟ 8
● Brunello di Montalcino '13	♟♟ 6
● Brunello di Montalcino '12	♟♟ 6
● Brunello di Montalcino '11	♟♟ 6
● Brunello di Montalcino '09	♟♟ 6
● Brunello di Montalcino '08	♟♟ 6
● Brunello di Montalcino '07	♟♟ 6
● Brunello di Montalcino Ris. '12	♟♟ 8
● Brunello di Montalcino Ris. '07	♟♟ 8
● Rosso di Montalcino Ginestreto '15	♟♟ 4
● Rosso di Montalcino Ginestreto '13	♟♟ 4
● S. J. '12	♟♟ 3

★Tenuta di Ghizzano

FRAZ. GHIZZANO
VIA DELLA CHIESA, 4
56037 PECCIOLI [PI]
TEL. +39 0587630096
www.tenutadighizzano.com

CELLAR SALES
PRE-BOOKED VISITS
ACCOMMODATION
ANNUAL PRODUCTION 80,000 bottles
HECTARES UNDER VINE 20.00
VITICULTURE METHOD Certified Organic

Tenuta di Ghizzano, one of Pisa's oldest agricultural producers, is an enchanted place that spans 300 hectares total, 20 of which are vineyards, and 20 of which are olive groves. The rest are dedicated to grains and, especially, woods, making for a balanced landscape. It comes as no surprise, therefore, that they've chosen certified organic and biodynamic cultivation. Their wines shine increasingly bright for their authenticity and grace, a good indication of their commitment and path forward. The new Nambrot needs a bit more time, so we'll review it in the next edition of Italian Wines. For now we'll settle for enjoying a Veneroso '16 that's truly super in its originality and class. This blend of Sangiovese and Cabernet mixes aromas of small black berry fruits and herbs, spices and sensations of rain-soaked earth. On the palate it's steady, velvety almost all the way through, just closed by assertive tannins.

● Terre di Pisa Veneroso '16	♟♟ 5
● Il Ghizzano Rosso '17	♟♟ 3
○ Il Ghizzano Bianco '18	♟ 4
● Nambrot '09	♟♟♟ 6
● Nambrot '08	♟♟♟ 6
● Nambrot '06	♟♟♟ 6
● Nambrot '05	♟♟♟ 6
● Nambrot '04	♟♟♟ 6
● Nambrot '03	♟♟♟ 6
● Terre di Pisa Nambrot '15	♟♟♟ 6
● Terre di Pisa Nambrot '13	♟♟♟ 6
● Terre di Pisa Nambrot '12	♟♟♟ 6
● Veneroso '10	♟♟♟ 5
● Veneroso '07	♟♟♟ 5
● Veneroso '04	♟♟♟ 5

Marchesi Ginori Lisci

Fraz. Ponteginori
Loc. Querceto
56040 Montecatini Val di Cecina [PI]
Tel. +39 058837443
www.marchesiginorilisci.it

CELLAR SALES
ACCOMMODATION AND RESTAURANT SERVICE
ANNUAL PRODUCTION 35,000 bottles
HECTARES UNDER VINE 17.00
VITICULTURE METHOD Certified Organic

Marchesi Ginori Lisci is situated halfway between Volterra and the sea. On the upper part of the hill, around Querceto castle, we find a medieval hamlet where it's still possible to lodge. This is the heart of the Ginori Lisci family's property. Over the past 20 years, their vineyards have undergone transformations, like new plots and a new cellar, which have contributed to its becoming a modern winery where Merlot, Cabernet Sauvignon, Sangiovese, Viognier and Vermentino are all cultivated. Their delicious Castello Ginori '16 delights with its notes of aromatic herbs, mint and rosemary, giving way to hints of blackcurrant and blueberries. On the palate it exhibits power, but not in excess, coming through pervasive, with nicely balanced tannins and alcohol followed by a juicy finish. The pencil lead, cherry and tobacco-scented Poderi Novi '16 performed well, proving rich, potent and full of vitality on the palate.

Giodo

Loc. Piazzini
53011 Montalcino [SI]
Tel. +39
carlo.ferrini27@gmail.com

ANNUAL PRODUCTION 8,000 bottles
HECTARES UNDER VINE 2.50
SUSTAINABLE WINERY

Carlo Ferrini and family's small property is situated in the heart of southern Montalcino, along the road that connects Sant'Angelo in Colle to Sant'Antimo, at elevations ranging from 300 to 400 meters. The celebrated winemaker personally chose the estate after extensive research in pursuit of agreeably modern Sangioveses, extrovert but rigorous, consistent but with some backbone. His wines leave technical details in the background so as to highlight the painstaking care that goes into their entire selection. In the last round of tastings we tried a Giodo Rosso '17 that impresses right out of the gate thanks to its aromatic profile of red fruit and balsams, the prelude to a soft, enfolding and highly pleasant palate. But it was their Brunello that most impressed. The 2014 is a bit less multifaceted with respect to its best years, but it's still a benchmark for clarity and structural soundness.

● Montescudaio Merlot Castello Ginori '16	🍷🍷 3*
● Montescudaio Cabernet Macchion del Lupo '17	🍷🍷 3
● Montescudaio Merlot Campordigno '17	🍷🍷 2*
● Poderi Novi Syrah '16	🍷🍷 5
○ Virgola Vermentino '18	🍷🍷 2*
⊙ Bacio Rosato '18	🍷 2
● Montescudaio Cabernet Macchion del Lupo '16	🍷🍷 3
● Montescudaio Cabernet Macchion del Lupo '14	🍷🍷 3*
● Montescudaio Cabernet Macchion del Lupo '13	🍷🍷 3
● Montescudaio Merlot Campordigno '16	🍷🍷 2*
● Montescudaio Merlot Castello Ginori '15	🍷🍷 3*
● Montescudaio Merlot Castello Ginori '14	🍷🍷 2*
● Montescudaio Rosso Campordigno '15	🍷🍷 2*

● Brunello di Montalcino Giodo '14	🍷🍷 8
● Giodo '17	🍷🍷 6
● Brunello di Montalcino Giodo '13	🍷🍷🍷 8
● Brunello di Montalcino Giodo '12	🍷🍷🍷 8
● Brunello di Montalcino Giodo '11	🍷🍷🍷 8
● Giodo '16	🍷🍷 6
● Giodo '15	🍷🍷 6
● Giodo '13	🍷🍷 6

Giusti & Zanza Vigneti

A DEI PUNTONI, 9
6043 FAUGLIA [PI]
EL. +39 058544354
www.igiustiezanza.it

CELLAR SALES
PRE-BOOKED VISITS
ACCOMMODATION
ANNUAL PRODUCTION 100,000 bottles
HECTARES UNDER VINE 17.00
VITICULTURE METHOD Certified Organic

This notable winery, founded in the 1990s, is a benchmark for the wines of the Tuscan coast. It belongs to the Giusti family and is situated in Fuaglia, along the hills that run from Pisa to Livorno. Their vineyards grow in clay-sandy soil (with a presence of gravel), and give rise to wines that, after a few years in slight decline, seem to have rebounded and are going through a comforting stage of stylistic consolidation. They're modern, though without renouncing a certain territorial identity. Their Dulcamara blend once again emerged as our favorite of the lot. The 2016 delivers thanks to its focused, dark aromas that are anything but redundant. To the contrary, its vegetal sensations and hints of rain-soaked leaves are delicate, accompanying a remarkable array of black fruit embellished by spicy nuances. The Nemorino '18 is aromatically intriguing and sapid on the palate, a jolly blend of Syrah and smaller shares Sangiovese, Merlot and Alicante.

Marchesi Gondi - Tenuta Bossi

LOC. BOSSI
VIA DELLO STRACCHINO, 32
50065 PONTASSIEVE [FI]
TEL. +39 0558317830
www.tenutabossi.com

CELLAR SALES
PRE-BOOKED VISITS
ACCOMMODATION
ANNUAL PRODUCTION 50,000 bottles
HECTARES UNDER VINE 19.00

We could define the Gondi family a piece of living history. They've owned the Bossi estate since the 16th century and continue with constance and commitment to develop its agricultural activities, concentrating especially on wine production. Bernardo Gondi, who's helped by his sons and his sister, owns the winery. Their products reflect a constant attention to tradition, though without forgoing innovation in the vineyard and cellar. Their Ris. Villa Bossi '16 landed a place in our finals by virtue of its fresh, clear, focused bouquet of cherry, blueberry together with balsamic hints. It exhibits a firm, but not weighty, body, delicate and well-integrate tannins, and a tasty finish. The Fiammae '16, a monovarietal Sangiovese made partially with dried grapes, offers up mature aromas, of plums and blackberries followed by mineral hints and slightly spicy notes. A succulent, well-layered structure follows before closing soft and long.

Dulcamara '16	♟♟ 8
Nemorino Rosso '18	♟♟ 5
Perbruno '17	♟♟ 6
Belcore '17	♟ 6
VignaVecchia '16	♟ 8
● Belcore '15	♟♟ 3
Belcore '13	♟♟ 3
Dulcamara '15	♟♟ 5
Dulcamara '13	♟♟ 5
Dulcamara '12	♟♟ 5
Nemorino Rosso '16	♟♟ 2*
Nemorino Rosso '15	♟♟ 2*
Perbruno '16	♟♟ 4
Perbruno '15	♟♟ 4
Perbruno '13	♟♟ 4

● Chianti Rufina Villa Bossi Ris. '16	♟♟ 4
● Chianti Rufina Pian dei Sorbi Ris. '16	♟♟ 3
● Chianti Rufina San Giuliano '17	♟♟ 3
● Fiammae '16	♟♟ 8
● Mazzaferrata '13	♟♟ 4
● Ser Amerigo '13	♟♟ 4
○ Sassobianco '18	♟ 2
● Chianti Rufina Pian dei Sorbi Ris. '15	♟♟ 3
● Chianti Rufina Pian dei Sorbi Ris. '12	♟♟ 3
● Chianti Rufina Pian dei Sorbi Ris. '11	♟♟ 3
● Chianti Rufina San Giuliano '16	♟♟ 2*
● Chianti Rufina San Giuliano '12	♟♟ 2*
● Mazzaferrata '09	♟♟ 4
○ Vin Santo del Chianti Rufina Cardinal de Retz Ris. '04	♟♟ 5
○ Vin Santo del Chianti Rufina Cardinal de Rez '06	♟♟ 5

★Grattamacco

LOC. LUNGAGNANO
57022 CASTAGNETO CARDUCCI [LI]
TEL. +39 0565765069
www.collemassari.it

CELLAR SALES
PRE-BOOKED VISITS
ANNUAL PRODUCTION 120,000 bottles
HECTARES UNDER VINE 16.00
VITICULTURE METHOD Certified Organic
SUSTAINABLE WINERY

Grattamacco is one of Bolgheri's star brands, a winery with a glorious, pioneering history behind them, and a radiant present. Founded in the 1970s, today the producer is masterfully (it must be said) managed by the Tipa brothers. As of late the property has been enlarged, and technically they appear to be living through a state of grace. Their vineyards, which are surrounded by woods, span various types of soil (though primarily sand and calcareous-marl). Their wines are as intriguing as they are complex. Their pair of Bolgheri Superiores is rock-solid. 2016 made for a Grattamacco marked by intensity, texture and complexity. It still exhibits its usual finesse, but with above-average aging power. Extraordinary. Their Alberello '16 is also exceptionally good — extremely fine in its aromas of small red berries — delicious and unpredictable in its vegetal-balsamic background, and bubbling with gustatory tension. We should also point out a successful Vermentino '17.

● Bolgheri Rosso Sup. Grattamacco '16	▼▼▼	8
● Bolgheri Rosso Sup. L'Alberello '16	▼▼	8
○ Bolgheri Vermentino '17	▼▼	5
● Bolgheri Rosso Sup. Grattamacco '05	♈♈♈	7
● Bolgheri Rosso Sup. Grattamacco '04	♈♈♈	7
● Bolgheri Sup. Grattamacco '15	♈♈♈	8
● Bolgheri Sup. Grattamacco '14	♈♈♈	8
● Bolgheri Sup. Grattamacco '13	♈♈♈	8
● Bolgheri Sup. Grattamacco '12	♈♈♈	8
● Bolgheri Sup. Grattamacco '10	♈♈♈	7
● Bolgheri Sup. Grattamacco '09	♈♈♈	7
● Bolgheri Sup. Grattamacco '07	♈♈♈	7
● Bolgheri Sup. Grattamacco '06	♈♈♈	7
● Bolgheri Sup. L'Alberello '11	♈♈♈	6

Guado al Melo

LOC. MURROTTO, 130A
57022 CASTAGNETO CARDUCCI [LI]
TEL. +39 0565763238
www.guadoalmelo.it

CELLAR SALES
PRE-BOOKED VISITS
ANNUAL PRODUCTION 120,000 bottles
HECTARES UNDER VINE 15.00
SUSTAINABLE WINERY

Michele Scienza's Guado al Melo is one of Bolgheri's most notable producers, even (and especially) considering the number of varieties cultivated (both Mediterranean and Caucasian). There's no shortage of experimentation, and it couldn't be any other way, considering the prestige the family enjoys in the world of Italian science. The lion's share of their vineyard are situated in a valley in the Bolgheri foothills, the rest are further west. The style of their wines is rigorous, clean, of impeccable extraction and texture. Their Criseo '17 confirms it's a top-notch white, almost Burgundian in its profile. The base level version comes from a vineyard whose various grapes are cultivated, harvested and fermented all together. On the nose it's truly elegant, smooth and precise, but by no means algid. On the palate it exhibits similar qualities, proving buttery and floral, finishing on a pleasant sensation of bitter almond. The recent reds tasted were less convincing.

○ Bolgheri Bianco Criseo '17	▼▼▼	
● Bolgheri Rosso Rute '17	▼	
● Bolgheri Rosso Sup. Atis '16	▼	
● Jassarte '16	▼	
● Bolgheri Rosso Sup. Atis '12	♈♈♈	
○ Bolgheri Bianco Criseo '16	♈♈	
● Bolgheri Rosso Antillo '15	♈♈	
● Bolgheri Rosso Rute '15	♈♈	
● Bolgheri Rosso Rute '13	♈♈	
● Bolgheri Rosso Sup. Atis '13	♈♈	
● Jassarte '15	♈♈	

Tenuta Guado al Tasso

Loc. Bolgheri
s.da Bolgherese km 3,9
57020 Castagneto Carducci [LI]
Tel. +39 0565749735
www.guadoaltasso.it

CELLAR SALES
ANNUAL PRODUCTION 1,500,000 bottles
HECTARES UNDER VINE 300.00

The Atinori family's Bolgheri estate comprises about a thousand hectares of terrain amidst vineyards, woods and Mediterranean scrub. Obviously this important, historic family have adopted the same approach and style as that of their main estate, resulting in impeccable and territorially correct wines. Naturally, it all starts with the vineyard and the grapes cultivated: Merlot, Cabernet Sauvignon, Petit Verdot and Sangiovese for their reds, and Vermentino especially for their whites. And it was a Vermentino, the 2018, that proved to be one of the more convincing wines in their selection. It's a delicate and floral wine with nice verve and a pleasant, elegant palate that's never too bitter or rich in alcohol. The reds tasted made for something of a chiaroscuro, with the Bolgheri Cont'Ugo 2016 emerging as our favorite. It's not a monument of vigor and dynamism, but it has its balance and completeness. We found the rest of the selection tasted to be fair.

Bolgheri Rosso Cont'Ugo '16	♈♈ 6
Bolgheri Rosso Guado al Tasso '16	♈♈ 8
Bolgheri Vermentino '18	♈♈ 3
Bolgheri Rosato Scalabrone '18	♈ 3
Bolgheri Rosso Il Bruciato '17	♈ 5
Bolgheri Sup. Guado al Tasso '01	♈♈♈ 8
Bolgheri Sup. Guado al Tasso '90	♈♈♈ 8
Bolgheri Rosato Scalabrone '16	♈♈ 3
Bolgheri Rosso Il Bruciato '16	♈♈ 5
Bolgheri Rosso Il Bruciato '15	♈♈ 5
Bolgheri Rosso Il Bruciato '14	♈♈ 5
Bolgheri Rosso Il Bruciato '13	♈♈ 5
Bolgheri Rosso Sup. Guado al Tasso '15	♈♈ 8
Bolgheri Sup. Guado al Tasso '13	♈♈ 8
Bolgheri Sup. Guado al Tasso '12	♈♈ 8
Bolgheri Vermentino '14	♈♈ 3

Gualdo del Re

Loc. Notri, 77
57028 Suvereto [LI]
Tel. +39 0565829888
www.gualdodelre.it

CELLAR SALES
PRE-BOOKED VISITS
ACCOMMODATION AND RESTAURANT SERVICE
ANNUAL PRODUCTION 100,000 bottles
HECTARES UNDER VINE 20.00
VITICULTURE METHOD Certified Organic

In the 1990s, Nico Rossi returned to the family winery and, accompanied by his wife (and now their children, as well), he transformed it into a modern example of ecological, quality viticulture. Thanks to his commitment, it supported the area's enological renaissance, while also endowing Gualdo del Re's wines with a clear identity. Red grapes from Sangiovese to Merlot, Cabernet Sauvignon and Franc are grown, as well as Aleatico. Pinot Bianco and Vermentino are the white grapes cultivated. The Quinto Re '16, a monovarietal Merlot, is introduced by jammy notes of blackberry and blackcurrant softened by spicy hints of cloves. On the palate it enters bold and broad, with nice pervasiveness. Tannins are silky and soft, with compelling flavor making for a truly long finish. The Eliseo '16 proves fresh and potent on the nose, marked by a foreground of raspberries and cherry. In the mouth it comes through dynamic and fluid, with adequate acidic vigor.

● Quinto Re '16	♈♈♈ 8
● Cabraia '16	♈♈ 6
○ Eliseo Rosso '16	♈♈ 3
● Suvereto Sangiovese Il Guardo '16	♈♈ 5
○ Valentina '18	♈♈ 3
☉ Shiny Rosato '18	♈ 3
● Val di Cornia Rosso I'Rennero '05	♈♈♈ 6
● Val di Cornia Rosso I'Rennero '01	♈♈♈ 7
● Cabraia '12	♈♈ 6
○ Eliseo Rosso '15	♈♈ 3
● Federico Primo '12	♈♈ 5
● Suvereto Merlot I'Rennero '15	♈♈ 5
● Suvereto Sangiovese Gualdo del Re '15	♈♈ 5
● Val di Cornia Rosso I'Rennero '12	♈♈ 7
● Val di Cornia Sangiovese Gualdo del Re '12	♈♈ 5
○ Vermentino Valentina '14	♈♈ 3

Conte Guicciardini

Loc. Poppiano
via Fezzana, 45/49
50025 Montespertoli [FI]
Tel. +39 05582315
www.conteguicciardini.it

CELLAR SALES
PRE-BOOKED VISITS
ANNUAL PRODUCTION 270,000 bottles
HECTARES UNDER VINE 130.00
SUSTAINABLE WINERY

Conte Guicciardini has ancient origins, with the Poppiano castle (their main site) going back to 1199. It's a true piece of history, considering that even back then they grew wine grapes here (a documented fact). Today the property is owned by Ferdinando Guicciardini, who's enlarged production. In addition to being one of the first to believe in Morellino, he also recently purchased an estate in Chianti Classico. The Syrah '17 opens with aromas of juniper and pepper, raspberry and blackcurrant, as well leathery hints. A firmly-structured but supple body follows, without excesses. Delicate tannins and proper acidity make for a clean, well-sustained finish. The interesting La Hystoria '16, a Merlot, plays on aromatic pleasantness with its balsamic, mineral hints before impressing with its pervasive (though not oppressive) body, refreshing acidity and focused finish. The Toscoforte '16, a Sangiovese, proves pleasantly fruity, characterized by a smooth, supple body.

● Syrah Castello di Poppiano '17	▼▼ 4
● Chianti Cl. Gran Selezione Il Tabernacolo Belvedere Campoli '15	▼▼ 6
● La Histuria Castello di Poppiano '16	▼▼ 5
● Morellino di Scansano Carbonile Massi di Mandorlaia '18	▼▼ 2*
● Toscoforte Castello di Poppiano '16	▼▼ 4
● Chianti Cl. Belvedere Campoli '17	▼ 4
● Chianti Cl. Principe Guicciardini Ris. Belvedere Campoli '15	▼ 5
● Chianti Colli Fiorentini Il Cortile Castello di Poppiano '17	▼ 3
● Chianti Colli Fiorentini Ris. Castello di Poppiano '16	▼ 4
● Maremma Toscana Scorfano Rosso Massi di Mandorlaia '18	▼ 3
● Morellino di Scansano Ris. Massi di Mandorlaia '16	▼ 4

Guicciardini Strozzi

Loc. Cusona, 5
53037 San Gimignano [SI]
Tel. +39 0577950028
www.guicciardinistrozzi.it

CELLAR SALES
PRE-BOOKED VISITS
ANNUAL PRODUCTION 500,000 bottles
HECTARES UNDER VINE 100.00

Theirs is a family history deeply bound to wine, one that began more than a thousand years ago on the 530-hectare Tenuta di Cusona, situated on the hills around San Gimignano (it's joined today by property in Maremma and Pantelleria). The turning point came in the early 20th century, when Francesco Guicciardini, minister of agriculture and later mayor of Florence, created the groundwork for a modern winery. Today it forges ahead thanks to the efforts of his grandson, and the winery's current owner, Girolamo Strozzi, who's brought out its production potential. The Vernaccia Riserva '16 is marked by classic notes of mature apple and almond, entering austere on the palate, where it shows a full structure and lovely freshness before closing long and sapid. The Vin Santo '09 features sensations of dried fruit and nuts, hazelnut and almond, accompanied by candied citrus. In the mouth it's smooth, soft, sweet and enticing with nice density and a delicately spicy aftertaste.

● Chianti Colli Senesi Titolato Strozzi '18	▼▼
○ San Gimignano Vin Santo '09	▼▼
○ Vernaccia di San Gimignano Ris. '16	▼▼
○ Arabesque '18	▼
○ Vernaccia di S. Gimignano Titolato Strozzi '18	▼
● Millanni '99	♈♈♈
○ Arabesque '17	♈♈
● Millanni '12	♈♈
● Sòdole '11	♈♈
○ Vernaccia di S. Gimignano '16	♈♈
○ Vernaccia di S. Gimignano Ris. '15	♈♈
○ Vernaccia di S. Gimignano Ris. '14	♈♈
○ Vernaccia di S. Gimignano Ris. '13	♈♈
○ Vernaccia di S. Gimignano Titolato Strozzi '16	♈♈

★★Isole e Olena

Loc. Isole, 1
50021 Barberino Val d'Elsa [FI]
Tel. +39 0558072763
www.isoleolena.it

CELLAR SALES
PRE-BOOKED VISITS
ANNUAL PRODUCTION 250,000 bottles
HECTARES UNDER VINE 56.00

Paolo De Marchi is a vigneron deeply committed to understanding the territory, and his wines are among Chianti Classico's most esteemed. Independent of the cultivars used, his selection proves capable of exhibiting personality and coherence, consistently earning it a place among the appellation's best. Theirs is an established style that pursues elegance, brought out by the generally discerning use of oak. Aromatic complexity accompanies an invigorating palate that's full of contrasts. Toasty and smoky notes accompanied by elegant fruity and floral hints feature in their Cepparello '16, which offers up its best on the palate, where it proves lean, dynamic and quite flavorful. The well-made Chianti Classico '16 exhibits a not banal aromatic profile, foremost flowery sensations, as well as lively, juicy, enticing flavor. The fragrant and intense Syrah Collezione Privata '16 is also well-crafted.

Cepparello '16	▼▼▼	8
● Chianti Cl. '16	▼▼	5
● Collezione Privata Syrah '16	▼▼	8
Collezione Privata Cabernet Sauvignon '15	▼	8
● Cepparello '15	♀♀♀	8
● Cepparello '13	♀♀♀	8
● Cepparello '12	♀♀♀	8
● Cepparello '09	♀♀♀	8
● Cepparello '07	♀♀♀	8
● Cepparello '06	♀♀♀	8
● Cepparello '05	♀♀♀	8
● Cepparello '03	♀♀♀	7
● Cepparello '01	♀♀♀	6
● Cepparello '00	♀♀♀	6
● Cepparello '99	♀♀♀	6
● Cepparello '98	♀♀♀	6

Istine

Loc. Istine
53017 Radda in Chianti [SI]
Tel. +39 0577733684
www.istine.it

CELLAR SALES
PRE-BOOKED VISITS
ANNUAL PRODUCTION 45,000 bottles
HECTARES UNDER VINE 26.00
VITICULTURE METHOD Certified Organic

Istine is one of the loveliest producers to emerge in Chianti Classico as of late. Maximum attention is paid to the territory's wines, starting with separate vinification for Sangiovese (according to the vineyard of origin). They avail themselves of 3 crus: Vigna Istine (Radda in Chianti), Vigna Casanova (Radda in Chianti) and Vigna Cavarchione (Gaiole in Chianti). Angela Fronti, who oversees the producer, proves to have precise ideas, as is testified to by a selection of wines aged in large wood barrels and characterized by a clear, coherent territorial identity. Their generally floral-scented Chianti Classico Vigna Istine '17 stands out for its characterful earthy sensations. On the palate it unfolds assertively, coming through juicy and sapid. Their Chianti Classico Casanova dell'Aia '17 exhibits the same flavorful and pleasant gustatory profile, though aromatically it's a bit too oak-laden. The highly drinkable and pleasant Chianti Classico '17 also performed well.

● Chianti Cl. V. Istine '17	▼▼	3*
● Chianti Cl. '17	▼▼	3
● Chianti Cl. Casanova dell'Aia '17	▼▼	4
● Chianti Cl. Le Vigne Ris. '16	▼▼	4
● Chianti Cl. V. Cavarchione '17	▼▼	5
● Chianti Cl. Le Vigne Ris. '13	♀♀♀	3*
● Chianti Cl. V. Cavarchione '16	♀♀♀	5
● Chianti Cl. V. Istine '15	♀♀♀	3*
● Chianti Cl. '16	♀♀	3
● Chianti Cl. '15	♀♀	3
● Chianti Cl. '14	♀♀	3*
● Chianti Cl. Le Vigne Ris. '15	♀♀	3*
● Chianti Cl. Le Vigne Ris. '14	♀♀	3
● Chianti Cl. V. Casanova '14	♀♀	3
● Chianti Cl. V. Cavarchione '15	♀♀	3*
● Chianti Cl. V. Istine '16	♀♀	3
● Chianti Cl. V. Istine '14	♀♀	3

Lamole di Lamole

LOC. LAMOLE
50022 GREVE IN CHIANTI [FI]
TEL. +39 0559331256
www.lamole.com

CELLAR SALES
PRE-BOOKED VISITS
RESTAURANT SERVICE
ANNUAL PRODUCTION 294,000 bottles
HECTARES UNDER VINE 57.00
SUSTAINABLE WINERY

Veneto's Santa Margherita group is one Italy's most important producers, with land holdings throughout the country. In Tuscany they own producers in Chianti Classico, Lamole di Lamole (in Greve in Chianti) and Villa Vistarenni, in Gaiole. Despite the production volumes, their Chianti wines are characterized by a modern style, especially when it comes to their Lamole selection. Hallmarks include clear personality and territorial identity — they're austere but never banal. Both large barrels and in small casks are used for aging. The Chianti Classico Etichetta Bianca '16 stands out for its lovely aromatic finesse, with red berries alternating with flowers, hints of grass and flint adorned by spices. On the palate it does even better, proving sapid, energetic and full of contrast before giving way to a rising finish. The solid Chianti Classico Etichetta Blu '17 is more aromatically approachable and fruit-forward, but equally delectable and drinkable.

Lanciola

FRAZ. POZZOLATICO
VIA IMPRUNETANA, 210
50023 IMPRUNETA [FI]
TEL. +39 055208324
www.lanciola.it

CELLAR SALES
PRE-BOOKED VISITS
ANNUAL PRODUCTION 250,000 bottles
HECTARES UNDER VINE 40.00

Situated just a few kilometers from Florence, on the hills of Impruneta, we find the Guarnieri family's winery. At the time of the Medicis it was owned by the Ricci family, to whom its roots in agriculture and wine can be traced. The recently acquired Villa Le Masse, situated in the heart of Chianti comprises 14 hectares of vineyards Several different grape varieties are cultivated on the two properties, even if Sangiovese dominates, and a number of different wines are produced. Their Chianti Classico wines most impressed, all from the same year (2016) but three different typologies. The Chianti Classico stands out for its bouquet of red berries, spicy notes of cloves and cinnamon, and a supple body marked by delicate tannins. The Riserva for its tertiaries of tanned leather and tobacco, and a full structure with discernible, but not excessive, tannins. The Gran Selezione for its aromas of blood-rich meat, its full attack and balanced acidity.

● Chianti Cl. Lamole di Lamole Et. Bianca '16	▼▼▼ 3*
● Chianti Cl. Lamole di Lamole Et. Blu '17	▼▼ 3*
● Chianti Cl. Gran Selezione Vign. di Campolungo '15	▼▼ 5
● Chianti Cl. Ris. '15	▼▼ 5
● Chianti Cl. Gran Sel. Vign. di Campolungo '10	♈♈♈ 5
● Chianti Cl. Lamole di Lamole Et. Bianca '13	♈♈♈ 3*
● Chianti Cl. Lamole di Lamole Et. Blu '15	♈♈♈ 3*
● Chianti Cl. Lamole di Lamole Et. Blu '14	♈♈♈ 3*
● Chianti Cl. Lamole di Lamole Et. Blu '12	♈♈♈ 3*

● Chianti Cl. Le Masse di Greve '16	▼▼ 4
● Chianti Cl. Le Masse di Greve Gran Selezione '16	▼▼ 4
● Chianti Cl. Le Masse di Greve Ris. '16	▼▼ 4
○ Ricciobianco Chardonnay '18	▼ 4
● Ricciotto Canaiolo '16	▼ 4
3	
● Chianti Cl. Le Masse di Greve '15	♈♈ 4
● Chianti Cl. Le Masse di Greve Ris. '12	♈♈ 4
● Chianti Colli Fiorentini Lanciola '15	♈♈ 3
● Ricciotto '13	♈♈ 4
● Terricci '15	♈♈ 5
● Terricci '11	♈♈ 5
● Vin Santo del Chianti Cl. Occhio di Pernice '09	♈♈ 6
○ Vin Santo del Chianti Colli Fiorentini '09	♈♈ 6

La Lastra

FRAZ. SANTA LUCIA
VIA R. DE GRADA, 9
53037 SAN GIMIGNANO [SI]
TEL. +39 0577941781
www.lalastra.it

CELLAR SALES
PRE-BOOKED VISITS
ANNUAL PRODUCTION 58,000 bottles
HECTARES UNDER VINE 7.00
SUSTAINABLE WINERY

Some forty years ago, Nadia Betti and her husband, Renato, created this small winery, now divided into two properties. On the one hand there's olive cultivation, vineyards with Canaiolo Nero, Merlot and Cabernet Franc, and an agritourism. On the other there's a vineyard of Vernaccia, Sangiovese, Cabernet Sauvignon and Merlot (in San Gimignano). Both are overseen by a small group of friends and relatives who operate according to the same care, emphasis on research, ethical principles and respect for the environment. Their Rovaio '16, a blend of Sangiovese, Cabernet Sauvignon and Merlot put in a good performance. An intriguing aromatic profile sees notes of forest floor join with blackberries and blueberries, all adorned by enticing hints of pepper and cinnamon. A meaty, fleshy and sapid palate is accompanied by fresh, compelling acidity. The pleasant Vernaccia '18 is redolent of medicinal herbs and fruity strokes of apple, coming through smooth and tasty on the palate.

● Rovaio '16	♟♟ 4
○ Vernaccia di S. Gimignano '18	♟♟ 2*
○ Vernaccia di S. Gimignano Ris. '17	♟ 3
○ Vernaccia di S. Gimignano Ris. '09	♟♟♟ 3*
● Chianti Colli Senesi '15	♟♟ 2*
● Rovaio '11	♟♟ 4
○ Vernaccia di S. Gimignano '17	♟♟ 2*
○ Vernaccia di S. Gimignano '13	♟♟ 2*
○ Vernaccia di S. Gimignano Ris. '16	♟♟ 3*
○ Vernaccia di S. Gimignano Ris. '15	♟♟ 3*
○ Vernaccia di S. Gimignano Ris. '14	♟♟ 3*
○ Vernaccia di S. Gimignano Ris. '12	♟♟ 3*

Fattoria Lavacchio

LOC. LAVACCHIO
VIA DI MONTEFIESOLE, 55
50065 PONTASSIEVE [FI]
TEL. +39 0558317472
www.fattorialavacchio.com

CELLAR SALES
PRE-BOOKED VISITS
ACCOMMODATION AND RESTAURANT SERVICE
ANNUAL PRODUCTION 120,000 bottles
HECTARES UNDER VINE 25.00
VITICULTURE METHOD Certified Organic
SUSTAINABLE WINERY

40 years ago, a winery with more than 300 years of experience behind it fell into the hands of the Lotteros. They reorganized it, bringing about a major shift in the production of grapes, olives, wheat, vegetables and truffle. Today it's all carried out with the utmost respect for the environment. For example, to identify disease, they planted hundreds of roses in their vineyards. They also make a wine without added sulfite, yeast or tannins — sulphur content is regulated using physical means, not chemical. Their unusual Chianti Rufina Cedro '17 sees notes of earth, blood-rich meat and ink, then plums. A nice entrance on the palate follows — firm and fleshy, it expands at the back, where it's more relaxed. The Ris. Cedro '16 sees aromas of cherry and blackberries, then supple structure, with integrated tannins and lovely persistence. The Fontegalli '14 blend impresses with its spicy notes. On the palate it comes through soft and creamy, closing on enticing, fruity fragrances.

● Chianti Rufina Cedro '17	♟♟ 2*
● Chianti Rufina Cedro Ris. '16	♟♟ 3
● Chianti Rufina Ludiè '13	♟♟ 7
● Fontegalli '14	♟♟ 4
○ Oro del Cedro V. T. '16	♟♟ 4
○ Vin Santo del Chianti Rufina '14	♟♟ 4
● Chianti Puro '17	♟ 2
○ Pachar '18	♟ 3
○ Puro Bianco Frizzante '18	♟ 2
● Chianti Rufina Cedro '16	♟♟ 2*
● Chianti Rufina Cedro '15	♟♟ 2*
● Chianti Rufina Cedro Ris. '15	♟♟ 3
● Chianti Rufina Cedro Ris. '13	♟♟ 3
● Chianti Rufina Ludiè Bio '11	♟♟ 7
○ Vin Santo del Chianti Rufina '11	♟♟ 4

Podere Le Bèrne

LOC. CERVOGNANO
VIA POGGIO GOLO, 7
53045 MONTEPULCIANO [SI]
TEL. +39 0578767328
www.leberne.it

CELLAR SALES
ANNUAL PRODUCTION 25,000 bottles
HECTARES UNDER VINE 6.00

Andrea Natalini hasn't let all the accolades go to his head. He's working his Cervognano vineyards, one of Montepulciano's most important crus, with the same commitment and passion. By now his wines are characterized by a precise style. They're elegant and complex, unafraid to age, but at the same time highly drinkable, exhibiting a strong typicity and pronounced character. The Nobile di Montepulciano '16 sees floral hints emerge from a spicy background. In the mouth a richly flavored and elegant development features clear, sapid and well-placed tannins. Multifaceted aromas of walnutskin and date, iodine and honey light up their Vin Santo Occhio di Pernice '07, a wine that manages to deliver breadth and vitality without ever being cloying.

● Nobile di Montepulciano '16	♟♟♟ 3*
○ Vin Santo di Montepulciano Occhio di Pernice '07	♟♟ 7
○ Vin Santo di Montepulciano '10	♟♟ 6
● Nobile di Montepulciano Ris. '15	♟ 5
● Rosso di Montepulciano '18	♟ 2
● Nobile di Montepulciano '15	♟♟♟ 3*
● Nobile di Montepulciano '11	♟♟♟ 3*
● Nobile di Montepulciano '06	♟♟♟ 3
● Nobile di Montepulciano '14	♟♟ 3
● Nobile di Montepulciano Ris. '12	♟♟ 5
● Rosso di Montepulciano '16	♟♟ 2*
○ Vin Santo di Montepulciano Occhio di Pernice '06	♟♟ 7

Tenuta Lenzini

FRAZ. GRAGNANO
VIA DELLA CHIESA, 44
55012 CAPANNORI [LU]
TEL. +39 0583974037
www.tenutalenzini.it

CELLAR SALES
PRE-BOOKED VISITS
ACCOMMODATION
ANNUAL PRODUCTION 60,000 bottles
HECTARES UNDER VINE 14.00
VITICULTURE METHOD Certified Organic

Situated in Gragnano di Capannori, a gorgeous corner of the Lucchesi hills, Tenuta Lenzini is, by now, and established winery, both in quality terms and in identity/style. Their vineyards host grapes common to the area: Merlot, Cabernet Sauvignon, Syrah, Alicante Bouschet. It's an estate cultivated biodynamically, in harmony with many of territory's producers. In the cellar they also opt for a minimally-invasive approach: spontaneous fermentation, limited sulfite use (to say the least) and maturation that's never forced. Their Syrah is increasingly delicious and on the mark. The 2016 is dominated by jubilant red and black berries accompanied by delicate and punctual spicy strokes. Its commendable palate proves rhythmic, with impeccable extraction. The Poggio de' Paoli '16 features herbaceous notes that are almost spicy hot. A linear palate gives way to an acute, unpredictable finish. Their white Vermignon '18 is a decidedly aromatic wine.

● La Syrah '16	♟♟ 5
● Poggio de' Paoli '16	♟♟ 4
○ Vermignon '18	♟♟ 4
● Colline Lucchesi Merlot Casa e Chiesa '17	♟ 3
● La Syrah '15	♟♟ 5
● La Syrah '13	♟♟ 5
● Poggio de' Paoli '13	♟♟ 4
● Syrah '12	♟♟ 5
● Syrah '11	♟♟ 5
○ Vermignon '17	♟♟ 3
○ Vermignon '15	♟♟ 3
○ Vermignon '14	♟♟ 3

Leuta

Via Pietraia, 21
52044 Cortona [AR]
Tel. +39 3385033560
www.leuta.it

CELLAR SALES
PRE-BOOKED VISITS
ANNUAL PRODUCTION 25,000 bottles
HECTARES UNDER VINE 12.60

About 20 years ago owner Denis Zenis decided to change his life, leaving his work in finance and, together with Enzo Berlanda (a former classmate), moving from Trentino to Tuscany to begin making wine (a passion he'd inherited from his grandfather). It brought him to Cortona, and in 2000 the two partners founded the winery. Their production philosophy centers on respect for the territory and their grapes, while using modern technology to craft harmonious, contemporary wines. The 2,618 put in a very good performance. Balsamic and minty aromas arise amidst fragrances of blueberries and blackcurrant, all accompanied by spicy hints. On the palate it's rich, smooth in its tannins, marked by sensations of red berries like cherry, and slight hints of clove. Its structure is broad and soft, giving way to an enticing, long finish. The velvet-smooth Vin Santo '07 is characterized by aromas of dried fruit and nuts.

● Cortona Cabernet Franc 2,618 '16	♟♟ 6
● Cortona Merlot 1.618 '15	♟♟ 5
○ Cortona Vin Santo '07	♟♟ 8
● Tau '14	♟♟ 4
● Cortona Syrah 0,618 '16	♟ 5
● Cortona Cabernet Franc 2,618 '15	♟♟ 6
● Cortona Merlot 1,618 '13	♟♟ 5
● Cortona Merlot 1.618 '14	♟♟ 5
● Cortona Sangiovese Solitario '13	♟♟ 6
● Cortona Sangiovese Solitario '12	♟♟ 6
● Cortona Sangiovese Solitario di Leuta '14	♟♟ 6
● Cortona Syrah 0,618 '15	♟♟ 5
○ Cortona Vin Santo '06	♟♟ 8
○ Cortona Vin Santo '05	♟♟ 8
● Nautilus '15	♟♟ 8
● Tau '12	♟♟ 4

Tenuta di Lilliano

Loc. Lilliano, 8
53011 Castellina in Chianti [SI]
Tel. +39 0577743070
www.lilliano.com

CELLAR SALES
PRE-BOOKED VISITS
ACCOMMODATION
ANNUAL PRODUCTION 150,000 bottles
HECTARES UNDER VINE 36.00
VITICULTURE METHOD Certified Organic

Tenuta di Lilliano represents a piece of history in Chianti Classico. Purchased by the Ruspoli family in 1920 (who still own it), the first bottles and sales came in 1958. Today Lilliano, whose vineyards can be found on the hills of Castellina in Chianti, produces classically-styled wines in which elegance remains intact. It's worth noting that, in recent years, the winery undertook efforts to modernize their selection, though they never lost sight of a stylistic identity that privileges nuance over extractive power. Lush fruit, hints of licorice, vanilla and coffee grind stand out in the intense aromatic profile of the Chianti Classico Gran Selezione '16, a soft, dense and multi-layered wine with nice fragrance. Aromas of sweet and spicy fruit feature in their Chianti Classico '17, a wine characterized by soft a development and, like the previous, sweet sensations. The Chianti Classico Riserva '16 is dense, and marked by somewhat immoderate oak.

● Chianti Cl. Gran Selezione '16	♟♟♟ 5
● Chianti Cl. '17	♟♟ 3*
● Anagallis '15	♟♟ 5
● Chianti Cl. Ris. '16	♟♟ 5
● Chianti Cl. '10	♟♟♟ 3*
● Chianti Cl. '09	♟♟♟ 3
● Chianti Cl. E. Ruspoli Berlingieri Ris. '85	♟♟♟ 8
● Chianti Cl. Gran Sel. '14	♟♟♟ 6
● Chianti Cl. Gran Sel. '11	♟♟♟ 5
● Chianti Cl. Gran Sel. Ris. '10	♟♟♟ 6
● Chianti Cl. Ris. '15	♟♟♟ 5
● Chianti Cl. Ris. '13	♟♟♟ 5
● Chianti Cl. '16	♟♟ 3
● Chianti Cl. '15	♟♟ 3
● Chianti Cl. Gran Sel. '12	♟♟ 5
● Chianti Cl. Gran Selezione '15	♟♟ 5

Lisini

FRAZ. SANT'ANGELO IN COLLE
POD. CASANOVA
53024 MONTALCINO [SI]
TEL. +39 0577844040
www.lisini.com

CELLAR SALES
PRE-BOOKED VISITS
ANNUAL PRODUCTION 90,000 bottles
HECTARES UNDER VINE 21.00

Situated primarily around their main facility, along the road that connects Sesta and Sant'Angelo in Colle, the Lisini-Clementi family's estate occupies an important part of south Montalcino. It's a decidedly sunny area that gives rise to dense, rigorous Brunellos aged in mid-sized oak barrels, and that typically offer up their best after a lengthy stay in the bottle. This is particularly true of their Urgolaia cru, an enclave that distinct for its tufaceous, iron-rich soils. The authoritative selection submitted for tasting by Lisini put in one of its best performances of late. Their Riserva and Ugolaia constitute the perfect pair of Brunellos when it comes to 2013. But the wine that really impressed, surprising, was the 2014. It's slow on the primaries, then opens to multiple registers of Mediterranean, woody aromas, finding persistence and thrust in a balanced and receptive palate — one that's certainly not lacking in contrast.

● Brunello di Montalcino '14	▼▼ 6
● Brunello di Montalcino Ris. '13	▼▼ 7
● Brunello di Montalcino Ugolaia '13	▼▼ 8
● Rosso di Montalcino '17	▼▼ 4
● Brunello di Montalcino '90	♈♈♈ 5
● Brunello di Montalcino '88	♈♈♈ 5
● Brunello di Montalcino Ugolaia '06	♈♈♈ 8
● Brunello di Montalcino Ugolaia '04	♈♈♈ 8
● Brunello di Montalcino Ugolaia '01	♈♈♈ 8
● Brunello di Montalcino Ugolaia '00	♈♈♈ 7
● Brunello di Montalcino Ugolaia '91	♈♈♈ 7
● Brunello di Montalcino '13	♈♈ 6
● Brunello di Montalcino '12	♈♈ 6
● Brunello di Montalcino Ris. '12	♈♈ 7
● Brunello di Montalcino Ris. '10	♈♈ 7
● Brunello di Montalcino Ugolaia '12	♈♈ 8
● Brunello di Montalcino Ugolaia '11	♈♈ 8

Lunadoro

FRAZ. VALIANO
VIA TERRA ROSSA
53045 MONTEPULCIANO [SI]
TEL. +39 348 2215188
www.nobilelunadoro.it

CELLAR SALES
PRE-BOOKED VISITS
ACCOMMODATION
ANNUAL PRODUCTION 60,000 bottles
HECTARES UNDER VINE 12.00
VITICULTURE METHOD Certified Organic
SUSTAINABLE WINERY

Lunadoro is situated near Valiano, a subzone of Nobile di Montepulciano. The Swiss giant Schenk Italian Wineries, its owner, was right to maintain the fundamental characteristics of the old management. Their wines still offer the qualities of a boutique winery, exhibiting a definite, though never banal, style and constant quality. The level of care shown in the vineyard and cellar are still high, which means avoiding useless shortcuts whenever possible. The result is a selection of classically-styled wines that are true to the territory but not lacking in brilliance either. The Nobile Quercione Riserva '15 features pleasantly herbaceous notes on the nose, which integrate with lush fruit well-supported by spicy and smoky hints. On the palate it enters soft, only to develop vigorous and full of contrast. The well-crafted Nobile Pagliareto '16 stands out for its clean aromas and sapid flavor. The Rosso di Montepulciano Prugnanello '17 is simple but well-made.

● Nobile di Montepulciano Quercione Ris. '15	▼▼ 4
● Nobile di Montepulciano Pagliareto '16	▼▼ 4
● Rosso di Montepulciano Prugnanello '17	▼ 3
● Nobile di Montepulciano Pagliareto '15	♈♈♈ 3*
● Nobile di Montepulciano Pagliareto '14	♈♈ 3*
● Nobile di Montepulciano Pagliareto '13	♈♈ 3
● Nobile di Montepulciano Quercione Ris. '14	♈♈ 4
● Nobile di Montepulciano Quercione Ris. '12	♈♈ 4
● Rosso di Montepulciano Prugnanello '16	♈♈ 3
● Rosso di Montepulciano Prugnanello '15	♈♈ 2*

I Luoghi

LOC. CAMPO AL CAPRIOLO, 201
57022 CASTAGNETO CARDUCCI [LI]
TEL. +39 0565777379
www.iluoghi.it

CELLAR SALES
ANNUAL PRODUCTION 15,000 bottles
HECTARES UNDER VINE 3.80
VITICULTURE METHOD Certified Organic

An idea, a dream, an intriguing project that hasn't ceased to evolve or seek out a way forward. A constant engine within an artisanal framework, authentic, extremely lived and passionate. It's all thanks to Stefano Granata and his wife, Paola. The journey began in 2000, i the vineyards: two distinct plots cultivated with respect for the environment, without pesticides or artificial chemicals. Their resulting wines are appealing, flavorful, outside preset patterns and schema. Their stylistic direction is evolving, however, and the wines submitted represent a coherent implementation of these path forward. The Bolgheri Superiore Campo al Fico '16 is redolent of topsoil, plowed earth and ripe fruit, with a woodland touch and intriguing herbaceous notes. It's full and juicy, just a bit set back by mouthdrying tannins. Podere Ritorti '16 features a similar profile — aromatically less defined, it convinces foremost on the palate.

● Bolgheri Rosso Sup. Campo al Fico '16	♟♟ 7
● Bolgheri Rosso Sup. Podere Ritorti '16	♟♟ 5
● Bolgheri Sup. Campo al Fico '10	♟♟♟ 7
● Bolgheri Sup. Campo al Fico '09	♟♟♟ 7
● Bolgheri Sup. Campo al Fico '08	♟♟♟ 7
● Bolgheri Sup. Podere Ritorti '13	♟♟♟ 5
● Bolgheri Sup. Campo al Fico '15	♟♟ 7
● Bolgheri Sup. Campo al Fico '13	♟♟ 7
● Bolgheri Sup. Podere Ritorti '15	♟♟ 5
● Bolgheri Sup. Podere Ritorti '14	♟♟ 5
● Bolgheri Sup. Podere Ritorti '12	♟♟ 5
● Bolgheri Sup. Podere Ritorti '11	♟♟ 5
● Bolgheri Sup. Podere Ritorti '10	♟♟ 5

★★Le Macchiole

LOC. BOLGHERI
VIA BOLGHERESE, 189A
57022 CASTAGNETO CARDUCCI [LI]
TEL. +39 0565766092
www.lemacchiole.it

PRE-BOOKED VISITS
ANNUAL PRODUCTION 165,000 bottles
HECTARES UNDER VINE 27.00

Le Macchiole was founded by Eugenio Campolmi and Cinzia Merli in 1983. It was still a pioneering era for Bolgheri, a territory that would develop thanks in part to their contribution. Indeed, from the outset, the producer proved capable of originality, vision, apt vineyard management and cultivar selection, as well as a discerning approach to winemaking. Looking back, we realize that these qualities persist today. The winery continues to evolve and bring together territorial roots with contemporary charm. The Paleo is still our favorite of the lot, with a splendid 2016 version redolent of dark fruit, vegetal wafts andvibrant spices. There's a bit of oak that needs to integrate still, but the palate is so thrilling that there are no doubts about its aging power in the bottle. Their Scrio '16 is also magnificent, proving it is, by now, a wine of great class and consistency, as is their Messorio '16, a wine that's plusher but no less outstanding.

● Paleo Rosso '16	♟♟♟ 8
● Scrio '16	♟♟ 8
● Bolgheri Rosso '17	♟♟ 4
● Messorio '16	♟♟ 8
● Bolgheri Sup. Paleo '14	♟♟♟ 8
● Messorio '07	♟♟♟ 8
● Messorio '06	♟♟♟ 8
● Paleo Rosso '15	♟♟♟ 8
● Paleo Rosso '13	♟♟♟ 8
● Paleo Rosso '12	♟♟♟ 8
● Paleo Rosso '11	♟♟♟ 8
● Paleo Rosso '10	♟♟♟ 8
● Paleo Rosso '09	♟♟♟ 8
● Paleo Rosso '03	♟♟♟ 8
● Scrio '08	♟♟♟ 8

Podere Il Macchione

FRAZ. GRACCIANO
VIA PROVINCIALE, 18
53045 MONTEPULCIANO [SI]
TEL. +39 0578 758595
www.podereilmacchione.it

CELLAR SALES
PRE-BOOKED VISITS
ANNUAL PRODUCTION 20,000 bottles
HECTARES UNDER VINE 6.00

Podere Il Macchione is owned by Trento's Leonardo and Simone Abram. The producer offers wines distinct for their uncommon verve and stylistic definition, in addition to a character that's firmly rooted in the appellation. It's a winery with undisputed potential, whose only weak point, a small one, may be lack of consistency. It's only a minor criticism when we consider the ageworthiness of their wines, which offer up their best only after a lengthy stay in the bottle. The Nobile di Montepulciano '15 may be a bit aromatically imprecise but it's more than compensated for by a lovely intensity on the palate and excellent rhythm, closing in crescendo with an encore of fruit. Even if it's the child of a difficult vintage, the Nobile di Montepulciano Riserva '14 stands out for its floral aromatic finesse and a precise palate that's not without some personality.

● Nobile di Montepulciano '15	♀♀ 5
● Nobile di Montepulciano Ris. '14	♀♀ 5
● Nobile di Montepulciano '14	♀♀ 5
● Nobile di Montepulciano '13	♀♀ 5
● Nobile di Montepulciano Ris. '13	♀♀ 5
● Rosso di Montepulciano '15	♀♀ 4

Le Macioche

S.DA PROV.LE 55 DI SANT'ANTIMO KM 4,850
53024 MONTALCINO [SI]
TEL. +39 0577849168
www.lemacioche.it

CELLAR SALES
PRE-BOOKED VISITS
ACCOMMODATION
ANNUAL PRODUCTION 18,000 bottles
HECTARES UNDER VINE 3.00

Recently taken over by the Cotarella family, Le Macioche gets its name from a local word that indicates the arbutus tree's roots (the woods surrounding the hillside vineyards of Sant'Antimo are full of them). Here, in the heart of southern Montalcino, at 450 meters elevation, the marly terrain is divided into four small parcels planted in the 1980s. Historically these give rise to elegant Sangiovese da Brunello wines that are almost lean in appearance. It will be interesting to follow their new stylistic direction. All it took was one wine for Le Macioche to blow us away in this round of tastings. It's thanks to a Brunello Ris. '13 that's distinct, to say the least, in its almost crepuscular notes of caramel, soil, dried herbs and iodine. It's an aromatic profile that perfectly anticipates a subtle but pounding palate supported by silky tannins, vigor and sweetness, all unwavering.

● Brunello di Montalcino Ris. '13	♀♀♀ 8
● Brunello di Montalcino '13	♀♀♀ 7
● Brunello di Montalcino Ris. '11	♀♀♀ 8
● Brunello di Montalcino '11	♀♀ 7
● Brunello di Montalcino '10	♀♀ 7
● Brunello di Montalcino '09	♀♀ 7
● Brunello di Montalcino '08	♀♀ 7
● Brunello di Montalcino '07	♀♀ 7
● Brunello di Montalcino '06	♀♀ 6
● Brunello di Montalcino '04	♀♀ 6
● Brunello di Montalcino Ris. '12	♀♀ 8
● Brunello di Montalcino Ris. '06	♀♀ 8
● Brunello di Montalcino Ris. '01	♀♀ 6
● Rosso di Montalcino '13	♀♀ 4
● Rosso di Montalcino '11	♀♀ 4
● Rosso di Montalcino '10	♀♀ 4
● Rosso di Montalcino '09	♀♀ 4

Fattoria Mantellassi

Loc. Banditaccia, 26
58051 Magliano in Toscana [GR]
Tel. +39 0564592037
www.fattoriamantellassi.it

CELLAR SALES
PRE-BOOKED VISITS
ANNUAL PRODUCTION 1,000,000 bottles
HECTARES UNDER VINE 99.00
SUSTAINABLE WINERY

The Mantellassi family's origins can be traced to the province of Pistoia, which they left around 1860 so as to move to Maremma (where they worked as grafters and pruners). The vineyards came in the 1960s, when the first four hectares were planted, those that today serve as the winery's core plots. Over time the estate expanded, reaching its current size of almost 100 hectares. Mostly native grapes are cultivated, with Sangiovese, which is used primarily for their Morellino di Scansano, making up the lion's share. The Maremma Toscana Maestrale '18, a wine made with Ciliegiolo, is redolent of crisp red berries accompanied by slightly spicy notes. On the palate it's tasty, with light tannins and a sweetness that's perfectly balanced by a restrained acidity. Their Maremma Vermentino '18, a fleshier and more citrusy Lucumone, moves along a similar stylistic track, as does the more mineral, taut and dynamic Scalandrino.

● Maremma Toscana Ciliegiolo Maestrale '18	♟♟ 2*
○ Maremma Toscana Vermentino Lucumone '18	♟♟ 2*
○ Maremma Toscana Vermentino Scalandrino '18	♟♟ 2*
● Maremma Toscana Alicante Querciolaia '15	♟ 4
● Maremma Toscana Cabernet Sauvignon Punton del Sorbo '16	♟ 3
● Morellino di scansano Il Mago di 03 '18	♟ 3
● Morellino di Scansano San Giuseppe '17	♟ 3
● Morellino di Scansano Sentinelle Ris. '15	♟ 4
● Maremma Toscana Ciliegiolo Maestrale '16	♟♟ 2*
○ Maremma Toscana Vermentino Lucumone '17	♟♟ 2*

Il Marroneto

Loc. Madonna delle Grazie, 307
53024 Montalcino [SI]
Tel. +39 0577849382
www.ilmarroneto.it

CELLAR SALES
PRE-BOOKED VISITS
ANNUAL PRODUCTION 30,000 bottles
HECTARES UNDER VINE 6.00
SUSTAINABLE WINERY

What was once an old farmstead equipped with a drying loft for chestnuts is today a highly sought after winery for those who love 'old-fashioned' Brunellos. Il Marroneto is home base for winemaker Alessandro Mori, north Montalcino's explosive interpreter of extraordinary crus like Madonna delle Grazie (as of 2013 available as a reserve as well). It's only one of a selection that's increasingly complete, the result of short maceration and lengthy aging in various sizes and types of barrels. It's a commitment that seems to have been fully realized with their latest releases. Their Rosso Ignaccio '16 impresses for its sunny whiffs of summer fruit and Mediterranean shrub, sensations that get deeper across its gradual, almost silent unfolding of flavor. But their 'vintage' 2014 Brunello is even more amazing. Delicate aromas of flowers, herbs and wood resin transform into sheer elegance on its silky, penetrating palate.

● Brunello di Montalcino '14	♟♟♟ 7
● Rosso di Montalcino Ignaccio '16	♟♟ 5
● Brunello di Montalcino Madonna delle Grazie '11	♟♟♟ 8
● Brunello di Montalcino Madonna delle Grazie '10	♟♟♟ 8
● Brunello di Montalcino Madonna delle Grazie '08	♟♟♟ 8
● Brunello di Montalcino '13	♟♟ 7
● Brunello di Montalcino '12	♟♟ 7
● Brunello di Montalcino '11	♟♟ 7
● Brunello di Montalcino '10	♟♟ 7
● Brunello di Montalcino Madonna delle Grazie '13	♟♟ 8
● Brunello di Montalcino Madonna delle Grazie '12	♟♟ 8
● Rosso di Montalcino Ignaccio '15	♟♟ 5

Cosimo Maria Masini

VIA POGGIO A PINO, 16
56028 SAN MINIATO [PI]
TEL. +39 0571465032
www.cosimomariamasini.it

CELLAR SALES
PRE-BOOKED VISITS
ANNUAL PRODUCTION 50,000 bottles
HECTARES UNDER VINE 14.00
VITICULTURE METHOD Certified Biodynamic
SUSTAINABLE WINERY

This 40-hectare estate is situated near San Miniato, an area characterized by olive groves and farmland. In the mid-19th century they adopted innovative techniques for vineyard cultivation, and the estate's current cellar was built. This long history continues today with the Masini family, who've owned the property since 2000. In addition to the region's classics, they grow international grapes as well, including lesser known varieties like Buonamico, San Colombano and Sanforte. The Daphné '18 is a pleasant, classic blend of Trebbiano and Malvasia whose character is delicately oxidative (evident from its amber color). Aromas of dried flowers are followed by apricot and apple. On the palate it's firm, slightly tannic even, sapid and flavorful, with a compelling finish. The Annick '18, a Sauvignon Blanc and Vermentino blend, opens on vegetal notes and aromatic herbs, lemon peel and then pleasantly tart fruit, like green damson. Both lively and edgy, it's an excellent, juicy drink.

○ Annick '18	♔♔ 2*
○ Daphné '18	♔♔ 4
● Nicole '18	♔♔ 3
● Sincero '18	♔♔ 3
○ Annick '16	♔♔ 2*
● Cosimo '15	♔♔ 5
○ Daphné '17	♔♔ 4
○ Daphné '16	♔♔ 4
○ Daphné '15	♔♔ 4
● Nicole '17	♔♔ 3
● Nicole '15	♔♔ 3
● San Forte Rosso '16	♔♔ 2*
● Sincero '17	♔♔ 3
○ Vin Santo del Chianti Fedardo '09	♔♔ 4

Masseto

FRAZ. BOLGHERI
LOC. ORNELLAIA, 191
57022 CASTAGNETO CARDUCCI [LI]
TEL. +39
www.masseto.com

ANNUAL PRODUCTION 33,000 bottles
HECTARES UNDER VINE 13.00
SUSTAINABLE WINERY

Masseto have always had a place among the ranks of important national and international wine producers, but now it's been made official. Masseto is no longer the name of a wine, it's an estate and, finally, an autonomous project in its own right operating independent of Ornellaia. In fact, it gets its own page in this guide. The cellar that represents it is magnificent, practical and as minimalist as it is elegant and sophisticated, making it worthy of one of Italy's most prestigious brands. Masseto is Masseto, there's not much you can do. The 2016 exhibits its usual profile, yet there's a more multifaceted and balanced quality to it, with aromas of great intensity that see ripe fruits mingling with sweet spices. The palate is monumental, dense and quite full in its tannic presence and alcohol. The surprise of the year is the birth of the Second Wine Massetino, the first is a 2017.

● Massetino '17	♔♔ 8
● Masseto '16	♔♔ 8

★Mastrojanni

FRAZ. CASTELNUOVO DELL'ABATE
POD. LORETO E SAN PIO
53024 MONTALCINO [SI]
TEL. +39 0577835681
www.mastrojanni.com

CELLAR SALES
PRE-BOOKED VISITS
ACCOMMODATION
ANNUAL PRODUCTION 110,000 bottles
HECTARES UNDER VINE 33.00

The Illy family has brought further international prestige to a winery founded by Gabriele Mastrojanni in the 1970s. It all revolves around Castelnuovo dell'Abate, a major outpost of southeast Montalcino that hosts their two historic Brunello crus. Long-lived and recognizable for their earthy, balsamic tones, these are interpreted through a varied approach in the cellar: tufaceous terrain and large wooden barrels for their Vigna Loreto, sandy soils and 1600 liter oak for their Vigna Schiena d'Asino. A 2013 version of this last leads the latest selection submitted by Mastrojanni. Understandable, it seems to have needed time to express all its potential. Nevertheless, its aromas of balsamic herbs, tobacco and spiciness configure it as a classic Brunello to the bone. This is also (and especially) true of its palate — still austere in this phase, it's rich in fiber and future prospects.

● Brunello di Montalcino '14	▼▼ 5
● Brunello di Montalcino V. Schiena d'Asino '13	▼▼ 8
● Rosso di Montalcino '17	▼ 4
● Brunello di Montalcino '97	♔♔♔ 7
● Brunello di Montalcino Schiena d'Asino '08	♔♔♔ 8
● Brunello di Montalcino Schiena d'Asino '93	♔♔♔ 7
● Brunello di Montalcino Schiena d'Asino '90	♔♔♔ 7
● Brunello di Montalcino V. Loreto '13	♔♔♔ 7
● Brunello di Montalcino V. Loreto '10	♔♔♔ 7
● Brunello di Montalcino V. Loreto '09	♔♔♔ 7
● Brunello di Montalcino V. Schiena d'Asino '12	♔♔♔ 8
● Brunello di Montalcino V. Schiena d'Asino '10	♔♔♔ 8

Fattorie Melini

LOC. GAGGIANO
53036 POGGIBONSI [SI]
TEL. +39 0577998511
www.cantinemelini.it

CELLAR SALES
PRE-BOOKED VISITS
ANNUAL PRODUCTION 3,000,000 bottles
HECTARES UNDER VINE 136.00

Melini di Poggibonsi and Fattoria Macchiavelli (San Casciano Val di Pesa) are Gruppo Italiano Vini's Chianti wineries. Their history coincides almost perfectly with that of Chianti. Indeed, it was Laborel Melini who, in 1860, first adopted the 'strapeso' wine bottle that, thanks to its durability, contributed to the wine's success. Today GIV's Gallo Nero wines exhibit personality, at times even excellence, in addition to praiseworthy technical precision. GIV's Tuscan winery submitted a pair of well-made Chianti Classicos. The Chianti Classico Granaio '17 offers up clear, fragrant aromas followed by a taut, juicy and highly pleasant palate. The Chianti Classico Machiavelli Solatio del Tani '16 exhibits a delicate, well-gauged, extremely clean aromatic profile, anticipating a sapid, vigorous and delicious palate. The rest of their selection also performed well.

● Chianti Cl. Granaio '17	▼▼ 3*
● Chianti Cl. Machiavelli Solatio del Tani '16	▼▼ 4
● Albergaccio Machiavelli '17	▼▼ 4
● Chianti Cl. Gran Selezione V. di Fontalle '15	▼▼ 5
● Il Principe Machiavelli '15	▼▼ 5
● I Coltri '18	▼ 2
● Chianti Cl. La Selvanella Ris. '06	♔♔♔ 5
● Chianti Cl. La Selvanella Ris. '03	♔♔♔ 4
● Chianti Cl. La Selvanella Ris. '01	♔♔♔ 4
● Chianti Cl. La Selvanella Ris. '00	♔♔♔ 4
● Chianti Cl. La Selvanella Ris. '99	♔♔♔ 5
● Chianti Cl. La Selvanella Ris. '90	♔♔♔ 3*
● Chianti Cl. La Selvanella Ris. '86	♔♔♔ 4*

Le Miccine

LOC. LE MICCINE
S.S. TRAVERSA CHIANTIGIANA
53013 GAIOLE IN CHIANTI [SI]
TEL. +39 0577749526
www.lemiccine.com

CELLAR SALES
PRE-BOOKED VISITS
ACCOMMODATION
ANNUAL PRODUCTION 25,000 bottles
HECTARES UNDER VINE 7.00
VITICULTURE METHOD Certified Organic

Le Miccine is one of Chianti Classico's best family-run artisanal wineries. Organic vineyard management is carried out without forced practices, while in the cellar they've adopted a minimally-invasive approach, with aging carried out in mid-sized casks and large wood barrels. Their wines have, by now, acquired a definite style and possess a territorial adherence that's coherent with the character of Gaiole in Chianti: forthright, flavorful and subtle. The Chianti Classico '17 does a nice job bringing out the best qualities of a complicated year. On the nose it's airy and sunny, with fruit in the foreground followed by spicy hints. On the palate it's simply delicious, subtle yet full, delivering a flavor that's almost irresistible. The Chianti Classico Riserva '16 exhibits great sapidity, there's just a bit of oak that needs integrating.

● Chianti Cl. '17	♟♟ 4
● Chianti Cl. Ris. '16	♟♟ 5
● Chianti Cl. '16	♟♟♟ 4*
● Chianti Cl. '15	♟♟♟ 4*
● Chianti Cl. Ris. '10	♟♟♟ 5
● Carduus '10	♟♟ 5
● Chianti Cl. '11	♟♟ 2*
● Chianti Cl. Ris. '15	♟♟ 5
● Chianti Cl. Ris. '13	♟♟ 5
● Chianti Cl. Ris. '12	♟♟ 5

Monte Rosola

LOC. PIGNANO
POD. LA ROSOLA
56048 VOLTERRA [PI]
TEL. +39 058835062
www.monterosola.com

ANNUAL PRODUCTION 8,000 bottles
HECTARES UNDER VINE

The estate's origins go back to the 15th century, when it served as an outpost of Pignano castle. Since then agriculture has thrived, foremost grape and olive cultivation. The turning point came 20 years ago, when Gottfried Schmitt and Carmen Vieytes purchased it and began renovation work on its buildings and land, replanting its olive trees and reviving its vineyards. Monte Rosola's current owners, Bent and Ewa Thomaeus, bought the estate in 2013, continuing the work of expansion and improvement. The Canto della Civetta '16 is a pleasant Merlot, aromatically delicate and complex, characterized by fruit and spices. On the palate it's soft, with notable length. Their interesting Crescendo '16, a Sangiovese, offers up minty, balsamic tones, and a supple, nicely structured palate, with well-integrated tannins. Their Corpo Notte '16 blend stands out for its delicate, elegant bouquet, fresh notes of fruit and medicinal herbs. On the palate it proves balanced and highly drinkable.

● Canto della Civetta '16	♟♟ 5
● Corpo Notte '16	♟♟ 4
● Crescendo '16	♟♟ 3
● Indomito '16	♟♟ 4
○ Primo Passo '17	♟ 3

Fattoria Montellori

VIA PISTOIESE, 1
50054 FUCECCHIO [FI]
TEL. +39 0571260641
www.fattoriamontellori.it

CELLAR SALES
PRE-BOOKED VISITS
ACCOMMODATION AND RESTAURANT SERVICE
ANNUAL PRODUCTION 250,000 bottles
HECTARES UNDER VINE 51.00
VITICULTURE METHOD Certified Organic
SUSTAINABLE WINERY

When the farm was purchased by the Nieri family in 1895 the garden already existed. Today, after meticulous renovation, we can once again appreciate its 19th-century Victorian facade and flower beds, which host various plants and flora. In addition to enlarging the vineyards and modernizing the cellar, they've changed stylistic course in favor of personality, with a selection of some 10 different wines, including a sparkler. The Salamartano '16 is a Bordeaux blend of Cabernet Sauvignon, Cabernet Franc and Merlot. On the nose it offers up intense aromas of grilled green pepper, then fresh balsamic and minty hints followed by coffee and toasty notes, all on a background of assorted wild berries. On the palate it's dense and docile, with elegant, well-integrated tannins, only to close soft, long and pervasive. The Riserva '13 version of their Pas Dosé features fragrant floral notes and nuances of bread crust, sensations that anticipate a spirited, well-balanced body.

○ Montellori Pas Dosé Ris. '13	♈♈	6
● Salamartano '16	♈♈	6
○ Bianco dell'Empolese Vin Santo '13	♈♈	5
● Dicatum '16	♈♈	5
○ Montellori Pas Dosé '15	♈♈	5
● Chianti '17	♈	2
○ Mandorlo '18	♈	2
○ Trebbiano '18	♈	2
○ Bianco dell'Empolese Vin Santo '12	♈♈	5
● Chianti Sup. Caselle '15	♈♈	2*
● Dicatum '15	♈♈	5
○ Montellori Pas Dosé '14	♈♈	5
○ Montellori Pas Dosé '13	♈♈	5
○ Montellori Pas Dosé Ris. '12	♈♈	6
● Moro '14	♈♈	3
● Salamartano '15	♈♈	6
● Salamartano '13	♈♈	6

Montenidoli

LOC. MONTENIDOLI
53037 SAN GIMIGNANO [SI]
TEL. +39 0577941565
www.montenidoli.com

CELLAR SALES
ACCOMMODATION
ANNUAL PRODUCTION 100,000 bottles
HECTARES UNDER VINE 24.00
VITICULTURE METHOD Certified Organic

When the first wine came, in 1971, Luigi Veronelli wrote that Elisabetta Fagiuoli, who founded the winery with Sergio Muratori more than 50 years ago, had the manner of San Gimignano's two battle towers. But Montenidoli, which means 'mountain of small nests', is more than just a winery focused on the environment and local grapes like Vernaccia, Sangiovese, Canaiolo, Trebbiano Gentile and Malvasia Bianca. It is foremost a meeting a place, for study, work and hospitality. The Vernaccia Carato '16, with its exceptional density of flavor, led a dazzling selection. Rich in smoky notes, almond and aniseed, it's a juicy, long wine (to say the least). Their Vernaccia Fiore '18 is fresher, more vibrant, a foil to the complex Templare '13 and its proud, elegant character. To close, we make note of the earthy, sylvan sensations of the Triassico '08, a sophisticated, limited-edition Sangiovese only available in magnums. It's an extraordinary wine that we won't score here.

○ Vernaccia di S. Gimignano Carato '16	♈♈♈	4*
○ Canaiuolo '18	♈♈	3*
○ Il Templare '13	♈♈	4
○ Vernaccia di S. Gimignano Fiore '18	♈♈	3*
○ Vernaccia di S. Gimignano Tradizionale '18	♈♈	2*
○ Vernaccia di S. Gimignano Carato '13	♈♈♈	4*
○ Vernaccia di S. Gimignano Carato '12	♈♈♈	4*
○ Vernaccia di S. Gimignano Carato '11	♈♈♈	4*
○ Vernaccia di S. Gimignano Carato '05	♈♈♈	5
○ Vernaccia di S. Gimignano Carato '02	♈♈♈	5
○ Vernaccia di S. Gimignano Fiore '09	♈♈♈	3
○ Vernaccia di S. Gimignano Tradizionale '15	♈♈♈	2*
○ Vernaccia di S. Gimignano Tradizionale '12	♈♈♈	2*

Montepeloso

LOC. MONTEPELOSO, 82
57028 SUVERETO [LI]
TEL. +39 0565828180
www.montepeloso.it

ANNUAL PRODUCTION 22,000 bottles
HECTARES UNDER VINE 7.00
SUSTAINABLE WINERY

The Tyrrhenian isn't far, and Bolgheri is near. But this southeast Suvereto producer's wines feature a clear personality, made possible thanks to Fabio Chiarellotto's efforts in managing the estate (first on his own, and later with the support of business partner Silvio Denz). Montepeloso reds and whites emerge from combinations and quantities of grapes that have found the right conditions for original wines. And so Fabio and Silvio have reached their goal of, 'Making wines that distinguish the Tuscan coast'. The Gabbro '16, a monovarietal Cabernet Sauvignon, earned a place in our finals, proving compelling in its notes of quinine, mineral hints, nuances of eucalyptus and blueberries. A nice initial impact is followed by a round, lively development. It's a dynamic, balanced red that closes with some energy. The Eneo '16 is a firm and balanced blend of Sangiovese, Montepulciano, Marselan and Alicante characterized by aromas of grilled pepper, blackberries and plums.

● Gabbro '16	♛♛ 8
● A Quo '16	♛♛ 5
● Eneo '16	♛♛ 5
● Nardo '16	♛♛ 8
● Gabbro '02	♛♛♛ 8
● Nardo '01	♛♛♛ 8
● Nardo '00	♛♛♛ 8
● A Quo '15	♛♛ 5
● Eneo '15	♛♛ 5
● Eneo '14	♛♛ 5
● Eneo '13	♛♛ 5
● Gabbro '15	♛♛ 8
● Gabbro '14	♛♛ 8
● Nardo '15	♛♛ 8
● Nardo '13	♛♛ 8
● Nardo '12	♛♛ 8

Montepepe

VIA SFORZA, 76
54038 MONTIGNOSO [MS]
TEL. +39 05851980363
www.montepepe.com

CELLAR SALES
PRE-BOOKED VISITS
ACCOMMODATION
ANNUAL PRODUCTION 25,000 bottles
HECTARES UNDER VINE 6.00

White grapes like Vermentino and Viognier, and reds like Syrah and Massaretta grow along the estate's terraced plots. Olives are also cultivated here between the Apuane Alps and the Tyrrhenian sea. Their few (but good) vineyards are in an elevated position with respect to the 18th-century villa that hosts their production facility (it's also used for hospitality). Their recently-built, basement wine cellar is overshadowed by an olive grove that helps naturally regulate the temperature below. The Grand Vintage '09, a blend of Vermentino and Viognier (a common combination for the winery), is a superb example of ageability. Aromatic herbs, thyme and sage, rise up on the nose along with lemon, then mature fruity notes of apple and peach. On the palate it proves juicy, enticing, with lovely roundness and a sapid, relaxed finish. Their intriguing Degeres '16 draws on the same grapes, though it's heavier on Viognier. The result is a subtle, delicate and elegant wine.

○ Candia dei Colli Apuani Vermentino Albèrico '17	♛♛ 3
○ Degeres '16	♛♛ 6
○ Montepepe Bianco '17	♛♛ 4
○ Montepepe Bianco Grand Vintage '09	♛♛ 8
● Montepepe Rosso '16	♛ 4
○ Candia dei Colli Apuani Vermentino Albèrico '16	♛♛ 3
○ Degeres '15	♛♛ 6
○ Degeres '12	♛♛ 6
○ Montepepe Bianco '16	♛♛ 4
○ Montepepe Bianco '14	♛♛ 4
○ Montepepe Bianco '13	♛♛ 4
○ Montepepe Bianco Vintage '10	♛♛ 5
○ Montepepe Bianco Vintage Magnum '12	♛♛ 8
● Montepepe Rosso '13	♛♛ 4

Monteraponi

Loc. Monteraponi
53017 Radda in Chianti [SI]
Tel. +39 0577738208
www.monteraponi.it

CELLAR SALES
PRE-BOOKED VISITS
ACCOMMODATION
ANNUAL PRODUCTION 50,000 bottles
HECTARES UNDER VINE 10.00
VITICULTURE METHOD Certified Organic

Owned by Michele Braganti, Monteraponi
has by now firmly established itself as
among the most important Radda wineries
in Chianti Classico. Care in the vineyards,
starting with organic cultivation, and a
minimally-invasive approach in the cellar
(with aging in large wooden barrels) make
for solid, decidedly territorial wines with a
clear identity and excellent personality.
They stand out for an aromatic profile that
alternates intense notes with more nuanced
hints, and a flavorful, highly energetic
palate. Aromas of flowers, flint and spices
characterize the Chianti Classico Il
Campitello Riserva '16. On the palate it
brings together sapidity and acidic
freshness, along with pleasantly spirited
tannins, making for a wine of decisive
character. The Baron'Ugo '15, a
monovarietal Sangiovese, is denser in its
development, offering up charming aromas
and tasty contrast of flavor. The delectable
and fragrant Chianti Classico '17 is also
well-made.

● Chianti Cl. Il Campitello Ris. '16	▼▼▼ 7
● Baron'Ugo '15	▼▼ 5
● Chianti Cl. '17	▼▼ 4
● Baron'Ugo '13	♈♈♈ 5
● Baron'Ugo '12	♈♈♈ 8
● Chianti Cl. Baron'Ugo Ris. '10	♈♈♈ 7
● Chianti Cl. Baron'Ugo Ris. '09	♈♈♈ 7
● Chianti Cl. Baron'Ugo Ris. '07	♈♈♈ 5
● Chianti Cl. Il Campitello Ris. '15	♈♈♈ 7
● Chianti Cl. '16	♈♈ 4
● Chianti Cl. '13	♈♈ 3
● Chianti Cl. Baron'Ugo Ris. '11	♈♈ 7
● Chianti Cl. Il Campitello Ris. '14	♈♈ 5
● Chianti Cl. Il Campitello Ris. '13	♈♈ 5
● Chianti Cl. Il Campitello Ris. '12	♈♈ 5
● Chianti Cl. Il Campitello Ris. '11	♈♈ 5

Monterinaldi

Loc. Lucarelli
53017 Radda in Chianti [SI]
Tel. +39 0577733533
www.monterinaldi.it

ANNUAL PRODUCTION 400,000 bottles
HECTARES UNDER VINE 65.00

Situated in Radda in Chianti, Castello
Monterinaldi boasts a history rooted entirely
in the district. Owned by the Ciampi family
since 1961, since 1991 it's been in the
hands of Daniele, who succeeded his
father, Remo, president of Viticola Tuscan
Meleto from 1972-1998 and founder of
Cooperative delle Storiche Cantine. After a
somewhat uncertain period, the winery
seems to have found its way, proving
capable of offering decidedly territorial
wines and a level of quality that clearly
strives for excellence. Their Chianti Classico
Vigneto Boscone '16 is a wine of lovely
definition, floral and citrusy in its aromas,
well-adorned by hints of spices and roots.
On the palate it's juicy and flavorful, with a
broad finish that sees an encore of fruit.
The Chianti Classico '16 is small but quite
pleasant. Fragrant aromas characterize the
Chianti Classico Riserva '16, a wine whose
palate proves balanced and sapid, just a bit
unrefined at the finish.

● Chianti Cl. Vign. Boscone '16	▼▼ 4
● Chianti Cl. '16	▼▼ 3
● Chianti Cl. Ris. '16	▼▼ 4
● Chianti Cl. '15	♈♈ 3
● Chianti Cl. Campopazzo '13	♈♈ 3
● Chianti Cl. Ris. '15	♈♈ 4
● Chianti Cl. Ris. '14	♈♈ 4
● Chianti Cl. Ris. '13	♈♈ 4
● Chianti Cl. Vign. Boscone '15	♈♈ 4
● Pesanella '00	♈♈ 5

Tenuta Monteti

S.DA DELLA SGRILLA, 6
58011 CAPALBIO [GR]
TEL. +39 0564896160
www.tenutamonteti.it

CELLAR SALES
PRE-BOOKED VISITS
ANNUAL PRODUCTION 130,000 bottles
HECTARES UNDER VINE 28.00
SUSTAINABLE WINERY

Owned by the Baratta family, Tenuta Monteti is situated in Capalbio, the southern part of Maremma. Founded in 1998, with the first bottles hitting the market in 2004, the winery has earned significant recognition. Exclusively international varieties are cultivated, from Petit Verdot to Cabernet Franc, Cabernet Sauvignon, Merlot and Alicante-Bouschet, all of which are aged in small wood barrels. Their style is clean, rich and modern, but also manages to preserve the Mediterranean traits that arise from the area's pedoclimate. Their Caburnio is once again the most successful wine of their selection. The 2015 reaffirms its status as a fragrant and highly pleasant red. Made with a field blend of Cabernet Sauvignon, Alicante Bouschet and Merlot, it has well-defined aromas and a lively palate marked by contrasting flavor. Their Maremma Toscana Monteti '15 also did well. It's more approachable on the nose, while on the palate it proves compact and well-supported by oak.

● Caburnio '15	♟♟♟ 4*
● Monteti '15	♟♟ 6
● Caburnio '14	♟♟♟ 3*
● Caburnio '13	♟♟ 3
● Caburnio '12	♟♟ 3
● Caburnio '11	♟♟ 3
● Monteti '13	♟♟ 6
● Monteti '12	♟♟ 5
● Monteti '11	♟♟ 5
☉ TM Rosé '14	♟♟ 3

Monteverro

S.DA AURELIA CAPALBIO, 11
58011 CAPALBIO [GR]
TEL. +39 0564890721
www.monteverro.com

CELLAR SALES
PRE-BOOKED VISITS
ANNUAL PRODUCTION 150,000 bottles
HECTARES UNDER VINE 40.00
VITICULTURE METHOD Certified Organic
SUSTAINABLE WINERY

Monteverro was founded in 2003 by businessman Georg Weber. The winery, situated between Capalbio and the sea, cultivates mostly international varieties (Cabernet Sauvignon, Franc, Merlot, Petit Verdot, Syrah, Grenache, Chardonnay, Sangiovese and Vermentino). In the cellar they use steel and barriques, making for a solid, modern style where mature fruit is accompanied by a conspicuous use of oak. The result is wines with a strong impact, though possibly somewhat lacking in personality. Their delicious Monteverro'16 is a Bordeaux blend of Cabernet Sauvignon and Franc, Merlot and Petit Verdot. It's a densely-colored wine, aromatically complex and spicy, with cloves and cinnamon rising up on a creamy background of wild berries. On the palate it's warm and firm, elegant, docile, soft and juicy, closing long. Their pleasant Chardonnay offers up buttery aromas enlivened by wood resin and aromatic herbs. A firm and creamy body characterizes the palate, with nice acidic vigor.

● Monteverro '16	♟♟ 8
☉ Chardonnay '16	♟♟ 8
● Terra di Monteverro '16	♟♟ 7
☉ Chardonnay '13	♟♟ 8
● Monteverro '14	♟♟ 8
● Monteverro '13	♟♟ 8
● Monteverro '12	♟♟ 8
● Terra di Monteverro '14	♟♟ 7
● Terra di Monteverro '13	♟♟ 7
● Terra di Monteverro '12	♟♟ 7
● Tinata '15	♟♟ 8
● Tinata '14	♟♟ 8
● Tinata '13	♟♟ 8
● Tinata '12	♟♟ 8

★★Montevertine

Loc. Montevertine
53017 Radda in Chianti [SI]
Tel. +39 0577738009
www.montevertine.it

PRE-BOOKED VISITS
ANNUAL PRODUCTION 85,000 bottles
HECTARES UNDER VINE 18.00

At Montevertine some of historic Chianti's most complete and representative wines continue to be produced, even if the winery doesn't use the 'Gallo Nero'. For many producers, these are model wines stylistically: delicate aromas, at times, somewhat austere and complex, a palate that's dominated by great contrast, absolute freshness and elegance. Martino Manetti's estate is situated among the hills of Radda in Chianti — it's highly improbable that you could understand this area's wine culture without them. The Le Pergole Torte submitted is one for the ages, thanks to a spectacular 2016. It's still finding its full focus, but exhibits the qualities possessed by only the best wines, masterfully bringing together intensity with elegance, and purity with a level of detail that's still not entirely revealed. In time it will thrill. Their Montevertine '16 is also amazing, proving floral and clearer aromatically, taut, mature and extremely flavorful on the palate.

● Le Pergole Torte '16	▼▼▼ 8
● Montevertine '16	▼▼ 6
● Pian del Ciampolo '17	▼▼ 4
● Le Pergole Torte '15	♈♈♈ 8
● Le Pergole Torte '13	♈♈♈ 8
● Le Pergole Torte '12	♈♈♈ 8
● Le Pergole Torte '11	♈♈♈ 8
● Le Pergole Torte '10	♈♈♈ 8
● Le Pergole Torte '09	♈♈♈ 8
● Le Pergole Torte '07	♈♈♈ 8
● Le Pergole Torte '04	♈♈♈ 8
● Montevertine '14	♈♈♈ 6
● Montevertine '04	♈♈♈ 5

Vignaioli del Morellino di Scansano

Loc. Saragiolo
58054 Scansano [GR]
Tel. +39 0564507288
www.vignaiolidiscansano.it

CELLAR SALES
PRE-BOOKED VISITS
ANNUAL PRODUCTION 2,500,000 bottles
HECTARES UNDER VINE 600.00
SUSTAINABLE WINERY

Cantina Cooperativa Vignaioli del Morellino di Scansano comprises 150 grower members and an equally sizable vineyard. It's a groundwork that, at least in numeric terms, makes it the largest producer in Morellino di Scansano. Their rich selection is centered on the appellation itself, but DOC Maremma is increasingly represented as well. Recently the cooperative's production has registered a rise in quality, with well-crafted wines that, on occasion, also exhibit nice personality. Their Sangiovese Scantianum '18 exhibits approachable aromatic pleasantness, with notes of fresh cherry, violet and slightly spicy hints anticipating a supple, juicy palate. Their Maremma Toscana Ciliegiolo Capoccia '18 is just as enjoyable. Flowery sensations are adorned with hints of pepper, while on the palate fruit and sapidity dominate, making for a decidedly gratifying and relaxed drink.

● Maremma Toscana Ciliegiolo Capoccia '18	▼▼ 2*
● Scantianum Sangiovese '18	▼▼ 2*
● Morellino di Scansano Roggiano Bio '18	▼ 2
● Morellino di Scansano Roggiano Ris. '16	▼ 3
○ Scantianum Viognier '18	▼ 2
○ Vigna Fiorini Vermentino V. T. '18	▼ 3
● Vin del Fattore Governo all'uso Toscano '18	▼ 3
● Morellino di Scansano Roggiano '15	♈♈ 2*
● Morellino di Scansano Roggiano Bio '15	♈♈ 2*
● Morellino di Scansano Roggiano Ris. '15	♈♈ 3*
● Morellino di Scansano Roggiano Ris. '14	♈♈ 3*
● Morellino di Scansano Sicomoro Ris. '15	♈♈ 4
● Morellino di Scansano Sicomoro Ris. '13	♈♈ 4
● Morellino di Scansano Vignabenefizio '17	♈♈ 3

Tenuta Moriniello

VIA SANTO STEFANO, 40
50050 MONTAIONE [FI]
TEL. +39 3483198880
www.tenutamoriniello.com

CELLAR SALES
PRE-BOOKED VISITS
ACCOMMODATION
ANNUAL PRODUCTION 50,000 bottles
HECTARES UNDER VINE 20.00
VITICULTURE METHOD Certified Organic

This family-run winery was founded thanks to the passion of Beniamino and his children. A few years ago they identified and purchased the estate. After studying the territory and the grapes, they launced the project, investing in improvements in the vineyards and cellar. Sangiovese makes up the lion's share. It's accompanied by Canaiolo, Ciliegiolo, Colorino, Cab Sauvignon, Franc, Merlot, Petit Verdot and Syrah. For their whites, they cultivate Sauvignon Blanc and Gewurztraminer. The delicious Gobbo Nero '16, a Syrah, offers up tantalizing aromas — minty hints accompany light nuances of pepper and cinnamon. Rich, fruity notes of raspberry and blackcurrant follow. On the palate it's close-knit, with tightly wound and nicely placed tannins giving way to a juicy, warm, long finish. The highly pleasant Chianti La Pieve '18 is characterized by lively, intense sensations of fruit, cherry and strawberry, while on the palate it proves lean and dynamic, closing sapid and juicy.

● Il Gobbo Nero '16	♟♟ 4
● Chianti Fortebraccio Ris. '16	♟♟ 3
● Chianti La Pieve '18	♟♟ 2*
○ Le Fate Furbe '18	♟ 3
● Chianti Fortebraccio Ris. '15	♀♀ 3
● Il Gobbo Nero '15	♀♀ 4
● Il Gobbo Nero '13	♀♀ 4
● Il Gobbo Nero '10	♀♀ 3
○ Le Fate Furbe '17	♀♀ 3
● Rosso del Pievano '13	♀♀ 4
● Syrah Gobbo Nero '11	♀♀ 3

Morisfarms

LOC. CURA NUOVA
FATTORIA POGGETTI
58024 MASSA MARITTIMA [GR]
TEL. +39 0566919135
www.morisfarms.it

CELLAR SALES
PRE-BOOKED VISITS
ACCOMMODATION
ANNUAL PRODUCTION 300,000 bottles
HECTARES UNDER VINE 70.00

Morisfarms, well-established among Maremma's most important producers, has contributed to the area's rise to the heights of regional excellence. Wines like their Avvoltore are part of the history and identity of the territory, which wouldn't be the same without them. Their clearly recognizable style, not lacking in character, oscillates between moderately modern and more solidly traditional, especially in terms of their premium wines. The rest of their selection exhibits a reliable standard of quality, though it's less intriguing. The Maremma Toscana Mandriolo '18 features intense, airy aromas, but finds its strong point on the palate where it's fragrant, enjoyable and flavorful. The Morellino di Scansano Riserva '16 is characterized by a detailed mix of fruit and toastiness, coming through austere and close-knit on the palate. The Morellino di Scansano '18, which is already open aromatically, proves well-made, especially in its flavor profile.

● Maremma Toscana Rosso Mandriolo '18	♟♟ 2*
● Morellino di Scansano Ris. '16	♟♟ 4
○ Maremma Toscana Bianco Santa Chiara '18	♟ 2
● Maremma Toscana Rosso Barbaspinosa '15	♟ 3
● Morellino di Scansano '18	♟ 2
○ Vermentino '18	♟ 2
● Avvoltore '06	♀♀♀ 5
● Avvoltore '04	♀♀♀ 5
● Avvoltore '01	♀♀♀ 5
● Avvoltore '00	♀♀♀ 5
● Avvoltore '99	♀♀♀ 5
● Avvoltore '15	♀♀ 6
○ Monteregio di Massa Marittima Santa Chiara '16	♀♀ 2*

Mormoraia

Loc. Sant'Andrea, 15
53037 San Gimignano [SI]
Tel. +39 0577940096
www.mormoraia.it

CELLAR SALES
PRE-BOOKED VISITS
ACCOMMODATION
ANNUAL PRODUCTION 230,000 bottles
HECTARES UNDER VINE 40.00

Almost forty years ago Pino Passoni and his
wife, Franca, between restoring the
buildings and land of this historic convent,
transforming it into their home and guest
accommodations, as well as a vineyard and
olive grove cultivated according to modern
norms. In addition to producing a
well-known extra-virgin olive oil, they
transform Vernaccia, Sangiovese, Cabernet
Sauvignon and Franc, Merlot and Syrah
grapes into increasingly appreciated wines.
The Vernaccia Ostrea '17 features a nice
aromatic profile, proving complex and rich
with notes of vanilla, a slight butteriness,
fragrances of mature fruit (melon foremost).
On the palate it opens firm, rich pleasantly
dense, and characterized by a fresh acidic
streak that carries it towards a sapid and
truly long finish. Tre Bicchieri. The
Vernaccia Antalis Riserva '16 proves
intense in its mineral notes before opening
on floral hints of potpourri, then pear. In the
mouth it exhibits structure and harmony,
with a fresh, deep finish.

○ Vernaccia di S. Gimignano Ostrea '17	♛♛♛	3*
○ Vernaccia di S. Gimignano Antalis Ris. '16	♛♛	3
○ Vernaccia di S. Gimignano Suavis '18	♛♛	2*
● Chianti Colli Senesi Ris. '15	♛	3
○ Vernaccia di S. Gimignano E' ReZet Mattia Barzaghi '11	♛♛♛	3*
● Chianti Colli Senesi '14	♛♛	2*
● Chianti Colli Senesi Haurio '16	♛♛	2*
● Chianti Colli Senesi Haurio '15	♛♛	2*
● Syrah '12	♛♛	3
○ Vernaccia di S. Gimignano '14	♛♛	2*
○ Vernaccia di S. Gimignano Ostrea '16	♛♛	3
○ Vernaccia di S. Gimignano Ostrea '15	♛♛	3
○ Vernaccia di S. Gimignano Ris. '14	♛♛	3*
○ Vernaccia di S. Gimignano Suavis '17	♛♛	2*
○ Vernaccia di S. Gimignano Suavis '16	♛♛	2*

Fabio Motta

Vigna al Cavaliere, 61
57022 Castagneto Carducci [LI]
Tel. +39 0565773041
www.mottafabio.it

CELLAR SALES
PRE-BOOKED VISITS
ANNUAL PRODUCTION 23,000 bottles
HECTARES UNDER VINE 6.50

Identified as one of Bolgheri's best
interpreters in the previous edition of our
guide, Fabio Motta has affirmed his
standing as a vigneron that's worth
watching. Bolstered by a degree in
agriculture, previous winemaking
experience (at Michele Satta) and now
experience on his own, he's carrying
forward at the foot of Castagneto Carducci,
in Le Pievi (red grapes) and Fornacelle
(white grapes, Vermentino foremost). The
house style is territorial, though also
capable of originality. Their Bolgheri Rosso
Superiore Le Gonnare confirms its
outstanding quality, this time with a
splendid 2016. Its less approachable than
the previous version, maybe a bit more
introverted and slow to reveal itself, and yet
it is unequivocally a 'grand' wine. This is
especially evident on the palate, where it
proves as elegant as it is rich in flavor. The
Rosso Pievi '17 is more rustic and sylvan,
while the Bianco Nova '18 proves redolent
of mint and aromatic herbs.

● Bolgheri Rosso Sup. Le Gonnare '16	♛♛♛	8
○ Bolgheri Bianco Nova '18	♛	4
● Bolgheri Rosso Pievi '17	♛	4
● Bolgheri Rosso Sup. Le Gonnare '15	♛♛♛	8
● Bolgheri Sup. Le Gonnare '13	♛♛♛	8
○ Bolgheri Bianco Nova '17	♛♛	4
○ Bolgheri Bianco Nova '16	♛♛	4
● Bolgheri Rosso Pievi '16	♛♛	4
● Bolgheri Rosso Pievi '15	♛♛	4

Muralia

LOC. IL POGGIARELLO
FRAZ. PIANETTO
VIA DEL SUGHERETO
58036 ROCCASTRADA [GR]
TEL. +39 0564577223
www.muralia.it

CELLAR SALES
PRE-BOOKED VISITS
ACCOMMODATION AND RESTAURANT SERVICE
ANNUAL PRODUCTION 65,000 bottles
HECTARES UNDER VINE 14.00
VITICULTURE METHOD Certified Organic
SUSTAINABLE WINERY

Stefano and Chiara Casali's enological adventure in Maremma began in 2003. Their core vineyards are situated in two areas, both in the DOC Maremma appellation: Poggiarelli, which is characterized by alluvial soils, and Sassofortino, which is calcareous-clay. Their winemaking style is modern but very well executed, with excellent balance. This Roccastrada winery's selection eschews forced tactics and excessive wood, making for a palate that's not lacking in suppleness or fragrance, qualities that are in keeping with the area's pedoclimate. The Maremma Toscana Babone '17 is redolent of small red berries and pepper, coming through dynamic, flavorful and a bit spicy hot on the palate. The Manolibera '17, made with Sangiovese, Cabernet Sauvignon and Merlot offers up lush aromas, foremost cherry, just slightly supported by toasty hints. On the palate it proves dense and nicely rhythmic. The Muralia '16, made with Cabernet Sauvignon, Syrah and Sangiovese, it just a bit clenched.

● Manolibera '17	🍷🍷 2*
● Maremma Toscana Babone '17	🍷🍷 3
● Muralia '16	🍷 5
○ Bianco Chiaraluna '13	🍷🍷 3
⊙ Corbizzo '17	🍷🍷 2*
● Manolibera '16	🍷🍷 2*
● Manolibera '15	🍷🍷 2*
● Manolibera '13	🍷🍷 2*
● Maremma Toscana Babone '13	🍷🍷 3
● Maremma Toscana Rosso Altana '16	🍷🍷 3*
● Monteregio di Massa Marittima Altana '15	🍷🍷 3*
● Monteregio di Massa Marittima Altana '11	🍷🍷 2*
● Muralia '10	🍷🍷 4

Tenute Silvio Nardi

LOC. CASALE DEL BOSCO
53024 MONTALCINO [SI]
TEL. +39 0577808332
www.tenutenardi.com

CELLAR SALES
PRE-BOOKED VISITS
ANNUAL PRODUCTION 250,000 bottles
HECTARES UNDER VINE 80.00

In his own way he was a pioneer. Indeed, Silvio Nardi was one of the first to bet on Montalcino, in an era very different from ours, the Second World War. It was a forward-thinking choice, to say the least, one that's being fully developed under Emilia, who manages the winery today. There are some thirty plots, situated primarily in Manachiara (to the east) and Casale del Bosco (northwest). After aging in mid-size casks and large barrels, these give rise to Sangiovese da Brunello wines that are classic in form and contemporary in substance. Their Brunello '14 isn't an extremely representative example. An austere aromatic profile sees fruity sensations, spices and soil. On the palate it unfolds supplely, proving poised and balanced. Their Rosso '17 follows a similar expressive track, though with an added share of Mediterranean sunniness on the nose, only to develop fluently and pervasively across the palate. Together they make a nice, reliable pair.

● Brunello di Montalcino '14	🍷🍷 6
● Rosso di Montalcino '17	🍷🍷 3
● Brunello di Montalcino Manachiara '99	🍷🍷🍷 7
● Brunello di Montalcino Manachiara '97	🍷🍷🍷 7
● Brunello di Montalcino '11	🍷🍷 6
● Brunello di Montalcino Poggio Doria '12	🍷🍷 8
● Brunello di Montalcino V. Manachiara '12	🍷🍷 8
● Brunello di Montalcino Vign. Poggio Doria '10	🍷🍷 8
● Brunello di Montalcino Vign. Poggio Doria Ris. '12	🍷🍷 8
● Brunello di Montalcino Vign. Poggio Doria Ris. '10	🍷🍷 8
● Rosso di Montalcino '16	🍷🍷 3
● Rosso di Montalcino '15	🍷🍷 3

★Orma

VIA BOLGHERESE
57022 CASTAGNETO CARDUCCI [LI]
TEL. +39 0575477857
www.ormawine.it

ANNUAL PRODUCTION 50,000 bottles
HECTARES UNDER VINE 5.50
SUSTAINABLE WINERY

Podere Orma is a branch of a rather major producer, designed and managed by Antonio Moretti (who also owns Tenuta Setteponti in Arezzo and Feudo Maccari in Sicily). It's a gem of a winery, just five hectares situated on clay soil rich in pebbles. Their production style is extremely appealing, inspired by the area's well-established traditions, but capable of expressing a personal quality that's both distinctive and sophisticated. Of course, the producer's most important wine is always presented quite young, which requires us to review it with an eye towards its aging prospects. That is the case for the 2017 version of their Rosso Sup. Orma, which is still in its early stages but absolute outstanding. Aromatically it's kaleidoscopic, while on the palate it's masterful in its share of oak and extraction, proving capable of continually changing pace. The Bolgheri Passi di Orma '17 is lighter, opting for aromas of red fruits such as pomegranate.

● Bolgheri Rosso Sup. Orma '17	♟♟♟ 8
● Bolgheri Rosso Passi di Orma '17	♟♟ 5
● Orma '16	♟♟♟ 8
● Orma '14	♟♟♟ 8
● Orma '13	♟♟♟ 8
● Orma '12	♟♟♟ 8
● Orma '11	♟♟♟ 8
● Orma '10	♟♟♟ 7
● Orma '09	♟♟♟ 6
● Orma '08	♟♟♟ 6
● Orma '07	♟♟♟ 5
● Orma '06	♟♟♟ 6
● Bolgheri Rosso '15	♟♟ 8
● Bolgheri Rosso Passi di Orma '16	♟♟ 5
● Orma '05	♟♟ 6

★★Ornellaia

FRAZ. BOLGHERI
LOC. ORNELLAIA, 191
57022 CASTAGNETO CARDUCCI [LI]
TEL. +39 056571811
www.ornellaia.it

PRE-BOOKED VISITS
ANNUAL PRODUCTION 930,000 bottles
HECTARES UNDER VINE 112.00

It's impossible to contain Ornellaia's fame, even Tuscany seems inadequate. Indeed, we're talking about one of Italian wine's most illustrious stars, a producer that's capable of shining like few in the world. It got its start in the 1980s and immediately made a name for itself. After a few changes in ownership it fell into the hands of Frescobaldi, who consolidated its position. Theirs are modern wines, monumental, with an intense, full-bodied character. It's a style for which the winery has always been known, but today is even more pronounced. Their Bolgheri Superiore Ornellaia 2016 is perfect for understanding their production philosophy. It's a compelling red for its impact and intensity, full of fruit and toasty sensations, yet also harmonious in its masterful play of balance, a feat made possible thanks to a favorable year. In short, it's an intelligible wine but also ageworthy — and decidedly so. Their Serre Nuove '17 and Ornellaia Bianco '16 are also both excellent.

● Bolgheri Rosso Sup. Ornellaia '16	♟♟♟ 8
○ Ornellaia Bianco '16	♟♟ 8
● Bolgheri Rosso Le Serre Nuove '17	♟♟ 6
○ Bolgheri Bianco Poggio alle Gazze '17	♟ 5
● Bolgheri Sup. Ornellaia '14	♟♟♟ 8
● Bolgheri Sup. Ornellaia '13	♟♟♟ 8
● Bolgheri Sup. Ornellaia '12	♟♟♟ 8
● Bolgheri Sup. Ornellaia '10	♟♟♟ 8
● Bolgheri Sup. Ornellaia '07	♟♟♟ 8
● Bolgheri Sup. Ornellaia '05	♟♟♟ 8
● Bolgheri Sup. Ornellaia '04	♟♟♟ 8
● Bolgheri Sup. Ornellaia '02	♟♟♟ 8
● Bolgheri Sup. Ornellaia '01	♟♟♟ 8

Siro Pacenti

LOC. PELAGRILLI, 1
53024 MONTALCINO [SI]
TEL. +39 0577848662
www.siropacenti.it

CELLAR SALES
PRE-BOOKED VISITS
ANNUAL PRODUCTION 60,000 bottles
HECTARES UNDER VINE 22.00

Siro Pacenti's winery was formed in the 1970s out of one of wine's great dynasties (and not just for Montalcino). Today Giancarlo is at the helm, a winemaker who's constantly remembered as one of the first 'modern' interpreters for his use of small barrels in aging, but especially for the idea of a Brunello more closely aligned with integrity and substance. This approach has gradually shifted according to the wines themselves, so as to more precisely express the unique attributes of Pelagrilli (to the north) and Piancornello (south). In this edition Siro Pacenti's wines convince, both their base level and premium offerings. We start with a pleasantly fragrant Rosso '17, a bottle in line with the characteristics of the vintage. The Brunello Pelagrilli '14 rises in intensity and nuance, proving potent and spicy. Last but not least, there's their Brunello Vecchie Vigne '14 — despite its mature, glyceric style, it exhibits a commendable development on the palate.

● Brunello di Montalcino V. V. '14	♟♟ 8
● Brunello di Montalcino Pelagrilli '14	♟♟ 6
● Rosso di Montalcino '17	♟♟ 5
● Brunello di Montalcino '97	♟♟♟ 7
● Brunello di Montalcino '96	♟♟♟ 7
● Brunello di Montalcino '95	♟♟♟ 7
● Brunello di Montalcino '88	♟♟♟ 7
● Brunello di Montalcino PS Ris. '07	♟♟♟ 8
● Brunello di Montalcino V. V. '10	♟♟♟ 8
● Brunello di Montalcino Pelagrilli '13	♟♟ 6
● Brunello di Montalcino Pelagrilli '12	♟♟ 6
● Brunello di Montalcino Pelagrilli '11	♟♟ 6
● Brunello di Montalcino PS Ris. '10	♟♟ 8
● Brunello di Montalcino V. V. '13	♟♟ 8
● Brunello di Montalcino V. V. '11	♟♟ 8
● Rosso di Montalcino '16	♟♟ 5
● Rosso di Montalcino '15	♟♟ 5

Il Palagione

LOC. PALAGIONE
VIA PER CASTEL SAN GIMIGNANO, 36
53037 SAN GIMIGNANO [SI]
TEL. +39 0577953134
www.ilpalagione.com

CELLAR SALES
PRE-BOOKED VISITS
ACCOMMODATION
ANNUAL PRODUCTION 60,000 bottles
HECTARES UNDER VINE 16.00
VITICULTURE METHOD Certified Organic

Palagione is a historic estate with roots that go back to 1594. In the mid-1990s it was purchased by Monica Rota and Giorgio Comotti. Their entrepreneurial efforts are characterized by passion and skill, which they deploy to the maximum in cultivating not just vineyards, but also olives, walnuts and cherries. They also offer guest accommodations. These were chosen for their elevated position, which offers views of both the valley and San Gimignano. The Vernaccia Hydra '18 opens with fresh vegetal aromas, notes of thyme and calamint, then lime peel and apple. On the palate it's racy, thanks to enjoyable acidity, marked by nice weight and a sapid finish. The Vernaccia Lyra '16 features a bouquet of mature fruit, with a foreground of yellow peaches and apricot adorned by hints of orange. In the mouth it's round, big and juicy, closing long and gratifying.

○ Vernaccia di S. Gimignano Hydra '18	♟♟ 2*
○ Vernaccia di San Gimignano Lyra '16	♟♟ 3
○ Vernaccia di San Gimignano Ori Ris. '17	♟♟ 3
● Antajr '15	♟ 4
● Chianti Colli Senesi Caelum '17	♟ 2
⊙ San Gimignano Rosato Sunrosé '18	♟ 2
● Chianti Colli Senesi Caelum '15	♟♟ 2*
● Chianti Colli Senesi Drago Ris. '14	♟♟ 3
○ Vernaccia di S. Gimignano Hydra '17	♟♟ 2*
○ Vernaccia di S. Gimignano Ori Ris. '15	♟♟ 3
○ Vernaccia di San Gimignano Lyra '15	♟♟ 3
○ Vernaccia di San Gimignano Ori Ris. '15	♟♟ 3

Palazzo

Loc. Palazzo, 144
53024 Montalcino [SI]
Tel. +39 0577849226
www.aziendapalazzo.it

CELLAR SALES
PRE-BOOKED VISITS
ANNUAL PRODUCTION 21,000 bottles
HECTARES UNDER VINE 4.00
VITICULTURE METHOD Certified Biodynamic

Angelo and Elia Loia oversee the winery launched in the 1980s by their parents Cosimo and Antonietta when the couple purchased Tenuta Palazzo. Characterized by elevations of around 300 meters and soil rich in sand and marl, the plots are situated in east Montalcino, an area well-defined in terms of pedoclimate. Their Sangiovese da Brunello wines are then aged in barriques and large barrels. The result is wines that are intense and clenched in youth, but that after bottle aging, gradually prove more radiant and relaxed. Reliability and constance prove to be Tenuta Palazzo's principal attributes. Their Rosso '17 features a delicate, airy stride, while their Brunello '14 exhibits a rougher quality, though without comprising on fruity energy and mobility on the palate. Their Brunello Ris. '13 impresses for its classic style — redolent of wild berries, licorice, plowed earth, on the palate its somewhat stiff tannins (in this stage) don't affect its breadth and juice.

● Brunello di Montalcino '14	♥♥ 6
● Brunello di Montalcino Ris. '13	♥♥ 7
● Rosso di Montalcino '17	♥♥ 3
● Rosso di Montalcino '15	♥♥♥ 3*
● Brunello di Montalcino '13	♀♀ 6
● Brunello di Montalcino '10	♀♀ 6
● Brunello di Montalcino '09	♀♀ 6
● Brunello di Montalcino '08	♀♀ 6
● Brunello di Montalcino '07	♀♀ 6
● Brunello di Montalcino Ris. '12	♀♀ 7
● Brunello di Montalcino Ris. '10	♀♀ 7
● Brunello di Montalcino Ris. '07	♀♀ 7
● Rosso di Montalcino '16	♀♀ 3
● Rosso di Montalcino '11	♀♀ 3

Panizzi

Loc. Santa Margherita, 34
53037 San Gimignano [SI]
Tel. +39 0577941576
www.panizzi.it

CELLAR SALES
PRE-BOOKED VISITS
ACCOMMODATION
ANNUAL PRODUCTION 210,000 bottles
HECTARES UNDER VINE 50.00

Giovanni Panizzi was one of the pioneers of San Gimignano's modern Vernaccia renaissance. For some years now his winery, which he built around the Santa Margherita estate in the late 1970s, has been in the hands of Simone Niccolai. He's expanded its vineyards and enlarged their selection of wines. In addition to vintage Vernaccia and a reserve, they're developing other wines as well, like Pinot Nero, a Sangiovese rosé and Merlot. Their extra-virgin olive oil and agritourism are also of increasing focus. The Vernaccia Riserva '15 features a bouquet in which attractive oak initially prevails only to give way to tobacco and aromatic herbs like marjoram and basil, all on a fruity backdrop of peach. On the palate it's complex, structured, big and properly dense, with a rising finish coming through sapid and lively. The Vernaccia Santa Margherita '17 offers up delicate nuances of lemon verbena and slightly citrusy notes, then apple, the prelude to a harmonious and long palate.

○ Vernaccia di S. Gimignano Ris. '15	♥♥ 5
○ Passito '17	♥♥ 4
○ Vernaccia di S. Gimignano '18	♥♥ 2*
○ Vernaccia di San Gimignano V. Santa Margherita '17	♥♥ 3
⊙ Ceraso Rosato '18	♥ 2
● Chianti Colli Senesi Vertunno Ris. '14	♥ 2
● San Gimignano Pinot Nero '17	♥ 2
● San Gimignano Rosso Folgore '15	♥ 5
○ Vernaccia di S. Gimignano Ris. '07	♀♀♀ 5
○ Vernaccia di S. Gimignano Ris. '05	♀♀♀ 5
○ Vernaccia di S. Gimignano Ris. '98	♀♀♀ 4*
○ Evoè '16	♀♀ 4
○ Vernaccia di S. Gimignano Ris. '14	♀♀ 5
○ Vernaccia di S. Gimignano Ris. '13	♀♀ 5
○ Vernaccia di San Gimignano V. Santa Margherita '16	♀♀ 3

Parmoleto

LOC. MONTENERO D'ORCIA
POD. PARMOLETONE, 44
58040 CASTEL DEL PIANO [GR]
TEL. +39 0564954131
www.parmoleto.it

CELLAR SALES
PRE-BOOKED VISITS
ACCOMMODATION AND RESTAURANT SERVICE
ANNUAL PRODUCTION 22,000 bottles
HECTARES UNDER VINE 6.00

Since 1990, the Sodi family have been producing wine here in Castel del Piano, on Monte Amiata, in one of Montecucco's most interesting districts. Theirs is a small vineyard of primarily Sangiovese, which gives rise to wines of good quality and personality. Today, this artisanal winery seems to have come into its own, offering a selection of notable wines that bring together a traditional approach with targeted forays into modern winemaking. This is especially true of their use of wood, which can, at times, be a bit excessive. The Montecucco Sangiovese Riserva '15 features clear, focused aromas of violet and fresh cherry on a background of flint and spices. On the palate it's lively, juicy and full-bodied. The Montecucco Rosso '16 also exhibits a lovely dynamic of flavor accompanied by intense and approachable aromas. The Vermentino Carabatto '18 is fragrant, but finds its strong point on the palate, where it develops sapid, well-sustained and fragrant.

● Montecucco Sangiovese Ris. '15	♟♟♟ 3*
● Montecucco Rosso '16	♟♟ 2*
○ Montecucco Vermentino Carabatto '18	♟♟ 2*
● Montecucco Sangiovese '14	♟♟ 3
● Montecucco Sangiovese '13	♟♟ 3
● Montecucco Sangiovese '12	♟♟ 3
● Montecucco Sangiovese '11	♟♟ 3
● Montecucco Sangiovese Ris. '13	♟♟ 3*
● Montecucco Sangiovese Ris. '12	♟♟ 3
● Montecucco Sangiovese Ris. '11	♟♟ 3*
● Montecucco Sangiovese Ris. '10	♟♟ 3

Tenuta La Parrina

FRAZ. ALBINIA
S.DA VICINALE DELLA PARRINA
58015 ORBETELLO [GR]
TEL. +39 0564862626
www.parrina.it

CELLAR SALES
PRE-BOOKED VISITS
ACCOMMODATION AND RESTAURANT SERVICE
ANNUAL PRODUCTION 100,000 bottles
HECTARES UNDER VINE 60.00
SUSTAINABLE WINERY

Managed by the Spinola family since the late 19th century, La Parrina, whose name comes from the Castilian 'Parra' (meaning 'pergola') is the only winery of the Parrina DOC designation (officially recognized in 1971). Their wide range comprises traditional grapes, like Sangiovese, Trebbiano and Ansonica, but international varieties also make a notable contribution, from Cab Sauvignon to Merlot, Chardonnay and Sauvignon. Their modern style privileges pleasantness and aromatic approachability, but they offer more ambitious wines as well. The Parrina Sangiovese '18 is a bottle that successfully plays on pleasantness. It has fragrant aromas and a sapid development of flavor, proving rhythmic and not without character. Their Ansonica Costa dell'Argentario '18 delivers, with its fresh aromas anticipating a penetrating and decisive palate. The succulent Parrina Rosso Muraccio '17 is notable, while the Parrina Sangiovese Ris. '16 and Parrina Merlot Radaia '16 prove more compact.

● Parrina Sangiovese '18	♟♟♟ 3*
○ Ansonica Costa dell'Argentario '18	♟♟ 3*
● Parrina Rosso Muraccio '17	♟♟ 4
● Parrina Sangiovese Ris. '16	♟♟ 5
○ Parrina Bianco Vialetto '18	♟ 3
● Parrina Merlot Radaia '16	♟ 7
○ Parrina Vermentino '18	♟ 3
○ Costa dell'Argentario Ansonica '17	♟♟♟ 3
○ Ansonica Costa dell'Argentario '16	♟♟ 3
○ Costa dell'Argentario Ansonica '15	♟♟ 3
● Parrina Merlot Radaia '15	♟♟ 6
● Parrina Rosso Muraccio '16	♟♟ 4
● Parrina Rosso Muraccio '14	♟♟ 3*
● Parrina Sangiovese '16	♟♟ 2*
○ Parrina Vermentino '16	♟♟ 3

Tenuta Perano

S.DA DI SAN DONATO IN PERANO
53013 GAIOLE IN CHIANTI [SI]
TEL. +39 0577749563
www.frescobaldi.com

ANNUAL PRODUCTION 500,000 bottles
HECTARES UNDER VINE 52.00

The Frescobaldis recently added a new estate, their seventh in Tuscany. Tenuta di Perano is a lovely 250-hectare property with 52 vineyards that had been rented and were subsequently purchased. Their vineyards, which grow in gravelly soil, form an amphitheater surrounded by woods. This, along with notable elevations (400-500 meters) sees to it that Sangiovese ripens late, making for elegant, expansive wines. Situated in Gaiole in Chianti, the new brand means that the family are fully within Chianti Classico. Three wines were submitted. The excellent Chianti Classico '16 is redolent of cherry and aromatic herbs. Smooth tannins and an expansive, fresh palate are supported by lovely acidity. The Riserva '16 is more firmly-structured. But the bottle that most speaks to the winery's potential is the Gran Selezione I Rialzi '15, the result of careful selection of the best grapes. It exhibits depth, complexity and elegance, closing extremely long.

● Chianti Cl. Gran Selezione I Rialzi '15	♛♛♛ 6
● Chianti Cl. '16	♛♛ 3
● Chianti Cl. Ris. '16	♛♛ 5

Perazzeta

FRAZ. MONTENERO D'ORCIA
VIA DELLA PIAZZA
58033 CASTEL DEL PIANO [GR]
TEL. +39 3803545477
www.perazzeta.it

CELLAR SALES
PRE-BOOKED VISITS
ANNUAL PRODUCTION 100,000 bottles
HECTARES UNDER VINE 19.00

Situated in Montenero d'Orcia, this winery was purchased in 2016 by the Narducci family. They make wines whose quality is generally more than respectable. Sangiovese takes center stage, as the Montecucco appellation requires, but in the cellar they also work with Cabernet Sauvignon, Merlot, Syrah and Vermentino. Their style, which is made possible thanks to the quality of the grapes used, is a measured mix of tradition and modern approaches, as is evident by their use of wood for aging (barriques and large barrels). Fermentation is carried out entirely in steel. The Montecucco Sangiovese Terra dei Bocci '15 offers up elegant floral and fruity aromas. It's a lean-structured wine but extremely sapid and tasty on the palate. The Montecucco Rosso Alfeno '17 features lush, intense fruit on the nose and a full, decisive development on the palate. The Montecucco Sangiovese Licurgo Riserva '15 is a bit held back by oak.

● Montecucco Rosso Alfeno '17	♛♛ 2*
● Montecucco Sangiovese Terre dei Bocci '15	♛♛ 3
● Montecucco Sangiovese Licurgo Ris. '15	♛ 4
○ Montecucco Vermentino '18	♛ 2
● Maremma Terre dei Bocci '11	♛♛ 3
● Montecucco Rosso Alfeno '15	♛♛ 2*
● Montecucco Rosso Alfeno '14	♛♛ 2*
● Montecucco Rosso Alfeno '12	♛♛ 2*
● Montecucco Rosso Alfeno '11	♛♛ 2*
● Montecucco Sangiovese Licurgo Ris. '13	♛♛ 5
● Montecucco Sangiovese Licurgo Ris. '11	♛♛ 4
● Montecucco Sangiovese Licurgo Ris. '09	♛♛ 5
● Montecucco Sangiovese Terre dei Bocci '14	♛♛ 3
○ Montecucco Vermentino '16	♛♛ 2*

Peteglia

LOC. PODERE PETEGLIA
FRAZ. MONTENERO D'ORCIA
58033 CASTEL DEL PIANO [GR]
TEL. +39 3498335438
www.peteglia.com

CELLAR SALES
PRE-BOOKED VISITS
ACCOMMODATION AND RESTAURANT SERVICE
ANNUAL PRODUCTION 30,000 bottles
HECTARES UNDER VINE 7.00

The Innocenti family perfectly represent
Montecucco's classic, small, family-run
producers, offering artisanal and
traditionally-styled wines. Sangiovese takes
center stage, and it's interpreted with nice
personality and character (despite the
occasional aromatic aberration). Aging is
carried out both in small wood barrels and
large casks, making for a coherent,
convincing mix. The Montecucco
Sangiovese '16 sees spices and smoky
notes rise up off an intensely fruity
background, while on the palate it exhibits
vitality and spirited tannins. The
Montecucco Sangiovese Riserva '15 is
more austere and marked by the
occasional hint of oak, though it's sapid
and tasty nevertheless. The Maremma
Toscana Cabernet '16 is held back by
somewhat immoderate oak, while the
Montecucco Vermentino '18 proves simple
and approachable.

● Montecucco Sangiovese '16	♟♟ 3
● Montecucco Sangiovese Ris. '15	♟♟ 5
● Maremma Toscana Cabernet '16	♟ 4
○ Montecucco Vermentino '18	♟ 2
● Maremma Toscana Sangiovese Mezzodì '16	♟♟ 2*
● Montecucco Sangiovese Ris. '13	♟♟ 5
● Montecucco Sangiovese Ris. '10	♟♟ 4

Petra

LOC. SAN LORENZO ALTO, 131
57028 SUVERETO [LI]
TEL. +39 0565845308
www.petrawine.it

CELLAR SALES
PRE-BOOKED VISITS
ANNUAL PRODUCTION 350,000 bottles
HECTARES UNDER VINE 94.00
SUSTAINABLE WINERY

Vittorio Moretti came to Tuscany after his
successes in Franciacorta. He chose an
area not far from the sea, and the hamlet
of Suvereto. It's a territory rich in cork oak,
Mediterranean shrubs, olive trees and
vineyards. Ultimately he called on a great
architect, Mario Botta, to design what
would become a wine monument, their
cellar. Today Francesca Moretti is at the
helm, bringing passion and experience to a
selection made with both native and
international grapes. Once again their
Petra '16, a Cab. Sauvignon and Merlot
blend, takes home Tre Bicchieri. Alluring
notes of berries greet the nose, enriched
by balsamic and spicy hints accompanied
by lovely nuances of cinnamon and
nutmeg. On the palate it enters big,
creamy, unfolding a delicate, subtle tannic
weave while letting through nice acidity.
The Colle al Fico '16, a Syrah, also
delivered with its lovely notes of tobacco,
its earthy and herbaceous hints on the
nose and a palate that exhibits lively, juicy,
healthy fruit.

● Petra Rosso '16	♟♟♟ 8
● Colle al Fico '16	♟♟ 6
● Alto '16	♟♟ 6
● Potenti '16	♟♟ 6
● Quercegobbe '16	♟♟ 6
● Suvereto Hebo '17	♟♟ 3
○ La Balena '17	♟ 6
● Petra Rosso '15	♟♟♟ 8
● Petra Rosso '14	♟♟♟ 8
● Petra Rosso '13	♟♟♟ 8
● Petra Rosso '12	♟♟♟ 8
● Petra Rosso '11	♟♟♟ 8
● Petra Rosso '04	♟♟♟ 7

★Fattoria Petrolo

LAZ. MERCATALE VALDARNO
A PETROLO, 30
2021 BUCINE [AR]
L. +39 0559911322
ww.petrolo.it

CELLAR SALES
PRE-BOOKED VISITS
ACCOMMODATION
ANNUAL PRODUCTION 85,000 bottles
HECTARES UNDER VINE 31.00
VITICULTURE METHOD Certified Organic

Luca Sanjust's estate spans 272 hectares
in Bucine, in Valdarno di Sopra. In recent
years they've focused on renovation of their
vineyards and upgrading their cellar, where
they make characterful wines with
Sangiovese, Merlot, Cabernet Sauvignon
and Trebbiano. There's also a selection in
which wines are fermented and aged in
terra-cotta amphoras, one of winemaking's
oldest techniques. Great attention is also
paid to their extra-virgin olive oil. The
delicious Galatrona '16, which is made
entirely with Merlot grapes, offers up a
subtle and complex bouquet in which clear
and focused fruity notes emerge, of cherry
and plums, ennobled by spicy hints of
pepper and cinnamon and topped off by
orice. On the palate it proves big, quite
balanced in its tannins, and fresh, before
giving way to an oaky finish. The interesting
Trebbiano Boggina B '17 features intense
fragrances of fruits and slightly citrusy
hints. It enters well in the mouth, where it's
juicy, warm and a dynamic.

Boggina B '17	▮▮ 6
Valdarno di Sopra Merlot Galatrona '16	▮▮ 8
Valdarno di Sopra Sangiovese Bòggina A '17	▮▮ 6
Valdarno di Sopra Sangiovese Bòggina C '17	▮▮ 6
Valdarno di Sopra Pietraviva Torrione '17	▮ 4
Galatrona '12	♈♈♈ 8
Galatrona '11	♈♈♈ 8
Galatrona '10	♈♈♈ 8
Galatrona '09	♈♈♈ 8
Galatrona '08	♈♈♈ 8
Torrione '11	♈♈♈ 5
Valdarno di Sopra Galatrona '14	♈♈♈ 8
Valdarno di Sopra Galatrona '13	♈♈♈ 8

★Piaggia

LOC. POGGETTO
VIA CEGOLI, 47
59016 POGGIO A CAIANO [PO]
TEL. +39 0558705401
www.piaggia.com

CELLAR SALES
PRE-BOOKED VISITS
ANNUAL PRODUCTION 75,000 bottles
HECTARES UNDER VINE 15.00

The winery that straddles Poggio a Caiano
and Carmignano was purchased in the
mid-1970s by Mauro Vannucci. Today it's
in the hands of his daughter, Silvia, who
oversees a selection centered on DOCG
Carmignano, as well as more experimental
wines, like their monovarietal Cab. Franc.
Their modern cellar is covered in earth,
grass and olives so as to maintain the right
temperature and humidity. Once again, Tre
Bicchieri for their Carmignano Ris.'16, a
wine whose intense aromas of cherry and
plum join with slightly balsamic hints and
delicate vanilla. On the palate it exhibits a
firm, harmonious body rich in fruit and
flesh, while silky tannins are supported by
an enticing acidity, making for a notably
long finish. It's our Red of the Year. Their
freshly acidic, long and gratifying Poggio
de' Colli '16, a Cab. Franc, offers up
sensations of blood-rich meat, then
blackberry fruit, fading to hints of mint and
licorice. It's warm in the mouth, with
delicate, well integrated tannins.

● Carmignano Ris. '16	▮▮▮ 6
● Poggio de' Colli '16	▮▮ 8
● Carmignano Il Sasso '17	▮▮ 4
● Carmignano Ris. '15	♈♈♈ 6
● Carmignano Ris. '14	♈♈♈ 6
● Carmignano Ris. '13	♈♈♈ 6
● Carmignano Ris. '12	♈♈♈ 6
● Carmignano Ris. '11	♈♈♈ 6
● Carmignano Ris. '08	♈♈♈ 5
● Carmignano Ris. '07	♈♈♈ 5
● Carmignano Ris. '99	♈♈♈ 5
● Carmignano Ris. '98	♈♈♈ 5
● Carmignano Sasso '07	♈♈♈ 4
● Il Sasso '01	♈♈♈ 4
● Poggio de' Colli '11	♈♈♈ 7
● Poggio de' Colli '10	♈♈♈ 6

Piancornello

Loc. Piancornello
53024 Montalcino [SI]
Tel. +39 0577844105
www.piancornello.it

CELLAR SALES
PRE-BOOKED VISITS
ANNUAL PRODUCTION 50,000 bottles
HECTARES UNDER VINE 10.00

The lovely estate that's belonged to the Monaci-Pieri family since the 1950s gets its name from the celebrated district that stretches towards Monte Amiata and two rivers, the Orcia and the Asso. Formed out of somewhat steep terrain, it's a territory that's strongly influenced by its warm, sunny microclimate, as well as relatively lower elevations (around 250 meters). Such conditions are perfect for lush, pervasive Sangiovese da Brunello aged primarily in small wood barrels. Piancornello's selection suggests a stage of mature awareness, with a host of interesting wines coming out year after year. This time it's their Brunello Ris. '13 leading the group, with its rich and fruity aromatic profile of black cherry and plums deepened by sensations of embers, black olive and curing spices. This openly Mediterranean character is confirmed across its broad, caressing palate.

● Brunello di Montalcino Ris. '13	🏆🏆 7
● Per Emma '15	🏆 3
● Rosso di Montalcino '17	🏆 3
● Brunello di Montalcino '13	🏆🏆🏆 6
● Brunello di Montalcino '10	🏆🏆🏆 6
● Brunello di Montalcino '06	🏆🏆🏆 6
● Brunello di Montalcino '99	🏆🏆🏆 6
● Brunello di Montalcino '12	🏆🏆 6
● Brunello di Montalcino '11	🏆🏆 6
● Brunello di Montalcino '09	🏆🏆 6
● Brunello di Montalcino '08	🏆🏆 6
● Brunello di Montalcino '07	🏆🏆 6
● Brunello di Montalcino Ris. '12	🏆🏆 7
● Brunello di Montalcino Ris. '06	🏆🏆 6
● Rosso di Montalcino '15	🏆🏆 3
● Rosso di Montalcino '11	🏆🏆 3

Piandaccoli

via Paganelle, 7
50041 Calenzano [FI]
Tel. +39 0550750005
www.piandaccoli.it

CELLAR SALES
PRE-BOOKED VISITS
ANNUAL PRODUCTION 100,000 bottles
HECTARES UNDER VINE 20.00

The work carried out by Giampaolo Bruni on his estate near Florence is aimed at respecting nature and rediscovering the area's roots. The use of toxic substances is kept to a minimum, while only 'natural' fertilizer (from his private stables) is employed, a choice that can attract insects. He loves lesser known grapes, like Barasaglina, Foglia Tonda, Mammolo and Pugnitello, which are cultivated alongside Colorino, Malvasia and Sangiovese (some 11 different clones of it). The Pugnitello '1 opens with sensations of blood-rich meat, then plums followed by notes of green tomato, bay leaf and aromatic herbs. On the palate it enters pleasant, meaty and firm, with nice power and a lively, tasty finish. The intriguing Mammolo '16 sees mature, jammy notes of black cherry dominate, followed by potpourri and tanned leather. In the mouth it's docile, well-gauged and relaxed, quite pleasant. The Barsaglina '16 is floral on the nose, fresh on the palate.

● Barsaglina del Rinascimento '16	🏆🏆
● Inprimis '16	🏆🏆
● Mammolo del Rinascimento '16	🏆🏆
● Pugnitello del Rinascimento '16	🏆🏆
● Chianti Ris. Cosmus '16	🏆
● Foglia Tonda del Rinascimento '16	🏆
● Maiorem '15	🏆
○ Vivendi '17	🏆
● Chianti Cosmus Ris. '14	🏆🏆
● Foglia Tonda del Rinascimento '15	🏆🏆
● Foglia Tonda del Rinascimento '13	🏆🏆
● Maiorem '13	🏆🏆
● Pugnitello del Rinascimento '15	🏆🏆
○ Vin Santo del Chianti Occhio di Pernice '14	🏆🏆

ianirossi

C. PORRONA
D. SANTA GENOVEFFA, 1
044 CINIGIANO [GR]
L. +39 0564990573
ww.pianirossi.it

ELLAR SALES
RE-BOOKED VISITS
CCOMMODATION AND RESTAURANT SERVICE
NNUAL PRODUCTION 50,000 bottles
ECTARES UNDER VINE 14.00

anirossi is situated on the Porrona hills, in
nigiano. Here Stefano Sincini has brought
life a modern selection made primarily
th international grape varieties. It's a
oice that, as of late, has led to wines that
e well crafted and constantly improving.
ven if his range centers on this approach,
ore recently his Montecucco designated
nes are also proving to be of high quality,
th a forthright sapidity and noteworthy
eshness. The Solus '16 exhibits a subtle,
ersonal character. It's a blend of
angiovese, Montepulciano and Alicante
aracterized by aromas of red fruits and
ices, sensations that pair well with its
cculent, rhythmic and elegant palate. The
ontecucco Sangiovese '16 is full and
brant, the Pianirossi '16 (a blend of Petit
rdot, Montepulciano and Cabernet
auvignon) more compact and oaky.

Solus '16	▼▼▼ 4*
Montecucco Sangiovese La Fonte '16	▼▼ 5
Pianirossi '16	▼▼ 6
Montecucco Rosso Sidus '16	♈ 2*
Montecucco Rosso Sidus '15	♈ 2*
Montecucco Sangiovese La Fonte '15	♈ 5
Montecucco Sidus '14	♈ 2*
Montecucco Sidus '13	♈ 2*
Montecucco Sidus '11	♈ 4
Pianirossi '12	♈ 6
Pianirossi '11	♈ 6
Solus '14	♈ 3
Solus '12	♈ 3
Solus '11	♈ 4
Solus '10	♈ 4

Tenute Piccini

LOC. PIAZZOLE, 25
53011 CASTELLINA IN CHIANTI [SI]
TEL. +39 057754011
www.tenutepiccini.it

ANNUAL PRODUCTION 15,000,000 bottles
HECTARES UNDER VINE 470.00

The Piccini family is now on its fourth
generation, following in the footsteps of
their forefather Angiolo, who began
cultivating grapes on a small Chianti
vineyard. Today Mario and his sisters
Martina and Elisa carry on, bringing the
same passion to their work. Today they
avail themselves of six estates, four of
which are in Tuscany: Fattoria di Valiano
(Castelnuovo Berardenga), Geografico
(Gaiole), Villa al Cortile (Montalcino) and
Tenuta Moraia (Maremma). Then there's
Regio Cantina in Basilicata, and Torre
Mora in Sicily. The Valiano farm's Gran
Selezione '15 6.38 performed well. It
offers up a fresh, complex bouquet, with
notes of aromatic herbs joining with wild
berries accented by pleasant spicy hints. In
the mouth it enters soft, with nice texture,
delicate, subtle tannins and a long finish.
Geografico's elegantly structured and
relaxed Ris. Montegiachi '16 features
mature aromas, tertiaries as well, of
tobacco and tanned leather on a jammy
background of cherries.

● Chianti Classico Gran Selezione Valiano 6.38 '15	▼▼▼ 5
● Chianti Cl. Montegiachi Ris. Geografico '16	▼▼ 4
● Chianti Cl. Valiano Poggio Teo '16	▼▼ 4
● Il Pacchia '16	▼▼ 2*
● Sasso al Poggio '16	▼▼ 3
● Bolgheri Gattabuia Tenuta Moraia '14	♈ 3
● Bolgheri Rosso Pietracupa Tenuta Moraia '12	♈ 3
○ Calasera Vermentino Tenuta Moraia '16	♈ 2*
● Chianti Cl. Contessa di Radda '15	♈ 2*
● Chianti Cl. Valiano '15	♈ 3*
● Chianti Cl. Valiano Poggio Teo '15	♈ 4
● Il Pacchia '15	♈ 2*
● Sasso al Poggio '15	♈ 3
● Vino in Musica '10	♈ 4

Pietroso

LOC. PIETROSO, 257
53024 MONTALCINO [SI]
TEL. +39 0577848573
www.pietroso.it

CELLAR SALES
PRE-BOOKED VISITS
ANNUAL PRODUCTION 30,000 bottles
HECTARES UNDER VINE 5.00

Supported by his wife and children, Gianni Pignattai is one of Montalcino's most highly-esteemed winemakers. His relaxed rigor is universally appreciated, a trait that's on full display in his selection of Sangioveses. The grapes are cultivated on four estates. Around his cellar (the western part of Collina Centrale) we find his Pietroso vineyards. Near to Sant'Antimo Abbey (to the south) are his Colombaiolo plots, while to the north we find his Fornello vineyards and the old parcel (now replanted) that gives rise to his Villa Montosoli. Pietroso's wines once again prove the producer's special gift for interpreting problematic vintages. Just look at the Brunello '14, a small gem of force and drinkability: vibrant fruit, medicinal herbs and spices emerge on the nose. On the palate it's kept together from beginning to end, freeing up a precious citrus and delicately salty stroke. Their Rosso '17 is no less notable, a 'faux simple' wine that offers up joy and flavor.

● Brunello di Montalcino '14	▼▼▼ 6
● Rosso di Montalcino '17	▼▼ 4
● Villa Montosoli '15	▼▼ 7
● Brunello di Montalcino '09	▽▽▽ 6
● Brunello di Montalcino '13	▽▽ 6
● Brunello di Montalcino '12	▽▽ 6
● Brunello di Montalcino '11	▽▽ 6
● Brunello di Montalcino '10	▽▽ 6
● Brunello di Montalcino '08	▽▽ 6
● Brunello di Montalcino '04	▽▽ 5
● Brunello di Montalcino Ris. '10	▽▽ 6
● Rosso di Montalcino '16	▽▽ 4
● Rosso di Montalcino '15	▽▽ 4
● Rosso di Montalcino '14	▽▽ 4
● Rosso di Montalcino '13	▽▽ 4
● Rosso di Montalcino '12	▽▽ 4
● Rosso di Montalcino '11	▽▽ 3*

Pieve Santo Stefano

LOC. SARDINI
55100 LUCCA
TEL. +39 0583394115
www.pievedisantostefano.com

CELLAR SALES
PRE-BOOKED VISITS
ACCOMMODATION
ANNUAL PRODUCTION 45,000 bottles
HECTARES UNDER VINE 10.60
SUSTAINABLE WINERY

Pieve Santo Stefano is situated on the hill that line Lucca. It's an area characterized by a cool climate, where the pursuit of high concentration seems like a fool's errand. Francesca Bogazzi and Antoine Hiriz have perfectly understood the situation, offering a selection comfortingly consistent in its grace, balance and drinkability. Sangiovese and Ciliegiolo take center stage, though they're supported by the discerning use of Cabernet Franc, Merlot and Syrah. Aging is entrusted to a mix of large wood and small wood barrels. The 2016 version of the Lippo, a blend of Merlot and Cabernet Franc, benefited from a niceyear, highlighting fragrant and varietal aromas well-adorned by spicy, smoky accents. On the palate it proves well-sustained, rhythmic and exhibits nice contrast (it's just a bit held back by oak at the finish). The pleasantly drinkable Colline Lucchesi Villa Sardini '17 stands out for it clear, clean aromas.

● Lippo '16	▼▼
● Colline Lucchesi Villa Sardini '17	▼▼
● Colline Lucchesi Ludovico Sardini '15	▽▽
● Colline Lucchesi Ludovico Sardini '13	▽▽
● Colline Lucchesi Villa Sardini '16	▽▽
● Colline Lucchesi Villa Sardini '15	▽▽
● Lippo '15	▽▽
● Lippo '14	▽▽

Pinino

LOC. PININO, 327
53024 MONTALCINO [SI]
TEL. +39 0577849381
www.pinino.com

CELLAR SALES
PRE-BOOKED VISITS
ANNUAL PRODUCTION 90,000 bottles
HECTARES UNDER VINE 16.00

It was 2003 when the Austrian couple of Andrea and Hannes Gamon decided to join forces with the Spanish couple Max and Silvia Hernandez. Their aim was to take over a winery founded by the notary Tito Costanti more than a century and a half ago. It was the beginning of Pinino's second life. It's a scenic estate situated in north Montalcino, along the slopes facing Montosoli. The Sangiovese cultivated here gives rise to three Brunellos ('vintage', Cupio and Pinone Riserva), all bound by a delectably visceral expressivity. Pinino's Brunellos didn't manage to repeat last year's splendid performance, but they still proved notable, even when it came to a year as difficult as 2014. The 'vintage' version features a spicy character that ties in with jammy sensations. It's all a prelude to a pleasantly lean palate. Their Cupio is more open in its Mediterranean and sylvan registers, with a flowery touch softening a palate that's a bit closed and rough at the end.

Brunello di Montalcino '14	▼▼	6
Brunello di Montalcino Cupio '14	▼▼	5
Rosso di Montalcino '17	▼	3
Brunello di Montalcino '13	♀♀	6
Brunello di Montalcino '11	♀♀	7
Brunello di Montalcino '10	♀♀	6
Brunello di Montalcino '09	♀♀	6
Brunello di Montalcino Cupio '13	♀♀	5
Brunello di Montalcino Pinino '07	♀♀	6
Brunello di Montalcino Pinone Ris. '12	♀♀	7
Brunello di Montalcino Pinone Ris. '10	♀♀	8
Brunello di Montalcino Pinone Ris. '07	♀♀	7
Brunello di Montalcino Pinone Ris. '06	♀♀	7
Brunello di Montalcino Pinone Ris. '04	♀♀	8
Rosso di Montalcino '16	♀♀	3*
Rosso di Montalcino '11	♀♀	3

Tenuta Podernovo

VIA PODERNUOVO, 13
56030 TERRICCIOLA [PI]
TEL. +39 0587655173
www.tenutapodernovo.it

CELLAR SALES
PRE-BOOKED VISITS
ACCOMMODATION
ANNUAL PRODUCTION 140,000 bottles
HECTARES UNDER VINE 25.00
VITICULTURE METHOD Certified Organic

Podernovo, a winery on a steady path of growth, belongs to the Lunellis, a family famous throughout Italy and the world for their Ferrari di Trento sparklers, but whose commitment to quality reaches beyond. In an area of rare beauty in Terricciola, along the Pisane hills, they cultivate Sangiovese and international classics. The resulting wines are increasingly precise and can surprise for their profile, style and authoritativeness. And their Auritea '16 does just that, beyond a shadow of a doubt. This Cab. Franc literally bewitched us. Toastiness is still pronounced, but its overall profile approaches perfection — time will see to it that its components integrate more fully. Aromatically dark, there's an herbaceous quality that's extraordinarily charming, while on the palate it's complex and enticing, never banal, decidedly deep. Their Teuto '16, a blend of Sangiovese, Merlot and Cabernet magnificent in its pulp and length, is right up there as well.

● Auritea '16	▼▼▼	8
● Teuto '16	▼▼	5
● Aliotto '16	♀♀	3
● Aliotto '15	♀♀	3
● Aliotto '06	♀♀	3
● Aliotto '05	♀♀	2
● Aliotto '04	♀♀	2
● Auritea '15	♀♀	8
● Teuto '15	♀♀	5
● Teuto '05	♀♀	4
● Teuto '03	♀♀	4

Poggerino

LOC. POGGERINO, 6
53017 RADDA IN CHIANTI [SI]
TEL. +39 0577738958
www.poggerino.com

CELLAR SALES
PRE-BOOKED VISITS
ACCOMMODATION
ANNUAL PRODUCTION 60,000 bottles
HECTARES UNDER VINE 12.20
VITICULTURE METHOD Certified Organic

Poggerino began producing Chianti
Classico in 1980. In 1999, Floriana Ginori
Conti left management in the hands of her
children Piero and Benedetto Lanza (who'd
been active since 1988). Today the winery
has firmly established itself among Radda
in Chianti's most notable producers, with
organically-cultivated vineyards and aging
in barriques and mid-size casks. Their
modern style generally pursues maturity of
fruit and generous extraction, qualities that
in no way detract from the personality and
character of this important winery's
selection. Their Chianti Classico Bugialla
Riserva continues to be a benchmark wine.
The 2016 features an intensely fruity and
spicy aromatic profile, and a juicy, deep
development, with sensations of fresh
cherry rising up at the finish. The Chianti
Classico '16 once again proves
fruit-forward, making for a delectable,
flavorful palate. The Prima Materia '16, a
blend of Sangiovese and Merlot, is also
well-made.

Poggio al Tesoro

FRAZ. BOLGHERI
VIA BOLGHERESE, 189B
57022 CASTAGNETO CARDUCCI [LI]
TEL. +39 0565773051
www.poggioaltesoro.it

CELLAR SALES
PRE-BOOKED VISITS
ANNUAL PRODUCTION 377,000 bottles
HECTARES UNDER VINE 67.50

The Allegrini family also bet on Bolgheri,
and the results were quick to follow. Not
that it was always easy, obviously, but we
can say that this project is hitting its stride
now that it's producing benchmark wines
for the territory. Their vineyards are situated
on various types of terrain, from soils rich
in stones and clay to more sandy
typologies. Their wines are growing
exponentially in terms of quality and style,
though without betraying their original aim.
Their Bolgheri Superiore Sondraia '16 is
simply spectacular. It's a blend of mostly
Cabernet Sauvignon with smaller shares of
Merlot and Franc, malolactically fermented
in steel and aged in barriques. It features
vibrant black fruit and aromas of
Mediterranean shrub, while the palate
comes through warm in alcohol. Dedicato
Walter '15 is on the same level, but clearer
and juicier — though their entire selection
performed well.

● Chianti Cl. Bugialla Ris. '16	♟♟ 6
● Chianti Cl. '16	♟♟ 4
● Primamateria '16	♟♟ 5
● Chianti Cl. Bugialla Ris. '13	♟♟♟ 5
● Chianti Cl. Bugialla Ris. '12	♟♟♟ 5
● Chianti Cl. Bugialla Ris. '09	♟♟♟ 5
● Chianti Cl. Bugialla Ris. '08	♟♟♟ 5
● Chianti Cl. Ris. '90	♟♟♟ 4*
● Primamateria '01	♟♟♟ 5
● Chianti Cl. '15	♟♟ 4
● Chianti Cl. '13	♟♟ 4
● Chianti Cl. '12	♟♟ 3*
● Chianti Cl. Bugialla Ris. '15	♟♟ 6
● Chianti Cl. Bugialla Ris. '14	♟♟ 6
● Primamateria '10	♟♟ 5
⊙ Spumante M. Cl. Sangiovese '11	♟♟ 5

● Bolgheri Rosso Sup. Sondraia '16	♟♟♟
● Bolgheri Rosso Sup. Dedicato a Walter '15	♟♟
⊙ Bolgheri Rosato Cassiopea Pagus Cerbaia '17	♟♟
● Bolgheri Rosso Il Seggio '16	♟♟
○ Bolgheri Vermentino Solosole '18	♟♟
● Mediterra '16	♟♟
● Bolgheri Rosso Sup. Sondraia '15	♟♟♟
● Bolgheri Sup. Sondraia '14	♟♟♟
● Bolgheri Sup. Sondraia '13	♟♟♟
● Bolgheri Sup. Sondraia '11	♟♟♟
● Bolgheri Sup. Sondraia '10	♟♟♟
● Dedicato a Walter '12	♟♟♟
● Dedicato a Walter '09	♟♟♟

attoria Poggio Capponi

Montelupo, 184
0025 Montespertoli [FI]
ᴇʟ. +39 0571671914
ww.poggiocapponi.it

ELLAR SALES
RE-BOOKED VISITS
CCOMMODATION
NNUAL PRODUCTION 200,000 bottles
ECTARES UNDER VINE 32.00

he Rousseau Colzi family's winery was
urchased by Giovanni in the 1930s. It was
e, a Florentine industrialist, who used it as
country residence for having parties and
unting. After WW II his son, also named
iovanni, launched the agricultural
usiness together with his children
lichelangelo and Gioconda. Replanting the
neyards took a long time, and they're still
utting on the finishing touches, but in the
eantime the agritourism has grown
otably. The Tinoroso '16 is an unusual
lend of Merlot and Syrah. Spicy notes of
epper and vanilla pair with cherry and
aspberry, with a slight hint of tobacco
tanding out. On the palate it's pleasant,
oming through soft and juicy, with a
ubtle, even tannic weave and a gratifying
nish. The Bianco di Binto '18, a blend of
ermentino, Trebbiano and Chardonnay,
urprises, offering up fruity whiffs of peach
nd apricot together with citrusy notes of
me. It's a racy, fresh, flavorful and
ppetizing drink.

Bianco di Binto '18	▼▼ 2*
Chianti Ris. '16	▼▼ 2*
Sovente Chardonnay '18	▼▼ 2*
Tinorso '16	▼▼ 3
Chianti Montespertoli Petriccio '16	▼ 3
Villa Capponi '18	▼ 2
Bianco di Binto '14	♀♀ 2*
Chianti Montespertoli Petriccio '13	♀♀ 3
Sovente '15	♀♀ 2*
Sovente '12	♀♀ 2*
Sovente Chardonnay '16	♀♀ 2*
Tinorso '15	♀♀ 3
Tinorso '11	♀♀ 3
Vin Santo del Chianti '16	♀♀ 6

★Poggio di Sotto

ꜰʀᴀᴢ. Castelnuovo dell'Abate
ʟᴏᴄ. Poggio di Sotto
53024 Montalcino [SI]
ᴛᴇʟ. +39 0577835502
www.collemassari.it

CELLAR SALES
PRE-BOOKED VISITS
ANNUAL PRODUCTION 30,000 bottles
HECTARES UNDER VINE 16.00
VITICULTURE METHOD Certified Organic
SUSTAINABLE WINERY

Rosso, Brunello and Brunello Riserva: this
splendid trio has, for thirty years, brought
global success to Poggio di Sotto. The Tipa
family, who purchased it in the early part of
the decade, are reinvigorating the estate
while also maintaining extraordinary
continuity with the era of Palmucci (its
founder). Its core vineyard is still
Castelnuovo dell'Abate, a property situated
in southeast Montalcino, at 450 meters
elevation, on clay and marl. The steep,
open slopes prove perfect for forging
suavely aristocratic wines. Poggio di Sotto's
magnificent trio once again shines, and it's
almost impossible to choose among them.
There's the flowery and citrusy grace of
their Rosso '16 and the warm depth of
their Brunello Ris. '13. Possibly we're
slightly partial to their Brunello '14 (taking
into account the year, as well). Strawberry
jelly, steeped herbs and wood resin all
make for an irresistible palate characterized
by sweet and savory development.

● Brunello di Montalcino '14	▼▼▼ 8
● Brunello di Montalcino Ris. '13	▼▼ 8
● Rosso di Montalcino '16	▼▼ 8
● Brunello di Montalcino '12	♀♀♀ 8
● Brunello di Montalcino '11	♀♀♀ 8
● Brunello di Montalcino '10	♀♀♀ 8
● Brunello di Montalcino '07	♀♀♀ 8
● Brunello di Montalcino '04	♀♀♀ 8
● Brunello di Montalcino '99	♀♀♀ 8
● Brunello di Montalcino Ris. '12	♀♀♀ 8
● Brunello di Montalcino Ris. '07	♀♀♀ 8
● Brunello di Montalcino Ris. '99	♀♀♀ 8
● Brunello di Montalcino Ris. '95	♀♀♀ 8
● Rosso di Montalcino '07	♀♀♀ 6

Poggio Landi

LOC. PODERE BELVEDERE
FRAZ. TORRENIERI
S.DA PROV.LE 71
53024 MONTALCINO [SI]
TEL. +39 0577042736

ANNUAL PRODUCTION 90,000 bottles
HECTARES UNDER VINE 74.00

One of the most noteworthy wineries to emerge of late in the competitive district of Montalcino, Poggio Landi is also the crown jewel of the Alejandro Bulgheroni Family Vineyards group. It's all thanks to a forward-thinking agricultural project grounded in a large estate that's purposefully spread throughout the area, spanning different elevations (from 175 to 500 meters) and pedoclimates. It's a veritable territorial puzzle that comes together in a contemporary Brunello aged in 3000 and 5400 liter French oak barrels. And that's not to mention their Rosso. The 2017 offers up a lovely combination of citrus and balsamic sensations. Aromas of forest undergrowth and iodine come forward on a pleasantly warm palate. Their Brunello Ris. '13 features a classic profile of black cherry, inflorescence and roots. On the palate it proves even airier in its development: flavorful, close-knit and well-sustained, making for a wine that's anything but bold, but extremely punchy nevertheless.

● Brunello di Montalcino Ris. '13	♟♟ 7
● Rosso di Montalcino '17	♟♟ 4
● Brunello di Montalcino '13	♟♟ 7
● Brunello di Montalcino '12	♟♟ 7
● Brunello di Montalcino Ris. '12	♟♟ 7
● Rosso di Montalcino '16	♟♟ 4

Poggio Sorbello

FRAZ. CENTOIA
LOC. CASE SPARSE, 168
52044 CORTONA [AR]
TEL. +39 3395447059
www.poggiosorbello.it

CELLAR SALES
ANNUAL PRODUCTION 10,000 bottles
HECTARES UNDER VINE 9.00
SUSTAINABLE WINERY

Owned by the Baldetti family since the early 20th century, this estate is situated on the hills of Cortona and Montepulciano, on the border of Arezzo, Siena and Perugia. Their vineyards were upgraded in the mid-1990s, with the introduction of native and international grape varieties (more recently they've also planted white grapes as well). All their vineyards are surrounded by woods, which create a unique microclimate that supports the proliferation of useful insects. The pleasant Syrah Gortinaia '16 features a broad-based aromatic profile, with whiffs of animal skins and leather melding with fruity notes of cherry and blackcurrant, then spicy hints of juniper. On the palate it exhibits nice fleshiness and crunchy tannins, proving succulent, fresh and lively right up through the end. The Fossa Granai '16 opens with balsamic aromas enriched by black fruits, like plums and blackberries. Its firm body features delicate tannins and a lovely, supporting acidity.

● Boschi ai Filari '16	♟♟ 3
● Cortona Cabernet Sauvignon Fossa Granai '16	♟♟ 4
● Cortona Syrah Gortinaia '16	♟♟ 4
● Cortona Merlot Donetto '16	♟ 4
● Boschi ai Filari '15	♟♟ 3
● Cortona Cabernet Sauvignon Fossa Granai '15	♟♟ 4
● Cortona Syrah Gortinaia '15	♟♟ 4

Tenuta Il Poggione

FRAZ. SANT'ANGELO IN COLLE
LOC. MONTEANO
3024 MONTALCINO [SI]
TEL. +39 0577844029
www.tenutailpoggione.it

CELLAR SALES
PRE-BOOKED VISITS
ACCOMMODATION
ANNUAL PRODUCTION 600,000 bottles
HECTARES UNDER VINE 127.00

A veritable majority shareholder of south Montalcino's wine sector (especially Sant'Angelo in Colle), Il Poggione has belonged to the Franceschi family for almost a century and a half. It's a historic winery that's been there throughout Brunello's rise to prominence, from the pioneering years to its international boom. Under Fabrizio Bindocci, they've consistently proposed a style that's recognizable for its union of sunniness and rigor, brought out by medium-long maceration and aging in 3000/5000 liter French oak barrels. The continuity of their selection makes Poggione a benchmark for the territory. Just take their Rosso '17 with its intense and meaty array of red fruits, Mediterranean herbs and sweet spices fully supported by a firm and robust palate. We find the same expressiveness reinforced in their Brunello '14. Sylvan notes are even more pronounced while sapidity supports its generous alcohol.

● Brunello di Montalcino '14	🏆🏆 7
● Rosso di Montalcino '17	🏆🏆 4
● Brunello di Montalcino Ris. '97	🏆🏆🏆 7
● Brunello di Montalcino '13	🏆🏆 7
● Brunello di Montalcino '12	🏆🏆 7
● Brunello di Montalcino '11	🏆🏆 7
● Brunello di Montalcino '10	🏆🏆 7
● Brunello di Montalcino '09	🏆🏆 6
● Brunello di Montalcino V. Paganelli Ris. '10	🏆🏆 8
● Brunello di Montalcino V. Paganelli Ris. '07	🏆🏆 7
● Rosso di Montalcino '16	🏆🏆 4
● Rosso di Montalcino '14	🏆🏆 4
● Rosso di Montalcino '13	🏆🏆 4
● Rosso di Montalcino '12	🏆🏆 3
● Toscana Rosso '13	🏆🏆 3

★★Poliziano

FRAZ. MONTEPULCIANO STAZIONE
VIA FONTAGO, 1
53045 MONTEPULCIANO [SI]
TEL. +39 0578738171
www.carlettipoliziano.com

CELLAR SALES
PRE-BOOKED VISITS
ANNUAL PRODUCTION 650,000 bottles
HECTARES UNDER VINE 145.00

Federico Carletti's Poliziano is a universally recognized benchmark for Tuscan wine. In the territory, it represents a symbol and a model for other producers, making it one of Nobile's undisputed leaders. In addition to consistently exhibiting an outstanding level of quality, year after year their wines confirm their excellence by demonstrating an ability to successfully exemplify various styles, from power to territorial elegance. Their Nobile di Montepulciano Le Caggiole '16 behaves like a great wine. It's young, though already expressive with its delicate, floral and spicy nose and a highly balanced, vigorous palate. The Nobile Asinone '16 is no less good, with its intense aromas of red berries and smoky hints, and a close-knit though succulent development. The well-made Nobile di Montepulciano '16 is a precise wine, to say the least.

● Nobile di Montepulciano Le Caggiole '16	🏆🏆🏆 4*
● Nobile di Montepulciano Asinone '16	🏆🏆 7
● Nobile di Montepulciano '16	🏆🏆 5
● Le Stanze '16	🏆 7
● Rosso di Montepulciano '17	🏆 3
● Nobile di Montepulciano '09	🏆🏆🏆 4*
● Nobile di Montepulciano Asinone '14	🏆🏆🏆 7
● Nobile di Montepulciano Asinone '12	🏆🏆🏆 7
● Nobile di Montepulciano Asinone '11	🏆🏆🏆 7
● Nobile di Montepulciano Asinone '07	🏆🏆🏆 6
● Nobile di Montepulciano Asinone '06	🏆🏆🏆 6
● Nobile di Montepulciano Le Caggiole '15	🏆🏆🏆 4*

Pomona

LOC. POMONA, 39
S.DA CHIANTIGIANA
53011 CASTELLINA IN CHIANTI [SI]
TEL. +39 0577740473
www.fattoriapomona.it

CELLAR SALES
PRE-BOOKED VISITS
ACCOMMODATION
ANNUAL PRODUCTION 16,000 bottles
HECTARES UNDER VINE 4.70
VITICULTURE METHOD Certified Organic

Castellina in Chianti is a notable example of artisanal winemaking in the territory. We find a style firmly rooted in classical tradition, starting with the use of large barrels for aging and a refusal to adopt shortcuts in the cellar, grounding their work, instead, in organically-cultivated vineyards. This rigorous approach gives rise to wines at times austere (and not always immediately discernible), but nonetheless original, characterful and capable of expressing a bond with the territory that's among the strongest of any producer operating in the area. The Chianti Classico Riserva '16 is a classic child of the typology. Aromatically it brings together meadow herbs and flowers with a slightly spicy register to complete the puzzle. On the palate it's juicy and highly flavorful, though without hiding a pleasant hardness that confers character and personality. The Piero Rosso '16, a Sangiovese, is well-made and stylistically different from their appellation designated wines.

● Chianti Cl. Ris. '16	♟♟♟ 4*
● Piero Rosso '16	♟♟ 3
● Chianti Cl. '13	♟♟♟ 3*
● Chianti Cl. '12	♟♟♟ 3*
● Chianti Cl. '14	♟♟♟ 4*
● Chianti Cl. '16	♟♟ 3*
● Chianti Cl. '15	♟♟ 3
● Chianti Cl. '14	♟♟ 3
● Chianti Cl. '11	♟♟ 3
● Chianti Cl. Ris. '15	♟♟ 4
● Chianti Cl. Ris. '13	♟♟ 4
● Chianti Cl. Ris. '12	♟♟ 4
● Chianti Cl. Ris. '11	♟♟ 4
● Chianti Cl. Ris. '10	♟♟ 4

Tenuta Le Potazzine

LOC. LE PRATA, 262
53024 MONTALCINO [SI]
TEL. +39 0577846168
www.lepotazzine.it

CELLAR SALES
PRE-BOOKED VISITS
RESTAURANT SERVICE
ANNUAL PRODUCTION 50,000 bottles
HECTARES UNDER VINE 4.70

Le Potazzine's vineyards represent a territorial patchwork, a situation that results in original Sangiovese wines. The core plots are in Le Prata, a part of eastern Montalcino that's well-suited to vine growing thanks to elevations approaching 500 meters and red soil. They also have plots in Torre, in the southern area that connects Sesta and Sant'Angelo in Colle. For some years now, young Viola and Sofia Gorelli have been tending to their vineyards along with their mother, Gigliola, giving rise to airy, streamlined Brunellos aged in 3000/5000 liter Slavonian oak. In many ways, Le Potazzine's Sangioveses had an open-ended year. The 2017 version of their Rosso is a bit less delectable than usual, conditioned by the occasional vegetal stroke and biting tannins that soften its sapid thrust. Their Brunello '14 performed on a somewhat similar track with a minimalist, essential palate accompanied by charming sensations of ginger, bouquet garni, dried fruit and nuts.

● Brunello di Montalcino '14	♟♟ 7
● Rosso di Montalcino '17	♟ 4
● Brunello di Montalcino '10	♟♟♟ 7
● Brunello di Montalcino '08	♟♟♟ 7
● Brunello di Montalcino Ris. '11	♟♟♟ 8
● Brunello di Montalcino Ris. '06	♟♟♟ 8
● Brunello di Montalcino '13	♟♟ 7
● Brunello di Montalcino '12	♟♟ 7
● Brunello di Montalcino '11	♟♟ 7
● Brunello di Montalcino '09	♟♟ 7
● Rosso di Montalcino '16	♟♟ 4
● Rosso di Montalcino '15	♟♟ 4
● Rosso di Montalcino '14	♟♟ 4
● Rosso di Montalcino '13	♟♟ 4
● Rosso di Montalcino '12	♟♟ 4

Fabrizio Pratesi

LOC. SEANO
VIA RIZZELLI, 10
59011 CARMIGNANO [PO]
TEL. +39 0558704108
www.pratesivini.it

CELLAR SALES
PRE-BOOKED VISITS
RESTAURANT SERVICE
ANNUAL PRODUCTION 80,000 bottles
HECTARES UNDER VINE 12.00

The winery got its start in 1875, when Piero Pratesi purchased the property of Lolocco in Camignano. Today they're on the fifth generation of family and Fabrizio, who's also the current president of the Carmignano Wine Consortium, is passionately carrying their work forward. Indeed, his tenure at the helm has brought about a sea change, with new, high-density vineyards planted, and a focus on the best areas and crus. Their Carmignano Il Circo Rosso Riserva '16 opens on the nose with intense aromas of licorice and ink accompanied by balsamic notes, before giving way to cherry and plums softened by cloves. On the palate it enters soft and fresh, with vitality, exhibiting mature, subtle tannins, long aromatic persistence and a finish that unfolds superbly. Their Carmignano Carmione '17 delights the nose with its hints of licorice and Mediterranean herbs, which adorn vibrant fruit. In the mouth it comes through soft, round and structured, with a sapid finish of fruit.

● Carmignano Il Circo Rosso Ris. '16	🍷🍷 6
● Carmignano Carmione '17	🍷🍷 4
● Barco Reale Locorosso '18	🍷 3
● Barco Reale '16	🍷🍷 2*
● Barco Reale di Carmignano Locorosso '17	🍷🍷 3
● Carmignano '13	🍷🍷 4
● Carmignano '12	🍷🍷 3
● Carmignano Carmione '15	🍷🍷 4
● Carmignano Circo Rosso Ris. '14	🍷🍷 3*
● Carmignano Circo Rosso Ris. '11	🍷🍷 5
● Carmignano Il Circo Rosso Ris. '15	🍷🍷 6
● Carmignano Il Circo Rosso Ris. '13	🍷🍷 6
● Carmignano Il Circo Rosso Ris. '12	🍷🍷 6
● Carmione '14	🍷🍷 6
● Merlot Barche di Bacchereto '12	🍷🍷 3

Tenuta Prima Pietra

LOC. I PRATI
56046 RIPARBELLA [PI]
TEL. +39 05771913750
www.tenutaprimapietra.com

ANNUAL PRODUCTION 40,000 bottles
HECTARES UNDER VINE 11.00

Prima Pietra was founded by Massimo Ferragamo, a well-known fashion entrepreneur who developed a taste for investing in wine, beginning with the splendid property of Castiglion del Bosco in Montalcino. The estate comprises 11 hectares situated at 450 meters elevation. Here they produce 40,000 bottles of a single wine, made primarily with Merlot and Cab. Sauvignon as well as smaller shares of Cab. Franc and Petit Verdot. Organic agriculture and an approach aimed at safeguarding biodiversity are indicative of their philosophy, while their wine draws on a singular terroir characterized by iron and mineral clay-rich terrain, as well as notable elevations. An excellent 2016 didn't betray our expectations. In the glass this red proves redolent of clearly discernible, fruity notes (blackcurrant, wild strawberry and sweet spices). On the palate it's supple and tight-knit, but rhythmic, with well-integrated oak and a deep, flavorful, but especially fresh, finish.

● Prima Pietra '16	🍷🍷 8
● Prima Pietra '15	🍷🍷 8

★Fattoria Le Pupille

FRAZ. ISTIA D'OMBRONE
LOC. PIAGGE DEL MAIANO, 92A
58100 GROSSETO
TEL. +39 0564409517
www.fattorialepupille.it

CELLAR SALES
PRE-BOOKED VISITS
ACCOMMODATION
ANNUAL PRODUCTION 450,000 bottles
HECTARES UNDER VINE 80.00

Elisabetta Geppetti is among Maremma's historic wine leaders, particularly when it comes to Morellino di Scansano. The first harvests came in the early 1980s, but what gave Fattoria Le Pupille's production a spark was the release of their Saffredi (1987), a wine that proved capable of standing shoulder-to-shoulder with the best Supertuscans of the time. Today the winery has consolidated its role as a leader, with a selection whose quality is recognized and constant, making it one of Italy's most important producers. The Morellino di Scansano Riserva '16 is a firm wine, in some ways austere, redolent of earth and fresh flowers, sensations accompanied by smoky notes and hints Mediterranean scrub. On the palate it's balanced, assertive, with properly spirited tannins and a punctual acidic verve that guarantees fragrance and intensity. As usual, the Morellino di Scansano versione '18 proves superbly drinkable.

● Morellino di Scansano Ris. '16	♥♥ 4
● Saffredi '16	♥♥ 8
● Morellino di Scansano '18	♥♥ 3
○ Poggio Argentato '18	♥ 2
● Poggio Valente '16	♥ 5
● Morellino di Scansano Poggio Valente '04	♀♀♀ 5
● Morellino di Scansano Poggio Valente '99	♀♀♀ 5
● Morellino di Scansano Ris. '15	♀♀♀ 4*
● Saffredi '14	♀♀♀ 8
● Saffredi '13	♀♀♀ 8
● Saffredi '05	♀♀♀ 8
● Saffredi '04	♀♀♀ 8
● Saffredi '03	♀♀♀ 8
● Saffredi '02	♀♀♀ 7
● Saffredi '01	♀♀♀ 7

La Querce

VIA IMPRUNETANA PER TAVARNUZZE, 41
50023 IMPRUNETA [FI]
TEL. +39 0552011380
www.laquerce.com

CELLAR SALES
PRE-BOOKED VISITS
ACCOMMODATION
ANNUAL PRODUCTION 35,000 bottles
HECTARES UNDER VINE 7.60

The Marchi family's winery is on a hill overlooking Impruneta near Florence. The vineyards have been almost entirely replanted in recent years, both with traditional grapes like Sangiovese and Colorino, as well as Merlot. Chemical treatment is kept to a minimum so as to guarantee ecological balance. There are two facilities, one for vinification, with an underground area used to hold the bottles during maturation, while the other, under the villa, is strictly for bottle aging. This time it's their La Querce '15, a Sangiovese blend, that lands a place in our finals. Its purple color anticipates aromas of aromatic herbs and peppers, then blackcurrant and blueberries. On the palate it enters well, proving juicy and pervasive, without excesses, closing long and sapid. The Riserva La Torretta '16 stands out on the nose for its fruity hints of cherry paired with jammy blackberry notes. In the mouth it's firmly structured, with integrated tannins, nice volume and a lengthy persistence.

● La Querce '15	♥♥ 5
● Chianti Colli Fiorentini La Torretta Ris. '16	♥♥ 3
● Belrosso '18	♥ 2
⊙ Rosa di Maggio '18	♥ 2
● Chianti Colli Fiorentini La Torretta Ris. '15	♀♀♀ 3*
● La Querce '11	♀♀♀ 5
● Belrosso '15	♀♀ 2*
● Belrosso Canaiolo '16	♀♀ 2*
● Chianti Colli Fiorentini La Torretta '13	♀♀ 2*
● Chianti Sorrettole '16	♀♀ 2*
● Chianti Sorrettole '15	♀♀ 2*
● La Querce '12	♀♀ 5
● M '13	♀♀ 6
● Terra di Vino '17	♀♀ 4

Le Ragnaie

LOC. LE RAGNAIE
53024 MONTALCINO [SI]
TEL. +39 0577848639
www.leragnaie.com

CELLAR SALES
PRE-BOOKED VISITS
ACCOMMODATION
ANNUAL PRODUCTION 80,000 bottles
HECTARES UNDER VINE 15.50
VITICULTURE METHOD Certified Organic

Riccardo Campinoti continues his unabated exploration of the Montalcino territory. New vineyards and new wines (such as Passo del Lume Spento) join the plots largely destined for Brunello, but are also used for Rosso coming from special vintages such as 2014. Ragnaie VV (from the section of plots near the cellar), Fornace (from the south-east sector of Loreto di Castelnuovo dell'Abate) and Petroso (on the western edge of the Colle Centrale) represent very different areas and interpretations that nonetheless maintain a clear fil rouge of vitality and elegance. Even without a Brunello this year, Le Ragnaie manages to carve out a prominent place for itself thanks especially to their Rosso '16. Crisp and nuanced in its sensations of small fruit, Asian spices, sylvan notes and balsamic herbs, it's a complete wine in every way, for fullness, energy and tension. Vibrant acidity and flavor, a subtle yet penetrating tannic weave give way to a radiant finish.

● Rosso di Montalcino '16	♟♟♟	5
● Passo del Lume Spento '15	♟♟	4
● Troncone '16	♟♟	4
● Brunello di Montalcino Fornace '08	♟♟♟	8
● Brunello di Montalcino V. V. '13	♟♟♟	8
● Brunello di Montalcino V. V. '11	♟♟♟	8
● Brunello di Montalcino V. V. '10	♟♟♟	8
● Brunello di Montalcino V. V. '07	♟♟♟	5
● Brunello di Montalcino '13	♟♟	7
● Brunello di Montalcino Fornace '13	♟♟	8
● Brunello di Montalcino Fornace '12	♟♟	8
● Brunello di Montalcino V. V. '12	♟♟	8
○ Ragnaie Bianco '16	♟♟	4
○ Rosato '16	♟♟	5
● Rosso di Montalcino '15	♟♟	5
● Rosso di Montalcino V. V. Ragnaie '14	♟♟	5

Podere La Regola

LOC. ALTAGRANDA
S.DA REG.LE 68 KM 6,400
56046 RIPARBELLA [PI]
TEL. +39 0586698145
www.laregola.com

CELLAR SALES
PRE-BOOKED VISITS
ANNUAL PRODUCTION 90,000 bottles
HECTARES UNDER VINE 20.00

An ancient Etruscan settlement and numerous amphorae testify to the fact that wine has been produced in Riparbella, a few kilometers from the sea, for at least 2500 years. The younger generations of the Nuti family have modernized the estate, starting with the planting of vineyards and the construction of a new cellar, which has greatly increased productivity. Quality wines and a pleasant setting have encouraged the winery to also become an agritourism. Their La Regola '16, a monovarietal Cabernet Franc, once again proves outstanding. A deep, complex bouquet spans fresh minty notes and whiffs of aromatic herbs, all on a fruity base of blackcurrant and blueberry, closing spicy. On the palate it's full, structured and succulent, with subtle tannins and a compelling, truly long finish. The Vallino'16, a blend of Cabernet Sauvignon and Sangiovese, is intense in its fruity aromas, smooth and harmonious on the palate.

● La Regola '16	♟♟♟	8
● Ligustro '17	♟♟	4
● Strido '15	♟♟	8
● Vallino '16	♟♟	5
○ Steccaia '18	♟	4
● La Regola '15	♟♟♟	7
● La Regola '14	♟♟	7
● La Regola '13	♟♟	6
○ Lauro '15	♟♟	5
○ Steccaia '17	♟♟	4
○ Steccaia Bianco '15	♟♟	3
● Strido '13	♟♟	8
● Strido '12	♟♟	8
● Vallino '15	♟♟	5
● Vallino '13	♟♟	5

Renieri

S.DA CONSORZIALE DELL'ASSO
53024 MONTALCINO [SI]
TEL. +39 0577359330
www.renierimontalcino.com

CELLAR SALES
PRE-BOOKED VISITS
ACCOMMODATION
ANNUAL PRODUCTION 301,200 bottles
HECTARES UNDER VINE 35.00

Magnificently restored at the end of the 1990s, the Renieri estate is the Montalcino headquarters of the Bacci family, leaders in the Tuscan wine scene. The family also owns Castello di Bossi in Chianti Classico and Terre di Talamo in Maremma. Dominated by Sangiovese (with some Merlot, Cabernet, Syrah and Petit Verdot), the property overlooks Mount Amiata to the south. This area favors the sweet, fruity expressiveness of their Brunello, aged in both small wood barrels and 3000-liter oak barrels. And, naturally, Montalcino's prince grape serves as the cornerstone of Renieri's small selection. If the 'vintage' 2014 is a bit limited in terms of texture and length, their Riserva '13 proves to be one of the best of its kind. Jammy notes of cherries, tanned leather, a touch of vanilla emerge on the nose. Its transparently modern character is well-supported by a generous palate that's not lacking in vigorous backbone.

● Brunello di Montalcino Ris. '13	♟♟ 8
● Brunello di Montalcino '14	♟ 7
● Brunello di Montalcino '13	♟♟ 7
● Brunello di Montalcino Ris. '12	♟♟ 8
● Re di Renieri '04	♟♟ 5
● Re di Renieri '03	♟♟ 5
● Regina di Renieri '05	♟♟ 6
● Regina di Renieri '03	♟♟ 5
● Rosso di Montalcino '15	♟♟ 3
● Rosso di Montalcino '04	♟♟ 3

★★Barone Ricasoli

LOC. MADONNA A BROLIO

53013 GAIOLE IN CHIANTI [SI]
TEL. +39 05777301
www.ricasoli.com

CELLAR SALES
PRE-BOOKED VISITS
ACCOMMODATION
ANNUAL PRODUCTION 2,500,000 bottles
HECTARES UNDER VINE 235.00
SUSTAINABLE WINERY

Barone Ricasoli has an enduring story in the Chianti area. It's now in the final stages of zoning varieties by ideal soil types, a process begun in 2008. The results are three specific crus for three Gran Selezioni: Collidilà, Roncicone and CeniPrimo. The last comes from the homonymous vineyard on clay and limestone soil at an elevation of 390 meters. Roncicone, comes from sandy soil mixed with stone and deep clay that, along with CeniPrimo (also from a homonymous vineyard), is at the property's southern extremity. Their Chianti Classico Castello di Brolio Gran Selezione '16 features a delicate, well-defined aromatic profile, the prelude to a dense, juicy development rich in contrast of flavor. The Chianti Classico Roncicone Gran Selezione '16 is also impeccable, especially on the palate where it exhibits superb sapidity. Nevertheless, the best seems to be their Chianti Classico Collidilà Gran Selezione '16, with its clear aromas and rhythmic palate.

● Chianti Cl. Gran Selezione Castello di Brolio '16	♟♟ 8
● Chianti Cl. Gran Selezione Collidilà '16	♟♟ 8
● Chianti Cl. Gran Selezione Roncicone '16	♟♟ 8
● Chianti Cl. Brolio '17	♟♟ 5
● Chianti Cl. Brolio Bettino '16	♟♟ 5
● Chianti Cl. Brolio Ris. '16	♟♟ 6
● Chianti Cl. Gran Selezione CeniPrimo '16	♟♟ 8
● Casalferro '08	♟♟♟ 8
● Chianti Cl. Brolio Bettino '15	♟♟♟ 5
● Chianti Cl. Castello di Brolio '07	♟♟♟ 8
● Chianti Cl. Collidilà '10	♟♟♟ 7
● Chianti Cl. Gran Selezione Collidilà '13	♟♟♟ 8
● Chianti Cl. Gran Selezione Collidilà '11	♟♟♟ 8
● Chianti Cl. Rocca Guicciarda Ris. '12	♟♟♟ 5

Riecine

LOC. RIECINE
53013 GAIOLE IN CHIANTI [SI]
TEL. +39 0577749098
www.riecine.it

CELLAR SALES
PRE-BOOKED VISITS
ANNUAL PRODUCTION 60,000 bottles
HECTARES UNDER VINE 11.00
VITICULTURE METHOD Certified Organic

Lana Frank has owned this estate in
Chianti's sub-area of Gaiole since 2011.
She has been busy revising its overall
structure and has directed it back along a
path more fitting with its reputation as a
leader in Chianti Classico. The overall
style has been refined with greater
precision and the resulting beautifully
clear, modern wines express both the
territory and a strong character,
representing a return to its storied heights.
The winery uses only organic viticulture
followed by aging in concrete vats and
small and medium wood barrels. The
Chianti Classico '17, which exhibits
absolute aromatic freshness and definition
on the nose, possesses a first-class
energy of flavor, coming through taut and
sapid on the palate. The Chianti Classico
Riserva '16 is no less good, with its
mineral aromas and sapid palate, it's just a
bit oakier at the finish. Their Riecine '15, a
monovarietal Sangiovese, speaks the same
delicious language. The La Gioia '15 is just
a step behind.

● Chianti Cl. '17	♟♟♟ 3*
● Chianti Cl. Ris. '16	♟♟ 5
● Riecine '15	♟♟ 3*
● La Gioia '15	♟♟ 6
● Chianti Cl. Ris. '15	♟♟♟ 5
● Chianti Cl. Ris. '99	♟♟♟ 7
● Chianti Cl. Ris. '88	♟♟♟ 6
● Chianti Cl. Ris. '86	♟♟♟ 6
● La Gioia '04	♟♟♟ 6
● La Gioia '01	♟♟♟ 6
● La Gioia '98	♟♟♟ 6
● La Gioia '95	♟♟♟ 6

Podere Le Ripi

LOC. LE RIPI
53021 MONTALCINO [SI]
TEL. +39 0577835641
www.podereleripi.it

CELLAR SALES
PRE-BOOKED VISITS
ANNUAL PRODUCTION 25,000 bottles
HECTARES UNDER VINE 12.00
VITICULTURE METHOD Certified Biodynamic
SUSTAINABLE WINERY

A few lines can't do justice to the vision
that animates Podere Le Ripi. It's a
'psychedelic dream', to use the words of
Francesco Illy, who, after a long search in
the late 1990s, chose to produce Brunello
(and more) in Castelnuovo dell'Abate, the
southeastern tip of Montalcino.
Sangiovese, Syrah and non-native varieties
are cultivated using biodynamic principles,
leading to a diverse range, which takes
shape in the winery's famous 'golden
cellar'. Deliciously anarchic wines result
from methods that could never be
considered dogmatic. It's an ambitious
direction that, in many ways, finds its full
realization in their Brunello Lupi e Sirene
Ris. '13. A blaze of red and black fruits,
smoky notes, aromas of light roots literally
explodes on the palate thanks to a
precious tannic weave made vigorous by
sapid energy. But their entire selection
shines, from the multifaceted and
close-knit Rosso Sogni e Follia '15 to the
more minimalist and elemental Cielo
d'Ulisse '14.

● Brunello di Montalcino Lupi e Sirene Ris. '13	♟♟♟ 8
● Cielo d'Ulisse '14	♟♟ 6
● Rosso di Montalcino Sogni e Follia '15	♟♟ 5
● Brunello di Montalcino Lupi e Sirene '12	♟♟ 6
● Brunello di Montalcino Lupi e Sirene Ris. '10	♟♟ 6
● Rosso di Montalcino '11	♟♟ 5

Rocca delle Macìe

LOC. LE MACÌE, 45
53011 CASTELLINA IN CHIANTI [SI]
TEL. +39 05777321
www.roccadellemacie.com

CELLAR SALES
PRE-BOOKED VISITS
ACCOMMODATION AND RESTAURANT SERVICE
ANNUAL PRODUCTION 2,000,000 bottles
HECTARES UNDER VINE 206.70
SUSTAINABLE WINERY

In 1973, film producer Italo Zingarelli founded Rocca delle Macìe in Castellina, a Chianti sub-zone. Today, the sturdy winery's production philosophy revolves around Chianti Classico. The estate has concentrated its efforts in two areas: first, with Sangiovese and the progressive abandonment of small barrels in favor of large ones; and, second, the stylistic fine-tuning of a range that reaches absolute excellence with assuring regularity and, even more promisingly, shows further potential for growth. Their Chianti Classico Famiglia Zingarelli Riserva '16 features delicate and well-defined aromas, the prelude to a well-balanced, vigorous and succulent palate. Their Chianti Classico Sant'Alfonso '17 is also well-made with its sweet, clear and focused aromas, and its soft, well-sustained flavor. Their Chianti Classico '17 is enjoyable, while their well-crafted Chianti Classico Riserva di Fizzano Gran Selezione '16 sees just a bit too much oak in the foreground.

● Chianti Cl. Famiglia Zingarelli Ris. '16	♟♟♟ 5
● Chianti Cl. Tenuta S. Alfonso '17	♟♟ 4
● Chianti Cl. '17	♟♟ 3
● Chianti Cl. Gran Selezione Riserva di Fizzano '16	♟ 6
● Chianti Cl. Gran Selezione Sergio Zingarelli '15	♟ 8
● Chianti Cl. Ser Gioveto Ris. '15	♟ 6
● Chianti Cl. '16	♟♟♟ 3*
● Chianti Cl. Gran Sel. Riserva di Fizzano '14	♟♟♟ 6
● Chianti Cl. Gran Sel. Riserva di Fizzano '13	♟♟♟ 6
● Chianti Cl. Gran Sel. Sergio Zingarelli '11	♟♟♟ 8

Rocca di Castagnoli

LOC. CASTAGNOLI
53013 GAIOLE IN CHIANTI [SI]
TEL. +39 0577731004
www.roccadicastagnoli.com

CELLAR SALES
PRE-BOOKED VISITS
ACCOMMODATION AND RESTAURANT SERVICE
ANNUAL PRODUCTION 500,000 bottles
HECTARES UNDER VINE 87.00
SUSTAINABLE WINERY

Lawyer Calogero Calì has owned this historic estate in Chianti's sub-zone of Gaiole since 1981. The wine produced here has one of the territory's most consistent levels of quality and and assured reliability that can achieve absolute excellence. The style captures the most intimate nuances of the terroir: it seeks without ever forcing the balance and elegance that are perhaps the most characteristic and elemental traits of Chianti products coming from this area in particular. The company also counts on the Maremma vineyards of Poggio Maestrino. The Chianti Classico Rocca di Castagnoli '17 impresses for its spicy and fruity nose, standing out on the palate for its subtlety and contrast of flavor. The Chianti Classico Capraia '17 is sunnier aromatically, still assertive, coming through fragrant and sapid on the palate. Their Cabernet Sauvignon Buriano '15 proves well-made, while oak dominates in their Chianti Classico Poggio ai Frati Riserva '16.

● Chianti Cl. Rocca di Castagnoli '17	♟♟♟ 3*
● Buriano '15	♟♟ 6
● Chianti Cl. Capraia '17	♟♟ 4
● Chianti Cl. Poggio a' Frati Ris. '16	♟♟ 5
● Chianti Cl. Gran Selezione Capraia Effe 55 '15	♟ 6
● Chianti Cl. Gran Selezione Stielle '15	♟ 6
● Chianti Cl. Capraia Ris. '07	♟♟♟ 4
● Chianti Cl. Poggio a' Frati Ris. '08	♟♟♟ 4
● Chianti Cl. Poggio a' Frati Ris. '06	♟♟♟ 4*
● Chianti Cl. Tenuta di Capraia Ris. '06	♟♟♟ 4*
● Chianti Cl. Tenuta di Capraia Ris. '05	♟♟♟ 4

★ Rocca di Frassinello

LOC. GIUNCARICO
58023 GAVORRANO [GR]
TEL. +39 056688400
www.roccadifrassinello.it

CELLAR SALES
PRE-BOOKED VISITS
ACCOMMODATION
ANNUAL PRODUCTION 400,000 bottles
HECTARES UNDER VINE 90.00
SUSTAINABLE WINERY

The owner of this producer is also a shareholder of Gambero Rosso spa. To avoid any conflict of interest, Paolo Panerai has subordinated the possible awarding of Tre Bicchieri (which, in any case, only occurs through a blind tasting) to the attainment of the same rating of excellence (upwards of 90/100) by an independent, international panel. This was the case here.

Rocca di Frassinello's cellar was designed by Renzo Piano and is representative of this well-conceived, ambitious enological endeavor, whose first wines arrived on the market with the 2004 vintage. The lovely 2017 version of their Maremma Toscana Rocca di Frassinello features a dark aromatic profile adorned by toasty and spicy notes. On the palate it proves full-bodied, big and decidedly gratifying. The Maremma Toscana Poggio alla Guardia '17 exhibits similar qualities, just at a slightly lower level. The Maremma Toscana Vermentino '18 also performed well.

● Maremma Toscana Rocca di Frassinello '17	♥♥♥ 8
● Maremma Toscana Poggio alla Guardia '17	♥♥ 3
○ Maremma Toscana Vermentino '18	♥ 3
● Baffo Nero '10	♥♥♥ 8
● Baffo Nero '09	♥♥♥ 8
● Baffonero '12	♥♥♥ 8
● Baffonero '11	♥♥♥ 8
● Le Sughere di Frassinello '10	♥♥♥ 4*
● Maremma Toscana Baffonero '16	♥♥♥ 8
● Maremma Toscana Baffonero '14	♥♥♥ 8
● Maremma Toscana Baffonero '13	♥♥♥ 8
● Maremma Toscana Rocca di Frassinello '15	♥♥♥ 6
● Rocca di Frassinello '12	♥♥♥ 6
● Rocca di Frassinello '11	♥♥♥ 6

Rocca di Montemassi

LOC. PIAN DEL BICHI
FRAZ. MONTEMASSI
S.DA PROV.LE SANT'ANNA
58036 ROCCASTRADA [GR]
TEL. +39 0564579700
www.roccadimontemassi.it

CELLAR SALES
PRE-BOOKED VISITS
ACCOMMODATION
ANNUAL PRODUCTION 480,000 bottles
HECTARES UNDER VINE 180.00
SUSTAINABLE WINERY

The Zonin 1821 Group's Maremma estate, Rocca di Montemassi is the realization of a project that was started in 1999 and that they've been growing with great patience. The winery and its vineyards are located in the district of Montemassi, in the heart of what writer Luciano Bianciardi called 'bitter' Maremma, an area made productive through sweat and toil, both above and below ground. Today the land is decidedly more generous, thanks especially to the rediscovery of winemaking here. They make modern, generous wines, at times approachable, at times complex and nuanced. Aromas of red berries, blueberries and eucalyptus characterize the Maremma Toscana Sassabruna '17, a well-balanced, flavorful and decisive wine. The pleasant and fragrant Maremma Toscana Rosso '16 features clear aromas and a docile, gratifying palate. The Maremma Toscana Sangiovese Le Focaie '18 stands out for its Mediterranean aromas, lush fruit and generous, full palate.

● Maremma Toscana Rosso Sassabruna '17	♥♥ 4
● Maremma Toscana Rosso '16	♥♥ 7
● Maremma Toscana Sangiovese Le Focaie '18	♥♥ 3
○ Maremma Toscana Vermentino Calasole '18	♥ 3
● Maremma Toscana Rocca di Montemassi '13	♥♥♥ 5
● Rocca di Montemassi '10	♥♥♥ 5
● Rocca di Montemassi '09	♥♥♥ 5
⊙ Maremma Toscana Rosato Syrosa '17	♥♥ 4
● Maremma Toscana Rosso Sassabruna '16	♥♥ 5
● Maremma Toscana Rosso Sassabruna '15	♥♥ 5
● Maremma Toscana Sangiovese Le Focaie '15	♥♥ 3

Roccapesta

LOC. MACERETO, 9
50854 SCANSANO [GR]
TEL. +39 0564599252
www.roccapesta.com

CELLAR SALES
PRE-BOOKED VISITS
ANNUAL PRODUCTION 100,000 bottles
HECTARES UNDER VINE 18.50

Of the more recently established wineries, Roccapesta is one of those making the biggest impact on the Morellino di Scansano wine scene. Owner Alberto Tanzini did not resort to easy sensationalism or 'pageant' wines, but instead immediately interpreted his terroir's potential by focusing on Sangiovese and traditional methods, starting with aging in large wood barrels. The linear, respectful path adopted for both the variety and territory has quickly born the fruits of success. Enticing aromas of small red berries adorned with smoky and spicy accents open the Morellino di Scansano Riserva '16, a wine that comes through firm, balanced and juicy on the palate. The Morellino di Scansano Calestaia Riserva '15 features aromas of dried flowers, earth and undergrowth, while in the mouth sweetness prevails. The Morellino di Scansano Ribeo '18 is characterized by pleasant flavor.

● Morellino di Scansano Ris. '16	▼▼▼ 5
● Morellino di Scansano Calestaia Ris. '15	▼▼ 6
● Morellino di Scansano Ribeo '18	▼▼ 3
● Morellino di Scansano Calestaia Ris. '11	♈♈♈ 5
● Morellino di Scansano Calestaia Ris. '10	♈♈♈ 5
● Morellino di Scansano Calestaia Ris. '09	♈♈♈ 5
● Morellino di Scansano Ribeo '15	♈♈♈ 3*
● Morellino di Scansano Ris. '13	♈♈♈ 4*
● Maremma Toscana Masca '14	♈♈ 2*
● Maremma Toscana Rosso Masca '16	♈♈ 2*
● Morellino di Scansano '15	♈♈ 3
● Morellino di Scansano '14	♈♈ 3
● Morellino di Scansano Ribeo '16	♈♈ 2*
● Morellino di Scansano Ribeo '14	♈♈ 3*
● Morellino di Scansano Ris. '15	♈♈ 5
● Pugnitello '14	♈♈ 6

★★Ruffino

P.LE RUFFINO, 1
50065 PONTASSIEVE [FI]
TEL. +39 05583605
www.ruffino.it

CELLAR SALES
PRE-BOOKED VISITS
ANNUAL PRODUCTION 18,000,000 bottles
HECTARES UNDER VINE 550.00

Purists often think of Ruffino, owned by the giant Constellation Brands, as a large-scale producer only. Nonetheless, their Chianti Classico Riserva Ducale Oro is now classified as a Gran Selezione and has 72 years of history behind it, a rare thing in the relatively young world of Italian enology. They have experienced ups and downs, with periods of inconsistency followed by quick recovery. The first 1947 vintage evolved from the Chianti Classico Riserva Ducale, in production since 1927, an era in which wine was largely used as sustenance for field workers. Great aromatic fragrance characterizes the Chianti Classico Riserva Ducale Oro Gran Selezione '15, a wine that's even better on the palate, where it proves well-sustained, succulent and deep. The floral and spicy Chianti Classico Romitorio di Santedame Gran Selezione '16 is less exuberant and a bit more marked by oak The Modus '16, a blend of Sangiovese, Cabernet Sauvignon and Merlot, is also well-made.

● Chianti Cl. Gran Selezione Riserva Ducale Oro '15	▼▼▼ 6
● Chianti Cl. Gran Selezione Romitorio di Santedame '16	▼▼ 6
● Modus '16	▼▼ 5
● Brunello di Montalcino Greppone Mazzi '05	♈♈♈ 6
● Chianti Cl. Gran Selezione Riserva Ducale Oro '14	♈♈♈ 6
● Chianti Cl. Riserva Ducale Oro '04	♈♈♈ 5
● Chianti Cl. Riserva Ducale Oro '01	♈♈♈ 5
● Chianti Cl. Riserva Ducale Oro '00	♈♈♈ 5
● Modus '04	♈♈♈ 5
● Romitorio di Santedame '00	♈♈♈ 7
● Romitorio di Santedame '99	♈♈♈ 7
● Romitorio di Santedame '98	♈♈♈ 7
● Romitorio di Santedame '97	♈♈♈ 7

Russo

LOC. LA METOCCHINA
VIA FORNI, 71
57028 SUVERETO [LI]
TEL. +39 0565845105
www.vinirusso.it

CELLAR SALES
PRE-BOOKED VISITS
ANNUAL PRODUCTION 80,000 bottles
HECTARES UNDER VINE 14.00

Podere La Metocchina, set in a hilly area of Suvereto, is an all-round operation including farm animals, in particular Friesian cows whose milk is conferred to a nearby dairy. They produce small amounts of cold cuts, cheeses, bread, fruit, vegetables, grains and olives. Similarly, winemaking began with small quantities and bottling only starting during the last years of the last century. The main cultivars are Claret, Chardonnay, Sangiovese Colorino, Canaiolo, Ciliegiolo, Merlot, Cabernet Sauvignon and Giacomino. The Poggio alle Vipere '15, a monovarietal Merlot, is a great drink, redolent of grilled peppers, then opening on rosemary across a fruity backdrop of blackcurrant and raspberry. On the palate it's pleasant and round, with delicate tannins. The Barbicone '16, made primarily with Sangiovese, is characterized by its notes of black cherry on the nose, and a smooth, harmonious balance on the palate.

● Barbicone '16	♥♥ 4
● Ceppitaio '17	♥♥ 2*
○ L'Isoletta Vermentino '18	♥♥ 2*
● Poggio alle Vipere '15	♥♥ 4
● Sassobucato '16	♥♥ 5
● Val di Cornia Rosso Barbicone '00	♥♥♥ 4*
● Barbicone '15	♀♀ 4
● Ceppitaio '16	♀♀ 2*
○ L'isoletta Vermentino '17	♀♀ 2*
La Mandria del Pari '15	♀♀ 8
○ Pietrasca '12	♀♀ 2*
Sassobucato '15	♀♀ 5
● Sassobucato '10	♀♀ 5
● Sassobucato '08	♀♀ 5
● Val di Cornia Rosso Ceppitaio '11	♀♀ 2*
● Val di Cornia Rosso Ceppitaio '08	♀♀ 2

Salcheto

VIA DI VILLA BIANCA, 15
53045 MONTEPULCIANO [SI]
TEL. +39 0578799031
www.salcheto.it

CELLAR SALES
PRE-BOOKED VISITS
ACCOMMODATION AND RESTAURANT SERVICE
ANNUAL PRODUCTION 350,000 bottles
HECTARES UNDER VINE 58.00
VITICULTURE METHOD Certified Organic
SUSTAINABLE WINERY

Salcheto's story may go back farther but it took its current form in 1997, when Michele Manelli got the reins and drove the winery along a path of environmental sustainability. The reds, from the simplest to the most prestigious, are all characterized by finesse, flavor and great drinkability. The wines go down easily, expressing the terroir while still leaving room for occasional pleasant surprises that point out the importance of avoiding preconceptions about style. The Nobile di Montepulciano '16 offers up a fragrant and floral aromatic suite adorned by spicy hints. It's a worthy introduction to a truly superb Sangiovese that shines with flavor and grace on the palate. The Nobile di Montepulciano Riserva '15 is denser, but no less accomplished in its airy and rich, fruity aromas. The Nobile Salco '15 and Rosso di Montepulciano '18 both prove well-made.

● Nobile di Montepulciano '16	♥♥♥ 4*
● Nobile di Montepulciano Ris. '15	♥♥ 5
● Nobile di Montepulciano V. V. del Salco '16	♥♥ 8
● Rosso di Montepulciano '18	♥♥ 3
● Nobile di Montepulciano '14	♀♀♀ 4*
● Nobile di Montepulciano '10	♀♀♀ 4*
● Nobile di Montepulciano Salco '11	♀♀♀ 6
● Nobile di Montepulciano Salco '10	♀♀♀ 5
● Nobile di Montepulciano Salco Evoluzione '06	♀♀♀ 6
● Nobile di Montepulciano '15	♀♀ 4
● Nobile di Montepulciano Vecchie Viti del Salco '15	♀♀ 8

Podere Salicutti

POD. SALICUTTI, 174
53024 MONTALCINO [SI]
TEL. +39 0577847003
www.poderesalicutti.it

CELLAR SALES
PRE-BOOKED VISITS
ACCOMMODATION
ANNUAL PRODUCTION 15,000 bottles
HECTARES UNDER VINE 4.00
VITICULTURE METHOD Certified Organic

Salicutti gets its name from the stream that delimits this property. It's located in the most evocative part of southeast Montalcino, on the road connecting Castelnuovo dell'Abate to Sant'Antimo. The Eichbauer family owns the estate, managing it with founder Francesco Leanza, the first producer in the appellation to obtain organic certification. Their Sorgente, Teatro and Piaggione vineyards give rise to flavorful and fruity Rosso and Brunello, which are aged in barrels of various sizes and origins. Salicutti's style is a personal one, and lately that style has seen some of its best expressions. Their Rosso '16 offers up aromas of raspberries, medicinal herbs and Mediterranean shrub. On the palate it does a nice job managing acidity thanks to a close-knit tannic weave. But it's their Brunello Piaggione Ris. '13 that most impresses, with its original combination of topsoil, red pepper and bath salts further amplified on woodland strokes across a full-bodied and flavorful palate.

● Brunello di Montalcino Piaggione Ris. '13	♥♥ 8
● Rosso di Montalcino '16	♥♥ 4
● Brunello di Montalcino '97	♥♥♥ 7
● Brunello di Montalcino '13	♥♥ 7
● Brunello di Montalcino '04	♥♥ 7
● Brunello di Montalcino '01	♥♥ 7
● Brunello di Montalcino '00	♥♥ 7
● Brunello di Montalcino Piaggione '07	♥♥ 7
● Brunello di Montalcino Piaggione Ris. '08	♥♥ 8
● Dopoteatro '09	♥♥ 5
● Rosso di Montalcino '15	♥♥ 4
● Rosso di Montalcino '04	♥♥ 4
● Rosso di Montalcino Sorgente '11	♥♥ 5

★Salvioni

P.ZZA CAVOUR, 19
53024 MONTALCINO [SI]
TEL. +39 0577848499
www.aziendasalvioni.com

PRE-BOOKED VISITS
RESTAURANT SERVICE
ANNUAL PRODUCTION 15,000 bottles
HECTARES UNDER VINE 4.00

La Cerbaiola, named after an old village in eastern Montalcino, is a virtually contiguous body of vineyards located at 400 meters elevation on stony soils rich in limestone and marl. The estate has belonged to the Salvioni family for at least three generations. Today Giulio and Mirella have the full-time support of their sons, who help to consolidate the powerful, untamed style that distinguishes their Rosso and Brunello, produced through spontaneous fermentation and maturation in 2000-liter Slavonian oak barrels. At Salvioni, it doesn't make much sense to distinguish between their base offering and premium wines, as their Rosso '17 testifies to in the best possible way. From the outset, the wine proves charming in its hints of dried flowers and orange peel. It finds oxygen in a warmer dimension amidst tobacco and curing spices. We find this dual track on its pervasive, yet austere palate, supported by robust backbone and sapid down to the last drop.

● Rosso di Montalcino '17	♥♥♥ 8
● Brunello di Montalcino '12	♥♥♥ 8
● Brunello di Montalcino '09	♥♥♥ 8
● Brunello di Montalcino '06	♥♥♥ 8
● Brunello di Montalcino '04	♥♥♥ 8
● Brunello di Montalcino '00	♥♥♥ 8
● Brunello di Montalcino '99	♥♥♥ 8
● Brunello di Montalcino '97	♥♥♥ 8
● Brunello di Montalcino '90	♥♥♥ 8
● Brunello di Montalcino '89	♥♥♥ 8
● Brunello di Montalcino '88	♥♥♥ 8
● Brunello di Montalcino '87	♥♥♥ 8
● Brunello di Montalcino '85	♥♥♥ 8

Podere San Cristoforo

FRAZ. BAGNO
VIA FORNI
58023 GAVORRANO [GR]
TEL. +39 3358212413
www.poderesancristoforo.it

CELLAR SALES
PRE-BOOKED VISITS
ACCOMMODATION
ANNUAL PRODUCTION 60,000 bottles
HECTARES UNDER VINE 17.00
VITICULTURE METHOD Certified Organic
SUSTAINABLE WINERY

Lorenzo Zonin has owned Podere San
Cristoforo since 2000. The biodynamic
estate in the district of Gavoranno quite
possibly produces the freshest, most
elegant Sangiovese in southern Toscana's
Maremma. This might at first seem
surprising given how difficult this Tuscan
grape variety can be and how hot the
climate of the area is, but the winery's
commitment to mastering both has resulted
in a range with a clearly legible style that is
never excessive or overpowering, but
instead has great grace and personality.
The San Cristoforo, a monovarietal Petit
Verdot, maintains its freshness and
fragrance even in a year as hot as 2017.
On the nose it calls up vanilla and toasty
notes, while on the palate it's full, not
without its rhythm. A supple, generally
sweet palate marks the red-berry and
spice-scented Maremma Sangiovese
Carandelle '17. The highly concentrated
Divita '17 is a blend of Sangiovese, Syrah
and Petit Verdot.

San Cristoforo '17	♟♟ 6
Maremma Toscana Sangiovese Carandelle '17	♟♟ 5
Ameri Governo all'Uso Toscano '17	♟ 7
Divita '17	♟ 5
Ameri Governo all'Uso Toscano '15	♟♟♟ 6
Maremma Toscana Podere San Cristoforo '13	♟♟♟ 3*
Maremma Toscana Sangiovese Carandelle '15	♟♟♟ 3*
Luminoso Dolce '09	♟♟ 5
Maremma Toscana Carandelle '16	♟♟ 3
Maremma Toscana Luminoso '15	♟♟ 3
Maremma Toscana Sangiovese Amaranto '16	♟♟ 3*
Maremma Toscana Sangiovese Amaranto '15	♟♟ 3

Tenute San Fabiano

VIA SAN FABIANO, 33
52100 AREZZO
TEL. +39 057524566
www.tenutesanfabiano.it

CELLAR SALES
PRE-BOOKED VISITS
ACCOMMODATION
ANNUAL PRODUCTION 1,000,000 bottles
HECTARES UNDER VINE 300.00

Tenute San Fabiano, the operational heart
of the Borghini Baldovinetti family's
business, is situated in Arezzo, extending
along the slopes of Castentino, northeast
of the city. But their Tenuta di Campriano
and Tregozzano (in Chianti and Poggio
Uliveto, in Nobile di Montepulciano) are
also an integral part of their production.
After a period that saw certain qualitative
and stylistic uncertainties emerging, this
Aretine producer seems to have found its
way, proposing a selection of supple wines
that more closely respect their territories of
origin. Clean and precise aromas of
fragrant red fruits and spices characterize
the Nobile di Montepulciano Poggio
Uliveto '16. On the palate it delivers,
proving juicy and flavorful. The Piocaia '16,
a Sangiovese and Merlot, performed well,
though it's just a bit too oak-laden. The
Chianti Riserva '16 is decidedly well-made,
while the Chianti Putto '18 proves highly
drinkable.

● Nobile di Montepulciano Poggio Uliveto '16	♟♟ 4
● Chianti Colli Aretini Putto San Fabiano '18	♟♟ 2*
● Chianti Ris. '16	♟♟ 3
● Piocaia '16	♟♟ 4
○ Vin Santo I Cannicci del Conte '08	♟♟ 5

★San Felice

LOC. SAN FELICE
53019 CASTELNUOVO BERARDENGA [SI]
TEL. +39 057739911
www.agricolasanfelice.it

CELLAR SALES
PRE-BOOKED VISITS
ACCOMMODATION AND RESTAURANT SERVICE
ANNUAL PRODUCTION 900,000 bottles
HECTARES UNDER VINE 140.00

San Felice, owned by the Allianz group, has left its mark on not only Tuscan but also national winemaking. The 'Super Tuscan' phenomenon began when the Castelnuovo Berardenga winery launched its Vigorello in 1968, and its role in conserving the genetic patrimony of traditionally cultivated grape varieties has also been pioneering. Today San Felice, active in Chianti Classico for over fifty years, produces a range of solid, reliable contemporary wines that are always faithful to the territory and often reach absolute excellence. Aromas of undergrowth, earth and mature red fruit characterize their Chianti Classico Poggio Rosso Gran Selezione '15, a well-sustained, succulent and complex wine. Their Chianti Classico Il Grigio Riserva '16 is somewhat limited by wood, but it's sapid and plucky nevertheless, marked by smoky and fruity sensations adorned with spices and toasty notes.

● Chianti Cl. Gran Selezione Poggio Rosso '15	▼▼▼ 5
● Chianti Cl. Il Grigio Ris. '16	▼▼ 3
● Chianti Cl. '17	▼ 3
● Vigorello '15	▼ 6
● Chianti Cl. '13	♀♀♀ 3*
● Chianti Cl. Gran Sel. Il Grigio da San Felice '11	♀♀♀ 5
● Chianti Cl. Gran Sel. Il Grigio da San Felice '10	♀♀♀ 5
● Chianti Cl. Il Grigio Ris. '15	♀♀♀ 3*
● Chianti Cl. Poggio Rosso Ris. '03	♀♀♀ 5
● Chianti Cl. Poggio Rosso Ris. '00	♀♀♀ 5
● Pugnitello '07	♀♀♀ 6
● Pugnitello '06	♀♀♀ 6
● Vigorello '13	♀♀♀ 6
● Vigorello '10	♀♀♀ 6

Fattoria San Felo

LOC. PAGLIATELLI DI SOTTO
58051 MAGLIANO IN TOSCANA [GR]
TEL. +39 05641950121
www.fattoriasanfelo.it

ANNUAL PRODUCTION 100,000 bottles
HECTARES UNDER VINE 30.00

Fattoria San Felo's soberly modern wines are aged in small and medium wood barrels. Selections are produced from international varieties (including ones that are challenging and unusual at these latitudes, such as Pinot Noir) and difficult types (such as sparkling versions) as well as the inevitable Morellino. As of late, the Magliano winery's range has shown a praiseworthy consistency of quality and impeccable workmanship that offer lovely character in harmony with the territory. The Maremma Toscana Balla la Vecchia '17 exhibits nice aromatic definition, but shows its best side in the mouth, where it proves rhythmic, sapid and fragrant. The mature and darkly fruity Morellino di Scansano Lampo '17 comes through generally tasty and vibrant on the palate. Their whites Maremma Toscana Vermentino Le Stoppie '18 and Maremma Toscana Viognier '18 are simple but well-made.

● Maremma Toscana Balla La Vecchia '17	▼▼ 3
● Morellino di Scansano Lampo '17	▼▼ 3
○ Maremma Toscana Vermentino Le Stoppie '18	▼ 3
○ Maremma Toscana Viognier '18	▼ 5
○ Chardonnay '15	♀♀ 3
● Maremma Toscana Rosso Balla La Vecchia '16	♀♀ 3
● Morellino di Scansano Lampo '16	♀♀ 3
● Morellino di Scansano Lampo '15	♀♀ 3
● Morellino di Scansano Lampo '13	♀♀ 3
● Pinot Nero '16	♀♀ 3
○ San Felo Brut M. Cl. '14	♀♀ 5

San Ferdinando

LOC. CIGGIANO
LA GARGAIOLO, 33
52041 CIVITELLA IN VAL DI CHIANA [AR]
TEL. +39 3287216738
www.sanferdinando.eu

CELLAR SALES
PRE-BOOKED VISITS
ACCOMMODATION
ANNUAL PRODUCTION 50,000 bottles
HECTARES UNDER VINE 10.00

San Ferdinando belongs to the Grifoni family and truly shines among the wineries of the Val di Chiana. Its discerning viticultural and enological approaches both respect the environment and emphasize the expressive naturalness of the wines. Only traditional Tuscan varieties are grown, including red Sangiovese, Ciliegiolo and Pugnitello, and among the whites, Vermentino. Brilliant and authentic, the wines respect the characteristics of each variety and of the terroir. 2018 gave rise to clear wines, certainly more honed — even if, possibly, they're in need of more time in the bottle. The Vermentino benefited from the vintage, making for a 'continental' white, even if it's intense aromatically and in its play of mature fruit and citrus. In any case, it's a truly delicious bottle. Their two Ciliegiolos are marvels, including the rosé. Their Chainti Podere Gamba '17 performed well, while the Pugnitello '15 is a bit more difficult to pin down.

Vermentino '18	🍷🍷 3*
Chianti Podere Gamba '17	🍷🍷 3
Ciliegiolo '18	🍷🍷 3
Ciliegiolo Rosato '18	🍷🍷 2*
Pugnitello '15	🍷 3
Vermentino '16	🍷🍷🍷 3*
Chianti Podere Gamba '16	🍷🍷 3
Chianti Podere Gamba '15	🍷🍷 3
Ciliegiolo '17	🍷🍷 3
Ciliegiolo '16	🍷🍷 3
Vermentino '17	🍷🍷 3*

San Filippo

LOC. SAN FILIPPO, 134
53024 MONTALCINO [SI]
TEL. +39 0577847176
www.sanfilippomontalcino.com

ANNUAL PRODUCTION 50,000 bottles
HECTARES UNDER VINE 10.50

Roberto Giannelli took over the estate in the early 2000s when he decided to leave city life behind and move to San Filippo. Surrounded by vineyards, olive groves and woods, the ancient village is the winery's center of operations. Worked separately, the plots of La Storta, Le Raffiche, Le Lucère and La Smarrita each lay at an elevation of about 400 meters on limestone marl and rocky clay. The eastern sector of Montalcino is historically suited for producing grippy, assertive Brunello aged in barriques and larger barrels. San Filippo doubles its satisfaction, earning itself a place among Montalcino's owners and landing two wines in our finals. Their Rosso Lo Scorno '17 is mobile and sophisticated in its aromas of fresh red fruits, meadow herbs and sweet spices, confirming its deliciously rustic profile on a supple and juicy palate. Their Brunello '14 is more intense and austere, though upholds its austere profile in the mouth.

● Brunello di Montalcino '14	🍷🍷 6
● Rosso di Montalcino Lo Scorno '17	🍷🍷 5
● Brunello di Montalcino Le Lucere '13	🍷🍷 6
● Brunello di Montalcino Le Lucere Ris. '04	🍷🍷🍷 6
● Brunello di Montalcino '09	🍷🍷 6
● Brunello di Montalcino '07	🍷🍷 6
● Brunello di Montalcino '06	🍷🍷 6
● Brunello di Montalcino Le Lucere '07	🍷🍷 6
● Brunello di Montalcino Le Lucere '06	🍷🍷 6
● Brunello di Montalcino Le Lucere Ris. '07	🍷🍷 6
● Brunello di Montalcino Le Lucere Ris. '06	🍷🍷 6
● Rosso di Montalcino Lo Scorno '10	🍷🍷 5

★★★Tenuta San Guido

FRAZ. BOLGHERI
LOC. LE CAPANNE, 27
57022 CASTAGNETO CARDUCCI [LI]
TEL. +39 0565762003
www.sassicaia.com

PRE-BOOKED VISITS
RESTAURANT SERVICE
ANNUAL PRODUCTION 780,000 bottles
HECTARES UNDER VINE 90.00

Sassicaia yesterday, today and tomorrow. The start of the new era in Italian winemaking, the producer created both a territory and a style, accompanied the first steps of modern Italian wine and made the country's potential known. The Marquises Incisa della Rocchetta, visionaries yesterday, innovators and wise conservators of a true treasure today, can claim the laurels for creating this absolutely essential masterpiece. Bolgheri, a terroir just waiting to be discovered and developed, did the rest. You didn't need a crystal ball to call out one of the best Sassicaias of all time (certainly in recent memory), though there have been plenty of other outstanding selections. The 2016 shines for its eleganceand flavor, bringing together (as no other wine in the area can) exuberance with grace, sophisticated and pure texture. There's nothing more and nothing less than what's needed, no frills or gimmicks. Just superb.

● Bolgheri Sup. Sassicaia '16	▼▼▼ 8
● Guidalberto '17	▼▼ 6
● Le Difese '17	▼ 4
● Bolgheri Sassicaia '15	♀♀♀ 8
● Bolgheri Sassicaia '14	♀♀♀ 8
● Bolgheri Sassicaia '13	♀♀♀ 8
● Bolgheri Sassicaia '12	♀♀♀ 8
● Bolgheri Sassicaia '11	♀♀♀ 8
● Bolgheri Sassicaia '10	♀♀♀ 8
● Bolgheri Sassicaia '09	♀♀♀ 8
● Bolgheri Sassicaia '08	♀♀♀ 8
● Bolgheri Sassicaia '07	♀♀♀ 8
● Bolgheri Sassicaia '06	♀♀♀ 8
● Bolgheri Sassicaia '05	♀♀♀ 8
● Bolgheri Sassicaia '04	♀♀♀ 8
● Guidalberto '08	♀♀♀ 6

Tenuta San Jacopo

LOC. CASTIGLIONCELLI, 151
52022 CAVRIGLIA [AR]
TEL. +39 055966003
www.tenutasanjacopo.it

CELLAR SALES
PRE-BOOKED VISITS
ACCOMMODATION
ANNUAL PRODUCTION 25,000 bottles
HECTARES UNDER VINE 40.00
VITICULTURE METHOD Certified Organic

The winery's history goes all the way back to the 18th century. Indeed, a period villa testifies to the fact, along with the presence of farmhouses (that now serve as an agritourism). It was 2002 when three brothers from Milan, Vanni, Carlo and Marco Cattaneo, decided to invest in Tuscany and began renovating the property. In addition to fixing up its buildings, they modernized the vineyards with the aim of creating quality wines that respect both territorial identity and the environment. The Orma del Diavolo '16 is a field blend of Sangiovese, Merlot and Cabernet Savignon redolent of wild fruit and fresh spices. On the palate it's warm, harmonious, closing sapid. Their Vigna del Mulinaccio '16 is a lean, racy and drinkable monovarietal Sangiovese that opens with fresh notes of cherry and Mediterranean scrub. Their Trebbiano Erboli '17 stands out for its floral aromas, then potpourri and fruity hints of apple. In the mouth it's fresh and tasty, with a long finish.

○ Erboli Trebbiano '17	▼▼ 3
● Orma Del Diavolo '16	▼▼ 4
○ Quarto di Luna '18	▼▼ 2
● Vigna del Mulinaccio '16	▼▼ 5
● Caprilus '15	▼ 4
● Orma del Diavolo '11	♀♀ 3
○ Quarto di Luna '14	♀♀ 2
○ Quarto di Luna '12	♀♀ 2

Fattoria San Michele a Torri

Via San Michele, 36
50018 Scandicci [FI]
Tel. +39 055769111
www.fattoriasanmichele.it

CELLAR SALES
PRE-BOOKED VISITS
ANNUAL PRODUCTION 200,000 bottles
HECTARES UNDER VINE 55.00
VITICULTURE METHOD Certified Organic

The estate embodies traditional ideas and therefore, in addition to vineyards and olive groves, has arable land, woodland and Cinta Senese pigs. In addition to wine and extra-virgin olive oil, for some years now small amounts of cold cuts, meat, eggs, vegetables, bread, legumes, honey, jams, flours, saffron, spelt and chickpeas are also produced. Tastings, visits and picnics are organized on the farm, with artisanal pasta workshops and tastings offered in Florence. Their interesting Vigna della Luna '18 is a field blend of primarily Chardonnay, plus smaller shares of Pinot Bianco and Petit Manseng. On the nose it offers up aromas of peach and mango, then citrusy hints of lime. On the palate it comes through full, pleasantly dense, with a sapid, appetizing finish. The Chianti Colli Fiorentini '17 opens with spicy aromas, hints of chocolate, then red fruits like plum and raspberry. It's a lively drink, with nice fresh and acidity, and good length.

Campotrovo '18	🍷🍷 2*
Chianti Colli Fiorentini San Michele a Torri '17	🍷🍷 2*
V. della Luna '18	🍷🍷 5
Chianti Colli Fiorentini S. Giovanni Novantasette Ris. '16	🍷 4
Murtas '16	🍷 5
Chianti Cl. Tenuta La Gabbiola '16	🍷🍷 3*
Chianti Cl. Tenuta La Gabbiola Ris. '14	🍷🍷 4
Chianti Colli Fiorentini '14	🍷🍷 2*
Chianti Colli Fiorentini S. Giovanni Novantasette Ris. '13	🍷🍷 4
Chicchirossi '16	🍷🍷 3
Colli dell'Etruria Centrale Vin Santo '11	🍷🍷 5
Murtas '15	🍷🍷 5

San Polo

Loc. Podernovi, 161
53024 Montalcino [SI]
Tel. +39 0577835101
www.poggiosanpolo.com

CELLAR SALES
PRE-BOOKED VISITS
ANNUAL PRODUCTION 150,000 bottles
HECTARES UNDER VINE 17.00

A decade ago, the San Polo estate in Montalcino became the newest addition to the Allegrini family's prestigious group. The estate is in the heart of Podernovi, the historical toponym of this central-south-eastern area, overlooking Sant'Antimo valley with Monte Amiata on the horizon. At an altitude of about 450 meters on calcareous, clay soils, the spot is ideal for Rosso and Brunello wines that are approachable right from the start. Vinification takes place in concrete with aging in both small barriques and oak barrels from Slavonia and Allier. We repeat: San Polo's selection seems to increase in quality and stylistic definition year after year. In this round of tastings we were particularly impressed with their Brunello Vignavecchia Ris. 13: mature fruit and hematic strokes rise up on the nose, on the palate it exhibits a certain tannic austerity that's well contrasted by sapid vigor. Their successful Rosso '17 and Brunello '14 follow a similar expressive track.

Brunello di Montalcino Vignavecchia Ris. '13	🍷🍷 8
Brunello di Montalcino '14	🍷🍷 7
Rosso di Montalcino '17	🍷🍷 3
Brunello di Montalcino '13	🍷🍷 7
Brunello di Montalcino '12	🍷🍷 6
Brunello di Montalcino '11	🍷🍷 6
Brunello di Montalcino '10	🍷🍷 6
Brunello di Montalcino '09	🍷🍷 6
Brunello di Montalcino '08	🍷🍷 6
Brunello di Montalcino '07	🍷🍷 6
Brunello di Montalcino Ris. '12	🍷🍷 8
Brunello di Montalcino Ris. '10	🍷🍷 7
Rosso di Montalcino '15	🍷🍷 3*
Rosso di Montalcino '13	🍷🍷 3
Rosso di Montalcino '12	🍷🍷 3
Rosso di Montalcino '11	🍷🍷 3

Podere Sanlorenzo

POD. SANLORENZO, 280
53024 MONTALCINO [SI]
TEL. +39 3396070930
www.poderesanlorenzo.net

CELLAR SALES
PRE-BOOKED VISITS
ANNUAL PRODUCTION 18,000 bottles
HECTARES UNDER VINE 4.50

Luciano Ciolfi has dedicated the Brunello produced at Podere Sanlorenzo to his grandfather, Bramante. The steep, sunny hills run from Poggio della Civitella towards the Ombrone River and the Maremma, and are marked by the best qualities of Montalcino's south-west side: lean, limestone marl soils,, a Mediterranean climate, constant ventilation and significant temperature fluctuations caused by the almost 500-meter elevation. These conditions help shape the vigorous, sanguine character of the estate's Sangiovese, aged in barriques and 3000-liter barrels. Luciano Ciolfi's stylistic work continues unwaveringlywith his Brunellos, always distinct for this mix of power and austerity. It's a style best represented by the Bramante Rls. '13. Here intense notes of dark fruit, pepper and licorice anticipate a large, meaty palate that finishes rougher in its tannins. Their 'vintage' Bramante '14 also performed exceptionally well — it's only a bit coarse at the finish.

● Brunello di Montalcino Bramante Ris. '13	🏆🏆 7
● Brunello di Montalcino Bramante '14	🏆🏆 6
● Rosso di Montalcino '17	🏆 3
● Brunello di Montalcino Bramante '07	🏆🏆🏆 6
● Brunello di Montalcino Bramante '07	🏆🏆🏆 8
● Brunello di Montalcino Bramante '13	🏆🏆 6
● Brunello di Montalcino Bramante '12	🏆🏆 6
● Brunello di Montalcino Bramante '11	🏆🏆 6
● Brunello di Montalcino Bramante '10	🏆🏆 6
● Brunello di Montalcino Bramante '09	🏆🏆 6
● Brunello di Montalcino Bramante '08	🏆🏆 6
● Rosso di Montalcino '15	🏆🏆 3
● Rosso di Montalcino '14	🏆🏆 3
● Rosso di Montalcino '13	🏆🏆 3
● Rosso di Montalcino '11	🏆🏆 3
● Rosso di Montalcino '10	🏆🏆 3

★Podere Sapaio

VIA DEL FOSSO, 31
57022 CASTAGNETO CARDUCCI [LI]
TEL. +39 0438430440
www.sapaio.it

CELLAR SALES
PRE-BOOKED VISITS
ANNUAL PRODUCTION 110,000 bottles
HECTARES UNDER VINE 26.00
VITICULTURE METHOD Certified Organic

Podere Sapaio is relatively young but already well-established and, in our opinion, one of the most interesting winery's in Bolgheri. Massimo Piccin acts as the face of the estate, but he's flanked and supported by his family in caring for their 40 hectares of vineyards (mainly sandy, calcareous soil). The style continues to evolve: no technically shocking changes but it follows a path that is more cognizant and focused with regard to extraction processes and aging in wood barrels. The most recent wines are purer and freed from the charred oak that they exhibited in the past. The current-vintage Sapaio will be released next year, so as to give the wine time to age and put its best foot forward. In the meantime we enjoyed a lovely version of their Rosso Volpolo. The 2017 exhibits the qualities of a great wine, both in terms of structure and aromatic intensity. Its toasty notes are still foregrounded and crowd out the rest, but the palate shows pluck and flavor, thus lending balance.

● Bolgheri Rosso Volpolo '17	🏆🏆 5
● Bolgheri Rosso Sup. '13	🏆🏆🏆
● Bolgheri Rosso Sup. '12	🏆🏆🏆
● Bolgheri Rosso Sup. '11	🏆🏆🏆
● Bolgheri Rosso Sup. Sapaio '16	🏆🏆🏆
● Bolgheri Sup. Sapaio '10	🏆🏆🏆
● Bolgheri Sup. Sapaio '09	🏆🏆🏆
● Bolgheri Sup. Sapaio '08	🏆🏆🏆
● Bolgheri Sup. Sapaio '07	🏆🏆🏆
● Bolgheri Sup. Sapaio '06	🏆🏆🏆
● Sapaio '15	🏆🏆🏆
● Bolgheri Volpolo '16	🏆🏆
● Bolgheri Volpolo '15	🏆🏆
● Bolgheri Volpolo '12	🏆🏆
● Bolgheri Volpolo '11	🏆🏆

Fattoria Sardi

FRAZ. MONTE SAN QUIRICO
VIA DELLA MAULINA, 747
55100 LUCCA
TEL. +39 0583341230
www.fattoriasardi.com

CELLAR SALES
PRE-BOOKED VISITS
ACCOMMODATION
ANNUAL PRODUCTION 120,000 bottles
HECTARES UNDER VINE 17.50
VITICULTURE METHOD Certified Organic

Fattoria Sardi is near Lucca, between the Apuan Alps, the Apennines and the Tyrrhenian Sea. The young owners manage it attentively in a modern way that maintains respect for family traditions using an agricultural approach based on sensitivity and sustainability. The vineyards are between the Freddana and Serchio rivers, where soils at the bottom are loamy, sandy and pebbly, becoming increasingly rich in clay and stone as they climb the slopes; due to these pedoclimatic characteristics the estate centers on the production of rosé wine. Their Mille968 '16 is a marvelous drink. The name brings together various leading Colline Lucchesi producers in a single collective project. Fattoria Sardi's version shines with its fresh aromas of wild berries and a decidedly herbaceous profile that's almost mossy. It's a springtime wine, tasty and easy to drink, while also exhibiting excellent complexity. Both their rosés delivered — it's a typology that the winery is particularly fond of.

● Colline Lucchesi Mille968 '16	🍷🍷 5
○ Colline Lucchesi Vermentino '18	🍷🍷 3
○ Le Cicale '18	🍷🍷 5
● Rosé '18	🍷🍷 3
● Colline Lucchesi Sebastiano '16	🍷 5
● Colline Lucchesi Merlot Sebastiano '12	🍷🍷 3
● Colline Lucchesi Rosso Sebastiano '13	🍷🍷 5
● Colline Lucchesi Sebastiano '15	🍷🍷 5
● Colline Lucchesi Vallebuia '16	🍷🍷 3
○ Colline Lucchesi Vermentino '14	🍷🍷 3
● Le Cicale '17	🍷🍷 5
● Le Cicale '16	🍷🍷 4
○ Pet-Nat Frizzante '16	🍷🍷 3

Sassotondo

FRAZ. SOVANA
LOC. PIAN DI CONATI, 52
58010 SORANO [GR]
TEL. +39 0564614218
www.sassotondo.it

CELLAR SALES
PRE-BOOKED VISITS
ANNUAL PRODUCTION 50,000 bottles
HECTARES UNDER VINE 12.00
VITICULTURE METHOD Certified Organic

Even if recent years were complicated in terms of climate, Carla and Edoardo are moving forward with the help of Cileno agronomist Pablo Parra in the work of zoning their vineyards. This research has given rise to a first bottle, which will soon be accompanied by others. It's their Ciliegiolo Poggio Pinzo (after the Poggio Pinzi volcano), a wine macerated on the skins for 11 months, fermented and matured in terra-cotta amphoras. Indeed, of late their direction pursues more marked flavor deriving from time-honored techniques like spontaneous fermentation and long maceration. Our tastings proved the value of the work being done with Ciliegiolo, with their historic, barrel-aged wine, the San Lorenzo, offering up aromas of black berries and cocoa powder before coming through rich in austere tannins on the palate. But the real standout is their Poggio Pinzo '17 — redolent of spicy and Mediterranean nuances on the nose, it pervades the palate with finesse and tannic naturalness.

● Maremma Toscana Ciliegiolo Poggio Pinzo '17	🍷🍷 6
● Maremma Toscana Ciliegiolo San Lorenzo '17	🍷🍷 6
○ Numero Sei '17	🍷🍷 7
● Tuforosso '17	🍷🍷 2*
○ Bianco di Pitigliano Isolina '18	🍷 4
● Maremma Toscana Ciliegiolo '18	🍷 3
○ Tufobianco '18	🍷 2
○ Bianco di Pitigliano Sup. Isolina '17	🍷🍷 4
● Maremma Toscana Ciliegiolo '17	🍷🍷 3
● Maremma Toscana Ciliegiolo Poggio Pinzo '16	🍷🍷 6
● Maremma Toscana Ciliegiolo San Lorenzo '15	🍷🍷 6
● Maremma Toscana Ciliegiolo San Lorenzo '13	🍷🍷 6

Sator

Fraz. Pomaia
via Macchia al Pino
56040 Santa Luce [PI]
Tel. +39 050740529
www.satorwines.com

CELLAR SALES
PRE-BOOKED VISITS
ANNUAL PRODUCTION 50,000 bottles
HECTARES UNDER VINE 9.50

The winery was founded in 2004 by Roberta and Gianna Moscardini. They decided to invest in the land that had been in their family for more than two centuries, pursuing a philosophy centered on respect for the territory, and the suitability of the grapes cultivated (in light of pedoclimatic characteristics). The name refers to the famed Sator Square, which contains a five-word Latin palindrome. Their intriguing Operaundici '17 blend offers up tertiaries of dried flowers and oak, then mineral notes and hints of blood-rich meat on a backdrop of red fruit. On the palate it enters intense, attractively nuanced amidst tannins and alcohol, with a lively acidity giving way to an appetizing finish. The Artume '18, a blend of Fiano and Vermentino, opens with notes of bay leaf and myrtle, fading into a lovely citrusy hint of lemon. It's a dense but harmonic wine, and pleasantly long in the mouth. The fruit and spice-scented Merlot Sileno '17 comes through soft and juicy on the palate.

○ Artume '18	♈♈ 7
● Montescudaio Merlot Sileno '17	♈♈ 4
● Montescudaio Operaundici '17	♈♈ 7
○ Vermentino '18	♈♈ 2*
● Montescudaio Rosso '18	♈ 2
● Montescudaio Sangiovese Sileno '17	♈ 4
○ Rosato '18	♈ 3
● Montescudaio Merlot Sileno '16	♈♈ 3
● Montescudaio Operaundici '15	♈♈ 6
● Sileno Ciliegiolo '16	♈♈ 3
● Sileno Ciliegiolo '15	♈♈ 3
○ Vermentino '16	♈♈ 2*

Michele Satta

loc. Vigna al Cavaliere, 61b
57022 Castagneto Carducci [LI]
Tel. +39 0565773041
www.michelesatta.com

CELLAR SALES
PRE-BOOKED VISITS
ANNUAL PRODUCTION 150,000 bottles
HECTARES UNDER VINE 20.00

Michele Satta is a father of Bolgheri wine. Established in 1983, his winery helped the terroir build its prestigious reputation. It's a producer with clear ideas in terms of style and varietals (sometimes even unconventional), making for unique Sangiovese in this part of Maremma. Today Michele's son Giacomo is choosing his own path forward. His first, surefooted, steps are resulting in wines that have their own identity. Once again we've got good things to say about their Bolgheri Rosso Superiore Marianova '16, a blend of Sangiovese and Syrah that's surprising for its profile and personality. It's a red that's not too 'bolgherese' inasmuch as it's difficult to correlate its style with that of most of the area's wines. It's earthy, moody and almost autumnal on the nose, it has crisp fruit and pluck. On the palate it finishes on a note of citron. Their Bianco Giovin Re '17 is just as original.

● Bolgheri Rosso Sup. Marianova '16	♈♈ 8
○ Bolgheri Bianco Giovin Re '17	♈♈ 6
● Bolgheri Rosso Piastraia '02	♈♈♈ 6
● Bolgheri Rosso Piastraia '01	♈♈♈ 6
○ Bolgheri Bianco Costa di Giulia '15	♈♈ 4
● Bolgheri Rosso '15	♈♈ 4
● Bolgheri Rosso '13	♈♈ 3
● Bolgheri Rosso Piastraia '12	♈♈ 5
● Bolgheri Rosso Piastraia '11	♈♈ 5
● Bolgheri Rosso Sup. I Castagni '12	♈♈ 8
● Bolgheri Rosso Sup. Marianova '15	♈♈ 8
● Bolgheri Rosso Sup. Piastraia '15	♈♈ 6
● Bolgheri Sup. Piastraia '14	♈♈ 6
● Cavaliere '15	♈♈ 6
● Syrah '12	♈♈ 5

La Selva

LOC. SAN DONATO
.DA PROV.LE 81 OSA, 7
8015 ORBETELLO [GR]
EL. +39 0564884820
www.laselva.bio

CELLAR SALES
PRE-BOOKED VISITS
ACCOMMODATION
ANNUAL PRODUCTION 200,000 bottles
HECTARES UNDER VINE 32.00
VITICULTURE METHOD Certified Organic

La Selva belongs to the historic nucleus of estates on which the success of Maremma wine rests. Owner Karl Egger is a pioneer of organic methods in the vineyard, cellar and other aspects of his operation. He was among the first to gamble on both red and white local varieties, as well as one of the first to strive for balance over power, thereby freeing himself from the stereotypes that had fundamentally defined local wines for years. Today, the range is enjoyable and qualitatively reliable. Freshness of flavor and aromatic cleanness characterize the Morellino di Scansano '18, a highly drinkable wine (as tradition would have it). The pleasant Maremma Toscana Ciliegiolo '16 offers up aromas of small red berries, coming through racy and flavorful on the palate. The Maremma Toscana Vermentino '18 is aromatically varietal, well-contoured on the palate, where it finds its fullest expression, closing with a delicately salty note and nice personality.

Maremma Toscana Ciliegiolo '16	♟♟ 4
Maremma Toscana Vermentino '18	♟♟ 3
Morellino di Scansano '18	♟♟ 3
Morellino di Scansano Colli dell'Uccellina Ris. '16	♟ 4
Sangiovese Bianco '18	♟ 3
Maremma Toscana Ciliegiolo '15	♟♟ 4
Maremma Toscana Ciliegiolo '13	♟♟ 3
Maremma Toscana Privo '16	♟♟ 2*
Maremma Toscana Vermentino '17	♟♟ 3
Morellino di Scansano '17	♟♟ 3
Morellino di Scansano '15	♟♟ 2*
Morellino di Scansano Colli dell'Uccellina Ris. '15	♟♟ 4
Morellino di Scansano Colli dell'Uccellina Ris. '13	♟♟ 3
Nudo Sangiovese '14	♟♟ 2*

Fattoria Selvapiana

LOC. SELVAPIANA, 43
50068 RUFINA [FI]
TEL. +39 0558369848
www.selvapiana.it

CELLAR SALES
PRE-BOOKED VISITS
ANNUAL PRODUCTION 220,000 bottles
HECTARES UNDER VINE 60.00

Silvia and Federico Giuntini oversee this historic estate, whose plots are spread throughout Rufina, Pelago and Pontassieve, and reach elevations of 350 meters at the edges of the Apennines. Most of the vineyards are around the Renaissance era villa, near their new cellar. In addition to the area's traditional grapes, they cultivate Cab. Sauvignon, Franc and Merlot, as well as rows of Syrah planted some years ago. Their Chianti Rufina Bucerchiale '16 earned a place in our finals, but it's the overall quality of their selection that impressed. A complex bouquet sees notes of animal skins and leather, then bitter hints and finally clear, focused plum. On the palate it has vigor, nice acidic verve, well-integrated tannins and a full finish. The Chianti Rufina '17 delivers with its fresh, mineral aromas and a lean, smooth body. The Rufina Vigneto Erci '16 is also pleasant, balsamic, minty and enticing on the nose, juicy and decisive on the palate, with a long finish.

● Chianti Rufina Vign. Bucerchiale Ris. '16	♟♟ 5
● Chianti Rufina '17	♟♟ 2*
● Chianti Rufina Vign. Erci '16	♟♟ 3
● Fornace '15	♟♟ 5
● Pomino Rosso Villa Petrognano '15	♟♟ 2*
○ Vin Santo del Chianti Rufina '10	♟♟ 4
● Chianti Rufina '16	♟♟ 2*
● Chianti Rufina '15	♟♟ 2*
● Chianti Rufina '14	♟♟ 2*
● Chianti Rufina Bucerchiale Ris. '13	♟♟ 5
● Chianti Rufina Bucerchiale Ris. '12	♟♟ 5
● Chianti Rufina Vign. Bucerchiale Ris. '15	♟♟ 5
● Pomino Rosso Villa Petrognano '13	♟♟ 2*

Sensi - Fattoria Calappiano

FRAZ. CERBAIA, 107
51035 LAMPORECCHIO [PT]
TEL. +39 057382910
www.sensivini.com

CELLAR SALES
PRE-BOOKED VISITS
ANNUAL PRODUCTION 2,000,000 bottles
HECTARES UNDER VINE 100.00
VITICULTURE METHOD Certified Organic
SUSTAINABLE WINERY

Fattoria di Calappiano is a historical and architectural treasure of the Florentine Medici family. The 200-hectare estate of vineyards, olive groves and woods is owned by the Sensi family, who have operated in various capacities in the world of wine for over 120 years. Along with Tenuta del Poggio, Calappiano is the centerpiece of a project that, through care in the vineyard, sophisticated winemaking and the use of select grapes, aims to rediscover the old style of Tuscan winemaking. The pleasant Collegonzi '16 is a monovarietal Sangiovese marked by a unique aromatic procession of mineral notes, then aromatic herbs, sage, mint, undergrowth and finally focused fruity hints of cherry. On the palate it's warm, with enjoyable acidity, nice weight and crunchy tannins. The Lungarno '16, a blend of Sangiovese and Colorino, opens with sweet hints of vanilla and cloves, then black cherry and finally faint, minty accents. In the mouth it's invigorating, lively and juicy.

● Collegonzi Sangiovese Fattoria Calappiano '16	♟♟ 6
● Chianti Vegante '17	♟♟ 3
● Governato '16	♟♟ 7
● Lungarno '16	♟♟ 7
● Ninfato '18	♟♟ 3
● Chianti Vinciano Ris. Fattoria di Calappiano '16	♟ 6
● Mantello '17	♟ 4
● Morellino di Scansano Pretorio '18	♟ 3
○ Vernaccia di San Gimignano Collegiata '18	♟ 2
● Chianti Dalcampo Ris. '14	♟♟ 3
● Collegonzi Sangiovese '15	♟♟ 6
● Governato '16	♟♟ 7
● Mantello Sangiovese Shiraz '16	♟♟ 4
● Ninfato '17	♟♟ 3

Serpaia

LOC. FONTEBLANDA
VIA GOLDONI, 15
58100 GROSSETO
TEL. +39 0461650129
www.endrizzi.it

ANNUAL PRODUCTION 135,000 bottles
HECTARES UNDER VINE 30.00

The historic Trentino winery Endrizzi has found in Maremma, as often happens, a spot for making reds with strong personality. The vineyards in Serpaia give rise to wines of overall high quality that are reliable, technically impeccable and in tune with the hot, sunny, Mediterranean climate of Magliano. The wines continue to improve, even if somewhat niavely in the occasional overabundance of oak and in a search for concentration, which at these latitudes can easily become excessive. The decisive Morellino di Scansano '18 pursues pleasantness. Aromatically it's fruit-forward while on the palate it proves soft, lively and not without contrast. The well-made Serpaiolo, a blend of Merlot, Cabernet Sauvignon and Sangiovese delivers nice aromatic cleanness and a soft, alluring palate. The Dono '13, a monovarietal Sangiovese, exhibits fragrance and gustatory force.

● Dono '13	♟♟ 4
● Morellino di Scansano '18	♟♟ 3
● Serpaiolo '17	♟♟ 3
● Morellino di Scansano '16	♟♟ 3
● Morellino di Scansano '15	♟♟ 3
● Morellino di Scansano '14	♟♟ 2
● Morellino di Scansano '13	♟♟ 2
● Morellino di Scansano '12	♟♟ 2
● Morellino di Scansano Dono Ris. '11	♟♟ 3
● Serpaiolo '16	♟♟ 3
● Serpaiolo '15	♟♟ 3
● Serpaiolo '14	♟♟ 2

Sesti - Castello di Argiano

FRAZ. SANT'ANGELO IN COLLE
LOC. CASTELLO DI ARGIANO
53024 MONTALCINO [SI]
TEL. +39 0577843921
www.sestiwine.com

CELLAR SALES
PRE-BOOKED VISITS
ANNUAL PRODUCTION 61,000 bottles
HECTARES UNDER VINE 9.00

Surrounded by scrub and woodlands on the southwestern border of the Montalcino territory, Castello di Argiano is a truly magical place, so it's not surprising that the Sestis chose it as their production center. But the decision was based on more than the quality of the vineyards here (marked by the sunny microclimate, breezes from the nearby sea and the light sandy-tufaceous soils). It is, even more, an ideal place for research, and the proof is a diverse range based more on the Sangiovese grape itself than on established theories of winemaking. The 2017 version of their Rosso di Sesti confirms that it's among Montalcino's best. Summer fruit, herb caramels, light roots — a warm year brought greater approachability to the wine's usual, delectable profile. Maybe it's just a bit lacking in vitality and breadth, but its charm is intact. It's an expressive track shared by their Brunello Phenomena Ris. '13, a wine that's just a bit more hurried in its development.

● Rosso di Montalcino '17	♟♟ 4
● Brunello di Montalcino Phenomena Ris. '13	♟♟ 8
● Brunello di Montalcino '14	♟ 6
● Grangiovese '17	♟ 2
● Brunello di Montalcino '06	♟♟♟ 6
● Brunello di Montalcino Phenomena Ris. '07	♟♟♟ 8
● Brunello di Montalcino Phenomena Ris. '01	♟♟♟ 8
● Brunello di Montalcino Ris. '04	♟♟♟ 8
● Rosso di Montalcino '16	♟♟♟ 4*
● Brunello di Montalcino '13	♟♟ 6
● Brunello di Montalcino Phenomena Ris. '12	♟♟ 8

★Tenuta Sette Ponti

VIA SETTE PONTI, 71
52029 CASTIGLION FIBOCCHI [AR]
TEL. +39 0575477857
www.tenutasetteponti.it

CELLAR SALES
PRE-BOOKED VISITS
ACCOMMODATION
ANNUAL PRODUCTION 250,000 bottles
HECTARES UNDER VINE 55.00
VITICULTURE METHOD Certified Organic
SUSTAINABLE WINERY

Wine is the great passion of Antonio Moretti, an entrepreneur in the fashion sector, who in the 1950s acquired this historic 330-hectare estate. He named it after the Via dei Sette Ponti (after the seven bridges that cross the Arno between the two Tuscan capitals). In addition to Sangiovese they cultivate international varieties, such as Cab. Sauvignon and Merlot. Moretti's general love of the land has led to breeding Chianina cattle and Cinta pigs on the estate. The 2017 version of their Oreno, a blend of Merlot, Cab. Sauvignon and Petit Verdot, is excellent, unveiling notes of wild berries softened by hints of cinnamon and cloves, then mineral accents. On the palate it enters pleasant, relaxed and soft, with nicely-woven tannins and a lovely, long finish. The Vigna dell'Impero '16 is more austere aromatically, with jammy notes of blackberries and cherry accompanied by Mediterranean scrub. In the mouth a solid body and delicate tannins give way to a truly juicy finish.

● Oreno '17	♟♟♟ 8
● Valdarno di Sopra Sangiovese Vigna dell'Impero '16	♟♟ 8
● Crognolo '17	♟♟ 5
● Oreno '16	♟♟♟ 8
● Oreno '15	♟♟♟ 8
● Oreno '12	♟♟♟ 7
● Oreno '11	♟♟♟ 7
● Oreno '10	♟♟♟ 7
● Oreno '09	♟♟♟ 7
● Oreno '05	♟♟♟ 7
● Oreno '00	♟♟♟ 5
● Valdarno di Sopra V. dell'Impero '13	♟♟♟ 8
● Chianti V. di Pallino Ris. '14	♟♟ 3
● Crognolo '15	♟♟ 5
● Valdarno di Sopra Sangiovese V. dell'Impero '15	♟♟ 8

Solaria - Cencioni Patrizia

POD. CAPANNA, 102
53024 MONTALCINO [SI]
TEL. +39 0577849426
www.solariacencioni.com

CELLAR SALES
PRE-BOOKED VISITS
ANNUAL PRODUCTION 35,500 bottles
HECTARES UNDER VINE 9.00

Solaria is a veteran family-run winery founded in the late 1980s by the Cencioni family and today led by the tenacious Patrizia. The estate is located about 300 meters elevation on clayey-tufaceous soil, in the southeastern part of Montalcino. Protected from the dampest and coolest air currents, the area is particularly suitable for shaping Sangiovese into consistent Brunello with backbone, aged in French and Slavonian oak of various sizes. Solaria's selection registered a veritable leap forward in what is the latest recognition of the district's quality. Their Brunello 123 Ris. '13 proves both airy and austere, intriguing for its procession of blackberry, bitter orange and dried herbs, all of which lend vigor to the palate with assertiveness and restraint. Their Rosso '17 sees even greater expressive substance. Its fruity aromatic profile proves meaty and fragrant, supported by a firm, well-sustained structure of flavor. It performed as a complete wine should.

● Rosso di Montalcino '17	🍷🍷 3*
● Brunello di Montalcino '14	🍷🍷 6
● Brunello di Montalcino 123 Ris. '13	🍷🍷 8
● Brunello di Montalcino '13	🍷🍷 6
● Brunello di Montalcino '12	🍷🍷 6
● Brunello di Montalcino '10	🍷🍷 5
● Brunello di Montalcino '09	🍷🍷 5
● Brunello di Montalcino '08	🍷🍷 5
● Brunello di Montalcino '07	🍷🍷 4
● Brunello di Montalcino '06	🍷🍷 5
● Brunello di Montalcino 123 Ris. '10	🍷🍷 8
● Rosso di Montalcino '16	🍷🍷 3
● Rosso di Montalcino '15	🍷🍷 3
● Rosso di Montalcino '12	🍷🍷 4
● Rosso di Montalcino '11	🍷🍷 4

Talenti

FRAZ. SANT'ANGELO IN COLLE
LOC. PIAN DI CONTE
53020 MONTALCINO [SI]
TEL. +39 0577844064
www.talentimontalcino.it

CELLAR SALES
PRE-BOOKED VISITS
ANNUAL PRODUCTION 100,000 bottles
HECTARES UNDER VINE 21.00

Pian di Conte is slightly below Sant'Angelo in Colle, overlooking the Orcia River valley at an elevation of between 200 and 400 meters. The well-established estate south-west of Montalcino has been owned by the Talenti family since Pierluigi (originally from Romagna) purchased it in 1980. His capable nephew Riccardo now runs it. He's moving toward even more well-structured and drinkable wines, attested to by the intense, layered Brunello he makes by tailored aging using both tonneau and medium oak barrels. Without a doubt, Talenti put in one of their best performances yet, starting with an irresistible Rosso '17. It's a subtle and delicate wine in its aromas of wild berries, Asian spices and balsamic herbs, on the palate the wine proves cosseting and gradual. But their Brunello Pian di Conte Ris. '13 took home Tre Bicchieri with a splendid version that plays on delicious Mediterranean and delicately salty strokes.

● Brunello di Montalcino Pian di Conte Ris. '13	🍷🍷🍷 7
● Rosso di Montalcino '17	🍷🍷 3*
● Brunello di Montalcino '14	🍷🍷 6
● Brunello di Montalcino '04	🍷🍷🍷 8
● Brunello di Montalcino '88	🍷🍷🍷 8
● Brunello di Montalcino Ris. '99	🍷🍷🍷 8
● Brunello di Montalcino Trentennale '11	🍷🍷🍷 8
● Brunello di Montalcino V. del Paretaio Ris. '01	🍷🍷🍷 6
● Brunello di Montalcino '13	🍷🍷 6
● Brunello di Montalcino '12	🍷🍷 6
● Brunello di Montalcino '10	🍷🍷 6
● Brunello di Montalcino '09	🍷🍷 6
● Brunello di Montalcino Pian di Conte Ris. '12	🍷🍷 7

★Tenimenti Luigi d'Alessandro

VIA MANZANO, 15
52042 CORTONA [AR]
TEL. +39 0575618667
www.tenimentidalessandro.it

CELLAR SALES
PRE-BOOKED VISITS
ACCOMMODATION AND RESTAURANT SERVICE
ANNUAL PRODUCTION 130,000 bottles
HECTARES UNDER VINE 37.00
VITICULTURE METHOD Certified Organic

The Cortona-based winery is in the midst of extensive agronomic and stylistic redefinition. Since passing into the hands of the Calabresi family, the multifaceted operation has become a truly intriguing pioneer following its own path. On the estate, numerous installations of contemporary art in the vineyards presage the experience that awaits within. The beautiful property boasts of exquisite hospitality in its resort, a welcoming bar and an interesting shop where you can buy traditional regional products. The Migliara '15, a Syrah from an estate cru characterized by clay soil and marine fossils, is sumptuous. A mixture of mature wild berries greets the nose before proceeding to spicy hints of cocoa powder and licorice. On the palate it's as potent as it is elegant, sweet in its fruity weave and extremely flavorful in its tannic texture. Almost all the rest of their wines also performed at very high levels.

● Migliara '15	♟♟ 8
● Cortona Syrah Il Bosco '15	♟♟ 6
● Syrah '17	♟♟ 3
○ Viognier '17	♟♟ 2*
● Cortona Il Bosco '09	♟♟♟ 6
● Cortona Il Bosco '06	♟♟♟ 6
● Cortona Il Bosco '04	♟♟♟ 5
● Cortona Il Bosco '03	♟♟♟ 5
● Cortona Il Bosco '01	♟♟♟ 6
● Cortona Syrah Il Bosco '12	♟♟♟ 6
● Cortona Syrah Migliara '08	♟♟♟ 8
● Cortona Syrah Migliara '07	♟♟♟ 8

Tenuta di Sesta

FRAZ. CASTELNUOVO DELL'ABATE
LOC. SESTA
53024 MONTALCINO [SI]
TEL. +39 0577835612
www.tenutadisesta.it

CELLAR SALES
PRE-BOOKED VISITS
ANNUAL PRODUCTION 150,000 bottles
HECTARES UNDER VINE 30.00

Founded by Giuseppe Ciacci in the 1960s, today Tenuta di Sesta is run by Andrea and Francesca, together with their father, Giovanni. The name comes from its prestigious location in the southern part of Montalcino, in turn named after the ancient milestone on the Via Roselle-Chiusi. The land is strongly characterized by elevations of around 350 meters and the calcareous soil with veins of clay and iron; these unique pedoclimatic peculiarities help form the almost airy quality of Brunello aged in medium oak barrels, capable of aging well over time. The Ciacci family doesn't miss a beat, as our last round of tastings confirms, with at least two standouts. Their Brunello '14 brings together various aromatic registers, ranging from plums and juniper to thermal wafts, effectively managing a slight lack of vigor and texture. Their Duelecci Est Ris. '13 is even deeper and more classic in its procession of forest undergrowth, topsoil and roots — sensations harmoniously revived on the palate.

● Brunello di Montalcino Duelecci Est Ris. '13	♟♟♟ 8
● Brunello di Montalcino '14	♟♟ 8
● Rosso di Montalcino '17	♟♟ 5
● Brunello di Montalcino Duelecci Ovest Ris. '12	♟♟♟ 7
● Brunello di Montalcino Ris. '10	♟♟♟ 7
● Brunello di Montalcino '13	♟♟ 8
● Brunello di Montalcino '10	♟♟ 5
● Brunello di Montalcino '09	♟♟ 5
● Brunello di Montalcino '08	♟♟ 5
● Brunello di Montalcino Ris. '11	♟♟ 7
● Brunello di Montalcino Ris. '09	♟♟ 7
● Brunello di Montalcino Ris. '07	♟♟ 7
● Rosso di Montalcino '15	♟♟ 3*
● Rosso di Montalcino '13	♟♟ 3
● Rosso di Montalcino '11	♟♟ 3

Tenuta di Trinoro

VIA VAL D'ORCIA, 15
53047 SARTEANO [SI]
TEL. +39 0578267110 0578267110
www.tenutaditrinoro.it

PRE-BOOKED VISITS
ANNUAL PRODUCTION 70,000 bottles
HECTARES UNDER VINE 20.00

Andrea Franchetti's beautiful Tuscan
operation continues to stand out for its
total originality. Started in the early
nineties, it really started to have a voice of
its own about a decade later when the Val
d'Orcia terroir he had chosen (considered
a gamble by many) began to exhibit the
complexity he sought. The estate's
vineyards are raised according to
biodynamic principles, with harvests
beginning as late as possible. In the cellar,
fermentation is done in cement tanks
using exclusively local yeasts with aging in
barriques. Aromatic intensity accompanied
by not secondary oak distinguishes their
Tenuta di Trinoro '16, a blend of Cabernet
Franc, Merlot, Cabernet Sauvignon and
Petit Verdot that's soft, deep and
full-bodied on the palate. The Palazzi '16,
a monovarietal Merlot, delivers lovely, lush
fruit on the nose, developing sweet and
alluring on the palate, accompanied by
nice supporting oak.

● Palazzi '16	▼▼ 8
● Tenuta di Trinoro '16	▼▼ 8
● Campo di Tenaglia '17	▼▼ 8
● Campo di Camagi '17	▼ 8
● Campo di Magnacosta '17	▼ 8
● Le Cupole '17	▼ 5
● Tenuta di Trinoro '08	▼▼▼ 8
● Tenuta di Trinoro '04	▼▼▼ 8
● Tenuta di Trinoro '03	▼▼▼ 8
● Le Cupole di Trinoro '16	▼▼ 5
● Palazzi '15	▼▼ 8
● Tenuta di Trinoro '15	▼▼ 8
● Tenuta di Trinoro '05	▼▼ 8

★Tenute del Cerro

FRAZ. ACQUAVIVA
VIA GRAZIANELLA, 5
53045 MONTEPULCIANO [SI]
TEL. +39 0578767722
www.fattoriadelcerro.it

CELLAR SALES
PRE-BOOKED VISITS
ACCOMMODATION AND RESTAURANT SERVICE
ANNUAL PRODUCTION 1,300,000 bottles
HECTARES UNDER VINE 181.00

Owned by Tenute del Cerro (Gruppo
Unipol's agricultural/viticultural branch),
Fattoria del Cerro represents one of
Montepulciano's most important producers.
The first steps, which came in 1978 under
different ownership, would eventually lead
to its becoming a regional leader. Today
their style leans modern, with primarily
small wood used for aging. Their
approach pursues generous concentration and
maturity of fruit, making for a selection of
wines defined by rather full structures.
Their Nobile di Montepulciano '16 put in a
delicious performance with its lush and
vibrant fruit accented by spices on the
nose. In the mouth it comes through dense,
well-sustained and succulent. Their
drinkable Manero '18, a blend of mostly
Sangiovese, features fragrant aromas,
while the Nobile di Montepulciano Antica
Chiusina '15 exhibits nuanced aromas and
full flavor, it's just a bit held back by
immoderate oak.

● Nobile di Montepulciano '16	▼▼▼ 4*
● Nobile di Montepulciano Antica Chiusina '15	▼▼ 6
● Manero Rosso '18	▼▼ 2*
● Nobile di Montepulciano Ris. '15	▼▼ 5
● Rosso di Montepulciano '18	▼▼ 2*
● Nobile di Montepulciano '15	▼▼▼ 4*
● Nobile di Montepulciano '14	▼▼▼ 3*
● Nobile di Montepulciano '11	▼▼▼ 3*
● Nobile di Montepulciano '10	▼▼▼ 3*
● Nobile di Montepulciano Ris. '12	▼▼▼ 4*
● Nobile di Montepulciano Ris. '11	▼▼▼ 4*
● Nobile di Montepulciano Ris. '06	▼▼▼ 4
● Nobile di Montepulciano Vign. Antica Chiusina '00	▼▼▼ 6

Terenzi

LOC. MONTEDONICO
58054 SCANSANO [GR]
TEL. +39 0564599601
www.terenzi.eu

CELLAR SALES
PRE-BOOKED VISITS
ACCOMMODATION
ANNUAL PRODUCTION 350,000 bottles
HECTARES UNDER VINE 60.00

Morellino di Scansano's continued
presence as a bold force in the rich,
competitive world of Tuscan appellations
over the last ten years is largely due to
wineries like that belonging to the Terenzi
family. Qualitative choices in both the
vineyard and cellar result in wines that are
well linked to the territory and interpreted
in a blend of tradition with modernity. The
range delivers consistent quality over time,
with the best versions firmly achieving
excellence. Their Morellino di Scansano
Purosangue Riserva '16 features nice
aromatic cleanness and a full, close-woven
and deep palate. The wild berry and
vanilla-scented Francesca Romana '16,
an aromatically clean blend of Cabernet
Sauvignon, Merlot and Cabernet Franc,
enters sweet and rhythmic on the palate.
The delectable Morellino di Scansano '18,
a wine that's well-crafted for the typology,
stands out for its alluring aromas and t
asty flavor.

● Francesca Romana '16	♟♟♟ 5
● Morellino di Scansano	
Purosangue Ris. '16	♟♟ 4
● Morellino di Scansano '18	♟♟ 3
○ Maremma Toscana Vermentino	
Balbino '18	♟ 3
○ Montedonico '18	♟ 3
● Morellino di Scansano	
Madrechiesa Ris. '15	♟♟♟ 5
● Morellino di Scansano	
Madrechiesa Ris. '14	♟♟♟ 5
● Morellino di Scansano	
Madrechiesa Ris. '13	♟♟♟ 5
● Morellino di Scansano	
Madrechiesa Ris. '12	♟♟♟ 5
● Morellino di Scansano	
Madrechiesa Ris. '11	♟♟♟ 5

Annalisa Terradonnà

LOC. NOTRI, 78
57028 SUVERETO [LI]
TEL. +39 0565829008
www.terradonna.it

CELLAR SALES
PRE-BOOKED VISITS
ANNUAL PRODUCTION 26,000 bottles
HECTARES UNDER VINE 6.00

Terradonnà refers to land donated from
one woman to another. Indeed, in the year
2000, Annalisa Rossi received these
vineyards from her mother. Today she
oversees them, together with her husband,
bringing the same passion to her work.
Here in the heart of the Cornia Valley, at
the foot of the Suvereto hills (and just a
few kilometers from the coast) they make
quality oils and wines. In addition to
Sangiovese and Trebbiano, they grow the
unusual Clarette grape along with the
rediscovered Ansonica and the recent
Vermentino. Their Prasio '16 blend put in a
nice performance, with its spicy and fresh
notes of juniper, minty hints, then fruity
sensations of strawberry and cherry. On
the palate it's soft, graceful, properly
fleshy, with an elegant, long finish. The
Spato '16, a Sangiovese, offers up clear,
focused aromas of blueberry and cherry
joined with a balsamic freshness. In the
mouth a balanced, juicy body and delicate
tannins give way to a long, gratifying finish.

● Giaietto '16	♟♟ 2*
○ Kalsi '18	♟♟ 2*
● Prasio '16	♟♟ 3
● Spato '16	♟♟ 3
● Bixbi '17	♟ 3
⊙ Sysa '18	♟ 3
● Val di Cornia Cabernet Sauvignon	
Okenio '16	♟ 5
● Bixbi '13	♟♟ 3
● Giaietto '12	♟♟ 2*
● Prasio '15	♟♟ 3*
● Prasio '11	♟♟ 3
● Spato '15	♟♟ 3
● Spato '12	♟♟ 3
● Val di Cornia Cabernet Sauvignon	
Okenio '15	♟♟ 5

Terre dell'Etruria
Il Poderone

LOC. PODERONE CA DE FRATI
58051 MAGLIANO IN TOSCANA [GR]
TEL. +39 0564593011
www.terretruria.it

CELLAR SALES
PRE-BOOKED VISITS
ANNUAL PRODUCTION 150,000 bottles
HECTARES UNDER VINE 97.00

Even if most of this 70-year-old cooperative's history concerns oil production in the province of Livorno, starting in 2014 (and through incorporation with the Agrimaremma coop), Terre dell'Etruria enlarged its operations to include winemaking (in the province of Grosseto), thanks to the contribution of its members and the Cantina di Magliano. In terms of style and quality their wines hit the mark, aiming for drinkability and pleasantness. The Morellino di Scansano Giogo '18 features airy, spicy aromas, calling up cherry and pepper. On the palate it's juicy, delicate, and well-paced. Their equally fragrant and pleasantly approachable Maremma Toscana Briglia '18 delivers clean, decisive aromas and sapid flavor. The Ansonica '18 is fresh, almost salty, while the Maremma Toscana Vermentino Marmato '18 is easier though enjoyable.

● Morellino di Scansano Giogo '18	♥♥	2*
○ Antico Borgo Ansonica '18	♥♥	2*
● Maremma Toscana Ciliegiolo Briglia '18	♥♥	2*
○ Maremma Toscana Vermentino Marmato '18	♥	2
● Briglia Ciliegiolo '14	♀♀	2*

Teruzzi

LOC. CASALE, 19
53037 SAN GIMIGNANO [SI]
TEL. +39 0577940143
www.teruzzieputhod.it

CELLAR SALES
PRE-BOOKED VISITS
ANNUAL PRODUCTION 1,000,000 bottles
HECTARES UNDER VINE 94.00

No private winery has larger vineyards of Vernaccia di San Gimignano. Founded by husband and wife Enrico Teruzzi and Carmen Puthod, the estate is now part of the Terra Moretti group, which is implementing modern, dynamic management of its organizational, production and distribution processes. Maniacal care is taken in the vineyards, where in addition to the white variety, red Sangiovese, Cabernet Sauvignon, Merlot, Petit Verdot, Alicante and Colorino are also grown. Their new labels with imaginary animals are beautiful. The Vernaccia '18 is pleasant on the nose, with its classic aromas of apple and almond accompanied by the occasional whiff of aromatic herbs. In the mouth it enters delicate, compact, with freshness balanced by alcohol and a serene, relaxed finish. The Vernaccia Isola Bianca '18 is characterized by citrus aromas joined with fruity fragrances of white peach. On the palate it proves properly rich and appetizing, standing out for its notable length.

○ Vernaccia di S. Gimignano '18	♥♥	2*
○ Vernaccia di San Gimignano Isola Bianca '18	♥♥	2*
○ Terre di Tufi '18	♥	4
○ Carmen Puthod '14	♀♀	3
● Melograni '15	♀♀	5
○ Terre di Tufi '16	♀♀	4
○ Terre di Tufi '15	♀♀	4
○ Vernaccia di S. Gimignano '16	♀♀	2*
○ Vernaccia di S. Gimignano '15	♀♀	2*
○ Vernaccia di S. Gimignano Ris. '11	♀♀	4
○ Vernaccia di S. Gimignano Sant'Elena '16	♀♀	3*
○ Vernaccia di S. Gimignano Sant'Elena '16	♀♀	3
○ Vernaccia di San Gimignano Isola Bianca '17	♀♀	2*

La Togata

FRAZ. SANT'ANGELO IN COLLE
LOC. TAVERNELLE
53024 MONTALCINO [SI]
TEL. +39 0668803000
www.brunellolatogata.com

CELLAR SALES
PRE-BOOKED VISITS
ANNUAL PRODUCTION 120,000 bottles
HECTARES UNDER VINE 21.50
VITICULTURE METHOD Certified Organic
SUSTAINABLE WINERY

La Togata is in the south-west sector of
Montalcino near Sant'Angelo in Colle and
the grapes of its main vineyards (Lavacchio,
Montosoli and Pietrafocaia) fill the winery's
cellar. Led by Jeanneth Angel along with
Stephania, Vanessa, Azzurra and her
husband Danilo Tonon, the winery has a
history of almost 30 years, but has further
strengthened its position in recent vintages
thanks to a range of both expansive and
compact Brunello, aged in small wood
barrels and 1500-2000-liter Slavonian
oak. It's hard to choose from a selection as
good as the one submitted by La Togata
this year, with each wine earning Due
Bicchieri. Each has its peculiarities
but they're held together by a common
stylistic approach that privileges maturity
of fruit and extractive precision. We were
slightly partial to their 2014 Brunellos
Jacopus and Carillon. The formed is darker
and broader, while the second is racier and
more lively in its aromas of wood resin and
forest undergrowth.

Brunello di Montalcino Carillon '14	♟♟ 6
Brunello di Montalcino Jacopus '14	♟♟ 6
Brunello di Montalcino La Togata '14	♟♟ 7
Rosso di Montalcino Carillon '17	♟♟ 4
Rosso di Montalcino Jacopus '17	♟♟ 4
Rosso di Montalcino La Togata '17	♟♟ 4
Brunello di Montalcino '06	♟♟♟ 7
Brunello di Montalcino '13	♟♟ 8
Brunello di Montalcino '08	♟♟ 7
Brunello di Montalcino La Togata '07	♟♟ 7
Brunello di Montalcino La Togata dei Togati '13	♟♟ 8
Brunello di Montalcino La Togata dei Togati '09	♟♟ 8
Brunello di Montalcino Notte di Note '13	♟♟ 8
Brunello di Montalcino Ris. '12	♟♟ 8

Tolaini

LOC. VALLENUOVA
S.DA PROV.LE 9 DI PIEVASCIATA, 28
53019 CASTELNUOVO BERARDENGA [SI]
TEL. +39 0577356972
www.tolaini.it

CELLAR SALES
PRE-BOOKED VISITS
ANNUAL PRODUCTION 250,000 bottles
HECTARES UNDER VINE 50.00
SUSTAINABLE WINERY

Pierluigi Tolaini established his winery in
1998 with the acquisition of the San
Giovanni and Montebello estates between
Pianella and Vagliagli. The first bottles
came in 2002; since then, having
adequately tailored the approach to a
not-so-simple territory like Chianti, it has
produced decidedly well-made wines.
However, the range still lacks a really
assertive Chianti Classico, something that
is surely in the works in the cellar in the
Castelnuovo Berardenga sub-zone. The
fleshy and pervasive Chianti Classico
Montebello Sette Gra Selezione '15
features toasty aromas and hints of
mature fruit. The close-knit and
well-coordinated Al Passo '16 is a
rhythmic, juicy blend of Sangiovese and
Merlot. The Val di Santi '15, a blend of
Cabernet Sauvignon, Cabernet Franc and
Sangiovese is tighter and more
concentrated, as is the Picconero '15, a
wine made with Merlot and Cabernet
Franc grapes.

Al Passo '16	♟♟ 4
Chianti Cl. Gran Selezione V. Montebello Sette '15	♟♟ 5
Picconero '15	♟♟ 8
Valdisanti '15	♟♟ 5
Chianti Cl. Vallenuova '17	♟ 3
Al Passo '14	♟♟♟ 4*
Picconero '10	♟♟♟ 8
Picconero '09	♟♟♟ 8
Valdisanti '08	♟♟♟ 8
Al Passo '15	♟♟ 4
Al Passo '12	♟♟ 4
Chianti Cl. Gran Selezione V. Montebello Sette '14	♟♟ 5
Chianti Cl. Valle Nuova '15	♟♟ 5
Chianti Cl. Vallenuova '16	♟♟ 3
Valdisanti '12	♟♟ 5

Torre a Cona

Loc. San Donato in Collina
via Torre a Cona, 49
50067 Rignano sull'Arno [FI]
Tel. +39 055699000
www.torreacona.com

CELLAR SALES
PRE-BOOKED VISITS
ACCOMMODATION
ANNUAL PRODUCTION 80,000 bottles
HECTARES UNDER VINE 18.00

Despite its placid beauty, the 18th-century villa has a rich history. During WW II it was a German headquarters and later a hospital for English soldiers. Works by Michelangelo and Donatello, including statues from the Medici Chapels and the Cathedral of Florence, were stored in its cellars. Owned by the Rossi di Montelera family, it's now a model of tourism and viticulture, firmly rooted in Sangiovese, Colorino, Merlot, Trebbiano and Malvasia del Chianti. Their Merlot '16, with its generous aromas, earned a place in our finals. Red berry sensations of cherry and strawberry fade to delicate notes of aromatic herbs and mineral hints. On the palate it enters pleasant, with a nice initial impact and then well-gauged freshness, fine tannins and a long, transparent finish. The Ris. Badia a Corte '16 features mature aromas of fruit preserves accompanied by medicinal herbs. In the mouth it exhibits structure, enjoyable freshness and a nice balance between tannins and alcohol.

● Chianti Colli Fiorentini Badia a Corte Ris. '16		♈♈♈ 4*
● Il Merlot '16		♈♈ 4
○ Vin Santo del Chianti Merlaia '12		♈♈ 6
● Vin Santo del Chianti Occhio di Pernice Fonti e Lecceta '16		♈♈ 7
● Chianti Colli Fiorentini '17		♈ 2
● Chianti Colli Fiorentini Badia a Corte Ris. '15		♈♈♈ 4*
● Chianti Colli Fiorentini Badia a Corte Ris. '13		♈♈♈ 4*
● Vin Santo del Chianti Occhio di Pernice Fonti e Lecceta '11		♈♈♈ 6
● Casamaggio '16		♈♈ 4
● Chianti Colli Fiorentini '15		♈♈ 2*
● Il Merlot '15		♈♈ 5
○ Vin Santo del Chianti Merlaia '11		♈♈ 6

Travignoli

via Travignoli, 78
50060 Pelago [FI]
Tel. +39 0558361098
www.travignoli.com

CELLAR SALES
PRE-BOOKED VISITS
ANNUAL PRODUCTION 250,000 bottles
HECTARES UNDER VINE 70.00

In this area, where the Arno and Sieve rivers meet, viticulture goes way back. The discovery of a 6th-century BC Etruscan stele that depicts a table with vases of wine testifies to the fact. The Busi family has owned the estate since the 19th century. Today Giovanni's at the helm, overseeing their vineyards of Sangiovese (the principal grape cultivated) as well as Cabernet Sauvignon, Merlot and Chardonnay. Their Tegolaia Riserva '16 delivers, with its tertiary notes of tobacco and tanned leather followed by mature cherry and hints of cloves. It's well-defined on the palate, firm and structured, with nicely coordinated tannins and a rising finish. The Governo '17 is fragrant in its flowery aromas, hints of blackberry and nuances of aromatic herbs, coming through lively, balanced and enticing on the palate. The Gavignano '17, mostly Chardonnay with a smaller share of Sauvignon, is fruity on the nose, fresh in flavor.

● Chianti Rufina Tegolaia Ris. '16	♈♈ 3
● Chianti Rufina '17	♈♈ 2
● Chianti Rufina Governo '17	♈♈ 2
○ Gavignano '17	♈♈ 2
⊙ Rosè Villa Travignoli '18	♈ 2
● Chianti Rufina '16	♈♈ 1
● Chianti Rufina Governo '16	♈♈ 2
● Chianti Rufina Tegolaia Ris. '15	♈♈ 2
● Chianti Rufina Tegolaia Ris. '13	♈♈ 3
● Chianti Rufina Tegolaia Ris. '12	♈♈ 3
● Chianti Rufina Tegolaia Ris. '11	♈♈ 3
○ Vin Santo Chianti Rufina '10	♈♈ 4

Tenuta Trerose

FRAZ. VALIANO
VIA DELLA STELLA, 3
53040 MONTEPULCIANO [SI]
TEL. +39 0577804101
www.tenutatrerose.it

CELLAR SALES
PRE-BOOKED VISITS
ANNUAL PRODUCTION 650,000 bottles
HECTARES UNDER VINE 102.00

Tenuta Trerose, a part of Bertani Domains (Angelini Group), is situated in Valiano, one of Nobile di Montepulciano's most important subzones. The winery's selection has been undergoing an overall stylistic reworking that today is bearing its first fruit. Their wines are decidedly more defined and not lacking in character or personality. It's the result of a more linear approach to vinification, without useless, forced maneuvers, and the careful use of wood barrels (only large ones) for aging. The Nobile di Montepulciano Simposio Riserva '15 features lush fruit of nice intensity, proving intriguing on the palate with a juicy, rhythmic development. Their well-crafted Nobile di Montepulciano Santa Caterina '16 offers up aromas of red fruits and smoky notes before a supple palate marked by contrast of flavor. The Rosso di Montepulciano Salterio '18 hits the mark in terms of pleasantness.

● Nobile di Montepulciano Simposio Ris. '15	♟♟♟ 6
● Nobile di Montepulciano Santa Caterina '16	♟♟ 4
● Rosso di Montepulciano Salterio '18	♟♟ 3
● Nobile di Montepulciano Simposio '97	♟♟♟ 5
● Nobile di Montepulciano S. Caterina '14	♟♟ 4
● Nobile di Montepulciano Santa Caterina '15	♟♟ 4

★Tua Rita

LOC. NOTRI, 81
57028 SUVERETO [LI]
TEL. +39 0565829237
www.tuarita.it

CELLAR SALES
PRE-BOOKED VISITS
ANNUAL PRODUCTION 250,000 bottles
HECTARES UNDER VINE 41.00

Just over thirty years ago, Rita and Virgilio purchased a bit of land and a house in Val di Cornia, between the Tyrrhenian and the hills. They weren't particularly interested in producing wine, but a return to nature evolved into a desire to do something with the few vineyards still growing. Those original two hectares became a winery that today is managed by their daughter and her husband. For some years they've also had a sister estate in Morellino di Scansano. The Giusto di Notri '16 is superb. Made with Cab. Sauvignon, Franc and Merlot, it offers up a vibrant bouquet in which red and black fruit exalt each other, enlivened by notes of aromatic herbs and floral hints of potpourri. On the palate it's exquisitely pervasive, juicy, with well-integrated tannins and a long, compelling finish. The tantalizing Vermentino Perlato del Bosco '18 is marked by fruity sensations of mango and lime, and aromatic herbs, anticipating a spirited, smooth and harmonious body.

● Giusto di Notri '16	♟♟ 8
● Perlato del Bosco '17	♟♟ 5
○ Perlato del Bosco Vermentino '18	♟♟ 3
● Redigaffi '08	♟♟♟ 8
● Redigaffi '07	♟♟♟ 8
● Redigaffi '06	♟♟♟ 8
● Redigaffi '04	♟♟♟ 8
● Redigaffi '03	♟♟♟ 8
● Redigaffi '02	♟♟♟ 8
● Redigaffi '01	♟♟♟ 8
● Redigaffi '00	♟♟♟ 7
● Redigaffi '99	♟♟♟ 8

Uccelliera

FRAZ. CASTELNUOVO DELL'ABATE
POD. UCCELLIERA, 45
53020 MONTALCINO [SI]
TEL. +39 0577835729
www.uccelliera-montalcino.it

CELLAR SALES
PRE-BOOKED VISITS
ANNUAL PRODUCTION 60,000 bottles
HECTARES UNDER VINE 6.00

Andrea Cortonesi's wines are among Montalcino's, and Castelnuovo del'Abate's most recognizable. Warm and flavorful, meaty and austere, his Sangioveses consistently offer up the Mediterranean atmosphere that characterizes his plots. These are situated on clay-sandy terrain at elevations below 250 meters. In the cellar they don't follow preset schema, relying instead of separate vinification for each parcel and an approach to aging that sees barriques and untoasted Slavonian oak used according to the characteristics of each vintage. Its extraordinary streak of awards doesn't carry over into this edition, but Uccelliera's Rosso remains an indispensable benchmark for the typology. The 2017 offers up the usual explosive aromas of red, ripe fruit, aromatic herbs and woodland sensations. With respect to its best versions, it comes across as a bit lacking in flavor, despite its generous and gutsy palate. Their Brunello '14 also performed at high levels.

● Rosso di Montalcino '17	♟♟ 4
● Brunello di Montalcino '14	♟♟ 6
● Brunello di Montalcino '10	♟♟♟ 6
● Brunello di Montalcino '08	♟♟♟ 7
● Brunello di Montalcino Ris. '97	♟♟♟ 8
● Rosso di Montalcino '16	♟♟♟ 4*
● Rosso di Montalcino '15	♟♟♟ 4*
● Rosso di Montalcino '14	♟♟♟ 4*
● Brunello di Montalcino '13	♟♟ 6
● Brunello di Montalcino '12	♟♟ 6
● Brunello di Montalcino '11	♟♟ 6
● Brunello di Montalcino '09	♟♟ 6
● Brunello di Montalcino Ris. '12	♟♟ 8
● Brunello di Montalcino Ris. '08	♟♟ 8
● Brunello di Montalcino Voliero '12	♟♟ 6
● Rosso di Montalcino Voliero '15	♟♟ 4

F.lli Vagnoni

LOC. PANCOLE, 82
53037 SAN GIMIGNANO [SI]
TEL. +39 0577955077
www.fratellivagnoni.com

CELLAR SALES
PRE-BOOKED VISITS
ACCOMMODATION
ANNUAL PRODUCTION 120,000 bottles
HECTARES UNDER VINE 17.00
VITICULTURE METHOD Certified Organic

For more than 60 years the Vagnoni family have dealt in agriculture in the village of Pancole, an area well-suited to cultivation and prosperous living, as testified to by th presence of Etruscan settlements in classical times. In addition to viticulture, they've maintained other crops, in particular grains and fruit orchards, which integrate with the production of extra-virgin oil and an agritourism. They show particular care when it comes to Vin Santo, having created a specific area for drying the grapes. The Riserva I Mocali '1(features an aromatic suite in which toasty notes of oak join with spicy hints of vanilla and buttery accents, then mature fruit, like melon and yellow peach refreshed by orange. On the palate it proves soft, with nice weight and an enjoyable acidity giving way to a juicy, appetizing finish. The slightly floral and fruity Vernaccia '18 is simple and linear on the palate, with a nice, saline finish.

● Rosso '18	♟♟ 1
○ Vernaccia di S. Gimignano I Mocali Ris. '16	♟♟ 3
○ Vernaccia di San Gimignano '18	♟♟ 2
● Chianti Colli Senesi '17	♟ 2
● Chianti Colli Senesi Capanneto Ris. '15	♟ 3
⊙ San Gimignano Rosato Il Pancolino '18	♟ 2
● San Gimignano Rosso San Biagio Bio '13	♟ 4
○ Vinbrusco Bianco '18	♟ 1
○ Vernaccia di S. Gimignano '17	♟♟ 2
○ Vernaccia di S. Gimignano '15	♟♟ 2'
○ Vernaccia di S. Gimignano Fontabuccio '17	♟♟ 2'
○ Vernaccia di S. Gimignano I Mocali Ris. '15	♟♟ 3

Val delle Corti

FRAZ. LA CROCE
LOC. VAL DELLE CORTI, 141
53017 RADDA IN CHIANTI [SI]
TEL. +39 0577738215
www.valdellecorti.it

CELLAR SALES
PRE-BOOKED VISITS
ACCOMMODATION
ANNUAL PRODUCTION 30,000 bottles
HECTARES UNDER VINE 6.00
VITICULTURE METHOD Certified Organic

Roberto Bianchi, who's overseen Val delle Corti since 1999, has managed to transform the producer into one of Radda in Chianti's best. His vineyards, which have been organically cultivated for some time now, are increasingly so with each passing year. In the cellar a minimally invasive approach is adopted and wines are aged in large wood barrels. The result is a selection that's one of the most significant in the area, with wines that offer up a rare depth of taste and territorial authenticity. The Chianti Classico Riserva '16 features floral and citrusy aromas, with whiffs of herbs and flint lending character. On the palate it's governed by a graceful and complex structure, exhibiting depth and great vitality. The deliciously fresh and rapid Chianti Classico '16 is characterized by aromas of violet and blueberry, while the Lo Straniero, a blend of Sangiovese and Merlot, proves pleasant.

● Chianti Cl. Ris. '16	♟♟♟ 5
● Chianti Cl. '16	♟♟ 4
● Lo Straniero	♟ 3
● Chianti Cl. '13	♟♟♟ 4*
● Chianti Cl. '12	♟♟♟ 4*
● Chianti Cl. '11	♟♟♟ 3*
● Chianti Cl. '10	♟♟♟ 3*
● Chianti Cl. '09	♟♟♟ 2*
● Chianti Cl. Ris. '14	♟♟♟ 5
● Chianti Cl. '15	♟♟ 4
● Chianti Cl. '14	♟♟ 4
● Chianti Cl. Ris. '15	♟♟ 5
● Chianti Cl. Ris. '13	♟♟ 5
● Chianti Cl. Ris. '11	♟♟ 5

Val di Suga

LOC. VAL DI CAVA
53024 MONTALCINO [SI]
TEL. +39 0577804101
www.valdisuga.it

CELLAR SALES
PRE-BOOKED VISITS
ANNUAL PRODUCTION 270,000 bottles
HECTARES UNDER VINE 55.00

The mapping work that began at Val di Suga some years ago, and that has gradually been implemented since Bertani Domains purchased the producer, continues to help them highlight Montalcino's unique territorial attributes. Three crus, Vigna del Lago (northeast), Vigna Spuntali (southwest), and Poggio al Granchio (south, near Sant'Antimo abbey), give rise to a commendable selection of Brunellos. Fermentation and maturation are tailored for the characteristics of each plot. At Val di Suga they're only missing a standout, but theirs is a selection that's appetizing, to say the least, in its quality and quantity. In particular, we were impressed with the multifaceted Brunello Vigna del Lago '13. It opens with delicate floral and balsamic notes, which give way to an energetic, delicately salty and citrusy stroke elegantly supported by a velvety tannic weave. But all their wines shine for clarity and territorial coherence.

● Brunello di Montalcino V. del Lago '13	♟♟ 8
● Brunello di Montalcino '14	♟♟ 6
● Brunello di Montalcino Poggio al Granchio '13	♟♟ 7
● Brunello di Montalcino Ris. '13	♟♟ 7
● Brunello di Montalcino V. Spuntali '13	♟♟ 8
● Rosso di Montalcino '17	♟♟ 4
● Brunello di Montalcino V. del Lago '95	♟♟♟ 8
● Brunello di Montalcino V. del Lago '93	♟♟♟ 8
● Brunello di Montalcino V. del Lago '90	♟♟♟ 8
● Brunello di Montalcino V. Spuntali '95	♟♟♟ 8
● Brunello di Montalcino V. Spuntali '93	♟♟♟ 8
● Brunello di Montalcino Val di Suga '07	♟♟♟ 5

Tenuta Valdipiatta

VIA DELLA CIARLIANA, 25A
53045 MONTEPULCIANO [SI]
TEL. +39 0578757930
www.valdipiatta.it

CELLAR SALES
PRE-BOOKED VISITS
ACCOMMODATION
ANNUAL PRODUCTION 100,000 bottles
HECTARES UNDER VINE 23.00
VITICULTURE METHOD Certified Organic
SUSTAINABLE WINERY

Year after year, Miriam Caporali's wines have continued to develop a recognizable style in which balance figures prominently. The result is a reliable selection (in qualitative terms) that exhibits nice coherence and isn't lacking personality either. Indeed, it's one of the clearest examples of Sangioves's potential in Montepulciano. However, with this type of production philosophy, you need a bit of patience. Indeed, their wines require adequate aging before offering up their best. The Nobile di Montepulciano Vigna d'Alfiero '16 brings together aromatic finesse and firmness of flavor, with sensations of flowers and slightly toasty hints accompanying a decisive palate before an encore of fruit. The Nobile di Montepulciano Riserva '15 is earthy on the nose and sapid on the palate, where tannins are maybe a bit over-edgy. The Rosso di Montepulciano '17 is a docile, balanced drink.

● Nobile di Montepulciano V. d'Alfiero '16	♟♟ 6
● Nobile di Montepulciano Ris. '15	♟♟ 6
● Rosso di Montepulciano '17	♟♟ 3
● Nobile di Montepulciano Ris. '90	♟♟♟ 5
● Nobile di Montepulciano V. d'Alfiero '99	♟♟♟ 5
● Chianti Colli Senesi Tosca '15	♟♟ 2*
● Nobile di Montepulciano Ris. '13	♟♟ 6
● Pinot Nero '15	♟♟ 4
● Rosso di Montepulciano '16	♟♟ 3
● Nobile di Montepulciano V. d'Alfiero '15	♀ 6

Valentini

LOC. VALPIANA
POD. FIORDALISO, 69
58024 MASSA MARITTIMA [GR]
TEL. +39 0566918058
www.agricolavalentini.it

CELLAR SALES
PRE-BOOKED VISITS
ACCOMMODATION
ANNUAL PRODUCTION 55,000 bottles
HECTARES UNDER VINE 7.00
SUSTAINABLE WINERY

The Valentini family winery offers reliable, well-crafted wines. Their style is characterized by aromatic precision and energy of taste, qualities that not all of Maremma's wines are capable of. There are, occasionally, cases of stylistic excess, but their current approach seems to be well-oriented towards drinkability and pleasantness, both when it comes to their reds and their whites. And they manage to avoid the occasional lapse that detectable in their selection a few years ago. Their Sangiovese '18 is characterized by an unembellished, model aromatic profile of cherries and herbs. It's in the mouth that it makes its mark, bringing together notable drinkability and freshness. Their denser an tighter Crebresco '16, a blend of Sangiovese, Merlot and Syrah, is characterized by intense, Mediterranean fragrances, while toasty notes dominate th Atunis '16, a monovarietal Merlot that's pervasive on the palate.

● Crebesco '16	♟♟ 5
● Sangiovese '18	♟♟ 2
● Atunis '16	♟ 5
● Maremma Toscana Vivoli '16	♟ 4
● Monteregio di Massa Marittima Rosso '17	♟ 3
● Atunis '12	♟♟ 5
○ Maremma Toscana Vermentino '16	♟♟ 2
● Monteregio di Massa Marittima '16	♟♟ 2
● Monteregio di Massa Marittima '14	♟♟ 2
● Monteregio di Massa Marittima Il Vivoli '15	♟♟ 4
● Monteregio di Massa Marittima Rosso '15	♟♟ 2
● Monteregio di Massa Marittima Vivoli '13	♟♟ 4
● Sangiovese '17	♟♟ 2

★Tenuta di Valgiano

VIA DI VALGIANO, 7
55015 LUCCA
TEL. +39 0583402271
www.valgiano.it

CELLAR SALES
PRE-BOOKED VISITS
ANNUAL PRODUCTION 60,000 bottles
HECTARES UNDER VINE 15.00
VITICULTURE METHOD Certified Biodynamic

Valgiano is an absolute benchmark for
Lucca, and Tuscan viticulture in general.
It's a place as magic as the winery built by
Moreno Petrini and Laura di Collobiano
(with the technical support of Saverio
Petrilli). They made courageous,
revolutionary decisions that in many ways
are possible to appreciate only today.
Indeed, the estate laid out a path
constituted of biodynamic viticulture and
an idea of 'living' wines, in the highest
sense of the term. It's a path that many
chose to follow, thus forming a veritable
district. Their Tenuta di Valgiano '16 will be
out next year, so we'll have to wait to taste
a wine that's become a benchmark for the
producer (and all of the Colline Lucchesi
hills). But it will be worth it if it performs at
the levels of their Palistorti Rosso, a blend
of Sangiovese and Merlot with a small
share of Syrah. Without a doubt, the 2017
proves brilliant, extremely elegant,
delectable and dynamic, unwavering in
terms of pulp and texture. It's a must.

● Palistorti Rosso '17	♟♟♟ 5
○ Palistorti Bianco '18	♟♟ 5
● Colline Lucchesi Tenuta di Valgiano '15	♟♟♟ 8
● Colline Lucchesi Tenuta di Valgiano '13	♟♟♟ 8
● Colline Lucchesi Tenuta di Valgiano '12	♟♟♟ 6
● Colline Lucchesi Tenuta di Valgiano '11	♟♟♟ 6
● Colline Lucchesi Tenuta di Valgiano '10	♟♟♟ 6
● Colline Lucchesi Tenuta di Valgiano '09	♟♟♟ 6
● Colline Lucchesi Tenuta di Valgiano '08	♟♟♟ 6
● Colline Lucchesi Tenuta di Valgiano '07	♟♟♟ 6
● Colline Lucchesi Tenuta di Valgiano '06	♟♟♟ 6
● Colline Lucchesi Tenuta di Valgiano '05	♟♟♟ 6
● Colline Lucchesi Tenuta di Valgiano '04	♟♟♟ 6

Vallepicciola

S.DA PROV.LE 9 DI PIEVASCIATA, 21
53019 CASTELNUOVO BERARDENGA [SI]
TEL. +39 05771698718
www.vallepicciola.com

CELLAR SALES
PRE-BOOKED VISITS
ANNUAL PRODUCTION 250,000 bottles
HECTARES UNDER VINE 95.00

Some years ago the entrepreneur Bruno
Bolfo fell in love with the Tuscan hills and
decided to found a lovely winery in Radda
in Chianti. Vallepicciola spans more than
265 hectares, 65 of which are vineyards
(40 more are currently being planted). The
southern part of Chianti Classico, and
Vallepicciola in particular, are characterized
by a variety of soils and microclimates,
making for an interesting and diverse
selection of wines. Vallepicciola's
enological team, supported by consultant
Riccardo Cotarella, submitted a valid
selection for tasting. The ruby-red Riserva
is a firmly-structured wine. On the nose
sensations of small fruits fade elegantly to
notes of spices and vanilla. On the palate it
exhibits structure and fullness, though it
still needs some time to come into its own.
The excellent Chianti Classico '17 is
subtler and more expansive, with its
irresistible bouquet of red fruits and cherry
anticipating a balanced, delicately tannic,
fresh and extremely long palate.

● Chianti Cl. '17	♟♟♟ 4*
● Boscobruno Pinot Nero '16	♟♟ 6
● Chianti Cl. Ris. '16	♟♟ 5
● Pievasciata '16	♟♟ 3
● Moredese '17	♟ 5
● Boscobruno Pinot Nero '15	♟♟ 6
● Chianti Cl. '16	♟♟ 4
● Chianti Cl. '15	♟♟ 4
● Chianti Cl. Gran Selezione '15	♟♟ 3*
● Quercegrosse Merlot '15	♟♟ 6

Varramista

LOC. VARRAMISTA
VIA RICAVO
56020 MONTOPOLI IN VAL D'ARNO [PI]
TEL. +39 057144711
www.varramista.it

CELLAR SALES
PRE-BOOKED VISITS
ACCOMMODATION
ANNUAL PRODUCTION 35,000 bottles
HECTARES UNDER VINE 13.00

Varramista's history goes way back to the 15th century, when it was built by Gino Capponi as an outpost against Pisa. The villa that still constitutes a central part of the property was completed in 1589. In the 20th century it was purchased by the Agnelli and Piaggio families, who developed it for agriculture and tourism. Their vineyards, which occupy only a limited part of the estate (though the best areas have been privileged), host Sangiovese and especially Syrah. The Varramista '13, a Syrah, offers up jammy notes of cherry, then sensations of fur and leather accompanied by tobacco and licorice. On the palate it proves soft, with resolved tannins and a relaxed, gratifying finish. The Frasca '15, a blend of Sangiovese, Merlot and Syrah, opens on fresh hints of mint and sage before proceeding to blackcurrant and tertiary aromas. In the mouth it's lively and vigorous, with well-integrated tannins and a warm, elegant development giving way to a truly pleasant finish.

● Chianti Monsonaccio '15	🍷🍷 3
● Frasca '15	🍷🍷 5
● Sterpato '16	🍷🍷 3
● Varramista '13	🍷🍷 7
● Chianti Monsonaccio '12	🍷🍷 2*
● Frasca '13	🍷🍷 4
● Frasca Rosso '11	🍷🍷 3
● Sterpato '12	🍷🍷 2*
● Sterpato '11	🍷🍷 2*
● Syrah '11	🍷🍷 6

I Veroni

VIA TIFARITI, 5
50065 PONTASSIEVE [FI]
TEL. +39 0558368886
www.iveroni.it

CELLAR SALES
PRE-BOOKED VISITS
ACCOMMODATION
ANNUAL PRODUCTION 110,000 bottles
HECTARES UNDER VINE 20.00
VITICULTURE METHOD Certified Organic

Here everything feels ancient, from the traces of the first decanters to the layout of the buildings. The name itself is redolent of history. Indeed, 'verone' is an old Tuscan term for 'terraces', which the estate once hosted. Then there's its historic 'vinsantaia', which is preserved within the loft of their 18th-century villa. The modern world can be detected in their approach to winemaking and management, which also features appealing accommodations in a perfectly renovated farm manor. The Chianti Rufina Riserva Vigneto Quona '16 earned a place in our finals, opening with mature aromas of wild berry preserves, then delicate, spicy hints followed by accents of aromatic herbs. On the palate it proves highly drinkable, coming through pervasive with crunchy tannins, and closing sapid and long. The Vin Santo '09 bewitches the nose with its aromas of figs and quince, then almonds. In the mouth it unfolds velvety, soft and round, giving way to a truly long and enjoyable finish.

● Chianti Rufina Vign. Quona Ris. '16	🍷🍷 5
● Vin Santo del Chianti Rufina Occhio di Pernice '09	🍷🍷 6
● Chianti Rufina I Domi '17	🍷🍷 3
⊙ I Veroni Rosé '18	🍷 3
● Chianti Rufina Vign. Quona Ris. '15	🍷🍷🍷 5
● Chianti Rufina I Domi '16	🍷🍷 3
● Chianti Rufina I Domi '15	🍷🍷 3
● Chianti Rufina Quona Ris. '14	🍷🍷 5
● Chianti Rufina Ris. '13	🍷🍷 5
⊙ Iveronirosé '16	🍷🍷 3
● Rosso Toscana '16	🍷🍷 2*
○ Vin Santo del Chianti Rufina '08	🍷🍷 5
○ Vin Santo del Chianti Rufina '07	🍷🍷 5
○ Vin Santo del Chianti Rufina Occhio di Pernice '08	🍷🍷 6

Vignamaggio

via Petriolo, 5
50022 Greve in Chianti [FI]
Tel. +39 055854661
www.vignamaggio.com

CELLAR SALES
PRE-BOOKED VISITS
ACCOMMODATION AND RESTAURANT SERVICE
ANNUAL PRODUCTION 250,000 bottles
HECTARES UNDER VINE 67.00
VITICULTURE METHOD Certified Organic
SUSTAINABLE WINERY

Active in Chianti Classico since 1987, and currently owned by Patrice Taravella, Vignamaggio is situated in the Greve subzone, among the territory's leading producers. Their selection features Sangiovese, but Vignamaggio owes much of its success to an international variety as well: Cabernet Franc. By now their style seems to enjoy a reassuring continuity in pursuit of finesse. But the careful use of wood, which calls for large barrels or barriques depending on the wine, has also made an important contribution. The aromatically elegant Cabernet Franc '15 offers up delicate herbaceous hints, notes of ivy and small red berries supported by smoky and toasty whiffs, as well as a peppery accent. On the palate it's well-sustained and balanced in its development, with an encore of fragrant, flavorful fruit lending rhythm, contrast and freshness.

● Cabernet Franc '15	🍷🍷 8
● Merlot '15	🍷 8
● Sangiovese '15	🍷 5
● Chianti Cl. Monna Lisa Ris. '99	🍷🍷🍷 5
● Chianti Cl. Monna Lisa Ris. '95	🍷🍷🍷 5
● Vignamaggio '06	🍷🍷🍷 7
● Vignamaggio '05	🍷🍷🍷 7
● Vignamaggio '04	🍷🍷🍷 6
● Vignamaggio '01	🍷🍷🍷 6
● Vignamaggio '00	🍷🍷🍷 6
● Chianti Cl. Gherardino Ris. '15	🍷🍷 5
● Chianti Cl. Gran Selezione Monna Lisa '15	🍷🍷 6
● Chianti Cl. Gran Selezione Monna Lisa Ris. '13	🍷🍷 6
● Chianti Cl. Terre di Prenzano '16	🍷🍷 3*
● Chianti Cl. Gherardino Ris. '14	🍷 3

Villa Le Corti

loc. Le Corti
via San Piero di Sotto, 1
50026 San Casciano in Val di Pesa [FI]
Tel. +39 055829301
www.principecorsini.com

CELLAR SALES
PRE-BOOKED VISITS
ACCOMMODATION
ANNUAL PRODUCTION 150,000 bottles
HECTARES UNDER VINE 50.00
VITICULTURE METHOD Certified Organic

The winery managed by Duccio Corsini is one of Chianti Classico's oldest (it also comprises plots in Maremma, Marsiliana). Today their production style centers on Chianti tradition, reinterpreted in a modern key, but with clarity and balance, focusing on liveliness and drinkability. Their work in the vineyards adheres to organic principles, and in the cellar they alternate between aging in concrete, large wood barrels and barriques. It's a discerning mix that makes for a consistent level of quality and a style characterized by noteworthy frankness. The well-crafted Chianti Classico Cortevecchia Riserva '16 exhibits a delicate aromatic profile marked by floral notes and smoky hints, and a juicy, well-sustained development on the palate. The Chianti Classico Le Corti '16 goes all in on drinkability, while the Chianti Classico Don Tommaso Gran Selezione '16 proves dense and rich in oak. Finally, the lo Zac '15 is a pleasant and fragrant monovarietal Sangiovese.

● Chianti Cl. Corte Vecchia Ris. '16	🍷🍷 4
● Chianti Cl. Le Corti '16	🍷🍷 3
● Chianti Cl.Gran Selezione Don Tommaso '16	🍷🍷 5
● Zac '15	🍷🍷 7
● Chianti Cl. '12	🍷🍷🍷 3*
● Chianti Cl. Cortevecchia Ris. '05	🍷🍷🍷 4
● Chianti Cl. Don Tommaso '99	🍷🍷🍷 4*
● Chianti Cl. Le Corti '10	🍷🍷🍷 3*
● Birillo Tenuta Marsiliana '15	🍷🍷 3
● Birillo Tenuta Marsiliana '13	🍷🍷 3
● Chianti Cl. '14	🍷🍷 3
● Chianti Cl. '13	🍷🍷 3*
● Chianti Cl. Corte Vecchia Ris. '15	🍷🍷 4
● Chianti Cl. Cortevecchia Ris. '14	🍷🍷 4
● Chianti Cl. Cortevecchia Ris. '13	🍷🍷 4

Acquabona

LOC. ACQUABONA, 1
57037 PORTOFERRAIO [LI]
TEL. +39 0565933013
www.acquabonaelba.it

CELLAR SALES
PRE-BOOKED VISITS
ANNUAL PRODUCTION 90,000 bottles
HECTARES UNDER VINE 18.00

○ Elba Ansonica '18	🍷🍷 3
○ Elba Bianco '18	🍷🍷 2*
● Voltraio '14	🍷🍷 4
● Elba Aleatico Passito '15	🍷 3

Agricola Del Nudo

VIA DELLE SANTE MARIA, 52
58100 GROSSETO
TEL. +39 3351304989
www.nudo.bio

CELLAR SALES
PRE-BOOKED VISITS
ACCOMMODATION
ANNUAL PRODUCTION 20,000 bottles
HECTARES UNDER VINE 4.00
VITICULTURE METHOD Certified Organic
SUSTAINABLE WINERY

● Maremma Toscana Rosso Nudo '17	🍷🍷 5
● Ivo '16	🍷 7
○ Maremma Toscana Vermentino Nudo '18	🍷 5

Agrisole - Podere Pellicciano

LOC. LA SERRA, 64
56028 SAN MINIATO [PI]
TEL. +39 0571409825
www.agri-sole.it

CELLAR SALES
PRE-BOOKED VISITS
ANNUAL PRODUCTION 30,000 bottles
HECTARES UNDER VINE 7.00

○ Mafefa Bianco '18	🍷🍷 3
● Mafefa Rosso '15	🍷🍷 4
○ Vin Santo del Chianti Griso '10	🍷🍷 5
● Chianti Sanminiatello '17	🍷 3

Podere Allocco

LOC. SEANO
VIA CAPEZZANA, 19
59015 CARMIGNANO [PO]
TEL. +39 0574622462
www.podereallocco.it

CELLAR SALES
PRE-BOOKED VISITS
ANNUAL PRODUCTION 9,000 bottles
HECTARES UNDER VINE 1.50

● Carmignano '16	🍷🍷 4
● Carmignano Ris. '15	🍷🍷 4

Amantis

FRAZ. MONTENERO D'ORCIA
LOC. COLOMBAIO BIRBE
58040 CASTEL DEL PIANO [GR]
TEL. +39 3461402687
www.agricolaamantis.com

ANNUAL PRODUCTION 55,000 bottles
HECTARES UNDER VINE 6.00
SUSTAINABLE WINERY

● Montecucco Sangiovese Ris. '15	🍷🍷 5
● Iperione '15	🍷 6

Argentaia

S.DA COLLE LUPO
58051 MAGLIANO IN TOSCANA [GR]
www.argentaia.com

○ Maremma Toscana Vermentino Monnallegra '18	🍷🍷 2*
● Morellino di Scansano Orto delle Monache Ris. '15	🍷🍷 5

Armilla

VIA TAVERNELLE, 6
53024 MONTALCINO [SI]
TEL. +39 0577816012
www.armillawine.com

ANNUAL PRODUCTION 12,000 bottles
HECTARES UNDER VINE 3.00

● Brunello di Montalcino '14	♥♥ 8
● Rosso di Montalcino '16	♥♥ 4

Arrighi

LOC. PIAN DEL MONTE, 1
57036 PORTO AZZURRO [LI]
TEL. +39 3356641793
www.arrighivigneolivi.it

CELLAR SALES
PRE-BOOKED VISITS
ANNUAL PRODUCTION 30,000 bottles
HECTARES UNDER VINE 6.00

● Elba Aleatico Passito Silosò '18	♥♥ 5
○ Elba Bianco Illagiù '18	♥♥ 3
● Tresse '16	♥♥ 5
○ Hermia '18	♥ 4

Fattoria di Bagnolo

LOC. BAGNOLO
VIA IMPRUNETANA PER TAVARNUZZE, 48
50023 IMPRUNETA [FI]
TEL. +39 0552313403
www.bartolinibaldelli.it

CELLAR SALES
PRE-BOOKED VISITS
ANNUAL PRODUCTION 25,000 bottles
HECTARES UNDER VINE 10.00

● Capro Rosso '16	♥♥ 7
● Chianti Colli Fiorentini '17	♥♥ 2*
● Chianti Colli Fiorentini Ris. '16	♥♥ 4

Alfonso Baldetti

LOC. PIETRAIA, 71A
52044 CORTONA [AR]
TEL. +39 057567077
CORTONA

CELLAR SALES
PRE-BOOKED VISITS
ANNUAL PRODUCTION 100,000 bottles
HECTARES UNDER VINE 15.00
SUSTAINABLE WINERY

○ Chagré '18	♥♥ 3
● Cortona Syrah Crano '15	♥♥ 5
○ Cortona Vin Santo Leopoldo '03	♥♥ 5
● Cortona Sangiovese Marius '16	♥ 3

I Balzini

LOC. PASTINE, 19
50021 BARBERINO VAL D'ELSA [FI]
TEL. +39 0558075503
www.ibalzini.it

CELLAR SALES
PRE-BOOKED VISITS
ANNUAL PRODUCTION 70,000 bottles
HECTARES UNDER VINE 12.00
SUSTAINABLE WINERY

● I Balzini Black Label '16	♥♥ 6
● I Balzini White Label '16	♥♥ 5

Il Balzo

VIA DEL POGGIOLO, 12
50068 RUFINA [FI]
TEL. +39 0558397556
www.ilbalzo.it

CELLAR SALES
PRE-BOOKED VISITS
ANNUAL PRODUCTION 9,000 bottles
HECTARES UNDER VINE 7.00

● Chianti Rufina Ris. '15	♥♥ 4
● Addiaccio '17	♥♥ 2*
● Chianti Rufina '16	♥♥ 2*

Fattoria di Basciano

V.LE DUCA DELLA VITTORIA, 159
50068 RUFINA [FI]
TEL. +39 0558397034
www.renzomasibasciano.it

CELLAR SALES
PRE-BOOKED VISITS
ANNUAL PRODUCTION 200,000 bottles
HECTARES UNDER VINE 35.00

● Chianti Rufina Ris. '15	♟♟	3
● Erta e China '17	♟♟	2*
● I Pini '17	♟♟	4
● Vigna Il Corto '17	♟	3

Batzella

LOC. BADIA, 227
57024 CASTAGNETO CARDUCCI [LI]
TEL. +39 3393975888
www.batzella.com

CELLAR SALES
PRE-BOOKED VISITS
ACCOMMODATION
ANNUAL PRODUCTION 55,000 bottles
HECTARES UNDER VINE 8.00

● Bolgheri Rosso Eccoci '17	♟♟	4
● Bolgheri Rosso Peàn '16	♟♟	4
● Vox Loci '16	♟♟	4
● Vox Loci Syrah '15	♟♟	4

Cantine Bellini

VIA PIAVE, 1
50068 RUFINA [FI]
TEL. +39 0558396025
www.bellinicantine.it

CELLAR SALES
ANNUAL PRODUCTION 900,000 bottles
HECTARES UNDER VINE 15.00

● Chianti Rufina Ris. '15	♟♟	2*
● Mamb-o Dominante '15	♟♟	2*
○ Vin Santo del Chianti Rufina '09	♟♟	4
● Comedia '15	♟	2

Le Bertille

VIA DELLE COLOMBELLE, 7
53045 MONTEPULCIANO [SI]
TEL. +39 0578758330
www.lebertille.com

CELLAR SALES
PRE-BOOKED VISITS
ACCOMMODATION
ANNUAL PRODUCTION 65,000 bottles
HECTARES UNDER VINE 14.00
SUSTAINABLE WINERY

● Nobile di Montepulciano '16	♟♟	4
● Nobile di Montepulciano Ris. '15	♟♟	5

La Biagiola

FRAZ. SOVANA
LOC. PIANETTI
58010 SORANO [GR]
TEL. +39 3666766400
www.labiagiola.it

CELLAR SALES
PRE-BOOKED VISITS
ANNUAL PRODUCTION 60,000 bottles
HECTARES UNDER VINE 8.50

● Maremma Toscana Rosso Tesan '17	♟♟	3
○ Maremma Toscana Vermentino Matan '17	♟♟	3
● Maremma Toscana Sangiovese Alideo '16	♟	3

Bindi Sergardi

LOC. POGGIOLO
FATTORIA I COLLI, 2
53035 MONTERIGGIONI [SI]
TEL. +39 0577309107
www.bindisergardi.it

CELLAR SALES
PRE-BOOKED VISITS
ACCOMMODATION AND RESTAURANT SERVICE
ANNUAL PRODUCTION 100,000 bottles
HECTARES UNDER VINE 103.00

● Chianti Cl. Ser Gardo '15	♟♟	4
● Nicolò '16	♟♟	4
● Chianti Cl. Ris. '15	♟	4

Borghetto

C. Montefiridolfi
Collina Sant'Angelo, 21
0026 San Casciano in Val di Pesa [FI]
.. +39 0558244442
w.borghetto.org

CELLAR SALES
PRE-BOOKED VISITS
ACCOMMODATION
ANNUAL PRODUCTION 14,000 bottles
HECTARES UNDER VINE 5.00

Bilaccio '15	♟♟ 5
Monte de Sassi '15	♟♟ 3
Clante '15	♟ 6

Tenuta del Buonamico

. Cercatoia
Provinciale di Montecarlo, 43
0015 Montecarlo [LU]
.. +39 058322038
w.buonamico.it

CELLAR SALES
PRE-BOOKED VISITS
ACCOMMODATION AND RESTAURANT SERVICE
ANNUAL PRODUCTION 350,000 bottles
HECTARES UNDER VINE 43.00
SUSTAINABLE WINERY

Cercatoja '16	♟♟ 5
Montecarlo Rosso Et. Blu '17	♟♟ 3
Dea Rosa '18	♟ 3

Caccia al Piano 1868

. Bolgheri
Bolgherese, 279
022 Castagneto Carducci [LI]
.. +39 0565763394
w.berlucchi.it

CELLAR SALES
PRE-BOOKED VISITS
ANNUAL PRODUCTION 127,000 bottles
HECTARES UNDER VINE 18.00
SUSTAINABLE WINERY

Grottaia Rosso '18	♟♟ 3*
Bolgheri Rosso Sup. Levia Gravia '16	♟♟ 7
Bolgheri Rosso Ruit Hora '17	♟ 4

Bulichella

Loc. Bulichella, 131
57028 Suvereto [LI]
Tel. +39 0565829892
www.bulichella.it

CELLAR SALES
PRE-BOOKED VISITS
ACCOMMODATION AND RESTAURANT SERVICE
ANNUAL PRODUCTION 60,000 bottles
HECTARES UNDER VINE 17.00
VITICULTURE METHOD Certified Organic

● Hyde '16	♟♟ 5
● Suvereto Coldipietre Rosse '16	♟♟ 5
● Suvereto Montecristo '16	♟♟ 2*
● Rubino '17	♟ 3

Ca' Marcanda

Loc. Santa Teresa, 272
57022 Castagneto Carducci [LI]
Tel. +39 0565763809
info@camarcanda.com

CELLAR SALES
PRE-BOOKED VISITS
ANNUAL PRODUCTION 450,000 bottles
HECTARES UNDER VINE 120.00

● Bolgheri Rosso Magari '17	♟♟ 6
● Promis '17	♟ 6

Cacciagrande

Fraz. Tirli
Loc. Ampio
58043 Castiglione della Pescaia [GR]
Tel. +39 0564944168
www.cacciagrande.com

CELLAR SALES
PRE-BOOKED VISITS
ANNUAL PRODUCTION 100,000 bottles
HECTARES UNDER VINE 20.00
SUSTAINABLE WINERY

● Castiglione '17	♟♟ 4
● Cortigliano '18	♟ 3
○ Maremma Toscana Vermentino '18	♟ 3

Campo al Pero

FRAZ. DONORATICO
VIA DEL CASONE UGOLINO, 12
57022 CASTAGNETO CARDUCCI [LI]
TEL. +39 0565774329
www.campoalpero.it

CELLAR SALES
PRE-BOOKED VISITS
ANNUAL PRODUCTION 30,000 bottles
HECTARES UNDER VINE 8.00

● Bolgheri Rosso '17	🍷🍷	5
● Bolgheri Sup. Dorianae '16	🍷🍷	5
○ Bolgheri Vermentino Mistral '18	🍷🍷	2*
● Bolgheri Sup. Dedicato a Vittorio '16	🍷	5

Campo alla Sughera

LOC. CACCIA AL PIANO
S.DA PROV.LE BOLGHERESE, 280
57020 BOLGHERI [LI]
TEL. +39 0565766936
www.campoallasughera.com

CELLAR SALES
PRE-BOOKED VISITS
ACCOMMODATION
ANNUAL PRODUCTION 110,000 bottles
HECTARES UNDER VINE 16.50

● Bolgheri Rosso Adeo '17	🍷🍷
● Campo alla Sughera Rosso '15	🍷🍷
○ Arioso '18	🍷
● Bolgheri Rosso Sup. Arnione '16	🍷

Campo del Monte
Eredi Benito Mantellini

VIA TRAIANA, 53A
52028 TERRANUOVA BRACCIOLINI [AR]
TEL. +39 0554684135
www.campodelmonte.it

CELLAR SALES
PRE-BOOKED VISITS
ACCOMMODATION
HECTARES UNDER VINE 7.50

● Valdarno di Sopra Cabernet Sauvignon Rodos '17	🍷🍷	4
● Valdarno di Sopra Sangiovese Bucapentoli '17	🍷🍷	4

Campogiovanni

FRAZ. SANT'ANGELO IN COLLE
LOC. CAMPOGIOVANNI
53020 MONTALCINO [SI]
TEL. +39 0577844001
www.agricolasanfelice.it

CELLAR SALES
PRE-BOOKED VISITS
ANNUAL PRODUCTION 130,000 bottles
HECTARES UNDER VINE 20.00

● Brunello di Montalcino '14	🍷🍷
● Rosso di Montalcino '16	🍷🍷
● Brunello di Montalcino Il Quercione Ris. '13	🍷

Canalicchio - Franco Pacenti

LOC. CANALICCHIO DI SOPRA, 6
53024 MONTALCINO [SI]
TEL. +39 0577849277
www.canalicchiofrancopacenti.it

CELLAR SALES
PRE-BOOKED VISITS
RESTAURANT SERVICE
ANNUAL PRODUCTION 40,000 bottles
HECTARES UNDER VINE 10.00

● Brunello di Montalcino '14	🍷🍷	7
● Rosso di Montalcino Gemma '15	🍷	3

Capanne Ricci

FRAZ. SANT'ANGELO IN COLLE
LOC. CASELLO
53024 MONTALCINO [SI]
TEL. +39 0564902063
www.tenimentiricci.it

ANNUAL PRODUCTION 40,000 bottles
HECTARES UNDER VINE 12.00

● Brunello di Montalcino '14	🍷🍷

appella Sant'Andrea

:. Casale, 26
037 San Gimignano [SI]
.. +39 0577940456
w.cappellasantandrea.it

CELLAR SALES
RE-BOOKED VISITS
ESTAURANT SERVICE
NNUAL PRODUCTION 45,000 bottles
ECTARES UNDER VINE 9.00
TICULTURE METHOD Certified Organic
STAINABLE WINERY

Vernaccia di S. Gimignano	
Prima Luce Ris. '16	♟ 5
Vernaccia di S. Gimignano Rialto '17	♟♟ 3
Vernaccia di S. Gimignano Clara Stella '18	♟ 2

Enzo Carmignani

via di Cercatoia Alta, 13b
55015 Montecarlo [LU]
Tel. +39 058322463
www.fattoriacarmignani.com

CELLAR SALES
PRE-BOOKED VISITS
ACCOMMODATION
ANNUAL PRODUCTION 1,970 bottles
HECTARES UNDER VINE 9.00
VITICULTURE METHOD Certified Organic
SUSTAINABLE WINERY

● Kapogiro '18	♟♟ 2*
○ Tentazione '17	♟♟ 4
○ Urano '18	♟♟ 3

odere Il Carnasciale

. San Leolino, 82
020 Mercatale Valdarno [AR]
.. +39 0559911142
ww.caberlot.eu

RE-BOOKED VISITS
NNUAL PRODUCTION 10,000 bottles
ECTARES UNDER VINE 4.50
STAINABLE WINERY

l Caberlot '16	♟♟ 8

Fattoria Casa di Terra

fraz. Bolgheri
loc. Le Ferruggini, 162a
57022 Castagneto Carducci [LI]
Tel. +39 0565749810
www.fattoriacasaditerra.com

CELLAR SALES
PRE-BOOKED VISITS
ACCOMMODATION
ANNUAL PRODUCTION 180,000 bottles
HECTARES UNDER VINE 44.50

● Bolgheri Rosso Moreccio '17	♟♟ 3
● Bolgheri Rosso Sup. Maronea '16	♟♟ 6
○ Bolgheri Vermentino '18	♟♟ 3

asa Emma

:. San Donato in Poggio
a prov.le di Castellina in Chianti, 3
021 Barberino Val d'Elsa [FI]
.. +39 0558072239
ww.casaemma.com

CELLAR SALES
RE-BOOKED VISITS
ESTAURANT SERVICE
NNUAL PRODUCTION 90,000 bottles
ECTARES UNDER VINE 31.00
TICULTURE METHOD Certified Organic
STAINABLE WINERY

Chianti Cl. Vigna al Parco Ris. '16	♟♟ 3*
Chianti Cl. '17	♟ 3
Chianti Cl. Gran Selezione '15	♟ 5

Tenuta Casadei

loc. San Rocco
57028 Suvereto [LI]
Tel. +39 0558300411
www.tenutacasadei.it

CELLAR SALES
PRE-BOOKED VISITS
ANNUAL PRODUCTION 125,000 bottles
HECTARES UNDER VINE 25.00
VITICULTURE METHOD Certified Biodynamic
SUSTAINABLE WINERY

● Filare 41 '17	♟♟ 6
● Filare 18 '17	♟♟ 6
● Sogno Mediterraneo '17	♟♟ 4

Casale Pozzuolo

LOC. BORGO SANTA RITA
58044 CINIGIANO [GR]
TEL. +39 0564902019
www.casalepozzuolo.it

CELLAR SALES
PRE-BOOKED VISITS
ACCOMMODATION
ANNUAL PRODUCTION 15,000 bottles
HECTARES UNDER VINE 4.50

● Montecucco Sangiovese Rosso della Porticcia Ris. '16	▼▼ 4
● Montecucco Sangiovese Rosso della Porticcia '16	▼ 3

Podere Casanova

S.DA PROV.LE 326 EST, 196
53045 MONTEPULCIANO [SI]
TEL. +39 0429841418
www.poderecasanovavini.com

CELLAR SALES
PRE-BOOKED VISITS
ACCOMMODATION
ANNUAL PRODUCTION 140,000 bottles
HECTARES UNDER VINE 18.00

● Nobile di Montepulciano '16	▼▼
● Nobile di Montepulciano Settecento Ris '15	▼▼

Castelgiocondo

LOC. CASTELGIOCONDO
53024 MONTALCINO [SI]
TEL. +39 057784131
www.frescobaldi.it

PRE-BOOKED VISITS
ANNUAL PRODUCTION 600,000 bottles
HECTARES UNDER VINE 235.00

● Brunello di Montalcino '14	▼▼ 6
● Brunello di Montalcino Ripe al Convento di Castelgiocondo Ris. '13	▼▼ 8

Castellinuzza

VIA PETRIOLO, 14
50022 GREVE IN CHIANTI [FI]
TEL. +39 0558549046
www.chianticlassicocastellinuzza.it

CELLAR SALES
PRE-BOOKED VISITS
ACCOMMODATION
ANNUAL PRODUCTION 7,000 bottles
HECTARES UNDER VINE 2.00

● Chianti Cl. '16	▼▼

Castello della Mugazzena

LOC. FOLA
VIA TRESANA PAESE, 103
54012 TRESANA [MS]
TEL. +39 3357906553
www.castellodellamugazzena.it

ANNUAL PRODUCTION 4,000 bottles
HECTARES UNDER VINE 3.00

● Gargantua '17	▼▼ 5
○ Pantagruel '17	▼▼ 4

Castello di Meleto

LOC. MELETO
53013 GAIOLE IN CHIANTI [SI]
TEL. +39 0577749217
www.castellomeleto.it

CELLAR SALES
PRE-BOOKED VISITS
ACCOMMODATION AND RESTAURANT SERVI▮
ANNUAL PRODUCTION 700,000 bottles
HECTARES UNDER VINE 144.00
SUSTAINABLE WINERY

● Chianti Cl. V. Casi Ris. '16	▼▼
● Chianti Cl. V. Poggiarso Ris. '16	▼▼
● Chianti Cl. '17	▼
● Chianti Cl. Castello di Meleto 1256 '16	▼

astello di Querceto

Alessandro Francois, 2
022 Greve in Chianti [FI]
.. +39 05585921
ww.castellodiquerceto.it

CELLAR SALES
RE-BOOKED VISITS
CCOMMODATION
NNUAL PRODUCTION 600,000 bottles
ECTARES UNDER VINE 60.00

Chianti Cl. Ris. '16	♥♥ 4
Chianti Cl. '17	♥♥ 3
Chianti Cl. Gran Selezione Il Picchio '16	♥♥ 5

Castello di Vicarello

loc. Vicarello, 1
58044 Cinigiano [GR]
Tel. +39 0564990718
www.castellodivicarellovini.com

CELLAR SALES
PRE-BOOKED VISITS
ACCOMMODATION AND RESTAURANT SERVICE
ANNUAL PRODUCTION 15,000 bottles
HECTARES UNDER VINE 6.50
VITICULTURE METHOD Certified Organic

● Castello di Vicarello '15	♥♥ 8
● Merah '17	♥♥ 5
● Terre di Vico '15	♥♥ 7

astello La Leccia

. La Leccia
011 Castellina in Chianti [SI]
.. +39 0577743148
ww.castellolaleccia.com

CELLAR SALES
RE-BOOKED VISITS
NNUAL PRODUCTION 30,000 bottles
ECTARES UNDER VINE 13.50

Chianti Cl. Giuliano Ris. '15	♥♥ 4
Chianti Cl. Gran Selezione Bruciagna '15	♥♥ 4
Chianti Cl. '16	♥ 3

Castello Sonnino

via Volterrana Nord, 6a
50025 Montespertoli [FI]
Tel. +39 0571609198
www.castellosonnino.it

CELLAR SALES
PRE-BOOKED VISITS
ACCOMMODATION
ANNUAL PRODUCTION 150,000 bottles
HECTARES UNDER VINE 40.00
SUSTAINABLE WINERY

● Cantinino '15	♥♥ 4
● Leone Rosso '18	♥♥ 2*
○ Vin Santo del Chianti '13	♥♥ 5
● Chianti Montespertoli '18	♥ 2

astelsina

. Osteria, 54a
048 Sinalunga [SI]
.. +39 0577663595
ww.castelsina.it

CELLAR SALES
RE-BOOKED VISITS
NNUAL PRODUCTION 2,000,000 bottles
ECTARES UNDER VINE 400.00

Chianti '18	♥♥ 2*
Chianti Ris. '16	♥♥ 2*
Governo all'Uso Toscano '18	♥♥ 2*
Toscano Rosso '18	♥ 1*

Cava d'Onice

pod. Colombaio 105
53024 Montalcino [SI]
Tel. +39 0577848405
www.cavadonice.it

CELLAR SALES
PRE-BOOKED VISITS
ACCOMMODATION
ANNUAL PRODUCTION 22,000 bottles
HECTARES UNDER VINE 3.60
VITICULTURE METHOD Certified Organic

● Brunello di Montalcino '14	♥♥ 7
● Rosso di Montalcino '17	♥ 4

Ceralti

VIA DEI CERALTI, 77
57022 CASTAGNETO CARDUCCI [LI]
TEL. +39 0565763989
www.ceralti.com

CELLAR SALES
PRE-BOOKED VISITS
ACCOMMODATION
ANNUAL PRODUCTION 50,000 bottles
HECTARES UNDER VINE 9.00
VITICULTURE METHOD Certified Organic

● Bolgheri Rosso Scirè '17	♥♥ 3
● Bolgheri Sup. Alfeo '16	♥♥ 5

Cantina Chiacchiera

FRAZ. CERVOGNANO
VIA POGGIO GOLO, 12
53045 MONTEPULCIANO [SI]
TEL. +39 3477969531
www.cantinachiacchiera.it

CELLAR SALES
PRE-BOOKED VISITS
RESTAURANT SERVICE
ANNUAL PRODUCTION 30,000 bottles
HECTARES UNDER VINE 18.00

● Nobile di Montepulciano Chiacchiera '16	♥♥
● Rosso di Montepulciano '17	♥♥
● Chiacchiera '18	♥

Podere La Chiesa

LOC. CASANOVA
VIA DI CASANOVA 66 A
56030 TERRICCIOLA [PI]
TEL. +39 0587635484
www.poderelachiesa.it

CELLAR SALES
PRE-BOOKED VISITS
ANNUAL PRODUCTION 40,000 bottles
HECTARES UNDER VINE 14.50
VITICULTURE METHOD Certified Organic
SUSTAINABLE WINERY

● Chianti Terre di Casanova '17	♥♥ 2*
○ Taigete '17	♥♥ 2*
● Terre di Pisa Sangiovese Opera in Rosso '14	♥♥ 7

La Ciarliana

FRAZ. GRACCIANO
VIA CIARLIANA, 31
53040 MONTEPULCIANO [SI]
TEL. +39 0578758423
www.laciarliana.it

CELLAR SALES
PRE-BOOKED VISITS
ANNUAL PRODUCTION 30,000 bottles
HECTARES UNDER VINE 12.00

● Nobile di Montepulciano V. Scianello '15	♥♥
● Rosso di Montepulciano '17	♥♥

Cipresso Roberto

FRAZ. CASTELNUOVO DELL'ABATE
VIA DELL'OLMO, 24
53024 MONTALCINO [SI]
TEL. +39 0577835511
rc@robertocipresso.it

CELLAR SALES
ACCOMMODATION
ANNUAL PRODUCTION 3,500 bottles
HECTARES UNDER VINE 7.00
SUSTAINABLE WINERY

● Brunello di Montalcino '14	♥♥ 8
● Rosso di Montalcino '17	♥ 5

La Cipriana

LOC. CAMPASTRELLO, 176B
57022 CASTAGNETO CARDUCCI [LI]
TEL. +39 0565775568
www.lacipriana.com

CELLAR SALES
PRE-BOOKED VISITS
ACCOMMODATION AND RESTAURANT SERVI
ANNUAL PRODUCTION 30,000 bottles
HECTARES UNDER VINE 8.00

● Bolgheri Rosso V. Scopaio '17	♥♥
● Bolgheri Rosso '17	♥♥
● Bolgheri Rosso Sup. San Martino '16	♥

Col di Lamo

POD. GROSSETO 28
53024 MONTALCINO [SI]
TEL. +39 0577834433
www.coldilamo.me

ANNUAL PRODUCTION 28,000 bottles
HECTARES UNDER VINE 7.50
VITICULTURE METHOD Certified Organic

● Rosso di Montalcino '16	♟♟	4

Il Colle

LOC. IL COLLE 102B
53024 MONTALCINO [SI]
TEL. +39 0577848295
ilcolledicarli@katamail.com

CELLAR SALES
PRE-BOOKED VISITS
ANNUAL PRODUCTION 18,000 bottles
HECTARES UNDER VINE 7.00

● Brunello di Montalcino '14	♟♟	6
● Rosso di Montalcino '16	♟	5

Colle delle 100 bottiglie

LOC. LA MAOLINA
FRAZ. SAN CONCORDIO DI MORIANO
VIA BEVILACQUA, 100
55100 LUCCA
TEL. +39 3924636248
www.colledelle100bottiglie.com

● Pigne Bordò '16	♟♟	3
● Segale '16	♟♟	4

Collelceto

LOC. CAMIGLIANO
POD. LA PISANA
53024 MONTALCINO [SI]
TEL. +39 0577816606
www.collelceto.it

CELLAR SALES
PRE-BOOKED VISITS
ANNUAL PRODUCTION 22,000 bottles
HECTARES UNDER VINE 6.00

● Brunello di Montalcino '14	♟♟	5
● Brunello di Montalcino Ris. '13	♟♟	6
● Rosso di Montalcino '17	♟	3

La Collina dei Lecci

LOC. VALLAFRICO
53024 MONTALCINO [SI]
TEL. +39 0577849287
collina@pacinimauro.com

SUSTAINABLE WINERY

● Brunello di Montalcino '14	♟♟	5
● Brunello di Montalcino Ris. '13	♟♟	6

Contucci

VIA DEL TEATRO, 1
53045 MONTEPULCIANO [SI]
TEL. +39 0578757006
www.contucci.it

CELLAR SALES
PRE-BOOKED VISITS
ACCOMMODATION
ANNUAL PRODUCTION 100,000 bottles
HECTARES UNDER VINE 21.00

● Nobile di Montepulciano Mulinvecchio '16	♟♟	5
● Nobile di Montepulciano Pietra Rossa '16	♟♟	5

Il Conventino

FRAZ. GRACCIANO
VIA DELLA CIARLIANA, 25B
53040 MONTEPULCIANO [SI]
TEL. +39 0578715371
www.ilconventino.it

CELLAR SALES
PRE-BOOKED VISITS
ANNUAL PRODUCTION 55,000 bottles
HECTARES UNDER VINE 12.00
VITICULTURE METHOD Certified Organic

● Nobile di Montepulciano '16	🍷🍷 4
● Nobile di Montepulciano Ris. '15	🍷🍷 5

Fattoria Corzano e Paterno

LOC. CORZANO
FRAZ. SAN PANCRAZIO
VIA SAN VITO DI SOPRA
50020 SAN CASCIANO IN VAL DI PESA [FI]
TEL. +39 0558248179
www.corzanoepaterno.com

CELLAR SALES
PRE-BOOKED VISITS
ACCOMMODATION
ANNUAL PRODUCTION 85,000 bottles
HECTARES UNDER VINE 19.00
VITICULTURE METHOD Certified Organic

● I Tre Borri '16	🍷🍷 5
● Il Corzano '16	🍷🍷 5
● Chianti Terre di Corzano '16	🍷 2
⊙ Rosato Corzanello '18	🍷 2

Diadema

VIA IMPRUNETANA PER TAVARNUZZE, 19
50023 IMPRUNETA [FI]
TEL. +39 0552311330
www.diadema-wine.com

CELLAR SALES
PRE-BOOKED VISITS
ACCOMMODATION
ANNUAL PRODUCTION 80,000 bottles
HECTARES UNDER VINE 40.00

○ Diadema Damare Bianco '18	🍷🍷 4
● Diadema Damare Rosso '17	🍷🍷 5
● Diadema Rosso '17	🍷🍷 8
● Imprunetis '16	🍷 4

Dianella

VIA DIANELLA, 48
50059 VINCI [FI]
TEL. +39 0571508166
www.dianella.wine

CELLAR SALES
PRE-BOOKED VISITS
ACCOMMODATION
ANNUAL PRODUCTION 130,000 bottles
HECTARES UNDER VINE 25.00
VITICULTURE METHOD Certified Organic
SUSTAINABLE WINERY

● Chianti Ris. '15	🍷🍷 4
● Il Matto delle Giuncaie '16	🍷🍷 5
○ Sereno e Nuvole '18	🍷🍷 3
⊙ All'Aria Aperta '18	🍷 3

Donna Olga

LOC. FRIGGIALI
S.DA MAREMMANA
53024 MONTALCINO [SI]
TEL. +39 0577849454
www.tenutedonnaolga.it

CELLAR SALES
PRE-BOOKED VISITS
ACCOMMODATION
ANNUAL PRODUCTION 25,000 bottles
HECTARES UNDER VINE 11.00

● Brunello di Montalcino Donna Olga '14	🍷🍷 8

Agricola Fabbriche - Palma

VIA FABBRICHE, 2-3A
52046 LUCIGNANO [AR]
TEL. +39 0575836152
www.agricolafabbriche.it

CELLAR SALES
PRE-BOOKED VISITS
ANNUAL PRODUCTION 15,000 bottles
HECTARES UNDER VINE 11.00

● Camargi '16	🍷🍷 4
● Merlot '16	🍷🍷 3
○ Ninis '18	🍷🍷 2
● Syrah '16	🍷 5

Falcone

ᴄ. Falcone, 186
7028 Suvereto [LI]
ᴇʟ. +39 0565829331
ww.ilfalcone.net

CELLAR SALES
PRE-BOOKED VISITS
ACCOMMODATION
ANNUAL PRODUCTION 40,000 bottles
HECTARES UNDER VINE 10.00

Falcorosso '17	🍷🍷 3
Suvereto Sangiovese Boccalupo '16	🍷🍷 5
Vallin dei Ghiri Syrah '17	🍷🍷 5

Fattoria di Fiano - Ugo Bing

ʟᴏᴄ. Fiano
ᴠɪᴀ Firenze, 11
50052 Certaldo [FI]
Tᴇʟ. +39 0571669048
www.ugobing.it

CELLAR SALES
PRE-BOOKED VISITS
ANNUAL PRODUCTION 150,000 bottles
HECTARES UNDER VINE 22.00

● Chianti Colli Fiorentini Ris. '16	🍷🍷 3
● Pugni d'Abrusco '16	🍷🍷 4
● Chianti Colli Fiorentini '17	🍷 2

Fietri

ᴄ. Fietri
3010 Gaiole in Chianti [SI]
ᴇʟ. +39 0577734048
ww.fietri.com

CELLAR SALES
ACCOMMODATION
ANNUAL PRODUCTION 15,000 bottles
HECTARES UNDER VINE 8.00
VITICULTURE METHOD Certified Organic

Chianti Cl. '17	🍷🍷 3
Dedicato a Benedetta '16	🍷🍷 4

La Fiorita

ꜰʀᴀᴢ. Castelnuovo dell'Abate
Podere Bellavista
53024 Montalcino [SI]
Tᴇʟ. +39 0577835657
www.lafiorita.com

CELLAR SALES
PRE-BOOKED VISITS
ANNUAL PRODUCTION 35,000 bottles
HECTARES UNDER VINE 7.00

● Brunello di Montalcino '14	🍷🍷 6
● Brunello di Montalcino Ris. '13	🍷🍷 7
● Rosso di Montalcino '17	🍷 5

Fontaleoni

ᴄ. Santa Maria, 39
3037 San Gimignano [SI]
ᴇʟ. +39 0577950193
ww.fontaleoni.com

CELLAR SALES
PRE-BOOKED VISITS
ACCOMMODATION AND RESTAURANT SERVICE
ANNUAL PRODUCTION 150,000 bottles
HECTARES UNDER VINE 35.00
VITICULTURE METHOD Certified Organic

● Vernaccia di S. Gimignano Ris. '16	🍷🍷 3*
● Chianti Colli Senesi '18	🍷🍷 2*
● Condorino Rosato '18	🍷 2
● Vernaccia di San Gimignano '18	🍷 2

Poderi Fontemorsi

ᴠɪᴀ ᴅᴇʟʟᴇ Colline
56040 Montescudaio [PI]
Tᴇʟ. +39 3356843438
www.fontemorsi.it

CELLAR SALES
ACCOMMODATION
ANNUAL PRODUCTION 50,000 bottles
HECTARES UNDER VINE 8.50
VITICULTURE METHOD Certified Organic

● Spazzavento '16	🍷🍷 2*
○ Tresassi Bianco '18	🍷🍷 2*
● Volterrano '15	🍷🍷 4
● Le Tinte '15	🍷 4

La Fornace

POD. FORNACE, 154A
53024 MONTALCINO [SI]
TEL. +39 0577848465
www.agricola-lafornace.it

CELLAR SALES
PRE-BOOKED VISITS
ANNUAL PRODUCTION 15,000 bottles
HECTARES UNDER VINE 4.50

● Brunello di Montalcino '14	♚♚ 6
● Rosso di Montalcino '17	♚♚ 4

Fortulla - Agrilandia

LOC. CASTIGLIONCELLO
S.DA VICINALE DELLE SPIANATE
57016 ROSIGNANO MARITTIMO [LI]
TEL. +39 3404524453
www.fortulla.it

CELLAR SALES
PRE-BOOKED VISITS
ACCOMMODATION AND RESTAURANT SERVIC
ANNUAL PRODUCTION 50,000 bottles
HECTARES UNDER VINE 7.00
VITICULTURE METHOD Certified Organic
SUSTAINABLE WINERY

● Sorpasso '14	♚♚
● Fortulla '16	♚
○ Serpentino '18	♚

Frank & Serafico

FRAZ. ALBERESE
S.DA SPERGOLAIA
58100 GROSSETO
TEL. +39 0564418491
www.frankeserafico.com

CELLAR SALES
PRE-BOOKED VISITS
RESTAURANT SERVICE
ANNUAL PRODUCTION 90,000 bottles
HECTARES UNDER VINE 25.00

● Maremma Toscana Sangiovese '16	♚♚ 4
● Frank '16	♚ 3
● Rosso di Redola '16	♚ 2

Gagliole

LOC. GAGLIOLE, 42
53011 CASTELLINA IN CHIANTI [SI]
TEL. +39 0577740369
www.gagliole.com

CELLAR SALES
PRE-BOOKED VISITS
ANNUAL PRODUCTION 35,000 bottles
HECTARES UNDER VINE 9.90

● Chianti Cl. Gallule Ris. '16	♚♚
● Chianti Cl. Rubiolo '17	♚
● Valletta '16	♚♚

Gentili

FRAZ. PIAZZE
VIA DEL TAMBURINO, 120
53040 CETONA [SI]
TEL. +39 0578244038
www.gentiliwine.com

CELLAR SALES
PRE-BOOKED VISITS
ANNUAL PRODUCTION 130,000 bottles
HECTARES UNDER VINE 15.00

○ Fleurs '18	♚♚ 2*
● Le Favorite '17	♚♚ 5
● Sinibaldo '17	♚♚ 3
○ Chardonnay '18	♚ 2

La Gerla

LOC. CANALICCHIO
POD. COLOMBAIO, 5
53024 MONTALCINO [SI]
TEL. +39 0577848599
www.lagerla.it

CELLAR SALES
PRE-BOOKED VISITS
ANNUAL PRODUCTION 80,000 bottles
HECTARES UNDER VINE 11.50

● Rosso di Montalcino Aisna '16	♚♚
● Brunello di Montalcino '14	♚
● Rosso di Montalcino '17	♚

Giardini Ripadiversilia

A ANGELINI
5047 LUCCA
TEL. +39 327 388 1106
www.giardinidiversilia.it

CELLAR SALES
PRE-BOOKED VISITS
ANNUAL PRODUCTION 4,500 bottles
HECTARES UNDER VINE 3.00
SUSTAINABLE WINERY

● Colli e Mare '17	🍷 6
● La Costa '16	🍷 8
● Vis Vitae '16	🍷 7

Fattoria di Grignano

IA DI GRIGNANO, 22
0065 PONTASSIEVE [FI]
TEL. +39 0558398490
www.fattoriadigrignano.com

CELLAR SALES
PRE-BOOKED VISITS
ANNUAL PRODUCTION 200,000 bottles
HECTARES UNDER VINE 53.00
VITICULTURE METHOD Certified Organic
SUSTAINABLE WINERY

● Chianti Rufina Poggio Gualtieri Ris. '15	🍷🍷 4
● Pietramaggio Rosso '16	🍷🍷 3
● Chianti Rufina '16	🍷 2
● Chianti Rufina Ritratto del Cardinale '16	🍷 2

Tenuta La Chiusa

LOC. MAGAZZINI, 93
7037 PORTOFERRAIO [LI]
TEL. +39 0565933046
lachiusa@elbalink.it

CELLAR SALES
PRE-BOOKED VISITS
ACCOMMODATION
ANNUAL PRODUCTION 25,000 bottles
HECTARES UNDER VINE 7.50

● Elba Aleatico Passito '17	🍷🍷 6
○ Elba Ansonica '18	🍷🍷 2*
● Elba Rosso Ginevra '17	🍷🍷 2*
○ Vermentino '18	🍷 2

Tenuta di Gracciano della Seta

FRAZ. GRACCIANO
VIA UMBRIA, 59
53045 MONTEPULCIANO [SI]
TEL. +39 0578708340
www.graccianodellaseta.com

CELLAR SALES
PRE-BOOKED VISITS
ANNUAL PRODUCTION 90,000 bottles
HECTARES UNDER VINE 18.00
SUSTAINABLE WINERY

● Nobile di Montepulciano '16	🍷🍷 4
● Nobile di Montepulciano Ris. '15	🍷🍷 5
● Rosso di Montepulciano '17	🍷🍷 3

Tenuta L' Impostino

LOC. IMPOSTINO, 95
58045 CIVITELLA PAGANICO [GR]
TEL. +39 0564900665
www.tenutaimpostino.it

CELLAR SALES
PRE-BOOKED VISITS
ACCOMMODATION AND RESTAURANT SERVICE
ANNUAL PRODUCTION 130,000 bottles
HECTARES UNDER VINE 20.00

● Montecucco Rosso Ris. '14	🍷🍷 3
● Montecucco Sangiovese Viandante Ris. '13	🍷🍷 5

Podere La Pace

FRAZ. VIVOLI
POD. BIANCOSPINO, 65
58024 MASSA MARITTIMA [GR]
TEL. +39 3336564195
www.poderelapace.com

CELLAR SALES
PRE-BOOKED VISITS
ACCOMMODATION
ANNUAL PRODUCTION 28,000 bottles
HECTARES UNDER VINE 5.00

● Maremma Toscana Rosso Black Label '16	🍷🍷 5
● Maremma Toscana Cabernet Gold Label '16	🍷 6
● Maremma Toscana Rosso Red Label '16	🍷 4

Fattoria Il Lago

FRAZ. CAMPAGNA, 23
50062 DICOMANO [FI]
TEL. +39 055838047
www.fattoriaillago.com

CELLAR SALES
PRE-BOOKED VISITS
ACCOMMODATION
ANNUAL PRODUCTION 50,000 bottles
HECTARES UNDER VINE 17.00
SUSTAINABLE WINERY

● Chianti Rufina '17	♟♟ 2*
● Chianti Rufina Ris. '16	♟♟ 3
● Pinot Nero '16	♟♟ 5

Maurizio Lambardi

LOC. CANALICCHIO DI SOTTO, 8
53024 MONTALCINO [SI]
TEL. +39 0577848476
www.lambardimontalcino.it

CELLAR SALES
PRE-BOOKED VISITS
ANNUAL PRODUCTION 17,000 bottles
HECTARES UNDER VINE 6.50

● Rosso di Montalcino '16	♟♟ 4

Podere Lamberto

VIA DEI POGGIARDELLI, 16
53045 MONTEPULCIANO [SI]
TEL. +39 3337896319
www.poderelamberto.com

CELLAR SALES
ACCOMMODATION AND RESTAURANT SERVICE
ANNUAL PRODUCTION 5,600 bottles
HECTARES UNDER VINE 80.60
VITICULTURE METHOD Certified Organic

● Nobile di Montepulciano '16	♟♟ 4

La Lecciaia

LOC. VALLAFRICO
53024 MONTALCINO [SI]
TEL. +39 0583928366
www.lecciaia.it

PRE-BOOKED VISITS
ANNUAL PRODUCTION 200,000 bottles
HECTARES UNDER VINE 16.00

● Brunello di Montalcino V. Manapetra Ris. '13	♟♟ 6
● Brunello di Montalcino '14	♟ 6
● Brunello di Montalcino Ris. '13	♟ 6

Cantine Leonardo da Vinci

VIA PROVINCIALE MERCATALE, 291
50059 VINCI [FI]
TEL. +39 0571902444
www.leonardodavinci.it

CELLAR SALES
PRE-BOOKED VISITS
ACCOMMODATION AND RESTAURANT SERVICE
ANNUAL PRODUCTION 4,500,000 bottles
HECTARES UNDER VINE 750.00

● Chianti Ris. '15	♟♟ 3
● Chianti Vergine delle Rocce Ris. '15	♟♟ 2*
○ Vermentino '18	♟♟ 2*
● Chianti Vergine delle Rocce '17	♟ 2

Luiano

LOC. MERCATALE VAL DI PESA
VIA DI LUIANO, 32
50024 SAN CASCIANO IN VAL DI PESA [FI]
TEL. +39 055821039
www.luiano.it

CELLAR SALES
PRE-BOOKED VISITS
ACCOMMODATION
ANNUAL PRODUCTION 160,000 bottles
HECTARES UNDER VINE 20.00

● Chianti Cl. Ris. '16	♟♟ 5
● Chianti Cl. Gran Selezione Ottantuno '16	♟♟ 6
● Lui '16	♟♟ 6
● Chianti Cl. '17	♟ 3

Maciarine

S.DA PROV.LE DI POGGIOFERRO
58038 SEGGIANO [GR]
TEL. +39 3487155650
www.maciarine.it

CELLAR SALES
PRE-BOOKED VISITS
ANNUAL PRODUCTION 15,000 bottles
HECTARES UNDER VINE 3.90
SUSTAINABLE WINERY

● Lunaio '15	♥♥ 5
● Maremma Toscana Tordaio '15	♥♥ 2*

La Madonnina

FRAZ. BOLGHERI
VIA BOLGHERESE, 193
57022 CASTAGNETO CARDUCCI [LI]
TEL. +39
www.lamadonninabolgheri.it

HECTARES UNDER VINE 7.00

● Bolgheri Sup. Opera Omnia '16	♥♥ 8
● La Madonnina '16	♥ 8
● Viator '16	♥ 8

La Magia

LOC. LA MAGIA
53024 MONTALCINO [SI]
TEL. +39 0577835667
www.fattorialamagia.it

ANNUAL PRODUCTION 80,000 bottles
HECTARES UNDER VINE 15.00

● Brunello di Montalcino '14	♥♥ 6
● Rosso di Montalcino '17	♥♥ 3

Fattoria di Magliano

FRAZ. MAGLIANO IN TOSCANA
LOC. STERPETI, 10
58051 MAGLIANO IN TOSCANA [GR]
TEL. +39 0564593040
www.fattoriadimagliano.it

CELLAR SALES
PRE-BOOKED VISITS
ACCOMMODATION AND RESTAURANT SERVICE
ANNUAL PRODUCTION 300,000 bottles
HECTARES UNDER VINE 50.00
VITICULTURE METHOD Certified Organic

● Maremma Toscana Rosso Altizi '16	♥♥ 5
● Maremma Toscana Sinarra '16	♥♥ 3
○ Maremma Toscana Vermentino Pagliatura '18	♥ 3

Malenchini

LOC. GRASSINA
VIA LILLIANO E MEOLI, 82
50015 BAGNO A RIPOLI [FI]
TEL. +39 055642602
www.malenchini.it

CELLAR SALES
PRE-BOOKED VISITS
ANNUAL PRODUCTION 120,000 bottles
HECTARES UNDER VINE 17.00

● Bruzzico '16	♥♥ 4
● Chianti Colli Fiorentini Ris. '16	♥♥ 2*
○ Vin Santo del Chianti '14	♥♥ 4
● Canaiolo '17	♥ 3

Podere Marcampo

LOC. SAN CIPRIANO
56048 VOLTERRA [PI]
TEL. +39 058885393
www.poderemarcampo.com

CELLAR SALES
PRE-BOOKED VISITS
ACCOMMODATION AND RESTAURANT SERVICE
ANNUAL PRODUCTION 18,000 bottles
HECTARES UNDER VINE 5.00
VITICULTURE METHOD Certified Organic
SUSTAINABLE WINERY

● Giusto alle Balze '16	♥♥ 5
● Marcampo '17	♥♥ 3
○ Terrablu '18	♥♥ 3
● Genuino '17	♥ 2

Martoccia

LOC. MARTOCCIA
53024 MONTALCINO [SI]
TEL. +39 0577848540
www.poderemartoccia.it

ANNUAL PRODUCTION 85,000 bottles
HECTARES UNDER VINE 15.00

● Brunello di Montalcino '14		▼▼ 6
● Brunello di Montalcino Ris. '13		▼▼ 7
● Rosso di Montalcino '17		▼ 3

Marzocco di Poppiano

FRAZ. POPPIANO
VIA FEZZANA, 36-38
50025 MONTESPERTOLI [FI]
TEL. +39 0555535259
www.marzoccopoppiano.it

CELLAR SALES
ANNUAL PRODUCTION 30,000 bottles
HECTARES UNDER VINE 35.00

● Pretale '15		▼▼ 4
● Vigna del Leone '15		▼▼ 5
● Chianti '17		▼ 3
● Chianti Ris. '16		▼ 4

Máté

LOC. SANTA RESTITUTA
53024 MONTALCINO [SI]
TEL. +39 0577847215
www.matewine.com

CELLAR SALES
PRE-BOOKED VISITS
ACCOMMODATION
ANNUAL PRODUCTION 25,000 bottles
HECTARES UNDER VINE 6.50
VITICULTURE METHOD Certified Organic

● Marinaia '16		▼▼ 6
● Banditone Syrah '15		▼ 7
● Mania Cabernet Sauvignon '16		▼ 7

Giorgio Meletti Cavallari

VIA CASONE UGOLINO, 12
57022 CASTAGNETO CARDUCCI [LI]
TEL. +39 0565775620
www.giorgiomeletticavallari.it

CELLAR SALES
PRE-BOOKED VISITS
ACCOMMODATION
ANNUAL PRODUCTION 40,000 bottles
HECTARES UNDER VINE 10.00

○ Bolgheri Bianco Borgeri '18		▼▼ 3
● Bolgheri Rosso Borgeri '17		▼▼ 3
● Bolgheri Rosso Sup. Impronte '16		▼▼ 5

Micheletti

MARCACCIO, 58
57022 CASTAGNETO CARDUCCI [LI]
TEL. +39 3803295193
www.michelettiwine.com

PRE-BOOKED VISITS
ANNUAL PRODUCTION 30,000 bottles
HECTARES UNDER VINE 5.00

● Bolgheri Rosso Dalleo '17		▼▼ 4
● Bolgheri Sup. Guardione '16		▼▼ 5
● Bolgheri Sup. Poggiomatto '16		▼▼ 5

Fattoria Migliarina & Montozzi

B.GO MIGLIARINA
52021 BUCINE [AR]
TEL. +39 0559789029
www.migliarina.it

CELLAR SALES
PRE-BOOKED VISITS
ACCOMMODATION
ANNUAL PRODUCTION 40,000 bottles
HECTARES UNDER VINE 23.00
VITICULTURE METHOD Certified Organic

● Chianti Sup. Villa Migliarina '17		▼▼ 2*
○ Trebbiano '18		▼▼ 2*
● Valdarno di Sopra Cavasonno '16		▼▼ 2*
● Vinile '16		▼▼ 2*

Mocali

Loc. Mocali
53024 Montalcino [SI]
Tel. +39 0577849485
www.mocali.eu

CELLAR SALES
PRE-BOOKED VISITS
ANNUAL PRODUCTION 120,000 bottles
HECTARES UNDER VINE 9.00
VITICULTURE METHOD Certified Organic
SUSTAINABLE WINERY

● Rosso di Montalcino '17	🍷🍷 3
● Brunello di Montalcino '14	🍷 6

Podere Monastero

Loc. Monastero
53011 Castellina in Chianti [SI]
Tel. +39 0577740436
www.poderemonastero.com

CELLAR SALES
PRE-BOOKED VISITS
ACCOMMODATION
ANNUAL PRODUCTION 7,000 bottles
HECTARES UNDER VINE 3.00

● La Pineta '17	🍷🍷 6
● Campanaio '17	🍷🍷 6

La Montanina

Loc. Monti in Chianti, 25
53020 Gaiole in Chianti [SI]
Tel. +39 0577280074
www.aziendaagricolalamontanina.it

● Chianti Cl. '16	🍷🍷 3*
● Nebbiano '16	🍷🍷 3

Montechiaro

s.da di Montechiaro, 3
53100 Siena
Tel. +39 0577363016
www.terredellagrigia.com

CELLAR SALES
PRE-BOOKED VISITS
ACCOMMODATION AND RESTAURANT SERVICE
ANNUAL PRODUCTION 50,000 bottles
HECTARES UNDER VINE 9.00
VITICULTURE METHOD Certified Organic

● Chianti Colli Senesi 345 Ris. '15	🍷🍷 4
● Primum Vinum '16	🍷🍷 4

Montemercurio

via di Totona, 25a
53045 Montepulciano [SI]
Tel. +39 0578716610
www.montemercurio.com

CELLAR SALES
PRE-BOOKED VISITS
ANNUAL PRODUCTION 40,000 bottles
HECTARES UNDER VINE 10.00
VITICULTURE METHOD Certified Organic

● Nobile di Montepulciano Messaggero '15	🍷🍷 5
● Tediccìolo '16	🍷 2

Monterò

Loc. Colle Lupo
58051 Magliano in Toscana [GR]
Tel. +39 3396024802
www.monterò.com

CELLAR SALES
PRE-BOOKED VISITS
ANNUAL PRODUCTION 13,000 bottles
HECTARES UNDER VINE 6.50
VITICULTURE METHOD Certified Organic
SUSTAINABLE WINERY

○ Maremma Toscana Vermentino '18	🍷🍷 4
⊙ Tetè '18	🍷🍷 3

Giacomo Mori

FRAZ. PALAZZONE
P.ZZA SANDRO PERTINI, 8
53040 SAN CASCIANO DEI BAGNI [SI]
TEL. +39 0578227005
www.giacomomori.it

CELLAR SALES
PRE-BOOKED VISITS
ACCOMMODATION
ANNUAL PRODUCTION 40,000 bottles
HECTARES UNDER VINE 12.00
VITICULTURE METHOD Certified Organic

● Chianti Castelrotto Ris. '16	♈♈ 3
● Chianti '17	♈ 2

Nittardi

LOC. NITTARDI
53011 CASTELLINA IN CHIANTI [SI]
TEL. +39 0577740269
www.nittardi.com

CELLAR SALES
PRE-BOOKED VISITS
ANNUAL PRODUCTION 100,000 bottles
HECTARES UNDER VINE 35.00
VITICULTURE METHOD Certified Organic

● Chianti Cl. V. Doghessa '17	♈♈ 6
● Chianti Cl. Belcanto '17	♈ 4
● Chianti Cl. Ris. '16	♈ 6

Famiglia Nunzi Conti

FRAZ. MERCATALE VAL DI PESA
VIA DI VILLA BARBERINO, 15
50020 SAN CASCIANO IN VAL DI PESA [FI]
TEL. +39 055 8218434
www.famiglianunziconti.it

CELLAR SALES
PRE-BOOKED VISITS
ACCOMMODATION
ANNUAL PRODUCTION 60,000 bottles
HECTARES UNDER VINE 23.00

● Chianti Cl. Gran Selezione V. Elisa '15	♈♈ 8
● Chianti Cl. Ris. '15	♈♈ 5
● Chianti Cl. '17	♈ 5

Oliviera

S.DA PROV.LE 102 DI VAGLIAGLI, 36
53019 CASTELNUOVO BERARDENGA [SI]
TEL. +39 3498950188
www.oliviera.it

ANNUAL PRODUCTION 30,000 bottles
HECTARES UNDER VINE 9.00

● Chianti Cl. Campo di Mansueto '17	♈♈ 3*
● Chianti Cl. Settantanove Ris. '16	♈♈ 3

Fattoria Ormanni

LOC. ORMANNI, 1
53036 POGGIBONSI [SI]
TEL. +39 0577937212
www.ormanni.it

CELLAR SALES
PRE-BOOKED VISITS
ACCOMMODATION
ANNUAL PRODUCTION 120,000 bottles
HECTARES UNDER VINE 68.00

● Julius '16	♈♈ 5
● Canaiolo '18	♈ 3
● Chianti Cl. '16	♈ 3

Ornina

S.DA ORNINA, 121
52016 CASTEL FOCOGNANO [AR]
TEL. +39 3939410053
www.ornina.it

CELLAR SALES
PRE-BOOKED VISITS
ACCOMMODATION
ANNUAL PRODUCTION 7,000 bottles
HECTARES UNDER VINE 3.00

● Ornina '15	♈♈ 3
● Ornoir '16	♈♈ 4
● Vallechiusa Rosso '16	♈♈ 2*
○ Vallechiusa Bianco '17	♈ 2

Orsumella

Loc. Montefiridolfi
via Collina 52
50026 San Casciano in Val di Pesa [FI]
Tel. +39 3395852557
www.orsumella.it

● Chianti Cl. '16	♟♟ 3*
● Rubereto '15	♟♟ 5
● Chianti Cl. Corte Rinieri Ris. '15	♟ 4

Padelletti

via Padelletti, 9
53024 Montalcino [SI]
Tel. +39 0577848314
www.padelletti.it

CELLAR SALES
PRE-BOOKED VISITS
ANNUAL PRODUCTION 30,000 bottles
HECTARES UNDER VINE 6.00

● Rosso di Montalcino '16	♟♟ 3

Pagani de Marchi

Loc. La Nocera
via della Camminata, 2
56040 Casale Marittimo [PI]
Tel. +39 0586653016
www.paganidemarchi.com

CELLAR SALES
PRE-BOOKED VISITS
ANNUAL PRODUCTION 35,000 bottles
HECTARES UNDER VINE 6.50

● Casa Nocera '15	♟♟ 5
● Casalvecchio '16	♟♟ 5
● Montescudaio Principe Guerriero '16	♟♟ 4
● Olmata '16	♟ 4

Fattoria Il Palagio

Fraz. Castel San Gimignano
Loc. Il Palagio
53030 Colle di Val d'Elsa [SI]
Tel. +39 0577953004
www.ilpalagio.it

CELLAR SALES
PRE-BOOKED VISITS
ANNUAL PRODUCTION 800,000 bottles
HECTARES UNDER VINE 79.00

○ Melaia Sauvignon '18	♟♟ 3
○ Vernaccia di S. Gimignano Ginestrelle '17	♟♟ 3
● Chianti Cellini '17	♟ 3
○ Wild Rose '17	♟ 3

La Palazzetta

Fraz. Castelnuovo dell'Abate
Podere La Palazzetta, 1p
53024 Montalcino [SI]
Tel. +39 0577835531
www.palazzettafanti.com

CELLAR SALES
PRE-BOOKED VISITS
ACCOMMODATION
ANNUAL PRODUCTION 70,000 bottles
HECTARES UNDER VINE 28.00
VITICULTURE METHOD Certified Organic
SUSTAINABLE WINERY

● Brunello di Montalcino Ris. '13	♟♟ 6
● Rosso di Montalcino '17	♟♟ 3
● Brunello di Montalcino '14	♟ 5

Pepi Lignana
Fattoria Il Casalone

via Aurelia, 18 km 140,5
58016 Orbetello [GR]
Tel. +39 0564 862160
www.pepilignanawine.com

CELLAR SALES
PRE-BOOKED VISITS
HECTARES UNDER VINE 11.00
SUSTAINABLE WINERY

● Maremma Cabernet Poggio Colombi '16	♟♟ 3*
● Maremma Toscana Cabernet Cucchetto '16	♟♟ 3
● Maremma Toscana Sangiovese Cerida '16	♟♟ 2*
○ Pitorsino '18	♟ 4

Pian delle Querci

VIA GIACOMO LEOPARDI, 10
53024 MONTALCINO [SI]
TEL. +39 0577834174
www.piandellequerci.it

CELLAR SALES
PRE-BOOKED VISITS
ANNUAL PRODUCTION 53,000 bottles
HECTARES UNDER VINE 8.50

● Brunello di Montalcino Ris. '13	🏆🏆 5
● Brunello di Montalcino '14	🏆 5
● Rosso di Montalcino '17	🏆 3

La Piana

VIA ROMA, 25
57032 CAPRAIA ISOLA [LI]
TEL. +39 3920592988
www.lapianacapraia.it

CELLAR SALES
PRE-BOOKED VISITS
ANNUAL PRODUCTION 11,000 bottles
HECTARES UNDER VINE 5.00
VITICULTURE METHOD Certified Organic

● Cristino '18	🏆🏆 5
○ Palmazio '18	🏆🏆 3
⊙ Rosa della Piana '18	🏆 3
● Zenobito '16	🏆 6

Le Pianore

FRAZ. MONTICELLO AMIATA
LOC. PODERE MALADINA, 1
58044 CINIGIANO [GR]
TEL. +39 3355371513
www.lepianore.it

CELLAR SALES
PRE-BOOKED VISITS
ACCOMMODATION AND RESTAURANT SERVICE
ANNUAL PRODUCTION 7,000 bottles
HECTARES UNDER VINE 1.30
VITICULTURE METHOD Certified Organic
SUSTAINABLE WINERY

● Montecucco Rosso Tiniatus '16	🏆🏆 3*
● Montecucco Rosso Tiniatus '17	🏆🏆 3

Piemaggio

LOC. FIORAIE
53011 CASTELLINA IN CHIANTI [SI]
TEL. +39 0577740658

CELLAR SALES
ANNUAL PRODUCTION 40,000 bottles
HECTARES UNDER VINE 11.50
SUSTAINABLE WINERY

● Chianti Cl. Le Fioraie Ris. '13	🏆🏆 4
● Chianti Cl. Le Fioraie '16	🏆🏆 4
● Chianti Cl. Le Fioraie '15	🏆 4

Agostina Pieri

FRAZ. SANT'ANGELO SCALO
LOC. PIANCORNELLO
53024 MONTALCINO [SI]
TEL. +39 0577844163
www.pieriagostina.it

ANNUAL PRODUCTION 45,000 bottles
HECTARES UNDER VINE 10.78

● Brunello di Montalcino '14	🏆🏆 6
● Rosso di Montalcino '17	🏆 3

Podere dell'Anselmo

LOC. ANSELMO
VIA ANSELMO PANFI, 12
50025 MONTESPERTOLI [FI]
TEL. +39 0571671951
www.poderedellanselmo.it

CELLAR SALES
PRE-BOOKED VISITS
ACCOMMODATION AND RESTAURANT SERVICE
ANNUAL PRODUCTION 40,000 bottles
HECTARES UNDER VINE 13.00
VITICULTURE METHOD Certified Organic
SUSTAINABLE WINERY

● Era Ora '15	🏆🏆 4
● Terre di Bracciatica '16	🏆🏆 2*
○ Vin Santo del Chianti Ris. '09	🏆🏆 5

Podere San Giacomo

LOC. VAL DI CAVA
S.DA VICINALE DEI COLLODI
53024 MONTALCINO [SI]
TEL. +39 0577 846050
www.poderesangiacomo.it

HECTARES UNDER VINE 5.00
SUSTAINABLE WINERY

Rosso di Montalcino '16	🍷🍷 5

Poderi del Paradiso

LOC. STRADA, 21A
53037 SAN GIMIGNANO [SI]
TEL. +39 0577941500
www.poderidelparadiso.it

CELLAR SALES
PRE-BOOKED VISITS
ACCOMMODATION
ANNUAL PRODUCTION 130,000 bottles
HECTARES UNDER VINE 27.00

● San Gimignano Rosso Bottaccio '16	🍷🍷 3
○ Vernaccia di S. Gimignano '18	🍷🍷 2*
○ Vernaccia di S. Gimignano Biscondola '17	🍷🍷 3

★Poggio Antico

LOC. POGGIO ANTICO
53024 MONTALCINO [SI]
TEL. +39 0577848044
www.poggioantico.com

CELLAR SALES
PRE-BOOKED VISITS
RESTAURANT SERVICE
ANNUAL PRODUCTION 120,000 bottles
HECTARES UNDER VINE 32.00

Rosso di Montalcino '17	🍷🍷 5
Madre '16	🍷 6

Poggio Bonelli

VIA DELL'ARBIA, 2
53019 CASTELNUOVO BERARDENGA [SI]
TEL. +39 057756661
www.poggiobonelli.it

CELLAR SALES
PRE-BOOKED VISITS
ACCOMMODATION
ANNUAL PRODUCTION 125,000 bottles
HECTARES UNDER VINE 87.00

● Chianti Cl. Ris. '16	🍷🍷 5
● Chianti Cl. '16	🍷 3
● Poggiassai '15	🍷 6

Poggio Grande

LOC. POGGIO GRANDE, 11
53023 CASTIGLIONE D'ORCIA [SI]
TEL. +39 3388677637
www.aziendapoggiogrande.it

CELLAR SALES
PRE-BOOKED VISITS
ANNUAL PRODUCTION 22,000 bottles
HECTARES UNDER VINE 6.50

Orcia Sangiovese Sesterzo Ris. '15	🍷🍷 5
Orcia Scorbutico '16	🍷🍷 3

Poggio La Noce

LOC. ONTIGNANO
VIA PAIATICI, 29
50014 FIESOLE [FI]
TEL. +39 0556549113
www.poggiolanoce.com

CELLAR SALES
PRE-BOOKED VISITS
ANNUAL PRODUCTION 10,000 bottles
HECTARES UNDER VINE 2.50
VITICULTURE METHOD Certified Organic

● Gigetto '16	🍷🍷 4
● Gigino '16	🍷🍷 5
● Gigiò '15	🍷🍷 6
● Paonazzo '14	🍷 7

Poggio Mandorlo

LOC. ANSIDONINA
58038 SEGGIANO [GR]
TEL. +39 3298825633
www.poggiomandorlo.it

CELLAR SALES
ANNUAL PRODUCTION 62,000 bottles
HECTARES UNDER VINE 12.00

● Il Guardiano '15	♟♟	3
● Montecucco Sangiovese La Querce '13	♟	4

Tenuta Poggio Rosso

FRAZ. POPULONIA
LOC. POGGIO ROSSO, 1
57025 PIOMBINO [LI]
TEL. +39 056529553
www.tenutapoggiorosso.it

CELLAR SALES
PRE-BOOKED VISITS
ACCOMMODATION
ANNUAL PRODUCTION 35,000 bottles
HECTARES UNDER VINE 6.00

○ Phylika '18	♟♟	3
● Tages '17	♟♟	4
● Velthune '16	♟♟	6
○ Feronia '18	♟	4

Podere Poggio Scalette

LOC. RUFFOLI
VIA BARBIANO, 7
50022 GREVE IN CHIANTI [FI]
TEL. +39 0558546108
www.poggioscalette.it

CELLAR SALES
PRE-BOOKED VISITS
ACCOMMODATION
ANNUAL PRODUCTION 60,000 bottles
HECTARES UNDER VINE 15.00

● Capogatto '16	♟♟	7
● Chianti Cl. '17	♟♟	3

Priorino

VIA MARTIRI DELLA LIBERTÀ, 16
53045 MONTEPULCIANO [SI]
TEL. +39 0578707841
www.cantinapriorino.com

ANNUAL PRODUCTION 18,000 bottles
HECTARES UNDER VINE 6.00

● Amore '15	♟♟	3
○ Solarina '18	♟♟	3
● Umore e Luce '15	♟♟	3
● Fonte al Giunco '18	♟	3

Provveditore

LOC. SALAIOLO, 174
58054 SCANSANO [GR]
TEL. +39 3487018670
www.provveditore.net

CELLAR SALES
PRE-BOOKED VISITS
RESTAURANT SERVICE
ANNUAL PRODUCTION 15,000 bottles
HECTARES UNDER VINE 40.00

○ Maremma Toscana Vermentino Il Bargaglino '18	♟♟	2*
● Morellino di Scansano Primo Ris. '16	♟	4

★Querciabella

VIA DI BARBIANO, 17
50022 GREVE IN CHIANTI [FI]
TEL. +39 05585927777
www.querciabella.com

CELLAR SALES
PRE-BOOKED VISITS
ANNUAL PRODUCTION 300,000 bottles
HECTARES UNDER VINE 112.00
VITICULTURE METHOD Certified Organic

● Camartina '15	♟♟	
● Chianti Cl. Ris. '16	♟♟	
● Chianti Cl. '17	♟	
● Palafreno '15	♟	

Ridolfi

LOC. MERCATALI
3024 MONTALCINO [SI]
TEL. +39 05771698333
www.ridolfimontalcino.it

ANNUAL PRODUCTION 110,000 bottles
HECTARES UNDER VINE 19.00

Rosso di Montalcino '17	▼▼ 4
Brunello di Montalcino '14	▼▼ 5
Brunello di Montalcino Donna Rebecca '14	▼▼ 5

Tenute delle Ripalte

LOC. RIPALTE
57031 CAPOLIVERI [LI]
TEL. +39 056594211
www.tenutadelleripalte.it

CELLAR SALES
PRE-BOOKED VISITS
ACCOMMODATION AND RESTAURANT SERVICE
ANNUAL PRODUCTION 60,000 bottles
HECTARES UNDER VINE 15.00
SUSTAINABLE WINERY

○ Bianco Mediterraneo Le Ripalte '18	▼▼ 3
● Elba Aleatico Passito Alea Ludendo '15	▼▼ 6
● Rosso Mediterraneo Alicante '18	▼▼ 3

Leonardo Salustri

AZ. POGGI DEL SASSO
LOC. LA CAVA, 7
3044 CINIGIANO [GR]
TEL. +39 0564990529
www.salustri.it

CELLAR SALES
PRE-BOOKED VISITS
ACCOMMODATION
ANNUAL PRODUCTION 80,000 bottles
HECTARES UNDER VINE 25.00
VITICULTURE METHOD Certified Organic
SUSTAINABLE WINERY

Montecucco Sangiovese Santa Marta '16	▼▼ 4
Montecucco Sangiovese Grotte Rosse '16	▼ 6

San Benedetto

LOC. SAN BENEDETTO, 4A
53037 SAN GIMIGNANO [SI]
TEL. +39 3386958705
www.agrisanbenedetto.com

CELLAR SALES
PRE-BOOKED VISITS
ACCOMMODATION
ANNUAL PRODUCTION 40,000 bottles
HECTARES UNDER VINE 25.00

○ Vermentino '18	▼▼ 2*
○ Vernaccia di San Gimignano Ris. '16	▼▼ 3
● Chianti '17	▼ 2
● Chianti Ris. '15	▼ 4

Tenuta San Giorgio

LOC. SAN GIORGIO
AZ. CASTELNUOVO DELL'ABATE
3024 MONTALCINO [SI]
TEL. +39 0577835502
www.collemassari.it

CELLAR SALES
PRE-BOOKED VISITS
ANNUAL PRODUCTION 50,000 bottles
HECTARES UNDER VINE 30.00

Brunello di Montalcino Ugolforte '14	▼▼ 6
Rosso di Montalcino Ciampoleto '17	▼ 4

Tenuta San Vito

VIA SAN VITO, 59
50056 MONTELUPO FIORENTINO [FI]
TEL. +39 057151411
www.san-vito.com

CELLAR SALES
PRE-BOOKED VISITS
ACCOMMODATION AND RESTAURANT SERVICE
ANNUAL PRODUCTION 150,000 bottles
HECTARES UNDER VINE 35.00
VITICULTURE METHOD Certified Organic

● Chianti Colli Fiorentini Darno '17	▼▼ 2*
● Colle dei Mandorli '16	▼▼ 6
● Chianti Colli Fiorentini Madiere Ris. '16	▼ 3
● Chianti San Vito '18	▼ 2

SanCarlo

FRAZ. TAVERNELLE
LOC. SAN CARLO
53024 MONTALCINO [SI]
TEL. +39 0577 848616
www.sancarlomontalcino.it

CELLAR SALES
PRE-BOOKED VISITS
ANNUAL PRODUCTION 10,000 bottles
HECTARES UNDER VINE 3.00
SUSTAINABLE WINERY

● Brunello di Montalcino '14	▼▼ 5
● Rosso di Montalcino '16	▼▼ 3

Sant'Agnese

LOC. CAMPO ALLE FAVE, 1
57025 PIOMBINO [LI]
TEL. +39 0565277069
www.santagnesefarm.it

CELLAR SALES
PRE-BOOKED VISITS
ANNUAL PRODUCTION 25,000 bottles
HECTARES UNDER VINE 6.00
SUSTAINABLE WINERY

● I Fiori Blu '13	▼▼ 6
○ Kalendamaia '18	▼▼ 2*
● Rubido '16	▼▼ 2*
● Spirto '13	▼ 5

Podere Santa Felicita

LOC. CIVETTAJA
FRAZ. CUNA
52015 PRATOVECCHIO STIA [AR]
TEL. +39 335453072
staderini@cuna.cloud

ANNUAL PRODUCTION 6,000 bottles
HECTARES UNDER VINE 4.00

● Cuna '16	▼▼ 7

SassodiSole

FRAZ. TORRENIERI
LOC. SASSO DI SOLE, 85
53024 MONTALCINO [SI]
TEL. +39 0577834303
www.sassodisole.it

CELLAR SALES
PRE-BOOKED VISITS
ANNUAL PRODUCTION 45,000 bottles
HECTARES UNDER VINE 10.00
SUSTAINABLE WINERY

● Brunello di Montalcino Ris. '13	▼▼ 8
● Rosso di Montalcino '17	▼▼ 4
● Brunello di Montalcino '14	▼ 8

Savignola Paolina

VIA PETRIOLO, 58
50022 GREVE IN CHIANTI [FI]
TEL. +39 0558546036
www.savignolapaolina.it

CELLAR SALES
PRE-BOOKED VISITS
ACCOMMODATION
ANNUAL PRODUCTION 35,000 bottles
HECTARES UNDER VINE 6.00

● Chianti Cl. Ris. '16	▼▼ 4
● Chianti Cl. Gran Selezione 360° '16	▼ 3

Fulvio Luigi Serni

LOC. LE LAME, 237
57022 CASTAGNETO CARDUCCI [LI]
TEL. +39 0565763585
www.sernifulvioluigi.it

CELLAR SALES
PRE-BOOKED VISITS
ANNUAL PRODUCTION 20,000 bottles
HECTARES UNDER VINE 3.50

● Bolgheri Rosso Acciderba '16	▼▼ 4
● Bolgheri Rosso Tegoleto '17	▼▼ 3
○ Bolgheri Bianco Le Lame '18	▼ 2

Serraiola

AZ. FRASSINE
LOC. SERRAIOLA
58025 MONTEROTONDO MARITTIMO [GR]
TEL. +39 0566910026
www.serraiola.it

CELLAR SALES
PRE-BOOKED VISITS
ANNUAL PRODUCTION 40,000 bottles
HECTARES UNDER VINE 12.00

Lentisco '17	♟♟	3
Vermentino '18	♟♟	3
Violina '18	♟	3

Tenuta Sette Cieli

FRAZ. LA CALIFORNIA
VIA SANDRO PERTINI
57020 BIBBONA [LI]
TEL. +39 0586677435
www.tenutasettecieli.com

ANNUAL PRODUCTION 92,000 bottles
HECTARES UNDER VINE 15.00
VITICULTURE METHOD Certified Organic
SUSTAINABLE WINERY

● Bolgheri Rosso Noi 4 '16	♟♟	5
● Indaco '15	♟♟	7
● Scipio '15	♟♟	8

Borgo La Stella

LOC. VAGLIAGLI
PODGO LA STELLA, 60
53017 RADDA IN CHIANTI [SI]
TEL. +39 0577740699
www.borgolastella.com

ANNUAL PRODUCTION 21,000 bottles
HECTARES UNDER VINE 4.50

Chianti Cl. Ris. '15	♟♟	5
Chianti Cl. Gran Selezione '16	♟♟	4
Chirone '15	♟♟	4
Chirone '16	♟	4

Stomennano

LOC. BORGO STOMENNANO
53035 MONTERIGGIONI [SI]
TEL. +39 0577304033
www.stomennano.it

CELLAR SALES
PRE-BOOKED VISITS
ACCOMMODATION
ANNUAL PRODUCTION 50,000 bottles
HECTARES UNDER VINE 25.00
SUSTAINABLE WINERY

● Chianti '18	♟♟	3
● Chianti Cl. '17	♟♟	5

Fattoria della Talosa

VIA TALOSA, 8
53045 MONTEPULCIANO [SI]
TEL. +39 0578758277
www.talosa.it

CELLAR SALES
PRE-BOOKED VISITS
ANNUAL PRODUCTION 100,000 bottles
HECTARES UNDER VINE 33.00

Nobile di Montepulciano Filai Lunghi '16	♟♟	6
Rosso di Montepulciano '18	♟♟	2*
Nobile di Montepulciano Alboreto '16	♟	4
Nobile di Montepulciano Ris. '15	♟	5

Agricola Tamburini

VIA CATIGNANO, 106
50050 GAMBASSI TERME [FI]
TEL. +39 0571680235
www.agricolatamburini.it

CELLAR SALES
PRE-BOOKED VISITS
ANNUAL PRODUCTION 90,000 bottles
HECTARES UNDER VINE 30.00

● Chianti Italo Ris. '15	♟♟	3
● Il Moraccio '15	♟♟	4
● Brunello di Montalcino Somnio '14	♟	6
● Chianti The Boss '16	♟	2

Tassi

v.le P. Strozzi, 1/3
53024 Montalcino [SI]
Tel. +39 0577848025
www.tassimontalcino.com

ANNUAL PRODUCTION 20,000 bottles
HECTARES UNDER VINE 5.00

● Brunello di Montalcino Franci Ris. '13	▼▼	8
● Rosso di Montalcino '16	▼▼	4
● Brunello di Montalcino '14	▼	7

Tenuta Buon Tempo

loc. Oliveto
53033 Montalcino [SI]
Tel. +39 3386707362
www.tenutabuontempo.it

HECTARES UNDER VINE 14.00
SUSTAINABLE WINERY

● Brunello di Montalcino '14	▼▼
● Brunello di Montalcino Oliveto P. 56 '14	▼▼
● Rosso di Montalcino '16	▼▼

Tenuta dello Scompiglio

via di Vorno, 67
55012 Capannori [LU]
Tel. +39 0583971438
www.delloscompiglio.org

CELLAR SALES
PRE-BOOKED VISITS
RESTAURANT SERVICE
ANNUAL PRODUCTION 8,000 bottles
HECTARES UNDER VINE 5.00
VITICULTURE METHOD Certified Organic
SUSTAINABLE WINERY

● Lavandaia Pura '16	▼▼	4
● Lavandaia Madre '16	▼	5

Tenuta di Castelfalfi

loc. Castelfalfi
50050 Montaione [FI]
Tel. +39 0571890190
www.castelfalfi.it

CELLAR SALES
PRE-BOOKED VISITS
ACCOMMODATION AND RESTAURANT SERVICE
ANNUAL PRODUCTION 50,000 bottles
HECTARES UNDER VINE 25.00
VITICULTURE METHOD Certified Organic

● Poggio alla Fame '15	▼▼
○ Poggio I Soli '18	▼▼
● Poggionero '15	▼▼
● Chianti Cerchiaia '17	▼

Tenute di Fraternita

via Vasari, 6
52100 Arezzo
Tel. +39 057524694
www.tenutedifraternita.it

PRE-BOOKED VISITS
HECTARES UNDER VINE 50.70

● Messer Angelo '15	▼▼	4
● Vin Santo del Chianti Occhio di Pernice '15	▼▼	4
○ Bianco Lya '18	▼	3
● Sangiovese '16	▼	3

Tenute Palagetto

via Monteoliveto, 46
53037 San Gimignano [SI]
Tel. +39 0577943090
www.palagetto.it

CELLAR SALES
PRE-BOOKED VISITS
ACCOMMODATION
ANNUAL PRODUCTION 250,000 bottles
HECTARES UNDER VINE 44.00

○ Vernaccia di S. Gimignano '18	▼▼
○ Vernaccia di S. Gimignano V. Santa Chiara '18	▼▼
● Chianti Colli Senesi Ris. '14	▼

Terre del Fondo

LOC. CASINO
53020 TREQUANDA [SI]
TEL. +39 0577662001
www.azienda-trequanda.it

CELLAR SALES
PRE-BOOKED VISITS
ACCOMMODATION AND RESTAURANT SERVICE
ANNUAL PRODUCTION 250,000 bottles
HECTARES UNDER VINE 55.00

● Colli del Trasimeno Sant'Anna Ris. '15	♟♟	3*
○ Colli del Trasimeno Vin Santo '14	♟♟	4
○ Ghirlandaia Sauvignon '18	♟♟	2*
● TreCalici '16	♟♟	3

Terre Nere

LOC. CASTELNUOVO DELL'ABATE
53024 MONTALCINO [SI]
TEL. +39 3490971713
www.terreneremontalcino.it

CELLAR SALES
PRE-BOOKED VISITS
ACCOMMODATION
ANNUAL PRODUCTION 50,000 bottles
HECTARES UNDER VINE 10.00

● Brunello di Montalcino Ris. '13	♟♟	6
● Rosso di Montalcino '17	♟♟	3
● Brunello di Montalcino '14	♟	6

Tiezzi

LOC. PODERE SOCCORSO
53024 MONTALCINO [SI]
TEL. +39 3479565201
www.tiezzivini.it

CELLAR SALES
PRE-BOOKED VISITS
ACCOMMODATION
ANNUAL PRODUCTION 30,000 bottles
HECTARES UNDER VINE 6.00
SUSTAINABLE WINERY

● Brunello di Montalcino V. Soccorso '14	♟♟	6
● Brunello di Montalcino V. Soccorso Ris. '13	♟♟	6
● Brunello di Montalcino Poggio Cerrino '14	♟	5

Tollena

VIA SAN GIOVANNI, 69
53037 SAN GIMIGNANO [SI]
TEL. +39 0577907178
www.tollena.it

CELLAR SALES
ACCOMMODATION
ANNUAL PRODUCTION 50,000 bottles
HECTARES UNDER VINE 22.00

○ Vernaccia di San Gimignano Signorina Vittoria Ris. '15	♟♟	3
○ Vernaccia San Gimignano Lunario '18	♟♟	2*

Torre a Cenaia

LOC. CENAIA
VIA DELLE COLLINE, 55
56040 CRESPINA LORENZANA [PI]
TEL. +39 050643739
www.torreacenaia.it

CELLAR SALES
PRE-BOOKED VISITS
ACCOMMODATION AND RESTAURANT SERVICE
ANNUAL PRODUCTION 150,000 bottles
HECTARES UNDER VINE 30.00
VITICULTURE METHOD Certified Organic

● Per Non Dormire '16	♟♟	8
● Pitti Sangiovese '17	♟♟	5
● Torre del Vajo '16	♟♟	6

Le Torri

VIA SAN LORENZO A VIGLIANO, 31
50021 BARBERINO VAL D'ELSA [FI]
TEL. +39 0558076161
www.letorri.net

CELLAR SALES
PRE-BOOKED VISITS
ACCOMMODATION AND RESTAURANT SERVICE
ANNUAL PRODUCTION 170,000 bottles
HECTARES UNDER VINE 28.00
SUSTAINABLE WINERY

● Magliano '16	♟♟	5
● Meridius '16	♟♟	2*
○ Soleluna '18	♟	2

Marchesi Torrigiani

FRAZ. VICO D'ELSA
P.ZZA TORRIGIANI, 15
50021 BARBERINO VAL D'ELSA [FI]
TEL. +39 0558073001
www.marchesitorrigiani.it

CELLAR SALES
PRE-BOOKED VISITS
ANNUAL PRODUCTION 140,000 bottles
HECTARES UNDER VINE 33.00

● Chianti '18	▼▼ 2*
● Guidaccio '15	▼▼ 5
● Torre di Ciardo '16	▼▼ 3

Castello Tricerchi

LOC. ALTESI
53024 MONTALCINO [SI]
TEL. +39 3472501884
www.castellotricerchi.com

CELLAR SALES
PRE-BOOKED VISITS
ANNUAL PRODUCTION 40,000 bottles
HECTARES UNDER VINE 13.00

● Rosso di Montalcino '17	▼▼
● Brunello di Montalcino Ris. '13	▼

Fattoria Uccelliera

VIA RONCIONE, 9
56042 CRESPINA LORENZANA [PI]
TEL. +39 050662747
www.uccelliera.com

CELLAR SALES
PRE-BOOKED VISITS
ACCOMMODATION
ANNUAL PRODUCTION 100,000 bottles
HECTARES UNDER VINE 16.00

● 7 Dieci Syrah '15	▼▼ 4
● Ginepraia Rosso '16	▼▼ 2*
○ Isola '18	▼▼ 3

Usiglian Del Vescovo

VIA USIGLIANO, 26
56036 PALAIA [PI]
TEL. +39 0587468000
www.usigliandelvescovo.it

CELLAR SALES
PRE-BOOKED VISITS
RESTAURANT SERVICE
ANNUAL PRODUCTION 130,000 bottles
HECTARES UNDER VINE 23.00
VITICULTURE METHOD Certified Organic
SUSTAINABLE WINERY

● Il Barbiglione '15	▼▼
● MilleEottantatre '15	▼▼
● Mora del Roveto '17	▼▼

Valle di Lazzaro

LOC. VALLE DI LAZZARO, 103
57037 PORTOFERRAIO [LI]
TEL. +39 0565916387
www.valledilazzaro.com

CELLAR SALES
PRE-BOOKED VISITS
ANNUAL PRODUCTION 12,000 bottles
HECTARES UNDER VINE 4.00

○ Chardonnay Lazarus '18	▼▼ 4
○ Elba Ansonica Lazarus '18	▼▼ 3
○ Elba Vermentino Lazarus '18	▼▼ 3
○ Elba Trebbiano Procanico '18	▼ 3

Valvirginio

VIA NUOVA DEL VIRGINIO, 34
50025 MONTESPERTOLI [FI]
TEL. +39 0571659127
www.collifiorentini.it

CELLAR SALES
PRE-BOOKED VISITS
ANNUAL PRODUCTION 1,000,000 bottles
HECTARES UNDER VINE 1500.00
VITICULTURE METHOD Certified Organic
SUSTAINABLE WINERY

● Baron del Nero '15	▼▼
○ Vin Santo del Chianti Santa Pazienza '09	▼▼
● Chianti Cl. Rifugio del Vescovo '15	▼
○ Vermentino '18	▼

Vecchia Cantina di Montepulciano

VIA PROVINCIALE, 7
53045 MONTEPULCIANO [SI]
TEL. +39 0578716092
www.vecchiacantinadimontepulciano.com

CELLAR SALES
PRE-BOOKED VISITS
ANNUAL PRODUCTION 4,500,000 bottles
HECTARES UNDER VINE 1000.00
VITICULTURE METHOD Certified Organic

● Nobile di Montepulciano Briareo Ris. Cantina dei Redi '15	▼▼ 5
● Orbaio Cantina dei Redi '16	▼▼ 5

Ventolaio

LOC. VENTOLAIO, 51
53024 MONTALCINO [SI]
TEL. +39 0577835779

CELLAR SALES
PRE-BOOKED VISITS
ANNUAL PRODUCTION 70,000 bottles
HECTARES UNDER VINE 14.00

● Brunello di Montalcino '14	▼▼ 6
● Rosso di Montalcino '17	▼ 4
● Sentiero del Fante '18	▼ 3

Verbena

LOC. VERBENA, 100
53024 MONTALCINO [SI]
TEL. +39 0577846035
www.aziendaverbena.it

CELLAR SALES
PRE-BOOKED VISITS
ANNUAL PRODUCTION 50,000 bottles
HECTARES UNDER VINE 10.00

● Rosso di Montalcino '17	▼▼ 4
● Brunello di Montalcino '14	▼ 5
● Brunello di Montalcino Ris. '13	▼ 7

I Vicini

FRAZ. PIETRAIA DI CORTONA
LOC. CASE SPARSE 38 A
52044 CORTONA [AR]
TEL. +39 0575678507
www.ivicinicortona.it

CELLAR SALES
PRE-BOOKED VISITS
ACCOMMODATION
ANNUAL PRODUCTION 66,000 bottles
HECTARES UNDER VINE 10.00

● Cortona Merlot Laudario '16	▼▼ 3
● Cortona Syrah Laudario '15	▼▼ 4
● Cortona Cabernet Sauvignon Laudario '16	▼ 3

Villa al Cortile

LOC. PODERUCCIO
53024 MONTALCINO [SI]
TEL. +39 057741011
www.tenutepiccini.it

ANNUAL PRODUCTION 45,000 bottles
HECTARES UNDER VINE 12.00

● Brunello di Montalcino Ris. '13	▼▼ 7
● Rosso di Montalcino '17	▼▼ 3

Villa Calcinaia

FRAZ. GRETI
VIA CITILLE, 84
50022 GREVE IN CHIANTI [FI]
TEL. +39 055853715
www.villacalcinaia.it

CELLAR SALES
PRE-BOOKED VISITS
ACCOMMODATION
ANNUAL PRODUCTION 90,000 bottles
HECTARES UNDER VINE 27.00
VITICULTURE METHOD Certified Organic

● Chianti Cl. Gran Selezione V. Contessa Luisa '16	▼▼ 6
● Chianti Cl. Gran Selezione V. La Fornace '16	▼▼ 5

Villa La Ripa

LOC. ANTRIA, 38
52100 AREZZO
TEL. +39 057523330
www.villalaripa.it

CELLAR SALES
PRE-BOOKED VISITS
ANNUAL PRODUCTION 10,000 bottles
HECTARES UNDER VINE 5.00
SUSTAINABLE WINERY

● Psyco '16	♟♟ 5
● Syrah '16	♟♟ 6
● Tiratari '16	♟♟ 5
○ Namastè '18	♟ 2

Villa Le Prata

LOC. LE PRATA, 261
53024 MONTALCINO [SI]
TEL. +39 0577848325
www.villaleprata.com

CELLAR SALES
PRE-BOOKED VISITS
ANNUAL PRODUCTION 15,000 bottles
HECTARES UNDER VINE 4.00

● Brunello di Montalcino '14	♟♟ 6
● Rosso di Montalcino '17	♟ 3

Villa Pillo

VIA VOLTERRANA, 24
50050 GAMBASSI TERME [FI]
TEL. +39 0571680212
www.villapillo.com

CELLAR SALES
PRE-BOOKED VISITS
ANNUAL PRODUCTION 350,000 bottles
HECTARES UNDER VINE 40.00

● Borgoforte '17	♟♟ 3
● Cypresses Sangiovese '17	♟♟ 3
● Sant'Adele Merlot '17	♟♟ 5
● Syrah '17	♟♟ 5

Villa Pinciana

S.DA VILLA PINCIANA, 2A
58011 CAPALBIO [GR]
TEL. +39 0564896598
www.villapinciana.com

CELLAR SALES
PRE-BOOKED VISITS
ANNUAL PRODUCTION 35,000 bottles
HECTARES UNDER VINE 8.50

○ Maremma Toscana Bianco Airali '18	♟♟ 3
● Tilaria '15	♟♟ 3

Fattoria Villa Saletta

LOC. MONTANELLI
VIA E. FERMI, 14
56036 PALAIA [PI]
TEL. +39 0587628121
www.villasaletta.com

ANNUAL PRODUCTION 50,000 bottles
HECTARES UNDER VINE 21.00

● 980 AD '15	♟♟ 8
● Saletta Giulia '15	♟♟ 8
● Chianti '15	♟ 5

Villanoviana

LOC. SANT'UBERTO
FRAZ. BOLGHERI
VIA SANTA MADDALENA, 172B
57022 CASTAGNETO CARDUCCI [LI]
TEL. +39 05861881227
www.villanoviana.it

ANNUAL PRODUCTION 30,000 bottles
HECTARES UNDER VINE 4.00
VITICULTURE METHOD Certified Organic

● Cabernet Franc '16	♟♟ 6
● Bolgheri Rosso Imeneo '17	♟♟ 5
● Bolgheri Sup. Sant'Uberto '16	♟♟ 8

MARCHE

A quick look through the list of Marche's Tre Bicchieri would make it seem as if the region's wine industry were stuck, or almost stuck. Verdicchio put in its usual good showing, with Matelica aptly confirming its importance, achieving four awards to Jesi's nine (which is, in realty, 10 times greater in size). In the region's south, there's the growing quality of Pecorino on the one hand and historically well-suited Montepulciano on the other at times blended with Sangiovese for Piceno Superiore). Lacrima di Morro d'Alba proves that the historic result achieved last year with Marotti Campi's exploit wasn't just a one off, and convincingly delivered. Unfortunately there was not much outstanding about Macerato this year (apart from the areas where Verdicchio is cultivated, naturally) and Pesaro. But in reality the situation is much more fluid than it would appear. An attentive eye would notice never-before recognized wineries, like Fattoria Nannì, Pantaleone, Tenuta dell'Ugolino and Vignamato. Others, like Valter 'Roccia' Mattoni and Montecappone, are back with Tre Bicchieri after going some years without one. Collestefano, Bucci, Dianetti, Pisci and Belisario savor their success after a brief pause. This is a clear sign that the region's various wineries are part of a generally positive trajectory that's increasingly difficult to evaluate and discern — at times the differences are small. And so we invite you to leaf through the following pages, reading attentively. In addition to the usual quality exhibited by Andrea Felici, Borgo Paglianetto, Le Caniette, Tenuta Santori, Tenuta Spinelli, Tenute San Sisto - Fazi Battaglia, Umani Ronchi and Velenosi, the reader will find a number of interesting producers, all capable of exquisite wines. In short, don't ignore those bottles marked with Due Bicchieri Rossi and you'll discover that many areas off the radar are growing steadily, often thanks to apt investments, good ideas and plenty of passion. To close, we'd like to make note of the good vibrations coming from Colli Maceratesi's Ribona, Metauro's Bianchello, the exquisiteness of Piceno's Bordò, and the elegant Montepulciano being made at the foot of Monte Conero, using grapes that breathe the salty Adriatic air.

MARCHE

Maria Letizia Allevi

VIA PESCOLLA
63081 CASTORANO [AP]
TEL. +39 3494063412
www.vinimida.it

CELLAR SALES
PRE-BOOKED VISITS
ANNUAL PRODUCTION 10,000 bottles
HECTARES UNDER VINE 5.00
VITICULTURE METHOD Certified Organic

Despite his involvement in other activities, Roberto Corradetti spends every minute of his spare time contributing to his wife Maria Letizia Allevi's winery. The results can be seen in the care with which he tends to the vineyards and the meticulous attention paid in the cellar, where the white and rosé wines mature in steel drums and the reds in wood barrels. Exclusively local varieties, no chemicals and strictly minimal protocols result in interpretations of vibrant authenticity and energy. The Offida Rosso Mida '16 exhibits all the flesh and generous texture of traditional Montepulciano, adorning it with fruity sensations and the occasional delicate vegetal note brought about by the cool season. The Arsi '16 features charming aromas of aromatic herbs, scrubland, licorice, myrtle and a profiled, gritty palate with balanced density. The Mida Pecorino '18 calls up aromas of candied grapefruit and wild herbs in a flavorful, invigorating, tasty palate.

● Arsi '16	♈♈ 8
● Offida Rosso Mida '16	♈♈ 4
○ Offida Pecorino Mida '18	♈♈ 3
● Mida Pecorino Pas Dosé M. Cl. '16	♈ 4
○ Offida Pecorino Mida '16	♈♈♈ 3*
⊙ Mida '13	♈♈ 3
⊙ Mida Rosato '16	♈♈ 3
○ Offida Pecorino Mida '17	♈♈ 3*
○ Offida Pecorino Mida '15	♈♈ 3
● Offida Rosso Mida '15	♈♈ 4
● Offida Rosso Mida '14	♈♈ 3
● Offida Rosso Mida '13	♈♈ 3
● Offida Rosso Mida '11	♈♈ 4

Aurora

LOC. SANTA MARIA IN CARRO
C.DA CIAFONE, 98
63073 OFFIDA [AP]
TEL. +39 0736810007
www.viniaurora.it

CELLAR SALES
PRE-BOOKED VISITS
ACCOMMODATION
ANNUAL PRODUCTION 53,300 bottles
HECTARES UNDER VINE 9.50
VITICULTURE METHOD Certified Organic

The years go by, the seasons change and Aurora's 'boys' have become a bit whiter at the temples, but they have not lost an ounce of their attachment to the values of rural culture grounded in human relations of friendship and mutual solidarity. Pioneers of organic farming and strenuous defenders of both local varieties and artisa practices, they create wines with a strong identity that is unlikely to compromise or bend to the fashions of the moment: they tell the story of the Offida territory with exceptional expressive fidelity. Barricadiero remains their best wine. The 2016 features fruit that's fresher than usual. The palate is racy and lively, despite its close-woven tannic weave, finishing on close-focused aromas of morello cherry. Their Rosso Piceno Superiore '17 follows a similar track, though with even greater tannic presence (grainy at this stage). The Offida Pecorino Fiobbo '17 is rustic and a bit acidulous on the nose, a result of its evident lift, but in the mouth it proves high flavorful and persistent with nice contrast.

● Barricadiero '16	♈♈ 4
○ Offida Pecorino Fiobbo '17	♈♈ 3
● Rosso Piceno Sup. '17	♈♈ 3
● Falerio '18	♈ 2
● Rosso Piceno '18	♈ 2
● Barricadiero '10	♈♈♈ 4
● Barricadiero '09	♈♈♈ 4
● Barricadiero '06	♈♈♈ 4
● Barricadiero '04	♈♈♈ 3
● Barricadiero '03	♈♈♈ 3
● Barricadiero '02	♈♈♈ 3
● Barricadiero '01	♈♈♈ 3
● Offida Rosso Barricadiero '11	♈♈♈ 4
○ Offida Pecorino Fiobbo '16	♈♈ 3
● Offida Rosso Barricadiero '15	♈♈ 4
● Rosso Piceno Sup. '16	♈♈ 2

Belisario

VIA ARISTIDE MERLONI, 12
62024 MATELICA [MC]
TEL. +39 0737787247
www.belisario.it

CELLAR SALES
PRE-BOOKED VISITS
ANNUAL PRODUCTION 1,000,000 bottles
HECTARES UNDER VINE 300.00

For almost fifty years, Belisario has been supporting the many small vintners in the upper Esino valley: the cooperative enables constant mapping and valuable coordination of work of its members' lands. At its historic headquarters, Matelica is treated with a strong personality and clear stylistic characterization that expresses itself on several eloquent registers: from wines with approachable fragrance to more complex versions induced by judicious maturation on the vine and patient aging in the cellar. Their Cambrugiano '16 proves to be a great version, fusing Verdicchio's sensual, creamy palate with Matelica's signature sapidity, intimate and long, making for a finish of extreme elegance. Their Meridia '16 also performs at a high level, bringing together Valbona's mineral nose with the supple flavor of Del Cerro and the delicately salty dynamics of Vigneti B.

○ Verdicchio di Matelica	
Cambrugiano Ris. '16	♀♀♀ 3*
○ Verdicchio di Matelica Meridia '16	♀♀ 3*
○ Verdicchio di Matelica Anfora '18	♀♀ 2*
○ Verdicchio di Matelica Del Cerro '18	♀♀ 2*
○ Verdicchio di Matelica	
Terre di Valbona '18	♀♀ 2*
○ Verdicchio di Matelica Vign. B. '18	♀♀ 3
● Colli Maceratesi Rosso Coll'Amato '18	♀ 2
○ Verdicchio di Matelica	
Cambrugiano Ris. '14	♀♀♀ 3*
○ Verdicchio di Matelica	
Cambrugiano Ris. '12	♀♀♀ 3*
○ Verdicchio di Matelica	
Cambrugiano Ris. '08	♀♀♀ 3*
○ Verdicchio di Matelica Meridia '10	♀♀♀ 3*
○ Verdicchio di Matelica Vign. B. '15	♀♀♀ 3*

Bisci

VIA FOGLIANO, 120
62024 MATELICA [MC]
TEL. +39 0737787490
www.bisci.it

CELLAR SALES
PRE-BOOKED VISITS
ACCOMMODATION
ANNUAL PRODUCTION 90,000 bottles
HECTARES UNDER VINE 20.00
VITICULTURE METHOD Certified Organic

Ten years of work by Mauro Bisci (heir of the founding family) and enologist Aroldo Bellelli have definitively pulled the company out of the transitional stylistic phase that seemed to characterize the start of the new century. Their current rigorous interpretations of the Matelica territory now make it a brand of great reliability that regularly offers an exceptionally clear reading of the 'mountain' origins of their whites, characterized by great flavor and crystalline aromatic profiles. Their Verdicchio di Matelica '18 stole the show from its more renowned brothers. A great year made for a memorable version in terms of transparency, territorial identity, sapidity and extraordinary drinkability. The Senex Riserva '10 is released only after 8 years of aging in concrete vats. It's an aromatically complex wine in its notes of rain-washed pebbles, almonds and delicately vegetal hints, sensations that reemerge on a relaxed palate with a balsamic finish. The Vigneto Fogliano '17 features a nice register of ripe fruit on a soft, caressing palate.

○ Verdicchio di Matelica '18	♀♀♀ 3*
○ Verdicchio di Matelica Senex Ris. '10	♀♀ 4
○ Verdicchio di Matelica	
Vign. Fogliano '17	♀♀ 4
● Villa Castiglioni '15	♀ 3
○ Verdicchio di Matelica	
Vign. Fogliano '15	♀♀♀ 4*
○ Verdicchio di Matelica	
Vign. Fogliano '13	♀♀♀ 3*
○ Verdicchio di Matelica	
Vign. Fogliano '10	♀♀♀ 3*
○ Verdicchio di Matelica	
Vign. Fogliano '08	♀♀♀ 3*
● Rosso Fogliano '15	♀♀ 2*
○ Verdicchio di Matelica '17	♀♀ 3*
○ Verdicchio di Matelica '16	♀♀ 3*
○ Verdicchio di Matelica	
Vign. Fogliano '16	♀♀ 4

Boccadigabbia

LOC. FONTESPINA
C.DA CASTELLETTA, 56
62012 CIVITANOVA MARCHE [MC]
TEL. +39 073370728
www.boccadigabbia.com

CELLAR SALES
PRE-BOOKED VISITS
ANNUAL PRODUCTION 100,000 bottles
HECTARES UNDER VINE 25.00

Elvio Alessandri has shaped two spirits that
live in harmony at Boccadigabbia. In the
vineyards nearer to the Adriatic Sea are
the international varieties that made the
winery famous at the end of the last
century and which even today represent its
productive backbone. Native varieties that
reflect the estate's new direction are
cultivated further inland on the La Floriana
estate near Macerata. Fermentation and
maturation, however, take place only in the
modern and efficient cellar in Civitanova
Marche. Le Grane '18 has never been so
good with its elegant nuances of aniseed
and its tasty, compellingly drinkable palate.
The Rosèo '18 moves on a similar track.
It's a Pinot Nero rosé that brings together
floral sensations and peach on a pleasant,
supple palate. The Akronte '15, made with
Cabernet Sauvignon, is still recalcitrant,
needing time to integrate its bounteous
alcohol, extract and tannins. A Chardonnay
aged in barriques, the Montalperti '17
exhibits fruity and buttery accents on a soft
palate that's not lacking in elegance.

○ Colli Maceratesi Ribona Le Grane '18	♟♟ 3*
● Akronte '15	♟♟ 8
○ Montalperti '17	♟♟ 4
⊙ Rosèo '18	♟♟ 2*
● Rosso Piceno '16	♟♟ 3
○ Colli Maceratesi Ribona '18	♟ 3
○ Garbì '18	♟ 2
● Akronte '13	♟♟ 8
● Pix '12	♟♟ 6
● Tenuta La Floriana Rosso '13	♟♟ 6

Borgo Paglianetto

LOC. PAGLIANO, 393
62024 MATELICA [MC]
TEL. +39 073785465
www.borgopaglianetto.it

CELLAR SALES
PRE-BOOKED VISITS
ANNUAL PRODUCTION 90,000 bottles
HECTARES UNDER VINE 28.50
VITICULTURE METHOD Certified Organic
SUSTAINABLE WINERY

Borgo Paglianetto is the result of the union
of two small Matelica area estates that
joined to form a single winery. The
insightful move by the five partners allows
them to combine fresh and loose soils with
different exposures, ensuring a
commendable consistency of quality. The
agronomic and enological management of
specialist Aroldo Bellelli creates intense yet
graceful Verdicchio that are well
differentiated in style. And the Matesis, a
Montepulciano-based red and their only
wine matured in wood, is not to be
overlooked. Jera Riserva '15 is a Matelica
of spectacular complexity. It has notes of
almond, aniseed and mineral strokes,
sensations that reemerge on a palate
made by vigorous by abundant sapidity
— it's an elegant, relaxed and deep drink.
But their Vertis '17, a wine with enticing
aromas of ripe fruit and a lively palate, also
shone bright. The Petrara '18 features a
full palate rich in notes of white fruit,
while the Matesis '16 offers substance
and somewhat austere tannins but of
nice grain.

○ Verdicchio di Matelica Jera Ris. '15	♟♟♟ 4*
○ Verdicchio di Matelica Petrara '18	♟♟ 2*
○ Verdicchio di Matelica Vertis '17	♟♟ 3*
● Matesis '16	♟♟ 3
○ Verdicchio di Matelica Ergon '18	♟♟ 3
○ Verdicchio di Matelica Terravignata '18	♟♟ 2
○ Verdicchio di Matelica Jera Ris. '10	♟♟♟ 4*
○ Verdicchio di Matelica Petrara '16	♟♟♟ 2*
○ Verdicchio di Matelica Vertis '16	♟♟♟ 3*
○ Verdicchio di Matelica Vertis '09	♟♟♟ 3*
● Matesis '15	♟♟ 3*
● Matesis '11	♟♟ 3*
○ Verdicchio di Matelica Ergon '16	♟♟ 3*
○ Verdicchio di Matelica M. Cl. Brut	♟♟ 5
○ Verdicchio di Matelica Petrara '17	♟♟ 2*
○ Verdicchio di Matelica Terravignata '17	♟♟ 2*

Brunori

V.LE DELLA VITTORIA, 103
60035 JESI [AN]
TEL. +39 0731207213
www.brunori.it

CELLAR SALES
PRE-BOOKED VISITS
ANNUAL PRODUCTION 50,000 bottles
HECTARES UNDER VINE 7.00

If we had to use just two terms to describe the work of Giorgio Brunori (and children Carlo and Cristina), we would choose "clarity" and 'longevity'. The first as much for the way they relate to one another as for the style of their wine - a classic ideal unaffected by fashion. The second refers to both their long work in the sector, which began in 1956, and the ability of their greatest successes to face time with ease: uncork a twenty-year-old bottle and you get the mettle and fiber of the best Verdicchio. An elegant hint of aniseed opens a broad array of aromas — the San Nicolò '18 proceeds with balsamic nuances and accents of almond, a fruity stroke softened by aromatic herbs. The palate is full, flavorful, very long. Highly recommended. Le Gemme '18 is more citrusy, with an acidic vigor that lends lightness and ease to the palate. The San Nicolò Riserva '17 is characterized by aromas of dried fruit and nuts — it's a wine not lacking in sapidity and aromatic cohesion.

○ Verdicchio dei Castelli di Jesi Cl. Sup. San Nicolò '18	♟♟ 2*
○ Verdicchio dei Castelli di Jesi Cl. Le Gemme '18	♟♟ 2*
○ Verdicchio dei Castelli di Jesi Cl. San Nicolò Ris. '17	♟ 3
○ Castelli di Jesi Verdicchio Cl. San Nicolò Ris. '15	♟♟ 3*
○ Verdicchio dei Castelli di Jesi Cl. San Nicolò Ris. '13	♟♟ 3*
○ Verdicchio dei Castelli di Jesi Cl. Sup. San Nicolò '17	♟♟ 2*

★Bucci

FRAZ. PONGELLI
VIA CONA, 30
60010 OSTRA VETERE [AN]
TEL. +39 071964179
www.villabucci.com

CELLAR SALES
PRE-BOOKED VISITS
ANNUAL PRODUCTION 120,000 bottles
HECTARES UNDER VINE 31.00
VITICULTURE METHOD Certified Organic

The Bucci brothers' farm was founded in 1700. Today the 350 hectares of cultivated land is used for activities ranging from arable crops to extra virgin olive oil. Less than 10% of the land is dedicated to winemaking, but this is the part that has given the brothers world fame. Old vineyards scattered over several municipalities on the left bank of the Esino River provide grapes for their iconic Verdicchio Ris. Villa Bucci, aged in large Slavonian oak barrels. The sparkling aromatic nuances of the Villa Bucci Riserva '17 seduce the nose, accurately calling up chamomile, sweet almond, wild herbs and hypnotic sensations of aniseed. On the mouth it's subtle and delicately salty, endowed with outstanding balance — a play of small details that transforms into a wonderful mosaic. Don't underestimate the Bucci '18. It has the class of its older brother but uses a simpler, more forthright language, and all without compromising its graceful varietal qualities.

○ Castelli di Jesi Verdicchio Cl. Villa Bucci Ris. '17	♟♟♟ 6
○ Verdicchio dei Castelli di Jesi Cl. Villa Bucci Ris. '18	♟♟ 2*
○ Castelli di Jesi Verdicchio Cl. Villa Bucci Ris. '14	♟♟♟ 6
○ Castelli di Jesi Verdicchio Cl. Villa Bucci Ris. '13	♟♟♟ 6
○ Castelli di Jesi Verdicchio Cl. Villa Bucci Ris. '12	♟♟♟ 6
○ Castelli di Jesi Verdicchio Cl. Villa Bucci Ris. '10	♟♟♟ 6
○ Verdicchio dei Castelli di Jesi Cl. Sup. '16	♟♟♟ 3*

La Calcinara

Fraz. Candia
via Calcinara, 102a
60131 Ancona
Tel. +39 3285552643
www.lacalcinara.it

CELLAR SALES
PRE-BOOKED VISITS
ANNUAL PRODUCTION 42,000 bottles
HECTARES UNDER VINE 13.00
SUSTAINABLE WINERY

Paolo and Eleanora, both enologists, follow a different path than their father Mario Berluti, a well-established large-scale producer in the Conero area. They have chosen to use only organically grown grapes from the estate, using spontaneous fermentation in their small cellar overlooking the vineyards, artisanal in size and craftsmanship. The resulting wines are full of personality, generous (sometimes excessively) in structure and energy. These are wines that never go unnoticed. The Conero Folle '15 put in a truly convincing performance. It's redolent of plums, morello cherry, a hint of burnt wood and noble spices. On the palate it's close-woven, extraordinarily effective at transmitting sensations of fleshy fruit enriched by sweet, mature tannins. The Terra Calcinara '16 is quite ripe in its fruit, but just manages to avoid overt super-ripeness, letting Montepulciano's fruity and meaty nature have the best of the palate. The Mun '18, a rosé made with Montepulciano grapes, is simply delicious.

● Conero Folle Ris. '15	♈♈ 5
● Conero Terra Calcinara Ris. '16	♈♈ 3
☉ Mun '18	♈♈ 3
○ Clochard '18	♈ 3
● Rosso Conero Il Cacciatore di Sogni '17	♈ 3
● Conero Folle Ris. '13	♈♈ 5
● Conero Folle Ris. '12	♈♈ 5
● Conero Folle Ris. '10	♈♈ 5
☉ Mun '16	♈♈ 3
● Rosso Conero Il Cacciatore di Sogni '16	♈♈ 3
● Rosso Conero Il Cacciatore di Sogni '15	♈♈ 3

Le Caniette

c.da Canali, 23
63065 Ripatransone [AP]
Tel. +39 07359200
www.lecaniette.it

CELLAR SALES
PRE-BOOKED VISITS
ANNUAL PRODUCTION 60,000 bottles
HECTARES UNDER VINE 16.00
VITICULTURE METHOD Certified Organic

Excellent exposure has enabled the Vagnoni brothers to manage their vineyards of entirely local varieties for many years using completely organic methods. The style is clear and modern, never excessive and above all never sacrificing the artisanal touch that makes each wine a benchmark in its respective appellation. Particular attention is reserved for their Pecorino (vinified in small oak casks), various Piceno wines (Montepulciano and smaller quantities of Sangiovese) and enthralling interpretations of Bordò reds (a Grenache clone). We open our tasting notes with an ovation for their Cinabro '15, a wine endowed with kaleidoscopic aromas and a sophisticated palate, amidst echoes of Mediterranean shrub, raspberries and Asian spices. But our highest honors go to their even more amazing Morellone '15. Crisp, healthy fruit and calibrated tannic extraction confer lightness, making for a relaxed but steady stride. Aromas of bitter orange rise up off their losonagaia '17, wine that features character and savoriness.

● Piceno Sup. Morellone '15	♈♈♈ 4
● Cinabro '15	♈♈ 8
○ Offida Pecorino losonagaia Nonsonolucrezia '17	♈♈ 5
○ Lucrezia '18	♈♈ 2
● Piceno Nero di Vite '11	♈ 6
● Piceno Rosso Bello '17	♈ 2
☉ Sinopia '18	♈ 3
● Piceno Morellone '10	♈♈♈ 4
● Piceno Sup. Morellone '13	♈♈♈ 4
● Piceno Sup. Morellone '12	♈♈♈ 4
● Cinabro '14	♈♈ 8
● Cinabro '13	♈♈ 8
● Piceno Nero di Vite '10	♈♈ 6

Carminucci

VIA SAN LEONARDO, 39
63013 GROTTAMMARE [AP]
TEL. +39 0735735869
www.carminucci.com

CELLAR SALES
ANNUAL PRODUCTION 350,000 bottles
HECTARES UNDER VINE 46.00
VITICULTURE METHOD Certified Organic

The large, well-organized winery on the Grottammare hills, overlooking the Tesino valley, gives an idea of the volume of grapes processed inside. However, not all the grapes that enter are destined to bear Carminucci labels: only the those from the best parcels, especially from dedicated plots near Offida planted primarily with traditional varieties, are used to create the varied range that Piero and son Giovanni have produced over the years. The Novanta, their most recent creation, is a blend of Montepulciano with smaller shares of Merlot and Cabernet aged in barriques. The 2014 offers up sensations of black cherry, licorice and plums, while the palate is persistent and mouthfilling from the primaries to the tertiaries. Somewhat healthier, fresher fruit characterizes their Piceno Superiore Naumakos '16. But the best wine of the batch is still their white Belato '18, a wine redolent of pink grapefruit whose tasty palate exhibits fruity sensations, with a slightly bitter finish of citrus peel.

○ Offida Pecorino Belato '18	🍷🍷 2*
○ Falerio Grotte sul Mare '18	🍷🍷 1*
● Novanta '14	🍷🍷 7
● Rosso Piceno Sup. Naumakos '16	🍷🍷 2*
○ Casta '18	🍷 2
○ Falerio Naumakos '18	🍷 2
⊙ Grotte sul Mare Rosato '18	🍷 2
● Rosso Piceno Grotte sul Mare '18	🍷 2
● Offida Pecorino Belato '17	🍷🍷 2*
● Offida Pecorino Belato '15	🍷🍷 2*
● Offida Pecorino Belato '14	🍷🍷 2*
● Rosso Piceno Sup. Naumakos '14	🍷🍷 2*

CasalFarneto

VIA FARNETO, 12
60030 SERRA DE' CONTI [AN]
TEL. +39 0731889001
www.casalfarneto.it

CELLAR SALES
PRE-BOOKED VISITS
ANNUAL PRODUCTION 80,000 bottles
HECTARES UNDER VINE 39.00

Paolo Togni's vineyards unfold around this modern winery in an area historically well-suited to the cultivation of Verdicchio. Jesi's famous white is the star here and the winery exploits its versatility by harvesting it at differing degrees of ripeness: from fresh young vintage versions to more stylized late harvest wines and true passito dessert wine. The versatile range offers ambitious selections such as Crisio, Cimaio and Ikòn, partially aged in small wood casks. Their Crisio Riserva '16 features elegant, smoky nuances and a rigorous palate that's complex yet docile. Their Grancasale '17 is notable for its ultra-precise balance and characteristic aromas, all at the service of a relaxed, tasty palate. Their Cimaio '16 is a late-harvest wine that's unabashedly sweet but with a sapid backbone so pronounced that it creates great contrasts and extremely long development. The Fontevecchia '18 features a pleasant palate with nice grip.

○ Castelli di Jesi Verdicchio Cl. Crisio Ris. '16	🍷🍷 3*
○ Cimaio '16	🍷🍷 4
○ Verdicchio dei Castelli di Jesi Cl. Sup. Grancasale '17	🍷🍷 3*
○ Verdicchio dei Castelli di Jesi Cl. Sup. Fontevecchia '18	🍷🍷 2*
○ Verdicchio dei Castelli di Jesi Passito Ikòn '15	🍷🍷 5
● Rosso Piceno Cimarè '14	🍷 3
○ Castelli di Jesi Verdicchio Cl. Crisio Ris. '13	🍷🍷🍷 3*
○ Verdicchio dei Castelli di Jesi Cl. Sup. Grancasale '16	🍷🍷🍷 3*
○ Verdicchio dei Castelli di Jesi Cl. Sup. Grancasale '13	🍷🍷🍷 3*

Castignano Cantine dal 1960

c.da San Venanzo, 31
63072 Castignano [AP]
Tel. +39 0736822216
www.cantinedicastignano.com

CELLAR SALES
PRE-BOOKED VISITS
ANNUAL PRODUCTION 600,000 bottles
HECTARES UNDER VINE 500.00
VITICULTURE METHOD Certified Organic

For over half a century this Castignano cooperative has been promoting viticulture in the inland areas of Piceno and its members' vineyards reach as far as the foothills of Monte Ascensione. This explains its specialization in Pecorino, which tends to thrive in cooler locations. For a few years now, President Omar Traini has been coordinating a young, close-knit team that supports him in his innovative work, the most recent being a line of organic wines embracing all the most significant denominations in the area. Their dual Pecorinos didn't disappoint. The Montemisio '18 offers up aromas of lemon leaves, and features a vibrant development. The Bio '18 exhibits an acidity that lends vigor and drinkability. Among their reds the Gran Maestro '14 stands out for its aromas of blackberries, black cherry and toasty nuances, sensations well-integrated in a palate that brings together firmness and commendable tension. Their Piceno Superiore Bio '17, an elegantly floral, taut and spicy wine, had a nice debut.

● Offida Rosso Gran Maestro '14	▼▼ 3*
○ Notturno	▼▼ 2
○ Offida Passerina Bio '18	▼▼ 3
○ Offida Pecorino Montemisio '18	▼▼ 2*
● Rosso Piceno Bio '18	▼▼ 3
● Rosso Piceno Sup. Bio '17	▼▼ 3
● Rosso Piceno Sup. Destriero '17	▼▼ 2*
○ Terre di Offida Passerina Brut '18	▼▼ 2*
○ Offida Pecorino Bio '18	▼ 3
○ Passerina '18	▼ 2
● Templaria '17	▼ 2
○ Offida Pecorino Montemisio '17	♀♀ 2*
○ Offida Pecorino Montemisio '16	♀♀ 2*
● Offida Rosso Gran Maestro '13	♀♀ 3*

Tenuta Cocci Grifoni

loc. San Savino
c.da Messieri, 12
63038 Ripatransone [AP]
Tel. +39 073590143
www.tenutacoccigrifoni.it

CELLAR SALES
PRE-BOOKED VISITS
ACCOMMODATION
ANNUAL PRODUCTION 400,000 bottles
HECTARES UNDER VINE 50.00
SUSTAINABLE WINERY

The profound renewal work carried out by sisters Marilena and Paola Cocci Grifoni has transformed the face of their winery. Considerable structural investments, marketing and communication have resulted in proper credit finally being given to the great work done by their father Guido, a patriarch of Piceno viticulture. The wines have an authentic sense of territory resulting in part from the patrimony of vineyards planted with local varieties as well as a never-abandoned traditions: whites aged in steel and reds aged for long periods in large wood barrels. The Grifone '13 is a dark, potent, extractive wine with a tannic weight that's still not entirely unraveled but a guarantee of great aging power. Their Piceno Superiore San Basso '15 is fruitier, with notes of black cherry made more graceful by an evident spiciness. On the palate it's robust but not without elegance. Their Colle Vecchio '17 features hints of dried fruit and nuts, wild flowers and a mouthfilling palate of commendable complexity.

○ Offida Pecorino Colle Vecchio '17	▼▼ 3
● Offida Rosso Il Grifone '13	▼▼ 5
● Rosso Piceno Sup. San Basso '15	▼▼ 2*
○ Terre di Offida Passerina Passito San Basso '13	▼▼ 2*
○ Falerio Pecorino Tarà '18	▼ 2
● Rosso Piceno Tarà '18	▼ 2
○ San Basso Passerina '18	▼ 2
○ Tarà Passerina Spumante Brut '18	▼ 3
⊙ Tarà Rosato '18	▼ 2
○ Offida Pecorino Guido Cocci Grifoni '14	♀♀♀ 6
○ Offida Pecorino Guido Cocci Grifoni '13	♀♀♀ 4*
● Rosso Piceno Sup. V. Messieri '13	♀♀ 4
● Rosso Piceno Sup. V. Messieri '11	♀♀ 4

ol di Corte

San Pietro, 19a
036 Montecarotto [AN]
. +39 073189435
ww.coldicorte.it

CELLAR SALES
RE-BOOKED VISITS
NNUAL PRODUCTION 40,000 bottles
ECTARES UNDER VINE 11.50
TICULTURE METHOD Certified Organic
USTAINABLE WINERY

2012, Giacomo Rossi and a couple of
low Roman friends decided to take over
model from scratch a winery that had
en abandoned for years. Adhering to
ganic principles and minimally invasive
ification, they have developed a style of
ne marked by a certain expressive
turalness that is both aromatically clear
d energetic on the palate. Enologist
audio Caldaroni from the Marche region
as supported them in their efforts, first
tting the vineyards back on track and
en reshaping some of the most
teresting wines on the Jesi scene today.
eir Sant'Ansovino Riserva '16 features a
mpelling nose, thanks to notes of
ndied citrus and an evident fruitiness. On
e palate it's marked by a punchy sapidity.
ne Vigneto di Tobia '17 is a firm white with
h expansive, supple texture. Anno Uno '18
as notable character — it's a highly
arietal wine with adequate depth of taste.
olume and calibrated tannic presence
haracterize their Sant'Ansovino '15, a
end of Montepulciano and Cabernet that's
ged in oak.

Castelli di Jesi Verdicchio Cl. Sant'Ansovino Ris. '16	♟♟ 5
Lancestrale	♟♟ 4
Sant'Ansovino '15	♟♟ 5
Verdicchio dei Castelli di Jesi Cl. Anno Uno '18	♟♟ 2*
Verdicchio dei Castelli di Jesi Cl. Sup. Vign. di Tobia '17	♟♟ 4
Castelli di Jesi Verdicchio Cl. Sant'Ansovino Ris. '15	♟♟ 5
Verdicchio dei Castelli di Jesi Cl. Anno Uno '17	♟♟ 2*
Verdicchio dei Castelli di Jesi Cl. Anno Uno '16	♟♟ 2*
Verdicchio dei Castelli di Jesi Cl. Sup. Vign. di Tobia '16	♟♟ 4

Collestefano

loc. Colle Stefano, 3
62022 Castelraimondo [MC]
Tel. +39 0737640439
www.collestefano.com

CELLAR SALES
PRE-BOOKED VISITS
ACCOMMODATION
ANNUAL PRODUCTION 120,000 bottles
HECTARES UNDER VINE 17.50
VITICULTURE METHOD Certified Organic

2016 and 2017 were difficult vintages for
Fabio Marchionni, because the character of
the territory is deeply inscribed in the
wines; this is true even during unstable
years of frost, reduced production, and out
of scale acidity. 2018 brrought redemption
and all of the signs indicate a positive
vintage. Verdicchio are pressed in whole
bunches and aged for a few months in
large steel tanks. As always, bottling will
bring out scents bearing unmistakable
mountain accents and a saline energy in
the mouth. The Collestefano '18 once again
gets a gold. And it does so with a masterful
version in terms of personality and aromatic
clarity, qualities that are already perfectly
developed yet capable of achieving further
levels of complexity thanks to its loyal
companion, time. Sophisticated aromas of
citrus, hawthorn blossom, and delicate
mineral hints are followed by a graceful,
delicately salty palate characterized by
unstoppable energy and contagious
drinkability.

○ Verdicchio di Matelica Collestefano '18	♟♟♟ 2*
○ Verdicchio di Matelica Collestefano '15	♟♟♟ 2*
○ Verdicchio di Matelica Collestefano '14	♟♟♟ 2*
○ Verdicchio di Matelica Collestefano '13	♟♟♟ 2*
○ Verdicchio di Matelica Collestefano '12	♟♟♟ 2*
○ Verdicchio di Matelica Collestefano '10	♟♟♟ 2*
○ Verdicchio di Matelica Collestefano '07	♟♟♟ 2*
○ Verdicchio di Matelica Collestefano '06	♟♟♟ 2*
○ Verdicchio di Matelica Collestefano '17	♟♟ 2*
○ Verdicchio di Matelica Collestefano '16	♟♟ 2*
○ Verdicchio di Matelica Collestefano '11	♟♟ 2*
○ Verdicchio di Matelica Collestefano '09	♟♟ 2*
○ Verdicchio di Matelica Extra Brut M. Cl. '14	♟♟ 4
○ Verdicchio di Matelica Extra Brut M. Cl. '13	♟♟ 3*

Cantina dei Colli Ripani

C.DA TOSCIANO, 28
63065 RIPATRANSONE [AP]
TEL. +39 07359505
www.colliripani.it

CELLAR SALES
PRE-BOOKED VISITS
ANNUAL PRODUCTION 1,300,000 bottles
HECTARES UNDER VINE 650.00
VITICULTURE METHOD Certified Organic

A strong wind of renewal has hit Colli
Ripani. The members of the cooperative
keep stewardship of the vineyards their top
priority, but changes are going forward in
the production and distribution sectors. To
wit, the different ranges sport new,
attractive graphics and highlight both the
organic segment and use of traditional
grape varieties. Ambitious quality is clearly
found in the new Line 508, named after the
elevation of the highest point of
Ripatransone and composed of modern,
fragrant and substantial wines. The toasty
attack of their Leo Ripano '13 is softened
by fruity sensations and strokes of aromatic
herbs. On the palate it proves pervasive,
bringing together extractive force and a
sapid complexity. Condividio '16 features
herbaceous notes well-integrated with
sensations of candied citrus, while on the
palate it's mature and relaxed. Their
full-bodied and tannic Diavolo e Vento '13
is also worth noting.

● Offida Rosso Leo Ripano '13	♥♥ 3*
● Diavolo e Vento '13	♥♥ 5
○ Offida Pecorino Condivio '16	♥♥ 5
○ Offida Pecorino Mercantino '18	♥♥ 2*
○ Offida Passerina Lajella '18	♥ 2
● Rosso Piceno Sup. Castellano '16	♥ 2
○ Falerio Pecorino Bio '15	♥♥ 2*
○ Falerio Pecorino Cap. 9 '17	♥♥ 2*
○ Offida Pecorino Rugaro Gold '15	♥♥ 2*
● Offida Rosso Leo Ripanus '11	♥♥ 3
● Rosso Piceno Sup. Castellano '13	♥♥ 2*
● Rosso Piceno Sup. Settantase77e '12	♥♥ 2*

Cològnola - Tenuta Musone

LOC. COLOGNOLA, 22A BIS
62011 CINGOLI [MC]
TEL. +39 0733616438
www.tenutamusone.it

CELLAR SALES
PRE-BOOKED VISITS
ANNUAL PRODUCTION 150,000 bottles
HECTARES UNDER VINE 25.00

Walter Darini and daughter Serena have ve
clear ideas: in 2015 they decided to follow
organic farming methods and for now they
want to produce wines that are obtained
only from Verdicchio and Montepulciano.
The many hectares available to them allow
for an excellent selection of the best grape
and the efficient, modern cellar enables the
technical staff led by Gabriele Villani to wor
at their best. Though lacking a stand-out
performer, the whole range shows a
reassuring level of quality. During our
tastings, the Ghiffa '17 once again proved
be the best of the lot. The fact of harvestin
the grapes only when completely ripe make
for sensations of toasted almond, and a sof
creamy palate that's not without a
compelling suppleness. Via Condotto '18
offers up citrusy sensations and a supple,
fragrant palate. Their cask-aged Labieno
Riserva '16 features notes of ripe summer
fruit and a relaxed palate that's not too dee
but appreciably pervasive. The Incauto '18
is subtle and flows quickly, while their Via
Rosa '18, made with Montepulciano,
exhibits a nice, fruity verve.

○ Castelli di Jesi Verdicchio Cl. Labieno Ris. '16	♥♥
○ Verdicchio dei Castelli di Jesi Cl. Sup. Ghiffa '17	♥♥
○ Verdicchio dei Castelli di Jesi Cl. Sup. Via Condotto '18	♥♥
⊙ Via Rosa '18	♥♥
● Cantamaggio '18	♥
○ Verdicchio dei Castelli di Jesi Cl. Sup. Incauto '18	♥
○ Verdicchio dei Castelli di Jesi Passito Cingulum '17	♥
○ Verdicchio dei Castelli di Jesi Cl. Sup. Ghiffa '16	♥♥
○ Verdicchio dei Castelli di Jesi Cl. Sup. Via Condotto '17	♥♥

olonnara

MANDRIOLE, 6
034 CUPRAMONTANA [AN]
.. +39 0731780273
ww.colonnara.it

ELLAR SALES
RE-BOOKED VISITS
NNUAL PRODUCTION 1,000,000 bottles
ECTARES UNDER VINE 120.00

elebrations for the 60th anniversary are
arting in grand form at Casa Colonnara.
nally reaping the fruit of its investment in
e Pesaro, appellations in the north of
arche (which are found in the Pisaurum
ne) now further enrich an already large
atalog that satisfies all budgets and
stes. And in the large Via Mandriole
ellar there is plenty to toast to and with
s sparkling wines are a recognized
pecialty, as is Verdicchio coming from the
ighly suitable Cupramontana area.
mong their sparkling wines, the Ubaldo
osi '13 shines as always. Despite
pending 60 months on the lees, it still
roves youthful and abundant in sapidity.
uigi Ghislieri is an extremely reliable
parkler, one that can evolve well in the
ottle, bringing together complexity with a
elicately-salty streak. We found their new
inot Nero Brut '15 interesting — it's a
avorful wine, rich in contrasts. Their
uprese '17 performed well thanks in part
o its almondy, varietal profile.

○ Verdicchio dei Castelli di Jesi Brut M. Cl. Ubaldo Rosi Ris. '13	🍷🍷 5
● Colli Pesaresi Cabernet Sauvignon Don Bartolo Pisaurum '16	🍷🍷 4
○ Pinot Nero Brut M. Cl. Pisaurum '15	🍷🍷 5
○ Verdicchio dei Castelli di Jesi Brut M. Cl. Luigi Ghislieri	🍷🍷 4
○ Verdicchio dei Castelli di Jesi Cl. Sup. Cuprese '17	🍷🍷 2*
○ Bianchello del Metauro Cleofe Pisaurum '18	🍷 2
● Colli Pesaresi Parco Naturale Monte San Bartolo Sangiovese Pisaurum '16	🍷 4
● Tornamagno '14	🍷 3
○ Verdicchio dei Castelli di Jesi Cl. Lyricus '18	🍷 2

Colpaola

LOC. COLPAOLA
FRAZ. BRACCANO

62024 MATELICA [MC]
TEL. +39 0737768300
www.cantinacolpaola.it

CELLAR SALES
ANNUAL PRODUCTION 18,000 bottles
HECTARES UNDER VINE 9.00
VITICULTURE METHOD Certified Organic

Tenuta Colpaola sits above the hamlet of
Braccano, on the shoulders of Monte San
Vicino, at an elevation of 650 meters. The
Apennines make their cold breath even
more felt here, especially during the
harvest. It's easy to understand why
Francesco Porcarelli and Stefania
Peppoloni's Matelica has such a
pronounced acid vigor and very clear,
mineral-like aromas. Processing in steel
and very intellegent bottling using screw
tops further enhance these characteristics.
Their Verdicchio Colpaola greatly reflects
the vintage, and when its grapes are
harvested at just at the right time, it comes
through in the bottle. An excellent 2018
gave rise to aromas of white-fleshed fruit,
almond, hints of aniseed and mineral
strokes. On the palate it proves complex
and juicy, full of flavor yet extraordinarily
supple and deep. It's a wine that will offer
up its best in the following years (given that
you can resist the temptation to drink it
straight away).

○ Verdicchio di Matelica '18	🍷🍷 2*
○ Verdicchio di Matelica '17	🍷🍷 2*
○ Verdicchio di Matelica '15	🍷🍷 2*
○ Verdicchio di Matelica '14	🍷🍷 2*

Il Conte Villa Prandone

C.DA COLLE NAVICCHIO, 28
63033 MONTEPRANDONE [AP]
TEL. +39 073562593
www.ilcontevini.it

CELLAR SALES
PRE-BOOKED VISITS
ANNUAL PRODUCTION 200,000 bottles
HECTARES UNDER VINE 50.00

Emanuel De Angelis coordinates the work of his large family, all of whom are involved with managing some 50 hectares on the hills of Monteprandone. The result is a complete, fairly wide range of modern, dense and glossy wines evincing an approachable pleasantness and fruity richness. In some cases, especially the more ambitious reds, the structural volume and wood could be lightened, but this generosity is typical of the winery's style. Among their whites, we appreciated their fresh, pleasant and fragrant Navicchio '18, while the Cavaceppo '18 proves subtle and supple. When it comes to their reds, the fruity and soft Marinus '17 put in a nice performance, as did the flavorful and spheric Zipolo '16 (a Montepulciano with smaller shares of Sangiovese and Merlot), and the spicy, fleshy IX Prandone '15, a Merlot. LuKont '16, a Montepulciano, reveals the occasional vegetal hint set on a toasty background and notes of black cherries — sensations that merge together on its dense, rather tannic palate.

● IX Prandone '15	♥♥ 8
○ L'Estro del Mastro Passerina Passito '17	♥♥ 5
○ Offida Pecorino Navicchio '18	♥♥ 3
● Piceno Sup. Marinus '17	♥♥ 3
⊙ Rosato '18	♥♥ 2*
● Zipolo '16	♥♥ 5
● Donello '18	♥ 3
○ Emmanuel Maria Passerina Brut	♥ 3
○ Falerio Pecorino Aurato '18	♥ 2
● LuKont '16	♥ 6
○ Offida Passerina Cavaceppo '18	♥ 3
● Rosso Piceno Conte Rosso '18	♥ 2
⊙ Venere&Azzurra Brut Rosé	♥ 3
○ Vizius '18	♥ 2

Fattoria Coroncino

C.DA CORONCINO, 7
60039 STAFFOLO [AN]
TEL. +39 0731779494
www.coroncino.it

CELLAR SALES
PRE-BOOKED VISITS
ANNUAL PRODUCTION 45,000 bottles
HECTARES UNDER VINE 9.50

Lucio Canestrari still speaks with a Roman rhythm, but he belongs to the small club of producers who in the mid-1980s changed the fate of Verdicchio by bringing it out of the 'dictatorship of the amphora' (i.e., anonymous wines sold at low prices). Since his first steps on the Staffolo hills, he has been a proponent of agricultural development and artisanal values: he has worked with many clones, compared stages of maturation and was one of the first to enthusiastically try both small wood barrels and long aging in steel. Today he's a cult producer, rightly collecting the fruit of his labor. Stragaio '15 enchants in its smoky notes and mineral primaries fused with hints of candied fruit, the prelude to a round palate of pure energy crossed by a long stroke of flavor. The Gaiospino '16 is redolent of summer fruit, while on the palate it exhibits a fleshy attack that's well-contrasted by a firm, acidic sinew. The Bacco '17 is a rustic wine (grains, hay) but irresistibly drinkable.

○ Verdicchio dei Castelli di Jesi Cl. Sup. Stragaio '15	♥♥ 5
● Ganzerello '16	♥♥ 4
○ Verdicchio dei Castelli di Jesi Cl. Sup. Gaiospino '16	♥♥ 4
○ Verdicchio dei Castelli di Jesi Cl. Sup. Il Bacco '17	♥♥ 3
○ Verdicchio dei Castelli di Jesi Cl. Sup. Il Coroncino '18	♥ 3
○ Verdicchio dei Castelli di Jesi Cl. Sup. Gaiospino '03	♥♥♥ 4
○ Verdicchio dei Castelli di Jesi Cl. Sup. Gaiospino '97	♥♥♥ 4
○ Verdicchio dei Castelli di Jesi Cl. Sup. Il Bacco '16	♥♥ 2

enuta De Angelis

San Francesco, 10
030 Castel di Lama [AP]
. +39 073687429
www.tenutadeangelis.it

CELLAR SALES
RE-BOOKED VISITS
ANNUAL PRODUCTION 500,000 bottles
HECTARES UNDER VINE 50.00

e Angelis was founded in 1958 as a
roducer of bulk wine. The first bottles date
ack to the early 1990s as a result of a
rategic choice made by Quinto Fausti. His
n Alighiero, grandson of the founder and
day the winery's soul, is improving this
egment more and more. A long-standing
ollaboration with enologist Roberto
otentini has resulted in wines expressive
the territory, obtained from some of
ceno's most beautiful vineyards, mostly
anted with traditional varietals. Each label
produced in suitable quantities, offering a
ood value for money. Their Oro '16 affirms
s status as their selection's most
xpressive wine thanks to its fruity and
picy tones, skilfully set on a close-woven,
ynamic palate — and it's still got room to
row in terms of complexity and finesse.
he Quiete '18 is an unfiltered Pecorino
hose citrusy and flavorful palate is
rinkable yet succulent. We also
ppreciated the toasty and fruity Piceno
uperiore '17 and the Anghelos '16, a
picy, mature wine that's quite intense on
e palate.

Rosso Piceno Sup. Oro '16	♛♛ 3*
Offida Pecorino '18	♛♛ 2*
Offida Pecorino Quiete '18	♛♛ 3
Offida Rosso Anghelos '16	♛♛ 4
Rosso Piceno Sup. '17	♛♛ 2*
Falerio '18	♛ 1*
Offida Passerina '18	♛ 2
Rosso Piceno '18	♛ 2
Anghelos '01	♛♛♛ 4
Anghelos '99	♛♛♛ 4*
Rosso Piceno Sup. Oro '15	♛♛♛ 3*
Offida Pecorino '17	♛♛ 2*
Offida Rosso Anghelos '15	♛♛ 4
Rosso Piceno '17	♛♛ 2*
Rosso Piceno Sup. '16	♛♛ 2*

Degli Azzoni

via Don Minzoni, 26
62010 Montefano [MC]
Tel. +39 0733850219
www.degliazzoni.it

CELLAR SALES
PRE-BOOKED VISITS
ANNUAL PRODUCTION 100,000 bottles
HECTARES UNDER VINE 130.00
SUSTAINABLE WINERY

Filippo, Valperto and Aldobrando Degli
Azzoni inherited the winery from their father
Roberto in 2000. The brothers have
ushered in a new season for one of
Macerata's greatest wineries, with
extensive vineyards and a cellar that can
work large volumes. Efforts are now largely
agronomic, shown by an increasingly
careful use of systemic pesticides and a
gradual shift to organic methods, and
enologic, with the implementation of many
experiments designed to assure the
recognizability and future quality of their
wines. The work done on their
Montepulciano proves right on the mark.
Their Passatempo '15 features an elegant
spiciness, fullness of fruit and tannins put
at the service of a full-bodied and flavorful
palate. The Merlot '16 exhibits volume and
nice tannic presence. Floral fragrance and
delicate fruit characterize their Rosso
Evasione '17, while among their whites the
delicious Ribona '18 stands out for its
well-defined aromas of citrus, and its nice,
sapid finish.

● Passatempo '15	♛♛ 4
○ Colli Maceratesi Ribona '18	♛♛ 2*
● Colli Maceratesi Rosso Evasione '17	♛♛ 2*
○ Grechetto '18	♛♛ 2*
● Merlot '16	♛♛ 2*
○ Beldiletto Brut	♛ 2
● Rosso Piceno San Donato '16	♛ 2
○ Colli Maceratesi Passito Sultano '16	♛♛ 4
○ Colli Maceratesi Ribona '17	♛♛ 2*
○ Grechetto '17	♛♛ 2*
● Passatempo '14	♛♛ 5
● Passatempo '13	♛♛ 5
● Rosso Piceno '15	♛♛ 2*
● Rosso Piceno '14	♛♛ 2*
● Rosso Piceno '13	♛♛ 2*

Fattoria Dezi

C.DA FONTEMAGGIO, 14
63839 SERVIGLIANO [FM]
TEL. +39 0734710090
fattoriadezi@hotmail.com

CELLAR SALES
PRE-BOOKED VISITS
ACCOMMODATION
ANNUAL PRODUCTION 45,000 bottles
HECTARES UNDER VINE 15.00

For many years Stefano and Davide Dezi have worked in the hills of Servigliano, a town with an ancient agricultural tradition. They are influenced by the wine-growing of Piceno and its tradition of Montepulciano, Sangiovese and Pecorino. Verdicchio (used in Solagne) is an exception, but is not really uncommon in an area where a tenant farming culture required diversification. Davide is a master at bringing grapes to perfect ripeness even in difficult years. Stefano transforms them into dense, full-bodied wines that are introverted when young but which find complexity and expansion over time. To fully appreciate their Regina del Bosco '16 you need patience. Let it rest in the glass and you'll discover a true, forthright, meaty Montepulciano with multifaceted aromas. The same holds for the Solo '16. Its tannins are still quite boisterous, while on the nose it already proves elegant in its smoky accents, and the earthy, fruity hints that characterize Piceno's Sangiovese. The Servigliano P. '17 put in an excellent performance with its aromas of candied citrus and its exceptionally long palate.

○ Falerio Pecorino Servigliano P. '17	♟♟ 3*
● Dezio '17	♟♟ 3
● Regina del Bosco '16	♟♟ 6
○ Solagne '17	♟♟ 3
● Solo '16	♟♟ 6
● Regina del Bosco '06	♟♟♟ 6
● Regina del Bosco '05	♟♟♟ 6
● Regina del Bosco '03	♟♟♟ 6
● Solo Sangiovese '05	♟♟♟ 6
● Solo Sangiovese '01	♟♟♟ 5
● Solo Sangiovese '00	♟♟♟ 6
● Dezio '16	♟♟ 3
○ Falerio Pecorino Servigliano P. '15	♟♟ 3
● Regina del Bosco '15	♟♟ 6
○ Solagne '16	♟♟ 3

Emanuele Dianetti

C.DA VALLEROSA, 25
63063 CARASSAI [AP]
TEL. +39 3383928439
www.dianettivini.it

CELLAR SALES
PRE-BOOKED VISITS
ANNUAL PRODUCTION 23,000 bottles
HECTARES UNDER VINE 4.00

A succession of vineyards, olive groves and fruit trees in a context that seems otherwise largely untouched by humans: the Menocchia Valley is a feast for the eyes. It lies on the northern border of the Offida DOC and is distinguished by its cooler microclimate. Emanuele Dianetti benefits by creating wines characterized by their acidity and well-balanced fruit, which are obtained through correct maturation and vinification, and by taking care not to eliminate the aromas naturally present in the skins of the local varieties. An artisanal touch completes the charm of this true 'boutique' Piceno winery. The Offida Rosso Vignagiulia is an exhilarating monovarietal Montepulciano. Elegant fruity sensations and spicy hints emerge clearly on a palate that impresses for its balance, energy, expressiveness and freshness. It's a truly contemporary wine: supple, territorial and complex all at once. The Pecorino Vignagiulia '18, a wine rich in citrus and thiols, with a saline, vigorous palate.

● Offida Rosso Vignagiulia '16	♟♟♟ 5
○ Offida Pecorino Vignagiulia '18	♟♟ 3
● Piceno '17	♟ 3
● Offida Rosso Vignagiulia '14	♟♟♟ 5
● Offida Rosso Vignagiulia '13	♟♟♟ 5
● Michelangelo Bordò '15	♟♟ 8
● Michelangelo Bordò '14	♟♟ 8
○ Offida Pecorino Vignagiulia '17	♟♟ 3
○ Offida Pecorino Vignagiulia '16	♟♟ 3
○ Offida Pecorino Vignagiulia '15	♟♟ 3
○ Offida Pecorino Vignagiulia '14	♟♟ 3
○ Offida Pecorino Vignagiulia '13	♟♟ 3
● Offida Rosso Vignagiulia '15	♟♟ 5
● Offida Rosso Vignagiulia '12	♟♟ 4
● Offida Rosso Vignagiulia '11	♟♟ 4

Andrea Felici

C.DA SANT'ISIDORO, 28
62021 APIRO [MC]
TEL. +39 0733611431
www.andreafelici.it

CELLAR SALES
PRE-BOOKED VISITS
ANNUAL PRODUCTION 96,000 bottles
HECTARES UNDER VINE 12.00

Leopardo Felici's wines have become unavoidable classics in the Verdicchio world. He's made his reputation by drawing on the attributes of Apiro, which, given its secluded position, combines the best qualities of Jesi with those of Matelica. He also has clear ideas on winemaking, both commercially and in terms of production, where he follows the theories of Aroldo Bellelli, one of the grape's great experts: ideal ripening ensures the presence of acidity and saline vigor, all of which may be enhanced by aging in steel and concrete vats. For these reasons, Leopardo is our Vine Grower of the Year. Vigna Il Cantico della Figura '16 features a transparent aromatic profile and a palate that's forceful in its expansion, leaving a deep, sapid sensation. It's a true masterpiece of finesse and style. Though their Andrea Felici '18 put in a performance that's second to none — it's probably the best version yet for its suppleness, energy and drinkability.

○ Castelli di Jesi Verdicchio Cl. V. Il Cantico della Figura Ris. '16	♈♈♈ 6
○ Verdicchio dei Castelli di Jesi Cl. Sup. Andrea Felici '18	♈♈ 3*
○ Castelli di Jesi Verdicchio Cl. Il Cantico della Figura Ris. '12	♈♈♈ 4*
○ Castelli di Jesi Verdicchio Cl. Il Cantico della Figura Ris. '11	♈♈♈ 4*
○ Castelli di Jesi Verdicchio Cl. Il Cantico della Figura Ris. '10	♈♈♈ 4*
○ Castelli di Jesi Verdicchio Cl. V. Il Cantico della Figura Ris. '15	♈♈♈ 6
○ Castelli di Jesi Verdicchio Cl. V. Il Cantico della Figura Ris. '13	♈♈♈ 6

Filodivino

VIA SERRA, 46
60030 SAN MARCELLO [AN]
TEL. +39 0731026139
www.filodivino.it

CELLAR SALES
PRE-BOOKED VISITS
ACCOMMODATION AND RESTAURANT SERVICE
ANNUAL PRODUCTION 52,000 bottles
HECTARES UNDER VINE 19.50

Now that the spectacular modern cellar is operational, Alberto Gandolfi and Gian Mario Bongini have put into place the last piece of a challenging project started in 2013: a refined country relais with guest accommodations surrounded by established vineyards. As is appropriate between Jesi and Morro d'Alba, only Verdicchio and Lacrima are found in the vineyards cared for with Luca Mercadante's agronomic experience. Matteo Chiucconi oversees winemaking and, with the owners, creates close-focused wines that fully respect each variety. Matto '18 offers up notably varietal aromas, while the palate is supple, guided by an acidity that's never harsh but rather at the service of flavor. The Fllotto '17 proves lip-smacking, not particularly complex but tasty, with a finish that calls up a delicious hint of sweet almond. The Filodivino Rosato '18 is yet another example of Lacrima's suitability for the typology, with its fruity hints, its freshness and appealing drinkability.

⊙ Filodivino Rosato '18	♈♈ 2*
○ Verdicchio dei Castelli di Jesi Cl. Sup. Filotto '17	♈♈ 3
○ Verdicchio dei Castelli di Jesi Cl. Sup. Matto '18	♈♈ 3
● Lacrima di Morro d'Alba Diana '17	♈ 3
○ Verdicchio dei Castelli di Jesi Cl. Serra 46 '18	♈ 2
○ Castelli di Jesi Verdicchio Cl. Dino Ris. '15	♈♈ 4
● Lacrima di Morro d'Alba Diana '15	♈♈ 3
○ Verdicchio dei Castelli di Jesi Cl. Sup. Filotto '15	♈♈ 3*
○ Verdicchio dei Castelli di Jesi Cl. Sup. Matto '17	♈♈ 3
○ Verdicchio dei Castelli di Jesi Cl. Sup. Matto '16	♈♈ 3

Fiorano

C.DA FIORANO, 19
63067 COSSIGNANO [AP]
TEL. +39 073598247
www.agrifiorano.it

CELLAR SALES
PRE-BOOKED VISITS
ACCOMMODATION
ANNUAL PRODUCTION 45,000 bottles
HECTARES UNDER VINE 8.50
VITICULTURE METHOD Certified Organic
SUSTAINABLE WINERY

Many things have changed since Paolo
Beretta left Lombardy to settle in Marche in
2003. For his wife Paola it was a
homecoming of sorts, for him a new life.
Today Fiorano is a gem: the old farmhouse
has been perfectly restored, the vineyards
are planted mostly with typical local varieties
and a grove of olive trees, and the
underground cellar is perfectly placed in the
agritourism's romantic, bucolic scenery. The
wines have personality and just the right
artisanal touch. Their Giulia Erminia '17 is a
truly delicious Pecorino aged in mid-size
casks. On the nose it proves citrusy and
complex, while on the palate it's driven by
a compelling acidic vigor. Their Donna
Orgilla '18 is a bit clenched, less racy than
usual. To compensate, the Ser Balduzio '13
has evolved well. It's a modern
Montepulciano with a complex, ripe palate.
More fruit-forward wines, like their
Sangiovese '18 and Rosato '18, also
performed well.

○ Giulia Erminia '17	⚑⚑ 5
⊙ Rosato '18	⚑⚑ 2*
● Sangiovese '18	⚑⚑ 2*
● Ser Balduzio '13	⚑⚑ 5
○ Offida Pecorino Donna Orgilla '18	⚑ 3
● Rosso Piceno Terre di Giobbe '16	⚑ 3
○ Offida Pecorino Donna Orgilla '14	⚑⚑⚑ 3*
○ Offida Pecorino Donna Orgilla '17	⚑⚑ 3
○ Offida Pecorino Donna Orgilla '16	⚑⚑ 3*
○ Offida Pecorino Giulia Erminia '16	⚑⚑ 5
⊙ Rosato '17	⚑⚑ 2*
● Rosso Piceno Sup. Terre di Giobbe '15	⚑⚑ 3
● Rosso Piceno Sup. Terre di Giobbe '14	⚑⚑ 3

Fiorini

FRAZ. BARCHI
VIA GIARDINO CAMPIOLI, 5
61038 TERRE ROVERESCHE
TEL. +39 072197151
www.fioriniwines.it

CELLAR SALES
PRE-BOOKED VISITS
ACCOMMODATION
ANNUAL PRODUCTION 200,000 bottles
HECTARES UNDER VINE 45.00
VITICULTURE METHOD Certified Organic

The estate, led by Carla Fiorini, is among the
most prominent in the Pesaro area due to
more than a century of history and the
reliability of its wines over the last two
decades. Not content to rest on its laurels,
however, the winery constantly experiments
with new ways to obtain increasingly
complex wines without sacrificing it ability to
express the territory. Most of the countryside
vineyards are dedicated to Bianchello, but
there is also Sangiovese Grosso and residual
amounts of Montepulciano, Cabernet and
Verdicchio. Their Tenuta Campioli '18 is
an exquisite wine with bold fruit and a
delicately saline stroke, sensations that
unfold across a palate marked by harmony
and varietal typicity. Its younger brother, the
Sant'Ilario '18, is acidulous and supple,
characterized by a more relaxed palate. The
Bartis '16 faithfully transmits its spicy
character, while on the palate it moves
gracefully (despite some evident tannic grip).
Their charming Monsavium '11 is made with
partially-dried Bianchello: aromas of walnut
husk, dried fruit and nuts give way to a
sweet palate revived by volatile acidity.

○ Bianchello del Metauro Sup. Tenuta Campioli '18	⚑⚑ 2
● Colli Pesaresi Rosso Bartis '16	⚑⚑ 3
Monsavium Passito '11	⚑⚑ 5
○ Bianchello del Metauro Sant'Ilario '18	⚑ 2
○ Bianchello del Metauro Sup. Andy '17	⚑ 3
● Colli Pesaresi Sangiovese Luigi Fiorini Ris. '15	⚑ 4
○ Keith '18	⚑ 3
○ Bianchello del Metauro Sant'Ilario '17	⚑⚑ 2
○ Bianchello del Metauro Sup. Andy '16	⚑⚑ 3
○ Bianchello del Metauro Sup. Tenuta Campioli '17	⚑⚑ 2
⊙ Colli Pesaresi Rosato Le Rose di Campioli '17	⚑⚑ 2
● Colli Pesaresi Rosso Bartis '15	⚑⚑ 3

Cantine Fontezoppa

C.DA SAN DOMENICO, 38
62012 CIVITANOVA MARCHE [MC]
TEL. +39 0733790504
www.cantinefontezoppa.it

CELLAR SALES
PRE-BOOKED VISITS
ACCOMMODATION AND RESTAURANT SERVICE
ANNUAL PRODUCTION 290,000 bottles
HECTARES UNDER VINE 38.00

Moses Ambrosi wants Fontezoppa wines to be the legitimate children of their terroir of provenance. . For this reason, the estate has increasingly relied on the most authentic traditional grapes and has not hesitated to adopt organic methods, thereby strengthen its territorial bonds. The hectares of vineyards wind between Serrapetrona, land of Vernaccia Nera, and the first hills of the Macerata coast. The winery's modern cellar and guesthouse are a few kilometers from the sea in a beautiful vineyard setting. La Ribona '18 confirms its status as the best of its kind, just falling short of a Tre Bicchieri. Aromas of aniseed and medlar, together with personal, subtly sulfurous notes rise up off the nose only to reemerge on a full, gratifying palate. Here, due to its young age, the wine may be just a bit lacking in complexity. Their Incrocio Bruni 54 '18 is lively and flavorful. The mobile and peppery Serrapetrona Morò '16 put in a nice performance, while both the Ribona Metodo Classico '15 and the Passito Cascià '09 prove charming and original.

○ Colli Maceratesi Ribona '18	🍷🍷 3*
○ Colli Maceratesi Ribona Dosaggio Zero M. Cl. '15	🍷🍷 4
● I Terreni di San Severino Passito Cascià '09	🍷🍷 6
○ Incrocio Bruni 54 '18	🍷🍷 2*
● Serrapetrona Morò '16	🍷🍷 5
● Colli Maceratesi Rosso Vardò Ris. '15	🍷 4
○ Frapiccì '18	🍷 2
● Serrapetrona Pepato '16	🍷 3
○ Carapetto '13	🍷🍷 5
○ Colli Maceratesi Ribona '16	🍷🍷 3*
○ Colli Maceratesi Ribona Dosaggio Zero M. Cl. '14	🍷🍷 4
○ Frapiccì '17	🍷🍷 2*
● Serrapetrona Carpignano '15	🍷🍷 2*
● Serrapetrona Morò '15	🍷🍷 5

★★Gioacchino Garofoli

VIA CARLO MARX, 123
60022 CASTELFIDARDO [AN]
TEL. +39 0717820162
www.garofolivini.it

CELLAR SALES
PRE-BOOKED VISITS
ANNUAL PRODUCTION 2,000,000 bottles
HECTARES UNDER VINE 42.00

Garofoli is one of Marche's best-known names in wine, with over a century of history and exemplary interpretations based on Verdicchio and Montepulciano. The vineyards include well-groomed vines from which the best selections are obtained, these include Serra de' Conti as well as an estate on calcareous soils at the foot of Mount Conero. Other grapes are supplied by long-trusted winegrowers. The cellar is fully equipped for complete range, from different versions of sparkling Metodo Classico through to sweet wines. The Podium '17 offers up enticing aromas of candied lemon, almond and mineral hints. On the palate it's pleasant, creamier than it is deep, but always quite harmonious. The Macrina '18 also exhibits great poise, a wine that opts for fresher tones, a bright, supple palate. The citrusy, saline and well-paced Garofoli Brut Riserva '13 performed well. Among their reds we appreciated the tight-knit Camerlano '16 and the vigorous Grosso Agontano Riserva '16.

○ Verdicchio dei Castelli di Jesi Brut M. Cl. Ris. '13	🍷🍷 4
○ Verdicchio dei Castelli di Jesi Cl. Sup. Macrina '18	🍷🍷 2*
○ Verdicchio dei Castelli di Jesi Cl. Sup. Podium '17	🍷🍷 4
● Camerlano '16	🍷🍷 4
○ Castelli di Jesi Verdicchio Cl. Serra Fiorese Ris. '15	🍷🍷 4
● Conero Grosso Agontano Ris. '16	🍷🍷 5
⊙ Kòmaros '18	🍷🍷 2*
● Rosso Conero Piancarda '16	🍷🍷 3
○ Verdicchio dei Castelli di Jesi Brut M. Cl. Delis '13	🍷🍷 4
⊙ Garofoli Brut M. Cl. Rosé '11	🍷 4
○ Verdicchio dei Castelli di Jesi Passito Brumato '08	🍷 4

Marco Gatti

VIA LAGUA E SAN MARTINO, 2
60043 CERRETO D'ESI [AN]
TEL. +39 0732677012
www.gattiagri.it

CELLAR SALES
PRE-BOOKED VISITS
ANNUAL PRODUCTION 10,000 bottles
HECTARES UNDER VINE 6.00

Marco Gatti' started as a nurseryman with a strong passion for viticulture. He started out with a hectare of vineyards, but pretty soon the plot became too small for his growing interest, so he began to rent additional land in the area. Today he has seven hectares of vineyards from which he obtains very well focused Matelica of a specific style: Marco loves full maturation without sacrificing the acidity that the land, at an elevation of about 400 meters and surrounded by the Apennines, guarantees. Steel tanks and aging on the fine lees imbue juiciness and clean approachability. Their Millo Riserva '16 entices: captivating aromas call up botrytis and candied orange, on the palate it's complex, multi-layered and exceptionally sapid. The only drawback is how few bottles are available. If you can't find it, you can still count on their Villa Marilla '18, an appealing wine on the nose where Verdicchio's signature timbres of aniseed and almond take center stage. On the palate it proves gratifyingly complete. Their Casale Venza '18 is a simpler, more accessible wine, but no less tasty.

○ Verdicchio di Matelica Millo Ris. '16	♀♀	3*
○ Verdicchio di Matelica Casale Venza '18	♀♀	2*
○ Verdicchio di Matelica Villa Marilla '18	♀♀	2*
○ Verdicchio di Matelica Casale Venza '17	♀♀	2*
○ Verdicchio di Matelica Casale Venza '16	♀♀	2*
○ Verdicchio di Matelica Millo Ris. '13	♀♀	3*
○ Verdicchio di Matelica Villa Marilla '17	♀♀	2*
○ Verdicchio di Matelica Villa Marilla '16	♀♀	2*
○ Verdicchio di Matelica Villa Marilla '15	♀♀	2*
○ Verdicchio di Matelica Villa Marilla '14	♀♀	2*
○ Verdicchio di Matelica Villa Marilla '13	♀♀	2*

Conte Leopardi Dittajuti

VIA MARINA II, 24
60026 NUMANA [AN]
TEL. +39 0717390116
www.conteleopardi.it

CELLAR SALES
PRE-BOOKED VISITS
ANNUAL PRODUCTION 350,000 bottles
HECTARES UNDER VINE 49.00

Piervittorio Leopardi's dedication to Montepulciano is long-standing: Conero's traditional grape has been vinified here for almost forty years. Today it forms the estate's backbone; the varietal is prominent in vineyards scattered between Sirolo and Numana, a few kilometers from the Adriatic, on cool soils formed of mixtures of marly clays and limestone. The large, well-equipped and mostly underground cellar houses an imposing quantity of small oak casks for aging wines that can sing on an international stage yet maintain their typical Ancona accent. Their Pigmento '16 calls up plums, black olives and burnt wood, sensations that reemerge on a close-knit, ripe palate where tannic presence is close to complete integration. Their Casirano '17 features a fruitier, fresher profile, and a palate characterized by pulp, volume and pronounced tannins. The Villa Marina '17 opens with a stroke of bottled cherries, but then on the palate the wine finds balance and softness. Thanks to its nice, juicy palate, the Castelverde '18 also delivered.

● Conero Pigmento Ris. '16	♀♀	5
○ Calcare '18	♀♀	3
● Conero Casirano Ris. '17	♀♀	4
● Rosso Conero Antichi Poderi del Conte '17	♀♀	2*
● Rosso Conero Villa Marina '17	♀♀	3
○ Verdicchio dei Castelli di Jesi Cl. Castelverde '17	♀♀	2*
○ Bianco del Coppo '18	♀	2
● Rosso Conero Fructus '18	♀	2
○ Verdicchio dei Castelli di Jesi Cl. Oltremare '18	♀	2
● Conero Pigmento Ris. '15	♀♀	5
● Conero Pigmento Ris. '13	♀♀	5
○ Verdicchio dei Castelli di Jesi Cl. Castelverde '16	♀♀	2*

Mario Lucchetti

VIA SANTA MARIA DEL FIORE, 17
60030 MORRO D'ALBA [AN]
TEL. +39 073163314
www.mariolucchetti.it

CELLAR SALES
PRE-BOOKED VISITS
ANNUAL PRODUCTION 150,000 bottles
HECTARES UNDER VINE 25.00

Mario Lucchetti was one of the first to believe in Lacrima and every now and then older bottles from his cellar give an idea of its long-term potential. Today production falls on his active and enthusiastic son Paolo who, with the help of consultants Pierluigi Donna and Alberto Mazzoni, carries out projects that are propelling the winery in a contemporary direction, such as organic conversion in the vineyards. The large and welcoming cellar is near the historic Santa Maria del Fiore cru. Their best wines are aged in concrete. The Guardengo '17 is a Lacrima dense in fruit, with a full, tasty palate that's just a bit short in suppleness due to its bulky structure. Their Vigna Vittoria '18, an unabashedly fruity and full wine with extremely persistent flavor, moves on a similar track. The Fiore '18 is very precise in its varietal character, boasting a lovely sapidity on the palate despite evident tannic grip. The Birbacciò '18 is a supple, easy drink.

● Lacrima di Morro d'Alba Fiore '18	🍷🍷 2*
● Lacrima di Morro d'Alba Sup. Guardengo '17	🍷🍷 3
○ Verdicchio dei Castelli di Jesi Cl. Sup. V. Vittoria '18	🍷🍷 2*
○ Verdicchio dei Castelli di Jesi Cl. Birbacciò '18	🍷 2
● Lacrima di Morro d'Alba '16	🍷🍷 2*
● Lacrima di Morro d'Alba '12	🍷🍷 2*
● Lacrima di Morro d'Alba Mariasole '16	🍷🍷 6
● Lacrima di Morro d'Alba Sup. Guardengo '16	🍷🍷 3
● Lacrima di Morro d'Alba Sup. Guardengo '15	🍷🍷 3
● Lacrima di Morro d'Alba Sup. Guardengo '11	🍷🍷 3
○ Verdicchio dei Castelli di Jesi Cl. Sup. '12	🍷🍷 3

Stefano Mancinelli

VIA ROMA, 62
60030 MORRO D'ALBA [AN]
TEL. +39 073163021
www.mancinellivini.it

CELLAR SALES
PRE-BOOKED VISITS
ACCOMMODATION
ANNUAL PRODUCTION 150,000 bottles
HECTARES UNDER VINE 25.00

Stefano Mancinelli not only created the modern image of Lacrima di Morro d'Alba, but also embodies the historical memory of the territory's agriculture. His estate integrates wine, oil, distilled spirits and hospitality; within its walls there is also a small but exhaustive museum of rural life that shows viticulture here over the years. The winery's production style sees long-aging reds resulting in rich, powerful wines, while whites are increasing in both freshness and drinkability. Their Lacrima Superiore '17 does a nice job managing abundant stuffing, making for vibrant, spicy aromas and characteristic floral accents. The palate is structured, but has length and nice grip. The Lacrima '17 features extended fruity strokes of black cherry amidst clear notes of rose and violet, sensations that reemerge on a juicy palate with a decisive finish. Their two 2018 Verdicchios prove supple, with pronounced acidity.

● Lacrima di Morro d'Alba Sup. '17	🍷🍷 3*
● Lacrima di Morro d'Alba '17	🍷🍷 2*
○ Verdicchio dei Castelli di Jesi Cl. '18	🍷🍷 2*
○ Verdicchio dei Castelli di Jesi Cl. Sup. '18	🍷🍷 2*
● Brut M. Cl.	🍷 5
● Lacrima di Morro d'Alba Sensazioni di Frutto '18	🍷 2
● Lacrima di Morro d'Alba '16	🍷🍷 2*
● Lacrima di Morro d'Alba '13	🍷🍷 2*
● Lacrima di Morro d'Alba Passito Re Sole '13	🍷🍷 5
● Lacrima di Morro d'Alba Sup. '15	🍷🍷 3
● Lacrima di Morro d'Alba Sup. '13	🍷🍷 3*
● Terre dei Goti '11	🍷🍷 5
○ Verdicchio dei Castelli di Jesi Cl. Sup. '17	🍷🍷 2*
○ Verdicchio dei Castelli di Jesi Passito Stell '13	🍷🍷 5

Clara Marcelli

VIA FONTE VECCHIA, 8
63081 CASTORANO [AP]
TEL. +39 073687289
www.claramarcelli.it

PRE-BOOKED VISITS
ANNUAL PRODUCTION 40,000 bottles
HECTARES UNDER VINE 14.00
VITICULTURE METHOD Certified Organic

Clara Marcelli's wines absorb all the energy of the sunny Castorano territory. Vineyards with vigorously organic management and spontaneous fermentation in the cellar, practiced for years, result in indomitable character, eloquent sincerity and a bit of roughness in the mouth that softens with time. A few rows of Cabernet are for the Corbu, but traditional varieties dominate with Montepulciano acting as the star. The more ambitious reds mature in barriques in the original, perfectly restored cellar. Their Bordò Ruggine '13 put in a performance for the ages: delicate notes of rhubarb, licorice and wet earth rise up on the nose, while on the palate it's an intricate weave of acidity, sweet tannins and harmony, making for a truly charming drink. The aggressive extractive force of their full-bodied K'Un '16, a genuine, no-nonsense Montepulciano, makes for an entirely different wine. Their Irata '17 is a vibrant, pervasive Pecorino that's original in its aromas of grain and hay.

● Ruggine '13	🍷🍷 8
● K'un '16	🍷🍷 3
○ Offida Pecorino Irata '17	🍷🍷 3
● Rosso Piceno Sup. '16	🍷🍷 3
● Corbù '16	🍷 2
● K'un '13	🍷🍷 3
● K'un '12	🍷🍷 3
● K'un '11	🍷🍷 3
● K'un '10	🍷🍷 3
○ Offida Pecorino Irata '11	🍷🍷 2*
● Rosso Piceno Sup. '10	🍷🍷 3
● Ruggine '11	🍷🍷 8

Maurizio Marchetti

FRAZ. PINOCCHIO
VIA DI PONTELUNGO, 166
60131 ANCONA
TEL. +39 071897386
www.marchettiwines.it

CELLAR SALES
PRE-BOOKED VISITS
ANNUAL PRODUCTION 65,000 bottles
HECTARES UNDER VINE 22.00

Maurizio Marchetti's vineyards comprise a single 22-hectare body that winds up the hill toward Candia. The clayey and calcareous soil has long been used for Montepulciano del Conero. Despite characateristically being late to ripen, grapes easily reach full maturity here thanks to their south-east exposure. In the cellar also used by Maurizio's father, Mario (one of the first winemakers of the appellation), there are several concrete tanks, while small barrels are exclusively for Riserva Villa Bonomi, one of the best Conero in circulation for many years now. Their 2016 is no exception. Its focused, vibrant, cherry profile is adorned with a spicy and smoky counterpoint, sensations that anticipate a profiled, energetic palate — it's a Conero that's not lacking in finesse, despite its weight. Their Castro di San Silvestro '18 also exhibits a certain gustatory density, even if it unfolds well, leaving a fruity trail in its wake. The Tenuta del Cavaligere '18 is characterized by late-harvest aromas and a juicy palate.

● Conero Villa Bonomi Ris. '16	🍷🍷 5
● Rosso Conero Castro di San Silvestro '18	🍷🍷 2*
○ Verdicchio dei Castelli di Jesi Cl. Sup. Tenuta del Cavaliere '18	🍷🍷 3
⊙ Rosato '18	🍷 1*
○ Verdicchio dei Castelli di Jesi Cl. '18	🍷 2
● Rosso Conero Villa Bonomi Ris. '02	🍷🍷🍷 4
● Conero Villa Bonomi Cento Vendemmie Mario Marchetti Ris. '13	🍷🍷 5
● Conero Villa Bonomi Ris. '15	🍷🍷 5
● Conero Villa Bonomi Ris. '14	🍷🍷 5
● Conero Villa Bonomi Ris. '13	🍷🍷 5
● Conero Villa Bonomi Ris. '12	🍷🍷 5
● Rosso Conero Castro di San Silvestro '16	🍷🍷 2*
● Rosso Conero Due Amici '17	🍷🍷 2*

...arotti Campi

SANT'AMICO, 14
...030 MORRO D'ALBA [AN]
. +39 0731618027
...w.marotticampi.it

...LLAR SALES
...E-BOOKED VISITS
...COMMODATION
...NUAL PRODUCTION 240,000 bottles
...CTARES UNDER VINE 71.00

...enzo Marotti Campi has moved into high
...ar in recent years and his winery is
...erating at never before seen levels of
...ality. This success is undoubtedly thanks
...his skill, with the help of long-time
...nsultant Roberto Potentini, at reading the
...engths of the territory where Lacrima is
...g and Verdicchio grows exuberantly. He
...es equal dignity to both cultivars and
...nks to many hectares of vineyards has
...uninterrupted supply of impeccable raw
...terial for expressive, modern wines,
...rfectly linked to the varietal ideal of each.
...eir Orgiolo '17 is a magnificent Lacrima,
...nonument built of characteristic floral
...mas softened by spicy hints of black
...oper, a brilliant palate in which a fine
...nic weave gives way to a complex,
...gant, extraordinarily long finish. The
...bico '18 is redolent of cherry and rose,
...d delicious on the palate, while their
...ris, another Lacrima, is an original sweet,
...mi-sparkling wine. In terms of their
...ites, the Salmariano '16 put in a
...mmendable performance with its
...essing, extremely tasty palate.

...acrima di Morro d'Alba Sup.	
...rgiolo '17	♥♥♥ 3*
...astelli di Jesi Verdicchio Cl.	
...almariano Ris. '16	♥♥ 3*
...acrima di Morro d'Alba Rubico '18	♥♥ 2*
...osato '18	♥♥ 2*
...erdicchio dei Castelli di Jesi Cl.	
...lbiano '18	♥♥ 1*
...erdicchio dei Castelli di Jesi Cl. Sup.	
...uzano '18	♥♥ 2*
...yris	♥♥ 2
...rut Rosé	♥ 3
...astelli di Jesi Verdicchio Cl.	
...almariano Ris. '14	♥♥♥ 3*
...astelli di Jesi Verdicchio Cl.	
...almariano Ris. '13	♥♥♥ 3*
...acrima di Morro d'Alba Sup.	
...rgiolo '16	♥♥♥ 3*

Poderi Mattioli

VIA FARNETO, 17A
60030 SERRA DE' CONTI [AN]
TEL. +39 0731878676
www.poderimattioli.it

CELLAR SALES
PRE-BOOKED VISITS
ANNUAL PRODUCTION 30,000 bottles
HECTARES UNDER VINE 6.50
VITICULTURE METHOD Certified Organic

Serra de' Conti can be seen as a sort of
Vosne-Romanée for Verdicchio not so much
for its soil and climatic characteristics as
for its domination of the territory. The
Mattioli had been winegrowers for
generations but Giordano, Giacomo and
Letizia decided to move into winemaking as
well. They have quickly established
themselves in the crowded Verdicchio
landscape as a result of vineyards cared for
like gardens, intimate familiarity with the
variety, a beautiful and efficient cellar, and
the correct amount of aging in steel. The
Lauro '16 is extraordinary. It opens on a
clear sensation of almonds, only to give
way to notes of white fruits and profuse
mineral hints. On the palate it's extremely
long, deep and multifaceted, exhibiting rare
harmony between its structural parts. And if
there were any need to probe Mattioli's skill
further, just try their Ylice '17, a child of
scorching year. The nose is perfectly
expressive and varietal, following through
to a streamlined, captivating palate, poised
and extraordinarily sapid.

○ Castelli di Jesi Verdicchio Cl.	
Lauro Ris. '16	♥♥♥ 4*
○ Verdicchio dei Castelli di Jesi Cl. Sup.	
Ylice '17	♥♥ 3*
○ Castelli di Jesi Verdicchio Cl.	
Lauro Ris. '15	♀♀♀ 4*
○ Castelli di Jesi Verdicchio Cl.	
Lauro Ris. '13	♀♀♀ 3*
○ Verdicchio dei Castelli di Jesi Cl. Sup.	
Ylice '16	♀♀♀ 3*
○ Verdicchio dei Castelli di Jesi Cl. Sup.	
Ylice '12	♀♀♀ 2*
○ Castelli di Jesi Verdicchio Cl.	
Lauro Ris. '14	♀♀ 4
○ Verdicchio dei Castelli di Jesi Cl. Sup.	
Lauro '10	♀♀ 3*
○ Verdicchio dei Castelli di Jesi Cl. Sup.	
Ylice '15	♀♀ 3*

Valter Mattoni

VIA PESCOLLA, 1
63030 CASTORANO [AP]
TEL. +39 073687329
www.valtermattoni.it

ANNUAL PRODUCTION 8,000 bottles
HECTARES UNDER VINE 8.50

Valter 'Roccia' Mattoni is one of the Piceno scene's best known characters: a decorator in life, he brings an authentic artisanal spirit to his a few acres of land planted with mature, local varieties. He follows the whole process personally (with the help of his nephew Andrea Bernabè) because of his personal passion for wine, which is inextricable from his attachment to family traditions. Advised by his friend Marco Casolanetti, he has for some time now produced wines that have achieved a real cult status, appreciated for their indomitable character and out-of-the-box character. Their Arshura '16 opens on notes of plums and morello cherry, only to explode into a thousand rivulets of flavor, filling the palate with tactile pleasure. Tannins are perfectly extracted, measured extraction and alcohol make for an authentic monument to Montepulciano. The arcadian Trebbién '17 proves highly drinkable thanks to its juicy, sapid palate.

● Arshura '16	♟♟♟ 5
○ Trebbien '17	♟♟ 4
● Cosecose '18	♟ 3
● Arshura '11	♟♟♟ 3*
● Arshura '14	♟♟ 5
● Arshura '13	♟♟ 5
● Cosecose '16	♟♟ 3
● Rosso Bordò '10	♟♟ 8
● Rossobordò '15	♟♟ 8
● Rossobordò '14	♟♟ 8
● Rossobordò '13	♟♟ 8
● Rossobordò '12	♟♟ 8
● Rossobordò '11	♟♟ 8
○ Trebbien '16	♟♟ 4
○ Trebbien '15	♟♟ 4
○ Trebbien '14	♟♟ 3

★La Monacesca

C.DA MONACESCA
62024 MATELICA [MC]
TEL. +39 0733672641
www.monacesca.it

CELLAR SALES
PRE-BOOKED VISITS
ANNUAL PRODUCTION 160,000 bottles
HECTARES UNDER VINE 28.00

A commemorative edition of Mirum reminds us that the wine, dedicated by A Cifola to the winery's founder, his father 'Miro', was born 30 years ago: a Matelica that has proven how Verdicchio can express complexity, with a stunning abilit to age. Over the years La Monacesca has kept the charm of small things done well Well-groomed vineyards, multiple passes during the harvest and judicial aging hav resulted in a well-established, recognizabl style that has also rubbed off on the red wines, which have never been so precise and territorial. Their Mirum Riserva '17 features appealing aromas of ripe yellow fruit, nuances of honey and candied orange. On the palate it has a soft, matur touch, with a graceful finish. The Mirum 3 Anni is a blend of various vintages from the last decade. It's complex and elegant even if it pursues a general atmosphere of pleasantness. The Terra di Mezzo '15 is extraordinarily rich and juicy, while their splendid Camerte '16 is earthy and fruity, with pervasive flavor and a multifaceted finish.

● Camerte '16	♟♟
○ Mirum 30 Anni	♟♟
○ Verdicchio di Matelica Mirum Ris. '17	♟♟
● Syrah '16	♟♟
○ Verdicchio di Matelica '17	♟♟
○ Verdicchio di Matelica Terra di Mezzo '15	♟♟
⊙ Camerte Rosé '18	♟
○ Verdicchio di Matelica Mirum Ris. '16	♟♟♟
○ Verdicchio di Matelica Mirum Ris. '15	♟♟♟
○ Verdicchio di Matelica Mirum Ris. '14	♟♟♟
○ Verdicchio di Matelica Mirum Ris. '12	♟♟♟
○ Verdicchio di Matelica Mirum Ris. '11	♟♟♟
○ Verdicchio di Matelica Mirum Ris. '10	♟♟♟
○ Verdicchio di Matelica Mirum Ris. '09	♟♟♟
○ Verdicchio di Matelica Mirum Ris. '08	♟♟♟

ontecappone

COLLE OLIVO, 2
035 JESI [AN]
. +39 0731205761
w.montecappone.com

LLAR SALES
E-BOOKED VISITS
NUAL PRODUCTION 150,000 bottles
CTARES UNDER VINE 42.50

anluca Mirizzi brings incredible energy to
ery aspect of his operations. He
ntinually acquires new vineyards,
periments with new methods like
mentation in amphora, and offers new
els. The family winery, Montecappone, is
e nucleus of his activity while his other
dependent projects bear the Mirizzi name.
rdicchio, the foundation of the entire
nge, is available in all types and for all
stes, but which all share a modern style
entive to overall freshness and
joyability. Their Utopia '16 once again
ds their selection. Captivating, fruity
omas, it exhibits smoothness and ease
the palate, together with extreme
pidity and volume — it's a complete
ne. But don't ignore the Federico II '17, a
btle wine redolent of aniseed that
atures austere elegance and supple
mmetry. Their Mirizzi Cogito A. '18 plays
nice contrast between softness and
pidity, while the Kylix '17 proves to be a
licate passito.

Castelli di Jesi Verdicchio Cl.	
Utopia Ris. '16	▼▼▼ 5
Verdicchio dei Castelli di Jesi Cl. Sup.	
Federico II A. D. 1194 '17	▼▼ 5
Kylix '17	▼▼ 5
Rosso Piceno '18	▼▼ 2*
Tabano '18	▼▼ 5
Verdicchio dei Castelli di Jesi Cl. '18	▼▼ 2*
Verdicchio dei Castelli di Jesi Cl. Sup.	
Cogito A. Mirizzi '18	▼▼ 3
Verdicchio dei Castelli di Jesi Cl. Sup.	
Muntobe '18	▼▼ 4
Madame Passerina '18	▼ 3
Passerina Brut	▼ 4
Verdicchio dei Castelli di Jesi Cl. Sup. Ergo	
Mirizzi '17	▼ 5
Verdicchio dei Castelli di Jesi M. Cl.	
Extra Brut Mirizzi '16	▼ 5

Alessandro Moroder

VIA MONTACUTO, 121
60029 ANCONA
TEL. +39 071898232
www.moroder-vini.it

CELLAR SALES
PRE-BOOKED VISITS
ANNUAL PRODUCTION 130,000 bottles
HECTARES UNDER VINE 18.00
VITICULTURE METHOD Certified Organic
SUSTAINABLE WINERY

Conero's recent story includes the insignia
of Moroder, Marche's first winery to be
awarded Tre Bicchieri. This is due to its
maniacal attachment to Montepulciano
grown on vineyards in Montacuto that
reach 70 years of age. The underground
cellar houses barrels of various ages and
volumes, where the four Conero mature
for different amounts of time. A complete
transition to organic farming has brought
even greater expressiveness to the wines,
whose production is followed by the
enologist Marco Gozzi. Their Dorico
Riserva '16 exhibits a superb
temperament. Precise sensations of black
cherry, plums, black olives and embers are
followed by a palate made exuberant by its
tannic presence, coming through
spontaneously, with a thrillingly authentic
varietal quality. Their Rosso Conero '16
needs a bit of time in the glass to
orchestrate its aromas, but its vivid,
characterful palate delivers unhesitatingly.
If you're looking for something more
approachable, trust in the fruity, grapey
fragrance of their Aiòn '18.

● Conero Dorico Ris. '16	▼▼ 5
● Conero Ris. '15	▼▼ 5
● Rosso Conero '16	▼▼ 2*
● Rosso Conero Aiòn '18	▼▼ 2*
○ Malvasia '18	▼ 2
● Conero Dorico Ris. '15	▼▼▼ 5
● Conero Dorico Ris. '05	▼▼▼ 5
● Rosso Conero Dorico '93	▼▼▼ 5
● Rosso Conero Dorico '90	▼▼▼ 5
● Rosso Conero Dorico '88	▼▼▼ 5
● Conero Dorico Ris. '13	▼▼ 5
● Conero Dorico Ris. '11	▼▼ 5
● Conero Ris. '13	▼▼ 5
● Rosso Conero '15	▼▼ 2*
● Rosso Conero Aiòn '17	▼▼ 2*
● Rosso Conero Aiòn '14	▼▼ 2*

Fattoria Nannì

c.da Arsicci
62021 Apiro [MC]
Tel. +39 3406225930
www.fattoriananni.it

CELLAR SALES
PRE-BOOKED VISITS
ANNUAL PRODUCTION 20,200 bottles
HECTARES UNDER VINE 8.50
VITICULTURE METHOD Certified Organic

In 2006, Roberto Cantori took over Gianni
Piersigilli's estate, known as Nannì,
comprised of an old ruin and six hectares
of vineyards reaching 50 years of age in a
wonderful place, situated at 450 meters
elevation, on Monte San Vicino. The 2018
vintage coming from all of the strictly
hand-harvested plots is the first in the new
cellar, equipped only with small-volume
steel. Territory, local cultivars and human
sensitivity, in a word, terroir, are at the
foundation of Fattoria Nannì's identity. The
Origini '18 is a masterpiece: Cantori drew
on his experience and a favorable year for
a Verdicchio with mountain sensations,
aromatically crystalline and delicate, racy
and rhythmic on the palate, with vigorous
acidity and a truly deep progression of
flavor. The Arsicci '18 is a masterful vin de
soif: nuanced and fragrant aromatically,
it's irresistible on the palate thanks to
well-gauged alcohol and a delicately
saline finish.

○ Verdicchio dei Castelli di Jesi Cl. Sup. Origini '18	♈♈♈ 5
○ Verdicchio dei Castelli di Jesi Cl. Sup. Arsicci '18	♈ 2*
○ Verdicchio dei Castelli di Jesi Cl. Sup. Origini '17	♈ 3
○ Verdicchio dei Castelli di Jesi Cl. Sup. Origini '16	♈ 3

★Oasi degli Angeli

c.da Sant'Egidio, 50
63012 Cupra Marittima [AP]
Tel. +39 0735778569
www.kurni.it

CELLAR SALES
PRE-BOOKED VISITS
ANNUAL PRODUCTION 5,000 bottles
HECTARES UNDER VINE 16.00

Seen from the outside, the vineyard with
40,000 Montepulciano vines per hectare
the now famous practice of aging the sam
wine twice in brand new barriques might
seem theatrical. In reality they are simply
examples of the experimental, avant-gard
techniques that allow their wines to obtain
personality and absolute recognizability.
The unique style finds a formidable ally in
time and in bottle aging, which bring new
nuances to the expression of Marco
Casolanetti and Eleonora Rossi's intuition
The Kurni '17 offers up manifold fruit and
spices, sensations that join together with
meaty palate. A sweetish attack is then
smoothed by the energy of its perfectly rip
tannins and exceptionally tight extraction.
It's one of the best versions in recent
memory for its clarity and aging prospects
The Kupra '16 alternates spices, balsamic
strokes, hints of Mediterranean shrub and
more complex, mineral notes. On the pala
it proves assertive, with a very long finish.

● Kupra '16	♈♈
● Kurni '17	♈♈
● Kupra '13	♈♈♈
● Kupra '12	♈♈♈
● Kupra '10	♈♈♈
● Kurni '10	♈♈♈
● Kurni '09	♈♈♈
● Kurni '08	♈♈♈
● Kurni '07	♈♈♈
● Kurni '04	♈♈♈
● Kurni '03	♈♈♈
● Kurni '02	♈♈♈
● Kurni '01	♈♈♈
● Kurni '00	♈♈♈
● Kurni '98	♈♈♈
● Kurni '97	♈♈♈

fficina del Sole

ᴠᴀ Montemilone, 1
842 Montegiorgio [FM]
. +39 0734967321
ww.officinadelsole.it

ᴺNUAL PRODUCTION 20,000 bottles
ᴇCTARES UNDER VINE 12.00

2009, the Beleggia family launched an
nbitious and somewhat revolutionary
oject for provincial Fermo: a luxury resort
rrounded by olive trees, vineyards and
uit trees. They acquired an entire hill, the
o of which offers an expansive view of
arche, and began a long process of
orks. After ten years, their wine has its
vn a very individual aspect despite the
x of international and traditional
ltivars, proof that enologist Davide Di
aiara's light hand has interpreted the
rritory's characteristics in the best
ssible way. Their Franco '18 put in an
ccellent performance, proving extremely
rusy, with vibrant acidity and a juicy,
adual palate that's at the service of a
ng, decidedly saline finish. Their Franco
anco '17, a more structured wine, is
rtainly not lacking in flavor and intensity.
e Tignium '16, a monovarietal Syrah,
es all in on elegance and balance,
fering up hints of black cherry and a
btle pepperiness on a supple palate with
ky smooth tannins.

Falerio Pecorino Franco '18	♈♈♈ 3*
Tignium '16	♈♈ 6
Falerio Pecorino Franco Franco '17	♈♈ 5
Leiè '18	♈ 3
Rosso Frutto '18	♈ 3
360 Brut	♈♈ 3
Falerio Pecorino Franco '17	♈♈ 3
Falerio Pecorino Franco Franco '15	♈♈ 5
Offida Pecorino Franco Franco '16	♈♈ 5
Tignium '15	♈♈ 6

Pantaleone

ᴠɪᴀ Colonnata Alta, 118
63100 Ascoli Piceno
Tᴇʟ. +39 3478757476
www.pantaleonewine.com

PRE-BOOKED VISITS
ANNUAL PRODUCTION 60,000 bottles
HECTARES UNDER VINE 16.00
VITICULTURE METHOD Certified Organic

A valley creeps into the side of the hills
north of Ascoli Piceno and arrives at Monte
Ascensione. Here, in an almost virgin
environment dominated by woods and
broom bushes, Nazzareno Pantaloni and
daughters Francesca and Federica have
planted vineyards according to the local
traditional methods. Giuseppe Infriccioli,
Francesca's husband, takes care of the
winemaking. The highly-stylized wines are
contemporary, with very fresh whites and
temperamental reds, which flow across the
palate in a manner that is far from banal.
After coming close in the past, their
Onirocep '18 finally takes home Tre
Bicchieri. It does so by transforming
buoyant acidity into pervasive, vibrant
flavor, a palate that's perfectly coherent
with its aromatic profile of citrus and wild
herbs, resolving on a crackling finish of sea
salt. The Chicca '18 a Passerina, is
decidedly fresh and tasty, thirst-quenching.
Their Boccascena '15, made with
Montepulciano grapes, features a
characterful but nicely sapid palate. The
Bordò La Ribalta '15 is a bit too evolved.

○ Falerio Pecorino Onirocep '18	♈♈♈ 3*
● Boccascena '15	♈♈ 3
○ Chicca '18	♈♈ 2*
● Atto I '18	♈ 2
● La Ribalta '15	♈ 8
○ Pivuàn '18	♈ 2
● Boccascena '12	♈♈ 3
○ Chicca '16	♈♈ 2*
○ Chicca '13	♈♈ 2*
○ Falerio Pecorino Onirocep '16	♈♈ 3*
○ Falerio Pecorino Onirocep '15	♈♈ 2*
○ Falerio Pecorino Onirocep '14	♈♈ 2*
○ Falerio Pecorino Onirocep '13	♈♈ 2*
● La Ribalta '13	♈♈ 8
● Ribalta '12	♈♈ 8

Tenute Pieralisi Monte Schiavo

FRAZ. MONTESCHIAVO
VIA VIVAIO
60030 MAIOLATI SPONTINI [AN]
TEL. +39 0731700385
www.monteschiavo.it

CELLAR SALES
PRE-BOOKED VISITS
ANNUAL PRODUCTION 950,000 bottles
HECTARES UNDER VINE 103.00
SUSTAINABLE WINERY

Monte Schiavo rose from the ashes of an old cooperative that was eventually taken over by the Pieralisi family. Its skin has changed several times to reach its current well-structured form, including a large wine cellar and considerable vineyards located in suitable areas of the Esino River's northern quadrant. The two most recent initiatives are the conversion to organic farming and the Tenuta Pieralisi line, which uses spontaneous fermentation and centers on highlighting the terroir. A number of Monte Schiavo's key wines were missing, but those submitted for tasting performed well. In particular, we appreciated the revived Pallio di San Floriano '18, a wine that's back to its previous, high standards thanks to an extremely sapid, supple and plucky version. Elegance and poise work in favor of their Villaia '18, a delicate and mineral wine that's just a bit lacking in length. The Tassanare Brut, a Verdicchio with a 10% share of Chardonnay vinified according to the long Charmat Method, is highly pleasant and on the mark, while the Molino '18 proves fragrant and smooth.

○ Verdicchio dei Castelli di Jesi Cl. Sup. Pallio di S. Floriano '18	♟♟ 3*
○ Tassanare Brut	♟♟ 2
○ Verdicchio dei Castelli di Jesi Cl. Sup. Villaia Tenute Pieralisi '18	♟♟ 3
● Lacrima di Morro d'Alba Marzaiola '18	♟ 2
● Rosso Piceno Sassaiolo '16	♟ 2
○ Verdicchio dei Castelli di Jesi Cl. Coste del Molino '18	♟ 2
○ Verdicchio dei Castelli di Jesi Cl. Sup. Pallio di S. Floriano '11	♟♟♟ 2*
○ Verdicchio dei Castelli di Jesi Cl. Sup. Pallio di S. Floriano '10	♟♟♟ 2*
○ Verdicchio dei Castelli di Jesi Cl. Sup. Pallio di S. Floriano '09	♟♟♟ 2*

Pievalta

VIA MONTESCHIAVO, 18
60030 MAIOLATI SPONTINI [AN]
TEL. +39 0731705199
www.baronepizzini.it

CELLAR SALES
PRE-BOOKED VISITS
ANNUAL PRODUCTION 125,000 bottles
HECTARES UNDER VINE 26.50
VITICULTURE METHOD Certified Biodynam
SUSTAINABLE WINERY

Since 2003, Pievalta has never wavered i its rigorous application of agronomic practices entirely based on biodynamics and today it's a touchstone of the Verdicch area. Its 29 hectares of vineyards are primarily Jesi, with smaller amounts of Malvasia, Trebbiano and Montepulciano. Last year saw the purchase of a vineyard adjacent to its San Paolo cru, an extremely suitable site in the municipality of the sam name and from which the company obtair the grapes for its celebrated Riserva. Dominé '18 offers up aromas of broom, orange peel and floral strokes. On the pala it exhibits balance while unveiling a close-focused almondy note. Their Verdicchio Pievalta '18 features herbaceo sensations amidst flowers and fresh almond. On the palate it's supple and racy with a refreshing quality. Their Curina '16 the best yet. Aromas of bitter citrus anticipate a palate that plays on contrasts sugars and acidic vigor. The Perlugo is a Verdicchio M.Cl. that's proving increasingl on the mark.

○ Verdicchio dei Castelli di Jesi Cl. Sup. Dominè Chiesa del Pozzo '18	♟♟
○ Verdicchio dei Castelli di Jesi Passito Curina '16	♟♟
● Campo del Noce '16	♟♟
○ Perlugo Dosaggio Zero M. Cl.	♟♟
○ Verdicchio dei Castelli di Jesi Cl. Sup. Pievalta '18	♟
○ Castelli di Jesi Verdicchio Cl. San Paolo Ris. '16	♟♟♟
○ Castelli di Jesi Verdicchio Cl. San Paolo Ris. '15	♟♟♟
○ Castelli di Jesi Verdicchio Cl. San Paolo Ris. '13	♟♟♟
○ Castelli di Jesi Verdicchio Cl. San Paolo Ris. '10	♟♟♟

Pollenza

A Casone, 4
*029 Tolentino [MC]
.. +39 0733961989
ww.ilpollenza.it

CELLAR SALES
PRE-BOOKED VISITS
ANNUAL PRODUCTION 300,000 bottles
HECTARES UNDER VINE 80.00
SUSTAINABLE WINERY

he estate founded by Aldo Brachetti
eretti is unparalleled in the region: its
derly vineyards unfold among ancient
las and fascinating artifacts. The cellar is
rt of a 16th century building designed by
ntonio da Sangallo the Younger. Despite
e enormous number of vineyards and
ailable technology, production is kept well
elow what it could be due to the
ilosophy that quality is integral to an
egant, sober style, far removed from the
shion of the moment. The Pollenza '16, a
ordeaux blend dominated by Cabernet
auvignon, features notes of peppers, spicy
ances and an elegant toasty stroke. On
e palate it's close-woven, still a bit stiff
ut poised. Their Cosmino '16, a Cabernet
anc, is more extrovert with its aromas of
owers and herbaceous notes, sensations
at reemerge on an earthy, characterful
alate. If you love fullness of fruit and
under sensations, there's the Porpora, a
ontepulciano with a 30% share of Merlot,
wine that features a meaty palate with
ocile tannins.

Cosmino '16	♥♥ 5
Il Pollenza '16	♥♥ 8
Colli Maceratesi Ribona Angera '18	♥♥ 3
Porpora '16	♥♥ 3
Brianello '18	♥ 3
Didì '18	♥ 3
Il Pollenza '15	♥♥♥ 8
Il Pollenza '12	♥♥♥ 8
Il Pollenza '11	♥♥♥ 7
Il Pollenza '10	♥♥♥ 7
Il Pollenza '09	♥♥♥ 7
Il Pollenza '07	♥♥♥ 7
Cosmino '15	♥♥ 5
Cosmino '14	♥♥ 5
Il Pollenza '14	♥♥ 8
Pius IX Mastai '15	♥♥ 6

Sabbionare

via Sabbionare, 10
60036 Montecarotto [AN]
Tel. +39 0731889004
www.sabbionare.it

CELLAR SALES
PRE-BOOKED VISITS
ANNUAL PRODUCTION 45,000 bottles
HECTARES UNDER VINE 24.00

Some of the Paolucci family's vineyards
are near the winery, in the district named
for the mighty sand bars that punctuate
the mostly clay soil. Verdicchio grows
vigorously here, reaching considerable
sugar levels without fail. Guided by the
experience of Sergio Paolucci (unrelated
to the owners) grapes are transformed
into robust but never excessive wines,
pulpy and respect the varietal. Their
Sabbionare '18 exhibits a vital energy
that characterizes the best Verdicchios.
This transforms into a background of sapid
echoes and almondy sensations. The
Filetto '18 is its young brother, made with
grapes cultivated in another area. It unveils
nice acidic tension, which facilitates
drinkability without sacrificing an ounce of
flavor.Their Cromìa '15 is a convincing,
personal interpretation of Montepulciano
(accompanied by a 10% share of Merlot)
that's redolent of plums and slightly
saltier notes on an expansive palate of
nice complexity.

● Cromìa '15	♥♥ 3
○ Verdicchio dei Castelli di Jesi Cl. Il Filetto '18	♥♥ 1*
○ Verdicchio dei Castelli di Jesi Cl. Sup. Sabbionare '18	♥♥ 3
○ Verdicchio dei Castelli di Jesi Pas Dosé M. Cl. Dune '15	♥ 5
○ Verdicchio dei Castelli di Jesi Cl. Sup. Sabbionare '15	♥♥♥ 2*
○ Verdicchio dei Castelli di Jesi Cl. Sup. Sabbionare '17	♥♥ 3
○ Verdicchio dei Castelli di Jesi Cl. Sup. Sabbionare '16	♥♥ 3*
○ Verdicchio dei Castelli di Jesi Cl. Sup. Sabbionare '12	♥♥ 2*

Saladini Pilastri

VIA SALADINI, 5
63078 SPINETOLI [AP]
TEL. +39 0736899534
www.saladinipilastri.it

CELLAR SALES
PRE-BOOKED VISITS
ANNUAL PRODUCTION 800,000 bottles
HECTARES UNDER VINE 150.00
VITICULTURE METHOD Certified Organic
SUSTAINABLE WINERY

The winery has very deep roots and today Saladino Saladini Pilastri manages substantial vineyards that wind through the gentle hills of Spinetoli and Monteprandone. Respect for tradition is central, with Sangiovese and Montepulciano coming together in different Rosso Piceno versions made of the best fruit from the oldest and best positioned vineyards. The reds all ferment in small wood barrels. Cooler positions on the slopes are reserved for Pecorino, Passerina and Trebbiano, helping to produce increasingly well-focused wines. Their Montetinello '17 put in a nice performance. At this stage it's particularly persuasive in its fruity sensations and invigorating, juicy development. The Vigna Monteprandone '17 is darker and more introverted aromatically, but its nice tannic grain and energy tell of good things to come. Among their whites, the Pecorino '18 offers up mineral hints and citrusy nuances on a full, cohesive, firm palate.

○ Offida Passerina '18	♟♟	3
○ Offida Pecorino '18	♟♟	3
● Rosso Piceno Sup. Montetinello '17	♟♟	4
● Rosso Piceno Sup. V. Monteprandone '17	♟♟	5
○ Falerio '18	♟	2
○ Falerio Palazzi '18	♟	3
● Pregio del Conte '17	♟	4
● Rosso Piceno '18	♟	2
● Rosso Piceno Piediprato '17	♟	3
● Rosso Piceno Sup. V. Monteprandone '00	♟♟♟	3
● Rosso Piceno Sup. Montetinello '16	♟♟	4
● Rosso Piceno Sup. V. Monteprandone '16	♟♟	5

San Filippo

LOC. BORGO MIRIAM
C.DA CIAFONE, 17A
63035 OFFIDA [AP]
TEL. +39 0736889828
www.vinisanfilippo.it

CELLAR SALES
PRE-BOOKED VISITS
ANNUAL PRODUCTION 100,000 bottles
HECTARES UNDER VINE 55.00
VITICULTURE METHOD Certified Organic

Brothers Lino and Fabrizio Stracci persona manage their sizable vineyards. Their attachment to country life and their own territory led them to embrace the practices of organic farming many years ago. The cellar and most of the vineyards, planted with local varieties, are in the intensely cultivated Contrada Ciafone, home to some of the most beautiful vineyards in the whole Piceno area. The style, created with enologist Roberto D'Angelo, centers on frank authenticity and varietal spontaneity, even if it means bringing along some rustic elements. The Lupo del Ciafone '15 is a monovarietal Montepulciano. In the glass it releases all the grape's signature energy, with clear sensations of plum and morello cherry, aromas that reemerge on its meaty tactile and highly persistent palate. Their Kàtharsis '17 features impetuous tannins and a floral profile that rises up amidst clear sensations of fruit, while the Pecorino '18 offers up aromas of country herbs and lemon peel on a dynamic palate.

○ Offida Pecorino '18	♟♟	1
● Offida Rosso Lupo del Ciafone '15	♟♟	4
● Rosso Piceno Sup. Kàtharsis '17	♟♟	2
○ Offida Passerina '18	♟	2
● Vi'Munn Rosso Senza Solfiti '18	♟	
○ Offida Pecorino '15	♟♟	2
○ Offida Pecorino '13	♟♟	2
● Offida Rosso Lupo del Ciafone '11	♟♟	3
● Rosso Piceno Sup. Kàtharsis '14	♟♟	2

Tenute San Sisto
Fazi Battaglia

Roma, 117
031 Castelplanio [AN]
L. +39 073181591
www.fazibattaglia.it

CELLAR SALES
PRE-BOOKED VISITS
ANNUAL PRODUCTION 1,000,000 bottles
HECTARES UNDER VINE 130.00

The Angelini family, owners of Bertani Domains, acquired the Fazi Battaglia property in 2015. The family spared no resources in immediately renewing and reorganizing a winery that is fundamental to the history of Verdicchio. The most important step, which took place in 2019, was the creation of Tenute San Sisto: the grapes of the best crus converge and are then vinified and aged in reserved spaces, using equipment suitable for small volumes and individual plots. Aged for a year in large casks, their San Sisto '17 features an elegant aromatic profile amidst almondy reflections, aromatic herbs, aniseed and a smoky echo. On the palate it exhibits a supple silhouette, a graceful stride and a lengthy finish that's rich in nuance. Their Massaccio '17, aged in concrete, is more well-defined, weighty and enticingly fruity. The Arkezia '17 is a balanced passito redolent of candied lemon, while the Titulus '18 proves to be a fragrant white, persuasive and tasty on the palate.

Castelli di Jesi Verdicchio Cl. San Sisto Ris. '17	♟♟♟ 5
Arkezia Muffo di San Sisto '17	♟♟ 5
Verdicchio dei Castelli di Jesi Cl. Sup. Massaccio '17	♟♟ 3*
Verdicchio dei Castelli di Jesi Cl. Titulus Fazi Battaglia '18	♟♟ 2*
Castelli di Jesi Verdicchio Cl. San Sisto Ris. '16	♟♟♟ 5
Castelli di Jesi Verdicchio Cl. San Sisto Ris. '15	♟♟♟ 5
Castelli di Jesi Verdicchio Cl. San Sisto Ris. '14	♟♟♟ 4*
Castelli di Jesi Verdicchio Cl. San Sisto Ris. '10	♟♟♟ 4*

Santa Barbara

b.go Mazzini 35
60010 Barbara [AN]
Tel. +39 0719674249
www.santabarbara.it

CELLAR SALES
PRE-BOOKED VISITS
ANNUAL PRODUCTION 900,000 bottles
HECTARES UNDER VINE 40.00

35 years have passed since Stefano Antonucci left his quiet bank job to found Santa Barbara. Today, as then, its operational base is in the historic center of the village of the same name. It has become one of Marche's best-known wineries, present in all the most developed markets and well distributed throughout the country. Credit must be given to the Stefano's intuition, which over the years has enabled him to a complete range made of highly pleasant, drinkable modern wines featuring full flavor and fruity fragrance. Among the many wines on their lengthy roster, our first choice is still their Tardivo ma non Tardo '17, with its intense aromatic weave — distinct notes of citrus, peach and almond stand out and then fuse on a soft, tasty yet extraordinarily supple palate. The Pathos '17, a blend of international grapes, features force and a fruity density made evident on a meaty palate characterized by docile tannins. The Lina '17 is a passito redolent of candied lemon, sensations that lend lightness to a creamy and extremely long palate.

○ Castelli di Jesi Verdicchio Cl. Tardivo ma non Tardo Ris. '17	♟♟ 6
● Pathos '17	♟♟ 6
○ Verdicchio dei Castelli di Jesi Cl. Le Vaglie '18	♟♟ 3*
○ Verdicchio dei Castelli di Jesi Passito Lina '17	♟♟ 5
● Lacrima di Morro d'Alba Pignocco '18	♟♟ 2*
● Mossone '17	♟♟ 8
● Stefano Antonucci Rosso '17	♟♟ 4
○ Verdicchio dei Castelli di Jesi Back to Basics '18	♟♟ 4
○ Verdicchio dei Castelli di Jesi Cl. Sup. Stefano Antonucci '17	♟♟ 4
○ Animale Celeste '18	♟ 3
● Mossi '17	♟ 5
⊙ Sensuade '18	♟ 3
○ Verdicchio dei Castelli di Jesi Ste' '18	♟ 2

Tenuta Santori

C.DA MONTEBOVE, 14
63065 RIPATRANSONE [AP]
TEL. +39 0735584189
www.tenutasantori.it

CELLAR SALES
ANNUAL PRODUCTION 45,000 bottles
HECTARES UNDER VINE 17.00
VITICULTURE METHOD Certified Organic

Marco comes from a family of nurserymen, so the subjects of arboreal maintenance and agronomic practices are second nature to him. His studies in enology led him to establish and develop his own winery in the Tesino Valley in 2012. The vineyards are planted with clear ideas and traditional vines; the coolest slopes are reserved for Passerina and Pecorino and the sunny slopes are for Montepulciano and Sangiovese. The efficient cellar provides ample space for steel vats and some small wood barrels for reds. Their Offida Pecorino '18 earns its third Tre Bicchieri in a row. It's a wine of extraordinary elegance: aromatic herbs and notes of aniseed lead the way to crystalline citrus, sensations that reemerge on a finish of spectacular development and staying power. But the good work they've been doing is also reflected in their Rosso Piceno Sup. '16, a gracefully crafted that carefully exalts aromas of morello cherry on a palate chiseled by ripe tannins and fresh vigor.

○ Offida Pecorino '18	♛♛♛ 3*
● Rosso Piceno Sup. '16	♛♛ 3*
○ Offida Passerina '18	♛♛ 2*
○ Offida Pecorino '17	♛♛♛ 3*
○ Offida Pecorino '16	♛♛♛ 3*
○ Offida Passerina '17	♛♛ 2*
○ Offida Passerina '16	♛♛ 2*
● Rosso Piceno Sup. '15	♛♛ 3

Sartarelli

VIA COSTE DEL MOLINO, 24
60030 POGGIO SAN MARCELLO [AN]
TEL. +39 073189732
www.sartarelli.com

CELLAR SALES
PRE-BOOKED VISITS
ANNUAL PRODUCTION 300,000 bottles
HECTARES UNDER VINE 55.00
SUSTAINABLE WINERY

The recent renovation of the Chiacchierini-Sartarelli family's cellar has made everything more efficient, multiplied the available spaces and made a Verdicchio museum possible. It's no coincidence that the spectacular vineyards, largely visible from the panoramic terrace on the cantina's roof, have always and exclusively been planted with Jesi's famous white variety. Dedication and specialization allow the winery to exploit the versatility of the cultivar in versions rangling from sparkling to sweet Passito wines. Also important is the complete absence of wood barrels, with production occurring entirely in steel vats. Their Balciana '17 is the usual explosion of enticing late-harvest aromas. An opening note of honey is followed by rivulets of candied orange, thyme, delicate saffron. This distinctly sweet attack is tempered by notable sapidity, making for a bewitching play of contrasts and chiaroscuro. The Sartarelli Classico '18 is marked by varietal character and subtleness, while the Brut proves tasty and technically faultless.

○ Verdicchio dei Castelli di Jesi Cl. Sup. Balciana '17	♛♛ 5
○ Sartarelli Brut	♛♛ 3
○ Verdicchio dei Castelli di Jesi Cl. Sartarelli '18	♛♛ 2
○ Verdicchio dei Castelli di Jesi Cl. Sup. Tralivio '17	♛ 3
○ Verdicchio dei Castelli di Jesi Cl. Sup. Balciana '09	♛♛♛ 5
○ Verdicchio dei Castelli di Jesi Cl. Sup. Balciana '04	♛♛♛ 5
○ Verdicchio dei Castelli di Jesi Cl. Sup. Contrada Balciana '98	♛♛♛ 5
○ Verdicchio dei Castelli di Jesi Cl. Sup. Contrada Balciana '97	♛♛♛ 5
○ Verdicchio dei Castelli di Jesi Cl. Sup. Contrada Balciana '95	♛♛♛ 5

lberto Serenelli

c. Pietralacroce
Bartolini, 2
0129 Ancona
l. +39 07135505
ww.albertoserenelli.com

CELLAR SALES
PRE-BOOKED VISITS
ANNUAL PRODUCTION 25,000 bottles
HECTARES UNDER VINE 7.00

lberto Serenelli is an explosive figure,
ctive for many years and famous for
imited-quantity reds made in his tiny
ncona cellar: a few years ago he might
ave been referred to as a 'garagista'
(working out of a garage). From the
oranico estate in Varano and the Candia
neyards, both fractions of Ancona, he
btains well-ripened grapes that he vinifies
 different sizes of quality wood barrels.
reat attention is paid to the bottling and
areful packaging of wines that defy time
ith ease. Whites result from
ollaborations in the Staffolo area. Their
iorgio Alberto '16, which brings together
qual parts Montepulciano and Syrah (the
rmer former from Conero, the latter from
iorgio Santini's Broccanera), is redolent of
omplex, fruity notes and delicate toasty
ints, sensations that give way to a palate
f great sapidity and length, as well as a
harming originality. Controlled tannins,
mooth pulp and healthy fruit mark the
Marro '15. Sensations of wood are evident
 the Boranico '17, but that doesn't affect
s fine texture.

Giorgio Alberto '16	🍷🍷 7
Biancospino '18	🍷🍷 4
Boranico '17	🍷🍷 7
Rosso Conero Marro '15	🍷🍷 4
Verdicchio dei Castelli di Jesi Cl. Sora Elvira '18	🍷🍷 4
Varano '16	🍷 7
Boranico '16	🍷🍷 6
Rosso Conero Marro '13	🍷🍷 4
Rosso Conero Varano '14	🍷🍷 7
Rosso Conero Varano '12	🍷🍷 6
Rosso Conero Varano '11	🍷🍷 6
Verdicchio dei Castelli di Jesi Cl. Sora Elvira '16	🍷🍷 4
Verdicchio dei Castelli di Jesi Cl. Sora Elvira '13	🍷🍷 3

Sparapani - Frati Bianchi

via Barchio, 12
60034 Cupramontana [AN]
Tel. +39 0731781216
www.fratibianchi.it

CELLAR SALES
PRE-BOOKED VISITS
RESTAURANT SERVICE
ANNUAL PRODUCTION 40,000 bottles
HECTARES UNDER VINE 18.00

A few years ago siblings Pino, Francesca
and Paolo Sparapani thought they had
permanently solved their space issues with
a new cellar. However, they had not
counted on the overwhelming success of
their Verdicchio wines, increasingly a
benchmark thanks to their ability to
precisely and intimately express the
cultivar's character, bringing out its natural
energy and sapidity. Enologist Sergio
Paolucci predominantly uses steel tanks to
good effect, while in another room medium
wood barrels are used for the Riserva
Donna Cloe. The fact that so few bottles of
the Donna Cloe Riserva '16 are available
shouldn't discourage you from finding one.
If you do, you'll discover a wine that mixes
hints of almond, smoky echoes and
captivating mineral notes. On the palate it
proves balanced in its density and
extremely pleasant. A hot year took off
some depth from their Priore '17, but early
harvest saved its acidic backbone and
varietal aromas.

○ Castelli di Jesi Verdicchio Cl. Donna Cloe Ris. '16	🍷🍷 5
○ Verdicchio dei Castelli di Jesi Cl. Salerna '18	🍷🍷 2*
○ Verdicchio dei Castelli di Jesi Cl. Sup. Il Priore '17	🍷🍷 3
○ Verdicchio dei Castelli di Jesi Cl. Sup. Il Priore '16	🍷🍷🍷 3*
○ Verdicchio dei Castelli di Jesi Cl. Sup. Il Priore '14	🍷🍷🍷 2*
○ Verdicchio dei Castelli di Jesi Cl. Sup. Il Priore '13	🍷🍷🍷 2*
○ Verdicchio dei Castelli di Jesi Cl. Sup. Il Priore '12	🍷🍷🍷 2*
○ Verdicchio dei Castelli di Jesi Cl. Sup. Il Priore '06	🍷🍷🍷 2*

Tenuta Spinelli

VIA LAGO, 2
63032 CASTIGNANO [AP]
TEL. +39 0736821489
www.tenutaspinelli.it

CELLAR SALES
PRE-BOOKED VISITS
ACCOMMODATION
ANNUAL PRODUCTION 57,000 bottles
HECTARES UNDER VINE 14.00

Simone Spinelli is young, enthusiastic and a tireless worker. Thanks to the help of his family and the advice of renowned professionals like Luca Severini and Pierluigi Lorenzetti, he has made a name for himself and his fresh and saline 'mountain' interpretations of classic Piceno white varieties. The style is strongly influenced by vineyards located at an elevation of almost 600 meters at the edge of Monte Ascensione. In recent years he has planted Pinot Nero for a new, interesting and difficult challenge. Their Artemisia bags yet another Tre Bicchieri. The 2018 offers up close-focused, enticing aromas of citrus and country herbs, while the palate's rich extracts are guided by a pronounced acidity all the way through its extremely long finish. Their Pinot Nero '16 had a nice debut, with its varietal sensations of small red berries and a subtle spicy nuance giving way to a palate marked by polished tannins and thorough harmony. It's a bit lacking in complexity but the result is more than satisfactory.

○ Offida Pecorino Artemisia '18	▼▼▼ 3*
○ Eden '18	▼▼ 2*
○ Mèroe Pecorino M. Cl.	▼▼ 4
● Simone Spinelli Pinot Nero '16	▼▼ 7
○ Offida Pecorino Artemisia '17	♈♈♈ 2*
○ Offida Pecorino Artemisia '16	♈♈♈ 2*
○ Offida Pecorino Artemisia '15	♈♈♈ 2*
○ Offida Pecorino Artemisia '14	♈♈♈ 2*
○ Offida Pecorino Artemisia '13	♈♈♈ 2*
○ Offida Pecorino Artemisia '12	♈♈♈ 2*
○ Eden '17	♈♈ 2*
○ Eden '15	♈♈ 2*
○ Eden '13	♈♈ 2*
○ Eden '16	♈ 2

La Staffa

VIA CASTELLARETTA, 19
60039 STAFFOLO [AN]
TEL. +39 0731779810
www.vinilastaffa.it

CELLAR SALES
PRE-BOOKED VISITS
ANNUAL PRODUCTION 45,000 bottles
HECTARES UNDER VINE 10.00
VITICULTURE METHOD Certified Organic

Riccardo may be much younger than his most important vineyard, planted in 1972, but he has understood from the beginning that for his wines to be successful they needed to be infused with clearly recognizable personality. He has found his own way by following the dictates of organic farming, producing in an authentic way that highlights craftsmanship, and rejecting alluring but ephemeral market trends. His tenacity and intuition are the reason that his Verdicchio is collected in the cellars of wine lovers around the world. Their Rincrocca '16 tickles the taste buds with sea salt, vigor and juicy vitality. On the palate it's resounding and hypnotic, adorned by aromas of ripe apple and toasted almond. Spontaneous fermentation makes its presence felt in the La Staffa '18 a wine characterized by hints of ripe fruit, acidity and a lively palate. The Aurora '18 is a credible Montepulciano rosé that exhibits sapidity and fruity verve.

○ Castelli di Jesi Verdicchio Cl. Rincrocca Ris. '16	▼▼ 4
○ L'Aurora '18	▼▼ 3
○ Verdicchio dei Castelli di Jesi Cl. Sup. La Staffa '18	▼▼ 3
○ Mai Sentito	▼ 2
○ Castelli di Jesi Verdicchio Cl. Rincrocca Ris. '15	♈♈ 4
○ Castelli di Jesi Verdicchio Cl. Selva di Sotto Ris. '15	♈♈ 8
○ L'Aurora '17	♈♈ 3
○ Verdicchio dei Castelli di Jesi Cl. Sup. La Staffa '17	♈♈ 3
○ Verdicchio dei Castelli di Jesi Cl. Sup. La Staffa '16	♈♈ 2*
○ Verdicchio dei Castelli di Jesi Cl. Sup. La Staffa '15	♈♈ 3

Tenuta di Tavignano

LOC. TAVIGNANO
2011 CINGOLI [MC]
TEL. +39 0733617303
www.tenutaditavignano.it

CELLAR SALES
PRE-BOOKED VISITS
ACCOMMODATION
ANNUAL PRODUCTION 100,000 bottles
HECTARES UNDER VINE 30.00
SUSTAINABLE WINERY

We have often mentioned the beauty of
Stefano Aymerich's estate on the high hill
of Tavignano overlooking the city of Jesi
(though formally situated in the province of
Macerata). The amphitheater of vineyards
with the striking profile of Monte San Vicino
behind are home to Verdicchio, while the
highest rows facing the Adriatic are
reserved for red varieties. All Verdicchio
wines are vinified in steel, differentiated by
the time of harvest and duration of aging
on fine lees. Their Misco '18 is elegant, as
usual, with aromas of citrus peel and
almonds. It's highly enjoyable in the mouth
thanks to a measured, sapid palate. A bit
more time in the bottle will bring out further
complexity. For now, enjoy the juicy verve of
their Villa Torre '18, a wine that features
aromas of yellow fruit and an irresistible
palate. The Misco Ris. '17 is fruity, broad
and flavorful, with nice tension despite the
scorching temperatures. On the palate, the
Cervidoni '17 is marked by meaty fruit.

○ Verdicchio dei Castelli di Jesi Cl. Sup. Misco '18	♈♈ 3*
○ Verdicchio dei Castelli di Jesi Cl. Sup. Villa Torre '18	♈♈ 3*
○ Castelli di Jesi Verdicchio Cl. Misco Ris. '17	♈♈ 5
● Rosso Piceno Cervidoni '17	♈♈ 3
○ Verdicchio dei Castelli di Jesi Cl. Sup. Misco '17	♈♈♈ 3*
○ Verdicchio dei Castelli di Jesi Cl. Sup. Misco '16	♈♈♈ 3*
○ Verdicchio dei Castelli di Jesi Cl. Sup. Misco '15	♈♈♈ 3*
○ Verdicchio dei Castelli di Jesi Cl. Sup. Misco '14	♈♈♈ 3*
○ Verdicchio dei Castelli di Jesi Cl. Sup. Misco '13	♈♈♈ 3*

Tenuta dell'Ugolino

LOC. CASTELPLANIO
VIA COPPARONI, 32
60031 CASTELPLANIO [AN]
TEL. +39 0731812569
www.tenutaugolino.it

CELLAR SALES
PRE-BOOKED VISITS
ANNUAL PRODUCTION 70,000 bottles
HECTARES UNDER VINE 12.00
SUSTAINABLE WINERY

In 1981, Andrea Petrini inherited the estate
that his father Costantino founded. He has
since expanded it to twelve hectares, with
vineyards partly located near the cellar and
other small plots scattered in neighboring
municipalities. Today in addtion to his
long-time enologist Aroldo Bellelli he has
the help of his young partner Matteo
Foroni. The winery specializes in Verdicchio;
the best grapes come from the cool
Balluccio cru and the resulting wine is
well-known by fans of wine for its
expressiveness. Finally, Andrea and Matteo
take home Tre Bicchieri. The Vigneto del
Balluccio does an excellent job managing
the hot 2017 summer, transforming it into
thrilling sensations of lime blossom, broom
and a quintessentially varietal note of
almond. On the palate it's penetrating and
vigorous without losing its sense of
proportion. Le Piaole '18 features aromas
of lime, almond and mineral notes,
sensations that emerge on its subtle,
spirited palate. Their Maltempo Brut is a
highly pleasant wine.

○ Verdicchio dei Castelli di Jesi Cl. Sup. Vign. del Balluccio '17	♈♈♈ 4*
○ Maltempo Brut	♈♈ 4
○ Verdicchio dei Castelli di Jesi Cl. Le Piaole '18	♈♈ 3
○ Verdicchio dei Castelli di Jesi Cl. Le Piaole '17	♈♈ 2*
○ Verdicchio dei Castelli di Jesi Cl. Le Piaole '16	♈♈ 2*
○ Verdicchio dei Castelli di Jesi Cl. Le Piaole '15	♈♈ 2*
○ Verdicchio dei Castelli di Jesi Cl. Sup. Vign. del Balluccio '16	♈♈ 3*
○ Verdicchio dei Castelli di Jesi Cl. Sup. Vign. del Balluccio '15	♈♈ 3*

Terra Fageto

VIA VALDASO, 52
63016 PEDASO [FM]
TEL. +39 0734931784
www.terrafageto.it

CELLAR SALES
PRE-BOOKED VISITS
ANNUAL PRODUCTION 100,000 bottles
HECTARES UNDER VINE 40.00
VITICULTURE METHOD Certified Organic

Campofilone is the oldest of the three estates that Claudio Di Ruscio and sons Angelo and Michele use for wine production. Located halfway up a hill, it's mostly home to white varieties. Red grapes are grown in the south-facing vineyard of Altidona and in the spectacular Monte Serrone di Pedaso, with rows overlooking the Adriatic. The large, efficient cellar is located in a central position of the Aso Valley. The winery's modern style and reliable quality are consistent traits, particularly its traditional whites. Their 500 '16 delivered during its debut. This limited-edition Pecorino is marked by well-calibrated density and elegant expressiveness. The fact that Pecorino is their specialty is confirmed by the Fenèsia '18, a citrusy, evenly developing wine that has room to grow over time. Their Falerio Eva '18 is fruit forward, while their Rusus '16, a wine made light by aromas of black cherry and graceful, spicy nuances, is characterized by a smooth tannic weave.

○ 500 '16	🍷🍷 5
○ Falerio Eva '18	🍷🍷 2*
○ Offida Pecorino Fenèsia '18	🍷🍷 3
● Rosso Piceno Rusus '16	🍷🍷 3
○ Letizia Passerina '18	🍷 2
● Rosso Piceno Colle del Buffo '18	🍷 3
● Serrone '17	🍷 5
○ Letizia Passerina '17	🍷🍷 2*
○ Letizia Passerina '16	🍷🍷 2*
○ Offida Pecorino Fenèsia '17	🍷🍷 3
○ Offida Pecorino Fenèsia '16	🍷🍷 3
○ Offida Pecorino Fenèsia '09	🍷🍷 3*
● Rosso Piceno Rusus '15	🍷🍷 3
● Rosso Piceno Rusus '14	🍷🍷 3
● Serrone '08	🍷🍷 4

Terracruda

VIA SERRE, 28
61040 FRATTE ROSA [PU]
TEL. +39 0721777412
www.terracruda.it

CELLAR SALES
PRE-BOOKED VISITS
ACCOMMODATION
ANNUAL PRODUCTION 130,000 bottles
HECTARES UNDER VINE 22.00

Fratte Rosa is at the crossroads of Pesaro's three wine districts: the Sangiovese district, the largest in the province, the Bianchello district and the Pergola microzone, the cradle of aromatic Aleatico. The Avenanti family has not limited itself to one single path and has a vast array of traditional varieties, including rare ones like Garofanata. The fully equipped, functional underground cellar contains only hand-harvested grapes. The wines have shown good personality and varietal adherence recently, renouncing excessive concentrations and precocious ambitions. Campodarchi '16 breaks through every prejudice about Bianchello's aging potential. Medlar, hazelnut and complex vegetal strokes introduce a palate that features personality and persistence, with a notably lengthy finish. Their Olpe '16 unveils the charming fané of evolved Sangiovese: undergrowth, flowers and wet earth merge on a relaxed palate. The Garofanata '18 offers up original floral sensations on a supple, fluent palate.

○ Bianchello del Metauro Campodarchi '16	🍷🍷 3
● Colli Pesaresi Sangiovese Olpe Ris. '16	🍷🍷 4
○ Garofanata '18	🍷🍷 3
● Pergola Rosso Vettina '17	🍷🍷 3
○ Bianchello del Metauro Boccalino '18	🍷 2
● Colli Pesaresi Sangiovese Profondo Ris. '15	🍷 5
○ Incrocio Bruni 54 '18	🍷 3
○ Bianchello del Metauro Boccalino '17	🍷🍷 2*
○ Bianchello del Metauro Campodarchi Argento '15	🍷🍷 3
○ Incrocio Bruni 54 '17	🍷🍷 3
● Pergola Aleatico Sup. Ortaia '16	🍷🍷 5

Fattoria Le Terrazze

VIA MUSONE, 4
60026 NUMANA [AN]
TEL. +39 0717390352
www.fattorialeterrazze.it

CELLAR SALES
PRE-BOOKED VISITS
ANNUAL PRODUCTION 100,000 bottles
HECTARES UNDER VINE 20.00

The estate has a centuries-long history, but already in the mid-1970s it was well known by those who love Montepulciano from Monte Conero's foothills. International fame arrived at the end of the century when Antonio and Giorgina Terni found a way to effectively and elegantly interpret the conspicuously fruity intensity imbued by the warm Numana territory. Today their wines are recognized as 'modern classics', reliable and smooth tasting, with evident traits of finesse despite the general bulk of the most ambitious wines. Their Vision of J, a wine that's only produced during certain years, was back in our tastings for this edition. Aromas of black cherry and Asian spices precede a palate marked by fruity vigor and a robust tannic weave. Energy of alcohol and abundant tannins also characterize their bold Sassi Neri '15, a wine that boasts an enviable balance of flavor. Their Chaos '15, a complete wine, reveals an excellent palate, while the Pink Fluid '18 and Donna Giulia Brut '16 both exhibit fragrant aromas and notable drinkability.

● Conero Sassi Neri Ris. '15	♟♟ 5
● Conero Visions of J Ris. '15	♟♟ 6
● Chaos '15	♟♟ 5
○ Donna Giulia Brut Rosé M. Cl. '16	♟♟ 4
○ Pink Fluid '18	♟♟ 2*
● Rosso Conero '16	♟♟ 2*
○ Le Cave Chardonnay '18	♟ 2
● Chaos '04	♟♟♟ 5
● Chaos '01	♟♟♟ 6
● Conero Sassi Neri Ris. '04	♟♟♟ 5
● Rosso Conero Sassi Neri '02	♟♟♟ 5
● Rosso Conero Sassi Neri '99	♟♟♟ 5
● Rosso Conero Sassi Neri '98	♟♟♟ 5
● Rosso Conero Visions of J '01	♟♟♟ 7
● Rosso Conero Visions of J '97	♟♟♟ 7

Terre Cortesi Moncaro

VIA PIANOLE, 7A
63036 MONTECAROTTO [AN]
TEL. +39 073189245
www.moncaro.com

CELLAR SALES
PRE-BOOKED VISITS
RESTAURANT SERVICE
ANNUAL PRODUCTION 7,500,000 bottles
HECTARES UNDER VINE 1200.00
VITICULTURE METHOD Certified Organic
SUSTAINABLE WINERY

For many years, Doriano Marchetti has been running the Marche region's largest winery, born out of a merger between the distant cooperative wineries of Montecarotto (Verdicchio area), Camerano (Conero area) and Acquaviva Picena in the south. The expansive vineyards available to the technical staff headed by Giuliano d'Ignazi and Danilo Coppa enable the creation of wines with a modern cadence, of which enjoyability, value for money and adequate volume are essential components. 2018 made for a supple and tasty Verde Ca' Ruptae, a wine redolent of the variety's most intimate sensations, like lime blossom and almond. The same impressions hold true for the Fondiglie '18, a wine that's just a bit softer on the palate. The V.Novali offers up notes of candied fruit, while the palate is quite creamy. A velvety touch, brought out by hints of honey and apricot jam lend charm to the Tordiruta '12. Among their reds, the fruitiness and delicate tannic weave distinguished the Conero Montescuro Res. '16.

● Conero Montescuro Ris. '16	♟♟ 3*
○ Verdicchio dei Castelli di Jesi Cl. Sup. Verde Ca' Ruptae '18	♟♟ 3*
○ Castelli di Jesi Verdicchio Cl. V. Novali Ris. '15	♟♟ 4
○ Madreperla Gran Cuvée Brut M. Cl.	♟♟ 5
○ Offida Pecorino Ofithe '18	♟♟ 3
● Piceno Sup. Roccaviva '16	♟♟ 2*
● Rosso Conero Montepasso '16	♟♟ 3
● Rosso Piceno Sup. Campo delle Mura '12	♟♟ 4
○ Verdicchio dei Castelli di Jesi Cl. Le Vele '18	♟♟ 3
○ Verdicchio dei Castelli di Jesi Cl. Sup. Fondiglie '18	♟♟ 3
○ Verdicchio dei Castelli di Jesi Passito Tordiruta '12	♟♟ 5
● Conero Nerone Ris. '15	♟ 6
● Rosso Conero Le Silve del Parco '18	♟ 3

★Umani Ronchi

VIA ADRIATICA, 12
60027 OSIMO [AN]
TEL. +39 0717108019
www.umanironchi.com

CELLAR SALES
PRE-BOOKED VISITS
ANNUAL PRODUCTION 2,900,000 bottles
HECTARES UNDER VINE 240.00
VITICULTURE METHOD Certified Organic
SUSTAINABLE WINERY

The winery led by Michele Bernetti holds the clear belief that territorial links, coming from many hectares of mostly traditional varieties, must be translated into modern, balanced wines that are never overdone and are capable of speaking to an international clientele. The technical team also infuses the character necessary to assure good quality and to form a complete a range that is further enriched by new wines derived from vineyards in Abruzzo. The Vecchie Vigne skillfully manages a hot 2017 thanks to great aromatic finesse and perfect proportions on the palate, making for a juicy, sapid and complex wine. It takes home Tre Bicchieri, easily surpassing the internal 'competition' from within their selection: the complex Plenio '16, the highly pleasant Casaldiserra '18 and a powerful, elegant Campo San Giorgio Ris. '15, a wine to buy and let sit. In the meantime try their Montepulciano Centovie '15, a wine that's already expressive in its vivid fruit.

○ Verdicchio dei Castelli di Jesi Cl. Sup. V. V. '17	♟♟♟ 4*
○ Castelli di Jesi Verdicchio Cl. Plenio Ris. '16	♟♟ 4
● Montepulciano d'Abruzzo Centovie '15	♟♟ 5
○ Verdicchio dei Castelli di Jesi Cl. Sup. Casal di Serra '18	♟♟ 3*
○ Centovie Pecorino '17	♟♟ 4
● Conero Campo San Giorgio Ris. '15	♟♟ 7
● Conero Cumaro Ris. '15	♟♟ 5
○ Extra Brut M. Cl.	♟♟ 4
⊙ La Hoz Nature M.Cl. Rosé	♟♟ 5
● Rosso Conero San Lorenzo '17	♟♟ 3
● Rosso Conero Serrano '18	♟♟ 2*
○ Trebbiano d'Abruzzo Montipagano '18	♟♟ 3
○ Verdicchio dei Castelli di Jesi Cl. Sup. Villa Bianchi '18	♟♟ 2*

La Valle del Sole

VIA SAN LAZZARO, 46
63035 OFFIDA [AP]
TEL. +39 0736889658
www.lavalledelsoleoffida.com

PRE-BOOKED VISITS
ANNUAL PRODUCTION 25,000 bottles
HECTARES UNDER VINE 11.00
VITICULTURE METHOD Certified Organic

In a few years, Valle del Sole has carved out a solid reputation among Piceno producers thanks to the Di Nicolò family's tireless work. Silvano takes care of the vineyards of traditional varieties, Alessia manages operations in the cellar and Valeria takes care of the small family agritourism. Entirely organic management and artisanal methods result in characterful wines, aromatically transparent and becoming increasingly balanced in structure, which in the past had always been rather generous. Kudos to their Offida Pecorino, a wine that delivers on the nose with fresh aromas of flowers and citrus, and convinces in the mouth even more, thanks to a delicately salty, flavorful palate and a lengthy finish. The Offida Rosso '15 features nice integration between alcohol and a close-knit tannic weave, with aromas of plums made light by spicy fragrances. If the Offida Passerina '18 is a timid wine, supple and drinkable, the Rosato '18 delivers for its fruity bravado, expressed across a pulpy palate.

○ Offida Pecorino '18	♟♟ 3*
● Offida Rosso '15	♟♟ 4
⊙ Rosato '18	♟♟ 2*
○ Offida Passerina '18	♟ 2
○ Offida Pecorino '17	♟♟ 3
○ Offida Pecorino '16	♟♟ 3
○ Offida Pecorino '15	♟♟ 2*
○ Offida Pecorino '11	♟♟ 2*
● Offida Rosso '14	♟♟ 4
○ Passerina '16	♟♟ 2*
● Rosso Piceno Sup. '16	♟♟ 3*
● Rosso Piceno Sup. '15	♟♟ 3
● Rosso Piceno Sup. '14	♟♟ 2*

★Velenosi

LOC. MONTICELLI
A DEI BIANCOSPINI, 11
3100 ASCOLI PICENO
TEL. +39 0736341218
www.velenosivini.com

CELLAR SALES
PRE-BOOKED VISITS
ANNUAL PRODUCTION 2,500,000 bottles
HECTARES UNDER VINE 192.00

In 1984 the young Ercole Velenosi and Angiolina Piotti could have not foreseen the impressive development of their newly created winery. The giant steps that have brought them to shops around the world have been achieved by the hard work put into improved quality. That persistence has forged a catalog of wines enviable for its variety, modernity and reliability, suitable for all budgets and supported by far-reaching distribution. In addition to Marche classics, the company makes impressive versions of Abruzzo wines on its new fifteen-hectare estate in nearby Controguerra. Roggio '16 does it again. A close-focused note of morello cherry, the complexity of its spicy fragrances, a tannic sweetness integrated with fruity pulp — it's love at first sip. The Solestà '17 moves on a similar track — though it's better suited to a pleasant drinkability. Ludi '16 is rich and flavorful, while among their Abruzzos we were impressed by the delectability of the Cerasuolo Prope '18 and the structural energy of the Verso Sera '17.

● Rosso Piceno Sup. Roggio del Filare '16	▼▼▼	6
⊙ Cerasuolo d'Abruzzo Prope '18	▼▼	2*
● Rosso Piceno Sup. Solestà '17	▼▼	4
● Lacrima di Morro d'Alba Sup. Querciantica '18	▼▼	3
● Montepulciano d'Abruzzo Colline Teramane Verso Sera '17	▼▼	6
● Montepulciano d'Abruzzo Prope '17	▼▼	3
○ Offida Pecorino Rêve '17	▼▼	5
○ Offida Pecorino Villa Angela '18	▼▼	3
● Offida Rosso Ludi '16	▼▼	6
● Rosso Piceno Sup. Brecciarolo '17	▼▼	2*
⊙ The Rose Brut M. Cl. '13	▼▼	5
○ Trebbiano d'Abruzzo Prope '18	▼▼	2*
○ Velenosi Gran Cuvée Brut M. Cl. '13	▼▼	5
○ Verdicchio dei Castelli di Jesi Cl. Querciantica '18	▼▼	3

Roberto Venturi

VIA CASE NUOVE, 1A
60010 CASTELLEONE DI SUASA [AN]
TEL. +39 3381855566
www.viniventuri.it

CELLAR SALES
PRE-BOOKED VISITS
ANNUAL PRODUCTION 60,000 bottles
HECTARES UNDER VINE 8.00

Castelleone di Suasa is in Val di Nevola, just outside what is considered the 'classic' Verdicchio area. Roberto Venturi has further developed the estate started by his father; in addition to the 'white grapes of Jesi', he also grows Montepulciano, Muscat and an ancient Aleatico clone locally called Balsamina. The best grapes are used to make both of the Qudì wines and come from a rented vineyard that the winery manages in Montecarotto. The beautiful, recently built cellar is extremely well equipped. Their Riserva Qudì '16 debuts with a bang: aniseed and appley aromas rise up off the nose, in the mouth it's exceptionally juicy, extremely smooth yet dense in flavor. The Qudì Classico Superiore '17 is fresh on the nose, with a note of pine needles that peeps out amidst citrusy sensations. In the mouth it expresses the softness and volume that characterize the vintage. Their Squarciafico '17 is a round and sufficiently persistent Montepulciano.

○ Castelli di Jesi Verdicchio Qudì Ris. '16	▼▼	5
○ Verdicchio dei Castelli di Jesi Cl. Sup. Qudì '17	▼▼	3*
● Squarciafico '16	▼▼	3
● Balsamino '17	▼	2
○ Desiderio '18	▼	3
○ Verdicchio dei Castelli di Jesi Cl. Sup. Qudì '15	▼▼▼	3*
○ Verdicchio dei Castelli di Jesi Cl. Sup. Qudì '13	▼▼▼	2*
● Balsamino '16	▼▼	2*
○ Desiderio '16	▼▼	2*
○ Verdicchio dei Castelli di Jesi Cl. Sup. Qudì '16	▼▼	3*
○ Verdicchio dei Castelli di Jesi Cl. Sup. Qudì '14	▼▼	2*

Vicari

via Pozzo Buono, 3
60030 Morro d'Alba [AN]
Tel. +39 073163164
www.vicarivini.it

CELLAR SALES
PRE-BOOKED VISITS
ANNUAL PRODUCTION 120,000 bottles
HECTARES UNDER VINE 28.00

Having 'Pozzo Buono', meaning Good Well, in the name of each Vicari wine may seem a bit affected; it actually reflects the winery's pride in its district, from the vineyards of Lacrima and Verdicchio to the recently renovated cellar. The estate's style is quite complex and full-bodied, especially its most ambitious selections, providing lip-smacking opulence in every glass. The challenge comes in finding the correct balance each year. The Riserva Oltretempo '15 had a nice debut, with its complex aromas of almond and candied citrus peel, sensations that reemerge on a pervasive, long palate that features slightly mature strokes. The Insolito '17 is the usual force of natura, both on the nose and on the palate, playing on the contrast between a soft attack and a sapid finish. The Capofila '18 moves on a similar track, though it's a simpler wine. Their entire Lacrima line is intensely aromatic and reliable.

● Lacrima di Morro d'Alba Dasempre del Pozzo Buono '18	🍷🍷 2*
○ Castelli di Jesi Verdicchio Cl. Oltretempo del Pozzo Buono Ris. '15	🍷🍷 5
● Lacrima di Morro d'Alba Passito Amaranto del Pozzo Buono '16	🍷🍷 5
● Lacrima di Morro d'Alba Sup. del Pozzo Buono '17	🍷🍷 5
○ Verdicchio dei Castelli di Jesi Cl. Capofila del Pozzo Buono '18	🍷🍷 2*
○ Verdicchio dei Castelli di Jesi Cl. Sup. L'Insolito del Pozzo Buono '17	🍷🍷 3
● Rosso Piceno Dueanime del Pozzo Buono '17	🍷 4
○ Verdicchio dei Castelli di Jesi Cl. Sup. Insolito del Pozzo Buono '15	🍷🍷🍷 3*

Vignamato

via Battinebbia, 4
60038 San Paolo di Jesi [AN]
Tel. +39 0731779197
www.vignamato.com

CELLAR SALES
PRE-BOOKED VISITS
ANNUAL PRODUCTION 100,000 bottles
HECTARES UNDER VINE 27.00

Young Andrea Ceci confidently leads the winery that his grandfather Amato established in 1952. He receives the support he needs from his father Maurizio and mother Serenella, who preceded him in the role. Another important contributor in his maturation as a winemaker has been enologist Pierluigi Lorenzetti, who has helped in the creation of dynamic, crystalline wines. The different exposures of the vineyards cultivated mostly with Verdicchio mean each one can be harvested at its peak. The Ambrosia lands the Ceci family, for the first time, a place among the region's Tre Bicchieri producers. A sumptuous 2016, aged for a year in 75% concrete and 25% mid-size wooden casks, offers up elegant notes of summer fruit, sweet almond, and delicate smoky strokes that render the palate complex, persistent and very long. Versiano '18 is a citrusy, tasty wine — it's a bit simpler but will gain in complexity with more time in the bottle.

○ Castelli di Jesi Verdicchio Cl. Ambrosia Ris. '16	🍷🍷🍷 3*
● Campalliano '17	🍷🍷 3
○ Verdicchio dei Castelli di Jesi Cl. Sup. Versiano '18	🍷🍷 3
○ Versus '18	🍷🍷 2*
○ Castelli di Jesi Verdicchio Cl. Ambrosia Ris. '15	🍷🍷 3*
○ Castelli di Jesi Verdicchio Cl. Ambrosia Ris. '13	🍷🍷 3*
○ Verdicchio dei Castelli di Jesi Cl. Sup. Versiano '17	🍷🍷 3*
○ Verdicchio dei Castelli di Jesi Cl. Valle delle Lame '17	🍷🍷 2*
○ Verdicchio dei Castelli di Jesi Passito Antares '15	🍷🍷 4

Accadia

FRAZ. CASTELLARO
C.DA AMMORTO, 19
60048 SERRA SAN QUIRICO [AN]
TEL. +39 073185172
www.accadiavini.it

CELLAR SALES
PRE-BOOKED VISITS
ANNUAL PRODUCTION 40,000 bottles
HECTARES UNDER VINE 9.00

○ Verdicchio dei Castelli di Jesi Cl. Sup. Conscio '17	♟♟ 3
○ Verdicchio dei Castelli di Jesi Cl. Sup. Cantorì '17	♟ 4

Bacelli

VIA COLOGNOLA, 1B
62011 CINGOLI [MC]
TEL. +39 3284259778
www.cantinabacelli.com

ANNUAL PRODUCTION 8,000 bottles
HECTARES UNDER VINE 4.00

○ Verdicchio dei Castelli di Jesi CL. Sup. Brejo '18	♟♟ 3
○ Verdicchio dei Castelli di Jesi CL. Sup. Monte Circe '18	♟♟ 2*

Le Canà

VIA MOLINO VECCHIO, 4
63063 CARASSAI [AP]
TEL. +39 0734930054
www.lecanà.it

ANNUAL PRODUCTION 9,000 bottles
HECTARES UNDER VINE 25.00
VITICULTURE METHOD Certified Organic

○ Doravera '18	♟♟ 2*
○ Offida pecorino Tornavento '18	♟♟ 3
● Rosso Piceno Sup. Davore '16	♟♟ 3
● Rosso Piceno Infernaccio '18	♟ 2

La Canosa

C.DA SAN PIETRO, 6
63071 ROTELLA [AP]
TEL. +39 0736374556
www.lacanosaagricola.it

CELLAR SALES
PRE-BOOKED VISITS
ACCOMMODATION
ANNUAL PRODUCTION 150,000 bottles
HECTARES UNDER VINE 28.00

○ Offida Passerina Servator '18	♟♟ 2*
○ Offida Pecorino Pekò '18	♟♟ 2*
● Musè '17	♟ 3
● Nullius '17	♟ 3

Castrum Morisci

VIA MOLINO, 16
63826 MORESCO [FM]
TEL. +39 3400820708
www.castrummorisci.it

CELLAR SALES
ANNUAL PRODUCTION 25,000 bottles
HECTARES UNDER VINE 7.00

○ Falerio Pecorino 003 '18	♟♟ 3
○ Falerio Pecorino Gallicano '18	♟♟ 5
○ 102 Passerina '18	♟ 2
● Piceno Sangiovese Testamozza '18	♟ 5

Giacomo Centanni

C.DA ASO, 159
63062 MONTEFIORE DELL'ASO [AP]
TEL. +39 0734938530
www.vinicentanni.it

CELLAR SALES
PRE-BOOKED VISITS
ACCOMMODATION
ANNUAL PRODUCTION 140,000 bottles
HECTARES UNDER VINE 35.00
VITICULTURE METHOD Certified Organic

○ Offida Pecorino '18	♟♟ 3
○ Offida Pecorino Affinato in Legno '17	♟♟ 4
⊙ Profumo di Rosa '18	♟ 2

Cherri d'Acquaviva

VIA ROMA, 40
63075 ACQUAVIVA PICENA [AP]
TEL. +39 0735764416
www.vinicherri.it

CELLAR SALES
PRE-BOOKED VISITS
ANNUAL PRODUCTION 160,000 bottles
HECTARES UNDER VINE 33.00

⊙ Ancella '18	♈♈ 2*
● Rosso Piceno Sup. '17	♈♈ 2*
○ Offida Pecorino Altissimo '18	♈ 3

Cignano

LOC. ISOLA DI FANO
VIA ADA NEGRI, 50
61034 FOSSOMBRONE [PU]
TEL. +39 0721727124
www.cantinacignano.it

ANNUAL PRODUCTION 25,000 bottles
HECTARES UNDER VINE 15.00

○ Bianchello del Metauro Sup. San Leone '17	♈♈
○ Bianchello del Metauro Sup. Superbo Ancestrale '17	♈♈

Colleminò

VIA MONTEGRANALE, 19
60035 JESI [AN]
TEL. +39 3331706220
www.collemino.it

CELLAR SALES
PRE-BOOKED VISITS
ANNUAL PRODUCTION 14,000 bottles
HECTARES UNDER VINE 5.50

○ Verdicchio dei Castelli di Jesi Cl. Mittera '18	♈♈ 2*
○ Veridio '18	♈♈ 3
● Theresia '18	♈ 2

Collevite

VIA VALLE CECCHINA, 9
63077 MONSAMPOLO DEL TRONTO [AP]
TEL. +39 0735767050
www.collevite.com

CELLAR SALES
PRE-BOOKED VISITS
ANNUAL PRODUCTION 300,000 bottles
HECTARES UNDER VINE 160.00
VITICULTURE METHOD Certified Organic

○ Falerio Pecorino Naturae '18	♈♈
○ Offida Pecorino Villa Piatti '18	♈♈
● Offida Rosso Villa Piatti '16	♈♈
○ Offida Passerina Villa Piatti '18	♈

Conventino Monteciccardo

LOC. CONVENTINO
VIA GIULIO TURCATO, 4
61024 MONTECICCARDO [PU]
TEL. +39 0721910574
www.conventinomonteciccardo.bio

CELLAR SALES
PRE-BOOKED VISITS
ANNUAL PRODUCTION 80,000 bottles
HECTARES UNDER VINE 10.00
VITICULTURE METHOD Certified Organic
SUSTAINABLE WINERY

○ Bianchello del Metauro Sup. Brecce di Tufo '17	♈♈ 3
● Corniale '18	♈♈ 2*
○ Extra Brut M. Cl. '15	♈ 4

Crespaia

LOC. PRELATO, 8
61032 FANO [PU]
TEL. +39 0721862383
www.crespaia.it

CELLAR SALES
PRE-BOOKED VISITS
ANNUAL PRODUCTION 25,000 bottles
HECTARES UNDER VINE 10.00
VITICULTURE METHOD Certified Organic

○ Bianchello del Metauro '18	♈♈
○ Bianchello del Metauro Sup. Chiaraluce '17	♈♈
○ Brut '18	♈

ioretti Brera

DELLA STAZIONE, 48
0022 CASTELFIDARDO [AN]
L. +39 335373896
www.fiorettibrera.it

ANNUAL PRODUCTION 10,000 bottles
ECTARES UNDER VINE 3.50
TICULTURE METHOD Certified Organic

Conero Rigo 23 Ris. '16	🍷🍷 5
L'Alba '18	🍷 2

esther Hauser

DA CORONCINO, 1A
039 STAFFOLO [AN]
. +39 0731770203
www.estherhauser.it

ELLAR SALES
RE-BOOKED VISITS
NNUAL PRODUCTION 6,000 bottles
ECTARES UNDER VINE 1.00

Il Ceppo '16	🍷🍷 4
Il Cupo '16	🍷🍷 5

oberto Lucarelli

. RIPALTA
PIANA, 20
030 CARTOCETO [PU]
. +39 0721893019
www.laripe.com

ELLAR SALES
RE-BOOKED VISITS
NNUAL PRODUCTION 200,000 bottles
ECTARES UNDER VINE 32.00

Bianchello del Metauro La Ripe '18	🍷🍷 2*
Bianchello del Metauro Sup. Rocho '18	🍷🍷 2*
Colli Pesaresi Sangiovese Goccione '16	🍷 3

Luca Guerrieri

VIA SAN FILIPPO, 24
61030 PIAGGE [PU]
TEL. +39 0721890152
www.aziendaguerrieri.it

CELLAR SALES
PRE-BOOKED VISITS
ACCOMMODATION
ANNUAL PRODUCTION 250,000 bottles
HECTARES UNDER VINE 44.53

○ Bianchello del Metauro Sup. Celso '18	🍷🍷 2*
● Colli Pesaresi Sangiovese Galileo Ris. '16	🍷🍷 3
○ Bianchello del Metauro '18	🍷 2
● Guerriero Nero '17	🍷 3

Laila Libenzi

VIA SAN FILIPPO SUL CESANO, 27
61040 MONDAVIO [PU]
TEL. +39 0721979353
www.lailalibenzi.it

CELLAR SALES
PRE-BOOKED VISITS
ANNUAL PRODUCTION 130,000 bottles
HECTARES UNDER VINE 33.00

○ Verdicchio dei Castelli di Jesi Baccaloro '18	🍷🍷 2*
○ Verdicchio dei Castelli di Jesi Poggio Casalta '16	🍷🍷 2*

Valerio Lucarelli

C.DA SAN COSTANZO, 43
62026 SAN GINESIO [MC]
TEL. +39 3661131022
www.cantinalucarelli.com

ANNUAL PRODUCTION 7,000 bottles
HECTARES UNDER VINE 2.00

● Sarnum '15	🍷🍷 5
● Lenòs '16	🍷🍷 3

Ma.Ri.Ca.

VIA ACQUASANTA, 7
60030 BELVEDERE OSTRENSE [AN]
TEL. +39 0731290091
www.cantinamarica.it

CELLAR SALES
PRE-BOOKED VISITS
ANNUAL PRODUCTION 50,000 bottles
HECTARES UNDER VINE 18.00
SUSTAINABLE WINERY

● Lacrima di Morro d'Alba Ramosceto '18	♼♼ 2*
○ Verdicchio dei Castelli di Jesi Cl. Sup. Tosius '17	♼♼ 3

Madonna Bruna

C.DA CAMERA, 100
63900 FERMO
TEL. +39 3381753801
www.madonnabruna.it

ANNUAL PRODUCTION 50,000 bottles
HECTARES UNDER VINE 13.50

○ Falerio Pecorino Maree '18	♼♼
● Moresco '15	♼♼

Mancini

FRAZ. MOIE
VIA PIANELLO, 5
60030 MAIOLATI SPONTINI [AN]
TEL. +39 0731702975
www.manciniwines.it

CELLAR SALES
PRE-BOOKED VISITS
RESTAURANT SERVICE
ANNUAL PRODUCTION 140,000 bottles
HECTARES UNDER VINE 20.00

○ Castelli di Jesi Verdicchio Cl. Ris. '16	♼♼ 5
○ Verdicchio dei Castelli di Jesi Cl. Santa Lucia '18	♼♼ 2*

La Marca di San Michele

VIA TORRE, 13
60034 CUPRAMONTANA [AN]
TEL. +39 0731781183
www.lamarcadisanmichele.com

CELLAR SALES
PRE-BOOKED VISITS
ACCOMMODATION
ANNUAL PRODUCTION 35,000 bottles
HECTARES UNDER VINE 6.00
VITICULTURE METHOD Certified Organic
SUSTAINABLE WINERY

○ Verdicchio dei Castelli di Jesi Cl. Sup. Capovolto '18	♼♼
○ Castelli di Jesi Verdicchio Cl. Passolento Ris. '17	♼

Mazzola

LOC. SCAPEZZANO
VIA BERARDINELLI, 297
60019 SENIGALLIA [AN]
TEL. +39 3490700546
www.cantinamazzola.it

CELLAR SALES
PRE-BOOKED VISITS
ANNUAL PRODUCTION 26,000 bottles
HECTARES UNDER VINE 3.20
VITICULTURE METHOD Certified Organic

● Bandita '15	♼♼ 4
○ Glarus '16	♼♼ 3
● Lacrima di Morro d'Alba Sup. Sangvineto '16	♼♼ 4

Enzo Mecella

VIA DANTE, 112
60044 FABRIANO [AN]
TEL. +39 073221680
www.enzomecella.com

CELLAR SALES
PRE-BOOKED VISITS
ANNUAL PRODUCTION 90,000 bottles
HECTARES UNDER VINE 12.00

○ Epilogo Brut M. Cl. '10	♼♼
○ Verdicchio di Matelica Godenzia '17	♼♼
● Braccano '15	♼
○ Verdicchio di Matelica Sainale '17	♼

ederico Mencaroni

OLMIGRANDI, 72
0013 CORINALDO [AN]
. +39 0717975625
ww.mencaroni.eu

RE-BOOKED VISITS
NNUAL PRODUCTION 30,000 bottles
ECTARES UNDER VINE 7.50

Verdicchio dei Castelli di Jesi Brut M. Cl. Contatto '14	🍷🍷 4
Verdicchio dei Castelli di Jesi Isola '17	🍷🍷 3

ilandro

Z. IL POZZETTO
GUGLIELMO OBERDAN, 03
031 CASTELPLANIO [AN]
. +39 0731814584
ww.ilpozzetto.net

NNUAL PRODUCTION 20,000 bottles
ECTARES UNDER VINE 35.00

Verdicchio dei Castelli di Jesi Cl. Il Pozzetto '18	🍷🍷 2*
Verdicchio dei Castelli di Jesi Cl. Sup. Passione '17	🍷🍷 3

oderi San Lazzaro

Z. B.GO MIRIAM
A SAN LAZZARO, 88
073 OFFIDA [AP]
. +39 0736889189
ww.poderisanlazzaro.it

ELLAR SALES
RE-BOOKED VISITS
NNUAL PRODUCTION 50,000 bottles
ECTARES UNDER VINE 7.50
TICULTURE METHOD Certified Organic

Bordò '15	🍷🍷 7
Rosso Piceno Sup. Podere 72 '16	🍷🍷 3
Offida Pecorino Pistillo '18	🍷 2
Renzo '17	🍷 3

Piersanti

ZONA IND.LE PONTEMAGNO
60034 CUPRAMONTANA [AN]
TEL. +39 0731703214
www.piersantivini.com

CELLAR SALES
ANNUAL PRODUCTION 4,000,000 bottles
HECTARES UNDER VINE 23.00
VITICULTURE METHOD Certified Organic
SUSTAINABLE WINERY

○ Verdicchio dei Castelli di Jesi Cl. Ottavio Piersanti '18	🍷🍷 1*
○ Verdicchio dei Castelli di Jesi Cl. Q311 '18	🍷🍷 2*

Podere sul Lago

LOC. BORGIANO
VIA CASTELLO, 20
62020 SERRAPETRONA [MC]
TEL. +39 3333017380
www.poderesullago.it

CELLAR SALES
PRE-BOOKED VISITS
ANNUAL PRODUCTION 10,000 bottles
HECTARES UNDER VINE 4.00
SUSTAINABLE WINERY

● Serrapetrona Torcular '16	🍷🍷 2*
● V. Adelaide '16	🍷🍷 5
● Serrapetrona Lacus '15	🍷 5

Fattoria San Lorenzo

VIA SAN LORENZO, 6
60036 MONTECAROTTO [AN]
TEL. +39 073189656
az-crognaletti@libero.it

CELLAR SALES
PRE-BOOKED VISITS
ACCOMMODATION AND RESTAURANT SERVICE
ANNUAL PRODUCTION 100,000 bottles
HECTARES UNDER VINE 30.00
VITICULTURE METHOD Certified Organic

● Artù '15	🍷🍷 3
● Rosso Piceno Burello '15	🍷 3
○ Verdicchio dei Castelli di Jesi Cl. Le Oche '17	🍷 3

Tenuta San Marcello

VIA MELANO, 30
60030 SAN MARCELLO [AN]
TEL. +39 0731267606
www.tenutasanmarcello.net

CELLAR SALES
ACCOMMODATION AND RESTAURANT SERVICE
ANNUAL PRODUCTION 4,000 bottles
HECTARES UNDER VINE 3.50
SUSTAINABLE WINERY

● Lacrima di Morro d'Alba Bastaro '18	♥♥	2*
○ Verdicchio dei Castelli di Jesi Cl. Sup. Cipriani '18	♥♥	3
○ Indisciplinato '18	♥	5

Cantina Sant'Isidoro

FRAZ. COLBUCCARO DI CORRIDONIA
C.DA COLLE SANT'ISIDORO, 5
62014 CORRIDONIA [MC]
TEL. +39 0733201283
www.cantinasantisidoro.it

ANNUAL PRODUCTION 19,000 bottles

○ Colli Maceratesi Ribona Paucis '17	♥♥
○ Colli Maceratesi Ribona Pausula '18	♥♥
○ Verdicchio di Matelica Piedicolle '18	♥♥
● Rosso Piceno Pinto '18	♥

Selvagrossa

FRAZ. BORGO S. MARIA
S.DA SELVAGROSSA, 37
61020 PESARO
TEL. +39 0721202923
www.selvagrossa.it

CELLAR SALES
PRE-BOOKED VISITS
ANNUAL PRODUCTION 32,000 bottles
HECTARES UNDER VINE 4.00

● Muschèn '17	♥♥	2*
● Poveriano '16	♥♥	5
● Trimpilin '15	♥♥	4

Tenuta di Fra'

VIA MARCIANO, 10B
60030 MORRO D'ALBA [AN]
TEL. +39 3397229846
www.tenutadifra.com

ANNUAL PRODUCTION 30,000 bottles
HECTARES UNDER VINE 7.50

● Lacrima di Morro d'Alba '18	♥♥
● Lacrima di Morro d'Alba Sup. Martalie '17	♥♥
○ Ros'Anna '18	♥♥

Vigneti Vallorani

C.DA LA ROCCA, 28
63079 COLLI DEL TRONTO [AP]
TEL. +39 3477305485
www.vignetivallorani.com

CELLAR SALES
PRE-BOOKED VISITS
ANNUAL PRODUCTION 25,000 bottles
HECTARES UNDER VINE 6.00
VITICULTURE METHOD Certified Organic

○ Falerio Avora '18	♥♥	3
○ LeFric '17	♥	3
● Piceno Sup. Konè '15	♥	4
● Piceno Sup. Polisia '15	♥	3

Le Vigne di Franca

C.DA SANTA PETRONILLA, 69
63900 FERMO
TEL. +39 3356512938
www.levignedifranca.it

CELLAR SALES
ANNUAL PRODUCTION 30,000 bottles
HECTARES UNDER VINE 4.50

● Crismon '16	♥♥
● Rubrum '16	♥

UMBRIA

When it comes to wine, Umbria is, by now, a juggernaut. Given its size that might seem like an oxymoron, but it's the truth. It's a region that not only demonstrates widespread quality, but manages to clearly transmit the character of its various territories. We start from the center, south of Perugia. Montefalco is standing out and not just for its Sagrantino. The great red grape continues to reign supreme, but we're pleased to note the exceptional quality of its Montefalco Rosso as well. It's certainly not an inferior wine with respect to those made with the region's king grape, just different (starting with the cultivars used, foremost Sangiovese) and capable of clearly expressing the territory's attributes. It's accompanied by two whites, the Montefalco Grechetto, made with grapes common to central Italy, and the Montefalco Bianco, which has led to increased focus on Trebbiano Spoletino. This last is showing great promise, including in Spoleto itself (where it has its own DOC zone). It's all thanks to charming wines marked by an incredible sapidity — wines that are ageworthy and unique when compared to the region's other whites. Staying on whites for the moment, we move to Orvieto, where the determined work of certain producers is bringing deserved recognition to one of Umbria's best areas for viticulture, both its dry and sweet wines, thanks to a unique microclimate capable of fostering botrytis. But as we've been saying, as of late some of Umbria's best wines have been coming out of smaller, lesser-known areas, which surprise both with native grapes and, in some cases, international varieties. Lake Trasimeno impresses more and more with its Gamay (which has nothing to do with the French variety, it's in the Grenache family), Torgiano is giving rise to some of the best Sangiovese around and Grechetto is back on center stage in Todi. And what to say about the juicy bottles of Ciliegiolo being made in Narni and Amelia? In short, it's a small but multifaceted region that this year saw a record number of Tre Bicchieri awarded, 14 in all. It's an outstanding achievement that testifies to the quality work being done over the years.

Adanti

via Belvedere, 2
06031 Bevagna [PG]
Tel. +39 0742360295
www.cantineadanti.com

CELLAR SALES
PRE-BOOKED VISITS
ANNUAL PRODUCTION 160,000 bottles
HECTARES UNDER VINE 30.00
SUSTAINABLE WINERY

Adanti exudes an air of tradition, from the manor house with cellar to the surrounding vineyards planted with the area's local varieties. Even the wines are designed with the past in mind, combining typicity and charm. Spontaneous fermentation, measured extraction and a masterly use of wood result in Sagrantino that age very well, reaching their best over time. Territorial adherence is, however, well expressed in both reds and whites throughout the entire Montefalco range. Their selection put in an excellent performance this year, especially their reds. Their Montefalco Rosso Arquata '15 led the pack, proving juicy and elegant with aromas of red fruits and spices. Their Montefalco Sagrantino '13 also delivered (aromas of blueberry, a tannic but supple palate) as did their Montefalco Rosso Riserva '14 (despite the difficult year, it exhibits a notable aromatic profile). We found their Montefalco Grechetto '18 a pleasant wine.

Antonelli - San Marco

loc. San Marco, 60
06036 Montefalco [PG]
Tel. +39 0742379158
www.antonellisanmarco.it

CELLAR SALES
PRE-BOOKED VISITS
ACCOMMODATION
ANNUAL PRODUCTION 300,000 bottles
HECTARES UNDER VINE 50.00
VITICULTURE METHOD Certified Organic
SUSTAINABLE WINERY

Antonelli, located in the prestigious San Marco sub-zone, one of the most suitable areas for wines from native varietals, is beyond question a benchmark in Montefalco. Of the estate's many hectares, 50 are cultivated for wine starting with Sagrantino, though Montefalco Rosso (where Sangiovese is the star) is also a favourite. Particularly in recent years there has been solid investment in whites, dominated by Trebbiano Spoletino. Elegance, finesse and a great territorial identity unite the whole range. This year it's truly difficult to choose the best wine submitted. We were impressed by the complexity, finesse and elegance of their Montefalco Rosso Riserva '15, a graceful, deep wine equipped with perfect tannins and exemplary acidity. On the nose it's a triumph of fragrances, from fruity and flowery to spices and herbaceous. Tre Bicchieri. Their Montefalco Sagrantino '14 also delivered. Their whites also performed well.

● Montefalco Rosso Arquata '15	♟♟ 2*
● Montefalco Rosso Ris. '14	♟♟ 4
● Montefalco Sagrantino '13	♟♟ 5
● Montefalco Sagrantino Arquata '13	♟♟ 6
○ Montefalco Grechetto '18	♟ 2
● Montefalco Sagrantino Arquata '08	♟♟♟ 6
● Montefalco Sagrantino Arquata '06	♟♟♟ 5
● Montefalco Sagrantino Arquata '05	♟♟♟ 5
○ Montefalco Grechetto '17	♟♟ 2*
● Montefalco Sagrantino '12	♟♟ 5
● Montefalco Sagrantino '11	♟♟ 5
● Montefalco Sagrantino '10	♟♟ 5
● Montefalco Sagrantino Passito '08	♟♟ 6

● Montefalco Rosso Ris. '15	♟♟♟
● Montefalco Rosso '16	♟♟
● Montefalco Sagrantino '14	♟♟
○ Montefalco Grechetto '18	♟♟
● Montefalco Sagrantino Chiusa di Pannone '12	♟♟
● Montefalco Sagrantino Passito '12	♟♟
○ Spoleto Trebbiano Spoletino Anteprima Tonda '17	♟♟
○ Spoleto Trebbiano Spoletino Trebium '18	♟♟
● Baiocco Sangiovese '18	♟
● Contrario '15	♟
○ Spoleto Trebbiano Spoletino Anteprima Tonda '16	♟♟♟

Barberani

LOC. VOCABOLO MIGNATTARO, 26
LOC. CERRETO
05023 BASCHI [TR]
TEL. +39 0763341820
www.barberani.it

CELLAR SALES
PRE-BOOKED VISITS
ACCOMMODATION
ANNUAL PRODUCTION 300,000 bottles
HECTARES UNDER VINE 55.00
VITICULTURE METHOD Certified Organic
SUSTAINABLE WINERY

Barberani is a major wine family and its name is synonymous with important bottles, not only in Orvieto but throughout the country. Bernardo and enologist Niccolò (the later also overseeing production) skillfully manage the estate under the watchful eye of parents Luigi and Giovanna, who over the years have created a modern and prestigious winery and to whom the most important white of the range is dedicated. The vineyards surround the cellar and feature traditional cultivars, which have for several years now been grown following organic farming dictates. Three years after vintage their Luigi e Giovanna '16 is a marvel. An Orvieto Superiore made with a fair share of botrytised grapes, it's a triumph of aromas, from yellow fruit to spices, saffron, candied lemon peel and dried apricot. The palate is fresh, pervasive and silky, with a long, clean finish. Tre Bicchieri. Their Calcaia, a benchmark for Italian passito wines, is another first-rate wine, but their entire selection proved well crafted.

Orvieto Cl. Sup. Luigi e Giovanna '16	♛♛♛ 5
Orvieto Cl. Sup. Muffa Nobile Calcaia '16	♛♛ 7
Grechetto '18	♛♛ 3
Moscato Passito '15	♛♛ 6
Orvieto Cl. Sup. Castagnolo '18	♛♛ 3
Foresco '17	♛ 3
Polvento '16	♛ 5
Lago di Corbara Rosso Villa Monticelli '04	♛♛♛ 4
Orvieto Cl. Sup. Luigi e Giovanna '13	♛♛♛ 5
Orvieto Cl. Sup. Luigi e Giovanna Villa Monticelli '11	♛♛♛ 5
Orvieto Cl. Sup. Muffa Nobile Calcaia '10	♛♛♛ 5
Orvieto Muffa Nobile Calcaia '15	♛♛♛ 6

Tenuta Bellafonte

LOC. TORRE DEL COLLE
VIA COLLE NOTTOLO, 2
06031 BEVAGNA [PG]
TEL. +39 0742710019
www.tenutabellafonte.it

CELLAR SALES
PRE-BOOKED VISITS
ACCOMMODATION
ANNUAL PRODUCTION 35,000 bottles
HECTARES UNDER VINE 11.00
SUSTAINABLE WINERY

Several years have passed since Peter Heilbron started a project that we immediately identified as one of the most original in terms of philosophy and qualitative ambitions. Now as manager, Peter lives in the countryside of Bevagna growing Sagrantino, Sangiovese and Trebbiano Spoletino. His wines offer great finesse with very measured extractions, incluing the maturation in wood. Everything is transformed to give extreme territorial fidelity and elegance. Over time, moreover, the potential for longevity of his most serious labels is becoming increasingly evident. Their Montefalco Sagrantino Collenottolo is the usual thoroughbred. The 2015 exhibits a structure and depth that are perfectly integrated with suppleness, juice and finesse. But the real surprise came from one of their recent additions, the Montefalco Rosso Pomontino '17. It's a graceful wine with great olfactive complexity, enjoyable from beginning to end. For us it's a Tre Bicchieri. Their Arnèto '17, made with Spoletino grapes, is always a sure bet.

● Montefalco Rosso Pomontino '17	♛♛♛ 6
● Montefalco Sagrantino Collenottolo '15	♛♛ 6
○ Arnèto '17	♛♛ 4
○ Montefalco Bianco Sperella '18	♛ 2
● Montefalco Sagrantino Collenottolo '14	♛♛♛ 6
● Montefalco Sagrantino Collenottolo '13	♛♛♛ 6
● Montefalco Sagrantino Collenottolo '11	♛♛♛ 6
● Montefalco Sagrantino Collenottolo '10	♛♛♛ 6

Bocale

LOC. MADONNA DELLA STELLA
VIA FRATTA ALZATURA
06036 MONTEFALCO [PG]
TEL. +39 0742399233
www.bocale.wine

CELLAR SALES
PRE-BOOKED VISITS
ANNUAL PRODUCTION 25,000 bottles
HECTARES UNDER VINE 4.20

Led by the Valentini family, the small Montefalco winery Bocale has been able to carve out a prominent place in the famous Umbrian appellation. In recent years production has shown incredible growth in terms of reliable quality expressed with elegance and drinkability. None of this is surprising given the progress made in the modulation of the use of wood and in extraction, which are fundamental in serious, structured wines like Sagrantino. A delicious Trebbiano Spoletino completes the Montefalco range. In any case it was their reds that most impressed during our tastings. The Montefalco Sagrantino '16 charms with its fruity notes of blackberry and wild strawberry. Tannins are present, and lend rhythm to the palate, but they're never bitter or mouth-drying. Their current vintage Montefalco Rosso is highly pleasant and great drinking. Another wine we recommend is their Ennio, a Sagrantino that stands out for its structure and depth. As mentioned, their Trebbiano Spoletino '18 is pleasant, as usual.

● Montefalco Rosso '17	♥♥ 3
● Montefalco Sagrantino '16	♥♥ 5
● Montefalco Sagrantino Ennio '15	♥♥ 7
○ Trebbiano Spoletino '18	♥ 3
● Montefalco Rosso '16	♀♀ 3*
● Montefalco Rosso '15	♀♀ 3
● Montefalco Rosso '14	♀♀ 3
● Montefalco Sagrantino '15	♀♀ 5
● Montefalco Sagrantino '14	♀♀ 5
● Montefalco Sagrantino '13	♀♀ 5
● Montefalco Sagrantino '12	♀♀ 5
● Montefalco Sagrantino '11	♀♀ 5
● Montefalco Sagrantino Passito '09	♀♀ 5
○ Trebbiano Spoletino '15	♀♀ 3

Briziarelli

VIA COLLE ALLODOLE, 10
06031 BEVAGNA [PG]
TEL. +39 0742360036
www.cantinebriziarelli.it

CELLAR SALES
PRE-BOOKED VISITS
ACCOMMODATION AND RESTAURANT SERVICE
ANNUAL PRODUCTION 70,000 bottles
HECTARES UNDER VINE 30.00

Founded in 2000, Cantine Briziarelli is an ambitious project with 30 hectares of vineyards. Everything, however, originated in 1906, when Pio Briziarelli moved to the Montefalco area and started his all-round farm. The new cellar, a modern structure with cutting-edge technology, was built in 2012 and since then there has been an evident qualitative leap with each vintage. The modern style, particularly in younger wines of recent years, attempts to highlight territorial characteristics. Their Rosso Mattone is the wine that most convinced during our tastings. It's a 2015 Montefalco Rosso Riserva redolent of black fruit and sweet spices. On the palate it exhibits nice structure. It's not missing tannic presence and the finish is clean, flavorful. Their Montefalco Rosso is very well-made, proving youthful with a creamy palate. Their Montefalco Sagrantino Vitruvio '11 was less convincing.

● Montefalco Rosso Mattone Ris. '16	♥♥♥ 5
● Montefalco Sagrantino '15	♥♥ 5
● Montefalco Sagrantino Vitruvio '11	♥ 6
● Montefalco Rosso '15	♀♀ 3
● Montefalco Rosso Mattone Ris. '15	♀♀ 5
● Montefalco Sagrantino '14	♀♀ 5
● Montefalco Sagrantino Vitruvio '11	♀ 6

Leonardo Bussoletti

LOC. MIRIANO
DA DELLE PRETARE, 62
05035 NARNI [TR]
TEL. +39 0744715687
www.leonardobussoletti.it

PRE-BOOKED VISITS
ANNUAL PRODUCTION 40,000 bottles
HECTARES UNDER VINE 9.00
VITICULTURE METHOD Certified Organic

Chatting with Leonardo Bussoletti is as pleasurable as drinking his wine. In only a few years' time, this humble, yet brilliant and enlightened winemaker has managed to greatly boost Narni's viticulture by means of the lovely red Ciliegiolo and the white Grechetto. Both are interpreted with full respect for the territory, offering a decadent nesse while always maintaining great technical skill. These expressive traits are common to the simplest wines, to be enjoyed young, as well as the more ambitious selections benefitting from prolonged aging. This year their entire selection put in a performance to remember. Among their Ciliegiolos (each better than the next, to be honest), their Ramici '16 stands out. Bolstered by a great year, it proves fresh and juicy, graceful on the palate with an elegant, clean finish. Tre Bicchieri. Their current-vintage version, 05035, also delivered, offering up vibrant aromas of wild berries. The Brecciaro is more full-bodied by still lean and supple. Among their whites their Colle Murello and Colle Ozio, made with Grechetto, both stood out.

Ramici Ciliegiolo '16	▼▼▼ 5
05035 Ciliegiolo '18	▼▼ 2
05035 Bianco '18	▼▼ 2*
05035 Rosato '18	▼▼ 2*
Brecciaro Ciliegiolo '17	▼▼ 3
Colle Murello '18	▼▼ 3
Colle Ozio Grechetto '18	▼▼ 3
05035 Rosso '16	♈♈♈ 2*
Brecciaro Ciliegiolo '14	♈♈♈ 3*
Colle Ozio Grechetto '12	♈♈♈ 3*
05035 Ciliegiolo '17	♈♈ 2*
Colle Ozio Grechetto '16	♈♈ 3*
Colle Ozio Grechetto '15	♈♈ 3*
Ramìci Ciliegiolo '15	♈♈ 5

★★Arnaldo Caprai

LOC. TORRE
06036 MONTEFALCO [PG]
TEL. +39 0742378802
www.arnaldocaprai.it

CELLAR SALES
PRE-BOOKED VISITS
ANNUAL PRODUCTION 1,000,000 bottles
HECTARES UNDER VINE 136.00
SUSTAINABLE WINERY

If there's one winery responsible for putting Montefalco (and Sagrantino) on the world wine map, it's undoubtedly Arnaldo Caprai, today directed by Marco Caprai. Established in the 1970s, it reached its peak in many ways in the 1990s, acquiring great notoriety. But entrepreneurs have never stop investing and so a few years ago the estate started on a new course advised by prestigious enologist Michel Rolland. Many wines are produced, starting from those obtained from local varieties and ending with the simplest, made with international cultivars. As usual they submitted a wide range of wines for tasting. Their reds, especially, stand out, thanks to a new selection of Montefalco Sagrantino, which won over our panel and earns Tre Bicchieri right of the bat. The 25 Anni '15 is a tight-knit, full-bodied wine marked by sensations of black fruit and spices. Despite its structure, it manages to be deep, elegant and highly drinkable. The Valdimaggio '15 is also top-notch.

● Montefalco Sagrantino 25 Anni '15	▼▼▼ 8
● Montefalco Rosso	
V. Flaminia Maremmana '17	▼▼ 4
● Montefalco Sagrantino	
Valdimaggio '15	▼▼ 7
● Montefalco Rosso '17	▼▼ 4
● Montefalco Rosso Ris. '16	▼▼ 6
● Montefalco Sagrantino Collepiano '15	▼▼ 7
○ Colli Martani Grechetto Grecante '18	▼ 4
● Montefalco Sagrantino Passito '15	▼ 7
● Montefalco Sagrantino 25 Anni '14	♈♈♈ 8
● Montefalco Sagrantino 25 Anni '10	♈♈♈ 8
● Montefalco Sagrantino Collepiano '13	♈♈♈ 7
● Montefalco Sagrantino Collepiano '12	♈♈♈ 7
● Montefalco Sagrantino Collepiano '11	♈♈♈ 7

La Carraia

LOC. TORDIMONTE, 56
05018 ORVIETO [TR]
TEL. +39 0763304013
www.lacarraia.it

CELLAR SALES
PRE-BOOKED VISITS
ANNUAL PRODUCTION 700,000 bottles
HECTARES UNDER VINE 119.00

Carraia was founded at the end of the 1980s thanks to the fruitful collaboration between well-known enologist Riccardo Cotarella and the Gialletti family. Despite the Orvieto winery's large production numbers, it has always made reliable wines at competitive prices. The very wide range includes both territorial wines and international varietals, all united in impeccable technical precision combined with the carefree drinkability that particularly characterizes the youngest wines. Four wines were submitted for tastings, three IGTs and an Orvieto. This last, the Poggio Calvelli '18, most impressed for its finesse and complexity. It goes all in on the quality of its aromatic profile, all notes of iodine, flowers, Mediterranean herbs and orange peel. It's not lacking in freshness on the palate, with a pure sapidity that together push the wine towards a nice, clean finish. Among their reds the Solcato '16, a blend of Sangiovese, Merlot and Cabernet Sauvignon, stood out.

○ Orvieto Cl. Sup. Poggio Calvelli '18	🍷🍷 2*
○ Le Basque '18	🍷🍷 3
● Merlot '18	🍷🍷 2*
● Solcato '16	🍷🍷 3
● Fobiano '03	🍷🍷🍷 4
○ Le Basque '17	🍷🍷 3*
○ Orvieto Cl. Sup. Poggio Calvelli '14	🍷🍷 2*
○ Orvieto Cl. Sup. Poggio Calvelli '13	🍷🍷 2*

★★★Castello della Sala

LOC. SALA
05016 FICULLE [TR]
TEL. +39 076386127
www.antinori.it

CELLAR SALES
PRE-BOOKED VISITS
ANNUAL PRODUCTION 760,000 bottles
HECTARES UNDER VINE 140.00

It was not by mere coincidence that Marquesi Antinori settled specifically in the Orvieto area of Umbria while searching for a good white wine country near their Tuscan home. This decision gave rise to Castello della Sala and Cervaro, the estate's most celebrated wines, were born. Its now famous formula involves Chardonnay flanked by traditional, local Grechetto and the Burgundy-style technique of using tonneau for both fermentation and maturation. The range is completed by an Orvieto, a Pinot Nero and the famous Muffato della Sala. And once again their Cervaro della Sala takes home gold. This important Italian white, fermented and aged in barrels, surprises for its bold structure, knowingly mitigated by freshness and sapidity. 2017 makes for a version rich in aromas of yellow flowers and apricot — it's not missing a touch of saffron either. The mouth is pervasive and flavorful, with a long, silky finish. Tre Bicchieri. Among the rest of their selection their Bramito '18, a monovarietal Chardonnay, stood out.

○ Cervaro della Sala '17	🍷🍷🍷
○ Bramito della Sala '18	🍷🍷
○ Conte della Vipera '18	🍷
○ Orvieto Cl. Sup. San Giovanni della Sala '18	🍷
○ Cervaro della Sala '16	🍷🍷🍷
○ Cervaro della Sala '15	🍷🍷🍷
○ Cervaro della Sala '14	🍷🍷🍷
○ Cervaro della Sala '13	🍷🍷🍷
○ Cervaro della Sala '12	🍷🍷🍷

antina Cenci

AZ. SAN BIAGIO DELLA VALLE
C. ANTICELLO, 52
6072 MARSCIANO [PG]
L. +39 3805198980
ww.cantinacenci.it

ELLAR SALES
RE-BOOKED VISITS
NNUAL PRODUCTION 25,000 bottles
ECTARES UNDER VINE 6.00
USTAINABLE WINERY

he Cenci winery is located a few
lometers south of Perugia and is now
anaged by the fourth generation of the
mily. The estate has about 40 hectares
f property of which six are vineyards. The
ayey and sandy soils are rich in
mestone and all fall within a territory
ettled at the end of the 1600s by the
livetan monks, known for their excellence
t selecting agricultural land. Production is
vided between central Italy's traditional
angiovese, Grechetto and Trebbiano
arieties and some international cultivars.
 highly respectable selection puts Cenci
 the club of regional notable regional
roducers. Their Piantata R led the way. It's
 monovarietal Sangiovese that made it to
ur final tastings. Fresh, with excellent
apidity, flavorful and with pervasive
romas — it's a well-calibrated wine of
are elegance. The 2017 version of their
iantata also delivered. Among their whites
eir Grechetto Anticello Laghetto '18
tood out.

Piantata R '16	♈♈ 6
Anticello Laghetto '18	♈♈ 3
Piantata '17	♈♈ 4
Sanbiagio '17	♈♈ 3
Anticello '18	♈ 3
Campo Maro '18	♈ 3
Giole '18	♈ 2
Anticello '16	♉♉ 2*
Anticello '14	♉♉ 2*
Ascheria '16	♉♉ 3
Piantata '16	♉♉ 4
Piantata '15	♉♉ 4
Piantata '13	♉♉ 4

Le Cimate

FRAZ. CASALE
LOC. CECAPECORE, 41
06036 MONTEFALCO [PG]
TEL. +39 0742290136
www.lecimate.it

CELLAR SALES
PRE-BOOKED VISITS
ACCOMMODATION AND RESTAURANT SERVICE
ANNUAL PRODUCTION 800,000 bottles
HECTARES UNDER VINE 20.00
SUSTAINABLE WINERY

The peaks of the Montefalco hills may have
inspired the name of the winery founded by
the Bartoloni family in 2011, but the
estate's agricultural origins extend back to
the 1800s. Paolo is in now charge of the
company, managing about 30 hectares of
vineyards with both local (for Montefalco
DOC) and international (used largely for
IGT) cultivars. The clayey and silty soils
feature limestone tongues, giving rise to
very enjoyable wines of great typicity. All
the wines submitted this year put in an
excellent performance. Their Montefalco
Sagrantino '18 led the selection and made
it into our final round, thanks to a charming
and complex olfactive spectrum, all dark
fruit, spices and sweet tobacco. The palate
is dynamic, crossed by ripe but never
aggressive tannins. Their supple and deep
Montefalco Rosso '15 proved well-crafted,
as did their Trebbiano Spoletino '18.

● Montefalco Sagrantino '14	♈♈ 5
● Montefalco Rosso '15	♈♈ 3
○ Trebbiano Spoletino '18	♈♈ 3
● Montefalco Sagrantino '13	♉♉ 5
● Montefalco Sagrantino '12	♉♉ 5
○ Trebbiano Spoletino '17	♉♉ 3
○ Trebbiano Spoletino '15	♉♉ 3

Colle Ciocco

VIA B. GOZZOLI 1/5
06036 MONTEFALCO [PG]
TEL. +39 0742379859
www.colleciocco.it

CELLAR SALES
PRE-BOOKED VISITS
ANNUAL PRODUCTION 45,000 bottles
HECTARES UNDER VINE 15.00

The positive results of its recent vintages
mean that Colle Ciocco clearly belongs
among the region's most important
wineries. Located in Montefalco on the hill
that shares the winery's name, it was
established in the 1930s by Settimio
Spacchetti and is now managed by his sons
Lamberto and Eliseo. Of the just over twenty
hectares, fifteen are vineyards, while the
remaining are planted with olive trees or are
arable land. Sagrantino dominates, flanked
by other 'black' grapes used in making
Montefalco Rosso. A masterful Montefalco
Sagrantino landed a place in our final round
of tastings. 2014 conferred impressive
aromas, with spices giving way to tobacco,
dark fruit and a citrusy touch. On the palate,
bolstered by its 5 years aging, it proves soft
and round, pervasive, long and clean.
Among the rest of their selection their sapid
and energetic Tempestivo, a 2018 Trebbiano
Spoletino, stood out, though all their wines
are well made.

● Montefalco Sagrantino '14	¶¶ 5
○ Montefalco Bianco '18	¶¶ 3
● Montefalco Rosso '15	¶¶ 3
○ Spoleto Trebbiano Spoletino Tempestivo '18	¶¶ 3
● Montefalco Sagrantino Passito '12	¶ 5
● Montefalco Sagrantino '11	¶¶ 5
○ Spoleto Trebbiano Spoletino Tempestivo '17	¶¶ 3

Fattoria Colleallodole

VIA COLLEALLODOLE, 3
06031 BEVAGNA [PG]
TEL. +39 0742361897
www.fattoriacolleallodole.com

CELLAR SALES
PRE-BOOKED VISITS
ANNUAL PRODUCTION 70,000 bottles
HECTARES UNDER VINE 25.00

Colleallodole is brilliantly managed by the
Antano family, which gives it a fully
artisanal signature style. The winery takes
its name from its position, one of the best
area's of the Montefalco district. The
vineyards are dedicated to the varieties th
typify the area, starting with Sagrantino,
giving shape to wines whose particular
charm comes from calibrated maceration
and a wise use of maturation in oak
barrels. Healthy imperfections help the
wines authentically express their territorial
identities more fully. We tasted some five
reds, all exceptionally well made. The mos
impressive is also the youngest, their
Montefalco Rosso '17. On the nose it offe
up aromas of violet and blackcurrant. On
the palate it's fresh and juicy with an
extremely clean finish. Another great wine
is their Montefalco Sagrantino Colleallodol
a 2016. It's still a bit young, but not lackin
in finesse. We should also point out their
Montefalco Sagrantino Passito, one of the
best of its kind.

● Montefalco Rosso '17	¶¶ 3
● Montefalco Sagrantino '16	¶¶ 6
● Montefalco Sagrantino Colleallodole '16	¶¶ 8
● Montefalco Sagrantino Passito '16	¶¶ 7
● Montefalco Rosso Ris. '16	¶ 5
● Montefalco Rosso Ris. '08	¶¶¶ 5
● Montefalco Sagrantino '12	¶¶¶ 6
● Montefalco Sagrantino Colleallodole '10	¶¶¶ 8
● Montefalco Sagrantino Colleallodole '09	¶¶¶ 8
● Montefalco Sagrantino Passito '15	¶¶ 7

Fattoria Colsanto

VIA MONTARONE
06031 BEVAGNA [PG]
TEL. +39 0742360412
www.livon.it

CELLAR SALES
PRE-BOOKED VISITS
ACCOMMODATION
ANNUAL PRODUCTION 50,000 bottles
HECTARES UNDER VINE 15.00

Colsanto is the Umbrian estate of the well-known and respected Livon family from Friuli. The winery is located on top of a promontory surrounded by vineyards and marked by a small cypress-lined road: a winsome scene that matches the wines, particularly those of recent years. Focused, non-invasive maturations are mainly in large wood barrels while macerations guarantee extremely enjoyable drinking without loss of typicity. The classics of the Montefalco territory take center stage, starting with Sagrantino. It's a Montefalco Sagrantino that distinguished itself in our last round of tastings. 2014 gave rise to aromas of embers and tobacco, anticipating hints of dark fruit and sweet spices. On the palate it's pervasive and silky, long, clean and marked by nice, ripe tannins. Without a doubt their Cantaluce '18 also convinced. A white made with Trebbiano Spoletino, it's redolent of wild flowers, with a sapid, rhythmic palate.

Montefalco Sagrantino '14	▼▼ 5
Cantaluce '18	▼▼ 5
CantaLuce '17	♀♀ 5
Montefalco Rosso '14	♀♀ 3
Montefalco Rosso '13	♀♀ 3
Montefalco Sagrantino '12	♀♀ 5
Montefalco Sagrantino '11	♀♀ 5
Montefalco Sagrantino '10	♀♀ 5
Montefalco Sagrantino '09	♀♀ 5
Montefalco Sagrantino Montarone Ris. '12	♀♀ 6
Ruris '14	♀♀ 2*

Decugnano dei Barbi

LOC. FOSSATELLO, 50
05018 ORVIETO [TR]
TEL. +39 0763308255
www.decugnano.it

CELLAR SALES
PRE-BOOKED VISITS
ANNUAL PRODUCTION 130,000 bottles
HECTARES UNDER VINE 32.00

Decugnano dei Barbi is definitely worth a visit. It's located in a landscape of unquestionable beauty, surrounded by marvelous vineyards whose soils are rich in shells and fossils. Do not miss a visit to the tufaceous cave used mainly for slow second fermentation of Metodo Classico, all 'done as it should be done' by the Barbi family. Production focuses on whites, starting with Orvieto, characterized by great stylistic precision, cleanliness and aromatic clarity, while never neglecting the territory's deepest voices. The Oriveto Classico Superiore Il Bianco is a benchmark for the appellation. A difficult 2018 still made for a wine redolent of white fruit, with citrus at the fore, followed by minty hints and aromatic herbs. The finish is sapid and extremely clean. We found both their Metodo Classicos very interesting, starting with their Brut, a wine of great balance and a prickle that's perfectly in line with texture.

○ Orvieto Cl. Sup. Il Bianco '18	▼▼ 4
○ Brut M. Cl. '14	▼▼ 5
○ Dosaggio Zero M. Cl. '14	▼▼ 5
○ Orvieto Cl. Villa Barbi '18	▼▼ 3
⊙ Tramonto d'Estate '18	▼ 4
○ Orvieto Cl. Sup. "IL" '11	♀♀♀ 3*
○ Orvieto Cl. Sup. Il Bianco '17	♀♀♀ 4*
○ Orvieto Cl. Sup. Il Bianco '16	♀♀♀ 4*
○ Orvieto Cl. Sup. Il Bianco '15	♀♀♀ 4*
○ Orvieto Cl. Sup. Il Bianco '12	♀♀♀ 3*
○ Orvieto Cl. Sup. Il Bianco '10	♀♀♀ 3
● Il Rosso A.D.1212 '16	♀♀ 4
○ Orvieto Cl. Sup. Muffa Nobile Pourriture Noble '15	♀♀ 6
○ Orvieto Cl. Villa Barbi '17	♀♀ 3

Di Filippo

voc. Conversino, 153
06033 Cannara [PG]
Tel. +39 0742731242
www.vinidifilippo.com

CELLAR SALES
PRE-BOOKED VISITS
ANNUAL PRODUCTION 227,000 bottles
HECTARES UNDER VINE 35.00
VITICULTURE METHOD Certified Organic
SUSTAINABLE WINERY

Enologist and skilled winemaker Roberto Di
Filippo founded this Cannara winery on
principles of sustainability and full support
for biodiversity. Organically run for some
time now, the estate is based in the two
different areas of Colli Martani and
Montefalco. The wide range puts traditional
varieties in the front lines, primarily
Sangiovese, Grechetto and Sagrantino. The
sincere wines are genuine, charming,
transmit identity of the territory well and are
all incredibly enjoyable to drink. This
Cannara producer put in an outstanding
performance this year. Their Montefalco
Rosso '17 stands out for its ability to bring
together finesse with a flavorful structure
and a very long finish. Their Vernaccia di
Cannara, one of the few out there, is
delicious and highly enjoyable. Their Villa
Conversino line also impressed, starting
with their Rosso. We've also ranked the
wines that Roberto Di Filippo produces at
another winery he founded, Plani Arche.

● Montefalco Rosso '17	♟♟ 3*
○ Colli Martani Grechetto Plani Arche '18	♟♟ 2*
● Colli Martani Vernaccia di Cannara '17	♟♟ 5
○ Grechetto '18	♟♟ 2*
● Sangiovese '18	♟♟ 2*
● Villa Conversino Rosso '18	♟♟ 2*
● Montefalco Sagrantino Plani Arche '16	♟ 5
○ Villa Conversino Bianco '18	♟ 2
☉ Villa Conversino Rosato '18	♟ 2
○ Colli Martani Grechetto '15	♟♟ 2*
● Montefalco Sagrantino Etnico '14	♟♟ 4
○ Villa Conversino Bianco '17	♟♟ 2*

Duca della Corgna

via Roma, 236
06061 Castiglione del Lago [PG]
Tel. +39 0759652493
www.ducadellacorgna.it

CELLAR SALES
PRE-BOOKED VISITS
ANNUAL PRODUCTION 300,000 bottles
HECTARES UNDER VINE 65.00

Duca della Corgna is a small cooperative
that brings together about 65 hectares of
vineyards near Lake Trasimeno, an area
just a stone's throw from Tuscany that has
always been used for viticulture. To its
great merit, the winery goes in heavily on
Trasimeno Gamay of the Grenache family,
producing different interpretations, from
the always juicy, fragrant young versions to
the most structured Riserva. The other
wines also have good typicity, prove very
drinkable and are all quite reasonably
priced, to say the least. Their Trasimeno
Gamay Divina Villa '18 is by the book. The
current vintage is fresh, vinified in steel
only, impressing with its Mediterranean
aromas, both herbaceous and fruity. The
palate is supple and highly drinkable,
never banal and made extremely long
thanks to a flavorful finish. Their two 2016
reserves exhibit more structure but
maintain grace and elegance. The Divina
Villa Etichetta Nera is more graceful and
pervasive, while the Corniolo is darker and
more austere. The rest of their selection
proved very well made.

● Trasimeno Gamay Divina Villa '18	♟♟ 3
○ Ascanio '18	♟♟ 2
● C. del Trasimeno Baccio del Rosso '18	♟♟ 2
○ C. del Trasimeno Grechetto	
Nuricante '18	♟♟ 2
● C. del Trasimeno Rosso Corniolo Ris. '16	♟♟ 4
● Trasimeno Gamay Divina Villa Ris. '16	♟♟ 3
○ C. del Trasimeno Baccio del Bianco '18	♟ 2
☉ Martavello '18	♟ 2
● C. del Trasimeno Gamay	
Divina Villa Et. Bianca '16	♟♟ 2
○ C. del Trasimeno Grechetto Nuricante '17	♟♟ 2
● C. del Trasimeno Rosso Corniolo Ris. '13	♟♟ 4

Tenute Lunelli - Castelbuono

LOC. CASTELLACCIO, 9
06031 BEVAGNA [PG]
TEL. +39 0742361670
www.tenutelunelli.it

CELLAR SALES
PRE-BOOKED VISITS
ANNUAL PRODUCTION 134,500 bottles
HECTARES UNDER VINE 32.00
VITICULTURE METHOD Certified Organic
SUSTAINABLE WINERY

Castelbuono is the Umbrian estate of the Lunelli family, known internationally for the Trentino sparkling wine of its Cantine Ferrari. It's worth visiting the winery, as much for the vineyards in the appellation of Montefalco as for Arnaldo Pomodoro's beautiful modern cellar, the Carapace. The latest vintages of local Sagrantino and Sangiovese have resulted in varietal, authentic wines that compromise on neither elegance nor depth of drink. Despite a hot 2017, the Ziguratt confirms that it's a great Montefalco Rosso and takes home a gold. Tre Bicchieri for a wine that's complex and multifaceted on the nose, starting with fruit. The palate is rhythmic in its stride, marked by acidic freshness and tannins — and the finish doesn't disappoint either. Their Lampante, a 2016 reserve, is more tight-knit and structured, while their Carapace '15 is well-made but still quite young.

● Montefalco Rosso Ziggurat '17	♥♥♥	4*
● Montefalco Rosso Lampante Ris. '16	♥♥	5
● Montefalco Rosso Sagrantino Carapace '15	♥♥	6
● Montefalco Rosso Ziggurat '16	♀♀♀	4*
● Montefalco Rosso Lampante Ris. '13	♀♀	5
● Montefalco Rosso Ziggurat '14	♀♀	3
● Montefalco Sagrantino Carapace '12	♀♀	5
● Montefalco Sagrantino Passito '12	♀♀	5

★Lungarotti

V.LE G. LUNGAROTTI, 2
06089 TORGIANO [PG]
TEL. +39 075988661
www.lungarotti.it

CELLAR SALES
PRE-BOOKED VISITS
ACCOMMODATION AND RESTAURANT SERVICE
ANNUAL PRODUCTION 2,500,000 bottles
HECTARES UNDER VINE 250.00
SUSTAINABLE WINERY

Lungarotti is symbolic in both the regional and national wine scenes. Since the 1960s it's produced high quality wines, investing heavily in vineyards and constantly renewing itself: over the decades the results have been quite obvious, so its global notoriety isn't terribly surprising. Many labels in the range come from the territory of the head office in Torgiano, as well as from Montefalco. In addition to traditional Umbrian varieties, a few international grapes have been cultivated here for a long time. And we start precisely with their San Giorgio, a blend of Cabernet Sauvignon and Sangiovese. A 2016 gave rise to a superb red, tight-knit and austere — we're sure it will age well. Their Vigna Monticchio is already enjoyable. A symbol of Togiano, it's redolent of pepper, red fruit and tobacco, anticipating a fresh, supple palate that's rhythmic in its stride, giving way to a very long, rapid finish. Tre Bicchieri. Finally, the Rosso '16 (made with grapes from their Montefalco vineyard), also deserves a mention.

● Torgiano Rosso Rubesco V. Monticchio '15	♥♥♥	6
● San Giorgio '16	♥♥	6
● ilBio '16	♥♥	3
● Montefalco Rosso '16	♥♥	4
○ Torgiano Bianco Torre di Giano V. Il Pino '17	♥♥	5
● Torgiano Rosso Rubesco '17	♥♥	3
○ Aurente '17	♥	4
● Montefalco Sagrantino '15	♥	5
○ Torgiano Bianco Torre di Giano '18	♥	2
● Torgiano Rosso Rubesco V. Monticchio Ris. '13	♀♀♀	6
● Torgiano Rosso Rubesco V. Monticchio Ris. '12	♀♀♀	6

La Madeleine

FRAZ. SCHIFANOIA
S.DA MONTINI, 38
05035 NARNI [TR]
TEL. +39 0744040427
www.cantinalamadeleine.it

CELLAR SALES
PRE-BOOKED VISITS
ANNUAL PRODUCTION 35,000 bottles
HECTARES UNDER VINE 6.40

The name hasn't changed since Linda and
Massimo D'Alema acquired it, but just
about everything else has. The winery is
now in the hands of their children Giulia
and Francesco, who manage the fifteen
hectares (of which about seven are
vineyards) between the hills of Narni and
Otricoli. Several varieties, starting with
international ones, are used to create
modern wines, based foremost on
authoritative technical control that aims to
highlight the character of this part of
Umbria. Two Metodo Classicos impressed
most during our tastings. Both have
well-calibrated prickle, which lends rhythm
to a supple, sapid palate. Their 60-month
version goes that extra mile. The nose is
more complex (wild berries and hints of
cake) while the palate proves deep and
very clean. Their reds are simple but well
made, starting with the Sfide, a
monovarietal Cabernet Franc IGT.

⊙ Nerosè60	🍷🍷 6
⊙ Nerosè Brut M. Cl.	🍷🍷 5
● Pinot Nero '17	🍷🍷 6
● Sfide '17	🍷🍷 3
● NarnOt '15	🍷🍷 6
● Pinot Nero '16	🍷🍷 6
● Pinot Nero '15	🍷🍷 6
● Sfide '14	🍷🍷 3*
● Sfide '13	🍷🍷 3*

Madrevite

LOC. VAIANO
VIA CIMBANO, 36
06061 CASTIGLIONE DEL LAGO [PG]
TEL. +39 0759527220
www.madrevite.com

CELLAR SALES
PRE-BOOKED VISITS
ACCOMMODATION AND RESTAURANT SERVICE
ANNUAL PRODUCTION 25,000 bottles
HECTARES UNDER VINE 11.00
SUSTAINABLE WINERY

Madrevite is a leading player in Lake
Trasimeno viticulture thanks above all to
artisan-inspired production that is highly
respectful of the environment. This results
in genuine, forthright wines that express the
territory. Both traditional and international
varieties are used, starting with one from
the Genache family called Gamay locally. In
recent years the range has arrived at a new
level of elegance and drinkability, adding to
its admirability. We started with the C'osa,
their most representative wine in our
opinion. Made with Gamay, the 2017 offers
up aromas of ripe red fruit and sweet
spices. It's not missing a floral touch (rose),
anticipating a warm but tonic and pervasive
palate. A truly great wine. Among their
whites we particularly appreciated the Èlvé,
a Grechetto that goes all in on sapidity
and crispness. Finally, an honorable
mention for their Futura, a charming and
enjoyable Metodo Ancestrale made with
Trebbiano Spoletino.

● Trasimeno Gamay C'osa '17	🍷🍷 5
○ Futura Metodo Ancestrale '18	🍷🍷 3
○ Il Reminore '18	🍷🍷 3
○ Trasimeno Grechetto Èlvé '18	🍷🍷 5
⊙ La Bisbetica Rosé '18	🍷 3
● C. del Trasimeno Glanio '10	🍷🍷 3*
○ Il Reminore '15	🍷🍷 3*
○ La Bisbetica Rosé '13	🍷🍷 3
○ Re Minore '11	🍷🍷 2*
● Trasimeno Gamay C'osa '16	🍷🍷 5

Cantine Neri

LOC. BARDANO, 28
05018 ORVIETO [TR]
TEL. +39 0763316196
www.neri-vini.it

CELLAR SALES
PRE-BOOKED VISITS
ACCOMMODATION
ANNUAL PRODUCTION 65,000 bottles
HECTARES UNDER VINE 50.00

The winery dates back to the Neri family's acquisition of 50 hectares of vineyards and olive groves in the 1950s. Harvests were conferred to others for winemaking until the 2000s, when it started producing and bottling wine. Credit goes to current owner and manager Enrico Neri, whose work has always focused on quality realized using local varieties and fully exalting Orvieto's territory. The style is based on highly artisanal production that is very intriguing with a compelling drink. And thanks to an outstanding Orivieto Classico Superiore, the winery earns itself a place among the guide's most important producers. The Ca' Viti '18 is a white of great sapidity, a multifaceted nose offers up floral and iodine aromas. On the palate it's long, clean, flavorful. Their Bardano '18 also delivered. It's another white that highlights the force of Grechetto. Among their reds we point out their America '16, a wine made with Merlot. It's tight-knit and austere but great drinking.

Orvieto Cl. Sup. Ca' Viti '18	♟♟ 2*
Americo '16	♟♟ 3
Bardano '18	♟♟ 3
Barrage Extra Brut '15	♟ 5
Bianco dei Neri '18	♟ 2
Oddone '15	♟ 3
Americo '14	♟♟ 3
Orvieto Cl. Sup. Ca' Viti '17	♟♟ 2*
Orvieto Cl. Sup. Ca' Viti '15	♟♟ 2*
Poggio Forno '15	♟♟ 5
Vardano '15	♟♟ 3

Palazzone

LOC. ROCCA RIPESENA, 68
05019 ORVIETO [TR]
TEL. +39 0763344921
www.palazzone.com

CELLAR SALES
PRE-BOOKED VISITS
ACCOMMODATION AND RESTAURANT SERVICE
ANNUAL PRODUCTION 130,000 bottles
HECTARES UNDER VINE 25.00
SUSTAINABLE WINERY

The winery is owned by the Dubini family, who bought the Palazzone property in the 1960s, and it's a true symbol of quality viticulture in the Orvieto area. Within the estate, the historic manor house from 1299 has been transformed into a charming hotel. The 25 hectares of vineyards are on clayey soils rich in fossil sediments, helping to produce wines that faithfully express the territory. In addition to traditional grapes used mainly for the Orvieto DOC, there are plots of Sangiovese, Sauvignon, Viognier and Cabernet Sauvignon. The Campo del Guardiano, a 2017 Orvieto Classico Superiore leads the way, offering up notes of grapefruit, curry plant and white flowers. The palate is lead, sapid — acidity and texture are well integrated. Their Vendemmia Tardia also performed notably. It's a week in which botrytis, common to Orvieto, characterizes both the nose and palate. Finally we mention the Musco, an artisanal wine made with white grapes cultivated on a tiny vineyard.

○ Orvieto Cl. Sup. Campo del Guardiano '17	♟♟ 4
○ Musco '16	♟♟ 6
○ Orvieto Cl. Sup. V. T. '17	♟♟ 4
○ Viognier '18	♟♟ 3
● Armaleo '17	♟ 5
○ Orvieto Cl. Sup. Terre Vineate '18	♟ 3
○ Orvieto Cl. Sup. Campo del Guardiano '14	♟♟♟ 3*
○ Orvieto Cl. Sup. Campo del Guardiano '11	♟♟♟ 2*
○ Orvieto Cl. Sup. Campo del Guardiano '09	♟♟♟ 3
○ Orvieto Cl. Sup. Terre Vineate '11	♟♟♟ 2*

F.lli Pardi

VIA G. PASCOLI, 7/9
06036 MONTEFALCO [PG]
TEL. +39 0742379023
www.cantinapardi.it

CELLAR SALES
PRE-BOOKED VISITS
ANNUAL PRODUCTION 56,000 bottles
HECTARES UNDER VINE 11.00

The name Pardi is well-known in the
Montefalco area and immediately brings
elegance and territorial recognition to
mind. The winery is located in the
municipality that gives its name to the
historic Umbrian appellation, within a
former textile factory, still the family's
primary activity. Vinification is done
vineyard by vineyard: for now there are two
versions of Sagrantino, a Montefalco Rosso
and white Grechetto, Chardonnay and
Trebbiano Spoletino. Sacrantino is this
Montefalco Sagrantino winery's highest
expression. We tasted a truly masterful
2015. A multifaceted nose offers up
blackcurrant, strokes of wild berry, aromas
of tobacco and orange. On the palate it's
silky but fresh, deep and sapid. Tannins
are present but well integrated with overall
mouthfeel. Tre Bicchieri. Their other
Sagrantino also proved excellent while,
among their whites, we point out both the
Grechetto and Spoletino.

● Montefalco Sagrantino Sacrantino '15	♟♟♟ 6
● Montefalco Rosso Ris. '16	♟♟ 4
○ Montefalco Grechetto '18	♟♟ 2*
● Montefalco Sagrantino '15	♟♟ 5
○ Spoleto Trebbiano Spoletino '17	♟♟ 4
○ Colle di Giove '18	♟ 2
● Montefalco Rosso '17	♟ 3
● Montefalco Sagrantino '13	♟♟♟ 5
● Montefalco Sagrantino '12	♟♟♟ 5
● Montefalco Sagrantino Sacrantino '14	♟♟♟ 6
● Montefalco Sagrantino '10	♟♟ 5
● Montefalco Sagrantino '09	♟♟ 5

Cantina Peppucci

LOC. SANT'ANTIMO
FRAZ. PETRORO, 4
06059 TODI [PG]
TEL. +39 0758947439
www.cantinapeppucci.com

CELLAR SALES
PRE-BOOKED VISITS
ACCOMMODATION
ANNUAL PRODUCTION 70,000 bottles
HECTARES UNDER VINE 12.50

In just a few short years, the Peppucci
family has built a beautiful winery that is
already a standard bearer of the Todi
district and Umbria in general. Young,
determined Filippo closely leads the estate
located in a stunning landscape of hills and
plains in which vineyards alternate with
untouched nature. Diverse local and
international varieties are used, but
Grechetto seems to be the most suitable
white grape for giving shape to deep,
excellently developed wines, while
Cabernet Sauvignon stands out among the
reds. Some two wines made it to our final
round of tastings. And even if neither
managed to earn Tre Bicchieri, I Rovi and
Giovanni are two outstanding wines. The
former, a white made with Grechetto,
suffered for the hot 2017. It's still
multifaceted on the nose, with aromas of
ripe white fruit and wild flowers. On the
palate it proves pervasive, supported by
nice freshness. The second is a very
tight-knit Bordeaux blend overall, though
it's lightened by a sapid freshness. The res
of their selection is also very well crafted.

● Giovanni '13	♟♟ 4
○ Todi Grechetto Sup. I Rovi '17	♟♟ 5
● Todi Rosso Petroro 4 '18	♟♟ 2
○ Todi Grechetto Montorsolo '18	♟ 2
○ Todi Grechetto I Rovi '16	♟♟♟ 5
● Altro Io '11	♟♟ 5
● Altro Io '10	♟♟ 5
● Giovanni '12	♟♟ 4
○ Todi Grechetto Sup. I Rovi '14	♟♟ 3
● Todi Rosso Petroro 4 '15	♟♟ 2

Perticaia

LOC. CASALE
06036 MONTEFALCO [PG]
TEL. +39 0742379014
www.perticaia.it

CELLAR SALES
PRE-BOOKED VISITS
ANNUAL PRODUCTION 120,000 bottles
HECTARES UNDER VINE 15.50
SUSTAINABLE WINERY

Perticaia is synonymous with quality even in a district as competitive as Montefalco. The winery founded in the Casale area by Guido Guardigli, is now owned by a group of Umbrian entrepreneurs with activities abroad. Production focuses exclusively on the cultivars of the area's most important appellation: not only the highly-prized Sagrantino and Montefalco Rosso reds, but also top quality whites obtained from Trebbiano Spoletino. Vintage after vintage, the extremely distinctive range never fails to win over the most demanding enthusiasts. And it was their whites that most convinced during our tastings. Both Trebbiano Spoletinos landed a place in our final round of tastings. The 2018 is simpler but never banal. It's fresh and gratifying on the palate, with an extremely long finish. The 2017 Del Posto is more complex, offering up iodine hints and aromatic herbs, while the palate is rhythmic in its sapidity, freshness and almost tannic presence. Their reds also proved well made.

○ Spoleto Trebbiano Spoletino '18	�♟ 2*
○ Spoleto Trebbiano Spoletino Del Posto '17	♟♟ 2*
● Montefalco Sagrantino '15	♟♟ 5
● Montefalco Rosso '16	♟ 3
● Montefalco Rosso Ris. '15	♟ 4
● Montefalco Sagrantino '11	♟♟♟ 5
● Montefalco Sagrantino '10	♟♟♟ 5
● Montefalco Sagrantino '09	♟♟♟ 5
● Montefalco Sagrantino '07	♟♟♟ 5
● Montefalco Sagrantino '06	♟♟♟ 5
● Montefalco Sagrantino '14	♟♟ 5
○ Spoleto Trebbiano Spoletino '15	♟♟ 2*

Pomario

LOC. POMARIO
06066 PIEGARO [PG]
TEL. +39 0758358579
www.pomario.it

CELLAR SALES
PRE-BOOKED VISITS
RESTAURANT SERVICE
ANNUAL PRODUCTION 15,000 bottles
HECTARES UNDER VINE 8.00
VITICULTURE METHOD Certified Organic
SUSTAINABLE WINERY

Pomario is located in an area of extreme environmental worth and beauty, near Monteleone di Orvieto on the Tuscan border. The main vineyards are almost 500 meters above sea level and the wines, shaped by an agricultural approach that is extremely respectful of the ecosystem, faithfully express the territory. The same principles are also applied in the beautiful stone cellar, completely self-sufficient in terms of energy thanks to the geothermal system. Varieties grown include those typical of central Italy as well as some international cultivars. A monovarietal Sangiovese most surprised during our tastings, and landed itself a place in our final tastings. Bolstered by an excellent 2016, the Sariano offers up complex, multifaceted aromas in which classic fruity notes alternated with forest undergrowth, mountain herbs and hints of mushrooms. The palate is fresh and dynamic, extremely subtle in its development, with a long, sapid finish. Their Rubicola also delivered, while the Muffato delle Streghe proves a charming wine in its delicate sweetness.

● Sariano '16	♟♟ 3*
○ Batticoda '18	♟♟ 2*
○ Muffato delle Streghe '16	♟♟ 6
○ Rubicola '18	♟♟ 2*
○ Arale '18	♟ 4
⊙ Rondirose '18	♟ 3
○ Arale '17	♟♟ 4
○ Arale '15	♟♟ 4
○ Muffato delle Streghe '15	♟♟ 6
● Rubicola '17	♟♟ 2*
● Sariano '15	♟♟ 3
● Sariano '13	♟♟ 3

Roccafiore

FRAZ. CHIOANO
VOC. COLLINA, 110A
06059 TODI [PG]
TEL. +39 0758942746
www.roccafiorewines.com

CELLAR SALES
PRE-BOOKED VISITS
ACCOMMODATION AND RESTAURANT SERVICE
ANNUAL PRODUCTION 120,000 bottles
HECTARES UNDER VINE 15.00
SUSTAINABLE WINERY

Roccafiore's innovative ideas of sustainability and respect for the environment extend far beyond wine production; it's also found in their guest reception and accommodations of a small hotel with adjoining spa and mini, wooden apartments scattered on the estate. The wines express remarkable delicacy and elegance, in recent year demonstrating great possibilities in terms of aging prospects. The vineyards are largely planted with Grechetto, the origin of diverse labels of white, and Sangiovese, the protagonist among reds. Once again a red and a white most convinced during our tastings. The Fiorfiore is a Grechetto redolent of yellow flowers and lemon peel — on the palate it's sapid and highly drinkable. But we preferred the Roccafiore, a monovarietal Sangiovese that, in the 2016 version, offers up its highest expression, from notes of small red fruits and spices to a subtle, elegant, fresh and extremely long palate. Tre Bicchieri. Their Prova d'Autore '16 is very good as well. We also make note of their Collina d'ora, a passito made with Moscato Giallo.

● Il Roccafiore '16	🍷🍷🍷 3*
○ Fiorfiore '17	🍷🍷 4
○ Bianco Fiordaliso '18	🍷🍷 2*
○ Collina d'Oro '18	🍷🍷 5
● Prova d'Autore '16	🍷🍷 5
⊙ Rosato Roccafiore '18	🍷 2
● Rosso Melograno '17	🍷 2
○ Fiorfiore '16	🍷🍷🍷 4*
○ Todi Grechetto Sup. Fiorfiore '14	🍷🍷🍷 3*
○ Fiorfiore '15	🍷🍷 4
● Il Roccafiore '15	🍷🍷 3*
● Il Roccafiore '14	🍷🍷 3*
● Prova d'Autore '13	🍷🍷 5
○ Todi Grechetto Sup. Fiorfiore '13	🍷🍷 3*

Romanelli

LOC. COLLE SAN CLEMENTE, 129A
06036 MONTEFALCO [PG]
TEL. +39 0742371245
www.romanelli.se

CELLAR SALES
PRE-BOOKED VISITS
ANNUAL PRODUCTION 48,000 bottles
HECTARES UNDER VINE 7.50
VITICULTURE METHOD Certified Organic

Agricola Romanelli is a solid operation capable of making the most of Colle San Clemente's heavily clay soils, which are home to the Montefalco area's typical varieties. Minimally intrusive work in the cellar also helps in giving rise to unadulterated wines that respect the varietal and territorial profile. The interpretations are characterized by a remarkable combination of firm structure and elegance, depth and drinkability. Sagrantino is the absolute protagonist now and destined to become even better with time. Their Medeo is the proof. It's a Sagrantino of great finesse and sophistication. The 2015 goes all in on freshness and rhythm, all made complete by exemplary tannins. Though simpler, the 'base' version of their Sagrantino is also excellent. Among their whites, both their Trebbiano Spoletino and their Grechetto are excellent. Finally we make notes of their delicious Montefalco Rosso '16.

● Montefalco Sagrantino Medeo '15	🍷🍷 8
○ Colli Martani Grechetto '18	🍷🍷 2
○ Le Tese Trebbiano Spoletino '17	🍷🍷 4
● Montefalco Rosso '16	🍷🍷 3
● Montefalco Rosso Molinetta Ris. '15	🍷🍷 5
● Montefalco Sagrantino '15	🍷🍷 5
● Montefalco Sagrantino '11	🍷🍷🍷 5
● Montefalco Sagrantino '10	🍷🍷🍷 5
● Montefalco Sagrantino '14	🍷🍷 5
● Montefalco Sagrantino '13	🍷🍷 5
● Montefalco Sagrantino Medeo '11	🍷🍷 8
● Montefalco Sagrantino Passito '13	🍷🍷 5

Scacciadiavoli

LOC. CANTINONE, 31
06036 MONTEFALCO [PG]
TEL. +39 0742371210
www.scacciadiavoli.it

CELLAR SALES
PRE-BOOKED VISITS
ANNUAL PRODUCTION 250,000 bottles
HECTARES UNDER VINE 40.00
SUSTAINABLE WINERY

The Panbuffetti family expertly manages Scacciadiavoli winery, a rare example of authentic industrial archaeology that deserves to be visited. In the 2000s, modernization began both in the vineyard and in the cellar. The vineyards are planted with the territory's traditional varietals: primarily Sagrantino, but also Sangiovese for Montefalco Rosso, with Grechetto and Trebbiano Spoletino (for whites) and small quantities of international cultivars. The range of wines is completed by two sparkling Metodo Classico in which Sagrantino is the star. Their Montefalco Sagrantino '15 put in an exemplary performance. It's a wine of structure and body, but also finesse and long sapidity. It amazes on the nose for its aromas of pipe tobacco and dark fruit. Their Metodo Classico Rosé (also Sagrantino, as mentioned) doesn't disappoint either. We found the Montefalco Bianco '17 interesting and pleasant in its sapidity and freshness.

○ Brut Rosé M. Cl.	♥♥ 4
○ Montefalco Bianco '17	♥♥ 3
● Montefalco Sagrantino '15	♥♥ 5
● Montefalco Rosso '16	♥ 3
● Montefalco Sagrantino Passito '15	♥ 5
● Montefalco Sagrantino '10	♥♥♥ 5
● Montefalco Rosso '09	♀♀ 3*
● Montefalco Sagrantino '11	♀♀ 5
● Montefalco Sagrantino '09	♀♀ 5
● Montefalco Sagrantino '08	♀♀ 5
● Montefalco Sagrantino Passito '12	♀♀ 5

Sportoletti

VIA LOMBARDIA, 1
06038 SPELLO [PG]
TEL. +39 0742651461
www.sportoletti.com

CELLAR SALES
PRE-BOOKED VISITS
ANNUAL PRODUCTION 210,000 bottles
HECTARES UNDER VINE 30.00
SUSTAINABLE WINERY

The name Sportoletti is well-known in Umbrian viticulture, with roots going back to the late 1970s when the company was founded; but its path has been one of modernization and continuous updating. Everything is based on strength of the vineyards located on the hills of Spello, planted with both traditional and international varieties. The very clean, modern wines always respect the varietals and the territory. In recent years, both the red and the white wines have been excellent. We tasted four wines this year, two of which impressed the most. The red is the 2017 Villa Fidelia. It's a wine redolent of pepper and blackberry — the palate exhibits structure, though it's mitigated by nice freshness. The white is their Assisi Grechetto '18, which features aromas of medlar and citrus peel. Their juicy Assisi Rosso, a simple wine on the palate, also proves well made.

○ Assisi Grechetto '18	♥♥ 1*
○ Villa Fidelia Bianco '17	♥♥ 3
● Villa Fidelia Rosso '17	♥♥ 4
● Assisi Rosso '18	♥ 2
● Assisi Rosso '15	♀♀ 2*
● Villa Fidelia Rosso '14	♀♀ 4
● Villa Fidelia Rosso '13	♀♀ 4
● Villa Fidelia Rosso '12	♀♀ 4

★Giampaolo Tabarrini

FRAZ. TURRITA
06036 MONTEFALCO [PG]
TEL. +39 0742379351
www.tabarrini.com

CELLAR SALES
PRE-BOOKED VISITS
ANNUAL PRODUCTION 70,000 bottles
HECTARES UNDER VINE 18.00
SUSTAINABLE WINERY

Gianpaolo Tabarrini is an explosive guy, and it only takes a few moments to understand his character: sometimes unpredictable, yet with very clear ideas about how to conduct work in the vineyard and cellar. A strong supporter of Sagrantino cru (producing three versions), he has shown in recent years that he can also do well with whites and his Trebbiano Spoletino has become an example of virtuosity in the category. The new functional, spacious underground cellar also produces other wine made with local varietals. Once again it was the Adarmando '17 that stood out during our tastings. It's a white made with Trebbiano Spoletino that offers up a truly unique aromatic profile, with iodine notes and Mediterranean shrub slowly giving way to yellow fruit. In the mouth it's sapid, almost savory, which lends a particular, deep rhythm to the palate. Among their Sagrantinos we particularly appreciate the Colle all Macchie '15.

○ Adarmando Trebbiano Spoletino '17	♀♀♀ 4*
● Montefalco Sagrantino Colle alle Macchie '15	♀♀ 6
● Montefalco Rosso Boccatone '16	♀♀ 3
● Montefalco Sagrantino Campo alla Cerqua '15	♀♀ 6
⊙ Bocca di Rosa '18	♀ 2
● Montefalco Sagrantino Colle Grimaldesco '15	♀ 5
○ Adarmando '16	♀♀♀ 4*
○ Adarmando '15	♀♀♀ 4*
● Montefalco Sagrantino Campo alla Cerqua '12	♀♀♀ 6
● Montefalco Sagrantino Campo alla Cerqua '11	♀♀♀ 6

Terre de la Custodia

LOC. PALOMBARA
06035 GUALDO CATTANEO [PG]
TEL. +39 0742929586
www.terredelacustodia.it

CELLAR SALES
PRE-BOOKED VISITS
ANNUAL PRODUCTION 1,000,000 bottles
HECTARES UNDER VINE 160.00
SUSTAINABLE WINERY

Terra de la Custodia is the wine brand of th Famiglia Farchioni, an internationally renowned agri-food group that also produces oil, beer and flour. Shaped by the Gualdo Cattaneo and Todi vineyards, the wines have shown in recent years that they are able to meet market demands. The modern, defined style primarily emphasizes technical precision using both traditional (especially those that grow in the Montefalco area) and international cultivars The Montefalco Sagrantino '15 is the wine that most surprised during our tastings. It's a modern style of red wine, with notes of spices and chocolate. On the palate it features pronounced tannins, coming through soft and pervasive. The Montefalco Rosso Riserva Rubium '16 is simpler and more supple on the palate, though the house style is also evident here. The rest of their selection proves generally well made.

● Montefalco Sagrantino '15	♀♀♀ 6
● Montefalco Rosso Rubium Ris. '16	♀♀ 5
○ Colli Martani Grechetto Duca Odoardo '18	♀ 2
○ Montefalco Bianco Plentis '18	♀ 3
○ Colli Martani Grechetto '14	♀♀ 2
○ Colli Martani Spumante Gladius Sublimis	♀♀ 4
● Montefalco Rosso Ris. '13	♀♀ 5

erre Margaritelli

AZ. CHIUSACCIA
C. MIRALDUOLO
6089 TORGIANO [PG]
EL. +39 0757824668
ww.terremargaritelli.com

ELLAR SALES
RE-BOOKED VISITS
CCOMMODATION
NNUAL PRODUCTION 120,000 bottles
ECTARES UNDER VINE 52.00
TICULTURE METHOD Certified Organic

he estate is named after the
ntrepreneurial family that skillfully runs
is Torgiano-based winery. Despite being
volvement in other sectors, the owners
ave shown a passion for the vineyards
at has led to gratifying results. Production
llows organic dictates and everything is
ased on sustainability, with only traditional
arietals starring in the single-body
neyard of about 50 hectares. The wines
re refreshing and flow across the palate
ith elegance, while clearly expressing the
ly territory from which they come. Both of
rgiano Rosso's reserves landed in our
nals. The Freccia deli Scacchi '16 is a
esh, supple wine, multifaceted on the
ose and deep on the palate. Their
inturicchio '16 is more complex and
ructured, with a bold texture that's
alanced out by acidic vigor and a sapid
nish — and it's all adorned with a rich,
narming palate. Tre Bicchieri. We
preciated the rest of their wines as well.

Torgiano Rosso Pinturicchio Ris. '16	▼▼▼ 5
Torgiano Rosso Freccia degli Scacchi Ris. '16	▼▼ 5
Torgiano Rosso Mirantico '17	▼▼ 2*
Greco di Renabianca '18	▼ 3
LAB '18	▼ 2
Malot '16	▼ 3
Simon de Brion '18	▼ 3
Thadea Rosato Spumante	▼ 3
Torgiano Bianco Costellato '18	▼ 2
Torgiano Rosato Venturosa '18	▼ 2
Torgiano Rosso Freccia degli Scacchi Ris. '12	♈ 5
Torgiano Rosso Freccia degli Scacchi Ris. '15	♈ 5

Todini

FRAZ. ROSCETO
VOC. COLLINA 29/1
06059 TODI [PG]
TEL. +39 075887122
www.cantinatodini.com

CELLAR SALES
PRE-BOOKED VISITS
ACCOMMODATION AND RESTAURANT SERVICE
ANNUAL PRODUCTION 220,000 bottles
HECTARES UNDER VINE 55.00

Todini was founded in the district of Todi at
the behest of entrepreneur Franco Todini in
the 1960s. The long-established estate is
divided into several activities that include
wine production, guest hospitality (with
both a Relais and a restaurant), several
hectares of arable land and a zoo with
many kinds of animals living in the ideal
environment. In recent years, wine
production has been undergoing a renewal
and the results can already be seen in the
most recent tastings. Everything here
happens under the slogan 'We are Todini'.
Two wines impressed the most, a white and
a red. The latter, their Rubro '16, is made
with Sangiovese and a share of other red
varieties. On the nose it offers up aromas
of dark fruit and forest undergrowth, while
the palate is tight-knit and soft. Their
Laudato '17, a top-notch white made with
Grechetto, proved even more convincing
thanks in part to its aging potential. We
found the Bianco del Cavaliere '18 simple
but pleasant and very well made.

○ Laudato '17	▼▼ 2*
○ Bianco del Cavaliere '18	▼▼ 3
● Rubro '16	▼▼ 3
● Consolare '15	▼ 3
● Nero della Cervara '13	♈ 5
● Sangiovese di Todi '15	♈ 1*
● Todi Sangiovese '14	♈ 4

Tudernum

Loc. Pian di Porto, 146
06059 Todi [PG]
Tel. +39 0758989403
www.tudernum.it

CELLAR SALES
PRE-BOOKED VISITS
ACCOMMODATION AND RESTAURANT SERVICE
ANNUAL PRODUCTION 1,000,000 bottles
HECTARES UNDER VINE 230.00

It's always a pleasure to see cooperatives guided by managerial foresight, able to renew themselves continually over the years, and keeping up with the times from the point of view of quality as well as sales and marketing. Tudernum is certainly one such winery and its growth has been particularly evident recently. The entire range is admirable, from the simplest wines, offered at honest prices (to say the least), to the most serious, which are standouts in their appellations. Once again their selection put in an outstanding performance, starting with their Montefalco Sagrantino Fidenzio '15. Notes of tanned leather, tobacco and undergrowth give way to dark fruit on the nose. The palate features close-knit, but never astringent, tannins — everything is mitigated by acidic vigor and a sapid finish. Their Montefalco Rosso '16 also delivered while among their whites we appreciated the Colle Nobile 17, a Todi Grechetto.

● Montefalco Sagrantino Fidenzio '15	🏆🏆	4
○ Colli Martani Grechetto di Todi Sup. Colle Nobile '17	🏆🏆	2*
● Montefalco Rosso Fidenzo '16	🏆🏆	4
● Todi Rosso '18	🏆🏆	2*
○ Todi Bianco '18	🏆	2
● Montefalco Sagrantino Fidenzio '12	🏆🏆🏆	4*
● Montefalco Sagrantino Fidenzio '14	🏆🏆	4
● Montefalco Sagrantino Fidenzio '11	🏆🏆	4
● Montefalco Sagrantino Fidenzio '10	🏆🏆	4
● Todi Rosso Sup. Rojano '13	🏆🏆	3*
● Todi Rosso Sup. Rojano '11	🏆🏆	3*

Tenuta Le Velette

Fraz. Canale di Orvieto
Loc. Le Velette, 23
05019 Orvieto [TR]
Tel. +39 076329090
www.levelette.it

CELLAR SALES
PRE-BOOKED VISITS
ANNUAL PRODUCTION 270,000 bottles
HECTARES UNDER VINE 109.00
SUSTAINABLE WINERY

Le Velette in Orvieto is a lovely operation that can count on over 100 hectares of vineyards in the more volcanic part of the appellation. The property is owned by the Bottai family, who over the years have been able to create impressive wines that satisfy market demands. The extremely functional cellar deserves a visit particularly for the suggestive aging caves which guarantee a peaceful resting place for the wines. Thanks to the use of many native and international varietals, the rang is wide and characterized by its modern style, aromatic cleanliness and pleasant drink. It was primarily their whites to shine during out tastings, starting with two Orvieto Classicos. The Lunato '18 is a Superiore redolent of medlar and citrus. It's not missing aromatic herbs either, sensations that anticipate a lean, fresh palate. Their Berganorio '18 is just a bit simpler, but very well made, featuring a floral fragrance and a supple palate. Finally, their Sole Uve '18 is a sapid Grechetto redolent of ripe yellow fruit.

○ Orvieto Cl. Berganorio '18	🏆🏆	2
○ Orvieto Cl. Sup. Lunato '18	🏆🏆	2
○ Sole Uve '18	🏆🏆	3
● Accordo Sangiovese '14	🏆	3
● Rosso Orvietano Rosso di Spicca '17	🏆	2
● Traluce '18	🏆	3
○ Orvieto Cl. Berganorio '15	🏆🏆	2
○ Orvieto Cl. Sup. Lunato '14	🏆🏆	2

Villa Mongalli

VIA DELLA CIMA, 52
06031 BEVAGNA [PG]
TEL. +39 0742360703
www.villamongalli.com

CELLAR SALES
ACCOMMODATION
ANNUAL PRODUCTION 70,000 bottles
HECTARES UNDER VINE 15.00

Villa Mongalli is masterfully run by the Menghini family in the middle of the Montefalco DOC. The splendid vineyards are in some of the most suitable areas of the territory and the grapes are vinified with both great attention and precision in the management of maceration and aging. The use of indigenous yeasts brings out personality, commendable craftsmanship and, last but not least, longevity that places the the wines at the top of the appellation. Some two wines landed in our finals this year. The first is their Montefalco Rosso Le Grazie '17, a wine that distinguishes itself for its fragrant aromas of wild berry, the prelude to a supple palate. The second is their Trebbiano Spoletino Minganna '17, a charming wine with fragrances of iodine, flowery notes and herbaceous hints. In the mouth it's rapid and lightly aromatic, in perfect keeping with its profile on the nose. Their Calicanto '18, another Trebbiano Spoletino, is simpler and more approachable.

Calicanto '18	♟♟ 5
Minganna '17	♟♟ 3*
Montefalco Rosso Le Grazie '17	♟♟ 5
Montefalco Sagrantino Pozzo del Curato '15	♟♟ 8
Montefalco Sagrantino Della Cima '15	♟ 8
Montefalco Sagrantino Della Cima '10	♟♟♟ 8
Montefalco Sagrantino Della Cima '06	♟♟♟ 6
Montefalco Sagrantino Pozzo del Curato '09	♟♟♟ 6
Montefalco Sagrantino Della Cima '13	♟♟ 8
Montefalco Sagrantino Pozzo del Curato '12	♟♟ 7
Trebbiano Spoletino Calicanto '14	♟♟ 5

Zanchi

S.DA PROV.LE AMELIA-ORTE KM 4,610
05022 AMELIA [TR]
TEL. +39 0744970011
www.cantinezanchi.it

CELLAR SALES
PRE-BOOKED VISITS
ANNUAL PRODUCTION 80,000 bottles
HECTARES UNDER VINE 35.00
SUSTAINABLE WINERY

Zanchi has been producing wine in Amelia, in southern Umbria, for more than 40 years. Sustainable agronomic practices in the vineyard and an artisanal approach in the cellar guarantee authentic, captivating wines that are characteristic of both this specific area and the vintage. Located near the cellar and manor house, the vineyards are planted with exclusively native varietals: Grechetto and Trebbiano for whites, and Aleatico and Ciliegiolo among the reds. And it's precisely a Ciliegiolo that surprises during our tastings. It landed a place in our finals thanks to its incredible simplicity (though never banal) — going all in on aromas of small red fruits, with a supple, fresh palate. Their Lu also delivered. It's an Aleatico that does a nice job balancing sugars and acidity. Among their whites we point out the Arvore, a flavorful 2018 Grechetto.

● Amelia Ciliegiolo Carmìno '18	♟♟ 2*
○ Arvore Grechetto '18	♟♟ 2*
● Lu Aleatico '16	♟♟ 3
○ Majolo '13	♟ 5
● Amelia Ciliegiolo Carmìno '17	♟♟ 2*
○ Amelia Grechetto Arvore '16	♟♟ 2*
● Amelia Rosso Armané '13	♟♟ 2*
○ Majolo '10	♟♟ 5

Cantina Altarocca

LOC. ROCCA RIPESENA, 62
05018 ORVIETO [TR]
TEL. +39 0763344210
www.cantinaaltarocca.com

CELLAR SALES
PRE-BOOKED VISITS
ACCOMMODATION AND RESTAURANT SERVICE
ANNUAL PRODUCTION 50,000 bottles
HECTARES UNDER VINE 11.00
VITICULTURE METHOD Certified Organic
SUSTAINABLE WINERY

● Rosso Orvietano Librato '18	♥♥ 3
○ Orvieto Cl. Arcosesto '18	♥ 2
○ Orvieto Cl. Sup. Albaco '18	♥ 3

Argillae

VOC. POMARRO, 45
05010 ALLERONA [TR]
TEL. +39 0763624604
www.argillae.eu

CELLAR SALES
PRE-BOOKED VISITS
ANNUAL PRODUCTION 70,000 bottles
HECTARES UNDER VINE 38.00
SUSTAINABLE WINERY

○ Orvieto Cl. Sup. Panata '18	♥♥ 4
○ Orvieto '18	♥♥ 2
○ Grechetto '18	♥ 3
● Vascellarus '16	♥ 3

Benedetti & Grigi

LOC. LA POLZELLA
06036 MONTEFALCO [PG]
TEL. +39 0742379136
www.benedettiegrigi.it

CELLAR SALES
ANNUAL PRODUCTION 400,000 bottles
HECTARES UNDER VINE 68.00

● Montefalco Sagrantino '15	♥♥ 5
● Montefalco Rosso La Gaita del Falco '17	♥♥ 2*
○ Spoleto Trebbiano Spoletino '18	♥ 3

Bigi

LOC. PONTE GIULIO
05018 ORVIETO [TR]
TEL. +39 0763315888
www.cantinebigi.it

PRE-BOOKED VISITS
ANNUAL PRODUCTION 3,500,000 bottles
HECTARES UNDER VINE 261.00

○ Orvieto Cl. Vign. Torricella '18	♥♥ 2
○ Orvieto Cl. '18	♥ 1
○ Vipra Bianca '18	♥ 2
● Vipra Rossa '18	♥ 2

Cardeto

FRAZ. SFERRACAVALLO
LOC. CARDETO
05018 ORVIETO [TR]
TEL. +39 0763341286
www.cardeto.com

CELLAR SALES
PRE-BOOKED VISITS
ANNUAL PRODUCTION 3,000,000 bottles
HECTARES UNDER VINE 700.00

○ Orvieto Cl. Sup. Febeo '17	♥♥ 3
● Nero della Greca Sangiovese '16	♥ 4
○ Orvieto Cl. '18	♥ 2

Carini

LOC. CANNETO
FRAZ. COLLE UMBERTO
S.DA DEL TEGOLARO, 3
06133 PERUGIA
TEL. +39 0756059495
www.agrariacarini.it

CELLAR SALES
PRE-BOOKED VISITS
ANNUAL PRODUCTION 40,000 bottles
HECTARES UNDER VINE 16.00
VITICULTURE METHOD Certified Organic

● C. del Trasimeno Òscano '17	♥♥ 2
○ C. del Trasimeno Rile '18	♥♥ 2
⊙ Le Cupe '18	♥ 3
○ Poggio Canneto '18	♥ 3

Castello delle Regine

loc. Le Regine
FRAZ. DI CASTELLUCCIO
05022 AMELIA [TR]
TEL. +39 0744702005
www.castellodelleregine.com

CELLAR SALES
PRE-BOOKED VISITS
ACCOMMODATION AND RESTAURANT SERVICE
ANNUAL PRODUCTION 400,000 bottles
HECTARES UNDER VINE 65.00

Rosso di Podernovo '16	♀♀ 2*
Sangiovese Sel. del Fondatore '15	♀♀ 5
● Bianco delle Regine '18	♀ 3

Castello di Corbara

loc. Corbara, 7
05018 Orvieto [TR]
TEL. +39 0763304035
www.castellodicorbara.it

CELLAR SALES
PRE-BOOKED VISITS
ANNUAL PRODUCTION 200,000 bottles
HECTARES UNDER VINE 100.00

● Lago di Corbara Merlot Cabernet Sauvignon '17	♀♀ 3
○ Orvieto Cl. Sup. '18	♀♀ 2*
○ Grechetto '18	♀ 2

Castello di Magione

loc. Le Cavalieri di Malta, 31
06063 Magione [PG]
TEL. +39 0755057319
www.sagrivit.it

CELLAR SALES
PRE-BOOKED VISITS
ANNUAL PRODUCTION 200,000 bottles
HECTARES UNDER VINE 42.00

○ C. del Trasimeno Grechetto Monterone '18	♀♀ 3
Moroneto '18	♀♀ 2*
Belfiore '18	♀ 2
Nero Cavalieri Pinot Nero '17	♀ 4

Chiorri

loc. Sant'Enea
via Todi, 100
06132 Perugia
TEL. +39 075607141
www.chiorri.it

CELLAR SALES
PRE-BOOKED VISITS
ACCOMMODATION AND RESTAURANT SERVICE
ANNUAL PRODUCTION 100,000 bottles
HECTARES UNDER VINE 25.00
SUSTAINABLE WINERY

● Sangiovese '17	♀♀ 2*
○ Colli Perugini Grechetto Sel. Antonio Chiorri '18	♀ 4
○ Titus Grechetto '18	♀ 2

Cocco

loc. Poggetto, 6c
06036 Montefalco [PG]
TEL. +39 3471916207
www.coccomontefalco.it

ANNUAL PRODUCTION 10,000 bottles
HECTARES UNDER VINE 3.50

● Montefalco Sagrantino Phonsano '14	♀♀ 4
● Montefalco Rosso Camorata '15	♀♀ 3
Montefalco Sagrantino Passito '15	♀ 5

Tenuta ColFalco

loc. Belvedere
fraz. Montepennino
via Valle Cupa
06036 Montefalco [PG]
TEL. +39 0742379679
www.tenutacolfalco.it

CELLAR SALES
PRE-BOOKED VISITS
ACCOMMODATION
ANNUAL PRODUCTION 35,000 bottles
HECTARES UNDER VINE 5.50
SUSTAINABLE WINERY

● Montefalco Sagrantino '15	♀♀ 5
● Giuliano R '16	♀♀ 3
⊙ La Rosa del Falco '18	♀ 2
● Montefalco Rosso '15	♀ 3

★Còlpetrone

FRAZ. MARCELLANO
VIA PONTE LA MANDRIA, 8/1
06035 GUALDO CATTANEO [PG]
TEL. +39 074299827
www.colpetrone.it

CELLAR SALES
PRE-BOOKED VISITS
ANNUAL PRODUCTION 350,000 bottles
HECTARES UNDER VINE 63.00

● Montefalco Sagrantino '12	♈♈	5
● Montefalco Sagrantino Sacer '10	♈♈	7
○ Grechetto '18	♈	2
● Montefalco Sagrantino '10	♈	5

Custodi

LOC. CANALE
V.LE VENERE
05018 ORVIETO [TR]
TEL. +39 076329053
www.cantinacustodi.com

CELLAR SALES
PRE-BOOKED VISITS
ANNUAL PRODUCTION 65,000 bottles
HECTARES UNDER VINE 40.00

○ Orvieto Cl. Belloro '18	♈♈	2

Fattoria di Monticello

FRAZ. RIPALVELLA
VOC. PONETRO
05010 SAN VENANZO [TR]
TEL. +39 3452550509
www.fattoriadimonticello.it

CELLAR SALES
PRE-BOOKED VISITS
ACCOMMODATION AND RESTAURANT SERVICE
ANNUAL PRODUCTION 70,000 bottles
HECTARES UNDER VINE 20.00

○ Giacchio '18	♈♈	2*
○ Ginestrello '18	♈♈	2*
○ Marièl '18	♈	2
○ Mi' Chicco '17	♈	5

Fongoli

LOC. SAN MARCO DI MONTEFALCO
06036 MONTEFALCO [PG]
TEL. +39 0742378930
www.fongoli.com

CELLAR SALES
PRE-BOOKED VISITS
ACCOMMODATION
ANNUAL PRODUCTION 100,000 bottles
HECTARES UNDER VINE 27.00
VITICULTURE METHOD Certified Organic

○ Maceratum '18	♈♈	6
● Montefalco Rosso '16	♈♈	3
● Montefalco Rosso Serpullo Ris. '15	♈	6
● Montefalco Sagrantino '13	♈	6

Goretti

LOC. PILA
S.DA DEL PINO, 4
06132 PERUGIA
TEL. +39 075607316
www.vinigoretti.com

PRE-BOOKED VISITS
ANNUAL PRODUCTION 300,000 bottles
HECTARES UNDER VINE 50.00

● Montefalco Sagrantino '15	♈♈	3*
● Colli Perugini Rosso L'Arringatore '16	♈♈	5
○ Il Moggio '18	♈	3
● Montefalco Rosso Le Mure Saracene '17	♈	3

Lamborghini

LOC. SODERI, 1
06064 PANICALE [PG]
TEL. +39 0758350029
www.tenutalamborghini.com

CELLAR SALES
PRE-BOOKED VISITS
ACCOMMODATION AND RESTAURANT SERVICE
ANNUAL PRODUCTION 150,000 bottles
HECTARES UNDER VINE 32.00

● Campoleone '16	♈♈	6
● Icon '16	♈♈	3
● Trescone '17	♈♈	3

antina Lapone

DEL LAPONE, 8
018 ORVIETO [TR]
+39 347 5472898
tinalapone.com

ANNUAL PRODUCTION 25,000 bottles
CTARES UNDER VINE 20.00
STAINABLE WINERY

rvieto Cl. L'Escluso '18	🍷🍷 4
aiano '18	🍷🍷 3
hardonnay '18	🍷 2
apone '18	🍷 3

oretti Omero

SAN SABINO, 20
30 GIANO DELL'UMBRIA [PG]
+39 074290426
w.morettiomero.it

LLAR SALES
E-BOOKED VISITS
COMMODATION AND RESTAURANT SERVICE
NUAL PRODUCTION 75,000 bottles
CTARES UNDER VINE 13.00
ICULTURE METHOD Certified Organic
STAINABLE WINERY

ontefalco Sagrantino Vignalunga '14	🍷🍷 7
ontefalco Rosso '16	🍷 3

Palazzola

VASCIGLIANO
39 STRONCONE [TR]
+39 0744609091
v.lapalazzola.it

LLAR SALES
NUAL PRODUCTION 150,000 bottles
CTARES UNDER VINE 28.00

nelia Vin Santo Caratelli al Pozzo '13	🍷🍷 5
ut Rosé M. Cl.	🍷🍷 4
esling Brut '15	🍷🍷 4
ut M. Cl.	🍷 4

Cantine Monrubio

FRAZ. MONTERUBIAGLIO
LOC. LE PRESE, 22
05014 CASTEL VISCARDO [TR]
TEL. +39 0763626064
www.monrubio.it

CELLAR SALES
PRE-BOOKED VISITS
ANNUAL PRODUCTION 200,000 bottles
HECTARES UNDER VINE 800.00

○ Orvieto Cl. Soana '18	🍷🍷 2*
● Palaia '16	🍷 3

Cantina Ninni

FRAZ. TERRAIA, 60A
06049 SPOLETO [PG]
TEL. +39 3355450523
www.cantinaninnispoleto.com

CELLAR SALES
PRE-BOOKED VISITS
ANNUAL PRODUCTION 12,000 bottles
HECTARES UNDER VINE 3.00

○ Longa '18	🍷🍷 2*
○ Misluli '18	🍷🍷 2*
● Sanbastiano '16	🍷 5

Sandonna

LOC. SELVE
S.DA DELLA STELLA POLARE
05024 GIOVE [TR]
TEL. +39 07441926176
www.cantinasandonna.com

CELLAR SALES
PRE-BOOKED VISITS
ANNUAL PRODUCTION 28,000 bottles
HECTARES UNDER VINE 6.20

● Ciliegiolo '18	🍷🍷 2*
○ Grechetto '18	🍷🍷 2*
● Selve di Giove '16	🍷 4

Santo Iolo

S.DA MONTINI, 30A
05035 NARNI [TR]
TEL. +39 0744796754
www.santoiolo.it

CELLAR SALES
PRE-BOOKED VISITS
ANNUAL PRODUCTION 20,000 bottles
HECTARES UNDER VINE 3.50
SUSTAINABLE WINERY

● Alicante '18	♟♟ 3
● Malbec '18	♟♟ 3
○ Pratalia '18	♟ 3
● Syrah '18	♟ 3

La Spina

FRAZ. SPINA
VIA EMILIO ALESSANDRINI, 1
06072 MARSCIANO [PG]
TEL. +39 0758738120
www.cantinalaspina.it

CELLAR SALES
PRE-BOOKED VISITS
ANNUAL PRODUCTION 17,000 bottles
HECTARES UNDER VINE 2.20
SUSTAINABLE WINERY

● A Fortiori '16	♟♟
● Rosso Spina '16	♟♟
○ Eburneo '18	♟
○ Rosato '18	♟

Tenuta di Salviano

LOC. CIVITELLA DEL LAGO
VOC. SALVIANO, 44
05020 BASCHI [TR]
TEL. +39 0744950459
www.titignano.it

CELLAR SALES
PRE-BOOKED VISITS
ACCOMMODATION AND RESTAURANT SERVICE
ANNUAL PRODUCTION 150,000 bottles
HECTARES UNDER VINE 70.00

○ Orvieto Cl. Sup. '18	♟♟ 2*
○ Orvieto Cl. Sup. Muffa Nobile '17	♟♟ 2*
○ Grechetto '18	♟ 2
○ Salviano di Salviano '18	♟ 3

Terre de' Trinci

VIA FIAMENGA, 57
06034 FOLIGNO [PG]
TEL. +39 0742320165
www.terredetrinci.com

CELLAR SALES
PRE-BOOKED VISITS
ANNUAL PRODUCTION 500,000 bottles
HECTARES UNDER VINE 300.00

● Montefalco Rosso '16	♟♟
● Montefalco Sagrantino '14	♟♟

Valdangius

LOC. S. MARCO
VIA CASE SPARSE, 84
06036 MONTEFALCO [PG]
TEL. +39 3334953595
www.cantinavaldangius.it

ANNUAL PRODUCTION 10,000 bottles
HECTARES UNDER VINE 5.60
SUSTAINABLE WINERY

○ Campo de Pico '18	♟♟ 3
● Montefalco Rosso Pippinello '16	♟ 5
● Montefalco Sagrantino Fortunato '15	♟ 5

La Veneranda

LOC. MONTEPENNINO SNC
06036 MONTEFALCO [PG]
TEL. +39 0742951630
www.laveneranda.com

PRE-BOOKED VISITS
ANNUAL PRODUCTION 100,000 bottles
HECTARES UNDER VINE 16.00
SUSTAINABLE WINERY

● Montefalco Rosso '16	♟♟
○ Aureo '18	♟
● Montefalco Sagrantino '15	♟

LAZIO

a region like Lazio, where white wines
minate, our overall assessment is often linked
the circumstances surrounding the previous
tage. In this case 2018 was somewhat
ficult. The result saw the region's more reliable
oducers (those that reward skill and passion) serve as
choring references. Olevano Romano earned its first Tre Bicchieri with Damiano
olli's Silene, a wine that interprets the grape in all its drinkability and fruity
shness. In terms of Cesanese del Piglio, historic wineries like Coletti Conti and
sale della Ioria confirmed their top positions. The first Tre Bicchieri was award
another historic producer, Castel de Paolis, thanks to their Frascati Superiore,
ile in the province of Rome, in addition to Tenuta di Fiorano's Fiorano Bianco,
ggio Le Volpi earned Tre Bicchieri with their Roma Rosso Edizione Limitata (the
nes of the Roma DOC zone keep getting better). The province of Latina Ponza,
th its Biancolella, also proves that it's one of the region's more interesting
stricts. This time Casale del Giglio's Faro della Guardia took home Tre Bicchieri,
t the Migliaccio family's wines (by now regulars in our final tastings), also
irmed their status as some of Lazio's best whites. Among the wines that most
ptured our attention, we can't forget two Bellones matured in amphoras,
sale del Giglio's Radix and Marco Carpineti's Nzu. It's a very promising
ection for finally realizing the grape's full potential. Finally, in Viterbo we saw
e usual names stand out, starting with Sergio Mottura and his Grechetto Poggio
lla Costa, the Cotarella family and Montana, and with wineries that are among
ly's national elite, like the Verdecchia family's Tenuta La Pazzaglia or Emanuele
ngrazi's San Giovenale. Speaking of, it's worth underlining how just being listed
our guide is a recognition of quality and how, even if all producers rightfully
pire to Tre Bicchieri, all the wines that make it to our final tastings can
gitimately be considered to be among Italy's best.

Marco Carpineti

s.da prov.le Velletri-Anzio, 3
04010 Cori [LT]
Tel. +39 069679860
www.marcocarpineti.com

CELLAR SALES
PRE-BOOKED VISITS
ANNUAL PRODUCTION 300,000 bottles
HECTARES UNDER VINE 52.00
VITICULTURE METHOD Certified Organic

Marco Carpineti has been running the family business since 1986. In that time he has brought it to the forefront of the southern Pontine area through conversion to organic production in 1994, the construction of a beautiful, modern cellar, and the continuous acquisition of vineyards in Cori and nearby Bassiano. There's no lack of bold experiments, such as their impressive 2016 Kius, the first Metodo Classico to be made with Bellone grapes. Their Kius Rosé '15, made with Nero Buono, Cori's other native grape, appears just as good. They have also fermented Bellone in amphorae to produce Nzù, which may only be in its second vintage but the gamble has already paid off. The 2016 easily reached our finals, thanks to its elegance, sapidity and length. It is joined by their two Capolemoles, which are among the best in the region for their price band, whereas the Moro '17, made from Greco Moro grapes, needs more time to reach its full potential. The rest of their vast range proves good.

Casale del Giglio

loc. Le Ferriere
s.da Cisterna-Nettuno km 13
04100 Latina
Tel. +39 0692902530
www.casaledelgiglio.it

CELLAR SALES
PRE-BOOKED VISITS
ANNUAL PRODUCTION 1,276,600 bottle
HECTARES UNDER VINE 164.00
SUSTAINABLE WINERY

The newly planted Pecorino vines near Amatrice, owner Antonio Santarelli's hometown, aren't yet producing, but do represent a step toward the estate's rediscovery of local varieties. After years ⬤ research and experimentation with enolog Paolo Tiefenthaler, the first, much anticipated version of Monti Lepini Cesanese finally debuts: Matidia '17 prov⬤ rich in fruit, with notes of black and red berries and good tannic elegance. But it w their territorial whites that we found most gratifying: Faro della Guardia '18, a splen⬤ tangy, mineral, salty Biancolella di Ponza that won our Tre Bicchieri, and Radix '15, which highlights Bellone's potential and th clever use of amphorae as aging vessels. Their high-level classic wines complete th range: Mater Matuta '15, Antinoo '17, Anthium '18 plus a base line, which includes their excellent Satrico '18.

○ Moro '17	♟♟ 3*
○ Nzù Bellone '16	♟♟ 5
○ Capolemole Bianco '18	♟♟ 2*
● Capolemole Rosso '16	♟♟ 3
○ Kius Brut '16	♟♟ 4
⊙ Kius Extra Brut Rosé '15	♟♟ 5
● Apolide '13	♟ 5
● Dithyrambus '13	♟ 5
○ Ludum '16	♟ 4
● Tufaliccio '18	♟ 2
● Apolide '12	♟♟ 5
○ Capolemole Bellone '17	♟♟ 5
○ Kius Brut '15	♟♟ 4
⊙ Kius Extra Brut Rosé '14	♟♟ 5
○ Moro '16	♟♟ 3*
○ Nzù Bellone '15	♟♟ 5
● Tufaliccio '17	♟♟ 2*

○ Faro della Guardia Biancolella '18	♟♟♟
● Mater Matuta '16	♟♟
○ Radix '15	♟♟
○ Antinoo '17	♟♟
○ Antium Bellone '18	♟♟
○ Aphrodisium '18	♟♟
● Matidia '17	♟♟
● Merlot '17	♟♟
● Petit Verdot '17	♟♟
○ Satrico '18	♟♟
○ Sauvignon '18	♟♟
● Tempranijo '17	♟♟
○ Viognier '18	♟♟
○ Antium Bellone '15	♟♟♟
○ Antium Bellone '14	♟♟♟
○ Biancolella Faro della Guardia '13	♟♟♟
○ Faro della Guardia Biancolella '16	♟♟♟

Casale della Ioria

LOC. LA GLORIA
STRADA PROV.LE 118 ANAGNI-PALIANO
03012 ANAGNI [FR]
TEL. +39 077556031
www.casaledellaioria.com

CELLAR SALES
PRE-BOOKED VISITS
ANNUAL PRODUCTION 65,000 bottles
HECTARES UNDER VINE 38.00
SUSTAINABLE WINERY

variety like Cesanese, in the past known
most exclusively locally, needed people
who could reinterpret it. Among those who
d, Paolo Perinelli, a forerunner in setting
is new course, deserves special mention.
Thanks to his passion, vineyards that are
articularly suitable for the variety, and his
esire to set new paths (such as Cesanese
ithout sulphites, which now in its final
ages of development), he continues to be
esanese's protagonist. Their 2017 Torre
el Piano stands out again this year as an
xample of what we said above: a
esanese coherent with its history, but
en to a rounder style at the same time,
th excellent raw materials and skilful use
wood. It's an unwaveringly good finalist.
enuta della Ioria '17 proves just a touch
ss concentrated, but follows the same
ilosophy, while their Colle Bianco '18
xhibits excellent quality, despite the
fficult vintage.

Cesanese del Piglio Sup. Torre del Piano Ris. '17	▼▼ 4
Cesanese del Piglio Sup. Tenuta della Ioria '17	▼▼ 3
Colle Bianco '18	▼ 2
Cesanese del Piglio Campo Novo '14	♔♔ 2*
Cesanese del Piglio Sup. Tenuta della Ioria '16	♔♔ 3
Cesanese del Piglio Sup. Tenuta della Ioria '15	♔♔ 3
Cesanese del Piglio Sup. Torre del Piano Ris. '16	♔♔ 4
Cesanese del Piglio Sup. Torre del Piano Ris. '15	♔♔ 4
Cesanese del Piglio Sup. Torre del Piano Ris. '13	♔♔ 4
Cesanese del Piglio Sup. Torre del Piano Ris. '12	♔♔ 4

Castel de Paolis

VIA VAL DE PAOLIS
00046 GROTTAFERRATA [RM]
TEL. +39 069412560
www.casteldepaolis.it

CELLAR SALES
PRE-BOOKED VISITS
RESTAURANT SERVICE
ANNUAL PRODUCTION 80,000 bottles
HECTARES UNDER VINE 11.00

Since its inception in 1985, Castel de Paolis
has drawn on the territory of Frascati. Today,
this established winery is still firmly rooted
in the territory, but it also manages to look
beyond, thanks not only to the combination
of international and traditional varieties
(ranging from Malvasia Puntinata to
Viognier, from Cesanese to Shiraz, from
Bellone to Bordolesi) but thanks also to solid
exports. The wines proposed combine a
traditional style with beautiful aromatic
precision. With the 2018 vintage, their
Frascati Superiore is back at the top of
regional winemaking. It opens on the nose
with exotic, ripe, yellow-fleshed fruit, while
the palate comes through mineral,
well-rounded and plush, with notable
length, typical of Malvasia Puntinata. Their
Frascati Campo Vecchio '18 also proves
pleasant and fresh with notes of almonds,
citron and bananas. The Quattro Mori '15
offers up sweet spices and black fruit, and
appears close-knit, with good body and
toasty notes at the finish.

○ Frascati Sup. '18	▼▼▼ 3*
○ Frascati Campo Vecchio '18	▼▼ 3
● I Quattro Mori '15	▼▼ 6
● Rosathea '16	▼▼ 5
○ Donna Adriana '17	♔♔ 4
○ Frascati Campo Vecchio '16	♔♔ 2*
○ Frascati Sup. '17	♔♔ 3*
○ Frascati Sup. '16	♔♔ 3
● I Quattro Mori '14	♔♔ 5
○ Muffa Nobile '16	♔♔ 5
○ Muffa Nobile '11	♔♔ 5

Cincinnato

VIA CORI - CISTERNA, KM 2
04010 CORI [LT]
TEL. +39 069679380
www.cincinnato.it

CELLAR SALES
PRE-BOOKED VISITS
ACCOMMODATION AND RESTAURANT SERVICE
ANNUAL PRODUCTION 900,000 bottles
HECTARES UNDER VINE 268.00
SUSTAINABLE WINERY

Founded in 1947, Cincinnato is one of the best examples of a cooperative winery in Lazio (and beyond), thanks to management that has always pursued quality over quantity, with the continued encouragement of about 130 members and the development of highly suitable terroir such as the Cori hills. Nonetheless, Nazareno Milita, recently confirmed as president, and enologist Carlo Morettini do not rest on their laurels, as demonstrated by the two new reserves, whose importance is also underlined by the special design of their bottles: Bellone Enyo '17 and Nero Buono Kora '15, the latter matured in wood barrels for four years, are already quite interesting, but destined for greater things. Pantaleo '18 achieved some important goals this year. This Greco Giallo deserved to reach our finals for the way it manages to combine elegance with structure and drinkability with complexity. Their Arcatura '17, the best version ever of a Cesanese, and Illirio '18, a blend of Bellone, Malvasia and Greco, also deserves a mention.

○ Pantaleo '18	♟♟ 2*
● Arcatura '17	♟♟ 2*
○ Cori Bianco Illirio '18	♟♟ 2*
○ Enyo Bellone '17	♟♟ 3
★ Kora Nero Buono '15	♟♟ 4
○ Castore '18	♟ 2
● Cori Rosso Raverosse '16	♟ 2
● Ercole Nero Buono '16	♟ 3
○ Puntinata '18	♟ 2
○ Brut di Bellone M. Cl. '15	♟♟ 2*
○ Castore '17	♟♟ 2*
○ Castore '16	♟♟ 2*
○ Cori Bianco Illirio '17	♟♟ 2*
○ Cori Bianco Illirio '16	♟♟ 2*
● Cori Rosso Raverosse '14	♟♟ 2*
● Ercole Nero Buono '15	♟♟ 3*
○ Pozzodorico Bellone '15	♟♟ 2*

Damiano Ciolli

VIA DEL CORSO
00035 OLEVANO ROMANO [RM]
TEL. +39 069563334
www.damianociolli.it

CELLAR SALES
PRE-BOOKED VISITS
ANNUAL PRODUCTION 25,000 bottles
HECTARES UNDER VINE 5.00
SUSTAINABLE WINERY

Damiano Ciolli has become a symbol of Cesanese and of a territory that is often overlooked and misunderstood. First with his father then with his wife Letizia, Damiano has managed to make his winery the flagbearer for local wines. Minimum treatment in both the vineyard and cellar, indigenous yeasts and careful selection of grapes characterize their work. A mixture experimentation, madness and far-sightedness results in wines that respect the territory, enhancing its character and potential. Tre Bicchieri for Cesanese di Olevano Romano Silene '17, which exhibit good body and plays on fruit. Vegetal and undergrowth notes give way to hints of blueberry and mulberry, which capture the fresh, long and pleasant palate. Their Cirsium Riserva '15 also proves good, with its rich and relaxed tasty notes of undergrowth. However it lacks a bit of drive and complexity on the palate.

● Cesanese di Olevano Romano Silene '17	♟♟♟
● Cesanese di Olevano Romano Cirsium Ris. '15	♟♟
● Cesanese di Olevano Cirsium '08	♟♟
● Cesanese di Olevano Romano Cirsium '11	♟♟
● Cesanese di Olevano Romano Cirsium Ris. '14	♟♟
● Cesanese di Olevano Romano Cirsium Ris. '13	♟♟
● Cesanese di Olevano Romano Sup. Cirsium Ris. '10	♟♟
● Cesanese di Olevano Romano Sup. Silene '16	♟♟
● Cesanese di Olevano Silene '11	♟♟

ntonello Coletti Conti

Vittorio Emanuele, 116
012 Anagni [FR]
. +39 0775728610
w.coletticonti.it

LLAR SALES
E-BOOKED VISITS
NNUAL PRODUCTION 20,000 bottles
CTARES UNDER VINE 20.00

tonello Coletti Conti is, more in
bstance than form, an independent
nemaker. He personally tends to both the
eyards (where he has never used any
e of fertilizer) and the cellar. The first
ferentiation between the two Cesanese
omanico and Hernicus) begins in the
eyard, with the former coming from the
canic soils of the highest cru on the La
etanella estate. It then continues in the
llar with the eighteen-month long
aturation of the same Romanico in
rriques. The result is two almost
mplementary wines. Hernicus '17
mes through more approachable,
spite its complex nose and palate. Their
manico '17 offers up concentrated fruit
h notes of rhubarb and coffee, which
ed more time in the bottle to produce a
sanese of substance. Their Cosmato '17
o proves interesting: this Bordeaux
nd is currently a triumph of youth, but
ssesses all the necessary potential for
g-term evolution.

Cesanese del Piglio Sup. Hernicus '17	♟♟ 3*
Cesanese del Piglio Sup. Romanico '17	♟♟ 5
Cosmato '17	♟♟ 5
Cesanese del Piglio Romanico '11	♟♟♟ 5
Cesanese del Piglio Romanico '07	♟♟♟ 5
Cesanese del Piglio Sup. Hernicus '14	♟♟♟ 3*
Cesanese del Piglio Sup. Hernicus '12	♟♟♟ 3*
Arcadia '16	♟♟ 3
Cesanese del Piglio Sup. Hernicus '16	♟♟ 3
Cesanese del Piglio Sup. Hernicus '15	♟♟ 3*
Cesanese del Piglio Sup. Romanico '16	♟♟ 5
Cesanese del Piglio Sup. Romanico '15	♟♟ 5
Cesanese del Piglio Sup. Romanico '14	♟♟ 5
Cosmato '16	♟♟ 5
Cosmato '15	♟♟ 5
Passerina del Frusinate Hernicus '17	♟♟ 3

★★Falesco
Famiglia Cotarella

s.s. Cassia Nord km 94,155
01027 Montefiascone [VT]
Tel. +39 07449556
www.falesco.it

CELLAR SALES
PRE-BOOKED VISITS
ACCOMMODATION
ANNUAL PRODUCTION 3,650,000 bottles
HECTARES UNDER VINE 330.00

The story began in the 1960s when
Monterubiaglio winegrowers Antonio and
Domenico Cotarella built the first cellar to
produce their own wine. Then, in 1979,
brothers Renzo and Riccardo established
the Falesco winery, which over time has
become one of Italy's most prestigious.
Now, the third generation, Dominga, Enrica
and Marta, are redesigning a line that more
than ever speaks of the family and its
name. The estate's wide range is notably
modern in style. Montiano, always fresh
and bright with good body, wins the Tre
Bicchieri once again. This monovarietal
Merlot reflects the stony volcanic soil the
grapes grow on, which enhances the
spectrum of aromatics marked by small red
fruit and sweet spices. Their whole range of
wines displays a good level, including the
whites, particularly their citrusy, pleasant
and gutsy Vitiano.

● Montiano '17	♟♟♟ 8
○ Ferentano '17	♟♟ 6
● Marciliano '16	♟♟ 8
● Sodale Merlot '17	♟♟ 3*
○ Appunto '18	♟♟ 2*
○ Est Est Est di Montefiascone Poggio dei Gelsi '18	♟♟ 2*
● Messidoro '18	♟♟ 2*
○ Soente Viognier '18	♟♟ 5
○ Tellus Rosè Syrah '18	♟♟ 3
● Tellus Syrah '18	♟♟ 3
● Trentanni '17	♟♟ 5
● Vitiano '18	♟♟ 2*
○ Vitiano Bianco '18	♟♟ 3
○ Brut M. Cl.	♟ 4
⊙ Brut Rosé M. Cl.	♟ 4
○ Tellus Chardonnay '18	♟ 4

LAZIO

Fontana Candida

VIA FONTANA CANDIDA, 11
00040 MONTE PORZIO CATONE [RM]
TEL. +39 069401881
www.fontanacandida.it

CELLAR SALES
PRE-BOOKED VISITS
RESTAURANT SERVICE
ANNUAL PRODUCTION 2,200,000 bottles
HECTARES UNDER VINE 210.00

Fontana Candida, owned by Gruppo Italiano
Vini, makes wines from over 200 hectares
of vineyards located between 200 and 400
meters above sea level on sandy and deep
volcanic soils. Traditional grapes such as
Malvasia di Candia and di Lazio, Tuscan
Trebbiano, Greco, Bombino and Cesanese
are cultivated along with international
varieties like Merlot and Syrah. Wines are
quite modern in style, technically well made
and have good qualitative consistency.
Once again, their whole range exhibits a
good level. For the reds, their monovorietal
Merlot, Kron '16, appears close-focused,
with good acidity and aromas of freshly-cut
grass and pepper, while the mature and
juicy palate offers up notes of plums and
red fruit. Of the whites, we liked the typicity
of their fruity and close-focused Frascati
Superiore Vigneto Santa Teresa '18, with its
notes of fresh white flowers, and the
complexity of Frascati Superiore Luna Mater
riserva '18.

○ Frascati Sup. Luna Mater Ris. '18	🏆🏆 4
○ Frascati Sup. Secco Vign. Santa Teresa '18	🏆🏆 3
● Kron '16	🏆🏆 4
○ Frascati Secco '18	🏆 2
○ Frascati Secco Terre dei Grifi '18	🏆 2
○ Frascati Sup. Luna Mater '11	🏆🏆 3*
○ Frascati Sup. Luna Mater Ris. '17	🏆🏆 3*
○ Frascati Sup. Luna Mater Ris. '16	🏆🏆 3*
○ Frascati Sup. Luna Mater Ris. '15	🏆🏆 3*
○ Frascati Sup. Luna Mater Ris. '12	🏆🏆 3*

Formiconi

LOC. FARINELLA
00021 AFFILE [RM]
TEL. +39 3470934541
www.cantinaformiconi.com

CELLAR SALES
PRE-BOOKED VISITS
ANNUAL PRODUCTION 13,000 bottles
HECTARES UNDER VINE 4.00
SUSTAINABLE WINERY

The winery may have been founded less
than twenty years ago but the family's
vineyards date back to the late nineteenth
century, when Domenico Formiconi bough
them after returning from the United State
Father Nazareno took care of them with
love and now sons Livio, Walter and Vito
take care of them despite coming from
other activities such as medicine and
music. Expert enologist Paolo Tiefenthaler
was intelligently brought in and the result
were immediately evident, so much so th
the winery became a leader in the
ambitious task of getting Cesanese d'Affi
recognized as a DOC. They presented two
complementary versions of Cesanese: the
more approachable Cisinianum '18, when
steel preserves fruit and tannins, and the
more complex Capozzano '17, which
spends 18 months in barriques and offer
up notes of bottled black cherries, spices
and undergrowth. Their brand new Enea
Malvasia '18, with its bitter and almondy
varietal finish, also proved interesting.

● Cesanese di Affile Capozzano Ris. '17	🏆🏆
● Cesanese di Affile Cisinianum '18	🏆🏆
○ Enea Malvasia '18	🏆
● Cesanese di Affile Capozzano '08	🏆
● Cesanese di Affile Capozzano Ris. '16	🏆
● Cesanese di Affile Capozzano Ris. '14	🏆
● Cesanese di Affile Cisinianum '17	🏆
● Cesanese di Affile Cisinianum '15	🏆
● Cesanese di Affile Cisinianum '14	🏆

Antiche Cantine Migliaccio

Pizzicato
4027 Ponza [LT]
L. +39 3392822252
www.antichecantinemigliaccio.it

CELLAR SALES
PRE-BOOKED VISITS
ANNUAL PRODUCTION 10,000 bottles
HECTARES UNDER VINE 3.00

Making wine in Ponza isn't easy. Here land carved out of the rocks into small handkerchief-sized plots reaching to the shore. The area's enormous potential was recognized by the Romans, who thought it perfect for growing grapes and making wine despite the inherent difficulties. The challenges did not deter Emanuele Vittorio Migliaccio either, who planted classic varieties from the islands of Campania (Biancolella to Forastera, Piedirosso to Aglianico) on the land his family was given by Carlo di Borbone. Biancolella is back on top of the range: fresh, gutsy and full-bodied, it affords aromas of mediterranean scrubland and citrus fruit. The palate expresses notes of capers and pome fruit, followed by a sapid finish where citrus fruits return to refresh the mouth. Their pleasant and fresh Fieno Bianco also proves good, with overtones of white flowers and iodine. Fieno Rosato and Fieno Rosso both come through notably drinkable and mostly play on approachability and pleasantness.

Biancolella di Ponza '18	▼▼ 5
Fieno di Ponza Bianco '18	▼▼ 4
Fieno di Ponza Rosato '18	▼▼ 4
Fieno di Ponza Rosso '18	▼▼ 4
Fieno di Ponza Bianco '17	♀♀♀ 4*
Biancolella di Ponza '17	♀♀ 5
Biancolella di Ponza '16	♀♀ 5
Biancolella di Ponza '14	♀♀ 5
Biancolella di Ponza '13	♀♀ 5
Biancolella di Ponza '12	♀♀ 5
Fieno di Ponza Bianco '16	♀♀ 4
Fieno di Ponza Bianco '15	♀♀ 4

★Sergio Mottura

LOC. Poggio della Costa, 1
01020 Civitella d'Agliano [VT]
TEL. +39 0761914533
www.motturasergio.it

CELLAR SALES
PRE-BOOKED VISITS
ACCOMMODATION AND RESTAURANT SERVICE
ANNUAL PRODUCTION 97,000 bottles
HECTARES UNDER VINE 37.00
VITICULTURE METHOD Certified Organic

A visceral love binds Sergio Mottura to Grechetto, the emblem of the area that spreads through upper Viterbo's clayey gullies. It's a difficult variety, whose unusual tannic component means that it must be managed with skill in order to guarantee the longevity that Sergio sensed and was then able to express in his wines. The winery's production is founded on organic cultivation that respects the territory. In addition to the other traditional cultivars, the vineyards are also planted with Chardonnay, Pinot Nero and Syrah. As usual, Grechetto is the winery's main grape variety. Poggio della Costa '18 appears superbly made: it features aromas of wild flowers, bergamot orange and light spices, while the rich palate is sustained by freshness and sapidity, with a long balsamic finish. Latour a Civitella '17 expresses notes of flowers and sweet citrus fruit, with a soft, almost buttery palate and good length. The rest of their range proves well made.

○ Poggio della Costa '18	▼▼▼ 4*
○ Latour a Civitella '17	▼▼ 5
● Civitella Rosso '17	▼▼ 3
● Magone '16	▼▼ 6
○ Orvieto Secco '18	▼▼ 3
○ Orvieto Tragugnano '18	▼▼ 3
○ Grechetto Latour a Civitella '11	♀♀♀ 3*
○ Grechetto Poggio della Costa '14	♀♀♀ 3*
○ Poggio della Costa '17	♀♀♀ 4*
○ Poggio della Costa '16	♀♀♀ 3*
○ Poggio della Costa '15	♀♀♀ 3*
○ Poggio della Costa '12	♀♀♀ 3*
○ Poggio della Costa '11	♀♀♀ 3*

Omina Romana

VIA FONTANA PARATA, 75
00049 VELLETRI [RM]
TEL. +39 0696430193
www.ominaromana.com

CELLAR SALES
PRE-BOOKED VISITS
ANNUAL PRODUCTION 130,000 bottles
HECTARES UNDER VINE 80.00
SUSTAINABLE WINERY

Omina Romana was born in 2007 out of the vision of Anton Borner, a German who decided to invest in 80 hectares on the volcanic hills south of Rome in Velletri. The pedoclimatic characteristics were evaluated, studied with attention and found to be 'good omens', hence the Latin name of the estate. His objective was to create a new, high-quality winery with a purely international style. His team, composed of enologists Simone Sarnà and Claudio Gori and agronomist Paula Pacheco, decided to focus mainly on red varietals. Ars Magna Merlot '15 impressed us the most, with good body and notes of sweet wood and tobacco, revealing good-quality tannin. However, it still needs a little longer to evolve. The same goes for Ceres Anesidora I, a fruity, spicy and balsamic blend of Cabernet Sauvignon and Franc. Their rich and pleasant Janus Geminus I offers up notes of sweet spices and good fruit.

● Ars Magna Merlot '15	♼♼ 8
● Ceres Anesidora I '15	♼♼ 8
● Janus Geminus I '15	♼♼ 8
● Ars Magna Cabernet Franc '15	♼ 8
● Ars Magna Cabernet Sauvignon '15	♼ 8
● Cesanese '15	♼ 6
○ Bellone Brut '14	♼♼ 4
● Cabernet Franc Linea Ars Magna '13	♼♼ 8
● Diana Nemorensis I '12	♼♼ 6
● Hermes Diactoros '13	♼♼ 4
● Merlot '13	♼♼ 7

Principe Pallavicini

VIA ROMA, 121
00030 COLONNA [RM]
TEL. +39 069438816
www.principepallavicini.com

CELLAR SALES
PRE-BOOKED VISITS
RESTAURANT SERVICE
ANNUAL PRODUCTION 600,000 bottles
HECTARES UNDER VINE 65.00

Wine tradition and culture are in the DNA of the noble Pallavicini family, a protagonist of regional enology since 1600. Located 25 km south-east of Rome on the remains of an ancient Lazio volcano, the estate consists of 50 hectares of vineyards planted with white varieties and fifteen hectares of red. The approach is based on respecting the territory, with low environmental impact cultivation and the use of natural yeasts. The winery continues to keep its sights on the future; the new cellar boasts truncated conical vats that allow for the separate vinification of individual vineyards, highlighting the best of the characteristics of each. Their long, fresh Frascati Superiore Poggio Verde '18 affords aromas of white flowers and citrus fruits. It opens up further on the palate, expressing mineral overtones, depth and pleasantness. Frascati '18 conveys nuances of tropical fruit and citrus. Syrah '17 was their most impressive red: crisp and fresh, with notes of black fruit and licorice. The rest of the range proved good.

○ Frascati '18	♼♼
○ Frascati Sup. Poggio Verde '18	♼♼
● Syrah '17	♼♼
● Amarasco Cesanese '17	♼
● Casa Romana '15	♼
○ Roma Malvasia Puntinata '18	♼
● Rubillo '18	♼
○ Frascati Sup. Poggio Verde '13	♼♼♼
○ Frascati Sup. Poggio Verde '15	♼♼
○ Frascati Sup. Poggio Verde '14	♼♼
○ Frascati Sup. Poggio Verde '12	♼♼
○ Stillato '13	♼♼

enuta La Pazzaglia

oa di Bagnoregio, 4
024 Castiglione in Teverina [VT]
l. +39 0761947114
ww.tenutalapazzaglia.it

ELLAR SALES
RE-BOOKED VISITS
CCOMMODATION
NNUAL PRODUCTION 56,000 bottles
ECTARES UNDER VINE 12.00

ne winery's story began in 1990, when
e Verdecchia family bought the
7-hectare La Pazzaglia Estate, seeing its
otential despite the state of abandonment.
eresa and her son-in-law Randolfo
ought the land bordering Lazio, Umbria
nd Tuscany back to life, initially focusing
n international and then turning to
aditional varieties, a change of direction
at marked a real turning point for the
inery. Today Grechetto is its top variety.
09 Grechetto '18 turned out well despite
e difficult vintage: pleasant and sapid,
ith notes of white fruit and jasmine, juicy
nd taut. Their other Grechetto, Poggio
riale '17, features hints of flowers and
anilla leading into a gutsy palate, where
annic nuances emerge. Miadimia '18, a
assic blend of native white grapes
rechetto, Procanico, Verdello and
alvasia), comes through pleasant,
romatic and citrusy.

109 Grechetto '18	🍷🍷 3*
Madimia '18	🍷🍷 3
Poggio Triaie '17	🍷🍷 3
Montijone Merlot '16	🍷 3
109 Grechetto '17	🍷🍷 3*
109 Grechetto '16	🍷🍷 3*
Grechetto 109 '13	🍷🍷 3*
Poggio Triale '16	🍷🍷 3
Poggio Triale '15	🍷🍷 3
Poggio Triale '14	🍷🍷 3*

Pietra Pinta

via Le Pastine km 20,200
04010 Cori [LT]
Tel. +39 069678001
www.pietrapinta.com

CELLAR SALES
PRE-BOOKED VISITS
ACCOMMODATION AND RESTAURANT SERVICE
ANNUAL PRODUCTION 300,000 bottles
HECTARES UNDER VINE 33.00
VITICULTURE METHOD Certified Organic
SUSTAINABLE WINERY

The Ferretti family's considerable property
extends across the territory of Cori, where
history, art and viticulture have lived together
for centuries (the stunning Ninfa gardens are
just a few kilometres away). Bruno Ferretti,
Cesare's son, runs the estate, which also
produces oil and cosmetics and runs a lovely
agritourism. The numerous varieties,
resulting from research done with the
Region of Lazio, are equally divided between
local and international reds and whites.
The various wines produced demonstrate
this. On one hand, their top wine Colle
Amato '15, excels once again. This
monovarietal Nero Buono features lovely
notes of cherry, red fruit and spice. On the
other, their fresh and pleasant Viognier '18
proves assertive. Costa Vecchia Rosso '17,
a blend of Nero Buono and Syrah, comes
through rich and spicy. Another more
approachable monovarietal Nero Buono,
some monovarietals and Costa Vecchia
Bianco '18 (a blend of Sauvignon,
Chardonnay and Malvasia) also appear
well made.

● Colle Amato Nero Buono '15	🍷🍷 3
● Costa Vecchia Rosso '17	🍷🍷 2*
○ Viognier '18	🍷🍷 2*
○ Chardonnay '18	🍷 2
○ Costa Vecchia Bianco '18	🍷 2
○ Malvasia Puntinata '18	🍷 2
● Nero Buono '17	🍷 2
● Shiraz '17	🍷 2
○ Chardonnay '15	🍷🍷 2*
● Colle Amato '13	🍷🍷 4
● Colle Amato '12	🍷🍷 4
○ Costa Vecchia Bianco '16	🍷🍷 2*
● Shiraz '16	🍷🍷 2*
○ Viognier '15	🍷🍷 2*

★Poggio Le Volpi

VIA COLLE PISANO, 27
00078 MONTE PORZIO CATONE [RM]
TEL. +39 069426980
www.poggiolevolpi.com

CELLAR SALES
PRE-BOOKED VISITS
RESTAURANT SERVICE
ANNUAL PRODUCTION 300,000 bottles
HECTARES UNDER VINE 145.00

Poggio Le Volpi was officially established in Monte Porzio Catone in 1996 by Felice Mergè. The first steps, howver, had been taken by his grandfather Manlio, who produced bulk wine in the 1920s, and by his father Armando, who first gave 'national' exposure to the previously 'local' estate. Today, the well-established winery makes the most of the diverse varieties on its almost 150 hectares of vineyards on Castelli Romani's volcanic soil. Roma Rosso Edizione Limitata '16 remains the winery's flagship wine. Aromas of black fruit and sweet spices pave the way for a close-knit and intense palate. Other well-made wines include Baccarossa '17, a Nero Buono with aromas of small black fruit and Mediteranean scrub, which offers up nuances of licorice and cloves on the palate, and Frascati Superiore Epos Riserva '18, with sage, medlar, candied lemon peel and an almondy finish typical of this appellation.

● Roma Rosso Ed. Limitata '16	♟♟♟ 5
● Baccarossa '17	♟♟ 6
○ Frascati Sup. Epos Ris. '18	♟♟ 5
○ Donnaluce '18	♟ 5
○ Roma Malvasia Puntinata '18	♟ 5
⊙ Roma Rosato '18	♟ 5
● Baccarossa '15	♟♟♟ 5
● Baccarossa '13	♟♟♟ 4*
● Baccarossa '11	♟♟♟ 4*
○ Frascati Sup. Epos '13	♟♟♟ 2*
○ Frascati Sup. Epos Ris. '15	♟♟♟ 3*
● Roma Rosso Ed. Limitata '15	♟♟♟ 5

San Giovenale

LOC. LA MACCHIA
01010 BLERA [VT]
TEL. +39 066877877
www.sangiovenale.it

CELLAR SALES
PRE-BOOKED VISITS
ACCOMMODATION AND RESTAURANT SERVIC
ANNUAL PRODUCTION 9,000 bottles
HECTARES UNDER VINE 10.00
VITICULTURE METHOD Certified Organic
SUSTAINABLE WINERY

Blera is about 400 meters above sea level has clayey soil, broad temperature fluctuations and constantly blowing winds. It was, therefore, a bold move by Emanuel Pangrazi to found his winery here in 2006 It also shows his great respect for the territory, exemplified by natural spring water, vegetable-based products in the vineyards and energy self-sufficiency coming from an innovative photovoltaic system. These meaningful choices are paired with an original selection of cultivars Syrah, Grenache, Carignano and Cabernet Franc that give life to two wines of unique character. Both their wines brush with excellence. Habemus '17, a blend of Grenache, Syrah and Carignano (a white wine) proves rich and close-knit, with juicy black fruit, Mediterranean scrub, sweeter notes, good grip and length. Habemus Cabernet '16 (red), a Cabernet Franc with notes of red cherry, blueberry, pepper and quinine, comes through lingering, but velvety and fresh at the same time.

● Habemus '17	♟♟ 7
● Habemus Cabernet '16	♟♟ 8
● Habemus '16	♟♟♟ 7
● Habemus '15	♟♟♟ 7
● Habemus '14	♟♟♟ 7
● Habemus Cabernet '15	♟♟ 8
● Habemus Cabernet '14	♟♟ 8
● Habemus Cabernet '13	♟♟ 8

Tenuta di Fiorano

VIA DI FIORANELLO, 19
00134 ROMA
TEL. +39 0679340093
www.tenutadifiorano.it

CELLAR SALES
PRE-BOOKED VISITS
ACCOMMODATION AND RESTAURANT SERVICE
ANNUAL PRODUCTION 30,000 bottles
HECTARES UNDER VINE 12.00
VITICULTURE METHOD Certified Organic

Close to Appia Antica stands the small but brilliant Tenuta di Fiorano, a winery with a prestigious past, rich in both its history and innovative insights. Alessandrojacopo Boncompagni Ludovisi inherited from his uncle Alberico not only the replanting rights but also a propensity for forward-looking choices. The twelve hectares of vineyards are under strict organic management and cultivated with Grechetto, Viognier, Merlot and Cabernet Sauvignon. More traditional, however, are both the manual harvesting of the grapes and the vinification, a process that still takes place in the estate's historic cellar. Fiorano Bianco confirms its place at the top of regional winemaking thanks to unmistakeable elegance. Great complexity on the palate, notes of white flowers, citrus fruit, Mediterranean scrub, cinnamon and nutmeg are all balanced by minerality that confers grip and depth. The close-focused, juicy, long and caressing Fiorano Rosso '14 also proves excellent, with red fruit and sweet spices, while their two Fioranellos come through fresh and pleasant.

○ Fiorano Bianco '17	♟♟♟ 6
● Fiorano Rosso '14	♟♟ 8
○ Fioranello Bianco '18	♟♟ 3
● Fioranello Rosso '17	♟♟ 4
○ Fiorano Bianco '16	♟♟♟ 6
○ Fiorano Bianco '13	♟♟♟ 5
○ Fiorano Bianco '12	♟♟♟ 4*
● Fiorano Rosso '12	♟♟♟ 7
● Fiorano Rosso '11	♟♟♟ 7
○ Fiorano Bianco '15	♟♟ 5
● Fiorano Rosso '13	♟♟ 8

Valle Vermiglia

VIA A. GRAMSCI, 7
00197 ROMA
TEL. +39 3487221073
www.vallevermiglia.it

CELLAR SALES
ANNUAL PRODUCTION 30,000 bottles
HECTARES UNDER VINE 8.00
SUSTAINABLE WINERY

Valle Vermiglia was founded in the 1950s on land next to the Camaldolese Hermitage of Monte Corona thanks to Pietro Campilli, who fought hard to gain recognition for the Frascati DOC. This legacy was inherited by his nephew Mario Masini, who over the last twenty years has not only given new impetus to the winery but who has also played a decisive role in the establishment of the Frascati Superiore DOCG. Eremo Tuscolano is the only wine produced here and it is the standard bearer for the appellation. Frascati Superiore Eremo Tuscolano always proves excellent and their 2018 manages to express territorial typicity despite the difficult vintage. Its delicate nose features citrus fruit, white-fleshed fruit, light spices and wild flowers. Though lacking the fullness and complexity of previous versions, the palate appears sapid, long, fresh and pleasant.

○ Frascati Sup. Eremo Tuscolano '18	♟♟ 3*
○ Frascati Sup. Eremo Tuscolano '17	♟♟♟ 3*
○ Frascati Sup. Eremo Tuscolano '16	♟♟♟ 3*
○ Frascati Sup. Eremo Tuscolano '13	♟♟♟ 3*
○ Frascati Sup. Eremo Tuscolano '15	♟♟ 3*
○ Frascati Sup. Eremo Tuscolano '14	♟♟ 3*
○ Frascati Sup. Eremo Tuscolano '12	♟♟ 3*

Masseria Barone

VIA BROILE, 267
03042 ATINA [FR]
TEL. +39 3494510581
www.masseriabarone.com

ANNUAL PRODUCTION 11,000 bottles
HECTARES UNDER VINE 2.00

● Atina Cabernet Ricucc' '16		🍷🍷 4
● Tèlina '16		🍷🍷 4

Capizucchi

VIA ARDEATINA
00134 ROMA
TEL. +39
www.capizzucchi.it

HECTARES UNDER VINE 25.00

● Merlot '18		🍷🍷 3
○ Roma Malvasia Puntinata '18		🍷🍷 2*
○ Extra Dry '18		🍷 3
● Syrah '18		🍷 3

Casa Divina Provvidenza

VIA DEI FRATI, 58
00048 NETTUNO [RM]
TEL. +39 069851366
www.casadivinaprovvidenza.it

CELLAR SALES
PRE-BOOKED VISITS
RESTAURANT SERVICE
ANNUAL PRODUCTION 100,000 bottles
HECTARES UNDER VINE 35.00
SUSTAINABLE WINERY

● Antica Fontana Cabernet Sauvignon '14		🍷🍷 5
○ Roma Bellone '18		🍷🍷 2*
● Cesanese '17		🍷 4
● Roma Rosso '18		🍷 3

Casale Marchese

VIA DI VERMICINO, 68
00044 FRASCATI [RM]
TEL. +39 069408932
www.casalemarchese.it

CELLAR SALES
PRE-BOOKED VISITS
ANNUAL PRODUCTION 150,000 bottles
HECTARES UNDER VINE 40.00

○ Frascati Sup. '18		🍷🍷 2*
○ Cannellino di Frascati '18		🍷 3
○ Frascati Sup. Quarto Marchese '18		🍷 3
● Rosso Eminenza '18		🍷 3

Casata Mergè

VIA DI FONTANA CANDIDA, 381
00132 ROMA
TEL. +39 0620609225
www.casatamerge.it

CELLAR SALES
PRE-BOOKED VISITS
ANNUAL PRODUCTION 500,000 bottles
HECTARES UNDER VINE 35.00

○ Frascati Sup. Sesto 21 Ris. '17		🍷🍷 5
● Sesto 21 Syrah '17		🍷🍷 5
○ Roma Bianco Cl. '18		🍷 5
● Roma Rosso Cl. '18		🍷 5

Tenuta Colfiorito

S.DA PROV.LE 40A
00024 CASTEL MADAMA [RM]
TEL. +39 0774449396
www.colfio.it

CELLAR SALES
PRE-BOOKED VISITS
ACCOMMODATION
ANNUAL PRODUCTION 20,000 bottles
HECTARES UNDER VINE 4.50
VITICULTURE METHOD Certified Organic

○ La Loggia '18		🍷🍷 3
○ Il Trovatore '18		🍷 3
○ Sorgente '18		🍷 3
● Villa Cocceia '16		🍷 3

Cordeschi

loc. Acquapendente
via Cassia km 137,400
00121 Acquapendente [VT]
Tel. +39 3356953547
www.cantinacordeschi.it

CELLAR SALES
PRE-BOOKED VISITS
ANNUAL PRODUCTION 35,000 bottles
HECTARES UNDER VINE 8.50

● Rufo '18	♟♟ 2*
○ Palea '18	♟ 2
● Saino '16	♟ 3
⊙ Siele '18	♟ 2

Paolo e Noemia D'Amico

loc. Palombaro
fraz. Vaiano
01024 Castiglione in Teverina [VT]
Tel. +39 0761948034
www.paoloenoemiadamico.it

CELLAR SALES
PRE-BOOKED VISITS
RESTAURANT SERVICE
ANNUAL PRODUCTION 150,000 bottles
HECTARES UNDER VINE 30.00
SUSTAINABLE WINERY

○ Falesia '17	♟♟ 5
○ Terre di Ala '17	♟♟ 3
● Atlante '13	♟ 6
○ Orvieto Noe dei Calanchi '18	♟ 2

Federici

via Santa Apollaria Vecchia, 30
00039 Zagarolo [RM]
Tel. +39 0695461022
www.vinifederici.com

CELLAR SALES
PRE-BOOKED VISITS
ANNUAL PRODUCTION 350,000 bottles
HECTARES UNDER VINE 3.00

○ Roma Malvasia Puntinata '18	♟♟ 3
● Roma Rosso '17	♟♟ 3
● Cesanese del Piglio Sapiens '18	♟ 3
○ Le Ripe '15	♟ 2

Corte dei Papi

loc. Colletonno
03012 Anagni [FR]
Tel. +39 0775769271
www.cortedeipapi.it

CELLAR SALES
PRE-BOOKED VISITS
ANNUAL PRODUCTION 40,000 bottles
HECTARES UNDER VINE 25.00

● Cesanese del Piglio San Magno '18	♟♟ 4
● Cesanese del Piglio Colle Ticchio '18	♟ 2
○ Passerina del Frusinate '18	♟ 2
○ Quattro Profeti '18	♟ 2

Doganieri Miyazaki

fraz. Vaiano, 3
01024 Castiglione in Teverina [VT]
Tel. +39 3332807985
doganierimiyazaki@gmail.com

CELLAR SALES
PRE-BOOKED VISITS
ANNUAL PRODUCTION 8,000 bottles
HECTARES UNDER VINE 1.30

○ Ame V. T. '16	♟♟ 5
● Poggio Eremo '16	♟♟ 3
● Confié '16	♟ 5

Alberto Giacobbe

c.da Colle San Giovenale
03018 Paliano [FR]
Tel. +39 3298738052
www.vinigiacobbe.it

CELLAR SALES
PRE-BOOKED VISITS
ACCOMMODATION
ANNUAL PRODUCTION 25,000 bottles
HECTARES UNDER VINE 10.00

● Cesanese del Piglio Sup. Lepanto Ris. '16	♟♟ 5
● Cesanese di Olevano Romano Sup. Giacobbe '17	♟♟ 3
○ Duchessa Passerina '18	♟ 2

Donato Giangirolami

FRAZ. LE FERRIERE
VIA DEL CAVALIERE, 1414
04100 LATINA
TEL. +39 3358394890
www.donatogiangirolami.it

CELLAR SALES
PRE-BOOKED VISITS
ANNUAL PRODUCTION 80,000 bottles
HECTARES UNDER VINE 38.00
VITICULTURE METHOD Certified Organic

● Lepino '17	🍷🍷 3
● Prodigo '17	🍷 2
○ Propizio '18	🍷 2
○ Regius '18	🍷 2

Iura et Arma

VIA COLLE ALTO
03034 CASALVIERI [FR]
TEL. +39 3355997255
www.iuretarma.com

ANNUAL PRODUCTION 12,000 bottles
HECTARES UNDER VINE 4.50

○ Armablanc Pas Dosé '16	🍷🍷 5
○ Armablanc Pas Dosé '15	🍷🍷 5
○ Armalike Brut	🍷 3

Antica Cantina Leonardi

VIA DEL PINO, 12
01027 MONTEFIASCONE [VT]
TEL. +39 0761826028
www.cantinaleonardi.it

CELLAR SALES
PRE-BOOKED VISITS
RESTAURANT SERVICE
ANNUAL PRODUCTION 150,000 bottles
HECTARES UNDER VINE 30.00

○ Est! Est!! Est!!! di Montefiascone Poggio del Cardinale '18	🍷🍷 2*
○ Le Muffe '17	🍷🍷 4
○ Pensiero '18	🍷 2

Le Macchie

FRAZ. CASTELFRANCO
VIA CASANUOVA, 5
02100 RIETI
TEL. +39 3384620702
www.cantinalemacchie.it

CELLAR SALES
PRE-BOOKED VISITS
RESTAURANT SERVICE
ANNUAL PRODUCTION 60,000 bottles
HECTARES UNDER VINE 8.00
SUSTAINABLE WINERY

○ Conubium '18	🍷🍷 2*
● L'Ultimo Baluardo '17	🍷🍷 4
● Campo dei Severi '17	🍷 2
○ Scarpe Toste '18	🍷 3

Merumalia

V.LO PRATAPORCI, 8
00044 FRASCATI [RM]
TEL. +39 069426324
www.merumalia.it

ANNUAL PRODUCTION 25,000 bottles
HECTARES UNDER VINE 7.00
VITICULTURE METHOD Certified Organic

○ Frascati Sup. Primo Ris. '18	🍷🍷 3
○ Frascati Terso '18	🍷🍷 2*
○ Fiano '18	🍷 2

Pileum

VIA CASALOTTO
03010 PIGLIO [FR]
TEL. +39 3663129910
www.pileum.it

CELLAR SALES
PRE-BOOKED VISITS
ACCOMMODATION
ANNUAL PRODUCTION 56,000 bottles
HECTARES UNDER VINE 15.00
VITICULTURE METHOD Certified Organic

● Cesanese del Piglio Sup. Bolla di Urbano Ris. '17	🍷🍷 5
● Cesanese del Piglio Sup. Massitium '17	🍷 3
○ Valle Bianca Passerina del Frusinate '18	🍷 2

Rapillo

VIA FORESE, 54
03010 SERRONE [FR]
TEL. +39 0775595467
www.vinirapillo.it

ANNUAL PRODUCTION 8,000 bottles
HECTARES UNDER VINE 3.50

● Cesanese del Piglio Sup. Sero Nero '17	🍷🍷 3
● Cesanese del Piglio Sup. Trasmondo '15	🍷 4
○ Passerina del Frusinate '18	🍷 2

Tenuta Ronci di Nepi

VIA RONCI, 2072
01036 NEPI [VT]
TEL. +39 0761555125
www.roncidinepi.it

CELLAR SALES
PRE-BOOKED VISITS
ANNUAL PRODUCTION 100,000 bottles
HECTARES UNDER VINE 17.00

○ Grechetto '18	🍷🍷 3
○ Manti '18	🍷 4
○ O' di Nè '18	🍷 3

Le Rose

VIA PONTE TRE ARMI, 25
00045 GENZANO DI ROMA [RM]
TEL. +39 0693709671
www.aziendaagricolalerose.com

CELLAR SALES
PRE-BOOKED VISITS
ANNUAL PRODUCTION 70,000 bottles
HECTARES UNDER VINE 10.00
VITICULTURE METHOD Certified Organic
SUSTAINABLE WINERY

○ Artemisia '18	🍷🍷 4
○ La Faiola Bianco '18	🍷🍷 5
● La Faiola Rosso '18	🍷🍷 5
○ Tre Armi '18	🍷 3

Sant'Andrea

LOC. BORGO VODICE
VIA RENIBBIO, 1720
04019 TERRACINA [LT]
TEL. +39 0773755028
www.cantinasantandrea.it

CELLAR SALES
PRE-BOOKED VISITS
ANNUAL PRODUCTION 1,000,000 bottles
HECTARES UNDER VINE 85.00

○ Moscato di Terracina Secco Oppidum '18	🍷🍷 2*
● Sogno '13	🍷🍷 3
● Circeo Rosso Incontro al Circeo '16	🍷 2
○ Moscato di Terracina Passito Capitolium '16	🍷 4

Tenuta Sant'Isidoro

LOC. PORTACCIA
01016 TARQUINIA [VT]
TEL. +39 0766869716
www.santisidoro.net

CELLAR SALES
PRE-BOOKED VISITS
ANNUAL PRODUCTION 65,000 bottles
HECTARES UNDER VINE 57.00

● Tarquinia Rosso Larth '18	🍷🍷 1*
● Terzolo '18	🍷🍷 2*
○ Soraluisa '18	🍷 3
● Soremidio '17	🍷 4

Stefanoni

VIA STEFANONI, 48
01027 MONTEFIASCONE [VT]
TEL. +39 0761825651
www.cantinastefanoni.it

CELLAR SALES
PRE-BOOKED VISITS
ANNUAL PRODUCTION 100,000 bottles
HECTARES UNDER VINE 10.00

○ Colle de' Poggeri Moscato '18	🍷🍷 2*
○ Colle de' Poggeri Roscetto '18	🍷 2
○ Est! Est!! Est!!! di Montefiascone Cl. Foltone '18	🍷 2

Giovanni Terenzi

FRAZ. LA FORMA
VIA FORESE, 13
03010 SERRONE [FR]
TEL. +39 0775594286
www.viniterenzi.com

CELLAR SALES
PRE-BOOKED VISITS
ANNUAL PRODUCTION 150,000 bottles
HECTARES UNDER VINE 12.00

● Cesanese del Piglio Sup. Vajoscuro Ris. '17	♔♔ 5
○ Zerli Passerina del Frusinate '17	♔♔ 5
● Cesanese del Piglio Velobra '17	♔ 3
○ Villa Santa Passerina del Frusinate '18	♔ 3

Casale Vallechiesa

VIA PIETRA PORZIA, 19/23
00044 FRASCATI [RM]
TEL. +39 069417270
www.casalevallechiesa.it

CELLAR SALES
PRE-BOOKED VISITS
ANNUAL PRODUCTION 500,000 bottles
HECTARES UNDER VINE 13.00

○ Frascati Sup. Heredio '18	♔♔ 2*
○ Ribello Bellone '18	♔ 2
● Roma Rosso 753 '17	♔ 3
● Soraya '16	♔ 3

Villa Gianna

LOC. BORGO SAN DONATO
S.DA MAREMMANA
04010 SABAUDIA [LT]
TEL. +39 0773250034
www.villagianna.it

PRE-BOOKED VISITS
ACCOMMODATION
ANNUAL PRODUCTION 1,000,000 bottles
HECTARES UNDER VINE 45.00
SUSTAINABLE WINERY

○ Vigne del Borgo Bellone '18	♔♔ 2*
● Vigne del Borgo Shiraz '18	♔♔ 2*
● Barriano '15	♔ 3
○ Bianco di Caprolace Chardonnay '18	♔ 2

Tenuta Tre Cancelli

LOC. DUE CASETTE
VIA DELLA PISCINA, 3
00052 CERVETERI [RM]
TEL. +39 069901664
www.tenutatrecancelli.com

CELLAR SALES
PRE-BOOKED VISITS
ANNUAL PRODUCTION 60,000 bottles
HECTARES UNDER VINE 18.00

● Roma Rosso 753 '17	♔ 2*
● Siborio '14	♔♔ 5
○ Flere '18	♔ 2
● Lituo '16	♔ 3

Villa Caviciana

LOC. TOJENA CAVICIANA
01025 GROTTE DI CASTRO [VT]
TEL. +39 0763798212
www.villacaviciana.com

CELLAR SALES
PRE-BOOKED VISITS
ANNUAL PRODUCTION 25,000 bottles
HECTARES UNDER VINE 16.00
VITICULTURE METHOD Certified Biodynamic

☉ Tadzio '18	♔ 2*
● Cassandra '14	♔ 4
○ Filippo '18	♔ 3
○ Lorenzo Brut '18	♔ 3

Villa Simone

VIA FRASCATI COLONNA, 29
00078 MONTE PORZIO CATONE [RM]
TEL. +39 069449717
www.villasimone.it

CELLAR SALES
PRE-BOOKED VISITS
ANNUAL PRODUCTION 200,000 bottles
HECTARES UNDER VINE 21.00
SUSTAINABLE WINERY

○ Frascati Sup. Vign. Filonardi Ris. '17	♔♔ 4
● La Torraccia '16	♔♔ 3
○ Frascati Sup. Villa dei Preti '18	♔ 3
● Syrah '17	♔ 3

ABRUZZO

Abruzzo's wine is certainly on an upward
trajectory. If its consortiums and economists are
responsible for tracking the numbers, it's our job
to evaluate its quality. Based on this year's
results, as laid out in the following pages, the
news is good. But a considerable number of wines were
tasted, almost 600 from around the region, from the north, and Tronto, all the
way to the south, with Vasto, and of course everything in between, with the
production areas of Gran Sasso and Majella. Obviously we don't have enough
space for them all, and the limited size of our guide forces us to carry out a
rigorous selection of those wines reviewed. The reader should remember that
every wine scored in this edition, whether it's one 'Bicchiere' or 'Tre Bicchieri',
represents a gem that should be sought out in wine bars and restaurant wine
lists. That being said, this year the number of Tre Bicchieri awarded topped last
year, with some 13 wines hitting the mark. Leading the way are eight
Montepulcianos, different vintages but different production visions as well. We
pass from the fresher 2018s (Feudo Antico and Villa Medoro) to more
concentrated, intense and modern wines (Agriverde, Castorani, Illuminati,
Codemi, Tollo) and the territorial qualities emphasized by Valle Reale. In terms of
the region's whites, Pecorino continues to reign supreme (myriad versions were
tasted), but in its annual rivalry with Trebbiano the cultivars finished in a tie (2-2).
The former earned Fauri another Tre Bicchieri, and we're pleased to give the
award to a new release by a historic producer, Cataldi Madonna, with their
Supergiulia. It's certainly not news to see yet another superb Trebbiano from
Valentini, this year accompanied by another classic producer, Masciarelli. We
conclude by mentioning Torre dei Beati's Rosa-ae. 2018 saw Fausto Albanesi
and Adriana Galasso bring a true masterpiece to life. For this reason it's our
'Rosé of the Year'.

Agriverde

LOC. CALDARI
VIA STORTINI, 32A
66026 ORTONA [CH]
TEL. +39 0859032101
www.agriverde.it

CELLAR SALES
PRE-BOOKED VISITS
RESTAURANT SERVICE
ANNUAL PRODUCTION 900,000 bottles
HECTARES UNDER VINE 65.00
VITICULTURE METHOD Certified Organic
SUSTAINABLE WINERY

Agriverde's vineyards are located in the Colline Teatine municipalities of Caldari, Ortona, Frisa and Crecchio. Owned by the Di Carlo family, the winery took a big stride forward in the 1980s under the management of Giannicola, a true visionary in the region, who decided to convert all of the vineyards to organic methods. The winery, guest accomodations and spa were built strictly guided by the dictates of bio-compatibility. The wide and versatile range is divided into different lines: Eikos, Piano di Maggio, Riseis, Solàrea and Natum Biovegan. Their Plateo Riserva '15 is at the top of its game. It's a Montepulciano that goes all in on dark notes of ripe plums, chocolate and toasty notes. In the mouth it unveils a tight-knit tannic weave, which does a nice job supporting its voluminous, warm palate. The Montepulciano Riseis '17 features signature dark aromas and a fresh palate, where fruity sensations come to the fore. Their Pecorino Eikos '18 also put in an excellent performance, with good signals coming from their entire selection.

● Montepulciano d'Abruzzo Plateo Ris. '15	🏆🏆🏆 6
● Montepulciano d'Abruzzo Riseis '17	🏆🏆 3*
○ Eikos Pecorino '18	🏆🏆 3
● Montepulciano d'Abruzzo Caldaria '16	🏆🏆 3
⊙ Cerasuolo d'Abruzzo Solàrea '18	🏆 3
⊙ Cuvée Prestige 830	🏆 5
● Montepulciano d'Abruzzo Eikos '17	🏆 3
○ Riseis Passerina '18	🏆 3
○ Riseis Pecorino '18	🏆 3
● Montepulciano d'Abruzzo Plateo '04	🏆🏆🏆 6
● Montepulciano d'Abruzzo Plateo '01	🏆🏆🏆 6
● Montepulciano d'Abruzzo Plateo '00	🏆🏆🏆 6
● Montepulciano d'Abruzzo Plateo '98	🏆🏆🏆 5
● Montepulciano d'Abruzzo Solàrea '03	🏆🏆🏆 4

F.lli Barba

LOC. SCERNE DI PINETO
S.DA ROTABILE PER CASOLI
64025 PINETO [TE]
TEL. +39 0859461020
www.fratellibarba.it

CELLAR SALES
PRE-BOOKED VISITS
ACCOMMODATION
ANNUAL PRODUCTION 300,000 bottles
HECTARES UNDER VINE 62.00
SUSTAINABLE WINERY

Fratelli Barba is one of the largest agricultural entities in Abruzzo. Giovanni, Domenico and Vincenzo carry on the wor∎ started by their father, Cavalier Luigi in th∎ 1950s. They manage over 680 hectares (including about seventy of vineyards in th∎ territories of Colle Morino, Casal Thaulero and Vignafranca) on the Colline Teramane between the Adriatic and Gran Sasso. In the modern cellar at Scerne di Pineto, the mostly local varieties of grapes, are transformed into wines with a modern imprint that is nevertheless recognizable and always convincing. Their Montepulciano Colline Teramane Yang landed a place in our finals with an excellent 2016 version. A fragrant, fruity profile of a black cherry merges with hint∎ of cinnamon and flowery whiffs. The pala∎ is light and airy thanks to an acidic stroke∎ that confers length and persistence. Their Montepulciano Collemorino '18 also got ∎ attention with its aromas of wild berries and bark, and its even, simple, juicy pala∎

● Montepulciano d'Abruzzo Colline Teramane Yang '16	🏆🏆
● Montepulciano d'Abruzzo Collemorino '18	🏆🏆
○ Trebbiano d'Abruzzo Vignafranca '18	🏆🏆
○ Collemorino Pecorino '18	🏆
● Montepulciano d'Abruzzo I Vasari '10	🏆🏆🏆
● Montepulciano d'Abruzzo I Vasari '09	🏆🏆🏆
● Montepulciano d'Abruzzo I Vasari '08	🏆🏆🏆
● Montepulciano d'Abruzzo Vignafranca '07	🏆🏆
● Montepulciano d'Abruzzo Vignafranca '06	🏆🏆
○ Trebbiano d'Abruzzo '06	🏆🏆
● Montepulciano d'Abruzzo Colle Morino Et. Bianca '13	🏆
● Montepulciano d'Abruzzo Vignafranca '15	🏆

arone Cornacchia
A Torri, 19
010 Torano Nuovo [TE]
+39 0861887412
w.baronecornacchia.it

LLAR SALES
E-BOOKED VISITS
COMMODATION
NUAL PRODUCTION 250,000 bottles
CTARES UNDER VINE 50.00
ICULTURE METHOD Certified Organic

e Cornacchia family received their
ronial title and the land surrounding the
tress of Civitella del Tronto from the
eroy of Naples toward the end of the
th century. They later moved to Torano
ovo, in the Torri district, where the core
the winery remains today, led by current
rs and siblings Filippo and Caterina. The
eyards are managed using certified
anic methods and are home to the
ssic local Abruzzo varieties of Trebbiano,
corino, Passerina and Montepulciano,
last of which is vinified in about ten
erent versions. Among their
ntepulcianos we were particularly
oressed with their Colline Teramane
zaro '15. On the nose notes of black fruit
chocolate merge with medicinal herbs
dark spices. In the mouth it's weighty
broad, finding vigor in its finish thanks
a slightly sapid stroke that endures right
to a pleasantly smokey closing note. It's
worth noting the fragrance of their
le Cupo '17, a wine that plays more on
kability and freshness.

ontroguerra Rosso Colle Cupo '17	♟♟ 5
Montepulciano d'Abruzzo Le Coste '16	♟♟ 5
Montepulciano d'Abruzzo olline Teramane Vizzaro '15	♟♟ 5
asanova Passerina '18	♟ 2
erasuolo d'Abruzzo Sup. Casanova '18	♟ 3
ontroguerra Pecorino Casanova '18	♟ 3
Montepulciano d'Abruzzo Casanova '17	♟ 3
rebbiano d'Abruzzo Sup. Casanova '18	♟ 3
ontroguerra Pecorino Casanova '17	♟♟ 3
ontroguerra Rosso Colle Lupo '16	♟♟ 5
Montepulciano d'Abruzzo olline Teramane Vizzarro '13	♟♟ 5
ontepulciano d'Abruzzo V. Le Coste '15	♟♟ 5
rebbiano d'Abruzzo Sup. Casanova '17	♟♟ 3

Tenute Barone di Valforte
c.da Piomba, 11
64028 Silvi Marina [TE]
Tel. +39 0859353432
www.baronedivalforte.it

CELLAR SALES
PRE-BOOKED VISITS
ANNUAL PRODUCTION 280,000 bottles
HECTARES UNDER VINE 50.00

Francesco and Guido Sorricchio di Valforte
are the current heirs of a family with roots
dating back to the 14th century. Together
with Guido's young daughter, Annamaria,
they look after vineyards that extend
between the territories of Atri, Multignano,
Casoli and the winery's home, Silvi Marina,
where they stand at the forefront of
vineyard management and environmental
sustainability. The rows of vines are mainly
planted with typical local varieties like
Montepulciano, Trebbiano, Passerina and
Pecorino, interpreted in ways that don't
readily conform to standard 'types' but that
are easily read. In this round of tastings the
best signs were coming from their whites.
The Pecorino '18, with its citrusy and juicy
verve, gave way to a fragrant, pleasantly
herbaceous and fresh Passerina (same
year). It's also worth noting the
performance put in by their Cerasuolo '18,
a wine whose lively vigor merges with an
intriguing smoky stroke.

○ Abruzzo Passerina '18	♟♟ 2*
○ Abruzzo Pecorino '18	♟♟ 2*
⊙ Cerasuolo d'Abruzzo Valforte Rosé '18	♟♟ 2*
○ Trebbiano d'Abruzzo Villa Chiara '18	♟♟ 2*
○ Abruzzo Pecorino '17	♟♟ 2*
● Montepulciano d'Abruzzo '15	♟♟ 2*
● Montepulciano d'Abruzzo Colle Sale '14	♟♟ 4
● Montepulciano d'Abruzzo Colline Teramane Colle Sale '13	♟♟ 3*
○ Passerina '14	♟♟ 2*
○ Pecorino '14	♟♟ 2*
○ Trebbiano d'Abruzzo Villa Chiara '17	♟♟ 2*
○ Trebbiano d'Abruzzo Villa Chiara '14	♟♟ 2*

Castorani

VIA CASTORANI, 5
65020 ALANNO [PE]
TEL. +39 3466355635
www.castorani.it

CELLAR SALES
PRE-BOOKED VISITS
ACCOMMODATION AND RESTAURANT SERVICE
ANNUAL PRODUCTION 600,000 bottles
HECTARES UNDER VINE 72.00
VITICULTURE METHOD Certified Organic

Located in the Colline Pescarasi between the Adriatic coast and the Majella, the long-established estate in Alanno is named after its famous first owner, surgeon Raffaele Castorani, who started it at the end of the 18th century. About twenty years ago a group of partners, including former Formula One driver Jarno Trulli, took over the winery and transformed it into a modern enterprise capable of combining both substantial volume and high quality. The vineyards are organically managed and are used to create a wide range of wines divided into different lines by price range and style. Once again Castorani submitted an exceptional selection in terms of aromatic precision and pleasantness of taste. Among their Montepulcianos, the first release of their Lupaia (vintage 2016) shines. Spices, aromatic herbs, black cherries give way to a palate that unfolds elegantly and firm. But it was overtaken by their new Podere Castorani Ris., an austere, close-woven and long 2015 Montepulciano.

● Montepulciano d'Abruzzo Podere Castorani Casauria Ris. '15	♟♟♟ 5
● Montepulciano d'Abruzzo Cadetto '17	♟♟ 2*
● Montepulciano d'Abruzzo Lupaia '16	♟♟ 2*
○ Abruzzo Pecorino Sup. Amorino '18	♟♟ 3
○ Cadetto Passerina '18	♟♟ 2*
○ Cadetto Pecorino '18	♟♟ 3
⊙ Cerasuolo d'Abruzzo Cadetto '18	♟♟ 2*
⊙ Cerasuolo d'Abruzzo Sup. Podere Castorani '18	♟♟ 3
● Montepulciano d'Abruzzo Amorino '15	♟♟ 3
○ Trebbiano d'Abruzzo Cadetto '18	♟♟ 2*
○ Trebbiano d'Abruzzo Sup. Amorino '18	♟♟ 2*
⊙ Cerasuolo d'Abruzzo Amorino '18	♟ 3
● Montepulciano d'Abruzzo Podere Castorani Ris. '14	♟♟♟ 5

★★Luigi Cataldi Madonna

LOC. PIANO
67025 OFENA [AQ]
TEL. +39 0862954252
www.cataldimadonna.com

CELLAR SALES
PRE-BOOKED VISITS
ANNUAL PRODUCTION 230,000 bottles
HECTARES UNDER VINE 30.00
VITICULTURE METHOD Certified Organic
SUSTAINABLE WINERY

The winery's centenary is just around the corner and Luigi Cataldi Madonna, now permanently supported by his daughter Giulia, carries on the work his father Antonio started in 1920. Ofena is in 'oven of Abruzzo', on the southern border of the Gran Sasso National Park, just below the Calderone: the only glacier in the Apennines, it's responsible for strong temperature ranges and a characteristic, say the least, microclimate. Wines speak the local dialect with Pecorino, Trebbiano and Montepulciano espressing their strong territorial and stylistic identity. Their Cerasuolo '18 does an excellent job representing the typology. In exhibits all the characteristics of Montepulciano, but it's even more sophisticated and light, with a lovely palate crossed by light tannins. It was their Supergiulia, a Pecorino on its f. release, that amazed however. The 2017 offers up sensations of yellow fruit and lemon that accompany an elegant mineral note. Delicately salty verve and acidic tension complete a great wine.

○ Supergiulia Pecorino '17	♟♟♟
⊙ Cerasuolo d'Abruzzo '18	♟♟
○ Giulia Pecorino '18	♟♟
● Montepulciano d'Abruzzo Malandrino '17	♟♟
○ Trebbiano d'Abruzzo '18	♟♟
⊙ Cataldino '17	♟
● Montepulciano d'Abruzzo Tonì '15	♟
⊙ Cerasuolo d'Abruzzo Piè delle Vigne '16	♟♟
⊙ Cerasuolo d'Abruzzo Piè delle Vigne '15	♟♟
● Montepulciano d'Abruzzo Malandrino '13	♟♟
● Montepulciano d'Abruzzo Malandrino '12	♟♟
○ Pecorino '11	♟♟
○ Pecorino '10	♟♟
○ Pecorino Frontone '13	♟♟

entorame

z. Casoli di Atri
delle Fornaci
030 Atri [TE]
. +39 0858709115
ww.centorame.it

LLAR SALES
E-BOOKED VISITS
NNUAL PRODUCTION 100,000 bottles
CTARES UNDER VINE 12.00
STAINABLE WINERY

mberto Vannucci and his family are the
rd generation to manage this winery,
nded in 2002 but with roots going back
the 1980s. The vineyards are located in
heart of the Calanchi Reserve, in Casoli
Atri on the Colline Teramane, not far
m the Adriatic, at an elevation of around
0 meters on mostly clayey soils. These
doclimatic characteristics reveal
emselves in the generous character of
e wines, divided into the lines of San
chele, Castellum Vetus, Scuderie Ducali
d Liberamente. Their Pecorino Scuderie
cali '18 seemed to be their strongest
ne during the last round of tastings.
rbs and lemon leaves, it exhibits a fresh
ofile both on the nose and on the palate.
eir Montepulciano '18, from the same
, also delivered. It's a meaty and earthy
ne on the nose, sapid and penetrating
the palate. Their Trebbiano Castellum
tus '17 is redolent of white, tropical fruit,
ile the palate unfolds broadly more than
oes vertically.

Cerulli Spinozzi

s.s. 150 del Vomano km 17,600
64020 Canzano [TE]
Tel. +39 086157193
www.cerullispinozzi.it

CELLAR SALES
PRE-BOOKED VISITS
ACCOMMODATION
ANNUAL PRODUCTION 200,000 bottles
HECTARES UNDER VINE 53.00

The company is the result of the union in
the early twentieth century between two
important Abruzzo families: the Cerulli Irelli
and the Spinozzi. The winery, as it stands
today, dates back to 2003 when it was
founded by brothers Vincenzo and
Francesco Cerulli Irelli. Management is now
entrusted to Enrico, Vincenzo's son, who for
about twenty years has been working the
organic vineyards divided into two bodies.
There are 35 hectares in the municipality of
Canzano and eighteen more in Mosciano,
both on alluvial land in the Vomano River
valley. Canzano's selection put in a nice
overall performance. The Trebbiano
d'Abruzzo Torre Migliori '17 stands out by
virtue of its aromas of yellow peach and
light nuances of vanilla. It's the prelude to a
flavorful palate with nice tension. Their
base line Trebbiano '18 also did well, as did
their Montepulcianos, both their 'base'
2018 (dark fruit, dried herbs, a supple
palate) and their Almorano '18, a fresh,
enjoyable wine.

Montepulciano d'Abruzzo Scuderie Ducali '18	2*
Scuderie Ducali Pecorino '18	2*
Trebbiano d'Abruzzo Castellum Vetus '17	3
Trebbiano d'Abruzzo Liberamente '18	2*
Cerasuolo d'Abruzzo Liberamente '18	2
Trebbiano d'Abruzzo San Michele '18	2
Tuapina Pecorino '18	2
Montepulciano d'Abruzzo Colline Teramane Castellum Vetus '15	4
Montepulciano d'Abruzzo S. Michele '16	2*
Montepulciano d'Abruzzo S. Michele '15	2*
Trebbiano d'Abruzzo Castellum Vetus '16	3*
Trebbiano d'Abruzzo S. Michele '17	2*
Tuapina Pecorino '16	2*

● Montepulciano d'Abruzzo '18	2*
● Montepulciano d'Abruzzo Almorano '18	1*
○ Trebbiano d'Abruzzo '18	2*
○ Trebbiano d'Abruzzo Torre Migliori '17	3
○ Almorano Pecorino '18	1*
⊙ Cerasuolo d'Abruzzo Almorano '18	1*
⊙ Cersauolo d'Abruzzo Sup. Cortalto '18	2
○ Trebbiano d'Abruzzo Almorano '18	1*
○ Almorano Pecorino '17	1*
○ Cortalto Pecorino '17	2*
○ Cortalto Pecorino '15	2*
● Montepulciano d'Abruzzo Colline Teramane Cortalto '15	2*
● Montepulciano d'Abruzzo Colline Teramane Torre Migliori '10	3
○ Trebbiano d'Abruzzo Almorano '16	2*

Cirelli

LOC. TRECIMINIERE
VIA COLLE SAN GIOVANNI, 1
64032 ATRI [TE]
TEL. +39 0858700106
www.agricolacirelli.com

CELLAR SALES
PRE-BOOKED VISITS
ACCOMMODATION AND RESTAURANT SERVICE
ANNUAL PRODUCTION 26,000 bottles
HECTARES UNDER VINE 5.00
VITICULTURE METHOD Certified Organic

Francesco Cirelli runs an all-purpose farm.
In just over fifteen years it has earned a
respectable place in the region's crowded
wine scene thanks to coherent ideas of
land management and wine production.
The organically cultivated vineyards are
concentrated on the hills of Atri, in the
heart of the Colline Teramane and just a
stone's throw from the Adriatic, giving life
to two lines that begin with spontaneous
fermentation: La Collina Biologica, with
screw caps, and Amphora, worked in
terracotta. In the absence of their Anfora
line, a lovely version of their Cerasuolo La
Collina Biologica led a nice overall
performance. On the nose red flowers,
cherry and slightly toasty touch emerge.
The mouth is delectable, fragrant and
flavorful, certainly versatile in terms of
pairings. Their Montepulciano '18 features
an earthy character that opens onto spices,
as well lively tannins — it's another good
wine for gastronomic pairings.

⊙ Cerasuolo d'Abruzzo La Collina Biologica '18	♥♥ 2*
● Montepulciano d'Abruzzo La Collina Biologica '18	♥♥ 2*
○ Trebbiano d'Abruzzo La Collina Biologica '18	♥♥ 2*
○ La Collina Biologica Pecorino '18	♥ 3
⊙ Cerasuolo d'Abruzzo Amphora '15	♀♀ 5
⊙ Cerasuolo d'Abruzzo La Collina Biologica '16	♀♀ 2*
○ La Collina Biologica Pecorino '17	♀♀ 3
○ Trebbiano d'Abruzzo Amphora '17	♀♀ 5
○ Trebbiano d'Abruzzo La Collina Biologica '17	♀♀ 2*

Codice Citra

C.DA CUCULLO
66026 ORTONA [CH]
TEL. +39 0859031342
www.citra.it

CELLAR SALES
PRE-BOOKED VISITS
ANNUAL PRODUCTION 18,000,000 bottle
HECTARES UNDER VINE 6000.00

Citra is among the most important names
in Abruzzo wine. It's a cooperative of
multiple winegrowers' associations (Pollu
Rocca San Giovanni, Lanciano, Ortona,
Paglieta, Crecchia, Torrevecchia Teatina,
Tollo) with about 3,000 members who
cultivate 6,000 hectares of vineyards and
produce about 18 million bottles annually
The very wide range is divided into severa
lines including easily enjoyed, ready to
drink wines alongside more ambitious
selections made to last over time.
Traditional Montepulciano, Trebbiano and
Pecorino dominate. Their Pecorino Sup.
Ferzo '18 came through with a truly lovel
version. Lemon, fennel and aniseed emer
on a fragrant and expressive aromatic
spectrum, anticipating a taut palate
crossed by a juicy stroke of citrus. Their
Montepulciano Caroso Ris. 15 also got ou
attention, with its notes of pencil led and
burnt embers suggesting a certain
austerity. Tannins set the rhythm of its
potent, warm palate.

○ Abruzzo Pecorino Sup. Ferzo '18	♥♥
● Montepulciano d'Abruzzo Caroso Ris. '15	♥♥
○ Abruzzo Passerina Sup. Ferzo '18	♥♥
⊙ Cerasuolo d'Abruzzo Sup. Ferzo '18	♥♥
● Montepulciano d'Abruzzo Teate Ferzo '16	♥♥
○ Fenaroli Brut 36 M. Cl. '14	♥
● Montepulciano d'Abruzzo Laus Vitae Ris. '14	♥
○ Abruzzo Pecorino Sup. Ferzo '17	♀♀
○ Abruzzo Pecorino Sup. Ferzo '16	♀♀
⊙ Cerasuolo d'Abruzzo Sup. Ferzo '17	♀♀
● Montepulciano d'Abruzzo Laus Vitae Ris. '12	♀♀

ontesa

A DELLE VIGNE, 28
010 Collecorvino [PE]
L. +39 0858205078
ww.contesa.it

ELLAR SALES
E-BOOKED VISITS
ESTAURANT SERVICE
NNUAL PRODUCTION 260,000 bottles
ECTARES UNDER VINE 45.00
USTAINABLE WINERY

e winery's name derives from a
st-unification era land dispute that
volved around the great-grandfather of
rrent owner, Rocco Passetti. Established
the Pescara hills in 2000 at the ancient
ngbard town of Collecorvino in the Terre
ei Vestini DOC subzone, the estate is
rrounded by its own vineyards planted
th the region's traditional varieties.
ontepulciano, Trebbiano, Pecorino and
sserina interpreted in agile, racy
nes divided into three lines: Vigna
rvino, Antica Persia and Contesa. Their
ebbiano d'Abruzzo Fermentazione
ontanea '18 made it to our finals and
st missed out on our highest honors.
ly steel is used to age a white that's
ghly expressive on the nose right from
e outset. Floral aromas call up jasmine
d broom, while nuances of aromatic
rbs complete the profile. On the palate
ese are transformed into fragrance and
eadth of taste with a lovely herbaceous
te at the finish. Their close-woven and
und Montepulciano Riserva '15 also got
r attention.

Trebbiano d'Abruzzo Fermentazione Spontanea '18	♥♥ 3*
Abruzzo Pecorino '18	♥♥ 3
Abruzzo Pecorino Sup. Aspetta Primavera '18	♥♥ 5
Montepulciano d'Abruzzo '17	♥♥ 2*
Montepulciano d'Abruzzo Ris. '15	♥♥ 4
Cerasuolo d'Abruzzo '18	♥ 2
Montepulciano d'Abruzzo Terre dei Vestini Chiedi alla Polvere Ris. '15	♥ 4
Montepulciano d'Abruzzo Ris. '08	♥♥♥ 3*
Montepulciano d'Abruzzo '16	♥♥ 2*
Montepulciano d'Abruzzo Ris. '13	♥♥ 4
Trebbiano d'Abruzzo Fermentazione Spontanea '17	♥♥ 3*

D'Alesio

VIA GAGLIERANO, 73
65013 Città Sant'Angelo [PE]
TEL. +39 08596713
www.sciarr.com

CELLAR SALES
PRE-BOOKED VISITS
RESTAURANT SERVICE
ANNUAL PRODUCTION 70,000 bottles
HECTARES UNDER VINE 16.00
VITICULTURE METHOD Certified Organic
SUSTAINABLE WINERY

The D'Alesio family winery is relatively
young; Lanfranco and Emiliano only took
over running their father Mario's estate in
2007. Today his grandchildren Mario and
Giovanni are at the helm, taking care of
the vineyards located on the Città
Sant'Angelo inlands, on the Colline
Pescaresi hills. Cultivated since inception
following an organic regime are classic
regional varietals, resulting in wines with a
strong territorial imprint that is anything
but banal. Their Trebbiano Tenuta del
Professore '14 didn't repeat last year's
stellar performance, but the result was
compensated for by a nice showing from
their reds. In fact, their Montepulciano '15
just fell short of Tre Bicchieri. Black and
red cherry, hints of spices and toasty notes
are enriched by a characteristic sensation
of embers. In the mouth it's warm,
flavorful, with sensations of red fruit and
close-knit but round tannins.

● Montepulciano d'Abruzzo '15	♥♥ 4
● Montepulciano d'Abruzzo '17	♥♥ 4
○ Trebbiano d'Abruzzo Tenuta del Professore '14	♥ 5
○ Abruzzo Pecorino Sup. '15	♥♥ 2*
● Montepulciano d'Abruzzo '13	♥♥ 4
○ Trebbiano d'Abruzzo Tenuta del Professore '13	♥♥ 5

Tenuta I Fauri

VIA FORO, 8
66010 ARI [CH]
TEL. +39 0871332627
www.tenutaifauri.it

CELLAR SALES
PRE-BOOKED VISITS
ANNUAL PRODUCTION 150,000 bottles
HECTARES UNDER VINE 35.00

Valentina and Luigi Di Camillo lead the
estate that their father Camillo founded in
1979 and today, with his help, they take
care of its significant vineyards. The plots
are distributed between Majella and
Adriatico, in the municipalities of Chieti,
Francavilla al Mare, Miglianico, Villamagna,
Bucchianico and Ari. In the vineyards
nature is fully respected with cultivation
following the criteria of integrated vineyard
management; in the cellar efforts are made
to enhance the territory's imprint and
natural expression in the wine using
spontaneous fermentation and maturation
in steel vats or cement tanks. Among the
2018 versions we tasted, Valentina and
Luigi's Pecorino is one of the region's most
convincing. A unique hint of wheat
illuminates an aromatic spectrum that
ranges from yellow flowers to peach and
mountain herbs. On the palate it's broad
and full, without ever becoming heavy
thanks to a long acidic and delicately salty
stroke that accompany's its flavor through
a long finish. Their Montepulciano
Baldovino '17 also delivered.

○ Abruzzo Pecorino '18	♟♟♟ 3*
● Montepulciano d'Abruzzo Baldovino '17	♟♟ 2*
⊙ Cerasuolo d'Abruzzo Baldovino '18	♟♟ 2*
⊙ Trebbiano d'Abruzzo Baldovino '18	♟♟ 2*
⊙ Albarosa Frizzante Rosé	♟ 2
● Montepulciano d'Abruzzo Ottobre Rosso '17	♟ 2
○ Passerina '18	♟ 2
○ Abruzzo Pecorino '14	♟♟♟ 2*
○ Abruzzo Pecorino '13	♟♟♟ 2*
⊙ Cerasuolo d'Abruzzo Baldovino '17	♟♟ 2*
⊙ Cerasuolo d'Abruzzo Baldovino '16	♟♟ 2*
● Montepulciano d'Abruzzo Ottobre Rosso '16	♟♟ 2*
● Montepulciano d'Abruzzo Rosso dei Fauri '15	♟♟ 5
○ Trebbiano d'Abruzzo Baldovino '17	♟♟ 2*

Feudo Antico

VIA CROCEVECCHIA, 101
66010 TOLLO [CH]
TEL. +39 0871969128
www.feudoantico.it

CELLAR SALES
ANNUAL PRODUCTION 80,000 bottles
HECTARES UNDER VINE 20.00
VITICULTURE METHOD Certified Organic

Compared to gigantic regional
cooperatives, Feudo Antico appears almost
Lilliputian. However, the ambitions of this
young operation within the Tullum DOC, of
which it is the standardbearer, are anything
but small. Locations at Pedine, Colle Secco
San Pietro, and Colle dei Campli provide
suitable plots for the organically managed
vineyards. Also noteworthy are its
collaborative experiments with
internationally renowned chef Niko Romito
in Casadonna di Castel di Sangro at around
800 meters above sea level. Their
Montepulciano Organic '18 is the wine that
unseats the producer's whites from their
place on the regional rankings. It's a young
version that plays on fruit and drinkability,
without giving up on a certain substance
thanks to close-knit but sweet tannins. It
shares a top place with their classic
Pecorino Casadonna — the 2018 version
proves linear and mineral. The rest of their
selection is more than reliable.

● Montepulciano d'Abruzzo Organic '18	♟♟♟
○ Casadonna Pecorino '18	♟♟
⊙ Rosato Biologico '18	♟♟
○ Tullum Passerina '18	♟♟
● Tullum Rosso Ris. '14	♟♟
● Tullum Rosso in Anfora '17	♟
○ Casadonna Pecorino '15	♟♟♟
○ Tullum Pecorino Biologico '17	♟♟♟
○ Casadonna Pecorino '17	♟♟
○ Casadonna Pecorino '14	♟♟
⊙ Rosato Biologico '16	♟♟
○ Tullum Pecorino '17	♟♟
○ Tullum Pecorino Biologico '16	♟♟
○ Tullum Pecorino Biologico '15	♟♟
● Tullum Rosso Biologico '15	♟♟

Feuduccio
Santa Maria D'Orni

C. FEUDUCCIO
6036 ORSOGNA [CH]
L. +39 0871891646
ww.ilfeuduccio.it

CELLAR SALES
PRE-BOOKED VISITS
ANNUAL PRODUCTION 150,000 bottles
HECTARES UNDER VINE 50.00

he winery takes its name from the Feudo
anta Maria d'Orni on which it sits. It's the
roject of Gaetano Lamaletto, who after a
uccessful career as an entrepreneur in
enezuela decided to return home to try his
and at Abruzzo wine. Orsogna is on the
olline Teatine, the border between the
art of the Majella and the Adriatic Sea.
amillo and his son Gaetano take care of
e estate and vineyards that speak in the
cal language of Trebbiano, Pecorino and
asserina for whites, and Montepulciano
r reds. This year their Pecorino Ursonia
d their selection. Fermented in wood and
ged in steel, the 2017 opens with aromas
f grass and aromatic herbs that move
wards lemon pulp. Its luminous palate
mazes, proving full of mineral and sapid
ounterpoint, with a lovely, characterful
ish. Similar sensations of rock and
tones, accompanied by a slightly smoky
ackground, characterize their linear
rebbiano '18.

Ursonia Pecorino '17	🍷🍷 6
Montepulciano d'Abruzzo '17	🍷🍷 3
Pecorino '18	🍷🍷 2*
Trebbiano d'Abruzzo '18	🍷🍷 3
Montepulciano d'Abruzzo '16	🍷 3
Montepulciano d'Abruzzo Margae '15	🍷 6
Montepulciano d'Abruzzo Ursonia '13	🍷🍷🍷 4*
Fonte Venna Pecorino '17	🍷🍷 2*
Fonte Venna Rosato '17	🍷🍷 2*
Montepulciano d'Abruzzo Ursonia '15	🍷🍷 5
Pecorino '16	🍷🍷 2*

Fontefico

VIA DIFENZA, 38
66054 VASTO [CH]
TEL. +39 3284113619
www.fontefico.it

CELLAR SALES
PRE-BOOKED VISITS
RESTAURANT SERVICE
ANNUAL PRODUCTION 45,000 bottles
HECTARES UNDER VINE 15.00
VITICULTURE METHOD Certified Organic
SUSTAINABLE WINERY

The winery is making its debut in the main
part of Italian Wines. Brothers Emanuele
and Nicola Altieri run the estate acquired by
their parents Alessandro and Miriam in
1996; its fifteen-hectare vineyard park
slopes down the hills towards Vasto, a few
kilometres from the Adriatic. Production is
based on traditional, local varieties
interpreted to respects each. The resulting
wines are seductive and captivating, as are
the labels designed by Emanuele. Their
Pecorino La Foia '16 is a special edition
wine that isn't released every year. It calls
for separate vinification of the bunches that
are most exposed after leaf removal. The
result is a wine rich in fragrances of honey,
apricot and saffron, whose alcohol in the
mouth is perfectly held at bay by a
calibrated acidity. Their Cerasuol
Fossimatto is also delicious in its rustic
sensations, and their Montepulciano and
Aglianico reds also hit the mark.

○ Abruzzo Pecorino Sup. La Foia '16	🍷🍷 5
⊙ Cerasuolo d'Abruzzo Sup. Fossimatto '18	🍷🍷 3
● Costetoste Aglianico '14	🍷🍷 5
● Montepulciano d'Abruzzo Cocca di Casa '16	🍷🍷 3
○ Abruzzo Pecorino Sup. La Canaglia '18	🍷 3
● Montepulciano d'Abruzzo Titinge Ris. '14	🍷 5
○ Abruzzo Pecorino Sup. La Canaglia '17	🍷🍷 3
○ Abruzzo Pecorino Sup. La Canaglia '16	🍷🍷 2*
● Montepulciano d'Abruzzo Cocca di Casa '14	🍷🍷 3
● Montepulciano d'Abruzzo Fontefico '13	🍷🍷 3
○ Trebbiano d'Abruzzo Sup. Portarispetto '15	🍷🍷 2*

★Dino Illuminati

C.DA SAN BIAGIO, 18
64010 CONTROGUERRA [TE]
TEL. +39 0861808008
www.illuminativini.it

CELLAR SALES
PRE-BOOKED VISITS
ANNUAL PRODUCTION 1,150,000 bottles
HECTARES UNDER VINE 130.00

Fattoria Nicò was started about 120 years ago by Nicola Illuminati and in the 1950s it passed to his grandson Dino who directed it with a clear vision of the future. In the 1970s, the estate began to bottle and expand, incorporating new vineyards entirely within the Controguerra and Montepulciano Colline Teramane appellations. The style is modern but never excessively so, ranging from major reds (aged in both 2500-liter barrels and smaller barriques) ideal for refreshing fragrant whites. In the absence of their Zanna, it's up to the Ilico '17 to lead this year's selection of Montepulcianos. After about a year of aging in wood barrels, it comes through meaty, earthy and woody, varietal in Montepulciano's signature dark tones. The palate is firm and close-knit, exhibiting great structure. Their Pieluni Ris. '13 also put in an excellent performance, and the great value for the money their Riparosso '18 represents shouldn't be discounted.

● Montepulciano d'Abruzzo Ilico '17	🍷🍷🍷 2*
● Montepulciano d'Abruzzo Colline Teramane Pieluni Ris. '13	🍷🍷 6
☉ Cerasuolo d'Abruzzo Lumeggio di Rosa '18	🍷🍷 2*
○ Controguerra Pecorino '18	🍷🍷 2*
○ Illuminati Brut M. Cl. '14	🍷🍷 4
● Montepulciano d'Abruzzo Riparosso '18	🍷🍷 2*
☉ Cerasuolo d'Abruzzo Campirosa '18	🍷 2
○ Controguerra Bianco Costalupo '18	🍷 2
○ Controguerra Bianco Lumeggio di Bianco '18	🍷 2
○ Controguerra Passerina '18	🍷 2
● Montepulciano d'Abruzzo Lumeggio di Rosso '18	🍷 2
● Montepulciano d'Abruzzo Colline Teramane Zanna Ris. '13	🍷🍷🍷 5

★★★Masciarelli

VIA GAMBERALE, 2
66010 SAN MARTINO SULLA MARRUCINA [CH]
TEL. +39 087185241
www.masciarelli.it

CELLAR SALES
PRE-BOOKED VISITS
ACCOMMODATION
ANNUAL PRODUCTION 2,500,000 bottles
HECTARES UNDER VINE 300.00
SUSTAINABLE WINERY

The vineyards of the estate, which was founded in 1981 by the late Gianni Masciarelli, wind through all four provinces of Abruzzo, as if trying to bring together the geography, soil and climate of the whole region. They go from the warm, gentle Colline Teramane to the continental climate of Ofena in the province of L'Aquila, passes through the vineyards of Loreto Aprutino (Colline Pescaresi) and finally reaches the province of Chieti, where the winery is located. The wide range of wine is divided into five lines: Classica, Gianni Masciarelli, Marina Cvetic, Castello di Semivicoli and Villa Gemma. Their Trebbiano Castello di Semivicoli repeats last year's successful performance, this time with a 2018 that's just as good: exotic fruit and citrus open an expressive profile refreshed by a stroke of aromatic herbs. On the palate it proves full-bodied and pulpy, broad and harmonious thanks to a pleasant mineral and sapid vein. Their Cerasuolo Villa Gemma '18, fresh, delectable and delicate, salty, also put in an excellent performance.

○ Trebbiano d'Abruzzo Castello di Semivicoli '18	🍷🍷🍷 5
☉ Cerasuolo d'Abruzzo Villa Gemma '18	🍷🍷 3
○ Abruzzo Malvasia Iskra Marina Cvetic '17	🍷🍷 4
☉ Cerasuolo d'Abruzzo Gianni Masciarelli '18	🍷🍷 2
● Montepulciano d'Abruzzo Iskra Ris. '16	🍷🍷 5
● Montepulciano d'Abruzzo San Martino Rosso Marina Cvetic Ris. '17	🍷🍷 4
● Montepulciano d'Abruzzo Villa Gemma Ris. '14	🍷🍷 8
○ Trebbiano d'Abruzzo Gianni Masciarelli '18	🍷🍷 2
○ Villa Gemma Bianco '18	🍷🍷 3
● Castello di Semivicoli Rosso '17	🍷 3

amillo Montori

c. Piane Tronto, 80
4010 Controguerra [TE]
L. +39 0861809900
ww.montorivini.it

ELLAR SALES
RE-BOOKED VISITS
CCOMMODATION AND RESTAURANT SERVICE
NNUAL PRODUCTION 600,000 bottles
ECTARES UNDER VINE 50.00

ontori is a well-known name in the Abruzzo
ine scene, both for the winery established
y the family at the end of the 1800s (one of
e oldest in the area), and for the solidity of
s range, which fluently speaks the local
nguage. A stone's throw from the border
ith Marche, the Controguerra vineyards are
ostly planted with Montepulciano, then
ebbiano and finally equal amounts of
ecorino, Passerina, Chardonnay, Sauvignon,
angiovese, Merlot and Cabernet. This
ssortment is presented in three distinct
es: Pillole di Magia, Camillo Montori and
e crown jewel, Fontecupa. Montori's
election this year was just a missing a
andout. Their Trebbiano Fonte Cupa '18
lly convinces by virtue of herbaceous notes
nd hints of hay enriched by a pleasant
ensation of white damson. On the palate it
alls up full fruit before gaining in delicacy
nd giving way to a sapid, pleasantly smoky
nish. Their Cerasuolo '18 is a bit rustic but
ets the job done.

⊙ Cerasuolo d'Abruzzo Fonte Cupa '18	🍷🍷 2*
● Montepulciano d'Abruzzo Colline Teramane Fonte Cupa Ris. '12	🍷🍷 5
⊙ Montepulciano d'Abruzzo Fonte Cupa '15	🍷🍷 2*
⊙ Trebbiano d'Abruzzo Fonte Cupa '18	🍷🍷 2*
⊙ Fonte Cupa Passerina '18	🍷 3
⊙ Fonte Cupa Pecorino '18	🍷 3
⊙ Cerasuolo d'Abruzzo Fonte Cupa '16	🍷🍷🍷 2*
⊙ Cerasuolo d'Abruzzo Fonte Cupa '17	🍷🍷 2*
⊙ Cerasuolo d'Abruzzo Fonte Cupa '15	🍷🍷 2*
⊙ Fonte Cupa Pecorino '17	🍷🍷 3
⊙ Pecorino Fonte Cupa '16	🍷🍷 3

Fattoria Nicodemi

c.da Veniglio, 8
64024 Notaresco [TE]
Tel. +39 085895493
www.nicodemi.com

CELLAR SALES
PRE-BOOKED VISITS
ANNUAL PRODUCTION 200,000 bottles
HECTARES UNDER VINE 30.00
VITICULTURE METHOD Certified Organic

Elena and Alessandro Nicodemi have taken
over the estate established by their father
Bruno, who in the 1970s left his previous
professional life and moved to the district of
Veniglio di Notaresco where he reinvented
himself as a winemaker. The winery can
count on roughly thirty organically farmed
hectares that face the nearby Adriatic and
are protected from behind by the Gran
Sasso. The range is an hommage to
Abruzzo: traditional Montepulciano,
Trebbiano and Pecorino are used to create
the Notàri and Le Murate lines. This
Notaresco winery is back with Tre Bicchieri
thanks to a sumptuous 2017 version of their
Montepulciano Colline Teramane Notàri.
After a moment in the glass it opens on a
slight note of tanned leather before giving
way to blackberry and ripe plum. On the
palate it's fragrant and fruity, with sweet,
round, well-crafted tannins. When it comes
to their whites the news is more than good,
with their Trebbiano Le Murate '18, Sup.
Notàri '17 and their new Cocciopesto '17.

● Montepulciano d'Abruzzo Colline Teramane Notàri '17	🍷🍷🍷 4*
⊙ Cerasuolo d'Abruzzo Le Murate '18	🍷🍷 2*
⊙ Trebbiano d'Abruzzo Cocciopesto '17	🍷🍷 3
⊙ Trebbiano d'Abruzzo Le Murate '18	🍷🍷 2*
⊙ Trebbiano d'Abruzzo Sup. Notàri '17	🍷🍷 3
⊙ Montepulciano d'Abruzzo Colline Teramane Neromoro Ris. '15	🍷 5
● Montepulciano d'Abuzzo Colline Teramane Le Murate '17	🍷 3
● Montepulciano d'Abruzzo Colline Teramane Neromoro Ris. '09	🍷🍷🍷 5
● Montepulciano d'Abruzzo Colline Teramane Neromoro Ris. '03	🍷🍷🍷 5
⊙ Trebbiano d'Abruzzo Sup. Notàri '15	🍷🍷🍷 3*

Orlandi Contucci Ponno

Loc. Piana degli Ulivi, 1
64026 Roseto degli Abruzzi [TE]
Tel. +39 0858944049
www.orlandicontucciponno.com

CELLAR SALES
PRE-BOOKED VISITS
ANNUAL PRODUCTION 185,000 bottles
HECTARES UNDER VINE 31.00

After focusing first on Franciacorta and
Chianti Classico, the Gussalli Beretta
family's wine group arrived in Abruzzo in
2007 (eventually also reaching Langa and
Alto Adige). Roseto degli Abruzzi, in the
Vomano River valley, is close to both the
Adriatic and the snowy peaks of the Gran
Sasso, which cools the warm evenings in
the hills around Teramo with its breezes.
The largest portion of the vineyard is
dedicated to local Montepulciano and
Trebbiano, but among the diverse cultivars
are also international varieties such as
Chardonnay or Cabernet Sauvignon. Aged
in 2000 liter oak and in steel, La Regia
Specula is a Montepulciano '15 that offers
up delicately salty notes before giving way
to more characteristic hints of dark fruit,
and a faint herbaceous, floral whiff. On the
palate it features close-knit but never
drying tannins accompanied by the return
of pleasant, fruity sensations. Their vibrant
Trebbiano Colle della Corte '18 offers up a
bouquet of aromatic herbs and hay.

● Montepulciano d'Abruzzo		
Colline Teramane La Regia Specula '16	♉♉ 3*	
● Montepulciano d'Abruzzo Rubiolo '18	♉♉ 2*	
○ Trebbiano d'Abruzzo Sup.		
Colle della Corte '18	♉♉ 2*	
☉ Cerasuolo d'Abruzzo Sup. Vermiglio '18	♉ 2	
● Montepulciano d'Abruzzo		
Colline Teramane Ris. '14	♉ 5	
○ Trebbiano d'Abruzzo Adrio '18	♉ 2	
○ Abruzzo Pecorino Sup. '17	♈♈ 3	
☉ Cerasuolo d'Abruzzo Sup. Vermiglio '17	♈♈ 2*	
● Montepulciano d'Abruzzo		
Colline Teramane La Regia Specula '15	♈♈ 3	
● Montepulciano d'Abruzzo		
Colline Teramane Ris. '13	♈♈ 5	
○ Trebbiano d'Abruzzo Sup.		
Colle della Corte '16	♈♈ 2*	

Emidio Pepe

Via Chiesi, 10
64010 Torano Nuovo [TE]
Tel. +39 0861856493
www.emidiopepe.com

CELLAR SALES
PRE-BOOKED VISITS
ACCOMMODATION AND RESTAURANT SERVIC
ANNUAL PRODUCTION 80,000 bottles
HECTARES UNDER VINE 15.00
VITICULTURE METHOD Certified Biodynam*
SUSTAINABLE WINERY

Organic and biodynamic farming,
spontaneous fermentation, no clarification c
filtration, and aging carried out exclusively i
cement tanks (or the bottle) are trademarks
of this estate. As a result, it's helped to writ
the history of Abruzzo wine and should be
counted as a leader of Italy's artisanal wine
movement. Sofia and Daniela have taken th
reins of the winery founded by their father i
the 1960s. The vineyards, on the hills of
Torano Nuovo in Teramo, give life to wines c
a traditional stamp that harken back to the
past and speak proudly of rural life. Their
Trebbiano '17 brings with it all the
sunniness and meatiness of the vintage. It'
a vibrant wine, to say the least, and
full-bodied, steadied by delicately salty,
smoky notes that call up toasted wheat and
almond peel. Their Montepulciano '17 is ric
and ripe, with its trademark spiciness on
notes of pepper and incense. It still needs
some time before fully expressing its
exuberant character. Their energetic and
extremely fresh Rosato '18, the rosé that
wasn't, is also excellent.

● Montepulciano d'Abruzzo '17	♉ 6	
☉ Rosato '18	♉ 5	
○ Trebbiano d'Abruzzo '17	♉♉ 5	
○ Pecorino '17	♉ 6	
● Montepulciano d'Abruzzo '98	♈♈♈ 8	
● Montepulciano d'Abruzzo '15	♈♈ 6	
● Montepulciano d'Abruzzo '13	♈♈ 6	
● Montepulciano d'Abruzzo '12	♈♈ 6	
○ Trebbiano d'Abruzzo '14	♈♈ 5	
○ Trebbiano d'Abruzzo '13	♈♈ 5	

an Lorenzo Vini

A PLAVIGNANO, 2
035 CASTILENTI [TE]
. +39 0861999325
ww.sanlorenzovini.com

CELLAR SALES
RE-BOOKED VISITS
NNUAL PRODUCTION 800,000 bottles
ECTARES UNDER VINE 150.00

ramano in Castilenti is equidistant
tween the mountains and the sea (twenty
ometers from both the Gran Sasso and
e Adriatic). This position guarantees ideal
matic conditions for a stylistically eclectic
nge of wines. Here since the end of the
th century, San Lorenzo is now led by
others Gianluca and Fabrizio Galasso,
o, along with their uncle, agronomist
anfranco Borbone, care for substantial
eyards planted with both traditional and
ernational varieties. Once again their
corino leads this Castilenti winery's
lection. Redolent of yellow fruit, lemon
lp and some kind of balsamic whiff, in
e mouth it's fresh, graceful, with the
turn of citrus accompanying a taut,
operly acidic palate. Their Casablanca
e features interesting experimentations
th spontaneous fermentation, both their
ebbiano '18 and their Pecorino-Passerina
end of the same year. When it comes to
eir reds, we point out their full-bodied
ontepulciano Oinos '15 and the suppler
tàres '16.

Abruzzo Pecorino Il Pecorino '18	♟♟ 2*
Casabianca Pecorino Passerina Fermentazione Spontanea '18	♟♟ 3
Montepulciano d'Abruzzo Colline Teramane Antàres '16	♟♟ 3
Montepulciano d'Abruzzo Colline Teramane Oinos '15	♟♟ 4
Trebbiano d'Abruzzo Casabianca Fermentazione Spontanea '18	♟♟ 2*
Montepulciano d'Abruzzo Colline Teramane Escol Ris. '14	♟ 5
Trebbiano d'Abruzzo Sirio '18	♟ 1*
Abruzzo Pecorino Il Pecorino '17	♟♟ 2*
Montepulciano d'Abruzzo Sirio '16	♟♟ 1*
Montepulciano d'Abruzzo Sirio '15	♟♟ 1*
Trebbiano d'Abruzzo Casabianca Fermentazione Spontanea '16	♟♟ 2*

Tenuta del Priore

VIA MASSERIA FLAIANI, 1
65010 COLLECORVINO [PE]
TEL. +39 0858207162
www.tenutadelpriore.it

CELLAR SALES
PRE-BOOKED VISITS
ANNUAL PRODUCTION 280,000 bottles
HECTARES UNDER VINE 39.00

The story of the Mazzocchetti cousins is
one of a family escaping the hectic capital
and returning to its roots in the 1970s. In
the process they rediscovered their
connection to the land and decided to
invest time and resources into wine
growing. Today Fabrizio takes care of the
Collecorvino-based estate, inland from
Pescara: the vineyards are located from
150 to 300 meters above sea level on hills
of clayey and calcareous soils. Five of the
approximately 40 hectares in Col del
Mondo are dedicated to the eponymously
named line of wines. Their Montepulciano
Terre dei Vestini Col del Mondo '16 led their
selection this year, exhibiting an array of
wild berries on a fresh, supple palate. In the
mouth the wine is supported by a graceful
tannic weave and refreshed at the end by
intriguing notes of medicinal herbs. Their
Montepulciano Il Fattore '16 is no less
interesting. Cherries and spices anticipate
a palate in which precise, sweet tannins
figure centrally.

○ Abruzzo Bianco Sunnae Col del Mondo '18	♟♟ 2*
⊙ Cerasuolo d'Abruzzo Col del Mondo '18	♟♟ 2*
● Montepulciano d'Abruzzo Campotino '18	♟♟ 2*
● Montepulciano d'Abruzzo Il Fattore '16	♟♟ 3
● Montepulciano d'Abruzzo Terre dei Vestini Col del Mondo '16	♟♟ 3
⊙ Campotino Pecorino '18	♟ 2
⊙ Cerasuolo d'Abruzzo Campotino '18	♟ 2
○ Kerrias Pecorino Col del Mondo '18	♟ 2
● Montepulciano d'Abruzzo Sunnae Col del Mondo '18	♟ 2

Tenuta Terraviva

via del Lago, 19
64018 Tortoreto [TE]
Tel. +39 0861786056
www.tenutaterraviva.it

CELLAR SALES
PRE-BOOKED VISITS
ANNUAL PRODUCTION 80,000 bottles
HECTARES UNDER VINE 22.00
VITICULTURE METHOD Certified Organic

Terraviva has quickly made a name for itself in the competitive area of Colline Teramane. This is especially true since it revised its agricultural and production philosophy to organic management in the vineyard, vinification using spontaneous fermentation, and aging in steel drums and wood barrels of various sizes. Pina Marano and Pietro Topi run the company with the vital help of their daughter Federica. They have a consciously artisanal approach in which Montepulciano, Trebbiano and Pecorino are interpreted with an easily recognizable style. Their Cerasuolo Giusi '18, one of Italy's best rosés, performs on an enchanting register. Gunpowder, freshly ground coffee and subtle notes of green tea emerge on a taut, lengthy palate of delicate flavor. Their Percorino '18 shines, coming through juicy and vibrant — it's outstanding value for the money. The 2017 version of their Mario's proves ripe and round. Their reds are less lively.

⊙ Cerasuolo d'Abruzzo Giusi '18	🍷🍷 2*
○ Abruzzo Passerina 12.1 '18	🍷🍷 3
○ Pecorino '18	🍷🍷 2*
○ Trebbiano d'Abruzzo '18	🍷🍷 2*
○ Trebbiano d'Abruzzo Mario's 45 '17	🍷🍷 3
○ Abruzzo Pecorino 'Ekwo '18	🍷 3
● Montepulciano d'Abruzzo Colline Teramane '17	🍷 2
● Montepulciano d'Abruzzo Colline Teramane Luì '16	🍷 3
● Montepulciano d'Abruzzo Luì '13	ỾỾỾ 3*
○ Trebbiano d'Abruzzo Sup. Mario's 44 '16	ỾỾỾ 3*
○ Abruzzo Pecorino 'Ekwo '16	ỾỾ 3*
○ Abruzzo Pecorino Ekwo '17	ỾỾ 3
● Montepulciano d'Abruzzo Luì '15	ỾỾ 3

Tiberio

c.da La Vota
65020 Cugnoli [PE]
Tel. +39 0858576744
www.tiberio.it

CELLAR SALES
PRE-BOOKED VISITS
ANNUAL PRODUCTION 90,000 bottles
HECTARES UNDER VINE 30.00

This dynamic operation in the Colline Pescaresi was founded in 2000 by Riccardo Tiberio. Getting ready to celebra twenty years of activity, the winery has been reinvigorated by the management o his children Cristiana and Antonio. Separated from the international varieties the vineyards near Cugnoli, between Majella and Gran Sasso (around 350 meters above sea level) are planted with only traditional local varieties taken from mass selections of mature plants. Montepulciano, Trebbiano and Pecorino a the heart of everything here. Vinification takes place exclusively in steel drums to produce agile, racy, versatile wines that fully express the territory. 2018 gave rise two great wines, a Pecorino and a Trebbiano. The former is redolent of white flowers and grassy herbs, with a racy palate whose blast of acidity drives its sensational citrusy verve towards the finis line. The latter is broader, both aromatical and on the palate, but it too features a vigorous mineral support and acidity. Thei Cerasuolo '18 is also excellent.

○ Pecorino '18	🍷🍷
○ Trebbiano d'Abruzzo '18	🍷🍷
⊙ Cerasuolo d'Abruzzo '18	🍷🍷
● Montepulciano d'Abruzzo '17	🍷
● Montepulciano d'Abruzzo '13	ỾỾỾ
○ Pecorino '16	ỾỾỾ
○ Pecorino '15	ỾỾỾ
○ Pecorino '13	ỾỾỾ
○ Pecorino '12	ỾỾỾ
○ Pecorino '11	ỾỾỾ
○ Pecorino '10	ỾỾỾ
⊙ Cerasuolo d'Abruzzo '17	ỾỾ
● Montepulciano d'Abruzzo '15	ỾỾ
○ Pecorino '17	ỾỾ
○ Trebbiano d'Abruzzo '17	ỾỾ
○ Trebbiano d'Abruzzo '16	ỾỾ

Cantina Tollo

ᴀ Garibaldi, 68
6010 Tollo [CH]
ᴛᴇʟ. +39 087196251
ᴡᴡw.cantinatollo.it

CELLAR SALES
ANNUAL PRODUCTION 13,000,000 bottles
HECTARES UNDER VINE 3200.00

The province of Chieti has one of the
world's highest concentrations of
cooperatives, and Cantina Tollo plays a
central role among them. Not only does it
operate on an impressive scale (3,200
hectares of vineyards of which almost 240
are organically grown, about 1,000
members, and 13 million bottles annually), it
also has an entrepreneurial vision that has
led to impressive growth in recent years.
Complementary lines characterized by a
recognizable style and offered at very
reasonable prices are largely responsible for
increasing international interest. Once again
we point out the excellent performance put
by this large cooperative's entire
selection. Their Montepulciano Mo Ris. '15
(complex and structured) and Trebbiano
Tre '18 (elegant, flavorful and close-knit)
are only the brightest stars of a selection
without weak points. Their organic Bio
line (Montepulciano, Cerasuolo and
Trebbiano '18) shine for aromatic cleanness
and precision of taste.

Montepulciano d'Abruzzo Mo Ris. '15	♈♈♈ 3*
Trebbiano d'Abruzzo Tre '18	♈♈ 3*
Cerasuolo d'Abruzzo Biologico '18	♈♈ 2*
Montepulciano d'Abruzzo Biologico '18	♈♈ 2*
Peco Pecorino '18	♈♈ 3
Trebbiano d'Abruzzo Biologico '18	♈♈ 2*
Cerasuolo d'Abruzzo Hedòs '18	♈ 3
Trebbiano d'Abruzzo C'Incanta '15	♈ 4
Montepulciano d'Abruzzo Cagiòlo Ris. '09	♈♈♈ 4*
Montepulciano d'Abruzzo Mo Ris. '13	♈♈♈ 3*
Montepulciano d'Abruzzo Mo Ris. '12	♈♈♈ 2*
Montepulciano d'Abruzzo Mo Ris. '11	♈♈♈ 3*
Montepulciano d'Abruzzo Mo' Ris. '14	♈♈♈ 3*
Trebbiano d'Abruzzo C'Incanta '11	♈♈♈ 4*
Trebbiano d'Abruzzo C'Incanta '10	♈♈♈ 4*

Torre dei Beati

c.ᴅᴀ Poggioragone, 56
65014 Loreto Aprutino [PE]
ᴛᴇʟ. +39 0854916069
www.torredeibeati.it

CELLAR SALES
PRE-BOOKED VISITS
ANNUAL PRODUCTION 100,000 bottles
HECTARES UNDER VINE 20.00
VITICULTURE METHOD Certified Organic
SUSTAINABLE WINERY

Adriana Galasso and Fausto Albanesi's
adventure began in 1999 when they both
decided to leave their professions to
produce wine with vineyards near Loreto
Aprutino. Today they take care of about
twenty organically farmed hectares at an
elevation of about 300 meters on the
foothills of the Apennines; the nearby Gran
Sasso and Adriatic Sea influence the
climate by generating strong daily
temperature swings. They create expressive,
spontaneous wines using Montepulciano,
Trebbiano and Pecorino. Torre dei Beati is
among the region's most top-performing
producers, as evidenced by an impressive
range of wines that features an incredible
Cerasuolo Rosa-ae '18. Flowers and red
fruits, pomegranate — it reveals
Montepulciano's smoky and earthy verve on
a juicy, spicy palate. For us it's the 'Rosé of
the Year'. Their Pecorino Giocheremo con i
Fiori '18, a veritable explosion of
aromatic herbs and salts, is just a hair's
breadth behind, as is their Trebbiano Bianchi
Grilli '17, a fragrant, expansive wine.

⊙ Cerasuolo d'Abruzzo Rosa-ae '18	♈♈♈ 2*
○ Abruzzo Pecorino Giocheremo con I Fiori '18	♈♈ 3*
● Montepulciano d'Abruzzo Mazzamurello '16	♈♈ 5
○ Trebbiano d'Abruzzo Bianchi Grilli per la Testa '17	♈♈ 3*
○ Abruzzo Pecorino Bianchi Grilli per la Testa '17	♈♈ 4
● Montepulciano d'Abruzzo Cocciapazza '16	♈♈ 5
● Montepulciano d'Abruzzo '17	♈ 3
○ Abruzzo Pecorino Giocheremo con I Fiori '17	♈♈♈ 3*
● Montepulciano d'Abruzzo Cocciapazza '11	♈♈♈ 4*
○ Trebbiano d'Abruzzo Bianchi Grilli per la Testa '14	♈♈♈ 4*

La Valentina

VIA TORRETTA, 52
65010 SPOLTORE [PE]
TEL. +39 0854478158
www.lavalentina.it

CELLAR SALES
PRE-BOOKED VISITS
ANNUAL PRODUCTION 350,000 bottles
HECTARES UNDER VINE 40.00
VITICULTURE METHOD Certified Organic
SUSTAINABLE WINERY

Brothers Sabatino, Roberto and Andrea Di Properzio have owned the estate since 1994, following principles of environmental sustainability from the start. The winery is increasingly showing its dynamism and originality. The organically managed vineyards extend across the municipalities of Spoltore and Cavaticchi, near the Adriatic coast, and Scafa, San Valentino and Alanno farther inland, near the Apennines. These differences in altitude and climate are reflected in a range divided into two lines: zesty, expressive Classica and the more energetic, prospective Terroir. Their Cerasuolo d'Abruzzo Spelt '18 unleashes fragrant aromas of wild strawberries, lemon grass and aromatic herbs. In the mouth it's vibrant and flavorful, exhibiting an entirely Mediterranean character. Their Montepulciano '17 also delivered: aromas of red and black fruits, close-knit tannins and a fresh stroke that lightens the palate. We also make note of their Montepulciano Spelt Riserva '16, a wine that's still evolving but has great potential.

⊙ Cerasuolo d'Abruzzo Sup. Spelt '18	🍷🍷 3*
● Montepulciano d'Abruzzo '17	🍷🍷 2*
● Montepulciano d'Abruzzo Binomio Ris. '15	🍷🍷 5
● Montepulciano d'Abruzzo Spelt Ris. '16	🍷🍷 4
⊙ Cerasuolo d'Abruzzo '18	🍷 2
● Montepulciano d'Abruzzo Terre dei Vestini Bellovedere Ris. '15	🍷 6
○ Pecorino '18	🍷 2
● Montepulciano d'Abruzzo Spelt '08	🍷🍷🍷 3*
● Montepulciano d'Abruzzo Spelt '07	🍷🍷🍷 3
● Montepulciano d'Abruzzo Spelt Ris. '15	🍷🍷🍷 4*
● Montepulciano d'Abruzzo Spelt Ris. '11	🍷🍷🍷 4*
● Montepulciano d'Abruzzo Spelt Ris. '10	🍷🍷🍷 3*

★★★Valentini

VIA DEL BAIO, 2
65014 LORETO APRUTINO [PE]
TEL. +39 0858291138
az.agr.valentini@gmail.com

ANNUAL PRODUCTION 50,000 bottles
HECTARES UNDER VINE 70.00

The Valentini family has deep agricultural roots going back to the 17th century — Francesco Paolo is the current heir of this long tradition. From his home/winery in Loreto Aprutino he produces a small range with an international cult following. The 70 hectares of vineyards rarely produce more than 50,000 bottles because of his extreme care; wines are released if and only if they live up to their incredible potential for longevity. Cerasuolo, Trebbiano and Montepulciano are worked using artisanal criteria that are difficult to pigeonhole technically. As of late we've noticed a careful pursuit of aromatically subtler, more measured wines. Their Trebbiano d'Abruzzo confirms the direction, opening slowly on sensations of ginger and wild grass — in the palate it's fresh, balsamic and harmonious. Their Cerasuolo '18 is another charming wine. Redolent of legumes and coffee with a slightly herbaceous stroke, on the palate proves warm and juicy.

○ Trebbiano d'Abruzzo '15	🍷🍷🍷
⊙ Cerasuolo d'Abruzzo '18	🍷🍷
● Montepulciano d'Abruzzo '13	🍷🍷🍷
● Montepulciano d'Abruzzo '12	🍷🍷🍷
● Montepulciano d'Abruzzo '06	🍷🍷🍷
⊙ Montepulciano d'Abruzzo Cerasuolo '09	🍷🍷🍷
○ Trebbiano d'Abruzzo '13	🍷🍷🍷
○ Trebbiano d'Abruzzo '12	🍷🍷🍷
○ Trebbiano d'Abruzzo '11	🍷🍷🍷
○ Trebbiano d'Abruzzo '10	🍷🍷🍷
○ Trebbiano d'Abruzzo '09	🍷🍷🍷
○ Trebbiano d'Abruzzo '08	🍷🍷🍷
○ Trebbiano d'Abruzzo '07	🍷🍷🍷
⊙ Cerasuolo d'Abruzzo '17	🍷🍷
⊙ Cerasuolo d'Abruzzo '16	🍷🍷
○ Trebbiano d'Abruzzo '14	🍷🍷

★Valle Reale

loc. San Calisto
65026 Popoli [PE]
tel. +39 0859871039
www.vallereale.it

CELLAR SALES
PRE-BOOKED VISITS
ANNUAL PRODUCTION 250,000 bottles
HECTARES UNDER VINE 46.00
VITICULTURE METHOD Certified Organic
SUSTAINABLE WINERY

The Pizzolo family estate is located in the magical town of Popoli, between the provinces of Pescara and L'Aquila, where the Gran Sasso, Majella and Sirente-Velino Natural Parks all meet. The vineyards in this unspoiled place are planted with organically managed local varieties: Trebbiano and Montepulciano are vinified with spontaneous fermentation, then aged in cement tanks and wood casks. Particular attention is paid to the carefully selected vineyards used for the company's cru: Sant'Eusanio, San Calisto, Vigneto di Popoli and Vigna del Convento di Capestrano. Their Montepulciano Vigneto Sant'Eusanio is their new star thanks to a successful 2017. A light rustic sensation doesn't impede the performance of a red that's varietal to the bone and full of character. On the nose it offers up aromas of dark fruit and pencil lead, while the palate is penetrating and taut, without concessions to redundant sweetness. Their Trebbiano Vigneto di Popoli '17 is also excellent, proving complex and stratified in flavor.

● Montepulciano d'Abruzzo Vign. Sant'Eusanio '17	♈♈♈ 4*
○ Trebbiano d'Abruzzo Vign. di Popoli '17	♈♈ 5
○ Cerasuolo d'Abruzzo Vign. Sant'Eusanio '18	♈♈ 4
● Montepulciano d'Abruzzo '18	♈♈ 3
○ Trebbiano d'Abruzzo '18	♈♈ 3
○ Trebbiano d'Abruzzo Vign. del Convento di Capestrano '18	♈♈ 6
● Montepulciano d'Abruzzo Vign. di Sant'Eusanio '16	♈♈♈ 4*
○ Trebbiano d'Abruzzo V. del Convento di Capestrano '15	♈♈♈ 6
○ Trebbiano d'Abruzzo V. del Convento di Capestrano '14	♈♈♈ 5

Valori

via Torquato al Salinello, 8
64027 Sant'Omero [TE]
tel. +39 087185241
www.vinivalori.it

PRE-BOOKED VISITS
ANNUAL PRODUCTION 150,000 bottles
HECTARES UNDER VINE 26.00
VITICULTURE METHOD Certified Organic
SUSTAINABLE WINERY

Energetic Abruzzo producer Luigi Valori has been cultivating his vineyards on the gentle slopes of the Colline Teramane at the border of Marche, between Sant'Omero and Controguerra, since 1996. In 2015, he switched to organic farming to enhance the richness and intensity of the grapes from his 26 hectares of vineyards situated between 150 and 300 meters above sea level. The wines, produced with native varieties and some incursions into international cultivars, reflect the Mediterranean warmth of this stretch of the Adriatic coast in a balanced and well-orchestrated way. Their Montepulciano Vigna Sant'Angelo is made with grapes from a vineyard that goes back more than 50 years. After about 20 months in barriques, the 2015 is already aromatically close-knit and vibrant, while on the palate it proves full-bodied, with structure to spare. Their Merlot Inkiostro '17 also has plenty of matière, while their Pecorino '18 features power and breadth. Their Cerasuolo '18, a wine that's more natural on the palate, also opts for greater delectability.

● Inkiostro Merlot '17	♈♈ 4
● Montepulciano d'Abruzzo Colline Teramane V. Sant'Angelo '15	♈♈ 4
○ Abruzzo Pecorino Chiamami Quando Piove '18	♈♈ 3
⊙ Cerasuolo d'Abruzzo Chiamami Quando Piove '18	♈♈ 2*
○ Abruzzo Pecorino '16	♈♈ 2*
○ Abruzzo Pecorino '15	♈♈ 2*
○ Abruzzo Pecorino Biologico '17	♈♈ 2*
● Montepulciano d'Abruzzo Bio '14	♈♈ 2*
● Montepulciano d'Abruzzo Colline Teramane V. Sant'Angelo '11	♈♈ 4
● Montepulciano d'Abruzzo V. Sant'Angelo '10	♈♈ 4
○ Trebbiano d'Abruzzo Bio '14	♈♈ 2*

★Villa Medoro

C.DA MEDORO
64030 ATRI [TE]
TEL. +39 0858708139
www.villamedoro.it

CELLAR SALES
PRE-BOOKED VISITS
ACCOMMODATION
ANNUAL PRODUCTION 300,000 bottles
HECTARES UNDER VINE 100.00

Over 40 years of experience (twenty 'official' and twenty 'experimental') has made the Morricone family estate one of the main entities of Colline Teramane. Based near the Adriatic in Atri, Villa Medoro has grown to some one hundred hectares of vineyards after acquiring the two prestigious estates of Fontanelle and Fonte Corvo. Trebbiano, Montepulciano, Pecorino and Montonico are expressed in a moderately modern style as a solid range of both basic single varietal wines and more ambitious selections. Their Pecorino 8½ '18 is one standout in a nice overall performance. Aromatic herbs, incense, ripe yellow fruit are among the complex nuances that anticipate a vibrant, flavorful palate with a lovely, lengthy finish. But this year the honors go to their Montepulciano '18, a vibrant, fragrant red in its notes of mature black fruit. On the palate it expresses all the grape's character. We also found their 2018 Trebbiano and Passerina noteworthy.

● Montepulciano d'Abruzzo '18	🍷🍷🍷 2*
○ 8½ Pecorino '18	🍷🍷 3*
⊙ Cerasuolo d'Abruzzo '18	🍷🍷 2*
○ Passerina '18	🍷🍷 2*
○ Trebbiano d'Abruzzo '18	🍷🍷 2*
● Montepulciano d'Abruzzo Colline Teramane Adrano '16	🍷 4
● Montepulciano d'Abruzzo Rosso del Duca '17	🍷 3
○ Pecorino '18	🍷 2
● Montepulciano d'Abruzzo '14	🍷🍷🍷 2*
● Montepulciano d'Abruzzo Colline Teramane Adrano '12	🍷🍷🍷 4*
● Montepulciano d'Abruzzo Rosso del Duca '12	🍷🍷🍷 3*
○ Pecorino '17	🍷🍷🍷 2*

Ciccio Zaccagnini

C.DA POZZO
65020 BOLOGNANO [PE]
TEL. +39 0858880195
www.cantinazaccagnini.it

CELLAR SALES
PRE-BOOKED VISITS
ANNUAL PRODUCTION 1,500,000 bottles
HECTARES UNDER VINE 300.00

It's been more than 40 years since Ciccio Zaccagnini founded the winery that carries his name in Bolognano, a town positioned between the first foothils of the Majella and the Adriatic. Today his son Marcello, with support from his cousin, enologist Concezio Marulli, leads an operation that has grown enormously over the years. Montepulciano, Trebbiano and Pecorino fill the main portion of the vineyards, giving shape to a varied range that goes from excellent entry level wines to bolder, more serious selections, while also experimenting with spumanti wines and wines without added sulfites. Their San Clemente Biano '17, a cuvée made with cask-aged Trebbiano, just fell short of Tre Bicchieri. A wine redolent of candied lemon, white and yellow fruit, on the palate it proves creamy and soft without being weighed down thanks to a juicy, sapid background. Their Montepulciano Chronicon '16 is also highly pleasant with its close-focused notes of ripe, black cherry and its tannic precision.

○ Abruzzo Bianco San Clemente '17	🍷🍷 4
○ Abruzzo Bianco Il Bianco di Ciccio '18	🍷🍷 2*
⊙ Cerasuolo d'Abruzzo Myosotis '18	🍷🍷 3
● Montepulciano d'Abruzzo Chronicon '16	🍷🍷 3
● Montepulciano d'Abruzzo Terre di Casauria S. Clemente Ris. '15	🍷🍷 5
⊙ Cerasuolo d'Abruzzo Il Vino dal Tralcetto '18	🍷 3
○ Ibisco Rosa '18	🍷 2
● Montepulciano d'Abruzzo Il Vino dal Tralcetto '17	🍷 2
⊙ Cerasuolo d'Abruzzo Myosotis '16	🍷🍷🍷 3*
● Montepulciano d'Abruzzo Chronicon '13	🍷🍷🍷 3*
● Montepulciano d'Abruzzo S. Clemente Ris. '12	🍷🍷🍷 5
● Montepulciano d'Abruzzo S. Clemente Ris. '11	🍷🍷🍷 5

usonia

A NOCELLA
032 ATRI [TE]
. +39 0859071026
ww.ausoniawines.com

ANNUAL PRODUCTION 35,000 bottles
ECTARES UNDER VINE 11.50

Abruzzo Pecorino Machaon '17	🏆🏆 3
Cerasuolo d'Abruzzo Apollo '18	🏆 3

Nestore Bosco

C.DA CASALI, 147
65010 NOCCIANO [PE]
TEL. +39 085847345
www.nestorebosco.com

CELLAR SALES
PRE-BOOKED VISITS
ANNUAL PRODUCTION 600,000 bottles
HECTARES UNDER VINE 75.00

○ Pecorino Linea Storica '18	🏆🏆 2*
○ Pecorino Linea Classica '18	🏆 2

ove

ROMA, 216
051 AVEZZANO [AQ]
. +39 086333133
o@cantinebove.it

ELLAR SALES
RE-BOOKED VISITS
NNUAL PRODUCTION 1,200,000 bottles
ECTARES UNDER VINE 60.00

Montepulciano d'Abruzzo	
Feudi d'Albe '17	🏆🏆 1*
Trebbiano d'Abruzzo Angeli '18	🏆🏆 2*
Montepulciano d'Abruzzo Indio '14	🏆 2

Casal Thaulero

C.DA CUCULLO
66026 ORTONA [CH]
TEL. +39 0859032533
www.casalthaulero.it

CELLAR SALES
PRE-BOOKED VISITS
ANNUAL PRODUCTION 1,300,000 bottles
HECTARES UNDER VINE 500.00
SUSTAINABLE WINERY

○ Abruzzo Pecorino Sup. Duca Thaulero '18	🏆🏆 3
● Montepulciano d'Abruzzo	
50 Anniversary Ris. '12	🏆🏆 2*
○ Orsetto Oro Pecorino '18	🏆🏆 2*

asalbordino

DA TERMINE, 38
021 CASALBORDINO [CH]
. +39 0873918107
ww.vinicasalbordino.com

ELLAR SALES
RE-BOOKED VISITS
NNUAL PRODUCTION 6,000,000 bottles
ECTARES UNDER VINE 1400.00

Montepulciano d'Abruzzo Sinello Ris. '16	🏆🏆 2*
Montepulciano d'Abruzzo ù	
rre Sabelli '16	🏆 1*

Cascina del Colle

VIA PIANA, 85A
66010 VILLAMAGNA [CH]
TEL. +39 0871301093
www.lacascinadelcolle.it

CELLAR SALES
PRE-BOOKED VISITS
ANNUAL PRODUCTION 150,000 bottles
HECTARES UNDER VINE 16.00
VITICULTURE METHOD Certified Organic

○ Abruzzo Pecorino Sup. Aimè '18	🏆🏆 3
⊙ Cerasuolo d'Abruzzo Cuvée 71 '18	🏆🏆 3
● Montepulciano d'Abruzzo Mammut '15	🏆🏆 4
○ La Canale Pecorino '18	🏆 3

Ciavolich

c.da Salmacina, 11
65014 Loreto Aprutino [PE]
Tel. +39 0858289200
www.ciavolich.com

CELLAR SALES
PRE-BOOKED VISITS
ACCOMMODATION AND RESTAURANT SERVICE
ANNUAL PRODUCTION 200,000 bottles
HECTARES UNDER VINE 30.00

⊙ Cerasuolo d'Abruzzo Fosso Cancelli '18	♟♟ 5
○ Fosso Cancelli Pecorino '16	♟♟ 5
● Montepulciano d'Abruzzo Antrum '14	♟♟ 5
○ Trebbiano d'Abruzzo Fosso Cancelli '15	♟♟ 2*

Colle Moro

loc. Guastameroli
via del Mare, 35/37
66030 Frisa [CH]
Tel. +39 087258128
www.collemoro.it

CELLAR SALES
PRE-BOOKED VISITS
ANNUAL PRODUCTION 750,000 bottles
HECTARES UNDER VINE 1500.00
VITICULTURE METHOD Certified Organic

● Montepulciano d'Abruzzo Alcàde '14	♟♟
○ Trebbiano d'Abruzzo Club '18	♟♟
○ Club Pecorino '18	♟
● Montepulciano d'Abruzzo Club '18	♟

Antonio Costantini

s.da Migliori, 20
65013 Città Sant'Angelo [PE]
Tel. +39 0859699169
www.costantinivini.it

CELLAR SALES
PRE-BOOKED VISITS
ACCOMMODATION AND RESTAURANT SERVICE
ANNUAL PRODUCTION 450,000 bottles
HECTARES UNDER VINE 60.00

● Montepulciano d'Abruzzo Febe '18	♟♟ 1*
○ Abruzzo Pecorino '18	♟ 2
⊙ Foglio Sei Rosato '18	♟ 2
○ Trebbiano d'Abruzzo Febe '18	♟ 1*

Eredi Legonziano

c.da Nasuti, 169
66034 Lanciano [CH]
Tel. +39 087245210
www.eredilegonziano.it

CELLAR SALES
PRE-BOOKED VISITS
ANNUAL PRODUCTION 200,000 bottles
HECTARES UNDER VINE 500.00

○ Abruzzo Spumante Bianco 36 Mesi M. Cl.	♟♟ 4
○ Abruzzo Spumante Bianco Carmine Festa M. Cl. '11	♟♟ 3
● Montepulciano d'Abruzzo Diocleziano '14	♟♟ 2

Fantini - Farnese Vini

loc. Castello Caldora
via dei Bastioni
66026 Ortona [CH]
Tel. +39 0859067388
www.farnese-vini.com

PRE-BOOKED VISITS
ANNUAL PRODUCTION 11,000,000 bottles
HECTARES UNDER VINE 250.00

● Cerasuolo d'Abruzzo Fantini '18	♟♟ 2*
● Edizione 5 Autoctoni	♟♟ 5
● Montepulciano d'Abruzzo Casale Vecchio Fantini '16	♟♟ 2*

Cantina Frentana

via Perazza, 32
66020 Rocca San Giovanni [CH]
Tel. +39 087260152
www.cantinafrentana.it

CELLAR SALES
PRE-BOOKED VISITS
ACCOMMODATION
ANNUAL PRODUCTION 800,000 bottles
HECTARES UNDER VINE 22.00

○ Abruzzo Pecorino Coste del Mulino '18	♟♟ 1
○ Abruzzo Pecorino Torre Vinaria '18	♟♟ 2
● Montepulciano d'Abruzzo Ris. '16	♟♟ 2
● Montepulciano d'Abruzzo Torre Vinaria '17	♟♟ 2

asci&Marchesani

Colli II, 3c
6054 Vasto [CH]
el. +39 0873364315
ww.jasciemarchesani.it

ELLAR SALES
RE-BOOKED VISITS
NNUAL PRODUCTION 350,000 bottles
ECTARES UNDER VINE 37.00
ITICULTURE METHOD Certified Organic

Montepulciano d'Abruzzo Nerubè '17	🍷🍷 3
Montepulciano d'Abruzzo Rudhir '16	🍷🍷 4
○ Abruzzo Pecorino Sup. '18	🍷 3
Cerasuolo d'Abruzzo '18	🍷 2

Marchesi De' Cordano

c.da Cordano, 43
65014 Loreto Aprutino [PE]
Tel. +39 0858289526
www.cordano.it

CELLAR SALES
PRE-BOOKED VISITS
ANNUAL PRODUCTION 250,000 bottles
HECTARES UNDER VINE 50.00
VITICULTURE METHOD Certified Organic
SUSTAINABLE WINERY

○ Diamine Pecorino '18	🍷🍷 3
○ Trebbiano d'Abruzzo Aida '18	🍷🍷 2*
⊙ Cerasuolo d'Abruzzo Puntarosa '18	🍷 3
● Montepulciano d'Abruzzo Trinità Ris. '14	🍷 4

Tommaso Masciantonio

da Caprafico, 35
6043 Casoli [CH]
el. +39 0871897457
ww.trappetodicaprafico.com

RE-BOOKED VISITS
CCOMMODATION
NNUAL PRODUCTION 8,000 bottles
ECTARES UNDER VINE 10.00
ITICULTURE METHOD Certified Organic

○ Abruzzo Pecorino Sup. Mantica V. Di Caprafico '15	🍷🍷 4
● Montepulciano d'Abruzzo Sciatò V. Di Caprafico '15	🍷🍷 3

Tommaso Olivastri

via Quercia del Corvo, 37
66038 San Vito Chietino [CH]
Tel. +39 087261543
www.viniolivastri.com

CELLAR SALES
PRE-BOOKED VISITS
ANNUAL PRODUCTION 30,000 bottles
HECTARES UNDER VINE 15.00

○ L'Ariosa Pecorino '18	🍷🍷 3
● Montepulciano D'Abruzzo La Grondaia '16	🍷🍷 3
○ Abruzzo Pecorino L'Ariosa '18	🍷 2
○ Trebbiano d'Abruzzo Santa Clara '18	🍷 2

Pasetti

loc. c.da Pretaro
via San Paolo, 21
66023 Francavilla al Mare [CH]
Tel. +39 08561875
www.pasettivini.it

CELLAR SALES
PRE-BOOKED VISITS
ACCOMMODATION
ANNUAL PRODUCTION 600,000 bottles
HECTARES UNDER VINE 75.00

○ Abruzzo Pecorino Colle Civetta '17	🍷🍷 3
● Montepulciano d'Abruzzo '16	🍷🍷 2*
○ Trebbiano d'Abruzzo Madonnella '17	🍷🍷 3
○ Abruzzo Pecorino '18	🍷 3

La Quercia

c.da Colle Croce
64020 Morro d'Oro [TE]
Tel. +39 0858959110
www.vinilaquercia.it

CELLAR SALES
PRE-BOOKED VISITS
ANNUAL PRODUCTION 200,000 bottles
HECTARES UNDER VINE 46.50
SUSTAINABLE WINERY

● Montepulciano d'Abruzzo Primamadre Ris. '13	🍷🍷 2*
○ Trebbiano d'Abruzzo Sup. La Quercia '18	🍷🍷 2*
● Montepulciano d'Abruzzo Peladi '18	🍷 1*

San Giacomo

C.DA NOVELLA, 51
66020 ROCCA SAN GIOVANNI [CH]
TEL. +39 0872620504
www.cantinasangiacomo.it

CELLAR SALES
PRE-BOOKED VISITS
ACCOMMODATION
ANNUAL PRODUCTION 60,000 bottles
HECTARES UNDER VINE 300.00
VITICULTURE METHOD Certified Organic

○ Casino Murri Pecorino '18	♥♥ 2*
○ Pecorino '18	♥♥ 2*
○ Trebbiano d'Abruzzo Casino Murri 14° '18	♥♥ 2*
⊙ Cerasuolo d'Abruzzo Casino Murri '18	♥ 2

Strappelli

VIA TORRI, 16
64010 TORANO NUOVO [TE]
TEL. +39 0861887402
www.cantinastrappelli.it

CELLAR SALES
PRE-BOOKED VISITS
ANNUAL PRODUCTION 65,000 bottles
HECTARES UNDER VINE 10.00
VITICULTURE METHOD Certified Organic

○ Trebbiano d'Abruzzo '18	♥♥ 2
⊙ Cerasuolo d'Abruzzo Sup. Colle Trà '18	♥ 3
○ Controguerra Pecorino Soprano '18	♥ 3

Terzini

VIA ROMA, 52
65028 TOCCO DA CASAURIA [PE]
TEL. +39 0859158147
www.cantinaterzini.it

CELLAR SALES
PRE-BOOKED VISITS
ANNUAL PRODUCTION 200,000 bottles
HECTARES UNDER VINE 22.00

○ Abruzzo Pecorino '18	♥♥ 3
⊙ Montepulciano d'Abruzzo Dumì '17	♥♥ 3
⊙ Cerasuolo d'Abruzzo '18	♥ 3
○ Dumì Pecorino '18	♥ 3

Tocco Vini

VIA S. PERTINI, 3
65020 ALANNO [PE]
TEL. +39 3400558624
www.toccovini.com

CELLAR SALES
ANNUAL PRODUCTION 25,000 bottles
HECTARES UNDER VINE 13.50

● Montepulciano d'Abruzzo Enisio Ris. '14	♥♥ 2*
⊙ Rosato '18	♥♥ 2
○ Trebbiano d'Abruzzo '18	♥♥ 2*
○ Pecorino '18	♥ 2

Tenuta Ulisse

VIA SAN POLO, 40
66014 CRECCHIO [CH]
TEL. +39 0871942007
www.tenutaulisse.it

CELLAR SALES
PRE-BOOKED VISITS
ANNUAL PRODUCTION 550,000 bottles
HECTARES UNDER VINE 75.00

● Montepulciano d'Abruzzo Nativae '17	♥♥ 4
● Montepulciano d'Abruzzo '17	♥ 4
○ Pecorino '18	♥ 3

Codice Vino

C.DA CUCULLO
66026 ORTONA [CH]
TEL. +39 0859031342
www.citra.it

● Montepulciano d'Abruzzo '17	♥♥ 3*
⊙ Cerasuolo d'Abruzzo '18	♥♥ 3

MOLISE

n small regions you drink good wine'. A play on
n old saying does a nice job describing our
eeling about this year's tastings. If once again
nly Di Majo Norante earned Tre Bicchieri, with
ne of its most convincing Don Luigi Riservas yet
a potent, compact red, modern but not excessively) we
nvite the reader to see how many (and which) wines reached our final tastings:
even (including the winner)! It's a record if we count the number of producers
eviewed. In a way this is something of a disappointment. The wineries
articipating in our tastings are still too few. In the following years we'll be
working to involve, and make space for, more of them so as to provide a more
omplete map of the region's enology. But to this end we're already seeing
positive signs. The most attentive will notice some movement, new releases, new
entries. While still small, we'd like to think that this mobility is the proof that the
egion isn't stuck, that it's carving out its own identity and that these steps will be
eflected in the quality of its wines. To achieve this goal, their best weapon is
'intilia. Among the seven finalists mentioned, six are made with Molise's native
grape, and finally we're seeing interpretations that are truly territorial and
nteresting, especially those that pursue lightness and vigor. There's still work to
do before the region will be free of a passé style centered on concentration and
extraction, but it seems as if, slowly, a new direction is taking shape. We're
confident in that direction and in the fact that soon we'll be able to enjoy further
encouraging results.

Borgo di Colloredo

FRAZ. NUOVA CLITERNIA
VIA COLLOREDO, 15
86042 CAMPOMARINO [CB]
TEL. +39 087557453
www.borgodicolloredo.com

CELLAR SALES
PRE-BOOKED VISITS
ACCOMMODATION AND RESTAURANT SERVICE
ANNUAL PRODUCTION 230,000 bottles
HECTARES UNDER VINE 80.00
SUSTAINABLE WINERY

In the 1960s, Silvio Di Giulio decided to purchase a one-hundred hectare estate near Campomarino. The current winery is named after a farmhouse on this land that was renovated as a place of worship for the D'Avalos D'Aragona family. Today, it is in the expert hands of brothers Enrico and Pasquale Di Giulio, who tend vineyards planted with native varieties, such as Montepulciano, Falanghina, Aglianico, Greco, Sangiovese and Malvasia, as well as the non-native Garganega, Chardonnay and Syrah. The range they presented for tasting this years contains hardly any weak points at all: Molise Rosso Campo Mare '16 leads their squad, with fragrant sweet spices and red fruits turning into a fresh, dynamic, succulent palate, thanks to its subtle sapid streak. Their Rosato Gironia '18 also comes through pleasant and drinkable.

○ Biferno Bianco Gironia '18	♟♟	3
⊙ Biferno Rosato Gironia '18	♟♟	3
● Molise Rosso Campo in Mare '16	♟♟	3
○ Greco '18	♟	3
○ Molise Falanghina Campo in Mare '18	♟	3
● Aglianico '10	♟♟♟	3*
● Aglianico '13	♟♟	3
○ Biferno Bianco Gironia '17	♟♟	3
○ Biferno Bianco Gironia '14	♟♟	3
⊙ Biferno Rosato Gironia '16	♟♟	3
⊙ Biferno Rosato Gironia '15	♟♟	2*
○ Molise Falanghina '17	♟♟	3

★Di Majo Norante

FRAZ. NUOVA CLITERNIA
VIA V. RAMITELLO, 4
86042 CAMPOMARINO [CB]
TEL. +39 087557208
www.dimajonorante.com

CELLAR SALES
PRE-BOOKED VISITS
ANNUAL PRODUCTION 800,000 bottles
HECTARES UNDER VINE 125.00
VITICULTURE METHOD Certified Organic

Three territories, southern Abruzzo, Daunia and Samnium, find a common thread in the Campomarino countryside. The Di Majo Norante family's property stands on the site where the estate of the Marquises of Santa Cristina used to be. Dating from the 1800s, this winery has been launched into the future by Alessio, who took over from his father, Luigi. This mixed territory is reflected in their organic vineyard, which is planted with the red varieties Montepulciano, Aglianico, Tintilia and Sangiovese, as well as the Trebbiano, Malvasia, Moscato, Falanghina and Greco white varieties. We tasted their succulent Tintilia '17 during this session. The more we taste it, the more we like it: a touch of pepper, red flowers, supple on the palate with a good tannic profile. But their Don Luigi Riserva '15 proves even better. This Montepulciano is modern without becoming a caricature, extractive but not excessive, tight-knit, dense and powerful.

● Molise Rosso Don Luigi Ris. '15	♟♟♟	5
● Molise Tintilia '17	♟♟	3*
○ Molise Falanghina '18	♟♟	2*
● Sangiovese '18	♟♟	2*
● Biferno Rosso Ramitello '15	♟	3
● Molise Aglianico Biorganic '15	♟	3
● Molise Aglianico Biorganic '11	♟♟♟	2*
● Molise Aglianico Contado Ris. '14	♟♟♟	3*
● Molise Aglianico Contado Ris. '10	♟♟♟	3*
● Molise Aglianico Contado Ris. '09	♟♟♟	3*
● Molise Aglianico Contado Ris. '07	♟♟♟	2*
● Molise Don Luigi Ris. '08	♟♟♟	5
● Molise Rosso Don Luigi Ris. '12	♟♟♟	5
● Molise Rosso Don Luigi Ris. '11	♟♟♟	5
● Molise Tintilia '16	♟♟♟	3*
● Molise Tintilia '13	♟♟♟	3*

enimenti Grieco

DA DIFENSOLA
6045 PORTOCANNONE [CB]
L. +39 0875590032
ww.tenimentigrieco.it

ELLAR SALES
RE-BOOKED VISITS
NNUAL PRODUCTION 700,000 bottles
ECTARES UNDER VINE 85.00

ntonio Grieco is an Apulian entrepreneur
ho decided to invest in winegrowing in
earby Molise, in 2013. He bought out the
neyards of what used to be Masseria
occo and began a complete renewal of
e vineyards, buildings, cellar technology
d marketing. He set off an escalation
at has never stopped since. His wide
nge of wines is produced with an ample
t of grape varieties and organized into 7
es, all linked by the same drinkability
d carefree taste. Their Tintilia 200 Metri
one such example: their winemaking
spects the fruity and floral notes of the
riety and preserves its characteristic
icy trait; acidity and pulp increase its
o and pleasantness. Their Triassi also
oves good; this Bordeaux blend of
abernet Sauvignon and Merlot, with a
sh of Aglianico, exhibits a refined
editerranean pace.

Molise Tintilia 200 Metri '18	♟♟ 2*
Molise Rosso I Costali '17	♟♟ 3
Triassi '15	♟♟ 5
Molise Falanghina Passo alle Tremiti '18	♟ 3
Molise Rosato Passo alle Tremiti '18	♟ 3
Biferno Bosco delle Guardie '14	♟♟ 3
Lenda Aglianico '15	♟♟ 5
Molise Rosato Passo alle Tremiti '15	♟♟ 3
Molise Rosso Monterosso I Costali '16	♟♟ 3*
Molise Rosso Passo alle Tremiti '15	♟♟ 3*
Molise Tintilia 200 Metri '17	♟♟ 2*
Molise Tintilia 200 Metri '16	♟♟ 2*
Molise Tintilia 200 Metri '15	♟♟ 2*

Cantine Salvatore

C.DA VIGNE
86049 URURI [CB]
TEL. +39 0874830656
www.cantinesalvatore.it

CELLAR SALES
PRE-BOOKED VISITS
ANNUAL PRODUCTION 80,000 bottles
HECTARES UNDER VINE 20.00
SUSTAINABLE WINERY

Pasquale Salvatore's winery is housed in a
perfectly-renovated old farmhouse,
surrounded by hundred-year-old olive
groves. Following on from his father
Donato, he tends an eighty-hectare estate,
including 20 of vineyards, arable land and
the above-said olive groves. Ururi is located
in Lower Molise, near the border with Puglia
and the Adriatic, whose influence is felt in
the hills at 300 m, where the vineyards are
planted. The wines they presented possess
a modern character and are made using a
clean and precise winemaking style. Rutilia
'16 is an excellent Tintilia: exclusive use of
steel affords aromas of black cherries
and ripe black fruit, a soft attack in the
mouth, tannins to steady the palate, lots of
flavor and a warm Mediterranean finish.
Biberius, a monovarietal Montepulciano,
expresses aromas of blueberry, raspberry,
vegetables, tight-knit tannins and a
fruit-dominated finish. Their IndoVINO
Rosso proves an interesting Montepulciano
with an earthy character.

● Molise Tintilia Rutilia '16	♟♟ 3*
● L'IndoVINO Rosso '16	♟♟ 2*
○ Molise Falanghina Nysias '18	♟♟ 3
● Molise Rosso Biberius '16	♟♟ 2*
⊙ Rosis '18	♟ 2
○ L'IndoVINO Falanghina '15	♟♟ 2*
● L'IndoVINO Rosso '14	♟♟ 2*
● L'IndoVINO Rosso '13	♟♟ 2*
● Molise Rosso Don Donà '13	♟♟ 3
● Molise Rosso Don Donà '11	♟♟ 3
⊙ Rosis '16	♟♟ 2*
● Ti.A.Mo. '14	♟♟ 3

Catabbo

C.DA PETRIERA
86046 SAN MARTINO IN PENSILIS [CB]
TEL. +39 0875604945
www.catabbo.it

CELLAR SALES
ANNUAL PRODUCTION 160,000 bottles
HECTARES UNDER VINE 54.00

● Molise Tintilia Ris, '14	🍷🍷 5
● Molise Tintilia S '16	🍷🍷 4
● Molise Tintilia Linea Classica '16	🍷 3
⊙ Petriera Rosé '18	🍷 3

Claudio Cipressi

C.DA MONTAGNA, 11B
86030 SAN FELICE DEL MOLISE [CB]
TEL. +39 3351244859
www.claudiocipressi.it

CELLAR SALES
PRE-BOOKED VISITS
ACCOMMODATION
ANNUAL PRODUCTION 40,000 bottles
HECTARES UNDER VINE 15.00
VITICULTURE METHOD Certified Organic
SUSTAINABLE WINERY

● Molise Tintilia 66 '12	🍷🍷
● Molise Tintilia Macchiarossa '14	🍷🍷
⊙ Molise Tintilia Rosato Collequinto '18	🍷

Angelo D'Uva

C.DA MONTE ALTINO, 23A
86035 LARINO [CB]
TEL. +39 0874822320
www.cantineduva.com

CELLAR SALES
PRE-BOOKED VISITS
ACCOMMODATION AND RESTAURANT SERVICE
ANNUAL PRODUCTION 70,000 bottles
HECTARES UNDER VINE 20.00
SUSTAINABLE WINERY

● Molise Tintilia Lagena '17	🍷🍷 3
⊙ Biferno Bianco Kantharos '18	🍷 2
⊙ Keres Falanghina '18	🍷 2

Tenute Martarosa

VIA MADONNA GRANDE, 11
86042 CAMPOMARINO [CB]
TEL. +39 087557156
www.tenutemartarosa.com

ANNUAL PRODUCTION 40,000 bottles
HECTARES UNDER VINE 17.00

● Molise Tintilia '16	🍷🍷
⊙ Molise Moscato '18	🍷
● Molise Rosso Antico Podere '17	🍷

Cantina San Zenone

C.DA PIANA DEI PASTINI
86036 MONTENERO DI BISACCIA [CB]
TEL. +39 3477998397
www.cantinasanzenone.it

CELLAR SALES
PRE-BOOKED VISITS
ANNUAL PRODUCTION 150,000 bottles
HECTARES UNDER VINE 300.00
VITICULTURE METHOD Certified Organic

⊙ Clivia Rosato '18	🍷🍷 2*
● Molilse Tintilia '16	🍷🍷 5
⊙ Clivia Falanghina '18	🍷 2
● Molise Cabernet Sauvignon Clivia '16	🍷 2

Terresacre

C.DA MONTEBELLO
86036 MONTENERO DI BISACCIA [CB]
TEL. +39 0875960191
www.terresacre.net

CELLAR SALES
PRE-BOOKED VISITS
ACCOMMODATION AND RESTAURANT SERVI
ANNUAL PRODUCTION 100,000 bottles
HECTARES UNDER VINE 35.00

● Molise Tintilia '18	🍷🍷
● Molise Rosso Neravite '16	🍷🍷
⊙ Molise Falanghina '18	🍷
● Molise Tintilia Selezione '16	🍷

CAMPANIA

What will it take for Campania to take that last, definitive step? It's certainly not a question of quality, or at least it's not only that, because it's already represented by so many outstanding wines (especially whites). And we're talking about evocative wines full of character, personality, flavor. It's that flavor that makes Campania a top destination for those who love great food and products made from the heart. And due to its diverse styles and territories, it has everything it needs to transmit all the region's charm and allure, for the curious and those in search of surprises. And yet this change in rhythm, especially in terms of image, in Italy and abroad, has been slower than thought. We're optimistic though. In terms of production you need the right dose of ambition, the will to improve day after day and to aim high, to bet it all, even while taking risks, with perseverance, on a simply extraordinary territory. Yeah, we'd like to see a bit more courage, projects of greater scope capable of projecting a new vision, to open the region up to the world and even cast doubt on certain cardinal rules of enology (for example the centrality of Aglianico and certain, set ways for approaching it). Moreover, we'd like to see more wineries focused on a certain direction and appellation. It's not obligatory to cover all typologies, maybe sourcing grapes to do so. The idea is to probe the longevity of Campania's great wines, of its Fiano di Avellino, its Greco di Tufo, its surprising Falanghinas and Taurasis capable of dazzling even 40 years after vintage. Finally, we'd like to see its enology conversing more directly with its gastronomy, as part of a tourism and hospitality initiative that's still, unfortunately, unable to get past its initial stages. In the meantime, we'll let the wines do the talking: some 23 Tre Bicchieri were awarded in this edition. Among the new entries we point out an absolute first for Bosco De' Medici, a winery operating on the slopes of Vesuvio, with an aromatically sophisticated and original Pompeii Bianco made with Caprettone grapes. From there, continuing with whites, we go from the smoky, thrilling and complex Fiano di Avellino VentitréFilari to the marine profile of Abbazia di Crapolla's Sireo, and Vallisassoli's 33/33/33, with its intense sensations of peat and pepper. When it comes to the reds, we make note of the carefree scents of rose and pomegranate offered by Giuseppe Apicella's Piedirosso and the potent, vibrant rhythm of Regina Viarum's Falerno Primitivo.

Abbazia di Crapolla

loc. Avigliano
via San Filippo, 2
80069 Vico Equense [NA]
Tel. +39 3383517280
www.abbaziadicrapolla.it

ANNUAL PRODUCTION 12,000 bottles
HECTARES UNDER VINE 2.00

Fulvio Alifano's vineyards in Vico Equense are situated in a veritable winemaking paradise. The winery is located in the former home of Cistercian monks, a place of extreme scenic beauty. Planted in 2007, the vineyards are on volcanic soils at elevations of 300 meters. Fiano, Falanghina, Sabato, Merlot and Pinot Nero provide the raw material for wines that are extremely fragrant and light, both supple and elegant. As with their Sireo '17, a blend of Fiano and Falangina that once again made a splash in our finals. It's fresh and pleasantly sapid, playing on sea breeze and Mediterranean sensations enriched by floral and fruity notes. It's a complex white, full on the palate, well-supported by acidity and creamy, delicate mouthfeel. Their Sabato, made with Sabato and Montepulciano grapes, features a juicy, racy development, making for a more accessible version with respect to the 2016 presented last year. The Nireo, made with Pinot Nero, is also excellent, exhibiting a lovely, Mediterranean character.

○ Sireo Bianco '17	🍷🍷 5
● Nireo '17	🍷🍷 5
○ Poizzo '18	🍷🍷 5
● Sabato	🍷🍷 5
● Noir '12	🍷🍷 5
● Pinot Nero '11	🍷🍷 5
● Sabato '17	🍷🍷 5
● Sabato '15	🍷🍷 5
● Sabato '12	🍷🍷 5
○ Sireo '15	🍷🍷 5
○ Sireo Bianco '14	🍷🍷 5
○ Sireo Bianco '13	🍷🍷 5
○ Sireo Bianco '11	🍷🍷 5
● Sireo Rosso '11	🍷🍷 5

Agnanum

via Vicinale Abbandonata agli Astroni, 3
80125 Napoli
Tel. +39 3385315272
www.agnanum.it

CELLAR SALES
PRE-BOOKED VISITS
ANNUAL PRODUCTION 25,000 bottles
HECTARES UNDER VINE 7.50

Raffaele Moccia has the keys to a unique enological area at the edge of Naples within the Natural Park of Vesuvius. The ungrafted vineyards inherited from his grandfather Gennaro are on the steep, sandy slopes of the hill of the Astroni on soils rich in phosphorus, magnesium and potassium. With a winemaker's stubbornness he has been able to pull quality from varieties such as Piedirosso and Falanghina on inaccessible terraces that require manual harvesting and have very low yields. The resulting wines show artisanal workmanship and clearly express the terroir. Our vigneron of the 'Phlegrean Fields' once again takes home Tre Bicchieri, proving capable of delivering a masterful version in an area still little known. His Campi Flegrei Falanghina '18 volcanic in every which way: flinty hints rise up on the nose along with smoky notes and Mediterranean scrub. On the palate it's creamy, yet sapid and deep. Meaty fruit and a poised tannic weave characterize the Pér 'è Palumm '18.

○ Campi Flegrei Falanghina '18	🍷🍷🍷
○ Campi Flegrei Falanghina	
V. delle Volpi '16	🍷🍷
● Campi Flegrei Pér 'e Palumm '18	🍷🍷
● Campi Flegrei Piedirosso '16	🍷🍷🍷
● Campi Flegrei Piedirosso '15	🍷🍷🍷
○ Campi Flegrei Falanghina '17	🍷🍷
○ Campi Flegrei Falanghina	
V. del Pino '15	🍷🍷
○ Campi Flegrei Falanghina	
V. del Pino '15	🍷🍷
○ Campi Flegrei Falanghina	
V. del Pino '14	🍷🍷
● Campi Flegrei Pér 'e Palumm '17	🍷🍷
● Campi Flegrei Piedirosso	
V. delle Volpi '15	🍷🍷
● Campi Flegrei Piedirosso	
V. delle Volpi '14	🍷🍷

Alois

C. Audelino
Ragazzano
040 Pontelatone [CE]
. +39 0823876710
www.vinialois.it

CELLAR SALES
PRE-BOOKED VISITS
ANNUAL PRODUCTION 300,000 bottles
HECTARES UNDER VINE 30.00
SUSTAINABLE WINERY

he Alois name brings to mind the fine
ks of San Leucio and the cultivation of
asavecchia, a red variety from Caserta
at risked disappearing after years of
eglect. Michele and Massimo, with
armine Valentino's help, have enriched
onti Caiatini's winemaking heritage by
nifying nine different grapes as
ono-varietals. The 30 hectares of
neyards can be found in some of the
ost suitable areas like Audalino, Morrone
ella Monica and Cesone in Pontelatone.
addition to production in Caserta, the
onna Paolina line comes from Irpinia.
eir Caiatì is always a sure bet. Made
th Pallagrello Bianco cultivated in
orrone della Monica, at the foot of Mt.
ento, it offers up citrusy notes and hints
Mediterranean scrub. On the palate it's
ucky and sapid, with a fresh, pleasant
ish. The Casavecchia di Pontelatone
ebulanum Riserva '13 is intensely
oncentrated, but closes generous in fruit
d sweet spices.

Caiatì Pallagrello Bianco '17	♔♔♔ 4*
Campole '17	♔♔ 3
Casavecchia di Pontelatone Trebulanum Ris. '13	♔♔ 5
Caulino '18	♔♔ 3
Cunto Pallagrello Nero '16	♔♔ 4
Ponte Pellegrino Aglianico '18	♔♔ 5
Ponte Pellegrino Falanghina '18	♔♔ 3
Fiano di Avellino Donna Paolina '18	♔ 4
Greco di Tufo Donna Paolina '18	♔ 3
Taurasi Donna Paolina '14	♔ 5
Caiatì Pallagrello Bianco '16	♔♔♔ 4*
Caiatì Pallagrello Bianco '15	♔♔♔ 3*
Caiatì Pallagrello Bianco '14	♔♔♔ 3*
Caiatì Pallagrello Bianco '13	♔♔♔ 2*

Giuseppe Apicella

Fraz. Capitignano
via Castello Santa Maria, 1
84010 Tramonti [SA]
Tel. +39 089876075
www.giuseppeapicella.it

CELLAR SALES
PRE-BOOKED VISITS
ANNUAL PRODUCTION 60,000 bottles
HECTARES UNDER VINE 7.00
VITICULTURE METHOD Certified Organic

Giuseppe Apicella's has one the oldest
ungrafted vineyards in the Amalfi Coast,
which feels the effects of both the
mountainous terrain and the influence of
the sea. The arbor-trained vineyards are in
Tramonti, in the Lattari mountains on
tuffaceous terraces and feature native,
local varieties like Tintore, Piedirosso,
Ginestra, Pepella, Falanghina and
Biancazita. Giuseppe, a true pioneer and
promoter of Tramonti wines, was among
the first to bet on the area's enormous
potential and to bottle his wines. A
Mediterranean streak accompanied by
sensations of figs, dates and orange peel
characterize their Costa d'Amalfi Tramonti
Bianco '18. It's a blend of Falangina and
Biancolella whose palate proves racy and
complex, finishing with a bang on a saline
note. Their Piedirosso '18 proves
enchanting in its airy accents of pepper
and fried peppers — on the palate it's
light, irresistible. A couple of minute in the
fridge bring out its pleasantness.

○ Costa d'Amalfi Tramonti Bianco '18	♔♔ 3*
● Costa d'Amalfi Tramonti Rosso a' Scippata Ris. '15	♔♔ 5
● Piedirosso '18	♔♔ 2*
○ Costa d'Amalfi Tramonti Bianco Colle Santa Marina '17	♔ 2
○ Costa d'Amalfi Tramonti Bianco '17	♕♔ 3
○ Costa d'Amalfi Tramonti Bianco Colle Santa Marina '15	♕♔ 2*
☉ Costa d'Amalfi Tramonti Rosato '16	♕♔ 3
● Costa d'Amalfi Tramonti Rosso a' Scippata Ris. '12	♕♔ 5
● Piedirosso '17	♕♔ 2*
● Piedirosso '16	♕♔ 2*

Cantine Astroni

VIA SARTANIA, 48
80126 NAPOLI
TEL. +39 0815884182
www.cantineastroni.com

CELLAR SALES
PRE-BOOKED VISITS
RESTAURANT SERVICE
ANNUAL PRODUCTION 330,000 bottles
HECTARES UNDER VINE 25.00
VITICULTURE METHOD Certified Organic
SUSTAINABLE WINERY

Astroni is one of the Phlegraean Fields area's most heavily engineered wineries due to the terracing of its 25-hectare vineyard park clinging to the external slopes of the Astroni crater. The powerful, rugged landscape, composed of layers of small volcanic rock and ash, makes its presence known in authentic wines such as the crus Vigna Astroni and Vigna Camaldoli. There are two additional two plots called Villa Imperatrice and Vigna Iossa. Gerardo Vernazzaro drives the work with the support of his wife Emanuela Russo and cousin Vincenzo. Their Campi Flegrei Piedirosso Tenuta Camaldoli Riserva '16, made with grapes cultivated in sandy, tuffaceous terrain, stood out during our tastings. It pours a garnet red, the prelude to vibrant, complex and multifaceted notes of quinine and pencil lead. Its fruit is meaty, interwoven with highly charming smoky sensations, only to close complex and assertive. Their 2018 Piedrosso Colle Rotondella and Falanghina Colle Imperatrice both represent excellent value for the money.

● Campi Flegrei Piedirosso Tenuta Camaldoli Ris. '16	♔♔ 3*
○ Campi Flegrei Falanghina Colle Imperatrice '18	♔♔ 2*
○ Campi Flegrei Falanghina V. Astroni '17	♔♔ 3
● Campi Flegrei Piedirosso Colle Rotondella '18	♔♔ 3
○ Strione '15	♔♔ 4
○ Campi Flegrei Falanghina V. Astroni '15	♔♔♔ 3*
○ Campi Flegrei Falanghina Colle Imperatrice '15	♔♔ 2*
● Campi Flegrei Piedirosso Colle Rotondella '17	♔♔ 3
● Campi Flegrei Piedirosso Colle Rotondella '16	♔♔ 3
● Campi Flegrei Piedirosso Colle Rotondella '15	♔♔ 3*

Bambinuto

VIA CERRO
83030 SANTA PAOLINA [AV]
TEL. +39 0825964634
www.cantinabambinuto.com

PRE-BOOKED VISITS
ANNUAL PRODUCTION 25,000 bottles
HECTARES UNDER VINE 6.00

This winery's story is similar to that of many small businesses in Irpinia. Bambinuto conferred grapes to more hilghly structured estates for years, until deciding to vinify for itself. It was Marilena Aufiero's intuition that convinced her parents Raffaele and Anna to make their own Greco wines. Production began in 2006 and now the winery owns six hectares of vineyards, producing 23000 bottles per year. The Greco di Tufo and Greco di Tufo Picoli come from small town in the municipality of Santa Paolina: the former from Paoloni at an elevation of 400 meters, and the latter from Picoli, at 500 meters, on clayey-calcareous soils. The 2017 version of their Greco di Tufo Picoli led their selection during our tastings. It's summery Greco in every which way, featuring smoky notes, fragrances of medlar and a glyceric palate softened by a lovely salinity, making for a lively drink. The Greco di Tufo '17 is less complex, but still maintains a pleasant palate.

○ Greco di Tufo Picoli '17	♔♔
○ Greco di Tufo '17	♔
○ Greco di Tufo '15	♔♔
○ Greco di Tufo '14	♔♔
○ Greco di Tufo '13	♔♔
○ Greco di Tufo '12	♔♔
○ Greco di Tufo Picoli '16	♔♔
○ Greco di Tufo Picoli '15	♔♔
○ Greco di Tufo Picoli '13	♔♔
○ Greco di Tufo Picoli '11	♔♔
○ Greco di Tufo Picoli '10	♔♔
○ Irpinia Falanghina Insania '15	♔♔
● Taurasi '07	♔♔

osco de' Medici

Antonio Segni, 43
045 Pompei [NA]
+39 3382828234
w.boscodemedici.com

NNUAL PRODUCTION 15,000 bottles
CTARES UNDER VINE 8.00

e winery's vineyards are on the southern
rt of Vesuvius and extend more than
ht hectares, in the heart of the
chaeological excavations of Pompeii.
re the ancient story of Roman wine
ertwines with that of the Florentine
edici dynasty. In 1567, when the area
as still part of the Kingdom of Naples,
igi de' Medici entrusted his beloved
andson Giuseppe with the task of
proving the quality of family's wines.
day that long tradition has been resumed
d fully showcased in a very original and
pressive range. For the first time the
oducer takes home Tre Bicchieri. It's all
anks to their Pompeii '18, a monovarietal
prettone white rich in personality. On the
se it exhibits mineral sensations
pported by aromas of wheat and
nonds. Complex and stylish, on the
late it's not without its force and flesh, all
t to a slow, extremely long pace. Their
essel 19.2 '17, a quality orange, is
rtainly not lacking in character.

Pompeii Bianco '18	♟♟♟ 3*
Dressel 19.2 '17	♟♟ 3
Lacryma Christi del Vesuvio Bianco Lavaflava '18	♟♟ 3
Pompeii Rosso '18	♟♟ 3
Lacryma Christi del Vesuvio Rosso Lavarubra '15	♀♀ 3
Pompeii Bianco '15	♀♀ 3*

Antonio Caggiano

c.da Sala
83030 Taurasi [AV]
Tel. +39 082774723
www.cantinecaggiano.it

CELLAR SALES
PRE-BOOKED VISITS
RESTAURANT SERVICE
ANNUAL PRODUCTION 165,000 bottles
HECTARES UNDER VINE 30.00

Many winemakers have helped pen the
story of Taurasi in Irpinia, and Antonio
Caggiano is one of its principal writers. A
true guardian of Irpinia's winemaking
tradition, in the 1990s he set his passion
for photography and travel aside and
began cultivating the Salae Domini family's
old vineyards. The cellar, with arches and
vaulted ceilings made of local stone,
houses barrels of different sizes, bottles
and other objects from local wine culture.
Outstanding reds like Taurasi Macchia dei
Goti, Salae Domini and Taurì age here. His
son Giuseppe (aka 'Pino') plays a
fundamental role in managing the winery.
Their historic Vigna Macchia dei Goti
proves that it's one of the Taurasi's most
potent and expressive crus. It's a red
redolent of quinine, black berries,
impenetrable in color. On the palate it
exhibits juice and excellent flesh, along
with tones of black olive and pencil lead,
finishing assertive and highly flavorful. The
Taurì feature a classic, highly pleasant
gustatory development.

● Taurasi V. Macchia dei Goti Ris. '15	♟♟♟ 6
● Irpinia Aglianico Taurì '18	♟♟ 2*
○ Mel	♟♟ 5
○ Fiano di Avellino Béchar '18	♟ 3
○ Greco di Tufo Devon '18	♟ 3
○ Fiano di Avellino Béchar '13	♀♀♀ 3*
● Taurasi V. Macchia dei Goti '14	♀♀♀ 6
● Taurasi V. Macchia dei Goti '08	♀♀♀ 5
● Taurasi V. Macchia dei Goti '04	♀♀♀ 5
● Taurasi V. Macchia dei Goti '99	♀♀♀ 5
○ Fiano di Avellino Béchar '17	♀♀ 3
○ Fiano di Avellino Béchar '16	♀♀ 3
○ Greco di Tufo Devon '16	♀♀ 3
● Irpinia Aglianico Taurì '17	♀♀ 2*
● Irpinia Aglianico Taurì '15	♀♀ 3*

Cantine dell'Angelo

VIA SANTA LUCIA, 32
83010 TUFO [AV]
TEL. +39 3384512965
www.cantinedellangelo.com

CELLAR SALES
PRE-BOOKED VISITS
ANNUAL PRODUCTION 18,000 bottles
HECTARES UNDER VINE 5.00

Angelo Muto and wife Maria Nuzzolo created a very original Greco di Tufo. The vineyards, over former sulfur mines in Tufo, give rise to vines with unique characteristics and wines rich in personality. The winery was founded in 1970 by Angelo Nuzzolo, who dedicated himself to enhancing the vineyard. His enthusiam passed to his nephew Angelo who since 2006 has been cultivating five hectares and producing two wines that are, to say the least, quite intriguing. Aromatically, the Greco di Tufo Torrefavale '17 is characterized by notes of citrus, aromatic herbs and almond. On the palate it's mature, deep and sapid. The Miniere '17 stands out for its varietal and territorial characteristics. Notes of sulfur give way to thyme, citrus and cereal sensations, making for a gratifying, savory and mineral drink. It's an impressive version, whose open fruit nicely reflects the vintage.

○ Greco di Tufo Miniere '17	♟♟ 4
○ Greco di Tufo Torrefavale '17	♟♟ 5
○ Greco di Tufo '09	♟♟♟ 3*
○ Greco di Tufo Miniere '16	♟♟♟ 4*
○ Greco di Tufo '14	♟♟ 3
○ Greco di Tufo '13	♟♟ 3
○ Greco di Tufo '11	♟♟ 3
○ Greco di Tufo '10	♟♟ 3
○ Greco di Tufo Torrefavale '16	♟♟ 5
○ Greco di Tufo Torrefavale '15	♟♟ 3
○ Greco di Tufo Torrefavale '14	♟♟ 3
○ Greco di Tufo Torrefavale '13	♟♟ 3*

Casa Setaro

VIA BOSCO DEL MONACO, 34
80040 TRECASE [NA]
TEL. +39 0818628956
www.casasetaro.it

CELLAR SALES
PRE-BOOKED VISITS
RESTAURANT SERVICE
ANNUAL PRODUCTION 75,000 bottles
HECTARES UNDER VINE 12.00
VITICULTURE METHOD Certified Organic
SUSTAINABLE WINERY

Massimo and Mariarosaria Setaro lead the small Trecase winery at the foot of Vesuvi with great love and dedication. The vineyards, which feature old, ungrafted vines, are located within the Parco Nazionale di Vesuvio, split between two distinct areas: Alto Torrione, located at an elevation of 350 meters, has a Guyot-trained system and soil rich in sand and lapilli; Bosco del Monaco, further downstream, has old vineyards trained on traditional Vesuvian arbors. Massimo's work with Caprettone, which he makes in both still and sparkling versions, is truly praiseworthy. The Pietrafumante Brut is a monovarietal Caprettone made with grapes cultivated in Alto Torrione. Floral, delicately salty and citrusy notes proceed quietly up out of the glass, accompanied sulfurous sensations. On the palate it reveals a nice freshness supported by a pleasant, flavorful development.

● Lacryma Christi del Vesuvio Rosso Don Vincenzo Ris. '14	♟♟
○ Pietrafumante Brut '16	♟♟
● Vesuvio Piedirosso Fuocoallegro '17	♟♟
● Lacryma Christi del Vesuvio Rosso Munazei '18	♟
○ Vesuvio Bianco Aryete '17	♟
○ Campanelle '17	♟♟
○ Caprettone Brut '12	♟♟
○ Caprettone Brut M. Cl. '14	♟♟
○ Caprettone Brut M. Cl. '13	♟♟
○ Caprettone Brut M. Cl. '13	♟♟
○ Falanghina Campanelle '16	♟♟
○ Falanghina Campanelle '16	♟♟
● Lacryma Christi del Vesuvio Rosso Don Vincenzo '14	♟♟

asebianche

CASE BIANCHE, 8
)76 TORCHIARA [SA]
. +39 0974843244
w.casebianche.eu

LLAR SALES
E-BOOKED VISITS
NUAL PRODUCTION 35,000 bottles
CTARES UNDER VINE 5.50
TICULTURE METHOD Certified Organic
STAINABLE WINERY

tty Iurio and Pasquale Amitrano's
erpretations of wines are among the
ost original around for their power,
pressiveness and extreme vibrance.
chitects by profession, in 2000 they
gan to take care of the family vineyards
Torchiara in Cilento. Soils rich in rocks
d clay located between Monte Stella,
quasanta Stream and the splendid
ento sea deliver organically vinified
lianico, Barbera, Piedirosso, Fiano,
ebbiano and Malvasia. Fiano and
lianico dominate the company's
oduction, offering wines such as La
atta, Il Fric and Pashkà, a nice trio of
nes refermented in the bottle. The
ic '18 features crisp aromas of raspberry
d blood orange. It's a monovarietal
glianico, delectable in its fresh, savory
mbres, closing just a bit less expansive
an usual. The Paskà '18 is pleasantly
stic with hints of geranium, blueberry and
ackberry. On the palate it proves fresh
d alluring in its tasty tannic stroke.

Tenuta Cavalier Pepe

VIA SANTA VARA
83050 SANT'ANGELO ALL'ESCA [AV]
TEL. +39 082773766
www.tenutapepe.it

CELLAR SALES
PRE-BOOKED VISITS
ACCOMMODATION AND RESTAURANT SERVICE
ANNUAL PRODUCTION 450,000 bottles
HECTARES UNDER VINE 60.00
SUSTAINABLE WINERY

The Sant'Angelo all'Esca winery was
founded by Angelo Pepe following his
famous activity as a restauranteur in
Belgium. Returning to Italy he was made a
Cavaliere della Repubblica (Knight of the
Republic) in recognition of his work
promoting the Italy's products. The 60
hectares of vineyards are spread among
Sant'Angelo all'Esca, Montefusco, Torrioni
and Luogosano, all villages of the
seventeen municipalities included in the
Taurasi appellation. Since 2005, the estate
has been managed by Milena Pepe, who,
by virtue of her studies and experience
abroad, is the real driving force behind the
enological activity. Aglianico continues to
deliver their best enological expressions, in
particular when it comes to their Taurasi La
Loggia del Cavaliere. The tight-woven, ruby
red Riserva '13, is adorned with jammy
nuances and balsamic hints. On the palate
it's spicy hot and assertive, closing austere
on pronounced, tightly wound tannins.

Cilento Rosso Dellemore '17	🍷🍷 3
Il Fric '18	🍷🍷 4
Pashkà '18	🍷🍷 4
Iscadoro '17	🍷 4
La Matta Dosaggio Zero '18	🍷 4
Il Fric '16	🍷🍷🍷 3*
Pashka' '17	🍷🍷🍷 4*
Cilento Rosso Dellemore '16	🍷🍷 3
Cilento Rosso Dellemore '15	🍷🍷 3
Il Fric '17	🍷🍷 4
Il Fric '15	🍷🍷 3
La Matta Dosaggio Zero '16	🍷🍷 3
Pashkà '16	🍷🍷 3

○ Fiano di Avellino Brancato '17	🍷🍷 5
○ Greco di Tufo Nestor '18	🍷🍷 5
● Taurasi La Loggia del Cavaliere Ris. '13	🍷🍷 8
● Irpinia Campi Taurisini Santo Stefano '14	🍷 3
○ Irpinia Coda di Volpe Bianco di Bellona '18	🍷 3
○ Irpinia Falanghina Santa Vara '18	🍷 5
● Taurasi Opera Mia '14	🍷 8
○ Fiano di Avellino Brancato '16	🍷🍷 3
○ Fiano di Avellino Refiano '16	🍷🍷 3
○ Greco di Tufo Grancare '15	🍷🍷 5
○ Greco di Tufo Grancare Sel. '16	🍷🍷 7
○ Greco di Tufo Nestor '17	🍷🍷 5
● Taurasi Opera Mia '13	🍷🍷 8
● Taurasi Opera Mia '12	🍷🍷 5

★Colli di Lapio

VIA ARIANIELLO, 47
83030 LAPIO [AV]
TEL. +39 0825982184
www.collidilapio.it

CELLAR SALES
PRE-BOOKED VISITS
ANNUAL PRODUCTION 60,000 bottles
HECTARES UNDER VINE 8.00

Clelia Romano grew up in the Lapio vineyards that her father Pasquale cultivated at the beginning of the twentieth century. A reserved woman, the undisputed 'Lady Fiano' takes care of the vineyards in Arianiello, a small village in the municipality of Lapio, about 600 meters above sea level. The microclimate, altitude and continuous temperature swings assure wines of a mountain character, with extraordinary depth and brilliance made possible by sapidity and acidic vigor. Fiano di Avellino and Greco di Tufo are aged in steel vats, while Taurasi, made with grapes from Venticano, are aged in oak barrels. The Fiano di Avellino '18 once again shines, exhibiting an extraordinary depth and sapid raciness. Lovely notes of fresh fruit, wild flowers and whiffs of aniseed make for a complex organoleptic profile. On the palate it's potent and rich, compelling in its drinkability and rhythm.

○ Fiano di Avellino '18	♟♟♟ 4*
○ Greco di Tufo Alèxandros '18	♟♟ 3
● Irpinia Campi Taurasini Donna Chiara '16	♟ 3
○ Fiano di Avellino '16	♟♟♟ 4*
○ Fiano di Avellino '15	♟♟♟ 4*
○ Fiano di Avellino '14	♟♟♟ 4*
○ Fiano di Avellino '13	♟♟♟ 4*
○ Fiano di Avellino '10	♟♟♟ 4
○ Fiano di Avellino '09	♟♟♟ 4
○ Fiano di Avellino '08	♟♟♟ 4*
○ Fiano di Avellino '07	♟♟♟ 4
○ Fiano di Avellino '05	♟♟♟ 4
○ Fiano di Avellino '04	♟♟♟ 4
○ Fiano di Avellino '17	♟♟ 4

Contrade di Taurasi

VIA MUNICIPIO, 41
83030 TAURASI [AV]
TEL. +39 082774483
www.cantinelonardo.it

CELLAR SALES
PRE-BOOKED VISITS
ANNUAL PRODUCTION 18,000 bottles
HECTARES UNDER VINE 5.00
VITICULTURE METHOD Certified Organic

For years, Aglianico has been the Lonardo family's undisputed star. The story begins in 1998 when Antonella Lonardo and her husband Flavio Castaldo abandoned their professions to start making wine in Taurasi. The vineyards are located on soil that are partly volcanic and partly clayey-calcareous around Taurasi, Bonito and Mirabella Eclano. They produce red wines with a powerful aromatic expression and an extreme varietal imprint. The five hectares of organically conducted vineyards give birth to two red Taurasi and the winery's only white, Grecomusc'. While waiting until next year to try their Taurasi crus, Coste and Vigne d'Alto, we delved into their juicy and extremely elegant Grecomusc' '17. It's a white that slowly reveals its aromatic profile. On the nose it enters on fragrances of helichrysum, melon, butter and wheat. In the mouth it unfolds airy, moved along by a highly persistent palate supported by lively acidity.

○ Grecomusc' '17	♟♟
● Irpinia Aglianico '16	♟♟
● Taurasi '15	♟♟
● Taurasi Ris. '11	♟
○ Grecomusc' '15	♟♟♟
○ Grecomusc' '12	♟♟♟
○ Grecomusc' '10	♟♟♟
● Taurasi '10	♟♟♟
● Taurasi '04	♟♟♟
● Taurasi Coste '11	♟♟♟
● Taurasi Coste '08	♟♟♟
● Taurasi Vigne d'Alto '12	♟♟♟
○ Grecomusc' '16	♟♟
● Taurasi Coste '12	♟♟

Marisa Cuomo

G. B. Lama, 16/18
84010 Furore [SA]
Tel. +39 089830348
www.marisacuomo.com

CELLAR SALES
PRE-BOOKED VISITS
RESTAURANT SERVICE
ANNUAL PRODUCTION 109,000 bottles
HECTARES UNDER VINE 18.00

Marisa Cuomo has succeeded in promoting
the Amalfi Coast's wines around the world
by producing a range strongly flavored by
Mediterranean lands and the sea. The
Furore vineyards feature soils rich in
limestone rocks held up by the dry stone
walls typical of the area. In 1980, as a
wedding gift, Marisa's husband Andrea
Ferraioli gave her the vineyards he had
inherited from his father. Today, together
with Andrea and children Dora and
Raffaele, they care for eighteen hectares
with varieties such as Ripoli, Fenile,
Ginestra, Piedirosso and Sciascinoso. Their
artisanal production includes whites vinified
in steel, except for the Fiorduva, and reds,
both entry-level and reserve versions, aged
in oak barrels. Their Costa d'Amalfi
Fiorduva '18 once again took home Tre
Bicchieri. It's a white that encapsulates the
essence of the sea, unleashing nuances of
white damson, Mediterranean scrub, sweet
and spicy sensations. Opulent and flavorful,
it delivers adequate acidity, conferring
harmony and force to a lengthy finish.

○ Costa d'Amalfi Furore Bianco Fiorduva '18	🍷🍷🍷 7
● Costa d'Amalfi Furore Rosso Ris. '16	🍷🍷 6
○ Costa d'Amalfi Furore Bianco '18	🍷🍷 4
● Costa d'Amalfi Furore Rosso '18	🍷🍷 3
○ Costa d'Amalfi Rosato '18	🍷🍷 4
● Costa d'Amalfi Ravello Rosso Ris. '16	🍷 5
○ Costa d'Amalfi Fiorduva '08	🍷🍷🍷 6
○ Costa d'Amalfi Furore Bianco '15	🍷🍷🍷 4*
○ Costa d'Amalfi Furore Bianco '10	🍷🍷🍷 4
○ Costa d'Amalfi Furore Bianco Fiorduva '17	🍷🍷🍷 7
○ Costa d'Amalfi Furore Bianco Fiorduva '16	🍷🍷🍷 7
○ Costa d'Amalfi Furore Bianco Fiorduva '14	🍷🍷🍷 7
○ Costa d'Amalfi Furore Bianco Fiorduva '10	🍷🍷🍷 6

D'Ambra Vini d'Ischia

Fraz. Panza
via Mario D'Ambra, 16
80077 Forio [NA]
Tel. +39 081907210
www.dambravini.com

CELLAR SALES
PRE-BOOKED VISITS
ANNUAL PRODUCTION 450,000 bottles
HECTARES UNDER VINE 14.00

This flagship winery on Ischia, founded in
1888 by Francesco d'Ambra, is now run
by Andrea and daughters Marina and Sara.
They continue a unique and ancient
heritage. The island was inhabited by the
Mycenaeans who brought grapes with
them, and in the nineteenth century Ischia
was one of the most densely-planted areas
in the Mediterranean, supplying the main
markets with grapes and wine. Traditional
varieties, such as Biancolella, Forastera,
Piedirosso and Guarnaccia, coexist with
other varieties from Campania, such as
Fiano and Aglianico. The family process its
grapes on the slopes of the extinct
Epomeo volcano. Tenuta Frassitelli, made
entirely with Biancolella grapes from their
Pietra Martone and Tifeo vineyards,
embodies the sea. On the nose it offers up
multifaceted hints of yellow-fleshed fruit,
broom and fresh herbs. It's elegant and
deep, bringing together softness and
sapidity. The Biancolella '18 is vibrant in its
citrusy tones.

○ Ischia Biancolella Tenuta Frassitelli '18	🍷🍷 5
○ Ischia Biancolella '18	🍷🍷 4
○ Ischia Bianco '18	🍷 3
○ Ischia Forastera '18	🍷 4
● Ischia Per' 'e Palummo '18	🍷 4
○ Ischia Biancolella Tenuta Frassitelli '12	🍷🍷🍷 3*
○ Ischia Biancolella Tenuta Frassitelli '90	🍷🍷🍷 3*
○ Ischia Bianco '16	🍷🍷 2*
○ Ischia Biancolella '17	🍷🍷 4
○ Ischia Biancolella '16	🍷🍷 3
○ Ischia Biancolella Tenuta Frassitelli '17	🍷🍷 5
○ Ischia Biancolella Tenuta Frassitelli '16	🍷🍷 4
○ Ischia Forastera '17	🍷🍷 4
○ Ischia Forastera '16	🍷🍷 3

Cantine Di Marzo

VIA GAETANO DI MARZO, 2
83010 TUFO [AV]
TEL. +39 0825998022
www.cantinedimarzo.it

CELLAR SALES
PRE-BOOKED VISITS
ANNUAL PRODUCTION 150,000 bottles
HECTARES UNDER VINE 23.00

Di Marzo has more than 370 years of enological history. In 1647, Scipione Di Marzo moved from Nola to Tufo to escape the plague and here he started producing wine. In 2009, the estate passed to Filippo Somma and children Ferrante and Maria Giovanna who renovated it and reorganized the picturesque seventeenth-century tuffstone cellars. The Greco di Tufo vineyards are in Santa Lucia and San Paolo di Tufo with some plots in Santa Paolina. The five versions of Greco, including a Metodo Classico, are all worked and aged in steel. Di Marzo's wines put in a nice performance, one characterized by a lively minerality. The Greco di Tufo '18 stands out for its citrusy and sulfurous impressions, in keeping with the territory. The Ortale '18 exhibits a smoky streak and malty fragrances, coming through full and tasty on the palate. Hints of flint and a mineral, broad profile characterize their Laure '17, a wine made with grapes from a Greco cru situated in the district of San Paolo.

○ Greco di Tufo '18	♛♛	2*
○ Greco di Tufo V. Laure '17	♛♛	3
○ Greco di Tufo V. Ortale '17	♛♛	3
○ Greco di Tufo '16	♛♛♛	2*
○ Fiano di Avellino Donatus '13	♛♛	3*
○ Greco di Tufo '15	♛♛	2*
○ Greco di Tufo Colle Serrone '16	♛♛	3*
○ Greco di Tufo Somnium Scipionis '13	♛♛	5
○ Greco di Tufo Somnium Scipionis '12	♛♛	5
○ Greco di Tufo V. Laure '16	♛♛	3*
○ Greco di Tufo V. Ortale '16	♛♛	3*

Di Meo

C.DA COCCOVONI, 1
83050 SALZA IRPINA [AV]
TEL. +39 0825981419
www.dimeo.it

CELLAR SALES
PRE-BOOKED VISITS
RESTAURANT SERVICE
ANNUAL PRODUCTION 380,000 bottles
HECTARES UNDER VINE 30.00
SUSTAINABLE WINERY

In 1980 the Di Meo siblings took over the parents' historic Salza Irpina estate and in 1986 they planted it with main appellations' local cultivars. It was a heady time for Erminia, Generoso and Roberto, who soon became recognized for the quality of their wines. The lovely eighteenth-century manor house, arising from the earlier hunting lodge of the Caracciolo family, the Princes of Avellino, surrounded by Fiano vineyards at an elevation of 550 meters on clay and limestone soils. Vineyards of Greco di Tufo are in Santa Paolina and Tufo, while the Taurasi are in Montemarano. It's Roberto (the family's winemaker) who deserves credit for betting on the longevity of Irpinia's whites, releasing them as much as 10-15 years after vintage. Black cherry jam and balsamic, spicy whiffs characterize their Aglianico A '16. On the palate it's soft with creamy, assertive tannins, closing sapid and fresh. We'll have to wait to try their Fiano di Avellino F '18 (it's still aging in the cellar).

● Aglianico A '16	♛♛	
○ Fiano di Avellino F '18	♛♛	
○ Greco di Tufo G '18	♛♛	
○ Falanghina S '18	♛	
○ Fiano di Avellino Alessandra '12	♛♛♛	
● Taurasi Ris. '06	♛♛♛	5
○ Coda di Volpe C '17	♛♛	2
○ Coda di Volpe C '16	♛♛	2
○ Fiano di Avellino F '15	♛♛	3
○ Greco di Tufo G '17	♛♛	3
○ Greco di Tufo G '07	♛♛	3
○ Greco di Tufo Vittoria '07	♛♛	4
● Taurasi Sel. Hamilton Ris. '09	♛♛	7
● Taurasi Sel. Hamilton Ris. '08	♛♛	7
● Taurasi V. Olmo Ris. '10	♛♛	5

onnachiara

. Pietracupa
Stazione
030 Montefalcione [AV]
. +39 0825977135
w.donnachiara.com

CELLAR SALES
PRE-BOOKED VISITS
ACCOMMODATION
ANNUAL PRODUCTION 200,000 bottles
HECTARES UNDER VINE 27.00

nnachiara is run by the hardworking
ria Petitto. Previously a lawyer, Ilaria took
er her father Umberto's winery,
structured it and modernized it with
chnological and innovative machinery.
e winery is named after her
andmother Chiara Mazzoleni, a
blewoman from Campania who as part
her dowery received the Torre Le
celle estate, planted with Aglianico.
pported by the enological advice of
ccardo Cotarella, Ilaria offers a wide
nge of Irpinia wines coming from grapes
the 27 hectares of estate property as
ll as with some grapes from targeted
rchases. The Fiano di Avellino Empatia
s all the makings of a great wine. The
18 is aromatically delicate and subtle,
oving from white peach to aniseed and
smine. On the palate it's rich in pulp and
eamy, exhibiting structure, and closing
ng and sapid.

Fiano di Avellino Empatia '18	♔♔♔ 4*
Aglianico '18	♔♔ 3
Falanghina Resilienza '17	♔♔ 2*
rpinia Aglianico '17	♔♔ 3
Greco di Tufo Aletheia '17	♔ 3
Taurasi '15	♔ 5
Aglianico '16	♔♔♔ 3*
Greco di Tufo '16	♔♔♔ 3*
Falanghina '15	♔♔ 2*
Falanghina '14	♔♔ 2*
Falanghina del Beneventano '13	♔♔ 2*
Fiano di Avellino '13	♔♔ 3
Greco di Tufo '14	♔♔ 2*
rpinia Coda di Volpe '14	♔♔ 2*
Taurasi Ris. '12	♔♔ 7

I Favati

p.zza Di Donato
83020 Cesinali [AV]
Tel. +39 0825666898
www.cantineifavati.it

CELLAR SALES
PRE-BOOKED VISITS
ANNUAL PRODUCTION 100,000 bottles
HECTARES UNDER VINE 21.00

Rosanna Petrozziello, a proud woman with
an Irpinian spirit, runs this Cesinali winery
with Piersabino and Giancarlo Favati. The
vineyards on the southern side of the
Sabato River are characterized by
clayey-calcareous soils that give rise to
full-bodied, expressive wines. The estate's
enological fame has been solidified over
the years by their Pietramara, a cru of
Fiano cultivated in Atripalda where the
climate is cooler. The Greco Terrantica
comes from Montefusco, while the
Cretarossa is vinified with Aglianico grapes
from San Mango sul Calore. The family gets
valuable help from enologist Vincenzo
Mercurio, who can truly read and interpret
the Irpinia territory. The Fiano di Avellino
Pietramara '18 is simply extraordinary,
once again taking home Tre Bicchieri.
Intriguing in its mineral profile, it exhibits an
elegant bouquet of aniseed, peach and
toasty echoes. On the palate it expresses
deep sapidity and lively freshness, finishing
long. The Taurasi TerzoTratto '14 features a
sapid palate and close-woven tannins.

○ Fiano di Avellino Pietramara '18	♔♔♔ 5
○ Cabrì Fiano Extra Brut	♔ 3
● irpinia Campi Taurasini Cretarossa '16	♔ 3
● Taurasi TerzoTratto '14	♔ 5
● Taurasi TerzoTratto Et. Bianca Ris. '13	♔ 7
○ Fiano di Avellino Pietramara '17	♔♔♔ 5
○ Fiano di Avellino Pietramara '16	♔♔♔ 5
○ Fiano di Avellino Pietramara '15	♔♔♔ 5
○ Fiano di Avellino Pietramara '13	♔♔♔ 3*
○ Fiano di Avellino Pietramara '12	♔♔♔ 3*
○ Fiano di Avellino Pietramara '14	♔♔ 3*
○ Greco di Tufo Terrantica '17	♔♔ 3*
○ Greco di Tufo Terrantica '16	♔♔ 3*
● Taurasi TerzoTratto Et. Bianca Ris. '10	♔♔ 7

Benito Ferrara

FRAZ. SAN PAOLO, 14A
83010 TUFO [AV]
TEL. +39 0825998194
www.benitoferrara.it

CELLAR SALES
PRE-BOOKED VISITS
ANNUAL PRODUCTION 55,000 bottles
HECTARES UNDER VINE 13.00

The estate's first Greco vines were planted in 1860 at San Paolo, the classic heart of the appellation. Gabriella Ferrara, great-granddaughter of the founder Benito, grew up in the vineyards and cellar, and today she runs the winery. She and her husband Sergio Ambrosino proudly carry on the family tradition of wine production. The thirteen hectares between Tufo and Montemiletto produce Greco di Tufo and Aglianico, respectively. The Vigna Cicogna '18 is a wine of great complexity and concentration. The first version of this noted cru, situated at 500 meters elevation on clay-sulfur soils, goes back to 1991. Aromatically intense, it offers up notes of meadow herbs, lemon, sage and mineral nuances. On the palate it's linear and potent. We also found the steel-fermented Greco Terra d'Uva and Fiano di Avello solid.

○ Greco di Tufo V. Cicogna '18	♟♟ 4	
○ Greco di Tufo Terra d'Uva '18	♟♟ 4	
○ Fiano d'Avellino Sequenzha '18	♟ 4	
○ Greco di Tufo V. Cicogna '15	♟♟♟ 4*	
○ Greco di Tufo V. Cicogna '14	♟♟♟ 4*	
○ Greco di Tufo V. Cicogna '13	♟♟♟ 5	
○ Greco di Tufo V. Cicogna '12	♟♟♟ 4*	
○ Greco di Tufo V. Cicogna '10	♟♟♟ 4	
○ Greco di Tufo V. Cicogna '09	♟♟♟ 4	
○ Fiano d'Avellino Sequenzha '17	♟♟ 4	
○ Greco di Tufo Terra d'Uva '17	♟♟ 4	
○ Greco di Tufo Terra d'Uva '16	♟♟ 4	
○ Greco di Tufo Terra d'Uva '15	♟♟ 4	
○ Greco di Tufo V. Cicogna '17	♟♟ 4	
○ Greco di Tufo V. Cicogna '16	♟♟ 4	

★★Feudi di San Gregorio

LOC. CERZA GROSSA
83050 SORBO SERPICO [AV]
TEL. +39 0825986683
www.feudi.it

CELLAR SALES
PRE-BOOKED VISITS
RESTAURANT SERVICE
ANNUAL PRODUCTION 3,500,000 bottles
HECTARES UNDER VINE 250.00
VITICULTURE METHOD Certified Organic

This is one of the most noteworthy operations in the Irpinia area. Since 1986 it has rewritten the story of the three great appellations: Fiano di Avellino, Greco di Tufo and Taurasi. The group, led by Antonio Capaldo, has extended its production over the years and now makes wine in Basilicata, with Basilisco, and in Bolgheri, with its 2006 acquisition of Campo alle Comete. The range is enhanced with the Dubl sparkling wine line, a project begun fourteen years ago to promote native varieties. A visit to the winery is highly recommended as is a meal in its excellent Marennà restaurant. The Taurasi Piano di Monte Vergine has the makings of a great wine. The 2014 Riserva pours a vibrant ruby red, the prelude to clear aromas of wild berries, delicate spices, sanguine notes and balsamic whiffs, all of which give way to a clean, lively finish. The Fiano di Avellino Pietracalda '18 proves complex, creamy and sapid.

● Taurasi Piano di Montevergine Ris. '14	♟♟♟	
○ Fiano di Avellino Pietracalda '18	♟♟	
○ Dubl Brut M.Cl.	♟♟	
○ Dubl Esse Dosaggio Zero	♟♟	
○ Greco di Tufo Cutizzi '18	♟♟	
● Taurasi '15	♟♟	
○ Dubl + Brut	♟	
⊙ Dubl Brut Rosé	♟	
○ Irpinia Bianco Campanaro '17	♟	
○ Fiano di Avellino Pietracalda '09	♟♟♟	
○ Greco di Tufo Cutizzi '12	♟♟♟	
○ Greco di Tufo Cutizzi '10	♟♟♟	
● Taurasi '13	♟♟♟	
● Taurasi Piano di Montevergine Ris. '13	♟♟♟	
● Taurasi Piano di Montevergine Ris. '07	♟♟♟	

iorentino

A BARBASSANO
052 PATERNOPOLI [AV]
.. +39 3473474869310

ELLAR SALES
RE-BOOKED VISITS
NNUAL PRODUCTION 12,000 bottles
ECTARES UNDER VINE 7.00
USTAINABLE WINERY

anni Fiorentino's cellar is futuristic, made
tirely of wood and fully respecting the
inciples of bio-architecture. The family
s long had winemaking in its blood;
andfather Luigi bought the Paternopoli
nery with the fruits of his work when he
turned from the United States. Now it has
en made modern and innovative by his
scendants. Only Aglianico is cultivated
re. The choice is partly family tradition,
t also one that based on the needs of the
riety: the most authentic Taurasi is born
d able to express its true character rising
m the family's vineyards on volcanic
ils. Taurasi is the bedrock of Fiorentino's
lection. The 2014 is redolent of vibrant,
d berry fruit, with hints of tanned leather,
bacco and cinnamon. On the palate it's
acious, cohesive and energetic. The
lsì, created in honor of Luigi, is a vibrant,
cculent drink.

Taurasi '14	▼▼ 5
rpinia Aglianico Celsì '14	▼▼ 3
rpinia Aglianico Celsì '12	♈▼ 3
Taurasi '13	♈▼ 5
Taurasi '12	♈▼ 5

Fontanavecchia

VIA FONTANAVECCHIA, 7
82030 TORRECUSO [BN]
TEL. +39 0824876275
www.fontanavecchia.info

CELLAR SALES
PRE-BOOKED VISITS
ACCOMMODATION AND RESTAURANT SERVICE
ANNUAL PRODUCTION 175,000 bottles
HECTARES UNDER VINE 20.00

Libero Rillo makes valuable contributions in
Sannio both as a producer and as president
of the local wine consortium. He, along with
brother Giuseppe, inherited the winery from
their father Horatio in 1990 and now vinify
Falanghina and Aglianico as well as
Piedirosso, Greco and Fiano. The cellar,
located at the foot of Monte Taburno,
counts on twenty hectares of its own
vineyards and some rented plots. The range
is extremely varied, next to refreshing
whites are more structured reds as well as
interesting Falanghina, from their
Vendemmia Tardiva to an aged version,
confirming the type's surprising longevity.
The Falanghina Del Sannio '18 brings
together penetrating acidic vigor and a
summery character. It's intense in its
mineral sensations and citrusy nuances of
grapefruit, while the palate is held up by a
firm supporting acidity and marked salinity,
only to close deep and elegant. The
Falanghina Libero '08 also delivered.

○ Falanghina del Sannio Taburno '18	▼▼▼ 3*
○ Taburno Falanghina Libero '08	▼▼ 3
⊙ Aglianico del Taburno Rosato '18	▼ 3
○ Sannio Fiano '18	▼ 3
○ Sannio Greco '18	▼ 3
○ Falanghina del Sannio Taburno '16	♈▼ 3*
○ Falanghina del Sannio Taburno '15	♈▼ 2*
○ Falanghina del Sannio Taburno '14	♈▼ 2*
○ Falanghina del Sannio Taburno '13	♈▼ 2*
○ Falanghina del Sannio Taburno '12	♈▼ 2*
○ Sannio Taburno Falanghina Libero '07	♈▼ 5
● Aglianico del Taburno V. Cataratte Ris. '10	♈▼ 5
○ Falanghina del Sannio Taburno '17	♈▼ 3*
○ Sannio Greco '16	♈▼ 3

Fonzone

LOC. SCORZAGALLINE
83052 PATERNOPOLI [AV]
TEL. +39 08271730100
www.fonzone.it

CELLAR SALES
PRE-BOOKED VISITS
ANNUAL PRODUCTION 57,000 bottles
HECTARES UNDER VINE 22.00
SUSTAINABLE WINERY

Lorenzo Fonzone Caccese, a surgeon by profession, began winemaking in 2005 in Paternopoli, an area dedicated to Taurasi. The grapes from the 22-hectare estate are processed in a highly technological, underground cellar of low environmental impact, which is perfectly integrated into the surrounding landscape. No herbicides are used between the rows where a natural mix of grasses, flowers and legumes grows perennially to preserve the biodiversity of the soil and flora. For the production of its seven wines, the winery consults with Arturo Erbaggio, who vinifies Greco di Tufo, Fiano di Avellino and Falanghina in steel vats, and the Taurasi in new wood barrels. The Fiano di Avellino '18 stands out for its fragrance and gustatory tension. On the nose it offers up aromas of exotic fruit and citrus, sensations accompanied by sweet spices and an almond finish. Vivid notes of blackberries and cherry mark a perky Irpinia Campi Taurasini '15, while the Greco di Tufo '18 proves linear and spirited.

○ Fiano di Avellino '18	🍷🍷 3*
○ Greco di Tufo '18	🍷🍷 3
● Irpinia Campi Taurasini '15	🍷🍷 3
○ Irpinia Falanghina '18	🍷 5
○ Fiano di Avellino '16	🍷🍷🍷 3*
○ Greco di Tufo '13	🍷🍷🍷 3*
○ Fiano di Avellino '17	🍷🍷 3
○ Fiano di Avellino '14	🍷🍷 3
○ Fiano di Avellino '13	🍷🍷 3*
○ Greco di Tufo '17	🍷🍷 3*
○ Greco di Tufo '16	🍷🍷 3
○ Greco di Tufo '14	🍷🍷 3*
● Irpina Aglianico '14	🍷🍷 3
○ Irpinia Fiano Sequoia '17	🍷🍷 5
● Taurasi Scorzagalline Ris. '10	🍷🍷 5

La Fortezza

LOC. TORA II, 20
82030 TORRECUSO [BN]
TEL. +39 0824886155
www.lafortezzasrl.it

CELLAR SALES
PRE-BOOKED VISITS
ANNUAL PRODUCTION 900,000 bottles
HECTARES UNDER VINE 65.00

Enzo Rillo is a successful entrepreneur in the textile, road safety and construction sectors and has been a passionate winemaker since 2006. The first vineyard he bought are in Torrecuso, in the Taburno Camposauro regional park, where Fiano and Falanghina are cultivated. Subsequently additional plots were added and the now 65 hectares of vineyards als contain Greco and Fiano. The wines are divided into two lines: the Classic line, traditional and substantial, and Noi Beviamo Con La Testa, simpler and more approachable. The entire proposed range offers reliable wines at attractive prices. The Falanghina del Sannio Taburno '18 stands out among the selection proposed Intense aromas of aromatic herbs and mi spring flowers and lime anticipate a rich palate supported by the cultivar's signatu acidic tension. Focused spicy flavors mar the Aglianico del Taburno Riserva '11, a wine that proves almost overpowering in pulpy palate and character.

○ Falanghina del Sannio Taburno '18	🍷🍷
● Aglianico del Taburno Ris. '11	🍷🍷
○ Falanghina Brut Maleventum	🍷
○ Sannio Fiano '18	🍷
○ Sannio Greco '18	🍷
● Aglianico del Taburno '14	🍷🍷
● Aglianico del Taburno '12	🍷🍷
● Aglianico del Taburno Ris. '10	🍷🍷
○ Falanghina del Sannio Taburno '17	🍷🍷
○ Falanghina del Sannio Taburno '15	🍷🍷
○ Sannio Fiano '17	🍷🍷
○ Sannio Fiano '15	🍷🍷
○ Sannio Greco '17	🍷🍷
○ Sannio Greco '16	🍷🍷
○ Sannio Greco '15	🍷🍷

Masseria Frattasi

FRAZ. VARONI
FRATTASI, 1
82016 MONTESARCHIO [BN]
TEL. +39 0824824392
www.masseriafrattasi.it

CELLAR SALES
PRE-BOOKED VISITS
ANNUAL PRODUCTION 200,000 bottles
HECTARES UNDER VINE 25.00

Masseria Frattasi is located in a white limestone building dating from 1779. The winery is managed by the Cecere family, a long-established Campania family that cultivated and produced wine in the Montesarchio estate as early as 1576. Winemaking here has gone on continuously even surviving phylloxera, in particular the famous Falanghina di Bonea from the slopes of Taburno; in fact, the southernmost point of the Taburno limestone massif is where Don Antonio Cecere saved the Falanghina of Montesarchio and Bonea from devastation in the 1950s. The steel-matured Falanghina del Sannio Bonea is their flagship wine. Made with biodynamically cultivated pre-phylloxera grapes, it comes through pleasant in its aromas of intense tropical fruit, rose flowers and mineral hints. On the palate it exhibits nice balance between freshness and sapidity. The Donnalaura moves on the same track, though it's marked by more open, softer fruit.

Aglianico del Taburno Iovi Tonant '16	▼▼ 6
Falanghina del Sannio Bonea '18	▼▼ 2*
Falanghina del Sannio Taburno Donnalaura '18	▼▼ 5
Chy 890 '18	▼ 5
Nymphis Sacrae Coda di Volpe '18	▼ 3
Aglianico del Taburno Iovi Tonant '15	♀♀ 6
Falanghina del Sannio Taburno Bonea '16	♀♀ 3
Taburno Falanghina '12	♀♀ 2*
Taburno Falanghina di Bonea '12	♀♀ 3
Taburno Falanghina di Bonea '11	♀♀ 2*

★Galardi

FRAZ. SAN CARLO
S.DA PROV.LE SESSA-MIGNANO
81037 SESSA AURUNCA [CE]
TEL. +39 08231440003
www.terradilavoro.it

CELLAR SALES
PRE-BOOKED VISITS
ANNUAL PRODUCTION 30,000 bottles
HECTARES UNDER VINE 10.00
VITICULTURE METHOD Certified Organic

Luisa Murena, Arturo and Dora Celentano and Francesco Catello, together with enologist Riccardo Cotarella, have created a bit of a cult in the Roccamonfina territory. We are talking, of course, about Terra di Lavoro, a multifaceted red Aglianico and Piedirosso wine with an elegant and deep color. The grapes are grown in the Vallemarina area of Sessa Aurunca, where volcanic and alluvial soils give the wines energy and a unique character. The vineyards are cultivated according to the criteria of biodiversity. To our surprise, it's their most recent creation that most impressed during our tastings, a wine that earned Galardi Tre Bicchieri. The Terra di Rosso '17, made with Piedirosso, is redolent of black figs, wild blackberries and violets. On the palate it's enlivened by acidity, delivering creamy tannins, meaty, pervasive fruit, and a long, clear finish. Darker notes of tobacco and wood tar characterize their alluring Terra di Lavoro '17, a generous wine of unquestionable charm.

● Terra di Rosso '17	▼▼▼ 5
● Terra di Lavoro '17	▼▼ 7
● Terra di Lavoro '13	♀♀♀ 7
● Terra di Lavoro '11	♀♀♀ 7
● Terra di Lavoro '10	♀♀♀ 7
● Terra di Lavoro '09	♀♀♀ 7
● Terra di Lavoro '08	♀♀♀ 7
● Terra di Lavoro '07	♀♀♀ 7
● Terra di Lavoro '06	♀♀♀ 7
● Terra di Lavoro '05	♀♀♀ 7
● Terra di Lavoro '04	♀♀♀ 7
● Terra di Lavoro '03	♀♀♀ 6
● Terra di Lavoro '02	♀♀♀ 6
● Terra di Lavoro '99	♀♀♀ 6

La Guardiense

C.DA SANTA LUCIA, 104/106
82034 GUARDIA SANFRAMONDI [BN]
TEL. +39 0824864034
www.laguardiense.it

CELLAR SALES
PRE-BOOKED VISITS
RESTAURANT SERVICE
ANNUAL PRODUCTION 4,500,000 bottles
HECTARES UNDER VINE 1500.00

The cooperative's impressive history dates back to 1960 when it had only 33 members and just a few hectares of vineyards. Today there are 1000 members and 1500 hectares. 600 hectares of the vineyards concentrated around Sannio are planted with local Falanghina, which is vinified in steel vats for wines of notable fragrance and acidity. Management is entrusted to enologist Riccardo Cotarella, who coordinates the winegrowers' production, creating wines without added sulfites obtained from very low yields. The new Aicon line, available both in Aglianico and Falanghina versions, joins the range this year. The Falanghina del Sannio Janare Senete '18 is a delight. On the nose it unleashes notes of tropical fruit and mint. On the palate it proves rich and opulent, with a long finish. The Falanghina Aicon '18 is intense and racy, with nice, focused fruit, then hints of green tea anticipating a vibrant and pleasant palate.

○ Falanghina del Sannio Janare Senete '18	▼▼▼ 3*
○ Falanghina del Sannio Aicon '18	▼▼ 2*
○ Brut Janare Quid	▼ 2
● Sannio Aglianico Aicon '17	▼ 2
● Sannio Aglianico Janare Lùcchero '15	▼ 2
⊙ Sannio Aglianico Rosato Ambra Rosa '18	▼ 3
○ Falanghina del Sannio Janare '15	▽▽▽ 2*
○ Falanghina del Sannio Janare '14	▽▽▽ 2*
○ Falanghina del Sannio Janare Senete '17	▽▽▽ 3*
○ Falanghina del Sannio Janare Senete '16	▽▽▽ 2*
○ Falanghina del Sannio Janare '17	▽▽ 2*
● Sannio Guardiolo Rosso Janare Ris. '15	▽▽ 2*

Salvatore Martusciello

VIA SPINELLI, 4
80010 QUARTO [NA]
TEL. +39 0818766123
www.salvatoremartusciello.it

ANNUAL PRODUCTION 70,000 bottles
HECTARES UNDER VINE 2.00

Salvatore Martusciello works to preserve and promote the Sorrento Peninsula's enological heritage. After his long experience at the Grotte del Sole winery, Salvatore has played many roles: not only as a winemaker but also as a vigneron and merchant. With the support of his wife Gilda Guida, he now produces local wines of great typicity on the Phlegrean Fields, in the Aversano area and in the Sorrento Peninsula. The latter, ideal for the production of delicious and fruity wines, provides the raw material for the Ottoue line in both Lettere and Gragnano versions. The Trentapioli is a sparkling wine made with Asprinio d'Aversa grapes cultivated in Casapessena using the area's traditional 'tree-trained' growing system. A Metodo Martinotti (Charmat), it features fresh citrusy notes and hints of flowering grass on the nose, proving delicately salty and lip-smacking on the palate. Piedirosso, Aglianico and Sciascinoso give rise to the Lettere Ottoue, a traditional Neapolitan sparkler that's just a bit subtler, but as delicious and approachable as its Gragnano brother.

○ Asprinio d'Aversa Trentapioli Brut	▼▼ 2
● Penisola Sorrentina Lettere Ottoue '18	▼▼ 3
○ Campi Flegrei Falanghina Settevulcani '18	▼ 3
● Campi Flegrei Piedirosso Settevulcani '18	▼ 3
● Penisola Sorrentina Gragnano Ottoue '18	▼ 3
● Campi Flegrei Piedirosso Settevulcani '15	▽▽ 3
● Penisola Sorrentina Gragnano Ottoue '17	▽▽ 3
● Penisola Sorrentina Lettere Ottoue '17	▽▽ 3
● Penisola Sorrentina Lettere Ottoue '16	▽▽ 3
● Penisola Sorrentina Lettere Ottoue '15	▽▽ 3

alvatore Molettieri

DA MUSANNI, 19B
3040 MONTEMARANO [AV]
L. +39 082763722
ww.salvatoremolettieri.com

CELLAR SALES
RE-BOOKED VISITS
NNUAL PRODUCTION 65,000 bottles
ECTARES UNDER VINE 13.00

alvatore Molettieri's winery, one of the
aurasi area's long-established interpreters,
turns to Italian Wines after a year's
xodus. The vineyards are at elevations that
an exceed 600 meters, resulting in very
ow ripening and harvesting that can
xtend into mid-November. The house style
elivers wines rich in pulp and body,
atured both in small and larger wood
arrels, whose exuberance can only be
med by long bottle aging. The Tauras
gna Cinque Querce Riserva '11 pays
omage to the producer's long tradition of
d wines. Potent and intense in its aromas
f mint and licorice, then coffee and roots,
n the palate it's dense, concentrated,
unctuated by an excellent, fruity pulp, only
 finish lively with complex earthy and spicy
uances. The Tauras Renonno '13 also
elivers, proving redolent of Mediterranean
hrub and black tea. On the palate it's
ustere, compact but surely ageworthy.
heir Aglianico Cinque Querce '15 exhibits
ce, focused fruit in its aromas of raspberry
nd blood orange.

Taurasi V. Cinque Querce Ris. '11	▼▼	7
Irpinia Aglianico Cinque Querce '15	▼▼	3
Taurasi Renonno '13	▼▼	5
Fiano di Avellino Apianum '17	▼	3
Greco di Tufo '17	▼	3
Taurasi Renonno '08	♀♀♀	5
Taurasi V. Cinque Querce '05	♀♀♀	6
Taurasi V. Cinque Querce '04	♀♀♀	6
Taurasi V. Cinque Querce '01	♀♀♀	5
Taurasi V. Cinque Querce Ris. '05	♀♀♀	7
Taurasi V. Cinque Querce Ris. '04	♀♀♀	7
Taurasi V. Cinque Querce Ris. '01	♀♀♀	7
Fiano di Avellino Apianum '15	♀♀	3
Irpinia Aglianico Cinque Querce '13	♀♀	3
Taurasi Renonno '11	♀♀	5
Taurasi V. Cinque Querce '10	♀♀	6

★★Montevetrano

LOC. NIDO
FRAZ. CAMPIGLIANO
VIA MONTEVETRANO, 3
84099 SAN CIPRIANO PICENTINO [SA]
TEL. +39 089882285
www.montevetrano.it

CELLAR SALES
PRE-BOOKED VISITS
ACCOMMODATION
ANNUAL PRODUCTION 76,000 bottles
HECTARES UNDER VINE 5.00

Silvia Imparato has changed the rhythm of
wine in Campania. Her success is bound
up with the Cabernet Sauvignon and
Aglianico vineyards in San Cipriano
Picentino that she planted on a bet (she
made the winning decision following the
advice of Riccardo Cotarella, who also
suggested leaving her own Aglianico
vineyards in production). In 1991 the first
bottles of Montevetrano, an Aglianico,
Cabernet Sauvignon and Merlot blend and
the winery's only offering for many years,
was born. Today, Silvia also produces two
wines named Core: red from Aglianico,
white from Fiano and Greco. Imparato
takes home Tre Bicchieri thanks to a
well-made Monevetrano '17. It's comes
through elegant and broad in its aromas of
blackberries, mulberries and cherries, all
enriched by notes of coffee and sweet
spices. On the palate it exhibits perfect
harmony between acidity and tannins,
proving generous and pervasive only to
close spicy and subtle.

● Montevetrano '17	▼▼▼	8
● Core Rosso '16	▼▼	5
● Montevetrano '16	♀♀♀	8
● Montevetrano '14	♀♀♀	7
● Montevetrano '12	♀♀♀	7
● Montevetrano '11	♀♀♀	7
● Montevetrano '10	♀♀♀	7
● Montevetrano '09	♀♀♀	7
● Montevetrano '08	♀♀♀	7
● Montevetrano '07	♀♀♀	7
● Montevetrano '06	♀♀♀	7
● Montevetrano '05	♀♀♀	7
● Montevetrano '04	♀♀♀	7
● Montevetrano '03	♀♀♀	7
● Montevetrano '02	♀♀♀	7

Mustilli

VIA CAUDINA, 10
82019 SANT'AGATA DE' GOTI [BN]
TEL. +39 0823718142
www.mustilli.com

CELLAR SALES
PRE-BOOKED VISITS
ACCOMMODATION AND RESTAURANT SERVICE
ANNUAL PRODUCTION 150,000 bottles
HECTARES UNDER VINE 21.00

The Sant'Agata dei Goti appellation is the result of work done by Leonardo Mustilli, who in 1993 was able to get the area recognized as one of the most suitable for Falanghina. The engineer realized the potential of this cultivar earlier and by 1979 had in fact already produced the first bottle, which is still held in the underground cellars of Palazzo Raione. Today, Paola and Anna Chiara, in addition to carrying their father's significant legacy on their shoulders, manage both the vineyards and cellar. Enologist Fortunato Sebastiano has helped them present enviable versions of Piedirosso and Falanghina. Their splendid Piedirosso Artus '17 pours a bright ruby red, the prelude to intense, enticing sensations of pepper and Ferrovia cherries. It enters alluringly and perky, and finishes long. The Falanghina Vigna Segreta '17 also had a great day, proving creamy and well-orchestrated.

● Sannio Sant'Agata dei Goti Piedirosso Artus '17	♥♥♥ 5
○ Falangina del Sannio Sant'Agata dei Goti V. Segreta '17	♥♥ 4
○ Falanghina del Sannio '18	♥♥ 3
☉ Regina Sofia Rosato '18	♥♥ 2*
● Sannio Aglianico '17	♥♥ 3
● Sannio Piedirosso '18	♥♥ 3
○ Sannio Greco '18	♥ 3
● Sannio Sant'Agata dei Goti Piedirosso Artus '16	♥♥♥ 5
● Sannio Sant'Agata dei Goti Piedirosso Artus '15	♥♥♥ 4*
○ Falanghina del Sannio Sant'Agata dei Goti '17	♥♥ 3
○ Falanghina del Sannio Sant'Agata dei Goti V. Segreta '16	♥♥ 5

Nanni Copè

VIA TUFO, 3
81041 VITULAZIO [CE]
TEL. +39 3487478459
www.nannicope.it

CELLAR SALES
PRE-BOOKED VISITS
ANNUAL PRODUCTION 7,500 bottles
HECTARES UNDER VINE 3.50
VITICULTURE METHOD Certified Organic
SUSTAINABLE WINERY

Giovanni Ascione loves to take on challenges and have some skin in the game. In 2008 he left his life as a manager and journalist behind to produce wine on the Colline Caiatine, where the ancient sandstone soils confer finesse and acidic vibrance. The first wine release was the Sabbie di Sopra al Bosco, a blend of Pallagrello Nero, Aglianico and Casavecchia. But, not satisfied with that, Giovanni added the white Vigna Scarrupat a blend of Fiano, Asprinio and Pallagrello Bianco, and this year enriched the range with a red offered seven years after the harvest. The Sabbie di Sopra il Bosco, one of Ascione's enological gems, mature in mid-sized casks. The 2017 features notes of wild rose and a charming spiciness in its suite of aromas. Sapid energy and exemplary tannic extraction make for a wine of extraordinary drinkability. Balsamic atmospheres and pencil lead mark their r12, a wine with a sublime tannic weave that comes through full, elegant and precise.

● Sabbie di Sopra il Bosco '17	♥♥♥ 6
● Sabbie di Sopra il Bosco r12 '12	♥♥ 6
● Sabbie di Sopra il Bosco '16	♥♥♥ 6
● Sabbie di Sopra il Bosco '15	♥♥♥ 6
● Sabbie di Sopra il Bosco '14	♥♥♥ 5
● Sabbie di Sopra il Bosco '12	♥♥♥ 5
● Sabbie di Sopra il Bosco '11	♥♥♥ 5
● Sabbie di Sopra il Bosco '10	♥♥♥ 5
● Sabbie di Sopra il Bosco '09	♥♥♥ 5
○ Polveri della Scarrupata '16	♥♥ 6
● Sabbie di Sopra il Bosco '13	♥♥ 5
● Sabbie di Sopra il Bosco '08	♥♥ 5

Ciro Picariello

VIA MARRONI, 18A
83010 SUMMONTE [AV]
TEL. +39 082533848
www.ciropicariello.it

PRE-BOOKED VISITS
ANNUAL PRODUCTION 55,000 bottles
HECTARES UNDER VINE 15.00
SUSTAINABLE WINERY

Ciro Picariello is a true artisan of Fiano di Avellino and long considered one of its most important interpreters. The winery's headquarters are in Summonte and the vineyards cover an area of fifteen hectares at an elevation of 650 meters. Those at Montefredane and Summonte are planted with Fiano for use in the classic version and in the Ciro 906. The soul of Ciro's winery is white, in fact, only one single hectare has Aglianico. Since 2004, with wife Rita and children Emma and Bruno, he has worked to obtain grapes of the highest quality for the production of linear whites with vibrant acidity. The Fiano di Avellino '18 is a bright, summery wine rich in musky aromas, sensations of flowers and Mediterranean scrub followed by balsamic and toasty whiffs. On the palate it leaves its mark by virtue of its savoriness and acidity. It's a soft and even white, just a bit less dazzling than other versions.

○ Fiano di Avellino '18	▼▼ 4
○ Fiano di Avellino '14	▼▼▼ 4*
○ Fiano di Avellino '10	▼▼▼ 3*
○ Fiano di Avellino '08	▼▼▼ 3*
○ Brut Contadino	▼▼ 4
○ Fiano di Avellino '17	▼▼ 4
○ Fiano di Avellino '15	▼▼ 4
○ Fiano di Avellino '13	▼▼ 4
○ Fiano di Avellino '11	▼▼ 3*
○ Fiano di Avellino '09	▼▼ 3
○ Fiano di Avellino '07	▼▼ 3*
○ Fiano di Avellino '06	▼▼ 3*
○ Fiano di Avellino Ciro 906 '13	▼▼ 4
○ Fiano di Avellino Ciro 906 '12	▼▼ 4

La Pietra di Tommasone

S.DA PROV.LE FANGO, 98
80076 LACCO AMENO [NA]
TEL. +39 0813330330
www.tommasonevini.it

CELLAR SALES
PRE-BOOKED VISITS
ANNUAL PRODUCTION 100,000 bottles
HECTARES UNDER VINE 11.00

Antonio Monti is an excellent interpreter of Ischia's winemaking and wine culture. It boasts a centuries-old tradition and a unique mix of native varieties, magical landscapes, volcanic elements and crystal clear waters. His efforts have led to the rediscovery of old plots that he works with the help of his daughter Lucia to create a wide, dependable range. This year they submitted a strong selection of wines, with an even distribution of quality across the board. The Biancolella Tenuta dei Preti '18 stands out for its aromas of basil and thyme. Subtle and soft, it unfolds notably on the palate towards a refreshing, delicately salty finish. Their succulent yet racy Epomeo Bianco Pithecusa '18 is just a bit richer, while the Per' 'e Palummo Tenuta Monte Zunta '17 is redolent of rose and pomegranate, finishing on sensations of wood resin and pepper.

○ Ischia Biancolella Tenuta dei Preti '18	▼▼ 4
○ Epomeo Bianco Pithecusa '18	▼▼ 3
○ Ischia Biancolella '18	▼▼ 2*
● Ischia Per' e Palummo Tenuta Monte Zunta '17	▼▼ 5
⊙ Rosamonti '18	▼▼ 2*
● Epomeo Rosso Pithecusa '16	▼ 3
● Ischia Per' e Palummo '18	▼ 3
○ Ischia Biancolella '17	▼▼▼ 2*
● Epomeo Rosso '14	▼▼ 3
○ Ischia Biancolella Tenuta dei Preti '17	▼▼ 4
● Ischia Per' e Palummo '17	▼▼ 3
● Ischia Per' e Palummo Tenuta Monte Zunta '16	▼▼ 5

★Pietracupa

C.DA VADIAPERTI, 17
83030 MONTEFREDANE [AV]
TEL. +39 0825607418
pietracupa@email.it

CELLAR SALES
PRE-BOOKED VISITS
ANNUAL PRODUCTION 50,000 bottles
HECTARES UNDER VINE 7.50

Sabino Loffredo is undoubtedly one of the most capable and consistent white wine producers in Italy. Pietracupa is proof: the winery he founded in the early 1990s has always shown amazing consistency. It makes high-quality Greco and Fiano wines with sharp, fragrant, mineral profiles that are all personally interpreted by this inspired Irpinia genius. Produced since 2008 at Torre delle Nocelle, the Taurasi also has an extremely territorial stamp and is never excessive in terms of extraction or tannic impetuosity. None of the wines that Sabino presented in this edition are designated within Irpinia. Downgraded to IGTs, they exhibited all their creator's uncompromising character. The Grego leads the way with its mineral profile and a jolt of aromatic herbs, peach, white pepper and flint. On the palate it's crisp, hard, taut and assertive to the say the least. The Falanghina '18 is more expressive and relaxed, while we'll have to wait for the 2018 version of their Fiano.

○ Greco '18	♟♟♟ 4*
○ Falanghina '18	♟♟ 3
○ Fiano '18	♟♟ 3
● Taurasi '14	♟♟ 5
○ Cupo '10	♟♟♟ 5
○ Cupo '08	♟♟♟ 5
○ Fiano di Avellino '13	♟♟♟ 3*
○ Fiano di Avellino '12	♟♟♟ 3*
○ Greco di Tufo '17	♟♟♟ 3*
○ Greco di Tufo '16	♟♟♟ 3*
○ Greco di Tufo '15	♟♟♟ 3*
○ Greco di Tufo '14	♟♟♟ 3*
○ Greco di Tufo '10	♟♟♟ 3*
○ Greco di Tufo '09	♟♟♟ 3*
● Taurasi '10	♟♟♟ 5

Fattoria La Rivolta

C.DA CONTRADA RIVOLTA
82030 TORRECUSO [BN]
TEL. +39 0824872921
www.fattorialarivolta.com

CELLAR SALES
PRE-BOOKED VISITS
ACCOMMODATION
ANNUAL PRODUCTION 180,000 bottles
HECTARES UNDER VINE 29.00
VITICULTURE METHOD Certified Organic

La Rivolta di Torrecuso is one of the Sannio area's leading wineries. Founded by the Cotroneo family in 1997, its production centers around Campania's principal varieties, which are planted on 29 organically managed hectares. There is a wide range of eleven wines including whites vinified in steel that stand out for their consistency and aromatic definition, and serious reds of more austere, essential character, aged in small oak casks. A step higher are great reserve wines like the Terre di Rivolta, of Aglianico, and Sogno di Rivolta, a Falanghina, Fiano and Greco blend. This last is a red that brings together juice and contrasting acidity. Suggestions of sour cherry, blackberry and violet rise up amidst quinine and sweet spices. On the palate it's long and mouthfilling, marked by sweet, fruity flavors and tannins at the same time. The Falanghina del Sannio '18 exhibits nice craft, with its nuances of broom, hawthorn and mineral hints, and its citrusy finish.

● Aglianico del Taburno Terra di Rivolta Ris. '16	♟♟ 6
○ Falanghina del Sannio Taburno '18	♟♟ 3
● Aglianico del Taburno '17	♟ 3
● Sannio Taburno Aglianico '18	♟ 3
○ Sogno di Rivolta '17	♟ 4
● Aglianico del Taburno '10	♟♟♟ 3*
● Aglianico del Taburno Terra di Rivolta Ris. '08	♟♟♟ 5
○ Falanghina del Sannio Taburno '16	♟♟♟ 2*
● Aglianico del Taburno '15	♟♟ 3
● Aglianico del Taburno Terra di Rivolta Ris. '15	♟♟ 5
● Sannio Taburno Piedirosso '17	♟♟ 3
● Sannio Taburno Piedirosso '16	♟♟ 3
● Simbiosi '16	♟♟ 5
● Simbiosi '15	♟♟ 5

Rocca del Principe

Via Arianiello, 9
83030 Lapio [AV]
Tel. +39 08251728013
www.roccadelprincipe.it

CELLAR SALES
PRE-BOOKED VISITS
ANNUAL PRODUCTION 30,000 bottles
HECTARES UNDER VINE 6.50

Since 2004, the winery has been a benchmark for original, character-laden Fiano di Avellino. Ercole Zarella and his wife Aurelia Fabrizio carry on the family tradition, producing wines from Lapio's clay-rich soils, which is recognized as being excellent for Fiano and Aglianico. Some of the most important Fiano vineyards are on the Arianello slopes, the district's highest point, where the cooler air results in a slightly delayed harvest, allowing the grapes to fully ripen. And once again their Fiano di Avellino Tognano proves to be in a league of its own, beating out the rest of Zarella's selection. The grapes are selected from a plot in their Togano vineyards, where the oldest vines are to be found. Rich in sapid nuances, it's an exceptionally deep wine in its marine sensations, while a palate of great concentration gives way to an extremely long finish. The Fiano '17 is airier with a delicately smoky hint that embraces juicy, fragrant yellow peach.

○ Fiano di Avellino Tognano '16	♥♥♥ 5
○ Fiano di Avellino '17	♥♥ 4
● Taurasi Aurelia '15	♥ 5
○ Fiano di Avellino '14	♥♥♥ 3*
○ Fiano di Avellino '13	♥♥♥ 3*
○ Fiano di Avellino '12	♥♥♥ 3*
○ Fiano di Avellino '10	♥♥♥ 3*
○ Fiano di Avellino '08	♥♥♥ 2*
○ Fiano di Avellino '07	♥♥♥ 2*
○ Fiano di Avellino Tognano '15	♥♥♥ 5
○ Fiano di Avellino '16	♥♥ 4
○ Fiano di Avellino '15	♥♥ 3*
○ Fiano di Avellino Tognano '14	♥♥ 3*
● Taurasi Ris. '10	♥♥ 5

Ettore Sammarco

Via Civita, 9
84010 Ravello [SA]
Tel. +39 089872774
www.ettoresammarco.it

CELLAR SALES
PRE-BOOKED VISITS
ANNUAL PRODUCTION 66,000 bottles
HECTARES UNDER VINE 13.00

Ettore Sammarco has one of the Amalfi Coasts most flourishing wineries and one of coastal wine's most intriguing stories. In 1962, the young Ettore started winemaking by buying some small terraces near Ravello that still dot the landscape. Today Ettore is 80 years old and supported in his work by son Bartolo, who takes care of the small plots of Selva delle Monache and Grotta Piana. The highest vineyard is on Mount Brusara at an elevation of 500 meters. The wines are all produced using grapes local to the Ravello sub-zones, often purchased from trusted, established growers. The producer submitted a compact, solid selection of wines. The Selva delle Monache '18, a blend of Biancolella and Falanghina stood out. On the nose it offers up hints of mint and white-fleshed fruit. On the palate it's delicately salty, exhibiting fullness and vigor. The rest of their wines proved extremely valid, confirming the serious of the work being done.

○ Costa d'Amalfi Ravello Bianco Selva delle Monache '18	♥♥ 3*
○ Costa D'Amalfi Bianco Terre Saracene '18	♥♥ 3
● Costa d'Amalfi Ravello Rosso Selva delle Monache Ris. '15	♥♥ 5
● Costa d'Amalfi Terre Saracene Rosato '18	♥♥ 3
● Costa d'Amalfi Terre Sarecene Rosso '17	♥♥ 3
○ Costa d'Amalfi Ravello Bianco Selva delle Monache '17	♥♥♥ 3*
○ Costa d'Amalfi Ravello Bianco V. Grotta Piana '15	♥♥♥ 4*
● Costa d'Amalfi Ravello Rosso Selva delle Monache Ris. '14	♥♥ 5

Tenuta San Francesco

FRAZ. CORSANO
VIA SOFILCIANO, 18
84010 TRAMONTI [SA]
TEL. +39 089876748
www.vinitenutasanfrancesco.com

CELLAR SALES
PRE-BOOKED VISITS
ACCOMMODATION
ANNUAL PRODUCTION 40,000 bottles
HECTARES UNDER VINE 10.00

The Bove, D'Avino and Giordano families founded this winery in 2004 with the aim of protecting and promoting Tramonti's historic wines. This is one of the most unforgiving areas of the Amalfi Coast's different sub-zones. The vineyards, on steeply sloping terraces ranging in elevations from 300 to 700 meters, are planted with ungrafted, local varieties trained on traditional arbors. They give life to austere, powerful reds of Tintore, Piedirosso and Aglianico, such as È Iss or Quattrospine, and to fresh, sapid whites of Falanghina, Pepella and Ginestra that unite in Per Eva. For the first time their E' Iss Tintore Prephilloxera took home Tre Bicchieri. The 2016 is dense, flavoursome, full of nuances and spicy sensations. On the nose earthy tones stand out amidst roots, crispy peppers and freshly ground pepper, while the finish comes through juicy and full of fruit. The rest of their selection also proves valid.

● È Iss Tintore Prephilloxera '16	▼▼▼ 5
○ Costa d'Amalfi Bianco Per Eva '17	▼▼ 4
● Costa d'Amalfi Tramonti Rosso '16	▼▼ 3
○ Costa d'Amalfi Tramonti Bianco '18	▼ 2
⊙ Costa d'Amalfi Tramonti Rosato '18	▼ 2
○ Costa d'Amalfi Bianco Per Eva '13	♈♈♈ 4*
○ Costa d'Amalfi Bianco Per Eva '14	♈♈ 4
○ Costa d'Amalfi Tramonti Bianco '17	♈♈ 2*
○ Costa d'Amalfi Tramonti Bianco Per Eva '16	♈♈ 4
○ Costa d'Amalfi Tramonti Bianco Per Eva '15	♈♈ 4
● Costa d'Amalfi Tramonti Rosso '14	♈♈ 3
● Costa d'Amalfi Tramonti Rosso Quattrospine Ris. '15	♈♈ 5
● È Iss Tintore Prephilloxera '14	♈♈ 5

San Giovanni

C.DA TRESINO
84048 CASTELLABATE [SA]
TEL. +39 0974965136
www.agricolasangiovanni.it

CELLAR SALES
PRE-BOOKED VISITS
ACCOMMODATION
ANNUAL PRODUCTION 20,000 bottles
HECTARES UNDER VINE 4.00

In 1993, Mario and Ida Corrado took the very bold step of settling in Punta Tresino i the Natural Park of Cilento, at that time lacking even a power supply. But the area is also one of the Tyrrhenian coast's most evocative places and the winery arrived a few years later. Their four hectares are planted with traditional, local cultivars that give rise to six wines, all with a pronounce sunny, marine character: Paestum, Tresinus and Aureus for whites, and Castellabate, Maroccia and Ficonero for reds. Be sure to taste their Tresinus '18, a wine full of fruity and iodine notes. It opens on aromas of yellow-fleshed fruit, peach, broom and ginger. On the palate it's broad and highly sapid, with a lovely, well-paced length. A slight touch of cherry and violet mark their Castellabate, a blend of Piedirosso and Aglianico.

○ Tresinus '18	▼▼ 4
● Castellabate '16	▼▼ 3
○ Paestum '18	▼ 3
○ Fiano Tresinus '12	♈♈♈ 3*
○ Paestum '15	♈♈♈ 2*
○ Aureus '15	♈♈ 5
○ Fiano Tresinus '15	♈♈ 3
○ Fiano Tresinus '14	♈♈ 3
○ Fiano Tresinus '13	♈♈ 3*
● Ficonera '14	♈♈ 5
○ Paestum '17	♈♈ 3
○ Paestum '16	♈♈ 3*
○ Paestum Bianco '14	♈♈ 2*
○ Tresinus '17	♈♈ 4
○ Tresinus '16	♈♈ 4

San Salvatore 1988

A DIONISIO
4050 GIUNGANO [SA]
TEL. +39 08281990900
www.sansalvatore1988.it

CELLAR SALES
ACCOMMODATION AND RESTAURANT SERVICE
ANNUAL PRODUCTION 160,000 bottles
HECTARES UNDER VINE 23.00
VITICULTURE METHOD Certified Biodynamic
SUSTAINABLE WINERY

The volcanic Giuseppe Pagano is one of the region's most versatile entrepreneurs – he works at full throttle, having created a model agricultural estate that makes organic wine, amazing buffalo mozzarella, as well as oil, grains, vegetables and an excellent array of traditional cuisine prepared according to classic, time-honored recipes. A photovoltaic system supplies part of the energy consumed. The range of wines is very wide but focuses on enhancing the characteristics of traditional varieties, mainly Fiano, Falanghina and Aglianico. Once again their excellent Pian di Stio '18 hits the mark and takes home the Bicchieri. It's a crisp wine in its aromas of citron and thyme, while the palate comes through creamy and assertive, accompanied by a long, delicate, sapid and smoky note. The Trentenare, another Fiano, also delivered, proving highly pleasant in its vibrant character. On the palate it unfolds with grace and confidence.

Sanpaolo
di Claudio Quarta Vignaiolo

FRAZ. C.DA SAN PAOLO
VIA AUFIERI, 25
83010 TORRIONI [AV]
TEL. +39 0832704398
www.claudioquarta.it

CELLAR SALES
PRE-BOOKED VISITS
ACCOMMODATION
ANNUAL PRODUCTION 115,000 bottles
HECTARES UNDER VINE 22.00

Entrepreneur Claudio Quarta and his daughter Alessandra have an increasingly extensive and complex operation. Stretching from Campania to Puglia, it is concerned about biodiversity and environmental sustainability, has invaluable research and innovation projects, and has been responsible for many social initiatives. The Sanpaolo estate is in Irpinia, in the heart of the Greco di Tufo DOC, the flagship wine of a range that includes Falanghina del Beneventano, Fiano Di Avellino, from Montefredane and Lapio, and some reds. Among the new entries in our guide, we point out an excellent debut by the line dedicated to the great Italian actor Totò, in particular the Rosso. A blend of Casavecchia and Piedirosso, it's redolent of pomegranate and geranium. On the palate it proves fruity, racy, truly pleasant and vivid. The Greco di Tufo Claudio Quarta is getting better. The 2018 features notes of aniseed and elderflower, a rich, dynamic palate and a noteworthy finish.

Pian di Stio '18	♟♟♟ 4*
Trentenare '18	♟♟ 3*
Calpazio '18	♟♟ 3
Ceraso '18	♟♟ 3
Jungano '17	♟♟ 3
Falanghina '18	♟ 3
Omaggio a Gillo Dorfles '15	♟ 6
Vetere Rosato '18	♟ 3
Pian di Stio '17	♟♟♟ 4*
Pian di Stio '14	♟♟♟ 4*
Pian di Stio '13	♟♟♟ 4*
Pian di Stio '12	♟♟♟ 3*
Trentenare '16	♟♟♟ 3*
Trentenare '15	♟♟♟ 3*

○ Greco di Tufo Claudio Quarta '18	♟♟ 4
○ Falanghina '18	♟♟ 2*
○ Totò Bianco '18	♟♟ 5
● Totò Rosso '17	♟♟ 5
○ Fiano di Avellino '18	♟ 3
○ Greco di Tufo Claudio Quarta '13	♟♟♟ 6
○ Greco di Tufo Claudio Quarta '12	♟♟♟ 6
○ Falanghina '16	♟♟ 2*
○ Falanghina '15	♟♟ 2*
○ Fiano di Avellino '15	♟♟ 2*
○ Greco di Tufo '17	♟♟ 3
○ Greco di Tufo Claudio Quarta '17	♟♟ 6
○ Greco di Tufo Claudio Quarta '16	♟♟ 6
○ Greco di Tufo Claudio Quarta '15	♟♟ 6
○ Suavemente '17	♟♟ 3

Tenuta Sarno 1860

c.da Serroni, 4b
83100 Avellino
Tel. +39 082526161
www.tenutasarno1860.it

ANNUAL PRODUCTION 15,000 bottles
HECTARES UNDER VINE 6.00

Maura Sarno continues to work with great passion and determination in Candida. The area is one of the best for Fiano di Avellino, and, as far white wines are concerned, one of the most awarded DOCGs in our guide. The soils are rich in clay and limestone, the harvest is often late. The rich flavor and fruity imprints pair beautifully with a driving sapid energy that will be even more enjoyed by those with the patience to leave them in the cellar. They are truly wines with great longevity, rich in the nuances reflecting the characteristics of the territory. This year, for the first time Maura proposed the Fiano di Avellino Erre '17, which she released after an extra year of aging (confirming the aging power of her wines). In the glass we find a wine that's still quite young, delicate in its aromas of freshly cut grass and lime, with a creamy, sapid palate well orchestrated by a vibrant acidity. A chalky finish lengthens the flavor of a wine that will offer up its best in a few more years.

○ Fiano di Avellino 1860 Erre '17	**ΨΨ**	4
○ Fiano di Avellino '15	ΨΨΨ	4*
○ Fiano di Avellino '17	ΨΨ	4
○ Fiano di Avellino '16	ΨΨ	4
○ Fiano di Avellino '14	ΨΨ	3*
○ Fiano di Avellino '13	ΨΨ	3*
○ Fiano di Avellino '12	ΨΨ	3*
○ Fiano di Avellino '11	ΨΨ	3
○ Fiano di Avellino '10	ΨΨ	3*
○ Sarno 1860 Pas Dosé '15	ΨΨ	4

Sclavia

loc. Marianello
via Case Sparse
81040 Liberi [CE]
Tel. +39 3357406773
www.sclavia.com

CELLAR SALES
PRE-BOOKED VISITS
ANNUAL PRODUCTION 50,000 bottles
HECTARES UNDER VINE 13.00
VITICULTURE METHOD Certified Organic
SUSTAINABLE WINERY

We anxiously await yet another leap in quality from the winery led by osteopathic physician Andrea Granito and art historian Lucia Ferrara. The thirteen certified organ hectares speak the broad dialect of this part of Caserta, with its strong and vibrant volcanic influences. The vineyards are planted with Casavecchia, which is also offered in a rosé version, and Pallagrello Bianco. The wines capture the essence of this intriguing land, full of angles and nuances, with a sometimes exuberant intensity. Redolent of rosemary and oregano, the Calù '18 is an aromatically intense Pallagrello Bianco that gradually moves towards citrus sensations. On the palate it's sapid and surefooted in its development, giving way to a juicy and pleasant finish marked by nice aromatic complexity. The Casavecchia di Pontelato Liberi '15 tantalizes with its almost spicy hot streak, while the palate proves peppe and penetrating, marked by austere tanni and nice overall balance.

○ Calù Pallagrello Bianco '18	**ΨΨ**
● Casavecchia di Pontelatone Liberi '15	**ΨΨ**
⊙ Sciròcco Rosato '18	**Ψ**
○ Calù Pallagrello Bianco '17	ΨΨ
○ Calù Pallagrello Bianco '16	ΨΨ
○ Calù Pallagrello Bianco '15	ΨΨ
○ Don Ferdinando '15	ΨΨ
● Granito '12	ΨΨ
● Granito Casavecchia '15	ΨΨ
● Liberi '14	ΨΨ
● Liberi '12	ΨΨ
○ Pallarè '15	ΨΨ

enuta Scuotto

ᴀ Campomarino, 2/3
030 Lapio [AV]
. +39 08251851965
ww.tenutascuotto.it

CELLAR SALES
RE-BOOKED VISITS
NNUAL PRODUCTION 40,000 bottles
ECTARES UNDER VINE 3.00

uardo Scuotto and son Adolfo's winery
Lapio is in great shape. Qualitative
owth has made it among the most
teresting in the Irpinia area. In 2009
uardo, a Neapolitan by birth, turned his
ttention to Campania's main appellations
d bought this winery on Mount Tuoro
ong with the surrounding plots and
eyards. The overall selection of wines
esented performed on a very high level.
e Fiano di Avellino '18 is an intense
ne in its notes of fresh herbs and
zelnut. A territorial Fiano, it proves
licate yet capable of changing direction
the palate, where it comes through
cy, with nice flesh and a long,
ltifaceted finish. The Greco di Tufo '18
atures a saline, savory and energetic
le adorned by aromas of aniseed and
sh almond. Both wines made it to our
al round of tastings, and we're willing to
t on their cellar lifespan.

Fiano di Avellino '18	♀♀ 2*
Greco di Tufo '18	♀♀ 3
Falanghina '16	♀♀ 3
Fiano di Avellino '16	♀♀ 2*
Greco di Tufo '17	♀♀ 3*
Greco di Tufo '16	♀♀ 3*
Di Nì '17	♀♀ 5
Taurasi '12	♀♀ 5

La Sibilla

ꜰʀᴀᴢ. Baia
ᴠɪᴀ Ottaviano Augusto, 19
80070 Bacoli [NA]
Tel. +39 0818688778
www.sibillavini.com

CELLAR SALES
PRE-BOOKED VISITS
ANNUAL PRODUCTION 70,000 bottles
HECTARES UNDER VINE 9.50

Vincenzo De Meo runs this solid winery in
the hills of Baia in the volcanic territory of
the Phlegraean Fields. Breezes from the
Gulf of Naples comb soils rich in lapilli
stones and ashes, conditions that have
allowed the ungrafted vineyards to survive.
Intriguing, centuries-old vines tell the story
of local varietals, mainly Falanghina and
Piedirosso with some rows of 'a Livella', 'a
Surcella' and 'a Marsigliese'. The Cruna
deLago '17, a Falnghina with an
unmistakably volcanic streak, handily
earned a place in our finals. A bold,
sulfurous intensity is nicely accompanied
by nuances of Mediterranean herbs. On the
palate it proves rich, big but nicely crafted,
finishing on pronounced notes of oregano
and ginger. The Piedirosso '18 is a great
drink, redolent of blackcurrant and violet.
It's fresh and perky, with a surefooted, fast
development — highly pleasant, especially
if enjoyed after 15 minutes in the fridge.

○ Campi Flegrei Falanghina Cruna deLago '17	♀♀ 5
● Campi Flegrei Piedirosso '18	♀♀ 4
● Campi Flegrei Piedirosso V. Madre '15	♀ 4
○ Campi Flegrei Falanghina '13	♀♀♀ 2*
○ Campi Flegrei Falanghina Cruna deLago '15	♀♀♀ 4*
○ Campi Flegrei Falanghina '17	♀♀ 3*
○ Campi Flegrei Falanghina '16	♀♀ 3
○ Campi Flegrei Falanghina '15	♀♀ 2*
○ Campi Flegrei Falanghina '14	♀♀ 3
○ Campi Flegrei Falanghina Cruna deLago '16	♀♀ 5
○ Campi Flegrei Falanghina Cruna deLago '14	♀♀ 4
● Campi Flegrei Piedirosso '16	♀♀ 4
● Campi Flegrei Piedirosso '15	♀♀ 3

Luigi Tecce

C.DA TRINITÀ, 6
83052 PATERNOPOLI [AV]
TEL. +39 3492957565
ltecce@libero.it

PRE-BOOKED VISITS
ANNUAL PRODUCTION 10,000 bottles
HECTARES UNDER VINE 5.00

Luigi Tecce is as unpredictable as his wines. He spends his time amid vineyards located between Paternopoli and Castelfranci where he cares for five hectares of Aglianico, some dating back to 1930 and trained on raggiera (wheel-spoked) systems. The very low-yield harvest is done manually and vineyards are managed in an entirely natural manner. No herbicides or other chemical products are used here, only copper and sulfur and vinification takes place in amphorae, mid-sized casks or chestnut tanks. The Taurasi Puro Sangue '15 bewitched during our tastings. It has the makings of a great wine, exhibiting power and energy, healthy fruit and a sapid thrust that's in a class of its own. Notes of blood orange and pepper rise up out of the glass, while on the palate it proves extremely long and flavorful. The Taurasi Vecchie Vigne is marked by intense, earthy sensations, echoes of roots and coffee. It's more mature but nevertheless charming.

● Taurasi Puro Sangue Ris. '14	♟♟♟ 6
● Taurasi Poliphemo V. V. Ris. '14	♟♟ 6
● Taurasi Poliphemo '08	♟♟♟ 6
● Taurasi Poliphemo '07	♟♟♟ 6
● Irpinia Campi Taurasini Satyricon '15	♟♟ 4
● Irpinia Campi Taurasini Satyricon '14	♟♟ 4
● Irpinia Campi Taurasini Satyricon '13	♟♟ 4
● Irpinia Campi Taurasini Satyricon '12	♟♟ 5
● Irpinia Campi Taurasini Satyricon '10	♟♟ 5
● Taurasi Poliphemo '13	♟♟ 6
● Taurasi Poliphemo '12	♟♟ 6
● Taurasi Poliphemo '11	♟♟ 6
● Taurasi Poliphemo '10	♟♟ 6
● Taurasi Poliphemo '09	♟♟ 7

Tenuta del Meriggio

C.DA SERRA, 79/81A
83038 MONTEMILETTO [AV]
TEL. +39 0825962282
www.tenutadelmeriggio.it

CELLAR SALES
PRE-BOOKED VISITS
ANNUAL PRODUCTION 65,000 bottles
HECTARES UNDER VINE 23.00
SUSTAINABLE WINERY

Founded in 2010, Bruno Pizza's 23-hecta winery is in great form and has managed establish a position for itself among the other excellent regional estates. This success can be attributed to high-quality advice and, above all, vineyards with optimal aspects that include some truly valuable, long-established plots. The classic trio of Irpinian appellations, Fiano di Avellino, Greco di Tufo and Taurasi are drawn on for wines characterized by their great freshness and clean taste. What we found during our tastings was a new, high-quality selection. In particular, the Fiano di Avellino '18 stands out for its fre and minty fragrances. It exhibits a decidedly balanced structure for a creamy sapid wine, while the finish features penetrating sensations of ginger and whit peach. The Greco di Tufo '18 also delivere with its notes of ripe wheat and aniseed. It's well-typed in its savory accents, sensations that reemerge in a characterfu finish. The mature and spicy Taurasi '14 i still a bit behind in terms of aromatic focu but it has nice prospects.

○ Fiano di Avellino '18	♟♟
○ Greco di Tufo '18	♟♟
● Taurasi '14	♟♟
○ Fiano di Avellino '17	♟♟♟
○ Greco di Tufo '18	♟♟
○ Greco di Tufo '17	♟♟

erre Stregate

: Santa Lucia
034 Guardia Sanframondi [BN]
. +39 0824817857
w.terrestregate.it

CLLAR SALES
RE-BOOKED VISITS
NNUAL PRODUCTION 130,000 bottles
CTARES UNDER VINE 22.00
STAINABLE WINERY

e Benevento winery is led by the volcanic
omena Iacobucci and her brother Carlo.
success can largely be attributed to their
termination, will, ambition, and courage.
ually important are the multiple versions
the multifaceted Falanghina that are
ered at decidedly good prices
nsidering their quality. It's no surprise,
erefore, that the wines are being enjoyed
ousands of kilometers from the Guardia
nframondi winery as they increasingly
vel around the world. Once again the
anghina del Sannio Svelato hits the
rk. The 2018 is full of character,
dolent of bergamot orange and green tea,
h a delicately smoky note that grows in
e glass. The palate is rich and dynamic,
h a long, clear and vivid finish. The
langhina Trama '18 is more citrusy and
ear, while the Falanghina Caracara '16
nvinces with its mature aromas of fruit
ticipating a palate rich in sensations of
megranate and citron.

Terredora Di Paolo

VIA SERRA
83030 Montefusco [AV]
Tel. +39 0825968215
www.terredora.com

CELLAR SALES
PRE-BOOKED VISITS
ACCOMMODATION
ANNUAL PRODUCTION 700,000 bottles
HECTARES UNDER VINE 200.00

The winery, founded in 1993 by Walter
Mastroberardino and now led by his
children Paolo and Daniela, is unique. Few
other producers in the area can count on
200 hectares of vineyards located in
Irpinia's most important appellations. Serra
di Montefusco and Santa Paolina are
planted with Greco di Tufo; Lapio and
Montemiletto provide Fiano and Aglianico;
Pietradeifusi gives rise to Taurasi; and
Falanghina comes from the estate of
Gesualdo. The diverse plots are the result
of astute, far-sighted choices that allow the
family to offer a wide range. The Taurasi
Fatica Contadina is made with select
grapes from their Lapio and Montemiletto
vineyards. It tantalizes with its spicy
accents, its aromas of wild berry and
licorice. On the palate it proves opulent,
with a clear, balsamic finish. The 2015
version of their Aglianico Corte di Giso also
proves quite valid.

Falanghina del Sannio Svelato '18	♟♟♟ 3*
Caracara Falanghina '16	♟♟ 6
Costa del Duca Aglianico '15	♟♟ 7
Falanghina Trama '18	♟♟ 2*
Sannio Aglianico Arcano Ris. '14	♟♟ 5
Sannio Fiano Genius Loci '18	♟ 3
Sannio Greco Aurora '18	♟ 3
Falanghina del Sannio Svelato '17	♟♟♟ 2*
Falanghina del Sannio Svelato '16	♟♟♟ 2*
Falanghina del Sannio Svelato '15	♟♟♟ 2*
Falanghina del Sannio Svelato '14	♟♟♟ 2*
Falanghina del Sannio Svelato '13	♟♟♟ 2*
Sannio Aglianico Manent '16	♟♟ 2*
Sannio Fiano Genius Loci '17	♟♟ 3

● Corte di Giso Aglianico '15	♟♟ 2*
● Taurasi Fatica Contadina '12	♟♟ 5
○ Fiano di Avellino '18	♟ 5
○ Fiano di Avellino Campore '15	♟ 5
○ Irpinia Coda di Volpe Le Starse '18	♟ 3
● Taurasi Fatica Contadina '08	♟♟♟ 5
○ Fiano di Avellino '17	♟♟ 5
○ Fiano di Avellino '16	♟♟ 3
○ Fiano di Avellino Terredora Di Paolo '15	♟♟ 3
○ Greco di Tufo Loggia della Serra '17	♟♟ 3
● Taurasi Pago dei Fusi '11	♟♟ 5
● Taurasi Pago dei Fusi '10	♟♟ 5

Traerte

c.da Vadiaperti
83030 Montefredane [AV]
Tel. +39 0825607270
info@traerte.it

CELLAR SALES
PRE-BOOKED VISITS
ANNUAL PRODUCTION 81,000 bottles
HECTARES UNDER VINE 6.00

Raffaele Troisi is a true, instinctive vigneron who safeguards the traditions and conscience of this corner of Irpinia. He gambled on the enormous potential of the slopes here and was one of Montefredane's first growers to vinify and bottle in his own cellar, interpreting local Fiano, Greco and Coda di Volpe. Raffaele's style is well defined and easily recognizable: austere, tight, with a great deal of acidity, rough when young but also capable of great evolution over time. The Greco di Tufo Tornante '18 has all the qualities of a great wine. It starts with unembellished sensations of flint, only to unleash hints of sesame and aniseed. On the palate it's a bolt of savoriness and flavor, proving dry and assertive, the groundwork for a linear, multi-layered, rhythmic development. It's a white that will age particularly well. The Coda di Volpe Torama '18, a wine redolent of coffee and mature lemon, is certainly not lacking in personality.

○ Greco di Tufo Tornante '18	🍷🍷🍷	5
○ Irpinia Coda di Volpe Torama '18	🍷🍷	5
○ Fiano di Avellino '18	🍷	3
○ Fiano di Avellino Aipierti '18	🍷	5
○ Greco di Tufo '18	🍷	3
○ Fiano di Avellino Aipierti '17	🍸🍸	5
○ Fiano di Avellino Aipierti '16	🍸🍸	5
○ Fiano di Avellino Aipierti '15	🍸🍸	5
○ Greco di Tufo '17	🍸🍸	3
○ Greco di Tufo Tornante '17	🍸🍸	5
○ Greco di Tufo Tornante '15	🍸🍸	5
○ Irpinia Coda di Volpe '17	🍸🍸	2*
○ Irpinia Coda di Volpe Torama '17	🍸🍸	5
○ Irpinia Coda di Volpe Torama '15	🍸🍸	5

Villa Dora

via Bosco Mauro, 1
80040 Terzigno [NA]
Tel. +39 0815295016
www.cantinevilladora.it

CELLAR SALES
PRE-BOOKED VISITS
RESTAURANT SERVICE
ANNUAL PRODUCTION 60,000 bottles
HECTARES UNDER VINE 15.00
VITICULTURE METHOD Certified Organic

Vincenzo Ambrosio returns to Italian Wine in a crown of laurels after a long period of absence. His winery is not far from Pompeii, in the heart of the Vesuvius National Park in Terzigno. Production here originally focused on groves of Frantoio, Leccino and Nocellara olives. Wine production was added in 1997 and today sees fifteen hectares of vineyards on the slopes of Vesuvius at an elevation of 250 meters. Coda di Volpe, Falanghina, Piedirosso and Aglianico are trained on traditional Vesuvian arbors in vineyards framed by brush, olive trees and ornamental plants. The Lacryma Christi d Vesuvio Vigna del Vulcano '17 landed a place in our final round of tastings. It has highly complex, fumé verve that calls up flint and roots on a sulfurous backdrop. It rich in mature fruit, with a development punctuated by salt, making for a wine of volcanic charm and personality, and an extremely long finish.

○ Lacryma Christi del Vesuvio Bianco V. del Vulcano '17	🍷🍷
● Lacryma Christi del Vesuvio Rosso Forgiato '16	🍷
● Lacryma Christi del Vesuvio Rosso Gelsonero '16	🍷
○ Vesuvio Lacryma Christi Bianco V. del Vulcano '09	🍸🍸

Villa Matilde Avallone

ɒa st.le Domitiana, 18
030 Cellole [CE]
ʟ. +39 0823932088
www.villamatilde.it

CELLAR SALES
PRE-BOOKED VISITS
ACCOMMODATION AND RESTAURANT SERVICE
ANNUAL PRODUCTION 700,000 bottles
HECTARES UNDER VINE 130.00
SUSTAINABLE WINERY

Salvatore and Maria Avallone are excellent interpreters and belong to Falerno's long winemaking tradition (which was already extraordinarily famous in ancient Roman times). The vineyards are not limited to the volcanic soils of the area, but also include Irpinia and Sannio, thanks to Tenute di Altavilla and Tenuta Rocca dei Leoni, respectively. The range is large, solid and complete. The Falerno del Massico Rosso '15 put in a nice performance by bringing together the vintage's summery, meaty character with notable freshness. Fragrant and full, it's marked by notes of blackberries and licorice, sensations that give way to a finish of printer's ink and pencil lead. Aromas of medlar adorned by sulfurous notes introduce the Falerno del Massico Bianco Vigna Caracci '16. On the palate it exhibits depth and rhythm, making for a finish characterized by notable sapidity. The rest of their selection proves reliable, the Vigna Camarato '14 standing out for its aromas of roots and its open, mature profile.

Falerno del Massico Bianco V. Caracci '16	♥♥ 5
Falerno del Massico Bianco '18	♥♥ 3
Falerno del Massico Rosso '15	♥♥ 3
Falerno del Massico Rosso V. Camarato Ris. '14	♥♥ 7
Sinuessa Falanghina '18	♥♥ 2*
Aglianico '16	♥ 2
Greco di Tufo Daltavilla '18	♥ 3
Mata Brut	♥ 5
Taurasi Fusonero '15	♥ 6
Falerno del Massico Bianco V. Caracci '08	♥♥♥ 3
Falerno del Massico Bianco V. Caracci '05	♥♥♥ 3
Falerno del Massico Bianco V. Caracci '04	♥♥♥ 3*

Villa Raiano

via Bosco Satrano, 1
83020 San Michele di Serino [AV]
Tel. +39 0825595663
www.villaraiano.com

CELLAR SALES
PRE-BOOKED VISITS
RESTAURANT SERVICE
ANNUAL PRODUCTION 300,000 bottles
HECTARES UNDER VINE 22.00
VITICULTURE METHOD Certified Organic

Villa Raiano was founded in 1996 by Sabino and Simone Basso. The winery sits on a hill that guards the Sabato River valley overlooking a unique landscape framed by chestnut forests and vineyards. Enologist Fortunato Sebastiano tends to the different crus; Marotta di Montefusco for Greco, Alimata di Montefredane and Ventidue di Lapio for Fiano, and Castelfranci for Aglianico. Much has happened at the winery since the last Guide, including the addition of plots in the Bosco Satrano area of San Michele di Serino and the Ponte dei Santi area of Altavilla. The Basso family submitted a dazzling selection. The Fiano di Avellino Bosco Satrano '17 features a multifaceted, poignant noise reminiscent of wood resin and citron, aromas that anticipate a creamy, delicately smoky palate of crystalline precision. Tre Bicchieri hands down. The Fiano Alimata proves it has plenty of character, while the new Greco Ponte dei Santi exhibits extraordinary gustatory depth.

○ Fiano di Avellino Bosco Satrano '17	♥♥♥ 4*
○ Fiano di Avellino Alimata '17	♥♥ 4
○ Greco di Tufo Ponte dei Santi '17	♥♥ 4
○ Fiano di Avellino '18	♥♥ 4
○ Fiano di Avellino Ventidue '17	♥♥ 4
○ Greco di Tufo '18	♥♥ 3
● Taurasi '14	♥♥ 5
○ Fiano di Avellino 22 '13	♥♥♥ 4*
○ Fiano di Avellino Alimata '15	♥♥♥ 4*
○ Fiano di Avellino Alimata '10	♥♥♥ 4
○ Fiano di Avellino Ventidue '16	♥♥♥ 4*
○ Fiano di Avellino '17	♥♥ 3
○ Fiano di Avellino Alimata '16	♥♥ 4
○ Greco di Tufo '17	♥♥ 3
● Irpinia Campi Taurasini Costa Baiano '15	♥♥ 3

Aia dei Colombi

C.DA SAPENZIE
82034 GUARDIA SANFRAMONDI [BN]
TEL. +39 0824817139
www.aiadeicolombi.it

CELLAR SALES
PRE-BOOKED VISITS
ANNUAL PRODUCTION 60,000 bottles
HECTARES UNDER VINE 10.00

○ Falanghina del Sannio Guardia Sanframondi Vignasuprema '18	♟♟ 2*
● Sannio Aglianico Guardia Sanframondi '16	♟ 3

Antico Castello

C.DA POPPANO, 11BIS
83050 SAN MANGO SUL CALORE [AV]
TEL. +39 3408062830
www.anticocastello.com

CELLAR SALES
PRE-BOOKED VISITS
ACCOMMODATION AND RESTAURANT SERVIC
ANNUAL PRODUCTION 50,000 bottles
HECTARES UNDER VINE 10.00
SUSTAINABLE WINERY

○ Irpinia Fiano Orfeo '18	♟♟
● Irpinia Aglianico Magis '15	♟
● Taurasi '14	♟

Cantine Barone

VIA GIARDINO, 2
84070 RUTINO [SA]
TEL. +39 0974830463
www.cantinebarone.it

CELLAR SALES
PRE-BOOKED VISITS
ACCOMMODATION
ANNUAL PRODUCTION 100,000 bottles
HECTARES UNDER VINE 12.00
VITICULTURE METHOD Certified Organic

○ Cilento Fiano Vignolella '18	♟♟ 3
● Pietralena Aglianico '17	♟♟ 2*
○ Marsia Bianco '18	♟ 1*
● Miles '16	♟ 5

Boccella

VIA SANT'EUSTACHIO
83040 CASTELFRANCI [AV]
TEL. +39 082772574
www.boccellavini.it

CELLAR SALES
PRE-BOOKED VISITS
ANNUAL PRODUCTION 10,000 bottles
HECTARES UNDER VINE 5.00
VITICULTURE METHOD Certified Organic

○ Casefatte Fiano '17	♟♟
● Irpinia Campi Taurasini Rasott '16	♟♟

Borgodangelo

C.DA BOSCO SELVA, S.P. 52 KM 10,00
83050 SANT'ANGELO ALL'ESCA [AV]
TEL. +39 082773027
www.borgodangelo.it

CELLAR SALES
PRE-BOOKED VISITS
RESTAURANT SERVICE
ANNUAL PRODUCTION 30,000 bottles
HECTARES UNDER VINE 9.00
SUSTAINABLE WINERY

○ Fiano di Avellino '18	♟♟ 2*
● Irpinia Campi Taurasini '14	♟♟ 3
◉ Irpinia Rosato '18	♟♟ 2*
● Taurasi '13	♟♟ 4

I Cacciagalli

P.ZZA DELLA VITTORIA, 27
81059 TEANO [CE]
TEL. +39 0823875216
www.icacciagalli.it

CELLAR SALES
PRE-BOOKED VISITS
ACCOMMODATION
ANNUAL PRODUCTION 20,000 bottles
HECTARES UNDER VINE 9.00
VITICULTURE METHOD Certified Organic

○ Aorivola '18	♟♟
○ Aorivola '18	♟♟

antina del Barone

Nocelleto, 21
3020 Cesinali [AV]
⌐. +39 0825666751
www.cantinadelbarone.it

CELLAR SALES
PRE-BOOKED VISITS
ANNUAL PRODUCTION 30,000 bottles
HECTARES UNDER VINE 2.50

Paone '18	♟♟ 3
Particella 928 '18	♟♟ 3

Casa Di Baal

C. Macchia
Tiziano, 14
-096 Montecorvino Rovella [SA]
⌐. +39 089981143
www.casadibaal.it

CELLAR SALES
PRE-BOOKED VISITS
ANNUAL PRODUCTION 25,000 bottles
HECTARES UNDER VINE 5.00
VITICULTURE METHOD Certified Organic
SUSTAINABLE WINERY

Fiano di Baal '17	♟♟ 3
Aglianico di Baal '18	♟ 3
Bianco di Baal '18	♟ 2
Rosso di Baal '18	♟ 2

enute Casoli

Roma, 28
3040 Candida [AV]
⌐. +39 3402958099
www.tenutecasoli.it

CELLAR SALES
PRE-BOOKED VISITS
ACCOMMODATION AND RESTAURANT SERVICE
ANNUAL PRODUCTION 65,000 bottles
HECTARES UNDER VINE 13.00

Greco di Tufo Cupavaticale '16	♟♟ 5
Fiano di Avellino Kryos '18	♟ 3

Cantine del Mare

via Cappella IV, trav. 6
80070 Monte di Procida [NA]
Tel. +39 0815233040
www.cantinedelmare.it

CELLAR SALES
PRE-BOOKED VISITS
ANNUAL PRODUCTION '35,000 bottles
HECTARES UNDER VINE 11.00

○ Campi Flegrei Falanghina Sorbo Bianco '16	♟♟ 3
● Campi Flegrei Piedirosso Sorbo Rosso Ris. '16	♟♟ 4

Case d'Alto

via Piave, 1
83035 Grottaminarda [AV]
Tel. +39 3397000779
www.casedalto.it

CELLAR SALES
ANNUAL PRODUCTION 10,000 bottles
HECTARES UNDER VINE 6.00
VITICULTURE METHOD Certified Organic

○ Fiano di Avellino Eclissi '17	♟♟ 3
● Taurasi '13	♟♟ 5

Castelle

s.da Nazionale Sannitica, 48
82037 Castelvenere [BN]
Tel. +39 0824940232
www.castelle.it

ANNUAL PRODUCTION 50,000 bottles
HECTARES UNDER VINE 4.00

○ Falanghina del Sannio '18	♟♟ 2*
○ Falanghina del Sannio Kidonia V. T. '16	♟ 3
● Sannio Aglianico '15	♟ 4
● Sannio Barbera '17	♟ 2

Cautiero

C.DA ARBUSTI
82030 FRASSO TELESINO [BN]
TEL. +39 3387640641
www.cautiero.it

CELLAR SALES
ACCOMMODATION
ANNUAL PRODUCTION 18,000 bottles
HECTARES UNDER VINE 4.00
VITICULTURE METHOD Certified Organic

○ Sannio Greco Trois '18	♟♟ 2*
○ Erba Bianca '17	♟ 2
○ Falanghina del Sannio Fois '18	♟ 2

Cenatiempo Vini d'Ischia

VIA BALDASSARRE COSSA, 84
80077 ISCHIA [NA]
TEL. +39 081981107
www.vinicenatiempo.it

CELLAR SALES
PRE-BOOKED VISITS
ANNUAL PRODUCTION 70,000 bottles
HECTARES UNDER VINE 4.00

○ Ischia Biancolella '18	♟♟
○ Ischia Forastera '18	♟♟
● Ischia Per' 'e Palummo '18	♟

Colle del Corsicano

C.DA FRANCO
84048 CASTELLABATE [SA]
TEL. +39 3398471226
www.ilcolledelcorsicano.it

ANNUAL PRODUCTION 4,000 bottles
HECTARES UNDER VINE 3.00

○ Cilento Fiano Licosa '18	♟♟ 3
● Patrinius '18	♟♟ 3

Colli di Castelfranci

C.DA BRAUDIANO
83040 CASTELFRANCI [AV]
TEL. +39 082772392
www.collidicastelfranci.com

CELLAR SALES
PRE-BOOKED VISITS
ACCOMMODATION AND RESTAURANT SERVIC●
ANNUAL PRODUCTION 150,000 bottles
HECTARES UNDER VINE 25.00

○ Fiano di Avellino Pendino '18	♟♟
○ Greco di Tufo Grotte '18	♟
● Irpinia Campi Taurasini Candriano '13	♟
● Taurasi Alta Valle '12	♟

Michele Contrada

C.DA TAVERNA, 31
83040 CANDIDA [AV]
TEL. +39 0825988434
www.vinicontrada.it

CELLAR SALES
PRE-BOOKED VISITS
ANNUAL PRODUCTION 60,000 bottles
HECTARES UNDER VINE 10.00

○ Fiano di Avellino '18	♟♟ 3
○ Fiano di Avellino Selvecorte '17	♟♟ 3
○ Greco di Tufo '18	♟ 3
● Taurasi '14	♟ 5

Contrada Salandra

FRAZ. COSTE DI CUMA
VIA TRE PICCIONI, 40
80078 POZZUOLI [NA]
TEL. +39 0815265258
contradasalandra@gmail.com

CELLAR SALES
PRE-BOOKED VISITS
ANNUAL PRODUCTION 20,000 bottles
HECTARES UNDER VINE 4.70

○ Campi Flegrei Falanghina '17	♟♟
● Campi Flegrei Piedirosso '16	♟♟

uomo - I Vini del Cavaliere

FEUDO LA PILA, 16
1047 CAPACCIO PAESTUM [SA]
L. +39 0828725376
www.vinicuomo.com

CELLAR SALES
PRE-BOOKED VISITS
RESTAURANT SERVICE
ANNUAL PRODUCTION 25,000 bottles
HECTARES UNDER VINE 4.00

Cilento Fiano Heraion '18	🍷🍷 3
Leukòs Fiano '18	🍷🍷 3
Cilento Aglianico Granatum '17	🍷 3

D'Antiche Terre

C.DA LO PIANO
83030 MANOCALZATI [AV]
TEL. +39 0825675358
www.danticheterre.it

CELLAR SALES
PRE-BOOKED VISITS
ACCOMMODATION AND RESTAURANT SERVICE
ANNUAL PRODUCTION 420,000 bottles
HECTARES UNDER VINE 40.00
SUSTAINABLE WINERY

● Irpinia Aglianico Macchia della Corte '12	🍷🍷 2*
○ Greco di Tufo Le Saure '18	🍷 3
● Taurasi Macchia della Corte '12	🍷 5

iticoltori De Conciliis

C. QUERCE, 1
1060 PRIGNANO CILENTO [SA]
L. +39 0974831090
www.viticoltorideconciliis.it

CELLAR SALES
PRE-BOOKED VISITS
ANNUAL PRODUCTION 200,000 bottles
HECTARES UNDER VINE 21.00
VITICULTURE METHOD Certified Organic
SUSTAINABLE WINERY

Bacioilcielo Bianco '18	🍷🍷 2*
Naima '11	🍷 6
Perella '15	🍷 3

De Falco Vini

VIA FIGLIOLA, 91
80040 SAN SEBASTIANO AL VESUVIO [NA]
TEL. +39 0817713755
www.defalco.it

CELLAR SALES
PRE-BOOKED VISITS
ANNUAL PRODUCTION 350,000 bottles
HECTARES UNDER VINE 8.00

○ Greco di Tufo '18	🍷🍷 3
○ Lacryma Christi Vesuvio Bianco '18	🍷 3
● Lacryma Christi Vesuvio Rosso '18	🍷 3
● Vesuvio Piedirosso Leali dell'Angelo '17	🍷 5

De Gaeta

A TOPPOLOCOZZETTO, 1
3040 CASTELVETERE SUL CALORE [AV]
EL. +39 081660552
www.degaeta.it

ANNUAL PRODUCTION 15,000 bottles
HECTARES UNDER VINE 5.00
VITICULTURE METHOD Certified Organic
SUSTAINABLE WINERY

Irpinia Campi Taurasini '15	🍷🍷 4
Aglianico Rosato '18	🍷 3
Taurasi Duecape '15	🍷 5

Drengot

VIA DELLE VIOLE, 12
AVERSA [CE]
TEL. +39 08119042955
www.drengot.com

ANNUAL PRODUCTION 20,000 bottles
HECTARES UNDER VINE 12.00

○ Asprinio d'Aversa Scalillo '17	🍷🍷 5
○ Asprinio d'Aversa Brut Terramasca	🍷 6

Dryas

VIA TOPPOLE, 10
83030 MONTEFREDANE [AV]
TEL. +39 3472392634
www.cantinadryas.it

ANNUAL PRODUCTION 7,400 bottles
HECTARES UNDER VINE 2.00

○ Brut Et. Bianca	🍷🍷 3
○ Brut Et. Verde	🍷🍷 3
○ Et. Nera M. Cl. '15	🍷🍷 5

Farro

LOC. FUSARO
VIA VIRGILIO, 16/24
80070 BACOLI [NA]
TEL. +39 0818545555
www.cantinefarro.it

CELLAR SALES
PRE-BOOKED VISITS
ANNUAL PRODUCTION 207,000 bottles
HECTARES UNDER VINE 20.00

○ Campi Flegrei Falanghina Le Cigliate '17	🍷🍷
⊙ Campi Flegrei Depié Rosé '18	🍷

Cantine Federiciane Monteleone

FRAZ. SAN ROCCO
VIA ANTICA CONSOLARE CAMPANA, 34
80016 MARANO DI NAPOLI [NA]
TEL. +39 0815765294
www.federiciane.it

CELLAR SALES
PRE-BOOKED VISITS
ANNUAL PRODUCTION 200,000 bottles
HECTARES UNDER VINE 15.00

● Penisola Sorrentina Gragnano '18	🍷🍷 2*
● Penisola Sorrentina Lettere '18	🍷🍷 2*
○ Campi Flegrei Falanghina '18	🍷 2

Cantina Fosso degli Angeli

C.DA ACQUARIO, 12
82027 CASALDUNI [BN]
TEL. +39 3492662936
www.fossodegliangeli.it

CELLAR SALES
PRE-BOOKED VISITS
ANNUAL PRODUCTION 40,000 bottles
HECTARES UNDER VINE 6.00
VITICULTURE METHOD Certified Organic

○ Falanghina del Sannio Biologico Cese '17	🍷🍷
○ Sannio Aglianico Safim Ris. '15	🍷

Raffaele Guastaferro

VIA A. GRAMSCI
83030 TAURASI [AV]
TEL. +39 3341551543
info@guastaferro.it

CELLAR SALES
ANNUAL PRODUCTION 10,000 bottles
HECTARES UNDER VINE 7.00

○ Fulgeo '18	🍷🍷 4
● Taurasi Primum '14	🍷🍷 6
● Irpinia Aglianico Memini '15	🍷 2

Historia Antiqua

VIA VARIANTE EST S.S 7BIS, 75
83030 MANOCALZATI [AV]
TEL. +39 0825675240
www.historiaantiqua.it

CELLAR SALES
PRE-BOOKED VISITS
ANNUAL PRODUCTION 90,000 bottles
HECTARES UNDER VINE 40.00

● Taurasi '14	🍷🍷
○ Fiano di Avellino '18	🍷
○ Greco di Tufo '18	🍷
● Irpinia Aglianico '15	🍷

unarossa

V. Fortunato P.I.P. Lotto 10
095 Giffoni Valle Piana [SA]
.. +39 0898021016
ww.viniepassione.it

CELLAR SALES
PRE-BOOKED VISITS
ANNUAL PRODUCTION 50,000 bottles
HECTARES UNDER VINE 4.50

Borgomastro '15	🏆🏆 6
Costacielo Bianco '18	🏆🏆 3
Costacielo Fiano '18	🏆🏆 3
Camporeale Falanghina '18	🏆 2

Masseria Felicia

Fraz. Carano
loc. San Terenzano
81037 Sessa Aurunca [CE]
Tel. +39 0823935095
www.masseriafelicia.it

CELLAR SALES
PRE-BOOKED VISITS
ANNUAL PRODUCTION 25,000 bottles
HECTARES UNDER VINE 5.00

○ Falerno del Massico Bianco Anthologia '18	🏆🏆 3
● Inpunta Dirosso '16	🏆🏆 3
● Falerno del Massico Rosso Et. Bronzo '15	🏆 5
○ Sinopea '18	🏆 2

Montesole

Serra
030 Montefusco [AV]
. +39 0825963972
ww.montesole.it

PRE-BOOKED VISITS
ACCOMMODATION AND RESTAURANT SERVICE
ANNUAL PRODUCTION 750,000 bottles
HECTARES UNDER VINE 50.00
SUSTAINABLE WINERY

Fiano di Avellino '18	🏆🏆 3
Fiano di Avellino V. Acquaviva '18	🏆 3
Greco di Tufo '18	🏆 3
Greco di Tufo V. Breccia '18	🏆 3

Le Ormere

via San Bernardino
83030 Santa Paolina [AV]
Tel. +39 32737322187
www.leormere.it

CELLAR SALES
ANNUAL PRODUCTION 7,000 bottles
HECTARES UNDER VINE 1.50

○ Greco di Tufo '18	🏆🏆 3

affaele Palma

. San Vito
Arsenale, 8
010 Maiori [SA]
. +39 3357601858
ww.raffaelepalma.it

CELLAR SALES
ANNUAL PRODUCTION 20,000 bottles
HECTARES UNDER VINE 6.00
VITICULTURE METHOD Certified Organic
SUSTAINABLE WINERY

Ginestra '18	🏆🏆 3
Costa d'Amalfi Bianco Puntacroce '17	🏆 6
Costa d'Amalfi Rosato Salicerchi '18	🏆 6

Gennaro Papa

p.zza Limata, 2
81030 Falciano del Massico [CE]
Tel. +39 0823931267
www.gennaropapa.it

CELLAR SALES
PRE-BOOKED VISITS
ANNUAL PRODUCTION 26,500 bottles
HECTARES UNDER VINE 6.00
SUSTAINABLE WINERY

● Falerno del Massico Primitivo Conclave '17	🏆🏆 4
● Falerno del Massico Primitivo Campantuono '16	🏆 6

Perillo

C.DA VALLE, 19
83040 CASTELFRANCI [AV]
TEL. +39 082772252
cantinaperillo@libero.it

CELLAR SALES
PRE-BOOKED VISITS
ANNUAL PRODUCTION 20,000 bottles
HECTARES UNDER VINE 5.00

● Taurasi '09   🏆🏆 6

Porto di Mola

S.S. 430, KM 16,200
81050 ROCCA D'EVANDRO [CE]
TEL. +39 0823925801
www.portodimola.it

CELLAR SALES
PRE-BOOKED VISITS
ANNUAL PRODUCTION 300,000 bottles
HECTARES UNDER VINE 50.00

● Galluccio Contra del Duca '13   🏆🏆
○ Galluccio Petratonda '18   🏆🏆
○ Collelepre '18   🏆
○ Montecamino '18   🏆

Andrea Reale

LOC. B.GO DI GETE
VIA CARDAMONE, 75
84010 TRAMONTI [SA]
TEL. +39 089856144
www.aziendaagricolareale.it

CELLAR SALES
PRE-BOOKED VISITS
ACCOMMODATION AND RESTAURANT SERVICE
ANNUAL PRODUCTION 16,000 bottles
HECTARES UNDER VINE 3.50
VITICULTURE METHOD Certified Organic

● Borgo di Gete '15   🏆🏆 6
○ Costa d'Amalfi Tramonti Rosato Getis '18   🏆🏆 4
○ Costa d'Amalfi Tramonti Bianco Aliseo '18   🏆 4

Regina Viarum

LOC. FALCIANO DEL MASSICO
VIA VELLARIA
81030 FALCIANO DEL MASSICO [CE]
TEL. +39 0823931299
www.reginaviarum.it

CELLAR SALES
PRE-BOOKED VISITS
ANNUAL PRODUCTION 19,000 bottles
HECTARES UNDER VINE 5.00
VITICULTURE METHOD Certified Organic
SUSTAINABLE WINERY

● Falerno del Massico Primitivo Zer05 '16   🏆🏆
● Falerno del Massico Primitivo
    V. Barone '15   🏆🏆
○ Petali Rosato '18   🏆

Santiquaranta

C.DA TORREPALAZZO
82030 TORRECUSO [BN]
TEL. +39 0824876128
www.santiquaranta.it

CELLAR SALES
PRE-BOOKED VISITS
ANNUAL PRODUCTION 45,000 bottles
HECTARES UNDER VINE 6.00
SUSTAINABLE WINERY

○ Sannio Moscato '18   🏆🏆 3
○ Falanghina del Sannio
    Tempo del Peccato '18   🏆 2
● Suono del Tempo Aglianico '13   🏆 3

Lorenzo Nifo Sarrapochiello

VIA PIANA, 62
82030 PONTE [BN]
TEL. +39 0824876450
www.nifo.eu

CELLAR SALES
PRE-BOOKED VISITS
ANNUAL PRODUCTION 90,000 bottles
HECTARES UNDER VINE 18.00
VITICULTURE METHOD Certified Organic

○ Falanghina del Sannio Alenta V. T. '17   🏆🏆
○ Sannio Fiano '18   🏆
● Sannio Taburno Rosso Serrone '16   🏆

Cantina di Solopaca

A Bebiana, 44
2036 Solopaca [BN]
TEL. +39 0824977921
www.cantinasolopaca.it

CELLAR SALES
PRE-BOOKED VISITS
ANNUAL PRODUCTION 700,000 bottles
HECTARES UNDER VINE 1300.00

Falanghina del Sannio '18	🏆 2*
Sannio Solopaca Rosso Sup. '16	🍷 2

Terre del Principe

C. CASTEL CAMPAGNANO
ZZA MUNICIPIO 4
1010 Castel Campagnano [CE]
EL. +39 0823867126
www.terredelprincipe.com

CELLAR SALES
PRE-BOOKED VISITS
ANNUAL PRODUCTION 20,000 bottles
HECTARES UNDER VINE 7.00
VITICULTURE METHOD Certified Organic
SUSTAINABLE WINERY

Ambruco '15	🏆 5
Centomoggia Casavecchia '15	🏆 3
Le Sèrole Pallagrello Bianco '17	🏆 5
Piancastelli '15	🏆 8

Torelle

C. TORELLE
NAZIONALE APPIA, 1
ESSA AURUNCA [CE]
EL. +39 392185208
www.vinitorelle.com

ANNUAL PRODUCTION 12,000 bottles
HECTARES UNDER VINE 4.00

Aglianico '17	🏆 3
Aglianico Rosato '18	🏆 3
Falerno del Massico Rosso '14	🏆 3
Falanghina '18	🍷 2

Sorrentino

VIA RIO, 26
80042 Boscotrecase [NA]
TEL. +39 0818584963
www.sorrentinovini.com

CELLAR SALES
PRE-BOOKED VISITS
ACCOMMODATION AND RESTAURANT SERVICE
ANNUAL PRODUCTION 250,000 bottles
HECTARES UNDER VINE 30.00
VITICULTURE METHOD Certified Organic

● Lacryma Christi del Vesuvio Rosso V. Lapillo '16	🏆 2*
○ Vesuvio Caprettone Benita '31 '18	🏆 2*
● Vesuvio Piedirosso 7 Moggi '18	🍷 2

Cantine Tora

VIA TORA II
82030 Torrecuso [BN]
TEL. +39 0824872406
www.cantinetora.it

CELLAR SALES
PRE-BOOKED VISITS
ANNUAL PRODUCTION 55,000 bottles
HECTARES UNDER VINE 10.00

● Aglianico del Taburno '15	🏆 3*
● Costa San Rocco Aglianico '17	🏆 2*
○ Falanghina del Sannio Kissòs '15	🏆 3
○ Falanghina del Sannio '18	🍷 2

Torre a Oriente

LOC. MERCURI I, 19
82030 Torrecuso [BN]
TEL. +39 0824874376
www.torreaoriente.eu

CELLAR SALES
PRE-BOOKED VISITS
ACCOMMODATION AND RESTAURANT SERVICE
ANNUAL PRODUCTION 40,000 bottles
HECTARES UNDER VINE 10.00
SUSTAINABLE WINERY

○ Falanghina del Sannio Taburno Siriana '18	🏆 2*

Vallisassoli

VIA TUFARA SCAUTIERI, 47
SAN MARTINO VALLE CAUDINA [AV]
TEL. +39 3339942832

ANNUAL PRODUCTION 5,000 bottles
HECTARES UNDER VINE 2.00
VITICULTURE METHOD Certified Biodynamic
SUSTAINABLE WINERY

○ Bianco 33/33/33 '13   ♟♟ 6

VentitréFilari

VIA PIANTE, 43
83030 MONTEFREDANE [AV]
TEL. +39 0825672482
www.ventitrefilari.com

ANNUAL PRODUCTION 4,000 bottles
HECTARES UNDER VINE 0.80
VITICULTURE METHOD Certified Organic
SUSTAINABLE WINERY

○ Fiano di Avellino Numero Primo
  Ventitréfilari '17   ♟♟

Vestini Campagnano Poderi Foglia

VIA COSTA DELL'AIA, 9
81044 CONCA DELLA CAMPANIA [CE]
TEL. +39 0823679087
www.vestinicampagnano.it

CELLAR SALES
PRE-BOOKED VISITS
ANNUAL PRODUCTION 80,000 bottles
HECTARES UNDER VINE 7.00
VITICULTURE METHOD Certified Organic

● Casavecchia di Pontelatone Ris. '15   ♟♟ 5
● Connubio '15   ♟ 7
○ Le Ortole Pallagrello Bianco '18   ♟ 4
○ Pallagrello Bianco '18   ♟ 3

Vigne Guadagno

VIA TAGLIAMENTO, 237
83100 AVELLINO
TEL. +39 08251686379
www.vigneguadagno.it

CELLAR SALES
PRE-BOOKED VISITS
ANNUAL PRODUCTION 20,000 bottles
HECTARES UNDER VINE 7.00

○ Fiano di Avellino '17   ♟♟
● Taurasi '15   ♟♟
○ Fiano di Avellino Contrada Sant'Aniello '16   ♟
○ Greco di Tufo '17   ♟

Villa Diamante

VIA TOPPOLE, 16
83030 MONTEFREDANE [AV]
TEL. +39 3476791469
villadiamante1996@gmail.com

CELLAR SALES
PRE-BOOKED VISITS
ANNUAL PRODUCTION 10,000 bottles
HECTARES UNDER VINE 4.50

○ Fiano di Avellino Clos d'Haut '18   ♟♟ 5

Pierluigi Zampaglione

S.S. 399, KM 6
83045 CALITRI [AV]
TEL. +39 082738851
www.ildonchisciotte.net

CELLAR SALES
PRE-BOOKED VISITS
ANNUAL PRODUCTION 8,000 bottles
HECTARES UNDER VINE 2.50
VITICULTURE METHOD Certified Organic

○ Don Chisciotte '18   ♟♟

BASILICATA

ive of Basilicata's wines earned Tre Bicchieri, ut the most impressive statistic may be that ome 18 earned a place in our final tastings. It's figure that points to the region's health, despite he difficulties of a less-than-receptive domestic market and an international market that only a small few ave been able to break into. 5 outstanding Aglianico del Vultures prove the mportance of Vulture to Basilicata's wine industry. Those awarded include the istoric Paternoster, with their classic Don Anselmo '16 (it beat out an excellent Synthesi '17 that almost stole the show). The same holds for Cantine del Notaio, vhose fragrant Repertorio '17 triumphed over the richer and more concentrated La Firma '14, and Terre degli Svevi, which saw a Re Manfredi '16 defeat their more complex, but evolved, Serpara '15. Elena Fucci's Titolo '17 shone, while Grifalco's Gricos '17 took home top honors once again (the Piccini family are roudly and enthusiastically carrying on, despite the recent death of the winery's ounder, Fabrizio). But there are many producers hot on their trail, both in Vulture and Matera, and deserving of recognition. 2019 saw Matera feature as Europe's apital of culture and the event brought millions to the 'City of Stones'. Visitors rom all over the world were able to taste the region's wines and gastronomic pecialities, and admire churches, museums, monuments and the region's many natural landscapes. We hope that the occasion represents a starting point or Basilicata's wine industry as well, and that the region is able to obtain the nternational visibility that it deserves for its extraordinary products. The arrival f major investors and wine groups from other regions, like Gruppo Italiano Vini, eudi di San Gregorio, Fantini and Piccini, is a positive sign, underlining the value f these terroirs, and we hope that they contribute to the popularity of Basilicata's vines. But most importantly, we hope that it serves as a catalyst for all the egion's producers, who have the potential to grow in both quantity and quality.

Basilisco

VIA DELLE CANTINE
85022 BARILE [PZ]
TEL. +39 3484932431
piazza caracciolo

CELLAR SALES
PRE-BOOKED VISITS
ANNUAL PRODUCTION 55,000 bottles
HECTARES UNDER VINE 25.00
VITICULTURE METHOD Certified Organic
SUSTAINABLE WINERY

The cellar is in the center of Barile and its 25 hectares of vineyards are between Macario and Gelosia. These highly suitable areas resulted from the continuous lava flows of the now inactive Vulture. The vineyards are located at an elevation of between 450 and 600 meters, enjoying temperature ranges beneficial to the old vineyards, some of which are planted with ungrafted cultivars. Viviana Malafarina manages the winery, part of Feudi di San Gregorio, with competence and the results are evident: exclusively manual harvesting, vinification by cru and great attention to viticulture. The Aglianico del Vulture Teodosio is a beautifully structured, full red. The 2016 vintage is dominated by aromas of dark berries with spicy nuances and tobacco; elegant despite slightly astringent tannins attributable to youth, it's certainly higlhy enjoyable and dynamic. Their Basilisco '13 is complex, deep and rich, with a ruby color, balsamic character and woody finish.

● Aglianico del Vulture Teodosio '16	🍷🍷 3*
● Aglianico del Vulture Basilisco '13	🍷 6
○ Sophia '18	🍷 3
● Aglianico del Vulture Basilisco '09	ΥΥΥ 5
● Aglianico del Vulture Basilisco '08	ΥΥΥ 5
● Aglianico del Vulture Basilisco '07	ΥΥΥ 5
● Aglianico del Vulture Basilisco '06	ΥΥΥ 5
● Aglianico del Vulture Basilisco '04	ΥΥΥ 5
● Aglianico del Vulture Basilisco '01	ΥΥΥ 5
● Aglianico del Vulture Sup. Cruà '13	ΥΥΥ 5
● Aglianico del Vulture Basilisco '12	ΥΥ 6
● Aglianico del Vulture Sup. Cruà '15	ΥΥ 5
● Aglianico del Vulture Sup. Fontanelle '15	ΥΥ 5
● Aglianico del Vulture Sup. Fontanelle '13	ΥΥ 5
● Aglianico del Vulture Teodosio '14	ΥΥ 3

Battifarano

C.DA CERROLONGO, 1
75020 NOVA SIRI [MT]
TEL. +39 0835536174
www.battifarano.com

CELLAR SALES
PRE-BOOKED VISITS
ACCOMMODATION
ANNUAL PRODUCTION 70,000 bottles
HECTARES UNDER VINE 33.00
SUSTAINABLE WINERY

Masseria Battifarano is a long-established estate on Basilicata's Ionian coast. Vincenzo Battifarano and his son Francesco Paolo manage the entire production process and the vineyards located in Cerrolongo, Torre Bollita and Santa Lania. Here in the heart of Matera, the soil and sunny climate mild winters, allow for the production of quality wine. Intimate knowledge of the land has allowed Battifarano to select the best methods of cultivation and to avoid fertilizers and pesticides. Matera Moro Torre Bollita '17, as indicated by the name, is a blend of Cabernet Sauvignon, Primitivo and Merlot offering hints of spices, ripe cherries and grass. Lithe and easy to drink it contracts at the end with a still chafing tannin. Matera Akratos '17 is pure Primitivo: juicy and rich on the palate with a refreshing, persistent finish.

● Matera Moro Torre Bollita '17	🍷🍷 2*
● Matera Primitivo Akratos '17	🍷🍷 2*
○ Matera Greco Le Paglie '18	🍷 2
○ Toccacielo Bianco '18	🍷 2
● Toccacielo Rosso '17	🍷 2
● Cerrolongo Rosso '06	ΥΥ 2*
● Matera Moro Curaffanni Ris. '16	ΥΥ 3*
● Matera Moro Torre Bollita '07	ΥΥ 2
● Matera Primitivo Akratos '15	ΥΥ 2*
● Matera Primitivo Akratos '14	ΥΥ 2*
● Matera Primitivo Akratos '11	ΥΥ 2*
● Toccaculo '16	ΥΥ 2*

Cantine del Notaio

Via Roma, 159
85028 Rionero in Vulture [PZ]
Tel. +39 0972723689
www.cantinedelnotaio.it

CELLAR SALES
PRE-BOOKED VISITS
ANNUAL PRODUCTION 450,000 bottles
HECTARES UNDER VINE 40.00

Gerardo Giuratrabocchetti knows very well that life is full of surprises. At the age of forty he, along with his wife Marcella, decided to follow in his grandfather's footsteps by cultivating the family vineyards. The project enhances the Aglianico in selected terroirs of the Vulture volcano area. Wines with names inspired by his father's work as a notary are created, produced in the modern cellar and then allowed to mature in the caves dug into tuff stone in the 17th century. Gerardo didn't pull any punches this year when he presented the splendidly formed, dark ruby Aglianico del Vulture Il Repertorio '17 with intense vanilla, morello cherry and spices. Its structured, balanced and dynamic, rapid, rich in fruit and with a well-defined finish. La Firma '14 also stands out as deep, opulent, harmonious and very intriguing. It offers notes of black mulberry, India ink and mint that lead into a silky, very persistent mouth.

Aglianico del Vulture Il Repertorio '17	♟♟♟ 4*
Aglianico del Vulture Macarico '17	♟♟ 3*
Aglianico del Vulture Sup. La Firma '14	♟♟ 6
Aglianico del Vulture Il Sigillo '14	♟♟ 6
L'Autentica '17	♟♟ 5
La Parcella '18	♟♟ 7
La Raccolta '18	♟♟ 3
Xjnestra Macarico '18	♟♟ 2*
Aglianico del Vulture Macarì '17	♟ 3
Aglianico del Vulture Il Repertorio '16	♟♟♟ 4*
Aglianico del Vulture Il Repertorio '15	♟♟♟ 4*
Aglianico del Vulture Il Repertorio '14	♟♟♟ 4*
Aglianico del Vulture Il Repertorio '13	♟♟♟ 4*
Aglianico del Vulture Il Repertorio '12	♟♟♟ 4*
Aglianico del Vulture La Firma '10	♟♟♟ 6

Masseria Cardillo

Loc. Cardillo
s.s. 407 Basentana, km 97,5
75012 Bernalda [MT]
Tel. +39 0835748992
www.masseriacardillo.it

CELLAR SALES
ACCOMMODATION AND RESTAURANT SERVICE
ANNUAL PRODUCTION 50,000 bottles
HECTARES UNDER VINE 20.00

Masseria Cardillo, managed by brothers Rocco and Giovanni Graziadei, is in the heart of Metapontino, in Bernalda, an area of great archaeological interest that has always been agricultural. The family itself has been involved in farming since 1600, producing grain, olives and cattle. The vineyards, on calcareous soils, enjoy a temperate climate and thanks to the proximity of the sea the wines acquire a pleasant sapidity. 50,000 bottles per year in a diverse range of wines are obtained from 20 hectares of vineyards. The Aglianico del Vulture Rubra '15 is intense and refined, with sweet, spicy wood and red berries successfully teaming up in this modern interpretation of a classic wine. Delicate, with a beautiful tannic texture, it delivers creaminess and persistence. Their Primativo Baruch and Matera Moro, both aged in French oak barrels, are well-styled and pleasant.

● Aglianico del Vulture Rubra '15	♟♟ 3*
● Baruch Primitivo '15	♟♟ 5
● Matera Moro Malandrina '15	♟♟ 3
● Tittà '15	♟♟ 2*
○ Burla Moscato '18	♟ 2
○ Ovo Di Elena '18	♟ 2
● Vigna Giadì '16	♟ 2
● Aglianico del Vulture Rubra '06	♟♟ 3
● Matera Moro Malandrina '06	♟♟ 3
● Tittà '10	♟♟ 2*
● Tittà '05	♟♟ 2*
● Vigna Giadì '08	♟♟ 2
● Vigna Giadì '06	♟♟ 2*

★Elena Fucci

c.da Solagna del Titolo
85022 Barile [PZ]
Tel. +39 3204879945
www.elenafuccivini.com

CELLAR SALES
PRE-BOOKED VISITS
ANNUAL PRODUCTION 28,000 bottles
HECTARES UNDER VINE 7.00
VITICULTURE METHOD Certified Organic
SUSTAINABLE WINERY

Grandfather Generoso bought his first vineyards in the 1960s, in Contrada Solagna in the Valle del Titolo di Barile, at the foot of Monte Vulture. Back then, wine was produced for personal consumption, while the rest of the grapes were sold to area producers. In 2000, management passed into the hands of the witty and passionate enologist Elena Fucci; her grandfather, father Salvatore and husband Andrea all work in the winery. The modern cellar is designed according to the dictates of sustainable architecture, using technology that reduces energy consumption and carbon dioxide emissions. Titolo, the winery's only wine, is absolute class. 2017 delivered a red of great structure and fullness with strong aromas of black currant and blackberry followed by spices, toasted smoky notes, tobacco and light hints of vanilla. It's refreshing and soothing, yet also deep and layered, with smooth tannins and extraordinarily well-balanced fruit.

● Aglianico del Vulture Titolo '17	♛♛♛ 8
● Aglianico del Vulture Titolo '16	♛♛♛ 6
● Aglianico del Vulture Titolo '15	♛♛♛ 6
● Aglianico del Vulture Titolo '14	♛♛♛ 6
● Aglianico del Vulture Titolo '13	♛♛♛ 6
● Aglianico del Vulture Titolo '12	♛♛♛ 5
● Aglianico del Vulture Titolo '11	♛♛♛ 5
● Aglianico del Vulture Titolo '10	♛♛♛ 5
● Aglianico del Vulture Titolo '09	♛♛♛ 5
● Aglianico del Vulture Titolo '08	♛♛♛ 6
● Aglianico del Vulture Titolo '07	♛♛♛ 6
● Aglianico del Vulture Titolo '06	♛♛♛ 5
● Aglianico del Vulture Titolo '05	♛♛♛ 5
● Aglianico del Vulture Titolo '02	♛♛♛ 5
● Aglianico del Vulture Titolo '04	♛♛ 5

Grifalco della Lucania

loc. Pian di Camera
85029 Venosa [PZ]
Tel. +39 097231002
www.grifalcovini.com

CELLAR SALES
PRE-BOOKED VISITS
ANNUAL PRODUCTION 65,000 bottles
HECTARES UNDER VINE 15.00
VITICULTURE METHOD Certified Organic
SUSTAINABLE WINERY

How does one tell the story of a winery that fell in love with and will continue to love this region wholeheartedly? In 2003, Fabrizio Cecilia Piccin, who unfortunately passed away a few months ago, and his wife, after having been involved in Tuscan wine is various roles, decided to establish new estate in Basilicata. In love with Aglianico, a variety that is very different th from Sangiovese grown in Chianti and Montepulciano, they bought vineyards that spread between Maschito, Ginestra, Rapolla and Venosa. Lorenzo and Andrea now carry on their father's legacy with the same great passion. Their Aglianico del Vulure Gricos '17 takes the medal: its intense, elegant nose is notable for nuances of ripe red berries and tobacco. The same finesse follows on its sapid, harmonious palate with delicate tannins and featuring a big finish. The Grifalco '17 delivers a concentration of fruit and dense tannic texture, closing with persistence and elegance.

● Aglianico del Vulture Gricos '17	♛♛♛
● Aglianico del Vulture Grifalco '17	♛♛
● Aglianico del Vulture Duemila11 '11	♛
● Aglianico del Vulture Gricos '14	♛♛♛
● Aglianico del Vulture Daginestra '11	♛♛
● Aglianico del Vulture Damaschito '12	♛♛
● Aglianico del Vulture Gricos '16	♛♛
● Aglianico del Vulture Gricos '15	♛♛
● Aglianico del Vulture Gricos '13	♛♛
● Aglianico del Vulture Gricos '12	♛♛
● Aglianico del Vulture Grifalco '16	♛♛
● Aglianico del Vulture Grifalco '15	♛♛
● Aglianico del Vulture Grifalco '14	♛♛
● Aglianico del Vulture Grifalco '13	♛♛
● Aglianico del Vulture Grifalco '12	♛♛

Cantine Madonna delle Grazie

C. VIGNALI
A APPIA
5029 VENOSA [PZ]
EL. +39 097235704
www.cantinemadonnadellegrazie.it

CELLAR SALES
PRE-BOOKED VISITS
ANNUAL PRODUCTION 18,000 bottles
HECTARES UNDER VINE 8.00
VITICULTURE METHOD Certified Organic

The Madonna delle Grazie Monastery in Venosa stands near the cellar of Giuseppe Latorraca, who in 2003 began vinifying the grapes of the family vineyards. The soil here, rich in trace elements, is ideal for Aglianico, which Giuseppe transforms into reds of character that defy time. His eight hectares of vineyards in four of Venosa's districts are all managed without pesticides or herbicides. A similar minimalist approach is taken in the cellar. Their garnet, ruby Aglianico del Vulture Messer Oto '16 opens with a complex cherry nose that fades into notes of tobacco. The palate is structured and harmonious, the finish warm and persistent. Liscone, on the other hand, made from Aglianico grapes of the homonymous vineyard, delivers a bouquet of red fruit jam and licorice followed by a soft and well-balanced attack on the palate. Well-structured, its evident tannins require more time to unwind.

Martino

VIA LA VISTA, 2A
85028 RIONERO IN VULTURE [PZ]
TEL. +39 0972721422
www.martinovini.com

CELLAR SALES
PRE-BOOKED VISITS
ANNUAL PRODUCTION 250,000 bottles
HECTARES UNDER VINE 50.00

The estate's history dates back to the end of the nineteenth century when Donato Martino started making wine in the Vulture area. Over the years the winery has been able to express all the facets of Aglianico del Vulture. Today, this success is consecrated by Armando Martino and his daughter Carolin, president of the Consorzio dell'Aglianico del Vulture. Production extends toward Matera allowing the winery to boast a range of white wines such as Greco, Malvasia, Muscat and Chardonnay. Their intense ruby red Aglianico del Vulture Oraziano '13 offers clearly defined tones of ripe red fruit, delicate spices and a solid, progressive palate that only lacks in its slightly drying finish. The Riserva '13 delivers a deep Mediterranean bouquet and soft tannins. Elegant notes of licorice, wood and balsam lead into a palate dominated by sour cherries and raspberries.

● Aglianico del Vulture Messer Oto '16	♟♟ 2*
Aglianico del Vulture Liscone '14	♟♟ 3
● Aglianico del Vulture Bauccio '13	♟♟ 4
● Aglianico del Vulture Bauccio '09	♟♟ 4
● Aglianico del Vulture Bauccio '08	♟♟ 4
● Aglianico del Vulture Bauccio '06	♟♟ 4
Aglianico del Vulture Bauccio '04	♟♟ 4
● Aglianico del Vulture Drogone d'Altavilla Ris. '07	♟♟ 4
● Aglianico del Vulture Liscone '09	♟♟ 3
● Aglianico del Vulture Liscone '08	♟♟ 3
● Aglianico del Vulture Liscone '07	♟♟ 3
● Aglianico del Vulture Liscone '06	♟♟ 3
● Aglianico del Vulture Messer Oto '08	♟♟ 2

● Aglianico del Vulture Oraziano '13	♟♟ 5
● Aglianico del Vulture Sup. Ris. '13	♟♟ 7
● Aglianico del Vulture '16	♟ 2
● Aglianico del Vulture Bel Poggio '13	♟ 2
○ Sincerità '18	♟ 2
● Aglianico del Vulture '14	♟♟ 3*
● Aglianico del Vulture '13	♟♟ 2*
● Aglianico del Vulture Bel Poggio '10	♟♟ 2*
● Aglianico del Vulture Oraziano '12	♟♟ 5
● Aglianico del Vulture Oraziano '10	♟♟ 5
● Aglianico del Vulture Pretoriano '10	♟♟ 5
● Aglianico del Vulture Sup. '13	♟♟ 7
● Aglianico del Vulture Sup. '12	♟♟ 7
● Aglianico del Vulture Sup. Ris. '12	♟♟ 7
○ I Sassi Greco '16	♟♟ 4

Musto Carmelitano

VIA PIETRO NENNI, 29
85020 MASCHITO [PZ]
TEL. +39 097233312
www.mustocarmelitano.it

CELLAR SALES
PRE-BOOKED VISITS
ACCOMMODATION AND RESTAURANT SERVICE
ANNUAL PRODUCTION 25,000 bottles
HECTARES UNDER VINE 6.00
VITICULTURE METHOD Certified Organic

Since 2006 Elisabetta Carmelitano and her brother Luigi have been running this Maschito winery. But its story begins in the mid-1980s when Francesco Carmelitano returned to Italy after years in England and decided to take over his father Vito Antonio's land. Four of the fourteen hectares of vineyards are planted in three different cru: Pian del Moro, Serra del Prete and Vernavà. The wines are artisanally produced by selecting only the best grapes, harvesting by hand, and avoiding intervention with selected yeasts or stabilization in the cellar. The Aglianico del Vulture Serra del Prete, from the homonymous vineyard, stood out among their offerings for this edition of the Guide. Enlivened by fresh fruit and a beautiful overall harmony, it opens with notes of spices, railway cherry, and smoke followed by a full-bodied and austere palate, rich in fruit and fine-grained tannins that ensure it will age well.

● Aglianico del Vulture Serra del Prete '16	♟♟ 4
● Aglianico del Vulture Pian del Moro '15	♟ 4
● Aglianico del Vulture Serra del Prete '09	♟♟♟ 2
● Aglianico del Vulture '13	♟♟ 6
● Aglianico del Vulture Maschitano Rosso '14	♟♟ 3
● Aglianico del Vulture Pian del Moro '13	♟♟ 4
● Aglianico del Vulture Serra del Prete '15	♟♟ 4
● Aglianico del Vulture Serra del Prete '13	♟♟ 4
● Aglianico del Vulture Serra del Prete '12	♟♟ 3
○ Maschitano Bianco '17	♟♟ 3
● Maschitano Rosso '16	♟♟ 3
● Maschitano Rosso '12	♟♟ 3

★Paternoster

C.DA VALLE DEL TITOLO
85022 BARILE [PZ]
TEL. +39 0972770224
Ronchetto

CELLAR SALES
PRE-BOOKED VISITS
ANNUAL PRODUCTION 150,000 bottles
HECTARES UNDER VINE 20.00
VITICULTURE METHOD Certified Organic

Anselmo Paternoster decided to focus on commercializing Aglianico del Vulture in 1925. His difficult yet far-sighted choice has ensured the wine's success (the sparkling version as well) in both domestic and foreign markets. Today, it's part of Tommasi, the important Venetian wine group, but Vito Paternoster and enologist Fabio Mecca are still in charge of the Barile operations. Grapes come mainly from Bari and Macarico. Their Don Anselmo '16 explodes with black fruit, spices and coffee and like their Rotondo comes from vineyards of Barile. Big and sumptuous, it delivers velvety tannins and a gutsy drink that earn Tre Bicchieri. Their Aglianico del Vulture Synthesi '17, supported by a refreshing acidic streak, proves powerful and well-orchestrated with beautiful fruity flesh and exceptional integrity.

● Aglianico del Vulture Don Anselmo '16	♟♟♟ 6
● Aglianico del Vulture Synthesi '17	♟♟ 3
● Aglianico del Vulture Rotondo '16	♟ 5
○ Vulcanico '18	♟ 3
● Aglianico del Vulture Don Anselmo '15	♟♟♟ 6
● Aglianico del Vulture Don Anselmo '13	♟♟♟ 6
● Aglianico del Vulture Don Anselmo '09	♟♟♟ 6
● Aglianico del Vulture Don Anselmo '94	♟♟♟ 6
● Aglianico del Vulture Don Anselmo Ris. '05	♟♟♟ 6
● Aglianico del Vulture Rotondo '11	♟♟♟ 5
● Aglianico del Vulture Rotondo '01	♟♟♟ 5
● Aglianico del Vulture Rotondo '00	♟♟♟ 5
● Aglianico del Vulture Rotondo '15	♟♟ 5
● Aglianico del Vulture Synthesi '16	♟♟ 3

★Re Manfredi
Cantina Terre degli Svevi

LOC. PIAN DI CAMERA
85029 VENOSA [PZ]
TEL. +39 097231263
www.cantineremanfredi.it

CELLAR SALES
PRE-BOOKED VISITS
RESTAURANT SERVICE
ANNUAL PRODUCTION 300,000 bottles
HECTARES UNDER VINE 110.00

Founded in 1998 and now part of the Gruppo Italiano Vini, the estate has 120 hectares in between Venosa, Maschito and Barile at elevations ranging from 400 to 650 meters. The dynamic, modern cellar is managed by Paolo Montrone who, together with Trentino-born enologist Pietro Bertè who has since adopted Basilicata as home), follows the whole production chain. Aglianico is the undisputed star here, with small quantities of Müller Thurgau and aromatic Traminer completing the range. Their Aglianico del Vulture Vigneto Serpara Cru, is produced from forty-year-old vineyards in Maschito, and the 2015 version proved deep and powerful. This year, however, Re Manfredi wins with its notes of forest undergrowth, sour cherry, wild rose and sweet spices leading into a complex, deep and balanced palate that is rich in fruit and delivers a sumptuous drink.

Terra dei Re

VIA MONTICCHIO KM 2,700
85028 RIONERO IN VULTURE [PZ]
TEL. +39 0972725116
www.terradeire.com

CELLAR SALES
PRE-BOOKED VISITS
ACCOMMODATION AND RESTAURANT SERVICE
ANNUAL PRODUCTION 70,000 bottles
HECTARES UNDER VINE 11.00
SUSTAINABLE WINERY

In 2000, the Rabasco and Leone families joined forces and ideas about winemaking, in the process creating a modern interpretation of Aglianico del Vulture and cultivating Pinot Nero, a variety almost unknown in the region. The vineyards are between Barile, Rapolla, Melfi and Rionero in Vulture in Piano di Carro, Colinelli, Calata delle Brecce and Querce di Annibale. The modern cellar is in Rionero, where wines mature 25 meters below ground in caves dug from Vulture's volcanic rock. Their Aglianico del Vulture Nocte '15 is an intense, compact red made of grapes from the Calata delle Brecce vineyard in Rionero. Notes of wild berries, spices and smoke open to a dense, juicy palate with hints of sapidity and strong-willed tannins. The Lerà Rosato '18 offers clear hints of blood orange, floral scents and zesty palate of wild berries.

● Aglianico del Vulture Re Manfredi '16	🍷🍷🍷 5
● Aglianico del Vulture Sup. Serpara '15	🍷🍷 5
● Aglianico del Vulture Taglio del Tralcio '17	🍷🍷 3
○ Re Manfredi Bianco '18	🍷🍷 3
● Aglianico del Vulture Re Manfredi '15	🍷🍷🍷 5
● Aglianico del Vulture Re Manfredi '13	🍷🍷🍷 6
● Aglianico del Vulture Re Manfredi '11	🍷🍷🍷 4*
● Aglianico del Vulture Re Manfredi '10	🍷🍷🍷 4*
● Aglianico del Vulture Re Manfredi '05	🍷🍷🍷 4
● Aglianico del Vulture Re Manfredi '99	🍷🍷🍷 4*
● Aglianico del Vulture Serpara '10	🍷🍷🍷 5
● Aglianico del Vulture Sup. Serpara '12	🍷🍷🍷 5
● Aglianico del Vulture Vign. Serpara '03	🍷🍷🍷 4*
● Aglianico del Vulture Taglio del Tralcio '16	🍷🍷 3*
○ Re Manfredi Bianco '17	🍷🍷 4

● Aglianico del Vulture Nocte '15	🍷🍷 4
⊙ Lerà Rosato '18	🍷🍷 2*
○ Lerà '18	🍷 2
● Aglianico del Vulture Divinus '05	🍷🍷 4
● Aglianico del Vulture Nocte '14	🍷🍷 4
● Aglianico del Vulture Nocte '13	🍷🍷 4
● Aglianico del Vulture Nocte '10	🍷🍷 4
● Aglianico del Vulture Sup. Divinus '13	🍷🍷 4
● Aglianico del Vulture Sup. Divinus '12	🍷🍷 4
● Aglianico del Vulture Vultur '14	🍷🍷 2*
● Aglianico del Vulture Vultur '13	🍷🍷 2*
● Aglianico del Vulture Vultur '06	🍷🍷 2*
● Pacus '06	🍷🍷 3*
● Vulcano 800 '15	🍷🍷 4
● Vulcano 800 Pinot Nero '17	🍷🍷 5

Cantina di Venosa

LOC. VIGNALI
VIA APPIA
85029 VENOSA [PZ]
TEL. +39 097236702
www.cantinadivenosa.it

CELLAR SALES
PRE-BOOKED VISITS
ANNUAL PRODUCTION 1,000,000 bottles
HECTARES UNDER VINE 800.00
SUSTAINABLE WINERY

The cooperative was founded in 1957 with 27 original members. Today there are 350, who care for 800 hectares of vineyards in Venosa, Ripacandida, Maschito and Ginestra. The operative headquarters are in Venosa, the most heavily planted commune in the region. This is where not only Aglianico is worked and given expression in multiple versions, but so are Moscato and Malvasia. For some time now, the winery has offered its new Matematico, a blend of Aglianico and Merlot, which, aged in barriques, is generous and has a wide range of aromas. Their Aglianico del Vulture Verbo '17, a well-structured red with Mediterranean notes, opens with hints of red berries and vanilla leading into a powerful palate of crunchy fruit and velvety tannins with a long finish. Their classic Terre di Orazio 2017 offers good structure and cocoa notes, full of fruity vitality and elegant tannins, qualities that translate into a great persistence and remarkable pleasantness.

● Aglianico del Vulture Verbo '17	♟♟ 3*
● Aglianico del Vulture Carato Venusio '13	♟♟ 6
● Aglianico del Vulture Terre di Orazio '17	♟♟ 4
○ Terre di Orazio Dry Muscat '18	♟♟ 3
○ Verbo Malvasia '18	♟ 3
⊙ Verbo Rosé '18	♟ 3
● Aglianico del Vulture Balì '13	♟♟ 2*
● Aglianico del Vulture Carato Venusio '12	♟♟ 6
● Aglianico del Vulture Gesualdo da Venosa '15	♟♟ 5
● Aglianico del Vulture Gesualdo da Venosa '13	♟♟ 5
● Aglianico del Vulture Sup. Carato Venusio '12	♟♟ 6
○ Terre di Orazio Dry Muscat '15	♟♟ 2*

Vigneti del Vulture

C.DA PIPOLI
85011 ACERENZA [PZ]
TEL. +39 0971749363
www.vignetidelvulture.it

PRE-BOOKED VISITS
ANNUAL PRODUCTION 100,000 bottles
HECTARES UNDER VINE 56.00

Internationally, the Fantini-Farnese group is one of the most famous names in Italian wines; it includes estates from Abruzzo, Tuscany, Campania, Puglia and Sicily. In 2010, it founded Vigneti del Vulture, creating an important winemaking center in Acerenza. The winegrowers' vineyards are at elevations between 600 and 800 meters on the different terroirs of the region, but largely around Vulture. Aglianico is the undisputed lord, but white and rosé wines also complete the Basilicata range. Their Aglianico del Vulture Pipoli Zero '17 is the result of long maceration obtained without the use of added sulfites (hence, the name Zero). Powerful scents of red fruits with shades of citrus hit the nose hard and become well-behaved, long and sapid on the palate. Their grippy and balsamic Aglianico del Vulture Piano del Cerro '16, on the other hand, offers alluring notes of red fruit and wood.

● Aglianico del Vulture Pipoli Zero '17	♟♟ 2*
● Aglianico del Vulture Piano del Cerro '16	♟♟ 5
● Aglianico del Vulture Pipoli '17	♟♟ 2*
○ Pipoli Greco Fiano '18	♟♟ 2*
○ Moscato Sensuale '18	♟ 2
⊙ Pipoli Rosato '18	♟ 2
● Aglianico del Vulture Piano del Cerro '13	♟♟ 5
● Aglianico del Vulture Pipoli '16	♟♟ 2*
● Aglianico del Vulture Pipoli '15	♟♟ 2*
● Aglianico del Vulture Pipoli '13	♟♟ 2*
● Aglianico del Vulture Pipoli Zero '15	♟♟ 2*
● Aglianico del Vulture Pipoli Zero '14	♟♟ 2*
○ Moscato Sensuale '16	♟♟ 2*

isceglia

A FINOCCHIARO
024 LAVELLO [PZ]
.. +39 0972877033
ww.vinibisceglia.it

CELLAR SALES
PRE-BOOKED VISITS
RESTAURANT SERVICE
ANNUAL PRODUCTION 250,000 bottles
HECTARES UNDER VINE 45.00

Aglianico del Vulture Terra di Vulcano '17	♥♥	3
Aglianico del Vulture Gudarrà '16	♥	2
Bosco delle Rose Merlot Rosato '18	♥	3

Cantine Cifarelli

C.DA SAN VITO
75024 MONTESCAGLIOSO [MT]
TEL. +39 3338535349
www.cantinecifarelli.it

CELLAR SALES
PRE-BOOKED VISITS
ANNUAL PRODUCTION 20,000 bottles
HECTARES UNDER VINE 30.00

○ Matera Greco di San Vito '18	♥♥	3
⊙ Matera Rosato di San Vito '18	♥	3

asa Vinicola D'Angelo

PADRE PIO, 8
028 RIONERO IN VULTURE [PZ]
.. +39 0972721517
ww.dangelowine.it

CELLAR SALES
PRE-BOOKED VISITS
ANNUAL PRODUCTION 300,000 bottles
HECTARES UNDER VINE 35.00

Aglianico del Vulture '17	♥♥	3
Aglianico del Vulture Caselle '15	♥	5
Aglianico del Vulture Tecum '15	♥	3

Donato D'Angelo
di Filomena Ruppi

VIA PADRE PIO, 10
85028 RIONERO IN VULTURE [PZ]
TEL. +39 0972724602
www.agrida.it

CELLAR SALES
PRE-BOOKED VISITS
ANNUAL PRODUCTION 80,000 bottles
HECTARES UNDER VINE 20.00

● Aglianico del Vulture '16	♥♥	4
● Aglianico del Vulture Calice '16	♥	2

ubea

A PROV.LE 8
020 RIPACANDIDA [PZ]
.. +39 3284312789
ww.agricolaeubea.com

CELLAR SALES
PRE-BOOKED VISITS
ANNUAL PRODUCTION 50,000 bottles
HECTARES UNDER VINE 16.00
VITICULTURE METHOD Certified Organic

Aglianico del Vulture Covo dei Briganti '17	♥♥	6
Aglianico del Vulture Ròinos '17	♥♥	8

Michele Laluce

VIA ROMA, 21
85020 GINESTRA [PZ]
TEL. +39 0972646145
www.vinilaluce.com

CELLAR SALES
PRE-BOOKED VISITS
ANNUAL PRODUCTION 40,000 bottles
HECTARES UNDER VINE 7.00
SUSTAINABLE WINERY

● Aglianico del Vulture Le Drude '13	♥♥	5
○ Morbino Bianco '17	♥	3

Tenuta Parco dei Monaci

C.DA PARCO DEI MONACI
75100 MATERA
TEL. +39 0835259546
www.tenutaparcodeimonaci.it

PRE-BOOKED VISITS
ACCOMMODATION
ANNUAL PRODUCTION 20,000 bottles
HECTARES UNDER VINE 5.00
SUSTAINABLE WINERY

● Matera Rosso Spaccasassi '16	♟♟ 5
● Matera Primitivo Monacello '17	♟♟ 4
☉ Matera Rosato Rosapersempre '18	♟ 3

Quarta Generazione

C.DA MACARICO
85022 BARILE [PZ]
TEL. +39 3342039805
www.quartagenerazione.com

ANNUAL PRODUCTION 20,000 bottles
HECTARES UNDER VINE 3.00
VITICULTURE METHOD Certified Organic

● Aglianico del Vulture '17	♟♟

Tenuta Le Querce

C.DA LE QUERCE
85022 BARILE [PZ]
TEL. +39 0971725102
www.tenutalequerce.com

CELLAR SALES
PRE-BOOKED VISITS
ANNUAL PRODUCTION 350,000 bottles
HECTARES UNDER VINE 70.00

● Aglianico del Vulture Viola '15	♟♟ 3
● Aglianico del Vulture Costanza '15	♟ 5
○ Costanza '17	♟ 2

Regio Cantina

LOC. PIANO REGIO
85029 VENOSA [PZ]
TEL. +39 057754011
www.tenutepiccini.it

CELLAR SALES
PRE-BOOKED VISITS
ANNUAL PRODUCTION 90,000 bottles
HECTARES UNDER VINE 15.00
VITICULTURE METHOD Certified Organic

● Aglianico del Vulture Genesi '17	♟♟
● Aglianico del Vulture Donpà '16	♟

Taverna

C.DA TRATTURO REGIO
75020 NOVA SIRI [MT]
TEL. +39 0835877310
www.cantinetaverna.wine

CELLAR SALES
PRE-BOOKED VISITS
ACCOMMODATION AND RESTAURANT SERVICE
ANNUAL PRODUCTION 50,000 bottles
HECTARES UNDER VINE 20.00

● Il Lucano '16	♟♟ 4
● Matera Primitivo I Sassi '17	♟♟ 3
● Senso2 Rosso '18	♟♟ 3
☉ Senso2 Rosato Frizzante '18	♟ 2

Vitis in Vulture

C.SO GIUSTINO FORTUNATO, 159
85024 LAVELLO [PZ]
TEL. +39 097283983
www.vitisinvulture.com

ANNUAL PRODUCTION 50,000 bottles
HECTARES UNDER VINE 100.00

● Aglianico del Vulture Labellum '17	♟♟
● Aglianico del Vulture Forentum '16	♟
○ Labellum '18	♟
○ Portarino '18	♟

PUGLIA

uglia received plenty of recognition in this year's
dition of Italian Wines, pointing up an overall
ath of growth that we've noticed for some time
ow, and that doesn't seem to be slowing down.
ndeed, it's to the point where, despite enlarging
ie number of wineries admitted last year, this year we
ad to apply draconian standards (and were forced to leave out many producers
ho were more than worthy). Primitivo once again affirmed its status as the
egion's leading cultivar, a tendency that we can longer consider mere fashion.
ndeed, the grape's qualities and its various interpretations are increasingly
ppreciated both nationally and abroad. This year we are pleased to announce
ie first Tre Bicchieri for a Primitivo rosé, Varvaglione's Idea, and Produttori di
Manduria's Primitivo di Manduria Lirica. While Gioia del Colle saw a decline in
ie number of Tre Bicchieri received, there's nice overall upward growth (this
ear some 11 of the appellation's wineries had at least one wine in our finals,
nd we'll never tire of reminding readers that just getting to our finals means
eing part of a national elite). In Salento we're pleased to see the return of the
aurino family's historic winery, with their Patriglione, but we should also point
ut a lack in growth for some of its most famous names, both in Salice Salentino
nd in Salento's Negroamaros. It appears like something's happening in the
rovince of Foggia, where a growth in quality is pointing to interesting, though
till unconfirmed, future prospects. At the risk of sounding repetitive (some might
ven say obsessive), we once again close by noting the excessive weight of many
f Puglia's most important bottles. This year we counted about 50 wines that
urpassed 1900 grams overall. That's almost two kilos for 750 ml. of wine. Can
omeone say 'grotesque'?

Amastuola

VIA APPIA KM 632,200
74016 MASSAFRA [TA]
TEL. +39 0998805668
www.amastuola.it

CELLAR SALES
PRE-BOOKED VISITS
ACCOMMODATION AND RESTAURANT SERVICE
ANNUAL PRODUCTION 360,000 bottles
HECTARES UNDER VINE 101.00
VITICULTURE METHOD Certified Organic

The Montanaro family acquired Masseria
Amastuola in 2003, adopting organic
methods from the start. They also
established the beautiful 'vineyard-garden'
designed by landscape architect Fernando
Caruncho, which he referred to as 'waves
of time'. Their eleven wines are made with
both local varieties, particularly Primitivo
but also Aglianico or Malvasia, and
international varieties like Cabernet
Sauvignon, Syrah, Merlot and Chardonnay.
The resulting interpretations have a modern
style and are technically well made. The
Lamarossa '15 is the wine that most
convinced this year. It's a monovarietal
Primitivo with notes of wild berry and a
close-focused, fresh palate. Their other
Primitivo, the Centosassi '16, is also well
made (though spicier and more
determined), as is the Onda del Tempo '16,
a generous blend of Primitivo, Aglianico,
Merlot and Caberneto Sauvignon.

● Lamarossa '15	♟♟ 2*
● Centosassi '15	♟♟ 5
● Onda del Tempo '16	♟♟ 3
○ Fiano - Malvasia '18	♟ 3
● Primitivo '16	♟ 3
● Vignatorta '16	♟ 2
● Aglianico '13	♟♟ 3
● Centosassi '11	♟♟ 2*
● Lamarossa '14	♟♟ 2*
● Vignatorta '13	♟♟ 2*
● Vignatorta '10	♟♟ 2*

Giuseppe Attanasio

VIA PER ORIA, 13
74024 MANDURIA [TA]
TEL. +39 0999737121
www.primitivo-attanasio.com

ANNUAL PRODUCTION 11,000 bottles
HECTARES UNDER VINE 6.00

The Attanasio family's winery has been or
of the most interesting in Manduria for
years. It focuses entirely on the productio
of wines from head-trained Primitivo
grapes, the only kind in its vineyards on
calcareous and tuffaceous land. Since
2000, winemaking has been carried out in
a modern cellar built inside a nineteenth-
century building. The limited number of
offerings are characterized by a traditiona
style with great adherence to territorial
typicity. Attanasio's Primitivo di Manduria
Dolce Naturale '18 is the best of its kind
tasted this year. On the nose it offers up
aromas of cherry preserves, gentian and
quinine, while the palate proves balanced
and pleasant, properly sweet, with nice
texture and freshness. Their Primitivo di
Manduria '16, a juicy wine with notes of
ripe, dark fruit, proves well made, as does
the refreshing, plucky Primitivo Rosato '18
a wide redolent of wild berry.

● Primitivo di Manduria Dolce Naturale '18	♟♟
● Primitivo di Manduria '15	♟♟
○ Primitivo Rosato '18	♟♟
● Primitivo di Manduria '13	♟♟
● Primitivo di Manduria '07	♟♟
● Primitivo di Manduria Dolce Naturale '13	♟♟
● Primitivo di Manduria Dolce Naturale '12	♟♟
● Primitivo di Manduria Dolce Naturale 15,5° '06	♟♟
● Primitivo di Manduria Dolce Naturale 15° '07	♟♟
● Primitivo di Manduria Ris. '13	♟♟
○ Primitivo Rosato '17	♟♟
○ Primitivo Rosato '16	♟♟

antele

ɪA PROV.ʟᴇ Sᴀʟɪᴄᴇ Sᴀʟᴇɴᴛɪɴᴏ-Sᴀɴ Dᴏɴᴀᴄɪ ᴋᴍ 35,600
010 Gᴜᴀɢɴᴀɴᴏ [LE]
. +39 0832705010
w.cantele.it

CELLAR SALES
RE-BOOKED VISITS
NNUAL PRODUCTION 16,000,000 bottles
ECTARES UNDER VINE 200.00

e Cantele family's winery has been a
ader in the Puglian wine scene for
veral years now. Its own plots, which
ver about 50 of the 200 hectares of
neyards that it works with, are located
tween Guagnano, Montemesola and San
etro Vernotico, on calcareous-clayey soils
minated by red earth. They are planted
ainly with traditional types, such as
egroamaro, Primitivo or Susumaniello,
t there is also Chardonnay, from which
me of the estate's historic wines are
rn. Amativo is a blend of Primitivo (60%)
d Negroamaro that, for some years now,
s served as Cantele's flagship. The
016 offers up aromas of dark fruit and
corice, sensations that anticipate a juicy
d energetic palate of nice fruit. But the
oducer offers several quality wines,
cluding the spicy and plucky Teresa
anara Negroamaro '16, the pulpy and
uity Teresa Manara Chardonnay '18, and
e Alticelli Fiano '18, a wine redolent of
trus and aromatic herbs.

Amativo '16	♟♟ 4
Alticelli Fiano '18	♟♟ 2*
Rohesia '18	♟♟ 3
Teresa Manara Chardonnay '18	♟♟ 3
Teresa Manara Negroamaro '16	♟♟ 3
Varius '17	♟♟ 2*
Verdeca '18	♟♟ 2*
Negroamaro Rosato '18	♟ 2
Salice Salentino Rosso Ris. '16	♟ 2
Teresa Manara Chardonnay Uno Settembre '17	♟ 4
Amativo '07	♟♟♟ 4*
Salice Salentino Rosso Ris. '09	♟♟♟ 2*
Amativo '15	♟♟ 4
Salice Salentino Rosso Ris. '15	♟♟ 2*

Carvinea

ʟᴏᴄ. Pᴇᴢᴢᴀ ᴅ'Aʀᴇɴᴀ
ᴠɪᴀ ᴘᴇʀ Sᴇʀʀᴀɴᴏᴠᴀ
72012 Cᴀʀᴏᴠɪɢɴᴏ [BR]
Tᴇʟ. +39 0805862345
www.carvinea.com

CELLAR SALES
PRE-BOOKED VISITS
ACCOMMODATION AND RESTAURANT SERVICE
ANNUAL PRODUCTION 35,000 bottles
HECTARES UNDER VINE 12.00
VITICULTURE METHOD Certified Organic

Beppe Di Maria's winery is located in a
sixteenth-century farmhouse a stone's
throw from the Torre Guaceto Nature
Reserve. After having focused on
non-traditional grapes for some years, the
estate has concentrated production efforts
on the area's native varieties, in particular
Negroamaro, Octavianello and Primitivo.
The vineyards are planted on the
calcareous, tufaceous soil that surround the
winery. The technically well-made wines
offer consistently good quality and great
aromatic precision. This year Carvinea's
Negroamaro '17 is the wine that most
convinced among their selection. On the
nose notes of red fruit and sweet spices
are followed by a juicy palate, with
well-integrated tannins and nice mouthfeel.
The Fiano Lucerna '18 is pleasant and
fresh in its notes of rosemary, citrus and
apple, while the approachable Primitivo '17
is supple and rich in fruit.

● Negroamaro '17	♟♟♟ 5
○ Lucerna '18	♟♟ 2*
● Primitivo '17	♟♟ 5
⊙ Brut Rosé M. Cl. '13	♟ 5
● Lunachiena '18	♟ 2
⊙ Merula Rosa '18	♟ 2
● Otto '17	♟ 4
● Merula '11	♟♟♟ 3*
● Negroamaro '14	♟♟♟ 5
● Negroamaro '13	♟♟♟ 5
● Negroamaro '11	♟♟♟ 3*
● Otto '16	♟♟♟ 4*
● Primitivo '15	♟♟♟ 5

Castello Monaci

VIA CASE SPARSE
73015 SALICE SALENTINO [LE]
TEL. +39 0831665700
www.castellomonaci.it

CELLAR SALES
PRE-BOOKED VISITS
RESTAURANT SERVICE
ANNUAL PRODUCTION 1,800,000 bottles
HECTARES UNDER VINE 210.00

Gruppo Italiano Vini has three estates: Masseria Flaminio, with vineyards of mainly Verdeca, Fiano and Chardonnay on sandy soil; Masseria Vittorio in Trepuzzi, with vineyards of Primitivo on iron-rich red soil; and, the estate of Salice Salentino, with vineyards of primarily Primitivo, Malvasia Nera di Lecce and Negroamaro located on clayey, tufaceous soil. The resulting wines are modern in style, with particular attention paid to their enjoyability and the fullness of the fruit. Once again, even if 2018 was a rather difficult year, Castello Monaci submitted a solid, well-crafted selection, from the Kreos, a pleasant, fresh and floral Negroamaro rosé, to Simera, an iodine, gutsy Chardonnay. The same holds for their Primitivo Pilùna, with its notes of wild berries, and their Negroamaro Maru, a highly drinkable wine with pronounced notes of Mediterranean shrub.

⊙ Kreos '18	🍷🍷 2*
● Maru '18	🍷🍷 2*
● Pilùna '18	🍷🍷 2*
○ Simera '18	🍷🍷 2*
○ Acante '18	🍷 2
● Artas '17	🍷 5
○ Charà '18	🍷 2
○ Heos '18	🍷 2
● Salice Salentino Aiace Ris. '16	🍷 4
● Salice Salentino Rosso Liante '18	🍷 2
● Artas '07	🍷🍷🍷 5
● Artas '06	🍷🍷🍷 4
● Artas '12	🍷🍷 5
● Salice Salentino Aiace Ris. '13	🍷🍷 3*

Giancarlo Ceci

C.DA SANT'AGOSTINO
76123 ANDRIA [BT]
TEL. +39 0883565220
www.giancarloceci.com

PRE-BOOKED VISITS
ANNUAL PRODUCTION 350,000 bottles
HECTARES UNDER VINE 60.00
VITICULTURE METHOD Certified Biodynam
SUSTAINABLE WINERY

The Ceci family has been making wine, oi fruit and vegetable products for eight generations. The company's vineyard is a single body located within a large estate c over 200 hectares between Andria and Castel del Monte at 250 meters above sea level and only twenty kilometers from the coast. Nero di Troia is the protagonist of th company's most important selections, but Bombino Bianco and Nero, Aglianico, Chardonnay, Montepulciano, Moscato, Fiano and Pampanuto also give life to elegant wines with great aromatic precision. This year Ceci's selection shone less than usual, the result of a difficult 2018, and its being without the Felice Ced Riserva. The Castel del Monte Rosso Parc Grande '18 offers up notes of red fruits accompanied by spicy nuances, sensation that anticipate a palate of nice length and persistence. The Moscato di Trans Dolce Naturale Dolce Rosalía '18 is fresh and pleasant, with aromas of candied orange peel, pomegranate and chestnut honey. T rest of their selection proved sound.

● Castel del Monte Rosso Parco Grande '18	🍷🍷
○ Moscato di Trani Dolce Rosalia '18	🍷🍷
● Almagia Senza Solfiti Aggiunti '18	🍷
○ Apnea Brut '17	🍷
○ Castel del Monte Bombino Bianco Penascio '18	🍷
○ Castel del Monte Chardonnay Pozzo Sorgente '18	🍷
● Castel del Monte Nero di Troia Parco Marano '16	🍷
● Castel del Monte Nero di Troia Felice Ceci Ris. '15	🍷🍷
● Castel del Monte Nero di Troia Felice Ceci Ris. '12	🍷🍷
● Castel del Monte Rosso Almagia '16	🍷🍷

Tenute Chiaromonte

ʋ Annunziata
ɔ21 Acquaviva delle Fonti [BA]
. +39 080768156
ʍw.tenutechiaromonte.com

CELLAR SALES
PRE-BOOKED VISITS
ANNUAL PRODUCTION 150,000 bottles
HECTARES UNDER VINE 45.00

icola Chiaromonte and Paolo Montanaro's
ɛw cellar is the most recent sign of their
ɔntinued success. They share a passion in
ɓuilding this winery, destined to remain at
ɪe top of the Puglian wine scene and
ɓeyond for a long time to come. The estate
ɖraws from its 45 hectares of vineyards
ɔcated on calcareous soils in Gioia del
ɔolle at an elevation of over 300 meters, of
ʋhich, ten hectares are planted with
ɛead-trained Primitivo over 60 years old.
ʰhe wines have extraordinary character,
ɛtriking that rare balance between power
ɑnd elegance. Their 2016 version of their
ɔioia del Colle Primitivo, the Muro
ɕant'Angelo Contrada Barbatto, also proves
ɕplendid, with complex aromas of black
ʍild berries and Mediterranean shrub. On
ʈhe palate it's rich, elegant and taut, with a
ɪong, notably sapid finish. The Gioia del
ɔolle Primitivo Risera '14 is a particularly
ɕuccessful version with aromas of black
ɖruits and licorice, and nice mouthfeel,
ɔoming through pulpy and sapid.

● Gioia del Colle Primitivo Muro Sant'Angelo Contrada Barbatto '16		♟♟♟ 5
● Gioia del Colle Primitivo Ris. '14		♟♟ 8
● Elè '17		♟♟ 3
● Gioia del Colle Primitivo Muro Sant'Angelo '17		♟♟ 4
● Primitivo '17		♟♟ 2*
○ Rosé M. Cl. '17		♟♟ 5
○ Kimìa Fiano '18		♟ 3
⊙ Kimìa Pinot Nero Rosato '18		♟ 3
⊙ Kimìa Primitivo Rosato '18		♟ 3
● Nigredo '17		♟ 5
● Gioia del Colle Primitivo Muro Sant'Angelo Contrada Barbatto '15		♟♟♟ 5

Coppi

s.da prov.le Turi - Gioia del Colle
70010 Turi [BA]
Tel. +39 0808915049
www.vinicoppi.it

CELLAR SALES
PRE-BOOKED VISITS
RESTAURANT SERVICE
ANNUAL PRODUCTION 900,000 bottles
HECTARES UNDER VINE 100.00
VITICULTURE METHOD Certified Organic

Founded in 1882, this long-established
winery was taken over in 1976 by the
Coppi family, who have transformed it
completely and turned it into one of the
area's most interesting. Located in the
so-called Agro del Marchesato, the
vineyards are between Turi and Gioia del
Colle. Traditional varieties are grown (50%
are head-trained vines), starting with
Primitivo and then Aleatico, Negroamaro,
Malvasia Nera, Malvasia Bianca, Falanghina
and Verdeca, resulting in well-made wines
with a modern touch. This year we most
preferred their Don Antonio Primitivo '17, a
wine that goes all in on approachability,
freshness and fruitiness, with nice
persistence and notable length. The Gioia
del Colle Primitivo Senatore '16 features
nice texture, it's just a bit less determined
than other versions. The rest of their
selection also proves solid and reliable,
from the pleasant Siniscalco Primitivo '17
to the sapid and fresh Guiscardo
Falanghina '18 and the Pellirosso
Negroamaro '18, a wine redolent of ripe,
black fruits.

● Don Antonio Primitivo '17		♟♟♟ 3*
● Gioia del Colle Primitivo Senatore '16		♟♟ 5
○ Guiscardo Falanghina '18		♟♟ 3
● Pellirosso Negroamaro '18		♟♟ 2*
● Siniscalco Primitivo '17		♟♟ 2*
● Cantonovo Primitivo Bio Organic '17		♟ 3
⊙ Coré '18		♟ 2
○ Isottèo Brut		♟ 3
● Peucetico Primitivo '15		♟ 3
● Sannace Malvasia Nera '17		♟ 2
○ Serralto Malvasia Bianca '18		♟ 2
● Vinaccero Aleatico '14		♟ 3
● Gioia del Colle Primitivo Senatore '15		♟♟♟ 5
● Gioia del Colle Primitivo Senatore '11		♟♟♟ 5

★Leone de Castris

via Senatore de Castris, 26
73015 Salice Salentino [LE]
Tel. +39 0832731112
www.leonedecastris.com

PRE-BOOKED VISITS
ACCOMMODATION AND RESTAURANT SERVICE
ANNUAL PRODUCTION 2,500,000 bottles
HECTARES UNDER VINE 300.00
SUSTAINABLE WINERY

Founded in 1665 by the Count of Lemos, Leone de Castris is well into its fifth century as a winery. In 1943, it became the first in Italy to bottle rosé, its Five Roses. This long history has not prevented it from developing modern, technically impeccable production methods and a range of over 40 wines. The company's 300 hectares of vineyards, a good half of which are head trained, are spread throughout Salice Salentino, Campi and Guagnano, where both international and traditionally local varieties are cultivated. The Salice Salentino Rosso Donna Lisa Riserva is back at the top of their selection. The 2016 offers up fragrances of spices and mulberry, followed by a bold palate that's rich, structured and long, with nicely managed tannins. Between the 2018 versions of their two historic rosés, we preferred the Five Roses, a sapid, fresh, long and pleasant wine, over the 75th anniversary edition, a supple and floral wine, but a bit less plucky and dynamic on the palate.

● Salice Salentino Rosso Donna Lisa Ris. '16	▼▼▼ 5
⊙ Five Roses '18	▼▼ 2*
○ Donna Lisa Malvasia Bianca '18	▼▼ 4
⊙ Five Roses 75° Anniversario '18	▼▼ 3
● Salice Salentino Rosso Per Lui Ris. '16	▼▼ 6
○ Messapia Verdeca '18	▼ 2
⊙ Salice Salentino Brut Rosé M.Cl. Five Roses '16	▼ 4
● Salice Salentino Rosso Ris. '17	▼ 3
⊙ Five Roses 74° Anniversario '17	▽▽▽ 3*
● Salice Salentino Rosso 50° Vendemmia Ris. '14	▽▽▽ 3*
● Salice Salentino Rosso Per Lui Ris. '15	▽▽▽ 6
● Salice Salentino Rosso Per Lui Ris. '13	▽▽▽ 6
● Elo Veni '17	▽▽ 2*
● Primitivo di Manduria Santera '17	▽▽ 3

★Cantine Due Palme

via San Marco, 130
72020 Cellino San Marco [BR]
Tel. +39 0831617865
www.cantineduepalme.it

CELLAR SALES
PRE-BOOKED VISITS
ACCOMMODATION AND RESTAURANT SERV
ANNUAL PRODUCTION 14,000,000 bottl
HECTARES UNDER VINE 2500.00

Since 1989, Due Palme has been makin wine from Salento's classic cultivars, suc as Negroamaro, Malvasia Nera, Primitivo and Susumaniello. The resulting range is technically well made, striking a success balance between a traditional approach and modern style. There are 1200 wine suppliers who work vineyards spread between the provinces of Brindisi, Tarant and Lecce. 90% of the plots are cultivate with mainly traditional red varieties, a significant proportion of which are head-trained. The Salice Salentino Rosso Selvarossa Riserva confirms its status as one of this historic appellation's best. The 2016 features aromas of spices and blac fruits, while the palate is juicy, long and balanced. The Salice Salentino Rosso Selvarossa Terra Riserva '14 is more concentrated, and just a bit less agile. Th rest of their selection also proves well made, from the Serre Susumaniello '17, a approachable wine in its notes of wild berry, to the 2018 versions of their new Doppio Nero line, like the Syrah, Sangiovese and Negroamaro.

● Salice Salentino Rosso Selvarossa Ris. '16	▼▼▼
● 1943 del Presidente '16	▼▼
● Salice Salentino Rosso Selvarossa Terra Ris. '14	▼▼
⊙ Corerosa Gold Edition '18	▼▼
● Doppio Nero Primitivo e Negroamaro '18	▼▼
● Doppio Nero Syrah '18	▼▼
● Serre Susumaniello '17	▼▼
● Doppio Nero Cabernet Sauvignon e Negroamaro '18	▼
● Doppio Nero Merlot '18	▼
⊙ Melarosa Rosé Extra Dry	▼
● Salice Salentino Rosso Selvarossa Ris. '14	▽▽▽
● Seraia Malvasia Nera '16	▽▽

enute Eméra
Claudio Quarta Vignaiolo

z. Marina di Lizzano
a Porvica
123 Lizzano [TA]
. +39 0832704398
w.claudioquarta.it

LLAR SALES
RE-BOOKED VISITS
CCOMMODATION
NNUAL PRODUCTION 550,000 bottles
CTARES UNDER VINE 50.00
STAINABLE WINERY

audio Quarta and his daughter
essandra are responsible for multiple
neries: in Irpinia there is Sanpaolo and in
glia there are Eméra and Moros. Tenute
néra's single body of almost 50 hectares
vineyards is located near Lizzano by the
nian coast, while Cantina Moros is a
eyard of just over a hectare in Guagnano
at produces about 6000 bottles of Salice
lentino. The range strives to combine a
ditional approach rich in fruit and
omatic clarity. As usual, the Quarta
mily's selection performed at a nice level
ring our tastings. The Lizzano
egroamaro Superiore Anima di
egroamaro '17 is fresh and plucky, long in
characteristic notes of ripe, black fruits.
e Sud del Sud '17, a blend of
egroamaro, Primitivo and Cabernet
uvignon, is a juicy and pleasant wine,
atures notes of red fruits, while the
egroamaro Rose '18 proves transparent,
sh and easy drinking.

Lizzano Negroamaro Sup. Anima di Negroamaro '17	♟♟ 2*
Rose '18	♟♟ 3
Salice Salentino Rosso Moros Ris. '16	♟♟ 4
Sud del Sud '17	♟♟ 3
Anima di Chardonnay R Revolution '17	♟ 3
Primitivo di Manduria Anima di Primitivo '17	♟ 3
Primitivo di Manduria Oro di Eméra '17	♟ 5
Qu.Ale '18	♟ 2
Lizzano Negroamaro Sup. Anima di Negroamaro '16	♟♟ 2*
Primitivo di Manduria Anima di Primitivo '16	♟♟ 3*
Salice Salentino Rosso '11	♟♟ 2*
Sud del Sud '16	♟♟ 3

Felline

via Santo Stasi Primo, 42b
74024 Manduria [TA]
Tel. +39 0999711660
www.agricolafelline.it

CELLAR SALES
PRE-BOOKED VISITS
ANNUAL PRODUCTION 1,000,000 bottles
HECTARES UNDER VINE 120.00
VITICULTURE METHOD Certified Organic
SUSTAINABLE WINERY

Gregory Perrucci's winery offers a wide
range that reconciles a modern emphasis
on the freshness of fruit and elegance
while maintaining more traditional
substance and richness of body. This has
largely been accomplished by reviving old
vineyards of head-trained grapevines.
Given the large area encompassed by the
estate (it owns 100 hectares of land and
rents another 20) its vineyards are situated
on various types of soil around Manduria,
from sandy to rocky and including both red
and black earth. The 2017 version of their
Primitivo di Manduria Singarosa Zinfandel
Terra Nera also takes home Tre Bicchieri.
It's a fresh wine, highly pleasant with
aromas of black fruits — on the palate it's
gutsy, long and sapid. Their Primitivo di
Manduria Giravolta '17 is also excellent,
while the plucky Malvasia Nera comes
through fresh with nice fruit. It's a well
made wine, despite a difficult 2018, as is
their Alcione Negroamaro, a wine redolent
of black fruits, and their spicy Primitivo di
Manduria Terra Rossa.

● Primitivo di Manduria Zinfandel Sinfarosa Terra Nera '17	♟♟♟ 4*
● Primitivo di Manduria Giravolta '17	♟♟ 3*
● Alberello '18	♟♟ 2*
● Alcione Negroamaro '18	♟♟ 2*
● I Monili '18	♟♟ 2*
● Malvasia Nera '18	♟♟ 3
● Primitivo di Manduria Terra Rossa '18	♟♟ 3
● Trullari Nero Di Troia '18	♟♟ 2*
○ Fiano '18	♟ 2
○ Verdeca '18	♟ 2
● Primitivo di Manduria '15	♟♟♟ 3*
● Primitivo di Manduria Sinfarosa Zinfandel '15	♟♟♟ 3*
● Primitivo di Manduria Zinfandel Sinfarosa Terra Nera '16	♟♟♟ 4*

Gianfranco Fino

VIA PIAVE, 12
74028 SAVA [TA]
TEL. +39 0997773970
www.gianfrancofino.it

PRE-BOOKED VISITS
ANNUAL PRODUCTION 20,000 bottles
HECTARES UNDER VINE 21.00
SUSTAINABLE WINERY

Gianfranco and Simona Fino's winery has
become the stuff of legend for Primitivo
lovers. Founded in 2004 with just over a
hectare of vineyard, today it works more
than twenty, many of which contain old
head-trained vines (which can reach 90
years of age) planted on red, calcareous
soil. Alongside Es, their calling card, they
produce several other wines: from
Negroamaro come Jo and Metodo Classico
Simona Natale; and, from Primitivo come
their sweet Es più Sole, the fresh and easy
to drink Sé, and their 'Riserva' Es Red.
Once again Gianfranco and Simona only
submitted their Es for tasting. The 2017
offers up jammy aromas of black fruits
together with sweet spices. On the
palate it's complex, notably compact
and well-supported by acidity. A long
finish features notes of undergrowth and
black fruits.

Tenute Girolamo

VIA NOCI, 314
74015 MARTINA FRANCA [TA]
TEL. +39 0804402141
www.tenutegirolamo.it

CELLAR SALES
PRE-BOOKED VISITS
ANNUAL PRODUCTION 400,000 bottles
HECTARES UNDER VINE 50.00

It has only taken a few years for the
Girolamo family's winery to become one
the most important in the Valle d'Itria. The
various vineyards located in this historic
Puglian wine area are on calcareous soils
mixed with red earth at elevations of
350-400 meters. The entire range has a
modern style that brings out the freshnes
and richness of fruit. Wines are divided ir
various lines and come from both
traditional and international varietals. This
year their Monte dei Cocci Negroamaro '
was the most convincing of the wines
submitted. Notes of cherry, black fruits ar
spices arise on the nose, while on the
palate it proves long with nice pulp and
tannins that are present, but well manage
The Primitivo Vendemmia Tardiva '17 of t
same line has nice juice, finding the right
balance between sweetness and freshnes
while the Verdeca '18 is fruity and supple
With respect to other versions, the Conte
Giangirolamo '16 was less impressive.

● Es '17	♛♛ 7
● Primitivo di Manduria Es '12	♛♛♛ 7
● Primitivo di Manduria Es '11	♛♛♛ 7
● Primitivo di Manduria Es '10	♛♛♛ 6
● Primitivo di Manduria Es '09	♛♛♛ 6
● Primitivo di Manduria Es '08	♛♛♛ 6
● Primitivo di Manduria Es '07	♛♛♛ 6
● Primitivo di Manduria Es '06	♛♛♛ 5
● Es '16	♛♛ 7
● Es '15	♛♛ 7
● Jo '08	♛♛ 6
● Primitivo di Manduria Dolce Naturale Es + Sole '12	♛♛ 7
● Primitivo di Manduria Es '14	♛♛ 7
● Primitivo di Manduria Es '13	♛♛ 7

● Monte dei Cocci Negroamaro '17	♛♛
● Monte dei Cocci Primitivo V. T. '17	♛♛
○ Monte dei Cocci Verdeca '18	♛♛
● Conte Giangirolamo '16	♛
● Pizzo Rosso '16	♛
● Codalunga '14	♛♛
● Conte Giangirolamo '15	♛♛
● Conte Giangirolamo '13	♛♛
● Conte Giangirolamo '12	♛♛
● Monte dei Cocci Negroamaro '16	♛♛
● Monte dei Cocci Negroamaro '15	♛♛
● Monte dei Cocci Negroamaro '13	♛♛
● Monte dei Cocci Primitivo V. T. '15	♛♛
○ Monte dei Cocci Verdeca '16	♛♛
● Primitivo La Voliera '16	♛♛

ito Donato Giuliani

Gioia Canale, 18
010 Turi [BA]
.. +39 0808915335
ww.vitivinicolagiuliani.com

ANNUAL PRODUCTION 100,000 bottles
ECTARES UNDER VINE 40.00

to Donato Giuliani leads the family estate
unded 80 years ago in the heart of the
urgia Barese. The signature karst soils of
s territory, with a rocky base of rich
inerals emerging from beneath a thin
ver of red soil, are home to vineyards
anted with a variety of cultivars. Next to
imitivo, the symbol of the winery, there
e also Aleatico, Negroamaro, Fiano,
alvasia Bianca and Chardonnay. The
nge highlights a strong connection to the
rritory and a modern style favoring
omatic clarity. This year the winery only
esented two wines. The 2016 version
their Gioia del Colle Primitivo
ronaggio Riserva offers up jammy
omas of black fruits along with quinine
d spices. On the palate it shows nice
rsistence and great concentration. With
st a bit more freshness and suppleness it
rely would have landed a gold. Their
ano Chiancaia '18 is pleasant and
rusy, with nice pulp.

Gioia del Colle Primitivo	
Baronaggio Ris. '16	🍷🍷 5
Chiancaia '18	🍷🍷 3
Gioia del Colle Primitivo	
Baronaggio Ris. '15	🍷🍷🍷 5
Chiancaia '17	🍷🍷 3
Gioia del Colle Aleatico	
Cantone di Cristo '15	🍷🍷 4
Gioia del Colle Baronaggio Ris. '13	🍷🍷 5
Gioia del Colle Primitivo Lavarossa '12	🍷🍷 3*

Cantine Paolo Leo

via Tuturano, 21
72025 San Donaci [BR]
Tel. +39 0831635073
www.paololeo.it

CELLAR SALES
PRE-BOOKED VISITS
ACCOMMODATION
ANNUAL PRODUCTION 1,300,000 bottles
HECTARES UNDER VINE 45.00

For thirty years now, Paolo Leo has been
running the family business with passion.
In addition to the wines from his own
vineyards, all located in the municipality of
San Donaci, the winery also functions as a
négociant, marketing wines produced
under its direct control in collaboration
with a group of trusted winemakers. The
range offers considerable technical
precision that brings out the best
characteristics of the varieties. This year
we particularly liked the Taccorosso
Negroamaro '15, a wine redolent of sweet
spices and orange peel. On the palate it
shows nice mouthfeel, proving expansive
with truly well-integrated tannins. Their
well-made Orfeo Negroamaro '17 offers
up fruity aromas and hints of
Mediterranean shrub. Notes of wood are
just a little too pronounced at this stage –
so we recommend waiting some. Their
highly enjoyable Primitivo di Manduria
Passo del Cardinale '18 is simpler and
more approachable in its aromas of
wild berries.

● Taccorosso Negroamaro '15	🍷🍷🍷 6
● Orfeo Negroamaro '17	🍷🍷 5
● Primitivo di Manduria	
Passo del Cardinale '18	🍷🍷 3
⊙ Alture Susumaniello Rosé '18	🍷 2
○ Numen '18	🍷 4
● Salice Salentino Ris. '12	🍷 4
○ Verdeca '18	🍷 2
● Orfeo Negroamaro '16	🍷🍷🍷 5
● Orfeo Negroamaro '15	🍷🍷🍷 4*
● Primitivo di Manduria	
Passo del Cardinale '14	🍷🍷🍷 3*

Masseria Li Veli

S.DA PROV.LE CELLINO-CAMPI, KM 1
72020 CELLINO SAN MARCO [BR]
TEL. +39 0831618259
www.liveli.it

CELLAR SALES
PRE-BOOKED VISITS
ANNUAL PRODUCTION 400,000 bottles
HECTARES UNDER VINE 33.00
SUSTAINABLE WINERY

The Falvo family acquired the Masseria Li
Veli in 1999 and began producing wine
here. Their range of about fifteen wines are
primarily made using Salento's local
varieties: from the well-known Negroamaro,
Primitivo, Aleatico and Verdeca, to cultivars
like Susumaniello or Malvasia Nera, whose
full potential have only recently become
broadly recognized and are now vinified on
their own. The vineyards are spread
between Cellino San Marco, for mainly red
varieties, and Valle d'Itria, for white. The
Askos Verdeca confirmed its exceptional
quality. Made with grapes cultivated in the
Itria Valley, the 2018 is redolent of white,
tropical fruit — its long, sapid palate
features nice mouthfeel, offering up citrusy
notes. The Masseria Li Veli '17, a blend of
Primitivo (40%), Negroamaro (30%) and
Cabernet Sauvignon exhibits great
concentration, a rich tannic weave and
fruit. We're sure it will reach its full
potential in a few years.

○ Askos Verdeca '18	🏆🏆🏆 4*
● Masseria Li Veli '17	🏆🏆 7
● Askos Susumaniello '18	🏆🏆 4
⊙ Askos Susumaniello Rosato '18	🏆🏆 3
● Askos Primitivo '17	🏆 4
○ Fiano '18	🏆 2
○ Askos Verdeca '17	🏆🏆🏆 3*
● Masseria Li Veli '10	🏆🏆🏆 5
● Aleatico Passito '10	🏆🏆 8
● Aleatico Passito '08	🏆🏆 6
● MLV '15	🏆🏆 5
● MLV '12	🏆🏆 5
● MLV '11	🏆🏆 5
● Salice Salentino Rosso Pezzo Morgana Ris. '16	🏆🏆 4

Masca del Tacco

VIA TRIPOLI, 5/7
72020 ERCHIE [BR]
TEL. +39 0831759786
www.mascadeltacco.com

ANNUAL PRODUCTION 300,000 bottles
HECTARES UNDER VINE 140.00

The Puglian company acquired by Felice
Mergè in 2010 manages a large number
vineyards in the provinces of Brindisi, Lec
and Taranto, some with plants that are
more than 50 years old. Local Negroama
Primitivo and Susumaniello are flanked by
a series of varieties that are international
somewhat uncommon here, including
Cabernet Sauvignon, Pinot Nero,
Chardonnay, Fiano, Syrah and Lambrusco
The wines have a very modern approach
driven by a quest for full body and rich fru
This year the Primitivo di Manduria Piano
Chiuso 26 27 63 Riserva '16, a proper cr
stood out during our tastings. Notes of
overripe black fruits and mulberry give wa
to a coherent, spicy palate, with a sweet
touch that's nicely balanced by a finish of
notable tension. Their Uetta '18 also prov
well made. It's a pleasant, characterful
Fiano that calls up Minutolo for its
pronounced aromas.

● Primitivo di Manduria Piano Chiuso 26 27 63 Ris. '16	🏆🏆🏆
○ L'Uetta '18	🏆🏆
⊙ Ro'Si '18	🏆
● Và dove ti porta il Vento Susumaniello '18	🏆
● Primitivo di Manduria Li Filitti Ris. '15	🏆🏆
● Primitivo di Manduria Lu Rappaio '17	🏆🏆
● Primitivo di Manduria Lu Rappaio '15	🏆🏆
● Primitivo di Manduria Piano Chiuso 26 27 63 Ris. '15	🏆🏆
⊙ Ro'si '17	🏆🏆

alamà

A. Diaz, 6
020 Cutrofiano [LE]
+39 0836542865
w.vinicolapalama.com

LLAR SALES
E-BOOKED VISITS
NUAL PRODUCTION 200,000 bottles
CTARES UNDER VINE 15.00
ICULTURE METHOD Certified Organic
STAINABLE WINERY

e Palamà family's estate offers a wide
ge made exclusively from traditional,
al cultivars, such as Negroamaro,
mitivo, Malvasia Nera, Malvasia Bianca
d Verdeca. The vineyards, planted with
erse head-trained varieties, are on
dium-textured land in the heart of
lento, between Cutrofiano and Matino.
e whole range combines a strong
ritorial imprint with careful cellar work
d considerable technical precision. The
18 version of their Metiusco Rosato also
rms its status as one of Puglia's best
sés. Made with Negroamaro, it's
matically flowery with notes of wild
rry, while its fresh, sophisticated and
rsistent palate proves sapid and
asant. The Mavro '17 also delivers. It's
other Negroamaro, intense in its aromas
red fruits and Mediterranean shrub, with
ong, expansive palate. It's also worth
ting their Biancoevoluto Collezione
vata '17, a blend of Verdeca and
lvasia Bianca de garde created by the
est generation of family.

Mavro '17	▼▼ 4
Metiusco Rosato '18	▼▼ 3*
Bianco Evoiuto '17	▼▼ 5
Albarossa '17	▼ 2
Vino d'Arcangelo '17	▼ 4
Metiusco Bianco '18	▼ 3
Metiusco Rosso '18	▼ 3
Nini Rosso '18	▼ 2
Nini Verdeca '18	▼ 2
'5 Vendemmie '11	▼▼▼ 4*
'5 Vendemmie '17	♈♈ 5
Mavro '16	♈♈ 4
Mavro '15	♈♈ 3*
Metiusco Bianco '17	♈♈ 3
Metiusco Rosato '17	♈♈ 3*
Metiusco Rosso '17	♈♈ 3

Pietraventosa

Loc. Parco Largo
s.da vic.le Latta Latta
70023 Gioia del Colle [BA]
Tel. +39 3355730274
www.pietraventosa.it

ANNUAL PRODUCTION 30,000 bottles
HECTARES UNDER VINE 5.40
VITICULTURE METHOD Certified Organic
SUSTAINABLE WINERY

Marianna Annio and Raffaele Leo have been
running this Gioia del Colle DOC winery for
fifteen years. The vineyards, at an elevation
of about 380 meters, are on two types of
soil, Gioia altarenite and Gravina limestone;
the two are so distinct that the color can
change from dark brown to almost white in
the middle of a row, causing the harvest
date to change accordingly. Primitivo,
Aglianico and Malvasia di Candia are used
to create wines with a modern style that are
developed to allow for the territory's
characteristics to be expressed at their best.
The Gioia del Colle Primitivo Riserva '13
made it to our finals thanks to aromas of
black fruits, incense and wood resin – and
to a vibrant but fresh, long and complex
palate that features a sapid, mineral finish.
The other wines proposed also prove truly
well made, especially their Primitivo (and
15% Aglianico) rosé, the Est Rosa '18, a
flowery, plucky wine with notes of red and
white fruit, and their Volere Volare '17, a
transparent, pleasant Primitivo.

● Gioia del Colle Primitivo Ris. '13	▼▼ 6
○ Apriti Cielo! '18	▼▼ 5
● Gioia del Colle Primitivo Allegoria '16	▼▼ 4
● Volere Volare '17	▼▼ 3
⊙ Est Rosa '18	▼ 4
● Ossimoro '16	▼ 4
● Gioia del Colle Primitivo Ris. '06	♈♈♈ 4
⊙ EstRosa '17	♈♈ 3*
⊙ EstRosa '16	♈♈ 3
⊙ EstRosa '14	♈♈ 3
● Gioia del Colle Primitivo Allegoria '13	♈♈ 3
● Gioia del Colle Primitivo Pietraventosa Ris. '12	♈♈ 5
● Gioia del Colle Primitivo Riserva di Pietraventosa '11	♈♈ 5
● Ossimoro '13	♈♈ 3

★Polvanera

S.DA VICINALE LAMIE MARCHESANA, 601
70023 GIOIA DEL COLLE [BA]
TEL. +39 080758900
www.cantinepolvanera.it

CELLAR SALES
RESTAURANT SERVICE
ANNUAL PRODUCTION 650,000 bottles
HECTARES UNDER VINE 120.00
VITICULTURE METHOD Certified Organic

The Cassano family's Polvanera is one of the wineries leading the new wave of Primitivo. Its vineyards are mostly in Gioia del Colle and Acquaviva delle Fonti on karst soil at an elevation of over 300 meters. In addition to Primitivo, there are other native and traditional cultivars, such as Aglianico, Aleatico, Bianco d'Alessano, Falanghina, Marchione, Minutolo, Moscato and Verdeca. The range is a fine example of the authentic expression of the territory and its potential. The Gioia del Colle Primitivo 17 Vigneto Montevella is back at the top. The 2016 is rich and concentrated, but also sapid and taut with notes of black fruits, roots and Mediterranean shrub. We also appreciated their Gioia del Colle Primitivo 14 Vigneto Marchesana, a plucky, fresh and juicy wine redolent of wild berries. We found very interesting their Primitivo 15 '18 (no added sulfites) — it's a pleasant wine that plays on notes of wild berries.

● Gioia del Colle Primitivo 17 Vign. Montevella '16	♥♥♥ 6
● Gioia del Colle Primitivo 14 Vign. Marchesana '16	♥♥ 3*
● Gioia del Colle Primitivo 16 Vign. San Benedetto '16	♥♥ 5
○ Minutolo '18	♥♥ 3
● Primitivo 15 Senza Solfiti Aggiunti '18	♥♥ 2*
● Gioia del Colle Primitivo 16 Vign. San Benedetto '15	♥♥♥ 5
● Gioia del Colle Primitivo 17 Vign. Montevella '14	♥♥♥ 6
● Gioia del Colle Primitivo 17 Vign. Montevella '12	♥♥♥ 6

Produttori di Manduria

VIA FABIO MASSIMO, 19
74024 MANDURIA [TA]
TEL. +39 0999735332
www.cpvini.com

CELLAR SALES
PRE-BOOKED VISITS
ANNUAL PRODUCTION 1,100,000 bottles
HECTARES UNDER VINE 900.00
SUSTAINABLE WINERY

Founded in 1932, the Produttori di Manduria cooperative has 400 members and plays a leading role in the Primitivo di Manduria DOC. Of the 900 planted hectares, more than half are dedicated to the production of Primitivo. The remaining vineyards are about 25% Negroamaro, which are accompanied by various other traditional and international cultivars. Production is oriented toward a modern style that highlights the best of the territory's characteristics. Moreover, the winery is deeply committed to sustainable cultivation. For this reasons, it receives our 'Award for Sustainable Viticulture'. Their Primitivo di Manduria Lirica '17 takes home Tre Bicchieri. It's a ripe, full wine rich in fruit and of notable length, but also sapid and gutsy. Their well-crafted Primitivo di Manduria Dolce Natural Madrigale '16 is pleasant in its notes of cherry and juniper, while the palate does a nice job balancing sweet tones thanks to a long, fresh finish. Another well-made wine is their Aka '18, a flowery and delicately spicy rosé made with Primitivo.

● Primitivo di Manduria Lirica '17	♥♥♥
○ Aka '18	♥♥
● Primitivo di Manduria Dolce Naturale Madrigale '16	♥♥
● Abatemasi Negroamaro '16	♥
○ Alica Verdeca '18	♥
● Primitivo di Manduria Elegia Ris. '16	♥
● Primitivo di Manduria Memoria '18	♥
● Primitivo di Manduria Sonetto Ris. '15	♥
○ Zin Fiano '17	♥
● Primitivo di Manduria Elegia Ris. '15	♥♥
● Primitivo di Manduria Elegia Ris. '13	♥♥
● Primitivo di Manduria Lirica '16	♥♥
● Primitivo di Manduria Lirica '15	♥♥
● Primitivo di Manduria Sonetto Ris. '14	♥♥

Rivera

VIA PROV.LE 231 KM 60,500
...123 ANDRIA [BT]
... +39 0883569510
...w.rivera.it

CELLAR SALES
PRE-BOOKED VISITS
ANNUAL PRODUCTION 1,200,000 bottles
HECTARES UNDER VINE 75.00

...e De Corato family's estate is one of the
...ost famous in Puglia's wine scene and a
...e standard bearer for the Castel del
...onte DOC. The four vineyards located
...thin the appellation are characterized by
...ferent soils and positions, all between
...0 and 350 meters above sea level and
...arked by a particularly cool climate. The
...nge offers remarkable character with
...rticular attention given to reds with good
...ing potential. And the proof can be found
...their Castel del Monte Rosso Il Falcone
...serva, a great classic. The 2014 is
...mplex, with notes of black fruits and
...ices — it may be just a bit lacking in
...nsion and acidity. We also appreciated
...e Castel del Monte Aglianico Cappellaccio
...serva '13, a full wine with nice mouthfeel
...d still slightly burred tannins, as well as
...eir Moscato di Trans Dolce Naturale Piani
...Tufara '17, an elegant and varietal wine.

Castel del Monte Rosso	
Il Falcone Ris. '14	♟♟ 4
Castel del Monte Aglianico	
Cappellaccio Ris. '13	♟♟ 2*
Castel del Monte Bombino Bianco	
Marese '18	♟♟ 2*
Castel del Monte Chardonnay	
Preludio n°1 '18	♟♟ 2*
Castel del Monte Nero di Troia	
Puer Apuliae Ris. '14	♟♟ 5
Moscato di Trani Dolce Naturale	
Piani di Tufara '17	♟♟ 2*
Castel del Monte Bombino Nero	
Pungirosa '18	♟ 2
Castel del Monte Chardonnay	
Lama dei Corvi '18	♟ 3
Castel del Monte Nero di Troia	
Violante '17	♟ 2

★Tenute Rubino

VIA E. FERMI, 50
72100 BRINDISI
TEL. +39 0831571955
www.tenuterubino.com

CELLAR SALES
PRE-BOOKED VISITS
ANNUAL PRODUCTION 1,200,000 bottles
HECTARES UNDER VINE 290.00

Luigi Rubino and his wife Romina manage
this Brindisi winery, which in only twenty
years has become a benchmark in both the
territory and beyond. The four estates extend
from the hills of the Adriatic ridge to
Brindisi's hinterland. The vineyards are
planted with traditional Salento varieties,
among which Susumaniello stands out, as
well as international varieties or those that
are atypical for the area, like Chardonnay
and Vermentino, respectively. The wines
exhibit considerable technical precision and
continue to move toward a strong expression
of their territorial identity. The 2018 version
of their Oltremè is at the top of its game. It's
a fresh and pleasant Susumaniello with nice
mouthfeel; spicy and rich in notes of red
fruit, it goes down like a charm. Their
Brindisi Negroamaro Rosso '17 also proved
excellent, with its notes of Mediterranean
shrub and black fruits — on the palate it's
fresh and sapid. The rest of their selection
also proves well made, especially the
plucky and supple Negroamaro Marmorelle
Rosso '17, and the citrusy, aromatic
Malvasia Bianca Giancola '18.

● Oltremé Susumaniello '18	♟♟♟ 3*
● Brindisi Negroamaro Rosso '17	♟♟ 4
○ Giancòla '18	♟♟ 3
● Marmorelle Rosso '17	♟♟ 2*
● Punta Aquila Primitivo '17	♟♟ 3
⊙ Brindisi Negroamaro Rosato	
Saturnino '18	♟ 2
● Brindisi Susumaniello Torre Testa '17	♟ 6
⊙ Brut Nature Sumaré M. Cl. '14	♟ 6
⊙ Torre Testa Susumaniello Rosato '18	♟ 3
● Oltremé '17	♟♟♟ 4*
● Oltremé '16	♟♟♟ 4*
● Torre Testa '13	♟♟♟ 6
● Torre Testa '12	♟♟♟ 6

San Marzano

VIA MONSIGNOR BELLO, 9
74020 SAN MARZANO DI SAN GIUSEPPE [TA]
TEL. +39 0999574181
www.sanmarzanowines.com

CELLAR SALES
ANNUAL PRODUCTION 10,000,000 bottles
HECTARES UNDER VINE 1500.00
VITICULTURE METHOD Certified Organic
SUSTAINABLE WINERY

Founded in 1962 at the initiative of nineteen winegrowers, San Marzano currently has 1200 contributing members and about 1500 hectares of vineyards. The wide range draws on both traditional and international varieties, but Primitivo-based wines stand out for their importance, starting with various versions of Primitivo di Manduria. The vineyards are mainly located in the municipalities of San Marzano, Sava and Francavilla Fontana, on mostly calcareous soil dominated dominated by red earth. The wines seek a balance between a traditional richness of alcohol and a modern approach. Their Primitivo di Manduria Sessantanni '16 exhibits the wine's characteristic qualities: it's rich and close-woven with jammy notes of black fruits; on the palate it exhibits nice texture, proving soft and pervasive. Though their selection features a number of well-crafted wines, like the spicy, long and juicy Primitivo di Manduria Anniversario 62° Riserva '16, or the Primitivo di Manduria Talò '17, a wine that's pleasant and fresh in its characteristic notes of plums.

● Primitivo di Manduria Sessantanni '16	♟♟♟ 5
● F Negroamaro '16	♟♟ 5
● Primitivo di Manduria Anniversario 62° Ris. '16	♟♟ 6
● Primitivo di Manduria Talò '18	♟♟ 3
● Talò Malvasia Nera '18	♟♟ 3
○ Talò Verdeca '18	♟♟ 3
☉ Tramari Rosé di Primitivo '18	♟♟ 3
○ Edda '18	♟ 4
● Talò Negroamaro '18	♟ 3
● Primitivo di Manduria Sessantanni '15	♟♟♟ 5
● Primitivo di Manduria Talò '13	♟♟♟ 3*

Conte Spagnoletti Zeuli

FRAZ. SAN DOMENICO
S.DA PROV.LE 231 KM 60,000
70031 ANDRIA [BT]
TEL. +39 0883569511
www.contespagnolettizeuli.it

CELLAR SALES
PRE-BOOKED VISITS
ANNUAL PRODUCTION 400,000 bottles
HECTARES UNDER VINE 120.00

This family winery, whose origins date back to the 16th century, is led with great passion by Onofrio Spagnoletti Zeuli. Vineyards are divided into two estates, San Domenico and Zagaria, both located within the Castel del Monte DOC. The calcareous soils of the Andria countryside host exclusively local varietals, ranging from Nero di Troia to Montepulciano, Aglianico, Bombino Nero and Fiano. The wines have a modern style, attentive to freshness and emphasizing fruit. Castel del Monte submitted a noteworthy selection, starting with their Pezzalaruca '16. It's fresh, long and gutsy with notes of red fruits, well-integrated tannins and crisp fruit. The Nero di Troia Il Rinzacco Riserva '16 offers up notes of black fruits, quinine and pepper, making for a soft and full palate, but nice acid and persistence. The Terranera Riserva '15 is still a bit closed, with notes of black fruits and tar, while the Rosso '18 proves fresh and approachable.

● Castel del Monte Rosso Pezzalaruca '16	♟♟ 2*
● Castel del Monte Nero di Troia Il Rinzacco Ris. '16	♟♟ 3
● Castel del Monte Rosso '18	♟♟ 3
● Castel del Monte Rosso Terranera Ris. '15	♟♟ 4
☉ Castel del Monte Bombino Nero Rosato Colombaio '18	♟ 3
● Castel del Monte Aglianico Ghiandara V. San Domenico '15	♟ 3
● Castel del Monte Rosso V. Grande Tenuta Zagaria '16	♟ 4
● Don Ferdinando Primitivo '17	♟ 3
○ Jody Fiano '18	♟ 2

osimo Taurino

A PROV.LE 365 KM 1,400
010 Guagnano [LE]
. +39 0832706490
ww.taurinovini.it

ELLAR SALES
RE-BOOKED VISITS
NNUAL PRODUCTION 900,000 bottles
ECTARES UNDER VINE 90.00

is long-established Guagnano winery
ntinues to be a benchmark of Puglian
nemaking. Its vineyards are situated on 90
ectares of mostly sandy, calcareous soils in
e countryside of Guagnano, Salice
alentino and San Donaci. 80 of these are
ultivated with Negroamaro and Malvasia
ero, while the remainder are divided
tween Chardonnay, Primitive, Cabernet,
esling and Semillon. The new cellar
ovides natural temperature control,
owing production methods to continue
ong the road that Cosimo Taurino staked
t years ago with his famous Patriglione. As
sual their Negroamaro reds stood out during
ur tastings. The Patriglione '14 affirms its
atus as one of the region's best, proving
xpansive with notes of rosemary and ripe
ack fruits. On the palate tannins show nice
nesse and give way to a long, juicy finish.
he Salice Salentino Rosso Riserva '14, a
ucky fruit-forward wine, proves well made,
s does the Kompà '16, with its flowery
nes and aromas of Mediterranean shrub,
nd the A64 Cosimo Taurino '13, a wine
at's tannic but also pulpy and harmonious.

Patriglione '14	♟♟ 7
A64 Cosimo Taurino '13	♟♟ 4
Kompà '16	♟♟ 2*
Salice Salentino Rosso Ris. '14	♟♟ 3
7° Ceppo '18	♟ 3
Antoros Extra Dry Rosé	♟ 3
I Sierri '18	♟ 2
Notarpanaro '14	♟ 3
Ricordanze '17	♟ 5
Scaloti '18	♟ 2
Stria Extra Dry	♟ 3
Patriglione '94	♟♟♟ 7
Patriglione '88	♟♟♟ 7
Patriglione '85	♟♟♟ 5
Notarpanaro '13	♟♟ 3
Scaloti '17	♟♟ 2*

Terrecarsiche1939

VIA MAESTRI DEL LAVORO 6/8
70013 CASTELLANA GROTTE [BA]
TEL. +39 0804962309
www.terrecarsiche.it

PRE-BOOKED VISITS
ANNUAL PRODUCTION 600,000 bottles
HECTARES UNDER VINE 12.00

Terrecarsiche1939 is both a newcomer and
a historic operation: it was officially founded
in 2011, but the family's agricultural roots
date back to 1939. The winery operates in
the area of the Murge, specifically within the
Gioia del Colle appellation and in Valle d'Itria.
In addition to its own twelve hectares of
vineyards, the winery collaborates year
round with a small group of winegrowers
whose vineyards it monitors. The fifteen or
so labels are modern in style and technically
well made. This year we particularly enjoyed
the Gioia del Colle Primitivo Fanova Riserva
'16, which features notes of blackberry,
blueberry and spices. The palate exhibits
nice freshness, proving sapid, pleasant and
long. The aromatic and juicy Passaturi
Minutolo '18 proves well-crafted, as does
the fresh and citrusy Verdeca '18 and their
Gioia del Colle Primitivo Fanova '17, a wine
redolent of ripe cherries with nice acidity and
pluck on the palate.

● Gioia del Colle Primitivo Fanova Ris. '16	♟♟ 3*
● Gioia del Colle Primitivo Fanova '17	♟♟ 3
○ Passaturi '18	♟♟ 2*
○ Verdeca '18	♟♟ 2*
○ Cava Bianca '18	♟ 3
● Gioia del Colle Primitivo Regula Magistri Ris. '15	♟ 6
⊙ Gioia Rosa '18	♟ 3
○ Locorotondo Sup. Padre Abate '18	♟ 2
● Gioia del Colle Primitivo Fanova '16	♟♟ 3*
● Gioia del Colle Primitivo Fanova Ris. '15	♟♟ 3
● Nero di Troia '15	♟♟ 3

★Tormaresca

LOC. TOFANO
C.DA TORRE D'ISOLA
76013 MINERVINO MURGE [BT]
TEL. +39 0883692631
www.tormaresca.it

CELLAR SALES
PRE-BOOKED VISITS
ACCOMMODATION
ANNUAL PRODUCTION 3,000,000 bottles
HECTARES UNDER VINE 380.00
VITICULTURE METHOD Certified Organic
SUSTAINABLE WINERY

The Antinori family's winery in Puglia, Tormaresca, has two vast estates. Bocca di Lupo is located on the Minervino Murge, in Alta Murgia, within the Castel del Monte DOC zone, while Masseria Maime is in San Pietro Vernotico, in Alto Salento. Many traditional varieties such as Aglianico, Negroamaro, Primitivo and Nero di Troia are cultivated, as are international cultivars, such as Chardonnay and Cabernet Sauvignon. The wines have a very modern stamp, based largely on their enjoyability and fullness of fruit. This year two 2017 Primitivos stood out. The Neprica offers up aromas of wild berries, with a fresh, pleasantly persistent palate, while the Torcicoda proves spicy with notes of Mediterranean shrub and chocolate. The Calafuria '18, a pleasant and floral rosé, delivers, as does the Castel del Monte Rosso Trentangeli '16, a wine with nice persistence and tension. The Masseria '15 and Castel del Monte Aglianico Bocca di Lupo '15 were less charming than usual.

⊙ Calafuria '18	♟♟ 3
○ Castel del Monte Chardonnay Pietrabianca '17	♟♟ 4
● Castel del Monte Rosso Trentangeli '16	♟♟ 3
● Nèprica Primitivo '17	♟♟ 2*
● Torcicoda '17	♟♟ 4
● Castel del Monte Aglianico Bocca di Lupo '15	♟ 5
● Masseria Maime '15	♟ 5
● Castel del Monte Rosso Trentangeli '11	♟♟♟ 3*
● Masseria Maime '12	♟♟♟ 5
● Torcicoda '11	♟♟♟ 4*
● Torcicoda '10	♟♟♟ 3*

★Torrevento

S.DA PROV.LE 234 KM 10.600
70033 CORATO [BA]
TEL. +39 0808980923
www.torrevento.it

CELLAR SALES
PRE-BOOKED VISITS
ACCOMMODATION AND RESTAURANT SERVI●
ANNUAL PRODUCTION 2,500,000 bottles●
HECTARES UNDER VINE 450.00
SUSTAINABLE WINERY

Francesco Liantonio's Torrevento can boa● a sizable estate, almost 250 hectares mostly within the Parco Rurale della Murgia, an area characterized by rocky limestone, karst-type soil. It also rents more than 200 hectares spanning from Valle d'Itria to the Primitivo region of Salento. Traditional varieties are almost exclusively grown, with Nero di Troia and Aglianico playing starring roles. The proposed range expresses respectful and● non-intrusive work in the cellar, resulting wines with finesse and elegance. The Castel del Monte Rosso Vigna Pedale Riserva '16 offers up notes of black fores● fruits and spices, while the palate impresses for its persistence and freshness, proving long and sapid. It's a Tre Bicchieri — no ifs, ands or buts. The Torre del Falco Nero di Troia '18 also performed well. With its notes of aromatic herbs and mulberry, it's fresh and comple● all at once. The rest of their selection was● also up to expectations.

● Castel del Monte Rosso V. Pedale Ris. '16	♟♟♟
● Torre del Falco Nero di Troia '18	♟♟
● Castel del Monte Rosso Bolonero '18	♟♟
● Kebir '18	♟♟
○ Bacca Rara Chardonnay '18	♟
● Castel del Monte Bombino Nero Veritas '18	♟
⊙ Castel del Monte Rosato Primaronda '18	♟
● Passione Reale '18	♟ 2
● Castel del Monte Nero di Troia Ottagono Ris. '14	♟♟♟
● Castel del Monte Rosso V. Pedale Ris. '15	♟♟♟
● Castel del Monte Rosso V. Pedale Ris. '14	♟♟♟

Cantine Tre Pini

LA VECCHIA PER ALTAMURA, S.DA PROV.LE 79 KM 16
70020 CASSANO DELLE MURGE [BA]
TEL. +39 080764911
www.cantinetrepini.com

CELLAR SALES
PRE-BOOKED VISITS
ACCOMMODATION AND RESTAURANT SERVICE
ANNUAL PRODUCTION 50,000 bottles
HECTARES UNDER VINE 9.00
VITICULTURE METHOD Certified Organic
SUSTAINABLE WINERY

The Plantamura family founded Cantine Tre Pini in 2012, and in these few years they have succeeded in making it one of the most interesting wineries not only of the Gioia del Colle DOC, but in all of Puglia. Vineyards are on moderately rocky, karst soil in the municipalities of Cassano delle Murge and Acquaviva delle Fonti, between 300 and 450 meters above sea level. Only traditional local vines are cultivated, specially Primitivo followed by Bombino Nero, Malvasia Bianca and Fiano. Production seeks finesse and elegance. The Gioia del Colle Primitivo Riserva '16 offers up aromas of red forest fruits, while on the palate it proves pleasant, with nice persistence and freshness. Their other Primitivos are all well made, from the juicy and pleasantly approachable Crae '18 to the pleasantly persistent Trullo di Carnevale '17 with its aromas of cherry and the Gioia del Colle Primitivo Piscina delle Monache '17, a wine rich in fruit.

Gioia del Colle Primitivo Ris. '16	▼▼ 5
● Crae '18	▼▼ 2*
Gioia del Colle Primitivo Piscina delle Monache '17	▼▼ 3
● Trullo di Carnevale '17	▼▼ 3
○ Domè '18	▼ 3
○ Donna Johanna '18	▼ 2
○ Ventifile Rosé '18	▼ 2
● Gioia del Colle Primitivo Ris. '14	▼▼▼ 5
Gioia del Colle Primitivo Ris. '13	▼▼▼ 4*
○ Donna Johanna '17	♈ 2*
● Gioia del Colle Primitivo Piscina delle Monache '16	♈ 3*
● Gioia del Colle Primitivo Ris. '15	♈ 5
● Trullo di Carnevale '16	♈ 3

Agricole Vallone

VIA XXV LUGLIO, 7
73100 LECCE
TEL. +39 0832308041
www.agricolevallone.it

PRE-BOOKED VISITS
ANNUAL PRODUCTION 424,000 bottles
HECTARES UNDER VINE 161.00
VITICULTURE METHOD Certified Organic
SUSTAINABLE WINERY

The Vallone family's estate is truly a standard bearer of Salento winemaking. Founded in 1934, the winery's vineyards are divided into three estates: one within the Brindisi DOC zone; a second within Salice Salentino, whose more than 90-year-old, head-trained Negroamaro vines produce Graticciaia, one of Puglia's most famous wines; and, a third in the countryside near Carovigno. The entire range is technically well made and highly enjoyable. The 2015 version of their Graticciaia delivered. It's a Negroamaro with aromas of ripe blackberries accompanied by spicy nuances. The palate is expansive, with nice persistence and a long finish in which new hints of rosemary meet a resurgence of black fruits. The Castel Serranova '15, a sapid, fresh and dynamic blend of Negroamaro and Susumainello with nice fruit, proves well-realized, as does their Susumaniello '17 with its pleasant hints of blackberry and mulberry.

● Graticciaia '15	▼▼ 7
● Castel Serranova '15	▼▼ 4
● Susumaniello '17	▼▼ 2*
⊙ Tenuta Serranova Susumaniello Rosè '18	▼ 2
● Graticciaia '03	▼▼▼ 6
● Castelserranova '14	♈ 4
● Graticciaia '13	♈ 7
● Graticciaia '12	♈ 7
⊙ Tenuta Serranova Susumaniello Rosè '17	♈ 2*
● Vigna Castello '11	♈ 5

Varvaglione 1921

C.DA SANTA LUCIA
74020 LEPORANO [TA]
TEL. +39 0995315370
www.varvaglione.com

CELLAR SALES
PRE-BOOKED VISITS
ACCOMMODATION
ANNUAL PRODUCTION 4,000,000 bottles
HECTARES UNDER VINE 400.00
SUSTAINABLE WINERY

The winery's centenary is quickly
approaching and, judging by the progress
we have seen, Varvaglione should celebrate
it in grand form. Including its own vineyards,
those rented and those of the associated
winegrowers, the estate draws from over
1,500 hectares largely planted with
traditional local grapes such as Primitivo,
Negroamaro, Aglianico, Verdeca and Fiano.
The wide range produced is united by a
style that seeks technical precision and
territorial expression. Their Idea '18 is a
fresh and fragrant rosé made with Primitivo.
On the nose it offers up flowery tones and
hints of red wild berries, while in the mouth
it proves highly pleasant — it goes down
like a charm. Other noteworthy tastes
include their Tatu '16, a full and persistent
Primitivo (with a 10% share of Aglianico)
that's redolent of plum and figs, their Salice
Salentino '17, a fruity wine with nice pulp,
their soft and spicy Primitivo di Manduria
Papale Linea Oro '17, and their 12 e Mezzo
Primitivo '18, which does a nice job
balancing softness and acidity.

⊙ Idea '18	♼♼♼ 3*
● 12 e Mezzo Primitivo '18	♼♼ 2*
● Negroamaro di Terra d'Otranto Varvaglione Collezione Privata Old Vines '16	♼♼ 6
● Primitivo di Manduria Papale Linea Oro '17	♼♼ 5
● Salice Salentino '17	♼♼ 4
● Tatu '16	♼♼ 2*
● Primitivo di Manduria Old Vines '16	♼ 3
● Primitivo di Manduria Papale '18	♼ 3
○ 12 e Mezzo Malvasia Bianca '17	♼♼ 2*
● 12 e mezzo Negroamaro '15	♼♼ 2*
● 12 e mezzo Primitivo '15	♼♼ 2*
● Primitivo di Manduria Papale Linea Oro '15	♼♼ 5
● Primitivo di Manduria Papale Oro '15	♼♼ 5

Vespa
Vignaioli per Passione

FRAZ. C.DA RENI
VIA MANDURIA - AVETRANA KM 3,8
74024 MANDURIA [TA]
TEL. +39 063722120
www.vespavignaioli.it

CELLAR SALES
ANNUAL PRODUCTION 165,000 bottles
HECTARES UNDER VINE 30.00
SUSTAINABLE WINERY

The Vespa family winery, with the continued
support of enologist Riccardo Cotarella,
manages about 30 hectares of vineyards on
the clayey and sandy soils of the Manduria
and Salice Salentino countryside. Primitivo
is the winery's principle variety, but there
there's also Aleatico, Fiano, Negroamaro
and Nero di Troia. The seven wines express
a resolutely modern approach, with
particular attention going to pleasantness
and full fruit. Their Primitivo di Manduria
Raccontami '17 features aromas of black
damson and Asian spices, while the palate
comes through long and juicy, with nice
persistence. Their Bruno dei Vespa '18,
another well-crafted wine, is a supple and
approachable Primitivo with notes of ripe
black fruit. The rest of their selection also
proves excellent, from their fresh Flarò Il
Rosa dei Vespa '18, a blend of Primitivo and
Aleatico, to the pleasant Primitivo di
Manduria Il Rosso dei Vespa '18 and their
Fiano Il Bianco dei Vespa '18, an
easy-drinking wine.

● Primitivo di Manduria Raccontami '17	♼♼♼ 5
● Il Bruno dei Vespa '18	♼♼ 2
⊙ Flarò Il Rosa dei Vespa '18	♼ 2
○ Il Bianco dei Vespa '18	♼ 2
● Primitivo di Manduria Il Rosso dei Vespa '18	♼ 3
○ Zoe	♼ 5
● Primitivo di Manduria Raccontami '16	♼♼♼ 5
● Primitivo di Manduria Raccontami '15	♼♼♼ 5
● Primitivo di Manduria Raccontami '14	♼♼♼ 5
● Primitivo di Manduria Raccontami '13	♼♼♼ 5
● Il Bruno dei Vespa '17	♼♼ 2

Tenuta Viglione

S.DA PROV.LE 140 KM 4,100
70029 SANTERAMO IN COLLE [BA]
TEL. +39 0802123661
www.tenutaviglione.it

CELLAR SALES
PRE-BOOKED VISITS
ACCOMMODATION AND RESTAURANT SERVICE
ANNUAL PRODUCTION 400,000 bottles
HECTARES UNDER VINE 60.00
VITICULTURE METHOD Certified Organic

The Zullo family founded Tenuta Viglione
between Gioia del Colle and Santeramo in
Colle, at the foot of the Murgia Barese
plateau. At an elevation of about 450
meters, the vineyards grow in thin layers of
red soil over clay and limestone soils rich in
minerals and shell fossils. They grow
traditional varieties, starting with Primitivo
and Aleatico, as well as international
cultivars, such as Chardonnay or Merlot.
The wines stand out for their pluck and
freshness, presenting the territory's
character at its finest. Their Gioia del Colle
Primitivo Marpione Riserva '16 performed
well during our tastings with its aromas of
wild berry, black olives and Mediterranean
shrub. On the palate it's close-focused, long
and dynamic. Their Gioia del Colle Primitivo
Sellato '16, which plays on spicy nuances
with notes of fruit and aromatic herbs,
proves well-made, as does their plucky
and fresh Nero di Troia Maioliche '18, and
their Negroamaro Maioliche '18, a wine
that's pleasant in its aromas of black fruits
and rosemary.

● Gioia del Colle Primitivo Marpione Ris. '16	🏆 3*
● Gioia del Colle Primitivo Sellato '17	🏆🏆 2*
● Negroamaro Maioliche '18	🏆🏆 2*
● Nero di Troia Maioliche '18	🏆🏆 2*
○ Falanghina '18	🏆 2
● Jesce Fiano '18	🏆 2
● Johe '17	🏆 2
⊙ Rosato '18	🏆 2
○ Verdeca '18	🏆 2
● Gioia del Colle Primitivo Marpione Ris. '15	🏆🏆🏆 3*
● Gioia del Colle Primitivo Marpione Ris. '13	🏆🏆🏆 3*

★Conti Zecca

VIA CESAREA
73045 LEVERANO [LE]
TEL. +39 0832925613
www.contizecca.it

CELLAR SALES
PRE-BOOKED VISITS
ANNUAL PRODUCTION 2,800,000 bottles
HECTARES UNDER VINE 320.00
SUSTAINABLE WINERY

The Zecca family's winery, founded in
1935, is a real institution of Salento
wine-growing. Its own four estates,
Saraceno, Donna Marzia and Santo Stefano
in Leverano, and Cantalupi in Salice
Salentino, give rise to a very wide range
dominated by traditional varieties. The
wines are divided in various lines that share
a modern style, technical skill, great
qualitative consistency, lovely freshness
and rich fruit. These year we most
preferred their two Primitivos. The
Cantalupi '18 features fresh notes of black
fruits with spicy nuances, and a surprisingly
tannic palate of notable acidity. Their
Rifugio '18 , on the other hand, is a juicy
and gutsy wine. Their approachable
Cantalupi Negroamaro '18 delivered with
its notes of ripe black fruits, as did the
Luna '18, a blend of equal shares
Malvasia Bianca and Chardonnay
fermented and aged in barriques. It's a
fresh wine rich in pulp.

● Cantalupi Primitivo '18	🏆 2*
● Cantalupi Negroamaro '18	🏆 2*
○ Luna '18	🏆 4
● Nero '16	🏆 6
● Rifugio '17	🏆 3
● Leverano Negroamaro Liranu Ris. '16	🏆 3
○ Luna Saracena '18	🏆 4
○ Mendola '18	🏆 3
● Terra '16	🏆 4
● Nero '09	🏆🏆🏆 5
● Nero '14	🏆🏆 6
● Salice Salentino Cantalupi Ris. '13	🏆🏆 3

A Mano

VIA SAN GIOVANNI, 41
70015 NOCI [BA]
TEL. +39 0803434872
www.amanowine.it

CELLAR SALES
PRE-BOOKED VISITS
ANNUAL PRODUCTION 235,000 bottles
SUSTAINABLE WINERY

○ A Mano Bianco '17	♀♀ 2*
● Imprint Susumaniello '17	♀♀ 2*
● Prima Mano Primitivo '16	♀♀ 5
⊙ Primitivo Rosé '18	♀ 2

Masseria Altemura

S.DA PROV.LE 69 MESAGNE
72028 TORRE SANTA SUSANNA [BR]
TEL. +39 0831740485
www.masseriaaltemura.it

CELLAR SALES
PRE-BOOKED VISITS
ACCOMMODATION
ANNUAL PRODUCTION 400,000 bottles
HECTARES UNDER VINE 150.00

● Sasseo '17	♀♀ 4
⊙ Zinzula Rosè '18	♀♀ 3
● Negroamaro '17	♀ 3
● Petravia '16	♀ 5

Antica Enotria

LOC. RISICATA
S.DA PROV.LE 65, KM 7
71042 CERIGNOLA [FG]
TEL. +39 0885418462
www.anticaenotria.it

CELLAR SALES
PRE-BOOKED VISITS
ANNUAL PRODUCTION 100,000 bottles
HECTARES UNDER VINE 14.00
VITICULTURE METHOD Certified Organic

○ Falanghina '18	♀♀ 2*
● Fiano '18	♀♀ 2*
● Contessa Staffa '18	♀ 2
Il Sale della Terra Nero di Troia '15	♀ 5

Cantina Albea

VIA DUE MACELLI, 8
70011 ALBEROBELLO [BA]
TEL. +39 0804323548
www.albeavini.com

CELLAR SALES
PRE-BOOKED VISITS
ANNUAL PRODUCTION 380,000 bottles
HECTARES UNDER VINE 40.00

● Lui '17	♀♀ 5
○ Locorotondo Sup. Il Selva '18	♀♀ 2*
● Petranera '17	♀♀ 3
● Sol '16	♀ 4

Donato Angiuli

FRAZ. MONTRONE
VIA PRINCIPE UMBERTO, 27
70010 ADELFIA [BA]
TEL. +39 0804597130
www.angiulidonato.com

CELLAR SALES
PRE-BOOKED VISITS
ANNUAL PRODUCTION 200,000 bottles
HECTARES UNDER VINE 6.00

⊙ Maccone Negroamaro Bianco '18	♀♀ 6
● Maccone Primitivo '17	♀♀ 4
○ Maccone Moscato Secco '18	♀ 1*
⊙ Maccone Primitivo Rosato '18	♀ 6

Bonsegna

VIA A. VOLTA, 17
73048 NARDÒ [LE]
TEL. +39 0833561483
www.vinibonsegna.it

CELLAR SALES
PRE-BOOKED VISITS
ANNUAL PRODUCTION 100,000 bottles
HECTARES UNDER VINE 20.00

● Nardò Rosso Barricato Danze della Contessa '16	♀♀ 3
● Nardò Rosso Danze della Contessa '17	♀♀ 2*
● Terra d'Otranto Rosso Baia di Uluzzo '17	♀ 2

Borgo Turrito

loc. Incoronata
71122 Foggia
Tel. +39 0881810141
www.borgoturrito.it

ANNUAL PRODUCTION 60,000 bottles
HECTARES UNDER VINE 12.00

○ Terra Cretosa Aleatico Rosato '18	♟♟ 3
○ TroQué '17	♟♟ 4
○ Terra Cretosa Falanghina '18	♟ 3

I Buongiorno

c.so Vittorio Emanuele II, 71
72012 Carovigno [BR]
Tel. +39 0831996286
www.ibuongiorno.com

ANNUAL PRODUCTION 50,000 bottles
HECTARES UNDER VINE 10.00

● Negroamaro '17	♟♟ 3
⊙ Rosalento '18	♟♟ 3
○ Fiano '18	♟ 2
● Primitivo '17	♟ 3

Caiaffa

c.da vicinale Le Torri
71042 Cerignola [FG]
Tel. +39 3293449555
www.caiaffavini.it

CELLAR SALES
PRE-BOOKED VISITS
ANNUAL PRODUCTION 100,000 bottles
HECTARES UNDER VINE 35.00
VITICULTURE METHOD Certified Organic

● Negroamaro '18	♟♟ 2*
⊙ Troia Rosato '18	♟♟ 2*
● Primitivo '18	♟ 3
⊙ Rosè Brut '18	♟ 3

Cannito

c.da Parco Bizzarro
70025 Grumo Appula [BA]
Tel. +39 080623529
www.agricolacannito.it

CELLAR SALES
PRE-BOOKED VISITS
ANNUAL PRODUCTION 60,000 bottles
HECTARES UNDER VINE 14.00
VITICULTURE METHOD Certified Organic
SUSTAINABLE WINERY

○ Drùmon Fiano '18	♟♟ 5
● Gioia del Colle Primitivo Drùmon '15	♟♟ 5
● Gioia del Colle Primitivo Drùmon Ris. '14	♟♟ 7
● Gioia del Colle Primitivo Drùmon S '15	♟♟ 6

Casa Primis

via Ortanova, km 0,500
71048 Stornarella [FG]
Tel. +39 0885433333
www.casaprimis.com

CELLAR SALES
PRE-BOOKED VISITS
ANNUAL PRODUCTION 160,000 bottles
HECTARES UNDER VINE 23.00
SUSTAINABLE WINERY

○ Fiano '18	♟♟ 2*
⊙ Monrose '18	♟♟ 2*
● Ciliegiolo '18	♟ 2
● Crusta '15	♟ 3

Centovignali

p.zza Aldo Moro, 10
70010 Sammichele di Bari [BA]
Tel. +39 0805768215
www.centovignali.it

CELLAR SALES
PRE-BOOKED VISITS
ANNUAL PRODUCTION 35,000 bottles
HECTARES UNDER VINE 25.00
VITICULTURE METHOD Certified Organic

● Gioia del Colle Primitivo Indellicato '17	♟♟ 5
● Gioia del Colle Primitivo Pentimone Ris. '17	♟♟ 7
○ Albiòre '18	♟ 2

Cantina Crifo

VIA MADONNA DELLE GRAZIE, 8A
70037 RUVO DI PUGLIA [BA]
TEL. +39 0803601611
www.cantinacrifo.it

CELLAR SALES
PRE-BOOKED VISITS
ANNUAL PRODUCTION 2,000,000 bottles

☉ Castel del Monte Rosato '18	♟♟ 1*
● Nero di Troia '18	♟♟ 3
☉ Castel del Monte Rosato Extra Dry Crifo	♟ 1*
● Squarcione '17	♟ 2

Masseria Cuturi

C.DA CUTURI
74024 MANDURIA [TA]
TEL. +39 0999711660
www.masseriacuturi.it

CELLAR SALES
PRE-BOOKED VISITS
ANNUAL PRODUCTION 100,000 bottles
HECTARES UNDER VINE 23.00
VITICULTURE METHOD Certified Organic

● Tumà Primitivo '17	♟♟ 4
● Zacinto '17	♟♟ 2
○ Segreto di Bianca Minutolo '17	♟ 4

D'Alfonso del Sordo

C.DA SANT'ANTONINO
71016 SAN SEVERO [FG]
TEL. +39 0882221444
www.dalfonsodelsordo.it

CELLAR SALES
PRE-BOOKED VISITS
ACCOMMODATION
ANNUAL PRODUCTION 250,000 bottles
HECTARES UNDER VINE 35.00

● Guado San Leo '16	♟♟ 4
● Montero '16	♟♟ 2*
○ Catapanus '18	♟ 2
○ Dammisole '18	♟ 2

De Falco

VIA MILANO, 25
73051 NOVOLI [LE]
TEL. +39 0832711597
www.cantinedefalco.it

CELLAR SALES
PRE-BOOKED VISITS
ACCOMMODATION
ANNUAL PRODUCTION 300,000 bottles
HECTARES UNDER VINE 20.00

● Bocca della Verità '16	♟♟ 2
● Negroamaro '18	♟♟ 1
○ Artiglio Bianco '18	♟ 3
● Artiglio Rosso '16	♟ 4

Ferri

VIA BARI, 347
70010 VALENZANO [BA]
TEL. +39 0804671753
www.cantineferri.it

CELLAR SALES
PRE-BOOKED VISITS
ANNUAL PRODUCTION 40,000 bottles
HECTARES UNDER VINE 5.00

● Memor '14	♟♟ 3
● Purpureus '15	♟♟ 3
● Ad Mira Chardonnay '16	♟ 5
● R2osso '15	♟ 2

Franco Ladogana

LOC. ORTA NOVA
FRAZ. LOC. PASSO D'ORTA
S.S. 16 KM 699+500
71045 ORTA NOVA [FG]
TEL. +39 0885784335
www.ladoganavini.it

CELLAR SALES
PRE-BOOKED VISITS
ANNUAL PRODUCTION 600,000 bottles
HECTARES UNDER VINE 40.00
VITICULTURE METHOD Certified Organic
SUSTAINABLE WINERY

● Nero di Troia Le Selezioni '18	♟♟ 2*
● Primitivo Le Selezioni '18	♟♟ 2*
○ Fiano Le Selezioni '18	♟ 2
● Negroamaro Le Selezioni '18	♟ 2

antine Massimo Leone

SPRECACENERE
121 FOGGIA
L. +39 0881723674
ww.cantinemassimoleone.it

ANNUAL PRODUCTION 100,000 bottles
HECTARES UNDER VINE 17.00

Forme Bianco '18	🍷🍷 2*
Forme Rosato '18	🍷🍷 3
Nero di Troia '17	🍷 3
Primitivo '17	🍷 3

Alberto Longo

S.DA PROV.LE 5 LUCERA-PIETRAMONTECORVINO KM 4
71036 LUCERA [FG]
TEL. +39 0881539057
www.albertolongo.it

CELLAR SALES
PRE-BOOKED VISITS
ANNUAL PRODUCTION 150,000 bottles
HECTARES UNDER VINE 35.00

● Le Cruste '16	🍷🍷 4
○ Le Fossette '18	🍷🍷 3
⊙ Brut Nature M. Cl. Rosé '13	🍷 4

Menhir Salento

SALVATORE NEGRO
020 BAGNOLO DEL SALENTO [LE]
. +39 0836818199
ww.menhirsalento.it

CELLAR SALES
PRE-BOOKED VISITS
RESTAURANT SERVICE
ANNUAL PRODUCTION 1,000,000 bottles
HECTARES UNDER VINE 45.00
SUSTAINABLE WINERY

Pietra Rosso '18	🍷🍷 2*
Pietra Susumaniello '17	🍷🍷 2*
Quota 29 '18	🍷🍷 2*
Calamuri Rosso '16	🍷 3

Cantine Miali

VIA MADONNINA, 11
74015 MARTINA FRANCA [TA]
TEL. +39 0804303222
www.cantinemiali.com

CELLAR SALES
PRE-BOOKED VISITS
ANNUAL PRODUCTION 160,000 bottles
HECTARES UNDER VINE 16.00

⊙ Ametys '18	🍷🍷 3
○ Falanghina Single Vineyard '18	🍷🍷 2*
○ Martina Franca Dolcimèlo '18	🍷🍷 2*
○ Verdeca Single Vineyard '18	🍷 2

Morella

PER UGGIANO, 147
024 MANDURIA [TA]
. +39 0999791482
ww.morellavini.com

CELLAR SALES
PRE-BOOKED VISITS
ANNUAL PRODUCTION 26,000 bottles
HECTARES UNDER VINE 20.00
VITICULTURE METHOD Certified Biodynamic

Old Vines Primitivo '16	🍷🍷 6

Mottura Vini del Salento

P.ZZA MELICA, 4
73058 TUGLIE [LE]
TEL. +39 0833596601
www.motturavini.it

PRE-BOOKED VISITS
ANNUAL PRODUCTION 2,500,000 bottles
HECTARES UNDER VINE 200.00

○ Fiano '18	🍷🍷 5
● Primitivo '18	🍷🍷 3
● Salice Salentino Rosso Le Pitre '17	🍷🍷 4
● Negroamaro '18	🍷 5

Tenute Nettis

VIA GIOVANNI XXIII, 12/A
70023 GIOIA DEL COLLE [BA]
TEL. +39 3319252274
www.tenutenettis.it

ANNUAL PRODUCTION 70,000 bottles
HECTARES UNDER VINE 7.00

● Gioia del Colle Primitivo '17	♥♥ 3
● Quattordici Primitivo '17	♥♥ 3
☉ Rosato '18	♥ 3

Cantine Paradiso

VIA MANFREDONIA, 39
71042 CERIGNOLA [FG]
TEL. +39 0885428720
www.cantineparadiso.it

ANNUAL PRODUCTION 200,000 bottles
HECTARES UNDER VINE 30.00

● 1954 Primitivo '17	♥♥
● Posta Piana Nero di Troia '17	♥♥
● Posta Piana Primitivo '17	♥♥
● Darione Podere Belmantello Primitivo '18	♥

Tenuta Patruno Perniola

C.DA MARZAGAGLIA
70023 GIOIA DEL COLLE [BA]
TEL. +39 3383940830
www.tenutapatrunoperniola.it

CELLAR SALES
PRE-BOOKED VISITS
ACCOMMODATION AND RESTAURANT SERVICE
ANNUAL PRODUCTION 12,000 bottles
HECTARES UNDER VINE 3.00
VITICULTURE METHOD Certified Organic

☉ Ghirigori '18	♥♥ 3
● Gioia del Colle Primitivo Marzagaglia '13	♥♥ 4
○ Striale '18	♥ 2

Plantamura

VIA V. BODINI, 9A
70023 GIOIA DEL COLLE [BA]
TEL. +39 3474711027
www.viniplantamura.it

CELLAR SALES
PRE-BOOKED VISITS
ANNUAL PRODUCTION 45,000 bottles
HECTARES UNDER VINE 8.00
VITICULTURE METHOD Certified Organic
SUSTAINABLE WINERY

● Gioia del Colle Primitivo Parco Largo '17	♥♥
● Gioia del Colle Primitivo Contrada San Pietro '17	♥♥
● Gioia del Colle Primitivo Ris. '16	♥

Podere 29

LOC. BORGO TRESSANTI
S.DA PROV.LE 544
76016 CERIGNOLA [FG]
TEL. +39 3471917291
www.podere29.it

CELLAR SALES
PRE-BOOKED VISITS
ACCOMMODATION
ANNUAL PRODUCTION 90,000 bottles
HECTARES UNDER VINE 15.00
VITICULTURE METHOD Certified Organic

● Avia Pervia '17	♥♥ 2*
● Gelso Nero '18	♥♥ 2*
● Gelso d'Oro '17	♥ 5
☉ Unio '18	♥ 2

Risveglio Agricolo

C.DA TORRE MOZZA
72100 BRINDISI
TEL. +39 0831519948
www.cantinerisveglio.it

CELLAR SALES
PRE-BOOKED VISITS
ANNUAL PRODUCTION 100,000 bottles
HECTARES UNDER VINE 44.00

● 72100 '17	♥♥
● Susu' '17	♥♥
● Gio 15° '16	♥
● Pecora Nera Nero di Troia '16	♥

osa del Golfo

GARIBALDI, 18
011 Alezio [LE]
, +39 0833281045
w.rosadelgolfo.com

LLAR SALES
E-BOOKED VISITS
NUAL PRODUCTION 300,000 bottles
CTARES UNDER VINE 40.00

rut Rosé M. Cl.	🍷🍷 4
egroamaro Rosato '18	🍷🍷 3
ortulano Negroamaro '16	🍷🍷 2*
rimitivo '17	🍷 2

Cantina Sociale Sampietrana

via Mare, 38
72027 San Pietro Vernotico [BR]
Tel. +39 0831671120
www.cantinasampietrana.com

CELLAR SALES
PRE-BOOKED VISITS
ACCOMMODATION
ANNUAL PRODUCTION 1,500,000 bottles
HECTARES UNDER VINE 140.00

● Squinzano Ris. '16	🍷🍷 2*
● Terre Cave '17	🍷🍷 2*
● Brindisi Rosso Since 1952 Ris. '16	🍷 2
● Settebraccia '16	🍷 3

antina San Donaci

MESAGNE, 62
025 San Donaci [BR]
, +39 0831681085
w.cantinasandonaci.eu

LLAR SALES
E-BOOKED VISITS
NUAL PRODUCTION 800,000 bottles
CTARES UNDER VINE 543.00

ulgeo '16	🍷🍷 5
ietra Cava Malvasia '17	🍷🍷 2*
alice Salentino Rosso Anticaia '18	🍷 3
alice Salentino Rosso Anticaia Ris. '16	🍷 3

Santa Barbara

via Maternità e Infanzia, 23
72027 San Pietro Vernotico [BR]
Tel. +39 0831652749
www.cantinesantabarbara.it

CELLAR SALES
PRE-BOOKED VISITS
ANNUAL PRODUCTION 2,000,000 bottles
HECTARES UNDER VINE 150.00

● Capirussu Susumaniello '17	🍷🍷 4
● Sumanero '17	🍷🍷 4
● Barbaglio '16	🍷 4
● Primitivo di Manduria '17	🍷 2

agaro

MONTETESSA, 63
10 Locorotondo [BA]
, +39 0802042313
w.tagaro.it

NUAL PRODUCTION 150,000 bottles
CTARES UNDER VINE 20.00

rimitivo di Manduria Muso Rosso '17	🍷🍷 3
alice Salentino Negroamaro	
ei Caselle '17	🍷🍷 3
inquenoci Primitivo '17	🍷 3

Teanum

via Croce Santa, 48
71016 San Severo [FG]
Tel. +39 0882336332
www.teanum.it

CELLAR SALES
PRE-BOOKED VISITS
RESTAURANT SERVICE
ANNUAL PRODUCTION 1,500,000 bottles
HECTARES UNDER VINE 190.00

● Gran Tiati '13	🍷🍷 5
● San Severo Rosso	
Gran Tiati Gold Vintage '13	🍷🍷 8
● Favùgne Sangiovese '17	🍷 3

Terre dei Vaaz

VIA AGOSTINO DE PRETIS, 9
70100 SAMMICHELE DI BARI [BA]
TEL. +39 3488013644
www.terredeivaaz.it

ANNUAL PRODUCTION 8,000 bottles
HECTARES UNDER VINE 3.00

● Ipnotico '17	♼♼ 7
● Onirico '17	♼♼ 6

La Vecchia Torre

VIA MARCHE, 1
73045 LEVERANO [LE]
TEL. +39 0832925053
www.cantinavecchiatorre.it

CELLAR SALES
PRE-BOOKED VISITS
ANNUAL PRODUCTION 3,000,000 bottles
HECTARES UNDER VINE 1300.00
SUSTAINABLE WINERY

● Primitivo di Manduria Auro '17	♼♼ 3*
● 50° Anniversario '16	♼♼ 3
● Leverano Rosso Ris. '14	♼ 2
● Salice Salentino Rosso Ris. '15	♼ 2

Le Vigne di Sammarco

VIA NICCOLÒ TOMMASEO, 15/19
72020 CELLINO SAN MARCO [BR]
TEL. +39 0831617776
www.levignedisammarco.com

CELLAR SALES
PRE-BOOKED VISITS
ANNUAL PRODUCTION 1,300,000 bottles
HECTARES UNDER VINE 180.00
SUSTAINABLE WINERY

● Archè Blend '14	♼♼ 5
● Somiero '16	♼♼ 5
● Alipasso '17	♼ 3
⊙ Susumà '18	♼ 3

Torrequarto

C.DA QUARTO, 5
71042 CERIGNOLA [FG]
TEL. +39 0885418453
www.torrequarto.com

CELLAR SALES
PRE-BOOKED VISITS
ACCOMMODATION AND RESTAURANT SERV
ANNUAL PRODUCTION 500,000 bottles
HECTARES UNDER VINE 70.00

○ Emilia '18	♼
● Rosso del Giudice '18	♼
● Primitivo di Manduria Regale '17	
● Tarabuso '17	

Vetrere

FRAZ. VETRERE
S.DA PROV.LE 80 MONTEIASI - MONTEMESOLA KM 16
74123 TARANTO
TEL. +39 3402977870
www.vetrere.it

CELLAR SALES
PRE-BOOKED VISITS
ACCOMMODATION
ANNUAL PRODUCTION 150,000 bottles
HECTARES UNDER VINE 37.00

⊙ Aureo Brut Rosè	♼
● Barone Pazzo '16	♼
⊙ Taranta '18	♼
○ Passito '17	

Vigneti Reale

VIA REALE, 55
73100 LECCE
TEL. +39 0832248433
www.vignetireale.it

PRE-BOOKED VISITS
ACCOMMODATION AND RESTAURANT SERV
ANNUAL PRODUCTION 180,000 bottles
HECTARES UNDER VINE 85.00
SUSTAINABLE WINERY

● Malvasia Nera '18	♼
● Norie '17	♼
○ Blasi '18	
● Rudiae '17	

CALABRIA

...labria's viticulture continues to grow, making
... pleasant surprises year after year, though
...ere's also cause for reflection. We greet, with
...eat pleasure, the return of a wine that in recent
...ars we'd heard so little from, Greco di Bianco, a
...ic of a millennium-old tradition that a group of passionate
...d prepared producers are trying to revive, with excellent results. But certain
...rò DOCs left us a bit confused. The choice by certain producers, in keeping with
...)C protocols, to enrich their wines with grapes like Cabernet Sauvignon and
...erlot adds little in terms of quality in our opinion, and actually flattens much of
...e typicity and elegance of which Gaglioppo is capable in its homeland. These
...nes may often be technically impeccable, but it's a style that belongs to a distant
...st. For some years now the world of wine has been moving in precisely the
...posite direction, that is a focus on native cultivars and territory in the name of
...picity. And Cirò provided two of Calabria's aces, the Cirò Riserva '15 is the first
...e Bicchieri for Francesco and Laura De Franco, two attentive and rigorous vine
...owers who were among the first to practice organic agriculture in Cirò. Cirò
...so spawned the Duca Sanfelice '17, a superb classic of Calabria and southern
...ly in general. Once again the Viola family's Moscato di Saracena '18 delivers
...at's 10 for them) and closing the list this year is Roberto Ceraudo's Grisara '18
...oberto is a pioneer of organic and biodynamic agriculture in Calabria). There's
...so interesting news from Reggino, where two wineries debuted with a bang,
...ariolino Baccellieri and Barone Macrì. Once again the number of producers that
...omitted wines for tasting increased — a lack of space forced us to move many
...at were nonetheless excellent into the second section — we'll make up for it in
...bsequent editions. The same holds for Criserà, De Mare, La Peschiera, Le Moire
...d Zito, who surely would have deserved more attention.

'A Vita

s.s. 106 km 279,800
88811 Cirò Marina [KR]
Tel. +39 3290732473
www.avitavini.it

CELLAR SALES
PRE-BOOKED VISITS
ANNUAL PRODUCTION 15,000 bottles
HECTARES UNDER VINE 8.00

From their first harvest, Francesco and Laura de Franco embraced sustainable agriculture, banning chemical products from their winery. Their vineyards, some of which are very old and head-trained, give life to the very territorial Cirò Rosso, easily recognizable by its austerity and poise. Thanks to the sober use of wood barrels it's never over-loaded or over-extracted, but always very elegant in style. In just a few years, the De Francos have set a new standard and now many, particularly younger Cirò winemakers, follow production philosophies that respect the environment by using organic or biodynamic methods. Cirò Rosso Classico Superiore Riserva '15 has won our Tre Bicchieri for the first time. Its sapid palate is well-governed by acidity and tannins, while the complex and richly multi-faceted nose flaunts lovely floral tones, followed by aromas of small ripe red berries and more scented grassy notes.

● Cirò Rosso Cl. Sup. Ris. '15	▼▼▼ 6
☉ 'A Vita Rosato '18	▼▼ 3
● Cirò Rosso Cl. Sup. '16	▼▼ 2*
☉ Cirò Rosato '16	♈♈ 2*
● Cirò Rosso Cl. Ris. '10	♈♈ 4
● Cirò Rosso Cl. Sup. '15	♈♈ 2*
● Cirò Rosso Cl. Sup. '14	♈♈ 2*
● Cirò Rosso Cl. Sup. Ris. '13	♈♈ 4
● Cirò Rosso Cl. Sup. Ris. '11	♈♈ 4
☉ Leukò '17	♈♈ 2*

Baccellieri

via Concordia, 4
89032 Bianco [RC]
Tel. +39 3355244570
www.baccellieri.net

ANNUAL PRODUCTION 25,000 bottles
HECTARES UNDER VINE 15.00
VITICULTURE METHOD Certified Organic
SUSTAINABLE WINERY

Mariolina Baccellieri's winery is located in Bianco on Calabria's Ionian coast, where the first Greek colonizers landed in Italy in the eighth century BCE. In addition to bringing their own varieties of grapes, the also introduced the method of head-training vines and the use of wine vessels during processing. However, by the end of World War Two there were so few producers of these millennia-old wines th Mantonico Passito and Greco di Bianco, among others, were at risk of disappearin The passionate, skillful Mariolina, whose vineyards have been certified organic sinc 1998, is one of the central actors in the rediscovery and revival of these ancient wines. Their Mantonico Passito '15 just missed our Tre Bicchieri. This wine of rare elegance offers a complex, deep nose combined with well-balanced acidity, fruit and sweetness on the palate. Greco di Bianco '12 also proves very good, with aromas of dates, lavender and gentian, ar a fresh, juicy, long palate.

○ Mantonico Passito '15	▼▼
○ Greco di Bianco '12	▼▼
○ Siccagno '18	▼▼
☉ Violet '18	▼

:oberto Ceraudo

:. Marina di Strongoli
:a Dattilo
:815 Crotone
:. +39 0962865613
ww.dattilo.it

:LLAR SALES
:E-BOOKED VISITS
:COMMODATION AND RESTAURANT SERVICE
NUAL PRODUCTION 70,000 bottles
:CTARES UNDER VINE 20.00
TICULTURE METHOD Certified Organic

berto Ceraudo's estate produces wine, oil d citrus fruits, according to biodynamic inciples (everything here has been gorously certified organic since 1973). It's t a coincidence that it has one of the best staurants in southern Italy and an ritourism. Roberto's children Susy, useppe and Caterina share ihis thusiasm, and have followed him into the mily business. They all fully embrace his lief in the value of the human dimension here respect for nature and the territory is nsidered not just useful but essential. eir very good Doro Bè '11 Passito is ade with Magliocco grapes. It affords nsual, bewitching aromas of bottled erries, licorice, bitter chocolate, tobacco d nuts; the full and dynamic palate proves veet but well balanced by acidity, making r a very long balsamic finish. Tre Bicchieri es to Pecorella Frisara '18, which atures an elegant floral, fruity bouquet, d a fresh, dense and gutsy palate.

Grisara Pecorello '18	▼▼▼ 4*
Doro Bè '11	▼▼ 3*
Dattilo '16	▼▼ 4
Grayasusi Argento '18	▼▼ 5
Grayasusi Et. Rame '18	▼▼ 3
Nanà '17	▼▼ 3
Imyr '18	▼ 5
Petelia '18	▼ 3
Grisara '17	▽▽▽ 4*
Grisara '16	▽▽▽ 4*
Grisara '15	▽▽▽ 4*
Grisara '14	▽▽▽ 3*
Grisara '13	▽▽▽ 3*
Grisara '12	▽▽▽ 3*

iGreco

loc. Salice
c.da Guardapiedi
87062 Cariati [CS]
Tel. +39 0983969441
www.igreco.it

CELLAR SALES
PRE-BOOKED VISITS
ACCOMMODATION AND RESTAURANT SERVICE
ANNUAL PRODUCTION 250,000 bottles
HECTARES UNDER VINE 80.00
SUSTAINABLE WINERY

The seven Greco brothers, despite all having brilliant careers in other sectors, have nevertheless continued to manage the operation founded by their father Tommaso in the 1960s. The charming estate of more than 1,500 hectares between the provinces of Crotone and Cosenza is mainly planted with olive trees, but since 2001 also includes about eighty hectares of vineyards. The wines produced by this beautiful and dynamic Cariati winery all share a modern style characterized by great cleanliness and territoriality. Masino '17, made with native Calabrian grapes, reached our finals. It offers up elegant, close-knit aromas of mulberries, blackberries and fresh herbs on a balsamic background. The palate proves soft, juicy and long. Savù '18, a rosé made with Gaglioppo grapes, reveals floral and mineral aromas, and appears spacious with a fresh, sapid drinkability on the palate.

● Masino '17	▼▼ 5
○ Filù '18	▼▼ 3
⊙ Savù '18	▼▼ 3
● Catà '17	▼ 3
● Masino '15	▽▽▽ 5
● Masino '14	▽▽▽ 5
● Masino '12	▽▽▽ 5
● Masino '11	▽▽▽ 5
● Masino '10	▽▽▽ 5
● Catà '15	▽▽ 3
○ Filù '17	▽▽ 3
● Masino '16	▽▽ 5

Ippolito 1845

via Tirone, 118
88811 Cirò Marina [KR]
Tel. +39 096231106
www.ippolito1845.it

CELLAR SALES
PRE-BOOKED VISITS
ANNUAL PRODUCTION 1,000,000 bottles
HECTARES UNDER VINE 100.00

Vincenzo and Gianluca Ippolito, and cousin Paolo, are the fifth generation to run the family winery founded by their great-great-grandfather Vincenzo in 1845. They have not only successfully made the generational change, but have also over the course of a decade been able to completely revolutionize the historic Ciró winery. The changes recorded by the wines are remarkable, resulting from work that began in the vineyard with revised management, yields and pruning, and then in the cellar, where great attention is paid to developing sharp definition and elegance. Their close-focused, elegant Cirò Rosso Classico Superiore Riserva Colli del Mancuso '16 made our finals. The old Gaglioppo vines are cultivated in the high hilly area between Cirò Maria and Cirò Superiore. Mineral and undergrowth notes merge with plums and spices in their Cirò Rosso Classico Superiore Liber Pater '17, and follow on to a fresh, fruity mouth, with balanced structure and acidity.

● Cirò Rosso Cl. Sup. Colli del Mancuso Ris. '16	▼▼ 3*
● Cirò Rosso Cl. Sup. Liber Pater '17	▼▼ 2*
● Cirò Rosso Cl. Sup. Ripe del Falco Ris. '11	▼▼ 5
○ Pecorello '18	▼▼ 2*
⊙ Pescanera Rosé '18	▼▼ 2*
● 160 Anni '16	▼ 5
● Calabrise '18	▼ 2
○ Cirò Bianco Mare Chiaro '18	▼ 2
⊙ Cirò Rosato Mabilia '18	▼ 2
○ Gemma del Sole '17	▼ 4
○ Pecorello '17	▽▽▽ 2*
⊙ Cirò Rosato Mabilia '17	▽▽ 2*

Cantine Lento

via del Progresso, 1
88040 Amato [CZ]
Tel. +39 096828028
www.cantinelento.it

CELLAR SALES
PRE-BOOKED VISITS
ANNUAL PRODUCTION 500,000 bottles
HECTARES UNDER VINE 70.00

Lento has three different areas of vineyar[ds] to draw from including the Romeo estate on the Tyrrhenian side, planted exclusively with Greco Bianco, and the older Caracciolo estate, where red varieties are planted. But it's truly worth a visit to the most recently acquired Tenuta Amato, wit[h] vineyards at elevations ranging from 500 to 700 meters. Villa Chimirri, a splendid nineteenth-century noble residence sits a[t] the highest point offering a breathtaking, sweeping view from the Ionian to the Tyrrhenian Sea. Perfectly integrated into the landscape at the center of the estate, the large new cellar was built to replace the previous one in the village of Lamezia. Federico II '15 is a good varietal, elegant Cabernet Sauvignon. Their Riserva Salvatore Lento '15, made with Magliocc[o], Greco Nero and Nerello, offers up an elegant floral and fruity bouquet that pave[s] the way for a deep palate with fine tannin[s]. Magliocco '15 proves spicy, juicy, round and appealing.

● Lamezia Rosso Salvatore Lento Ris. '15	▼▼
● Dragone Rosso '17	▼▼
● Federico II '15	▼▼
○ Lamezia Greco '18	▼▼
● Magliocco '15	▼▼
○ Contessa Emburga '18	▼
○ Contessa Emburga '17	▽▽
○ Dragone Bianco '17	▽▽
● Federico II '14	▽▽
● Federico II '10	▽▽
● Lamezia Rosso Salvatore Lento Ris. '14	▽▽

Librandi

C. San Gennaro
S. Jonica, 106
811 Cirò Marina [KR]
. +39 096231518
ww.librandi.it

CELLAR SALES
PRE-BOOKED VISITS
ANNUAL PRODUCTION 2,200,000 bottles
HECTARES UNDER VINE 232.00

he second generation of the Librandi
mily is at the head of this important
outhern Italian winery, and everything is
 track. The long study made on local
rietals and subsequent selection of
ones has born the desired fruit, which is
creasingly seen in the quality of the
ines. At the same time, careful, almost
aniacal, management in the vineyards
as significantly reduced interventions in
e cellar. The result is a signature style
ased on enjoyability and elegance that
ms at enhancing the entire range's
romatic complexity and territoriality.
onsistent with their strong opposition to
anges in the DOC rules, Librandi have
ecided not to resort to using other grapes
 their Cirò, which remains proudly 100%
aglioppo. Their elegant and complex Duca
an Felice '17 conveys aromas of small red
uit and balsam, leading to a graceful,
apid palate with good balance between
uit, silky tannins and acidity.

Cirò Rosso Cl. Sup. Duca San Felice Ris. '17	♟♟♟ 3*
Gravello '17	♟♟ 5
Cirò Bianco '18	♟♟ 2*
Cirò Rosato '18	♟♟ 2*
Cirò Rosso Cl. '18	♟♟ 2*
Critone '18	♟♟ 2*
Efeso '18	♟♟ 4
Magno Megonio '17	♟♟ 4
Terre Lontane '18	♟♟ 2*
Melissa Asylia Rosso '18	♟ 2
Melissa Bianco Asylia '18	♟ 2
Gravello '16	♟♟♟ 5
Gravello '14	♟♟♟ 5

Russo & Longo

Loc. Serpito
88816 Strongoli [KR]
Tel. +39 09621905782
www.russoelongo.it

CELLAR SALES
PRE-BOOKED VISITS
ANNUAL PRODUCTION 100,000 bottles
HECTARES UNDER VINE 16.00

Since the earliest Greek colonizations,
Strongoli (originally called Petèlia), like
nearby Ciró, has been considered one of
the most suitable areas for wine production
in Calabria. Both are hills that rapidly
descend towards the sea and, as evidenced
by the many millstones found during
various archaeological digs, were already
being cultivated before the arrival of the
Greeks. The colonizers did, however,
introduce head-trained vines and some
cultivars that still retain their name, such as
Greco Bianco and Greco Nero. This historic
two-hundred-year-old winery performed
very well and saw their assertive Pecorello
Ois '18 reach our finals. It exhibits an
elegant nose where fruity aromas merge
with lemony and mineral tones that follow
through onto the fresh, tangy palate with a
deep citrus finish. Their Gaglioppo
Decennio '16 stands out among the reds:
its fruity aromas are enhanced by spices
and tobacco, while the palate comes
through juicy and well-supported by acidity
and tannins.

○ Ois '18	♟♟ 3*
● Decennio '16	♟♟ 3
○ Malvasia e Sauvignon '18	♟♟ 3
○ Passo del Gelso '18	♟♟ 2*
○ Terre di Trezzi '18	♟♟ 2*
⊙ Colli di Ginestra '18	♟ 2
● Jachello '16	♟ 5
● Pietra di Tesauro '17	♟ 3
⊙ Colli di Ginestra Rosato '17	♟♟ 2*
● Jachello '15	♟♟ 5

Santa Venere

LOC. TENUTA VOLTA GRANDE
S.DA PROV.LE 04 KM 10,00
88813 CIRÒ [KR]
TEL. +39 096238519
www.santavenere.com

CELLAR SALES
PRE-BOOKED VISITS
ANNUAL PRODUCTION 125,000 bottles
HECTARES UNDER VINE 25.00
VITICULTURE METHOD Certified Organic

Santa Venere's very long roots are documented back to the sixteenth century when it became the Scala family's property. Now, as then, olive trees and grape vines are cultivated. One of the first in Cirò to switch to organic methods, the estate, run by Giuseppe Scala, is converting to strictly biodynamic methods. Today the winery is so deeply connected to the territory and the area's traditions that it resumed growing native Calabrian grapes like Marsiliana Nera and Guardavalle, with excellent results. Their wines always meet our expectations: Cirò Rosso Classico Superiore '18 proves stylish and elegant with overtones of tea rose and red fruit paving the way for a juicy palate well-supported by acidity. Their Speziale '18, made with native Marsigliana Nera grapes, appears pleasantly drinkable. Its well-paced palate features a vibrant acidity that enhances the crunchy fruit.

○ Cirò Bianco '18	♟♟ 2*
● Cirò Rosso Cl. Sup. '18	♟♟ 2*
● Speziale '18	♟♟ 3
○ Vescovado '18	♟♟ 3
● Cirò Cl. Sup. Federico Scala Ris. '17	♟ 5
⊙ Scassabarile '18	♟ 3
○ VoltaGrande '16	♟ 5
● Vurgadà '17	♟ 4
○ Cirò Bianco '17	♟♟ 2*
● Cirò Cl. Sup. Federico Scala Ris. '16	♟♟ 5
● Vurgadà '16	♟♟ 4

Spiriti Ebbri

VIA ROMA, 96
87050 SPEZZANO PICCOLO [CS]
TEL. +39 0984408992
www.spiritiebbri.com

CELLAR SALES
PRE-BOOKED VISITS
ANNUAL PRODUCTION 20,000 bottles
HECTARES UNDER VINE 2.50

Pierpaolo Greco, Damiano Mele and Michele Scrivano, friends who shared a passion for wine, decided to make some of their personal consumption using an old vineyard belonging to a grandfather. The experiment went well so the natural next step was to transform their hobby into something more. Thus was born a small winery based on two dictates: organic methods in the vineyards and bare-bone practices in the cellar. The rest is history and in just a few years it earned a prominent place in the Calabrian wine scene. Their wines are always distinctive, elegant and territorial but never over the top. Neostòs Rosso '17, a blend of Greco Nero, Guarnaccia Nera and Merlot, possesses an intense, refined nose of red fruit, herbs and spices leading into a dense but dynamic palate with a fresh blasamic finish. Neostòs Bianco '18, made with Pecorello grapes, proves tangy on the palate, with aromas of yellow-fleshed fruit and flowers.

● Neostòs Rosso '17	♟♟
⊙ Appianum Rosato '18	♟♟
● Appianum Rosso '17	♟♟
○ Neostòs Bianco '18	♟♟
○ Cotidie Bianco '18	♟
● Cotidie Rosato '18	♟
● Cotidie Rosso '17	♟
⊙ Neostòs Rosato '18	♟
○ Neostòs Bianco '17	♟♟♟
○ Neostòs Bianco '16	♟♟♟
● Cotidie Neostòs Rosso '16	♟♟
● Neostòs Rosso '16	♟♟
● See... '16	♟♟

tatti

ᴅᴀ Lᴇɴᴛɪ
046 Lᴀᴍᴇᴢɪᴀ Tᴇʀᴍᴇ [CZ]
ʟ. +39 0968456138
ww.statti.com

CELLAR SALES
RE-BOOKED VISITS
ESTAURANT SERVICE
NNUAL PRODUCTION 500,000 bottles
ECTARES UNDER VINE 100.00

e Statti brothers' large, dynamic
mpany has a very modern cellar and
ore than 100 hectares of vineyards
anaged with the utmost respect for the
vironment, as is the rest of the estate.
ere, in fact, all the waste created from
gricultural processing and the large cattle
rm is used to make energy from biogas.
e wines at our regional tastings this year
e certainly better than in the past though
ere is still room for growth, less with
gard to the already high quality than
th the elegance of the details. Lamezia
osso '15 comes through very pleasant
d spicy in the mouth, with balanced
cidity and tannins. Its generous and
any-sided bouquet reveals dark citrus
uit, blueberries, mulberries and herbs.
heir Mantonico '17 also proves very
easant, with a complex nose of
llow-fleshed fruit and aniseed. Juicy ripe
uit on the palate appears well-supported
a fresh note, making for a long,
atifying finish.

Gaglioppo '18	🍷🍷 3
Greco '18	🍷🍷 3
Lamezia Batasarro Ris. '15	🍷🍷 4
Lamezia Rosso '18	🍷🍷 2*
Mantonico '17	🍷🍷 3
Greco Nero '18	🍷 3
Lamezia Bianco '18	🍷 2
Batasarro '13	🍷🍷 4
Gaglioppo '17	🍷🍷 3
Greco '16	🍷🍷 2*
Lamezia Greco Nosside '16	🍷🍷 4
Mantonico '16	🍷🍷 3

★Luigi Viola

ᴠɪᴀ Rᴏᴍᴀ, 18
87010 Sᴀʀᴀᴄᴇɴᴀ [CS]
Tᴇʟ. +39 098134722
www.cantineviola.it

CELLAR SALES
PRE-BOOKED VISITS
ANNUAL PRODUCTION 15,000 bottles
HECTARES UNDER VINE 3.00
VITICULTURE METHOD Certified Organic

Twenty years have passed since Luigi Viola
began to produce and bottle Moscato di
Saracena in 1999. The sweet passito wine
had been lost to memory earlier despite its
illustrious past; documents show that in
the sixteenth century it was part of the
Enoteca Pontificia during Pius IV's reign.
Now Luigi is helped by his sons Roberto,
Alessandro and Claudio, and the Moscato
di Saraceno has not only come out of
oblivion, but today it's successfully
produced and marketed by many others.
With this year's Tre Bicchieri, Viola can
sport the Star indicating wineries that have
won our most desirable award 10 times.
What a way to celebrate their splendid and
intriguing Moscato Passito '18. Aromas of
apricots, candied orange and spices pave
the way for a creamy, delicately sweet
palate, rich in juicy fruit, but balanced by
very fresh acidity. The finish proves very
long and elegant.

○ Moscato Passito '18	🍷🍷🍷 6
○ Bianco Margherita '17	🍷🍷 3
● Rosso Viola '15	🍷🍷 3
○ Moscato Passito '17	🍷🍷🍷 6
○ Moscato Passito '14	🍷🍷🍷 6
○ Moscato Passito '13	🍷🍷🍷 6
○ Moscato Passito '12	🍷🍷🍷 6
○ Moscato Passito '11	🍷🍷🍷 6
○ Moscato Passito '10	🍷🍷🍷 6
○ Moscato Passito '09	🍷🍷🍷 6

Sergio Arcuri

VIA ROMA VICO PRIMO
88811 CIRÒ MARINA [KR]
TEL. +39 3280250255
www.sergioarcuri.it

CELLAR SALES
PRE-BOOKED VISITS
ANNUAL PRODUCTION 15,000 bottles
HECTARES UNDER VINE 3.68
VITICULTURE METHOD Certified Organic

● Cirò Rosso Cl. Sup. Aris '16	♥♥ 6
● Cirò Rosso Cl. Sup. Più Vite Ris. '13	♥♥ 5

Brigante

VIA SANT'ELIA
88813 CIRÒ [KR]
TEL. +39 3334135843
www.vinocirobrigante.it

ANNUAL PRODUCTION 32,000 bottles
HECTARES UNDER VINE 10.00

● Gaglioppo Zero '18	♥♥ 3
● Cirò Rosso Cl. Sup 0727 '16	♥♥ 3
○ Cirò Bianco Phemina '18	♥ 2
● Gaglioppo Zero Rosato '18	♥ 3

Cantine Bruni

LOC. LA SOBRIA
VIA COSENZA, 1
88814 MELISSA [KR]
TEL. +39 0962835383
info@cantinebruni.it

ANNUAL PRODUCTION 150,000 bottles
HECTARES UNDER VINE 20.00

● Cirò Rosso Cl. '17	♥♥ 2*
● Survia '16	♥♥ 4
● Nobili Melissesi '16	♥ 3

Caparra & Siciliani

S.S. 106
88811 CIRÒ MARINA [KR]
TEL. +39 0962373319
www.caparraesiciliani.com

CELLAR SALES
PRE-BOOKED VISITS
ANNUAL PRODUCTION 800,000 bottles
HECTARES UNDER VINE 180.00
VITICULTURE METHOD Certified Organic

☉ Cirò Rosato Le Formelle '18	♥♥ 2*
● Cirò Rosso Cl. Solagi '17	♥♥ 2*
● Cirò Rosso Cl. Sup. Ris. '16	♥♥ 2*
● Cirò Rosso Cl. Sup. Volvito Ris. '16	♥♥ 2*

Massimiliano Capoano

C.DA CERAMIDIO
88811 CIRÒ MARINA [KR]
TEL. +39 096235801
www.capoano.it

CELLAR SALES
ANNUAL PRODUCTION 100,000 bottles
HECTARES UNDER VINE 20.00

○ Cirò Bianco Antea '18	♥♥ 3
● Aeternum '17	♥ 4
○ Cirò Rosato '18	♥ 2
● Cirò Rosso Cl. Sup. Don Raffaele Ris. '16	♥ 5

Casa Comerci

FRAZ. BADIA DI NICOTERA
C.DA COMERCI, 6
89844 NICOTERA [VV]
TEL. +39 09631976077
www.casacomerci.it

CELLAR SALES
PRE-BOOKED VISITS
ANNUAL PRODUCTION 45,000 bottles
HECTARES UNDER VINE 15.00
VITICULTURE METHOD Certified Organic

● Libìci '17	♥♥ 4
○ Rèfulu '18	♥♥ 3
☉ Granàtu '18	♥ 3

...olacino Wines

...COLLE MANCO
...050 MARZI [CS]
+39 09841900252
...w.colacino.it

CELLAR SALES
PRE-BOOKED VISITS
ANNUAL PRODUCTION 125,000 bottles
HECTARES UNDER VINE 21.00

...uarto '18	🍷🍷 2*
...avuto Cl. Colle Barabba '18	🍷🍷 3
...avuto Rosso Si '18	🍷🍷 2*
...avuto Bianco Si '18	🍷 2

...antine Elisium

...Z. BORGO PARTENOPE
...A SERRE, 8
...00 COSENZA
+39 3281143418
...w.cantineelisium.it

CELLAR SALES
PRE-BOOKED VISITS
ACCOMMODATION AND RESTAURANT SERVICE
ANNUAL PRODUCTION 10,000 bottles
HECTARES UNDER VINE 4.50

...spico '18	🍷🍷 3
...etrara '18	🍷 3
...erra Torzano '17	🍷 3

...rrocinto

...Z. VIGNE
...FERROCINTO
...12 CASTROVILLARI [CS]
+39 0981415122
...w.ferrocinto.it

CELLAR SALES
PRE-BOOKED VISITS
ANNUAL PRODUCTION 700,000 bottles
HECTARES UNDER VINE 45.00
VITICULTURE METHOD Certified Organic

...erre di Cosenza Pollino Bianco '18	🍷🍷 3
...erre di Cosenza Pollino Rosato '18	🍷🍷 4
...erre di Cosenza Pollino Rosso '17	🍷 3

Cote di Franze

LOC. PIANA DI FRANZE
88811 CIRÒ MARINA [KR]
TEL. +39 3926911606
www.cotedifranze.it

CELLAR SALES
PRE-BOOKED VISITS
ANNUAL PRODUCTION 18,000 bottles
HECTARES UNDER VINE 9.00
VITICULTURE METHOD Certified Organic

⊙ Cirò Rosato '18	🍷🍷 2*
○ Kom'è '18	🍷🍷 2*
⊙ Cirò Bianco '18	🍷 2

Cantina Enotria

C.DA SAN GENNARO, SS JONICA, 106
88811 CIRÒ MARINA [KR]
TEL. +39 0962371181
www.cantinaenotria.wine

CELLAR SALES
PRE-BOOKED VISITS
ANNUAL PRODUCTION 450,000 bottles
HECTARES UNDER VINE 170.00

○ 91 '18	🍷🍷 3
○ Cirò Bianco '18	🍷🍷 2*
● Cirò Rosso Cl. '17	🍷🍷 2*
⊙ Cirò Rosato '18	🍷 2

Feudo dei Sanseverino

VIA VITTORIO EMANUELE, 108/110
87010 SARACENA [CS]
TEL. +39 098121461
www.feudodeisanseverino.it

CELLAR SALES
PRE-BOOKED VISITS
ANNUAL PRODUCTION 20,000 bottles
HECTARES UNDER VINE 6.00
VITICULTURE METHOD Certified Organic
SUSTAINABLE WINERY

○ Moscato Passito al Governo di Saracena '14	🍷🍷 5
○ Terre di Cosenza Pollino Moscato Passito Mastro Terenzio '16	🍷🍷 5

Tenuta Iuzzolini

LOC. FRASSÀ
88811 CIRÒ MARINA [KR]
TEL. +39 0962373893
www.tenutaiuzzolini.it

CELLAR SALES
PRE-BOOKED VISITS
ANNUAL PRODUCTION 1,000,000 bottles
HECTARES UNDER VINE 100.00

● Artino '17	♙♙ 3
● Cirò Rosso Cl. Sup. Maradea Ris. '15	♙♙ 3
○ Donna Giovanna '18	♙ 5
⊙ Lumare '18	♙ 3

Cantine Lucà

VIA MARCHESE, 34
89032 BIANCO [RC]
TEL. +39 09641903179
www.cantineluca.it

ANNUAL PRODUCTION 30,000 bottles
HECTARES UNDER VINE 15.00

○ Greco di Bianco '15	♙♙
○ Mantonico '14	

Barone Macrì

C.DA MODI
89040 GERACE [RC]
TEL. +39 0964356497
www.baronemacri.it

CELLAR SALES
PRE-BOOKED VISITS
ACCOMMODATION AND RESTAURANT SERVICE
ANNUAL PRODUCTION 25,000 bottles
HECTARES UNDER VINE 11.00

⊙ Centocamere Rosè Brut M. Cl. '17	♙♙ 5
○ Greco di Bianco Passito Centocamere '16	♙♙ 4
○ Terre di Gerace Bianco '18	♙♙ 2*
⊙ Terre di Gerace Rosato '18	♙ 2

Maisano

VIA GARIBALDI, 18
89032 BIANCO [RC]
TEL. +39 333 243 4863
f.maisano@gotmail.com

ANNUAL PRODUCTION 7,000 bottles
HECTARES UNDER VINE 5.00
SUSTAINABLE WINERY

○ Greco di Bianco '07	♙♙

Malena

LOC. PETRARO
S.S. JONICA 106
88811 CIRÒ MARINA [KR]
TEL. +39 096231758
www.malena.it

CELLAR SALES
PRE-BOOKED VISITS
ANNUAL PRODUCTION 220,000 bottles
HECTARES UNDER VINE 16.00

⊙ Cirò Rosato '18	♙♙ 2*
● Cirò Rosso Cl. Sup. Pian della Corte Ris. '16	♙♙ 3
● Magna Grecia '18	♙♙ 2*

Poderi Marini

LOC. SANT'AGATA
87069 SAN DEMETRIO CORONE [CS]
TEL. +39 3683525028
www.poderimarini.it

CELLAR SALES
PRE-BOOKED VISITS
ANNUAL PRODUCTION 50,000 bottles
HECTARES UNDER VINE 7.00
VITICULTURE METHOD Certified Organic

● Basileus '16	♙♙
○ Collimarini Passito '17	♙♙
● Elaphe '16	
● Koronè Rosso '17	

Masseria Falvo 1727

ᴸᴼᶜ. Garga
87010 Saracena [CS]
ᴛᴇʟ. +39 098138127
www.masseriafalvo.com

CELLAR SALES
ANNUAL PRODUCTION 80,000 bottles
HECTARES UNDER VINE 26.00
VITICULTURE METHOD Certified Organic

Terre di Cosenza Pollino Magliocco Graneta Ris. '15	♟♟ 2*
Terre di Cosenza Bianco Spart '17	♟ 3
Terre di Cosenza Rosato Cjviz '18	♟ 3

Tenute Pacelli

ᶜ.ᴰᴬ Rose
87010 Malvito [CS]
ᴛᴇʟ. +39 09841634348
www.tenutepacelli.it

CELLAR SALES
PRE-BOOKED VISITS
ACCOMMODATION
ANNUAL PRODUCTION 18,000 bottles
HECTARES UNDER VINE 9.00
VITICULTURE METHOD Certified Organic
SUSTAINABLE WINERY

● Tèmeso '15	♟♟ 3
● Terra Rossa '17	♟♟ 3

La Pizzuta del Principe

ᴸᴼᶜ.ᴰᴬ Pizzuta
88816 Strongoli [KR]
ᴛᴇʟ. +39 096288252
www.lapizzutadelprincipe.it

CELLAR SALES
PRE-BOOKED VISITS
ACCOMMODATION AND RESTAURANT SERVICE
ANNUAL PRODUCTION 80,000 bottles
HECTARES UNDER VINE 13.00
VITICULTURE METHOD Certified Organic

Molarella '18	♟♟ 3
Zingamaro '15	♟♟ 3
Melissa Rosso Jacca Ventu '17	♟ 3
Scavello Bianco Chardonnay '18	♟ 2

Fattoria San Francesco

ᴸᴼᶜ. Quattromani
88813 Cirò [KR]
ᴛᴇʟ. +39 096232228
www.fattoriasanfrancesco.it

CELLAR SALES
PRE-BOOKED VISITS
ANNUAL PRODUCTION 224,000 bottles
HECTARES UNDER VINE 40.00

☉ Donna Rosa '18	♟♟ 3
● Vigna Corta '18	♟♟ 3
☉ Cirò Bianco '18	♟ 2
● Cirò Rosso Cl. '17	♟ 2

Luigi Scala

ᴸᴼᶜ. Torricella San Biagio
88811 Cirò Marina [KR]
ᴛᴇʟ. +39 3389320696
www.cantinascala.it

CELLAR SALES
ANNUAL PRODUCTION 35,000 bottles
HECTARES UNDER VINE 15.00
VITICULTURE METHOD Certified Organic
SUSTAINABLE WINERY

Cirò Rosso Cl. Sup. Ris. '14	♟♟ 3*
Cirò Bianco '18	♟♟ 3
Cirò Rosso Cl. Sup. '16	♟♟ 2*
Cirò Rosato '18	♟ 4

Senatore Vini

ᴸᴼᶜ. San Lorenzo
88811 Cirò Marina [KR]
ᴛᴇʟ. +39 096232350
www.senatorevini.com

CELLAR SALES
PRE-BOOKED VISITS
ANNUAL PRODUCTION 280,000 bottles
HECTARES UNDER VINE 32.00
VITICULTURE METHOD Certified Organic
SUSTAINABLE WINERY

☉ Cirò Rosato Puntalice '18	♟♟ 3
● Negrus Bio '18	♟♟ 3
☉ Alikia Bio '18	♟ 3
☉ Cirò Bianco Alalei '18	♟ 2

Serracavallo

C.DA SERRACAVALLO
87043 BISIGNANO [CS]
TEL. +39 098421144
www.viniserracavallo.com

CELLAR SALES
PRE-BOOKED VISITS
RESTAURANT SERVICE
ANNUAL PRODUCTION 80,000 bottles
HECTARES UNDER VINE 32.00
VITICULTURE METHOD Certified Organic

○ Petramola '18	♟♟ 3
⊙ Terre di Cosenza Rosato Filì '18	♟♟ 2*
● Terre di Cosenza Rosso Quattro Lustri '18	♟♟ 3
● Terre di Cosenza Rosso Sette Chiese '18	♟♟ 2*

Tenuta del Travale

VIA TRAVALE, 13
87050 ROVITO [CS]
TEL. +39 3937150240
www.tenutadeltravale.it

CELLAR SALES
PRE-BOOKED VISITS
ANNUAL PRODUCTION 14,000 bottles
HECTARES UNDER VINE 2.00
SUSTAINABLE WINERY

● Eleuteria '16	♟♟

Terre del Gufo - Muzzillo

C.DA ALBO SAN MARTINO, 22A
87100 COSENZA
TEL. +39 0984780364
www.terredelgufo.it

CELLAR SALES
PRE-BOOKED VISITS
ANNUAL PRODUCTION 25,500 bottles
HECTARES UNDER VINE 3.00

⊙ Terre di Cosenza Rosato Chiaroscuro '18	♟♟ 3
● Timpamara '17	♟♟ 5
● Kaulos '18	♟ 3
● Terre di Cosenza Portapiana '17	♟ 4

Terre di Balbia

C.DA MONTINO
87042 ALTOMONTE [CS]
TEL. +39 098435359
www.terredibalbia.it

CELLAR SALES
PRE-BOOKED VISITS
ANNUAL PRODUCTION 12,000 bottles
HECTARES UNDER VINE 8.00
VITICULTURE METHOD Certified Organic
SUSTAINABLE WINERY

● Fervore '17	♟♟
● Blandus '17	♟
⊙ Ligrezza '18	♟

Val di Neto

LOC. MARGHERITA
VIA DELLE MAGNOLIE, 71
88900 CROTONE
TEL. +39 0962930185
www.cantinavaldineto.com

CELLAR SALES
PRE-BOOKED VISITS
ACCOMMODATION AND RESTAURANT SERVICE
ANNUAL PRODUCTION 50,000 bottles
HECTARES UNDER VINE 20.00

● Arkè '13	♟♟ 3
● Arkè Barrique '17	♟♟ 4
● Melissa Rosso Sup. Mutrò '14	♟♟ 3
● V. delle Volpi '18	♟♟ 2*

Vulcano Wine

VIA INDIPENDENZA, 11
88811 CIRÒ MARINA [KR]
TEL. +39 096235381
www.vulcanowine.com

CELLAR SALES
ANNUAL PRODUCTION 250,000 bottles
HECTARES UNDER VINE 4.00

○ Cirò Bianco Beppe Vulcano '18	♟♟
● Cirò Rosso Cl. Cordòne '17	♟♟

SICILY

he 26 Tre Bicchieri awarded to Sicily points up a rend that we've been observing for some time ow. We can affirm the increasing stylistic recision of the region's individual wines and the ndisputed quality that ties together all its roducers, big and small, reputable and lesser-known, as roof of their outstanding skill and market sensibility. You can't only explain such uccess in terms of the value for money that the island offers. The numbers speak o a DOC Sicilia that's as dazzling as ever — in July 60 million bottles were roduced, meaning that 100 million by year's end is a reasonable prediction, a estament to its extraordinary success. It's been a gradual process that started ome 20 years ago, but it's brought great expertise in terms of enology, agronomy nd marketing, professionals and professionalism, a success that's had a snowball ffect and helped develop the entire sector. Once again, its cooperatives shine hanks to a virtuous cycle that's made them front-runners in terms of know-how, ommercial capacity, and a vision of the world and its markets. It's almost edundant to point out how Etna and its wines have become true gems for this sland-continent, forcefully expressing its unique and original volcanic terrain. But ve're sure that all the areas and extraordinary traditional grapes (and non-native nes as well) are in one or another represented in the guide. Speaking of, we warded a well-deserved Tre Bicchieri to the Nero d'Avola Fontanelle '14, an Eloro ull of personality, deep and true to type, produced by the historic winery Curto. Centopassi's Terre Rosse di Giabbascio '18 also took home top marks — it's a nagnificent Catarratto for its clear, focused fruit, drinkability and exuberant haracter. The history of the winery is bound up with a struggle against the Sicilian nafia, and an example that we hope everyone will follow. As a result we decided o give the staff at Centopassi our special 'Solidarity Award'. Day after day, their ommitment demonstrates that change is possible.

Abbazia Santa Anastasia

LOC. CASTELBUONO
C.DA SANTA ANASTASIA
90013 CASTELBUONO [PA]
TEL. +39 0921671959
www.abbaziasantanastasia.com

CELLAR SALES
PRE-BOOKED VISITS
ACCOMMODATION AND RESTAURANT SERVICE
ANNUAL PRODUCTION 400,000 bottles
HECTARES UNDER VINE 67.50
VITICULTURE METHOD Certified Organic
SUSTAINABLE WINERY

In 1982, engineer Franco Lena purchased this extraordinary 300-hectare estate on the slopes of Madonie Park. Here, as far back as the 12th century, powerful sovereigns and monks oversaw the territory, leaving behind a superb abbey. Lena has shown the utmost dedication, transforming the historic building into a charming relais, raising livestock and developing 70 hectares of vineyards according to organic and biodynamic techniques. Thanks in part to an exceptional microclimate, their wines exhibit strong and uncommon personality. Their excellent Montenero '16, a blend of Syrah and Cabernet Franc, put in a sparkling performance. It's a classy wine, deep and multifaceted, with nuances of morello cherry, plums, chocolate and sweet spices, all adorned by an intriguing balsamic note. Their Sens(i)nverso Syrah '16, with its aromas of ripe pomegranate, is also noteworthy, as is their Passomaggio (Nero d'Avola, Merlot and Cabernet Sauvignon), a fruity, quaffable 2016.

● Montenero '16		♟♟ 4
● Passomaggio '16		♟♟ 4
○ Santa Anastasia Zibibbo Traminer '18		♟♟ 4
● Sens(i)nverso Syrah '16		♟♟ 6
● Litra '16		♟ 6
● Sens(i)nverso Nero d'Avola '16		♟ 6
○ Zurrica '18		♟ 4
● Litra '04		♟♟♟ 6
● Litra '01		♟♟♟ 7
● Montenero '04		♟♟♟ 4
● Litra '14		♟♟ 6
○ Zurrica '17		♟♟ 4

Alessandro di Camporeale

C.DA MANDRANOVA
90043 CAMPOREALE [PA]
TEL. +39 092437038
www.alessandrodicamporeale.it

CELLAR SALES
PRE-BOOKED VISITS
ANNUAL PRODUCTION 240,000 bottles
HECTARES UNDER VINE 40.00
VITICULTURE METHOD Certified Organic

Alessandro di Camporeale, founded in the early 20th century, is among Sicily's 'cult' wineries for its artisanal style. Recently Natale, Nino and Rosolino have shown foresight and entrepreneurial vision, bringing about a qualitative breakthrough and earning their selection praise among among critics and fans of 'tailor-made' wines. The arrival of their children, fresh off their studies in law, enology and marking, along with the purchase of an estate on Etna, are bringing added value to the producer. Their Grillo Vigna di Mandranova '18 took home a our highest honors. It's a wine of great finesse and elegance, with vibrant nuances of mountain herbs, citron peel and almonds. On the palate it's sensual and compelling, mineral and pulpy, charming and very long. The Syrah Kaid '17 is very close behind, with its lovely, fruity aromas of ripe mulberry. On the palate it proves taut and vibrant, plush, with velvet-smooth tannins and plenty of personality.

○ Sicilia Grillo V. di Mandranova '18		♟♟♟ 3*
● Sicilia Syrah Kaid '17		♟♟ 4
○ Monreale Syrah V. di Mandranova '16		♟♟ 4
● Sicilia Catarratto Benedè '18		♟♟ 2*
● Sicilia Nero d'Avola Donnatà '18		♟♟ 2*
○ Sicilia Sauvignon Blanc '18		♟♟ 3
○ Sicilia Catarratto V. di Mandranova '16		♟♟♟ 4*
● Sicilia Syrah Kaid '16		♟♟♟ 4*
○ Sicilia Grillo V. di Mandranova '17		♟♟ 3*
● Sicilia Syrah Kaid '15		♟♟ 4

Alta Mora

LOC. PIETRAMARINA
CDA VERZELLA
95012 CASTIGLIONE DI SICILIA [CT]
TEL. +39 0918908713
www.altamora.it

PRE-BOOKED VISITS
ANNUAL PRODUCTION 70,000 bottles
HECTARES UNDER VINE 18.00
SUSTAINABLE WINERY

Alberto and Diego Cusumano were also seduced by Etna's indescribable charm. They accepted the challenge of a unique terroir where varying soil compositions, positions and wind patterns give rise to a kaleidoscope of elegant wines that are never alike. That's how Alta Mora came to be, a tribute to the districts and their diversity. Here the pursuit of the absolute purity of local cultivars and each volcanic plot is carried out without forced methods or gimmicks. This because, at 600 meters above sea level in Verzella, and 1,000 in Guardiola, 'Beauty is truth and truth beauty'. Their Guardiola '15 is true to type, territorial, extremely delicate and elegant. It delivers for its complex, layered personality, with vibrant nuances calling up peach tobacco and medicinal herbs. The palate is fresh and dynamic, with silky, charming tannins. Fragrances of cherry and licorice characterize the Feudo di Mezzo '15, while the Etna Bianco '18 exhibits a class and precious, transparent phrasing that are still worthy of Tre Bicchieri.

Etna Bianco Alta Mora '18	▼▼▼ 4*
Etna Rosso Alta Mora Feudo di Mezzo '15	▼▼ 4
Etna Rosso Alta Mora Guardiola '15	▼▼ 4
Etna Rosato Alta Mora '18	▼▼ 3
Etna Rosso Alta Mora '17	▼▼ 4
Etna Bianco Alta Mora '17	♀♀♀ 4*
Etna Bianco Alta Mora '16	♀♀♀ 4*
Etna Bianco Alta Mora '14	♀♀♀ 3*
Etna Rosato Alta Mora '17	♀♀ 3
Etna Rosso Alta Mora '16	♀♀ 4

Assuli

C.DA CARCITELLA
91026 MAZARA DEL VALLO [TP]
TEL. +39 0923547267
www.assuli.it

CELLAR SALES
ANNUAL PRODUCTION 100,000 bottles
HECTARES UNDER VINE 100.00

The winery created and overseen by Roberto Caruso is a tribute to the entrepreneurial foresight of his father, Giacomo. Indeed, it's been made entirely with Sicilian Perlato, the marble that paved the way for the success of Sicilmarmi, the business Giacomo founded in 1948. Assuli avails itself of more than 100 hectares of vineyards in Trapani, at elevations ranging from 100 to 250 meters. 40 hectares are in Carcitella, in Mazara del Vallo (where their main facility is also located), 17 in Besi, Castelvetrano, 56 in Fontanabianca, Salemi, and 3 are in Conca, Calatafimi-Segesta. Tre Bicchieri for their elegant Perricone Furioso '16, a vibrant and focused wine in its fruity notes and iodine nuances. On the palate it's soft and tight-knit, with a long finish. The other finalist, a reserve, the Nero d'Avola Lorlando '16, features lovely, mature aromas of black mulberries, and a delicate, firm, persistent palate. The notable Insolia Carinda '18 is fresh and pleasant, while the Catarratto Lucido Donna Angelica '17, another noteworthy selection, proves floral and citrusy.

● Sicilia Perricone Furioso '16	▼▼▼ 5
● Sicilia Nero d'Avola Lorlando Ris. '16	▼▼ 5
○ Passito di Grillo '16	▼▼ 5
○ Sicilia Grillo Fiordiligi '18	▼▼ 2*
○ Sicilia Inzolia Carinda '18	▼▼ 2*
○ Sicilia Lucido Donna Angelica '17	▼▼ 3
● Sicilia Nero d'Avola Besi '16	▼▼ 5
● Sicilia Nero d'Avola Lorlando '18	▼▼ 3
● Sicilia Syrah Ruggiero '18	▼▼ 2*
○ Sicilia Grillo Astolfo '17	▼ 4
○ Astolfo '15	♀♀♀ 4*
● Lorlando '15	♀♀♀ 2*
● Sicilia Nero d'Avola Lorlando '17	♀♀♀ 3*
○ Sicilia Grillo Fiordiligi '17	♀♀ 2*

Baglio del Cristo di Campobello

LOC. C.DA FAVAROTTA
S.DA ST.LE 123 KM 19,200
92023 CAMPOBELLO DI LICATA [AG]
TEL. +39 0922 877709
www.cristodicampobello.it

PRE-BOOKED VISITS
ANNUAL PRODUCTION 300,000 bottles
HECTARES UNDER VINE 30.00

This lovely Campobello di Licata winery is certainly well-established, thanks to the passion and skill that the Bonetta family have shown for generations. From above, their more than 30 hectares of vineyards seem like lush gardens embedded in the white earth, sparkling rich in limestone and quartz. From the outset their wines, which are technically impeccable, have proven distinct for their ability to exhibit a modern, captivating quality while also highlighting unique, varietal attributes and terroir of origin. Even if their selection was without a key player, all the wines submitted handily passed through our regional selections, in particular the Syrah Lusirà '17, which easily landed a place in our finals thanks to its elegant, varietal aromatic profile. On the palate, in addition to a crystal-clear return of its spicy, balsamic fragrances, it's marked by round, juicy fruit.

● Sicilia Syrah Lusirà '17	♥♥ 5
○ C'D'C' Cristo di Campobello Bianco '18	♥♥ 2*
○ C'D'C' Cristo di Campobello Rosato '18	♥♥ 2*
● C'D'C' Cristo di Campobello Rosso '18	♥♥ 2*
○ Sicilia Bianco Adènzia '18	♥♥ 3
○ Sicilia Chardonnay Laudàri '17	♥♥ 4
○ Sicilia Grillo Lalùci '18	♥♥ 3
● Sicilia Nero d'Avola Lu Patri '17	♥♥ 5
● Sicilia Rosso Adènzia '17	♥♥ 3
● Lu Patri '09	♥♥♥ 5
○ C'D'C' Bianco Cristo di Campobello '17	♥♥ 2*
○ Sicilia Bianco Adènzia '17	♥♥ 3
○ Sicilia Grillo Lalùci '17	♥♥ 3*
● Sicilia Nero d'Avola Lu Patri '16	♥♥ 5

Baglio di Pianetto

LOC. PIANETTO
VIA FRANCIA
90030 SANTA CRISTINA GELA [PA]
TEL. +39 0918570002
www.bagliodipianetto.it

CELLAR SALES
PRE-BOOKED VISITS
ACCOMMODATION AND RESTAURANT SERVIC
ANNUAL PRODUCTION 550,000 bottles
HECTARES UNDER VINE 104.00
SUSTAINABLE WINERY

Founded in 1997, Paolo Marzotto's lovely Santa Cristina Gela and Pachino vineyards (100+ hectares) represent some of Sicily's most eco-sustainable. Since 2013 the entire estate (more than 160 hectares in all) was converted to organic and, as of 2016, all their grapes have been certified. Moreover, the installation of a latest-generation solar power system, a drastic reduction in CO2 emissions, and rigorous protocols for the use of water, make it one of the island's greenest producers. Their Viafrancia Riserva Rosso '14, a classic Bordeaux blend redolent of fruit and spice earned a place in our finals. Its austere palate is well-managed by a close-knit, elegant tannic weave. Their Viognier Viafrancia Riserva '16 is also noteworthy, proving that the cultivar is well-suited to Sicily's climate and terroir. On the nose it offers up fragrances of ripe medlar, hazelnut and saffron, while on the palate it proves invigorating and highly pleasant.

○ Sicilia Bianco Viafrancia Ris. '16	♥♥
● Sicilia Rosso Viafrancia Ris. '14	♥♥
○ Sicilia Ficiligno '18	♥♥
○ Sicilia Grillo Timeo '18	♥♥
○ Monreale Bianco Murriali '18	♥
● Shymer '14	♥♥♥
● Shymer '13	♥♥♥
● Sicilia Rosso Ramione '13	♥♥♥
● Cembali '11	♥♥
● Shymer '15	♥♥
● Sicilia Nero d'Avola '16	♥♥
● Syraco '15	♥♥

Barone di Villagrande

A DEL BOSCO, 25
5025 MILO [CT]
EL. +39 0957082175
www.villagrande.it

CELLAR SALES
PRE-BOOKED VISITS
ACCOMMODATION AND RESTAURANT SERVICE
ANNUAL PRODUCTION 80,000 bottles
HECTARES UNDER VINE 19.00
VITICULTURE METHOD Certified Organic

After graduating in enology in Milan, Marco Nicolosi returned to Milo to take over the reigns of his family's historic winery. Of course, he had to keep up with the great interest in Etna that was shaking up its wine industry. It's to his credit that Marco was able, in just a few short years, to give a decidedly positive boost to the producer, innovating in both technical terms and its image. The result was to open the winery to an increasingly large number of enotourists interested in Etna through a lovely wine resort and restaurant. Their Etna Bianco Superiore Contrada Villagrande '15 earned a place in our finals. It was certainly the volcano that endowed it with the spirited personality of a fresh, sapid palate that's just reigned in by fruit. On the nose, signature aromas of iron and smoky notes follow citrusy hints, flowers and fragrances of yellow-fleshed fruit. Their Etna Rosso '17 also delivered, with its close-woven tannins nicely invigorated by round, yet tonic fruit.

○ Etna Bianco Sup. Contrada Villagrande '15	🍷🍷 6
○ Etna Bianco Sup. '18	🍷🍷 3
● Etna Rosso '18	🍷🍷 3
○ Salina Bianco '18	🍷 3
○ Etna Bianco Sup. '17	🍷🍷 3
● Etna Rosso '16	🍷🍷 3
● Etna Rosso Contrada Villagrande '14	🍷🍷 6
● Etna Rosso Contrada Villagrande '13	🍷🍷 6
○ Malvasia delle Lipari Passito '14	🍷🍷 5

Tenuta Bastonaca

C.DA BASTONACA
97019 VITTORIA [RG]
TEL. +39 0932686480
www.tenutabastonaca.it

CELLAR SALES
PRE-BOOKED VISITS
ACCOMMODATION
ANNUAL PRODUCTION 48,000 bottles
HECTARES UNDER VINE 17.00
VITICULTURE METHOD Certified Organic
SUSTAINABLE WINERY

With vigor and enthusiasm, Silvana Raniolo and Giovanni Calcaterra (both with family backgrounds in agriculture) founded this small winery. In addition to property in one of Cerasuolo di Vittoria's best areas, they now avail themselves of two hectares on Etna. Their head-trained vineyards are cultivated organically, and purposefully without irrigation. The result is a 'natural' wine produced with a deep respect for nature and consumers, qualities further evidenced by the use of natural, recyclable materials. Their 18th-century palmento and lovely tasting areas are also noteworthy. Their Etna Rosso '16 just fell short of our highest honors. Elegant nuances rise up off the nose, calling up black cherries, rose petals, tobacco and sweet spices. On the palate it exhibits a noble tannic weave, with a sensual, enticing freshness. But their entire selection impresses for its territorial expressiveness, in pursuit of precision and rich, sophisticated composition.

● Etna Rosso '16	🍷🍷 5
● Cerasuolo di Vittoria '17	🍷🍷 3
○ Etna Bianco '17	🍷🍷 5
● Frappato '18	🍷🍷 3
○ Sicilia Grillo '18	🍷🍷 3
● Sicilia Nero d'Avola '18	🍷🍷 3
● Sud '17	🍷🍷 5
● Cerasuolo di Vittoria '16	🍷🍷 3
● Etna Rosso '15	🍷🍷 4
○ Sicilia Grillo '17	🍷🍷 3
● Sicilia Nero d'Avola '17	🍷🍷 3
● Sud '16	🍷🍷 5

★Benanti

VIA GIUSEPPE GARIBALDI, 361
95029 VIAGRANDE [CT]
TEL. +39 0957893399
www.benanti.it

CELLAR SALES
PRE-BOOKED VISITS
RESTAURANT SERVICE
ANNUAL PRODUCTION 160,000 bottles
HECTARES UNDER VINE 28.00
SUSTAINABLE WINERY

After a long period of training alongside their father, Giuseppe (one of Etna's wine pioneers), for a couple of years now Antonio and Salvino Benanti have been firmly in control of the family winery. After selling off certain non-strategic assets, they dedicated themselves entirely to upgrading the cellar and, especially, purchasing new vineyards in some of the volcano's best areas. Their production philosophy, however, hasn't changed, which is to say, their focus remains making outstanding wines that are absolutely true to their terroir of origin. A superb varietal, their Contrada Monte Serra '17, brings Benanti back in the Tre Bicchieri club. Its smoky notes and territorial qualities are on display, merging with aromas of yellow peach and citrus, then giving way to elegant hints of balsamic and medicinal herbs. On the palate it exhibits a close-knit tannic weave that does a nice job supporting its full, juicy fruit, all enlivened by a highly fresh streak of acidity.

● Etna Rosso Contrada Monte Serra '17	♟♟♟ 6
● Etna Rosso '17	♟♟ 3
● Etna Rosso Contrada Cavaliere '17	♟♟ 5
○ Etna Bianco Contrada Cavaliere '17	♟ 5
⊙ Etna Rosato '18	♟ 4
○ Etna Bianco Sup. Pietramarina '09	♟♟♟ 5
○ Etna Bianco Sup. Pietramarina '04	♟♟♟ 6
● Etna Rosso Serra della Contessa '06	♟♟♟ 7
● Etna Rosso Serra della Contessa '04	♟♟♟ 7
● Il Drappo '04	♟♟♟ 5

Bonavita

LOC. FARO SUPERIORE
C.DA CORSO
98158 MESSINA
TEL. +39 3471754683
www.bonavitafaro.com

PRE-BOOKED VISITS
ANNUAL PRODUCTION 10,000 bottles
HECTARES UNDER VINE 2.50

Bonavita is situated in Faro Superiore, on the slopes of Peloritani, a wooded hillside between the Ionian and Tyrrhenian seas dense in oaks and chestnuts. Here Giovanni Scarfone follows in the footsteps of his father, cultivating 2.5 hectares of terraced plots. They cultivate exclusively Nerello Mascalese, Cappuccio and Nocero head-trained and vertical-trellised vineyards that, in some cases, go back more than 80 years. Both in the vineyards and in their historic cellar, they apply a production philosophy aimed at bringing out the natural attributes and biodiversity of the grapes. Their Faro once again lands a place in our finals. 2017 conferred an elegantly mature bouquet in which clear notes of capers Mediterranean shrub emerge on a delicately mineral background. On the palate it's crisp, exhibiting full, lively consistence, and closing clean and long. Their Rosato '18, dedicated to Carmelo, expresses a generous intensity in its earthy character, as well as a gutsy, rustic pleasantness.

● Faro '17	♟♟ 5
⊙ Rosato '18	♟♟ 2
● Faro '16	♟♟ 5
● Faro '15	♟♟ 5
● Faro '14	♟♟ 5
⊙ Rosato '17	♟♟ 2
⊙ Rosato '16	♟♟ 2
⊙ Rosato '15	♟♟ 2

Tenute Bosco

S.DA PROV.LE 64 SOLICCHIATA
95012 CASTIGLIONE DI SICILIA [CT]
TEL. +39 0957658856
www.tenutebosco.com

CELLAR SALES
PRE-BOOKED VISITS
ANNUAL PRODUCTION 50,000 bottles
HECTARES UNDER VINE 10.00
VITICULTURE METHOD Certified Organic

Sofia and Concetto Bosco's Piano dei Daini and its lovely palmento have existed for at least three centuries. Testifying to the fact is a front-page appearance on the June 21st, 1879 edition of the celebrated French magazine L'Illustration (reporting on one of Etna's many eruptions). The Boscos have started out with clear ideas, focusing immediately on elegant, territorial wines produced with the utmost respect for the environment. Indeed, as Sofia says, 'If you want the territory to be at its best in your wines, you have to love it and respect it'. Their Vigna Vico '16 took home a well-deserved Tre Bicchieri. It's an Etna Rosso made with grapes grown in the centuries-old vineyard of the same name, a true monument to viticulture with its mostly ungrafted vines. On the nose the wine is close-woven and generous amidst aromas of pomegranate, gentian, blackberries, pennyroyal, dark citrus and rust. A palate of rare complexity stands out more for the noble harmony of its tannins, fruit and acidity than for its force.

● Etna Rosso Vico Prephylloxera '16	🍷🍷🍷	8
○ Etna Bianco Piano dei Daini '18	🍷🍷	5
⊙ Etna Rosato Piano dei Daini '18	🍷🍷	5
● Etna Rosso Piano dei Daini '17	🍷🍷	5
● Etna Rosso Vico Prephylloxera '15	🍷🍷🍷	8
○ Etna Bianco Piano dei Daini '17	🍷🍷	5
○ Etna Bianco Piano dei Daini '16	🍷🍷	5
⊙ Etna Rosato Piano dei Daini '17	🍷🍷	5
● Etna Rosso Piano dei Daini '16	🍷🍷	5
● Etna Rosso Vigna Vico '14	🍷🍷	8

Paolo Calì

FRAZ. C.DA SALMÉ
VIA DEL FRAPPATO, 100
97019 VITTORIA [RG]
TEL. +39 0932510082
www.vinicali.it

CELLAR SALES
PRE-BOOKED VISITS
ANNUAL PRODUCTION 90,000 bottles
HECTARES UNDER VINE 15.00

Paolo Calì is a genuine guy, a pharmacist who rediscovered a passion for the vineyard in light of a family tradition of viticulture and winemaking. His land is also particular, because it's marked by a strong presence of sand (even if it's not near the sea), and gives rise to elegant, subtle wines that know neither select yeasts nor filtration or stabilizers. Furthermore, from the beginning Paolo has chosen to cultivate only local grapes, which he looks after with painstaking care, convinced of the importance of allowing them to express, without invasive practices, both cultivar and terroir. Their entire selection put in a standout performance. The Nero d'Avola Violino '16 is mature with fruit flavors, highly pleasant and true to type. The elegant, refined Frappato Mandragola '16 exhibits commendable persistence, while the nose offers up Mediterranean herbs and pomegranate invigorated by iodine nuances. Their elegant, expansive Forfice '15 is in great form, proving tantalizing on the palate, while the lively Grillo Blues '18 proves citrusy and almondy fresh.

○ Blues '18	🍷🍷	3
● Cerasuolo di Vittoria Cl. Forfice '15	🍷🍷	4
● Jazz '16	🍷🍷	3
⊙ Osa! Frappato Rosato '18	🍷🍷	4
● Vittoria Frappato Mandragola '17	🍷🍷	3
● Vittoria Nero d'Avola Violino '16	🍷🍷	3
● Cerasuolo di Vittoria Cl. Manene '17	🍷	4
● Vittoria Frappato Pruvenza '16	🍷	6
○ Blues '17	🍷🍷	3
● Cerasuolo di Vittoria Cl. Forfice '13	🍷🍷	6
● Vittoria Frappato Mandragola '16	🍷🍷	3
● Vittoria Frappato Pruvenza '15	🍷🍷	6

Caravaglio

VIA NAZIONALE, 33
98050 MALFA [ME]
TEL. +39 3398115953
caravagliovini@virgilio.it

CELLAR SALES
PRE-BOOKED VISITS
ANNUAL PRODUCTION 50,000 bottles
HECTARES UNDER VINE 12.00
VITICULTURE METHOD Certified Organic
SUSTAINABLE WINERY

Since his winemaking debut on Salina, back in 1992, Nino Caravaglio has always managed to make discerning decisions without resting on his laurels. Thus he always reinvested profit back in the winery, growing its vineyards to the point of becoming autonomous and improving their management (including yields and pruning). Today, in addition to 15-hectares on Salina, they've added 5 newly-planted hectares on Stromboli. And Nino is already working to build a new cellar with spaces and technology that are better suited to his new production needs. Once again the Malvasia delle Lipari Passito '18 proves that it's one of Italy's most interesting and intriguing wines. Transparent and complex on the nose amidst aromas of citrus, white figs, aromatic herbs and delicate iodine nuances. A rock solid palate proves fresh, with sweetness and acidity well balanced — it's just sapid, with a lovely return of citrus on its extremely long finish. Hats off and Tre Bicchieri.

○ Malvasia delle Lipari Passito '18	🍷🍷🍷 5
● Chianu Cruci '15	🍷🍷 3
○ Infatata '18	🍷🍷 3
○ Malvasia '18	🍷🍷 5
● Palmento di Salina '18	🍷🍷 4
○ Rossi di Salina '18	🍷🍷 3
○ Malvasia delle Lipari Passito '17	🍷🍷🍷 5
○ Malvasia delle Lipari Passito '16	🍷🍷🍷 5
○ Infatata '17	🍷🍷 3
○ Malvasia '17	🍷🍷 5

Le Casematte

LOC. FARO SUPERIORE
C.DA CORSO
98163 MESSINA
TEL. +39 0906409427
www.lecasematte.it

CELLAR SALES
ANNUAL PRODUCTION 40,000 bottles
HECTARES UNDER VINE 11.00
VITICULTURE METHOD Certified Organic
SUSTAINABLE WINERY

The small winery managed by Gianfranco Sabbatino, a well-known accountant, and Andrea Barzagli, a famous footballer, represents an excellent example of heroic agriculture. Its terraced plots are situated on the high, steep hills that overlook the Strait of Messina, an area where strong winds rich in iodine meet and clash incessantly, beating the three WW II military forts ('casematte') that still rise here. Their entire selection exhibits great elegance and class, perfectly embodying the prestigious Faro DOC appellation thanks to their stylistic perfection and artisanal cut. Yet another outstanding performance for their Faro. The 2017 is a sumptuous wine, deep and refined. It takes home Tre Bicchieri for its limpid nuances of topsoil, small red berries, aromatic herbs, nuances of licorice and pepper. On the palate it's compelling, iodine, full and highly fresh, supple, with pronounced personality. Their excellent Nanuci '17, made with Nocera grapes, offers up a truly enticing, foral and fruity bouquet.

● Faro '17	🍷🍷🍷 5
● Nanuci '17	🍷🍷 3
○ Peloro Bianco '18	🍷🍷 3
● Peloro Rosso '17	🍷🍷 3
⊙ Rosematte Nerello Mascalese '18	🍷🍷 3
● Faro '16	🍷🍷🍷 5
● Faro '15	🍷🍷🍷 5
● Faro '14	🍷🍷🍷 5
● Faro '13	🍷🍷🍷 5
○ Peloro Bianco '17	🍷🍷 3
● Peloro Rosso '16	🍷🍷 3
● Peloro Rosso '15	🍷🍷 2*
⊙ Rosematte Nerello Mascalese '17	🍷🍷 3

entopassi

Porta Palermo, 132
948 San Giuseppe Jato [PA]
+39 0918577655
w.centopassisicilia.it

LLAR SALES
E-BOOKED VISITS
COMMODATION AND RESTAURANT SERVICE
NNUAL PRODUCTION 450,000 bottles
CTARES UNDER VINE 65.00
ICULTURE METHOD Certified Organic
STAINABLE WINERY

ntopassi, a project of the 'Free Land'
nsortium, is a cooperative winery that
anically cultivates 94 hectares of
eyards confiscated from the mafia. The
ncipal property is in Alto Belice
leonese, hillsides in Monreale,
mporeale and San Giuseppe Jato (where
winery itself, also confiscated, is located).
eir line of crus, which has grown over the
rs, now comprises 10 wines, each an
ression of its respective cultivars, soil and
croclimate. The result is a selection that
resses, with personality and elegance,
biodiversity of a superb territory. Their
es put in a respectable performance in
suit of a commendable continuity of
ality. The Cimento di Perricone '17 is
used in its varietal character, while the
oyant Nero d'Avola Argille di Tagghia Via
is characterized by fresh strawberry. The
ly Catarratto Terre Rosse di Giabbascio
proves sapid, solid and linear in its
getal notes, juicy and highly drinkable on
palate, with iodine nuances and a nice
rbaceous profile. It takes home Tre
chieri and our special Solidarity award.

Sicilia Catarratto	
Terre Rosse di Giabbascio '18	🍷🍷🍷 3*
Cimento di Perricone '17	🍷🍷 3
Nero d'Avola Argille di Tagghia Via '18	🍷🍷 3
Sicilia Giato Catarratto '18	🍷🍷 2*
Sicilia Giato Nero d'Avola Perricone '18	🍷🍷 2*
Pietre a Purtedda da Ginestra '16	🍷 5
R14 Terre Rosse di Giabbascio '14	🍷 5
Sicilia Grillo Rocce di Pietra Longa '18	🍷 3
Sulla Via Francigena Merlot '16	🍷 3
Tendoni di Trebbiano '17	🍷 3
Pietre a Purtedda da Ginestra '15	🍷🍷 5
Sicilia Catarratto	
Terre Rosse di Giabbascio '17	🍷🍷 3*
Tendoni di Trebbiano '16	🍷🍷 3

Terra Costantino

via Garibaldi, 417
95029 Viagrande [CT]
Tel. +39 095434288
www.terracostantino.it

CELLAR SALES
PRE-BOOKED VISITS
ANNUAL PRODUCTION 40,000 bottles
HECTARES UNDER VINE 7.00
VITICULTURE METHOD Certified Organic

Fabio inherited a love for vineyards and wine
from his father, Dino. It couldn't have been
otherwise, considering that the Costantino
family own an estate that they've cultivated
since 1699. The year is etched on the
entranceway to the estate's historic
palmento in Contrada Blandano, Viagrande,
on the southeast side of Etna (the side that
directly faces the Ionian Sea). You can smell
the salty sea air when the wind blows up
towards the mountain, regulating the area's
temperature, especially during the warm
summer months. The de Aetna '17 is
superb, transparent on the nose with clear,
focused aromas of yellow peach. On the
palate it's sophisticated, rich in tannins that
integrate confidently with ripe, juicy fruit, and
closing extremely clean and persistent. The
Etna Rosso Contrada Blandano '16 also
delivers. It's austere and aristocratic, offering
up mineral notes and hints of forest berries,
making for a harmonious palate of lengthy
aromatic persistence.

● Etna Rosso Contrada Blandano '16	🍷🍷 5
● Etna Rosso De Aetna '17	🍷🍷 3*
○ Etna Bianco Contrada Blandano '16	🍷🍷 5
○ Etna Bianco De Aetna '17	🍷🍷 3
⊙ Etna Rosato De Aetna '18	🍷🍷 3
⊙ Rasola '18	🍷🍷 3
○ Etna Bianco Contrada Blandano '15	🍷🍷 5
○ Etna Bianco Contrada Blandano '14	🍷🍷 5
⊙ Etna Rosato De Aetna '16	🍷🍷 3
● Etna Rosso Contrada Blandano '15	🍷🍷 5
● Etna Rosso De Aetna '16	🍷🍷 3*

★Cottanera

LOC. IANNAZZO
S.DA PROV.LE 89
95030 CASTIGLIONE DI SICILIA [CT]
TEL. +39 0942963601
www.cottanera.it

CELLAR SALES
PRE-BOOKED VISITS
ANNUAL PRODUCTION 350,000 bottles
HECTARES UNDER VINE 65.00

One of Etna's most noteworthy wineries in terms of vineyard size and quality, the result of unequalled, meticulous management, Iannazzo produces a range of extraordinarily elegant wines (using primarily native cultivars). Designed and realized by the forward-thinking Guglielmo Cambria, today Iannazzo is overseen by his brother Enzo, who's been there from the beginning, and Guglielmo's children, Emanuele, Francesco and Mariangela, a young and skilled team. Their modern cellar allows them to make wines of notable personality, exemplary expressions of the terroir's multifaceted charm. The Etna Rosso Feudo di Mezzo '16 handily earned Tre Bicchieri. It's a wine of character and strong personality, complex and elegant, a perfect icon of one of Etna's great crus. Redolent of violent, peach and red berries, on the palate it exhibits fat, compelling tannins. Their sophisticated and multifaceted Diciassettesalme '17 is also at the top of its game. Pleasant and vibrant, it's exemplary in the way it brings together fruit, acidity and tannins. The rest of their selection also proves exceptional.

● Etna Rosso Feudo di Mezzo '16	🍷🍷🍷 6
● Etna Rosso Diciassettesalme '17	🍷🍷 3*
○ Etna Bianco '18	🍷🍷 3
○ Etna Bianco Calderara '17	🍷🍷 5
⊙ Etna Rosato '18	🍷🍷 2*
● Etna Rosso Barbazzale '18	🍷🍷 3
● Etna Rosso Zottorinoto Ris. '15	🍷🍷 8
● Sicilia L'Ardenza '16	🍷🍷 4
● Sicilia Sole di Sesta '16	🍷🍷 4
● Etna Rosso '11	🍷🍷🍷 5
● Etna Rosso Zottorinoto Ris. '14	🍷🍷🍷 8
● Etna Rosso Zottorinoto Ris. '13	🍷🍷🍷 8
● Etna Rosso Zottorinoto Ris. '12	🍷🍷🍷 8
● Etna Rosso Zottorinoto Ris. '11	🍷🍷🍷 8

Curto

LOC. CONTRADA SULLA
S.DA ST.LE 115 ISPICA - ROSOLINI KM 358
97014 ISPICA [RG]
TEL. +39 0932950161
www.curto.it

CELLAR SALES
PRE-BOOKED VISITS
ANNUAL PRODUCTION 70,000 bottles
HECTARES UNDER VINE 30.00

For 350 years the Curtos, a family with ancient, noble roots, have been cultivating vines in Ispica. Here, between Ragusa and Syracuse and in the heart of Eloro, Nero d'Avola expresses its original character. Francesca, who studied enology at prestigious Bordeaux wineries before taking over the reins of the family business, oversees vineyard management. Their head-trained or upwards-trained vertical-trellised vines go back anywhere form 20 to 50 years. In addition to Nero d'Avola they grow Moscato Bianco, Inzolia, Syrah and Merlot. An even but continued development earned the Eloro Fontanelle cru Tre Bicchieri. 2014 conferred a nose of extreme finesse, with fruity notes of plum and cherry fused with pleasant nuances of herbs. On the palate it's elegant and confident, highly persistent and clear in its finish. The Inzolia Poiano '18, with its corpulent, fresh fruit, is also a nice surprise, proving intense and deep in its iodine hints.

● Eloro Nero d'Avola Fontanelle '14	🍷🍷🍷
● Eloro Nero d'Avola '16	🍷🍷
● Ikano '16	🍷🍷
○ Poiano '18	🍷🍷
⊙ Eloro Nero d'Avola Eos '18	🍷
● Eloro Nero d'Avola '15	🍷🍷🍷
⊙ Eloro Nero d'Avola Eos '16	🍷🍷🍷
● Eloro Nero d'Avola Fontanelle '13	🍷🍷🍷
● Eloro Nero d'Avola Fontanelle '12	🍷🍷🍷
● Ikano '14	🍷🍷🍷
○ Moscato Passito Dulce Netum '14	🍷🍷🍷

★★Cusumano

C. C.DA SAN CARLO
DA ST.LE 113 KM 307
)047 PARTINICO [PA]
L. +39 0918908713
www.cusumano.it

CELLAR SALES
PRE-BOOKED VISITS
ANNUAL PRODUCTION 2,500,000 bottles
HECTARES UNDER VINE 520.00
SUSTAINABLE WINERY

berto and Diego's new slogan is
Difference and Diversity'. These two values
ave always distinguished Cusumano's
ines, whether it's Ficuzza (700 meters
evation — Insolia, Chardonnay and Pinot
ero), the white soils of San Giacomo (Nero
Avola), or Partinico, which hosts their
nuta San Carlo (Moscato dello Zucco)
d cellar. We also shouldn't forget their
ots in Monreale, Presti and Pegni, where
imarily non-native grapes are cultivated,
d Monte Pietroso, homeland for Grillo
amaris. And the 2018 version of the
illo Shamaris impressed with its extreme
omatic finesse. On the palate it exhibits
esh, crisp fruit, proving sapid and
ersisten. The Noà '17, a blend of Nero
Avola, Merlot and Cabernet Sauvignon,
companied it in our final tastings.
ose-woven and deep aromatically, it has
ce texture on the palate. As always, the
st of their selection excelled for its
nsistently high level of quality.

★★Donnafugata

VIA S. LIPARI, 18
91025 MARSALA [TP]
TEL. +39 0923724200
www.donnafugata.it

CELLAR SALES
PRE-BOOKED VISITS
ANNUAL PRODUCTION 2,500,000 bottles
HECTARES UNDER VINE 405.00
SUSTAINABLE WINERY

Sicilian wine owes much to the late, great
Giacomo Rallo, a brilliant, forward-thinking
entrepreneur and man of culture who
founded, along with his wife, this winery of
international renown and prestige. It was he
who paved the way for a production style in
which the important values of tradition and
respect for terroir could coexist with
modern sensibilities and innovation.
Following in his footsteps, his wife and
sons are carrying forward, seeing to it that
the winery produces deep, elegant wines
with grapes cultivated in various districts,
from Cerasuolo to Etna, Pantelleria,
Contessa Entellina and Marsala. Prolonged
aging of the 2016 version of their Ben Ryé
made for a spectacular passito with highly
elegant aromas of dried apricots, figs,
dates and lavender. It's a wine of extreme
fullness, depth and character that, also in
light of a well-balanced sweetness and
acidity, earns itself Tre Bicchieri. Their
Etna Rosso Fragore '16 is also in a class
of its own thanks to its alluring complexity
and freshness.

Sicilia Grillo Shamaris '18	♀♀♀ 3*
Sicilia Noà '17	♀♀ 5
Angimbè Tenuta Ficuzza '18	♀♀ 3
Sicilia Benuara	
Tenuta Presti e Pegni '18	♀♀ 3
Insolia '18	♀♀ 2*
Merlot '18	♀♀ 2*
Ramusa '18	♀♀ 3
Sicilia Lucido '18	♀♀ 3
Sicilia Nero d'Avola '18	♀♀ 4
Sicilia Nero d'Avola Disueri '18	♀♀ 3
Moscato dello Zucco '10	♀♀♀ 5
Sàgana '12	♀♀♀ 4*
Sàgana '11	♀♀♀ 4*
Sicilia Nero d'Avola Sàgana '16	♀♀♀ 4*
Sicilia Noà '13	♀♀♀ 4*

○ Passito di Pantelleria Ben Ryé '16	♀♀♀ 7
● Etna Rosso Fragore '16	♀♀ 8
○ Contessa Entellina Chiarandà '16	♀♀ 5
● Mille e una Notte '15	♀♀ 7
○ Moscato di Pantelleria Kabir '18	♀♀ 3
○ Sicilia Grillo SurSur '18	♀♀ 3
● Sicilia Nero d'Avola Sherazade '18	♀♀ 3
○ Sicilia Zibibbo Lighea '18	♀♀ 3
● Tancredi '16	♀♀ 5
● Mille e una Notte '14	♀♀♀ 7
○ Passito di Pantelleria Ben Ryé '15	♀♀♀ 7
○ Passito di Pantelleria Ben Ryé '14	♀♀♀ 7
○ Passito di Pantelleria Ben Ryé '12	♀♀♀ 7
● Tancredi '11	♀♀♀ 5

Duca di Salaparuta

VIA NAZIONALE, S.S. 113
90014 CASTELDACCIA [PA]
TEL. +39 091945201
www.duca.it

PRE-BOOKED VISITS
ANNUAL PRODUCTION 9,000,000 bottles
HECTARES UNDER VINE 155.00
SUSTAINABLE WINERY

You can understand modern Sicilian history
(not only its wine) by studying Corvo, Duca
di Salaparuta and Florio, historic,
established brands owned today by
Saronno's ILLVA group. They represent,
chronologically, the first wine bottled in Italy
(in 1824), the first high-quality
monovarietal Nero d'Avola (Duca Enrico del
1984), the rise of Marsala and the Florio
family. Today we should commend their
commitment to further develop these three
businesses through innovative, successful
models, foremost enotourism. We quite
enjoyed a number of their offerings. The
2007 version of their Marsa Targa 1840
exhibits a refined, oxidative bouquet, while
on the palate it proves summery, complex
and harmonious, with a riveting finish. The
rich and pulpy Bianca di Valguarnera '17 is
an Inzolia of notable class. We also
appreciated the invigorating, lingering,
deep and sophisticated Marsala Vergine
Baglio Florio '13, and the delicious,
tantalizing Marsala Superiore Secco
Vecchio Florio '15.

○ Marsala Sup.Targa 1840 Ris. '07	♟♟	4
○ Bianca di Valguarnera '17	♟♟	6
● Calanica Nero d'Avola Merlot '17	♟♟	3
○ Colomba Platino Risignolo '18	♟♟	4
○ Marsala Sup. Secco Vecchio Florio '15	♟♟	3
○ Marsala Sup. Semisecco Ambra Donna Franca Ris.	♟♟	6
○ Marsala Vergine Baglio Florio '03	♟♟	5
● Passo delle Mule Suor Marchesa '17	♟♟	3
● Sciaranera Pinot Nero '17	♟♟	4
● Triskelè '16	♟♟	4
● Calanica Frappato Syrah '17	♟	3
○ Calanica Grillo Viognier '18	♟	3
○ Calanica Insolia Chardonnay '18	♟	3
○ Kados '18	♟	3
○ Morsi di Luce	♟	5

★Feudi del Pisciotto

C.DA PISCIOTTO
93015 NISCEMI [CL]
TEL. +39 09331935186
www.feudidelpisciotto.it

CELLAR SALES
PRE-BOOKED VISITS
ACCOMMODATION
ANNUAL PRODUCTION 200,000 bottles
HECTARES UNDER VINE 45.00

*The owner of this producer is also a
shareholder of Gambero Rosso spa. To
avoid any conflict of interest, Paolo Paner
has subordinated the possible awarding o
Tre Bicchieri (which, in any case, only
occurs through a blind tasting), to the
attainment of the same rating of excellen
(upwards of 90/100) by an independent,
international panel. This was the case he*

Feudi is a lovely winery endowed with a
modern and up-to-date cellar, and
bolstered by more than 45 hectares of
vineyards, all of which are painstakingly
looked after by Alessandro Cellai and his
valid technical staff. Once again they hit t
Tre Bicchieri mark thanks to a refined (an
not just in its label) Cerasuolo di Vittoria
Giambattista Valli Paris '17, a wine that's
elegant in its aromas of small wild berries
and wild rose, fresh in its balsamic hints.
On the palate, where tannins and fruit me
without either overwhelming the other, it's
spicy and well-distributed.

● Cerasuolo di Vittoria Giambattista Valli '17	♟♟♟	
○ Sicilia Grillo Carolina Marengo Kisa '17	♟♟	
● Alberta Ferretti Chardonnay '17	♟♟	
● Baglio del Sole Nero d'Avola '17	♟♟	
● Carolina Marengo Kisa Frappato '17	♟♟	
○ Gurra di Mare Tirsat '17	♟♟	
● L'Eterno '17	♟♟	
● Missoni Cabernet Sauvignon '17	♟♟	
● Versace Nero d'Avola '17	♟♟	
○ Baglio del Sole Inzolia '18	♟	
○ Baglio del Sole Inzolia Catarratto '18	♟	
● Baglio del Sole Merlot Syrah '17	♟	

eudo Arancio

A Portella Misilbesi
017 Sambuca di Sicilia [AG]
. +39 0925579000
w.feudoarancio.it

ELLAR SALES
RE-BOOKED VISITS
CCOMMODATION
NNUAL PRODUCTION 6,000,000 bottles
ECTARES UNDER VINE 750.00
USTAINABLE WINERY

unded in 1904 and today a large
ternational player, Trentino's Mezzacorona
ve invested heavily in two Sicilian areas,
cate (Ragusa province) and Sambuca di
cilia (near Lake Arancio). The idea was to
eate high-quality, characterful wines from
o excellent territories while respecting
adition and reducing environmental
pact to a minimum. The beauty of their
mbuca estate, which stretches along
chanting, wind-swept hills, is also worth
ting. Their Hedonis '16 (Nero d'Avola and
rah) is a dark and deep wine, with clear,
ense nuances that call up black
ulberries, chocolate and Asian spices, all
livened by refreshing balsamic hints. It
ows the qualities of its excellent caliber,
inging it within a hair of a gold. Their
esh and gratifying Grillo '18, a wine
dolent of spring flowers, pear,
editerranean herbs, is also top-notch.

Sicilia Hedonis Ris. '16	🍷🍷 4
Cantodoro Ris. '16	🍷🍷 3
Sicilia Dalila Ris. '17	🍷🍷 4
Sicilia Grillo '18	🍷🍷 3
Sicilia Grillo Tinchitè '18	🍷🍷 3
Sicilia Inzolia '18	🍷🍷 3
Barone d'Albius '15	🍷🍷 5
Sicilia Dalila Riserva '16	🍷🍷 4
Sicilia Grillo '17	🍷🍷 3
Sicilia Hedonis Ris. '15	🍷🍷 4
Sicilia Inzolia '17	🍷🍷 3
Sicilia Nero d'Avola '16	🍷🍷 5

★Feudo Maccari

s.da prov.le Pachino-Noto km 13,500
96017 Noto [SR]
Tel. +39 0931596894
www.feudomaccari.it

CELLAR SALES
PRE-BOOKED VISITS
ANNUAL PRODUCTION 280,000 bottles
HECTARES UNDER VINE 60.00
VITICULTURE METHOD Certified Organic
SUSTAINABLE WINERY

The Moretti family's estate is situated in
Noto and Pachina, in that part of eastern
Sicily that's always been considered choice
territory for Nero d'Avola. Here Sicily's
crown prince grape exhibits varietal
characteristics that are completely different
with respect to the western part of the
island, almost certainly due to a
combination of mineral-rich, calcareous
terrain, its proximity to the sea (just a
couple of kilometers) and the presence of
head-trained vines. Despite the fact that
temperatures during summer can be quite
elevated, their vines go into water stress,
even if it's a part of Sicily that sees little
rainfall. Once again the 2017 version of
their Nero d'Avola Saia proves that it's
probably their best yet, taking home Tre
Bicchieri by virtue of its pervasive and
multifaceted aromas, focused notes of
cherries, spices, medicinal herbs and
iodine. On the palate it's alluring yet firm
and fresh.

● Sicilia Nero d'Avola Saia '17	🍷🍷🍷 4*
○ Family and Friends '18	🍷🍷 5
⊙ Rosè di Nerè '18	🍷🍷 3
○ Sicilia Grillo Olli '18	🍷🍷 3
● Sicilia Nero d'Avola Nerè '17	🍷 3
● Saia '14	🍷🍷🍷 4*
● Saia '13	🍷🍷🍷 4*
● Saia '12	🍷🍷🍷 4*
● Saia '11	🍷🍷🍷 4*
● Saia '10	🍷🍷🍷 4*
● Sicilia Nero d'Avola Saia '16	🍷🍷🍷 4*
● Sicilia Saia '15	🍷🍷🍷 4*
● Sicilia Maharis '15	🍷🍷 5

Feudo Montoni

C.DA MONTONI VECCHI
92022 CAMMARATA [AG]
TEL. +39 091513106
www.feudomontoni.it

CELLAR SALES
PRE-BOOKED VISITS
ANNUAL PRODUCTION 215,000 bottles
HECTARES UNDER VINE 30.00
VITICULTURE METHOD Certified Organic
SUSTAINABLE WINERY

Feudo Montoni's baglio is situated in the
heart of Sicily, in the territory of the historic
Villanova princedom. It was built 550 years
by the noble and Aragon Abatellis family.
The estates viticultural roots go back to
then, an uninterrupted tradition all the way
up to 1800, when Rosario Sireci purchased
the property and began the delicate work of
selection the plants. That work was carried
on by his son Elio and grandson Fabio, its
current owner. Fabio also began producing
his own wines, using grapes from
organically cultivated head-trained vines.
The Nero d'Avola Vrucara once again
demonstrates its unmistakable character.
The 2015's mature and complex aromatic
profile proves elegant, austere and
charming, sensations that follow through
on a nobly textured palate. The Grillo Vigna
della TImpa '18 opts for lovely, fruity notes
of apple and grapefruit, with a pleasantly
fresh palate. The delicate and highly
persistent Catarratto Vigna del Masso '18,
another notable selection, is more mature
and complex.

○ Sicilia Catarratto V. del Masso '18	♟♟ 4
○ Sicilia Grillo V. della Timpa '18	♟♟ 3
○ Sicilia Inzolia dei Fornelli '18	♟♟ 3
● Sicilia Nero d'Avola Vrucara '15	♟♟ 5
☉ Sicilia Nerello Mascalese Rose di Adele '18	♟ 4
● Sicilia Nero d'Avola V. Lagnusa '17	♟ 4
● Sicilia Perricone V. del Core '17	♟ 4
○ Sicilia Catarratto V. del Masso '17	♟♟ 4
○ Sicilia Grillo V. della Timpa '17	♟♟ 3
○ Sicilia Inzolia dei Fornelli '17	♟♟ 3
☉ Sicilia Nerello Mascalese Rose di Adele '17	♟♟ 4

★Firriato

VIA VIA TRAPANI, 4
91027 PACECO [TP]
TEL. +39 0923882755
www.firriato.it

CELLAR SALES
PRE-BOOKED VISITS
ANNUAL PRODUCTION 4,500,000 bottles
HECTARES UNDER VINE 380.00
VITICULTURE METHOD Certified Organic
SUSTAINABLE WINERY

The winery managed by Salvatore and
Vinzia Di Gaetano, along with their daught
Irene and her husband, has passed an
important milestone. Thanks to a continue
commitment on behalf of the environment
Firriato was the first Italian winery to have
eradicated their carbon footprint, a feat
made possible by reducing emissions,
reforestation and the use of renewable
energy sources. Their wines express three
distinct Sicilian terroirs: the hills of Trapani
the sea of Favignano (a small but prized
selection) and the heroic viticulture that
characterizes Etna, in Cavanera. Another
Etna proved at the top of its game, this tim
it's their Bianco Ripa di Scorciavacca '17.
On the nose it's highly elegant and focuse
revealing extremely pleasant fruit and
length. Two white blends of native cultivars
also landed in our finals. The Favinia La
Muciara '17 is rich in aromas of aromatic
herbs, sensations fused with extraordinaril
delicate mineral hints. Their Quater Vitis '1
features lovely nuances of lavender and a
lively freshness.

○ Etna Bianco Cavanera Ripa di Scorciavacca '17	♟♟♟ 6
○ Favinia La Muciara '17	♟♟ 6
○ Quater Vitis Bianco '18	♟♟ 4
● Altavilla della Corte Syrah '16	♟♟ 3
● Camelot '14	♟♟ 5
○ Etna Bianco Le Sabbie dell'Etna '18	♟♟ 3
● Etna Rosso Cavanera Rovo delle Coturnie '15	♟♟ 6
○ Jasmin Zibibbo '18	♟♟ 3
○ Sicilia Bianco Santagostino Baglio Sorià '18	♟♟ 4
● Etna Rosso Cavanera Rovo delle Coturnie '14	♟♟♟ 6
○ Favinia La Muciara '14	♟♟♟ 5
● Quater Vitis Rosso '14	♟♟♟ 4

◗ndo Antico

◗. Rilievo
◗ Fiorame, 54a
◗00 Trapani
◗ +39 0923864339
◗w.fondoantico.it

◗LLAR SALES
◗E-BOOKED VISITS
◗NUAL PRODUCTION 350,000 bottles
◗CTARES UNDER VINE 80.00

◗ce the early 20th century, the Polizzotti
◗nily have cultivated grapes in the district
◗ Portelli, in Trapani. What was once just a
◗w hectares has grown to 80, all in a
◗gle, contiguous estate that stretches
◗m sea level all the way up to 350 meters
◗vation. Near sea level, the terrain is
◗aracterized by marl and clay, but as it
◗ves up to to higher elevations, it
◗comes increasingly marked by stony,
◗careous earth. As usual, all the wines
◗sented to our regional selections proved
◗ecise and pleasant. Their Baccadoro '16,
◗rillo and Zibibbo passito, just fell short
◗Tre Bicchieri. On the nose it offers up
◗mas of orange blossom, lavender and
◗hee, while on the palate it nicely
◗ances acidity, fruit and sweetness. Their
◗gant Grillo Parlante '18 also performed
◗ll, with its deep, multifaceted aromas of
◗ples and pears, sweet almond and
◗dlars. On the palate it develops well
◗nks to acidity and a punctual
◗ow-through of fruit.

◗accadoro '16	♟♟ 3*
◗ello Mio Zibibbo '18	♟♟ 3
◗emorie '16	♟♟ 4
◗icilia Grillo Parlante '18	♟♟ 3
◗icilia Nero d'Avola Nenè '17	♟♟ 2*
◗icilia Syrah '17	♟♟ 2*
◗prile '18	♟ 2
◗ Coro '18	♟ 3
◗umière '18	♟ 1*
◗er Te Perricone '18	♟ 3
◗icilia Grillo Parlante '17	♟♟ 3*

Tenuta Gorghi Tondi

c.da San Nicola
91026 Mazara del Vallo [TP]
Tel. +39 0923719741
www.gorghitondi.it

CELLAR SALES
PRE-BOOKED VISITS
ACCOMMODATION AND RESTAURANT SERVICE
ANNUAL PRODUCTION 1,300,000 bottles
HECTARES UNDER VINE 130.00
VITICULTURE METHOD Certified Organic

In 2020 Annamaria and Clara Sala's Gorghi
Tondi will celebrate its twentieth birthday.
The winery is situated amidst a
kaleidoscope of colors in Mazara del Vallo,
a beautiful territory that lies between the
nearby sea and the Lake Preola-Gorghi
Tondi Reserve. Here they organically
cultivate 130 hectares of vineyards. The
grapes are fermented in their modern
baglio-cellar and give rise to a multifaceted
selection: five Crus, three sparkling wines,
their fresh and youthful Maioliche line, their
Territoriali wines and, finally, their Contrade,
a white and a red without added sulfites.
Once again the Grillo Kheirè delivers, with a
2018 that stretches its long streak of
successes. It offers up elegant fragrances,
with white-fleshed fruit at the fore, and an
elegant aromatic profile that follows
through on a pleasantly fresh palate. Their
Syrah Segreante '16 exhibits lovely aromas
of cherry accompanied by a successful
gustatory development, while the Frappato
Dumè '18 stands out for its aromatic
cleanness amidst notes of strawberry.

○ Sicilia Grillo Kheirè '18	♟♟ 4
○ Palmarés Brut	♟♟ 3
● Sicilia Frappato Dumè '18	♟♟ 3
● Sicilia Syrah Segreante '16	♟♟ 4
○ Sicilia Zibibbo Rajah '18	♟♟ 4
○ Coste a Preola Bianco '18	♟ 2
● Coste a Preola Rosso '18	♟ 2
○ Sicilia Catarratto Midor '18	♟ 2
● Sicilia Nero d'Avola Sorante '16	♟ 3
● Coste a Preola Rosso '11	♟♟ 2*
○ Sicilia Zibibbo Rajah '17	♟♟ 4

Graci

LOC. PASSOPISCIARO
C.DA FEUDO DI MEZZO
95012 CASTIGLIONE DI SICILIA [CT]
TEL. +39 3487016773
www.graci.eu

CELLAR SALES
PRE-BOOKED VISITS
ANNUAL PRODUCTION 65,000 bottles
HECTARES UNDER VINE 18.00
VITICULTURE METHOD Certified Organic

Alberto Graci's cellar can be found in a carefully renovated, historic palmento just a stone's throw from the main vineyard: 15.5 hectares of Nerello Mascalese and 2.5 of Carricante and Catarratto. Then there's an 80-year-old vineyard in Feudo di Mezzo (a more recent acquisition), and finally, their crown jewel, 1.5 hectares of centuries-old, ungrafted head-trained vines in Barbabecchi, where the terraced plots are cultivated at 1000-1100 meters. Their approach is as minimally-invasive and ecological as possible, thus guaranteeing the full expression of their precious grapes. A spectacular Etna Rosso Arcuria '17 earned Tre Bicchieri. Its complex, multi-layered bouquet follows through on a palate marked by elegantly mineral fruit, with a flesh of exceptional consistence and length. The fresh and sapid Etna Bianco '18 features lovely notes of citrus and Mediterranean scrub on a smoky background. Their Bianco Arcuria '17 is more austere and evolved, while the fruit-forward Rosato '18 proves highly pleasant.

● Etna Rosso Arcuria '17	▼▼▼ 6
○ Etna Bianco '18	▼▼ 3
○ Etna Bianco Arcuria '17	▼▼ 6
⊙ Etna Rosato '18	▼▼ 3
● Etna Rosso '17	▼▼ 3
● Etna Rosso Feudo di Mezzo '17	▼▼ 6
○ Etna Bianco Arcuria '11	♈♈♈ 5
○ Etna Bianco Quota 600 '10	♈♈♈ 5
● Etna Rosso '16	♈♈♈ 3*
● Etna Rosso Arcuria '13	♈♈♈ 6
● Etna Rosso Arcuria '12	♈♈♈ 6
○ Etna Bianco '17	♈♈ 3*
● Etna Rosso Feudo di Mezzo '15	♈♈ 6

Hauner

LOC. SANTA MARIA
VIA G.GRILLO, 61
98123 MESSINA
TEL. +39 0906413029
www.hauner.it

CELLAR SALES
PRE-BOOKED VISITS
ANNUAL PRODUCTION 80,000 bottles
HECTARES UNDER VINE 18.00

In addition to his art, the architect, design and world-famous painter Carlo Hauner i known for his wines, Malvasia in particula It was during the 1960s when Carlo, whi on vacation in Salina, that he came to kn and appreciate that noble wine, sensing potential. Being the visionary artist that h was, he got it in his head that he would produce Malvasia delle Lipari, thus savin from extinction. It was immediately a success. Just think that Carlo Hauner's Malvasia delle Lipari 1985 was one of or 32 Tre Bicchieri awarded in the first editi of this guide, way back in 1988. Their Malvasia delle Lipari Passito Riserva Carl Hauner '16 just fell short of Tre Bicchieri. On the nose it offers up generous and pervasive aromas in which oven-baked figs, fresh aromatic herbs, pineapple and fruits in syrup emerge along with candied orange and Parma violet. Rich and highly sophisticated, it has nice acidity to suppo a great encore of fruit, coming through fresh and juicy. Too bad that it closes dee but too sweet.

○ Malvasia delle Lipari Passito Carlo Hauner Ris. '16	▼▼
⊙ Hierà Rosato '18	▼▼
● Hierà Rosso '17	▼▼
○ Iancura '18	▼▼
○ Malvasia delle Lipari Naturale '17	▼▼
○ Malvasia delle Lipari Passito '17	▼▼
● Rosso Antonello '15	▼
○ Salina Bianco Carlo Hauner '17	▼
○ Malvasia delle Lipari Naturale '85	♈♈♈
○ Malvasia delle Lipari Ris. '11	♈♈♈
○ Malvasia delle Lipari Ris. '10	♈♈♈
○ Malvasia delle Lipari Passito Carlo Hauner Ris. '15	♈♈

antine Mothia

Giovanni Falcone, 22
025 Marsala [TP]
. +39 0923737295
ww.cantinemothia.it

CLLAR SALES
RE-BOOKED VISITS
NNUAL PRODUCTION 100,000 bottles
ECTARES UNDER VINE 25.00

antine Mothia is owned by the Bonomos,
family that's dealt in wine for more than
0 years. Their main facility goes back to
e late 1990s, when they purchased a
aglio built in the early 20th century for the
apes cultivated on the island of Mozia
d Stagnone. At their barrel loft, a real
mily treasure, their Marsala and Stella
enicia reserve age (this last is a precious,
rillo-based Perpetuo). Their vineyards are
tuated on the coastal strip around
arsala, where the unique, wind-beaten
ndscapes undergo significant day-night
mperature swings, allowing for grapes to
ature perfectly. Their Nero d'Avola
edicato a Francesco '16 made it back into
ur finals, and just fell short of a second Tre
icchieri. It has nice, mature fruit and a
alate of elegant consistence. The Grillo
osaikon '18 is vibrant in its varietal notes
f fresh almond, rich and juicy on the
alate. The Hammon '18, a blend of Nero
Avola and Frappato, features a subtle
romatic typicity on the nose, with distinct
ea and herbaceous sensations following
rough on a fresh, pleasant palate.

Dedicato a Francesco '16	♥♥ 4
Hammon '18	♥♥ 2*
Sicilia Grillo Mosaikon '18	♥♥ 2*
Vela Latina '18	♥♥ 2*
Sicilia Nero d'avola Mosaikon '17	♥ 2
Dedicato a Francesco '15	♥♥♥ 4*
Mosaikon Grillo '17	♀♀ 2*
Mulsum Passito di Zibibbo '16	♀♀ 4
Vela Latina '17	♀♀ 2*
Vela Latina Grillo Damaschino '16	♀♀ 2*

Cantine Nicosia

via Luigi Capuana, 65
95039 Trecastagni [CT]
Tel. +39 0957806767
www.cantinenicosia.it

CELLAR SALES
PRE-BOOKED VISITS
RESTAURANT SERVICE
ANNUAL PRODUCTION 1,800,000 bottles
HECTARES UNDER VINE 240.00
VITICULTURE METHOD Certified Organic
SUSTAINABLE WINERY

Talking about history and traditions at
Nicosia is almost too easy, considering that
this lovely winery's roots go back to 1898,
the year in which they first began
operating in the sector. Today they're on
their fifth generation of family, pursuing
organic and vegan agriculture here on
Etna, a benchmark terroir for winemaking.
Nicosia is one of the area's leading
producers in terms of size and quality,
though they also avail themselves of a vast
estate in Cerasuolo di Vittoria. Their
selection stands out for its elegance,
respect for territorial models, character
and personality. Their Etna Rosso Vigneto
Monte Gorna Riserva '13 confirms its great
class, handily repeating last year's Tre
Bicchieri performance thanks to an
impeccably varietal/territorial profile that
features refined hints of wild rose, topsoil,
quinine and peach preserves. On the
palate it's enlivened by balsamic nuances
and well-integrated tannins. Their
sophisticated and intense Etna Bianco
Monte Gorno '18 is also excellent.

● Etna Rosso Vign. Monte Gorna Ris. '13	♥♥♥ 6
○ Etna Bianco Contrada Monte Gorna '18	♥♥ 6
● Cerasuolo di Vittoria Cl. Fondo Filara '17	♥♥ 4
○ Etna Bianco Vign. Monte Gorna '15	♥♥ 6
● Etna Rosso Sosta Tre Santi Collezione di Famiglia '13	♥♥ 4
● Etna Rosso Vulkà '18	♥♥ 2*
● Sicilia Frappato Fondo Filara '18	♥♥ 2*
● Sicilia Nero d'Avola Fondo Filara '18	♥♥ 2*
○ Etna Bianco Fondo Filara Contrada Monte Gorna '16	♀♀♀ 4*
● Etna Rosso Vign. Monte Gorna Ris. '12	♀♀♀ 6
● Nero d'Avola Sosta Tre Santi '10	♀♀♀ 5

Arianna Occhipinti

FRAZ. PEDALINO
S.DA PROV.LE 68 VITTORIA-PEDALINO KM 3,3
97019 VITTORIA [RG]
TEL. +39 09321865519
www.agricolaocchipinti.it

CELLAR SALES
PRE-BOOKED VISITS
ANNUAL PRODUCTION 130,000 bottles
HECTARES UNDER VINE 22.00
VITICULTURE METHOD Certified Organic
SUSTAINABLE WINERY

A deep knowledge of enology, a passion for vineyards and wine, and a 'hard-headed' determination have all allowed this young, talented woman to establish a presence on global markets for some time now. This because Arianna is also capable of going beyond modish tendencies, remaining proudly outside the debate between 'natural' and 'unnatural'. A couple things are for sure: her respect for nature and the environment is unquestionable, her wines are delicious, highly drinkable, respectful of terroir and cultivar, original, authentic and full of character. And that's not bad. The gratifying and clearly focused Nero d'Avola Siccagno '16 put in a noteworthy performance, with its lovely fruity notes of cherry and black mulberries. The rest of their range is also of notable quality and a pleasantly 'tailored' style, from their highly pleasant Frappato '17, a fresh wine marked by vitality and iodine sensations, to their juicy and elegant Cerasuolo di Vittoria Classico Grotte Alte '14 — aromas of black plums and rain-soaked earth give way to a palate characterized by plush tannins.

● Cerasuolo di Vittoria Cl. Grotte Alte '14	♟♟ 7
● Il Frappato '17	♟♟ 5
● Siccagno '16	♟♟ 6
○ SP 68 Bianco '18	♟♟ 3
● SP 68 Rosso '18	♟ 3
● Il Frappato '12	♟♟♟ 5
● Il Frappato '11	♟♟♟ 5
● SP 68 Rosso '15	♟♟♟ 3*
● Cerasuolo di Vittoria Cl. Grotte Alte '13	♀♀ 7
● Cerasuolo di Vittoria Cl. Grotte Alte '10	♀♀ 7
● Il Frappato '16	♀♀ 5
● SP 68 Rosso '17	♀♀ 3

Tenute Orestiadi

V.LE SANTA NINFA
91024 GIBELLINA [TP]
TEL. +39 092469124
www.tenuteorestiadi.it

PRE-BOOKED VISITS
ACCOMMODATION AND RESTAURANT SERVI
ANNUAL PRODUCTION 1,200,000 bottles
HECTARES UNDER VINE 120.00
VITICULTURE METHOD Certified Organic
SUSTAINABLE WINERY

High production volumes and revenue, Tenute Orestiadi represents a successful model of quality cooperative winemaking. Founded in the wake of the Belice Valley earthquake in 1968 so as to restore faith and hope to the territory, it has over the years worked felicitously with the Orestiad Foundation, one of the Mediterranean's most important cultural sponsors. Togethe they've miraculously put together a selection of modern, well-crafted wines tie to the territory. Expressions of identity, cultivar and great skill, they've also been highly appreciated by the market. Their non-vintage Pacènzia earned itself a well-deserved place in our finals. It pours magnificent, brilliant amber, the prelude to a lovely bouquet in which vibrant nuances of dates converse with orange blossom honey and apricot. On the palate it's harmonious, balanced, summery, closing long and smooth. Their fragrant and fresh Zibbio Secco '18 opts for citrusy tones an rose, while their pleasant Perricone '17 proves a lovely, elegant drink.

○ Pacènzia Zibibbo V. T.	♟♟ 4
● Sicilia Frappato '17	♟♟ 3
● Sicilia Perricone '17	♟♟ 3
○ Sicilia Zibibbo '18	♟♟ 3
● Paxmentis Syrah Passito '17	♟ 4
● Ludovico '12	♀♀ 4
● Paxmentis Syrah Passito '16	♀♀ 4
● Sicilia Frappato '16	♀♀ 3
● Sicilia Nero d'Avola '16	♀♀ 3
● Sicilia Perricone '16	♀♀ 3

★Palari

C. SANTO STEFANO BRIGA
DA BARNA
3137 MESSINA
L. +39 090630194
ww.palari.it

NNUAL PRODUCTION 50,000 bottles
ECTARES UNDER VINE 7.00

or the moment Salvatore and Giampiero
eraci don't seem to be distracted by their
ew adventure on Etna. The esteemed
inemaking pair purchased a tiny, historic
amlet on the volcano surrounded by an
d plot of ungrafted vines, as well as a
earby tract (after careful study) where they
st planted the most well-suited
ootstocks, Nerello and Carricante clones.
Ve're still waiting for the first arrivals, but
 the meantime their two prized Palari
ines, made with grapes cultivated on the
teep, sunny hills overlooking the Strait of
essina, didn't disappoint (as usual). Even
 it didn't earn Tre Bicchieri, the Faro '15
dn't disappoint. Its grapes are cultivated
n the sunny, steep hills of Messina, in
neyards looking down over the Strait. It's
om here that it draws its iodine
ensations, detectable on the nose along
ith blackberries and mulberries, spicy
uances of cinnamon and balsamic hints.
n the palate it's austere and elegant, just
 bit static.

Faro Palari '15	🍷🍷 6
Faro Palari '14	🍷🍷🍷 6
Faro Palari '12	🍷🍷🍷 6
Faro Palari '11	🍷🍷🍷 6
Faro Palari '09	🍷🍷🍷 6
Faro Palari '08	🍷🍷🍷 6
Rosso del Soprano '15	🍷🍷🍷 4*
Rosso del Soprano '11	🍷🍷🍷 4*
Rosso del Soprano '10	🍷🍷🍷 4*

Palmento Costanzo

LOC. PASSOPISCIARO
C.DA SANTO SPIRITO
95012 CASTIGLIONE DI SICILIA [CT]
TEL. +39 0942983239
www.palmentocostanzo.com

CELLAR SALES
PRE-BOOKED VISITS
RESTAURANT SERVICE
ANNUAL PRODUCTION 90,000 bottles
HECTARES UNDER VINE 20.00
VITICULTURE METHOD Certified Organic
SUSTAINABLE WINERY

The Costanzo family's estate is made up of
single, centuries-old terraced plots
situated in Santo Spirito (Passopisciaro,
Castiglione di Sicilia) at elevations ranging
from 650-800 meters. The mix of old and
modern, expressed by the presence of a
perfectly renovated palmento and a
well-equipped, modern cellar, makes a
notable impact. The property also hosts
historic pre-phylloxera vines, true
viticultural gems. Their wines are aimed at
bringing out the nuances of the single
plots and their respective cultivars. Their
Mofete '18, a great rosé, earned our
accolades and Tre Bicchieri with its
charming and complex aromas of peach,
small red berries, Mediterranean herbs
and jasmine. On the palate, intriguing
mineral sensations emerge, and the wine
proves highly persistent and elegant.
Their refined Prefillossera '16, a deep
wine full of personality, also put in an
excellent performance.

⊙ Etna Rosato Mofete '18	🍷🍷🍷 3*
● Etna Rosso Prefillossera '16	🍷🍷 8
○ Etna Bianco di Sei '18	🍷🍷 5
○ Etna Bianco Monfete '18	🍷🍷 3
● Etna Rosso Contrada Santo Spirito '16	🍷🍷 6
● Etna Rosso Nero di Sei '15	🍷🍷 5
○ Etna Bianco di Sei '17	🍷🍷🍷 5
○ Etna Bianco Mofete '17	🍷🍷 3
● Etna Rosso Mofete '15	🍷🍷 3
● Etna Rosso Mofete '14	🍷🍷 3*

Passopisciaro

LOC. PASSOPISCIARO
C.DA GUARDIOLA
95030 CASTIGLIONE DI SICILIA [CT]
TEL. +39 0578267110
www.vinifranchetti.com

CELLAR SALES
ANNUAL PRODUCTION 75,000 bottles
HECTARES UNDER VINE 26.00

Passopisciaro, a winery inspired by Andrea Franchetti's love for a unique territory, is turning 20. It's worth remembering, at this important milestone, that the winery was a driving force behind the Etna Renaissance. This constantly active terroir features a singular climate. Rich in potential, it finds its fullest expression in the 'Contrade', the historic feudal properties. It's a true palimpsest that Franchetti has been working with patience and wisdom, bringing out the unique attributes of each cru. Their vineyards are situated at elevations ranging from 550-1000 meters in 6 different Contrade. Contrada C '17 handily takes home Tre Bicchieri. On the nose it exhibits extreme finesse and depth, with mineral nuances and focused aromas of incense pushing to the fore. On the palate it delivers juicy fruit, proving smooth and persistent. Their Contrada S '17 also earned a place in our finals, thanks to lovely smoky notes, aromas of small red berries and a full gustatory development. Asian spices characterize their Contrada G '17 — the palate comes through full, with a certain austere quality.

● Contrada C '17	♥♥♥	6
● Contrada S '17	♥♥	6
● Contrada G '17	♥♥	7
● Contrada R '17	♥♥	6
● Etna Rosso Passorosso '17	♥♥	5
● Franchetti '16	♥♥	8
○ Passobianco '17	♥♥	5
● Contrada P '17	♥	7
● Contrada G '11	♥♥♥	8
● Contrada P '10	♥♥♥	7
● Contrada P '09	♥♥♥	7
● Contrada Sciaranuova '15	♥♥♥	6
● Passopisciaro '04	♥♥♥	5

Carlo Pellegrino

VIA DEL FANTE, 39
91025 MARSALA [TP]
TEL. +39 0923719911
www.carlopellegrino.it

CELLAR SALES
PRE-BOOKED VISITS
ANNUAL PRODUCTION 6,900,000 bottles
HECTARES UNDER VINE 150.00
SUSTAINABLE WINERY

Founded in 1880 by Paolo Pellegrino, a notary and passionate wine-grower, today the estate is managed by Pietro Algna and Benedetto Renda. From the beginning, theirs has been a continued path of growth, resulting in what is now an example of dedication and commitment, as well as high-quality, healthy entrepreneurship that's in-step with the times. Their main vineyards are in Trapani and the island of Pantelleria. They've chosen to focus on specific grapes and plots, in a logic that's grounded in the concept of cru, an interesting and modern approach. Their Nes '17 confirms that it's an undisputed icon of Pantelleria passito. It pours a trademark intense gold, tending towards amber. On the nose it's marked by sensual nuances that range from orange blossom honey to dates, medicinal herbs and jammy notes of mature apricot. Their delicate and fresh Gibelè '18, a highly charming and exceptionally drinkable dry Zibibbo, is redolent of mint and lavender.

○ Passito di Pantelleria Nes '17	♥♥	7
● Gazzerotta '16	♥♥	4
○ Gibelè '18	♥♥	4
Marsala Sup. Semisecco Old John Ris. '98	♥♥	5
○ Marsala Vergine Soleras Dry	♥♥	4
● Rinazzo '16	♥♥	4
○ Sicilia Grillo Il Salinaro '18	♥♥	3
○ Kelbi '18	♥	5
○ Marsala Sup. Ambra Semisecco Ris. '85	♥♥♥	4*
● Tripudium Rosso Duca di Castelmonte '13	♥♥♥	5
● Tripudium Rosso Duca di Castelmonte '09	♥♥♥	4*
○ Passito di Pantelleria Nes '16	♥♥	5
○ Passito di Pantelleria Nes '15	♥♥	7

Pietradolce

z. Solicchiata
a Rampante
012 Castiglione di Sicilia [CT]
. +39 3484037792
w.pietradolce.it

NNUAL PRODUCTION 50,000 bottles
CTARES UNDER VINE 20.00

hen, as was the case with Mario and
chele Faro, passion is rewarded with
traordinary results in such a short time,
kindles your desire to grow further. And
it was that the two brothers decided to
ild a new, beautiful, technologically
vanced cellar that integrates well with
e territory. Then, with the encouragement
their supportive parents, they purchased
enty more hectares (comprising old and
w plots) and established one of Etna's
gest properties. Three wines made it to
r finals, all of which had a chance at our
hest honors. The sumptuous, faded but
lliant ruby-colored Vigna Barbagalli '16
ok home Tre Bicchieri, proving vibrant
d extremely elegant both on the nose
d the palate. Their superb Contrada
nto Sprito '17 is also in form, exhibiting
highly elegant and complex nose, and a
ate marked by vitality, depth and
table length.

Etna Rosso V. Barbagalli '16	♈♈♈ 8
Etna Rosso Archineri '17	♈♈ 6
Etna Rosso Contrada Santo Spirito '17	♈♈ 6
Etna Bianco Archineri '18	♈♈ 6
Etna Bianco Pietradolce '18	♈♈ 4
Etna Rosato Pietradolce '18	♈♈ 3
Etna Rosso Contrada Rampante '17	♈♈ 6
Etna Rosso Pietradolce '18	♈♈ 4
Sant'Andrea Carricante '16	♈♈ 8
Etna Rosso Archineri '10	♈♈♈ 5
Etna Rosso Contrada Rampante '16	♈♈♈ 6
Etna Rosso V. Barbagalli '14	♈♈♈ 8
Etna Rosso V. Barbagalli '13	♈♈♈ 8
Etna Rosso V. Barbagalli '12	♈♈♈ 8
Etna Rosso V. Barbagalli '11	♈♈♈ 8

★★★Planeta

c.da Dispensa
92013 Menfi [AG]
Tel. +39 091327965
www.planeta.it

PRE-BOOKED VISITS
ACCOMMODATION AND RESTAURANT SERVICE
ANNUAL PRODUCTION 3,500,000 bottles
HECTARES UNDER VINE 395.00
SUSTAINABLE WINERY

Francesca, Alessio and Santi's 35-year
adventure in winemaking has been full of
emotions, discoveries and beauty. It's also
forever changed the way of doing business
in Sicily, serving as a model that's still
capable of innovating and channeling
positive energy. The 'journey' undertaken
by Planeta touches all of Sicily's top
winemaking districts, from Samba and
Menfi, where it all began, to Noto, Vittoria,
Etna and finally Trinacria, Capo Milazzo.
Every stop offers elegant, personal wines
that are deeply tied to their terroir of origin.
Casa Planeta's premium Nero d'Avola, the
Santa Cecilia '16, triumphs with the
extreme elegance of its focused, pervasive
bouquet. Tantalizing balsamic nuances
meet spices before opening to extremely
vibrant and persistent fruit. Their highly
pleasant and peachy Etna Rosso '18
also made it in our finals, as did their
Piumbago '17, a mature, deep and
linear expression of another terroir for
growing Nero d'Avola.

● Noto Nero d'Avola Santa Cecilia '16	♈♈♈ 5
● Etna Rosso '18	♈♈ 3*
● Sicilia Nero d'Avola Plumbago '17	♈♈ 3*
● Cerasuolo di Vittoria '17	♈♈ 3
○ Etna Bianco '18	♈♈ 3
○ Moscato di Noto Allemanda '18	♈♈ 2*
● Noto Controdanza '16	♈♈ 3
○ Passito di Noto '18	♈♈ 5
○ Sicilia Carricante Eruzione 1614 '17	♈♈ 4
○ Sicilia Menfi Alastro '18	♈♈ 3
○ Sicilia Menfi Cometa '18	♈♈ 5
● Sicilia Nocera '17	♈♈ 3
○ Etna Bianco '16	♈♈♈ 3*
● Menfi Syrah Maroccoli '14	♈♈♈ 4*

Poggio di Bortolone

FRAZ. ROCCAZZO
VIA BORTOLONE, 19
97010 CHIARAMONTE GULFI [RG]
TEL. +39 0932921161
www.poggiodibortolone.it

CELLAR SALES
PRE-BOOKED VISITS
ACCOMMODATION AND RESTAURANT SERVICE
ANNUAL PRODUCTION 80,000 bottles
HECTARES UNDER VINE 15.00
SUSTAINABLE WINERY

For more than two centuries, the Cosenza family have cultivate their land at the meeting of the Para Para and Mazzarronello rivers. Testifying to their historic presence is a 19th-century palmento and a water-powered, wood and stone olive press. The turning point came in the 1980s when Ignazio, father of Pierluigi (its current owner) began bottling his own wine. Their 15 hectares of vineyards, which host exclusively red grapes, are situated in the best parts of the estate, the hill ridge and stony terrain that runs along the river. Their Pigi '17, a blend of 60% Syrah and 40% Cabernet Sauvignon earned a place in our finals. On the nose it offers up charming fragrances of mulberry and pomegranate, with lovely green nuances — on the palate it proves highly pleasant and persistent. The Para '16, a Cerasuolo cru aged in mid-size casks, features a full, balsamic bouquet and fruit of elegant consistency. Clear, fruity notes of strawberries and cherry rise up off their fresh and drinkable Frappato '18.

● Sicilia Rosso Pigi '17	♟♟ 5
● Cerasuolo di Vittoria Cl. Poggio di Bortolone '17	♟♟ 3
● Cerasuolo di Vittoria Il Para Para '16	♟♟ 4
● Petiverdò '18	♟♟ 3
● Vittoria Frappato '18	♟♟ 3
● Cerasuolo di Vittoria Cl. Contessa Costanza '17	♟ 3
⊙ Sicilia Rosato Rosachiara '18	♟ 3
● Cerasuolo di Vittoria V. Para Para '05	♟♟♟ 4
● Cerasuolo di Vittoria V. Para Para '02	♟♟♟ 4*
● Addamanera '17	♟♟ 3*
⊙ Sicilia Rosato Rosachiara '17	♟♟ 3

Principi di Butera

C.DA DELIELLA
93011 BUTERA [CL]
TEL. +39 0934347726
www.feudobutera.it

CELLAR SALES
PRE-BOOKED VISITS
ANNUAL PRODUCTION 800,000 bottles
HECTARES UNDER VINE 180.00
SUSTAINABLE WINERY

The history of this 'Feudo' is bound up with that of Sicily itself, having once belonged to one of the the island's wealthiest and most powerful families, the Branciforte (declared rulers of Butera by Spain's Philip II). In 1997 the Zonin family gave the Feudo back its identity, renovating its ancient baglio and reviving its vineyards in Licata and Gela, hills of calcareous terra not far from sea. Here a beneficial combination of microclimate and soil favors the production of wines with a pronounced Mediterranean character. While waiting for their cru wines, which are being aged, we registered an excellent performance by their monovarietals. The Syrah '17 features fruity notes of cherry, pleasant vegetal hints, and a plush, juicy palate. The fresh and fruit-rich Grillo '18 vibrant and focused in its fragrances of medlar and wild flowers, while the pleasant and easy-drinking Insolia '18 offers up delicate herbaceous and fruity aromas. Their solid Cabernet Sauvignon '17 features a nice, varietal aromatic profile.

● Sicilia Cabernet Sauvignon '17	♟♟
○ Sicilia Grillo '18	♟♟
○ Sicilia Insolia '18	♟♟
● Sicilia Syrah '17	♟♟
○ Sicilia Chardonnay '18	♟
● Sicilia Nero d'Avola Amira '17	♟
● Deliella '12	♟♟♟
● Deliella '05	♟♟♟
● Deliella '02	♟♟♟
● Sicilia Deliella '13	♟♟♟
● Sicilia Nero d'Avola Deliella '16	♟♟♟
● Sicilia Syrah '15	♟♟♟

allo

Vincenzo Florio, 2
025 Marsala [TP]
. +39 0923721633
w.cantinerallo.it

ELLAR SALES
RE-BOOKED VISITS
NNUAL PRODUCTION 420,000 bottles
ECTARES UNDER VINE 110.00
TICULTURE METHOD Certified Organic

unded in 1860 by Don Diego Rallo, it
as he who, thanks to the quality of their
nes, made this esteemed winery an
ternationally recognized brand. A turning
int came in 1997, when the Vesco
mily took over the estate and
mediately began working to grow its
estige. Today young and determined
drea Vesco is at the helm. He's made
llo a cornerstone of finesse, elegance
d pleasantness, and he's done it with an
ological sensibility that's seen the
oducer successfully establish itself as a
oducer of 'natural' wine. Among a
lection that consistently performs at a
gh qualitative level, once again the
anco Maggiore emerges and takes home
e Bicchieri. The 2018 version of this
llo pours a brilliant straw yellow-gold
lor, the prelude to intense aromas of
ron peel, tropical fruit, jasmine and fresh
mond. It's a wine of great class, elegant
d juicy. Their succulent and delicate
ro d'Avola La Zisa '15 is also excellent.

Tenute Rapitalà

c.da Rapitalà
90043 Camporeale [PA]
Tel. +39 092437233
www.rapitala.it

CELLAR SALES
PRE-BOOKED VISITS
ANNUAL PRODUCTION 2,600,000 bottles
HECTARES UNDER VINE 163.00

Tenuta Rapitalà was founded in 1968.
Today it's part of Gruppo Italiano Vini and
managed by Laurent de La Gatinais, son of
founders Hugues and Gigi. With the
exception of a small, recently added parcel
on Etna, the vineyards can be found on the
hills that run from Camporeale to Alcamo,
at elevations of 300-600 meters.
Alternating layers of clay and sand, along
with day-night temperature swings,
contribute to making it the perfect terroir
for viticulture, giving rise to wine of
unmistakably Mediterranean character. In
the cellar, their wines are looked after by
expert Silvio Centonze. A blend of Cabernet
Sauvignon and Nero d'Avola landed a
place in our finals. The Hugonis '16 is
intense and balsamic on the nose, while
on the palate it proves full-bodied, with
lingering toasty notes. The Alcamo Vigna
Casalj '18, a fresh and sapid monovarietal
Catarratto, is focused and elegant in its
citrusy fragrances. Their Grillo Viviri '18 is
also very well-crafted, with a tantalizing
nuance of lavender and a streak of
pleasantly fruity flavor.

Sicilia Bianco Maggiore '18	♔♔♔ 3*
La Zisa '15	♔♔ 2*
Orange AV 01 Catarratto '18	♔♔ 4
Sicilia La Clarissa '18	♔♔ 2*
Sicilia La Cuba '17	♔♔ 3
Sicilia Rujari '17	♔♔ 4
Alcamo Beleda '17	♔♔♔ 4*
Alcamo Beleda '15	♔♔♔ 4*
Alcamo Beleda '13	♔♔♔ 2*
Bianco Maggiore '12	♔♔♔ 3*
Sicilia Bianco Maggiore '16	♔♔♔ 3*
Sicilia Bianco Maggiore '14	♔♔♔ 3*
Passito di Pantelleria '14	♔♔ 5

● Hugonis '16	♔♔ 5
○ Alcamo Cl. V. Casalj '18	♔♔ 3
○ Conte Hugues Bernard de la Gatinais	
Grand Cru '17	♔♔ 4
○ Piano Maltese Bianco '18	♔♔ 2*
○ Sicilia Grillo '18	♔♔ 2*
○ Sicilia Grillo Viviri '18	♔♔ 2*
● Sicilia Nero d'Avola Alto Nero '17	♔♔ 3
○ Alcamo Bianco '18	♔ 2
○ Bouquet '18	♔ 2
● Sicilia Syrah Sire Nero '18	♔ 2
○ Conte Hugues Bernard de la Gatinais	
Grand Cru '10	♔♔♔ 4*

Girolamo Russo

LOC. PASSOPISCIARO
VIA REGINA MARGHERITA, 78
95012 CASTIGLIONE DI SICILIA [CT]
TEL. +39 3283840247
www.girolamorusso.it

CELLAR SALES
PRE-BOOKED VISITS
ANNUAL PRODUCTION 65,000 bottles
HECTARES UNDER VINE 15.00
VITICULTURE METHOD Certified Organic

Fifteen years ago Giuseppe Russo decided to put aside his literature and piano studies so as to throw himself into viticulture. It was a legacy he inherited from his family (originally from Passopisciaro). The winery, which is in the name of his father, Girolamo, avails itself of excellent vineyards, with some plots going back more than a century. These are situated in Passopisciaro, in San Lorenzo and Feudo (Randazzo and Feudo di Mezzo). Their head-trained vines are cultivated organically, only by hand, and vinified so as to bring out the expressivity of the cru of origin. Two wines in their selection made it to our final round of tastings. The Feudo di mezzo '17 is elegant in its nuances of Mediterranean shrub, expansive, rich in pulp and very persistent. The Il Feudo '17 is intense in its fruity sensations of small red berries and peach. On the palate it exhibits a firm yet creamy texture all at once. Their fresh and sapid Rosato '18, another highly notable wine, offers up distinct aromas of grapefruit and bergamot, all on an elegant mineral background.

● Etna Rosso Feudo '17	♟♟ 6
● Etna Rosso Feudo di Mezzo '17	♟♟ 6
○ Etna Bianco Nerina '18	♟♟ 5
⊙ Etna Rosato '18	♟♟ 4
● Etna Rosso 'A Rina '17	♟♟ 4
● Etna Rosso San Lorenzo '17	♟♟ 6
● Etna Rosso 'A Rina '15	♟♟♟ 4*
● Etna Rosso 'A Rina '12	♟♟♟ 3*
● Etna Rosso Feudo '11	♟♟♟ 5
● Etna Rosso Feudo '10	♟♟♟ 5
● Etna Rosso Feudo di Mezzo '16	♟♟♟ 6
● Etna Rosso San Lorenzo '14	♟♟♟ 6
● Etna Rosso San Lorenzo '13	♟♟♟ 5

Emanuele Scammacca del Murgo

VIA ZAFFERANA, 13
95010 SANTA VENERINA [CT]
TEL. +39 095950520
www.murgo.it

CELLAR SALES
PRE-BOOKED VISITS
ACCOMMODATION AND RESTAURANT SERVIC
ANNUAL PRODUCTION 230,000 bottles
HECTARES UNDER VINE 35.00

It was 1981 when Emanuele Scammacca del Murgo decided to transform Tenuta San Michele into a modern agricultural business for producing wines and, especially, a Metodo Classico sparkler that bears the family's coat of arms on its label. As a result they built a modern, underground facility next to the historic cellar (built in 1860), so as to use gravity to make exclusively Metodo Classico with Nerello Mascalese. For some years now, the Tenuta has also featured a lovely reception area and a restaurant that offers good, local food. This year their Etna Rosso Tenuta San Michele '16, a wine redolent of peach and medicinal herbs, stands out for its noble, authentically territorial elegance. On the palate it's austere, crisp and silky, with transparent, crisp fruit enriched by a close-woven tannic weave. Their Etna Rosso '17, another wine of rare pleasantness, proves generous and complex on the nose, while on the palate it exhibits freshness, vitality and richness of fruit.

● Etna Rosso Tenuta San Michele '16	♟♟ 5*
● Etna Rosso '17	♟♟ 2*
● Etna Rosso Tenuta San Michele '17	♟♟ 2*
○ Murgo Brut '17	♟♟ 3
⊙ Murgo Brut Rosé '16	♟♟ 4
○ Murgo Extra Brut '11	♟♟ 5
○ Etna Bianco '18	♟ 2
○ Moscato Passito Tenuta San Michele '16	♟ 4
○ Etna Bianco '13	♟♟ 2*
○ Etna Bianco Tenuta San Michele '16	♟♟ 5
○ Etna Bianco Tenuta San Michele '15	♟♟ 5
⊙ Murgo Extra Brut Rosé '14	♟♟ 4

Cantine Settesoli

s. 115
2013 Menfi [AG]
Tel. +39 092577111
www.cantinesettesoli.it

CELLAR SALES
PRE-BOOKED VISITS
ANNUAL PRODUCTION 20,000,000 bottles
HECTARES UNDER VINE 6000.00

A glimpse at this formidable winery's numbers reveals its economic and social importance for the territory. But in some ways it doesn't give you the full picture. There's a sense of belonging that also matters for its 2,000 grower members, as well as pride in being part of a forward-thinking project grounded in values and responsibility. It was the wise Diego Planeta who brought their wines to international markets. Today, after having the chance to see the quality of their products, with respect to territory and cultivar, first hand, Giuseppe Bursi is carrying on in his work. Their Nero d'Avola Cartagho '17 impresses right off the bat with its dark, ruby color and purplish highlights. It earns itself Tre Bicchieri by virtue of its intense, elegant aromas, which call up black mulberries, wild blackberries, cloves and quinine. On the palate it's magnificent, juicy and persistent, bolstered by extremely classy, well-rounded tannins. The focused, mature and spicy Cavadiserpe '18, a Merlot and Alicante Bouschet blend, is also noteworthy.

● Sicilia Mandrarossa Cartagho '17	♟♟♟ 3*
● Mandrarossa Cavadiserpe '18	♟♟ 3
● Mandrarossa Timperosse '18	♟♟ 3
● Sicilia Bertolino Soprano '17	♟♟ 3
● Sicilia Mandrarossa Bonera '18	♟♟ 3
○ Sicilia Mandrarossa Urra di Mare '18	♟ 2
● Sicilia Nero d'Avola Terre del Sommacco '16	♟ 2
● Cartagho Mandrarossa '09	♟♟♟ 3*
● Mandrarossa Cavadiserpe '16	♟♟♟ 3*
● Sicilia Mandrarossa Cartagho '16	♟♟♟ 3*
● Sicilia Mandrarossa Cartagho '14	♟♟♟ 3*
● Timperosse Mandrarossa '14	♟♟♟ 3*

★★Tasca d'Almerita

C.DA REGALEALI
90129 Sclafani Bagni [PA]
Tel. +39 0916459711
www.tascadalmerita.it

CELLAR SALES
PRE-BOOKED VISITS
ACCOMMODATION AND RESTAURANT SERVICE
ANNUAL PRODUCTION 2,500,000 bottles
HECTARES UNDER VINE 388.00
SUSTAINABLE WINERY

With the recent technological upgrades made to their cellar, and the purchase of 8 more plots in Passopisciaro, this historic Sicilian winery, led by Alberto Tasca, has completed a long journey that began some 15 years with the purchase of their first estate on Etna. Now Tasca's wines can finally boast not only Etna DOC designation, but also (and this is important) a territorial mention of the 'contrade' where their grapes are cultivated: Rampante, Sciara Nuova and Pianodario, all on the northern side of the volcano. Their Nozze d'Oro '17, which earned Tre Bicchieri, is a great classic of Sicilian winemaking. In fact, it goes back to 1984, the first harvest of what was at the time a new and highly innovative blend of Inzolia and Sauvignon. On the nose it's complex and elegant amidst mineral hints, tropical fruit, citrus and lavender. On the palate it's rock solid, harmoniously bringing together fruit, sapidity and acidic tension.

○ Sicilia Bianco Nozze d'Oro '17	♟♟♟ 4*
● Etna Rosso Tascante Contrada Sciaranuova '16	♟♟ 5
● Contea di Sclafani Rosso del Conte '15	♟♟ 6
○ Diamante d'Almerita '18	♟♟ 5
○ Didyme '18	♟♟ 3
○ Etna Bianco Tascante Buonora '18	♟♟ 3
● Etna Rosso Tascante Contrada Rampante '16	♟♟ 5
● Etna Rosso Tascante Ghiaia Nera '17	♟♟ 5
○ Malvasia Tenuta Capofaro '18	♟♟ 5
● Sicilia Cabernet Sauvignon V. San Francesco '16	♟♟ 5
○ Sicilia Catarratto Antisa '18	♟♟ 3
○ Sicilia Chardonnay V. San Francesco '17	♟♟ 5
● Sicilia Rosso Cygnus '16	♟♟ 4

Tenuta di Fessina

VIA NAZIONALE 120, 22
95012 CASTIGLIONE DI SICILIA [CT]
TEL. +39 3357220021
www.tenutadifessina.com

CELLAR SALES
PRE-BOOKED VISITS
ANNUAL PRODUCTION 70,000 bottles
HECTARES UNDER VINE 13.00
SUSTAINABLE WINERY

Silvia Maestrelli was the first female 'outsider' to arrive on Etna. Her love for this difficult but fascinating terroir goes back to 2006, then, after a tiring year of negotiations and acquisitions, the estate was born. It's headquartered in Contrada Rovittello, Castiglione, in a valley between two 'wakes', that is, two ancient lava trails that here and elsewhere have shaped this unique territory. A carefully renovated, 17th-century palmento serves as the cellar, as well as an enchanting reception area. Their other vineyards are situated in Milo, S. Maria di Licodia and Noto. Another recognition for A' Puddara '17, a highly elegant wine in its mineral notes, it thrills with fruit of enchanting concentration. Their Musmeci Bianco '15 also earned a place in our finals, proving vibrant in its fruit, with a palate of commendable harmony. Just a few steps behind it is their other white, Erse '18, with its lovely, crisp, fruity flavors of peach and citrus. The subtle and deep Laeneo '17 is a Nerello Cappuccio with a long, smoky finish.

○ Etna Bianco A' Puddara '17	♆♆♆ 5
○ Etna Bianco Il Musmeci '15	♆♆ 5
○ Etna Bianco Erse '18	♆♆ 4
● Etna Rosso Erse '17	♆♆ 4
● Sicilia Nerello Cappuccio Laeneo '17	♆♆ 4
○ Etna Bianco A' Puddara '16	♆♆♆ 5
○ Etna Bianco A' Puddara '13	♆♆♆ 5
○ Etna Bianco A' Puddara '12	♆♆♆ 5
○ Etna Bianco A' Puddara '11	♆♆♆ 5
○ Etna Bianco A' Puddara '10	♆♆♆ 5
○ Etna Bianco A' Puddara '09	♆♆♆ 5

Terrazze dell'Etna

C.DA BOCCA D'ORZO
95036 RANDAZZO [CT]
TEL. +39 0916236343
www.terrazzedelletna.it

CELLAR SALES
PRE-BOOKED VISITS
ANNUAL PRODUCTION 120,000 bottles
HECTARES UNDER VINE 38.00

Nino Bevilacqua's dream came true in January of 2008. While searching for the perfect place to start his venture on Etna, he came across Bocca d'Orzo, Randazzo, where the vineyards grow in ancient, terraced plots carved out of the lava at elevations of 600-950 meters above sea level. Great care has been shown to reviving the existing vineyards, as well as replanting. Nerello Mascalese is accompanied by Chardonnay and Pinot Noir, which serve as the basis for elegant, Metodo Classico sparkling wines. As of 2014, Nino has been accompanied by his daughter in managing the estate. Their Cuvée 50 mesi '14 found itself in our finals, displaying aromatic precision and cleanness amidst notes of grapefruit, pineapple and lavender. On the palate it's creamy yet invigorating and vital all at once. In the end leaves an impression for the persistence of its fruit and sapidity. Lovely citrus notes, aromas of raspberries and mineral nuances rise up off their Rosé Brut 50 mesi '14, a wine with elegant, lingering sparkle. The pleasantly drinkable Etna Rosso Carusu '17 exhibits nice nose-palate symmetry.

○ Cuvée Brut 50 Mesi '14	♆♆ 5
○ Ciuri '18	♆♆ 3
○ Cuvée Brut '16	♆♆ 5
● Etna Rosso Carusu '17	♆♆ 4
⊙ Rosé Brut '16	♆♆ 5
⊙ Rosé Brut 50 Mesi '14	♆♆ 5
● Etna Rosso Cirneco '08	♆♆♆ 5
○ Ciuri '17	♆ 3
● Etna Rosso Cirneco '12	♆ 6
⊙ Rosé Brut 50 Mesi '12	♆ 5

Girolamo Tola & C.

VIA GIACOMO MATTEOTTI, 2
90047 PARTINICO [PA]
TEL. +39 0918781591
www.vinitola.it

ANNUAL PRODUCTION 180,000 bottles
HECTARES UNDER VINE 55.00

Girolamo Tola & C. is a family-run winery
that's still anchored to the territory's
agricultural traditions. Over time they've
developed an organic approach to
cultivation, which is accompanied by a
modern cellar with spacious tasting areas.
Young Francesco Tola's entrance as a
member of staff, fresh off his economy and
management studies, has brought new life
to a producer that's highly valued on
international markets for its distinct,
artisanal style. Their main vineyards are
situated in Bosco Falconeria, Giambascio
and Grassuri Daioroldi, at more than 400
meters elevation. Year after year this
prestigious winery demonstrates admirable
growth in quality. Standing out among their
selection is the Nero d'Avola '18, a wine
with intense notes of black mulberries and
rhubarb, their mature and territorial/varietal
Black Label '17, and their juicy, plush
Syrah '18. Among their whites we
appreciated their Catarratto Insolia '18, with
its lovely sensations of fruit and aromatic
herbs, and the citrusy, appley notes of the
delicate Grillo '18.

○ Catarratto '18	♀♀	2*
○ Catarratto Insolia '18	♀♀	2*
○ Chardonnay Insolia '17	♀♀	2*
● Nero d'Avola Black Label '17	♀♀	3
● Nero D'Avola Syrah '16	♀♀	3
● Pinot Nero '18	♀♀	2*
○ Rosé '18	♀♀	3
○ Sicilia Grillo '18	♀♀	2*
● Sicilia Nero d'Avola '18	♀♀	3
Syrah '18	♀♀	2*
● Nero d'Avola Black Label '15	♀♀	3
● Sicilia Nero d'Avola '17	♀♀	3

Tornatore

FRAZ. VERZELLA
VIA PIETRAMARINA, 8A
95012 CASTIGLIONE DI SICILIA [CT]
TEL. +39 3339195793
www.tornatorewine.com

CELLAR SALES
PRE-BOOKED VISITS
ANNUAL PRODUCTION 120,000 bottles
HECTARES UNDER VINE 45.00

Francesco Tornatore has always been
proud of his deep agricultural roots. Back in
the 19th century his grandfather cultivated
vines in Contrada Trimarchisa, while his
father, Giuseppe, in the mid-20th century,
enlarged the estate, cultivating fruit
orchards and olives. And so, when Etna
was suddenly thrust back in the limelight,
Francesco was well prepared. With the
instincts of a great entrepreneur, he'd
already enlarged their vineyards tenfold,
half Nerello and half Carricante, and then
built a second cellar so as to vinify whites
and reds separately. Their noteworthy Etna
Rosso '17, a wine that's also excellent
value for the money, handily took home Tre
Bicchieri. It's highly elegant in its aromas of
red fruit berries and peach tobacco, all
fused with mineral nuances reminiscent of
red salt, and ultimately giving way to
balsam herbs and orange blossom. On the
palate it's fresh and silky, led by a
close-knit tannic weave that delicately
enfolds sweet, juicy fruit.

● Etna Rosso '17	♀♀♀	4*
○ Etna Bianco '18	♀♀	4
● Etna Rosso Pietrarizzo '17	♀♀	5
○ Etna Bianco Pietrarizzo '18	♀♀	5
● Etna Rosso Ris. '14	♀♀	4
● Etna Rosso Trimarchisa '17	♀♀	6
● Etna Rosso '15	♀♀♀	4*
● Etna Rosso Trimarchisa '16	♀♀♀	6
○ Etna Bianco '17	♀♀	4
○ Etna Bianco '16	♀♀	4
● Etna Rosso '16	♀♀	4

Valle dell'Acate

C.DA BIDINI
97011 ACATE [RG]
TEL. +39 0932874166
www.valledellacate.it

CELLAR SALES
PRE-BOOKED VISITS
ACCOMMODATION
ANNUAL PRODUCTION 350,000 bottles
HECTARES UNDER VINE 80.00
VITICULTURE METHOD Certified Organic
SUSTAINABLE WINERY

The winery managed by Gaetana Jacono represents one of Cerasuolo di Vittoria's crown jewels. It's situated in the historic Feudo Bidini, on the hills that develop along the path of the Dirillo river. Within its 100 hectares of vineyards, 7 different types of soil have been identified, making for a surprising amount of biodiversity in a relatively small area. It's a fact reflected in the organoleptic qualities of their grapes, most notably the red-orange terrain on the Bidine Soprano plateau, which hosts their Ire da Ire cru. While waiting for this last, we once again appreciated the nice performance put in by their Frappato '18, an authentic classic. Gorgeous, fresh fruit of black cherry accompany green sensations. In the mouth it's invigorating, deliciously drinkable with a long finish. The Cerasuolo Classico '17 offers up clear, floral notes of cherry and bay leaf, aromas that reemerge on the palate amidst highly pleasant fruit. We also enjoyed the close-focused, fresh and sapid Bellifolli Insola '18.

● Cerasuolo di Vittoria Cl. '17	♟♟ 4
○ Sicilia Grillo Zagra '18	♟♟ 3
○ Sicilia Insolia Bellifolli '18	♟♟ 3
● Sicilia Nero d'Avola Tanè '15	♟♟ 6
● Sicilia Nero d'Avola Bellifolli '18	♟♟ 3
● Vittoria Frappato Il Frappato '18	♟♟ 3
○ Sicilia Chardonnay Bidis '16	♟ 4
● Sicilia Nero d'Avola Il Moro '17	♟ 4
● Cerasuolo di Vittoria Cl. '14	♟♟ 4
● Cerasuolo di Vittoria Cl. Iri da Iri '13	♟♟ 5
● Vittoria Frappato Il Frappato '15	♟♟ 3*

Zisola

C.DA ZISOLA
96017 NOTO [SR]
TEL. +39 057773571
www.mazzei.it

CELLAR SALES
PRE-BOOKED VISITS
ANNUAL PRODUCTION 120,000 bottles
HECTARES UNDER VINE 21.00
SUSTAINABLE WINERY

When he first saw Zisola, Filippo Mazzei didn't think that the largely abandoned, sun-beaten terrain, or its three run-down baglios and sheds could become what it is today: a lush garden, elegant country residence and wine cellar overlooking Noto. Filippo planted 20 hectares of the 50-hectare estate with vineyards, all head-trained, while leaving the preexisting citrus orchards, almond trees and olive groves all intact. This year Zisola's premium offerings weren't submitted for tasting. Filippo Mazzei decided they weren't ready and to let them age a while longer in the cellar. The Zisola '17 performed well, nonetheless. It's a Nero d'Avola redolent of red berries, blood orange and sea salt. On the palate it proves highly pleasant thanks to freshness, fruity flavors and nice balance

● Noto Nero d'Avola Zisola '17	♟♟ 4
○ Sicilia Azisa '18	♟♟ 3
● Achilles '16	♟♟ 6
● Achilles '15	♟♟ 4
● Effe Emme '15	♟♟ 6
● Effe Emme '12	♟♟ 7
● Noto Doppiozeta '15	♟♟ 6
● Noto Doppiozeta '14	♟♟ 6
● Noto Zisola '14	♟♟ 4
○ Sicilia Azisa '17	♟♟ 3

Al Cantàra

VIA ANTONIO CECCHI, 23
95100 CATANIA
TEL. +39 095222644
www.al-cantara.it

CELLAR SALES
PRE-BOOKED VISITS
ANNUAL PRODUCTION 50,000 bottles
HECTARES UNDER VINE 14.00

● Etna Rosso O' Scuru O' Scuru '16	♥♥ 5
○ Etna Bianco Occhi di Ciumi '18	♥♥ 4
○ Etna Rosato Amuri di Fimmina e Amuri di Matri '18	♥♥ 4

Alberelli di Giodo

LOC. SOLICCHIATA
CASTIGLIONE DI SICILIA [CT]
carlo.ferrini27@gmail.com

ANNUAL PRODUCTION 6,000 bottles
HECTARES UNDER VINE 1.50
SUSTAINABLE WINERY

● Sicilia Alberelli di Giodo '17	♥♥ 7

Augustali

FRAZ. BOSCO FALCONERIA
S.DA ST.LE 113 ALCAMO-PARTINICO KM 318,700
90047 PARTINICO [PA]
TEL. +39 3396132334
www.augustali.com

ANNUAL PRODUCTION 25,000 bottles
HECTARES UNDER VINE 15.50

○ Catarratto '18	♥♥ 3
● Contrasto del Rosso Nero d'Avola '14	♥♥ 5
● Syrah '18	♥♥ 3
○ Sicilia Grillo '18	♥ 2

Alagna

VIA SALEMI, 752
91025 MARSALA [TP]
TEL. +39 0923981022
www.alagnavini.com

CELLAR SALES
PRE-BOOKED VISITS
ACCOMMODATION
ANNUAL PRODUCTION 500,000 bottles
HECTARES UNDER VINE 50.00

○ Marsala Sup. Secco S.O.M.	♥♥ 3
○ Marsala Vergine Baglio Baiata	♥♥ 5
○ Marsala Fine	♥ 2
○ Marsala Sup. Dolce Garibaldi	♥ 3

Ampelon

C.DA CALDERARA
95036 RANDAZZO [CT]
TEL. +39 3459196437
www.viniampelon.it

CELLAR SALES
ANNUAL PRODUCTION 50,000 bottles
HECTARES UNDER VINE 7.00
SUSTAINABLE WINERY

○ Etna Bianco Ampelon '18	♥♥ 3
● Etna Rosso Le Caldere '15	♥ 5
● Etna Rosso Passo alle Sciare '16	♥ 4

Avide - Vigneti & Cantine

C.DA MASTRELLA, 346
97013 COMISO [RG]
TEL. +39 0932967456
www.avide.it

CELLAR SALES
PRE-BOOKED VISITS
ANNUAL PRODUCTION 250,000 bottles
HECTARES UNDER VINE 68.00

● 1607 Frappato '18	♥♥ 3
● Cerasuolo di Vittoria Cl. Etichetta Nera '16	♥♥ 3
○ Maria Stella '18	♥ 4
○ Riflessi di Sole '17	♥ 4

Birgi

C.DA BIRGI NIVALORO
91025 MARSALA [TP]
TEL. +39 0923966736
www.cantinebirgi.it

CELLAR SALES
PRE-BOOKED VISITS
ACCOMMODATION AND RESTAURANT SERVICE
ANNUAL PRODUCTION 1,300,000 bottles
HECTARES UNDER VINE 3000.00
VITICULTURE METHOD Certified Organic

● Sicilia Frappato Trisole '18	▼▼ 2*
○ Sicilia Grillo Trisole '18	▼▼ 2*
○ Sicilia Merlot Kinisia '17	▼▼ 3
○ Sicilia Zibibbo Trisole '18	▼ 2

Biscaris

VIA MARESCIALLO GIUDICE, 52
97011 ACATE [RG]
TEL. +39 0932990762
www.biscaris.it

CELLAR SALES
ANNUAL PRODUCTION 50,000 bottles
HECTARES UNDER VINE 10.00
VITICULTURE METHOD Certified Biodynamic

● Cerasuolo di Vittoria Principuzzu '18	▼▼ 3
● Frappato '18	▼▼ 2

Calcagno

FRAZ. PASSOPISCIARO
VIA REGINA MARGHERITA, 153
95012 CASTIGLIONE DI SICILIA [CT]
TEL. +39 3387772780
www.vinicalcagno.it

CELLAR SALES
PRE-BOOKED VISITS
ANNUAL PRODUCTION 13,000 bottles
HECTARES UNDER VINE 3.00

○ Etna Bianco Ginestra '18	▼▼ 5
◉ Etna Rosato Romice delle Sciare '18	▼ 5

Cambria

C.DA SAN FILIPPO - VIA VILLA ARANGIA
98054 FURNARI [ME]
TEL. +39 0941840214
www.cambriavini.com

PRE-BOOKED VISITS
ANNUAL PRODUCTION 100,000 bottles
HECTARES UNDER VINE 25.00

● Kio Nocera Passito '16	▼▼ 5
● Sicilia Rosso del Levriero '15	▼▼ 5
● Sicilia Syrah '16	▼▼ 4
● Masseria '17	▼ 3

CVA Canicattì

C.DA AQUILATA
92024 CANICATTÌ [AG]
TEL. +39 0922829371
www.cvacanicatti.it

CELLAR SALES
PRE-BOOKED VISITS
ANNUAL PRODUCTION 900,000 bottles
HECTARES UNDER VINE 1,000.00

● Aquilae Nero d'Avola '17	▼▼ 2*
○ Sicilia Grillo Aquilae Bio '18	▼▼ 2*
○ Sicilia Grillo Fileno '18	▼▼ 2*
● Scialo '16	▼ 3

Caruso & Minini

VIA SALEMI, 3
91025 MARSALA [TP]
TEL. +39 0923982356
www.carusoeminini.it

CELLAR SALES
PRE-BOOKED VISITS
ANNUAL PRODUCTION 1,200,000 bottles
HECTARES UNDER VINE 120.00
VITICULTURE METHOD Certified Organic
SUSTAINABLE WINERY

● Naturalmente Bio Perricone '17	▼▼ 3
● Sicilia Nero d'Avola Cutaja Ris. '16	▼▼ 3
● Terre di Giumara Frappato Nerello Mascalese '18	▼▼ 2*

Casa di Grazia

C.DA PROV.LE 51 KM 3
93012 GELA [CL]
TEL. +39 0933919465
www.casadigrazia.com

CELLAR SALES
ANNUAL PRODUCTION 50,000 bottles
HECTARES UNDER VINE 30.00

○ Cerasuolo di Vittoria Victorya '17	♥♥ 4
● Sicilia Cabernet Sauvignon Vi Veri '16	♥♥ 3
○ Sicilia Grillo Zahara '18	♥ 4
○ Sicilia Moscato Adorè '18	♥ 4

Case Alte

LOC. MACELLAROTTO
VIA PISCIOTTA, 27
90043 CAMPOREALE [PA]
TEL. +39 3297130750
www.casealte.it

ACCOMMODATION
ANNUAL PRODUCTION 17,000 bottles
HECTARES UNDER VINE 8.00
VITICULTURE METHOD Certified Organic

● Sicilia Nero d'Avola 16 Filari '17	♥♥ 4
○ Sicilia Catarratto 12 Filari '18	♥♥ 3
○ Sicilia Grillo 4 Filari '18	♥♥ 3
● Sicilia Syrah di Macellarotto '17	♥ 5

Colomba Bianca

VIA GIOVANNI FALCONE, 72
91026 MAZARA DEL VALLO [TP]
TEL. +39 0923942747
www.cantinecolombabianca.it

ANNUAL PRODUCTION 2,000,000 bottles
HECTARES UNDER VINE 7,700.00

○ Sicilia Grillo Resilience '18	♥♥ 2*
● Sicilia Perricone Resilience '18	♥♥ 2*
○ Sicilia Zibibbo Vitese '18	♥♥ 2*
○ Sicilia Grillo Vitese '18	♥ 2

Cantine Colosi

LOC. PACE DEL MELA
FRAZ. GIAMMORO
98042 MESSINA
TEL. +39 0909385549
www.cantinecolosi.it

PRE-BOOKED VISITS
ANNUAL PRODUCTION 100,000 bottles
HECTARES UNDER VINE 10.00

● Colosi Rosso '17	♥♥ 2*
⊙ Salina Rosato '18	♥♥ 2*
○ Sicilia Grillo '18	♥♥ 2*
○ Secca del Capo Malvasia '18	♥ 3

Cortese

C.DA SABUCI, S.P. 3 KM 11
97019 VITTORIA [RG]
TEL. +39 09321846555
www.agricolacortese.com

CELLAR SALES
PRE-BOOKED VISITS
ANNUAL PRODUCTION 70,000 bottles
HECTARES UNDER VINE 12.00
VITICULTURE METHOD Certified Organic
SUSTAINABLE WINERY

○ Nostru Carricante '18	♥♥ 3
○ Nostru Catarratto '18	♥♥ 3
○ Vanedda '17	♥♥ 4
● Cerasuolo di Vittoria Cl. Sabuci '17	♥ 4

Cossentino

VIA PRINCIPE UMBERTO, 241
90047 PARTINICO [PA]
TEL. +39 0918782569
www.cossentino.it

CELLAR SALES
PRE-BOOKED VISITS
ANNUAL PRODUCTION 70,000 bottles
HECTARES UNDER VINE 17.00
VITICULTURE METHOD Certified Organic

○ Muscarò	♥♥ 5
○ Sicilia Catarratto Gadì '18	♥♥ 2*
● Sicilia Nero d'Avola '17	♥♥ 4
○ Sicilia Grillo '18	♥ 2

I Custodi delle Vigne dell'Etna

LOC. SOLICCHIATA
C.DA MOGANAZZI
95012 CASTIGLIONE DI SICILIA [CT]
TEL. +39 3931898430
www.icustodi.it

CELLAR SALES
PRE-BOOKED VISITS
ANNUAL PRODUCTION 40,000 bottles
HECTARES UNDER VINE 12.50
VITICULTURE METHOD Certified Organic
SUSTAINABLE WINERY

○ Etna Bianco Ante '17	🍷🍷 5
⊙ Etna Rosato Alnus '18	🍷🍷 4
● Etna Rosso Aetneus '12	🍷 5
● Etna Rosso Pistus '17	🍷 4

Di Giovanna

C.DA SAN GIACOMO
92017 SAMBUCA DI SICILIA [AG]
TEL. +39 3206583904
www.di-giovanna.com

CELLAR SALES
PRE-BOOKED VISITS
ANNUAL PRODUCTION 250,000 bottles
HECTARES UNDER VINE 56.00
VITICULTURE METHOD Certified Organic

○ Sicilia Grillo Vurria... '18	🍷🍷 3
⊙ Vurria Nerello Mascalese Rosato '18	🍷🍷 3
● Helios Rosso '16	🍷 5
● Sicilia Nero d'Avola Vurria... '17	🍷 3

Gaspare Di Prima

VIA G. GUASTO, 27
92017 SAMBUCA DI SICILIA [AG]
TEL. +39 0925941201
www.diprimavini.it

CELLAR SALES
PRE-BOOKED VISITS
ANNUAL PRODUCTION 50,000 bottles
HECTARES UNDER VINE 38.00
VITICULTURE METHOD Certified Organic

● Janub Rosso '17	🍷🍷 3
○ Janub Moscato Bianco '18	🍷 2
○ Sicilia Bianco Pepita '18	🍷 2
● Syrah '17	🍷 2

Feudo Disisa

FRAZ. GRISÌ
C.DA DISISA
90046 MONREALE [PA]
TEL. +39 0919127109
www.vinidisisa.it

CELLAR SALES
PRE-BOOKED VISITS
ANNUAL PRODUCTION 150,000 bottles
HECTARES UNDER VINE 150.00
VITICULTURE METHOD Certified Organic

○ Chara '18	🍷🍷 3
⊙ Sicilia Grecu di Livanti '18	🍷🍷 3
○ Sicilia Grillo '18	🍷🍷 3
● Sicilia Syrah Adhara '17	🍷 3

Fazio Wines

FRAZ. FULGATORE
VIA CAPITANO RIZZO, 39
91010 ERICE [TP]
TEL. +39 0923811700
www.faziowines.it

CELLAR SALES
ANNUAL PRODUCTION 750,000 bottles
HECTARES UNDER VINE 100.00
SUSTAINABLE WINERY

○ Erice Müller Thurgau '18	🍷🍷 3
● Erice Syrah Luce d' Oriente '17	🍷🍷 3
● Cartesiano Rosso '17	🍷 5
● Erice Torre dei Venti '18	🍷 3

Ferreri

C.DA SALINELLA
91029 SANTA NINFA [TP]
TEL. +39 092461871
www.ferrerivini.it

CELLAR SALES
PRE-BOOKED VISITS
ANNUAL PRODUCTION 70,000 bottles
HECTARES UNDER VINE 30.00

● Brasi '14	🍷🍷 5
● Pignatello Rosè '18	🍷🍷 2*
○ Zibibbo '18	🍷🍷 3

...eudo di Santa Tresa

..DA SANTA TERESA
...019 VITTORIA [RG]
...L. +39 09321846555
...w.santatresa.it

CELLAR SALES
...RE-BOOKED VISITS
...NNUAL PRODUCTION 250,000 bottles
...ECTARES UNDER VINE 39.00
...TICULTURE METHOD Certified Organic

Cerasuolo di Vittoria '17		🍷🍷 3
Frappato '18		🍷🍷 3
Nivuro '16		🍷 4
Rina Lanca '18		🍷 3

...oderà

...A GIARDINELLO, 154
...025 MARSALA [TP]
... +39 0923712776
...nafodera@libero.it

CELLAR SALES
...RE-BOOKED VISITS
...NNUAL PRODUCTION 10,000 bottles
...ECTARES UNDER VINE 2.45

Grillo '18		🍷🍷 5
Grillo Tardivo '16		🍷🍷 5
Grillo '14		🍷 5

...a Gelsomina

...C. PRESA
... SAN GIOVANNI BOSCO, 26
...EDIMONTE ETNEO [CT]
... +39 092469124
...jelsomina.it

Etna Bianco '18		🍷🍷 3
Etna Rosso '15		🍷🍷 3
Etna M. Cl. Blanc de Noir Brut		🍷 5
Moscato Passito '14		🍷 5

Feudo Ramaddini

FRAZ. MARZAMEMI
C.DA LETTIERA
96018 PACHINO [SR]
TEL. +39 09311847100
www.feudoramaddini.com

CELLAR SALES
PRE-BOOKED VISITS
RESTAURANT SERVICE
ANNUAL PRODUCTION 90,000 bottles
HECTARES UNDER VINE 20.00

○ Perla Marina Brut		🍷🍷 4
○ Quattroventi '18		🍷🍷 4
○ Sicilia Grillo Nassa '18		🍷🍷 2*
● Sicilia Nero d'Avola Note Nere '17		🍷 3

Cantina Antonio Gabriele

VIA DEI SESI 20, 9
91017 PANTELLERIA [TP]
TEL. +39 3286878105
www.cantinagabrieleantonio.com

CELLAR SALES
PRE-BOOKED VISITS
ACCOMMODATION
ANNUAL PRODUCTION 5,000 bottles
HECTARES UNDER VINE 3.00
SUSTAINABLE WINERY

○ Pantelleria Bianco Don Klocks '17		🍷🍷 5
○ Passito di Pantelleria Bagghiu '17		🍷🍷 7

Gulfi

C.DA PATRIA
97012 CHIARAMONTE GULFI [RG]
TEL. +39 0932921654
www.gulfi.it

CELLAR SALES
PRE-BOOKED VISITS
ACCOMMODATION AND RESTAURANT SERVICE
ANNUAL PRODUCTION 280,000 bottles
HECTARES UNDER VINE 70.00
VITICULTURE METHOD Certified Organic

● Nero d'Avola Nerobaronj '16		🍷🍷 5
● Nerobufaleffj '16		🍷🍷 6
● Nerosanlorè '16		🍷🍷 6
● Neromàccarj '16		🍷 6

Gurrieri

V.LE DELLA RESISTENZA, 81
97013 COMISO [RG]
TEL. +39 0932968106
www.gurrieri.net

ANNUAL PRODUCTION 30,000 bottles
HECTARES UNDER VINE 6.30
VITICULTURE METHOD Certified Organic

⊙ Sicilia Rosato Donna Grazia '18	🍷🍷	3
● Vittoria Frappato '18	🍷🍷	3
● Cerasuolo di Vittoria Cl. Don Vicè '15	🍷	3
● Syrah '17	🍷	3

Hibiscus

C.DA TRAMONTANA
90010 USTICA [PA]
TEL. +39 0918449543
www.agriturismohibiscus.com

CELLAR SALES
PRE-BOOKED VISITS
ACCOMMODATION
ANNUAL PRODUCTION 10,000 bottles
HECTARES UNDER VINE 3.00

⊙ L'Isola Rosato '18	🍷🍷
⊙ Onde di Sole '18	🍷🍷
⊙ Zhabib Passito '18	🍷🍷
⊙ Grotta dell'Oro '18	🍷

Tenuta Enza La Fauci

C.DA MEZZANA-SPARTÀ
98163 MESSINA
TEL. +39 3476854318
www.tenutaenzalafauci.com

CELLAR SALES
ACCOMMODATION
ANNUAL PRODUCTION 14,000 bottles
HECTARES UNDER VINE 5.00

○ Case Bianche '18	🍷🍷	4
● Faro Obli '14	🍷🍷	5
● Maestro '16	🍷🍷	4
● Vignadorata '16	🍷	4

Lisciandrello

VIA CASE NUOVE, 31
90048 SAN GIUSEPPE JATO [PA]
TEL. +39 3395917618
www.aziendalisciandrello.com

ANNUAL PRODUCTION 30,000 bottles
HECTARES UNDER VINE 6.00

● Nerello Mascalese '16	🍷🍷
○ Sicilia Carricante '17	🍷🍷
○ Sicilia Chardonnay '17	🍷🍷
● Perricone '17	🍷

Maggiovini

VIA FILIPPO BONETTI, 35
97019 VITTORIA [RG]
TEL. +39 0932984771
www.maggiovini.com

CELLAR SALES
PRE-BOOKED VISITS
ACCOMMODATION
ANNUAL PRODUCTION 270,000 bottles
HECTARES UNDER VINE 45.00
VITICULTURE METHOD Certified Organic
SUSTAINABLE WINERY

● Cerasuolo di Vittoria V. di Pettineo '16	🍷🍷	2*
● Vittoria Frappato V. di Pettineo '18	🍷🍷	3
● Sicilia Nero d'Avola V. di Pettineo '17	🍷	3
○ Vittoria Grillo V. di Pettineo '17	🍷	3

Marino Vini

VIA ALFIERI, 51
90043 CAMPOREALE [PA]
TEL. +39 3886537642
www.marinovini.com

CELLAR SALES
PRE-BOOKED VISITS
RESTAURANT SERVICE
ANNUAL PRODUCTION 50,000 bottles
HECTARES UNDER VINE 15.00
VITICULTURE METHOD Certified Organic
SUSTAINABLE WINERY

● Sicilia Nero d'Avola Grintoso '17	🍷🍷
● Sontuoso '17	🍷🍷
○ Sublime '18	🍷🍷
○ Sicilia Grillo Armonioso '18	🍷

Masseria del Feudo

C.DA GROTTAROSSA
93100 CALTANISSETTA
TEL. +39 0934830885
www.masseriadelfeudo.it

CELLAR SALES
PRE-BOOKED VISITS
ACCOMMODATION
ANNUAL PRODUCTION 100,000 bottles
HECTARES UNDER VINE 12.00
VITICULTURE METHOD Certified Organic

○ Sicilia Grillo '18	♟♟ 2*
○ Sicilia Grillo Haermosa '18	♟♟ 3
● Sicilia Rosso delle Rose '17	♟ 3
● Sicilia Syrah '18	♟ 2

Cantina Modica di San Giovanni

C.DA BUFALEFI
96017 NOTO [SR]
TEL. +39 09311805181
www.vinidinoto.it

CELLAR SALES
PRE-BOOKED VISITS
RESTAURANT SERVICE
ANNUAL PRODUCTION 80,000 bottles
HECTARES UNDER VINE 40.00
SUSTAINABLE WINERY

● Dolcenero	♟♟ 5
○ Moscato di Noto Dolcenoto '18	♟♟ 3
○ SATIS faction	♟♟ 4
● Eloro Nero d'Avola Filinona '13	♟ 2

Monteleone

C.DA SCIAMBRO
95012 CASTIGLIONE DI SICILIA [CT]
TEL. +39 334 5772 422
giulia@monteleonetna.com

ANNUAL PRODUCTION 6,000 bottles
HECTARES UNDER VINE 3.00

● Etna Rosso Cuba '17	♟♟ 6
● Etna Bianco Anthemis '18	♟♟ 6
● Etna Rosso '17	♟♟ 6

Morgante

C.DA RACALMARE
92020 GROTTE [AG]
TEL. +39 0922945579
www.morgantevini.it

CELLAR SALES
ANNUAL PRODUCTION 310,000 bottles
HECTARES UNDER VINE 52.00

○ Bianco di Morgante '18	♟♟ 2*
● Sicilia Nero d'Avola '17	♟♟ 2*
● Sicilia Nero d'Avola Don Antonio '16	♟♟ 6
◎ Sicilia Rosè di Morgante '18	♟ 2

Tenuta Morreale Agnello

C.DA FAUMA
92100 AGRIGENTO
TEL. +39 347 6028029
www.tenutamorrealeagnello.it

ANNUAL PRODUCTION 50,000 bottles
HECTARES UNDER VINE 60.00
VITICULTURE METHOD Certified Organic
SUSTAINABLE WINERY

● Terre di Fauma Nero d'Avola '16	♟♟ 2*
● Sephora Syrah '18	♟ 3
● Sicilia Nero d'Avola Sephora '18	♟ 3
● Terre di Fauma Insolia '18	♟ 2

Ottoventi

C.DA TORREBIANCA - FICO
91019 VALDERICE [TP]
TEL. +39 0923 1877151
www.cantinaottoventi.wine

CELLAR SALES
PRE-BOOKED VISITS
ACCOMMODATION
ANNUAL PRODUCTION 300,000 bottles
HECTARES UNDER VINE 35.00

● Sicilia Nero d'Avola Wow '18	♟♟ 3
○ Sicilia Zibibbo '18	♟♟ 4
● Nerello Mascalese '14	♟ 4
○ Zibibbo Passito Scibà '17	♟ 5

Tenute dei Paladini

VIA PALESTRO, 23
91025 MARSALA [TP]
TEL. +39 3463513366
www.tenutedeipaladini.com

ANNUAL PRODUCTION 40,000 bottles
HECTARES UNDER VINE 45.00

○ Palatium '18	♔♔ 3
○ Sicilia Grillo Palatium '18	♔♔ 3
○ Emà '18	♔ 3

Tenuta Palmeri

C.DA BOCHINI - FIUMARELLA
96012 AVOLA [SR]
TEL. +39 3345646866
www.tenutapalmeri.it

CELLAR SALES
PRE-BOOKED VISITS
ACCOMMODATION
ANNUAL PRODUCTION 28,000 bottles
HECTARES UNDER VINE 11.00
VITICULTURE METHOD Certified Organic

○ Palmeri Bianco '17	♔♔ 6
● Palmeri Celeste '17	♔♔ 5
● Palmeri Verde '17	♔♔ 6
● Palmeri Blu '17	♔ 5

Papa Maria

LOC. SOLICCHIATA
C.DA MARCHESA
95012 CASTIGLIONE DI SICILIA [CT]
TEL. +39 3929708495

HECTARES UNDER VINE 3.00
SUSTAINABLE WINERY

○ Etna Bianco Cuore di Marchesa '18	♔♔ 5
● Etna Rosso Cuore di Marchesa '17	♔♔ 5

Pietracava

VIA LUIGI STURZO, 16
93011 BUTERA [CL]
TEL. +39 3392410117
www.pietracavawines.it

ANNUAL PRODUCTION 30,000 bottles
HECTARES UNDER VINE 15.00

● Manaar '16	♔♔ 4
○ Pioggia di Luce Grillo '18	♔♔ 3
○ Sicilia Sauvignon Blanc '18	♔ 3

Pupillo

C.DA LA TARGIA
96100 SIRACUSA
TEL. +39 0931494029
www.pupillowines.com

CELLAR SALES
PRE-BOOKED VISITS
ANNUAL PRODUCTION 35,000 bottles
HECTARES UNDER VINE 20.00

○ Moscato di Siracusa Pollio '18	♔♔ 5
○ Moscato di Siracusa Solacium '17	♔♔ 4
○ Siracusa Cyane '18	♔♔ 3
● Sicilia Rosso Baronessa di Canseria '17	♔ 3

Riofavara

LOC. ISPICA
S.DA PROV.LE 49 ISPICA-PACHINO
97014 ISPICA [RG]
TEL. +39 0932705130
www.riofavara.it

CELLAR SALES
PRE-BOOKED VISITS
ACCOMMODATION
ANNUAL PRODUCTION 70,000 bottles
HECTARES UNDER VINE 20.00
VITICULTURE METHOD Certified Organic
SUSTAINABLE WINERY

● Eloro Nero d'Avola Sciavè '16	♔♔ 5
○ Marzaiolo '18	♔♔ 3
○ Moscato di Noto Mizzica '18	♔♔ 3
● Eloro Nero d'Avola Spaccaforno '16	♔ 4

enuta Sallier de La Tour

z. Camporeale
a Pernice
046 Monreale [PA]
. +39 0916459711
ww.tascadalmerita.it

RE-BOOKED VISITS
NNUAL PRODUCTION 395,000 bottles
ECTARES UNDER VINE 44.00
USTAINABLE WINERY

Madamarosè '18	🍷🍷 1*
Syrah '17	🍷🍷 2*

La Solidea

c.da Kaddiuggia
91017 Pantelleria [TP]
Tel. +39 0923913016
www.solideavini.it

CELLAR SALES
PRE-BOOKED VISITS
ANNUAL PRODUCTION 12,000 bottles
HECTARES UNDER VINE 5.00

○ Ilios '18	🍷🍷 3
○ Passito di Pantelleria '18	🍷🍷 5

alvatore Tamburello

Borsellino, 22
020 Poggioreale [TP]
. +39 3398605865
ww.salvatoretamburello.it

NNUAL PRODUCTION 10,000 bottles
ECTARES UNDER VINE 12.00
TICULTURE METHOD Certified Organic

306 Nero d'Avola Biologico '15	🍷🍷 3
Sicilia Grillo 204 '18	🍷🍷 2*
Sicilia Grillo 204 N '18	🍷🍷 3

Terre di Giurfo

via Palestro, 536
97019 Vittoria [RG]
Tel. +39 0957221551
www.terredigiurfo.it

CELLAR SALES
PRE-BOOKED VISITS
ANNUAL PRODUCTION 100,000 bottles
HECTARES UNDER VINE 40.00

● Etna Rosso Nardalici '16	🍷🍷 4
⊙ Pian della Signora '18	🍷🍷 3
● Sicilia Nero d'Avola Kudyah '17	🍷🍷 3
○ Sicilia Grillo Suliccènti '18	🍷 3

erre di Shemir

. Guarrato
100 Trapani
. +39 0923865323
ww.terredishemir.com

ELLAR SALES
RE-BOOKED VISITS
NNUAL PRODUCTION 40,000 bottles
ECTARES UNDER VINE 9.00

Erede Grillo '17	🍷🍷 3
Fedire Grillo Zibibbo '17	🍷🍷 3
Paradiso di Lara '17	🍷🍷 3

Terresikane

c.da Turchiotto
93011 Butera [CL]
Tel. +39 3273872386
www.terresikane.com

CELLAR SALES
PRE-BOOKED VISITS
ACCOMMODATION
ANNUAL PRODUCTION 90,000 bottles
HECTARES UNDER VINE 21.00

● Sicilia Nero d'Avola Il Sikano '18	🍷🍷 3
● Turchiotto '18	🍷🍷 4
○ Sicilia Chardonnay Frasciano '18	🍷 3
○ Sicilia Grillo Turchiotto '18	🍷 3

Todaro

C.DA FEOTTO
90048 SAN GIUSEPPE JATO [PA]
TEL. +39 3461056393
www.todarowinery.com

PRE-BOOKED VISITS
ANNUAL PRODUCTION 80,000 bottles
HECTARES UNDER VINE 25.00
VITICULTURE METHOD Certified Organic

● 4 Elementa '16	♟♟ 4
● Sicilia Nero d'Avola Shadir '17	♟♟ 3
○ Sicilia Grillo Nihal '18	♟ 2
● Virgo '17	♟ 4

Torre Mora

LOC. ROVITTELLO
95012 CASTIGLIONE DI SICILIA [CT]
TEL. +39 057754011
www.tenutepiccini.it

PRE-BOOKED VISITS
ANNUAL PRODUCTION 76,000 bottles
HECTARES UNDER VINE 13.00
VITICULTURE METHOD Certified Organic

● Etna Rosso Cauru '18	♟♟ 3*
○ Etna Bianco Scalunera '18	♟♟ 5
⊙ Etna Rosato Scalunera '18	♟♟ 5
● Etna Rosso Scalunera '16	♟ 5

Virgona

VIA BANDIERA, 2
98050 MALFA [ME]
TEL. +39 0909844430
www.malvasiadellelipari.it

PRE-BOOKED VISITS
ANNUAL PRODUCTION 30,000 bottles
HECTARES UNDER VINE 5.00

○ Malvasia delle Lipari Passito '17	♟♟ 6
○ Salina Bianco '18	♟♟ 3
○ Ruffiano	♟ 3

Torre Favara

VIA CANNADA, 1
93013 MAZZARINO [CL]
TEL. +39 0934384064
www.torrefavara.com

CELLAR SALES
PRE-BOOKED VISITS
ACCOMMODATION
ANNUAL PRODUCTION 50,600 bottles
HECTARES UNDER VINE 10.00

○ Trenta Filari '18	♟♟
○ Conca del Principe '18	♟
○ Pian del Grigno '18	♟
● Torre Favara '15	♟

Vinisola

C.DA KAZZEN, 11
91017 PANTELLERIA [TP]
TEL. +39 0923912078
http://www.vinisola.it

ANNUAL PRODUCTION 40,000 bottles
HECTARES UNDER VINE 5.60

○ Pantelleria Bianco A'mmare '11	♟♟
○ Pantelleria Bianco Zefiro '17	♟♟
○ Passito di Pantelleria Arbaria '16	♟♟
○ A Mano Libera '18	♟

Vivera

LOC. MARTINELLA
S.DA PROV.LE 59 IV
95015 LINGUAGLOSSA [CT]
TEL. +39 095643837
www.vivera.it

CELLAR SALES
PRE-BOOKED VISITS
ANNUAL PRODUCTION 120,000 bottles
HECTARES UNDER VINE 30.00
VITICULTURE METHOD Certified Organic

○ A'Mami '16	♟♟
⊙ Etna Rosato di Martinella '18	♟♟
● Terra dei Sogni '16	♟♟

SARDINIA

previous editions of Italian Wines we underlined Sardinia's continued growth, independent of the year. Some could argue that if we were to do so again this year it wouldn't be credible. But we can't do otherwise. From the more than 600 wines tasted the snapshot is one of a region in great form. The quality detected is increasingly high, but not just in terms of sensorial profile (balance, harmony, complexity). The whites and reds proposed are increasingly authentic, territorial, respectful of the grapes and their terroirs of origin. The work in the vineyard is the most arduous kind (and as a result, it has to be more respectful of the environment, making for greater sustainability). In the cellar they follow practices increasingly aimed at bringing out the best of what nature produces. The time has passed when strict regimes would be allowed in the name of international tastes, resulting in wines unable to fully express the region's territories. Yes, territories. Because Sardinia's beauty doesn't only lie in its native grapes, it lies in its diverse soils and microclimates, from its sandy, seaside terrain to its granitic hills and the steep slopes reaching almost 00 meters elevation. Despite the fact that we're seeing this diversity expressed with greater frequency, it's in no way required by DOC protocols, which are stuck in the past. There are too few territorial DOCs, and regional regimes for their most representative cultivars (Cannonau, Moscato and Vermentino) don't account for terroir. Now would be the time for the entire sector to take control and afford Sardinia the place it deserves. Concerning the wines awarded this year, there's more good news. 14 Tre Bicchieri is a record and testifies to the results achieved. Three of them are absolutely outstanding: the Nuracada is the young winery Audarya di Serdinia's Bovale. The Terresicci is a Barbera Sarda made by Cantina Dolianova. The Pro Vois is Nepente's lovely version of Oliena Riserva. Three different terroirs, three cultivars, one superb outcome.

★★Argiolas

via Roma, 28/30
09040 Serdiana [CA]
Tel. +39 070740606
www.argiolas.it

CELLAR SALES
PRE-BOOKED VISITS
ANNUAL PRODUCTION 2,200,000 bottles
HECTARES UNDER VINE 230.00

Argiolas is a great wine family, now on its third generation. The winery has contributed to making Sardinian wine known throughout the world and done it by investing in high quality projects as far back as the 1980s. Decades later, the producer continues to invest and experiment, drawing on an exceptional estate and the region's traditional cultivars. Their extremely wide range comprises both daily-drinking wine (that are excellent value for money) and premium selections characterized by personality and good ageing prospects. This year this Serdiana winery put in a performance for the ages. We begin with their Turriga, a wine that's in a class of its own for its ability to combine the complexity of a great Mediterranean red with textbook finesse and elegance. Notes of Mediterranean shrub give way to a fresh, sapid palate with mature and pliant tannins, and a very long finish. Tre Bicchieri. Their Senes (a Cannonau reserve) and the Anglialis (a Nasco passito) are also both top-notch. The rest of their selection delivers as well, starting with their Korem (Bovale), Is Solinas (Carignano) and Cerdena.

● Turriga '15	♟♟♟ 8
● Cannonau di Sardegna Senes Ris. '16	♟♟ 5
○ Vermentino di Sardegna Cerdeña '16	♟♟ 7
○ Cannonau di Sardegna Passito Antonio Argiolas '16	♟♟ 5
● Carignano del Sulcis Is Solinas Ris. '16	♟♟ 4
● Korem Bovale '16	♟♟ 5
○ Nasco di Cagliari Iselis '18	♟♟ 3
○ Vermentino di Sardegna Is Argiolas '18	♟♟ 3
● Monica di Sardegna Sup. Is Selis '17	♟ 3
● Cannonau di Sardegna Senes Ris. '13	♟♟♟ 5
● Cannonau di Sardegna Senes Ris. '12	♟♟♟ 5
● Turriga '11	♟♟♟ 8
● Turriga '14	♟♟ 8

Audarya

loc. Sa Perdera
s.s. 466 KM 10,100
09040 Serdiana [CA]
Tel. +39 070 740437
www.audarya.it

CELLAR SALES
PRE-BOOKED VISITS
ANNUAL PRODUCTION 280,000 bottles
HECTARES UNDER VINE 40.00

Audarya is just over five years old, but in a short time it's managed to make a name for itself among southern Sardinia's quality wine growers. The winery is managed by the young and passionate team of Nicoletta and Salvatore Pala, descendants of a great family of producers. Only traditional grape varieties are cultivated, starting with Vermentino and Cannonau (these are accompanied by Bovale, Malvasia, Nasco and Nuragus). The gentle hills that host their vineyards are characterized by calcareous-clay soil, while in the cellar, they only work to bring out the best of what their grapes have to offer. If you work hard, the results won't be slow in coming. The proof is in their undeniably strong overall selection, and in particular a red of incredible complexity and finesse. The Nuracada is a Bovale with close-focused notes of blackberries and pepper, as well as a touch of tobacco. The palate is caressing, fresh and highly sapid, with a charming pace of development. And so it is that the winery takes home Tre Bicchieri for the first time. Their deep and iodine Vermentino Camminera '17 is also top-notch.

● Nuracada Bovale '17	♟♟♟
○ Bisai '18	♟♟
○ Vermentino di Sardegna Camminera '18	♟♟
● Cannonau di Sardegna '18	♟♟
○ Malvasia di Cagliari Estissa '18	♟♟
○ Vermentino di Sardegna '18	♟♟
● Monica di Sardegna '18	♟
○ Nuragus di Cagliari '18	♟
● Cannonau di Sardegna '17	♟♟
● Nuracada Bovale '16	♟♟
○ Nuragus di Cagliari '17	♟♟
○ Vermentino di Sardegna Camminera '17	♟♟

antina di Calasetta

ROMA, 134
011 CALASETTA [SU]
. +39 078188413
ww.cantinadicalasetta.it

CELLAR SALES
RE-BOOKED VISITS
NNUAL PRODUCTION 100,000 bottles
ECTARES UNDER VINE 300.00

he small cooperative producer of Calasetta
back in the main section of our guide. It
eems that they've managed to regain the
uality that we were used to seeing in the
ast. They're located in Calasetta, on the
and of Sant'Antioco. Here the vines are old
d ungrafted, and grow in sand. Carignano
el Sulcis is the primary grape cultivated
ere, and their selection centers on the
ariety. It gives rise to a number of different
ines divided according to the prestige of
e vineyard and the manner in which the
ine was produced. A Vermentino di
ardegna and a passito Moscato round out
e selection. Their Piedefranco '17, a red
rmented exclusively in steel, put in a
p-notch performance, proving aromatically
uthentic and highly pleasant on the palate.
s the name says, it's a Carignano made
ith grapes ungrafted on American vines.
n the nose it offers up aromas of
ackberries and Mediterranean shrub, with
acidic freshness that's well-integrated
ith a sapid rhythm. The other three
arignanos also delivered, starting with their
ose-woven and austere Riserva Aina '16.

Carignano del Sulcis Piede Franco '17	♥♥ 2*
Carignano del Sulcis Àina Ris. '16	♥♥ 4
Carignano del Sulcis Maccòri '18	♥♥ 2*
Carignano del Sulcis Rosato Rassetto '18	♥♥ 2*
Carignano del Sulcis Tupei '17	♥♥ 2*
Moscato di Cagliari In Fundu '17	♥♥ 3
Vermentino di Sardegna Cala di Seta '18	♥♥ 2*
Carignano del Sulcis Tupei '10	♀♀♀ 2*
Carignano del Sulcis Piede Franco '15	♀♀ 2*
Carignano del Sulcis Tupei '16	♀♀ 2*
Carignano del Sulcis Tupei '15	♀♀ 2*

★Capichera

S.S. ARZACHENA-SANT'ANTONIO, KM 4
07021 ARZACHENA [SS]
TEL. +39 078980612
www.capichera.it

CELLAR SALES
PRE-BOOKED VISITS
ANNUAL PRODUCTION 250,000 bottles
HECTARES UNDER VINE 50.00
SUSTAINABLE WINERY

Capichera is a true benchmark in Sardinia. It
was in the past, when they blazed a trail with
their focus on quality and successful
marketing initiatives, and they are today,
thanks to the exceptional quality of their
wines and an ageability (starting with their
whites) that surprises every time you uncork
a bottle with a few years under its belt. Their
vineyards, which are situated along the
gentle hills of Arzachena, are gorgeous and
tended to down to the last detail. These enjoy
both the sea breeze and the granite-based
soil here — you can taste the result for
yourselves. It's difficult to choose the best
wine in their selection, especially when it
comes to their whites. In the end it was those
that had a little more time to age that
prevailed. Their Vendemmia Tardiva '16 put
in a first-rate performance. It's extraordinary
for its notes of fresh almonds, aromatic
herbs, quinces and summer flowers. In the
mouth it's broad and pervasive, never heavy
or cloying. Sapidity and freshness make for a
lean palate and deep finish. Tre Bicchieri.
Both the Santigaini '15 and Capichera '17
also performed well.

○ Capichera V. T. '16	♥♥♥ 8
○ Capichera '17	♥♥ 6
○ Santigaini '15	♥♥ 8
● Albori di Lampata '15	♥♥ 8
● Assajé '16	♥♥ 6
⊙ També V.T '18	♥♥ 4
○ Vermentino di Gallura Vigna'Ngena '18	♥♥ 5
● Lianti '15	♥ 4
○ Vermentino di Sardegna Lintori '18	♥ 4
○ Capichera '14	♀♀♀ 6
○ Capichera '13	♀♀♀ 6
○ Capichera '12	♀♀♀ 6
○ Capichera '11	♀♀♀ 6
○ Vermentino di Gallura Vigna'Ngena '17	♀♀♀ 5

Giovanni Maria Cherchi

LOC. SA PALA E SA CHESSA
07049 USINI [SS]
TEL. +39 079380273
www.vinicolacherchi.it

CELLAR SALES
PRE-BOOKED VISITS
ANNUAL PRODUCTION 170,000 bottles
HECTARES UNDER VINE 30.00

Cherchi is a historic producer situated in the northwestern part of the region. It's renowned and appreciated for having brought prestige to Usini, thanks to its focus on two cultivars, Vermentino and Cagnulari. This success had by the latter, which is only cultivated here, is undoubtedly thanks to the work of Giovannia Maria Cherchi, the winery's founder. But even Vermentino has thrived here, with elevation, soil and the sea breeze conferring elegance, finesse and longevity to their wines. As proof that even before the cultivar it's important to identify the right territory, this year we particularly appreciated their Cannonau di Sardegna. An excellent year, 2016, conferred freshness and vitality, making for an elegant and deep palate. Their Tuvaoes and Cagnulari, both 2018s, also proved excellent. Our final comment concerns their Luzzana, a full-bodied and close-knit blend of Cagnulari and Cannonau. The rest of their selection is also well-crafted.

● Cannonau di Sardegna '16	♟♟ 3*
● Cagnulari '18	♟♟ 3
● Luzzana '17	♟♟ 4
○ Vermentino di Sardegna Filighe M. Cl '14	♟♟ 3
○ Vermentino di Sardegna Tuvaoes '18	♟♟ 3
○ Tokaterra	♟ 3
○ Vermentino di Sardegna Billia '18	♟ 2
○ Vermentino di Sardegna Tuvaoes '16	♟♟♟ 3*
○ Vermentino di Sardegna Tuvaoes '17	♟♟ 3*

Chessa

VIA SAN GIORGIO
07049 USINI [SS]
TEL. +39 3283747069
www.cantinechessa.it

CELLAR SALES
PRE-BOOKED VISITS
ANNUAL PRODUCTION 43,000 bottles
HECTARES UNDER VINE 15.00

Giovanni Chessa is a young producer who operates in Ursini, an excellent territory for wine-growing. The combination of limeston and clay rich soil here, together with a climate mitigated by the sea breeze, makes for sophisticated wines that exhibit finesse and great balance. Obviously, behind it all is the steady hand of Giovanna, a passionate vine grower and expert winemaker. They focus on two cultivars: Vermentino (which thrives in the area) and the traditional variet Cagnulari. A Moscato passito completes their selection. Their Cagnulari '18 landed a place in our final round of tastings by virtue of its textbook complexity, starting with the nose and finishing with a long, flavorful palate. Aromas of small red berries and hint of tobacco give way to sweet spices and minty notes. The palate exhibits vigor and vitality, as well as a reviving acidity. Their Mattariga '18, a wine redolent of citrus and almond, features sapidity and vitality. Tastin of their current vintage Kentales and IGT re has been postponed until next year.

● Cagnulari '18	♟♟ 3
○ Vermentino di Sardegna Mattariga '18	♟♟ 3
● Cagnulari '16	♟♟ 3
● Cagnulari '15	♟♟ 3
● Cagnulari '14	♟♟ 3
● Cagnulari '10	♟♟ 3
○ Kentàles	♟♟ 5
● Lugherra '16	♟♟ 5
○ Vermentino di Sardegna Mattariga '16	♟♟ 3
○ Vermentino di Sardegna Mattariga '15	♟♟ 3

Attilio Contini

A Genova, 48/50
09072 Cabras [OR]
Tel. +39 0783290806
www.vinicontini.it

CELLAR SALES
PRE-BOOKED VISITS
ANNUAL PRODUCTION 1,000,000 bottles
HECTARES UNDER VINE 110.00
VITICULTURE METHOD Certified Organic
SUSTAINABLE WINERY

Contini is a great wine family, and its name is tied not only to quality wines, but especially to the production of Vernaccia di Oristano, a unique wine in the world, particular and oxidative, and capable of evolving for decades. It's no coincidence that in their old cellar you can taste wines that go back to the 1950s, right out of the barrel. But Contini's selection is vast, and comprises whites, reds, sparkling wines and sweet wines, all characterized by a focus on traditional grapes and territorial identity. Both of the two Vernaccia di Oristanos presented are top-notch performers. The Riserva '95 is a triumph of aromas amidst dried flowers, toasted almonds, iodine and smoky notes. On the palate it's dry, sapid and very long — a great meditation wine. Their Antico Gregori (it's a non-vintage that was awarded many years ago, and for us continues to be a great Tre Bicchieri) is more pervasive and round. An oxidative touch integrates well with sweeter sensations, making for great charm overall. Among the reds we found both the Sartiglia '17 and I Giganti Rossi '16 to be noteworthy.

○ Vernaccia di Oristano Antico Gregori	♥♥ 8
○ Vernaccia di Oristano Ris. '95	♥♥ 7
● Cannonau di Sardegna Sartiglia '17	♥♥ 3
● I Giganti Rosso '16	♥♥ 5
⊙ Nieddera Rosato '18	♥♥ 2*
○ Vernaccia di Oristano Flor '07	♥♥ 4
○ I Giganti Bianco '18	♥ 5
○ Karmis Cuvée '18	♥ 3
○ Vermentino di Sardegna Pariglia '18	♥ 2
● Barrile '13	♥♥♥ 7
● Barrile '11	♥♥♥ 6
○ Vernaccia di Oristano Antico Gregori	♥♥♥ 7

Antonella Corda

s.s. 466 Km 6,8
09040 Serdiana [CA]
Tel. +39 0707966300
www.antonellacorda.it

CELLAR SALES
PRE-BOOKED VISITS
ANNUAL PRODUCTION 30,000 bottles
HECTARES UNDER VINE 14.50

Antonella Corda was one of the guide's most newsworthy stories last year, debuting with a bang and earning Tre Bicchieri right off the bat. Actually, it's not surprising, considering the project's credibility and a family history of vine growing in Serdinia that goes way back. Three wines are produced, now on their third vintage, a Cannonau, a Nuragus and a Vermentino. All are released while still young, and seek to transmit the characteristics of the grapes cultivated on the area's sandy and clay-rich terrain. They're accompanied by new, highly interesting selections that we'll taste in the coming months. For now we 'settle' for tasting the new vintages submitted last year. We confirm our opinion of their Cannonau di Sardegna. For us it's exemplary of the typology, fresh, sapid and elegant with notes of small wild berries and delicate spicy nuances. On the palate it proves deep and linear. Tre Bicchieri. Their two whites also delivered, especially the Vermentino di Sardegna, a complex, delicious wine. Finally, it's worth noting their highly pleasant Nuragus di Cagliari '18.

● Cannonau di Sardegna '17	♥♥♥ 3*
○ Nuragus di Cagliari '18	♥♥ 2*
○ Vermentino di Sardegna '18	♥♥ 3
● Cannonau di Sardegna '16	♥♥♥ 3*
○ Nuragus di Cagliari '17	♥♥ 2*
○ Vermentino di Sardegna '17	♥♥ 3

Ferruccio Deiana

Loc. Su Leunaxi
via Gialeto, 7
09040 Settimo San Pietro [CA]
Tel. +39 070749117
www.ferrucciodeiana.it

CELLAR SALES
PRE-BOOKED VISITS
ANNUAL PRODUCTION 520,000 bottles
HECTARES UNDER VINE 120.00

Ferruccio Deiana is a skilled vine grower and enologist who's managed to build a major winery in terms of production volumes and estate size. His vineyards are situated primarily on two tracts of land. One is near the cellar, Su Leunaxiu, the other in Sibiola, in Serdinia, a district historically well-suited to viticulture. The focus is on traditional cultivars, often times monovarietal selections, except for some of their premium offerings, which are blends. At the time of our tastings some of their reserve wines weren't ready, so we settled for their younger selections. The only exception was their Pluminus '17, a white fermented and aged in wood that's released two years after vintage. Its full aromatic profile and body do a nice job managing sensations of wood. Their Monica di Sardegna Karel '17, a fresh and vinous wine, also performed well. Among their sweet wines, their Oirad, made primarily with Nasco grapes, is a perennial standout.

● Monica di Sardegna Karel '17	♛♛ 2*
○ Oirad '17	♛♛ 5
⊙ Pluminus '17	♛♛ 6
⊙ Bellarosa '18	♛ 2
● Cannonau di Sardegna Sileno '17	♛ 3
○ Vermentino di Sardegna Arvali '18	♛ 3
○ Vermentino di Sardegna Donnikalia '18	♛ 2
● Cannonau di Sardegna Sileno Ris. '10	♛♛♛ 3*
● Ajana '15	♛♛ 6
● Cannonau di Sardegna Sileno Ris. '15	♛♛ 4
● Monica di Sardegna Sup. Karel '16	♛♛ 3
○ Oirad '16	♛♛ 5
○ Vermentino di Sardegna Donnikalia '17	♛♛ 2*

Cantine di Dolianova

Loc. Sant'Esu
s.s. 387 km 17,150
09041 Dolianova [SU]
Tel. +39 070744101
www.cantinedidolianova.it

CELLAR SALES
PRE-BOOKED VISITS
ANNUAL PRODUCTION 4,000,000 bottles
HECTARES UNDER VINE 1200.00

Today one of Sardinia's largest social cooperatives, Cantine di Dolianova was founded in the 1950s (as is the case for many of the island's coops). In recent years the producer has undergone an image restyling that's in line with their recent growth in quality. It's a quality that we find among their premium wines, but also their daily-drinking offerings, which can be found in wine shops at very reasonable prices. South Sardinia's traditional grapes are used, but they've also bet on varieties that once risked extinction, like Nasco, Nuragus and Barbera Sarda. And it's a Barbera Sarda that most surprised our tasting panel. The Terresicci '14 is a close-woven and austere red redolent of red fruit, myrtle, tanned leather and tobacco leaves. On the palate it's marked by a tannic sensation that's never astringent, and held together by acidity and sapidity. Tre Bicchieri. Another convincing red is their Blasio, a Cannonau reserve, while among their whites we were pleasantly suprised by their Perlas, Prendas and Montesicci, a great monovarietal Nasco.

● Terresicci '14	♛♛♛ 5
● Cannonau di Sardegna Blasio Ris. '13	♛♛ 3
○ Càralis Brut Nature M. Cl. '17	♛♛ 3
○ Nasco di Cagliari Montesicci '17	♛♛ 3
○ Nuragus di Cagliari Perlas '18	♛♛ 2*
○ Vermentino di Sardegna Prendas '18	♛♛ 2*
● Cannonau di Sardegna Anzenas '17	♛ 2
○ Malvasia Scaleri Demi Sec	♛ 3
● Falconaro '11	♛♛♛ 3*
● Cannonau di Sardegna Anzenas '15	♛♛ 2*
⊙ Cannonau di Sardegna Rosato Rosada '17	♛♛ 2*
○ Moscato di Sardegna Passito	♛♛ 5
○ Vermentino di Sardegna Naeli '17	♛♛ 2*

antina Dorgali

Piemonte, 11
022 Dorgali [NU]
.. +39 078496143
ww.cantinadorgali.com

CELLAR SALES
RE-BOOKED VISITS
NNUAL PRODUCTION 1,500,000 bottles
ECTARES UNDER VINE 600.00
USTAINABLE WINERY

we know, Cannonau is cultivated on the
tire island, but each area has its
culiarities. On the eastern coast, the
apes benefit from a Mediterranean climate
anks to the Tyrrhenian breezes that caress
e vineyards. Cantina di Dorgali operates
re, in the district after which it was named,
ying on the work of the many vine growers
o cultivate Cannonau, especially. In
dition to enjoying the favorable conditions
entioned above, the grape also benefits
m a geography characterized by slopes,
lleys and plateaus. Dorgali's wines, which
and out for their excellent prices, also draw
Vermentino, the occasional aromatic
ape and some international varieties as
ell. Two wines stood out for their complexity
d territorial expressiveness. The Cannonau
Sardegna Classico D53 '15 offers up
omas of violet, blackberries and forest
dergrowth. On the palate it's rhythmic in
alternating sapidity and freshness. The
gna di Isalle, a young, fresh and graceful
annonau, is deliberately simpler. Once
ain we found the IGT Hortos, a Cannonau
th a share of Syrah, interesting.

Cannonau di Sardegna Cl. D 53 '15	� 5
Cannonau di Sardegna Tunila '17	� 2*
Cannonau di Sardegna Vigna di Isalle '17	♮ 2*
Fuili '14	♧ 4
Hortos '13	♩ 6
Cannonau di Sardegna Icorè '17	♪ 2
Cannonau di Sardegna Rosato Filieri '18	♫ 2
Rosa e Luna Brut	♬ 3
Vermentino di Sardegna Filine '18	♭ 2
Vermentino di Sardegna Isalle '18	♮ 2
Cannonau di Sardegna Cl. D53 '13	♯♯♯ 4*
Cannonau di Sardegna Cl. D53 '12	♯♯♯ 4*
Cannonau di Sardegna Vinìola Ris. '10	♯♯♯ 4*

Fradiles

Loc. Creccherì
08030 Atzara [NU]
Tel. +39 3331761683
www.fradiles.it

CELLAR SALES
PRE-BOOKED VISITS
ANNUAL PRODUCTION 20,000 bottles
HECTARES UNDER VINE 12.00
SUSTAINABLE WINERY

Paolo Savoldo is a somewhat timid vigneron.
He may be a man of few words, but he has
very clear ideas about how to manage his
vineyards. He operates here in Atzara,
immersed in the Mandrolisai, a subregion in
the heart of Sardinia that's also a DOC
designated area. Three grapes are cultivated
(Cannonau, Bovale and Monica) on granite
and shale rich soils. Their wines are
artisanally styled, testifying to the work done
in the vineyards and simple winemaking
practices. Of the many wines produced, we're
especially partial to their young, fresh and
vital selections, a true testimony to the value
of old vineyards cultivated at more than
600 meters elevations. The Mandrolisai
Fradiles '17 is a tight-knit wine, warm and
pervasive, with aromas of dark fruit and
spices. On the palate it features acidic
backbone, which guarantees drinkability and
finesse, and a clean, flavorful finish. Their
excellent Mandrolisai Antiogu, in a 2015
Superiore version, proves more complex on
the nose, but slightly more clenched on the
palate. It's also worth mentioning their highly
drinkable Bagadiu '17, a monovarietal Bovale.

● Mandrolisai Fradiles '17	♟ 3*
● Bagadiu '17	♟ 3
● Mandrolisai Sup. Antiogu '15	♟ 4
● Mandrolisai Sup. Istentu '15	♙ 5
● Mandrolisai Sup. Antiogu '11	♟♟♟ 5
● Bagadiu '16	♟♟ 3
● Bagadiu '13	♟♟ 4
● Mandrolisai Azzàra '16	♟♟ 2*
● Mandrolisai Fradiles '16	♟♟ 3
● Mandrolisai Fradiles '15	♟♟ 3*
● Mandrolisai Sup. Antiogu '14	♟♟ 4
● Mandrolisai Sup. Istentu '11	♟♟ 8

★Giuseppe Gabbas

VIA TRIESTE, 59
08100 NUORO
TEL. +39 078433745
www.gabbas.it

CELLAR SALES
PRE-BOOKED VISITS
ANNUAL PRODUCTION 70,000 bottles
HECTARES UNDER VINE 15.00

Giuseppe Gabbas is an expert vigneron, a meticulous man of the fields who oversees his vines with great dedication. By now Cannonau is the dominant grape cultivated, though there are also a few rows of Muristellu. Vermentino, which gives rise to their Manzanile, rounds out the selection. Three Cannonaus, divided according to the age and location of the vineyard, are produced in all. During the best years they also produce a Passito (with Cannonanu). Their wines are complex and long-lived, highly respectful of the terroir of origin. They always feature great drinkability, finesse and elegance. A fantastic 2016 made for two memorable reds. Once again their Dule lands a gold, with its complex aromas of Mediterranean shrub, blackberries, myrtle and cistus. On the palate it's fresh, supple, marked by sapidity and pliant, pervasive tannins. Their excellent Arbore is warmer and silkier, soft, with a deep finish. Finally, we were also impressed by their Lillové '18, a wine that's deliberately simpler, but with a pleasantness unseen in prior versions.

● Cannonau di Sardegna Cl. Dule '16	▼▼▼	4*
● Cannonau di Sardegna Cl. Arbòre '16	▼▼	4
● Cannonau di Sardegna Lillové '18	▼▼	2*
○ Vermentino di Sardegna Manzanile '18	▼	3
● Cannonau di Sardegna Cl. Dule '15	♀♀♀	4*
● Cannonau di Sardegna Cl. Dule '13	♀♀♀	4*
● Cannonau di Sardegna Cl. Dule '12	♀♀♀	4*
● Cannonau di Sardegna Cl. Dule '11	♀♀♀	4*
● Cannonau di Sardegna Dule Ris. '10	♀♀♀	4*
● Cannonau di Sardegna Dule Ris. '09	♀♀♀	3*
● Cannonau di Sardegna Cl. Arbòre '15	♀♀	4
● Cannonau di Sardegna Cl. Arbòre '13	♀♀	4

Cantina Giba

VIA PRINCIPE DI PIEMONTE, 16
09010 GIBA [SU]
TEL. +39 0781689718
www.cantinagiba.it

CELLAR SALES
ANNUAL PRODUCTION 100,000 bottles
HECTARES UNDER VINE 15.00

Giba was founded in the early part of the century under the name 6Mura, a brand that can still be found on the labels of the two most important wines. Today, with a change in ownership, they've chosen to identify themselves with the area in which they're located, in the name of territorial identity (expressed year after year in their wines). Two grapes are cultivated, Carignano and Vermentino, and both transmit Sulcis's sandy soil and warmth. Their artisanally-styled wines are capable of intriguing imperfections, rendering them even more charming. Once again, the Carignano del Sulcis 6Mura Risera is superb. Bolstered by a great year, 2016, it offers up notes of myrtle, Mediterranean shrubs, hints of plums and a smoky touch as well. On the palate it's highly sapid, with pliant, appealing tannins and a clean, flavorful finish. Tre Bicchieri. Their two whites also delivered. The Giba '18 is fresh and graceful, the 6Mura complex and pervasive in its yellow-gold color.

● Carignano del Sulcis 6Mura Ris. '16	▼▼▼
○ Vermentino di Sardegna 6Mura '18	▼▼
○ Vermentino di Sardegna Giba '18	▼▼
● Carignano del Sulcis Giba '18	▼
⊙ Carignano del Sulcis Rosato '18	▼
● Carignano del Sulcis 6Mura '12	♀♀♀
● Carignano del Sulcis 6Mura '11	♀♀♀
● Carignano del Sulcis 6Mura '10	♀♀♀
● Carignano del Sulcis 6Mura '09	♀♀♀
● Carignano del Sulcis 6Mura Ris. '15	♀♀♀

Antichi Poderi Jerzu

Via Umberto I, 1
08044 Jerzu [OG]
Tel. +39 078270028
www.jerzuantichipoderi.it

CELLAR SALES
PRE-BOOKED VISITS
ANNUAL PRODUCTION 1,500,000 bottles
HECTARES UNDER VINE 750.00

Antichi Poderi di Jerzu is the name of a great winery, but it's also a subszone of Cannonau di Sardegna DOC. This cooperative producer avails itself of 700 hectares, thanks to the growers that work here in the eastern part of the region. Cannonau takes center stage, but other native grapes are also cultivated. Years ago the winery launched a propitious zoning project, and their selection followed suit (all in the name of the quality). Their wines pursue territorial expression, and are available at good prices. As is often the case, it's their simple, current vintage Cannonau that surprises with its finesse and elegance. The Bantu '18 is fresh and sapid, especially in its finish, with aromas of rose and spices. The Riserva Chuerra '16 is different, but still quite good, close-woven and austere, redolent of dark fruit, tanned leather and undergrowth. On the palate it's pervasive, deep, with a tannic (though never astringent) finish. The rest of their selection also proves well-crafted, with a special mention for their Telavé '18 (Vermentino) and Camalda '18 (Monica).

● Cannonau di Sardegna Bantu '18	♟♟ 2*
● Cannonau di Sardegna Chuèrra Ris. '16	♟♟ 5
● Cannonau di Sardegna Passito Akràtos '13	♟♟ 5
● Monica di Sardegna Camalda '18	♟♟ 2*
○ Vermentino di Sardegna Telavè '18	♟♟ 2*
● Cannonau di Sardegna Jerzu Marghìa '17	♟ 4
● Cannonau di Sardegna Josto Miglior Ris. '16	♟ 5
○ Vermentino di Sardegna Lucean le Stelle '18	♟ 3
● Cannonau di Sardegna Josto Miglior Ris. '09	♟♟♟ 4*

Andrea Ledda

Via Musio, 13
07043 Bonnanaro [SS]
Tel. 079845060
www.vitivinicolaledda.com

CELLAR SALES
PRE-BOOKED VISITS
ANNUAL PRODUCTION 25,000 bottiglie
HECTARES UNDER VINE 24.00

Andrea Ledda is a successful entrepreneur who some years back decided to invest in quality agriculture. He did it through a serious project aimed at developing three different estates. One is situated in Bonnanaro, where his cellar is also located, one sits atop an extinguished volcano (here his grapes grow at higher elevations), while the third, in Gallura, saw the purchase of a historic vineyard called Matteu. They're different terroirs, but all distinctly represented in wines that stand out for their finesse and drinkability. Once again Ledda's whites performed at high levels. Their Tenuta Matteu Vermentino, cultivated in one of Gallura's most beautiful vineyards, is a cut above the rest. A subtle 2018 vintage highlighted all the nuances of this granitic terroir, making for a fresh and sapid wine redolent of aromatic herbs and curry plant. Their Azzesu, a unique Vermentino made with grapes cultivated at more than 700 meters elevation, also delivered. The Giaru, from their Tenuta Monte Santu plots, proves fuller and more aromatic. We found their reds pleasant and well-crafted as well.

○ Vermentino di Gallura Sup. Soliànu - Tenuta Matteu '18	♟♟♟ 5
○ Vermentino di Sardegna Azzesu - Tenuta del Vulcano Pelao '18	♟♟ 7
● Cannonau di Sardegna Cerasa - Tenuta Monte Santu '16	♟♟ 6
○ Vermentino di Sardegna Giaru - Tenuta Monte Santu '18	♟♟ 3
○ Vermentino di Sardegna Azzesu - Tenuta del Vulcano Pelao '17	♟♟♟ 7
● Cannonau di Sardegna Cerasa - Tenuta Monte Santu '15	♟ 6
● Ruju - Tenuta Monte Santu '14	♟ 5
○ Vermentino di Gallura Sup. Soliànu - Tenuta Matteu '17	♟ 5
○ Vermentino di Sardegna Giaru - Tenuta Monte Santu '17	♟♟ 3

Cantina del Mandrolisai

C.SO IV NOVEMBRE, 20
08038 SORGONO [NU]
TEL. +39 078460113
www.cantinadelmandrolisai.com

CELLAR SALES
PRE-BOOKED VISITS
ANNUAL PRODUCTION 200,000 bottles
HECTARES UNDER VINE 80.00

For the first time, Cantina del Mandrolisai is listed among the guide's most important producers. It does so by virtue of a selection that's improved greatly in recent years and that finally shines a light on all the territory's potential. Mandrolisai is one of Sardinia's subzones, but it's also a DOC appellation. Here they cultivate on high, at 700 meters elevation. Their vineyards, which are primarily head-trained (some of them very old), grow in granite and shale rich soil. The cultivares used in Mandrolisai are Cannonau, Bovale and Monica, with a number of vine growers contributing to their production. The two wines submitted, both from the Kent'Annos line, performed quite well. The Mandrolisai Sup. '15 is austere, with aromas of dark fruit. It's still just a bit marked by oak, but that's doesn't obscure its complexity. On the palate it's tight-knit, with notable tannic presence. The 2016 is more elegant, delicate and graceful. Here red berries are more in evidence, while the palate comes through fresh and dynamic.

● Mandrolisai Kent'Annos '16	♥♥ 4
● Mandrolisai Rosato 100 Kent'Annos '18	♥♥ 4
● Mandrolisai Sup. Kent'Annos '15	♥♥ 4
● Mandrolisai Kent'Annos '12	♡♡ 4
● Mandrolisai Sup. Kent'Annos Gold '13	♡♡ 4
● Mandrolisai Sup. V. V. '13	♡♡ 2*

Masone Mannu

LOC. SU CANALE
S.S. 199 KM 48
07020 MONTI [SS]
TEL. +39 078947140
www.masonemannu.com

CELLAR SALES
PRE-BOOKED VISITS
ANNUAL PRODUCTION 100,000 bottles
HECTARES UNDER VINE 19.00

Massone Mannu has always been a lovely Gallura winery, standing out for its high quality selection. After various changes in ownership, in recent years the producer seems to have found the right proprietor, a passionate entrepreneur from Rimini who also owns Mara, in Romagna. Vermentino di Gallura is still at the fore, even if they've always made very interesting reds. Like their whites, these exhibit a strong territorial affiliation; moreover, they're never lacking in drinkability or great aging power. This year we only tasted 2018 versions, so they were all wines produced by the new technical staff. The Costarenas Superiore i top-notch. It's a white of great sapidity and finesse, characterized by citrusy notes and aromatic herbs; it's delicate in its development, deep on the palate. Tre Bicchieri. Their Petrizza also delivered. It's simpler, more approachable Vermentino di Gallura, though it's still complex and multifaceted. Both their red and rosé prove pleasant and well-made.

○ Vermentino di Gallura Sup. Costarenas '18	♥♥♥ 4
○ Vermentino di Gallura Petrizza '18	♥♥ 3
● Cannonau di Sardegna Zòjosu '18	♥ 3
⊙ Zeluiu '18	♥ 3
○ Vermentino di Gallura Sup. Costarenas '16	♡♡♡ 3
● Cannonau di Sardegna Zòjosu '15	♡♡ 3
○ Vermentino di Gallura Sup. Costarenas '17	♡♡ 4
○ Vermentino di Gallura Sup. Costarenas '15	♡♡ 3
○ Vermentino di Gallura Sup. Costarenas '14	♡♡ 3

Mesa

loc. Su Baroni
09010 Sant'Anna Arresi [CA]
tel. +39 0781965057
www.cantinamesa.it

CELLAR SALES
PRE-BOOKED VISITS
ANNUAL PRODUCTION 750,000 bottles
HECTARES UNDER VINE 70.00

Mesa is a Sulcis winery that's part of the Santa Margherita group. It was founded years ago by Gavino Sanna with the idea of drawing on and promoting this extraordinary patch of the region's southwest corner. The estate is beautiful not only for its vineyards, but for its entire natural landscape, indeed, it's one of the best terroirs for growing Carignano, which is produced in various versions according to the vineyard and its age. But their selection is vast and comprises other grapes, like Vermentino and international varieties that have integrated perfectly with the territory. Two versions of their Carignano del Sulcis were presented this year, both the result of a rigorous grape selection process, the Gavino and the Buio Buio. We preferred the latter, which landed a place in our final tastings thanks to its intense, clean aromas of red fruit and scrub. On the palate it's plush, pervasive and silky, with a particularly spicy finish. The Gavino is more concentrated. Especially in youth, it's a bit clenched on the palate. We also mention their Giunco '18, a fresh and delicate Vermentino di Sardegna that's quite good.

● Carignano del Sulcis Buio Buio Ris. '16	♥♥ 5
● Carignano del Sulcis Sup. Gavino '16	♥♥ 5
○ Vermentino di Sardegna Giunco '18	♥♥ 3
● Brama Syrah '17	♥ 4
○ Vermentino di Sardegna Opale '18	♥ 4
● Buio Buio '10	♥♥♥ 4*
● Carignano del Sulcis Buio Buio Ris. '13	♥♥♥ 5
● Carignano del Sulcis Buio Buio Ris. '12	♥♥♥ 5
● Carignano del Sulcis Buio Buio Ris. '14	♥♥ 5
● Carignano del Sulcis Gavino Ris. '15	♥♥ 5
● Carignano del Sulcis Gavino Ris. '14	♥♥ 5
○ Vermentino di Sardegna Opale '17	♥♥ 4
○ Vermentino di Sardegna Opale '16	♥♥ 4

Cantina di Mogoro
Il Nuraghe

s.s. 131 km 62
09095 Mogoro [OR]
tel. +39 0783990285
www.cantinadimogoro.it

CELLAR SALES
PRE-BOOKED VISITS
ANNUAL PRODUCTION 850,000 bottles
HECTARES UNDER VINE 480.00

Nuraghe is a cooperative in Mogoro, the town in upper Campidano after which the appellation is named. Here Semidano, an indigenous grape, reigns. For some years their commitment to quality, through grower education and efforts to identify the best vineyards, has been unquestionable. They make a number of wines but focus on traditional cultivars: Semidano (as already mentioned) but also Bovale, Nuragus, Monica and Cannonau. It's also worth mentioning their prices, which are quite reasonable — this is true of their premium wines, and especially of their simpler offerings. The Puistèris represents the highest expression of Semidano. Released two years after vintage, it exhibits all the aging power of the cultivar. The 2017 offers up aromas of candied lemon peel and summer flowers, white peach and Mediterranean herbs. On the palate it's fresh, invigorating, with nice depth. Their Anastasia (a standard-label, 2018 Semidano) is much simpler but still quite well-crafted. Among their reds, it's worth nothing their Vignaruja, Cannonau di Sardegna '15.

○ Semidano di Mogoro Sup. Puistèris '17	♥♥ 4
● Cannonau di Sardegna Vignaruja '15	♥♥ 2*
○ Semidano di Mogoro Anastasia '18	♥♥ 2*
○ Vermentino di Sardegna Don Giovanni '18	♥♥ 2*
● Cannonau di Sardegna Chio Ris. '15	♥ 5
● Monica di Sardegna Sup. Nabui '15	♥ 5
○ Mora Bianca '18	♥ 1*
○ Nuragus di Cagliari Ajò '18	♥ 2
○ T'Amo Cuvée '18	♥ 3
○ Semidano di Mogoro Sup. Puistèris '16	♥♥♥ 4*
○ Semidano di Mogoro Sup. Puistèris '10	♥♥♥ 4*

Mura

loc. Azzanidò, 1
07020 Loiri Porto San Paolo [SS]
Tel. +39 078941070
www.vinimura.it

CELLAR SALES
PRE-BOOKED VISITS
RESTAURANT SERVICE
ANNUAL PRODUCTION 50,000 bottles
HECTARES UNDER VINE 12.00

Mura is a small winery of 12 hectares managed by siblings Marianna (enologist) and Salvatore (who takes care of sales). Their wines are a true expression of Gallura, distinguished by their sapidity and freshness. But tasting some of their older vintage wines is turning out to be quite interesting indeed. Their selection is led Vermentino di Gallura, though it's accompanied by fresh, and highly drinkable reds. Subsoil rich in granite is aromatically well-expressed, guaranteeing character and authenticity. Three wines were presented this year, all 2018s. The best, in our opinion, is the Sienda, a high expression of Vermentino di Gallura that charms with its aromas of yellow-fleshed fruit and aromatic herbs. On the palate it proves fresh and dynamic, with nice sapidity and length. It's good now, but we think it will continue to improve over time. Their Cheremi is another Gallura, simpler and more accessible in this case, gratifying on the palate. Their pleasant and juicy Cannonau di Sardegna Cortes also performed well.

○ Vermentino di Gallura Sup. Sienda '18	🏆🏆 3*
○ Vermentino di Gallura Cheremi '18	🏆🏆 3
● Cannonau di Sardegna Cortes '18	🏆 3
○ Vermentino di Gallura Sup. Sienda '13	🏆🏆🏆 3*
● Cannonau di Sardegna Cortes '16	🏆🏆 3
○ Vermentino di Gallura Cheremi '16	🏆🏆 3
○ Vermentino di Gallura Sienda '15	🏆🏆 4
○ Vermentino di Gallura Sup. Sienda '14	🏆🏆 3*
○ Vermentino di Gallura Sup. Sienda '12	🏆🏆 3*
○ Vermentino di Gallura Sup. Sienda Il Decennio '11	🏆🏆 3*

Olianas

loc. Porruddu
08030 Gergei [CA]
Tel. +39 0558300411
www.olianas.it

CELLAR SALES
PRE-BOOKED VISITS
ANNUAL PRODUCTION 170,000 bottles
HECTARES UNDER VINE 23.00
VITICULTURE METHOD Certified Organic
SUSTAINABLE WINERY

This Gergei winery is the result of a collaboration between Artemio Olianas and Sefano Casadei, enologist and owner of various estates in Tuscany. Olianas's philosophy is rooted in sustainability and carried out according to a system called 'biointegrale'. In addition to organic principles, it calls for only animals to be used in the vineyard (horses instead of tractors, and geese as weed control) along with other practices aimed at protecting the ecosystem. Depending on the cultivar, their wines are fermented and aged in wood, steel or amphoras. Two reds and a white were submitted for tasting. The Cannonau and Vermentino di Sategna are young, but well-made. Their Riserva di Cannonau, on the other hand, moves on a very different track, proving sophisticated in its complexity and depth. A favorable 2016 conferred spicy notes and hints of forest undergrowth. On the palate it's sapid and rhythmic, thanks to nice acidity. It landed in our finals, but didn't get further. Possibly because of its youth, the palate is just a bit held back by rough tannins. It's still a great Mediterranean wine.

● Cannonau di Sardegna Ris. '16	🏆🏆 4
● Cannonau di Sardegna '18	🏆 3
○ Vermentino di Sardegna '18	🏆🏆 3
● Cannonau di Sardegna '16	🏆🏆 3
● Cannonau di Sardegna '15	🏆🏆 3
● Cannonau di Sardegna Ris. '15	🏆🏆 4
● Cannonau di Sardegna Ris. '14	🏆🏆 4
⊙ Cannonau di Sardegna Rosato '15	🏆🏆 3
● Perdixi '16	🏆🏆 4
⊙ Rosato '17	🏆🏆 3

...ala

Via Verdi, 7
...040 Serdiana [CA]
...L. +39 070740284
...ww.pala.it

CELLAR SALES
PRE-BOOKED VISITS
ANNUAL PRODUCTION 490,000 bottles
HECTARES UNDER VINE 98.00

...la is one of the most well-established
...neries in Sardinia (for quality) and the
...orld (for their prestige). Credit goes to
...ario Pala who, supported by his family,
...anaged to create a cutting-edge winery,
...oth in terms of production and when it
...mes to marketing/communication. A
...mber of wines are made, primarily with
...tive grapes, while their approach centers
... freshness and drinkability. And that's not
... mention territorial identity, which is
...ident throughout their selection. We
...sted three sophisticated reds, all the
...sult of the excellent 2016 vintage.
...remost is their S'Arai, a close-woven and
...ep blend. Then there's their Riserva di
...nnonau, with its aromas of tanned
...ather and tobacco, and finally their
...temari, a full, pervasive white. We're still
...nvinced that the Stellato is one of
...uthern Italy's great whites, and so the
...018 version takes home Tre Bicchieri. And
...does so thanks to a rich aromatic profile
...dolent of aromatic herbs and floral
...cents, and a palate that amazes for its
...pid freshness.

Vermentino di Sardegna Stellato '18	▼▼▼ 4*
Cannonau di Sardegna Ris. '16	▼▼ 3*
Essentija '15	▼▼ 3*
S'Arai '15	▼▼ 5
Cannonau di Sardegna I Fiori '18	▼▼ 5
Entemari '16	▼▼ 5
Vermentino di Sardegna I Fiori '18	▼▼ 3
Chiaro di Stelle '18	▼ 3
Monica di Sardegna I Fiori '18	▼ 3
Nuragus di Cagliari I Fiori '18	▼ 2
Siyr '16	▼ 4
Cannonau di Sardegna Ris. '12	▼▼▼ 3*
Vermentino di Sardegna Stellato '17	▼▼▼ 4*
Vermentino di Sardegna Stellato '16	▼▼▼ 4*
Vermentino di Sardegna Stellato '15	▼▼▼ 4*
Vermentino di Sardegna Stellato '14	▼▼▼ 3*

Cantina Pedres

Via Mincio 42 z.i. sett.7
07026 Olbia
Tel. +39 0789595075
www.cantinapedres.it

CELLAR SALES
PRE-BOOKED VISITS
ANNUAL PRODUCTION 400,000 bottles
HECTARES UNDER VINE 80.00

Antonella Mancini, with the critical support
of her enologist husband, brings great
determination to her work of overseeing
Pedres. Antonella descends from the
Mancini family, who are known throughout
the island as a great wine family. Her wines
are a mirror of Gallura, proving
Mediterranean but also fresh, delicate and
extremely clean. The granite-rich subsoil
and northeastern climate are particularly
evident in their Vermentino di Gallura. It's a
selection rounded out by certain young
reds and Charmat method sparkling wines
(both dry and sweet). Some three versions
of Vermentino di Gallura are produced, all
of them appreciable for their craft and
splendid drinkability. The new addition this
year is called Thilibas Excellence, a wine
that surprises for its acidic backbone and
linear development. Aromas of meldar and
citrus are followed by a vibrant, stylish
palate. Their Brino also delivered. It's more
light-bodied but deep on the palate. It's
also worth noting their excellent Sangusta,
a wine that features sapidity and vitality.
The rest of their selection is solid.

○ Vermentino di Gallura Brino '18	▼▼ 3
○ Vermentino di Gallura Sangusta '18	▼▼ 3
○ Vermentino di Gallura Sup. Thilibas Exellence '18	▼▼ 4
● Cannonau di Sardegna Cerasio '18	▼ 4
● Cannonau di Sardegna Sulità '17	▼ 3
○ Moscato di Sardegna '18	▼ 4
● Muros '16	▼ 3
○ Vermentino di Gallura Colline '18	▼ 2
○ Vermentino di Gallura Sup. Thilibas '10	▼▼▼ 3*
○ Vermentino di Gallura Sup. Thilibas '09	▼▼▼ 3*

F.lli Puddu

Loc. Orbuddai
08025 Oliena [NU]
Tel. +39 0784288457
azienda.puddu@tiscali.it

ANNUAL PRODUCTION 70,000 bottles
HECTARES UNDER VINE 30.00
VITICULTURE METHOD Certified Organic

The Puddu brothers' winery is situated in Oliena, at the foot of Monte Corrasi. It avails itself of 50 hectares of terrain, 30 of which are vineyards (the rest dedicated primarily to olives). Cannonau takes center stage in a territory that comprises the Nepente subzone of Oliena. Organic principles, hard work in the vineyard and a minimally-invasive approach in the cellar give rise to artisanal wines, highly charming (especially aromatically) — elegant and supple on the palate. The producer is also specialized in excellent cured pork charcuterie. A great 2014 made for a Nepente Riserva of exceptional craft, playing on notes of red fruit, dried roses, sweet spices and forest undergrowth. The Pro Vois exhibits a lean, caressing palate that's both relaxed and invigorating, with supple tannins and an unbelievable freshness. It's the right direction for pointing up the elegance and sophistication of which Cannonau is capable, and for this reason it earns Tre Bicchieri. Their Tiscoli, another 2017 Nepente, also performed well.

● Cannonau di Sardegna		
Nepente di Oliena Pro Vois Ris. '14	♛♛♛	5
● Cannonau di Sardegna		
Nepente di Oliena Tiscali '17	♛♛	3
☉ Cannonau di Sardegna Rosato		
Nepente di Oliena Biriai '18	♛♛	3
○ Gioias su Sole '18	♛	3
● Cannonau di Sardegna		
Nepente di Oliena '07	♛♛	3*
● Cannonau di Sardegna		
Nepente di Oliena Pro Vois Ris. '06	♛♛	5
● Cannonau di Sardegna		
Nepente di Oliena Tiscali '16	♛♛	3*

Quartomoro di Sardegna

via Dino Poli, 31
09092 Arborea [OR]
Tel. +39 3467643522
www.quartomoro.it

CELLAR SALES
PRE-BOOKED VISITS
ANNUAL PRODUCTION 35,000 bottles
HECTARES UNDER VINE 2.50

Quartomoro is the project created a few years ago by Piero Cella, a skilled enologist known and esteemed throughout Sardinia. It all centers on old, rented vineyards scattered throughout Sardinia, cultivated o behalf of the region's most important grapes. In the cellar, their work is kept to a minimum, with an artisanal approach that highlights the various terroirs (for better or for worse). The result is authentic, genuine wines that, despite the occasional defect, offer undisputed charm. For some years now Cella's winery has surprised our tasting panel, which is why we've decided to list it in the main part of our guide. All the wines in their Memorie di Vite line thrilled, starting with their Bovale, which reached our final round of tastings. The BVL '17 is sapid, redolent of dark fruit, with a dynamic, long palate. Their VRM '16 also delivered — it's a Vermentino di Sardegna that shows you the cultivar's aging power. Both the CNS (Cannonau) and SMD (Semidano) are also noteworthy.

● BVL Memorie di Vite '17	♛♛	4
● Cannonau di Sardegna CNS		
Memorie di Vite '16	♛♛	4
○ Orriu Vernaccia sulle Bucce '18	♛♛	3
○ SMD Memorie di Vite '18	♛♛	3
○ Vermentino di Sardegna VRM		
Memorie di Vite '16	♛♛	4
○ Q Brut M. Cl.	♛	4
● MAI Intrecci di Vite '12	♛♛	6
○ Vermentino di Sardegna VRM		
Memorie di Vite '14	♛♛	4

Santa Maria La Palma

FRAZ. SANTA MARIA LA PALMA
07041 ALGHERO [SS]
TEL. +39 079999008
www.santamarialapalma.it

CELLAR SALES
PRE-BOOKED VISITS
ANNUAL PRODUCTION 4,000,000 bottles
HECTARES UNDER VINE 650.00

This Alghero cooperative took its name from the township. It draws on the efforts of dozens of growers, who cultivate both native grapes and the international cultivars that have, for some time now, thrived here. Strategic decisions of late have brought the winery to a high level of quality, both with their premium wines and, especially, their daily-drinking selections, which are always recommended considering their price. One of these is the Aragosta, a DOC that's among the most widely circulated in Italy. It's worth pointing out their Vermentino sparklers, which they've invested heavily in. Some two wines landed in our final round tastings, thus confirming the great work. They're both 2016 reds on their first release. The Redit is a Cannonau di Sardegna Riserva that's graceful and elegant, lean and dynamic, with a long, gratifying finish. On the nose it offers up aromas of red berries and rose. Their Recònta, a Riserva di Cagnular, is more full-bodied, dense, as is fitting, with assertive tannins, aromas of dark fruit and spices.

● Alghero Cagnulari Recònta Ris. '16	🍷🍷 4
● Cannonau di Sardegna Redit Ris. '16	🍷🍷 3*
● Cannonau di Sardegna '17	🍷🍷 3
○ Vermentino di Sardegna Ràfia '17	🍷🍷 5
○ Vermentino di Sardegna Aragosta '18	🍷 2
● Cannonau di Sardegna R Ris. '15	🍷🍷🍷 3*
● Alghero Cagnulari '16	🍷🍷 3
● Cannonau di Sardegna Valmell '17	🍷🍷 2*

★★Cantina di Santadi

VIA CAGLIARI, 78
09010 SANTADI [SU]
TEL. +39 0781950127
www.cantinadisantadi.it

CELLAR SALES
PRE-BOOKED VISITS
ANNUAL PRODUCTION 1,740,000 bottles
HECTARES UNDER VINE 603.00

There's no doubt that Cantina di Santadi was and is a benchmark for Sardinian wine, especially if we're talking about cooperatives. It's gotten here by creating a positive relationship with its growers, one based on the quality of the grapes cultivated and adequate payment for them. It continues by maintaining high standards, while offering their wines at the right prices and providing a product that's appreciated the world over. Carignano, the cornerstone of their selection, is cultivated on dozens of hectares of old head-trained vineyards that grow in the area's sandy soil. Two wines made it to our final tastings this year. The Latinia is a barrel-aged passito made with Nasco grapes. The result is evident from the outset, with lovely, charming oxidative notes combining with more aromatic, fruitier fragrances. On the palate it's sweet but never cloying. The Terre Brune '15 is a tight-knit and austere Carignano del Sulcis Superiore with plush, caressing, sapid and deep tannins. This last convinced the entire panel and once again took home Tre Bicchieri.

● Carignano del Sulcis Sup. Terre Brune '15	🍷🍷🍷 7
● Cannonau di Sardegna Noras '16	🍷🍷 4
⊙ Carignano del Sulcis Rosato Tre Torri '18	🍷🍷 2*
○ Nuragus di Cagliari Pedraia '18	🍷🍷 2*
○ Solais M. Cl. '18	🍷🍷 5
○ Vermentino di Sardegna Cala Silente '18	🍷🍷 3
● Araja '17	🍷 3
● Carignano del Sulcis Grotta Rossa '17	🍷 2
● Carignano del Sulcis Rocca Rubia Ris. '16	🍷 4
● Monica di Sardegna Antigua '18	🍷 2
● Carignano del Sulcis Sup. Terre Brune '14	🍷🍷🍷 7

Sardus Pater

VIA RINASCITA, 46
09017 SANT'ANTIOCO [SU]
TEL. +39 0781800274
www.cantinesarduspater.com

CELLAR SALES
PRE-BOOKED VISITS
ANNUAL PRODUCTION 600,000 bottles
HECTARES UNDER VINE 295.00

Sardus Pater is Sant'Antioco's cooperative winery. It's an island southeast of the region, connected to Sardinia by an artificial isthmus. Here in the in the sandy soil of DOC Carignano del Sulcis wine country, there's no lack of old vineyards, some of them ungrafted. Their selection is vast and, in addition to Carignano (made in various versions, from vintage wines fermented entirely in steel to reserves and passitos), it draws on Vermentino (including a notable sparkling wine). They also make sweet wines from Moscato and Nasco grapes. The two wines we appreciated most are both 2017s. The Nur is a fresh and juicy Carignano del Sulcis that impresses with its aromas of red fruit berries, and its sapid, supple palate. Is Arenas is a Riserva (Carignano) redolent of spices, undergrowth and balsamic hints. The palate's tight-knit, but it's not lacking in drinkability and length. The rest of the wines tasted all proved pleasant and well-made.

● Carignano del Sulcis Is Arenas Ris. '17	♟♟ 5
● Carignano del Sulcis Nur '17	♟♟ 3
● Carignano del Sulcis Sup. Arruga '16	♟♟ 5
○ Elat '17	♟ 3
○ Vermentino di Sardegna Lugore '18	♟ 4
○ Vermentino di Sardegna Terre Fenicie '18	♟ 2
● Carignano del Sulcis Is Arenas Ris. '09	♟♟♟ 4*
● Carignano del Sulcis Is Arenas Ris. '08	♟♟♟ 4*
● Carignano del Sulcis Sup. Arruga '09	♟♟♟ 6
● Carignano del Sulcis Sup. Arruga '07	♟♟♟ 5

Giuseppe Sedilesu

VIA VITTORIO EMANUELE II, 64
08024 MAMOIADA [NU]
TEL. +39 078456791
www.giuseppesedilesu.com

CELLAR SALES
PRE-BOOKED VISITS
ANNUAL PRODUCTION 120,000 bottles
HECTARES UNDER VINE 17.00

Sedilesu is a symbol in Mamoiada for many reasons. Foremost, they have managed to make great artisanal wines, which express and pay homage to their territory of origin. They've also given a voice to, and supported, many small vine growers in producing their own wines, thus founding a true territorial movement. Here the terroir is marked by its elevation, by the age of its vineyards, by a particular microclimate and by lean terrain of which broken down granitic rock is a key feature. These characteristics give rise to their various Cannonaus, which are accompanied by Granazza di Mamoiada, a particular white variety of grape. The Cannonau di Sardegna Ballu Tundu Riserva put in an impressive performance. It's a 2014 (an excellent year in the region) redolent of ripe fruit, minty hints, a touch of forest undergrowth and tobacco. On the palate it proves pervasive, warm, silky, punctuated by a nice acidity that brings us back to the highlands. Even if it's much simpler, the Mamuthone '16 (a Cannonau fermented entirely in steel) is just delicious.

● Cannonau di Sardegna Ballu Tundu Ris. '14	♟♟ 6
● Cannonau di Sardegna Mamuthone '16	♟♟ 3
● Cannonau di Sardegna Carnevale Ris. '15	♟ 5
○ Perda Pintà '17	♟ 5
● Cannonau di Sardegna Mamuthone '15	♟♟♟ 3
● Cannonau di Sardegna Mamuthone '12	♟♟♟ 3
● Cannonau di Sardegna Mamuthone '11	♟♟♟ 3
● Cannonau di Sardegna Mamuthone '08	♟♟♟ 3
○ Perda Pintà '09	♟♟♟ 4
● Cannonau di Sardegna Ballu Tundu Ris. '14	♟♟ 6

★★Tenute Sella & Mosca

Loc. I Piani
07041 Alghero [SS]
Tel. +39 079997700
www.sellaemosca.com

CELLAR SALES
PRE-BOOKED VISITS
ANNUAL PRODUCTION 6,700,000 bottles
HECTARES UNDER VINE 541.00

Some years have passed since the Moretti family (established producers in Franciacorta and Tuscany) purchased this estate, and the results are evident. The quality here is extremely high, both with their premium wines and their daily-drinking selections, but their presence is most felt in terms of a growth path worthy of a historic winery like Sella & Mosca. Four new wines (not tasted this year) are among the most newsworthy developments. They're part of a project that features a close collaboration with the designer Antonio Marras. Two wines, a red and white, put in first-rate performances. Both, for different reasons, are important for the winery's history. The Marchese di Villamarina is one of their premium offerings. Made with Cabernet Sauvigon, it offers up herbaceous notes and aromas of black berries, along with a touch of spices and minty hints. On the palate it's close-woven, but also smooth and deep. The other is their Terre Bianche Cuvée 161, an elegant and balanced monovarietal Torbato. Yellow summer flowers and citrus are the prelude to a lean, vital palate.

○ Alghero Torbato Terre Bianche Cuvée 161 '18	▼▼▼ 3*
● Alghero Marchese di Villamarina '15	▼▼ 6
○ Alghero Torbato Brut	▼▼ 3
○ Vermentino di Gallura Sup. Monteoro '18	▼▼ 3
○ Vermentino di Sardegna Cala Reale '18	▼▼ 3
● Alghero Marchese di Villamarina '09	♀♀♀ 6
● Alghero Rosso Marchese di Villamarina '08	♀♀♀ 6
○ Alghero Torbato Catore '17	♀♀♀ 5
○ Alghero Torbato Terre Bianche Cuvée 161 '16	♀♀♀ 3*
○ Alghero Torbato Terre Bianche Cuvée 161 '15	♀♀♀ 4*
○ Vermentino di Gallura Sup. Monteoro '14	♀♀♀ 3*

Siddùra

Loc. Siddùra

07020 Luogosanto [SS]
Tel. +39 0796513027
www.siddura.com

CELLAR SALES
PRE-BOOKED VISITS
ACCOMMODATION AND RESTAURANT SERVICE
ANNUAL PRODUCTION 200,000 bottles
HECTARES UNDER VINE 37.00
SUSTAINABLE WINERY

The Luogosanto winery is beautiful for its structure and the planting of its vineyards. In just a few short years it has carved out an important space among more substantial estates in Gallura and throughout the island. This success can be attributed to the quality of the wines, as well as to good marketing, distribution and communication. Vermentino, produced in three different types, is the star, but the range also includes some reds, made from both traditional varietals grown near the winery and from plots outside the Gallura area. The very precise, clean and crystalline style exalts the territory as much as possible. Their Màia, a Vermentino di Gallura Superiore fermented entirely in steel, earned itself a place in our finals. Clean and transparent in its aromas of hedgerow and fruit, the palate proves lean and supple, technically precise but possibly just a bit lacking in personality. Their Spero, another elegant and gratifying Gallura, is close behind. The rest of their selection is all well-made.

○ Vermentino di Gallura Sup. Màia '17	▼▼ 4
○ Vermentino di Gallura Spèra '18	▼▼ 3
● Bàcco Cagnulari '16	▼ 5
● Cannonau di Sardegna Fòla Ris. '16	▼ 5
● Tiros '15	▼ 6
○ Vermentino di Gallura Sup. Màia '15	♀♀♀ 4*
○ Vermentino di Gallura Sup. Màia '14	♀♀♀ 4*
○ Vermentino di Gallura Sup. Màia '16	♀♀ 4
○ Vermentino di Gallura Sup. Màia '13	♀♀ 5

Su Entu

S.DA PROV.LE KM 1,800
09025 SANLURI
TEL. +39 070 93571206
www.cantinesuentu.com

CELLAR SALES
PRE-BOOKED VISITS
ANNUAL PRODUCTION 240,000 bottles
HECTARES UNDER VINE 32.00

The Pilloni family launched this high-level, entrepreneurial operation a few years ago. Its primary aim was to revitalize this marvellous territory, the Marmilla, through agricultural production and upgraded reception and accommodation facilities. It's truly a pleasure to visit the winery, taste the wines, enjoy the unique natural environment, and take part in the many organized events. As the vines have grown older, the wines have become increasingly centered and intriguing, more fully reflecting the territory. Some two wines earned a place in our finals this year. One is a recent addition, their Su'Oltre '16, a notable wine whose ambitions are just as notable. On its first year after release, it's still just a bit young, and its oak needs time to integrate, but there's no doubt that this is a wine to keep an eye on. On the other hand the Su'Orma, Vermentino di Sardegna '17 surprised. Released two years after vintage, it proves that a southern Sardinian wine can have great aging prospects.

● Su'Oltre '16		♥♥ 3*
○ Vermentino di Sardegna Su'Orma '17		♥♥ 3*
● Bovale '17		♥♥ 5
○ Vermentino di Sardegna Su'Imari '18		♥♥ 3
● Cannonau di Sardegna Su'Anima '17		♥ 3
○ Su'Aro '18		♥ 3
● Su'Diterra '17		♥ 3
● Bovale '16		♥♥♥ 5
● Bovale '15		♥♥ 3*
● Mediterraneo '16		♥♥ 3*
● Mediterraneo '14		♥♥ 3*

Surrau

S.DA PROV.LE ARZACHENA - PORTO CERVO
07021 ARZACHENA [SS]
TEL. +39 078982933
www.vignesurrau.it

CELLAR SALES
PRE-BOOKED VISITS
ANNUAL PRODUCTION 300,000 bottles
HECTARES UNDER VINE 50.00
SUSTAINABLE WINERY

Surrau is at the vanguard, both technically and in terms of guest facilities. One of the most beautiful wineries in Sardinia, it's open twelve months per year for a purchase or a tasting, but also for the chance to enjoy the extraordinary architecture surrounded by granite outcropping and Mediterranean scrubbrush. The vineyards are planted with tradition varietals, including Vermentino and different red grapes that have found an ideal habitat here. The range is completed by sparkling Metodo Classico of unquestionable merit. And once again, their Sciala proves to be one of the best wines in its category. It's a 2018 Vermentino di Gallura Superiore redolent of almond, aromatic herbs and yellow summer flowers, while the palate exhibits plenty of sapidity and depth. Tre Bicchieri. Simplicity, together with a supple, fresh palate, figure centrally in their Branu '18. Among their reds, we found the fruity and floral Sincaru Riserva '16 quite interesting, with its sapid palate and ripe tannins.

○ Vermentino di Gallura Sup. Sciala '18		♥♥♥ 5
● Cannonau di Sardegna Sincaru Ris. '16		♥♥ 5
○ Vermentino di Gallura Branu '18		♥♥ 3
● Cannonau di Sardegna Sincaru '17		♥ 5
○ Vermentino di Gallura Sciala V.T. '17		♥ 5
● Cannonau di Sardegna Sincaru Ris. '14		♥♥♥ 5
○ Vermentino di Gallura Sup. Sciala '17		♥♥♥ 5
○ Vermentino di Gallura Sup. Sciala '15		♥♥♥ 5
○ Vermentino di Gallura Sup. Sciala '14		♥♥♥ 5
○ Vermentino di Gallura Sup. Sciala '13		♥♥♥ 5
○ Vermentino di Gallura Sup. Sciala '12		♥♥♥ 5

Cantina Trexenta

LE PIEMONTE, 40
09040 SENORBÌ [CA]
TEL. +39 0709808863
www.cantinatrexenta.it

CELLAR SALES
ANNUAL PRODUCTION 1,000,000 bottles
HECTARES UNDER VINE 250.00

Cantina Trexenta is a large cooperative founded in the 1950s that gets its name from its territory. The 200 members work about 350 hectares of vineyards with production reaching one million bottles. The many wines are all characterized by excellent value for money. Cannonau dominates and is bottled in different versions depending on the quality of the grapes and the vineyard of origin; generally speaking, it's the most complete and authentic wine they produce, a unique expression of the variety in South Sardinia. The range is completed by Monica, Nuragus, Vermentino and some more aromatic varieties. Their delicious Bingias '18 is a complex Cannonau, though it's also lean and graceful. The Goimajor '17 is more tight-knit and mature. The Corte Auda, another young Cannonau (2017), proves pleasant. Among their whites we appreciated the Bingias, a 2018 Vermentino di Sardegna.

● Cannonau di Sardegna Bingias '17	♀♀ 2*
● Cannonau di Sardegna Goimajor '17	♀♀ 2*
○ Vermentino di Sardegna Bingias '18	♀♀ 2*
● Cannonau di Sardegna Corte Auda '17	♀ 2
● Cannonau di Sardegna Tanca su Conti Ris. '15	♀ 4
○ Nuragus di Cagliari Tenute San Mauro '18	♀ 2
○ Vermentino di Sardegna Donna Leonora '18	♀ 2
○ Vermentino di Sardegna Monteluna '18	♀ 2
● Cannonau di Sardegna Corte Auda '11	♀♀ 2*
● Cannonau di Sardegna Baione '16	♀ 2

Cantina Sociale della Vernaccia

LOC. RIMEDIO
VIA ORISTANO, 6A
09170 ORISTANO
TEL. +39 078333383
www.vinovernaccia.com

CELLAR SALES
PRE-BOOKED VISITS
ANNUAL PRODUCTION 260,000 bottles
HECTARES UNDER VINE 120.00

Formerly known as Cantina del Rimedio, the cooperative is now called Cantina della Vernaccia after Oristano's important wine. Small but very dynamic, it's specialized in the territory's oxidative wines as well as in classic vinification of traditional varietals. It's no coincidence that recently the range has been expanded and a new pricing policy has been implemented, paying homage to the great amber wine. The range also includes Cannonau, Monica, Vermentino and Niedera, the other varieties native to the area. The Terresinis is just delicious. It's made with Vernaccia, but it's young and fresh, without resorting to oxidation. The 2018 is highly fresh and sapid — long, elegant and deep on the palate. Their Maimone is a delicate and supple 2017 Cannonau di Sardegna. But once again it's their charming Riserva di Vernaccia Judikes '03 that steals the show, with its aromas of dried fruit and nuts, and its smoky notes.

○ Vernaccia di Oristano Judikes Ris. '03	♀♀ 3*
○ Aristanis M. Cl. Brut	♀♀ 3
● Cannonau di Sardegna Maimone '17	♀♀ 2*
⊙ Seu '18	♀♀ 2*
○ Terresinis Vernaccia '18	♀♀ 2*
● Monica di Sardegna Sup. Don Efisio '16	♀ 2
● Niedera Montiprama '16	♀ 1*
○ Vermentino di Sardegna Benas '18	♀ 1*
○ Vermentino di Sardegna Is Arutas '18	♀ 2
○ Vernaccia di Oristano Sup. Jughissa '08	♀♀♀ 3*
○ Vermentino di Sardegna Benas '17	♀♀ 1*
○ Vernaccia di Oristano Jughissa '09	♀♀ 3

1Sorso

Loc. Trunconi
07037 Sorso [SS]
Tel. +39 3471274211
www.1sorso.it

CELLAR SALES
PRE-BOOKED VISITS
ANNUAL PRODUCTION 15,000 bottles
HECTARES UNDER VINE 12.00
SUSTAINABLE WINERY

● Cannonau di Sardegna '18	🍷🍷 4
○ Millenovecento64 '18	🍷 5

Cantina Arvisionadu

Loc. Luzzanas
07010 Benetutti [SS]
Tel. +39 3489989260
www.cantina-arvisionadu.it

CELLAR SALES
PRE-BOOKED VISITS
ANNUAL PRODUCTION 9,000 bottles
HECTARES UNDER VINE 2.00

● Bene Tutti '18	🍷🍷
○ G'oceano '18	🍷

Cantina Berritta

Loc. Vallata di Oddoene
via Kennedy, 108
08022 Dorgali [NU]
Tel. +39 078495372
www.cantinaberritta.it

CELLAR SALES
PRE-BOOKED VISITS
ANNUAL PRODUCTION 25,000 bottles
HECTARES UNDER VINE 11.00
SUSTAINABLE WINERY

● Cannonau di Sardegna Cl. Monte Tundu '16	🍷🍷 4
● Cannonau di Sardegna Nostranu '17	🍷🍷 3
● Don Baddore '17	🍷 5

Biomar - Tenuta La Sabbiosa

via Garibaldi, 119
09011 Calasetta [SU]
Tel. +39 3921493397
www.biomar.bio

ANNUAL PRODUCTION 10,000 bottles
HECTARES UNDER VINE 4.00
VITICULTURE METHOD Certified Organic

● Carignano del Sulcis Il Bio '17	🍷🍷
● Carignano del Sulcis Il Doc '17	🍷🍷

Cantina Canneddu

via Manno, 69
08024 Mamoiada [NU]
Tel. +39 3496852916
www.cantinacanneddu.it

ACCOMMODATION
ANNUAL PRODUCTION 8,000 bottles
HECTARES UNDER VINE 2.50
VITICULTURE METHOD Certified Organic

● Cannonau di Sardegna Zibbo '17	🍷🍷 5
○ Delissia	🍷 5

Carboni

via Umberto 163
08036 Ortueri [NU]
Tel. +39 078466213
www.vinicarboni.it

ANNUAL PRODUCTION 30,000 bottles
HECTARES UNDER VINE 12.00

● Balente '17	🍷🍷
● Mandrolisai Sup. Balente '15	🍷🍷
○ Helios '18	🍷
● Pin8 '17	🍷

Carpante

VIA GARIBALDI, 151
07049 USINI [SS]
TEL. +39 079380614
www.carpante.it

CELLAR SALES
PRE-BOOKED VISITS
ANNUAL PRODUCTION 30,000 bottles
HECTARES UNDER VINE 8.00

Cagnulari '17	♟♟ 3
Carignano del Sulcis '17	♟♟ 4
Vermentino di Sardegna Longhera '18	♟♟ 2*

Cantina Castiadas

LOC. OLIA SPECIOSA
09040 CASTIADAS [CA]
TEL. +39 0709949004
www.cantinacastiadas.com

CELLAR SALES
PRE-BOOKED VISITS
ANNUAL PRODUCTION 120,000 bottles
HECTARES UNDER VINE 150.00

⊙ Cannonau di Sardegna Rosato Capo Ferrato '18	♟♟ 2*
○ Vermentino di Sardegna Praidis '18	♟♟ 2*
○ Vermentino di Sardegna Notteri '18	♟ 3

Francesco Fiori

VIA OSSI, 10
07049 USINI [SS]
TEL. +39 3381949246
www.vinifiori.it

CELLAR SALES
HECTARES UNDER VINE 6.00

Cannonau di Sardegna Torricla '18	♟♟ 4
Cagnulari Serra Juales '16	♟ 3
Vermentino di Sardegna Serra Aspridda '18	♟ 3

Cantina Gallura

VIA VAL DI COSSU, 9
07029 TEMPIO PAUSANIA
TEL. +39 079631241
www.cantinagallura.com

CELLAR SALES
PRE-BOOKED VISITS
ANNUAL PRODUCTION 1,300,000 bottles
HECTARES UNDER VINE 350.00

⊙ Campos '18	♟♟ 2*
○ Vermentino di Gallura Piras '18	♟♟ 2*
○ Vermentino di Gallura Sup. Canayli '18	♟♟ 2*
○ Vermentino di Gallura Gemellae '18	♟ 2

Garagisti di Sorgono

VIA LOGUDORO, 1
08038 SORGONO [NU]
TEL. +39 3470868122
www.garagistidisorgono.com

ANNUAL PRODUCTION 6,000 bottles
HECTARES UNDER VINE 10.00

Manca '16	♟♟ 6
Murru '16	♟♟ 5
Uras '16	♟♟ 6

Luca Gungui

C.SO VITTORIO EMANUELE, 21
08024 MAMOIADA [NU]
TEL. +39 3473320735
cantinagungui@tiscali.it

ANNUAL PRODUCTION 3,437 bottles
HECTARES UNDER VINE 2.30

● Cannonau di Sardegna Berteru '18	♟♟ 6
⊙ Cannonau di Sardegna Berteru En Rose '18	♟♟ 8

Antonella Ledà d'Ittiri

FRAZ. FERTILIA
LOC. ARENOSU, 23
07041 ALGHERO [SS]
TEL. +39 079999263
www.ledadittiri.it

CELLAR SALES
PRE-BOOKED VISITS
ACCOMMODATION
ANNUAL PRODUCTION 18,000 bottles
HECTARES UNDER VINE 5.50
SUSTAINABLE WINERY

⊙ Encant '18	♟♟ 3
● Alghero Cagnulari Cigala '18	♟ 3
● Ginjol '18	♟ 3
● Margallò '18	♟ 3

Li Duni

LOC. LI PARISI
07030 BADESI [SS]
TEL. +39 0799144480
www.cantinaliduni.it

CELLAR SALES
PRE-BOOKED VISITS
ANNUAL PRODUCTION 40,000 bottles
HECTARES UNDER VINE 20.00
SUSTAINABLE WINERY

● Nalboni '16	♟♟
○ Vermentino di Gallura Amabile Nozzinà '18	♟♟
● Tajanu '15	♟
○ Vermentino di Gallura Sup. Renabianca '18	♟

Alberto Loi

S.S. 125 KM124,1
08040 CARDEDU [OG]
TEL. +39 070240866
www.albertoloi.it

CELLAR SALES
PRE-BOOKED VISITS
ACCOMMODATION
ANNUAL PRODUCTION 250,000 bottles
HECTARES UNDER VINE 61.00

● Cannonau di Sardegna Jerzu '17	♟♟ 4
○ Leila '16	♟♟ 5
○ NàNà '14	♟♟ 5
● Cannonau di Sardegna Cardedo Ris. '16	♟ 5

Meana - Terre del Mandrolisa

VIA ROMA, 129
08030 MEANA SARDO [NU]
TEL. +39 3498797817
www.cantinameana.it

ANNUAL PRODUCTION 35,000 bottles
HECTARES UNDER VINE 12.00

● Mandrolisai Parèda '16	♟♟

Abele Melis

VIA SANTA SUINA, 3
09098 TERRALBA [OR]
TEL. +39 0783851090
melis.vini@tiscali.it

CELLAR SALES
PRE-BOOKED VISITS
ANNUAL PRODUCTION 100,000 bottles
HECTARES UNDER VINE 35.00

● Terralba Bovale Dominariu '16	♟♟ 3
○ Vermentino di Sardegna Ereb '18	♟♟ 3
○ Vermentino di Sardegna localia '18	♟ 2

Mora&Memo

VIA GIUSEPPE VERDI, 9
09040 SERDIANA [CA]
TEL. +39 3311972266
www.moraememo.it

CELLAR SALES
PRE-BOOKED VISITS
ANNUAL PRODUCTION 35,000 bottles
HECTARES UNDER VINE 37.00
VITICULTURE METHOD Certified Organic

● Cannonau di Sardegna Nau '18	♟♟
○ È '18	♟♟
○ Vermentino di Sardegna Tino '18	♟♟
● Monica di Sardegna Ica '18	♟

Nuraghe Crabioni

c. Lu Crabioni
037 Sorso [SS]
.. +39 3468292457
ww.nuraghecrabioni.com

CELLAR SALES
PRE-BOOKED VISITS
ANNUAL PRODUCTION 60,000 bottles
HECTARES UNDER VINE 35.00
SUSTAINABLE WINERY

Cannonau di Sardegna Crabioni '17	▼▼ 3
Moscato di Sorso-Sennori '16	▼ 4
Sussinku '17	▼ 3
Vermentino di Sardegna Kanimari '18	▼ 3

Cantina Oliena

via Nuoro, 112
08025 Oliena [NU]
Tel. +39 0784287509
www.cantinasocialeoliena.it

ANNUAL PRODUCTION 300,000 bottles
HECTARES UNDER VINE 180.00

● Cannonau di Sardegna Nepente di Oliena Irilai '14	▼▼ 3
⊙ Onorosa Brut Rosè	▼▼ 5

Cantine di Orgosolo

Ilole
027 Orgosolo [NU]
.. +39 0784403096
ww.cantinediorgosolo.it

CELLAR SALES
PRE-BOOKED VISITS
RESTAURANT SERVICE
ANNUAL PRODUCTION 17,000 bottles
HECTARES UNDER VINE 16.00
VITICULTURE METHOD Certified Organic

Cannonau di Sardegna Neale '18	▼▼ 3
Cannonau di Sardegna Urùlu '18	▼▼ 4
Cannonau di Sardegna Luna Vona '18	▼ 4

Gabriele Palmas

v.le Italia, 3
07100 Sassari
Tel. +39 079233721
gabrielepalmas@tiscali.it

CELLAR SALES
PRE-BOOKED VISITS
ANNUAL PRODUCTION 20,000 bottles
HECTARES UNDER VINE 10.00

● Alghero Cabernet '15	▼▼ 4
● Alghero Cabernet Riserva di Palmas '14	▼▼ 4
● Cannonau di Sardegna '17	▼▼ 3
● Syrah '15	▼▼ 3

Poderi Parpinello

c. Janna de Mare
s. 291
100 Sassari
L. +39 3465915194
ww.poderiparpinello.it

ANNUAL PRODUCTION 110,000 bottles
HECTARES UNDER VINE 20.00

Alghero Torbato '18	▼▼ 4
Vermentino di Sardegna Ala Blanca '18	▼▼ 4
Alghero Torbato Cento Gemme '18	▼ 4
Torbato Brut Centogemme '18	▼ 4

Giuliana Puligheddu

p.zza Collegio, 5
08025 Oliena [NU]
Tel. +39 0784287734
www.agricolapuligheddu.it

CELLAR SALES
PRE-BOOKED VISITS
ANNUAL PRODUCTION 5,000 bottles
HECTARES UNDER VINE 3.00
VITICULTURE METHOD Certified Organic
SUSTAINABLE WINERY

● Cannonau di Sardegna Cupanera '17	▼▼ 5

Rigàtteri

LOC. SANTA MARIA LA PALMA
REG. FLUMELONGU, 56
07041 ALGHERO [SS]
TEL. +39 3408636375
www.rigatteri.com

CELLAR SALES
PRE-BOOKED VISITS
ANNUAL PRODUCTION 15,000 bottles
HECTARES UNDER VINE 10.00
SUSTAINABLE WINERY

● Alghero Cagnulari Graffiante '17	💯💯 3
○ Vermentino di Sardegna Ardelia '17	💯💯 3
○ Vermentino di Sardegna Bramassa '17	💯💯 2*
○ Vermentino di Sardegna Yiòs '18	💯 2

Viticoltori Romangia

VIA MARINA, 5
07037 SORSO [SS]
TEL. +39 079351666
www.cantinaromangia.it

CELLAR SALES
PRE-BOOKED VISITS
ANNUAL PRODUCTION 60,000 bottles
HECTARES UNDER VINE 60.00

● Cannonau di Sardegna Radice Ris. '16	💯💯
● Oro Dry '18	💯💯
● Cannonau di Sardegna Radice '17	💯
○ Moscato di Sorso Sennori Oro Oro '18	💯

Tenute Smeralda

VIA KENNEDY, 21
09040 DONORI [CA]
TEL. +39 3387446524
www.tenutesmeralda.it

ANNUAL PRODUCTION 45,000 bottles
HECTARES UNDER VINE 7.00

● Rubìnus '17	💯💯 5
○ Vermentino di Sardegna Terramea '18	💯💯 3
● Cannonau di Sardegna D'Onore '18	💯 3
○ Vermentino di Sardegna Smeralda '18	💯 3

Agricola Soi

VIA CUCCHESÌ, 1
08030 NURAGUS [CA]
TEL. +39 0782818262
www.agricolasoi.it

CELLAR SALES
PRE-BOOKED VISITS
ANNUAL PRODUCTION 14,000 bottles
HECTARES UNDER VINE 4.00

● Cannonau di Sardegna '15	💯💯
● Lun '17	💯💯
○ Nuragus di Cagliari Nurà '18	💯

Tenute Soletta

LOC. SIGNOR'ANNA
07040 CODRONGIANOS [SS]
TEL. +39 079435067
www.tenutesoletta.it

CELLAR SALES
PRE-BOOKED VISITS
ACCOMMODATION AND RESTAURANT SERVICE
ANNUAL PRODUCTION 100,000 bottles
HECTARES UNDER VINE 15.00
VITICULTURE METHOD Certified Organic
SUSTAINABLE WINERY

● Cannonau di Sardegna Sardo '16	💯💯 3
⊘ Prius '18	💯💯 3
● Keramos '16	💯 5
○ Vermentino di Sardegna Chimera '18	💯 4

Cantina Tani

LOC. CONCA SA RAIGHINA, 2
07020 MONTI [SS]
TEL. +39 3386432055
www.cantinatani.it

CELLAR SALES
PRE-BOOKED VISITS
ACCOMMODATION AND RESTAURANT SERVIC
ANNUAL PRODUCTION 65,000 bottles
HECTARES UNDER VINE 18.00

● Cannonau di Sardegna Donosu '18	💯💯 3
○ Vermentino di Gallura Meoru '18	💯 3
○ Vermentino di Gallura Sup. Taerra '17	💯 4

nuta l'Ariosa

PREDDA NIEDDA SUD
15
00 SASSARI
+39 079261905
w.lariosa.it

ANNUAL PRODUCTION 40,000 bottles
HECTARES UNDER VINE 9.00

Cannonau di Sardegna Assolo '18	🏆🏆 3
Vermentino di Sardegna Galatea '18	🏆🏆 3
Cannonau di Sardegna Llunes Ris. '16	🏆 3
Vermentino di Sardegna Arenu '18	🏆 3

Tabarka Tanca Gioia

GIOIA
014 CARLOFORTE [SU]
+39 3356359329
w.u-tabarka.it

CELLAR SALES
PRE-BOOKED VISITS
RESTAURANT SERVICE
ANNUAL PRODUCTION 40,000 bottles
HECTARES UNDER VINE 7.00

Novale Ciù Roussou '18	🏆🏆 3
Verdigiournou '18	🏆 3
Vermentino di Sardegna Bentou de Ma '18	🏆 3

gna du Bertin

Agostino Tagliafico, 49
014 CARLOFORTE [SU]
+39 347 1375548
w.vignadubertincarloforte.com

CELLAR SALES
ANNUAL PRODUCTION 8,000 bottles
HECTARES UNDER VINE 1.20
SUSTAINABLE WINERY

Carignano del Sulcis Mandediu Ris. '15	🏆🏆 5
Carignano del Sulcis Bertin '17	🏆🏆 3
Vermentino di Sardegna Ribotta '15	🏆🏆 3

Cantina Tondini

LOC. SAN LEONARDO
07023 CALANGIANUS [SS]
TEL. +39 079661359
www.cantinatondini.it

CELLAR SALES
PRE-BOOKED VISITS
ANNUAL PRODUCTION 80,000 bottles
HECTARES UNDER VINE 25.00

○ Lajcheddu '15	🏆🏆 5
○ Vermentino di Gallura Sup. Karagnanj '18	🏆🏆 4
○ Vermentino di Gallura Sup. Katala '18	🏆🏆 3
● Siddaju '16	🏆 5

Cantina del Vermentino Monti

VIA SAN PAOLO, 2
07020 MONTI [SS]
TEL. +39 078944012
www.vermentinomonti.it

CELLAR SALES
PRE-BOOKED VISITS
ANNUAL PRODUCTION 2,000,000 bottles
HECTARES UNDER VINE 500.00

○ Moscato di Sardegna Spumante V. del Portale	🏆🏆 3
○ Vermentino di Gallura Sup. Aghiloia Oro '18	🏆🏆 2*

Vigne Rada

LOC. ALGHERO
FRAZ. MONTE PEDROSU
REG. GUARDIA GRANDE, 12
07041 ALGHERO [SS]
TEL. +39 3274259136
www.vignerada.com

ANNUAL PRODUCTION 28,000 bottles
HECTARES UNDER VINE 7.00

● Alghero Cagnulari Arsenale '16	🏆🏆 6
● Cannonau di Sardegna Riviera '17	🏆🏆 5
○ Vermentino Passito 3 Nodi '16	🏆🏆 7

INDEXES
wineries in alphabetical order
wineries by region

WINERIES IN ALPHABETICAL ORDER

WINERIES BY REGION